Natural Resources
Canada

Ressources naturelles
Canada

CONCISE GAZETTEER OF CANADA

RÉPERTOIRE TOPONYMIQUE CONCIS DU CANADA

CPCGN·CPCNG
1897-1997

Published for the Canadian Permanent Committee on Geographical Names by the Centre for Topographic Information, Geomatics Canada, Natural Resources Canada.

Publié pour le Comité permanent canadien des noms géographiques par le Centre d'information topographique, Géomatique Canada, Ressources naturelles Canada.

OTTAWA 1997

FIRST EDITION   PREMIÈRE ÉDITION

Compilation, data, verification and editing:
Geographical Names Section,
Mapping and Services Branch

Map of Canada:
GeoAccess, Canada Centre for Remote Sensing

Cover artwork:
Kostron Graphics

Compilation, vérification des données et révisions :
Section des noms géographiques,
Division des services cartographiques

Carte du Canada :
GéoAccès, Centre canadien de télédétection

Couverture :
Kostron Graphics

Canadian Cataloguing in Publication Data

Main entry under title:
Concise Gazetteer of Canada = Répertoire
toponymique concis du Canada

Text in English and French.
ISBN 0-660-60185-0
Catalogue No. M86-16/1997-1

1. Canada -- Gazetteers. I. Canadian Permanent
Committee on Geographical Names. II. Title.
III. Title: Répertoire toponymique concis du Canada.

FC35.C66 1997   917.1'003   C97-9000032-7E
                             F1004.C66 1997

Données de catalogage avant publication (Canada)

Vedette principale au titre :
Concise Gazetteer of Canada = Répertoire
toponymique concis du Canada

Texte en anglais et en français.
ISBN 0-660-60185-0
N° de catalogue M86-16/1997-1

1. Canada -- Répertoires. I. Comité permanent canadien
des noms géographiques. II. Titre. III. Titre : Répertoire
toponymique concis du Canada.

FC35.C66 1997   917.1'003   C97-9000032-7F
F1004.C66 1997

MINISTER'S FOREWORD

I am delighted to have the opportunity in this first national volume of the *Gazetteer of Canada* to extend my congratulations to the Canadian Permanent Committee on Geographical Names (CPCGN) on the occasion of its 100th anniversary.

A century of service to Canadians

One of many important organizations at Natural Resources Canada, the CPCGN has provided an invaluable service to the people of Canada since it was founded as the Geographic Board of Canada one hundred years ago. With every decision made on the name of a community or geographical feature listed in this gazetteer, the CPCGN makes an important contribution to Canada's national identity.

The wonderful diversity of names for our communities and landmarks reflects the cultural and linguistic roots that help define what it means to be Canadian. Our common heritage is expressed in the words we use to describe the cities, towns, and rural communities of Canada. Together, they depict a rich mosaic that has provided the foundation for a quality of life that is second to none in the world.

Other countries benefit from the experience of the CPCGN and its work in creating and distributing a national registry, in keeping with recommendations of the United Nations. In addition, this work responds to a key priority at Natural Resources Canada by contributing to the development of a solid knowledge infrastructure for our nation.

The names of our communities and landmarks also remind us that Canada was built on our natural resource wealth. Petrolia, Ontario was the first place in Canada where oil was discovered. In the Northwest Territories, the Coppermine area was named for the efforts by an 18th century explorer who was looking for sources of native copper. The name was changed in January 1996 to Kugluktuk. The Quebec hamlet of Montauban-les-Mines derives part of its name from mining activity in the area. And in Nova Scotia, several communities have been named Forest Glen as a descriptive link to the beauty of their geographic surroundings.

AVANT-PROPOS DE LA MINISTRE

C'est avec beaucoup de fierté que je vous présente le tout premier volume national du *Répertoire géographique du Canada* et que, par la même occasion, je félicite le Comité permanent canadien des noms géographiques (CPCNG), qui célèbre cette année son 100ᵉ anniversaire.

Un siècle au service des Canadiennes et des Canadiens

L'un des nombreux organismes importants de Ressources naturelles Canada, le CPCNG fournit depuis sa création il y a 100 ans — sous le nom de Commission de géographie du Canada — un service inestimable à la population du Canada. En effet, chaque fois qu'il répertorie un nouveau nom de lieu ou d'entité géographique, c'est l'identité nationale du Canada que le CPCNG renforce un peu plus.

La diversité remarquable de nos noms de lieux et d'entités naturelles est à l'image des racines culturelles et linguistiques qui contribuent à définir l'identité canadienne. Notre patrimoine s'exprime par les mots que nous employons pour décrire les villes, les villages et les collectivités rurales du Canada. Ensemble, tous ces mots dépeignent une riche mosaïque qui nous a donné une qualité de vie incomparable dans le monde entier.

D'autres pays bénéficient de l'expérience du CPCNG et du précieux travail qu'il accomplit en établissant et en diffusant un répertoire national basé sur les recommandations des Nations Unies. Ce travail s'inscrit également dans l'une des principales priorités de Ressources naturelles Canada en contribuant à l'établissement d'une infrastructure de connaissances solides pour notre pays.

Les noms donnés à nos lieux et à nos entités naturelles nous rappellent aussi que le Canada doit son développement à l'abondance de ses richesses naturelles. Au Canada, on a découvert le premier champ de pétrole à Petrolia, en Ontario. La région de Coppermine, dans les Territoires du Nord-Ouest, a été nommée ainsi en l'honneur des efforts d'un explorateur du XVIIIᵉ siècle à la recherche de cuivre natif. En janvier 1996, on a changé son nom pour Kugluktuk. Au Québec, le hameau de Montauban-les-Mines tire partiellement son nom des activités minières de la région. Et, en Nouvelle-Écosse, plusieurs collectivités ont été appelées Forest Glen pour décrire la beauté de l'espace environnant.

Today, we are strengthening our commitment to the responsible stewardship of our birthright through progress toward sustainable development.

Demonstrating the federal commitment to partnerships

Key to this progress is the Government of Canada's determination to encourage cooperative approaches to the challenges we face. That is why representatives from provincial, territorial and federal governments work in partnership through the CPCGN to adopt names officially. The priority given to public consultation emphasizes the commitment to cooperation that further defines our nation. This serves to boost a strong sense of identity in communities across Canada — in rural and urban areas alike.

I am confident that the CPCGN will maintain its significant role in adopting and disseminating meaningful names for our communities and geographical features as we move together toward the next century and beyond.

Aujourd'hui, nous réitérons notre engagement à gérer de façon responsable les richesses qui nous ont été confiées, en nous efforçant de les mettre en valeur selon les principes du développement durable.

L'engagement du gouvernement fédéral envers les partenariats

Nos progrès en ce sens dépendent de la détermination du gouvernement du Canada à favoriser le recours à la collaboration pour relever les défis. Voilà pourquoi des représentants des gouvernements provinciaux, territoriaux et fédéral travaillent en partenariat, par l'intermédiaire du CPCNG, pour adopter officiellement les noms géographiques. La priorité accordée aux consultations publiques souligne bien cette volonté de collaboration qui définit notre pays. Ce travail contribue à consolider le fort sentiment d'identité des collectivités du Canada tout entier, dans les régions rurales comme dans les zones urbaines.

Je ne doute pas que le CPCNG continuera de jouer un rôle prépondérant en adoptant et en faisant connaître les noms importants qui sont donnés à nos lieux et à nos entités géographiques, et ce bien après le tournant du siècle.

A. Anne McLellan

PREFACE

Every day we use geographical names as a frame of reference in describing the events of our lives. These names identify the features of our land and water areas and allow us to communicate effectively with each other.

Geographical names reflect the culture and history of our country and embrace the various languages spoken across Canada. Some names undoubtedly reveal the regional diversity of the country, yet others illustrate the common bonds from coast to coast.

Since 1952, the Government of Canada has published various regional and provincial/territorial volumes of the *Gazetteer of Canada Series*. To make geographical names from across the country available in one volume, and yet create a manageable edition, we have selected some 47 000 of the 350 000 names currently recognized by the Canadian Permanent Committee on Geographical Names (CPCGN), to create the first *Concise Gazetteer of Canada*. In addition to current names, some names that were formerly official have been included for information purposes.

Names for places across Canada and for features in Canada and the surrounding waters are made official by the various provincial, territorial, and federal jurisdictions, under the umbrella of the CPCGN. The first use of many names can, of course, be traced back centuries before the existence of a names board, whereas others have become established only in recent years.

The CPCGN today has 25 members from federal, provincial and territorial governments, and academia. Its chair is from the private sector and the Secretariat is provided by Natural Resources Canada. Some provinces and territories (Newfoundland, Quebec, Ontario, Saskatchewan, Alberta, Yukon Territory) now have their own names boards to undertake the decision-making process. Others (Prince Edward Island, Nova Scotia, New Brunswick, Manitoba, British Columbia, Northwest Territories) have an administrative process in place for this purpose. Names of features lying wholly or partly within

PRÉFACE

Tous les jours, nous avons recours aux toponymes comme cadre de référence pour décrire les événements de notre vie. Ces noms géographiques désignent des entités, qu'elles soient situées à la surface de la Terre ou sous l'eau, et ils facilitent notre communication avec les autres.

Les toponymes reflètent la culture et l'histoire de notre pays et dérivent de l'une des différentes langues parlées au Canada. Certains noms révèlent sans aucun doute la diversité régionale du pays, alors que d'autres illustrent les liens qui nous unissent d'un océan à l'autre.

Depuis 1952, le gouvernement du Canada a publié plusieurs volumes du *Répertoire géographique du Canada* qui portent sur différentes régions et provinces ou territoires. Pour réunir des toponymes du pays en un seul volume d'une taille qui puisse être gérée, nous avons choisi quelque 47 000 des 350 000 noms actuellement approuvés par le Comité permanent canadien des noms géographiques (CPCNG), d'où le titre de *Répertoire toponymique concis du Canada*. En plus des noms actuels, d'anciennes appellations officielles sont indiquées pour fins d'information.

Les noms de lieux canadiens et les noms des entités situées au Canada et le long du littoral canadien ont acquis un caractère officiel par le biais des divers gouvernements provinciaux, territoriaux et fédéral et sous la coordination du CPCNG. Le premier usage de nombreux toponymes remonte parfois à plusieurs siècles avant l'existence d'une autorité toponymique; d'autres toponymes, par contre, sont d'origine très récente.

Le CPCNG compte aujourd'hui 25 membres représentant les gouvernements fédéral, provinciaux et territoriaux et les institutions d'enseignement. La présidence est occupée par un représentant du secteur privé et le Secrétariat est assuré par Ressources naturelles Canada. Certaines provinces et territoires (Terre-Neuve, Québec, Ontario, Saskatchewan, Alberta, Yukon) ont créé leur propre commission de toponymie qui est à même de prendre des décisions. D'autres (Île-du-Prince-Édouard, Nouvelle-Écosse, Nouveau-Brunswick, Manitoba, Colombie-Britannique, Territoires du Nord-Ouest) ont mis sur

federal lands (e.g., national parks) are the joint responsibility of federal and provincial/territorial jurisdictions.

When names have been approved through these channels they become (without further action) decisions of the CPCGN and are recorded in the Canadian Geographical Names Data Base (CGNDB) maintained by Natural Resources Canada.

Names from the CGNDB are disseminated for Canadian and international use. Distribution of digital files, our World Wide Web reference gazetteer, and inclusion of names on maps and in paper copy gazetteers all help to increase the availability of information. The use of the officially recognized names are in this way promoted, in line with United Nations standardization programmes.

The cooperation of each provincial and territorial government, as well as various federal departments, in the work of the Committee has been essential to ensure the accuracy of the data included in the *Concise Gazetteer of Canada*. As naming is a dynamic process, the Committee welcomes reliable information concerning additions and corrections to Canada's geographical names.

pied un processus administratif à cette fin. Les noms d'entités qui s'étendent en tout ou en partie sur les terres fédérales (p. ex. parcs nationaux) relèvent à la fois du gouvernement fédéral et de la province ou du territoire.

Lorsqu'on a approuvé des noms en suivant cette filière, ils sont adoptés (sans autre étape) par le CPCNG et consignés dans la Base de données toponymiques du Canada (BDTC) gérée par Ressources naturelles Canada.

Les noms contenus dans la BDTC sont diffusés pour une utilisation canadienne et internationale. La distribution des fichiers numériques, la présence d'un répertoire de référence sur le World Wide Web et l'inclusion des noms sur les cartes et dans les répertoires sur support papier contribuent à accroître l'accès aux données. L'emploi des noms entérinés est de cette façon favorisé, conformément aux programmes de normalisation des Nations Unies.

La collaboration de chaque province et territoire et de divers ministères fédéraux aux travaux du Comité a été essentielle pour assurer l'exactitude des données retenues pour le *Répertoire toponymique concis du Canada*. Comme le processus de dénomination est dynamique, le Comité accepte toute information fiable ayant trait à des corrections et à des ajouts relatifs aux toponymes du Canada

E. Anthony Price
Chairman / Président
Canadian Permanent Committee on Geographical Names /
Comité permanent canadien des noms géographiques
1997

TABLE OF CONTENTS

Map of Canada - see inside back cover

TABLE DES MATIÈRES

Carte du Canada - voir à l'intérieur de la couverture arrière

GENERAL INFORMATION

Contact addresses

Names and policies

Queries about specific names and the policies and practices relating to the origin and use of geographical names or terminology, should be directed to the:

Secretariat
Canadian Permanent Committee on
 Geographical Names
6th Floor, 615 Booth Street
Ottawa, Ontario K1A 0E9

Fax: (613) 943-8282
E-mail: geonames@NRCan.gc.ca

Digital toponymic information

For information about the availability of data in this gazetteer volume in digital form, please contact:

Geographical Names Section
Natural Resources Canada
Room 634, 615 Booth Street
Ottawa, Ontario K1A 0E9

Fax: (613) 943-8282
E-mail: geonames@NRCan.gc.ca

World Wide Web sites

- **GeoNames: Canadian geographical names reference site**
  http://www-nais.ccm.NRCan.gc.ca/cgndb/

- **SchoolNet: name origins and teaching materials**
  http://www-nais.ccm.NRCan.gc.ca/
  cgndb/english/schoolnet/

Where to find related information

Index maps and National Topographic System (NTS) maps

Canada Map Office
615 Booth Street
Ottawa, Ontario K1A 0E9

Phone: (613) 952-7000
Fax: (613) 957-8861

RENSEIGNEMENTS GÉNÉRAUX

Adresses utiles

Toponymes et lignes directrices

Prière d'adresser les questions relatives aux toponymes, à la politique et aux pratiques concernant l'origine et l'usage des noms géographiques ou la terminologie au :

Secrétariat
Comité permanent canadien des
 noms géographiques
615, rue Booth, 6e étage
Ottawa (Ontario) K1A 0E9

Téléc. :   (613) 943-8282
Courrier électr. : geonames@RNCan.gc.ca

Données toponymiques numériques

Pour savoir comment obtenir, sous forme numérique, les données figurant dans le présent volume, veuillez contacter la :

Section des noms géographiques
Ressources naturelles Canada
615, rue Booth, pièce 634
Ottawa (Ontario) K1A 0E9

Téléc. :   (613) 943-8282
Courrier électr. : geonames@RNCan.gc.ca

Sites du World Wide Web

- **Toponymie : site de référence des noms géographiques du Canada**
  http://www-nais.ccm.RNCan.gc.ca/cgndb/

- **Rescol : origine des toponymes et matériel didactique**
  http://www-nais.ccm.RNCan.gc.ca/
  cgndb/francais/schoolnet/

Où trouver des renseignements connexes

Index de cartes et cartes du Système national de référence cartographique (SNRC)

Bureau des cartes
615, rue Booth
Ottawa (Ontario) K1A 0E9

Tél. :   (613) 952-7000
Téléc. : (613) 957-8861

CHS charts and maps

Canadian Hydrographic Service
Fisheries and Oceans Canada
1675 Russell Road
P.O. Box 8080
Ottawa, Ontario K1G 3H6

Phone: (613) 998-4931
Fax: (613) 998-1217

Air photos

National Air Photo Library
1st Floor, 615 Booth Street
Ottawa, Ontario K1A 0E9

Phone: (613) 995-4560
Fax: (613) 995-4568
WWW site:
http:/www.geocan.NRCan.gc.ca/napl-pha/

Cartes hydrographiques

Service hydrographique du Canada
Pêches et Océans Canada
1675, chemin Russell
B.P. 8080
Ottawa (Ontario) K1G 3H6

Tél. :   (613) 998-4931
Téléc. : (613) 998-1217

Photos aériennes

Phototèque nationale de l'air
615, rue Booth, 1ᵉʳ étage
Ottawa (Ontario) K1A 0E9

Tél. :   (613) 995-4560
Téléc. : (613) 995-4568
Site WWW :
http:www.geocan.RNCan.gc.ca/napl-pha/

Some abbreviations used in this publication
Quelques abréviations utilisées dans cette publication

Abbreviation/Abréviation	Meaning/Sens
CPCGN	Canadian Permanent Committee on Geographical Names
CPCNG	Comité permanent canadien des noms géographiques
Lat	Latitude
Loc 1	Location 1
Loc 2	Location 2
Long	Longitude

HISTORY OF THE CPCGN

During the last quarter of the nineteenth century, surveyors, geographers, geologists, and mapmakers realized the need for a single authority to which questions of geographical nomenclature and orthography could be addressed. Such advice and decision-making would help avoid errors and inconsistencies in spelling and applications of geographical names. In 1890, a position was set up in the Department of the Interior to compile lists of names and establish uniformity of use in government publications. However, it was not until the end of 1897 that an Order in Council created the Geographic Board of Canada (GBC). Chaired by F. Gourdeau (Deputy Minister of Marine and Fisheries), the board had members from six federal departments and a Secretary (A.H. Whitcher, from the Department of the Interior).

Within a few years the participation of the provinces was encouraged. These early days of the Board saw considerable publication of geographical names material. Individuals such as James White (Chief Geographer of Canada) and Robert Douglas (Board Secretary) wrote names studies for many parts of Canada.

During World War II activities were cut back to the minimum, with name approval being the only task undertaken. However, by 1948 a new Order in Council had been drawn up and under the title of the Canadian Board on Geographical Names (CBGN) the board was reconstituted and completely revised its principles and procedures.

As early as the 1930s, there were proposals that the provinces should take responsibility for approving names. Nevertheless, it was not until the federal Order in Council of 1961 that this authority was recognized, with all provinces designating members to sit on the national board - now the Canadian Permanent Committee on Geographical Names (CPCGN) - to recommend common policies, principles and procedures.

In 1984, the responsibility for naming in the Northwest Territories and Yukon Territory was devolved from the federal Department of Indian and Northern Affairs to the territorial governments.

The mandate of the Committee is today set out by Order in Council P.C. 1990-549 of 22 March 1990. The CPCGN meets annually and its work is facilitated by four advisory committees that address undersea features, nomenclature and delineation, toponymy research, and digital toponymic services.

HISTORIQUE DU CPCNG

Au cours du dernier quart du XIXe siècle, les arpenteurs, les géographes, les géologues et les cartographes ont pris conscience de la nécessité de créer un organisme central pour acheminer les questions de nomenclature géographique et d'orthographie. En offrant des conseils et en prenant des décisions, cet organisme devait permettre d'éviter des erreurs et des incohérences dans l'orthographe et l'application des toponymes. En 1890, était créé un poste au ministère de l'Intérieur pour compiler des listes de noms et uniformiser leur emploi dans les publications du gouvernement. Ce ne fut toutefois pas avant la fin de 1897 qu'un décret a été promulgué pour la création de la Commission de géographie du Canada. Présidée par F. Gourdeau (sous-ministre de la Marine et des Pêcheries), la commission comptait des membres de six ministères fédéraux et un secrétaire (A.H. Whitcher, du ministère de l'Intérieur).

En quelques années, la participation des provinces a été sollicitée. Dès ses débuts, la Commission a publié de nombreux ouvrages sur la toponymie. Certaines personnes, comme James White (géographe en chef du Canada) et Robert Douglas (secrétaire de la Commission) ont rédigé des études toponymiques sur de nombreuses régions du pays.

Durant la Deuxième Guerre mondiale, les activités ont été réduites à leur plus simple expression, l'approbation des noms étant la seule tâche accomplie. Dès 1948, cependant, un nouveau décret avait été passé et, sous l'appellation de Commission canadienne des noms géographiques (CCNG), la commission était reconstituée et ses principes et directives générales complètement restructurés.

Dès les années 30, des propositions pour que la responsabilité d'approuver les toponymes soit confiée aux provinces ont été formulées. Néanmoins, il a fallu attendre le décret fédéral de 1961 pour que cette compétence soit reconnue et que toutes les provinces désignent les membres devant faire partie de la commission nationale - le Comité permanent canadien des noms géographiques - afin de recommander des politiques, des principes et des directives communes.

En 1984, la responsabilité d'adopter les toponymes en usage dans les Territoires du Nord-Ouest et au Yukon est passée du ministère fédéral des Affaires indiennes et du Nord canadien aux territoires.

Le mandat du comité actuel a été établi par décret le 22 mars 1990. Le CPCNG se réunit à chaque année et l'avancement de ses travaux est facilité par quatre comités consultatifs qui traitent des entités sous-marines, de la nomenclature et de la délimitation, de la recherche toponymique et des services toponymiques numériques.

One hundred years of national standardization has created a single authoritative reference set of geographical names in Canada and so helps avoid ambiguity and confusion in communication. This experience has also made Canada a leading participant in the work of the United Nations Economic and Social Council (ECOSOC) in promoting international standardization. Canadians have contributed to the six conferences held since 1961 and to the ongoing technical work of the United Nations Group of Experts on Geographical Names (UNGEGN).

Un siècle de normalisation nationale a permis de créer une seule base de référence faisant autorité et contenant les toponymes canadiens, de manière à éviter toute ambiguïté et toute confusion dans les communications. L'expérience acquise par le Canada lui permet d'être un chef de file dans les travaux du Conseil économique et social des Nations Unies en faisant la promotion d'une normalisation à l'échelle internationale. Les Canadiens ont contribué aux six conférences tenues depuis 1961 et aux travaux techniques en cours du Groupe d'experts des Nations Unies pour les noms géographiques.

COMMITTEE MEMBERSHIP

The Canadian Permanent Committee on Geographical Names is composed of representatives from federal government departments concerned with mapping, archives, translation, defence, Indian lands, and statistics, and appointed representatives from each province and territory of Canada, as well as chairs of advisory committees.

Chairman

PRICE, E.A.
Canadian Permanent Committee on Geographical Names, Ottawa K1A 0E9

Federal Members

EVERELL, M.D.
Assistant Deputy Minister, Earth Sciences Sector, Natural Resources Canada, Ottawa K1A 0E4

COREY, M.
Director General, Mapping Services Branch, Geomatics Canada, Natural Resources Canada, Ottawa K1A 0E4

WALLOT, J.-P.
National Archivist, National Archives of Canada, Ottawa K1A 0N3

MONNET, D.
Chief Executive Officer, Translation Bureau, Public Works and Government Services Canada Ottawa K1A 0M5

QUINN, M.
Director, Lands Directorate, Lands and Environment Branch, Department of Indian and Northern Affairs, Ottawa K1A 0H4

DAWSON, COL. J.W.
Director, J2 Geo, National Defence Headquarters, Ottawa K1A 0K2

MacPHEE, S.B.
Dominion Hydrographer, Canadian Hydrographic Service, Department of Fisheries and Oceans, Ottawa K1A 0E6

BUGGEY, S.
Director, Historical and Built Environment Research, National Historic Sites Directorate, Parks Canada, Ottawa K1A 0M5

DAVIS, T.
Director, Geography Division, Statistics Canada, Ottawa K1A 0T6

COMPOSITION DU COMITÉ

Le Comité permanent canadien des noms géographiques est composé de représentants des ministères fédéraux, en poste dans les domaines de la cartographie, des archives, de la traduction, de la défense, des terres indiennes, des statistiques, et d'un représentant de chacune des provinces et de chacun des territoires du Canada ainsi que des présidents des comités consultatifs.

Président

PRICE, E.A.
Comité permanent canadien des noms géographiques, Ottawa K1A 0E9

Représentants du gouvernement fédéral

EVERELL, M.D.
Sous-ministre adjoint, Secteur des sciences de la Terre, Ressources naturelles Canada, Ottawa K1A 0E4

COREY, M.
Directeur général, Direction des services cartographiques, Géomatique Canada, Ressources naturelles Canada, Ottawa K1A 0E4

WALLOT, J.-P.
Archiviste national, Archives nationales du Canada, Ottawa K1A 0N3

MONNET, D.
Présidente-directrice générale, Services de traduction, Travaux publics et Services gouvernementaux Canada, Ottawa K1A 0M5

QUINN, M.
Directeur, Direction des terres et de l'environnement, Direction des réserves et des fidéicommis, ministère des Affaires indiennes et du Nord canadien, Ottawa K1A 0H4

DAWSON, COL. J.W.
Directeur, J2 Géo, Quartier général de la défense nationale, Ottawa K1A 0K2

MacPHEE, S.B.
Hydrographe fédéral, Service hydrographique du Canada, ministère des Pêches et des Océans, Ottawa K1A 0E6

BUGGEY, S.
Directrice, Direction de la recherche historique et de l'environnement bâti, Direction générale des lieux historiques, Parcs Canada, Ottawa K1A 0M5

DAVIS, T.
Directeur, Division de la géographie, Statistique Canada, Ottawa K1A 0T6

OKULITCH, A.V.
    Research Scientist, Geological Survey of
    Canada, Natural Resources Canada, Calgary T2L
    2A7

Provincial and territorial members

MacNAUGHTON, N.
    Director of Surveys and Mapping, Department of
    Government Services and Lands, St. John's,
    Newfoundland A1B 4J6

RAMSAY, J.
    Provincial Tax Commissioner, Provincial
    Treasury, Charlottetown, Prince Edward Island
    C1A 7N8

AuCOIN, K.
    Director of Surveys, Department of Natural
    Resources, Dartmouth, Nova Scotia B3B 1T3

RAE, D.
    Municipalities, Culture and Housing,
    Fredericton, New Brunswick E3B 5H1

VALLIÈRES, A.
    Président intérimaire, Commission de
    toponymie, Québec, Quebec G1R 5V8

FINOS, P.L.
    Surveyor General, Natural Resources
    Information Management Branch, Ministry of
    Natural Resources, Peterborough, Ontario
    K9J 8M5

HOLM, G.F.
    Provincial Toponymist, Manitoba Geographical
    Names Program, Department of Natural
    Resources, Winnipeg, Manitoba R3H 0W4

TURNBULL, J.
    General Manager, SaskGeomatics Division,
    Saskatchewan Property Management
    Corporation, Regina, Saskatchewan S4P 3V7

PANNEKOEK, F.
    Director, Historic Sites and Archives Service,
    Alberta Community Development, Edmonton,
    Alberta T6G 2P8

SAWAYAMA, G.T.
    Director, Geographic Data BC, Ministry of
    Environment, Lands and Parks, Victoria, British
    Columbia V8V 1X4

HUNSTON, J.
    Director, Heritage Branch, Department of
    Tourism, Whitehorse, Yukon Y1A 2C6

OKULITCH, A.V.
    Chercheur scientifique, Commission géologique
    du Canada, Ressources naturelles Canada,
    Calgary T2L 2A7

Représentants des provinces et territoires

MacNAUGHTON, N.
    Director of Surveys and Mapping, Department of
    Government Services and Lands, St. John's
    (Terre-Neuve) A1B 4J6

RAMSAY, J.
    Provincial Tax Commissioner, Provincial
    Treasury, Charlottetown (Île-du-Prince-Édouard)
    C1A 7N8

AuCOIN, K.
    Director of Surveys, Department of Natural
    Resources, Dartmouth (Nouvelle-Écosse)
    B3B 1T3

RAE, D.
    Municipalités, Culture et Habitation, Fredericton
    (Nouveau-Brunswick) E3B 5H1

VALLIÈRES, A.
    Président intérimaire, Commission de
    toponymie, Québec (Québec) G1R 5V8

FINOS, P.L.
    Arpenteur général, Direction de l'information sur
    les ressources naturelles, ministère des Richesses
    naturelles, Peterborough (Ontario) K9J 8M5

HOLM, G.F.
    Toponymiste provincial, Programme des noms
    géographiques du Manitoba, ministère des
    Ressources naturelles, Winnipeg (Manitoba)
    R3H 0W4

TURNBULL, J.
    General Manager, SaskGeomatics Division,
    Saskatchewan Property Management
    Corporation, Regina (Saskatchewan) S4P 3V7

PANNEKOEK, F.
    Director, Historic Sites and Archives Services,
    Alberta Community Development, Edmonton
    (Alberta) T6G 2P8

SAWAYAMA, G.T.
    Director, Geographic Data BC, Ministry of
    Environment, Lands and Parks, Victoria
    (Colombie-Britannique) V8V 1X4

HUNSTON, J.
    Director, Heritage Branch, Department of
    Tourism, Whitehorse (Yukon) Y1A 2C6

FREEMAN, R.
　　Territorial Toponymist, Geographical Names
　　Program, Department of Education, Culture and
　　Employment, Yellowknife, Northwest Territories
　　X1A 2L9

Advisory committee chairs

MacPHEE, S.B.
　　Chairman, Advisory Committee on Names for
　　Undersea and Maritime Features

LAPIERRE, A.
　　Chairman, Advisory Committee on Toponymy
　　Research

OKULITCH, A.V.
　　Chairman, Advisory Committee on
　　Nomenclature and Delineation

PITBLADO, J.R.
　　Chairman, Advisory Committee on Canadian
　　Digital Toponymic Services

FREEMAN, R.
　　Territorial Toponymist, Geographical Names
　　Program, Department of Education, Culture and
　　Employment, Yellowknife (Territoires du Nord-
　　Ouest) X1A 2L9

Présidents des comités consultatifs

MacPHEE, S.B.
　　Président, Comité consultatif des noms d'entités
　　sous-marines et marines

LAPIERRE, A.
　　Président, Comité consultatif de la recherche
　　toponymique

OKULITCH, A.V.
　　Président, Comité consultatif de la nomenclature
　　et de la délimitation

PITBLADO, J.R.
　　Président, Comité consultatif sur les services
　　canadiens de données toponymiques numériques

PRINCIPLES OF NOMENCLATURE

The principles of nomenclature which guide the decisions of the Canadian Permanent Committee on Geographical Names are summarized as follows:

1. Names created by legislation are accepted by the Committee.

2. First consideration is given to names with well-established local usage. Unless there are good reasons to the contrary, this principle prevails.

3. Names for facilities established by postal authorities, railway companies and major public utilities are accepted, if they are in keeping with the other principles. Such agencies are encouraged to have open communication with the appropriate names authorities.

4. A name decision for a physical or cultural feature should specify the geographical limits of the feature to which the name applies. Future approval of different names with the same generic for a part of the same feature should be avoided.

5. The application of a personal name is not made unless it can be demonstrated that exceptional circumstances exist and it is in the public interest to do so.

6. Where no local names are in use, preferred sources for names are: descriptive names appropriate to the features; pioneers, explorers and historical events connected with the area; names from native languages formerly identified with the general area; and names of persons who died during war service.

7. Names should be euphonious and in good taste.

8. A name is usually adopted in a single language form, and where possible, written in the Roman alphabet. Other forms in use may also be sanctioned by the appropriate names authority. A name derived from languages other than English or French should be written

PRINCIPES DE NOMENCLATURE

Résumé des principes de nomenclature qui orientent les décisions du Comité permanent canadien des noms géographiques :

1. Le Comité reconnaît les noms créés par une loi.

2. Les noms qui sont depuis longtemps implantés dans l'usage local ont la priorité. Ce principe doit prévaloir à moins de bonnes raisons contraires.

3. Les noms d'installations établis par les autorités postales, les compagnies de chemins de fer et les principaux services publics sont acceptés pourvu qu'ils soient conformes aux autres principes. Ces organismes sont encouragés à communiquer librement avec les autorités toponymiques compétentes.

4. Une décision prise à la suite d'une proposition de nom pour une entité naturelle ou un élément anthropique doit préciser les limites géographiques de l'entité ou de l'élément auquel le nom se rapporte. Par la suite, on évitera d'approuver des noms différents comportant le même générique pour désigner une partie de la même entité.

5. L'emploi d'anthroponymes (noms de personnes) est déconseillé, à moins que l'on ne fasse état de circonstances exceptionnelles et qu'il n'y aille de l'intérêt public.

6. Lorsqu'aucun toponyme local n'existe déjà, les toponymes choisis devraient être de préférence des noms descriptifs convenant aux éléments considérés, des noms de pionniers, d'explorateurs ou d'évènements historiques qui ont un lien avec la région, des noms tirés des langues autochtones assimilés autrefois avec la région environnante, ou encore des noms de personnes mortes à la guerre.

7. Les noms doivent être euphoniques et de bon goût.

8. De façon générale, un nom est adopté dans une seule forme linguistique, et autant que possible, écrit dans l'alphabet romain. D'autres formes peuvent aussi être sanctionnées par les autorités toponymiques compétentes. Un nom dérivé d'une langue autre que le français ou

in the best recognized orthography. Names of selected geographical entities of pan-Canadian significance are recognized in both English and French for use on federal maps and in federal texts.

9. The spelling and accenting of names are in accordance with the rules of the language in which they are written.

10. Names of the same origin applying to various service facilities in a community should conform in spelling with the official name of the community. Names with the same specific for associated features should agree in form and spelling.

11. Duplication of names to the extent that confusion may result should be avoided.

12. A geographical name usually includes both a specific and a generic element. The generic term should be appropriate to the nature of the feature and will be recorded in English or in French, by the names authority concerned.

13. Qualifying words such as "upper", "west branch", and "nouveau" may be used in an area to distinguish two or more features with identical specific forms.

14. Except where local and historic usage dictates, the official approval of a name of a minor feature is guided by the relative significance of the feature, the familiarity of the name, and the scale of mapping available.

l'anglais doit avoir la meilleure orthographe reconnue. Les noms de certaines entités géographiques d'intérêt pancanadien ont, dans les deux langues officielles, une forme consacrée qu'il faut respecter sur les cartes et dans les textes produits par le gouvernement fédéral.

9. L'orthographe des noms géographiques ainsi que l'emploi des accents appropriés sont conformes aux règles de la langue utilisée.

10. Les noms de même origine donnés à diverses installations de service dans une localité, doivent avoir une orthographe conforme à celle du nom officiel de la localité. Les mêmes spécifiques qui se retrouvent dans des noms différents employés pour désigner des entités parentes ou voisines doivent respecter une orthographe unique.

11. Le double emploi d'un nom doit être évité lorsque ce nom peut prêter à confusion.

12. De manière générale, un toponyme comprend à la fois un terme spécifique et un terme générique. Le générique devrait correspondre à la nature de l'entité géographique qu'il désigne et doit être enregistré en français ou en anglais par l'autorité toponymique compétente.

13. On peut utiliser des termes qualificatifs tels que «upper», «west branch», et «nouveau» pour distinguer deux ou plusieurs entités comportant des formes spécifiques identiques.

14. Sauf lorsque l'impose l'usage local et historique, l'approbation officielle de noms pour de petites entités s'appuie sur l'importance relative de l'entité, son usage et l'échelle des cartes disponibles.

PROCEDURES CONCERNING THE SUBMISSION OF GEOGRAPHICAL NAMES

Proposals and changes

Only in exceptional circumstances does the Committee itself initiate naming. Most new names approved by the Committee, through the jurisdictions of its provincial, territorial and federal members, are submitted by the general public and by organizations. Such names should be for specific geographical features.

Individuals or organizations contemplating the publication of geographical names should submit proposals to the provincial or territorial authority, well in advance of publication dates. The consideration of new names may require considerable time, particularly when local investigation is required. The publication of unauthorized names will not necessarily result in official recognition.

Descriptive names, local names, and names relating to the history of an area are preferred. The following information accompanied by adequate documentation will facilitate the decision-making process:

- location by latitude and longitude, specifying map consulted
- identification on a map indicating precise extent of the feature
- photographs or sketches
- reasons for proposals
- origin and meaning of name

Reliable, preferably documented, information concerning corrections in the use, spelling, or application of toponyms on maps and charts is welcomed by the Committee.

Inquiries

Inquiries concerning geographical nomenclature in Canada, proposals concerning new names, or changes in the form, spelling or application of existing names may be submitted in writing to the appropriate CPCGN member, as listed on pages x to xii, or the:

Executive Secretary, CPCGN
6th Floor, 615 Booth Street
Ottawa, Ontario K1A 0E9

DIRECTIVES POUR LA PRÉSENTATION DE NOMS GÉOGRAPHIQUES

Propositions et modifications

À moins de circonstances exceptionnelles, le Comité n'amorce pas lui-même le mécanisme de désignation des lieux. Les nouveaux noms approuvés par le Comité, par l'entremise de ses membres provinciaux, territoriaux et fédéraux, sont pour la plupart proposés par un particulier ou par un organisme. Ces noms doivent s'appliquer à des éléments géographiques précis.

Les particuliers ou les organismes qui envisagent de faire publier des noms géographiques doivent présenter leurs propositions longtemps à l'avance à l'autorité toponymique provinciale ou territoriale pertinente. L'examen des nouveaux noms peut demander du temps, surtout s'il faut procéder à des enquêtes sur place. Un nom ne reçoit pas forcément la sanction officielle parce qu'il a déjà été publié.

Il faut proposer de préférence des noms descriptifs, d'usage local ou des noms qui évoquent une page de l'histoire de la région. Il est souhaitable de soumettre les renseignements suivants et la documentation pertinente afin de faciliter les procédures de décision :

- la latitude et la longitude du lieu considéré, en indiquant la carte consultée
- l'identification de l'élément sur une carte en indiquant son étendue exacte
- des photographies ou des croquis
- les raisons motivant la proposition
- l'origine et le sens du nom

Le Comité accueille favorablement tout renseignement sûr, et de préférence documenté, relatif aux corrections à apporter à l'utilisation, à l'orthographe ou à l'application de toponymes sur les cartes géographiques.

Demandes de renseignements

Les demandes de renseignements concernant la toponymie du Canada, les propositions de nouveaux noms ou les modifications à apporter à la forme, à l'orthographe ou à l'application de noms existants doivent être présentées par écrit au membre pertinent du CPCNG (voir la liste aux pages x à xii) ou au :

Secrétaire exécutif, CPCNG
615, rue Booth, 6e étage
Ottawa (Ontario) K1A 0E9

SELECTION CRITERIA FOR NAMES IN THIS *GAZETTEER*

The CPCGN appointed a working group to recommend an appropriate selection of names for a "concise" national gazetteer. To suit the needs of Canadian and international users, both objective and subjective selection criteria were developed, and as a result 47 000 names are included.

A core of names was chosen using **objective** criteria. All names in the following categories are included systematically:

- incorporated populated places and administrative areas
- unincorporated populated places
- Indian reserves
- national parks, national park reserves, national historic sites, and international parks
- world heritage sites
- geographical areas
- features of "pan-Canadian significance"[1]
- physical features (both terrain and hydrographic) named on 1:2 million scale maps produced by Natural Resources Canada
- features crossing the United States - Canada boundary and shown in the *United States Concise National Gazetteer, 1990*

---

[1] pan-Canadian names

Pan-Canadian names are names of Canadian geographical entities with well-known forms in both official languages of Canada, including the largest entities in and around Canada, as well as those with national historical significance. These names are considered part of the Canadian national heritage and have been listed in the Government of Canada Treasury Board Circular No. 1983-58 (of November 23, 1983). They are to be used on federal government maps: in both forms on a bilingual map, or, in the case of separate English and French versions of a map, in the form appropriate to the language of the map. (Refer to *Principles and Procedures for Geographical Naming*, 1990, Appendix 3.) Eighty such names are listed, with the English and French versions of the names cross-referenced to each other.

CRITÈRES DE SÉLECTION TOPONYMIQUE POUR CE *RÉPERTOIRE*

Le CPCNG a nommé un groupe de travail qui avait pour tâche de recommander une sélection toponymique pertinente pour un répertoire toponymique national «concis». Afin de répondre aux besoins d'utilisateurs nationaux et internationaux, des critères de sélection objectifs et subjectifs furent développés; le résultat est ce volume contenant plus de 47 000 toponymes.

Les critères de sélection **objectifs** ont déterminé l'essentiel du volume. Tous les toponymes dans les catégories suivantes furent inclus de façon systématique :

- lieux habités constitués en corporation et zones administratives
- lieux habités non organisés
- réserves indiennes
- parcs nationaux, réserves de parcs nationaux, lieux historiques nationaux et parcs internationaux
- sites du patrimoine mondial
- zones géographiques
- entités d'intérêt pancanadien[1]
- entités physiques (de terrain et hydrographiques) sur les cartes à l'échelle 1/2 million produites par Ressources naturelles Canada
- entités transfrontalières entre le Canada et les États-Unis montrées dans le *United States Concise National Gazetteer, 1990*

---

[1] Noms d'intérêt pancanadien

Les noms d'intérêt pancanadien représentent les entités géographiques du Canada qui ont deux formes bien connues dans les deux langues officielles du pays, englobant tant les principales entités géographiques à l'intérieur et aux environs du Canada, que celles d'intérêt historique à l'échelle nationale. On considère que ces toponymes font partie du patrimoine national canadien. Ils sont inscrits sur la liste de la Circulaire n° 1983-58 du Conseil du trésor du gouvernement du Canada (datée du 23 novembre 1983). Ces noms sont autorisés aux fins d'usage sur les cartes du gouvernement fédéral; dans le cas d'une carte bilingue, les deux formes sont utilisées et dans le cas de versions linguistiques distinctes, le nom pertinent à la version sera utilisé. (Se référer aux *Principes et directives pour la dénomination des lieux*, 1990, Annexe 3.) Quatre-vingt noms d'intérêt pancanadien font donc partie du corps de ce volume accompagnés de leur renvoi dans l'autre forme linguistique officielle.

In addition to the above, **subjective** selections of names were made in the following categories:

- some 1000 urban community names

- Canadian Forces bases and stations

- terrain features from the 1:1 million scale *International Map of the World* (IMW) series (particularly mountain ranges and peaks)

- physical features (hydrographic and terrain) based on various scales of maps in the *Canada Gazetteer Atlas*, 1980; the scales range from 1:4 million to 1:250,000 in urban areas

- undersea features around the coasts of Canada, chosen by the Canadian Hydrographic Service (CHS) from the 1:1 million scale *National Earth Science Series*

- places and features considered important by CPCGN members in their own jurisdictions

- major mountain passes and waterfalls

- major ice caps and glaciers

- cross-references to previously official names, changed during the last ten years

Note:

Nunavut

The territory of Nunavut will come into existence on 1 April 1999, or earlier. For reference purposes, it is listed in this *Gazetteer*. The limits of the new territory have been indicated in purple on the map of Canada at the back of the *Gazetteer*.

En plus des critères de sélection susmentionnés, une sélection toponymique **subjective** fut faite parmi les catégories suivantes :

- quelque 1 000 toponymes de communautés urbaines

- bases et stations des Forces canadiennes

- entités de terrain tirées de la série *Carte internationale du monde* (CIM) à l'échelle 1/1 million (en particulier, les chaînes de montagnes et les sommets)

- entités physiques (hydrographiques et de terrain) tirées de cartes à diverses échelles de la publication *Canada Atlas toponymique,* 1980; l'échelle des cartes varie du 1/4 million au 1/250 000 dans les zones urbaines

- entités sous-marines le long des côtes du Canada, choisies par le Service hydrographique du Canada et tirées de la série à l'échelle 1/1 million *Série nationale de la science de la terre*

- lieux et entités choisis par les membres du CPCNG pour leur importance dans leur autorité compétente

- cols et chutes d'importance

- principaux glaciers et calottes glaciaires

- renvois aux noms anciennement approuvés qui ont changé depuis les dix dernières années

Note :

Nunavut

Le territoire de Nunavut entrera officiellement en vigueur au plus tard le 1er avril 1999. À titre de renseignements, ce toponyme est inclus dans le *Répertoire*. Les limites du nouveau territoire sont indiquées en pourpre sur la carte du Canada à la fin du volume.

HOW TO USE THIS *GAZETTEER*

The *Concise Gazetteer of Canada* lists the selected names in alphabetical order (Column 1 - Name), followed by information on the type of feature (Column 2 - Entity), the province or territory in which the name is situated (Column 3 - Loc 1), and, where relevant, a land division of that area (Column 4 - Loc 2), the map or chart on which the feature can be found (Column 5 - Map), and the geographical coordinates (Column 6 - Lat, Column 7 - Long). Specific details follow.

Column 1 - Name

Name status, typefaces, and cross-references

Typeface is used to indicate the official status of a name:

- officially approved names, including those which are cross-referenced to the other official language version of the name, are shown in a combination of upper and lower case, upright characters
- formerly approved names, which have been changed to another name, are in *italics*; a "see-voir" reference is provided to the current name, which is shown in regular type
- names which have been rescinded and no longer exist are in *italics*, preceded by an asterisk (*)

- equivalent names (used in Manitoba) are preceded by a "+" sign[2]
- pan-Canadian names appear in **bold** type

---

[2] Equivalent names

In Manitoba, certain areas of the province are designated as French Language Services Areas. Within these areas, there are sixteen flowing-water features which have well-known names in English and French. These names are authorized for use on bilingual maps, signs, and other official documents affecting these French Language Services Areas. In the case of separate English and French versions, the name appropriate to the language of the map, sign, or document should be used.

COMMENT UTILISER CE *RÉPERTOIRE*

Le *Répertoire toponymique concis du Canada* présente la liste des toponymes choisis de façon alphabétique (Colonne 1 - Nom), suivie des renseignements relatifs au genre d'entité (Colonne 2 - Entité), de la province ou du territoire où se trouve l'entité (Colonne 3 - Lieu 1), et, s'il y a lieu, le nom d'une division territoriale s'y rattachant (Colonne 4 - Lieu 2), la carte où l'on retrouve l'entité (Colonne 5 - Carte), et les coordonnées géographiques (Colonne 6 - Lat, Colonne 7 - Long). Pour plus de renseignements, veuillez lire ce qui suit.

Colonne 1 - Nom

Statuts toponymiques, typographie et renvois

La typographie est utilisée dans ce volume pour déterminer le statut officiel d'un toponyme :

- les noms officiellement appouvés, englobant ceux qui renvoient à l'autre forme linguistique officielle, sont indiqués en lettres majuscules et minuscules et en caractères droits
- les noms anciennement approuvés, qui ont maintenant une autre forme officielle, sont en *italique*; la référence «see-voir» précède la forme officielle à jour qui apparaît en caractères droits
- les noms qui ont été abrogés et qui sont maintenant disparus sont en *italique*, précédés d'une astérisque (*)
- les noms équivalents (retrouvés au Manitoba) sont précédés du symbole «+»[2]
- les noms d'intérêt pancanadien sont indiqués en caractères **gras**

---

[2] Noms équivalents

Certaines régions du Manitoba sont désignées comme zones desservant les collectivités francophones. À l'intérieur de ces zones, seize entités de cours d'eau ont des formes bien connues en français et en anglais. Ces noms sont autorisés aux fins d'usage sur les cartes bilingues, la signalisation et tout autre document touchant aux zones désignées qui desservent les collectivités de langue française. Lorsque les cartes sont préparées dans deux versions linguistiques distinctes, le nom pertinent à la version utilisée sur la carte, le panneau de signalisation ou le document devrait être utilisé.

- "also-aussi" references are provided for names which have both English and French forms; these include names of Department of National Defence (DND) bases and stations, some undersea features, names for some features crossing provincial/territorial boundaries, national parks, national historic sites, world heritage sites, equivalent names, and pan-Canadian names

Examples of these are shown in Table 1.

- la référence «also-aussi» accompagne les toponymes qui sont approuvés officiellement en français et en anglais; ces derniers englobent les noms de bases et de stations du ministère de la Défense nationale, quelques entités sous-marines, les entités interprovinciales/territoriales, les parcs nationaux, les lieux historiques nationaux, les sites du patrimoine mondial, les noms équivalents et noms d'intérêt pancanadien

Voir le Tableau 1 pour des exemples illustrant les catégories de toponymes susmentionnés.

Table 1. **Name status, typefaces, and cross-references**
Tableau 1. **Les statuts toponymiques, la typographie utilisée et les renvois**

Name Nom	Entity Entité	Loc 1 Lieu 1	Loc 2 Lieu 2	Map Carte	Position Lat	Long
Alkali Creek	RIV/CDE	SK	27-23-27-W3	72 K/13	50°59'	109°41'
Américains, Banc des - also-aussi - American Bank	SEAU/SMER	--		4485	48°36'	63°54'
*Clermont Station	UNP/LNO	PE	Prince	11 L/5	46°26'	63°40'
Grand View - see-voir - Browns Flat	UNP/LNO	NB		21 G/8	45°28'	66°08'
Greenhorn Lakes	LAKE/LAC	NT	Mackenzie	86 M	67°05'	119°03'
+Morris, Rivière - also-aussi - Morris River	RIV/RIV	MB		62 H/6	49°21'	97°21'
Winnipeg, Lake - also-aussi - **Winnipeg, Lac**	LAKE/LAC	MB		63 A/3	52°08'	97°16'

Alphabetization and language treatment

Information is presented in a manner designed to serve the needs of both English- and French-speaking readers in a single volume. Except as noted below, alphabetization is letter-by-letter rather than word by word. For example, "Adamsdale" precedes "Adams Gulch".

(a) general considerations relating to all names

Punctuation, such as comma (,), hyphen (-), apostrophe ('), does not affect alphabetization.

Where an **abbreviation** is used, such as "No.", "St.", "Ste.", or "Rev.", the alphabetical arrangement proceeds as though the abbreviated word were *spelled in full*. For example, "St. Eustache" precedes "Saint-Évariste-de-Forsyth".

Names with an **ampersand** (&) are arranged as if the ampersand were spelled "and".

Classement alphabétique et usage linguistique

Les renseignements sont présentés de manière à pouvoir répondre en un seul volume aux besoins des lecteurs francophones et anglophones. À l'exception des considérations indiquées ci-dessous, les toponymes sont classés par ordre alphabétique, lettre par lettre plutôt que mot par mot. Par exemple, «Adamsdale» précède «Adams Gulch».

(a) considérations d'ordre général relatives aux toponymes

La **ponctuation** telle que la virgule (,), le trait d'union (-) et l'apostrophe (') n'influe pas sur le classement alphabétique.

Dans le cas où l'on utilise des **abréviations** telles que «No.», «St.», «Ste.» ou «Rev.», le classement alphabétique s'effectue comme si le terme abrégé était écrit en toutes lettres. Ainsi, «St. Eustache» précède «Saint-Évariste-de-Forsyth».

L'**esperluète** (&) dans les toponymes se lit comme si le terme était épelé «and» (forme anglaise de «et»).

Names beginning with a **number** are arranged as if the number were spelled out in English, so that "70 Mile House" is listed as though it were *Seventy Mile House*. "12 Mile" precedes "Twelve Mile Stream".

Identical names are listed in the following sequence: populated places; geographical features, sorted by province/territory, longitude, and latitude.

(b) populated places and administrative areas

Most populated place and administrative area names are listed in natural language order, for example, "The Bluff", "Lake Edward", "Point Gardiner", "Cape Breton Highlands National Park" and "The Forks National Historic Site" and "Les Éboulements".

Exceptions:

- Some unincorporated entities in Quebec, as in "Greens, Le".

- When, in French, the generic precedes the specific, as in "Wood Buffalo, Parc national" and as in "Grands-Ormes, Réserve écologique des".

- Names of military bases and stations in both English and French, as in "Kingston, Canadian Forces Base" and "Alert, Station des Forces canadiennes".

- Several administrative areas in Alberta and Ontario, as in "Northern Lights No. 22, Municipal District of" and as in "Prescott and Russell, United Counties of".

(c) physical features

The names of most physical features consist of a **specific**, for example, "Pokemouche" in Pokemouche River and "Holland" in Holland Marsh, and of a **generic**, for example, "Hill" in Mosquito Berry Hill. These names are listed in alphabetical order, letter by letter, regardless of the number of words in the name, so that, for example, "Peter's River" precedes "Peter Strides Pond".

Exceptions:

- When a name begins with a generic, the word order is inverted, for example, "Doré, Lake"; "Bon-Secours, Lac de"; "False, Rivière".

- Certain well-known names where the generic precedes the specific, as in "Lake Ontario", have

Les toponymes commençant avec un **chiffre** se lisent comme si le chiffre était écrit en toutes lettres dans la langue anglaise; ainsi, «70 Mile House» se lit comme s'il était épelé «*Seventy* Mile House» et «12 Mile House» précède «Twelve Mile Stream».

Les **noms identiques** sont classés selon l'ordre suivant : premièrement, les lieux habités; et deuxièmement, les entités géographiques qui sont par la suite triées selon la province ou le territoire, la longitude et finalement la latitude.

(b) lieux habités et zones administratives

La plupart des noms de lieux habités et de zones administratives sont classés selon leur forme naturelle comme dans le cas de «The Bluff», «Lake Edward», «Point Gardiner», «Cape Breton Highlands National Park», «The Forks National Historic Site» et «Les Éboulements».

Exceptions :

- Quelques lieux non organisés au Québec, comme dans «Greens, Le».

- Quand, en français, le terme générique précède le nom propre, comme dans «Wood Buffalo, Parc national» et «Grands-Ormes, Réserve écologique des».

- Noms français et anglais de bases et de stations militaires, comme dans «Kingston, Canadian Forces Base» et «Alert, Station des Forces canadiennes».

- Plusieurs zones administratives en Alberta et en Ontario, comme dans «Northern Lights No. 22, Municipal District of» et «Prescott and Russell, United Counties of».

(c) entités physiques

Les noms de la plupart des entités physiques sont constitués d'un nom propre, le **spécifique**, comme *Pokemouche* dans «Pokemouche River» et *Holland* dans «Holland Marsh»; et d'un **générique**, comme *Hill* dans «Mosquito Berry Hill». Ces noms complets d'entités physiques sont utilisés lettre par lettre pour le classement alphabétique, ne tenant pas compte du nombre de mots formant le toponyme; ainsi, «Peter's River» précède «Peter Strides Pond».

Exceptions :

- Quand le terme générique précède le spécifique, l'ordre de classement des mots est inversé comme dans «Doré, Lake», «Bon-Secours, Lac de» et «False, Rivière».

- Certains noms bien connus dont le générique précède le spécifique, par exemple «Lake

been provided in natural language order as well as in their inverted form, "Ontario, Lake".

- When the name begins with a definite article, as in "The Beast", it is listed as "Beast, The". Similarly, "La Grande Rivière" is listed as "Grande Rivière, La".

- When French particles such as "à" or "du" occur in physical feature names, they are placed with the generic, resulting in listings such as "Chasse, Pointe à la" and "Prince-de-Galles, Cap du".

Column 2 - Entity

This column contains a three- or four-letter code indicating the general feature class to which a named place or feature has been assigned. The terms used for these categories ("entities") are applied in a general sense and not perhaps as narrowly as such a term might be used in a glossary of generics. The codes and the terms used here were examined by the Advisory Committee on Nomenclature and Delineation and approved by the CPCGN.

The tables below list the codes and terms used to refer to 34 designated categories. Examples of generics included in each category are shown. See the Glossary (page xxvii) for a definition of each category.

Ontario», sont inscrits et classés dans leur forme naturelle ainsi que sous leur forme inversée, «Ontario, Lake».

- Quand le nom commence par un article défini, comme dans «The Beast», il est inscrit et classé comme «Beast, The». De même, le toponyme «La Grande Rivière» sera inscrit et classé comme «Grande Rivière, La».

- Lorsque le nom d'une entité physique contient une particule française, comme «à» ou «du», cette particule accompagne le générique, de sorte que le nom est classé comme «Chasse, Pointe à la» et «Prince-de-Galles, Cap du».

Colonne 2 - Entité

Cette colonne contient un code à trois ou quatre lettres indiquant la classe d'entité générale où l'on a groupé les noms de lieux ou d'entités physiques. Ces catégories («entités») sont utilisées au sens large du terme et non de façon aussi précise que les termes retrouvés dans un glossaire de génériques. Les codes et les termes utilisés furent revus par le Comité consultatif de la nomenclature et de la délimitation et approuvés par le CPCNG.

Le tableau ci-dessous dresse la liste des codes et des termes utilisés pour référer aux 34 catégories d'entités désignées, accompagné d'exemples de génériques inclus dans chaque catégorie. Voir le Glossaire (à la page xxvii) pour la définition de chaque catégorie.

Table 2. Populated places, administration and geographical areas
Tableau 2. Lieux habités, zones administratives et géographiques

Entity code / Code d'entité	Entity term / Terme d'entité	Generics included / Génériques inclus
PROV / PROV	Province / Province	province
TERR / TERR	Territory / Territoire	territory, territoire
CITY / VIL1	City / Ville	city, cité, ville
TOWN / VIL2	Town / Ville	town, borough, separated town, municipality, municipalité de village
VILG / VILG	Village / Village	village, community, summer village, municipalité, resort municipality, resort village, northern village, urban community, municipalité de canton, municipalité de cantons unis, municipalité de paroisse, municipalité de village cri, municipalité de village naskapi, municipalité de village nordique
HAM / HAM	Hamlet / Hameau	hamlet, organized hamlet, northern hamlet, northern settlement, charter community
MUN1 / AZM1	Other municipal / district area - major agglomeration / Autre zone municipale / de district - agglomération majeure	metropolitan municipality, municipal district, district municipality, regional district, county, region, county municipality, restructured county, communauté urbaine, municipalité régionale de comté, municipal county, région administrative

Code	Entity term	Generics included
MUN2 / AZM2	Other municipal / district area - miscellaneous / Autre zone municipale / de district - divers	local government district, township municipality, rural municipality, improvement district, territoire non organisé, Indian government district
UNP / LNO	Unincorporated place / Lieu non organisé	hamlet, police village, rural village, settlement, compact rural community, resort, locality, lieu-dit, railway point, station, post office, landing, abandoned locality, community, dispersed rural community, hameau, northern community, unincorporated village district, vacated or seasonal settlement, station de chemin de fer, établissement amérindien, neighbourhood, suburban community, metropolitan area, secteur, local service district
IR / RI	Indian Reserve / Réserve indienne	Indian reserve, réserve indienne
GEOG / GÉOG	Geographical area / Zone géographique	county, parish, geographic district, district, royalty, settlement, territoire, geographic county, region
PARK / PARC	Conservation area / Zone de préservation	réserve de la biosphère, world heritage site, site du patrimoine mondial, national historic site, lieu historique national, national park, provincial park, parc de conservation, parc de récréation, international park, parc international, réserve écologique, parc national, réserve faunique, provincial historic site, national park reserve, réserve de parc national, waterway, voie navigable, canal
MIL / MIL	Military area / Réserve militaire	Canadian Forces Base, Base des Forces canadiennes, Canadian Forces Station, Station des Forces canadiennes

Table 3. **Physical features**
Tableau 3. **Entités physiques**

Entity code / Code d'entité	Entity term / Terme d'entité	Generics included / Génériques inclus
BAY / BAIE	Bay / Baie	bay, cove, estuaire, fjord, gulf, havre, sound
BCH / PLAG	Beach / Plage	beach, bar, dune
CAPE / CAP	Cape / Cap	cape, head, peninsula, côte, presqu'île, cap, promontoire, foreland, spit, point
CAVE / CAV	Cave / Caverne	grotte
CHAN / CHEN	Channel / Chenal	channel, chenal, pass, passage, narrows, strait, détroit, basin
CLF / ESC	Cliff / Escarpement	bank, cliff, bluff, falaise, blow-me-down, berge, escarpement
FALL / CHUT	Falls / Chute	falls, cascade, cascades, fall, chute, sault, waterfall
GLAC / GLAC	Glacier / Glacier	glacier, icefield, ice cap / icecap
ISL / ÎLE	Island / Île	island, isle, archipelago, group, île, archipel, rocher
LAKE / LAC	Lake / Lac	lake, pond, reservoir, lagoon, barasway, flowage, loch, mal bay, lac, lagune, réservoir
MISC / DIV	Miscellaneous / Divers	centrale hydroélectrique, port, dam, drain, barrage, canal de dérivation, floodway, canal
MTN / MNT	Mountain / Mont	range, mountain, peak, hill, ridge, bluff, dune, butte, pinnacles, mount, mont, foothills, dome, tower, colline, sommet, sand hills, montagnes, massif, chaîne, paroi
PLN / PLNE	Plain / Plaine	plateau, plain, uplands
RAP / RAP	Rapids / Rapides	rapids, rapides, rapide, run
RIV / CDE	River / Cours d'eau	river, brook, creek, fleuve, branch, millstream, ruisseau, stream, rivière, fork, channel
RIVF / EFLV	River feature / Entité fluviale	bend, reach, stillwater, courant, stretch
SEA / MER	Sea / Mer	ocean, sea, mer, océan
SEAU / SMER	Undersea feature /	abyssal plain, plaine, bank, banc, basin, bassin, canyon, continental

	Entité sous-marine	margin, marge continentale, escarpment, talus, fan, cône, pingos, fracture zone, zone de fractures, gap, passage, guyot, knoll, dôme, marginal trough, cuvette marginale, median valley, vallée axiale, pass, col, seamount chain, chaîne de monts, seamounts, monts sous-marins, ridge, dorsale, rise, massif, saddle, shoal, haut-fond, sill, seuil, shelf, plate-forme continentale, slope, pente, spur, éperon, terrace, terrasse, trough, cuvette, valley, vallée
SHL / H-FD	Shoal / Haut-fond	ledge, rock, récifs
VALL / VALL	Valley / Vallée	valley, canyon, pass, trench, vallée, coulee
VEGL / VÉGB	Low vegetation / Végétation basse	meadow, marsh

Column 3 - Location 1 (Loc 1)

This column shows the first level of locational information for geographical names in Canada: province, territory, or undersea, each identified by a two-letter code. The code and full name of each are shown in Table 4 on page xxiv. As of 1997 there are ten provinces and two territories. (Nunavut, which will exist as a territory after 1 April 1999, is today still part of the Northwest Territories.)

In most cases, only one province or territory is listed for each name. However, there are some features which cross one or more provincial and/or territorial boundary and in such cases, each of these locational codes is included.

Four populated places in Canada straddle the boundary between two provinces: Lloydminster, Flin Flon, Pointe-Fortune, and Crowsnest. How they are listed depends on their administrative status within each province.

Column 4 - Location 2 (Loc 2)

The second level of locational information (i.e., a land division within the province or territory) is shown in Column 4. Newfoundland, Yukon Territory, and undersea do not have land divisions, therefore, the column remains blank.

Provincial and territorial land divisions

- Most of Alberta, Manitoba, and Saskatchewan is divided into **Sections, Townships**, and **Ranges**, relative to one of seven meridians. Where available, this information is shown in Arabic numerals separated by hyphens.

Colonne 3 - Lieu 1 (Lieu 1)

Cette colonne montre le premier niveau de référence relatif à l'emplacement des toponymes du Canada : la province, le territoire ou une entité sous-marine, tous identifiés à l'aide d'un code à deux lettres. On retrouve les codes et le noms complet au Tableau 4 à la page xxiv. En 1997, le Canada se compose de dix provinces et de deux territoires. (Nunavut, un territoire qui entrera en vigueur le 1er avril 1999, fait encore partie aujourd'hui des Territoires du Nord-Ouest.)

Dans la plupart des cas, une seule province ou un seul territoire accompagne chaque toponyme. Il y a toutefois des entités qui traversent plus d'une province ou plus d'un territoire et, dans ces cas-là, tous les codes pertinents sont indiqués.

Quatre lieux habités au Canada chevauchent la frontière entre deux provinces : Lloydminster, Flin Flon, Pointe-Fortune et Crowsnest. Leur statut administratif à l'intérieur de chaque province détermine leur traitement dans ce volume.

Colonne 4 - Lieu 2 (Lieu 2)

Cette colonne montre le deuxième niveau de référence relatif à l'emplacement des toponymes, c'est-à-dire les divisions territoriales à l'intérieur des provinces ou territoires. Puisque Terre-Neuve, le Territoire du Yukon et les entités sous-marines n'ont pas de divisions territoriales, il n'y a pas d'entrée dans cette colonne.

Divisions territoriales dans les provinces et les territoires

- Les provinces de l'Alberta, du Manitoba et de la Saskatchewan sont divisées en grande majorité en «**sections**», «**cantons**» et «**rangs**» selon leur relation à un des sept méridiens. Lorsque disponibles, ces données sont montrées en chiffres arabes séparés par un trait d'union.

Examples:

49-11-W4	Township 49, Range 11, west of the Fourth Meridian
22,23-23-W2	Townships 22 and 23, Range 23, west of the Second Meridian
11-9-24-W	Section 11, Township 9, Range 24, west of the Principal Meridian
7-11-14-E	Section 7, Township 11, Range 14, east of the Principal Meridian
25,27,36-8-16,17-E	Sections 25, 27, and 36, Township 8, Ranges 16 and 17, east of the Principal Meridian

Exemples :

49-11-W4	Canton 49, Rang 11, à l'ouest du quatrième méridien
22,23-23-W2	Cantons 22 et 23, Rang 23, à l'ouest du deuxième méridien
11-9-24-W	Section 11, Canton 9, Rang 24, à l'ouest du premier méridien
7-11-14-E	Section 7, Canton 11, Rang 14, à l'est du premier méridien
25,27,36-8-16,17-E	Sections 25, 27, et 36, Canton 8, Rangs 16 et 17, à l'est du premier méridien

- British Columbia is divided into **Land Districts**.

- New Brunswick, Nova Scotia, and Prince Edward Island use **County** as their primary land division.

- Northwest Territories: the names of the three historic **Districts**, created when the territory was established at its present size, are used.

- Ontario uses **County** in the southern part of the province and **District** in the northern part.

- For Quebec, the administrative division, **Municipalité régionale de comté** (County Regional Municipality), rather than a geographic division, is shown for most entries.

- La Colombie-Britannique est divisée en «**Land Districts**» (districts des terres).

- Le Nouveau-Brunswick, la Nouvelle-Écosse et l'Île-du-Prince-Édouard utilisent le «**County**» (comté) comme principale division territoriale.

- Les Territoires du Nord-Ouest utilisent les noms des trois **districts** historiques créés lors de l'établissement du territoire actuel.

- Ontario utilise le **comté** dans la partie sud de la province et le **district** dans sa partie nord.

- Au Québec, une division administrative, la **municipalité régionale de comté**, plutôt qu'une division géographique est indiquée pour la plupart des entrées.

Table 4. Codes and locational information
Tableau 4. Codes et renseignements d'emplacement

Code	Location 1 / Lieu 1	Location 2 / Lieu 2
AB	Alberta	Section, Township, Range / Section, Canton, Rang
BC	British Columbia / Colombie-Britannique	Land District / District des terres
MB	Manitoba	Section, Township, Range / Section, Canton, Rang
NB	New Brunswick / Nouveau-Brunswick	County / Comté
NF	Newfoundland / Terre-Neuve	----
NS	Nova Scotia / Nouvelle-Écosse	County / Comté
NT	Northwest Territories / Territoires du Nord-Ouest	District
ON	Ontario	County, District / Comté, District
PE	Prince Edward Island / Île-du-Prince-Édouard	County / Comté
QC	Quebec / Québec	County Regional Municipality / Municipalité régionale de comté
SK	Saskatchewan	Section, Township, Range / Section, Canton, Rang
SM	Undersea areas / Zones sous-marines	----
YT	Yukon Territory / Territoire du Yukon	----

Column 5 - Map

Column 5 indicates the National Topographic System (NTS) map, Canadian Hydrographic Service (CHS) chart, or other map or chart on which a feature is located. Maps or charts are not cited for a few international water features.

An **NTS** map is labelled by an alpha-numeric identifier, such as 1 C/6, 11 L/5, 93 A/4, and 105 A/1.

Some large features are referenced to Map Compilation and Reproduction (**MCR**) maps; these are indicated with the letters MCR and followed by two or three numbers, for example, MCR 77 and MCR 130.

Undersea features appear on several different kinds of maps and charts:

- A **CHS** chart is identified by a series of four numbers, as in 4485.

- A three-digit number, sometimes followed by a letter, for example, 850 or 811A, indicates a CHS **non-series bathymetric** map.

- A **Natural Resource Map (Bathymetry)** has an alpha-numeric identifier with five numbers followed by one letter, such as 15182A.

- A General Bathymetric Chart of the Oceans (**GEBCO**) chart has a three-digit decimal number, for example, 5.17 or 5.04.

- A Geological Survey of Canada (**GSC**) map has an alpha-numeric identifier with four numbers followed by a letter, such as 1399A.

- A National Earth Science Series (**NESS**) map is identified either by two letters followed by two or four numbers, (e.g., NK23, NT1216) or by two letters followed by two numbers and a letter, for example NK21 B.

These maps and charts have a variety of scales.

Colonne 5 - Carte

Dans la colonne 5, on peut retrouver soit le numéro d'une carte du Système national de référence cartographique (SNRC), soit le numéro d'une carte hydrographique du Service hydrographique du Canada (SHC) ou soit une variété de cartes de référence qui donne l'emplacement du toponyme. Dans le cas des entités hydrographiques internationales, aucun renseignement cartographique ne sera fourni.

Une carte du **SNRC** est identifiée par un code alphanumérique tel que 1 C/6, 11 L/5, 93 A/4 et 105 A/1.

Quelques entités importantes sont identifiées par une carte de la série «Map Compilation and Reproduction» (**MCR**); à la colonne 5 de l'entrée, il y aura donc les lettres MCR suivies de deux ou trois chiffres, comme dans MCR 77 et MCR 130.

Les entités sous-marines se retrouvent sur plusieurs types de cartes :

- Une carte hydrographique du **SHC** est représentée par une série de quatre chiffres, comme dans 4485.

- Un code à trois chiffres, parfois suivi d'une lettre, comme dans 850 ou 811A, indique une carte bathymétrique hors-série.

- Une **carte des ressources naturelles (Bathymétrique)** se compose d'un code alphanumérique de cinq chiffres suivi d'une lettre, comme dans 15182A.

- Une carte **GEBCO** («General Bathymetric Chart of the Oceans») est représentée par trois chiffres avec des décimales, comme dans 5.17 ou 5.04.

- Une carte de la Commission géologique du Canada (**C G C**) se compose d'un code alphanumérique de quatre chiffres suivis d'une lettre, comme dans 1399A.

- Une carte de la Série nationale de la science de la Terre (**SNST**) est identifiée soit par deux lettres suivies de deux ou quatre chiffres (comme dans NK23 et NT1216), ou de deux lettres suivies de deux chiffres et d'une lettre, comme dans NK21 B.

Ces cartes sont représentées à une variété d'échelles.

Table 5. Map and chart scales
Tableau 5. Échelles des cartes

Type	Examples / Exemples	Scales / Échelles
CHS / SHC	8010	various / diverses
GEBCO	5.03 / 5.04 / 5.07	1: 10 000 000
GEBCO	5.17	1: 6 000 000
GSC/CGC	1399A	1: 2 000 000
MCR	MCR 77	various / diverses
NESS / SNST	NK23	1: 1 000 000
NRM / CRN	15182A	1: 250 000
NTS / SNRC	64 H	1: 250 000
NTS / SNRC	30 M/11	1: 50 000
Non-series maps / Cartes hors-série	800 / 814A	1: 1 000 000 - 1: 6 750 000

Columns 6 - Latitude (Lat) and Column - 7 Longitude (Long)

Position information is provided by the latitude and longitude coordinates in Columns 6 and 7. The geographic coordinates indicate the **centre** of each feature, except in the following circumstances:

- for flowing water features (coded as RIV/CDE), the coordinates are those of the **mouth**

- for glaciers, the coordinates are those of the **tongue** of the glacier

- for undersea canyons, the position of the **head** of the canyon is given

Latitude is measured in degrees and minutes north and south of the Equator (for example, 57°40' N). Longitude is measured east and west of 0° meridian at Greenwich, England (for example, 113°50' W). As all of Canada is north of the Equator and west of Greenwich, the "N" and "W" have been omitted from the latitude and longitude columns.

Most new name decisions made by CPCGN members now include coordinates in degrees, minutes, and seconds, but the majority of earlier CPCGN records remain in degrees and minutes only. For consistency, coordinates shown in Columns 6 and 7 are all rounded to the nearest minute.

Colonne 6 - Latitude (Lat) et colonne 7 - Longitude (Long)

Les coordonnées de longitude et de latitude donnent la position des toponymes. Les coordonnées géographiques correspondent au **point central** de chaque entité, sauf dans les cas suivants :

- pour les entités de cours d'eau (code RIV/CDE), les coordonnées représentent l'**embouchure**

- pour les glaciers, les coordonnées sont celles de la **langue** glaciaire

- pour les canyons sous-marins, les coordonnées de la **tête** du canyon sont indiquées

La latitude se mesure en degrés et minutes utilisant l'équateur comme ligne de division entre le nord et le sud (par exemple 57°40' N). La longitude utilise le méridien 0° situé à Greenwich, Angleterre comme ligne de division entre l'est et l'ouest (par exemple 113°50' O). Comme tout le Canada se trouve au nord de l'équateur et à l'ouest de Greenwich, le «N» et le «O» ne sont pas inclus dans les colonnes de longitude et de latitude.

Par souci d'uniformité, les coordonnées montrées dans les colonnes 6 et 7 sont toutes à la minute près. La plupart des nouveaux toponymes approuvés par les membres du CPCNG sont maintenant à la seconde près; toutefois, la majorité des entrées toponymiques consignées dans le passé le furent seulement à la minute près et n'ont pas encore été mise à jour à la seconde près.

GLOSSARY OF ENTITY TERMS

This glossary includes a broad range of generic terms grouped together under entity terms (i.e., feature categories). The groupings incorporate the generic terms as used in officially approved geographical names in Canada.

For each entry, the **entity code** appears first, followed by the **entity** to which the code is assigned, its **definition**, and some **examples of the generic terms** included in the category.

BAY
bay: water area in an indentation of the shoreline of seas, lakes, and rivers (bay, cove, estuaire, fjord, gulf, havre, sound)

BCH
beach: gently sloping shore of unconsolidated material along the margins of a sea, lake, or river (beach, bar, dune)

CAPE
cape: elevated projection of land extending into a body of water (cape, head, peninsula, côte, presqu'île, cap, promontoire, foreland, spit, point)

CAVE
cave: natural subterranean chamber open to the surface; may be inland or in coastal cliffs (grotte)

CHAN
channel: narrow stretch of water; an inlet or a connection between two bodies of water (channel, chenal, pass, passage, narrows, strait, détroit, basin)

CITY
city: populated place with legally-defined boundaries, usually incorporated under a provincial or territorial Municipal Act; the highest level of municipal incorporation (city, cité, ville)

CLF
cliff: high steep face of rock and/or unconsolidated material (bluff, falaise, escarpement, cliffs, escarpment, coteau)

FALL
falls: perpendicular or steep descent of water; may be confined within steep walls and flow quickly (falls, chute, chutes)

GLOSSAIRE DES TERMES RELATIFS AUX ENTITÉS

Ce glossaire comprend une gamme plus large de termes génériques regroupés dans des catégories d'entités. Ces regroupements contiennent les génériques utilisés dans la toponymie officielle du Canada.

Chaque entrée comprend : le **code d'entité** suivi du **terme d'entité** associée au code, sa **définition** et quelques **exemples de génériques** compris dans la catégorie.

BAIE
baie : partie d'une mer, d'un lac ou d'un grand cours d'eau occupant une échancrure du littoral (bay, cove, estuaire, fjord, gulf, havre, sound)

PLAG
plage : partie du rivage d'un lac, d'une mer ou d'un cours d'eau, de faible pente et constituée de matériaux non consolidés (beach, bar, dune)

CAP
cap : saillie de terre élevée qui s'avance dans une étendue d'eau (cape, head, peninsula, côte, presqu'île, cap, promontoire, foreland, spit, point)

CAV
caverne : cavité naturelle souterraine et ouverte sur l'extérieur; peut être creusée dans les terres ou dans des falaises côtières (grotte)

CHEN
chenal : bande d'eau étroite et allongée, qui prolonge une étendue d'eau ou qui met en communication deux étendues d'eau (channel, chenal, pass, passage, narrows strait, détroit, basin)

VIL1
ville : lieu habité dont les limites sont définies par la loi, habituellement constitué en vertu de la Loi sur les municipalités de la province ou du territoire; le niveau le plus élevé de constitution municipale (city, cité, ville)

ESC
escarpement : paroi abrupte et élevée, constituée de roc ou de matériaux non consolidés, ou des deux (bluff, falaise, escarpement, cliffs, escarpment, coteau)

CHUT
chute : rupture de pente perpendiculaire ou brusque d'où tombe une masse d'eau; peut être enserrée entre des berges abruptes où l'eau s'écoule brusquement (falls, chute, chutes)

GEOG
geographical area: legally-designated land subdivision of a province or territory (county, comté, parish, paroisse, geographic district, district, royalty, settlement, territoire, geographic county, region)

GLAC
glacier: mass of permanent snow and ice (glacier, icefield, ice cap / icecap)

HAM
hamlet: populated place with legally-defined boundaries, usually incorporated under a provincial or territorial Municipal Act, of lesser status than a town (hamlet, organized hamlet, northern hamlet, northern settlement, charter community)

IR
indian reserve: tract of land set apart for the use and benefit of a particular Indian band (Indian reserve, réserve indienne)

ISL
island: land area surrounded by water or marsh (island, isle, archipelago, group, île, archipel, rocher)

LAKE
lake: inland body of standing water or an expansion of a river; body of water separated from a lake, river, or sea by a narrow land barrier (lake, pond, reservoir, lagoon, barasway, flowage, loch, mal bay, lac, lagune, réservoir)

MIL
military area: established base or station for the operations of the armed forces (Canadian Forces Base, Base des Forces canadiennes, Canadian Forces Station, Station des Forces canadiennes)

MISC
miscellaneous: constructed features used in shipping, agriculture, resource development, or flood control (centrale hydroélectrique, port, dam, drain, barrage, canal de dérivation, floodway, canal)

MTN
mountain: mass of land prominently elevated above the surrounding terrain, bounded by steep slopes and rising to a summit and/or peaks; in plural may refer to a whole region including peaks, mountains, and intervening valleys (range, mountain, peak, hill, ridge, bluff, dune, butte, pinnacles, mount, mont, foothills, dome, tower, colline, sommet, sand hills, montagnes, massif, chaîne, paroi)

GÉOG
zone géographique : subdivision territoriale d'une province ou d'un territoire dont les limites sont définies par la loi (county, comté, parish, paroisse, geographic district, district, royalty, settlement, territoire, geographic county, region)

GLAC
glacier : masse de neige et de glace éternelles (glacier, icefield, ice cap / icecap)

HAM
hameau : lieu habité dont les limites sont définies par la loi, habituellement constitué en vertu de la Loi des municipalités de la province ou du territoire, et de statut moindre qu'une ville (hamlet, organized hamlet, northern hamlet, northern settlement, charter community)

RI
réserve indienne : étendue de terrain réservée à l'usage et au profit d'une tribu spécifique d'Autochtones (Indian reserve, réserve indienne)

ÎLE
île : masse de terre entourée d'eau ou de marécages (island, isle, archipelago, group, île, archipel, rocher)

LAC
lac : nappe d'eau dormante dans les terres ou un élargissement d'une rivière; étendue d'eau complètement ou partiellement isolée d'un lac, d'une rivière ou d'une mer par une étroite barrière de terre (lake, pond, reservoir, lagoon, barasway, flowage, loch, mal bay, lac, lagune, réservoir)

MIL
réserve militaire : base ou station établies pour les activités des Forces armées (Canadian Forces Base, Base des Forces canadiennes, Canadian Forces Station, Station des Forces canadiennes)

DIV
divers : entités artificielles relatives à la navigation, à l'agriculture, au développement des ressources ou au contrôle de la crue des eaux (centrale hydroélectrique, port, dam, drain, barrage, canal de dérivation, floodway, canal)

MNT
mont : élévation de terrain aux versants raides se détachant du relief environnant et se terminant par un sommet ou un ou plusieurs pics; au pluriel, le mot s'applique parfois à l'ensemble des pics des montagnes et des vallées intermédiaires d'une région donnée (range, mountain, peak, hill, ridge, bluff, dune, butte, pinnacles, mount, mont, foothills, dome, tower, colline, sommet, sand hills, montagnes, massif, chaîne, paroi)

MUN1

other municipal / district area - major agglomeration: a legally-defined land area ; larger in area than a city, town, or village, usually an upper tier administrative division of a province (metropolitan municipality, municipal district, district municipality, regional district, county, region, county municipality, restructured county, communauté urbaine, municipalité régionale de comté, municipal county, région administrative)

MUN2

other municipal / district area - miscellaneous: legally-defined land area; administrative division of a province (local government district, township municipality, rural municipality, improvement district, territoire non organisé, Indian government district)

PARK

conservation area: property, whether a site of nature or a work of man, that is of interest for its architectural, historical, cultural, environmental, aesthetic, or scientific value (réserve de la biosphère, world heritage site, site du patrimoine mondial, national historic site, lieu historique national, national park, provincial park, parc de conservation, parc de récréation, international park, parc international, réserve écologique, parc national, réserve faunique, provincial historic site, national park reserve, réserve de parc national, waterway, voie navigable, canal)

PLN

plain: area of flat or gently rolling terrain (plateau, plain, uplands)

PROV

province: the principal administrative division of Canada, it is a legally-defined area, as established by Articles of Confederation or Constitutional Amendment (province)

RAP

rapids: fast-flowing section of a watercourse, usually with turbulent water or exposed rocks (rapids, rapides, rapide, run)

RIV

river: watercourse of varying size which flows into another body of water (river, brook, creek, fleuve, branch, millstream, ruisseau, stream, rivière, fork, channel)

RIVF

river feature: a part of a watercourse (bend, reach, stillwater, courant, stretch)

AZM1

autre zone municipale / de district - agglomération majeure : une division territoriale définie par la loi; sa superficie est plus grande que celle d'une ville ou d'un village, et habituellement un niveau plus élevé de division administrative d'une province (metropolitan municipality, municipal district, district municipality, regional district, county, region, county municipality, restructured county, communauté urbaine, municipalité régionale de comté, municipal county, région administrative)

AZM2

autre zone municipale / de district - divers : une division territoriale définie par la loi; division administrative d'une province (local government district, township municipality, rural municipality, improvement district, territoire non organisé, Indian government district)

PARC

zone de préservation : propriété, site de la nature résultant du travail de l'homme, ayant une valeur architecturale, historique, culturelle, environnementale, esthétique ou scientifique (réserve de la biosphère, world heritage site, site du patrimoine mondial, national historic site, lieu historique national, national park, provincial park, parc de conservation, parc de récréation, international park, parc international, réserve écologique, parc national, réserve faunique, provincial historic site, national park reserve, réserve de parc national, waterway, voie navigable, canal)

PLNE

plaine : étendue de terrain à surface plane ou légèrement ondulée (plateau, plain, uplands)

PROV

province : la principale division administrative du Canada; il s'agit d'une zone délimitée par voie légale et établie par des articles de la Confédération ou une modification de la Constitution (province)

RAP

rapides : partie d'un cours d'eau généralement hérissée de rochers, où le courant est rapide et souvent turbulent (rapids, rapides, rapide, run)

CDE

cours d'eau : cours d'eau de dimension variable et se déversant dans une nappe d'eau ou un autre cours d'eau plus important (river, brook, creek, fleuve, branch, millstream, ruisseau, stream, rivière, fork, channel)

EFLV

entité fluviale : partie d'un cours d'eau (bend, reach, stillwater, courant, stretch)

SEA

sea: large body of salt water (ocean, sea, mer, océan)

SEAU

undersea feature: part of the ocean floor or seabed that has measurable relief or is delimited by relief and is submerged at low tide (abyssal plain, plaine, bank, banc, basin, bassin, canyon, continental margin, marge continentale, escarpment, talus, fan, cône, pingos, fracture zone, zone de fractures, gap, passage, guyot, knoll, dôme, marginal trough, cuvette marginale, median valley, vallée axiale, pass, seamount chain, chaîne de monts, seamounts, monts sous-marins, ridge, dorsale, rise, massif, saddle, col, shoal, haut-fond, sill, seuil, shelf, plate-forme continentale, slope, pente, spur, éperon, terrace, terrasse, trough, cuvette, valley, vallée)

SHL

shoal: elevation of the bed of a body of water; composed of unconsolidated material and posing a hazard to surface navigation (ledge, rock, récifs)

TERR

territory: administrative division of Canada, not yet admitted to the full rights of a province (territory, territoire)

TOWN

town: a populated place with legally-defined boundaries, usually incorporated under a provincial Municipal Act; of lesser status than a city (town, borough, separated town, municipality, municipalité de village)

UNP

unincorporated place: an unincorporated place, sometimes with a semi-official status (hamlet, police village, rural village, settlement, compact rural community, resort, locality, lieu-dit, railway point, station, post office, landing, abandoned locality, community, dispersed rural community, hameau, northern community, unincorporated village district, vacated or seasonal settlement, station de chemin de fer, établissement amérindien, neighbourhood, suburban community, metropolitan area, secteur, local service district)

VALL

valley: long relatively narrow depression, commonly containing a river or other water feature (valley, canyon, pass, trench, vallée, coulee)

VEGL

vegetation, low: area of low-lying land, flooded (often or seasonally), and usually characterized by grass and/or reeds (meadow, marsh)

MER

mer : vaste étendue d'eau salée (ocean, sea, mer, océan)

SMER

entité sous-marine : partie du fond de l'océan ou du lit océanique qui a un relief mesurable ou est délimitée par un relief, et qui est submergée à marée basse (abyssal plain, plaine, bank, banc, basin, bassin, canyon, continental margin, marge continentale, escarpment, talus, fan, cône, pingos, fracture zone, zone de fractures, gap, passage, guyot, knoll, dôme, marginal trough, cuvette marginale, median valley, vallée axiale, pass, seamount chain, chaîne de monts, seamounts, monts sous-marins, ridge, dorsale, rise, massif, saddle, col, shoal, haut-fond, sill, seuil, shelf, plate-forme continentale, slope, pente, spur, éperon, terrace, terrasse, trough, cuvette, valley, vallée)

H-FD

haut-fond : élévation du lit d'une étendue d'eau constituée de matériaux non consolidés et présentant un risque pour la navigation de surface (ledge, rock, récifs)

TERR

territoire : division administrative du Canada, n'ayant pas encore le statut d'une province (territory, territoire)

VIL2

ville : un lieu habité dont les limites sont définies par la loi, habituellement constitué en vertu de la Loi sur les municipalités de la province ou du territoire; de moindre statut qu'une ville plus importante (town, borough, separated town, municipality, municipalité de village)

LNO

lieu non organisé : un lieu non organisé dont le statut est parfois semi-officiel (hamlet, police village, rural village, settlement, compact rural community, resort, locality, lieu-dit, railway point, station, post office, landing, abandoned locality, community, dispersed rural community, hameau, northern community, unincorporated village district, vacated or seasonal settlement, station de chemin de fer, établissement amérindien, neighbourhood, suburban community, metropolitan area, secteur, local service district)

VALL

vallée : dépression de forme allongée et relativement étroite, souvent parcourue par un cours d'eau (valley, canyon, pass, trench, vallée, coulee)

VÉGB

végétation basse : terrain bas, plat et inondé (souvent ou de façon saisonnière) et occupé par une végétation herbeuse et/ou de roseaux (meadow, marsh)

village: populated place with legally-defined boundaries, usually incorporated under the Municipal Act of the province or territory in which it is found; of lesser status than a town (village, community, summer village, municipalité, resort municipality, resort village, northern village, urban community, municipalité de canton, municipalité de canton unis, municipalité de paroisse, municipalité de village cri, municipalité de village naskapi, municipalité de village nordique)

village : lieu habité dont les limites sont définies par la loi, habituellement constitué en vertu de la Loi sur les municipalités de la province ou du territoire; de statut moindre qu'une ville (village, community, summer village, municipalité, resort municipality, resort village, northern village, urban community, municipalité de canton, municipalité de canton unis, municipalité de paroisse, municipalité de village cri, municipalité de village naskapi, municipalité de village nordique)

CONCISE GAZETTEER OF CANADA

RÉPERTOIRE TOPONYMIQUE CONCIS DU CANADA

NAME NOM	ENTITY ENTITÉ	LOC 1 LIEU 1	LOC 2 LIEU 2	MAP CARTE	POSITION LAT	POSITION LONG

A

NAME NOM	ENTITY ENTITÉ	LOC 1 LIEU 1	LOC 2 LIEU 2	MAP CARTE	LAT	LONG
Aalders Landing	UNP/LNO	NS	Annapolis	21 A/15	44°50′	64°55′
Aasiwaskwasich	UNP/LNO	QC	Kativik	33 N/2	55°06′	76°53′
Aass 3	IR/RI	BC	Nootka	92 E/10	49°37′	126°49′
Abamasagi Lake	LAKE/LAC	ON	Thunder Bay	42 L/6	50°28′	87°15′
Abamategwia Lake	LAKE/LAC	ON	Kenora	52 G/12	49°40′	91°54′
Abana	UNP/LNO	QC	Abitibi-Ouest	32 D/14	48°57′	79°21′
Abattis, L′	UNP/LNO	QC	Charlevoix	21 M/2	47°14′	70°36′
Abbé-Huard, Rivière de l′	RIV/CDE	QC	Minganie	12 L/14	50°59′	63°17′
Abbey	VILG/VILG	SK	31-20-20-W3	72 K/10	50°44′	108°45′
Abbot Pass Refuge Cabin National Historic Site - also-aussi - Refuge-du-Col-Abbot, Lieu historique national du	PARK/PARC	AB		82 N/8	51°22′	116°17′
Abbotsford	CITY/VIL1	BC	New Westminster	92 G/1	49°04′	122°15′
Abbotsford	UNP/LNO	BC	New Westminster	92 G/1	49°03′	122°17′
Abbott	UNP/LNO	SK	21-7-18-W2	72 H/9	49°35′	104°24′
Abbott′s Corner	UNP/LNO	QC	Brome-Missisquoi	31 H/2	45°02′	72°48′
Abee	UNP/LNO	AB	1-61-21-W4	83 I/3	54°14′	113°02′
Abénakis	UNP/LNO	QC	Bellechasse	21 L/10	46°35′	70°49′
Abenakis Springs	UNP/LNO	QC	Nicolet-Yamaska	31 I/2	46°05′	72°52′
Abénaquis, Lac des	LAKE/LAC	QC	Les Etchemins	21 L/1	46°10′	70°22′
Abénaquis, Rivière des	RIV/CDE	QC	Bellechasse	21 L/10	46°35′	70°49′
Aberarder	UNP/LNO	ON	Lambton	40 O/1	43°03′	82°06′
Abercorn	TOWN/VIL2	QC	Brome-Missisquoi	31 H/2	45°02′	72°40′
Abercrombie	UNP/LNO	NS	Pictou	11 E/10	45°38′	62°41′
Aberdeen	TOWN/VIL2	SK	6-39-2-W3	73 B/8	52°19′	106°17′
Aberdeen	UNP/LNO	NS	Inverness	11 F/14	45°59′	61°03′
Aberdeen	UNP/LNO	ON	Prescott	31 G/7	45°30′	74°40′
Aberdeen	UNP/LNO	ON	Grey	41 A/2	44°12′	80°52′
Aberdeen	UNP/LNO	BC	Kamloops Division Yale	92 I/9	50°39′	120°22′
Aberdeen	UNP/LNO	BC	New Westminster	92 G/1	49°03′	122°25′
Aberdeen	GEOG/GÉOG	NB	Carleton	21 J/11	46°30′	67°18′
Aberdeen Lake	LAKE/LAC	BC	Osoyoos Division Yale	82 L/3	50°07′	119°03′
Aberdeen Lake	LAKE/LAC	NT	Keewatin	66 B	64°30′	99°00′
Aberdeen No. 373	MUN2/AZM2	SK		73 B/8	52°20′	106°15′
Aberfeldy	UNP/LNO	ON	Lambton	40 I/13	42°45′	81°56′
Aberfeldy	UNP/LNO	SK	28-49-27-W3	73 F/5	53°15′	109°53′
Aberfoyle	UNP/LNO	ON	Wellington	40 P/8	43°28′	80°09′
Abernethy	VILG/VILG	SK	25-20-11-W2	62 L/11	50°45′	103°25′
Abernethy No. 186	MUN2/AZM2	SK	25-20-11-W2	62 L/11	50°45′	103°30′
Abijévis, Collines	MTN/MNT	QC	Rouyn-Noranda	32 D/7	48°29′	78°46′
Abilene	UNP/LNO	AB	18-59-10-W4	73 L/3	54°07′	111°30′
Abingdon	UNP/LNO	ON	Lincoln	30 M/4	43°05′	79°41′
Abino, Point	CAPE/CAP	ON	Welland	30 L/14	42°50′	79°06′
Abitau Lake	LAKE/LAC	NT	Mackenzie	75 B	60°27′	107°15′
Abitau River	RIV/CDE	SK/NT		74 N/14	59°53′	109°03′
Abitibi	MUN1/AZM1	QC	Abitibi	32 D/9	48°34′	78°00′
Abitibi	UNP/LNO	ON	Cochrane	42 H/2	49°02′	80°53′
Abitibi 70	IR/RI	ON	Cochrane	32 D/12	48°35′	79°59′
Abitibi Canyon	UNP/LNO	ON	Cochrane	42 H/13	49°52′	81°34′
Abitibi, Lac - also-aussi - **Abitibi, Lake**	LAKE/LAC	ON/QC		32 D/13	48°42′	79°44′
Abitibi, Lake - also-aussi - **Abitibi, Lac**	LAKE/LAC	ON/QC		32 D/13	48°42′	79°44′
Abitibi-Ouest	MUN1/AZM1	QC	Abitibi-Ouest	32 D/11	48°45′	79°10′
Abitibi River	RIV/CDE	ON	Cochrane	42 P/2	51°03′	80°55′
Abitibi-Témiscamingue	MUN1/AZM1	QC	Vallée-de-l′Or	32 C/4	48°06′	77°47′
Abiwin	UNP/LNO	ON	Rainy River	52 B/11	48°44′	91°04′
Abney	UNP/LNO	PE	Kings	11 E/15	45°59′	62°34′
Abound	UNP/LNO	SK	34-15-28-W2	72 I/5	50°19′	105°46′
Aboushagan Road	UNP/LNO	NB	Westmorland	21 H/16	45°59′	64°21′
Abraham Bay	BAY/BAIE	NT	Franklin	26 H	65°07′	64°26′
Abraham-Bell, Rivière	RIV/CDE	QC	Les Basques	22 C/2	48°00′	69°00′
Abraham Lake	LAKE/LAC	AB	37,38-17,18-W5	83 C/1	52°13′	116°26′
Abrahams Cove	UNP/LNO	NF		12 B/10	48°32′	58°55′
Abrams River	UNP/LNO	NS	Yarmouth	20 P/13	43°50′	65°57′
Abrams Village	VILG/VILG	PE	Prince	21 I/8	46°27′	64°05′
Abri-du-Vent-de-Nord, L′	UNP/LNO	QC	Le Haut-Richelieu	31 H/3	45°06′	73°17′
Abuntlet Lake 4	IR/RI	BC	Range 3 Coast	93 C/11	52°34′	125°24′
Acaciaville	UNP/LNO	NS	Digby	21 A/12	44°35′	65°46′
Academy	UNP/LNO	NS	Pictou	11 E/10	45°36′	62°36′
Academy	UNP/LNO	AB	10-22-1-W5	82 J/16	50°51′	114°03′
Acadia, Cape	CAPE/CAP	NT	Keewatin	35 E	61°33′	79°48′
Acadia Cove	BAY/BAIE	NT	Franklin	25 H	61°20′	64°54′
Acadia No. 34, Municipal District of	MUN1/AZM1	AB		72 M/1	51°06′	110°13′
Acadia Valley	UNP/LNO	AB	27-25-2-W4	72 M/1	51°09′	110°13′
Acadieville	UNP/LNO	NB	Kent	21 I/11	46°44′	65°16′

NAME NOM	ENTITY ENTITÉ	LOC 1 LIEU 1	LOC 2 LIEU 2	MAP CARTE	POSITION	
					LAT	LONG
Acadieville	GEOG/GÉOG	NB	Kent	21 I/11	46°43′	65°20′
Acamac	UNP/LNO	NB	Saint John	21 G/8	45°16′	66°09′
Acanthus	UNP/LNO	ON	Nipissing	31 L/1	46°02′	78°24′
Acasta Lake	LAKE/LAC	NT	Mackenzie	86 G	65°22′	115°33′
Acasta River	RIV/CDE	NT	Mackenzie	86 C	64°47′	116°20′
Achakakunikach	UNP/LNO	QC	Kativik	33 O/2	55°12′	74°58′
Acheninni Lake	LAKE/LAC	SK	63,64-7-W2	63 L/6	54°30′	103°00′
Acheron Head	CAPE/CAP	NT	Franklin	69 B	76°27′	101°54′
Acheson	UNP/LNO	AB	4-53-26-W4	83 H/12	53°34′	113°46′
Achigan	UNP/LNO	ON	Algoma	41 K/16	46°53′	84°10′
Achigan, Lac de l'	LAKE/LAC	QC	Pontiac	31 K/3	46°15′	77°06′
Achill	UNP/LNO	ON	Simcoe	31 D/4	44°01′	79°55′
Achilles Lake	LAKE/LAC	NT	Mackenzie	76 D	64°57′	110°54′
Achimasahitunanuch	UNP/LNO	QC	Kativik	33 O/10	55°44′	74°41′
Achipaschiwikuyasinanuch	UNP/LNO	QC	Kativik	33 O/3	55°06′	75°13′
Achiwapaschikisit	UNP/LNO	QC	Jamésie	33 D/15	52°58′	78°57′
Achray	UNP/LNO	ON	Nipissing	31 F/13	45°52′	77°45′
Acland Bay	BAY/BAIE	NT	Franklin	68 B	72°11′	100°45′
Acland Point	CAPE/CAP	NT	Keewatin	57 B	68°37′	93°45′
Acme	VILG/VILG	AB	19-29-25-W4	82 P/5	51°30′	113°30′
Aconi, Point	CAPE/CAP	NS	Cape Breton	11 K/8	46°20′	60°17′
Acous 1	IR/RI	BC	Nootka	92 L/4	50°06′	127°35′
Acquin, Mount	MTN/MNT	NB	Northumberland	21 O/8	47°21′	66°28′
Acropole des Draveurs, L'	MTN/MNT	QC	Charlevoix-Est	21 M/16	47°54′	70°28′
Actinolite	UNP/LNO	ON	Hastings	31 C/11	44°33′	77°20′
Active Pass	CHAN/CHEN	BC	Cowichan	92 B/14	48°52′	123°18′
Acton	MUN1/AZM1	QC	Acton	31 H/10	45°39′	72°34′
Acton	UNP/LNO	NB	York	21 G/10	45°44′	66°57′
Acton	UNP/LNO	ON	Halton	40 P/9	43°37′	80°02′
Actons Corners	UNP/LNO	ON	Grenville	31 B/13	44°59′	75°43′
Acton Vale	CITY/VIL1	QC	Acton	31 H/10	45°39′	72°34′
Acworth, Cape	CAPE/CAP	NT	Franklin	68 B	72°36′	102°26′
Ada	UNP/LNO	SK	6-13-1-W3	72 J/1	50°04′	106°08′
Adagio, Mont	MTN/MNT	QC	La Jacques-Cartier	21 M/3	47°13′	71°25′
Adair, Cape	CAPE/CAP	NT	Franklin	27 G	71°30′	71°34′
Adalômkamek	UNP/LNO	QC	Nicolet-Yamaska	31 I/2	46°05′	72°49′
Adamant Mountain	MTN/MNT	BC	Kootenay	82 N/12	51°44′	117°54′
Adami, Mount	MTN/MNT	YT		115 O/8	63°19′	138°02′
Adam Lake	LAKE/LAC	NT	Mackenzie	86 K	66°16′	116°15′
Adam Range	MTN/MNT	NT	Franklin	69 B	76°09′	103°30′
Adam River	RIV/CDE	BC	Rupert	92 L/8	50°28′	126°17′
Adam River	RIV/CDE	NT	Franklin	98 C	73°24′	124°23′
Adams	UNP/LNO	SK	30-17-21-W2	72 I/7	50°28′	104°52′
Adams Cove	UNP/LNO	NF		1 N/14	47°52′	53°06′
Adamsdale	UNP/LNO	ON	Sudbury	41 I/7	46°30′	80°55′
Adams Gulch	UNP/LNO	NB	Restigouche	21 O/14	47°50′	67°03′
Adams Island	ISL/ÎLE	NT	Franklin	37 H	71°27′	73°05′
Adams Lake	UNP/LNO	BC	Kamloops Division Yale	82 L/13	50°58′	119°41′
Adams Lake	LAKE/LAC	BC	Kamloops Division Yale	82 L/13	51°00′	119°43′
Adams Landing	UNP/LNO	AB	108-7-W5	84 J/6	58°23′	115°04′
Adams River	RIV/CDE	BC	Kamloops Division Yale	82 L/13	50°54′	119°33′
Adams Sound	CHAN/CHEN	NT	Franklin	48 B	72°52′	84°45′
Adamsville	UNP/LNO	NB	Kent	21 I/6	46°24′	65°11′
Adamsville	UNP/LNO	QC	La Haute-Yamaska	31 H/7	45°17′	72°47′
Adamsville	UNP/LNO	ON	Bruce	41 A/14	44°52′	81°10′
Adanac	VILG/VILG	SK	23-40-22-W3	73 C/6	52°27′	109°05′
Adanac	UNP/LNO	ON	Nipissing	41 I/16	46°58′	80°01′
Adanac	UNP/LNO	ON	Parry Sound	41 H/8	45°26′	80°23′
Ad Astra Ice Cap	GLAC/GLAC	NT	Franklin	340 D	81°36′	76°15′
Adderley	UNP/LNO	QC	L'Érable	21 L/4	46°12′	71°35′
Addington	GEOG/GÉOG	NB	Restigouche	21 O/10	47°44′	66°45′
Addington Forks	UNP/LNO	NS	Antigonish	11 E/9	45°34′	62°06′
Addison	UNP/LNO	ON	Leeds	31 B/12	44°40′	75°53′
Adelaide	MUN2/AZM2	ON	Middlesex	40 I/13	42°58′	81°40′
Adelaide	UNP/LNO	ON	Middlesex	40 P/4	43°00′	81°42′
Adelaide, Cape	CAPE/CAP	NT	Franklin	67 C	69°24′	101°54′
Adelaide Park	UNP/LNO	SK		73 B/2	52°06′	106°38′
Adelaide Peninsula	CAPE/CAP	NT	Keewatin	67 A/2	68°15′	97°30′
Adéla-Lessard, Mont	MTN/MNT	QC	La Haute-Côte-Nord	22 C/4	48°09′	69°45′
Adelard	UNP/LNO	ON	Renfrew	31 L/1	46°13′	78°02′
Aden	UNP/LNO	AB	8-1-10-W4	72 E/3	49°02′	111°19′
Adeytown	UNP/LNO	NF		2 C/4	48°05′	53°56′
Adies Pond	LAKE/LAC	NF		12 H/6	49°25′	57°17′
Adjala - see-voir - Adjala-Tosorontio	MUN2/AZM2	ON		31 D/4	44°08′	79°56′
Adjala-Tosorontio	MUN2/AZM2	ON	Simcoe	31 D/4	44°08′	79°56′

NAME / NOM	ENTITY / ENTITÉ	LOC 1 / LIEU 1	LOC 2 / LIEU 2	MAP / CARTE	POSITION LAT	LONG
Adlatok Bay	BAY/BAIE	NF		13 N/2	55°14′	60°30′
Adlatovusek	UNP/LNO	NF		13 N/8	55°15′	60°30′
Adlavik Bay	BAY/BAIE	NF		13 J/15	54°55′	58°55′
Adlavik Islands	ISL/ÎLE	NF		13 O/2	55°00′	58°40′
Admaston	MUN2/AZM2	ON	Renfrew	31 F/7	45°25′	76°50′
Admaston	UNP/LNO	ON	Renfrew	31 F/7	45°29′	76°49′
Admiral	VILG/VILG	SK	5-9-15-W3	72 F/9	49°43′	108°01′
Admiral Collinson, Cape	CAPE/CAP	NT	Franklin	67 F	70°19′	101°39′
Admiral Lake	LAKE/LAC	NS	Halifax	11 D/14	44°49′	63°08′
Admiral M'Clintock, Cape	CAPE/CAP	NT	Franklin	58 E	74°01′	91°05′
Admiral Rock	UNP/LNO	NS	Hants	11 E/3	45°10′	63°24′
Admiral's Beach	VILG/VILG	NF		1 N/4	47°00′	53°39′
Admiral's Cove	UNP/LNO	NF		1 N/2	47°06′	52°55′
Admiralty Inlet	BAY/BAIE	NT	Franklin	48 B	72°30′	86°00′
Admiralty Island	ISL/ÎLE	NT	Franklin	67 C	69°28′	101°10′
Admiralty Trough	SEAU/SMER	—		5.17	73°15′	86°00′
Adolphus Reach	RIVF/EFLV	ON	Lennox and Addington	31 C/2	44°05′	76°55′
Adolphustown	MUN2/AZM2	ON	Lennox and Addington	31 C/3	44°05′	77°04′
Adolphustown	UNP/LNO	ON	Lennox and Addington	31 C/3	44°04′	77°00′
Adonis, Lac	LAKE/LAC	QC	Antoine-Labelle	31 O/7	47°25′	74°41′
Adstock, Mont	MTN/MNT	QC	L'Amiante	21 L/3	46°03′	71°12′
Advance	UNP/LNO	ON	Manitoulin	41 G/16	45°52′	82°26′
Advocate Bay	BAY/BAIE	NS	Cumberland	21 H/7	45°20′	64°50′
Advocate Harbour	UNP/LNO	NS	Cumberland	21 H/7	45°20′	64°47′
*Aero	UNP/LNO	BC	Queen Charlotte	103 G/4	53°03′	131°58′
Aerobus Lake	LAKE/LAC	ON	Kenora	52 K/6	50°19′	93°24′
Aetna	UNP/LNO	AB	23-2-25-W4	82 H/3	49°08′	113°15′
Afridi Lake	LAKE/LAC	NT	Mackenzie	76 C	64°20′	109°19′
Afrique, L'	UNP/LNO	QC	Maria-Chapdelaine	32 A/16	48°52′	72°20′
Afton	VILG/VILG	PE	Queens	11 L/3	46°11′	63°11′
Afton	UNP/LNO	NS	Antigonish	11 F/12	45°37′	61°43′
Afton Road	UNP/LNO	PE	Queens	11 L/7	46°23′	62°56′
Agamemnon Channel	CHAN/CHEN	BC	New Westminster	92 F/9	49°42′	124°04′
Agassiz	UNP/LNO	BC	Yale Division Yale	92 H/4	49°14′	121°46′
Agassiz Ice Cap	GLAC/GLAC	NT	Franklin	340 A	80°15′	76°00′
Agassiz Lake	LAKE/LAC	NT	Mackenzie	85 P	63°11′	112°47′
Agate	UNP/LNO	ON	Algoma	42 B/10	48°31′	82°58′
Agate	UNP/LNO	BC	Kamloops Division Yale	92 I/6	50°16′	121°07′
Agatha	UNP/LNO	AB	4-14-10-W4	72 L/3	50°08′	111°17′
Agats Meadow 8	IR/RI	BC	Range 3 Coast	93 C/8	52°17′	124°10′
Agawa	UNP/LNO	ON	Algoma	41 N/10	47°40′	84°30′
Agawa Bay	UNP/LNO	ON	Algoma	41 N/7	47°21′	84°38′
Agawa Canyon	VALL/VALL	ON	Algoma	41 N/8	47°27′	84°29′
Agawa River	RIV/CDE	ON	Algoma	41 N/7	47°21′	84°38′
Agency 1	IR/RI	ON	Rainy River	52 C/11	48°38′	93°22′
Agency 30	IR/RI	ON	Kenora	52 E/7	49°22′	94°37′
Agerton	UNP/LNO	ON	Halton	30 M/12	43°33′	79°48′
Aggautik, Lac	LAKE/LAC	QC	Kativik	35 B/7	60°20′	74°45′
Aggie	UNP/LNO	AB	36-74-18-W5	83 N/7	55°27′	116°38′
Aghaming	UNP/LNO	MB	4-26-9-E	62 P/1	51°11′	96°17′
Agimak Lake	LAKE/LAC	ON	Kenora	52 G/5	49°23′	91°41′
Agincourt	UNP/LNO	ON	York	30 M/14	43°47′	79°17′
Agincourt North	UNP/LNO	ON	York	30 M/14	43°48′	79°16′
Aglakumna 4A	IR/RI	BC	Range 1 Coast	92 L/10	50°33′	126°39′
Aglakumna-la 2	IR/RI	BC	Range 1 Coast	92 L/10	50°34′	126°31′
Agnes Lake	LAKE/LAC	ON	Rainy River	52 B/3	48°15′	91°20′
Agnes River	RIV/CDE	ON	Sudbury	41 I/12	46°40′	81°46′
Agnew Lake	LAKE/LAC	ON	Sudbury	41 I/5	46°22′	81°45′
Agonzon	UNP/LNO	ON	Thunder Bay	42 C/13	48°59′	85°54′
Aguanish	VILG/VILG	QC	Minganie	12 L/1	50°13′	62°05′
Aguanish Nord-Ouest, Rivière	RIV/CDE	QC	Minganie	12 M/10	51°33′	62°35′
Aguanish Nord, Rivière	RIV/CDE	QC	Minganie	12 M/8	51°16′	62°27′
Aguanish, Rivière	RIV/CDE	QC	Minganie	12 L/1	50°13′	62°05′
Aguasabon River	RIV/CDE	ON	Thunder Bay	42 D/14	48°47′	87°07′
Aguathuna	UNP/LNO	NF		12 B/10	48°33′	58°46′
Agu Bay	BAY/BAIE	NT	Franklin	47 F	70°18′	86°45′
Aguenier, Lac	LAKE/LAC	QC	Manicouagan	22 K/9	50°42′	68°13′
Agusk Lake	LAKE/LAC	ON	Kenora	53 I/11	54°40′	89°30′
Agwedin 3	IR/RI	BC	Cassiar	93 M/5	55°23′	127°41′
Ahahswinis 1	IR/RI	BC	Alberni	92 F/7	49°16′	124°49′
Ahaminaquus 12	IR/RI	BC	Nootka	92 E/9	49°41′	126°07′
Ahbau	UNP/LNO	BC	Cariboo	93 G/8	53°22′	122°03′
Ahbau	UNP/LNO	BC	Cariboo	93 G/1	53°13′	122°24′
Ahbau Lake	LAKE/LAC	BC	Cariboo	93 G/8	53°16′	122°06′
Ahmacinnit 3	IR/RI	BC	Rupert	92 L/3	50°01′	127°24′

NAME NOM	ENTITY ENTITÉ	LOC 1 LIEU 1	LOC 2 LIEU 2	MAP CARTE	POSITION LAT	LONG
Ahmic Harbour	UNP/LNO	ON	Parry Sound	31 E/12	45°40′	79°47′
Ahmic Lake	UNP/LNO	ON	Parry Sound	31 E/12	45°37′	79°43′
Ahmic Lake	LAKE/LAC	ON	Parry Sound	31 E/12	45°37′	79°42′
Ahmitsa 5	IR/RI	BC	Clayoquot	92 C/14	48°58′	125°03′
Ahnighito, Cape	CAPE/CAP	NT	Franklin	79 D	77°44′	106°07′
Ahnuhati 6	IR/RI	BC	Range 1 Coast	92 K/13	50°54′	125°38′
Ahnuhati Point	CAPE/CAP	BC	Range 1 Coast	92 K/13	50°53′	125°38′
Ahnuhati River	RIV/CDE	BC	Range 1 Coast	92 K/13	50°53′	125°38′
Ahous 16	IR/RI	BC	Clayoquot	92 E/1	49°01′	126°01′
Ahousat	UNP/LNO	BC	Clayoquot	92 E/8	49°17′	126°04′
Ahous Bay	BAY/BAIE	BC	Clayoquot	92 E/1	49°11′	126°01′
Ahpokum 9	IR/RI	BC	Range 1 Coast	92 K/2	50°14′	124°35′
Ahpukto 3	IR/RI	BC	Nootka	92 E/15	49°49′	126°57′
Ahta 3	IR/RI	BC	Range 1 Coast	92 L/16	50°52′	126°10′
Ahtahkakoop 104	IR/RI	SK		73 G/7	53°24′	106°54′
Ahuk 1	IR/RI	BC	Barclay	92 C/10	48°43′	124°53′
Ahuntsic	UNP/LNO	QC	Communauté urbaine de Montréal	31 H/12	45°33′	73°39′
Ahwachanjeesh Pond	LAKE/LAC	NF		12 A/1	48°04′	56°05′
Ah-we-cha-ol-to 16	IR/RI	BC	Rupert	92 L/12	50°32′	127°58′
Ahwhichaolto Inlet	BAY/BAIE	BC	Rupert	92 L/12	50°32′	127°55′
Aigle-à-Tête-Blanche, Réserve écologique de l'	PARK/PARC	QC	Pontiac	31 K/4	46°12′	77°41′
Aigle, Lac à l'	LAKE/LAC	QC	Minganie	22 P/3	51°12′	65°25′
Aigle, Lac de l'	LAKE/LAC	QC	Jamésie	23 E/15	53°47′	70°42′
Aigle, Rivière de l'	RIV/CDE	QC	La Vallée-de-la-Gatineau	31 K/8	46°27′	76°03′
Aigles, Lac des	LAKE/LAC	QC	Témiscouata	21 N/15	47°57′	68°42′
Aigles, Lac des	LAKE/LAC	QC	Maria-Chapdelaine	22 E/4	49°06′	71°44′
Aigneau, Lac	LAKE/LAC	QC	Kativik	24 E/1	57°13′	70°08′
Aigneau, Rivière	RIV/CDE	QC	Kativik	24 F/12	57°35′	69°52′
Aigremont, Lac	LAKE/LAC	QC	Le Domaine-du-Roy	32 H/5	49°19′	73°49′
Aiguebelle, Parc de conservation d'	PARK/PARC	QC	Rouyn-Noranda	32 D/10	48°30′	78°45′
Aiguebelle, Réserve faunique d'	PARK/PARC	QC	Rouyn-Noranda	32 D/7	48°26′	78°51′
Aikens Lake	LAKE/LAC	MB	25,26-15,16-E	52 M/3	51°12′	95°21′
Aikensville	UNP/LNO	ON	Wellington	40 P/8	43°26′	80°14′
Aikins	UNP/LNO	SK	10-16-13-W3	72 J/5	50°20′	107°42′
Aikwucks 15	IR/RI	BC	New Westminster	92 G/14	49°46′	123°10′
Aillik	UNP/LNO	NF		13 O/3	55°13′	59°13′
Ailsa Craig	VILG/VILG	ON	Middlesex	40 P/4	43°08′	81°33′
Ain 6	IR/RI	BC	Queen Charlotte	103 F/9	53°44′	132°25′
Ainslie Creek	RIV/CDE	BC	Yale Division Yale	92 H/14	49°57′	121°28′
Ainslie Glen	UNP/LNO	NS	Inverness	11 K/3	46°01′	61°08′
Ainslie, Lake	LAKE/LAC	NS	Inverness	11 K/3	46°08′	61°11′
Ainsworth Hot Springs	UNP/LNO	BC	Kootenay	82 F/10	49°44′	116°55′
Aird	UNP/LNO	QC	Le Haut-Richelieu	31 H/3	45°02′	73°12′
Aird Island	ISL/ÎLE	ON	Algoma	41 J/1	46°08′	82°25′
Airdrie	CITY/VIL1	AB	12-27-1-W5	82 O/8	51°18′	114°02′
Air Force Island	ISL/ÎLE	NT	Franklin	36 O/16	67°58′	74°05′
Airlie	UNP/LNO	ON	Simcoe	41 A/8	44°16′	80°01′
Air Ronge	VILG/VILG	SK		73 P/3	55°05′	105°19′
Airy	MUN2/AZM2	ON	Nipissing	31 E/9	45°32′	78°13′
Airy	UNP/LNO	ON	Nipissing	31 E/8	45°30′	78°16′
Airy, Cape	CAPE/CAP	NT	Franklin	57 G	71°27′	93°11′
Aishihik	UNP/LNO	YT		115 H/12	61°36′	137°31′
Aishihik Lake	LAKE/LAC	YT		115 H/6	61°26′	137°15′
Aishihik River	RIV/CDE	YT		115 A/14	60°50′	137°05′
Aitchelitch 9	IR/RI	BC	New Westminster	92 H/4	49°09′	121°59′
Aitken Creek	RIV/CDE	BC	Peace River	94 A/11	56°41′	121°14′
Aivirsiuvik, Caps	CAPE/CAP	QC	Kativik	35 F/12	61°41′	77°59′
Aiyansh	UNP/LNO	BC	Cassiar	103 P/6	55°16′	129°05′
Aiyansh 1	IR/RI	BC	Cassiar	103 P/3	55°15′	129°06′
Aiyansh 83	IR/RI	BC	Cassiar	103 P/3	55°14′	129°06′
Aiyansh 87	IR/RI	BC	Cassiar	103 P/3	55°13′	129°08′
Ajax	TOWN/VIL2	ON	Ontario	30 M/14	43°51′	79°02′
Ajax Lake	LAKE/LAC	ON	Kenora	52 F/6	49°20′	93°25′
Ajax Lake	LAKE/LAC	NT	Mackenzie	76 D	64°59′	110°35′
Akaitcho Lake	LAKE/LAC	NT	Mackenzie	75 L	63°53′	111°15′
Akaiyesseh Lake	LAKE/LAC	NT	Mackenzie	86 A	64°48′	113°28′
Akamiht Uahakutet	UNP/LNO	QC	Côte-Nord-du-Golfe-Saint-Laurent	12 K/2	50°13′	60°53′
Akanekau Kauitshiht	UNP/LNO	QC	Côte-Nord-du-Golfe-Saint-Laurent	12 K/8	50°21′	60°11′
Akehurst Lake	LAKE/LAC	BC	Kamloops Division Yale	92 P/8	51°20′	120°28′
Akenside	UNP/LNO	AB	25-53-23-W4	83 H/11	53°36′	113°15′
Akie River	RIV/CDE	BC	Cassiar	94 F/3	57°02′	125°07′
Akiliniq Hills	MTN/MNT	NT	Keewatin	66 C	64°45′	100°50′
Akimiski Island	ISL/ÎLE	NT	Keewatin	43 H	53°00′	81°20′
Akimiski Strait	CHAN/CHEN	NT	Keewatin	43 G	53°05′	82°10′
Aklavik	HAM/HAM	NT	Mackenzie	107 B	68°13′	135°00′

4

NAME NOM	ENTITY ENTITÉ	LOC 1 LIEU 1	LOC 2 LIEU 2	MAP CARTE	POSITION LAT	LONG
Akosane	UNP/LNO	SK	26-43-4-W2	63 D/9	52°44'	102°29'
Akpatok Island	ISL/ÎLE	NT	Franklin	25 C	60°25'	68°08'
Akron	UNP/LNO	ON	Algoma	42 C/16	48°55'	84°07'
Aktaklin Lake	LAKE/LAC	BC	Range 3 Coast	93 C/2	52°12'	124°55'
Aktijartukan Fiord	BAY/BAIE	NT	Franklin	16 E	65°06'	63°55'
Akuliaqattak Peninsula	CAPE/CAP	NT	Franklin	27 B	68°50'	68°10'
Akuliaqattaq, Territoire	GEOG/GÉOG	QC	Kativik	35 F/4	61°08'	77°37'
Akulivik	VILG/VILG	QC	Kativik	35 D/16	60°48'	78°12'
Akwesasne 15	IR/RI	QC	Le Haut-Saint-Laurent	31 G/2	45°03'	74°34'
Akwesasne 59	IR/RI	ON	Stormont	31 G/2	45°03'	74°34'
Alalco 8	IR/RI	BC	Range 2 Coast	92 M/2	51°04'	126°32'
Alameda	TOWN/VIL2	SK	1-4-3-W2	62 E/8	49°16'	102°17'
Alareak Island	ISL/ÎLE	NT	Franklin	36 B	64°19'	75°36'
Alaska	UNP/LNO	PE	Prince	21 I/9	46°37'	64°06'
Alastair 80	IR/RI	BC	Range 5 Coast	103 I/3	54°08'	129°11'
Alastair 81	IR/RI	BC	Range 5 Coast	103 I/3	54°06'	129°10'
Alastair 82	IR/RI	BC	Range 5 Coast	103 I/3	54°04'	129°11'
Alastair Lake	LAKE/LAC	BC	Range 5 Coast	103 I/3	54°06'	129°11'
Alba	UNP/LNO	NS	Inverness	11 F/14	45°56'	61°01'
Alban	UNP/LNO	ON	Sudbury	41 I/2	46°06'	80°37'
Albanel	VILG/VILG	QC	Maria-Chapdelaine	32 A/16	48°53'	72°27'
Albanel, Lac	LAKE/LAC	QC	Jamésie	32 I/14	50°54'	73°18'
Albany	UNP/LNO	PE	Prince	11 L/5	46°17'	63°39'
Albany	UNP/LNO	NS	Annapolis	21 A/14	44°48'	65°03'
Albany Corner	UNP/LNO	PE	Prince	11 L/5	46°17'	63°38'
Albany Cross	UNP/LNO	NS	Annapolis	21 A/11	44°43'	65°01'
Albany Forks	UNP/LNO	ON	Algoma	42 F/1	49°07'	84°11'
Albany Island	ISL/ÎLE	ON	Cochrane	43 A/4	52°15'	81°34'
Albany River	RIV/CDE	ON	Kenora	43 A/5	52°17'	81°31'
Albas	UNP/LNO	BC	Kamloops Division Yale	82 M/3	51°12'	119°01'
Albatross	UNP/LNO	SK	23-18-20-W2	72 I/10	50°32'	104°40'
Albemarle	MUN2/AZM2	ON	Bruce	41 A/14	44°50'	81°13'
Albemarle, Mount	MTN/MNT	BC	Clayoquot	92 E/9	49°35'	126°28'
Alberni	UNP/LNO	BC	Alberni	92 F/7	49°15'	124°48'
Alberni 2	IR/RI	BC	Alberni	92 F/2	49°13'	124°49'
Alberni-Clayoquot	MUN1/AZM1	BC	Clayoquot	92 F/3	49°15'	125°20'
Alberni Inlet	BAY/BAIE	BC	Barclay	92 F/2	49°05'	124°49'
Alberni Land District	GEOG/GÉOG	BC		92 F	49°16'	124°45'
Alberni, Port	BAY/BAIE	BC	Alberni	92 F/2	49°14'	124°50'
Alberry Plains	UNP/LNO	PE	Queens	11 L/2	46°13'	62°48'
Albert	MUN2/AZM2	MB		62 F/6	49°27'	101°07'
Albert	UNP/LNO	ON	Hastings	31 C/6	44°19'	77°08'
Albert	UNP/LNO	SK		73 B/2	52°07'	106°39'
Albert	GEOG/GÉOG	NB		21 H/15	45°50'	64°55'
Alberta	PROV/PROV	AB		MCR27	52°17'	117°28'
Alberta Beach	VILG/VILG	AB	22-54-3-W5	83 G/9	53°40'	114°21'
Alberta, Cape	CAPE/CAP	NT	Franklin	36 G	65°31'	74°12'
Alberta, Mount	MTN/MNT	AB	38-25-W5	83 C/5	52°18'	117°28'
Albert Beach	UNP/LNO	MB	19,20-7-E	62 I/10	50°41'	96°31'
Albert Bridge	UNP/LNO	NS	Cape Breton	11 K/1	46°01'	60°04'
Albert Canyon	UNP/LNO	BC	Kootenay	82 N/4	51°08'	117°53'
Albert, Cape	CAPE/CAP	NT	Franklin	39 H	79°03'	74°24'
Albert Dease, Mount	MTN/MNT	BC	Cassiar	94 E/12	57°45'	127°36'
Albert Edward Bay	BAY/BAIE	NT	Franklin	67 C	69°32'	102°25'
Albert Edward, Cape	CAPE/CAP	NT	Franklin	340 H	83°07'	72°36'
Albert Flat 5	IR/RI	BC	Yale Division Yale	92 H/11	49°31'	121°25'
Albert Head	UNP/LNO	BC	Esquimalt	92 B/6	48°23'	123°30'
Albert Head	CAPE/CAP	BC	Esquimalt	92 B/6	48°23'	123°29'
Albertine	UNP/LNO	NB	Madawaska	21 N/8	47°18'	68°24'
Albert Islands	ISL/ÎLE	NT	Franklin	87 F	70°33'	116°45'
Albert, Lac	LAKE/LAC	QC	Le Fjord-du-Saguenay	22 D/16	48°54'	70°19'
Albert Lake	LAKE/LAC	ON	Rainy River	52 C/13	48°55'	93°44'
Albert-Low, Mont	MTN/MNT	QC	Kativik	35 H/9	61°43'	72°13'
Albert Mines	UNP/LNO	NB	Albert	21 H/15	45°52'	64°40'
Albert Mines	UNP/LNO	QC	Sherbrooke	21 E/5	45°19'	71°55'
Albert, Mont	MTN/MNT	QC	Denis-Riverin	22 B/16	48°55'	66°11'
Alberton	TOWN/VIL2	PE	Prince	21 I/16	46°49'	64°04'
Alberton	MUN2/AZM2	ON	Rainy River	52 C/11	48°35'	93°30'
Alberton	UNP/LNO	ON	Wentworth	40 P/1	43°11'	80°05'
Alberton South	UNP/LNO	PE	Prince	21 I/16	46°48'	64°05'
Albert Park	UNP/LNO	SK		72 I/7	50°24'	104°38'
Albert Park	UNP/LNO	AB	24-29-W4	82 P/4	51°02'	114°00'
Albert Park South	UNP/LNO	SK		72 I/7	50°24'	104°38'
Albert Peak	MTN/MNT	BC	Kootenay	82 N/4	51°02'	117°52'
Alberts Lake	LAKE/LAC	SK	68-23-W3	73 K/14	54°54'	109°29'

NAME / NOM	ENTITY / ENTITÉ	LOC 1 / LIEU 1	LOC 2 / LIEU 2	MAP / CARTE	POSITION LAT	POSITION LONG
Albertville	VILG/VILG	SK	12,13-51-25-W2	73 H/5	53°24′	105°33′
Albertville	UNP/LNO	QC	La Matapédia	22 B/6	48°20′	67°22′
Albertville	UNP/LNO	SK	19-51-24-W2	73 H/5	53°25′	105°32′
Albion	UNP/LNO	PE	Kings	11 L/2	46°08′	62°33′
Albion	UNP/LNO	ON	Peel	30 M/13	43°54′	79°51′
Albion	UNP/LNO	BC	New Westminster	92 G/2	49°11′	122°33′
Albion Cross	UNP/LNO	PE	Kings	11 L/8	46°20′	62°29′
Albion Falls	UNP/LNO	ON	Wentworth	30 M/4	43°12′	79°49′
Albreda	UNP/LNO	BC	Cariboo	83 D/11	52°38′	119°10′
Albright	UNP/LNO	AB	29-72-10-W6	83 M/6	55°16′	119°30′
Albrights Corner	UNP/LNO	NB	Sunbury	21 J/1	46°01′	66°11′
Albro Lake	UNP/LNO	NS	Halifax	11 D/12	44°41′	63°35′
Albuna	UNP/LNO	ON	Essex	40 J/2	42°08′	82°38′
Albury	UNP/LNO	ON	Prince Edward	31 C/4	44°05′	77°31′
Alcantara Lake	LAKE/LAC	NT	Mackenzie	75 C	60°57′	108°09′
Alces River	RIV/CDE	BC	Peace River	94 A/1	56°08′	120°03′
Alcida	UNP/LNO	NB	Gloucester	21 P/13	47°46′	65°50′
Alcock Island	ISL/ÎLE	NF		2 E/11	49°31′	55°25′
Alcomdale	UNP/LNO	AB	5-57-26-W4	83 H/13	53°54′	113°50′
Alcona	UNP/LNO	ON	Simcoe	31 D/5	44°19′	79°33′
Alcona	UNP/LNO	ON	Kenora	52 J/4	50°04′	91°45′
Alcove	UNP/LNO	QC	Les Collines-de-l'Outaouais	31 G/12	45°41′	75°56′
Alcurve	UNP/LNO	AB	27-52-1-W4	73 E/9	53°31′	110°03′
Alcyone Bay	BAY/BAIE	NT	Mackenzie	96 H	65°12′	121°37′
Aldborough	MUN2/AZM2	ON	Elgin	40 I/12	42°35′	81°40′
Aldborough	MUN2/AZM2	ON	Elgin	40 I/12	42°36′	81°41′
Alden	UNP/LNO	ON	Algoma	42 C/2	48°12′	84°33′
Alder	UNP/LNO	ON	York	31 D/3	44°11′	79°23′
Alderburn	UNP/LNO	NF		2 E/3	49°07′	55°15′
Alder Creek	UNP/LNO	BC	New Westminster	92 G/7	49°21′	122°54′
Alder Creek 70	IR/RI	BC	Range 5 Coast	103 I/3	54°14′	129°25′
Alderdale	UNP/LNO	ON	Nipissing	31 L/3	46°06′	79°15′
Alder Flats	UNP/LNO	AB	4-46-7-W5	83 B/15	52°56′	114°57′
Aldergrove	UNP/LNO	BC	New Westminster	92 G/1	49°03′	122°28′
Aldermac	UNP/LNO	QC	Rouyn-Noranda	32 D/3	48°13′	79°13′
Alder Point	UNP/LNO	NS	Cape Breton	11 K/8	46°18′	60°17′
Alder River	UNP/LNO	NS	Guysborough	11 F/5	45°29′	61°44′
Aldershot	UNP/LNO	NS	Kings	21 H/2	45°06′	64°31′
Aldershot	UNP/LNO	ON	Wentworth	30 M/5	43°18′	79°51′
Alderslea	UNP/LNO	ON	Simcoe	31 D/5	44°20′	79°32′
Alderson	UNP/LNO	AB	20-15-10-W4	72 L/6	50°17′	111°20′
Aldersville	UNP/LNO	NS	Lunenburg	21 A/15	44°49′	64°30′
Aldersyde	UNP/LNO	AB	7-20-28-W4	82 I/12	50°41′	113°52′
Alderville	UNP/LNO	ON	Northumberland	31 D/1	44°11′	78°03′
Alderville 37	IR/RI	ON	Northumberland	31 D/1	44°11′	78°03′
Alderwood	UNP/LNO	NB	Gloucester	21 P/10	47°31′	65°00′
Alderwood	UNP/LNO	ON	York	30 M/12	43°36′	79°33′
Aldina	UNP/LNO	SK		73 G/2	53°00′	106°53′
Aldouane	UNP/LNO	NB	Kent	21 I/11	46°38′	65°04′
Aldred's Beach	UNP/LNO	ON	Ontario	31 D/2	44°10′	78°51′
Aldrich, Cape	CAPE/CAP	NT	Franklin	120 G	83°07′	69°35′
Aldrich, Cape	CAPE/CAP	NT	Franklin	79 A	76°06′	104°23′
Aldridge Lake	LAKE/LAC	ON	Thunder Bay	52 I/4	50°08′	89°48′
Alert	UNP/LNO	NT	Franklin	120 E	82°30′	62°22′
Alert Bay	VILG/VILG	BC	Rupert	92 L/10	50°35′	126°55′
Alert Bay 1A	IR/RI	BC	Rupert	92 L/10	50°35′	126°57′
Alert Bay 1	IR/RI	BC	Rupert	92 L/10	50°35′	126°56′
Alert, Canadian Forces Station - also-aussi - Alert, Station des Forces canadiennes	MIL/MIL	NT	Franklin	120 E/5	82°30′	62°21′
Alert Point	CAPE/CAP	NT	Franklin	340 F	82°28′	85°55′
Alert, Station des Forces canadiennes - also-aussi - Alert, Canadian Forces Station	MIL/MIL	NT	Franklin	120 E/5	82°30′	62°21′
Alexander	MUN2/AZM2	MB		62 I/8	50°29′	96°03′
Alexander	UNP/LNO	MB	17-10-21-W	62 F/16	49°50′	100°18′
Alexander 134	IR/RI	AB	4-56-27-W4	83 H/13	53°49′	113°57′
Alexander Bay	UNP/LNO	NF		2 D/9	48°41′	54°07′
Alexander Bay	BAY/BAIE	NF		2 C/12	48°43′	53°56′
Alexander Bay	BAY/BAIE	NT	Franklin	27 D	69°06′	67°47′
Alexander, Cape	CAPE/CAP	NT	Franklin	67 E	70°25′	96°24′
Alexander, Cape	CAPE/CAP	NT	Mackenzie	77 A	68°56′	106°12′
Alexander-Graham-Bell, Lieu historique national - also-aussi - Alexander Graham Bell National Historic Site	PARK/PARC	NS		11 K/2	46°06′	60°45′
Alexander Graham Bell National Historic Site - also-aussi - Alexander-Graham-Bell, Lieu historique national	PARK/PARC	NS		11 K/2	46°06′	60°45′
Alexander Island	ISL/ÎLE	NT	Franklin	68 G	75°52′	102°37′
Alexander Milne Point	CAPE/CAP	NT	Franklin	97 H	71°33′	120°29′

NAME NOM	ENTITY ENTITÉ	LOC 1 LIEU 1	LOC 2 LIEU 2	MAP CARTE	POSITION LAT	LONG
Alexandra	VILG/VILG	PE	Queens	11 L/3	46°12′	63°02′
Alexandra - see-voir - Stratford	VILG/VILG	PE		11 L/3	46°13′	63°05′
Alexandra	UNP/LNO	PE	Queens	11 L/3	46°12′	63°02′
Alexandra Falls	UNP/LNO	NT	Mackenzie	85 C	60°22′	116°26′
Alexandra Falls	FALL/CHUT	NT	Mackenzie	85 C	60°30′	116°18′
Alexandra Fiord	UNP/LNO	NT	Franklin	39 E	78°53′	75°48′
Alexandra Island	ISL/ÎLE	ON	Thunder Bay	52 H/9	49°32′	88°26′
Alexandra Strait	CHAN/CHEN	NT	Franklin	67 D	69°03′	99°46′
Alexandria	TOWN/VIL2	ON	Glengarry	31 G/7	45°19′	74°38′
Alexandria	UNP/LNO	BC	Cariboo	93 B/9	52°38′	122°27′
Alexandria 1	IR/RI	BC	Cariboo	93 B/9	52°33′	122°28′
Alexandria 3	IR/RI	BC	Cariboo	93 B/9	52°35′	122°30′
Alexandria 3A	IR/RI	BC	Cariboo	93 B/10	52°34′	122°30′
Alexandria 10	IR/RI	BC	Cariboo	93 B/10	52°40′	122°36′
Alexandria 11	IR/RI	BC	Cariboo	93 B/10	52°38′	122°37′
Alexandria 12	IR/RI	BC	Cariboo	93 B/9	52°31′	122°19′
Alexandria Bay	BAY/BAIE	ON	Rainy River	52 C/14	48°52′	93°25′
Alexandria Island	ISL/ÎLE	ON	Kenora	52 E/2	49°13′	94°40′
Alexandrina	UNP/LNO	NB	Kent	21 I/7	46°19′	64°47′
Alex Graham, Mount	MTN/MNT	BC	Cariboo	93 B/2	52°05′	122°57′
Alexis 9	IR/RI	BC	Similkameen Division Yale	82 E/4	49°13′	119°54′
Alexis 133	IR/RI	AB	55-4-W5	83 G/15	53°44′	114°31′
Alexis Bay	BAY/BAIE	NF		13 A/9	52°33′	56°05′
Alexis Creek	UNP/LNO	BC	Cariboo	93 B/3	52°05′	123°17′
Alexis Creek 6	IR/RI	BC	Range 3 Coast	93 C/8	52°21′	124°05′
Alexis Creek 12	IR/RI	BC	Range 3 Coast	93 C/1	52°14′	124°14′
Alexis Creek 13	IR/RI	BC	Range 3 Coast	93 C/1	52°13′	124°17′
Alexis Creek 14	IR/RI	BC	Range 3 Coast	93 C/1	52°12′	124°18′
Alexis Creek 15	IR/RI	BC	Range 3 Coast	93 C/1	52°12′	124°19′
Alexis Creek 16	IR/RI	BC	Range 3 Coast	93 C/1	52°11′	124°19′
Alexis Creek 17	IR/RI	BC	Range 3 Coast	93 C/1	52°12′	124°22′
Alexis Creek 18	IR/RI	BC	Range 3 Coast	93 C/1	52°13′	124°22′
Alexis Creek 20	IR/RI	BC	Range 3 Coast	93 C/8	52°19′	124°15′
Alexis Creek 21	IR/RI	BC	Range 3 Coast	93 C/8	52°18′	124°17′
Alexis Creek 22	IR/RI	BC	Range 3 Coast	93 C/8	52°19′	124°19′
Alexis Creek 23	IR/RI	BC	Range 3 Coast	93 C/8	52°18′	124°20′
Alexis Creek 24	IR/RI	BC	Range 3 Coast	93 C/8	52°18′	124°21′
Alexis Creek 25	IR/RI	BC	Range 3 Coast	93 C/8	52°18′	124°23′
Alexis Creek 26	IR/RI	BC	Range 3 Coast	93 C/8	52°18′	124°26′
Alexis Creek 27	IR/RI	BC	Range 3 Coast	93 C/8	52°19′	124°25′
Alexis Creek 28	IR/RI	BC	Range 3 Coast	93 C/8	52°22′	124°22′
Alexis Creek 29	IR/RI	BC	Range 3 Coast	93 C/8	52°22′	124°24′
Alexis Creek 30	IR/RI	BC	Range 3 Coast	93 C/8	52°23′	124°25′
Alexis Creek 31	IR/RI	BC	Range 3 Coast	93 C/8	52°25′	124°24′
Alexis Creek 32	IR/RI	BC	Range 3 Coast	93 C/8	52°27′	124°26′
Alexis Creek 33	IR/RI	BC	Range 3 Coast	93 C/8	52°27′	124°28′
Alexis Creek 34	IR/RI	BC	Range 3 Coast	93 C/8	52°29′	124°17′
Alexis Creek 35	IR/RI	BC	Range 3 Coast	93 C/8	52°26′	124°14′
Alexis River	RIV/CDE	NF		13 A/9	52°33′	56°09′
Alexis Thomas 1A	IR/RI	BC	Range 4 Coast	93 F/11	53°44′	125°15′
Alex, Lac	LAKE/LAC	QC	Maria-Chapdelaine	22 E/6	49°15′	71°28′
Alexo	UNP/LNO	ON	Cochrane	42 A/10	48°40′	80°49′
Alexo	UNP/LNO	AB	27-40-13-W5	83 B/5	52°28′	115°48′
Alex, Rivière	RIV/CDE	QC	Lac-Saint-Jean-Est	22 D/13	48°50′	71°46′
Aleza Lake	UNP/LNO	BC	Cariboo	93 J/1	54°07′	122°02′
Alfred	VILG/VILG	ON	Prescott	31 G/10	45°33′	74°53′
Alfred	MUN2/AZM2	ON	Prescott	31 G/10	45°35′	74°55′
Alfred, Cape	CAPE/CAP	NT	Franklin	67 C	69°40′	101°19′
Alfred-DesRochers, Mont	MTN/MNT	QC	Memphrémagog	31 H/8	45°19′	72°15′
Alfred-De Vigny, Lac	LAKE/LAC	QC	Sept-Rivières	22 J/4	50°06′	67°37′
Alfred, Lac	LAKE/LAC	QC	Témiscamingue	31 M/9	47°31′	78°02′
Alfred Lake	LAKE/LAC	ON	Thunder Bay	42 E/15	49°51′	86°46′
Alfred, Mount	MTN/MNT	BC	New Westminster	92 K/1	50°12′	124°05′
Alfred Station	UNP/LNO	ON	Prescott	31 G/10	45°32′	74°53′
Algar	UNP/LNO	MB	11-9-24-W	62 F/10	49°44′	100°37′
Algerine Passage	CHAN/CHEN	BC	New Westminster	92 F/15	49°49′	124°38′
Algerine Seamount	SEAU/SMER	—		NK22 B	40°54′	52°30′
Alger, Mount	MTN/MNT	BC	Cassiar	104 A/13	56°57′	129°55′
Algo	UNP/LNO	ON	Sudbury	41 I/10	46°31′	80°59′
Algoma	UNP/LNO	ON	Algoma	41 J/2	46°11′	82°49′
Algoma	GEOG/GÉOG	ON		41 N/16	48°00′	84°00′
Algoma Mills	UNP/LNO	ON	Algoma	41 J/2	46°11′	82°49′
Algonquin	UNP/LNO	ON	Grenville	31 B/12	44°42′	75°40′
Algonquin, Lac	LAKE/LAC	QC	Témiscamingue	31 N/4	47°07′	78°00′
Algonquin Park	UNP/LNO	ON	Nipissing	31 E/10	45°33′	78°35′

NAME NOM	ENTITY ENTITÉ	LOC 1 LIEU 1	LOC 2 LIEU 2	MAP CARTE	POSITION LAT	LONG
Algonquin Park	UNP/LNO	MB		62 H/14	49°57'	97°03'
Algrove	UNP/LNO	SK	40-14-W2	63 D/5	52°29'	103°53'
Alhambra	UNP/LNO	AB	9-39-5-W5	83 B/7	52°20'	114°40'
Alice	UNP/LNO	ON	Renfrew	31 F/14	45°45'	77°17'
Alice and Fraser	MUN2/AZM2	ON	Renfrew	31 F/11	45°44'	77°15'
Alice Arm	UNP/LNO	BC	Cassiar	103 P/6	55°29'	129°28'
Alice Arm	BAY/BAIE	BC	Cassiar	103 P/5	55°27'	129°35'
Alice Beach	VILG/VILG	SK	22,23-23-W2	72 I/14	50°56'	105°10'
Alice Creek	RIV/CDE	AB	107-20-W4	84 I/6	58°18'	113°12'
Alice Lake	LAKE/LAC	AB	49-11-W4	73 E/4	53°13'	111°34'
Alice Lake	LAKE/LAC	BC	Rupert	92 L/6	50°28'	127°25'
Alice Peak	MTN/MNT	BC	Range 5 Coast	103 I/10	54°38'	128°56'
Alice Siding	UNP/LNO	BC	Kootenay	82 F/2	49°07'	116°31'
Alida	VILG/VILG	SK	16-5-33-W	62 F/5	49°23'	101°52'
Alikdjuak Island	ISL/ÎLE	NT	Franklin	27 A	68°04'	65°28'
Alix	VILG/VILG	AB	36-39-23-W4	83 A/6	52°24'	113°11'
Alix, Lac	LAKE/LAC	QC	Minganie	12 K/9	50°43'	60°16'
Alix South Junction	UNP/LNO	AB	22-39-23-W4	83 A/6	52°21'	113°12'
Alixton 5	IR/RI	BC	Lillooet	92 O/16	51°48'	122°08'
Alkali Creek	RIV/CDE	SK	27-23-27-W3	72 K/13	50°59'	109°41'
Alkali Creek	RIV/CDE	AB	22-4-W4	72 L/16	50°52'	110°30'
Alkali Creek	RIV/CDE	BC	Lillooet	92 O/9	51°43'	122°22'
Alkali Lake	UNP/LNO	BC	Lillooet	92 O/16	51°47'	122°14'
Alkali Lake	LAKE/LAC	BC	Lillooet	92 O/16	51°47'	122°17'
Alkali Lake 1	IR/RI	BC	Lillooet	92 O/16	51°47'	122°14'
Alkali Lake 4A	IR/RI	BC	Lillooet	92 O/16	51°49'	122°07'
Alkhili 2	IR/RI	BC	Lillooet	92 O/16	51°49'	122°07'
Allains Creek	UNP/LNO	NS	Annapolis	21 A/12	44°43'	65°32'
Allainville	UNP/LNO	NB	Northumberland	21 P/6	47°18'	65°15'
Allan	TOWN/VIL2	SK	34-1-W3	72 O/16	51°53'	106°04'
Allan	UNP/LNO	ON	Hastings	31 C/11	44°37'	77°29'
Allanburg	UNP/LNO	ON	Welland	30 M/3	43°05'	79°12'
Allan Cot	UNP/LNO	NB	Saint John	21 G/1	45°13'	66°11'
Allan Creek	RIV/CDE	YT		105 A/12	60°30'	129°45'
Allandale	UNP/LNO	NB	York	21 G/14	45°54'	67°18'
Allan Hills	UNP/LNO	SK	16-31-1-W3	72 O/9	51°39'	106°05'
Allan Lake	LAKE/LAC	BC	Kamloops Division Yale	92 P/1	51°14'	120°21'
Allan Mills	UNP/LNO	ON	Northumberland	31 C/5	44°24'	77°43'
Allan Park	UNP/LNO	ON	Grey	41 A/2	44°10'	80°56'
Allan's Corners	UNP/LNO	QC	Le Haut-Saint-Laurent	31 H/4	45°10'	73°56'
Allans Corners	UNP/LNO	ON	Renfrew	31 F/11	45°41'	77°06'
Allan's Island	UNP/LNO	NF		1 L/13	46°51'	55°48'
Allan Water	UNP/LNO	ON	Thunder Bay	52 J/1	50°14'	90°12'
Allan Water	RIV/CDE	ON	Thunder Bay	52 I/12	50°33'	89°45'
Allanwater Bridge	UNP/LNO	ON	Thunder Bay	52 J/1	50°14'	90°10'
Allard	UNP/LNO	QC	Avignon	22 B/1	48°10'	66°23'
Allard, Lac	LAKE/LAC	QC	Minganie	12 L/12	50°31'	63°31'
Allard, Lac	LAKE/LAC	QC	Témiscamingue	31 M/7	47°20'	78°50'
Allard, Rivière	RIV/CDE	QC	Jamésie	32 F/13	49°50'	77°45'
Allardville	UNP/LNO	NB	Gloucester	21 P/6	47°28'	65°29'
Allardville	GEOG/GÉOG	NB	Gloucester	21 P/6	47°25'	65°25'
Allardville East	UNP/LNO	NB	Gloucester	21 P/11	47°30'	65°23'
Allegra	UNP/LNO	MB	14-9-E	62 I/1	50°13'	96°22'
Alle Harbour	BAY/BAIE	NT	Keewatin	34 L	58°49'	78°33'
Allely Lake	LAKE/LAC	ON	Thunder Bay	52 G/9	49°37'	90°20'
Allemand, Lac	LAKE/LAC	QC	Kativik	35 G/4	61°04'	75°47'
Allen Bay	BAY/BAIE	NT	Franklin	58 F	74°47'	95°18'
Allenby	UNP/LNO	BC	Similkameen Division Yale	92 H/7	49°25'	120°31'
Allendale	UNP/LNO	NS	Shelburne	20 P/11	43°45'	65°06'
Allenford	UNP/LNO	ON	Bruce	41 A/11	44°33'	81°10'
Allen Heights	UNP/LNO	NS	Halifax	11 D/12	44°41'	63°54'
Allen Hill	UNP/LNO	NS	Cumberland	21 H/7	45°24'	64°43'
Allen Island	ISL/ÎLE	NT	Franklin	25 P	63°28'	64°54'
Allen Lake	LAKE/LAC	MB	39-12-W	63 B/6	52°22'	99°09'
Allen Lake	LAKE/LAC	NT	Mackenzie	65 D	60°56'	103°48'
Allenou, Lac	LAKE/LAC	QC	Maria-Chapdelaine	22 M/3	51°02'	71°24'
Allen's Corners	UNP/LNO	ON	Lincoln	30 M/4	43°07'	79°35'
Allen's Mill	UNP/LNO	QC	Portneuf	21 L/13	46°55'	71°58'
Allensville	UNP/LNO	ON	Muskoka	31 E/3	45°15'	79°18'
Allenwood	UNP/LNO	ON	Simcoe	31 D/12	44°35'	79°57'
Allenwood Beach	UNP/LNO	ON	Simcoe	31 D/12	44°34'	80°00'
Alleyn-et-Cawood	VILG/VILG	QC	Pontiac	31 F/16	45°55'	76°14'
Alleys Pond	LAKE/LAC	NF		2 E/1	49°07'	54°08'
Alliance	VILG/VILG	AB	15-40-13-W4	73 D/5	52°26'	111°47'
Alliford Bay	UNP/LNO	BC	Queen Charlotte	103 G/4	53°12'	131°59'

NAME NOM	ENTITY ENTITÉ	LOC 1 LIEU 1	LOC 2 LIEU 2	MAP CARTE	POSITION LAT	LONG
Alligator, L'	UNP/LNO	QC	Pontiac	31 K/11	46°34'	77°14'
Allimil	UNP/LNO	ON	Simcoe	31 D/4	44°06'	79°47'
Allingham	UNP/LNO	AB	34-31-26-W4	82 P/12	51°42'	113°36'
Allioux, Lac	LAKE/LAC	QC	La Côte-de-Beaupré	21 M/7	47°27'	70°56'
Allisary	UNP/LNO	PE	Queens	11 L/7	46°22'	62°51'
Allison	UNP/LNO	NB	Westmorland	21 I/2	46°04'	64°55'
Allison Bay 219	IR/RI	AB	112-6-W4	74 L/14	58°47'	111°02'
Allison Creek	RIV/CDE	BC	Similkameen Division Yale	92 H/8	49°28'	120°28'
Allison Inlet	BAY/BAIE	NT	Franklin	68 H	75°03'	99°24'
Allison Lake	UNP/LNO	BC	Kamloops Division Yale	92 H/10	49°41'	120°36'
Allisonville	UNP/LNO	ON	Prince Edward	31 C/3	44°02'	77°22'
Alliston	UNP/LNO	PE	Kings	11 L/2	46°04'	62°36'
Alliston	UNP/LNO	ON	Simcoe	31 D/4	44°09'	79°52'
Alliston, Beeton, Tecumseth and Tottenham - see-voir - New Tecumseth	TOWN/VIL2	ON		31 D/4	44°05'	79°46'
Allman Bay	BAY/BAIE	NT	Franklin	39 H	79°30'	73°50'
Alloa	UNP/LNO	ON	Peel	30 M/12	43°42'	79°51'
Allsaw	UNP/LNO	ON	Haliburton	31 D/15	44°59'	78°36'
All Seasons Estates	UNP/LNO	MB		62 H/14	49°56'	97°03'
Allumette Lake	LAKE/LAC	ON	Renfrew	31 F/14	45°53'	77°13'
Allumettes, Île aux	ISL/ÎLE	QC	Pontiac	31 F/14	45°51'	77°04'
Allumettes, Lac aux	LAKE/LAC	QC	Pontiac	31 F/14	45°51'	77°07'
Alluviaq Fiord	BAY/BAIE	NT	Franklin	24 P/6	59°30'	65°09'
Alluviaq, Rivière	RIV/CDE	QC	Kativik	24 P/6	59°23'	65°00'
Alma	CITY/VIL1	QC	Lac-Saint-Jean-Est	22 D/12	48°33'	71°39'
Alma	VILG/VILG	NB	Albert	21 H/10	45°36'	64°57'
Alma	UNP/LNO	PE	Prince	21 I/16	46°52'	64°07'
Alma	UNP/LNO	NS	Pictou	11 E/10	45°35'	62°46'
Alma	UNP/LNO	ON	Wellington	40 P/10	43°44'	80°30'
Alma	GEOG/GÉOG	NB	Albert	21 H/10	45°38'	65°00'
Alma, Lake	LAKE/LAC	NS	Halifax	11 D/15	44°59'	62°45'
Alma Lake	LAKE/LAC	NS	Annapolis	21 A/11	44°37'	65°07'
Alma Peak	MTN/MNT	BC	Cassiar	94 D/13	56°46'	127°30'
Alma Russell Islands	ISL/ÎLE	BC	Barclay	92 C/14	48°57'	125°12'
Alma Station	UNP/LNO	ON	Wellington	40 P/9	43°43'	80°30'
Almdals Cove	UNP/LNO	MB	21-17-7-E	62 I/7	50°28'	96°35'
Almira	UNP/LNO	ON	York	30 M/14	43°56'	79°20'
Almond Gardens	UNP/LNO	BC	Similkameen Division Yale	82 E/1	49°01'	118°30'
Almond Mountain	MTN/MNT	BC	Similkameen Division Yale	82 E/7	49°19'	118°36'
Almonte	TOWN/VIL2	ON	Lanark	31 F/1	45°14'	76°12'
Alness	UNP/LNO	AB	13-31-13-W4	72 M/12	51°39'	111°44'
Alnwick	MUN2/AZM2	ON	Northumberland	31 D/1	44°13'	78°05'
Alnwick	GEOG/GÉOG	NB	Northumberland	21 P/3	47°15'	65°13'
Alonsa	MUN2/AZM2	MB		62 J/14	50°59'	99°03'
Alonsa	UNP/LNO	MB	7-21-11-W	62 J/15	50°48'	98°58'
Alouette Lake	LAKE/LAC	BC	New Westminster	92 G/8	49°20'	122°25'
Alouette River	RIV/CDE	BC	New Westminster	92 G/7	49°16'	122°42'
Alouettes, Pointe aux	CAPE/CAP	QC	Charlevoix-Est	22 C/4	48°06'	69°42'
Alpen	UNP/LNO	AB	2-63-20-W4	83 I/7	54°26'	112°55'
Alpena	UNP/LNO	NS	Annapolis	21 A/14	44°50'	65°03'
Alpen Siding	UNP/LNO	AB	4-63-20-W4	83 I/7	54°26'	112°55'
Alpha, Dorsale - also-aussi - Alpha Ridge	SEAU/SMER	—		800A	85°30'	110°00'
Alpha Ridge - also-aussi - Alpha, Dorsale	SEAU/SMER	—		800A	85°30'	110°00'
Alphonse Tommy 7	IR/RI	BC	Cassiar	93 M/7	55°18'	126°38'
Alpine	UNP/LNO	MB	22-32-29-W	62 N/14	51°45'	101°30'
Alpine Meadows	UNP/LNO	BC	New Westminster	92 J/2	50°09'	122°58'
Alpine Ridge	UNP/LNO	NS	Inverness	11 K/3	46°01'	61°25'
Alpine Village	UNP/LNO	ON	Peterborough	31 D/9	44°35'	78°28'
Alpine Village	UNP/LNO	ON	Waterloo	40 P/8	43°25'	80°29'
Alpland	UNP/LNO	BC	Cariboo	83 E/3	53°02'	119°11'
Alport	UNP/LNO	ON	Muskoka	31 E/3	45°01'	79°21'
Alsace	UNP/LNO	ON	Parry Sound	31 L/4	46°02'	79°33'
Alsask	VILG/VILG	SK	10-28-29-W3	72 N/5	51°21'	109°59'
Alsek Ranges	MTN/MNT	BC/YT		114 O/16	59°35'	137°09'
Alsek River	RIV/CDE	BC/YT		114 P/5	59°26'	137°58'
Alsfeldt	UNP/LNO	ON	Grey	41 A/2	44°01'	80°56'
Alsike	UNP/LNO	AB	36-48-4-W5	83 G/1	53°11'	114°29'
Alsops Beach	UNP/LNO	ON	Ontario	31 D/6	44°26'	79°09'
Alstead Lake	LAKE/LAC	SK	76,77-9,10-W3	73 O/11	55°38'	107°23'
Alstead River	RIV/CDE	SK	79-10-W3	73 O/14	55°50'	107°26'
Alston Creek	RIV/CDE	MB	54 L/9	58°34'	94°06'
Alstonvale	UNP/LNO	QC	Vaudreuil-Soulanges	31 G/8	45°28'	74°11'
Alta Lake	UNP/LNO	BC	New Westminster	92 J/2	50°06'	122°59'
Altamont	UNP/LNO	MB	21-5-8-W	62 G/8	49°24'	98°30'
Altamont	UNP/LNO	BC	New Westminster	92 G/6	49°20'	123°12'
Altario	UNP/LNO	AB	13-34-2-W4	72 M/16	51°55'	110°09'

NAME NOM	ENTITY ENTITÉ	LOC 1 LIEU 1	LOC 2 LIEU 2	MAP CARTE	POSITION LAT	LONG
Alta Vista	HAM/HAM	SK	22-21-22-W2	72 I/15	50°48′	104°58′
Altawan	UNP/LNO	SK	23-3-30-W3	72 F/4	49°14′	109°56′
Altbergthal	UNP/LNO	MB	1-2-2-W	62 H/4	49°06′	97°37′
Althorpe	UNP/LNO	ON	Lanark	31 C/16	44°46′	76°28′
Alticane	UNP/LNO	SK	26-45-11-W3	73 B/14	52°54′	107°29′
Alton	UNP/LNO	NS	Colchester	11 E/3	45°11′	63°18′
Alton	UNP/LNO	ON	Peel	40 P/16	43°52′	80°04′
Altona	TOWN/VIL2	MB	5,8-2-1-W	62 H/4	49°06′	97°34′
Altona	UNP/LNO	ON	Ontario	30 M/14	43°58′	79°12′
Altona	UNP/LNO	BC	Peace River	94 A/15	56°54′	120°54′
Alukpaluk Bay	BAY/BAIE	NT	Franklin	24 J	58°23′	67°06′
Alva	UNP/LNO	QC	Brome-Missisquoi	31 H/2	45°04′	72°39′
Alva	UNP/LNO	ON	Algoma	41 N/1	47°02′	84°02′
Alva, Loch	LAKE/LAC	NB	Saint John	21 G/8	45°18′	66°19′
Alvanley	UNP/LNO	ON	Grey	41 A/11	44°32′	81°07′
Alvena	VILG/VILG	SK	12-41-1-W3	73 B/9	52°31′	106°01′
Alvin	UNP/LNO	BC	New Westminster	92 G/10	49°36′	122°38′
Alvinston	VILG/VILG	ON	Lambton	40 I/13	42°49′	81°52′
Alward	UNP/LNO	NB	Queens	21 I/3	46°12′	65°26′
Alward Brook	RIV/CDE	NB	Queens	21 I/3	46°04′	65°28′
Amabel	MUN2/AZM2	ON	Bruce	41 A/11	44°40′	81°12′
Amadjuak	UNP/LNO	NT	Franklin	36 A	64°01′	72°39′
Amadjuak Bay	BAY/BAIE	NT	Franklin	35 P	63°59′	72°40′
Amadjuak Lake	LAKE/LAC	NT	Franklin	26 D	65°00′	71°08′
Amadjuak River	RIV/CDE	NT	Franklin	26 E	65°55′	71°18′
Amai 15	IR/RI	BC	Rupert	92 L/3	50°02′	127°05′
Amai Inlet	BAY/BAIE	BC	Rupert	92 L/3	50°01′	127°07′
Amaral 46 & 47	IR/RI	BC	Cassiar	103 P/3	55°12′	129°12′
Amaranth	MUN2/AZM2	ON	Dufferin	40 P/16	43°58′	80°15′
Amaranth	UNP/LNO	MB	1-19-10-W	62 J/10	50°36′	98°44′
Amaranth Station	UNP/LNO	ON	Dufferin	40 P/16	43°54′	80°14′
Amariton, Lac	LAKE/LAC	QC	Manicouagan	22 F/16	49°52′	68°04′
Amatal 5	IR/RI	BC	Cassiar	103 P/3	55°12′	129°11′
Amatal 6	IR/RI	BC	Cassiar	103 P/3	55°12′	129°12′
Amazon	UNP/LNO	SK	9-30-25-W2	72 P/11	51°33′	105°27′
Ambassador	UNP/LNO	SK	15-30-22-W2	72 P/11	51°34′	105°01′
Ambassador Beach	UNP/LNO	ON	Essex	40 J/2	42°01′	82°59′
Amberley	UNP/LNO	ON	Bruce	41 A/4	44°03′	81°43′
Amber River	RIV/CDE	AB	113-6-W6	84 L/15	58°52′	118°55′
Amber River 211	IR/RI	AB	16-114-6-W6	84 L/15	58°54′	118°57′
Amber Valley	UNP/LNO	AB	23-66-20-W4	83 I/10	54°44′	112°55′
Ambition Mountain	MTN/MNT	BC	Cassiar	104 G/6	57°23′	131°28′
Ambleside	UNP/LNO	ON	Bruce	41 A/3	44°01′	81°12′
Ambleside	UNP/LNO	BC	New Westminster	92 G/6	49°19′	123°09′
Ambrose, Lake	LAKE/LAC	NF		12 A/10	48°33′	56°39′
Amedroz Island	ISL/ÎLE	ON	Algoma	41 J/1	46°03′	82°09′
Ameer	UNP/LNO	MB	5-15-17-W	62 J/4	50°15′	99°46′
Amelia	UNP/LNO	AB	3-57-21-W4	83 H/14	53°54′	113°03′
Ameliasburg	UNP/LNO	ON	Prince Edward	31 C/3	44°04′	77°26′
Ameliasburgh	MUN2/AZM2	ON	Prince Edward	31 C/3	44°04′	77°27′
Américains, Banc des - also-aussi - American Bank	SEAU/SMER	—		801	48°36′	63°54′
American Bank - also-aussi - Américains, Banc des	SEAU/SMER	—		801	48°36′	63°54′
Amer Lake	LAKE/LAC	NT	Mackenzie	66 H	65°35′	97°10′
Amery	UNP/LNO	MB	87-22-E	54 D/9	56°34′	94°04′
Amesbury	UNP/LNO	AB	26-70-17-W4	83 P/1	55°05′	112°29′
Amesdale	UNP/LNO	ON	Kenora	52 K/2	50°01′	92°56′
Ames Lake	LAKE/LAC	NT	Mackenzie	85 P	63°30′	113°10′
Ameson	UNP/LNO	ON	Cochrane	42 F/15	49°48′	84°34′
Amethyst Harbour	UNP/LNO	ON	Thunder Bay	52 A/10	48°32′	88°52′
Amethyst Lakes	LAKE/LAC	AB	43-2-W6	83 D/9	52°42′	118°16′
Ameto Lake	LAKE/LAC	NT	Keewatin	65 H	61°39′	97°12′
Amet Sound	BAY/BAIE	NS	Pictou	11 E/14	45°47′	63°10′
Amherst	TOWN/VIL2	NS	Cumberland	21 H/16	45°50′	64°12′
Amherst	VILG/VILG	QC	Les Laurentides	31 J/2	46°03′	74°46′
Amherstburg	TOWN/VIL2	ON	Essex	40 J/3	42°06′	83°06′
Amherst Cove	UNP/LNO	NF		2 C/11	48°34′	53°12′
Amherst Head	UNP/LNO	NS	Cumberland	11 E/13	45°53′	64°00′
Amherst Island	MUN2/AZM2	ON	Lennox and Addington	31 C/2	44°10′	76°40′
Amherst Island	ISL/ÎLE	ON	Lennox and Addington	31 C/2	44°08′	76°43′
Amherst Island	ISL/ÎLE	NT	Franklin	47 D	69°47′	83°44′
Amherst Point	UNP/LNO	NS	Cumberland	21 H/16	45°47′	64°16′
Amherst Pointe	UNP/LNO	ON	Essex	40 J/3	42°03′	83°07′
Amherst Shore	UNP/LNO	NS	Cumberland	11 E/13	45°58′	63°54′
Amherstview	UNP/LNO	ON	Lennox and Addington	31 C/2	44°13′	76°38′
Amiens	UNP/LNO	SK	50-9-W3	73 G/6	53°19′	107°15′

NAME NOM	ENTITY ENTITÉ	LOC 1 LIEU 1	LOC 2 LIEU 2	MAP CARTE	POSITION LAT	LONG
Amigari Downs	UNP/LNO	ON	Welland	30 L/15	42°56′	78°57′
Amigo Beach	UNP/LNO	ON	Simcoe	31 D/11	44°42′	79°24′
Amik Lake	LAKE/LAC	ON	Kenora	52 G/13	49°50′	91°56′
Amikougami Lake	LAKE/LAC	ON	Timiskaming	42 A/1	48°12′	80°05′
Aminapiskasich	UNP/LNO	QC	Jamésie	33 D/2	52°13′	78°32′
Aminapustasich	UNP/LNO	QC	Kativik	33 N/1	55°07′	76°02′
Amiraults Corner	UNP/LNO	NS	Digby	21 A/5	44°27′	65°51′
Amiraults Hill	UNP/LNO	NS	Yarmouth	20 P/13	43°49′	65°59′
Amisk	VILG/VILG	AB	26-41-8-W4	73 D/11	52°33′	111°04′
Amisk Lake	LAKE/LAC	MB	54-22,23-W	63 F/10	53°39′	100°43′
Amisk Lake	LAKE/LAC	SK		63 L/9	54°35′	102°15′
Amisk Lake 184	IR/RI	SK		63 L/9	54°34′	102°25′
Amisk River	RIV/CDE	AB	20-63-12-W4	73 L/5	54°27′	111°46′
Amisquioumisca, Lac	LAKE/LAC	QC	Jamésie	32 K/8	50°28′	76°13′
Amitapanuch, Chute	FALL/CHUT	QC	Kativik	33 N/3	55°10′	77°23′
Amitioke Peninsula	CAPE/CAP	NT	Franklin	47 A	68°09′	82°03′
Amituryouak Lake	LAKE/LAC	NT	Franklin	57 G	71°30′	94°46′
Ammalurtuq Lake	LAKE/LAC	NT	Franklin	87 D/10	69°37′	113°25′
Ammon	UNP/LNO	NB	Westmorland	21 I/2	46°10′	64°51′
Ammonite Mountain	MTN/MNT	NT	Franklin	49 C	77°49′	87°31′
Amor Lake	LAKE/LAC	BC	Sayward	92 K/4	50°10′	125°33′
Amor Point	CAPE/CAP	BC	Range 1 Coast	92 K/10	50°32′	124°59′
Amos	CITY/VIL1	QC	Abitibi	32 D/9	48°34′	78°07′
Amostown	UNP/LNO	NB	Northumberland	21 J/9	46°32′	66°12′
Amour, Pointe	CAPE/CAP	NF		12 P/7	51°27′	56°52′
Amphitrite Point	CAPE/CAP	BC	Clayoquot	92 C/13	48°55′	125°33′
Amqui	CITY/VIL1	QC	La Matapédia	22 B/6	48°28′	67°26′
Amsbury	UNP/LNO	BC	Range 5 Coast	103 I/7	54°28′	128°46′
Amsterdam	HAM/HAM	SK	14-32-4-W2	62 M/9	51°45′	102°28′
Amulet	UNP/LNO	QC	Rouyn-Noranda	32 D/6	48°18′	79°01′
Amulet	UNP/LNO	SK	2-8-21-W2	72 H/10	49°37′	104°45′
Amulree	UNP/LNO	ON	Perth	40 P/7	43°25′	80°50′
Amund Ringnes Island	ISL/ÎLE	NT	Franklin	69 E	78°20′	96°25′
Amundsen Gulf	BAY/BAIE	NT	Franklin	97 D	71°00′	124°00′
Amundsen Island	ISL/ÎLE	NT	Franklin	67 B	68°26′	100°45′
Amundsen Trough	SEAU/SMER	—		7000	70°30′	123°00′
Amundson	UNP/LNO	AB	4-63-3-W6	83 L/8	54°25′	118°23′
Amwri	UNP/LNO	ON	Thunder Bay	42 C/13	48°50′	85°51′
Amy Corners	UNP/LNO	QC	Memphrémagog	31 H/1	45°07′	72°09′
Amyot	UNP/LNO	ON	Algoma	42 C/7	48°29′	84°57′
Amyot Lake	LAKE/LAC	SK	54-5-W3	73 G/10	53°42′	106°38′
Anabusko River	RIV/CDE	MB		54 G/1	57°12′	90°30′
Anacla 12	IR/RI	BC	Barclay	92 C/14	48°48′	125°07′
Anaconda	UNP/LNO	BC	Similkameen Division Yale	82 E/2	49°05′	118°41′
Anagance	UNP/LNO	NB	Kings	21 H/14	45°52′	65°15′
Anagance Ridge	UNP/LNO	NB	Kings	21 H/14	45°53′	65°19′
Anagance River	RIV/CDE	NB	Westmorland	21 H/14	45°56′	65°11′
Anahareo Lake	LAKE/LAC	ON	Algoma	42 C/10	48°37′	84°41′
Anahim 3	IR/RI	BC	Cariboo	93 B/3	52°12′	123°04′
Anahim 4	IR/RI	BC	Cariboo	93 B/3	52°13′	123°04′
Anahim 5	IR/RI	BC	Cariboo	93 B/3	52°13′	123°01′
Anahim 6	IR/RI	BC	Cariboo	93 B/3	52°13′	123°00′
Anahim 7	IR/RI	BC	Cariboo	93 B/2	52°12′	122°58′
Anahim 8	IR/RI	BC	Cariboo	93 B/2	52°13′	122°57′
Anahim 9	IR/RI	BC	Cariboo	93 B/2	52°13′	122°57′
Anahim 10	IR/RI	BC	Cariboo	93 B/7	52°15′	122°56′
Anahim 11	IR/RI	BC	Cariboo	93 B/7	52°17′	122°57′
Anahim 12	IR/RI	BC	Cariboo	93 B/7	52°18′	122°58′
Anahim 13	IR/RI	BC	Cariboo	93 B/6	52°16′	123°00′
Anahim 14	IR/RI	BC	Cariboo	93 B/6	52°17′	123°00′
Anahim 15	IR/RI	BC	Cariboo	93 B/6	52°17′	123°02′
Anahim 16	IR/RI	BC	Cariboo	93 B/6	52°20′	123°05′
Anahim 17	IR/RI	BC	Cariboo	93 B/6	52°22′	123°04′
Anahim 18	IR/RI	BC	Cariboo	93 B/6	52°26′	123°12′
Anahim Creek	RIV/CDE	BC	Cariboo	93 B/3	52°01′	123°12′
Anahim Lake	UNP/LNO	BC	Range 3 Coast	93 C/6	52°28′	125°19′
Anahim's Flat 1	IR/RI	BC	Cariboo	93 B/3	52°02′	123°10′
Anahim's Meadow 2	IR/RI	BC	Cariboo	93 B/3	52°07′	123°14′
Anahim's Meadow 2A	IR/RI	BC	Cariboo	93 B/3	52°06′	123°13′
Anaktalik Brook	RIV/CDE	NF		14 D/8	56°29′	62°06′
Analta	UNP/LNO	AB	11-62-25-W4	83 I/5	54°22′	113°38′
Anastasia	UNP/LNO	AB	30-20-22-W4	82 I/11	50°44′	113°02′
Anaukaskayach	UNP/LNO	QC	Kativik	33 O/3	55°01′	75°21′
Anaunethad Lake	LAKE/LAC	NT	Mackenzie	75 A	60°55′	104°25′
Anayapuskauch	UNP/LNO	QC	Kativik	33 O/6	55°25′	75°05′

NAME NOM	ENTITY ENTITÉ	LOC 1 LIEU 1	LOC 2 LIEU 2	MAP CARTE	POSITION	
					LAT	LONG
Ancaster	TOWN/VIL2	ON	Wentworth	30 M/4	43°13′	79°59′
Ancaster Heights	UNP/LNO	ON	Wentworth	30 M/4	43°14′	79°58′
Anchor Lake	LAKE/LAC	BC	Range 4 Coast	103 H/2	53°04′	128°47′
Anchor Point	VILG/VILG	NF		12 P/2	51°14′	56°48′
Ancienne-Cale-de-l'Étang-des-Caps, L'	UNP/LNO	QC	Les Îles-de-la-Madeleine	11 M/8	47°15′	62°01′
Ancien-Quai, L'	UNP/LNO	QC	Les Îles-de-la-Madeleine	11 N/4	47°14′	61°50′
Ancliff	UNP/LNO	ON	Thunder Bay	52 A/10	48°42′	88°35′
Ancona	UNP/LNO	AB	23-40-12-W5	83 B/5	52°27′	115°36′
Ancona Point	UNP/LNO	ON	Victoria	31 D/10	44°30′	78°37′
Ancrum	UNP/LNO	SK	33-27-W2	72 P/13	51°52′	105°47′
Andak 9	IR/RI	BC	Cassiar	93 M/5	55°27′	127°37′
Andegulay 8	IR/RI	BC	Cassiar	103 P/3	55°05′	129°25′
Andegulay 8A	IR/RI	BC	Cassiar	103 P/3	55°05′	129°27′
Anderdon	MUN2/AZM2	ON	Essex	40 J/3	42°11′	83°03′
Andersen Point	CAPE/CAP	NT	Franklin	69 G	79°54′	100°09′
Anderson	UNP/LNO	QC	Le Haut-Saint-Laurent	31 G/1	45°04′	74°03′
Anderson	UNP/LNO	ON	Lennox and Addington	31 C/2	44°12′	76°56′
Anderson	UNP/LNO	ON	Perth	40 P/6	43°18′	81°14′
Anderson	UNP/LNO	BC	Cariboo	93 G/8	53°21′	122°03′
Anderson Bay	BAY/BAIE	NT	Franklin	77 A	68°55′	104°22′
Anderson Channel	CHAN/CHEN	NT	Franklin	25 P	63°45′	64°40′
Anderson Creek	RIV/CDE	YT		105 H/11	61°34′	129°25′
Anderson Headland	CAPE/CAP	NT	Franklin	26 L	66°22′	71°12′
Anderson Island	ISL/ÎLE	NT	Keewatin	34 C	56°18′	76°41′
Anderson Lake	UNP/LNO	ON	Sudbury	41 I/4	46°14′	81°44′
Anderson Lake	LAKE/LAC	ON	Nipissing	31 L/11	46°32′	79°20′
Anderson Lake	LAKE/LAC	MB	36-6-W	63 B/1	52°05′	98°17′
Anderson Lake	LAKE/LAC	BC	Kamloops Division Yale	83 D/4	52°11′	119°47′
Anderson Lake	LAKE/LAC	BC	Lillooet	92 J/9	50°38′	122°25′
Anderson Lake 5	IR/RI	BC	Lillooet	92 J/10	50°33′	122°31′
Anderson Lake Station	UNP/LNO	ON	Sudbury	41 I/4	46°14′	81°43′
Anderson Mountain	UNP/LNO	NS	Pictou	11 E/10	45°37′	62°34′
Anderson River	UNP/LNO	NT	Mackenzie	107 D	69°42′	128°58′
Anderson River	RIV/CDE	BC	Yale Division Yale	92 H/14	49°50′	121°26′
Anderson River	RIV/CDE	NT	Mackenzie	107 D	69°43′	129°00′
Anderson Road	UNP/LNO	NB	Victoria	21 J/13	46°52′	67°30′
Anderson's Cove	UNP/LNO	NF		1 M/11	47°36′	55°07′
Anderson Settlement	UNP/LNO	NB	Westmorland	21 I/1	46°07′	64°15′
Andersons Landing	UNP/LNO	NT	Mackenzie	106 I	66°43′	129°49′
Andersonville	UNP/LNO	NB	Charlotte	21 G/6	45°25′	67°15′
Andesite Peak	MTN/MNT	BC	Range 5 Coast	103 I/8	54°15′	128°04′
Andimaul	UNP/LNO	BC	Cassiar	93 M/4	55°06′	127°57′
Andimaul 1	IR/RI	BC	Cassiar	93 M/4	55°06′	127°56′
Andou, Lac	LAKE/LAC	QC	Vallée-de-l'Or	31 N/7	47°23′	76°45′
Andover	GEOG/GÉOG	NB	Victoria	21 J/12	46°42′	67°45′
Andreasen, Cape	CAPE/CAP	NT	Franklin	89 C	77°21′	118°46′
Andrecyk Lake	LAKE/LAC	NT	Mackenzie	75 H	61°05′	105°10′
André-Grenier, Rivière	RIV/CDE	QC	Kativik	24 I/10	58°36′	64°47′
André Lake	LAKE/LAC	NF		23 I/12	54°38′	65°40′
André-Linteau, Réserve écologique	PARK/PARC	QC	Pontiac	31 K/4	46°13′	77°47′
André-Michaux, Réserve écologique	PARK/PARC	QC	La Vallée-de-la-Gatineau	31 G/13	45°50′	75°53′
Andrew	VILG/VILG	AB	32-56-16-W4	83 H/16	53°53′	112°21′
Andrew Bay	BAY/BAIE	ON	Kenora	52 E/9	49°36′	94°20′
Andrew Gordon Bay	BAY/BAIE	NT	Franklin	36 B	64°27′	75°30′
Andrew Island	ISL/ÎLE	NS	Guysborough	11 F/7	45°18′	60°58′
Andrew Lake	LAKE/LAC	SK		74 N/8	59°28′	108°20′
Andrew Lake	LAKE/LAC	AB	125,126-1-W4	74 M/16	59°55′	110°05′
Andrew River	RIV/CDE	NT	Mackenzie	107 A	68°23′	128°58′
Andrews Head	CAPE/CAP	NS	Queens	21 A/2	44°04′	64°33′
Andrews Lake	LAKE/LAC	NT	Mackenzie	55 M	63°53′	94°35′
Andrews Pond	LAKE/LAC	NF		2 D/1	48°14′	54°09′
Andrewsville	UNP/LNO	ON	Lanark	31 B/13	44°57′	75°49′
Andy Cahoose Meadow 16	IR/RI	BC	Range 3 Coast	93 C/13	52°53′	125°44′
Andy's Corners	UNP/LNO	ON	Norfolk	40 I/15	42°45′	80°32′
Anerley	UNP/LNO	SK	28-10-W3	72 O/6	51°22′	107°19′
Aneroid	VILG/VILG	SK	9-9-10-W3	72 G/11	49°43′	107°18′
Anfield	UNP/LNO	NB	Victoria	21 J/13	46°56′	67°31′
Angajurjualuk Lake	LAKE/LAC	NT	Franklin	37 G	71°07′	79°00′
Angekum Lake	LAKE/LAC	ON	Kenora	53 F/5	53°18′	93°46′
Angéline	UNP/LNO	QC	Rouville	31 H/7	45°20′	72°52′
Angels Cove	UNP/LNO	NF		1 M/1	47°00′	54°09′
Anger Island	ISL/ÎLE	BC	Range 4 Coast	103 G/8	53°31′	129°56′
Angers	UNP/LNO	QC	Communauté urbaine de l'Outaouais	31 G/11	45°31′	75°29′
Angevine Lake	LAKE/LAC	NS	Cumberland	11 E/12	45°44′	63°31′
Angijak Island	ISL/ÎLE	NT	Franklin	16 E/9	65°40′	62°18′

NAME NOM	ENTITY ENTITÉ	LOC 1 LIEU 1	LOC 2 LIEU 2	MAP CARTE	POSITION LAT	LONG
Angikuni Lake	LAKE/LAC	NT	Keewatin	65 J	62°12'	99°59'
Angimajuq River	RIV/CDE	NT	Mackenzie	77 A	68°11'	106°20'
Anglais, Baie des	BAY/BAIE	QC	Manicouagan	22 F/8	49°15'	68°07'
Anglais, Pointe aux	CAPE/CAP	QC	Sept-Rivières	22 G/11	49°40'	67°10'
Anglais, Rivière aux	RIV/CDE	QC	Manicouagan	22 F/8	49°15'	68°08'
Anglais, Rivière des	RIV/CDE	QC	Le Haut-Saint-Laurent	31 H/4	45°13'	73°50'
Anglemont	UNP/LNO	BC	Kamloops Division Yale	82 L/14	50°58'	119°10'
Anglia	UNP/LNO	SK	30-16-W3	72 N/9	51°34'	108°10'
Angliers	TOWN/VIL2	QC	Témiscamingue	31 M/11	47°33'	79°14'
Angling Lake	UNP/LNO	ON	Kenora	53 H/13	53°50'	89°31'
Angling Lake	LAKE/LAC	ON	Kenora	53 H/13	53°49'	89°30'
Angling Lake	LAKE/LAC	MB		53 F/13	53°55'	93°51'
Angling Lake	LAKE/LAC	AB	60-3-W4	73 L/1	54°12'	110°19'
Angling River	RIV/CDE	MB	28-89-3-E2	54 C/13	56°45'	93°37'
Anglin Lake	UNP/LNO	SK	54-27-W2	73 H/12	53°42'	105°57'
Anglin Lake	LAKE/LAC	SK		73 H/12	53°44'	105°56'
Anglo-Rouyn Mine Site	UNP/LNO	SK		73 P/6	55°18'	105°00'
Anglo Rustico	UNP/LNO	PE	Queens	11 L/6	46°27'	63°18'
Anglo Tignish	UNP/LNO	PE	Prince	11 L/13	46°59'	64°00'
Anguille, Cape	CAPE/CAP	NF		11 O/14	47°55'	59°24'
Anguille Mountains	MTN/MNT	NF		12 B/3	48°00'	59°11'
Anguille Trough	SEAU/SMER	—		801-A	48°09'	59°14'
Angus	UNP/LNO	ON	Simcoe	31 D/5	44°19'	79°53'
Angus Horne	UNP/LNO	BC	Kamloops Division Yale	83 D/3	52°03'	119°20'
Angus Horne Creek	RIV/CDE	BC	Kamloops Division Yale	83 D/5	52°23'	119°59'
Angus Horne Lake	LAKE/LAC	BC	Kamloops Division Yale	83 D/5	52°21'	119°46'
Angusko Point	CAPE/CAP	NT	Keewatin	55 F	61°46'	93°16'
Angusmac	UNP/LNO	BC	Cariboo	93 J/10	54°36'	122°42'
Angusville	UNP/LNO	MB	21,22-20-26-W	62 K/11	50°44'	101°01'
Anialik River	RIV/CDE	NT	Mackenzie	76 M	67°46'	111°04'
Anicinabe	UNP/LNO	QC	Vallée-de-l'Or	32 B/4	48°12'	75°48'
Anicinabe Ecitacikewapan	UNP/LNO	QC	Témiscamingue	31 M/2	47°11'	78°52'
Anicinabe Tcipekamik	UNP/LNO	QC	Témiscamingue	31 L/15	46°50'	78°49'
Anima Nipissing Lake	LAKE/LAC	ON	Nipissing	31 M/4	47°14'	79°57'
Anishinabi Lake	LAKE/LAC	ON	Kenora	52 K/6	50°26'	93°28'
Anistusikwasich	UNP/LNO	QC	Jamésie	33 C/5	52°17'	77°45'
Aniutarvik	UNP/LNO	QC	Kativik	34 K/5	58°16'	77°39'
Anjigami	UNP/LNO	ON	Algoma	41 N/15	47°53'	84°33'
Anjigami Lake	LAKE/LAC	ON	Algoma	41 N/15	47°50'	84°35'
Anjou	CITY/VIL1	QC	Communauté urbaine de Montréal	31 H/12	45°36'	73°33'
Anker, Cape	CAPE/CAP	NT	Franklin	67 F	70°46'	103°52'
Ankerton	UNP/LNO	AB	25-43-17-W4	83 A/9	52°44'	112°19'
Anlaw 4	IR/RI	BC	Cassiar	93 M/5	55°18'	127°41'
Anmore	VILG/VILG	BC	New Westminster	92 G/7	49°19'	122°51'
Annabel Lake	LAKE/LAC	SK	67-1,2-W2	63 L/16	54°50'	102°10'
Annabelle-Beach	UNP/LNO	QC	Roussillon	31 H/5	45°24'	73°43'
Annable Settlement	UNP/LNO	ON	Dundas	31 G/3	45°06'	75°21'
Annacis	UNP/LNO	BC	New Westminster	92 G/2	49°10'	122°56'
Annaheim	VILG/VILG	SK	4-39-20-W2	73 A/7	52°19'	104°49'
Annan	UNP/LNO	ON	Grey	41 A/10	44°37'	80°51'
Annandale	UNP/LNO	PE	Kings	11 L/8	46°16'	62°25'
Annandale-Little Pond-Howe Bay	VILG/VILG	PE	Kings	11 L/8	46°18'	62°25'
Annapolis	MUN1/AZM1	NS	Annapolis	21 A/11	44°35'	65°10'
Annapolis	GEOG/GÉOG	NS		21 A/11	44°35'	65°10'
Annapolis Basin	BAY/BAIE	NS	Digby	21 A/12	44°39'	65°42'
Annapolis River	RIV/CDE	NS	Annapolis	21 A/12	44°42'	65°36'
Annapolis Royal	TOWN/VIL2	NS	Annapolis	21 A/12	44°45'	65°31'
Annapolis Valley	VALL/VALL	NS	Annapolis	21 H/2	45°00'	64°55'
Anne, Cape	CAPE/CAP	NT	Franklin	58 F	74°06'	94°45'
Annex	UNP/LNO	ON	Thunder Bay	52 B/9	48°37'	90°00'
Annidale	UNP/LNO	NB	Queens	21 H/13	45°48'	65°47'
Anniedale	UNP/LNO	BC	New Westminster	92 G/2	49°10'	122°43'
Annieopsquotch Mountains	MTN/MNT	NF		12 A/5	48°20'	57°30'
Annieville - see-voir - North Delta	UNP/LNO	BC		92 G/2	49°10'	122°55'
Annis	UNP/LNO	BC	Kamloops Division Yale	82 L/14	50°48'	119°05'
Ann Island 7	IR/RI	BC	Range 2 Coast	92 M/5	51°16'	127°48'
Anokswok 59	IR/RI	BC	Cassiar	103 P/6	55°23'	129°02'
Anola	UNP/LNO	MB	36-10-6-E	62 H/15	49°53'	96°38'
Anoma Lea	UNP/LNO	ON	Leeds	31 B/12	44°38'	75°55'
Anse-aux-Amérindiens, L'	UNP/LNO	QC	La Côte-de-Gaspé	22 A/16	48°46'	64°12'
Anse-aux-Fraises, L'	UNP/LNO	QC	Minganie	22 H/16	49°50'	64°27'
Anse-Blanchette, L'	UNP/LNO	QC	La Côte-de-Gaspé	22 A/16	48°47'	64°13'
Anse-Bleue	UNP/LNO	NB	Gloucester	21 P/14	47°50'	65°05'
Anse-des-Mères, L'	UNP/LNO	QC	Communauté urbaine de Québec	21 L/14	46°48'	71°12'
Anse-des-Quinze-Collets, L'	UNP/LNO	QC	Denis-Riverin	22 G/1	49°10'	66°22'

NAME / NOM	ENTITY / ENTITÉ	LOC 1 / LIEU 1	LOC 2 / LIEU 2	MAP / CARTE	POSITION LAT	POSITION LONG
Ansell	UNP/LNO	AB	12-53-18-W5	83 F/10	53°33′	116°31′
Anselmo	UNP/LNO	AB	2-57-10-W5	83 G/14	53°53′	115°23′
Anse-Saint-Georges, L'	UNP/LNO	QC	La Côte-de-Gaspé	22 A/16	48°47′	64°13′
Ansnorveldt	UNP/LNO	ON	York	31 D/4	44°05′	79°33′
Anson	UNP/LNO	ON	Hastings	31 C/5	44°18′	77°35′
Anson, Hindon and Minden	MUN2/AZM2	ON	Haliburton	31 E/2	45°00′	78°45′
Ansonia	UNP/LNO	ON	Algoma	41 J/5	46°19′	83°37′
Ansonville	UNP/LNO	ON	Cochrane	42 A/15	48°45′	80°41′
Anstey Arm	BAY/BAIE	BC	Kamloops Division Yale	82 M/2	51°04′	118°56′
Anstey River	RIV/CDE	BC	Kamloops Division Yale	82 M/2	51°08′	118°55′
Anstice	UNP/LNO	ON	Sudbury	41 I/14	46°54′	81°02′
Anstruther Lake	UNP/LNO	ON	Peterborough	31 D/9	44°44′	78°12′
Anstruther Lake	LAKE/LAC	ON	Peterborough	31 D/16	44°45′	78°12′
Antelope	UNP/LNO	SK	1-14-18-W3	72 K/1	50°09′	108°20′
Antelope Lake	LAKE/LAC	SK	15-18-W3	72 K/8	50°16′	108°24′
Antelope Park No. 322	MUN2/AZM2	SK		72 N/12	51°45′	109°50′
Anten Mills	UNP/LNO	ON	Simcoe	31 D/5	44°29′	79°50′
Anthony	UNP/LNO	ON	Cochrane	42 A/10	48°32′	80°34′
Anthony Island (South Moresby) World Heritage Site - also-aussi - Île Anthony (Moresby-Sud), Site du patrimoine mondial de l'	PARK/PARC	BC		103 B/3	52°06′	131°13′
Anthonys Cove	UNP/LNO	NB	Saint John	21 G/1	45°14′	66°01′
Anthracite	UNP/LNO	AB	5-26-11-W5	82 O/3	51°12′	115°30′
Anticline Mountain	MTN/MNT	YT		105 E/5	61°21′	135°36′
Anticosti Channel - also-aussi - Anticosti, Chenal d'	SEAU/SMER	—		801	49°30′	61°00′
Anticosti, Chenal d' - also-aussi - Anticosti Channel	SEAU/SMER	—		801	49°30′	61°00′
Anticosti, Île d' - also-aussi - Anticosti Island	ISL/ÎLE	QC	Minganie	12 E/11	49°30′	63°00′
Anticosti Island - also-aussi - Anticosti, Île d'	ISL/ÎLE	QC	Minganie	12 E/11	49°30′	63°00′
Anticosti Platform	SEAU/SMER	—		811A	49°33′	63°10′
Anti Dam Flowage	LAKE/LAC	NS	Halifax	11 E/2	45°07′	62°30′
Antigonish	TOWN/VIL2	NS	Antigonish	11 F/12	45°37′	62°00′
Antigonish	MUN1/AZM1	NS	Antigonish	11 F/12	45°40′	61°55′
Antigonish	GEOG/GÉOG	NS		11 F/12	45°40′	61°55′
Antigonish Harbour	UNP/LNO	NS	Antigonish	11 F/12	45°43′	61°55′
Antigonish Harbour	BAY/BAIE	NS	Antigonish	11 F/12	45°39′	61°55′
Antigonish Landing	UNP/LNO	NS	Antigonish	11 F/12	45°38′	61°58′
Antinouri Lake	LAKE/LAC	NB	Restigouche	21 P/13	47°48′	65°59′
Antiquois, Lac	LAKE/LAC	QC	Témiscamingue	31 N/4	47°10′	77°51′
Antler	VILG/VILG	SK	14-7-30-W	62 F/11	49°34′	101°27′
Antler No. 61	MUN2/AZM2	SK		62 F/12	49°38′	101°40′
Antler River	RIV/CDE	MB/SK		62 F/3	49°08′	101°00′
Antoine-Labelle	MUN1/AZM1	QC	Antoine-Labelle	31 J/14	46°53′	75°20′
Antoine, Lac	LAKE/LAC	QC	Le Fjord-du-Saguenay	22 D/14	48°46′	71°04′
Antoine Lake	LAKE/LAC	BC	Cariboo	93 A/5	52°25′	121°30′
Antoine Lake	LAKE/LAC	NT	Mackenzie	95 H	61°42′	121°41′
Antoinette Bay	BAY/BAIE	NT	Franklin	340 A	80°51′	76°40′
Antonio	UNP/LNO	AB	14-10-14-W4	72 E/13	49°49′	111°48′
Anton Lake	UNP/LNO	AB	4-60-23-W4	83 I/3	54°09′	113°24′
Antrim	UNP/LNO	NS	Halifax	11 D/14	44°58′	63°23′
Antrim	UNP/LNO	ON	Carleton	31 F/8	45°22′	76°13′
Antross	UNP/LNO	AB	22-47-4-W5	83 G/2	53°05′	114°30′
Anuc, Lac	LAKE/LAC	QC	Kativik	34 O/6	59°20′	75°10′
Anurikallak	UNP/LNO	QC	Kativik	24 J/5	58°22′	67°50′
Anvil Island	UNP/LNO	BC	New Westminster	92 G/11	49°31′	123°18′
Anvil Island	ISL/ÎLE	BC	New Westminster	92 G/11	49°32′	123°18′
Anvil Mountain	MTN/MNT	BC	Lillooet	92 O/6	51°20′	123°25′
Anvil Range	MTN/MNT	YT		105 K/6	62°20′	133°00′
Anyox	UNP/LNO	BC	Cassiar	103 P/5	55°25′	129°49′
Anyutawl 31	IR/RI	BC	Cassiar	103 P/3	55°08′	129°24′
Anzac	UNP/LNO	AB	9-86-7-W4	74 D/6	56°27′	111°02′
Anzac	UNP/LNO	BC	Cariboo	93 J/15	54°46′	122°30′
Anzac River	RIV/CDE	BC	Cariboo	93 J/15	54°48′	122°32′
Apamitaukasich	UNP/LNO	QC	Kativik	33 O/13	55°56′	75°40′
Apeganau Lake	LAKE/LAC	MB	76-14-W	63 O/12	55°35′	99°34′
Apex	UNP/LNO	NT	Franklin	25 N/9	63°43′	68°27′
Apex Mountain	MTN/MNT	BC	Similkameen Division Yale	82 E/5	49°21′	119°54′
Apex Mountain	MTN/MNT	YT		115 J/8	62°28′	138°04′
Apica, Rivière	RIV/CDE	QC	Charlevoix	21 M/14	47°59′	71°25′
Apohaqui	UNP/LNO	NB	Kings	21 H/12	45°42′	65°36′
Appalaches, Les - also-aussi - Appalachian Mountains	MTN/MNT	QC	L'Islet	21 M/1	47°00′	70°00′
Appalachian Mountains - also-aussi - Appalaches, Les	MTN/MNT	QC	L'Islet	21 M/1	47°00′	70°00′
Appelo	UNP/LNO	ON	Sudbury	41 P/3	47°12′	81°24′
Appin	UNP/LNO	ON	Middlesex	40 I/13	42°48′	81°39′
Appin Road	UNP/LNO	PE	Queens	11 L/3	46°15′	63°24′
Appleby	UNP/LNO	ON	Halton	30 M/5	43°23′	79°46′
Appledale	UNP/LNO	BC	Kootenay	82 F/12	49°39′	117°32′
Appledore	UNP/LNO	ON	Kent	40 J/9	42°31′	82°09′

NAME NOM	ENTITY ENTITÉ	LOC 1 LIEU 1	LOC 2 LIEU 2	MAP CARTE	POSITION LAT	LONG
Applegrove	UNP/LNO	QC	Memphrémagog	31 H/1	45°05′	72°11′
Applegrove	UNP/LNO	BC	Kootenay	82 E/16	49°47′	118°05′
Apple Hill	UNP/LNO	QC	Argenteuil	31 G/9	45°34′	74°15′
Apple Hill	UNP/LNO	ON	Glengarry	31 G/2	45°13′	74°46′
Apple River	UNP/LNO	NS	Cumberland	21 H/7	45°28′	64°47′
Apple River	RIV/CDE	BC	Range 1 Coast	92 K/11	50°43′	125°25′
Appleton	TOWN/VIL2	NF		2 D/15	48°59′	54°52′
Appleton	UNP/LNO	ON	Lanark	31 F/1	45°11′	76°08′
Applewood Acres	UNP/LNO	ON	Peel	30 M/12	43°36′	79°35′
Applewood Heights	UNP/LNO	ON	Peel	30 M/12	43°37′	79°36′
Applewood Hills	UNP/LNO	ON	Peel	30 M/12	43°37′	79°36′
Apps Lake	LAKE/LAC	SK	74-15-W3	73 N/8	55°25′	108°18′
Apsagayu 1A	IR/RI	BC	Range 1 Coast	92 L/9	50°44′	126°29′
Apsey Lake	LAKE/LAC	ON	Sudbury	41 I/4	46°13′	81°47′
Apsley	UNP/LNO	ON	Peterborough	31 D/16	44°45′	78°06′
Apto	UNP/LNO	ON	Simcoe	31 D/12	44°31′	79°48′
Aquadell	UNP/LNO	SK	29-19-6-W3	72 J/10	50°38′	106°47′
Aquadeo	VILG/VILG	SK	16-48-17-W3	73 F/1	53°08′	108°25′
Aquadeo Beach - see-voir - Aquadeo	HAM/HAM	SK		73 F/1	53°08′	108°25′
Aquaforte	VILG/VILG	NF		1 N/2	47°00′	52°58′
Aquaforte Harbour	BAY/BAIE	NF		1 N/2	47°00′	52°56′
Aquatuk River	RIV/CDE	ON	Kenora	43 K/16	54°58′	84°06′
Aqueduc, Lac de l'	LAKE/LAC	QC	Côte-Nord-du-Golfe-Saint-Laurent	12 J/15	50°50′	58°59′
Aquiatulavik Point	UNP/LNO	NT	Franklin	36 B	64°22′	74°42′
Aqvik Trough	SEAU/SMER	—		7053	69°43′	66°45′
Arabella	UNP/LNO	SK	35-1-W2	63 D/1	52°03′	102°03′
Arabella Bay	BAY/BAIE	NT	Franklin	68 D	73°44′	99°11′
Arabian, Lac	LAKE/LAC	QC	Côte-Nord-du-Golfe-Saint-Laurent	12 J/14	50°55′	59°27′
Araignées, Lac aux	LAKE/LAC	QC	Le Granit	21 E/7	45°28′	70°49′
Ara Lake	LAKE/LAC	ON	Thunder Bay	42 L/11	50°33′	87°28′
Arbakka	UNP/LNO	MB	20-1-8-E	62 H/1	49°03′	96°29′
Arbeau Settlement	UNP/LNO	NB	Northumberland	21 I/12	46°38′	65°51′
Arborfield	TOWN/VIL2	SK	3-48-12-W2	63 E/4	53°06′	103°39′
Arborfield No. 456	MUN2/AZM2	SK		63 E/3	53°00′	103°30′
Arborg	VILG/VILG	MB	23-22-2-E	62 I/14	50°54′	97°13′
Arbor Vitae	UNP/LNO	ON	Rainy River	52 D/16	48°54′	94°18′
Arbre-à-Spring, L'	UNP/LNO	QC	Les Îles-de-la-Madeleine	11 N/14	47°47′	61°29′
Arbuckle	UNP/LNO	NB	Victoria	21 J/14	46°54′	67°23′
Arbury	UNP/LNO	SK	27-25-17-W2	72 P/1	51°09′	104°17′
Arbuthnot	UNP/LNO	SK	9-10-7-W3	72 G/15	49°49′	106°54′
Arbuthnot Island	ISL/ÎLE	NT	Franklin	57 F	70°45′	92°33′
Arbutus Ridge	UNP/LNO	BC	New Westminster	92 G/3	49°15′	123°10′
Arcadia	UNP/LNO	NS	Yarmouth	20 O/16	43°50′	66°04′
Arcadia	UNP/LNO	AB	8-74-14-W5	83 N/8	55°24′	116°08′
Ar-ce-wy-ee 4	IR/RI	BC	Rupert	92 L/11	50°33′	127°01′
Archambault, Lac	LAKE/LAC	QC	Matawinie	31 J/8	46°19′	74°15′
Archer	UNP/LNO	ON	Dundas	31 B/14	44°59′	75°06′
Archer Creek	RIV/CDE	BC	Kamloops Division Yale	93 A/8	52°18′	120°15′
Archer Fiord	BAY/BAIE	NT	Franklin	120 C	81°25′	67°00′
Archerwill	VILG/VILG	SK	18-40-13-W2	63 D/5	52°26′	103°51′
Archibald Lake	LAKE/LAC	NS	Guysborough	11 F/4	45°12′	61°57′
Archibald Lake	LAKE/LAC	SK	60-1-W2	63 L/1	54°11′	102°07′
Archibald Lake	LAKE/LAC	SK		74 N/2	59°01′	108°35′
Archibald, Mount	MTN/MNT	YT		115 A/13	60°47′	137°52′
Archibald Settlement	UNP/LNO	NB	Restigouche	21 O/16	47°53′	66°03′
Archibalds Mill	UNP/LNO	NS	Guysborough	11 E/8	45°19′	62°07′
Archibalds Mill Lake	LAKE/LAC	NS	Guysborough	11 E/8	45°20′	62°09′
Archie	MUN2/AZM2	MB		62 K/3	50°10′	101°15′
Archipel-de-Mingan, Réserve de parc national de l' - also-aussi - Mingan Archipelago National Park Reserve	PARK/PARC	QC	Minganie	12 L/3	50°13′	63°10′
Archive	UNP/LNO	SK	23-15-27-W2	72 I/5	50°17′	105°37′
Archydal	UNP/LNO	SK	35-17-28-W2	72 I/5	50°29′	105°45′
Arcola	TOWN/VIL2	SK	9-8-4-W2	62 E/9	49°38′	102°29′
Arctic Bay	HAM/HAM	NT	Franklin	48 C	73°02′	85°10′
Arctic Ocean - also-aussi - **Arctique, Océan**	SEA/MER	—				
Arctic Red River - see-voir - Tsiigehtchic	HAM/HAM	NT		106 N/5	67°27′	133°44′
Arctic Red River	RIV/CDE	NT	Mackenzie	106 N	67°27′	133°45′
Arctic Sound	CHAN/CHEN	NT	Mackenzie	76 N	67°32′	108°51′
Arctique, Océan - also-aussi - **Arctic Ocean**	SEA/MER	—				
Ardath	UNP/LNO	SK	33-30-9-W3	72 O/11	51°37′	107°14′
Ardbeg	UNP/LNO	ON	Parry Sound	41 H/9	45°38′	80°05′
Arden	UNP/LNO	ON	Frontenac	31 C/10	44°43′	76°56′
Arden	UNP/LNO	MB	13-15-14-W	62 J/6	50°17′	99°16′
Ardendale	UNP/LNO	ON	Frontenac	31 C/10	44°43′	76°57′
Ardenode	UNP/LNO	AB	21-25-25-W4	82 P/3	51°08′	113°26′
Ardenville	UNP/LNO	AB	10-7-26-W4	82 H/11	49°33′	113°27′

NAME NOM	ENTITY ENTITÉ	LOC 1 LIEU 1	LOC 2 LIEU 2	MAP CARTE	POSITION LAT	LONG
Ardgowan, Lieu historique national - also-aussi - Ardgowan National Historic Site	PARK/PARC	PE	Queens	11 L/6	46°15′	63°08′
Ardgowan National Historic Site - also-aussi - Ardgowan, Lieu historique national	PARK/PARC	PE	Queens	11 L/6	46°15′	63°08′
Ardill	HAM/HAM	SK	25-11-29-W2	72 H/13	49°56′	105°51′
Ardley	UNP/LNO	AB	16-38-23-W4	83 A/6	52°16′	113°14′
Ardmore	UNP/LNO	AB	1-62-4-W4	73 L/8	54°20′	110°29′
Ardmore	UNP/LNO	BC	North Saanich	92 B/11	48°38′	123°28′
Ardmore Beach	UNP/LNO	ON	Simcoe	41 A/9	44°42′	80°00′
Ardness	UNP/LNO	NS	Pictou	11 E/9	45°42′	62°14′
Ardoch	UNP/LNO	ON	Frontenac	31 C/15	44°56′	76°55′
Ardoise	UNP/LNO	NS	Hants	11 D/13	44°57′	63°56′
Ardrossan	UNP/LNO	AB	2-53-22-W4	83 H/11	53°33′	113°08′
Ardtrea	UNP/LNO	ON	Simcoe	31 D/11	44°41′	79°25′
Ardwick	UNP/LNO	SK	13-8-1-W3	72 G/9	49°38′	106°01′
Arelee	VILG/VILG	SK	10-38-11-W3	73 B/5	52°15′	107°30′
Argenta	UNP/LNO	BC	Kootenay	82 K/2	50°10′	116°55′
Argentenay, Pointe	CAPE/CAP	QC	L'Île-d'Orléans	21 M/2	47°01′	70°48′
Argenteuil	MUN1/AZM1	QC	Argenteuil	31 G/9	45°41′	74°25′
Argentia	UNP/LNO	NF		1 N/5	47°18′	53°59′
Argentia Beach	VILG/VILG	AB	13,14-47-1-W5	83 G/1	53°03′	114°01′
Argentine Mountain	MTN/MNT	BC	Kootenay	82 N/12	51°32′	117°54′
Argent, Lac d'	LAKE/LAC	QC	Kativik	23 O/14	55°58′	67°05′
Argent, Rivière à l'	RIV/CDE	QC	Manicouagan	22 K/6	50°22′	69°16′
Argo	UNP/LNO	SK	17-35-15-W3	73 C/1	52°01′	108°06′
Argo Bay	BAY/BAIE	NT	Franklin	97 C	69°23′	124°29′
Argo Lake	LAKE/LAC	ON	Rainy River	52 B/5	48°15′	91°48′
Argolis	UNP/LNO	ON	Algoma	42 B/11	48°42′	83°27′
Argon	UNP/LNO	ON	Thunder Bay	52 B/16	48°54′	90°01′
Argosy	UNP/LNO	NB	Victoria	21 J/13	46°59′	67°43′
Argue	UNP/LNO	MB	6-6-22-W	62 F/8	49°27′	100°27′
Arguyartu Point	CAPE/CAP	NT	Franklin	27 D	69°01′	67°43′
Argyle	MUN1/AZM1	NS	Yarmouth	20 P/13	43°56′	65°46′
Argyle	MUN2/AZM2	MB		62 G/6	49°21′	99°15′
Argyle	UNP/LNO	NS	Guysborough	11 F/5	45°23′	61°56′
Argyle	UNP/LNO	NS	Yarmouth	20 P/13	43°48′	65°51′
Argyle	UNP/LNO	NS	Yarmouth	20 P/13	43°49′	65°51′
Argyle	UNP/LNO	NB	Carleton	21 J/11	46°31′	67°20′
Argyle	UNP/LNO	ON	Victoria	31 D/6	44°27′	79°01′
Argyle	UNP/LNO	MB	7,18-14-1-E	62 I/3	50°11′	97°27′
Argyle Head	UNP/LNO	NS	Yarmouth	20 P/13	43°49′	65°51′
Argyle No. 1	MUN2/AZM2	SK		62 F/3	49°10′	101°30′
Argyle Park	UNP/LNO	SK		72 I/7	50°29′	104°38′
Argyle Shore	UNP/LNO	PE	Queens	11 L/3	46°10′	63°21′
Argyle Sound	UNP/LNO	NS	Yarmouth	20 P/12	43°41′	65°49′
Arichat	UNP/LNO	NS	Richmond	11 F/11	45°31′	61°01′
Arisaig	UNP/LNO	NS	Antigonish	11 E/16	45°45′	62°10′
Arisaig Point	CAPE/CAP	NS	Antigonish	11 E/16	45°46′	62°10′
Ariss	UNP/LNO	ON	Wellington	40 P/9	43°35′	80°22′
Aristazabal Island	ISL/ÎLE	BC	Range 3 Coast	103 A/6	52°38′	129°05′
Arizona	UNP/LNO	MB	9,10,15,16-10-12-W	62 G/14	49°50′	99°02′
Arjay, Lac	LAKE/LAC	QC	Kativik	23 P/3	55°00′	65°27′
Arkell	UNP/LNO	ON	Wellington	40 P/9	43°32′	80°10′
Arkell, Mount	MTN/MNT	YT		105 D/12	60°36′	135°37′
Arklan	UNP/LNO	ON	Lanark	31 F/1	45°05′	76°21′
Arkona	VILG/VILG	ON	Lambton	40 P/4	43°04′	81°50′
Arkwood	UNP/LNO	ON	Kent	40 J/8	42°29′	82°07′
Arkwright	UNP/LNO	ON	Bruce	41 A/6	44°28′	81°14′
Arlagnuk Point	CAPE/CAP	NT	Franklin	47 D	69°12′	81°18′
Arlington	UNP/LNO	PE	Prince	11 L/12	46°32′	63°54′
Arlington	UNP/LNO	NS	Kings	21 H/1	45°12′	64°26′
Arlington	UNP/LNO	YT		116 B/3	64°02′	139°10′
Arlington Beach	HAM/HAM	SK	25-26-24-W2	72 P/3	51°15′	105°14′
Arlington No. 79	MUN2/AZM2	SK		72 F/10	49°40′	108°40′
Arlington West	UNP/LNO	NS	Annapolis	21 A/14	44°55′	65°17′
Arma	UNP/LNO	SK	4-42-3-W3	73 B/9	52°35′	106°22′
Armada	UNP/LNO	AB	12-17-21-W4	82 I/7	50°25′	112°46′
Armadale	UNP/LNO	ON	York	30 M/14	43°50′	79°15′
Armagh	VILG/VILG	QC	Bellechasse	21 L/10	46°45′	70°35′
Armagh Station	UNP/LNO	QC	Bellechasse	21 L/10	46°43′	70°35′
Armark Lake	LAKE/LAC	NT	Mackenzie	66 K	66°29′	100°50′
Armark River	RIV/CDE	NT	Keewatin	66 N	67°45′	101°05′
Armbro Heights	UNP/LNO	ON	Peel	30 M/12	43°40′	79°45′
Armdale	UNP/LNO	NS	Halifax	11 D/12	44°38′	63°38′
Armena	UNP/LNO	AB	12-48-21-W4	83 H/2	53°07′	112°57′
Armi Lake	LAKE/LAC	NT	Mackenzie	85 O	63°43′	114°07′
Armilla	UNP/LNO	SK	11-8-5-W2	62 E/10	49°38′	102°35′

NAME NOM	ENTITY ENTITÉ	LOC 1 LIEU 1	LOC 2 LIEU 2	MAP CARTE	POSITION LAT	POSITION LONG
Armit	UNP/LNO	SK	32-44-30-W	63 C/13	52°50′	101°47′
Armitage	UNP/LNO	ON	York	31 D/3	44°02′	79°29′
Armit Lake	LAKE/LAC	ON	Kenora	52 J/7	50°28′	90°56′
Armit Lake	LAKE/LAC	MB/SK		63 C/12	52°33′	101°35′
Armit Lake	LAKE/LAC	NT	Keewatin	56 B	64°10′	91°32′
Armit River	RIV/CDE	MB/SK		63 C/13	52°55′	101°30′
Armley	UNP/LNO	SK	6-48-14-W2	73 H/1	53°07′	104°02′
Armond	UNP/LNO	NB	Carleton	21 J/6	46°25′	67°23′
Armour	MUN2/AZM2	ON	Parry Sound	31 E/11	45°39′	79°20′
Armour	UNP/LNO	SK	12-18-20-W2	72 I/10	50°31′	104°37′
Armour Heights	UNP/LNO	ON	York	30 M/11	43°45′	79°26′
Armour, Mount	MTN/MNT	BC	Cassiar	114 O/15	59°55′	138°42′
Armow	UNP/LNO	ON	Bruce	41 A/4	44°12′	81°31′
Arm River	RIV/CDE	SK	18-21-22-W2	72 I/14	50°47′	105°02′
Arm River No. 252	MUN2/AZM2	SK		72 P/4	51°15′	105°50′
Arms	UNP/LNO	ON	Thunder Bay	42 E/9	49°34′	86°00′
Armstrong	CITY/VIL1	BC	Kamloops Division Yale	82 L/6	50°27′	119°12′
Armstrong	MUN2/AZM2	ON	Timiskaming	31 M/12	47°43′	79°49′
Armstrong	MUN2/AZM2	MB		62 I/11	50°40′	97°27′
Armstrong	UNP/LNO	QC	Beauce-Sartigan	21 E/16	45°57′	70°27′
Armstrong	UNP/LNO	ON	Thunder Bay	52 I/6	50°18′	89°02′
Armstrong	UNP/LNO	YT		105 N/3	63°03′	133°24′
Armstrong Brook	UNP/LNO	NB	Restigouche	21 P/13	47°55′	65°58′
Armstrong, Cape	CAPE/CAP	NT	Franklin	560 E	82°06′	88°03′
Armstrong Junction	UNP/LNO	BC	Kamloops Division Yale	82 L/6	50°27′	119°12′
Armstrong Lake	LAKE/LAC	MB	77,78-4-E	63 P/10	55°43′	96°56′
Armstrong Mills	UNP/LNO	ON	Wellington	40 P/9	43°38′	80°16′
Armstrong Point	CAPE/CAP	NT	Franklin	88 B	72°56′	117°17′
Armstrongs Corners	UNP/LNO	ON	Lanark	31 C/16	44°56′	76°18′
Armstrongs Point	UNP/LNO	MB		62 H/14	49°53′	97°09′
Arnaud	UNP/LNO	MB	27,34-3-3-E	62 H/6	49°15′	97°06′
Arnaud, Rivière	RIV/CDE	QC	Kativik	24 N/13	59°59′	69°46′
Arner	UNP/LNO	ON	Essex	40 J/2	42°02′	82°49′
Arnes	UNP/LNO	MB	8-21-4-E	62 I/15	50°48′	97°00′
Arneson	UNP/LNO	AB	4-26-1-W4	72 M/1	51°12′	110°04′
Arnheim Place	UNP/LNO	SK		72 I/7	50°26′	104°35′
Arnold	UNP/LNO	NS	Shelburne	20 P/11	43°43′	65°02′
Arnold	UNP/LNO	BC	New Westminster	92 G/1	49°09′	122°03′
Arnold	UNP/LNO	BC	New Westminster	92 G/1	49°01′	122°09′
Arnold's Cove	TOWN/VIL2	NF		1 N/13	47°46′	53°59′
Arnolds Cove Station	UNP/LNO	NF		1 N/13	47°47′	53°58′
Arnot	UNP/LNO	MB	19-78-6-E	63 P/15	55°46′	96°41′
Arnot Lake	LAKE/LAC	NT	Mackenzie	65 E	61°18′	103°17′
Arnott	UNP/LNO	ON	Grey	41 A/7	44°26′	80°51′
Arnott Strait	CHAN/CHEN	NT	Franklin	69 B	76°18′	103°34′
Arnprior	TOWN/VIL2	ON	Renfrew	31 F/8	45°26′	76°21′
Arnstein	UNP/LNO	ON	Parry Sound	31 E/13	45°55′	79°56′
Arntfield	VILG/VILG	QC	Rouyn-Noranda	32 D/3	48°12′	79°15′
Aroland	UNP/LNO	ON	Thunder Bay	42 L/2	50°14′	86°59′
Aroland 83	IR/RI	ON	Thunder Bay	42 L/2	50°13′	87°00′
Aroma Lake	LAKE/LAC	SK		73 C/7	52°18′	108°33′
Aroostook	VILG/VILG	NB	Victoria	21 J/13	46°48′	67°43′
Aroostook River	RIV/CDE	NB	Victoria	21 J/13	46°49′	67°43′
Arpiers	UNP/LNO	SK	34-17-W2	72 P/13	51°57′	105°47′
Arpin	UNP/LNO	ON	Cochrane	42 A/15	48°56′	80°43′
Arqusiugaq	UNP/LNO	QC	Kativik	25 C/12	60°33′	69°46′
Arran	VILG/VILG	SK	6-34-30-W	62 N/13	51°53′	101°43′
Arran	MUN2/AZM2	ON	Bruce	41 A/6	44°28′	81°14′
*Arrandale	UNP/LNO	BC	Range 5 Coast	103 J/15	54°59′	130°00′
Arran Lake	LAKE/LAC	ON	Bruce	41 A/6	44°29′	81°15′
Arranvale	UNP/LNO	ON	Bruce	41 A/6	44°27′	81°09′
Arras	UNP/LNO	BC	Peace River	93 P/10	55°45′	120°32′
Arrondissement historique de Québec, Site du patrimoine mondial de l' - also-aussi - The Historic District of Québec World Heritage Site	PARK/PARC	QC		21 L/14	46°49′	71°13′
Arrow Creek	UNP/LNO	BC	Kootenay	82 F/1	49°08′	116°27′
Arrowhead	UNP/LNO	BC	Kootenay	82 K/12	50°43′	117°55′
Arrowhead Lake	LAKE/LAC	AB	123-22-W4	84 P/12	59°42′	113°38′
Arrowhead River	RIV/CDE	NT	Mackenzie	95 B	60°21′	123°03′
Arrow Lake	LAKE/LAC	ON	Thunder Bay	52 B/1	48°09′	90°16′
Arrow Lake	LAKE/LAC	ON	Kenora	52 E/8	49°19′	94°25′
Arrow Park Lake - see-voir - Mosquito Lake	LAKE/LAC	BC		82 L/8	50°19′	118°04′
Arrow River	UNP/LNO	MB	31-13-25-W	62 K/2	50°09′	100°54′
Arrow River	RIV/CDE	ON	Thunder Bay	52 A/4	48°01′	89°44′
Arrow River	RIV/CDE	MB	10-13-26-W	62 K/2	50°05′	100°57′
Arrowsmith	UNP/LNO	BC	Alberni	92 F/7	49°15′	124°42′
Arrowsmith Bay	BAY/BAIE	NT	Keewatin	57 B	68°04′	94°52′

NAME / NOM	ENTITY / ENTITÉ	LOC 1 / LIEU 1	LOC 2 / LIEU 2	MAP / CARTE	POSITION LAT	POSITION LONG
Arrowsmith, Mount	MTN/MNT	BC	Cameron	92 F/2	49°13'	124°36'
Arrowsmith River	RIV/CDE	NT	Keewatin	57 A	68°22'	90°17'
Arrowview Heights	UNP/LNO	BC	Alberni	92 F/2	49°14'	124°46'
Arrowwood	VILG/VILG	AB	32-20-23-W4	82 I/11	50°44'	113°09'
Arsenault Lake	LAKE/LAC	SK	70,71-17-W3	73 N/2	55°06'	108°32'
Arseneault	UNP/LNO	QC	Les Îles-de-la-Madeleine	11 N/5	47°25'	61°46'
Artemesia	MUN2/AZM2	ON	Grey	41 A/2	44°15'	80°31'
Arthabaska	MUN1/AZM1	QC	Arthabaska	31 H/16	45°55'	72°05'
Arthabaska, Lac	LAKE/LAC	QC	Charlevoix	21 M/10	47°40'	70°47'
Arthur	VILG/VILG	ON	Wellington	40 P/15	43°50'	80°32'
Arthur	MUN2/AZM2	ON	Wellington	40 P/15	43°55'	80°40'
Arthur	MUN2/AZM2	MB		62 F/2	49°10'	101°00'
Arthurette	UNP/LNO	NB	Victoria	21 J/14	46°47'	67°29'
Arthur Fiord	BAY/BAIE	NT	Franklin	59 B	76°30'	93°24'
Arthur, Lac	LAKE/LAC	QC	Minganie	12 M/1	51°09'	62°23'
Arthur Laing Peninsula	CAPE/CAP	NT	Franklin	120 F	82°53'	68°47'
Arthur Lake	LAKE/LAC	BC	Kamloops Division Yale	82 L/11	50°32'	119°28'
Arthur-LeBlanc, Mont	MTN/MNT	QC	Le Fjord-du-Saguenay	22 D/8	48°24'	70°12'
Arthur's Corners	UNP/LNO	ON	Oxford	40 I/15	42°54'	80°35'
Arthurville	UNP/LNO	QC	Bellechasse	21 L/15	46°49'	70°45'
Artifice, L'	UNP/LNO	QC	Le Haut-Saint-Laurent	31 H/4	45°05'	73°51'
Artillery Lake	LAKE/LAC	NT	Mackenzie	75 O/4	63°09'	107°52'
Artillery Park National Historic Site - also-aussi - Parc-de-l'Artillerie, Lieu historique national du	PARK/PARC	QC	Communauté urbaine de Québec	21 L/14	46°49'	71°13'
Artimon, Banc d' - also-aussi - Artimon Bank	SEAU/SMER	—		8008	45°10'	58°00'
Artimon Bank - also-aussi - Artimon, Banc d'	SEAU/SMER	—		8008	45°10'	58°00'
Artland	UNP/LNO	SK	7-43-27-W3	73 C/12	52°42'	109°53'
Artlish 12	IR/RI	BC	Rupert	92 L/3	50°07'	127°05'
Artlish River	RIV/CDE	BC	Rupert	92 L/3	50°07'	127°05'
Arundel	VILG/VILG	QC	Les Laurentides	31 G/15	45°58'	74°37'
Arva	UNP/LNO	ON	Middlesex	40 P/3	43°03'	81°17'
Arvalik Islands	ISL/ÎLE	NT	Franklin	24 J	58°36'	66°39'
Arvert, Lac - see-voir - Arvert Lake	LAKE/LAC	NF		13 C/5	52°17'	61°45'
Arvert Lake	LAKE/LAC	NF		13 C/5	52°17'	61°45'
Arviat	HAM/HAM	NT	Keewatin	55 E/1	61°07'	94°04'
Arvida	UNP/LNO	QC	Le Fjord-du-Saguenay	22 D/6	48°25'	71°11'
Arvilla	UNP/LNO	AB	12-58-1-W5	83 G/16	53°59'	114°00'
Asahal Lake 2	IR/RI	BC	Cariboo	93 B/1	52°09'	122°01'
Asakioyo Lake - see-voir - Asakiyo Lake	LAKE/LAC	MB		54 D/11	56°44'	95°10'
Asakiyo Lake	LAKE/LAC	MB		54 D/11	56°44'	95°10'
Asati	UNP/LNO	QC	Le Haut-Saint-Maurice	31 P/5	47°25'	73°57'
Asbestos	CITY/VIL1	QC	Asbestos	21 E/13	45°46'	71°56'
Asbestos	MUN1/AZM1	QC	Asbestos	21 E/12	45°44'	71°48'
Ascalon	UNP/LNO	ON	Nipissing	31 L/2	46°05'	78°49'
Ascension	UNP/LNO	PE	Prince	21 I/16	46°57'	64°04'
Ascension Islands	ISL/ÎLE	NT	Keewatin	46 A	64°22'	81°41'
Ascot	VILG/VILG	QC	Sherbrooke	21 E/5	45°21'	71°50'
Ascot Corner	VILG/VILG	QC	Le Haut-Saint-François	21 E/5	45°27'	71°46'
Ash	UNP/LNO	ON	Halton	30 M/5	43°26'	79°49'
Asham Point	UNP/LNO	MB	12-26-12-W	62 O/3	51°14'	99°03'
Ash Bay	BAY/BAIE	ON	Rainy River	52 C/14	48°54'	93°27'
Ashburn	UNP/LNO	ON	Ontario	31 D/2	44°00'	79°00'
Ashburnham	UNP/LNO	ON	Peterborough	31 D/8	44°18'	78°18'
Ashburton	UNP/LNO	ON	Nipissing	41 I/9	46°31'	80°01'
Ashburton Bay	BAY/BAIE	ON	Thunder Bay	42 D/15	48°47'	86°43'
Ashbury	UNP/LNO	MB	3-10-22-W	62 F/16	49°48'	100°23'
Ashby	UNP/LNO	NS	Cape Breton	11 K/1	46°08'	60°10'
Ashby Lake	LAKE/LAC	ON	Lennox and Addington	31 F/3	45°05'	77°21'
Ashby Mill	UNP/LNO	ON	Peterborough	31 C/5	44°28'	77°50'
Ash Creek	RIV/CDE	BC	Cassiar	104 O/2	59°22'	130°57'
Ashcroft	VILG/VILG	BC	Kamloops Division Yale	92 I/11	50°43'	121°17'
Ashcroft 4	IR/RI	BC	Kamloops Division Yale	92 I/11	50°43'	121°19'
Ashdad	UNP/LNO	ON	Renfrew	31 F/7	45°21'	76°45'
Ashdale	UNP/LNO	NS	Antigonish	11 E/9	45°31'	62°02'
Ashdale	UNP/LNO	NS	Hants	11 E/4	45°00'	63°56'
*Ashdod	UNP/LNO	ON	Renfrew	31 F/7	45°21'	76°45'
Ashe Inlet	BAY/BAIE	NT	Franklin	25 L	62°34'	70°36'
Ashern	UNP/LNO	MB	23-25-7-W	62 O/1	51°11'	98°21'
Asheweig River	RIV/CDE	ON	Kenora	43 L/6	54°17'	87°12'
Ashfield	MUN2/AZM2	ON	Huron	40 P/13	43°55'	81°40'
Ashfield	UNP/LNO	NS	Inverness	11 F/14	45°55'	61°10'
Ashgrove	UNP/LNO	ON	Halton	30 M/12	43°36'	79°53'
Ashigami Lake	LAKE/LAC	ON	Sudbury	41 I/10	46°39'	80°34'
Ash Lake	LAKE/LAC	ON	Rainy River	52 C/14	48°57'	93°27'
Ashland	UNP/LNO	NB	Carleton	21 J/6	46°19'	67°28'
Ashley Lake	LAKE/LAC	MB		64 I/4	58°06'	97°48'

NAME NOM	ENTITY ENTITÉ	LOC 1 LIEU 1	LOC 2 LIEU 2	MAP CARTE	POSITION LAT	LONG
Ashlu Creek	RIV/CDE	BC	New Westminster	92 G/14	49°54′	123°17′
Ashmont	UNP/LNO	AB	27-59-11-W4	73 L/4	54°08′	111°34′
Ashmore	UNP/LNO	NS	Digby	21 A/5	44°28′	65°58′
Ashnola 10	IR/RI	BC	Similkameen Division Yale	82 E/4	49°13′	120°00′
Ashnola River	RIV/CDE	BC	Similkameen Division Yale	82 E/4	49°13′	119°58′
Ash River	RIV/CDE	ON	Cochrane	42 K/8	50°29′	84°30′
Ash River	RIV/CDE	BC	Alberni	92 F/7	49°22′	124°59′
Ashton	UNP/LNO	ON	Carleton	31 F/1	45°09′	76°02′
Ashton Creek	UNP/LNO	BC	Kamloops Division Yale	82 L/1	50°33′	119°01′
Ashton Station	UNP/LNO	ON	Lanark	31 F/1	45°10′	76°03′
Ashuanipi	UNP/LNO	NF		23 B/16	52°46′	66°05′
Ashuanipi Lake	LAKE/LAC	NF		23 B/9	52°45′	66°15′
Ashuanipi River	RIV/CDE	NF		23 H/14	53°58′	65°24′
Ashuapmushuan, Lac	LAKE/LAC	QC	Le Domaine-du-Roy	32 H/4	49°10′	73°45′
Ashuapmushuan, Réserve faunique	PARK/PARC	QC	Le Domaine-du-Roy	32 H/4	49°05′	73°32′
Ashuapmushuan, Rivière	RIV/CDE	QC	Le Domaine-du-Roy	32 A/9	48°37′	72°20′
Ashville	UNP/LNO	MB	24-25-21-W	62 N/1	51°11′	100°18′
Ashworth	UNP/LNO	ON	Muskoka	31 E/6	45°21′	79°24′
Asiak River	RIV/CDE	NT	Mackenzie	86 O	67°46′	114°25′
Asikunitakupuch	UNP/LNO	QC	Jamésie	33 D/10	52°30′	78°33′
Asimakaniseekan Askiy 102A	IR/RI	SK		73 B/15	53°00′	106°54′
Asinich Aatiwapich	UNP/LNO	QC	Jamésie	33 K/9	54°42′	76°28′
Asinich Ausapich	UNP/LNO	QC	Jamésie	33 L/16	54°57′	78°16′
Asinkaanumevatt	UNP/LNO	MB		63 A/7	52°15′	96°51′
Asipoquobah Lake	LAKE/LAC	ON	Kenora	53 G/11	53°40′	91°15′
Asipwayasich	UNP/LNO	QC	Jamésie	33 D/7	52°16′	78°32′
Askey Lake	LAKE/LAC	MB		64 O/10	59°39′	98°43′
Askikkapit	UNP/LNO	MB		53 L/12	54°37′	95°56′
Askilton	UNP/LNO	NS	Inverness	11 F/11	45°42′	61°18′
Askwasimwakwanan	UNP/LNO	QC	Jamésie	33 D/15	52°58′	78°57′
Askwataskupich	UNP/LNO	QC	Kativik	24 F/12	57°41′	69°33′
Aspdin	UNP/LNO	ON	Muskoka	31 E/6	45°18′	79°22′
Aspen	UNP/LNO	NF		2 C/4	48°10′	53°45′
Aspen	UNP/LNO	NS	Guysborough	11 E/8	45°18′	62°03′
Aspen Beach	UNP/LNO	AB	22-40-28-W4	83 A/5	52°27′	113°56′
Aspen Beach Provincial Park	PARK/PARC	AB	21,28-40-28-W4	83 A/5	52°28′	113°58′
Aspen Cove	UNP/LNO	NF		2 E/8	49°27′	54°06′
Aspen Cove	UNP/LNO	SK	2-53-19-W3	73 F/10	53°33′	108°41′
Aspen Cove	BAY/BAIE	NF		2 E/8	49°28′	54°06′
Aspen Grove	UNP/LNO	BC	Kamloops Division Yale	92 H/15	49°56′	120°37′
Aspen Park	UNP/LNO	MB	18-19-4-E	62 I/11	50°38′	97°02′
Aspey Brook	UNP/LNO	NF		2 C/4	48°10′	53°51′
Asphodel	MUN2/AZM2	ON	Peterborough	31 C/5	44°20′	78°00′
Aspotogan	UNP/LNO	NS	Lunenburg	21 A/9	44°31′	64°03′
Aspy Bay	UNP/LNO	NS	Victoria	11 K/16	46°55′	60°29′
Aspy Bay	BAY/BAIE	NS	Victoria	11 K/16	46°56′	60°24′
Asquith	TOWN/VIL2	SK	33-36-9-W3	73 B/3	52°08′	107°13′
Asquith	UNP/LNO	SK	27-36-9-W3	73 B/3	52°07′	107°13′
Assaikwatamo River	RIV/CDE	MB		54 D/13	56°52′	95°50′
Assean Lake	LAKE/LAC	MB		64 A/2	56°13′	96°30′
Assean River	RIV/CDE	MB		54 D/5	56°18′	95°55′
Asselstine	UNP/LNO	ON	Lennox and Addington	31 C/2	44°14′	76°44′
Assemetquagan, Rivière	RIV/CDE	QC	Avignon	22 B/3	48°05′	67°06′
Assiginack	MUN2/AZM2	ON	Manitoulin	41 H/13	45°49′	81°55′
Assigny, Lac	LAKE/LAC	NF		22 P/14	52°00′	65°20′
Assineau	UNP/LNO	AB	32-73-8-W5	83 O/6	55°22′	115°11′
Assineau River 150F	IR/RI	AB	5-74-8-W5	83 O/6	55°23′	115°11′
Assineweetasataypawin	UNP/LNO	MB		63 A/1	52°12′	96°25′
Assiniboia	TOWN/VIL2	SK	10-8-30-W2	72 H/12	49°38′	105°59′
Assiniboia	VILG/VILG	MB		62 H/14	49°52′	97°16′
Assiniboia	UNP/LNO	MB		62 H/14	49°54′	97°21′
Assiniboia East	UNP/LNO	SK		72 I/7	50°26′	104°35′
Assiniboine 76	IR/RI	SK		62 L/6	50°20′	103°28′
Assiniboine, Mount	MTN/MNT	AB/BC		82 J/13	50°52′	115°38′
Assiniboine Park - Fort Garry - see-voir - Assiniboia	VILG/VILG	MB		62 H/14	49°52′	97°16′
Assiniboine Park - Fort Garry - see-voir - Headingley	VILG/VILG	MB		62 H/14	49°52′	97°23′
Assiniboine River - also-aussi - +Assiniboine, Rivière	RIV/CDE	MB/SK		62 H/14	49°53′	97°08′
+Assiniboine, Rivière - also-aussi - Assiniboine River	RIV/CDE	MB		62 H/14	49°53′	97°08′
Assinica, Lac	LAKE/LAC	QC	Jamésie	32 J/11	50°30′	75°16′
Assinica, Réserve faunique	PARK/PARC	QC	Jamésie	32 J/11	50°37′	75°14′
Assiniview Park	UNP/LNO	MB		62 G/13	49°51′	99°59′
Assumption	UNP/LNO	ON	Peterborough	31 D/8	44°16′	78°16′
Assumption	UNP/LNO	AB	1-112-5-W6	84 L/10	58°40′	118°36′
Astle	UNP/LNO	NB	York	21 J/8	46°25′	66°28′
Aston Bay	BAY/BAIE	NT	Franklin	58 C	73°44′	95°00′

NAME NOM	ENTITY ENTITÉ	LOC 1 LIEU 1	LOC 2 LIEU 2	MAP CARTE	POSITION LAT	LONG
Aston, Cape	CAPE/CAP	NT	Franklin	27 D	70°00′	67°15′
Aston-Jonction	TOWN/VIL2	QC	Nicolet-Yamaska	31 I/1	46°10′	72°14′
Aston River	RIV/CDE	NT	Franklin	58 C	73°40′	94°38′
Aston Station	UNP/LNO	QC	Nicolet-Yamaska	31 I/1	46°11′	72°16′
Astorville	UNP/LNO	ON	Nipissing	31 L/3	46°11′	79°17′
Astray	UNP/LNO	NF		23 J/10	54°36′	66°42′
Astray Lake	LAKE/LAC	NF		23 J/9	54°33′	66°30′
Astrolabe Lake	LAKE/LAC	SK		74 P/12	59°39′	105°50′
Astron Bay	BAY/BAIE	ON	Kenora	52 E/7	49°27′	94°34′
Astronomical Society Islands	ISL/ÎLE	NT	Franklin	57 D	69°50′	91°34′
Asuwapamatikunan	UNP/LNO	QC	Jamésie	32 L/14	50°47′	79°23′
Atakakup 104 - see-voir - Ahtahkakoop 104	IR/RI	SK		73 G/7	53°24′	106°54′
Atbara	UNP/LNO	BC	Kootenay	82 F/11	49°36′	117°10′
Atchelitz	UNP/LNO	BC	New Westminster	92 G/1	49°07′	122°01′
Athabasca	TOWN/VIL2	AB	16-66-22-W4	83 I/11	54°43′	113°17′
Athabasca Falls	FALL/CHUT	AB	4-27-W5	83 C/12	52°40′	117°52′
Athabasca, Lac - also-aussi - **Athabasca, Lake**	LAKE/LAC	SK/AB		74 N/2	59°13′	108°40′
Athabasca, Lake - also-aussi - **Athabasca, Lac**	LAKE/LAC	SK/AB		74 N/2	59°13′	108°40′
Athabasca Landing Provincial Historic Site (Undeveloped)	PARK/PARC	AB	66-22-W4	83 I/11	54°43′	113°17′
Athabasca, Mount	MTN/MNT	AB	37-23-W5	83 C/3	52°11′	117°13′
Athabasca No. 12, County of	MUN1/AZM1	AB	66-21-W4	83 I/11	54°44′	113°03′
Athabasca Pass National Historic Site - also-aussi - Col-Athabasca, Lieu historique national du	PARK/PARC	AB		83 D/8	52°23′	118°11′
Athabasca River - also-aussi - **Athabasca, Rivière**	RIV/CDE	AB		74 L/10	58°40′	110°50′
Athabasca, Rivière - also-aussi - **Athabasca River**	RIV/CDE	AB		74 L/10	58°40′	110°50′
Athalmer	UNP/LNO	BC	Kootenay	82 K/9	50°31′	116°01′
Athapap	UNP/LNO	MB	31-64-28-W	63 K/12	54°34′	101°41′
Athapapuskow Lake	LAKE/LAC	MB/SK		63 K/12	54°37′	101°39′
Atha Road	UNP/LNO	ON	Ontario	30 M/14	43°56′	79°10′
Athelstan	UNP/LNO	QC	Le Haut-Saint-Laurent	31 G/1	45°02′	74°11′
Athelstane Lake	LAKE/LAC	ON	Thunder Bay	52 B/16	48°46′	90°12′
Athenia Lake	LAKE/LAC	NT	Mackenzie	75 M	63°38′	111°30′
Athens	VILG/VILG	ON	Leeds	31 B/12	44°38′	75°57′
Atherley	UNP/LNO	ON	Ontario	31 D/11	44°36′	79°22′
Atherton	UNP/LNO	ON	Norfolk	40 I/16	42°49′	80°27′
Athlone	UNP/LNO	ON	Simcoe	31 D/4	44°02′	79°53′
Athlone Island	ISL/ÎLE	BC	Range 3 Coast	103 A/1	52°11′	128°26′
Athlow Bay	BAY/BAIE	BC	Queen Charlotte	103 F/10	53°38′	132°59′
Athol	MUN2/AZM2	ON	Prince Edward	30 N/14	43°55′	77°11′
Athol	UNP/LNO	NS	Cumberland	21 H/9	45°40′	64°13′
Athol	UNP/LNO	ON	Glengarry	31 G/7	45°19′	74°53′
Athol	UNP/LNO	ON	Prince Edward	30 N/14	43°55′	77°14′
Athol Bay	BAY/BAIE	ON	Prince Edward	30 N/14	43°53′	77°15′
Athol Road	UNP/LNO	NS	Cumberland	21 H/9	45°38′	64°05′
Athol Station	UNP/LNO	NS	Cumberland	21 H/9	45°41′	64°13′
Atholville	VILG/VILG	NB	Restigouche	21 O/15	47°59′	66°43′
Aticonipi, Lac	LAKE/LAC	QC	Minganie	12 O/14	51°52′	59°22′
Atik	UNP/LNO	MB	23-61-27-W	63 K/6	54°18′	101°24′
Atikamakw Pachistiwakan	UNP/LNO	QC	Jamésie	33 J/15	54°53′	74°37′
Atikameg	UNP/LNO	AB	8-80-11-W5	83 O/13	55°56′	115°39′
Atikameg Lake	UNP/LNO	MB	3-58-24-W	63 F/15	53°59′	100°56′
Atikameg River	RIV/CDE	ON	Kenora	43 B/7	52°30′	82°46′
Atikkamek Creek	RIV/CDE	AB	65-19-W5	83 K/10	54°36′	116°51′
Atik Lake - see-voir - Utik Lake	LAKE/LAC	MB		53 M/5	55°16′	95°58′
Atik Lake	LAKE/LAC	MB	60-27,28-W	63 K/3	54°14′	101°30′
Atikokan	MUN2/AZM2	ON	Rainy River	52 B/13	48°46′	91°37′
Atikokan	UNP/LNO	ON	Rainy River	52 B/13	48°45′	91°37′
Atikonak Lake	LAKE/LAC	NF		23 A/10	52°40′	64°32′
Atikonak River	RIV/CDE	NF		23 H/2	53°14′	64°43′
Atik River - see-voir - Utik River	RIV/CDE	MB		53 M/11	55°32′	95°21′
Atikwa Lake	LAKE/LAC	ON	Kenora	52 F/6	49°27′	93°34′
Atironto	UNP/LNO	ON	Lanark	31 C/16	44°54′	76°00′
Atitikwapustasich	UNP/LNO	QC	Kativik	33 O/3	55°04′	75°11′
Atkins Lake	LAKE/LAC	ON	Leeds	31 B/13	44°45′	75°51′
Atkinson	UNP/LNO	NS	Cumberland	11 E/12	45°39′	63°43′
Atkinson	UNP/LNO	ON	Frontenac	31 C/8	44°23′	76°17′
Atkinson Lake - see-voir - Fox Lake	LAKE/LAC	MB		53 M/15	56°00′	94°48′
Atkinson Lake	LAKE/LAC	NT	Mackenzie	75 A	60°52′	105°52′
Atkinson, Point	CAPE/CAP	BC	New Westminster	92 G/6	49°20′	123°16′
Atkinson Point	CAPE/CAP	NT	Mackenzie	66 M	67°55′	102°55′
Atkinson Point	CAPE/CAP	NT	Franklin	107 D	69°57′	131°27′
Atlanta	UNP/LNO	NS	Kings	21 H/2	45°09′	64°31′
Atlantic	UNP/LNO	NS	Shelburne	20 P/11	43°35′	65°20′
Atlantic Ocean - also-aussi - **Atlantique, Océan**	SEA/MER	—				
Atlantique, Océan - also-aussi - **Atlantic Ocean**	SEA/MER	—				
Atlee	UNP/LNO	AB	5-22-7-W4	72 L/15	50°50′	110°57′

NAME / NOM	ENTITY / ENTITÉ	LOC 1 / LIEU 1	LOC 2 / LIEU 2	MAP / CARTE	POSITION LAT	POSITION LONG
Atlin	UNP/LNO	BC	Cassiar	104 N/12	59°34′	133°42′
Atlin Lake	LAKE/LAC	BC/YT		104 N/4	59°33′	133°43′
Atlin Mountain	MTN/MNT	BC	Cassiar	104 N/12	59°32′	133°52′
Atlin-Teslin Indian Cemetery 4	IR/RI	BC	Cassiar	104 N/12	59°34′	133°41′
Atluck	UNP/LNO	BC	Rupert	92 L/2	50°12′	126°59′
Atluck Lake	LAKE/LAC	BC	Rupert	92 L/2	50°13′	126°58′
Atmore	UNP/LNO	AB	20-67-17-W4	83 I/15	54°49′	112°33′
Atna Lake	LAKE/LAC	BC	Range 5 Coast	93 L/4	54°02′	127°47′
Atna Range	MTN/MNT	BC	Cassiar	93 M/13	55°54′	127°30′
Atnarko	UNP/LNO	BC	Range 3 Coast	93 C/5	52°24′	125°50′
Atnarko River	RIV/CDE	BC	Range 3 Coast	93 D/8	52°22′	126°06′
Attachie	UNP/LNO	BC	Peace River	94 A/3	56°13′	121°25′
Attawapiskat	UNP/LNO	ON	Kenora	43 B/16	52°56′	82°24′
Attawapiskat 91	IR/RI	ON	Kenora	43 F/9	53°33′	84°21′
Attawapiskat 91A	IR/RI	ON	Kenora	43 B/16	52°56′	82°25′
Attawapiskat Lake	LAKE/LAC	ON	Kenora	43 D/5	52°18′	87°54′
Attawapiskat River	RIV/CDE	ON	Kenora	43 B/16	52°57′	82°18′
Attercliffe	UNP/LNO	ON	Haldimand	30 L/13	42°59′	79°36′
Attercliffe Station	UNP/LNO	ON	Haldimand	30 L/13	42°58′	79°36′
Attica	UNP/LNO	SK	29-34-22-W2	72 P/14	51°57′	105°06′
Attic, Lac	LAKE/LAC	QC	Vallée-de-l'Or	32 C/8	48°17′	76°23′
Atticoupi, Lac	LAKE/LAC	QC	Caniapiscau	23 C/12	52°39′	69°56′
Attikamagen Lake	LAKE/LAC	NF		23 J/16	55°00′	66°30′
Attikuan, Pointe	CAPE/CAP	QC	Jamésie	33 L/6	54°16′	79°27′
Attitti Lake	LAKE/LAC	SK		63 M/1	55°08′	102°28′
Attwood Lake	LAKE/LAC	ON	Thunder Bay	52 P/2	51°15′	88°30′
Attwood River	RIV/CDE	ON	Thunder Bay	42 M/5	51°25′	87°49′
Atwater	VILG/VILG	SK	4-21-2-W2	62 L/16	50°47′	102°13′
Atwood	MUN2/AZM2	ON	Rainy River	52 D/15	48°46′	94°37′
Atwood	UNP/LNO	ON	Perth	40 P/11	43°40′	81°01′
Atwood Point	CAPE/CAP	NT	Franklin	340 B	80°33′	83°47′
Atwoods Brook	UNP/LNO	NS	Shelburne	20 P/12	43°30′	65°40′
Atzinging Lake	LAKE/LAC	NT	Mackenzie	65 D	60°13′	103°10′
Aua River	RIV/CDE	NT	Franklin	46 J/9	66°43′	82°22′
Auassat Kapmehenhiht	UNP/LNO	QC	Minganie	12 M/13	51°50′	63°43′
Auberge-de-Ski-Skoki, Lieu historique national de l' - also-aussi - Skoki Ski Lodge National Historic Site	PARK/PARC	AB		82 N/9	51°31′	116°05′
Aubert-Gallion	VILG/VILG	QC	Beauce-Sartigan	21 L/2	46°05′	70°45′
Aubichon Arm	BAY/BAIE	SK		73 O/5	55°33′	108°00′
Aubigny	UNP/LNO	MB		62 H/6	49°27′	97°15′
Aubinadong River	RIV/CDE	ON	Algoma	41 J/14	46°51′	83°22′
Aubrey	UNP/LNO	QC	Le Haut-Saint-Laurent	31 H/4	45°08′	73°48′
Aubry Lake	LAKE/LAC	NT	Mackenzie	96 M	67°24′	126°27′
Auburn	UNP/LNO	PE	Queens	11 L/7	46°18′	62°54′
Auburn	UNP/LNO	NS	Kings	21 H/2	45°01′	64°52′
Auburn	UNP/LNO	ON	Huron	40 P/13	43°47′	81°33′
Auburndale	UNP/LNO	NS	Lunenburg	21 A/7	44°24′	64°36′
Auburndale	UNP/LNO	AB	18-47-6-W4	73 E/2	53°03′	110°52′
Auburn Mills	UNP/LNO	ON	Peterborough	31 D/8	44°19′	78°19′
Auburnton	UNP/LNO	SK	21-5-1-W2	62 E/8	49°24′	102°05′
Auburnton Creek	RIV/CDE	SK	14-4-34-W	62 F/5	49°18′	101°58′
Auburnville	UNP/LNO	NB	Northumberland	21 P/3	47°00′	65°08′
Aubut	UNP/LNO	QC	Témiscouata	21 N/6	47°27′	69°00′
Auchistikunapasunanuch	UNP/LNO	QC	Jamésie	33 K/13	54°52′	77°51′
Auclair	VILG/VILG	QC	Témiscouata	21 N/10	47°44′	68°39′
Auden	UNP/LNO	ON	Thunder Bay	42 L/4	50°14′	87°53′
Auden Park	UNP/LNO	ON	Frontenac	31 C/2	44°14′	76°35′
Audet	VILG/VILG	QC	Le Granit	21 E/10	45°39′	70°44′
Audhild Bay	BAY/BAIE	NT	Franklin	560 D	81°34′	90°30′
Audiepvre, Lac	LAKE/LAC	QC	Kativik	13 M/12	55°40′	63°55′
Audley	UNP/LNO	ON	Ontario	30 M/14	43°54′	79°01′
Audoin, Lac	LAKE/LAC	QC	Témiscamingue	31 L/15	46°54′	78°48′
Audy	UNP/LNO	QC	Mékinac	31 I/16	46°56′	72°28′
Augers Lake	LAKE/LAC	BC	Lillooet	92 O/12	51°31′	123°57′
Augier Lake	LAKE/LAC	BC	Range 5 Coast	93 K/5	54°25′	125°35′
Augier Lake 22	IR/RI	BC	Range 5 Coast	93 K/5	54°27′	125°37′
Augsburg	UNP/LNO	ON	Renfrew	31 F/11	45°31′	77°11′
Auguet, Cape	CAPE/CAP	NS	Richmond	11 F/6	45°28′	61°00′
Augusta	MUN2/AZM2	ON	Leeds	31 B/13	44°45′	75°36′
Augusta, Mount	MTN/MNT	YT		115 C/8	60°18′	140°27′
Augustine Cove	UNP/LNO	PE	Prince	11 L/4	46°14′	63°37′
Augustines, Lac des	LAKE/LAC	QC	La Vallée-de-la-Gatineau	31 O/12	47°37′	75°57′
Augustus Island	ISL/ÎLE	NT	Franklin	25 O	63°35′	67°41′
Augustus Lake	LAKE/LAC	NT	Mackenzie	86 K	66°21′	116°43′
Aukpar River	RIV/CDE	NT	Franklin	36 H	65°30′	73°58′
Aulac	UNP/LNO	NB	Westmorland	21 H/16	45°52′	64°17′

NAME NOM	ENTITY ENTITÉ	LOC 1 LIEU 1	LOC 2 LIEU 2	MAP CARTE	POSITION LAT	LONG
Aulac River	RIV/CDE	NB	Westmorland	21 H/16	45°52'	64°19'
Aulassivik, Pointe	CAPE/CAP	QC	Kativik	35 L/8	62°16'	78°10'
Aulavik National Park - also-aussi - Aulavik, Parc national	PARK/PARC	NT	Franklin	88 C/12	73°42'	119°55'
Aulavik, Parc national - also-aussi - Aulavik National Park	PARK/PARC	NT	Franklin	88 C/12	73°42'	119°55'
Aulds Cove	UNP/LNO	NS	Antigonish	11 F/11	45°39'	61°27'
Aulitivik Island	ISL/ÎLE	NT	Franklin	27 C	69°36'	68°01'
Aulitiving Island	ISL/ÎLE	NT	Franklin	27 D	69°33'	67°33'
Aulnaies, Rivière des	RIV/CDE	QC	Le Fjord-du-Saguenay	22 D/6	48°29'	71°19'
Aulneau Peninsula	CAPE/CAP	ON	Kenora	52 E/8	49°23'	94°29'
Aulneuse, Rivière	RIV/CDE	QC	Les Chutes-de-la-Chaudière	21 L/11	46°43'	71°23'
Aumond	VILG/VILG	QC	La Vallée-de-la-Gatineau	31 J/12	46°30'	75°50'
Aumond	UNP/LNO	QC	La Vallée-de-la-Gatineau	31 J/5	46°28'	75°53'
Aumond, Lacs	LAKE/LAC	QC	Pontiac	31 K/12	46°34'	77°33'
Aunor	UNP/LNO	ON	Cochrane	42 A/6	48°26'	81°17'
Aupaluk	VILG/VILG	QC	Kativik	24 N/5	59°18'	69°36'
Aupaluktut Island	ISL/ÎLE	NT	Franklin	26 G	65°24'	66°50'
Aupasich	UNP/LNO	QC	Jamésie	33 D/7	52°16'	78°33'
Aupe 6A	IR/RI	BC	Range 1 Coast	92 K/6	50°20'	125°04'
Aupe 6	IR/RI	BC	Range 1 Coast	92 K/6	50°20'	125°04'
Auriol Range	MTN/MNT	YT		115 A/12	60°38'	137°38'
Aurland Fiord	BAY/BAIE	NT	Franklin	560 D	81°04'	94°25'
Aurora	TOWN/VIL2	ON	York	31 D/3	44°00'	79°28'
Aurore, Pic de l'	CAPE/CAP	QC	Pabok	22 A/9	48°32'	64°14'
Ausable River	RIV/CDE	ON	Lambton	40 P/4	43°19'	81°46'
Austin	VILG/VILG	QC	Memphrémagog	31 H/1	45°11'	72°17'
Austin	UNP/LNO	ON	Sudbury	41 I/7	46°29'	80°51'
Austin	UNP/LNO	MB	29-11-11-W	62 G/15	49°57'	98°56'
Austin Bay	BAY/BAIE	NT	Franklin	87 A	68°33'	113°10'
Austin Channel	CHAN/CHEN	NT	Franklin	68 G	75°26'	103°16'
Austin Heights	UNP/LNO	BC	New Westminster	92 G/7	49°15'	122°52'
Austin Island	ISL/ÎLE	NT	Keewatin	55 F	61°20'	94°00'
Austin's Flat 3	IR/RI	BC	Yale Division Yale	92 H/14	49°47'	121°27'
Australia Mountain	MTN/MNT	YT		115 O/9	63°37'	138°08'
Australian	UNP/LNO	BC	Cariboo	93 B/9	52°44'	122°27'
Auteuil	UNP/LNO	QC	Laval	31 H/12	45°38'	73°46'
Authier	VILG/VILG	QC	Abitibi-Ouest	32 D/10	48°44'	78°51'
Authier-Nord	VILG/VILG	QC	Abitibi-Ouest	32 D/15	48°50'	78°52'
Autridge Bay	BAY/BAIE	NT	Franklin	47 F	70°03'	85°15'
Auvergne No. 76	MUN2/AZM2	SK		72 G/11	49°40'	107°25'
Auyuittuq National Park Reserve - also-aussi - Auyuittuq, Réserve de parc national	PARK/PARC	NT	Franklin	26 P/5	67°30'	66°00'
Auyuittuq, Réserve de parc national - also-aussi - Auyuittuq National Park Reserve	PARK/PARC	NT	Franklin	26 P/5	67°30'	66°00'
Ava	UNP/LNO	SK	33-19-W3	72 N/15	51°51'	108°37'
Ava Inlet	BAY/BAIE	NT	Franklin	25 M	63°49'	71°55'
Avalon	UNP/LNO	SK		73 B/2	52°06'	106°39'
Avalon Channel - also-aussi - Avalon, Chenal d'	SEAU/SMER	—		8014	46°30'	53°00'
Avalon, Chenal d' - also-aussi - Avalon Channel	SEAU/SMER	—		8014	46°30'	53°00'
Avalon Park	UNP/LNO	ON	Norfolk	40 I/16	42°46'	80°15'
Avalon Peninsula	CAPE/CAP	NF		1 N/6	47°30'	53°30'
Avayalik Islands	ISL/ÎLE	NF		25 A/1	60°07'	64°14'
Avebury	UNP/LNO	SK	17-48-7-W3	73 G/2	53°09'	106°59'
Avening	UNP/LNO	ON	Simcoe	41 A/8	44°18'	80°04'
Avenir	UNP/LNO	AB	6-70-15-W4	83 P/1	55°02'	112°16'
Averil, Mount	MTN/MNT	BC	Cariboo	93 J/8	54°25'	122°25'
Avery	UNP/LNO	SK	28-49-14-W3	73 G/4	53°15'	107°59'
Avery Island 92	IR/RI	BC	Range 5 Coast	103 J/2	54°13'	130°46'
Avery Point	UNP/LNO	ON	Victoria	31 D/11	44°40'	79°07'
Avignon	MUN1/AZM1	QC	Avignon	22 B/2	48°06'	66°51'
Aviron Bay	BAY/BAIE	NF		11 P/10	47°34'	56°49'
Aviron Point	CAPE/CAP	NF		11 P/10	47°32'	56°49'
Avoca	UNP/LNO	QC	Argenteuil	31 G/10	45°43'	74°42'
Avola	UNP/LNO	BC	Kamloops Division Yale	82 M/14	51°47'	119°19'
Avon	UNP/LNO	NB	Queens	21 J/1	46°04'	66°03'
Avon	UNP/LNO	ON	Middlesex	40 I/15	42°54'	80°56'
Avonbank	UNP/LNO	ON	Perth	40 P/6	43°20'	81°08'
Avondale	TOWN/VIL2	NF		1 N/6	47°25'	53°12'
Avondale	UNP/LNO	PE	Queens	11 L/2	46°15'	62°50'
Avondale	UNP/LNO	NS	Pictou	11 E/9	45°38'	62°18'
Avondale	UNP/LNO	NS	Hants	21 H/1	45°01'	64°07'
Avondale	UNP/LNO	NB	Carleton	21 J/5	46°19'	67°39'
Avondale	UNP/LNO	ON	Glengarry	31 G/2	45°13'	74°41'
Avondale Road	UNP/LNO	NB	Carleton	21 J/5	46°18'	67°40'
Avondale Station	UNP/LNO	NS	Pictou	11 E/9	45°37'	62°18'
Avonhurst	UNP/LNO	SK	26-19-16-W2	72 I/9	50°38'	104°08'
Avonlea	VILG/VILG	SK	22-12-23-W2	72 I/3	50°01'	105°04'
Avonlea Creek	RIV/CDE	SK	4-14-22-W2	72 I/2	50°09'	104°57'

NAME / NOM	ENTITY / ENTITÉ	LOC 1 / LIEU 1	LOC 2 / LIEU 2	MAP / CARTE	POSITION LAT	LONG
Avonmore	UNP/LNO	ON	Stormont	31 G/2	45°10'	74°58'
Avonport	UNP/LNO	NS	Kings	21 H/1	45°06'	64°15'
Avonport Station	UNP/LNO	NS	Kings	21 H/1	45°07'	64°14'
Avon River	RIV/CDE	NS	Hants	21 H/1	45°07'	64°13'
Avon River	RIV/CDE	ON	Perth	40 P/6	43°18'	81°10'
Avonry	UNP/LNO	ON	Lambton	40 J/16	42°45'	82°21'
Avonton	UNP/LNO	ON	Perth	40 P/6	43°21'	81°05'
Awagakama River	RIV/CDE	ON	Cochrane	42 O/4	51°06'	83°33'
Aweme	UNP/LNO	MB	32-8-16-W	62 G/12	49°43'	99°36'
Awikwaschiskach	UNP/LNO	QC	Kativik	33 O/3	55°02'	75°04'
Awikwataukach	UNP/LNO	QC	Kativik	34 B/2	56°08'	74°44'
Awikwataukach	UNP/LNO	QC	Kativik	33 N/2	55°06'	76°51'
Awry Lake	LAKE/LAC	NT	Mackenzie	85 J	62°56'	114°55'
Axe Lake	UNP/LNO	ON	Parry Sound	31 E/5	45°24'	79°32'
Axe Lake	LAKE/LAC	ON	Parry Sound	31 E/5	45°23'	79°30'
Axel Heiberg Island	ISL/ÎLE	NT	Franklin	59 H	79°45'	91°00'
Axe Point	UNP/LNO	NT	Mackenzie	85 E	61°18'	118°41'
Axford	UNP/LNO	SK	17-8-18-W2	72 H/9	49°39'	104°25'
Ayde, Lac	LAKE/LAC	QC	Jamésie	33 A/6	52°20'	73°25'
Ayer's Cliff	TOWN/VIL2	QC	Memphrémagog	31 H/1	45°10'	72°03'
Ayers Lake	LAKE/LAC	NB	Carleton	21 J/3	46°12'	67°20'
Aylechootlook 5	IR/RI	BC	New Westminster	92 G/1	49°07'	122°06'
Aylen	UNP/LNO	ON	Renfrew	31 L/1	46°13'	78°13'
Aylen Lake	UNP/LNO	ON	Nipissing	31 F/12	45°36'	77°52'
Aylen Lake	LAKE/LAC	ON	Nipissing	31 F/12	45°37'	77°51'
Aylen Lake Station	UNP/LNO	ON	Nipissing	31 F/12	45°33'	77°50'
Aylesbury	VILG/VILG	SK	10-23-27-W2	72 I/13	50°56'	105°41'
Ayles Fiord	BAY/BAIE	NT	Franklin	340 F	82°45'	80°00'
Aylesford	VILG/VILG	NS	Kings	21 H/2	45°02'	64°50'
Aylesford East	UNP/LNO	NS	Kings	21 H/2	45°02'	64°48'
Aylesford Lake	LAKE/LAC	NS	Kings	21 A/15	44°57'	64°40'
Aylesford Mountain	UNP/LNO	NS	Kings	21 H/2	45°04'	64°51'
Aylesworth	UNP/LNO	ON	Frontenac	31 C/7	44°17'	76°32'
Aylesworth, Mount	MTN/MNT	BC	Cassiar	114 O/15	59°56'	138°47'
Aylmer	CITY/VIL1	QC	Communauté urbaine de l'Outaouais	31 G/5	45°24'	75°50'
Aylmer	TOWN/VIL2	ON	Elgin	40 I/15	42°46'	80°59'
Aylmer, Barrage	MISC/DIV	QC	Le Haut-Saint-François	21 E/14	45°46'	71°24'
Aylmer, Lac	LAKE/LAC	QC	L'Amiante	21 E/14	45°49'	71°21'
Aylmer Lake	LAKE/LAC	BC	Kamloops Division Yale	82 L/13	50°51'	119°43'
Aylmer Lake	LAKE/LAC	NT	Mackenzie	76 C	64°05'	108°30'
Aylmer, Mount	MTN/MNT	AB	27-11-W5	82 O/6	51°19'	115°27'
Aylmer Sound	UNP/LNO	QC	Côte-Nord-du-Golfe-Saint-Laurent	12 J/11	50°37'	59°27'
Aylsham	VILG/VILG	SK	2-49-13-W2	63 E/4	53°12'	103°49'
Aylsworth	UNP/LNO	ON	Rainy River	52 C/12	48°33'	93°49'
Aylwin	UNP/LNO	QC	La Vallée-de-la-Gatineau	31 F/16	45°59'	76°01'
Aylwin Station	UNP/LNO	QC	La Vallée-de-la-Gatineau	31 F/16	45°59'	76°03'
Ayr	UNP/LNO	ON	Waterloo	40 P/8	43°17'	80°27'
Ayr Lake	LAKE/LAC	NT	Franklin	27 F	70°24'	70°15'
Ayrness	UNP/LNO	QC	Le Haut-Saint-Laurent	31 H/4	45°11'	73°52'
Aysiwataukach	UNP/LNO	QC	Kativik	33 O/4	55°03'	75°34'
Aytiwawastach	UNP/LNO	QC	Kativik	33 O/1	55°04'	74°30'
Ayton	UNP/LNO	ON	Grey	41 A/2	44°03'	80°55'
Ayton Siding	UNP/LNO	ON	Grey	41 A/2	44°02'	80°56'
Aywawwis 15	IR/RI	BC	Yale Division Yale	92 H/6	49°24'	121°25'
Azen	UNP/LNO	ON	Nipissing	41 I/9	46°38'	80°15'
Azilda	UNP/LNO	ON	Sudbury	41 I/11	46°33'	81°06'
Azouzetta	UNP/LNO	BC	Cariboo	93 O/7	55°24'	122°37'
Azure	UNP/LNO	AB	12-18-29-W4	82 I/12	50°30'	113°52'
Azure Lake	LAKE/LAC	BC	Kamloops Division Yale	93 A/8	52°23'	120°07'
Azure Mountain	MTN/MNT	BC	Kamloops Division Yale	93 A/8	52°18'	120°05'
Azu Ski Village	UNP/LNO	BC	Cariboo	93 O/7	55°23'	122°38'

B

NAME / NOM	ENTITY / ENTITÉ	LOC 1 / LIEU 1	LOC 2 / LIEU 2	MAP / CARTE	POSITION LAT	LONG
Baad Fiord	BAY/BAIE	NT	Franklin	49 B	76°28'	86°30'
Babbage River	RIV/CDE	YT		117 D/3	69°14'	138°27'
Babbitt	UNP/LNO	NB	Sunbury	21 G/16	45°51'	66°20'
Babcock	UNP/LNO	MB	11-6-8-W	62 G/8	49°28'	98°27'
Babel, Mont	MTN/MNT	QC	Manicouagan	22 N/7	51°27'	68°42'
Babiche, La	UNP/LNO	QC	Antoine-Labelle	31 J/5	46°15'	75°42'
Babine 6	IR/RI	BC	Cassiar	93 M/7	55°19'	126°38'
Babine 16	IR/RI	BC	Cassiar	93 M/7	55°19'	126°39'
Babine 17	IR/RI	BC	Cassiar	93 M/3	55°02'	127°20'

NAME NOM	ENTITY ENTITÉ	LOC 1 LIEU 1	LOC 2 LIEU 2	MAP CARTE	POSITION LAT	POSITION LONG
Babine 18	IR/RI	BC	Cassiar	93 M/3	55°02′	127°23′
Babine 25	IR/RI	BC	Range 5 Coast	93 L/16	54°52′	126°08′
Babine 26	IR/RI	BC	Range 5 Coast	93 L/16	54°57′	126°08′
Babine Lake	LAKE/LAC	BC	Range 5 Coast	93 L/16	54°45′	126°00′
Babine Lake 20	IR/RI	BC	Cassiar	93 M/1	55°04′	126°28′
Babine Lake 21B	IR/RI	BC	Range 5 Coast	93 K/5	54°29′	125°39′
Babine Range	MTN/MNT	BC	Range 5 Coast	93 M/6	55°16′	127°15′
Babine River	RIV/CDE	BC	Cassiar	93 M/12	55°41′	127°42′
Babine River 21	IR/RI	BC	Cassiar	93 M/7	55°25′	126°41′
Babine River 21A	IR/RI	BC	Cassiar	93 M/7	55°25′	126°40′
Baby, Lac	LAKE/LAC	QC	Témiscamingue	31 M/11	47°30′	79°19′
Baby Point	UNP/LNO	ON	York	30 M/11	43°39′	79°30′
Babys Point	UNP/LNO	ON	Lambton	40 J/10	42°39′	82°30′
Bacalhao Island	ISL/ÎLE	NF		2 E/10	49°42′	54°33′
Baccalieu Island	UNP/LNO	NF		2 C/2	48°09′	52°48′
Baccalieu Island	ISL/ÎLE	NF		2 C/2	48°08′	52°48′
Baccaro	UNP/LNO	NS	Shelburne	20 P/6	43°29′	65°28′
Baccaro, Banc de - also-aussi - Baccaro Bank	SEAU/SMER	—		4474	43°00′	64°45′
Baccaro Bank - also-aussi - Baccaro, Banc de	SEAU/SMER	—		4474	43°00′	64°45′
Baccaro Point	CAPE/CAP	NS	Shelburne	20 P/6	43°27′	65°28′
Bacchus, Lac	LAKE/LAC	QC	Kativik	23 O/7	55°23′	66°53′
Bache Peninsula	CAPE/CAP	NT	Franklin	39 H	79°08′	76°00′
Back	UNP/LNO	MB		54 E/9	57°42′	94°14′
Back Bay	UNP/LNO	NB	Charlotte	21 G/2	45°03′	66°52′
Back Bay	BAY/BAIE	NT	Franklin	68 D	73°32′	97°20′
Backbone Ranges	MTN/MNT	NT/YT		105 P/15	63°53′	128°45′
Back Brook	RIV/CDE	NF		1 K/11	46°45′	53°17′
Back, Cape	CAPE/CAP	NT	Franklin	87 F	70°09′	116°46′
Back Centre	UNP/LNO	NS	Lunenburg	21 A/8	44°22′	64°22′
Back Clarendon	UNP/LNO	NB	Charlotte	21 G/7	45°26′	66°34′
Back Cove	UNP/LNO	NF		12 H/15	49°50′	56°34′
Back Cove	BAY/BAIE	NF		11 P/9	47°38′	56°15′
Back Harbour	UNP/LNO	NF		2 E/10	49°40′	54°47′
Back Lake	LAKE/LAC	MB		53 L/14	54°58′	95°14′
Back Lake	LAKE/LAC	NT	Mackenzie	75 N	63°48′	109°21′
Back Lots	UNP/LNO	NB	Northumberland	21 P/4	47°03′	65°31′
Back Point	CAPE/CAP	NT	Franklin	77 A	68°53′	104°30′
Backport	UNP/LNO	QC	Memphrémagog	31 H/1	45°10′	72°11′
Back River	RIV/CDE	NT	Keewatin	56 M	67°15′	95°15′
Back Settlement	UNP/LNO	NS	Antigonish	11 F/13	45°50′	61°58′
Back Shore	UNP/LNO	NF		1 K/12	46°37′	53°36′
Back-up Pond	LAKE/LAC	NF		2 E/1	49°05′	54°11′
Backway, The	BAY/BAIE	NF		13 J/1	54°55′	58°17′
Bacon Cove	UNP/LNO	NF		1 N/6	47°29′	53°10′
Bacon Ridge	UNP/LNO	MB	23-11,12-W	62 O/3	51°00′	99°00′
Bacon's Bay	UNP/LNO	QC	Memphrémagog	31 H/1	45°11′	72°02′
Bacqueville, Lac	LAKE/LAC	QC	Kativik	34 I/4	58°07′	73°50′
Bad Bay	BAY/BAIE	NF		12 I/11	50°32′	57°24′
Baddeck	VILG/VILG	NS	Victoria	11 K/2	46°06′	60°45′
Baddeck Bay	UNP/LNO	NS	Victoria	11 K/2	46°08′	60°42′
Baddeck Bridge	UNP/LNO	NS	Victoria	11 K/2	46°07′	60°48′
Baddeck River	RIV/CDE	NS	Victoria	11 K/2	46°05′	60°52′
Baddow	UNP/LNO	ON	Victoria	31 D/10	44°36′	78°46′
Baden	UNP/LNO	ON	Waterloo	40 P/7	43°24′	80°39′
Baden	UNP/LNO	MB	7-44-26-W	63 C/14	52°47′	101°13′
Badenoch	UNP/LNO	ON	Wellington	40 P/8	43°28′	80°06′
Badgeley Island	ISL/ÎLE	ON	Manitoulin	41 H/13	45°56′	81°36′
Badgeley Point	CAPE/CAP	ON	Manitoulin	41 H/13	45°58′	81°38′
Badger	TOWN/VIL2	NF		12 A/16	48°59′	56°02′
Badger	UNP/LNO	MB	6-3-12-E	52 E/4	49°11′	95°58′
Badger Bay	BAY/BAIE	NF		2 E/5	49°26′	55°40′
Badger Lake	LAKE/LAC	BC	Kamloops Division Yale	92 P/1	51°02′	120°08′
Badger's Corners	UNP/LNO	ON	Parry Sound	41 H/8	45°23′	80°01′
Badger's Quay	UNP/LNO	NF		2 F/4	49°07′	53°35′
Badger's Quay-Valleyfield-Pool's Island-Wesleyville-Newtown - see-voir - New-Wes-Valley	TOWN/VIL2	NF		2 F/4	49°09′	53°34′
Badgerville	UNP/LNO	SK	34-30-32-W	62 N/12	51°38′	101°55′
Badham, Mount	MTN/MNT	YT		115 B/13	60°51′	139°52′
Bad Heart	UNP/LNO	AB	17-75-2-W6	83 M/8	55°30′	118°18′
Bad Heart River	RIV/CDE	AB	2-76-2-W6	83 M/9	55°33′	118°12′
Badjeros	UNP/LNO	ON	Grey	41 A/8	44°16′	80°17′
Bad Lake	LAKE/LAC	SK	28-18-W3	72 N/8	51°23′	108°26′
Badlands No. 7, Municipal District of	MUN1/AZM1	AB	27,28,29-18,19,20-W4	82 P/7	51°25′	112°37′
Bad Vermilion Lake	LAKE/LAC	ON	Rainy River	52 C/10	48°44′	92°40′
Badwater River	RIV/CDE	SK		74 I/12	58°35′	105°44′
Bad Weather Cape	CAPE/CAP	NT	Franklin	560 B	80°09′	96°40′

NAME NOM	ENTITY ENTITÉ	LOC 1 LIEU 1	LOC 2 LIEU 2	MAP CARTE	POSITION LAT	LONG
Baelstadt	UNP/LNO	ON	Renfrew	31 F/14	45°55'	77°21'
Baezaeko River	RIV/CDE	BC	Cariboo	93 G/4	53°08'	123°40'
Baezaeko River 25	IR/RI	BC	Cariboo	93 B/13	52°59'	123°48'
Baezaeko River 26	IR/RI	BC	Cariboo	93 B/13	52°58'	123°48'
Baezaeko River 27	IR/RI	BC	Cariboo	93 B/13	52°59'	123°48'
Baffin, Baie de - also-aussi - **Baffin Bay**	BAY/BAIE	NT	Franklin	38 A	74°00'	68°00'
Baffin Basin	SEAU/SMER	—		800A	66°00'	72°00'
Baffin Bay - also-aussi - **Baffin, Baie de**	BAY/BAIE	NT	Franklin	38 A	74°00'	68°00'
Baffin, Cape	CAPE/CAP	NT	Keewatin	46 G	65°42'	83°10'
Baffin, Île de - also-aussi - **Baffin Island**	ISL/ÎLE	NT	Franklin	37 A	68°00'	75°00'
Baffin Island - also-aussi - **Baffin, Île de**	ISL/ÎLE	NT	Franklin	37 A	68°00'	75°00'
Bagdad	UNP/LNO	NB	Queens	21 H/13	45°55'	65°51'
Bagnall	UNP/LNO	ON	Kent	40 J/8	42°21'	82°22'
Bagot	UNP/LNO	MB	33-11-9-W	62 G/15	49°58'	98°38'
Bagot and Blythfield	MUN2/AZM2	ON	Renfrew	31 F/7	45°18'	76°42'
Bagot, Mount	MTN/MNT	BC	Cassiar	104 M/6	59°21'	135°01'
Bagotville	UNP/LNO	QC	Le Fjord-du-Saguenay	22 D/7	48°21'	70°53'
Bagotville, Base des Forces canadiennes - also-aussi - Bagotville, Canadian Forces Base	MIL/MIL	QC	Le Fjord-du-Saguenay	22 D/7	48°20'	70°59'
Bagotville, Canadian Forces Base - also-aussi - Bagotville, Base des Forces canadiennes	MIL/MIL	QC	Le Fjord-du-Saguenay	22 D/7	48°20'	70°59'
Bague Bay	BAY/BAIE	SK		73 P/6	55°25'	105°21'
Baie-Atibenne	MUN2/AZM2	QC	Matawinie	31 O/8	47°23'	74°27'
Baie-Carrière	UNP/LNO	QC	Vallée-de-l'Or	31 M/16	47°50'	78°01'
Baie-Comeau	CITY/VIL1	QC	Manicouagan	22 F/1	49°13'	68°09'
Baie-de-la-Bouteille	MUN2/AZM2	QC	Matawinie	31 I/13	46°46'	73°40'
Baie-de-l'Ours	UNP/LNO	QC	Papineau	31 G/14	45°52'	75°07'
Baie-des-Bacon	UNP/LNO	QC	La Haute-Côte-Nord	22 C/11	48°31'	69°17'
Baie-des-Brises	UNP/LNO	QC	Beauharnois-Salaberry	31 G/1	45°12'	74°10'
Baie-des-Capucins	UNP/LNO	QC	Denis-Riverin	22 G/2	49°02'	66°51'
Baie-des-Cèdres	UNP/LNO	QC	Témiscamingue	31 M/6	47°18'	79°28'
Baie-des-Chaloupes	MUN2/AZM2	QC	Antoine-Labelle	31 J/10	46°35'	74°32'
Baie-des-Ha! Ha!	UNP/LNO	QC	Côte-Nord-du-Golfe-Saint-Laurent	12 J/15	50°56'	58°58'
Baie-de-Shawinigan	TOWN/VIL2	QC	Le Centre-de-la-Mauricie	31 I/10	46°32'	72°46'
Baie-des-Homards	UNP/LNO	QC	Sept-Rivières	22 G/14	49°50'	67°07'
Baie-des-Rochers	UNP/LNO	QC	Charlevoix-Est	21 N/13	47°58'	69°51'
Baie-des-Sables	VILG/VILG	QC	Matane	22 B/12	48°43'	67°51'
Baie-d'Hudson	MUN2/AZM2	QC	Kativik	34 J/11	58°30'	75°00'
Baie-Dorval	UNP/LNO	QC	Témiscamingue	31 L/14	46°59'	79°15'
Baie Du Doré	UNP/LNO	ON	Bruce	41 A/5	44°20'	81°33'
Baie-du-Febvre	VILG/VILG	QC	Nicolet-Yamaska	31 I/2	46°08'	72°43'
Baie-d'Urfé	CITY/VIL1	QC	Communauté urbaine de Montréal	31 H/5	45°25'	73°55'
Baie-James	VILG/VILG	QC	Jamésie	33 C/1	52°00'	76°00'
Baie-Johan-Beetz	VILG/VILG	QC	Minganie	12 L/7	50°17'	62°48'
Baie-Jolie	UNP/LNO	QC	Francheville	31 I/7	46°17'	72°38'
Baie, La	UNP/LNO	QC	Portneuf	31 I/9	46°43'	72°01'
Baie-Laperrière	UNP/LNO	QC	Témiscamingue	31 M/6	47°17'	79°27'
Baie-Laval	UNP/LNO	QC	La Haute-Côte-Nord	22 C/14	48°46'	69°03'
Baie-Noire	UNP/LNO	QC	Papineau	31 G/11	45°36'	75°11'
Baie-Obaoca	MUN2/AZM2	QC	Matawinie	31 O/9	47°31'	74°18'
Baie-Rouge	UNP/LNO	QC	Côte-Nord-du-Golfe-Saint-Laurent	12 J/15	50°49'	58°58'
Baie-Sainte-Anne	UNP/LNO	NB	Northumberland	21 P/2	47°03'	64°57'
Baie-Sainte-Catherine	VILG/VILG	QC	Charlevoix-Est	22 C/4	48°06'	69°44'
Baie-Sainte-Claire	UNP/LNO	QC	Minganie	22 H/16	49°54'	64°30'
Baie-Saint-Ludger	UNP/LNO	QC	Manicouagan	22 F/1	49°05'	68°19'
Baie-Saint-Paul	CITY/VIL1	QC	Charlevoix	21 M/7	47°27'	70°30'
Baie St. Paul	GEOG/GÉOG	MB		62 I/4	50°01'	97°48'
Baies, Lac des	LAKE/LAC	QC	Rimouski-Neigette	22 C/2	48°10'	68°40'
Baies, Lac des	LAKE/LAC	QC	La Haute-Côte-Nord	22 C/5	48°20'	69°46'
Baies, Lac des	LAKE/LAC	QC	Le Fjord-du-Saguenay	22 E/1	49°12'	70°05'
Baies, Lac des	LAKE/LAC	QC	Vallée-de-l'Or	31 N/5	47°18'	77°40'
Baie-Trinité	TOWN/VIL2	QC	Manicouagan	22 G/6	49°25'	67°18'
Baie-Trinité-Est	UNP/LNO	QC	Manicouagan	22 G/6	49°26'	67°17'
Baie-Trinité-Ouest	UNP/LNO	QC	Manicouagan	22 G/6	49°25'	67°19'
Baie Verte	TOWN/VIL2	NF		12 H/16	49°56'	56°11'
Baie Verte	UNP/LNO	NB	Westmorland	21 I/1	46°01'	64°06'
Baie Verte Road	UNP/LNO	NB	Westmorland	21 H/16	45°59'	64°09'
Baikie Lake	LAKE/LAC	NF		23 H/7	53°27'	64°37'
Baildon	UNP/LNO	SK	24-15-26-W2	72 I/6	50°16'	105°28'
Baildon No. 131	MUN2/AZM2	SK		72 I/3	50°10'	105°30'
Baile Lake	LAKE/LAC	BC	New Westminster	92 K/2	50°15'	124°52'
Bailey	UNP/LNO	NB	Sunbury	21 G/10	45°38'	66°35'
Bailey Corners	UNP/LNO	ON	Sudbury	41 I/10	46°37'	80°49'
Bailey Creek	RIV/CDE	ON	Simcoe	31 D/4	44°07'	79°47'
Bailey Lake	LAKE/LAC	SK		64 M/14	59°54'	103°02'
Bailey Point	CAPE/CAP	NT	Franklin	88 E	74°58'	115°02'
Baileys Brook	UNP/LNO	NS	Pictou	11 E/9	45°40'	62°16'

NAME NOM	ENTITY ENTITÉ	LOC 1 LIEU 1	LOC 2 LIEU 2	MAP CARTE	POSITION	
					LAT	LONG
Bailieboro	UNP/LNO	ON	Northumberland	31 D/1	44°08′	78°21′
Baillarge Bay	BAY/BAIE	NT	Franklin	48 C	73°17′	84°30′
Baillargeon, Lac	LAKE/LAC	QC	La Côte-de-Gaspé	22 A/15	48°47′	64°50′
Baillie	UNP/LNO	NB	Charlotte	21 G/6	45°23′	67°16′
Baillie	UNP/LNO	NT	Mackenzie	107 E	70°33′	128°00′
Baillie-Hamilton Island	ISL/ÎLE	NT	Franklin	58 G	75°52′	94°35′
Baillie Islands	ISL/ÎLE	NT	Franklin	107 E	70°35′	128°10′
Baillie Knolls	SEAU/SMER	—		7606	70°46′	128°42′
Baillie River	RIV/CDE	NT	Mackenzie	76 H/2	65°07′	104°36′
Bain	UNP/LNO	AB	6-4-3-W4	72 E/8	49°17′	110°24′
Baine Harbour	VILG/VILG	NF		1 M/7	47°22′	54°54′
Bains Corner	UNP/LNO	NB	Saint John	21 H/5	45°20′	65°39′
Bainsville	UNP/LNO	ON	Glengarry	31 G/1	45°11′	74°25′
Baintree	UNP/LNO	AB	35-25-24-W4	82 P/3	51°10′	113°15′
Baird	UNP/LNO	ON	Thunder Bay	52 A/6	48°25′	89°25′
Baird	UNP/LNO	SK	16-12-W3	72 J/5	50°21′	107°39′
Baird Bay	BAY/BAIE	NT	Keewatin	55 J	62°55′	90°56′
Baird, Cape	CAPE/CAP	NT	Franklin	120 C	81°32′	64°30′
Baird Inlet	BAY/BAIE	NT	Franklin	39 E/5	78°28′	75°50′
Baird, Mount	MTN/MNT	YT		106 F/5	65°20′	133°49′
Baird Peninsula	CAPE/CAP	NT	Franklin	37 B	68°55′	76°04′
Bairds	UNP/LNO	ON	Elgin	40 I/14	42°46′	81°20′
Bairdsville	UNP/LNO	NB	Victoria	21 J/12	46°38′	67°43′
Bait Range	MTN/MNT	BC	Cassiar	93 M/9	55°40′	126°30′
Bajo Point	CAPE/CAP	BC	Nootka	92 E/10	49°37′	126°49′
Baker	UNP/LNO	BC	Kootenay	82 G/5	49°30′	115°35′
Baker	UNP/LNO	BC	Cariboo	93 G/2	53°00′	122°30′
Baker Brook	VILG/VILG	NB	Madawaska	21 N/7	47°18′	68°31′
Baker Brook	GEOG/GÉOG	NB	Madawaska	21 N/7	47°23′	68°32′
Baker Brook	RIV/CDE	NB	Sunbury	21 G/15	45°54′	66°33′
Baker Cove	UNP/LNO	NF		1 M/9	47°34′	54°13′
Baker Creek	UNP/LNO	BC	Cariboo	93 B/14	52°56′	123°01′
Baker Creek	RIV/CDE	BC	Cariboo	93 B/15	52°58′	122°30′
Baker Foreland	CAPE/CAP	NT	Keewatin	55 J	62°55′	90°48′
Baker Island	ISL/ÎLE	BC	Range 1 Coast	92 L/10	50°45′	126°35′
Baker Island	ISL/ÎLE	NT	Franklin	68 H	75°01′	97°38′
Baker, Lac	LAKE/LAC	NB/QC		21 N/7	47°22′	68°41′
Baker Lake	HAM/HAM	NT	Keewatin	66 A/8	64°19′	96°01′
Baker Lake	LAKE/LAC	NT	Keewatin	56 D	64°10′	95°30′
Baker, Mount	MTN/MNT	YT		115 K/9	62°34′	140°09′
Baker Passage	CHAN/CHEN	BC	Sayward	92 K/2	50°01′	124°56′
Bakers Brook	UNP/LNO	NF		12 H/12	49°39′	57°58′
Bakers Dozen Islands	ISL/ÎLE	NT	Keewatin	34 D	56°45′	78°45′
Baker's Island	ISL/ÎLE	NF		11 O/10	47°36′	58°50′
Bakers Narrows	UNP/LNO	MB	5-66-28-W	63 K/12	54°41′	101°40′
Bakers Settlement	UNP/LNO	NS	Lunenburg	21 A/7	44°24′	64°41′
Bala	UNP/LNO	ON	Muskoka	31 E/4	45°01′	79°37′
Balaclava	UNP/LNO	ON	Renfrew	31 F/7	45°23′	76°57′
Balaclava	UNP/LNO	ON	Grey	41 A/10	44°41′	80°47′
Balaklava Island	ISL/ÎLE	BC	Rupert	92 L/13	50°51′	127°37′
Bala Park	UNP/LNO	ON	Muskoka	31 E/4	45°01′	79°35′
Bala Road	UNP/LNO	ON	Muskoka	31 E/4	45°02′	79°38′
Balaton Beach	UNP/LNO	MB	32-22-4-E	62 I/15	50°57′	96°57′
Balcarres	TOWN/VIL2	SK	13-21-12-W2	62 L/13	50°48′	103°33′
Balcom Inlet	BAY/BAIE	NT	Franklin	25 K	62°22′	68°42′
Balderson	UNP/LNO	ON	Lanark	31 C/16	44°57′	76°20′
Baldock Lake	LAKE/LAC	MB		64 A/12	56°32′	97°57′
Baldonnel	UNP/LNO	BC	Peace River	94 A/2	56°12′	120°41′
Baldoon	UNP/LNO	ON	Kent	40 J/8	42°30′	82°21′
Bald Peak	MTN/MNT	NB	Victoria	21 O/3	47°10′	67°07′
Bald, Pic	MTN/MNT	QC	Le Val-Saint-François	21 E/12	45°34′	71°41′
Bald Rock	UNP/LNO	NS	Halifax	11 D/5	44°28′	63°35′
Baldur	UNP/LNO	MB	13-5-14-W	62 G/6	49°23′	99°15′
Baldwin	MUN2/AZM2	ON	Sudbury	41 I/5	46°18′	81°45′
Baldwin	UNP/LNO	ON	York	31 D/6	44°16′	79°21′
Baldwin Mills	UNP/LNO	QC	Coaticook	21 E/4	45°02′	71°55′
Baldwin River	RIV/CDE	NT	Franklin	78 H	75°27′	105°35′
Baldwin Road	UNP/LNO	PE	Kings	11 L/7	46°16′	62°44′
Baldwins Bridge	UNP/LNO	ON	Dundas	31 G/3	45°00′	75°25′
Baldwinton	UNP/LNO	SK	15-44-23-W3	73 C/14	52°47′	109°16′
Baldwin Walker Range	MTN/MNT	NT	Franklin	78 H	75°47′	106°15′
Baldy	UNP/LNO	MB	19-66-20-W	63 K/9	54°44′	100°29′
Baldy Hughes	UNP/LNO	BC	Cariboo	93 G/10	53°37′	122°56′
Baldy Mountain	MTN/MNT	MB	29-24-W	62 N/7	51°28′	100°44′
Baldy Mountain	MTN/MNT	BC	Similkameen Division Yale	82 E/3	49°10′	119°15′

NAME NOM	ENTITY ENTITÉ	LOC 1 LIEU 1	LOC 2 LIEU 2	MAP CARTE	POSITION LAT	LONG
Baleine	UNP/LNO	NS	Cape Breton	11 G/13	45°57′	59°49′
Baleine, Banc de la - also-aussi - Whale Bank	SEAU/SMER	—		8011	45°20′	53°20′
Baleine, Grande rivière de la	RIV/CDE	QC	Kativik	33 N/5	55°16′	77°47′
Baleine, La	UNP/LNO	QC	Minganie	22 I/7	50°16′	64°57′
Baleine, Petite rivière de la	RIV/CDE	QC	Kativik	34 C/2	56°00′	76°45′
Baleine, Rivière à la	RIV/CDE	QC	Kativik	24 J/5	58°15′	67°35′
Baleine, Trou de la - also-aussi - Whale Deep	SEAU/SMER	—		8011	45°20′	52°45′
Balfour	UNP/LNO	BC	Kootenay	82 F/10	49°37′	116°58′
Balfour Bay	BAY/BAIE	NT	Keewatin	57 C	69°06′	94°14′
Balfour Beach	UNP/LNO	ON	York	31 D/6	44°16′	79°30′
Balfron	UNP/LNO	NS	Colchester	11 E/11	45°40′	63°14′
Balgonie	TOWN/VIL2	SK	3-18-17-W2	72 I/9	50°29′	104°16′
Baliol	UNP/LNO	SK	18-35-23-W3	73 C/3	52°01′	109°17′
Baljennie	UNP/LNO	SK	24-41-14-W3	73 B/12	52°33′	107°54′
Ballantine	UNP/LNO	AB	17-57-4-W5	83 G/15	53°55′	114°34′
Ballantrae	UNP/LNO	ON	York	31 D/3	44°02′	79°18′
Ballantyne Bay	BAY/BAIE	SK		63 L/12	54°40′	103°33′
Ballantyne, Lac	LAKE/LAC	QC	Kativik	24 K/11	58°37′	69°10′
Ballantyne River	RIV/CDE	SK	65-12-W2	63 L/12	54°38′	103°43′
Ballantynes Cove	UNP/LNO	NS	Antigonish	11 F/13	45°52′	61°55′
Ballantyne Strait	CHAN/CHEN	NT	Franklin	89 D	77°35′	115°06′
Balla Philip	UNP/LNO	NB	Kent	21 I/7	46°29′	64°55′
Ballarat Creek	UNP/LNO	YT		115 J/15	62°55′	138°58′
Ballard, Banc - also-aussi - Ballard Bank	SEAU/SMER	—		4817	46°38′	52°55′
Ballard Bank - also-aussi - Ballard, Banc	SEAU/SMER	—		4817	46°38′	52°55′
Ballard, Cape	CAPE/CAP	NF		1 K/15	46°47′	52°57′
Ballast Brook	RIV/CDE	NT	Franklin	98 E	74°27′	123°13′
Ball, Cape	CAPE/CAP	BC	Queen Charlotte	103 G/12	53°43′	131°52′
Ballenas Channel	CHAN/CHEN	BC	Nanaimo	92 F/8	49°20′	124°10′
Ballenas Islands	ISL/ÎLE	BC	Nanaimo	92 F/8	49°21′	124°09′
Ballenden Lake	LAKE/LAC	NT	Keewatin	57 A	68°32′	88°37′
Ballinafad	UNP/LNO	ON	Wellington	40 P/9	43°42′	80°01′
Ball Lake	LAKE/LAC	ON	Kenora	52 K/5	50°18′	94°00′
Balls Creek	UNP/LNO	NS	Cape Breton	11 K/1	46°09′	60°18′
Balls Lake	LAKE/LAC	NB	Saint John	21 H/4	45°14′	65°54′
Ballycanoe	UNP/LNO	ON	Leeds	31 B/12	44°32′	75°54′
Ballycroy	UNP/LNO	ON	Simcoe	30 M/13	43°58′	79°52′
Ballydown Beach	UNP/LNO	ON	Simcoe	31 D/4	44°15′	79°32′
Ballyduff	UNP/LNO	ON	Durham	31 D/2	44°08′	78°39′
Ballyhack	UNP/LNO	NF		1 N/6	47°26′	53°13′
Bally Haly	UNP/LNO	NF		1 N/10	47°35′	52°43′
Ballymote	UNP/LNO	ON	Middlesex	40 P/3	43°04′	81°14′
Balm	UNP/LNO	AB	10-57-9-W5	83 G/14	53°55′	115°16′
Balm Beach	UNP/LNO	ON	Simcoe	41 A/9	44°42′	80°00′
Balmertown - see-voir - Golden	MUN2/AZM2	ON		52 N/4	51°05′	93°43′
Balmertown	UNP/LNO	ON	Kenora	52 N/4	51°04′	93°44′
Balmoral	VILG/VILG	NB	Restigouche	21 O/16	47°58′	66°27′
Balmoral	UNP/LNO	NS	Richmond	11 F/11	45°40′	61°04′
Balmoral	UNP/LNO	ON	Haldimand	30 L/13	42°55′	79°58′
Balmoral	UNP/LNO	MB	6-15-2-E	62 I/6	50°15′	97°19′
Balmoral	UNP/LNO	BC	Kamloops Division Yale	82 L/14	50°51′	119°21′
Balmoral	GEOG/GÉOG	NB	Restigouche	21 O/16	47°45′	66°30′
Balmoral Beach	UNP/LNO	BC	Comox	92 F/10	49°40′	124°54′
Balmoral Mills	UNP/LNO	NS	Colchester	11 E/11	45°39′	63°12′
Balmoral Park	UNP/LNO	ON	Frontenac	31 C/2	44°15′	76°36′
Balmy Beach	UNP/LNO	ON	Grey	41 A/10	44°37′	80°56′
Balmy Beach	UNP/LNO	MB	32,5-4,5-16-W	62 G/5	49°21′	99°35′
Balone Beach	HAM/HAM	SK	31,5-42,43-25-W2	73 A/12	52°40′	105°36′
Balsam	UNP/LNO	ON	Ontario	30 M/14	43°59′	79°04′
Balsam Bay	UNP/LNO	MB	32-17-7-E	62 I/7	50°29′	96°35′
Balsam Creek	UNP/LNO	ON	Nipissing	31 L/6	46°25′	79°12′
Balsam Grove	UNP/LNO	ON	Frontenac	31 C/2	44°15′	76°32′
Balsam Hill	UNP/LNO	ON	Renfrew	31 F/7	45°29′	76°49′
Balsam Lake	LAKE/LAC	ON	Victoria	31 D/10	44°35′	78°50′
Balsam Lake	LAKE/LAC	SK	64-3,4-W2	63 L/9	54°31′	102°27′
Bals Fiord	BAY/BAIE	NT	Franklin	560 A	80°24′	95°45′
Baltic	UNP/LNO	PE	Kings	11 L/8	46°26′	62°10′
Baltic	UNP/LNO	PE	Prince	11 L/11	46°31′	63°39′
Baltics Corners	UNP/LNO	ON	Glengarry	31 G/7	45°20′	74°47′
Baltimore	UNP/LNO	NB	Albert	21 H/15	45°53′	64°49′
Baltimore	UNP/LNO	ON	Northumberland	31 D/1	44°02′	78°09′
Balvenie	UNP/LNO	ON	Renfrew	31 F/6	45°17′	77°04′
Balzac	UNP/LNO	AB	13-26-1-W5	82 O/1	51°13′	114°01′
Bamaji Lake	LAKE/LAC	ON	Kenora	52 O/3	51°09′	91°25′
Bamberg	UNP/LNO	ON	Waterloo	40 P/7	43°29′	80°41′

NAME NOM	ENTITY ENTITÉ	LOC 1 LIEU 1	LOC 2 LIEU 2	MAP CARTE	POSITION LAT	LONG
Bamberton	UNP/LNO	BC	Malahat	92 B/12	48°35′	123°31′
Bamfield	UNP/LNO	BC	Barclay	92 C/14	48°50′	125°08′
Banbury	UNP/LNO	ON	Parry Sound	31 E/5	45°27′	79°32′
Banc, Le	UNP/LNO	QC	Antoine-Labelle	31 J/3	46°14′	75°09′
Bancroft	TOWN/VIL2	ON	Hastings	31 F/4	45°03′	77°51′
Bancroft, Île	ISL/ÎLE	QC	Jamésie	32 F/12	49°42′	77°34′
Banda	UNP/LNO	ON	Dufferin	41 A/8	44°17′	80°04′
Banff	TOWN/VIL2	AB	25-12-W5	82 O/4	51°10′	115°34′
Banff National Park - also-aussi - Banff, Parc national	PARK/PARC	AB		82 N/9	51°36′	116°03′
Banff, Parc national - also-aussi - Banff National Park	PARK/PARC	AB		82 N/9	51°36′	116°03′
Banff Park Museum National Historic Site - also-aussi - Musée-du-Parc-Banff, Lieu historique national du	PARK/PARC	AB		82 O/4	51°10′	115°34′
Bangor	VILG/VILG	SK	15-21-3-W2	62 L/16	50°48′	102°20′
Bangor	UNP/LNO	PE	Kings	11 L/7	46°22′	62°41′
Bangor	UNP/LNO	NS	Digby	21 B/1	44°13′	66°06′
Bangor Lodge	UNP/LNO	ON	Muskoka	31 E/3	45°02′	79°23′
Bangor, Wicklow and McClure	MUN2/AZM2	ON	Hastings	31 F/5	45°17′	77°55′
Bangs Falls	UNP/LNO	NS	Queens	21 A/2	44°15′	64°50′
Bank Bay	UNP/LNO	AB	34-64-2-W4	73 L/9	54°34′	110°13′
Bankeir	UNP/LNO	BC	Kamloops Division Yale	92 H/9	49°43′	120°14′
Bankend	HAM/HAM	SK	13-29-14-W2	62 M/12	51°31′	103°51′
Bankfield	UNP/LNO	ON	Thunder Bay	42 E/11	49°42′	87°05′
Bankhead	UNP/LNO	AB	12-26-12-W5	82 O/4	51°12′	115°32′
Bank Head	CAPE/CAP	NF		12 B/7	48°22′	58°41′
Banko Junction	UNP/LNO	AB	17-55-24-W4	83 H/12	53°45′	113°32′
Banks	UNP/LNO	ON	Grey	41 A/8	44°29′	80°21′
Banks Island	ISL/ÎLE	BC	Range 4 Coast	103 G/1	53°25′	130°10′
Banks Island	ISL/ÎLE	NT	Franklin	98 A	72°45′	121°30′
Banks Lake	LAKE/LAC	NT	Keewatin	55 M	63°08′	94°28′
Banks Peninsula	CAPE/CAP	NT	Mackenzie	76 N	67°19′	108°17′
Banner	UNP/LNO	ON	Oxford	40 P/2	43°00′	80°59′
Banning	UNP/LNO	ON	Rainy River	52 B/12	48°44′	91°59′
Banning Lake	LAKE/LAC	NT	Franklin	77 C	69°35′	110°10′
Bannock	UNP/LNO	SK	18-45-8-W2	63 D/14	52°52′	103°09′
Bannockburn	UNP/LNO	ON	Hastings	31 C/12	44°39′	77°33′
Bannock Lake	LAKE/LAC	SK		64 L/15	58°51′	102°42′
Bannon	UNP/LNO	NB	Carleton	21 J/6	46°22′	67°28′
Banquereau	SEAU/SMER	—		4013	44°30′	58°30′
Bantalor	UNP/LNO	NB	York	21 J/8	46°16′	66°17′
Bantam Banks	SEAU/SMER	—		4817	46°55′	52°50′
Banting Lake	LAKE/LAC	NF		2 F/5	49°18′	53°57′
Bantry	UNP/LNO	AB	5-18-13-W4	72 L/5	50°29′	111°45′
Bapaume	UNP/LNO	SK	51-12-W3	73 G/5	53°23′	107°40′
Baptiste	UNP/LNO	ON	Hastings	31 F/4	45°06′	77°59′
Baptiste Island	ISL/ÎLE	NS	Halifax	11 D/16	44°55′	62°18′
Baptiste, Lac	LAKE/LAC	QC	Le Haut-Saint-Maurice	32 B/15	48°57′	74°47′
Baptiste Lake	UNP/LNO	AB	27-66-24-W4	83 I/12	54°43′	113°34′
Baptiste Lake	LAKE/LAC	ON	Hastings	31 E/1	45°07′	78°03′
Baptiste Lake	LAKE/LAC	AB	66,67-24-W4	83 I/12	54°45′	113°33′
Baptiste Louis 8	IR/RI	BC	Range 4 Coast	93 F/14	53°45′	125°24′
Baptiste Meadow 2	IR/RI	BC	Lillooet	92 O/15	52°00′	122°33′
Baptiste River	UNP/LNO	AB	3-43-8-W5	83 B/11	52°40′	115°04′
Baptiste River	RIV/CDE	AB	42-8-W5	83 B/11	52°41′	115°05′
Baptiste Smith 1A	IR/RI	BC	New Westminster	92 J/2	50°07′	122°32′
Baptiste Smith 1B	IR/RI	BC	New Westminster	92 J/2	50°03′	122°32′
Barachois	UNP/LNO	NF		1 K/13	46°52′	53°35′
Barachois	UNP/LNO	NB	Westmorland	21 I/1	46°13′	64°26′
Barachois	UNP/LNO	QC	Côte-Nord-du-Golfe-Saint-Laurent	12 J/11	50°33′	59°28′
Barachois	UNP/LNO	QC	Pabok	22 A/9	48°37′	64°16′
Barachois	UNP/LNO	QC	Pabok	22 A/9	48°37′	64°17′
Barachois Brook	UNP/LNO	NF		12 B/8	48°27′	58°26′
Barachois-Nord	UNP/LNO	QC	Pabok	22 A/9	48°38′	64°18′
Barachois-Ouest	UNP/LNO	QC	Pabok	22 A/9	48°37′	64°19′
Barachoix	UNP/LNO	NF		1 M/12	47°39′	55°42′
Baragar	UNP/LNO	MB	30-10-18-W	62 G/13	49°52′	99°55′
Baralzon Lake	LAKE/LAC	MB/NT		64 O/16	60°00′	98°03′
Barasway Bay	BAY/BAIE	NF		11 P/12	47°38′	57°44′
Barasway de Plate	UNP/LNO	NF		1 M/6	47°29′	55°05′
Barasway Island	ISL/ÎLE	NF		11 O/9	47°40′	58°16′
Barasway Point	CAPE/CAP	NF		11 P/12	47°37′	57°47′
Barasway, The	BAY/BAIE	NF		11 O/10	47°36′	58°45′
Barb	UNP/LNO	ON	Prescott	31 G/10	45°31′	74°32′
Barbara Lake	LAKE/LAC	ON	Thunder Bay	42 E/5	49°20′	87°47′
Barbara Lake	LAKE/LAC	AB	64-6-W4	73 L/10	54°32′	110°52′
Barbeau Peak	MTN/MNT	NT	Franklin	340 D	81°55′	75°02′
Barbel, Lac	LAKE/LAC	QC	Caniapiscau	22 N/16	51°55′	68°12′

NAME NOM	ENTITY ENTITÉ	LOC 1 LIEU 1	LOC 2 LIEU 2	MAP CARTE	POSITION LAT	LONG
Barber Dam	UNP/LNO	NB	Charlotte	21 G/6	45°29′	67°14′
Barberie	UNP/LNO	NB	Restigouche	21 O/14	47°47′	67°14′
Barbers Bay	UNP/LNO	ON	Cochrane	42 A/10	48°37′	80°54′
Barber's Beach	UNP/LNO	ON	Wellington	40 P/8	43°25′	80°16′
Barbour Bay	BAY/BAIE	NT	Keewatin	55 N/9	63°35′	92°15′
Barclay	MUN2/AZM2	ON	Kenora	52 F/15	49°47′	92°43′
Barclay	UNP/LNO	ON	Simcoe	31 D/5	44°18′	79°37′
Barclay, Cape	CAPE/CAP	NT	Keewatin	56 M	67°44′	95°42′
Barclay Land District	GEOG/GÉOG	BC		92 C	48°54′	124°58′
Barcovan Beach	UNP/LNO	ON	Northumberland	31 C/4	44°01′	77°38′
Bar-de-Cocagne	UNP/LNO	NB	Kent	21 I/7	46°25′	64°37′
Bardney Lake	LAKE/LAC	ON	Sudbury	41 O/8	47°15′	82°28′
Bardo	UNP/LNO	AB	10-50-19-W4	83 H/7	53°18′	112°41′
Bardoux, Lac	LAKE/LAC	QC	Sept-Rivières	22 O/4	51°09′	67°50′
Bardsville	UNP/LNO	ON	Muskoka	31 E/3	45°06′	79°26′
Barehead	UNP/LNO	ON	Thunder Bay	42 F/4	49°04′	85°54′
Bare Island 9	IR/RI	BC	Cowichan	92 B/11	48°38′	123°17′
Bare Lake	LAKE/LAC	BC	Kamloops Division Yale	92 P/2	51°11′	120°32′
Barella Creek	RIV/CDE	BC	Kamloops Division Yale	93 A/8	52°20′	120°16′
Bareneed	UNP/LNO	NF		1 N/11	47°35′	53°15′
Barford	VILG/VILG	QC	Coaticook	21 E/4	45°08′	71°44′
Barford	UNP/LNO	SK	25-41-14-W2	63 D/12	52°33′	103°54′
Bargain Bay	BAY/BAIE	BC	New Westminster	92 F/9	49°37′	124°02′
Barge Bay	UNP/LNO	NF		12 P/16	51°48′	56°13′
Barge Bay	BAY/BAIE	NF		12 P/16	51°48′	56°12′
Bargrave	UNP/LNO	AB	9-30-25-W4	82 P/11	51°33′	113°28′
Bar Haven	UNP/LNO	NF		1 M/9	47°43′	54°14′
Bar Haven Island	ISL/ÎLE	NF		1 M/9	47°43′	54°14′
Barhead - see-voir - Barrhead	UNP/LNO	ON		41 A/7	44°18′	80°40′
Barhead Creek - see-voir - Barrhead Creek	RIV/CDE	ON		41 A/7	44°18′	80°40′
Baribeau	UNP/LNO	QC	Le Haut-Saint-Maurice	31 P/7	47°17′	72°43′
Barich	UNP/LNO	AB	16-60-18-W4	83 I/2	54°12′	112°38′
Baril Lake	LAKE/LAC	AB	112,113-10,11-W4	74 L/13	58°46′	111°42′
Baring	UNP/LNO	SK	9-15-8-W2	62 L/3	50°15′	103°03′
Baring Bay	BAY/BAIE	NT	Franklin	58 G	75°40′	92°03′
Baring, Cape	CAPE/CAP	NT	Franklin	87 F	70°02′	117°21′
Baring Channel	CHAN/CHEN	NT	Franklin	68 D	73°48′	98°50′
Baring Island	ISL/ÎLE	NT	Franklin	58 G	75°56′	95°50′
Barkenhouse Lake	LAKE/LAC	AB	30,31-17-18-22-W4	82 I/16	50°54′	112°22′
Barker Lake	LAKE/LAC	MB	39-13-W	63 B/6	52°20′	99°12′
Barkers Point	UNP/LNO	NB	York	21 G/15	45°57′	66°37′
Barkerville	UNP/LNO	BC	Cariboo	93 H/4	53°04′	121°31′
Barkfield	UNP/LNO	MB	31-4-6-E	62 H/7	49°20′	96°48′
Barkhouse Settlement	UNP/LNO	NS	Halifax	11 D/16	44°57′	62°23′
Bark Lake	LAKE/LAC	ON	Nipissing	31 F/5	45°27′	77°51′
Bark Lake	LAKE/LAC	ON	Algoma	41 J/16	46°54′	82°28′
Barkley Canyon	SEAU/SMER	—		3602	48°25′	125°53′
Barkley Sound	CHAN/CHEN	BC	Barclay	92 C/14	48°51′	125°23′
Barkmere	CITY/VIL1	QC	Les Laurentides	31 J/2	46°00′	74°35′
Barkway	UNP/LNO	ON	Muskoka	31 D/14	44°54′	79°11′
Bar Lake	LAKE/LAC	SK	74,75-3-W3	73 O/8	55°27′	106°26′
Barlee Junction	UNP/LNO	AB	14-47-20-W4	83 H/2	53°03′	112°49′
Barlochan	UNP/LNO	ON	Muskoka	31 E/3	45°02′	79°29′
Barlow	UNP/LNO	AB	34-23-29-W4	82 P/4	51°00′	113°58′
Barlow	UNP/LNO	BC	Cariboo	93 G/1	53°03′	122°24′
Barlow	UNP/LNO	YT		115 P/12	63°44′	137°39′
Barlow Creek	UNP/LNO	BC	Cariboo	93 G/1	53°02′	122°26′
Barlow Lake	LAKE/LAC	ON	Sudbury	41 I/7	46°17′	80°34′
Barlow Lake	LAKE/LAC	NT	Mackenzie	65 E	62°00′	103°00′
Barnaby River	UNP/LNO	NB	Northumberland	21 I/13	46°53′	65°31′
Barnaby River	RIV/CDE	NB	Northumberland	21 I/13	46°54′	65°37′
Barnard Point	CAPE/CAP	NT	Franklin	88 D	73°01′	113°05′
Barnegat	UNP/LNO	AB	8-67-12-W4	73 L/13	54°47′	111°49′
Barner, Mount	MTN/MNT	BC	Range 1 Coast	92 K/7	50°27′	124°35′
Barnes Creek	RIV/CDE	BC	Kootenay	82 E/16	49°54′	118°07′
Barnes Creek	RIV/CDE	BC	Kamloops Division Yale	92 I/11	50°45′	121°14′
Barnesdale	UNP/LNO	ON	Lincoln	30 M/3	43°11′	79°17′
Barnes Ice Cap	GLAC/GLAC	NT	Franklin	37 D	70°00′	73°30′
Barnes Lake	LAKE/LAC	MB		64 B/8	56°23′	98°06′
Barnes Lake	LAKE/LAC	SK	53-12-W3	73 G/12	53°33′	107°45′
Barnesville	UNP/LNO	NB	Kings	21 H/5	45°27′	65°44′
Barnet	UNP/LNO	BC	New Westminster	92 G/7	49°18′	122°55′
Barnettville	UNP/LNO	NB	Northumberland	21 I/13	46°46′	65°48′
Barneys Brook	UNP/LNO	NS	Hants	11 D/14	45°00′	63°28′
Barneys Brook	RIV/CDE	NF		12 H/8	49°25′	56°10′

NAME NOM	ENTITY ENTITÉ	LOC 1 LIEU 1	LOC 2 LIEU 2	MAP CARTE	POSITION	
					LAT	LONG
Barneys River	RIV/CDE	NS	Pictou	11 E/9	45°40'	62°21'
Barneys River Station	UNP/LNO	NS	Pictou	11 E/9	45°36'	62°16'
Barnhart	UNP/LNO	ON	Rainy River	52 C/12	48°44'	93°48'
Barnhartvale	UNP/LNO	BC	Kamloops Division Yale	92 I/9	50°39'	120°10'
Barn Range	MTN/MNT	YT		117 A/11	68°30'	138°20'
Barnsley	UNP/LNO	MB	30-7-4-W1	62 H/12	49°36'	97°59'
Barnston	VILG/VILG	QC	Coaticook	21 E/4	45°06'	71°53'
Barnston Island	UNP/LNO	BC	New Westminster	92 G/2	49°12'	122°43'
Barnston Island 3	IR/RI	BC	New Westminster	92 G/2	49°11'	122°42'
Barnston-Ouest	VILG/VILG	QC	Coaticook	21 E/4	45°06'	71°58'
Barnwell	VILG/VILG	AB	28-9-17-W4	82 H/16	49°46'	112°15'
Baronet Passage	CHAN/CHEN	BC	Range 1 Coast	92 L/10	50°33'	126°35'
Baron Island	ISL/ÎLE	BC	Range 5 Coast	103 J/7	54°28'	130°49'
Barons	VILG/VILG	AB	16-12-23-W4	82 H/14	50°00'	113°05'
Barony	UNP/LNO	NB	York	21 G/14	45°58'	67°12'
Bar Point	UNP/LNO	ON	Essex	40 J/3	42°03'	83°07'
Barrachois	UNP/LNO	NS	Cape Breton	11 K/1	46°08'	60°26'
Barrachois	UNP/LNO	NS	Colchester	11 E/11	45°44'	63°16'
Barrachois Harbour	UNP/LNO	NS	Cape Breton	11 K/1	46°09'	60°25'
Barrage-de-Saint-Narcisse	UNP/LNO	QC	Francheville	31 I/9	46°33'	72°25'
Barrage-du-Grand-Remous	UNP/LNO	QC	Portneuf	21 L/13	46°47'	71°40'
Barrage-Hopkins	UNP/LNO	QC	Coaticook	21 E/4	45°09'	71°49'
Barrage-McLaren	UNP/LNO	QC	Papineau	31 G/13	45°51'	75°39'
Barrage-Mistigougèche	UNP/LNO	QC	Rimouski-Neigette	22 C/1	48°11'	68°01'
Barrage-Sainte-Marguerite	UNP/LNO	QC	Sept-Rivières	22 J/2	50°13'	66°40'
Barra Glen	UNP/LNO	NS	Victoria	11 F/15	45°58'	60°51'
Barra Head	UNP/LNO	NS	Richmond	11 F/10	45°41'	60°47'
Barraute	VILG/VILG	QC	Abitibi	32 C/5	48°26'	77°38'
Barr'd Harbour	UNP/LNO	NF		12 I/14	50°49'	57°04'
Barr'd Islands	UNP/LNO	NF		2 E/9	49°44'	54°11'
Barré, Cap	CAPE/CAP	QC	La Côte-de-Gaspé	22 H/3	49°14'	65°08'
Barrel Lake	LAKE/LAC	ON	Kenora	52 G/12	49°39'	91°33'
Barren Hill	UNP/LNO	NS	Richmond	11 F/10	45°42'	60°35'
Barren Hill Lake	LAKE/LAC	NS	Richmond	11 F/10	45°42'	60°35'
Barren Island	ISL/ÎLE	NS	Guysborough	11 D/16	44°57'	62°02'
Barren Lake	LAKE/LAC	NF		12 A/10	48°32'	56°49'
Barrett	UNP/LNO	BC	Range 5 Coast	93 L/7	54°25'	126°46'
Barrett Chute	UNP/LNO	ON	Renfrew	31 F/2	45°15'	76°46'
Barrette	UNP/LNO	QC	Roussillon	31 H/5	45°24'	73°32'
Barrett Lake	UNP/LNO	BC	Range 5 Coast	93 L/7	54°27'	126°45'
Barretville	UNP/LNO	ON	Essex	40 J/2	42°06'	82°51'
Barrhead	TOWN/VIL2	AB	59-3-W5	83 J/1	54°08'	114°24'
Barrhead	UNP/LNO	ON	Grey	41 A/7	44°18'	80°40'
Barrhead No. 11, County of	MUN1/AZM1	AB	59-4-W5	83 J/2	54°09'	114°32'
Barricade Creek	RIV/CDE	BC	Kamloops Division Yale	92 I/15	50°56'	120°59'
Barrie	CITY/VIL1	ON	Simcoe	31 D/5	44°24'	79°40'
Barrie	MUN2/AZM2	ON	Frontenac	31 C/14	44°51'	77°06'
Barrieau	UNP/LNO	NB	Kent	21 I/14	46°46'	65°16'
Barriefield	UNP/LNO	ON	Frontenac	31 C/1	44°14'	76°28'
Barrie Island	MUN2/AZM2	ON	Manitoulin	41 G/15	45°55'	82°40'
Barrie Island	ISL/ÎLE	ON	Manitoulin	41 G/15	45°56'	82°39'
Barrier Bay	UNP/LNO	MB	13,14-14-13-E	52 L/4	50°11'	95°43'
Barrière	UNP/LNO	QC	Vallée-de-l'Or	31 N/7	47°30'	76°42'
Barrière	UNP/LNO	BC	Kamloops Division Yale	92 P/1	51°11'	120°07'
Barrière-Béthanie	UNP/LNO	QC	Le Fjord-du-Saguenay	22 D/6	48°18'	71°08'
Barrière-Caribou	UNP/LNO	QC	Matawinie	31 J/8	46°23'	74°06'
Barrière-de-la-Chaîne, La	UNP/LNO	QC	Matane	22 B/15	48°48'	66°35'
Barrière-de-Laterrière	UNP/LNO	QC	Le Fjord-du-Saguenay	22 D/3	48°15'	71°15'
Barrière-de-Stoneham	UNP/LNO	QC	La Jacques-Cartier	21 M/3	47°09'	71°16'
Barrière, La	UNP/LNO	QC	Charlevoix	21 M/7	47°17'	70°39'
Barrière, Lac	LAKE/LAC	QC	Rouyn-Noranda	31 M/14	47°57'	79°07'
Barrière-Mésy	UNP/LNO	QC	Lac-Saint-Jean-Est	22 D/5	48°16'	71°41'
Barrière River	RIV/CDE	BC	Kamloops Division Yale	92 P/1	51°11'	120°08'
Barriere River 3A	IR/RI	BC	Kamloops Division Yale	92 P/1	51°11'	120°07'
Barrier Ford	HAM/HAM	SK	19,20-41-12-2	63 D/12	52°32'	103°42'
Barrier Inlet	BAY/BAIE	NT	Franklin	25 K	62°28'	68°46'
Barrier Islands	ISL/ÎLE	BC	Rupert	92 E/14	49°57'	127°19'
Barrier River	RIV/CDE	SK	10-42-12-W2	63 D/12	52°36'	103°39'
Barrier Valley No. 397	MUN2/AZM2	SK		73 A/8	52°30'	104°00'
Barrillia Park	UNP/LNO	ON	Simcoe	31 D/5	44°27'	79°30'
Barrington	MUN1/AZM1	NS	Shelburne	20 P/12	43°41'	65°33'
Barrington	UNP/LNO	NS	Shelburne	20 P/12	43°34'	65°34'
Barrington	UNP/LNO	QC	Les Jardins-de-Napierville	31 H/4	45°06'	73°35'
Barrington Bay	BAY/BAIE	NS	Shelburne	20 P/5	43°30'	65°32'
Barrington Head	UNP/LNO	NS	Shelburne	20 P/12	43°34'	65°35'

NAME NOM	ENTITY ENTITÉ	LOC 1 LIEU 1	LOC 2 LIEU 2	MAP CARTE	POSITION LAT	LONG
Barrington Lake	LAKE/LAC	ON	Thunder Bay	52 J/8	50°16′	90°18′
Barrington Lake	LAKE/LAC	MB		64 C/16	56°57′	100°15′
Barrington Passage	UNP/LNO	NS	Shelburne	20 P/12	43°32′	65°37′
Barrington River	RIV/CDE	NS	Shelburne	20 P/12	43°34′	65°35′
Barrington River	RIV/CDE	MB		64 B/13	56°46′	99°44′
Barrington West	UNP/LNO	NS	Shelburne	20 P/12	43°34′	65°36′
Barrin, Lac	LAKE/LAC	QC	Minganie	12 M/8	51°21′	62°10′
Barrin, Lac	LAKE/LAC	QC	Le Fjord-du-Saguenay	22 D/15	48°54′	70°36′
Barrio Lake	LAKE/LAC	NS	Digby	21 A/4	44°13′	65°48′
Barrios Beach	UNP/LNO	NS	Antigonish	11 F/12	45°38′	61°37′
Bar River	UNP/LNO	ON	Algoma	41 K/8	46°26′	84°02′
Barr Lake	LAKE/LAC	NT	Mackenzie	65 D	60°27′	102°56′
Bar Road	UNP/LNO	NB	Charlotte	21 G/3	45°06′	67°03′
Barron Lake	LAKE/LAC	NF		13 H/12	53°43′	57°43′
Barron River	RIV/CDE	ON	Renfrew	31 F/14	45°53′	77°24′
Barronsfield	UNP/LNO	NS	Cumberland	21 H/16	45°45′	64°21′
Barrow Bay	UNP/LNO	ON	Bruce	41 A/14	44°57′	81°13′
Barrow Bay	BAY/BAIE	ON	Bruce	41 A/14	44°58′	81°11′
Barrow, Cape	CAPE/CAP	NT	Mackenzie	77 B	68°01′	110°08′
Barrow Harbour	BAY/BAIE	NF		2 C/12	48°40′	53°39′
Barrow Harbour	BAY/BAIE	NT	Franklin	59 B	76°33′	95°57′
Barrow Inlet	BAY/BAIE	NT	Franklin	67 A	68°09′	96°29′
Barrow Lake	LAKE/LAC	NT	Keewatin	57 A	68°24′	89°31′
Barrow Peninsula	CAPE/CAP	NT	Franklin	25 O	63°03′	66°15′
Barrow River	RIV/CDE	NT	Franklin	46 P/6	67°19′	81°20′
Barrows	UNP/LNO	MB	27,34-44-28-W	63 C/14	52°50′	101°26′
Barrow Strait	CHAN/CHEN	NT	Franklin	58 F	74°24′	94°10′
Barrowtown	UNP/LNO	BC	New Westminster	92 G/1	49°06′	122°06′
Barr Settlement	UNP/LNO	NS	Hants	11 E/4	45°08′	63°38′
Barry Bay	BAY/BAIE	NT	Franklin	88 H	75°10′	112°35′
Barrydowne	UNP/LNO	ON	Sudbury	41 I/10	46°31′	80°56′
Barry Islands	ISL/ÎLE	NT	Franklin	76 N	67°32′	108°10′
Barry, Lac	LAKE/LAC	QC	Vallée-de-l'Or	32 B/13	48°59′	75°37′
Barrymere	UNP/LNO	ON	Hastings	31 F/5	45°23′	77°40′
Barry's Bay	VILG/VILG	ON	Renfrew	31 F/5	45°29′	77°41′
Barrys Corner	UNP/LNO	NS	Lunenburg	21 A/8	44°26′	64°29′
Barry's Ponds	LAKE/LAC	NF		2 E/8	49°16′	54°23′
Barryvale	UNP/LNO	ON	Renfrew	31 F/7	45°17′	76°44′
Barryville	UNP/LNO	NB	Northumberland	21 P/3	47°09′	65°15′
Barss Corner	UNP/LNO	NS	Lunenburg	21 A/10	44°34′	64°41′
Barter Settlement	UNP/LNO	NB	Charlotte	21 G/3	45°12′	67°20′
Bar, The	BCH/PLAG	NF		12 B/10	48°44′	58°50′
Barthel	UNP/LNO	SK	3-57-21-W3	73 F/14	53°55′	109°03′
Bartholomew	UNP/LNO	NB	Northumberland	21 I/12	46°43′	65°54′
Bartholomew River	RIV/CDE	NB	Northumberland	21 I/12	46°44′	65°50′
Bartibog	UNP/LNO	NB	Northumberland	21 P/3	47°11′	65°24′
Bartibog Bridge	UNP/LNO	NB	Northumberland	21 P/3	47°06′	65°21′
Bartibog River	RIV/CDE	NB	Northumberland	21 P/3	47°06′	65°21′
Bartibog Station	UNP/LNO	NB	Gloucester	21 P/5	47°17′	65°37′
Bartlett Bay	BAY/BAIE	NT	Franklin	39 H	79°10′	74°45′
Bartlett, Cape	CAPE/CAP	NT	Keewatin	34 D/7	56°26′	78°40′
Bartlett Island	ISL/ÎLE	NT	Keewatin	34 K	58°09′	77°33′
Bartlett Island 7	IR/RI	BC	Range 1 Coast	92 K/6	50°19′	125°05′
Bartlett Island 32	IR/RI	BC	Clayoquot	92 E/1	49°13′	126°05′
Bartlett Lake	LAKE/LAC	SK		74 K/12	58°35′	109°51′
Bartlett Lake	LAKE/LAC	NT	Franklin	85 M	63°05′	118°20′
Bartlett Point	CAPE/CAP	NT	Franklin	37 B	68°56′	79°25′
Bartletts Harbour	UNP/LNO	NF		12 I/15	50°57′	57°00′
Bartletts Mills	UNP/LNO	NB	Charlotte	21 G/3	45°12′	67°08′
Barton	UNP/LNO	NF		2 C/4	48°13′	53°54′
Barton	UNP/LNO	NS	Digby	21 A/12	44°32′	65°52′
Barton	UNP/LNO	NB	York	21 J/3	46°08′	67°02′
Barton Lake	LAKE/LAC	ON	Kenora	52 M/16	52°00′	94°06′
Bartonville	UNP/LNO	ON	Wentworth	30 M/4	43°14′	79°48′
Bartstow	UNP/LNO	AB	22-23-W4	82 I/14	50°53′	113°09′
Bar U Ranch National Historic Site - also-aussi - Ranch-Bar U, Lieu historique national du	PARK/PARC	AB	8-17-2-W5	82 J/8	50°25′	114°15′
Barvas	UNP/LNO	SK	32-25-1-W2	62 M/1	51°12′	102°06′
Barville	UNP/LNO	QC	Abitibi	32 C/12	48°31′	77°41′
Barwick	UNP/LNO	ON	Rainy River	52 C/12	48°39′	93°59′
Bas-Cap-Pelé	UNP/LNO	NB	Westmorland	21 I/1	46°14′	64°15′
Bas-Caraquet	VILG/VILG	NB	Gloucester	21 P/15	47°48′	64°50′
Bas-de-Champlain, Le	UNP/LNO	QC	Francheville	31 I/8	46°27′	72°19′
Bas-de-la-Baie	UNP/LNO	QC	Charlevoix	21 M/7	47°25′	70°31′
Bas-de-la-Montagne, Le	UNP/LNO	QC	La Rivière-du-Nord	31 G/9	45°43′	74°06′
Bas-de-l'Anse	UNP/LNO	QC	Charlevoix-Est	21 M/9	47°42′	70°02′

NAME NOM	ENTITY ENTITÉ	LOC 1 LIEU 1	LOC 2 LIEU 2	MAP CARTE	POSITION LAT	LONG
Bas-de-Sainte-Rose	UNP/LNO	QC	Laval	31 H/12	45°39′	73°45′
Bas-du-Cournoyer, Le	UNP/LNO	QC	Bécancour	31 I/8	46°23′	72°24′
Baseline Bay	BAY/BAIE	SK		73 J/3	54°13′	107°10′
Base Line Road	UNP/LNO	NS	Kings	21 H/2	45°08′	64°45′
Bas-Fond, Le	UNP/LNO	QC	Maskinongé	31 I/7	46°23′	72°59′
Basford	UNP/LNO	BC	Cariboo	93 G/15	53°55′	122°42′
Bashaw	TOWN/VIL2	AB	4-42-21-W4	83 A/10	52°35′	112°58′
Basil Bay	BAY/BAIE	NT	Mackenzie	87 A	68°14′	114°51′
Basil Point	CAPE/CAP	ON	Kenora	52 E/2	49°05′	94°44′
Basin Depot	UNP/LNO	ON	Nipissing	31 F/12	45°43′	77°47′
Basingstoke	UNP/LNO	ON	Lincoln	30 M/4	43°06′	79°37′
Basin Lake	LAKE/LAC	SK	42-23-W2	73 A/11	52°38′	105°17′
Basin Mines	UNP/LNO	ON	Sudbury	41 I/10	46°37′	80°40′
Basin Road	UNP/LNO	NS	Richmond	11 F/11	45°48′	61°11′
Baskatong, Réservoir	LAKE/LAC	QC	La Vallée-de-la-Gatineau	31 J/13	46°48′	75°50′
Basket Lake	LAKE/LAC	ON	Kenora	52 F/9	49°43′	92°00′
Basket Lake	LAKE/LAC	MB	32-11-12-W	62 O/14	51°47′	99°01′
Baskin's Beach	UNP/LNO	ON	Carleton	31 F/8	45°29′	76°01′
Basler Lake	LAKE/LAC	NT	Mackenzie	85 O	63°57′	115°58′
Basque	UNP/LNO	BC	Kamloops Division Yale	92 I/11	50°38′	121°18′
Basque 18	IR/RI	BC	Kamloops Division Yale	92 I/11	50°38′	121°19′
Basque, Cap du	CAPE/CAP	QC	Charlevoix-Est	22 C/4	48°00′	69°46′
Basques, Île aux	ISL/ÎLE	QC	Les Basques	22 C/3	48°09′	69°15′
Bas-Saint-Laurent	MUN1/AZM1	QC	Rimouski-Neigette	22 C/7	48°20′	68°40′
Bassano	TOWN/VIL2	AB	17-21-18-W4	82 I/16	50°47′	112°28′
Bass Creek	UNP/LNO	ON	Manitoulin	41 G/16	45°48′	82°01′
Basse-Aboujagane	UNP/LNO	NB	Westmorland	21 I/1	46°09′	64°25′
Basserode, Lac	LAKE/LAC	QC	Rouyn-Noranda	31 M/15	47°56′	78°50′
Basse Terre Point	CAPE/CAP	NF		11 P/8	47°28′	56°08′
Basset Lake	LAKE/LAC	AB	107-3,4-W6	84 L/8	58°20′	118°28′
Basse-Ville	UNP/LNO	QC	Communauté urbaine de Québec	21 L/14	46°49′	71°14′
Bassin	UNP/LNO	QC	Les Îles-de-la-Madeleine	11 N/4	47°13′	61°56′
Bassin-du-Lièvre	UNP/LNO	QC	Communauté urbaine de l'Outaouais	31 G/11	45°32′	75°26′
Bassin, Le	UNP/LNO	QC	Beauharnois-Salaberry	31 G/8	45°15′	74°05′
Bass Lake	UNP/LNO	ON	Renfrew	31 K/4	46°06′	77°36′
Bass Lake	LAKE/LAC	ON	Leeds	31 C/16	44°49′	76°08′
Bass Lake	LAKE/LAC	ON	Simcoe	31 D/12	44°36′	79°30′
Bass Lake	LAKE/LAC	ON	Parry Sound	31 L/4	46°07′	79°48′
Bass Lake	LAKE/LAC	ON	Grey	41 A/11	44°43′	81°00′
Bass Lake	LAKE/LAC	ON	Manitoulin	41 H/13	45°53′	81°57′
Bass Lake Park	UNP/LNO	ON	Simcoe	31 D/11	44°37′	79°28′
Bass River	UNP/LNO	NS	Colchester	11 E/5	45°25′	63°47′
Bass River	UNP/LNO	NB	Kent	21 I/11	46°33′	65°07′
Bass River	UNP/LNO	NB	Gloucester	21 P/12	47°39′	65°35′
Bass River	RIV/CDE	NS	Colchester	11 E/5	45°24′	63°47′
Bass River	RIV/CDE	NB	Kent	21 I/11	46°32′	65°03′
Bass River	RIV/CDE	NB	Gloucester	21 P/12	47°40′	65°35′
Bass River Lake	LAKE/LAC	NB	Gloucester	21 P/5	47°23′	65°36′
Bass River Point	UNP/LNO	NB	Kent	21 I/11	46°33′	65°02′
Basswood	UNP/LNO	MB	28-15-19-W	62 K/8	50°18′	100°02′
Basswood Lake	LAKE/LAC	ON	Algoma	41 J/6	46°19′	83°24′
Basswood Lake	LAKE/LAC	ON	Rainy River	52 B/3	48°05′	91°35′
Basswood Ridge	UNP/LNO	NB	Charlotte	21 G/6	45°19′	67°22′
Bastarache	UNP/LNO	NB	Kent	21 I/7	46°27′	64°53′
Bastard and South Burgess	MUN2/AZM2	ON	Leeds	31 C/9	44°43′	76°08′
Bastien, Le	UNP/LNO	QC	Le Haut-Saint-Maurice	31 P/2	47°07′	72°40′
Bastille, Lac	LAKE/LAC	QC	Minganie	12 N/14	51°46′	61°11′
Bastion Bay	UNP/LNO	BC	Kamloops Division Yale	82 L/14	50°51′	119°05′
Bastions, The	CLF/ESC	NT	Franklin	37 H	71°50′	74°15′
Bataille-de-Fish Creek, Lieu historique national de la - also-aussi - Battle of Fish Creek National Historic Site	PARK/PARC	SK		73 B/9	52°33′	106°11′
Bataille-de-la-Châteauguay, Lieu historique national de la - also-aussi - Battle of the Châteauguay National Historic Site	PARK/PARC	QC	Le Haut-Saint-Laurent	31 H/4	45°10′	73°56′
Bataille-de-la-Ristigouche, Lieu historique national de la - also-aussi - Battle of the Restigouche National Historic Site	PARK/PARC	QC	Avignon	22 B/2	48°01′	66°44′
Bataille-du-Moulin-à-Vent, Lieu historique national de la - also-aussi - Battle of the Windmill National Historic Site	PARK/PARC	ON	Grenville	31 B/11	44°43′	75°29′
Batawa	UNP/LNO	ON	Hastings	31 C/4	44°10′	77°36′
Batchawana Bay	UNP/LNO	ON	Algoma	41 K/15	46°56′	84°36′
Batchawana Bay	BAY/BAIE	ON	Algoma	41 K/16	46°53′	84°29′
Batchawana Island	ISL/ÎLE	ON	Algoma	41 K/16	46°53′	84°30′
Batchawana Mountain	MTN/MNT	ON	Algoma	41 N/1	47°04′	84°24′
Batchawana River	RIV/CDE	ON	Algoma	41 K/15	46°55′	84°32′

NAME NOM	ENTITY ENTITÉ	LOC 1 LIEU 1	LOC 2 LIEU 2	MAP CARTE	POSITION LAT	POSITION LONG
Batchelor Hills	UNP/LNO	BC	Kamloops Division Yale	92 I/9	50°43'	120°22'
Batchewana	UNP/LNO	ON	Algoma	41 N/1	47°11'	84°17'
Bateau Channel	CHAN/CHEN	ON	Frontenac	31 C/8	44°17'	76°16'
Bateau Island	ISL/ÎLE	ON	Parry Sound	41 H/8	45°18'	80°18'
Bate Lake	ISL/ÎLE	NT	Keewatin	65 G	61°38'	99°00'
Bateman	HAM/HAM	SK	22-12-6-W3	72 J/2	50°01'	106°45'
Bateman Point	CAPE/CAP	BC	Range 2 Coast	92 N/1	51°15'	124°04'
Batemans Mills	UNP/LNO	NB	Westmorland	21 I/2	46°14'	64°37'
Bates Lake	LAKE/LAC	YT		115 A/4	60°15'	137°36'
Bates Peak	MTN/MNT	BC	Cassiar	104 K/3	58°02'	133°01'
Bates River	RIV/CDE	YT		115 A/4	60°07'	137°56'
Bates Settlement	UNP/LNO	NB	York	21 J/3	46°00'	67°20'
Bateston	UNP/LNO	NS	Cape Breton	11 J/4	46°00'	59°54'
Bath	VILG/VILG	NB	Carleton	21 J/12	46°31'	67°36'
Bath	VILG/VILG	ON	Lennox and Addington	31 C/2	44°11'	76°47'
Bathing Lake	LAKE/LAC	NT	Mackenzie	106 N	67°40'	132°24'
Bathurst	CITY/VIL1	NB	Gloucester	21 P/12	47°36'	65°39'
Bathurst	MUN2/AZM2	ON	Lanark	31 C/16	44°54'	76°24'
Bathurst	UNP/LNO	ON	Lanark	31 C/16	44°52'	76°23'
Bathurst	GEOG/GÉOG	NB	Gloucester	21 P/5	47°25'	65°55'
Bathurst Bay	BAY/BAIE	NT	Franklin	38 C	73°21'	77°00'
Bathurst, Cape	CAPE/CAP	NT	Franklin	107 E	70°34'	128°00'
Bathurst Harbour	BAY/BAIE	NB	Gloucester	21 P/12	47°38'	65°39'
Bathurst Inlet	UNP/LNO	NT	Mackenzie	76 K/16	66°50'	108°03'
Bathurst Inlet	BAY/BAIE	NT	Mackenzie	76 N/9	67°35'	108°30'
Bathurst Island	ISL/ÎLE	NT	Franklin	68 H/12	75°45'	100°00'
Bathurst Lake	LAKE/LAC	NT	Mackenzie	76 J	66°16'	107°13'
Bathurst Mines	UNP/LNO	NB	Gloucester	21 P/5	47°25'	65°48'
Batiscan	VILG/VILG	QC	Francheville	31 I/8	46°30'	72°15'
Batiscan, Lac	LAKE/LAC	QC	La Jacques-Cartier	21 M/5	47°22'	71°55'
Batiscan, Rivière	RIV/CDE	QC	Francheville	31 I/9	46°31'	72°14'
Bat-l-ki 3	IR/RI	BC	Range 1 Coast	92 L/16	50°54'	126°24'
Batoche	UNP/LNO	SK	8-43-1-W3	73 B/9	52°44'	106°06'
*Batoche Ferry	UNP/LNO	SK		73 B/9	52°40'	106°08'
Batoche, Lieu historique national de - also-aussi - Batoche National Historic Site	PARK/PARC	SK		73 B/16	52°45'	106°07'
Batoche National Historic Site - also-aussi - Batoche, Lieu historique national de	PARK/PARC	SK		73 B/16	52°45'	106°07'
Batteau	UNP/LNO	NF		3 E/5	53°25'	55°47'
Batteaux	UNP/LNO	ON	Simcoe	41 A/8	44°28'	80°11'
Batteaux Creek	RIV/CDE	ON	Simcoe	41 A/8	44°29'	80°10'
Batter Junction	UNP/LNO	AB	8-31-13-W4	72 M/12	51°38'	111°49'
Battersea	UNP/LNO	ON	Frontenac	31 C/8	44°26'	76°23'
Battery	UNP/LNO	NF		1 N/2	47°02'	52°53'
Battery Bay	BAY/BAIE	NT	Keewatin	46 E	65°21'	86°07'
Battle Bend	UNP/LNO	AB	7-40-10,11-W4	73 D/6	52°26'	111°27'
Battle Creek	UNP/LNO	SK	33-5-29-W3	72 F/5	49°26'	109°51'
Battle Creek	RIV/CDE	SK/AB		72 F/3	49°00'	109°25'
Battleford	TOWN/VIL2	SK	30-43-17-W3	73 C/9	52°44'	108°19'
Battleford Junction	UNP/LNO	SK	35-44-17-W3	73 C/16	52°50'	108°21'
Battle Glacier	GLAC/GLAC	BC	Cassiar	114 O/9	59°39'	138°19'
Battle Harbour	UNP/LNO	NF		3 D/5	52°16'	55°35'
Battle Heights	UNP/LNO	SK	2-51-10-W2	63 E/6	53°22'	103°23'
Battle Islands	ISL/ÎLE	NF		3 D/5	52°16'	55°39'
Battle Lake	UNP/LNO	AB	46-1-W5	83 B/16	52°58'	114°11'
Battle Lake	LAKE/LAC	AB	46-2-W5	83 B/16	52°58'	114°11'
Battle Lake	LAKE/LAC	BC	Range 1 Coast	92 L/9	50°43'	126°21'
Battle of Fish Creek National Historic Site - also-aussi - Bataille-de-Fish Creek, Lieu historique national de la	PARK/PARC	SK		73 B/9	52°33'	106°11'
Battle of the Châteauguay National Historic Site - also-aussi - Bataille-de-la-Châteauguay, Lieu historique national de la	PARK/PARC	QC	Le Haut-Saint-Laurent	31 H/4	45°10'	73°56'
Battle of the Restigouche National Historic Site - also-aussi - Bataille-de-la-Ristigouche, Lieu historique national de la	PARK/PARC	QC	Avignon	22 B/2	48°01'	66°44'
Battle of the Windmill National Historic Site - also-aussi - Bataille-du-Moulin-à-Vent, Lieu historique national de la	PARK/PARC	ON	Grenville	31 B/11	44°43'	75°29'
Battle Pond	LAKE/LAC	NF		12 A/5	48°29'	57°45'
Battle River	UNP/LNO	AB	4-38-14-W4	73 D/4	52°14'	111°56'
Battle River	RIV/CDE	SK/AB		73 C/9	52°43'	108°15'
Battle River No. 438	MUN2/AZM2	SK		73 C/15	52°50'	108°35'
Battrum	UNP/LNO	SK	30-18-17-W3	72 K/9	50°33'	108°20'
Batture-Agômbama	UNP/LNO	QC	Maskinongé	31 I/2	46°13'	72°55'
Batture-d'Argent, La	UNP/LNO	QC	Les Laurentides	31 J/2	46°07'	74°40'
Batture-de-Roche	UNP/LNO	QC	Antoine-Labelle	31 J/14	46°58'	75°22'
Batty Bay	BAY/BAIE	NT	Franklin	58 D	73°14'	91°25'
Batty Lake	LAKE/LAC	MB		63 N/2	55°09'	100°39'

NAME NOM	ENTITY ENTITÉ	LOC 1 LIEU 1	LOC 2 LIEU 2	MAP CARTE	POSITION LAT	LONG
Batty Lake	LAKE/LAC	SK	67-2-W2	63 L/16	54°48′	102°14′
Batwing Lake	LAKE/LAC	ON	Thunder Bay	52 B/8	48°26′	90°10′
Baudeau, Lac	LAKE/LAC	QC	Jamésie	32 P/14	51°45′	73°07′
Bauld, Cape	CAPE/CAP	NF		2 M/11	51°38′	55°26′
Bauline	TOWN/VIL2	NF		1 N/10	47°43′	52°50′
Bauline East	UNP/LNO	NF		1 N/2	47°11′	52°51′
Baumann Fiord	BAY/BAIE	NT	Franklin	49 C	77°40′	85°35′
Bawk	UNP/LNO	ON	Thunder Bay	42 E/15	49°58′	86°40′
Bawlf	VILG/VILG	AB	31-45-17-W4	83 A/16	52°55′	112°28′
Baxter	UNP/LNO	ON	Simcoe	31 D/4	44°15′	79°50′
Baxter Creek	RIV/CDE	ON	Northumberland	31 D/1	44°12′	78°21′
Baxter Lakes	LAKE/LAC	AB	45-5,6-W4	73 D/15	52°53′	110°43′
Baxters Corner	UNP/LNO	NB	Saint John	21 H/5	45°23′	65°49′
Baxters Corners	UNP/LNO	ON	Carleton	31 G/4	45°10′	75°47′
Baxters Harbour	UNP/LNO	NS	Kings	21 H/2	45°13′	64°31′
Bayard	HAM/HAM	SK	25-12-25-W2	72 I/3	50°01′	105°17′
Bayard	UNP/LNO	NB	Charlotte	21 G/8	45°26′	66°20′
Bayard	UNP/LNO	QC	Antoine-Labelle	31 J/7	46°22′	74°49′
Bayard Station - see-voir - Bayard	HAM/HAM	SK		72 I/3	50°01′	105°17′
Bay Beach	UNP/LNO	ON	Welland	30 L/14	42°52′	79°05′
Bay Bulls	TOWN/VIL2	NF		1 N/7	47°19′	52°49′
Bay Bulls Big Pond	LAKE/LAC	NF		1 N/7	47°24′	52°47′
Bay de l'Eau	UNP/LNO	NF		1 M/10	47°38′	54°55′
Bay de Loup	UNP/LNO	NF		11 P/12	47°40′	57°31′
Bay de Loup Brook	RIV/CDE	NF		11 P/12	47°40′	57°31′
Bay de Verde	TOWN/VIL2	NF		2 C/2	48°05′	52°54′
Bay de Verde Peninsula	CAPE/CAP	NF		2 C/2	48°07′	52°56′
Bay du Nord	UNP/LNO	NF		1 M/11	47°43′	55°25′
Bay du Nord River	RIV/CDE	NF		1 M/11	47°43′	55°25′
Bay du Vin	UNP/LNO	NB	Northumberland	21 P/3	47°02′	65°08′
Bay du Vin Beach	UNP/LNO	NB	Northumberland	21 P/3	47°03′	65°08′
Bay du Vin Island	ISL/ÎLE	NB	Northumberland	21 P/3	47°06′	65°06′
Bay du Vin River	RIV/CDE	NB	Northumberland	21 P/3	47°03′	65°08′
Bayend	UNP/LNO	MB	13-26-12-W	62 O/3	51°15′	99°02′
Bayeuville, Lac	LAKE/LAC	QC	Le Fjord-du-Saguenay	22 E/8	49°15′	70°21′
Bayfield	VILG/VILG	ON	Huron	40 P/12	43°34′	81°42′
Bayfield	UNP/LNO	PE	Kings	11 L/8	46°28′	62°12′
Bayfield	UNP/LNO	NS	Antigonish	11 F/12	45°38′	61°45′
Bayfield	UNP/LNO	NB	Westmorland	11 L/4	46°08′	63°49′
Bayfield, Île	ISL/ÎLE	QC	Côte-Nord-du-Golfe-Saint-Laurent	12 O/1	51°13′	58°23′
Bayfield Inlet	UNP/LNO	ON	Parry Sound	41 H/9	45°37′	80°30′
Bayfield River	RIV/CDE	ON	Huron	40 P/12	43°34′	81°42′
Bayfield Road	UNP/LNO	NS	Antigonish	11 F/12	45°36′	61°45′
Bayfield Sound	BAY/BAIE	ON	Manitoulin	41 G/15	45°53′	82°40′
Bay Fiord	BAY/BAIE	NT	Franklin	49 F	78°55′	83°30′
Bay Fortune	UNP/LNO	PE	Kings	11 L/8	46°20′	62°22′
Bayham	MUN2/AZM2	ON	Elgin	40 I/10	42°45′	80°46′
Bayhead	UNP/LNO	NS	Colchester	11 E/11	45°44′	63°22′
Bay Island	ISL/ÎLE	ON	Kenora	52 E/7	49°17′	94°44′
Bay, Lac	LAKE/LAC	QC	Témiscamingue	31 M/8	47°25′	78°17′
Bay Lake	LAKE/LAC	ON	Timiskaming	31 M/5	47°21′	79°51′
Bay L'Argent	TOWN/VIL2	NF		1 M/10	47°33′	54°54′
Bayly Lake	LAKE/LAC	MB		53 L/15	54°49′	94°35′
Bay Mill	UNP/LNO	QC	La Haute-Côte-Nord	22 C/5	48°15′	69°57′
Bayne No. 371	MUN2/AZM2	SK		73 A/4	52°15′	105°35′
Baynes Lake	UNP/LNO	BC	Kootenay	82 G/3	49°14′	115°13′
Baynes Sound	CHAN/CHEN	BC	Nanaimo	92 F/7	49°29′	124°45′
Baynham	UNP/LNO	MB	23-4-9-E	62 H/8	49°19′	96°16′
Bayonne	UNP/LNO	QC	Kamouraska	21 N/5	47°24′	69°46′
Bayonne, Rivière	RIV/CDE	QC	D'Autray	31 I/3	46°05′	73°10′
Bayport	UNP/LNO	NS	Lunenburg	21 A/8	44°19′	64°19′
Bayridge	UNP/LNO	ON	Frontenac	31 C/2	44°14′	76°35′
Bay Road	UNP/LNO	NB	Charlotte	21 G/3	45°13′	67°14′
Bay Road Valley	UNP/LNO	NS	Victoria	11 K/16	46°58′	60°29′
Bay Roberts	TOWN/VIL2	NF		1 N/11	47°36′	53°16′
Bay St. George South	UNP/LNO	NF		12 B/2	48°14′	58°51′
Bay St. Lawrence	UNP/LNO	NS	Victoria	11 N/1	47°00′	60°28′
Bayshore	UNP/LNO	NB	Northumberland	21 P/7	47°23′	64°56′
Bay Shore	UNP/LNO	NB	Saint John	21 G/1	45°14′	66°04′
Bayshore Estates	UNP/LNO	ON	Simcoe	31 D/5	44°22′	79°37′
Bay Shore Heights	UNP/LNO	MB	4-21-4-E	62 I/15	50°47′	97°00′
Bayshore Village	UNP/LNO	ON	Simcoe	31 D/11	44°33′	79°17′
Bayside	UNP/LNO	NF		12 H/10	49°34′	56°53′
Bayside	UNP/LNO	PE	Prince	11 L/12	46°31′	63°54′
Bayside	UNP/LNO	NS	Halifax	11 D/12	44°32′	63°48′

NAME / NOM	ENTITY / ENTITÉ	LOC 1 / LIEU 1	LOC 2 / LIEU 2	MAP / CARTE	POSITION LAT	POSITION LONG
Bayside	UNP/LNO	NB	Westmorland	21 I/1	46°04′	64°01′
Bayside	UNP/LNO	NB	Charlotte	21 G/3	45°08′	67°07′
Bayside	UNP/LNO	ON	Hastings	31 C/4	44°07′	77°30′
Bays, Lake of	LAKE/LAC	ON	Muskoka	31 E/3	45°15′	79°04′
Bays, Lake of	LAKE/LAC	ON	Kenora	52 J/3	50°00′	91°16′
Baysville	UNP/LNO	ON	Muskoka	31 E/3	45°09′	79°07′
Bayswater	UNP/LNO	NS	Lunenburg	21 A/8	44°30′	64°04′
Bayswater	UNP/LNO	NB	Kings	21 G/8	45°21′	66°08′
Bayswater	UNP/LNO	ON	Sudbury	41 I/2	46°05′	80°45′
Baytona	VILG/VILG	NF		2 E/7	49°20′	54°46′
Bay Trail	UNP/LNO	SK	24-36-23-W2	73 A/3	52°07′	105°09′
Bay Tree	UNP/LNO	AB	2-79-13-W6	83 M/13	55°49′	119°54′
Bayview	UNP/LNO	NF		2 E/10	49°37′	54°45′
Bay View	UNP/LNO	NF		1 M/3	47°05′	55°13′
Bayview	UNP/LNO	PE	Queens	11 L/6	46°28′	63°26′
Bay View	UNP/LNO	NS	Pictou	11 E/10	45°43′	62°40′
Bay View	UNP/LNO	NS	Digby	21 A/12	44°41′	65°47′
Bay View	UNP/LNO	NB	Saint John	21 H/6	45°23′	65°30′
Bayview	UNP/LNO	ON	Lennox and Addington	31 C/2	44°13′	76°40′
Bayview	UNP/LNO	ON	Halton	30 M/5	43°18′	79°52′
Bayview	UNP/LNO	ON	Grey	41 A/10	44°36′	80°42′
Bayview	UNP/LNO	ON	Algoma	41 K/9	46°31′	84°23′
Bayview Beach	UNP/LNO	ON	Simcoe	31 D/4	44°14′	79°32′
Bayview Heights	HAM/HAM	SK	15-48-17-W3	73 F/1	53°08′	108°24′
Bayview Park	UNP/LNO	ON	Muskoka	31 D/13	44°51′	79°49′
Bayview Point	UNP/LNO	ON	Grey	41 A/10	44°37′	80°36′
Bayview Village	UNP/LNO	ON	York	30 M/14	43°47′	79°23′
Baywood Park	UNP/LNO	ON	Simcoe	31 D/11	44°31′	79°26′
Bazentin	UNP/LNO	SK	50-13-W3	73 G/5	53°19′	107°54′
Bazile, Lac	LAKE/LAC	QC	Charlevoix-Est	21 M/16	47°59′	70°23′
Bazil, Lac	LAKE/LAC	QC	Caniapiscau	23 J/11	54°43′	67°27′
Bazin, Rivière	RIV/CDE	QC	Antoine-Labelle	31 O/6	47°29′	75°22′
Beachburg	VILG/VILG	ON	Renfrew	31 F/10	45°44′	76°51′
Beachcomber Bay	UNP/LNO	BC	Osoyoos Division Yale	82 L/3	50°15′	119°23′
Beach Corner	UNP/LNO	AB	5-53-1-W5	83 G/9	53°32′	114°07′
Beach Grove	UNP/LNO	BC	New Westminster	92 G/3	49°02′	123°03′
Beach Hill Farms - see-voir - Beech Hill Farms	UNP/LNO	NS		20 P/15	43°56′	64°47′
Beach Junction	UNP/LNO	MB		62 H/14	49°53′	97°04′
Beach Meadows	UNP/LNO	NS	Queens	21 A/2	44°04′	64°38′
Beach O'Pines	UNP/LNO	ON	Lambton	40 P/5	43°18′	81°47′
Beach Point	UNP/LNO	PE	Kings	11 L/1	46°01′	62°29′
Beach Point	CAPE/CAP	NT	Keewatin	46 K	66°12′	85°11′
Beachside	VILG/VILG	NF		2 E/12	49°38′	55°54′
Beachville	UNP/LNO	ON	Oxford	40 P/2	43°05′	80°49′
Beachy Cove	UNP/LNO	NF		1 N/11	47°36′	53°15′
Beacon Corner	UNP/LNO	AB	9-60-8-W4	73 L/3	54°11′	111°09′
Beacon Hill	UNP/LNO	SK	62-25-W3	73 K/5	54°21′	109°39′
Beaconia	UNP/LNO	MB	15-17-7-E	62 I/7	50°27′	96°33′
Beaconsfield	CITY/VIL1	QC	Communauté urbaine de Montréal	31 H/5	45°26′	73°52′
Beaconsfield	UNP/LNO	NS	Annapolis	21 A/14	44°51′	65°20′
Beaconsfield	UNP/LNO	NB	Charlotte	21 G/6	45°24′	67°24′
Beaconsfield	UNP/LNO	NB	Victoria	21 J/12	46°41′	67°47′
Beaconsfield	UNP/LNO	ON	Oxford	40 P/2	43°04′	80°36′
Beadle	UNP/LNO	SK	11-29-22-W3	72 N/7	51°28′	109°00′
Beadle Lake	LAKE/LAC	ON	Rainy River	52 C/13	48°56′	93°52′
Beak Creek	RIV/CDE	BC	Kamloops Division Yale	82 L/4	50°07′	119°59′
Beale, Cape	CAPE/CAP	BC	Barclay	92 C/14	48°47′	125°13′
Beale Mountain	MTN/MNT	BC	Cassiar	104 I/14	58°55′	129°12′
Beales Mills	UNP/LNO	ON	Leeds	31 B/12	44°35′	75°58′
Bealton	UNP/LNO	ON	Norfolk	40 I/16	43°00′	80°13′
Beamsville	UNP/LNO	ON	Lincoln	30 M/3	43°10′	79°29′
Bear Bay	BAY/BAIE	MB		64 F/5	57°29′	101°56′
Bear Bay	BAY/BAIE	BC	Range 1 Coast	92 K/15	50°48′	124°58′
Bear Bay	BAY/BAIE	NT	Franklin	48 G	75°47′	87°00′
Bear Bay 8	IR/RI	BC	Range 1 Coast	92 K/15	50°50′	124°57′
Bearberry	UNP/LNO	AB	27-33-7-W5	82 O/15	51°51′	114°54′
Bearbone Lake	LAKE/LAC	ON	Kenora	53 G/10	53°44′	90°55′
Bearbrook	UNP/LNO	ON	Russell	31 G/6	45°23′	75°20′
Bear Brook	RIV/CDE	NB	Sunbury	21 J/1	46°05′	66°18′
Bear Brook	RIV/CDE	ON	Prescott	31 G/6	45°25′	75°04′
Bear Camp	UNP/LNO	BC	Cassiar	114 P/15	59°55′	136°48′
Bear Canyon	UNP/LNO	AB	27-83-12-W6	84 D/4	56°13′	119°49′
Bear Cave	UNP/LNO	ON	Muskoka	31 E/5	45°19′	79°36′
Bear Cove	UNP/LNO	NF		12 H/15	49°50′	56°34′
Bear Cove	UNP/LNO	NF		12 P/7	51°16′	56°46′

NAME NOM	ENTITY ENTITÉ	LOC 1 LIEU 1	LOC 2 LIEU 2	MAP CARTE	POSITION LAT	LONG
Bear Cove	UNP/LNO	NF		12 H/12	49°36′	57°56′
Bear Cove	UNP/LNO	NS	Halifax	11 D/12	44°32′	63°33′
Bear Cove	UNP/LNO	NS	Digby	21 B/1	44°08′	66°11′
Bear Cove	BAY/BAIE	NF		12 G/1	49°01′	58°29′
Bear Cove	BAY/BAIE	NT	Keewatin	45 N	63°35′	84°15′
Bear Cove Point	CAPE/CAP	NF		1 K/15	46°57′	52°54′
Bear Cove Point	CAPE/CAP	NT	Keewatin	45 N	63°35′	84°06′
Bear Creek	HAM/HAM	SK		74 C/7	56°18′	108°58′
Bear Creek	UNP/LNO	SK	22-17-32-W	62 K/5	50°28′	101°49′
Bear Creek	UNP/LNO	BC	Kootenay	82 N/6	51°21′	117°28′
Bear Creek	UNP/LNO	BC	Yale Division Yale	92 H/12	49°32′	121°45′
Bear Creek	UNP/LNO	YT		115 A/13	60°48′	137°40′
Bear Creek	UNP/LNO	YT		116 B/3	64°02′	139°15′
Bear Creek	RIV/CDE	ON	Lambton	40 J/9	42°44′	82°21′
Beardmore	MUN2/AZM2	ON	Thunder Bay	42 E/12	49°37′	87°57′
Beardmore	UNP/LNO	ON	Thunder Bay	42 E/12	49°36′	87°57′
Beardy's 97 and Okemasis 96	IR/RI	SK		73 B/16	52°48′	106°28′
Bear Flat	UNP/LNO	BC	Peace River	94 A/6	56°17′	121°14′
Bear Head	CAPE/CAP	NF		11 P/9	47°36′	56°26′
Bear Head	CAPE/CAP	NF		11 P/11	47°35′	57°20′
Bear Head	CAPE/CAP	NF		12 G/1	49°01′	58°29′
Bear Head	CAPE/CAP	NS	Richmond	11 F/11	45°33′	61°17′
Bearhead Creek	RIV/CDE	AB	18-81-19-W5	84 C/2	56°02′	116°58′
Bear Head Lake	LAKE/LAC	ON	Kenora	53 C/13	52°47′	93°43′
Bear Head Lake	LAKE/LAC	MB		63 P/9	55°33′	96°08′
Bearhills Lake	LAKE/LAC	AB	45,46-25-W4	83 A/13	52°56′	113°37′
Bear Hills, The	MTN/MNT	SK		72 N/16	51°52′	108°12′
Bear Island	UNP/LNO	NB	York	21 G/14	45°55′	67°02′
Bear Island	UNP/LNO	ON	Nipissing	41 I/16	46°58′	80°05′
Bear Island	ISL/ÎLE	NF		11 P/11	47°37′	57°22′
Bear Island	ISL/ÎLE	ON	Kenora	52 E/2	49°13′	94°47′
Bear Island	ISL/ÎLE	MB		63 J/16	54°53′	98°04′
Bear Island	ISL/ÎLE	NT	Keewatin	43 I	54°22′	81°05′
Bear Island 1	IR/RI	ON	Nipissing	41 I/16	46°59′	80°03′
Bear Lake	UNP/LNO	ON	Parry Sound	31 E/5	45°27′	79°35′
Bear Lake	UNP/LNO	AB	4-73-7-W6	83 M/7	55°17′	118°59′
Bear Lake	UNP/LNO	BC	Cariboo	93 J/7	54°30′	122°40′
Bear Lake	UNP/LNO	BC	Cassiar	94 D/2	56°12′	126°51′
Bear Lake	LAKE/LAC	ON	Parry Sound	31 E/5	45°26′	79°35′
Bear Lake	LAKE/LAC	ON	Sudbury	41 I/3	46°12′	81°27′
Bear Lake	LAKE/LAC	MB		63 P/1	55°07′	96°00′
Bear Lake	LAKE/LAC	AB	72-7-W6	83 M/6	55°15′	119°00′
Bear Lake	LAKE/LAC	BC	Cassiar	94 D/2	56°06′	126°49′
Bear Lake (Fort Connelly) 4	IR/RI	BC	Cassiar	94 D/2	56°12′	126°51′
Bear Lake (Tsaytut Bay) 1B	IR/RI	BC	Cassiar	94 D/2	56°06′	126°47′
Bear Lake (Upper Driftwood River) 1A	IR/RI	BC	Cassiar	93 M/15	55°58′	126°39′
Bear Landing	UNP/LNO	NB	Gloucester	21 P/6	47°21′	65°19′
Bear Line	UNP/LNO	ON	Kent	40 J/8	42°27′	82°17′
Béarn	VILG/VILG	QC	Témiscamingue	31 M/6	47°17′	79°20′
Bear Pass	UNP/LNO	ON	Rainy River	52 C/10	48°44′	92°57′
Bear Point	UNP/LNO	NS	Shelburne	20 P/5	43°29′	65°40′
Bear Point	UNP/LNO	ON	Simcoe	31 D/5	44°24′	79°33′
Bear River	UNP/LNO	PE	Kings	11 L/8	46°24′	62°21′
Bear River	UNP/LNO	NS	Digby	21 A/12	44°34′	65°39′
Bear River	RIV/CDE	NS	Digby	21 A/12	44°37′	65°41′
Bear River	RIV/CDE	SK	64-13-W2	63 L/12	54°33′	103°57′
Bear River	RIV/CDE	AB	107-9-W5	84 J/6	58°18′	115°25′
Bear River	RIV/CDE	AB	36-70-4-W6	83 M/1	55°06′	118°28′
Bear River	RIV/CDE	BC	Range 1 Coast	92 K/15	50°50′	124°57′
Bear River 6	IR/RI	NS	Annapolis	21 A/12	44°33′	65°38′
Bear River 6A	IR/RI	NS	Annapolis	21 A/11	44°40′	65°29′
Bear River 6B	IR/RI	NS	Annapolis	21 A/11	44°43′	65°30′
Bear River East	UNP/LNO	NS	Annapolis	21 A/12	44°36′	65°36′
Bear River Station	UNP/LNO	NS	Digby	21 A/12	44°37′	65°42′
Bear River (Sustut River) 3	IR/RI	BC	Cassiar	94 D/7	56°17′	126°58′
Bears Gut	BAY/BAIE	NF		14 L/10	58°42′	63°00′
Bearskin Lake	UNP/LNO	ON	Kenora	53 G/15	53°55′	90°58′
Bearskin Lake	LAKE/LAC	ON	Kenora	53 G/12	53°45′	91°42′
Bearskin Lake	IR/RI	ON	Kenora	53 G/15	53°53′	90°57′
Bearspaw	UNP/LNO	AB	14-25-3-W5	82 O/1	51°08′	114°18′
Bears Rump Island	ISL/ÎLE	ON	Bruce	41 H/5	45°19′	81°33′
Bear Valley	UNP/LNO	ON	Parry Sound	31 E/13	45°58′	79°43′
Beasley	UNP/LNO	BC	Kootenay	82 F/6	49°29′	117°27′
Beast, The	MTN/MNT	BC	Lillooet	92 O/4	51°03′	123°45′
Beaton	UNP/LNO	BC	Kootenay	82 K/12	50°44′	117°44′

NAME / NOM	ENTITY / ENTITÉ	LOC 1 / LIEU 1	LOC 2 / LIEU 2	MAP / CARTE	POSITION LAT	POSITION LONG
Beaton Arm	BAY/BAIE	BC	Kootenay	82 K/12	50°43′	117°48′
Beaton River	RIV/CDE	ON	Algoma	42 F/2	49°07′	84°39′
Beaton Road	UNP/LNO	PE	Prince	21 I/9	46°38′	64°09′
Beatrice	UNP/LNO	ON	Muskoka	31 E/3	45°09′	79°23′
Beatrice Point	CAPE/CAP	NT	Franklin	38 F	74°49′	79°52′
Beatrix Bay	BAY/BAIE	NT	Franklin	120 C	81°10′	69°55′
Beatton	UNP/LNO	BC	Peace River	94 H/3	57°14′	121°27′
Beatton Ranch	UNP/LNO	BC	Peace River	94 B/10	56°44′	122°35′
Beatton River	RIV/CDE	BC	Peace River	94 A/1	56°06′	120°23′
Beatty	VILG/VILG	SK	23-45-20-W2	73 A/15	52°54′	104°48′
Beatty	UNP/LNO	ON	Frontenac	31 F/2	45°02′	76°45′
Beatty Creek	RIV/CDE	BC	Cassiar	104 J/3	58°06′	131°11′
Beatty Lake	LAKE/LAC	AB	125-1-W6	84 M/16	59°52′	118°03′
Beatty Saugeen River	RIV/CDE	ON	Grey	41 A/3	44°08′	81°02′
Beaubears Island National Historic Site - also-aussi - Île-Beaubears, Lieu historique national de l'	PARK/PARC	NB	Northumberland	21 I/13	46°58′	65°34′
Beaubier	HAM/HAM	SK	16-2-16-W2	72 H/1	49°08′	104°05′
Beau Bois	UNP/LNO	NF		1 M/3	47°08′	55°06′
Beaucage	UNP/LNO	ON	Nipissing	31 L/5	46°21′	79°39′
Beaucage Point	CAPE/CAP	ON	Nipissing	31 L/5	46°21′	79°40′
Beaucanton	UNP/LNO	QC	Jamésie	32 E/3	49°02′	79°15′
Beauce-Sartigan	MUN1/AZM1	QC	Beauce-Sartigan	21 E/15	45°58′	70°39′
Beauceville	CITY/VIL1	QC	Robert-Cliche	21 L/2	46°12′	70°47′
Beauceville-Est	UNP/LNO	QC	Robert-Cliche	21 L/2	46°12′	70°46′
Beauchamp	UNP/LNO	QC	Montmagny	21 L/9	46°35′	70°08′
Beauchampville	UNP/LNO	QC	Communauté urbaine de l'Outaouais	31 G/11	45°34′	75°25′
Beauchastel, Lac	LAKE/LAC	QC	Rouyn-Noranda	32 D/3	48°09′	79°07′
Beauchemin Channel	CHAN/CHEN	BC	Range 3 Coast	103 A/11	52°37′	129°15′
Beauchemin Lake	LAKE/LAC	MB	11,12-16-E	52 E/14	49°58′	95°23′
Beauchêne, Lac	LAKE/LAC	QC	Témiscamingue	31 L/10	46°39′	78°56′
Beaucours, Lac	LAKE/LAC	QC	Jamésie	32 G/2	49°06′	74°31′
Beaudette, Rivière	RIV/CDE	QC/ON		31 G/1	45°12′	74°19′
Beaudoin-Centre	UNP/LNO	QC	Arthabaska	21 E/13	45°53′	71°34′
Beaudry	VILG/VILG	QC	Rouyn-Noranda	32 D/3	48°06′	79°09′
Beaudry	UNP/LNO	MB		62 H/14	49°52′	97°30′
Beaudry, Lac	LAKE/LAC	QC	Témiscamingue	31 M/10	47°44′	78°55′
Beaufield	UNP/LNO	SK	18-32-22-W3	72 N/11	51°45′	109°06′
Beaufort	UNP/LNO	NB	Carleton	21 J/11	46°35′	67°17′
Beaufort, Mer de - also-aussi - **Beaufort Sea**	SEA/MER	NT/YT		MCR130	72°50′	132°30′
Beaufort Rise	SEAU/SMER	—		7000	72°00′	143°30′
Beaufort Sea - also-aussi - **Beaufort, Mer de**	SEA/MER	NT/YT		MCR130	72°50′	132°30′
Beaufort Shelf	SEAU/SMER	—		5.17	70°00′	142°30′
Beaufort Slope	SEAU/SMER	—			71°00′	145°00′
Beaugé, Banc	SEAU/SMER	—		4025	49°45′	60°10′
Beauglen	UNP/LNO	QC	Bonaventure	22 A/5	48°16′	65°57′
Beauharnois	CITY/VIL1	QC	Beauharnois-Salaberry	31 H/5	45°19′	73°52′
Beauharnois, Canal de	CHAN/CHEN	QC	Beauharnois-Salaberry	31 H/5	45°19′	73°55′
Beauharnois-Salaberry	MUN1/AZM1	QC	Beauharnois-Salaberry	31 H/5	45°19′	73°56′
Beaujon, Lac	LAKE/LAC	QC	Jamésie	23 E/12	53°40′	71°32′
Beaulac	TOWN/VIL2	QC	L'Amiante	21 E/14	45°50′	71°23′
Beaulac	UNP/LNO	QC	Matawinie	31 I/4	46°02′	73°53′
Beau Lac, Le	LAKE/LAC	QC	Témiscouata	21 N/6	47°21′	69°03′
Beaulieu River	RIV/CDE	NT	Mackenzie	85 I	62°03′	113°11′
Beauly	UNP/LNO	NS	Antigonish	11 F/12	45°31′	61°49′
Beaumaris	UNP/LNO	ON	Muskoka	31 E/3	45°04′	79°29′
Beaumesnil, Lac	LAKE/LAC	QC	Témiscamingue	31 M/14	47°46′	79°04′
Beaumonde Heights	UNP/LNO	ON	York	30 M/12	43°44′	79°34′
Beaumont	TOWN/VIL2	AB	34-50-24-W4	83 H/6	53°21′	113°25′
Beaumont	UNP/LNO	NF		2 E/12	49°37′	55°41′
Beaumont	UNP/LNO	NB	Westmorland	21 H/15	45°53′	64°35′
Beaumont	UNP/LNO	QC	Bellechasse	21 L/14	46°50′	71°01′
Beaumont	UNP/LNO	MB		62 H/14	49°51′	97°10′
Beaumont-Est	UNP/LNO	QC	Bellechasse	21 L/15	46°48′	70°58′
Beaumont Harbour	BAY/BAIE	NT	Franklin	25 L	62°56′	70°50′
Beaumont, Lac	LAKE/LAC	QC	Bellechasse	21 L/15	46°47′	70°59′
Beaumont-la-Ronce	UNP/LNO	QC	L'Islet	21 M/1	47°10′	70°18′
Beaumont North	UNP/LNO	NF		2 E/12	49°37′	55°42′
Beaumont, Ruisseau	RIV/CDE	QC	Bellechasse	21 L/15	46°51′	70°57′
Beauport	CITY/VIL1	QC	Communauté urbaine de Québec	21 L/14	46°52′	71°11′
Beauport, Lac	LAKE/LAC	QC	La Jacques-Cartier	21 L/14	46°57′	71°17′
Beaupré	CITY/VIL1	QC	La Côte-de-Beaupré	21 M/2	47°03′	70°54′
Beaupré, Lac	LAKE/LAC	QC	Kativik	13 M/4	55°13′	63°36′
Beaupré Lake	LAKE/LAC	SK	64-9-W3	73 J/11	54°32′	107°10′
Beauregard, Île	ISL/ÎLE	QC	Lajemmerais	31 H/14	45°45′	73°25′
Beaurepaire	UNP/LNO	QC	Communauté urbaine de Montréal	31 H/5	45°25′	73°53′
Beaurivage, Rivière	RIV/CDE	QC	Les Chutes-de-la-Chaudière	21 L/11	46°42′	71°16′

NAME / NOM	ENTITY / ENTITÉ	LOC 1 / LIEU 1	LOC 2 / LIEU 2	MAP / CARTE	POSITION LAT	POSITION LONG
Beausejour	TOWN/VIL2	MB	12,13-7-E	62 I/2	50°04′	96°31′
Beauséjour	UNP/LNO	QC	Rimouski-Neigette	22 C/7	48°24′	68°32′
Beauséjour	UNP/LNO	QC	Témiscouata	21 N/10	47°36′	68°58′
Beauséjour, Lac	LAKE/LAC	QC	Le Fjord-du-Saguenay	22 D/15	48°59′	70°44′
Beauséjour, Lac	LAKE/LAC	QC	La Côte-de-Beaupré	21 M/11	47°35′	71°18′
Beausoleil Island	ISL/ÎLE	ON	Muskoka	31 D/13	44°53′	79°52′
Beauvais Lake	LAKE/LAC	NT	Mackenzie	75 A	60°27′	105°31′
Beauvais Lake Provincial Park	PARK/PARC	AB	5-1,2-W5	82 G/8	49°25′	114°06′
Beauval	VILG/VILG	SK	71-11-W3	73 O/4	55°09′	107°37′
Beauvallon	UNP/LNO	AB	14-54-10-W4	73 E/11	53°40′	111°22′
Beaux-Rivages	VILG/VILG	QC	Antoine-Labelle	31 J/11	46°32′	75°18′
Beaver	UNP/LNO	NF		12 B/16	48°49′	58°10′
Beaver	UNP/LNO	MB	31-12-9-W	62 J/2	50°04′	98°42′
*Beaver	UNP/LNO	BC	Range 2 Coast	92 M/12	51°33′	127°36′
Beaverbank	UNP/LNO	NS	Halifax	11 D/13	44°48′	63°41′
Beaverbank Villa	UNP/LNO	NS	Halifax	11 D/13	44°54′	63°43′
Beaver Brook	UNP/LNO	NS	Colchester	11 E/6	45°19′	63°25′
Beaver Brook	UNP/LNO	NB	Albert	21 H/10	45°42′	64°48′
Beaver Brook	RIV/CDE	NF		2 D/12	48°38′	55°44′
Beaver Brook	RIV/CDE	NF		12 I/16	50°54′	56°09′
Beaver Brook	RIV/CDE	NF		11 P/16	47°45′	56°20′
Beaver Brook Lake	LAKE/LAC	NB	York	21 J/10	46°44′	66°54′
Beaver Brook Station	UNP/LNO	NB	Northumberland	21 P/4	47°08′	65°36′
Beaver Cove	UNP/LNO	NF		2 E/8	49°25′	54°23′
Beaver Cove	UNP/LNO	NS	Cape Breton	11 K/2	46°04′	60°34′
Beaver Cove	UNP/LNO	BC	Rupert	92 L/10	50°32′	126°52′
Beaver Creek	HAM/HAM	SK		72 O/15	51°58′	106°40′
Beaver Creek	UNP/LNO	BC	Alberni	92 F/7	49°19′	124°54′
Beaver Creek	UNP/LNO	YT		115 K/7	62°23′	140°53′
Beaver Creek	RIV/CDE	ON	Frontenac	31 C/10	44°44′	76°58′
Beaver Creek	RIV/CDE	AB	8-28-W4	82 H/12	49°39′	113°42′
Beaver Creek	RIV/CDE	BC	Cariboo	93 B/9	52°44′	122°07′
Beaver Crossing	UNP/LNO	QC	Le Haut-Saint-Laurent	31 G/1	45°01′	74°22′
Beaver Crossing	UNP/LNO	AB	15-62-2-W4	73 L/8	54°21′	110°13′
Beaverdale	UNP/LNO	ON	Grey	41 A/7	44°25′	80°36′
Beaver Dale	UNP/LNO	SK	15-26-7-W2	62 M/2	51°15′	102°54′
Beaver Dam	UNP/LNO	NB	York	21 G/15	45°48′	66°42′
Beaverdam	UNP/LNO	AB	24-60-3-W4	73 L/1	54°12′	110°18′
Beaverdam Lake	LAKE/LAC	BC	Lillooet	92 P/5	51°16′	121°37′
Beaver Dams	UNP/LNO	ON	Welland	30 M/3	43°06′	79°13′
Beaverdell	UNP/LNO	BC	Similkameen Division Yale	82 E/6	49°26′	119°05′
Beaverdell Creek	RIV/CDE	BC	Similkameen Division Yale	82 E/6	49°26′	119°05′
Beaverdell Range	MTN/MNT	BC	Similkameen Division Yale	82 E/10	49°35′	118°57′
Beaver Falls	UNP/LNO	BC	Kootenay	82 F/4	49°05′	117°35′
Beaver Flat	VILG/VILG	SK		72 J/12	50°39′	107°40′
Beaver Harbour	UNP/LNO	NS	Halifax	11 D/16	44°54′	62°25′
Beaver Harbour	UNP/LNO	NB	Charlotte	21 G/2	45°04′	66°45′
Beaver Harbour	BAY/BAIE	NS	Halifax	11 D/16	44°53′	62°23′
Beaver Harbour	BAY/BAIE	BC	Rupert	92 L/11	50°42′	127°24′
Beaverhill	UNP/LNO	AB	35-55-20-W4	83 H/15	53°48′	112°52′
Beaverhill Creek	RIV/CDE	AB	5-57-20-W4	83 H/15	53°54′	112°57′
Beaver Hill Lake	LAKE/LAC	MB		53 L/7	54°15′	94°54′
Beaverhill Lake	LAKE/LAC	AB	51,52-17,18-W4	83 H/7	53°27′	112°32′
Beaverhill Lake	LAKE/LAC	NT	Mackenzie	75 I	62°49′	104°23′
Beaver Hills	MTN/MNT	SK		62 M/6	51°18′	103°26′
Beaverhouse Lake	LAKE/LAC	ON	Rainy River	52 C/9	48°33′	92°06′
Beaverhouse Lake	LAKE/LAC	ON	Kenora	52 F/11	49°34′	93°25′
Beaver Island	ISL/ÎLE	SK		64 E/8	57°26′	102°10′
Beaver Islands 8	IR/RI	BC	Range 5 Coast	93 K/8	54°28′	124°31′
Beaver Lake	UNP/LNO	ON	Timiskaming	32 D/4	48°08′	79°39′
Beaver Lake	UNP/LNO	AB	32-66-13-W4	73 L/13	54°46′	111°55′
Beaver Lake	UNP/LNO	BC	Lake	92 B/11	48°31′	123°24′
Beaver Lake	LAKE/LAC	ON	Lennox and Addington	31 C/11	44°30′	77°02′
Beaver Lake	LAKE/LAC	AB	66-12,13-W4	73 L/12	54°43′	111°50′
Beaver Lake	LAKE/LAC	BC	Cariboo	93 B/2	52°15′	123°00′
Beaver Lake	LAKE/LAC	NT	Mackenzie	85 F	61°07′	117°08′
Beaver Lake 131	IR/RI	AB	34-65-13-W4	73 L/12	54°40′	111°52′
Beaver Lake 17	IR/RI	NS	Halifax	11 E/2	45°02′	62°46′
Beaverley	UNP/LNO	BC	Cariboo	93 G/15	53°49′	122°53′
Beaverlodge	TOWN/VIL2	AB	2-72-10-W6	83 M/3	55°13′	119°26′
Beaverlodge Lake	LAKE/LAC	SK		74 N/10	59°31′	108°35′
Beaverlodge Lake	LAKE/LAC	NT	Mackenzie	86 D	64°42′	118°12′
Beaverlodge River	RIV/CDE	AB/BC		83 M/3	55°03′	119°22′
Beaver Meadow	UNP/LNO	NS	Antigonish	11 E/9	45°33′	62°06′
Beaver Meadow	UNP/LNO	ON	Lambton	40 J/9	42°43′	82°14′

NAME / NOM	ENTITY / ENTITÉ	LOC 1 / LIEU 1	LOC 2 / LIEU 2	MAP / CARTE	POSITION LAT	LONG
Beaver Mines	UNP/LNO	AB	10-6-2-W5	82 G/8	49°27′	114°12′
Beavermouth	UNP/LNO	BC	Kootenay	82 N/11	51°31′	117°23′
Beaver No. 9, County of	MUN1/AZM1	AB	49-16-W4	83 H/1	53°13′	112°12′
Beaver Pass House	UNP/LNO	BC	Cariboo	93 H/4	53°05′	121°52′
Beaver Point	UNP/LNO	BC	Saltspring Island	92 B/14	48°46′	123°23′
Beaver Point	CAPE/CAP	NS	Halifax	11 D/16	44°52′	62°24′
Beaver Point	CAPE/CAP	SK		74 N/2	59°08′	108°56′
Beaver Ranch 163	IR/RI	AB	3-109-11-W5	84 J/5	58°27′	115°45′
Beaver River	UNP/LNO	NS	Digby	21 B/1	44°01′	66°09′
Beaver River	UNP/LNO	AB	17-62-2-W4	73 L/8	54°22′	110°15′
Beaver River	RIV/CDE	NF		13 F/10	53°44′	60°56′
Beaver River	RIV/CDE	ON	Durham	31 D/6	44°26′	79°10′
Beaver River	RIV/CDE	ON	Grey	41 A/9	44°34′	80°27′
Beaver River	RIV/CDE	ON	Kenora	43 M/13	55°55′	87°48′
Beaver River	RIV/CDE	SK/AB		73 O/5	55°26′	107°45′
Beaver River	RIV/CDE	BC	Kootenay	82 N/11	51°32′	117°26′
Beaver River	RIV/CDE	BC/YT		94 N/16	59°43′	124°19′
Beaver River	RIV/CDE	YT		105 N/13	63°58′	133°54′
Beaver River Metis Settlement - see-voir - Kikino Metis Settlement	UNP/LNO	AB		83 I/9	54°24′	112°09′
Beaver River Metis Settlement - see-voir - Buffalo Lake Metis Settlement	UNP/LNO	AB		83 I/8	54°30′	112°20′
Beaver River No. 622	MUN2/AZM2	SK		73 K/6	54°22′	109°23′
Beavers Corner	UNP/LNO	ON	Brant	40 P/1	43°04′	80°01′
Beaverstone Bay	UNP/LNO	ON	Manitoulin	41 I/3	46°00′	81°09′
Beaverstone Bay	BAY/BAIE	ON	Manitoulin	41 H/14	45°58′	81°11′
Beaver Stone River	RIV/CDE	ON/MB		53 I/14	54°59′	89°25′
Beavertail Lake	LAKE/LAC	BC	Cariboo	93 B/7	52°22′	122°57′
Beavertail Lake	LAKE/LAC	BC	Comox	92 F/13	49°59′	125°30′
Beaverton	UNP/LNO	NF		2 E/10	49°31′	54°35′
Beaverton	UNP/LNO	ON	Ontario	31 D/6	44°26′	79°09′
Beaverton River - see-voir - Beaver River	RIV/CDE	ON		31 D/6	44°26′	79°10′
Beavertrap Creek	RIV/CDE	ON	Kenora	43 M/14	55°55′	87°13′
Beaver Valley	UNP/LNO	SK	18-6-13-W3	72 G/5	49°28′	107°45′
Beaver Valley	VALL/VALL	ON	Grey	41 A/7	44°26′	80°32′
Beazer	UNP/LNO	AB	13-2-27-W4	82 H/3	49°07′	113°29′
Bebensee Lake	LAKE/LAC	NT	Mackenzie	86 M	67°29′	118°33′
Becaguimec Lake	LAKE/LAC	NB	York	21 J/6	46°16′	67°11′
Becaguimec Stream	RIV/CDE	NB	Carleton	21 J/5	46°18′	67°32′
Bécancour	CITY/VIL1	QC	Bécancour	31 I/8	46°20′	72°26′
Bécancour	MUN1/AZM1	QC	Bécancour	31 I/8	46°19′	72°11′
Bécancour, Rivière	RIV/CDE	QC	Bécancour	31 I/8	46°22′	72°27′
Bécard, Lac	LAKE/LAC	QC	Kativik	35 A/4	60°02′	73°45′
Bechard	UNP/LNO	SK	2-13-17-W2	72 I/1	50°03′	104°13′
Becher	UNP/LNO	ON	Lambton	40 J/9	42°39′	82°21′
Becher Bay 1	IR/RI	BC	Metchosin	92 B/5	48°20′	123°35′
Becher Bay 2	IR/RI	BC	Metchosin	92 B/5	48°19′	123°35′
Becher, Cape	CAPE/CAP	NT	Franklin	59 B	76°13′	95°23′
Becher House	UNP/LNO	BC	Lillooet	92 O/15	51°57′	122°31′
Becher Peninsula	CAPE/CAP	NT	Franklin	25 O	63°30′	67°50′
Beck	UNP/LNO	ON	Thunder Bay	52 A/10	48°36′	88°52′
Beck Bay	BAY/BAIE	NF		11 P/8	47°30′	56°11′
Becker	UNP/LNO	ON	Algoma	42 F/2	49°13′	84°42′
Becketts Bridge	UNP/LNO	ON	Welland	30 L/14	42°58′	79°22′
Becketts Creek	UNP/LNO	ON	Russell	31 G/11	45°31′	75°22′
Becketts Landing	UNP/LNO	ON	Carleton	31 G/4	45°03′	75°41′
Becketville	UNP/LNO	NB	Restigouche	21 P/13	47°54′	66°00′
Beckford Head	CAPE/CAP	NF		1 K/13	46°54′	53°54′
Beckfords	UNP/LNO	NF		1 K/13	46°54′	53°55′
Beckim Settlement	UNP/LNO	NB	Carleton	21 J/5	46°19′	67°43′
Beckstead	UNP/LNO	ON	Dundas	31 G/3	45°03′	75°11′
Beckwith	MUN2/AZM2	ON	Lanark	31 F/1	45°05′	76°06′
Beckwith	UNP/LNO	NS	Cumberland	11 E/13	45°50′	63°50′
Beckwith	UNP/LNO	ON	Lanark	31 F/1	45°05′	76°06′
Beckwith Island	ISL/ÎLE	ON	Simcoe	41 A/16	44°52′	80°07′
Bédard	UNP/LNO	QC	Antoine-Labelle	31 J/11	46°30′	75°15′
Bedard Creek	RIV/CDE	SK	9-52-18-W2	73 H/7	53°29′	104°35′
Bédard, Lac	LAKE/LAC	QC	Sept-Rivières	22 J/13	50°56′	67°58′
Bedareh Lake	LAKE/LAC	NT	Mackenzie	75 C	60°19′	110°00′
Beddington	UNP/LNO	AB	23-25-1-W5	82 O/1	51°09′	114°03′
Bede	UNP/LNO	MB	18,19-5-26-W	62 F/7	49°24′	100°58′
Bedec	UNP/LNO	NB	Kent	21 I/10	46°41′	64°47′
Bede Creek	RIV/CDE	AB	108-18-W5	84 K/7	58°24′	116°53′
Bedell	UNP/LNO	ON	Grenville	31 B/13	45°00′	75°38′
Bedell Settlement	UNP/LNO	NB	Carleton	21 J/4	46°08′	67°39′
Bedeque	VILG/VILG	PE	Prince	11 L/5	46°20′	63°44′
Bedeque Bay	BAY/BAIE	PE	Prince	11 L/5	46°22′	63°53′

NAME / NOM	ENTITY / ENTITÉ	LOC 1 / LIEU 1	LOC 2 / LIEU 2	MAP / CARTE	POSITION LAT	LONG
Bedford	CITY/VIL1	QC	Brome-Missisquoi	31 H/2	45°07′	72°59′
Bedford	VILG/VILG	QC	Brome-Missisquoi	31 H/2	45°08′	72°58′
Bedford	MUN2/AZM2	ON	Frontenac	31 C/10	44°38′	76°31′
Bedford	UNP/LNO	NS	Halifax	11 D/12	44°44′	63°40′
Bedford	UNP/LNO	NB	Kings	21 G/8	45°26′	66°09′
Bedford	UNP/LNO	ON	Frontenac	31 C/10	44°37′	76°34′
Bedford	UNP/LNO	MB	9-5-9-E	62 H/8	49°22′	96°19′
Bedford Basin	BAY/BAIE	NS	Halifax	11 D/12	44°42′	63°38′
Bedford Corner	UNP/LNO	PE	Queens	11 L/6	46°20′	63°01′
Bedford Island	ISL/ÎLE	ON	Manitoulin	41 J/1	46°02′	82°07′
Bedford Island	ISL/ÎLE	SK		64 E/7	57°28′	102°44′
Bedford Lake	LAKE/LAC	NT	Mackenzie	75 K	63°00′	109°30′
Bedford Mills	UNP/LNO	ON	Frontenac	31 C/9	44°36′	76°24′
Bedford Park	UNP/LNO	ON	York	30 M/11	43°44′	79°25′
Bedford Road	UNP/LNO	NB	Victoria	21 J/14	46°53′	67°29′
Bedford Station	UNP/LNO	PE	Queens	11 L/6	46°20′	63°01′
Bedivere Lake	LAKE/LAC	ON	Thunder Bay	52 B/15	48°52′	90°51′
*Bednesti	UNP/LNO	BC	Cariboo	93 G/14	53°51′	123°05′
Bedodid Lake	LAKE/LAC	NT	Mackenzie	75 D	60°20′	110°12′
Bedwell Harbour	UNP/LNO	BC	Cowichan	92 B/11	48°44′	123°13′
Bedwell River	RIV/CDE	BC	Clayoquot	92 F/5	49°22′	125°46′
Bedwell Sound	BAY/BAIE	BC	Clayoquot	92 F/5	49°17′	125°49′
Beebe Plain	UNP/LNO	QC	Memphrémagog	31 H/1	45°01′	72°09′
Beece Creek	RIV/CDE	BC	Lillooet	92 O/5	51°23′	123°38′
Beecham Settlement	UNP/LNO	NS	Cumberland	11 E/13	45°58′	63°59′
Beech Beach	UNP/LNO	ON	Algoma	41 J/4	46°07′	83°54′
Beech Corners	UNP/LNO	ON	Frontenac	31 C/14	44°57′	77°04′
Beech Glen	UNP/LNO	NB	Victoria	21 J/12	46°42′	67°41′
Beech Grove	UNP/LNO	QC	Les Collines-de-l'Outaouais	31 F/9	45°33′	76°10′
Beech Hill	UNP/LNO	NS	Antigonish	11 F/12	45°35′	61°58′
Beech Hill	UNP/LNO	NS	Halifax	11 D/15	44°46′	62°55′
Beech Hill	UNP/LNO	NS	Lunenburg	21 A/9	44°36′	64°24′
Beech Hill	UNP/LNO	NB	Albert	21 H/15	45°55′	64°45′
Beech Hill Farms	UNP/LNO	NS	Queens	20 P/15	43°56′	64°47′
Beechmont	UNP/LNO	NS	Cape Breton	11 K/1	46°05′	60°23′
Beechmont North	UNP/LNO	NS	Cape Breton	11 K/1	46°07′	60°20′
Beechmount	UNP/LNO	ON	Hastings	31 F/4	45°04′	77°58′
Beechville	UNP/LNO	NS	Halifax	11 D/12	44°38′	63°41′
Beechwood	UNP/LNO	NB	Carleton	21 J/12	46°33′	67°40′
Beechwood	UNP/LNO	ON	Waterloo	40 P/7	43°28′	80°32′
Beechwood	UNP/LNO	ON	Huron	40 P/11	43°33′	81°18′
Beechwood	UNP/LNO	ON	Middlesex	40 P/4	43°04′	81°36′
Beechwood	UNP/LNO	ON	Kent	40 I/5	42°28′	81°54′
Beechwood Park	UNP/LNO	NS	Halifax	11 D/12	44°40′	63°38′
Beechy	VILG/VILG	SK	18-22-10-W3	72 J/14	50°53′	107°23′
Beekman Peninsula	CAPE/CAP	NT	Franklin	25 P	63°33′	64°40′
Beersville	UNP/LNO	NB	Kent	21 I/6	46°27′	65°05′
Bees 6	IR/RI	BC	Range 4 Coast	103 H/15	53°55′	128°45′
Beeton	UNP/LNO	ON	Simcoe	31 D/4	44°05′	79°47′
Beetz, Lac	LAKE/LAC	QC	Minganie	12 L/10	50°34′	62°43′
Bégin	VILG/VILG	QC	Le Fjord-du-Saguenay	22 D/11	48°40′	71°20′
Bégon, Lac	LAKE/LAC	QC	Minganie	12 M/16	51°55′	62°22′
Behan	UNP/LNO	AB	35-72-10-W4	73 M/6	55°16′	111°26′
Behan Lake	LAKE/LAC	AB	73-11-W4	73 M/5	55°17′	111°35′
Behnke Wood	UNP/LNO	ON	Renfrew	31 F/14	45°55′	77°21′
Beinn Bhreagh	UNP/LNO	NS	Victoria	11 K/2	46°06′	60°43′
Beinn Scalpie	UNP/LNO	NS	Victoria	11 K/2	46°12′	60°34′
Beirnes Lake	LAKE/LAC	NT	Mackenzie	75 M	63°22′	110°02′
Beirnes, Mount	MTN/MNT	BC	Cassiar	104 A/15	56°58′	128°35′
Beiseker	VILG/VILG	AB	12-28-26-W4	82 P/5	51°23′	113°32′
Beith	UNP/LNO	QC	Le Haut-Saint-Laurent	31 G/1	45°01′	74°14′
Beitstad Fiord	BAY/BAIE	NT	Franklin	39 G	79°04′	78°10′
Bekanon	UNP/LNO	ON	Parry Sound	41 H/15	45°51′	80°33′
Bekere Lake	LAKE/LAC	NT	Franklin	97 B	68°53′	126°22′
Bekevar	UNP/LNO	SK	27-12-5-W2	62 L/2	50°02′	102°37′
Belair	UNP/LNO	NB	Westmorland	21 I/2	46°04′	64°50′
Bélair	UNP/LNO	QC	Communauté urbaine de Québec	21 L/14	46°51′	71°26′
Bélair	UNP/LNO	QC	Communauté urbaine de Québec	21 L/14	46°46′	71°29′
Bélair	UNP/LNO	MB	9-19-7-E	62 I/10	50°36′	96°33′
Bélair, Mont	MTN/MNT	QC	Communauté urbaine de Québec	21 L/14	46°49′	71°30′
Béland	UNP/LNO	QC	Beauce-Sartigan	21 E/15	45°48′	70°37′
Bélanger	UNP/LNO	QC	Témiscouata	21 N/7	47°23′	68°50′
Belanger	UNP/LNO	ON	Sudbury	41 I/11	46°34′	81°08′
Bélanger	UNP/LNO	SK	78-2-W3	73 O/16	55°47′	106°13′
Belanger	UNP/LNO	SK	16-7-25-W3	72 F/11	49°34′	109°19′

NAME NOM	ENTITY ENTITÉ	LOC 1 LIEU 1	LOC 2 LIEU 2	MAP CARTE	POSITION LAT	LONG
Bélanger Island	ISL/ÎLE	NT	Keewatin	34 C	56°08′	76°45′
Belanger Lake	LAKE/LAC	SK	57-31-W	63 F/13	53°55′	102°00′
Bélanger Point	CAPE/CAP	MB		63 H/5	53°25′	97°41′
Bélanger River	RIV/CDE	MB		63 H/5	53°27′	97°40′
Bélanger River	RIV/CDE	SK	78-2-W3	73 O/16	55°47′	106°11′
Belangers Corner	UNP/LNO	ON	Renfrew	31 F/7	45°24′	76°43′
Bel Ayr Park	UNP/LNO	NS	Halifax	11 D/12	44°40′	63°30′
Belbeck	UNP/LNO	SK	31-17-26-W2	72 I/5	50°28′	105°34′
Belbutte	UNP/LNO	SK	51-13-W3	73 G/5	53°22′	107°49′
Belcarra	VILG/VILG	BC	New Westminster	92 G/7	49°19′	122°56′
Belcher	UNP/LNO	MB		54 E/16	57°56′	94°10′
Belcher Channel	CHAN/CHEN	NT	Franklin	59 C/4	77°15′	95°00′
Belcher Islands	ISL/ÎLE	NT	Keewatin	34 D	56°15′	79°15′
Belcher Lake	LAKE/LAC	SK		63 M/7	55°16′	102°33′
Belcher Point	CAPE/CAP	NT	Franklin	48 H	75°46′	81°06′
Belcher Street	UNP/LNO	NS	Kings	21 H/1	45°05′	64°27′
Belcourt	VILG/VILG	QC	Vallée-de-l'Or	32 C/6	48°24′	77°21′
Belcourt Creek	RIV/CDE	BC	Peace River	93 I/9	54°41′	120°06′
Belcreft Beach	UNP/LNO	ON	Essex	40 J/2	42°01′	82°59′
Belfast	VILG/VILG	PE	Queens	11 L/2	46°04′	62°53′
Belfast	UNP/LNO	PE	Queens	11 L/2	46°05′	62°53′
Belfast	UNP/LNO	ON	Huron	40 P/13	43°55′	81°33′
Belford	UNP/LNO	ON	Ontario	30 M/14	43°53′	79°10′
Belford	UNP/LNO	BC	Kootenay	82 F/6	49°29′	117°22′
Belfountain	UNP/LNO	ON	Peel	40 P/16	43°48′	80°01′
Belfry	UNP/LNO	NF		13 H/11	53°43′	57°01′
Belfry Lake	LAKE/LAC	NS	Cape Breton	11 F/16	45°47′	60°11′
Belgiumtown	UNP/LNO	NS	Cape Breton	11 K/1	46°11′	60°01′
Belgo Creek	RIV/CDE	BC	Osoyoos Division Yale	82 E/14	49°52′	119°10′
Belgoville	UNP/LNO	QC	Le Centre-de-la-Mauricie	31 I/10	46°32′	72°46′
Belgrave	UNP/LNO	ON	Huron	40 P/14	43°49′	81°22′
Belhaven	UNP/LNO	ON	York	31 D/6	44°16′	79°26′
Bel-Horizon	UNP/LNO	QC	Sherbrooke	21 E/5	45°22′	71°54′
Belize Inlet	BAY/BAIE	BC	Range 2 Coast	92 M/3	51°08′	127°09′
Bella Bella - see-voir - Old Bella Bella	UNP/LNO	BC		103 A/1	52°09′	128°07′
Bella Bella 1	IR/RI	BC	Range 3 Coast	103 A/1	52°09′	128°09′
Bella Coola	UNP/LNO	BC	Range 3 Coast	93 D/7	52°23′	126°45′
Bella Coola 1	IR/RI	BC	Range 3 Coast	93 D/7	52°22′	126°43′
Bella Coola River	RIV/CDE	BC	Range 3 Coast	93 D/7	52°23′	126°45′
Bella Lake	LAKE/LAC	ON	Muskoka	31 E/6	45°26′	79°02′
Bellamys	UNP/LNO	ON	Leeds	31 B/12	44°42′	75°48′
Bellamys Lake	LAKE/LAC	ON	Leeds	31 C/9	44°43′	76°02′
Bellamys Mill	UNP/LNO	ON	Leeds	31 C/9	44°43′	76°01′
Bellanca, Lac	LAKE/LAC	QC	Minganie	22 P/9	51°38′	64°25′
Bellarmin	UNP/LNO	QC	Le Granit	21 E/15	45°45′	70°35′
Bell Bay	BAY/BAIE	NT	Franklin	47 G	71°00′	84°54′
Bellburns	VILG/VILG	NF		12 I/5	50°20′	57°32′
Belle Air Beach	UNP/LNO	ON	Simcoe	31 D/5	44°17′	79°32′
Belle-Anse	UNP/LNO	QC	Pabok	22 A/9	48°37′	64°14′
Belle Bay	BAY/BAIE	NF		1 M/11	47°37′	55°18′
Bellechasse	MUN1/AZM1	QC	Bellechasse	21 L/10	46°44′	70°43′
Bellecombe	VILG/VILG	QC	Rouyn-Noranda	32 D/2	48°04′	78°56′
Belle Côte	UNP/LNO	NS	Inverness	11 K/6	46°27′	61°06′
Belledune	VILG/VILG	NB	Gloucester	21 P/13	47°53′	65°59′
Belledune	UNP/LNO	NB	Gloucester	21 P/13	47°54′	65°49′
Belledune Point	CAPE/CAP	NB	Gloucester	21 P/13	47°55′	65°50′
Belledune River	UNP/LNO	NB	Gloucester	21 P/13	47°55′	65°53′
Belledune Station	UNP/LNO	NB	Gloucester	21 P/13	47°52′	65°49′
Belle-eau-Claire Beach	UNP/LNO	ON	Simcoe	41 A/9	44°44′	80°03′
Bellefeuille	VILG/VILG	QC	La Rivière-du-Nord	31 G/16	45°47′	74°05′
Bellefeuille	UNP/LNO	QC	Le Haut-Saint-François	21 E/6	45°18′	71°18′
Bellefeuille	UNP/LNO	QC	Abitibi-Ouest	32 D/15	48°47′	78°52′
Bellefleur	UNP/LNO	NB	Madawaska	21 O/4	47°07′	67°53′
Bellefleur Station	UNP/LNO	NB	Madawaska	21 O/4	47°06′	67°53′
Bellefond	UNP/LNO	NB	Northumberland	21 P/4	47°07′	65°39′
Bellegarde	HAM/HAM	SK	36-6-31W	62 F/12	49°32′	101°33′
Belle Harbour	BAY/BAIE	NF		1 M/11	47°41′	55°19′
Belle Isle	UNP/LNO	NF		3 D/3	52°01′	55°17′
Belleisle	UNP/LNO	NS	Annapolis	21 A/14	44°48′	65°24′
Belle Isle	ISL/ÎLE	NF		2 M/14	51°57′	55°21′
Belle Isle Bank	SEAU/SMER	—		813	52°20′	52°30′
Belleisle Bay	BAY/BAIE	NB	Kings	21 H/12	45°35′	65°55′
Belleisle Creek	UNP/LNO	NB	Kings	21 H/12	45°43′	65°45′
Belle Isle, Détroit de - also-aussi - **Belle Isle, Strait of**	CHAN/CHEN	NF/QC		12 P/9	51°39′	56°14′
Belleisle Sound	CHAN/CHEN	BC	Range 1 Coast	92 L/16	50°53′	126°25′

NAME NOM	ENTITY ENTITÉ	LOC 1 LIEU 1	LOC 2 LIEU 2	MAP CARTE	POSITION LAT	LONG
Belle Isle, Strait of - also-aussi - Belle Isle, Détroit de	CHAN/CHEN	NF/QC		12 P/9	51°39′	56°14′
Belle-Marche	UNP/LNO	NS	Inverness	11 K/10	46°37′	60°59′
Belleoram	TOWN/VIL2	NF		1 M/11	47°31′	55°25′
Belle Plaine	VILG/VILG	SK	31-16-23-W2	72 I/6	50°24′	105°09′
Belle River	TOWN/VIL2	ON	Essex	40 J/7	42°18′	82°43′
Belle River	UNP/LNO	PE	Queens	11 E/15	45°59′	62°50′
Belle River	RIV/CDE	ON	Essex	40 J/7	42°18′	82°43′
Bellerive-sur-le-Lac	UNP/LNO	QC	Antoine-Labelle	31 J/7	46°24′	74°59′
Belle-Rivière	MUN2/AZM2	QC	Lac-Saint-Jean-Est	22 D/4	48°10′	71°46′
Belle-Rivière	UNP/LNO	QC	Mirabel	31 G/9	45°37′	74°06′
Belle Rivière, La	RIV/CDE	QC	Lac-Saint-Jean-Est	22 D/5	48°29′	71°48′
Belle Rivière, Lac de la	LAKE/LAC	QC	Lac-Saint-Jean-Est	22 D/4	48°14′	71°44′
Belleterre	CITY/VIL1	QC	Témiscamingue	31 M/7	47°23′	78°42′
Belle Vallée	UNP/LNO	ON	Timiskaming	31 M/12	47°39′	79°35′
Belleview	UNP/LNO	MB	30-7-25-W	62 F/10	49°36′	100°51′
Belleview	UNP/LNO	BC	Kootenay	82 F/13	50°00′	117°55′
Belleview Beach	UNP/LNO	ON	Welland	30 L/14	42°52′	79°21′
Belleville	CITY/VIL1	ON	Hastings	31 C/3	44°10′	77°23′
Belleville	UNP/LNO	NS	Yarmouth	20 P/13	43°52′	65°56′
Belleville	UNP/LNO	NB	Carleton	21 J/4	46°12′	67°42′
Belleville North	UNP/LNO	NS	Yarmouth	20 P/13	43°52′	65°56′
Belleville South	UNP/LNO	NS	Yarmouth	20 P/13	43°51′	65°55′
Bellevue	UNP/LNO	NF		1 N/12	47°38′	53°44′
Bellevue	UNP/LNO	PE	Queens	11 L/2	46°06′	62°45′
Bellevue	UNP/LNO	QC	L'Érable	21 L/4	46°15′	71°49′
Bellevue	UNP/LNO	QC	Le Domaine-du-Roy	32 A/9	48°40′	72°27′
Bellevue	UNP/LNO	QC	Vaudreuil-Soulanges	31 H/5	45°21′	73°55′
Bellevue	UNP/LNO	ON	Algoma	41 K/9	46°42′	84°13′
Bellevue	UNP/LNO	AB	21-7-3-W5	82 G/9	49°35′	114°22′
Bellevue, Baie	BAY/BAIE	QC	Le Fjord-du-Saguenay	22 L/15	50°55′	70°57′
Bellevue Beach	UNP/LNO	NF		1 N/12	47°37′	53°47′
Bellevue Creek	RIV/CDE	BC	Osoyoos Division Yale	82 E/13	49°49′	119°30′
Bellevue House National Historic Site - also-aussi - Villa-Bellevue, Lieu historique national de la	PARK/PARC	ON	Frontenac	31 C/2	44°13′	76°30′
Bellevue, Lac	LAKE/LAC	QC	Le Haut-Saint-Maurice	32 A/4	48°02′	73°52′
Bellevue, Lac	LAKE/LAC	AB	56-9,10-W4	73 E/14	53°49′	111°20′
Bellevue Mountain	MTN/MNT	NT	Franklin	48 A	72°25′	81°27′
Bell Ewart	UNP/LNO	ON	Simcoe	31 D/5	44°16′	79°33′
Belley	UNP/LNO	QC	Charlevoix	21 M/9	47°33′	70°29′
Belley, Lac	LAKE/LAC	QC	Maria-Chapdelaine	22 D/13	48°51′	71°37′
Bell Falls	UNP/LNO	QC	Argenteuil	31 G/15	45°46′	74°41′
Bell Grove	UNP/LNO	NB	Victoria	21 J/13	46°55′	67°34′
Bell Grove	UNP/LNO	ON	Sudbury	41 I/7	46°28′	81°00′
Bellheck	UNP/LNO	ON	Lennox and Addington	31 C/10	44°31′	76°58′
Bell II	UNP/LNO	BC	Cassiar	104 A/12	56°45′	129°48′
Bellinger, Lac	LAKE/LAC	QC	Jamésie	32 O/8	51°20′	74°08′
Bellingham	UNP/LNO	ON	Algoma	41 J/6	46°24′	83°17′
Bell-Irving River	RIV/CDE	BC	Cassiar	104 A/3	56°10′	129°02′
Bellis	UNP/LNO	AB	34-59-15-W4	83 I/1	54°09′	112°09′
Bell Island	UNP/LNO	NF		1 N/10	47°38′	52°58′
Bell Island	ISL/ÎLE	NF		1 N/10	47°38′	52°58′
Bell Island	ISL/ÎLE	NF		2 L/12	50°45′	55°35′
Bell Island	ISL/ÎLE	ON	Kenora	52 E/8	49°20′	94°11′
Bell Island	ISL/ÎLE	BC	Rupert	92 L/13	50°50′	127°32′
Bell Island	ISL/ÎLE	NT	Mackenzie	86 D/15	64°58′	118°30′
Bell Island Front	UNP/LNO	NF		1 N/10	47°38′	52°56′
Belliveau	UNP/LNO	NS	Digby	21 B/8	44°22′	66°03′
Belliveau Lake	LAKE/LAC	NS	Digby	21 B/8	44°20′	66°03′
Belliveaus Cove	UNP/LNO	NS	Digby	21 B/8	44°23′	66°03′
Belliveau Village	UNP/LNO	NB	Westmorland	21 H/15	45°56′	64°37′
Bell Lake	LAKE/LAC	ON	Kenora	52 G/15	49°48′	90°58′
Bellmans Cove	UNP/LNO	NF		12 B/10	48°33′	58°45′
Bellman's Pond	LAKE/LAC	NF		2 E/2	49°10′	54°40′
Bell Mount	UNP/LNO	QC	Pontiac	31 F/15	45°51′	76°31′
Bell, Mount	MTN/MNT	BC	Range 2 Coast	92 N/6	51°25′	125°26′
Bell Neck	UNP/LNO	NS	Yarmouth	20 P/13	43°52′	65°55′
Belloni Point	CAPE/CAP	NB	Gloucester	21 P/12	47°40′	65°34′
Bellos	UNP/LNO	BC	Cariboo	93 G/1	53°07′	122°21′
Bellot Island	ISL/ÎLE	NT	Franklin	120 C	81°42′	65°05′
Bellot Strait	CHAN/CHEN	NT	Franklin	57 G	72°00′	94°48′
Belloy	UNP/LNO	AB	15-78-2-W6	83 M/16	55°45′	118°15′
Bell Peninsula	CAPE/CAP	NT	Keewatin	45 P	63°47′	81°21′
Bell Point	CAPE/CAP	PE	Queens	11 E/15	45°58′	62°50′
Bell Rapids	UNP/LNO	ON	Hastings	31 F/5	45°23′	77°48′
Bell River	RIV/CDE	YT		116 P/5	67°17′	137°47′
Bell, Rivière	RIV/CDE	QC	Jamésie	32 F/13	49°49′	77°39′

NAME NOM	ENTITY ENTITÉ	LOC 1 LIEU 1	LOC 2 LIEU 2	MAP CARTE	POSITION LAT	LONG
Bellrock	UNP/LNO	ON	Frontenac	31 C/7	44°28′	76°46′
Bell Rock	UNP/LNO	NT	Mackenzie	85 A	60°01′	112°06′
Bells Corners	UNP/LNO	ON	Carleton	31 G/5	45°19′	75°50′
Bells Corners	UNP/LNO	ON	Lanark	31 C/16	44°56′	76°21′
Bells Corners Station	UNP/LNO	ON	Carleton	31 G/5	45°20′	75°48′
Bells Crossing	UNP/LNO	ON	Leeds	31 B/13	44°45′	75°50′
Bellshill	UNP/LNO	AB	41,42-11-W4	73 D/12	52°34′	111°31′
Bellshill Lake	LAKE/LAC	AB	42-11-W4	73 D/12	52°36′	111°33′
Bellsite	UNP/LNO	MB	6-42-25-W	63 C/11	52°36′	101°04′
Bells Junction	UNP/LNO	ON	Carleton	31 G/5	45°20′	75°50′
Bells Lake	LAKE/LAC	ON	Grey	41 A/7	44°19′	80°45′
Bells Mills	UNP/LNO	NB	Kent	21 I/10	46°38′	64°48′
Bells Point	CAPE/CAP	PE	Prince	11 L/4	46°13′	63°39′
Bellwood	UNP/LNO	ON	Nipissing	31 E/9	45°30′	78°15′
Belly River	RIV/CDE	AB		82 H/14	49°46′	113°02′
Belmeade	UNP/LNO	ON	Dundas	31 G/3	45°08′	75°30′
Belmina	UNP/LNO	QC	L'Amiante	21 E/14	45°59′	71°28′
Belmont	VILG/VILG	ON	Elgin	40 I/14	42°53′	81°05′
Belmont	UNP/LNO	NS	Colchester	11 E/6	45°25′	63°23′
Belmont	UNP/LNO	NS	Hants	21 H/1	45°03′	64°06′
Belmont	UNP/LNO	NB	Saint John	21 G/8	45°17′	66°10′
Belmont	UNP/LNO	MB	20-5-15-W	62 G/6	49°25′	99°27′
Belmont and Methuen	MUN2/AZM2	ON	Peterborough	31 C/12	44°35′	77°55′
Belmont, Lacs	LAKE/LAC	QC	Minganie	22 P/10	51°42′	64°53′
Belmont Lake	LAKE/LAC	ON	Peterborough	31 C/12	44°31′	77°49′
Belmont Lot 16	UNP/LNO	PE	Prince	11 L/5	46°29′	63°49′
Belmont Park	UNP/LNO	BC	Esquimalt	92 B/6	48°26′	123°28′
Belmore	UNP/LNO	ON	Bruce	40 P/14	43°58′	81°11′
Belnan	UNP/LNO	NS	Hants	11 D/13	45°00′	63°32′
Beloeil	CITY/VIL1	QC	La Vallée-du-Richelieu	31 H/11	45°34′	73°12′
Belot, Lac	LAKE/LAC	NT	Mackenzie	96 L	66°53′	126°16′
Belton	UNP/LNO	ON	Middlesex	40 P/3	43°10′	81°08′
Belval	UNP/LNO	QC	Bellechasse	21 L/10	46°32′	70°49′
Belvédère	UNP/LNO	QC	Vaudreuil-Soulanges	31 H/5	45°21′	73°55′
Belvedere	UNP/LNO	AB	10-58-3-W5	83 G/16	54°00′	114°21′
Belvedere	UNP/LNO	BC	New Westminster	92 G/7	49°20′	122°53′
Belvédère-Heights	UNP/LNO	QC	Sherbrooke	21 E/5	45°21′	71°53′
Belwood	UNP/LNO	ON	Wellington	40 P/16	43°47′	80°19′
Belwood, Lake	LAKE/LAC	ON	Wellington	40 P/16	43°46′	80°20′
Belyeas Cove	UNP/LNO	NB	Queens	21 G/9	45°43′	66°00′
Bemersyde	UNP/LNO	SK	36-12-8-W2	62 L/2	50°03′	102°59′
Benacadie	UNP/LNO	NS	Cape Breton	11 F/15	45°57′	60°43′
Benacadie Point	CAPE/CAP	NS	Cape Breton	11 F/15	45°54′	60°43′
Benacadie Pond	UNP/LNO	NS	Cape Breton	11 F/15	45°55′	60°43′
Benacadie West	UNP/LNO	NS	Cape Breton	11 F/15	45°56′	60°44′
Benallen	UNP/LNO	ON	Grey	41 A/10	44°37′	80°59′
Benalto	UNP/LNO	AB	31-38-2-W5	83 B/8	52°18′	114°17′
Bénard	UNP/LNO	MB	17,18-11-2-W	62 H/13	49°55′	97°51′
Bénard	UNP/LNO	MB	18-11-3-W	62 H/13	49°55′	97°51′
Benbow	UNP/LNO	AB	14-59-18-W5	83 K/2	54°06′	116°35′
Bencas Island	ISL/ÎLE	NT	Keewatin	45 J	63°00′	82°41′
Bend	UNP/LNO	BC	Cariboo	93 H/14	53°46′	121°04′
Bendale	UNP/LNO	ON	York	30 M/14	43°46′	79°15′
Bender	UNP/LNO	MB	1-20-1-W	62 I/11	50°41′	97°28′
Bender	UNP/LNO	SK	7-13-4-W2	62 L/2	50°04′	102°32′
Benedict Glacier	GLAC/GLAC	NT	Franklin	39 G	79°22′	78°04′
Benedict, Mount	MTN/MNT	NF		13 J/10	54°43′	58°32′
Benedict Mountains	MTN/MNT	NF		13 J/10	54°45′	58°45′
Ben Eoin	UNP/LNO	NS	Cape Breton	11 F/16	45°58′	60°26′
Bengough	TOWN/VIL2	SK	23-5-24-W2	72 H/6	49°24′	105°08′
Bengough No. 40	MUN2/AZM2	SK		72 H/6	49°25′	105°00′
Beniah Lake	LAKE/LAC	NT	Mackenzie	85 P	63°24′	112°17′
Benito	VILG/VILG	MB	17-34-29-W	62 N/13	51°55′	101°33′
Benjamin Bridge	UNP/LNO	NS	Kings	21 H/1	45°04′	64°23′
Benjamin Lake	LAKE/LAC	NT	Mackenzie	75 M	63°13′	110°45′
Benjamin River	UNP/LNO	NB	Restigouche	21 O/16	47°58′	66°10′
Benjamin River	RIV/CDE	NB	Restigouche	21 O/16	47°58′	66°10′
Benjamins Mill	UNP/LNO	NS	Hants	21 A/16	44°56′	64°18′
Benledi	UNP/LNO	BC	Kamloops Division Yale	92 I/9	50°41′	120°24′
Ben Lomond	UNP/LNO	NB	Saint John	21 H/5	45°20′	65°54′
Benmiller	UNP/LNO	ON	Huron	40 P/12	43°44′	81°37′
Bennett	UNP/LNO	AB	13-23-28-W4	82 I/13	50°58′	113°47′
Bennett	UNP/LNO	BC	Cassiar	104 M/15	59°51′	135°00′
Bennett, Banc de - also-aussi - Bennett Bank	SEAU/SMER	—		15182A	48°05′	62°29′
Bennett Bank - also-aussi - Bennett, Banc de	SEAU/SMER	—		15182A	48°05′	62°29′

NAME NOM	ENTITY ENTITÉ	LOC 1 LIEU 1	LOC 2 LIEU 2	MAP CARTE	POSITION LAT	LONG
Bennett Bay	BAY/BAIE	NT	Keewatin	56 H	65°55'	89°45'
Bennett Lake	LAKE/LAC	ON	Lanark	31 C/16	44°55'	76°28'
Bennett Lake	LAKE/LAC	MB		63 H/8	53°28'	96°05'
Bennett Lake	LAKE/LAC	YT/BC		105 D/2	60°02'	134°54'
Bennies Corners	UNP/LNO	ON	Lanark	31 F/8	45°15'	76°16'
Bennington	UNP/LNO	ON	Oxford	40 P/2	43°12'	80°57'
Bennington Heights	UNP/LNO	ON	York	30 M/11	43°42'	79°22'
Benny	UNP/LNO	ON	Sudbury	41 I/13	46°47'	81°38'
Benoit	UNP/LNO	NB	Gloucester	21 P/7	47°29'	64°58'
Benoit	UNP/LNO	ON	Russell	31 G/6	45°18'	75°10'
Benoît, Lac	LAKE/LAC	QC	Le Fjord-du-Saguenay	22 M/11	51°31'	71°07'
Benoit Lake	LAKE/LAC	NT	Mackenzie	86 K	66°22'	116°15'
Benoit's Cove	UNP/LNO	NF		12 G/1	49°01'	58°08'
Benoits Siding	UNP/LNO	NF		11 O/14	47°52'	59°07'
Bensfort Bridge	UNP/LNO	ON	Northumberland	31 D/1	44°12'	78°17'
Bensfort Corners	UNP/LNO	ON	Northumberland	31 D/1	44°11'	78°16'
Bensham	UNP/LNO	SK	43-13-W3	63 D/12	52°42'	103°49'
Benson	VILG/VILG	SK	10-6-8-W2	62 E/6	49°27'	103°01'
Benson Corner	UNP/LNO	NB	Charlotte	21 G/3	45°13'	67°12'
Benson Island	ISL/ÎLE	BC	Barclay	92 C/14	48°53'	125°23'
Benson Lake	UNP/LNO	BC	Rupert	92 L/6	50°22'	127°14'
Benson No. 35	MUN2/AZM2	SK		62 E/6	49°25'	103°00'
Benson River	RIV/CDE	BC	Rupert	92 L/6	50°25'	127°22'
Bentinck	MUN2/AZM2	ON	Grey	41 A/2	44°14'	80°57'
Bentinck	UNP/LNO	ON	Grey	41 A/7	44°15'	80°52'
Bentinck Island	ISL/ÎLE	BC	Metchosin	92 B/5	48°19'	123°32'
Bentinck Point	CAPE/CAP	NS	Victoria	11 K/8	46°26'	60°27'
Bentley	VILG/VILG	AB	26-40-1-W5	83 B/8	52°28'	114°04'
Bentley Bay	BAY/BAIE	SK		73 O/15	55°49'	106°53'
Bentley Lake	LAKE/LAC	SK		64 L/14	58°51'	103°22'
Benton	UNP/LNO	NF		2 D/16	48°54'	54°25'
Benton	UNP/LNO	NB	Carleton	21 G/13	45°59'	67°36'
Benton Station	UNP/LNO	AB	34-27-3-W4	72 M/8	51°21'	110°22'
Bentpath	UNP/LNO	ON	Lambton	40 J/9	42°42'	82°11'
Bent River	UNP/LNO	ON	Muskoka	31 E/4	45°13'	79°32'
Bents	UNP/LNO	SK	13-33-13-W3	72 O/13	51°49'	107°44'
Benvoulin	UNP/LNO	BC	Osoyoos Division Yale	82 E/14	49°53'	119°26'
Beothuk Knoll	SEAU/SMER	—		8012	46°10'	46°30'
Béranger	UNP/LNO	QC	Brome-Missisquoi	31 H/2	45°11'	72°50'
Bérard, Lac	LAKE/LAC	QC	Kativik	24 L/8	58°28'	70°07'
Berceau-de-Kamouraska	UNP/LNO	QC	Kamouraska	21 N/12	47°35'	69°50'
Berdinskies	UNP/LNO	AB	23-104-9-W4	74 L/3	58°03'	111°22'
Bere Bay	BAY/BAIE	NT	Franklin	59 B	76°54'	94°13'
Berens, Cape	CAPE/CAP	NT	Keewatin	57 D	69°05'	90°38'
Berens Island	ISL/ÎLE	MB		63 A/6	52°19'	97°18'
Berens Islands	ISL/ÎLE	NT	Mackenzie	86 O	67°56'	114°00'
Berens Landing	UNP/LNO	NT	Mackenzie	95 H	61°50'	120°56'
Berens River	UNP/LNO	MB		63 A/6	52°22'	97°02'
Berens River	RIV/CDE	MB/ON		63 A/6	52°21'	97°03'
Berens River 13	IR/RI	MB		63 A/7	52°21'	96°59'
Beresford	TOWN/VIL2	NB	Gloucester	21 P/12	47°42'	65°42'
Beresford	UNP/LNO	MB	12-9-21-W	62 F/9	49°44'	100°12'
Beresford	UNP/LNO	BC	Kamloops Division Yale	92 I/9	50°35'	120°15'
Beresford	GEOG/GÉOG	NB	Gloucester	21 P/13	47°45'	65°55'
Beresford Bay	BAY/BAIE	BC	Queen Charlotte	103 K/3	54°03'	133°06'
Beresford Island	ISL/ÎLE	BC	Rupert	102 I/15	50°47'	128°46'
Beresina	UNP/LNO	SK	29-23-31-W	62 N/4	51°01'	101°46'
Berford Lake	LAKE/LAC	ON	Bruce	41 A/14	44°48'	81°11'
Bergen	UNP/LNO	MB	29-11-2-E	62 H/14	49°57'	97°17'
Bergen	UNP/LNO	AB	3-32-5-W5	82 O/10	51°42'	114°38'
Bergeron, Lac	LAKE/LAC	QC	Le Fjord-du-Saguenay	22 E/2	49°06'	70°42'
Bergeronnes	VILG/VILG	QC	La Haute-Côte-Nord	22 C/5	48°20'	69°35'
Bergerville	UNP/LNO	QC	Communauté urbaine de Québec	21 L/14	46°47'	71°15'
Bergheim	UNP/LNO	SK	37-3-W3	73 B/1	52°12'	106°25'
Bergland	UNP/LNO	ON	Rainy River	52 D/16	48°57'	94°23'
Berichan	UNP/LNO	NS	Colchester	11 E/11	45°35'	63°06'
Berkeley	UNP/LNO	ON	Grey	41 A/7	44°22'	80°43'
Berkeley, Cape	CAPE/CAP	NT	Franklin	68 C	73°55'	100°15'
Berkeley Islands	ISL/ÎLE	NT	Franklin	69 B	76°43'	100°40'
Berkeley Point	CAPE/CAP	NT	Franklin	87 G	71°35'	118°52'
Berkeley Trough	SEAU/SMER	—		7951	76°57'	100°50'
Berkinshaw	UNP/LNO	AB	2-40-13-W4	73 D/5	52°25'	111°46'
Berkshire Village	UNP/LNO	ON	Middlesex	40 I/14	42°57'	81°17'
Berland River	RIV/CDE	AB		83 K/2	54°00'	116°50'
Berlett's Corners	UNP/LNO	ON	Waterloo	40 P/7	43°28'	80°43'

NAME NOM	ENTITY ENTITÉ	LOC 1 LIEU 1	LOC 2 LIEU 2	MAP CARTE	POSITION LAT	LONG
Berlinguet Inlet	BAY/BAIE	NT	Franklin	47 G	71°10′	85°50′
Berlinguet, Lac	LAKE/LAC	QC	Le Haut-Saint-Maurice	32 B/9	48°41′	74°07′
Berlo	UNP/LNO	MB	27-20-3-E	62 I/11	50°45′	97°06′
Bermen, Lac	LAKE/LAC	QC	Caniapiscau	23 F/10	53°35′	68°55′
Bernabé, Lac	LAKE/LAC	QC	Maria-Chapdelaine	22 D/13	48°55′	71°37′
Bernard	UNP/LNO	SK	28-21-8-W3	72 J/14	50°49′	107°04′
Bernard Brook	RIV/CDE	NF		2 D/4	48°00′	55°36′
Bernard Harbour	BAY/BAIE	NT	Mackenzie	87 A	68°46′	114°42′
Bernard House	UNP/LNO	NT	Mackenzie	106 K	66°30′	133°04′
Bernard Island	ISL/ÎLE	NT	Franklin	98 C	73°36′	124°14′
Bernard, Lac	LAKE/LAC	QC	Les Collines-de-l'Outaouais	31 G/13	45°45′	75°59′
Bernard Lake	LAKE/LAC	ON	Parry Sound	31 E/11	45°45′	79°23′
Bernard Lake	LAKE/LAC	MB	12-16,17-E	52 E/14	49°59′	95°17′
Bernard River	RIV/CDE	NT	Franklin	98 C	73°34′	124°05′
Bernards Pond	LAKE/LAC	NF		2 D/4	48°07′	55°40′
Bernatchez	UNP/LNO	QC	Montmagny	21 L/9	46°38′	70°07′
Bernecher, Mont	MTN/MNT	QC	Le Haut-Saint-Maurice	32 A/5	48°15′	73°52′
Bernetz, Rivière	RIV/CDE	QC	Jamésie	32 F/3	49°04′	77°22′
Bernheimer Bay	BAY/BAIE	NT	Keewatin	56 A	64°02′	89°06′
Bernice	UNP/LNO	MB	14-5-26-W	62 F/7	49°24′	100°53′
Bernic Lake	UNP/LNO	MB	15-17-15-E	52 L/6	50°26′	95°27′
Bernier Bay	BAY/BAIE	NT	Franklin	57 H	71°05′	88°15′
Bernières	UNP/LNO	QC	Les Chutes-de-la-Chaudière	21 L/11	46°41′	71°22′
Bernières — Saint-Nicolas	CITY/VIL1	QC	Les Chutes-de-la-Chaudière	21 L/11	46°42′	71°24′
Bernier, Pointe	CAPE/CAP	QC	Kativik	35 F/5	61°28′	77°49′
Bernierville	TOWN/VIL2	QC	L'Érable	21 L/4	46°06′	71°34′
Berriedale	UNP/LNO	ON	Parry Sound	31 E/11	45°40′	79°23′
Berry	VILG/VILG	QC	Abitibi	32 D/16	48°49′	78°16′
Berry Creek	UNP/LNO	AB	36-28-12-W4	72 M/5	51°27′	111°35′
Berry Creek	RIV/CDE	AB	22-12-W4	72 L/13	50°50′	111°37′
Berry Creek	RIV/CDE	AB	118-22-W4	84 P/5	59°17′	113°38′
Berryer	UNP/LNO	QC	L'Islet	21 M/8	47°17′	70°10′
Berry Head - see-voir - Port au Port East	VILG/VILG	NF		12 B/10	48°33′	58°43′
Berry Head	CAPE/CAP	NS	Guysborough	11 F/3	45°11′	61°19′
Berry Hill Pond	LAKE/LAC	NF		2 D/6	48°20′	55°26′
Berry Lake	LAKE/LAC	ON	Kenora	52 F/5	49°28′	93°58′
Berry Mills	UNP/LNO	NB	Westmorland	21 I/2	46°07′	64°57′
Berry Mills Heights	UNP/LNO	NB	Westmorland	21 I/2	46°06′	64°51′
Berry, Monts	MTN/MNT	QC	La Matapédia	22 B/9	48°38′	66°14′
Berrymoor	UNP/LNO	AB	1-50-6-W5	83 G/7	53°17′	114°45′
Berrys	UNP/LNO	ON	Carleton	31 G/5	45°26′	75°56′
Berryton	UNP/LNO	NB	Albert	21 H/15	45°53′	64°53′
Berryton	UNP/LNO	ON	Leeds	31 C/8	44°28′	76°12′
Bersimis 3 - see-voir - Betsiamites 3	IR/RI	QC		22 C/15	48°56′	68°38′
Bersimis-Deux, Barrage	MISC/DIV	QC	La Haute-Côte-Nord	22 F/3	49°10′	69°15′
Bersimis-Un, Barrage	MISC/DIV	QC	La Haute-Côte-Nord	22 F/5	49°18′	69°33′
Berté, Lac	LAKE/LAC	QC	Manicouagan	22 K/15	50°48′	68°30′
Berthelot, Lac	LAKE/LAC	QC	Vallée-de-l'Or	32 C/9	48°33′	76°08′
Berthet, Lac	LAKE/LAC	QC	Kativik	24 K/7	58°28′	68°30′
Berthier-sur-Mer	VILG/VILG	QC	Montmagny	21 L/15	46°55′	70°44′
Berthierville	CITY/VIL1	QC	D'Autray	31 I/3	46°05′	73°11′
Bertrame	UNP/LNO	QC	Antoine-Labelle	31 J/6	46°27′	75°07′
Bertrand	VILG/VILG	NB	Gloucester	21 P/14	47°45′	65°04′
Bertrand	UNP/LNO	ON	Thunder Bay	42 C/12	48°41′	85°35′
Bertrand Creek	RIV/CDE	BC	New Westminster	92 G/2	49°00′	122°31′
Bertwell	UNP/LNO	SK	6-42-4-W2	63 D/10	52°35′	102°34′
Bérubé Lake	LAKE/LAC	SK	52-7-W3	73 G/7	53°29′	106°57′
Bervie	UNP/LNO	ON	Bruce	41 A/4	44°08′	81°30′
Berwick	TOWN/VIL2	NS	Kings	21 H/2	45°03′	64°44′
Berwick	UNP/LNO	NB	Kings	21 H/13	45°47′	65°36′
Berwick	UNP/LNO	ON	Stormont	31 G/3	45°11′	75°07′
Berwick North	UNP/LNO	NS	Kings	21 H/2	45°04′	64°44′
Berwick West	UNP/LNO	NS	Kings	21 H/2	45°02′	64°45′
Berwyn	VILG/VILG	AB	31-82-24-W5	84 C/4	56°09′	117°44′
Beryl Prairie	UNP/LNO	BC	Peace River	94 B/1	56°05′	122°02′
Berylvale	UNP/LNO	ON	Cochrane	42 A/15	48°57′	81°00′
Besa River	RIV/CDE	BC	Peace River	94 G/11	57°40′	123°18′
Besnard Lake	LAKE/LAC	SK		73 P/5	55°25′	106°00′
Bessborough	UNP/LNO	BC	Peace River	93 P/15	55°49′	120°30′
Bessemer	UNP/LNO	ON	Hastings	31 F/4	45°03′	77°38′
Bessette Creek	RIV/CDE	BC	Osoyoos Division Yale	82 L/7	50°18′	118°49′
Best's Harbour	UNP/LNO	NF		1 M/9	47°35′	54°13′
Bestwick	UNP/LNO	BC	Kamloops Division Yale	92 I/9	50°34′	120°05′
Betalock	UNP/LNO	SK	20-29-8-W3	72 O/6	51°30′	107°06′
Bétaux, Lac	LAKE/LAC	QC	Minganie	12 O/13	51°56′	59°57′

NAME NOM	ENTITY ENTITÉ	LOC 1 LIEU 1	LOC 2 LIEU 2	MAP CARTE	POSITION LAT	LONG
Betchie, Lac	LAKE/LAC	QC	La Haute-Côte-Nord	22 F/12	49°39'	69°59'
Betchouane	UNP/LNO	QC	Minganie	12 L/3	50°14'	63°11'
Betchouane, Havre de	BAY/BAIE	QC	Minganie	12 L/3	50°14'	63°10'
Béthanie	VILG/VILG	QC	Acton	31 H/9	45°30'	72°26'
Bethany	UNP/LNO	ON	Lennox and Addington	31 C/3	44°11'	77°01'
Bethany	UNP/LNO	ON	Durham	31 D/2	44°11'	78°34'
Bethany	UNP/LNO	MB	28-15-17-W	62 J/5	50°19'	99°45'
Bethel	UNP/LNO	PE	Queens	11 L/2	46°15'	62°58'
Bethel	UNP/LNO	NB	Charlotte	21 G/2	45°10'	66°55'
Béthel	UNP/LNO	QC	Le Val-Saint-François	31 H/9	45°35'	72°21'
Bethel	UNP/LNO	ON	Leeds	31 B/12	44°39'	75°41'
Bethel	UNP/LNO	ON	Prince Edward	31 C/3	44°03'	77°12'
Bethel	UNP/LNO	ON	Victoria	31 D/8	44°20'	78°29'
Bethel	UNP/LNO	ON	Welland	30 L/14	42°56'	79°12'
Bethesda	UNP/LNO	ON	Prince Edward	31 C/3	44°07'	77°08'
Bethesda	UNP/LNO	ON	York	30 M/14	43°58'	79°21'
Bethesda	UNP/LNO	ON	Simcoe	31 D/4	44°14'	79°41'
Bethléem	UNP/LNO	QC	Le Haut-Saint-François	21 E/6	45°22'	71°17'
Bethnal	UNP/LNO	ON	Sudbury	41 P/13	47°47'	81°49'
Béthoulat, Lac	LAKE/LAC	QC	Jamésie	32 P/8	51°27'	72°15'
Bethune	VILG/VILG	SK	24-20-24-W2	72 I/11	50°43'	105°13'
Bethune Bush	UNP/LNO	ON	Dundas	31 G/3	45°04'	75°15'
Bethune Inlet	BAY/BAIE	NT	Franklin	48 E	74°53'	80°20'
Bethune Memorial House National Historic Site - also-aussi - Maison commémorative Bethune, Lieu historique national de la	PARK/PARC	ON		31 D/14	44°55'	79°23'
Betsey, Barrage	MISC/DIV	QC	Le Fjord-du-Saguenay	22 D/11	48°43'	71°10'
Betsiamites	UNP/LNO	QC	Manicouagan	22 C/15	48°56'	68°39'
Betsiamites 3	IR/RI	QC	Manicouagan	22 C/15	48°56'	68°38'
Betsiamites, Barrage	MISC/DIV	QC	La Haute-Côte-Nord	22 F/5	49°21'	69°46'
Betsiamites, Lac	LAKE/LAC	QC	Le Fjord-du-Saguenay	22 D/10	48°43'	70°32'
Betsiamites, Pointe de	CAPE/CAP	QC	Manicouagan	22 C/15	48°56'	68°39'
Betsiamites, Rivière	RIV/CDE	QC	Manicouagan	22 C/15	48°56'	68°38'
Bettsburg	UNP/LNO	NB	Northumberland	21 J/8	46°28'	66°15'
Betts Cove	BAY/BAIE	NF		2 E/13	49°49'	55°47'
Betty Creek 18	IR/RI	BC	Range 3 Coast	93 C/14	52°52'	125°25'
Betty Island	ISL/ÎLE	NS	Halifax	11 D/5	44°27'	63°46'
Betula Beach	VILG/VILG	AB	4,5-53-5-W5	83 G/10	53°33'	114°41'
Betula Lake	UNP/LNO	MB	13-14-E	52 L/4	50°04'	95°35'
Betula Lake	LAKE/LAC	MB	13-14-E	52 L/4	50°05'	95°35'
Between Lake	LAKE/LAC	SK	55,56-1-W2	63 E/16	53°48'	102°03'
Beuchat, Cape	CAPE/CAP	NT	Franklin	89 D/10	77°31'	113°10'
Beulah	UNP/LNO	NB	Kings	21 G/9	45°37'	66°01'
Beulah	UNP/LNO	MB	8-15-26-W	62 K/6	50°16'	101°02'
Bevan	UNP/LNO	BC	Comox	92 F/11	49°40'	125°05'
Beveridge	UNP/LNO	NB	Victoria	21 J/14	46°50'	67°25'
Beveridge Locks	UNP/LNO	ON	Lanark	31 C/16	44°53'	76°08'
Beverley	UNP/LNO	SK	15-15-W3	72 J/5	50°16'	107°58'
Beverley Acres	UNP/LNO	ON	York	30 M/14	43°53'	79°25'
Beverley Head	CAPE/CAP	NF		12 G/8	49°18'	58°15'
Beverley Hills	UNP/LNO	ON	York	31 D/3	44°12'	79°29'
Beverley Inlet	BAY/BAIE	NT	Franklin	78 H	75°04'	107°43'
Beverley Isles	UNP/LNO	ON	York	31 D/3	44°12'	79°28'
Beverly Lake	LAKE/LAC	NT	Keewatin	66 C	64°36'	100°30'
Bewdley	UNP/LNO	ON	Northumberland	31 D/1	44°05'	78°19'
Bewick Lake	LAKE/LAC	NT	Mackenzie	75 I	62°29'	105°42'
Bexhill	UNP/LNO	SK	14-7-1-W3	72 G/9	49°34'	106°02'
Bexley	MUN2/AZM2	ON	Victoria	31 D/10	44°36'	78°51'
Bexley	UNP/LNO	ON	Victoria	31 D/10	44°39'	78°55'
Bexley, Cape	CAPE/CAP	NT	Mackenzie	87 D	69°01'	115°55'
Beynon	UNP/LNO	AB	29-27-20-W4	82 P/7	51°20'	112°47'
Bezanson	UNP/LNO	AB	10-72-3-W6	83 M/1	55°14'	118°22'
Bhreac, Sgurra	MTN/MNT	NS	Cape Breton	11 F/16	45°56'	60°26'
Bibby Island	ISL/ÎLE	NT	Keewatin	55 F	61°53'	93°05'
Bible Hill	VILG/VILG	NS	Colchester	11 E/6	45°22'	63°17'
Biche, Lac la	LAKE/LAC	AB	67-14-W4	83 I/16	54°50'	112°03'
Bic, Île du	ISL/ÎLE	QC	Rimouski-Neigette	22 C/7	48°24'	68°52'
Bickerdike	UNP/LNO	AB	6-53-18-W5	83 F/10	53°33'	116°37'
Bickerton Lake	LAKE/LAC	SK		64 M/3	59°07'	103°06'
Bickerton West	UNP/LNO	NS	Guysborough	11 F/4	45°06'	61°44'
Bickford	UNP/LNO	ON	Lambton	40 J/16	42°46'	82°26'
Bickleigh	UNP/LNO	SK	12-27-18-W3	72 N/8	51°17'	108°24'
Bicknor, Cape	CAPE/CAP	NT	Franklin	340 F	82°49'	81°18'
Bic, Parc de conservation du	PARK/PARC	QC	Rimouski-Neigette	22 C/7	48°21'	68°47'
Bic, Rivière du	RIV/CDE	QC	Rimouski-Neigette	22 C/7	48°22'	68°43'
Bicroft	MUN2/AZM2	ON	Haliburton	31 D/16	45°00'	78°03'
Biddison Lake	LAKE/LAC	ON	Rainy River	52 C/13	48°58'	93°38'

NAME NOM	ENTITY ENTITÉ	LOC 1 LIEU 1	LOC 2 LIEU 2	MAP CARTE	POSITION	
					LAT	LONG
Biddulph	MUN2/AZM2	ON	Middlesex	40 P/3	43°14′	81°20′
Biddy's Hole	UNP/LNO	QC	Pontiac	31 F/15	45°55′	76°56′
Bide Arm	VILG/VILG	NF		12 I/16	50°49′	56°06′
Bide Arm	BAY/BAIE	NF		12 I/16	50°47′	56°07′
Bideford	UNP/LNO	PE	Prince	11 L/12	46°36′	63°55′
Bidwell	UNP/LNO	ON	Manitoulin	41 H/13	45°48′	81°59′
Bield	UNP/LNO	MB	2-26-27-W	62 N/3	51°13′	101°09′
Bieler Lake	LAKE/LAC	NT	Franklin	37 E	70°23′	73°05′
Bieman's Corners	UNP/LNO	ON	Grey	41 A/2	44°00′	80°59′
Biencourt	VILG/VILG	QC	Témiscouata	21 N/15	47°56′	68°36′
Bienfait	TOWN/VIL2	SK	19-2-6-W2	62 E/2	49°09′	102°49′
Bienvenu	UNP/LNO	QC	Abitibi-Ouest	32 D/14	48°48′	79°14′
Bienville, Lac	LAKE/LAC	QC	Kativik	33 P/2	55°05′	72°40′
Bifrost	MUN2/AZM2	MB		62 I/14	50°50′	97°10′
Big Arm No. 251	MUN2/AZM2	SK		72 P/3	51°15′	105°25′
Big Baddeck	UNP/LNO	NS	Victoria	11 K/2	46°09′	60°47′
Big Bald Mountain	MTN/MNT	NB	Northumberland	21 O/1	47°12′	66°25′
Big Bank	UNP/LNO	NS	Victoria	11 K/1	46°13′	60°30′
Big Barasway	LAKE/LAC	NF		11 P/12	47°39′	57°44′
Big Bar Creek	UNP/LNO	BC	Lillooet	92 O/1	51°11′	122°08′
Big Bar Creek	RIV/CDE	BC	Lillooet	92 O/1	51°11′	122°07′
Big Bar Lake	LAKE/LAC	BC	Lillooet	92 P/5	51°19′	121°48′
Big Basin, The	BAY/BAIE	NS	Richmond	11 F/11	45°35′	61°12′
Big Bay	UNP/LNO	ON	Grey	41 A/15	44°47′	80°57′
Big Bay	UNP/LNO	BC	Range 1 Coast	92 K/6	50°24′	125°08′
Big Bay	BAY/BAIE	NF		13 N/10	55°43′	60°35′
Big Bay Point	UNP/LNO	ON	Simcoe	31 D/5	44°24′	79°30′
Big Beach	UNP/LNO	NS	Cape Breton	11 K/2	46°01′	60°41′
Big Bear Cave Pond	LAKE/LAC	NF		2 E/1	49°07′	54°00′
Big Bear Cove Pond - see-voir - Big Bear Cave Pond	LAKE/LAC	NF		2 E/1	49°07′	54°00′
Big Beaver	HAM/HAM	SK	5-2-24-W2	72 H/3	49°06′	105°10′
Big Beaver Falls	FALL/CHUT	ON	Cochrane	42 G/7	49°18′	82°32′
Big Beaver House	UNP/LNO	ON	Kenora	53 A/13	52°57′	89°53′
Big Bight	BAY/BAIE	NF		13 O/3	55°02′	59°00′
Big Birch Island	ISL/ÎLE	MB		62 J/15	50°51′	98°34′
Big Black River	UNP/LNO	MB	48-1-E	63 H/3	53°10′	97°25′
Big Blue Hill Pond	LAKE/LAC	NF		1 M/14	47°50′	55°14′
Big Bon Mature Lake	LAKE/LAC	NS	Queens	21 A/2	44°05′	64°53′
Big Bras d'Or	UNP/LNO	NS	Victoria	11 K/8	46°16′	60°26′
Big Brook	UNP/LNO	NF		12 P/9	51°31′	56°09′
Big Brook	UNP/LNO	NS	Cape Breton	11 K/2	46°00′	60°41′
Big Brook	UNP/LNO	NS	Inverness	11 K/6	46°17′	61°02′
Big Brook	UNP/LNO	NS	Inverness	11 F/14	45°48′	61°14′
Big Bullhead Point	CAPE/CAP	MB	30-6-E	62 P/10	51°37′	96°44′
Big Burnt Island	ISL/ÎLE	ON	Manitoulin	41 H/13	45°53′	81°37′
Big Campbell Creek	RIV/CDE	YT		105 G/14	61°46′	131°07′
Big Canon Lake	LAKE/LAC	ON	Kenora	52 K/4	50°04′	93°46′
Big Caribou Lake	LAKE/LAC	ON	Parry Sound	41 H/16	45°56′	80°04′
Big Caribou River	RIV/CDE	NS	Pictou	11 E/15	45°45′	62°46′
Big Cedar	UNP/LNO	ON	Peterborough	31 D/9	44°35′	78°11′
Big Cedar Brook	RIV/CDE	NB	Restigouche	21 O/6	47°27′	67°03′
Big Cedar Lake	LAKE/LAC	ON	Peterborough	31 D/9	44°36′	78°10′
Big Cedar Point	UNP/LNO	ON	Simcoe	31 D/5	44°18′	79°32′
Big Chute	UNP/LNO	ON	Simcoe	31 D/13	44°53′	79°41′
Big Clear Lake	LAKE/LAC	ON	Frontenac	31 C/10	44°43′	76°55′
Big Conne	BAY/BAIE	NF		1 M/11	47°36′	55°02′
Big Coulee	UNP/LNO	AB	10-68-22-W4	83 I/14	54°53′	113°17′
Big Cove	UNP/LNO	NB	Kent	21 I/10	46°35′	64°59′
Big Cove	UNP/LNO	NB	Queens	21 H/13	45°46′	65°57′
Big Cove	BAY/BAIE	NF		12 B/6	48°30′	59°15′
Big Creek	UNP/LNO	BC	Lillooet	92 O/11	51°43′	123°02′
Big Creek	RIV/CDE	ON	Brant	40 P/1	43°06′	80°02′
Big Creek	RIV/CDE	ON	Norfolk	40 I/9	42°36′	80°27′
Big Creek	RIV/CDE	ON	Essex	40 J/8	42°19′	82°27′
Big Creek	RIV/CDE	BC	Lillooet	92 O/15	51°51′	122°41′
Big Creek	RIV/CDE	YT		115 I/10	62°37′	137°00′
Big Crow Lake	LAKE/LAC	ON	Nipissing	31 E/16	45°49′	78°26′
Big Dam	UNP/LNO	QC	La Jacques-Cartier	21 L/13	46°53′	71°31′
Big Duck Island	ISL/ÎLE	NS	Lunenburg	21 A/8	44°21′	64°09′
Big East River	RIV/CDE	ON	Muskoka	31 E/6	45°20′	79°17′
Big Eddy	UNP/LNO	BC	Kootenay	82 L/16	51°00′	118°13′
Big Eddy Settlement	GEOG/GÉOG	MB	56-26-W	63 F/14	53°52′	101°20′
Bigelow	UNP/LNO	ON	Timiskaming	31 M/5	47°18′	79°31′
Big Farm	UNP/LNO	NS	Victoria	11 K/2	46°06′	60°49′
Big Five Bridge Lake	LAKE/LAC	NS	Halifax	11 D/12	44°35′	63°49′

NAME NOM	ENTITY ENTITÉ	LOC 1 LIEU 1	LOC 2 LIEU 2	MAP CARTE	POSITION LAT	POSITION LONG
Big Flat Lake	LAKE/LAC	MB		64 F/16	58°00′	100°18′
Big Fork	UNP/LNO	ON	Rainy River	52 C/12	48°31′	93°40′
Big Forks Stream	RIV/CDE	NB	Kent	21 I/5	46°20′	65°37′
Biggar	TOWN/VIL2	SK		73 B/4	52°04′	108°00′
Biggar, Lac	LAKE/LAC	QC	Jamésie	32 O/13	51°54′	75°35′
Biggar Lake	LAKE/LAC	ON	Nipissing	31 E/15	45°57′	78°55′
Biggar No. 347	MUN2/AZM2	SK		73 B/4	52°00′	108°00′
Biggar Ridge	UNP/LNO	NB	Carleton	21 J/11	46°33′	67°17′
Biggars Lake	LAKE/LAC	NS	Yarmouth	20 P/13	43°55′	65°46′
Big Gaspereaux Lake	LAKE/LAC	NS	Guysborough	11 E/1	45°06′	62°04′
Big Glace Bay	UNP/LNO	NS	Cape Breton	11 J/4	46°11′	59°55′
Big Glen	UNP/LNO	NS	Cape Breton	11 F/16	45°50′	60°28′
Big Glen	UNP/LNO	NS	Victoria	11 K/2	46°14′	60°41′
Big Grassy River	RIV/CDE	ON	Rainy River	52 E/1	49°05′	94°20′
Big Grassy River 35G	IR/RI	ON	Rainy River	52 E/1	49°03′	94°20′
Biggs Point	CAPE/CAP	NT	Franklin	78 B	72°34′	111°15′
Big Gull Lake	LAKE/LAC	NS	Yarmouth	20 P/13	43°53′	65°42′
Big Gull Lake	LAKE/LAC	ON	Frontenac	31 C/15	44°50′	76°58′
Big Gull Pond	LAKE/LAC	NF		12 B/9	48°45′	58°04′
Big Gully Creek	RIV/CDE	SK/AB		73 F/3	53°12′	109°03′
Big Harbour	UNP/LNO	NS	Victoria	11 K/2	46°09′	60°36′
Big Harbour Centre	UNP/LNO	NS	Inverness	11 F/15	45°52′	60°59′
Big Harbour Island	UNP/LNO	NS	Inverness	11 F/15	45°52′	60°57′
Big Harbour Island	ISL/ÎLE	NS	Inverness	11 F/15	45°52′	60°57′
Big Hawk Lake	LAKE/LAC	ON	Haliburton	31 E/2	45°10′	78°44′
Big Hay Lake	LAKE/LAC	AB	48,49-22,23-W4	83 H/3	53°10′	113°12′
Big Head	CAPE/CAP	NF		12 H/16	49°58′	56°24′
Big Head 124 - see-voir - Bighead 124	IR/RI	SK		73 K/5	54°25′	109°35′
Bighead 124	IR/RI	SK		73 K/5	54°25′	109°35′
Bighead River	RIV/CDE	ON	Grey	41 A/10	44°36′	80°35′
Big Hill	UNP/LNO	NS	Victoria	11 K/2	46°10′	60°38′
Big Hill Springs Provincial Park	PARK/PARC	AB	29-26-3-W5	82 O/8	51°15′	114°23′
Big Hole	UNP/LNO	NB	Northumberland	21 P/4	47°02′	65°50′
Big Hole Brook	UNP/LNO	NB	Northumberland	21 J/9	46°35′	66°13′
Big Hole Tract 8	IR/RI	NB	Northumberland	21 P/4	47°03′	65°48′
Big Horn 144A	IR/RI	AB	21-39-16-W5	83 C/8	52°22′	116°15′
Bighorn Creek	RIV/CDE	BC	Kootenay	82 G/2	49°11′	114°58′
Bighorn Improvement District No. 8 - see-voir - Bighorn No. 8, Municipal District of	MUN2/AZM2	AB		82 O/3	51°21′	115°05′
Bighorn No. 8, Municipal District of	MUN1/AZM1	AB	27-8-W5	82 O/6	51°21′	115°05′
Big Indian Lake	LAKE/LAC	NS	Hants	11 D/13	44°48′	63°56′
Big Interior Mountain	MTN/MNT	BC	Clayoquot	92 F/5	49°28′	125°34′
Big Intervale	UNP/LNO	NS	Inverness	11 K/7	46°27′	60°56′
Big Intervale Cape North	UNP/LNO	NS	Victoria	11 K/15	46°51′	60°36′
Big Island	UNP/LNO	NS	Pictou	11 E/9	45°39′	62°26′
Big Island	ISL/ÎLE	NF		14 C/4	56°14′	61°51′
Big Island	ISL/ÎLE	NF		14 L/10	58°33′	62°42′
Big Island	ISL/ÎLE	ON	Prince Edward	31 C/3	44°07′	77°15′
Big Island	ISL/ÎLE	ON	Kenora	52 K/7	50°27′	92°51′
Big Island	ISL/ÎLE	ON	Kenora	52 E/2	49°09′	94°40′
Big Island	ISL/ÎLE	MB		63 N/3	55°12′	101°13′
Big Island	ISL/ÎLE	SK		73 J/14	54°49′	107°23′
Big Island	ISL/ÎLE	NT	Franklin	25 L	62°43′	70°43′
Big Island	ISL/ÎLE	NT	Mackenzie	85 F	61°07′	116°42′
Big Island 31D	IR/RI	ON	Kenora	52 E/2	49°06′	94°38′
Big Island 31E	IR/RI	ON	Kenora	52 E/2	49°07′	94°37′
Big Island 31F	IR/RI	ON	Kenora	52 E/2	49°09′	94°39′
Big Island 37	IR/RI	ON	Kenora	52 E/2	49°10′	94°46′
Big Island Lake	LAKE/LAC	MB	66,67-29-W	63 K/12	54°45′	101°46′
Big Island Landing	UNP/LNO	MB	35-9-17-E	52 E/14	49°47′	95°11′
Big Island Mainland 93	IR/RI	ON	Rainy River	52 E/1	49°05′	94°20′
Big Joe's Meadow 7	IR/RI	BC	Cariboo	93 B/7	52°26′	122°37′
Big Kalzas Lake	LAKE/LAC	YT		105 M/2	63°15′	134°35′
Big Kedron Lake	LAKE/LAC	NB	York	21 G/11	45°30′	67°00′
Big Knife Provincial Park	PARK/PARC	AB	34,35-40-16-W4	83 A/8	52°30′	112°13′
Big LaHave Lake	LAKE/LAC	NS	Annapolis	21 A/10	44°39′	64°57′
Big Lake	UNP/LNO	ON	Manitoulin	41 G/9	45°45′	82°03′
Big Lake	LAKE/LAC	NS	Cumberland	11 E/12	45°43′	63°43′
Big Lake	LAKE/LAC	ON	Thunder Bay	52 I/6	50°24′	89°00′
Big Lake	LAKE/LAC	AB	53-25,26-W4	83 H/12	53°37′	113°42′
Big Lake	LAKE/LAC	BC	Lillooet	92 P/11	51°40′	121°27′
Big Lake	LAKE/LAC	BC	Cariboo	93 A/5	52°23′	121°50′
Big Lake	LAKE/LAC	NT	Mackenzie	86 A	64°51′	113°00′
Big Lake Ranch	UNP/LNO	BC	Cariboo	93 A/5	52°25′	121°51′
Big Lakes No. 125, Municipal District of	MUN1/AZM1	AB		83 N/8	55°17′	116°00′
Big Liscomb Lake	LAKE/LAC	NS	Guysborough	11 E/1	45°14′	62°28′

NAME NOM	ENTITY ENTITÉ	LOC 1 LIEU 1	LOC 2 LIEU 2	MAP CARTE	POSITION LAT	LONG
Big Lorraine	UNP/LNO	NS	Cape Breton	11 G/13	45°56′	59°56′
Big Lots	UNP/LNO	NS	Lunenburg	21 A/8	44°26′	64°26′
Big Marsh	UNP/LNO	NS	Inverness	11 F/14	45°54′	61°12′
Big Marsh	UNP/LNO	NS	Antigonish	11 E/9	45°44′	62°01′
Big Meadow	UNP/LNO	AB	27-62-5-W4	73 L/7	54°24′	110°40′
Big Merigomish Island	ISL/ÎLE	NS	Pictou	11 E/9	45°40′	62°25′
Big Mesh	UNP/LNO	QC	Côte-Nord-du-Golfe-Saint-Laurent	12 O/7	51°18′	58°40′
Big Molly Upsim Lake	LAKE/LAC	NS	Annapolis	21 A/11	44°40′	65°03′
Big Mossy Point	CAPE/CAP	MB		63 G/9	53°41′	98°01′
Big Muddy	UNP/LNO	SK	10-1-22-W2	72 H/2	49°02′	104°52′
Big Muddy Lake	LAKE/LAC	SK		72 H/2	49°09′	104°51′
Big Mushamush Lake	LAKE/LAC	NS	Lunenburg	21 A/10	44°30′	64°33′
Bigney	UNP/LNO	NS	Pictou	11 E/10	45°43′	62°59′
Bigniba, Rivière	RIV/CDE	QC	Jamésie	32 F/6	49°18′	77°20′
Bigoray River	RIV/CDE	AB	16-51-8-W5	83 G/6	53°24′	115°07′
Bigot, Lac	LAKE/LAC	QC	Sept-Rivières	22 I/13	50°50′	65°39′
Big Otter Creek	RIV/CDE	ON	Elgin	40 I/10	42°39′	80°49′
Big Pine Lake	LAKE/LAC	NS	Digby	21 A/5	44°18′	65°39′
Big Piskwamish Point	CAPE/CAP	ON	Cochrane	42 P/10	51°42′	80°35′
Big Plate Island	ISL/ÎLE	NF		11 P/1	47°12′	56°03′
Big Point	CAPE/CAP	PE	Queens	11 L/2	46°00′	62°54′
Big Point	CAPE/CAP	MB	16-8-W	62 J/7	50°24′	98°31′
Big Pond	UNP/LNO	NF		1 N/7	47°25′	52°46′
Big Pond	UNP/LNO	PE	Kings	11 L/8	46°28′	62°15′
Big Pond	UNP/LNO	NS	Cape Breton	11 F/15	45°54′	60°32′
Big Pond	LAKE/LAC	NF		1 N/6	47°16′	53°27′
Big Pond	LAKE/LAC	NF		2 C/5	48°17′	53°49′
Big Pond	LAKE/LAC	NF		13 A/1	52°14′	56°06′
Big Pond	LAKE/LAC	NF		11 O/16	47°51′	58°14′
Big Pond Centre	UNP/LNO	NS	Cape Breton	11 F/15	45°53′	60°34′
Big Prairie Settlement	UNP/LNO	AB	76-15,16-W5	83 N/9	55°36′	116°19′
Big Quill Lake	LAKE/LAC	SK		72 P/16	51°55′	104°22′
Big Quill No. 308	MUN2/AZM2	SK		72 P/9	51°40′	104°20′
Bigras-Island	UNP/LNO	QC	Laval	31 H/12	45°31′	73°51′
Big Rideau Lake	LAKE/LAC	ON	Leeds	31 C/16	44°46′	76°13′
Big Ridge	UNP/LNO	NS	Cape Breton	11 F/16	45°57′	60°13′
Big Ridge South	UNP/LNO	NS	Cape Breton	11 F/16	45°56′	60°14′
Big Ridge, The	MTN/MNT	NS	Inverness	11 F/14	45°53′	61°19′
Big River	TOWN/VIL2	SK		73 G/14	53°50′	107°01′
Big River	UNP/LNO	NB	Gloucester	21 P/12	47°34′	65°40′
Big River	RIV/CDE	NF		13 J/15	54°50′	58°26′
Big River	RIV/CDE	SK	56-7-W2	73 G/14	53°50′	107°02′
Big River	RIV/CDE	NT	Franklin	98 B	72°30′	125°14′
Big River 118	IR/RI	SK		73 G/11	53°34′	107°10′
Big River 118A	IR/RI	SK		73 G/6	53°28′	107°04′
Big River No. 555	MUN2/AZM2	SK		73 G/14	53°55′	107°16′
Big Rocky Lake	LAKE/LAC	NT	Mackenzie	65 L	62°17′	102°15′
Big St. Margarets Bay Lake	LAKE/LAC	NS	Hants	21 A/16	44°47′	64°05′
Big Salmon	UNP/LNO	YT		105 E/15	61°53′	134°55′
Big Salmon Range	MTN/MNT	YT		105 F/4	61°10′	133°45′
Big Salmon River	RIV/CDE	NB	Saint John	21 H/6	45°25′	65°24′
Big Salmon River	RIV/CDE	YT		105 E/15	61°53′	134°55′
Big Sand Lake	LAKE/LAC	ON	Kenora	52 L/2	50°07′	94°38′
Big Sand Lake	LAKE/LAC	MB		64 G/12	57°45′	99°45′
Big Sandy Lake	LAKE/LAC	ON	Kenora	52 F/16	49°49′	92°21′
Big Sandy Lake	LAKE/LAC	MB	12-1-22-W	62 F/1	49°01′	100°18′
Big Sandy Lake	LAKE/LAC	SK		73 I/8	54°27′	104°06′
Big Sandy Point	CAPE/CAP	MB	31-14-W	62 O/11	51°39′	99°19′
Bigsby Island	ISL/ÎLE	ON	Kenora	52 E/2	49°04′	94°34′
Bigsby Point	CAPE/CAP	ON	Kenora	52 E/2	49°02′	94°38′
Big Sevogle River	RIV/CDE	NB	Northumberland	21 P/4	47°03′	65°50′
Big Shannon Island	ISL/ÎLE	MB		63 F/1	53°06′	100°28′
Big Shell	VILG/VILG	SK		73 G/3	53°12′	107°08′
Big Silver Creek	RIV/CDE	BC	Yale Division Yale	92 H/12	49°35′	121°50′
Big Slough	UNP/LNO	AB	113-19,20-W4	84 I/14	58°49′	113°09′
Big Smith Creek	RIV/CDE	NT	Mackenzie	96 C	64°35′	124°54′
Big Spruce River	RIV/CDE	MB		64 I/15	58°58′	96°47′
Big Spruce River	RIV/CDE	NT	Mackenzie	96 I	66°46′	121°22′
Bigstick Lake	LAKE/LAC	SK	15-24,25-W3	72 K/6	50°16′	109°20′
Big Stick No. 141	MUN2/AZM2	SK		72 K/3	50°10′	109°30′
Big Stillwater	RIVF/EFLV	NS	Guysborough	11 E/1	45°03′	62°07′
Big Stone	UNP/LNO	AB	10-26-9-W4	72 M/3	51°12′	111°12′
Bigstone Bay	BAY/BAIE	ON	Kenora	52 E/9	48°46′	94°19′
Bigstone Lake	LAKE/LAC	MB		53 M/5	55°18′	95°36′
Bigstone Lake	LAKE/LAC	MB		53 E/12	53°41′	95°43′

NAME NOM	ENTITY ENTITÉ	LOC 1 LIEU 1	LOC 2 LIEU 2	MAP CARTE	POSITION LAT	POSITION LONG
Bigstone Lake	LAKE/LAC	SK	64,65-7,8-W2	63 L/11	54°38′	103°05′
Bigstone Lake	LAKE/LAC	SK		73 P/3	55°04′	105°24′
Big Stone Lake	LAKE/LAC	NT	Mackenzie	106 N	67°33′	132°22′
Bigstone River	RIV/CDE	MB		53 M/15	55°54′	94°37′
Bigstone River	RIV/CDE	SK	57-3-W2	63 E/16	53°55′	102°21′
Big Sturgeon Island	ISL/ÎLE	MB		63 A/5	52°16′	97°45′
Big Tancook Island	ISL/ÎLE	NS	Lunenburg	21 A/8	44°27′	64°10′
Big Timber Creek	RIV/CDE	YT		105 J/4	62°05′	131°45′
Big Timothy Mountain	MTN/MNT	BC	Cariboo	93 A/2	52°06′	120°56′
Big Tom Wallace Lake	LAKE/LAC	NS	Digby	21 A/5	44°29′	65°43′
Big Tracadie	UNP/LNO	NS	Antigonish	11 F/12	45°37′	61°38′
Big Tracadie River	RIV/CDE	NB	Gloucester	21 P/7	47°29′	64°52′
Big Tracadie River Gully	CHAN/CHEN	NB	Gloucester	21 P/7	47°29′	64°52′
Big Traverse Bay	BAY/BAIE	MB	1,2-17-E	52 E/3	49°06′	95°12′
Big Trout Lake	UNP/LNO	ON	Kenora	53 H/13	53°49′	89°53′
Big Trout Lake	LAKE/LAC	ON	Nipissing	31 E/15	45°46′	78°37′
Big Trout Lake	LAKE/LAC	ON	Kenora	53 G/16	53°45′	90°00′
Big Trout Lake	IR/RI	ON	Kenora	53 H/13	53°50′	90°00′
Big Turtle River	RIV/CDE	ON	Rainy River	52 C/15	48°51′	92°45′
Big Tusket Island	ISL/ÎLE	NS	Yarmouth	20 O/9	43°39′	66°01′
Big Valley	VILG/VILG	AB	26-35-20-W4	83 A/2	52°02′	112°46′
Big Vermilion Lake	LAKE/LAC	ON	Kenora	52 K/1	50°03′	92°13′
Big White Mountain	MTN/MNT	BC	Similkameen Division Yale	82 E/10	49°45′	118°56′
Big Whiteshell Lake	UNP/LNO	MB	13-16-E	52 L/3	50°05′	95°22′
Big Whiteshell Lake	LAKE/LAC	MB	9,16,20,28-13-16-E	52 L/3	50°05′	95°20′
Big Willow-Bed	UNP/LNO	QC	Minganie	12 P/12	51°44′	57°36′
Bigwin	UNP/LNO	ON	Muskoka	31 E/3	45°14′	79°01′
Bigwood	UNP/LNO	ON	Sudbury	41 I/2	46°02′	80°36′
Big Woody	UNP/LNO	MB	25,26-36-29-W	63 C/3	52°08′	101°28′
Bihlk'a 6	IR/RI	BC	Range 5 Coast	93 K/10	54°34′	124°54′
Bihl′ K′ A 18	IR/RI	BC	Cassiar	93 K/14	55°00′	125°23′
Bihl K'a Chah 20	IR/RI	BC	Range 5 Coast	93 K/10	54°35′	125°00′
Bilby	UNP/LNO	AB	33-54-1-W5	83 G/6	53°42′	114°06′
Billimun	UNP/LNO	SK	1-6-10-W3	72 G/6	49°27′	107°13′
Billings	MUN2/AZM2	ON	Manitoulin	41 G/16	45°53′	82°14′
Billings	UNP/LNO	ON	Carleton	31 G/5	45°23′	75°40′
Billings	UNP/LNO	ON	Manitoulin	41 G/16	45°51′	82°13′
Billings	UNP/LNO	BC	Similkameen Division Yale	82 E/1	49°01′	118°14′
Billings Bay	UNP/LNO	BC	New Westminster	92 F/9	49°42′	124°12′
Billings Bridge	UNP/LNO	ON	Carleton	31 G/5	45°23′	75°41′
Billings, Mount	MTN/MNT	YT		105 H/2	61°11′	128°54′
Bill Lake 37	IR/RI	BC	Range 5 Coast	103 J/8	54°24′	130°04′
Bill's Corners	UNP/LNO	ON	Norfolk	40 I/16	42°58′	80°16′
Bill's Corners	UNP/LNO	ON	Norfolk	40 I/16	42°49′	80°22′
Billtown	UNP/LNO	NS	Kings	21 H/2	45°07′	64°34′
Billygoat Creek	RIV/CDE	BC	New Westminster	92 J/2	50°03′	122°32′
Billy Lake	LAKE/LAC	NT	Mackenzie	97 C	69°10′	124°09′
Bilodeau	UNP/LNO	QC	Le Domaine-du-Roy	32 A/8	48°20′	72°10′
Bilodeau, Pointe	CAPE/CAP	QC	Minganie	12 E/2	49°09′	62°38′
Bilson, Lac	LAKE/LAC	QC	Kativik	35 F/10	61°31′	76°58′
Binamé Lake	LAKE/LAC	NT	Mackenzie	97 C	69°03′	124°32′
Binbrook	UNP/LNO	ON	Wentworth	30 M/4	43°07′	79°48′
Binche 2	IR/RI	BC	Range 5 Coast	93 K/9	54°34′	124°30′
Binche 10	IR/RI	BC	Range 5 Coast	93 K/9	54°35′	124°16′
Binche 12	IR/RI	BC	Range 5 Coast	93 K/9	54°37′	124°27′
Binche Bun 7	IR/RI	BC	Range 5 Coast	93 K/9	54°37′	124°26′
Bindloss	UNP/LNO	AB	19-22-2-W4	72 L/16	50°52′	110°16′
Bingle	UNP/LNO	ON	Cochrane	42 A/16	48°57′	80°24′
Bingley	UNP/LNO	AB	22-40-6-W5	83 B/7	52°28′	114°47′
Binkham	UNP/LNO	ON	Wellington	40 P/16	43°49′	80°06′
Binney	UNP/LNO	MB	34-3-9-W	62 G/7	49°16′	98°36′
Binscarth	VILG/VILG	MB	10,15-19-28-W	62 K/11	50°38′	101°17′
Binta Lake	LAKE/LAC	BC	Range 4 Coast	93 F/14	53°53′	125°29′
Binta Lake 2	IR/RI	BC	Range 4 Coast	93 F/14	53°52′	125°26′
Biota	UNP/LNO	ON	Thunder Bay	52 B/16	48°59′	90°23′
Birch	UNP/LNO	NT	Mackenzie	85 B	60°44′	115°25′
Bircham	UNP/LNO	AB	3-29-25-W4	82 P/6	51°27′	113°25′
Birchbank	UNP/LNO	BC	Kootenay	82 F/4	49°11′	117°43′
Birchbark Lake	LAKE/LAC	SK	52,53-21,22-W2	73 H/11	53°33′	105°07′
Birch Bay	UNP/LNO	MB	17-29-8-W	62 O/7	51°29′	98°32′
Birch Bay	BAY/BAIE	MB		64 K/4	58°08′	101°48′
Birchcliff	VILG/VILG	AB	17,18,19,20-39-1-W5	83 B/8	52°22′	114°07′
Birch Cliff	UNP/LNO	ON	York	30 M/11	43°41′	79°16′
Birch Cove	VILG/VILG	AB	27-57-3-W5	83 G/16	53°57′	114°22′
Birch Cove	UNP/LNO	NS	Halifax	11 D/12	44°41′	63°40′

NAME NOM	ENTITY ENTITÉ	LOC 1 LIEU 1	LOC 2 LIEU 2	MAP CARTE	POSITION LAT	LONG
Birchdale	UNP/LNO	BC	Kootenay	82 K/2	50°02′	116°52′
Birch Grove	UNP/LNO	NS	Cape Breton	11 J/4	46°07′	59°57′
Birch Haven	UNP/LNO	ON	Nipissing	31 L/6	46°19′	79°25′
Birch Head	CAPE/CAP	NS	Cumberland	11 E/13	45°55′	63°49′
Birch Hill	UNP/LNO	PE	Queens	11 L/2	46°13′	62°57′
Birch Hill	UNP/LNO	PE	Prince	11 L/12	46°33′	63°52′
Birch Hill	UNP/LNO	NS	Colchester	11 E/3	45°12′	63°11′
Birch Hill	UNP/LNO	NS	Colchester	11 E/5	45°24′	63°46′
Birch Hills	TOWN/VIL2	SK	21-46-24-W2	73 A/14	52°59′	105°25′
Birch Hills	UNP/LNO	NF		1 N/11	47°35′	53°18′
Birch Hills	MTN/MNT	AB	77-2,3-W6	83 M/9	55°39′	118°15′
Birch Hills No. 19, Municipal District of	MUN1/AZM1	AB		83 M/9	55°43′	118°05′
Birch Hills No. 460	MUN2/AZM2	SK		73 H/3	53°00′	105°20′
Birch Island	UNP/LNO	ON	Manitoulin	41 I/4	46°03′	81°47′
Birch Island	UNP/LNO	BC	Kamloops Division Yale	82 M/12	51°36′	119°55′
Birch Island	ISL/ÎLE	MB		63 B/5	52°27′	99°55′
Birch Lake	UNP/LNO	SK	5-51-14-W3	73 F/8	53°28′	108°02′
Birch Lake	LAKE/LAC	ON	Sudbury	41 I/5	46°18′	81°58′
Birch Lake	LAKE/LAC	ON	Kenora	52 N/8	51°23′	92°18′
Birch Lake	LAKE/LAC	MB	3-7-14-E	52 E/12	49°32′	95°36′
Birch Lake	LAKE/LAC	MB	56-29-W	63 F/13	53°53′	101°39′
Birch Lake	LAKE/LAC	SK	51-15-W3	73 F/8	53°27′	108°10′
Birch Lake	LAKE/LAC	AB	50-11,12-W4	73 E/5	53°19′	111°35′
Birch Lake	LAKE/LAC	AB	55-4-W5	83 G/10	53°45′	114°32′
Birch Lake	LAKE/LAC	BC	Kamloops Division Yale	92 P/7	51°27′	120°30′
Birch Lake	LAKE/LAC	NT	Mackenzie	85 K	62°04′	116°33′
Birch Lake	LAKE/LAC	NT	Franklin	96 A	64°21′	121°58′
Birchland Manor	UNP/LNO	BC	New Westminster	92 G/7	49°16′	122°45′
Birch Manor	UNP/LNO	QC	Communauté urbaine de l'Outaouais	31 G/5	45°26′	75°46′
Birch Mountain	MTN/MNT	BC	Cassiar	104 N/5	59°26′	133°49′
Birch Mountains	MTN/MNT	AB	97-19-W4	84 H/6	57°30′	113°10′
Birchmount Park	UNP/LNO	ON	York	30 M/11	43°43′	79°16′
Birch Plain	UNP/LNO	NS	Victoria	11 K/9	46°31′	60°26′
Birch Point	UNP/LNO	ON	Victoria	31 D/10	44°31′	78°36′
Birch Point	CAPE/CAP	PE	Prince	11 L/4	46°12′	63°32′
Birch Portage 184A	IR/RI	SK		63 L/15	54°53′	102°36′
Birch Rapids	UNP/LNO	SK		73 P/11	55°34′	105°23′
Birch Ridge	UNP/LNO	NB	Kent	21 I/6	46°19′	65°07′
Birch Ridge	UNP/LNO	NB	Victoria	21 J/14	46°45′	67°28′
Birch River	UNP/LNO	MB	35-39-26-W	63 C/6	52°24′	101°06′
Birch River	RIV/CDE	MB	10-10-12-E	52 E/13	49°49′	95°53′
Birch River	RIV/CDE	AB	110-14-W4	84 I/9	58°35′	112°17′
Birchton	UNP/LNO	QC	Le Haut-Saint-François	21 E/5	45°22′	71°40′
Birchtown	UNP/LNO	NS	Shelburne	20 P/11	43°45′	65°23′
Birchview	UNP/LNO	MB	22-23-24-W	62 K/15	51°00′	100°45′
Birchwood	UNP/LNO	NS	Cumberland	11 E/12	45°42′	63°47′
Birchwood	UNP/LNO	ON	Peel	30 M/12	43°31′	79°38′
Birchwood	UNP/LNO	MB		62 H/14	49°52′	97°15′
Birchy Bay	TOWN/VIL2	NF		2 E/7	49°21′	54°44′
Birchy Bay	BAY/BAIE	NF		2 E/7	49°21′	54°45′
Birchy Cove	UNP/LNO	NF		2 C/11	48°36′	53°11′
Birchy Cove	UNP/LNO	NF		12 H/9	49°41′	56°01′
Birchy Head	UNP/LNO	NF		12 H/5	49°27′	57°54′
Birchy Head	UNP/LNO	NS	Lunenburg	21 A/9	44°35′	64°03′
Birchy Island	ISL/ÎLE	NF		2 E/7	49°22′	55°00′
Birchy Lake	LAKE/LAC	NF		12 H/7	49°18′	56°45′
Birchy Nap	UNP/LNO	NF		1 N/10	47°39′	52°45′
Bird	UNP/LNO	MB	86-21-E	54 D/9	56°30′	94°13′
Bird Cove	VILG/VILG	NF		12 P/2	51°03′	56°56′
Birdell	UNP/LNO	ON	Grey	41 A/2	44°10′	80°30′
Bird Fiord	BAY/BAIE	NT	Franklin	49 C	77°10′	87°00′
Birdinia	UNP/LNO	MB	27-21-12-W	62 J/14	50°51′	99°04′
Bird Islands	ISL/ÎLE	NS	Victoria	11 K/8	46°22′	60°23′
Bird River	UNP/LNO	MB	12-17-13-E	52 L/5	50°25′	95°41′
Bird River	RIV/CDE	MB/ON		52 L/5	50°24′	95°45′
Birdsalls	UNP/LNO	ON	Peterborough	31 D/8	44°17′	78°03′
Birds Creek	UNP/LNO	ON	Hastings	31 F/4	45°06′	77°53′
Birds Hill	UNP/LNO	MB		62 H/14	49°59′	97°00′
Bird's Point	VILG/VILG	SK	22,27,28,29-18-3-W2	62 L/9	50°33′	102°21′
Birdtail	UNP/LNO	MB	21-20-25-W	62 K/10	50°44′	100°53′
Birdtail Creek	RIV/CDE	MB	7-15-27-W	62 K/6	50°16′	101°12′
Birdtail Creek 57	IR/RI	MB		62 K/6	50°16′	101°10′
Birdtail Hay Lands 57A	IR/RI	MB		62 K/3	50°13′	101°07′
Birdtail Sioux	UNP/LNO	MB	8,9-15-27-W	62 K/6	50°16′	101°09′
Birdton	UNP/LNO	NB	York	21 J/2	46°07′	66°50′

NAME NOM	ENTITY ENTITÉ	LOC 1 LIEU 1	LOC 2 LIEU 2	MAP CARTE	POSITION LAT	LONG
Birge Mills	UNP/LNO	ON	Wellington	40 P/9	43°40′	80°15′
Birken	UNP/LNO	BC	Lillooet	92 J/7	50°29′	122°37′
Birkendale	UNP/LNO	ON	Muskoka	31 E/7	45°18′	78°58′
Birkenhead Lake	LAKE/LAC	BC	Lillooet	92 J/10	50°32′	122°41′
Birkenhead River	RIV/CDE	BC	Lillooet	92 J/7	50°19′	122°36′
Birling	UNP/LNO	SK	15-47-22-W3	73 F/3	53°03′	109°09′
Birma Seamount	SEAU/SMER	—		NK22 B	40°52′	52°04′
Birmingham	UNP/LNO	SK	9-23-7-W2	62 L/15	50°58′	102°56′
Birmingham Junction	UNP/LNO	SK	31-22-6-W2	62 L/15	50°56′	102°50′
Birnam	UNP/LNO	ON	Lambton	40 P/4	43°03′	81°53′
Birnie	UNP/LNO	MB	14-17-15-W	62 J/6	50°27′	99°26′
Birnie Island 18	IR/RI	BC	Range 5 Coast	103 J/9	54°36′	130°28′
Biron	UNP/LNO	QC	Avignon	22 B/1	48°12′	66°16′
Birr	UNP/LNO	ON	Middlesex	40 P/3	43°07′	81°20′
Birsay	VILG/VILG	SK	6-25-7-W3	72 O/2	51°06′	106°59′
Birson	UNP/LNO	SK	13-48-24-W2	73 H/3	53°11′	105°24′
Birtle	TOWN/VIL2	MB	6-17-26-W	62 K/6	50°25′	101°03′
Birtle	MUN2/AZM2	MB		62 K/7	50°28′	101°00′
Biscayan Cove	UNP/LNO	NF		1 N/15	47°48′	52°47′
Biscay Bay	VILG/VILG	NF		1 K/11	46°44′	53°18′
Biscay Bay	BAY/BAIE	NF		1 K/11	46°43′	53°17′
Biscay Bay River	RIV/CDE	NF		1 K/14	46°46′	53°17′
Biscotasi Lake	LAKE/LAC	ON	Sudbury	41 O/8	47°19′	82°07′
Biscotasing	UNP/LNO	ON	Sudbury	41 O/8	47°17′	82°06′
Bishop Bluffs 5	IR/RI	BC	Range 4 Coast	93 F/1	53°04′	124°19′
Bishop Bluffs 6	IR/RI	BC	Range 4 Coast	93 F/1	53°05′	124°19′
Bishop Bluffs 10	IR/RI	BC	Range 4 Coast	93 F/1	53°06′	124°20′
Bishop Corners	UNP/LNO	ON	Frontenac	31 C/14	44°47′	77°10′
Bishop Island	ISL/ÎLE	NT	Franklin	25 N	63°38′	68°45′
Bishop Lake	LAKE/LAC	ON	Thunder Bay	52 G/9	49°38′	90°29′
Bishop Lake	LAKE/LAC	NT	Mackenzie	86 F	65°31′	116°08′
Bishopric	UNP/LNO	SK	21-12-28-W2	72 I/4	50°00′	105°47′
Bishop River	RIV/CDE	BC	Range 1 Coast	92 K/16	50°59′	124°22′
Bishops Beach	UNP/LNO	NF		1 N/11	47°37′	53°13′
Bishop's Cove	VILG/VILG	NF		1 N/11	47°38′	53°14′
Bishop's Falls	TOWN/VIL2	NF		2 E/3	49°01′	55°29′
Bishops Falls South	UNP/LNO	NF		2 E/3	49°01′	55°29′
Bishopsgate	UNP/LNO	ON	Brant	40 P/1	43°06′	80°24′
Bishop's Harbour	UNP/LNO	NF		2 C/12	48°41′	53°38′
Bishops Mills	UNP/LNO	ON	Grenville	31 B/13	44°52′	75°42′
Bishops Mitre	MTN/MNT	NF		14 F/13	57°53′	61°59′
Bishopville	UNP/LNO	NS	Kings	21 H/1	45°02′	64°15′
Bismarck	UNP/LNO	ON	Lincoln	30 M/4	43°03′	79°30′
Bison Lake	UNP/LNO	AB	35-94-14-W5	84 F/1	57°12′	116°08′
Bison Lake	LAKE/LAC	AB	94,95-14-W5	84 F/1	57°13′	116°10′
Bisseltown	UNP/LNO	ON	Grenville	31 B/12	44°41′	75°41′
Bisset Creek	RIV/CDE	SK	24-51-18-W2	73 H/7	53°25′	104°32′
Bissett	UNP/LNO	MB	24-13-E	52 M/4	51°02′	95°41′
Bissett Creek	UNP/LNO	ON	Renfrew	31 L/1	46°13′	78°04′
Bissett Lake	LAKE/LAC	MB	89-7-E	64 A/9	56°43′	96°25′
Bissett Lake	LAKE/LAC	NT	Keewatin	55 M	63°46′	95°20′
Bisson, Lac	LAKE/LAC	QC	Kativik	34 I/12	58°36′	73°55′
Bistcho Lake	LAKE/LAC	AB		84 M/10	59°45′	118°50′
Bistcho Lake 213	IR/RI	AB	33-122-3-W6	84 M/9	59°39′	118°28′
Bitter Lake	LAKE/LAC	SK	13-28,29-W3	72 K/4	50°07′	109°48′
Bittern Lake	VILG/VILG	AB	36-46-21-W4	83 H/3	53°01′	113°03′
Bittern Lake	LAKE/LAC	SK	57,58-26-W2	73 H/13	53°56′	105°45′
Bittern Lake	LAKE/LAC	AB	46,47-21,22-W4	83 H/3	53°03′	113°05′
Bittern Lake 218	IR/RI	SK		73 H/13	53°55′	105°48′
Bitumount	UNP/LNO	AB	1-97-11-W4	74 E/5	57°23′	111°38′
Bitumount Provincial Historic Site (Undeveloped)	PARK/PARC	AB	1-97-11-W4	74 E/5	57°23′	111°38′
Bizard, Île	ISL/ÎLE	QC	Communauté urbaine de Montréal	31 H/5	45°29′	73°54′
Bjarni, Lac	LAKE/LAC	QC	Kativik	23 P/16	55°51′	64°08′
Bjorkdale	VILG/VILG	SK	43-12-W2	63 D/12	52°43′	103°39′
Bjorkdale No. 426	MUN2/AZM2	SK		63 D/11	52°40′	103°30′
Bjork Lake	LAKE/LAC	SK	43-11-W2	63 D/11	52°43′	103°30′
Bjorne Peninsula	CAPE/CAP	NT	Franklin	49 C	77°37′	87°00′
Black Angus Creek	RIV/CDE	BC	Cassiar	104 P/16	59°51′	128°14′
Black Avon	UNP/LNO	NS	Antigonish	11 F/12	45°33′	61°47′
Black Bank	UNP/LNO	ON	Dufferin	41 A/1	44°14′	80°09′
Black Banks	UNP/LNO	PE	Prince	21 I/9	46°44′	64°00′
Black Bay	UNP/LNO	ON	Renfrew	31 F/14	45°52′	77°21′
Black Bay	BAY/BAIE	NF		12 P/16	51°46′	56°20′
Black Bay	BAY/BAIE	ON	Thunder Bay	52 A/9	48°40′	88°25′
Black Bay	BAY/BAIE	SK		73 O/12	55°38′	107°53′

NAME NOM	ENTITY ENTITÉ	LOC 1 LIEU 1	LOC 2 LIEU 2	MAP CARTE	POSITION	
					LAT	LONG
Black Bay	BAY/BAIE	SK		74 N/7	59°28′	108°55′
Black Bay Peninsula	CAPE/CAP	ON	Thunder Bay	52 A/9	48°38′	88°21′
Black Beach	UNP/LNO	NB	Saint John	21 G/1	45°09′	66°14′
Black Bear Bay	BAY/BAIE	NF		3 E/5	53°19′	55°50′
Blackbear Island	ISL/ÎLE	ON	Cochrane	42 O/11	51°44′	83°08′
Black Bear Island Lake	LAKE/LAC	SK		73 P/12	55°38′	105°40′
Blackbear Lake	LAKE/LAC	ON	Kenora	53 J/3	54°11′	91°28′
Black Bear River	RIV/CDE	NF		3 E/5	53°18′	55°55′
Blackbear River	RIV/CDE	ON	Kenora	53 I/12	54°33′	89°48′
Black Birch Lake	LAKE/LAC	SK		74 B/13	56°54′	107°45′
Black Bluff	MTN/MNT	NT	Franklin	25 H	61°56′	65°06′
Black Bridge	UNP/LNO	ON	Muskoka	31 D/14	44°59′	79°16′
Black Brook	UNP/LNO	NS	Cape Breton	11 K/1	46°13′	60°26′
Black Brook	UNP/LNO	NB	Victoria	21 O/5	47°22′	67°38′
Black Brook	RIV/CDE	NS	Victoria	11 K/16	46°46′	60°21′
Black Brook Cove	BAY/BAIE	NS	Victoria	11 K/16	46°46′	60°20′
Blackburn	UNP/LNO	QC	Le Domaine-du-Roy	32 A/8	48°24′	72°05′
Blackburn	UNP/LNO	ON	Carleton	31 G/5	45°26′	75°33′
Blackburn Hamlet	UNP/LNO	ON	Carleton	31 G/5	45°26′	75°34′
Blackburn Station	UNP/LNO	ON		31 G/5	45°26′	75°33′
Black Cape	UNP/LNO	QC	Bonaventure	22 A/4	48°08′	65°50′
Black Cliffs Bay	BAY/BAIE	NT	Franklin	120 E	82°32′	62°50′
Black Creek	UNP/LNO	ON	Prince Edward	30 N/14	43°58′	77°02′
Black Creek	UNP/LNO	ON	Welland	30 L/14	42°59′	79°02′
Black Creek	UNP/LNO	BC	Cariboo	93 A/6	52°18′	121°06′
Black Creek	UNP/LNO	BC	Comox	92 F/14	49°50′	125°08′
Black Creek	RIV/CDE	ON	Norfolk	40 I/16	42°47′	80°12′
Black Creek	RIV/CDE	ON	Perth	40 P/6	43°22′	81°12′
Black Creek	RIV/CDE	ON	Lambton	40 J/9	42°44′	82°21′
Black Creek	RIV/CDE	BC	Peace River	94 H/3	57°14′	121°18′
Black Creek	RIV/CDE	BC	Comox	92 F/14	49°51′	125°06′
Blackdale	UNP/LNO	MB	4-13-3-E	62 I/3	50°04′	97°08′
Black Diamond	TOWN/VIL2	AB	8-20-2-W5	82 J/9	50°42′	114°14′
Black Donald	UNP/LNO	ON	Renfrew	31 F/2	45°14′	76°55′
Black Donald Lake	LAKE/LAC	ON	Renfrew	31 F/2	45°13′	76°57′
Black Duck	UNP/LNO	NF		12 B/9	48°35′	58°23′
Black Duck Brook	UNP/LNO	NF		12 B/10	48°42′	58°54′
Black Duck Brook-Winterhouse	UNP/LNO	NF		12 B/10	48°42′	58°55′
Black Duck Cove	UNP/LNO	NF		2 C/4	48°13′	53°30′
Black Duck Cove	UNP/LNO	NF		2 E/10	49°36′	54°44′
Black Duck Cove	UNP/LNO	NF		1 M/3	47°03′	55°11′
Black Duck Cove	UNP/LNO	NF		12 P/2	51°12′	56°48′
Black Duck Pond	UNP/LNO	NF		1 N/11	47°34′	53°15′
Black Duck River	RIV/CDE	MB/ON		54 A/14	56°51′	89°02′
Black Duck Siding	UNP/LNO	NF		12 B/9	48°35′	58°23′
Blacketts Lake	UNP/LNO	NS	Cape Breton	11 K/1	46°04′	60°20′
Blacketts Lake	LAKE/LAC	NS	Cape Breton	11 K/1	46°04′	60°18′
Blackfalds	TOWN/VIL2	AB	26-39-27-W4	83 A/5	52°23′	113°47′
Blackfish Lake	LAKE/LAC	MB		64 O/4	59°10′	99°32′
Blackfoot	UNP/LNO	AB	1-50-2-W4	73 E/8	53°17′	110°10′
Blackfoot 146 - see-voir - Siksika 146	IR/RI	AB		82 I/15	50°47′	112°57′
Black Hawk	UNP/LNO	ON	Rainy River	52 C/13	48°48′	93°59′
Blackhead	UNP/LNO	NF		1 N/10	47°32′	52°39′
Blackhead	UNP/LNO	NF		1 N/14	47°51′	53°06′
Black Head	CAPE/CAP	NF		1 K/15	46°49′	52°56′
Black Head	CAPE/CAP	NF		2 C/11	48°37′	53°10′
Blackhead Bay	BAY/BAIE	NF		2 C/11	48°35′	53°16′
Black Head North	CAPE/CAP	NF		1 N/15	47°46′	52°43′
Blackheath	UNP/LNO	ON	Haldimand	30 M/4	43°04′	79°49′
Black Hills	UNP/LNO	YT		115 O/7	63°28′	138°50′
Black Horse	UNP/LNO	ON	Peel	30 M/13	43°59′	79°48′
Black Horse Corner	UNP/LNO	ON	Welland	30 M/3	43°05′	79°12′
Blackie	VILG/VILG	AB	13-19-27-W4	82 I/12	50°36′	113°37′
Blackies Landing	UNP/LNO	NB	Carleton	21 G/13	45°59′	67°39′
Black Island	UNP/LNO	NF		2 E/10	49°35′	54°43′
Black Island	UNP/LNO	NF		2 E/10	49°32′	54°59′
Black Island	ISL/ÎLE	NF		2 E/10	49°33′	54°59′
Black Island	ISL/ÎLE	NF		13 H/16	53°45′	56°22′
Black Island	ISL/ÎLE	NF		13 I/5	54°22′	57°47′
Black Island	ISL/ÎLE	MB		62 P/1	51°12′	96°30′
Black Lake	CITY/VIL1	QC	L'Amiante	21 L/3	46°03′	71°22′
Black Lake	UNP/LNO	SK		74 P/4	59°08′	105°36′
Black Lake	LAKE/LAC	NF		12 H/10	49°34′	56°33′
Black Lake	LAKE/LAC	ON	Lanark	31 C/16	44°46′	76°18′
Black Lake	LAKE/LAC	ON	Kenora	52 E/9	49°32′	94°05′

NAME NOM	ENTITY ENTITÉ	LOC 1 LIEU 1	LOC 2 LIEU 2	MAP CARTE	POSITION	
					LAT	LONG
Black Lake	LAKE/LAC	SK		74 P/3	59°12′	105°15′
Black Lake	LAKE/LAC	BC	New Westminster	92 K/2	50°09′	124°48′
Blackland	UNP/LNO	NB	Restigouche	21 O/16	47°58′	66°14′
Blackland	UNP/LNO	NB	Charlotte	21 G/3	45°14′	67°17′
Blacklead Island	ISL/ÎLE	NT	Franklin	26 B	64°59′	66°12′
Blackley Haven	BAY/BAIE	NT	Franklin	89 B	76°01′	116°32′
Black Lichen Lake	LAKE/LAC	NT	Mackenzie	86 C	64°26′	116°15′
Blackloam	UNP/LNO	BC	Kamloops Division Yale	92 I/9	50°39′	120°15′
Black, Mount	MTN/MNT	YT		105 E/1	61°13′	134°04′
Black Mountains	MTN/MNT	NB	Victoria	21 O/3	47°08′	67°05′
Black Pines	UNP/LNO	BC	Kamloops Division Yale	92 I/16	50°56′	120°15′
Black Point	HAM/HAM	SK		74 C/6	56°22′	109°27′
Black Point	UNP/LNO	NS	Victoria	11 N/2	47°01′	60°32′
Black Point	UNP/LNO	NS	Pictou	11 E/10	45°40′	62°33′
Black Point	UNP/LNO	NS	Halifax	11 D/12	44°39′	63°59′
Black Point	UNP/LNO	NB	Restigouche	21 O/16	47°56′	66°06′
Black Point	CAPE/CAP	NF		1 M/1	47°12′	54°03′
Black Point	CAPE/CAP	NF		11 P/10	47°37′	56°30′
Black Point	CAPE/CAP	PE	Queens	11 L/3	46°10′	63°24′
Black Point	CAPE/CAP	NS	Richmond	11 F/10	45°37′	60°36′
Black Point	CAPE/CAP	NS	Guysborough	11 F/6	45°21′	61°08′
Black Point	CAPE/CAP	NS	Queens	20 P/15	43°58′	64°43′
Black Point	CAPE/CAP	NS	Queens	20 P/15	43°51′	64°48′
Black Point	CAPE/CAP	NS	Digby	21 B/1	44°02′	66°10′
Black Point	CAPE/CAP	ON	Kenora	52 E/2	49°00′	94°34′
Black Point	CAPE/CAP	NT	Franklin	68 H	75°41′	97°21′
Black Point 11	IR/RI	BC	Range 5 Coast	103 I/13	54°59′	129°41′
Blackpool	UNP/LNO	QC	Les Jardins-de-Napierville	31 H/3	45°01′	73°27′
Blackpool	UNP/LNO	BC	Kamloops Division Yale	92 P/9	51°35′	120°07′
Black Rapids	UNP/LNO	ON	Leeds	31 C/9	44°31′	76°05′
Black River	UNP/LNO	NF		1 M/16	47°53′	54°10′
Black River	UNP/LNO	NS	Inverness	11 K/3	46°08′	61°19′
Black River	UNP/LNO	NS	Pictou	11 E/10	45°40′	62°59′
Black River	UNP/LNO	NS	Kings	21 H/1	45°01′	64°25′
Black River	UNP/LNO	NB	Northumberland	21 I/14	46°58′	65°20′
Black River	UNP/LNO	NB	Saint John	21 H/5	45°17′	65°46′
Black River	UNP/LNO	ON	Stormont	31 G/2	45°05′	74°52′
Black River	RIV/CDE	NB	Northumberland	21 P/3	47°03′	65°13′
Black River	RIV/CDE	NB	Saint John	21 H/5	45°16′	65°49′
Black River	RIV/CDE	ON	Hastings	31 C/11	44°32′	77°22′
Black River	RIV/CDE	ON	Ontario	31 D/14	44°45′	79°19′
Black River	RIV/CDE	ON	York	31 D/6	44°19′	79°21′
Black River	RIV/CDE	ON	Cochrane	42 A/10	48°42′	80°38′
Black River	RIV/CDE	ON	Thunder Bay	42 D/9	48°38′	86°16′
Black River	RIV/CDE	MB		62 I/16	50°49′	96°21′
Black River	RIV/CDE	YT		105 B/9	60°44′	130°08′
Black River 9	IR/RI	MB		62 I/16	50°50′	96°19′
Black River Bridge	UNP/LNO	NB	Northumberland	21 P/3	47°00′	65°17′
Black River Lake	LAKE/LAC	NS	Kings	21 A/16	44°56′	64°24′
Black River-Matheson	MUN2/AZM2	ON	Cochrane	42 A/8	48°27′	80°20′
Black River Pond	LAKE/LAC	NF		2 D/1	48°01′	54°08′
Black River Road	UNP/LNO	NS	Cumberland	11 E/12	45°41′	63°59′
Black River Road	UNP/LNO	NB	Saint John	21 H/5	45°16′	65°58′
Black Road	UNP/LNO	ON	Parry Sound	31 E/5	45°16′	79°53′
Black Rock	UNP/LNO	NS	Victoria	11 K/8	46°18′	60°23′
Black Rock	UNP/LNO	NS	Colchester	11 E/6	45°19′	63°29′
Black Rock	UNP/LNO	NS	Cumberland	21 H/8	45°23′	64°25′
Black Rock	UNP/LNO	NS	Kings	21 H/2	45°10′	64°46′
Black Rock	UNP/LNO	NB	Gloucester	21 P/11	47°45′	65°14′
Black Rock Point	CAPE/CAP	NF		25 A/1	60°02′	64°10′
Blackrock Point	CAPE/CAP	NS	Cape Breton	11 G/13	45°53′	59°58′
Blacks Brook	RIV/CDE	NS	Shelburne	20 P/14	43°46′	65°20′
Blacks Corners	UNP/LNO	ON	Lanark	31 F/1	45°06′	76°06′
Blacks Corners	UNP/LNO	ON	Wentworth	30 M/5	43°20′	79°57′
Blacks Corners	UNP/LNO	ON	Dufferin	41 A/1	44°00′	80°14′
Blacks Harbour	VILG/VILG	NB	Charlotte	21 G/2	45°03′	66°47′
Black Slate 11	IR/RI	BC	Queen Charlotte	103 F/1	53°14′	132°16′
Blacks Point	UNP/LNO	MB	7-26-6-E	62 P/2	51°14′	96°44′
Blacks Point	CAPE/CAP	ON	Huron	40 P/12	43°42′	81°44′
Blackstock	UNP/LNO	ON	Durham	31 D/2	44°06′	78°49′
Blackstock Point	CAPE/CAP	ON	Manitoulin	41 G/15	45°58′	82°35′
Blackstone	UNP/LNO	NS	Inverness	11 K/3	46°08′	61°18′
Blackstone	UNP/LNO	ON	Parry Sound	31 E/5	45°15′	79°50′
Blackstone Lake	UNP/LNO	ON	Parry Sound	31 E/4	45°15′	79°52′
Blackstone Lake	LAKE/LAC	ON	Parry Sound	31 E/4	45°14′	79°53′

NAME NOM	ENTITY ENTITÉ	LOC 1 LIEU 1	LOC 2 LIEU 2	MAP CARTE	POSITION LAT	LONG
Blackstone River	RIV/CDE	AB	44-15-W5	83 C/16	52°50'	116°07'
Blackstone River	RIV/CDE	YT		116 H/14	65°51'	137°15'
Blackstone River	RIV/CDE	NT	Mackenzie	95 G	61°05'	122°55'
Black Sturgeon	IR/RI	MB	90,91-20-W1	64 C/15	56°50'	100°34'
Black Sturgeon Lake	LAKE/LAC	ON	Thunder Bay	52 H/7	49°20'	88°53'
Black Sturgeon Lakes	LAKE/LAC	ON	Kenora	52 E/16	49°51'	94°25'
Black Sturgeon River	RIV/CDE	ON	Thunder Bay	52 A/16	48°50'	88°23'
Black Sturgeon River	RIV/CDE	ON	Kenora	52 E/15	49°55'	94°33'
Black Tickle	UNP/LNO	NF		3 E/5	53°27'	55°45'
Black Tickle-Domino	UNP/LNO	NF		3 E/5	53°27'	55°45'
Blackville	VILG/VILG	NB	Northumberland	21 I/12	46°44'	65°50'
Blackville	GEOG/GÉOG	NB	Northumberland	21 I/12	46°40'	65°44'
Blackwater	UNP/LNO	ON	Ontario	31 D/3	44°14'	79°03'
Blackwater	UNP/LNO	BC	Cariboo	93 G/6	53°17'	123°08'
Blackwater Junction	UNP/LNO	ON	Ontario	31 D/3	44°14'	79°03'
Blackwater Lake	LAKE/LAC	NT	Mackenzie	95 O	64°00'	123°05'
Blackwater Meadow 11	IR/RI	BC	Range 3 Coast	93 C/12	52°44'	125°32'
Blackwater River	RIV/CDE	ON	Thunder Bay	52 H/9	49°31'	88°09'
Blackwater River	RIV/CDE	NT	Mackenzie	95 N	63°57'	124°10'
Blackwelder Mountains	MTN/MNT	NT	Franklin	340 B	80°39'	84°25'
Blackwell	UNP/LNO	ON	Lambton	40 O/1	43°01'	82°19'
Blackwood	UNP/LNO	SK	1-19-11-W2	62 L/11	50°36'	103°25'
Bladworth	VILG/VILG	SK	6-28-1-W3	72 O/8	51°22'	106°08'
Blaeberry	UNP/LNO	BC	Kootenay	82 N/6	51°26'	117°04'
Blaeberry River	RIV/CDE	BC	Kootenay	82 N/6	51°25'	117°05'
Blagdon	UNP/LNO	NB	Kings	21 G/8	45°25'	66°19'
Blagousse	UNP/LNO	QC	Charlevoix	21 M/8	47°29'	70°23'
Blaine Lake	TOWN/VIL2	SK		73 B/15	52°50'	106°54'
Blaine Lake No. 434	MUN2/AZM2	SK		73 B/10	52°45'	106°50'
Blaine Lakes	LAKE/LAC	SK	44-7,8-W3	73 B/15	52°50'	106°59'
Blainville	CITY/VIL1	QC	Thérèse-De Blainville	31 H/12	45°40'	73°53'
Blair	UNP/LNO	ON	Waterloo	40 P/8	43°23'	80°23'
Blair Athol	UNP/LNO	NB	Restigouche	21 O/15	47°56'	66°33'
Blairhampton	UNP/LNO	ON	Haliburton	31 E/2	45°02'	78°39'
Blairmore	UNP/LNO	AB	35-7-4-W5	82 G/9	49°36'	114°26'
Blairs	UNP/LNO	NB	Kings	21 H/5	45°25'	65°57'
Blairs Settlement	UNP/LNO	ON	Leeds	31 C/9	44°38'	76°24'
Blairton	UNP/LNO	ON	Peterborough	31 C/5	44°27'	77°46'
Blairton Station	UNP/LNO	ON	Peterborough	31 C/5	44°26'	77°48'
Blake	UNP/LNO	ON	Huron	40 P/5	43°27'	81°39'
Blake	UNP/LNO	BC	Kootenay	82 F/10	49°32'	116°51'
Blake Bay	BAY/BAIE	NT	Franklin	46 J	66°32'	82°56'
Blakely Lake	LAKE/LAC	NT	Keewatin	55 M	63°18'	94°56'
Blakeney	UNP/LNO	ON	Lanark	31 F/8	45°16'	76°15'
Blake Point	CAPE/CAP	ON	Manitoulin	41 G/10	45°44'	82°59'
Blaketown	UNP/LNO	NF		1 N/5	47°29'	53°34'
Blakiston, Mount	MTN/MNT	AB	2-1-W5	82 G/1	49°05'	114°02'
Blalock	UNP/LNO	ON	Rainy River	52 B/14	48°45'	91°19'
Blanc, Cap	CAPE/CAP	QC	Pabok	22 A/9	48°30'	64°13'
Blanchard Road	UNP/LNO	NS	Pictou	11 E/8	45°28'	62°29'
Blanchard Settlement	UNP/LNO	NB	Gloucester	21 P/10	47°44'	64°54'
Blanchards Hill	UNP/LNO	ON	Leeds	31 C/16	44°47'	76°06'
Blanchard's Landing	UNP/LNO	ON	Nipissing	31 L/6	46°17'	79°02'
Blanche	UNP/LNO	NS	Shelburne	20 P/11	43°30'	65°24'
Blanche	UNP/LNO	QC	Papineau	31 G/11	45°45'	75°21'
Blanche	UNP/LNO	ON	Cochrane	42 K/4	50°05'	85°44'
Blanche, Baie	BAY/BAIE	QC	La Haute-Côte-Nord	22 C/15	48°49'	68°55'
Blanche Island	ISL/ÎLE	NS	Shelburne	20 P/6	43°28'	65°24'
Blanche, Lac la	LAKE/LAC	QC	Papineau	31 G/11	45°43'	75°19'
Blanche-Mills	UNP/LNO	QC	Papineau	31 G/11	45°37'	75°15'
Blanche, Petite rivière	RIV/CDE	QC	Communauté urbaine de l'Outaouais	31 G/12	45°30'	75°31'
Blanche River	RIV/CDE	ON	Timiskaming	31 M/12	47°34'	79°32'
Blanche, Rivière	RIV/CDE	QC	Matane	22 B/13	48°47'	67°42'
Blanche, Rivière	RIV/CDE	QC	Bécancour	31 I/8	46°17'	72°23'
Blanche, Rivière	RIV/CDE	QC	Communauté urbaine de l'Outaouais	31 G/5	45°30'	75°33'
Blanches, Montagnes	MTN/MNT	QC	Le Haut-Saint-François	21 E/6	45°15'	71°15'
Blanchet Island	ISL/ÎLE	NT	Mackenzie	85 H	62°00'	112°23'
Blanchet, Lac	LAKE/LAC	QC	La Côte-de-Gaspé	22 H/2	49°06'	64°46'
Blanchet Lake	LAKE/LAC	BC	Range 4 Coast	93 E/8	53°23'	126°19'
Blanchfield Lake	LAKE/LAC	NT	Franklin	37 D	69°40'	73°10'
Blanc, Mont	MTN/MNT	QC	Matane	22 B/15	48°47'	66°53'
Blanc, Réservoir	LAKE/LAC	QC	Le Haut-Saint-Maurice	31 P/14	47°45'	73°15'
Blanc-Sablon	VILG/VILG	QC	Côte-Nord-du-Golfe-Saint-Laurent	12 P/6	51°25'	57°07'
Blanc-Sablon	UNP/LNO	QC	Côte-Nord-du-Golfe-Saint-Laurent	12 P/6	51°25'	57°08'
Blandford	UNP/LNO	NS	Lunenburg	21 A/8	44°29'	64°07'

NAME NOM	ENTITY ENTITÉ	LOC 1 LIEU 1	LOC 2 LIEU 2	MAP CARTE	POSITION LAT	LONG
Blandford Bay	BAY/BAIE	NT	Franklin	25 M	63°33'	71°25'
Blandford-Blenheim	MUN2/AZM2	ON	Oxford	40 P/2	43°10'	80°35'
Blandford Station	UNP/LNO	ON	Oxford	40 P/2	43°13'	80°38'
Blaney Ridge	UNP/LNO	NB	York	21 G/14	45°48'	67°09'
Blanley Bay	BAY/BAIE	NT	Franklin	48 F	74°30'	87°25'
Blanshard	MUN2/AZM2	ON	Perth	40 P/6	43°17'	81°15'
Blanshard	MUN2/AZM2	MB		62 K/1	50°11'	100°21'
Blanshard, Mount	MTN/MNT	BC	New Westminster	92 G/7	49°21'	122°30'
Blantyre	UNP/LNO	ON	Grey	41 A/10	44°30'	80°38'
Blatchford Lake	LAKE/LAC	NT	Mackenzie	85 I/2	62°11'	112°35'
Blatz-Nolin - see-voir - Turtle Lake South Bay	HAM/HAM	SK		73 F/10	53°31'	108°42'
Blenheim	TOWN/VIL2	ON	Kent	40 J/8	42°20'	82°00'
Blenheim Junction	UNP/LNO	ON	Kent	40 J/8	42°20'	82°01'
Blessington	UNP/LNO	ON	Hastings	31 C/6	44°16'	77°16'
Blessington Creek	RIV/CDE	ON	Hastings	31 C/3	44°10'	77°20'
Bleue, Rivière	RIV/CDE	QC	Témiscouata	21 N/6	47°26'	69°03'
Bleues, Montagnes	MTN/MNT	QC	Le Granit	21 E/7	45°25'	70°39'
Bleuets, Rivière aux	RIV/CDE	QC	Antoine-Labelle	31 O/11	47°36'	75°06'
Bleu, Lac	LAKE/LAC	QC	Témiscamingue	31 L/9	46°37'	78°24'
Blevins Lake	LAKE/LAC	MB		64 O/15	59°53'	98°50'
Blewett	UNP/LNO	SK	12-5-10-W2	62 E/6	49°23'	103°14'
Blewett	UNP/LNO	BC	Kootenay	82 F/6	49°29'	117°25'
Blezard	UNP/LNO	ON	Peterborough	31 D/8	44°18'	78°06'
Blezard Valley	UNP/LNO	ON	Sudbury	41 I/11	46°37'	81°03'
Blezard Valley	VALL/VALL	ON	Sudbury	41 I/11	46°38'	81°10'
Bligh Island	ISL/ÎLE	BC	Nootka	92 E/10	49°39'	126°31'
Blind Bay	UNP/LNO	BC	Kamloops Division Yale	82 L/14	50°53'	119°23'
Blind Bay	BAY/BAIE	ON	Kenora	52 F/11	49°41'	93°24'
Blind Bay	BAY/BAIE	BC	New Westminster	92 F/9	49°44'	124°11'
Blind Channel	UNP/LNO	BC	Range 1 Coast	92 K/5	50°25'	125°30'
Blind Creek	RIV/CDE	BC	Peace River	93 P/5	55°22'	121°44'
Blind Creek 6	IR/RI	BC	Similkameen Division Yale	82 E/4	49°11'	119°44'
Blind Creek 6A	IR/RI	BC	Similkameen Division Yale	82 E/4	49°11'	119°45'
Blind Fiord	BAY/BAIE	NT	Franklin	49 F	78°14'	86°16'
Blindfold Lake	LAKE/LAC	ON	Kenora	52 E/9	49°40'	94°15'
Blindman River	RIV/CDE	AB	13-39-27-W4	83 A/5	52°22'	113°46'
Blind River	TOWN/VIL2	ON	Algoma	41 J/2	46°10'	82°58'
Blink Bonnie	UNP/LNO	ON	Oxford	40 P/7	43°18'	80°39'
Blissfield	UNP/LNO	NB	Northumberland	21 J/9	46°35'	66°03'
Blissfield	GEOG/GÉOG	NB	Northumberland	21 J/9	46°37'	66°05'
Bliss Landing	UNP/LNO	BC	New Westminster	92 K/2	50°02'	124°49'
Blissville	UNP/LNO	NB	Sunbury	21 G/10	45°36'	66°34'
Blissville	GEOG/GÉOG	NB	Sunbury	21 G/10	45°35'	66°35'
Blister Ice Cap	GLAC/GLAC	NT	Franklin	340 D	81°52'	72°05'
Blizzard Pond	LAKE/LAC	NF		12 A/7	48°20'	56°53'
Block 14	UNP/LNO	NB	Kent	21 I/14	46°45'	65°20'
Blockhaus-de-St. Andrews, Lieu historique national du - also-aussi - St. Andrews Blockhouse National Historic Site	PARK/PARC	NB	Charlotte	21 G/3	45°05'	67°04'
Blockhouse	UNP/LNO	NS	Lunenburg	21 A/8	44°27'	64°25'
Bloedel	UNP/LNO	BC	Sayward	92 K/3	50°07'	125°23'
Blomidon	UNP/LNO	NS	Kings	21 H/1	45°13'	64°22'
Blomidon, Cape	CAPE/CAP	NS	Kings	21 H/8	45°18'	64°20'
Blood 148	IR/RI	AB	6-24-W4	82 H/6	49°31'	113°11'
Blood 148A	IR/RI	AB	20-1-28-W4	82 H/4	49°04'	113°44'
Blood Indian Creek	RIV/CDE	AB	22-8-W4	72 L/14	50°55'	111°03'
Bloodsucker Lake	LAKE/LAC	SK	56-4-W2	63 E/15	53°51'	102°34'
Bloodvein	UNP/LNO	MB	28,32,33-32-6-E	62 P/15	51°47'	96°42'
Bloodvein 12	IR/RI	MB		62 P/15	51°47'	96°41'
Bloodvein River	RIV/CDE	MB/ON		62 P/15	51°47'	96°43'
Bloody Creek	RIV/CDE	NS	Shelburne	20 P/12	43°43'	65°31'
Bloody Reach	RIVF/EFLV	NF		2 C/13	48°47'	53°50'
Bloody River	RIV/CDE	NT	Mackenzie	96 I	66°56'	120°34'
Bloom	UNP/LNO	MB	3-12-8-W	62 G/16	49°59'	98°29'
Bloomfield	VILG/VILG	ON	Prince Edward	30 N/14	43°59'	77°14'
Bloomfield	UNP/LNO	NF		2 C/5	48°23'	53°54'
Bloomfield	UNP/LNO	PE	Prince	21 I/16	46°46'	64°14'
Bloomfield	UNP/LNO	NS	Digby	21 A/12	44°32'	65°50'
Bloomfield	UNP/LNO	NB	Kings	21 H/12	45°35'	65°45'
Bloomfield	UNP/LNO	NB	Carleton	21 J/5	46°19'	67°46'
Bloomfield Corner	UNP/LNO	PE	Prince	21 I/16	46°46'	64°11'
Bloomfield Ridge	UNP/LNO	NB	Kings	21 H/12	45°34'	65°41'
Bloomfield Ridge	UNP/LNO	NB	York	21 J/8	46°29'	66°29'
Blooming	UNP/LNO	SK	33-2-18-W2	72 H/1	49°09'	104°21'
Bloomingdale	UNP/LNO	ON	Waterloo	40 P/9	43°31'	80°27'
Blooming Point	UNP/LNO	PE	Queens	11 L/7	46°23'	62°59'
Bloomington	UNP/LNO	NS	Annapolis	21 A/14	44°53'	65°00'

NAME NOM	ENTITY ENTITÉ	LOC 1 LIEU 1	LOC 2 LIEU 2	MAP CARTE	POSITION LAT	LONG
Bloomington	UNP/LNO	ON	Stormont	31 G/7	45°16′	74°53′
Bloomington	UNP/LNO	ON	York	31 D/3	44°00′	79°16′
Bloomsburg	UNP/LNO	ON	Norfolk	40 I/16	42°53′	80°18′
Bloomsbury	UNP/LNO	AB	24-60-4-W5	83 J/1	54°13′	114°27′
Bloordale Gardens	UNP/LNO	ON	York	30 M/12	43°38′	79°34′
Blossom Park	UNP/LNO	ON	Carleton	31 G/5	45°21′	75°37′
Blouin	UNP/LNO	QC	Desjardins	21 L/11	46°42′	71°00′
Blouin, Lac	LAKE/LAC	QC	Vallée-de-l'Or	32 C/4	48°11′	77°46′
Blount	UNP/LNO	ON	Dufferin	40 P/16	43°58′	80°02′
Blount	UNP/LNO	ON	Cochrane	42 H/6	49°16′	81°02′
Blouse, La	UNP/LNO	QC	Vaudreuil-Soulanges	31 G/8	45°25′	74°23′
Blowdown	UNP/LNO	NB	Carleton	21 J/4	46°02′	67°46′
Blowhole	UNP/LNO	BC	Nootka	92 E/15	49°50′	126°40′
Blow Me Down	UNP/LNO	NF		1 N/11	47°36′	53°11′
Blow River	RIV/CDE	YT		117 A/15	68°56′	137°08′
Bloxsome Bay	BAY/BAIE	NT	Franklin	99 A	76°07′	122°36′
Blubber Bay	UNP/LNO	BC	Texada Island	92 F/15	49°47′	124°37′
Blucher	UNP/LNO	SK	15-35-2-W3	73 B/1	52°01′	106°12′
Blucher Hall	UNP/LNO	BC	Kamloops Division Yale	92 P/1	51°06′	120°01′
Blucher No. 343	MUN2/AZM2	SK		73 B/1	52°00′	106°10′
Blue	MUN2/AZM2	ON	Rainy River	52 D/16	48°46′	94°25′
Blue Acres	UNP/LNO	NS	Pictou	11 E/10	45°33′	62°39′
Blue Beach	UNP/LNO	NF		12 B/15	48°47′	58°46′
Blue Bell	UNP/LNO	NB	Victoria	21 J/13	46°57′	67°32′
Blue Bell	UNP/LNO	SK	60-21-W3	73 K/2	54°13′	109°00′
Blue Bell Corner	UNP/LNO	NB	Victoria	21 J/13	46°56′	67°37′
Blueberry Creek	UNP/LNO	BC	Kootenay	82 F/4	49°15′	117°40′
Blueberry Mountain	UNP/LNO	AB	10-80-8-W6	83 M/14	55°56′	119°09′
Blueberry River	RIV/CDE	BC	Peace River	94 A/10	56°44′	120°49′
Blueberry River 205	IR/RI	BC	Peace River	94 A/11	56°43′	121°06′
Blue, Cape	CAPE/CAP	NS	Antigonish	11 F/12	45°40′	61°35′
Blue Church	UNP/LNO	ON	Grenville	31 B/12	44°41′	75°33′
Blue Corners	UNP/LNO	ON	Prescott	31 G/10	45°35′	74°48′
Blue Cove	UNP/LNO	NF		12 P/2	51°06′	56°52′
Blue Fiord	BAY/BAIE	NT	Franklin	49 C	77°16′	87°05′
Bluefish River	RIV/CDE	YT		116 N/8	67°29′	140°15′
Bluefish River	RIV/CDE	NT	Mackenzie	106 I	66°24′	128°12′
Bluegoose Prairie	VEGL/VÉGB	NT	Franklin	36 H/11	65°32′	73°30′
Bluegoose River	RIV/CDE	NT	Franklin	36 H	65°27′	73°32′
Blue Gull Pond	LAKE/LAC	NF		2 C/5	48°21′	53°32′
Blue Heron	UNP/LNO	SK	52-4-W3	73 G/7	53°30′	106°31′
Blue Hill	UNP/LNO	NB	Victoria	21 J/12	46°38′	67°47′
Blue Hills	UNP/LNO	QC	Les Pays-d'en-Haut	31 G/16	45°53′	74°17′
Blue Hills	UNP/LNO	BC	Peace River	94 A/11	56°39′	121°13′
Blue Hills	MTN/MNT	NT	Franklin	88 H	75°34′	114°30′
Blue Hills of Couteau	MTN/MNT	NF		11 P/13	47°57′	57°52′
Blue Island	ISL/ÎLE	NS	Shelburne	20 P/11	43°41′	65°11′
Blue Island	ISL/ÎLE	SK		64 L/6	58°17′	103°25′
Blue Island	ISL/ÎLE	NT	Mackenzie	65 E	61°44′	102°13′
Blue Jay	UNP/LNO	SK	50,51-11-W2	63 E/5	53°22′	103°33′
Blue Jay Creek	RIV/CDE	ON	Manitoulin	41 G/9	45°35′	82°06′
Blue Lake	LAKE/LAC	ON	Kenora	52 F/13	49°54′	93°30′
Blue Man Cape	CAPE/CAP	NT	Franklin	49 G	79°45′	86°20′
Blue Mountain	UNP/LNO	NS	Pictou	11 E/8	45°29′	62°26′
Blue Mountain	UNP/LNO	NS	Kings	21 A/15	44°53′	64°32′
Blue Mountain	UNP/LNO	ON	Peterborough	31 C/12	44°41′	77°57′
Blue Mountain	MTN/MNT	NB	Restigouche	21 O/16	47°48′	66°18′
Blue Mountain Bend	UNP/LNO	NB	Victoria	21 O/3	47°06′	67°16′
Blue Mountains	MTN/MNT	ON	Grey	41 A/8	44°27′	80°21′
Blue Mountains	MTN/MNT	NT	Franklin	340 B	80°44′	85°35′
Blue Mountain Settlement	UNP/LNO	NB	Gloucester	21 P/12	47°33′	65°41′
Bluenose Lake	LAKE/LAC	NT	Mackenzie	87 B/5	68°25′	119°45′
Blue Point	CAPE/CAP	ON	Lambton	40 O/1	43°06′	82°09′
Blue Ridge	UNP/LNO	AB	26-59-10-W5	83 J/3	54°08′	115°22′
Blueridge	UNP/LNO	BC	New Westminster	92 G/7	49°20′	123°00′
Blue River	UNP/LNO	BC	Kamloops Division Yale	83 D/3	52°06′	119°18′
Blue River	RIV/CDE	BC	Kamloops Division Yale	83 D/3	52°06′	119°17′
Blue River	RIV/CDE	BC	Cassiar	104 P/10	59°42′	128°58′
Blue River 1	IR/RI	BC	Cassiar	104 P/10	59°42′	128°58′
Blue River East	UNP/LNO	BC	Kamloops Division Yale	83 D/3	52°07′	119°18′
Blue River West	UNP/LNO	BC	Kamloops Division Yale	83 D/3	52°05′	119°18′
Blue Rocks	UNP/LNO	NS	Lunenburg	21 A/8	44°21′	64°15′
Blue Sac Road	UNP/LNO	NS	Cumberland	21 H/8	45°24′	64°06′
Blue Sea	VILG/VILG	QC	La Vallée-de-la-Gatineau	31 K/1	46°12′	76°05′
Blue Sea Corner	UNP/LNO	NS	Cumberland	11 E/14	45°47′	63°18′

NAME NOM	ENTITY ENTITÉ	LOC 1 LIEU 1	LOC 2 LIEU 2	MAP CARTE	POSITION LAT	LONG
Blue Sea, Lac	LAKE/LAC	QC	La Vallée-de-la-Gatineau	31 K/1	46°13′	76°03′
Bluesky	UNP/LNO	AB	4-82-2-W6	84 D/1	56°04′	118°14′
Blues Mills	UNP/LNO	NS	Inverness	11 F/14	45°56′	61°11′
Blue Springs	UNP/LNO	ON	Halton	40 P/9	43°37′	80°05′
Blue Springs	UNP/LNO	BC	Osoyoos Division Yale	82 L/7	50°15′	118°51′
Bluevale	UNP/LNO	ON	Huron	40 P/14	43°51′	81°15′
Bluevale Siding	UNP/LNO	ON	Huron	40 P/14	43°50′	81°15′
Bluewater Beach	UNP/LNO	ON	Simcoe	31 D/12	44°37′	80°00′
Blue Water Beach	UNP/LNO	ON	Huron	40 P/12	43°43′	81°43′
Bluff	UNP/LNO	BC	Cassiar	93 M/9	55°30′	126°01′
Bluff, Cape	CAPE/CAP	NF		3 D/13	52°50′	55°49′
Bluff Creek	UNP/LNO	MB	20-21-10-W	62 J/15	50°49′	98°50′
Bluff Head	CAPE/CAP	NF		2 C/4	48°11′	53°45′
Bluff Head	CAPE/CAP	NF		2 E/14	49°56′	55°30′
Bluff Head	CAPE/CAP	NF		12 B/15	48°47′	58°38′
Bluff Head Cove	UNP/LNO	NF		2 E/10	49°38′	54°46′
Bluff Head Cove	BAY/BAIE	NF		13 I/5	54°24′	57°35′
Bluffpoint Lake	LAKE/LAC	ON	Kenora	52 F/3	49°10′	93°22′
Bluffton	UNP/LNO	AB	31-43-2-W5	83 B/9	52°45′	114°17′
Bluffy Lake	LAKE/LAC	ON	Kenora	52 K/15	50°48′	92°55′
Blumenfeld	UNP/LNO	MB	20-1-4-W	62 H/4	49°03′	97°58′
Blumengart	UNP/LNO	MB	15,16-2-3-W	62 H/4	49°08′	97°48′
Blumenheim	UNP/LNO	SK	31-39-3-W3	73 B/8	52°24′	106°25′
Blumenhof	UNP/LNO	SK	27-12-13-W3	72 J/4	50°01′	107°42′
Blumenort	UNP/LNO	MB	27,34-7-6-E	62 H/10	49°36′	96°41′
Blumenort	UNP/LNO	MB	3-1-2-W	62 H/4	49°00′	97°39′
Blumenort	UNP/LNO	SK	17-12-13-W3	72 G/13	50°00′	107°45′
Blumenthal	HAM/HAM	SK	33-40-3-W3	73 B/8	52°29′	106°22′
Blunden Point	CAPE/CAP	BC	Nanoose	92 F/8	49°15′	124°05′
Blundons Siding	UNP/LNO	NF		2 C/5	48°21′	53°54′
Blunt Peninsula	CAPE/CAP	NT	Franklin	25 I	62°42′	65°08′
Blustry Mountain	MTN/MNT	BC	Kamloops Division Yale	92 I/12	50°37′	121°42′
Blyth	VILG/VILG	ON	Huron	40 P/11	43°44′	81°26′
Blytheswood	UNP/LNO	ON	Essex	40 J/2	42°07′	82°36′
Boakview	UNP/LNO	ON	Parry Sound	41 H/9	45°34′	80°02′
Board Dam	UNP/LNO	QC	Pontiac	31 K/5	46°26′	77°43′
Boars Head	CAPE/CAP	NS	Digby	21 B/8	44°24′	66°13′
Boas River	RIV/CDE	NT	Keewatin	46 C	63°43′	85°45′
Boat Basin	UNP/LNO	BC	Clayoquot	92 E/8	49°29′	126°25′
Boat Harbour	UNP/LNO	NF		1 M/7	47°26′	54°50′
Boat Harbour	UNP/LNO	BC	Cedar	92 G/4	49°05′	123°48′
Boat Harbour	BAY/BAIE	NF		1 M/7	47°24′	54°50′
Boat Harbour West	UNP/LNO	NF		1 M/7	47°26′	54°50′
Boat Harbour West 37	IR/RI	NS	Pictou	11 E/10	45°39′	62°40′
Boat Lake	LAKE/LAC	ON	Bruce	41 A/11	44°44′	81°14′
Boat Point	CAPE/CAP	NT	Franklin	59 A	76°00′	89°56′
Boatswain Bay	BAY/BAIE	NT	Keewatin	32 M	51°50′	78°55′
Bobbie Burns Creek	RIV/CDE	BC	Kootenay	82 K/15	50°55′	116°32′
Bobby Cove	UNP/LNO	NF		2 E/13	49°50′	55°45′
Bobbys Pond	LAKE/LAC	NF		12 A/10	48°39′	56°50′
Bobcaygeon	VILG/VILG	ON	Victoria	31 D/10	44°33′	78°33′
Bob Lake	LAKE/LAC	ON	Haliburton	31 D/15	44°55′	78°47′
Bob Quinn Lake	UNP/LNO	BC	Cassiar	104 B/16	56°58′	130°15′
Bobs Lake	UNP/LNO	ON	Frontenac	31 C/10	44°39′	76°35′
Bobs Lake	LAKE/LAC	ON	Frontenac	31 C/10	44°41′	76°35′
Bocabec	UNP/LNO	NB	Charlotte	21 G/2	45°10′	66°59′
Bocabec Cove	UNP/LNO	NB	Charlotte	21 G/3	45°10′	67°01′
Bocage, Le	UNP/LNO	QC	Témiscouata	21 N/6	47°29′	69°17′
Bodmin	UNP/LNO	SK	16-55-7-W3	73 G/15	53°45′	107°00′
Bodo	UNP/LNO	AB	4-37-1-W4	73 D/1	52°09′	110°05′
Boeste, Lac	LAKE/LAC	QC	Caniapiscau	22 O/15	51°58′	66°58′
Boffin Lake	LAKE/LAC	ON	Rainy River	52 C/14	48°45′	93°29′
Bog-à-Lanières, Réserve écologique du	PARK/PARC	QC	Le Haut-Saint-Maurice	31 P/9	47°36′	72°15′
Bogart	UNP/LNO	ON	Hastings	31 C/6	44°30′	77°15′
Bogarttown	UNP/LNO	ON	York	31 D/3	44°03′	79°26′
Boger Point	CAPE/CAP	NT	Franklin	39 C	77°19′	78°50′
Boggy Creek	UNP/LNO	MB	32,33-29-28-W	62 N/11	51°32′	101°21′
Boggy Hall	UNP/LNO	AB	34-46-9-W5	83 G/3	53°01′	115°14′
Boggy River	RIV/CDE	MB	32,7-14-E	52 E/12	49°37′	95°38′
Bogies Beach	UNP/LNO	ON	Huron	40 P/13	43°49′	81°43′
Bog Lake	LAKE/LAC	SK	55-2-W2	63 E/16	53°46′	102°12′
Bognor	UNP/LNO	ON	Grey	41 A/10	44°31′	80°45′
Bog River	RIV/CDE	MB	21-13-11-E	62 I/1	50°06′	96°02′
Bogton	UNP/LNO	QC	Les Jardins-de-Napierville	31 H/4	45°04′	73°31′
Boharm	UNP/LNO	SK	6-17-27-W2	72 I/5	50°24′	105°43′

NAME NOM	ENTITY ENTITÉ	LOC 1 LIEU 1	LOC 2 LIEU 2	MAP CARTE	POSITION LAT	LONG
Bohier, Lac	LAKE/LAC	QC	Minganie	12 N/3	51°10'	61°04'
Bohn Lake	LAKE/LAC	AB	73-11-W4	73 M/15	55°54'	110°41'
Boiestown	UNP/LNO	NB	Northumberland	21 J/8	46°27'	66°25'
Boileau	VILG/VILG	QC	Papineau	31 G/15	45°55'	74°46'
Boileau	UNP/LNO	QC	Papineau	31 G/15	45°54'	74°46'
Boiler, Le	UNP/LNO	QC	Témiscamingue	31 L/15	46°55'	78°56'
Boilleau	UNP/LNO	QC	Le Fjord-du-Saguenay	22 D/2	48°05'	70°50'
Bois-Blanc	UNP/LNO	NB	Gloucester	21 P/11	47°37'	65°05'
Bois-Blanc	UNP/LNO	QC	Maskinongé	31 I/3	46°15'	73°08'
Bois Blanc Island Lighthouse National Historic Site - also-aussi - Phare-de-l'Île-Bois Blanc, Lieu historique national du	PARK/PARC	ON	Essex	40 J/3	42°05'	83°07'
Boisbouscache, Rivière	RIV/CDE	QC	Les Basques	22 C/3	48°01'	69°07'
Boisbriand	CITY/VIL1	QC	Thérèse-De Blainville	31 H/12	45°37'	73°50'
Boisbriand, Lac	LAKE/LAC	QC	Jamésie	23 E/3	53°00'	71°19'
Bois-Brûlé	UNP/LNO	QC	La Côte-de-Gaspé	22 A/9	48°43'	64°18'
Bois Brûlé, Cap du	CAPE/CAP	QC	La Côte-de-Gaspé	22 A/9	48°42'	64°16'
Boischatel	VILG/VILG	QC	La Côte-de-Beaupré	21 L/14	46°54'	71°09'
Boisdale	UNP/LNO	NS	Cape Breton	11 K/2	46°06'	60°30'
Bois-des-Bel	UNP/LNO	QC	Rivière-du-Loup	21 N/14	47°57'	69°26'
Bois-des-Filion	CITY/VIL1	QC	Thérèse-De Blainville	31 H/12	45°40'	73°45'
Bois-du-Curé	UNP/LNO	QC	Lajemmerais	31 H/14	45°51'	73°14'
Boisé-des-Muir, Réserve écologique du	PARK/PARC	QC	Le Haut-Saint-Laurent	31 G/1	45°05'	74°07'
Bois-Franc	VILG/VILG	QC	La Vallée-de-la-Gatineau	31 J/12	46°30'	75°59'
Bois Franc, Lac	LAKE/LAC	QC	Témiscamingue	31 L/15	46°45'	78°37'
Bois-Franc, Le	UNP/LNO	QC	Vaudreuil-Soulanges	31 G/8	45°27'	74°21'
Bois-Gagnon	UNP/LNO	NB	Gloucester	21 P/11	47°31'	65°10'
Boishébert	UNP/LNO	NB	Gloucester	21 P/10	47°34'	65°00'
Bois, Île au	ISL/ÎLE	QC	Côte-Nord-du-Golfe-Saint-Laurent	12 P/6	51°23'	57°09'
Bois Island	ISL/ÎLE	NF		1 M/12	47°44'	56°00'
Boisjoli	UNP/LNO	NB	Kent	21 I/7	46°28'	64°45'
Bois, Lac des - also-aussi - **Woods, Lake of the**	LAKE/LAC	ON/MB		52 E/7	49°16'	94°40'
Bois, Lac des	LAKE/LAC	NT	Mackenzie	96 K	66°50'	125°09'
Bois, Lac du	LAKE/LAC	NT	Mackenzie	75 P	63°36'	105°45'
Bois Long, Lac du	LAKE/LAC	QC	Manicouagan	22 K/15	50°55'	68°57'
Boissevain	TOWN/VIL2	MB	24-3-20-W	62 F/1	49°14'	100°03'
Boissonneault, Lac	LAKE/LAC	QC	Le Val-Saint-François	21 E/12	45°36'	71°54'
Boisvert, Pointe à	CAPE/CAP	QC	La Haute-Côte-Nord	22 C/11	48°34'	69°09'
Boisvert, Rivière	RIV/CDE	QC	Le Domaine-du-Roy	32 G/9	49°32'	74°08'
Boisville	UNP/LNO	QC	Les Îles-de-la-Madeleine	11 N/5	47°23'	61°56'
Boitano Lake	LAKE/LAC	BC	Lillooet	92 O/16	51°57'	122°07'
Boiteuse, Lac de la	LAKE/LAC	QC	Le Fjord-du-Saguenay	22 D/14	48°54'	71°16'
Boivin, Lac	LAKE/LAC	QC	Le Fjord-du-Saguenay	22 M/15	51°53'	70°30'
Boland Brook	RIV/CDE	NB	Restigouche	21 O/15	47°47'	66°53'
Boland Lake	LAKE/LAC	NT	Keewatin	65 G	61°41'	99°38'
Boland River	RIV/CDE	ON	Algoma	41 J/10	46°36'	82°53'
Boland's Bay	UNP/LNO	ON	Sudbury	41 I/10	46°39'	80°46'
Bold Point	UNP/LNO	BC	Sayward	92 K/3	50°10'	125°10'
Bold Point	CAPE/CAP	ON	Manitoulin	41 H/13	45°54'	81°40'
Bolduc, Mount	MTN/MNT	BC	Renfrew	92 C/9	48°43'	124°18'
Bolean Creek	RIV/CDE	BC	Kamloops Division Yale	82 L/5	50°30'	119°34'
Bolean Lake	LAKE/LAC	BC	Kamloops Division Yale	82 L/11	50°32'	119°30'
Bolger	UNP/LNO	ON	Parry Sound	41 H/9	45°41'	80°08'
Bolger Bridge	UNP/LNO	ON	Parry Sound	41 H/9	45°41'	80°08'
Bolingbroke	UNP/LNO	ON	Lanark	31 C/15	44°46'	76°31'
Bolingbroke Siding	UNP/LNO	ON	Lanark	31 C/15	44°46'	76°32'
Bolkow	UNP/LNO	ON	Sudbury	42 B/4	48°07'	83°55'
Bolney	UNP/LNO	SK	34-52-23-W3	73 F/11	53°32'	109°18'
Bolsover	UNP/LNO	ON	Victoria	31 D/11	44°32'	79°03'
Bolton	UNP/LNO	ON	Peel	30 M/13	43°53'	79°44'
Bolton Centre	UNP/LNO	QC	Memphrémagog	31 H/1	45°12'	72°21'
Bolton Creek	RIV/CDE	ON	Lanark	31 C/16	44°58'	76°23'
Bolton-Est	VILG/VILG	QC	Memphrémagog	31 H/1	45°12'	72°21'
Bolton Forest	UNP/LNO	QC	Memphrémagog	31 H/8	45°18'	72°17'
Bolton Glen	UNP/LNO	QC	Brome-Missisquoi	31 H/1	45°13'	72°26'
Bolton Lake	LAKE/LAC	NB	York	21 G/12	45°42'	67°35'
Bolton Lake	LAKE/LAC	MB		53 L/5	54°16'	95°47'
Bolton, Mount	MTN/MNT	NT	Franklin	39 E	78°20'	75°15'
Bolton-Ouest	VILG/VILG	QC	Brome-Missisquoi	31 H/1	45°14'	72°27'
Bolton River	RIV/CDE	MB		53 L/6	54°28'	95°28'
Bolton Station	UNP/LNO	ON		30 M/13	43°52'	79°45'
Bompas Lake	LAKE/LAC	SK		74 P/10	59°59'	104°57'
Bon Accord	TOWN/VIL2	AB	18-56-23-W4	83 H/14	53°50'	113°25'
Bon Accord	UNP/LNO	NB	Victoria	21 J/12	46°39'	67°35'
Bon Air	UNP/LNO	ON	Parry Sound	41 I/2	46°01'	80°34'
Bon Ami, Cap	CAPE/CAP	QC	La Côte-de-Gaspé	22 A/16	48°48'	64°12'
Bonanza	UNP/LNO	AB	9-80-12-W6	83 M/13	55°55'	119°49'

NAME NOM	ENTITY ENTITÉ	LOC 1 LIEU 1	LOC 2 LIEU 2	MAP CARTE	POSITION LAT	LONG
Bonanza Lake	LAKE/LAC	BC	Rupert	92 L/7	50°22′	126°46′
Bonaparte 3	IR/RI	BC	Kamloops Division Yale	92 I/14	50°51′	121°22′
Bonaparte Lake	LAKE/LAC	BC	Kamloops Division Yale	92 P/7	51°15′	120°34′
Bonaparte River	RIV/CDE	BC	Lillooet	92 I/11	50°44′	121°16′
Bonar	UNP/LNO	AB	8-31-13-W4	72 M/12	51°38′	111°48′
Bonarlaw	UNP/LNO	ON	Hastings	31 C/5	44°26′	77°37′
Bonaventure	VILG/VILG	QC	Bonaventure	22 A/3	48°03′	65°29′
Bonaventure	MUN1/AZM1	QC	Bonaventure	22 A/3	48°03′	65°29′
Bonaventure	UNP/LNO	QC	Bonaventure	22 A/3	48°04′	65°28′
Bonaventure, Cuvette	SEAU/SMER	—		801-A	48°28′	62°50′
Bonaventure-Est	UNP/LNO	QC	Bonaventure	22 A/3	48°02′	65°28′
Bonaventure Head	CAPE/CAP	NF		2 C/6	48°16′	53°23′
Bonaventure, Île	ISL/ÎLE	QC	Pabok	22 A/9	48°30′	64°10′
Bonaventure Ouest, Rivière	RIV/CDE	QC	Bonaventure	22 A/5	48°25′	65°30′
Bonaventure, Pointe	CAPE/CAP	QC	Bonaventure	22 A/3	48°00′	65°27′
Bonaventure, Rivière	RIV/CDE	QC	Bonaventure	22 A/3	48°03′	65°28′
Bonavista	TOWN/VIL2	NF		2 C/11	48°39′	53°07′
Bona Vista	UNP/LNO	ON	Muskoka	31 E/6	45°16′	79°04′
Bonavista Bay	BAY/BAIE	NF		2 C/11	48°45′	53°30′
Bonavista, Cape	CAPE/CAP	NF		2 C/11	48°42′	53°05′
Bond	UNP/LNO	BC	Peace River	93 P/14	55°50′	121°26′
Bon-Désir	UNP/LNO	QC	La Haute-Côte-Nord	22 C/6	48°17′	69°29′
Bon-Désir, Cap de	CAPE/CAP	QC	La Haute-Côte-Nord	22 C/6	48°16′	69°28′
Bond Head	UNP/LNO	ON	Simcoe	31 D/4	44°05′	79°41′
Bondiss	VILG/VILG	AB	6-65-18-W4	83 I/10	54°36′	112°42′
Bondi Village	UNP/LNO	ON	Muskoka	31 E/6	45°18′	79°01′
Bond's Corners	UNP/LNO	ON	Oxford	40 P/2	43°08′	80°42′
Bond Sound	CHAN/CHEN	BC	Range 1 Coast	92 L/16	50°50′	126°10′
Bon Echo	UNP/LNO	ON	Frontenac	31 C/14	44°54′	77°12′
Bone Creek	RIV/CDE	SK	17-10-19-W3	72 F/15	49°49′	108°33′
Bone Creek	RIV/CDE	BC	Kamloops Division Yale	83 D/6	52°15′	119°11′
Bone Creek No. 108	MUN2/AZM2	SK		72 F/16	49°50′	108°15′
Bonell Creek	RIV/CDE	BC	Nanoose	92 F/8	49°16′	124°11′
*Bones Bay	UNP/LNO	BC	Range 1 Coast	92 L/9	50°35′	126°21′
Bonfield	MUN2/AZM2	ON	Nipissing	31 L/3	46°13′	79°05′
Bonfield	UNP/LNO	ON	Nipissing	31 L/3	46°14′	79°09′
Bongard	UNP/LNO	ON	Prince Edward	31 C/2	44°03′	76°57′
Bongard Corners	UNP/LNO	ON	Prince Edward	31 C/2	44°03′	76°56′
Bonheur	UNP/LNO	ON	Kenora	52 G/6	49°19′	91°20′
Bonhomme, Lac	LAKE/LAC	QC	Communauté urbaine de Québec	21 L/13	46°50′	71°31′
Bonhomme, Ruisseau	RIV/CDE	QC	La Jacques-Cartier	21 L/13	46°51′	71°34′
Bonilla Island	ISL/ÎLE	BC	Range 4 Coast	103 G/7	53°30′	130°37′
Boninville	UNP/LNO	ON	Sudbury	41 I/11	46°36′	81°05′
Bonlea	UNP/LNO	AB	33-45-14-W4	73 D/13	52°56′	111°58′
Bonnard, Baie de	BAY/BAIE	QC	Kativik	24 N/12	59°43′	69°35′
Bonne Bay	UNP/LNO	NF		12 H/5	49°30′	57°55′
Bonne Bay	BAY/BAIE	NF		11 P/9	47°39′	56°13′
Bonne Bay	BAY/BAIE	NF		12 H/12	49°33′	57°56′
Bonne Bay Big Pond	LAKE/LAC	NF		12 H/5	49°19′	57°35′
Bonnécamps Canyon - also-aussi - Bonnécamps, Canyon	SEAU/SMER	—		8007	43°05′	60°25′
Bonnécamps, Canyon - also-aussi - Bonnécamps Canyon	SEAU/SMER	—		8007	43°05′	60°25′
Bonnechere	UNP/LNO	ON	Renfrew	31 F/12	45°39′	77°34′
Bonnechere River	RIV/CDE	ON	Renfrew	31 F/10	45°31′	76°33′
Bonne-Espérance	VILG/VILG	QC	Côte-Nord-du-Golfe-Saint-Laurent	12 P/5	51°28′	57°43′
Bonne-Espérance	UNP/LNO	QC	Côte-Nord-du-Golfe-Saint-Laurent	12 P/5	51°23′	57°40′
Bonne Madone	UNP/LNO	SK	36-42-25-W2	73 A/11	52°40′	105°29′
Bonnet Flamand - also-aussi - Flemish Cap	SEAU/SMER	—		8013	47°00′	44°50′
Bonnet Hill	UNP/LNO	BC	Cariboo	93 G/15	53°54′	122°37′
Bonnet, Lac du	LAKE/LAC	MB		52 L/5	50°22′	95°54′
Bonnet Lake	LAKE/LAC	NS	Guysborough	11 F/6	45°17′	61°25′
Bonnet Plume Pass	VALL/VALL	YT		106 C/6	64°21′	133°17′
Bonnet Plume River	RIV/CDE	YT		106 E/15	65°56′	134°56′
Bonney, Mount	MTN/MNT	BC	Kootenay	82 N/4	51°13′	117°32′
Bonney Road	UNP/LNO	NB	Kings	21 H/5	45°29′	65°51′
Bonnie Beach	UNP/LNO	ON	Ontario	31 D/11	44°34′	79°18′
Bonnington Falls	UNP/LNO	BC	Kootenay	82 F/6	49°28′	117°29′
Bonny River	UNP/LNO	NB	Charlotte	21 G/2	45°13′	66°51′
Bonny River	RIV/CDE	NB	Charlotte	21 G/2	45°12′	66°51′
Bonnyville	TOWN/VIL2	AB	7,18-61-5-W4	73 L/7	54°16′	110°44′
Bonnyville Beach	VILG/VILG	AB	32-60-6-W4	73 L/2	54°14′	110°52′
Bonnyville No. 87, Municipal District of	MUN1/AZM1	AB	68-8-W4	73 L/14	54°54′	111°13′
Bonnyville No. 87, Municipal District of - see-voir - Cold Lake	MUN1/AZM1	AB		73 L/8	54°27′	110°12′
Bonokoski Lake	LAKE/LAC	SK		64 M/11	59°44′	103°23′
Bonsecours	VILG/VILG	QC	Le Val-Saint-François	31 H/8	45°25′	72°17′
Bon-Secours	UNP/LNO	NB	Kent	21 I/6	46°22′	65°02′

NAME / NOM	ENTITY / ENTITÉ	LOC 1 / LIEU 1	LOC 2 / LIEU 2	MAP / CARTE	POSITION LAT	LONG
Bon Secours Beach	UNP/LNO	ON	Simcoe	31 D/5	44°20′	79°32′
Bonshaw	VILG/VILG	PE	Queens	11 L/3	46°12′	63°21′
Bonshaw	UNP/LNO	PE	Queens	11 L/3	46°12′	63°21′
Bonville	UNP/LNO	ON	Stormont	31 G/2	45°08′	74°49′
Bonwick Island	ISL/ÎLE	BC	Range 1 Coast	92 L/10	50°42′	126°39′
Boofus, Mount	MTN/MNT	BC	Cassiar	104 N/14	59°57′	133°03′
Bookton	UNP/LNO	ON	Norfolk	40 I/15	42°57′	80°30′
Boom Camp	UNP/LNO	QC	Témiscamingue	31 M/10	47°42′	78°43′
Boom Island	ISL/ÎLE	NS	Inverness	11 F/15	45°54′	61°00′
Boom Island	ISL/ÎLE	ON	Sudbury	41 I/2	46°02′	80°50′
Boom Road	UNP/LNO	NB	Northumberland	21 I/13	46°57′	65°47′
Boon	UNP/LNO	ON	Algoma	42 G/5	49°23′	83°57′
Bootahnie 15	IR/RI	BC	Kamloops Division Yale	92 I/5	50°24′	121°32′
Booth	UNP/LNO	ON	Nipissing	31 L/3	46°12′	79°20′
Booth	UNP/LNO	SK	21-28-19-W2	72 P/7	51°25′	104°38′
Boothia, Gulf of	BAY/BAIE	NT	Franklin	57 E	70°40′	91°00′
Boothia Isthmus	CAPE/CAP	NT	Keewatin	57 C/10	69°35′	93°05′
Boothia Peninsula	CAPE/CAP	NT	Franklin	57 F	71°00′	94°00′
Booth Island	ISL/ÎLE	NT	Keewatin	44 P	59°56′	79°56′
Booth Island	ISL/ÎLE	NT	Franklin	97 F	70°08′	125°03′
Booth Islands	ISL/ÎLE	NT	Franklin	97 F	70°09′	125°03′
Booth Lake	LAKE/LAC	ON	Nipissing	31 E/9	45°39′	78°12′
Booth Lake	LAKE/LAC	MB	Sudbury	64 O/5	59°23′	99°36′
Booth Landing	UNP/LNO	ON	Nipissing	31 L/3	46°08′	79°13′
Booth River	RIV/CDE	NT	Mackenzie	76 K	66°58′	108°56′
Boothroyd 5A	IR/RI	BC	Yale Division Yale	92 H/14	49°58′	121°29′
Boothroyd 5B	IR/RI	BC	Yale Division Yale	92 H/14	49°58′	121°30′
Boothroyd 5C	IR/RI	BC	Yale Division Yale	92 H/14	49°58′	121°29′
Boothroyd 6A	IR/RI	BC	Yale Division Yale	92 H/13	50°00′	121°30′
Boothroyd 6B	IR/RI	BC	Yale Division Yale	92 I/4	50°01′	121°31′
Boothroyd 8A	IR/RI	BC	Yale Division Yale	92 I/4	50°03′	121°32′
Boothroyd 13	IR/RI	BC	Yale Division Yale	92 H/14	49°59′	121°29′
Booth's Beach	UNP/LNO	QC	Sherbrooke	21 E/5	45°20′	71°50′
Boothville	UNP/LNO	ON	Grey	41 A/2	44°09′	80°37′
Boot Island	ISL/ÎLE	NS	Kings	21 H/1	45°08′	64°16′
Boot Lake	LAKE/LAC	BC	Sayward	92 K/4	50°03′	125°32′
Borden	VILG/VILG	SK	33-39-9-W3	73 B/6	52°24′	107°14′
Borden	UNP/LNO	PE	Prince	11 L/5	46°15′	63°42′
Borden	UNP/LNO	ON	Simcoe	31 D/5	44°16′	79°53′
Borden, Base des Forces canadiennes - also-aussi - Borden, Canadian Forces Base	MIL/MIL	ON	Simcoe	31 D/5	44°16′	79°55′
Borden, Canadian Forces Base - also-aussi - Borden, Base des Forces canadiennes	MIL/MIL	ON	Simcoe	31 D/5	44°16′	79°55′
Borden-Carleton	VILG/VILG	PE	Prince	11 L/5	46°16′	63°40′
Borden Island	ISL/ÎLE	NT	Franklin	79 F	78°30′	111°16′
Borden Lake	LAKE/LAC	ON	Sudbury	41 O/14	47°50′	83°17′
Borden Peninsula	CAPE/CAP	NT	Franklin	48 A	73°00′	83°00′
Borden River	RIV/CDE	NT	Keewatin	56 A	64°06′	88°21′
Bordenwood	UNP/LNO	ON	Frontenac	31 C/11	44°43′	77°03′
Border Beacon	UNP/LNO	QC	Kativik	13 M/5	55°15′	63°40′
Borderland	UNP/LNO	SK	8-1-1-W3	72 G/1	49°01′	106°06′
Border Ranges	MTN/MNT	AB		82 G/7	49°20′	114°30′
Border Ranges	MTN/MNT	BC	Kootenay	82 G/1	49°00′	114°30′
Borgels Point	UNP/LNO	NS	Lunenburg	21 A/9	44°33′	64°19′
Borgles Island	ISL/ÎLE	NS	Halifax	11 D/15	44°46′	62°43′
Boring Ranch	UNP/LNO	BC	Peace River	94 B/15	56°57′	122°42′
Borneo	UNP/LNO	NS	Guysborough	11 F/5	45°17′	61°55′
Borney Lake	LAKE/LAC	NF		2 D/14	48°56′	55°26′
Bornholm	UNP/LNO	ON	Perth	40 P/11	43°32′	81°09′
Bornish	UNP/LNO	ON	Middlesex	40 P/4	43°06′	81°41′
Borradaile	UNP/LNO	AB	29-50-5-W4	73 E/7	53°21′	110°42′
Borup Fiord	BAY/BAIE	NT	Franklin	340 B	80°37′	83°25′
Borups Corners	UNP/LNO	ON	Kenora	52 F/9	49°35′	92°19′
Bosanquet	MUN2/AZM2	ON	Lambton	40 P/4	43°10′	81°56′
Boscobel	UNP/LNO	QC	Le Val-Saint-François	31 H/9	45°30′	72°24′
Boscombe	UNP/LNO	AB	4-60-10-W4	73 L/3	54°09′	111°27′
Boscoville	UNP/LNO	QC	Matawinie	31 I/4	46°08′	73°37′
Boshkung Lake	LAKE/LAC	ON	Haliburton	31 E/2	45°04′	78°44′
Bosk Lake	LAKE/LAC	BC	Cariboo	93 A/2	52°10′	120°48′
Boskung	UNP/LNO	ON	Haliburton	31 E/2	45°05′	78°45′
Boss Creek	RIV/CDE	BC	Lillooet	92 P/15	51°53′	120°39′
Boss Mountain	MTN/MNT	BC	Cariboo	93 A/2	52°10′	120°34′
Boston	UNP/LNO	ON	Halton	30 M/12	43°33′	79°55′
Boston	UNP/LNO	ON	Norfolk	40 I/16	42°59′	80°16′
Boston Bar	UNP/LNO	BC	Yale Division Yale	92 H/14	49°52′	121°26′
Boston Bar 1A	IR/RI	BC	Yale Division Yale	92 H/14	49°49′	121°25′
Boston Bar 8	IR/RI	BC	Yale Division Yale	92 H/14	49°51′	121°26′

NAME NOM	ENTITY ENTITÉ	LOC 1 LIEU 1	LOC 2 LIEU 2	MAP CARTE	POSITION LAT	LONG
Boston Bar 9	IR/RI	BC	Yale Division Yale	92 H/14	49°52′	121°26′
Boston Bar 10	IR/RI	BC	Yale Division Yale	92 H/14	49°51′	121°24′
Boston Bar 11	IR/RI	BC	Yale Division Yale	92 H/14	49°49′	121°27′
Boston Creek	UNP/LNO	ON	Timiskaming	32 D/4	48°00′	79°56′
Boston Creek	RIV/CDE	ON	Haldimand	30 M/4	43°01′	79°56′
Boston Flats	UNP/LNO	BC	Kamloops Division Yale	92 I/14	50°46′	121°18′
Boston Mills	UNP/LNO	ON	Peel	30 M/13	43°46′	79°56′
Bostonnais, Grand lac	LAKE/LAC	QC	Le Haut-Saint-Maurice	31 P/16	47°54′	72°14′
Bostonnais, Rivière	RIV/CDE	QC	Le Haut-Saint-Maurice	31 P/7	47°28′	72°47′
Boswarlos	UNP/LNO	NF		12 B/10	48°34′	58°49′
Boswell	UNP/LNO	BC	Kootenay	82 F/7	49°27′	116°46′
Boswell River	RIV/CDE	YT		105 E/1	61°03′	134°13′
Bosworth	UNP/LNO	ON	Wellington	40 P/15	43°47′	80°39′
Botanie Creek	RIV/CDE	BC	Kamloops Division Yale	92 I/5	50°15′	121°33′
Botanie Mountain	MTN/MNT	BC	Kamloops Division Yale	92 I/5	50°22′	121°36′
Botanist Lake	LAKE/LAC	ON	Kenora	52 L/1	50°05′	94°18′
Botany	UNP/LNO	ON	Kent	40 I/5	42°29′	81°59′
Botha	VILG/VILG	AB	33-38-18-W4	83 A/7	52°18′	112°32′
Botha River	RIV/CDE	AB	95-24-W5	84 F/5	57°17′	117°52′
Bothwell	TOWN/VIL2	ON	Kent	40 I/12	42°38′	81°52′
Bothwell	UNP/LNO	PE	Kings	11 L/8	46°24′	62°05′
Bothwell's Corner	UNP/LNO	ON	Grey	41 A/10	44°35′	80°52′
Bothwell Station	UNP/LNO	ON	Kent	40 I/12	42°39′	81°54′
Botrel	UNP/LNO	QC	L'Islet	21 M/8	47°16′	70°07′
Botsford	GEOG/GÉOG	NB	Westmorland	21 I/1	46°07′	64°00′
Botsford Lake	LAKE/LAC	ON	Kenora	52 J/4	50°08′	91°38′
Botsford Portage	UNP/LNO	NB	Westmorland	21 I/1	46°11′	64°15′
Botten	UNP/LNO	AB	24-60-5-W6	83 L/2	54°11′	118°37′
Bottle Lake	LAKE/LAC	NF		12 A/5	48°28′	57°38′
Bottle Lake	LAKE/LAC	MB	18,19-19-W	62 K/9	50°37′	100°05′
Bottle Lake 61B	IR/RI	MB		62 K/9	50°38′	100°11′
Bottle Point	CAPE/CAP	ON	Thunder Bay	42 D/10	48°45′	86°52′
Bottom Brook	RIV/CDE	NF		11 P/16	47°48′	56°20′
Bottom Brook	RIV/CDE	NF		12 B/9	48°31′	58°16′
Bottrel	UNP/LNO	AB	21-28-4-W5	82 O/8	51°24′	114°29′
Botwood	TOWN/VIL2	NF		2 E/3	49°09′	55°21′
Boucher	VILG/VILG	QC	Mékinac	31 P/2	47°00′	72°45′
Boucher	UNP/LNO	NB	Madawaska	21 N/8	47°24′	68°21′
Boucher, Lac	LAKE/LAC	QC	Minganie	12 O/4	51°07′	59°34′
Boucher Lake	LAKE/LAC	SK	40-26-W2	73 A/5	52°27′	105°40′
Boucher Point	CAPE/CAP	ON	Grey	41 A/10	44°35′	80°31′
Boucher, Pointe	CAPE/CAP	QC	Kativik	34 N/12	59°37′	77°47′
Boucher, Rivière	RIV/CDE	QC	La Haute-Côte-Nord	22 F/3	49°10′	69°06′
Boucherville	CITY/VIL1	QC	Lajemmerais	31 H/11	45°36′	73°27′
Boucherville, Îles de	ISL/ÎLE	QC	Lajemmerais	31 H/11	45°37′	73°28′
Boucherville, Port de	BAY/BAIE	NT	Franklin	35 N	63°12′	77°33′
Bouchette	VILG/VILG	QC	La Vallée-de-la-Gatineau	31 J/4	46°13′	75°58′
Bouchette, Lac	LAKE/LAC	QC	Le Domaine-du-Roy	32 A/1	48°15′	72°12′
Bouchette Point	CAPE/CAP	ON	Durham	30 M/16	43°54′	78°29′
Bouchie Lake	UNP/LNO	BC	Cariboo	93 G/2	53°01′	122°36′
Bouchier, Lac	LAKE/LAC	QC	Jamésie	32 K/4	50°06′	77°48′
Boucks Hill	UNP/LNO	ON	Dundas	31 B/14	44°59′	75°13′
Boucle-des-Rapides	UNP/LNO	QC	La Matapédia	22 B/6	48°27′	67°12′
Bouctouche	TOWN/VIL2	NB	Kent	21 I/7	46°28′	64°43′
Boudart, Lac	LAKE/LAC	QC	Sept-Rivières	22 O/10	51°38′	66°40′
Boudreau	UNP/LNO	NB	Westmorland	21 I/1	46°13′	64°29′
Boudreau-Corners	UNP/LNO	QC	Coaticook	21 E/4	45°11′	71°46′
Boudreau Road	UNP/LNO	NB	Gloucester	21 P/10	47°38′	64°57′
Boudreau Village	UNP/LNO	NB	Westmorland	21 H/15	45°55′	64°36′
Boudreauville	UNP/LNO	NS	Richmond	11 F/10	45°30′	60°58′
Bouée-Gagnon, La	UNP/LNO	QC	La Vallée-de-la-Gatineau	31 K/9	46°45′	76°01′
Bouffard, Lac	LAKE/LAC	QC	Sept-Rivières	22 J/12	50°39′	67°46′
Bougainville	UNP/LNO	QC	Pabok	22 A/9	48°39′	64°16′
Boughey Bay	BAY/BAIE	BC	Range 1 Coast	92 L/9	50°31′	126°11′
Boughton Bay	BAY/BAIE	PE	Kings	11 L/8	46°15′	62°24′
Boughton Island	ISL/ÎLE	PE	Kings	11 L/1	46°11′	62°25′
Boughton River	RIV/CDE	PE	Kings	11 L/8	46°15′	62°25′
Boulain, Lac	LAKE/LAC	QC	Minganie	12 K/14	50°59′	61°24′
Boularderie	UNP/LNO	NS	Victoria	11 K/2	46°10′	60°34′
Boularderie Centre	UNP/LNO	NS	Victoria	11 K/2	46°12′	60°30′
Boularderie East	UNP/LNO	NS	Victoria	11 K/1	46°15′	60°27′
Boularderie West	UNP/LNO	NS	Cape Breton	11 K/1	46°11′	60°28′
Boulay	UNP/LNO	QC	La Matapédia	22 B/6	48°25′	67°24′
Boulder	UNP/LNO	BC	Kamloops Division Yale	92 P/8	51°28′	120°10′
Boulder, Baie	BAY/BAIE	QC	Kativik	24 N/3	59°00′	69°22′

NAME NOM	ENTITY ENTITÉ	LOC 1 LIEU 1	LOC 2 LIEU 2	MAP CARTE	POSITION LAT	LONG
Boulder City	UNP/LNO	BC	Cassiar	104 I/6	58°24′	129°00′
Boulder Creek	RIV/CDE	BC	Lillooet	92 J/11	50°38′	123°25′
Boulder Creek 5	IR/RI	BC	Kamloops Division Yale	92 P/8	51°28′	120°08′
Boulder Lake	LAKE/LAC	NT	Mackenzie	85 P	63°46′	113°04′
Boulderwood	UNP/LNO	NS	Halifax	11 D/12	44°37′	63°35′
Bouleau Lake	LAKE/LAC	BC	Osoyoos Division Yale	82 L/5	50°17′	119°39′
Bouleau, Rivière au	RIV/CDE	QC	Minganie	22 I/5	50°17′	65°31′
Bouleaux-Gris, Les	UNP/LNO	QC	Brome-Missisquoi	31 H/3	45°14′	73°00′
Bouleaux, Les	UNP/LNO	QC	Le Val-Saint-François	31 H/9	45°33′	72°02′
Boule, Baie de la	BAY/BAIE	QC	Sept-Rivières	22 J/1	50°11′	66°16′
Boullais, Les	UNP/LNO	QC	La Côte-de-Beaupré	21 M/2	47°02′	70°55′
Boullé, Lac	LAKE/LAC	QC	Kativik	24 B/13	56°55′	67°45′
Boulogne	UNP/LNO	QC	Drummond	31 H/15	45°51′	72°39′
Boulogne Lake	LAKE/LAC	NT	Mackenzie	85 F	61°19′	116°20′
Boulter	UNP/LNO	ON	Hastings	31 F/4	45°13′	77°38′
Boulton	MUN2/AZM2	MB		62 K/14	51°00′	101°00′
Boundary	UNP/LNO	NB	Madawaska	21 N/7	47°22′	68°43′
Boundary	UNP/LNO	YT		116 C/10	64°41′	140°59′
Boundary Bay	UNP/LNO	BC	New Westminster	92 G/3	49°00′	123°02′
Boundary Bay	BAY/BAIE	BC	New Westminster	92 G/2	49°02′	122°56′
Boundary Creek	UNP/LNO	NB	Westmorland	21 I/3	46°03′	65°00′
Boundary Creek	RIV/CDE	BC	Similkameen Division Yale	82 E/2	49°00′	118°46′
Boundary Dam Reservoir	LAKE/LAC	SK	1,2-8-W2	62 E/3	49°03′	103°02′
Boundary Falls	UNP/LNO	BC	Similkameen Division Yale	82 E/2	49°02′	118°42′
Boundary Island	ISL/ÎLE	MB/SK		64 F/12	57°40′	102°02′
Boundary Park	UNP/LNO	MB	4-18-4-E	62 I/10	50°31′	96°58′
Boundary Ranges	MTN/MNT	BC/YT		104 G/6	57°23′	131°15′
Boundary Road	UNP/LNO	BC	New Westminster	92 G/3	49°12′	123°01′
Bounty	VILG/VILG	SK	33-29-10-W3	72 O/11	51°31′	107°22′
Bounty, Cape	CAPE/CAP	NT	Franklin	78 F	74°52′	109°32′
Bourassa Bay	BAY/BAIE	NT	Franklin	57 H	71°32′	90°00′
Bourbonnais	UNP/LNO	QC	Bellechasse	21 L/11	46°36′	71°01′
Bourbon, Rivière	RIV/CDE	QC	L'Érable	21 L/5	46°17′	71°55′
Bourdages	UNP/LNO	QC	Bonaventure	22 A/4	48°07′	65°46′
Bourdages Corner	UNP/LNO	ON	Algoma	41 K/9	46°44′	84°18′
Bourdeau	UNP/LNO	ON	Parry Sound	31 E/12	45°30′	79°33′
Bourdel, Lac	LAKE/LAC	QC	Kativik	34 B/9	56°43′	74°10′
Bourdon, Lac	LAKE/LAC	QC	Caniapiscau	23 I/15	54°52′	64°36′
Bourgault	UNP/LNO	QC	L'Islet	21 M/1	47°12′	70°17′
Bourgeois	UNP/LNO	NB	Kent	21 I/7	46°21′	64°32′
Bourgeois Mills	UNP/LNO	NB	Westmorland	21 I/1	46°10′	64°25′
Bourget	UNP/LNO	ON	Russell	31 G/6	45°26′	75°09′
Bourg-la-Reine	UNP/LNO	QC	Communauté urbaine de Québec	21 L/14	46°54′	71°15′
Bourg-Louis-Station	UNP/LNO	QC	Portneuf	21 L/13	46°51′	71°46′
Bourg-Royal	UNP/LNO	QC	Communauté urbaine de Québec	21 L/14	46°53′	71°15′
Bourjoli, Pointe	CAPE/CAP	QC	Kativik	34 N/5	59°24′	77°55′
Bourkes	UNP/LNO	ON	Cochrane	42 A/8	48°17′	80°14′
Bourlamaque	UNP/LNO	QC	Vallée-de-l'Or	32 C/4	48°06′	77°46′
Bourne, Cape	CAPE/CAP	NT	Franklin	560 D	81°52′	90°35′
Bournemouth	UNP/LNO	SK	32-48-13-W3	73 G/4	53°10′	107°54′
Bourniol, Monts	MTN/MNT	QC	Rouyn-Noranda	32 D/6	48°23′	79°17′
Bournival	UNP/LNO	QC	Maskinongé	31 I/7	46°25′	72°52′
Bourque Lake	LAKE/LAC	AB	65,66-4-W4	73 L/10	54°40′	110°33′
Bousso River	RIV/CDE	NT	Mackenzie	85 O	63°12′	115°41′
Bout-de-l'Île	UNP/LNO	QC	Communauté urbaine de Montréal	31 H/11	45°42′	73°29′
Bout-du-Monde	UNP/LNO	QC	Maskinongé	31 I/6	46°25′	73°03′
Boutiliers Point	UNP/LNO	NS	Halifax	11 D/12	44°39′	63°57′
Boutin, Rivière	RIV/CDE	QC	Kativik	33 N/15	55°56′	76°37′
Bow City	UNP/LNO	AB	14-17-17-W4	82 I/8	50°26′	112°14′
Bowden	TOWN/VIL2	AB	23-34-1-W5	82 O/16	51°55′	114°02′
Bowden Lake	LAKE/LAC	ON	Kenora	52 F/14	49°58′	93°27′
Bowell	UNP/LNO	AB	6-14-7-W4	72 L/2	50°08′	110°57′
Bowell Islands	ISL/ÎLE	NT	Keewatin	56 D/1	64°01′	94°04′
Bowen Bay	UNP/LNO	BC	New Westminster	92 G/6	49°21′	123°25′
Bowen Corner	UNP/LNO	ON	Hastings	31 F/4	45°04′	77°42′
Bowen Island	UNP/LNO	BC	New Westminster	92 G/6	49°23′	123°20′
Bowen Island	ISL/ÎLE	BC	New Westminster	92 G/6	49°23′	123°22′
Bowermans	UNP/LNO	ON	Prince Edward	31 C/3	44°01′	77°22′
Bowers Beach	UNP/LNO	ON	Simcoe	41 A/8	44°29′	80°09′
Bowers Lake	LAKE/LAC	BC	Lillooet	92 P/10	51°41′	120°41′
Bowes Point	CAPE/CAP	NT	Keewatin	66 N	67°48′	101°56′
Bowesville	UNP/LNO	ON	Carleton	31 G/5	45°19′	75°40′
Bowie Seamount	SEAU/SMER	—		5.03	53°18′	135°38′
Bow Island	TOWN/VIL2	AB	36-10-11-W4	72 E/14	49°52′	111°22′
Bowker	UNP/LNO	ON	Thunder Bay	52 A/10	48°43′	88°38′

NAME NOM	ENTITY ENTITÉ	LOC 1 LIEU 1	LOC 2 LIEU 2	MAP CARTE	POSITION LAT	LONG
Bowker, Lac	LAKE/LAC	QC	Memphrémagog	31 H/8	45°25′	72°13′
Bowles Bay	BAY/BAIE	NT	Franklin	38 G	75°18′	79°35′
Bowling Green	UNP/LNO	ON	Dufferin	40 P/16	43°56′	80°16′
Bowman	VILG/VILG	QC	Papineau	31 G/13	45°55′	75°40′
Bowman Bay	BAY/BAIE	NT	Franklin	36 H	65°30′	73°40′
Bowman Head	CAPE/CAP	NS	Antigonish	11 F/12	45°39′	61°40′
Bowmanton	UNP/LNO	AB	4-15-14-W4	72 L/1	50°13′	110°29′
Bowmanville	UNP/LNO	ON	Durham	30 M/15	43°55′	78°41′
Bowmanville Creek	RIV/CDE	ON	Durham	30 M/15	43°53′	78°40′
Bown	UNP/LNO	QC	Le Haut-Saint-François	21 E/6	45°29′	71°25′
Bowood	UNP/LNO	ON	Middlesex	40 P/4	43°05′	81°32′
Bow Pass	VALL/VALL	AB	32-18-W5	82 N/9	51°43′	116°30′
Bow River	RIV/CDE	ON	Kenora	52 O/9	51°38′	90°20′
Bow River	RIV/CDE	SK	68-22-W2	73 I/14	54°56′	105°13′
Bow River	RIV/CDE	AB	22-11-13-W4	72 E/13	49°57′	111°41′
Bowron Lake	LAKE/LAC	BC	Cariboo	93 H/3	53°14′	121°23′
Bowron River	RIV/CDE	BC	Cariboo	93 I/4	54°03′	121°49′
Bowser	UNP/LNO	BC	Newcastle	92 F/7	49°26′	124°40′
Bowser Lake	LAKE/LAC	BC	Cassiar	104 A/5	56°25′	129°30′
Bowser River	RIV/CDE	BC	Cassiar	104 A/6	56°22′	129°19′
Bowser's Corner	UNP/LNO	ON	Manitoulin	41 G/16	45°50′	82°13′
Bowsman	VILG/VILG	MB	2-38-27-W	63 C/3	52°14′	101°12′
Bow Valley Provincial Park	PARK/PARC	AB	28-8-W5	82 O/3	51°05′	115°05′
Box Alder	UNP/LNO	ON	Rainy River	52 C/12	48°34′	93°41′
Boxelder Creek	RIV/CDE	AB/SK		72 L/1	50°05′	110°02′
Boxey	UNP/LNO	NF		1 M/5	47°27′	55°34′
Boxey Point	CAPE/CAP	NF		1 M/5	47°24′	55°35′
Box Grove	UNP/LNO	ON	York	30 M/14	43°51′	79°14′
Box Lake	UNP/LNO	BC	Kootenay	82 K/4	50°13′	117°43′
Box Lake	LAKE/LAC	SK		74 O/10	59°38′	106°40′
Box Lake	LAKE/LAC	NT	Mackenzie	75 N	63°56′	109°24′
Boyd	UNP/LNO	MB	33-79-7-E	63 P/16	55°53′	96°28′
Boyd, Lac	LAKE/LAC	QC	Jamésie	33 C/15	52°46′	76°42′
Boyd Lake	LAKE/LAC	NT	Mackenzie	65 E	61°30′	103°23′
Boyd Point	CAPE/CAP	BC	Range 1 Coast	92 K/10	50°44′	124°53′
Boyds	UNP/LNO	ON	Lanark	31 F/1	45°05′	76°15′
Boyds Corner	UNP/LNO	NB	York	21 J/7	46°16′	66°49′
Boyd's Cove	UNP/LNO	NF		2 E/7	49°27′	54°39′
Boyer	UNP/LNO	QC	Bellechasse	21 L/15	46°51′	70°52′
Boyer	UNP/LNO	QC	Antoine-Labelle	31 J/11	46°33′	75°14′
Boyer	UNP/LNO	AB	11-109-13-W5	84 K/8	58°28′	116°05′
Boyer 164	IR/RI	AB	109-14-W5	84 K/8	58°27′	116°15′
Boyer Nord, Rivière	RIV/CDE	QC	Bellechasse	21 L/10	46°44′	70°58′
Boyer River	RIV/CDE	AB	109-12-W5	84 J/5	58°27′	115°57′
Boyer, Rivière	RIV/CDE	QC	Bellechasse	21 L/15	46°53′	70°52′
Boyer Settlement	UNP/LNO	AB	109-13-W5	84 K/8	58°27′	116°02′
Boyer Strait	CHAN/CHEN	NT	Franklin	68 G	75°55′	103°00′
Boyer Sud, Rivière	RIV/CDE	QC	Bellechasse	21 L/10	46°44′	70°58′
Boyle	VILG/VILG	AB	4-65-19-W4	83 I/10	54°35′	112°49′
Boyle	UNP/LNO	ON	Lincoln	30 M/3	43°01′	79°25′
Boyle Drain	MISC/DIV	ON	Kent	40 J/8	42°26′	82°25′
Boyle Point	CAPE/CAP	BC	Nanaimo	92 F/7	49°28′	124°41′
Boyles Point	CAPE/CAP	BC	Range 1 Coast	92 L/14	50°49′	127°01′
Boylston	UNP/LNO	NS	Guysborough	11 F/5	45°26′	61°30′
Boyne	UNP/LNO	ON	Halton	30 M/5	43°29′	79°50′
Boyne Lake	UNP/LNO	AB	1-61-12-W4	73 L/4	54°14′	111°41′
Boyne River	RIV/CDE	ON	Simcoe	31 D/4	44°10′	79°49′
Boyne River	RIV/CDE	MB	19-7-1-W	62 H/12	49°35′	97°35′
Boynton	UNP/LNO	QC	Coaticook	31 H/1	45°07′	72°05′
Braaten	UNP/LNO	AB	27-67-5-W6	83 L/15	54°50′	118°40′
Brabant	HAM/HAM	SK		64 D/4	56°07′	103°45′
Brabant Lake	LAKE/LAC	SK		63 M/13	56°00′	103°43′
Bracebridge	TOWN/VIL2	ON	Muskoka	31 E/3	45°02′	79°19′
Bracebridge Inlet	BAY/BAIE	NT	Franklin	68 G	75°35′	100°20′
Bracken	VILG/VILG	SK	3-3-16-W3	72 F/1	49°11′	108°06′
Brackendale	UNP/LNO	BC	New Westminster	92 G/14	49°46′	123°09′
Bracken Lake	LAKE/LAC	MB	53,54-17-W	63 G/12	53°38′	99°53′
Brackenrig	UNP/LNO	ON	Muskoka	31 E/4	45°07′	79°31′
Brackett Lake	LAKE/LAC	NT	Mackenzie	96 F	65°13′	125°20′
Brackley	VILG/VILG	PE	Queens	11 L/6	46°19′	63°09′
Brackley	UNP/LNO	PE	Queens	11 L/6	46°19′	63°09′
Brackley Beach	UNP/LNO	PE	Queens	11 L/6	46°25′	63°11′
Brackley Point	UNP/LNO	PE	Queens	11 L/6	46°23′	63°11′
Brada	UNP/LNO	SK	24-43-16-W3	73 C/9	52°43′	108°11′
Bradburn Subdivision	UNP/LNO	ON	Oxford	40 I/15	42°53′	80°45′

NAME NOM	ENTITY ENTITÉ	LOC 1 LIEU 1	LOC 2 LIEU 2	MAP CARTE	POSITION LAT	LONG
Braddock	UNP/LNO	SK	24-13-11-W3	72 J/3	50°06′	107°23′
Bradelle, Banc - also-aussi - Bradelle Bank	SEAU/SMER	—		801	47°26′	62°54′
Bradelle Bank - also-aussi - Bradelle, Banc	SEAU/SMER	—		801	47°26′	62°54′
Bradelle Est, Vallée de	SEAU/SMER	—		4024	47°50′	62°30′
Bradelle Ouest, Vallée de	SEAU/SMER	—		4024	48°00′	62°45′
Bradens Bay	UNP/LNO	ON	Simcoe	31 D/6	44°28′	79°30′
Bradford	UNP/LNO	ON	Simcoe	31 D/4	44°07′	79°34′
Bradford West Gwillimbury	TOWN/VIL2	ON	Simcoe	31 D/4	44°07′	79°37′
Bradley	UNP/LNO	ON	Bruce	41 A/3	44°15′	81°18′
Bradley	UNP/LNO	ON	Kent	40 J/8	42°20′	82°25′
Bradley Corner	UNP/LNO	NB	Carleton	21 J/5	46°23′	67°42′
Bradley Creek	RIV/CDE	BC	Lillooet	92 P/15	51°52′	120°53′
Bradleys Cove	UNP/LNO	NF		1 N/14	47°52′	53°04′
Bradlo	UNP/LNO	ON	Cochrane	42 G/12	49°36′	83°39′
Bradner	UNP/LNO	BC	New Westminster	92 G/1	49°06′	122°25′
Brador	UNP/LNO	QC	Côte-Nord-du-Golfe-Saint-Laurent	12 P/6	51°28′	57°15′
Brador, Baie de	BAY/BAIE	QC	Côte-Nord-du-Golfe-Saint-Laurent	12 P/6	51°28′	57°17′
Bradore Marginal Trough	SEAU/SMER	—		813	52°45′	55°35′
Bradshaw	UNP/LNO	ON	Frontenac	31 C/10	44°41′	76°39′
Bradshaw	UNP/LNO	ON	Lambton	40 J/16	42°45′	82°16′
Bradshaw Lake	LAKE/LAC	MB		54 E/11	57°42′	95°04′
Bradwardine	UNP/LNO	MB	7-12-22-W	62 F/16	50°00′	100°28′
Bradwell	VILG/VILG	SK	28-34-2-W3	72 O/16	51°57′	106°14′
Brady Lake	UNP/LNO	ON	Haliburton	31 E/2	45°03′	78°50′
Brady Ranch	UNP/LNO	BC	Peace River	94 B/15	56°50′	122°38′
Brae	UNP/LNO	PE	Prince	21 I/9	46°40′	64°12′
Brae Bay	BAY/BAIE	NT	Franklin	48 H	75°47′	83°15′
Braeburn	UNP/LNO	AB	29-75-5-W6	83 M/10	55°32′	118°44′
Braeburn	UNP/LNO	YT		105 E/12	61°31′	135°50′
Brae Harbour	UNP/LNO	PE	Prince	21 I/9	46°37′	64°11′
Braeheid Survey	UNP/LNO	ON	Wentworth	30 M/5	43°20′	79°55′
Braeloch	UNP/LNO	BC	Osoyoos Division Yale	82 E/13	49°47′	119°31′
Braemar	UNP/LNO	ON	Oxford	40 P/2	43°11′	80°51′
Braemar Heights	UNP/LNO	BC	Metchosin	92 B/5	48°25′	123°30′
Braeshore	UNP/LNO	NS	Pictou	11 E/10	45°42′	62°39′
Braeside	VILG/VILG	ON	Renfrew	31 F/8	45°28′	76°24′
Braeside	UNP/LNO	MB		62 H/14	49°55′	97°05′
Braeside	UNP/LNO	BC	Range 5 Coast	93 K/1	54°05′	124°15′
Bragg Creek	UNP/LNO	AB	12-23-5-W5	82 J/15	50°57′	114°35′
Bragg Creek Provincial Park	PARK/PARC	AB	11,12-23-5-W5	82 J/15	50°56′	114°35′
Bragg's Island	ISL/ÎLE	NF		2 C/13	48°56′	53°40′
Brainard	UNP/LNO	AB	2-74-12-W6	83 M/5	55°23′	119°44′
Brainard, Cape	CAPE/CAP	NT	Franklin	340 B	80°33′	83°06′
Brainerd	UNP/LNO	MB		62 I/2	50°08′	96°51′
Brake's Cove	UNP/LNO	NF		12 G/1	49°08′	58°06′
Bralorne	UNP/LNO	BC	Lillooet	92 J/15	50°46′	122°49′
Bramalea	UNP/LNO	ON	Peel	30 M/12	43°44′	79°43′
Bramalea Woods	UNP/LNO	ON	Peel	30 M/12	43°43′	79°44′
Bramber	UNP/LNO	NS	Hants	21 H/1	45°10′	64°09′
Bramham Island	ISL/ÎLE	BC	Range 2 Coast	92 M/4	51°04′	127°34′
Bramley	UNP/LNO	ON	Simcoe	31 D/5	44°19′	79°36′
Brampton	CITY/VIL1	ON	Peel	30 M/12	43°41′	79°46′
Brancepeth	HAM/HAM	SK	34-46-23-W2	73 H/3	53°00′	105°16′
Branch	VILG/VILG	NF		1 K/13	46°53′	53°57′
Branch LaHave	UNP/LNO	NS	Lunenburg	21 A/7	44°27′	64°38′
Branch River	RIV/CDE	NF		1 K/13	46°53′	53°57′
Branchton	UNP/LNO	ON	Waterloo	40 P/8	43°18′	80°15′
Brandon	CITY/VIL1	MB		62 G/13	49°51′	99°57′
Brandon	UNP/LNO	BC	Kootenay	82 F/14	49°45′	117°27′
Brandon Hills	UNP/LNO	MB	17,21-9-18-W	62 G/13	49°45′	99°52′
Brandon Junction	UNP/LNO	MB	6-10-14-W	62 G/14	49°49′	99°21′
Brandon North	UNP/LNO	MB	7-12-18-W	62 G/13	50°00′	99°56′
Brandy Head	CAPE/CAP	NF		11 P/10	47°33′	56°45′
Brandy Point	UNP/LNO	ON	Perth	40 P/6	43°26′	81°14′
Brandywine	UNP/LNO	BC	New Westminster	92 J/3	50°02′	123°07′
Brandywine Falls	FALL/CHUT	BC	New Westminster	92 J/3	50°02′	123°05′
Brant	MUN1/AZM1	ON	Brant	40 P/1	43°10′	80°20′
Brant	MUN2/AZM2	ON	Grey	41 A/3	44°12′	81°10′
Brant	UNP/LNO	AB	16-18-26-W4	82 I/12	50°31′	113°30′
Brant	GEOG/GÉOG	ON		40 P/1	43°10′	80°20′
Brantford	CITY/VIL1	ON	Brant	40 P/1	43°08′	80°16′
Brantford	MUN2/AZM2	ON	Brant	40 P/1	43°06′	80°18′
Brant Hills	UNP/LNO	ON	Halton	30 M/5	43°22′	79°51′
Brantville	UNP/LNO	NB	Northumberland	21 P/7	47°22′	64°58′
Bras Coupé, Lac du	LAKE/LAC	QC	Jamésie	32 G/11	49°33′	75°00′

NAME NOM	ENTITY ENTITÉ	LOC 1 LIEU 1	LOC 2 LIEU 2	MAP CARTE	POSITION LAT	LONG
Bras-d'Apic	UNP/LNO	QC	L'Islet	21 L/16	46°57′	70°11′
Bras d'Or	UNP/LNO	NS	Cape Breton	11 K/1	46°15′	60°17′
Bras d'Or Lake	LAKE/LAC	NS	Cape Breton	11 F/15	45°50′	60°50′
Bras d'Or Lake	LAKE/LAC	NT	Mackenzie	85 J	62°24′	115°44′
Bras, Le	RIV/CDE	QC	Desjardins	21 L/11	46°43′	71°07′
Brass	UNP/LNO	SK	6-39-19-W3	73 C/7	52°20′	108°44′
Brasset	UNP/LNO	QC	La Côte-de-Gaspé	22 A/15	48°49′	64°35′
Brass Hill	UNP/LNO	NS	Shelburne	20 P/12	43°33′	65°36′
Bratnober, Mount	MTN/MNT	YT		115 A/10	60°44′	136°40′
Bratton	UNP/LNO	SK	2-28-9-W3	72 O/6	51°25′	107°10′
Bratt's Lake No. 129	MUN2/AZM2	SK		72 I/2	50°10′	104°40′
Braund Port	UNP/LNO	ON	Peterborough	31 D/8	44°16′	78°20′
Brawny	UNP/LNO	ON	Nipissing	31 F/13	45°54′	77°57′
Bray Island	ISL/ÎLE	NT	Franklin	37 C	69°16′	77°00′
Bray, Lac de	LAKE/LAC	QC	Jamésie	33 A/16	52°59′	72°05′
Bray Lake	UNP/LNO	ON	Parry Sound	31 E/14	45°53′	79°26′
Bray Lake	LAKE/LAC	ON	Parry Sound	31 E/14	45°54′	79°28′
Brazeau	UNP/LNO	AB	27-40-15-W5	83 C/8	52°28′	116°05′
Brazeau Dam	UNP/LNO	AB	17-46-11-W5	83 B/13	52°58′	115°34′
Brazeau Lake	LAKE/LAC	AB	39-22-W5	83 C/6	52°25′	117°05′
Brazeau, Mount	MTN/MNT	AB	41-24-W5	83 C/11	52°33′	117°21′
Brazeau No. 77, Municipal District of	MUN1/AZM1	AB	48-8-W5	83 G/3	53°11′	115°13′
Brazeau River	RIV/CDE	AB	45-9-W5	83 B/14	52°55′	115°14′
Brazel Neighbourhood	UNP/LNO	QC	Le Haut-Saint-François	21 E/5	45°23′	71°43′
Brazil Lake	UNP/LNO	NS	Yarmouth	20 O/16	44°00′	66°00′
Brazza, Lac	LAKE/LAC	QC	Le Fjord-du-Saguenay	22 E/2	49°02′	70°30′
Breac Brook	UNP/LNO	NS	Cape Breton	11 F/15	45°54′	60°31′
Breadalbane	VILG/VILG	PE	Queens	11 L/5	46°21′	63°30′
Breadalbane	UNP/LNO	NB	Northumberland	21 I/12	46°44′	65°53′
Breadalbane	UNP/LNO	NB	Charlotte	21 G/2	45°08′	66°52′
Breadalbane	UNP/LNO	ON	Glengarry	31 G/7	45°28′	74°36′
Bread and Cheese	UNP/LNO	NF		1 N/7	47°19′	52°47′
Breakenridge, Mount	MTN/MNT	BC	Yale Division Yale	92 H/12	49°43′	121°56′
Breakeyville	UNP/LNO	QC	Les Chutes-de-la-Chaudière	21 L/11	46°40′	71°14′
Breakheart Point	CAPE/CAP	NF		2 C/2	48°10′	52°58′
Breau Creek	UNP/LNO	NB	Westmorland	21 H/15	45°58′	64°31′
Breault	UNP/LNO	QC	Nicolet-Yamaska	31 I/1	46°12′	72°20′
Breau Road	UNP/LNO	NB	Northumberland	21 P/6	47°18′	65°07′
Breau-Village	UNP/LNO	NB	Kent	21 I/7	46°22′	64°38′
Brébeuf	VILG/VILG	QC	Les Laurentides	31 J/2	46°04′	74°40′
Brébeuf	UNP/LNO	QC	Avignon	22 B/1	48°14′	66°24′
Brébeuf, Lac	LAKE/LAC	QC	Le Fjord-du-Saguenay	22 D/2	48°11′	70°36′
Brèche-à-Manon	UNP/LNO	QC	Pabok	22 A/8	48°24′	64°26′
Brechin	UNP/LNO	ON	Ontario	31 D/11	44°32′	79°10′
Brechin Beach	UNP/LNO	ON	Ontario	31 D/11	44°32′	79°12′
Brechin East	UNP/LNO	ON	Ontario	31 D/11	44°33′	79°11′
Brechin Point	UNP/LNO	ON	Ontario	31 D/11	44°33′	79°12′
Breckenridge	UNP/LNO	QC	Les Collines-de-l'Outaouais	31 G/5	45°29′	75°57′
Bredenbury	TOWN/VIL2	SK	35-22-1-W2	62 L/16	50°57′	102°03′
Bredin	UNP/LNO	AB	25-72-7-W6	83 M/7	55°16′	118°56′
Breeches, Lac	LAKE/LAC	QC	L'Amiante	21 E/14	45°54′	71°28′
Breeze	UNP/LNO	SK	36-4-6-W2	62 E/7	49°20′	102°41′
Breezy Point	UNP/LNO	MB	9-15-5-E	62 I/7	50°16′	96°51′
Breezy's Corners	UNP/LNO	ON	Wentworth	40 P/8	43°23′	80°00′
Bréhat, Lac	LAKE/LAC	QC	Jamésie	23 D/10	52°33′	70°47′
Breithaupt Lake	LAKE/LAC	NT	Mackenzie	75 I	62°38′	105°23′
Bremen	UNP/LNO	SK	20-39-26-W2	73 A/5	52°22′	105°42′
Breme, Point	CAPE/CAP	NF		1 L/16	47°00′	54°10′
Bremner	UNP/LNO	ON	Thunder Bay	42 C/11	48°40′	85°29′
Bremner	UNP/LNO	AB	7-53-22-W4	83 H/11	53°34′	113°15′
Bremner River	RIV/CDE	ON	Thunder Bay	42 C/12	48°41′	85°31′
Brem River	UNP/LNO	BC	Range 1 Coast	92 K/7	50°26′	124°40′
Brem River	RIV/CDE	BC	Range 1 Coast	92 K/7	50°26′	124°40′
Brenda	MUN2/AZM2	MB		62 F/2	49°11′	100°41′
Brennan Harbour	UNP/LNO	ON	Algoma	41 J/1	46°03′	82°23′
Brennan Hills	UNP/LNO	QC	Communauté urbaine de l'Outaouais	31 G/13	45°47′	75°57′
Brennan Lake	LAKE/LAC	ON	Thunder Bay	52 I/5	50°29′	89°55′
Brent	UNP/LNO	ON	Nipissing	31 L/1	46°02′	78°29′
Brentford Bay	BAY/BAIE	NT	Franklin	57 G	71°54′	94°08′
Brentha	UNP/LNO	ON	Timiskaming	31 M/13	47°47′	79°54′
Brent Islands	ISL/ÎLE	NF		2 M/5	51°16′	55°57′
Brent, Mount	MTN/MNT	BC	Osoyoos Division Yale	82 E/5	49°29′	119°54′
Brenton	UNP/LNO	NS	Yarmouth	20 O/16	43°58′	66°03′
Brent's Cove	VILG/VILG	NF		2 E/13	49°56′	55°43′
Brentwood	UNP/LNO	NS	Colchester	11 E/3	45°13′	63°17′

NAME NOM	ENTITY ENTITÉ	LOC 1 LIEU 1	LOC 2 LIEU 2	MAP CARTE	POSITION LAT	LONG
Brentwood	UNP/LNO	ON	Simcoe	31 D/5	44°20′	79°56′
Brentwood Bay	UNP/LNO	BC	South Saanich	92 B/11	48°35′	123°27′
Brentwood Park	UNP/LNO	BC	New Westminster	92 G/7	49°17′	123°00′
Brereton Lake	UNP/LNO	MB	11-14-15-E	52 E/13	49°55′	95°32′
Brereton Lake	UNP/LNO	MB	31-10-15-E	52 E/13	49°53′	95°32′
Brereton Lake	LAKE/LAC	MB	11-14,15-E	52 E/13	49°54′	95°33′
Bresaylor	UNP/LNO	SK	13-46-20-W3	73 C/15	52°58′	108°46′
Breslau	UNP/LNO	ON	Waterloo	40 P/8	43°28′	80°25′
Brésolettes	UNP/LNO	QC	Communauté urbaine de Québec	21 L/14	46°53′	71°10′
Brésolles, Lac	LAKE/LAC	QC	Kativik	23 M/4	55°04′	71°48′
Brest	UNP/LNO	NB	Kent	21 I/7	46°28′	65°00′
Bretagne	UNP/LNO	QC	Kamouraska	21 N/5	47°22′	69°43′
Bretagneville	UNP/LNO	NB	Kent	21 I/11	46°43′	65°03′
Brethour	MUN2/AZM2	ON	Timiskaming	31 M/12	47°40′	79°34′
Brethour	UNP/LNO	ON	Timiskaming	31 M/12	47°44′	79°34′
Breton	VILG/VILG	AB	2-48-4-W5	83 G/1	53°07′	114°28′
Bretona	UNP/LNO	AB	33-51-23-W4	83 H/6	53°27′	113°20′
Breton, Cape	CAPE/CAP	NS	Cape Breton	11 G/13	45°57′	59°47′
Breton Cove	UNP/LNO	NS	Victoria	11 K/8	46°27′	60°27′
Breton, Harbour	BAY/BAIE	NF		1 M/5	47°30′	55°48′
Brettell Point	CAPE/CAP	BC	Range 1 Coast	92 K/7	50°19′	124°44′
Bretville Junction	UNP/LNO	AB	17-53-23-W4	83 H/11	53°34′	113°22′
Brevoort Island	ISL/ÎLE	NT	Franklin	25 P	63°30′	64°20′
Brevoort Park	UNP/LNO	SK		73 B/2	52°07′	106°37′
Brew Bay	UNP/LNO	BC	New Westminster	92 F/16	49°46′	124°23′
Brew Creek	RIV/CDE	BC	Range 2 Coast	92 N/3	51°06′	125°01′
Brewer	UNP/LNO	SK	19-23-5-W2	62 L/15	50°59′	102°42′
Brewer Creek	UNP/LNO	YT		115 O/2	63°11′	139°00′
Brewer Lake	UNP/LNO	ON	Frontenac	31 C/8	44°24′	76°20′
Brewers Mills	UNP/LNO	NB	York	21 J/3	46°04′	67°01′
Brewers Mills	UNP/LNO	ON	Frontenac	31 C/8	44°25′	76°19′
Brew, Mount	MTN/MNT	BC	Lillooet	92 I/12	50°35′	121°58′
Brewster Lake	LAKE/LAC	BC	Sayward	92 K/4	50°06′	125°35′
Brexton	UNP/LNO	BC	Lillooet	92 J/15	50°50′	122°49′
Breynat	UNP/LNO	AB	13-71-17-W4	83 P/1	55°08′	112°28′
Briar Lake	UNP/LNO	NS	Digby	21 A/4	44°08′	65°58′
Briarlea	UNP/LNO	SK	50-1-W3	73 G/8	53°18′	106°05′
Briar Ridge	UNP/LNO	BC	Peace River	93 P/16	55°47′	120°02′
Briars Park	UNP/LNO	ON	York	31 D/6	44°20′	79°20′
Bricailles, Les	UNP/LNO	QC	Bécancour	31 I/9	46°33′	72°08′
Brichta Lake	LAKE/LAC	NT	Mackenzie	76 P	67°46′	104°50′
Brickburn	UNP/LNO	AB	23,24-24-2-W5	82 O/1	51°04′	114°10′
Brickley	UNP/LNO	ON	Northumberland	31 C/5	44°15′	77°56′
Brick, Rivière du	RIV/CDE	QC	Minganie	12 E/6	49°21′	63°24′
Brickton	UNP/LNO	NS	Annapolis	21 A/14	44°55′	65°08′
Brickyard Road	UNP/LNO	NS	Cape Breton	11 K/1	46°01′	60°01′
Briçonnet, Lac	LAKE/LAC	QC	Minganie	12 N/8	51°21′	60°10′
Bridal Falls	UNP/LNO	BC	Yale Division Yale	92 H/4	49°11′	121°44′
Bridal Veil Falls	FALL/CHUT	BC	Yale Division Yale	92 H/4	49°11′	121°44′
Bridesville	UNP/LNO	BC	Similkameen Division Yale	82 E/3	49°02′	119°09′
Bridgar	UNP/LNO	MB	3-77-3-E	63 P/11	55°38′	97°04′
Bridgar, Lac	LAKE/LAC	QC	Jamésie	33 F/8	53°16′	76°00′
Bridge	UNP/LNO	BC	Cariboo	93 G/15	53°55′	122°41′
Bridge Creek	RIV/CDE	SK	15-18-W3	72 K/1	50°15′	108°24′
Bridge Creek	RIV/CDE	BC	Lillooet	92 P/15	51°46′	120°54′
Bridgedale	UNP/LNO	NB	Albert	21 I/2	46°04′	64°45′
Bridge End	UNP/LNO	ON	Glengarry	31 G/8	45°16′	74°26′
Bridgeford	UNP/LNO	SK	7-23-3-W3	72 J/16	50°56′	106°25′
Bridge Glacier	GLAC/GLAC	BC	Lillooet	92 J/13	50°50′	123°34′
Bridge Lake	UNP/LNO	BC	Lillooet	92 P/7	51°29′	120°43′
Bridge Lake	LAKE/LAC	BC	Lillooet	92 P/7	51°30′	120°45′
Bridgenorth	UNP/LNO	ON	Peterborough	31 D/8	44°23′	78°23′
Bridgeport	UNP/LNO	NF		2 E/10	49°33′	54°52′
Bridgeport	UNP/LNO	NS	Cape Breton	11 J/4	46°13′	60°00′
Bridgeport	UNP/LNO	ON	Waterloo	40 P/8	43°29′	80°29′
Bridgeport	UNP/LNO	BC	New Westminster	92 G/3	49°12′	123°07′
Bridge River	RIV/CDE	BC	Lillooet	92 I/13	50°45′	121°56′
Bridge River 1	IR/RI	BC	Lillooet	92 I/12	50°45′	122°00′
Bridge River 2	IR/RI	BC	Lillooet	92 I/13	50°48′	121°52′
Bridgetown	TOWN/VIL2	NS	Annapolis	21 A/14	44°51′	65°18′
Bridgetown	UNP/LNO	PE	Kings	11 L/7	46°18′	62°32′
Bridgetown	UNP/LNO	QC	Le Haut-Saint-Laurent	31 H/4	45°02′	73°57′
Bridgetown Wye	UNP/LNO	NS	Annapolis	21 A/14	44°51′	65°18′
Bridgeview	UNP/LNO	NS	Halifax	11 D/12	44°40′	63°39′
Bridgeview	UNP/LNO	ON	Essex	40 J/6	42°17′	83°03′

NAME NOM	ENTITY ENTITÉ	LOC 1 LIEU 1	LOC 2 LIEU 2	MAP CARTE	POSITION	
					LAT	LONG
Bridgeview	UNP/LNO	AB	9-77-6-W6	83 M/10	55°39′	118°51′
Bridgeview	UNP/LNO	BC	New Westminster	92 G/2	49°13′	122°52′
Bridgeview Survey	UNP/LNO	ON	Wentworth	30 M/5	43°18′	79°54′
Bridgeville	UNP/LNO	NS	Pictou	11 E/7	45°26′	62°36′
Bridgeville	UNP/LNO	QC	Pabok	22 A/9	48°36′	64°20′
Bridgewater	TOWN/VIL2	NS	Lunenburg	21 A/7	44°23′	64°31′
Bridport Inlet	BAY/BAIE	NT	Franklin	78 G	75°02′	108°45′
Briens	UNP/LNO	NF		1 N/6	47°24′	53°07′
Brient	UNP/LNO	ON	Algoma	41 N/15	47°58′	84°53′
Briercrest	VILG/VILG	SK	18-14-24-W2	72 I/3	50°10′	105°16′
Brièreville	UNP/LNO	AB	28-63-12-W4	73 L/5	54°28′	111°46′
Brier Hill	UNP/LNO	ON	Leeds	31 C/9	44°33′	76°10′
Brier Island	ISL/ÎLE	NS	Digby	21 B/8	44°16′	66°22′
Brierly Brook	UNP/LNO	NS	Antigonish	11 E/9	45°36′	62°04′
Brierly Brook Back Road	UNP/LNO	NS	Antigonish	11 E/9	45°37′	62°03′
Brigade Lake	UNP/LNO	BC	Kamloops Division Yale	92 I/9	50°30′	120°18′
Brig Bay	UNP/LNO	NF		12 P/2	51°04′	56°55′
Brigden	UNP/LNO	ON	Lambton	40 J/16	42°49′	82°17′
Briggs	UNP/LNO	AB	10-39-28-W4	83 A/5	52°21′	113°57′
Briggs, Cape	CAPE/CAP	NT	Franklin	59 C	77°04′	95°43′
Briggs, Cape	CAPE/CAP	NT	Franklin	68 D	73°38′	96°57′
Briggs Corner	UNP/LNO	NB	Queens	21 I/4	46°13′	65°54′
Briggs Corner	UNP/LNO	NB	Carleton	21 J/3	46°15′	67°18′
Briggs Corner	UNP/LNO	NB	Carleton	21 J/4	46°14′	67°41′
Briggs Spur	UNP/LNO	MB	36-23-W	63 C/2	52°05′	100°39′
Brigham	VILG/VILG	QC	Brome-Missisquoi	31 H/2	45°15′	72°51′
Brigham Creek 3	IR/RI	BC	Lillooet	92 O/14	51°46′	123°18′
Brig Harbour Island	ISL/ÎLE	NF		13 I/11	54°33′	57°10′
Brighouse	UNP/LNO	BC	New Westminster	92 G/3	49°10′	123°08′
Bright	UNP/LNO	ON	Oxford	40 P/7	43°16′	80°39′
Bright	GEOG/GÉOG	NB	York	21 J/3	46°08′	67°03′
Brightbank	UNP/LNO	AB	23-51-2-W5	83 G/8	53°25′	114°11′
Brightholme	UNP/LNO	SK	47-4-W3	73 G/1	53°02′	106°27′
Bright Land District	GEOG/GÉOG	BC		92 G	49°01′	123°55′
Brightmore	UNP/LNO	SK	26-9-16-W2	72 H/16	49°46′	104°05′
Bright Oaks	UNP/LNO	MB		62 H/14	49°50′	97°07′
Brighton	TOWN/VIL2	ON	Northumberland	31 C/4	44°02′	77°44′
Brighton	VILG/VILG	NF		2 E/12	49°33′	55°38′
Brighton	MUN2/AZM2	ON	Northumberland	31 C/4	44°09′	77°47′
Brighton	UNP/LNO	PE	Queens	11 L/3	46°14′	63°09′
Brighton	UNP/LNO	NS	Shelburne	20 P/11	43°42′	65°08′
Brighton	UNP/LNO	NS	Digby	21 A/12	44°33′	65°51′
Brighton	GEOG/GÉOG	NB	Carleton	21 J/6	46°18′	67°23′
Brighton Beach	UNP/LNO	ON	York	31 D/6	44°17′	79°29′
Brighton Beach	UNP/LNO	ON	Essex	40 J/6	42°16′	83°05′
Brighton Beach	UNP/LNO	BC	New Westminster	92 G/7	49°22′	122°54′
Bright Sand	UNP/LNO	SK	20-54-20-W3	73 F/10	53°41′	108°56′
Brightsand Lake	LAKE/LAC	SK	53-20-W3	73 F/10	53°36′	108°53′
Brights Grove	UNP/LNO	ON	Lambton	40 O/1	43°02′	82°15′
Brightside	UNP/LNO	ON	Lanark	31 F/1	45°07′	76°30′
Brightstone	UNP/LNO	MB	16-15-10-E	62 I/8	50°17′	96°10′
Brightview	UNP/LNO	AB	7-46-25-W4	83 A/13	52°57′	113°37′
Brignall	UNP/LNO	ON	Parry Sound	31 E/5	45°15′	79°50′
Brigus	TOWN/VIL2	NF		1 N/11	47°32′	53°13′
Brigus	UNP/LNO	NF		1 N/11	47°32′	53°13′
Brigus Gullies	UNP/LNO	NF		1 N/11	47°32′	53°14′
Brigus Head	CAPE/CAP	NF		1 N/2	47°06′	52°52′
Brigus Junction	UNP/LNO	NF		1 N/6	47°23′	53°18′
Brigus South	UNP/LNO	NF		1 N/2	47°07′	52°53′
Brill	UNP/LNO	QC	Brome-Missisquoi	31 H/8	45°16′	72°26′
Brillant, Mont	MTN/MNT	QC	Communauté urbaine de Québec	21 L/14	46°54′	71°27′
Brilliant	UNP/LNO	BC	Kootenay	82 F/5	49°19′	117°39′
Brimstone	UNP/LNO	ON	Peel	40 P/16	43°48′	80°00′
Brindle Crossing	UNP/LNO	ON	Renfrew	31 F/14	45°56′	77°20′
Bringadin, Lac	LAKE/LAC	QC	Caniapiscau	23 J/13	54°50′	67°43′
Brinka	UNP/LNO	ON	Kenora	52 L/1	50°00′	94°18′
Brinklow	UNP/LNO	ON	Hastings	31 C/13	44°54′	77°42′
Brinkman's Corners	UNP/LNO	ON	Bruce	41 H/3	45°09′	81°24′
Brinks Pond	LAKE/LAC	NF		2 E/2	49°13′	54°54′
Brinsley	UNP/LNO	ON	Middlesex	40 P/4	43°12′	81°32′
Brinston	UNP/LNO	ON	Dundas	31 B/14	44°56′	75°21′
Brion, Île	ISL/ÎLE	QC	Les Îles-de-la-Madeleine	11 N/14	47°48′	61°28′
Brion, Lac	LAKE/LAC	QC	Jamésie	23 L/9	54°43′	70°08′
Brisay, Lac	LAKE/LAC	QC	Jamésie	23 L/8	54°23′	70°24′
Brisbane	UNP/LNO	ON	Wellington	40 P/9	43°44′	80°04′

NAME / NOM	ENTITY / ENTITÉ	LOC 1 / LIEU 1	LOC 2 / LIEU 2	MAP / CARTE	POSITION LAT	LONG
Brisbin	UNP/LNO	SK	31-12-W3	72 O/12	51°40′	107°40′
Brisco	UNP/LNO	BC	Kootenay	82 K/16	50°50′	116°16′
Brisebois, Lac	LAKE/LAC	QC	Témiscamingue	31 M/6	47°17′	79°04′
Brise-Culotte	UNP/LNO	QC	Francheville	31 I/8	46°29′	72°16′
Brise-du-Lac	UNP/LNO	QC	Matawinie	31 J/1	46°07′	74°03′
Brise-Lame, Le	UNP/LNO	QC	Les Îles-de-la-Madeleine	11 N/12	47°33′	61°34′
Brisson	UNP/LNO	ON	Russell	31 G/6	45°18′	75°20′
Brisson, Lac	LAKE/LAC	QC	Kativik	24 A/8	56°18′	64°20′
Bristol	VILG/VILG	NB	Carleton	21 J/5	46°28′	67°35′
Bristol	VILG/VILG	QC	Pontiac	31 F/9	45°32′	76°28′
Bristol	UNP/LNO	PE	Kings	11 L/7	46°25′	62°44′
Bristol	UNP/LNO	NS	Queens	21 A/2	44°03′	64°43′
Bristol	UNP/LNO	MB	8-6-6-E	62 H/7	49°28′	96°44′
Bristol Mines	UNP/LNO	QC	Pontiac	31 F/8	45°30′	76°21′
Bristol Ridge	UNP/LNO	QC	Pontiac	31 F/9	45°37′	76°25′
Bristol's Hope	UNP/LNO	NF		1 N/11	47°43′	53°12′
Britainville	UNP/LNO	ON	Manitoulin	41 G/9	45°44′	82°24′
Britannia	UNP/LNO	NF		2 C/4	48°09′	53°43′
Britannia	UNP/LNO	ON	Muskoka	31 E/6	45°18′	79°04′
Britannia	UNP/LNO	ON	Peel	30 M/12	43°37′	79°41′
Britannia Bay	UNP/LNO	ON	Carleton	31 G/5	45°22′	75°48′
Britannia Bay	BAY/BAIE	ON	Carleton	31 G/5	45°22′	75°49′
Britannia Beach	UNP/LNO	BC	New Westminster	92 G/11	49°38′	123°12′
Britannia Creek	UNP/LNO	YT		115 J/15	62°52′	138°40′
Britannia Heights	UNP/LNO	ON	Carleton	31 G/5	45°21′	75°48′
Britannia No. 502	MUN2/AZM2	SK		73 F/5	53°25′	109°45′
Britannia Road	UNP/LNO	ON	Muskoka	31 E/6	45°16′	79°11′
British Columbia - also-aussi - **Colombie-Britannique**	PROV/PROV	BC		MCR3	54°00′	125°00′
British Empire Range	MTN/MNT	NT	Franklin	340 E	82°21′	77°30′
British Harbour	UNP/LNO	NF		2 C/5	48°16′	53°30′
British Mountains	MTN/MNT	YT		117 C/1	69°00′	140°30′
British Properties	UNP/LNO	BC	New Westminster	92 G/6	49°21′	123°08′
British Settlement	UNP/LNO	NB	Westmorland	21 H/16	45°52′	64°24′
Britt	UNP/LNO	ON	Parry Sound	41 H/15	45°46′	80°33′
Brittain River	RIV/CDE	BC	New Westminster	92 F/16	50°00′	124°01′
Britt Brook Lake	LAKE/LAC	NB	Victoria	21 O/2	47°05′	66°53′
Britton	UNP/LNO	ON	Perth	40 P/10	43°41′	80°56′
Britton Lake	LAKE/LAC	MB		63 N/13	55°55′	101°51′
Britt Station	UNP/LNO	ON	Parry Sound	41 H/15	45°48′	80°32′
Brizley Stream	RIV/CDE	NB	Sunbury	21 G/10	45°40′	66°34′
Broadacres	UNP/LNO	SK	32-35-21-W3	73 C/2	52°03′	108°59′
Broadback, Rivière	RIV/CDE	QC	Jamésie	32 M/7	51°21′	78°52′
Broadbent	UNP/LNO	ON	Parry Sound	31 E/5	45°27′	79°50′
Broad Cove	UNP/LNO	NF		1 N/14	47°50′	53°06′
Broad Cove	UNP/LNO	NF		1 N/12	47°33′	53°33′
Broad Cove	UNP/LNO	NF		1 M/9	47°35′	54°14′
Broad Cove	UNP/LNO	NS	Lunenburg	21 A/1	44°11′	64°29′
Broad Cove	BAY/BAIE	NF		2 C/11	48°36′	53°22′
Broad Cove Banks	UNP/LNO	NS	Inverness	11 K/3	46°13′	61°20′
Broad Cove Brook	RIV/CDE	NF		11 O/9	47°44′	58°23′
Broad Cove Chapel	UNP/LNO	NS	Inverness	11 K/6	46°15′	61°16′
Broad Cove Head	CAPE/CAP	NF		1 M/7	47°19′	54°55′
Broad Cove Marsh	UNP/LNO	NS	Inverness	11 K/6	46°18′	61°15′
Broad Cove Point	CAPE/CAP	NF		12 B/15	48°45′	58°39′
Broad Creek	RIV/CDE	SK	2-68-15-W3	73 K/16	54°52′	108°11′
Broad Island	ISL/ÎLE	NF		2 C/13	48°46′	53°49′
Broad Lake	LAKE/LAC	NT	Mackenzie	75 H	61°37′	104°15′
Broadlands	UNP/LNO	QC	Avignon	22 B/2	48°00′	66°46′
Broadmoor	UNP/LNO	BC	New Westminster	92 G/3	49°09′	123°08′
Broad River	RIV/CDE	NS	Queens	20 P/15	43°57′	64°49′
Broad River	RIV/CDE	MB		54 K/2	58°08′	92°51′
Broad River Lake	LAKE/LAC	NS	Queens	21 A/3	44°05′	65°03′
Broad Valley	UNP/LNO	MB	15-23-2-W	62 I/13	50°59′	97°39′
Broadview	TOWN/VIL2	SK	25-16-5-W2	62 L/7	50°22′	102°35′
Broadview	UNP/LNO	BC	Kamloops Division Yale	82 L/11	50°43′	119°15′
Broadview Gardens	UNP/LNO	ON	Algoma	41 K/9	46°32′	84°23′
Broadway	UNP/LNO	NS	Pictou	11 E/9	45°35′	62°22′
Brochant, Baie	BAY/BAIE	QC	Kativik	24 N/13	59°54′	69°42′
Brochant, Baie	BAY/BAIE	NT	Franklin	24 N/13	59°54′	69°42′
Brochant, Rivière	RIV/CDE	QC	Kativik	24 N/13	59°55′	69°45′
Brochet	UNP/LNO	MB		64 F/13	57°53′	101°40′
Brochet 197	IR/RI	MB		64 F/13	57°54′	101°35′
Brochet Bay	BAY/BAIE	MB		64 F/13	57°50′	101°36′
Brochet, Lac	LAKE/LAC	MB		64 K/12	58°37′	101°35′
Brochet, Lac au	LAKE/LAC	QC	La Haute-Côte-Nord	22 F/12	49°40′	69°36′

NAME / NOM	ENTITY / ENTITÉ	LOC 1 / LIEU 1	LOC 2 / LIEU 2	MAP / CARTE	POSITION LAT	POSITION LONG
Brochet, Rivière au	RIV/CDE	QC	La Haute-Côte-Nord	22 F/5	49°23'	69°37'
Brochets, Rivière aux	RIV/CDE	QC	Le Haut-Richelieu	31 H/3	45°04'	73°06'
Brock	VILG/VILG	SK	35-28-20-W3	72 N/7	51°26'	108°43'
Brock	MUN2/AZM2	ON	Ontario	31 D/6	44°17'	79°06'
Brocket	UNP/LNO	AB	8-7-28-W4	82 H/12	49°34'	113°44'
Brock Gardens	UNP/LNO	ON	Wentworth	40 P/8	43°17'	80°00'
Brockington	UNP/LNO	SK	3-48-19-W2	73 H/2	53°06'	104°42'
Brock Island	ISL/ÎLE	NT	Franklin	89 D	77°52'	114°19'
Brock Lake	LAKE/LAC	AB	56-6-W5	83 G/15	53°49'	114°50'
Brocklehurst	UNP/LNO	BC	Kamloops Division Yale	92 I/9	50°42'	120°25'
Brockley	UNP/LNO	ON	Middlesex	40 I/14	42°55'	81°12'
Brock No. 64	MUN2/AZM2	SK		62 E/10	49°40'	102°35'
Brock River	RIV/CDE	NT	Mackenzie	97 D	69°27'	123°24'
Brock, Rivière	RIV/CDE	QC	Jamésie	32 J/3	50°01'	75°05'
Brock Road	UNP/LNO	ON	Ontario	30 M/14	43°53'	79°05'
Brocks Beach	UNP/LNO	ON	Simcoe	41 A/8	44°27'	80°06'
Brocksden	UNP/LNO	ON	Perth	40 P/7	43°23'	80°53'
Brockton	UNP/LNO	PE	Prince	21 I/16	46°48'	64°15'
Brockville	CITY/VIL1	ON	Leeds	31 B/12	44°35'	75°41'
Brockway	UNP/LNO	NB	York	21 G/11	45°32'	67°07'
Broderick	VILG/VILG	SK	16-29-7-W3	72 O/7	51°30'	106°55'
Broders Annex	UNP/LNO	SK		72 I/7	50°27'	104°35'
Brodeur	UNP/LNO	QC	La Vallée-de-la-Gatineau	31 K/9	46°30'	76°04'
Brodeur Island	ISL/ÎLE	ON	Thunder Bay	52 A/9	48°33'	88°18'
Brodeur Peninsula	CAPE/CAP	NT	Franklin	58 A	72°30'	88°00'
Brodhagen	UNP/LNO	ON	Perth	40 P/11	43°33'	81°12'
Brodie	UNP/LNO	ON	Glengarry	31 G/7	45°25'	74°33'
Brodie	UNP/LNO	ON	Sudbury	41 I/7	46°29'	80°59'
Brodie Bay	BAY/BAIE	NT	Franklin	27 A	68°08'	66°10'
Brodie, Cape	CAPE/CAP	NT	Franklin	68 A	72°25'	96°16'
Brodtkorb, Lac	LAKE/LAC	QC	La Vallée-de-la-Gatineau	31 K/10	46°32'	76°37'
Brokenhead	MUN2/AZM2	MB		62 I/1	50°05'	96°30'
Brokenhead	UNP/LNO	MB	1-15-7-E	62 I/1	50°14'	96°29'
Brokenhead 4	IR/RI	MB		62 I/7	50°21'	96°36'
Brokenhead Reserve	UNP/LNO	MB	16-6,7-E	62 I/7	50°22'	96°38'
Brokenhead River - also-aussi - +Brokenhead, Rivière	RIV/CDE	MB	26-16-6-E	62 I/7	50°24'	96°40'
+Brokenhead, Rivière - also-aussi - Brokenhead River	RIV/CDE	MB	26-16-6-E	62 I/7	50°24'	96°40'
Brokenshell No. 68	MUN2/AZM2	SK		72 H/9	49°40'	104°15'
Broken Skull River	RIV/CDE	NT	Mackenzie	95 L	62°16'	127°39'
Broman Lake	UNP/LNO	BC	Range 5 Coast	93 L/8	54°25'	126°08'
Broman Lake	UNP/LNO	BC	Range 5 Coast	93 L/8	54°24'	126°10'
Brome	TOWN/VIL2	QC	Brome-Missisquoi	31 H/2	45°12'	72°34'
Brome-Centre	UNP/LNO	QC	Brome-Missisquoi	31 H/2	45°13'	72°36'
Brome, Lac	LAKE/LAC	QC	Brome-Missisquoi	31 H/7	45°15'	72°30'
Brome-Missisquoi	MUN1/AZM1	QC	Brome-Missisquoi	31 H/2	45°08'	72°48'
Brome, Mont	MTN/MNT	QC	La Haute-Yamaska	31 H/7	45°17'	72°38'
Bromhead	UNP/LNO	SK	3-3-13-W2	62 E/4	49°11'	103°40'
Bromley	MUN2/AZM2	ON	Renfrew	31 F/10	45°35'	76°57'
Bromley	UNP/LNO	ON	Renfrew	31 F/10	45°32'	76°53'
Bromley Island	ISL/ÎLE	NT	Franklin	340 E	82°56'	78°18'
Bromley Lake	LAKE/LAC	ON	Sudbury	42 A/5	48°26'	81°59'
Bromley Lake	LAKE/LAC	NT	Keewatin	66 I	66°19'	97°42'
Bromont	CITY/VIL1	QC	La Haute-Yamaska	31 H/7	45°19'	72°39'
Brompton	VILG/VILG	QC	Sherbrooke	21 E/12	45°31'	71°59'
Brompton, Lac	LAKE/LAC	QC	Memphrémagog	31 H/8	45°26'	72°09'
Bromptonville	CITY/VIL1	QC	Sherbrooke	21 E/5	45°28'	71°57'
Broncho	UNP/LNO	SK	21-5-11-W3	72 G/6	49°24'	107°25'
Bronson	UNP/LNO	NB	Queens	21 I/4	46°11'	65°45'
Bronson	UNP/LNO	ON	Hastings	31 F/4	45°04'	77°47'
Bronson, Île	ISL/ÎLE	QC	La Vallée-de-la-Gatineau	31 N/7	47°25'	76°30'
Bronson Island	ISL/ÎLE	NT	Keewatin	44 P	59°57'	79°52'
Bronson Lake	LAKE/LAC	SK	56-25-W3	73 F/13	53°52'	109°42'
Bronson Settlement	UNP/LNO	NB	Queens	21 I/4	46°13'	65°43'
Bronson Station	UNP/LNO	ON	Hastings	31 F/4	45°02'	77°48'
Bronte	UNP/LNO	ON	Halton	30 M/5	43°24'	79°43'
Bronte Creek	RIV/CDE	ON	Halton	30 M/5	43°24'	79°43'
Bronte Station	UNP/LNO	ON	Halton	30 M/5	43°25'	79°44'
Bronx	UNP/LNO	MB		62 H/14	49°55'	97°07'
Brooch, Lac	LAKE/LAC	QC	Sept-Rivières	22 J/12	50°44'	67°58'
Brookbury	UNP/LNO	QC	Le Haut-Saint-François	21 E/12	45°32'	71°32'
Brookdale	UNP/LNO	NS	Cumberland	21 H/16	45°48'	64°10'
Brookdale	UNP/LNO	QC	Papineau	31 G/15	45°56'	74°49'
Brookdale	UNP/LNO	MB	26-12-16-W	62 J/4	50°03'	99°34'
Brooke	MUN2/AZM2	ON	Lambton	40 I/13	42°50'	81°55'
Brooke	UNP/LNO	ON	Lanark	31 C/16	44°51'	76°26'

NAME NOM	ENTITY ENTITÉ	LOC 1 LIEU 1	LOC 2 LIEU 2	MAP CARTE	POSITION LAT	LONG
Brooke	UNP/LNO	ON	Grey	41 A/10	44°35'	80°57'
Brookfield	UNP/LNO	NF		2 F/4	49°08'	53°35'
Brookfield	UNP/LNO	PE	Queens	11 L/6	46°20'	63°17'
Brookfield	UNP/LNO	NS	Colchester	11 E/6	45°15'	63°17'
Brookfield	UNP/LNO	ON	Welland	30 L/14	42°57'	79°10'
Brookfield	UNP/LNO	ON	Algoma	41 K/9	46°32'	84°23'
Brookfield	UNP/LNO	MB	14-11-E	62 I/1	50°08'	96°04'
Brookfield Creek	RIV/CDE	BC	Kamloops Division Yale	92 P/9	51°39'	120°05'
Brooking	UNP/LNO	SK	31-6-18-W2	72 H/9	49°30'	104°25'
Brookland	UNP/LNO	NS	Pictou	11 E/10	45°33'	62°56'
Brooklands	UNP/LNO	MB		62 H/14	49°55'	97°12'
Brooklet	UNP/LNO	QC	Le Haut-Saint-Laurent	31 G/1	45°00'	74°03'
Brooklin	UNP/LNO	ON	Ontario	30 M/15	43°57'	78°57'
Brooklyn	UNP/LNO	NF		2 C/5	48°23'	53°52'
Brooklyn	UNP/LNO	PE	Kings	11 L/2	46°06'	62°40'
Brooklyn	UNP/LNO	PE	Prince	21 I/16	46°48'	64°07'
Brooklyn	UNP/LNO	NS	Hants	21 H/1	45°01'	64°01'
Brooklyn	UNP/LNO	NS	Queens	21 A/2	44°03'	64°42'
Brooklyn	UNP/LNO	NS	Annapolis	21 A/14	44°56'	65°08'
Brooklyn	UNP/LNO	NS	Yarmouth	20 O/16	43°52'	66°05'
Brooklyn	UNP/LNO	NB	Westmorland	21 I/1	46°01'	64°13'
Brooklyn Corner	UNP/LNO	NS	Kings	21 H/2	45°05'	64°35'
Brooklyn Road	UNP/LNO	NB	Westmorland	21 H/16	45°59'	64°16'
Brooklyn Street	UNP/LNO	NS	Kings	21 H/2	45°05'	64°38'
Brookmere	UNP/LNO	BC	Yale Division Yale	92 H/15	49°49'	120°53'
Brook Road	UNP/LNO	NS	Pictou	11 E/11	45°44'	63°04'
Brooks	TOWN/VIL2	AB	32-18-14-W4	72 L/12	50°35'	111°53'
Brooks Arm	BAY/BAIE	YT		115 G/6	61°28'	139°01'
Brooks Bay	BAY/BAIE	ON	Kenora	52 F/6	49°17'	93°29'
Brooks Bay	BAY/BAIE	BC	Rupert	92 L/4	50°13'	127°53'
Brooks Brook	UNP/LNO	YT		105 C/6	60°25'	133°12'
Brooksby	UNP/LNO	SK	30-46-16-W2	73 A/16	53°00'	104°19'
Brooksdale	UNP/LNO	ON	Oxford	40 P/2	43°14'	80°56'
Brookside	UNP/LNO	NF		1 M/7	47°26'	54°49'
Brookside	UNP/LNO	NS	Colchester	11 E/6	45°24'	63°14'
Brookside	UNP/LNO	NS	Halifax	11 D/12	44°33'	63°43'
Brookside	UNP/LNO	ON	Northumberland	30 M/16	43°59'	78°05'
Brooks Lake	LAKE/LAC	ON	Kenora	52 F/4	49°13'	93°34'
Brooks Lake	LAKE/LAC	NT	Mackenzie	75 G	61°54'	106°35'
Brooks Landing	UNP/LNO	ON	Parry Sound	41 H/8	45°26'	80°20'
Brooks Mill	UNP/LNO	ON	Muskoka	31 E/6	45°25'	79°01'
Brooks Peninsula	CAPE/CAP	BC	Rupert	92 L/4	50°10'	127°45'
Brookswood	UNP/LNO	BC	New Westminster	92 G/2	49°04'	122°40'
Brookvale	UNP/LNO	PE	Queens	11 L/6	46°17'	63°25'
Brookvale	UNP/LNO	NS	Halifax	11 E/3	45°02'	63°07'
Brookvale	UNP/LNO	NB	Queens	21 H/13	45°59'	65°41'
Brook Village	UNP/LNO	NS	Inverness	11 K/3	46°03'	61°18'
Brookville	UNP/LNO	NS	Pictou	11 E/7	45°29'	62°35'
Brookville	UNP/LNO	NS	Cumberland	21 H/7	45°24'	64°36'
Brookville	UNP/LNO	NB	Albert	21 H/10	45°43'	64°48'
Brookville	UNP/LNO	NB	Saint John	21 G/8	45°20'	66°02'
Brookville	UNP/LNO	NB	Carleton	21 J/5	46°20'	67°44'
Brookville	UNP/LNO	ON	Halton	40 P/9	43°32'	80°03'
Broomclose Head	CAPE/CAP	NF		2 C/12	48°41'	53°37'
Broom, Grande baie	BAY/BAIE	QC	Minganie	12 E/8	49°24'	62°11'
Broomhill	UNP/LNO	MB	17-5-27-W1	62 F/6	49°24'	101°05'
Broom Point	CAPE/CAP	NF		12 H/13	49°50'	57°52'
Brooms Brook	RIV/CDE	NF		11 O/14	47°51'	59°18'
Brophy	UNP/LNO	NS	Antigonish	11 F/12	45°44'	61°57'
Brora	UNP/LNO	SK	3-19-20-W2	72 I/10	50°35'	104°41'
Brossard	CITY/VIL1	QC	Champlain	31 H/6	45°27'	73°28'
Brosseau	UNP/LNO	QC	Champlain	31 H/6	45°26'	73°28'
Brosseau	UNP/LNO	AB	3-56-12-W4	73 E/13	53°47'	111°41'
Brothers Peaks	MTN/MNT	BC	Cassiar	94 E/3	57°09'	127°26'
Brotherston	UNP/LNO	ON	Perth	40 P/15	43°49'	80°57'
Brough	UNP/LNO	SK	10-9-12-W2	62 E/12	49°43'	103°33'
Brougham	MUN2/AZM2	ON	Renfrew	31 F/7	45°16'	76°57'
Brougham	UNP/LNO	ON	Ontario	30 M/14	43°55'	79°06'
Broughdale	UNP/LNO	ON	Middlesex	40 P/3	43°01'	81°16'
Broughton	UNP/LNO	NS	Cape Breton	11 J/4	46°05'	59°58'
Broughton, Cape	CAPE/CAP	NT	Franklin	16 M	67°39'	63°56'
Broughton Island	HAM/HAM	NT	Franklin	26 P	67°33'	64°02'
Broughton Island	ISL/ÎLE	BC	Range 1 Coast	92 L/15	50°49'	126°45'
Broughton Island	ISL/ÎLE	NT	Franklin	16 M	67°34'	63°54'
Broughton Island	ISL/ÎLE	NT	Keewatin	34 F	57°21'	76°47'

NAME NOM	ENTITY ENTITÉ	LOC 1 LIEU 1	LOC 2 LIEU 2	MAP CARTE	POSITION	
					LAT	LONG
Broughton Station	UNP/LNO	QC	L'Amiante	21 L/3	46°10'	71°08'
Broughton Strait	CHAN/CHEN	BC	Rupert	92 L/11	50°37'	127°03'
Broulan Reef	UNP/LNO	ON	Cochrane	42 A/11	48°31'	81°08'
Brouse	UNP/LNO	BC	Kootenay	82 K/4	50°13'	117°45'
Brouseville	UNP/LNO	ON	Grenville	31 B/14	44°50'	75°25'
Brower	UNP/LNO	ON	Cochrane	42 H/2	49°01'	80°50'
Brown	UNP/LNO	MB	22-1-6-W	62 G/1	49°03'	98°11'
Brown, Banc de - also-aussi - Browns Bank	SEAU/SMER	—		8006	42°37'	65°55'
Brown Bluff	CAPE/CAP	NT	Franklin	89 B	76°35'	116°18'
Brown Creek	RIV/CDE	ON	Lambton	40 I/13	42°50'	81°51'
Browne Bay	BAY/BAIE	NT	Franklin	68 D	73°08'	97°30'
Browne Island	ISL/ÎLE	NT	Franklin	68 E	74°49'	96°21'
Brownell Lake	LAKE/LAC	SK		63 M/4	55°00'	103°45'
Brownfield	UNP/LNO	AB	6-39-10-W4	73 D/6	52°19'	111°26'
Brown Hill	UNP/LNO	ON	York	31 D/3	44°13'	79°20'
Brown House Corner	UNP/LNO	ON	Glengarry	31 G/2	45°13'	74°34'
Browning	UNP/LNO	SK	4-6-5-W2	62 E/7	49°27'	102°38'
Browning Entrance	CHAN/CHEN	BC	Range 4 Coast	103 G/9	53°40'	130°31'
Browning Island	UNP/LNO	ON	Muskoka	31 D/14	45°00'	79°25'
Browning No. 34	MUN2/AZM2	SK		62 E/7	49°25'	102°35'
Brownings Landing	UNP/LNO	NT	Mackenzie	85 E	61°18'	119°48'
Brown Inlet	BAY/BAIE	NT	Franklin	26 G	65°29'	67°20'
Brown Lake	LAKE/LAC	NT	Keewatin	56 G	65°54'	91°15'
Brown Lake	LAKE/LAC	NT	Keewatin	55 M	63°39'	94°04'
Brown Lake	LAKE/LAC	NT	Mackenzie	85 P	63°24'	112°58'
Brownlee	VILG/VILG	SK	36-20-1-W3	72 J/9	50°44'	106°01'
Brown-Lowery Provincial Park	PARK/PARC	AB	21-4-W5	82 J/16	50°49'	114°26'
Brown Passage	CHAN/CHEN	BC	Range 5 Coast	103 J/7	54°20'	130°53'
Brown Point	CAPE/CAP	NT	Mackenzie	77 A	68°15'	104°33'
Brownrigg	UNP/LNO	ON	Cochrane	42 H/12	49°41'	81°31'
Brown River	RIV/CDE	NT	Keewatin	56 G	65°56'	90°56'
Brown's Arm	UNP/LNO	NF		2 E/6	49°15'	55°10'
Brown's Arm-Porterville	UNP/LNO	NF		2 E/6	49°15'	55°11'
Browns Bank - also-aussi - Brown, Banc de	SEAU/SMER	—		8006	42°37'	65°55'
Browns Brae	UNP/LNO	ON	Muskoka	31 E/3	45°13'	79°02'
Brownsburg	TOWN/VIL2	QC	Argenteuil	31 G/9	45°41'	74°25'
Browns Corner	UNP/LNO	NB	Kings	21 G/9	45°31'	66°09'
Browns Corners	UNP/LNO	ON	York	30 M/14	43°48'	79°15'
Brown's Corners	UNP/LNO	ON	York	30 M/14	43°51'	79°22'
Brown's Corners	UNP/LNO	ON	Oxford	40 I/15	42°56'	80°35'
Brown's Corners	UNP/LNO	ON	Oxford	40 P/3	43°11'	81°05'
Browns Cove	UNP/LNO	NF		12 H/10	49°38'	56°49'
Brownsdale	UNP/LNO	NF		2 C/3	48°02'	53°07'
Browns Flat	UNP/LNO	NB	Kings	21 G/8	45°28'	66°08'
Brown's Hill	UNP/LNO	QC	Memphrémagog	31 H/1	45°08'	72°07'
Browns Point	UNP/LNO	NS	Pictou	11 E/10	45°40'	62°44'
Browns River	RIV/CDE	BC	Comox	92 F/11	49°41'	125°03'
Brownsville	UNP/LNO	NS	Pictou	11 E/9	45°39'	62°23'
Brownsville	UNP/LNO	ON	Oxford	40 I/15	42°52'	80°50'
Brownsville	UNP/LNO	BC	New Westminster	92 G/2	49°12'	122°54'
Brownsville Station	UNP/LNO	ON	Oxford	40 I/15	42°51'	80°50'
Browns Yard	UNP/LNO	NB	Kent	21 I/11	46°31'	65°04'
Brownvale	UNP/LNO	AB	19-82-25-W5	84 C/4	56°08'	117°53'
Broxburn	UNP/LNO	AB	6-9-20-W4	82 H/10	49°43'	112°42'
Broyle, Cape	CAPE/CAP	NF		1 N/2	47°03'	52°52'
Bruce	MUN1/AZM1	ON	Bruce	41 A/6	44°30'	81°15'
Bruce	MUN2/AZM2	ON	Bruce	41 A/6	44°18'	81°29'
Bruce	UNP/LNO	NB	Gloucester	21 P/5	47°29'	65°38'
Bruce	UNP/LNO	AB	30-48-14-W4	83 H/1	53°10'	112°02'
Bruce	GEOG/GÉOG	ON		41 A/6	44°30'	81°15'
Brucedale	UNP/LNO	ON	Wellington	40 P/9	43°39'	80°11'
Brucefield	UNP/LNO	ON	Huron	40 P/12	43°31'	81°31'
Bruce Island	ISL/ÎLE	NT	Franklin	25 O	63°19'	67°25'
Bruce, Lac	LAKE/LAC	QC	Pontiac	31 K/11	46°44'	77°20'
Bruce Lake	UNP/LNO	ON	Kenora	52 K/14	50°48'	93°24'
Bruce Lake	LAKE/LAC	ON	Kenora	52 K/14	50°49'	93°20'
Bruce Mines	TOWN/VIL2	ON	Algoma	41 J/5	46°18'	83°48'
Bruce Mountains	MTN/MNT	NT	Franklin	37 H	71°10'	72°30'
Bruce Park	UNP/LNO	MB		62 H/14	49°53'	97°13'
Bruce Peninsula	CAPE/CAP	ON	Bruce	41 A/14	44°55'	81°15'
Bruce Peninsula National Park - also-aussi - Péninsule-Bruce, Parc national de la	PARK/PARC	ON	Bruce	41 H/4	45°14'	81°36'
Bruces	UNP/LNO	ON	Brant	40 P/8	43°16'	80°16'
Bruce Station	UNP/LNO	ON	Algoma	41 J/5	46°19'	83°46'
Bruceton	UNP/LNO	ON	Renfrew	31 F/3	45°13'	77°23'
Brucy	UNP/LNO	QC	Vaudreuil-Soulanges	31 H/5	45°24'	73°57'

NAME NOM	ENTITY ENTITÉ	LOC 1 LIEU 1	LOC 2 LIEU 2	MAP CARTE	POSITION LAT	LONG
Brudenell	VILG/VILG	PE	Kings	11 L/2	46°11'	62°37'
Brudenell	UNP/LNO	PE	Kings	11 L/2	46°11'	62°39'
Brudenell	UNP/LNO	ON	Renfrew	31 F/6	45°27'	77°24'
Brudenell and Lyndoch	MUN2/AZM2	ON	Renfrew	31 F/6	45°20'	77°22'
Bruderheim	TOWN/VIL2	AB	32-55-20-W4	83 H/15	53°47'	112°56'
Bruin, Cape	CAPE/CAP	NB	Westmorland	11 L/4	46°11'	63°59'
Brule	UNP/LNO	NS	Colchester	11 E/11	45°45'	63°10'
Brûlé	UNP/LNO	AB	3-50-27-W5	83 F/5	53°17'	117°53'
Brûlé, Cape	CAPE/CAP	NF		2 E/13	49°59'	55°51'
Brule Corner	UNP/LNO	NS	Colchester	11 E/11	45°44'	63°10'
Brûlée, Pointe	CAPE/CAP	NS	Richmond	11 F/10	45°37'	60°52'
Brule Harbour	BAY/BAIE	NS	Colchester	11 E/14	45°45'	63°11'
Brûlé, Lac	LAKE/LAC	QC	Minganie	13 D/5	52°17'	63°52'
Brûlé, Lac	LAKE/LAC	QC	Sept-Rivières	22 O/4	51°04'	67°43'
Brûlé, Lac	LAKE/LAC	QC	Manicouagan	22 F/10	49°31'	68°30'
Brûlé, Lac	LAKE/LAC	QC	Pontiac	31 K/14	46°57'	77°12'
Brûlé, Lac	LAKE/LAC	NT	Mackenzie	75 B	60°45'	106°02'
Brule Lake	LAKE/LAC	ON	Frontenac	31 F/3	45°03'	77°03'
Brûlé Lake	LAKE/LAC	AB	49,50-27-W5	83 F/5	53°17'	117°51'
Brule Point	UNP/LNO	NS	Colchester	11 E/14	45°45'	63°12'
Brulé Point	CAPE/CAP	ON	Algoma	41 N/15	47°49'	84°57'
Brule Shore	UNP/LNO	NS	Colchester	11 E/11	45°44'	63°14'
Brûlis-à-Thyme, Le	UNP/LNO	QC	Minganie	12 L/4	50°13'	63°36'
Brumes, Lac aux	LAKE/LAC	QC	Le Fjord-du-Saguenay	22 D/9	48°40'	70°26'
Brumlie	UNP/LNO	MB	2-15-22-W	62 K/1	50°15'	100°24'
Brumsfield	UNP/LNO	ON	Renfrew	31 F/14	45°49'	77°08'
Brundage, Mount	MTN/MNT	BC	Cassiar	104 K/6	58°17'	133°20'
Bruneau Lake	LAKE/LAC	MB	69,70-4-W	63 P/4	55°02'	97°56'
Brune, Lac	LAKE/LAC	QC	Jamésie	33 G/7	53°25'	74°37'
Brunel, Lac	LAKE/LAC	QC	Kativik	34 O/9	59°38'	74°20'
Brunet	UNP/LNO	QC	Antoine-Labelle	31 J/11	46°31'	75°27'
Brunette Creek	UNP/LNO	BC	New Westminster	92 G/2	49°14'	122°53'
Brunette Island	ISL/ÎLE	NF		1 M/5	47°16'	55°55'
Brunetville	UNP/LNO	ON	Cochrane	42 G/8	49°26'	82°25'
Brunkild	UNP/LNO	MB	30-7-1-W	62 H/12	49°36'	97°34'
Brunner	UNP/LNO	ON	Perth	40 P/10	43°31'	80°55'
Bruno	TOWN/VIL2	SK	16-38-25-W2	73 A/5	52°16'	105°31'
Brunskill	UNP/LNO	SK		73 B/2	52°08'	106°39'
Brunswick	UNP/LNO	ON	Durham	31 D/2	44°12'	78°35'
Brunswick	UNP/LNO	BC	Range 2 Coast	92 M/12	51°38'	127°33'
Brunswick	GEOG/GÉOG	NB	Queens	21 I/4	46°05'	65°35'
Brunswick Beach	UNP/LNO	BC	New Westminster	92 G/6	49°28'	123°15'
Brunswick Lake	LAKE/LAC	ON	Algoma	42 B/14	48°58'	83°23'
Brunswick Mines	UNP/LNO	NB	Gloucester	21 P/5	47°28'	65°54'
Brunswick Mountain	MTN/MNT	BC	New Westminster	92 G/6	49°29'	123°12'
Brussels	VILG/VILG	ON	Huron	40 P/11	43°44'	81°15'
Bruxelles	UNP/LNO	MB	17-6-11-W	62 G/7	49°29'	98°55'
Bryanston	UNP/LNO	ON	Middlesex	40 P/3	43°07'	81°16'
Bryant	UNP/LNO	SK	12-5-9-W2	62 E/6	49°23'	103°06'
Bryants Corner	UNP/LNO	NB	Kent	21 I/6	46°28'	65°12'
Bryant's Cove	VILG/VILG	NF		1 N/11	47°41'	53°11'
Bryant's Landing	UNP/LNO	QC	Memphrémagog	31 H/1	45°11'	72°14'
Bryce, Mount	MTN/MNT	AB/BC		83 C/3	52°03'	117°19'
Bryce, Mount	MTN/MNT	BC	Kootenay	83 C/3	52°03'	117°19'
Bryd	UNP/LNO	MB	14-17-24-W	62 K/7	50°27'	100°40'
Bryde Island	ISL/ÎLE	NT	Franklin	67 B	68°37'	100°50'
Bryde, Mount	MTN/MNT	YT		105 C/3	60°06'	133°11'
Bryenton	UNP/LNO	NB	Northumberland	21 I/13	46°52'	65°41'
Bryn	UNP/LNO	BC	Nanoose	92 F/8	49°17'	124°13'
Bryson	TOWN/VIL2	QC	Pontiac	31 F/10	45°41'	76°37'
Bryson	UNP/LNO	QC	Le Haut-Saint-Laurent	31 H/4	45°09'	73°56'
Bryson, Barrage de	MISC/DIV	QC	Pontiac	31 F/10	45°40'	76°38'
Bryson, Lac	LAKE/LAC	QC	Pontiac	31 K/6	46°28'	77°01'
B-Say-Tah	VILG/VILG	SK	23-21-14-W2	62 L/13	50°48'	103°51'
Buade, Lac	LAKE/LAC	QC	Le Domaine-du-Roy	32 G/1	49°05'	74°11'
Buccaneer Bay	UNP/LNO	BC	New Westminster	92 G/5	49°29'	123°59'
Buccleugh	UNP/LNO	SK	2-41-24-W3	73 C/6	52°30'	109°21'
Buchanan	VILG/VILG	SK	23-31-6-W2	62 M/10	51°42'	102°45'
Buchanan	UNP/LNO	ON	Wentworth	30 M/4	43°14'	79°54'
Buchanan Bay	BAY/BAIE	NT	Franklin	39 E/13	78°58'	75°11'
Buchanan Lake	LAKE/LAC	ON	Cochrane	42 G/3	49°12'	83°14'
Buchanan Lake	LAKE/LAC	NT	Franklin	49 G	79°28'	87°40'
Buchanan No. 304	MUN2/AZM2	SK		62 M/10	51°45'	102°40'
Buchan Bay	BAY/BAIE	NT	Mackenzie	76 O	67°56'	107°46'
Buchan Gulf	BAY/BAIE	NT	Franklin	37 H	71°46'	74°21'

NAME NOM	ENTITY ENTITÉ	LOC 1 LIEU 1	LOC 2 LIEU 2	MAP CARTE	POSITION LAT	LONG
Buchan Lake	LAKE/LAC	AB/NT		84 O/15	60°00′	114°57′
Buchans	TOWN/VIL2	NF		12 A/15	48°50′	56°51′
Buchans	UNP/LNO	NF		12 A/15	48°49′	56°52′
Buchans Island	ISL/ÎLE	NF		12 A/15	48°46′	56°50′
Buchans Junction	UNP/LNO	NF		12 A/16	48°51′	56°28′
Buchans Lake	LAKE/LAC	NF		12 A/15	48°51′	56°52′
Bûché-à-Louis-Rehel, Le	UNP/LNO	QC	Bonaventure	22 A/6	48°25′	65°07′
Bûché-à-Médé, Le	UNP/LNO	QC	Pabok	22 A/10	48°34′	64°38′
Buchholz Channel	CHAN/CHEN	BC	Rupert	92 L/5	50°30′	127°38′
Buck Creek	UNP/LNO	AB	36-47-7-W5	83 G/2	53°06′	114°54′
Buck Creek	RIV/CDE	BC	Range 5 Coast	93 L/7	54°24′	126°39′
Buckfield	UNP/LNO	NS	Queens	21 A/7	44°18′	64°47′
Buckham Lake	LAKE/LAC	NT	Mackenzie	85 I	62°18′	112°38′
Buckham's Bay	UNP/LNO	ON	Carleton	31 F/8	45°30′	76°06′
Buckhorn	UNP/LNO	ON	Peterborough	31 D/9	44°33′	78°21′
Buckhorn	UNP/LNO	BC	Cariboo	93 G/15	53°48′	122°39′
Buckhorn Lake	LAKE/LAC	ON	Peterborough	31 D/8	44°29′	78°23′
Buckingham	CITY/VIL1	QC	Communauté urbaine de l'Outaouais	31 G/11	45°35′	75°25′
Buckingham Heights	UNP/LNO	BC	New Westminster	92 G/2	49°14′	122°57′
Buckingham Island	ISL/ÎLE	NT	Franklin	59 D	77°12′	91°00′
Buckinghorse River	UNP/LNO	BC	Peace River	94 G/7	57°23′	122°51′
Buckinghorse River	RIV/CDE	BC	Peace River	94 G/8	57°29′	122°07′
Buck Lake	UNP/LNO	ON	Frontenac	31 C/9	44°32′	76°27′
Buck Lake	UNP/LNO	AB	11-46-6-W5	83 B/15	52°57′	114°47′
Buck Lake	LAKE/LAC	ON	Frontenac	31 C/9	44°32′	76°26′
Buck Lake	LAKE/LAC	AB	46-6-W5	83 B/15	52°59′	114°46′
Buck Lake	LAKE/LAC	AB	41-26-W5	83 C/12	52°33′	117°39′
Buck Lake 133C	IR/RI	AB	45-5-W5	83 B/15	52°54′	114°41′
Buckland	UNP/LNO	QC	Bellechasse	21 L/10	46°37′	70°33′
Buckland	UNP/LNO	SK	32-48-27-W2	73 H/4	53°11′	105°56′
Buckland-Est	UNP/LNO	QC	Bellechasse	21 L/9	46°38′	70°30′
Buckland Lake	LAKE/LAC	MB		64 H/10	57°39′	96°48′
Buckland No. 491	MUN2/AZM2	SK		73 H/5	53°20′	105°45′
Bucklaw	UNP/LNO	NS	Victoria	11 K/2	46°01′	60°59′
Buckles Point	UNP/LNO	NF		12 P/7	51°29′	56°56′
Buckley	UNP/LNO	ON	Algoma	41 K/9	46°32′	84°22′
Buckley Bay	UNP/LNO	BC	Nelson	92 F/10	49°32′	124°51′
Buckley Lake	LAKE/LAC	BC	Cassiar	104 G/15	57°54′	130°57′
Buckleys Corner	UNP/LNO	NS	Kings	21 H/2	45°06′	64°42′
Buckley Settlement	UNP/LNO	NB	Kings	21 H/14	45°54′	65°16′
Buck Point	CAPE/CAP	BC	Queen Charlotte	103 F/2	53°06′	132°34′
Buckshot Lake	LAKE/LAC	ON	Frontenac	31 F/3	45°00′	77°04′
Buckskin	UNP/LNO	ON	Simcoe	31 D/13	44°52′	79°36′
Bucktum 4	IR/RI	BC	Yale Division Yale	92 H/14	49°55′	121°27′
Buckwheat Corner	UNP/LNO	NS	Victoria	11 K/2	46°06′	60°52′
Buctouche - see-voir - Bouctouche	VILG/VILG	NB		21 I/7	46°28′	64°43′
Buctouche 16	IR/RI	NB	Kent	21 I/7	46°27′	64°46′
Buctouche, Baie de	BAY/BAIE	NB	Kent	21 I/7	46°28′	64°40′
Buctouche, Dune de	BCH/PLAG	NB	Kent	21 I/7	46°29′	64°38′
Buctouche River	RIV/CDE	NB	Kent	21 I/7	46°28′	64°42′
Buctouche-Sud	UNP/LNO	NB	Kent	21 I/7	46°28′	64°42′
Bucyrus	UNP/LNO	ON	Algoma	41 K/16	46°55′	84°13′
Buda	UNP/LNO	ON	Thunder Bay	52 A/12	48°40′	89°49′
Budd	UNP/LNO	MB	18-59-22-W	63 K/2	54°06′	100°45′
Budd Mills	UNP/LNO	ON	Renfrew	31 F/11	45°38′	77°15′
Budd's Point 20D	IR/RI	SK		63 E/16	53°58′	102°10′
Bueil, Lac	LAKE/LAC	QC	Jamésie	32 J/16	50°53′	74°14′
Buena Vista	VILG/VILG	SK	13,14-21-22-2	72 I/15	50°47′	104°57′
Buena Vista	UNP/LNO	SK		73 B/2	52°07′	106°40′
Buena Vista Park	UNP/LNO	ON	Simcoe	31 D/11	44°42′	79°24′
Buena Vista Park - see-voir - Buena Vista	UNP/LNO	SK		72 I/15	50°47′	104°57′
Buerger Point	CAPE/CAP	NT	Franklin	25 J	62°20′	66°13′
Buet, Rivière	RIV/CDE	QC	Kativik	25 D/1	60°02′	70°21′
Buffalo	UNP/LNO	AB	30-21-5-W4	72 L/15	50°48′	110°40′
Buffalo-Ankerite	UNP/LNO	ON	Cochrane	42 A/6	48°26′	81°16′
Buffalo Bay	BAY/BAIE	MB		52 E/3	49°07′	95°13′
Buffalo Bay	BAY/BAIE	AB	76-14,15-W5	83 N/9	55°34′	116°10′
Buffalo Creek	UNP/LNO	BC	Lillooet	92 P/11	51°44′	121°09′
Buffalo Gap	UNP/LNO	SK	10-2-25-W2	72 H/3	49°07′	105°16′
Buffalo Head Hills	MTN/MNT	AB	98-12-W5	84 G/5	57°25′	115°55′
Buffalo Head Prairie	UNP/LNO	AB	26-104-15-W5	84 K/1	58°03′	116°21′
Buffalo Heights	UNP/LNO	ON	Welland	30 L/15	42°53′	79°00′
Buffalo Horn	UNP/LNO	SK	21-6-12-W3	72 G/5	49°29′	107°33′
Buffalo Lake	UNP/LNO	AB	4-74-7-W6	83 M/6	55°23′	119°01′
Buffalo Lake	LAKE/LAC	AB	44-8-W4	73 D/14	52°46′	111°00′

NAME NOM	ENTITY ENTITÉ	LOC 1 LIEU 1	LOC 2 LIEU 2	MAP CARTE	POSITION LAT	LONG
Buffalo Lake	LAKE/LAC	AB	40,41-20,21-W4	83 A/7	52°27′	112°54′
Buffalo Lake	LAKE/LAC	BC	Lillooet	92 P/11	51°42′	121°04′
Buffalo Lake	LAKE/LAC	NT	Mackenzie	85 B	60°13′	115°30′
Buffalo Lake Metis Settlement	UNP/LNO	AB		83 I/8	54°29′	112°26′
Buffalo Narrows	VILG/VILG	SK		73 N/16	55°51′	108°29′
Buffalo No. 409	MUN2/AZM2	SK		73 C/10	52°35′	108°45′
Buffalo Point	UNP/LNO	MB	3,4,10-1-16,17-E	52 E/3	49°01′	95°14′
Buffalo Point 36	IR/RI	MB		52 E/3	49°01′	95°16′
Buffalo Pound Lake	LAKE/LAC	SK	19,20-25,26-W2	72 I/11	50°39′	105°30′
Buffalo River	UNP/LNO	NT	Mackenzie	85 B	60°53′	115°02′
Buffalo River	RIV/CDE	AB	102-19-W5	84 F/14	57°50′	117°01′
Buffalo River	RIV/CDE	NT/AB		85 B/14	60°53′	115°03′
Buffalo Rock	UNP/LNO	ON	Nipissing	31 M/3	47°01′	79°22′
Buffalo View	UNP/LNO	AB	10-42-6-W4	73 D/10	52°36′	110°46′
Buffer Lake	LAKE/LAC	SK		73 B/8	52°23′	106°00′
Buffett Head	CAPE/CAP	NF		1 M/8	47°29′	54°05′
Buford	UNP/LNO	AB	19-49-27-W4	83 H/4	53°15′	113°55′
Bugaboo Creek	RIV/CDE	BC	Kootenay	82 K/16	50°53′	116°22′
Bugeaud	UNP/LNO	QC	Bonaventure	22 A/3	48°03′	65°14′
Buick	UNP/LNO	BC	Peace River	94 A/14	56°46′	121°17′
Buit, Lac	LAKE/LAC	QC	Minganie	12 L/14	50°59′	63°13′
Bujeault River - also-aussi - Bujeault, Rivière	RIV/CDE	NF		12 P/12	51°41′	57°36′
Bujeault, Rivière - also-aussi - Bujeault River	RIV/CDE	QC	Minganie	12 P/12	51°41′	57°36′
Bukken Fiord	BAY/BAIE	NT	Franklin	560 A	80°43′	94°55′
Bulger Lake	LAKE/LAC	MB	70-1,2-E	63 P/3	55°03′	97°19′
Bulgers Corners	UNP/LNO	ON	Renfrew	31 F/11	45°36′	77°01′
Bulkley 1	IR/RI	BC	Cassiar	93 M/3	55°13′	127°24′
Bulkley Canyon	UNP/LNO	BC	Cassiar	93 M/3	55°15′	127°27′
Bulkley House	UNP/LNO	BC	Cassiar	93 M/9	55°42′	126°14′
Bulkley-Nechako	MUN1/AZM1	BC	Range 5 Coast	93 K/12	54°30′	125°40′
Bulkley Ranges	MTN/MNT	BC	Range 5 Coast	93 L/12	54°40′	127°40′
Bulkley River	RIV/CDE	BC	Cassiar	93 M/4	55°15′	127°40′
Bulkley River 19	IR/RI	BC	Cassiar	93 M/3	55°02′	127°19′
Bull Arm	BAY/BAIE	NF		1 N/13	47°49′	53°52′
Bull Creek	RIV/CDE	NB	Carleton	21 G/13	45°57′	67°43′
Bull Creek	RIV/CDE	SK	9-9-13-W3	72 G/12	49°43′	107°42′
Bullen River	RIV/CDE	NT	Mackenzie	66 E	65°51′	102°03′
Buller	UNP/LNO	ON	Hastings	31 C/6	44°27′	77°22′
Buller	UNP/LNO	ON	Haliburton	31 D/15	44°48′	78°45′
Buller Siding	UNP/LNO	ON	Hastings	31 C/6	44°27′	77°23′
Bulley's Cove	UNP/LNO	NF		2 E/6	49°21′	55°22′
Bull Harbour	UNP/LNO	BC	Rupert	92 L/13	50°55′	127°56′
Bullhead	UNP/LNO	MB	30-6-E	62 P/10	51°37′	96°44′
Bull Island	ISL/ÎLE	NF		1 N/13	47°47′	53°47′
Bull Island Point	CAPE/CAP	NF		1 L/16	46°47′	54°07′
Bull Lake	UNP/LNO	NB	York	21 J/3	46°06′	67°23′
Bull Lake	LAKE/LAC	NT	Mackenzie	75 H	61°24′	105°15′
Bullmoose Creek	RIV/CDE	BC	Peace River	93 P/3	55°08′	121°05′
Bull Moose Hill	UNP/LNO	NB	Kings	21 H/12	45°44′	65°47′
Bullock	UNP/LNO	ON	Lanark	31 F/1	45°06′	76°28′
Bullock Lake	LAKE/LAC	BC	Lillooet	92 P/5	51°27′	121°30′
Bullock, Mount	MTN/MNT	NT	Franklin	68 G	75°12′	100°20′
Bullocks Corners	UNP/LNO	ON	Wentworth	30 M/5	43°17′	79°59′
Bull Pen	UNP/LNO	QC	La Jacques-Cartier	21 L/14	46°56′	71°28′
Bull Pen, The	SEAU/SMER	—		8007	44°15′	61°35′
Bullpound	UNP/LNO	AB	35-24-15-W4	72 M/4	51°05′	111°59′
Bullpound Creek	RIV/CDE	AB	25-15-W4	72 M/4	51°04′	111°58′
Bull River	UNP/LNO	BC	Kootenay	82 G/6	49°28′	115°27′
Bull River	RIV/CDE	BC	Kootenay	82 G/6	49°28′	115°27′
Bull Rock	SHL/H-FD	NB	Charlotte	21 B/10	44°30′	66°57′
Bulls Cove	UNP/LNO	NF		1 M/3	47°03′	55°10′
Bulls Creek	UNP/LNO	NB	Carleton	21 J/4	46°06′	67°34′
Bullshead	UNP/LNO	AB	22-11-6-W4	72 E/15	49°55′	110°45′
Bullshead Creek	RIV/CDE	AB	32-12-5-W4	72 L/2	50°00′	110°37′
Bulman, Mount	MTN/MNT	BC	Kamloops Division Yale	92 I/8	50°26′	120°05′
Bulmer Lake	LAKE/LAC	NT	Mackenzie	95 I/15	62°48′	120°45′
Bulstrode, Rivière	RIV/CDE	QC	Arthabaska	31 I/1	46°03′	72°15′
Bulwark	UNP/LNO	AB	1-38-12-W4	73 D/4	52°15′	111°35′
Bulwer	UNP/LNO	QC	Le Haut-Saint-François	21 E/5	45°21′	71°42′
Bulyea	VILG/VILG	SK	27-23-21-W2	72 I/15	50°59′	104°52′
Bulyea River	RIV/CDE	SK		74 O/7	59°21′	106°55′
Bummers Flat 6	IR/RI	BC	Kootenay	82 G/12	49°39′	115°41′
Bummers' Roost	UNP/LNO	ON	Parry Sound	31 E/13	45°49′	79°37′
Bumpus, Mount	MTN/MNT	NT	Franklin	87 D/9	69°33′	112°40′
Bunbury	UNP/LNO	PE	Queens	11 L/3	46°14′	63°05′

NAME NOM	ENTITY ENTITÉ	LOC 1 LIEU 1	LOC 2 LIEU 2	MAP CARTE	POSITION LAT	LONG
Bunclody	UNP/LNO	MB	1-7-20-W	62 F/9	49°32'	100°03'
Bunde Fiord	BAY/BAIE	NT	Franklin	560 A	80°36'	94°55'
Bunder Lake	LAKE/LAC	AB	61-12-W4	73 L/5	54°16'	111°42'
Bunessan	UNP/LNO	ON	Grey	41 A/2	44°12'	80°43'
Bungalow G	UNP/LNO	BC	Kamloops Division Yale	83 D/3	52°04'	119°19'
Bungay	UNP/LNO	PE	Queens	11 L/6	46°22'	63°19'
Bunker Hill	UNP/LNO	ON	Stormont	31 G/3	45°03'	75°02'
Bunker Hill Brook	RIV/CDE	NF		11 O/16	47°52'	58°15'
Bunoz, Mount	MTN/MNT	YT		116 H/6	65°29'	137°11'
Bunsby Islands	ISL/ÎLE	BC	Rupert	92 L/3	50°06'	127°30'
Buntzen Bay	UNP/LNO	BC	New Westminster	92 G/7	49°23'	122°52'
Buntzen Lake	LAKE/LAC	BC	New Westminster	92 G/7	49°21'	122°51'
Bunyan	UNP/LNO	ON	Lambton	40 J/16	42°56'	82°16'
Bunyan's Cove	UNP/LNO	NF		2 D/8	48°24'	54°01'
Buoyant	UNP/LNO	AB	26-29-25-W4	82 P/11	51°31'	113°25'
Burchell Lake	UNP/LNO	ON	Thunder Bay	52 B/10	48°36'	90°36'
Burchell Lake	LAKE/LAC	ON	Thunder Bay	52 B/10	48°35'	90°38'
Burchills Flats	UNP/LNO	NB	Saint John	21 H/5	45°23'	65°35'
Bur Creek	UNP/LNO	ON	Frontenac	31 C/7	44°18'	76°33'
Burden, Mount	MTN/MNT	BC	Peace River	94 B/3	56°10'	123°25'
Burdett	VILG/VILG	AB	23-10-12-W4	72 E/13	49°50'	111°32'
Burdick	UNP/LNO	SK	4-17-25-W2	72 I/6	50°24'	105°24'
Burditt Lake	UNP/LNO	ON	Rainy River	52 C/13	48°55'	93°48'
Burditt Lake	LAKE/LAC	ON	Rainy River	52 C/13	48°57'	93°46'
Burdwood Point	CAPE/CAP	BC	Clayoquot	92 E/10	49°35'	126°34'
Bures	UNP/LNO	SK	36-8-22-W2	72 H/10	49°41'	104°52'
Burford	MUN2/AZM2	ON	Brant	40 P/1	43°05'	80°30'
Burford	UNP/LNO	ON	Brant	40 P/1	43°06'	80°26'
Burgeo	TOWN/VIL2	NF		11 P/12	47°37'	57°37'
Burgeo, Banc - also-aussi - Burgeo Bank	SEAU/SMER	—		4015	47°10'	57°55'
Burgeo Bank - also-aussi - Burgeo, Banc	SEAU/SMER	—		4015	47°10'	57°55'
Burgeo Islands	ISL/ÎLE	NF		11 P/12	47°35'	57°38'
Burgerville	UNP/LNO	QC	La Vallée-de-la-Gatineau	31 J/4	46°10'	75°50'
Burgess Mines	UNP/LNO	ON	Hastings	31 F/5	45°16'	77°42'
Burgess, Mount	MTN/MNT	YT		116 J/4	66°03'	139°38'
Burgess Settlement	UNP/LNO	NB	Victoria	21 O/4	47°05'	67°35'
Burgessville	UNP/LNO	ON	Oxford	40 P/2	43°01'	80°39'
Burgis	UNP/LNO	SK	36-29-4-W2	62 M/9	51°33'	102°27'
Burgoyne	UNP/LNO	ON	Bruce	41 A/6	44°27'	81°20'
Burgoyne Bay	BAY/BAIE	NT	Franklin	25 E	61°14'	71°30'
Burgoyne, Cape	CAPE/CAP	NT	Franklin	59 A/14	76°47'	90°34'
Burgoynes Cove	UNP/LNO	NF		2 C/4	48°11'	53°43'
Burgoynes Cove	UNP/LNO	NF		2 C/4	48°11'	53°43'
Burial Ground 6	IR/RI	BC	Nanaimo	92 G/4	49°08'	123°43'
Burin	TOWN/VIL2	NF		1 M/3	47°02'	55°10'
Burin Bay	UNP/LNO	NF		1 M/3	47°01'	55°11'
Burin Bay Arm	UNP/LNO	NF		1 M/3	47°05'	55°12'
Burin Inlet	BAY/BAIE	NF		1 M/3	47°04'	55°12'
Burin Island	ISL/ÎLE	NF		1 M/3	47°01'	55°09'
Burin Peninsula	CAPE/CAP	NF		1 M/4	47°00'	55°40'
Burke Channel	CHAN/CHEN	BC	Range 2 Coast	92 M/13	51°55'	127°53'
Burke Road	UNP/LNO	BC	New Westminster	92 G/2	49°08'	122°51'
Burke Settlement	UNP/LNO	ON	Frontenac	31 C/15	44°51'	76°44'
Burketon Station	UNP/LNO	ON	Durham	31 D/2	44°03'	78°47'
Burkeville	UNP/LNO	BC	New Westminster	92 G/3	49°11'	123°09'
Burks Corners	UNP/LNO	QC	Papineau	31 G/11	45°40'	75°09'
Burk's Falls	VILG/VILG	ON	Parry Sound	31 E/11	45°37'	79°24'
Burleigh and Anstruther	MUN2/AZM2	ON	Peterborough	31 D/9	44°42'	78°10'
Burleigh Falls	UNP/LNO	ON	Peterborough	31 D/9	44°33'	78°13'
Burlington	CITY/VIL1	ON	Halton	30 M/5	43°19'	79°47'
Burlington	VILG/VILG	NF		12 H/16	49°45'	56°01'
Burlington	UNP/LNO	PE	Prince	11 L/5	46°29'	63°36'
Burlington	UNP/LNO	NS	Kings	21 H/2	45°07'	64°49'
Burlington Beach	UNP/LNO	ON	Halton	30 M/5	43°18'	79°48'
Burman River	RIV/CDE	BC	Clayoquot	92 E/9	49°37'	126°03'
Burmis	UNP/LNO	AB	13-7-3-W5	82 G/9	49°33'	114°17'
Burnaby	CITY/VIL1	BC	New Westminster	92 G/7	49°16'	122°57'
Burnaby	UNP/LNO	ON	Welland	30 L/14	42°52'	79°20'
Burnaby	UNP/LNO	BC	New Westminster	92 G/2	49°15'	122°54'
Burnaby Heights	UNP/LNO	BC	New Westminster	92 G/6	49°17'	123°00'
Burnaby Island	ISL/ÎLE	BC	Queen Charlotte	103 B/6	52°23'	131°19'
Burnbrae	UNP/LNO	ON	Northumberland	31 C/5	44°19'	77°42'
Burnet	UNP/LNO	QC	Les Collines-de-l'Outaouais	31 G/12	45°34'	75°51'
Burnett Bay	BAY/BAIE	BC	Range 2 Coast	92 M/4	51°07'	127°41'
Burnett Bay	BAY/BAIE	NT	Franklin	98 C	73°45'	124°00'

NAME NOM	ENTITY ENTITÉ	LOC 1 LIEU 1	LOC 2 LIEU 2	MAP CARTE	POSITION	
					LAT	LONG
Burnett Inlet	BAY/BAIE	NT	Franklin	48 F	74°32'	86°12'
Burnett Lake	LAKE/LAC	SK		64 M/1	59°02'	102°18'
Burnett, Mount	MTN/MNT	BC	Kootenay	82 F/7	49°17'	116°52'
Burnett Point	CAPE/CAP	NT	Franklin	78 H	75°43'	105°22'
Burney, Cape	CAPE/CAP	NT	Franklin	38 C	73°06'	76°15'
Burnham	UNP/LNO	SK	16-15-11-W3	72 J/6	50°15'	107°28'
Burnhamthorpe	UNP/LNO	ON	Peel	30 M/12	43°37'	79°36'
Burnie Lake	LAKE/LAC	MB		64 K/16	58°55'	100°25'
Burnie River	RIV/CDE	BC	Range 5 Coast	93 L/4	54°10'	127°50'
Burnley	UNP/LNO	ON	Northumberland	31 D/1	44°10'	78°00'
Burnley Creek	RIV/CDE	ON	Northumberland	31 C/4	44°13'	77°51'
Burns	UNP/LNO	ON	Perth	40 P/10	43°37'	80°51'
Burns Cove	UNP/LNO	NF		1 M/7	47°24'	54°52'
Burnside	UNP/LNO	NF		2 C/12	48°43'	53°48'
Burnside	UNP/LNO	NS	Colchester	11 E/7	45°18'	62°59'
Burnside	UNP/LNO	NS	Halifax	11 D/12	44°42'	63°36'
Burnside	UNP/LNO	ON	Simcoe	31 D/13	44°45'	79°32'
Burnside	UNP/LNO	MB	35-11-8-W	62 G/16	49°58'	98°28'
Burnside River	RIV/CDE	NT	Mackenzie	76 K	66°51'	108°04'
Burnside-St. Chads	UNP/LNO	NF		2 C/12	48°43'	53°48'
Burns Lake	VILG/VILG	BC	Range 5 Coast	93 K/4	54°14'	125°45'
Burns Lake	LAKE/LAC	ON	Renfrew	31 F/6	45°19'	77°05'
Burns Lake	LAKE/LAC	NT	Franklin	77 G/6	71°24'	110°00'
Burns Lake 18	IR/RI	BC	Range 5 Coast	93 K/4	54°14'	125°46'
Burnstown	UNP/LNO	ON	Renfrew	31 F/7	45°23'	76°35'
Burnsville	UNP/LNO	NB	Gloucester	21 P/11	47°42'	65°09'
Burnt Arm	UNP/LNO	NF		2 E/3	49°11'	55°17'
Burnt Arm	BAY/BAIE	NF		2 E/3	49°10'	55°17'
Burnt Bay	BAY/BAIE	NF		2 E/3	49°15'	55°00'
Burnt Berry Brook	RIV/CDE	NF		12 H/9	49°30'	56°07'
Burntbush River	RIV/CDE	ON	Cochrane	32 E/5	49°29'	79°33'
Burnt Church	UNP/LNO	NB	Northumberland	21 P/3	47°12'	65°09'
Burnt Church 14	IR/RI	NB	Northumberland	21 P/3	47°14'	65°08'
Burnt Cliff Islands 20	IR/RI	BC	Range 5 Coast	103 J/8	54°29'	130°28'
Burntcoat	UNP/LNO	NS	Hants	11 E/5	45°19'	63°47'
Burntcoat Head	CAPE/CAP	NS	Hants	11 E/5	45°18'	63°49'
Burnt Cove	UNP/LNO	NF		1 N/2	47°12'	52°51'
Burnt Creek	UNP/LNO	QC	Caniapiscau	23 J/15	54°49'	66°53'
Burnt Hill	UNP/LNO	NB	Charlotte	21 G/3	45°10'	67°21'
Burnthill Brook	RIV/CDE	NB	York	21 J/10	46°35'	66°49'
Burnt Hills	UNP/LNO	ON	Frontenac	31 C/8	44°27'	76°18'
Burnt Island	UNP/LNO	NF		1 M/7	47°23'	54°42'
Burnt Island	UNP/LNO	ON	Manitoulin	41 G/15	45°49'	82°57'
Burnt Island	ISL/ÎLE	NF		2 C/13	48°51'	53°49'
Burnt Island	ISL/ÎLE	NF		2 E/10	49°41'	54°45'
Burnt Island	ISL/ÎLE	NF		2 E/6	49°27'	55°24'
Burnt Island	ISL/ÎLE	ON	Nipissing	31 L/4	46°13'	79°51'
Burnt Island Brook	RIV/CDE	NF		11 O/10	47°37'	58°52'
Burnt Island Harbour	BAY/BAIE	ON	Manitoulin	41 G/15	45°50'	82°57'
Burnt Island Lake	LAKE/LAC	ON	Nipissing	31 E/10	45°39'	78°39'
Burnt Islands	TOWN/VIL2	NF		11 O/10	47°36'	58°53'
Burnt Lake	LAKE/LAC	NF		2 E/7	49°15'	54°37'
Burnt Lake	LAKE/LAC	NF		2 D/14	48°53'	55°26'
Burnt Lake	LAKE/LAC	AB	67-3-W4	73 L/16	54°48'	110°26'
Burnt Lake	LAKE/LAC	AB	66-16-W4	83 I/9	54°41'	112°19'
Burnt Lake	LAKE/LAC	NT	Mackenzie	106 P/8	67°26'	128°10'
Burntland Brook	UNP/LNO	NB	Victoria	21 J/14	46°59'	67°20'
Burntout Brook	RIV/CDE	SK	30-48-11-W2	63 E/4	53°11'	103°35'
Burnt Point	UNP/LNO	NF		1 N/14	47°58'	53°02'
Burnt Point	UNP/LNO	PE	Kings	11 L/2	46°11'	62°30'
Burnt Pond	LAKE/LAC	NF		12 H/1	49°14'	56°04'
Burnt Pond	LAKE/LAC	NF		12 A/3	48°11'	57°24'
Burnt Pond River	RIV/CDE	NF		12 A/3	48°06'	57°22'
Burnt River	UNP/LNO	ON	Victoria	31 D/10	44°41'	78°42'
Burnt River	RIV/CDE	ON	Victoria	31 D/10	44°35'	78°46'
Burnt River	RIV/CDE	BC	Peace River	93 P/5	55°20'	121°43'
Burntroot Lake	LAKE/LAC	ON	Nipissing	31 E/15	45°52'	78°40'
Burnt Stump	UNP/LNO	NF		1 N/6	47°24'	53°09'
Burnt Village	UNP/LNO	NF		2 M/4	51°10'	55°59'
Burntwood Island	ISL/ÎLE	AB	114-4-W4	74 L/15	58°55'	110°37'
Burntwood Lake	LAKE/LAC	MB		63 N/8	55°22'	100°26'
Burntwood River	RIV/CDE	MB		64 A/2	56°08'	96°34'
Burpee	MUN2/AZM2	ON	Manitoulin	41 G/15	45°47'	82°40'
Burpee	UNP/LNO	NB	York	21 G/11	45°34'	67°22'
Burpee	UNP/LNO	ON	Manitoulin	41 G/15	45°47'	82°34'

NAME NOM	ENTITY ENTITÉ	LOC 1 LIEU 1	LOC 2 LIEU 2	MAP CARTE	POSITION LAT	LONG
Burpee, Cape	CAPE/CAP	NT	Franklin	37 B	68°40′	76°35′
Burpee Lake	LAKE/LAC	NT	Mackenzie	75 G/7	61°28′	106°40′
Burpees Corner	UNP/LNO	NB	Sunbury	21 G/16	45°52′	66°20′
Burquitlam	UNP/LNO	BC	New Westminster	92 G/7	49°16′	122°53′
Burr	UNP/LNO	ON	Prince Edward	31 C/3	44°03′	77°23′
Burr	UNP/LNO	SK	31-35-22-W2	73 A/3	52°03′	105°08′
Burrage Creek	RIV/CDE	BC	Cassiar	104 G/8	57°16′	130°16′
Burrard Inlet	BAY/BAIE	BC	New Westminster	92 G/6	49°18′	123°12′
Burrard Inlet 3	IR/RI	BC	New Westminster	92 G/7	49°19′	122°59′
Burrell Creek	RIV/CDE	BC	Similkameen Division Yale	82 E/8	49°22′	118°28′
Burridge	UNP/LNO	ON	Frontenac	31 C/10	44°39′	76°32′
Burriss	UNP/LNO	ON	Rainy River	52 C/12	48°41′	93°40′
Burritts Rapids	UNP/LNO	ON	Grenville	31 B/13	44°59′	75°48′
Burrows	UNP/LNO	SK	31-15-1-W2	62 L/8	50°19′	102°08′
Burrows Lake	LAKE/LAC	ON	Thunder Bay	42 E/15	49°57′	86°44′
Burstall	TOWN/VIL2	SK	35-19-29-W3	72 K/12	50°39′	109°54′
Burstall Lake	LAKE/LAC	AB	119-2-W4	74 M/8	59°20′	110°11′
Bursting Brook	RIV/CDE	NT	Keewatin	45 N	63°37′	84°17′
Burt	UNP/LNO	SK	8-17-27-W2	72 I/5	50°25′	105°40′
Burtch	UNP/LNO	ON	Brant	40 P/1	43°03′	80°16′
Burt Lake	LAKE/LAC	ON	Rainy River	52 B/5	48°18′	91°33′
Burton	UNP/LNO	PE	Prince	21 I/16	46°46′	64°20′
Burton	UNP/LNO	NB	Sunbury	21 G/16	45°52′	66°27′
Burton	UNP/LNO	ON	Durham	31 D/2	44°07′	78°44′
Burton	UNP/LNO	ON	Parry Sound	41 H/9	45°43′	80°12′
Burton	UNP/LNO	BC	Kootenay	82 F/13	49°59′	117°53′
Burton	GEOG/GÉOG	NB	Sunbury	21 G/16	45°48′	66°25′
Burton Bay	BAY/BAIE	NT	Franklin	25 N	63°39′	68°14′
Burton, Lac	LAKE/LAC	QC	Jamésie	33 L/16	54°45′	78°25′
Burton Lake	UNP/LNO	SK		73 A/6	52°16′	105°07′
Burtons	UNP/LNO	NS	Hants	11 E/4	45°14′	63°34′
Burtons Cove	UNP/LNO	NF		12 H/10	49°33′	56°52′
Burtonsville	UNP/LNO	AB	28-50-4-W5	83 G/7	53°20′	114°31′
Burtonville	UNP/LNO	QC	Le Haut-Richelieu	31 H/3	45°06′	73°22′
Burtts Corner	UNP/LNO	NB	York	21 J/2	46°03′	66°52′
Burwash	UNP/LNO	ON	Sudbury	41 I/2	46°14′	80°51′
Burwash Bay	BAY/BAIE	NT	Franklin	26 E	65°59′	71°12′
Burwash Lake	LAKE/LAC	ON	Sudbury	41 P/3	47°08′	81°03′
Burwash Landing	UNP/LNO	YT		115 G/7	61°21′	139°00′
Bury	VILG/VILG	QC	Le Haut-Saint-François	21 E/5	45°28′	71°30′
Burys Green	UNP/LNO	ON	Victoria	31 D/10	44°36′	78°40′
Busby	UNP/LNO	NB	Northumberland	21 P/4	47°12′	65°38′
Busby	UNP/LNO	AB	24-57-27-W4	83 H/13	53°57′	113°53′
Bush	UNP/LNO	SK	6-40-19-W3	73 C/7	52°25′	108°44′
Bushby Point	CAPE/CAP	ON	Muskoka	31 D/13	44°58′	79°57′
Bushell	UNP/LNO	SK		74 N/10	59°31′	108°45′
Bushell Park	UNP/LNO	SK	7,8-16-26-W2	72 I/5	50°20′	105°33′
Bushe River	RIV/CDE	AB	109-17-W5	84 K/7	58°26′	116°48′
Bushe River 207	IR/RI	AB	110-18-W5	84 K/7	58°29′	116°58′
Bush Glen	UNP/LNO	ON	Stormont	31 G/3	45°03′	75°06′
Bush Island	UNP/LNO	NS	Lunenburg	21 A/1	44°14′	64°22′
Bush, Lac	LAKE/LAC	QC	Kativik	34 G/13	57°50′	75°58′
Bushnan, Cape	CAPE/CAP	NT	Franklin	37 C	69°28′	78°49′
Bushnan Island	ISL/ÎLE	NT	Franklin	46 K	66°09′	84°37′
Bushnell	UNP/LNO	ON	Nipissing	31 L/13	46°48′	79°34′
Bush River	RIV/CDE	BC	Kootenay	82 N/14	51°49′	117°20′
Bushville	UNP/LNO	NB	Northumberland	21 P/4	47°01′	65°31′
Bushy Head Corner	UNP/LNO	AB	21-43-8-W4	73 D/11	52°43′	111°06′
Buskegau	UNP/LNO	ON	Cochrane	42 H/3	49°06′	81°12′
Buskegau River	RIV/CDE	ON	Cochrane	42 H/3	49°07′	81°09′
Bussy, Lac	LAKE/LAC	QC	Jamésie	22 M/12	51°30′	71°46′
Bustard Island	ISL/ÎLE	AB	113-5-W4	74 L/15	58°47′	110°44′
Bustard Islands	ISL/ÎLE	ON	Parry Sound	41 H/15	45°53′	80°54′
Busteed	UNP/LNO	ON	Kenora	52 E/15	49°45′	94°46′
Busy Bee Corners	UNP/LNO	ON	Essex	40 J/3	42°06′	83°02′
Butchers	UNP/LNO	NF		1 N/14	47°53′	53°23′
Butedale	UNP/LNO	BC	Range 4 Coast	103 H/2	53°09′	128°42′
Bute Inlet	BAY/BAIE	BC	Range 1 Coast	92 K/6	50°21′	125°06′
Bute, Mount	MTN/MNT	BC	Range 1 Coast	92 K/15	50°56′	124°42′
Buteux, Lac	LAKE/LAC	QC	Kativik	24 F/1	57°06′	68°10′
Buteux, Lac	LAKE/LAC	QC	Charlevoix-Est	22 C/4	48°03′	69°55′
Butler	UNP/LNO	ON	Kenora	52 G/5	49°28′	91°49′
Butler	UNP/LNO	MB	33-9-29-W	62 F/14	49°48′	101°22′
Butler Bay	BAY/BAIE	NT	Franklin	25 P	63°11′	64°56′
Butler, Ruisseau	RIV/CDE	QC	Avignon	22 B/7	48°16′	66°30′

NAME NOM	ENTITY ENTITÉ	LOC 1 LIEU 1	LOC 2 LIEU 2	MAP CARTE	POSITION LAT	LONG
Butler's Barracks National Historic Site - also-aussi - Casernes-de-Butler, Lieu historique national des	PARK/PARC	ON	Lincoln	30 M/3	43°15′	79°04′
Butlerville	UNP/LNO	NF		1 N/11	47°35′	53°20′
Butnau River	RIV/CDE	MB		54 D/7	56°19′	94°47′
Butte	UNP/LNO	AB	13-37-6-W5	83 B/2	52°11′	114°44′
Butte-à-Chandonnet, La	UNP/LNO	QC	Francheville	31 I/9	46°33′	72°09′
Butte-à-Julie, La	UNP/LNO	QC	Charlevoix-Est	21 M/9	47°43′	70°07′
Butte-D'Or	UNP/LNO	NB	Gloucester	21 P/11	47°32′	65°12′
Butter Cove	UNP/LNO	NF		2 C/4	48°02′	53°39′
Buttereau-du-Nègre, Le	UNP/LNO	QC	Les Îles-de-la-Madeleine	11 N/12	47°31′	61°44′
Buttereau-Vert, Le	UNP/LNO	QC	Les Îles-de-la-Madeleine	11 N/12	47°34′	61°38′
Butterfly Lake	LAKE/LAC	MB		63 I/6	54°27′	97°17′
Buttermilk Falls	UNP/LNO	ON	Haliburton	31 E/2	45°06′	78°45′
Butternut Bay	UNP/LNO	ON	Leeds	31 B/12	44°31′	75°47′
Butternut Flat	UNP/LNO	QC	Memphrémagog	31 H/1	45°12′	72°02′
Butter Porridge Point	CAPE/CAP	NT	Franklin	340 B	80°24′	87°38′
Butter Pot	MTN/MNT	NF		1 K/14	46°58′	53°03′
Butterton	UNP/LNO	SK	15-24-20-W2	72 P/2	51°02′	104°42′
Butte-St-Pierre	UNP/LNO	SK	36-51-23-W3	73 F/6	53°27′	109°22′
Butt Lake	LAKE/LAC	ON	Nipissing	31 E/10	45°42′	78°57′
Buttle Lake	LAKE/LAC	BC	Nootka	92 F/12	49°41′	125°33′
Button	UNP/LNO	MB	1-66-11-W	63 J/10	54°41′	99°00′
Button Bay	BAY/BAIE	NT	Keewatin	54 L/9	58°45′	94°23′
Button Channel	SEAU/SMER	—		1399A	60°00′	93°30′
Button Islands	ISL/ÎLE	NT	Franklin	25 A/10	60°38′	64°42′
Button's Corners	UNP/LNO	ON	Timiskaming	31 M/5	47°28′	79°48′
Buttonville	UNP/LNO	ON	York	30 M/14	43°52′	79°22′
Buttress	UNP/LNO	SK	28-14-27-W2	72 I/4	50°12′	105°38′
Butts	UNP/LNO	NF		2 D/16	48°49′	54°17′
Butts Lake	LAKE/LAC	NT	Keewatin	55 N	63°43′	92°44′
Butts Pond	LAKE/LAC	NF		2 D/16	48°49′	54°16′
Buzwah	UNP/LNO	ON	Manitoulin	41 H/13	45°45′	81°47′
Buzzard	UNP/LNO	SK	1-47-27-W3	73 F/4	53°01′	109°49′
Byam Channel	CHAN/CHEN	NT	Franklin	78 H	75°15′	105°15′
Byam Martin, Cape	CAPE/CAP	NT	Franklin	38 C	73°29′	77°08′
Byam Martin Channel	CHAN/CHEN	NT	Franklin	79 A	76°15′	105°45′
Byam Martin Island	ISL/ÎLE	NT	Franklin	78 H	75°15′	104°15′
Byam Martin Mountains	MTN/MNT	NT	Franklin	38 C	73°23′	78°35′
Byam River	RIV/CDE	NT	Franklin	78 H/2	75°04′	106°00′
Bydand Bay	BAY/BAIE	NT	Mackenzie	96 F	66°00′	124°55′
Byemoor	UNP/LNO	AB	6-35-16-W4	82 P/16	51°59′	112°17′
Byersville	UNP/LNO	ON	Peterborough	31 D/8	44°17′	78°21′
Bylot	UNP/LNO	MB		54 L/8	58°25′	94°08′
Bylot, Cape	CAPE/CAP	NT	Keewatin	46 F	65°20′	84°08′
Bylot Island	ISL/ÎLE	NT	Franklin	38 C	73°13′	78°34′
Bylot, Lac	LAKE/LAC	QC	Kativik	35 C/16	60°53′	76°23′
Byng	UNP/LNO	ON	Haldimand	30 L/13	42°53′	79°37′
Byng Inlet	UNP/LNO	ON	Parry Sound	41 H/15	45°46′	80°33′
Byng Inlet	BAY/BAIE	ON	Parry Sound	41 H/15	45°46′	80°32′
Byng, Mount	MTN/MNT	YT		105 D/16	60°55′	134°20′
Byrd, Lac	LAKE/LAC	QC	La Vallée-de-la-Gatineau	31 N/2	47°03′	76°53′
Byrnedale	UNP/LNO	ON	Essex	40 J/2	42°15′	82°40′
*Byrne Road	UNP/LNO	BC	New Westminster	92 G/2	49°12′	122°59′
Byrnes Road	UNP/LNO	PE	Kings	11 L/7	46°20′	62°45′
Byron	UNP/LNO	ON	Middlesex	40 I/14	42°57′	81°20′
Byron Bay	BAY/BAIE	NF		13 I/12	54°40′	57°40′
Byron Bay	BAY/BAIE	NT	Franklin	77 B	68°55′	108°30′

C

Caamaño Passage	CHAN/CHEN	BC	Queen Charlotte	103 J/10	54°35′	131°00′
Caamaño Sound	CHAN/CHEN	BC	Range 3 Coast	103 A/13	52°54′	129°22′
Cabana	UNP/LNO	SK	59-16-W3	73 K/1	54°05′	108°15′
Cabanage, Le	UNP/LNO	QC	Le Fjord-du-Saguenay	22 D/1	48°12′	70°09′
Cabane d'Automne, Lac à la	LAKE/LAC	QC	Portneuf	21 M/4	47°10′	71°59′
Cabane-Noire, La	UNP/LNO	QC	Les Îles-de-la-Madeleine	11 N/12	47°33′	61°41′
Cabane-Ronde	UNP/LNO	QC	Les Moulins	31 H/13	45°47′	73°33′
Cabano	CITY/VIL1	QC	Témiscouata	21 N/10	47°41′	68°53′
Cabano, Rivière	RIV/CDE	QC	Témiscouata	21 N/10	47°41′	68°52′
Cabbagetown	UNP/LNO	ON	York	30 M/11	43°40′	79°22′
Cabin Lake	UNP/LNO	AB	20-24-9-W4	72 M/3	51°04′	111°13′
Cabin Lake	LAKE/LAC	MB	12-14-E	52 E/13	50°00′	95°34′
Cabituquimats, Lac	LAKE/LAC	QC	La Haute-Côte-Nord	22 F/12	49°35′	69°32′
Cable Head	CAPE/CAP	PE	Kings	11 L/7	46°28′	62°37′
Cable Head East	UNP/LNO	PE	Kings	11 L/7	46°28′	62°35′

NAME NOM	ENTITY ENTITÉ	LOC 1 LIEU 1	LOC 2 LIEU 2	MAP CARTE	POSITION	
					LAT	LONG
Cable Head West	UNP/LNO	PE	Kings	11 L/7	46°27′	62°38′
Cabonga, Réservoir	LAKE/LAC	QC	Vallée-de-l'Or	31 N/7	47°20′	76°35′
Cabot	UNP/LNO	MB		62 H/13	49°52′	97°35′
Cabot, Détroit de - also-aussi - **Cabot Strait**	CHAN/CHEN	NF/NS		11 O/5	47°21′	59°22′
Cabot Head	CAPE/CAP	ON	Bruce	41 H/3	45°15′	81°17′
Cabot Islands	ISL/ÎLE	NF		2 F/3	49°10′	53°22′
Cabot, Lac	LAKE/LAC	QC	Caniapiscau	23 I/16	54°55′	64°25′
Cabot Lake	LAKE/LAC	NF		14 D/2	56°09′	62°37′
Cabot Strait - also-aussi - **Cabot, Détroit de**	CHAN/CHEN	NF/NS		11 O/5	47°21′	59°22′
Cabri	TOWN/VIL2	SK	20-19-18-W3	72 K/9	50°37′	108°28′
Cabri Lake	LAKE/LAC	SK	24,25-27-W3	72 N/4	51°06′	109°44′
Cacaoni, Lac	LAKE/LAC	QC	Sept-Rivières	22 I/12	50°40′	65°54′
Cacaoui, Lac	LAKE/LAC	QC	Sept-Rivières	22 J/15	50°54′	66°58′
Cache Bay	TOWN/VIL2	ON	Nipissing	31 L/5	46°22′	79°59′
Cache Bay	BAY/BAIE	ON	Nipissing	41 I/8	46°21′	80°00′
Cache-Canada	UNP/LNO	QC	Portneuf	21 M/4	47°11′	71°50′
Cache-Cinq	UNP/LNO	QC	Manicouagan	22 F/8	49°26′	68°00′
Cache Creek	VILG/VILG	BC	Kamloops Division Yale	92 I/14	50°48′	121°19′
Cache Creek	RIV/CDE	AB	100-18-W5	84 F/10	57°39′	116°50′
Cache Creek	RIV/CDE	NT	Mackenzie	106 A	64°39′	129°12′
Cache-Douze	UNP/LNO	QC	Manicouagan	22 G/5	49°24′	67°50′
Cachée, Rivière	RIV/CDE	QC	La Jacques-Cartier	21 M/3	47°07′	71°22′
Cache, La	UNP/LNO	QC	Bonaventure	22 B/8	48°16′	66°03′
Cache, La	UNP/LNO	QC	Rouyn-Noranda	32 D/2	48°03′	78°53′
*Cache Lake	UNP/LNO	ON	Nipissing	31 E/10	45°33′	78°34′
Cache Lake	LAKE/LAC	ON	Nipissing	41 I/8	46°27′	80°06′
Cache Lake	LAKE/LAC	AB	59-12-W4	73 L/4	54°06′	111°47′
Cache Lake	LAKE/LAC	NT	Mackenzie	75 M/3	63°05′	111°24′
Cache Point	CAPE/CAP	NT	Franklin	87 A	68°39′	113°27′
Cache-Quatre	UNP/LNO	QC	Manicouagan	22 G/5	49°23′	67°57′
Cachet	UNP/LNO	ON	York	30 M/14	43°53′	79°21′
Cache-Trois	UNP/LNO	QC	Manicouagan	22 G/5	49°21′	67°50′
Cachette-chez-Ringuette, La	UNP/LNO	QC	Le Domaine-du-Roy	32 A/8	48°22′	72°01′
Cachisca, Lac	LAKE/LAC	QC	Jamésie	32 J/6	50°28′	75°00′
Cacouna 22	IR/RI	QC	Rivière-du-Loup	21 N/13	47°55′	69°31′
Cacouna-Est	UNP/LNO	QC	Rivière-du-Loup	21 N/14	48°00′	69°26′
Cacouna-Station	UNP/LNO	QC	Rivière-du-Loup	21 N/14	47°53′	69°28′
Cacouna-Sud	UNP/LNO	QC	Rivière-du-Loup	21 N/14	47°57′	69°28′
Cactus Lake	HAM/HAM	SK	29-36-27-W3	73 C/4	52°07′	109°49′
Cadboro Bay	UNP/LNO	BC	Victoria	92 B/6	48°28′	123°18′
Cadboro Point	CAPE/CAP	BC	Victoria	92 B/6	48°27′	123°16′
Caddy Lake	UNP/LNO	MB	10-17-E	52 E/14	49°49′	95°14′
Caddy Lake	LAKE/LAC	MB	10-17-E	52 E/14	49°49′	95°13′
Caderette	UNP/LNO	ON	Nipissing	41 I/8	46°23′	80°02′
Cadillac	CITY/VIL1	QC	Rouyn-Noranda	32 D/1	48°14′	78°23′
Cadillac	VILG/VILG	SK	8-9-13-W3	72 G/12	49°44′	107°45′
Cadman Corner	UNP/LNO	NB	Westmorland	21 I/1	46°11′	64°01′
Cadmus	UNP/LNO	ON	Durham	31 D/2	44°07′	78°47′
Cadogan	UNP/LNO	AB	1-39-4-W4	73 D/8	52°19′	110°27′
Cadogan Glacier	GLAC/GLAC	NT	Franklin	39 F	78°14′	77°04′
Cadogan Inlet	BAY/BAIE	NT	Franklin	39 F	78°12′	76°10′
Cadomin	UNP/LNO	AB	5-47-23-W5	83 F/3	53°02′	117°20′
Cadot	UNP/LNO	QC	Montcalm	31 H/13	45°55′	73°42′
Cadotte Lake	UNP/LNO	AB	24-86-16-W5	84 C/8	56°28′	116°22′
Cadotte Lake	LAKE/LAC	AB	86-15,16-W5	84 C/8	56°26′	116°23′
Cadotte River	RIV/CDE	AB	18-89-20-W5	84 C/11	56°43′	117°10′
Cadurcis	UNP/LNO	MB	33,4-14,15-19-W	62 K/1	50°14′	100°01′
Cadwallader Creek	RIV/CDE	BC	Lillooet	92 J/15	50°48′	122°50′
Caen Lake	LAKE/LAC	NT	Mackenzie	85 F	61°39′	116°58′
Caesarea	UNP/LNO	ON	Durham	31 D/2	44°09′	78°50′
Caesars	UNP/LNO	BC	Osoyoos Division Yale	82 L/3	50°04′	119°30′
Café	UNP/LNO	QC	Vallée-de-l'Or	32 C/6	48°25′	77°26′
Cages, Les	UNP/LNO	QC	Rimouski-Neigette	22 C/1	48°01′	68°12′
Cagnet, Cape	CAPE/CAP	NF		2 E/13	49°57′	55°47′
Cahill	UNP/LNO	NB	York	21 J/3	46°08′	67°08′
Cahill Point	UNP/LNO	NF		1 N/10	47°34′	52°41′
Cahilty	UNP/LNO	BC	Kamloops Division Yale	92 I/16	50°57′	120°01′
Cahoose 8	IR/RI	BC	Range 3 Coast	93 C/13	52°53′	125°42′
Cahoose 10	IR/RI	BC	Range 3 Coast	93 C/13	52°52′	125°38′
Cahoose 12	IR/RI	BC	Range 3 Coast	93 C/13	52°54′	125°39′
Cahore	UNP/LNO	ON	Stormont	31 G/3	45°11′	75°12′
Cailleteau, Lac	LAKE/LAC	QC	Caniapiscau	23 B/3	52°05′	67°27′
Caillet, Rivière	RIV/CDE	QC	Jamésie	33 E/10	53°33′	78°53′
Caillou-du-Pied-de-Saint-Roch, Le	UNP/LNO	QC	L'Île-d'Orléans	21 L/14	46°51′	71°08′
Cails Mills	UNP/LNO	NB	Kent	21 I/6	46°29′	65°09′

NAME NOM	ENTITY ENTITÉ	LOC 1 LIEU 1	LOC 2 LIEU 2	MAP CARTE	POSITION LAT	LONG
Cains Island	UNP/LNO	NF		11 O/10	47°36′	58°42′
Cains Mountain	UNP/LNO	NS	Victoria	11 F/15	45°58′	60°55′
Cains Point	UNP/LNO	NB	Northumberland	21 P/6	47°20′	65°06′
Cains River	RIV/CDE	NB	Northumberland	21 I/12	46°40′	65°47′
Cainsville	UNP/LNO	ON	Brant	40 P/1	43°09′	80°12′
Caintown	UNP/LNO	ON	Leeds	31 B/12	44°32′	75°53′
Cairn-de-Glengarry, Lieu historique national du - also-aussi - Glengarry Cairn National Historic Site	PARK/PARC	ON	Glengarry	31 G/1	45°07′	74°29′
Cairnes, Mount	MTN/MNT	YT		115 B/16	60°52′	138°17′
Cairngorm	UNP/LNO	ON	Middlesex	40 I/13	42°54′	81°40′
Cairn, Île	ISL/ÎLE	QC	Kativik	34 C/1	56°08′	76°17′
Cairn Needle	MTN/MNT	BC	New Westminster	92 H/13	49°49′	121°59′
Cairns	UNP/LNO	AB	8-39-4-W4	73 D/7	52°21′	110°33′
Cairns Lake	LAKE/LAC	ON	Kenora	52 M/10	51°43′	94°30′
Cairns Lake	LAKE/LAC	SK		64 E/11	57°39′	103°19′
Cairo	UNP/LNO	ON	Lambton	40 I/12	42°42′	81°54′
Cairo, Cape	CAPE/CAP	NT	Franklin	69 F/16	78°50′	100°21′
Caissie Cape - also-aussi - Cap-des-Caissie	UNP/LNO	NB	Kent	21 I/7	46°20′	64°32′
Caissie-Village	UNP/LNO	NB	Kent	21 I/10	46°34′	64°45′
Caistor Centre	UNP/LNO	ON	Lincoln	30 M/4	43°04′	79°39′
Caistorville	UNP/LNO	ON	Lincoln	30 M/4	43°03′	79°44′
Caithness	UNP/LNO	NB	Charlotte	21 G/2	45°07′	66°50′
Caithness	UNP/LNO	BC	Kootenay	82 G/6	49°19′	115°10′
Calabogie	UNP/LNO	ON	Renfrew	31 F/7	45°18′	76°43′
Calabogie Lake	LAKE/LAC	ON	Renfrew	31 F/7	45°16′	76°45′
Calahoo	UNP/LNO	AB	31-54-27-W4	83 H/12	53°43′	113°58′
Calais Lake	LAKE/LAC	NT	Mackenzie	85 F	61°32′	116°45′
Calamity Corners	UNP/LNO	ON	Middlesex	40 P/3	43°02′	81°17′
Calcaire, Chute du	FALL/CHUT	QC	Kativik	24 F/6	57°29′	69°19′
Calder	VILG/VILG	SK	15,16-25-31-W	62 N/4	51°09′	101°45′
Calderbank	UNP/LNO	SK	23-19-7-W3	72 J/10	50°37′	106°51′
Calder Lake	LAKE/LAC	ON	Rainy River	52 C/13	48°57′	93°32′
Calder, Mount	MTN/MNT	BC	New Westminster	92 G/13	49°52′	123°59′
Calder No. 241	MUN2/AZM2	SK		62 N/4	51°15′	101°50′
Calder River	RIV/CDE	SK/AB		73 N/4	55°01′	109°45′
Calder River	RIV/CDE	NT	Mackenzie	86 F	65°34′	117°37′
Calders Dock	UNP/LNO	MB	17-30-6-E	62 P/10	51°34′	96°44′
Calderwood	UNP/LNO	ON	Grey	41 A/2	44°01′	80°52′
Caldwell	MUN2/AZM2	ON	Nipissing	41 I/8	46°22′	80°06′
Caldwell	UNP/LNO	NB	Victoria	21 O/4	47°04′	67°42′
Caldwell	UNP/LNO	QC	Pontiac	31 F/9	45°35′	76°25′
Cale	UNP/LNO	BC	Cariboo	93 G/10	53°45′	122°40′
Cale-à-Ben, La	UNP/LNO	QC	Les Îles-de-la-Madeleine	11 N/12	47°34′	61°31′
Cale-à-Fatima, La	UNP/LNO	QC	Les Îles-de-la-Madeleine	11 N/12	47°33′	61°33′
Cale-à-Will, La	UNP/LNO	QC	Les Îles-de-la-Madeleine	11 N/12	47°33′	61°33′
Caledon	TOWN/VIL2	ON	Peel	30 M/13	43°52′	79°51′
Caledon East	UNP/LNO	ON	Peel	30 M/13	43°52′	79°52′
Caledonia	MUN2/AZM2	ON	Prescott	31 G/7	45°28′	74°47′
Caledonia	UNP/LNO	PE	Queens	11 L/2	46°04′	62°43′
Caledonia	UNP/LNO	NS	Cape Breton	11 J/4	46°11′	59°57′
Caledonia	UNP/LNO	NS	Guysborough	11 E/8	45°17′	62°23′
Caledonia	UNP/LNO	NS	Queens	21 A/6	44°22′	65°02′
Caledonia	UNP/LNO	ON	Haldimand	30 M/4	43°04′	79°56′
Caledonia, Cape	CAPE/CAP	NT	Franklin	79 B	76°33′	108°29′
Caledonia Front	UNP/LNO	ON	Prescott	31 G/10	45°32′	74°44′
Caledonia Junction	UNP/LNO	NS	Lunenburg	21 A/10	44°32′	64°42′
Caledonia Mills	UNP/LNO	NS	Antigonish	11 F/5	45°30′	61°49′
Caledonia Mountain	UNP/LNO	NB	Albert	21 H/15	45°51′	64°48′
Caledonia No. 99	MUN2/AZM2	SK		72 H/15	49°55′	104°35′
Caledonia Springs	UNP/LNO	ON	Prescott	31 G/10	45°33′	74°48′
Caledon Mountain	MTN/MNT	ON	Peel	30 M/13	43°51′	79°59′
Caledon Village	UNP/LNO	ON	Peel	30 M/13	43°52′	80°00′
Calf Island	ISL/ÎLE	NT	Franklin	59 A	76°27′	89°30′
Calgary	CITY/VIL1	AB	24-1-W5	82 O/1	51°03′	114°05′
Calhoun	UNP/LNO	NB	Westmorland	21 I/2	46°04′	64°35′
Calhoun Lake	LAKE/LAC	NT	Keewatin	65 F	61°20′	100°27′
Caliento	UNP/LNO	MB	14-2-8-E	62 H/1	49°08′	96°25′
California	UNP/LNO	ON	Leeds	31 C/9	44°33′	76°16′
California	UNP/LNO	ON	Lanark	31 F/1	45°13′	76°29′
Californie	UNP/LNO	QC	D'Autray	31 I/6	46°21′	73°14′
Caliper Lake	UNP/LNO	ON	Rainy River	52 F/4	49°04′	93°54′
Caliper Lake	LAKE/LAC	ON	Rainy River	52 F/4	49°03′	93°55′
Calixa-Lavallée	VILG/VILG	QC	Lajemmerais	31 H/11	45°45′	73°17′
Callaghan Creek	RIV/CDE	BC	New Westminster	92 J/3	50°03′	123°06′
Callaghan Lake	LAKE/LAC	BC	New Westminster	92 J/3	50°12′	123°11′
Callaghan, Mount	MTN/MNT	BC	New Westminster	92 J/3	50°14′	123°16′

NAME NOM	ENTITY ENTITÉ	LOC 1 LIEU 1	LOC 2 LIEU 2	MAP CARTE	POSITION LAT	LONG
Callander	UNP/LNO	ON	Parry Sound	31 L/3	46°13′	79°22′
Calley	UNP/LNO	SK	32-25-3-W2	62 M/1	51°12′	102°24′
Calling Lake	UNP/LNO	AB	20-72-21-W4	83 P/3	55°15′	113°12′
Calling Lake	LAKE/LAC	AB	72-22-W4	83 P/3	55°15′	113°20′
Calling Lake	LAKE/LAC	BC	Kamloops Division Yale	92 I/6	50°28′	121°06′
Calling Lake Provincial Park	PARK/PARC	AB	71-21-W4	83 P/3	55°10′	113°16′
Calling River	UNP/LNO	AB	30-70-19-W4	83 P/2	55°05′	112°53′
Calling River	RIV/CDE	AB	30-70-19-W4	83 P/2	55°05′	112°53′
Call Inlet	BAY/BAIE	BC	Range 1 Coast	92 L/9	50°37′	126°05′
Callison Ranch	UNP/LNO	BC	Cassiar	104 J/12	58°38′	131°41′
Call's Mills	UNP/LNO	QC	Brome-Missisquoi	31 H/2	45°11′	72°37′
Callum	UNP/LNO	ON	Sudbury	41 I/10	46°31′	80°38′
Calmar	TOWN/VIL2	AB	25-49-27-W4	83 H/5	53°16′	113°49′
Calm Channel	CHAN/CHEN	BC	Range 1 Coast	92 K/6	50°19′	125°05′
Calme, Lac	LAKE/LAC	QC	Kativik	35 B/9	60°32′	74°15′
Calmer	UNP/LNO	NF		1 L/13	46°54′	55°54′
Calm Lake	UNP/LNO	ON	Rainy River	52 C/9	48°45′	92°10′
Calm Lake	LAKE/LAC	ON	Rainy River	52 C/16	48°46′	92°04′
Calmus Passage	CHAN/CHEN	BC	Clayoquot	92 E/1	49°13′	126°00′
Calong	UNP/LNO	ON	Thunder Bay	42 E/15	49°46′	86°32′
Calrin	UNP/LNO	MB		62 H/14	49°50′	97°28′
Calstock	UNP/LNO	ON	Cochrane	42 F/16	49°47′	84°09′
Calthorpe	UNP/LNO	AB	13-31-2-W4	72 M/9	51°40′	110°08′
Calthorpe Islands	ISL/ÎLE	NT	Franklin	47 D	69°28′	80°15′
Calton	UNP/LNO	ON	Elgin	40 I/10	42°43′	80°52′
Calumet	TOWN/VIL2	QC	Argenteuil	31 G/10	45°39′	74°39′
Calumet	UNP/LNO	YT		105 M/14	63°55′	135°23′
Calvaire, Le	UNP/LNO	QC	Communauté urbaine de Québec	21 L/11	46°44′	71°25′
Calvaire, Le	UNP/LNO	QC	Bécancour	31 I/9	46°33′	72°05′
Calvert	UNP/LNO	NF		1 N/2	47°03′	52°55′
Calvert, Cape	CAPE/CAP	BC	Range 2 Coast	92 M/5	51°25′	127°54′
Calvert Island	ISL/ÎLE	BC	Range 2 Coast	102 P/9	51°35′	128°03′
Calves Nose	CAPE/CAP	NF		2 C/11	48°37′	53°26′
Calvin	MUN2/AZM2	ON	Nipissing	31 L/2	46°14′	78°55′
Calvin Park	UNP/LNO	ON	Frontenac	31 C/2	44°14′	76°31′
Calway	UNP/LNO	QC	Robert-Cliche	21 L/7	46°16′	70°49′
Calway, Rivière	RIV/CDE	QC	Robert-Cliche	21 L/7	46°16′	70°50′
Camachigama, Lac	LAKE/LAC	QC	Vallée-de-l'Or	31 N/16	47°50′	76°20′
Camachigama, Rivière	RIV/CDE	QC	Vallée-de-l'Or	31 N/10	47°40′	76°32′
Cambie	UNP/LNO	BC	Kamloops Division Yale	82 L/15	50°54′	118°52′
Camborne	UNP/LNO	ON	Northumberland	31 D/1	44°02′	78°14′
Camborne	UNP/LNO	BC	Kootenay	82 K/13	50°47′	117°38′
Cambray	UNP/LNO	ON	Peterborough	31 D/7	44°25′	78°50′
Cambria	UNP/LNO	AB	15-28-19-W4	82 P/7	51°24′	112°36′
Cambria Icefield	GLAC/GLAC	BC	Cassiar	103 P/13	55°48′	129°40′
Cambrian Heights	UNP/LNO	ON	Sudbury	41 I/10	46°31′	80°59′
Cambria No. 6	MUN2/AZM2	SK		62 E/3	49°10′	103°25′
Cambridge	CITY/VIL1	ON	Waterloo	40 P/8	43°23′	80°19′
Cambridge	MUN2/AZM2	ON	Russell	31 G/6	45°19′	75°07′
Cambridge	UNP/LNO	PE	Kings	11 L/2	46°04′	62°31′
Cambridge	UNP/LNO	NS	Hants	21 H/1	45°12′	64°07′
Cambridge	UNP/LNO	NS	Kings	21 H/2	45°04′	64°38′
Cambridge	GEOG/GÉOG	NB	Queens	21 G/16	45°50′	66°02′
Cambridge 32	IR/RI	NS	Kings	21 H/2	45°04′	64°39′
Cambridge Bay	HAM/HAM	NT	Franklin	77 D/2	69°07′	105°03′
Cambridge Bay	BAY/BAIE	NT	Franklin	77 D	69°03′	105°07′
Cambridge Fiord	BAY/BAIE	NT	Franklin	37 H	71°26′	74°45′
Cambridge Forest Estates	UNP/LNO	ON	Russell	31 G/6	45°21′	75°15′
Cambridge-Narrows	VILG/VILG	NB	Queens	21 H/13	45°50′	65°57′
Cambrien, Lac	LAKE/LAC	QC	Kativik	24 C/6	56°23′	69°07′
Cam, Cape	CAPE/CAP	NT	Franklin	98 H	75°49′	120°16′
Camden	MUN2/AZM2	ON	Kent	40 J/9	42°35′	82°05′
Camden	UNP/LNO	NS	Colchester	11 E/6	45°19′	63°12′
Camden East	MUN2/AZM2	ON	Lennox and Addington	31 C/7	44°24′	76°55′
Camden East	UNP/LNO	ON	Lennox and Addington	31 C/7	44°20′	76°50′
Camden Lake	LAKE/LAC	ON	Lennox and Addington	31 C/7	44°25′	76°52′
Camel Back Mountain	MTN/MNT	NB	Restigouche	21 O/9	47°32′	66°24′
Camel Chute	UNP/LNO	ON	Renfrew	31 F/3	45°11′	77°07′
Camelot Beach	UNP/LNO	ON	Welland	30 L/14	42°53′	79°18′
Camelsfoot Range	MTN/MNT	BC	Lillooet	92 O/1	51°08′	122°17′
Cameo	UNP/LNO	SK	49-4-W3	73 G/2	53°15′	106°32′
Cameron - see-voir - Papineau-Cameron	MUN2/AZM2	ON		31 L/2	46°14′	78°34′
Cameron	MUN2/AZM2	MB		62 F/7	49°25′	100°35′
Cameron	UNP/LNO	ON	Peterborough	31 D/8	44°19′	78°06′
Cameron	UNP/LNO	ON	Victoria	31 D/7	44°26′	78°46′

NAME NOM	ENTITY ENTITÉ	LOC 1 LIEU 1	LOC 2 LIEU 2	MAP CARTE	POSITION LAT	LONG
Cameron	UNP/LNO	MB	31-1-27-W	62 F/3	49°05'	101°05'
Cameron Bar 13	IR/RI	BC	Kamloops Division Yale	92 I/5	50°22'	121°41'
Cameron Bay	BAY/BAIE	NT	Franklin	69 B	76°32'	103°23'
Cameron Beach	UNP/LNO	NS	Cumberland	11 E/13	45°52'	63°44'
Cameron Canyon	SEAU/SMER	—		8010	43°00'	49°35'
Cameron Falls	UNP/LNO	ON	Thunder Bay	52 H/1	49°09'	88°21'
Cameron Heights	UNP/LNO	BC	Alberni	92 F/2	49°13'	124°48'
Cameron Hills	UNP/LNO	NT	Mackenzie	85 C	60°00'	116°59'
Cameron Hills	MTN/MNT	AB/NT		84 M/16	59°54'	117°46'
Cameron Island	ISL/ÎLE	NT	Franklin	69 B	76°30'	103°50'
Cameron Island Rise	SEAU/SMER	—		7951	76°45'	105°40'
Cameron Lake	UNP/LNO	NS	Hants	11 D/13	44°56'	63°55'
Cameron Lake	UNP/LNO	BC	Cameron	92 F/7	49°17'	124°35'
Cameron Lake	LAKE/LAC	ON	Victoria	31 D/10	44°33'	78°46'
Cameron Lake	LAKE/LAC	ON	Algoma	42 F/1	49°01'	84°17'
Cameron Lake	LAKE/LAC	ON	Kenora	52 F/5	49°16'	93°42'
Cameron Lake	LAKE/LAC	BC	Cameron	92 F/7	49°18'	124°37'
Cameron Land District	GEOG/GÉOG	BC		92 F	49°15'	124°32'
Cameron, Mount	MTN/MNT	BC	Cassiar	104 M/8	59°24'	134°05'
Cameron River	RIV/CDE	BC	Peace River	94 A/5	56°23'	121°40'
Cameron River	RIV/CDE	BC	Alberni	92 F/7	49°18'	124°39'
Cameron River	RIV/CDE	NT	Mackenzie	85 J	62°35'	114°09'
Cameron River	RIV/CDE	NT	Mackenzie	85 C	60°26'	117°28'
Cameron Settlement	UNP/LNO	NS	Guysborough	11 E/8	45°17'	62°27'
Camerons Mill	UNP/LNO	NB	Kent	21 I/11	46°41'	65°07'
Camerons Mountain	UNP/LNO	NS	Richmond	11 F/11	45°41'	61°02'
Camerons Point	UNP/LNO	ON	Glengarry	31 G/2	45°05'	74°32'
Camilla	UNP/LNO	ON	Dufferin	41 A/1	44°00'	80°07'
Camille-Pouliot, Mont	MTN/MNT	QC	La Côte-de-Beaupré	21 M/11	47°34'	71°14'
Camlachie	UNP/LNO	ON	Lambton	40 O/1	43°02'	82°09'
Camlaren	UNP/LNO	NT	Mackenzie	85 I/14	62°59'	113°12'
Camousitchouane, Lac	LAKE/LAC	QC	Jamésie	32 O/3	51°05'	75°25'
Camp Acouchiching	UNP/LNO	ON	Nipissing	41 I/16	46°51'	80°04'
Camp Agamik	UNP/LNO	ON	Nipissing	41 I/16	46°55'	80°01'
Campania	UNP/LNO	ON	Dufferin	40 P/16	43°59'	80°18'
Campania Island	ISL/ÎLE	BC	Range 4 Coast	103 A/14	53°05'	129°25'
Camp Artaban	UNP/LNO	BC	New Westminster	92 G/6	49°29'	123°21'
Camp Bay	UNP/LNO	NF		3 D/4	52°10'	55°39'
Camp-Beauregard, Le	UNP/LNO	QC	La Vallée-de-la-Gatineau	31 J/13	46°50'	75°48'
Campbell	UNP/LNO	AB	24,25,26-17-13-W4	72 L/5	50°29'	111°40'
Campbell	UNP/LNO	AB	12-54-25-W4	83 H/12	53°38'	113°34'
Campbell Bay	BAY/BAIE	NT	Franklin	67 B	68°08'	104°00'
Campbell Corners	UNP/LNO	QC	Brome-Missisquoi	31 H/2	45°03'	72°58'
Campbell Creek	UNP/LNO	BC	Kamloops Division Yale	92 I/9	50°39'	120°05'
Campbell Creek	RIV/CDE	BC	Kamloops Division Yale	92 I/9	50°39'	120°05'
Campbell Creek Junction - see-voir - Campbell Creek	UNP/LNO	BC		92 I/9	50°39'	120°05'
Campbellcroft	UNP/LNO	ON	Durham	31 D/1	44°04'	78°22'
Campbelldale	UNP/LNO	NS	Cape Breton	11 F/16	45°54'	60°15'
Campbellford	TOWN/VIL2	ON	Northumberland	31 C/5	44°18'	77°48'
Campbell Island	UNP/LNO	BC	Range 3 Coast	103 A/1	52°10'	128°09'
Campbell Island	ISL/ÎLE	BC	Range 3 Coast	103 A/1	52°07'	128°12'
Campbell Island	ISL/ÎLE	NT	Mackenzie	107 D	69°35'	130°44'
Campbell Lake	LAKE/LAC	MB		64 A/11	56°33'	97°17'
Campbell Lake	LAKE/LAC	SK	4-51-16-W2	73 H/8	53°22'	104°18'
Campbell Lake	LAKE/LAC	SK		73 P/13	55°46'	105°30'
Campbell Lake	LAKE/LAC	BC	Kamloops Division Yale	92 I/9	50°33'	120°06'
Campbell Lake	LAKE/LAC	BC	Sayward	92 K/3	50°01'	125°27'
Campbell Lake	LAKE/LAC	NT	Mackenzie	75 O	63°14'	106°55'
Campbell Lake	LAKE/LAC	NT	Mackenzie	107 B	68°13'	133°27'
Campbell Maxwell Front	UNP/LNO	ON	Frontenac	31 C/8	44°18'	76°15'
Campbell Park	UNP/LNO	AB	4-12-54-24-W4	83 H/12	53°39'	113°34'
Campbell Point	CAPE/CAP	ON	Thunder Bay	42 D/9	48°35'	86°18'
Campbell Range	MTN/MNT	YT		105 H/4	61°15'	129°45'
Campbell River	MUN1/AZM1	BC	Sayward	92 K/3	50°01'	125°15'
Campbell River	RIV/CDE	BC	New Westminster	92 G/2	49°01'	122°47'
Campbell River 11	IR/RI	BC	Sayward	92 K/3	50°02'	125°15'
Campbell's Bay	TOWN/VIL2	QC	Pontiac	31 F/10	45°44'	76°36'
Campbells Beach	UNP/LNO	ON	Victoria	31 D/11	44°37'	79°07'
Campbell's Corner	UNP/LNO	QC	L'Érable	21 L/6	46°17'	71°30'
Campbells Corners	UNP/LNO	ON	Grenville	31 B/13	44°55'	75°34'
Campbells Cove	UNP/LNO	PE	Kings	11 L/8	46°29'	62°08'
Campbells Creek	UNP/LNO	NF		12 B/10	48°31'	58°52'
Campbells Cross	UNP/LNO	ON	Peel	30 M/13	43°47'	79°52'
Campbell Settlement	UNP/LNO	NB	Kings	21 H/12	45°36'	65°32'
Campbell Settlement	UNP/LNO	NB	York	21 J/3	46°01'	67°21'

NAME / NOM	ENTITY / ENTITÉ	LOC 1 / LIEU 1	LOC 2 / LIEU 2	MAP / CARTE	POSITION LAT	POSITION LONG
Campbell Settlement	UNP/LNO	NB	Carleton	21 J/4	46°08′	67°43′
Campbells Mountain	UNP/LNO	NS	Inverness	11 K/3	46°01′	61°13′
Campbells Siding	UNP/LNO	NS	Colchester	11 E/7	45°27′	62°59′
Campbellton	CITY/VIL1	NB	Restigouche	21 O/15	48°00′	66°40′
Campbellton	TOWN/VIL2	NF		2 E/7	49°17′	54°56′
Campbellton	UNP/LNO	PE	Queens	11 L/6	46°29′	63°29′
Campbellton	UNP/LNO	PE	Prince	21 I/16	46°47′	64°18′
Campbellton	UNP/LNO	ON	Elgin	40 I/12	42°41′	81°35′
Campbellton	UNP/LNO	BC	Sayward	92 K/3	50°02′	125°16′
Campbellton Road	UNP/LNO	NS	Inverness	11 K/3	46°15′	61°15′
Campbelltown	UNP/LNO	ON	Peterborough	31 D/1	44°13′	78°14′
Campbellville	UNP/LNO	ON	Halton	30 M/5	43°29′	79°59′
Camp Bigwee	UNP/LNO	ON	Nipissing	41 P/1	47°01′	80°07′
Camp Boggy	UNP/LNO	NF		1 M/13	47°59′	55°48′
Camp Cayuga	UNP/LNO	ON	Nipissing	41 P/1	47°01′	80°07′
Camp Champlain	UNP/LNO	ON	Nipissing	31 L/6	46°19′	79°18′
Camp Chimo	UNP/LNO	ON	Nipissing	41 I/16	46°55′	80°05′
Camp-C.I.P.	UNP/LNO	QC	Témiscamingue	31 M/9	47°40′	78°04′
Camp Cochrane	UNP/LNO	ON	Nipissing	41 I/16	46°54′	80°05′
Camp-Comfort	UNP/LNO	QC	L'Amiante	21 E/14	45°49′	71°24′
Camp Creek	UNP/LNO	AB	6-61-4-W5	83 J/7	54°15′	114°35′
Camp-Cyprès	UNP/LNO	QC	Matawinie	31 J/9	46°36′	74°10′
Campden	UNP/LNO	ON	Lincoln	30 M/3	43°08′	79°26′
Camp Dundurn	UNP/LNO	SK	33-4-W3	72 O/15	51°51′	106°34′
Camp-du-Prospecteur, Le	UNP/LNO	QC	Lac-Saint-Jean-Est	22 D/12	48°41′	71°55′
Camp-du-Vieillard, Le	UNP/LNO	QC	Denis-Riverin	22 H/4	49°00′	65°52′
Camper	UNP/LNO	MB	17-24-6-W	62 O/1	51°04′	98°16′
Camperdown	UNP/LNO	NS	Lunenburg	21 A/7	44°16′	64°36′
Camperdown	UNP/LNO	ON	Grey	41 A/9	44°32′	80°24′
Camperville	UNP/LNO	MB	35-19-W	62 N/16	51°59′	100°09′
Camp Farewell	UNP/LNO	NT	Mackenzie	107 C	69°17′	134°55′
Camp-Faribault, Le	UNP/LNO	QC	Matane	22 B/15	48°48′	66°32′
Camp Gagetown	UNP/LNO	NB	Sunbury	21 G/16	45°51′	66°27′
Camp-Garde-Feu, Le	UNP/LNO	QC	Vallée-de-l'Or	31 M/9	47°44′	78°03′
Camp Harmony	UNP/LNO	NB	Restigouche	21 O/15	47°53′	66°57′
Camping Islands	ISL/ÎLE	MB		63 C/8	52°16′	100°07′
Camp-Isaac	UNP/LNO	QC	Témiscamingue	31 M/9	47°42′	78°11′
Camp-Johnson, Le	UNP/LNO	QC	La Côte-de-Gaspé	22 A/14	48°55′	65°17′
Camp Kagawong	UNP/LNO	ON	Victoria	31 D/10	44°33′	78°50′
Camp Kenda	UNP/LNO	ON	Sudbury	41 P/13	47°50′	81°53′
Camp Kenogaming	UNP/LNO	ON	Sudbury	41 P/13	47°58′	81°57′
Camp Ketchini	UNP/LNO	ON	Sudbury	41 P/13	47°52′	81°54′
Camp Lake	LAKE/LAC	ON	Thunder Bay	52 B/9	48°45′	90°25′
Camp-Marcel	UNP/LNO	QC	Matawinie	31 I/4	46°14′	73°39′
Camp McKinney	UNP/LNO	BC	Similkameen Division Yale	82 E/3	49°07′	119°11′
Camp-Mercier	UNP/LNO	QC	La Côte-de-Beaupré	21 M/3	47°14′	71°13′
Camp-Michaud	UNP/LNO	QC	Antoine-Labelle	31 J/13	46°58′	75°46′
Camp Morton	UNP/LNO	MB	8-20-4-E	62 I/10	50°43′	96°59′
Camp-Nector, Le	UNP/LNO	QC	Matane	22 B/15	48°55′	66°43′
Campobello	GEOG/GÉOG	NB	Charlotte	21 B/15	44°53′	66°52′
Campobello Island	ISL/ÎLE	NB	Charlotte	21 B/15	44°53′	66°55′
Camp Oconto	UNP/LNO	ON	Frontenac	31 C/10	44°41′	76°41′
Camp-Ouareau	UNP/LNO	QC	Matawinie	31 J/8	46°15′	74°07′
Camp-Quatre, Le	UNP/LNO	QC	Denis-Riverin	22 H/4	49°08′	65°44′
Camp-Quatre, Le	UNP/LNO	QC	Témiscamingue	31 L/15	46°48′	78°38′
Camp Robinson	UNP/LNO	ON	Kenora	52 K/3	50°08′	93°13′
Campsall Lake	LAKE/LAC	NT	Franklin	78 A	72°32′	106°51′
Campsie	UNP/LNO	AB	26-59-5-W5	83 J/2	54°08′	114°39′
Camp-Trente-Cinq, Le	UNP/LNO	QC	Témiscamingue	31 L/10	46°36′	78°33′
Camp-Trente-Neuf, Le	UNP/LNO	QC	Pabok	22 A/10	48°41′	64°55′
Camp-Trente-Six, Le	UNP/LNO	QC	Pabok	22 A/10	48°33′	64°47′
Camp-Vingt-Cinq, Le	UNP/LNO	QC	Témiscamingue	31 L/10	46°39′	78°40′
Camp Wanapitei	UNP/LNO	ON	Nipissing	41 P/1	47°10′	80°04′
Camp Wegesegum	UNP/LNO	NB	Queens	21 I/4	46°08′	65°56′
Camp White Bear	UNP/LNO	ON	Nipissing	41 I/16	46°53′	80°09′
Camp Whitney	UNP/LNO	MB	31-64-28-W	63 K/12	54°36′	101°41′
Camp Wigwasati	UNP/LNO	ON	Nipissing	41 I/16	46°55′	80°08′
Camrose	CITY/VIL1	AB	46,47-20-W4	83 H/2	53°01′	112°50′
Camrose No. 22, County of	MUN1/AZM1	AB	45-20-W4	83 A/12	52°54′	112°44′
Camsell Bay	BAY/BAIE	NT	Franklin	26 K	66°28′	69°40′
Camsell Bend	RIVF/EFLV	NT	Mackenzie	95 J/6	62°17′	123°22′
Camsell Lake	LAKE/LAC	NT	Mackenzie	75 M	63°35′	111°15′
Camsell Lake 30	IR/RI	BC	Range 5 Coast	93 K/10	54°31′	124°51′
Camsell, Mount	MTN/MNT	NT	Mackenzie	95 J	62°15′	123°29′
Camsell Portage	HAM/HAM	SK		74 N/11	59°37′	109°15′

NAME NOM	ENTITY ENTITÉ	LOC 1 LIEU 1	LOC 2 LIEU 2	MAP CARTE	POSITION LAT	LONG
Camsell Range	MTN/MNT	NT	Mackenzie	95 J/12	62°35′	123°50′
Camsell River	RIV/CDE	NT	Mackenzie	86 E	65°40′	118°07′
Cana	UNP/LNO	SK	9-22-5-W2	62 L/15	50°53′	102°39′
Canaan	UNP/LNO	NS	Lunenburg	21 A/9	44°41′	64°14′
Canaan	UNP/LNO	NS	Kings	21 H/1	45°02′	64°29′
Canaan	UNP/LNO	NS	Yarmouth	20 P/13	43°58′	65°52′
Canaan	UNP/LNO	NB	Westmorland	21 I/6	46°15′	65°04′
Canaan	UNP/LNO	ON	Russell	31 G/6	45°27′	75°18′
Canaan Forks	UNP/LNO	NB	Queens	21 I/4	46°03′	65°33′
Canaan No. 225	MUN2/AZM2	SK		72 J/14	50°55′	107°10′
Canaan Rapids	UNP/LNO	NB	Queens	21 H/13	45°56′	65°45′
Canaan River	RIV/CDE	NB	Queens	21 H/13	45°55′	65°47′
Canaan Road	UNP/LNO	NB	Kings	21 I/3	46°02′	65°21′
Canada Abyssal Plain	SEAU/SMER	—		897	78°00′	150°00′
Canada Basin - also-aussi - Canada, Bassin	SEAU/SMER	—		800A	78°00′	144°00′
Canada, Bassin - also-aussi - Canada Basin	SEAU/SMER	—		800A	78°00′	144°00′
Canada Bay	BAY/BAIE	NF		12 I/9	50°43′	56°08′
Canada Creek	UNP/LNO	NS	Kings	21 H/2	45°10′	64°45′
Canada Harbour	UNP/LNO	NF		12 I/9	50°41′	56°08′
Canada Hill Lake	LAKE/LAC	NS	Shelburne	20 P/14	43°49′	65°08′
Canada Point	CAPE/CAP	NT	Franklin	48 D	73°17′	80°46′
Canadian Heights	UNP/LNO	NB	Westmorland	21 I/2	46°07′	64°50′
Cana Junction	UNP/LNO	SK	28-22-6-W2	62 L/15	50°55′	102°47′
Canal	UNP/LNO	NB	Charlotte	21 G/2	45°10′	66°50′
Canal	UNP/LNO	ON	Muskoka	31 E/6	45°20′	79°08′
Canal Bay	BAY/BAIE	ON	Kenora	52 F/11	49°30′	93°25′
Canal Flats	UNP/LNO	BC	Kootenay	82 J/4	50°09′	115°49′
Canal Lake	LAKE/LAC	ON	Victoria	31 D/11	44°34′	79°03′
Cananée, Lac	LAKE/LAC	QC	Kativik	24 A/1	56°04′	64°10′
Cana No. 214	MUN2/AZM2	SK		62 M/2	51°00′	102°40′
Canard	UNP/LNO	NS	Kings	21 H/1	45°08′	64°26′
Canard, Lac au	LAKE/LAC	QC	Arthabaska	21 E/13	45°48′	71°31′
Canard River	RIV/CDE	ON	Essex	40 J/3	42°09′	83°06′
Canards, Lac aux	LAKE/LAC	QC	Charlevoix-Est	21 N/13	47°59′	69°57′
Canards, Lac aux	LAKE/LAC	QC	Bellechasse	21 L/15	46°50′	70°49′
Canavoy	UNP/LNO	PE	Kings	11 L/7	46°24′	62°49′
Canborough	UNP/LNO	ON	Haldimand	30 L/13	42°59′	79°41′
Candiac	CITY/VIL1	QC	Roussillon	31 H/5	45°23′	73°31′
Candiac	HAM/HAM	SK	35-14-10-W2	62 L/3	50°13′	103°15′
Candle Lake	VILG/VILG	SK	18-55-22-W2	73 H/11	53°45′	105°15′
Candle Lake	LAKE/LAC	SK		73 H/14	53°50′	105°18′
Cando	VILG/VILG	SK	22-39-16-W3	73 C/8	52°23′	108°14′
Candyville	UNP/LNO	ON	Elgin	40 I/10	42°42′	80°59′
Cane	UNP/LNO	ON	Timiskaming	41 P/9	47°38′	80°04′
Canfield	UNP/LNO	ON	Haldimand	30 L/13	42°58′	79°45′
Canfield Junction	UNP/LNO	ON	Haldimand	30 L/13	42°58′	79°44′
Canford	UNP/LNO	BC	Kamloops Division Yale	92 I/2	50°09′	121°00′
Caniapiscau	MUN1/AZM1	QC	Caniapiscau	23 B/14	52°47′	67°05′
Caniapiscau	MUN2/AZM2	QC	Caniapiscau	23 K/13	54°52′	69°55′
Caniapiscau	UNP/LNO	QC	Caniapiscau	23 K/13	54°52′	69°55′
Caniapiscau, Lac	LAKE/LAC	QC	Caniapiscau	23 K/4	54°10′	69°50′
Caniapiscau, Réservoir de	LAKE/LAC	QC	Jamésie	23 K/4	54°10′	69°50′
Caniapiscau, Rivière	RIV/CDE	QC	Kativik	24 F/11	57°40′	69°29′
Canica, Île	ISL/ÎLE	QC	Jamésie	32 F/6	49°21′	77°17′
Canim	UNP/LNO	BC	Lillooet	92 P/11	51°37′	121°17′
Canimina, Lac	LAKE/LAC	QC	Vallée-de-l'Or	31 N/3	47°13′	77°06′
Canim Lake	UNP/LNO	BC	Lillooet	92 P/15	51°46′	120°54′
Canim Lake	LAKE/LAC	BC	Lillooet	92 P/15	51°51′	120°45′
Canim Lake 1	IR/RI	BC	Lillooet	92 P/14	51°47′	121°00′
Canim Lake 2	IR/RI	BC	Lillooet	92 P/11	51°44′	121°08′
Canim Lake 3	IR/RI	BC	Lillooet	92 P/14	51°46′	121°13′
Canim Lake 4	IR/RI	BC	Lillooet	92 P/14	51°48′	121°28′
Canim Lake 5	IR/RI	BC	Lillooet	92 P/15	51°53′	120°38′
Canim Lake 6	IR/RI	BC	Lillooet	92 P/15	51°54′	120°37′
Canimred Creek	RIV/CDE	BC	Lillooet	92 P/15	51°52′	120°38′
Cankerville	UNP/LNO	ON	Northumberland	31 C/4	44°04′	77°46′
Canmore	TOWN/VIL2	AB	32-24-10-W4	82 O/3	51°05′	115°21′
Cann	UNP/LNO	QC	Le Haut-Saint-Maurice	31 P/13	47°54′	73°53′
Cannamore	UNP/LNO	ON	Dundas	31 G/3	45°12′	75°15′
Cannell	UNP/LNO	AB	21-53-25-W4	83 H/12	53°36′	113°37′
Cannes	UNP/LNO	NS	Richmond	11 F/10	45°38′	60°58′
Cannes-de-Roches	UNP/LNO	QC	Pabok	22 A/9	48°33′	64°17′
Cannifton	UNP/LNO	ON	Hastings	31 C/3	44°12′	77°23′
Canning	VILG/VILG	NS	Kings	21 H/1	45°09′	64°25′
Canning	UNP/LNO	ON	Oxford	40 P/1	43°12′	80°28′

NAME NOM	ENTITY ENTITÉ	LOC 1 LIEU 1	LOC 2 LIEU 2	MAP CARTE	POSITION LAT	LONG
Canning	GEOG/GÉOG	NB	Queens	21 G/16	45°56′	66°07′
Canning, Cape	CAPE/CAP	NT	Franklin	89 B	76°25′	118°03′
Canning, Mount	MTN/MNT	BC	Cassiar	104 M/2	59°15′	134°42′
Cannings Brook	RIV/CDE	NF		2 D/12	48°39′	55°32′
Cannings Cove	UNP/LNO	NF		2 C/5	48°27′	53°51′
Cannington	UNP/LNO	ON	Ontario	31 D/6	44°21′	79°02′
Cannington Lake	HAM/HAM	SK	36-9-2-W2	62 E/16	49°47′	102°10′
Cann Island	ISL/ÎLE	NF		2 E/9	49°35′	54°11′
Canobie	UNP/LNO	NB	Gloucester	21 P/11	47°41′	65°22′
Canobie South	UNP/LNO	NB	Gloucester	21 P/11	47°40′	65°20′
Canoe	UNP/LNO	BC	Kamloops Division Yale	82 L/14	50°45′	119°14′
Canoe Cove	UNP/LNO	PE	Queens	11 L/3	46°09′	63°18′
Canoe Creek	RIV/CDE	BC	Lillooet	92 O/8	51°27′	122°14′
Canoe Creek 1	IR/RI	BC	Lillooet	92 O/8	51°28′	122°08′
Canoe Creek 2	IR/RI	BC	Lillooet	92 O/8	51°26′	122°03′
Canoe Creek 3	IR/RI	BC	Lillooet	92 O/9	51°32′	122°15′
Canoe Lake	UNP/LNO	NS	Cape Breton	11 F/16	45°52′	60°13′
Canoe Lake	UNP/LNO	ON	Nipissing	31 E/10	45°34′	78°44′
Canoe Lake	UNP/LNO	SK	70-16-W3	73 N/1	55°06′	108°20′
Canoe Lake	LAKE/LAC	ON	Frontenac	31 C/10	44°35′	76°33′
Canoe Lake	LAKE/LAC	ON	Nipissing	31 E/10	45°33′	78°43′
Canoe Lake	LAKE/LAC	SK		73 N/1	55°10′	108°15′
Canoe Lake	LAKE/LAC	AB	69-3-W4	73 L/16	54°58′	110°23′
Canoe Lake 165	IR/RI	SK		73 N/1	55°07′	108°10′
Canoe Lake 165A	IR/RI	SK		73 N/1	55°08′	108°23′
Canoe Lake 165B	IR/RI	SK		73 N/1	55°11′	108°07′
Canoe Narrows	UNP/LNO	SK	71-14-W3	73 N/1	55°10′	108°09′
Canoe Reach	RIVF/EFLV	BC	Cariboo	83 D/10	52°30′	118°48′
Canoe River	UNP/LNO	SK	72-14-W3	73 N/1	55°14′	108°10′
Canoe River	UNP/LNO	BC	Cariboo	83 D/11	52°44′	119°16′
Canoe River	RIV/CDE	SK	74-13-W3	73 O/5	55°23′	107°56′
Canoe River	RIV/CDE	BC	Cariboo	83 D/14	52°47′	119°10′
Canol	UNP/LNO	NT	Mackenzie	96 E/3	65°14′	127°06′
Cañon Fiord	BAY/BAIE	NT	Franklin	39 G	80°00′	82°35′
Canon Inlet	BAY/BAIE	NT	Franklin	25 M	63°06′	71°23′
Canonto	UNP/LNO	ON	Frontenac	31 F/2	45°03′	76°47′
Canonto Lake	LAKE/LAC	ON	Frontenac	31 F/2	45°03′	76°47′
Canoona 2	IR/RI	BC	Range 4 Coast	103 H/2	53°04′	128°35′
Canoose	UNP/LNO	NB	Charlotte	21 G/6	45°22′	67°21′
Canoose Flowage	LAKE/LAC	NB	Charlotte	21 G/6	45°25′	67°20′
Canoose Stream	RIV/CDE	NB	Charlotte	21 G/6	45°23′	67°25′
Canopus	UNP/LNO	SK	9-3-2-W3	72 G/1	49°12′	106°12′
Canora	TOWN/VIL2	SK		62 M/9	51°38′	102°26′
Canotaicane, Lac	LAKE/LAC	QC	Jamésie	32 O/2	51°05′	74°40′
Canot Lake	LAKE/LAC	NT	Mackenzie	106 P	67°26′	128°46′
Canots, Lac aux	LAKE/LAC	QC	Le Fjord-du-Saguenay	22 E/6	49°19′	71°02′
Canrobert Hills	MTN/MNT	NT	Franklin	89 A	76°01′	115°50′
Canso	TOWN/VIL2	NS	Guysborough	11 F/7	45°20′	61°00′
Canso, Banc de - also-aussi - Canso Bank	SEAU/SMER	—		4003	45°09′	60°17′
Canso Bank - also-aussi - Canso, Banc de	SEAU/SMER	—		4003	45°09′	60°17′
Canso, Cape	CAPE/CAP	NS	Guysborough	11 F/7	45°18′	60°56′
Canso, Strait of	CHAN/CHEN	NS		11 F/11	45°37′	61°22′
Cantal	UNP/LNO	SK	36-5-34-W	62 F/5	49°26′	101°56′
Cantara Bay	BAY/BAIE	SK		74 N/2	59°07′	108°51′
Canterbury	VILG/VILG	NB	York	21 G/14	45°53′	67°29′
Canterbury	UNP/LNO	QC	Le Haut-Saint-François	21 E/11	45°30′	71°21′
Canterbury	GEOG/GÉOG	NB	York	21 G/14	45°50′	67°30′
Canterbury Park	UNP/LNO	MB		62 H/15	49°54′	96°58′
Cantic	UNP/LNO	QC	Le Haut-Richelieu	31 H/3	45°04′	73°21′
Cantin	UNP/LNO	QC	Les Chutes-de-la-Chaudière	21 L/11	46°37′	71°10′
Cantin Lake	LAKE/LAC	MB		53 E/6	53°27′	95°10′
Cantley	VILG/VILG	QC	Les Collines-de-l'Outaouais	31 G/12	45°34′	75°47′
Canton	UNP/LNO	NB	Victoria	21 O/4	47°04′	67°36′
Canton	UNP/LNO	ON	Durham	30 M/16	44°00′	78°21′
Canton-Arnaud	UNP/LNO	QC	Sept-Rivières	22 J/2	50°15′	66°30′
Canton-des-Roches	UNP/LNO	QC	Kamouraska	21 N/5	47°21′	69°56′
Canton-Jetté	UNP/LNO	QC	La Matapédia	22 B/5	48°16′	67°34′
Canton-Pelletier	UNP/LNO	QC	Maria-Chapdelaine	32 H/1	49°01′	72°18′
Cantor	UNP/LNO	NB	Sunbury	21 J/1	46°09′	66°04′
Cantuar	UNP/LNO	SK	28-16-15-W3	72 K/8	50°23′	108°00′
Cantyre	UNP/LNO	SK	36-50-31-W	63 F/5	53°22′	101°51′
Canuck	UNP/LNO	SK	10-3-17-W3	72 F/1	49°12′	108°13′
Canusio, Lac	LAKE/LAC	QC	Vallée-de-l'Or	32 B/12	48°34′	75°48′
Canwood	VILG/VILG	SK	36-50-5-W3	73 G/7	53°22′	106°36′
Canwood No. 494	MUN2/AZM2	SK		73 G/7	53°30′	106°45′

NAME NOM	ENTITY ENTITÉ	LOC 1 LIEU 1	LOC 2 LIEU 2	MAP CARTE	POSITION	
					LAT	LONG
Canyon	UNP/LNO	ON	Algoma	41 N/8	47°25′	84°29′
Canyon	UNP/LNO	ON	Kenora	52 F/13	49°59′	93°45′
Canyon	UNP/LNO	BC	Kootenay	82 F/1	49°05′	116°27′
Canyon	UNP/LNO	YT		115 A/14	60°52′	137°03′
Canyon Alpine	UNP/LNO	BC	Yale Division Yale	92 H/14	49°55′	121°27′
Canyon City	UNP/LNO	YT		115 F/15	61°49′	140°46′
Canyon Creek	UNP/LNO	AB	36-73-8-W5	83 O/6	55°22′	115°05′
Canyon Creek	RIV/CDE	YT		116 H/16	65°54′	136°01′
Canyon Crescent	UNP/LNO	YT		105 D/11	60°40′	135°02′
Canyon Heights	UNP/LNO	BC	New Westminster	92 G/6	49°21′	123°06′
Canyon Hot Springs	UNP/LNO	BC	Kootenay	82 N/4	51°08′	117°51′
Canyon Lake	LAKE/LAC	ON	Kenora	52 F/13	49°58′	93°40′
Canyon Lake (Ormonde Lake) 7	IR/RI	BC	Range 5 Coast	93 K/2	54°12′	124°41′
Canyon Ranges	MTN/MNT	YT/NT		96 D/2	64°37′	127°15′
Caopacho, Lac	LAKE/LAC	QC	Sept-Rivières	23 B/1	52°00′	66°09′
Caopacho, Rivière	RIV/CDE	QC	Sept-Rivières	22 O/8	51°18′	66°18′
Caopatina, Lac	LAKE/LAC	QC	Jamésie	32 G/7	49°27′	74°46′
Caotibi, Grand lac	LAKE/LAC	QC	Sept-Rivières	22 J/12	50°44′	67°34′
Caotibi, Petit lac	LAKE/LAC	QC	Sept-Rivières	22 J/13	50°52′	67°33′
Cap-à-la-Baleine	UNP/LNO	QC	Matane	22 B/14	48°55′	67°15′
Cap-à-la-Branche	UNP/LNO	QC	Charlevoix	21 M/8	47°23′	70°26′
Cap-à-l'Aigle	TOWN/VIL2	QC	Charlevoix-Est	21 M/9	47°40′	70°07′
Cap-à-l'Orignal	UNP/LNO	QC	Rimouski-Neigette	22 C/7	48°21′	68°49′
Capaotigamau, Lac	LAKE/LAC	QC	Manicouagan	22 K/8	50°19′	68°13′
Capasin	UNP/LNO	SK	53-10-W3	73 G/11	53°36′	107°23′
Cap-au-Renard	UNP/LNO	QC	Denis-Riverin	22 G/1	49°12′	66°14′
Cap-aux-Corbeaux	UNP/LNO	QC	Charlevoix	21 M/8	47°26′	70°28′
Cap-aux-Meules	TOWN/VIL2	QC	Les Îles-de-la-Madeleine	11 N/5	47°23′	61°52′
Cap aux Meules, Île du	ISL/ÎLE	QC	Les Îles-de-la-Madeleine	11 N/5	47°23′	61°54′
Cap-aux-Oies	UNP/LNO	QC	Charlevoix	21 M/8	47°29′	70°14′
Cap-aux-Os	UNP/LNO	QC	La Côte-de-Gaspé	22 A/16	48°50′	64°21′
Cap-Bateau	UNP/LNO	NB	Gloucester	21 P/15	47°49′	64°32′
Cap-Bon-Ami	UNP/LNO	QC	La Côte-de-Gaspé	22 A/16	48°49′	64°13′
Cap Breton, Cuvette du - also-aussi - Cape Breton Trough	SEAU/SMER	—		15160A	46°50′	60°50′
Cap-Breton, Île du - also-aussi - **Cape Breton Island**	ISL/ÎLE	NS	Victoria	11 K/2	46°10′	60°45′
Cap-Brûlé	UNP/LNO	NB	Westmorland	21 I/1	46°14′	64°29′
Cap-Brûlé	UNP/LNO	QC	La Côte-de-Beaupré	21 M/2	47°06′	70°43′
Cap-Chat	CITY/VIL1	QC	Denis-Riverin	22 G/2	49°06′	66°41′
Cap-Chat-Est	UNP/LNO	QC	Denis-Riverin	22 G/2	49°06′	66°40′
Cap-Chat, Pointe de	CAPE/CAP	QC	Denis-Riverin	22 G/2	49°07′	66°39′
Cap-Chat, Rivière	RIV/CDE	QC	Denis-Riverin	22 G/2	49°06′	66°41′
Cap-de-Cocagne	UNP/LNO	NB	Kent	21 I/7	46°21′	64°34′
Cap-de-la-Madeleine	CITY/VIL1	QC	Francheville	31 I/7	46°22′	72°31′
Cap-de-Rabast	UNP/LNO	QC	Minganie	22 H/16	49°57′	64°09′
Cap-de-Roche, Le	UNP/LNO	QC	Asbestos	21 E/13	45°48′	71°54′
Cap-de-Saint-Louis	UNP/LNO	NB	Kent	21 I/15	46°46′	64°55′
Cap-des-Caissie - also-aussi - Caissie Cape	UNP/LNO	NB	Kent	21 I/7	46°20′	64°32′
Cap-des-Pilotes, Le	UNP/LNO	QC	Matane	22 B/13	48°51′	67°32′
Cap-d'Espoir	UNP/LNO	QC	Pabok	22 A/8	48°26′	64°20′
Cap-des-Rosiers	UNP/LNO	QC	La Côte-de-Gaspé	22 A/16	48°52′	64°13′
Cap des Rosiers, Anse du	BAY/BAIE	QC	La Côte-de-Gaspé	22 A/16	48°49′	64°13′
Cap-des-Rosiers-Est	UNP/LNO	QC	La Côte-de-Gaspé	22 A/16	48°51′	64°13′
Cape Anguille	UNP/LNO	NF		11 O/14	47°54′	59°25′
Cape Auguet	UNP/LNO	NS	Richmond	11 F/6	45°29′	61°01′
Cape Bathurst	UNP/LNO	NT	Mackenzie	107 E	70°32′	128°00′
Cape Breton	MUN1/AZM1	NS	Cape Breton	11 K/1	46°00′	60°19′
Cape Breton	UNP/LNO	NB	Westmorland	21 I/2	46°12′	64°45′
Cape Breton	GEOG/GÉOG	NS		11 K/1	46°00′	60°19′
Cape Breton Highlands National Park - also-aussi - Hautes-Terres-du-Cap-Breton, Parc national des	PARK/PARC	NS	Victoria	11 K/10	46°45′	60°39′
Cape Breton Island - also-aussi - **Cap-Breton, Île du**	ISL/ÎLE	NS	Victoria	11 K/2	46°10′	60°45′
Cape Breton Trough - also-aussi - Cap Breton, Cuvette du	SEAU/SMER	—		15160A	46°50′	60°50′
Cape Broyle	VILG/VILG	NF		1 N/2	47°06′	52°57′
Cape Broyle Harbour	BAY/BAIE	NF		1 N/2	47°05′	52°54′
Cape Charles	UNP/LNO	NF		3 D/4	52°13′	55°38′
Cape Chidley Islands	ISL/ÎLE	NT	Franklin	25 A/8	60°26′	64°28′
Cape Chin	UNP/LNO	ON	Bruce	41 H/3	45°04′	81°19′
Cape Chin North	UNP/LNO	ON	Bruce	41 H/3	45°07′	81°19′
Cape Chin South	UNP/LNO	ON	Bruce	41 H/3	45°06′	81°17′
Cape Cove	UNP/LNO	NF		2 E/9	49°39′	54°03′
Cape Cove	UNP/LNO	QC	Pabok	22 A/8	48°26′	64°20′
Cape Cove	BAY/BAIE	NF		2 E/9	49°39′	54°03′
Cape Croker	UNP/LNO	ON	Bruce	41 A/14	44°56′	81°01′
Cape Croker 27 - see-voir - Neyaashiinigmiing 27	IR/RI	ON		41 A/14	44°55′	81°02′
Cape Croker Hunting Ground 60B	IR/RI	ON	Bruce	41 H/3	45°10′	81°30′
Cape Dauphin	UNP/LNO	NS	Victoria	11 K/8	46°20′	60°25′

NAME NOM	ENTITY ENTITÉ	LOC 1 LIEU 1	LOC 2 LIEU 2	MAP CARTE	POSITION LAT	LONG
Cape Dog	UNP/LNO	NF		1 N/4	47°05′	53°42′
Cape Dorset	HAM/HAM	NT	Franklin	36 C/2	64°14′	76°33′
Cape Dyer	UNP/LNO	NT	Franklin	16 K	66°40′	61°22′
Cape Egmont	UNP/LNO	PE	Prince	21 I/8	46°24′	64°06′
Cape Enrage	UNP/LNO	NB	Albert	21 H/10	45°37′	64°47′
Cape Forchu	UNP/LNO	NS	Yarmouth	20 O/16	43°48′	66°09′
Cape Freels North	UNP/LNO	NF		2 F/5	49°16′	53°30′
Cape Freels South	UNP/LNO	NF		2 F/6	49°15′	53°29′
Cape George	UNP/LNO	NS	Antigonish	11 F/13	45°50′	61°55′
Cape George Point	UNP/LNO	NS	Antigonish	11 F/13	45°53′	61°55′
Cape George Point	CAPE/CAP	NS	Antigonish	11 F/13	45°52′	61°54′
Cape Hope Islands	ISL/ÎLE	NT	Keewatin	33 D/7	52°26′	78°47′
Cape Hopes Advance	UNP/LNO	QC	Kativik	25 F/4	61°05′	69°34′
Cape Island	UNP/LNO	NF		2 F/3	49°14′	53°28′
Cape Jack	UNP/LNO	NS	Antigonish	11 F/12	45°41′	61°34′
Cape John	UNP/LNO	NS	Pictou	11 E/14	45°47′	63°06′
Cape LaHave Island	ISL/ÎLE	NS	Lunenburg	21 A/1	44°12′	64°22′
Cape la Hune	UNP/LNO	NF		11 P/10	47°33′	56°52′
Capelton	UNP/LNO	QC	Sherbrooke	21 E/5	45°19′	71°54′
Cape Mudge 10	IR/RI	BC	Sayward	92 F/14	50°00′	125°11′
Cape Negro	UNP/LNO	NS	Shelburne	20 P/11	43°33′	65°27′
Cape Negro Island	ISL/ÎLE	NS	Shelburne	20 P/11	43°31′	65°22′
Cape Norman	UNP/LNO	NF		2 M/12	51°37′	55°54′
Cape North	UNP/LNO	NS	Victoria	11 K/15	46°53′	60°31′
Cape Parry	UNP/LNO	NT	Franklin	97 F	70°09′	124°40′
Cape Pond	LAKE/LAC	NF		1 N/3	47°12′	53°05′
Cape Race	UNP/LNO	NF		1 K/11	46°39′	53°04′
Cape Ray	UNP/LNO	NF		11 O/11	47°38′	59°17′
Cape Sable Island	ISL/ÎLE	NS	Shelburne	20 P/5	43°28′	65°36′
Cape St. George	UNP/LNO	NF		12 B/6	48°28′	59°15′
Cape St. George-Petit Jardin-Grand Jardin-De Grau-Marches Point-Loretto	VILG/VILG	NF		12 B/6	48°29′	59°11′
Cape St. Mary's	UNP/LNO	NF		1 L/16	46°49′	54°12′
Cape St. Marys	UNP/LNO	NS	Digby	21 B/1	44°05′	66°12′
Cape Smith	UNP/LNO	NT	Keewatin	35 D	60°44′	78°28′
Cape Spear	UNP/LNO	NB	Westmorland	11 L/4	46°05′	63°49′
Cape Spear National Historic Site - also-aussi - Cap-Spear, Lieu historique national du	PARK/PARC	NF		1 N/10	47°31′	52°38′
Cape Spencer	UNP/LNO	NB	Saint John	21 H/4	45°12′	65°55′
Cape Station	UNP/LNO	NB	Albert	21 H/15	45°49′	64°37′
Cape Tormentine	UNP/LNO	NB	Westmorland	11 L/4	46°08′	63°47′
Cape Traverse	UNP/LNO	PE	Prince	11 L/4	46°14′	63°38′
Cape Traverse Landing	UNP/LNO	PE	Prince	11 L/4	46°14′	63°39′
Cape Wolfe	UNP/LNO	PE	Prince	21 I/9	46°43′	64°24′
Cap-Gaspé	UNP/LNO	QC	La Côte-de-Gaspé	22 A/16	48°45′	64°10′
Capilano 5	IR/RI	BC	New Westminster	92 G/6	49°19′	123°08′
Capilano Highlands	UNP/LNO	BC	New Westminster	92 G/6	49°21′	123°06′
Capilano River	RIV/CDE	BC	New Westminster	92 G/6	49°19′	123°08′
Capimitchigama, Lac	LAKE/LAC	QC	La Vallée-de-la-Gatineau	31 O/12	47°36′	75°46′
Capitachouane, Lac	LAKE/LAC	QC	Vallée-de-l'Or	32 B/4	48°05′	75°55′
Capitachouane, Rivière	RIV/CDE	QC	Vallée-de-l'Or	31 N/10	47°35′	76°54′
Capital	MUN1/AZM1	BC	Goldstream	92 B/5	48°25′	123°35′
Capitol Hill	UNP/LNO	BC	New Westminster	92 G/7	49°17′	122°59′
Caplan	VILG/VILG	QC	Bonaventure	22 A/4	48°06′	65°41′
Caplan-Ouest	UNP/LNO	QC	Bonaventure	22 A/4	48°08′	65°44′
Cap La Ronde	UNP/LNO	NS	Richmond	11 F/10	45°34′	60°54′
Cap, Le	UNP/LNO	QC	Communauté urbaine de Québec	21 L/14	46°51′	71°22′
Cap Le Moine	UNP/LNO	NS	Inverness	11 K/11	46°30′	61°04′
Cap Lemoyne	UNP/LNO	NS	Inverness	11 K/11	46°30′	61°04′
Caplin Bay	BAY/BAIE	NF		3 D/12	52°37′	55°46′
Caplin Bay	BAY/BAIE	NF		3 E/4	53°06′	55°50′
Caplin Cove	UNP/LNO	NF		2 C/2	48°02′	52°59′
Caplin Cove	UNP/LNO	NF		2 C/4	48°01′	53°44′
Caplin Gulch	UNP/LNO	NF		2 M/12	51°36′	55°31′
Cap-Lumière	UNP/LNO	NB	Kent	21 I/10	46°40′	64°43′
Cap Mountain	MTN/MNT	YT		105 D/15	60°46′	134°44′
Cap Mountain	MTN/MNT	NT	Mackenzie	95 O	63°24′	123°13′
Capot Blanc, Lac	LAKE/LAC	NT	Mackenzie	75 M	63°35′	110°35′
Cap-Ouest	UNP/LNO	QC	Le Fjord-du-Saguenay	22 D/7	48°23′	70°47′
Cappahayden	UNP/LNO	NF		1 K/15	46°52′	52°57′
Cap-Pele	VILG/VILG	NB	Westmorland	21 I/1	46°13′	64°16′
Cap-Pelé - see-voir - Cap-Pele	VILG/VILG	NB		21 I/1	46°13′	64°16′
Cappon	UNP/LNO	AB	2-25-5-W4	72 M/2	51°06′	110°36′
Capreol	TOWN/VIL2	ON	Sudbury	41 I/10	46°43′	80°56′
Caprona	UNP/LNO	AB	14-36-20-W4	83 A/2	52°06′	112°45′
Cap-Rouge	CITY/VIL1	QC	Communauté urbaine de Québec	21 L/14	46°45′	71°22′
Cap Rouge, Rivière du	RIV/CDE	QC	Communauté urbaine de Québec	21 L/11	46°45′	71°21′

NAME NOM	ENTITY ENTITÉ	LOC 1 LIEU 1	LOC 2 LIEU 2	MAP CARTE	POSITION LAT	LONG
Cap-Saint-Ignace	VILG/VILG	QC	Montmagny	21 M/1	47°02′	70°28′
Cap-Saint-Ignace-Station	UNP/LNO	QC	Montmagny	21 M/1	47°02′	70°26′
Cap-Saint-Jacques	UNP/LNO	QC	Communauté urbaine de Montréal	31 H/5	45°28′	73°55′
Cap-Santé	VILG/VILG	QC	Portneuf	21 L/12	46°40′	71°47′
Caps-de-Maria	UNP/LNO	QC	Avignon	22 B/1	48°08′	66°03′
Cap-Seize	UNP/LNO	QC	Denis-Riverin	22 G/1	49°01′	66°24′
Cap-Spear, Lieu historique national du - also-aussi - Cape Spear National Historic Site	PARK/PARC	NF		1 N/10	47°31′	52°38′
Caps-Saint-Fidèle	UNP/LNO	QC	Charlevoix-Est	21 N/12	47°43′	70°00′
Capstan, Cape	CAPE/CAP	NS	Cumberland	21 H/7	45°28′	64°51′
Capstan Island	UNP/LNO	NF		12 P/10	51°34′	56°44′
Capstick	UNP/LNO	NS	Victoria	11 N/2	47°00′	60°31′
Captain Ball Rock	SEAU/SMER	—		4625	46°42′	55°47′
Captain Island	ISL/ÎLE	NF		11 O/9	47°41′	58°02′
Cap-Tourmente	UNP/LNO	QC	La Côte-de-Beaupré	21 M/2	47°04′	70°48′
Capucins	VILG/VILG	QC	Denis-Riverin	22 G/2	49°03′	66°50′
Capweak	UNP/LNO	QC	Le Haut-Saint-Maurice	31 P/13	47°54′	73°49′
Caradoc	MUN2/AZM2	ON	Middlesex	40 I/13	42°52′	81°30′
Caradoc	UNP/LNO	ON	Middlesex	40 I/13	42°55′	81°31′
Caradoc 42 - see-voir - Chippewas of the Thames First Nation 42	IR/RI	ON		40 I/13	42°50′	81°30′
	UNP/LNO	ON	Thunder Bay	42 E/9	49°37′	86°09′
Caramat	TOWN/VIL2	NB	Gloucester	21 P/15	47°47′	64°57′
Caraquet	GEOG/GÉOG	NB	Gloucester	21 P/15	47°45′	64°55′
Caraquet, Baie de	BAY/BAIE	NB	Gloucester	21 P/14	47°48′	65°01′
Caraquet Island	ISL/ÎLE	NB	Gloucester	21 P/15	47°50′	64°53′
Caraquet, Rivière	RIV/CDE	NB	Gloucester	21 P/14	47°47′	65°04′
Carberry	TOWN/VIL2	MB	30-10-14-W	62 G/14	49°52′	99°22′
Carberry Junction	UNP/LNO	MB	30-10-14-W	62 G/14	49°52′	99°21′
Carberry Junction	UNP/LNO	MB	24-13-15-W	62 J/3	50°07′	99°23′
Carbon	VILG/VILG	AB	15-29-23-W4	82 P/6	51°29′	113°09′
Carbon Creek	RIV/CDE	BC	Peace River	93 O/15	55°59′	122°41′
Carbondale	UNP/LNO	AB	8-55-24-W4	83 H/12	53°45′	113°32′
Carbonear	TOWN/VIL2	NF		1 N/11	47°44′	53°13′
Carcajou	UNP/LNO	AB	32-101-19-W5	84 F/14	57°47′	117°06′
Carcajou Lake	LAKE/LAC	NT	Mackenzie	96 D	64°41′	127°54′
Carcajou Lake	LAKE/LAC	NT	Mackenzie	106 P	67°17′	128°40′
Carcajou River	RIV/CDE	NT	Mackenzie	106 H/10	65°37′	128°43′
Carcross	UNP/LNO	YT		105 D/2	60°10′	134°42′
Carcross 4	IR/RI	YT		105 D/2	60°04′	134°50′
Carcross Cutoff	UNP/LNO	YT		105 D/10	60°36′	134°53′
Cardale	UNP/LNO	MB	32-14-21-W	62 K/1	50°14′	100°19′
Cardell	UNP/LNO	SK	23-11-25-W3	72 F/14	49°56′	109°19′
Carden	MUN2/AZM2	ON	Victoria	31 D/11	44°40′	79°04′
Cardiff	MUN2/AZM2	ON	Haliburton	31 D/16	45°00′	78°07′
Cardiff	UNP/LNO	ON	Haliburton	31 E/1	45°01′	78°01′
Cardiff	UNP/LNO	AB	26-55-25-W4	83 H/13	53°47′	113°36′
Cardigan	VILG/VILG	PE	Kings	11 L/2	46°14′	62°37′
Cardigan	UNP/LNO	PE	Kings	11 L/2	46°14′	62°37′
Cardigan	UNP/LNO	NB	York	21 J/2	46°09′	66°47′
Cardigan Bay	BAY/BAIE	PE	Kings	11 L/1	46°10′	62°28′
Cardigan North	UNP/LNO	PE	Kings	11 L/2	46°14′	62°34′
Cardigan Strait	CHAN/CHEN	NT	Franklin	59 A	76°38′	90°40′
Cardinal	VILG/VILG	ON	Grenville	31 B/14	44°47′	75°23′
Cardinal	UNP/LNO	MB	24-6-9-W	62 G/7	49°30′	98°33′
Cardinal Heights	UNP/LNO	ON	Carleton	31 G/5	45°27′	75°37′
Cardinal Lake	LAKE/LAC	AB	83-24-W5	84 C/4	56°14′	117°44′
Cardinal River	RIV/CDE	AB	45-18-W5	83 C/15	52°52′	116°35′
Card Lake	LAKE/LAC	NS	Lunenburg	21 A/9	44°45′	64°17′
Cardross	UNP/LNO	PE	Kings	11 L/7	46°16′	62°38′
Cardross	UNP/LNO	SK	16-10-27-W2	72 H/13	49°49′	105°37′
Card's Harbour	UNP/LNO	NF		2 E/12	49°31′	55°38′
Cardston	TOWN/VIL2	AB	9-3-25-W4	82 H/3	49°12′	113°18′
Cardston No. 6, Municipal District of	MUN1/AZM1	AB	4-24-W4	82 H/6	49°17′	113°10′
Cardtable Mountain	MTN/MNT	BC	Lillooet	92 O/2	51°06′	122°57′
Cardwell	UNP/LNO	ON	Dufferin	40 P/16	43°58′	80°06′
Cardwell	GEOG/GÉOG	NB	Kings	21 H/14	45°48′	65°19′
Cardwell, Cape	CAPE/CAP	NT	Franklin	97 H	71°23′	121°23′
Careen Lake	LAKE/LAC	SK		74 C/16	57°00′	108°11′
Careless Brook	RIV/CDE	NF		2 D/15	48°55′	54°57′
Carew Bay	BAY/BAIE	NT	Franklin	25 K	62°36′	69°24′
Carey	UNP/LNO	MB	5,6-4-E	62 H/6	49°27′	97°03′
Carey Island	ISL/ÎLE	NT	Keewatin	32 M	52°00′	79°12′
Carey Lake	LAKE/LAC	NT	Mackenzie	65 L	62°12′	103°00′
Careys Hill	UNP/LNO	QC	Bonaventure	22 A/4	48°07′	65°47′
Cargenholm, Cape	CAPE/CAP	NT	Franklin	37 H	71°46′	73°35′
Carghill Island	ISL/ÎLE	MB		53 L/13	54°50′	95°40′

NAME NOM	ENTITY ENTITÉ	LOC 1 LIEU 1	LOC 2 LIEU 2	MAP CARTE	POSITION LAT	LONG
Cargill	UNP/LNO	ON	Bruce	41 A/3	44°12′	81°15′
Cargill Siding	UNP/LNO	ON	Bruce	41 A/3	44°12′	81°14′
Carheil, Lac	LAKE/LAC	QC	Caniapiscau	23 B/11	52°40′	67°05′
Carholme	UNP/LNO	ON	Norfolk	40 I/10	42°44′	80°31′
Cariboo	MUN1/AZM1	BC	Cariboo	93 B/6	52°20′	123°10′
Cariboo	UNP/LNO	BC	Cariboo	93 G/8	53°25′	122°03′
Cariboo	UNP/LNO	BC	New Westminster	92 G/2	49°15′	122°53′
Cariboo	UNP/LNO	BC	Range 5 Coast	93 J/4	54°01′	123°57′
Cariboo Falls	FALL/CHUT	BC	Cariboo	93 H/3	53°02′	121°10′
Cariboo Lake	LAKE/LAC	BC	Cariboo	93 A/11	52°45′	121°26′
Cariboo Land District	GEOG/GÉOG	BC		93 H	53°15′	121°15′
Cariboo Meadows	UNP/LNO	BC	Cassiar	104 J/2	58°15′	130°37′
Cariboo Mountains	MTN/MNT	BC	Cariboo	93 A/16	52°55′	120°15′
Cariboo River	RIV/CDE	BC	Peace River	93 A/12	52°40′	121°40′
Caribou	UNP/LNO	NS	Pictou	11 E/10	45°44′	62°42′
Caribou	UNP/LNO	YT		115 O/15	63°50′	138°45′
Caribou Depot	UNP/LNO	NB	Restigouche	21 O/9	47°34′	66°16′
Caribou Falls	UNP/LNO	ON	Kenora	52 L/7	50°16′	94°58′
Caribou Ferry	UNP/LNO	NS	Pictou	11 E/10	45°44′	62°41′
Caribou Harbour	BAY/BAIE	NS	Pictou	11 E/10	45°44′	62°42′
Caribou Heights	UNP/LNO	SK		72 I/5	50°24′	105°35′
Caribou Island	UNP/LNO	NS	Pictou	11 E/10	45°45′	62°43′
Caribou Island	ISL/ÎLE	NS	Pictou	11 E/10	45°45′	62°44′
Caribou Island	ISL/ÎLE	ON	Thunder Bay	41 N/5	47°22′	85°49′
Caribou Island	ISL/ÎLE	ON	Thunder Bay	52 H/10	49°40′	88°51′
Caribou Island	ISL/ÎLE	NT	Keewatin	46 A	64°12′	81°28′
Caribou Islands	ISL/ÎLE	NT	Mackenzie	85 H	61°55′	113°32′
Caribou, Lac du	LAKE/LAC	QC	Le Centre-de-la-Mauricie	31 I/11	46°43′	73°05′
Caribou Lake	LAKE/LAC	NF		2 D/11	48°38′	55°01′
Caribou Lake	LAKE/LAC	NS	Lunenburg	21 A/10	44°32′	64°33′
Caribou Lake	LAKE/LAC	ON	Thunder Bay	52 I/6	50°25′	89°05′
Caribou Lake	LAKE/LAC	ON	Kenora	52 J/3	50°12′	91°04′
Caribou Lake	LAKE/LAC	MB	65-27-W	63 K/11	54°40′	101°26′
Caribou Lake	LAKE/LAC	AB	70-6-W4	73 M/2	55°04′	110°52′
Caribou Lake	LAKE/LAC	NT	Mackenzie	106 N	67°59′	132°52′
Caribou Landing	UNP/LNO	MB	1-23-13-E	52 L/13	50°56′	95°40′
Caribou Marsh	UNP/LNO	NS	Cape Breton	11 K/1	46°03′	60°12′
Caribou Marsh 29	IR/RI	NS	Cape Breton	11 K/1	46°03′	60°13′
Caribou Mines	UNP/LNO	NS	Halifax	11 E/2	45°04′	62°57′
Caribou Mountain	MTN/MNT	YT		105 F/11	61°36′	133°15′
Caribou Mountains	MTN/MNT	AB	117-10-W5	84 O/4	59°12′	115°40′
Caribou Point	CAPE/CAP	NT	Mackenzie	85 G	61°31′	115°40′
Caribou River	UNP/LNO	NS	Pictou	11 E/15	45°45′	62°50′
Caribou River	RIV/CDE	MB		54 M/7	59°20′	94°44′
Caribou River	RIV/CDE	YT		106 L/8	66°30′	134°11′
Caribou River	RIV/CDE	NT	Mackenzie	95 F/5	61°27′	125°47′
Caribou Run	UNP/LNO	NF		3 D/5	52°16′	55°39′
Caribous-de-Jourdan, Réserve écologique des	PARK/PARC	QC	Vallée-de-l'Or	31 N/13	47°48′	77°54′
Carievale	VILG/VILG	SK	31-2-31-W	62 F/4	49°10′	101°38′
Carignan	CITY/VIL1	QC	La Vallée-du-Richelieu	31 H/6	45°27′	73°19′
Carignan	UNP/LNO	QC	Le Haut-Saint-Maurice	31 P/7	47°20′	72°47′
Carillon	TOWN/VIL2	QC	Argenteuil	31 G/9	45°34′	74°22′
Carillon Barracks National Historic Site - also-aussi - Caserne-de-Carillon, Lieu historique national de la	PARK/PARC	QC	Argenteuil	31 G/9	45°34′	74°22′
Carillon Canal - also-aussi - Carillon, Canal de	PARK/PARC	QC	Argenteuil	31 G/9	45°34′	74°23′
Carillon, Canal de - also-aussi - Carillon Canal	PARK/PARC	QC	Argenteuil	31 G/9	45°34′	74°23′
Carl Bay	BAY/BAIE	ON	Kenora	52 E/10	49°32′	94°51′
Carlea	UNP/LNO	SK	19-48-13-W2	63 E/4	53°09′	103°54′
Carleton	CITY/VIL1	QC	Avignon	22 B/1	48°06′	66°08′
Carleton	UNP/LNO	PE	Prince	11 L/5	46°15′	63°40′
Carleton	UNP/LNO	PE	Prince	21 I/9	46°42′	64°09′
Carleton	UNP/LNO	NS	Yarmouth	21 A/4	44°00′	65°56′
Carleton	UNP/LNO	QC	Avignon	22 B/1	48°07′	66°08′
Carleton	GEOG/GÉOG	NB	Kent	21 I/15	46°53′	64°58′
Carleton	GEOG/GÉOG	NB		21 J/6	46°20′	67°25′
Carleton	GEOG/GÉOG	ON		31 G/5	45°20′	75°35′
Carleton Centre	UNP/LNO	QC	Avignon	22 B/1	48°06′	66°07′
Carleton Corner	UNP/LNO	NS	Annapolis	21 A/14	44°49′	65°17′
Carleton Heights	UNP/LNO	ON	Carleton	31 G/5	45°21′	75°43′
Carleton Martello Tower National Historic Site - also-aussi - Tour-Martello-de-Carleton, Lieu historique national de la	PARK/PARC	NB	Saint John	21 G/8	45°15′	66°05′
Carleton, Mount	MTN/MNT	NB	Northumberland	21 O/7	47°23′	66°53′
Carleton-Ouest	UNP/LNO	QC	Avignon	22 B/1	48°07′	66°11′
Carleton Place	TOWN/VIL2	ON	Lanark	31 F/1	45°08′	76°09′
Carleton, Pointe	CAPE/CAP	QC	Minganie	12 E/10	49°44′	62°56′
Carleton Siding	UNP/LNO	PE	Prince	11 L/5	46°16′	63°40′
Carleton Village	UNP/LNO	NS	Shelburne	20 P/11	43°40′	65°20′

NAME NOM	ENTITY ENTITÉ	LOC 1 LIEU 1	LOC 2 LIEU 2	MAP CARTE	POSITION LAT	LONG
Carley	UNP/LNO	ON	Simcoe	31 D/12	44°36′	79°38′
Carleys Corner	UNP/LNO	ON	Grenville	31 B/13	44°52′	75°48′
Carlin	UNP/LNO	QC	Argenteuil	31 G/10	45°45′	74°32′
Carlin	UNP/LNO	BC	Kamloops Division Yale	82 L/14	50°49′	119°19′
Carling	MUN2/AZM2	ON	Parry Sound	41 H/8	45°25′	80°15′
Carling	UNP/LNO	ON	Parry Sound	41 H/8	45°24′	80°10′
Carlingford	UNP/LNO	NB	Victoria	21 J/13	46°45′	67°45′
Carlingford	UNP/LNO	ON	Perth	40 P/6	43°23′	81°09′
Carling Lake	LAKE/LAC	ON	Kenora	52 J/11	50°35′	91°16′
Carlington	UNP/LNO	ON	Carleton	31 G/5	45°23′	75°44′
Carlisle	UNP/LNO	NB	Carleton	21 J/6	46°21′	67°23′
Carlisle	UNP/LNO	ON	Wentworth	30 M/5	43°23′	79°59′
Carlisle	UNP/LNO	ON	Middlesex	40 P/3	43°07′	81°29′
Carlos	UNP/LNO	AB	27-41-5-W5	83 B/10	52°33′	114°38′
Carlow	MUN2/AZM2	ON	Hastings	31 F/4	45°14′	77°42′
Carlow	UNP/LNO	NB	Carleton	21 J/12	46°31′	67°31′
Carlow	UNP/LNO	ON	Huron	40 P/13	43°47′	81°37′
Carlowrie	UNP/LNO	MB	34,35-3-4-E	62 H/7	49°15′	96°58′
Carl Ritter Bay	BAY/BAIE	NT	Franklin	120 B	80°55′	67°30′
Carlsbad Springs	UNP/LNO	ON	Carleton	31 G/6	45°22′	75°28′
Carlson Landing	UNP/LNO	AB	16-115-11-W4	74 L/13	58°58′	111°48′
Carlsruhe	UNP/LNO	ON	Bruce	41 A/3	44°07′	81°03′
Carlton	UNP/LNO	SK	27-44-4-W3	73 B/15	52°50′	106°30′
Carlton Park	UNP/LNO	ON	Lincoln	30 M/3	43°11′	79°13′
Carluke	UNP/LNO	ON	Wentworth	30 M/4	43°08′	79°59′
Carlyle	TOWN/VIL2	SK	7-8-2-W2	62 E/9	49°38′	102°16′
Carlyle Lake Resort	UNP/LNO	SK		62 E/16	49°45′	102°16′
Carlyle, Mount	MTN/MNT	BC	Kootenay	82 F/14	49°56′	117°07′
Carlyon	UNP/LNO	ON	Simcoe	31 D/11	44°43′	79°30′
Carmacks	VILG/VILG	YT		115 I/1	62°05′	136°17′
Carmacks 11	IR/RI	YT		115 I/1	62°05′	136°18′
Carmacks Landing	IR/RI	YT		115 I/1	62°05′	136°18′
Carman	TOWN/VIL2	MB	6-4,5-W	62 G/8	49°30′	98°00′
Carman	UNP/LNO	ON	Northumberland	31 C/4	44°07′	77°45′
Carmanah 6	IR/RI	BC	Renfrew	92 C/10	48°37′	124°44′
Carmanah Creek	RIV/CDE	BC	Renfrew	92 C/10	48°36′	124°44′
Carmanah Point	CAPE/CAP	BC	Renfrew	92 C/10	48°37′	124°45′
Carmangay	VILG/VILG	AB	32-13-23-W4	82 I/3	50°08′	113°07′
Carman Junction	UNP/LNO	MB		62 H/14	49°50′	97°17′
Carmanville	TOWN/VIL2	NF		2 E/8	49°24′	54°18′
Carmanville Arm	BAY/BAIE	NF		2 E/8	49°25′	54°16′
Carm Creek 38	IR/RI	BC	Range 5 Coast	103 I/12	54°37′	129°47′
Carmel	UNP/LNO	QC	Drummond	31 H/16	45°58′	72°23′
Carmel	UNP/LNO	ON	Northumberland	31 C/4	44°05′	78°00′
Carmel	UNP/LNO	ON	Durham	31 D/1	44°06′	78°26′
Carmel	UNP/LNO	SK	34-37-24-W2	73 A/3	52°14′	105°21′
Carmi	UNP/LNO	BC	Similkameen Division Yale	82 E/6	49°30′	119°07′
Carmichael	VILG/VILG	SK	34-12-20-W3	72 K/2	50°03′	108°39′
Carmichael No. 109	MUN2/AZM2	SK		72 F/15	49°55′	108°40′
Carmunnock	UNP/LNO	ON	Perth	40 P/11	43°37′	81°09′
Carnaby	UNP/LNO	BC	Cassiar	93 M/4	55°10′	127°46′
Carnagh	UNP/LNO	SK	33-9-22-W3	72 F/15	49°47′	108°56′
Carnarvon	MUN2/AZM2	ON	Manitoulin	41 G/9	45°41′	82°14′
Carnarvon	UNP/LNO	ON	Haliburton	31 E/2	45°03′	78°42′
Carnduff	TOWN/VIL2	SK	35-2-33-W	62 F/4	49°10′	101°48′
Carnecksluck Lake	LAKE/LAC	NT	Keewatin	65 G	61°54′	98°15′
Carnegie	UNP/LNO	MB	36-11-20-W	62 F/16	49°58′	100°05′
Carnegie Beach	UNP/LNO	ON	Ontario	31 D/2	44°12′	78°51′
Carnwath River	RIV/CDE	NT	Mackenzie	107 A	68°26′	128°52′
Caroline	VILG/VILG	AB	14-36-6-W5	83 B/2	52°05′	114°45′
Caroline Village	UNP/LNO	ON	Lanark	31 C/16	44°54′	76°15′
Carol Richard Park	UNP/LNO	ON	Sudbury	41 I/11	46°37′	81°01′
Carolside	UNP/LNO	AB	16-26-12-W4	72 M/4	51°13′	111°38′
Caron	HAM/HAM	SK	25-17-29-W2	72 I/5	50°28′	105°52′
Caron	UNP/LNO	QC	Rouyn-Noranda	32 D/3	48°15′	79°05′
Caron, Baie	LAKE/LAC	QC	Rouyn-Noranda	32 D/2	48°00′	78°55′
Caron Brook	UNP/LNO	NB	Madawaska	21 N/7	47°17′	68°35′
Caron, Lac	LAKE/LAC	QC	Sept-Rivières	22 J/13	50°57′	67°43′
Caron No. 162	MUN2/AZM2	SK		72 I/5	50°25′	105°50′
Caronport	VILG/VILG	SK	29-17-28-W2	72 I/5	50°27′	105°49′
Carp	UNP/LNO	ON	Carleton	31 F/8	45°21′	76°02′
Carp	UNP/LNO	BC	Cariboo	93 J/5	54°28′	123°39′
Carpathia Seamount	SEAU/SMER	—		NK22 B	41°06′	49°33′
Carpenter	UNP/LNO	NB	Queens	21 G/9	45°40′	66°04′
Carpenter	UNP/LNO	SK	1-42-28-W2	73 A/12	52°35′	105°55′

NAME NOM	ENTITY ENTITÉ	LOC 1 LIEU 1	LOC 2 LIEU 2	MAP CARTE	POSITION LAT	LONG
Carpenter Bay	BAY/BAIE	BC	Queen Charlotte	103 B/3	52°14′	131°07′
Carpenter Bay	BAY/BAIE	NT	Mackenzie	76 C	64°14′	108°19′
Carpenter Lake	LAKE/LAC	BC	Lillooet	92 J/15	50°51′	122°30′
Carpenter Mountain 15	IR/RI	BC	Cariboo	93 A/4	52°11′	121°58′
Carpin Beach	UNP/LNO	ON	Algoma	41 K/9	46°30′	84°28′
Carp Lake	LAKE/LAC	BC	Cariboo	93 J/14	54°46′	123°21′
Carp Lake 3	IR/RI	BC	Cariboo	93 J/14	54°47′	123°25′
Carp River	RIV/CDE	ON	Carleton	31 F/8	45°29′	76°14′
Carquile	UNP/LNO	BC	Kamloops Division Yale	92 I/14	50°33′	121°25′
Carr	UNP/LNO	NB	Carleton	21 J/3	46°11′	67°23′
Carr	UNP/LNO	ON	Parry Sound	31 L/4	46°01′	79°39′
Carragana	VILG/VILG	SK	33-41-8-W2	63 D/11	52°35′	103°06′
Carraholly	UNP/LNO	BC	New Westminster	92 G/7	49°18′	122°55′
Carrick	MUN2/AZM2	ON	Bruce	41 A/3	44°04′	81°06′
Carrick	UNP/LNO	MB	28-3-11-E	62 H/1	49°15′	96°03′
Carrière, Baie	BAY/BAIE	QC	Vallée-de-l'Or	31 M/16	47°50′	78°00′
Carrière, La	UNP/LNO	QC	Acton	31 H/10	45°41′	72°40′
Carrière, Lac	LAKE/LAC	QC	Vallée-de-l'Or	31 N/3	47°14′	77°12′
Carrier-Jonction	UNP/LNO	QC	Desjardins	21 L/11	46°44′	71°06′
Carrier Lake 15	IR/RI	BC	Cariboo	93 J/12	54°31′	123°53′
Carrington	UNP/LNO	NS	Cumberland	11 E/13	45°50′	63°46′
Carr Lake	LAKE/LAC	NT	Keewatin	55 L/4	62°05′	95°42′
Carroll	UNP/LNO	QC	Pontiac	31 F/15	45°55′	77°00′
Carroll	UNP/LNO	MB	31-7-19-W	62 F/9	49°36′	100°02′
Carroll Glacier	GLAC/GLAC	BC	Cassiar	114 P/2	59°10′	136°45′
Carroll Lake	LAKE/LAC	MB		52 M/3	51°05′	95°09′
Carroll Lake	LAKE/LAC	SK		63 M/4	55°07′	103°56′
Carroll Ridge	UNP/LNO	NB	York	21 G/14	45°51′	67°28′
Carrolls Corner	UNP/LNO	NS	Halifax	11 E/3	45°01′	63°23′
Carrolls Cove	UNP/LNO	NF		3 D/4	52°09′	55°42′
Carrolls Crossing	UNP/LNO	NB	Northumberland	21 J/9	46°31′	66°15′
Carrolls Landing	UNP/LNO	BC	Kootenay	82 K/4	50°02′	117°54′
Carron Point	UNP/LNO	NB	Gloucester	21 P/12	47°39′	65°36′
Carrot Creek	UNP/LNO	AB	28-53-13-W5	83 G/12	53°37′	115°51′
Carrot River	TOWN/VIL2	SK	5-50-11-W2	63 E/5	53°17′	103°35′
Carrot River	RIV/CDE	MB		63 I/16	54°49′	96°02′
Carrot River	RIV/CDE	MB/SK		63 F/14	53°50′	101°18′
Carrot River 29A	IR/RI	SK		63 E/7	53°28′	102°50′
Carrs	UNP/LNO	QC	Le Haut-Saint-Laurent	31 G/1	45°03′	74°17′
Carrs	UNP/LNO	BC	Osoyoos Division Yale	82 L/3	50°08′	119°27′
Carrs Brook	UNP/LNO	NS	Colchester	11 E/5	45°24′	63°57′
Carr's Landing	UNP/LNO	ON	Sudbury	41 I/10	46°40′	80°46′
Carruthers	UNP/LNO	SK	10-45-23-W3	73 C/14	52°52′	109°16′
Carruthers Lake	LAKE/LAC	NT	Keewatin	65 K	62°32′	100°20′
Carrville	UNP/LNO	ON	York	30 M/14	43°51′	79°27′
Carry	UNP/LNO	ON	Algoma	42 C/1	48°13′	84°04′
Carrying Place	UNP/LNO	ON	Northumberland	31 C/4	44°03′	77°35′
Carscallen Point	CAPE/CAP	MB	37-5-W	63 B/1	52°13′	98°08′
Carseland	UNP/LNO	AB	7-22-25-W4	82 I/14	50°51′	113°28′
Carson	UNP/LNO	ON	Sudbury	41 I/4	46°10′	81°44′
Carson	UNP/LNO	BC	Similkameen Division Yale	82 E/1	49°00′	118°29′
Carsonby	UNP/LNO	ON	Carleton	31 G/4	45°11′	75°43′
Carson Canyon	SEAU/SMER	—		8012	45°26′	48°38′
Carson-Pegasus Provincial Park	PARK/PARC	AB	61-11,12-W5	83 J/5	54°18′	115°39′
Carsonville	UNP/LNO	NB	Kings	21 H/13	45°51′	65°31′
Carsoosat 5 - see-voir - Carsoosat 17	IR/RI	BC		93 K/10	54°41′	124°57′
Carsoosat 17	IR/RI	BC	Range 5 Coast	93 K/10	54°41′	124°57′
Carss	UNP/LNO	ON	Parry Sound	31 E/11	45°39′	79°24′
Carstairs	TOWN/VIL2	AB	17-30-1-W5	82 O/9	51°34′	114°06′
Carstens Lake	LAKE/LAC	ON	Kenora	52 E/8	49°21′	94°22′
Carswell Lake	LAKE/LAC	SK		74 K/11	58°37′	109°20′
Carter Basin	BAY/BAIE	NF		13 G/5	53°29′	59°50′
Carter Bay	BAY/BAIE	NT	Franklin	88 G	75°58′	119°37′
Carter, Cape	CAPE/CAP	NT	Franklin	25 I	62°25′	64°56′
Carteret, Lac	LAKE/LAC	QC	Manicouagan	22 F/14	49°48′	69°17′
Carter Lake	LAKE/LAC	BC	Range 3 Coast	103 A/16	52°53′	128°22′
Carter Lake	LAKE/LAC	NT	Mackenzie	75 I	62°57′	104°18′
Carters Corners	UNP/LNO	ON	Thunder Bay	52 A/6	48°23′	89°28′
Carter's Cove	UNP/LNO	NF		2 E/10	49°32′	54°48′
Carters Cove	UNP/LNO	NS	Richmond	11 F/10	45°41′	60°50′
Carters Point	UNP/LNO	NB	Kings	21 G/8	45°24′	66°11′
Carterton	UNP/LNO	ON	Algoma	41 J/4	46°12′	83°57′
Carthage	UNP/LNO	ON	Perth	40 P/10	43°40′	80°51′
Carthew Bay	UNP/LNO	ON	Simcoe	31 D/11	44°32′	79°26′
Cartier	MUN2/AZM2	MB		62 H/13	49°53′	97°41′

NAME NOM	ENTITY ENTITÉ	LOC 1 LIEU 1	LOC 2 LIEU 2	MAP CARTE	POSITION LAT	LONG
Cartier	UNP/LNO	ON	Sudbury	41 I/12	46°42′	81°33′
Cartier	UNP/LNO	MB		62 H/11	49°41′	97°08′
Cartier-Brébeuf, Lieu historique national - also-aussi - Cartier-Brébeuf National Historic Site	PARK/PARC	QC	Communauté urbaine de Québec	21 L/14	46°50′	71°14′
Cartier-Brébeuf National Historic Site - also-aussi - Cartier-Brébeuf, Lieu historique national	PARK/PARC	QC	Communauté urbaine de Québec	21 L/14	46°50′	71°14′
Cartier Lake	LAKE/LAC	SK		73 P/1	55°05′	104°17′
Cartmel, Mount	MTN/MNT	BC	Cassiar	104 H/11	57°43′	129°18′
Cartwright	VILG/VILG	NF		13 H/11	53°42′	57°01′
Cartwright	VILG/VILG	MB	6-2-14-W	62 G/3	49°06′	99°20′
Cartwright Saddle	SEAU/SMER	—		8047	54°40′	55°55′
Cartwright Sound	CHAN/CHEN	BC	Queen Charlotte	103 F/2	53°12′	132°40′
Carty Lake	LAKE/LAC	ON	Sudbury	42 B/2	48°10′	82°42′
Cartyville	UNP/LNO	NF		12 B/2	48°14′	58°48′
Caruso	UNP/LNO	AB	24-25-W4	82 P/3	51°03′	113°28′
Carvel	UNP/LNO	AB	34-52-2-W5	83 G/9	53°32′	114°13′
Carvel Corner	UNP/LNO	AB	4-53-2-W5	83 G/9	53°33′	114°13′
Carvell	UNP/LNO	NB	Carleton	21 J/5	46°21′	67°46′
Carway	UNP/LNO	AB	2-1-26-W4	82 H/3	49°00′	113°23′
Carye, Lac	LAKE/LAC	QC	Kativik	35 F/3	61°09′	77°14′
Carys Swan Nest	CAPE/CAP	NT	Keewatin	45 J	62°10′	83°07′
Casa-Berardi, Mont	MTN/MNT	QC	La Jacques-Cartier	21 L/13	46°55′	71°35′
Casault	UNP/LNO	QC	Montmagny	21 L/15	46°57′	70°39′
Casault, Lac	LAKE/LAC	QC	La Matapédia	22 B/11	48°30′	67°09′
Cascade	UNP/LNO	BC	Similkameen Division Yale	82 E/1	49°01′	118°12′
Cascade	UNP/LNO	BC	New Westminster	92 G/7	49°21′	122°54′
Cascade Heights	UNP/LNO	BC	New Westminster	92 G/6	49°15′	123°01′
Cascade Inlet	BAY/BAIE	BC	Range 3 Coast	93 D/5	52°30′	127°30′
Cascade Mountains	MTN/MNT	BC	Yale Division Yale	92 H/11	49°45′	121°00′
Cascade River	RIV/CDE	AB	25-11-W5	82 O/3	51°10′	115°29′
Cascades	UNP/LNO	QC	Les Collines-de-l'Outaouais	31 G/12	45°35′	75°52′
Cascades-Malignes	MUN2/AZM2	QC	La Vallée-de-la-Gatineau	31 N/1	47°07′	76°06′
Cascadia Basin - also-aussi - Cascadia, Bassin	SEAU/SMER	—		15787A	46°30′	127°30′
Cascadia, Bassin - also-aussi - Cascadia Basin	SEAU/SMER	—		15787A	46°30′	127°30′
Cascapédia, Baie de	BAY/BAIE	QC	Avignon	22 A/4	48°10′	65°56′
Cascapédia Est, Petite rivière	RIV/CDE	QC	Bonaventure	22 A/5	48°22′	65°46′
Cascapédia, Lac	LAKE/LAC	QC	Denis-Riverin	22 B/16	48°55′	66°20′
Cascapédia Ouest, Petite rivière	RIV/CDE	QC	Bonaventure	22 A/5	48°22′	65°46′
Cascapédia, Petite rivière	RIV/CDE	QC	Bonaventure	22 A/4	48°09′	65°51′
Cascapédia, Rivière	RIV/CDE	QC	Bonaventure	22 A/4	48°11′	65°54′
Cascouia, Baie	BAY/BAIE	QC	Le Fjord-du-Saguenay	22 D/5	48°24′	71°31′
Cascumpec	UNP/LNO	PE	Prince	21 I/9	46°45′	64°05′
Cascumpec Bay	BAY/BAIE	PE	Prince	21 I/16	46°46′	64°03′
Casdeded 8	IR/RI	BC	Cassiar	93 M/7	55°18′	126°37′
Case River	RIV/CDE	ON	Cochrane	32 E/5	49°17′	79°53′
Caserne-de-Carillon, Lieu historique national de la - also-aussi - Carillon Barracks National Historic Site	PARK/PARC	QC	Argenteuil	31 G/9	45°34′	74°22′
Casernes-de-Butler, Lieu historique national des - also-aussi - Butler's Barracks National Historic Site	PARK/PARC	ON	Lincoln	30 M/3	43°15′	79°04′
Case Settlement	UNP/LNO	NB	Kings	21 H/12	45°41′	65°44′
Casey	MUN2/AZM2	ON	Timiskaming	31 M/12	47°38′	79°35′
Casey	UNP/LNO	QC	Le Haut-Saint-Maurice	31 O/16	47°53′	74°11′
Casey Corner	UNP/LNO	NS	Kings	21 H/2	45°01′	64°33′
Casgrain	UNP/LNO	QC	La Côte-de-Beaupré	21 M/2	47°01′	70°57′
Cashel	UNP/LNO	ON	York	30 M/14	43°55′	79°19′
Cashions Glen	UNP/LNO	ON	Glengarry	31 G/2	45°06′	74°41′
Cashtown Corners	UNP/LNO	ON	Simcoe	41 A/8	44°20′	80°05′
Casimiel Meadows 15A	IR/RI	BC	Range 3 Coast	93 C/11	52°40′	125°29′
Casimir	UNP/LNO	ON	Sudbury	41 I/8	46°20′	80°25′
Casimir Island	ISL/ÎLE	NT	Mackenzie	65 E	61°28′	102°36′
Casimir, Jennings and Appleby	MUN2/AZM2	ON	Sudbury	41 I/8	46°20′	80°29′
Casimir Lake	LAKE/LAC	NT	Keewatin	65 E	61°28′	102°38′
Casino	UNP/LNO	BC	Kootenay	82 F/4	49°03′	117°40′
Caslan	UNP/LNO	AB	16-65-17-W4	83 I/10	54°38′	112°31′
Cass Bridge	UNP/LNO	ON	Dundas	31 G/3	45°03′	75°19′
Cassburn	UNP/LNO	ON	Prescott	31 G/10	45°35′	74°42′
Cassel	UNP/LNO	ON	Oxford	40 P/7	43°17′	80°46′
Casselman	VILG/VILG	ON	Russell	31 G/6	45°19′	75°05′
Cassels Lake	LAKE/LAC	ON	Nipissing	31 M/4	47°04′	79°43′
Casse-Pierre, Le	UNP/LNO	QC	La Mitis	22 C/9	48°40′	68°04′
Cassette, Lac	LAKE/LAC	QC	La Haute-Côte-Nord	22 C/14	48°47′	69°18′
Cassiar Land District	GEOG/GÉOG	BC		104 H	57°30′	129°00′
Cassiar Mountains	MTN/MNT	BC/YT		104 P/3	59°07′	129°15′
Cassidy	UNP/LNO	BC	Cranberry	92 G/4	49°03′	123°53′
Cassilis	UNP/LNO	NB	Northumberland	21 I/13	46°57′	65°46′
Cassils	UNP/LNO	AB	5-19-15-W4	82 I/9	50°35′	112°02′

NAME NOM	ENTITY ENTITÉ	LOC 1 LIEU 1	LOC 2 LIEU 2	MAP CARTE	POSITION LAT	LONG
Cassimayooks (Mayook) 5	IR/RI	BC	Kootenay	82 G/5	49°30′	115°34′
Cassville	UNP/LNO	QC	Coaticook	31 H/1	45°06′	72°03′
Castagnier	UNP/LNO	QC	Abitibi	32 C/12	48°44′	77°50′
Castagnier, Lac	LAKE/LAC	QC	Abitibi	32 C/12	48°44′	77°46′
Castagnier, Rivière	RIV/CDE	QC	Abitibi	32 C/14	48°59′	77°23′
Castalia	UNP/LNO	NB	Charlotte	21 B/10	44°44′	66°45′
Castaway	UNP/LNO	NB	Queens	21 I/5	46°18′	65°44′
Castel Bay	BAY/BAIE	NT	Franklin	88 F/4	74°12′	119°35′
Castelnau, Lac	LAKE/LAC	QC	Manicouagan	22 F/8	49°16′	68°13′
Castignon, Lac	LAKE/LAC	QC	Kativik	24 C/7	56°20′	68°37′
Castile	UNP/LNO	ON	Renfrew	31 F/6	45°30′	77°19′
Castlebar	UNP/LNO	QC	Asbestos	21 E/13	45°49′	71°59′
Castlebar Lake	LAKE/LAC	ON	Thunder Bay	42 E/16	49°49′	86°03′
Castle Bay	UNP/LNO	NS	Cape Breton	11 F/15	45°55′	60°39′
Castle Cove	BAY/BAIE	NF		2 C/11	48°36′	53°25′
Castle Creek	RIV/CDE	BC	Cariboo	93 H/1	53°14′	120°02′
Castledale	UNP/LNO	BC	Kootenay	82 N/2	51°01′	116°32′
Castlederg	UNP/LNO	ON	Peel	30 M/13	43°55′	79°46′
Castleford	UNP/LNO	ON	Renfrew	31 F/10	45°31′	76°35′
Castlegar	CITY/VIL1	BC	Kootenay	82 F/5	49°18′	117°40′
Castle Glen Estates	UNP/LNO	ON	Grey	41 A/8	44°28′	80°20′
Castle Green	UNP/LNO	ON	Halton	30 M/5	43°28′	79°42′
Castle Hill, Lieu historique national de - also-aussi - Castle Hill National Historic Site	PARK/PARC	NF		1 N/5	47°15′	53°59′
Castle Hill National Historic Site - also-aussi - Castle Hill, Lieu historique national de	PARK/PARC	NF		1 N/5	47°15′	53°58′
Castle Island	VILG/VILG	AB	35-54-3-W5	83 G/9	53°43′	114°20′
Castle Island	ISL/ÎLE	NF		2 M/13	51°59′	55°51′
Castle Island	ISL/ÎLE	NT	Keewatin	33 N	55°37′	77°17′
Castlemore	UNP/LNO	ON	Peel	30 M/13	43°47′	79°41′
Castle Mountain	UNP/LNO	AB	33-26-14-W5	82 O/5	51°16′	115°55′
Castle Mountain	MTN/MNT	AB	27-14-W5	82 O/5	51°19′	115°57′
Castle Mountain	MTN/MNT	BC	Cassiar	104 C/16	56°53′	132°11′
Castlereagh	UNP/LNO	NS	Colchester	11 E/12	45°31′	63°40′
Castle River	RIV/CDE	AB	27-7-30-W4	82 H/12	49°36′	113°59′
Castle Rock	UNP/LNO	BC	Cariboo	93 B/9	52°32′	122°29′
Castleton	UNP/LNO	ON	Northumberland	31 C/4	44°05′	77°56′
Castle Towers Mountain	MTN/MNT	BC	New Westminster	92 G/15	49°56′	122°56′
Castonguay, Lac	LAKE/LAC	QC	Vallée-de-l'Or	32 C/16	48°51′	76°26′
Castor	TOWN/VIL2	AB	35-37-14-W4	73 D/4	52°13′	111°53′
Castor Creek	RIV/CDE	AB	2-39-12-W4	73 D/5	52°20′	111°37′
Castor Lake	LAKE/LAC	NT	Mackenzie	86 B	64°28′	115°57′
Castor River	RIV/CDE	ON	Russell	31 G/6	45°18′	75°07′
Castor, Rivière au	RIV/CDE	QC	Jamésie	33 E/7	53°24′	78°58′
Castors Harbour	BAY/BAIE	NF		12 I/15	50°55′	56°59′
Castors, Les	UNP/LNO	QC	Lac-Saint-Jean-Est	22 D/12	48°41′	71°54′
Castors River	UNP/LNO	NF		12 I/15	50°55′	56°57′
Castors River North	UNP/LNO	NF		12 I/15	50°56′	56°58′
Casummit Lake	UNP/LNO	ON	Kenora	52 N/8	51°28′	92°24′
Caswell	UNP/LNO	BC	Cariboo	93 O/2	55°12′	122°44′
Caswell Hill	UNP/LNO	SK		73 B/2	52°08′	106°41′
Caswell's Beach	UNP/LNO	ON	Simcoe	31 D/12	44°44′	79°45′
Catala Island	ISL/ÎLE	BC	Nootka	92 E/14	49°50′	127°03′
Catalans, Mont des	MTN/MNT	QC	La Matapédia	22 B/7	48°25′	66°45′
Catalina	TOWN/VIL2	NF		2 C/11	48°31′	53°05′
Catalina Harbour	BAY/BAIE	NF		2 C/11	48°31′	53°04′
Catalogne, Lac	LAKE/LAC	QC	Jamésie	23 E/14	53°45′	71°15′
Catalone	UNP/LNO	NS	Cape Breton	11 G/13	45°59′	59°59′
Catalone Gut	UNP/LNO	NS	Cape Breton	11 J/4	46°01′	59°57′
Catalone Road	UNP/LNO	NS	Cape Breton	11 G/13	45°59′	59°56′
Catamount	UNP/LNO	NB	Westmorland	21 I/2	46°10′	64°59′
Cataract	UNP/LNO	ON	Peel	40 P/16	43°49′	80°01′
Cataraqui	UNP/LNO	ON	Frontenac	31 C/7	44°16′	76°32′
Cataraqui, Domaine	MISC/DIV	QC	Communauté urbaine de Québec	21 L/14	46°46′	71°15′
Cataraqui River	RIV/CDE	ON	Frontenac	31 C/1	44°14′	76°28′
Cataraqui River (Rideau Canal) - see-voir - Cataraqui River	RIV/CDE	ON		31 C/1	44°14′	76°28′
Cat Arm River	RIV/CDE	NF		12 I/2	50°08′	56°45′
Catastrophe Lake	LAKE/LAC	ON	Kenora	52 E/15	49°54′	94°47′
Cat Bay	BAY/BAIE	NF		2 C/13	48°47′	54°00′
Cat Brook	RIV/CDE	NF		2 D/6	48°28′	55°29′
Catchacoma	UNP/LNO	ON	Peterborough	31 D/9	44°44′	78°20′
Catchacoma Lake	LAKE/LAC	ON	Peterborough	31 D/9	44°45′	78°19′
Cater	UNP/LNO	SK	6-51-14-W3	73 F/8	53°22′	108°02′
Catfish Creek	RIV/CDE	ON	Elgin	40 I/11	42°39′	81°00′
Catfish Lake	LAKE/LAC	ON	Nipissing	31 E/15	45°57′	78°33′
Catfish Point	CAPE/CAP	MB	37-3-E	63 A/3	52°09′	97°03′
Cathcart	UNP/LNO	ON	Brant	40 P/2	43°06′	80°31′

NAME NOM	ENTITY ENTITÉ	LOC 1 LIEU 1	LOC 2 LIEU 2	MAP CARTE	POSITION LAT	LONG
Cathedral	UNP/LNO	BC	Kootenay	82 N/8	51°26′	116°25′
Cathedral Glacier	GLAC/GLAC	YT		115 B/2	60°14′	138°57′
Cathedral Mountain	MTN/MNT	BC	New Westminster	92 G/6	49°28′	123°01′
Catherine, Lac	LAKE/LAC	QC	Le Fjord-du-Saguenay	22 E/8	49°23′	70°10′
Catherwood	UNP/LNO	SK	6-35-11-W3	72 O/13	51°58′	107°34′
Cathkin	UNP/LNO	SK	7-38-19-W3	73 C/7	52°15′	108°42′
Cat Island	ISL/ÎLE	ON	Kenora	52 N/3	51°08′	93°23′
Cat Lake	UNP/LNO	ON	Kenora	52 O/12	51°44′	91°49′
Cat Lake	LAKE/LAC	ON	Kenora	52 O/12	51°40′	91°50′
Cat Lake 63C	IR/RI	ON	Kenora	52 O/12	51°43′	91°50′
Cat River	RIV/CDE	ON	Kenora	52 J/14	50°58′	91°17′
Catt, Mount	MTN/MNT	BC	Range 5 Coast	103 I/7	54°21′	128°47′
Caubvick, Mount - also-aussi - D'Iberville, Mont	MTN/MNT	NF		14 L/3	58°53′	63°43′
Cauchon Lake	LAKE/LAC	MB		63 P/8	55°30′	96°27′
Cauchy, Lac	LAKE/LAC	QC	Minganie	12 K/10	50°36′	60°46′
Caughnawaga 14 - see-voir - Kahnawake 14	IR/RI	QC		31 H/5	45°25′	73°41′
Caugnawana, Lac	LAKE/LAC	QC	Témiscamingue	31 L/9	46°33′	78°19′
Caulfeild	UNP/LNO	BC	New Westminster	92 G/6	49°21′	123°15′
Caumont, Lac	LAKE/LAC	QC	Minganie	12 K/10	50°33′	60°47′
Cauouatstacau, Rivière	RIV/CDE	QC	Jamésie	32 P/13	51°59′	73°35′
Causapscal	CITY/VIL1	QC	La Matapédia	22 B/6	48°22′	67°14′
Causapscal, Rivière	RIV/CDE	QC	La Matapédia	22 B/6	48°21′	67°13′
Caution, Cape	CAPE/CAP	BC	Range 2 Coast	92 M/4	51°10′	127°47′
Cautley Creek	RIV/CDE	BC	Peace River	94 H/15	57°54′	120°48′
Cavalier	UNP/LNO	SK	27-47-18-W3	73 F/2	53°05′	108°33′
Cavan	MUN2/AZM2	ON	Peterborough	31 D/1	44°10′	78°29′
Cavan	UNP/LNO	ON	Durham	31 D/1	44°12′	78°28′
Cavanagh	UNP/LNO	NF		23 J/1	54°02′	66°26′
Cavanagh Mills	UNP/LNO	NS	Colchester	11 E/11	45°36′	63°16′
Cavan Creek	RIV/CDE	ON	Peterborough	31 D/1	44°13′	78°21′
Cavan Station	UNP/LNO	ON	Durham	31 D/1	44°13′	78°27′
Cave and Basin, Lieu historique national - also-aussi - Cave and Basin National Historic Site	PARK/PARC	AB		82 O/4	51°10′	115°35′
Cave and Basin National Historic Site - also-aussi - Cave and Basin, Lieu historique national	PARK/PARC	AB		82 O/4	51°10′	115°35′
Cavée, La	UNP/LNO	QC	Le Domaine-du-Roy	32 A/8	48°19′	72°06′
Cave, La	UNP/LNO	QC	Coaticook	21 E/4	45°02′	71°43′
Cavell	UNP/LNO	ON	Thunder Bay	42 L/3	50°14′	87°02′
Cavell	UNP/LNO	SK	12-38-19-W3	73 C/7	52°16′	108°35′
Cavendish	UNP/LNO	NF		1 N/11	47°43′	53°29′
Cavendish	UNP/LNO	PE	Queens	11 L/6	46°29′	63°23′
Cavendish	UNP/LNO	AB	26-21-4-W4	72 L/16	50°49′	110°27′
Cave Point	CAPE/CAP	ON	Bruce	41 H/3	45°14′	81°29′
Caverhill	UNP/LNO	NB	York	21 J/3	46°04′	67°12′
Caverhill Lake	LAKE/LAC	BC	Kamloops Division Yale	92 P/8	51°20′	120°24′
Caverlys Landing	UNP/LNO	ON	Lennox and Addington	31 F/3	45°04′	77°26′
Cavernes, Les	UNP/LNO	QC	La Mitis	22 B/5	48°27′	67°52′
Cavers	UNP/LNO	ON	Thunder Bay	42 D/13	48°54′	87°41′
Caviar Lake	LAKE/LAC	ON	Kenora	52 F/5	49°23′	93°46′
Cavignac	UNP/LNO	QC	Les Maskoutains	31 H/15	45°50′	72°50′
Cawachagamite, Lac	LAKE/LAC	QC	Jamésie	32 O/9	51°42′	74°08′
Cawaja Beach	UNP/LNO	ON	Simcoe	41 A/9	44°42′	80°01′
Cawatose, Lac	LAKE/LAC	QC	Vallée-de-l'Or	31 N/6	47°19′	77°06′
Cawker Lake	LAKE/LAC	MB	39-12-W	63 B/6	52°22′	99°05′
Cawood	UNP/LNO	QC	Pontiac	31 F/16	45°50′	76°12′
Cawston	UNP/LNO	BC	Similkameen Division Yale	82 E/4	49°11′	119°46′
Caxton	UNP/LNO	SK	27-8-9-W2	62 E/11	49°41′	103°09′
Cayamant	VILG/VILG	QC	La Vallée-de-la-Gatineau	31 K/1	46°08′	76°15′
Cayamant, Lac	LAKE/LAC	QC	La Vallée-de-la-Gatineau	31 K/1	46°06′	76°16′
Caycuse	UNP/LNO	BC	Cowichan Lake	92 C/16	48°53′	124°22′
Caycuse River	RIV/CDE	BC	Renfrew	92 C/15	48°48′	124°41′
Caye	UNP/LNO	MB	5-12-9-W	62 G/15	49°59′	98°40′
Cayenne Creek	RIV/CDE	BC	Kamloops Division Yale	82 M/6	51°21′	119°15′
Cayer	UNP/LNO	MB	31-26-12-W	62 O/6	51°18′	99°08′
Cayilth 5	IR/RI	BC	Rupert	92 L/6	50°20′	127°26′
Cayley	UNP/LNO	AB	19-17-28-W4	82 I/5	50°27′	113°51′
Cayley, Mount	MTN/MNT	BC	New Westminster	92 J/3	50°07′	123°17′
Cayoosh Creek	RIV/CDE	BC	Lillooet	92 I/12	50°40′	121°58′
Cayoosh Creek 1	IR/RI	BC	Lillooet	92 I/12	50°40′	121°56′
Cayuga	UNP/LNO	ON	Haldimand	30 L/13	42°56′	79°51′
*Cayuga Station	UNP/LNO	ON	Haldimand	30 L/13	42°58′	79°52′
Cayuse 6	IR/RI	BC	Rupert	92 L/6	50°23′	127°28′
Cazalet	UNP/LNO	SK	28-35-13-W3	73 B/4	52°02′	107°48′
Cazaville	UNP/LNO	QC	Le Haut-Saint-Laurent	31 G/1	45°05′	74°22′
Cazeau, Rivière	RIV/CDE	QC	La Côte-de-Beaupré	21 L/14	46°57′	71°03′
Ceba	UNP/LNO	SK	28-47-2-W2	63 E/1	53°05′	102°13′
Cecebe	UNP/LNO	ON	Parry Sound	31 E/12	45°38′	79°33′

NAME NOM	ENTITY ENTITÉ	LOC 1 LIEU 1	LOC 2 LIEU 2	MAP CARTE	POSITION LAT	LONG
Cecebe, Lake	LAKE/LAC	ON	Parry Sound	31 E/12	45°39'	79°34'
Cecil	UNP/LNO	SK	21-48-24-W2	73 H/3	53°12'	105°29'
Cecil	UNP/LNO	AB	29-13-12-W4	72 L/4	50°07'	111°36'
Cecil Lake	UNP/LNO	BC	Peace River	94 A/7	56°18'	120°35'
Cecil Lake	LAKE/LAC	ON	Kenora	52 G/11	49°32'	91°24'
Cedar	UNP/LNO	BC	Cranberry	92 G/4	49°07'	123°51'
Cedar Bay	UNP/LNO	ON	Welland	30 L/14	42°53'	79°11'
Cedar Beach	UNP/LNO	ON	Renfrew	31 F/14	45°49'	77°05'
Cedar Beach	UNP/LNO	ON	Ontario	31 D/6	44°25'	79°10'
Cedar Beach	UNP/LNO	ON	Essex	40 J/2	42°00'	82°47'
Cedarbrae	UNP/LNO	ON	York	31 D/3	44°15'	79°18'
Cedarbrook	UNP/LNO	QC	Vaudreuil-Soulanges	31 G/8	45°24'	74°10'
Cedar Camp	UNP/LNO	NB	Kings	21 H/11	45°42'	65°20'
Cedar Creek	UNP/LNO	ON	Northumberland	31 C/4	44°06'	77°46'
Cedar Croft	UNP/LNO	ON	Parry Sound	31 E/12	45°39'	79°43'
Cedardale	UNP/LNO	ON	Lanark	31 F/1	45°07'	76°28'
Cedar Dale	UNP/LNO	ON	Ontario	30 M/15	43°53'	78°51'
Cedardale	UNP/LNO	BC	New Westminster	92 G/6	49°20'	123°08'
Cedar Glen	UNP/LNO	ON	Victoria	31 D/7	44°29'	78°39'
Cedar Grove	UNP/LNO	ON	Stormont	31 B/14	45°00'	75°03'
Cedar Grove	UNP/LNO	ON	York	30 M/14	43°51'	79°12'
Cedar Grove	UNP/LNO	BC	Osoyoos Division Yale	82 L/3	50°08'	119°27'
Cedar Harbour	UNP/LNO	ON	Simcoe	31 D/5	44°19'	79°32'
Cedar Heights	UNP/LNO	ON	Algoma	41 K/9	46°33'	84°18'
Cedar Hill	UNP/LNO	ON	Lanark	31 F/8	45°16'	76°18'
Cedarhurst Beach	UNP/LNO	ON	Ontario	31 D/6	44°24'	79°10'
Cedarhurst Park	UNP/LNO	ON	Essex	40 J/2	42°01'	82°47'
Cedar Lake	UNP/LNO	NS	Digby	21 B/1	44°02'	66°06'
Cedar Lake	UNP/LNO	ON	Frontenac	31 C/8	44°25'	76°24'
Cedar Lake	LAKE/LAC	ON	Nipissing	31 L/1	46°01'	78°28'
Cedar Lake	LAKE/LAC	ON	Kenora	52 K/3	50°10'	93°10'
Cedar Lake	LAKE/LAC	MB		63 F/8	53°20'	100°10'
Cedar Land District	GEOG/GÉOG	BC		92 G	49°06'	123°49'
Cedar Mills	UNP/LNO	ON	Peel	30 M/13	43°55'	79°48'
Cedarmont Beach	UNP/LNO	ON	Simcoe	31 D/11	44°32'	79°25'
Cedar Mount	UNP/LNO	ON	Simcoe	31 D/5	44°23'	79°34'
Cedar Nook	UNP/LNO	ON	Muskoka	31 D/13	44°55'	79°46'
Cedar Park	UNP/LNO	QC	Communauté urbaine de Montréal	31 H/5	45°27'	73°49'
Cedar Point	UNP/LNO	ON	Simcoe	41 A/16	44°49'	80°07'
Cedar Point	UNP/LNO	ON	Lambton	40 O/1	43°08'	82°04'
Cedar River	RIV/CDE	ON	Kenora	52 K/11	50°35'	93°24'
Cedar River	RIV/CDE	BC	Range 5 Coast	103 I/15	54°50'	128°50'
Cedar Shores	UNP/LNO	ON	Ontario	31 D/2	44°08'	78°55'
Cedarside	UNP/LNO	BC	Cariboo	83 D/14	52°47'	119°15'
Cedar Springs	UNP/LNO	ON	Halton	30 M/5	43°25'	79°55'
Cedar Springs	UNP/LNO	ON	Kent	40 J/8	42°17'	82°02'
Cedartree Lake	LAKE/LAC	ON	Kenora	52 F/5	49°05'	93°52'
Cedarvale	UNP/LNO	ON	York	30 M/11	43°42'	79°26'
Cedarvale	UNP/LNO	BC	Cassiar	103 P/1	55°01'	128°19'
Cedar Valley	UNP/LNO	ON	Peterborough	31 D/1	44°11'	78°25'
Cedar Valley	UNP/LNO	ON	York	31 D/3	44°04'	79°21'
Cedar Valley	UNP/LNO	ON	Wellington	40 P/16	43°46'	80°10'
Cedar Villa Estates	HAM/HAM	SK	15-36-6-W3	73 B/2	52°06'	106°46'
Cedar Village	UNP/LNO	ON	Muskoka	31 E/3	45°03'	79°23'
Cedarville	UNP/LNO	QC	Memphrémagog	31 H/1	45°01'	72°13'
Cedarville	UNP/LNO	ON	Simcoe	30 M/13	44°00'	79°52'
Cedarville	UNP/LNO	ON	Grey	41 A/2	44°02'	80°34'
Cedarwood Lake	LAKE/LAC	NS	Digby	21 A/4	44°14'	65°52'
Cedoux	UNP/LNO	SK	4-11-14-W2	62 E/13	49°53'	103°52'
Cèdres, Barrage des	MISC/DIV	QC	Vaudreuil-Soulanges	31 G/8	45°19'	74°02'
Cèdres, Grand lac des	LAKE/LAC	QC	La Vallée-de-la-Gatineau	31 K/8	46°18'	76°07'
Cèdres, Lac aux	LAKE/LAC	QC	Caniapiscau	23 B/3	52°02'	67°07'
Cèdres, Lac des	LAKE/LAC	QC	La Haute-Côte-Nord	22 C/11	48°36'	69°18'
Cèdres, Lac des	LAKE/LAC	QC	Le Fjord-du-Saguenay	22 D/2	48°14'	70°44'
Cèdres, Rivière des	RIV/CDE	QC	La Haute-Côte-Nord	22 C/11	48°41'	69°20'
Cédrière, La	UNP/LNO	QC	La Côte-de-Gaspé	22 H/3	49°12'	65°10'
Cédrière, La	UNP/LNO	QC	Montmagny	21 M/2	47°02'	70°33'
Ceepee	UNP/LNO	SK	29-39-8-W3	73 B/6	52°23'	107°08'
Ceepeecee	UNP/LNO	BC	Nootka	92 E/15	49°52'	126°42'
Celista	UNP/LNO	BC	Kamloops Division Yale	82 L/14	50°57'	119°21'
Celista Creek	RIV/CDE	BC	Kamloops Division Yale	82 M/3	51°12'	119°00'
Celista Mountain	MTN/MNT	BC	Kamloops Division Yale	82 M/6	51°25'	119°02'
Celtic	UNP/LNO	SK	2-52-23-W3	73 F/6	53°27'	109°17'
Cent-Ans, Le	UNP/LNO	QC	L'Amiante	21 L/4	46°04'	71°33'
Centennial	UNP/LNO	NS	Inverness	11 F/14	45°49'	61°28'

NAME NOM	ENTITY ENTITÉ	LOC 1 LIEU 1	LOC 2 LIEU 2	MAP CARTE	POSITION	
					LAT	LONG
Centennial	UNP/LNO	ON	York	30 M/14	43°47′	79°10′
Centennial	UNP/LNO	MB		62 H/14	49°54′	97°09′
Centennial	UNP/LNO	MB		62 G/13	49°50′	99°59′
Centennial Lake	LAKE/LAC	ON	Renfrew	31 F/3	45°09′	77°03′
Centennial Place	UNP/LNO	NB	Westmorland	21 I/2	46°05′	64°49′
Centennial Range	MTN/MNT	YT		115 C/15	60°58′	140°39′
Central	UNP/LNO	ON	Wentworth	30 M/5	43°16′	79°52′
Central Argyle	UNP/LNO	NS	Yarmouth	20 P/13	43°46′	65°50′
Central Bedeque	VILG/VILG	PE	Prince	11 L/5	46°20′	63°42′
Central Bedeque	UNP/LNO	PE	Prince	11 L/5	46°20′	63°42′
Central Blissville	UNP/LNO	NB	Sunbury	21 G/10	45°38′	66°35′
Central Business District	UNP/LNO	SK		73 B/2	52°08′	106°40′
Central Butte	TOWN/VIL2	SK	21-21-4-W3	72 J/15	50°48′	106°31′
Central Cambridge	UNP/LNO	NB	Queens	21 G/9	45°44′	66°02′
Central Caribou	UNP/LNO	NS	Pictou	11 E/10	45°43′	62°42′
Central Channel	CHAN/CHEN	NF		1 M/9	47°32′	54°08′
Central Chebogue	UNP/LNO	NS	Yarmouth	20 O/16	43°47′	66°05′
Central Clarence	UNP/LNO	NS	Annapolis	21 A/14	44°54′	65°13′
Central Coast	MUN1/AZM1	BC	Range 3 Coast	93 D/2	52°10′	127°00′
Central Fraser Valley	MUN1/AZM1	BC	New Westminster	92 G/2	49°10′	122°45′
Central Greenwich	UNP/LNO	NB	Kings	21 G/9	45°31′	66°07′
Central Grove	UNP/LNO	NS	Digby	21 B/8	44°21′	66°16′
Central Hainesville	UNP/LNO	NB	York	21 J/3	46°07′	67°06′
Central Hampstead	UNP/LNO	NB	Queens	21 G/9	45°38′	66°07′
Centralia	UNP/LNO	ON	Huron	40 P/6	43°17′	81°28′
Central Kildare	UNP/LNO	PE	Prince	21 I/16	46°52′	64°00′
Central Kings	VILG/VILG	PE	Kings	11 L/7	46°19′	62°30′
Central Kingsclear	UNP/LNO	NB	York	21 G/15	45°56′	66°52′
Central Kootenay	MUN1/AZM1	BC	Kootenay	82 F/14	49°55′	117°30′
Central Lot 16	VILG/VILG	PE	Prince	11 L/5	46°29′	63°52′
Central Lot 16	UNP/LNO	PE	Prince	11 L/5	46°29′	63°52′
Central New Annan	UNP/LNO	NS	Colchester	11 E/11	45°38′	63°19′
Central North River	UNP/LNO	NS	Colchester	11 E/6	45°28′	63°13′
Central Norton	UNP/LNO	NB	Kings	21 H/12	45°34′	65°48′
Central Okanagan	MUN1/AZM1	BC	Osoyoos Division Yale	82 E/14	50°00′	119°25′
Central Onslow	UNP/LNO	NS	Colchester	11 E/6	45°23′	63°22′
Central Patricia	UNP/LNO	ON	Kenora	52 O/8	51°30′	90°09′
Central Port Mouton	UNP/LNO	NS	Queens	20 P/15	43°55′	64°51′
Central Saanich	MUN1/AZM1	BC	South Saanich	92 B/11	48°34′	123°25′
Central Tower Hill	UNP/LNO	NB	Charlotte	21 G/6	45°19′	67°13′
Central Waterville	UNP/LNO	NB	York	21 J/3	46°05′	67°17′
Central West River	UNP/LNO	NS	Pictou	11 E/10	45°35′	62°50′
Central Woods Harbour	UNP/LNO	NS	Shelburne	20 P/12	43°33′	65°44′
Centre	UNP/LNO	NS	Lunenburg	21 A/8	44°23′	64°22′
Centre	UNP/LNO	ON	Prince Edward	31 C/3	44°05′	77°26′
Centre-Acadie	UNP/LNO	NB	Kent	21 I/11	46°43′	65°18′
Centre Burlington	UNP/LNO	NS	Hants	21 H/1	45°04′	64°06′
Centre-d'Accueil-du-Parc-Jasper, Lieu historique national du - also-aussi - Jasper Park Information Centre National Historic Site	PARK/PARC	AB		83 D/16	52°53′	118°05′
Centredale	UNP/LNO	NS	Pictou	11 E/7	45°25′	62°39′
Centre-d'Inscription-de-l'Entrée-Est-du-Parc-du-Mont-Riding, Lieu historique national du - also-aussi - Riding Mountain Park East Gate Registration Complex National Historic Site	PARK/PARC	MB	19,20-16-W1	62 J/12	50°41′	99°33′
Centre Dummer	UNP/LNO	ON	Peterborough	31 D/8	44°28′	78°01′
Centre East Pubnico	UNP/LNO	NS	Yarmouth	20 P/12	43°38′	65°46′
Centrefield	UNP/LNO	ON	Prescott	31 G/11	45°31′	75°03′
Centre Glassville	UNP/LNO	NB	Carleton	21 J/11	46°33′	67°25′
Centre Inn	UNP/LNO	ON	Wellington	40 P/9	43°38′	80°12′
Centre Island	ISL/ÎLE	ON	Manitoulin	41 H/13	45°56′	81°40′
Centre Island	ISL/ÎLE	BC	Nootka	92 E/15	49°51′	126°56′
Centre Lake Junction	UNP/LNO	ON	Renfrew	31 F/13	45°56′	77°31′
Centrelea	UNP/LNO	NS	Annapolis	21 A/14	44°49′	65°19′
Centre Musquodoboit	UNP/LNO	NS	Halifax	11 E/3	45°06′	63°02′
Centre Napan	UNP/LNO	NB	Northumberland	21 P/3	47°01′	65°24′
Centre Rawdon	UNP/LNO	NS	Hants	11 E/4	45°03′	63°50′
Centre-Saint-François	UNP/LNO	QC	Le Haut-Saint-Laurent	31 G/1	45°11′	74°16′
Centre-Saint-Simon	UNP/LNO	NB	Gloucester	21 P/10	47°44′	64°50′
Centreton	UNP/LNO	NB	Kings	21 G/8	45°26′	66°05′
Centreton	UNP/LNO	ON	Northumberland	31 D/1	44°05′	78°02′
Centreview	UNP/LNO	ON	Hastings	31 F/5	45°22′	77°45′
Centre Village	UNP/LNO	NB	Westmorland	21 I/1	46°03′	64°17′
Centreville	VILG/VILG	NB	Carleton	21 J/5	46°26′	67°43′
Centreville	UNP/LNO	NF		2 F/4	49°01′	53°53′
Centreville	UNP/LNO	NS	Cape Breton	11 K/1	46°13′	60°13′
Centreville	UNP/LNO	NS	Inverness	11 K/3	46°04′	61°14′

NAME NOM	ENTITY ENTITÉ	LOC 1 LIEU 1	LOC 2 LIEU 2	MAP CARTE	POSITION LAT	LONG
Centreville	UNP/LNO	NS	Kings	21 H/2	45°08′	64°32′
Centreville	UNP/LNO	NS	Shelburne	20 P/5	43°29′	65°36′
Centreville	UNP/LNO	NS	Digby	21 B/9	44°33′	66°01′
Centreville	UNP/LNO	NB	Kings	21 H/13	45°48′	65°36′
Centreville	UNP/LNO	NB	York	21 J/7	46°21′	66°44′
Centreville	UNP/LNO	ON	Lennox and Addington	31 C/7	44°24′	76°54′
Centreville	UNP/LNO	ON	Waterloo	40 P/8	43°26′	80°26′
Centreville	UNP/LNO	ON	Grey	41 A/10	44°37′	80°37′
Centreville	UNP/LNO	ON	Oxford	40 P/2	43°03′	80°51′
Centreville	UNP/LNO	ON	Bruce	41 A/14	44°57′	81°16′
Centreville	UNP/LNO	BC	Cassiar	104 P/6	59°17′	129°24′
Centreville Reserve Mines	UNP/LNO	NS	Cape Breton	11 K/1	46°11′	60°02′
Centreville-Wareham-Trinity	TOWN/VIL2	NF		2 C/13	48°59′	53°59′
Centurion	UNP/LNO	ON	Muskoka	31 E/6	45°24′	79°19′
Cereal	VILG/VILG	AB	28-28-6-W4	72 M/7	51°25′	110°48′
Cerf, Grand lac du	LAKE/LAC	QC	Antoine-Labelle	31 J/6	46°17′	75°30′
Cesar Trough	SEAU/SMER	—		897	85°56′	120°00′
Cessford	UNP/LNO	AB	36-23-12-W4	72 M/4	51°01′	111°33′
Ceylon	VILG/VILG	SK	11-6-20-W2	72 H/7	49°27′	104°36′
Ceylon	UNP/LNO	ON	Grey	41 A/2	44°15′	80°34′
Chaatl	UNP/LNO	BC	Queen Charlotte	103 F/2	53°07′	132°32′
Chaatl Island	ISL/ÎLE	BC	Queen Charlotte	103 F/1	53°07′	132°28′
Chabot	UNP/LNO	QC	Papineau	31 G/11	45°36′	75°01′
Chaboullié, Lac	LAKE/LAC	QC	Jamésie	32 K/13	50°53′	77°50′
Chachukew Lake	LAKE/LAC	SK		63 M/7	55°15′	102°58′
Chads Point	CAPE/CAP	NT	Franklin	79 B	76°12′	109°54′
Chaffeys Locks	UNP/LNO	ON	Leeds	31 C/9	44°35′	76°19′
Chagoness	UNP/LNO	SK	21-42-16-W2	73 A/9	52°38′	104°13′
Chaigneau, Lac	LAKE/LAC	QC	Caniapiscau	23 J/13	54°50′	67°50′
Chaillot, Sommet de	MTN/MNT	QC	Charlevoix	21 M/15	47°48′	70°52′
Chain Lakes	LAKE/LAC	AB	33-16-W4	82 P/16	51°50′	112°09′
Chain Lakes Provincial Park	PARK/PARC	AB	14,15-2-W5	82 J/1	50°13′	114°12′
Chain Pond	LAKE/LAC	NF		2 D/9	48°33′	54°15′
Chakonipau, Lac	LAKE/LAC	QC	Kativik	24 C/7	56°18′	68°30′
Chalet Beach	UNP/LNO	MB	1-17-4-E	62 I/7	50°25′	96°55′
Chaleur Bay	BAY/BAIE	NF		11 P/10	47°36′	56°45′
Chaleur Bay - also-aussi - **Chaleurs, Baie des**	BAY/BAIE	QC/NB		22 A/3	48°00′	65°08′
Chaleur Harbour	BAY/BAIE	NF		11 P/10	47°35′	56°40′
Chaleurs	UNP/LNO	QC	Bonaventure	22 A/4	48°10′	65°50′
Chaleurs, Baie des - also-aussi - **Chaleur Bay**	BAY/BAIE	QC/NB		22 A/3	48°00′	65°08′
Chaleurs, Baie des	BAY/BAIE	QC	Antoine-Labelle	31 J/14	46°59′	75°24′
Chaleurs, Vallée des - also-aussi - Chaleur Trough	SEAU/SMER	—		1399A	48°00′	65°00′
Chaleur Trough - also-aussi - Chaleurs, Vallée des	SEAU/SMER	—		1399A	48°00′	65°00′
Chalifoux	UNP/LNO	QC	La Vallée-de-la-Gatineau	31 J/4	46°13′	75°56′
Chalk River	VILG/VILG	ON	Renfrew	31 K/3	46°01′	77°27′
Challenger Mountains	MTN/MNT	NT	Franklin	340 E	82°41′	76°12′
Challetkohum 5	IR/RI	BC	New Westminster	92 J/2	50°03′	122°32′
Challetkohum 9	IR/RI	BC	New Westminster	92 J/2	50°03′	122°32′
Chaloupe, Rivière de la	RIV/CDE	QC	Minganie	12 E/2	49°08′	62°32′
Chalto	UNP/LNO	QC	Le Granit	21 E/10	45°41′	70°55′
Chambeaux, Lac	LAKE/LAC	QC	Caniapiscau	23 F/10	53°42′	68°37′
Chamberlain	VILG/VILG	SK	8-22-26-W2	72 I/13	50°51′	105°34′
Chamberlain	MUN2/AZM2	ON	Timiskaming	31 M/13	47°53′	79°59′
Chamberlain	UNP/LNO	ON	Timiskaming	31 M/13	47°51′	79°54′
Chamberlaine, Lac	LAKE/LAC	QC	Kativik	35 B/12	60°41′	75°50′
Chamberlain Island	ISL/ÎLE	NT	Franklin	36 A	64°06′	73°42′
Chamberlains	UNP/LNO	NF		1 N/10	47°32′	52°57′
Chamberlain Settlement	UNP/LNO	NB	Gloucester	21 P/12	47°34′	65°38′
Chamberlin River	RIV/CDE	NT	Keewatin	65 N	63°41′	100°33′
Chambers	UNP/LNO	SK	30-33-8-W3	72 O/14	51°52′	107°07′
Chambers Corners	UNP/LNO	ON	Welland	30 L/14	42°57′	79°23′
Chambers Island	ISL/ÎLE	NF		1 M/9	47°37′	54°20′
Chambers Point	CAPE/CAP	NF		1 L/14	46°52′	55°26′
Chambers Settlement	UNP/LNO	NB	Kings	21 H/11	45°41′	65°19′
Chambly	CITY/VIL1	QC	La Vallée-du-Richelieu	31 H/6	45°27′	73°17′
Chambly Canal - also-aussi - Chambly, Canal de	PARK/PARC	QC	La Vallée-du-Richelieu	31 H/6	45°23′	73°15′
Chambly, Canal de - also-aussi - Chambly Canal	PARK/PARC	QC	La Vallée-du-Richelieu	31 H/6	45°23′	73°15′
Chambord	VILG/VILG	QC	Le Domaine-du-Roy	32 A/8	48°26′	72°04′
Chambord-Jonction	UNP/LNO	QC	Le Domaine-du-Roy	32 A/8	48°25′	72°03′
Chambres Corner	UNP/LNO	NB	Queens	21 H/13	45°54′	65°49′
Chambure, Lac	LAKE/LAC	QC	Jamésie	23 E/15	53°52′	70°44′
Chamcook	UNP/LNO	NB	Charlotte	21 G/3	45°07′	67°04′
Chamcook Lake	UNP/LNO	NB	Charlotte	21 G/3	45°08′	67°04′
Chamiss 7	IR/RI	BC	Rupert	92 L/3	50°05′	127°17′
Chamiss Bay	UNP/LNO	BC	Rupert	92 L/3	50°04′	127°17′

NAME	ENTITY	LOC 1	LOC 2	MAP	POSITION	
NOM	ENTITÉ	LIEU 1	LIEU 2	CARTE	LAT	LONG
Champagne	UNP/LNO	YT		115 A/16	60°47′	136°29′
Champagne Landing 10	IR/RI	YT		115 A/16	60°50′	136°18′
Champcoeur	UNP/LNO	QC	Abitibi	32 C/12	48°41′	77°38′
Champ-des-Gouffres	UNP/LNO	QC	Minganie	12 E/7	49°27′	62°47′
Champdoré	UNP/LNO	NB	Kent	21 I/7	46°24′	64°47′
Champdoré, Lac	LAKE/LAC	QC	Kativik	23 P/13	55°55′	65°49′
Champigny	UNP/LNO	QC	Communauté urbaine de Québec	21 L/14	46°47′	71°21′
Champion	VILG/VILG	AB	7-15-23-W4	82 I/3	50°14′	113°09′
Champlain	VILG/VILG	QC	Francheville	31 I/8	46°27′	72°21′
Champlain	MUN1/AZM1	QC	Champlain	31 H/6	45°29′	73°29′
Champlain	UNP/LNO	NB	Charlotte	21 G/3	45°10′	67°11′
Champlain Heights	UNP/LNO	NB	Saint John	21 G/8	45°17′	66°00′
Champlain, Lac - also-aussi - **Champlain, Lake**	LAKE/LAC	QC	Le Haut-Richelieu	31 H/3	45°03′	73°09′
Champlain, Lake - also-aussi - **Champlain, Lac**	LAKE/LAC	QC	Le Haut-Richelieu	31 H/3	45°03′	73°09′
Champlain Park	UNP/LNO	ON	Nipissing	31 L/3	46°15′	79°26′
Champlain, Pic	MTN/MNT	QC	Rimouski-Neigette	22 C/7	48°20′	68°50′
Champlain, Rivière	RIV/CDE	QC	Francheville	31 I/8	46°27′	72°17′
Champneuf	VILG/VILG	QC	Abitibi	32 C/11	48°35′	77°30′
Champney's	UNP/LNO	NF		2 C/6	48°23′	53°17′
Champney's Arm	UNP/LNO	NF		2 C/6	48°24′	53°19′
Champney's West	UNP/LNO	NF		2 C/6	48°23′	53°18′
Chance Cove	TOWN/VIL2	NF		1 N/12	47°41′	53°50′
Chance Cove	BAY/BAIE	NF		1 K/14	46°45′	53°00′
Chance Cove Brook	RIV/CDE	NF		1 K/14	46°46′	53°00′
Chance Cove Head	CAPE/CAP	NF		1 K/15	46°45′	52°59′
Chance Creek	RIV/CDE	YT		116 J/8	66°25′	138°24′
Chance Harbour	UNP/LNO	NS	Pictou	11 E/10	45°40′	62°35′
Chance Harbour	UNP/LNO	NB	Saint John	21 G/1	45°07′	66°21′
Chance Head	CAPE/CAP	NF		2 C/12	48°32′	53°38′
Chancellor	UNP/LNO	AB	35-24-21-W4	82 P/2	51°05′	112°50′
Chancellor Channel	CHAN/CHEN	BC	Range 1 Coast	92 K/5	50°25′	125°42′
Chanceport	UNP/LNO	NF		2 E/10	49°33′	54°49′
Chandindu River	RIV/CDE	YT		116 B/5	64°15′	139°43′
Chandler	CITY/VIL1	QC	Pabok	22 A/7	48°21′	64°41′
Chandler Fiord	BAY/BAIE	NT	Franklin	120 C	81°38′	68°46′
Chandler Lake	LAKE/LAC	MB	15,16-11-W	62 J/7	50°19′	98°53′
Chandler-Ouest	UNP/LNO	QC	Pabok	22 A/7	48°20′	64°43′
Chandler Reach	RIVF/EFLV	NF		2 C/5	48°30′	53°47′
Chandonnet	UNP/LNO	QC	L'Érable	21 L/4	46°12′	71°40′
Chandos	MUN2/AZM2	ON	Peterborough	31 C/13	44°50′	78°00′
Chandos Lake	UNP/LNO	ON	Peterborough	31 D/16	44°48′	78°03′
Chandos Lake	LAKE/LAC	ON	Peterborough	31 D/16	44°48′	78°00′
Change Islands	TOWN/VIL2	NF		2 E/9	49°40′	54°25′
Change Islands	ISL/ÎLE	NF		2 E/9	49°40′	54°24′
Channel	UNP/LNO	QC	Memphrémagog	31 H/1	45°13′	72°14′
Channel Island	ISL/ÎLE	MB		63 F/1	53°00′	100°25′
Channel Islands 33	IR/RI	BC	Range 5 Coast	103 J/10	54°31′	130°49′
Channel-Port aux Basques	TOWN/VIL2	NF		11 O/11	47°34′	59°09′
Channing	UNP/LNO	MB	31-66-29-W	63 K/13	54°45′	101°50′
Chanoodandidalch 14	IR/RI	BC	Cassiar	93 M/1	55°03′	126°27′
Chantelle	UNP/LNO	QC	Matawinie	31 I/4	46°07′	73°54′
Chantler	UNP/LNO	ON	Welland	30 M/3	43°00′	79°20′
Chantrey Inlet	BAY/BAIE	NT	Keewatin	56 M/12	67°45′	95°54′
Chantry	UNP/LNO	ON	Leeds	31 C/9	44°40′	76°06′
Chantry Island	ISL/ÎLE	NT	Franklin	87 A	68°46′	114°39′
Chapais	CITY/VIL1	QC	Jamésie	32 G/15	49°47′	74°51′
Chapais	UNP/LNO	QC	L'Islet	21 N/4	47°00′	69°51′
Chapeau	TOWN/VIL2	QC	Pontiac	31 F/14	45°55′	77°04′
Chapel Arm	TOWN/VIL2	NF		1 N/12	47°31′	53°40′
Chapel Arm	BAY/BAIE	NF		1 N/12	47°32′	53°39′
Chapel Cove	UNP/LNO	NF		1 N/6	47°26′	53°08′
Chapel Grove	UNP/LNO	NB	Kings	21 G/8	45°23′	66°05′
Chapel Island	ISL/ÎLE	NF		2 E/7	49°26′	54°43′
Chapel Island	ISL/ÎLE	NF		1 M/11	47°33′	55°22′
Chapel Island 5	IR/RI	NS	Richmond	11 F/10	45°42′	60°46′
Chapell Inlet	BAY/BAIE	NT	Franklin	25 I	62°35′	65°00′
Chapel Park 28	IR/RI	BC	Range 5 Coast	93 K/4	54°13′	125°45′
*Chapel Road	UNP/LNO	NS	Richmond	11 F/11	45°37′	61°14′
Chapel's Corner	UNP/LNO	QC	Brome-Missisquoi	31 H/2	45°09′	72°48′
Chapiteau, Lac	LAKE/LAC	QC	Kativik	13 M/5	55°23′	63°41′
Chapleau	MUN2/AZM2	ON	Sudbury	41 O/11	47°48′	83°27′
Chapleau	UNP/LNO	ON	Sudbury	41 O/14	47°50′	83°24′
Chapleau 61	IR/RI	ON	Sudbury	41 O/14	47°49′	83°24′
Chapleau 61A	IR/RI	ON	Sudbury	41 O/14	47°49′	83°24′
Chapleau 74	IR/RI	ON	Sudbury	41 O/14	47°49′	83°24′

NAME NOM	ENTITY ENTITÉ	LOC 1 LIEU 1	LOC 2 LIEU 2	MAP CARTE	POSITION LAT	LONG
Chapleau 74A	IR/RI	ON	Sudbury	41 O/14	47°49′	83°24′
Chapleau 75	IR/RI	ON	Sudbury	41 O/14	47°49′	83°24′
Chapleau Cree Fox Lake	IR/RI	ON	Chapleau	41 O/14	47°49′	83°27′
Chapleau River	RIV/CDE	ON	Algoma	42 B/7	48°29′	82°57′
Chaplin	VILG/VILG	SK	17-5-W3	72 J/7	50°28′	106°40′
Chaplin	UNP/LNO	NS	Halifax	11 E/2	45°12′	62°51′
Chaplin Island Road	UNP/LNO	NB	Northumberland	21 P/4	47°04′	65°41′
Chaplin Lake	LAKE/LAC	SK		72 J/7	50°22′	106°36′
Chaplin No. 164	MUN2/AZM2	SK		72 J/7	50°25′	106°35′
Chapman	MUN2/AZM2	ON	Parry Sound	31 E/12	45°42′	79°35′
Chapman	UNP/LNO	ON	Hastings	31 C/6	44°26′	77°19′
Chapman Camp	UNP/LNO	BC	Kootenay	82 G/12	49°40′	115°58′
Chapman, Cape	CAPE/CAP	NT	Keewatin	57 D	69°17′	89°05′
Chapman Corner	UNP/LNO	NB	Westmorland	21 I/2	46°13′	64°34′
Chapman Creek	RIV/CDE	BC	New Westminster	92 G/5	49°26′	123°43′
Chapman Islands	ISL/ÎLE	NT	Franklin	76 N	67°54′	109°15′
Chapman Lake	LAKE/LAC	MB		64 B/16	56°57′	98°10′
Chapman Lake	LAKE/LAC	BC	Range 5 Coast	93 L/15	54°56′	126°40′
Chapman, Mont	MTN/MNT	QC	Le Val-Saint-François	21 E/12	45°34′	71°40′
Chapman, Mount	MTN/MNT	BC	Kootenay	82 M/16	51°55′	118°18′
Chapmans	UNP/LNO	BC	Yale Division Yale	92 H/11	49°43′	121°25′
Chapman's Bar 10	IR/RI	BC	Yale Division Yale	92 H/11	49°43′	121°24′
Chapmans Corner	UNP/LNO	NB	Westmorland	21 I/1	46°08′	64°05′
Chapman Settlement	UNP/LNO	NS	Cumberland	11 E/13	45°57′	63°56′
Chapman's Landing	UNP/LNO	ON	Parry Sound	31 L/4	46°06′	79°32′
Chapmanville	UNP/LNO	NB	Carleton	21 J/11	46°37′	67°27′
Chappell	UNP/LNO	SK	1-36-6-W3	73 B/2	52°06′	106°43′
Chapperon Creek	RIV/CDE	BC	Kamloops Division Yale	92 I/1	50°10′	120°08′
Chapperon Creek 6	IR/RI	BC	Kamloops Division Yale	92 I/1	50°12′	120°03′
Chapperon Lake	LAKE/LAC	BC	Kamloops Division Yale	92 I/1	50°12′	120°03′
Chapperon Lake 5	IR/RI	BC	Kamloops Division Yale	92 I/1	50°13′	120°04′
Chapple	MUN2/AZM2	ON	Rainy River	52 C/12	48°45′	94°00′
Chaput Hughes	UNP/LNO	ON	Timiskaming	42 A/1	48°08′	80°04′
Charbonneau River	RIV/CDE	SK		74 K/16	58°48′	108°21′
Charcoal Creek	RIV/CDE	BC	Kamloops Division Yale	82 L/12	50°38′	119°40′
Charcoal Lake	LAKE/LAC	SK		64 L/16	58°49′	102°22′
Chard	UNP/LNO	AB	17-79-6-W4	73 M/15	55°50′	110°55′
Chardon, Lac du	LAKE/LAC	QC	Manicouagan	22 F/7	49°26′	68°52′
Charella Garden	UNP/LNO	BC	Cariboo	93 G/15	53°53′	122°46′
Charest, Rivière	RIV/CDE	QC	Francheville	31 I/9	46°35′	72°14′
Charette	VILG/VILG	QC	Le Centre-de-la-Mauricie	31 I/7	46°27′	72°56′
Charing Cross	UNP/LNO	ON	Kent	40 J/8	42°20′	82°06′
Charland, Lac	LAKE/LAC	QC	Matawinie	31 J/16	46°52′	74°11′
Charlebois	UNP/LNO	MB	89-22-E	54 D/9	56°41′	94°04′
Charlemagne	CITY/VIL1	QC	L'Assomption	31 H/11	45°43′	73°29′
Charlemont	UNP/LNO	ON	Lambton	40 J/9	42°38′	82°17′
Charles	UNP/LNO	MB		63 N/11	55°32′	101°01′
Charles	UNP/LNO	BC	Cariboo	83 D/14	52°52′	119°18′
Charles Bay	BAY/BAIE	NT	Franklin	35 J	62°41′	74°20′
Charlesbourg	CITY/VIL1	QC	Communauté urbaine de Québec	21 L/14	46°51′	71°16′
Charles Brook	UNP/LNO	NF		2 E/6	49°20′	55°15′
Charles Brook	RIV/CDE	NF		2 E/6	49°20′	55°15′
Charles Creek 2	IR/RI	BC	Range 1 Coast	92 L/16	50°56′	126°22′
Charles Dickens Point	CAPE/CAP	NT	Franklin	67 H	71°32′	98°03′
Charles Francis Hall Bay	BAY/BAIE	NT	Franklin	25 J	62°38′	66°43′
Charles Inlet	BAY/BAIE	ON	Parry Sound	41 H/10	45°38′	80°34′
Charles Island	ISL/ÎLE	NT	Franklin	35 J	62°39′	74°15′
Charles Lake	LAKE/LAC	AB/NT		74 M/15	59°53′	110°34′
Charles Lake 225	IR/RI	AB	125-4-W4	74 M/15	59°54′	110°36′
Charles-Lynch Place	UNP/LNO	QC	Pontiac	31 F/15	45°54′	76°57′
Charleston	UNP/LNO	NF		2 C/5	48°23′	53°40′
Charleston	UNP/LNO	NS	Queens	21 A/2	44°10′	64°40′
Charleston	UNP/LNO	NB	Carleton	21 J/5	46°22′	67°39′
Charleston	UNP/LNO	ON	Leeds	31 B/12	44°34′	76°00′
Charleston Lake	LAKE/LAC	ON	Leeds	31 C/9	44°32′	76°00′
Charlesville	UNP/LNO	NS	Shelburne	20 P/12	43°35′	65°47′
Charleswood	UNP/LNO	MB		62 H/14	49°51′	97°17′
Charles Yorke, Cape	CAPE/CAP	NT	Franklin	48 D	73°44′	82°49′
Charleville	UNP/LNO	ON	Grenville	31 B/13	44°45′	75°37′
Charlevoix	MUN1/AZM1	QC	Charlevoix	21 M/8	47°29′	70°29′
Charlevoix-Est	MUN1/AZM1	QC	Charlevoix-Est	21 N/12	47°44′	69°59′
Charlevoix, Réserve de la biosphère de	PARK/PARC	QC	Charlevoix	21 M/15	47°45′	70°45′
Charley Boy's Meadow 3	IR/RI	BC	Range 3 Coast	93 C/8	52°18′	124°13′
Charlie-Gibbs Fracture Zone	SEAU/SMER	—		5.04	52°00′	31°00′
Charlie Lake	UNP/LNO	BC	Peace River	94 A/7	56°17′	120°57′

NAME / NOM	ENTITY / ENTITÉ	LOC 1 / LIEU 1	LOC 2 / LIEU 2	MAP / CARTE	POSITION LAT	POSITION LONG
Charlie Lake	LAKE/LAC	NT/MB		65 C/2	60°02′	100°36′
Charlie Lake	LAKE/LAC	BC	Peace River	94 A/6	56°20′	121°00′
Charlo	VILG/VILG	NB	Restigouche	21 O/16	48°00′	66°19′
Charloit, Lac de	LAKE/LAC	NT	Mackenzie	75 O/13	63°50′	107°57′
Charlo River	RIV/CDE	NB	Restigouche	21 O/16	47°59′	66°17′
Charlos Cove	UNP/LNO	NS	Guysborough	11 F/3	45°15′	61°20′
Charlot Island	ISL/ÎLE	SK		74 N/11	59°35′	109°15′
Charlotte	GEOG/GÉOG	NB		21 G/2	45°10′	66°50′
Charlotte, Lake	LAKE/LAC	NS	Halifax	11 D/15	44°50′	62°58′
Charlotte Lake	LAKE/LAC	BC	Range 3 Coast	93 C/3	52°12′	125°20′
Charlottenburgh	MUN2/AZM2	ON	Glengarry	31 G/2	45°10′	74°40′
Charlottetown	CITY/VIL1	PE	Queens	11 L/3	46°14′	63°08′
Charlottetown	VILG/VILG	NF		13 A/16	52°46′	56°07′
Charlottetown	UNP/LNO	NF		2 D/8	48°26′	54°01′
Charlottetown	GEOG/GÉOG	PE	Queens	11 L/3	46°15′	63°08′
Charlton	TOWN/VIL2	ON	Timiskaming	31 M/13	47°48′	79°59′
*Charlton	UNP/LNO	SK		73 C/9	52°34′	108°18′
Charlton Bay	BAY/BAIE	NT	Mackenzie	75 K	62°42′	109°07′
Charlton Depot	UNP/LNO	NT	Keewatin	32 M	51°58′	79°19′
Charlton Island	ISL/ÎLE	NT	Keewatin	32 M	52°00′	79°30′
Charnois, Lac	LAKE/LAC	QC	Le Fjord-du-Saguenay	22 D/6	48°24′	71°25′
Charnwood	UNP/LNO	ON	Halton	30 M/5	43°28′	79°40′
Charny	CITY/VIL1	QC	Les Chutes-de-la-Chaudière	21 L/11	46°43′	71°16′
Charrington	UNP/LNO	QC	Le Haut-Saint-François	21 E/4	45°11′	71°34′
Charron Lake	LAKE/LAC	MB		53 D/11	52°45′	95°15′
Charron Lake	LAKE/LAC	AB	67,68-17-W4	83 I/15	54°50′	112°31′
Charteris	UNP/LNO	QC	Pontiac	31 F/9	45°41′	76°27′
Charters Settlement	UNP/LNO	NB	York	21 G/15	45°51′	66°45′
Chartersville	UNP/LNO	NB	Westmorland	21 I/2	46°05′	64°44′
Chartier Lake	LAKE/LAC	ON	Parry Sound	31 E/13	45°51′	79°51′
Chartierville	VILG/VILG	QC	Le Haut-Saint-François	21 E/6	45°18′	71°12′
Chartrand Corner	UNP/LNO	ON	Sudbury	41 I/1	46°08′	80°23′
Chase	VILG/VILG	BC	Kamloops Division Yale	82 L/13	50°49′	119°41′
Chase Corners	UNP/LNO	ON	Peterborough	31 C/5	44°28′	77°48′
Chase Creek	RIV/CDE	BC	Kamloops Division Yale	82 L/13	50°50′	119°42′
Chase Island	ISL/ÎLE	NT	Franklin	25 O	63°03′	66°55′
Chase River	UNP/LNO	BC	Nanaimo	92 G/4	49°08′	123°55′
Chasm	UNP/LNO	BC	Lillooet	92 P/3	51°13′	121°29′
Chasse, Île à la	ISL/ÎLE	QC	Minganie	12 L/3	50°13′	63°09′
Chasse, Pointe à la	CAPE/CAP	QC	Sept-Rivières	22 J/1	50°08′	66°28′
Chasseurs, Lac des	LAKE/LAC	QC	La Mitis	22 B/4	48°13′	67°52′
Chassignolle, Lac	LAKE/LAC	QC	Abitibi	32 D/8	48°18′	78°29′
Chastrier, Lac	LAKE/LAC	QC	Caniapiscau	23 F/14	53°58′	69°13′
Chaswood	UNP/LNO	NS	Halifax	11 E/3	45°03′	63°13′
Chatboro	UNP/LNO	QC	Argenteuil	31 G/9	45°38′	74°29′
Chateau	UNP/LNO	NF		2 M/13	51°59′	55°54′
Chateau Bay	BAY/BAIE	NF		2 M/13	51°58′	55°53′
Château-Bigot	UNP/LNO	QC	Communauté urbaine de Québec	21 L/14	46°54′	71°16′
Château-d'Eau	UNP/LNO	QC	Communauté urbaine de Québec	21 L/14	46°52′	71°22′
Châteauguay	CITY/VIL1	QC	Roussillon	31 H/5	45°23′	73°45′
Châteauguay-Centre	UNP/LNO	QC	Roussillon	31 H/5	45°21′	73°45′
Châteauguay, Lac	LAKE/LAC	QC	Kativik	24 D/8	56°27′	70°03′
Châteauguay, Rivière	RIV/CDE	QC	Kativik	24 C/11	56°39′	69°08′
Châteauguay, Rivière	RIV/CDE	QC	Roussillon	31 H/5	45°24′	73°45′
Chateau Pond	LAKE/LAC	NF		13 A/1	52°04′	56°16′
Château-Richer	CITY/VIL1	QC	La Côte-de-Beaupré	21 L/14	46°58′	71°01′
Château-Richer-Station	UNP/LNO	QC	La Côte-de-Beaupré	21 L/14	46°58′	71°01′
Châteauvert, Lac	LAKE/LAC	QC	Le Haut-Saint-Maurice	31 P/12	47°39′	73°55′
Châtelain, Lac	LAKE/LAC	QC	Kativik	35 B/8	60°23′	74°10′
Chater	UNP/LNO	MB	27-10-18-W	62 G/13	49°52′	99°50′
Chatfield	UNP/LNO	MB	5-21-1-W	62 I/13	50°47′	97°34′
Chatfield Island	ISL/ÎLE	BC	Range 3 Coast	103 A/1	52°16′	128°05′
Chatham	CITY/VIL1	ON	Kent	40 J/8	42°24′	82°11′
Chatham	VILG/VILG	QC	Argenteuil	31 G/9	45°40′	74°26′
Chatham	MUN2/AZM2	ON	Kenora	40 J/9	42°31′	82°14′
Chatham	UNP/LNO	NB	Northumberland	21 P/3	47°02′	65°28′
Chatham	GEOG/GÉOG	NB	Northumberland	21 P/3	47°02′	65°26′
Chatham Head	UNP/LNO	NB	Northumberland	21 I/13	47°00′	65°33′
Chatham Islands	ISL/ÎLE	BC	Victoria	92 B/6	48°26′	123°15′
Chatham Islands 4	IR/RI	BC	Victoria	92 B/6	48°26′	123°15′
Chatham Sound	BAY/BAIE	BC	Range 5 Coast	103 J/7	54°22′	130°35′
Chatscah 2	IR/RI	BC	Range 3 Coast	93 D/14	52°53′	127°05′
Chats Haven	UNP/LNO	ON	Renfrew	31 F/8	45°26′	76°21′
Chatsworth	VILG/VILG	ON	Grey	41 A/7	44°27′	80°54′
Chattan Park	UNP/LNO	NS	Pictou	11 E/10	45°36′	62°40′

NAME NOM	ENTITY ENTITÉ	LOC 1 LIEU 1	LOC 2 LIEU 2	MAP CARTE	POSITION LAT	LONG
Chatterton	UNP/LNO	ON	Hastings	31 C/3	44°15′	77°29′
Chatwin Lake	LAKE/LAC	MB		64 K/15	58°54′	100°48′
Chaudière-Appalaches	MUN1/AZM1	QC	Bellechasse	21 L/7	46°29′	70°37′
Chaudière, Chutes de la	FALL/CHUT	QC	Les Chutes-de-la-Chaudière	21 L/11	46°43′	71°17′
Chaudière Dam	MISC/DIV	ON	Parry Sound	41 I/1	46°08′	80°01′
Chaudière, Lac	LAKE/LAC	QC	Kamouraska	21 N/5	47°18′	69°46′
Chaudière, Rivière	RIV/CDE	QC	Les Chutes-de-la-Chaudière	21 L/11	46°45′	71°17′
Chaudron, Le	UNP/LNO	QC	Montmagny	21 L/16	46°46′	70°04′
Chaufferie, La	UNP/LNO	QC	Lac-Saint-Jean-Est	22 D/12	48°39′	71°49′
Chaumox	UNP/LNO	BC	Yale Division Yale	92 H/14	49°57′	121°29′
Chaumox 11	IR/RI	BC	Yale Division Yale	92 H/14	49°56′	121°29′
Chaussée-de-Castors, La	UNP/LNO	QC	Montmagny	21 L/9	46°43′	70°07′
Chaussée-du-Moulin, La	UNP/LNO	QC	Les Îles-de-la-Madeleine	11 N/5	47°23′	61°57′
Chauve, Mont	MTN/MNT	QC	Denis-Riverin	22 B/16	48°50′	66°16′
Chauvigny	UNP/LNO	QC	Le Fjord-du-Saguenay	22 D/6	48°25′	71°14′
Chauvin	VILG/VILG	AB	7-43-1-W4	73 D/9	52°42′	110°07′
Chauvreulx, Rivière	RIV/CDE	QC	Jamésie	33 J/5	54°21′	75°44′
Chavannes, Lac	LAKE/LAC	QC	Pontiac	31 K/14	46°51′	77°09′
Chavigny, Lac	LAKE/LAC	QC	Kativik	34 J/3	58°12′	75°08′
Chawathil 4	IR/RI	BC	Yale Division Yale	92 H/5	49°22′	121°33′
Chazel	VILG/VILG	QC	Abitibi-Ouest	32 D/14	48°52′	79°03′
Cheadle	UNP/LNO	AB	2-24-26-W4	82 P/4	51°01′	113°32′
Cheakamus	UNP/LNO	BC	New Westminster	92 G/14	49°50′	123°09′
Cheakamus 11	IR/RI	BC	New Westminster	92 G/14	49°48′	123°11′
Cheakamus Lake	LAKE/LAC	BC	New Westminster	92 G/15	50°00′	122°54′
Cheakamus River	RIV/CDE	BC	New Westminster	92 G/14	49°47′	123°10′
Cheam 1	IR/RI	BC	New Westminster	92 H/4	49°12′	121°46′
Cheam View	UNP/LNO	BC	Yale Division Yale	92 H/5	49°17′	121°40′
Cheam View	UNP/LNO	BC	Yale Division Yale	92 H/5	49°15′	121°41′
Cheapside	UNP/LNO	ON	Haldimand	30 L/13	42°50′	79°59′
Chebogue Harbour	BAY/BAIE	NS	Yarmouth	20 O/9	43°45′	66°06′
Chebogue Point	UNP/LNO	NS	Yarmouth	20 O/16	43°45′	66°07′
Chebogue Point	CAPE/CAP	NS	Yarmouth	20 O/9	43°44′	66°07′
Chécatica, Rivière	RIV/CDE	QC	Côte-Nord-du-Golfe-Saint-Laurent	12 O/8	51°23′	58°17′
Checkaklis Island 9	IR/RI	BC	Rupert	92 L/4	50°05′	127°33′
Checleset Bay	BAY/BAIE	BC	Rupert	92 L/4	50°06′	127°40′
Chedabucto Bay	BAY/BAIE	NS	Guysborough	11 F/6	45°24′	61°08′
Chedabucto Lake	LAKE/LAC	NT	Mackenzie	85 J	62°23′	115°32′
Cheddar	UNP/LNO	ON	Haliburton	31 D/16	44°59′	78°08′
Chedderville	UNP/LNO	AB	17-37-6-W5	83 B/2	52°10′	114°50′
Chedoke Park	UNP/LNO	ON	Wentworth	30 M/4	43°15′	79°55′
Cheecham	UNP/LNO	AB	15-84-6-W4	74 D/7	56°17′	110°52′
Cheekye	UNP/LNO	BC	New Westminster	92 G/14	49°48′	123°09′
Cheepash River	RIV/CDE	ON	Cochrane	42 P/2	51°03′	80°59′
Cheepay River	RIV/CDE	ON	Cochrane	42 O/6	51°28′	83°24′
Cheeseborough	UNP/LNO	ON	Leeds	31 C/8	44°22′	76°11′
Cheese Factory Corner	UNP/LNO	NS	Hants	11 E/4	45°05′	63°39′
Cheeseman Lake - also-aussi - Des Marets, Lac	LAKE/LAC	NF		12 M/16	51°58′	62°01′
Cheeseman Lake	LAKE/LAC	ON	Thunder Bay	52 H/6	49°27′	89°20′
Cheesish 15	IR/RI	BC	Nootka	92 E/9	49°40′	126°28′
Cheetsum's Farm 1	IR/RI	BC	Kamloops Division Yale	92 I/11	50°41′	121°19′
Cheewat 4A	IR/RI	BC	Renfrew	92 C/10	48°39′	124°49′
Chef, Rivière du	RIV/CDE	QC	Le Domaine-du-Roy	32 H/6	49°20′	73°24′
Chehalis 5	IR/RI	BC	New Westminster	92 H/5	49°18′	121°54′
Chehalis 6	IR/RI	BC	New Westminster	92 H/5	49°17′	121°53′
Chehalis Lake	LAKE/LAC	BC	New Westminster	92 G/8	49°27′	122°01′
Chehalis River	RIV/CDE	BC	New Westminster	92 H/5	49°16′	121°56′
Chekwelp 26	IR/RI	BC	New Westminster	92 G/6	49°25′	123°30′
Chekwelp 26A	IR/RI	BC	New Westminster	92 G/6	49°25′	123°29′
Chelan	HAM/HAM	SK	16-42-10-W2	63 D/11	52°37′	103°23′
Chelan Seamount	SEAU/SMER	—		3000	49°45′	131°32′
Chelaslie Arm	BAY/BAIE	BC	Range 4 Coast	93 F/5	53°27′	125°36′
Chelaslie River	RIV/CDE	BC	Range 4 Coast	93 F/5	53°28′	125°42′
Chelmsford	UNP/LNO	NB	Northumberland	21 I/13	46°53′	65°39′
Chelmsford	UNP/LNO	ON	Sudbury	41 I/11	46°35′	81°12′
Chelsea	VILG/VILG	QC	Les Collines-de-l'Outaouais	31 G/12	45°30′	75°47′
Chelsea	UNP/LNO	NS	Lunenburg	21 A/7	44°22′	64°45′
Chelsea	UNP/LNO	QC	Les Collines-de-l'Outaouais	31 G/12	45°30′	75°47′
Chelsea, Barrage	MISC/DIV	QC	Les Collines-de-l'Outaouais	31 G/12	45°31′	75°47′
Chelsea Green	UNP/LNO	ON	Middlesex	40 I/14	42°58′	81°13′
Chelsea, Ruisseau	RIV/CDE	QC	Les Collines-de-l'Outaouais	31 G/5	45°29′	75°45′
Cheltenham	UNP/LNO	ON	Peel	30 M/13	43°45′	79°55′
Chelton	UNP/LNO	PE	Prince	11 L/5	46°18′	63°45′
Chemainus	UNP/LNO	BC	Chemainus	92 B/13	48°55′	123°43′
Chemainus 13	IR/RI	BC	Oyster	92 B/13	49°00′	123°47′

NAME NOM	ENTITY ENTITÉ	LOC 1 LIEU 1	LOC 2 LIEU 2	MAP CARTE	POSITION	
					LAT	LONG
Chemainus Land District	GEOG/GÉOG	BC		92 B	48°54′	123°47′
Chemainus River	RIV/CDE	BC	Chemainus	92 B/13	48°54′	123°41′
Chemawawin 1	IR/RI	MB		63 F/8	53°19′	100°23′
Chemawawin 2	IR/RI	MB		63 G/4	53°06′	99°48′
Chemawawin 3	IR/RI	MB	45,46-16,17-W	63 B/13	52°57′	99°44′
Chemical Road	UNP/LNO	NB	Albert	21 H/15	45°47′	64°40′
Chemin-Craig	UNP/LNO	QC	Les Chutes-de-la-Chaudière	21 L/11	46°38′	71°22′
Chemin-des-Buttes	UNP/LNO	QC	Les Îles-de-la-Madeleine	11 N/5	47°24′	61°47′
Chemin des Canots, Rivière du	RIV/CDE	QC	Charlevoix	21 M/15	47°46′	70°48′
Chemin-des-Pins	UNP/LNO	QC	Les Collines-de-l'Outaouais	31 G/12	45°35′	75°52′
Chemin-du-Lac	UNP/LNO	QC	Rivière-du-Loup	21 N/12	47°45′	69°33′
Chemin-Guay	UNP/LNO	QC	Matawinie	31 J/1	46°13′	74°15′
Cheminis	UNP/LNO	ON	Timiskaming	32 D/4	48°10′	79°32′
Chemin-Neuf	UNP/LNO	QC	Bellechasse	21 L/7	46°26′	70°36′
Chemong	UNP/LNO	SK	5-49-1-W2	63 E/1	53°12′	102°06′
Chemong Heights	UNP/LNO	ON	Peterborough	31 D/8	44°24′	78°23′
Chemong Lake	LAKE/LAC	ON	Peterborough	31 D/8	44°24′	78°23′
Chemong Park	UNP/LNO	ON	Peterborough	31 D/8	44°23′	78°23′
Chenahkint 12	IR/RI	BC	Nootka	92 E/15	49°53′	126°58′
Chenail-du-Moine	UNP/LNO	QC	Le Bas-Richelieu	31 I/2	46°05′	72°58′
Chenatha 4	IR/RI	BC	Clayoquot	92 C/14	48°57′	125°27′
Chenaux	UNP/LNO	ON	Renfrew	31 F/10	45°34′	76°43′
Chenaux, Les	UNP/LNO	QC	Lac-Saint-Jean-Est	32 A/9	48°44′	72°04′
Chêne, Rivière du	RIV/CDE	QC	Lotbinière	21 L/12	46°34′	72°00′
Chêne, Rivière du	RIV/CDE	QC	Deux-Montagnes	31 H/12	45°33′	73°53′
Chénéville	TOWN/VIL2	QC	Papineau	31 G/14	45°53′	75°03′
Cheney	UNP/LNO	ON	Russell	31 G/6	45°25′	75°15′
Cheney Island	ISL/ÎLE	NB	Charlotte	21 B/10	44°39′	66°43′
Chénier	UNP/LNO	QC	La Vallée-de-la-Gatineau	31 K/1	46°06′	76°07′
Chenil, Lac	LAKE/LAC	QC	Minganie	12 O/13	51°51′	59°41′
Chenon, Lac	LAKE/LAC	QC	Témiscamingue	31 M/8	47°19′	78°28′
Chensagi, Lac	LAKE/LAC	QC	Jamésie	32 K/2	50°05′	76°45′
Chepstow	UNP/LNO	PE	Kings	11 L/8	46°21′	62°13′
Chepstow	UNP/LNO	ON	Bruce	41 A/3	44°09′	81°16′
Chequis 3	IR/RI	BC	Clayoquot	92 C/14	48°59′	125°24′
Cherbourg	UNP/LNO	QC	Matane	22 B/15	48°55′	67°00′
Cherbourg-Centre	UNP/LNO	QC	Matane	22 B/14	48°55′	67°04′
Cherbourg-Ouest	UNP/LNO	QC	Matane	22 B/14	48°51′	67°10′
Cherhill	UNP/LNO	AB	9-56-5-W5	83 G/15	53°49′	114°41′
Cherpeta Creek	RIV/CDE	SK	73-20-W3	73 N/11	55°35′	109°03′
Cherrier, Lac	LAKE/LAC	QC	Vallée-de-l'Or	32 B/12	48°43′	75°47′
Cherry	UNP/LNO	ON	York	30 M/14	43°58′	79°29′
Cherry Brook	UNP/LNO	NS	Halifax	11 D/11	44°43′	63°29′
Cherry Burton	UNP/LNO	NB	Westmorland	21 H/16	45°54′	64°29′
Cherry Creek	UNP/LNO	BC	Alberni	92 F/7	49°17′	124°47′
Cherry Creek	RIV/CDE	BC	Osoyoos Division Yale	82 L/7	50°16′	118°38′
Cherry Creek	RIV/CDE	BC	Kamloops Division Yale	92 I/10	50°43′	120°38′
Cherryfield	UNP/LNO	NS	Lunenburg	21 A/10	44°37′	64°48′
Cherryfield	UNP/LNO	NB	Westmorland	21 I/2	46°08′	64°48′
Cherryfield Road	UNP/LNO	NS	Annapolis	21 A/10	44°39′	64°48′
Cherry Grove	UNP/LNO	ON	Middlesex	40 P/3	43°11′	81°11′
Cherry Grove	UNP/LNO	AB	9-62-1-W4	73 L/8	54°22′	110°06′
Cherry Heights	UNP/LNO	ON	Wentworth	30 M/4	43°13′	79°45′
Cherry Hill	UNP/LNO	PE	Kings	11 L/7	46°22′	62°49′
Cherry Hill	UNP/LNO	NS	Lunenburg	21 A/2	44°09′	64°30′
Cherry Hill	UNP/LNO	NB	Queens	21 G/16	45°48′	66°02′
Cherry Lane Estates	UNP/LNO	ON	Essex	40 J/2	42°02′	82°36′
Cherry Point	UNP/LNO	AB	10-83-13-W6	84 D/4	56°11′	119°57′
Cherry Ridge	UNP/LNO	SK	8-51-15-W2	73 H/8	53°24′	104°10′
Cherry River	UNP/LNO	QC	Memphrémagog	31 H/8	45°19′	72°10′
Cherryvale	UNP/LNO	NB	Queens	21 I/3	46°03′	65°29′
Cherry Valley	UNP/LNO	PE	Queens	11 L/2	46°10′	62°55′
Cherry Valley	UNP/LNO	ON	Prince Edward	30 N/14	43°56′	77°09′
Cherryville	UNP/LNO	BC	Osoyoos Division Yale	82 L/2	50°15′	118°37′
Cherrywood	UNP/LNO	ON	Ontario	30 M/14	43°51′	79°09′
Cherrywood Acres	UNP/LNO	ON	Welland	30 M/3	43°06′	79°06′
Cherrywood Station	UNP/LNO	ON	Ontario	30 M/14	43°51′	79°08′
Chertsey	VILG/VILG	QC	Matawinie	31 I/4	46°10′	73°55′
Ches-la-kee 3	IR/RI	BC	Rupert	92 L/10	50°34′	126°59′
Cheslatta	UNP/LNO	BC	Range 4 Coast	93 F/13	53°49′	125°48′
Cheslatta 1 - see-voir - Unasaorta 1	IR/RI	BC		93 F/13	53°57′	125°45′
Cheslatta Lake	LAKE/LAC	BC	Range 4 Coast	93 F/11	53°44′	125°22′
Chesley	TOWN/VIL2	ON	Bruce	41 A/6	44°17′	81°05′
Chesley Lake	LAKE/LAC	ON	Bruce	41 A/11	44°33′	81°14′
Chesnaye	UNP/LNO	MB		54 L/1	58°12′	94°09′

NAME NOM	ENTITY ENTITÉ	LOC 1 LIEU 1	LOC 2 LIEU 2	MAP CARTE	POSITION LAT	LONG
Chesney Bay	BAY/BAIE	ON	Cochrane	42 A/16	48°46'	80°06'
Chester	VILG/VILG	NS	Lunenburg	21 A/9	44°33'	64°15'
Chester	MUN1/AZM1	NS	Lunenburg	21 A/9	44°41'	64°22'
Chester	UNP/LNO	NB	Albert	21 H/15	45°47'	64°44'
Chester	UNP/LNO	NB	Saint John	21 H/5	45°21'	65°34'
Chester Acres	UNP/LNO	NS	Lunenburg	21 A/9	44°35'	64°11'
Chester Basin	UNP/LNO	NS	Lunenburg	21 A/9	44°34'	64°19'
Chester Bay	BAY/BAIE	NT	Keewatin	66 M	67°45'	102°15'
Chester-Est	VILG/VILG	QC	Arthabaska	21 L/4	46°02'	71°42'
Chesterfield	UNP/LNO	ON	Oxford	40 P/7	43°18'	80°40'
Chesterfield Inlet	HAM/HAM	NT	Keewatin	55 O/7	63°20'	90°42'
Chesterfield Inlet	BAY/BAIE	NT	Keewatin	55 O/12	63°43'	92°00'
Chesterfield No. 261	MUN2/AZM2	SK		72 N/3	51°10'	109°30'
Chester Grant	UNP/LNO	NS	Lunenburg	21 A/9	44°37'	64°19'
Chestermere	TOWN/VIL2	AB	3-24-28-W4	82 P/4	51°02'	113°49'
Chestermere Lake - see-voir - Chestermere	VILG/VILG	AB		82 P/4	51°02'	113°49'
Chester No. 125	MUN2/AZM2	SK		62 L/2	50°10'	103°00'
Chesterville	VILG/VILG	QC	Arthabaska	21 E/13	45°58'	71°49'
Chesterville	VILG/VILG	ON	Dundas	31 G/3	45°06'	75°14'
Chestnut Hills	UNP/LNO	ON	York	30 M/12	43°40'	79°31'
Chetarpe	UNP/LNO	BC	Clayoquot	92 E/1	49°15'	126°00'
Chetarpe 17	IR/RI	BC	Clayoquot	92 E/1	49°14'	126°01'
Chéticamp	UNP/LNO	NS	Inverness	11 K/11	46°38'	61°01'
Chéticamp Harbour	BAY/BAIE	NS	Inverness	11 K/11	46°38'	61°01'
Chéticamp Island - see-voir - La Pointe	UNP/LNO	NS		11 K/11	46°37'	61°03'
Chéticamp Island	ISL/ÎLE	NS	Inverness	11 K/11	46°38'	61°03'
Chéticamp Lake	LAKE/LAC	NS	Victoria	11 K/10	46°39'	60°36'
Chéticamp River	RIV/CDE	NS	Inverness	11 K/10	46°40'	60°57'
Chettleburgh Peak	MTN/MNT	BC	Cassiar	94 D/13	56°48'	127°53'
Chetwynd	MUN1/AZM1	BC	Peace River	93 P/12	55°42'	121°38'
Chetwynd	UNP/LNO	ON	Parry Sound	31 E/11	45°37'	79°19'
Chevalier Bay	BAY/BAIE	NT	Franklin	78 G	75°05'	111°24'
Cheverie	UNP/LNO	NS	Hants	21 H/1	45°09'	64°10'
Chevery	UNP/LNO	QC	Côte-Nord-du-Golfe-Saint-Laurent	12 J/5	50°28'	59°36'
Cheves Creek	RIV/CDE	BC	Peace River	94 J/10	58°33'	122°50'
Cheviot	UNP/LNO	SK	28-35-3-W3	73 B/1	52°02'	106°22'
Chevrefils	UNP/LNO	QC	Asbestos	21 E/12	45°43'	71°49'
Cheyne Point	CAPE/CAP	NT	Franklin	58 F	74°30'	95°14'
Cheyne Settlement	UNP/LNO	NB	Kings	21 G/8	45°26'	66°14'
Chezacut	UNP/LNO	BC	Range 3 Coast	93 C/8	52°24'	124°02'
Chezacut Cemetery 5	IR/RI	BC	Range 3 Coast	93 C/8	52°21'	124°03'
Chez David	UNP/LNO	QC	La Haute-Côte-Nord	22 C/15	48°54'	68°46'
Chez Geoffrion	UNP/LNO	QC	Deux-Montagnes	31 G/8	45°28'	74°06'
Chez Norbert	UNP/LNO	QC	La Haute-Côte-Nord	22 C/15	48°54'	68°39'
Cheztainya Lake 11	IR/RI	BC	Cassiar	93 M/9	55°37'	126°05'
Chiasson	UNP/LNO	NB	Gloucester	21 P/10	47°44'	64°38'
Chiblow Lake	LAKE/LAC	ON	Algoma	41 J/6	46°21'	83°03'
Chibouet, Rivière	RIV/CDE	QC	Les Maskoutains	31 H/15	45°47'	72°52'
Chibougamau	CITY/VIL1	QC	Jamésie	32 G/16	49°55'	74°22'
Chibougamau, Lac	LAKE/LAC	QC	Jamésie	32 G/16	49°50'	74°15'
Chibougamau, Rivière	RIV/CDE	QC	Jamésie	32 G/12	49°42'	75°57'
Chic-Chocs, Monts	MTN/MNT	QC	Denis-Riverin	22 B/16	48°55'	66°00'
Chic-Chocs, Réserve faunique des	PARK/PARC	QC	Denis-Riverin	22 A/13	48°58'	65°45'
Chichester	VILG/VILG	QC	Pontiac	31 F/14	45°55'	77°07'
Chicken 224	IR/RI	SK		74 P/4	59°15'	105°40'
Chicken 225	IR/RI	SK		74 P/5	59°20'	105°45'
Chicken 226	IR/RI	SK		74 P/2	59°15'	104°55'
Chicken Lake	LAKE/LAC	MB	87-21-W	64 C/10	56°31'	100°41'
Chicken Lake	LAKE/LAC	SK/MB		63 M/9	55°33'	102°02'
Chick Lake	LAKE/LAC	NT	Mackenzie	106 H	65°52'	128°06'
Chicobi, Lac	LAKE/LAC	QC	Abitibi	32 D/15	48°53'	78°30'
Chicomo, Lac	LAKE/LAC	QC	Sept-Rivières	22 P/12	51°35'	65°49'
Chicot	UNP/LNO	QC	Deux-Montagnes	31 H/12	45°36'	73°56'
Chicot, Rivière	RIV/CDE	QC	D'Autray	31 I/3	46°08'	73°07'
Chicot, Rivière du	RIV/CDE	QC	Deux-Montagnes	31 H/12	45°35'	73°51'
Chicoutai, Pointe	CAPE/CAP	QC	Côte-Nord-du-Golfe-Saint-Laurent	12 K/2	50°11'	60°57'
Chicoutillette	UNP/LNO	QC	La Haute-Côte-Nord	22 C/4	48°15'	69°47'
Chicoutimi	CITY/VIL1	QC	Le Fjord-du-Saguenay	22 D/6	48°26'	71°04'
Chicoutimi-Centre	UNP/LNO	QC	Le Fjord-du-Saguenay	22 D/6	48°26'	71°04'
Chicoutimi-Est	UNP/LNO	QC	Le Fjord-du-Saguenay	22 D/6	48°26'	71°02'
Chicoutimi-Nord	UNP/LNO	QC	Le Fjord-du-Saguenay	22 D/6	48°27'	71°04'
Chicoutimi-Ouest	UNP/LNO	QC	Le Fjord-du-Saguenay	22 D/6	48°26'	71°05'
Chicoutimi, Rivière	RIV/CDE	QC	Le Fjord-du-Saguenay	22 D/6	48°26'	71°05'
Chidley, Cape	CAPE/CAP	NF		25 A/8	60°23'	64°26'
Chidley, Cape	CAPE/CAP	NT	Franklin	25 A	60°23'	64°26'

NAME NOM	ENTITY ENTITÉ	LOC 1 LIEU 1	LOC 2 LIEU 2	MAP CARTE	POSITION LAT	LONG
Chidliak Bay	BAY/BAIE	NT	Franklin	26 B	64°57′	66°40′
Chief Bay	BAY/BAIE	ON	Thunder Bay	52 H/11	49°33′	89°01′
Chief Lake	LAKE/LAC	BC	Cariboo	93 J/3	54°08′	123°00′
Chief Louis Lake	LAKE/LAC	BC	Range 4 Coast	93 E/9	53°32′	126°03′
Chief Morris 13	IR/RI	BC	Range 4 Coast	93 F/1	53°04′	124°21′
Chiefs Point	CAPE/CAP	ON	Bruce	41 A/11	44°41′	81°18′
Chief's Point 28	IR/RI	ON	Bruce	41 A/11	44°40′	81°17′
Chienne, Lac à la	LAKE/LAC	QC	Mékinac	31 P/4	47°02′	73°31′
Chiens, Rivière aux	RIV/CDE	QC	Thérèse-De Blainville	31 H/12	45°39′	73°46′
Chiganois River	RIV/CDE	NS	Colchester	11 E/6	45°22′	63°25′
Chig-in-kaht 8	IR/RI	BC	Range 5 Coast	103 I/16	54°51′	128°21′
Chignecto	UNP/LNO	NS	Cumberland	21 H/9	45°44′	64°12′
Chignecto Bay	BAY/BAIE	NS	Cumberland	21 H/10	45°35′	64°40′
Chignecto Bay	BAY/BAIE	NB		21 H/10	45°35′	64°45′
Chignecto, Cape	CAPE/CAP	NS	Cumberland	21 H/7	45°20′	64°57′
Chignecto Isthmus	CAPE/CAP	NS	Cumberland	21 H/16	45°55′	64°10′
Chigoubiche, Lac	LAKE/LAC	QC	Le Domaine-du-Roy	32 H/4	49°05′	73°32′
Chigwell	UNP/LNO	AB	33-40-25-W4	83 A/5	52°29′	113°32′
Chikopi	UNP/LNO	ON	Parry Sound	31 E/12	45°39′	79°43′
Chilako River	RIV/CDE	BC	Cariboo	93 G/15	53°53′	122°59′
Chilanko Forks	UNP/LNO	BC	Range 3 Coast	93 C/1	52°07′	124°04′
Chilanko River	RIV/CDE	BC	Cariboo	93 B/4	52°07′	123°41′
Chilco Lake 1	IR/RI	BC	Range 3 Coast	92 N/8	51°25′	124°07′
Chilco Lake 1A	IR/RI	BC	Range 3 Coast	92 N/8	51°25′	124°06′
Chilcotin Forest	UNP/LNO	BC	Cariboo	93 B/2	52°07′	122°34′
Chilcotin Ranges	MTN/MNT	BC	Range 2 Coast	92 O/3	51°10′	123°15′
Chilcotin River	RIV/CDE	BC	Lillooet	92 O/9	51°44′	122°24′
Child Lake 164A	IR/RI	AB	15-109-16-W5	84 K/7	58°29′	116°35′
Childs Lake	LAKE/LAC	MB	30-26-W	62 N/11	51°36′	101°05′
Childs Mines	UNP/LNO	ON	Hastings	31 F/4	45°05′	77°37′
Chilhil 6	IR/RI	BC	Lillooet	92 I/12	50°38′	121°48′
Chilkat River	RIV/CDE	BC	Cassiar	104 M/12	59°41′	135°52′
Chilko Lake	LAKE/LAC	BC	Range 2 Coast	92 N/8	51°16′	124°04′
Chilkoot Pass	VALL/VALL	BC	Cassiar	104 M/11	59°42′	135°14′
Chilkoot Trail National Historic Site - also-aussi - Piste-Chilkoot, Lieu historique national de la	PARK/PARC	BC	Cassiar	104 M/15	59°45′	134°58′
Chilko River	RIV/CDE	BC	Cariboo	93 B/3	52°06′	123°27′
Chilliwack	MUN1/AZM1	BC	New Westminster	92 H/4	49°11′	121°57′
Chilliwack	UNP/LNO	BC	New Westminster	92 H/4	49°10′	121°57′
Chilliwack Lake	LAKE/LAC	BC	Yale Division Yale	92 H/3	49°03′	121°25′
Chilliwack River	RIV/CDE	BC	New Westminster	92 H/4	49°06′	121°58′
Chillon	UNP/LNO	MB	27-18-28-W	62 K/11	50°35′	101°13′
Chiman Uchimaskwaw	UNP/LNO	QC	Jamésie	33 D/10	52°31′	78°38′
Chimdimash 2	IR/RI	BC	Range 5 Coast	103 I/9	54°40′	128°22′
Chimdimash 2A	IR/RI	BC	Range 5 Coast	103 I/9	54°41′	128°21′
Chimney Bay	BAY/BAIE	NF		12 I/16	50°48′	56°09′
Chimney Corner	UNP/LNO	NS	Inverness	11 K/6	46°24′	61°09′
Chimney Cove	UNP/LNO	NF		12 G/8	49°22′	58°13′
Chimney Creek	RIV/CDE	BC	Cariboo	93 B/1	52°04′	122°16′
Chimney Creek 5	IR/RI	BC	Cariboo	93 B/1	52°04′	122°17′
Chimney Lake	LAKE/LAC	BC	Lillooet	92 P/13	51°55′	121°57′
Chimney Tickle	UNP/LNO	NF		3 D/4	52°10′	55°42′
Chin	UNP/LNO	AB	25-9-19-W4	82 H/16	49°46′	112°27′
China Bar	UNP/LNO	BC	Yale Division Yale	92 H/14	49°48′	121°27′
China Creek	RIV/CDE	BC	Alberni	92 F/2	49°09′	124°48′
China Point	UNP/LNO	PE	Queens	11 L/2	46°08′	62°55′
Chin, Cape	CAPE/CAP	ON	Bruce	41 H/3	45°07′	81°17′
Chinchaga River	RIV/CDE	AB/BC		84 L/16	58°53′	118°20′
Chin Coulee	VALL/VALL	AB	9-18-W4	82 H/9	49°39′	112°16′
Chineside	UNP/LNO	BC	New Westminster	92 G/7	49°16′	122°50′
Chiniguchi Lake	LAKE/LAC	ON	Sudbury	41 I/15	46°57′	80°42′
Chin Lakes	LAKE/LAC	AB	7,8,9-16,17,18-W4	82 H/9	49°37′	112°13′
Chinook	UNP/LNO	AB	4-29-7-W4	72 M/7	51°27′	110°55′
Chinook Cove	UNP/LNO	BC	Kamloops Division Yale	92 P/8	51°15′	120°09′
Chinook Cove	UNP/LNO	BC	Kamloops Division Yale	92 P/1	51°14′	120°10′
Chinook Valley	UNP/LNO	AB	24-86-24-W5	84 C/5	56°29′	117°39′
Chin River	RIV/CDE	ON	Cochrane	42 H/2	49°14′	80°52′
Chinusaw Pachistiwakan	UNP/LNO	QC	Jamésie	33 I/13	54°54′	73°49′
Chipai Lake	LAKE/LAC	ON	Kenora	43 D/13	52°56′	87°53′
Chipai River	RIV/CDE	ON	Kenora	43 D/13	52°51′	87°53′
Chipewyan 201	IR/RI	AB	109,110,111-6,7-W4	74 L/10	58°33′	110°58′
Chipewyan 201A	IR/RI	AB	21-111-4-W4	74 L/10	58°39′	110°36′
Chipewyan 201B	IR/RI	AB	33-110-5-W5	74 L/10	58°36′	110°47′
Chipewyan 201C	IR/RI	AB		74 L/7	58°27′	110°55′
Chipewyan 201D	IR/RI	AB	27-108-6-W4	74 L/7	58°23′	110°55′
Chipewyan 201E	IR/RI	AB	20-108-6-W4	74 L/7	58°23′	110°59′

NAME NOM	ENTITY ENTITÉ	LOC 1 LIEU 1	LOC 2 LIEU 2	MAP CARTE	POSITION LAT	LONG
Chipewyan 201F	IR/RI	AB	13-104-9-W4	74 L/3	58°03'	111°20'
Chipewyan 201G	IR/RI	AB	3-103-9-W4	74 E/14	57°54'	111°25'
Chipewyan Lake	UNP/LNO	AB	33-34-91-22-W4	84 A/14	56°56'	113°27'
Chipewyan Lake	LAKE/LAC	MB		64 G/16	57°59'	98°27'
Chip Lake	UNP/LNO	AB	32-53-10-W5	83 G/11	53°37'	115°26'
Chip Lake	LAKE/LAC	AB	53,54-9,10-W5	83 G/11	53°40'	115°23'
Chipman	VILG/VILG	NB	Queens	21 I/4	46°10'	65°53'
Chipman	VILG/VILG	AB	30-54-18-W4	83 H/10	53°42'	112°38'
Chipman	GEOG/GÉOG	NB	Queens	21 I/4	46°10'	65°50'
Chipman Brook	UNP/LNO	NS	Kings	21 H/2	45°11'	64°41'
Chipman Creek	RIV/CDE	BC	Cowichan Lake	92 B/13	48°51'	123°56'
Chipman Lake	LAKE/LAC	ON	Thunder Bay	42 E/16	49°58'	86°15'
Chipman River	RIV/CDE	SK		74 P/6	59°17'	105°16'
Chipmans Corner	UNP/LNO	NS	Kings	21 H/1	45°06'	64°29'
*Chipmunk	UNP/LNO	BC	Cassiar	94 D/12	56°42'	127°49'
Chippawa	UNP/LNO	ON	Welland	30 M/3	43°04'	79°03'
Chippawa Hill	UNP/LNO	ON	Bruce	41 A/11	44°31'	81°20'
Chipperfield	UNP/LNO	SK	12-27-17-W3	72 N/8	51°17'	108°15'
Chippewa	UNP/LNO	ON	Lennox and Addington	31 C/7	44°30'	76°50'
Chippewa Island 4	IR/RI	ON	Muskoka	41 H/1	45°05'	80°02'
Chippewa River	RIV/CDE	ON	Algoma	41 K/16	46°56'	84°26'
Chippewas of Georgina Island First Nation	IR/RI	ON	York	31 D/6	44°24'	79°18'
Chippewas of Georgina Island First Nation 33A	IR/RI	ON	York	31 D/6	44°24'	79°18'
Chippewas of the Thames First Nation 42	IR/RI	ON	Middlesex	40 I/14	42°49'	81°30'
Chiputachikwan	UNP/LNO	QC	Kativik	24 G/13	57°57'	67°44'
Chiputneticook Lakes	LAKE/LAC	NB	York	21 G/12	45°37'	67°40'
Chisasibi	VILG/VILG	QC	Jamésie	33 E/9	53°40'	78°20'
Chiselhurst	UNP/LNO	ON	Perth	40 P/6	43°26'	81°26'
Chisel Lake	UNP/LNO	MB	34-67-18-W	63 K/16	54°50'	100°07'
Chiseuquis 9	IR/RI	BC	Nootka	92 E/14	49°50'	127°02'
Chisholm	MUN2/AZM2	ON	Nipissing	31 L/3	46°08'	79°15'
Chisholm	UNP/LNO	AB	26-28-2-W5	83 J/16	54°55'	114°10'
Chisholm's Mills	UNP/LNO	ON	Hastings	31 C/6	44°21'	77°19'
Chiswick	UNP/LNO	ON	Nipissing	31 L/3	46°07'	79°11'
Chitek	UNP/LNO	SK	55-12-W3	73 G/13	53°48'	107°45'
Chitek Lake	VILG/VILG	SK	16-55-12-W3	73 G/12	53°45'	107°43'
Chitek Lake	LAKE/LAC	MB	39,40-14-W	63 B/6	52°25'	99°24'
Chitek Lake	LAKE/LAC	SK		73 G/12	53°45'	107°47'
Chitek Lake 191	IR/RI	SK		73 G/12	53°42'	107°47'
Chitek River	RIV/CDE	SK	59-16-W3	73 K/1	54°06'	108°16'
Chiyask Bay	BAY/BAIE	NT	Keewatin	32 M/5	51°29'	79°33'
Chiyask Point	CAPE/CAP	ON	Cochrane	32 M/5	51°29'	79°35'
Choate	UNP/LNO	BC	Yale Division Yale	92 H/6	49°28'	121°25'
Chochocouane, Rivière	RIV/CDE	QC	Vallée-de-l'Or	31 N/11	47°36'	77°08'
Chockpish	UNP/LNO	NB	Kent	21 I/10	46°34'	64°44'
Chocolate Cove	UNP/LNO	NB	Charlotte	21 B/15	44°57'	66°59'
Choelquoit Lake	LAKE/LAC	BC	Range 2 Coast	92 N/9	51°42'	124°12'
Choiceland	TOWN/VIL2	SK	17,18-52-17-W2	73 H/8	53°29'	104°29'
Choisy	UNP/LNO	QC	Vaudreuil-Soulanges	31 G/8	45°29'	74°13'
Chokio	UNP/LNO	AB	24-7-28-W4	82 H/13	49°36'	113°39'
Chomedey	UNP/LNO	QC	Laval	31 H/12	45°32'	73°45'
Chopaka	UNP/LNO	BC	Similkameen Division Yale	82 E/4	49°00'	119°43'
Chopaka 7 & 8	IR/RI	BC	Similkameen Division Yale	82 E/4	49°03'	119°43'
Chorkbak Inlet	BAY/BAIE	NT	Franklin	36 B	64°30'	74°25'
Chorney Beach	VILG/VILG	SK	6-33-11-W2	62 M/13	51°48'	103°33'
Chortitz	HAM/HAM	SK	19-13-12-W3	72 J/4	50°06'	107°39'
Chortitz	UNP/LNO	MB	18,20-2-4-W	62 H/4	49°08'	97°59'
Chortitz	UNP/LNO	SK	5-41-4-W3	73 B/7	52°30'	106°33'
Chowade River	RIV/CDE	BC	Peace River	94 B/10	56°42'	122°33'
Chown, Mount	MTN/MNT	AB	51-10-W6	83 E/6	53°24'	119°25'
Christensen Point	CAPE/CAP	BC	Rupert	102 I/16	50°50'	128°13'
Christian Island	UNP/LNO	ON	Simcoe	41 A/16	44°49'	80°11'
Christian Island	ISL/ÎLE	ON	Simcoe	41 A/16	44°50'	80°12'
Christian Island 30	IR/RI	ON	Simcoe	41 A/16	44°50'	80°12'
Christian Island 30A	IR/RI	ON	Simcoe	41 A/16	44°48'	80°08'
Christian Valley	UNP/LNO	ON	Nipissing	31 L/3	46°04'	79°29'
Christian Valley	UNP/LNO	BC	Similkameen Division Yale	82 E/10	49°33'	118°49'
Christie	MUN2/AZM2	ON	Parry Sound	31 E/5	45°22'	79°46'
Christie Bay	BAY/BAIE	NT	Mackenzie	75 L/11	62°32'	111°10'
Christie Beach	UNP/LNO	ON	Grey	41 A/10	44°36'	80°31'
Christie Island	ISL/ÎLE	NT	Keewatin	34 F	57°02'	76°41'
Christie Lake	UNP/LNO	ON	Lanark	31 C/16	44°49'	76°25'
Christie Lake	LAKE/LAC	ON	Lanark	31 C/16	44°48'	76°26'
Christie Lake	LAKE/LAC	MB		64 A/15	56°55'	96°57'
Christie Lake	LAKE/LAC	SK		74 H/11	57°38'	105°02'

NAME NOM	ENTITY ENTITÉ	LOC 1 LIEU 1	LOC 2 LIEU 2	MAP CARTE	POSITION LAT	LONG
Christie Lake	LAKE/LAC	NT	Keewatin	46 L	66°45′	87°07′
Christie, Mount	MTN/MNT	YT		105 P/4	63°01′	129°41′
Christie Pass	VALL/VALL	YT		105 P/4	63°04′	129°41′
Christie Ridge	UNP/LNO	NB	York	21 G/11	45°38′	67°09′
Christies Corner	UNP/LNO	ON	Wentworth	40 P/8	43°16′	80°02′
Christies Landing	UNP/LNO	NB	Northumberland	21 P/6	47°21′	65°12′
Christina	UNP/LNO	ON	Middlesex	40 I/14	42°52′	81°29′
Christina Crossing	UNP/LNO	AB	6-84-3-W4	74 D/8	56°16′	110°27′
Christina Falls	FALL/CHUT	BC	Peace River	94 B/11	56°33′	123°06′
Christina Lake	UNP/LNO	BC	Similkameen Division Yale	82 E/1	49°02′	118°13′
Christina Lake	LAKE/LAC	AB	76-6,7-W4	73 M/10	55°38′	110°55′
Christina Lake	LAKE/LAC	BC	Similkameen Division Yale	82 E/1	49°07′	118°15′
Christina Range	MTN/MNT	BC	Similkameen Division Yale	82 E/8	49°30′	118°20′
Christina River	RIV/CDE	AB	88-7-W4	74 D/11	56°40′	111°03′
Christmas Island	UNP/LNO	NS	Cape Breton	11 F/15	45°58′	60°45′
Christo, Mont	MTN/MNT	QC	Arthabaska	21 L/4	46°02′	71°54′
Christophe-Colomb, Pointe	CAPE/CAP	QC	Minganie	12 E/10	49°37′	62°34′
Christopher	UNP/LNO	NB	Restigouche	21 O/15	47°56′	66°48′
Christopher Cross	UNP/LNO	PE	Prince	21 I/16	46°59′	64°03′
Christopher Falls	FALL/CHUT	ON	Cochrane	42 J/1	50°03′	82°29′
Christopher Hall Island	ISL/ÎLE	NT	Franklin	26 A	64°29′	65°01′
Christopher Island	ISL/ÎLE	NT	Keewatin	56 D/2	64°04′	94°32′
Christopher Lake	VILG/VILG	SK	52,53-26-W2	73 H/12	53°32′	105°48′
Christopher Lakes	LAKE/LAC	NS	Queens	21 A/6	44°18′	65°00′
Christopher Peninsula	CAPE/CAP	NT	Franklin	69 F	78°58′	101°50′
Chrysler	UNP/LNO	SK	20-25-3-W2	62 M/1	51°10′	102°24′
Chub Lake	LAKE/LAC	BC	Lillooet	92 P/14	51°48′	121°17′
Chuchakacook 4	IR/RI	BC	Clayoquot	92 F/2	49°05′	124°50′
Chuchhriaschin 5	IR/RI	BC	Kamloops Division Yale	92 I/6	50°28′	121°20′
Chuchhriaschin 5A	IR/RI	BC	Kamloops Division Yale	92 I/6	50°27′	121°21′
Chuchi Lake	LAKE/LAC	BC	Cassiar	93 N/2	55°10′	124°33′
Chu Chua	UNP/LNO	BC	Kamloops Division Yale	92 P/8	51°21′	120°10′
Chuchummisapo 15	IR/RI	BC	Renfrew	92 C/15	48°52′	124°37′
Chuchuwayha 2	IR/RI	BC	Similkameen Division Yale	92 H/8	49°21′	120°04′
Chuchuwayha 2C	IR/RI	BC	Similkameen Division Yale	92 H/8	49°19′	120°08′
Chuckchuck 8	IR/RI	BC	New Westminster	92 G/14	49°58′	123°18′
Chuckwalla River	RIV/CDE	BC	Range 2 Coast	92 M/11	51°43′	127°20′
Chudleigh	UNP/LNO	ON	Sudbury	41 I/9	46°38′	80°23′
Chudliasi Bay	BAY/BAIE	NT	Franklin	25 M	63°15′	71°40′
Chukachida River	RIV/CDE	BC	Cassiar	94 E/12	57°41′	127°35′
Chukcheetso 7	IR/RI	BC	Yale Division Yale	92 I/4	50°00′	121°32′
Chukotat, Lac	LAKE/LAC	QC	Kativik	35 G/5	61°22′	75°51′
Chukotat, Rivière	RIV/CDE	QC	Kativik	35 C/13	60°47′	77°59′
Chukuni River	RIV/CDE	ON	Kenora	52 K/11	50°39′	93°25′
Chumah	UNP/LNO	MB	9-14-24-W	62 K/2	50°10′	100°42′
Chum Creek 2	IR/RI	BC	Kamloops Division Yale	82 L/13	50°52′	119°35′
Chundoo Lh'tan La 45	IR/RI	BC	Range 5 Coast	93 K/10	54°34′	124°34′
Churchbridge	TOWN/VIL2	SK	17-22-32-W	62 K/13	50°54′	101°54′
Churchbridge No. 211	MUN2/AZM2	SK		62 N/4	51°00′	101°50′
Church Hill	UNP/LNO	NB	Albert	21 H/11	45°45′	65°07′
Church House	UNP/LNO	BC	Range 1 Coast	92 K/6	50°20′	125°04′
Churchill	MUN2/AZM2	MB		54 L/9	58°44′	94°07′
Churchill	UNP/LNO	PE	Queens	11 L/3	46°13′	63°20′
Churchill	UNP/LNO	ON	Simcoe	31 D/5	44°15′	79°35′
Churchill	UNP/LNO	ON	Wellington	40 P/9	43°39′	80°03′
Churchill	UNP/LNO	MB		54 L/16	58°47′	94°11′
Churchill	UNP/LNO	SK		73 B/2	52°06′	106°39′
Churchill 1	IR/RI	MB		64 J/9	58°43′	98°29′
Churchill, Cape	CAPE/CAP	MB		54 K/14	58°46′	93°13′
Churchill Downs	UNP/LNO	SK		72 I/7	50°29′	104°36′
Churchill Falls	UNP/LNO	NF		23 H/9	53°33′	64°01′
Churchill Falls	FALL/CHUT	NF		23 H/9	53°36′	64°19′
Churchill, Fleuve - also-aussi - **Churchill River**	RIV/CDE	NF		13 F/8	53°22′	60°10′
Churchill Heights	UNP/LNO	NB	Saint John	21 G/1	45°14′	66°07′
Churchill Heights	UNP/LNO	ON	Stormont	31 G/2	45°04′	74°46′
Churchill Lake	LAKE/LAC	ON	Kenora	52 J/14	50°50′	91°10′
Churchill Lake	LAKE/LAC	SK		73 N/16	55°55′	108°20′
Churchill Lake 193A	IR/RI	SK		74 C/1	56°09′	108°12′
Churchill, Mount	MTN/MNT	BC	New Westminster	92 G/13	49°58′	123°51′
Churchill Park	UNP/LNO	NF		1 N/10	47°34′	52°43′
Churchill Park	UNP/LNO	SK		72 I/5	50°23′	105°32′
Churchill Peak	MTN/MNT	BC	Peace River	94 K/3	58°15′	125°11′
Churchill Ridge	SEAU/SMER	—		1399A	59°50′	93°00′
Churchill River - also-aussi - **Churchill, Fleuve**	RIV/CDE	NF		13 F/8	53°22′	60°10′
Churchill River - also-aussi - **Churchill, Rivière**	RIV/CDE	MB/SK		54 L/16	58°48′	94°12′

NAME NOM	ENTITY ENTITÉ	LOC 1 LIEU 1	LOC 2 LIEU 2	MAP CARTE	POSITION LAT	LONG
Churchill, Rivière - also-aussi - **Churchill River**	RIV/CDE	MB/SK		54 L/16	58°48′	94°12′
Churchills	UNP/LNO	NF		1 N/13	47°59′	53°58′
Churchill Sound	CHAN/CHEN	NT	Keewatin	33 M	55°57′	80°04′
Churchland Road	UNP/LNO	NB	Saint John	21 H/5	45°21′	65°56′
Churchover	UNP/LNO	NS	Shelburne	20 P/11	43°43′	65°22′
Church Point	UNP/LNO	NS	Digby	21 B/8	44°20′	66°07′
Church Point	CAPE/CAP	BC	Metchosin	92 B/5	48°19′	123°35′
Church Point	CAPE/CAP	NT	Franklin	25 M	63°31′	71°30′
Church Point Station	UNP/LNO	NS	Digby	21 B/8	44°18′	66°05′
Church Road	UNP/LNO	PE	Kings	11 L/7	46°22′	62°37′
Churchs Corner	UNP/LNO	NB	Albert	21 H/14	45°45′	65°05′
Church Street	UNP/LNO	NS	Kings	21 H/1	45°07′	64°26′
Churchview	UNP/LNO	NS	Inverness	11 F/14	45°59′	61°08′
Churchville	UNP/LNO	NS	Pictou	11 E/10	45°31′	62°38′
Churchville	UNP/LNO	ON	Peel	30 M/12	43°38′	79°45′
Churchville	UNP/LNO	ON	Elgin	40 I/12	42°34′	81°37′
Chute-à-Blondeau	UNP/LNO	ON	Prescott	31 G/9	45°35′	74°29′
Chute-à-Caron	UNP/LNO	QC	Le Fjord-du-Saguenay	22 D/6	48°27′	71°15′
Chute-aux-Galets	UNP/LNO	QC	Le Fjord-du-Saguenay	22 D/11	48°39′	71°12′
Chute-aux-Galets, Barrage de la	MISC/DIV	QC	Le Fjord-du-Saguenay	22 D/11	48°39′	71°11′
Chute-aux-Outardes	TOWN/VIL2	QC	Manicouagan	22 F/1	49°07′	68°24′
Chute-aux-Outardes, Barrage de	MISC/DIV	QC	Manicouagan	22 F/1	49°09′	68°24′
Chute-des-Georges	UNP/LNO	QC	Le Fjord-du-Saguenay	22 D/11	48°43′	71°09′
Chute-des-Passes	MUN2/AZM2	QC	Maria-Chapdelaine	22 L/4	50°00′	71°35′
Chute-des-Passes	UNP/LNO	QC	Le Fjord-du-Saguenay	22 E/14	49°50′	71°10′
Chute-des-Passes, Barrage de	MISC/DIV	QC	Maria-Chapdelaine	22 E/14	49°54′	71°15′
Chute-du-Diable, Barrage de la	MISC/DIV	QC	Lac-Saint-Jean-Est	22 D/13	48°47′	71°42′
Chute-du-Grand-Calumet	UNP/LNO	QC	Pontiac	31 F/10	45°40′	76°38′
Chute-du-Pin-Rouge	UNP/LNO	QC	Témiscamingue	31 L/15	46°51′	78°37′
Chute Lake	UNP/LNO	BC	Similkameen Division Yale	82 E/12	49°41′	119°32′
Chute-Panet	UNP/LNO	QC	Portneuf	21 L/13	46°51′	71°51′
Chute-Rouge	UNP/LNO	QC	La Vallée-de-la-Gatineau	31 K/9	46°35′	76°03′
Chute-Saint-Philippe	VILG/VILG	QC	Antoine-Labelle	31 J/11	46°39′	75°14′
Chutes-de-Sainte-Ursule	UNP/LNO	QC	Maskinongé	31 I/6	46°18′	73°05′
Chute-Victoria	UNP/LNO	QC	Antoine-Labelle	31 J/11	46°39′	75°17′
Chutine	UNP/LNO	BC	Cassiar	104 G/12	57°40′	131°35′
Chutine River	RIV/CDE	BC	Cassiar	104 G/12	57°39′	131°37′
Chuwanten Mountain	MTN/MNT	BC	Yale Division Yale	92 H/2	49°02′	120°38′
Chuwels Mountain	MTN/MNT	BC	Kamloops Division Yale	92 I/10	50°33′	120°35′
Chuz Ghun 8	IR/RI	BC	Range 5 Coast	93 K/9	54°38′	124°23′
Chuz Teeslee 41	IR/RI	BC	Range 5 Coast	93 K/15	54°46′	124°37′
Cigâk Octigwân	UNP/LNO	QC	Vallée-de-l'Or	31 N/6	47°28′	77°03′
Cigonicinanik Pokodinan	UNP/LNO	QC	Témiscamingue	31 N/5	47°19′	77°58′
Cimetière-à-Chevreuils, Le	UNP/LNO	QC	Pabok	22 A/10	48°33′	64°31′
Cimetière, Le	UNP/LNO	QC	Pabok	22 A/8	48°30′	64°11′
Cinconsine, Lac	LAKE/LAC	QC	Le Haut-Saint-Maurice	31 P/6	47°25′	73°04′
Cinema	UNP/LNO	BC	Cariboo	93 G/1	53°14′	122°27′
Cinnabar Valley	UNP/LNO	BC	Cranberry	92 G/4	49°06′	123°55′
Cinq Cerf Bay	BAY/BAIE	NF		11 O/9	47°41′	58°07′
Cinq Cerf Brook	RIV/CDE	NF		11 O/9	47°42′	58°08′
Cinq-Fourches, Les	UNP/LNO	QC	La Haute-Yamaska	31 H/7	45°22′	72°33′
Cinq Islands Bay	BAY/BAIE	NF		1 M/11	47°38′	55°27′
Cinq, Rivière du	RIV/CDE	QC	Robert-Cliche	21 L/2	46°09′	70°56′
Cinquante-Sept, Le	UNP/LNO	QC	La Matapédia	22 B/10	48°35′	66°37′
Ciquart	UNP/LNO	NB	Madawaska	21 N/9	47°30′	68°18′
Circle River	RIV/CDE	ON	Cochrane	42 A/16	48°55′	80°09′
Cirque Mountain	MTN/MNT	NF		14 L/13	58°56′	63°33′
Cisco	UNP/LNO	BC	Kamloops Division Yale	92 I/4	50°09′	121°34′
Citadelle-d'Halifax, Lieu historique national de la - also-aussi - Halifax Citadel National Historic Site	PARK/PARC	NS	Halifax	11 D/12	44°39′	63°35′
Cité-de-la-Mode	UNP/LNO	QC	Communauté urbaine de Montréal	31 H/12	45°32′	73°39′
Cité-des-Jeunes	UNP/LNO	QC	Vaudreuil-Soulanges	31 G/8	45°24′	74°02′
Cité-du-Havre	UNP/LNO	QC	Communauté urbaine de Montréal	31 H/5	45°30′	73°33′
Citeyats 9	IR/RI	BC	Range 4 Coast	103 H/3	53°15′	129°30′
City Centre	VILG/VILG	MB		62 H/14	49°53′	97°10′
City Centre	UNP/LNO	MB		62 H/14	49°54′	97°10′
City Centre - Fort Rouge - see-voir - City Centre	VILG/VILG	MB		62 H/14	49°53′	97°10′
City Park North	UNP/LNO	SK		73 B/2	52°08′	106°39′
City Park South	UNP/LNO	SK		73 B/2	52°08′	106°39′
City View	UNP/LNO	ON	Carleton	31 G/5	45°21′	75°45′
City View	UNP/LNO	SK		72 I/7	50°29′	104°37′
City View	UNP/LNO	SK		72 I/5	50°24′	105°34′
Clachan	UNP/LNO	ON	Kent	40 I/12	42°35′	81°48′
Clachnacudainn Icefield	GLAC/GLAC	BC	Kootenay	82 M/1	51°07′	118°02′
Claggett	UNP/LNO	SK	22,27-44-20-W2	73 A/15	52°49′	104°49′
Clair	VILG/VILG	NB	Madawaska	21 N/7	47°15′	68°36′

NAME NOM	ENTITY ENTITÉ	LOC 1 LIEU 1	LOC 2 LIEU 2	MAP CARTE	POSITION	
					LAT	LONG
Clair	UNP/LNO	SK	22-35-15-W2	73 A/1	52°01′	104°05′
Clair	GEOG/GÉOG	NB	Madawaska	21 N/7	47°18′	68°38′
Clairambault, Lac	LAKE/LAC	QC	Caniapiscau	23 K/6	54°29′	69°05′
Claire-Fontaine	UNP/LNO	NB	Kent	21 I/15	46°50′	64°59′
Claire, Lake	LAKE/LAC	AB	110-13-W4	84 I/9	58°35′	112°05′
Claireville	UNP/LNO	ON	York	30 M/13	43°45′	79°38′
Clair, Lac	LAKE/LAC	QC	Rouyn-Noranda	31 M/14	47°58′	79°10′
Clairlea	UNP/LNO	ON	York	30 M/11	43°43′	79°18′
Clairmont	UNP/LNO	AB	25-72-6-W6	83 M/7	55°16′	118°47′
Clairmont	UNP/LNO	BC	Peace River	94 A/7	56°15′	120°54′
Clairvaux-de-Bagot	UNP/LNO	QC	Les Maskoutains	31 H/10	45°43′	72°51′
Clairville	UNP/LNO	NB	Kent	21 I/6	46°23′	65°06′
Clakamucus 2	IR/RI	BC	Clayoquot	92 C/13	48°59′	125°35′
Clam Bay	UNP/LNO	NS	Halifax	11 D/10	44°44′	62°55′
Clam Bay	BAY/BAIE	NS	Halifax	11 D/10	44°43′	62°55′
Clam Harbour	UNP/LNO	NS	Halifax	11 D/10	44°44′	62°53′
Clam Lake	LAKE/LAC	SK		73 P/5	55°19′	105°43′
Clam Point	UNP/LNO	NS	Shelburne	20 P/5	43°29′	65°34′
Clanbrassil	UNP/LNO	ON	Haldimand	30 L/13	42°57′	79°57′
Clandeboye	UNP/LNO	ON	Middlesex	40 P/3	43°12′	81°27′
Clandeboye	UNP/LNO	MB	3-15-4-E	62 I/2	50°15′	96°58′
Clandonald	UNP/LNO	AB	17-53-5-W4	73 E/10	53°34′	110°44′
Clanwilliam	MUN2/AZM2	MB		62 J/12	50°30′	99°45′
Clanwilliam	UNP/LNO	MB	13-16-18-W	62 J/5	50°22′	99°49′
Clanwilliam	UNP/LNO	BC	Kootenay	82 L/16	50°58′	118°21′
Claoose 4	IR/RI	BC	Renfrew	92 C/10	48°40′	124°50′
Clapham	UNP/LNO	QC	L'Amiante	21 L/3	46°09′	71°29′
Clapperton	UNP/LNO	QC	Avignon	22 B/1	48°09′	66°01′
Clapperton	UNP/LNO	BC	Kamloops Division Yale	92 I/6	50°20′	121°13′
Clapperton Channel	RIV/CDE	ON	Manitoulin	41 G/16	46°00′	82°15′
Clapperton Creek	RIV/CDE	BC	Kamloops Division Yale	92 I/2	50°10′	120°40′
Clapperton Island	ISL/ÎLE	ON	Manitoulin	41 J/1	46°00′	82°14′
Clapperton Island	ISL/ÎLE	NT	Franklin	97 D/12	69°42′	123°57′
Clappison's Corners	UNP/LNO	ON	Wentworth	30 M/5	43°19′	79°55′
Clara Belle	UNP/LNO	ON	Sudbury	41 I/6	46°30′	81°03′
Claraday	UNP/LNO	ON	Peterborough	31 D/8	44°17′	78°19′
Clardon Beach	UNP/LNO	ON	York	31 D/3	44°14′	79°28′
Clare	MUN1/AZM1	NS	Digby	21 B/1	44°13′	66°00′
Clare	UNP/LNO	ON	Wellington	40 P/15	43°59′	80°38′
Claremont	UNP/LNO	NS	Cumberland	11 E/12	45°41′	63°58′
Claremont	UNP/LNO	ON	Ontario	30 M/14	43°58′	79°07′
Clarence	MUN2/AZM2	ON	Russell	31 G/6	45°30′	75°14′
Clarence	UNP/LNO	NS	Annapolis	21 A/14	44°54′	65°14′
Clarence	UNP/LNO	ON	Russell	31 G/11	45°34′	75°15′
Clarence, Cape	CAPE/CAP	NT	Franklin	58 D	73°54′	90°10′
Clarence Creek	UNP/LNO	ON	Russell	31 G/11	45°30′	75°13′
Clarence East	UNP/LNO	NS	Annapolis	21 A/14	44°55′	65°11′
Clarence Head	CAPE/CAP	NT	Franklin	39 B	76°47′	77°47′
Clarence Islands	ISL/ÎLE	NT	Franklin	67 D	69°55′	97°20′
Clarence Ridge	UNP/LNO	NB	Charlotte	21 G/6	45°19′	67°00′
Clarence West	UNP/LNO	NS	Annapolis	21 A/14	44°52′	65°17′
Clarendon	VILG/VILG	QC	Pontiac	31 F/10	45°39′	76°31′
Clarendon	UNP/LNO	NB	Queens	21 G/8	45°29′	66°26′
Clarendon	GEOG/GÉOG	NB	Charlotte	21 G/7	45°25′	66°38′
Clarendon and Miller	MUN2/AZM2	ON	Frontenac	31 C/15	44°59′	76°59′
Clarendon, Cape	CAPE/CAP	NT	Franklin	78 F	74°30′	111°37′
Clarendon Front	UNP/LNO	QC	Pontiac	31 F/10	45°33′	76°35′
Clarendon Station	UNP/LNO	QC	Pontiac	31 F/10	45°34′	76°35′
Clarendon Station	UNP/LNO	ON	Frontenac	31 C/15	44°52′	76°42′
Clarenville	UNP/LNO	NF		2 C/4	48°10′	53°58′
Clarenville-Shoal Harbour	TOWN/VIL2	NF		2 C/4	48°11′	53°58′
Clarenville South	UNP/LNO	NF		2 C/4	48°09′	53°58′
Claresholm	TOWN/VIL2	AB	26-12-27-W4	82 I/4	50°02′	113°35′
Clarina	UNP/LNO	ON	Peterborough	31 D/9	44°33′	78°04′
Clarington	TOWN/VIL2	ON	Durham	30 M/15	44°00′	78°41′
Clark Bay	BAY/BAIE	SK		64 L/7	58°20′	102°50′
Clark Bay	BAY/BAIE	SK		73 I/7	54°23′	104°31′
Clarkboro	UNP/LNO	SK	36-38-4-W3	73 B/8	52°19′	106°27′
Clark Bridge	UNP/LNO	SK	3-4-27-W2	72 H/5	49°16′	105°34′
Clarkdon	UNP/LNO	ON	Kenora	52 G/14	49°46′	91°15′
Clarke	UNP/LNO	ON	Durham	30 M/15	43°58′	78°33′
Clarke, Cape	CAPE/CAP	NT	Franklin	46 K	66°15′	85°09′
Clarke City	UNP/LNO	QC	Sept-Rivières	22 J/2	50°12′	66°38′
Clarke Head	CAPE/CAP	NS	Cumberland	21 H/8	45°23′	64°15′
Clarke Hills	MTN/MNT	YT		105 M/2	63°07′	134°45′

NAME NOM	ENTITY ENTITÉ	LOC 1 LIEU 1	LOC 2 LIEU 2	MAP CARTE	POSITION	
					LAT	LONG
Clarke Island	ISL/ÎLE	NT	Keewatin	34 C	56°27′	76°40′
Clarke Lake	LAKE/LAC	SK		73 J/7	54°24′	106°54′
Clarke Lake	LAKE/LAC	AB	48-3-W4	73 E/1	53°08′	110°20′
Clarke Marsh	VEGL/VÉGB	SK	11-1-W3	72 G/16	49°56′	106°02′
Clarke Peak	MTN/MNT	YT		105 M/3	63°02′	135°05′
Clarke River	RIV/CDE	NT	Mackenzie	75 P	63°37′	104°27′
Clarke's Beach	TOWN/VIL2	NF		1 N/11	47°33′	53°17′
Clarke's Corners	UNP/LNO	ON	Bruce	41 H/3	45°02′	81°22′
Clarke's Head	UNP/LNO	NF		2 E/8	49°18′	54°30′
Clarkes Hollow	UNP/LNO	ON	Ontario	30 M/14	43°52′	79°07′
Clarke Sound	CHAN/CHEN	NT	Franklin	37 A	68°35′	74°25′
Clark Fiord	BAY/BAIE	NT	Franklin	27 G	71°00′	72°00′
Clarkie, Lac	LAKE/LAC	QC	Jamésie	33 B/3	52°14′	75°30′
Clarkin	UNP/LNO	PE	Queens	11 L/2	46°15′	62°53′
Clarkleigh	UNP/LNO	MB	1-19-5-W	62 J/9	50°36′	98°01′
Clark, Mount	MTN/MNT	NT	Mackenzie	96 C	64°25′	124°13′
Clark, Point	CAPE/CAP	ON	Bruce	41 A/4	44°04′	81°45′
Clarksburg	UNP/LNO	ON	Grey	41 A/9	44°33′	80°27′
Clarks Church	UNP/LNO	ON	Bruce	41 A/4	44°07′	81°34′
Clarks Corners	UNP/LNO	NB	Queens	21 G/16	45°57′	66°08′
Clarks Corners	UNP/LNO	ON	York	30 M/14	43°48′	79°18′
Clark's Crossing	UNP/LNO	SK	38-5-W3	73 B/2	52°15′	106°37′
Clarksdale	UNP/LNO	ON	Halton	30 M/5	43°22′	79°48′
Clark's Harbour	TOWN/VIL2	NS	Shelburne	20 P/5	43°27′	65°38′
Clarkson	UNP/LNO	ON	Peel	30 M/12	43°31′	79°37′
Clarkson Valley	UNP/LNO	AB	9-71-25-W5	83 N/4	55°07′	117°46′
Clarks Point	CAPE/CAP	MB	36-5-W	63 B/1	52°07′	98°04′
Clarksville	UNP/LNO	NS	Hants	11 E/4	45°06′	63°50′
Clarkville	UNP/LNO	NB	York	21 J/3	46°07′	67°22′
Clashmoor	UNP/LNO	SK	1-46-13-W2	63 D/13	52°56′	103°45′
Classy Creek 8	IR/RI	BC	Cassiar	104 J/2	58°11′	130°48′
Clatse 5	IR/RI	BC	Range 3 Coast	93 D/5	52°20′	127°50′
Clattice Harbour	UNP/LNO	NF		1 M/8	47°29′	54°28′
Clattice South West	UNP/LNO	NF		1 M/8	47°28′	54°28′
Clatto Creek	RIV/CDE	SK	78-26-W3	73 N/12	55°43′	109°56′
Clatux 9	IR/RI	BC	Rupert	92 L/5	50°30′	127°50′
Claude	UNP/LNO	ON	Peel	30 M/13	43°47′	79°54′
Claude-Mélançon, Réserve écologique	PARK/PARC	QC	Bellechasse	21 L/9	46°36′	70°26′
Claude, Rivière à	RIV/CDE	QC	Denis-Riverin	22 H/4	49°13′	65°54′
Claverhouse	UNP/LNO	NS	Inverness	11 K/3	46°04′	61°09′
Clavering	UNP/LNO	ON	Grey	41 A/11	44°41′	81°09′
Clavet	VILG/VILG	SK	9-35-3-W3	72 O/16	52°00′	106°23′
Claw Lake	UNP/LNO	MB	28-66-22-W	63 K/10	54°44′	100°43′
Claybank	HAM/HAM	SK	33-12-24-W2	72 I/3	50°03′	105°14′
Clay Bank	UNP/LNO	ON	Renfrew	31 F/8	45°23′	76°25′
Clayburn	UNP/LNO	BC	New Westminster	92 G/1	49°05′	122°16′
Clayburn	UNP/LNO	BC	New Westminster	92 G/1	49°05′	122°17′
Claydon	UNP/LNO	SK	9-3-22-W3	72 F/2	49°12′	108°54′
Clay Hills	UNP/LNO	ON	Bruce	41 A/14	44°54′	81°03′
Clayhurst	UNP/LNO	BC	Peace River	94 A/1	56°11′	120°03′
Clay Lake	LAKE/LAC	ON	Kenora	52 K/3	50°03′	93°29′
Clayoqua 6	IR/RI	BC	Clayoquot	92 F/4	49°11′	125°32′
Clayoquot	UNP/LNO	BC	Clayoquot	92 F/4	49°10′	125°56′
Clayoquot Arm	BAY/BAIE	BC	Clayoquot	92 F/4	49°08′	125°34′
Clayoquot Land District	GEOG/GÉOG	BC		92 F	49°20′	125°35′
Clayoquot River	RIV/CDE	BC	Clayoquot	92 F/4	49°11′	125°32′
Clayoquot Sound	CHAN/CHEN	BC	Clayoquot	92 E/1	49°12′	126°06′
Clayridge	UNP/LNO	SK	10-17-1-W2	62 L/8	50°26′	102°05′
Claysmore	UNP/LNO	AB	30-50-7-W4	73 E/6	53°21′	111°01′
Clayton	UNP/LNO	ON	Lanark	31 F/1	45°11′	76°20′
Clayton Lake	LAKE/LAC	ON	Lanark	31 F/1	45°10′	76°20′
Clayton No. 333	MUN2/AZM2	SK		63 D/1	52°05′	102°15′
Clayton Park	UNP/LNO	NS	Halifax	11 D/12	44°39′	63°38′
Claytonville	UNP/LNO	SK	26-49-24-W2	73 H/3	53°15′	105°24′
Clay Valley	UNP/LNO	ON	Renfrew	31 F/8	45°25′	76°26′
Clear Bay	BAY/BAIE	MB	50-17,18,19-W1	63 F/8	53°23′	100°01′
Clearbrook	UNP/LNO	AB	36-60-23-W4	83 I/3	54°14′	113°19′
Clearbrook	UNP/LNO	BC	New Westminster	92 G/1	49°03′	122°20′
Clear Creek	UNP/LNO	ON	Norfolk	40 I/10	42°35′	80°36′
Clear Creek	UNP/LNO	YT		115 P/14	63°47′	137°17′
Clear Creek	RIV/CDE	YT		115 P/12	63°37′	137°39′
Cleardale	UNP/LNO	ON	Middlesex	40 I/14	42°57′	81°15′
Cleardale	UNP/LNO	AB	1-85-11-W6	84 D/5	56°20′	119°35′
Clearfield	UNP/LNO	SK	4-7-16-W2	72 H/9	49°31′	104°07′
Clear Hills	UNP/LNO	AB	10-87-25-W5	84 C/12	56°33′	117°53′

NAME NOM	ENTITY ENTITÉ	LOC 1 LIEU 1	LOC 2 LIEU 2	MAP CARTE	POSITION LAT	LONG
Clear Hills	MTN/MNT	AB	88-10-W6	84 D/11	56°40′	119°30′
Clear Hills 152C	IR/RI	AB	12-87-6-W6	84 D/10	56°32′	118°48′
Clear Hills No. 21, Municipal District of	MUN1/AZM1	AB		84 D/14	56°46′	119°02′
Clear Lake	UNP/LNO	ON	Muskoka	31 E/3	45°00′	79°01′
Clear Lake	UNP/LNO	ON	Parry Sound	31 E/11	45°31′	79°16′
Clear, Lake	LAKE/LAC	ON	Renfrew	31 F/6	45°26′	77°12′
Clear Lake	LAKE/LAC	ON	Peterborough	31 D/9	44°30′	78°12′
Clear Lake	LAKE/LAC	MB	27,28-8-W	62 O/7	51°22′	98°33′
Clear Lake	LAKE/LAC	MB	19,20-18,19-W	62 J/12	50°41′	100°00′
Clear Lake	LAKE/LAC	BC	Sayward	92 K/3	50°14′	125°15′
Clearland	UNP/LNO	NS	Lunenburg	21 A/8	44°29′	64°25′
Clear Prairie	UNP/LNO	AB	28-87-10-W6	84 D/12	56°34′	119°31′
Clear River	RIV/CDE	AB	83-11-W6	84 D/4	56°11′	119°42′
Clearsand Beach	UNP/LNO	SK	18-53-26-W2	73 H/12	53°34′	105°51′
Clearsand Lake	LAKE/LAC	SK	56-24,25-W2	73 H/13	53°50′	105°34′
Clearspring	UNP/LNO	PE	Kings	11 L/8	46°27′	62°21′
Clear Springs	UNP/LNO	MB	10,11-7-6-E	62 H/10	49°34′	96°41′
Clearview	MUN2/AZM2	ON	Simcoe	41 A/8	44°24′	80°04′
Clearview	UNP/LNO	NB	Carleton	21 J/12	46°35′	67°43′
Clearview	UNP/LNO	ON	Carleton	31 G/5	45°20′	75°42′
Clearview	UNP/LNO	ON	Halton	30 M/12	43°30′	79°40′
Clearview Estates	UNP/LNO	ON	Wentworth	30 M/4	43°14′	80°00′
Clearview Heights	UNP/LNO	ON	York	30 M/13	43°55′	79°31′
Clearville	UNP/LNO	ON	Kent	40 I/5	42°28′	81°43′
Clearwater - see-voir - Sarnia	TOWN/VIL2	ON		40 J/16	42°58′	82°23′
Clearwater	UNP/LNO	NB	York	21 J/7	46°23′	66°31′
Clearwater	UNP/LNO	MB	20-2-12-W	62 G/3	49°08′	99°02′
Clearwater	UNP/LNO	BC	Kamloops Division Yale	92 P/9	51°39′	120°02′
Clearwater 175	IR/RI	AB	88-7-W4	74 D/11	56°39′	111°02′
Clearwater Bay	UNP/LNO	ON	Kenora	52 E/10	49°43′	94°49′
Clearwater Bay	BAY/BAIE	NT	Mackenzie	96 I/11	66°45′	121°27′
Clearwater Beach	UNP/LNO	ON	Simcoe	31 D/13	44°51′	79°55′
Clearwater Brook	RIV/CDE	NB	York	21 J/10	46°35′	66°43′
Clearwater Creek	RIV/CDE	BC	Peace River	93 O/14	55°54′	123°10′
Clearwater Creek	RIV/CDE	NT	Mackenzie	95 F	61°35′	125°34′
Clearwater Fiord	BAY/BAIE	NT	Franklin	26 J	66°34′	67°27′
Clearwater Lake	UNP/LNO	MB	5-58-24-W	63 F/15	53°59′	100°59′
Clearwater Lake	LAKE/LAC	ON	Kenora	52 F/14	49°45′	93°26′
Clearwater Lake	LAKE/LAC	MB	53-16-W	63 G/12	53°33′	99°49′
Clearwater Lake	LAKE/LAC	MB	58,59-24,25-W	63 K/3	54°05′	101°00′
Clearwater Lake	LAKE/LAC	BC	Kamloops Division Yale	93 A/8	52°16′	120°14′
Clearwater No. 99, Municipal District of	MUN1/AZM1	AB	37-12-W5	83 B/5	52°17′	115°43′
Clearwater River	RIV/CDE	AB/SK		74 D/11	56°44′	111°23′
Clearwater River	RIV/CDE	AB	16-39-7-W5	83 B/7	52°22′	114°57′
Clearwater River	RIV/CDE	BC	Kamloops Division Yale	92 P/9	51°38′	120°05′
Clearwater River Dene Band 221	IR/RI	SK		74 C/5	56°20′	109°35′
Clearwater River Dene Band 222	IR/RI	SK		74 C/7	56°23′	108°54′
Clearwater River Dene Band 223	IR/RI	SK		74 C/2	56°05′	108°45′
Clearwater West Lake	LAKE/LAC	ON	Rainy River	52 G/4	49°00′	91°57′
Clearys	UNP/LNO	QC	La Haute-Yamaska	31 H/7	45°26′	72°34′
Cleeves	UNP/LNO	SK	5-52-21-W3	73 F/6	53°28′	109°03′
Cleho 6	IR/RI	BC	Barclay	92 C/14	48°56′	125°14′
Clematis	UNP/LNO	MB	19-1-W	62 I/12	50°37′	97°35′
Clemenceau	HAM/HAM	SK	33-42-4-W2	63 D/10	52°40′	102°32′
Clemenceau Icefield	GLAC/GLAC	BC	Kootenay	83 C/4	52°11′	117°48′
Clemenceau, Mount	MTN/MNT	BC	Kootenay	83 C/4	52°15′	117°57′
Clemens	UNP/LNO	SK	8-44-18-W2	73 A/15	52°47′	104°35′
Clément	UNP/LNO	QC	La Vallée-de-la-Gatineau	31 J/4	46°07′	75°56′
Clements Markham Inlet	BAY/BAIE	NT	Franklin	120 F	82°45′	67°00′
Clementsport	UNP/LNO	NS	Annapolis	21 A/12	44°40′	65°37′
Clementsvale	UNP/LNO	NS	Annapolis	21 A/12	44°37′	65°34′
*Clemina	UNP/LNO	BC	Kamloops Division Yale	83 D/11	52°35′	119°06′
Clemina East	UNP/LNO	BC	Kamloops Division Yale	83 D/11	52°35′	119°06′
Clemina West	UNP/LNO	BC	Kamloops Division Yale	83 D/11	52°32′	119°06′
Clemow	UNP/LNO	QC	La Vallée-de-la-Gatineau	31 K/1	46°09′	76°03′
Clemretta	UNP/LNO	BC	Range 5 Coast	93 L/1	54°00′	126°17′
Clemville	UNP/LNO	QC	Pabok	22 A/3	48°11′	65°01′
Clendenning Creek - see-voir - Clendinning Creek	RIV/CDE	BC		92 J/5	50°20′	123°35′
Clendenning River	RIV/CDE	ON	Kenora	43 L/6	54°18′	87°10′
Clendinning Creek	RIV/CDE	BC	Lillooet	92 J/5	50°20′	123°35′
Clephane Bay	BAY/BAIE	NT	Franklin	16 E	65°59′	62°27′
Cléricy	UNP/LNO	QC	Rouyn-Noranda	32 D/7	48°22′	78°52′
Clérion, Lac	LAKE/LAC	QC	Témiscamingue	31 M/15	47°50′	78°40′
Clerke Point	CAPE/CAP	BC	Rupert	92 L/4	50°05′	127°48′
Clermont	CITY/VIL1	QC	Charlevoix-Est	21 M/9	47°41′	70°14′

NAME NOM	ENTITY ENTITÉ	LOC 1 LIEU 1	LOC 2 LIEU 2	MAP CARTE	POSITION LAT	LONG
Clermont	VILG/VILG	QC	Abitibi-Ouest	32 D/14	48°55′	79°10′
Clermont	UNP/LNO	PE	Prince	11 L/5	46°27′	63°41′
*Clermont Station	UNP/LNO	PE	Prince	11 L/5	46°26′	63°40′
Clerval	VILG/VILG	QC	Abitibi-Ouest	32 D/11	48°45′	79°26′
Clesbaoneecheck 3	IR/RI	BC	Cariboo	93 G/15	53°58′	122°57′
Clestrain Point	CAPE/CAP	NT	Franklin	67 B	68°35′	101°48′
Cleveland	VILG/VILG	QC	Le Val-Saint-François	31 H/9	45°40′	72°05′
Cleveland	UNP/LNO	NS	Richmond	11 F/11	45°40′	61°14′
Cleveland Park	UNP/LNO	BC	New Westminster	92 G/6	49°22′	123°06′
Cleveland River	RIV/CDE	NT	Keewatin	46 F	65°13′	84°48′
Cleverly Point	CAPE/CAP	NT	Franklin	89 A	76°29′	114°09′
Clienna 14	IR/RI	BC	Rupert	92 L/12	50°32′	128°00′
Cliff, Cape	CAPE/CAP	NS	Cumberland	11 E/14	45°52′	63°28′
Cliffcrest	UNP/LNO	ON	York	30 M/11	43°43′	79°16′
Cliff Island	ISL/ÎLE	ON	Kenora	52 E/8	49°30′	94°27′
Cliff Lake	LAKE/LAC	ON	Kenora	52 K/3	50°10′	93°18′
Clifford	VILG/VILG	ON	Wellington	40 P/15	43°58′	80°58′
Clifford Smith Canyon	SEAU/SMER	—		8010	44°35′	49°10′
Cliffside	UNP/LNO	ON	York	30 M/11	43°42′	79°15′
Cliffside	UNP/LNO	BC	Malahat	92 B/12	48°37′	123°37′
Clifton	UNP/LNO	NF		2 C/4	48°11′	53°44′
Clifton	UNP/LNO	NS	Colchester	11 E/6	45°20′	63°27′
Clifton	UNP/LNO	NB	Gloucester	21 P/11	47°44′	65°24′
Clifton	UNP/LNO	ON	Welland	30 M/3	43°07′	79°05′
Clifton Lake	LAKE/LAC	MB		64 J/11	58°44′	99°13′
Clifton-Partie-Est	VILG/VILG	QC	Le Haut-Saint-François	21 E/5	45°15′	71°33′
Clifton Point	CAPE/CAP	NT	Mackenzie	87 C/3	69°13′	118°38′
Clifton Royal	UNP/LNO	NB	Kings	21 G/8	45°27′	66°00′
Cli Lake	LAKE/LAC	NT	Mackenzie	95 G	61°59′	123°18′
Climax	VILG/VILG	SK	17-3-18-W3	72 F/1	49°12′	108°23′
Cline River	UNP/LNO	AB	23-37-18-W5	83 C/1	52°12′	116°28′
Cline River	RIV/CDE	AB	38-18-W5	83 C/1	52°10′	116°29′
Clinton	TOWN/VIL2	ON	Huron	40 P/12	43°37′	81°32′
Clinton	VILG/VILG	BC	Lillooet	92 P/4	51°05′	121°35′
Clinton	UNP/LNO	PE	Queens	11 L/5	46°27′	63°33′
Clinton 1	IR/RI	BC	Lillooet	92 P/4	51°06′	121°36′
Clinton-Colden Lake	LAKE/LAC	NT	Mackenzie	75 O	63°55′	107°29′
Clinton Creek	UNP/LNO	YT		116 C/7	64°24′	140°36′
Clinton Point	CAPE/CAP	NT	Franklin	97 D	69°31′	120°34′
Clinworth No. 230	MUN2/AZM2	SK		72 K/14	50°50′	109°05′
Clio Channel	CHAN/CHEN	BC	Range 1 Coast	92 L/9	50°35′	126°24′
Clipper Point	CAPE/CAP	BC	Range 1 Coast	92 K/10	50°33′	124°57′
Clisbako River	RIV/CDE	BC	Cariboo	93 B/13	52°49′	123°33′
Clivale	UNP/LNO	AB	26-16-W4	82 P/8	51°16′	112°09′
Clive	VILG/VILG	AB	31-40-24-W4	83 A/6	52°28′	113°27′
Clive Lake	LAKE/LAC	NT	Mackenzie	85 M	63°12′	118°52′
Clive, Mount	MTN/MNT	BC	Cassiar	104 M/9	59°44′	134°21′
Cloan	UNP/LNO	SK	11-42-20-W3	73 C/10	52°37′	108°46′
Clode	UNP/LNO	BC	Kootenay	82 J/2	50°00′	114°51′
Clode Sound	BAY/BAIE	NF		2 C/5	48°25′	54°00′
Clonmel	UNP/LNO	SK	20-24-2-W2	62 M/1	51°05′	102°16′
Clontarf	UNP/LNO	ON	Renfrew	31 F/6	45°25′	77°08′
Cloolthpich 12	IR/RI	BC	Clayoquot	92 F/4	49°12′	125°56′
Clo-oose	UNP/LNO	BC	Renfrew	92 C/10	48°39′	124°49′
Clore River	RIV/CDE	BC	Range 5 Coast	103 I/8	54°27′	128°02′
Cloridorme	VILG/VILG	QC	La Côte-de-Gaspé	22 H/2	49°10′	64°55′
Cloridorme	UNP/LNO	QC	La Côte-de-Gaspé	22 H/2	49°11′	64°50′
Cloridorme-Ouest	UNP/LNO	QC	La Côte-de-Gaspé	22 H/2	49°11′	64°51′
Clos-des-Ormes, Le	UNP/LNO	QC	Avignon	22 B/1	48°14′	66°02′
Close Lake	LAKE/LAC	SK		74 H/15	57°53′	104°57′
Clotalairquot 4	IR/RI	BC	Cassiar	93 M/7	55°22′	126°38′
Cloud Bay	UNP/LNO	ON	Thunder Bay	52 A/3	48°08′	89°26′
Cloud Bay	BAY/BAIE	NT	Mackenzie	96 H	65°04′	121°40′
Cloud Lake	LAKE/LAC	NS	Annapolis	21 A/15	44°52′	64°53′
Cloud Lake	LAKE/LAC	ON	Thunder Bay	52 A/4	48°08′	89°32′
Cloud River	RIV/CDE	NF		12 I/16	50°51′	56°12′
Cloudslee	UNP/LNO	ON	Algoma	41 J/5	46°19′	83°42′
Cloue Patches	SEAU/SMER	—		4653	49°14′	58°17′
Cloué, Roche - also-aussi - Cloué Rock	SEAU/SMER	—		4624	46°48′	55°17′
Cloué Rock - also-aussi - Cloué, Roche	SEAU/SMER	—		4624	46°48′	55°17′
Clouston	UNP/LNO	SK	13-47-27-W2	73 H/4	53°06′	105°51′
Clouston Bay	BAY/BAIE	NT	Franklin	87 D/2	69°03′	113°33′
Cloutier	VILG/VILG	QC	Rouyn-Noranda	32 D/3	48°01′	79°09′
Clova	UNP/LNO	QC	Le Haut-Saint-Maurice	32 B/3	48°07′	75°22′
Clover Bar	UNP/LNO	AB	8-53-23-W4	83 H/11	53°34′	113°21′

NAME / NOM	ENTITY / ENTITÉ	LOC 1 / LIEU 1	LOC 2 / LIEU 2	MAP / CARTE	POSITION LAT	POSITION LONG
Cloverdale	UNP/LNO	NS	Colchester	11 E/3	45°11′	63°13′
Cloverdale	UNP/LNO	NB	Carleton	21 J/6	46°18′	67°22′
Cloverdale	UNP/LNO	ON	Dundas	31 G/3	45°07′	75°24′
Cloverdale	UNP/LNO	MB	4-14-4-E	62 I/3	50°10′	97°00′
Cloverdale	UNP/LNO	BC	New Westminster	92 G/2	49°07′	122°44′
Clover Hill	UNP/LNO	NB	Kings	21 H/12	45°34′	65°35′
Cloverleaf	UNP/LNO	MB	9,10-12-7-E	62 H/15	49°59′	96°34′
Clover Valley	UNP/LNO	ON	Bruce	41 A/4	44°01′	81°35′
Clover Valley	UNP/LNO	ON	Manitoulin	41 H/12	45°43′	81°49′
Cloverville	UNP/LNO	NS	Antigonish	11 E/9	45°40′	62°01′
Clowel 13	IR/RI	BC	Range 4 Coast	103 H/5	53°26′	129°50′
Clowhom Lake	LAKE/LAC	BC	New Westminster	92 G/11	49°45′	123°30′
Clowns Cove	UNP/LNO	NF		1 N/14	47°46′	53°11′
Cloyne	UNP/LNO	ON	Frontenac	31 C/14	44°49′	77°11′
Club Island	ISL/ÎLE	ON	Manitoulin	41 H/12	45°34′	81°36′
Cluchuta Lake 10A	IR/RI	BC	Range 3 Coast	93 C/14	52°58′	125°04′
Cluchuta Lake 10B	IR/RI	BC	Range 3 Coast	93 C/14	52°58′	125°05′
Cluculz Creek	RIV/CDE	BC	Cariboo	93 G/13	53°59′	123°38′
Cluculz Lake	LAKE/LAC	BC	Cariboo	93 G/13	53°53′	123°34′
Cludolicum 9	IR/RI	BC	Lillooet	92 O/16	51°52′	122°02′
Cludolicum 9A	IR/RI	BC	Lillooet	92 O/16	51°52′	122°01′
Cluny	UNP/LNO	AB	5-22-21-W4	82 I/15	50°50′	112°52′
Clusko River	RIV/CDE	BC	Range 3 Coast	93 C/8	52°25′	124°04′
Clustalach 5	IR/RI	BC	Range 4 Coast	93 F/16	53°57′	124°16′
Clute	UNP/LNO	ON	Cochrane	42 H/3	49°11′	81°05′
Clut Lake	LAKE/LAC	NT	Mackenzie	86 F/12	65°33′	117°41′
Clutterbuck Head	CAPE/CAP	NT	Franklin	25 C	60°12′	68°22′
Clutus 11	IR/RI	BC	Barclay	92 C/14	48°46′	125°09′
Cluxewe River	RIV/CDE	BC	Rupert	92 L/11	50°37′	127°10′
Clyde	VILG/VILG	AB	35-59-25-W4	83 I/4	54°09′	113°39′
Clyde	UNP/LNO	ON	Wentworth	40 P/8	43°22′	80°14′
Clyde Corners	UNP/LNO	QC	Le Haut-Saint-Laurent	31 G/1	45°05′	74°15′
Clyde Forks	UNP/LNO	ON	Lanark	31 F/2	45°08′	76°41′
Clydegale Lake	LAKE/LAC	ON	Haliburton	31 E/8	45°24′	78°22′
Clyde Inlet	BAY/BAIE	NT	Franklin	27 F/2	70°12′	69°30′
Clyde Lake	LAKE/LAC	AB	73-10-W4	73 M/6	55°18′	111°28′
Clyde River	VILG/VILG	PE	Queens	11 L/3	46°13′	63°16′
Clyde River	HAM/HAM	NT	Franklin	27 F	70°28′	68°36′
Clyde River	UNP/LNO	PE	Queens	11 L/3	46°13′	63°15′
Clyde River	UNP/LNO	NS	Shelburne	20 P/11	43°38′	65°29′
Clyde River	RIV/CDE	NS	Shelburne	20 P/11	43°35′	65°27′
Clyde River	RIV/CDE	ON	Lanark	31 C/16	44°59′	76°22′
Clyde River	RIV/CDE	AB	71-12-W4	73 M/4	55°10′	111°42′
Clyde River	RIV/CDE	NT	Franklin	27 C	69°51′	70°27′
Clydesdale	UNP/LNO	NS	Antigonish	11 E/9	45°39′	62°03′
Clydesdale	UNP/LNO	NS	Colchester	11 E/11	45°37′	63°11′
Clydesville	UNP/LNO	ON	Lanark	31 F/1	45°02′	76°24′
Coachman's Cove	VILG/VILG	NF		12 I/1	50°04′	56°07′
Coacoachou, Lac	LAKE/LAC	QC	Minganie	12 K/8	50°25′	60°14′
Coady Road	UNP/LNO	NS	Inverness	11 K/6	46°19′	61°08′
Coal All Island	ISL/ÎLE	NF		2 E/7	49°24′	54°47′
Coal Branch	UNP/LNO	NB	Kent	21 I/6	46°21′	65°09′
Coal Branch River	RIV/CDE	NB	Kent	21 I/11	46°31′	65°05′
Coal Brook	UNP/LNO	NF		11 O/15	47°56′	58°59′
Coalburn	UNP/LNO	NS	Pictou	11 E/10	45°34′	62°35′
Coal Creek	UNP/LNO	NB	Queens	21 I/4	46°06′	65°53′
*Coal Creek	UNP/LNO	BC	Kootenay	82 G/7	49°29′	114°59′
Coal Creek	RIV/CDE	NB	Queens	21 I/4	46°06′	65°53′
Coaldale	TOWN/VIL2	AB	11-9-20-W4	82 H/10	49°43′	112°37′
Coalfields	UNP/LNO	SK	3-2-6-W2	62 E/2	49°06′	102°44′
Coalfields No. 4	MUN2/AZM2	SK		62 E/2	49°10′	102°35′
Coal Harbour	UNP/LNO	BC	Rupert	92 L/12	50°36′	127°35′
Coal Harbour Point	CAPE/CAP	NF		2 F/4	49°09′	53°33′
Coalhurst	TOWN/VIL2	AB	21-9-22-W4	82 H/10	49°45′	112°56′
Coal Island	ISL/ÎLE	BC	Cowichan	92 B/11	48°41′	123°22′
Coal Lake	LAKE/LAC	AB	46,48-23-W4	83 H/3	53°05′	113°17′
Coalmont	UNP/LNO	BC	Yale Division Yale	92 H/10	49°31′	120°42′
Coalpit Bay	UNP/LNO	QC	Témiscamingue	31 L/15	46°46′	79°00′
Coal River	UNP/LNO	BC	Cassiar	94 M/10	59°39′	126°56′
Coal River	RIV/CDE	BC/YT		94 M/10	59°39′	125°56′
Coalspur	UNP/LNO	AB	33-48-21-W5	83 F/3	53°11′	117°01′
Coal Valley	UNP/LNO	AB	26-47-20-W5	83 F/2	53°05′	116°48′
Coast Mountains - also-aussi - **Côtière, Chaîne**	MTN/MNT	BC/YT		103 I/15	54°53′	128°48′
Coast Point	CAPE/CAP	NT	Franklin	87 F	70°51′	118°12′
Coates Mills	UNP/LNO	NB	Kent	21 I/7	46°22′	64°52′

NAME / NOM	ENTITY / ENTITÉ	LOC 1 / LIEU 1	LOC 2 / LIEU 2	MAP / CARTE	POSITION LAT	POSITION LONG
Coaticook	CITY/VIL1	QC	Coaticook	21 E/4	45°08′	71°48′
Coaticook	MUN1/AZM1	QC	Coaticook	21 E/4	45°08′	71°48′
Coaticook-Nord	UNP/LNO	QC	Coaticook	21 E/4	45°09′	71°48′
Coaticook, Rivière	RIV/CDE	QC	Sherbrooke	21 E/5	45°19′	71°54′
Coats Bay	BAY/BAIE	NT	Keewatin	34 D/6	56°20′	79°25′
Coats Island	ISL/ÎLE	NT	Keewatin	45 J	62°30′	83°00′
Coats, Rivière	RIV/CDE	QC	Kativik	33 N/7	55°19′	76°55′
Coatsworth	UNP/LNO	ON	Kent	40 J/1	42°10′	82°21′
Cobalt	TOWN/VIL2	ON	Timiskaming	31 M/5	47°24′	79°41′
Cobaz, Lac	LAKE/LAC	QC	Minganie	12 N/8	51°15′	60°21′
Cobb	UNP/LNO	NF		1 N/13	47°50′	53°58′
Cobble Hill	UNP/LNO	ON	Middlesex	40 P/3	43°07′	81°05′
Cobble Hill	UNP/LNO	BC	Shawnigan	92 B/12	48°41′	123°36′
Cobble Lake	LAKE/LAC	ON	Kenora	52 F/13	49°53′	93°37′
Cobbs Arm	UNP/LNO	NF		2 E/10	49°37′	54°35′
Cobden	VILG/VILG	ON	Renfrew	31 F/10	45°38′	76°53′
Cobequid Bay	BAY/BAIE	NS	Colchester	11 E/5	45°21′	63°45′
Cobequid Mountains	MTN/MNT	NS	Cumberland	21 H/9	45°31′	64°05′
Cobham River	RIV/CDE	ON/MB		53 F/4	53°14′	93°58′
Coboconk	UNP/LNO	ON	Victoria	31 D/10	44°39′	78°48′
Cobourg	TOWN/VIL2	ON	Northumberland	30 M/16	43°58′	78°10′
Coburg	UNP/LNO	NB	Westmorland	21 I/1	46°01′	64°08′
Coburg Island	ISL/ÎLE	NT	Franklin	38 G/13	75°57′	79°26′
Coburn	UNP/LNO	NB	York	21 G/11	45°41′	67°03′
Cocagne	UNP/LNO	NB	Kent	21 I/7	46°20′	64°37′
Cocagne Cove	UNP/LNO	NB	Kent	21 I/7	46°20′	64°33′
Cocagne Harbour	BAY/BAIE	NB	Kent	21 I/7	46°21′	64°36′
Cocagne Island	ISL/ÎLE	NB	Kent	21 I/7	46°23′	64°36′
Cocagne-Nord	UNP/LNO	NB	Kent	21 I/7	46°20′	64°41′
Cocagne River	RIV/CDE	NB	Kent	21 I/7	46°20′	64°37′
Cocagne-Sud	UNP/LNO	NB	Kent	21 I/7	46°19′	64°38′
Cochenour	UNP/LNO	ON	Kenora	52 N/4	51°05′	93°48′
Cochin	VILG/VILG	SK	30-47-16-W3	73 F/1	53°05′	108°20′
Cochrane	TOWN/VIL2	ON	Cochrane	42 H/3	49°04′	81°01′
Cochrane	TOWN/VIL2	AB	2,3-26-4-W5	82 O/1	51°11′	114°28′
Cochrane	GEOG/GÉOG	ON		42 J/3	50°00′	83°00′
Cochrane Corner	UNP/LNO	NB	Kings	21 G/8	45°29′	66°09′
Cochrane Ranche Provincial Historic Site (Developed)	PARK/PARC	AB		82 O/1	51°12′	114°29′
Cochrane River	RIV/CDE	MB		64 F/13	57°53′	101°34′
Cochrane River	RIV/CDE	SK		64 L/16	58°58′	102°00′
Cockburn Bay	BAY/BAIE	NT	Keewatin	56 M	67°18′	95°12′
Cockburn, Cape	CAPE/CAP	BC	New Westminster	92 F/9	49°40′	124°12′
Cockburn, Cape	CAPE/CAP	NT	Franklin	68 G	75°02′	100°22′
Cockburn Island	MUN2/AZM2	ON	Manitoulin	41 G/14	45°55′	83°22′
Cockburn Island	ISL/ÎLE	ON	Manitoulin	41 G/14	45°55′	83°22′
Cockburn Island 19	IR/RI	ON	Manitoulin	41 G/14	45°58′	83°25′
Cockburn Island 19A	IR/RI	ON	Manitoulin	41 G/15	45°57′	82°53′
Cockburn Islands	ISL/ÎLE	NT	Franklin	77 B	68°05′	108°23′
Cockmi 3	IR/RI	BC	Range 2 Coast	92 M/12	51°31′	127°41′
Cockram Strait	CHAN/CHEN	NT	Franklin	37 A	68°02′	74°55′
Cockscomb Mountain	MTN/MNT	NT	Franklin	27 F	70°30′	70°32′
Cod Bank	SEAU/SMER	—		3728	52°16′	128°26′
Coddles Harbour	UNP/LNO	NS	Guysborough	11 F/4	45°10′	61°32′
Coddles Island	ISL/ÎLE	NS	Guysborough	11 F/4	45°09′	61°32′
Coderre	VILG/VILG	SK	5-14-3-W3	72 J/1	50°08′	106°23′
Codesa	UNP/LNO	AB	22-78-1-W6	83 M/16	55°46′	118°04′
Codes Corner	UNP/LNO	ON	Frontenac	31 C/8	44°18′	76°25′
Codette	VILG/VILG	SK	6-50-14-W2	73 H/8	53°17′	104°02′
Codiac Heights	UNP/LNO	NB	Westmorland	21 I/2	46°04′	64°51′
Cod Island	ISL/ÎLE	NF		14 F/13	57°47′	61°47′
Codner	UNP/LNO	NF		1 N/10	47°31′	53°00′
Codner	UNP/LNO	AB	28-39-6-W5	83 B/7	52°23′	114°48′
Codrington	UNP/LNO	ON	Northumberland	31 C/4	44°10′	77°48′
Codroy	UNP/LNO	NF		11 O/14	47°53′	59°24′
Codroy Island	ISL/ÎLE	NF		11 O/14	47°52′	59°24′
Codroy Pond	UNP/LNO	NF		12 B/2	48°04′	58°52′
Codroy Pond	LAKE/LAC	NF		12 B/2	48°04′	58°53′
Cody	UNP/LNO	BC	Kootenay	82 F/14	49°58′	117°12′
Cody Creek	RIV/CDE	ON	Carleton	31 F/8	45°21′	76°16′
Cody Creek	RIV/CDE	YT		116 J/9	66°32′	138°25′
Codys	UNP/LNO	NB	Queens	21 H/13	45°53′	65°49′
Cody's Corners	UNP/LNO	ON	Oxford	40 P/2	43°07′	80°52′
Coe Hill	UNP/LNO	ON	Hastings	31 C/13	44°52′	77°50′
Coeurs, Lac des	LAKE/LAC	QC	La Haute-Côte-Nord	22 C/12	48°42′	69°57′
Coffee Cove	UNP/LNO	NF		2 E/12	49°35′	55°57′

NAME NOM	ENTITY ENTITÉ	LOC 1 LIEU 1	LOC 2 LIEU 2	MAP CARTE	POSITION LAT	LONG
Coffee Creek	UNP/LNO	YT		115 J/14	62°55′	139°05′
Coffey	UNP/LNO	QC	Le Haut-Saint-Laurent	31 G/1	45°04′	74°18′
Coffin Cove	UNP/LNO	NF		1 M/9	47°31′	54°05′
Coffin Island 3	IR/RI	BC	Range 1 Coast	92 L/9	50°34′	126°30′
Coffinscroft	UNP/LNO	NS	Shelburne	20 P/12	43°33′	65°33′
Cogburn Creek	RIV/CDE	BC	Yale Division Yale	92 H/12	49°32′	121°46′
Coghill	UNP/LNO	AB	8-39-23-W4	83 A/6	52°21′	113°17′
Coglistiko River	RIV/CDE	BC	Cariboo	93 G/4	53°00′	123°48′
Coglistiko River 29	IR/RI	BC	Cariboo	93 B/13	52°59′	123°51′
Cogmagun River	UNP/LNO	NS	Hants	21 H/1	45°06′	64°03′
Cogmagun River	RIV/CDE	NS	Hants	21 H/1	45°04′	64°09′
Cognashene	UNP/LNO	ON	Muskoka	31 D/13	44°55′	79°56′
Cohoe Point 20	IR/RI	BC	Queen Charlotte	103 K/2	54°14′	132°58′
Coiffier, Lac	LAKE/LAC	QC	Kativik	24 A/6	56°20′	65°03′
Coigny, Rivière	RIV/CDE	QC	Jamésie	32 E/1	49°06′	78°03′
Coin-chez-Leblanc	UNP/LNO	QC	Pontiac	31 F/14	45°52′	77°10′
Coin-de-la-Petite-Mine	UNP/LNO	QC	Arthabaska	21 E/13	45°50′	71°51′
Coin-des-Îles	UNP/LNO	QC	Lac-Saint-Jean-Est	22 D/12	48°31′	71°46′
Coin-des-Soeurs, Le	UNP/LNO	QC	Argenteuil	31 G/9	45°34′	74°20′
Coin-Douglas	UNP/LNO	QC	Les Jardins-de-Napierville	31 H/3	45°12′	73°27′
Coin-du-Banc	UNP/LNO	QC	Pabok	22 A/9	48°34′	64°18′
Coin-du-Bonjour, Le	UNP/LNO	QC	Matane	22 B/10	48°43′	66°53′
Coin-du-Quatre	UNP/LNO	QC	Abitibi-Ouest	32 D/10	48°38′	78°59′
Coin-Guérin, Le	UNP/LNO	QC	Brome-Missisquoi	31 H/2	45°14′	72°57′
Coin-Lavigne	UNP/LNO	QC	Matawinie	31 I/5	46°23′	73°54′
Coin-Racey	UNP/LNO	QC	Le Haut-Saint-François	21 E/5	45°20′	71°47′
Coin-Rond	UNP/LNO	QC	La Vallée-du-Richelieu	31 H/11	45°38′	73°13′
Coin-Saint-Philippe	UNP/LNO	QC	Arthabaska	21 E/13	45°56′	71°47′
Coins Gratton	UNP/LNO	ON	Prescott	31 G/10	45°37′	74°56′
Coin-Simoneau, Le	UNP/LNO	QC	La Matapédia	22 B/10	48°45′	66°39′
Cokato	UNP/LNO	BC	Kootenay	82 G/6	49°28′	115°04′
Colan, Cape	CAPE/CAP	NT	Franklin	120 F	82°55′	66°20′
Col-Athabasca, Lieu historique national du - also-aussi - Athabasca Pass National Historic Site	PARK/PARC	AB		83 D/8	52°23′	118°11′
Colbeck	UNP/LNO	ON	Dufferin	40 P/16	43°59′	80°22′
Colborne	VILG/VILG	ON	Northumberland	31 C/4	44°00′	77°53′
Colborne	MUN2/AZM2	ON	Huron	40 P/13	43°46′	81°40′
Colborne	UNP/LNO	ON	Norfolk	40 I/16	42°51′	80°19′
Colborne	GEOG/GÉOG	NB	Restigouche	21 O/16	47°45′	66°15′
Colborne, Cape	CAPE/CAP	NT	Franklin	77 A	68°58′	105°14′
Colby	UNP/LNO	MB	8-17-12-W	62 J/6	50°27′	99°05′
Colby Village	UNP/LNO	NS	Halifax	11 D/11	44°40′	63°29′
Colchester	MUN1/AZM1	NS	Colchester	11 E/6	45°20′	63°15′
Colchester	UNP/LNO	ON	Essex	40 G/15	41°59′	82°56′
Colchester	GEOG/GÉOG	NS		11 E/6	45°20′	63°15′
Colchester North	MUN2/AZM2	ON	Essex	40 J/2	42°08′	82°55′
Colchester South	MUN2/AZM2	ON	Essex	40 J/2	42°04′	82°55′
Cold Brook	UNP/LNO	NF		12 B/10	48°36′	58°32′
Coldbrook	UNP/LNO	NS	Kings	21 H/2	45°04′	64°35′
Coldbrook	UNP/LNO	NB	Saint John	21 G/8	45°19′	66°02′
Cold Creek	RIV/CDE	ON	Hastings	31 C/4	44°12′	77°36′
Cold Lake	TOWN/VIL2	AB	24-63-2-W4	73 L/8	54°27′	110°12′
Cold Lake	UNP/LNO	MB		63 N/3	55°08′	101°07′
Cold Lake	LAKE/LAC	AB/SK		73 L/9	54°32′	110°02′
Cold Lake 149	IR/RI	AB	61-2,3-W4	73 L/8	54°18′	110°18′
Cold Lake 149A	IR/RI	AB	19-63-1-W4	73 L/8	54°27′	110°09′
Cold Lake 149B	IR/RI	AB	32-63-2-W4	73 L/9	54°31′	110°15′
Cold Lake, Base des Forces canadiennes - also-aussi - Cold Lake, Canadian Forces Base	MIL/MIL	AB	62,63-2,3-W4	73 L/8	54°24′	110°17′
Cold Lake, Canadian Forces Base - also-aussi - Cold Lake, Base des Forces canadiennes	MIL/MIL	AB	62,63-2,3-W4	73 L/8	54°24′	110°17′
Cold Lake Provincial Park	PARK/PARC	AB	63-1-W4	73 L/8	54°28′	110°07′
Coldscaur Lake	LAKE/LAC	BC	Kamloops Division Yale	92 P/9	51°43′	120°23′
Coldspring Head	CAPE/CAP	NS	Cumberland	11 E/13	45°58′	63°52′
Coldspring House	UNP/LNO	BC	Cariboo	93 G/1	53°01′	122°05′
Cold Spring Pond	LAKE/LAC	NF		12 A/1	48°11′	56°18′
Cold Springs	UNP/LNO	ON	Northumberland	31 D/1	44°04′	78°13′
Coldsprings	UNP/LNO	ON	Peterborough	31 D/8	44°17′	78°18′
Cold Springs	UNP/LNO	ON	Manitoulin	41 G/16	45°52′	82°06′
Coldstream	MUN1/AZM1	BC	Osoyoos Division Yale	82 L/3	50°13′	119°12′
Coldstream	UNP/LNO	NS	Colchester	11 E/3	45°04′	63°19′
Coldstream	UNP/LNO	NB	Carleton	21 J/6	46°21′	67°28′
Coldstream	UNP/LNO	ON	Middlesex	40 P/4	43°01′	81°30′
Coldstream Creek	RIV/CDE	BC	Osoyoos Division Yale	82 L/3	50°14′	119°15′
Coldwater	UNP/LNO	ON	Simcoe	31 D/12	44°43′	79°39′
Coldwater 1	IR/RI	BC	Kamloops Division Yale	92 I/2	50°02′	120°50′
Coldwater River	RIV/CDE	BC	Kamloops Division Yale	92 I/2	50°07′	120°48′
Coldwell	MUN2/AZM2	MB		62 I/12	50°39′	97°54′

NAME / NOM	ENTITY / ENTITÉ	LOC 1 / LIEU 1	LOC 2 / LIEU 2	MAP / CARTE	POSITION LAT	POSITION LONG
Coldwell	UNP/LNO	ON	Thunder Bay	42 D/15	48°46′	86°32′
Coldwell Beach	UNP/LNO	BC	New Westminster	92 G/7	49°24′	122°53′
Colebank	UNP/LNO	BC	Cariboo	93 G/7	53°18′	122°31′
Cole Bay	VILG/VILG	SK	35-70-16-W3	73 N/1	55°06′	108°20′
Cole Bay 3	IR/RI	BC	North Saanich	92 B/11	48°37′	123°27′
Colebrook	UNP/LNO	ON	Lennox and Addington	31 C/7	44°23′	76°46′
Colebrook	UNP/LNO	BC	New Westminster	92 G/2	49°06′	122°52′
Colebrooke Settlement	UNP/LNO	NB	Restigouche	21 O/15	47°56′	66°43′
Colebrooke West	UNP/LNO	NB	Victoria	21 O/4	47°02′	67°47′
Cole Harbour	UNP/LNO	NS	Guysborough	11 F/6	45°16′	61°16′
Cole Harbour	UNP/LNO	NS	Halifax	11 D/11	44°40′	63°29′
Cole Harbour 30	IR/RI	NS	Halifax	11 D/11	44°39′	63°30′
Cole Lake	UNP/LNO	ON	Frontenac	31 C/10	44°35′	76°40′
Coleman	MUN2/AZM2	ON	Timiskaming	31 M/5	47°22′	79°50′
Coleman	UNP/LNO	PE	Prince	21 I/9	46°41′	64°10′
Coleman	UNP/LNO	ON	Timiskaming	31 M/5	47°23′	79°41′
Coleman	UNP/LNO	AB	8,9-8-4-W5	82 G/9	49°38′	114°30′
Coleman Creek	RIV/CDE	BC	Barclay	92 F/2	49°01′	124°52′
Coleman Lake	LAKE/LAC	AB	28,29-14-W4	72 M/5	51°26′	111°52′
Colemans	UNP/LNO	ON	Lincoln	30 M/3	43°14′	79°08′
Coleman's Shore	UNP/LNO	ON	Lanark	31 F/1	45°03′	76°10′
Colen Lakes	LAKE/LAC	MB		53 L/11	54°34′	95°25′
Coleraine	UNP/LNO	NB	Saint John	21 H/5	45°18′	65°41′
Coleraine	UNP/LNO	QC	L'Amiante	21 E/14	45°58′	71°22′
Coleraine	UNP/LNO	ON	Peel	30 M/13	43°49′	79°41′
Colesdale Park	HAM/HAM	SK	16-23-23-W2	72 I/14	50°57′	105°09′
Coles Island	UNP/LNO	NB	Westmorland	21 H/16	45°53′	64°19′
Coles Island	UNP/LNO	NB	Queens	21 H/13	45°55′	65°47′
Coles Lake	LAKE/LAC	BC	Range 4 Coast	93 E/6	53°29′	127°17′
Coles Pond	LAKE/LAC	NF		2 L/13	51°00′	56°00′
Coleville	VILG/VILG	SK	6-32-23-W3	72 N/11	51°43′	109°15′
Cole Wharf	UNP/LNO	ON	Prince Edward	31 C/3	44°08′	77°04′
Coley's Point	UNP/LNO	NF		1 N/11	47°35′	53°16′
Coley's Point South	UNP/LNO	NF		1 N/11	47°35′	53°16′
Colfax	UNP/LNO	SK	33-11-15-W2	62 E/13	49°57′	103°59′
Colgan	UNP/LNO	ON	Simcoe	31 D/4	44°02′	79°51′
Colgate	VILG/VILG	SK	24-5-15-W2	62 E/5	49°24′	103°53′
Colgate, Cape	CAPE/CAP	NT	Franklin	560 D	81°49′	91°02′
Colin Archer Peninsula	CAPE/CAP	NT	Franklin	59 A	76°15′	90°20′
Colindale	UNP/LNO	NS	Inverness	11 K/4	46°03′	61°31′
Colinet	VILG/VILG	NF		1 N/4	47°13′	53°33′
Colinet Arm	BAY/BAIE	NF		1 N/4	47°11′	53°35′
Colinet River	RIV/CDE	NF		1 N/4	47°13′	53°33′
Colin Lake	LAKE/LAC	SK		73 P/16	55°49′	104°15′
Colin Lake	LAKE/LAC	AB	121,122-1,2-W4	74 M/9	59°34′	110°08′
Colinton	UNP/LNO	AB	15,-65-22-W4	83 I/11	54°37′	113°15′
Colinville	UNP/LNO	ON	Lambton	40 J/16	42°52′	82°21′
Col-Kicking Horse, Lieu historique national du - also-aussi - Kicking Horse Pass National Historic Site	PARK/PARC	AB/BC		82 N/8	51°27′	116°17′
Collas, Lac	LAKE/LAC	QC	Minganie	22 I/16	50°45′	64°22′
College Bridge	UNP/LNO	NB	Westmorland	21 H/15	45°59′	64°33′
College Grant	UNP/LNO	NS	Antigonish	11 E/8	45°24′	62°05′
College Grant	UNP/LNO	NS	Pictou	11 E/11	45°38′	63°06′
College Heights	UNP/LNO	AB	31-40-26-W4	83 A/5	52°29′	113°44′
College Heights	UNP/LNO	BC	Cariboo	93 G/15	53°52′	122°46′
College Park	UNP/LNO	SK		73 B/2	52°07′	106°36′
College Park East	UNP/LNO	SK		73 B/2	52°07′	106°35′
Collette	UNP/LNO	NB	Northumberland	21 I/14	46°47′	65°27′
Collette-Village	UNP/LNO	NB	Kent	21 I/10	46°30′	64°43′
Collettville	UNP/LNO	BC	Kamloops Division Yale	92 I/2	50°06′	120°48′
Colleymount	UNP/LNO	BC	Range 5 Coast	93 L/1	54°02′	126°09′
Collicutt	UNP/LNO	AB	26-28-1-W5	82 O/8	51°25′	114°02′
Collier Bay	BAY/BAIE	NF		1 N/12	47°36′	53°42′
Colliers	TOWN/VIL2	NF		1 N/6	47°28′	53°13′
Colliers Point	CAPE/CAP	NF		1 N/11	47°30′	53°10′
Collier's Riverhead	UNP/LNO	NF		1 N/6	47°28′	53°13′
Collies Head	CAPE/CAP	NS	Halifax	11 D/11	44°41′	63°10′
Collina	UNP/LNO	NB	Kings	21 H/13	45°47′	65°40′
Collines-du-Basque	MUN2/AZM2	QC	La Côte-de-Gaspé	22 A/14	48°55′	65°09′
Collingwood	TOWN/VIL2	ON	Simcoe	41 A/8	44°29′	80°13′
Collingwood	MUN2/AZM2	ON	Grey	41 A/8	44°27′	80°24′
Collingwood Channel	CHAN/CHEN	BC	New Westminster	92 G/6	49°23′	123°25′
Collingwood Corner	UNP/LNO	NS	Cumberland	11 E/12	45°37′	63°56′
Collingwood Range	MTN/MNT	NT	Franklin	87 G	71°30′	116°45′
Collin Lake 223	IR/RI	AB	12-122-1,2-W4	74 M/9	59°35′	110°11′
Collins	UNP/LNO	ON	Thunder Bay	52 I/6	50°17′	89°27′

NAME NOM	ENTITY ENTITÉ	LOC 1 LIEU 1	LOC 2 LIEU 2	MAP CARTE	POSITION LAT	LONG
Collins Bay	UNP/LNO	ON	Frontenac	31 C/2	44°15'	76°36'
Collins Bay	BAY/BAIE	SK		64 L/5	58°17'	103°38'
Collins Cove	UNP/LNO	NF		1 M/3	47°02'	55°10'
Collins Creek	RIV/CDE	ON	Frontenac	31 C/2	44°14'	76°37'
Collins Inlet	UNP/LNO	ON	Manitoulin	41 I/3	46°00'	81°12'
Collins Inlet	BAY/BAIE	ON	Manitoulin	41 H/14	45°59'	81°18'
Collins Lake	LAKE/LAC	NB	Westmorland	21 I/1	46°07'	64°09'
Collins Lake	LAKE/LAC	ON	Frontenac	31 C/8	44°22'	76°28'
Collinson, Cape	CAPE/CAP	NT	Franklin	120 B	80°05'	70°26'
Collinson, Cape	CAPE/CAP	NT	Franklin	97 H	71°17'	122°05'
Collinson Inlet	BAY/BAIE	NT	Franklin	67 D	69°31'	98°10'
Collinson Peninsula	CAPE/CAP	NT	Franklin	67 C	69°58'	101°24'
Collison Heights	UNP/LNO	ON	Peterborough	31 D/8	44°17'	78°19'
Colmer	UNP/LNO	SK	19-22-7-W2	62 L/15	50°55'	102°58'
Colombet, Lac	LAKE/LAC	QC	Kativik	24 C/15	56°57'	68°55'
Colombie-Britannique - also-aussi - **British Columbia**	PROV/PROV	BC		MCR3	54°00'	125°00'
Colombier	VILG/VILG	QC	La Haute-Côte-Nord	22 C/15	48°52'	68°51'
Colombier, Cap	CAPE/CAP	QC	La Haute-Côte-Nord	22 C/15	48°49'	68°53'
Colombière	UNP/LNO	QC	Vallée-de-l'Or	32 C/4	48°05'	77°35'
Colombines, Les	SHL/H-FD	QC	Les Îles-de-la-Madeleine	11 N/11	47°32'	61°29'
Colombourg	VILG/VILG	QC	Abitibi-Ouest	32 D/11	48°45'	79°09'
Colombourg-Station	UNP/LNO	QC	Abitibi-Ouest	32 D/14	48°47'	79°08'
Colonie-Cinq	UNP/LNO	QC	Rouyn-Noranda	32 D/7	48°23'	78°52'
Colonie-du-Quinze, La	UNP/LNO	QC	Pabok	22 A/7	48°28'	64°51'
Colonie-du-Vingt-et-Un, La	UNP/LNO	QC	Pabok	22 A/7	48°30'	64°49'
Colonie-Fournière	UNP/LNO	QC	Vallée-de-l'Or	32 D/1	48°05'	78°09'
Colonna Lake	LAKE/LAC	ON	Kenora	52 K/4	50°07'	93°53'
Colonsay	TOWN/VIL2	SK	1-35-28-W2	72 P/13	51°59'	105°53'
Colonsay No. 342	MUN2/AZM2	SK		73 A/4	52°00'	105°57'
Colpitts	UNP/LNO	NB	Saint John	21 G/1	45°14'	66°10'
Colpitts Settlement	UNP/LNO	NB	Albert	21 H/15	45°59'	64°58'
Colpoy's Bay	UNP/LNO	ON	Bruce	41 A/14	44°47'	81°08'
Colpoy's Bay	BAY/BAIE	ON	Grey	41 A/14	44°47'	81°06'
Colpton	UNP/LNO	NS	Lunenburg	21 A/7	44°27'	64°51'
Colquhoun	UNP/LNO	ON	Dundas	31 G/3	45°01'	75°08'
Colquhoun, Cape	CAPE/CAP	NT	Franklin	79 B	76°44'	108°23'
Colquhoun River	RIV/CDE	NT	Franklin	98 E	74°32'	121°52'
Colquitz	UNP/LNO	BC	Victoria	92 B/6	48°29'	123°25'
Col-Rogers, Lieu historique national du - also-aussi - Rogers Pass National Historic Site	PARK/PARC	BC	Kootenay	82 N/5	51°18'	117°31'
Columbia, Cape	CAPE/CAP	NT	Franklin	120 G/3	83°07'	69°57'
Columbia, Fleuve - also-aussi - **Columbia River**	RIV/CDE	BC	Kootenay	82 F/4	49°00'	117°38'
Columbia Gardens	UNP/LNO	BC	Kootenay	82 F/4	49°04'	117°35'
Columbia Icefield	GLAC/GLAC	BC/AB		83 C/3	52°08'	117°23'
Columbia Lake	LAKE/LAC	BC	Kootenay	82 J/4	50°13'	115°51'
Columbia Lake 3	IR/RI	BC	Kootenay	82 J/5	50°25'	115°55'
Columbia, Mount	MTN/MNT	AB/BC		83 C/3	52°09'	117°27'
Columbia Mountains	MTN/MNT	BC	Kootenay	82 L/16	51°00'	118°00'
Columbia Reach	RIVF/EFLV	BC	Kootenay	82 N/13	51°50'	117°47'
Columbia River - also-aussi - **Columbia, Fleuve**	RIV/CDE	BC	Kootenay	82 F/4	49°00'	117°38'
Columbia-Shuswap	MUN1/AZM1	BC	Kootenay	82 N/5	51°25'	117°40'
Columbus	UNP/LNO	ON	Ontario	30 M/15	43°59'	78°55'
Colvalli	UNP/LNO	BC	Kootenay	82 G/6	49°22'	115°22'
Colvile Mountains	MTN/MNT	NT	Franklin	87 D	69°37'	115°15'
Colville Bay	BAY/BAIE	PE	Kings	11 L/8	46°21'	62°16'
Colville, Cape	CAPE/CAP	NT	Keewatin	57 B	68°45'	94°37'
Colville Lake	UNP/LNO	NT	Mackenzie	96 M/1	67°02'	126°07'
Colville Lake	LAKE/LAC	NF		23 H/12	53°41'	65°38'
Colville Lake	LAKE/LAC	NT	Mackenzie	96 M	67°10'	126°00'
Colwell	UNP/LNO	ON	Simcoe	31 D/5	44°20'	79°47'
Colwood	CITY/VIL1	BC	Esquimalt	92 B/6	48°26'	123°29'
Col-Yellowhead, Lieu historique national du - also-aussi - Yellowhead Pass National Historic Site	PARK/PARC	AB		83 D/16	52°54'	118°28'
Comber	UNP/LNO	ON	Essex	40 J/2	42°14'	82°33'
Combermere	UNP/LNO	ON	Renfrew	31 F/5	45°22'	77°37'
Combermere, Cape	CAPE/CAP	NT	Franklin	39 C	77°01'	78°06'
Comb Islands	ISL/ÎLE	NT	Keewatin	33 E	53°17'	79°00'
Comeau	UNP/LNO	MB	23-11-W	62 O/2	51°02'	98°59'
Comeau Point	UNP/LNO	NB	Westmorland	21 I/1	46°10'	64°09'
Comeau Ridge	UNP/LNO	NB	Madawaska	21 O/4	47°09'	67°42'
Comeau Settlement	UNP/LNO	NB	Northumberland	21 P/6	47°17'	65°02'
Comeaus Hill	UNP/LNO	NS	Yarmouth	20 O/9	43°42'	66°01'
Comeauville	UNP/LNO	NS	Digby	21 B/8	44°17'	66°08'
Come By Chance	TOWN/VIL2	NF		1 N/13	47°51'	53°59'
Come By Chance	BAY/BAIE	NF		1 M/16	47°48'	54°01'
Comencho, Lac	LAKE/LAC	QC	Jamésie	32 J/6	50°20'	75°10'
Comer	UNP/LNO	BC	Cariboo	93 B/1	52°10'	122°13'

NAME NOM	ENTITY ENTITÉ	LOC 1 LIEU 1	LOC 2 LIEU 2	MAP CARTE	POSITION LAT	LONG
Comer Strait	CHAN/CHEN	NT	Keewatin	46 F	65°45′	85°05′
Comestock Corners	UNP/LNO	QC	Memphrémagog	31 H/1	45°03′	72°08′
Comet	UNP/LNO	ON	Essex	40 J/2	42°01′	82°59′
Comet	UNP/LNO	AB	7-33-14-W4	72 M/13	51°49′	111°59′
Comfort Bight	UNP/LNO	NF		3 E/4	53°09′	55°48′
Comfort, Cape	CAPE/CAP	NT	Keewatin	46 G	65°08′	83°23′
Comfort Cove-Newstead	VILG/VILG	NF		2 E/7	49°24′	54°52′
Comfort Head	CAPE/CAP	NF		2 E/7	49°25′	54°51′
Comiaken Land District	GEOG/GÉOG	BC		92 B	48°50′	123°38′
Comi, Mont	MTN/MNT	QC	La Mitis	22 C/8	48°28′	68°13′
Cominco	UNP/LNO	SK	32-17-20-W2	72 I/7	50°28′	104°44′
Comins Mills	UNP/LNO	QC	Coaticook	21 E/4	45°01′	71°30′
Comma Island	ISL/ÎLE	NF		13 N/8	55°20′	60°20′
Commanda	UNP/LNO	ON	Parry Sound	31 E/13	45°57′	79°36′
Commanda Lake	LAKE/LAC	ON	Parry Sound	31 L/4	46°01′	79°43′
Commerce-de-la-Fourrure-à-Lachine, Lieu historique national du - also-aussi - The Fur Trade at Lachine National Historic Site	PARK/PARC	QC	Communauté urbaine de Montréal	31 H/5	45°26′	73°41′
Commercial Cross	UNP/LNO	PE	Kings	11 L/2	46°08′	62°38′
Commerell Point	CAPE/CAP	BC	Rupert	102 I/9	50°34′	128°15′
Commissaires, Lac des	LAKE/LAC	QC	Le Domaine-du-Roy	32 A/1	48°10′	72°16′
Commissioner Island	ISL/ÎLE	MB		63 A/3	52°10′	97°16′
Committee Bay	BAY/BAIE	NT	Franklin	47 B	68°16′	86°54′
Commodore, Cape	CAPE/CAP	ON	Grey	41 A/15	44°47′	80°55′
Commodore Heights	UNP/LNO	BC	Cariboo	93 B/1	52°10′	122°08′
Commodore Park	UNP/LNO	NS	Halifax	11 D/12	44°41′	63°31′
Commons	UNP/LNO	NS	Lunenburg	21 A/9	44°33′	64°14′
Commonwealth Mountain	MTN/MNT	NT	Franklin	340 E	82°24′	76°45′
Communauté Atikamekw de Manawan	IR/RI	QC	Matawinie	31 O/1	47°13′	74°23′
Communauté de Wemotaci	IR/RI	QC	Le Haut-Saint-Maurice	31 P/13	47°54′	73°47′
Communauté montagnaise Essipit	IR/RI	QC	La Haute-Côte-Nord	22 C/6	48°20′	69°24′
Commune-de-la-Baie-du-Febvre	UNP/LNO	QC	Nicolet-Yamaska	31 I/2	46°10′	72°43′
Commune, La	UNP/LNO	QC	Rivière-du-Loup	21 N/14	47°59′	69°29′
Community Beach	UNP/LNO	ON	Wentworth	30 M/4	43°14′	79°44′
Como	UNP/LNO	QC	Vaudreuil-Soulanges	31 G/8	45°27′	74°07′
Como Lake	LAKE/LAC	NS	Halifax	11 E/2	45°05′	62°41′
Como Lake	LAKE/LAC	ON	Sudbury	41 O/13	47°55′	83°30′
Comox	TOWN/VIL2	BC	Comox	92 F/10	49°41′	124°56′
Comox 1	IR/RI	BC	Comox	92 F/10	49°41′	124°57′
Comox, Base des Forces canadiennes - also-aussi - Comox, Canadian Forces Base	MIL/MIL	BC	Comox	92 F/10	49°43′	124°54′
Comox, Canadian Forces Base - also-aussi - Comox, Base des Forces canadiennes	MIL/MIL	BC	Comox	92 F/10	49°43′	124°54′
Comox Lake	LAKE/LAC	BC	Nelson	92 F/11	49°37′	125°10′
Comox Land District	GEOG/GÉOG	BC		92 F	49°49′	124°17′
Comox-Strathcona	MUN1/AZM1	BC	Sayward	92 K/6	50°20′	125°20′
Compeer	UNP/LNO	AB	25-33-1-W4	72 M/16	51°52′	110°00′
Compton	VILG/VILG	QC	Coaticook	21 E/4	45°14′	71°49′
Compton Island 6	IR/RI	BC	Range 1 Coast	92 L/10	50°36′	126°41′
Compton Névé	GLAC/GLAC	BC	Range 1 Coast	92 K/16	50°49′	124°11′
Compton Station	VILG/VILG	QC	Coaticook	21 E/4	45°14′	71°51′
Compulsion Bay	BAY/BAIE	SK		64 E/11	57°45′	103°16′
Comstock Seamount	SEAU/SMER	—		5.03	48°15′	156°55′
Conception Bay	BAY/BAIE	NF		1 N/10	47°45′	53°00′
Conception Bay South	TOWN/VIL2	NF		1 N/10	47°30′	53°00′
Conception Harbour	TOWN/VIL2	NF		1 N/6	47°27′	53°13′
Concession	UNP/LNO	NS	Digby	21 B/8	44°17′	66°04′
Concession-de-Baker-Brook	UNP/LNO	NB	Madawaska	21 N/7	47°20′	68°33′
Concession-des-Bouchard	UNP/LNO	NB	Madawaska	21 N/7	47°16′	68°41′
Concession-des-Jaunes	UNP/LNO	NB	Madawaska	21 N/2	47°14′	68°48′
Concession-des-Lang	UNP/LNO	NB	Madawaska	21 N/7	47°17′	68°38′
Concession-des-Ouellette	UNP/LNO	NB	Madawaska	21 N/7	47°19′	68°35′
Concession-des-Vasseur	UNP/LNO	NB	Madawaska	21 N/7	47°16′	68°40′
Concession-des-Viel	UNP/LNO	NB	Madawaska	21 N/7	47°15′	68°45′
Conche	VILG/VILG	NF		2 L/13	50°53′	55°54′
Concord	UNP/LNO	NS	Pictou	11 E/7	45°27′	62°47′
Concord	UNP/LNO	ON	York	30 M/14	43°48′	79°29′
Concord Point	UNP/LNO	ON	Ontario	31 D/11	44°32′	79°12′
Condie	UNP/LNO	SK	30-18-20-W2	72 I/10	50°33′	104°44′
Condor	UNP/LNO	AB	5-39-4-W5	83 B/7	52°20′	114°33′
Conestogo	UNP/LNO	ON	Waterloo	40 P/10	43°32′	80°30′
Conestogo River	RIV/CDE	ON	Waterloo	40 P/9	43°32′	80°29′
Coney Arm	UNP/LNO	NF		12 H/15	49°58′	56°47′
Coney Head	CAPE/CAP	NF		12 H/15	49°57′	56°44′
Confederation Lake	LAKE/LAC	ON	Kenora	52 N/2	51°05′	92°44′
Confederation Park	UNP/LNO	ON	Wentworth	30 M/4	43°15′	79°45′
Confederation Park	UNP/LNO	SK		73 B/2	52°08′	106°44′
Confusion Bay	BAY/BAIE	NF		2 E/13	49°57′	55°45′
Congresbury	UNP/LNO	AB	32-37-7-W5	83 B/2	52°14′	114°58′

NAME NOM	ENTITY ENTITÉ	LOC 1 LIEU 1	LOC 2 LIEU 2	MAP CARTE	POSITION LAT	LONG
Congress	HAM/HAM	SK	24-9-1-W3	72 G/16	49°46′	106°01′
Conibear Lake	LAKE/LAC	AB	122-19,20-W4	84 P/11	59°37′	113°17′
Coningham Bay	BAY/BAIE	NT	Franklin	67 H	71°48′	96°50′
Coningsby	UNP/LNO	ON	Wellington	40 P/9	43°44′	80°07′
Coniston	UNP/LNO	ON	Sudbury	41 I/7	46°29′	80°51′
Conjuror Bay	BAY/BAIE	NT	Mackenzie	86 E	65°43′	118°07′
Conkle Lake	LAKE/LAC	BC	Similkameen Division Yale	82 E/3	49°10′	119°06′
Conklin	UNP/LNO	AB	31-76-7-W4	73 M/11	55°38′	111°05′
Conlin Lake Camp	UNP/LNO	MB	67-8-W	63 J/15	54°49′	98°37′
Conmee	MUN2/AZM2	ON	Thunder Bay	52 A/5	48°28′	89°40′
Conmee	UNP/LNO	ON	Thunder Bay	52 A/12	48°32′	89°38′
Conn	UNP/LNO	ON	Wellington	40 P/15	44°00′	80°34′
Connaigre Bay	BAY/BAIE	NF		1 M/5	47°30′	55°55′
Connaigre Head	CAPE/CAP	NF		1 M/5	47°26′	55°56′
Connaught	UNP/LNO	ON	Dundas	31 G/3	45°09′	75°13′
Connaught	UNP/LNO	ON	Renfrew	31 F/10	45°38′	77°00′
Connaught	UNP/LNO	ON	Cochrane	42 A/10	48°37′	80°56′
*Connaught	UNP/LNO	BC	Kootenay	82 N/6	51°20′	117°27′
Connaught Heights	UNP/LNO	BC	New Westminster	92 G/2	49°12′	122°57′
Connaught Hill	UNP/LNO	ON	Cochrane	42 A/6	48°28′	81°12′
Connaught Lake	LAKE/LAC	NS	Lunenburg	21 A/9	44°40′	64°12′
Connaught No. 457	MUN2/AZM2	SK		63 E/4	53°00′	104°00′
Connaught Shore	UNP/LNO	ON	Peterborough	31 D/8	44°27′	78°22′
Connecting Point	CAPE/CAP	NF		2 C/5	48°28′	53°49′
Connell	UNP/LNO	NB	Carleton	21 J/5	46°24′	67°37′
Connell Creek	UNP/LNO	SK	23-48-10-W2	63 E/3	53°09′	103°22′
*Connelly	UNP/LNO	BC	Cassiar	94 D/2	56°13′	126°52′
Connellys	UNP/LNO	ON	Northumberland	31 C/5	44°21′	77°49′
Connemara	UNP/LNO	AB	32-16-28-W4	82 I/5	50°24′	113°49′
Conne River	TOWN/VIL2	NF		1 M/13	47°52′	55°45′
Conne River	RIV/CDE	NF		1 M/13	47°55′	55°42′
Conne River Pond	LAKE/LAC	NF		2 D/3	48°11′	55°29′
Conn Lake	LAKE/LAC	NT	Franklin	37 E	70°32′	73°34′
Connoire Bay	BAY/BAIE	NF		11 P/12	47°40′	57°55′
Connoire Head	CAPE/CAP	NF		11 P/12	47°39′	57°55′
Connolly Bay	BAY/BAIE	MB		63 F/7	53°27′	100°54′
Connor	UNP/LNO	ON	Simcoe	30 M/13	43°59′	79°56′
Connor Creek	UNP/LNO	AB	16-59-8-W5	83 J/3	54°06′	115°08′
Connors	UNP/LNO	NB	Madawaska	21 N/2	47°13′	68°50′
Conn, Rivière	RIV/CDE	QC	Jamésie	33 D/7	52°22′	78°30′
Conns Mills	UNP/LNO	NS	Cumberland	11 E/13	45°45′	63°43′
Conolly Bay	BAY/BAIE	NT	Franklin	77 A	68°12′	104°30′
Conover	UNP/LNO	ON	Dufferin	41 A/1	44°11′	80°13′
Conquerall	UNP/LNO	NS	Lunenburg	21 A/7	44°18′	64°34′
Conquerall Bank	UNP/LNO	NS	Lunenburg	21 A/8	44°22′	64°28′
Conquerall Mills	UNP/LNO	NS	Lunenburg	21 A/7	44°18′	64°32′
Conquest	VILG/VILG	SK	32-29-9-W3	72 O/11	51°32′	107°14′
Conrad	UNP/LNO	AB	32-6-15-W4	72 E/12	49°31′	111°58′
Conrad	UNP/LNO	BC	Kamloops Division Yale	92 I/4	50°08′	121°34′
Conrad	UNP/LNO	YT		105 D/2	60°04′	134°33′
Conrich	UNP/LNO	AB	5-25-28-W4	82 P/4	51°06′	113°52′
Conrod Settlement	UNP/LNO	NS	Halifax	11 D/14	44°46′	63°14′
Conroy	UNP/LNO	ON	Perth	40 P/6	43°18′	81°03′
Conroy Creek	RIV/CDE	BC	Peace River	94 I/4	58°00′	121°32′
Conroy Island	ISL/ÎLE	BC	Range 3 Coast	103 A/11	52°31′	129°24′
Consecon	UNP/LNO	ON	Prince Edward	30 N/13	44°00′	77°31′
Consecon Lake	LAKE/LAC	ON	Prince Edward	31 C/3	44°00′	77°27′
Consol	MUN2/AZM2	MB		63 K/3	54°10′	101°23′
Consort	VILG/VILG	AB	15-35-6-W3	73 D/2	52°01′	110°46′
Constance	UNP/LNO	SK	11-3-29-W2	72 H/4	49°12′	105°49′
Constance Bay	UNP/LNO	ON	Carleton	31 F/8	45°30′	76°05′
Constance Lake	LAKE/LAC	ON	Carleton	31 G/5	45°24′	75°59′
Constance Lake 92	IR/RI	ON	Cochrane	42 F/16	49°50′	84°07′
Constant Creek	UNP/LNO	ON	Renfrew	31 F/6	45°25′	77°01′
Constantine, Mount	MTN/MNT	YT		115 F/7	61°25′	140°34′
Constant Lake	LAKE/LAC	ON	Renfrew	31 F/7	45°24′	76°59′
Consul	VILG/VILG	SK	13-4-27-W3	72 F/5	49°18′	109°31′
Consul Lake	LAKE/LAC	NT	Mackenzie	66 E	65°06′	102°20′
Consul River	RIV/CDE	NT	Mackenzie	66 E	65°42′	102°03′
Content Reach	RIVF/EFLV	NF		2 C/13	48°50′	53°58′
Contour	UNP/LNO	MB	35-10-10-E	62 H/16	49°53′	96°07′
Contracosta Lake	LAKE/LAC	AB	31-11,12-M/12	72 M/12	51°42′	111°34′
Contrecoeur	VILG/VILG	QC	Lajemmerais	31 H/14	45°51′	73°14′
Control	UNP/LNO	AB	6-24-14-W4	72 M/4	51°01′	111°57′
Contwoyto Lake	LAKE/LAC	NT	Mackenzie	76 E	65°42′	110°50′

NAME NOM	ENTITY ENTITÉ	LOC 1 LIEU 1	LOC 2 LIEU 2	MAP CARTE	POSITION LAT	LONG
Contwoyto River	RIV/CDE	NT	Mackenzie	76 C	64°43'	108°07'
Conuma Peak	MTN/MNT	BC	Nootka	92 E/16	49°50'	126°19'
Conuma River	RIV/CDE	BC	Nootka	92 E/16	49°48'	126°26'
Convoy Place	UNP/LNO	NS	Halifax	11 D/12	44°40'	63°37'
Conway	UNP/LNO	PE	Prince	11 L/12	46°40'	63°59'
Conway	UNP/LNO	NS	Digby	21 A/12	44°36'	65°46'
Conway	UNP/LNO	ON	Lennox and Addington	31 C/2	44°07'	76°55'
Conybeare Fiord	BAY/BAIE	NT	Franklin	120 C	81°34'	67°35'
Conybeare, Mount	MTN/MNT	YT		117 C/8	69°30'	140°07'
Cook Bank	SEAU/SMER	—		3605	49°58'	128°47'
Cook, Cape	CAPE/CAP	BC	Rupert	92 L/4	50°08'	127°55'
Cooke	UNP/LNO	NF		12 B/16	48°54'	58°03'
Cooke Creek	RIV/CDE	BC	Kamloops Division Yale	82 L/10	50°36'	118°50'
Cooke's Shore	UNP/LNO	ON	Lanark	31 F/1	45°03'	76°13'
Cooking Lake	UNP/LNO	AB	13-51-22-W4	83 H/6	53°25'	113°08'
Cooking Lake	LAKE/LAC	AB	51-21,22-W4	83 H/6	53°26'	113°02'
Cook Lake	LAKE/LAC	NT	Mackenzie	75 N	63°13'	108°45'
Cook Peninsula	CAPE/CAP	NT	Franklin	39 G	79°24'	76°30'
Cook's Bay	BAY/BAIE	ON	Simcoe	31 D/4	44°15'	79°31'
Cooks Brook	UNP/LNO	NS	Halifax	11 E/3	45°02'	63°17'
Cooks Brook	UNP/LNO	NB	Westmorland	21 I/2	46°08'	64°42'
Cooks Brook	RIV/CDE	NF		12 B/16	48°59'	58°04'
Cooks Cove	UNP/LNO	NS	Guysborough	11 F/6	45°22'	61°29'
Cooks Cove	BAY/BAIE	NF		2 C/3	48°06'	53°00'
Cooks Creek	UNP/LNO	MB	13-12-5-E	62 I/2	50°01'	96°46'
Cooks Creek	RIV/CDE	MB		62 I/2	50°11'	96°50'
Cooks Crossing	UNP/LNO	NB	Restigouche	22 B/1	48°04'	66°25'
Cook's Harbour	TOWN/VIL2	NF		2 M/12	51°36'	55°52'
Cookshire	CITY/VIL1	QC	Le Haut-Saint-François	21 E/5	45°25'	71°38'
Cooks Mills	UNP/LNO	ON	Welland	30 L/14	43°00'	79°11'
Cooks Mills	UNP/LNO	ON	Nipissing	31 L/6	46°24'	79°28'
Cookson	UNP/LNO	SK	53-3-W3	73 G/9	53°32'	106°19'
Cookstown	UNP/LNO	ON	Simcoe	31 D/4	44°11'	79°42'
Cooksville	UNP/LNO	ON	Peel	30 M/12	43°34'	79°37'
Cook Trough	SEAU/SMER	—		19318A	51°06'	128°18'
Cookville	UNP/LNO	NS	Lunenburg	21 A/7	44°25'	64°33'
Cookville	UNP/LNO	NB	Westmorland	21 I/1	46°02'	64°20'
Coombe	UNP/LNO	BC	New Westminster	92 G/7	49°19'	122°55'
Coombes Road	UNP/LNO	NB	Madawaska	21 O/4	47°12'	67°46'
Coombs	UNP/LNO	BC	Nanoose	92 F/8	49°18'	124°25'
Coomb's Cove	UNP/LNO	NF		1 M/5	47°27'	55°37'
Cooper	UNP/LNO	ON	Hastings	31 C/11	44°39'	77°28'
Cooperage	UNP/LNO	NF		1 N/11	47°40'	53°15'
Cooper Brook	RIV/CDE	NF		2 D/11	48°42'	55°12'
Cooper Creek	UNP/LNO	BC	Kootenay	82 K/2	50°12'	116°58'
Cooper Creek	RIV/CDE	MB		54 F/4	57°11'	93°53'
Cooper, Mount	MTN/MNT	BC	Kootenay	82 K/3	50°11'	117°12'
Cooper Reach	RIVF/EFLV	BC	Range 1 Coast	92 K/11	50°41'	125°28'
Cooper's Cove	UNP/LNO	NF		1 M/9	47°35'	54°12'
Coopers Falls	UNP/LNO	ON	Ontario	31 D/14	44°47'	79°14'
Cooper's Trailer Park	UNP/LNO	ON	Peterborough	31 D/8	44°19'	78°12'
Coopte 9	IR/RI	BC	Nootka	92 E/10	49°42'	126°35'
Cootes Paradise	UNP/LNO	ON	Wentworth	30 M/5	43°17'	79°56'
Cootes Pond	UNP/LNO	NF		1 K/13	46°57'	53°31'
Coothill	UNP/LNO	SK	35-14-33-W	62 K/4	50°14'	101°53'
Copeau River	RIV/CDE	SK	33-43-7-W2	63 D/10	52°45'	102°58'
Copeland	UNP/LNO	SK	20-30-18-W2	72 P/10	51°35'	104°31'
Copeland Islands	ISL/ÎLE	BC	New Westminster	92 F/15	50°00'	124°48'
Copenhagen	UNP/LNO	ON	Elgin	40 I/10	42°41'	80°59'
Copes Bay	BAY/BAIE	NT	Franklin	39 G	79°25'	76°30'
Copetown	UNP/LNO	ON	Wentworth	40 P/1	43°14'	80°04'
Copp	UNP/LNO	ON	Renfrew	31 F/6	45°28'	77°27'
Coppell	UNP/LNO	ON	Cochrane	42 G/12	49°32'	83°50'
Coppen	UNP/LNO	SK	33-11-5-W3	72 G/15	49°57'	106°38'
Copper Bay	BAY/BAIE	BC	Queen Charlotte	103 G/4	53°10'	131°47'
Copper Cliff	UNP/LNO	ON	Sudbury	41 I/6	46°28'	81°04'
Copper Creek	UNP/LNO	BC	Kootenay	82 J/4	50°05'	115°47'
Copper Creek	UNP/LNO	BC	Kamloops Division Yale	92 I/15	50°47'	120°46'
Copper Creek	RIV/CDE	BC	Yale Division Yale	92 H/2	49°11'	120°33'
Coppercrown Mountain	MTN/MNT	BC	Kootenay	82 K/8	50°18'	116°21'
Copperhead	UNP/LNO	ON	Parry Sound	41 H/1	45°09'	80°08'
Copper Island	ISL/ÎLE	NF		2 F/12	49°33'	53°58'
Copper Island	ISL/ÎLE	ON	Thunder Bay	42 D/14	48°46'	87°24'
Copper Island	ISL/ÎLE	BC	Cassiar	104 N/5	59°18'	133°59'
Copper Johnny Meadow 8	IR/RI	BC	Lillooet	92 P/5	51°23'	121°45'

NAME NOM	ENTITY ENTITÉ	LOC 1 LIEU 1	LOC 2 LIEU 2	MAP CARTE	POSITION LAT	POSITION LONG
Copperkettle	UNP/LNO	ON	Grey	41 A/11	44°39'	81°00'
Copper Lake	UNP/LNO	NS	Antigonish	11 F/5	45°24'	61°59'
Coppermine - see-voir - Kugluktuk	HAM/HAM	NT		86 O/14	67°51'	115°06'
Coppermine Mountains	MTN/MNT	NT	Mackenzie	86 N	67°18'	116°00'
Coppermine Point	CAPE/CAP	ON	Algoma	41 K/15	46°59'	84°47'
Coppermine River	RIV/CDE	NT	Mackenzie	86 O/14	67°49'	115°04'
Copperneedle River	RIV/CDE	NT	Keewatin	55 F	61°53'	93°37'
Copper River	UNP/LNO	BC	Range 5 Coast	103 I/9	54°32'	128°30'
Coppett	UNP/LNO	NF		11 P/11	47°36'	57°15'
Coppett Harbour	BAY/BAIE	NF		11 P/11	47°36'	57°16'
Coppin's Corners	UNP/LNO	ON	Ontario	31 D/3	44°03'	79°09'
Copp Lake	LAKE/LAC	NT	Mackenzie	85 B	60°14'	114°41'
Coq-Rond, Le	UNP/LNO	QC	Deux-Montagnes	31 G/8	45°30'	74°01'
Coquihalla Mountain	MTN/MNT	BC	Yale Division Yale	92 H/11	49°31'	121°04'
Coquihalla River	RIV/CDE	BC	Yale Division Yale	92 H/6	49°24'	121°26'
Coquitlam	CITY/VIL1	BC	New Westminster	92 G/7	49°17'	122°45'
Coquitlam	UNP/LNO	BC	New Westminster	92 G/7	49°16'	122°47'
Coquitlam 1	IR/RI	BC	New Westminster	92 G/2	49°14'	122°48'
Coquitlam 2	IR/RI	BC	New Westminster	92 G/2	49°15'	122°48'
Coquitlam Lake	LAKE/LAC	BC	New Westminster	92 G/7	49°24'	122°47'
Coquitlam Mountain	MTN/MNT	BC	New Westminster	92 G/7	49°24'	122°42'
Coquitlam River	RIV/CDE	BC	New Westminster	92 G/2	49°14'	122°48'
Coral	UNP/LNO	ON	Cochrane	42 I/4	50°13'	81°41'
Coral Bay	BAY/BAIE	NT	Franklin	26 L	66°16'	71°07'
Coral Harbour	HAM/HAM	NT	Keewatin	46 B	64°08'	83°10'
Corbeau, Baie du	BAY/BAIE	QC	Jamésie	32 K/15	50°50'	76°43'
Corbeil	UNP/LNO	ON	Nipissing	31 L/6	46°16'	79°18'
Corbeil Point	CAPE/CAP	ON	Algoma	41 K/15	46°55'	84°37'
Corberrie	UNP/LNO	NS	Digby	21 A/4	44°14'	65°56'
Corbett	UNP/LNO	ON	Middlesex	40 P/4	43°15'	81°41'
Corbett Creek	UNP/LNO	AB	7-61-8-W5	83 J/6	54°16'	115°12'
Corbett Inlet	BAY/BAIE	NT	Keewatin	55 K	62°28'	92°20'
Corbett Lake	LAKE/LAC	NT	Keewatin	65 H	61°19'	96°27'
Corbetton	UNP/LNO	ON	Dufferin	41 A/1	44°08'	80°20'
Corbière, Lac	LAKE/LAC	QC	Sept-Rivières	22 O/9	51°34'	66°29'
Corbin	UNP/LNO	NF		1 L/14	46°58'	55°14'
Corbin	UNP/LNO	NF		1 M/11	47°35'	55°25'
Corbin	UNP/LNO	BC	Kootenay	82 G/10	49°31'	114°39'
Corbin Bay	BAY/BAIE	NF		1 M/11	47°36'	55°25'
Corbin Head	CAPE/CAP	NF		1 L/14	46°57'	55°14'
Corbin Head	CAPE/CAP	NF		1 M/11	47°37'	55°24'
Corbold Creek	RIV/CDE	BC	New Westminster	92 G/10	49°37'	122°39'
Corbyville	UNP/LNO	ON	Hastings	31 C/3	44°13'	77°23'
Corcoran Point	CAPE/CAP	NT	Franklin	47 B	68°28'	85°43'
Cordel	UNP/LNO	AB	20-40-15-W4	83 A/8	52°27'	112°09'
Cordelia Deeps	SEAU/SMER	—		4574	47°43'	52°35'
Cordero Channel	CHAN/CHEN	BC	Range 1 Coast	92 K/5	50°26'	125°33'
Cordingley Lake	LAKE/LAC	ON	Thunder Bay	42 L/2	50°15'	86°39'
Cordova	UNP/LNO	MB	27-13-17-W	62 J/4	50°08'	99°43'
Cordova Bay	UNP/LNO	BC	Lake	92 B/11	48°31'	123°22'
Cordova Channel	CHAN/CHEN	BC	Cowichan	92 B/11	48°36'	123°22'
Cordova Mines	UNP/LNO	ON	Hastings	31 C/12	44°32'	77°47'
Corfu Island, Le	UNP/LNO	QC	Les Îles-de-la-Madeleine	11 N/5	47°20'	61°57'
Coriander	UNP/LNO	SK	16-4-12-W3	72 G/5	49°18'	107°34'
Corinne	UNP/LNO	SK	2-13-20-W2	72 I/2	50°03'	104°37'
Corinth	UNP/LNO	ON	Elgin	40 I/15	42°49'	80°50'
Coristine	UNP/LNO	ON	Nipissing	31 L/2	46°05'	78°53'
Cork	UNP/LNO	NB	York	21 G/10	45°43'	66°56'
Corkery	UNP/LNO	ON	Carleton	31 F/8	45°17'	76°06'
Corkscrew Creek	RIV/CDE	BC	Range 3 Coast	93 C/6	52°29'	125°21'
Corkscrew Creek 9	IR/RI	BC	Range 4 Coast	93 F/16	53°57'	124°21'
Corkscrew Creek 10	IR/RI	BC	Range 4 Coast	93 F/16	53°53'	124°13'
Corkscrew Island	ISL/ÎLE	ON	Kenora	52 E/10	49°41'	94°41'
Corktown	UNP/LNO	ON	Wentworth	30 M/5	43°15'	79°52'
Corkums Island	UNP/LNO	NS	Lunenburg	21 A/8	44°21'	64°19'
Corliss	UNP/LNO	QC	Coaticook	21 E/4	45°04'	71°55'
Cormac	UNP/LNO	ON	Renfrew	31 F/6	45°28'	77°18'
Cormack	VILG/VILG	NF		12 H/6	49°18'	57°23'
Cormack Lake	LAKE/LAC	NT	Mackenzie	95 A	60°56'	121°40'
Cormack, Mount	MTN/MNT	NF		2 D/5	48°24'	55°57'
Cormacks Lake	LAKE/LAC	NF		12 A/5	48°16'	57°53'
Corman Park No. 344	MUN2/AZM2	SK		73 B/2	52°00'	106°40'
Cormier Cove	UNP/LNO	NB	Westmorland	21 H/15	45°57'	64°34'
Cormier, Lac	LAKE/LAC	QC	Minganie	12 N/4	51°03'	61°50'
Cormier-Village	UNP/LNO	NB	Westmorland	21 I/1	46°10'	64°21'

NAME NOM	ENTITY ENTITÉ	LOC 1 LIEU 1	LOC 2 LIEU 2	MAP CARTE	POSITION LAT	POSITION LONG
Cormierville	UNP/LNO	NB	Kent	21 I/7	46°24′	64°37′
Cormorandière, La	UNP/LNO	QC	Les Îles-de-la-Madeleine	11 N/5	47°29′	61°42′
Cormoran, Pointe au	CAPE/CAP	QC	Minganie	12 F/4	49°04′	61°50′
Cormorant	UNP/LNO	MB	31-60-21-W	63 K/2	54°13′	100°36′
Cormorant Channel	CHAN/CHEN	BC	Rupert	92 L/10	50°36′	126°54′
Cormorant Island	ISL/ÎLE	BC	Rupert	92 L/10	50°35′	126°55′
Cormorant Lake	LAKE/LAC	MB		63 K/2	54°15′	100°50′
Corneille Lake	LAKE/LAC	SK	69-5-W2	63 L/15	54°58′	102°40′
Corneille, Rivière de la	RIV/CDE	QC	Pontiac	31 K/11	46°32′	77°02′
Cornelius Grinnell Bay	BAY/BAIE	NT	Franklin	25 P	63°20′	64°50′
Cornelius Island	ISL/ÎLE	NF		11 P/12	47°36′	57°40′
Cornell	UNP/LNO	ON	Oxford	40 I/15	42°54′	80°38′
Corner Brook	CITY/VIL1	NF		12 A/13	48°58′	57°57′
Corner Brook	RIV/CDE	NF		12 A/13	48°57′	57°57′
Corner Brook Lake	LAKE/LAC	NF		12 A/13	48°50′	57°50′
Corner Lake	LAKE/LAC	ON	Kenora	52 F/14	49°53′	93°29′
Cornfield	UNP/LNO	NF		1 N/2	47°02′	52°53′
Cornfield Pond	LAKE/LAC	NF		2 E/4	49°01′	55°56′
Cornhill	UNP/LNO	NB	Kings	21 H/14	45°55′	65°21′
Cornhill East	UNP/LNO	NB	Kings	21 H/14	45°55′	65°18′
Corning	HAM/HAM	SK	36-11-8-W2	62 E/15	49°58′	102°58′
Corn Lake	LAKE/LAC	ON	Kenora	52 E/16	49°59′	94°26′
Cornwall	CITY/VIL1	ON	Stormont	31 G/2	45°02′	74°44′
Cornwall	TOWN/VIL2	PE	Queens	11 L/3	46°14′	63°13′
Cornwall	MUN2/AZM2	ON	Stormont	31 G/2	45°07′	74°49′
Cornwall Centre	UNP/LNO	ON	Stormont	31 G/2	45°03′	74°48′
Cornwallis	MUN2/AZM2	MB		62 G/13	49°48′	99°51′
Cornwallis	UNP/LNO	NS	Annapolis	21 A/12	44°39′	65°38′
Cornwallis Island	ISL/ÎLE	NT	Franklin	58 G/3	75°08′	95°00′
Cornwall Island	UNP/LNO	ON	Stormont	31 G/2	45°01′	74°41′
Cornwall Island	ISL/ÎLE	NT	Franklin	59 C	77°37′	94°38′
Cornwallis Square	VILG/VILG	NS	Kings	21 H/2	45°05′	64°40′
Cornwall Lake	LAKE/LAC	AB	121,122-4-W4	74 M/10	59°36′	110°35′
Cornwall Lake 224	IR/RI	AB	15-122-4-W4	74 M/10	59°36′	110°35′
Coromonie	UNP/LNO	NS	Pictou	11 E/7	45°27′	62°35′
Coronach	TOWN/VIL2	SK	11-2-27-W2	72 H/4	49°07′	105°31′
Coronado	UNP/LNO	AB	36-56-23-W4	83 H/14	53°53′	113°18′
Coronation	TOWN/VIL2	AB	13-36-11-W4	73 D/3	52°05′	111°27′
Coronation Boundary Marker Provincial Historic Site (Undeveloped)	PARK/PARC	AB	SW6-35-10-W4	72 M/14	51°58′	111°26′
Coronation Fiord	BAY/BAIE	NT	Franklin	26 P	67°14′	64°35′
Coronation Gardens	UNP/LNO	ON	Ontario	30 M/14	43°57′	79°00′
Coronation Gulf	BAY/BAIE	NT	Franklin	77 B	68°08′	112°00′
Coronation Park	UNP/LNO	ON	Lambton	40 J/16	42°58′	82°22′
Coronation Park	UNP/LNO	SK		72 I/7	50°29′	104°38′
Corps-Mort, Le	ISL/ÎLE	QC	Les Îles-de-la-Madeleine	11 M/8	47°16′	62°12′
Corra Linn	UNP/LNO	BC	Kootenay	82 F/6	49°28′	117°29′
Corran Ban	UNP/LNO	PE	Queens	11 L/6	46°23′	63°02′
Corraville	UNP/LNO	PE	Kings	11 L/7	46°19′	62°36′
Corrigall Lake	LAKE/LAC	AB	72-18-W5	83 P/2	55°13′	112°38′
Corris	UNP/LNO	QC	Le Val-Saint-François	31 H/9	45°37′	72°05′
Corriveau	UNP/LNO	QC	L'Amiante	21 L/3	46°08′	71°02′
Corson Lake	LAKE/LAC	SK		64 L/12	58°44′	103°45′
Corsons	UNP/LNO	ON	Victoria	31 D/10	44°37′	78°53′
Corte-Real	UNP/LNO	QC	La Côte-de-Gaspé	22 A/15	48°54′	64°36′
Cortes Bay	UNP/LNO	BC	Sayward	92 K/2	50°04′	124°56′
Cortes Island	ISL/ÎLE	BC	Sayward	92 K/2	50°07′	124°59′
Corunna	UNP/LNO	ON	Lambton	40 J/16	42°53′	82°26′
Corvette, Lac de la	LAKE/LAC	QC	Jamésie	33 G/8	53°25′	74°03′
Corvette, Rivière de la	RIV/CDE	QC	Jamésie	33 G/7	53°24′	74°41′
Corwhin	UNP/LNO	ON	Wellington	40 P/9	43°31′	80°06′
Corwin Crescent	UNP/LNO	ON	Welland	30 M/3	43°05′	79°06′
Cory	UNP/LNO	SK	36-6-W3	73 B/2	52°07′	106°50′
Coryatsaqua (Moricetown) 2	IR/RI	BC	Cassiar	93 M/3	55°02′	127°20′
Cory Bay	BAY/BAIE	NT	Franklin	36 G	65°25′	74°30′
Cosby, Mason and Martland	MUN2/AZM2	ON	Sudbury	41 I/1	46°07′	80°29′
Cosine	UNP/LNO	SK	33-36-28-W3	73 C/4	52°08′	109°56′
Cosman Settlement	UNP/LNO	NB	Kings	21 H/14	45°54′	65°28′
Cosmo	UNP/LNO	AB	23-57-6-W5	83 G/15	53°56′	114°48′
Cossette, Lac	LAKE/LAC	QC	Rimouski-Neigette	22 C/2	48°09′	68°43′
Cossetteville	UNP/LNO	QC	Mékinac	31 I/10	46°41′	72°32′
Costebelle, Lac	LAKE/LAC	QC	Minganie	12 L/8	50°24′	62°18′
Coste Island	ISL/ÎLE	BC	Range 4 Coast	103 H/15	53°50′	128°45′
Costello Lake	LAKE/LAC	MB		64 C/1	56°13′	100°08′
Costes Lake	LAKE/LAC	MB	55-2-E	63 H/14	53°48′	97°16′
Costigan	UNP/LNO	NB	Victoria	21 J/13	46°54′	67°45′

NAME NOM	ENTITY ENTITÉ	LOC 1 LIEU 1	LOC 2 LIEU 2	MAP CARTE	POSITION LAT	LONG
Costigan Lake	LAKE/LAC	NF		12 A/11	48°30′	57°05′
Costigan Lake	LAKE/LAC	SK		74 A/13	56°57′	105°54′
Costley Lake	LAKE/LAC	NS	Guysborough	11 F/5	45°19′	61°43′
Cosway	UNP/LNO	AB	32-29-25-W4	82 P/11	51°31′	113°28′
Cosy Cove	UNP/LNO	ON	Hastings	31 C/6	44°29′	77°17′
Cosy Cove	UNP/LNO	BC	New Westminster	92 G/7	49°20′	122°55′
Coté	UNP/LNO	SK	16-29-31-W	62 N/12	51°31′	101°48′
Cote 64	IR/RI	SK		62 N/12	51°37′	101°55′
Coteau, Barrages du	MISC/DIV	QC	Vaudreuil-Soulanges	31 G/8	45°16′	74°10′
Coteau Beach	VILG/VILG	SK	29,30-25-6-W3	72 O/2	51°10′	106°49′
Coteau-des-Hêtres	UNP/LNO	QC	Argenteuil	31 G/9	45°36′	74°19′
Coteau-du-Lac	VILG/VILG	QC	Vaudreuil-Soulanges	31 G/8	45°18′	74°11′
Coteau-du-Lac, Lieu historique national de - also-aussi - Coteau-du-Lac National Historic Site	PARK/PARC	QC	Vaudreuil-Soulanges	31 G/8	45°17′	74°11′
Coteau-du-Lac National Historic Site - also-aussi - Coteau-du-Lac, Lieu historique national de	PARK/PARC	QC	Vaudreuil-Soulanges	31 G/8	45°17′	74°11′
Coteau-Landing	UNP/LNO	QC	Vaudreuil-Soulanges	31 G/8	45°15′	74°13′
Coteau, Le	UNP/LNO	QC	L'Érable	21 L/5	46°22′	71°33′
Coteau-Mauvais-Riz	UNP/LNO	QC	Montmagny	21 M/1	47°01′	70°26′
Coteau No. 255	MUN2/AZM2	SK		72 O/2	51°11′	107°00′
Coteau Road	UNP/LNO	NB	Gloucester	21 P/15	47°50′	64°34′
Coteau-Station	UNP/LNO	QC	Vaudreuil-Soulanges	31 G/8	45°17′	74°14′
Coteau, The	CLF/ESC	SK		72 J/13	51°00′	107°30′
Côte-Cachée	UNP/LNO	QC	Le Centre-de-la-Mauricie	31 I/7	46°28′	72°41′
Côte-d'en-Bas	UNP/LNO	QC	Lajemmerais	31 H/14	45°48′	73°19′
Côte-des-Perron	UNP/LNO	QC	Laval	31 H/12	45°39′	73°44′
Côte-d'Or	UNP/LNO	NB	Kent	21 I/7	46°21′	64°37′
Côte-du-Lac	UNP/LNO	QC	Communauté urbaine de Québec	21 L/14	46°56′	71°12′
Côte-Girard	UNP/LNO	QC	Abitibi	32 C/11	48°45′	77°23′
Côte-McLean	UNP/LNO	QC	La Côte-de-Beaupré	21 M/2	47°10′	70°40′
Côte-Nord	MUN1/AZM1	QC	Sept-Rivières	22 I/13	50°52′	65°49′
Côte-Nord-du-Golfe-Saint-Laurent	VILG/VILG	QC	Côte-Nord-du-Golfe-Saint-Laurent	12 J/5	50°28′	59°36′
Cote No. 271	MUN2/AZM2	SK		62 N/5	51°30′	101°50′
Côte-Sainte-Anne	UNP/LNO	NB	Kent	21 I/10	46°35′	64°43′
Côte-Saint-Joseph	UNP/LNO	QC	Sherbrooke	31 H/8	45°29′	72°01′
Côte-Saint-Luc	CITY/VIL1	QC	Communauté urbaine de Montréal	31 H/5	45°28′	73°40′
Côte-Saint-Pierre	UNP/LNO	QC	Papineau	31 G/14	45°49′	75°04′
Cotes Landing	UNP/LNO	MB		63 J/12	54°39′	99°48′
Cotham	UNP/LNO	SK	12-19-5-W2	62 L/10	50°37′	102°35′
Côtière, Chaîne - also-aussi - **Coast Mountains**	MTN/MNT	BC/YT		103 I/15	54°53′	128°48′
Cotieville	UNP/LNO	ON	Renfrew	31 F/7	45°29′	76°43′
Cotnam Island	UNP/LNO	ON	Renfrew	31 F/14	45°48′	77°03′
Cotonou, Sommet de	MTN/MNT	QC	Charlevoix	21 M/15	47°47′	70°49′
Cotswold	UNP/LNO	ON	Wellington	40 P/15	43°52′	80°47′
Cottage-Hawthorne, Lieu historique national du - also-aussi - Hawthorne Cottage National Historic Site	PARK/PARC	NF		1 N/11	47°33′	53°13′
Cottam	UNP/LNO	ON	Essex	40 J/2	42°08′	82°45′
Cottel Island	ISL/ÎLE	NF		2 C/13	48°51′	53°42′
Cottel Reach	RIVF/EFLV	NF		2 C/13	48°52′	53°42′
Cotter Island	ISL/ÎLE	NT	Keewatin	34 F	57°46′	77°01′
Cotter Lake	LAKE/LAC	SK	75-2,3-W3	73 O/9	55°31′	106°18′
Cottesloe	UNP/LNO	ON	Peterborough	31 D/8	44°24′	78°05′
Cottlesville	TOWN/VIL2	NF		2 E/10	49°30′	54°51′
Cottlesville	UNP/LNO	NF		2 E/10	49°31′	54°52′
Cotton Lake	LAKE/LAC	MB	70-4,5-E	63 P/2	55°04′	96°49′
Cottonwood	UNP/LNO	BC	Cariboo	93 G/1	53°03′	122°10′
Cottonwood Flats	UNP/LNO	BC	Kamloops Division Yale	82 M/14	51°51′	119°19′
Cottonwood River	RIV/CDE	BC	Cariboo	93 G/2	53°07′	122°36′
Cottonwood River	RIV/CDE	BC	Cassiar	104 P/4	59°05′	129°42′
Cottrell	UNP/LNO	NB	York	21 G/11	45°41′	67°21′
Cottrell's Cove	UNP/LNO	NF		2 E/6	49°29′	55°17′
Cotwood	UNP/LNO	BC	Cariboo	93 G/1	53°04′	122°22′
Couchepaganiche, Réserve écologique de	PARK/PARC	QC	Lac-Saint-Jean-Est	22 D/5	48°22′	71°50′
Couchiching 16A	IR/RI	ON	Rainy River	52 C/11	48°42′	93°25′
Couchiching, Lake	LAKE/LAC	ON	Simcoe	31 D/11	44°40′	79°22′
Coucoucache 24A	IR/RI	QC	Le Haut-Saint-Maurice	31 P/14	47°45′	73°14′
Coucou, Rivière du	RIV/CDE	QC	La Vallée-de-la-Gatineau	31 O/11	47°35′	75°24′
Coude-de-la-Rivière-Moisie	UNP/LNO	QC	Sept-Rivières	22 J/8	50°15′	66°04′
Coudres, Île aux	ISL/ÎLE	QC	Charlevoix	21 M/8	47°24′	70°23′
Coughlan	UNP/LNO	NB	Northumberland	21 I/13	46°46′	65°46′
Coughlin	UNP/LNO	ON	Thunder Bay	52 A/16	48°53′	88°23′
Coulée-des-Adolphe	MUN2/AZM2	QC	Denis-Riverin	22 B/15	48°58′	66°39′
Coulée, La	UNP/LNO	QC	Matane	22 B/11	48°42′	67°17′
Coulee No. 136	MUN2/AZM2	SK		72 J/3	50°10′	107°25′
Coulonge, Chutes	FALL/CHUT	QC	Pontiac	31 F/15	45°52′	76°41′
Coulonge, Lac	LAKE/LAC	ON/QC		31 F/15	45°53′	76°50′
Coulonge, Rivière	RIV/CDE	QC	Pontiac	31 F/15	45°52′	76°46′
Coulson	UNP/LNO	ON	Simcoe	31 D/12	44°34′	79°37′

NAME NOM	ENTITY ENTITÉ	LOC 1 LIEU 1	LOC 2 LIEU 2	MAP CARTE	POSITION LAT	LONG
Coulson's Hill	UNP/LNO	ON	Simcoe	31 D/4	44°10'	79°35'
Coulter	UNP/LNO	MB	2-2-27-w	62 F/2	49°05'	100°59'
Coulterville	UNP/LNO	ON	Peel	40 P/16	43°50'	80°02'
Countess	UNP/LNO	AB	15-21-17-W4	82 I/16	50°47'	112°17'
Country Harbour	BAY/BAIE	NS	Guysborough	11 F/4	45°12'	61°43'
Country Harbour Head	CAPE/CAP	NS	Guysborough	11 F/4	45°07'	61°39'
Country Harbour Lake	UNP/LNO	NS	Guysborough	11 F/5	45°18'	61°54'
Country Harbour Mines	UNP/LNO	NS	Guysborough	11 F/4	45°15'	61°48'
Country Hills	UNP/LNO	ON	Waterloo	40 P/8	43°25'	80°28'
Country Pond	LAKE/LAC	NF		1 N/7	47°20'	52°55'
Country Road	UNP/LNO	NF		1 N/11	47°35'	53°18'
County Line	UNP/LNO	NS	Queens	21 A/2	44°11'	64°36'
County Line	UNP/LNO	NB	York	21 J/3	46°10'	67°20'
Coupe-de-Pierre, La	UNP/LNO	QC	Les Pays-d'en-Haut	31 G/16	46°00'	74°08'
Couper Islands	ISL/ÎLE	NT	Mackenzie	86 O	67°56'	114°33'
Courageous Lake	LAKE/LAC	NT	Mackenzie	76 D	64°10'	111°15'
Courcelles	VILG/VILG	QC	Le Granit	21 E/15	45°52'	70°59'
Courcellette	UNP/LNO	QC	Charlevoix-Est	21 M/9	47°43'	70°03'
Courchesne	UNP/LNO	QC	Témiscouata	21 N/7	47°23'	68°48'
Court	UNP/LNO	SK	22-33-28-W3	72 N/13	51°51'	109°52'
Courtenay	CITY/VIL1	BC	Comox	92 F/10	49°41'	124°59'
Courtice	UNP/LNO	ON	Durham	30 M/15	43°55'	78°46'
Courtland	UNP/LNO	ON	Norfolk	40 I/15	42°51'	80°38'
Courtney Lake	LAKE/LAC	BC	Kamloops Division Yale	92 I/2	50°00'	120°36'
Courtois, Lac	LAKE/LAC	QC	Le Fjord-du-Saguenay	22 M/11	51°42'	71°10'
Courtright	UNP/LNO	ON	Lambton	40 J/16	42°49'	82°28'
Courval	HAM/HAM	SK	7-14-2-W3	72 J/1	50°10'	106°15'
Courville	UNP/LNO	QC	Communauté urbaine de Québec	21 L/14	46°53'	71°10'
Cous 3	IR/RI	BC	Alberni	92 F/2	49°11'	124°50'
Cousineau	UNP/LNO	QC	Communauté urbaine de l'Outaouais	31 G/12	45°33'	75°33'
Cousins	UNP/LNO	AB	33-37-5-W4	73 D/2	52°14'	110°39'
Cousins	UNP/LNO	AB	2-13-6-W4	72 L/2	50°04'	110°43'
Cousins Lake	LAKE/LAC	MB		64 B/15	56°49'	98°33'
Couteau Bay	BAY/BAIE	NF		11 O/9	47°41'	58°02'
Couteau Brook	RIV/CDE	NF		11 O/9	47°43'	58°03'
Couteau Head	CAPE/CAP	NF		11 O/9	47°41'	58°05'
Coutlee	UNP/LNO	BC	Kamloops Division Yale	92 I/2	50°08'	120°49'
Coutnac Beach	UNP/LNO	ON	Simcoe	31 D/13	44°50'	79°55'
Coutts	VILG/VILG	AB	4-1-15-W4	72 E/4	49°00'	111°57'
Coutts, Cape	CAPE/CAP	NT	Franklin	38 A	72°15'	74°55'
Coutts Inlet	BAY/BAIE	NT	Franklin	37 H	71°54'	75°36'
Coutts River	RIV/CDE	AB	68-4-W5	83 J/16	54°53'	114°30'
Couttsville	UNP/LNO	ON	Timiskaming	31 M/12	47°40'	79°41'
Couture, Lac	LAKE/LAC	QC	Kativik	35 B/3	60°06'	75°20'
Couturier	UNP/LNO	QC	Témiscouata	21 N/11	47°42'	69°13'
Couturier Siding	UNP/LNO	NB	Madawaska	21 N/8	47°18'	68°29'
Couturval	UNP/LNO	QC	La Matapédia	22 B/5	48°28'	67°30'
Cove Beach	UNP/LNO	QC	Pabok	22 A/9	48°30'	64°10'
Cove Beach	UNP/LNO	ON	Prince Edward	30 N/14	43°55'	77°11'
Cove Beach	UNP/LNO	ON	Simcoe	41 A/9	44°45'	80°07'
Cove Cliff	UNP/LNO	BC	New Westminster	92 G/7	49°19'	122°56'
Covedell	UNP/LNO	NB	Northumberland	21 P/6	47°19'	65°01'
Covehead	UNP/LNO	PE	Queens	11 L/6	46°23'	63°07'
Covehead Road	UNP/LNO	PE	Queens	11 L/6	46°21'	63°07'
Cove Inlet	UNP/LNO	ON	Thunder Bay	52 H/8	49°21'	88°08'
Cove Island	ISL/ÎLE	ON	Bruce	41 H/5	45°17'	81°44'
Coventry	UNP/LNO	ON	Peel	30 M/13	43°54'	79°44'
Coventry Lake	LAKE/LAC	NT	Mackenzie	75 G	61°10'	106°10'
Coventry Place	UNP/LNO	SK		72 I/7	50°28'	104°39'
Coverdale	UNP/LNO	NB	Albert	21 I/2	46°03'	64°54'
Coverdale	UNP/LNO	ON	Northumberland	30 M/16	43°58'	78°09'
Coverdale	GEOG/GÉOG	NB	Albert	21 I/2	46°00'	64°50'
Covered Bridge	UNP/LNO	NB	York	21 J/2	46°14'	66°37'
Cove Road	UNP/LNO	NS	Colchester	11 E/5	45°23'	63°53'
Covey Hill	UNP/LNO	QC	Le Haut-Saint-Laurent	31 H/4	45°01'	73°45'
Cowan	UNP/LNO	QC	Le Haut-Saint-Laurent	31 H/4	45°04'	73°42'
Cowan	UNP/LNO	MB	26-35-23-W	63 C/2	52°02'	100°39'
Cowan Lake	LAKE/LAC	SK		73 J/3	54°00'	107°15'
Cowan River	RIV/CDE	SK		73 J/5	54°25'	107°51'
Cowan's Bay	UNP/LNO	ON	Victoria	31 D/7	44°20'	78°33'
Cowans Creek	UNP/LNO	NB	Gloucester	21 P/10	47°39'	64°55'
Cowans Point	UNP/LNO	BC	New Westminster	92 G/6	49°20'	123°21'
Cowansville	CITY/VIL1	QC	Brome-Missisquoi	31 H/2	45°12'	72°45'
Cow Bay	UNP/LNO	NS	Halifax	11 D/11	44°37'	63°25'
Cowessess 73	IR/RI	SK		62 L/10	50°32'	102°42'

NAME NOM	ENTITY ENTITÉ	LOC 1 LIEU 1	LOC 2 LIEU 2	MAP CARTE	POSITION LAT	LONG
Cow Head	TOWN/VIL2	NF		12 H/13	49°55′	57°49′
Cow Head	CAPE/CAP	NF		2 C/12	48°42′	53°39′
Cowichan 1	IR/RI	BC	Cowichan Lake	92 B/12	48°45′	123°30′
Cowichan 9	IR/RI	BC	Cowichan	92 B/13	48°45′	123°39′
Cowichan Bay	UNP/LNO	BC	Cowichan	92 B/12	48°44′	123°37′
Cowichan Bay	UNP/LNO	BC	Cowichan	92 B/12	48°45′	123°37′
Cowichan Bay	BAY/BAIE	BC	Cowichan	92 B/12	48°45′	123°37′
Cowichan Lake	LAKE/LAC	BC	Cowichan	92 C/16	48°52′	124°16′
Cowichan Lake	IR/RI	BC	Cowichan	92 C/16	48°50′	124°04′
Cowichan Lake Land District	GEOG/GÉOG	BC		92 C	48°51′	124°07′
Cowichan Land District	GEOG/GÉOG	BC		92 B	48°52′	123°19′
Cowichan River	RIV/CDE	BC	Cowichan	92 B/13	48°46′	123°38′
Cowichan Station	UNP/LNO	BC	Cowichan	92 B/12	48°44′	123°40′
Cowichan Valley	MUN1/AZM1	BC	Renfrew	92 C/16	48°50′	124°13′
Cowie Hill	UNP/LNO	NS	Halifax	11 D/12	44°37′	63°37′
Cowie Seamount	SEAU/SMER	—		5.03	54°15′	149°30′
Cowishil 1	IR/RI	BC	Clayoquot	92 C/14	48°59′	125°00′
Cow Lake	LAKE/LAC	AB	38-8-W5	83 B/6	52°16′	115°01′
Cowlest BaraswAy	LAKE/LAC	NF		11 P/12	47°38′	57°47′
Cowley	VILG/VILG	AB	21-7-1-W5	82 G/9	49°34′	114°05′
Cowley	UNP/LNO	YT		105 D/10	60°31′	134°54′
Cowoki Lake	LAKE/LAC	AB	18,19-13-W4	72 L/12	50°35′	111°42′
Cow Pen, The	SEAU/SMER	—		8007	44°17′	61°22′
Cowper	UNP/LNO	SK	19-8-1-W2	62 E/9	49°40′	102°07′
Cowper Point	CAPE/CAP	NT	Franklin	78 B	72°48′	111°33′
Cow River	RIV/CDE	ON	Algoma	41 O/5	47°23′	83°59′
Coxby	UNP/LNO	SK	12-48-23-W2	73 H/3	53°07′	105°14′
Coxheath	UNP/LNO	NS	Cape Breton	11 K/1	46°07′	60°14′
Coxipi, Lac	LAKE/LAC	QC	Minganie	12 O/9	51°33′	58°23′
Coxipi, Rivière	RIV/CDE	QC	Côte-Nord-du-Golfe-Saint-Laurent	12 O/8	51°18′	58°28′
Cox Island	ISL/ÎLE	BC	Rupert	102 I/15	50°48′	128°36′
Cox Island	ISL/ÎLE	NT	Keewatin	34 L	58°39′	78°41′
Cox Point	UNP/LNO	NB	Queens	21 I/4	46°01′	65°58′
Cox Point	CAPE/CAP	BC	Clayoquot	92 F/4	49°06′	125°53′
Cox's Cove	VILG/VILG	NF		12 G/1	49°07′	58°05′
Coxvale	UNP/LNO	ON	Frontenac	31 C/15	44°53′	76°52′
Coykendahl	UNP/LNO	BC	Kootenay	82 E/8	49°23′	118°01′
Coyle	UNP/LNO	ON	Welland	30 L/14	42°58′	79°16′
Coyle	UNP/LNO	BC	Kamloops Division Yale	92 I/2	50°09′	120°53′
Coyne Lake	LAKE/LAC	NT	Mackenzie	75 H	61°30′	105°05′
Coy Pond	LAKE/LAC	NF		2 D/5	48°22′	55°37′
Coytown	UNP/LNO	NB	Queens	21 G/16	45°50′	66°12′
Cozy Corners	UNP/LNO	ON	Rainy River	52 D/16	48°57′	94°18′
CPR	UNP/LNO	SK		72 I/5	50°24′	105°33′
Crabbes River	RIV/CDE	NF		12 B/2	48°13′	58°52′
Crabclaw Lake	LAKE/LAC	ON	Kenora	52 F/13	49°47′	93°37′
Crab River (Crab Harbour) 18	IR/RI	BC	Range 4 Coast	103 H/10	53°34′	128°46′
Crabtree	VILG/VILG	QC	Joliette	31 H/14	45°58′	73°28′
Cracknell	UNP/LNO	MB	1-22-28-W	62 K/14	50°52′	101°14′
Cracroft	UNP/LNO	BC	Range 1 Coast	92 L/9	50°32′	126°23′
Cracroft Bay	BAY/BAIE	NT	Franklin	97 C	69°49′	125°06′
Cracroft, Cape	CAPE/CAP	NT	Franklin	25 I	62°42′	65°20′
Cracroft Islands	ISL/ÎLE	BC	Range 1 Coast	92 L/9	50°33′	126°20′
Craddock	UNP/LNO	AB	11-6-19-W4	82 H/8	49°28′	112°27′
Crafts Cove	UNP/LNO	NB	Queens	21 H/12	45°44′	66°00′
Craig	UNP/LNO	NB	Restigouche	22 B/1	48°00′	66°21′
Craigavon	UNP/LNO	SK	19-46-14-W3	73 C/16	52°59′	108°01′
Craigdhu	UNP/LNO	AB	12-27-26-W4	82 P/5	51°17′	113°31′
Craigellachie	UNP/LNO	BC	Kamloops Division Yale	82 L/15	50°58′	118°43′
Craig Harbour	UNP/LNO	NT	Franklin	49 A	76°12′	81°00′
Craighurst	UNP/LNO	ON	Simcoe	31 D/12	44°32′	79°43′
Craig Lake	LAKE/LAC	NT	Franklin	120 C	81°52′	68°47′
Craigleith	UNP/LNO	ON	Grey	41 A/9	44°32′	80°19′
Craigmawr Beach	UNP/LNO	ON	York	31 D/3	44°14′	79°28′
Craigmillar	UNP/LNO	AB	35-38-7-W4	73 D/7	52°18′	110°54′
Craigmont	UNP/LNO	ON	Hastings	31 F/5	45°18′	77°38′
Craigmore	UNP/LNO	NS	Inverness	11 F/14	45°46′	61°28′
Craigmyle	UNP/LNO	AB	20-31-16-W4	82 P/9	51°40′	112°15′
Craig River	RIV/CDE	BC	Cassiar	104 B/11	56°42′	131°17′
Craigs	UNP/LNO	BC	New Westminster	92 G/2	49°09′	122°52′
Craigsford	UNP/LNO	MB	37,38-26-W	63 C/3	52°14′	101°04′
Craigsholme	UNP/LNO	ON	Dufferin	40 P/16	43°47′	80°17′
Craig Shore	UNP/LNO	ON	Lanark	31 F/1	45°03′	76°10′
Craigville	UNP/LNO	NB	Northumberland	21 I/13	46°58′	65°32′
Craik	TOWN/VIL2	SK	14-24-28-W2	72 P/4	51°03′	105°49′

NAME NOM	ENTITY ENTITÉ	LOC 1 LIEU 1	LOC 2 LIEU 2	MAP CARTE	POSITION LAT	POSITION LONG
Craik No. 222	MUN2/AZM2	SK		72 I/13	50°55′	105°50′
Cramahe	MUN2/AZM2	ON	Northumberland	31 C/4	44°05′	77°53′
Cramersburg	UNP/LNO	SK	30-22-20-W3	72 K/15	50°54′	108°46′
Crammond	UNP/LNO	AB	29-35-5-W5	83 B/2	52°02′	114°40′
Crammond Islands	ISL/ÎLE	NS	Inverness	11 F/14	45°45′	61°05′
Cramoisy, Lac	LAKE/LAC	QC	Jamésie	32 O/14	51°54′	75°25′
Cramolet, Lac	LAKE/LAC	QC	Kativik	23 O/13	55°50′	67°38′
Crampe, Lac de la	LAKE/LAC	QC	Le Domaine-du-Roy	32 A/11	48°33′	73°27′
Crampton	UNP/LNO	ON	Middlesex	40 I/15	42°57′	80°57′
Cranberry	UNP/LNO	QC	L'Amiante	21 L/3	46°04′	71°27′
Cranberry	UNP/LNO	ON	Parry Sound	41 H/15	45°55′	80°34′
Cranberry	UNP/LNO	BC	New Westminster	92 F/15	49°53′	124°32′
Cranberry Island	ISL/ÎLE	ON	Bruce	41 A/11	44°44′	81°18′
Cranberry Junction	UNP/LNO	BC	Cassiar	103 P/10	55°34′	128°36′
Cranberry Lake	LAKE/LAC	NB	Queens	21 I/4	46°07′	65°38′
Cranberry Lake	LAKE/LAC	ON	Grenville	31 B/13	44°48′	75°49′
Cranberry Land District	GEOG/GÉOG	BC		92 G	49°07′	123°55′
Cranberry Mountain	MTN/MNT	BC	Kootenay	82 L/9	50°42′	118°12′
Cranberry Point	CAPE/CAP	NS	Yarmouth	20 O/16	43°54′	66°10′
Cranberry Portage	UNP/LNO	MB	31-64-26-W	63 K/11	54°35′	101°23′
Cranberry River	RIV/CDE	BC	Cassiar	103 P/10	55°32′	128°50′
Cranbourne	UNP/LNO	QC	Robert-Cliche	21 L/7	46°23′	70°42′
Cranbrook	CITY/VIL1	BC	Kootenay	82 G/5	49°30′	115°46′
Cranbrook	UNP/LNO	ON	Huron	40 P/11	43°42′	81°12′
Crandall	UNP/LNO	MB	35-13-25-W	62 K/2	50°09′	100°47′
Crandall Road	UNP/LNO	NS	Inverness	11 F/11	45°40′	61°20′
Crane Bay	BAY/BAIE	MB		62 O/11	51°33′	99°16′
Crane Junction	UNP/LNO	SK	18-45-12-W2	63 D/13	52°53′	103°43′
Crane Lake	LAKE/LAC	SK		72 K/3	50°05′	109°05′
Crane Lake	LAKE/LAC	AB	10-64-4-W4	73 L/10	54°31′	110°31′
Crane River	UNP/LNO	MB	30-29-13-W	62 O/11	51°32′	99°17′
Crane River 51	IR/RI	MB		62 O/6	51°30′	99°14′
Crane Valley	UNP/LNO	SK	30-9-26-W2	72 H/13	49°45′	105°32′
Cranford	UNP/LNO	AB	27-9-18-W4	82 H/16	49°46′	112°21′
Cranmer	UNP/LNO	MB	1-2-25-W	62 F/2	49°06′	100°41′
Cran, Rivière du	RIV/CDE	QC	Le Domaine-du-Roy	32 A/15	48°52′	72°50′
Crans-Serrés, Les	UNP/LNO	QC	Sept-Rivières	22 J/3	50°07′	67°11′
Cranston	UNP/LNO	ON	Haldimand	30 L/13	43°00′	79°56′
Cranstone Peninsula	CAPE/CAP	NT	Franklin	340 E	82°55′	72°20′
*Cranstons Beach	UNP/LNO	ON	Frontenac	31 C/7	44°22′	76°34′
Cranswick River	RIV/CDE	NT	Mackenzie	106 K/1	66°05′	132°09′
Crapaud	VILG/VILG	PE	Queens	11 L/3	46°14′	63°30′
Crater Mountain	MTN/MNT	BC	Similkameen Division Yale	92 H/1	49°11′	120°05′
Crathie	UNP/LNO	ON	Middlesex	40 P/4	43°02′	81°38′
Crauford, Cape	CAPE/CAP	NT	Franklin	48 C	73°44′	84°51′
Craven	VILG/VILG	SK	23-20-21-W2	72 I/10	50°42′	104°48′
Craven, Lac	LAKE/LAC	QC	Jamésie	33 K/7	54°20′	76°56′
Crawfish Lake	LAKE/LAC	BC	Nootka	92 E/10	49°41′	126°48′
Crawford	UNP/LNO	QC	La Mitis	22 C/9	48°38′	68°04′
Crawford	UNP/LNO	ON	Grey	41 A/7	44°15′	80°56′
Crawford Bay	UNP/LNO	BC	Kootenay	82 F/10	49°41′	116°49′
Crawford Park	UNP/LNO	MB	5-20-19-W	62 K/9	50°41′	100°05′
Crawford's Grove	UNP/LNO	ON	Peterborough	31 D/8	44°17′	78°20′
Crawley Island	UNP/LNO	NF		1 N/5	47°26′	53°52′
Crean Hill	UNP/LNO	ON	Sudbury	41 I/6	46°26′	81°21′
Crean Lake	LAKE/LAC	SK		73 J/1	54°05′	106°09′
Crean River	RIV/CDE	SK	60-26-W2	73 I/4	54°13′	105°50′
Crease Island	ISL/ÎLE	BC	Range 1 Coast	92 L/10	50°37′	126°39′
Crediton	UNP/LNO	ON	Huron	40 P/5	43°17′	81°33′
Credit River	RIV/CDE	ON	Peel	30 M/12	43°33′	79°35′
Creditville	UNP/LNO	ON	Oxford	40 P/2	43°09′	80°37′
Cree	UNP/LNO	ON	Algoma	42 F/2	49°13′	84°43′
Creek Bank	UNP/LNO	ON	Wellington	40 P/10	43°42′	80°32′
Creek Beach	UNP/LNO	QC	Laval	31 H/12	45°35′	73°51′
Creekland	UNP/LNO	AB	12-50-4-W5	83 G/8	53°18′	114°26′
Creek Road	UNP/LNO	NB	Kings	21 H/14	45°56′	65°23′
Creekside	UNP/LNO	BC	Lillooet	92 J/7	50°24′	122°42′
Cree Lake	UNP/LNO	SK		74 G/7	57°22′	106°50′
Cree Lake	LAKE/LAC	SK		74 G/7	57°30′	106°30′
Creelman	VILG/VILG	SK	16-10-10-W2	62 E/14	49°49′	103°18′
Creelmans Crossing	UNP/LNO	NS	Halifax	11 E/2	45°07′	62°41′
Creemore	UNP/LNO	ON	Simcoe	41 A/8	44°24′	80°04′
Creemorne	UNP/LNO	QC	Pontiac	31 F/16	45°49′	76°28′
Cree River	RIV/CDE	SK		74 I/13	58°57′	105°47′
Creighton	TOWN/VIL2	SK	66-30-W	63 K/12	54°45′	101°54′

NAME NOM	ENTITY ENTITÉ	LOC 1 LIEU 1	LOC 2 LIEU 2	MAP CARTE	POSITION LAT	LONG
Creighton	UNP/LNO	ON	Simcoe	31 D/12	44°36′	79°35′
Creighton	UNP/LNO	ON	Sudbury	41 I/6	46°28′	81°11′
Creighton Creek	RIV/CDE	BC	Osoyoos Division Yale	82 L/2	50°15′	118°57′
Creighton Heights	UNP/LNO	ON	Northumberland	31 D/1	44°01′	78°09′
Creighton Valley	UNP/LNO	BC	Osoyoos Division Yale	82 L/2	50°13′	118°47′
Creignish	UNP/LNO	NS	Inverness	11 F/11	45°44′	61°27′
Creignish Rear	UNP/LNO	NS	Inverness	11 F/11	45°43′	61°25′
Cremona	VILG/VILG	AB	3-30-4-W5	82 O/9	51°33′	114°29′
Creosote	UNP/LNO	ON	Sudbury	41 I/6	46°30′	81°03′
Crépeau, Lac	LAKE/LAC	QC	Jamésie	23 E/15	53°56′	70°36′
Crerar	UNP/LNO	ON	Sudbury	41 I/10	46°38′	80°34′
Crescent	UNP/LNO	BC	New Westminster	92 G/2	49°03′	122°51′
Crescent Bay	UNP/LNO	ON	Norfolk	40 I/16	42°47′	80°07′
Crescent Bay	UNP/LNO	MB		62 I/8	50°20′	96°02′
Crescent Bay	UNP/LNO	BC	Kootenay	82 F/11	49°37′	117°09′
Crescent Bay	BAY/BAIE	BC	Texada Island	92 F/15	49°46′	124°38′
Crescent Beach	UNP/LNO	NS	Lunenburg	21 A/1	44°14′	64°25′
Crescent Beach	UNP/LNO	QC	Communauté urbaine de Québec	21 L/11	46°45′	71°18′
Crescent Beach	UNP/LNO	ON	Welland	30 L/15	42°53′	78°58′
Crescent Beach	UNP/LNO	ON	York	31 D/6	44°19′	79°27′
Crescent Beach	UNP/LNO	BC	Osoyoos Division Yale	82 E/12	49°37′	119°39′
Crescent Beach	UNP/LNO	BC	New Westminster	92 G/2	49°03′	122°53′
Crescent Creek	RIV/CDE	SK	35-23-4-W2	62 M/1	51°01′	102°28′
Crescent Grove	UNP/LNO	NS	Victoria	11 K/2	46°07′	60°44′
Crescent Harbour	UNP/LNO	ON	Simcoe	31 D/5	44°22′	79°32′
Crescent Heights	UNP/LNO	SK		72 I/6	50°23′	105°29′
Crescent Island	ISL/ÎLE	NT	Franklin	69 A	76°59′	97°20′
Crescent Lake	UNP/LNO	SK	15,22-23-4-W2	62 L/16	50°59′	102°29′
Crescent Lake	LAKE/LAC	NF		2 E/5	49°28′	55°52′
Crescent Park	UNP/LNO	ON	Welland	30 L/15	42°53′	78°58′
Crescent Park	UNP/LNO	MB		62 H/14	49°50′	97°09′
Crescent Spur	UNP/LNO	BC	Cariboo	93 H/10	53°35′	120°41′
Crescent Town	UNP/LNO	ON	York	30 M/11	43°42′	79°18′
Crescent Valley	UNP/LNO	BC	Kootenay	82 F/5	49°27′	117°33′
Crescent View	UNP/LNO	SK		72 I/5	50°24′	105°30′
Crescentwood	UNP/LNO	MB		62 H/14	49°52′	97°10′
Cressday	UNP/LNO	AB	31-3-2-W4	72 E/1	49°15′	110°16′
Cresswell	UNP/LNO	ON	Victoria	31 D/7	44°17′	78°58′
Cresswell, Cape	CAPE/CAP	NT	Franklin	120 E	82°38′	63°15′
Cressy	UNP/LNO	ON	Prince Edward	31 C/2	44°05′	76°52′
Cresthill	UNP/LNO	QC	La Vallée-de-la-Gatineau	31 J/5	46°19′	75°52′
Crestomere	UNP/LNO	AB	6-43-27-W4	83 A/12	52°40′	113°55′
Creston	TOWN/VIL2	BC	Kootenay	82 F/1	49°06′	116°30′
Creston	UNP/LNO	NF		1 M/3	47°09′	55°11′
Creston 1	IR/RI	BC	Nelson	82 F/2	49°03′	116°32′
Creston North	UNP/LNO	NF		1 M/3	47°09′	55°12′
Crestview	UNP/LNO	ON	Carleton	31 G/5	45°20′	75°44′
Crestview	UNP/LNO	MB		62 H/14	49°53′	97°18′
Crestview	UNP/LNO	MB	28-36-29-W	63 C/4	52°08′	101°34′
Crestview	UNP/LNO	YT		105 D/14	60°47′	135°10′
Crestwynd	UNP/LNO	SK	30-13-27-W2	72 I/4	50°06′	105°41′
Creswell Bay	BAY/BAIE	NT	Franklin	58 B	72°41′	93°25′
Creswell River	RIV/CDE	NT	Franklin	58 B	72°49′	93°24′
Crewe	UNP/LNO	ON	Huron	40 P/13	43°54′	81°39′
Crewsons Corners	UNP/LNO	ON	Wellington	40 P/9	43°37′	80°05′
Cribbons Point	CAPE/CAP	NS	Antigonish	11 F/13	45°45′	61°54′
Crichton	UNP/LNO	SK	8-9-14-W3	72 G/12	49°44′	107°53′
Crichton Park	UNP/LNO	NS	Halifax	11 D/12	44°41′	63°34′
Cridge, Mount	MTN/MNT	BC	Range 1 Coast	92 K/14	50°57′	125°27′
Crieff	UNP/LNO	ON	Wellington	40 P/8	43°26′	80°09′
Crilly	UNP/LNO	ON	Rainy River	52 C/16	48°45′	92°17′
Crimson Lake	UNP/LNO	AB	13-40-8-W5	83 B/6	52°27′	115°02′
Crimson Lake Provincial Park	PARK/PARC	AB	40-7,8-W5	83 B/6	52°28′	115°03′
Crinan	UNP/LNO	ON	Elgin	40 I/12	42°39′	81°40′
Cripple Cove Point	CAPE/CAP	NF		1 K/11	46°38′	53°06′
Crippsdale	UNP/LNO	AB	19-59-21-W4	83 I/3	54°07′	113°09′
Crique-Clair	UNP/LNO	QC	Le Haut-Saint-Maurice	31 P/7	47°17′	72°51′
Crique-La Corne	UNP/LNO	QC	Vallée-de-l'Or	32 C/5	48°15′	77°58′
Crique-Rouillé, Le	UNP/LNO	QC	Antoine-Labelle	31 J/13	46°50′	75°47′
Criss Creek	UNP/LNO	BC	Kamloops Division Yale	92 P/2	51°03′	120°44′
Criss Creek	RIV/CDE	BC	Kamloops Division Yale	92 I/15	50°53′	120°58′
Critchell-Bullock Arm	BAY/BAIE	NT	Mackenzie	75 O	63°27′	107°00′
Croal Lake	LAKE/LAC	ON	Kenora	43 E/12	53°32′	87°52′
Croche-à-Gaby, Le	UNP/LNO	QC	L'Islet	21 N/4	47°02′	69°55′
Croche-des-Maires, Le	UNP/LNO	QC	Le Domaine-du-Roy	32 A/9	48°43′	72°24′

NAME NOM	ENTITY ENTITÉ	LOC 1 LIEU 1	LOC 2 LIEU 2	MAP CARTE	POSITION LAT	LONG
Croche, Lac	LAKE/LAC	QC	Témiscouata	21 N/15	47°47′	68°47′
Croche, Lac	LAKE/LAC	QC	La Jacques-Cartier	21 M/5	47°24′	71°47′
Croche, Rivière	RIV/CDE	QC	Le Haut-Saint-Maurice	31 P/7	47°30′	72°46′
Crocker Hill	UNP/LNO	NB	Charlotte	21 G/3	45°11′	67°15′
Crocker Lake	LAKE/LAC	NB	Northumberland	21 I/13	46°53′	65°44′
Crockers Cove	UNP/LNO	NF		1 N/11	47°44′	53°12′
Crockets Corner	UNP/LNO	NB	Kings	21 H/14	45°47′	65°21′
Crocus	UNP/LNO	MB	3-17-18-W	62 J/5	50°25′	99°51′
Croft	UNP/LNO	NS	Antigonish	11 F/12	45°30′	61°50′
Crofton	UNP/LNO	ON	Prince Edward	31 C/3	44°04′	77°19′
Crofton	UNP/LNO	BC	Chemainus	92 B/13	48°52′	123°39′
Croix, La	UNP/LNO	QC	Les Îles-de-la-Madeleine	11 N/11	47°37′	61°24′
Croix, La	UNP/LNO	QC	Le Domaine-du-Roy	32 A/8	48°28′	72°14′
Croix, Lac à la	LAKE/LAC	QC	Le Fjord-du-Saguenay	22 M/8	51°16′	70°13′
Croix, Lac de la	LAKE/LAC	QC	Le Fjord-du-Saguenay	22 D/16	48°48′	70°09′
Croix, Lac la	LAKE/LAC	ON	Rainy River	52 C/8	48°21′	92°09′
Croker Bay	BAY/BAIE	NT	Franklin	48 E	74°42′	83°15′
Croker, Cape	CAPE/CAP	ON	Bruce	41 A/15	44°58′	80°59′
Croker Island	ISL/ÎLE	ON	Algoma	41 J/1	46°05′	82°13′
Croker River	RIV/CDE	NT	Mackenzie	87 C/5	69°18′	119°19′
Croll	UNP/LNO	MB	36-4-21-W	62 F/8	49°20′	100°11′
Croll Lake	LAKE/LAC	MB		64 O/9	59°34′	98°23′
Cromar	UNP/LNO	ON	Lambton	40 J/16	42°47′	82°16′
Cromarty	UNP/LNO	ON	Perth	40 P/6	43°26′	81°21′
Cromarty	UNP/LNO	MB		54 L/1	58°04′	94°09′
Crombies	UNP/LNO	ON	Dufferin	41 A/1	44°01′	80°11′
Crombie Settlement	UNP/LNO	NB	Victoria	21 J/14	46°57′	67°30′
Cromer	UNP/LNO	MB	8-9-28-W	62 F/11	49°44′	101°14′
Cromwell	UNP/LNO	MB	30,31-13-8-E	62 I/1	50°07′	96°30′
Cronin, Mount	MTN/MNT	BC	Range 5 Coast	93 L/15	54°56′	126°52′
Crooked Bay	UNP/LNO	ON	Muskoka	31 D/13	44°55′	79°46′
Crooked Creek	UNP/LNO	ON	Durham	30 M/15	43°58′	78°30′
Crooked Creek	UNP/LNO	AB	26-71-26-W5	83 N/4	55°10′	117°52′
Crooked Creek	RIV/CDE	NB	Albert	21 H/10	45°44′	64°45′
Crooked Falls	FALL/CHUT	MB	19-37-10E	63 A/1	52°12′	96°10′
Crooked Lake	LAKE/LAC	NF		12 H/1	49°08′	56°04′
Crooked Lake	LAKE/LAC	NF		12 A/8	48°24′	56°17′
Crooked Lake	LAKE/LAC	ON	Rainy River	52 B/4	48°12′	91°46′
Crooked Lake	LAKE/LAC	SK		62 L/10	50°36′	102°44′
Crooked Lake	LAKE/LAC	BC	Cariboo	93 A/2	52°15′	120°41′
Crooked Lake	LAKE/LAC	NT	Franklin	68 A	72°38′	98°36′
Crooked Pine Lake	LAKE/LAC	ON	Rainy River	52 B/14	48°47′	91°04′
Crooked River	HAM/HAM	SK	6-45-12-W2	63 D/13	52°51′	103°44′
Crooked River	RIV/CDE	NF		13 F/15	53°48′	60°51′
Crooked River	RIV/CDE	ON	Kenora	43 F/9	53°32′	84°24′
Crooked River	RIV/CDE	BC	Cariboo	93 J/15	54°50′	122°53′
Crooked Turn	UNP/LNO	MB		63 H/13	53°57′	97°51′
Crooks	UNP/LNO	ON	Thunder Bay	52 A/4	48°05′	89°31′
Crooks Inlet	BAY/BAIE	NT	Franklin	25 M	63°03′	71°00′
Crookston	UNP/LNO	ON	Hastings	31 C/6	44°26′	77°27′
Croque	UNP/LNO	NF		2 M/4	51°04′	55°50′
Croque Harbour	BAY/BAIE	NF		2 M/4	51°03′	55°48′
Crosby	UNP/LNO	ON	Leeds	31 C/9	44°39′	76°16′
Crosby Lake	LAKE/LAC	ON	Leeds	31 C/16	44°45′	76°26′
Crosbys Mill	UNP/LNO	PE	Queens	11 L/3	46°12′	63°21′
Cross	UNP/LNO	SK	4-12-24-W3	72 F/14	49°58′	109°14′
Cross Bay	BAY/BAIE	MB		63 G/4	53°13′	99°30′
Cross Bay	BAY/BAIE	NT	Keewatin	55 N	63°54′	93°30′
Crossburn	UNP/LNO	NS	Kings	21 A/10	44°45′	64°49′
Cross Country Pond	LAKE/LAC	NF		12 H/9	49°45′	56°12′
Cross Creek	UNP/LNO	NB	York	21 J/7	46°19′	66°43′
Cross Creek Station	UNP/LNO	NB	York	21 J/7	46°16′	66°38′
Crossfield	TOWN/VIL2	AB	26-28-1-W5	82 O/8	51°26′	114°02′
Crossfield Creek	RIV/CDE	AB	27-27-26-W4	82 P/5	51°20′	113°34′
Cross (Grass) Island	ISL/ÎLE	NF		1 M/7	47°21′	54°50′
Crosshill	UNP/LNO	ON	Waterloo	40 P/10	43°31′	80°45′
Crossing Bay	BAY/BAIE	MB		63 F/16	53°48′	100°26′
Crossing-Labrecque	UNP/LNO	QC	La Nouvelle-Beauce	21 L/7	46°25′	70°59′
Crossing Place River	RIV/CDE	NF		1 K/14	46°56′	53°28′
Cross Island	ISL/ÎLE	NF		13 O/5	55°23′	60°00′
Cross Island	ISL/ÎLE	NS	Lunenburg	21 A/8	44°19′	64°11′
Cross Lake	UNP/LNO	ON	Nipissing	31 F/5	45°25′	77°55′
Cross Lake	UNP/LNO	MB	15-10-17-E	52 E/14	49°50′	95°12′
Cross Lake	UNP/LNO	MB	65-3-W	63 I/12	54°38′	97°47′
Cross Lake	LAKE/LAC	NS	Halifax	11 E/1	45°03′	62°27′

NAME NOM	ENTITY ENTITÉ	LOC 1 LIEU 1	LOC 2 LIEU 2	MAP CARTE	POSITION LAT	LONG
Cross Lake	LAKE/LAC	ON	Nipissing	31 L/13	46°53′	79°57′
Cross Lake	LAKE/LAC	MB		63 I/12	54°45′	97°30′
Cross Lake	LAKE/LAC	SK	58-1-W2	63 E/16	54°00′	102°04′
Cross Lake 19	IR/RI	MB		63 I/12	54°37′	97°50′
Cross Lake 19A	IR/RI	MB		63 I/12	54°39′	97°46′
Cross Lake 19B	IR/RI	MB		63 I/12	54°35′	97°45′
Cross Lake 19C	IR/RI	MB		63 I/12	54°36′	97°47′
Cross Lake 19D	IR/RI	MB	65,66-3,4,5-W1	63 I/12	54°37′	97°57′
Cross Lake Provincial Park	PARK/PARC	AB	65-25,26-W4	83 I/12	54°39′	113°47′
Crossland	UNP/LNO	ON	Simcoe	31 D/12	44°32′	79°55′
Crossley Hunter	UNP/LNO	ON	Elgin	40 I/14	42°51′	81°02′
Crossley Lakes	LAKE/LAC	NT	Mackenzie	107 A	68°38′	129°32′
Cross Point	UNP/LNO	NS	Cape Breton	11 K/2	46°04′	60°34′
Cross Point	CAPE/CAP	NF		1 L/16	46°56′	54°11′
Cross Point	CAPE/CAP	ON	Parry Sound	31 L/4	46°12′	79°42′
Cross Point Station	UNP/LNO	QC	Avignon	22 B/2	48°02′	66°42′
Cross Pond	LAKE/LAC	NF		12 B/8	48°22′	58°03′
Cross River	UNP/LNO	PE	Prince	11 L/5	46°30′	63°58′
Cross River	RIV/CDE	BC	Kootenay	82 J/12	50°38′	115°48′
Cross Road	UNP/LNO	QC	Témiscamingue	31 M/9	47°38′	78°01′
Cross Roads - see-voir - Stratford	VILG/VILG	PE		11 L/3	46°13′	63°05′
Crossroads	UNP/LNO	NF		1 N/14	47°52′	53°22′
Cross Roads	UNP/LNO	NF		1 N/5	47°27′	53°33′
Cross Roads	UNP/LNO	PE	Queens	11 L/3	46°13′	63°05′
Crossroads - see-voir - Cross Roads	UNP/LNO	PE		11 L/3	46°13′	63°05′
Cross Roads	UNP/LNO	NB	Northumberland	21 P/4	47°01′	65°35′
Cross Roads	UNP/LNO	NB	Gloucester	21 P/12	47°38′	65°41′
Cross Roads Country Harbour	UNP/LNO	NS	Guysborough	11 F/5	45°17′	61°53′
Crossroads Lake	LAKE/LAC	NF		23 I/11	54°45′	65°04′
Cross Roads Ohio	UNP/LNO	NS	Antigonish	11 E/8	45°29′	62°03′
Crossroute Lake	LAKE/LAC	ON	Kenora	52 F/3	49°12′	93°26′
Crotchet Lake	LAKE/LAC	ON	Victoria	31 D/15	44°57′	78°56′
Crotch Lake	LAKE/LAC	ON	Frontenac	31 C/15	44°55′	76°48′
Croton	UNP/LNO	ON	Kent	40 J/9	42°37′	82°03′
Crouchers Forks	UNP/LNO	NS	Halifax	11 D/12	44°38′	63°53′
Crouses Settlement	UNP/LNO	NS	Lunenburg	21 A/8	44°21′	64°24′
Crousetown	UNP/LNO	NS	Lunenburg	21 A/8	44°15′	64°29′
Crowchild	UNP/LNO	AB	17-23-2-W5	82 J/16	50°57′	114°14′
Crowduck Lake	LAKE/LAC	ON	Kenora	52 E/11	49°40′	95°02′
Crowduck Lake	LAKE/LAC	MB	13,14-17-E	52 L/3	50°08′	95°15′
Crowe Bridge	UNP/LNO	ON	Northumberland	31 C/5	44°23′	77°45′
Crowe Lake	LAKE/LAC	NF		2 D/14	48°45′	55°22′
Crowe Lake	LAKE/LAC	ON	Peterborough	31 C/5	44°29′	77°44′
Crowell	UNP/LNO	NS	Shelburne	20 P/12	43°33′	65°36′
Crowell	UNP/LNO	AB	1-79-20-W5	83 N/15	55°49′	116°59′
Crowell Basin - also-aussi - Crowell, Bassin de	SEAU/SMER	—		4003	42°54′	67°20′
Crowell, Bassin de - also-aussi - Crowell Basin	SEAU/SMER	—		4003	42°54′	67°20′
Crowe River	RIV/CDE	ON	Northumberland	31 C/5	44°22′	77°46′
Crowes Landing	UNP/LNO	ON	Peterborough	31 D/9	44°34′	78°04′
Crowes Mills	UNP/LNO	NS	Colchester	11 E/6	45°24′	63°22′
Crowfoot	UNP/LNO	AB	25-21-20-4	82 I/15	50°49′	112°39′
Crowfoot Creek	RIV/CDE	AB	21-20-W4	82 I/15	50°48′	112°39′
Crow Harbour	UNP/LNO	NB	Charlotte	21 G/2	45°06′	66°37′
Crow Head	VILG/VILG	NF		2 E/10	49°41′	54°48′
Crow Head	CAPE/CAP	NF		1 M/5	47°27′	55°56′
Crow Head	CAPE/CAP	NF		12 B/11	48°36′	59°09′
Crow Indian Lake	LAKE/LAC	AB	5-13-W4	72 E/5	49°22′	111°48′
Crow Lake	UNP/LNO	ON	Frontenac	31 C/10	44°44′	76°36′
Crow Lake	UNP/LNO	ON	Kenora	52 F/4	49°10′	93°56′
Crow Lake	LAKE/LAC	ON	Frontenac	31 C/10	44°42′	76°37′
Crow Lake	LAKE/LAC	MB		63 N/6	55°19′	101°22′
Crowland	UNP/LNO	ON	Welland	30 L/14	42°58′	79°15′
Crown Hill	UNP/LNO	ON	Simcoe	31 D/5	44°26′	79°39′
Crown Mountain	MTN/MNT	BC	Nootka	92 F/13	49°57′	125°49′
Crown Prince Frederik Island	ISL/ÎLE	NT	Franklin	47 F/3	70°02′	86°50′
Crow River	RIV/CDE	BC/YT		94 N/16	59°50′	124°20′
Crows Nest	UNP/LNO	NS	Guysborough	11 E/1	45°15′	62°04′
Crowsnest	UNP/LNO	AB	12-8-5-W5	82 G/10	49°38′	114°42′
Crowsnest	UNP/LNO	BC	Kootenay	82 G/10	49°38′	114°42′
Crowsnest Mountain	MTN/MNT	AB	9-5-W5	82 G/10	49°42′	114°34′
Crowsnest Pass	TOWN/VIL2	AB	7-4-W5	82 G/10	49°36′	114°31′
Crowther Canyon	SEAU/SMER	—		3604	49°58′	127°41′
Croydon	UNP/LNO	ON	Lennox and Addington	31 C/7	44°25′	76°58′
Croydon	UNP/LNO	BC	Cariboo	83 E/4	53°04′	119°43′
Crozier	UNP/LNO	ON	Rainy River	52 C/12	48°37′	93°31′

NAME NOM	ENTITY ENTITÉ	LOC 1 LIEU 1	LOC 2 LIEU 2	MAP CARTE	POSITION LAT	LONG
Crozier Channel	CHAN/CHEN	NT	Franklin	89 D	76°10′	118°30′
Crozier Channel	CHAN/CHEN	NT	Franklin	88 G	75°55′	119°00′
Crozier Island	ISL/ÎLE	NT	Franklin	68 H	75°47′	96°33′
Crozier River	RIV/CDE	NT	Franklin	47 D	69°31′	83°12′
Crozier Strait	CHAN/CHEN	NT	Franklin	68 H	75°30′	97°12′
Cruickshank	UNP/LNO	ON	Grey	41 A/11	44°36′	81°03′
Cruickshank River	RIV/CDE	BC	Nelson	92 F/11	49°35′	125°11′
Cruiser, Lac	LAKE/LAC	QC	Maria-Chapdelaine	22 D/14	48°59′	71°28′
Cruisers	UNP/LNO	NF		2 D/13	48°59′	55°35′
Crumlin	UNP/LNO	ON	Middlesex	40 P/3	43°01′	81°09′
Crutch, The	UNP/LNO	QC	Les Jardins-de-Napierville	31 H/4	45°07′	73°34′
Crutwell	HAM/HAM	SK	49-1-W3	73 G/1	53°13′	106°04′
Cryderman Subdivision	UNP/LNO	ON	Sudbury	41 I/10	46°41′	80°45′
Cry Lake	LAKE/LAC	BC	Cassiar	104 I/11	58°44′	129°02′
Crysdale	UNP/LNO	BC	Cariboo	93 G/10	53°35′	122°40′
Crysdale, Mount	MTN/MNT	BC	Peace River	93 O/14	55°56′	123°25′
Crysler	UNP/LNO	ON	Stormont	31 G/3	45°13′	75°09′
Crystal	UNP/LNO	ON	Leeds	31 B/13	44°47′	75°54′
Crystal Bay	UNP/LNO	ON	Carleton	31 G/5	45°22′	75°51′
Crystal Bay-Sunset	HAM/HAM	SK		73 F/10	55°33′	108°52′
Crystal Beach	UNP/LNO	NB	Kings	21 G/8	45°21′	66°13′
Crystal Beach	UNP/LNO	ON	Welland	30 L/14	42°52′	79°04′
Crystal Beach	UNP/LNO	SK	3-32-12-W3	72 O/12	51°43′	107°36′
Crystal City	VILG/VILG	MB	24-2-12-W	62 G/2	49°09′	98°57′
Crystal Creek	RIV/CDE	SK	47-16-W3	73 F/1	53°01′	108°18′
Crystal Falls	UNP/LNO	QC	Les Laurentides	31 J/2	46°03′	74°36′
Crystal Falls	UNP/LNO	ON	Nipissing	31 L/5	46°27′	79°54′
Crystal Hill	UNP/LNO	SK	19-10-24-W2	72 H/14	49°50′	105°15′
Crystal Island	ISL/ÎLE	NT	Mackenzie	75 O	63°04′	107°57′
Crystal Lake	HAM/HAM	SK		62 M/16	51°51′	102°26′
Crystal Lake	LAKE/LAC	ON	Peterborough	31 D/16	44°46′	78°29′
Crystal Peak	MTN/MNT	NT	Franklin	27 F	70°32′	70°55′
Crystal Rock	UNP/LNO	ON	Grenville	31 B/14	44°48′	75°30′
Crystal Springs	VILG/VILG	AB	23-46-1-W5	83 B/16	52°58′	114°02′
Crystal Springs	HAM/HAM	SK	24-44-24-W2	73 A/14	52°48′	105°22′
Crystal Springs	UNP/LNO	ON	Peterborough	31 D/1	44°14′	78°19′
Cub Hills	MTN/MNT	SK		73 I/1	54°15′	104°30′
Cuckold Head	CAPE/CAP	NF		2 C/11	48°32′	53°02′
Cuddle Lake	LAKE/LAC	MB		53 M/5	55°25′	95°50′
Cudsaskwa Beach	HAM/HAM	SK	46-26-W2	73 A/12	52°39′	105°37′
Cudworth	TOWN/VIL2	SK	31-40-26-W2	73 A/5	52°30′	105°44′
Cudworth Junction	UNP/LNO	SK	18-48-25-W2	73 H/4	53°11′	105°41′
Cuffley	UNP/LNO	SK	20-53-19-W3	73 F/10	53°36′	108°46′
Culbertson Island	ISL/ÎLE	NT	Franklin	25 O	63°23′	67°56′
Culbute Channel - also-aussi - Culbute, Chenal de la	RIV/CDE	ON	Renfrew	31 F/14	45°55′	77°05′
Culbute, Chenal de la - also-aussi - Culbute Channel	CHAN/CHEN	QC	Pontiac	31 F/14	45°55′	77°05′
Culbute, La	UNP/LNO	QC	Vaudreuil-Soulanges	31 G/8	45°25′	74°16′
Culchillum	UNP/LNO	BC	Cowichan Lake	92 B/13	48°47′	123°56′
Cul-de-la-Baie, Le	UNP/LNO	QC	Maskinongé	31 I/3	46°11′	73°01′
Cul de Sac West	UNP/LNO	NF		11 P/10	47°33′	56°51′
Cullen	UNP/LNO	SK	7-5-7-W2	62 E/7	49°22′	102°57′
Cullens Brook	UNP/LNO	QC	Bonaventure	22 A/3	48°03′	65°26′
Culligan	UNP/LNO	NB	Gloucester	21 P/13	47°55′	65°56′
Cullite 3	IR/RI	BC	Renfrew	92 C/10	48°36′	124°42′
Cullivan Creek	RIV/CDE	BC	Cassiar	104 H/14	57°56′	129°05′
Culloden	UNP/LNO	PE	Queens	11 L/2	46°01′	62°47′
Culloden	UNP/LNO	NS	Digby	21 A/12	44°39′	65°51′
Culloden	UNP/LNO	ON	Oxford	40 I/15	42°53′	80°51′
Culloden Lake	LAKE/LAC	ON	Kenora	52 E/15	49°50′	94°44′
Culls Harbour	UNP/LNO	NF		2 C/12	48°41′	53°57′
Culp	UNP/LNO	AB	17-78-23-W5	83 N/13	55°45′	117°32′
Culross	MUN2/AZM2	ON	Bruce	41 A/3	44°02′	81°18′
Culross	UNP/LNO	MB	2-9-4-W	62 H/12	49°43′	97°55′
Cultus	UNP/LNO	ON	Norfolk	40 I/10	42°38′	80°37′
Cultus Lake	UNP/LNO	BC	New Westminster	92 H/4	49°04′	121°58′
Cultus Lake	LAKE/LAC	BC	New Westminster	92 H/4	49°03′	121°59′
Culver	UNP/LNO	MB	7-11-14-E	52 E/13	49°54′	95°40′
Cumberland	VILG/VILG	BC	Nelson	92 F/11	49°37′	125°02′
Cumberland	MUN1/AZM1	NS	Cumberland	21 H/9	45°45′	64°10′
Cumberland	MUN2/AZM2	ON	Russell	31 G/6	45°26′	75°26′
Cumberland	UNP/LNO	PE	Queens	11 L/3	46°10′	63°10′
Cumberland	UNP/LNO	ON	Russell	31 G/11	45°31′	75°24′
Cumberland	GEOG/GÉOG	NS		21 H/9	45°45′	64°10′
Cumberland 20	IR/RI	SK		63 E/16	53°56′	102°14′
Cumberland 100A	IR/RI	SK		73 H/2	53°03′	104°50′

NAME NOM	ENTITY ENTITÉ	LOC 1 LIEU 1	LOC 2 LIEU 2	MAP CARTE	POSITION LAT	LONG
Cumberland Basin	BAY/BAIE	NB	Westmorland	21 H/16	45°48'	64°23'
Cumberland Bay	UNP/LNO	NB	Queens	21 I/4	46°02'	65°52'
Cumberland Bay	BAY/BAIE	NB	Queens	21 I/4	46°01'	65°56'
Cumberland Beach	UNP/LNO	ON	Simcoe	31 D/11	44°41'	79°23'
Cumberland Cove	BAY/BAIE	PE	Prince	11 L/4	46°13'	63°34'
Cumberland House	VILG/VILG	SK	57-2-W2	63 E/16	53°58'	102°16'
Cumberland Lake	LAKE/LAC	SK		63 E/16	54°03'	102°18'
Cumberland Mills	UNP/LNO	QC	Beauce-Sartigan	21 L/2	46°12'	70°37'
Cumberland Peninsula	CAPE/CAP	NT	Franklin	26 I	66°30'	64°30'
Cumberland Sound	CHAN/CHEN	NT	Franklin	26 H/3	65°10'	65°30'
Cumberland Station	UNP/LNO	QC	Les Etchemins	21 L/7	46°15'	70°38'
Cumines Island	ISL/ÎLE	SK		64 E/16	57°47'	102°09'
Cuming Inlet	BAY/BAIE	NT	Franklin	48 F	74°35'	85°00'
Cumins Lake	LAKE/LAC	SK	76-19-W3	73 N/10	55°34'	108°50'
Cummings	UNP/LNO	SK	19-12-29-W3	72 K/4	50°00'	109°57'
Cummings Cove	UNP/LNO	NB	Charlotte	21 B/15	44°56'	66°59'
Cummings, Mont	MTN/MNT	QC	Jamésie	32 G/16	49°57'	74°12'
Cumnock	UNP/LNO	ON	Wellington	40 P/16	43°45'	80°27'
Cumshewa	UNP/LNO	BC	Queen Charlotte	103 G/4	53°02'	131°41'
Cumshewa Head	CAPE/CAP	BC	Queen Charlotte	103 G/4	53°02'	131°36'
Cumshewa Inlet	BAY/BAIE	BC	Queen Charlotte	103 G/4	53°03'	131°47'
Cumshewas 7	IR/RI	BC	Queen Charlotte	103 G/4	53°02'	131°40'
Cundles	UNP/LNO	ON	Simcoe	31 D/5	44°24'	79°43'
Cunliffe	UNP/LNO	SK	20-53-9-W3	73 G/11	53°36'	107°17'
Cunning Bay	BAY/BAIE	SK		64 L/5	58°25'	103°35'
Cunningham, Barrage	MISC/DIV	QC	Le Fjord-du-Saguenay	22 D/11	48°39'	71°10'
Cunningham Inlet	BAY/BAIE	NT	Franklin	58 F	74°07'	93°50'
Cunningham Island	ISL/ÎLE	BC	Range 3 Coast	93 D/4	52°14'	127°59'
Cunningham Lake	LAKE/LAC	BC	Lillooet	92 P/5	51°21'	121°30'
Cunningham Lake	LAKE/LAC	BC	Range 5 Coast	93 K/11	54°36'	125°22'
Cunningham Lake 11 - see-voir - Ye Koos Lee 11	IR/RI	BC		93 K/11	54°34'	125°16'
Cunningham Landing	UNP/LNO	NT	Mackenzie	85 A	60°02'	112°08'
Cunningham Mountains	MTN/MNT	NT	Franklin	48 E	74°40'	81°10'
Cunningham Point	CAPE/CAP	ON	Manitoulin	41 G/15	45°59'	82°50'
Cunningham River	RIV/CDE	NT	Franklin	58 F	74°05'	93°48'
Cunningham's Corners	UNP/LNO	ON	Victoria	31 D/7	44°20'	78°41'
Cupar	TOWN/VIL2	SK	8-23-16-W2	72 I/16	50°57'	104°13'
Cupar No. 218	MUN2/AZM2	SK		72 I/16	50°55'	104°15'
Cupids	TOWN/VIL2	NF		1 N/11	47°33'	53°13'
Cupids Crossing	UNP/LNO	NF		1 N/11	47°32'	53°15'
*Curle	UNP/LNO	SK	36-16-27-W2	72 I/5	50°23'	105°35'
Curlew	UNP/LNO	AB	2-33-25-W4	82 P/14	51°48'	113°27'
Curlew, Pointe	CAPE/CAP	QC	Côte-Nord-du-Golfe-Saint-Laurent	12 K/3	50°11'	61°11'
Curran	UNP/LNO	ON	Prescott	31 G/7	45°30'	75°00'
Current Island	UNP/LNO	NF		12 P/2	51°11'	56°49'
Current Island	ISL/ÎLE	NF		12 P/2	51°11'	56°50'
Current River	RIV/CDE	ON	Thunder Bay	52 A/6	48°27'	89°11'
Currie	UNP/LNO	NB	Victoria	21 J/13	46°46'	67°35'
Currieburg	UNP/LNO	NB	York	21 J/7	46°18'	66°49'
Currie Heights	UNP/LNO	SK		72 I/5	50°23'	105°33'
Currie Lake	LAKE/LAC	MB		64 H/13	57°46'	97°33'
Currie Road	UNP/LNO	NB	Victoria	21 J/13	46°52'	67°35'
Curries	UNP/LNO	ON	Oxford	40 P/2	43°04'	80°43'
Curry Hill	UNP/LNO	ON	Glengarry	31 G/1	45°13'	74°24'
Curry Island	ISL/ÎLE	NT	Franklin	38 B	72°24'	79°35'
Currys Corner	UNP/LNO	NS	Hants	21 A/16	44°59'	64°08'
Curryville	UNP/LNO	NB	Albert	21 H/15	45°50'	64°38'
Curtis	UNP/LNO	MB	19-11-5-W	62 G/16	49°56'	98°09'
Curtis Lake	LAKE/LAC	NT	Keewatin	56 I	66°41'	89°10'
Curtis Park	UNP/LNO	NB	Northumberland	21 P/3	47°01'	65°27'
Curtis Park - see-voir - Southport	UNP/LNO	MB		62 G/16	49°55'	98°17'
Curtis River	RIV/CDE	NT	Keewatin	46 M	67°12'	87°20'
Curve Lake	UNP/LNO	ON	Peterborough	31 D/8	44°28'	78°22'
Curve Lake 35 - see-voir - Curve Lake First Nation 35	IR/RI	ON		31 D/8	44°29'	78°21'
Curve Lake 35A	IR/RI	ON	Peterborough	31 D/8	44°28'	78°25'
Curve Lake First Nation 35	IR/RI	ON	Peterborough	31 D/8	44°29'	78°21'
Curventon	UNP/LNO	NB	Northumberland	21 P/4	47°03'	65°50'
Curzon	UNP/LNO	BC	Kootenay	82 F/1	49°05'	116°08'
Curzon Village	UNP/LNO	NF		12 H/12	49°31'	57°55'
Cushendall	UNP/LNO	ON	Frontenac	31 C/8	44°19'	76°23'
Cushing	UNP/LNO	QC	Argenteuil	31 G/9	45°36'	74°28'
Cushing Lake	LAKE/LAC	AB	58-3-W4	73 L/1	54°03'	110°26'
Cushing, Mount	MTN/MNT	BC	Cassiar	94 E/10	57°37'	126°51'
Cuslett	UNP/LNO	NF		1 L/16	46°58'	54°10'
Cussed Creek	RIV/CDE	SK	6-28-4-W2	62 M/7	51°24'	102°33'

NAME NOM	ENTITY ENTITÉ	LOC 1 LIEU 1	LOC 2 LIEU 2	MAP CARTE	POSITION LAT	LONG
Cusson, Pointe	CAPE/CAP	QC	Kativik	35 C/5	60°24'	77°46'
Custeau	UNP/LNO	QC	L'Amiante	21 L/3	46°13'	71°15'
Cutarm	UNP/LNO	SK	34-19-32-W	62 K/12	50°40'	101°51'
Cutarm Creek	RIV/CDE	SK	10-18-31-W	62 K/12	50°31'	101°40'
Cutbank	UNP/LNO	SK	12-27-7-W3	72 O/7	51°18'	106°51'
Cutbank Creek	RIV/CDE	AB	50-27-W4	83 H/5	53°20'	113°53'
Cutbank Lake	LAKE/LAC	SK		72 N/6	51°18'	109°08'
Cutbank River	RIV/CDE	AB	66-4-W6	83 L/10	54°43'	118°32'
Cut Beaver Lake	LAKE/LAC	SK	55-4,5-W2	63 E/15	53°47'	102°38'
Cuthbert	UNP/LNO	SK	22-26-29-W3	72 N/4	51°14'	109°58'
Cut Knife	TOWN/VIL2	SK	32-43-21-W3	73 C/11	52°45'	109°01'
Cut Knife No. 439	MUN2/AZM2	SK		73 C/14	52°50'	109°00'
Cutlar Fergusson Point	CAPE/CAP	NT	Franklin	57 G	71°06'	92°50'
Cutler	UNP/LNO	ON	Algoma	41 J/1	46°12'	82°28'
Cutler Head	CAPE/CAP	NF		2 C/12	48°32'	53°36'
Cutoff	UNP/LNO	SK	43-21-W3	73 C/10	52°44'	109°00'
Cutts	UNP/LNO	MB	30-20-15W	62 J/14	50°45'	99°29'
Cutts Brook	RIV/CDE	NF		11 P/12	47°40'	57°51'
Cuve, La	UNP/LNO	QC	Le Fjord-du-Saguenay	22 D/11	48°37'	71°12'
Cuvier	UNP/LNO	SK	28-39-15-W2	73 A/8	52°23'	104°05'
Cuvillier, Lac	LAKE/LAC	QC	Vallée-de-l'Or	32 C/15	48°54'	76°35'
Cyclops, Cape	CAPE/CAP	NT	Franklin	88 G	75°07'	116°40'
Cygnet	UNP/LNO	AB	16-38-28-W4	83 A/5	52°16'	113°57'
Cygnet Lake	LAKE/LAC	ON	Kenora	52 E/15	50°00'	94°53'
Cygnet Lake	LAKE/LAC	MB		54 D/15	56°46'	94°56'
Cymbria	UNP/LNO	PE	Queens	11 L/6	46°24'	63°15'
Cymric	UNP/LNO	SK	27-26-22-W2	72 P/2	51°14'	104°59'
Cymri No. 36	MUN2/AZM2	SK		62 E/6	49°25'	103°25'
Cynthia	UNP/LNO	AB	32-49-10-W5	83 G/6	53°17'	115°25'
Cypre River	RIV/CDE	BC	Clayoquot	92 F/5	49°17'	125°55'
Cypress Bay	BAY/BAIE	BC	Clayoquot	92 F/5	49°16'	125°53'
Cypress Creek	RIV/CDE	BC	Peace River	94 B/15	56°49'	122°36'
Cypress Hills	MTN/MNT	SK/AB		72 E/9	49°34'	109°40'
Cypress Hills Park	UNP/LNO	SK	20-8-26-W3	72 F/11	49°39'	109°30'
Cypress Hills Provincial Park	PARK/PARC	AB	7,8-1,2,3-W4	72 E/9	49°38'	110°12'
Cypress Lake	LAKE/LAC	SK		72 F/6	49°28'	109°28'
Cypress, Municipal District of	MUN1/AZM1	AB	11-6-W4	72 E/15	49°52'	110°41'
Cypress No. 1, Municipal District of - see-voir - Cypress, Municipal District of	MUN1/AZM1	AB		72 E/15	49°52'	110°41'
Cypress Park	UNP/LNO	BC	New Westminster	92 G/6	49°21'	123°15'
Cypress Point	CAPE/CAP	AB	117-2-W4	74 M/1	59°12'	110°09'
Cypress River	UNP/LNO	MB	7-7-12-W	62 G/11	49°33'	99°05'
Cypress River - also-aussi - +Cypress, Rivière	RIV/CDE	MB	28-8-11-W	62 G/10	49°41'	98°55'
+Cypress, Rivière - also-aussi - Cypress River	RIV/CDE	MB	28-8-11-W	62 G/10	49°41'	98°55'
Cyr	UNP/LNO	QC	Bonaventure	22 A/4	48°08'	65°42'
Cyriac, Rivière	RIV/CDE	QC	Le Fjord-du-Saguenay	22 D/6	48°18'	71°18'
Cyril Lake	LAKE/LAC	MB	80,81-15,16-E	53 M/14	55°59'	95°09'
Cyril River	RIV/CDE	MB	81-17-E	53 M/15	55°59'	94°54'
Cyr Junction	UNP/LNO	NB	Madawaska	21 O/4	47°07'	67°54'
Cyrus Field Bay	BAY/BAIE	NT	Franklin	25 I	62°50'	64°55'
Cyrville	UNP/LNO	ON	Carleton	31 G/5	45°25'	75°38'
Czar	VILG/VILG	AB	20-40-6-W4	73 D/7	52°27'	110°50'

D

NAME NOM	ENTITY ENTITÉ	LOC 1 LIEU 1	LOC 2 LIEU 2	MAP CARTE	POSITION LAT	LONG
Daaquam	UNP/LNO	QC	Montmagny	21 L/9	46°35'	70°04'
Daaquam-Nord	UNP/LNO	QC	Montmagny	21 L/9	46°37'	70°05'
Daaquam, Rivière	RIV/CDE	QC	Montmagny	21 L/9	46°35'	70°01'
Dablon	UNP/LNO	QC	Le Domaine-du-Roy	32 A/8	48°19'	72°10'
Dacer	UNP/LNO	SK	4-43-16-W3	73 C/9	52°41'	108°16'
Dachlabah 30	IR/RI	BC	Cassiar	103 P/3	55°04'	129°29'
Dack	MUN2/AZM2	ON	Timiskaming	31 M/13	47°48'	79°58'
Dacotah	UNP/LNO	MB	35-10-2-W	62 H/13	49°53'	97°38'
Dacre	UNP/LNO	ON	Renfrew	31 F/7	45°22'	76°58'
Dafoe	VILG/VILG	SK	20-32-18-W2	72 P/10	51°45'	104°32'
Dafoe Lake	LAKE/LAC	MB		63 P/9	55°44'	96°15'
Dafoe River	RIV/CDE	MB	16-80-18-E	53 M/15	55°56'	94°48'
Daggitt Lake	LAKE/LAC	MB		64 I/13	58°56'	98°00'
Dagmar	UNP/LNO	ON	Ontario	31 D/3	44°00'	79°02'
Dahadinni, Mount	MTN/MNT	NT	Mackenzie	95 N	63°40'	125°00'
Dahadinni River	RIV/CDE	NT	Mackenzie	95 N	63°59'	124°22'
Dahinda	UNP/LNO	SK	15-9-23-W2	72 H/11	49°44'	105°03'
Dahl Creek	RIV/CDE	BC	Peace River	94 H/15	57°51'	120°45'

NAME NOM	ENTITY ENTITÉ	LOC 1 LIEU 1	LOC 2 LIEU 2	MAP CARTE	POSITION LAT	LONG
Dahlia	UNP/LNO	ON	Nipissing	31 F/13	45°47′	77°33′
Dahlton	UNP/LNO	SK	22-40-16-W2	73 A/8	52°27′	104°06′
Daigneault	UNP/LNO	QC	Le Granit	21 E/15	45°50′	70°57′
D'Aiguillon	UNP/LNO	QC	La Côte-de-Gaspé	22 A/16	48°50′	64°19′
D'Ailleboust, Lac	LAKE/LAC	QC	Maria-Chapdelaine	22 E/11	49°34′	71°28′
Dain City	UNP/LNO	ON	Welland	30 L/14	42°57′	79°15′
Dairy Valley	UNP/LNO	QC	Le Haut-Richelieu	31 H/3	45°04′	73°13′
Dakar, Sommet de	MTN/MNT	QC	Charlevoix	21 M/15	47°47′	70°50′
Dakiulis 7	IR/RI	BC	Range 1 Coast	92 L/10	50°44′	126°34′
Dakota Crossing	UNP/LNO	MB		62 H/14	49°49′	97°05′
Dakota Plains	UNP/LNO	MB	8-10-8-W	62 G/15	49°49′	98°32′
Dakota Plains 6A	IR/RI	MB		62 G/15	49°49′	98°31′
Dakota Tipi	UNP/LNO	MB	27-11-7-W	62 G/16	49°57′	98°21′
Dakota Tipi 1	IR/RI	MB		62 G/16	49°57′	98°21′
Dala River	RIV/CDE	BC	Range 4 Coast	103 H/15	53°51′	128°31′
Dalayee Lake	LAKE/LAC	YT		105 C/5	60°20′	133°38′
Dale	UNP/LNO	ON	Durham	30 M/16	43°59′	78°17′
Dalehurst	UNP/LNO	AB	28-52-23-W5	83 F/11	53°32′	117°20′
D'Alembert	VILG/VILG	QC	Rouyn-Noranda	32 D/6	48°22′	79°01′
Dalemead	UNP/LNO	AB	14-22-27-W4	82 I/13	50°52′	113°38′
Dalesville	UNP/LNO	QC	Argenteuil	31 G/9	45°42′	74°24′
Dalgleish, Mount	MTN/MNT	BC	Lillooet	92 J/12	50°41′	123°50′
Dalhousie	TOWN/VIL2	NB	Restigouche	22 B/1	48°04′	66°23′
Dalhousie	UNP/LNO	QC	Vaudreuil-Soulanges	31 G/8	45°18′	74°27′
Dalhousie	GEOG/GÉOG	NB	Restigouche	21 O/15	48°00′	66°30′
Dalhousie, Cape	CAPE/CAP	NT	Mackenzie	107 E	70°15′	129°40′
Dalhousie Crossing	UNP/LNO	NS	Annapolis	21 A/10	44°42′	64°56′
Dalhousie Junction	UNP/LNO	NB	Restigouche	22 B/2	48°03′	66°30′
Dalhousie Lake	UNP/LNO	ON	Lanark	31 C/15	44°57′	76°36′
Dalhousie Lake	LAKE/LAC	ON	Lanark	31 C/15	44°58′	76°34′
Dalhousie Mills	UNP/LNO	ON	Glengarry	31 G/8	45°19′	74°28′
Dalhousie Road	UNP/LNO	NS	Kings	21 A/10	44°44′	64°42′
Dalibaire-Ouest	UNP/LNO	QC	Matane	22 B/15	48°56′	66°53′
Dalkeith	UNP/LNO	ON	Glengarry	31 G/7	45°27′	74°35′
Dalk-ka-gila-quoeux 2	IR/RI	BC	Range 5 Coast	103 I/10	54°35′	128°39′
Dallas	UNP/LNO	MB	28-1-W	62 P/6	51°24′	97°29′
Dallas	UNP/LNO	BC	Kamloops Division Yale	92 I/9	50°40′	120°10′
Dalling	UNP/LNO	QC	Le Val-Saint-François	31 H/9	45°33′	72°18′
Dall Mountain	MTN/MNT	YT		105 O/4	63°15′	131°41′
Dall River	RIV/CDE	BC	Cassiar	94 L/13	58°47′	127°45′
Dalmas, Lac	LAKE/LAC	QC	Jamésie	23 E/5	53°28′	71°52′
Dalmeny	TOWN/VIL2	SK	10-39-6-W3	73 B/7	52°20′	106°46′
Dalmeny	UNP/LNO	ON	Carleton	31 G/4	45°09′	75°32′
Dalny	UNP/LNO	MB	4-2-26-W	62 F/2	49°06′	100°54′
Dalpe Lake	LAKE/LAC	NT	Keewatin	65 B	60°26′	98°38′
Dalroy	UNP/LNO	AB	14-25-27-W4	82 P/4	51°08′	113°40′
Dalrymple	UNP/LNO	ON	Victoria	31 D/11	44°38′	79°06′
Dalrymple Lake	LAKE/LAC	ON	Victoria	31 D/11	44°38′	79°07′
Dalston	UNP/LNO	ON	Simcoe	31 D/5	44°29′	79°41′
Dalton	MUN2/AZM2	ON	Victoria	31 D/14	44°46′	79°05′
Dalton	UNP/LNO	ON	Algoma	42 C/1	48°09′	84°02′
Dalton Mills	UNP/LNO	ON	Algoma	42 C/1	48°07′	84°04′
Dalton, Mount	MTN/MNT	BC	Cassiar	104 I/13	58°58′	129°31′
Dalton Post	UNP/LNO	YT		115 A/3	60°07′	137°02′
Dalton Range	MTN/MNT	YT		115 A/6	60°29′	137°10′
Dalum	UNP/LNO	AB	8,9,16,17-27-19-W4	82 P/7	51°18′	112°38′
Dalvay by the Sea	UNP/LNO	PE	Queens	11 L/6	46°25′	63°05′
Dalvay-by-the-Sea Hotel National Historic Site - also-aussi - Hôtel-Dalvay-by-the-Sea, Lieu historique national de l'	PARK/PARC	PE	Queens	11 L/6	46°25′	63°04′
Daly	MUN2/AZM2	MB		62 F/16	49°58′	100°15′
Daly Bay	BAY/BAIE	NT	Keewatin	55 P	64°00′	89°45′
Daly Lake	LAKE/LAC	MB	67-18-W	63 K/16	54°48′	100°10′
Daly Lake	LAKE/LAC	SK		74 A/12	56°32′	105°39′
Daly River	RIV/CDE	NT	Franklin	120 C	81°13′	65°52′
Dalzell	UNP/LNO	SK	33-13-6-W2	62 L/2	50°07′	102°45′
Damant Lake	LAKE/LAC	NT	Mackenzie	75 H	61°45′	105°05′
Damascus	UNP/LNO	NB	Kings	21 H/5	45°27′	65°48′
Damascus	UNP/LNO	ON	Wellington	40 P/16	43°55′	80°29′
Dame-à-Blanchet, La	UNP/LNO	QC	Bonaventure	22 A/6	48°20′	65°10′
Dame-à-Thivierge	UNP/LNO	QC	Les Laurentides	31 J/2	46°11′	74°32′
Dame-du-Curé-Chenel, La	UNP/LNO	QC	Pabok	22 A/3	48°11′	65°02′
Dame-du-Line	UNP/LNO	QC	Antoine-Labelle	31 O/2	47°10′	74°49′
Dame-Neuve	UNP/LNO	QC	Argenteuil	31 G/9	45°38′	74°21′
Dame-Plate	UNP/LNO	QC	Antoine-Labelle	31 J/6	46°22′	75°19′
Damfino Creek	RIV/CDE	BC	Similkameen Division Yale	82 E/10	49°42′	118°46′
Damnable Bay	BAY/BAIE	NF		2 C/12	48°42′	53°45′

NAME NOM	ENTITY ENTITÉ	LOC 1 LIEU 1	LOC 2 LIEU 2	MAP CARTE	POSITION LAT	LONG
Damour	UNP/LNO	SK	17-47-7-W3	73 G/2	53°04′	107°00′
Dana	UNP/LNO	ON	Algoma	42 C/16	48°50′	84°09′
Dana	UNP/LNO	SK	30-38-26-W2	73 A/5	52°18′	105°42′
Dana, Lac	LAKE/LAC	QC	Jamésie	32 K/14	50°53′	77°20′
Danbury	UNP/LNO	SK	36-2-W2	63 D/1	52°03′	102°15′
Danby	UNP/LNO	QC	Drummond	31 H/9	45°41′	72°25′
Danby Island	ISL/ÎLE	NT	Keewatin	32 M	51°57′	79°17′
Dancaster Courts	UNP/LNO	ON	Wentworth	30 M/4	43°13′	79°59′
Dance	UNP/LNO	ON	Rainy River	52 C/13	48°46′	93°40′
Dancing Point	CAPE/CAP	MB	40-7-W	63 B/8	52°30′	98°27′
Dand	UNP/LNO	MB	34-4-23-W	62 F/8	49°20′	100°30′
Dandonneau	UNP/LNO	SK	23-6-17-W2	72 H/8	49°29′	104°12′
Dandurand, Lac	LAKE/LAC	QC	Le Haut-Saint-Maurice	31 O/15	47°50′	74°30′
Dane	UNP/LNO	ON	Timiskaming	42 A/1	48°05′	80°01′
Danesville	UNP/LNO	NS	Queens	21 A/2	44°12′	64°37′
Danford Lake	UNP/LNO	QC	Pontiac	31 F/16	45°55′	76°10′
Danforth Station	UNP/LNO	ON	York	30 M/11	43°41′	79°18′
Dangereuses, Passes	CHAN/CHEN	QC	Maria-Chapdelaine	22 E/14	49°52′	71°13′
Daniel-Johnson, Barrage	MISC/DIV	QC	Manicouagan	22 K/10	50°39′	68°44′
Daniel, Lac	LAKE/LAC	QC	Caniapiscau	22 N/15	52°00′	68°38′
Daniel Moore Bay	BAY/BAIE	NT	Mackenzie	76 N	67°45′	109°34′
Daniel, Rivière	RIV/CDE	QC	Jamésie	32 F/6	49°25′	77°30′
Daniel's Cove	UNP/LNO	NF		2 C/2	48°08′	52°58′
Daniel's Harbour	VILG/VILG	NF		12 I/4	50°14′	57°35′
Daniels Lake	LAKE/LAC	ON	Kenora	52 F/13	49°55′	93°50′
Daniel's Point	UNP/LNO	NF		1 K/14	46°45′	53°23′
Daniels River	RIV/CDE	BC	Range 1 Coast	92 K/8	50°16′	124°24′
Daningay 12	IR/RI	BC	Queen Charlotte	103 K/2	54°05′	132°34′
Danish Island	ISL/ÎLE	NT	Keewatin	46 G	65°53′	83°36′
Danish Strait	CHAN/CHEN	NT	Franklin	69 F	78°02′	101°45′
Dankin	UNP/LNO	SK	15-26-24-W3	72 N/3	51°13′	109°17′
Danseur, Rapide	RAP/RAP	QC	Abitibi-Ouest	32 D/11	48°33′	79°18′
Danskin	UNP/LNO	BC	Range 4 Coast	93 F/13	53°59′	125°48′
Dans Pond	LAKE/LAC	NF		2 E/2	49°08′	54°57′
Dantzic Point	CAPE/CAP	NF		1 L/13	47°00′	55°59′
Danube	UNP/LNO	AB	22-62-21-W4	83 I/6	54°22′	113°03′
Danvers	UNP/LNO	NS	Digby	21 A/5	44°23′	65°54′
Danville	CITY/VIL1	QC	Asbestos	31 H/16	45°47′	72°01′
Daoust	UNP/LNO	QC	Antoine-Labelle	31 J/7	46°20′	74°47′
Daphne	UNP/LNO	SK	34-37-18-W2	73 A/1	52°14′	104°30′
Dapp	UNP/LNO	AB	12-62-27-W4	83 I/5	54°21′	113°55′
Darby	UNP/LNO	QC	La Haute-Yamaska	31 H/7	45°25′	72°39′
Darby Lake	LAKE/LAC	NT	Keewatin	56 N	67°50′	92°30′
Darbys Harbour	UNP/LNO	NF		1 M/7	47°28′	54°32′
Darbyville	UNP/LNO	ON	Halton	40 P/9	43°33′	80°04′
Darch Island	ISL/ÎLE	ON	Algoma	41 J/1	46°05′	82°25′
D'Arcy	UNP/LNO	SK	12-29-19-W3	72 N/7	51°28′	108°32′
D'Arcy	UNP/LNO	BC	Lillooet	92 J/9	50°33′	122°29′
Darcy Corners	UNP/LNO	QC	Rouville	31 H/7	45°25′	72°55′
D'Arcy Island	ISL/ÎLE	BC	Cowichan	92 B/11	48°34′	123°17′
Dardanelles	UNP/LNO	QC	Pontiac	31 F/10	45°34′	76°39′
Darfield	UNP/LNO	BC	Kamloops Division Yale	92 P/8	51°18′	120°11′
D'Argenson, Pointe	CAPE/CAP	QC	Kativik	25 E/1	61°05′	70°24′
Dargie Lake	LAKE/LAC	NS	Annapolis	21 A/11	44°40′	65°19′
Dark Cove	UNP/LNO	NF		2 C/12	48°40′	53°43′
Darke Lake	LAKE/LAC	BC	Osoyoos Division Yale	82 E/12	49°43′	119°52′
Dark Harbour	BAY/BAIE	NB	Charlotte	21 B/10	44°45′	66°50′
Darlens, Rivière	RIV/CDE	QC	Rouyn-Noranda	31 M/15	47°57′	78°31′
Darling	MUN2/AZM2	ON	Lanark	31 F/2	45°12′	76°30′
Darling	UNP/LNO	ON	Muskoka	31 D/13	44°57′	79°38′
Darlingford	UNP/LNO	MB	8-3-7-W	62 G/1	49°12′	98°23′
Darling Peninsula	CAPE/CAP	NT	Franklin	29 G	79°47′	71°51′
Darling Road	UNP/LNO	ON	Haldimand	30 L/13	42°58′	79°42′
Darlings Beach	HAM/HAM	SK	12-12-15-W3	72 G/13	49°59′	107°56′
Darlingside	UNP/LNO	ON	Leeds	31 B/5	44°22′	75°58′
Darlings Lake	UNP/LNO	NS	Yarmouth	20 O/16	43°57′	66°08′
Darlings Lake	LAKE/LAC	NB	Kings	21 H/12	45°30′	65°52′
Darlington	VILG/VILG	PE	Queens	11 L/6	46°19′	63°19′
Darlington	UNP/LNO	PE	Queens	11 L/6	46°19′	63°20′
Darlington	UNP/LNO	NB	Restigouche	22 B/1	48°03′	66°23′
Darlington	UNP/LNO	ON	Durham	30 M/15	43°53′	78°46′
Darmody	UNP/LNO	SK	24-20-3-W3	72 J/9	50°43′	106°17′
Darnley	UNP/LNO	PE	Prince	11 L/12	46°32′	63°38′
Darnley Bay	BAY/BAIE	NT	Franklin	97 D/12	69°35′	123°40′
Darrell	UNP/LNO	ON	Kent	40 J/8	42°29′	82°11′

NAME NOM	ENTITY ENTITÉ	LOC 1 LIEU 1	LOC 2 LIEU 2	MAP CARTE	POSITION LAT	LONG
Darrell Bay	UNP/LNO	BC	New Westminster	92 G/11	49°40'	123°10'
Darrell Lake	LAKE/LAC	NT	Mackenzie	75 P	63°47'	105°39'
Darrell River	RIV/CDE	NT	Mackenzie	75 P	63°40'	105°09'
D'Artagnan	UNP/LNO	QC	Desjardins	21 L/11	46°41'	71°03'
Dartford	UNP/LNO	ON	Northumberland	31 C/4	44°13'	77°56'
Dartmoor	UNP/LNO	BC	New Westminster	92 G/2	49°15'	122°49'
Dartmouth	UNP/LNO	NS	Halifax	11 D/12	44°40'	63°34'
Dartmouth, Mount	MTN/MNT	BC	Range 2 Coast	92 N/8	51°16'	124°20'
Dartmouth Point	CAPE/CAP	NS	Digby	21 B/1	44°15'	66°20'
Dartmouth, Rivière	RIV/CDE	QC	La Côte-de-Gaspé	22 A/15	48°53'	64°33'
Darwell	UNP/LNO	AB	13-54-5-W5	83 G/10	53°40'	114°35'
Darwin	UNP/LNO	MB	13-11-12-E	52 E/13	49°56'	95°50'
Darwin Sound	CHAN/CHEN	BC	Queen Charlotte	103 B/12	52°40'	131°43'
Dash Creek	RIV/CDE	BC	Lillooet	92 O/7	51°16'	122°43'
Dashken 22	IR/RI	BC	Range 5 Coast	103 J/1	54°07'	130°09'
Dash Lake	LAKE/LAC	ON	Rainy River	52 F/4	49°06'	93°36'
Dashwood	UNP/LNO	ON	Huron	40 P/5	43°21'	81°38'
Dashwood	UNP/LNO	BC	Newcastle	92 F/7	49°22'	124°31'
Dashwoods Pond	LAKE/LAC	NF		12 B/1	48°02'	58°18'
Dasserat	UNP/LNO	QC	Rouyn-Noranda	32 D/3	48°10'	79°25'
Dasserat, Lac	LAKE/LAC	QC	Rouyn-Noranda	32 D/6	48°15'	79°24'
Daulnay	UNP/LNO	NB	Gloucester	21 P/6	47°25'	65°28'
Dauphin	TOWN/VIL2	MB		62 N/1	51°09'	100°03'
Dauphin	MUN2/AZM2	MB		62 N/1	51°12'	100°04'
Dauphin Beach	UNP/LNO	MB	7-25-17-W	62 O/4	51°09'	99°50'
Dauphin, Cape	CAPE/CAP	NS	Victoria	11 K/8	46°21'	60°25'
Dauphinees Mill Lake	LAKE/LAC	NS	Halifax	21 A/9	44°40'	64°07'
Dauphiné, Rivière	RIV/CDE	QC	Minganie	12 E/1	49°07'	62°28'
Dauphin Lake	LAKE/LAC	MB		62 O/5	51°17'	99°47'
Dauphin, Péninsule du	CAPE/CAP	QC	Jamésie	32 P/3	51°12'	73°00'
Dauphin River	UNP/LNO	MB	26,35-34-5-W1	62 O/16	51°58'	98°04'
Dauphin River	RIV/CDE	MB		62 O/16	51°58'	98°04'
Dauphin River 48A	IR/RI	MB		62 O/16	51°57'	98°03'
D'Auteuil, Lac	LAKE/LAC	QC	Minganie	12 K/11	50°38'	61°17'
D'Autray	MUN1/AZM1	QC	D'Autray	31 I/3	46°10'	73°10'
Dauversière	UNP/LNO	NB	Gloucester	21 P/13	47°46'	65°52'
Davangus	UNP/LNO	QC	Rouyn-Noranda	32 D/7	48°28'	78°53'
D'Avaugour, Pointe	CAPE/CAP	QC	Kativik	25 E/1	61°04'	70°25'
Daveluyville	VILG/VILG	QC	Arthabaska	31 I/1	46°12'	72°08'
Daventry	UNP/LNO	ON	Nipissing	31 L/2	46°04'	78°40'
David Lake	LAKE/LAC	ON	Sudbury	41 I/3	46°08'	81°18'
David, Rivière	RIV/CDE	QC	Le Bas-Richelieu	31 H/15	45°58'	72°54'
Davidson	TOWN/VIL2	SK	33-26-29-W2	72 P/5	51°16'	105°59'
Davidson	UNP/LNO	QC	Pontiac	31 F/15	45°52'	76°46'
Davidson	UNP/LNO	BC	Cariboo	93 G/14	53°55'	123°15'
Davidson, Cape	CAPE/CAP	NT	Franklin	67 B	68°46'	100°35'
Davidson Corner	UNP/LNO	QC	Communauté urbaine de l'Outaouais	31 G/12	45°30'	75°40'
Davidson Hill	UNP/LNO	QC	Le Val-Saint-François	31 H/9	45°35'	72°22'
Davidson Lake	UNP/LNO	NB	York	21 G/14	45°56'	67°08'
Davidson Lake	LAKE/LAC	NB	York	21 G/14	45°56'	67°09'
Davidson Lake	LAKE/LAC	MB	55-15-W	63 G/13	53°47'	99°36'
Davidson, Mount	MTN/MNT	BC	Range 4 Coast	93 F/2	53°09'	124°53'
Davidsons Beach	UNP/LNO	ON	Frontenac	31 C/7	44°22'	76°33'
Davidson's Corners	UNP/LNO	ON	Durham	31 D/1	44°03'	78°18'
Davidsville	UNP/LNO	NF		2 E/8	49°22'	54°26'
Davieau Island	ISL/ÎLE	NT	Keewatin	34 F	57°08'	76°41'
Davie Lake	LAKE/LAC	BC	Cariboo	93 J/10	54°32'	122°45'
Davies Gilbert, Mount	MTN/MNT	YT		117 A/9	68°32'	136°43'
Davies Island	ISL/ÎLE	NT	Franklin	35 I	62°14'	72°51'
Davies River	RIV/CDE	NT	Franklin	98 F	74°09'	124°25'
Davin	HAM/HAM	SK	35-16-16-W2	72 I/8	50°23'	104°07'
Davin Lake	LAKE/LAC	SK		64 D/13	56°50'	103°40'
Davis	UNP/LNO	SK	20-47-25-W2	73 H/4	53°07'	105°39'
Davis Bay	UNP/LNO	BC	New Westminster	92 G/5	49°26'	123°44'
Davis, Cape	CAPE/CAP	NT	Franklin	69 B	76°39'	103°56'
Davis Cove	UNP/LNO	NF		1 M/9	47°38'	54°21'
Davis, Détroit de - also-aussi - **Davis Strait**	CHAN/CHEN	NT	Franklin	25 I	65°00'	58°00'
Davis House	UNP/LNO	NF		12 P/7	51°28'	56°53'
Davis Inlet	VILG/VILG	NF		13 N/15	55°53'	60°54'
Davis Island	UNP/LNO	NF		1 M/7	47°16'	54°55'
Davis Lake	LAKE/LAC	ON	Haliburton	31 D/15	44°47'	78°43'
Davis Lock	UNP/LNO	ON	Leeds	31 C/9	44°34'	76°17'
Davis Mill	UNP/LNO	NB	Victoria	21 O/4	47°02'	67°36'
Davis Mill	UNP/LNO	NB	Madawaska	21 N/8	47°21'	68°08'
Davis Mills	UNP/LNO	ON	Renfrew	31 F/14	45°46'	77°12'

NAME NOM	ENTITY ENTITÉ	LOC 1 LIEU 1	LOC 2 LIEU 2	MAP CARTE	POSITION	
					LAT	LONG
Davison, Point	CAPE/CAP	NT	Franklin	67 E	70°40′	96°22′
Davison Street	UNP/LNO	NS	Kings	21 H/1	45°01′	64°21′
Davis Point	UNP/LNO	MB	27-31-10-W1	62 O/10	51°41′	98°48′
Davis Pond	LAKE/LAC	NF		12 H/9	49°33′	56°04′
Davis River	RIV/CDE	NS	Shelburne	20 P/13	43°55′	65°31′
Davis River	RIV/CDE	BC	Cassiar	94 C/9	56°33′	124°28′
Davis Sill	SEAU/SMER	—		800A	65°30′	57°00′
Davis Strait - also-aussi - **Davis, Détroit de**	CHAN/CHEN	NT	Franklin	25 I	65°00′	58°00′
Davisville	UNP/LNO	ON	York	30 M/11	43°42′	79°23′
Davy Lake	LAKE/LAC	SK		74 K/16	58°53′	108°18′
Davyroyd	UNP/LNO	SK	8,9-28-W2	72 H/12	49°42′	105°44′
Dawes Pond	LAKE/LAC	NF		12 H/1	49°07′	56°12′
Dawn	MUN2/AZM2	ON	Lambton	40 J/9	42°41′	82°07′
Dawn Mills	UNP/LNO	ON	Kent	40 J/9	42°35′	82°08′
Dawn Valley	UNP/LNO	ON	Lambton	40 J/9	42°39′	82°14′
Dawson	TOWN/VIL2	YT		116 B/3	64°04′	139°26′
Dawson Bay	UNP/LNO	MB	23-46-25-W1	63 C/15	52°59′	100°59′
Dawson Bay	BAY/BAIE	MB		63 C/15	52°53′	100°49′
Dawson Bay 65A - see-voir - Shoal River 65A	IR/RI	MB		63 C/10	52°45′	100°41′
Dawson Bay 65B - see-voir - Shoal River 65B	IR/RI	MB		63 C/15	52°50′	100°40′
Dawson Bay 65F - see-voir - Shoal River 65F	IR/RI	MB		63 C/15	52°48′	100°39′
Dawson Canyon	SEAU/SMER	—		8007	43°00′	61°05′
Dawson City Buildings National Historic Site - also-aussi - Édifices-de-Dawson City, Lieu historique national des	PARK/PARC	YT		116 B/3	64°03′	139°26′
Dawson Creek	CITY/VIL1	BC	Peace River	93 P/16	55°46′	120°14′
Dawson Inlet	BAY/BAIE	NT	Keewatin	55 F	61°50′	93°25′
Dawson Island	ISL/ÎLE	ON	Kenora	52 E/2	49°07′	94°31′
Dawson Landing	UNP/LNO	NT	Franklin	85 B	60°59′	114°10′
Dawson, Mount	MTN/MNT	BC	Kootenay	82 N/3	51°09′	117°25′
Dawson Peaks	MTN/MNT	BC	Cassiar	104 N/15	59°57′	132°30′
Dawson Range	MTN/MNT	YT		115 J/9	62°35′	138°20′
Dawson River	RIV/CDE	ON	Kenora	53 C/15	52°58′	92°38′
Dawson's Cove	UNP/LNO	NF		1 M/12	47°32′	55°56′
Dawson Settlement	UNP/LNO	NB	Albert	21 H/15	45°57′	64°45′
Dawsons Landing	UNP/LNO	BC	Range 2 Coast	92 M/12	51°35′	127°35′
Dawsonville	UNP/LNO	NB	Restigouche	21 O/15	47°56′	66°54′
Day and Bright Additional	MUN2/AZM2	ON	Algoma	41 J/3	46°18′	83°23′
Day Hill	UNP/LNO	NB	York	21 G/14	45°59′	67°09′
Daylesford	UNP/LNO	SK	2-41-21-W2	73 A/10	52°30′	104°55′
Day Mills	UNP/LNO	ON	Algoma	41 J/6	46°18′	83°21′
Dayohessarah Lake	LAKE/LAC	ON	Algoma	42 C/14	47°44′	85°02′
Day Point	CAPE/CAP	BC	Range 3 Coast	103 A/7	52°16′	128°40′
Day's Beach	HAM/HAM	SK	47-16,17-W3	73 F/1	53°03′	108°21′
Days Corner	UNP/LNO	PE	Prince	11 L/5	46°27′	63°59′
Days Corner	UNP/LNO	NB	Kings	21 G/8	45°28′	66°11′
Daysland	TOWN/VIL2	AB	9-45-16-W4	83 A/16	52°52′	112°15′
Days Landing	UNP/LNO	NB	Kings	21 G/8	45°22′	66°13′
Dayspring	UNP/LNO	NS	Lunenburg	21 A/8	44°22′	64°29′
Days Ranch	UNP/LNO	BC	Cassiar	104 J/2	58°02′	130°53′
Day Star 87	IR/RI	SK		72 P/9	51°33′	104°17′
Daysville	UNP/LNO	SK	28-50-19-W3	73 F/7	53°20′	108°43′
Dayton	UNP/LNO	NS	Yarmouth	20 O/16	43°52′	66°06′
Dayton	UNP/LNO	ON	Algoma	41 J/6	46°15′	83°21′
Daytonia Beach	UNP/LNO	ON	Victoria	31 D/7	44°29′	78°44′
Dayton Station	UNP/LNO	ON	Algoma	41 J/3	46°14′	83°21′
Daytown	UNP/LNO	ON	Leeds	31 C/9	44°38′	76°06′
Deacon	UNP/LNO	ON	Renfrew	31 F/11	45°36′	77°22′
Deacon	UNP/LNO	MB	23,24-10-4-E	62 H/15	49°51′	96°56′
Deacon Lake	LAKE/LAC	ON	Kenora	52 E/16	49°54′	94°21′
Deacons Corner	UNP/LNO	MB	12-10-4-E	62 H/15	49°49′	96°56′
Dead Creek	UNP/LNO	NB	York	21 G/13	45°52′	67°31′
Dead Duck Bay	BAY/BAIE	NT	Keewatin	33 E	53°34′	79°00′
Deadhorse Lake	LAKE/LAC	AB	24-19,20-W4	82 P/2	51°05′	112°40′
Dead Islands	UNP/LNO	NF		3 D/13	52°48′	55°50′
Deadman River	RIV/CDE	BC	Kamloops Division Yale	92 I/10	50°45′	120°55′
Deadman's Bay	UNP/LNO	NF		2 F/5	49°21′	53°42′
Deadman's Bay	BAY/BAIE	NF		2 F/5	49°20′	53°40′
Deadmans Bight	BAY/BAIE	NF		1 M/5	47°27′	55°53′
Deadman's Brook	RIV/CDE	NF		2 F/5	49°21′	53°43′
Deadmans Cove	UNP/LNO	NF		12 P/7	51°15′	56°47′
Deadman's Creek - see-voir - Skeetchestn	IR/RI	BC		92 I/15	50°48′	120°57′
Dead Man's Flats	UNP/LNO	AB	13-24-10-W5	82 O/3	51°02′	115°16′
Deadmans Harbour	UNP/LNO	NB	Charlotte	21 G/2	45°03′	66°46′
Deadman's Point	CAPE/CAP	NF		2 F/5	49°21′	53°41′
Deadmans Pond	LAKE/LAC	NF		2 D/15	48°55′	54°32′
Dead Point 5	IR/RI	BC	Range 1 Coast	92 L/10	50°36′	126°35′

NAME NOM	ENTITY ENTITÉ	LOC 1 LIEU 1	LOC 2 LIEU 2	MAP CARTE	POSITION LAT	LONG
Dead Poplar Point	CAPE/CAP	ON	Thunder Bay	52 H/10	49°33′	88°34′
Dead Wolf Brook	RIV/CDE	NF		2 D/10	48°43′	54°58′
Dead Wolf Pond	LAKE/LAC	NF		2 D/10	48°40′	54°48′
Deadwood	UNP/LNO	AB	29-89-22-W5	84 C/11	56°44′	117°27′
Deadwood	UNP/LNO	BC	Similkameen Division Yale	82 E/2	49°06′	118°42′
Deadwood River	RIV/CDE	BC	Cassiar	104 P/8	59°24′	128°13′
Dealtown	UNP/LNO	ON	Kent	40 J/1	42°15′	82°06′
Dealy Island	ISL/ÎLE	NT	Franklin	78 F	74°57′	108°44′
Dean	UNP/LNO	NS	Halifax	11 E/2	45°12′	62°53′
Dean Channel	CHAN/CHEN	BC	Range 3 Coast	93 D/5	52°19′	127°31′
Dean Lake	UNP/LNO	ON	Algoma	41 J/3	46°13′	83°10′
Dean Lake	LAKE/LAC	NS	Queens	21 A/6	44°27′	65°04′
Deanlea Beach	UNP/LNO	ON	Simcoe	31 D/12	44°37′	80°00′
Dean River	RIV/CDE	BC	Range 3 Coast	93 D/15	52°48′	126°58′
Deans	UNP/LNO	ON	Parry Sound	31 E/14	45°54′	79°21′
Deans Corner	UNP/LNO	NS	Lunenburg	21 A/8	44°24′	64°20′
Deans Dundas Bay	BAY/BAIE	NT	Franklin	88 B	72°16′	118°19′
Dearlock	UNP/LNO	ON	Rainy River	52 D/16	48°50′	94°05′
Dease Arm	BAY/BAIE	NT	Mackenzie	86 L	66°52′	119°37′
Dease Lake	UNP/LNO	BC	Cassiar	104 J/8	58°26′	130°01′
Dease Lake	LAKE/LAC	BC	Cassiar	104 J/9	58°38′	130°04′
Dease Lake 9	IR/RI	BC	Cassiar	104 J/8	58°28′	130°02′
Dease River	RIV/CDE	BC	Cassiar	104 P/16	59°55′	128°29′
Dease River	RIV/CDE	NT	Mackenzie	86 L	66°53′	119°02′
Dease River 2	IR/RI	BC	Cassiar	104 P/10	59°43′	128°55′
Dease River 3	IR/RI	BC	Cassiar	104 P/6	59°19′	129°02′
Dease Strait	CHAN/CHEN	NT	Franklin	77 A	68°50′	107°30′
D'East, Bay	BAY/BAIE	NF		1 M/10	47°36′	54°51′
Deas Thompson Point	CAPE/CAP	NT	Mackenzie	97 D/15	69°46′	121°24′
Deauville	TOWN/VIL2	QC	Sherbrooke	31 H/8	45°20′	72°02′
DeBaies Cove	UNP/LNO	NS	Halifax	11 D/15	44°45′	62°49′
deBartok Lake	LAKE/LAC	NT	Keewatin	65 B	60°14′	99°00′
Debden	VILG/VILG	SK	30-52-6-W3	73 G/10	53°31′	106°53′
De Beaujeu	UNP/LNO	QC	Vaudreuil-Soulanges	31 G/8	45°20′	74°20′
Debec	UNP/LNO	NB	Carleton	21 J/4	46°04′	67°42′
Debec Junction	UNP/LNO	NB	Carleton	21 J/4	46°04′	67°42′
Debert	UNP/LNO	NS	Colchester	11 E/6	45°26′	63°28′
Debert River	RIV/CDE	NS	Colchester	11 E/5	45°23′	63°32′
DeBlois	UNP/LNO	PE	Prince	21 I/16	46°55′	64°07′
DeBolt	UNP/LNO	AB	12-71-1-W6	83 M/1	55°13′	118°01′
De Bonnard, Baie	BAY/BAIE	NT	Franklin	24 N/12	59°43′	69°35′
Deborah	UNP/LNO	SK	32-3-4-W2	62 E/7	49°15′	102°31′
Decelles, Lac	LAKE/LAC	QC	Le Haut-Saint-Maurice	32 B/1	48°05′	74°26′
Decelles, Réservoir	LAKE/LAC	QC	Témiscamingue	31 M/9	47°42′	78°08′
Déception	UNP/LNO	QC	Kativik	35 J/2	62°07′	74°38′
Deception Bay	BAY/BAIE	SK		64 L/10	58°32′	102°56′
Deception Bay	BAY/BAIE	NT	Franklin	35 J	62°10′	74°42′
Deception Creek	RIV/CDE	BC	Kamloops Division Yale	92 P/16	51°53′	120°28′
Deception Lake	LAKE/LAC	NS	Shelburne	20 P/14	43°54′	65°23′
Deception Lake	LAKE/LAC	ON	Kenora	52 E/10	49°44′	94°50′
Deception Lake	LAKE/LAC	SK		74 A/9	56°33′	104°14′
DeCew Falls	UNP/LNO	ON	Lincoln	30 M/3	43°06′	79°16′
Decewsville	UNP/LNO	ON	Haldimand	30 L/13	42°56′	79°55′
Dechêne, Lac	LAKE/LAC	QC	Sept-Rivières	22 O/5	51°15′	67°51′
Decimal	UNP/LNO	MB	36-10-15-E	52 E/14	49°53′	95°25′
Decker	UNP/LNO	MB	7-15-24-W	62 K/7	50°16′	100°47′
Decker Hollow	UNP/LNO	ON	Durham	31 D/1	44°01′	78°28′
Decker Lake	UNP/LNO	BC	Range 5 Coast	93 K/5	54°18′	125°50′
Decker Lake	LAKE/LAC	BC	Range 5 Coast	93 K/5	54°18′	125°49′
Decker Lake 10A - see-voir - Palling 1	IR/RI	BC		93 K/5	54°20′	125°54′
Deckers Hill	UNP/LNO	ON	Ontario	30 M/14	43°52′	79°05′
Déclin, Le	UNP/LNO	QC	Vaudreuil-Soulanges	31 G/8	45°24′	74°01′
Decoigne	UNP/LNO	AB	16-45-3-W6	83 D/16	52°53′	118°22′
De Courcy Group	ISL/ÎLE	BC	Nanaimo	92 G/4	49°06′	123°45′
Découverte, Côte de la	CAPE/CAP	QC	Minganie	12 E/10	49°39′	62°40′
Decoy, Chute	FALL/CHUT	QC	Kativik	35 A/4	60°12′	73°40′
Decrene	UNP/LNO	AB	1-72-2-W5	83 O/1	55°12′	114°10′
Dedegaus 8	IR/RI	BC	Range 2 Coast	92 M/4	51°06′	127°31′
Dee Bank	UNP/LNO	ON	Muskoka	31 E/4	45°11′	79°31′
Deekyakus 2	IR/RI	BC	Clayoquot	92 F/3	49°03′	125°21′
Deemerton	UNP/LNO	ON	Bruce	41 A/3	44°03′	81°05′
Deena 3	IR/RI	BC	Queen Charlotte	103 F/1	53°09′	132°07′
Deep Bay	UNP/LNO	NF		2 E/9	49°40′	54°18′
Deep Bay	UNP/LNO	ON	Haliburton	31 D/15	44°51′	78°49′
Deep Bay	UNP/LNO	BC	Newcastle	92 F/7	49°28′	124°43′

NAME / NOM	ENTITY / ENTITÉ	LOC 1 / LIEU 1	LOC 2 / LIEU 2	MAP / CARTE	POSITION LAT	POSITION LONG
Deep Bay	BAY/BAIE	ON	Kenora	52 E/2	49°02′	94°36′
Deep Bay	BAY/BAIE	SK		64 D/6	56°25′	103°00′
Deep Bay	BAY/BAIE	NT	Mackenzie	85 F	61°17′	116°40′
Deep Bight	UNP/LNO	NF		2 C/4	48°06′	53°57′
Deep Brook	UNP/LNO	NS	Annapolis	21 A/12	44°38′	65°39′
Deep Brook	RIV/CDE	NF		11 O/16	47°54′	58°15′
Deep Cove	UNP/LNO	NF		1 M/7	47°25′	54°30′
Deep Cove	UNP/LNO	NB	Charlotte	21 B/10	44°37′	66°52′
Deep Cove	UNP/LNO	BC	New Westminster	92 G/7	49°20′	122°57′
Deep Cove	UNP/LNO	BC	North Saanich	92 B/11	48°41′	123°28′
Deep Cove Island	UNP/LNO	NS	Yarmouth	20 O/9	43°40′	66°02′
Deep Creek	UNP/LNO	AB	7-69-21-W4	83 I/14	54°57′	113°13′
Deep Creek	UNP/LNO	BC	Kamloops Division Yale	82 L/11	50°37′	119°13′
Deep Creek	RIV/CDE	BC	Osoyoos Division Yale	82 L/6	50°21′	119°19′
Deep Creek 2	IR/RI	BC	Cariboo	93 B/8	52°16′	122°05′
Deep Creek 5	IR/RI	BC	Cariboo	93 G/6	53°18′	123°07′
Deepdale	UNP/LNO	NS	Inverness	11 K/3	46°14′	61°16′
Deepdale	UNP/LNO	MB	13-27-29A-W	62 N/6	51°18′	101°25′
Deep Inlet	BAY/BAIE	NF		13 N/8	55°22′	60°14′
Deep River	TOWN/VIL2	ON	Renfrew	31 K/4	46°06′	77°30′
Deep Rose Lake	LAKE/LAC	NT	Mackenzie	66 G	65°44′	98°40′
Deep Valley 5	IR/RI	BC	Range 1 Coast	92 K/7	50°23′	124°56′
Deep Valley Creek	RIV/CDE	AB	64-25-W5	83 K/12	54°33′	117°44′
Deepwater Point	CAPE/CAP	ON	Parry Sound	31 L/3	46°12′	79°30′
Deer	UNP/LNO	MB	5-12-10-W	62 G/15	49°59′	98°47′
Deer Bay	UNP/LNO	ON	Peterborough	31 D/9	44°32′	78°17′
Deer Bay	BAY/BAIE	ON	Peterborough	31 D/9	44°32′	78°16′
Deer Bay	BAY/BAIE	NT	Franklin	79 E/16	78°45′	104°10′
Deerbrook	UNP/LNO	ON	Essex	40 J/7	42°17′	82°37′
Deer Creek	UNP/LNO	SK	23-52-25-W3	73 F/12	53°31′	109°34′
Deer Creek	RIV/CDE	ON	Bruce	41 A/6	44°16′	81°13′
Deerfield	UNP/LNO	NS	Yarmouth	20 P/13	43°57′	65°59′
Deer Forks No. 232	MUN2/AZM2	SK		72 K/12	50°45′	109°50′
Deer Ground	UNP/LNO	QC	Minganie	12 P/13	51°54′	57°49′
Deer Harbour	UNP/LNO	NF		2 C/4	48°08′	53°34′
Deer Harbour	BAY/BAIE	NF		1 N/13	47°54′	53°44′
Deer Hill	UNP/LNO	AB	13-84-3-W6	84 D/8	56°17′	118°20′
Deerholme	UNP/LNO	BC	Quamichan	92 B/13	48°45′	123°46′
Deerhorn	UNP/LNO	MB	1-21-5-W	62 J/16	50°47′	98°02′
Deerhorn Creek	RIV/CDE	MB/SK		62 K/11	50°32′	101°23′
Deerhurst	UNP/LNO	ON	Simcoe	31 D/4	44°11′	79°35′
Deering Island	ISL/ÎLE	NT	Mackenzie	65 D	60°13′	103°11′
Deer Island	UNP/LNO	NF		2 C/13	48°56′	53°43′
Deer Island	UNP/LNO	NF		11 P/11	47°37′	57°22′
Deer Island	ISL/ÎLE	NF		2 C/12	48°33′	53°40′
Deer Island	ISL/ÎLE	NF		2 C/13	48°56′	53°44′
Deer Island	ISL/ÎLE	NB	Charlotte	21 G/2	45°00′	66°58′
Deer Island	ISL/ÎLE	MB		62 P/7	51°18′	96°32′
Deer Island	ISL/ÎLE	BC	Rupert	92 L/11	50°43′	127°23′
Deer, Lacs	LAKE/LAC	QC	Pontiac	31 F/15	45°55′	76°32′
Deer Lake	TOWN/VIL2	NF		12 H/3	49°10′	57°26′
Deer Lake	UNP/LNO	NB	York	21 G/14	45°49′	67°24′
Deer Lake	UNP/LNO	ON	Haliburton	31 E/1	45°03′	78°05′
Deer Lake	UNP/LNO	ON	Kenora	53 D/9	52°37′	94°05′
Deer Lake	LAKE/LAC	NF		12 H/4	49°06′	57°35′
Deer Lake	LAKE/LAC	ON	Haliburton	31 E/1	45°02′	78°06′
Deer Lake	LAKE/LAC	ON	Parry Sound	31 E/13	45°49′	79°34′
Deer Lake	LAKE/LAC	ON	Nipissing	41 I/8	46°28′	80°13′
Deer Lake	LAKE/LAC	ON	Kenora	53 D/9	52°38′	94°15′
Deer Lake	IR/RI	ON	Kenora	53 D/1	52°07′	94°00′
Deer Lodge	UNP/LNO	MB		62 H/14	49°53′	97°14′
Deer Park	UNP/LNO	ON	York	30 M/11	43°41′	79°25′
Deer Park	UNP/LNO	BC	Kootenay	82 E/8	49°25′	118°03′
Deer Passage	CHAN/CHEN	BC	New Westminster	92 K/7	50°17′	124°58′
Deerpass Bay	BAY/BAIE	NT	Mackenzie	96 G	65°56′	122°16′
Deer Pond	LAKE/LAC	NF		2 D/7	48°30′	54°45′
Deer Ridge	UNP/LNO	SK	52-1-W3	73 G/8	53°27′	106°06′
Deer River	RIV/CDE	MB		54 L/8	58°23′	94°13′
Deersdale	UNP/LNO	NB	York	21 J/6	46°30′	67°02′
Deerville	UNP/LNO	NB	Carleton	21 J/5	46°18′	67°40′
Deerwood	UNP/LNO	MB	17-5-7-W	62 G/8	49°24′	98°23′
Defeat Lake	LAKE/LAC	NT	Mackenzie	85 I	62°00′	113°38′
Defence Island 28	IR/RI	BC	New Westminster	92 G/11	49°35′	123°16′
De Forceville	UNP/LNO	QC	Pabok	22 A/9	48°32′	64°21′
Defosse, Cape	CAPE/CAP	NT	Franklin	120 C	81°14′	65°36′

NAME NOM	ENTITY ENTITÉ	LOC 1 LIEU 1	LOC 2 LIEU 2	MAP CARTE	POSITION LAT	LONG
Defot	UNP/LNO	BC	Cassiar	104 J/16	58°54′	130°27′
Defoy	UNP/LNO	QC	Arthabaska	31 I/1	46°08′	72°08′
De Freneuse, Lac	LAKE/LAC	QC	Kativik	24 K/6	58°23′	69°15′
Dégelis	CITY/VIL1	QC	Témiscouata	21 N/10	47°33′	68°39′
Dégelis, Lac du	LAKE/LAC	QC	Le Fjord-du-Saguenay	22 E/1	49°04′	70°10′
De Grasse	UNP/LNO	QC	Sept-Rivières	22 J/1	50°13′	66°13′
De Grassi Point	UNP/LNO	ON	Simcoe	31 D/5	44°15′	79°32′
De Grau	UNP/LNO	NF		12 B/6	48°29′	59°12′
DeGros Marsh	UNP/LNO	PE	Kings	11 L/1	46°13′	62°29′
De Haven Point	CAPE/CAP	NT	Franklin	67 C	69°00′	101°46′
Dehoux Bay	BAY/BAIE	NT	Mackenzie	65 D	60°25′	103°08′
Dejong	UNP/LNO	ON	Middlesex	40 P/4	43°00′	81°46′
Deka Lake	LAKE/LAC	BC	Lillooet	92 P/10	51°39′	120°47′
De la Beche Bay	BAY/BAIE	NT	Franklin	68 G	75°16′	100°24′
De La Blache, Lac	LAKE/LAC	QC	Manicouagan	22 K/3	50°05′	69°29′
Delacour	UNP/LNO	AB	24-25-28-W4	82 P/4	51°09′	113°46′
De Lacy Head	CAPE/CAP	NT	Franklin	59 A	76°50′	89°59′
Delage, Lac	LAKE/LAC	QC	La Jacques-Cartier	21 L/14	46°58′	71°24′
De la Guiche Point	CAPE/CAP	NT	Keewatin	57 B	68°59′	94°34′
Delahey, Lac	LAKE/LAC	QC	La Vallée-de-la-Gatineau	31 K/15	46°50′	76°38′
Délaissés, Les	UNP/LNO	QC	D'Autray	31 I/6	46°20′	73°24′
Delamere	UNP/LNO	ON	Sudbury	41 I/2	46°10′	80°43′
Delaney	UNP/LNO	AB	17-39-26-W4	83 A/5	52°21′	113°42′
Delaney Lake	LAKE/LAC	ON	Kenora	52 L/1	50°05′	94°03′
Delano Bay	BAY/BAIE	NT	Franklin	25 J	62°40′	66°59′
De La Noue, Lac	LAKE/LAC	QC	Kativik	23 L/13	54°45′	71°44′
Delaps Cove	UNP/LNO	NS	Annapolis	21 A/13	44°46′	65°38′
Delaronde Lake	LAKE/LAC	SK		73 J/3	54°03′	107°03′
Delaware	MUN2/AZM2	ON	Middlesex	40 I/14	42°52′	81°22′
Delaware	UNP/LNO	ON	Middlesex	40 I/14	42°55′	81°25′
Delaware West	UNP/LNO	ON	Middlesex	40 I/14	42°54′	81°26′
Delay, Rivière	RIV/CDE	QC	Kativik	24 D/14	56°56′	71°28′
Del Bonita	UNP/LNO	AB	18-1-21-W4	82 H/2	49°02′	112°48′
Delbrook	UNP/LNO	BC	New Westminster	92 G/6	49°21′	123°05′
Delburne	VILG/VILG	AB	21-37-23-W4	83 A/3	52°12′	113°14′
Delbys Cove	UNP/LNO	NF		2 C/4	48°14′	53°32′
Déléage	VILG/VILG	QC	La Vallée-de-la-Gatineau	31 J/5	46°23′	75°55′
Deleau	UNP/LNO	MB	20-7-23-W	62 F/10	49°35′	100°35′
De Lesseps	UNP/LNO	QC	Les Laurentides	31 J/2	46°08′	74°33′
De Lesseps Lake	LAKE/LAC	ON	Thunder Bay	52 J/10	50°43′	90°42′
Delestres, Rivière	RIV/CDE	QC	Vallée-de-l'Or	32 C/15	48°47′	76°54′
Delhaven	UNP/LNO	NS	Kings	21 H/1	45°12′	64°23′
Delhi	MUN2/AZM2	ON	Norfolk	40 I/16	42°50′	80°25′
Delhi	UNP/LNO	ON	Norfolk	40 I/16	42°51′	80°30′
Delia	VILG/VILG	AB	5-31-17-W4	82 P/9	51°38′	112°23′
Delight Lake	LAKE/LAC	NT	Mackenzie	75 C	60°37′	108°14′
Délįne	HAM/HAM	NT	Mackenzie	96 G/3	65°11′	123°25′
De Lionne, Lac	LAKE/LAC	QC	Jamésie	23 E/11	53°40′	71°22′
Delisle	TOWN/VIL2	SK	34-8-W3	72 O/14	51°55′	107°08′
Delisle	VILG/VILG	QC	Lac-Saint-Jean-Est	22 D/12	48°38′	71°42′
Delisle, Rivière	RIV/CDE	QC/ON		31 G/8	45°17′	74°11′
Delisle's Corners	UNP/LNO	ON	Essex	40 J/3	42°11′	83°01′
Delkatla	UNP/LNO	BC	Queen Charlotte	103 K/1	54°01′	132°08′
Dell	UNP/LNO	QC	Le Granit	21 E/11	45°35′	71°11′
Della Falls	FALL/CHUT	BC	Clayoquot	92 F/5	49°27′	125°32′
Dellwood Basin	SEAU/SMER	—		19400A	50°42′	130°32′
Dellwood Knolls	SEAU/SMER	—		3744	50°45′	130°25′
Dellwood Seamount Chain	SEAU/SMER	—		3744	50°30′	130°38′
Dellwood Valley	SEAU/SMER	—		19400A	50°49′	130°25′
Delmas	HAM/HAM	SK	31-45-18-W3	73 C/15	52°56′	108°36′
Delmer	UNP/LNO	ON	Oxford	40 I/15	42°52′	80°48′
Delmont	UNP/LNO	QC	Le Haut-Saint-Laurent	31 G/1	45°08′	74°16′
Delnite	UNP/LNO	QC	Cochrane	42 A/6	48°26′	81°18′
Deloraine	TOWN/VIL2	MB	3-3-23-W	62 F/1	49°11′	100°30′
Delorme Beach	UNP/LNO	SK	35-47-17-W3	73 F/1	53°06′	108°23′
Delorme, Lac	LAKE/LAC	QC	Caniapiscau	23 K/12	54°31′	69°52′
Deloro	VILG/VILG	ON	Hastings	31 C/12	44°31′	77°37′
Delph	UNP/LNO	AB	18-58-18-W4	83 I/2	54°00′	112°40′
Del Ray	UNP/LNO	ON	York	30 M/11	43°42′	79°28′
Delrex	UNP/LNO	ON	Halton	30 M/12	43°39′	79°55′
Delson	CITY/VIL1	QC	Roussillon	31 H/5	45°22′	73°33′
Delta	MUN1/AZM1	BC	New Westminster	92 G/3	49°05′	123°05′
Delta	UNP/LNO	ON	Leeds	31 C/9	44°37′	76°08′
Delta Beach	UNP/LNO	MB	14-14-7-W	62 J/1	50°11′	98°19′
Delta Marsh	VEGL/VÉGB	MB		62 J/1	50°12′	98°12′

NAME NOM	ENTITY ENTITÉ	LOC 1 LIEU 1	LOC 2 LIEU 2	MAP CARTE	POSITION LAT	LONG
Delta Peak	MTN/MNT	BC	Cassiar	104 A/12	56°39′	129°34′
Del-Val	UNP/LNO	QC	Denis-Riverin	22 G/2	49°05′	66°44′
Demaine	HAM/HAM	SK	24-22-10-W3	72 J/14	50°54′	107°15′
De Martigny, Promontoire	CAPE/CAP	QC	Kativik	35 I/2	62°07′	72°41′
Demay	UNP/LNO	AB	8-48-19-W4	83 H/2	53°07′	112°44′
Demay Lake	LAKE/LAC	AB	48-19-W4	83 H/2	53°07′	112°42′
Demean	UNP/LNO	BC	Peace River	93 P/14	55°47′	121°29′
Demers	UNP/LNO	QC	Pontiac	31 F/14	45°51′	77°04′
Demers-Centre	UNP/LNO	QC	Pontiac	31 F/14	45°52′	77°04′
Demers, Lac	LAKE/LAC	QC	Sept-Rivières	22 O/7	51°19′	66°49′
Demers, Mount	MTN/MNT	BC	Malahat	92 C/9	48°37′	124°05′
Demers, Pointe	CAPE/CAP	QC	Kativik	35 C/12	60°39′	77°50′
Demmitt	UNP/LNO	AB	35-74-13-W6	83 M/5	55°27′	119°54′
Demoiselle Creek	UNP/LNO	NB	Albert	21 H/15	45°51′	64°39′
De Montigny, Lac	LAKE/LAC	QC	Vallée-de-l'Or	32 C/4	48°08′	77°54′
De Morbihan, Lac	LAKE/LAC	QC	Minganie	12 M/15	51°50′	62°54′
Demorestville	UNP/LNO	ON	Prince Edward	31 C/3	44°06′	77°12′
Dempseys Corner	UNP/LNO	NS	Kings	21 H/2	45°03′	64°51′
Denard	UNP/LNO	AB	16-57-7-W6	83 E/15	53°55′	118°59′
Denare Beach	VILG/VILG	SK	65-1-W2	63 L/9	54°40′	102°05′
Denbeigh Point	UNP/LNO	MB	45-16-W	63 B/13	52°54′	99°47′
Denbeigh Point	CAPE/CAP	MB	45-17-W	63 B/13	52°54′	99°46′
Denbigh	UNP/LNO	ON	Lennox and Addington	31 F/3	45°08′	77°16′
Denbigh, Abinger and Ashby	MUN2/AZM2	ON	Lennox and Addington	31 F/3	45°04′	77°18′
Denbigh Island	ISL/ÎLE	NF		3 D/12	52°33′	55°50′
Denbow	UNP/LNO	MB	24-7-23-W	62 F/9	49°35′	100°29′
Dencross	UNP/LNO	MB	12-15-7-E	62 I/8	50°16′	96°29′
Dendron	UNP/LNO	SK	25-13-9-W3	72 J/3	50°07′	107°07′
Denetiah Lake	LAKE/LAC	BC	Cassiar	94 L/6	58°28′	127°33′
Denfield	UNP/LNO	ON	Middlesex	40 P/3	43°07′	81°26′
Dengy Place	UNP/LNO	QC	Côte-Nord-du-Golfe-Saint-Laurent	12 O/2	51°02′	58°52′
Denhart	UNP/LNO	AB	2-20-11-W4	72 L/11	50°40′	111°25′
Denholm	VILG/VILG	QC	La Vallée-de-la-Gatineau	31 G/13	45°49′	75°45′
Denholm	VILG/VILG	SK	31-42-14-W3	73 C/9	52°39′	108°01′
Deniau	UNP/LNO	QC	L'Islet	21 N/4	47°05′	69°56′
Denison	UNP/LNO	ON	Thunder Bay	42 C/11	48°36′	85°26′
Denison Lake	LAKE/LAC	MB		64 G/5	57°30′	99°30′
Denison Mills	UNP/LNO	QC	Asbestos	31 H/9	45°45′	72°06′
Denis-Riverin	MUN1/AZM1	QC	Denis-Riverin	22 G/1	49°13′	66°04′
Denman Island	UNP/LNO	BC	Nanaimo	92 F/10	49°32′	124°49′
Denman Island	ISL/ÎLE	BC	Nanaimo	92 F/10	49°33′	124°48′
Denmark	UNP/LNO	NS	Colchester	11 E/11	45°42′	63°10′
Denmark	GEOG/GÉOG	NB	Victoria	21 O/3	47°10′	67°30′
Denmark Bay	BAY/BAIE	NT	Franklin	67 F	70°40′	103°22′
Denmark Lake	LAKE/LAC	ON	Kenora	52 F/5	49°23′	93°39′
Dennis	UNP/LNO	NB	Northumberland	21 J/16	46°53′	66°01′
Dennis Hill	UNP/LNO	NF		11 O/11	47°36′	59°11′
Dennis Lake	UNP/LNO	MB	2-18-1-E	62 I/11	50°31′	97°22′
Dennis Pond	LAKE/LAC	NF		12 B/8	48°24′	58°10′
Denny	UNP/LNO	SK	16-29-9-W3	72 O/6	51°29′	107°13′
Denny Island	ISL/ÎLE	BC	Range 3 Coast	93 D/4	52°08′	128°00′
De Nouë, Lac	LAKE/LAC	QC	Kativik	24 C/5	56°20′	69°45′
Densmores Mills	UNP/LNO	NS	Hants	11 E/5	45°18′	63°42′
Dent, Mount	MTN/MNT	BC	Range 3 Coast	93 C/9	52°43′	124°11′
Dentville	UNP/LNO	BC	New Westminster	92 G/11	49°43′	123°09′
Denver	UNP/LNO	NS	Guysborough	11 E/8	45°20′	62°06′
Denver Canyon	UNP/LNO	BC	Kootenay	82 F/14	50°00′	117°21′
Denys Basin	BAY/BAIE	NS	Inverness	11 F/14	45°53′	61°02′
Denys Canyon	SEAU/SMER	—		8010	42°48′	50°14′
Denys, Lac	LAKE/LAC	QC	Jamésie	33 K/15	54°55′	76°47′
Denys, River	RIV/CDE	NS	Inverness	11 F/14	45°51′	61°05′
Denys, Rivière	RIV/CDE	QC	Kativik	33 N/3	55°09′	77°23′
Denzil	VILG/VILG	SK	33-37-26-W3	73 C/4	52°14′	109°39′
Departure Bay	UNP/LNO	BC	Nanaimo	92 G/4	49°12′	123°58′
Departure Lake	UNP/LNO	ON	Cochrane	42 H/5	49°17′	81°48′
De Pas, Rivière	RIV/CDE	QC	Kativik	23 P/15	55°53′	64°45′
Depew	UNP/LNO	ON	Algoma	42 C/11	48°32′	85°12′
Dépôt-Baskatong	UNP/LNO	QC	La Vallée-de-la-Gatineau	31 J/13	46°47′	75°52′
Dépôt-Davidson	UNP/LNO	QC	Pontiac	31 F/15	45°59′	76°41′
Dépôt-de-la-Savane	UNP/LNO	QC	Mékinac	31 P/4	47°12′	73°47′
Dépôt-de-l'Île	UNP/LNO	QC	Antoine-Labelle	31 J/13	46°55′	75°48′
Dépôt-des-Lacs-Obatogamau	UNP/LNO	QC	Jamésie	32 G/9	49°34′	74°20′
Dépôt-des-Loutres	UNP/LNO	QC	Maria-Chapdelaine	32 H/9	49°30′	72°11′
Dépôt-Dix-Sept-Milles	UNP/LNO	QC	Le Haut-Saint-Maurice	31 O/9	47°41′	74°07′
Dépôt-du-Lac-Chibougamau	UNP/LNO	QC	Jamésie	32 G/16	49°45′	74°15′

NAME NOM	ENTITY ENTITÉ	LOC 1 LIEU 1	LOC 2 LIEU 2	MAP CARTE	POSITION LAT	LONG
Dépôt-du-Lac-Devenyns	UNP/LNO	QC	Matawinie	31 P/4	47°02′	73°49′
Dépôt-Échouani	MUN2/AZM2	QC	La Vallée-de-la-Gatineau	31 O/13	47°50′	75°35′
Dépôt-Esturgeon	UNP/LNO	QC	Antoine-Labelle	31 O/4	47°01′	75°43′
Depot Harbour	UNP/LNO	ON	Parry Sound	41 H/8	45°19′	80°06′
Dépôt-Mungo	UNP/LNO	QC	Témiscamingue	31 L/15	46°47′	78°40′
Depot Point	CAPE/CAP	NT	Franklin	49 G	79°37′	85°45′
Depot Point	CAPE/CAP	NT	Franklin	58 F	74°55′	93°23′
Dépôt-Sunnyside	UNP/LNO	QC	Témiscamingue	31 L/15	46°55′	78°55′
De Quen-Nord	UNP/LNO	QC	Le Domaine-du-Roy	32 A/8	48°20′	72°08′
Derby	MUN2/AZM2	ON	Grey	41 A/10	44°32′	81°00′
Derby	UNP/LNO	PE	Prince	21 I/9	46°38′	64°11′
Derby	UNP/LNO	NB	Northumberland	21 I/13	46°53′	65°39′
Derby	GEOG/GÉOG	NB	Northumberland	21 I/13	46°53′	65°42′
Derby Junction	UNP/LNO	NB	Northumberland	21 I/13	46°58′	65°36′
Derby Lake	LAKE/LAC	NT	Keewatin	55 K	62°43′	93°39′
Dereham Centre	UNP/LNO	ON	Oxford	40 I/15	42°55′	80°49′
*Derek	UNP/LNO	BC	Range 5 Coast	93 L/7	54°23′	126°41′
De Ré, Lac	LAKE/LAC	QC	Minganie	12 K/16	50°54′	60°22′
Dering	UNP/LNO	MB	9,10-61-21-W	63 K/7	54°15′	100°32′
Derland	UNP/LNO	ON	Nipissing	31 L/3	46°13′	79°21′
Dermid	UNP/LNO	ON	Rainy River	52 C/12	48°40′	93°45′
Dernic	UNP/LNO	SK	12-32-7-W2	62 M/10	51°44′	102°52′
Deroche	UNP/LNO	BC	New Westminster	92 G/1	49°11′	122°04′
De Rozière, Baie	BAY/BAIE	NT	Franklin	25 C	60°30′	69°45′
Derrynane	UNP/LNO	ON	Wellington	40 P/15	43°56′	80°35′
Derrys Corner	UNP/LNO	NB	Albert	21 H/10	45°44′	64°44′
Derryville	UNP/LNO	ON	Ontario	31 D/6	44°19′	79°05′
Derry West	UNP/LNO	ON	Peel	30 M/12	43°39′	79°42′
Derwent	VILG/VILG	AB	9-54-7-W4	73 E/10	53°39′	110°58′
Derwent	UNP/LNO	ON	Middlesex	40 I/14	42°56′	81°06′
DeSable	UNP/LNO	PE	Queens	11 L/3	46°12′	63°25′
De Saint-Just	UNP/LNO	QC	Kamouraska	21 M/8	47°27′	70°00′
De Salaberry	MUN2/AZM2	MB		62 H/6	49°24′	97°01′
De Salis Bay	BAY/BAIE	NT	Franklin	97 H	71°26′	121°40′
De Salis River	RIV/CDE	NT	Franklin	97 H	71°29′	121°42′
Des Antons, Lac	LAKE/LAC	QC	Jamésie	33 A/13	52°53′	73°34′
Désaulniers	UNP/LNO	ON	Nipissing	41 I/9	46°33′	80°07′
Desbarats	UNP/LNO	ON	Algoma	41 J/5	46°20′	83°56′
Desbarats Basin	SEAU/SMER	—		7951	76°40′	103°00′
Desbarats Strait	CHAN/CHEN	NT	Franklin	69 B	76°52′	104°10′
DesBarres Canyon	SEAU/SMER	—		15042A	44°15′	53°05′
DesBarres Spur	SEAU/SMER	—		4045	43°58′	59°12′
Desbergères, Lac	LAKE/LAC	QC	Kativik	24 D/15	56°52′	70°52′
Desbiens	CITY/VIL1	QC	Lac-Saint-Jean-Est	22 D/5	48°25′	71°57′
Desboro	UNP/LNO	ON	Grey	41 A/7	44°24′	81°00′
Desceliers, Lac	LAKE/LAC	QC	Jamésie	23 D/16	52°55′	70°11′
Descente-aux-Enfers, La	UNP/LNO	QC	Rimouski-Neigette	22 C/7	48°16′	68°32′
Descente des Femmes, Anse de la	BAY/BAIE	QC	Le Fjord-du-Saguenay	22 D/7	48°23′	70°34′
Deschaillons-sur-Saint-Laurent	VILG/VILG	QC	Bécancour	31 I/9	46°33′	72°07′
Deschambault	VILG/VILG	QC	Portneuf	21 L/12	46°39′	71°56′
Deschambault Lake	HAM/HAM	SK	68-9-W2	63 L/14	54°55′	103°22′
Deschambault Lake	LAKE/LAC	SK		63 L/14	54°47′	103°25′
Deschambault, Pointe	CAPE/CAP	QC	Communauté urbaine de Québec	21 L/11	46°44′	71°22′
Deschambault River	RIV/CDE	SK	67-12-W2	63 L/13	54°47′	103°46′
Deschambault-Station	UNP/LNO	QC	Portneuf	21 L/12	46°40′	71°57′
Descharme Lake	HAM/HAM	SK		74 F/3	57°06′	109°12′
Descharme Lake	LAKE/LAC	SK		74 F/3	57°05′	109°13′
Descharme River	RIV/CDE	SK		74 C/14	56°51′	109°13′
Deschênes	UNP/LNO	QC	Communauté urbaine de l'Outaouais	31 G/5	45°23′	75°48′
Deschênes, Lac	LAKE/LAC	QC	Charlevoix-Est	21 M/16	47°57′	70°04′
Deschênes, Lac	LAKE/LAC	QC/ON		31 G/5	45°22′	75°51′
D'Escousse	UNP/LNO	NS	Richmond	11 F/10	45°35′	60°58′
Deseronto	TOWN/VIL2	ON	Hastings	31 C/3	44°12′	77°03′
Desert	UNP/LNO	NS	Halifax	11 D/11	44°41′	63°16′
Désert-à-Brave-Homme, Le	UNP/LNO	QC	Portneuf	31 I/9	46°42′	72°14′
Désert-à-Clément	UNP/LNO	QC	Antoine-Labelle	31 G/13	46°00′	75°43′
Désert-Brûlé	UNP/LNO	QC	Minganie	12 E/11	49°30′	63°00′
Deserters Group	ISL/ÎLE	BC	Range 1 Coast	92 L/14	50°53′	127°29′
Deserters Peak	MTN/MNT	BC	Cassiar	94 C/15	56°58′	124°54′
Désert, Lac	LAKE/LAC	QC	La Vallée-de-la-Gatineau	31 K/9	46°35′	76°19′
Desert Lake	UNP/LNO	ON	Frontenac	31 C/10	44°31′	76°36′
Desert Lake	LAKE/LAC	ON	Frontenac	31 C/10	44°32′	76°35′
Désert, Le	UNP/LNO	QC	Lac-Saint-Jean-Est	22 D/5	48°24′	71°46′
Désert, Le	UNP/LNO	QC	Portneuf	21 L/13	46°51′	72°00′
Désert, Le	UNP/LNO	QC	Portneuf	31 I/9	46°40′	72°04′

NAME NOM	ENTITY ENTITÉ	LOC 1 LIEU 1	LOC 2 LIEU 2	MAP CARTE	POSITION	
					LAT	LONG
Désert, Rivière	RIV/CDE	QC	La Vallée-de-la-Gatineau	31 J/5	46°23′	75°58′
Des Groseilliers, Presqu'île	CAPE/CAP	QC	Jamésie	32 P/4	51°05′	73°38′
Desherbiers	UNP/LNO	NB	Kent	21 I/11	46°39′	65°14′
Desjardins	MUN1/AZM1	QC	Desjardins	21 L/14	46°45′	71°07′
Desjardins Road	UNP/LNO	NB	Victoria	21 O/4	47°00′	67°41′
Desjardinsville	UNP/LNO	QC	Pontiac	31 F/14	45°51′	77°07′
Deskenatlata Lake	LAKE/LAC	NT	Mackenzie	85 A	60°55′	112°03′
Desliens, Lac	LAKE/LAC	NF		23 J/6	54°18′	67°23′
Desmarais Lake	LAKE/LAC	MB		64 O/6	59°29′	99°25′
Desmarais Lake	LAKE/LAC	NT	Mackenzie	75 A	60°37′	105°35′
Desmarais, Pointe	CAPE/CAP	NT	Mackenzie	85 F	61°01′	116°29′
Desmaraisville	UNP/LNO	QC	Jamésie	32 F/9	49°30′	76°11′
Des Marets, Lac - also-aussi - Cheeseman Lake	LAKE/LAC	QC	Minganie	12 M/16	51°58′	62°01′
Desmond	UNP/LNO	ON	Lennox and Addington	31 C/7	44°24′	76°50′
Desolation Sound	BAY/BAIE	BC	New Westminster	92 K/2	50°07′	124°47′
Des Ormeaux	UNP/LNO	QC	Bécancour	31 I/7	46°20′	72°31′
Despair, Lake	LAKE/LAC	ON	Rainy River	52 C/13	48°53′	93°40′
Desperation Lake	LAKE/LAC	NT	Mackenzie	85 I	62°35′	112°25′
Despinassy	UNP/LNO	QC	Abitibi	32 C/14	48°46′	77°26′
Despins, Pointe	CAPE/CAP	QC	Kativik	34 M/1	59°08′	78°12′
D'Espoir Brook	RIV/CDE	NF		11 P/16	47°52′	56°10′
D'Espoir Lake	LAKE/LAC	NF		11 P/16	47°59′	56°12′
Després-Village	UNP/LNO	NB	Kent	21 I/7	46°24′	64°39′
Des Rivières	UNP/LNO	QC	Communauté urbaine de Québec	21 L/14	46°50′	71°18′
Des Rivières	UNP/LNO	QC	Brome-Missisquoi	31 H/3	45°09′	73°03′
Desrosiers	UNP/LNO	QC	Matane	22 B/12	48°45′	67°49′
Des Ruisseaux	VILG/VILG	QC	Antoine-Labelle	31 J/12	46°35′	75°38′
Dessaint	UNP/LNO	QC	Kamouraska	21 N/12	47°34′	69°46′
Desserte-du-Lac-d'Argent, La	UNP/LNO	QC	Antoine-Labelle	31 O/3	47°02′	75°21′
De Stael Point	CAPE/CAP	NT	Keewatin	57 A	68°22′	90°16′
Desteffany Lake	LAKE/LAC	NT	Mackenzie	76 D	64°37′	111°42′
Dester Lake	LAKE/LAC	BC	Cariboo	93 B/1	52°12′	122°26′
Destor	VILG/VILG	QC	Rouyn-Noranda	32 D/7	48°27′	78°57′
Destruction Bay	UNP/LNO	YT		115 G/7	61°15′	138°48′
Des Voeux, Lac	LAKE/LAC	QC	Jamésie	33 H/15	53°56′	72°38′
Detah	UNP/LNO	NT	Mackenzie	85 J/8	62°25′	114°18′
Detention Harbour	BAY/BAIE	NT	Mackenzie	76 N	67°52′	109°57′
Detlor	UNP/LNO	ON	Hastings	31 F/4	45°02′	77°44′
Détour-à-Philippon, Le	UNP/LNO	QC	Pabok	22 A/10	48°31′	64°33′
Detour River - also-aussi - Détour, Rivière du	RIV/CDE	ON	Cochrane	32 E/14	49°56′	79°26′
Détour, Rivière du - also-aussi - Detour River	RIV/CDE	QC	Jamésie	32 E/14	49°56′	79°26′
De Tracy, Pointe	CAPE/CAP	QC	Kativik	25 E/2	61°05′	70°45′
Detroit River	RIV/CDE	ON	Essex	40 J/3	42°03′	83°09′
De Troyes, Rivière	RIV/CDE	QC	Kativik	34 B/4	56°12′	75°57′
Deux Décharges, Lac aux	LAKE/LAC	QC	Le Fjord-du-Saguenay	22 M/15	51°58′	70°40′
Deuxième-Sault	UNP/LNO	NB	Madawaska	21 N/8	47°28′	68°14′
Deux Loutres, Lac aux	LAKE/LAC	QC	Minganie	12 M/9	51°31′	62°28′
Deux-Milles, Le	UNP/LNO	QC	Témiscouata	21 N/10	47°43′	68°50′
Deux-Montagnes	CITY/VIL1	QC	Deux-Montagnes	31 H/12	45°32′	73°53′
Deux-Montagnes	MUN1/AZM1	QC	Deux-Montagnes	31 G/8	45°28′	74°06′
Deux Montagnes, Lac des	LAKE/LAC	QC	Deux-Montagnes	31 G/8	45°27′	74°00′
Deux-Rivières	UNP/LNO	ON	Renfrew	31 L/1	46°15′	78°17′
Devastation Channel	CHAN/CHEN	BC	Range 4 Coast	103 H/10	53°40′	128°50′
Devault	UNP/LNO	QC	Maskinongé	31 I/7	46°18′	72°55′
Développement-Blais	UNP/LNO	QC	Le Haut-Saint-François	21 E/5	45°27′	71°47′
Développement-de-Sainte-Clothilde	UNP/LNO	QC	Arthabaska	31 H/16	45°57′	72°14′
Développement-la-Terre	UNP/LNO	QC	Asbestos	21 E/13	45°48′	71°50′
Développement-Malaga	UNP/LNO	QC	Memphrémagog	31 H/8	45°15′	72°16′
Développement-Nadeau	UNP/LNO	QC	Le Haut-Saint-François	21 E/5	45°19′	71°48′
Développement-Quatre-Saisons	UNP/LNO	QC	Memphrémagog	31 H/8	45°15′	72°21′
Développement-Webster	UNP/LNO	QC	Memphrémagog	31 H/8	45°16′	72°16′
Devenish	UNP/LNO	AB	33-75-8-W4	73 M/11	55°32′	111°12′
Devenyns, Lac	LAKE/LAC	QC	Matawinie	31 P/4	47°05′	73°50′
Devereaux	UNP/LNO	NB	Gloucester	21 P/13	47°49′	65°44′
Devereux Lake	LAKE/LAC	BC	Range 2 Coast	92 N/4	51°14′	125°36′
Devil Bay	BAY/BAIE	NF		11 P/10	47°38′	56°37′
Devil Brook	RIV/CDE	NF		1 M/6	47°17′	55°19′
Devil Lake	LAKE/LAC	ON	Frontenac	31 C/9	44°35′	76°27′
Devil Lake	LAKE/LAC	SK		73 P/10	55°40′	104°45′
Deville	UNP/LNO	AB	32-51-20-W4	83 H/7	53°27′	112°55′
Deville Névé	GLAC/GLAC	BC	Kootenay	82 N/3	51°07′	117°22′
Devil Point	CAPE/CAP	NF		12 I/8	50°15′	56°29′
Devil's Cove	BAY/BAIE	NF		12 I/1	50°02′	56°02′
Devils Creek	RIV/CDE	MB	15-5-E	62 I/7	50°19′	96°49′
Devil's Gate 220	IR/RI	AB	11-113-8-W4	74 L/14	58°49′	111°13′

NAME NOM	ENTITY ENTITÉ	LOC 1 LIEU 1	LOC 2 LIEU 2	MAP CARTE	POSITION LAT	LONG
Devils Island	UNP/LNO	NS	Halifax	11 D/11	44°35′	63°28′
Devils Kitchen	UNP/LNO	NF		1 N/2	47°04′	52°56′
Devils Thumb	MTN/MNT	BC	Cassiar	104 F/1	57°06′	132°22′
Devine	UNP/LNO	BC	Lillooet	92 J/9	50°31′	122°29′
Devine Corner	UNP/LNO	NB	Kings	21 H/12	45°32′	65°33′
De Vitré, Lac	LAKE/LAC	QC	Minganie	12 O/12	51°39′	59°52′
Devizes	UNP/LNO	ON	Middlesex	40 P/3	43°09′	81°14′
Devlin	UNP/LNO	ON	Rainy River	52 C/12	48°37′	93°41′
Devlin, Lac	LAKE/LAC	QC	Témiscamingue	31 M/7	47°28′	78°38′
Devon	TOWN/VIL2	AB	34-50-26-W4	83 H/5	53°22′	113°44′
Devon	UNP/LNO	NS	Halifax	11 D/14	44°55′	63°24′
Devon	UNP/LNO	NB	York	21 G/15	45°58′	66°37′
Devon	UNP/LNO	ON	Sudbury	41 O/14	47°46′	83°22′
Devon 30	IR/RI	NB	York	21 G/15	46°00′	66°37′
Devona	UNP/LNO	AB	15-48-1-W6	83 F/4	53°09′	118°00′
Devon Ice Cap	GLAC/GLAC	NT	Franklin	48 H	75°20′	82°30′
Devon Island	ISL/ÎLE	NT	Franklin	48 G	75°15′	88°00′
Devon Shelf	SEAU/SMER	—		7000	75°30′	74°00′
Devonshire	UNP/LNO	ON	Cochrane	42 A/15	48°49′	80°50′
Devon Slope	SEAU/SMER	—		7000	74°00′	70°00′
Devon Trough	SEAU/SMER	—		7220	75°30′	79°30′
Dewar Lake	UNP/LNO	SK	4-31-26-W3	72 N/12	51°38′	109°38′
Dewar Lake	LAKE/LAC	SK	30-26-W3	72 N/12	51°36′	109°37′
Dewar Lakes	LAKE/LAC	NT	Franklin	27 B	68°30′	71°20′
Dewars	UNP/LNO	ON	Renfrew	31 F/8	45°29′	76°29′
Dewberry	VILG/VILG	AB	21-53-4-W4	73 E/10	53°35′	110°32′
Dewdney	UNP/LNO	BC	New Westminster	92 G/1	49°10′	122°12′
Dewdney-Alouette	MUN1/AZM1	BC	New Westminster	92 G/9	49°30′	122°20′
Dewdney Island	ISL/ÎLE	BC	Range 4 Coast	103 A/13	52°59′	129°37′
De Wette	UNP/LNO	YT		105 D/7	60°22′	134°49′
Dewey	UNP/LNO	BC	Cariboo	93 I/4	54°02′	121°43′
Dewey Point	CAPE/CAP	ON	Huron	40 P/5	43°26′	81°43′
De Winton	UNP/LNO	AB	36-21-1-W5	82 J/16	50°49′	114°01′
DeWitts Corners	UNP/LNO	ON	Lanark	31 C/16	44°51′	76°22′
Dewittville	UNP/LNO	QC	Le Haut-Saint-Laurent	31 G/1	45°07′	74°05′
DeWolfe	UNP/LNO	NB	Charlotte	21 G/6	45°20′	67°17′
Dexter	UNP/LNO	ON	Elgin	40 I/11	42°41′	81°08′
Dexterity Fiord	BAY/BAIE	NT	Franklin	37 H/2	71°15′	73°02′
Dexterity Island	ISL/ÎLE	NT	Franklin	37 H	71°36′	72°50′
Dezadeash	UNP/LNO	YT		115 A/6	60°22′	137°03′
Dezadeash Lake	LAKE/LAC	YT		115 A/7	60°28′	136°59′
Dezadeash Range	MTN/MNT	YT		115 A/10	60°42′	136°55′
Dezadeash River	RIV/CDE	YT		115 A/12	60°39′	137°47′
Diable, Cap au	CAPE/CAP	QC	Kamouraska	21 N/12	47°32′	69°56′
Diable, Cape	CAPE/CAP	NF		12 P/10	51°35′	56°42′
Diable, Lac au	LAKE/LAC	QC	Denis-Riverin	22 H/3	49°10′	65°24′
Diable, Rivière du	RIV/CDE	QC	Les Laurentides	31 J/2	46°03′	74°38′
Diamain Lake	LAKE/LAC	YT		115 I/16	62°55′	136°19′
Diamant, Cap	CAPE/CAP	QC	Manicouagan	22 K/2	50°01′	68°47′
Diamant, Cap	CAPE/CAP	QC	Communauté urbaine de Québec	21 L/14	46°48′	71°12′
Diamond	UNP/LNO	NS	Pictou	11 E/11	45°37′	63°00′
Diamond	UNP/LNO	QC	Les Chutes-de-la-Chaudière	21 L/11	46°43′	71°13′
Diamond	UNP/LNO	MB		62 H/14	49°50′	97°25′
Diamond City	UNP/LNO	AB	6-10-21-W4	82 H/15	49°48′	112°51′
Diamond Cove	UNP/LNO	NF		11 O/10	47°37′	58°43′
Diamond Islands	ISL/ÎLE	NT	Franklin	36 A	64°19′	73°56′
Diamond Jenness Peninsula	CAPE/CAP	NT	Franklin	87 E	70°55′	116°00′
Diamond Lake	UNP/LNO	ON	Timiskaming	32 D/4	48°07′	79°45′
Diamond Lake	LAKE/LAC	ON	Nipissing	41 P/1	47°12′	80°15′
Diana	UNP/LNO	SK	4-14-21-W2	72 I/2	50°08′	104°48′
Diana Bay	BAY/BAIE	NT	Franklin	25 C	60°55′	69°55′
Diana Island	ISL/ÎLE	BC	Barclay	92 C/14	48°51′	125°11′
Diana Island	ISL/ÎLE	NT	Franklin	25 C	60°59′	69°58′
Diana, Lac	LAKE/LAC	QC	Kativik	24 K/7	58°23′	68°58′
Diana Lake	LAKE/LAC	NT	Keewatin	55 K	62°58′	92°45′
Dibblee	UNP/LNO	NB	Carleton	21 J/4	46°06′	67°35′
D'Iberville, Lac	LAKE/LAC	QC	Kativik	33 P/14	55°55′	73°15′
D'Iberville, Mont - also-aussi - Caubvick, Mount	MTN/MNT	QC	Kativik	14 L/13	58°53′	63°43′
Dickey Lake	LAKE/LAC	ON	Hastings	31 C/13	44°47′	77°44′
Dickey River	RIV/CDE	ON	Kenora	43 M/13	55°55′	87°57′
Dickie - see-voir - Sea Side	UNP/LNO	NB		21 O/16	47°57′	66°08′
Dickie Mountain	UNP/LNO	NB	Kings	21 H/12	45°38′	65°44′
*Dickinsons Landing	UNP/LNO	ON	Stormont	31 G/2	45°01′	74°56′
Dickins Seamount	SEAU/SMER	—		5.03	54°30′	137°00′
Dickison Lake	LAKE/LAC	ON	Thunder Bay	42 E/3	49°11′	87°19′

NAME NOM	ENTITY ENTITÉ	LOC 1 LIEU 1	LOC 2 LIEU 2	MAP CARTE	POSITION LAT	LONG
Dickson	UNP/LNO	AB	1-36-3-W5	83 B/1	52°03'	114°19'
Dickson Canyon	VALL/VALL	NT	Mackenzie	75 P	63°44'	104°43'
Dickson Hill	UNP/LNO	ON	York	30 M/14	43°57'	79°17'
Dickson Lake	LAKE/LAC	ON	Nipissing	31 E/16	45°47'	78°12'
Dickson Lake	LAKE/LAC	BC	New Westminster	92 G/8	49°19'	122°06'
Dickson Lake	LAKE/LAC	BC	Newcastle	92 F/6	49°24'	125°05'
Dickson Peak	MTN/MNT	BC	Lillooet	92 J/15	50°54'	122°59'
Dicksons Corners	UNP/LNO	ON	Oxford	40 P/2	43°03'	80°57'
Dicksons Hill - see-voir - Dickson Hill	UNP/LNO	ON		30 M/14	43°57'	79°17'
Dickstone	UNP/LNO	MB	66-21-W1	63 K/10	54°44'	100°36'
Didsbury	TOWN/VIL2	AB	18-31-1-W5	82 O/9	51°40'	114°08'
Didyme	UNP/LNO	QC	Maria-Chapdelaine	32 A/15	48°54'	72°40'
Diefenbaker, Lake	LAKE/LAC	SK		72 J/11	50°43'	107°30'
Dieppe	TOWN/VIL2	NB	Westmorland	21 I/2	46°06'	64°45'
Dieppe Lake	LAKE/LAC	NT	Mackenzie	85 F	61°37'	116°31'
Dieppe Place	UNP/LNO	SK		72 I/7	50°27'	104°41'
Dietrichsen Point	CAPE/CAP	NT	Franklin	77 E/16	70°58'	104°10'
Digby	TOWN/VIL2	NS	Digby	21 A/12	44°37'	65°46'
Digby	MUN1/AZM1	NS	Digby	21 A/5	44°22'	65°42'
Digby	GEOG/GÉOG	NS		21 A/5	44°18'	65°48'
Digby Corner	UNP/LNO	NB	Carleton	21 J/5	46°23'	67°46'
Digby Gut	CHAN/CHEN	NS	Digby	21 A/12	44°41'	65°46'
Digby Island	UNP/LNO	BC	Range 5 Coast	103 J/8	54°17'	130°23'
Digby Island	ISL/ÎLE	BC	Range 5 Coast	103 J/8	54°17'	130°25'
Digby Neck	CAPE/CAP	NS	Digby	21 B/8	44°30'	66°05'
Digdeguash	UNP/LNO	NB	Charlotte	21 G/2	45°11'	66°58'
Digdeguash Lake	LAKE/LAC	NB	Charlotte	21 G/2	45°13'	66°55'
Digdeguash River	RIV/CDE	NB	Charlotte	21 G/2	45°09'	66°58'
Digges	UNP/LNO	MB		54 L/9	58°32'	94°08'
Digges Basin	SEAU/SMER	—		1399A	62°45'	78°00'
Digges Islands	ISL/ÎLE	NT	Keewatin	35 K	62°35'	77°50'
Digges Sound	CHAN/CHEN	NT	Keewatin	35 K	62°30'	77°45'
Dihourse, Lac	LAKE/LAC	QC	Kativik	24 A/8	56°26'	64°19'
Dildo	UNP/LNO	NF		1 N/12	47°34'	53°33'
Dildo	UNP/LNO	NF		1 N/12	47°34'	53°33'
Dildo Arm	BAY/BAIE	NF		1 N/12	47°33'	53°34'
Dildo Pond	LAKE/LAC	NF		1 N/5	47°29'	53°33'
Dildo Pond	LAKE/LAC	NF		2 E/7	49°15'	54°53'
Dildo Run	RAP/RAP	NF		2 E/10	49°32'	54°38'
Dildo South - see-voir - South Dildo	UNP/LNO	NF		1 N/12	47°31'	53°33'
Diligent River	UNP/LNO	NS	Cumberland	21 H/8	45°25'	64°27'
Dilke	VILG/VILG	SK	15-22-24-W2	72 I/14	50°52'	105°15'
Dilke	MUN2/AZM2	ON	Rainy River	52 D/9	48°43'	94°16'
Dillabough	UNP/LNO	SK	23-41-6-W2	63 D/10	52°33'	102°46'
Dillberry Lake Provincial Park	PARK/PARC	AB	41,42-1-W4	73 D/9	52°35'	110°02'
Dillon	UNP/LNO	ON	Parry Sound	41 H/8	45°26'	80°19'
Dillon	UNP/LNO	SK		73 N/15	55°56'	108°56'
Dillon Lake	LAKE/LAC	SK	78-23-W3	73 N/11	55°45'	109°30'
Dillon Point	CAPE/CAP	BC	Rupert	92 L/11	50°45'	127°24'
Dillon River	RIV/CDE	SK/AB		73 N/15	55°55'	108°56'
Dill Siding	UNP/LNO	ON	Sudbury	41 I/7	46°25'	80°50'
Dilly Creek	RIV/CDE	BC	Peace River	94 P/13	59°51'	121°50'
Dil-ma-sow 5	IR/RI	BC	Range 3 Coast	103 A/10	52°34'	128°58'
Dimma Lake	LAKE/LAC	NT	Keewatin	65 F	61°36'	100°37'
Dimock Creek	UNP/LNO	QC	Avignon	22 A/4	48°12'	65°55'
Dimsdale	UNP/LNO	AB	10-71-7-W6	83 M/2	55°08'	118°59'
Dina	UNP/LNO	AB	33-45-1-W4	73 D/16	52°56'	110°05'
Dinant	UNP/LNO	AB	12-48-20-W4	83 H/2	53°08'	112°49'
Dînette, La	UNP/LNO	QC	Caniapiscau	23 F/10	53°44'	68°37'
Dingley	UNP/LNO	SK	11-18-12-W2	62 L/12	50°31'	103°33'
Dingman Creek	RIV/CDE	ON	Middlesex	40 I/14	42°55'	81°25'
Dingwall	UNP/LNO	NS	Victoria	11 K/16	46°54'	60°28'
Dingwell	UNP/LNO	PE	Kings	11 L/7	46°25'	62°40'
Dingwells Mills	UNP/LNO	PE	Kings	11 L/8	46°22'	62°27'
Dinner Point Depot	UNP/LNO	ON	Manitoulin	41 H/13	46°00'	81°44'
Dinorwic	UNP/LNO	ON	Kenora	52 F/9	49°41'	92°30'
Dinorwic Lake	LAKE/LAC	ON	Kenora	52 F/10	49°37'	92°33'
Dinosaur	UNP/LNO	AB	10-30-20-W4	82 P/10	51°34'	112°43'
Dinosaur Provincial Park	PARK/PARC	AB	20,21-10,11,12-W4	72 L/13	50°47'	111°30'
Dinosaur Provincial Park World Heritage Site - also-aussi - Parc provincial Dinosaur, Site du patrimoine mondial du	PARK/PARC	AB		72 L/13	50°47'	111°30'
Dinsmore	VILG/VILG	SK	26-27-11-W3	72 O/6	51°20'	107°26'
Dionne, Lac	LAKE/LAC	QC	Manicouagan	22 G/12	49°36'	67°54'
Dipper Harbour East	UNP/LNO	NB	Saint John	21 G/1	45°06'	66°25'
Dipper Harbour West	UNP/LNO	NB	Saint John	21 G/1	45°06'	66°26'
Dipper Lake	LAKE/LAC	SK	80,81-9-W3	73 O/14	55°56'	107°20'

NAME NOM	ENTITY ENTITÉ	LOC 1 LIEU 1	LOC 2 LIEU 2	MAP CARTE	POSITION LAT	LONG
Dipper Rapids 192C	IR/RI	SK		73 O/14	55°57'	107°17'
Dipper Seamount	SEAU/SMER	—		NK23	43°28'	45°15'
Direct Lake	LAKE/LAC	ON	Kenora	52 L/1	50°03'	94°14'
Dirleton	UNP/LNO	ON	Carleton	31 F/8	45°30'	76°09'
Dirom, Mount	MTN/MNT	BC	Cassiar	104 K/13	58°52'	133°30'
Disappointment Lake	LAKE/LAC	NF		13 E/15	53°49'	62°31'
Disappointment Lake	LAKE/LAC	AB	120-5-W4	74 M/7	59°25'	110°47'
Disappointment Lake	LAKE/LAC	NT	Mackenzie	75 D	60°05'	110°27'
Discovery	UNP/LNO	NT	Mackenzie	85 P	63°11'	113°54'
Discovery, Cape	CAPE/CAP	NT	Franklin	340 E	83°00'	77°24'
Discovery Harbour	BAY/BAIE	NT	Franklin	120 C	81°42'	65°20'
Discovery Island	ISL/ÎLE	BC	Victoria	92 B/6	48°25'	123°14'
Discovery Island 3	IR/RI	BC	Victoria	92 B/6	48°26'	123°14'
Discovery Mountain	MTN/MNT	NT	Franklin	59 B	76°33'	93°20'
Discovery Passage	CHAN/CHEN	BC	Sayward	92 K/3	50°10'	125°21'
Discovery Point	CAPE/CAP	NT	Franklin	89 C	77°02'	120°00'
Dishnish	UNP/LNO	ON	Algoma	42 B/13	48°51'	83°43'
Disley	VILG/VILG	SK	30-19-22-W2	72 I/11	50°38'	105°03'
Dismal Creek	RIV/CDE	AB	47-11-W5	83 G/4	53°05'	115°34'
Dismal Lakes	LAKE/LAC	NT	Mackenzie	86 N	67°26'	117°07'
Disraeli	CITY/VIL1	QC	L'Amiante	21 E/14	45°54'	71°21'
Disraeli	VILG/VILG	QC	L'Amiante	21 E/14	45°55'	71°22'
Disraeli Fiord	BAY/BAIE	NT	Franklin	340 E	82°49'	73°21'
Disraeli Glacier	GLAC/GLAC	NT	Franklin	340 E	82°40'	72°28'
Diss	UNP/LNO	AB	7-48-20-W5	83 F/2	53°08'	116°55'
Dissection River	RIV/CDE	NT	Franklin	88 C/5	73°15'	119°36'
Dissimieux, Lac	LAKE/LAC	QC	La Haute-Côte-Nord	22 F/13	49°52'	69°48'
Ditchfield	UNP/LNO	QC	Le Granit	21 E/10	45°33'	70°50'
Ditton	VILG/VILG	QC	Le Haut-Saint-François	21 E/6	45°25'	71°15'
Ditton Park	UNP/LNO	SK	4-48-13-W2	63 E/4	53°06'	103°50'
Diver	UNP/LNO	ON	Nipissing	31 L/12	46°43'	79°30'
Diversion Lake	LAKE/LAC	NF		2 D/13	48°49'	55°53'
Divide	UNP/LNO	NB	Carleton	21 J/11	46°33'	67°20'
Divide	UNP/LNO	SK	27-2-24-W3	72 F/3	49°09'	109°08'
Dixie	UNP/LNO	ON	Ontario	30 M/14	43°52'	79°07'
Dixie	UNP/LNO	ON	Peel	30 M/12	43°36'	79°36'
Dix Milles, Lac	LAKE/LAC	QC	Pontiac	31 K/13	46°47'	77°45'
Dix Milles, Lac des	LAKE/LAC	QC	Le Haut-Saint-Maurice	31 O/15	47°54'	74°49'
Dixon	UNP/LNO	ON	Stormont	31 G/2	45°05'	74°59'
Dixon	UNP/LNO	SK	28-37-23-W2	73 A/3	52°12'	105°13'
Dixon Entrance	CHAN/CHEN	BC	Queen Charlotte	103 K/1	54°25'	132°00'
Dixon Island	ISL/ÎLE	NT	Franklin	67 H	71°40'	96°52'
Dixons Corners	UNP/LNO	ON	Dundas	31 B/14	44°55'	75°21'
Dixonville	UNP/LNO	AB	13-87-24-W5	84 C/12	56°32'	117°40'
Dixville	VILG/VILG	QC	Coaticook	21 E/4	45°04'	71°46'
Dizzy Creek	RIV/CDE	AB	122-19-W5	84 N/11	59°37'	117°09'
Dlah Koh 31	IR/RI	BC	Cassiar	93 N/3	55°02'	125°06'
Dneiper	UNP/LNO	SK	27-28-2-W2	62 M/8	51°27'	102°12'
Doak Settlement	UNP/LNO	NB	York	21 G/15	45°54'	66°38'
Doaktown	VILG/VILG	NB	Northumberland	21 J/9	46°33'	66°08'
Doan	UNP/LNO	AB	34-34-1-W5	82 O/16	51°58'	114°03'
Dobbin Bay	BAY/BAIE	NT	Franklin	39 H	79°45'	73°45'
Dobbinton	UNP/LNO	ON	Bruce	41 A/6	44°23'	81°08'
Dobbs, Cape	CAPE/CAP	NT	Keewatin	46 E	65°14'	87°00'
Dobie	UNP/LNO	ON	Timiskaming	32 D/4	48°08'	79°49'
Dobie Lake	LAKE/LAC	ON	Kenora	52 O/6	51°27'	91°03'
Dobie River	RIV/CDE	ON	Kenora	52 O/9	51°41'	90°29'
Dobsons Corner	UNP/LNO	NB	Westmorland	21 I/3	46°02'	65°13'
Dochsupple 3	IR/RI	BC	Barclay	92 C/14	48°53'	125°03'
Dock	UNP/LNO	MB	4-12-11-W	62 G/15	49°59'	98°55'
Dock Corner	UNP/LNO	PE	Prince	21 I/16	46°49'	64°05'
Dock Cove	UNP/LNO	NF		2 C/13	48°52'	53°38'
Dock, Le	UNP/LNO	QC	Minganie	22 I/7	50°16'	64°41'
Dockmure	UNP/LNO	ON	Parry Sound	31 E/5	45°18'	79°58'
Dock Siding	UNP/LNO	ON	Parry Sound	31 E/4	45°11'	79°47'
Doctor Island	ISL/ÎLE	NT	Franklin	25 E	61°40'	71°35'
Doctors Brook	UNP/LNO	NS	Antigonish	11 E/16	45°46'	62°08'
Doctors Cove	UNP/LNO	NS	Shelburne	20 P/12	43°31'	65°38'
Doctors Harbour	UNP/LNO	NF		1 M/11	47°40'	55°19'
Doctors Harbour	UNP/LNO	NF		11 P/12	47°38'	57°46'
Doda, Lac	LAKE/LAC	QC	Jamésie	32 G/6	49°25'	75°13'
Dodd Creek	RIV/CDE	ON	Elgin	40 I/14	42°47'	81°13'
Dodd Island	ISL/ÎLE	BC	Barclay	92 C/14	48°55'	125°20'
Dodd Lake	LAKE/LAC	BC	New Westminster	92 F/16	49°58'	124°18'
Doddridge	UNP/LNO	NS	Hants	11 E/4	45°13'	63°38'

NAME NOM	ENTITY ENTITÉ	LOC 1 LIEU 1	LOC 2 LIEU 2	MAP CARTE	POSITION LAT	LONG
Dodds	UNP/LNO	QC	Les Collines-de-l'Outaouais	31 G/12	45°44′	75°36′
Dodds	UNP/LNO	AB	15-49-18-W4	83 H/2	53°13′	112°33′
Dodge Lake	LAKE/LAC	SK		74 P/13	59°50′	105°36′
Dodge River	RIV/CDE	NT	Franklin	120 C	81°31′	68°40′
Dodier, Lac	LAKE/LAC	QC	La Haute-Côte-Nord	22 F/11	49°33′	69°24′
Dodsland	VILG/VILG	SK	6-33-20-W3	72 N/15	51°48′	108°49′
Doe Lake	UNP/LNO	ON	Parry Sound	31 E/11	45°33′	79°26′
Doe Lake	LAKE/LAC	ON	Parry Sound	31 E/11	45°32′	79°24′
Doe River	UNP/LNO	BC	Peace River	93 P/16	56°00′	120°05′
Dog Bay	BAY/BAIE	NF		2 E/7	49°30′	54°30′
Dog Bay Islands	ISL/ÎLE	NF		2 E/9	49°32′	54°25′
Dog Bay Point	CAPE/CAP	NF		2 E/8	49°29′	54°27′
Dog, Cape	CAPE/CAP	NF		1 N/4	47°05′	53°42′
Dog Cove	UNP/LNO	NF		11 P/11	47°37′	57°08′
Dog Creek	UNP/LNO	MB	22-9-W	62 J/15	50°55′	98°36′
Dog Creek	UNP/LNO	BC	Cariboo	93 B/1	52°06′	122°08′
Dog Creek	UNP/LNO	BC	Lillooet	92 O/9	51°35′	122°14′
Dog Creek	UNP/LNO	BC	Range 5 Coast	93 K/8	54°17′	124°16′
Dog Creek	RIV/CDE	BC	Kootenay	82 E/8	49°26′	118°06′
Dog Creek	RIV/CDE	BC	Lillooet	92 O/9	51°35′	122°18′
Dog Creek 1	IR/RI	BC	Lillooet	92 O/9	51°35′	122°13′
Dog Creek 2	IR/RI	BC	Lillooet	92 O/9	51°36′	122°05′
Dog Creek 3	IR/RI	BC	Lillooet	92 O/9	51°37′	122°04′
Dog Creek 4	IR/RI	BC	Lillooet	92 O/9	51°36′	122°18′
Dog Creek 46	IR/RI	MB		62 J/15	50°55′	98°34′
Dogface Lake	LAKE/LAC	NT	Mackenzie	85 D	60°17′	119°06′
Dog Falls	FALL/CHUT	ON	Thunder Bay	52 A/12	48°40′	89°36′
Dogfish Bay 42	IR/RI	BC	Cassiar	103 O/1	55°04′	130°08′
Dog Head 218	IR/RI	AB	7-112-7-W4	74 L/11	58°42′	111°11′
Doghide River	RIV/CDE	SK	35-46-14-W2	73 H/1	53°01′	104°04′
Dog Island	ISL/ÎLE	NF		14 C/11	56°38′	61°10′
Dog Island	ISL/ÎLE	MB		63 C/15	52°48′	100°43′
Dog Islands	ISL/ÎLE	NF		13 J/15	54°52′	58°40′
Dog Lake	LAKE/LAC	ON	Algoma	42 C/8	48°17′	84°08′
Dog Lake	LAKE/LAC	ON	Thunder Bay	52 A/12	48°46′	89°32′
Dog Lake	LAKE/LAC	MB	7,18-14-5-W	62 J/1	50°11′	98°08′
Dog Lake	LAKE/LAC	MB	23-7,8,9-W	62 O/2	51°01′	98°31′
Dogpaw Lake	LAKE/LAC	ON	Kenora	52 F/5	49°23′	93°53′
Dogpound	UNP/LNO	AB	5-29-3-W5	82 O/8	51°28′	114°24′
Dogpound Creek	RIV/CDE	AB	9-33-3-W5	82 O/16	51°48′	114°22′
Dog River	RIV/CDE	ON	Algoma	41 N/14	47°58′	85°12′
Dog River	RIV/CDE	ON	Thunder Bay	52 A/13	48°51′	89°37′
Dogskin Lake	LAKE/LAC	MB		52 M/11	51°43′	95°12′
Dogskin River	RIV/CDE	MB		52 M/14	51°56′	95°24′
Dogs Nest	UNP/LNO	ON	Norfolk	40 I/16	42°48′	80°10′
Dogtooth Lake	LAKE/LAC	ON	Kenora	52 E/9	49°43′	94°11′
Dog (University) River - see-voir - Dog River	RIV/CDE	ON		41 N/14	47°58′	85°12′
Dogwood	UNP/LNO	NF		12 A/13	48°57′	57°50′
Dogwood Valley	UNP/LNO	BC	Yale Division Yale	92 H/6	49°29′	121°25′
Doheny	UNP/LNO	QC	Mékinac	31 P/2	47°04′	72°36′
Doherty	UNP/LNO	QC	Pontiac	31 F/9	45°39′	76°20′
Doherty	UNP/LNO	ON	Nipissing	31 L/3	46°58′	79°44′
Doidge Bay	BAY/BAIE	NT	Franklin	120 F	82°59′	68°45′
Doig River	RIV/CDE	BC/AB		94 A/7	56°25′	120°39′
Doig River 206	IR/RI	BC	Peace River	94 A/9	56°34′	120°30′
Dokie	UNP/LNO	BC	Peace River	93 P/12	55°39′	121°43′
Dokie Siding	UNP/LNO	BC	Peace River	93 P/12	55°39′	121°44′
Dokis	UNP/LNO	ON	Parry Sound	41 I/1	46°08′	80°02′
Dokis 9	IR/RI	ON	Parry Sound	41 I/1	46°04′	80°03′
Dokis Point	CAPE/CAP	ON	Nipissing	31 L/5	46°18′	79°51′
Dolbeau	CITY/VIL1	QC	Maria-Chapdelaine	32 A/16	48°53′	72°14′
Dolbel, Lac	LAKE/LAC	QC	Minganie	22 P/11	51°33′	65°06′
Dolby Lake	LAKE/LAC	NT	Mackenzie	65 E	61°28′	103°48′
Dolland Bight	BAY/BAIE	NF		1 M/12	47°44′	55°50′
Dolland Brook	RIV/CDE	NF		11 P/10	47°44′	56°35′
Dolland Pond	LAKE/LAC	NF		12 A/1	48°00′	56°30′
Dollard	VILG/VILG	SK	1-8-20-W3	72 F/10	49°37′	108°35′
Dollard-des-Ormeaux	CITY/VIL1	QC	Communauté urbaine de Montréal	31 H/5	45°29′	73°49′
Dollard, Lac	LAKE/LAC	QC	Sept-Rivières	22 J/15	50°48′	66°36′
Dollar Lake	LAKE/LAC	NS	Halifax	11 D/14	44°55′	63°19′
Dollars Lake	LAKE/LAC	ON	Parry Sound	41 H/16	45°56′	80°13′
Dollarton	UNP/LNO	BC	New Westminster	92 G/7	49°19′	122°57′
Dolly Bay	UNP/LNO	MB	4-25-9-W	62 O/2	51°08′	98°40′
Dolly Bay	BAY/BAIE	MB		62 O/2	51°07′	98°42′
Dolphin and Union Strait	CHAN/CHEN	NT	Mackenzie	87 C	69°08′	116°00′

NAME NOM	ENTITY ENTITÉ	LOC 1 LIEU 1	LOC 2 LIEU 2	MAP CARTE	POSITION	
					LAT	LONG
Dolphin Beach	UNP/LNO	BC	Nanoose	92 F/8	49°18′	124°09′
Dolphin Island	ISL/ÎLE	BC	Range 4 Coast	103 G/16	53°47′	130°26′
Dolphin Island 1	IR/RI	BC	Range 4 Coast	103 G/16	53°47′	130°26′
Dolu, Lac	LAKE/LAC	QC	Caniapiscau	23 K/15	54°45′	68°54′
Domagaya Lake	LAKE/LAC	NF		22 P/15	51°53′	64°38′
Domain	UNP/LNO	MB	31-7-2-E	62 H/11	49°37′	97°19′
Domaine-à-Martin	UNP/LNO	QC	Vaudreuil-Soulanges	31 G/8	45°27′	74°21′
Domaine-Bastien	UNP/LNO	QC	Les Pays-d'en-Haut	31 G/16	45°57′	74°17′
Domaine-Beauchesne	UNP/LNO	QC	Maskinongé	31 I/6	46°29′	73°16′
Domaine-Beaumont	UNP/LNO	QC	Deux-Montagnes	31 G/9	45°31′	74°06′
Domaine-Belle-Rivière	UNP/LNO	QC	Les Laurentides	31 J/1	46°09′	74°29′
Domaine-Brunet	UNP/LNO	QC	Vaudreuil-Soulanges	31 G/8	45°27′	74°20′
Domaine-Cloutier	UNP/LNO	QC	La Rivière-du-Nord	31 G/16	45°45′	74°04′
Domaine-Condor	UNP/LNO	QC	Asbestos	21 E/13	45°46′	71°52′
Domaine-de-la-Châtelaine	UNP/LNO	QC	Les Pays-d'en-Haut	31 G/16	45°56′	74°20′
Domaine-de-la-Halte	UNP/LNO	QC	Arthabaska	21 E/13	45°56′	71°47′
Domaine-de-la-Petite-Coulée	UNP/LNO	QC	Arthabaska	31 H/16	45°57′	72°14′
Domaine-des-Lacs-Boisés	UNP/LNO	QC	Les Pays-d'en-Haut	31 J/1	46°00′	74°20′
Domaine-des-Pins	UNP/LNO	QC	L'Amiante	21 E/14	45°57′	71°22′
Domaine-des-Pyramides	UNP/LNO	QC	Les Laurentides	31 J/1	46°09′	74°25′
Domaine-Desrosiers	UNP/LNO	QC	Les Laurentides	31 J/1	46°06′	74°07′
Domaine-des-Sapins	UNP/LNO	QC	Asbestos	21 E/13	45°48′	71°51′
Domaine-des-Sources	UNP/LNO	QC	La Rivière-du-Nord	31 G/16	45°45′	74°05′
Domaine-du-Lac-des-Cyprès	UNP/LNO	QC	Arthabaska	31 H/16	45°57′	72°12′
Domaine-Entrelacs	UNP/LNO	QC	Matawinie	31 J/1	46°06′	74°01′
Domaine-Filion	UNP/LNO	QC	Les Pays-d'en-Haut	31 G/16	45°55′	74°11′
Domaine-Fortier	UNP/LNO	QC	La Rivière-du-Nord	31 G/16	45°46′	74°08′
Domaine-Francoeur	UNP/LNO	QC	Drummond	31 H/16	45°48′	72°15′
Domaine-Frontiersman	UNP/LNO	QC	Jamésie	32 G/16	49°52′	74°25′
Domaine-Gaybois	UNP/LNO	QC	Drummond	31 H/16	45°49′	72°15′
Domaine-Grenon	UNP/LNO	QC	Argenteuil	31 G/16	45°46′	74°13′
Domaine-Guindon	UNP/LNO	QC	Les Laurentides	31 J/1	46°05′	74°18′
Domaine, Le	UNP/LNO	QC	Nicolet-Yamaska	31 I/2	46°14′	72°39′
Domaine, Le	UNP/LNO	QC	Maskinongé	31 I/2	46°13′	72°55′
Domaine-Lemieux	UNP/LNO	QC	Arthabaska	31 H/16	45°52′	72°07′
Domaine-Lemire	UNP/LNO	QC	Drummond	31 H/16	45°53′	72°22′
Domaine-Malard	UNP/LNO	QC	L'Érable	21 L/4	46°12′	71°33′
Domaine-Mont-Blanc	UNP/LNO	QC	Les Laurentides	31 G/16	45°57′	74°26′
Domaine-Parent	UNP/LNO	QC	Arthabaska	31 H/16	45°53′	72°14′
Domaine-Parent	UNP/LNO	QC	Les Pays-d'en-Haut	31 G/16	45°50′	74°07′
Domaine-Pharand	UNP/LNO	QC	Vaudreuil-Soulanges	31 G/8	45°18′	74°11′
Domaine-Philippe	UNP/LNO	QC	Le Domaine-du-Roy	32 A/9	48°35′	72°16′
Domaine-Roger	UNP/LNO	QC	Les Laurentides	31 J/1	46°08′	74°29′
Dome	UNP/LNO	ON	Cochrane	42 A/6	48°28′	81°15′
Dome Bay	BAY/BAIE	NT	Franklin	69 F	78°18′	103°16′
Dome Creek	UNP/LNO	BC	Cariboo	93 H/11	53°45′	121°02′
Dome Extension	UNP/LNO	ON	Cochrane	42 A/6	48°28′	81°14′
Dôme, Mont	MTN/MNT	QC	Jamésie	32 K/9	50°37′	76°27′
Dome Mountain	MTN/MNT	BC	Range 5 Coast	93 L/10	54°45′	126°39′
Domett Point	CAPE/CAP	NT	Franklin	79 A/3	76°04′	106°39′
Domex	UNP/LNO	SK	20-4-5-W2	62 E/7	49°19′	102°39′
Dominion	UNP/LNO	NS	Cape Breton	11 K/1	46°13′	60°01′
Dominion	UNP/LNO	YT		115 O/10	63°40′	138°39′
Dominion, Cape	CAPE/CAP	NT	Franklin	36 J	66°10′	74°28′
Dominion City	UNP/LNO	MB	20-2-3-E	62 H/3	49°09′	97°09′
Dominion Heights	UNP/LNO	SK		72 I/7	50°26′	104°34′
Dominion Lake	LAKE/LAC	NF		13 C/12	52°40′	61°45′
Dominion Mountain	MTN/MNT	BC	Kamloops Division Yale	83 D/7	52°26′	118°57′
Dominion Point	CAPE/CAP	ON	Manitoulin	41 G/9	45°42′	82°26′
Dominionville	UNP/LNO	ON	Glengarry	31 G/7	45°16′	74°50′
Domino	UNP/LNO	NF		3 E/5	53°27′	55°45′
Domremy	VILG/VILG	SK	17-44-26-W2	73 A/13	52°47′	105°44′
Domville	UNP/LNO	ON	Grenville	31 B/13	44°46′	75°33′
Donagh	UNP/LNO	PE	Queens	11 L/7	46°16′	62°57′
Donahue Lake	LAKE/LAC	NS	Guysborough	11 F/6	45°18′	61°30′
Donald	UNP/LNO	ON	Haliburton	31 D/15	44°59′	78°32′
Donald	UNP/LNO	BC	Kootenay	82 N/6	51°30′	117°10′
Donalda	VILG/VILG	AB	6-42-18-W4	83 A/10	52°35′	112°34′
Donald Gunn	UNP/LNO	SK	17-29-5-W2	62 M/10	51°31′	102°40′
Donald Lake	LAKE/LAC	ON	Kenora	52 M/2	51°02′	94°55′
Donald Landing	UNP/LNO	BC	Range 5 Coast	93 K/5	54°29′	125°39′
Donaldson	UNP/LNO	ON	Frontenac	31 C/15	44°59′	76°44′
Donaldson, Mount	MTN/MNT	BC	New Westminster	92 G/11	49°43′	123°27′
Donaldston	UNP/LNO	PE	Queens	11 L/6	46°21′	63°00′
Donatville	UNP/LNO	AB	33-66-19-W4	83 I/10	54°45′	112°48′

NAME / NOM	ENTITY / ENTITÉ	LOC 1 / LIEU 1	LOC 2 / LIEU 2	MAP / CARTE	POSITION LAT	POSITION LONG
Donavon	UNP/LNO	SK	6-33-8-W3	72 O/14	51°48'	107°08'
Doncaster 17	IR/RI	QC	Les Laurentides	31 J/1	46°09'	74°07'
Doncrest	UNP/LNO	SK	42-6-W2	63 D/10	52°37'	102°46'
Donegal	UNP/LNO	NB	Kings	21 H/11	45°42'	65°16'
Donegal	UNP/LNO	ON	Renfrew	31 F/11	45°30'	77°09'
Donegal	UNP/LNO	ON	Perth	40 P/10	43°37'	80°57'
Donegal	UNP/LNO	SK	2-38-25-W3	73 C/3	52°14'	109°28'
Donegal Head	CAPE/CAP	BC	Rupert	92 L/10	50°38'	126°49'
Dongola	UNP/LNO	ON	Victoria	31 D/10	44°44'	78°46'
Donjek Glacier	GLAC/GLAC	YT		115 G/4	61°04'	139°43'
Donjek River	RIV/CDE	YT		115 J/12	62°36'	140°00'
Donkin	UNP/LNO	NS	Cape Breton	11 J/4	46°11'	59°52'
Don Lita	UNP/LNO	ON	Sudbury	41 I/10	46°31'	80°55'
Don Mills	UNP/LNO	ON	York	30 M/11	43°44'	79°20'
Donnacona	CITY/VIL1	QC	Portneuf	21 L/12	46°40'	71°45'
Donnegana Lake	LAKE/LAC	ON	Sudbury	41 P/5	47°22'	81°35'
Donnelly	VILG/VILG	AB	78-20,21-W5	83 N/11	55°44'	117°06'
Donnelly River	RIV/CDE	NT	Mackenzie	106 H/15	65°50'	128°51'
Donnelly Settlement	UNP/LNO	NB	York	21 G/14	45°50'	67°02'
Donnely Landing	UNP/LNO	BC	New Westminster	92 F/9	49°37'	124°02'
Donner Lake	LAKE/LAC	BC	Nootka	92 F/12	49°43'	125°54'
Donnybrook	UNP/LNO	ON	Huron	40 P/14	43°50'	81°29'
Donohue	UNP/LNO	QC	La Côte-de-Beaupré	21 M/2	47°03'	70°53'
Donovans	UNP/LNO	NF		1 N/10	47°32'	52°50'
Don Peninsula	CAPE/CAP	BC	Range 3 Coast	103 A/8	52°30'	128°10'
Donquan, Lac - also-aussi - Donquan Lake	LAKE/LAC	QC	Minganie	13 C/1	52°00'	60°15'
Donquan Lake - also-aussi - Donquan, Lac	LAKE/LAC	NF		13 C/1	52°00'	60°15'
Don Vale	UNP/LNO	ON	York	30 M/11	43°40'	79°22'
Donwell	UNP/LNO	SK	27-29-3-W2	62 M/9	51°32'	102°21'
Donwood	UNP/LNO	ON	Peterborough	31 D/8	44°19'	78°18'
Doobah 10	IR/RI	BC	Renfrew	92 C/10	48°44'	124°44'
Dookqua 5	IR/RI	BC	Clayoquot	92 C/13	48°55'	125°31'
Dookqua 5A - see-voir - Stuart Bay 6	IR/RI	BC		92 C/13	48°56'	125°31'
Doolittle, Lac	LAKE/LAC	QC	Pontiac	31 K/10	46°41'	76°48'
Doon	UNP/LNO	ON	Waterloo	40 P/8	43°23'	80°26'
Doonside	UNP/LNO	SK	16-11-32-W	62 F/13	49°55'	101°49'
Doran Creek	RIV/CDE	BC	Range 2 Coast	92 N/7	51°19'	124°49'
Doran Lake	LAKE/LAC	ON	Thunder Bay	52 J/15	50°58'	90°35'
Doran Lake	LAKE/LAC	BC	Clayoquot	92 F/6	49°19'	125°17'
Doran Lake	LAKE/LAC	NT	Mackenzie	75 F	61°13'	108°06'
Dorcas Bay	BAY/BAIE	ON	Bruce	41 H/4	45°11'	81°35'
Dorchester	VILG/VILG	NB	Westmorland	21 H/15	45°54'	64°31'
Dorchester	UNP/LNO	ON	Middlesex	40 I/14	42°59'	81°04'
Dorchester	GEOG/GÉOG	NB	Westmorland	21 H/15	45°58'	64°35'
Dorchester Bay	BAY/BAIE	NT	Franklin	36 F	65°25'	77°03'
Dorchester Cape	UNP/LNO	NB	Westmorland	21 H/15	45°52'	64°32'
Dorchester, Cape	CAPE/CAP	NT	Franklin	36 F	65°27'	77°27'
Dorea	UNP/LNO	QC	Le Haut-Saint-Laurent	31 H/4	45°00'	73°55'
Doré, Baie du	BAY/BAIE	ON	Bruce	41 A/5	44°20'	81°34'
Doré Bay	UNP/LNO	ON	Renfrew	31 F/11	45°39'	77°13'
Dore Lake	HAM/HAM	SK	14-65-10-W3	73 J/11	54°38'	107°24'
Doré, Lake	LAKE/LAC	ON	Renfrew	31 F/11	45°37'	77°07'
Doré Lake	LAKE/LAC	SK		73 J/14	54°46'	107°17'
Dorenlee	UNP/LNO	AB	14-43-21-W4	83 A/10	52°42'	112°57'
Doré River	RIV/CDE	SK		73 J/13	54°56'	107°45'
Dorés, Lac aux	LAKE/LAC	QC	Jamésie	32 G/16	49°52'	74°20'
Dorintosh	VILG/VILG	SK	9,10,15,16-62-18-W3	73 K/7	54°22'	108°38'
Dorion	MUN2/AZM2	ON	Thunder Bay	52 A/15	48°47'	88°39'
Dorion	UNP/LNO	ON	Thunder Bay	52 A/15	48°47'	88°32'
Dorion Landing	UNP/LNO	ON	Thunder Bay	52 A/15	48°47'	88°32'
Doris	UNP/LNO	AB	10-63-5-W5	83 J/7	54°27'	114°39'
Doriston	UNP/LNO	BC	New Westminster	92 G/12	49°43'	123°53'
Dorking	UNP/LNO	ON	Waterloo	40 P/10	43°38'	80°45'
Dorland	UNP/LNO	ON	Lennox and Addington	31 C/3	44°05'	77°01'
Dorland	UNP/LNO	ON	Oxford	40 P/2	43°07'	80°48'
Dornie	UNP/LNO	ON	Glengarry	31 G/7	45°19'	74°43'
Dornoch	UNP/LNO	ON	Grey	41 A/7	44°18'	80°51'
Dorn Ridge	UNP/LNO	NB	York	21 J/2	46°08'	66°56'
Dorothy	UNP/LNO	AB	4-27-17-W4	82 P/8	51°18'	112°19'
Dorothy Creek	RIV/CDE	BC	Range 2 Coast	92 N/5	51°25'	125°40'
Dorothy Lake	UNP/LNO	MB	14-13-E	52 L/4	50°10'	95°44'
Dorothy Lake	LAKE/LAC	MB	14-13-E	52 L/4	50°10'	95°45'
Dorothy Lake	LAKE/LAC	BC	Lillooet	92 O/4	51°12'	123°55'
Dorreen	UNP/LNO	BC	Range 5 Coast	103 I/16	54°50'	128°21'
Dorrington Hill	UNP/LNO	NB	York	21 G/14	45°56'	67°26'

NAME NOM	ENTITY ENTITÉ	LOC 1 LIEU 1	LOC 2 LIEU 2	MAP CARTE	POSITION LAT	LONG
Dorscheid	UNP/LNO	AB	5-67-4-W6	83 L/15	54°46′	118°35′
Dorset	UNP/LNO	ON	Haliburton	31 E/2	45°14′	78°54′
Dorset Park	UNP/LNO	ON	York	30 M/14	43°45′	79°17′
Dorset Park	UNP/LNO	ON	Halton	30 M/12	43°32′	79°53′
Dorts Cove	UNP/LNO	NS	Guysborough	11 F/6	45°21′	61°27′
Dorval	CITY/VIL1	QC	Communauté urbaine de Montréal	31 H/5	45°27′	73°45′
Dorval-Lodge	UNP/LNO	QC	Vallée-de-l'Or	31 N/6	47°27′	77°05′
Dorwin, Chutes	FALL/CHUT	QC	Matawinie	31 I/4	46°02′	73°42′
Dos-d'Âne, Le	UNP/LNO	QC	Pabok	22 A/7	48°27′	64°48′
Dosquet	UNP/LNO	QC	Lotbinière	21 L/5	46°28′	71°32′
Dot	UNP/LNO	BC	Kamloops Division Yale	92 I/3	50°14′	121°06′
Doting Cove	UNP/LNO	NF		2 F/5	49°27′	53°57′
Double Island	ISL/ÎLE	NF		13 I/11	54°32′	57°13′
Double Island	ISL/ÎLE	NF		13 J/16	54°52′	58°23′
Double, Lac	LAKE/LAC	QC	Le Fjord-du-Saguenay	22 L/16	50°48′	70°24′
Double Mer	BAY/BAIE	NF		13 J/3	54°04′	59°10′
Doucet Lake	LAKE/LAC	NT	Mackenzie	75 E	61°41′	111°30′
Doucetteville	UNP/LNO	NS	Digby	21 A/5	44°27′	65°49′
Doughfig Point	CAPE/CAP	NF		2 C/6	48°24′	53°07′
Douglas	UNP/LNO	NB	York	21 G/15	45°59′	66°44′
Douglas	UNP/LNO	ON	Renfrew	31 F/10	45°31′	76°56′
Douglas	UNP/LNO	MB	3-11-17-W	62 G/13	49°54′	99°43′
Douglas	UNP/LNO	BC	New Westminster	92 G/2	49°00′	122°44′
Douglas	GEOG/GÉOG	NB	York	21 J/7	46°15′	66°55′
Douglas 8	IR/RI	BC	New Westminster	92 G/16	49°45′	122°10′
Douglas Bay	BAY/BAIE	NT	Franklin	67 A	68°32′	97°00′
Douglas Bay	BAY/BAIE	NT	Mackenzie	96 I	66°06′	121°32′
Douglas Channel	CHAN/CHEN	BC	Range 4 Coast	103 H/6	53°37′	129°12′
Douglas Creek	RIV/CDE	BC	New Westminster	92 G/16	49°46′	122°09′
Douglasfield	UNP/LNO	NB	Northumberland	21 I/14	46°59′	65°29′
Douglas Harbour	UNP/LNO	NB	Queens	21 G/16	45°55′	66°06′
Douglas Harbour	BAY/BAIE	NT	Franklin	35 H	61°55′	72°38′
Douglas Harbour	BAY/BAIE	NT	Keewatin	56 H	65°39′	88°40′
Douglas Island	ISL/ÎLE	NT	Franklin	87 A	68°28′	113°29′
Douglas Lake	UNP/LNO	BC	Kamloops Division Yale	92 I/1	50°10′	120°12′
Douglas Lake	LAKE/LAC	BC	Kamloops Division Yale	92 I/1	50°09′	120°14′
Douglas Lake	LAKE/LAC	NT	Mackenzie	75 O	63°19′	107°15′
Douglas Lake 3	IR/RI	BC	Kamloops Division Yale	92 I/1	50°10′	120°15′
Douglas Land District	GEOG/GÉOG	BC		92 F	49°04′	124°02′
Douglas No. 436	MUN2/AZM2	SK		73 B/13	52°50′	107°45′
Douglas Peninsula	CAPE/CAP	NT	Mackenzie	75 L	62°43′	110°10′
Douglas Place	UNP/LNO	SK		72 I/7	50°26′	104°35′
Douglas Point	CAPE/CAP	ON	Bruce	41 A/5	44°19′	81°37′
Douglas River	RIV/CDE	AB/SK		74 L/8	58°23′	110°02′
Douglas Road	UNP/LNO	NS	Annapolis	21 A/14	44°58′	65°08′
Douglaston	UNP/LNO	SK	20-5-3-W2	62 E/8	49°24′	102°24′
Douglastown	UNP/LNO	NB	Northumberland	21 P/4	47°02′	65°30′
Douglastown	UNP/LNO	QC	La Côte-de-Gaspé	22 A/16	48°46′	64°23′
Douglastown	UNP/LNO	ON	Welland	30 L/14	42°58′	79°01′
Doumic, Lac	LAKE/LAC	QC	Le Fjord-du-Saguenay	22 D/10	48°44′	70°38′
Douro	MUN2/AZM2	ON	Peterborough	31 D/8	44°24′	78°13′
Douro	UNP/LNO	ON	Peterborough	31 D/8	44°23′	78°12′
Douro Range	MTN/MNT	NT	Franklin	59 B	76°20′	92°44′
Douville	UNP/LNO	QC	Les Maskoutains	31 H/10	45°36′	72°59′
Douze, Le	UNP/LNO	QC	Pabok	22 A/7	48°19′	64°55′
Dove Brook	UNP/LNO	NF		13 H/11	53°39′	57°26′
Dove Island 12	IR/RI	BC	Range 1 Coast	92 L/14	50°56′	127°09′
Dover	TOWN/VIL2	NF		2 C/13	48°52′	53°58′
Dover	VILG/VILG	NS	Guysborough	11 F/6	45°17′	61°03′
Dover	MUN2/AZM2	ON	Kent	40 J/8	42°25′	82°21′
Dover	UNP/LNO	PE	Kings	11 L/2	46°01′	62°39′
Dover	UNP/LNO	NB	Westmorland	21 I/2	46°00′	64°42′
Dover Bay	BAY/BAIE	NS	Guysborough	11 F/6	45°16′	61°01′
Dover Centre	UNP/LNO	ON	Kent	40 J/8	42°29′	82°19′
Dovercourt	UNP/LNO	AB	6-38-6-W5	83 B/2	52°15′	114°51′
Dover Heights	UNP/LNO	ON	Stormont	31 G/2	45°01′	74°45′
Dover Hill	UNP/LNO	NB	Victoria	21 J/12	46°37′	67°45′
Dover Island	ISL/ÎLE	NS	Guysborough	11 F/3	45°14′	61°03′
Dover Island	ISL/ÎLE	NS	Halifax	11 D/5	44°29′	63°52′
Dovetail Lake	LAKE/LAC	ON	Rainy River	52 C/16	48°53′	92°02′
Dowager Island	ISL/ÎLE	BC	Range 3 Coast	103 A/8	52°25′	128°22′
Dowdell Point	CAPE/CAP	NT	Mackenzie	86 L/1	66°01′	118°09′
Dowling	UNP/LNO	ON	Sudbury	41 I/11	46°35′	81°20′
Dowling	UNP/LNO	AB	25-32-15-W4	72 M/13	51°47′	112°00′
Dowling Lake	UNP/LNO	AB	34-32-16-W4	82 P/16	51°47′	112°11′

NAME NOM	ENTITY ENTITÉ	LOC 1 LIEU 1	LOC 2 LIEU 2	MAP CARTE	POSITION LAT	LONG
Dowling Lake	LAKE/LAC	AB	32-14-W4	72 M/12	51°44'	112°00'
Downard	UNP/LNO	ON	Cochrane	42 A/15	48°59'	80°56'
Downe	UNP/LNO	SK	29-33-18-W3	72 N/15	51°51'	108°32'
Downer Lake	LAKE/LAC	NT	Keewatin	65 A	60°36'	96°56'
Downers Corners	UNP/LNO	ON	Peterborough	31 D/8	44°17'	78°18'
Downeys	UNP/LNO	ON	Wellington	40 P/8	43°29'	80°14'
Downeyville	UNP/LNO	ON	Victoria	31 D/7	44°22'	78°35'
Downie	MUN2/AZM2	ON	Perth	40 P/6	43°20'	81°04'
Downie	UNP/LNO	BC	Kootenay	82 N/4	51°09'	117°49'
*Downie Creek	UNP/LNO	BC	Kootenay	82 M/8	51°27'	118°27'
Downie Creek	RIV/CDE	BC	Kootenay	82 M/9	51°30'	118°22'
Downing Basin	SEAU/SMER	—		8014	47°05'	50°57'
Downsview	UNP/LNO	ON	York	30 M/11	43°43'	79°29'
Downton Creek	RIV/CDE	BC	Lillooet	92 J/9	50°36'	122°06'
Downton Lake	LAKE/LAC	BC	Lillooet	92 J/15	50°50'	122°59'
Downton, Mount	MTN/MNT	BC	Range 3 Coast	93 C/10	52°42'	124°51'
Downtown	UNP/LNO	MB		62 H/14	49°53'	97°08'
Dow Settlement	UNP/LNO	NB	York	21 G/14	45°57'	67°29'
Doyle Island	ISL/ÎLE	BC	Rupert	92 L/14	50°48'	127°28'
Doyles	UNP/LNO	NF		1 N/7	47°27'	52°46'
Doyles	UNP/LNO	NF		11 O/14	47°50'	59°11'
Doyles	UNP/LNO	ON	Kent	40 J/8	42°20'	82°10'
Doyles Brook	UNP/LNO	NB	Northumberland	21 I/13	46°50'	65°45'
Doyleville	UNP/LNO	NB	Restigouche	21 O/16	47°54'	66°06'
Dozois	UNP/LNO	QC	Les Laurentides	31 J/1	46°02'	74°18'
Dozois, Réservoir	LAKE/LAC	QC	Vallée-de-l'Or	31 N/11	47°30'	77°05'
Drachm Point	CAPE/CAP	MB		54 L/9	58°40'	94°12'
Dracon	UNP/LNO	ON	Wellington	40 P/16	43°49'	80°23'
Drag Lake	LAKE/LAC	ON	Haliburton	31 E/1	45°05'	78°24'
Dragon	UNP/LNO	QC	Vaudreuil-Soulanges	31 G/8	45°29'	74°15'
Dragon	UNP/LNO	BC	Cariboo	93 B/16	52°51'	122°25'
Dragon Lake 3	IR/RI	BC	Cariboo	93 B/16	52°58'	122°26'
Drague-Numéro-Quatre, Lieu historique national de la - also-aussi - Dredge No. 4 National Historic Site	PARK/PARC	YT		115 O/14	63°57'	139°20'
Drake	VILG/VILG	SK	14-32-22-W2	72 P/11	51°45'	105°01'
Drake Bay	BAY/BAIE	NT	Franklin	68 C	73°32'	100°40'
Drake Island	ISL/ÎLE	BC	Rupert	92 L/5	50°30'	127°40'
Drake Point	CAPE/CAP	NT	Franklin	79 B	76°28'	108°24'
Draney Inlet	BAY/BAIE	BC	Range 2 Coast	92 M/5	51°27'	127°30'
Dranoel	UNP/LNO	ON	Durham	31 D/2	44°10'	78°32'
Drapeau	UNP/LNO	QC	Avignon	22 B/1	48°07'	66°17'
Draper	UNP/LNO	AB	28-88-8-W4	74 D/11	56°40'	111°15'
Drayton	VILG/VILG	ON	Wellington	40 P/15	43°46'	80°40'
Drayton Valley	TOWN/VIL2	AB	17-49-7-W5	83 G/2	53°13'	114°59'
Dreau	UNP/LNO	AB	11-78-22-W5	83 N/11	55°45'	117°17'
Dredge Creek	UNP/LNO	YT		115 O/6	63°25'	139°12'
Dredge No. 4 National Historic Site - also-aussi - Drague-Numéro-Quatre, Lieu historique national de la	PARK/PARC	YT		115 O/14	63°57'	139°20'
Drefal	UNP/LNO	ON	Sudbury	41 O/8	47°16'	82°03'
Dreghorn	UNP/LNO	SK	17-17-18-W2	72 I/8	50°26'	104°27'
Dresden	TOWN/VIL2	ON	Kent	40 J/9	42°35'	82°11'
Drew	UNP/LNO	ON	Wellington	40 P/15	43°59'	80°53'
Drew Harbour 9	IR/RI	BC	Sayward	92 K/3	50°05'	125°11'
Drew Passage	CHAN/CHEN	BC	Sayward	92 K/6	50°16'	125°03'
Drewry	UNP/LNO	BC	Kootenay	82 F/7	49°26'	116°49'
Drewry Lake	LAKE/LAC	BC	Lillooet	92 P/10	51°43'	120°50'
Drewry River	RIV/CDE	NT	Franklin	37 D	69°40'	75°16'
Driedmeat Creek	RIV/CDE	AB	6-45-19-W4	83 A/15	52°52'	112°44'
Driedmeat Lake	LAKE/LAC	AB	44,45-19-W4	83 A/15	52°52'	112°45'
Drifting River	UNP/LNO	MB	30-27-22-W	62 N/7	51°20'	100°33'
Driftpile	UNP/LNO	AB	22-73-12-W5	83 O/5	55°20'	115°46'
Driftpile River	RIV/CDE	AB	74-11-W5	83 O/5	55°23'	115°40'
Drift Pile River 150	IR/RI	AB	74-12-W5	83 O/5	55°22'	115°46'
Drift River	RIV/CDE	MB		64 I/3	58°13'	97°05'
Driftwood	UNP/LNO	ON	Cochrane	42 H/3	49°08'	81°23'
*Driftwood	UNP/LNO	BC	Cassiar	93 M/16	55°49'	126°25'
Driftwood Creek	UNP/LNO	BC	Range 5 Coast	93 L/14	54°49'	127°05'
Driftwood Island	ISL/ÎLE	NT	Keewatin	34 E	57°18'	78°25'
Driftwood Lake	LAKE/LAC	MB	54,55-21-W	63 F/10	53°44'	100°31'
Driftwood River	RIV/CDE	BC	Cassiar	93 M/9	55°42'	126°15'
Driftwood River	RIV/CDE	YT		116 O/9	67°34'	138°30'
Driftwood River (Kastberg Creek) 1	IR/RI	BC	Cassiar	93 M/15	55°55'	126°34'
Drinkwater	VILG/VILG	SK	32-15-23-W2	72 I/6	50°18'	105°08'
Drinkwater Creek	RIV/CDE	BC	Clayoquot	92 F/6	49°24'	125°25'
Driscol Lake	UNP/LNO	SK	13-7-14-W3	72 G/12	49°33'	107°47'
Drisdelle	UNP/LNO	NB	Westmorland	21 I/1	46°08'	64°24'
Drisdelle Settlement	UNP/LNO	NB	Northumberland	21 P/3	47°14'	65°12'

NAME NOM	ENTITY ENTITÉ	LOC 1 LIEU 1	LOC 2 LIEU 2	MAP CARTE	POSITION LAT	LONG
Driver	UNP/LNO	SK	20-31-24-W3	72 N/11	51°41′	109°23′
Drobot	UNP/LNO	SK	32-29-6-W2	62 M/10	51°33′	102°50′
Drocourt	UNP/LNO	ON	Parry Sound	41 H/16	45°46′	80°21′
Drolet, Lac	LAKE/LAC	QC	Le Granit	21 E/10	45°44′	70°53′
Dromedary Mountain	MTN/MNT	YT		105 L/15	62°53′	134°44′
Dromore	UNP/LNO	PE	Queens	11 L/7	46°18′	62°50′
Dromore	UNP/LNO	ON	Grey	41 A/2	44°07′	80°40′
Drook	UNP/LNO	NF		1 K/11	46°41′	53°15′
Drook Point	CAPE/CAP	NF		1 K/11	46°40′	53°15′
Dropmore	UNP/LNO	MB	26-23-29-W	62 N/3	51°01′	101°27′
Droppingwater Creek	RIV/CDE	BC	Kamloops Division Yale	92 I/8	50°24′	120°19′
Drowning River	RIV/CDE	ON	Cochrane	42 K/15	50°54′	84°34′
Droxford	UNP/LNO	SK	10-16-6-W3	72 J/7	50°20′	106°46′
Druid	UNP/LNO	SK	5-33-20-W3	72 N/15	51°48′	108°48′
Drumbo	UNP/LNO	ON	Oxford	40 P/2	43°14′	80°33′
Drum Head	UNP/LNO	NS	Guysborough	11 F/4	45°09′	61°36′
Drumheller	CITY/VIL	AB	29-20-W4	82 P/7	51°28′	112°42′
Drum Islands	ISL/ÎLE	NT	Franklin	26 J	66°05′	67°00′
Drummond	VILG/VILG	NB	Victoria	21 O/4	47°02′	67°41′
Drummond	MUN1/AZM1	QC	Drummond	31 H/16	45°53′	72°29′
Drummond	MUN2/AZM2	ON	Lanark	31 C/16	44°58′	76°14′
Drummond	UNP/LNO	ON	Peterborough	31 D/8	44°15′	78°13′
Drummond	GEOG/GÉOG	NB	Victoria	21 O/5	47°15′	67°35′
Drummond Centre	UNP/LNO	ON	Lanark	31 C/16	45°00′	76°14′
Drummond Heights	UNP/LNO	ON	Welland	30 M/3	43°04′	79°06′
Drummond Station	UNP/LNO	NB	Victoria	21 O/4	47°03′	67°40′
Drummondville	CITY/VIL1	QC	Drummond	31 H/16	45°53′	72°29′
Drumquin	UNP/LNO	ON	Halton	30 M/12	43°32′	79°47′
Drunken Harbour	BAY/BAIE	NF		13 O/4	55°11′	59°33′
Drunken Point	CAPE/CAP	MB	22-21-4-E	62 I/15	50°50′	96°57′
Drury	UNP/LNO	ON	Sudbury	41 I/5	46°23′	81°30′
Drury Cove	UNP/LNO	NB	Saint John	21 G/8	45°20′	66°02′
Drury Inlet	BAY/BAIE	BC	Range 1 Coast	92 L/14	50°54′	127°03′
Drury Lake	LAKE/LAC	YT		105 L/7	62°20′	134°42′
Drurys Cove	UNP/LNO	NB	Kings	21 H/12	45°41′	65°33′
Dry Bay	BAY/BAIE	NT	Franklin	25 C	60°25′	69°44′
Dryberry Lake	LAKE/LAC	ON	Kenora	52 F/12	49°32′	93°50′
Drybones Lake	LAKE/LAC	NT	Mackenzie	85 P	63°30′	112°25′
Drybrough	UNP/LNO	MB		64 C/11	56°31′	101°12′
Dry Creek	UNP/LNO	YT		115 K/2	62°10′	140°41′
Dryden	TOWN/VIL2	ON	Kenora	52 F/15	49°47′	92°50′
Dryden	UNP/LNO	ON	Perth	40 P/15	43°48′	80°53′
Dryden's Corner	UNP/LNO	ON	Manitoulin	41 G/9	45°43′	82°16′
Dry Gulch	UNP/LNO	BC	Kootenay	82 K/9	50°35′	116°02′
Dry Island Buffalo Jump Provincial Park	PARK/PARC	AB	29-34-21-W4	82 P/15	51°57′	112°57′
Drylake	UNP/LNO	NF		23 A/12	52°38′	65°59′
Drynoch	UNP/LNO	BC	Kamloops Division Yale	92 I/6	50°21′	121°24′
Dry Pond	LAKE/LAC	NF		11 P/13	47°51′	57°32′
Dry River	UNP/LNO	MB	21-4-12-W	62 G/6	49°19′	99°01′
Dry Salmon 7	IR/RI	BC	Lillooet	92 I/13	50°45′	121°55′
Drysdale	UNP/LNO	ON	Huron	40 P/5	43°27′	81°42′
Drywood	UNP/LNO	AB	24-4-29-W4	82 H/5	49°18′	113°47′
Duagh	UNP/LNO	AB	5-55-23-W4	83 H/11	53°43′	113°23′
Duart	UNP/LNO	ON	Kent	40 I/5	42°30′	81°45′
Dubawnt Lake	LAKE/LAC	NT	Keewatin	65 N/4	63°04′	101°42′
Dubawnt River	RIV/CDE	NT	Keewatin	66 C	64°33′	100°06′
Dubee Settlement	UNP/LNO	NB	Kings	21 H/14	45°55′	65°29′
Dublin	UNP/LNO	ON	Perth	40 P/11	43°31′	81°17′
Dublin	UNP/LNO	ON	Thunder Bay	42 D/13	48°56′	87°55′
Dublin Shore	UNP/LNO	NS	Lunenburg	21 A/8	44°16′	64°22′
Dubonnet	UNP/LNO	QC	Montmagny	21 L/9	46°41′	70°12′
DuBose	UNP/LNO	BC	Range 5 Coast	103 I/7	54°17′	128°38′
Dubreuilville	MUN2/AZM2	ON	Algoma	42 C/7	48°21′	84°32′
Dubuc	VILG/VILG	SK	3-20-4-W2	62 L/9	50°41′	102°28′
Dubuisson	VILG/VILG	QC	Vallée-de-l'Or	32 C/4	48°07′	77°57′
Duchemin	UNP/LNO	QC	Francheville	31 I/10	46°39′	72°34′
Duchesnau, Pointe	CAPE/CAP	QC	Kativik	25 E/1	61°04′	70°07′
Duchess	VILG/VILG	AB	32-20-14-W4	72 L/12	50°43′	111°55′
Duck Bay	UNP/LNO	MB	17-37-19-W	63 C/1	52°11′	100°09′
Duckbill Point	CAPE/CAP	NF		12 I/9	50°36′	56°12′
Duck Cove	UNP/LNO	NB	Saint John	21 G/1	45°15′	66°06′
Duck Island	ISL/ÎLE	NF		2 C/3	48°10′	53°29′
Duck Island	ISL/ÎLE	NF		2 F/12	49°32′	53°56′
Duck Island	ISL/ÎLE	NF		2 E/10	49°39′	54°30′
Duck Island	ISL/ÎLE	NF		2 E/5	49°28′	55°39′

NAME / NOM	ENTITY / ENTITÉ	LOC 1 / LIEU 1	LOC 2 / LIEU 2	MAP / CARTE	POSITION LAT	POSITION LONG
Duck Island	ISL/ÎLE	NT	Keewatin	33 N	55°45′	77°12′
Duck Lake	TOWN/VIL2	SK	4-45-2-W3	73 B/16	52°49′	106°14′
Duck Lake	LAKE/LAC	ON	Rainy River	52 B/11	48°44′	91°14′
Duck Lake	LAKE/LAC	ON	Kenora	52 E/15	49°52′	94°58′
Duck Lake	LAKE/LAC	MB	67,68-5,6-W	63 J/16	54°52′	98°10′
Duck Lake	LAKE/LAC	SK	43,44-2-W3	73 B/16	52°48′	106°16′
Duck Lake 7	IR/RI	BC	Osoyoos Division Yale	82 E/14	50°00′	119°24′
Duck Lake 76B	IR/RI	ON	Sudbury	41 O/14	47°50′	83°17′
Duck Lake No. 463	MUN2/AZM2	SK		73 G/1	53°00′	106°10′
Duck Lake Post	UNP/LNO	MB		64 P/5	59°25′	97°44′
Duck Meadow	UNP/LNO	BC	Kamloops Division Yale	82 L/12	50°35′	119°54′
Duck Mountain	MTN/MNT	MB/SK		62 N/10	51°35′	101°05′
Duck Range	UNP/LNO	BC	Kamloops Division Yale	82 L/12	50°37′	119°50′
Duck River	UNP/LNO	MB	9-34-20-W	62 N/16	51°54′	100°15′
Ducks, The	ISL/ÎLE	ON	Prince Edward	30 N/15	43°56′	76°36′
Duclos	UNP/LNO	QC	Les Collines-de-l'Outaouais	31 F/9	45°41′	76°07′
Duclos Point	UNP/LNO	ON	York	31 D/6	44°21′	79°15′
Duclos Point	CAPE/CAP	ON	York	31 D/6	44°21′	79°15′
Duder Lake	LAKE/LAC	NF		2 E/7	49°18′	54°41′
Dudidontu River	RIV/CDE	BC	Cassiar	104 J/5	58°47′	131°59′
Dudley	UNP/LNO	ON	Muskoka	31 E/4	45°03′	79°37′
Dudley	UNP/LNO	SK	4-23-9-W3	72 J/14	50°56′	107°11′
Dudswell	VILG/VILG	QC	Le Haut-Saint-François	21 E/12	45°35′	71°35′
Dudswell-Jonction	UNP/LNO	QC	Le Haut-Saint-François	21 E/12	45°34′	71°35′
Dufault, Lac	LAKE/LAC	QC	Rouyn-Noranda	32 D/6	48°19′	79°00′
Dufaultville	UNP/LNO	QC	La Mitis	22 B/12	48°33′	67°56′
Duff	VILG/VILG	SK	8-22-8-W2	62 L/14	50°53′	103°05′
Duff Corners	UNP/LNO	ON	Hastings	31 C/6	44°24′	77°18′
Dufferin	MUN1/AZM1	ON	Dufferin	41 A/1	44°05′	80°15′
Dufferin	MUN2/AZM2	MB	62 G/9	62 G/9	49°32′	98°04′
Dufferin	UNP/LNO	NS	Pictou	11 E/10	45°41′	62°53′
Dufferin	UNP/LNO	NB	Queens	21 I/4	46°08′	65°50′
Dufferin	UNP/LNO	ON	Haldimand	30 L/13	42°58′	79°58′
Dufferin	UNP/LNO	BC	Kamloops Division Yale	92 I/9	50°40′	120°23′
Dufferin	GEOG/GÉOG	NB	Charlotte	21 G/3	45°11′	67°14′
Dufferin	GEOG/GÉOG	ON		41 A/1	44°05′	80°15′
Dufferin 10	IR/RI	BC	Kamloops Division Yale	92 I/4	50°04′	121°33′
Dufferin Bridge	UNP/LNO	ON	Parry Sound	31 E/5	45°29′	79°41′
Dufferin, Cape	CAPE/CAP	NT	Keewatin	34 L	58°38′	78°42′
Dufferin Heights	UNP/LNO	QC	Coaticook	31 H/1	45°04′	72°04′
Dufferin Island	ISL/ÎLE	BC	Range 3 Coast	103 A/1	52°12′	128°20′
Dufferin Mines	UNP/LNO	NS	Halifax	11 D/16	44°57′	62°24′
Dufferin No. 190	MUN2/AZM2	SK		72 I/14	50°40′	105°20′
Duffey Lake	LAKE/LAC	BC	Lillooet	92 J/8	50°24′	122°19′
Duffield	UNP/LNO	AB	26-52-3-W5	83 G/9	53°32′	114°21′
Duffin Lakes	LAKE/LAC	MB		64 P/4	59°03′	97°43′
Duffs	UNP/LNO	NF		1 N/6	47°27′	53°07′
Duff's Corners	UNP/LNO	ON	Wentworth	40 P/1	43°12′	80°01′
Duffy	UNP/LNO	ON	Welland	30 L/15	43°56′	78°58′
Duffy	UNP/LNO	ON	Muskoka	31 E/4	45°05′	79°42′
Duffy Lake	LAKE/LAC	NT	Keewatin	55 L	62°48′	94°52′
Duffys Corner	UNP/LNO	NB	Sunbury	21 J/1	46°11′	66°02′
Duffyville	UNP/LNO	QC	Pontiac	31 F/10	45°42′	76°41′
Dufour	UNP/LNO	QC	Charlevoix	21 M/7	47°25′	70°33′
Dufournel	UNP/LNO	QC	La Côte-de-Beaupré	21 L/14	46°55′	71°05′
Dufourville	UNP/LNO	NB	Kent	21 I/7	46°17′	64°46′
Dufreboy, Lac	LAKE/LAC	QC	Kativik	24 L/2	58°06′	70°40′
Dufreboy, Ruisseau	RIV/CDE	QC	Kativik	24 L/6	58°17′	71°14′
Dufresne	UNP/LNO	MB	9-9-6-E	62 H/10	49°44′	96°43′
Dufresne, Lac	LAKE/LAC	QC	Sept-Rivières	22 P/5	51°24′	65°45′
Dufresnoy, Lac	LAKE/LAC	QC	Rouyn-Noranda	32 D/7	48°26′	79°00′
Dufrost	UNP/LNO	MB	1-5-3-E	62 H/6	49°22′	97°03′
Dufrost, Pointe	CAPE/CAP	QC	Kativik	35 C/4	60°04′	77°39′
Dugald	UNP/LNO	MB	3-11-5-E	62 H/15	49°53′	96°50′
Dugan Lake	UNP/LNO	BC	Cariboo	93 A/4	52°10′	121°56′
Dugas	UNP/LNO	NB	Gloucester	21 P/14	47°48′	65°07′
Du Gas, Lac	LAKE/LAC	QC	Minganie	12 N/1	51°02′	60°04′
Dug-da-myse 12	IR/RI	BC	Range 2 Coast	92 M/2	51°02′	126°31′
Duggan Lake	LAKE/LAC	NT	Mackenzie	76 H	65°35′	104°56′
Du Glas, Lac	LAKE/LAC	QC	Jamésie	32 O/14	51°55′	75°12′
Dugré, Lac	LAKE/LAC	QC	Le Haut-Saint-Maurice	32 B/2	48°09′	74°50′
Duguayville	UNP/LNO	NB	Gloucester	21 P/11	47°36′	65°03′
Du Gué, Rivière	RIV/CDE	QC	Kativik	24 E/7	57°21′	70°45′
Duguesclin	UNP/LNO	QC	Pabok	22 A/8	48°26′	64°26′
Dugwal	UNP/LNO	ON	Cochrane	42 A/11	48°35′	81°01′

NAME NOM	ENTITY ENTITÉ	LOC 1 LIEU 1	LOC 2 LIEU 2	MAP CARTE	POSITION LAT	LONG
Duhamel	VILG/VILG	QC	Papineau	31 J/3	46°01′	75°05′
Duhamel	UNP/LNO	AB	27-45-21-W4	83 A/15	52°55′	112°58′
Duhamel, Lac	LAKE/LAC	NT	Mackenzie	75 L	62°19′	110°45′
Duhamel-Ouest	VILG/VILG	QC	Témiscamingue	31 M/6	47°22′	79°26′
Duhesme, Lac	LAKE/LAC	QC	Jamésie	23 E/12	53°34′	71°55′
Duke Crossing	UNP/LNO	ON	Renfrew	31 F/14	45°58′	77°22′
Duke of York Archipelago	ISL/ÎLE	NT	Franklin	87 A	68°15′	112°45′
Duke of York Bay	BAY/BAIE	NT	Keewatin	46 F	65°25′	84°50′
Dulcemaine	UNP/LNO	ON	Leeds	31 C/8	44°27′	76°03′
Dulhut, Lac	LAKE/LAC	QC	Kativik	24 L/10	58°41′	70°38′
Duluth Junction	UNP/LNO	ON	Rainy River	52 C/11	48°37′	93°23′
Dulwich	UNP/LNO	SK	34-49-20-W3	73 F/7	53°16′	108°50′
Dumas	UNP/LNO	SK	26-11-2-W2	62 E/16	49°57′	102°10′
Dumbarton	UNP/LNO	NB	Charlotte	21 G/6	45°23′	67°08′
Dumbarton	GEOG/GÉOG	NB	Charlotte	21 G/6	45°25′	67°03′
Dumbell Lake	LAKE/LAC	NF		23 A/5	52°28′	65°45′
Dumbell Lake	LAKE/LAC	BC	Range 2 Coast	92 N/7	51°23′	124°57′
Dumble	UNP/LNO	SK	21-54-7-W3	73 G/10	53°40′	106°57′
Dumfries	UNP/LNO	NB	York	21 G/14	45°58′	67°08′
Dumfries	GEOG/GÉOG	NB	York	21 G/14	45°50′	67°13′
Dummer	MUN2/AZM2	ON	Peterborough	31 D/8	44°29′	78°05′
Dummer	UNP/LNO	SK	30-10-21-W2	72 H/15	49°51′	104°50′
Dummer Lake	LAKE/LAC	ON	Peterborough	31 D/9	44°32′	78°06′
Dumoine	UNP/LNO	QC	Pontiac	31 K/5	46°22′	77°40′
Dumoine, Lac	LAKE/LAC	QC	Témiscamingue	31 K/13	46°55′	77°54′
Dumoine, Rivière	RIV/CDE	QC	Pontiac	31 K/4	46°13′	77°51′
Dumond River	RIV/CDE	ON	Kenora	53 A/6	52°20′	89°23′
Dumont, Lac	LAKE/LAC	QC	Pontiac	31 K/1	46°04′	76°27′
Dumpling Harbour	UNP/LNO	NF		13 H/15	53°51′	56°59′
Dunakin	UNP/LNO	NS	Inverness	11 F/14	45°57′	61°16′
Dunany	UNP/LNO	QC	Argenteuil	31 G/9	45°45′	74°20′
Dunbar	UNP/LNO	ON	Dundas	31 G/3	45°03′	75°14′
Dunbar	UNP/LNO	AB	14-53-23-W4M	83 H/11	53°35′	113°17′
Dunbar-Southlands	UNP/LNO	BC	New Westminster	92 G/3	49°15′	123°11′
Dunbarton	UNP/LNO	ON	Ontario	30 M/14	43°49′	79°06′
Dunblane	UNP/LNO	PE	Prince	21 I/9	46°39′	64°20′
Dunblane	UNP/LNO	ON	Bruce	41 A/6	44°23′	81°18′
Dunblane	UNP/LNO	SK	11-26-7-W3	72 O/2	51°11′	106°52′
Dunboro	UNP/LNO	QC	Brome-Missisquoi	31 H/2	45°09′	72°44′
Dunboyne	UNP/LNO	ON	Elgin	40 I/10	42°43′	80°59′
Duncairn	UNP/LNO	SK	17-13-15-W3	72 K/1	50°05′	108°02′
Duncan	CITY/VIL1	BC	Quamichan	92 B/13	48°47′	123°42′
Duncan	UNP/LNO	QC	Drummond	31 H/15	45°47′	72°38′
Duncan	UNP/LNO	ON	Grey	41 A/8	44°25′	80°29′
Duncan Bay	UNP/LNO	BC	Sayward	92 K/3	50°04′	125°17′
Duncanby Landing	UNP/LNO	BC	Range 2 Coast	92 M/5	51°24′	127°38′
Duncan, Cape	CAPE/CAP	NT	Keewatin	43 A	52°40′	80°43′
Duncan, Lac	LAKE/LAC	QC	Jamésie	33 F/5	53°29′	77°56′
Duncan Lake	LAKE/LAC	ON	Timiskaming	41 P/15	47°46′	80°58′
Duncan Lake	LAKE/LAC	BC	Kootenay	82 K/7	50°26′	116°59′
Duncan Lake	LAKE/LAC	NT	Mackenzie	85 I	62°51′	113°58′
Duncan Lake 2	IR/RI	BC	Range 5 Coast	93 L/8	54°26′	126°08′
Duncan Lake 12 - see-voir - Duncan Lake 2	IR/RI	BC		93 L/8	54°26′	126°08′
Duncan Ranges	MTN/MNT	BC	Kootenay	82 K/13	50°45′	117°30′
Duncan River	RIV/CDE	BC	Kootenay	82 K/2	50°11′	116°57′
Duncan's 151A	IR/RI	AB	9-82-25-W5	84 C/4	56°06′	117°51′
Duncans Cove	UNP/LNO	NS	Halifax	11 D/5	44°30′	63°32′
Dunchurch	UNP/LNO	ON	Parry Sound	31 E/12	45°39′	79°51′
Duncrief	UNP/LNO	ON	Middlesex	40 P/3	43°04′	81°28′
Dundalk	VILG/VILG	ON	Grey	41 A/1	44°10′	80°24′
Dundalk	UNP/LNO	YT		105 D/2	60°04′	134°50′
Dundarave	UNP/LNO	BC	New Westminster	92 G/6	49°20′	123°11′
Dundas	TOWN/VIL2	ON	Wentworth	30 M/5	43°16′	79°58′
Dundas	UNP/LNO	PE	Kings	11 L/7	46°19′	62°31′
Dundas	UNP/LNO	NB	Kent	21 I/7	46°17′	64°52′
Dundas	GEOG/GÉOG	NB	Kent	21 I/7	46°20′	64°42′
Dundas	GEOG/GÉOG	ON		31 B/14	45°00′	75°20′
Dundas, Cape	CAPE/CAP	NT	Franklin	68 D	73°56′	99°46′
Dundas, Cape	CAPE/CAP	NT	Franklin	88 E	74°27′	113°42′
Dundas Harbour	UNP/LNO	NT	Franklin	48 E	74°32′	82°23′
Dundas Harbour	BAY/BAIE	NT	Franklin	48 E	74°33′	82°30′
Dundas Island	ISL/ÎLE	BC	Range 5 Coast	103 J/10	54°33′	130°52′
Dundas Island	ISL/ÎLE	NT	Franklin	59 B	76°05′	94°58′
Dundas Island 32B	IR/RI	BC	Range 5 Coast	103 J/10	54°35′	130°55′
Dundas Islands	ISL/ÎLE	BC	Range 5 Coast	103 J/7	54°30′	130°50′

NAME NOM	ENTITY ENTITÉ	LOC 1 LIEU 1	LOC 2 LIEU 2	MAP CARTE	POSITION LAT	LONG
Dundas Peninsula	CAPE/CAP	NT	Franklin	78 F	74°50′	111°30′
Dundee	VILG/VILG	QC	Le Haut-Saint-Laurent	31 G/2	45°00′	74°30′
Dundee	UNP/LNO	PE	Kings	11 L/7	46°24′	62°46′
Dundee	UNP/LNO	NS	Richmond	11 F/11	45°42′	61°06′
Dundee	UNP/LNO	NB	Restigouche	22 B/1	48°00′	66°29′
Dundee	UNP/LNO	QC	Le Haut-Saint-Laurent	31 G/2	45°00′	74°31′
Dundee Bight	BAY/BAIE	NT	Franklin	69 B	76°04′	100°10′
Dundee Centre	UNP/LNO	QC	Le Haut-Saint-Laurent	31 G/1	45°02′	74°25′
Dundela	UNP/LNO	ON	Dundas	31 B/14	44°56′	75°18′
Dundonald	UNP/LNO	ON	Northumberland	31 C/4	44°04′	77°52′
Dundonald	UNP/LNO	MB	9-13-8W	62 J/1	50°05′	98°30′
Dundonald	UNP/LNO	SK		73 B/2	52°09′	106°44′
Dundurn	TOWN/VIL2	SK	9-33-4-W3	72 O/15	51°49′	106°30′
Dundurn	UNP/LNO	ON	Norfolk	40 I/16	42°58′	80°18′
Dundurn No. 314	MUN2/AZM2	SK		72 O/15	51°50′	106°35′
Dunedin	UNP/LNO	PE	Queens	11 L/3	46°12′	63°17′
Dunedin	UNP/LNO	ON	Simcoe	41 A/8	44°17′	80°10′
Dunedin River	RIV/CDE	BC	Peace River	94 N/9	59°31′	124°05′
Dune-du-Sud	UNP/LNO	QC	Les Îles-de-la-Madeleine	11 N/5	47°25′	61°46′
Dune, Lac	LAKE/LAC	QC	Kativik	34 I/12	58°31′	73°46′
Dunelm	UNP/LNO	SK	14-14-W3	72 J/4	50°11′	107°49′
Dunes-de-la-Moraine-d'Harricana, Réserve écologique des	PARK/PARC	QC	Rouyn-Noranda	31 M/16	47°47′	78°15′
Dunfermline	UNP/LNO	SK	36-8-W3	73 B/3	52°08′	107°02′
Dunfield	UNP/LNO	NF		2 C/6	48°21′	53°23′
Dungannon	MUN2/AZM2	ON	Hastings	31 F/4	45°03′	77°45′
Dungannon	UNP/LNO	ON	Huron	40 P/13	43°51′	81°36′
Dungarry	UNP/LNO	NS	Inverness	11 K/4	46°01′	61°31′
Dungarvon River	RIV/CDE	NB	Northumberland	21 I/13	46°49′	65°54′
Dungeness, Cape	CAPE/CAP	NT	Franklin	58 F	74°39′	93°43′
Dunham	CITY/VIL1	QC	Brome-Missisquoi	31 H/2	45°08′	72°48′
Dunière, Réserve faunique de	PARK/PARC	QC	La Matapédia	22 B/10	48°38′	66°45′
Dunira Island	ISL/ÎLE	BC	Range 5 Coast	103 J/7	54°26′	130°46′
Dunkeld	UNP/LNO	ON	Bruce	41 A/3	44°10′	81°12′
Dunkerron	UNP/LNO	ON	Simcoe	31 D/4	44°02′	79°40′
Dunkin	UNP/LNO	QC	Memphrémagog	31 H/1	45°03′	72°28′
Dunkirk	UNP/LNO	SK	36-12-28-W2	72 I/4	50°02′	105°43′
Dunkirk River	RIV/CDE	AB	31-89-16-W4	84 A/15	56°46′	112°32′
Dunkley	UNP/LNO	BC	Cariboo	93 G/8	53°17′	122°28′
Dunks Point	CAPE/CAP	ON	Bruce	41 H/5	45°16′	81°38′
Dunleath	UNP/LNO	SK	33,34-25-2-W2	62 M/1	51°13′	102°13′
Dunlop	UNP/LNO	NB	Gloucester	21 P/12	47°41′	65°44′
Dunlop	UNP/LNO	ON	Huron	40 P/13	43°47′	81°42′
Dunlop	UNP/LNO	MB	26-66-10-W	63 J/10	54°45′	98°52′
Dunlop Lake	LAKE/LAC	ON	Algoma	41 J/7	46°29′	82°42′
Dunmore	UNP/LNO	NS	Inverness	11 F/14	46°00′	61°30′
Dunmore	UNP/LNO	NS	Antigonish	11 F/12	45°32′	61°56′
Dunmore	UNP/LNO	SK		72 I/5	50°24′	105°35′
Dunmore	UNP/LNO	AB	3-12-5-W4	72 E/15	49°58′	110°36′
Dunn	UNP/LNO	AB	21-43-3-W4	73 D/9	52°43′	110°22′
Dunnage Island	ISL/ÎLE	NF		2 E/10	49°30′	54°38′
Dunne Foxe Island	ISL/ÎLE	NT	Keewatin	55 K	62°18′	92°13′
Dunne River	RIV/CDE	NT	Franklin	36 D/16	64°59′	78°03′
Dunnet's Corner	UNP/LNO	ON	Sudbury	41 I/8	46°23′	80°21′
Dunnette Landing	UNP/LNO	ON	Northumberland	31 D/1	44°12′	78°06′
Dunning	UNP/LNO	ON	Cochrane	42 H/2	49°03′	80°50′
Dunning	UNP/LNO	SK	24-5-16-W2	72 H/8	49°24′	104°03′
Dunning Lake	LAKE/LAC	SK		74 F/16	57°57′	108°11′
Dunn Lake	LAKE/LAC	BC	Kamloops Division Yale	92 P/8	51°26′	120°08′
Dunnottar	VILG/VILG	MB	15-17-4E	62 I/7	50°27′	96°57′
Dunn Peak	MTN/MNT	BC	Kamloops Division Yale	82 M/5	51°26′	119°57′
Dunn Point	CAPE/CAP	NT	Franklin	37 B	68°55′	78°48′
Dunns Brook	RIV/CDE	NF		1 M/10	47°44′	54°33′
Dunns Corner	UNP/LNO	NS	Hants	11 E/4	45°12′	63°38′
Dunn's Corner	UNP/LNO	ON	Oxford	40 P/2	43°05′	80°54′
Dunns Mountain Pond	LAKE/LAC	NF		1 M/15	47°52′	54°44′
Dunns Valley	UNP/LNO	ON	Algoma	41 J/5	46°28′	83°38′
Dunnville	TOWN/VIL2	ON	Haldimand	30 L/13	42°54′	79°36′
Du Nort, Lac	LAKE/LAC	QC	Minganie	12 N/11	51°32′	61°22′
Dunphy	UNP/LNO	AB	14-29-21-W4	82 P/7	51°28′	112°52′
Dunphy, Lac	LAKE/LAC	QC	Kativik	24 B/4	56°02′	67°42′
Dunphy Lakes	LAKE/LAC	MB		64 C/12	56°41′	101°34′
Dunphys Pond	LAKE/LAC	NF		2 D/8	48°28′	54°06′
Dunrankin	UNP/LNO	ON	Algoma	42 B/11	48°35′	83°07′
Dunrankin River	RIV/CDE	ON	Algoma	42 B/15	48°47′	82°51′
Dunraven	UNP/LNO	QC	Pontiac	31 F/10	45°45′	76°40′

NAME NOM	ENTITY ENTITÉ	LOC 1 LIEU 1	LOC 2 LIEU 2	MAP CARTE	POSITION LAT	LONG
Dunrea	UNP/LNO	MB	20-5-17-W	62 G/5	49°24′	99°44′
Dunrobin	UNP/LNO	ON	Carleton	31 F/8	45°25′	76°01′
Dunrobin Shore	UNP/LNO	ON	Carleton	31 G/5	45°27′	75°58′
Dunsford	UNP/LNO	ON	Victoria	31 D/7	44°27′	78°39′
Dunshalt	UNP/LNO	AB	20-25-24-W4	82 P/3	51°09′	113°18′
Dunsheath Lake	LAKE/LAC	MB		64 F/2	57°03′	100°46′
Dunsinane	UNP/LNO	NB	Kings	21 H/14	45°50′	65°21′
Dunsmuir	UNP/LNO	BC	Newcastle	92 F/7	49°23′	124°36′
Dunsmuir Land District	GEOG/GÉOG	BC		92 F	49°06′	124°17′
Dunstable	UNP/LNO	AB	26-57-2-W5	83 G/16	53°57′	114°12′
Dunstaffnage	UNP/LNO	PE	Queens	11 L/6	46°20′	63°02′
Dunster	UNP/LNO	BC	Cariboo	83 E/4	53°07′	119°50′
Dunsterville, Cape	CAPE/CAP	NT	Franklin	39 D	77°57′	75°53′
Duntara	VILG/VILG	NF		2 C/11	48°36′	53°22′
Duntroon	UNP/LNO	ON	Simcoe	41 A/8	44°23′	80°11′
Dunvegan	UNP/LNO	NS	Inverness	11 K/6	46°18′	61°13′
Dunvegan	UNP/LNO	ON	Glengarry	31 G/7	45°22′	74°49′
Dunvegan	UNP/LNO	AB	7-80-4-W6	83 M/15	55°55′	118°36′
Dunvegan Lake	LAKE/LAC	NT	Mackenzie	75 B	60°08′	107°10′
Dunvegan Provincial Park	PARK/PARC	AB	80-4-W4	83 M/15	55°55′	118°36′
Dunville	UNP/LNO	NF		1 N/5	47°16′	53°54′
Dunwich	MUN2/AZM2	ON	Elgin	40 I/12	42°41′	81°30′
Du Parc, Lac	LAKE/LAC	QC	Kativik	24 B/10	56°44′	66°47′
Duparquet	CITY/VIL1	QC	Abitibi-Ouest	32 D/11	48°30′	79°14′
Duparquet, Lac	LAKE/LAC	QC	Abitibi-Ouest	32 D/6	48°28′	79°16′
Dupas, Île	ISL/ÎLE	QC	D'Autray	31 I/3	46°07′	73°07′
Duperow	UNP/LNO	SK	9-35-16-W3	72 N/16	51°59′	108°14′
Dupire, Lac	LAKE/LAC	QC	Kativik	34 H/3	57°05′	73°20′
Duplessis	UNP/LNO	QC	Le Haut-Saint-Maurice	31 P/11	47°42′	73°13′
Duplin	UNP/LNO	QC	Le Val-Saint-François	21 E/12	45°34′	71°47′
Duport River	RIV/CDE	NT	Mackenzie	85 K	62°50′	116°12′
Duprat	UNP/LNO	QC	Rouyn-Noranda	32 D/6	48°19′	79°03′
Dupuis Corner	UNP/LNO	NB	Westmorland	21 I/1	46°13′	64°19′
Dupuy	VILG/VILG	QC	Abitibi-Ouest	32 D/14	48°50′	79°21′
Dupuy	UNP/LNO	QC	Abitibi-Ouest	32 D/14	48°50′	79°21′
Duquet, Lac	LAKE/LAC	QC	Kativik	35 B/6	60°21′	75°18′
Durand Creek	RIV/CDE	BC	Kamloops Division Yale	92 I/15	50°46′	120°49′
Durban	UNP/LNO	MB	24-34-29-W	62 N/14	51°56′	101°26′
Durban Island	ISL/ÎLE	NT	Franklin	16 M	67°05′	62°13′
D'Urban, Mont	MTN/MNT	QC	Le Granit	21 E/6	45°18′	71°06′
Durells Island	UNP/LNO	NS	Guysborough	11 F/6	45°20′	61°01′
Durells Island	ISL/ÎLE	NS	Guysborough	11 F/6	45°21′	61°01′
Duret	UNP/LNO	QC	Bonaventure	22 A/3	48°03′	65°15′
Durgin Guyot	SEAU/SMER	—		5.03	55°45′	141°50′
Durham	TOWN/VIL2	ON	Grey	41 A/2	44°10′	80°49′
Durham	MUN1/AZM1	ON	Durham	31 D/2	44°12′	79°00′
Durham	UNP/LNO	NS	Pictou	11 E/10	45°37′	62°49′
Durham	GEOG/GÉOG	NB	Restigouche	21 O/16	47°45′	66°04′
Durham	GEOG/GÉOG	ON		31 D/2	44°05′	78°35′
Durham Bridge	UNP/LNO	NB	York	21 J/2	46°07′	66°36′
Durham Centre	UNP/LNO	NB	Restigouche	21 O/16	47°55′	66°02′
Durham Heights	CAPE/CAP	NT	Franklin	97 H	71°07′	122°58′
Durham-Sud	VILG/VILG	QC	Drummond	31 H/9	45°40′	72°20′
Duricle	UNP/LNO	NF		1 M/3	47°07′	55°05′
Durieu	UNP/LNO	BC	New Westminster	92 G/1	49°13′	122°15′
Durlingville	UNP/LNO	AB	14-61-5-W4	73 L/7	54°17′	110°39′
Durocher, Lac	LAKE/LAC	QC	Minganie	12 K/14	50°52′	61°12′
Durocher Lake	LAKE/LAC	SK	68,69-12,13-W3	73 J/13	54°56′	107°51′
Durrell	UNP/LNO	NF		2 E/10	49°40′	54°44′
Durward	UNP/LNO	AB	30-15-27-W4	82 I/5	50°18′	113°43′
Dusey River	RIV/CDE	ON	Cochrane	42 M/1	51°11′	86°21′
Dusterlo, Lac	LAKE/LAC	QC	Caniapiscau	23 C/14	52°58′	69°05′
Dusty Glacier	GLAC/GLAC	YT		115 B/8	60°24′	138°23′
Dusty Lake	LAKE/LAC	AB	48-17,18-W4	83 H/1	53°08′	112°29′
Du Tast, Lac	LAKE/LAC	QC	Jamésie	32 N/3	51°00′	77°22′
Dutch Brook	UNP/LNO	NS	Cape Breton	11 K/1	46°04′	60°12′
Dutch Creek	RIV/CDE	BC	Kootenay	82 J/5	50°18′	115°52′
Dutcher Lake	LAKE/LAC	NT	Keewatin	65 B	60°36′	98°55′
Dutch Line	UNP/LNO	ON	Haliburton	31 D/15	44°52′	78°38′
Dutch Settlement	UNP/LNO	NS	Halifax	11 D/14	44°59′	63°27′
Dutch Valley	UNP/LNO	NB	Kings	21 H/11	45°42′	65°28′
Duteau Creek	RIV/CDE	BC	Osoyoos Division Yale	82 L/2	50°15′	118°57′
Duthil	UNP/LNO	AB	13-25-11-W5	82 O/3	51°08′	115°25′
Duthill	UNP/LNO	ON	Lambton	40 J/9	42°41′	82°23′
Duti River	RIV/CDE	BC	Cassiar	94 D/13	56°46′	127°56′

NAME NOM	ENTITY ENTITÉ	LOC 1 LIEU 1	LOC 2 LIEU 2	MAP CARTE	POSITION LAT	LONG
Dutton	VILG/VILG	ON	Elgin	40 I/12	42°40′	81°30′
Dutton	UNP/LNO	MB	11-25-23-W	62 N/2	51°09′	100°35′
Duttona Beach	UNP/LNO	ON	Elgin	40 I/11	42°35′	81°28′
Duval	VILG/VILG	SK	27-25-22-W2	72 P/2	51°09′	105°00′
Duval Island	ISL/ÎLE	BC	Rupert	92 L/13	50°46′	127°30′
Duval, Lac	LAKE/LAC	QC	Pontiac	31 K/7	46°19′	76°55′
Duval Lake	LAKE/LAC	MB	70-27-W	63 N/4	55°03′	101°34′
Duvar	UNP/LNO	PE	Prince	21 I/9	46°45′	64°14′
Duvernay	UNP/LNO	QC	Laval	31 H/12	45°35′	73°40′
Duvernay	UNP/LNO	AB	26-55-12-W4	73 E/13	53°47′	111°41′
Duvert, Lac	LAKE/LAC	QC	Kativik	34 H/9	57°37′	72°07′
Duvivier, Lac	LAKE/LAC	QC	Matane	22 B/11	48°43′	67°10′
Duxbury, Lac	LAKE/LAC	QC	Jamésie	33 C/6	52°27′	77°28′
Dwarf Birch Creek	RIV/CDE	YT		115 G/16	61°56′	138°07′
Dwight	UNP/LNO	ON	Muskoka	31 E/6	45°20′	79°01′
Dwyer Hill	UNP/LNO	ON	Carleton	31 G/4	45°07′	75°56′
Dwyer Lake	LAKE/LAC	SK		64 E/13	57°57′	103°53′
Dyce	UNP/LNO	MB	13-62-19-W	63 K/8	54°22′	100°09′
Dyer	UNP/LNO	ON	Stormont	31 G/7	45°16′	74°55′
Dyer Bay	BAY/BAIE	NT	Franklin	98 H	75°53′	121°42′
Dyer, Cape	CAPE/CAP	NT	Franklin	16 K	66°37′	61°16′
Dyer, Mount	MTN/MNT	BC	Range 1 Coast	92 K/13	51°00′	125°38′
Dyer's Bay	UNP/LNO	ON	Bruce	41 H/3	45°10′	81°20′
Dyer's Bay	BAY/BAIE	ON	Bruce	41 H/3	45°10′	81°18′
Dyke Acland Bay	BAY/BAIE	NT	Franklin	68 H	75°01′	98°54′
Dyke Lake	LAKE/LAC	NF		23 J/9	54°30′	66°18′
Dyment	UNP/LNO	ON	Kenora	52 F/9	49°37′	92°19′
Dymond	MUN2/AZM2	ON	Timiskaming	31 M/12	47°35′	79°42′
Dymond	UNP/LNO	ON	Timiskaming	31 M/12	47°32′	79°40′
Dymond Lake	LAKE/LAC	NT	Mackenzie	75 G	61°25′	106°14′
Dynes	UNP/LNO	ON	Halton	30 M/5	43°21′	79°47′
D'Youville, Monts	MTN/MNT	QC	Kativik	35 F/3	61°00′	77°20′
Dysart	VILG/VILG	SK	9-23-15-W2	72 I/16	50°57′	104°02′
Dysart, Dudley, Harcourt, Guilford, Harburn, Bruton, Havelock, Eyre and Clyde	MUN2/AZM2	ON	Haliburton	31 E/2	45°15′	78°50′
Dzagayap 73	IR/RI	BC	Range 5 Coast	103 I/6	54°18′	129°18′
Dzagayap 74	IR/RI	BC	Range 5 Coast	103 I/6	54°19′	129°15′
Dzin Tl'At 46	IR/RI	BC	Range 5 Coast	93 K/14	54°46′	125°24′
Dzitline Lee 9	IR/RI	BC	Range 5 Coast	93 K/14	54°52′	125°08′

E

NAME NOM	ENTITY ENTITÉ	LOC 1 LIEU 1	LOC 2 LIEU 2	MAP CARTE	POSITION LAT	LONG
Eabamet Lake	LAKE/LAC	ON	Kenora	42 M/12	51°32′	87°46′
Eades	UNP/LNO	ON	Cochrane	32 D/13	48°56′	79°53′
Eads Bush	UNP/LNO	ON	Manitoulin	41 H/13	45°57′	81°57′
Eady	UNP/LNO	ON	Simcoe	31 D/12	44°39′	79°37′
Eagan Lake	LAKE/LAC	BC	Lillooet	92 P/7	51°22′	120°44′
Eager Lake	LAKE/LAC	MB		64 C/12	56°33′	101°38′
Eagle	UNP/LNO	QC	La Vallée-de-la-Gatineau	31 K/1	46°05′	76°05′
Eagle	UNP/LNO	ON	Elgin	40 I/12	42°34′	81°34′
Eagle Bay	UNP/LNO	BC	Kamloops Division Yale	82 L/14	50°56′	119°13′
Eagle Bluff	UNP/LNO	BC	Similkameen Division Yale	82 E/5	49°16′	119°30′
Eagle Butte	UNP/LNO	AB	36-7-4-W4	72 E/9	49°36′	110°26′
Eagle Creek	UNP/LNO	BC	Lillooet	92 P/15	51°52′	120°52′
Eagle Creek	RIV/CDE	SK	8-39-10-W3	73 B/6	52°21′	107°24′
Eagle Creek	RIV/CDE	BC	Kootenay	82 E/16	49°46′	118°09′
Eagle Creek	RIV/CDE	BC	Lillooet	92 P/15	51°52′	120°51′
Eagle Creek 6 - see-voir - Bihl' K' A 18	IR/RI	BC		93 K/14	55°00′	125°23′
Eagle Creek No. 376	MUN2/AZM2	SK		73 B/3	52°15′	107°30′
Eagle Harbour	UNP/LNO	BC	New Westminster	92 G/6	49°21′	123°16′
Eagle Head	UNP/LNO	NS	Queens	21 A/2	44°04′	64°37′
Eagle Head	UNP/LNO	QC	Côte-Nord-du-Golfe-Saint-Laurent	12 P/11	51°34′	57°15′
Eaglehead Lake	LAKE/LAC	ON	Thunder Bay	52 H/3	49°02′	89°12′
Eagle Heights	UNP/LNO	BC	Quamichan	92 B/13	48°46′	123°43′
Eagle Hill	UNP/LNO	AB	6-34-3-W5	82 O/16	51°53′	114°26′
Eagle Island	ISL/ÎLE	ON	Algoma	41 J/1	46°07′	82°18′
Eagle Island	ISL/ÎLE	MB		63 G/10	53°39′	98°54′
Eagle Lake	UNP/LNO	ON	Haliburton	31 E/2	45°08′	78°31′
Eagle Lake	UNP/LNO	ON	Parry Sound	31 E/14	45°48′	79°29′
Eagle Lake	LAKE/LAC	ON	Frontenac	31 C/10	44°41′	76°42′
Eagle Lake	LAKE/LAC	ON	Parry Sound	31 E/13	45°50′	79°30′
Eagle Lake	LAKE/LAC	ON	Kenora	52 F/11	49°42′	93°13′
Eagle Lake	LAKE/LAC	AB	23-24-W4	82 P/3	51°00′	113°19′
Eagle Lake	LAKE/LAC	BC	Range 2 Coast	92 N/16	51°54′	124°23′
Eagle Lake 27	IR/RI	ON	Kenora	52 F/11	49°44′	93°02′

NAME NOM	ENTITY ENTITÉ	LOC 1 LIEU 1	LOC 2 LIEU 2	MAP CARTE	POSITION LAT	LONG
Eagle Mountain	UNP/LNO	ON	Thunder Bay	52 H/2	49°03′	88°36′
Eagle (Murphy) Lake	LAKE/LAC	BC	Cariboo	93 A/3	52°03′	121°14′
Eaglenest Creek	RIV/CDE	BC	Cassiar	104 H/11	57°37′	129°28′
Eaglenest Lake	LAKE/LAC	MB/ON		52 L/6	50°16′	95°13′
Eagle Place	UNP/LNO	ON	Brant	40 P/1	43°08′	80°16′
Eagle Plains	UNP/LNO	YT		116 I/7	66°22′	136°44′
Eagle Point	CAPE/CAP	ON	Bruce	41 H/4	45°09′	81°36′
Eagle Ridge	UNP/LNO	BC	New Westminster	92 G/7	49°17′	122°49′
Eagle River	UNP/LNO	NF		13 H/11	53°34′	57°26′
Eagle River	UNP/LNO	ON	Kenora	52 F/14	49°48′	93°12′
Eagle River	RIV/CDE	NF		13 H/11	53°34′	57°27′
Eagle River	RIV/CDE	BC	Kamloops Division Yale	82 L/14	50°51′	119°00′
Eagle River	RIV/CDE	BC	Cassiar	104 P/4	59°06′	129°33′
Eagle River	RIV/CDE	YT		116 P/6	67°18′	137°08′
Eagle Run	UNP/LNO	BC	New Westminster	92 G/14	49°45′	123°08′
Eaglesham	UNP/LNO	AB	25-78-26-W5	83 N/13	55°47′	117°53′
Eagles Lake 165C	IR/RI	SK	58-15-W3	73 K/1	54°07′	108°03′
Eagles Nest	UNP/LNO	ON	Manitoulin	41 H/12	45°43′	81°55′
Eaglesons Corners	UNP/LNO	ON	Carleton	31 G/5	45°18′	75°52′
Eagle Village First Nation-Kipawa	IR/RI	QC	Témiscamingue	31 L/15	46°47′	78°59′
Eakin Creek	RIV/CDE	BC	Kamloops Division Yale	92 P/8	51°27′	120°13′
Eamers Corners	UNP/LNO	ON	Stormont	31 G/2	45°04′	74°46′
Eames River	RIV/CDE	NT	Franklin	98 E	74°19′	120°18′
Earchman	UNP/LNO	MB	23-71-5-W	63 O/1	55°09′	98°07′
Eardley	UNP/LNO	QC	Les Collines-de-l'Outaouais	31 F/9	45°33′	76°06′
Eardley, Escarpement d'	CLF/ESC	QC	Les Collines-de-l'Outaouais	31 F/9	45°33′	76°01′
Eardley Lake	LAKE/LAC	MB		63 A/9	52°32′	96°07′
Ear Falls	MUN2/AZM2	ON	Kenora	52 K/11	50°42′	93°17′
Ear Falls	UNP/LNO	ON	Kenora	52 K/11	50°38′	93°13′
Ear Lake	LAKE/LAC	SK	38-23-W3	73 C/6	52°17′	109°13′
Earle Wharf	UNP/LNO	NB	Kings	21 H/12	45°37′	65°55′
Earl Grey	VILG/VILG	SK	10-23-20-W2	72 I/15	50°56′	104°43′
Earl Island	ISL/ÎLE	NF		13 H/11	53°41′	57°07′
Earls Cove	UNP/LNO	BC	New Westminster	92 F/16	49°45′	124°00′
Earlstown	UNP/LNO	QC	Sherbrooke	21 E/5	45°20′	71°53′
Earlton	UNP/LNO	ON	Timiskaming	31 M/12	47°43′	79°49′
Earltown	UNP/LNO	NS	Colchester	11 E/11	45°35′	63°08′
Early Gardens	UNP/LNO	AB	6-82-23-W5	84 C/4	56°05′	117°36′
Earn Lake	LAKE/LAC	YT		105 L/16	62°49′	134°16′
Earnscliffe	UNP/LNO	PE	Queens	11 L/2	46°09′	62°57′
Earnscliffe	UNP/LNO	ON	Dufferin	41 A/1	44°08′	80°03′
Earnscliffe	UNP/LNO	SK		72 I/5	50°25′	105°32′
Easey Lake	LAKE/LAC	ON	Algoma	42 C/8	48°24′	84°03′
East Advocate	UNP/LNO	NS	Cumberland	21 H/7	45°20′	64°46′
East Aldfield	UNP/LNO	QC	Les Collines-de-l'Outaouais	31 F/9	45°45′	76°11′
East Amherst	UNP/LNO	NS	Cumberland	21 H/16	45°51′	64°11′
East Anderson River	RIV/CDE	BC	Yale Division Yale	92 H/14	49°47′	121°23′
East Anglia	UNP/LNO	SK	17-51-17-W3	73 F/8	53°24′	108°28′
East Angus	CITY/VIL1	QC	Le Haut-Saint-François	21 E/5	45°29′	71°40′
East Apple River	UNP/LNO	NS	Cumberland	21 H/7	45°28′	64°47′
East Arlington	UNP/LNO	NS	Annapolis	21 A/14	44°56′	65°12′
East Arm - see-voir - Southeast Arm	BAY/BAIE	NF		13 H/11	53°33′	57°10′
East Arm	BAY/BAIE	YT		105 H/6	61°25′	129°22′
East Arrow Park	UNP/LNO	BC	Kootenay	82 K/4	50°05′	117°55′
East Baccaro	UNP/LNO	NS	Shelburne	20 P/6	43°28′	65°28′
East Barrière Lake	LAKE/LAC	BC	Kamloops Division Yale	82 M/5	51°17′	119°47′
East Barrière River	RIV/CDE	BC	Kamloops Division Yale	82 M/4	51°15′	119°55′
East Bathurst	UNP/LNO	NB	Gloucester	21 P/12	47°37′	65°37′
East Bay	UNP/LNO	NF		11 O/16	47°46′	58°15′
East Bay	UNP/LNO	NS	Cape Breton	11 K/1	46°01′	60°22′
East Bay	UNP/LNO	MB	18,19-26-15-W	62 O/5	51°16′	99°34′
East Bay - see-voir - D'East, Bay	BAY/BAIE	NF		1 M/10	47°36′	54°51′
East Bay	BAY/BAIE	NF		1 M/11	47°42′	55°23′
East Bay	BAY/BAIE	NF		11 P/16	47°46′	56°04′
East Bay	BAY/BAIE	NF		12 B/10	48°37′	58°45′
East Bay	BAY/BAIE	NS	Cape Breton	11 F/15	45°56′	60°33′
East Bay	BAY/BAIE	ON	Thunder Bay	52 H/16	49°51′	88°07′
East Bay	BAY/BAIE	ON	Thunder Bay	52 H/11	49°43′	89°03′
East Bay	BAY/BAIE	ON	Thunder Bay	52 A/14	48°47′	89°24′
East Bay	BAY/BAIE	NT	Keewatin	46 A	64°04′	81°40′
East Bay Hills	MTN/MNT	NS	Cape Breton	11 F/15	45°55′	60°30′
East Beaver Brook	UNP/LNO	NB	Northumberland	21 P/4	47°08′	65°35′
East Berlin	UNP/LNO	NS	Queens	21 A/2	44°04′	64°34′
East Bideford	UNP/LNO	PE	Prince	11 L/12	46°37′	63°55′
East Bluff	MTN/MNT	NT	Franklin	25 H	61°53′	65°57′

NAME NOM	ENTITY ENTITÉ	LOC 1 LIEU 1	LOC 2 LIEU 2	MAP CARTE	POSITION LAT	LONG
Eastbourne	UNP/LNO	ON	York	31 D/6	44°18′	79°29′
Eastbourne	UNP/LNO	BC	New Westminster	92 G/6	49°24′	123°26′
East Braintree	UNP/LNO	MB	33-7-14-E	52 E/12	49°37′	95°37′
East Branch	UNP/LNO	NB	Kent	21 I/10	46°32′	64°53′
East Branch Indian Brook	RIV/CDE	NS	Victoria	11 K/7	46°26′	60°33′
East Branch River John	UNP/LNO	NS	Pictou	11 E/11	45°40′	63°03′
East Branch Sabbies River	RIV/CDE	NB	Northumberland	21 I/12	46°34′	65°43′
East Brighton	UNP/LNO	NB	Carleton	21 J/6	46°16′	67°26′
East Broad River	RIV/CDE	NS	Queens	20 P/15	43°58′	64°52′
East Broughton	VILG/VILG	QC	L'Amiante	21 L/3	46°13′	71°04′
Eastburg	UNP/LNO	AB	16-59-1-W5	83 J/1	54°07′	114°06′
Eastburn	UNP/LNO	BC	New Westminster	92 G/2	49°13′	122°56′
East Cape	UNP/LNO	QC	Les Îles-de-la-Madeleine	11 N/11	47°37′	61°28′
East Catfish Creek	RIV/CDE	ON	Middlesex	40 I/14	42°47′	81°05′
East Centreville	UNP/LNO	NB	Carleton	21 J/5	46°27′	67°40′
East Channel	CHAN/CHEN	NT	Mackenzie	107 B/2	69°21′	133°54′
East Chester	UNP/LNO	NS	Lunenburg	21 A/9	44°34′	64°13′
East Chezzetcook	UNP/LNO	NS	Halifax	11 D/11	44°43′	63°14′
East Clifford	UNP/LNO	NS	Lunenburg	21 A/7	44°26′	64°44′
East Clifton	UNP/LNO	QC	Le Haut-Saint-François	21 E/5	45°16′	71°34′
East Cloverdale	UNP/LNO	NB	Carleton	21 J/6	46°16′	67°20′
East Colborne	UNP/LNO	ON	Northumberland	31 C/4	44°01′	77°52′
East Coldstream	UNP/LNO	NB	Carleton	21 J/6	46°25′	67°27′
East Collette	UNP/LNO	NB	Northumberland	21 I/14	46°48′	65°26′
East Coulee	UNP/LNO	AB	28,29-27-18-W4	82 P/8	51°20′	112°29′
East Cracroft Island	ISL/ÎLE	BC	Range 1 Coast	92 L/9	50°35′	126°15′
East Creighton	UNP/LNO	ON	Sudbury	41 I/6	46°28′	81°11′
East Creswell River	RIV/CDE	NT	Franklin	58 B	72°51′	93°25′
East Cross Creek	RIV/CDE	ON	Victoria	31 D/7	44°17′	78°44′
East Dalhousie	UNP/LNO	NS	Kings	21 A/10	44°43′	64°45′
East Dover	UNP/LNO	NS	Halifax	11 D/5	44°30′	63°51′
East Dunham	UNP/LNO	QC	Brome-Missisquoi	31 H/2	45°07′	72°45′
East Earltown	UNP/LNO	NS	Colchester	11 E/11	45°39′	63°08′
East Edmonton	UNP/LNO	AB	6-53-23-W4	83 H/11	53°33′	113°22′
East Elmwood	UNP/LNO	MB		62 H/14	49°54′	97°05′
Eastend	TOWN/VIL2	SK	31-6-21-W3	72 F/10	49°31′	108°49′
East End	UNP/LNO	MB		62 G/13	49°51′	99°55′
East End	CAPE/CAP	NS	Pictou	11 E/15	45°49′	62°31′
Easter Cape	CAPE/CAP	NT	Franklin	57 E	70°55′	89°26′
Easter Head	CAPE/CAP	SK		74 N/6	59°29′	109°04′
East Erinville	UNP/LNO	NS	Guysborough	11 F/5	45°22′	61°44′
Easter Island	ISL/ÎLE	NT	Franklin	39 C	77°49′	77°50′
Easter Lake	LAKE/LAC	BC	Clayoquot	92 E/8	49°26′	126°10′
Eastern Arm	BAY/BAIE	NF		2 E/8	49°24′	54°11′
Eastern Blue Pond	LAKE/LAC	NF		12 I/6	50°27′	57°07′
Eastern Bradelle Valley	SEAU/SMER	—		4024	47°50′	62°30′
Eastern Channel	CHAN/CHEN	NF		1 M/8	47°23′	54°05′
Eastern Corner	UNP/LNO	NF		1 N/11	47°42′	53°29′
Eastern Hare Hills	MTN/MNT	NF		1 L/13	46°59′	55°49′
Eastern Head	CAPE/CAP	NF		1 K/12	46°37′	53°36′
Eastern Head - see-voir - Mortier Head	CAPE/CAP	NF		1 M/3	47°05′	55°05′
Eastern Head	CAPE/CAP	NF		12 I/4	50°11′	57°37′
Eastern Indian Island	ISL/ÎLE	NF		2 E/9	49°32′	54°14′
Eastern Island	ISL/ÎLE	NF		2 L/4	50°13′	55°45′
Eastern Island 13	IR/RI	BC	Range 4 Coast	93 F/13	53°56′	125°40′
Eastern Kings	VILG/VILG	PE	Kings	11 L/8	46°26′	62°06′
Eastern Meelpaeg	LAKE/LAC	NF		2 D/2	48°11′	54°56′
Eastern Passage	UNP/LNO	NS	Halifax	11 D/11	44°37′	63°29′
Eastern Peninsula	CAPE/CAP	ON	Kenora	52 E/9	49°34′	94°21′
Eastern Point	CAPE/CAP	NF		11 O/9	47°39′	58°22′
Eastern Points	UNP/LNO	NS	Lunenburg	21 A/8	44°21′	64°13′
Eastern Pond	LAKE/LAC	NF		2 D/11	48°35′	55°15′
Eastern Shoals	SEAU/SMER	—		4049	46°25′	50°30′
Eastern Tickle	UNP/LNO	NF		2 E/9	49°43′	54°15′
Eastern Wolf Island	ISL/ÎLE	NB	Charlotte	21 B/15	44°58′	66°42′
Easter Sound	CHAN/CHEN	NT	Franklin	47 G	71°20′	84°50′
Easterville	UNP/LNO	MB	48-17-W	63 G/4	53°06′	99°49′
East Fairwell	UNP/LNO	SK	6-8-23-W3	72 F/11	49°37′	109°06′
East Farnham	TOWN/VIL2	QC	Brome-Missisquoi	31 H/2	45°14′	72°46′
East Ferris	MUN2/AZM2	ON	Nipissing	31 L/3	46°12′	79°17′
East Ferry	UNP/LNO	NS	Digby	21 B/8	44°23′	66°12′
East Folly Mountain	UNP/LNO	NS	Colchester	11 E/6	45°29′	63°29′
Eastford	UNP/LNO	ON	Cochrane	42 H/6	49°15′	81°06′
East Fraserville	UNP/LNO	NS	Cumberland	21 H/7	45°24′	64°39′
East Galloway	UNP/LNO	NB	Kent	21 I/10	46°35′	64°48′

NAME / NOM	ENTITY / ENTITÉ	LOC 1 / LIEU 1	LOC 2 / LIEU 2	MAP / CARTE	POSITION LAT	POSITION LONG
East Garafraxa	MUN2/AZM2	ON	Dufferin	40 P/16	43°51'	80°15'
East Gate	UNP/LNO	BC	Kootenay	82 N/6	51°25'	117°28'
Eastgate	UNP/LNO	BC	Yale Division Yale	92 H/2	49°08'	120°37'
East Glassville	UNP/LNO	NB	Carleton	21 J/11	46°31'	67°23'
East Goose Lake	LAKE/LAC	NS	Yarmouth	20 P/12	43°45'	65°49'
East Gore	UNP/LNO	NS	Hants	11 E/4	45°07'	63°41'
East Green Harbour	UNP/LNO	NS	Shelburne	20 P/11	43°43'	65°08'
East Gwillimbury	TOWN/VIL2	ON	York	31 D/3	44°08'	79°25'
East Halls Harbour Road	UNP/LNO	NS	Kings	21 H/2	45°11'	64°35'
East Hansford	UNP/LNO	NS	Cumberland	11 E/12	45°43'	63°43'
East Hants	MUN1/AZM1	NS	Hants	11 E/4	45°05'	63°45'
East Harrow	UNP/LNO	ON	Essex	40 J/2	42°02'	82°53'
East Havre Boucher	UNP/LNO	NS	Antigonish	11 F/11	45°41'	61°30'
East Hawkesbury	MUN2/AZM2	ON	Prescott	31 G/7	45°30'	74°30'
East Head	CAPE/CAP	NF		1 K/13	46°57'	53°51'
East Head	CAPE/CAP	NB	Saint John	21 H/5	45°17'	65°40'
East Hereford	VILG/VILG	QC	Coaticook	21 E/4	45°05'	71°30'
East Hereford	UNP/LNO	QC	Coaticook	21 E/4	45°05'	71°30'
East Hill	UNP/LNO	QC	Brome-Missisquoi	31 H/1	45°09'	72°29'
East Humber River	RIV/CDE	ON	York	30 M/13	43°47'	79°35'
East Hungerford	UNP/LNO	ON	Hastings	31 C/11	44°30'	77°09'
East Inglisville	UNP/LNO	NS	Annapolis	21 A/14	44°52'	65°05'
East Ironbound Island	ISL/ÎLE	NS	Lunenburg	21 A/8	44°26'	64°05'
East Jeddore	UNP/LNO	NS	Halifax	11 D/10	44°44'	63°00'
East Jordan	UNP/LNO	NS	Shelburne	20 P/14	43°46'	65°13'
East Kelowna	UNP/LNO	BC	Osoyoos Division Yale	82 E/14	49°51'	119°25'
East Kemptville	UNP/LNO	NS	Yarmouth	21 A/4	44°05'	65°46'
East Kildonan	UNP/LNO	MB		62 H/14	49°55'	97°06'
East Kildonan - Transcona	VILG/VILG	MB		62 H/14	49°55'	97°03'
East Knowlesville	UNP/LNO	NB	Carleton	21 J/6	46°28'	67°20'
East Kootenay	MUN1/AZM1	BC	Kootenay	82 G/13	49°55'	115°45'
East Korah	UNP/LNO	ON	Algoma	41 K/9	46°34'	84°21'
East LaHave	UNP/LNO	NS	Lunenburg	21 A/8	44°19'	64°22'
East Lake	LAKE/LAC	ON	Prince Edward	30 N/14	43°55'	77°12'
East Lake	LAKE/LAC	ON	Rainy River	52 B/3	48°11'	91°23'
East Lake	LAKE/LAC	ON	Kenora	53 F/11	53°42'	93°10'
East Lake Ainslie	UNP/LNO	NS	Inverness	11 K/3	46°08'	61°08'
East Landing	UNP/LNO	NF		1 K/11	46°40'	53°04'
East Leicester	UNP/LNO	NS	Cumberland	11 E/13	45°47'	63°58'
Eastleigh	UNP/LNO	SK	27-15-2-W3	72 J/8	50°17'	106°12'
East Linden	UNP/LNO	NS	Cumberland	11 E/13	45°54'	63°49'
East Linton	UNP/LNO	ON	Grey	41 A/10	44°39'	80°56'
East Long Lake	LAKE/LAC	NB	Charlotte	21 G/7	45°23'	66°32'
East Luther - see-voir - East Luther Grand Valley	MUN2/AZM2	ON		40 P/16	43°55'	80°20'
East Luther Grand Valley	MUN2/AZM2	ON	Dufferin	40 P/16	43°55'	80°20'
Eastmain	VILG/VILG	QC	Jamésie	33 D/1	52°11'	78°10'
Eastmain, Rivière	RIV/CDE	QC	Jamésie	33 D/7	52°15'	78°35'
Eastman	TOWN/VIL2	QC	Memphrémagog	31 H/8	45°18'	72°19'
East Mapleton	UNP/LNO	NS	Cumberland	21 H/9	45°33'	64°07'
East Margaretsville	UNP/LNO	NS	Annapolis	21 H/3	45°03'	65°01'
East McKirdy	UNP/LNO	ON	Thunder Bay	52 H/8	49°16'	88°08'
East Meadows	UNP/LNO	NF		1 N/10	47°36'	52°42'
East Milford	UNP/LNO	NS	Hants	11 E/3	45°01'	63°26'
East Mines	UNP/LNO	NS	Colchester	11 E/6	45°26'	63°29'
East Mines Station	UNP/LNO	NS	Colchester	11 E/5	45°26'	63°31'
East Moberly Lake 169	IR/RI	BC	Peace River	93 P/13	55°50'	121°38'
Eastmount	UNP/LNO	NB	Saint John	21 G/8	45°18'	66°02'
East Mountain	UNP/LNO	NS	Colchester	11 E/6	45°25'	63°11'
East Natashquan River - also-aussi - Natashquan Est, Rivière	RIV/CDE	NF		12 N/5	51°20'	61°40'
East New Annan	UNP/LNO	NS	Colchester	11 E/11	45°37'	63°17'
East Newbridge	UNP/LNO	NB	Carleton	21 J/3	46°09'	67°27'
East Noel	UNP/LNO	NS	Hants	11 E/5	45°18'	63°42'
Eastnor	MUN2/AZM2	ON	Bruce	41 A/14	44°57'	81°16'
East Oakland	UNP/LNO	ON	Brant	40 P/1	43°02'	80°17'
Easton	UNP/LNO	NS	Digby	21 A/5	44°19'	65°52'
Eastons Corners	UNP/LNO	ON	Grenville	31 B/13	44°50'	75°53'
East Oro	UNP/LNO	ON	Simcoe	31 D/11	44°32'	79°30'
East Osoyoos	UNP/LNO	BC	Similkameen Division Yale	82 E/3	49°01'	119°26'
East Oxford	UNP/LNO	ON	Grenville	31 B/13	44°55'	75°39'
East Peace No. 131, Municipal District of	MUN1/AZM1	AB		84 C/9	56°38'	116°04'
East Pen Island	ISL/ÎLE	NT	Keewatin	54 A	56°45'	88°40'
East Pennant	UNP/LNO	NS	Halifax	11 D/5	44°28'	63°38'
East Petpeswick	UNP/LNO	NS	Halifax	11 D/11	44°45'	63°09'
East Pine	UNP/LNO	BC	Peace River	93 P/11	55°43'	121°13'
East Pinnacle	UNP/LNO	QC	Brome-Missisquoi	31 H/2	45°02'	72°43'

NAME NOM	ENTITY ENTITÉ	LOC 1 LIEU 1	LOC 2 LIEU 2	MAP CARTE	POSITION LAT	LONG
East Point	UNP/LNO	PE	Kings	11 K/5	46°27'	62°00'
East Point	CAPE/CAP	NF		2 C/12	48°37'	53°41'
East Point	CAPE/CAP	NF		11 P/11	47°36'	57°11'
East Point	CAPE/CAP	PE	Kings	11 K/5	46°27'	61°58'
East Point	CAPE/CAP	NS	Halifax	10 O/13	43°58'	59°45'
East Point	CAPE/CAP	NS	Shelburne	20 P/11	43°32'	65°21'
East Pond	LAKE/LAC	NF		12 H/16	49°50'	56°27'
East Poplar	UNP/LNO	SK	26-1-26-W2	72 H/3	49°04'	105°23'
East Porcupine River	RIV/CDE	SK		74 P/8	59°30'	104°12'
Eastport	TOWN/VIL2	NF		2 C/12	48°39'	53°45'
Eastport Bay	BAY/BAIE	NF		2 C/12	48°41'	53°43'
East Port Medway	UNP/LNO	NS	Queens	21 A/2	44°09'	64°34'
Eastport North	UNP/LNO	NF		2 C/12	48°40'	53°45'
East Prairie Metis Settlement	UNP/LNO	AB		83 N/1	55°10'	116°10'
East Prairie River	RIV/CDE	AB	35-75-16-W5	83 N/9	55°33'	116°22'
East Preston	UNP/LNO	NS	Halifax	11 D/11	44°43'	63°25'
East Preston	UNP/LNO	ON	Waterloo	40 P/8	43°23'	80°21'
East Pubnico	UNP/LNO	NS	Yarmouth	20 P/12	43°40'	65°46'
East Quinan	UNP/LNO	NS	Yarmouth	20 P/13	43°56'	65°49'
East Quoddy	UNP/LNO	NS	Halifax	11 D/16	44°55'	62°20'
East Random Head	CAPE/CAP	NF		2 C/4	48°06'	53°33'
East Redonda Island	ISL/ÎLE	BC	New Westminster	92 K/2	50°13'	124°43'
East Ridge	SEAU/SMER	—		15787A	48°20'	128°20'
East River	UNP/LNO	NS	Lunenburg	21 A/9	44°35'	64°10'
East River	RIV/CDE	NF		12 I/11	50°38'	57°10'
East River	RIV/CDE	NT	Mackenzie	86 K/13	67°00'	117°51'
East River of Pictou	RIV/CDE	NS	Pictou	11 E/10	45°39'	62°42'
East River Point	UNP/LNO	NS	Lunenburg	21 A/9	44°34'	64°10'
East River St. Marys	UNP/LNO	NS	Pictou	11 E/8	45°24'	62°10'
East River St. Marys	RIV/CDE	NS	Guysborough	11 E/8	45°15'	62°04'
East River St. Marys West Side	UNP/LNO	NS	Pictou	11 E/8	45°23'	62°09'
East River Sheet Harbour	UNP/LNO	NS	Halifax	11 D/15	44°55'	62°31'
East Riverside-Kinghurst	VILG/VILG	NB	Kings	21 G/8	45°22'	66°00'
East Riverside-Kinghurst - see-voir - East Riverside-Kinghurst	VILG/VILG	NB	Kings	21 G/8	45°22'	66°00'
East Roman Valley	UNP/LNO	NS	Guysborough	11 F/5	45°27'	61°42'
East Rous Island	ISL/ÎLE	ON	Manitoulin	41 I/4	46°02'	82°00'
East Royalty	UNP/LNO	PE	Queens	11 L/6	46°17'	63°06'
East Saanich 2	IR/RI	BC	South Saanich	92 B/11	48°35'	123°23'
East Sable River	UNP/LNO	NS	Shelburne	20 P/14	43°46'	65°00'
East St. Paul	MUN2/AZM2	MB		62 H/14	49°48'	97°02'
East St. Paul	UNP/LNO	MB		62 H/14	49°59'	97°03'
East Scotch Settlement	UNP/LNO	NB	Kings	21 H/13	45°46'	65°48'
East Selkirk	UNP/LNO	MB		62 I/2	50°08'	96°50'
East Selkirk Station	UNP/LNO	MB		62 I/2	50°08'	96°49'
East Shediac	UNP/LNO	NB	Westmorland	21 I/2	46°14'	64°32'
East Shining Tree Lake	LAKE/LAC	ON	Sudbury	41 P/11	47°33'	81°04'
East Ship Harbour	UNP/LNO	NS	Halifax	11 D/15	44°47'	62°48'
East Shoal Lake	LAKE/LAC	MB	15,16-1,2-W	62 I/5	50°22'	97°37'
East Side	UNP/LNO	NS	Yarmouth	20 O/8	43°24'	66°01'
Eastside	UNP/LNO	ON	Algoma	41 K/9	46°31'	84°15'
East Side of Ragged Island	UNP/LNO	NS	Shelburne	20 P/11	43°42'	65°05'
East Side Port L'Hebert	UNP/LNO	NS	Queens	20 P/15	43°49'	64°56'
East Sister Island	ISL/ÎLE	ON	Essex	40 G/15	41°49'	82°52'
East Skye Glen	UNP/LNO	NS	Inverness	11 K/3	46°03'	61°12'
East Slope	UNP/LNO	NS	Cape Breton	11 J/4	46°11'	60°00'
East Sooke	UNP/LNO	BC	Sooke	92 B/5	48°22'	123°41'
East Southampton	UNP/LNO	NS	Cumberland	21 H/9	45°35'	64°12'
East Spanish River	RIV/CDE	ON	Sudbury	41 P/4	47°02'	81°51'
East Sullivan Mines	UNP/LNO	QC	Vallée-de-l'Or	32 C/4	48°04'	77°42'
East Thurlow Island	ISL/ÎLE	BC	Sayward	92 K/6	50°24'	125°25'
East Tracadie	UNP/LNO	NS	Antigonish	11 F/12	45°38'	61°37'
East Trail	UNP/LNO	BC	Kootenay	82 F/4	49°06'	117°42'
East Tremont	UNP/LNO	NS	Kings	21 A/15	44°57'	64°54'
East Trout Lake	LAKE/LAC	SK	62-21-W2	73 I/6	54°22'	105°05'
East Uniacke	UNP/LNO	NS	Halifax	11 D/13	44°55'	63°46'
East Valley	SEAU/SMER	—		15787A	48°20'	128°30'
Eastview	UNP/LNO	ON	Frontenac	31 C/8	44°16'	76°23'
Eastview	UNP/LNO	ON	Nipissing	31 L/6	46°19'	79°26'
Eastview	UNP/LNO	ON	Cochrane	42 G/8	49°25'	82°25'
Eastview	UNP/LNO	SK		72 I/7	50°28'	104°35'
Eastview	UNP/LNO	SK	18-17-24-W2	72 I/6	50°26'	105°17'
Eastview	UNP/LNO	SK		73 B/2	52°06'	106°37'
East Village	UNP/LNO	NS	Colchester	11 E/5	45°26'	63°34'
Eastville	UNP/LNO	NS	Colchester	11 E/7	45°16'	62°53'
East Wallace	UNP/LNO	NS	Cumberland	11 E/14	45°48'	63°26'

NAME NOM	ENTITY ENTITÉ	LOC 1 LIEU 1	LOC 2 LIEU 2	MAP CARTE	POSITION LAT	LONG
East Walton	UNP/LNO	NS	Hants	11 E/5	45°15′	63°57′
East Waterville	UNP/LNO	NB	York	21 J/3	46°04′	67°18′
East Wawanosh	MUN2/AZM2	ON	Huron	40 P/14	43°50′	81°25′
East Wellington	UNP/LNO	BC	Mountain	92 F/1	49°11′	124°01′
East Wentworth	UNP/LNO	NS	Cumberland	11 E/11	45°37′	63°29′
East Williams	MUN2/AZM2	ON	Middlesex	40 P/4	43°05′	81°35′
East Wiltshire	UNP/LNO	PE	Queens	11 L/6	46°15′	63°13′
East Windsor	UNP/LNO	ON	Essex	40 J/7	42°19′	82°59′
Eastwood	UNP/LNO	ON	Oxford	40 P/2	43°08′	80°40′
East York	TOWN/VIL2	ON	York	30 M/11	43°42′	79°20′
East Zorra-Tavistock	MUN2/AZM2	ON	Oxford	40 P/2	43°15′	80°50′
Easyford	UNP/LNO	AB	6-50-8-W5	83 G/6	53°07′	115°09′
Eaton	VILG/VILG	QC	Le Haut-Saint-François	21 E/5	45°23′	71°39′
Eaton, Canyon	VALL/VALL	QC	Kativik	23 N/9	55°33′	68°12′
Eaton Corner	UNP/LNO	QC	Le Haut-Saint-François	21 E/5	45°22′	71°36′
Eatonia	TOWN/VIL2	SK	26-25-W3	72 N/3	51°13′	109°23′
Eaton Nord, Rivière	RIV/CDE	QC	Le Haut-Saint-François	21 E/5	45°24′	71°35′
Eaton, Rivière	RIV/CDE	QC	Le Haut-Saint-François	21 E/5	45°28′	71°39′
Eatonville	UNP/LNO	NS	Cumberland	21 H/7	45°24′	64°53′
Eatonville	UNP/LNO	QC	Kamouraska	21 N/5	47°20′	69°41′
Eatonville	UNP/LNO	ON	Kent	40 I/5	42°22′	81°54′
Eau, Bay de l′	BAY/BAIE	NF		1 M/7	47°23′	54°48′
Eau Claire	UNP/LNO	ON	Nipissing	31 L/2	46°14′	78°53′
Eau-Claire, Lac à l′	LAKE/LAC	NF		23 A/12	52°36′	65°50′
Eau Claire, Lac à l′	LAKE/LAC	QC	Le Centre-de-la-Mauricie	31 I/11	46°33′	73°03′
Eau Claire, Lac à l′	LAKE/LAC	QC	Kativik	34 B/1	56°10′	74°25′
Eau Claire, Lac à l′	LAKE/LAC	QC	Jamésie	32 J/3	50°10′	75°10′
Eau Claire, Rivière à l′	RIV/CDE	QC	Kativik	34 C/1	56°13′	76°01′
Eau Claire Station	UNP/LNO	ON	Nipissing	31 L/7	46°16′	78°55′
Eau Froide, Lac à l′	LAKE/LAC	QC	Jamésie	32 I/16	50°53′	72°27′
Eau Jaune, Lac à l′	LAKE/LAC	QC	Jamésie	32 G/10	49°38′	74°42′
Eaux Mortes, Lac des	LAKE/LAC	QC	Rimouski-Neigette	22 C/1	48°14′	68°05′
Eaux-Mortes, Les	UNP/LNO	QC	Charlevoix-Est	21 M/16	47°57′	70°27′
Eaux-Mortes, Les	UNP/LNO	QC	Beauce-Sartigan	21 L/2	46°03′	70°31′
Eaux-Mortes, Les	UNP/LNO	QC	Robert-Cliche	21 L/2	46°10′	70°55′
Ebb and Flow	UNP/LNO	MB	32-23-11-W	62 O/3	51°02′	99°04′
Ebb and Flow 52	IR/RI	MB		62 O/2	51°03′	99°00′
Ebb and Flow Lake	LAKE/LAC	MB	30,31-3,4-E	62 P/11	51°37′	97°02′
Ebb and Flow Lake	LAKE/LAC	MB		62 O/2	51°04′	98°57′
Ebbs Shore	UNP/LNO	ON	Lanark	31 F/1	45°03′	76°12′
Ebbutt Hills	MTN/MNT	NT	Mackenzie	95 J/8	62°20′	122°05′
Ebenezer	VILG/VILG	SK	25-27-4-W2	62 M/8	51°22′	102°27′
Ebenezer	UNP/LNO	PE	Queens	11 L/6	46°21′	63°15′
Ebenezer	UNP/LNO	ON	Leeds	31 C/8	44°23′	76°03′
Ebenezer	UNP/LNO	ON	Hastings	31 C/6	44°19′	77°06′
Ebenezer	UNP/LNO	ON	Peel	30 M/13	43°46′	79°40′
Ebenezer	UNP/LNO	ON	Simcoe	31 D/12	44°41′	79°49′
Eberts	UNP/LNO	ON	Kent	40 J/9	42°30′	82°11′
Ebierbing Bay	BAY/BAIE	NT	Franklin	25 P	63°14′	64°55′
Ebor	UNP/LNO	MB	15-9-29-W	62 F/11	49°44′	101°20′
Éboulements, Mont des	MTN/MNT	QC	Charlevoix	21 M/9	47°32′	70°17′
Éboulis, L′	UNP/LNO	QC	Le Fjord-du-Saguenay	22 D/7	48°19′	70°57′
Écart-du-Bras, L′	UNP/LNO	QC	Charlevoix	21 M/7	47°26′	70°36′
Eccles Hill	UNP/LNO	QC	Brome-Missisquoi	31 H/2	45°01′	72°54′
Echachis 2	IR/RI	BC	Clayoquot	92 F/4	49°08′	125°56′
Echechempisut	UNP/LNO	QC	Jamésie	33 D/2	52°02′	78°41′
Echo	UNP/LNO	ON	Frontenac	31 C/10	44°36′	76°45′
Echo Bay	VILG/VILG	SK		73 G/3	53°13′	107°08′
Echo Bay	UNP/LNO	ON	Algoma	41 K/8	46°29′	84°04′
Echo Bay	UNP/LNO	BC	Range 1 Coast	92 L/16	50°45′	126°30′
Echo Bay	UNP/LNO	NT	Mackenzie	86 L/1	66°05′	118°02′
Echo Bay	BAY/BAIE	NT	Mackenzie	86 K/4	66°02′	117°53′
Echo Beach	UNP/LNO	ON	Muskoka	31 E/3	45°12′	79°28′
Echoing Lake	LAKE/LAC	ON	Kenora	53 K/9	54°31′	92°15′
Echoing River	RIV/CDE	MB/ON		53 N/16	55°51′	92°05′
Echo Island	ISL/ÎLE	BC	Yale Division Yale	92 H/5	49°21′	121°47′
Écho, Lac	LAKE/LAC	QC	Papineau	31 G/14	45°55′	75°27′
Echo Lake	LAKE/LAC	ON	Algoma	41 J/12	46°34′	83°59′
Echo Lake	LAKE/LAC	MB	14,15-16-E	52 L/3	50°13′	95°23′
Echo Lake	LAKE/LAC	SK	65-1-W2	63 L/9	54°39′	102°00′
Echo Place	UNP/LNO	ON	Brant	40 P/1	43°09′	80°13′
Echo River	UNP/LNO	ON	Algoma	41 K/9	46°31′	84°02′
Échouani, Lac	LAKE/LAC	QC	La Vallée-de-la-Gatineau	31 O/13	47°45′	75°42′
Échouerie, Pointe de l′	CAPE/CAP	QC	La Côte-de-Gaspé	22 H/1	49°03′	64°28′
Echo Vale	UNP/LNO	QC	Le Granit	21 E/10	45°35′	70°55′

NAME NOM	ENTITY ENTITÉ	LOC 1 LIEU 1	LOC 2 LIEU 2	MAP CARTE	POSITION LAT	LONG
Ecklund Lake	LAKE/LAC	NT	Mackenzie	65 L	62°27′	103°07′
Eckner	UNP/LNO	SK	34-59-16-W3	73 K/1	54°09′	108°19′
Eckville	TOWN/VIL2	AB	16-39-3-W5	83 B/8	52°21′	114°22′
Eclipse	UNP/LNO	MB	5,6,7,8-25-18-W	62 O/4	51°08′	99°59′
Eclipse Channel	CHAN/CHEN	NF		24 P/9	59°42′	64°10′
Eclipse Harbour	BAY/BAIE	NF		24 P/16	59°50′	64°08′
Eclipse Pond	LAKE/LAC	NF		12 H/2	49°00′	56°47′
Eclipse Sound	CHAN/CHEN	NT	Franklin	38 B	72°38′	79°00′
Écluse-à-Tardif, L'	UNP/LNO	QC	Témiscouata	21 N/6	47°27′	69°10′
Écluse, L'	UNP/LNO	QC	La Matapédia	22 B/6	48°27′	67°25′
Écluse, L'	UNP/LNO	QC	Le Fjord-du-Saguenay	22 D/1	48°14′	70°13′
Écluse, L'	UNP/LNO	QC	Charlevoix-Est	21 M/16	47°53′	70°29′
Economy	UNP/LNO	NS	Colchester	11 E/5	45°23′	63°55′
Economy Lake	LAKE/LAC	NS	Colchester	11 E/5	45°29′	63°52′
Economy Point	UNP/LNO	NS	Colchester	11 E/5	45°23′	63°54′
Economy Point	CAPE/CAP	NS	Colchester	11 E/5	45°21′	63°53′
Ecoole	UNP/LNO	BC	Barclay	92 C/14	48°58′	125°04′
Écorce, Lac de l'	LAKE/LAC	QC	Matawinie	31 J/16	46°52′	74°16′
Écorce, Lac de l'	LAKE/LAC	QC	La Vallée-de-la-Gatineau	31 N/1	47°05′	76°24′
Écorces, Lac aux	LAKE/LAC	QC	La Côte-de-Beaupré	21 M/13	47°54′	71°44′
Écorces Nord-Est, Rivière aux	RIV/CDE	QC	La Côte-de-Beaupré	21 M/13	47°48′	71°43′
Écorces, Rivière aux	RIV/CDE	QC	Le Fjord-du-Saguenay	22 D/6	48°17′	71°29′
Écorces, Rivière aux	RIV/CDE	QC	Maskinongé	31 I/6	46°27′	73°09′
Écorceur, L'	UNP/LNO	QC	Le Fjord-du-Saguenay	22 D/7	48°21′	70°52′
Ecstall River	RIV/CDE	BC	Range 5 Coast	103 I/4	54°10′	129°57′
Écueils, Pointe aux	CAPE/CAP	QC	Kativik	34 N/12	59°42′	77°48′
Ecum Secum	UNP/LNO	NS	Guysborough	11 D/16	44°58′	62°08′
Ecum Secum Bridge	UNP/LNO	NS	Halifax	11 D/16	44°58′	62°10′
Ecum Secum River	RIV/CDE	NS	Halifax	11 D/16	44°59′	62°10′
Ecum Secum West	UNP/LNO	NS	Halifax	11 D/16	44°58′	62°10′
Eda Lake	LAKE/LAC	NT	Mackenzie	76 D	64°55′	112°00′
Edam	VILG/VILG	SK		73 F/2	53°11′	108°46′
Edberg	VILG/VILG	AB	14-44-20-W4	83 A/15	52°47′	112°47′
Eddies Cove	UNP/LNO	NF		12 P/8	51°25′	56°27′
Eddies Cove West	UNP/LNO	NF		12 I/14	50°45′	57°10′
Eddontenajon	UNP/LNO	BC	Cassiar	104 H/13	57°49′	129°57′
Eddontenajon Lake	LAKE/LAC	BC	Cassiar	104 H/13	57°46′	129°58′
Eddy	UNP/LNO	BC	Cariboo	93 H/1	53°14′	120°04′
Eddy Island	ISL/ÎLE	NT	Keewatin	44 P	59°26′	80°28′
Eddy Point	CAPE/CAP	NS	Guysborough	11 F/11	45°31′	61°15′
Eddystone	UNP/LNO	ON	Northumberland	31 D/1	44°04′	78°01′
Eddystone	UNP/LNO	MB	19-24-12-W	62 O/3	51°05′	99°09′
Edehon Lake	LAKE/LAC	NT	Keewatin	65 A	60°23′	97°15′
Edelweiss	UNP/LNO	BC	Kootenay	82 N/7	51°19′	116°58′
Eden	UNP/LNO	NS	Inverness	11 F/14	45°51′	61°08′
Eden	UNP/LNO	ON	Elgin	40 I/15	42°48′	80°45′
Eden	UNP/LNO	MB	21-16-15-W	62 J/6	50°23′	99°28′
Eden Bay	BAY/BAIE	NT	Franklin	79 B	76°37′	108°34′
Edenburg	UNP/LNO	MB	11-1-1-W	62 H/3	49°01′	97°29′
Eden, Cape	CAPE/CAP	NT	Franklin	68 C	73°47′	101°02′
Eden Grove	UNP/LNO	ON	Leeds	31 C/8	44°24′	76°06′
Eden Grove	UNP/LNO	ON	Bruce	41 A/3	44°13′	81°14′
Edenhurst	UNP/LNO	ON	Bruce	41 A/14	44°55′	81°16′
Eden Island	ISL/ÎLE	BC	Range 1 Coast	92 L/10	50°45′	126°40′
Eden Lake	UNP/LNO	NS	Pictou	11 E/8	45°24′	62°18′
Eden Lake	LAKE/LAC	NS	Pictou	11 E/8	45°24′	62°18′
Eden Lake	LAKE/LAC	MB		64 C/9	56°38′	100°15′
Eden Lake	LAKE/LAC	BC	Queen Charlotte	103 F/15	53°51′	132°45′
Eden Mills	UNP/LNO	ON	Wellington	40 P/9	43°35′	80°09′
Edenvale	UNP/LNO	ON	Simcoe	31 D/5	44°27′	79°54′
Eden Valley 216	IR/RI	AB	17-4-W5	82 J/8	50°29′	114°15′
Edenwold	VILG/VILG	SK	26-19-17-W2	72 I/9	50°38′	104°15′
Edenwold No. 158	MUN2/AZM2	SK		72 I/8	50°30′	104°20′
Edfield	UNP/LNO	SK	29-32-11-W2	62 M/13	51°46′	103°32′
Edgar	UNP/LNO	ON	Simcoe	31 D/12	44°31′	79°37′
Edgars	UNP/LNO	ON	Essex	40 J/2	42°09′	82°55′
Edge Hill	UNP/LNO	ON	Grey	41 A/2	44°14′	80°48′
Edgeley	HAM/HAM	SK	27-19-15-W2	62 L/12	50°38′	103°59′
Edgeley	UNP/LNO	ON	York	30 M/13	43°48′	79°31′
Edgell	UNP/LNO	SK	24-10-23-W3	72 F/14	49°50′	109°01′
Edgell Island	ISL/ÎLE	NT	Franklin	25 H	61°50′	65°00′
Edgerton	VILG/VILG	AB	1-44-4-W4	73 D/16	52°45′	110°27′
Edgetts Landing	UNP/LNO	NB	Albert	21 H/15	45°54′	64°38′
Edgewater	UNP/LNO	BC	Kootenay	82 K/9	50°42′	116°08′
Edgewater Beach	UNP/LNO	ON	Essex	40 J/3	42°09′	83°07′

NAME / NOM	ENTITY / ENTITÉ	LOC 1 / LIEU 1	LOC 2 / LIEU 2	MAP / CARTE	POSITION LAT	LONG
Edgewood	UNP/LNO	NS	Colchester	11 E/5	45°25′	63°48′
Edgewood	UNP/LNO	BC	Kootenay	82 E/16	49°47′	118°09′
Edgewood Park	UNP/LNO	ON	Peterborough	31 D/8	44°17′	78°26′
Edgewood Park	UNP/LNO	ON	Welland	30 L/15	42°54′	78°59′
Edgeworth	UNP/LNO	SK	8-9-22-W2	72 H/10	49°44′	104°57′
Edgeworth Island	ISL/ÎLE	NT	Franklin	68 D	73°53′	97°12′
Édifices-de-Dawson City, Lieu historique national des - also-aussi - Dawson City Buildings National Historic Site	PARK/PARC	YT		116 B/3	64°03′	139°26′
Edillen	UNP/LNO	MB	16-28-15-W	62 O/5	51°24′	99°32′
Edina	UNP/LNO	QC	Argenteuil	31 G/10	45°43′	74°30′
Edinburgh Mountain	MTN/MNT	BC	Renfrew	92 C/9	48°39′	124°25′
Edison	UNP/LNO	ON	Kenora	52 F/13	49°48′	93°33′
Edith Cavell, Mount	MTN/MNT	AB	42,43-1-W6	83 D/9	52°40′	118°03′
Edmison Heights	UNP/LNO	ON	Peterborough	31 D/8	44°20′	78°19′
Edmond Creek	RIV/CDE	BC	Range 2 Coast	92 N/1	51°04′	124°01′
Edmonton	CITY/VIL1	AB		83 H/11	53°33′	113°28′
Edmonton Beach	VILG/VILG	AB	30-52-1-W5	83 G/9	53°31′	114°07′
Edmore	UNP/LNO	SK	2-30-12-W2	62 M/12	51°34′	103°35′
Edmore Beach	UNP/LNO	ON	Simcoe	41 A/9	44°36′	80°01′
Edmund Lake	LAKE/LAC	MB		53 K/11	54°45′	93°17′
Edmund Lake	LAKE/LAC	BC	Lillooet	92 P/11	51°36′	121°24′
Edmundston	CITY/VIL1	NB	Madawaska	21 N/8	47°22′	68°20′
Edmundston-Est	UNP/LNO	NB	Madawaska	21 N/8	47°22′	68°19′
Edmund Walker Island	ISL/ÎLE	NT	Franklin	79 D	77°07′	104°11′
Édouard, Lac	LAKE/LAC	QC	Le Haut-Saint-Maurice	31 P/9	47°35′	72°21′
Edrans	UNP/LNO	MB	35-12-13-W	62 J/3	50°03′	99°08′
Edson	TOWN/VIL2	AB	53-17-W5	83 F/9	53°35′	116°26′
Edson River	RIV/CDE	AB	54-16-W5	83 F/9	53°40′	116°17′
Edville	UNP/LNO	ON	Northumberland	31 C/4	44°03′	77°50′
Edwand	UNP/LNO	AB	36-59-16-W4	83 I/1	54°09′	112°17′
Edward	MUN2/AZM2	MB		62 F/3	49°11′	101°14′
Edward Island	ISL/ÎLE	ON	Thunder Bay	52 A/7	48°22′	88°37′
Edward Lake	LAKE/LAC	SK	54-12-W3	73 G/12	53°39′	107°45′
Edwards	UNP/LNO	ON	Carleton	31 G/6	45°19′	75°28′
Edwardsburgh	MUN2/AZM2	ON	Leeds	31 B/13	44°50′	75°30′
Edwards, Cape	CAPE/CAP	NT	Franklin	26 A	64°54′	65°55′
Edwards, Cape	CAPE/CAP	NT	Franklin	88 H	75°08′	112°25′
Edwards Corner	UNP/LNO	NB	Charlotte	21 G/3	45°07′	67°05′
Edwards Lake	LAKE/LAC	BC	Lillooet	92 P/11	51°42′	121°01′
Edwards, Mount	MTN/MNT	YT		105 M/9	63°43′	134°15′
Edwardsville	UNP/LNO	NS	Cape Breton	11 K/1	46°10′	60°14′
Edwin	UNP/LNO	MB	4-11-8-W	62 G/15	49°53′	98°31′
Edye 93	IR/RI	BC	Range 5 Coast	103 J/2	54°04′	130°34′
Edys Mills	UNP/LNO	ON	Lambton	40 J/9	42°44′	82°07′
Edzell	UNP/LNO	SK	23-37-6-W3	73 B/2	52°11′	106°46′
Edziza, Mount	MTN/MNT	BC	Cassiar	104 G/10	57°44′	130°40′
Edzo	UNP/LNO	NT	Mackenzie	85 K/16	62°45′	116°02′
Eel Ground	UNP/LNO	NB	Northumberland	21 I/13	46°58′	65°38′
Eel Ground 2	IR/RI	NB	Northumberland	21 I/13	46°59′	65°38′
Eel River	RIV/CDE	NB	York	21 G/14	46°00′	67°30′
Eel River 3	IR/RI	NB	Northumberland	22 B/1	48°02′	66°23′
Eel River Bridge	UNP/LNO	NB	Northumberland	21 P/3	47°02′	65°01′
Eel River Cove	UNP/LNO	NB	Restigouche	22 B/1	48°01′	66°23′
Eel River Crossing	VILG/VILG	NB	Restigouche	22 B/1	48°01′	66°25′
Eel River Lake	UNP/LNO	NB	York	21 G/13	45°50′	67°39′
Eels Creek	RIV/CDE	ON	Peterborough	31 D/9	44°35′	78°04′
Eelseuklis 10	IR/RI	BC	Clayoquot	92 F/4	49°13′	125°41′
Eels Lake	LAKE/LAC	ON	Peterborough	31 D/16	44°54′	78°08′
Effiat, Lac	LAKE/LAC	QC	Kativik	24 B/3	56°00′	67°28′
Effie, Mount	MTN/MNT	NT	Mackenzie	96 E	65°57′	127°51′
Effingham	UNP/LNO	ON	Welland	30 M/3	43°04′	79°18′
Effingham Inlet	BAY/BAIE	BC	Clayoquot	92 F/3	49°02′	125°09′
Effingham Island	ISL/ÎLE	BC	Barclay	92 C/14	48°52′	125°19′
Effingham Lake	LAKE/LAC	ON	Lennox and Addington	31 F/3	45°00′	77°23′
Effingham River	RIV/CDE	BC	Clayoquot	92 F/3	49°06′	125°12′
Égalité, Cap	CAPE/CAP	QC	Le Fjord-du-Saguenay	22 D/8	48°19′	70°16′
Egan Creek	UNP/LNO	ON	Hastings	31 F/4	45°03′	77°43′
Egan Creek	UNP/LNO	ON	Hastings	31 C/13	44°58′	77°44′
Egan-Sud	VILG/VILG	QC	La Vallée-de-la-Gatineau	31 J/5	46°26′	76°00′
Eganville	VILG/VILG	ON	Renfrew	31 F/11	45°32′	77°06′
Egbert	UNP/LNO	ON	Simcoe	31 D/4	44°14′	79°46′
Egenolf Lake	LAKE/LAC	MB		64 O/4	59°03′	100°00′
Egeria Bay 19	IR/RI	BC	Queen Charlotte	103 K/2	54°13′	132°59′
Egerton	UNP/LNO	NS	Pictou	11 E/9	45°36′	62°29′
Egerton	UNP/LNO	ON	Wellington	41 A/2	44°01′	80°31′
Egerton, Cape	CAPE/CAP	NT	Franklin	340 F	82°48′	81°33′

NAME NOM	ENTITY ENTITÉ	LOC 1 LIEU 1	LOC 2 LIEU 2	MAP CARTE	POSITION LAT	LONG
Egg Lake	LAKE/LAC	MB	62-27-W	63 K/6	54°22′	101°27′
Egg Lake	LAKE/LAC	SK	56,57-2,3-W2	63 E/16	53°53′	102°20′
Egg Lake	LAKE/LAC	SK		73 P/3	55°05′	105°30′
Egg River	RIV/CDE	MB		54 M/15	59°55′	94°50′
Egg River	RIV/CDE	NT	Franklin	98 B	72°27′	124°36′
Egina River	RIV/CDE	NT	Franklin	98 D	73°25′	122°16′
Églefin, Chenal de l' - also-aussi - Haddock Channel	SEAU/SMER	—		4016	45°30′	54°20′
Eglington	UNP/LNO	PE	Kings	11 L/8	46°19′	62°22′
Eglinton, Cape	CAPE/CAP	NT	Franklin	27 F	70°47′	69°25′
Eglinton Fiord	BAY/BAIE	NT	Franklin	27 F	70°40′	70°03′
Eglinton Island	ISL/ÎLE	NT	Franklin	88 G	75°48′	118°20′
Église, Arrondissement de l'	UNP/LNO	QC	Robert-Cliche	21 L/2	46°13′	70°47′
Egmondville	UNP/LNO	ON	Huron	40 P/11	43°32′	81°24′
Egmont	UNP/LNO	BC	New Westminster	92 G/12	49°45′	123°56′
Egmont Bay	UNP/LNO	PE	Prince	21 I/8	46°29′	64°06′
Egmont Bay	BAY/BAIE	PE	Prince	21 I/9	46°34′	64°14′
Egmont, Cape	CAPE/CAP	PE	Prince	21 I/8	46°24′	64°08′
Egremont	MUN2/AZM2	ON	Grey	41 A/2	44°05′	80°43′
Egremont	UNP/LNO	AB	25-58-22-W4	83 I/3	54°02′	113°08′
Egypt	UNP/LNO	ON	York	31 D/6	44°16′	79°18′
Égypte	UNP/LNO	QC	Les Maskoutains	31 H/10	45°32′	72°43′
Egypt Road	UNP/LNO	NS	Inverness	11 K/7	46°20′	60°57′
Ehatis 11	IR/RI	BC	Nootka	92 E/15	49°59′	126°52′
Ehatisaht	UNP/LNO	BC	Nootka	92 E/15	49°53′	126°51′
Ehkuapustet	UNP/LNO	QC	Minganie	22 I/16	50°52′	64°04′
Eholt	UNP/LNO	BC	Similkameen Division Yale	82 E/2	49°10′	118°33′
Eidsbotn	BAY/BAIE	NT	Franklin	59 A	76°10′	91°00′
Eids Fiord	BAY/BAIE	NT	Franklin	49 C	77°21′	87°06′
Eight Bears Island	ISL/ÎLE	NT	Franklin	89 D	77°06′	113°22′
Eighteen Mile Bay	BAY/BAIE	ON	Sudbury	41 I/2	46°05′	80°34′
Eighteen Mile Island	ISL/ÎLE	ON	Sudbury	41 I/1	46°05′	80°23′
Eighteen Mile River	RIV/CDE	ON	Huron	41 A/4	44°01′	81°44′
Eight Foot Falls	UNP/LNO	MB	15-15-E	52 L/5	50°17′	95°32′
Eight Island Lake	UNP/LNO	NS	Guysborough	11 F/5	45°22′	61°57′
Eight Mile Lake	LAKE/LAC	NS	Queens	21 A/2	44°10′	64°48′
Eight Mile Point	UNP/LNO	ON	Simcoe	31 D/11	44°31′	79°26′
Eileen Lake	LAKE/LAC	NT	Mackenzie	75 J	62°16′	107°37′
Eileen River	RIV/CDE	NT	Mackenzie	75 K	62°32′	108°23′
Eirik Ridge	SEAU/SMER	—		814A	58°15′	45°00′
Eka Kamahkauatihk	UNP/LNO	QC	Minganie	12 K/7	50°22′	60°50′
Ekalluk River	RIV/CDE	NT	Franklin	77 D	69°24′	106°18′
Ekalugad Fiord	BAY/BAIE	NT	Franklin	27 B	68°46′	68°37′
Ekapo Lake	LAKE/LAC	SK		62 L/7	50°19′	102°34′
Ekatuk River	RIV/CDE	NT	Franklin	77 H/5	71°27′	107°45′
Ekblaw Glacier	GLAC/GLAC	NT	Franklin	39 F	78°30′	76°50′
Ekblaw Lake	LAKE/LAC	NT	Franklin	340 D	81°40′	75°40′
Ekfrid	MUN2/AZM2	ON	Middlesex	40 I/13	42°46′	81°38′
Ekfrid	UNP/LNO	ON	Middlesex	40 I/13	42°46′	81°36′
Ekins Island	ISL/ÎLE	NT	Franklin	59 C	77°09′	95°48′
Ekins Point	UNP/LNO	BC	New Westminster	92 G/11	49°32′	123°23′
Ekka Island	ISL/ÎLE	NT	Mackenzie	96 J	66°19′	122°29′
Ekwan	UNP/LNO	BC	Peace River	94 I/5	58°23′	121°59′
Ekwan Point	CAPE/CAP	ON	Kenora	43 G/8	53°16′	82°07′
Ekwan River	RIV/CDE	ON	Kenora	43 G/1	53°12′	82°15′
Ekwi River	RIV/CDE	NT	Mackenzie	106 A	64°05′	128°08′
Eladesor	UNP/LNO	AB	12-28-19-W4	82 P/7	51°24′	112°35′
Elaho River	RIV/CDE	BC	New Westminster	92 J/3	50°07′	123°24′
Elaine Lake	LAKE/LAC	SK	63-3-W3	73 J/8	54°27′	106°22′
Elak Dase 192A	IR/RI	SK		73 O/15	55°51′	106°47′
Elba	UNP/LNO	ON	Dufferin	41 A/1	44°03′	80°08′
Elbourne	UNP/LNO	SK	20-25-19-W2	72 P/2	51°08′	104°38′
Elbow	VILG/VILG	SK	11-25-5-W3	72 O/2	51°07′	106°35′
Elbow Lake	HAM/HAM	SK		63 C/5	52°29′	101°43′
Elbow Lake	LAKE/LAC	ON	Thunder Bay	42 L/4	50°08′	87°47′
Elbow Lake	LAKE/LAC	MB	67,68-23-W	63 K/15	54°50′	100°52′
Elbow Lake	LAKE/LAC	BC	Cariboo	93 A/2	52°14′	120°50′
Elbow River	RIV/CDE	AB	14-24-1-W5	82 O/1	51°03′	114°02′
Elbridge	UNP/LNO	AB	22-60-22-W4	83 I/3	54°13′	113°14′
Elcapo No. 154	MUN2/AZM2	SK		62 L/7	50°25′	102°45′
Elcho	UNP/LNO	ON	Lincoln	30 M/4	43°01′	79°33′
Elcho 6	IR/RI	BC	Range 3 Coast	93 D/5	52°24′	127°32′
Elco Beach	UNP/LNO	ON	Welland	30 L/14	42°53′	79°09′
Elcott	UNP/LNO	SK	24-1-3-W2	62 E/1	49°03′	102°18′
Eldee	UNP/LNO	ON	Nipissing	31 L/11	46°39′	79°05′
Elder	UNP/LNO	ON	Dufferin	41 A/1	44°04′	80°03′

NAME NOM	ENTITY ENTITÉ	LOC 1 LIEU 1	LOC 2 LIEU 2	MAP CARTE	POSITION LAT	LONG
Elderbank	UNP/LNO	NS	Halifax	11 D/14	44°59′	63°13′
Elder Mills	UNP/LNO	ON	York	30 M/13	43°49′	79°38′
Eldersley	HAM/HAM	SK	45-13-W2	63 D/13	52°52′	103°49′
Elderslie	MUN2/AZM2	ON	Bruce	41 A/6	44°20′	81°12′
Elder Station	UNP/LNO	ON	York	30 M/13	43°49′	79°38′
Eldon	MUN2/AZM2	ON	Victoria	31 D/7	44°30′	79°00′
Eldon	UNP/LNO	PE	Queens	11 L/2	46°06′	62°53′
Eldon	UNP/LNO	ON	Victoria	31 D/11	44°31′	79°01′
Eldon	UNP/LNO	AB	23-27-15-W5	82 N/8	51°19′	116°02′
Eldon	GEOG/GÉOG	NB	Restigouche	21 O/11	47°40′	67°05′
Eldon No. 471	MUN2/AZM2	SK		73 F/3	53°10′	109°18′
Eldorado	UNP/LNO	ON	Hastings	31 C/12	44°35′	77°31′
Eldorado	UNP/LNO	SK		74 N/9	59°33′	108°30′
Eldorado Bay	BAY/BAIE	ON	Kenora	52 F/11	49°38′	93°22′
Eldorado Park	UNP/LNO	ON	Peel	30 M/12	43°39′	79°46′
Eldred	UNP/LNO	SK	21-53-7-W3	73 G/10	53°35′	106°58′
Eldred River	RIV/CDE	BC	New Westminster	92 K/1	50°05′	124°14′
Eldridge Bay	BAY/BAIE	NT	Franklin	79 B/2	76°04′	109°40′
Eleanor Lake	LAKE/LAC	MB	13-12-E	52 L/4	50°07′	95°50′
Electric	UNP/LNO	ON	Kent	40 J/9	42°31′	82°21′
Elephant Crossing	UNP/LNO	BC	Rupert	102 I/9	50°40′	128°03′
Elephant Lake	LAKE/LAC	ON	Haliburton	31 E/1	45°08′	78°08′
Éléphant, Mont	MTN/MNT	QC	Les Laurentides	31 J/1	46°14′	74°29′
Elephant Point	CAPE/CAP	BC	New Westminster	92 F/16	49°50′	124°02′
Eleven Mile Lake	LAKE/LAC	NS	Annapolis	21 A/11	44°32′	65°17′
Eley	UNP/LNO	ON	Algoma	41 J/3	46°13′	83°14′
Elf Lake	LAKE/LAC	ON	Thunder Bay	52 I/12	50°30′	89°41′
Elford	UNP/LNO	ON	Essex	40 J/2	42°06′	82°49′
Elfrida	UNP/LNO	ON	Wentworth	30 M/4	43°10′	79°47′
Elfros	VILG/VILG	SK	13-32-14-W2	62 M/12	51°45′	103°52′
Elfros No. 307	MUN2/AZM2	SK		62 M/12	51°45′	103°55′
Elgin	VILG/VILG	QC	Le Haut-Saint-Laurent	31 G/1	45°01′	74°14′
Elgin	MUN1/AZM1	ON	Elgin	40 I/5	42°30′	81°40′
Elgin	UNP/LNO	NS	Pictou	11 E/7	45°26′	62°40′
Elgin	UNP/LNO	NB	Albert	21 H/14	45°48′	65°07′
Elgin	UNP/LNO	QC	Le Haut-Saint-Laurent	31 G/1	45°01′	74°16′
Elgin	UNP/LNO	ON	Leeds	31 C/9	44°36′	76°13′
Elgin	UNP/LNO	MB	5-6-21-W	62 F/8	49°27′	100°16′
Elgin	UNP/LNO	BC	New Westminster	92 G/2	49°04′	122°49′
Elgin	GEOG/GÉOG	NB	Albert	21 H/14	45°50′	65°03′
Elgin	GEOG/GÉOG	ON	Elgin	40 I/5	42°30′	81°40′
Elginburg	UNP/LNO	ON	Frontenac	31 C/7	44°19′	76°32′
Elginfield	UNP/LNO	ON	Middlesex	40 P/3	43°10′	81°22′
Elgin, Lac	LAKE/LAC	QC	Le Granit	21 E/14	45°45′	71°20′
Elgin Mills	UNP/LNO	ON	York	30 M/14	43°53′	79°27′
Elhlateese 2	IR/RI	BC	Clayoquot	92 F/3	49°01′	125°02′
Elie	UNP/LNO	MB	1,2-11-3-W	62 H/13	49°54′	97°46′
Élie, Mont	MTN/MNT	QC	Charlevoix-Est	21 M/16	47°55′	70°22′
Elimere Point	UNP/LNO	ON	Simcoe	31 D/13	44°45′	79°51′
Elimville	UNP/LNO	ON	Huron	40 P/6	43°19′	81°24′
Elinor Lake	LAKE/LAC	AB	65-11-W4	73 L/12	54°40′	111°39′
Eliot, Mount	MTN/MNT	NF		14 M/4	59°11′	63°48′
Elizabeth	UNP/LNO	ON	Rainy River	52 B/12	48°44′	91°50′
Elizabeth Bay	UNP/LNO	ON	Manitoulin	41 G/15	45°49′	82°43′
Elizabeth Bay	BAY/BAIE	ON	Manitoulin	41 G/15	45°50′	82°45′
Elizabeth Falls	FALL/CHUT	SK		74 P/4	59°11′	105°33′
Elizabeth Gardens	UNP/LNO	ON	Halton	30 M/5	43°22′	79°44′
Elizabeth Harbour	BAY/BAIE	NT	Franklin	57 F	70°36′	92°15′
Elizabeth, Lac	LAKE/LAC	QC	Kativik	33 O/11	55°36′	75°28′
Elizabeth Metis Settlement	UNP/LNO	AB		73 L/1	54°07′	110°05′
Elizabeth, Point	CAPE/CAP	NT	Franklin	46 J	66°42′	82°06′
Elizabeth, Port	BAY/BAIE	BC	Range 1 Coast	92 L/9	50°40′	126°28′
Elizabethtown	MUN2/AZM2	ON	Grenville	31 B/12	44°42′	75°47′
Elizabethville	UNP/LNO	ON	Durham	31 D/1	44°03′	78°28′
Eliza, Lake	LAKE/LAC	AB	6-56-8,9-W4	73 E/14	53°48′	111°12′
Eliza, Port	BAY/BAIE	BC	Nootka	92 E/14	49°53′	127°01′
Elk Bay	UNP/LNO	BC	Sayward	92 K/6	50°17′	125°26′
Elkford	MUN1/AZM1	BC	Kootenay	82 J/2	50°03′	114°53′
Elk Hill	UNP/LNO	SK	36-49-16-W2	73 H/8	53°17′	104°13′
Elkhorn	VILG/VILG	MB	11,12-28-W	62 F/14	49°59′	101°14′
Elkhorn Mountain	MTN/MNT	BC	Nootka	92 F/13	49°47′	125°50′
Elk Island	UNP/LNO	AB	25-55-21-W4	83 H/15	53°47′	112°59′
Elk Island	ISL/ÎLE	MB		53 L/9	54°40′	94°07′
Elk Island	ISL/ÎLE	MB		62 I/15	50°46′	96°33′
Elk Island National Park - also-aussi - Elk Island, Parc national	PARK/PARC	AB	53-20-W4	83 H/10	53°36′	112°53′

NAME NOM	ENTITY ENTITÉ	LOC 1 LIEU 1	LOC 2 LIEU 2	MAP CARTE	POSITION LAT	LONG
Elk Island, Parc national - also-aussi - Elk Island National Park	PARK/PARC	AB	53-20-W4	83 H/10	53°36'	112°53'
Elk Lake	UNP/LNO	ON	Timiskaming	41 P/9	47°44'	80°20'
Elk Lake	LAKE/LAC	BC	Lake	92 B/11	48°32'	123°24'
Elko	UNP/LNO	BC	Kootenay	82 G/6	49°18'	115°07'
Elk Point	TOWN/VIL2	AB	57-7-W4	73 E/15	53°54'	110°54'
Elk Prairie	UNP/LNO	BC	Kootenay	82 G/15	49°46'	114°53'
Elk Ranch	UNP/LNO	MB	13-17-16-W	62 J/5	50°27'	99°34'
Elk River	RIV/CDE	BC	Kootenay	82 G/3	49°10'	115°13'
Elk River	RIV/CDE	BC	Comox	92 F/13	49°52'	125°45'
Elk River	RIV/CDE	NT	Mackenzie	75 I/7	62°25'	104°48'
Elkton	UNP/LNO	AB	17-31-4-W5	82 O/10	51°39'	114°32'
Elkview	UNP/LNO	BC	Kootenay	82 G/10	49°44'	114°53'
Elkwater	UNP/LNO	AB	24-8-3-W4	72 E/9	49°40'	110°17'
Ella Bay	BAY/BAIE	NT	Franklin	120 C	81°07'	69°50'
Ellard	UNP/LNO	QC	La Vallée-de-la-Gatineau	31 K/1	46°13'	76°02'
Ellard Lake	LAKE/LAC	ON	Kenora	53 J/12	54°33'	91°55'
Ellaton - see-voir - Rattlesnake Harbour	UNP/LNO	ON		40 I/16	42°53'	80°25'
Ell Bay	BAY/BAIE	NT	Keewatin	46 D	64°08'	86°16'
Ellef Ringnes Island	ISL/ÎLE	NT	Franklin	69 F	78°30'	102°15'
Elleh	UNP/LNO	BC	Peace River	94 J/9	58°32'	122°05'
Elleh Creek	RIV/CDE	BC	Peace River	94 J/8	58°30'	122°05'
Ellen Creek	RIV/CDE	BC	Range 2 Coast	92 M/14	51°50'	127°18'
Ellengowan	UNP/LNO	ON	Bruce	41 A/6	44°16'	81°14'
Ellenvale	UNP/LNO	NS	Halifax	11 D/12	44°40'	63°31'
Ellenwood Lake	LAKE/LAC	NS	Yarmouth	20 P/13	43°56'	65°59'
Ellershouse	UNP/LNO	NS	Hants	21 A/16	44°57'	64°00'
Ellerslie	UNP/LNO	PE	Prince	11 L/12	46°36'	63°57'
Ellerslie-Bideford	VILG/VILG	PE	Prince	11 L/12	46°36'	63°57'
Ellerslie Lake	LAKE/LAC	BC	Range 3 Coast	93 D/12	52°33'	127°58'
Ellesmere	UNP/LNO	ON	York	30 M/14	43°46'	79°17'
Ellesmere, Île d' - also-aussi - **Ellesmere Island**	ISL/ÎLE	NT	Franklin	39 G	79°50'	78°00'
Ellesmere Island - also-aussi - **Ellesmere, Île d'**	ISL/ÎLE	NT	Franklin	39 G	79°50'	78°00'
Ellesmere Island National Park Reserve - also-aussi - Île-d'Ellesmere, Réserve de parc national de l'	PARK/PARC	NT	Franklin	340 E/1	82°13'	72°13'
Ellice	MUN2/AZM2	ON	Perth	40 P/6	43°29'	81°00'
Ellice	MUN2/AZM2	MB		62 K/6	50°28'	101°20'
Ellice Hills	MTN/MNT	NT	Keewatin	56 P	67°50'	88°30'
Ellice Island	ISL/ÎLE	NT	Mackenzie	107 C	69°07'	135°48'
Ellice River	RIV/CDE	NT	Keewatin	67 B/4	68°02'	103°58'
Ellington Lake	LAKE/LAC	NT	Mackenzie	86 F/3	65°03'	117°18'
Elliot Bay	BAY/BAIE	NT	Keewatin	66 P	67°31'	96°14'
Elliot Creek	RIV/CDE	BC	Range 1 Coast	92 K/15	50°52'	124°40'
Elliot Lake	CITY/VIL1	ON	Algoma	41 J/7	46°23'	82°38'
Elliot Lake	LAKE/LAC	ON	Algoma	41 J/7	46°23'	82°42'
Elliot Lake	LAKE/LAC	MB		53 D/14	52°55'	95°19'
Elliott	UNP/LNO	ON	Lanark	31 C/16	44°50'	76°24'
Elliott Brook	RIV/CDE	NB	Carleton	21 J/11	46°34'	67°17'
Elliott Lake	LAKE/LAC	NT	Keewatin	65 G	61°07'	99°29'
Elliotts	UNP/LNO	PE	Queens	11 L/6	46°22'	63°28'
Elliotts Corners	UNP/LNO	ON	Simcoe	31 D/12	44°43'	79°49'
Elliott's Cove	UNP/LNO	NF		2 C/4	48°09'	53°54'
Elliott's Cove-Snook's Harbour-Aspey Brook - see-voir - Random Island West	UNP/LNO	NF		2 C/4	48°08'	53°53'
Elliotvale	UNP/LNO	PE	Kings	11 L/7	46°15'	62°47'
Ellis	UNP/LNO	ON	Thunder Bay	52 A/12	48°34'	89°42'
Ellisboro	UNP/LNO	SK	17-18-9-W2	62 L/11	50°32'	103°14'
Ellis Creek	RIV/CDE	BC	Similkameen Division Yale	82 E/5	49°29'	119°36'
Ellis Lake	LAKE/LAC	BC	New Westminster	92 K/2	50°14'	124°52'
Ellison	UNP/LNO	BC	Osoyoos Division Yale	82 E/14	49°56'	119°22'
Elliston	TOWN/VIL2	NF		2 C/11	48°38'	53°03'
Ellisville	UNP/LNO	ON	Leeds	31 C/8	44°29'	76°10'
Ell, Lac	LAKE/LAC	QC	Jamésie	33 C/9	52°40'	76°07'
Ell, Ruisseau	RIV/CDE	QC	Avignon	22 B/7	48°16'	66°30'
Ellscott	UNP/LNO	AB	1-64-20-W4	83 I/10	54°30'	112°54'
Ellsmere Village	UNP/LNO	ON	Nipissing	31 L/12	46°35'	79°38'
Ells River	RIV/CDE	AB	96-11-W4	74 E/5	57°18'	111°40'
Ellwood	UNP/LNO	ON	Carleton	31 G/5	45°22'	75°40'
Elm	UNP/LNO	ON	Carleton	31 F/8	45°21'	76°05'
Elma	MUN2/AZM2	ON	Perth	40 P/10	43°38'	81°00'
Elma	UNP/LNO	ON	Dundas	31 G/3	45°01'	75°14'
Elma	UNP/LNO	MB	28,29,32,33-10-12-E	52 E/13	49°53'	95°54'
Elmbank	UNP/LNO	ON	Peel	30 M/12	43°41'	79°37'
Elm Brook	UNP/LNO	NB	Kings	21 H/12	45°42'	65°47'
Elmbrook	UNP/LNO	ON	Prince Edward	31 C/3	44°04'	77°08'
Elm Creek	UNP/LNO	MB	19-8-4-W	62 H/12	49°41'	98°00'
Elmdale	UNP/LNO	ON	Essex	40 J/1	42°03'	82°29'
Elmer, Lac	LAKE/LAC	QC	Jamésie	33 C/5	52°23'	77°40'

NAME NOM	ENTITY ENTITÉ	LOC 1 LIEU 1	LOC 2 LIEU 2	MAP CARTE	POSITION LAT	LONG
Elmerson Peninsula	CAPE/CAP	NT	Franklin	340 B	80°40′	82°00′
Elmfield	UNP/LNO	NS	Pictou	11 E/10	45°38′	62°56′
Elmgrove	UNP/LNO	ON	Leeds	31 C/16	44°50′	76°12′
Elmgrove	UNP/LNO	ON	Simcoe	31 D/4	44°11′	79°49′
Elmhedge	UNP/LNO	ON	Grey	41 A/10	44°34′	80°41′
Elm Hill	UNP/LNO	NB	Queens	21 G/9	45°43′	66°09′
Elmhurst	UNP/LNO	NB	Kings	21 H/12	45°34′	65°56′
Elmhurst	UNP/LNO	MB		62 H/14	49°51′	97°16′
Elmhurst	UNP/LNO	SK	9-54-19-W3	73 F/10	53°39′	108°44′
Elmhurst Beach	UNP/LNO	ON	York	31 D/3	44°13′	79°28′
Elmira	UNP/LNO	PE	Kings	11 L/8	46°27′	62°04′
Elmira	UNP/LNO	ON	Waterloo	40 P/10	43°36′	80°33′
Elmore	UNP/LNO	SK	1-1-32-W	62 F/4	49°00′	101°38′
Elm Park	UNP/LNO	MB		62 H/14	49°51′	97°07′
Elmsdale	UNP/LNO	PE	Prince	21 I/16	46°49′	64°08′
Elmsdale	UNP/LNO	NS	Hants	11 D/13	44°58′	63°30′
Elmside	UNP/LNO	QC	Pontiac	31 F/9	45°32′	76°24′
Elm Springs	UNP/LNO	SK	14-5-2-W3	72 G/8	49°22′	106°12′
Elmstead	UNP/LNO	ON	Essex	40 J/7	42°17′	82°51′
Elmsthorpe No. 100	MUN2/AZM2	SK		72 H/14	49°55′	105°00′
Elmsvale	UNP/LNO	NS	Halifax	11 E/3	45°05′	63°04′
Elmsville	UNP/LNO	NB	Charlotte	21 G/6	45°16′	67°01′
Elmtree	UNP/LNO	NB	Northumberland	21 I/13	46°50′	65°45′
Elm Tree	UNP/LNO	ON	Frontenac	31 C/11	44°41′	77°00′
Elm Tree Corners	UNP/LNO	ON	Victoria	31 D/7	44°19′	78°47′
Elmvale	UNP/LNO	ON	Simcoe	31 D/12	44°35′	79°52′
Elmview	UNP/LNO	ON	Sudbury	41 I/10	46°39′	81°00′
Elmwood	UNP/LNO	PE	Queens	11 L/3	46°15′	63°19′
Elmwood	UNP/LNO	NS	Lunenburg	21 A/10	44°35′	64°38′
Elmwood	UNP/LNO	NB	Carleton	21 J/4	46°04′	67°43′
Elmwood	UNP/LNO	ON	Frontenac	31 C/2	44°14′	76°38′
Elmwood	UNP/LNO	ON	Grey	41 A/3	44°14′	81°03′
Elmwood	UNP/LNO	MB		62 H/14	49°55′	97°06′
Elmwood Estates	UNP/LNO	NB	Westmorland	21 I/2	46°07′	64°46′
Elmwood Station	UNP/LNO	NB	Carleton	21 J/4	46°05′	67°43′
Elmworth	UNP/LNO	AB	9-70-11-W6	83 M/4	55°03′	119°37′
Elnora	VILG/VILG	AB	10-35-23-W4	82 P/14	51°59′	113°12′
Eloida	UNP/LNO	ON	Leeds	31 B/12	44°41′	75°58′
Eloida, Lake	LAKE/LAC	ON	Leeds	31 B/12	44°40′	75°58′
Elora	VILG/VILG	ON	Wellington	40 P/9	43°41′	80°26′
Elphin	UNP/LNO	ON	Lanark	31 C/15	44°55′	76°37′
Elphinstone	UNP/LNO	MB	8,9-18-21-W	62 K/9	50°32′	100°19′
Elphinstone, Mount	MTN/MNT	BC	New Westminster	92 G/5	49°28′	123°32′
Elrose	TOWN/VIL2	SK	9-26-15-W3	72 N/1	51°12′	108°02′
Elsa	UNP/LNO	YT		105 M/14	63°55′	135°29′
Elsas	UNP/LNO	ON	Algoma	42 B/10	48°31′	82°54′
Elsie Island	ISL/ÎLE	NT	Keewatin	34 L	58°50′	78°55′
Elsie, Lac	LAKE/LAC	QC	Kativik	23 O/9	55°32′	66°05′
Elsie Lake	LAKE/LAC	BC	Newcastle	92 F/6	49°27′	125°09′
Elsinore	UNP/LNO	ON	Bruce	41 A/11	44°31′	81°15′
Elson, Lac	LAKE/LAC	QC	Caniapiscau	23 I/16	54°50′	64°25′
Elspeth	UNP/LNO	AB	33-38-2-W5	83 B/8	52°19′	114°13′
Elstow	VILG/VILG	SK	10-35-1-W3	72 O/16	51°59′	106°04′
Eltham	UNP/LNO	AB	4-19-26-W4	82 I/12	50°35′	113°33′
Elton	MUN2/AZM2	MB		62 G/13	49°58′	99°50′
Elton Lake	LAKE/LAC	BC	Kamloops Division Yale	92 J/1	50°08′	122°10′
Eltrut Lake	LAKE/LAC	ON	Kenora	52 F/1	49°01′	92°25′
Elu Inlet	BAY/BAIE	NT	Mackenzie	77 A	68°30′	106°05′
Elva	UNP/LNO	MB	18-3-27-W	62 F/3	49°13′	101°07′
Elvina Island	ISL/ÎLE	NT	Franklin	78 D	73°21′	107°29′
Elwin Bay	BAY/BAIE	NT	Franklin	58 D	73°32′	90°55′
Elwin Inlet	BAY/BAIE	NT	Franklin	48 D/5	73°25′	83°45′
Elzevir	UNP/LNO	ON	Hastings	31 C/11	44°38′	77°16′
Elzevir and Grimsthorpe	MUN2/AZM2	ON	Hastings	31 C/11	44°43′	77°23′
Émard	UNP/LNO	QC	Beauharnois-Salaberry	31 G/1	45°11′	74°04′
Embar	UNP/LNO	NF		23 A/5	52°18′	65°41′
Embarras	UNP/LNO	AB	8-50-20-W5	83 F/7	53°18′	116°54′
Embarras, Lac	LAKE/LAC	QC	La Vallée-de-la-Gatineau	31 K/15	46°54′	76°30′
Embarras Portage	UNP/LNO	AB	109-9-W4	74 L/6	58°27′	111°28′
Embarras River	RIV/CDE	AB	52-18-W5	83 F/7	53°27′	116°37′
Emblem	UNP/LNO	MB	36-5-24-W	62 F/7	49°27′	100°35′
Embree	TOWN/VIL2	NF		2 E/6	49°18′	55°03′
Embro	UNP/LNO	ON	Oxford	40 P/2	43°09′	80°54′
Embrun	UNP/LNO	ON	Russell	31 G/6	45°16′	75°17′
Embury Lake	LAKE/LAC	MB	67-29-W	63 K/13	54°49′	101°48′

NAME NOM	ENTITY ENTITÉ	LOC 1 LIEU 1	LOC 2 LIEU 2	MAP CARTE	POSITION LAT	LONG
Emerald	UNP/LNO	NS	Inverness	11 K/6	46°19′	61°02′
Emerald	UNP/LNO	ON	Lennox and Addington	31 C/2	44°09′	76°46′
Emerald Bank - also-aussi - Émeraude, Banc d'	SEAU/SMER	—		8006	43°35′	62°30′
Emerald Basin - also-aussi - Émeraude, Bassin d'	SEAU/SMER	—		8007	44°00′	62°50′
Emerald Isle	ISL/ÎLE	NT	Franklin	89 A	76°48′	114°10′
Emerald Junction	UNP/LNO	PE	Queens	11 L/5	46°22′	63°33′
Emerald Lake	LAKE/LAC	ON	Sudbury	41 I/16	46°54′	80°19′
Emerald Lake	LAKE/LAC	ON	Algoma	41 J/7	46°18′	82°52′
Emerald No. 277	MUN2/AZM2	SK		62 M/5	51°30′	103°55′
Emerald Shoal	SEAU/SMER	—		4579	46°44′	53°22′
Emerald Vale	UNP/LNO	NF		1 N/11	47°31′	53°18′
Émeraude, Banc d' - also-aussi - Emerald Bank	SEAU/SMER	—		8006	43°35′	62°30′
Émeraude, Bassin d' - also-aussi - Emerald Basin	SEAU/SMER	—		8007	44°00′	62°50′
Emeraude Shoal	SEAU/SMER	—		4505	50°23′	56°32′
Emeric Point	CAPE/CAP	ON	Lennox and Addington	31 C/2	44°06′	76°42′
Emeril	UNP/LNO	NF		23 G/1	53°05′	66°13′
Emerson	TOWN/VIL2	MB		62 H/3	49°00′	97°13′
Emerson	UNP/LNO	NB	Kent	21 I/6	46°28′	65°07′
Emerson Junction	UNP/LNO	MB	3-1-2-E	62 H/3	49°01′	97°14′
Emery	UNP/LNO	ON	Leeds	31 C/8	44°23′	76°08′
Emery	UNP/LNO	ON	York	30 M/13	43°45′	79°33′
Emeryville	UNP/LNO	ON	Essex	40 J/7	42°18′	82°45′
Emesville	UNP/LNO	MB	20-12-3-E	62 I/3	50°02′	97°08′
Emile River	RIV/CDE	NT	Mackenzie	85 N/7	63°18′	116°35′
Émileville	UNP/LNO	QC	Les Maskoutains	31 H/7	45°29′	72°54′
Emily	MUN2/AZM2	ON	Victoria	31 D/7	44°23′	78°35′
Emily Creek	RIV/CDE	ON	Victoria	31 D/7	44°30′	78°37′
Emily Harbour	UNP/LNO	NF		13 I/11	54°33′	57°11′
Emily Lake	LAKE/LAC	ON	Victoria	31 D/7	44°26′	78°35′
Emma Fiord	BAY/BAIE	NT	Franklin	560 D	81°29′	89°00′
Emma Lake	UNP/LNO	SK	11-53-27-W2	73 H/12	53°34′	105°53′
Emma Lake	LAKE/LAC	SK	53,54-27-W2	73 H/12	53°36′	105°54′
Emmanuel, Lac	LAKE/LAC	QC	Jamésie	33 A/16	52°53′	72°00′
Emmaville	UNP/LNO	SK	52-22-W3	73 F/11	53°31′	109°08′
Emm Bay	BAY/BAIE	ON	Kenora	52 F/5	49°17′	93°56′
Emmeline Lake	LAKE/LAC	SK	69-3-W3	73 J/16	55°00′	106°22′
Emmerson Island	ISL/ÎLE	NT	Franklin	38 B	72°24′	78°56′
Emmuraillé, Lac	LAKE/LAC	QC	Le Fjord-du-Saguenay	22 D/16	48°59′	70°08′
Emo	MUN2/AZM2	ON	Rainy River	52 C/12	48°39′	93°46′
Emo	UNP/LNO	ON	Rainy River	52 C/12	48°38′	93°50′
Empey Hill	UNP/LNO	ON	Hastings	31 C/6	44°15′	77°04′
Empire Corners	UNP/LNO	ON	Haldimand	30 M/4	43°02′	79°47′
Empire Lake	LAKE/LAC	ON	Thunder Bay	52 G/9	49°43′	90°15′
Empress	VILG/VILG	AB	8-13-23-1-W4	72 L/16	50°57′	110°00′
Emsdale	UNP/LNO	ON	Parry Sound	31 E/11	45°32′	79°19′
Emyvale	UNP/LNO	PE	Queens	11 L/6	46°17′	63°22′
Ena Lake	UNP/LNO	ON	Kenora	52 E/15	49°59′	94°31′
Ena Lake	LAKE/LAC	ON	Kenora	52 E/15	49°59′	94°31′
Ena Lake	LAKE/LAC	SK		74 N/16	59°55′	108°12′
Ena River	RIV/CDE	NT/SK		75 C/1	60°00′	108°09′
Enchant	UNP/LNO	AB	17-14-18-W4	82 I/1	50°10′	112°25′
Enchanteresse, Île	ISL/ÎLE	QC	La Jacques-Cartier	21 L/14	46°58′	71°12′
Encombe	UNP/LNO	BC	Range 5 Coast	93 K/2	54°04′	124°43′
Endako	UNP/LNO	BC	Range 5 Coast	93 K/3	54°05′	125°01′
Endcliffe	UNP/LNO	MB	6-22-28-W	62 K/14	50°52′	101°22′
Endeavour	VILG/VILG	SK	37-5-W2	63 D/2	52°10′	102°39′
Endeavour Seamount	SEAU/SMER	—		15789A	48°16′	129°05′
Endeavour Trough	SEAU/SMER	—		15789A	48°18′	129°00′
Enderby	CITY/VIL1	BC	Kamloops Division Yale	82 L/11	50°33′	119°09′
Enderby 2	IR/RI	BC	Kamloops Division Yale	82 L/11	50°33′	119°08′
Endiang	UNP/LNO	AB	26-34-16-W4	82 P/16	51°57′	112°10′
Endikai Lake	LAKE/LAC	ON	Algoma	41 J/11	46°35′	83°02′
Enemy, Lake of the	LAKE/LAC	NT	Mackenzie	46 F	63°47′	110°15′
Enfield	UNP/LNO	NS	Hants	11 D/13	44°57′	63°32′
Enfield	UNP/LNO	ON	Durham	31 D/2	44°02′	78°50′
Enfield No. 194	MUN2/AZM2	SK		72 J/10	50°40′	106°35′
Enfin	UNP/LNO	SK	16-25-4-W2	62 M/2	51°10′	102°31′
Engemann Lake	LAKE/LAC	SK		74 G/15	57°55′	106°55′
Engen	UNP/LNO	BC	Range 5 Coast	93 K/1	54°02′	124°18′
Engineer	UNP/LNO	BC	Cassiar	104 M/8	59°29′	134°15′
Englee	TOWN/VIL2	NF		12 I/9	50°44′	56°06′
Englefeld	VILG/VILG	SK	9-37-19-W2	73 A/2	52°10′	104°39′
Englefield Bay	BAY/BAIE	BC	Queen Charlotte	103 C/16	52°59′	132°25′
Englefield, Cape	CAPE/CAP	NT	Franklin	47 C	69°49′	85°34′
Englehart	TOWN/VIL2	ON	Timiskaming	31 M/13	47°49′	79°52′

NAME NOM	ENTITY ENTITÉ	LOC 1 LIEU 1	LOC 2 LIEU 2	MAP CARTE	POSITION LAT	LONG
Englehart River	RIV/CDE	ON	Timiskaming	31 M/13	47°51′	79°50′
Engler Lake	LAKE/LAC	SK		74 O/2	59°08′	106°52′
Englewood	UNP/LNO	SK		72 I/7	50°30′	104°37′
*Englewood	UNP/LNO	BC	Rupert	92 L/10	50°32′	126°53′
English, Cape	CAPE/CAP	NF		1 K/13	46°47′	53°40′
English Chief River	RIV/CDE	NT	Mackenzie	95 J	62°52′	123°52′
English Corner	UNP/LNO	NS	Halifax	11 D/12	44°44′	63°47′
English Harbour	UNP/LNO	NF		2 C/6	48°22′	53°16′
English Harbour East	VILG/VILG	NF		1 M/10	47°38′	54°54′
English Harbour West	UNP/LNO	NF		1 M/6	47°28′	55°30′
English Lake	LAKE/LAC	BC	Lillooet	92 P/10	51°35′	120°39′
English Line	UNP/LNO	ON	Northumberland	31 C/5	44°16′	77°44′
Englishman River	RIV/CDE	BC	Nanoose	92 F/8	49°20′	124°17′
Englishmans Range	MTN/MNT	YT		105 C/8	60°25′	132°01′
English Point	UNP/LNO	NF		12 P/7	51°29′	56°56′
English River	UNP/LNO	ON	Kenora	52 G/2	49°12′	90°58′
English River	UNP/LNO	ON	Kenora	52 G/2	49°13′	90°58′
English River	RIV/CDE	ON	Kenora	52 L/3	50°12′	95°00′
English River	RIV/CDE	MB	7-14-13-E	52 L/4	50°09′	95°49′
English River 21	IR/RI	ON	Kenora	52 L/1	50°11′	94°02′
English River 66	IR/RI	ON	Cochrane	42 K/8	50°28′	84°25′
English Settlement	UNP/LNO	NB	York	21 J/7	46°15′	66°44′
Englishtown	UNP/LNO	NS	Victoria	11 K/7	46°17′	60°33′
Enhalt 11	IR/RI	BC	Kamloops Division Yale	92 I/6	50°20′	121°19′
Enid	UNP/LNO	SK	18-25-14-W2	62 M/4	51°08′	103°57′
Enid Creek	RIV/CDE	ON	Cochrane	42 A/12	48°38′	81°37′
Enilda	UNP/LNO	AB	13-74-16-W5	83 N/8	55°25′	116°18′
Enlaugra	UNP/LNO	QC	Brome-Missisquoi	31 H/2	45°09′	72°36′
Enmore	UNP/LNO	PE	Prince	21 I/9	46°35′	64°03′
Ennadai	UNP/LNO	NT	Keewatin	65 F	61°08′	100°53′
Ennadai Lake	LAKE/LAC	NT	Keewatin	65 C	60°58′	101°20′
Ennemond	UNP/LNO	NB	Madawaska	21 N/8	47°24′	68°26′
Ennisclare Park	UNP/LNO	ON	Halton	30 M/5	43°28′	79°39′
Ennishone	UNP/LNO	NB	Victoria	21 O/4	47°05′	67°41′
Ennishore	UNP/LNO	NB	Victoria	21 O/4	47°02′	67°39′
Enniskerry	UNP/LNO	ON	Carleton	31 G/4	45°12′	75°34′
Enniskillen	MUN2/AZM2	ON	Lambton	40 J/16	42°51′	82°07′
Enniskillen	UNP/LNO	NB	Queens	21 G/9	45°33′	66°30′
Enniskillen	UNP/LNO	ON	Durham	31 D/2	44°01′	78°46′
Enniskillen No. 3	MUN2/AZM2	SK		62 E/1	49°10′	102°10′
Ennismore	MUN2/AZM2	ON	Peterborough	31 D/8	44°25′	78°27′
Ennismore	UNP/LNO	ON	Peterborough	31 D/8	44°25′	78°26′
Ennotville	UNP/LNO	ON	Wellington	40 P/9	43°39′	80°20′
Enon	UNP/LNO	NS	Cape Breton	11 F/15	45°48′	60°32′
Enquocto 14	IR/RI	BC	Kamloops Division Yale	92 I/7	50°28′	120°57′
Enragé, Cap	CAPE/CAP	QC	Rimouski-Neigette	22 C/7	48°22′	68°45′
Enrage, Cape	CAPE/CAP	NB	Albert	21 H/10	45°36′	64°47′
Enragée, Pointe	CAPE/CAP	NF		11 O/11	47°35′	59°14′
Ens	UNP/LNO	SK	16-43-26-W2	73 A/12	52°42′	105°43′
Ensheshese 13	IR/RI	BC	Range 5 Coast	103 J/9	54°31′	130°13′
Ensheshese 53	IR/RI	BC	Range 5 Coast	103 J/9	54°31′	130°14′
Ensign	UNP/LNO	AB	31-17-25-W4	82 I/6	50°28′	113°26′
Ensleigh	UNP/LNO	AB	6-33-8-W4	72 M/14	51°51′	111°08′
Enterprise	UNP/LNO	NB	Victoria	21 J/14	46°58′	67°23′
Enterprise	UNP/LNO	ON	Lennox and Addington	31 C/7	44°28′	76°52′
Enterprise	UNP/LNO	BC	Lillooet	92 P/13	51°58′	121°49′
Enterprise	UNP/LNO	NT	Mackenzie	85 C/9	60°33′	116°08′
Enterprise No. 142	MUN2/AZM2	SK		72 K/5	50°20′	109°50′
Entiako River	RIV/CDE	BC	Range 4 Coast	93 F/6	53°24′	125°17′
Entice	UNP/LNO	AB	14-29-24-W4	82 P/6	51°29′	113°17′
Entlqwekkinh 19	IR/RI	BC	Kamloops Division Yale	92 I/6	50°28′	121°19′
Entrance	UNP/LNO	AB	1-51-26-W5	83 F/5	53°22′	117°41′
Entrée, Île d'	ISL/ÎLE	QC	Les Îles-de-la-Madeleine	11 N/5	47°17′	61°42′
Entrelacs	VILG/VILG	QC	Matawinie	31 J/1	46°07′	74°00′
Entwine Lake	LAKE/LAC	ON	Kenora	52 F/2	49°08′	92°41′
Entwistle	VILG/VILG	AB	20-53-7-W5	83 G/10	53°36′	115°00′
Enukso Point	CAPE/CAP	NT	Franklin	36 D	64°34′	78°12′
Envies, Rivière des	RIV/CDE	QC	Francheville	31 I/9	46°36′	72°23′
Environ	UNP/LNO	SK	34-37-10-W3	73 B/3	52°14′	107°19′
Eokuk Lake	LAKE/LAC	NT	Mackenzie	86 P	67°24′	112°56′
Épaule, Lac à l'	LAKE/LAC	QC	La Côte-de-Beaupré	21 M/6	47°15′	71°14′
Épaule, Rivière à l'	RIV/CDE	QC	La Jacques-Cartier	21 M/3	47°07′	71°22′
Épave-Fayette-Brown, L'	UNP/LNO	QC	Minganie	12 E/12	49°36′	63°47′
Epemistikwepichinanuch	UNP/LNO	QC	Jamésie	32 M/16	51°48′	78°08′
Éphrem, Lac	LAKE/LAC	QC	La Haute-Côte-Nord	22 C/14	48°52′	69°26′

NAME NOM	ENTITY ENTITÉ	LOC 1 LIEU 1	LOC 2 LIEU 2	MAP CARTE	POSITION LAT	POSITION LONG
Epimichischiskach Eseyau	UNP/LNO	QC	Jamésie	32 N/5	51°26′	77°51′
Epinette Creek	RIV/CDE	MB	6-9-13-W	62 G/11	49°43′	99°13′
Epping	UNP/LNO	ON	Grey	41 A/7	44°27′	80°33′
Epping	UNP/LNO	SK	30-47-27-W3	73 F/4	53°05′	109°57′
Epsom	UNP/LNO	ON	Ontario	31 D/3	44°06′	79°02′
Epworth	UNP/LNO	NF		1 M/3	47°02′	55°12′
Epworth and Great Salmonier	UNP/LNO	NF		1 M/3	47°02′	55°12′
Epworth Park	UNP/LNO	NB	Kings	21 G/8	45°19′	66°12′
Eqe Bay	BAY/BAIE	NT	Franklin	37 C	69°37′	76°24′
Équerre, L'	UNP/LNO	QC	Témiscouata	21 N/6	47°28′	69°16′
Équerre, L'	UNP/LNO	QC	L'Islet	21 K/13	46°52′	69°54′
Équerre, L'	UNP/LNO	QC	Charlevoix-Est	21 M/16	47°57′	70°27′
Équerres-à-Campbell, Les	UNP/LNO	QC	Lotbinière	21 L/6	46°21′	71°22′
Équerres, Les	UNP/LNO	QC	Le Haut-Saint-Maurice	31 P/9	47°44′	72°29′
Equesis Creek	RIV/CDE	BC	Osoyoos Division Yale	82 L/6	50°17′	119°24′
Equis 8	IR/RI	BC	Clayoquot	92 C/14	48°58′	125°17′
Equity	UNP/LNO	AB	31-32-23-W4	82 P/14	51°47′	113°14′
Érablière-du-Trente-et-Un-Milles, Réserve écologique de l'	PARK/PARC	QC	La Vallée-de-la-Gatineau	31 J/4	46°09′	75°52′
Era Island	ISL/ÎLE	NT	Franklin	37 B	68°15′	78°35′
Eramosa	MUN2/AZM2	ON	Wellington	40 P/9	43°38′	80°14′
Eramosa	UNP/LNO	ON	Wellington	40 P/9	43°37′	80°13′
Eramosa River	RIV/CDE	ON	Wellington	40 P/9	43°32′	80°14′
Erbs Cove	UNP/LNO	NB	Kings	21 H/12	45°35′	65°55′
Erb Settlement	UNP/LNO	NB	Kings	21 H/12	45°40′	65°37′
Erbsville	UNP/LNO	ON	Waterloo	40 P/7	43°29′	80°36′
Erebus and Terror Bay	BAY/BAIE	NT	Franklin	58 E	74°43′	91°45′
Erebus Bay	BAY/BAIE	NT	Franklin	67 D	69°18′	98°55′
Erichsen Lake	LAKE/LAC	NT	Franklin	47 E	70°40′	80°41′
Erickson	VILG/VILG	MB	32-17-18-W	62 J/5	50°30′	99°55′
Erickson	UNP/LNO	BC	Kootenay	82 F/1	49°05′	116°28′
Erickson Lake	LAKE/LAC	SK	58-8-W2	63 L/3	54°02′	103°06′
Éric, Lac	LAKE/LAC	QC	Sept-Rivières	22 P/13	51°55′	65°36′
Erie	UNP/LNO	ON	Haldimand	40 I/16	42°54′	80°01′
Erie	UNP/LNO	BC	Kootenay	82 F/3	49°11′	117°20′
Erieau	VILG/VILG	ON	Kent	40 I/5	42°16′	81°56′
Erie Beach	VILG/VILG	ON	Kent	40 I/5	42°16′	82°00′
Erie Beach	UNP/LNO	ON	Welland	30 L/15	42°53′	78°57′
Erie Curve	UNP/LNO	ON	Essex	40 J/2	42°02′	82°36′
Érié, Lac - also-aussi - **Erie, Lake**	LAKE/LAC	ON		40 I	42°15′	81°00′
Erie, Lake - also-aussi - **Érié, Lac**	LAKE/LAC	ON		40 I	42°15′	81°00′
Erie Rest	UNP/LNO	ON	Elgin	40 I/11	42°40′	81°14′
Erie View	UNP/LNO	ON	Norfolk	40 I/10	42°36′	80°31′
Erik Cove	BAY/BAIE	NT	Franklin	35 K	63°32′	77°25′
Erik Point	CAPE/CAP	NT	Franklin	27 F	70°53′	69°53′
Eriksdale	MUN2/AZM2	MB		62 J/16	50°50′	98°10′
Eriksdale	UNP/LNO	MB	4-22-5-W	62 J/16	50°52′	98°06′
Erin	VILG/VILG	ON	Wellington	40 P/16	43°46′	80°04′
Erin	MUN2/AZM2	ON	Wellington	40 P/9	43°45′	80°07′
Erindale	UNP/LNO	ON	Peel	30 M/12	43°32′	79°39′
*Erindale Station	UNP/LNO	ON		30 M/12	43°34′	79°39′
Erindale Woodlands	UNP/LNO	ON	Peel	30 M/12	43°34′	79°39′
Erinferry	UNP/LNO	SK	8-54-7-W3	73 G/11	53°39′	107°01′
Eringate	UNP/LNO	ON	York	30 M/12	43°40′	79°35′
Erin Lodge	UNP/LNO	AB	21-80-2-W6	83 M/16	55°57′	118°15′
Erin Mills	UNP/LNO	ON	Peel	30 M/12	43°33′	79°41′
Erinsville	UNP/LNO	ON	Lennox and Addington	31 C/6	44°29′	77°03′
Erinview	UNP/LNO	MB	13-16-1-W	62 I/6	50°22′	97°29′
Erinville	UNP/LNO	NS	Guysborough	11 F/5	45°22′	61°44′
Erith	UNP/LNO	AB	14-51-19-W5	83 F/7	53°24′	116°41′
Erith River	RIV/CDE	AB	51-19-W5	83 F/7	53°23′	116°40′
Erle	UNP/LNO	QC	Le Haut-Saint-François	21 E/12	45°42′	71°36′
Ermine	UNP/LNO	SK	14-33-22-W3	72 N/14	51°50′	109°00′
Ermineskin 138	IR/RI	AB	45-24,25-W4	83 A/14	52°52′	113°31′
Ernest Kendall, Cape	CAPE/CAP	NT	Franklin	87 C/9	69°36′	116°53′
Ernest-Lepage, Réserve écologique	PARK/PARC	QC	Bonaventure	22 A/12	48°32′	65°43′
Ernestown	MUN2/AZM2	ON	Lennox and Addington	31 C/7	44°15′	76°45′
Ernestown	UNP/LNO	ON	Lennox and Addington	31 C/2	44°13′	76°45′
Ernfold	VILG/VILG	SK	21-17-7-W3	72 J/7	50°28′	106°53′
Ernie Lake	LAKE/LAC	NT	Mackenzie	65 M	63°16′	102°20′
Errettsville	UNP/LNO	ON	Timiskaming	31 M/13	47°50′	79°52′
Errington	UNP/LNO	BC	Nanoose	92 F/8	49°17′	124°22′
Errol	UNP/LNO	ON	Lambton	40 O/1	43°03′	82°12′
Erskine	UNP/LNO	AB	6-39-20-W4	83 A/7	52°20′	112°53′
Erskine Inlet	BAY/BAIE	NT	Franklin	69 B	76°02′	102°05′
Ervick	UNP/LNO	AB	1-47-21-W4	83 H/2	53°01′	112°57′

NAME / NOM	ENTITY / ENTITÉ	LOC 1 / LIEU 1	LOC 2 / LIEU 2	MAP / CARTE	POSITION LAT	POSITION LONG
Erwood	HAM/HAM	SK	11-45-2-W2	63 D/16	52°51′	102°11′
Esayoo Bay	BAY/BAIE	NT	Franklin	340 B	80°44′	82°35′
Escalante Point	CAPE/CAP	BC	Clayoquot	92 E/10	49°32′	126°34′
Escalante River	RIV/CDE	BC	Clayoquot	92 E/10	49°32′	126°33′
Escalier, Réservoir l′	LAKE/LAC	QC	Papineau	31 G/13	45°52′	75°39′
Esclaves, Grand lac des - also-aussi - **Great Slave Lake**	LAKE/LAC	NT	Mackenzie	85 G	61°30′	114°00′
Escott	UNP/LNO	ON	Leeds	31 B/5	44°27′	75°56′
Escoumins, Baie des	BAY/BAIE	QC	La Haute-Côte-Nord	22 C/6	48°21′	69°24′
Escoumins, Rivière des	RIV/CDE	QC	La Haute-Côte-Nord	22 C/6	48°21′	69°24′
Escuminac	VILG/VILG	QC	Avignon	22 B/1	48°07′	66°29′
Escuminac	UNP/LNO	NB	Northumberland	21 P/2	47°05′	64°54′
Escuminac, Baie d′	BAY/BAIE	QC	Avignon	22 B/1	48°05′	66°26′
Escuminac East	UNP/LNO	QC	Avignon	22 B/1	48°08′	66°26′
Escuminac Flats	UNP/LNO	QC	Avignon	22 B/1	48°07′	66°27′
Escuminac Glen	UNP/LNO	QC	Avignon	22 B/1	48°08′	66°30′
Escuminac-Nord	UNP/LNO	QC	Avignon	22 B/2	48°10′	66°30′
Escuminac, Point	CAPE/CAP	NB	Northumberland	21 P/2	47°04′	64°48′
Escuminac, Rivière	RIV/CDE	QC	Avignon	22 B/1	48°07′	66°28′
Esdraelon	UNP/LNO	NB	Carleton	21 J/6	46°26′	67°25′
Esher	UNP/LNO	ON	Sudbury	41 O/13	47°52′	83°34′
Esk	UNP/LNO	SK	12-33-21-W2	72 P/15	51°49′	104°51′
Eskasoni	UNP/LNO	NS	Cape Breton	11 F/15	45°56′	60°36′
Eskasoni 3	IR/RI	NS	Cape Breton	11 F/15	45°57′	60°37′
Eskasoni 3A	IR/RI	NS	Cape Breton	11 F/15	45°57′	60°34′
Eskbank	UNP/LNO	SK	1-20-2-W3	72 J/9	50°40′	106°09′
*Eskdale	UNP/LNO	ON	Bruce	41 A/3	44°14′	81°28′
Esker	UNP/LNO	NF		23 G/16	53°53′	66°25′
Esker Point	CAPE/CAP	NT	Keewatin	65 I	62°33′	97°31′
Eskimo Inlet	BAY/BAIE	NT	Franklin	38 B	72°12′	80°00′
Eskimo Lakes	LAKE/LAC	NT	Mackenzie	107 C/1	69°15′	132°17′
Eskimo Point - see-voir - Arviat	HAM/HAM	NT		55 E/1	61°07′	94°04′
Eskimo Point	CAPE/CAP	MB		54 L/16	58°49′	94°13′
Esk Lake	LAKE/LAC	NT	Mackenzie	75 B	60°41′	107°37′
Esler	UNP/LNO	BC	Cariboo	93 B/1	52°07′	122°11′
Esme	UNP/LNO	SK	2-11-9-W3	72 G/14	49°53′	107°08′
Esmonde	UNP/LNO	ON	Renfrew	31 F/6	45°23′	77°04′
Esnagami Lake	LAKE/LAC	ON	Thunder Bay	42 L/7	50°19′	86°50′
Esnagami River	RIV/CDE	ON	Cochrane	42 L/9	50°43′	86°04′
Esnagi Lake	LAKE/LAC	ON	Algoma	42 C/10	48°36′	84°33′
Esnault, Lac	LAKE/LAC	QC	Minganie	22 I/9	50°40′	64°10′
Esowista 3	IR/RI	BC	Clayoquot	92 F/4	49°04′	125°47′
Esowista Peninsula	CAPE/CAP	BC	Clayoquot	92 F/4	49°05′	125°50′
Esox Lake	LAKE/LAC	ON	Kenora	52 F/3	49°07′	93°15′
Espanola	TOWN/VIL2	ON	Sudbury	41 I/5	46°15′	81°46′
Esperanza	UNP/LNO	BC	Nootka	92 E/15	49°52′	126°44′
Esperanza Canyon	SEAU/SMER			3603	49°40′	127°30′
Esperanza Inlet	BAY/BAIE	BC	Nootka	92 E/15	49°49′	126°56′
Espeseth Cove	HAM/HAM	SK	30-18-3-W2	62 L/9	50°33′	102°24′
Espinosa Inlet	BAY/BAIE	BC	Nootka	92 E/15	49°55′	126°56′
Espoir, Bay d′	BAY/BAIE	NF		11 P/9	47°40′	56°07′
Espoir, Cap d′	CAPE/CAP	QC	Pabok	22 A/8	48°25′	64°19′
Esprit-Saint	VILG/VILG	QC	Rimouski-Neigette	22 C/2	48°04′	68°34′
Esquimalt	MUN1/AZM1	BC	Esquimalt	92 B/6	48°27′	123°25′
Esquimalt	UNP/LNO	BC	Esquimalt	92 B/6	48°27′	123°26′
Esquimalt, Base des Forces canadiennes - also-aussi - Esquimalt, Canadian Forces Base	MIL/MIL	BC	Esquimalt	92 B/6	48°26′	123°26′
Esquimalt, Canadian Forces Base - also-aussi - Esquimalt, Base des Forces canadiennes	MIL/MIL	BC	Esquimalt	92 B/6	48°26′	123°26′
Esquimalt Harbour	BAY/BAIE	BC	Esquimalt	92 B/6	48°26′	123°26′
Esquimalt	IR/RI	BC	Esquimalt	92 B/6	48°26′	123°26′
Esquimalt Land District	GEOG/GÉOG	BC		92 B	48°26′	123°29′
Esquiman Channel - also-aussi - Esquiman, Chenal d′	SEAU/SMER	—		4025	49°45′	59°00′
Esquiman, Chenal d′ - also-aussi - Esquiman Channel	SEAU/SMER	—		4025	49°45′	59°00′
Essa	MUN2/AZM2	ON	Simcoe	31 D/5	44°15′	79°47′
Essa	UNP/LNO	ON	Simcoe	31 D/5	44°20′	79°50′
Essex	TOWN/VIL2	ON	Essex	40 J/2	42°10′	82°49′
Essex	MUN1/AZM1	ON	Essex	40 J/2	42°10′	82°50′
Essex	GEOG/GÉOG	ON		40 J/2	42°10′	82°50′
Essex Centre - see-voir - Essex	VILG/VILG	ON		40 J/2	42°10′	82°49′
Essondale	UNP/LNO	BC	New Westminster	92 G/2	49°14′	122°49′
Essonville	UNP/LNO	ON	Haliburton	31 E/1	45°00′	78°18′
Estabrook Lake	LAKE/LAC	NT	Mackenzie	96 O	67°54′	123°48′
Estaire	UNP/LNO	ON	Sudbury	41 I/7	46°18′	80°48′
Est, Cap à l′	CAPE/CAP	QC	Le Fjord-du-Saguenay	22 D/7	48°22′	70°42′

NAME / NOM	ENTITY / ENTITÉ	LOC 1 / LIEU 1	LOC 2 / LIEU 2	MAP / CARTE	POSITION LAT	POSITION LONG
Estcourt	UNP/LNO	QC	Témiscouata	21 N/6	47°28′	69°14′
Esten Lake	LAKE/LAC	ON	Algoma	41 J/7	46°22′	82°40′
Estérel	CITY/VIL1	QC	Les Pays-d'en-Haut	31 J/1	46°03′	74°02′
Esterhazy	TOWN/VIL2	SK	28-19-1-W2	62 L/9	50°39′	102°05′
Estero Basin	BAY/BAIE	BC	Range 1 Coast	92 K/3	50°31′	125°11′
Estero Peak	MTN/MNT	BC	Range 1 Coast	92 K/6	50°28′	125°11′
Estevan	CITY/VIL1	SK		62 E/2	49°08′	102°59′
Estevan Airport	UNP/LNO	SK	1-8-W2	62 E/2	49°05′	103°00′
Estevan Group	ISL/ÎLE	BC	Range 4 Coast	103 H/4	53°03′	129°38′
Estevan No. 5	MUN2/AZM2	SK		62 E/2	49°10′	103°00′
Estevan Point	UNP/LNO	BC	Clayoquot	92 E/7	49°23′	126°33′
Estevan Sound	CHAN/CHEN	BC	Range 4 Coast	103 H/4	53°05′	129°32′
Esther	UNP/LNO	AB	29-31-2-W4	72 M/9	51°42′	110°16′
Est, Île de l'	ISL/ÎLE	QC	Les Îles-de-la-Madeleine	11 N/11	47°37′	61°26′
Est, Lac de l'	LAKE/LAC	QC	Kamouraska	21 N/4	47°12′	69°34′
Estlin	UNP/LNO	SK	15-15-19-W2	72 I/7	50°15′	104°32′
Estmere	UNP/LNO	NS	Victoria	11 F/15	45°55′	60°58′
Eston	TOWN/VIL2	SK	20-25-20-W3	72 N/2	51°09′	108°45′
Est-patrolas 4	IR/RI	BC	Shawnigan	92 B/12	48°43′	123°36′
Est, Pointe de l'	CAPE/CAP	QC	Les Îles-de-la-Madeleine	11 N/11	47°37′	61°24′
Est, Pointe de l'	CAPE/CAP	QC	Minganie	12 F/4	49°08′	61°40′
Estrie	MUN1/AZM1	QC	Le Haut-Saint-François	21 E/5	45°29′	71°40′
Est, Roches de l'	SEAU/SMER	—		802	46°25′	50°30′
Estuary	UNP/LNO	SK	3-23-28-W3	72 K/13	50°56′	109°49′
Établissement-Ryan, Lieu historique national de l' - also-aussi - Ryan Premises National Historic Site	PARK/PARC	NF		2 C/11	48°39′	53°07′
Etacho Point	CAPE/CAP	NT	Mackenzie	96 I	66°03′	121°15′
Etagaulet Bay	BAY/BAIE	NF		13 G/11	53°43′	59°10′
Etagaulet Point	CAPE/CAP	NF		13 G/14	53°47′	59°04′
Étamamiou	UNP/LNO	QC	Côte-Nord-du-Golfe-Saint-Laurent	12 J/5	50°16′	59°58′
Étamamiou, Rivière	RIV/CDE	QC	Côte-Nord-du-Golfe-Saint-Laurent	12 J/5	50°17′	59°58′
Etawney Lake	LAKE/LAC	MB		64 H/15	57°50′	96°50′
Etchemin, Lac	LAKE/LAC	QC	Les Etchemins	21 L/7	46°23′	70°30′
Etchemin, Rivière	RIV/CDE	QC	Les Chutes-de-la-Chaudière	21 L/14	46°46′	71°14′
Éternité, Cap	CAPE/CAP	QC	Le Fjord-du-Saguenay	22 D/8	48°18′	70°17′
Éternité, Lac	LAKE/LAC	QC	Le Fjord-du-Saguenay	22 D/2	48°13′	70°33′
Éternité, Rivière	RIV/CDE	QC	Le Fjord-du-Saguenay	22 D/8	48°18′	70°20′
Ethel	UNP/LNO	ON	Huron	40 P/11	43°43′	81°08′
Ethelbert	VILG/VILG	MB	30,31-29-21-W	62 N/9	51°32′	100°24′
Ethelbert	MUN2/AZM2	MB		62 N/9	51°32′	100°30′
Ethel Lake	UNP/LNO	AB	35-63-3-W4	73 L/8	54°30′	110°22′
Ethel Lake	LAKE/LAC	AB	64-3-W4	73 L/9	54°32′	110°21′
Ethel Lake	LAKE/LAC	YT		115 P/8	63°22′	136°05′
Ethelma Lake	LAKE/LAC	ON	Kenora	52 F/12	49°42′	93°58′
Ethel Park	UNP/LNO	ON	Victoria	31 D/6	44°26′	79°10′
Ethel Siding	UNP/LNO	ON	Huron	40 P/11	43°43′	81°09′
Ethelton	UNP/LNO	SK	14-44-21-W2	73 A/15	52°47′	104°56′
Étienniche, Lac	LAKE/LAC	QC	Maria-Chapdelaine	22 E/11	49°31′	71°22′
Etin Kahinikuauminan	UNP/LNO	QC	Minganie	12 O/7	51°29′	58°41′
Etiwaskuhikan Meskanu	UNP/LNO	QC	Jamésie	32 M/8	51°18′	78°26′
Etna Lake	LAKE/LAC	NT	Mackenzie	86 D	64°27′	119°28′
Etobicoke	CITY/VIL1	ON	York	30 M/12	43°42′	79°34′
Etobicoke	UNP/LNO	ON	York	30 M/12	43°39′	79°34′
Etomami	UNP/LNO	SK	43-3-W2	63 D/9	52°44′	102°19′
Etomami River	RIV/CDE	SK	28-44-3-W2	63 D/16	52°49′	102°23′
Eton	UNP/LNO	ON	Algoma	41 N/9	47°31′	84°29′
Eton Court	UNP/LNO	ON	Lambton	40 O/1	43°03′	82°13′
Etonia	UNP/LNO	ON	Brant	40 P/1	43°10′	80°28′
Eton-Rugby	UNP/LNO	ON	Kenora	52 F/14	49°53′	93°00′
Etowamami River	RIV/CDE	ON	Kenora	52 P/11	51°32′	89°04′
Etsekin 1	IR/RI	BC	Range 1 Coast	92 L/9	50°34′	126°12′
Etters Beach	VILG/VILG	SK	21-26-24-W2	72 P/3	51°14′	105°18′
Etter Settlement	UNP/LNO	NS	Hants	11 D/13	44°52′	63°48′
Etthen Island	ISL/ÎLE	NT	Mackenzie	75 L	62°15′	111°41′
Etthithun River	RIV/CDE	BC	Peace River	94 I/7	58°17′	120°38′
Ettington	UNP/LNO	SK	33-10-1-W3	72 G/16	49°52′	106°05′
Ettrick	UNP/LNO	ON	Middlesex	40 P/3	43°02′	81°21′
Ettyville	UNP/LNO	ON	Prescott	31 G/6	45°26′	75°05′
Etwell	UNP/LNO	ON	Muskoka	31 E/6	45°20′	79°21′
Etzikom	UNP/LNO	AB	14-6-9-W4	72 E/6	49°29′	111°06′
Etzikom Coulee	VALL/VALL	AB	6-16,17-W4	82 H/8	49°28′	112°08′
Euchinico Creek 17	IR/RI	BC	Cariboo	93 G/3	53°13′	123°30′
Euchinico Creek 18	IR/RI	BC	Cariboo	93 G/4	53°12′	123°32′
Euchinico Creek 19	IR/RI	BC	Cariboo	93 G/5	53°15′	123°33′
Euchiniko River	RIV/CDE	BC	Cariboo	93 G/4	53°14′	123°30′
Euchu Reach	RIVF/EFLV	BC	Range 4 Coast	93 F/6	53°24′	125°25′

NAME / NOM	ENTITY / ENTITÉ	LOC 1 / LIEU 1	LOC 2 / LIEU 2	MAP / CARTE	POSITION LAT	POSITION LONG
Eudistes, Lac des	LAKE/LAC	QC	Minganie	22 I/11	50°30′	65°15′
Eugene Lake	LAKE/LAC	BC	Lillooet	92 P/7	51°27′	120°42′
Eugène-Rouillard, Lac	LAKE/LAC	QC	Sept-Rivières	22 J/11	50°43′	67°15′
Eugenia	UNP/LNO	ON	Grey	41 A/7	44°19′	80°31′
Eugenia Lake	LAKE/LAC	ON	Grey	41 A/8	44°19′	80°30′
Eugenie Glacier	GLAC/GLAC	NT	Franklin	39 H	79°51′	75°10′
Eulas Lake	LAKE/LAC	SK		73 P/13	55°54′	105°38′
Euphemia	MUN2/AZM2	ON	Lambton	40 I/11	42°43′	81°27′
Euphemia Hill	MTN/MNT	NT	Keewatin	57 A	68°30′	91°09′
Euphrasia	MUN2/AZM2	ON	Grey	41 A/7	44°26′	80°35′
Eureka	UNP/LNO	NS	Pictou	11 E/7	45°30′	62°41′
Eureka	UNP/LNO	ON	Sudbury	41 P/4	47°12′	82°00′
Eureka River	UNP/LNO	AB	9-86-5-W6	84 D/7	56°27′	118°44′
Eureka River	RIV/CDE	AB	85-10-W6	84 D/5	56°23′	119°30′
Eureka Sound	CHAN/CHEN	NT	Franklin	49 G	79°00′	85°00′
Europa Lake	LAKE/LAC	BC	Range 4 Coast	103 H/8	53°21′	128°23′
Eustis	UNP/LNO	QC	Sherbrooke	21 E/5	45°18′	71°55′
Eutsuk Lake	LAKE/LAC	BC	Range 4 Coast	93 E/7	53°16′	126°37′
Évain	VILG/VILG	QC	Rouyn-Noranda	32 D/3	48°14′	79°08′
Eva Lake	LAKE/LAC	ON	Rainy River	52 B/11	48°43′	91°10′
Eva Lake	LAKE/LAC	AB	114-7,8-W5	84 J/14	58°54′	115°10′
Evandale	UNP/LNO	NB	Kings	21 G/9	45°35′	66°02′
Evangeline	UNP/LNO	NB	Westmorland	21 I/2	46°13′	64°42′
Evangeline	UNP/LNO	NB	Gloucester	21 P/10	47°42′	64°51′
Evans	UNP/LNO	NB	Westmorland	21 H/16	45°52′	64°27′
Evans	UNP/LNO	BC	Lillooet	92 J/7	50°19′	122°43′
Evansburg	VILG/VILG	AB	30-53-7-W5	83 G/11	53°36′	115°01′
Evans, Cape	CAPE/CAP	NT	Franklin	340 F	82°39′	82°16′
Evans Corner	UNP/LNO	ON	Simcoe	31 D/12	44°44′	79°49′
Evans Island	ISL/ÎLE	NS	Richmond	11 F/15	45°45′	60°46′
Evans, Lac	LAKE/LAC	QC	Jamésie	32 K/14	50°55′	77°00′
Evans Lake	LAKE/LAC	BC	Kootenay	82 F/13	49°51′	117°39′
Evans, Mount	MTN/MNT	AB	40-1-W6	83 D/8	52°26′	118°07′
Evans, Mount	MTN/MNT	BC	Kootenay	82 F/9	49°33′	116°18′
Evans Point	CAPE/CAP	ON	Haldimand	30 L/13	42°49′	79°45′
Evans Strait	CHAN/CHEN	NT	Keewatin	45 O	63°15′	82°00′
Evanston	UNP/LNO	NS	Richmond	11 F/11	45°37′	61°13′
Evansville	UNP/LNO	ON	Nipissing	31 L/5	46°23′	79°54′
Evansville	UNP/LNO	ON	Manitoulin	41 G/15	45°49′	82°34′
Evanturel	MUN2/AZM2	ON	Timiskaming	31 M/13	47°47′	79°48′
Evanturel	UNP/LNO	ON	Prescott	31 G/10	45°37′	74°47′
Evarts	UNP/LNO	AB	7-38-2-W5	83 B/8	52°16′	114°16′
Evelyn	UNP/LNO	ON	Middlesex	40 P/3	43°03′	81°05′
Evelyn	UNP/LNO	BC	Range 5 Coast	93 L/14	54°53′	127°16′
Evening Lake	LAKE/LAC	ON	Kenora	52 K/3	50°06′	93°22′
Everard	UNP/LNO	ON	Thunder Bay	52 A/16	48°54′	88°21′
Everard, Mount	MTN/MNT	BC	Range 2 Coast	92 N/4	51°01′	125°42′
Everett	UNP/LNO	NB	Victoria	21 O/3	47°03′	67°19′
Everett	UNP/LNO	ON	Simcoe	31 D/4	44°11′	79°57′
Everett Mountains	MTN/MNT	NT	Franklin	25 J	62°45′	67°12′
Evergreen	UNP/LNO	AB	5-38-4-W5	83 B/2	52°14′	114°32′
Evergreen Acres	HAM/HAM	SK	36-52-19-W3	73 F/10	53°31′	108°39′
Evergreen Brightsand	HAM/HAM	SK	26-53-20	73 F/10	53°37′	108°50′
Evergreen Village	UNP/LNO	NF		1 N/10	47°32′	52°50′
Eve River	RIV/CDE	BC	Rupert	92 L/8	50°26′	126°15′
Eversley	UNP/LNO	ON	York	30 M/13	43°57′	79°30′
Everton	UNP/LNO	ON	Wellington	40 P/9	43°40′	80°09′
Evesham	VILG/VILG	SK	32-39-27-W3	73 C/5	52°24′	109°51′
Ewan	UNP/LNO	ON	Peterborough	31 D/16	44°48′	78°30′
Ewariege Lake	LAKE/LAC	NT	Mackenzie	97 B	68°08′	125°07′
Ewart	UNP/LNO	MB	9-8-28-W	62 F/11	49°39′	101°13′
Ewart Creek	RIV/CDE	BC	Similkameen Division Yale	92 H/1	49°08′	120°02′
Ewart Lake	LAKE/LAC	BC	Nootka	92 E/10	49°43′	126°50′
Ewing	UNP/LNO	BC	Osoyoos Division Yale	82 L/4	50°10′	119°30′
Ewing Lake	LAKE/LAC	AB	37-20,21-W4	83 A/2	52°10′	112°52′
Ewing, Mount	MTN/MNT	BC	Cassiar	104 N/14	59°53′	133°24′
Exaluin Fiord	BAY/BAIE	NT	Franklin	16 E	65°40′	62°54′
Excel	UNP/LNO	AB	13-28-5-W4	72 M/7	51°23′	110°35′
Excel No. 71	MUN2/AZM2	SK		72 H/11	49°40′	105°25′
Excelsior	UNP/LNO	AB	28-55-24-W4	83 H/14	53°47′	113°30′
Excelsior No. 166	MUN2/AZM2	SK		72 J/5	50°30′	107°30′
Exchamsiks River	RIV/CDE	BC	Range 5 Coast	103 I/6	54°20′	129°18′
Exeter	TOWN/VIL2	ON	Huron	40 P/6	43°21′	81°29′
Exeter	UNP/LNO	BC	Lillooet	92 P/11	51°39′	121°20′
Exeter Bay	BAY/BAIE	NT	Franklin	16 K/5	66°30′	61°30′

NAME NOM	ENTITY ENTITÉ	LOC 1 LIEU 1	LOC 2 LIEU 2	MAP CARTE	POSITION LAT	LONG
Exeter Lake	LAKE/LAC	NT	Mackenzie	76 D	64°50'	110°50'
Exeter Sound	CHAN/CHEN	NT	Franklin	16 L	66°14'	62°00'
Exhibition	UNP/LNO	SK		73 B/2	52°06'	106°41'
Exira	UNP/LNO	MB	6-12-12-W	62 G/15	49°59'	98°58'
Exlou	UNP/LNO	BC	Kamloops Division Yale	92 P/1	51°07'	120°08'
Exmoor	UNP/LNO	NB	Northumberland	21 I/13	46°59'	65°50'
Exmouth Island	ISL/ÎLE	NT	Franklin	59 C	77°13'	95°54'
Exmouth Lake	LAKE/LAC	NT	Mackenzie	86 G/4	65°03'	115°54'
Expanse	UNP/LNO	SK	12-12-29-W2	72 H/13	49°59'	105°51'
Exploits	UNP/LNO	NF		2 E/11	49°31'	55°04'
Exploits, Bay of	BAY/BAIE	NF		2 E/6	49°20'	55°10'
Exploits Islands	ISL/ÎLE	NF		2 E/11	49°32'	55°04'
Exploits River	RIV/CDE	NF		2 E/3	49°05'	55°20'
Explorer Median Valley	SEAU/SMER	—		15789A	49°27'	130°35'
Explorer Ridge	SEAU/SMER	—		15890A	49°27'	130°35'
Explorer Seamount	SEAU/SMER	—		3000	49°04'	130°56'
Exshaw	UNP/LNO	AB	22-24-9-W5	82 O/3	51°03'	115°09'
Exstew	UNP/LNO	BC	Range 5 Coast	103 I/6	54°23'	129°06'
Exstew River	RIV/CDE	BC	Range 5 Coast	103 I/6	54°24'	129°03'
Extension	UNP/LNO	BC	Cranberry	92 G/4	49°06'	123°57'
Exton	UNP/LNO	ON	Thunder Bay	42 L/2	50°11'	86°48'
Eyapamikama Lake	LAKE/LAC	ON	Kenora	53 B/15	52°57'	90°50'
Eyeberry Lake	LAKE/LAC	NT	Mackenzie	75 P	63°08'	104°43'
Eyebrow	VILG/VILG	SK	24-21-2-W3	72 J/16	50°48'	106°09'
Eyebrow No. 193	MUN2/AZM2	SK		72 J/9	50°40'	106°15'
Eyehill Creek	RIV/CDE	SK/AB		73 C/12	52°41'	109°39'
Eye Hill No. 382	MUN2/AZM2	SK		73 C/4	52°15'	109°45'
Eyre	UNP/LNO	SK	1-27-28-W3	72 N/5	51°16'	109°49'
Eyre, Cape	CAPE/CAP	NT	Franklin	67 H	71°50'	96°31'
Eyre Corners	UNP/LNO	ON	Leeds	31 C/9	44°42'	76°07'
Eyrie Lake	LAKE/LAC	MB		64 F/10	57°35'	100°51'

F

Faber Lake	LAKE/LAC	NT	Mackenzie	85 N	63°56'	117°15'
Fabre	UNP/LNO	QC	Témiscamingue	31 M/3	47°12'	79°22'
Fabre-Station	UNP/LNO	QC	Témiscamingue	31 M/3	47°12'	79°20'
Fabreville	UNP/LNO	QC	Laval	31 H/12	45°34'	73°51'
Fabyan	UNP/LNO	AB	18-45-7-W4	73 D/15	52°53'	111°00'
Facer	UNP/LNO	ON	Lincoln	30 M/3	43°11'	79°13'
Facheux Bay	BAY/BAIE	NF		11 P/9	47°42'	56°19'
Factorydale	UNP/LNO	NS	Kings	21 A/15	45°00'	64°47'
Factory Island 1	IR/RI	ON	Cochrane	42 P/7	51°16'	80°35'
Factory Point	UNP/LNO	QC	Côte-Nord-du-Golfe-Saint-Laurent	12 P/5	51°25'	57°38'
Fadden Corner	UNP/LNO	QC	Le Haut-Richelieu	31 H/3	45°03'	73°18'
Faden	UNP/LNO	NF		23 J/2	54°11'	66°30'
Faillon, Lac	LAKE/LAC	QC	Vallée-de-l'Or	32 C/7	48°21'	76°39'
Fair and False Bay	BAY/BAIE	NF		2 C/12	48°43'	53°49'
Fairbairn Lake	LAKE/LAC	NT	Mackenzie	75 L	62°15'	111°00'
Fairbairn Meadows	UNP/LNO	ON	Peterborough	31 D/8	44°20'	78°21'
Fairbank	UNP/LNO	NF		2 E/10	49°33'	54°45'
Fairbank	UNP/LNO	ON	York	30 M/11	43°42'	79°27'
Fairbank Lake	LAKE/LAC	ON	Sudbury	41 I/6	46°28'	81°26'
Fairbanks	UNP/LNO	NF		2 E/10	49°33'	54°45'
Fairbanks East	UNP/LNO	NF		2 E/10	49°33'	54°45'
Fairbridge	UNP/LNO	BC	Quamichan	92 B/12	48°45'	123°42'
Fairchild Creek	RIV/CDE	ON	Brant	40 P/1	43°07'	80°07'
Fairchild Lake	LAKE/LAC	ON	Thunder Bay	52 J/7	50°23'	90°55'
Fairfax	UNP/LNO	QC	Coaticook	31 H/1	45°05'	72°01'
Fairfax	UNP/LNO	ON	Leeds	31 C/8	44°25'	76°03'
Fairfax	UNP/LNO	MB	32-5-20-W	62 F/8	49°26'	100°08'
Fairfield	UNP/LNO	PE	Kings	11 L/8	46°28'	62°07'
Fairfield	UNP/LNO	NB	Westmorland	21 H/16	45°55'	64°28'
Fairfield	UNP/LNO	NB	Saint John	21 H/5	45°20'	65°41'
Fairfield	UNP/LNO	ON	Leeds	31 B/12	44°39'	75°44'
Fairfield	UNP/LNO	BC	New Westminster	92 H/4	49°11'	121°57'
Fairfield	UNP/LNO	BC	Victoria	92 B/6	48°25'	123°21'
Fairfield East	UNP/LNO	ON	Leeds	31 B/12	44°40'	75°43'
Fairfield Park	UNP/LNO	MB		62 H/14	49°48'	97°10'
Fairfield Plain	UNP/LNO	ON	Brant	40 P/1	43°03'	80°24'
Fairford	UNP/LNO	MB		62 O/10	51°35'	98°43'
Fairford 50	IR/RI	MB		62 O/10	51°37'	98°38'
Fairford Reserve	UNP/LNO	MB	30-9-W	62 O/10	51°36'	98°42'

NAME NOM	ENTITY ENTITÉ	LOC 1 LIEU 1	LOC 2 LIEU 2	MAP CARTE	POSITION LAT	POSITION LONG
Fairground	UNP/LNO	ON	Norfolk	40 I/10	42°39′	80°40′
Fair Harbour	UNP/LNO	BC	Rupert	92 L/3	50°04′	127°07′
Fair Haven	UNP/LNO	NF		1 N/12	47°32′	53°54′
Fairhaven	UNP/LNO	NB	Charlotte	21 B/14	44°58′	67°00′
Fairhaven	UNP/LNO	ON	York	30 M/12	43°42′	79°33′
Fairhaven	UNP/LNO	SK		73 B/2	52°07′	106°44′
Fair Haven Point	CAPE/CAP	NF		1 N/12	47°31′	53°55′
Fairholme	HAM/HAM	SK	26-51-18-W3	73 F/7	53°26′	108°32′
Fairholme	UNP/LNO	ON	Parry Sound	31 E/12	45°34′	79°55′
Fairholme Park	UNP/LNO	ON	Lanark	31 C/16	44°54′	76°15′
Fair Islands	ISL/ÎLE	NF		2 C/13	48°59′	53°42′
Fairisle	UNP/LNO	NB	Northumberland	21 P/6	47°17′	65°07′
Fairlight	VILG/VILG	SK	31-10-31-W	62 F/13	49°53′	101°41′
Fairloch	UNP/LNO	ON	Thunder Bay	52 H/8	49°28′	88°06′
Fairmont	UNP/LNO	NS	Antigonish	11 F/12	45°42′	61°59′
Fairmont	UNP/LNO	ON	Middlesex	40 I/14	42°59′	81°11′
Fairmont	UNP/LNO	BC	Kootenay	82 J/5	50°19′	115°52′
Fairmont Hot Springs	UNP/LNO	BC	Kootenay	82 J/5	50°20′	115°51′
Fairmount	UNP/LNO	NS	Halifax	11 D/12	44°39′	63°38′
Fairmount	UNP/LNO	ON	Frontenac	31 C/8	44°19′	76°28′
Fairmount	UNP/LNO	ON	Durham	31 D/1	44°15′	78°27′
Fairmount	UNP/LNO	ON	Grey	41 A/7	44°29′	80°34′
Fairmount	UNP/LNO	SK	22-28-24-W3	72 N/6	51°25′	109°18′
Fair Ness	CAPE/CAP	NT	Franklin	35 P	63°24′	72°05′
Fairplay	UNP/LNO	ON	Essex	40 J/7	42°16′	82°54′
Fairport	UNP/LNO	ON	Ontario	30 M/14	43°49′	79°05′
Fairport Beach	UNP/LNO	ON	Ontario	30 M/14	43°48′	79°06′
Fairvale	VILG/VILG	NB	Kings	21 H/5	45°25′	66°00′
Fair Valley	UNP/LNO	ON	Simcoe	31 D/12	44°39′	79°36′
Fairview	TOWN/VIL2	AB	34-81-3-W6	84 D/1	56°04′	118°23′
Fairview	UNP/LNO	PE	Queens	11 L/3	46°11′	63°12′
Fairview	UNP/LNO	NS	Halifax	11 D/12	44°39′	63°38′
Fair View	UNP/LNO	NB	Saint John	21 H/6	45°24′	65°30′
Fairview	UNP/LNO	ON	Renfrew	31 F/14	45°47′	77°08′
Fairview	UNP/LNO	ON	Peel	30 M/12	43°35′	79°38′
Fairview	UNP/LNO	ON	Brant	40 P/1	43°10′	80°17′
Fairview	UNP/LNO	ON	Elgin	40 I/10	42°44′	80°53′
Fairview	UNP/LNO	ON	Oxford	40 P/7	43°17′	80°57′
Fairview	UNP/LNO	MB	13-11-15-W	62 G/14	49°55′	99°24′
Fairview	UNP/LNO	SK		72 I/5	50°24′	105°30′
Fairview	UNP/LNO	BC	Similkameen Division Yale	82 E/4	49°11′	119°36′
Fairview	UNP/LNO	BC	New Westminster	92 G/6	49°16′	123°08′
Fairview Island	UNP/LNO	ON	Muskoka	31 E/3	45°13′	79°04′
Fairview Knoll	UNP/LNO	NB	Westmorland	21 I/2	46°07′	64°46′
Fairview No. 136, Municipal District of	MUN1/AZM1	AB	81-3-W6	84 D/1	56°02′	118°27′
Fairville Plateau	UNP/LNO	NB	Saint John	21 G/1	45°15′	66°06′
Fairway Island	ISL/ÎLE	NT	Keewatin	55 O	63°15′	90°33′
Fairweather Lake	LAKE/LAC	YT		105 N/1	63°12′	132°27′
Fairweather Mountain	MTN/MNT	BC	Cassiar	114 I/13	58°54′	137°31′
Fairwind, Lac	LAKE/LAC	QC	Kativik	35 A/5	60°17′	73°50′
Fairydell	UNP/LNO	AB	8-58-24-W4	83 I/4	54°01′	113°33′
Fairy Glen	HAM/HAM	SK	10-47-18-W2	73 H/2	53°03′	104°33′
Fairy Hill	UNP/LNO	SK	27-21-19-W2	72 I/15	50°49′	104°34′
Fairy Lake	LAKE/LAC	ON	Muskoka	31 E/6	45°20′	79°11′
Fairy Lake River	RIV/CDE	NT	Mackenzie	86 J	66°10′	114°16′
Faith, Mount	MTN/MNT	BC	Similkameen Division Yale	82 E/8	49°22′	118°15′
Falaise, Lac	LAKE/LAC	QC	Caniapiscau	23 K/8	54°15′	68°15′
Falaise Lake	LAKE/LAC	NT	Mackenzie	85 F	61°27′	116°12′
Falcon	UNP/LNO	SK	9-17-9-W2	62 L/6	50°25′	103°11′
Falconbridge	UNP/LNO	ON	Sudbury	41 I/10	46°35′	80°48′
Falconbridge	UNP/LNO	ON	Middlesex	40 I/13	42°54′	81°32′
Falcon Island	ISL/ÎLE	ON	Kenora	52 E/7	49°23′	94°45′
Falcon Lake	UNP/LNO	MB	25,27,36-8-16,17-E	52 E/11	49°41′	95°20′
Falcon Lake	LAKE/LAC	MB	8-17-E	52 E/11	49°42′	95°15′
Falcon River	RIV/CDE	MB	4-8-17-E	52 E/11	49°37′	95°13′
Falcoz, Rivière	RIV/CDE	QC	Kativik	24 A/15	56°56′	65°00′
Falding	UNP/LNO	ON	Parry Sound	31 E/5	45°18′	79°55′
Falgarwood	UNP/LNO	ON	Halton	30 M/5	43°29′	79°41′
Falher	TOWN/VIL2	AB	4-78-21-W5	83 N/11	55°44′	117°12′
Falkenburg Station	UNP/LNO	ON	Muskoka	31 E/3	45°06′	79°21′
Falk Lake	LAKE/LAC	BC	New Westminster	92 G/13	49°56′	123°36′
Falkland	UNP/LNO	ON	Brant	40 P/1	43°10′	80°26′
Falkland	UNP/LNO	BC	Kamloops Division Yale	82 L/5	50°30′	119°33′
Falkland Ridge	UNP/LNO	NS	Annapolis	21 A/10	44°40′	64°51′
Fallaize Lake	LAKE/LAC	NT	Mackenzie	97 B	68°55′	124°18′

NAME NOM	ENTITY ENTITÉ	LOC 1 LIEU 1	LOC 2 LIEU 2	MAP CARTE	POSITION LAT	POSITION LONG
Fallbrook	UNP/LNO	ON	Lanark	31 C/16	44°57′	76°24′
Fallentimber Creek	RIV/CDE	AB	32-5-W5	82 O/10	51°45′	114°39′
Fallis	UNP/LNO	AB	23-53-5-W5	83 G/10	53°35′	114°38′
Fallis Lake	LAKE/LAC	MB		64 P/6	59°28′	97°19′
Fallison	UNP/LNO	MB	15-1-11-W	62 G/2	49°02′	98°52′
Fall, Le	UNP/LNO	QC	Bonaventure	22 A/5	48°17′	65°35′
Fallowfield	UNP/LNO	ON	Carleton	31 G/5	45°16′	75°50′
Fallowfield Station	UNP/LNO	ON	Carleton	31 G/5	45°16′	75°47′
Fall River	UNP/LNO	NS	Halifax	11 D/13	44°49′	63°37′
Fall River	RIV/CDE	NT	Franklin	47 G	71°14′	84°41′
Fall River West	UNP/LNO	NS	Halifax	11 D/13	44°48′	63°38′
Falls	UNP/LNO	BC	Peace River	93 O/9	55°36′	122°16′
Falls Brook	RIV/CDE	NB	Restigouche	21 O/12	47°43′	67°35′
Falls Creek	UNP/LNO	BC	Kamloops Division Yale	92 I/4	50°04′	121°33′
Falls Creek	RIV/CDE	BC	Kamloops Division Yale	93 A/1	52°08′	120°11′
Falls, Les	UNP/LNO	QC	La Matapédia	22 B/6	48°27′	67°13′
Falls River	RIV/CDE	BC	Lillooet	92 O/4	51°08′	123°33′
Falls River	RIV/CDE	BC	Range 4 Coast	103 H/16	53°49′	128°31′
Falls View	UNP/LNO	ON	Welland	30 M/3	43°05′	79°05′
Falmouth	UNP/LNO	NS	Hants	21 A/16	45°00′	64°10′
Faloma	UNP/LNO	MB	5,6-9-17-E	52 E/11	49°43′	95°15′
False Bay	UNP/LNO	BC	Nanaimo	92 F/8	49°30′	124°21′
False Cape	CAPE/CAP	NF		13 I/13	54°50′	57°51′
False Detour Channel	CHAN/CHEN	ON	Manitoulin	41 G/14	45°57′	83°28′
False Ducks Islands	ISL/ÎLE	ON	Prince Edward	30 N/15	43°57′	76°49′
False Head	CAPE/CAP	BC	Rupert	92 L/11	50°40′	127°17′
Falsen Island	ISL/ÎLE	NT	Franklin	67 F	70°43′	103°22′
False Passage Peninsula	CAPE/CAP	NT	Franklin	26 J	66°29′	67°48′
False, Rivière	RIV/CDE	QC	Kativik	24 J/5	58°28′	67°50′
Falun	UNP/LNO	AB	10-46-27-W4	83 A/13	52°57′	113°50′
Fame Point	UNP/LNO	QC	La Côte-de-Gaspé	22 H/2	49°06′	64°36′
Family Lake	LAKE/LAC	MB	34,35-14-15-E	52 M/14	51°54′	95°27′
Famine, Rivière	RIV/CDE	QC	Beauce-Sartigan	21 L/2	46°08′	70°42′
Fanning Brook	UNP/LNO	PE	Kings	11 L/7	46°20′	62°49′
Fanny Bay	UNP/LNO	BC	Newcastle	92 F/7	49°29′	124°49′
Fannystelle	UNP/LNO	MB	15-9-3-W	62 H/12	49°45′	97°47′
Fanshawe	UNP/LNO	ON	Middlesex	40 P/3	43°03′	81°14′
Fanshawe, Cape	CAPE/CAP	NT	Franklin	38 C	73°32′	77°25′
Fanshawe Lake	LAKE/LAC	ON	Middlesex	40 P/3	43°04′	81°11′
Fanshawe Martin, Cape	CAPE/CAP	NT	Franklin	340 F	82°55′	80°12′
Fansher Creek	RIV/CDE	ON	Lambton	40 J/9	42°39′	82°00′
Fanson Lake	LAKE/LAC	SK		64 M/4	59°15′	103°43′
Faraday	MUN2/AZM2	ON	Hastings	31 F/4	45°00′	77°55′
Faraday	UNP/LNO	ON	Hastings	31 C/13	44°55′	77°55′
Faraday, Cape	CAPE/CAP	NT	Franklin	39 C	77°52′	76°46′
Faraud Lake	LAKE/LAC	SK		74 P/14	59°47′	105°04′
Farewell	UNP/LNO	ON	Wellington	40 P/15	43°54′	80°43′
Farewell Cove	UNP/LNO	QC	La Côte-de-Gaspé	22 A/16	48°52′	64°28′
Fargo	UNP/LNO	ON	Kent	40 J/8	42°21′	82°04′
Faribault, Lac	LAKE/LAC	QC	Kativik	24 M/4	59°03′	71°58′
Faride, Lac	LAKE/LAC	QC	Minganie	12 J/13	50°58′	59°56′
Faris Island	ISL/ÎLE	NT	Franklin	25 N/10	63°35′	68°44′
Farlain Lake	UNP/LNO	ON	Simcoe	31 D/13	44°49′	79°58′
Farlane	UNP/LNO	ON	Kenora	52 L/1	50°00′	94°12′
Farley	UNP/LNO	QC	La Vallée-de-la-Gatineau	31 K/8	46°18′	76°01′
Farley	UNP/LNO	SK	36-6-W3	73 B/2	52°07′	106°49′
Farleys Corners	UNP/LNO	ON	Parry Sound	31 E/13	45°59′	79°39′
Farlinger	UNP/LNO	ON	Thunder Bay	52 H/8	49°27′	88°08′
Farmborough	UNP/LNO	QC	Rouyn-Noranda	32 D/2	48°13′	78°51′
Farmer Island	ISL/ÎLE	NT	Keewatin	44 I	58°24′	80°47′
Farmers Island	ISL/ÎLE	NF		2 E/7	49°28′	54°50′
Farmers Rapids	UNP/LNO	QC	Communauté urbaine de l'Outaouais	31 G/5	45°30′	75°46′
Farmingdale	UNP/LNO	SK	39-11-W2	63 D/6	52°21′	103°28′
Farmington	UNP/LNO	PE	Kings	11 L/8	46°23′	62°29′
Farmington	UNP/LNO	NS	Cumberland	11 E/12	45°34′	63°54′
Farmington	UNP/LNO	NS	Lunenburg	21 A/10	44°37′	64°40′
Farmington	UNP/LNO	ON	Dufferin	40 P/16	43°56′	80°10′
Farmington	UNP/LNO	BC	Peace River	93 P/15	55°54′	120°30′
Far Mountain	MTN/MNT	BC	Range 3 Coast	93 C/14	52°47′	125°19′
Farm Point	UNP/LNO	QC	Les Collines-de-l'Outaouais	31 G/12	45°36′	75°54′
Farmville	UNP/LNO	NS	Lunenburg	21 A/8	44°28′	64°28′
Farnam's Corner	UNP/LNO	QC	Brome-Missisquoi	31 H/2	45°07′	72°44′
Farnham	CITY/VIL1	QC	Brome-Missisquoi	31 H/7	45°17′	72°59′
Farnham	UNP/LNO	ON	Wellington	40 P/9	43°32′	80°10′
Farnham Centre	UNP/LNO	QC	Brome-Missisquoi	31 H/2	45°14′	72°52′

NAME NOM	ENTITY ENTITÉ	LOC 1 LIEU 1	LOC 2 LIEU 2	MAP CARTE	POSITION LAT	LONG
Farnham, Mount	MTN/MNT	BC	Kootenay	82 K/8	50°29′	116°29′
Faro	TOWN/VIL2	YT		105 K/3	62°14′	133°20′
Farquhar	UNP/LNO	ON	Huron	40 P/6	43°22′	81°22′
Farquhar Lake	LAKE/LAC	ON	Haliburton	31 E/1	45°05′	78°12′
Farrant	UNP/LNO	AB	31-39-26-W4	83 A/5	52°24′	113°44′
Farrant Island	ISL/ÎLE	BC	Range 4 Coast	103 H/6	53°21′	129°23′
Farrell Corners	UNP/LNO	ON	Hastings	31 C/6	44°27′	77°08′
Farrell Creek	UNP/LNO	BC	Peace River	94 A/4	56°07′	121°43′
Farrell Creek	RIV/CDE	BC	Peace River	94 A/4	56°07′	121°44′
Farrell Lake	LAKE/LAC	AB	33-17-W4	82 P/16	51°52′	112°20′
Farrellton	UNP/LNO	QC	Les Collines-de-l'Outaouais	31 G/12	45°45′	75°55′
Farrerdale	UNP/LNO	SK	27-29-28-W2	72 P/5	51°30′	105°51′
Farrington	UNP/LNO	ON	Rainy River	52 C/15	48°46′	92°50′
Farrington, Cape	CAPE/CAP	NT	Franklin	25 I	62°51′	64°45′
Farron	UNP/LNO	BC	Kootenay	82 E/8	49°16′	118°08′
Farrow	UNP/LNO	AB	9-20-25-W4	82 I/11	50°41′	113°24′
Farwell Creek	RIV/CDE	BC	Lillooet	92 O/15	51°50′	122°34′
Farwell Lake	LAKE/LAC	MB	64-18,19-W	63 K/9	54°33′	100°11′
Far West Point 34	IR/RI	BC	Range 5 Coast	103 J/7	54°26′	130°50′
Fassett	VILG/VILG	QC	Papineau	31 G/10	45°39′	74°52′
Fassifern	UNP/LNO	ON	Glengarry	31 G/7	45°21′	74°40′
Father Charles Canyon	SEAU/SMER	—		3602	48°49′	126°25′
Father, Lac	LAKE/LAC	QC	Jamésie	32 G/6	49°18′	75°29′
Father Lacombe Chapel Provincial Historic Site (Developed)	PARK/PARC	AB	4-54-25-W4	83 H/12	53°38′	113°38′
Fathom Five, Aire marine nationale de conservation - also-aussi - Fathom Five National Marine Conservation Area	PARK/PARC	ON	Bruce	41 H/5	45°17′	81°40′
Fathom Five National Marine Conservation Area - also-aussi - Fathom Five, Aire marine nationale de conservation	PARK/PARC	ON	Bruce	41 H/5	45°17′	81°40′
Fatima	VILG/VILG	QC	Les Îles-de-la-Madeleine	11 N/5	47°24′	61°53′
Fatima	UNP/LNO	QC	Témiscouata	21 N/7	47°27′	68°50′
Fatima	UNP/LNO	QC	Le Granit	21 E/10	45°34′	70°52′
Fat Lake	LAKE/LAC	NT	Mackenzie	75 M/5	63°24′	111°38′
Faubourg-des-Tuyaux	UNP/LNO	QC	L'Île-d'Orléans	21 L/15	46°55′	70°53′
Faubourg-du-Moulin	UNP/LNO	QC	Bellechasse	21 L/10	46°44′	70°52′
Faubourg, Le	UNP/LNO	QC	Pontiac	31 F/10	45°44′	76°38′
Faulder	UNP/LNO	BC	Osoyoos Division Yale	82 E/12	49°36′	119°46′
Faulkner	UNP/LNO	MB	28-28-9-W	62 O/7	51°25′	98°40′
Fault Range	MTN/MNT	YT		105 O/10	63°45′	130°55′
Fauna	UNP/LNO	SK	16-11-W3	72 J/5	50°23′	107°30′
Fauquier	UNP/LNO	ON	Cochrane	42 G/8	49°19′	82°02′
Fauquier	UNP/LNO	BC	Kootenay	82 E/16	49°52′	118°04′
Fauquier-Strickland	MUN2/AZM2	ON	Cochrane	42 H/5	49°19′	81°57′
Faust	UNP/LNO	AB	16-73-11-W5	83 O/5	55°19′	115°38′
Fauvel	UNP/LNO	QC	Bonaventure	22 A/3	48°00′	65°25′
Fauxburg	UNP/LNO	NS	Lunenburg	21 A/8	44°26′	64°24′
Faux-Canals, Les	UNP/LNO	QC	Maria-Chapdelaine	32 A/9	48°44′	72°19′
Favard, Lac	LAKE/LAC	QC	Kativik	23 M/10	55°30′	70°51′
Favel	UNP/LNO	ON	Kenora	52 F/13	49°59′	93°56′
Favery, Lac	LAKE/LAC	QC	Kativik	23 M/8	55°26′	70°10′
Favourable Lake	LAKE/LAC	ON	Kenora	53 C/13	52°55′	93°57′
Fawcett	UNP/LNO	NB	Westmorland	21 H/14	45°59′	65°12′
Fawcett	UNP/LNO	AB	16-64-1-W5	83 J/9	54°32′	114°05′
Fawcett Hill	UNP/LNO	NB	Westmorland	21 H/14	45°59′	65°13′
Fawcett Lake	LAKE/LAC	ON	Kenora	52 O/5	51°21′	91°49′
Fawcett Lake	LAKE/LAC	AB	73-26-W4	83 P/5	55°19′	113°53′
Fawcett River	RIV/CDE	AB	27-72-2-W5	83 O/8	55°15′	114°14′
Fawcett River	RIV/CDE	NT	Franklin	98 F	74°04′	124°22′
Fawcettville	UNP/LNO	ON	Prince Edward	31 C/3	44°01′	77°08′
Fawn Bay	UNP/LNO	ON	Ontario	31 D/11	44°38′	79°21′
Fawnie Range	MTN/MNT	BC	Range 4 Coast	93 F/6	53°15′	125°05′
Fawn Lake	UNP/LNO	AB	23-58-1-W5	83 J/1	54°03′	114°02′
Fawn Lake	LAKE/LAC	NT	Mackenzie	85 K	62°11′	117°32′
Fawn River	RIV/CDE	ON	Kenora	53 P/8	55°22′	88°20′
Fay Islands	ISL/ÎLE	NT	Franklin	69 H	79°37′	97°25′
Fay Lake	UNP/LNO	MB	69-24-W	63 N/3	55°00′	101°06′
Fearney Point	CAPE/CAP	BC	New Westminster	92 F/9	49°39′	124°06′
Featherstone	UNP/LNO	ON	Haldimand	30 L/13	42°49′	79°51′
Featherstone Point	CAPE/CAP	ON	Haldimand	30 L/13	42°49′	79°51′
Fecteau, Île	ISL/ÎLE	QC	Côte-Nord-du-Golfe-Saint-Laurent	12 J/15	50°56′	58°55′
Federal	UNP/LNO	ON	Carleton	31 G/5	45°20′	75°42′
Federal	UNP/LNO	AB	19-36-11-W4	73 D/4	52°07′	111°34′
Federal Ranch	UNP/LNO	BC	Peace River	94 B/8	56°24′	122°23′
Fedorah	UNP/LNO	AB	14-57-23-W4	83 H/14	53°56′	113°20′
Feeder	UNP/LNO	ON	Welland	30 L/14	42°57′	79°19′

NAME NOM	ENTITY ENTITÉ	LOC 1 LIEU 1	LOC 2 LIEU 2	MAP CARTE	POSITION LAT	POSITION LONG
Feeners Corner	UNP/LNO	NS	Lunenburg	21 A/7	44°28'	64°35'
Fee Peninsula	CAPE/CAP	NT	Franklin	37 A	68°08'	74°19'
Fee's Landing	UNP/LNO	ON	Victoria	31 D/7	44°21'	78°32'
Fee Spur	UNP/LNO	ON	Thunder Bay	52 I/5	50°16'	89°46'
Fehet Lake	LAKE/LAC	NT	Keewatin	56 C	64°17'	92°19'
Feilden Peninsula	CAPE/CAP	NT	Franklin	120 E	82°47'	63°50'
Feir Mill	UNP/LNO	ON	Victoria	31 D/7	44°16'	78°37'
Feist Lake	LAKE/LAC	ON	Kenora	52 F/13	49°48'	93°50'
Felix	UNP/LNO	ON	Sudbury	41 P/3	47°12'	81°25'
Félix-Antoine-Savard, Mont	MTN/MNT	QC	Charlevoix-Est	21 M/15	47°53'	70°30'
Felix, Cape	CAPE/CAP	NT	Franklin	67 D	69°54'	97°58'
Felix Cove	UNP/LNO	NF		12 B/10	48°32'	58°47'
Felix George 3 - see-voir - Felix George 7	IR/RI	BC		93 L/2	54°07'	126°45'
Felix George 7	IR/RI	BC	Range 5 Coast	93 L/2	54°07'	126°45'
Felker Lake	LAKE/LAC	BC	Lillooet	92 O/16	51°57'	122°00'
Fell	UNP/LNO	ON	Victoria	31 D/10	44°36'	78°43'
Fellers Heights	UNP/LNO	BC	Peace River	93 P/10	55°36'	120°34'
Fellfoot Point	CAPE/CAP	NT	Franklin	58 E	74°30'	88°35'
Felton	UNP/LNO	ON	Russell	31 G/3	45°12'	75°20'
Feltzen South	UNP/LNO	NS	Lunenburg	21 A/8	44°20'	64°17'
Femme	UNP/LNO	NF		1 M/10	47°36'	54°59'
Fenaghvale	UNP/LNO	ON	Prescott	31 G/7	45°28'	74°49'
Fenella	UNP/LNO	ON	Northumberland	31 D/1	44°09'	78°05'
Fenelon	MUN2/AZM2	ON	Victoria	31 D/10	44°31'	78°47'
Fenelon Falls	VILG/VILG	ON	Victoria	31 D/10	44°32'	78°45'
*Fenerty's	UNP/LNO	NS	Halifax	11 D/13	44°49'	63°43'
Fenn	UNP/LNO	AB	35-36-20-W4	83 A/2	52°08'	112°45'
Fennell	UNP/LNO	ON	Simcoe	31 D/4	44°13'	79°35'
Fennell Creek	RIV/CDE	BC	Kamloops Division Yale	82 M/5	51°21'	119°43'
Fenton	UNP/LNO	SK	32-46-25-W2	73 H/4	53°01'	105°35'
Fenton Lake	LAKE/LAC	BC	Range 4 Coast	93 E/8	53°30'	126°27'
Fenton Lake	LAKE/LAC	NT	Franklin	85 P/2	63°02'	112°57'
Fentons	UNP/LNO	NB	Queens	21 G/9	45°44'	66°08'
Fenwick	UNP/LNO	NS	Cumberland	21 H/16	45°46'	64°11'
Fenwick	UNP/LNO	ON	Welland	30 M/3	43°01'	79°22'
Fenwick	UNP/LNO	BC	Kootenay	82 G/5	49°29'	115°31'
Fenwood	VILG/VILG	SK	27-23-8-W2	62 M/3	51°01'	103°03'
Fenwood Gardens	UNP/LNO	ON	Prince Edward	31 C/3	44°07'	77°23'
Fer-à-Cheval, Le	UNP/LNO	QC	Pabok	22 A/10	48°32'	64°36'
Fer-à-Cheval, Le	UNP/LNO	QC	Manicouagan	22 G/5	49°24'	67°34'
Fer-à-Cheval, Le	UNP/LNO	QC	Bellechasse	21 L/10	46°34'	70°35'
Fer-à-Cheval, Le	UNP/LNO	QC	Le Fjord-du-Saguenay	22 D/7	48°19'	70°57'
Fer-à-Cheval, Le	UNP/LNO	QC	Le Fjord-du-Saguenay	22 D/11	48°38'	71°06'
Fer-à-Cheval, Le	UNP/LNO	QC	Les Pays-d'en-Haut	31 G/16	45°59'	74°07'
Fergus	TOWN/VIL2	ON	Wellington	40 P/9	43°42'	80°22'
Fergus Hill Estate	UNP/LNO	ON	Simcoe	31 D/11	44°35'	79°28'
Ferguslea	UNP/LNO	ON	Renfrew	31 F/7	45°26'	76°45'
Ferguson	UNP/LNO	QC	Le Haut-Saint-Maurice	31 P/14	47°49'	73°25'
Ferguson	UNP/LNO	BC	Kootenay	82 K/11	50°41'	117°29'
Ferguson Bay	BAY/BAIE	ON	Nipissing	41 P/1	47°09'	80°05'
Ferguson Corners	UNP/LNO	ON	Lennox and Addington	31 F/3	45°05'	77°17'
Ferguson Creek	RIV/CDE	MB	68-10-W	63 J/15	54°56'	98°52'
Ferguson Island	ISL/ÎLE	SK		73 I/4	54°11'	105°45'
Ferguson Lake	LAKE/LAC	NT	Keewatin	65 I	62°55'	96°53'
Ferguson Lake	LAKE/LAC	NT	Franklin	77 D	69°25'	105°15'
Ferguson River	RIV/CDE	NT	Keewatin	55 K	62°03'	93°20'
Fergusons Beach	UNP/LNO	ON	Renfrew	31 F/10	45°31'	76°34'
Fergusons Cove	UNP/LNO	NS	Halifax	11 D/12	44°36'	63°34'
Fergusons Falls	UNP/LNO	ON	Lanark	31 F/1	45°03'	76°17'
Fergusons Lake	UNP/LNO	NS	Richmond	11 F/10	45°39'	60°36'
Fergusonvale	UNP/LNO	ON	Simcoe	31 D/12	44°32'	79°49'
Ferintosh	VILG/VILG	AB	3-44-21-W4	83 A/15	52°46'	112°58'
*Ferland	VILG/VILG	SK	1-6-8-W3	72 G/7	49°27'	106°57'
Ferland	UNP/LNO	QC	Le Fjord-du-Saguenay	22 D/2	48°11'	70°51'
Ferland	UNP/LNO	ON	Thunder Bay	52 I/8	50°18'	88°25'
Ferland-et-Boilleau	VILG/VILG	QC	Le Fjord-du-Saguenay	22 D/2	48°06'	70°50'
Ferlow Junction	UNP/LNO	AB	6-46-20-W4	83 A/15	52°57'	112°53'
Ferme-à-Rosanna, La	UNP/LNO	QC	Charlevoix-Est	21 M/9	47°37'	70°29'
Ferme-Jeunesse, La	UNP/LNO	QC	Matane	22 B/11	48°43'	67°28'
Ferme-Joseph	UNP/LNO	QC	La Vallée-de-la-Gatineau	31 J/5	46°25'	75°49'
Ferme, La	UNP/LNO	QC	Bonaventure	22 A/5	48°18'	65°59'
Ferme, La	UNP/LNO	QC	Abitibi	32 D/9	48°36'	78°13'
Ferme-Lefebvre	UNP/LNO	QC	La Vallée-de-la-Gatineau	31 J/4	46°13'	75°56'
Ferme-Neuve	TOWN/VIL2	QC	Antoine-Labelle	31 J/11	46°42'	75°27'
Ferme-Neuve	VILG/VILG	QC	Antoine-Labelle	31 J/11	46°43'	75°28'

NAME NOM	ENTITY ENTITÉ	LOC 1 LIEU 1	LOC 2 LIEU 2	MAP CARTE	POSITION LAT	LONG
Ferme-Rouge	UNP/LNO	QC	Antoine-Labelle	31 J/6	46°26′	75°26′
Ferme-Tapani	UNP/LNO	QC	Antoine-Labelle	31 J/14	46°56′	75°08′
Fermeuse	VILG/VILG	NF		1 K/15	46°59′	52°58′
Fermeuse	UNP/LNO	NF		1 K/15	46°59′	52°58′
Fermont	CITY/VIL1	QC	Caniapiscau	23 B/14	52°47′	67°05′
Fermoy	UNP/LNO	ON	Frontenac	31 C/10	44°38′	76°31′
Fernald, Réserve écologique	PARK/PARC	QC	Matane	22 B/15	48°53′	66°41′
Fernand-Seguin, Mont	MTN/MNT	QC	Denis-Riverin	22 B/16	48°58′	66°11′
Fernbank	UNP/LNO	ON	Leeds	31 B/12	44°33′	75°43′
Fernbank	UNP/LNO	ON	Perth	40 P/10	43°36′	80°49′
Fern Creek	UNP/LNO	AB	32-47-2-W5	83 G/1	53°06′	114°15′
Ferndale	UNP/LNO	NF		1 N/5	47°16′	53°57′
Ferndale	UNP/LNO	NB	Albert	21 H/15	45°46′	65°00′
Ferndale	UNP/LNO	ON	Muskoka	31 E/4	45°08′	79°36′
Ferndale	UNP/LNO	ON	Peel	30 M/13	43°46′	79°55′
Ferndale	UNP/LNO	ON	Bruce	41 A/14	44°58′	81°17′
Ferndale	UNP/LNO	MB	9-1-W	62 H/12	49°43′	97°31′
Ferndale	UNP/LNO	BC	Cariboo	93 G/6	53°59′	122°29′
Ferndell	UNP/LNO	ON	Elgin	40 I/12	42°37′	81°41′
Ferndon	UNP/LNO	QC	Brome-Missisquoi	31 H/7	45°15′	72°54′
Fern Glen	UNP/LNO	ON	Parry Sound	31 E/6	45°28′	79°22′
Fern Hill	UNP/LNO	NS	Halifax	11 D/15	44°49′	62°38′
Fernhill	UNP/LNO	ON	Middlesex	40 P/4	43°03′	81°34′
Fernie	CITY/VIL1	BC	Kootenay	82 G/6	49°30′	115°04′
Fernlee	UNP/LNO	ON	Manitoulin	41 G/15	45°51′	82°48′
Fernlee	UNP/LNO	BC	New Westminster	92 G/7	49°21′	122°54′
Fernleigh	UNP/LNO	NS	Halifax	11 D/12	44°42′	63°40′
Fernleigh	UNP/LNO	ON	Frontenac	31 C/15	44°54′	76°59′
Fernmount	UNP/LNO	NB	Sunbury	21 G/16	45°57′	66°19′
Fernow Lake	LAKE/LAC	ON	Thunder Bay	42 E/16	49°55′	86°03′
Fern Ridge	UNP/LNO	BC	New Westminster	92 G/2	49°03′	122°39′
Fernwood	UNP/LNO	PE	Prince	11 L/5	46°19′	63°48′
Fernwood	UNP/LNO	BC	Saltspring Island	92 B/13	48°55′	123°32′
Feronia	UNP/LNO	ON	Nipissing	31 L/6	46°22′	79°19′
Ferraille-à-Willie, La	UNP/LNO	QC	Le Val-Saint-François	31 H/9	45°40′	72°00′
Ferrer Point	CAPE/CAP	BC	Nootka	92 E/10	49°45′	126°59′
Ferrier	UNP/LNO	AB	22-39-8-W5	83 B/6	52°23′	115°04′
Ferris	UNP/LNO	ON	Nipissing	31 L/6	46°18′	79°28′
Ferris Glacier	GLAC/GLAC	BC	Cassiar	114 P/3	59°04′	137°13′
*Ferrona	UNP/LNO	NS	Pictou	11 E/7	45°30′	62°41′
*Ferrona Junction	UNP/LNO	NS	Pictou	11 E/10	45°30′	62°41′
Ferru, Lac	LAKE/LAC	QC	Minganie	12 O/6	51°16′	59°12′
Ferry Creek	RIV/CDE	BC	Osoyoos Division Yale	82 L/2	50°15′	118°39′
Ferryland	VILG/VILG	NF		1 N/2	47°02′	52°53′
Ferryland Head	CAPE/CAP	NF		1 N/2	47°01′	52°51′
Ferryland Head	CAPE/CAP	NF		1 L/14	46°52′	55°24′
Ferry, Rivière	RIV/CDE	QC	La Côte-de-Beaupré	21 L/14	46°54′	71°10′
Ferry Road	UNP/LNO	NB	Northumberland	21 P/3	47°02′	65°29′
Fertile	UNP/LNO	SK	15-5-30-W	62 F/6	49°23′	101°27′
Fertile Belt No. 183	MUN2/AZM2	SK		62 L/9	50°45′	102°10′
Fertile Valley No. 285	MUN2/AZM2	SK		72 O/6	51°25′	107°10′
Fesserton	UNP/LNO	ON	Simcoe	31 D/12	44°44′	79°41′
Festubert	UNP/LNO	QC	Le Haut-Saint-Maurice	31 P/2	47°14′	72°41′
Feudal	UNP/LNO	SK	3-34-23-W3	72 O/13	51°53′	107°36′
Feuilles, Lac aux	LAKE/LAC	QC	Kativik	24 K/13	58°48′	69°50′
Feuilles, Rivière aux	RIV/CDE	QC	Kativik	24 L/16	58°47′	70°04′
Feu, Lac du	LAKE/LAC	QC	Minganie	12 K/9	50°31′	60°03′
Feversham	UNP/LNO	ON	Grey	41 A/8	44°20′	80°22′
Ficko	UNP/LNO	ON	Carleton	31 G/5	45°17′	75°38′
Fiddlers Head	CAPE/CAP	NS	Guysborough	11 F/4	45°04′	61°45′
Fidler	UNP/LNO	AB	24-47-23-W5	83 F/3	53°04′	117°15′
Fidler Bay	BAY/BAIE	SK		64 L/2	58°10′	102°58′
Fidler Lake	LAKE/LAC	MB		64 H/2	57°11′	96°57′
Fidler Point	CAPE/CAP	AB	116-3-W4	74 M/1	59°06′	110°26′
Fiedmont, Lac	LAKE/LAC	QC	Abitibi	32 C/5	48°21′	77°39′
Fief, Le	UNP/LNO	QC	Vaudreuil-Soulanges	31 G/8	45°27′	74°12′
Field	MUN2/AZM2	ON	Nipissing	31 L/5	46°30′	79°56′
Field	UNP/LNO	ON	Nipissing	41 I/9	46°31′	80°01′
Field	UNP/LNO	BC	Kootenay	82 N/8	51°24′	116°29′
Fielder Point	CAPE/CAP	NT	Franklin	49 A/11	76°31′	82°08′
Fielding	UNP/LNO	NB	Carleton	21 J/5	46°28′	67°33′
Fielding	UNP/LNO	ON	Cochrane	42 A/10	48°39′	80°52′
Fielding	UNP/LNO	SK	8-41-11-W3	73 B/12	52°31′	107°32′
Fieldville	UNP/LNO	QC	La Vallée-de-la-Gatineau	31 F/16	45°49′	76°01′
Fife	UNP/LNO	BC	Similkameen Division Yale	82 E/1	49°04′	118°12′

NAME NOM	ENTITY ENTITÉ	LOC 1 LIEU 1	LOC 2 LIEU 2	MAP CARTE	POSITION LAT	LONG
Fife Island	ISL/ÎLE	SK		64 L/6	58°28′	103°15′
Fife Lake	VILG/VILG	SK	8-3-28-W2	72 H/4	49°12′	105°44′
Fife Lake	LAKE/LAC	SK		72 H/4	49°14′	105°53′
Fife's Bay	UNP/LNO	ON	Peterborough	31 D/8	44°21′	78°26′
Fife Sound	CHAN/CHEN	BC	Range 1 Coast	92 L/15	50°47′	126°38′
Fifteenmile River	RIV/CDE	YT		116 B/5	64°17′	139°48′
Fifth Cabin	UNP/LNO	BC	Cassiar	94 D/5	56°26′	127°57′
Fifth Depot Lake	LAKE/LAC	ON	Frontenac	31 C/10	44°36′	76°52′
Fifth Lake	LAKE/LAC	NB	York	21 G/11	45°43′	67°25′
Fifth Lake Flowage	LAKE/LAC	NS	Digby	21 A/5	44°23′	65°38′
Fifth Meridian	UNP/LNO	AB	24-111-1-W5	84 J/9	58°38′	114°00′
Fiji Island	ISL/ÎLE	NT	Franklin	97 F	70°11′	125°03′
Fildegrand, Rivière	RIV/CDE	QC	Témiscamingue	31 K/5	46°18′	77°51′
File Axe, Lac	LAKE/LAC	QC	Maria-Chapdelaine	32 I/5	50°18′	73°34′
File Lake	LAKE/LAC	MB	68-19,20-W	63 K/16	54°53′	100°20′
Filer Creek	RIV/CDE	BC	Range 1 Coast	92 K/9	50°34′	124°09′
Filer Glacier	GLAC/GLAC	BC	Range 1 Coast	92 K/16	50°47′	124°17′
File River	RIV/CDE	MB		63 N/8	55°20′	100°24′
Filer, Mount	MTN/MNT	BC	Range 1 Coast	92 K/16	50°47′	124°21′
Filey Beach	UNP/LNO	ON	York	31 D/6	44°19′	79°24′
Filion Lake	LAKE/LAC	SK	52-5-W3	73 G/10	53°31′	106°37′
Filkars, Rivière	RIV/CDE	QC	Lotbinière	21 L/6	46°25′	71°18′
Fill	UNP/LNO	BC	Lillooet	92 P/3	51°11′	121°30′
Fillmore	VILG/VILG	SK	3-11-11-W2	62 E/14	49°53′	103°26′
Fillmore No. 96	MUN2/AZM2	SK		62 E/14	49°55′	103°25′
Fils, Lac du	LAKE/LAC	QC	Témiscamingue	31 L/9	46°37′	78°08′
Fincastle	UNP/LNO	AB	8-10-15-W4	82 H/16	49°48′	112°00′
Finch	VILG/VILG	ON	Stormont	31 G/3	45°08′	75°05′
Finch	MUN2/AZM2	ON	Stormont	31 G/3	45°12′	75°07′
Finchley	UNP/LNO	ON	Renfrew	31 F/15	45°46′	76°59′
Findlater	VILG/VILG	SK	16-21-25-W2	72 I/14	50°47′	105°24′
Findlay	UNP/LNO	MB	13-7-25-W	62 F/10	49°34′	100°45′
Findlay Creek	RIV/CDE	BC	Kootenay	82 J/4	50°06′	115°57′
Findlay Crossing	UNP/LNO	MB	15-7-25-W	62 F/10	49°34′	100°47′
Findlay Group	ISL/ÎLE	NT	Franklin	79 D	77°24′	104°46′
Findlay, Mount	MTN/MNT	BC	Kootenay	82 K/1	50°05′	116°30′
Fingal	UNP/LNO	ON	Elgin	40 I/11	42°43′	81°19′
Finger	UNP/LNO	MB	18-58-23-W	63 K/2	54°00′	100°52′
Fingerboard	UNP/LNO	ON	Victoria	31 D/2	44°14′	78°55′
Finger Lake	LAKE/LAC	ON	Kenora	53 F/4	53°09′	93°30′
Finger Lake	LAKE/LAC	BC	Range 4 Coast	93 F/9	53°34′	124°17′
Finger Land	CAPE/CAP	NT	Franklin	26 A	64°28′	65°11′
Fin Island	ISL/ÎLE	BC	Range 4 Coast	103 H/6	53°16′	129°21′
Finland	UNP/LNO	ON	Rainy River	52 C/13	48°51′	93°55′
Finlay Point	CAPE/CAP	NS	Inverness	11 K/3	46°07′	61°28′
Finlay Ranges	MTN/MNT	BC	Cassiar	94 C/7	56°20′	124°45′
Finlay Reach	RIVF/EFLV	BC	Cassiar	94 C/10	56°40′	124°45′
Finlay River	RIV/CDE	BC	Cassiar	94 C/15	56°54′	124°57′
Finlayson Channel	CHAN/CHEN	BC	Range 3 Coast	103 A/9	52°38′	128°28′
Finlayson Island	ISL/ÎLE	BC	Range 5 Coast	103 J/9	54°32′	130°28′
Finlayson Island 19	IR/RI	BC	Range 5 Coast	103 J/9	54°32′	130°28′
Finlayson Islands	ISL/ÎLE	NT	Franklin	77 D	69°05′	105°58′
Finlayson Lake	LAKE/LAC	ON	Rainy River	52 B/13	48°55′	91°34′
Finlayson Lake	LAKE/LAC	YT		105 G/10	61°41′	130°38′
Finlayson River	RIV/CDE	YT		105 H/5	61°29′	129°41′
Finmark	UNP/LNO	ON	Thunder Bay	52 A/12	48°35′	89°45′
Finmoore	UNP/LNO	BC	Cariboo	93 G/13	53°59′	123°36′
Finn Creek	RIV/CDE	BC	Kamloops Division Yale	82 M/14	51°54′	119°19′
Finnegan	UNP/LNO	AB	18-25-15-W4	82 P/1	51°07′	112°04′
Finnie	UNP/LNO	SK	33-21-9-W2	62 L/14	50°51′	103°12′
Finnie Bay	BAY/BAIE	NT	Franklin	36 F	65°13′	77°30′
Finns	UNP/LNO	MB	21,22-4-E	62 I/15	50°52′	97°00′
Finntown	UNP/LNO	ON	Cochrane	42 A/6	48°29′	81°13′
Fintry	UNP/LNO	BC	Osoyoos Division Yale	82 L/3	50°08′	119°30′
Firdale	UNP/LNO	MB	6-12-12-W	62 G/14	49°59′	99°07′
Firebag Island	ISL/ÎLE	ON	Kenora	52 E/7	49°17′	94°35′
Firebag River	RIV/CDE	AB/SK		74 E/11	57°45′	111°21′
Fire Creek	RIV/CDE	BC	New Westminster	92 G/16	49°47′	122°13′
Fire Creek	RIV/CDE	BC	Lillooet	92 O/6	51°28′	123°08′
Firedrake Lake	LAKE/LAC	NT	Mackenzie	75 H	61°25′	104°30′
Fire, Lac	LAKE/LAC	QC	Jamésie	33 A/11	52°38′	73°05′
Fire Lake	UNP/LNO	QC	Caniapiscau	23 B/6	52°20′	67°22′
Fire Lake	LAKE/LAC	BC	New Westminster	92 G/16	49°50′	122°23′
Fire Ranger Camp	UNP/LNO	QC	Rouyn-Noranda	31 M/9	47°43′	78°23′
Fire River	UNP/LNO	ON	Algoma	42 B/13	48°46′	83°36′

NAME NOM	ENTITY ENTITÉ	LOC 1 LIEU 1	LOC 2 LIEU 2	MAP CARTE	POSITION LAT	LONG
Fire River	RIV/CDE	ON	Algoma	42 B/14	48°52′	83°21′
Fireside	UNP/LNO	BC	Cassiar	94 M/11	59°40′	127°09′
Firesteel River	RIV/CDE	ON	Thunder Bay	52 G/2	49°02′	90°57′
Firesteel River	RIV/CDE	BC	Cassiar	94 E/2	57°08′	126°55′
Fir Island	ISL/ÎLE	SK		74 P/3	59°11′	105°25′
Fir Mountain	UNP/LNO	SK	13-5-5-W3	72 G/7	49°28′	106°32′
Fir Ridge	UNP/LNO	SK	12-48-24-W2	73 H/3	53°11′	105°25′
Fir River	RIV/CDE	SK		63 D/16	52°49′	102°23′
First Brook	RIV/CDE	NF		11 P/16	47°46′	56°08′
First Burnt Pond	LAKE/LAC	NF		2 D/16	48°46′	54°23′
First Double Pond	LAKE/LAC	NF		2 F/4	49°13′	53°57′
First Eel Lake	LAKE/LAC	NB	York	21 G/13	45°51′	67°40′
First Lake	LAKE/LAC	NB	Madawaska	21 N/9	47°38′	68°17′
First Oil Well in Western Canada National Historic Site - also-aussi - Premier-Puits-de-Pétrole-de-l'Ouest-Canadien, Lieu historique national du	PARK/PARC	AB		82 H/4	49°04′	113°59′
First Peninsula	UNP/LNO	NS	Lunenburg	21 A/8	44°23′	64°19′
First Pond	LAKE/LAC	NF		2 F/4	49°03′	53°59′
First Pond	LAKE/LAC	NF		2 E/7	49°25′	54°37′
First South	UNP/LNO	NS	Lunenburg	21 A/8	44°22′	64°21′
Firth River	RIV/CDE	YT		117 D/12	69°33′	139°32′
Firth's Corners	UNP/LNO	ON	Simcoe	31 D/12	44°44′	79°54′
Firvale	UNP/LNO	BC	Range 3 Coast	93 D/8	52°26′	126°17′
Fischells	UNP/LNO	NF		12 B/7	48°19′	58°42′
Fischells Brook	RIV/CDE	NF		12 B/7	48°19′	58°43′
Fischot Islands	UNP/LNO	NF		2 M/4	51°11′	55°41′
Fisgard Lighthouse National Historic Site - also-aussi - Phare-de-Fisgard, Lieu historique national du	PARK/PARC	BC	Esquimalt	92 B/6	48°26′	123°27′
Fishbasket Lake	LAKE/LAC	ON	Kenora	53 A/9	52°36′	88°00′
Fishbasket River	RIV/CDE	ON	Kenora	43 D/13	52°46′	87°37′
Fish Cove Point	CAPE/CAP	NF		13 I/3	54°08′	57°22′
Fish Creek	UNP/LNO	SK	7-42A-1-W3	73 B/9	52°37′	106°09′
Fish Creek	RIV/CDE	ON	Perth	40 P/3	43°13′	81°13′
Fish Creek	RIV/CDE	AB	25-22-1-W5	82 J/16	50°54′	114°01′
Fish Creek No. 402	MUN2/AZM2	SK		73 A/12	52°35′	105°55′
Fish Creek Provincial Park	PARK/PARC	AB	22,23-29,1-W4,5	82 J/16	50°55′	114°02′
Fish Egg Inlet	BAY/BAIE	BC	Range 2 Coast	92 M/12	51°37′	127°45′
Fishem Lake	LAKE/LAC	BC	Lillooet	92 O/4	51°14′	123°40′
Fisher	MUN2/AZM2	MB		62 P/4	51°05′	97°35′
Fisher	UNP/LNO	QC	Abitibi	32 C/5	48°29′	77°48′
Fisher	UNP/LNO	SK	2,3-47A-24-W2	73 H/3	53°02′	105°27′
Fisher Bay	UNP/LNO	MB	7-29-2-E	62 P/6	51°29′	97°18′
Fisher Bay	BAY/BAIE	MB		62 P/11	51°35′	97°13′
Fisher Bay	BAY/BAIE	NT	Franklin	35 H/16	61°47′	72°10′
Fisher Branch	UNP/LNO	MB	24-24-2-W	62 P/4	51°05′	97°37′
Fisher, Cape	CAPE/CAP	NT	Keewatin	46 B	64°41′	82°06′
Fisher, Cape	CAPE/CAP	NT	Franklin	46 J/2	66°12′	82°59′
Fisher, Cape	CAPE/CAP	NT	Franklin	78 G	75°51′	111°24′
Fisher Channel	CHAN/CHEN	BC	Range 3 Coast	93 D/4	52°08′	127°53′
Fisher Creek	RIV/CDE	AB	23-66-8-W4	73 L/11	54°43′	111°06′
Fisher Glacier	GLAC/GLAC	YT		115 B/1	60°06′	138°18′
Fisher Heights	UNP/LNO	ON	Carleton	31 G/5	45°22′	75°44′
Fisher Home	UNP/LNO	AB	14-47-2-W5	83 G/1	53°03′	114°10′
Fisher Lake	LAKE/LAC	NS	Annapolis	21 A/11	44°33′	65°21′
Fisher Lake	LAKE/LAC	ON	Kenora	52 F/12	49°33′	93°33′
Fisher Lake	LAKE/LAC	MB	13-15-E	52 L/4	50°06′	95°31′
Fisher Lake	LAKE/LAC	NT	Franklin	68 A	72°12′	98°00′
Fisherman Lake	LAKE/LAC	NT	Mackenzie	95 B	60°20′	123°45′
Fisherman River	RIV/CDE	BC	Rupert	102 I/16	50°46′	128°21′
*Fishermans Cove	UNP/LNO	BC	New Westminster	92 G/6	49°22′	123°16′
Fishermans Harbour	UNP/LNO	NS	Guysborough	11 F/4	45°07′	61°41′
Fisher Mills	UNP/LNO	NS	Guysborough	11 F/5	45°19′	61°55′
Fisher Mills	UNP/LNO	ON	Waterloo	40 P/8	43°27′	80°20′
Fisher, Mount	MTN/MNT	BC	Kootenay	82 G/11	49°39′	115°29′
Fisher River	UNP/LNO	MB	34,35-28-1-E	62 P/6	51°26′	97°22′
Fisher River	RIV/CDE	MB	28-1-E	62 P/6	51°26′	97°17′
Fisher River 44	IR/RI	MB		62 P/6	51°26′	97°21′
Fisher River 44A	IR/RI	MB		62 P/5	51°24′	97°32′
Fishers Glen	UNP/LNO	ON	Norfolk	40 I/9	42°43′	80°18′
Fisher's Grant 24	IR/RI	NS	Pictou	11 E/10	45°40′	62°39′
Fisher's Grant 24G	IR/RI	NS	Pictou	11 E/10	45°39′	62°39′
Fishers Island	ISL/ÎLE	NT	Franklin	76 N	67°55′	108°07′
Fisher's Point	UNP/LNO	QC	Brome-Missisquoi	31 H/1	45°15′	72°30′
Fisher Strait	CHAN/CHEN	NT	Franklin	45 O/5	63°15′	83°30′
Fisherton	UNP/LNO	MB	13-25-3-W	62 P/4	51°09′	97°46′

NAME NOM	ENTITY ENTITÉ	LOC 1 LIEU 1	LOC 2 LIEU 2	MAP CARTE	POSITION LAT	LONG
Fisherville	UNP/LNO	ON	York	30 M/14	43°47'	79°28'
Fisherville	UNP/LNO	ON	Haldimand	30 L/13	42°52'	79°54'
Fishing Branch	RIV/CDE	YT		116 J/7	66°27'	138°35'
Fishing Eagle Lake	LAKE/LAC	MB		53 L/15	54°54'	94°32'
Fishing Islands	ISL/ÎLE	ON	Bruce	41 A/14	44°46'	81°19'
Fishing Lake	UNP/LNO	SK	11-33-12-W2	62 M/13	51°49'	103°36'
Fishing Lake	LAKE/LAC	MB		53 D/3	52°08'	95°24'
Fishing Lake	LAKE/LAC	SK	33-11,12-W2	62 M/13	51°50'	103°32'
Fishing Lake	LAKE/LAC	AB	57-2-W4	73 E/16	53°54'	110°13'
Fishing Lake 89	IR/RI	SK		62 M/13	51°51'	103°40'
Fishing Lake 89A	IR/RI	SK		62 M/13	51°50'	103°34'
Fishing Lake Metis Settlement	UNP/LNO	AB		73 E/16	54°00'	110°10'
Fishing Lakes, The	LAKE/LAC	SK		62 L/12	50°45'	103°51'
Fishing River	UNP/LNO	MB	33-28-19-W	62 N/8	51°27'	100°05'
Fishing Ships Harbour	UNP/LNO	NF		3 D/12	52°36'	55°47'
Fishing Station 62A	IR/RI	MB		62 K/10	50°44'	100°42'
Fish Island	ISL/ÎLE	NF		14 F/6	57°28'	61°25'
Fish Island	ISL/ÎLE	NF		14 L/8	58°21'	62°27'
Fish Lake	LAKE/LAC	ON	Prince Edward	31 C/3	44°06'	77°10'
Fish Lake	LAKE/LAC	YT		105 D/11	60°37'	135°14'
Fish Lake	LAKE/LAC	NT	Mackenzie	95 O	63°11'	122°35'
Fish Lake 5	IR/RI	BC	Lillooet	92 P/5	51°29'	121°58'
Fish Lake 7	IR/RI	BC	Lillooet	92 I/12	50°36'	121°48'
Fish Point	CAPE/CAP	NF		12 H/16	49°54'	56°28'
Fish Point	CAPE/CAP	ON	Essex	40 G/10	41°43'	82°40'
Fishpot Lake 24	IR/RI	BC	Cariboo	93 B/13	52°57'	123°46'
Fishtail Lake	LAKE/LAC	ON	Haliburton	31 E/1	45°09'	78°12'
Fishtrap Lake	LAKE/LAC	ON	Kenora	43 D/8	52°21'	86°24'
Fishtrap Lake	LAKE/LAC	NT	Mackenzie	86 E	65°29'	118°25'
Fiske	HAM/HAM	SK	13-29-18-W3	72 N/8	51°29'	108°24'
Fiskes Corners	UNP/LNO	ON	Glengarry	31 G/7	45°23'	74°46'
Fitch Bay	UNP/LNO	QC	Memphrémagog	31 H/1	45°07'	72°11'
Fitton, Mount	MTN/MNT	YT		117 A/6	68°29'	138°02'
Fitton Point	CAPE/CAP	NT	Mackenzie	97 F	70°11'	127°05'
Fitzallen	UNP/LNO	AB	6-53-14-W4	83 H/9	53°33'	112°03'
Fitzgerald	UNP/LNO	AB	7-11-6-W4	72 E/15	49°53'	110°50'
Fitzgerald	UNP/LNO	AB	125-10-W4	74 M/13	59°51'	111°36'
Fitzgerald Bay	BAY/BAIE	NT	Franklin	58 A	72°09'	89°45'
Fitzgerald Islands	ISL/ÎLE	NT	Mackenzie	77 A	68°13'	104°20'
Fitz Hugh Sound	CHAN/CHEN	BC	Range 2 Coast	92 M/12	51°40'	127°50'
Fitzmaurice	UNP/LNO	SK	18-27-8-W2	62 M/6	51°20'	103°07'
Fitzpatrick	UNP/LNO	NS	Pictou	11 E/11	45°44'	63°02'
Fitzpatrick	UNP/LNO	QC	Le Haut-Saint-Maurice	31 P/7	47°29'	72°46'
Fitzpatrick Lake	LAKE/LAC	NT	Keewatin	65 B	60°50'	98°36'
Fitzpatricks Mountain	UNP/LNO	NS	Pictou	11 E/10	45°38'	62°52'
Fitzroy	UNP/LNO	ON	Carleton	31 F/8	45°28'	76°12'
Fitz Roy, Cape	CAPE/CAP	NT	Franklin	38 G	75°32'	79°56'
Fitzroy Harbour	UNP/LNO	ON	Carleton	31 F/8	45°28'	76°13'
Fitz Roy Inlet	BAY/BAIE	NT	Franklin	58 B	72°09'	95°00'
Fitzsimmons	UNP/LNO	AB	22-73-3-W6	83 M/8	55°20'	118°22'
Fitzwilliam	UNP/LNO	BC	Cariboo	83 D/15	52°52'	118°40'
Fitzwilliam Channel	CHAN/CHEN	ON	Manitoulin	41 H/5	45°26'	81°47'
Fitzwilliam Island	ISL/ÎLE	ON	Manitoulin	41 H/5	45°29'	81°45'
Fitzwilliam Owen Island	ISL/ÎLE	NT	Franklin	89 D	77°07'	113°47'
Fitzwilliam Strait	CHAN/CHEN	NT	Franklin	89 B/8	76°25'	116°10'
Five Corners	UNP/LNO	NB	Charlotte	21 G/3	45°12'	67°18'
Five Corners	UNP/LNO	ON	Peterborough	31 D/8	44°22'	78°14'
Five Corners	UNP/LNO	MB	26,27-5-7-W	62 G/8	49°26'	98°19'
Five Fathom Hole	UNP/LNO	NB	Saint John	21 G/1	45°11'	66°15'
Five Fingers	UNP/LNO	NB	Restigouche	21 O/11	47°31'	67°22'
Five Houses	UNP/LNO	PE	Kings	11 L/7	46°25'	62°32'
Five Houses	UNP/LNO	NS	Colchester	11 E/5	45°24'	63°44'
Five Houses	UNP/LNO	NS	Lunenburg	21 A/8	44°17'	64°20'
Five Island Lake	UNP/LNO	NS	Halifax	11 D/12	44°40'	63°49'
Five Islands	UNP/LNO	NS	Colchester	21 H/8	45°25'	64°02'
Five Islands	ISL/ÎLE	NS	Cumberland	21 H/8	45°23'	64°06'
Five Mile	UNP/LNO	BC	Kootenay	82 K/11	50°40'	117°27'
Five Mile 3	IR/RI	BC	Cariboo	93 A/4	52°10'	121°58'
Five Mile Bay	BAY/BAIE	ON	Parry Sound	41 H/8	45°16'	80°07'
Five Mile Lake	LAKE/LAC	NS	Hants	11 D/13	44°53'	63°58'
Five Mile Lake	LAKE/LAC	ON	Sudbury	41 O/11	47°34'	83°16'
Five Mile Plains	UNP/LNO	NS	Hants	21 A/16	44°58'	64°05'
Five Mile Point 3	IR/RI	BC	Cassiar	104 N/5	59°30'	133°40'
Five Mile River	UNP/LNO	NS	Hants	11 E/4	45°13'	63°36'
Five Points	UNP/LNO	NB	Albert	21 I/3	46°01'	65°01'

NAME NOM	ENTITY ENTITÉ	LOC 1 LIEU 1	LOC 2 LIEU 2	MAP CARTE	POSITION LAT	LONG
Five Points	UNP/LNO	NB	Kings	21 H/14	45°49′	65°18′
Five River Lake	LAKE/LAC	NS	Shelburne	20 P/11	43°43′	65°27′
Five Rivers	RIV/CDE	NS	Queens	20 P/15	43°58′	64°44′
Flack Lake	LAKE/LAC	ON	Algoma	41 J/10	46°35′	82°47′
Flagler Bay	BAY/BAIE	NT	Franklin	39 G	79°10′	77°00′
Flagstaff No. 29, County of	MUN1/AZM1	AB	43-5-W4	73 D/12	52°40′	111°48′
Flagstaff Point	CAPE/CAP	ON	Kenora	43 N/6	55°16′	85°00′
Flaherty Island	ISL/ÎLE	NT	Keewatin	34 D	56°14′	79°17′
Flake	UNP/LNO	ON	Sudbury	41 I/11	46°37′	81°02′
Flamande, Passe - also-aussi - Flemish Pass	SEAU/SMER	—		8012	47°00′	46°45′
Flamand, Lac	LAKE/LAC	QC	Le Haut-Saint-Maurice	31 P/11	47°33′	73°25′
Flamboro	UNP/LNO	ON	Wentworth	30 M/5	43°24′	79°58′
Flamboro Centre	UNP/LNO	ON	Wentworth	30 M/5	43°22′	79°56′
Flamborough	TOWN/VIL2	ON	Wentworth	30 M/5	43°17′	79°57′
Flanagan Lake	LAKE/LAC	SK		63 M/9	55°36′	102°30′
Flanagan River	RIV/CDE	ON	Kenora	53 C/14	52°50′	93°28′
Flanders	UNP/LNO	QC	Le Haut-Saint-François	21 E/5	45°22′	71°33′
Flanders	UNP/LNO	ON	Rainy River	52 C/9	48°44′	92°05′
Flanders Heights	UNP/LNO	ON	Leeds	31 B/12	44°37′	75°42′
Flannigan Corners	UNP/LNO	ON	Perth	40 P/7	43°20′	80°57′
Flash, Le	UNP/LNO	QC	La Vallée-de-la-Gatineau	31 J/13	46°49′	75°54′
Flat Bay	UNP/LNO	NF		12 B/7	48°24′	58°35′
Flat Bay	BAY/BAIE	NF		12 B/7	48°26′	58°33′
Flat Bay Brook	RIV/CDE	NF		12 B/7	48°24′	58°35′
Flat Bay West	UNP/LNO	NF		12 B/7	48°24′	58°36′
Flatbush	UNP/LNO	AB	1-66-2-W5	83 J/9	54°42′	114°09′
Flat Creek	UNP/LNO	BC	Kootenay	82 N/4	51°13′	117°41′
Flat Creek	UNP/LNO	YT		115 O/15	63°57′	138°37′
Flat Creek	RIV/CDE	ON	Perth	40 P/6	43°17′	81°10′
Flathead	UNP/LNO	BC	Kootenay	82 G/1	49°00′	114°29′
Flathead	UNP/LNO	BC	Kootenay	82 G/7	49°21′	114°37′
Flathead River	RIV/CDE	BC	Kootenay	82 G/1	49°00′	114°28′
Flat Island	UNP/LNO	NF		1 M/7	47°17′	54°55′
Flat Island	ISL/ÎLE	NF		12 B/7	48°26′	58°34′
Flat Island	ISL/ÎLE	NS	Lunenburg	21 A/8	44°25′	64°08′
Flat Island	ISL/ÎLE	NS	Yarmouth	20 O/9	43°30′	66°00′
Flat Islands	ISL/ÎLE	NF		2 C/13	48°48′	53°38′
Flat Lake	UNP/LNO	AB	28-59-8-W4	73 L/3	54°08′	111°09′
Flat Lake	LAKE/LAC	AB	65,66-19,20-W4	83 I/10	54°38′	112°54′
Flat Lake	LAKE/LAC	BC	Lillooet	92 P/5	51°29′	121°32′
Flat Landing	UNP/LNO	NB	Northumberland	21 I/13	46°50′	65°57′
Flatland Island	ISL/ÎLE	ON	Thunder Bay	52 H/9	49°44′	88°19′
Flatlands	UNP/LNO	NB	Restigouche	21 O/15	47°59′	66°53′
Flat, Le	UNP/LNO	QC	Pontiac	31 F/14	45°52′	77°05′
Flat Point	CAPE/CAP	NT	Keewatin	55 N	64°00′	93°27′
Flat River	UNP/LNO	PE	Queens	11 L/2	46°01′	62°52′
Flat River	RIV/CDE	BC	Cassiar	103 P/14	55°55′	129°17′
Flat River	RIV/CDE	NT	Mackenzie	95 F/11	61°32′	125°22′
Flatrock	TOWN/VIL2	NF		1 N/10	47°42′	52°43′
Flatrock	UNP/LNO	NF		1 N/10	47°43′	52°50′
Flat Rock	UNP/LNO	NF		1 N/2	47°00′	52°59′
Flatrock	UNP/LNO	NF		1 N/14	47°46′	53°11′
Flatrock	UNP/LNO	BC	Peace River	94 A/8	56°16′	120°17′
Flatrock Lake	LAKE/LAC	MB		63 N/10	55°37′	100°48′
Flat Sound	CHAN/CHEN	NT	Franklin	560 A/1	80°15′	88°52′
Flatstone Lake	LAKE/LAC	SK		74 B/4	56°15′	107°43′
Flat Top	MTN/MNT	YT		115 P/3	63°14′	137°23′
Flat Top, Mont	MTN/MNT	QC	Le Granit	21 E/7	45°29′	70°44′
Flat Valley	UNP/LNO	SK	61-22-W3	73 K/6	54°18′	109°14′
Flat Water Pond	LAKE/LAC	NF		12 H/16	49°47′	56°18′
Flaxcombe	VILG/VILG	SK	16-29-26-W3	72 N/5	51°29′	109°36′
Fléché, Lac	LAKE/LAC	QC	Manicouagan	22 K/1	50°02′	68°11′
Flee Island	UNP/LNO	MB		62 J/1	50°10′	98°10′
Fleet	UNP/LNO	AB	1-37-13-W4	73 D/4	52°09′	111°44′
Fleet Lake	LAKE/LAC	ON	Kenora	52 K/3	50°14′	93°23′
Fleet Peak	MTN/MNT	BC	Cassiar	94 D/16	56°47′	126°16′
Fleet River	RIV/CDE	BC	Malahat	92 C/9	48°35′	124°04′
Fleet Settlement	UNP/LNO	NS	Guysborough	11 D/16	44°59′	62°10′
Fleetwood	UNP/LNO	ON	Durham	31 D/2	44°13′	78°37′
Fleetwood	UNP/LNO	BC	New Westminster	92 G/2	49°10′	122°48′
Fleetwood, Cape	CAPE/CAP	NT	Franklin	69 B	76°34′	103°32′
Fleming	TOWN/VIL2	SK	3-13-30-W	62 K/4	50°04′	101°31′
Fleming	UNP/LNO	BC	Cassiar	93 M/5	55°15′	127°34′
Fleming Creek	RIV/CDE	ON	Elgin	40 I/12	42°38′	81°47′
Flemingdon Park	UNP/LNO	ON	York	30 M/11	43°43′	79°20′

NAME NOM	ENTITY ENTITÉ	LOC 1 LIEU 1	LOC 2 LIEU 2	MAP CARTE	POSITION LAT	LONG
Fleming Inlet	BAY/BAIE	NT	Franklin	48 B	72°25′	84°55′
Fleming Island	ISL/ÎLE	BC	Barclay	92 C/14	48°53′	125°08′
Fleming Lake	LAKE/LAC	ON	Thunder Bay	42 L/2	50°07′	86°56′
Fleming's Landing	UNP/LNO	ON	Parry Sound	41 H/16	45°54′	80°09′
Flemish Cap - also-aussi - Bonnet Flamand	SEAU/SMER	—		8013	47°00′	44°50′
Flemish Pass - also-aussi - Flamande, Passe	SEAU/SMER	—		8012	47°00′	46°45′
Flemming	UNP/LNO	NB	Madawaska	21 O/5	47°17′	67°52′
Flesherton	VILG/VILG	ON	Grey	41 A/7	44°16′	80°33′
Flesherton Station	UNP/LNO	ON	Grey	41 A/2	44°15′	80°34′
Flétan, Chenal du - also-aussi - Halibut Channel	SEAU/SMER	—		4016	46°00′	55°15′
Fletcher	UNP/LNO	ON	Kent	40 J/8	42°18′	82°18′
Fletcher Island	ISL/ÎLE	NT	Franklin	25 O	63°12′	67°47′
Fletcher Lake	LAKE/LAC	MB		54 K/4	58°11′	93°51′
Fletcher Lake	LAKE/LAC	SK		63 M/4	55°12′	103°45′
Fletcher Lake	LAKE/LAC	NT	Mackenzie	75 N	63°35′	108°45′
Fletchers Lake	UNP/LNO	NS	Halifax	11 D/13	44°50′	63°36′
Flett	UNP/LNO	ON	Thunder Bay	52 A/12	48°36′	89°46′
Flett Lake	LAKE/LAC	NT	Mackenzie	75 A	60°25′	104°08′
Flett Springs	UNP/LNO	SK	9,16-44-20-W2	73 A/15	52°47′	104°51′
Flett's Springs No. 429	MUN2/AZM2	SK		73 A/15	52°50′	104°45′
Fleurant	UNP/LNO	QC	Avignon	22 B/1	48°06′	66°24′
Fleur de Lys	TOWN/VIL2	NF		12 I/1	50°07′	56°08′
Fleur-de-May, Lac	LAKE/LAC	NF		22 P/14	52°00′	65°05′
Fleurimont	CITY/VIL1	QC	Sherbrooke	21 E/5	45°25′	71°52′
Fleury Bight	UNP/LNO	NF		2 E/11	49°32′	55°18′
Flindt Landing	UNP/LNO	ON	Thunder Bay	52 J/1	50°14′	90°26′
Flin Flon	CITY/VIL1	MB/SK		63 K/13	54°46′	101°52′
Flin Flon Junction	UNP/LNO	MB	34-56-26-W	63 F/14	53°53′	101°14′
Flint	UNP/LNO	ON	Thunder Bay	52 A/5	48°20′	89°41′
Flintdale	UNP/LNO	ON	Cochrane	42 K/4	50°04′	85°36′
Flint Lake	LAKE/LAC	ON	Thunder Bay	42 F/13	49°52′	85°53′
Flint Lake	LAKE/LAC	ON	Kenora	52 F/5	49°20′	93°50′
Flint Lake	LAKE/LAC	NT	Franklin	37 D	69°16′	74°15′
Flintoft	UNP/LNO	SK	9-6-3-W3	72 G/8	49°28′	106°21′
Flinton	UNP/LNO	ON	Lennox and Addington	31 C/11	44°41′	77°13′
Flinton Corner	UNP/LNO	ON	Lennox and Addington	31 C/11	44°43′	77°09′
Flint River	RIV/CDE	ON	Cochrane	42 K/3	50°14′	85°18′
Floatingstone Lake	LAKE/LAC	AB	60-11-W4	73 L/4	54°13′	111°38′
Flodden	UNP/LNO	QC	Le Val-Saint-François	31 H/9	45°31′	72°12′
Floods	UNP/LNO	BC	Yale Division Yale	92 H/5	49°22′	121°31′
Flood's Landing	UNP/LNO	ON	Peterborough	31 D/8	44°26′	78°29′
Floors	UNP/LNO	MB	21-13-21-W	62 K/1	50°07′	100°18′
Floradale	UNP/LNO	ON	Waterloo	40 P/10	43°37′	80°35′
Floral	UNP/LNO	SK	36-4-W3	73 B/1	52°04′	106°28′
Floral Park	UNP/LNO	ON	Ontario	31 D/11	44°42′	79°20′
Florence	UNP/LNO	NS	Cape Breton	11 K/8	46°16′	60°16′
Florence	UNP/LNO	ON	Lambton	40 J/9	42°39′	82°00′
Florence Lake	LAKE/LAC	ON	Sudbury	41 P/2	47°15′	80°33′
Florence Lake	LAKE/LAC	BC	Sayward	92 K/6	50°24′	125°15′
Florenceville	VILG/VILG	NB	Carleton	21 J/5	46°27′	67°38′
Florencia Bay	BAY/BAIE	BC	Clayoquot	92 C/13	48°59′	125°38′
Flores Island	ISL/ÎLE	BC	Clayoquot	92 E/8	49°20′	126°10′
Florida	UNP/LNO	ON	Frontenac	31 C/7	44°20′	76°41′
Florida	UNP/LNO	ON	Cochrane	42 H/2	49°06′	80°51′
Florze	UNP/LNO	MB	4-12-E	52 E/5	49°19′	95°57′
Flos - see-voir - Springwater	MUN2/AZM2	ON		31 D/12	44°30′	79°51′
Flotten Lake	LAKE/LAC	SK	65-17-W3	73 K/10	54°37′	108°32′
Flour Mill	UNP/LNO	ON	Sudbury	41 I/10	46°30′	80°59′
Flower Pot Farm	UNP/LNO	QC	Minganie	12 P/12	51°40′	57°36′
Flowerpot Island	ISL/ÎLE	ON	Bruce	41 H/5	45°18′	81°38′
Flowers Bay	BAY/BAIE	NF		13 N/15	55°46′	60°42′
Flower's Cove	TOWN/VIL2	NF		12 P/7	51°18′	56°44′
Flowers Cove	UNP/LNO	NB	Queens	21 J/1	46°02′	66°02′
Flowers Island	ISL/ÎLE	NF		2 F/3	49°08′	53°28′
Flowers Point	CAPE/CAP	NF		2 C/11	48°36′	53°00′
Flower Station	UNP/LNO	ON	Lanark	31 F/2	45°10′	76°41′
Flowing Well	UNP/LNO	SK	18-15-7-W3	72 J/7	50°15′	106°58′
Fluke Lake	LAKE/LAC	ON	Kenora	52 K/3	50°10′	93°28′
Flume Ridge	UNP/LNO	NB	Charlotte	21 G/6	45°29′	67°04′
Fluor Island	ISL/ÎLE	ON	Thunder Bay	52 A/9	48°40′	88°05′
Fluorite	UNP/LNO	ON	Sudbury	41 I/13	46°59′	81°49′
Fly Creek	RIV/CDE	BC	Lillooet	92 P/3	51°14′	121°12′
Flying Point	CAPE/CAP	NS	Guysborough	11 F/3	45°12′	61°12′
Flying Point	CAPE/CAP	NS	Halifax	11 D/11	44°41′	63°06′
Flying Post 73	IR/RI	ON	Cochrane	42 B/9	48°32′	82°02′

NAME NOM	ENTITY ENTITÉ	LOC 1 LIEU 1	LOC 2 LIEU 2	MAP CARTE	POSITION LAT	LONG
Flyingshot Lake Settlement	UNP/LNO	AB	71-6-W6	83 M/2	55°08′	118°52′
Flying U	UNP/LNO	BC	Lillooet	92 P/6	51°28′	121°15′
Fly Lake	LAKE/LAC	MB		54 E/7	57°25′	94°36′
Flynn	UNP/LNO	QC	Pabok	22 A/9	48°30′	64°16′
Flynns Turn	UNP/LNO	ON	Peterborough	31 D/9	44°37′	78°23′
Flyway Lake	LAKE/LAC	NT	Franklin	37 D	69°27′	72°14′
Foam Lake	TOWN/VIL2	SK	32-30-11-W2	62 M/12	51°39′	103°32′
Foam Lake	LAKE/LAC	SK	31,32-12-W2	62 M/12	51°43′	103°37′
Foam Lake No. 276	MUN2/AZM2	SK		62 M/5	51°30′	103°30′
Foch Lagoon	LAKE/LAC	BC	Range 4 Coast	103 H/14	53°48′	129°05′
Foch Lake	LAKE/LAC	BC	Range 4 Coast	103 H/14	53°47′	129°12′
Foch River	RIV/CDE	ON	Algoma	42 F/6	49°25′	85°05′
Fodhla	UNP/LNO	PE	Queens	11 L/2	46°06′	62°49′
Foeda	UNP/LNO	SK	30-2-6-W2	62 E/2	49°09′	102°49′
Fog Bay	BAY/BAIE	NT	Franklin	69 D	77°55′	97°10′
Fogo	TOWN/VIL2	NF		2 E/9	49°43′	54°17′
Fogo, Cape	CAPE/CAP	NF		2 F/12	49°40′	54°00′
Fogo Island	ISL/ÎLE	NF		2 E/9	49°40′	54°10′
Fogo Island Region	MUN1/AZM1	NF		2 E/9	49°40′	54°11′
Fogo Seamounts	SEAU/SMER	—		NK22 B	41°15′	51°00′
Foins, Lac aux	LAKE/LAC	QC	Témiscamingue	31 M/1	47°05′	78°11′
Foisy	UNP/LNO	AB	4-57-11-W4	73 E/13	53°53′	111°35′
Foldens	UNP/LNO	ON	Oxford	40 P/2	43°02′	80°48′
Foley	MUN2/AZM2	ON	Parry Sound	31 E/5	45°17′	79°58′
Foley	UNP/LNO	MB	15-18-3-E	62 I/11	50°33′	97°05′
Foley Brook	UNP/LNO	NB	Victoria	21 O/4	47°02′	67°35′
Foleyet	UNP/LNO	ON	Sudbury	42 B/1	48°15′	82°26′
Foley Island	ISL/ÎLE	NT	Franklin	37 A	68°32′	75°05′
Folger	UNP/LNO	ON	Lanark	31 F/2	45°04′	76°43′
Folly Lake	UNP/LNO	NS	Colchester	11 E/12	45°33′	63°33′
Folly Lake Station	UNP/LNO	NS	Colchester	11 E/12	45°31′	63°33′
Folly Mountain	UNP/LNO	NS	Colchester	11 E/5	45°28′	63°32′
Folson Lake	LAKE/LAC	ON	Algoma	41 J/8	46°25′	82°15′
Fond-à-Patoche	UNP/LNO	QC	Bellechasse	21 L/10	46°42′	70°50′
Fond-de-la-Baie	UNP/LNO	QC	Côte-Nord-du-Golfe-Saint-Laurent	12 P/11	51°30′	57°15′
Fond-d'Ormes	UNP/LNO	QC	Rimouski-Neigette	22 C/1	48°13′	68°28′
Fond-du-Lac	UNP/LNO	SK		74 O/6	59°19′	107°12′
Fond du Lac	BAY/BAIE	SK		74 O/8	59°17′	106°12′
Fond du Lac 227	IR/RI	SK		74 O/6	59°19′	107°12′
Fond du Lac 228	IR/RI	SK		74 O/6	59°18′	107°12′
Fond du Lac 229	IR/RI	SK		74 O/5	59°26′	107°42′
Fond du Lac 231	IR/RI	SK		74 O/4	59°01′	107°54′
Fond du Lac 232	IR/RI	SK		74 O/3	59°08′	107°25′
Fond du Lac 233	IR/RI	SK		74 O/6	59°18′	107°12′
Fond du Lac River	RIV/CDE	SK		74 O/8	59°17′	106°00′
Fonderie, La	UNP/LNO	QC	Denis-Riverin	22 G/2	49°04′	66°46′
Fondeur 9	IR/RI	BC	Range 5 Coast	93 K/1	54°09′	124°25′
Fond Noir, Le	UNP/LNO	QC	La Haute-Côte-Nord	22 C/11	48°38′	69°09′
Fonds, Les	UNP/LNO	QC	Beauce-Sartigan	21 L/2	46°02′	70°59′
Fonehill	UNP/LNO	SK	31-25-5-W2	62 M/2	51°13′	102°41′
Fontaine	UNP/LNO	NB	Kent	21 I/15	46°51′	64°58′
Fontainebleau	VILG/VILG	QC	Le Haut-Saint-François	21 E/11	45°41′	71°23′
Fontainebleau	UNP/LNO	ON	Essex	40 J/7	42°18′	82°59′
Fontaine Lake	LAKE/LAC	SK		74 O/9	59°42′	106°27′
Fontaine's Landing	UNP/LNO	ON	Cochrane	42 G/13	49°49′	83°46′
Fontarabie, Lac	LAKE/LAC	QC	Sept-Rivières	22 O/1	51°10′	66°25′
Fontas	UNP/LNO	BC	Peace River	94 I/5	58°17′	121°44′
Fontas 1	IR/RI	BC	Peace River	94 I/5	58°17′	121°42′
Fontas River	RIV/CDE	BC/AB		94 I/5	58°17′	121°45′
Fontbonne, Lac	LAKE/LAC	QC	Abitibi	32 D/8	48°21′	78°26′
Fonteneau, Lac - also-aussi - Fonteneau Lake	LAKE/LAC	QC	Minganie	12 N/13	51°56′	61°31′
Fonteneau Lake - also-aussi - Fonteneau, Lac	LAKE/LAC	NF		12 N/13	51°56′	61°31′
Fontenelle	UNP/LNO	QC	La Côte-de-Gaspé	22 A/15	48°53′	64°33′
Fontenoy	UNP/LNO	QC	Le Val-Saint-François	31 H/9	45°37′	72°14′
Fonthill	UNP/LNO	ON	Welland	30 M/3	43°02′	79°17′
Foot Cape	UNP/LNO	NS	Inverness	11 K/3	46°11′	61°18′
Foothills	UNP/LNO	AB	24-47-20-W5	83 F/2	53°04′	116°47′
Foothills Creek	RIV/CDE	NT	Mackenzie	97 C/10	69°34′	125°15′
Foothills No. 31, Municipal District of	MUN1/AZM1	AB	19-1-W5	82 J/9	50°37′	114°01′
Footner Lake	UNP/LNO	AB	5,8-111-19-W5	84 K/11	58°37′	117°09′
Footprint Lake	LAKE/LAC	ON	Rainy River	52 C/13	48°54′	93°36′
Footprint Lake	LAKE/LAC	MB	78,79-9,10-W	63 O/15	55°47′	98°53′
Footprint River	RIV/CDE	MB	78-10-W	63 O/10	55°44′	98°55′
Foot's Bay	UNP/LNO	ON	Muskoka	31 E/4	45°08′	79°45′
Forbes Creek	RIV/CDE	BC	Range 1 Coast	92 K/2	50°15′	124°35′

NAME NOM	ENTITY ENTITÉ	LOC 1 LIEU 1	LOC 2 LIEU 2	MAP CARTE	POSITION LAT	LONG
Forbes, Lac	LAKE/LAC	QC	Matawinie	31 J/9	46°31′	74°12′
Forbes Lake	LAKE/LAC	MB	15-15-E	52 L/3	50°15′	95°26′
Forbes, Mount	MTN/MNT	AB	33-21-W5	82 N/15	51°52′	116°55′
Forbes Point	UNP/LNO	NS	Shelburne	20 P/12	43°33′	65°45′
Forbes Sound	CHAN/CHEN	NT	Franklin	25 A/7	60°23′	64°48′
Ford	UNP/LNO	NF		14 C/6	56°28′	61°12′
Ford Bank	UNP/LNO	NB	Kent	21 I/7	46°30′	65°00′
Ford Bay	BAY/BAIE	NT	Mackenzie	96 K	66°00′	124°37′
Forde	UNP/LNO	BC	Kootenay	82 N/6	51°27′	117°06′
Forde Lake	LAKE/LAC	NT	Keewatin	65 P	63°20′	96°20′
Ford Falls	FALL/CHUT	NT	Mackenzie	75 P	63°43′	104°42′
Fording	UNP/LNO	BC	Kootenay	82 J/2	50°11′	114°52′
Fording River	RIV/CDE	BC	Kootenay	82 G/15	49°53′	114°53′
Ford Lake	LAKE/LAC	NT	Keewatin	56 G	65°54′	90°33′
Ford Lake	LAKE/LAC	NT	Mackenzie	75 O	63°08′	107°24′
Ford River	RIV/CDE	NT	Keewatin	46 B	64°11′	82°59′
Ford, Rivière	RIV/CDE	QC	Kativik	24 I/4	58°10′	65°47′
Fords Mills	UNP/LNO	NB	Kent	21 I/6	46°29′	65°06′
Fordview	UNP/LNO	NS	Inverness	11 K/6	46°22′	61°05′
Fordwich	UNP/LNO	ON	Huron	40 P/14	43°52′	81°02′
Fordyce	UNP/LNO	ON	Huron	40 P/14	43°52′	81°27′
Fordyce Corners	UNP/LNO	QC	Brome-Missisquoi	31 H/2	45°13′	72°48′
Foreman	UNP/LNO	BC	Cariboo	93 G/15	53°57′	122°41′
Foreman Island	ISL/ÎLE	NT	Franklin	35 J	62°36′	74°01′
Foremost	VILG/VILG	AB	17-6-11-W4	72 E/6	49°29′	111°25′
Forest	TOWN/VIL2	ON	Lambton	40 P/4	43°06′	82°00′
Forest	UNP/LNO	ON	Frontenac	31 C/7	44°22′	76°37′
Forest Bank	UNP/LNO	SK	49-24-W3	73 F/3	53°13′	109°26′
Forestburg	VILG/VILG	AB	2-42-15-W4	83 A/9	52°35′	112°04′
Forest City	UNP/LNO	NB	York	21 G/12	45°40′	67°44′
Forest Corner	UNP/LNO	NB	Northumberland	21 P/3	47°03′	65°25′
Forestdale	UNP/LNO	BC	Range 5 Coast	93 L/8	54°25′	126°12′
Foresters Falls	UNP/LNO	ON	Renfrew	31 F/10	45°41′	76°47′
Forest Estates	UNP/LNO	ON	Oxford	40 P/2	43°11′	80°39′
Forest Farm	UNP/LNO	SK	17-17-1-W2	62 L/8	50°26′	102°07′
Forest Field	UNP/LNO	NF		1 N/3	47°09′	53°27′
Forest Field-New Bridge	UNP/LNO	NF		1 N/3	47°09′	53°27′
Forest Gate	UNP/LNO	SK	21-53-25-W2	73 H/12	53°36′	105°37′
Forest Glade	UNP/LNO	NS	Annapolis	21 H/3	45°01′	65°02′
Forest Glade	UNP/LNO	ON	Essex	40 J/7	42°18′	82°55′
Forest Glen	UNP/LNO	NS	Inverness	11 K/7	46°28′	60°55′
Forest Glen	UNP/LNO	NS	Colchester	11 E/3	45°12′	63°14′
Forest Glen	UNP/LNO	NS	Yarmouth	21 A/4	44°05′	65°55′
Forest Grove	UNP/LNO	SK		73 B/2	52°09′	106°35′
Forest Grove	UNP/LNO	BC	Lillooet	92 P/14	51°46′	121°06′
Forest Harbour	UNP/LNO	ON	Simcoe	31 D/13	44°47′	79°43′
Forest Heights	UNP/LNO	ON	Waterloo	40 P/7	43°25′	80°31′
Forest Hill	UNP/LNO	PE	Kings	11 L/7	46°22′	62°34′
Forest Hill	UNP/LNO	NS	Guysborough	11 F/5	45°18′	61°46′
Forest Hill	UNP/LNO	NS	Kings	21 H/1	45°03′	64°21′
Forest Hill	UNP/LNO	NB	Albert	21 H/14	45°52′	65°02′
Forest Hill	UNP/LNO	ON	York	30 M/11	43°42′	79°25′
Forest Hills	UNP/LNO	NS	Halifax	11 D/11	44°40′	63°28′
Forest Hills	UNP/LNO	NB	Saint John	21 G/8	45°19′	66°01′
Forest Hills	UNP/LNO	ON	Waterloo	40 P/7	43°26′	80°31′
Forest Hills	UNP/LNO	BC	New Westminster	92 G/6	49°21′	123°05′
Forest Home	UNP/LNO	NS	Kings	21 A/15	44°56′	64°31′
Forest Home	UNP/LNO	ON	Simcoe	31 D/11	44°34′	79°27′
Forest Knolls	UNP/LNO	BC	New Westminster	92 G/2	49°09′	122°35′
Forest Lawn	UNP/LNO	AB	24-29-W4	82 P/4	51°02′	113°58′
Forest Lea	UNP/LNO	ON	Renfrew	31 F/14	45°49′	77°13′
Forest Mills	UNP/LNO	ON	Lennox and Addington	31 C/6	44°20′	77°03′
Foreston	UNP/LNO	NB	Carleton	21 J/11	46°32′	67°18′
Forest Park	UNP/LNO	ON	Russell	31 G/6	45°18′	75°13′
Forestview	UNP/LNO	PE	Prince	21 I/9	46°43′	64°17′
Forestview	UNP/LNO	YT		105 D/14	60°49′	135°12′
Forestville	CITY/VIL1	QC	La Haute-Côte-Nord	22 C/11	48°44′	69°05′
Forestville	UNP/LNO	ON	Norfolk	40 I/9	42°42′	80°23′
Forfar	UNP/LNO	ON	Leeds	31 C/9	44°40′	76°13′
Forgan	UNP/LNO	SK	31-26-13-W3	72 O/5	51°16′	107°48′
Forgan Lake	LAKE/LAC	ON	Thunder Bay	52 H/8	49°22′	88°18′
Forges-du-Saint-Maurice, Lieu historique national des - also-aussi - Forges du Saint-Maurice National Historic Site	PARK/PARC	QC	Francheville	31 I/7	46°24′	72°40′
Forges du Saint-Maurice National Historic Site - also-aussi - Forges-du-Saint-Maurice, Lieu historique national des	PARK/PARC	QC	Francheville	31 I/7	46°24′	72°40′
Forget	VILG/VILG	SK	15-8-7-W2	62 E/10	49°39′	102°52′
Forget	UNP/LNO	ON	Russell	31 G/3	45°14′	75°16′

NAME NOM	ENTITY ENTITÉ	LOC 1 LIEU 1	LOC 2 LIEU 2	MAP CARTE	POSITION	
					LAT	LONG
Forgotten Lake	LAKE/LAC	ON	Kenora	52 L/1	50°04′	94°21′
Forillon National Park - also-aussi - Forillon, Parc national	PARK/PARC	QC	La Côte-de-Gaspé	22 A/16	48°54′	64°21′
Forillon, Parc national - also-aussi - Forillon National Park	PARK/PARC	QC	La Côte-de-Gaspé	22 A/16	48°54′	64°21′
Forillon, Péninsule de	CAPE/CAP	QC	La Côte-de-Gaspé	22 A/16	48°53′	64°20′
Forked Pond	LAKE/LAC	NF		2 E/1	49°09′	54°02′
Fork Lake	UNP/LNO	AB	19-63-11-W4	73 L/5	54°27′	111°37′
Fork Lake	LAKE/LAC	AB	63-11-W4	73 L/5	54°28′	111°35′
Fork River	UNP/LNO	MB	26-29-19-W	62 N/9	51°31′	100°01′
Forks	UNP/LNO	ON	Sudbury	41 P/4	47°03′	81°52′
Forks Baddeck	UNP/LNO	NS	Victoria	11 K/2	46°11′	60°46′
Forks of the Credit	UNP/LNO	ON	Peel	30 M/13	43°48′	80°00′
Forks Road	UNP/LNO	ON	Welland	30 L/14	42°57′	79°28′
Forks Stream	UNP/LNO	NB	Queens	21 I/4	46°07′	65°34′
Forks Stream	RIV/CDE	NB	Queens	21 I/4	46°03′	65°33′
Formosa	UNP/LNO	ON	Bruce	41 A/3	44°04′	81°13′
Formosa Creek	RIV/CDE	ON	Bruce	41 A/3	44°04′	81°20′
Forrest	UNP/LNO	MB	36-11-19W	62 G/13	49°58′	99°56′
Forresters Point	UNP/LNO	NF		12 P/2	51°11′	56°48′
Forrest, Lac	LAKE/LAC	QC	La Haute-Côte-Nord	22 F/3	49°02′	69°20′
Forrest Lake	LAKE/LAC	SK		74 F/11	57°35′	109°15′
Forrest Station - see-voir - Forrest	UNP/LNO	MB		62 G/13	49°58′	99°56′
Forshee	UNP/LNO	AB	25-41-2-W5	83 B/9	52°33′	114°09′
Forslund	UNP/LNO	SK	12-34-28-W2	72 P/13	51°55′	105°51′
*Forslund	UNP/LNO	BC	Kootenay	82 E/16	49°50′	118°07′
Forster Seamount	SEAU/SMER	—		3000	48°57′	133°50′
Forsyth Bay	BAY/BAIE	NT	Franklin	87 D/2	69°12′	113°37′
Forsythe	UNP/LNO	QC	Vallée-de-l'Or	32 C/1	48°14′	76°26′
Forsyth Lake	LAKE/LAC	SK		74 I/10	58°37′	104°42′
Forsyth Lake	LAKE/LAC	SK		74 O/11	59°36′	107°12′
Fort Albany	UNP/LNO	ON	Cochrane	43 A/4	52°12′	81°40′
Fort Albany 67	IR/RI	ON	Kenora	43 A/5	52°20′	81°45′
Fort Alexander	UNP/LNO	MB		62 I/9	50°37′	96°18′
Fort Alexander 3	IR/RI	MB		62 I/9	50°36′	96°18′
Fort Amherst — Port-la-Joye, Lieu historique national du - also-aussi - Fort Amherst—Port-la-Joye National Historic Site	PARK/PARC	PE	Queens	11 L/3	46°12′	63°08′
Fort Amherst—Port-la-Joye National Historic Site - also-aussi - Fort Amherst — Port-la-Joye, Lieu historique national du	PARK/PARC	PE	Queens	11 L/3	46°12′	63°08′
Fort-Anne, Lieu historique national du - also-aussi - Fort Anne National Historic Site	PARK/PARC	NS	Annapolis	21 A/12	44°45′	65°31′
Fort Anne National Historic Site - also-aussi - Fort-Anne, Lieu historique national du	PARK/PARC	NS	Annapolis	21 A/12	44°45′	65°31′
Fort Assiniboine	UNP/LNO	AB	1-62-6-W5	83 J/7	54°20′	114°46′
Fort Augustus	UNP/LNO	PE	Queens	11 L/7	46°19′	62°56′
Fort Babine	UNP/LNO	BC	Cassiar	93 M/7	55°19′	126°37′
Fort-Battleford, Lieu historique national du - also-aussi - Fort Battleford National Historic Site	PARK/PARC	SK		73 C/9	52°44′	108°18′
Fort Battleford National Historic Site - also-aussi - Fort-Battleford, Lieu historique national du	PARK/PARC	SK		73 C/9	52°44′	108°18′
Fort-Beauséjour, Lieu historique national du - also-aussi - Fort Beauséjour National Historic Site	PARK/PARC	NB		21 H/16	45°52′	64°17′
Fort Beauséjour National Historic Site - also-aussi - Fort-Beauséjour, Lieu historique national du	PARK/PARC	NB	Westmorland	21 H/16	45°52′	64°17′
Fort Belcher	UNP/LNO	NS	Colchester	11 E/6	45°22′	63°25′
Fort Black	UNP/LNO	SK	74-12-W3	73 O/5	55°25′	107°48′
Fort-Chambly, Lieu historique national du - also-aussi - Fort Chambly National Historic Site	PARK/PARC	QC	La Vallée-du-Richelieu	31 H/6	45°27′	73°17′
Fort Chambly National Historic Site - also-aussi - Fort-Chambly, Lieu historique national du	PARK/PARC	QC	La Vallée-du-Richelieu	31 H/6	45°27′	73°17′
Fort Chipewyan	UNP/LNO	AB	8-112-7-W4	74 L/11	58°42′	111°08′
Fort Churchill	UNP/LNO	MB		54 L/16	58°45′	94°05′
Fort Collinson	UNP/LNO	NT	Franklin	87 G	71°37′	117°52′
Fort Conger	UNP/LNO	NT	Franklin	120 C	81°45′	64°45′
Fort-Coulonge	TOWN/VIL2	QC	Pontiac	31 F/15	45°51′	76°44′
Fort Creek	UNP/LNO	ON	Algoma	41 K/9	46°32′	84°20′
Forteau	VILG/VILG	NF		12 P/7	51°28′	56°58′
Forteau Bay	BAY/BAIE	NF		12 P/7	51°28′	56°56′
Fort-Edward, Lieu historique national du - also-aussi - Fort Edward National Historic Site	PARK/PARC	NS	Hants	21 A/16	45°00′	64°08′
Fort Edward National Historic Site - also-aussi - Fort-Edward, Lieu historique national du	PARK/PARC	NS	Hants	21 A/16	45°00′	64°08′
Fort Ellis	UNP/LNO	NS	Colchester	11 E/3	45°09′	63°23′
Fort Enterprise	UNP/LNO	NT	Mackenzie	86 A	64°28′	113°09′

NAME NOM	ENTITY ENTITÉ	LOC 1 LIEU 1	LOC 2 LIEU 2	MAP CARTE	POSITION LAT	LONG
Forteresse-de-Louisbourg, Lieu historique national de la - also-aussi - Fortress of Louisbourg National Historic Site	PARK/PARC	NS	Cape Breton	11 F/16	45°55′	60°30′
Fort Erie	TOWN/VIL2	ON	Welland	30 L/15	42°54′	78°56′
Fort Erie Beach	UNP/LNO	ON	Welland	30 L/15	42°54′	78°55′
Fort Erie North	UNP/LNO	ON	Welland	30 L/15	42°56′	78°56′
Fort Erie West	UNP/LNO	ON	Welland	30 L/15	42°54′	78°56′
Fortescue	UNP/LNO	ON	Haliburton	31 D/16	44°50′	78°28′
Fort-Espérance, Lieu historique national du - also-aussi - Fort Espérance National Historic Site	PARK/PARC	SK		62 K/5	50°30′	101°35′
Fort Espérance National Historic Site - also-aussi - Fort-Espérance, Lieu historique national du	PARK/PARC	SK		62 K/5	50°30′	101°35′
Fort Folly 1	IR/RI	NB	Albert	21 H/15	45°53′	64°35′
Fort Folly Point	CAPE/CAP	NB	Westmorland	21 H/15	45°52′	64°34′
Fort Frances	TOWN/VIL2	ON	Rainy River	52 C/11	48°36′	93°24′
Fort Franklin - see-voir - Déline	HAM/HAM	NT		96 G/3	65°11′	123°25′
Fort Fraser	UNP/LNO	BC	Range 5 Coast	93 K/2	54°04′	124°33′
Fort Garry	UNP/LNO	MB		62 I/2	50°07′	96°56′
Fort Garry	UNP/LNO	MB		62 H/14	49°50′	97°09′
Fort-Gaspareaux, Lieu historique national du - also-aussi - Fort Gaspareaux National Historic Site	PARK/PARC	NB	Westmorland	21 I/1	46°02′	64°04′
Fort Gaspareaux National Historic Site - also-aussi - Fort-Gaspareaux, Lieu historique national du	PARK/PARC	NB	Westmorland	21 I/1	46°02′	64°04′
Fort George	UNP/LNO	QC	Jamésie	33 E/14	53°50′	79°00′
Fort George Cemetery 1A	IR/RI	BC	Cariboo	93 G/15	53°55′	122°45′
Fort-George, Lieu historique national du - also-aussi - Fort George National Historic Site	PARK/PARC	ON	Lincoln	30 M/3	43°15′	79°03′
Fort George National Historic Site - also-aussi - Fort-George, Lieu historique national du	PARK/PARC	ON	Lincoln	30 M/6	43°15′	79°03′
Fort George (Shelley) 2	IR/RI	BC	Cariboo	93 J/2	54°01′	122°38′
Fort Good Hope	HAM/HAM	NT	Mackenzie	106 I/7	66°15′	128°38′
Forth	UNP/LNO	AB	8-38-27-W4	83 A/4	52°15′	113°49′
Fort Hall	UNP/LNO	MB		64 N/6	59°24′	101°19′
Fort Henry Heights	UNP/LNO	ON	Frontenac	31 C/1	44°14′	76°27′
Fort Hope	UNP/LNO	ON	Kenora	42 M/12	51°33′	87°58′
Fort Hope	UNP/LNO	NT	Franklin	46 L/10	66°32′	86°42′
Fort Hope 64	IR/RI	ON	Kenora	42 M/12	51°37′	87°55′
Forthton	UNP/LNO	ON	Leeds	31 B/12	44°38′	75°52′
Fortier	UNP/LNO	MB	22,23-11-4-W	62 H/13	49°56′	97°55′
Fortier, Rivière	RIV/CDE	QC	Antoine-Labelle	31 O/12	47°45′	75°32′
Fortierville	TOWN/VIL2	QC	Bécancour	31 I/8	46°29′	72°02′
Forties	UNP/LNO	NS	Lunenburg	21 A/10	44°44′	64°33′
Fortifications-de-Québec, Lieu historique national des - also-aussi - Fortifications of Québec National Historic Site	PARK/PARC	QC	Communauté urbaine de Québec	21 L/14	46°49′	71°13′
Fortifications of Québec National Historic Site - also-aussi - Fortifications-de-Québec, Lieu historique national des	PARK/PARC	QC	Communauté urbaine de Québec	21 L/14	46°49′	71°13′
Fortin, Lac	LAKE/LAC	QC	Sept-Rivières	22 J/13	50°50′	67°46′
Fortin, Lac	LAKE/LAC	QC	Robert-Cliche	21 L/2	46°07′	70°51′
Fortin Lake	LAKE/LAC	YT		105 G/15	61°59′	130°34′
Fort Irwin	UNP/LNO	ON	Haliburton	31 E/1	45°11′	78°25′
Fort Kent	UNP/LNO	AB	25-61-5-W4	73 L/7	54°19′	110°37′
Fort-Kitwanga, Lieu historique national du - also-aussi - Kitwanga Fort National Historic Site	PARK/PARC	BC	Cassiar	103 P/1	55°07′	128°01′
Fort La Cloche	UNP/LNO	ON	Algoma	41 J/1	46°07′	82°05′
Fort Langley	UNP/LNO	BC	New Westminster	92 G/2	49°10′	122°35′
Fort-Langley, Lieu historique national du - also-aussi - Fort Langley National Historic Site	PARK/PARC	BC	New Westminster	92 G/2	49°10′	122°35′
Fort Langley National Historic Site - also-aussi - Fort-Langley, Lieu historique national du	PARK/PARC	BC	New Westminster	92 G/2	49°10′	122°35′
Fort la Reine	UNP/LNO	MB	26-11-7-W	62 G/16	49°57′	98°20′
Fort Lawrence	UNP/LNO	NS	Cumberland	21 H/16	45°51′	64°15′
Fort-Lennox, Lieu historique national du - also-aussi - Fort Lennox National Historic Site	PARK/PARC	QC	Le Haut-Richelieu	31 H/3	45°07′	73°16′
Fort Lennox National Historic Site - also-aussi - Fort-Lennox, Lieu historique national du	PARK/PARC	QC	Le Haut-Richelieu	31 H/3	45°07′	73°16′
Fort Liard	HAM/HAM	NT	Mackenzie	95 B/3	60°14′	123°28′
Fort-Livingstone, Lieu historique national du - also-aussi - Fort Livingstone National Historic Site	PARK/PARC	SK		62 N/13	51°54′	101°58′
Fort Livingstone National Historic Site - also-aussi - Fort-Livingstone, Lieu historique national du	PARK/PARC	SK		62 N/13	51°54′	101°58′
Fort MacKay	UNP/LNO	AB	25-94-11-W4	74 E/4	57°11′	111°37′
Fort Mackenzie	UNP/LNO	QC	Kativik	24 C/15	56°50′	68°57′
Fort Macleod	TOWN/VIL2	AB	12-9-26-W4	82 H/11	49°43′	113°25′
Fort-Malden, Lieu historique national du - also-aussi - Fort Malden National Historic Site	PARK/PARC	ON	Essex	40 J/3	42°07′	83°07′

NAME NOM	ENTITY ENTITÉ	LOC 1 LIEU 1	LOC 2 LIEU 2	MAP CARTE	POSITION LAT	LONG
Fort Malden National Historic Site - also-aussi - Fort-Malden, Lieu historique national du	PARK/PARC	ON	Essex	40 J/3	42°07'	83°07'
Fort McKay 174	IR/RI	AB	94-11-W4	74 E/4	57°09'	111°38'
Fort McMurray	UNP/LNO	AB	89-9-W4	74 D/11	56°44'	111°23'
Fort McMurray Oil Sands Interpretive Centre Provincial Historic Site (Developed)	PARK/PARC	AB	27,34-88-9-W4	74 D/11	56°44'	111°23'
Fort-McNab, Lieu historique national du - also-aussi - Fort McNab National Historic Site	PARK/PARC	NS	Halifax	11 D/12	44°36'	63°31'
Fort McNab National Historic Site - also-aussi - Fort-McNab, Lieu historique national du	PARK/PARC	NS	Halifax	11 D/12	44°36'	63°31'
Fort McPherson	HAM/HAM	NT	Mackenzie	106 M/7	67°26'	134°53'
Fort-Mississauga, Lieu historique national du - also-aussi - Fort Mississauga National Historic Site	PARK/PARC	ON	Lincoln	30 M/6	43°16'	79°05'
Fort Mississauga National Historic Site - also-aussi - Fort-Mississauga, Lieu historique national du	PARK/PARC	ON	Lincoln	30 M/6	43°16'	79°05'
Fort Nelson	TOWN/VIL2	BC	Peace River	94 J/15	58°48'	122°43'
Fort Nelson 2	IR/RI	BC	Peace River	94 J/15	58°45'	122°35'
Fort Nelson-Liard	MUN1/AZM1	BC	Peace River	94 O/4	59°00'	123°45'
Fort Nelson River	RIV/CDE	BC	Peace River	94 N/9	59°32'	124°00'
Fort No. 1 at Pointe de Lévy National Historic Site - also-aussi - Fort-Numéro-Un-de-la-Pointe-de-Lévy, Lieu historique national du	PARK/PARC	QC	Desjardins	21 L/14	46°10'	71°49'
Fort Norman - see-voir - Tulita	HAM/HAM	NT		96 C/13	64°54'	125°35'
Fort-Numéro-Un-de-la-Pointe-de-Lévy, Lieu historique national du - also-aussi - Fort No. 1 at Pointe de Lévy National Historic Site	PARK/PARC	QC	Desjardins	21 L/14	46°10'	71°49'
Fort Pelly	UNP/LNO	SK	30-32-32-W	62 N/13	51°46'	102°00'
Fort-Pelly, Lieu historique national du - also-aussi - Fort Pelly National Historic Site	PARK/PARC	SK		62 N/13	51°47'	102°00'
Fort Pelly National Historic Site - also-aussi - Fort-Pelly, Lieu historique national du	PARK/PARC	SK		62 N/13	51°47'	102°00'
Fort Pitt	UNP/LNO	SK	11-54-26-W3	73 F/12	53°39'	109°45'
Fort-Prince-de-Galles, Lieu historique national du - also-aussi - Prince of Wales Fort National Historic Site	PARK/PARC	MB		54 L/16	58°48'	94°13'
Fort Providence	HAM/HAM	NT	Mackenzie	85 F/5	61°21'	117°39'
Fort Qu'Appelle	TOWN/VIL2	SK	7-21-13-W2	62 L/13	50°46'	103°48'
Fort Reliance	UNP/LNO	YT		116 B/3	64°09'	139°29'
Fort Resolution	UNP/LNO	NT	Mackenzie	85 H/4	61°10'	113°40'
Fortress	UNP/LNO	MB	35-9-2-E	62 H/14	49°47'	97°14'
Fortress Lake	LAKE/LAC	BC	Kootenay	83 C/5	52°22'	117°48'
Fortress of Louisbourg National Historic Site - also-aussi - Forteresse-de-Louisbourg, Lieu historique national de la	PARK/PARC	NS	Cape Breton	11 F/16	45°55'	60°30'
Fort Richmond	UNP/LNO	MB		62 H/14	49°48'	97°09'
Fort Rodd Hill, Lieu historique national - also-aussi - Fort Rodd Hill National Historic Site	PARK/PARC	BC		92 B/6	48°26'	123°27'
Fort Rodd Hill National Historic Site - also-aussi - Fort Rodd Hill, Lieu historique national	PARK/PARC	BC		92 B/6	48°26'	123°27'
Fort Ross	UNP/LNO	NT	Franklin	58 B	72°00'	94°14'
Fort Rouge	UNP/LNO	MB		62 H/14	49°52'	97°09'
Fort-Rupert	VILG/VILG	QC	Jamésie	32 M/2	51°12'	78°46'
Fort Rupert	UNP/LNO	BC	Rupert	92 L/11	50°42'	127°25'
Fort Rupert 1	IR/RI	BC	Rupert	92 L/11	50°42'	127°24'
Fort St. James	MUN1/AZM1	BC	Range 5 Coast	93 K/8	54°27'	124°15'
Fort-St. James, Lieu historique national du - also-aussi - Fort St. James National Historic Site	PARK/PARC	BC	Range 5 Coast	93 K/8	54°26'	124°15'
Fort St. James National Historic Site - also-aussi - Fort-St. James, Lieu historique national du	PARK/PARC	BC	Range 5 Coast	93 K/8	54°26'	124°15'
Fort St. John	CITY/VIL1	BC	Peace River	94 A/2	56°15'	120°51'
Fort-St. Joseph, Lieu historique national du - also-aussi - Fort St. Joseph National Historic Site	PARK/PARC	ON	Algoma	41 J/4	46°04'	83°57'
Fort St. Joseph National Historic Site - also-aussi - Fort-St. Joseph, Lieu historique national du	PARK/PARC	ON	Algoma	41 J/4	46°04'	83°57'
Fort San	VILG/VILG	SK	18,24,26-21-13,14-W2	62 L/13	50°48'	103°49'
Fort Saskatchewan	CITY/VIL1	AB	32-54-22-W4	83 H/11	53°43'	113°13'
Fort Selkirk	UNP/LNO	YT		115 I/14	62°47'	137°23'
Fort Severn	UNP/LNO	ON	Kenora	43 M/13	55°59'	87°38'
Fort Severn 89	IR/RI	ON	Kenora	43 M/13	55°59'	87°38'
Fort Simpson	VILG/VILG	NT	Mackenzie	95 H	61°52'	121°21'
Fort Smith	TOWN/VIL2	NT	Mackenzie	75 D/4	60°00'	111°53'
Fort Smith Settlement	UNP/LNO	AB	126-11-W4	74 M/13	60°00'	111°51'
Fort Steele	UNP/LNO	BC	Kootenay	82 G/12	49°37'	115°38'

NAME NOM	ENTITY ENTITÉ	LOC 1 LIEU 1	LOC 2 LIEU 2	MAP CARTE	POSITION LAT	LONG
Fort Stewart	UNP/LNO	ON	Hastings	31 F/4	45°10′	77°37′
Fort-Témiscamingue, Lieu historique national du - also-aussi - Fort Témiscamingue National Historic Site	PARK/PARC	QC	Témiscamingue	31 M/6	47°18′	79°27′
Fort Témiscamingue National Historic Site - also-aussi - Fort-Témiscamingue, Lieu historique national du	PARK/PARC	QC	Témiscamingue	31 M/6	47°18′	79°27′
Fort Townshend	UNP/LNO	NF		1 N/10	47°34′	52°44′
Fortune	TOWN/VIL2	NF		1 M/4	47°04′	55°50′
Fortune	UNP/LNO	SK	30-14-W3	72 O/12	51°33′	107°53′
Fortune Bay	BAY/BAIE	NF		1 M/5	47°15′	55°30′
Fortune Bridge	UNP/LNO	PE	Kings	11 L/8	46°21′	62°23′
Fortune, Cape	CAPE/CAP	NT	Franklin	69 B	76°30′	103°14′
Fortune Channel	CHAN/CHEN	BC	Clayoquot	92 F/4	49°11′	125°46′
Fortune Cove	UNP/LNO	PE	Prince	21 I/16	46°45′	64°08′
Fortune Harbour	UNP/LNO	NF		2 E/11	49°31′	55°15′
Fortune Harbour	UNP/LNO	PE	Kings	11 L/8	46°20′	62°21′
Fortune Head	CAPE/CAP	NF		1 M/4	47°05′	55°51′
Fortune Lake	LAKE/LAC	ON	Frontenac	31 F/3	45°06′	77°02′
Fort Vermilion	UNP/LNO	AB	24-108-13-W5	84 K/8	58°24′	116°00′
Fort Vermilion (Paint Creek House) Provincial Historic Site (Undeveloped)	PARK/PARC	AB	14-54-3-W4	73 E/9	53°40′	110°20′
Fort Vermilion Settlement	UNP/LNO	AB	108-12,13-W5	84 J/5	58°23′	116°00′
Fort Walsh	UNP/LNO	SK	21-7-29-W3	72 F/12	49°34′	109°53′
Fort-Walsh, Lieu historique national du - also-aussi - Fort Walsh National Historic Site	PARK/PARC	SK		72 F/12	49°34′	109°53′
Fort Walsh National Historic Site - also-aussi - Fort-Walsh, Lieu historique national du	PARK/PARC	SK		72 F/12	49°34′	109°53′
Fort Ware 1	IR/RI	BC	Cassiar	94 F/5	57°26′	125°38′
Fort-Wellington, Lieu historique national du - also-aussi - Fort Wellington National Historic Site	PARK/PARC	ON	Leeds	31 B/12	44°43′	75°31′
Fort Wellington National Historic Site - also-aussi - Fort-Wellington, Lieu historique national du	PARK/PARC	ON	Leeds	31 B/12	44°43′	75°31′
Fort White Earth (Lower Terre Blanche House) Provincial Historic Site (Undeveloped)	PARK/PARC	AB	35-58-16-W4	83 I/1	54°03′	112°17′
Fort Whyte	UNP/LNO	MB		62 H/14	49°49′	97°12′
Fort William	UNP/LNO	NF		1 N/10	47°34′	52°43′
Fort William	UNP/LNO	QC	Pontiac	31 F/14	45°57′	77°16′
Fort William 52	IR/RI	ON	Thunder Bay	52 A/6	48°20′	89°20′
48 Road	UNP/LNO	PE	Kings	11 L/7	46°15′	62°43′
Forty Mile	UNP/LNO	YT		115 P/10	63°41′	136°42′
Forty Mile	UNP/LNO	YT		116 C/7	64°25′	140°32′
Forty Mile Brook	RIV/CDE	NB	Northumberland	21 O/8	47°24′	66°07′
Forty Mile Creek	RIV/CDE	ON	Lincoln	30 M/4	43°12′	79°33′
40 Mile Flats	UNP/LNO	BC	Cassiar	104 G/16	57°56′	130°02′
Forty Mile No. 8, County of	MUN1/AZM1	AB	8-8-W4	72 E/11	49°31′	111°10′
Forward	UNP/LNO	ON	Dundas	31 G/3	45°06′	75°15′
Forward	UNP/LNO	SK	12-8-19-W2	72 H/9	49°38′	104°28′
Forward Harbour	BAY/BAIE	BC	Range 1 Coast	92 K/5	50°29′	125°44′
Forward Inlet	BAY/BAIE	BC	Rupert	102 I/8	50°30′	128°02′
Fosheim Peninsula	CAPE/CAP	NT	Franklin	49 H/12	79°40′	83°45′
Foss	UNP/LNO	BC	Peace River	93 P/14	55°46′	121°10′
Fossambault-sur-le-Lac	CITY/VIL1	QC	La Jacques-Cartier	21 L/13	46°52′	71°37′
Fosse-à-Raiche, La	UNP/LNO	QC	La Mitis	22 C/8	48°19′	68°10′
Foss Fiord	BAY/BAIE	NT	Franklin	47 F	70°22′	87°00′
Fossmill	UNP/LNO	ON	Nipissing	31 L/3	46°05′	79°07′
Fosston	VILG/VILG	SK	21-37-13-W2	63 D/4	52°12′	103°49′
Foster	UNP/LNO	QC	Brome-Missisquoi	31 H/8	45°17′	72°30′
Foster	UNP/LNO	BC	Cariboo	83 E/3	53°01′	119°08′
Foster Bay	BAY/BAIE	NT	Franklin	47 A	68°57′	81°30′
Foster Island	ISL/ÎLE	BC	Range 1 Coast	92 L/10	50°42′	126°50′
Foster Lake	LAKE/LAC	NT	Mackenzie	75 H	61°54′	104°19′
Foster, Mont	MTN/MNT	QC	Memphrémagog	31 H/1	45°14′	72°24′
Foster River	RIV/CDE	SK		73 P/13	55°47′	105°49′
Fosterton	UNP/LNO	SK	34-17-18-W3	72 K/8	50°29′	108°23′
Fosterville	UNP/LNO	NB	York	21 G/13	45°48′	67°46′
Fosthall	UNP/LNO	BC	Kootenay	82 K/5	50°21′	117°56′
Fosthall Creek	RIV/CDE	BC	Kootenay	82 K/5	50°22′	117°56′
Fougère Rouge, Pointe de la	CAPE/CAP	QC	Jamésie	32 M/11	51°38′	79°22′
Foul Inlet	BAY/BAIE	NT	Franklin	25 N/10	63°44′	68°54′
Founds Mills	UNP/LNO	PE	Queens	11 L/6	46°26′	63°30′
Fountain	UNP/LNO	BC	Lillooet	92 I/13	50°45′	121°53′
Fountain 1	IR/RI	BC	Lillooet	92 I/12	50°44′	121°51′
Fountain 1A	IR/RI	BC	Lillooet	92 I/12	50°44′	121°50′
Fountain 1B	IR/RI	BC	Lillooet	92 I/12	50°45′	121°53′
Fountain 1C	IR/RI	BC	Lillooet	92 I/12	50°45′	121°53′
Fountain 1D	IR/RI	BC	Lillooet	92 I/12	50°45′	121°52′
Fountain 2	IR/RI	BC	Lillooet	92 I/13	50°46′	121°54′
Fountain 3A	IR/RI	BC	Lillooet	92 I/13	50°46′	121°50′

NAME NOM	ENTITY ENTITÉ	LOC 1 LIEU 1	LOC 2 LIEU 2	MAP CARTE	POSITION LAT	LONG
Fountain 3	IR/RI	BC	Lillooet	92 I/13	50°47′	121°51′
Fountain 4	IR/RI	BC	Lillooet	92 I/12	50°42′	121°48′
Fountain 9	IR/RI	BC	Lillooet	92 I/12	50°44′	121°52′
Fountain 10	IR/RI	BC	Lillooet	92 I/13	50°46′	121°55′
Fountain 11	IR/RI	BC	Lillooet	92 I/12	50°43′	121°55′
Fountain 12	IR/RI	BC	Lillooet	92 I/12	50°41′	121°49′
Fountain Beach	UNP/LNO	ON	Ontario	31 D/11	44°36′	79°20′
Fountain Creek 8	IR/RI	BC	Lillooet	92 I/12	50°42′	121°50′
Fountain Road	UNP/LNO	NS	Cumberland	11 E/13	45°48′	63°35′
Fountain Valley	UNP/LNO	BC	Lillooet	92 I/12	50°44′	121°52′
Fouquet, Lac	LAKE/LAC	QC	Sept-Rivières	22 O/10	51°30′	66°53′
4 1/2 Mile 2	IR/RI	BC	Yale Division Yale	92 H/11	49°36′	121°25′
Fourche-à-Cellard, La	UNP/LNO	QC	Avignon	22 B/2	48°10′	66°33′
Fourche-à-Clark	UNP/LNO	NB	Madawaska	21 O/5	47°21′	67°55′
Fourche-à-Hélène, La	UNP/LNO	QC	Témiscouata	21 N/10	47°32′	68°47′
Fourche-du-Bout-d'en-Bas, La	UNP/LNO	QC	Rimouski-Neigette	22 C/7	48°29′	68°33′
Fourché Harbour	BAY/BAIE	NF		12 I/9	50°31′	56°18′
Fourche, La	UNP/LNO	QC	Lotbinière	21 L/6	46°28′	71°25′
Fourche, La	UNP/LNO	QC	Maria-Chapdelaine	32 I/8	50°15′	72°09′
Fourche, La	UNP/LNO	QC	Vaudreuil-Soulanges	31 G/8	45°28′	74°24′
Fourche, Lieu historique national de la - also-aussi - The Forks National Historic Site	PARK/PARC	MB		62 H/14	49°53′	97°08′
Fourche, Rivière de la	RIV/CDE	QC	Bellechasse	21 L/10	46°44′	70°33′
Fourches, Lac des	LAKE/LAC	QC	Témiscamingue	31 M/9	47°33′	78°29′
Fourches, Les	UNP/LNO	QC	Lotbinière	21 L/5	46°25′	71°46′
Fourches, Les	UNP/LNO	QC	Matawinie	31 J/8	46°18′	74°16′
Fourches, Les	UNP/LNO	QC	Antoine-Labelle	31 O/3	47°04′	75°07′
Fourchette, Ruisseau	RIV/CDE	QC	Desjardins	21 L/11	46°41′	71°07′
Fourchu	UNP/LNO	NS	Richmond	11 F/9	45°43′	60°15′
Fourchu Bay	BAY/BAIE	NS	Cape Breton	11 F/16	45°46′	60°10′
Fourchu Head	CAPE/CAP	NS	Richmond	11 F/9	45°43′	60°14′
Four Corners	UNP/LNO	NB	Charlotte	21 G/3	45°11′	67°19′
Four Corners	UNP/LNO	SK	60-18-W3	73 K/2	54°11′	108°38′
Four Falls	UNP/LNO	NB	Victoria	21 J/13	46°50′	67°44′
Four Harbour	UNP/LNO	NF		2 M/4	51°11′	55°44′
Four Mile Brook	UNP/LNO	NS	Pictou	11 E/10	45°36′	62°52′
Four Mile Lake	LAKE/LAC	NS	Kings	21 A/15	44°55′	64°37′
Four Mile Lake	LAKE/LAC	ON	Victoria	31 D/10	44°41′	78°45′
Four Mile Pond	LAKE/LAC	NF		2 F/4	49°15′	53°58′
Four Mile Pond	LAKE/LAC	NF		2 E/1	49°05′	54°02′
Four Mile River	RIV/CDE	BC	Cassiar	104 P/3	59°12′	129°09′
Fourmont, Lac - see-voir - Fourmont Lake	LAKE/LAC	NF		13 C/1	52°04′	60°26′
Fourmont Lake	LAKE/LAC	NF		13 C/1	52°04′	60°26′
Fourneau, Pointe à	CAPE/CAP	QC	Vaudreuil-Soulanges	31 H/5	45°22′	73°51′
Fourneaux, Les	UNP/LNO	QC	Les Basques	22 C/3	48°09′	69°15′
Fournel, Lac	LAKE/LAC	QC	Côte-Nord-du-Golfe-Saint-Laurent	12 P/12	51°34′	57°58′
Fournier	UNP/LNO	ON	Prescott	31 G/7	45°26′	74°54′
Fournière, Lac	LAKE/LAC	QC	Vallée-de-l'Or	32 D/1	48°04′	78°03′
Fournier, Lac	LAKE/LAC	QC	Minganie	22 P/11	51°33′	65°25′
Four Ponds Corners	UNP/LNO	ON	Brant	40 P/1	43°01′	80°24′
Four Portages 157C	IR/RI	SK		73 P/7	55°17′	104°47′
Four Rivers Bay	BAY/BAIE	NT	Franklin	58 B	72°45′	95°37′
Four Roads	UNP/LNO	NB	Gloucester	21 P/10	47°36′	64°49′
Fourth Cabin	UNP/LNO	BC	Cassiar	94 D/4	56°15′	127°56′
Fourth Chute	UNP/LNO	ON	Renfrew	31 F/11	45°31′	77°00′
Fourth Lake Flowage	LAKE/LAC	NS	Digby	21 A/5	44°22′	65°42′
Fourth Line	UNP/LNO	ON	Lambton	40 J/16	42°57′	82°19′
Fowler	UNP/LNO	ON	Kenora	52 J/2	50°14′	90°58′
Fowler	UNP/LNO	BC	Cassiar	104 B/13	56°50′	131°46′
Fowlers Corner	UNP/LNO	NB	Queens	21 I/4	46°12′	65°56′
Fowlers Corners	UNP/LNO	NB	Queens	21 G/8	45°30′	66°20′
Fowlers Corners	UNP/LNO	ON	Peterborough	31 D/8	44°20′	78°27′
Fowlies Mill	UNP/LNO	NB	Northumberland	21 P/3	47°01′	65°13′
Foxboro	UNP/LNO	ON	Hastings	31 C/3	44°15′	77°26′
Fox Brook	UNP/LNO	NS	Pictou	11 E/10	45°32′	62°43′
Fox, Cape	CAPE/CAP	NF		2 L/13	50°52′	55°54′
Fox Corners	UNP/LNO	ON	Hastings	31 C/12	44°36′	77°32′
Fox Cove	UNP/LNO	NF		1 M/3	47°06′	55°06′
Fox Cove-Mortier	TOWN/VIL2	NF		1 M/3	47°05′	55°07′
Fox Creek	TOWN/VIL2	AB	32-62-19-W5	83 K/7	54°24′	116°48′
Fox Creek	UNP/LNO	NB	Westmorland	21 I/2	46°03′	64°41′
Foxdale	UNP/LNO	SK	23-51-3-W3	73 G/8	53°25′	106°19′
Foxe Basin	CHAN/CHEN	NT	Franklin	36 E	65°56′	77°55′
Foxe Channel	SEAU/SMER	—		1399A	64°30′	81°00′
Foxe Channel	CHAN/CHEN	NT	Franklin	36 C	65°00′	80°00′
Foxe Peninsula	CAPE/CAP	NT	Franklin	36 B	65°00′	76°00′

NAME / NOM	ENTITY / ENTITÉ	LOC 1 / LIEU 1	LOC 2 / LIEU 2	MAP / CARTE	LAT	LONG
Foxey	UNP/LNO	ON	Manitoulin	41 G/15	45°53'	82°31'
Foxford	UNP/LNO	SK	1-52-22-W2	73 H/6	53°28'	105°07'
Fox Harbour	VILG/VILG	NF		1 N/5	47°19'	53°55'
Fox Harbour	UNP/LNO	NS	Cumberland	11 E/14	45°51'	63°28'
Fox Harbour	BAY/BAIE	NS	Cumberland	11 E/14	45°51'	63°28'
Fox Hill	UNP/LNO	NB	Kings	21 H/12	45°43'	65°34'
Fox Hills	UNP/LNO	SK	14-24-16-W2	72 P/1	51°03'	104°08'
Fox Island	ISL/ÎLE	NF		12 B/10	48°44'	58°42'
Fox Island	ISL/ÎLE	NS	Guysborough	11 F/6	45°21'	61°06'
Fox Island	ISL/ÎLE	NB	Northumberland	21 P/3	47°06'	65°00'
Fox Island Harbour	UNP/LNO	NF		11 P/11	47°36'	57°17'
Fox Island Main	UNP/LNO	NS	Guysborough	11 F/6	45°20'	61°06'
Fox Island River	UNP/LNO	NF		12 B/10	48°42'	58°41'
Fox Island River	RIV/CDE	NF		12 B/10	48°42'	58°41'
Fox Island River-Point au Mal	UNP/LNO	NF		12 B/10	48°40'	58°41'
Fox Lake	UNP/LNO	ON	Sudbury	41 I/4	46°10'	81°44'
Fox Lake	UNP/LNO	AB	14-109-4-W5	84 J/7	58°28'	114°31'
Fox Lake	LAKE/LAC	ON	Sudbury	41 I/12	46°35'	81°44'
Fox Lake	LAKE/LAC	ON	Kenora	52 E/15	49°58'	94°47'
Fox Lake	LAKE/LAC	MB	80,81-17,18-E	53 M/15	56°00'	94°48'
Fox Lake 1	IR/RI	MB		54 D/2	56°01'	94°47'
Fox Lake 2	IR/RI	MB	10,11-87-21-1-E	54 D/9	56°30'	94°12'
Fox Lake 162	IR/RI	AB	109,110-3,4-W5	84 J/7	58°30'	114°32'
Fox Lake West 3	IR/RI	MB		63 P/10	55°44'	96°51'
Foxley River	UNP/LNO	PE	Prince	21 I/9	46°42'	64°01'
Fox Marsh	UNP/LNO	NF		1 N/6	47°24'	53°23'
Foxmead	UNP/LNO	ON	Simcoe	31 D/12	44°42'	79°33'
Fox Mine	UNP/LNO	MB		64 C/12	56°38'	101°39'
Fox Mountain	MTN/MNT	YT		105 F/14	61°55'	133°22'
Fox Point	UNP/LNO	NS	Lunenburg	21 A/9	44°37'	64°04'
Fox Point	UNP/LNO	ON	Muskoka	31 E/7	45°16'	79°00'
Fox Point - see-voir - Colesdale Park	UNP/LNO	SK		72 I/14	50°57'	105°09'
Fox Point	CAPE/CAP	NT	Mackenzie	96 G	65°21'	122°45'
Fox Point 157D	IR/RI	SK		73 I/15	54°59'	104°54'
Fox Point 157E	IR/RI	SK		73 I/15	54°59'	104°54'
Fox Pond	LAKE/LAC	NF		2 D/16	48°56'	54°06'
Fox River	UNP/LNO	NS	Cumberland	21 H/7	45°25'	64°32'
Fox River	RIV/CDE	NS	Cumberland	21 H/7	45°24'	64°32'
Fox River	RIV/CDE	MB		54 C/3	56°03'	93°18'
Fox River	RIV/CDE	BC	Cassiar	94 F/5	57°26'	125°41'
Fox Roost	UNP/LNO	NF		11 O/11	47°34'	59°03'
Fox Roost-Margaree	UNP/LNO	NF		11 O/11	47°34'	59°03'
Fox's Corners	UNP/LNO	ON	Victoria	31 D/7	44°23'	78°36'
Foxtrap	UNP/LNO	NF		1 N/10	47°31'	52°59'
Fox Valley	VILG/VILG	SK	26-17-26-W3	72 K/6	50°28'	109°29'
Fox Valley No. 171	MUN2/AZM2	SK		72 K/5	50°25'	109°30'
Foxville	UNP/LNO	ON	Cochrane	42 I/4	50°04'	81°38'
Foxwarren	UNP/LNO	MB	4-18-27-W	62 K/11	50°31'	101°09'
Foxy Creek 6	IR/RI	BC	Range 5 Coast	93 L/8	54°20'	126°08'
Foxy Creek 11B - see-voir - Foxy Creek 6	IR/RI	BC		93 L/8	54°20'	126°08'
Foymount	UNP/LNO	ON	Renfrew	31 F/6	45°26'	77°18'
Fraine	UNP/LNO	BC	Kootenay	82 N/6	51°29'	117°30'
*Fraine	UNP/LNO	BC	Kootenay	82 F/5	49°27'	117°32'
Fraley Island	ISL/ÎLE	NT	Keewatin	34 L/8	58°21'	78°03'
Fralick's Beach	UNP/LNO	ON	Ontario	31 D/2	44°12'	78°53'
Framboise	UNP/LNO	NS	Richmond	11 F/9	45°43'	60°22'
Framboise Cove	BAY/BAIE	NS	Richmond	11 F/9	45°42'	60°20'
Framboise Intervale	UNP/LNO	NS	Richmond	11 F/9	45°41'	60°26'
Frames	UNP/LNO	BC	New Westminster	92 G/7	49°22'	122°53'
Framnes	UNP/LNO	MB	31-22-2-E	62 I/14	50°56'	97°18'
Frampton	UNP/LNO	QC	La Nouvelle-Beauce	21 L/7	46°28'	70°49'
Fram Sound	CHAN/CHEN	NT	Franklin	59 A	76°25'	89°45'
Frances Bay	BAY/BAIE	BC	Range 1 Coast	92 K/6	50°20'	125°02'
Frances Lake	UNP/LNO	YT		105 H/6	61°17'	129°17'
Frances Lake	LAKE/LAC	MB	21-9-16-E	52 E/14	49°46'	95°20'
Frances Lake	LAKE/LAC	YT		105 H/5	61°23'	129°35'
Frances River	RIV/CDE	YT		105 A/6	60°16'	129°11'
Franceville	UNP/LNO	ON	Muskoka	31 D/13	44°56'	79°54'
Franchere	UNP/LNO	AB	8-61-7-W4	73 L/6	54°16'	111°02'
Franchère, Lac	LAKE/LAC	QC	Antoine-Labelle	31 J/15	46°47'	75°00'
Franchetot, Lac	LAKE/LAC	QC	Sept-Rivières	22 O/1	51°04'	66°01'
Francheville	MUN1/AZM1	QC	Francheville	31 I/9	46°30'	72°25'
Francis	TOWN/VIL2	SK	21-13-14-W2	62 L/4	50°06'	103°52'
Francisco Point	CAPE/CAP	BC	Sayward	92 K/3	50°01'	125°09'
Francis Harbour	UNP/LNO	NF		3 D/12	52°33'	55°43'

NAME / NOM	ENTITY / ENTITÉ	LOC 1 / LIEU 1	LOC 2 / LIEU 2	MAP / CARTE	POSITION LAT	LONG
Francis Lake	LAKE/LAC	ON	Grey	41 A/11	44°40'	81°02'
Francis, Lake	LAKE/LAC	MB	15-4-W	62 I/5	50°18'	97°58'
Francis Lake	LAKE/LAC	AB	2,11-69-11-W4	73 L/13	54°57'	111°34'
Francis No. 127	MUN2/AZM2	SK		62 L/3	50°15'	103°50'
Francoeur	UNP/LNO	NB	Madawaska	21 N/8	47°24'	68°17'
Francoeur	UNP/LNO	QC	Lotbinière	21 L/12	46°37'	71°31'
Francoeurville	UNP/LNO	QC	Drummond	31 H/16	45°47'	72°10'
François	UNP/LNO	NF		11 P/10	47°35'	56°45'
François Bay	BAY/BAIE	NF		11 P/10	47°34'	56°45'
François-De Laval, Mont	MTN/MNT	QC	La Côte-de-Beaupré	21 M/6	47°23'	71°13'
François, Lac	LAKE/LAC	QC	Charlevoix-Est	22 C/4	48°06'	69°50'
François, Lacs à	LAKE/LAC	QC	Sept-Rivières	22 P/12	51°40'	65°49'
François Lake	UNP/LNO	BC	Range 5 Coast	93 K/4	54°03'	125°45'
François Lake	LAKE/LAC	BC	Range 4 Coast	93 K/4	54°03'	125°45'
François Lake	LAKE/LAC	NT	Mackenzie	85 I	62°27'	112°22'
François Lake 7	IR/RI	BC	Range 4 Coast	93 K/4	54°01'	125°57'
Franey Corner	UNP/LNO	NS	Lunenburg	21 A/10	44°44'	64°40'
Frank	UNP/LNO	AB	31-7-3-W5	82 G/9	49°36'	114°24'
Frankford	VILG/VILG	ON	Hastings	31 C/4	44°12'	77°36'
Frankfurt Seamount	SEAU/SMER	—		NK22 B	42°16'	53°00'
Frank Lake	LAKE/LAC	ON	Thunder Bay	42 L/4	50°10'	87°53'
Frank Lake	LAKE/LAC	AB	18,19-27,28-W4	82 I/12	50°34'	113°43'
Frank Lake	LAKE/LAC	AB	30-7-3-W5M	82 G/9	49°35'	114°24'
Franklin	VILG/VILG	QC	Le Haut-Saint-Laurent	31 H/4	45°02'	73°55'
Franklin	MUN2/AZM2	MB		62 H/3	49°10'	97°00'
Franklin	UNP/LNO	ON	Durham	31 D/2	44°14'	78°35'
Franklin	UNP/LNO	MB	6-15-16-W	62 J/4	50°15'	99°40'
Franklin Basin	SEAU/SMER	—		8005	42°10'	68°00'
Franklin Bay	BAY/BAIE	NT	Franklin	47 C/6	69°26'	85°25'
Franklin Bay	BAY/BAIE	NT	Franklin	97 C/10	69°45'	126°00'
Franklin Beach	UNP/LNO	ON	York	31 D/6	44°19'	79°23'
Franklin Centre	UNP/LNO	QC	Le Haut-Saint-Laurent	31 H/4	45°02'	73°55'
Franklin, District de - also-aussi - **Franklin, District of**	GEOG/GÉOG	NT		MCR130	74°00'	85°00'
Franklin, District of - also-aussi - **Franklin, District de**	GEOG/GÉOG	NT		MCR130	74°00'	85°00'
Franklin Glacier	GLAC/GLAC	BC	Range 2 Coast	92 N/6	51°16'	125°23'
Franklin Inlet	BAY/BAIE	NT	Franklin	57 D	69°34'	91°15'
Franklin Island	ISL/ÎLE	ON	Parry Sound	41 H/8	45°24'	80°20'
Franklin Island	ISL/ÎLE	ON	Bruce	41 H/3	45°04'	81°30'
Franklin, Lake	LAKE/LAC	NS	Digby	21 A/5	44°27'	65°31'
Franklin Lake	LAKE/LAC	MB	27-89-23-W	64 C/11	56°45'	101°02'
Franklin Lake	LAKE/LAC	SK		64 M/6	59°22'	103°21'
Franklin Lake	LAKE/LAC	NT	Keewatin	66 I/16	66°56'	96°03'
Franklin Manor 22	IR/RI	NS	Cumberland	21 H/9	45°33'	64°24'
Franklin Mountains	MTN/MNT	NT	Mackenzie	96 B/4	64°15'	124°00'
Franklin Pierce Bay	BAY/BAIE	NT	Franklin	39 H	79°26'	74°50'
Franklin Point	CAPE/CAP	NT	Franklin	67 D	69°35'	98°32'
Franklin River	RIV/CDE	BC	Range 2 Coast	92 N/4	51°05'	125°34'
Franklins Corners	UNP/LNO	ON	Prescott	31 G/7	45°26'	74°56'
Franklin Strait	CHAN/CHEN	NT	Franklin	67 H	71°30'	96°51'
Franklin Trough	SEAU/SMER	—		5.17	71°40'	96°00'
Franklyn Arm	BAY/BAIE	BC	Range 2 Coast	92 N/1	51°13'	124°08'
Frank Mackie Glacier	GLAC/GLAC	BC	Cassiar	104 B/8	56°19'	130°10'
Franks 10	IR/RI	BC	New Westminster	92 G/16	49°53'	122°18'
Frankslake	UNP/LNO	SK	18-19-17-W2	72 I/9	50°36'	104°22'
Frank Slide Interpretive Centre Provincial Historic Site (Developed)	PARK/PARC	AB	7-3-W5	82 G/9	49°36'	114°24'
Franks Pond	LAKE/LAC	NF		1 N/3	47°08'	53°12'
Franktown	UNP/LNO	ON	Lanark	31 F/1	45°02'	76°04'
Franktown Station	UNP/LNO	ON	Lanark	31 F/1	45°01'	76°04'
Frankville	UNP/LNO	NS	Antigonish	11 F/12	45°39'	61°31'
Frankville	UNP/LNO	ON	Leeds	31 B/12	44°43'	75°58'
Franquelin	VILG/VILG	QC	Manicouagan	22 G/5	49°22'	67°50'
Franquelin, Lac	LAKE/LAC	QC	Manicouagan	22 F/9	49°31'	68°05'
Franz	UNP/LNO	ON	Algoma	42 C/8	48°28'	84°25'
Frapeau Point	CAPE/CAP	NF		1 K/13	46°56'	53°38'
Fraser	UNP/LNO	NB	Victoria	21 J/14	46°56'	67°29'
Fraser	UNP/LNO	ON	Welland	30 M/3	43°03'	79°07'
Fraser	UNP/LNO	BC	Kootenay	82 F/10	49°37'	116°59'
Fraserburg	UNP/LNO	ON	Muskoka	31 E/3	45°04'	79°09'
Fraser, Cape	CAPE/CAP	NT	Franklin	29 G	79°47'	71°06'
Fraser-Cheam	MUN1/AZM1	BC	Yale Division Yale	92 H/12	49°35'	121°40'
Fraserdale	UNP/LNO	ON	Cochrane	42 H/13	49°51'	81°37'
Fraser, Fleuve - also-aussi - **Fraser River**	RIV/CDE	BC	New Westminster	92 G/3	49°07'	123°11'
Fraser-Fort George	MUN1/AZM1	BC	Cariboo	93 H/11	53°42'	121°15'
Fraser Heights	UNP/LNO	BC	New Westminster	92 G/2	49°12'	122°47'
Fraser Island	ISL/ÎLE	NT	Franklin	35 M	63°29'	78°30'

NAME / NOM	ENTITY / ENTITÉ	LOC 1 / LIEU 1	LOC 2 / LIEU 2	MAP / CARTE	POSITION LAT	POSITION LONG
Fraser Island 6	IR/RI	BC	Metchosin	92 B/5	48°20'	123°36'
Fraser Lake	VILG/VILG	BC	Range 5 Coast	93 K/2	54°03'	124°51'
Fraser Lake	LAKE/LAC	NF		13 L/5	54°24'	63°40'
Fraser Lake	LAKE/LAC	ON	Hastings	31 F/4	45°11'	77°39'
Fraser Lake	LAKE/LAC	BC	Range 5 Coast	93 K/2	54°05'	124°45'
Fraser Lake	LAKE/LAC	BC	Range 1 Coast	92 L/9	50°41'	126°19'
Fraser Lake	LAKE/LAC	NT	Mackenzie	75 B	61°00'	106°07'
Fraser Lake 2	IR/RI	BC	Range 5 Coast	93 K/2	54°06'	124°38'
Fraser Landing	UNP/LNO	QC	Pontiac	31 K/4	46°10'	77°35'
Fraser Mills	UNP/LNO	BC	New Westminster	92 G/2	49°14'	122°51'
Fraser Reach	RIVF/EFLV	BC	Range 4 Coast	103 H/2	53°14'	128°47'
Fraser River	RIV/CDE	NF		14 D/9	56°37'	62°15'
Fraser River - also-aussi - **Fraser, Fleuve**	RIV/CDE	BC	New Westminster	92 G/3	49°07'	123°11'
Fraser River Junction	UNP/LNO	BC	New Westminster	92 G/2	49°12'	122°53'
Frasers Corners	UNP/LNO	ON	Peel	30 M/12	43°42'	79°42'
Fraser Settlement	UNP/LNO	NS	Halifax	11 E/2	45°06'	62°58'
Frasers Grant	UNP/LNO	NS	Antigonish	11 F/12	45°34'	61°46'
Frasers Mills	UNP/LNO	NS	Antigonish	11 F/5	45°29'	61°56'
Frasers Mountain	UNP/LNO	NS	Pictou	11 E/10	45°36'	62°37'
Frasertown	UNP/LNO	NS	Annapolis	21 A/12	44°38'	65°32'
Fraserview	UNP/LNO	BC	Cariboo	93 G/15	53°59'	122°42'
Fraserville	UNP/LNO	NS	Cumberland	21 H/7	45°23'	64°40'
Fraserville	UNP/LNO	QC	Charlevoix-Est	21 M/9	47°41'	70°08'
Fraserville	UNP/LNO	ON	Northumberland	31 D/1	44°12'	78°23'
Fraserwood	UNP/LNO	MB	23-19-2-E	62 I/11	50°38'	97°13'
Fraspur	UNP/LNO	AB	10-47-4-W5	83 G/1	53°02'	114°30'
Frater	UNP/LNO	ON	Algoma	41 N/7	47°20'	84°33'
Fraternité, Cap	CAPE/CAP	QC	Le Fjord-du-Saguenay	22 D/8	48°19'	70°15'
Fraxa Junction	UNP/LNO	ON	Dufferin	40 P/16	43°55'	80°10'
Fraxville	UNP/LNO	NS	Lunenburg	21 A/15	44°46'	64°34'
Fraye, Lac	LAKE/LAC	QC	Manicouagan	22 L/1	50°01'	70°02'
Frayn's Landing	UNP/LNO	ON	Grenville	31 C/16	44°48'	76°07'
Frazer Bay	BAY/BAIE	ON	Manitoulin	41 H/13	46°00'	81°40'
Frazer Lake	LAKE/LAC	ON	Thunder Bay	52 H/2	49°15'	88°32'
Frazier Island	ISL/ÎLE	NT	Keewatin	34 K/5	58°18'	77°53'
Freakly Point	CAPE/CAP	NT	Keewatin	33 M	55°47'	79°48'
Fréchette	UNP/LNO	QC	L'Érable	21 L/4	46°06'	71°38'
Fréchette, Lac	LAKE/LAC	QC	Rouyn-Noranda	31 M/14	48°00'	79°10'
Frechette Lake	LAKE/LAC	ON	Sudbury	41 O/7	47°20'	82°32'
Fréchette, Rivière	RIV/CDE	QC	Minganie	22 P/7	51°23'	64°42'
Freda Creek	RIV/CDE	BC	New Westminster	92 F/16	49°52'	124°16'
Freda Lake	LAKE/LAC	BC	New Westminster	92 F/16	50°00'	124°10'
Freda Point 4	IR/RI	BC	Range 1 Coast	92 K/12	50°41'	125°46'
Freddie Charley Boy 7	IR/RI	BC	Range 3 Coast	93 C/8	52°21'	124°07'
Freddie's Meadow 8	IR/RI	BC	Cariboo	93 B/7	52°29'	122°36'
Fredensthal	UNP/LNO	MB	13-1-3-E	62 H/3	49°03'	97°05'
Fredensthal West	UNP/LNO	MB	19-1-3-E	62 H/3	49°03'	97°10'
Frederick	UNP/LNO	ON	Cochrane	42 H/3	49°05'	81°09'
Frederick	UNP/LNO	BC	Kamloops Division Yale	92 I/10	50°45'	120°38'
Frederick Arm	BAY/BAIE	BC	Range 1 Coast	92 K/6	50°29'	125°16'
Frederickhouse	UNP/LNO	ON	Cochrane	42 H/3	49°05'	81°10'
Frederick House Lake	LAKE/LAC	ON	Cochrane	42 A/10	48°39'	80°55'
Frederick House River	RIV/CDE	ON	Cochrane	42 H/6	49°18'	81°16'
Frederick Island	ISL/ÎLE	BC	Queen Charlotte	103 F/14	53°56'	133°11'
Fredericksburg	UNP/LNO	NB	York	21 J/7	46°16'	66°52'
Frederickton	UNP/LNO	NF		2 E/8	49°26'	54°22'
Fredericton	CITY/VIL1	NB	York	21 G/15	45°58'	66°39'
Fredericton	UNP/LNO	PE	Queens	11 L/6	46°22'	63°26'
Fredericton Junction	VILG/VILG	NB	Sunbury	21 G/10	45°40'	66°37'
Fredericton Road	UNP/LNO	NB	Westmorland	21 I/3	46°04'	65°11'
Frederiksen Point	CAPE/CAP	BC	Rupert	102 I/16	50°48'	128°21'
Fredrikshald Bay	BAY/BAIE	NT	Franklin	77 H/8	71°20'	104°22'
Fredrikson Lake	LAKE/LAC	BC	Cassiar	94 D/15	56°57'	126°31'
Freedale	UNP/LNO	MB	2-28-16-W	62 O/5	51°22'	99°37'
Freedom	UNP/LNO	AB	2-60-2-W5	83 J/1	54°09'	114°13'
Free Grant	UNP/LNO	NB	Gloucester	21 P/12	47°44'	65°51'
Freeland	UNP/LNO	PE	Prince	11 L/12	46°41'	63°58'
Freeland	UNP/LNO	ON	Leeds	31 C/9	44°41'	76°14'
Freels, Cape	CAPE/CAP	NF		2 F/5	49°15'	53°30'
Freelton	UNP/LNO	ON	Wentworth	40 P/8	43°24'	80°02'
Freeman	UNP/LNO	ON	Timiskaming	31 M/4	47°14'	79°44'
Freeman	UNP/LNO	ON	Halton	30 M/5	43°20'	79°49'
Freeman 150B	IR/RI	AB	31-75-14-W5	83 N/9	55°33'	116°09'
Freeman Corners	UNP/LNO	ON	Peterborough	31 C/5	44°29'	77°47'
Freeman Lake	LAKE/LAC	AB	66-11-W5	83 J/12	54°42'	115°32'

NAME NOM	ENTITY ENTITÉ	LOC 1 LIEU 1	LOC 2 LIEU 2	MAP CARTE	POSITION LAT	LONG
Freeman River	UNP/LNO	AB	34-62-6-W5	83 J/7	54°24′	114°49′
Freeman River	RIV/CDE	AB	61-6-W5	83 J/7	54°19′	114°47′
Freemans Cove	BAY/BAIE	NT	Franklin	68 H	75°10′	98°00′
Freemont	UNP/LNO	SK	31-44-24-W3	73 C/14	52°50′	109°30′
Freeport	VILG/VILG	NS	Digby	21 B/8	44°17′	66°19′
Freeport	UNP/LNO	QC	Brome-Missisquoi	31 H/2	45°13′	72°46′
Freeport	UNP/LNO	ON	Waterloo	40 P/8	43°25′	80°25′
Freetown	UNP/LNO	PE	Prince	11 L/5	46°22′	63°37′
Frégate, Lac de la	LAKE/LAC	QC	Jamésie	33 G/2	53°12′	74°45′
Freil Lake	LAKE/LAC	BC	New Westminster	92 G/13	49°52′	123°58′
Frelighsburg	VILG/VILG	QC	Brome-Missisquoi	31 H/2	45°03′	72°50′
Fremantle	UNP/LNO	SK	17-8-3-W2	62 E/9	49°38′	102°23′
Fremo Corners	UNP/LNO	ON	Renfrew	31 F/7	45°26′	76°50′
French Bar Creek	RIV/CDE	BC	Lillooet	92 O/1	51°14′	122°10′
French Bay	UNP/LNO	ON	Algoma	41 K/9	46°33′	84°11′
French Cove	UNP/LNO	NS	Richmond	11 F/10	45°42′	60°50′
French Creek	UNP/LNO	BC	Nanoose	92 F/8	49°21′	124°21′
French Creek	RIV/CDE	MB		54 F/1	57°01′	92°14′
Frenchfort	UNP/LNO	PE	Queens	11 L/6	46°19′	63°01′
French Headland	CAPE/CAP	NT	Franklin	25 I	62°43′	64°56′
French Hill	UNP/LNO	ON	Russell	31 G/6	45°28′	75°23′
French Lake	UNP/LNO	NB	Sunbury	21 G/15	45°46′	66°32′
French Lake	LAKE/LAC	NB	Sunbury	21 G/16	45°55′	66°16′
French Lake	LAKE/LAC	NB	Sunbury	21 G/15	45°47′	66°32′
French Line	UNP/LNO	ON	Lanark	31 F/2	45°08′	76°32′
Frenchman Butte	HAM/HAM	SK	21-53-25-W3	73 F/12	53°35′	109°38′
Frenchman Butte, Lieu historique national de - also-aussi - Frenchman Butte National Historic Site	PARK/PARC	SK		73 F/12	53°38′	109°35′
Frenchman Butte National Historic Site - also-aussi - Frenchman Butte, Lieu historique national de	PARK/PARC	SK		73 F/12	53°38′	109°35′
Frenchman Butte No. 501	MUN2/AZM2	SK		73 F/11	53°35′	109°30′
Frenchman Lake	LAKE/LAC	AB	64-10-W4	73 L/11	54°32′	111°27′
Frenchman Point	CAPE/CAP	NS	Yarmouth	20 O/9	43°38′	66°01′
Frenchman Point	CAPE/CAP	ON	Bruce	41 A/11	44°35′	81°18′
Frenchman River	RIV/CDE	SK	5-1-10-W3	72 G/3	49°00′	107°18′
Frenchman's Bay	BAY/BAIE	ON	Ontario	30 M/14	43°49′	79°05′
Frenchman's Cove	VILG/VILG	NF		1 M/3	47°13′	55°24′
Frenchman's Cove	UNP/LNO	NF		12 G/1	49°03′	58°11′
Frenchman's Cove	BAY/BAIE	NF		1 K/11	46°45′	53°02′
Frenchman's Cove Barasway	LAKE/LAC	NF		1 M/3	47°13′	55°24′
Frenchmans Creek	UNP/LNO	NB	Saint John	21 G/1	45°10′	66°13′
Frenchman's Creek	RIV/CDE	ON	Welland	30 L/15	42°57′	78°56′
Frenchman's Head	UNP/LNO	ON	Kenora	52 K/1	50°07′	92°12′
Frenchmans Island	UNP/LNO	NF		3 E/4	53°13′	55°44′
Frenchmans Pond	LAKE/LAC	NF		12 H/4	49°05′	57°58′
Frenchmans Road	UNP/LNO	NS	Halifax	11 D/13	44°55′	63°34′
French Portage	UNP/LNO	ON	Kenora	52 E/7	49°25′	94°42′
French River	UNP/LNO	PE	Queens	11 L/12	46°31′	63°31′
French River	UNP/LNO	NS	Victoria	11 K/8	46°29′	60°26′
French River	UNP/LNO	NS	Pictou	11 E/9	45°34′	62°26′
French River	UNP/LNO	NS	Colchester	11 E/11	45°43′	63°20′
French River	UNP/LNO	ON	Sudbury	41 I/2	46°02′	80°34′
French River	UNP/LNO	ON	Parry Sound	41 H/15	45°58′	80°54′
French River	RIV/CDE	ON	Parry Sound	41 H/15	45°56′	80°54′
French River 13	IR/RI	ON	Parry Sound	41 H/15	46°00′	80°30′
French River Main Channel - see-voir - Main Channel (French River)	CHAN/CHEN	ON		41 I/2	46°01′	80°50′
French River North Channel - see-voir - North Channel (French River)	RIV/CDE	ON		41 I/2	46°06′	80°34′
French Road	UNP/LNO	NS	Cape Breton	11 F/16	45°54′	60°13′
Frenchs Cove	UNP/LNO	NF		1 N/11	47°37′	53°13′
French Settlement	UNP/LNO	ON	Renfrew	31 F/11	45°44′	77°04′
Frenchvale	UNP/LNO	NS	Cape Breton	11 K/1	46°06′	60°23′
French Village	UNP/LNO	PE	Queens	11 L/7	46°24′	62°53′
French Village	UNP/LNO	PE	Queens	11 L/6	46°24′	63°25′
French Village	UNP/LNO	NS	Halifax	11 D/12	44°41′	63°53′
French Village	UNP/LNO	NS	Halifax	11 D/12	44°38′	63°55′
French Village	UNP/LNO	NB	Kings	21 H/5	45°26′	65°52′
French Village	UNP/LNO	NB	York	21 G/15	45°57′	66°50′
Frenchville	UNP/LNO	SK	12-7-15-W3	72 G/12	49°33′	107°55′
Freppel	UNP/LNO	QC	L'Islet	21 N/4	47°01′	69°56′
Freshfield Icefield	GLAC/GLAC	AB	32-21-W5	82 N/10	51°45′	116°54′
Freshford	UNP/LNO	MB	54-26-W	63 F/11	53°41′	101°14′
Freshwater	UNP/LNO	NF		1 N/2	47°02′	52°54′
Freshwater	UNP/LNO	NF		1 K/15	46°51′	52°57′
Freshwater	UNP/LNO	NF		1 N/11	47°36′	53°01′

NAME NOM	ENTITY ENTITÉ	LOC 1 LIEU 1	LOC 2 LIEU 2	MAP CARTE	POSITION LAT	POSITION LONG
Freshwater	UNP/LNO	NF		1 N/14	47°45′	53°11′
Freshwater	UNP/LNO	NF		1 N/14	47°46′	53°11′
Freshwater	UNP/LNO	NF		1 N/5	47°15′	53°59′
Freshwater	UNP/LNO	QC	Pontiac	31 F/15	45°46′	76°38′
Freshwater Bay	BAY/BAIE	NF		2 D/16	54°49′	54°05′
Freshwater Lake	LAKE/LAC	SK/AB		73 C/12	52°37′	109°59′
Freshwater Point	CAPE/CAP	NF		1 K/11	46°38′	53°14′
Freshwater Pond	LAKE/LAC	NF		1 M/3	47°06′	55°16′
Fresnoy	UNP/LNO	AB	35-60-6-W4	73 L/2	54°14′	110°48′
Fressel, Lac	LAKE/LAC	QC	Kativik	33 O/6	55°27′	75°12′
Freuchen Bay	BAY/BAIE	NT	Franklin	46 I	66°58′	81°50′
Fricker	UNP/LNO	ON	Nipissing	31 L/6	46°20′	79°26′
Friday Bay	BAY/BAIE	NF		2 E/10	49°35′	54°45′
Friday Creek	RIV/CDE	ON	Cochrane	42 J/8	50°16′	82°24′
Friday Lake	LAKE/LAC	ON	Sudbury	41 I/14	46°57′	81°21′
Fridays	UNP/LNO	ON	Nipissing	41 I/16	46°59′	80°02′
Friedensfeld	UNP/LNO	MB	14-6-6-E	62 H/7	49°28′	96°40′
Friedensfeld	UNP/LNO	MB	21,28-1-4-W	62 H/4	49°03′	97°56′
Friedensruh	UNP/LNO	MB	13,24-2-4-W	62 H/4	49°08′	97°52′
Friedenstal	UNP/LNO	AB	25-81-3-W6	84 D/1	56°03′	118°20′
Friendly Corners	UNP/LNO	ON	Middlesex	40 P/3	43°07′	81°07′
Friendly Lake	LAKE/LAC	BC	Kamloops Division Yale	92 P/9	51°35′	120°27′
Frigid, Cape	CAPE/CAP	NT	Keewatin	46 K	66°05′	85°05′
Froatburn	UNP/LNO	ON	Dundas	31 B/14	44°57′	75°09′
Frobisher	VILG/VILG	SK	13-3-4-W2	62 E/1	49°12′	102°26′
Frobisher Bay - see-voir - Iqaluit	TOWN/VIL2	NT		25 N/10	63°45′	68°31′
Frobisher Bay	BAY/BAIE	NT	Franklin	25 J	62°50′	66°35′
Frobisher Lake	LAKE/LAC	MB		63 I/16	54°54′	96°18′
Frobisher Lake	LAKE/LAC	SK		74 C/8	56°20′	108°15′
Frobisher's Farthest	ISL/ÎLE	NT	Franklin	25 O	63°30′	68°00′
Frodsham Lake	LAKE/LAC	NT	Mackenzie	85 P	63°38′	113°36′
Froggetts Corners	UNP/LNO	ON	Elgin	40 I/10	42°43′	80°47′
Frog Lake	UNP/LNO	NB	York	21 G/11	45°40′	67°03′
Frog Lake	UNP/LNO	AB	17-56-3-W4	73 E/16	53°50′	110°25′
Frog Lake	LAKE/LAC	NS	Kings	21 A/15	44°50′	64°51′
Frog Lake	LAKE/LAC	AB	56,57-2,3-W4	73 E/16	53°55′	110°20′
Frog Lake Massacre Provincial Historic Site (Undeveloped)	PARK/PARC	AB	10,17-56-3-W4	73 E/16	53°50′	110°22′
Frog Marsh	UNP/LNO	NF		1 N/11	47°32′	53°12′
Frogmoore Lakes	LAKE/LAC	BC	Kamloops Division Yale	92 I/7	50°24′	120°33′
Frogmore	UNP/LNO	ON	Norfolk	40 I/10	42°41′	80°40′
Frogpond Lake	LAKE/LAC	BC	New Westminster	92 K/1	50°03′	124°25′
Frog River	RIV/CDE	ON	Kenora	43 E/13	53°57′	87°42′
Frog River	RIV/CDE	BC	Cassiar	94 L/10	58°41′	126°53′
Froid, Ruisseau	RIV/CDE	QC	Antoine-Labelle	31 J/7	46°22′	74°46′
Frome	UNP/LNO	ON	Elgin	40 I/14	42°46′	81°19′
Fromenteau, Lac	LAKE/LAC	QC	La Côte-de-Gaspé	22 A/15	48°48′	64°35′
Fromenteau, Lac	LAKE/LAC	QC	Jamésie	32 P/6	51°26′	73°22′
Front Centre	UNP/LNO	NS	Lunenburg	21 A/8	44°23′	64°21′
Frontenac	VILG/VILG	QC	Le Granit	21 E/10	45°35′	70°50′
Frontenac	MUN1/AZM1	ON	Frontenac	31 C/10	44°40′	76°45′
Frontenac	GEOG/GÉOG	ON		31 C/10	44°40′	76°45′
Frontenac, Parc de récréation de	PARK/PARC	QC	L'Amiante	21 E/14	45°52′	71°13′
Frontier	VILG/VILG	SK	13-3-20-W3	72 F/2	49°12′	108°34′
Frontier Creek	RIV/CDE	BC	Range 2 Coast	92 N/12	51°33′	125°32′
Frontière, Lac	LAKE/LAC	QC	Montmagny	21 L/9	46°43′	70°00′
Frontier No. 19	MUN2/AZM2	SK		72 F/2	49°10′	108°35′
Front Lake	UNP/LNO	NS	Cape Breton	11 K/1	46°03′	60°10′
Front of Escott	MUN2/AZM2	ON	Grenville	31 B/5	44°28′	75°58′
Front of Leeds and Lansdowne	MUN2/AZM2	ON	Grenville	31 C/8	44°25′	76°05′
Front of Yonge	MUN2/AZM2	ON	Grenville	31 B/12	44°30′	75°50′
Frood Mine	UNP/LNO	ON	Sudbury	41 I/11	46°32′	81°01′
Froomfield	UNP/LNO	ON	Lambton	40 J/16	42°54′	82°27′
Frost Village	UNP/LNO	QC	La Haute-Yamaska	31 H/8	45°20′	72°29′
Frosty Hollow	UNP/LNO	NB	Westmorland	21 H/16	45°53′	64°24′
Frotet, Lac	LAKE/LAC	QC	Jamésie	32 J/15	50°45′	74°40′
Froude	UNP/LNO	SK	27-8-10-W2	62 E/11	49°41′	103°17′
Frozen Ocean Lake	LAKE/LAC	NF		2 D/14	48°54′	55°21′
Frozen Ocean Lake	LAKE/LAC	NF		2 E/4	49°11′	55°41′
Frozen Ocean Lake	LAKE/LAC	NS	Annapolis	21 A/6	44°27′	65°21′
Frozen Strait	CHAN/CHEN	NT	Keewatin	46 F	65°45′	84°20′
Fruitland	UNP/LNO	ON	Wentworth	30 M/4	43°13′	79°43′
Fruitvale	VILG/VILG	BC	Kootenay	82 F/4	49°07′	117°33′
Frustration Bay	BAY/BAIE	NT	Franklin	37 C	69°09′	78°56′
Fryatt	UNP/LNO	ON	Cochrane	42 G/11	49°38′	83°18′
Fryatt, Mount	MTN/MNT	AB	41-28-W5	83 C/12	52°33′	117°54′

NAME / NOM	ENTITY / ENTITÉ	LOC 1 / LIEU 1	LOC 2 / LIEU 2	MAP / CARTE	POSITION LAT	POSITION LONG
Fry Creek	UNP/LNO	BC	Kootenay	82 K/2	50°04′	116°52′
Fry Creek	RIV/CDE	BC	Kootenay	82 K/2	50°03′	116°53′
Frye Island	ISL/ÎLE	NB	Charlotte	21 G/2	45°03′	66°51′
Fry Lake	LAKE/LAC	ON	Kenora	52 O/3	51°14′	91°19′
Frys	UNP/LNO	SK	14-7-31-W	62 F/12	49°34′	101°35′
Fugèreville	VILG/VILG	QC	Témiscamingue	31 M/6	47°24′	79°12′
Fulda	UNP/LNO	SK	14-39-23-W2	73 A/6	52°21′	105°13′
Fulford	UNP/LNO	QC	Brome-Missisquoi	31 H/7	45°18′	72°34′
Fulford Harbour	UNP/LNO	BC	Saltspring Island	92 B/14	48°46′	123°27′
Fulford Harbour 5	IR/RI	BC	Cowichan	92 B/14	48°45′	123°25′
Fullarton	MUN2/AZM2	ON	Perth	40 P/6	43°24′	81°13′
Fullarton	UNP/LNO	ON	Perth	40 P/6	43°23′	81°14′
Fuller	UNP/LNO	ON	Hastings	31 C/6	44°24′	77°25′
Fullerton	UNP/LNO	NT	Keewatin	55 P	64°00′	88°59′
Fullerton, Cape	CAPE/CAP	NT	Keewatin	55 P	63°58′	88°46′
Fullerton Corner	UNP/LNO	QC	Memphrémagog	31 H/1	45°02′	72°20′
Fulmore Lake	LAKE/LAC	BC	Range 1 Coast	92 K/12	50°35′	125°57′
Fulton	UNP/LNO	ON	Lincoln	30 M/4	43°08′	79°40′
Fulton	UNP/LNO	MB	21-13-7-W	62 J/1	50°07′	98°23′
Fulton Lake	LAKE/LAC	BC	Range 5 Coast	93 L/16	54°49′	126°22′
Fulton River	RIV/CDE	BC	Range 5 Coast	93 L/16	54°48′	126°09′
Fultons	UNP/LNO	ON	Wellington	40 P/15	43°57′	80°57′
Fundian Channel	SEAU/SMER	—		8005	42°15′	67°00′
Fundy, Baie de - also-aussi - **Fundy, Bay of**	BAY/BAIE	NB/NS		21 H/4	45°10′	65°38′
Fundy Basin	SEAU/SMER	—		1399A	45°00′	66°00′
Fundy, Bay of - also-aussi - **Fundy, Baie de**	BAY/BAIE	NB/NS		21 H/4	45°10′	65°38′
Fundy Heights	UNP/LNO	NB	Saint John	21 G/8	45°15′	66°05′
Fundy National Park - also-aussi - Fundy, Parc national	PARK/PARC	NB	Albert	21 H/11	45°37′	65°02′
Fundy, Parc national - also-aussi - Fundy National Park	PARK/PARC	NB	Albert	21 H/11	45°37′	65°02′
Funk Island	ISL/ÎLE	NF		2 F/14	49°45′	53°11′
Funk Island Bank	SEAU/SMER	—		8015	50°30′	52°00′
Furby's Cove	UNP/LNO	NF		1 M/12	47°36′	55°50′
Furdale	HAM/HAM	SK	8-36-5-W3	73 B/2	52°05′	106°41′
Furnace Falls	UNP/LNO	ON	Haliburton	31 D/15	44°49′	78°33′
Furness	UNP/LNO	SK	1-48-28-W3	73 F/4	53°07′	109°58′
Fury and Hecla Channel	SEAU/SMER	—		1399A	69°54′	84°00′
Fury and Hecla Strait	CHAN/CHEN	NT	Franklin	47 D	69°50′	83°00′
Fury Point	CAPE/CAP	NT	Franklin	58 B	72°42′	92°16′
Fushimi Lake	LAKE/LAC	ON	Cochrane	42 G/13	49°50′	83°54′
Fusilier	UNP/LNO	SK	21-33-27-W3	72 N/13	51°51′	109°46′
F.-X.-Lemieux, Lac	LAKE/LAC	QC	La Jacques-Cartier	21 M/12	47°32′	71°40′
Fyfe, Mount	MTN/MNT	YT		116 H/7	65°17′	136°52′

G

NAME / NOM	ENTITY / ENTITÉ	LOC 1 / LIEU 1	LOC 2 / LIEU 2	MAP / CARTE	POSITION LAT	POSITION LONG
Gabarus	UNP/LNO	NS	Cape Breton	11 F/16	45°50′	60°09′
Gabarus Bay	BAY/BAIE	NS	Cape Breton	11 F/16	45°51′	60°07′
Gabarus, Cape	CAPE/CAP	NS	Cape Breton	11 F/16	45°49′	60°05′
Gabarus Lake	UNP/LNO	NS	Cape Breton	11 F/16	45°49′	60°14′
Gabarus Lake	LAKE/LAC	NS	Cape Breton	11 F/16	45°49′	60°12′
Gabbro Peninsula	CAPE/CAP	NT	Franklin	69 F/13	78°48′	104°00′
Gable Creek	RIV/CDE	BC	Similkameen Division Yale	82 E/7	49°24′	118°30′
Gable Mountain	MTN/MNT	BC	Cariboo	93 I/12	54°30′	121°40′
Gable Mountain	MTN/MNT	BC	Range 4 Coast	93 E/2	53°10′	126°58′
Gaboury	UNP/LNO	QC	Témiscamingue	31 M/6	47°19′	79°20′
Gabriel Island	ISL/ÎLE	NT	Franklin	25 J	62°53′	66°30′
Gabriel, Lac	LAKE/LAC	QC	Kativik	24 K/2	58°13′	68°40′
Gabriel, Lac	LAKE/LAC	QC	Jamésie	32 G/8	49°18′	74°28′
Gabrielle-Roy, Mont	MTN/MNT	QC	Charlevoix	21 M/7	47°23′	70°35′
Gabriel Strait	CHAN/CHEN	NT	Franklin	25 H	61°45′	65°30′
Gabriola	UNP/LNO	BC	Nanaimo	92 G/4	49°10′	123°51′
Gabriola Island	ISL/ÎLE	BC	Nanaimo	92 G/4	49°10′	123°48′
Gabriola Island 5	IR/RI	BC	Nanaimo	92 G/4	49°08′	123°43′
Gadds Harbour	UNP/LNO	NF		12 H/12	49°31′	57°53′
Gadelle, La	UNP/LNO	QC	Charlevoix-Est	21 M/9	47°37′	70°20′
Gadsby	VILG/VILG	AB	27-38-17-W4	83 A/8	52°18′	112°21′
Gads Hill	UNP/LNO	ON	Perth	40 P/7	43°26′	80°55′
Gaetz Brook	UNP/LNO	NS	Halifax	11 D/14	44°46′	63°13′
Gaffaret, Lac - see-voir - Gaffaret Lake	LAKE/LAC	NF		13 C/4	52°14′	61°55′
Gaffaret Lake	LAKE/LAC	NF		13 C/4	52°14′	61°55′
Gaff Point	CAPE/CAP	NS	Lunenburg	21 A/1	44°15′	64°17′
Gaff Topsail	UNP/LNO	NF		12 H/2	49°08′	56°39′

NAME NOM	ENTITY ENTITÉ	LOC 1 LIEU 1	LOC 2 LIEU 2	MAP CARTE	POSITION LAT	LONG
Gage	UNP/LNO	AB	26-82-4-W6	84 D/1	56°08′	118°30′
Gage, Cape	CAPE/CAP	PE	Prince	21 I/16	46°54′	64°14′
Gagetown	VILG/VILG	NB	Queens	21 G/16	45°47′	66°09′
Gagetown	GEOG/GÉOG	NB	Queens	21 G/16	45°45′	66°15′
Gagetown, Base des Forces canadiennes - also-aussi - Gagetown, Canadian Forces Base	MIL/MIL	NB	Sunbury	21 G/16	45°50′	66°27′
Gagetown, Canadian Forces Base - also-aussi - Gagetown, Base des Forces canadiennes	MIL/MIL	NB	Sunbury	21 G/16	45°50′	66°27′
Gagné	UNP/LNO	QC	Avignon	22 A/4	48°12′	65°57′
Gagnon	UNP/LNO	QC	Caniapiscau	22 N/16	51°54′	68°10′
Gagnon	UNP/LNO	ON	Russell	31 G/6	45°20′	75°12′
Gagnon, Lac	LAKE/LAC	QC	Papineau	31 J/3	46°07′	75°07′
Gagnon Lake	LAKE/LAC	NT	Mackenzie	75 E/16	61°58′	110°23′
Gagnon-Siding	UNP/LNO	QC	Vallée-de-l'Or	32 C/8	48°15′	76°09′
Gahern	UNP/LNO	AB	30-4-8-W4	72 E/6	49°19′	111°05′
Gaichbin 5 - see-voir - Gaichbin 8	IR/RI	BC		93 L/2	54°01′	126°40′
Gaichbin 8	IR/RI	BC	Range 5 Coast	93 L/2	54°01′	126°40′
Gaillarbois, Lac	LAKE/LAC	QC	Caniapiscau	22 O/14	52°00′	67°27′
Gaillard, Lac	LAKE/LAC	QC	Manicouagan	22 K/2	50°06′	68°47′
Gaines	UNP/LNO	SK	30-28-12-W3	72 O/5	51°25′	107°41′
Gainford	UNP/LNO	AB	14-53-6-W5	83 G/10	53°35′	114°47′
Gainsborough	VILG/VILG	SK	33-2-30-W	62 F/3	49°10′	101°27′
Gainsborough Creek	RIV/CDE	MB/SK		62 F/3	49°10′	101°02′
Galahad	VILG/VILG	AB	10-41-14-W4	73 D/12	52°31′	111°56′
Galarneauville	UNP/LNO	AB	23-25-15-W4	82 P/1	51°09′	112°00′
Galbraith	UNP/LNO	ON	Lanark	31 F/1	45°10′	76°14′
Galeairy Lake	LAKE/LAC	ON	Haliburton	31 E/8	45°30′	78°17′
Galena	UNP/LNO	BC	Kootenay	82 K/12	50°37′	117°52′
Galena Bay	UNP/LNO	BC	Kootenay	82 K/12	50°40′	117°51′
Galena Hill	UNP/LNO	ON	Victoria	31 D/10	44°41′	78°37′
Gale Point	CAPE/CAP	NT	Franklin	39 E	78°13′	75°28′
Gale, Rivière	RIV/CDE	QC	Jamésie	32 E/8	49°19′	78°12′
Galesburg	UNP/LNO	ON	Peterborough	31 D/8	44°28′	78°12′
Galet-Beaudry, Le	UNP/LNO	QC	Portneuf	21 L/12	46°42′	71°35′
Galeton	UNP/LNO	ON	Cochrane	42 P/2	51°08′	80°55′
Galet-Plat, Le	UNP/LNO	QC	Les Îles-de-la-Madeleine	11 N/5	47°21′	61°53′
Galet-Robitaille, Le	UNP/LNO	QC	Portneuf	21 L/12	46°42′	71°35′
Galetta	UNP/LNO	ON	Carleton	31 F/8	45°25′	76°15′
Galette, La	UNP/LNO	QC	Charlevoix	21 M/10	47°44′	70°43′
Galeville	UNP/LNO	NF		12 H/10	49°33′	56°51′
Galiano Island	ISL/ÎLE	BC	Cowichan	92 B/14	48°56′	123°27′
Galiano Island 9	IR/RI	BC	Chemainus	92 G/4	49°01′	123°35′
Galibois, Îles	ISL/ÎLE	QC	Côte-Nord-du-Golfe-Saint-Laurent	12 J/5	50°18′	59°47′
Galilee	UNP/LNO	SK	30-11-26-W2	72 H/13	49°56′	105°32′
Gallagher Ridge	UNP/LNO	NB	Westmorland	21 I/3	46°12′	65°01′
Gallant	UNP/LNO	QC	La Haute-Côte-Nord	22 C/15	48°53′	68°52′
Gallants	VILG/VILG	NF		12 B/9	48°42′	58°14′
Gallants	UNP/LNO	NF		12 B/9	48°42′	58°14′
Gallant Settlement	UNP/LNO	NB	Westmorland	21 I/1	46°11′	64°22′
Gallardin Point	UNP/LNO	NF		1 N/5	47°16′	53°59′
Gallas Point	CAPE/CAP	PE	Queens	11 L/2	46°07′	62°58′
Gallatin, Mount	MTN/MNT	BC	Cassiar	104 B/13	56°45′	131°55′
Gallet, Lac	LAKE/LAC	QC	Minganie	12 O/16	51°48′	58°25′
Gallichan	VILG/VILG	QC	Abitibi-Ouest	32 D/11	48°36′	79°17′
Gallingertown	UNP/LNO	ON	Stormont	31 G/3	45°01′	75°05′
Gallivan	UNP/LNO	SK	34-43-20-W3	73 C/15	52°45′	108°50′
Gallix	VILG/VILG	QC	Sept-Rivières	22 J/2	50°08′	66°37′
Galloway	UNP/LNO	NB	Kent	21 I/10	46°36′	64°49′
Galloway	UNP/LNO	AB	34-52-20-W5	83 F/10	53°32′	116°53′
Galloway	UNP/LNO	BC	Kootenay	82 G/6	49°23′	115°13′
Gallows Cove	UNP/LNO	NF		1 N/6	47°27′	53°09′
Gallup Hill	UNP/LNO	QC	Le Val-Saint-François	31 H/9	45°38′	72°11′
Galt	UNP/LNO	ON	Waterloo	40 P/8	43°22′	80°19′
Galts Corner	UNP/LNO	ON	Lennox and Addington	31 C/2	44°11′	76°52′
Galuchon, Île	ISL/ÎLE	QC	Côte-Nord-du-Golfe-Saint-Laurent	12 J/11	50°39′	59°09′
Galway and Cavendish	MUN2/AZM2	ON	Peterborough	31 D/9	44°45′	78°30′
Gamache, Baie	BAY/BAIE	QC	Minganie	22 H/16	49°48′	64°22′
Gamart, Lac	LAKE/LAC	QC	Caniapiscau	23 F/3	53°07′	69°00′
Gambier Harbour	UNP/LNO	BC	New Westminster	92 G/6	49°23′	123°26′
Gambier Island	ISL/ÎLE	BC	New Westminster	92 G/6	49°30′	123°23′
Gamble Lake	LAKE/LAC	BC	Range 4 Coast	103 H/11	53°31′	129°24′
Gambler	UNP/LNO	MB	19-29-W	62 K/11	50°36′	101°23′
Gambler 63	IR/RI	MB		62 K/11	50°36′	101°23′
Gambles Corner	UNP/LNO	PE	Prince	11 L/5	46°16′	63°31′
Gambo	TOWN/VIL2	NF		2 D/16	48°47′	54°13′
Gambo	UNP/LNO	NF		2 D/16	48°47′	54°13′
Gambo Pond	UNP/LNO	NF		2 D/9	48°45′	54°13′

NAME / NOM	ENTITY / ENTITÉ	LOC 1 / LIEU 1	LOC 2 / LIEU 2	MAP / CARTE	POSITION LAT	POSITION LONG
Gambo Pond	LAKE/LAC	NF		2 D/9	48°40′	54°20′
Gambo South	UNP/LNO	NF		2 D/16	48°46′	54°14′
Gamebridge	UNP/LNO	ON	Ontario	31 D/6	44°30′	79°09′
Gamebridge Beach	UNP/LNO	ON	Ontario	31 D/11	44°30′	79°12′
Gamebridge East	UNP/LNO	ON	Ontario	31 D/6	44°30′	79°09′
Gamebridge Station	UNP/LNO	ON	Ontario	31 D/6	44°30′	79°10′
Gameland	UNP/LNO	ON	Rainy River	52 D/16	48°50′	94°25′
Gammon River	RIV/CDE	MB/ON		52 M/5	51°24′	95°45′
Gamsby	UNP/LNO	ON	Thunder Bay	42 F/12	49°33′	85°52′
Gamsby Lake	LAKE/LAC	ON	Thunder Bay	42 E/11	49°31′	87°11′
Gamsby River	RIV/CDE	BC	Range 4 Coast	93 E/6	53°28′	127°26′
Gananoque	TOWN/VIL2	ON	Leeds	31 C/8	44°20′	76°10′
Gananoque Junction	UNP/LNO	ON	Leeds	31 C/8	44°22′	76°10′
Gananoque Lake	LAKE/LAC	ON	Leeds	31 C/8	44°27′	76°09′
Gananoque River	RIV/CDE	ON	Leeds	31 C/8	44°20′	76°10′
Ganaraska River	RIV/CDE	ON	Durham	30 M/16	43°57′	78°18′
Gander	TOWN/VIL2	NF		2 D/15	48°57′	54°37′
Gander, Base des Forces canadiennes - also-aussi - Gander, Canadian Forces Base	MIL/MIL	NF		2 D/15	48°57′	54°35′
Gander Bay	UNP/LNO	NF		2 E/8	49°18′	54°29′
Gander Bay	BAY/BAIE	NF		2 E/8	49°25′	54°28′
Gander Bay North	UNP/LNO	NF		2 E/8	49°21′	54°29′
Gander Bay South	UNP/LNO	NF		2 E/8	49°17′	54°29′
Gander Bay South	UNP/LNO	NF		2 E/8	49°17′	54°29′
Gander, Canadian Forces Base - also-aussi - Gander, Base des Forces canadiennes	MIL/MIL	NF		2 D/15	48°57′	54°35′
Gander Island	ISL/ÎLE	NF		2 E/8	49°28′	54°24′
Gander Island 14	IR/RI	BC	Range 3 Coast	103 A/11	52°40′	129°25′
Gander Lake	LAKE/LAC	NF		2 D/15	48°55′	54°35′
Gander River	RIV/CDE	NF		2 E/8	49°16′	54°30′
Ganges	UNP/LNO	BC	Saltspring Island	92 B/14	48°51′	123°30′
Gang Ranch	UNP/LNO	BC	Lillooet	92 O/9	51°33′	122°20′
Gannet Point	CAPE/CAP	NS	Guysborough	11 F/7	45°17′	60°57′
Gannet Rock	SHL/H-FD	NB	Charlotte	21 B/10	44°31′	66°47′
Gannett Creek	RIV/CDE	BC	Kamloops Division Yale	82 M/6	51°24′	119°25′
Gannon Beach	UNP/LNO	ON	Peterborough	31 D/8	44°28′	78°27′
Gannon Road	UNP/LNO	NS	Cape Breton	11 K/1	46°13′	60°15′
Gannon Village	UNP/LNO	ON	Peterborough	31 D/8	44°28′	78°27′
Gaotanaga, Lac	LAKE/LAC	QC	Témiscamingue	31 N/12	47°38′	77°36′
Gap	UNP/LNO	AB	24-9-W5	82 O/3	51°03′	115°16′
Gap Creek	RIV/CDE	SK	29-11-26-W3	72 F/13	49°56′	109°31′
Gap-E, La	UNP/LNO	QC	Antoine-Labelle	31 O/4	47°01′	75°48′
Gap, La	UNP/LNO	QC	La Matapédia	22 B/12	48°35′	67°35′
Gapview	UNP/LNO	SK	1-10-7-W2	62 E/15	49°48′	102°50′
Garafraxa Woods	UNP/LNO	ON	Dufferin	40 P/16	43°54′	80°08′
Garbitt	UNP/LNO	BC	Peace River	93 O/7	55°29′	122°47′
Garde, Lac la	LAKE/LAC	QC	Témiscamingue	31 L/16	46°46′	78°15′
Garde Lake	LAKE/LAC	NT	Mackenzie	75 J	62°50′	106°15′
Garden 2	IR/RI	BC	Range 3 Coast	92 N/8	51°29′	124°03′
Garden 2A	IR/RI	BC	Range 3 Coast	92 N/8	51°26′	124°03′
Garden Bay	UNP/LNO	BC	New Westminster	92 F/9	49°38′	124°02′
Garden City	UNP/LNO	MB		62 H/14	49°57′	97°09′
Garden Cove	UNP/LNO	NF		1 M/16	47°51′	54°10′
Garden Creek	UNP/LNO	NB	York	21 G/15	45°58′	66°42′
Garden Creek	UNP/LNO	AB	7-112-23-W4	84 I/12	58°42′	113°53′
Garden Grove	UNP/LNO	MB		62 H/14	49°57′	97°13′
Garden Head	UNP/LNO	SK	10-10-20-W3	72 F/15	49°48′	108°38′
Garden Hill	UNP/LNO	ON	Durham	31 D/1	44°03′	78°24′
Garden Hill	UNP/LNO	MB		53 E/15	53°53′	94°39′
Gardenia Lake	LAKE/LAC	NT	Mackenzie	75 I	62°00′	105°59′
Garden Lake	LAKE/LAC	ON	Thunder Bay	52 H/12	49°32′	89°48′
Garden Lots	UNP/LNO	NS	Lunenburg	21 A/8	44°22′	64°18′
Garden of Eden	UNP/LNO	NS	Pictou	11 E/8	45°26′	62°19′
Garden of Eden	UNP/LNO	ON	Renfrew	31 F/10	45°33′	76°45′
Garden Plain	UNP/LNO	AB	32-33-13-W4	72 M/13	51°52′	111°47′
Garden River	UNP/LNO	ON	Algoma	41 K/9	46°33′	84°10′
Garden River	RIV/CDE	ON	Algoma	41 K/9	46°32′	84°09′
Garden River	RIV/CDE	SK	20-49-23-W2	73 H/3	53°15′	105°19′
Garden River 14	IR/RI	ON	Algoma	41 K/9	46°33′	84°06′
Garden River No. 490	MUN2/AZM2	SK		73 H/6	53°20′	105°20′
Garden Road	UNP/LNO	NB	Northumberland	21 I/13	46°56′	65°51′
Gardenton	UNP/LNO	MB	35-1-6-E	62 H/2	49°05′	96°42′
Gardenview	UNP/LNO	AB	32-57-4-W5	83 G/15	53°59′	114°33′
Garden Village	UNP/LNO	ON	Nipissing	31 L/5	46°19′	79°52′
Garden Village	UNP/LNO	BC	New Westminster	92 G/3	49°14′	123°00′
Gardenville	UNP/LNO	ON	Prince Edward	31 C/4	44°02′	77°35′
Gardiner	UNP/LNO	ON	Cochrane	42 H/6	49°18′	81°02′

NAME NOM	ENTITY ENTITÉ	LOC 1 LIEU 1	LOC 2 LIEU 2	MAP CARTE	POSITION LAT	LONG
Gardiner Dam	MISC/DIV	SK		72 O/7	51°16′	106°52′
Gardiner Heights	UNP/LNO	SK		72 I/7	50°26′	104°33′
Gardiner Lake	LAKE/LAC	NT	Mackenzie	75 A	60°32′	105°55′
Gardiner Lakes	LAKE/LAC	AB	98,99-16-W4	84 H/9	57°32′	112°30′
Gardiner Mines	UNP/LNO	NS	Cape Breton	11 K/1	46°13′	60°03′
Gardiner Park	UNP/LNO	SK		72 I/7	50°27′	104°33′
Gardiner Point	CAPE/CAP	NT	Franklin	89 B	76°07′	117°40′
Gardner Brook	RIV/CDE	NF		2 D/5	48°22′	55°42′
Gardner Canal	CHAN/CHEN	BC	Range 4 Coast	103 H/8	53°27′	128°25′
Gardner Creek	UNP/LNO	NB	Saint John	21 H/5	45°16′	65°44′
Gardner Creek	RIV/CDE	NB	Saint John	21 H/5	45°17′	65°43′
Gardners Mills	UNP/LNO	NS	Yarmouth	21 A/4	44°02′	65°58′
Gardom Lake	LAKE/LAC	BC	Kamloops Division Yale	82 L/11	50°36′	119°11′
Garemand, Lac	LAKE/LAC	QC	Sept-Rivières	22 O/3	51°06′	67°12′
Garfield	UNP/LNO	PE	Queens	11 L/2	46°03′	62°52′
Garfield	UNP/LNO	AB	20-30-3-W5	82 O/9	51°35′	114°23′
Garfield Range	MTN/MNT	NT	Franklin	340 D	81°48′	72°40′
Gargamelle	UNP/LNO	NF		12 I/11	50°42′	57°21′
Gargantua	UNP/LNO	ON	Algoma	41 N/10	47°34′	84°58′
Gargantua, Cape	CAPE/CAP	ON	Algoma	41 N/11	47°36′	85°02′
Garia Bay	BAY/BAIE	NF		11 O/10	47°41′	58°33′
Garia Brook	RIV/CDE	NF		11 O/10	47°44′	58°32′
Garibaldi	UNP/LNO	BC	New Westminster	92 G/14	49°58′	123°09′
Garibaldi Estates	UNP/LNO	BC	New Westminster	92 G/11	49°44′	123°08′
Garibaldi Lake	LAKE/LAC	BC	New Westminster	92 G/14	49°56′	123°02′
Garibaldi, Mount	MTN/MNT	BC	New Westminster	92 G/14	49°51′	123°00′
Garibaldi Névé	GLAC/GLAC	BC	New Westminster	92 G/15	49°51′	122°59′
Garin	UNP/LNO	QC	Bonaventure	22 A/3	48°11′	65°27′
Garin, Rivière	RIV/CDE	QC	Bonaventure	22 A/6	48°18′	65°29′
Garland	UNP/LNO	NS	Kings	21 H/2	45°06′	64°46′
Garland	UNP/LNO	MB	12,13-31-22-W	62 N/9	51°39′	100°28′
Garland River	RIV/CDE	MB	9-34-20-W	62 N/16	51°55′	100°14′
Garlands Crossing	UNP/LNO	NS	Hants	21 A/16	44°58′	64°06′
Garlep Point	CAPE/CAP	NF		1 N/14	47°55′	53°23′
Garneau, Lac	LAKE/LAC	QC	Minganie	12 M/11	51°43′	63°22′
Garneau, Rivière	RIV/CDE	QC	Minganie	12 M/6	51°18′	63°24′
Garner Lake	LAKE/LAC	AB	60-12-W4	73 L/4	54°12′	111°44′
Garner Lake Provincial Park	PARK/PARC	AB	16-60-12-W4	73 L/4	54°11′	111°44′
Garners Corners	UNP/LNO	ON	Wentworth	30 M/4	43°12′	79°57′
Garnet	UNP/LNO	ON	Haldimand	40 I/16	42°55′	80°05′
Garnet Bay	BAY/BAIE	NT	Franklin	36 G	65°18′	75°22′
Garnett Settlement	UNP/LNO	NB	Saint John	21 H/5	45°18′	65°51′
Garnet Valley	UNP/LNO	BC	Osoyoos Division Yale	82 E/12	49°39′	119°43′
Garnham Lake	LAKE/LAC	ON	Thunder Bay	42 F/3	49°01′	85°29′
Garnier	UNP/LNO	QC	Antoine-Labelle	31 J/11	46°39′	75°29′
Garnier Bay	BAY/BAIE	NT	Franklin	58 F	74°00′	92°10′
Garnish	TOWN/VIL2	NF		1 M/3	47°08′	55°06′
Garnish Pond	LAKE/LAC	NF		1 M/3	47°12′	55°13′
Garrett Island	ISL/ÎLE	NT	Franklin	68 E	74°45′	98°15′
Garrett Lake	LAKE/LAC	ON	Kenora	53 G/10	53°39′	90°59′
Garretton	UNP/LNO	ON	Grenville	31 B/13	44°50′	75°40′
Garretts Cove	UNP/LNO	NF		1 N/13	47°51′	53°44′
Garrick	HAM/HAM	SK	17-52-16-W2	73 H/8	53°29′	104°20′
Garrick Corners	UNP/LNO	QC	Brome-Missisquoi	31 H/2	45°07′	72°50′
Garrington	UNP/LNO	AB	24-34-4-W5	82 O/16	51°56′	114°26′
Garry Bay	BAY/BAIE	NT	Franklin	47 B	68°55′	85°10′
Garry, Cape	CAPE/CAP	NT	Franklin	58 B	72°28′	93°25′
Garry Island	ISL/ÎLE	NT	Mackenzie	107 C	69°26′	135°41′
Garry Lake	LAKE/LAC	NT	Keewatin	66 F	65°58′	100°18′
Garry, Loch	LAKE/LAC	ON	Glengarry	31 G/7	45°15′	74°43′
Garry No. 245	MUN2/AZM2	SK		62 M/2	51°15′	103°00′
Garryowen	UNP/LNO	ON	Grey	41 A/10	44°37′	80°49′
Garson	VILG/VILG	MB	4,9-13-6-E	62 I/2	50°05′	96°42′
Garson	UNP/LNO	ON	Sudbury	41 I/10	46°33′	80°52′
Garson Junction	UNP/LNO	ON	Sudbury	41 I/10	46°32′	80°55′
Garson Lake	HAM/HAM	SK		74 C/5	56°19′	109°58′
Garson Lake	LAKE/LAC	AB/SK		74 D/8	56°19′	110°02′
Garson Mine - see-voir - Garson	UNP/LNO	ON		41 I/10	46°33′	80°52′
Garson Quarry Station	UNP/LNO	MB	13-13-5-E	62 I/2	50°06′	96°42′
Garson River	RIV/CDE	SK		74 C/3	56°14′	109°29′
Garth	UNP/LNO	AB	12-39-8-W5	83 B/6	52°21′	115°01′
Garthby	VILG/VILG	QC	L'Amiante	21 E/14	45°50′	71°23′
Garthland	UNP/LNO	SK	22-46-3-W3	73 B/16	52°59′	106°20′
Gartly	UNP/LNO	AB	11-30-19-W4	82 P/10	51°34′	112°35′
Garwood	UNP/LNO	SK	1-8-14-W2	62 E/12	49°37′	103°47′

NAME / NOM	ENTITY / ENTITÉ	LOC 1 / LIEU 1	LOC 2 / LIEU 2	MAP / CARTE	POSITION LAT	LONG
Gascoigne	UNP/LNO	SK	27-20-28-W3	72 K/12	50°44′	109°47′
Gascons-Est	UNP/LNO	QC	Pabok	22 A/2	48°13′	64°48′
Gascons-Ouest	UNP/LNO	QC	Pabok	22 A/2	48°11′	64°54′
Gasket Island	ISL/ÎLE	NT	Keewatin	43 A	52°25′	80°15′
Gaskiers	UNP/LNO	NF		1 K/13	46°52′	53°37′
Gaskiers-Point La Haye	VILG/VILG	NF		1 K/13	46°53′	53°37′
Gasline	UNP/LNO	ON	Welland	30 L/14	42°53′	79°11′
Gaspard Creek	RIV/CDE	BC	Lillooet	92 O/9	51°34′	122°18′
Gasparin, Lac	LAKE/LAC	QC	Jamésie	33 A/13	52°59′	73°45′
Gaspé	CITY/VIL1	QC	La Côte-de-Gaspé	22 A/16	48°50′	64°29′
Gaspé, Baie de	BAY/BAIE	QC	La Côte-de-Gaspé	22 A/16	48°46′	64°17′
Gaspé, Cap	CAPE/CAP	QC	La Côte-de-Gaspé	22 A/16	48°45′	64°10′
Gaspé, Cuvette de	SEAU/SMER	—		801-A	48°43′	64°10′
Gaspé Harbour	UNP/LNO	QC	La Côte-de-Gaspé	22 A/16	48°49′	64°29′
Gaspé, Havre de	BAY/BAIE	QC	La Côte-de-Gaspé	22 A/16	48°51′	64°27′
Gaspé-Ouest	UNP/LNO	QC	La Côte-de-Gaspé	22 A/15	48°49′	64°32′
Gaspereau	UNP/LNO	NS	Kings	21 H/1	45°04′	64°21′
Gaspereau	UNP/LNO	NB	Gloucester	21 P/10	47°36′	64°58′
Gaspereau Forks	UNP/LNO	NB	Queens	21 I/4	46°14′	65°51′
Gaspereau Lake	LAKE/LAC	NS	Kings	21 A/15	44°58′	64°33′
Gaspereau Lake	LAKE/LAC	NS	Digby	21 B/1	44°06′	66°07′
Gaspereau Mountain	UNP/LNO	NS	Kings	21 H/1	45°03′	64°20′
Gaspereau River	RIV/CDE	NS	Kings	21 H/1	45°07′	64°17′
Gaspereau River	RIV/CDE	NB	Westmorland	21 I/1	46°03′	64°05′
Gaspereau River	RIV/CDE	NB	Queens	21 I/4	46°14′	65°51′
Gaspereaux	UNP/LNO	PE	Kings	11 L/1	46°06′	62°28′
Gaspésie — Îles-de-la-Madeleine	MUN1/AZM1	QC	La Côte-de-Gaspé	22 A/11	48°42′	65°25′
Gaspésie, Parc de conservation de la	PARK/PARC	QC	Denis-Riverin	22 A/13	48°52′	65°58′
Gaspésie, Péninsule de la	CAPE/CAP	QC	Denis-Riverin	22 A/12	48°40′	66°00′
Gassend Lake	LAKE/LAC	NT	Mackenzie	97 B	68°00′	126°06′
Gasters	UNP/LNO	NF		1 N/6	47°27′	53°10′
Gatacre Point	CAPE/CAP	ON	Manitoulin	41 H/15	45°45′	82°38′
Gataga Mountain	MTN/MNT	BC	Cassiar	94 L/10	58°39′	126°50′
Gataga River	RIV/CDE	BC	Cassiar	94 L/10	58°35′	126°55′
Gatchell	UNP/LNO	ON	Sudbury	41 I/6	46°29′	81°02′
Gates	UNP/LNO	BC	Lillooet	92 J/10	50°30′	122°32′
Gates Creek	RIV/CDE	BC	Osoyoos Division Yale	82 L/9	50°38′	118°22′
Gateshead Island	ISL/ÎLE	NT	Franklin	67 F	70°36′	100°26′
Gateway	UNP/LNO	ON	Nipissing	31 L/6	46°20′	79°28′
Gateway	UNP/LNO	BC	Lillooet	92 P/11	51°40′	121°13′
Gathto Creek	RIV/CDE	BC	Peace River	94 J/5	58°16′	123°37′
Gatine	UNP/LNO	AB	7-29-21-W4	82 P/7	51°28′	112°55′
Gatineau	CITY/VIL1	QC	Communauté urbaine de l'Outaouais	31 G/12	45°30′	75°39′
Gatineau, Parc de la - also-aussi - Gatineau Park	PARK/PARC	QC	Les Collines-de-l'Outaouais	31 G/12	45°34′	75°57′
Gatineau Park - also-aussi - Gatineau, Parc de la	PARK/PARC	QC	Les Collines-de-l'Outaouais	31 G/12	45°34′	75°57′
Gatineau, Rivière	RIV/CDE	QC	Communauté urbaine de l'Outaouais	31 G/5	45°27′	75°42′
Gatineau, Ruisseau	RIV/CDE	QC	La Vallée-de-la-Gatineau	31 G/13	45°57′	75°49′
Gaud Corners	UNP/LNO	ON	Durham	30 M/15	43°56′	78°43′
Gaudreault, Lac	LAKE/LAC	QC	Minganie	12 L/16	50°52′	62°15′
Gauer Lake	LAKE/LAC	MB		64 H/4	57°00′	97°50′
Gauer River	RIV/CDE	MB		64 H/5	57°22′	97°33′
Gaulin	UNP/LNO	QC	Le Haut-Saint-François	21 E/5	45°22′	71°48′
Gaultois	TOWN/VIL2	NF		1 M/12	47°36′	55°54′
Gauthier	MUN2/AZM2	ON	Timiskaming	32 D/4	48°09′	79°49′
Gauthier	UNP/LNO	QC	Pabok	22 A/7	48°23′	64°39′
Gautier	UNP/LNO	MB	23-13-20-W	62 K/1	50°07′	100°06′
Gautreau Village	UNP/LNO	NB	Westmorland	21 H/15	45°58′	64°39′
Gauvin	UNP/LNO	QC	Avignon	22 B/1	48°12′	66°02′
Gauvreau	UNP/LNO	NB	Gloucester	21 P/10	47°32′	64°59′
Gavelton	UNP/LNO	NS	Yarmouth	20 P/13	43°54′	65°57′
Gayford	UNP/LNO	AB	28-26-25-W4	82 P/3	51°14′	113°26′
Gayhurst-Partie-Sud-Est	VILG/VILG	QC	Le Granit	21 E/10	45°44′	70°44′
Gayna River	RIV/CDE	NT	Mackenzie	106 H/6	65°25′	129°07′
Gayot, Lac	LAKE/LAC	QC	Kativik	23 M/10	55°43′	70°52′
Gayside - see-voir - Baytona	VILG/VILG	NF		2 E/7	49°20′	54°46′
Gays River	UNP/LNO	NS	Colchester	11 E/3	45°02′	63°21′
Gaythorne	UNP/LNO	NB	Northumberland	21 P/6	47°21′	65°04′
Gaytons	UNP/LNO	NB	Westmorland	21 I/2	46°02′	64°34′
Geary	UNP/LNO	NB	Sunbury	21 G/16	45°46′	66°29′
Geco	UNP/LNO	ON	Thunder Bay	42 F/4	49°10′	85°46′
Geelmuyden, Cape	CAPE/CAP	NT	Franklin	77 H/16	71°58′	104°46′
Gegogan, Cape	CAPE/CAP	NS	Guysborough	11 F/4	45°02′	61°55′
Geikie	UNP/LNO	AB	17-45-2-W6	83 D/16	52°52′	118°16′
Geikie Island	ISL/ÎLE	ON	Thunder Bay	52 I/2	50°00′	88°35′
Geikie River	RIV/CDE	SK		64 E/12	57°45′	103°52′

NAME NOM	ENTITY ENTITÉ	LOC 1 LIEU 1	LOC 2 LIEU 2	MAP CARTE	POSITION LAT	LONG
Geillini Lake	LAKE/LAC	NT	Keewatin	55 D	60°16′	95°35′
Geillini River	RIV/CDE	NT	Keewatin	55 D	60°10′	94°43′
Gelangle 1 - see-voir - Dzitline Lee 9	IR/RI	BC		93 K/14	54°52′	125°08′
Gelert	UNP/LNO	ON	Haliburton	31 D/15	44°54′	78°37′
Gellatly	UNP/LNO	BC	Osoyoos Division Yale	82 E/13	49°49′	119°37′
Gem	UNP/LNO	AB	8-23-16-W4	82 I/16	50°57′	112°11′
Gendreau	UNP/LNO	QC	Témiscamingue	31 L/14	46°47′	79°01′
Gendron	UNP/LNO	QC	Maskinongé	31 I/6	46°25′	73°08′
Genelle	UNP/LNO	BC	Kootenay	82 F/4	49°13′	117°42′
Général-Allard, Mont du	MTN/MNT	QC	La Jacques-Cartier	21 M/4	47°01′	71°35′
Generator Lake	LAKE/LAC	NT	Franklin	27 C/12	69°36′	71°50′
Genesee	UNP/LNO	AB	27-50-3-W5	83 G/8	53°21′	114°20′
Geneva	UNP/LNO	QC	Argenteuil	31 G/9	45°36′	74°21′
Geneva	UNP/LNO	ON	Sudbury	41 I/13	46°45′	81°34′
Geneva Park	UNP/LNO	ON	Ontario	31 D/11	44°40′	79°21′
Genévrier-Farm	UNP/LNO	QC	Minganie	12 P/12	51°42′	57°36′
Genévriers, Île des	ISL/ÎLE	QC	Côte-Nord-du-Golfe-Saint-Laurent	12 O/8	51°15′	58°26′
Genier	UNP/LNO	ON	Cochrane	42 H/3	49°10′	81°01′
Genoa Bay	UNP/LNO	BC	Cowichan	92 B/13	48°46′	123°36′
Gensart, Lac	LAKE/LAC	QC	Caniapiscau	23 B/13	52°45′	67°53′
Gens de Terre, Rivière	RIV/CDE	QC	Antoine-Labelle	31 K/16	46°53′	76°01′
Gentilly	UNP/LNO	QC	Bécancour	31 I/8	46°24′	72°17′
Gentilly, Rivière	RIV/CDE	QC	Bécancour	31 I/8	46°24′	72°21′
Geoffroy	UNP/LNO	QC	Témiscamingue	31 M/6	47°29′	79°13′
Geologist Bay	BAY/BAIE	NT	Franklin	59 F	78°33′	95°56′
George	UNP/LNO	ON	Thunder Bay	52 G/1	49°13′	90°29′
George Bay	BAY/BAIE	NT	Franklin	25 M	63°29′	71°28′
George, Cape	CAPE/CAP	NS	Antigonish	11 F/13	45°52′	61°58′
George, Cape	CAPE/CAP	BC	Range 5 Coast	103 G/15	53°51′	130°42′
Georgefield	UNP/LNO	NS	Hants	11 E/4	45°12′	63°33′
George Fraser Islands	ISL/ÎLE	BC	Clayoquot	92 C/13	48°54′	125°31′
George Island	ISL/ÎLE	NF		13 I/6	54°16′	57°20′
George Island	ISL/ÎLE	ON	Manitoulin	41 H/13	45°58′	81°31′
George Island	ISL/ÎLE	SK		64 L/3	58°15′	103°12′
George Island	ISL/ÎLE	SK		63 L/14	54°55′	103°13′
George Island	ISL/ÎLE	NT	Franklin	77 F	70°18′	112°00′
George, Lake	LAKE/LAC	NS	Digby	21 B/1	44°00′	66°03′
George, Lake	LAKE/LAC	NB	York	21 G/14	45°49′	67°03′
George, Lake	LAKE/LAC	ON	Algoma	41 K/8	46°26′	84°06′
George Lake	LAKE/LAC	MB	14,15-15-E	52 L/6	50°15′	95°30′
George Lake	LAKE/LAC	SK		74 B/1	56°14′	106°20′
George Lake	LAKE/LAC	SK	17-40-25-W3	73 C/5	52°27′	109°34′
George-Nother Ground	UNP/LNO	QC	Minganie	12 P/13	51°49′	57°40′
George Passage	CHAN/CHEN	BC	Range 1 Coast	92 L/10	50°41′	126°50′
George Richards, Cape	CAPE/CAP	NT	Franklin	79 B	76°51′	108°45′
George River	UNP/LNO	BC	Range 1 Coast	92 K/12	50°34′	125°32′
George, Rivière	RIV/CDE	QC	Kativik	24 J/16	58°49′	66°10′
Georges, Banc de - also-aussi - Georges Bank	SEAU/SMER	—		8005	41°45′	67°00′
Georges Bank - also-aussi - Georges, Banc de	SEAU/SMER	—		8005	41°45′	67°00′
Georges Basin - also-aussi - Georges, Bassin de	SEAU/SMER	—		8005	42°25′	67°00′
Georges, Bassin de - also-aussi - Georges Basin	SEAU/SMER	—		8005	42°25′	67°00′
Georges Brook	UNP/LNO	NF		2 C/4	48°14′	53°58′
Georges Brook	RIV/CDE	NF		2 C/4	48°14′	53°58′
Georges-Côté, Lac	LAKE/LAC	QC	Vallée-de-l'Or	32 C/16	48°48′	76°09′
Georges Cove	UNP/LNO	NF		3 D/12	52°34′	55°46′
Georges Cove	UNP/LNO	NF		12 H/10	49°34′	56°50′
Georges Island National Historic Site - also-aussi - Île-Georges, Lieu historique national de l'	PARK/PARC	NS	Halifax	11 D/12	44°38′	63°34′
Georges Lake	UNP/LNO	NF		12 B/9	48°44′	58°11′
Georges Lake	LAKE/LAC	NF		12 B/9	48°45′	58°10′
Georges Pond	LAKE/LAC	NF		2 D/8	48°16′	54°04′
Georges Pond	LAKE/LAC	NF		2 D/5	48°20′	55°59′
Georges River	UNP/LNO	NS	Cape Breton	11 K/1	46°12′	60°20′
Georgestown	UNP/LNO	NF		1 N/10	47°34′	52°44′
Georgetown	TOWN/VIL2	PE	Kings	11 L/2	46°11′	62°32′
Georgetown	UNP/LNO	NF		1 N/11	47°30′	53°13′
Georgetown	UNP/LNO	NF		12 B/16	48°57′	58°01′
Georgetown	UNP/LNO	ON	Halton	30 M/12	43°39′	79°55′
Georgetown	GEOG/GÉOG	PE	Kings	11 L/2	46°12′	62°32′
Georgetown Mills	UNP/LNO	BC	Range 5 Coast	103 J/8	54°28′	130°24′
Georgeville	UNP/LNO	NS	Antigonish	11 E/16	45°49′	62°02′
Georgeville	UNP/LNO	QC	Memphrémagog	31 H/1	45°08′	72°15′
Georgian Bay	MUN2/AZM2	ON	Muskoka	31 E/4	45°00′	79°50′
Georgian Bay - also-aussi - **Georgienne, Baie**	BAY/BAIE	ON		41 H	45°15′	80°45′
Georgian Bay Islands National Park - also-aussi - Îles-de-la-Baie-Georgienne, Parc national des	PARK/PARC	ON	Muskoka	31 D/13	44°53′	79°52′
Georgian Beach	UNP/LNO	ON	Grey	41 A/10	44°39′	80°38′

NAME NOM	ENTITY ENTITÉ	LOC 1 LIEU 1	LOC 2 LIEU 2	MAP CARTE	POSITION LAT	LONG
Georgian Heights	UNP/LNO	ON	Simcoe	41 A/9	44°36′	80°00′
Georgian Highlands	UNP/LNO	ON	Simcoe	41 A/16	44°46′	80°08′
Georgian Inlet	UNP/LNO	ON	Parry Sound	41 H/10	45°37′	80°31′
Georgian Sands Beach	UNP/LNO	ON	Simcoe	41 A/9	44°44′	80°05′
Georgia, Strait of	CHAN/CHEN	BC	Nanaimo	92 F/8	49°30′	124°00′
Georgie 17	IR/RI	BC	Cassiar	103 O/9	55°42′	130°06′
Georgie Lake	LAKE/LAC	BC	Rupert	92 L/12	50°45′	127°40′
Georgienne, Baie - also-aussi - **Georgian Bay**	BAY/BAIE	ON		41 H	45°15′	80°45′
Georgina	TOWN/VIL2	ON	York	31 D/3	44°15′	79°19′
Georgina Beach	UNP/LNO	ON	Simcoe	31 D/12	44°38′	79°59′
Georgina Island	UNP/LNO	ON	York	31 D/6	44°22′	79°19′
Georgina Island	ISL/ÎLE	ON	York	31 D/6	44°22′	79°17′
Gerald	VILG/VILG	SK	25-19-32-W	62 K/12	50°40′	101°48′
Gerald Island	ISL/ÎLE	BC	Nanaimo	92 F/8	49°19′	124°10′
Geraldton	TOWN/VIL2	ON	Thunder Bay	42 E/10	49°44′	86°57′
Gérard-Morisset, Mont	MTN/MNT	QC	La Côte-de-Beaupré	21 M/3	47°12′	71°01′
Gergovia	UNP/LNO	SK		72 G/3	49°11′	107°25′
Gerido, Lac	LAKE/LAC	QC	Kativik	24 K/4	58°05′	69°50′
Gérin	UNP/LNO	QC	Maskinongé	31 I/6	46°16′	73°07′
Germaine, Lac	LAKE/LAC	QC	Caniapiscau	23 G/4	53°02′	67°40′
Germaine Lake	LAKE/LAC	NT	Mackenzie	85 O	63°18′	114°35′
Germain, Grand lac	LAKE/LAC	QC	Sept-Rivières	22 O/2	51°12′	66°40′
Germania	UNP/LNO	ON	Muskoka	31 D/14	44°57′	79°13′
Germanicus	UNP/LNO	ON	Renfrew	31 F/11	45°36′	77°11′
German Landing	UNP/LNO	ON	Northumberland	31 C/5	44°15′	77°40′
German Mills	UNP/LNO	ON	York	30 M/14	43°49′	79°22′
Germansen Lake	LAKE/LAC	BC	Cassiar	93 N/10	55°42′	124°49′
Germansen Landing	UNP/LNO	BC	Cassiar	93 N/15	55°47′	124°42′
German Settlement	UNP/LNO	ON	Renfrew	31 F/11	45°31′	77°27′
Germantown	UNP/LNO	NB	Albert	21 H/10	45°40′	64°49′
Germany	UNP/LNO	NB	Sunbury	21 G/10	45°34′	66°38′
Gernon Bay	BAY/BAIE	NT	Franklin	67 B	68°01′	103°15′
Gerrard	UNP/LNO	BC	Kootenay	82 K/11	50°31′	117°17′
Gerrish Valley	UNP/LNO	NS	Colchester	11 E/5	45°25′	63°59′
Gerrow's Beach	UNP/LNO	ON	Ontario	31 D/2	44°07′	78°56′
Gesgapegiag 2	IR/RI	QC	Avignon	22 A/4	48°12′	65°56′
Gesto	UNP/LNO	ON	Essex	40 J/2	42°08′	82°53′
Gething, Mount	MTN/MNT	BC	Peace River	94 B/1	56°02′	122°27′
Geyser	UNP/LNO	MB	23-22-3-E	62 I/14	50°55′	97°05′
Ghost Lake	VILG/VILG	AB	9-26-6-W5	82 O/2	51°12′	114°46′
Ghost Lake	LAKE/LAC	BC	Cariboo	93 A/15	52°56′	120°51′
Ghost Lake	LAKE/LAC	NT	Mackenzie	85 O/14	63°51′	115°10′
Ghost Pine Creek	UNP/LNO	AB	5-32-22-W4	82 P/11	51°43′	113°04′
Ghostpine Creek	RIV/CDE	AB	14-30-22-W4	82 P/10	51°34′	112°59′
Ghost River	UNP/LNO	ON	Cochrane	42 O/6	51°29′	83°25′
Ghost River	UNP/LNO	ON	Kenora	52 J/3	50°10′	91°27′
Ghost River	RIV/CDE	ON	Cochrane	32 D/12	48°37′	79°55′
Ghurka Lake	LAKE/LAC	NT	Mackenzie	76 F/3	65°01′	109°05′
Ghyvelde Lake	LAKE/LAC	NF		13 D/13	52°55′	63°51′
Giacomini Seamount	SEAU/SMER	—		5.03	56°25′	146°25′
Giants Causeway	CAPE/CAP	NT	Franklin	98 H	75°46′	121°17′
Giants Glen	UNP/LNO	NB	York	21 J/7	46°18′	66°47′
Giants Lake	UNP/LNO	NS	Guysborough	11 F/5	45°23′	61°51′
Giants Tomb Island	ISL/ÎLE	ON	Simcoe	31 D/13	44°55′	80°00′
Gibbon	UNP/LNO	NS	Cape Breton	11 K/1	46°06′	60°13′
Gibbon	UNP/LNO	NB	Kings	21 H/13	45°52′	65°33′
Gibbons	TOWN/VIL2	AB	10-56-23-W4	83 H/14	53°50′	113°20′
Gibbs	UNP/LNO	SK	28-22-21-W2	72 I/15	50°54′	104°52′
Gibbs	UNP/LNO	BC	Lillooet	92 I/12	50°45′	121°52′
Gibbs Fiord	BAY/BAIE	NT	Franklin	27 F	70°49′	71°55′
Giberson Settlement	UNP/LNO	NB	Carleton	21 J/12	46°33′	67°34′
Gibi Lake	LAKE/LAC	ON	Kenora	52 E/9	49°36′	94°08′
Gibraltar	UNP/LNO	QC	La Jacques-Cartier	21 L/13	46°54′	71°37′
Gibraltar	UNP/LNO	ON	Grey	41 A/8	44°26′	80°21′
Gibraltar	UNP/LNO	ON	Manitoulin	41 G/16	45°45′	82°06′
Gibraltar	UNP/LNO	BC	Cariboo	93 B/8	52°27′	122°24′
Gibraltar Island	ISL/ÎLE	BC	Barclay	92 C/14	48°55′	125°15′
Gibraltar Lake	LAKE/LAC	NS	Halifax	11 D/14	44°52′	63°15′
Gibraltar Point	CAPE/CAP	ON	York	30 M/11	43°36′	79°23′
Gibs Fiord	BAY/BAIE	NT	Franklin	49 G	79°53′	87°15′
Gibson	UNP/LNO	ON	Simcoe	31 D/12	44°37′	79°59′
Gibson 31 - see-voir - **Wahta Mohawk Territory**	IR/RI	ON		31 E/4	45°02′	79°44′
Gibson Bay	BAY/BAIE	NT	Franklin	36 F	65°16′	76°00′
Gibson Cove	BAY/BAIE	NT	Keewatin	46 L	66°31′	86°44′
Gibson Creek	UNP/LNO	BC	Kootenay	82 F/5	49°22′	117°40′

NAME NOM	ENTITY ENTITÉ	LOC 1 LIEU 1	LOC 2 LIEU 2	MAP CARTE	POSITION LAT	LONG
Gibson Creek	RIV/CDE	NB	Carleton	21 J/4	46°03′	67°33′
Gibson Island	ISL/ÎLE	NT	Franklin	57 G	71°47′	95°22′
Gibson Lake	LAKE/LAC	NT	Mackenzie	55 N	63°30′	93°12′
Gibson Peninsula	CAPE/CAP	NT	Franklin	57 B	68°48′	95°25′
Gibsons	TOWN/VIL2	BC	New Westminster	92 G/5	49°24′	123°30′
Gib, The	UNP/LNO	QC	Minganie	12 P/13	51°49′	57°32′
Giddie Point	CAPE/CAP	NT	Franklin	89 A	76°41′	115°53′
Giddy River	RIV/CDE	NT	Franklin	88 H	75°29′	116°17′
Gidley Point	CAPE/CAP	ON	Simcoe	41 A/9	44°45′	80°07′
Giffard	UNP/LNO	QC	Communauté urbaine de Québec	21 L/14	46°51′	71°12′
Giffard, Lac	LAKE/LAC	QC	Jamésie	32 N/2	51°08′	76°55′
Gifford	UNP/LNO	BC	New Westminster	92 G/1	49°06′	122°20′
Gifford Fiord	BAY/BAIE	NT	Franklin	47 E	70°10′	82°30′
Gifford Peninsula	CAPE/CAP	BC	New Westminster	92 K/2	50°04′	124°45′
Gifford Point	CAPE/CAP	NT	Franklin	58 F	74°10′	93°43′
Gifford River	RIV/CDE	NT	Franklin	47 E	70°19′	83°03′
Gift Lake	UNP/LNO	AB	28,33-79-12-W5	83 O/13	55°53′	115°49′
Gift Lake Metis Settlement	UNP/LNO	AB		83 O/13	55°52′	115°50′
Gignac	UNP/LNO	QC	Bonaventure	22 A/3	48°04′	65°08′
Gilbert Bay	BAY/BAIE	NF		13 A/9	52°38′	56°00′
Gilbert Lake	LAKE/LAC	NF		13 A/9	52°41′	56°14′
Gilbert Mills	UNP/LNO	ON	Prince Edward	31 C/3	44°03′	77°15′
Gilbert, Mount	MTN/MNT	BC	Range 1 Coast	92 K/16	50°52′	124°16′
Gilbert Mountain	UNP/LNO	NS	Cumberland	21 H/9	45°31′	64°13′
Gilbert Plains	VILG/VILG	MB	9-25-22-W	62 N/1	51°09′	100°29′
Gilbert Plains	MUN2/AZM2	MB		62 N/1	51°11′	100°25′
Gilbert River	RIV/CDE	NF		13 A/9	52°40′	56°07′
Gilberts Corner	UNP/LNO	NB	Westmorland	21 I/2	46°14′	64°34′
Gilberts Cove	UNP/LNO	NS	Digby	21 A/5	44°29′	65°57′
Gilbert Seamounts	SEAU/SMER	—		5.03	52°15′	149°00′
Gilberts Landing	UNP/LNO	NS	Digby	21 B/8	44°20′	66°17′
Gilberts Point	CAPE/CAP	NS	Digby	21 A/5	44°29′	65°57′
Gilbertville	UNP/LNO	ON	Norfolk	40 I/16	42°50′	80°29′
Gilby	UNP/LNO	AB	20-40-3-W5	83 B/8	52°28′	114°23′
Gilchrist	UNP/LNO	ON	Simcoe	31 D/5	44°27′	79°35′
Gilchrist Bay	UNP/LNO	ON	Peterborough	31 D/9	44°33′	78°06′
Gildale	UNP/LNO	ON	Grey	41 A/2	44°04′	80°32′
Gildersleve Lake	LAKE/LAC	BC	Range 2 Coast	92 M/13	51°57′	127°35′
Giles Lake	LAKE/LAC	SK		74 I/13	58°55′	105°48′
Gilford	UNP/LNO	ON	Simcoe	31 D/4	44°13′	79°33′
Gilford Beach	UNP/LNO	ON	Simcoe	31 D/4	44°14′	79°32′
Gilford Island	ISL/ÎLE	BC	Range 1 Coast	92 L/9	50°45′	126°20′
Gil Island	ISL/ÎLE	BC	Range 4 Coast	103 H/3	53°12′	129°14′
Gill	UNP/LNO	ON	Haldimand	30 L/13	42°56′	79°59′
Gillam	MUN2/AZM2	MB		54 D/8	56°28′	94°13′
Gillam	UNP/LNO	MB		54 D/7	56°21′	94°42′
Gillams	VILG/VILG	NF		12 G/1	49°01′	58°04′
Gillard's Cove	UNP/LNO	NF		2 E/10	49°37′	54°45′
Gillespie	UNP/LNO	SK	24-21-11-W2	62 L/14	50°49′	103°24′
Gillespie Lake	LAKE/LAC	AB	39,40-2-W4	73 D/8	52°25′	110°11′
Gillespie Settlement	UNP/LNO	NB	Victoria	21 J/13	46°57′	67°46′
Gillesport	UNP/LNO	NF		2 E/10	49°40′	54°45′
Gillfillan Lake	LAKE/LAC	NS	Yarmouth	20 P/13	43°57′	65°48′
Gillian, Lake	LAKE/LAC	NT	Franklin	37 D	69°33′	75°30′
Gillies	MUN2/AZM2	ON	Thunder Bay	52 A/5	48°16′	89°41′
Gillies	UNP/LNO	ON	Timiskaming	31 M/5	47°23′	79°45′
Gillies, Baie	BAY/BAIE	QC	Témiscamingue	31 M/6	47°27′	79°06′
Gillies Bay	UNP/LNO	BC	Texada Island	92 F/9	49°41′	124°29′
Gillies Corners	UNP/LNO	ON	Lanark	31 F/1	45°00′	76°06′
Gillies Depot	UNP/LNO	ON	Timiskaming	31 M/5	47°22′	79°45′
Gillies Hill	UNP/LNO	ON	Bruce	41 A/6	44°20′	81°11′
Gillies Island	ISL/ÎLE	NT	Keewatin	34 C/10	56°37′	76°39′
Gillies Lake	UNP/LNO	ON	Bruce	41 H/3	45°02′	81°20′
Gillies Lake	LAKE/LAC	ON	Bruce	41 H/3	45°12′	81°20′
Gilliland, Mount	MTN/MNT	YT		95 D/3	60°13′	127°21′
Gilling	UNP/LNO	NF		23 J/10	54°45′	66°47′
Gillinghams Pond	LAKE/LAC	NF		2 D/15	48°54′	54°45′
Gillis Cove	UNP/LNO	NS	Inverness	11 F/14	45°55′	61°03′
Gillisdale	UNP/LNO	NS	Inverness	11 K/3	46°14′	61°08′
Gillis Lake	UNP/LNO	NS	Cape Breton	11 K/1	46°03′	60°24′
Gill Island 2	IR/RI	BC	Range 4 Coast	103 H/11	53°39′	129°17′
Gillis Point	UNP/LNO	NS	Victoria	11 K/2	46°00′	60°48′
Gillis Point East	UNP/LNO	NS	Victoria	11 K/2	46°01′	60°47′
Gill Lake	LAKE/LAC	NT	Keewatin	55 K	62°27′	93°08′
Gillman, Cape	CAPE/CAP	NT	Franklin	78 H	75°02′	104°13′

NAME NOM	ENTITY ENTITÉ	LOC 1 LIEU 1	LOC 2 LIEU 2	MAP CARTE	POSITION	
					LAT	LONG
Gillson's Point	UNP/LNO	ON	Victoria	31 D/2	44°12′	78°55′
Gilman Corner	UNP/LNO	QC	Brome-Missisquoi	31 H/2	45°12′	72°40′
Gilmans Corner	UNP/LNO	NB	Charlotte	21 G/3	45°12′	67°08′
Gilmour	UNP/LNO	ON	Hastings	31 C/13	44°49′	77°37′
Gilmour Island	ISL/ÎLE	NT	Keewatin	44 P	59°48′	80°02′
Gilpin	UNP/LNO	BC	Similkameen Division Yale	82 E/1	49°01′	118°19′
Gilroy	UNP/LNO	SK	26-22-6-W3	72 J/15	50°54′	106°44′
Giltoyees 13	IR/RI	BC	Range 4 Coast	103 H/14	53°54′	129°01′
Gilttoyees Inlet	BAY/BAIE	BC	Range 4 Coast	103 H/15	53°50′	128°58′
Gimli	TOWN/VIL2	MB		62 I/10	50°38′	96°59′
Gimli	MUN2/AZM2	MB		62 I/11	50°40′	97°03′
Gin Cove	UNP/LNO	NF		2 C/4	48°12′	53°49′
Ginoogaming First Nation 77	IR/RI	ON	Thunder Bay	42 E/10	49°44′	86°31′
Gipouloux, Rivière	RIV/CDE	QC	Jamésie	33 B/12	52°36′	75°56′
Gipsy Lake	LAKE/LAC	AB	85,86-2-W4	74 D/8	56°25′	110°14′
Girard Creek	RIV/CDE	SK	20-1-26-W2	72 H/3	49°03′	105°27′
Girardin, Lac	LAKE/LAC	QC	Kativik	24 J/1	58°00′	66°02′
Girardville	VILG/VILG	QC	Maria-Chapdelaine	32 H/2	49°00′	72°33′
Girdwood	UNP/LNO	ON	Algoma	42 C/7	48°28′	84°46′
Girouard, Lac	LAKE/LAC	QC	La Haute-Côte-Nord	22 C/15	48°53′	68°58′
Girouard, Lac	LAKE/LAC	QC	Vallée-de-l'Or	32 C/8	48°28′	76°20′
Girouard Lake	LAKE/LAC	MB		63 N/6	55°29′	101°26′
Girouardville	UNP/LNO	NB	Kent	21 I/7	46°29′	64°44′
Giroux	UNP/LNO	MB	15,22-7-7-E	62 H/10	49°34′	96°34′
Giroux Lake	LAKE/LAC	ON	Parry Sound	41 H/9	45°43′	80°30′
Giroux Lake	LAKE/LAC	AB	65-20-W5	83 K/10	54°37′	116°58′
Giroux River	RIV/CDE	ON	Parry Sound	41 H/10	45°42′	80°36′
Girouxville	VILG/VILG	AB	16-78-22-W5	83 N/14	55°45′	117°20′
Girvin	VILG/VILG	SK	25-25-29-W2	72 P/4	51°09′	105°55′
Gisborne Lake	LAKE/LAC	NF		1 M/15	47°48′	54°49′
Giscome	UNP/LNO	BC	Cariboo	93 J/1	54°04′	122°22′
Gish Creek 45	IR/RI	BC	Cassiar	103 P/3	55°13′	129°11′
Gitandoiks 75	IR/RI	BC	Range 5 Coast	103 I/6	54°19′	129°13′
Gitandoiks 76	IR/RI	BC	Range 5 Coast	103 I/6	54°19′	129°12′
Gitanmaax 1	IR/RI	BC	Cassiar	93 M/5	55°16′	127°41′
Gitanyow 1	IR/RI	BC	Cassiar	103 P/8	55°16′	128°04′
Gitanyow 2	IR/RI	BC	Cassiar	103 P/1	55°10′	128°02′
Gitanyow 3A	IR/RI	BC	Cassiar	103 P/8	55°19′	128°06′
Gitche Lake	LAKE/LAC	ON	Kenora	52 O/12	51°30′	91°40′
Gitche River	RIV/CDE	ON	Kenora	52 O/11	51°39′	91°00′
Gîte-du-Mont-Albert, Le	UNP/LNO	QC	Denis-Riverin	22 B/16	48°57′	66°07′
Gitquinmiyaue 76	IR/RI	BC	Cassiar	103 P/6	55°25′	129°01′
Gitsegukla 1	IR/RI	BC	Cassiar	93 M/4	55°05′	127°49′
Gitsegukla Logging 3	IR/RI	BC	Cassiar	93 M/4	55°05′	127°50′
Gitsheoaksit 68	IR/RI	BC	Cassiar	103 P/7	55°28′	128°57′
Gitwangak 1	IR/RI	BC	Cassiar	103 P/1	55°06′	128°04′
Gitwangak 2	IR/RI	BC	Cassiar	103 P/1	55°05′	128°01′
Gitwinksihlkw	UNP/LNO	BC	Cassiar	103 P/3	55°12′	129°13′
Gitwinksihlkw 7	IR/RI	BC	Cassiar	103 P/3	55°12′	129°13′
Gitzault 24	IR/RI	BC	Cassiar	103 P/6	55°29′	129°29′
Gjoa Haven	HAM/HAM	NT	Franklin	57 B/12	68°38′	95°53′
Glace Bay	UNP/LNO	NS	Cape Breton	11 J/4	46°12′	59°57′
Glaces-Éternelles, Les	UNP/LNO	QC	Vallée-de-l'Or	32 C/6	48°16′	77°17′
Glacial Mountain	MTN/MNT	BC	Cassiar	104 I/3	58°15′	129°27′
Glacier	UNP/LNO	BC	Kootenay	82 N/5	51°16′	117°31′
Glacier Camp	UNP/LNO	BC	Cassiar	114 P/15	59°47′	136°36′
Glacière, La	UNP/LNO	QC	La Jacques-Cartier	21 L/13	46°55′	71°30′
Glacière, La	UNP/LNO	QC	Jamésie	32 G/9	49°33′	74°20′
Glacier Fiord	BAY/BAIE	NT	Franklin	59 E	78°22′	89°29′
Glacier Lake	LAKE/LAC	BC	New Westminster	92 G/16	49°53′	122°27′
Glacier National Park - also-aussi - Glaciers, Parc national des	PARK/PARC	BC	Kootenay	82 N/5	51°16′	117°31′
Glaciers, Parc national des - also-aussi - Glacier National Park	PARK/PARC	BC	Kootenay	82 N/5	51°16′	117°31′
Glacier Strait	CHAN/CHEN	NT	Franklin	39 B	76°12′	79°30′
Glackmeyer	MUN2/AZM2	ON	Cochrane	42 H/2	49°08′	81°00′
Glade	UNP/LNO	BC	Kootenay	82 F/5	49°24′	117°33′
Gladeside	UNP/LNO	NB	Kent	21 I/7	46°18′	64°53′
Gladmar	VILG/VILG	SK	34-2-19-W2	72 H/1	49°10′	104°27′
Gladmer	UNP/LNO	SK		73 B/2	52°06′	106°40′
Gladsheim Peak	MTN/MNT	BC	Kootenay	82 F/13	49°47′	117°38′
Gladstone	TOWN/VIL2	MB	14-11-W	62 J/2	50°14′	98°57′
Gladstone	UNP/LNO	PE	Kings	11 L/2	46°01′	62°34′
Gladstone	UNP/LNO	ON	Middlesex	40 I/14	42°55′	81°03′
Gladstone	GEOG/GÉOG	NB	Sunbury	21 G/10	45°37′	66°45′
Gladue Lake 105B	IR/RI	SK		73 K/8	54°28′	108°15′
Gladwick	UNP/LNO	ON	Sudbury	42 A/4	48°01′	81°59′

NAME NOM	ENTITY ENTITÉ	LOC 1 LIEU 1	LOC 2 LIEU 2	MAP CARTE	POSITION LAT	POSITION LONG
Gladwin	UNP/LNO	BC	Kamloops Division Yale	92 I/6	50°15′	121°30′
Gladwyn	UNP/LNO	NB	Victoria	21 J/13	46°46′	67°32′
Gladys	UNP/LNO	AB	29-20-27-W4	82 I/12	50°43′	113°42′
Gladys Lake	LAKE/LAC	BC	Cassiar	104 N/14	59°54′	132°52′
Gladys River	RIV/CDE	BC	Cassiar	104 N/7	59°48′	132°17′
Glaises, Les	UNP/LNO	QC	Denis-Riverin	22 G/1	49°02′	66°29′
Glamis	UNP/LNO	SK	7-28-13-W3	72 O/5	51°23′	107°50′
Glammis	UNP/LNO	ON	Bruce	41 A/3	44°12′	81°23′
Glamorgan	MUN2/AZM2	ON	Haliburton	31 D/16	44°54′	78°28′
Glamorgan	UNP/LNO	ON	Durham	31 D/2	44°06′	78°31′
Glamor Lake	LAKE/LAC	ON	Haliburton	31 D/16	44°57′	78°22′
Glanbrook	MUN2/AZM2	ON	Wentworth	30 M/4	43°08′	79°51′
Glandine	UNP/LNO	ON	Victoria	31 D/7	44°19′	78°48′
Glanford Station	UNP/LNO	ON	Wentworth	30 M/4	43°07′	79°53′
Glanmire	UNP/LNO	ON	Hastings	31 C/13	44°45′	77°41′
Glanworth	UNP/LNO	ON	Middlesex	40 I/14	42°52′	81°12′
Glascott	UNP/LNO	ON	Grey	41 A/7	44°19′	80°46′
Glasgow	UNP/LNO	NS	Cape Breton	11 K/2	46°03′	60°35′
Glasgow	UNP/LNO	ON	Ontario	30 M/14	44°00′	79°12′
Glasgow	UNP/LNO	ON	Peel	30 M/13	43°53′	79°46′
Glasgow Bay	BAY/BAIE	NT	Franklin	25 K	62°47′	69°46′
Glasgow Head	CAPE/CAP	NS	Guysborough	11 F/7	45°19′	60°58′
Glasgow Station	UNP/LNO	ON	Renfrew	31 F/7	45°27′	76°31′
Glaslyn	VILG/VILG	SK	36-50-17-W3	73 F/8	53°22′	108°21′
Glasnevin	UNP/LNO	SK	10-7-23-W2	72 H/11	49°33′	105°03′
Glass	UNP/LNO	MB	33-10-6-E	62 H/15	49°53′	96°44′
Glassburn	UNP/LNO	NS	Antigonish	11 F/12	45°31′	61°46′
Glassville	UNP/LNO	NB	Carleton	21 J/6	46°29′	67°25′
Glastonbury	UNP/LNO	ON	Lennox and Addington	31 C/11	44°44′	77°08′
Glatheli Lake	LAKE/LAC	BC	Range 4 Coast	93 E/9	53°37′	126°25′
Glaude	UNP/LNO	NB	Westmorland	21 I/1	46°11′	64°25′
Glazier Creek 12	IR/RI	BC	New Westminster	92 G/16	49°52′	122°27′
Gleam	UNP/LNO	BC	Peace River	94 H/11	57°32′	121°13′
Gleason, Cape	CAPE/CAP	NT	Franklin	340 D	81°10′	78°25′
Gleason Road	UNP/LNO	NB	Charlotte	21 G/6	45°19′	67°25′
Glebe Farm 40B	IR/RI	ON	Brant	40 P/1	43°08′	80°14′
Gledhow	UNP/LNO	SK	32-6-W3	72 O/15	51°47′	106°50′
Gleichen	TOWN/VIL2	AB	13-22-23-W4	82 I/14	50°52′	113°03′
Glen	UNP/LNO	ON	Grey	41 A/2	44°11′	80°41′
Glen Afton	UNP/LNO	ON	Sudbury	41 I/9	46°38′	80°17′
Glen Agar	UNP/LNO	ON	York	30 M/12	43°40′	79°33′
Glen Alda	UNP/LNO	ON	Peterborough	31 C/13	44°51′	77°57′
Glen Allan	UNP/LNO	ON	Wellington	40 P/10	43°39′	80°42′
Glen Almond	UNP/LNO	QC	Les Collines-de-l'Outaouais	31 G/11	45°42′	75°29′
Glen Alpine	UNP/LNO	NS	Antigonish	11 E/8	45°29′	62°00′
Glen Andrew	UNP/LNO	ON	Prescott	31 G/7	45°27′	74°31′
Glenannan	UNP/LNO	ON	Bruce	40 P/14	43°56′	81°17′
Glenannan	UNP/LNO	BC	Range 5 Coast	93 K/3	54°01′	125°00′
Glenarm	UNP/LNO	ON	Victoria	31 D/7	44°29′	78°53′
Glenavon	VILG/VILG	SK	26-14-9-W2	62 L/3	50°12′	103°08′
Glenbain	UNP/LNO	SK	27-10-8-W3	72 G/14	49°51′	107°01′
Glen Bain No. 105	MUN2/AZM2	SK		72 G/14	49°55′	107°00′
Glenbank	UNP/LNO	BC	Kootenay	82 K/5	50°15′	117°48′
Glen Bard	UNP/LNO	NS	Antigonish	11 E/9	45°35′	62°10′
Glen Bay	UNP/LNO	MB	33-20-4-E	62 I/15	50°46′	96°59′
Glen Becker	UNP/LNO	ON	Dundas	31 B/14	44°56′	75°13′
Glenbervie - see-voir - Pembroke	UNP/LNO	NS		11 E/7	45°16′	62°56′
Glenbogie	UNP/LNO	SK	21-54-23-W3	73 F/11	53°41′	109°19′
Gienboro	VILG/VILG	MB		62 G/11	49°33′	99°17′
Glenbow	UNP/LNO	AB	29-25-3-W5	82 O/1	51°10′	114°23′
Glenboyle	UNP/LNO	YT		115 O/15	63°58′	138°43′
Glenbrea	UNP/LNO	SK	17-21-20-W2	72 I/15	50°47′	104°43′
Glenbrook	UNP/LNO	ON	Glengarry	31 G/2	45°07′	74°39′
Glenbrooke North	UNP/LNO	BC	New Westminster	92 G/2	49°13′	122°55′
Glen Buell	UNP/LNO	ON	Leeds	31 B/12	44°38′	75°51′
Glenburn	UNP/LNO	ON	Prescott	31 G/6	45°29′	75°05′
Glenburnie	UNP/LNO	NF		12 H/5	49°26′	57°54′
Glenburnie	UNP/LNO	ON	Frontenac	31 C/8	44°19′	76°29′
Glenburnie-Birchy Head-Shoal Brook	VILG/VILG	NF		12 H/5	49°27′	57°55′
Glenbush	UNP/LNO	SK	49-14-W3	73 F/8	53°15′	108°00′
Glen Cairn	UNP/LNO	NB	Westmorland	21 I/2	46°07′	64°51′
Glen Cairn	UNP/LNO	ON	Carleton	31 G/5	45°17′	75°52′
Glencairn	UNP/LNO	ON	Simcoe	41 A/8	44°18′	80°01′
Glencairn	UNP/LNO	MB	23-19-14-W	62 J/11	50°39′	99°18′
Glencairn	UNP/LNO	SK		72 I/7	50°27′	104°33′

NAME NOM	ENTITY ENTITÉ	LOC 1 LIEU 1	LOC 2 LIEU 2	MAP CARTE	POSITION	
					LAT	LONG
Glencairn Village	UNP/LNO	SK		72 I/7	50°27′	104°33′
Glen Cairn Woods	UNP/LNO	ON	Middlesex	40 I/14	42°58′	81°12′
Glen Campbellton	UNP/LNO	NS	Inverness	11 K/3	46°13′	61°13′
Glenchristie	UNP/LNO	ON	Wellington	40 P/8	43°28′	80°17′
Glencoe	VILG/VILG	ON	Middlesex	40 I/12	42°45′	81°43′
Glencoe	UNP/LNO	PE	Queens	11 L/2	46°12′	62°49′
Glencoe	UNP/LNO	NS	Inverness	11 F/14	45°57′	61°20′
Glencoe	UNP/LNO	NS	Guysborough	11 F/5	45°25′	61°44′
Glencoe	UNP/LNO	NS	Pictou	11 E/7	45°25′	62°33′
Glencoe	UNP/LNO	NB	York	21 J/7	46°16′	66°34′
Glencoe	UNP/LNO	NB	Restigouche	21 O/15	47°57′	66°48′
Glencoe Island	ISL/ÎLE	NT	Franklin	25 M	63°04′	71°28′
Glencoe Mills	UNP/LNO	NS	Inverness	11 F/14	45°58′	61°19′
Glencoe Station	UNP/LNO	NS	Inverness	11 F/14	45°59′	61°27′
Glencolin	UNP/LNO	ON	Elgin	40 I/15	42°48′	80°56′
Glencorradale	UNP/LNO	PE	Kings	11 L/8	46°27′	62°11′
Glen Cross	UNP/LNO	ON	Dufferin	40 P/16	43°59′	80°01′
Glencross	UNP/LNO	MB	11-2-5-W	62 G/1	49°07′	98°01′
Glendale	UNP/LNO	NF		1 N/10	47°31′	52°48′
Glendale	UNP/LNO	NS	Inverness	11 F/14	45°49′	61°18′
Glendale	UNP/LNO	ON	Glengarry	31 G/2	45°04′	74°41′
Glendale	UNP/LNO	ON	Middlesex	40 I/14	42°56′	81°15′
Glendale	UNP/LNO	ON	Algoma	41 K/9	46°44′	84°03′
Glendale	UNP/LNO	BC	Cariboo	93 B/1	52°09′	122°10′
Glendale Beach	UNP/LNO	ON	Lambton	40 O/1	43°08′	82°04′
Glendale Cove	UNP/LNO	BC	Range 1 Coast	92 K/12	50°40′	125°43′
Glendale Lake	LAKE/LAC	BC	Range 1 Coast	92 K/12	50°37′	125°38′
Glendon	VILG/VILG	AB	5-61-8-W4	73 L/6	54°15′	111°10′
Glendon Cove	UNP/LNO	NF		1 M/9	47°42′	54°14′
Glendower	UNP/LNO	ON	Frontenac	31 C/10	44°34′	76°38′
Glendyer	UNP/LNO	NS	Inverness	11 K/3	46°05′	61°21′
Glendyer Station	UNP/LNO	NS	Inverness	11 K/3	46°05′	61°21′
Glendyne	UNP/LNO	QC	Témiscouata	21 N/7	47°24′	68°56′
Gleneagle	UNP/LNO	QC	Les Collines-de-l'Outaouais	31 G/12	45°32′	75°48′
Gleneagles	UNP/LNO	BC	New Westminster	92 G/6	49°22′	123°17′
Glen Echo	UNP/LNO	ON	Muskoka	31 D/14	44°59′	79°28′
Glen Eden	UNP/LNO	ON	Essex	40 J/3	42°04′	83°07′
Gleneden	UNP/LNO	BC	Kamloops Division Yale	82 L/11	50°44′	119°21′
Glen Elbe	UNP/LNO	ON	Leeds	31 B/12	44°38′	75°53′
Glenelg	MUN2/AZM2	ON	Grey	41 A/2	44°15′	80°45′
Glenelg	UNP/LNO	NS	Guysborough	11 E/8	45°16′	62°05′
Glenelg	GEOG/GÉOG	NB	Northumberland	21 I/14	46°56′	65°18′
Glenelg Centre	UNP/LNO	ON	Grey	41 A/2	44°14′	80°42′
Glenelg Lake	LAKE/LAC	NS	Guysborough	11 E/8	45°16′	62°04′
Glenella	MUN2/AZM2	MB		62 J/11	50°35′	99°05′
Glenella	UNP/LNO	MB	21-18-13-W	62 J/11	50°33′	99°12′
Glenellen	UNP/LNO	SK	12-33-17-W3	72 N/16	51°49′	108°16′
Glenelm	UNP/LNO	QC	Le Haut-Saint-Laurent	31 G/1	45°02′	74°12′
Glen Elmo	UNP/LNO	MB	12-21-25-W	62 K/15	50°48′	100°50′
Glenelm Park	UNP/LNO	SK		72 I/7	50°27′	104°34′
Glen Emma	UNP/LNO	QC	La Matapédia	22 B/3	48°07′	67°09′
Glenemma	UNP/LNO	BC	Kamloops Division Yale	82 L/6	50°28′	119°21′
Glenevis	UNP/LNO	AB	34-55-4-W5	83 G/15	53°48′	114°31′
Glen Ewen	VILG/VILG	SK	13-3-1-W2	62 E/1	49°12′	102°01′
Glen Falloch	UNP/LNO	ON	Glengarry	31 G/2	45°07′	74°43′
Glen Falls	UNP/LNO	NB	Saint John	21 G/8	45°19′	66°01′
Glenfanning	UNP/LNO	PE	Kings	11 L/7	46°16′	62°35′
Glenfield	UNP/LNO	ON	Lennox and Addington	31 F/3	45°07′	77°11′
Glenfinnan	UNP/LNO	PE	Queens	11 L/7	46°17′	62°59′
Glenford	UNP/LNO	AB	1-56-2-W5	83 G/16	53°48′	114°10′
Glenforsa	UNP/LNO	MB	1-18-22-W	62 K/9	50°31′	100°23′
Glen Fraser	UNP/LNO	BC	Lillooet	92 I/13	50°49′	121°51′
Glengarry	UNP/LNO	PE	Prince	21 I/16	46°46′	64°19′
Glengarry	UNP/LNO	NS	Inverness	11 K/3	46°03′	61°27′
Glengarry	UNP/LNO	NS	Lunenburg	21 A/9	44°43′	64°27′
Glengarry	GEOG/GÉOG	ON		31 G/2	45°15′	74°40′
Glengarry Cairn National Historic Site - also-aussi - Cairn-de-Glengarry, Lieu historique national du	PARK/PARC	ON	Glengarry	31 G/1	45°07′	74°29′
Glengarry Station	UNP/LNO	NS	Pictou	11 E/7	45°25′	62°46′
Glengarry Valley	UNP/LNO	NS	Cape Breton	11 F/15	45°52′	60°31′
Glen-gla-ouch 5	IR/RI	BC	Rupert	92 L/13	50°50′	127°37′
Glen Gordon	UNP/LNO	ON	Glengarry	31 G/2	45°11′	74°32′
Glen Grove	UNP/LNO	ON	Ontario	30 M/14	43°50′	79°05′
Glen Harbour	VILG/VILG	SK	23-22-23-W2	72 I/14	50°53′	105°06′
Glen Haven	UNP/LNO	NS	Halifax	11 D/12	44°38′	63°55′
Glenhaven Beach	UNP/LNO	ON	Simcoe	31 D/5	44°23′	79°31′

NAME NOM	ENTITY ENTITÉ	LOC 1 LIEU 1	LOC 2 LIEU 2	MAP CARTE	POSITION LAT	POSITION LONG
Glenholme	UNP/LNO	NS	Colchester	11 E/5	45°24′	63°32′
Glen Huron	UNP/LNO	ON	Simcoe	41 A/8	44°21′	80°11′
Glen Island	ISL/ÎLE	NT	Franklin	47 B	68°24′	85°45′
Glenister	UNP/LNO	AB	20-58-6-W5	83 J/2	54°02′	114°52′
Glenkeen	UNP/LNO	NS	Guysborough	11 F/6	45°25′	61°29′
Glen Kerr	UNP/LNO	SK	11-19-8-W3	72 J/11	50°36′	107°01′
Glen Lake	UNP/LNO	BC	Esquimalt	92 B/5	48°26′	123°31′
Glenlawn	UNP/LNO	MB		62 H/14	49°52′	97°06′
Glenlea	UNP/LNO	MB		62 H/11	49°38′	97°08′
Glenlee	UNP/LNO	ON	Wellington	40 P/15	43°53′	80°47′
Glen Leslie	UNP/LNO	AB	1-72-4-W6	83 M/1	55°12′	118°28′
Glen Leven	UNP/LNO	ON	Peel	30 M/12	43°31′	79°36′
Glen Levit	UNP/LNO	NB	Restigouche	21 O/15	47°58′	66°51′
Glenlily	UNP/LNO	BC	Kootenay	82 F/1	49°03′	116°10′
Glen Lloyd	UNP/LNO	QC	L'Érable	21 L/6	46°17′	71°26′
Glenlochar	UNP/LNO	MB	22-13-26-W	62 K/2	50°07′	100°58′
Glenlyon Peak	MTN/MNT	YT		105 L/9	62°32′	134°29′
Glenlyon Range	MTN/MNT	YT		105 L/8	62°25′	134°20′
Glen Major	UNP/LNO	ON	Ontario	31 D/3	44°00′	79°04′
Glen Margaret	UNP/LNO	NS	Halifax	11 D/12	44°35′	63°55′
Glenmartin	UNP/LNO	PE	Kings	11 L/2	46°04′	62°40′
Glen McPherson	UNP/LNO	SK	31-5-11-W3	72 G/6	49°26′	107°28′
Glen McPherson No. 46	MUN2/AZM2	SK		72 G/6	49°25′	107°25′
Glenmerry	UNP/LNO	BC	Kootenay	82 F/4	49°06′	117°40′
Glen Meyer	UNP/LNO	ON	Norfolk	40 I/10	42°44′	80°41′
Glen Miller	UNP/LNO	ON	Hastings	31 C/4	44°08′	77°35′
Glen Moir	UNP/LNO	NS	Halifax	11 D/12	44°43′	63°40′
Glenmont	UNP/LNO	NS	Kings	21 H/1	45°11′	64°30′
Glenmoor	UNP/LNO	MB	34-15-8-E	62 I/8	50°19′	96°25′
Glenmore	UNP/LNO	NS	Halifax	11 E/3	45°04′	63°09′
Glenmore	UNP/LNO	ON	Grenville	31 B/12	44°44′	75°39′
Glenmore	UNP/LNO	BC	New Westminster	92 G/6	49°22′	123°07′
Glenmore Mountain	MTN/MNT	NS	Colchester	11 E/3	45°05′	63°12′
Glen Morris	UNP/LNO	ON	Leeds	31 B/12	44°35′	75°58′
Glen Morris	UNP/LNO	ON	Brant	40 P/8	43°16′	80°21′
Glen Morrison	UNP/LNO	NS	Cape Breton	11 F/16	46°00′	60°19′
Glenmount	UNP/LNO	ON	Muskoka	31 E/3	45°13′	79°02′
Glen Murray	UNP/LNO	QC	L'Érable	21 L/6	46°18′	71°29′
Glenn	UNP/LNO	MB	6-8-15-E	52 E/12	49°38′	95°32′
Glen Nevis	UNP/LNO	ON	Glengarry	31 G/8	45°17′	74°29′
Glennie Lake	LAKE/LAC	SK		63 M/12	55°44′	103°54′
Glen Norman	UNP/LNO	ON	Glengarry	31 G/7	45°18′	74°32′
Glen Oak	UNP/LNO	ON	Middlesex	40 I/13	42°53′	81°36′
Glenogle	UNP/LNO	BC	Kootenay	82 N/7	51°17′	116°49′
Glenomo	UNP/LNO	ON	Cochrane	42 G/11	49°40′	83°28′
Glenora	UNP/LNO	NS	Inverness	11 F/11	45°44′	61°18′
Glenora	UNP/LNO	ON	Prince Edward	31 C/3	44°02′	77°03′
Glenora	UNP/LNO	MB	33-3-13-W	62 G/6	49°15′	99°09′
Glenora	UNP/LNO	BC	Cassiar	104 G/14	57°50′	131°23′
Glenora Falls	UNP/LNO	NS	Inverness	11 K/3	46°07′	61°22′
Glen Orchard	UNP/LNO	ON	Muskoka	31 E/4	45°05′	79°39′
Glenorchy	UNP/LNO	ON	Halton	30 M/5	43°29′	79°46′
Glenorchy	UNP/LNO	ON	Rainy River	52 C/16	48°45′	92°25′
Glen Otter	UNP/LNO	ON	Algoma	41 J/5	46°17′	83°39′
Glen Park	UNP/LNO	NB	Saint John	21 G/8	45°19′	66°01′
Glen Park	UNP/LNO	AB	5-49-7-W4	83 H/4	53°12′	113°55′
Glen Payne	UNP/LNO	SK	29-15-W3	72 N/8	51°30′	108°01′
Glen Rae	UNP/LNO	ON	Lambton	40 J/16	42°49′	82°02′
Glenrest Beach	UNP/LNO	ON	Ontario	31 D/11	44°34′	79°15′
Glenridge	UNP/LNO	ON	Lincoln	30 M/3	43°09′	79°14′
Glenridge	UNP/LNO	ON	Oxford	40 I/15	42°52′	80°45′
Glenridge Crescent	UNP/LNO	NF		1 N/10	47°34′	52°42′
Glen Road	UNP/LNO	NS	Antigonish	11 E/9	45°33′	62°01′
Glen Robertson	UNP/LNO	ON	Glengarry	31 G/7	45°21′	74°30′
Glenrosa	UNP/LNO	BC	Osoyoos Division Yale	82 E/13	49°51′	119°40′
Glen Ross	UNP/LNO	ON	Hastings	31 C/5	44°16′	77°36′
Glenroy	UNP/LNO	PE	Queens	11 L/7	46°21′	62°55′
Glenroy	UNP/LNO	NS	Antigonish	11 F/12	45°32′	61°52′
Glenroy	UNP/LNO	ON	Glengarry	31 G/2	45°14′	74°38′
Glen Sandfield	UNP/LNO	ON	Glengarry	31 G/7	45°24′	74°32′
Glenshee	UNP/LNO	ON	Norfolk	40 I/16	42°46′	80°29′
Glenside	VILG/VILG	SK	5-29-6-W3	72 O/7	51°27′	106°48′
Glenside No. 377	MUN2/AZM2	SK		73 B/5	52°20′	107°55′
Glen Smail	UNP/LNO	ON	Grenville	31 B/13	44°49′	75°31′
Glen Stewart	UNP/LNO	ON	Dundas	31 B/14	44°55′	75°25′

NAME NOM	ENTITY ENTITÉ	LOC 1 LIEU 1	LOC 2 LIEU 2	MAP CARTE	POSITION LAT	LONG
Glen Sutton	UNP/LNO	QC	Brome-Missisquoi	31 H/2	45°02'	72°33'
Glentanna	UNP/LNO	BC	Range 5 Coast	93 L/14	54°52'	127°08'
Glen Tay	UNP/LNO	ON	Lanark	31 C/16	44°53'	76°18'
Glenton	UNP/LNO	QC	Brome-Missisquoi	31 H/2	45°02'	72°32'
Glen Tosh	UNP/LNO	NS	Victoria	11 K/2	46°10'	60°37'
Glentworth	VILG/VILG	SK	36-5-6-W3	72 G/7	49°26'	106°41'
Glenvale	UNP/LNO	NB	Westmorland	21 H/14	45°56'	65°14'
Glenvale	UNP/LNO	ON	Frontenac	31 C/7	44°19'	76°37'
Glenvale	UNP/LNO	ON	Timiskaming	41 P/16	47°52'	80°09'
Glenvale Station	UNP/LNO	ON	Frontenac	31 C/7	44°19'	76°35'
Glen Valley	UNP/LNO	PE	Queens	11 L/6	46°21'	63°27'
Glen Valley	UNP/LNO	BC	New Westminster	92 G/1	49°10'	122°28'
Glenview	UNP/LNO	NF		1 N/13	47°53'	53°58'
Glenview	UNP/LNO	ON	Lanark	31 C/16	44°57'	76°06'
Glenview Heights	UNP/LNO	ON	Stormont	31 G/2	45°01'	74°42'
Glenvilla Court	UNP/LNO	NF		1 N/10	47°37'	52°43'
Glenville	UNP/LNO	NS	Inverness	11 K/3	46°09'	61°19'
Glenville	UNP/LNO	NS	Cumberland	11 E/12	45°41'	63°58'
Glenville	UNP/LNO	ON	York	31 D/4	44°03'	79°31'
Glen Vowell	UNP/LNO	BC	Cassiar	93 M/5	55°19'	127°40'
Glen Walter	UNP/LNO	ON	Glengarry	31 G/2	45°02'	74°37'
Glenwater	UNP/LNO	ON	Thunder Bay	52 A/12	48°33'	89°47'
Glenway Village	UNP/LNO	ON	Victoria	31 D/7	44°27'	78°37'
Glenwilliam	UNP/LNO	PE	Kings	11 L/2	46°03'	62°39'
Glen Williams	UNP/LNO	ON	Halton	30 M/12	43°40'	79°55'
Glenwood	TOWN/VIL2	NF		2 D/15	48°59'	54°53'
Glenwood	VILG/VILG	AB	1,12-5-27-W4	82 H/5	49°22'	113°31'
Glenwood	MUN2/AZM2	MB		62 F/9	49°37'	100°15'
Glenwood	UNP/LNO	PE	Prince	21 I/9	46°39'	64°19'
Glenwood	UNP/LNO	NS	Yarmouth	20 P/13	43°48'	65°53'
Glenwood	UNP/LNO	NB	Northumberland	21 I/14	46°59'	65°22'
Glenwood	UNP/LNO	NB	Kings	21 G/8	45°29'	66°07'
Glenwood	UNP/LNO	NB	Restigouche	21 O/14	47°51'	67°01'
Glenwood	UNP/LNO	ON	Kent	40 J/1	42°13'	82°16'
Glenwood	UNP/LNO	ON	Cochrane	42 G/8	49°26'	82°25'
Glenwood Beach	UNP/LNO	ON	York	31 D/3	44°13'	79°29'
Glenwood Beach	UNP/LNO	ON	Simcoe	31 D/5	44°21'	79°32'
Glenwood Heights	UNP/LNO	ON	Wentworth	30 M/5	43°16'	80°00'
Glenwood Park	UNP/LNO	ON	Halton	30 M/5	43°21'	79°48'
Gleyka 6	IR/RI	BC	Range 1 Coast	92 L/14	50°58'	127°02'
Glidden	VILG/VILG	SK	21-26-23-W3	72 N/3	51°14'	109°10'
Glide Brook	RIV/CDE	NF		12 H/3	49°10'	57°20'
Glide Lake	LAKE/LAC	NF		12 H/3	49°06'	57°24'
Glines Corner	UNP/LNO	QC	Memphrémagog	31 H/1	45°01'	72°11'
Gloria Rise	SEAU/SMER	—		814A	55°30'	45°00'
Gloria Village	UNP/LNO	QC	Le Haut-Richelieu	31 H/3	45°03'	73°11'
Glossop	UNP/LNO	MB	22-16-21-W	62 K/8	50°23'	100°18'
Glossy Mountain	MTN/MNT	BC	Kamloops Division Yale	92 I/11	50°38'	121°09'
Gloucester	CITY/VIL1	ON	Carleton	31 G/5	45°21'	75°38'
Gloucester	UNP/LNO	ON	Carleton	31 G/5	45°18'	75°38'
Gloucester	GEOG/GÉOG	NB		21 P/11	47°35'	65°25'
Gloucester Glen	UNP/LNO	ON	Carleton	31 G/5	45°17'	75°42'
Gloucester Junction	UNP/LNO	NB	Gloucester	21 P/12	47°33'	65°39'
Glover Island	ISL/ÎLE	NF		12 A/13	48°46'	57°43'
Glovers Harbour	UNP/LNO	NF		2 E/6	49°27'	55°30'
Glovertown	TOWN/VIL2	NF		2 D/9	48°41'	54°02'
Glovertown South	UNP/LNO	NF		2 D/9	48°40'	54°01'
Glowworm Lake	LAKE/LAC	NT	Mackenzie	76 C	64°38'	109°15'
Glundebery Creek	RIV/CDE	BC	Cassiar	104 O/4	59°10'	131°51'
Gnadenfeld	UNP/LNO	MB	27-1-1-W	62 H/4	49°04'	97°32'
Gnadenthal	UNP/LNO	MB	3,4-2-3-W	62 H/4	49°06'	97°48'
Gnat Mountain	MTN/MNT	NF		13 J/1	54°10'	58°08'
Gnawed Mountain	MTN/MNT	BC	Kamloops Division Yale	92 I/7	50°26'	120°59'
Goan	UNP/LNO	NB	Sunbury	21 G/16	45°52'	66°25'
Go Ashore, Le	UNP/LNO	QC	Matane	22 B/15	48°51'	66°34'
Goatfell	UNP/LNO	BC	Kootenay	82 F/1	49°07'	116°11'
Goatherd Mountain	MTN/MNT	YT		115 A/5	60°16'	137°51'
Goat Island	ISL/ÎLE	BC	New Westminster	92 K/1	50°03'	124°26'
Goat Lake	LAKE/LAC	BC	New Westminster	92 K/1	50°03'	124°15'
Goat River	UNP/LNO	BC	Cariboo	93 H/10	53°32'	120°36'
Goat River	RIV/CDE	ON	Cochrane	42 G/4	49°14'	83°37'
Goat River	RIV/CDE	BC	Kootenay	82 F/2	49°05'	116°34'
Goat River	RIV/CDE	BC	Cariboo	93 H/10	53°32'	120°34'
Goatskin Creek	RIV/CDE	BC	Similkameen Division Yale	82 E/10	49°42'	118°42'
Gobeil	UNP/LNO	QC	Charlevoix	21 M/8	47°26'	70°30'

NAME NOM	ENTITY ENTITÉ	LOC 1 LIEU 1	LOC 2 LIEU 2	MAP CARTE	POSITION LAT	LONG
Gobles	UNP/LNO	ON	Oxford	40 P/2	43°09'	80°34'
Goblin	UNP/LNO	NF		11 P/9	47°43'	56°07'
God Bay	BAY/BAIE	NF		11 O/10	47°36'	58°53'
Godbout	TOWN/VIL2	QC	Manicouagan	22 G/5	49°19'	67°36'
Godbout Est, Rivière	RIV/CDE	QC	Sept-Rivières	22 G/12	49°38'	67°44'
Godbout, Mornes de	MTN/MNT	QC	Manicouagan	22 G/5	49°20'	67°30'
Godbout, Rivière	RIV/CDE	QC	Manicouagan	22 G/5	49°19'	67°36'
Goddenville	UNP/LNO	NF		1 N/11	47°36'	53°21'
Goderich	TOWN/VIL2	ON	Huron	40 P/12	43°45'	81°43'
Goderich	MUN2/AZM2	ON	Huron	40 P/12	43°38'	81°37'
Godfrey	UNP/LNO	ON	Frontenac	31 C/10	44°32'	76°41'
Goding Bay	BAY/BAIE	NT	Franklin	39 C	77°58'	76°14'
Godmanchester	VILG/VILG	QC	Le Haut-Saint-Laurent	31 G/1	45°05'	74°15'
Godolphin	UNP/LNO	ON	Northumberland	31 C/5	44°17'	77°53'
Gods Lake	UNP/LNO	MB		53 L/9	54°40'	94°09'
Gods Lake	LAKE/LAC	MB		53 L/9	54°40'	94°15'
God's Lake 23	IR/RI	MB		53 L/10	54°32'	94°35'
Gods Lake Narrows	UNP/LNO	MB		53 L/9	54°33'	94°29'
God's Mercie, Islands of	ISL/ÎLE	NT	Franklin	35 P	63°30'	72°00'
Gods Mercy, Bay of	BAY/BAIE	NT	Keewatin	45 M	63°30'	86°10'
Gods River	UNP/LNO	MB		53 L/16	54°51'	94°05'
Gods River	RIV/CDE	MB		54 C/7	56°22'	92°51'
God's River 86A	IR/RI	MB		53 L/16	54°50'	94°03'
Goéland, Lac au	LAKE/LAC	QC	Jamésie	32 F/15	49°47'	76°48'
Goéland, Lac du	LAKE/LAC	QC	Maria-Chapdelaine	22 E/13	49°47'	71°41'
Goélands, Lac aux	LAKE/LAC	QC	Kativik	23 P/8	55°27'	64°17'
Goffs	UNP/LNO	NS	Halifax	11 D/14	44°53'	63°29'
Gogama	UNP/LNO	ON	Sudbury	41 P/12	47°40'	81°43'
Gohere Bay	BAY/BAIE	ON	Rainy River	52 F/4	49°04'	93°58'
Go Home	UNP/LNO	ON	Muskoka	31 D/13	45°00'	79°56'
Go Home Lake	LAKE/LAC	ON	Muskoka	31 E/4	45°01'	79°51'
Goisard, Lac	LAKE/LAC	QC	Maria-Chapdelaine	22 L/4	50°05'	71°31'
Golburn	UNP/LNO	SK	6-44-14-W2	73 A/16	52°46'	104°01'
Goldboro	UNP/LNO	NS	Guysborough	11 F/4	45°11'	61°39'
Gold Bottom	UNP/LNO	YT		115 O/15	63°58'	138°58'
Gold Bridge	UNP/LNO	BC	Lillooet	92 J/15	50°51'	122°50'
Gold Brook	UNP/LNO	NS	Victoria	11 K/2	46°14'	60°55'
Gold Centre	UNP/LNO	ON	Cochrane	42 A/6	48°28'	81°17'
Gold Cove	UNP/LNO	NF		12 H/10	49°34'	56°51'
Gold Creek	RIV/CDE	BC	Kootenay	82 G/3	49°04'	115°14'
Gold Creek	RIV/CDE	BC	Kamloops Division Yale	82 M/11	51°45'	119°10'
Golden	TOWN/VIL2	BC	Kootenay	82 N/7	51°18'	116°58'
Golden	MUN2/AZM2	ON	Kenora	52 N/4	51°05'	93°43'
Golden Bay	UNP/LNO	MB	1-13-8-E	62 I/1	50°04'	96°23'
Golden Bay	BAY/BAIE	NF		1 L/16	46°49'	54°09'
Golden Beach	UNP/LNO	ON	Muskoka	31 E/3	45°02'	79°24'
Goldenburgh	UNP/LNO	ON	Algoma	41 J/6	46°21'	83°21'
Golden City	UNP/LNO	ON	Cochrane	42 A/6	48°30'	81°10'
Golden Days	VILG/VILG	AB	15-47-1-W5	83 G/1	53°03'	114°03'
Golden Grove	UNP/LNO	NB	Saint John	21 H/5	45°22'	65°58'
Golden Hill	UNP/LNO	ON	Prescott	31 G/10	45°31'	74°36'
Golden Hinde	MTN/MNT	BC	Nootka	92 F/12	49°40'	125°45'
Golden Lake	UNP/LNO	ON	Renfrew	31 F/11	45°35'	77°14'
Golden Lake	LAKE/LAC	ON	Renfrew	31 F/11	45°34'	77°21'
Golden Lake 39	IR/RI	ON	Renfrew	31 F/11	45°33'	77°15'
Golden Prairie	VILG/VILG	SK	33-14-27-W3	72 K/4	50°13'	109°38'
Golden Ridge	UNP/LNO	SK	62-21-W3	73 K/6	54°20'	109°06'
Golden Spike	UNP/LNO	AB	21-51-27-W4	83 H/5	53°25'	113°55'
Golden Stream	UNP/LNO	MB	4-14-11-W	62 J/2	50°09'	98°54'
Goldenvale	UNP/LNO	SK		62 M/10	51°35'	102°54'
Golden Valley	UNP/LNO	ON	Parry Sound	31 E/13	45°56'	79°48'
Goldenville	UNP/LNO	NS	Guysborough	11 E/1	45°07'	62°01'
Golden West No. 95	MUN2/AZM2	SK		62 E/14	49°55'	103°00'
Goldfield	UNP/LNO	ON	Stormont	31 G/3	45°07'	75°08'
Goldfields	UNP/LNO	SK		74 N/8	59°28'	108°29'
Goldie Lake	LAKE/LAC	ON	Sudbury	42 B/4	48°03'	83°54'
Gold Lake	LAKE/LAC	BC	Nootka	92 F/13	49°59'	125°59'
Goldpines	UNP/LNO	ON	Kenora	52 K/11	50°38'	93°12'
Gold River	VILG/VILG	BC	Nootka	92 E/9	49°41'	126°07'
Gold River	UNP/LNO	NS	Lunenburg	21 A/9	44°32'	64°19'
Gold River	RIV/CDE	NS	Lunenburg	21 A/9	44°33'	64°19'
Gold River	RIV/CDE	BC	Nootka	92 E/9	49°41'	126°06'
Gold River 21	IR/RI	NS	Lunenburg	21 A/9	44°34'	64°21'
Gold Rock	UNP/LNO	ON	Kenora	52 F/7	49°27'	92°43'
Gold Room at Bear Creek National Historic Site - also-aussi - Salle-d'Affinage-de-l'Or-de-Bear Creek, Lieu historique national de la	PARK/PARC	YT		116 B/3	64°02'	139°14'

NAME NOM	ENTITY ENTITÉ	LOC 1 LIEU 1	LOC 2 LIEU 2	MAP CARTE	POSITION LAT	LONG
Gold Run	UNP/LNO	YT		115 O/10	63°42′	138°36′
Goldsand Lake	LAKE/LAC	MB		64 F/3	57°02′	101°09′
Goldsmith	UNP/LNO	ON	Essex	40 J/2	42°07′	82°32′
Goldsmith Channel	CHAN/CHEN	NT	Franklin	57 G	71°47′	95°20′
Goldsmith Channel	CHAN/CHEN	NT	Franklin	78 D/3	73°10′	106°05′
Goldstone	UNP/LNO	ON	Wellington	40 P/10	43°43′	80°35′
Goldstream 13	IR/RI	BC	Goldstream	92 B/5	48°29′	123°33′
Goldstream Land District	GEOG/GÉOG	BC		92 B	48°26′	123°36′
Goldstream River	RIV/CDE	BC	Kootenay	82 M/10	51°39′	118°37′
Goldthorpe	UNP/LNO	ON	Timiskaming	42 A/1	48°08′	80°10′
Goldwin	UNP/LNO	QC	Pontiac	31 F/15	45°47′	76°39′
Goletas Channel	CHAN/CHEN	BC	Rupert	92 L/13	50°49′	127°44′
Golet, Lac	LAKE/LAC	QC	Minganie	12 N/15	51°48′	60°32′
Golf Side Gardens	UNP/LNO	ON	Leeds	31 B/12	44°35′	75°43′
Gollen Creek	RIV/CDE	BC	Kamloops Division Yale	82 M/6	51°26′	119°28′
Golspie	UNP/LNO	ON	Oxford	40 P/2	43°08′	80°51′
Gondola Point	VILG/VILG	NB	Kings	21 H/5	45°26′	65°59′
Gonor	UNP/LNO	MB		62 I/2	50°04′	96°57′
Gonor Station	UNP/LNO	MB		62 I/2	50°03′	96°55′
Goobies	UNP/LNO	NF		1 N/13	47°56′	53°58′
Goobies Siding	UNP/LNO	NF		1 N/13	47°57′	53°58′
Goobies Station	UNP/LNO	NF		1 N/13	47°55′	53°57′
Good Corner	UNP/LNO	NB	Carleton	21 J/5	46°23′	67°44′
Good Corner	UNP/LNO	NB	Victoria	21 J/12	46°37′	67°47′
Gooderham	UNP/LNO	ON	Haliburton	31 D/16	44°54′	78°23′
Goodeve	VILG/VILG	SK	10-24-9-W2	62 M/3	51°04′	103°11′
Goodfare	UNP/LNO	AB	25-72-12-W6	83 M/5	55°16′	119°43′
Goodfellow Beach	UNP/LNO	ON	Simcoe	31 D/5	44°20′	79°32′
Goodfish Lake	UNP/LNO	AB	26-61-13-W4	73 L/5	54°18′	111°50′
Goodfish Lake	LAKE/LAC	AB	61-13-W4	73 L/5	54°17′	111°49′
Good Friday Bay	BAY/BAIE	NT	Franklin	59 F	78°33′	92°24′
Good Harbour	UNP/LNO	MB	32-36-19-W	63 C/1	52°08′	100°09′
Good Hope	UNP/LNO	BC	Range 2 Coast	92 M/12	51°34′	127°31′
Good Hope Bay	BAY/BAIE	NT	Mackenzie	96 K	66°18′	124°18′
Good Hope Lake	UNP/LNO	BC	Cassiar	104 P/6	59°17′	129°18′
Good Hope Mountain	MTN/MNT	BC	Range 2 Coast	92 N/1	51°09′	124°11′
Good Lake No. 274	MUN2/AZM2	SK		62 M/7	51°30′	102°40′
Goodlands	UNP/LNO	MB	3-2-24-W	62 F/2	49°06′	100°36′
Goodlow	UNP/LNO	BC	Peace River	94 A/8	56°20′	120°08′
Good Point	CAPE/CAP	NT	Franklin	120 G	83°01′	68°30′
Goodridge	UNP/LNO	AB	30-62-9-W4	73 L/6	54°23′	111°22′
Goodsir Inlet	BAY/BAIE	NT	Franklin	68 H	75°45′	97°45′
Goodsir, Mount	MTN/MNT	BC	Kootenay	82 N/1	51°12′	116°25′
Goodsoil	VILG/VILG	SK	27,28-62-22-W3	73 K/6	54°24′	109°13′
Goodspeed Lake	LAKE/LAC	NT	Mackenzie	75 N	63°06′	109°32′
Good Spirit Lake	LAKE/LAC	SK		62 M/10	51°34′	102°40′
Goodstown	UNP/LNO	ON	Carleton	31 G/4	45°09′	75°48′
Goodwater	VILG/VILG	SK	21-5-13-W2	62 E/5	49°24′	103°42′
Goodwin	UNP/LNO	ON	Cochrane	32 D/13	48°54′	79°41′
Goodwin	UNP/LNO	AB	12-72-2-W6	83 M/1	55°13′	118°11′
Goodwin, Banc	SEAU/SMER	—		4002	47°28′	61°24′
Goodwin Island	ISL/ÎLE	NT	Franklin	25 A/10	60°41′	64°39′
Goodwin Lake	LAKE/LAC	AB	74-11-W4	73 M/5	55°25′	111°39′
Goodwood	UNP/LNO	NS	Halifax	11 D/12	44°37′	63°40′
Goodwood	UNP/LNO	ON	Ontario	31 D/3	44°02′	79°12′
Goodwood, Rivière	RIV/CDE	QC	Kativik	23 N/9	55°35′	68°09′
Goo-ewe 8	IR/RI	BC	Range 3 Coast	103 A/7	52°28′	128°44′
Goose Arm	UNP/LNO	NF		12 H/4	49°07′	57°56′
Goose Arm	BAY/BAIE	NF		12 H/4	49°09′	57°55′
Goose Bay	UNP/LNO	BC	Range 2 Coast	92 M/5	51°23′	127°40′
Goose Bay	BAY/BAIE	NF		2 C/5	48°25′	53°50′
Goose Bay	BAY/BAIE	NF		13 F/8	53°24′	60°10′
Goose Bay	BAY/BAIE	NT	Keewatin	33 E	53°55′	79°02′
Goose Bay, Base des Forces canadiennes - also-aussi - Goose Bay, Canadian Forces Base	MIL/MIL	NF		13 F/8	53°19′	60°26′
Goose Bay, Canadian Forces Base - also-aussi - Goose Bay, Base des Forces canadiennes	MIL/MIL	NF		13 F/8	53°19′	60°26′
Gooseberry Brook	RIV/CDE	ON	Kenora	43 N/6	55°23′	85°20′
Gooseberry Cove	UNP/LNO	NF		2 C/4	48°02′	53°38′
Gooseberry Cove	UNP/LNO	NF		1 M/1	47°04′	54°06′
Gooseberry Cove	UNP/LNO	NB	Saint John	21 G/1	45°09′	66°16′
Gooseberry Island	UNP/LNO	NF		2 C/13	48°53′	53°37′
Gooseberry Lake	LAKE/LAC	SK	11,12-9-W2	62 E/14	49°57′	103°12′
Gooseberry Lake Provincial Park	PARK/PARC	AB	26-36-6-W6	73 D/2	52°07′	110°46′
Goose Cove	UNP/LNO	NF		2 C/6	48°22′	53°23′
Goose Cove	UNP/LNO	NF		1 M/16	47°52′	54°06′
Goose Cove	UNP/LNO	NF		2 M/5	51°18′	55°38′

NAME NOM	ENTITY ENTITÉ	LOC 1 LIEU 1	LOC 2 LIEU 2	MAP CARTE	POSITION LAT	LONG
Goose Cove	UNP/LNO	NS	Victoria	11 K/7	46°15′	60°37′
Goose Cove East	VILG/VILG	NF		2 M/5	51°18′	55°38′
Goose Creek	RIV/CDE	ON	Kenora	43 M/13	55°57′	87°22′
Goose Fiord	BAY/BAIE	NT	Franklin	59 A/8	76°36′	88°35′
Goose Group	ISL/ÎLE	BC	Range 2 Coast	102 P/16	51°57′	128°27′
Goose Harbour Lake	LAKE/LAC	NS	Guysborough	11 F/11	45°33′	61°25′
Goosehunting Creek	RIV/CDE	SK		73 H/2	53°02′	104°51′
Goose Island	ISL/ÎLE	NS	Guysborough	11 F/4	45°07′	61°34′
Goose Island	ISL/ÎLE	NS	Guysborough	11 D/16	44°56′	62°05′
Goose Island	ISL/ÎLE	BC	Range 2 Coast	102 P/16	51°57′	128°26′
Goose Island Bank	SEAU/SMER	—		19318A	51°40′	129°15′
Goose Islands	ISL/ÎLE	ON	Nipissing	31 L/5	46°15′	79°43′
Goose, Lac	LAKE/LAC	QC	Jamésie	33 G/1	53°00′	74°30′
Goose Lake	LAKE/LAC	ON	Victoria	31 D/7	44°25′	78°52′
Goose Lake	LAKE/LAC	ON	Lambton	40 J/10	42°32′	82°31′
Goose Lake	LAKE/LAC	ON	Kenora	52 N/15	51°46′	93°00′
Goose Lake	LAKE/LAC	MB		53 L/7	54°16′	94°35′
Goose Lake	LAKE/LAC	MB	39,40-9-W	63 B/7	52°24′	98°46′
Goose Lake	LAKE/LAC	MB/NT		64 N/15	59°58′	100°30′
Goose Lake	LAKE/LAC	MB	63-27,28-W	63 K/6	54°28′	101°30′
Goose Lake	LAKE/LAC	SK	53-4-W2	63 E/9	53°37′	102°30′
Goose Lake	LAKE/LAC	SK	32-10-W3	72 O/11	51°45′	107°23′
Goose Lake	LAKE/LAC	SK	38-17-W3	73 C/8	52°19′	108°16′
Goose Lake	LAKE/LAC	AB	31-10-W4	72 M/11	51°41′	111°20′
Goose Point	CAPE/CAP	NT	Franklin	59 D	77°51′	88°13′
Goose Pond	LAKE/LAC	NF		2 D/8	48°15′	54°20′
Goose Pond	LAKE/LAC	NF		12 H/2	49°05′	57°00′
Goose River	UNP/LNO	PE	Kings	11 L/7	46°27′	62°31′
Goose River	RIV/CDE	NF		13 F/8	53°22′	60°22′
Goose River	RIV/CDE	AB	69-21-W5	83 K/14	54°58′	117°11′
Goose Spit 3	IR/RI	BC	Comox	92 F/10	49°40′	124°55′
Gopher Creek	RIV/CDE	MB	20-10-25-W	62 F/15	49°51′	100°51′
Gorden Bay	BAY/BAIE	NT	Keewatin	45 P	63°53′	80°35′
Gordon	MUN2/AZM2	ON	Manitoulin	41 G/16	45°53′	82°29′
Gordon	UNP/LNO	MB	11,12-12-1-E	62 H/14	50°00′	97°21′
Gordon	GEOG/GÉOG	NB	Victoria	21 J/14	46°50′	67°10′
Gordon 86	IR/RI	SK		72 P/1	51°15′	104°15′
Gordon Bay	UNP/LNO	ON	Parry Sound	31 E/4	45°13′	79°48′
Gordon Bay	BAY/BAIE	NT	Franklin	76 J	67°00′	107°20′
Gordon Corner	UNP/LNO	QC	Memphrémagog	31 H/1	45°04′	72°20′
Gordondale	UNP/LNO	AB	17-79-10-W6	83 M/13	55°50′	119°33′
Gordon Head	UNP/LNO	BC	Victoria	92 B/6	48°29′	123°19′
Gordon Head	CAPE/CAP	BC	Victoria	92 B/6	48°30′	123°18′
Gordon Horne Peak	MTN/MNT	BC	Kootenay	82 M/15	51°47′	118°49′
Gordon Island	ISL/ÎLE	NT	Keewatin	34 C/15	56°52′	76°40′
Gordon Lake	UNP/LNO	ON	Algoma	41 J/5	46°25′	83°52′
Gordon Lake	LAKE/LAC	ON	Algoma	41 J/5	46°25′	83°50′
Gordon Lake	LAKE/LAC	ON	Kenora	52 F/13	49°54′	93°43′
Gordon Lake	LAKE/LAC	SK	78,79-3,4-W3	73 O/16	55°50′	106°28′
Gordon Lake	LAKE/LAC	AB	86,87-3,4-W4	74 D/8	56°30′	110°25′
Gordon Lake	LAKE/LAC	NT	Mackenzie	85 P/3	63°05′	113°11′
Gordon Landing	UNP/LNO	YT		105 M/11	63°38′	135°27′
Gordon McKenzie Arm	BAY/BAIE	SK		72 O/2	51°02′	106°32′
Gordon, Mount	MTN/MNT	BC	Cassiar	104 G/14	57°46′	131°14′
Gordon Point	CAPE/CAP	NT	Franklin	88 B	72°11′	118°31′
Gordon River	UNP/LNO	BC	Cowichan Lake	92 C/16	48°46′	124°20′
Gordon River	RIV/CDE	BC	Renfrew	92 C/9	48°35′	124°25′
Gordon River	RIV/CDE	NT	Keewatin	46 D	64°31′	87°49′
Gordon River 2	IR/RI	BC	Renfrew	92 C/9	48°35′	124°24′
Gordon Summit	UNP/LNO	NS	Pictou	11 E/7	45°26′	62°51′
Gordonsville	UNP/LNO	NB	Carleton	21 J/5	46°29′	67°31′
Gordon Vale	UNP/LNO	NB	York	21 J/7	46°28′	66°32′
Gordonville	UNP/LNO	QC	La Rivière-du-Nord	31 G/9	45°42′	74°09′
Gordonville	UNP/LNO	ON	Wellington	40 P/15	43°54′	80°33′
Gore	VILG/VILG	QC	Argenteuil	31 G/16	45°46′	74°15′
Gore	UNP/LNO	NS	Hants	11 E/4	45°07′	63°43′
Gore	UNP/LNO	QC	Drummond	31 H/9	45°39′	72°14′
Gore Bay	TOWN/VIL2	ON	Manitoulin	41 G/16	45°55′	82°28′
Gore Bay	BAY/BAIE	NT	Franklin	46 K	66°19′	84°24′
Gore Island	ISL/ÎLE	BC	Nootka	92 E/9	49°39′	126°24′
Gore Islands	ISL/ÎLE	NT	Franklin	98 F	74°19′	124°57′
Gore Point	CAPE/CAP	NT	Keewatin	46 A	64°05′	81°24′
Gores Landing	UNP/LNO	ON	Northumberland	31 D/1	44°07′	78°14′
Gorewood Acres	UNP/LNO	ON	Peel	30 M/12	43°45′	79°39′
Gorgotton, Lac	LAKE/LAC	QC	La Haute-Côte-Nord	22 C/12	48°39′	69°59′

NAME NOM	ENTITY ENTITÉ	LOC 1 LIEU 1	LOC 2 LIEU 2	MAP CARTE	POSITION LAT	LONG
Goring	UNP/LNO	ON	Grey	41 A/7	44°27'	80°40'
Gorlitz	UNP/LNO	SK	25-28-4-W2	62 M/8	51°28'	102°27'
Gormanville	UNP/LNO	NS	Hants	11 E/5	45°15'	63°45'
Gormley	UNP/LNO	ON	York	30 M/14	43°56'	79°23'
Gorrie	UNP/LNO	ON	Huron	40 P/14	43°52'	81°06'
Gort	UNP/LNO	NB	Westmorland	21 I/2	46°05'	64°51'
G.-Oscar-Villeneuve, Réserve écologique	PARK/PARC	QC	Le Fjord-du-Saguenay	22 D/8	48°29'	70°30'
Goschen Island	ISL/ÎLE	BC	Range 4 Coast	103 G/15	53°49'	130°35'
Gosfield - see-voir - Gosfield South	MUN2/AZM2	ON		40 J/2	42°04'	82°44'
Gosfield - see-voir - Gosfield North	MUN2/AZM2	ON		40 J/2	42°09'	82°44'
Gosfield North	MUN2/AZM2	ON	Essex	40 J/2	42°09'	82°44'
Gosfield South	MUN2/AZM2	ON	Essex	40 J/2	42°04'	82°44'
Gosford, Mont	MTN/MNT	QC	Le Granit	21 E/7	45°18'	70°52'
Goshen	UNP/LNO	NS	Guysborough	11 F/5	45°23'	61°59'
Goshen	UNP/LNO	NS	Colchester	11 E/2	45°10'	62°57'
Goshen	UNP/LNO	NS	Hants	21 H/1	45°10'	64°04'
Goshen	UNP/LNO	NB	Albert	21 H/14	45°47'	65°10'
Goshen	UNP/LNO	NB	Queens	21 H/13	45°52'	65°43'
Goshen	UNP/LNO	ON	Renfrew	31 F/7	45°27'	76°35'
Goshen	UNP/LNO	ON	Huron	40 P/5	43°29'	81°38'
Gosnell	UNP/LNO	BC	Kamloops Division Yale	83 D/6	52°30'	119°07'
Gosnell Creek	RIV/CDE	BC	Range 5 Coast	93 L/3	54°13'	127°20'
Gosport	UNP/LNO	ON	Lennox and Addington	31 C/3	44°07'	77°02'
Gosport	UNP/LNO	ON	Northumberland	31 C/4	44°01'	77°43'
Gossage River	RIV/CDE	NT	Mackenzie	106 J	66°57'	130°18'
Gosselin-Mills	UNP/LNO	QC	Coaticook	21 E/4	45°23'	71°40'
Gotham	UNP/LNO	ON	Perth	40 P/10	43°39'	80°57'
Gothe Island	ISL/ÎLE	NT	Keewatin	65 D/8	60°23'	102°15'
Gott Creek	RIV/CDE	BC	Lillooet	92 J/9	50°32'	122°08'
Gottfriedsen, Mount	MTN/MNT	BC	Kamloops Division Yale	82 E/13	49°56'	119°57'
Gott Peak	MTN/MNT	BC	Lillooet	92 J/8	50°22'	122°10'
Goudalie	UNP/LNO	NB	Kent	21 I/7	46°22'	64°41'
Goudie	UNP/LNO	SK	35-30-10-W2	62 M/11	51°39'	103°19'
Goudreau	UNP/LNO	ON	Algoma	42 C/7	48°16'	84°32'
Gouffre, Rivière du	RIV/CDE	QC	Charlevoix	21 M/8	47°26'	70°29'
Gough Lake	LAKE/LAC	AB	35-18-W4	83 A/1	52°02'	112°28'
Gouin, Lac	LAKE/LAC	QC	Le Fjord-du-Saguenay	22 E/9	49°33'	70°14'
Gouin, Réservoir	LAKE/LAC	QC	Le Haut-Saint-Maurice	32 B/10	48°38'	74°54'
Goulais Bay	UNP/LNO	ON	Algoma	41 K/9	46°43'	84°25'
Goulais Bay	BAY/BAIE	ON	Algoma	41 K/9	46°43'	84°30'
Goulais Bay 15A	IR/RI	ON	Algoma	41 K/10	46°43'	84°32'
Goulais Lake	LAKE/LAC	ON	Algoma	41 O/4	47°10'	83°40'
Goulais Mission	UNP/LNO	ON	Algoma	41 K/10	46°42'	84°31'
Goulais Point	CAPE/CAP	ON	Nipissing	41 I/8	46°19'	80°02'
Goulais Point	CAPE/CAP	ON	Algoma	41 K/10	46°41'	84°34'
Goulais River	UNP/LNO	ON	Algoma	41 K/9	46°43'	84°23'
Goulais River	RIV/CDE	ON	Algoma	41 K/9	46°43'	84°27'
Goulbourn	MUN2/AZM2	ON	Carleton	31 G/4	45°10'	75°56'
Goulbourne	UNP/LNO	MB	34-24-8-W	62 O/2	51°07'	98°31'
Gould	UNP/LNO	QC	Le Haut-Saint-François	21 E/11	45°35'	71°22'
Goulden Lake	LAKE/LAC	SK	62,63-10-W2	63 L/6	54°24'	103°26'
Gould Lake	LAKE/LAC	ON	Frontenac	31 C/7	44°28'	76°35'
Gould Lake	LAKE/LAC	ON	Bruce	41 A/11	44°35'	81°12'
Goulds	UNP/LNO	NF		1 N/7	47°29'	52°46'
Goulds	UNP/LNO	ON	Haliburton	31 E/2	45°01'	78°32'
Gould Station	UNP/LNO	QC	Le Haut-Saint-François	21 E/11	45°32'	71°22'
Gouldtown	UNP/LNO	SK	17-19-9-W3	72 J/11	50°37'	107°13'
Goulet-du-Nord, Le	UNP/LNO	QC	Les Îles-de-la-Madeleine	11 N/5	47°27'	61°48'
Goulet Lake	LAKE/LAC	MB		63 P/8	55°24'	96°17'
Goulet, Le - also-aussi - Gully, The	SEAU/SMER	—		4013	44°08'	59°12'
Gounamitz River	RIV/CDE	NB	Victoria	21 O/12	47°31'	67°39'
Goupil	UNP/LNO	QC	Matane	22 B/11	48°43'	67°19'
Goupil, Lac	LAKE/LAC	QC	Caniapiscau	23 C/16	52°55'	68°08'
Gourd	UNP/LNO	QC	Abitibi	32 D/9	48°31'	78°22'
Gourdeau Point	CAPE/CAP	NT	Franklin	68 E	74°27'	97°38'
Gourlay Lake	LAKE/LAC	ON	Algoma	42 C/15	48°52'	84°55'
Gouverneur	UNP/LNO	SK	30-9-12-W3	72 G/13	49°45'	107°37'
Govan	TOWN/VIL2	SK	14-27-22-W2	72 P/6	51°18'	105°00'
Govan Lake	LAKE/LAC	ON	Frontenac	31 F/2	45°08'	76°48'
Govenlock	UNP/LNO	SK	23-3-29-W3	72 F/4	49°14'	109°49'
Gover Lake	LAKE/LAC	NB	Northumberland	21 O/2	47°03'	66°44'
Government Landing	UNP/LNO	ON	Rainy River	52 C/13	48°50'	93°39'
Government Park	UNP/LNO	ON	Nipissing	31 L/2	46°03'	78°33'
Government Road	UNP/LNO	ON	Renfrew	31 F/14	45°46'	77°03'
Governor Lake	LAKE/LAC	NS	Halifax	11 E/2	45°13'	62°40'

NAME / NOM	ENTITY / ENTITÉ	LOC 1 / LIEU 1	LOC 2 / LIEU 2	MAP / CARTE	POSITION LAT	LONG
Governors Island	ISL/ÎLE	NF		12 G/1	49°04′	58°20′
Governors Island	ISL/ÎLE	PE	Queens	11 L/3	46°08′	63°04′
Gowanbrae	UNP/LNO	PE	Kings	11 L/8	46°23′	62°18′
Gowan Creek	RIV/CDE	BC	New Westminster	92 G/16	49°55′	122°22′
Gowan River	RIV/CDE	MB		53 M/16	55°49′	94°09′
Gowanstown	UNP/LNO	ON	Perth	40 P/15	43°46′	80°55′
Gower Point	UNP/LNO	BC	New Westminster	92 G/5	49°23′	123°32′
Gower Point	CAPE/CAP	BC	New Westminster	92 G/5	49°23′	123°32′
Gowgaia Bay	BAY/BAIE	BC	Queen Charlotte	103 B/5	52°25′	131°35′
Gowganda	UNP/LNO	ON	Timiskaming	41 P/10	47°39′	80°46′
Gowganda Lake	LAKE/LAC	ON	Timiskaming	41 P/10	47°38′	80°47′
Gow Lake	LAKE/LAC	SK		74 A/8	56°28′	104°29′
Gowland Mountain	UNP/LNO	NB	Albert	21 H/14	45°49′	65°03′
Goyeau, Pointe	CAPE/CAP	QC	Jamésie	32 M/14	51°47′	79°03′
Goyelle, Lac	LAKE/LAC	QC	Minganie	12 K/15	50°47′	60°45′
Gozdz Lake	LAKE/LAC	NT	Mackenzie	75 H/4	61°07′	105°54′
Gracefield	TOWN/VIL2	QC	La Vallée-de-la-Gatineau	31 K/1	46°06′	76°03′
Grâce, Île de	ISL/ÎLE	QC	Le Bas-Richelieu	31 I/3	46°05′	73°02′
Grace Lake	UNP/LNO	MB	56-26-W	63 F/14	53°49′	101°12′
Grace Lake	LAKE/LAC	NF		23 A/4	52°13′	65°37′
Gracieville	UNP/LNO	NS	Richmond	11 F/10	45°35′	60°43′
Grady Harbour	UNP/LNO	NF		13 H/16	53°48′	56°25′
Grady Island	ISL/ÎLE	NF		13 H/16	53°49′	56°25′
Grafton	UNP/LNO	NS	Kings	21 H/2	45°06′	64°42′
Grafton	UNP/LNO	NB	Carleton	21 J/4	46°09′	67°34′
Grafton	UNP/LNO	ON	Northumberland	30 M/16	44°00′	78°01′
Grafton Hill	UNP/LNO	NB	Carleton	21 J/4	46°08′	67°34′
Graham	UNP/LNO	ON	Thunder Bay	52 G/2	49°15′	90°34′
Graham	UNP/LNO	MB	29-5-4-W	62 H/5	49°25′	97°58′
Graham	UNP/LNO	BC	Lillooet	92 P/6	51°24′	121°19′
Graham Bay	BAY/BAIE	NT	Franklin	68 H/1	75°12′	96°24′
Graham Corner	UNP/LNO	NB	York	21 G/13	45°50′	67°41′
Graham Creek	RIV/CDE	MB/SK		62 F/7	49°16′	100°59′
Grahamdale	MUN2/AZM2	MB		62 O/7	51°23′	98°33′
Grahamdale	UNP/LNO	MB	15-28-8-W	62 O/8	51°24′	98°30′
Graham Gore Peninsula	CAPE/CAP	NT	Franklin	67 A	69°00′	99°12′
Graham Head	CAPE/CAP	NS	Halifax	11 D/11	44°38′	63°17′
Graham Hill	UNP/LNO	NS	Colchester	11 E/7	45°17′	62°59′
Graham Island	ISL/ÎLE	BC	Queen Charlotte	103 F/8	53°20′	132°25′
Graham Island	ISL/ÎLE	NT	Franklin	59 D	77°25′	90°30′
Graham Lake	LAKE/LAC	ON	Leeds	31 B/12	44°34′	75°53′
Graham Lake	LAKE/LAC	AB	87,88-4-W5	84 B/10	56°35′	114°33′
Graham Lake	LAKE/LAC	NT	Mackenzie	85 I/13	62°54′	113°48′
Graham Moore Bay	BAY/BAIE	NT	Franklin	68 G	75°26′	101°25′
Graham Moore, Cape	CAPE/CAP	NT	Franklin	38 B	72°52′	76°04′
Graham Reach	RIVF/EFLV	BC	Range 4 Coast	103 H/2	53°04′	128°34′
Graham River	RIV/CDE	BC	Peace River	94 B/9	56°30′	122°14′
Grahams Corner	UNP/LNO	NS	Halifax	11 D/12	44°41′	63°33′
Grahams Road	UNP/LNO	PE	Queens	11 L/5	46°26′	63°32′
Grahamsville	UNP/LNO	ON	Peel	30 M/12	43°43′	79°40′
Grahamvale	UNP/LNO	ON	Nipissing	31 L/3	46°08′	79°15′
Grainfield	UNP/LNO	NB	Northumberland	21 I/13	46°49′	65°53′
Grainger	UNP/LNO	AB	20-29-24-W4	82 P/6	51°30′	113°20′
Grainger River	RIV/CDE	NT	Mackenzie	95 G/3	61°08′	123°04′
Grainland	UNP/LNO	SK	19-23-4-W3	72 J/15	50°59′	106°33′
Gramont	UNP/LNO	QC	Papineau	31 G/15	45°54′	74°49′
Gramsons	UNP/LNO	BC	Lillooet	92 J/7	50°27′	122°41′
Granada	UNP/LNO	QC	Rouyn-Noranda	32 D/3	48°12′	79°03′
Granada	UNP/LNO	AB	25-53-10-W5	83 G/11	53°37′	115°21′
Granary Lake	LAKE/LAC	ON	Algoma	41 J/7	46°17′	82°50′
Granby	CITY/VIL1	QC	La Haute-Yamaska	31 H/7	45°24′	72°44′
Granby	VILG/VILG	QC	La Haute-Yamaska	31 H/7	45°24′	72°44′
Granby Island	UNP/LNO	NF		12 H/10	49°44′	56°44′
Granby-Ouest	UNP/LNO	QC	La Haute-Yamaska	31 H/7	45°25′	72°46′
Granby River	RIV/CDE	BC	Similkameen Division Yale	82 E/1	49°02′	118°26′
Grand-Aigle, Le	UNP/LNO	QC	La Vallée-de-la-Gatineau	31 K/1	46°13′	76°12′
Grand Banc - also-aussi - Grand Bank	SEAU/SMER	—		8014	45°25′	51°25′
Grand Banc, Queue du - also-aussi - Tail of the Bank	SEAU/SMER	—		8010	43°13′	50°03′
Grand Bank	TOWN/VIL2	NF		1 M/4	47°06′	55°46′
Grand Bank - also-aussi - Grand Banc	SEAU/SMER	—		8014	45°25′	51°25′
Grand Bank Head	CAPE/CAP	NF		1 M/4	47°07′	55°47′
Grand Banks of Newfoundland, The - also-aussi - Grands Bancs de Terre-Neuve, Les	SEAU/SMER	—		4016	45°30′	52°30′
Grand Bay	TOWN/VIL2	NB	Kings	21 G/8	45°18′	66°12′
Grand Bay	BAY/BAIE	NF		11 O/11	47°36′	59°10′
Grand Bay	BAY/BAIE	ON	Thunder Bay	52 H/10	49°34′	88°50′

NAME / NOM	ENTITY / ENTITÉ	LOC 1 / LIEU 1	LOC 2 / LIEU 2	MAP / CARTE	LAT	LONG
Grand Bay East	UNP/LNO	NF		11 O/11	47°35′	59°10′
Grand Bay River	RIV/CDE	NF		11 O/11	47°36′	59°09′
Grand Bay West	UNP/LNO	NF		11 O/11	47°35′	59°11′
Grand Beach	UNP/LNO	NF		1 M/4	47°08′	55°31′
Grand Beach	UNP/LNO	MB	24,18-6—E	62 I/10	50°33′	96°38′
Grand Bend	VILG/VILG	ON	Lambton	40 P/5	43°19′	81°45′
Grandbois	UNP/LNO	QC	Rivière-du-Loup	21 N/14	47°50′	69°12′
Grand-Bois-de-l'Ail, Le	UNP/LNO	QC	Portneuf	21 L/12	46°42′	71°45′
Grand-Bras	UNP/LNO	QC	Kamouraska	21 N/5	47°25′	69°48′
Grand Bruit	UNP/LNO	NF		11 O/9	47°40′	58°14′
Grand-Brûlé, Le	UNP/LNO	QC	Antoine-Labelle	31 J/4	46°09′	75°40′
Grand-Calumet	VILG/VILG	QC	Pontiac	31 F/10	45°44′	76°41′
Grand Calumet, Île du	ISL/ÎLE	QC	Pontiac	31 F/10	45°44′	76°41′
Grand Canyon of the Stikine	VALL/VALL	BC	Cassiar	104 J/1	58°07′	130°38′
Grand Centre - see-voir - Cold Lake	TOWN/VIL2	AB		73 L/8	54°25′	110°13′
Grand Codroy River	RIV/CDE	NF		11 O/14	47°50′	59°20′
Grand-Côtoyage, Le	UNP/LNO	QC	Pabok	22 A/10	48°35′	64°49′
Grand Coulee	VILG/VILG	SK	15-17-21-W2	72 I/7	50°26′	104°49′
Grand Desert	UNP/LNO	NS	Halifax	11 D/11	44°41′	63°16′
Grand-Détour	UNP/LNO	QC	Matane	22 B/13	48°48′	67°32′
Grand-Détour	UNP/LNO	QC	Le Domaine-du-Roy	32 A/8	48°22′	72°11′
Grand-Détour	UNP/LNO	QC	Témiscamingue	31 N/11	47°36′	77°29′
Grand Détour, Lac du	LAKE/LAC	QC	Le Fjord-du-Saguenay	22 E/15	49°58′	70°32′
Grande-Aldouane	UNP/LNO	NB	Kent	21 I/10	46°42′	64°56′
Grande-Anse	VILG/VILG	NB	Gloucester	21 P/14	47°48′	65°11′
Grande Anse	UNP/LNO	NS	Richmond	11 F/11	45°37′	61°04′
Grande-Anse	UNP/LNO	QC	Mékinac	31 P/2	47°05′	72°55′
Grande-Baie	UNP/LNO	QC	Le Fjord-du-Saguenay	22 D/7	48°19′	70°51′
Grande Baie, La	BAY/BAIE	QC	Le Fjord-du-Saguenay	22 L/10	50°36′	70°41′
Grande Cache	TOWN/VIL2	AB	56,57-8-W6	83 E/14	53°53′	119°08′
Grande-Cascapédia	VILG/VILG	QC	Bonaventure	22 A/5	48°15′	65°54′
Grande-Clairière	UNP/LNO	MB	30-6-24-W	62 F/10	49°30′	100°42′
Grande Décharge, La	LAKE/LAC	QC	Lac-Saint-Jean-Est	22 D/12	48°37′	71°43′
Grande-Digue	UNP/LNO	NB	Kent	21 I/7	46°18′	64°34′
Grande-Eau-Morte, La	UNP/LNO	QC	Le Domaine-du-Roy	32 A/8	48°17′	72°12′
Grande-Entrée	VILG/VILG	QC	Les Îles-de-la-Madeleine	11 N/12	47°33′	61°33′
Grande Entrée, Havre de la	BAY/BAIE	QC	Les Îles-de-la-Madeleine	11 N/12	47°35′	61°33′
Grande Entrée, Île de la	ISL/ÎLE	QC	Les Îles-de-la-Madeleine	11 N/12	47°34′	61°31′
Grande Fourche, La	RIV/CDE	QC	La Côte-de-Gaspé	22 A/15	48°49′	64°49′
Grande-Fresnière, La	UNP/LNO	QC	Deux-Montagnes	31 G/9	45°34′	74°00′
Grande-Grave	UNP/LNO	QC	La Côte-de-Gaspé	22 A/16	48°48′	64°14′
Grande-Grave, Lieu historique national de - also-aussi - Grande-Grave National Historic Site	PARK/PARC	QC	La Côte-de-Gaspé	22 A/16	48°48′	64°14′
Grande-Grave National Historic Site - also-aussi - Grande-Grave, Lieu historique national de	PARK/PARC	QC	La Côte-de-Gaspé	22 A/16	48°48′	64°14′
Grande Greve	UNP/LNO	NS	Richmond	11 F/10	45°38′	60°51′
Grande-Île	VILG/VILG	QC	Beauharnois-Salaberry	31 G/8	45°17′	74°08′
Grande Île, La	ISL/ÎLE	QC	Minganie	12 L/4	50°13′	63°54′
Grande-Ligne	UNP/LNO	QC	Le Haut-Richelieu	31 H/3	45°13′	73°18′
Grande Passe, Île de la	ISL/ÎLE	QC	Côte-Nord-du-Golfe-Saint-Laurent	12 O/2	51°08′	58°30′
Grande-Pointe	UNP/LNO	QC	Charlevoix	21 M/7	47°16′	70°35′
Grande Pointe	UNP/LNO	ON	Kent	40 J/8	42°26′	82°21′
Grande Pointe	UNP/LNO	MB		62 H/14	49°46′	97°03′
Grande Pointe, La	CAPE/CAP	QC	Minganie	12 L/3	50°12′	63°27′
Grande Pointe, Lac	LAKE/LAC	QC	Jamésie	33 G/13	53°51′	75°39′
Grande Point Settlement	GEOG/GÉOG	MB		62 H/14	49°46′	97°03′
Grande Prairie	CITY/VIL1	AB	71-6-W6	83 M/2	55°10′	118°48′
Grande Prairie No. 1, County of	MUN1/AZM1	AB	72-7-W6	83 M/6	55°16′	119°09′
Grande-Presqu'île	UNP/LNO	QC	Papineau	31 G/11	45°36′	75°02′
Grande-Quatre, La	UNP/LNO	QC	Jamésie	33 H/13	53°50′	73°32′
Grande-Rivière	CITY/VIL1	QC	Pabok	22 A/8	48°24′	64°30′
Grande Rivière, La	RIV/CDE	NB	Madawaska	21 O/4	47°11′	67°57′
Grande Rivière, La	RIV/CDE	QC	Pabok	22 A/7	48°24′	64°30′
Grande Rivière, La	RIV/CDE	QC	Kamouraska	21 N/5	47°21′	69°56′
Grande Rivière, La	RIV/CDE	QC	Jamésie	33 E/14	53°50′	79°00′
Grande-Rivière-Ouest	UNP/LNO	QC	Pabok	22 A/7	48°24′	64°31′
Grande Rivière Ouest	RIV/CDE	QC	Pabok	22 A/7	48°27′	64°32′
Grandes-Bergeronnes	TOWN/VIL2	QC	La Haute-Côte-Nord	22 C/4	48°15′	69°32′
Grandes-Piles	TOWN/VIL2	QC	Mékinac	31 I/10	46°41′	72°44′
Grandes Pointes, Lac aux	LAKE/LAC	QC	Maria-Chapdelaine	22 E/4	49°08′	71°34′
Grand Étang	UNP/LNO	NS	Inverness	11 K/11	46°33′	61°02′
Grand-Étang	UNP/LNO	QC	La Côte-de-Gaspé	22 H/2	49°08′	64°45′
Grande Traversée, Côte de la	CAPE/CAP	QC	Minganie	12 E/6	49°18′	63°16′
Grande-Trois, La	UNP/LNO	QC	Jamésie	33 G/12	53°44′	75°59′
Grande-Vallée	VILG/VILG	QC	La Côte-de-Gaspé	22 H/3	49°13′	65°08′
Grande-Vallée-des-Monts	UNP/LNO	QC	La Côte-de-Gaspé	22 H/3	49°10′	65°11′
Grand Falls - also-aussi - Grand-Sault	TOWN/VIL2	NB	Victoria	21 O/4	47°03′	67°44′

NAME NOM	ENTITY ENTITÉ	LOC 1 LIEU 1	LOC 2 LIEU 2	MAP CARTE	POSITION	
					LAT	LONG
Grand Falls	UNP/LNO	NF		2 D/13	48°56′	55°40′
Grand Falls	GEOG/GÉOG	NB	Victoria	21 J/13	46°55′	67°45′
Grand Falls Portage	UNP/LNO	NB	Victoria	21 O/4	47°01′	67°45′
Grand Falls Station	UNP/LNO	NB	Madawaska	21 O/4	47°04′	67°45′
Grand Falls-Windsor	TOWN/VIL2	NF		2 D/13	48°56′	55°40′
Grand-Fonds	UNP/LNO	QC	Denis-Riverin	22 G/2	49°03′	66°41′
Grand-Fonds	UNP/LNO	QC	Charlevoix-Est	21 M/16	47°45′	70°07′
Grand Fonds, Mont	MTN/MNT	QC	Charlevoix-Est	21 M/16	47°46′	70°05′
Grand Forks	CITY/VIL1	BC	Similkameen Division Yale	82 E/1	49°02′	118°26′
Grand Forks	UNP/LNO	YT		115 O/14	63°55′	139°19′
Grand Harbour	UNP/LNO	NB	Charlotte	21 B/10	44°41′	66°46′
Grand Haven	UNP/LNO	BC	Peace River	94 A/2	56°14′	120°54′
Grandin, Lac	LAKE/LAC	NT	Mackenzie	85 M	63°59′	119°00′
Grandin, Rivière	RIV/CDE	NT	Mackenzie	85 M	63°32′	118°20′
Grandique Ferry	UNP/LNO	NS	Richmond	11 F/11	45°36′	61°02′
Grand Island	ISL/ÎLE	MB	44,45-18-W	63 C/16	52°52′	100°00′
Grand Jardin	UNP/LNO	NF		12 B/6	48°28′	59°13′
Grand John	UNP/LNO	NF		1 M/6	47°29′	55°04′
Grand, Lac	LAKE/LAC	QC	Les Collines-de-l'Outaouais	31 G/12	45°41′	75°39′
Grand, Lac	LAKE/LAC	QC	La Vallée-de-la-Gatineau	31 N/2	47°10′	76°56′
Grand-Lac-Neigette	UNP/LNO	QC	La Mitis	22 C/8	48°16′	68°10′
Grand-Lac-Salé, Réserve écologique du	PARK/PARC	QC	Minganie	12 E/6	49°20′	63°15′
Grand-Lac-Touradi	MUN2/AZM2	QC	Rimouski-Neigette	22 C/2	48°07′	68°40′
Grand-Lac-Victoria	UNP/LNO	QC	Vallée-de-l'Or	31 N/11	47°32′	77°27′
Grand Lake	LAKE/LAC	NF		12 H/3	49°00′	57°20′
Grand Lake	LAKE/LAC	NF		13 F/9	53°40′	60°30′
Grand Lake	LAKE/LAC	NS	Halifax	11 D/15	44°55′	62°36′
Grand Lake	LAKE/LAC	NS	Halifax	11 D/14	44°54′	63°09′
Grand Lake	LAKE/LAC	NB	Queens	21 G/16	45°55′	66°05′
Grand Lake	LAKE/LAC	NB	York	21 G/12	45°42′	67°48′
Grand Lake	LAKE/LAC	ON	Nipissing	31 F/13	45°53′	77°49′
Grand Lake Road	UNP/LNO	NS	Cape Breton	11 K/1	46°09′	60°08′
Grand Lake Road	UNP/LNO	NB	Northumberland	21 J/9	46°32′	66°06′
Grand Lake Station	UNP/LNO	NS	Halifax	11 D/13	44°53′	63°36′
Grand Le Pierre	VILG/VILG	NF		1 M/10	47°41′	54°47′
Grandmaison	UNP/LNO	NB	Madawaska	21 N/9	47°31′	68°23′
Grand Manan	VILG/VILG	NB	Charlotte	21 B/10	44°42′	66°49′
Grand Manan	GEOG/GÉOG	NB	Charlotte	21 B/10	44°40′	66°45′
Grand Manan, Bancs - also-aussi - Grand Manan Banks	SEAU/SMER	—		4003	44°10′	67°05′
Grand Manan Banks - also-aussi - Grand Manan, Bancs	SEAU/SMER	—		4003	44°10′	67°05′
Grand Manan Basin - also-aussi - Grand Manan, Bassin	SEAU/SMER	—		4011	44°25′	66°35′
Grand Manan, Bassin - also-aussi - Grand Manan Basin	SEAU/SMER	—		4011	44°25′	66°35′
Grand Manan Channel	CHAN/CHEN	NB	Charlotte	21 B/10	44°45′	66°52′
Grand Manan Island	ISL/ÎLE	NB	Charlotte	21 B/10	44°43′	66°47′
Grand Marais	UNP/LNO	MB	18-18-7-E	62 I/10	50°33′	96°37′
Grand-Maria, La	UNP/LNO	QC	Le Bas-Richelieu	31 I/3	46°01′	73°07′
Grand-Mère	CITY/VIL1	QC	Le Centre-de-la-Mauricie	31 I/10	46°37′	72°42′
Grandmesnil, Lac	LAKE/LAC	QC	Sept-Rivières	22 O/5	51°19′	67°33′
Grand-Métis	VILG/VILG	QC	La Mitis	22 C/9	48°38′	68°08′
Grand Mira North	UNP/LNO	NS	Cape Breton	11 F/16	45°52′	60°19′
Grand Mira South	UNP/LNO	NS	Cape Breton	11 F/16	45°53′	60°17′
Grandmother's Bay 219	IR/RI	SK		73 P/10	55°36′	104°35′
Grand Narrows	UNP/LNO	NS	Cape Breton	11 F/15	45°57′	60°47′
Grand Nord, Le	SEAU/SMER	—		4049	47°10′	49°30′
Grand Nord, Ruisseau	RIV/CDE	QC	Bonaventure	22 B/8	48°19′	66°01′
Grandois	UNP/LNO	NF		2 M/4	51°06′	55°45′
Grandora	UNP/LNO	SK	36-7-W3	73 B/2	52°07′	106°59′
Grand-Pabos	UNP/LNO	QC	Pabok	22 A/7	48°21′	64°38′
Grand Pabos, Baie du	BAY/BAIE	QC	Pabok	22 A/7	48°20′	64°42′
Grand-Pabos-Ouest	UNP/LNO	QC	Pabok	22 A/7	48°19′	64°44′
Grand Pabos, Rivière du	RIV/CDE	QC	Pabok	22 A/7	48°21′	64°42′
Grand Pacific Glacier	GLAC/GLAC	BC	Cassiar	114 P/3	59°11′	137°18′
Grand Passage	CHAN/CHEN	NS	Digby	21 B/8	44°16′	66°20′
Grand-Plaqué, Le	UNP/LNO	QC	Denis-Riverin	22 G/1	49°04′	66°29′
Grand Pré	UNP/LNO	NS	Kings	21 H/1	45°06′	64°18′
Grand-Pré	UNP/LNO	QC	Asbestos	21 E/12	45°39′	71°51′
Grand-Pré, Lieu historique national de - also-aussi - Grand-Pré National Historic Site	PARK/PARC	NS	Kings	21 H/1	45°07′	64°19′
Grand-Pré National Historic Site - also-aussi - Grand-Pré, Lieu historique national de	PARK/PARC	NS	Kings	21 H/1	45°07′	64°19′
Grand Rapide 5 - see-voir - Kuz Che 5	IR/RI	BC		93 K/15	54°47′	124°53′
Grand Rapids	MUN2/AZM2	MB		63 G/3	53°13′	99°18′
Grand Rapids	UNP/LNO	MB		63 G/3	53°11′	99°16′
Grand Rapids	UNP/LNO	BC	Range 5 Coast	93 K/15	54°47′	124°53′

NAME NOM	ENTITY ENTITÉ	LOC 1 LIEU 1	LOC 2 LIEU 2	MAP CARTE	POSITION LAT	LONG
Grand Rapids 33	IR/RI	MB		63 G/3	53°10′	99°14′
Grand-Remous	VILG/VILG	QC	La Vallée-de-la-Gatineau	31 J/12	46°37′	75°54′
Grand-Remous	UNP/LNO	QC	La Vallée-de-la-Gatineau	31 J/12	46°37′	75°55′
Grand River	UNP/LNO	PE	Prince	11 L/12	46°30′	63°55′
Grand River	UNP/LNO	NS	Richmond	11 F/10	45°39′	60°40′
Grand River	UNP/LNO	NB	Madawaska	21 O/5	47°17′	67°47′
Grand River	RIV/CDE	NS	Richmond	11 F/10	45°37′	60°38′
Grand River	RIV/CDE	ON	Haldimand	30 L/13	42°51′	79°34′
Grand River Falls	UNP/LNO	NS	Richmond	11 F/10	45°42′	60°38′
Grand-Ruisseau	UNP/LNO	NB	Madawaska	21 O/4	47°12′	67°52′
Grand-Ruisseau	UNP/LNO	QC	Les Îles-de-la-Madeleine	11 N/5	47°24′	61°53′
Grand-Ruisseau	UNP/LNO	QC	Sept-Rivières	22 G/11	49°44′	67°10′
Grand-Saint-Esprit	VILG/VILG	QC	Nicolet-Yamaska	31 I/1	46°11′	72°30′
Grand-Saint-Louis	UNP/LNO	QC	Bécancour	31 I/8	46°19′	72°21′
Grand-Sault - also-aussi - Grand Falls	TOWN/VIL2	NB	Victoria	21 O/4	47°03′	67°44′
Grands Bancs de Terre-Neuve, Les - also-aussi - Grand Banks of Newfoundland, The	SEAU/SMER	—		4016	45°30′	52°30′
Grands-Jardins, Parc de conservation des	PARK/PARC	QC	Charlevoix	21 M/10	47°41′	70°51′
Grands-Ormes, Réserve écologique des	PARK/PARC	QC	Charlevoix-Est	21 M/16	47°53′	70°28′
Grands Voiliers, Chenal des	CHAN/CHEN	QC	Bellechasse	21 L/15	46°52′	70°58′
Grand Tracadie	VILG/VILG	PE	Queens	11 L/6	46°24′	63°02′
Grand Tracadie	UNP/LNO	PE	Queens	11 L/6	46°24′	63°03′
Grand Trunk	UNP/LNO	BC	Range 5 Coast	103 I/16	54°54′	128°24′
Granduc	UNP/LNO	BC	Cassiar	104 B/1	56°14′	130°06′
Grand Valley	UNP/LNO	ON	Dufferin	40 P/16	43°54′	80°19′
Grand Valley Creek	RIV/CDE	YT		115 O/1	63°15′	138°19′
Grand Valley Roadhouse	UNP/LNO	YT		115 P/4	63°06′	137°46′
Grandview	TOWN/VIL2	MB	24-25-24-W	62 N/2	51°10′	100°42′
Grandview	VILG/VILG	AB	22,27,28-46-1-W5	83 B/16	52°59′	114°04′
Grandview	MUN2/AZM2	MB		62 N/2	51°12′	100°49′
Grandview	UNP/LNO	PE	Queens	11 L/2	46°07′	62°46′
Grand View - see-voir - Browns Flat	UNP/LNO	NB		21 G/8	45°28′	66°08′
Grandview	UNP/LNO	ON	Muskoka	31 E/3	45°12′	79°03′
Grand View	UNP/LNO	SK		72 I/5	50°23′	105°33′
Grandview	UNP/LNO	BC	New Westminster	92 G/2	49°03′	122°44′
Grandview Beach	VILG/VILG	SK	15-22-23-W2	72 I/14	50°52′	105°06′
Grandview Beach	UNP/LNO	ON	Simcoe	31 D/13	44°46′	79°49′
Grandview Bench	UNP/LNO	BC	Kamloops Division Yale	82 L/11	50°39′	119°09′
Grandview Gardens	UNP/LNO	ON	Algoma	41 K/9	46°31′	84°16′
Grandview No. 349	MUN2/AZM2	SK		73 C/2	52°00′	108°40′
*Grandview Station	UNP/LNO	PE	Queens	11 L/2	46°08′	62°48′
Grandview-Woodlands	UNP/LNO	BC	New Westminster	92 G/6	49°17′	123°04′
Grandy Brook	RIV/CDE	NF		11 P/12	47°38′	57°42′
Grandys Brook	RIV/CDE	NF		11 O/10	47°37′	58°51′
Grandy Sound	CHAN/CHEN	NF		11 O/10	47°36′	58°50′
Granet, Lac	LAKE/LAC	QC	Vallée-de-l'Or	31 N/13	47°47′	77°31′
Granet Lake	LAKE/LAC	NT	Franklin	97 B	68°42′	125°35′
Granger	UNP/LNO	ON	Dufferin	41 A/1	44°04′	80°06′
Granger Lake	LAKE/LAC	SK		74 I/11	58°33′	105°12′
Granger, Mount	MTN/MNT	YT		105 D/11	60°33′	135°15′
Grangeville	UNP/LNO	NB	Kent	21 I/6	46°25′	65°12′
Granisle	VILG/VILG	BC	Range 5 Coast	93 L/16	54°53′	126°13′
Granite	UNP/LNO	BC	Kootenay	82 F/6	49°29′	117°22′
Granite Bay	UNP/LNO	BC	Sayward	92 K/3	50°14′	125°18′
Granite Canyon	VALL/VALL	YT		115 I/16	62°51′	136°13′
Granite, Cape	CAPE/CAP	NT	Franklin	58 C	73°43′	95°41′
Granite, Chute au	FALL/CHUT	QC	Kativik	23 N/16	55°51′	68°25′
Granite Creek	RIV/CDE	BC	Yale Division Yale	92 H/7	49°30′	120°41′
Granite Falls	UNP/LNO	BC	New Westminster	92 G/7	49°27′	122°52′
Granite Hill	UNP/LNO	NB	York	21 G/14	45°57′	67°06′
Granitehill Lake	LAKE/LAC	ON	Algoma	42 F/3	49°06′	85°15′
Granite Island 4	IR/RI	BC	Rupert	92 L/3	50°02′	127°25′
Granite Lake	UNP/LNO	ON	Kenora	52 E/10	49°43′	94°51′
Granite Lake	LAKE/LAC	NF		12 A/3	48°10′	57°07′
Granite Lake	LAKE/LAC	ON	Thunder Bay	52 I/5	50°29′	89°46′
Granite Lake	LAKE/LAC	SK	68-4-W2	63 L/15	54°53′	102°32′
Granite Peak	MTN/MNT	BC	Range 1 Coast	92 K/10	50°43′	124°58′
Granite Point	CAPE/CAP	NF		12 I/9	50°31′	56°17′
Granite Village	UNP/LNO	NS	Queens	20 P/15	43°52′	64°58′
Graniteville	UNP/LNO	QC	Memphrémagog	31 H/1	45°01′	72°11′
Graniteville	UNP/LNO	ON	Nipissing	31 L/6	46°20′	79°26′
Grant	UNP/LNO	ON	Cochrane	42 L/1	50°08′	86°18′
Grant	UNP/LNO	SK	17-18-18-W3	72 K/9	50°31′	108°27′
Grant Brook	UNP/LNO	BC	Cariboo	83 D/15	52°54′	118°46′
Grantham	UNP/LNO	ON	Lincoln	30 M/3	43°12′	79°13′
Grantham	UNP/LNO	AB	8-13-15-W4	82 I/1	50°04′	112°00′

NAME NOM	ENTITY ENTITÉ	LOC 1 LIEU 1	LOC 2 LIEU 2	MAP CARTE	POSITION LAT	LONG
Grantham	UNP/LNO	BC	Comox	92 F/14	49°46'	125°01'
Granthams Landing	UNP/LNO	BC	New Westminster	92 G/6	49°25'	123°30'
Grant Ice Cap	GLAC/GLAC	NT	Franklin	120 F	82°25'	66°45'
Grant Lake	LAKE/LAC	NT	Keewatin	65 N	63°38'	100°30'
Grant Lake	LAKE/LAC	NT	Mackenzie	86 C	64°54'	116°30'
Grantley	UNP/LNO	ON	Dundas	31 G/3	45°04'	75°09'
Grant No. 372	MUN2/AZM2	SK		73 A/5	52°20'	105°50'
Granton	UNP/LNO	NS	Pictou	11 E/10	45°37'	62°44'
Granton	UNP/LNO	ON	Middlesex	40 P/3	43°13'	81°18'
Grant Park	UNP/LNO	MB		62 H/14	49°51'	97°10'
Grant Point	CAPE/CAP	ON	Haldimand	30 L/13	42°50'	79°38'
Grant Point	CAPE/CAP	NT	Keewatin	67 A	68°24'	98°40'
Grant Point	CAPE/CAP	NT	Mackenzie	85 H/6	61°29'	113°04'
Grants	UNP/LNO	NF		2 D/9	48°44'	54°11'
Grants Corners	UNP/LNO	ON	Stormont	31 G/2	45°05'	74°42'
Grants Cut	UNP/LNO	MB	13-12-21-W	62 K/1	50°01'	100°13'
Grant Settlement	UNP/LNO	NB	Queens	21 I/4	46°01'	65°51'
Grants Lake	LAKE/LAC	NB	Northumberland	21 O/8	47°20'	66°14'
Grants Settlement	UNP/LNO	ON	Renfrew	31 F/10	45°42'	76°44'
Grant-Suttie Bay	BAY/BAIE	NT	Franklin	37 C	69°47'	77°15'
Grant Valley	UNP/LNO	NS	Hants	11 E/4	45°08'	63°40'
Grantville	UNP/LNO	NS	Richmond	11 F/11	45°39'	61°14'
Granum	TOWN/VIL2	AB	31-10-26-W4	82 H/13	49°52'	113°30'
Granville	UNP/LNO	PE	Queens	11 L/6	46°26'	63°28'
Granville	UNP/LNO	YT		115 O/10	63°40'	138°37'
Granville Beach	UNP/LNO	NS	Annapolis	21 A/12	44°44'	65°34'
Granville Centre	UNP/LNO	NS	Annapolis	21 A/14	44°47'	65°27'
Granville Ferry	UNP/LNO	NS	Annapolis	21 A/12	44°45'	65°31'
Granville Lake	UNP/LNO	MB		64 C/2	56°14'	100°34'
Granville Lake	LAKE/LAC	MB		64 C/8	56°18'	100°29'
Graphite	UNP/LNO	ON	Hastings	31 F/4	45°12'	77°53'
Gras, Lac	LAKE/LAC	QC	Caniapiscau	23 B/6	52°18'	67°06'
Gras, Lac de	LAKE/LAC	NT	Mackenzie	76 D	64°30'	110°30'
Grasmere	UNP/LNO	BC	Kootenay	82 G/3	49°06'	115°05'
Grass 15	IR/RI	BC	New Westminster	92 H/4	49°08'	121°53'
Grassberry River	RIV/CDE	SK	59-6-W2	63 L/2	54°07'	102°51'
Grass Cove	UNP/LNO	NS	Cape Breton	11 F/15	45°59'	60°49'
Grassdale	UNP/LNO	SK	20-7-15-W2	72 H/9	49°35'	104°00'
Grasset, Lac	LAKE/LAC	QC	Jamésie	32 E/16	49°57'	78°10'
Grassham Lake	LAKE/LAC	BC	Range 5 Coast	93 K/7	54°30'	124°47'
Grasshill	UNP/LNO	ON	Victoria	31 D/7	44°25'	78°55'
Grassie	UNP/LNO	ON	Lincoln	30 M/4	43°09'	79°37'
Grass Lake No. 381	MUN2/AZM2	SK		73 C/3	52°15'	109°20'
Grassland	UNP/LNO	AB	28-67-18-W4	83 I/15	54°49'	112°41'
Grasslands 7	IR/RI	BC	New Westminster	92 I/14	50°48'	121°24'
Grasslands National Park - also-aussi - Prairies, Parc national des	PARK/PARC	SK		72 G/3	49°07'	107°26'
Grassmere	UNP/LNO	ON	Muskoka	31 E/6	45°22'	79°07'
Grass Point 13	IR/RI	BC	Rupert	102 I/9	50°31'	128°02'
Grass River	UNP/LNO	MB	12-18-12-W	62 J/10	50°31'	99°00'
Grass River	RIV/CDE	MB		64 A/2	56°03'	96°33'
Grasswood	HAM/HAM	SK	3,4-36-5-3	73 B/2	52°03'	106°39'
Grassy, Cape	CAPE/CAP	NT	Franklin	89 A	76°17'	113°00'
Grassy Creek No. 78	MUN2/AZM2	SK		72 F/9	49°35'	108°10'
Grassy Island 17	IR/RI	BC	Nootka	92 E/14	49°55'	127°15'
Grassy Island Lake	LAKE/LAC	AB	33-3-W4	72 M/16	51°50'	110°20'
Grassy Island National Historic Site - also-aussi - Île-Grassy, Lieu historique national de l'	PARK/PARC	NS	Guysborough	11 F/7	45°20'	60°58'
Grassy Islet 2	IR/RI	BC	Range 4 Coast	103 G/16	53°48'	130°22'
Grassy Lake	UNP/LNO	AB	16-10-13-W4	72 E/13	49°49'	111°43'
Grassy Lake	LAKE/LAC	NB	York	21 G/14	45°49'	67°29'
Grassy Narrow	UNP/LNO	QC	Témiscamingue	31 M/10	47°39'	78°50'
Grassy Narrows	UNP/LNO	ON	Kenora	52 L/1	50°09'	94°02'
Grassy Narrows Lake	LAKE/LAC	ON	Kenora	52 L/1	50°09'	94°02'
Grassy Plains	UNP/LNO	BC	Range 4 Coast	93 F/13	53°58'	125°53'
Grassy Point	CAPE/CAP	NF		1 M/16	47°46'	54°01'
Grassy River	RIV/CDE	ON	Cochrane	42 A/6	48°22'	81°27'
Grates Cove	UNP/LNO	NF		2 C/2	48°10'	52°56'
Grates Point	CAPE/CAP	NF		2 C/2	48°10'	52°57'
Grattan	MUN2/AZM2	ON	Renfrew	31 F/6	45°28'	77°01'
Grave Flats	UNP/LNO	AB	45-21-W5	83 C/15	52°53'	116°50'
Gravel	UNP/LNO	QC	Bonaventure	22 A/4	48°07'	65°35'
Gravel	UNP/LNO	ON	Thunder Bay	42 D/13	48°55'	87°46'
Gravelbourg	TOWN/VIL2	SK	1-11-5-W3	72 G/15	49°53'	106°33'
Gravelbourg Junction	UNP/LNO	SK	27-12-23-W2	72 I/3	50°02'	105°05'
Gravelbourg No. 104	MUN2/AZM2	SK		72 G/15	49°55'	106°35'
Gravel Hill	UNP/LNO	NB	Restigouche	21 O/16	47°55'	66°08'

NAME NOM	ENTITY ENTITÉ	LOC 1 LIEU 1	LOC 2 LIEU 2	MAP CARTE	POSITION LAT	LONG
Gravel Hill	UNP/LNO	ON	Stormont	31 G/2	45°13′	74°54′
Gravel Hill Lake	LAKE/LAC	NT	Mackenzie	65 L/4	62°10′	103°52′
Gravel Island	ISL/ÎLE	NS	Lunenburg	21 A/9	44°30′	64°02′
Gravel Lake	UNP/LNO	YT		115 P/13	63°49′	137°54′
Gravelle	UNP/LNO	QC	La Vallée-de-la-Gatineau	31 K/1	46°12′	76°03′
Gravelle Ferry	UNP/LNO	BC	Cariboo	93 B/16	52°51′	122°14′
Gravell Point	CAPE/CAP	NT	Franklin	36 N	67°13′	76°42′
Gravelly Point	CAPE/CAP	ON	Prince Edward	30 N/15	43°55′	76°56′
Gravel River	RIV/CDE	ON	Thunder Bay	42 D/13	48°55′	87°46′
Graven Bank	UNP/LNO	NF		1 K/13	46°58′	53°32′
Gravenhurst	TOWN/VIL2	ON	Muskoka	31 D/14	44°55′	79°22′
Graves Strait	CHAN/CHEN	NT	Franklin	25 H	61°43′	65°00′
Graveyard 5	IR/RI	BC	New Westminster	92 G/2	49°13′	122°39′
Gravier, Le	UNP/LNO	QC	Bellechasse	21 L/15	46°47′	70°42′
Gray	HAM/HAM	SK	18-14-18-W2	72 I/1	50°10′	104°26′
Grayburn	UNP/LNO	SK	19-18-28-W2	72 I/12	50°32′	105°50′
Gray Creek	UNP/LNO	BC	Kootenay	82 F/10	49°38′	116°47′
Gray Lake	LAKE/LAC	NT	Mackenzie	75 F	61°52′	108°15′
Grayling Fork	RIV/CDE	YT		116 K/2	66°09′	141°00′
Grayling River	RIV/CDE	BC	Peace River	94 N/6	59°21′	125°02′
Gray Point	CAPE/CAP	BC	Queen Charlotte	103 G/4	53°06′	131°39′
Gray Rapids	UNP/LNO	NB	Northumberland	21 I/13	46°47′	65°45′
Grays	UNP/LNO	ON	Lambton	40 I/13	42°47′	81°51′
Grays Bay	UNP/LNO	ON	Ontario	31 D/11	44°39′	79°21′
Grays Bay	BAY/BAIE	NT	Franklin	76 M	67°49′	111°03′
Gray's Beach	UNP/LNO	ON	Grenville	31 C/8	44°20′	76°07′
Grays Mills	UNP/LNO	NB	Kings	21 G/8	45°29′	66°04′
Grayson	VILG/VILG	SK	16-20-5-W2	62 L/10	50°43′	102°39′
Grayson Lake	LAKE/LAC	ON	Thunder Bay	52 I/14	50°53′	89°25′
Grayson No. 184	MUN2/AZM2	SK		62 L/10	50°45′	102°35′
Gray Strait	CHAN/CHEN	NT	Franklin	25 A/10	60°32′	64°40′
Graysville	UNP/LNO	MB	25-6-6-W	62 G/9	49°31′	98°09′
Gray Valley	UNP/LNO	QC	Les Laurentides	31 G/15	45°57′	74°41′
Graywood	UNP/LNO	NS	Annapolis	21 A/11	44°39′	65°27′
Grease River	RIV/CDE	SK/NT		74 O/7	59°22′	106°48′
Greasy Lake	LAKE/LAC	NT	Mackenzie	95 J/16	62°57′	122°15′
Greata	UNP/LNO	BC	Osoyoos Division Yale	82 E/12	49°42′	119°45′
Great Barasway	UNP/LNO	NF		1 M/1	47°08′	54°04′
Great Barren Lake	LAKE/LAC	NS	Yarmouth	20 P/13	43°51′	65°44′
Great Bay de l'Eau	BAY/BAIE	NF		1 M/5	47°28′	55°42′
Great Bear Cape	CAPE/CAP	NT	Franklin	49 C	77°23′	87°45′
Great Bear Lake - also-aussi - **Ours, Grand lac de l'**	LAKE/LAC	NT	Mackenzie	96 H	65°50′	120°45′
Great Bear Lake 16	IR/RI	BC	Cariboo	93 J/5	54°28′	123°42′
Great Bear River	RIV/CDE	NT	Mackenzie	96 C/13	64°54′	125°36′
Great Beaver Lake	LAKE/LAC	BC	Cariboo	93 J/5	54°28′	123°44′
Great Bend No. 405	MUN2/AZM2	SK		73 B/6	52°30′	107°10′
Great Black Island	ISL/ÎLE	NF		2 C/13	48°49′	53°37′
Great Bona	UNP/LNO	NF		1 M/7	47°23′	54°32′
Great Bras d'Or	CHAN/CHEN	NS	Victoria	11 K/8	46°16′	60°27′
Great Brehat	UNP/LNO	NF		2 M/5	51°26′	55°30′
Great Brule	UNP/LNO	NF		1 M/9	47°40′	54°08′
Great Burnt Lake	LAKE/LAC	NF		12 A/8	48°20′	56°13′
Great Caribou Island	ISL/ÎLE	NF		3 D/5	52°16′	55°38′
Great Cat Arm	BAY/BAIE	NF		12 I/2	50°07′	56°39′
Great Central	UNP/LNO	BC	Alberni	92 F/7	49°19′	124°59′
Great Central Lake	LAKE/LAC	BC	Clayoquot	92 F/6	49°21′	125°15′
Great Chance Harbour	BAY/BAIE	NF		2 C/5	48°31′	53°41′
Great Codroy	UNP/LNO	NF		11 O/14	47°51′	59°16′
Great Colinet Island	ISL/ÎLE	NF		1 K/13	47°00′	53°42′
Great Cormorandier Island	ISL/ÎLE	NF		2 M/4	51°13′	55°40′
Great Deer	UNP/LNO	SK	35-41-8-W3	73 B/11	52°35′	107°03′
Great Desert	UNP/LNO	ON	Nipissing	31 L/3	46°13′	79°01′
Great Duck Island	ISL/ÎLE	NB	Charlotte	21 B/10	44°41′	66°42′
Great Duck Island	ISL/ÎLE	ON	Manitoulin	41 G/10	45°40′	82°57′
Greater Vancouver	MUN1/AZM1	BC	New Westminster	92 G/6	49°20′	123°00′
Great Falls	UNP/LNO	MB	27-17-11-E	62 I/8	50°28′	96°01′
Great Glacier	GLAC/GLAC	BC	Cassiar	104 B/13	56°51′	131°53′
Great Gull Lake	LAKE/LAC	NF		2 D/6	48°19′	55°22′
Great Gull Lake	LAKE/LAC	NF		12 H/1	49°12′	56°09′
Great Gull River	RIV/CDE	NF		2 D/11	48°36′	55°21′
Great Harbour	UNP/LNO	NF		1 M/12	47°31′	55°51′
Great Harbour Deep	VILG/VILG	NF		12 I/7	50°22′	56°31′
Great Harbour Deep	BAY/BAIE	NF		12 I/8	50°22′	56°27′
Great Hill	UNP/LNO	NS	Queens	21 A/2	44°04′	64°43′
Great Island	ISL/ÎLE	NF		1 N/2	47°14′	52°47′

NAME NOM	ENTITY ENTITÉ	LOC 1 LIEU 1	LOC 2 LIEU 2	MAP CARTE	POSITION	
					LAT	LONG
Great Island	ISL/ÎLE	NF		11 P/11	47°32′	57°21′
Great Island	ISL/ÎLE	NS	Queens	21 A/2	44°08′	64°32′
Great Island	ISL/ÎLE	MB		64 I/15	58°53′	96°35′
Great Islets Harbour	BAY/BAIE	NF		2 M/4	51°09′	55°45′
Great Jervais	UNP/LNO	NF		1 M/6	47°28′	55°09′
Great Jervis Harbour	UNP/LNO	NF		11 P/9	47°40′	56°10′
Great La Cloche Island	ISL/ÎLE	ON	Manitoulin	41 I/4	46°01′	81°53′
Great North	SEAU/SMER	—		4049	47°10′	49°30′
Great North Bay	BAY/BAIE	ON	Nipissing	31 L/5	46°20′	79°43′
Great Paradise	UNP/LNO	NF		1 M/8	47°21′	54°36′
Great Pinchgut	BAY/BAIE	NF		1 N/12	47°36′	53°55′
Great Plain of the Koukdjuak	PLN/PLNE	NT	Franklin	36 I	66°25′	72°50′
Great Pubnico Lake	LAKE/LAC	NS	Yarmouth	20 P/12	43°42′	65°43′
Great Rattling Brook	RIV/CDE	NF		2 D/13	48°58′	55°33′
Great Salmonier	UNP/LNO	NF		1 M/3	47°02′	55°12′
Great Sand Hills	MTN/MNT	SK		72 K/11	50°30′	109°00′
Great Seal Island	ISL/ÎLE	NF		1 M/8	47°28′	54°08′
Great Slave Lake - also-aussi - **Esclaves, Grand lac des**	LAKE/LAC	NT	Mackenzie	85 G	61°30′	114°00′
Great Snow Mountain	MTN/MNT	BC	Peace River	94 F/8	57°27′	124°06′
Great Village	UNP/LNO	NS	Colchester	11 E/5	45°25′	63°36′
Greaves Island	ISL/ÎLE	BC	Range 2 Coast	92 M/5	51°18′	127°30′
Greece's Point	UNP/LNO	QC	Argenteuil	31 G/10	45°36′	74°30′
Greeley	UNP/LNO	BC	Kootenay	82 M/1	51°01′	118°05′
Greeleytown	UNP/LNO	NF		1 N/10	47°30′	52°59′
Greely	UNP/LNO	ON	Carleton	31 G/5	45°16′	75°33′
Greely Fiord	BAY/BAIE	NT	Franklin	340 B	80°30′	81°40′
Greely Haven	BAY/BAIE	NT	Franklin	77 H/16	71°56′	104°50′
Green	UNP/LNO	ON	Thunder Bay	52 I/7	50°17′	88°40′
Green Acres	UNP/LNO	NS	Halifax	11 D/12	44°35′	63°36′
Green Acres	UNP/LNO	NS	Kings	21 H/2	45°00′	64°55′
Green Acres	UNP/LNO	ON	Northumberland	31 C/5	44°16′	77°41′
Greenacres	UNP/LNO	MB		62 G/13	49°50′	99°56′
Greenan	UNP/LNO	SK	9-26-17-W3	72 N/1	51°12′	108°19′
Greenbank	UNP/LNO	ON	Ontario	31 D/3	44°09′	79°01′
Green Bank - also-aussi - Vert, Banc à	SEAU/SMER	—		4016	45°40′	54°40′
Green Bay	UNP/LNO	PE	Queens	11 L/6	46°15′	63°22′
Green Bay	UNP/LNO	NS	Lunenburg	21 A/1	44°13′	64°26′
Green Bay	UNP/LNO	ON	Manitoulin	41 G/16	45°52′	82°01′
Green Bay	UNP/LNO	MB	16-13-8-E	62 I/1	50°06′	96°26′
Green Bay	BAY/BAIE	NF		2 C/6	48°22′	53°11′
Green Bay	BAY/BAIE	NF		2 E/13	49°42′	56°00′
Green Bay	BAY/BAIE	NS	Lunenburg	21 A/1	44°13′	64°25′
Green Bay	BAY/BAIE	ON	Manitoulin	41 G/16	45°51′	82°03′
Green Bay	BAY/BAIE	SK		74 I/6	58°28′	105°12′
Green Bay	BAY/BAIE	NT	Franklin	89 B	76°30′	118°45′
Green Bay Island	ISL/ÎLE	NF		2 E/12	49°43′	55°53′
Greenbrier	UNP/LNO	SK	32-23-8-W3	72 J/14	50°56′	107°02′
Greenbush	UNP/LNO	ON	Leeds	31 B/12	44°41′	75°51′
Greenbush	UNP/LNO	SK	5-45-5-W2	63 D/15	52°51′	102°42′
Greenbush Lake	LAKE/LAC	ON	Thunder Bay	52 J/16	50°56′	90°05′
Greenbush River	RIV/CDE	SK	29-44-5-W2	63 D/15	52°49′	102°42′
Green Canyon	UNP/LNO	SK	46-12-W3	73 B/13	52°58′	107°39′
Green Court	UNP/LNO	AB	14-58-9-W5	83 J/3	54°01′	115°14′
Green Cove	UNP/LNO	NF		2 E/10	49°38′	54°35′
Green Cove	UNP/LNO	BC	Clayoquot	92 C/15	48°59′	124°59′
Green Cove	BAY/BAIE	NF		2 M/14	51°56′	55°24′
Green Creek	UNP/LNO	NS	Colchester	11 E/3	45°15′	63°25′
Greendale	UNP/LNO	NB	Saint John	21 G/8	45°15′	66°06′
Greendale	UNP/LNO	BC	New Westminster	92 G/1	49°07′	122°03′
Greene	UNP/LNO	SK	33-30-28-W3	72 N/12	51°37′	109°52′
Greene Island	ISL/ÎLE	ON	Manitoulin	41 G/14	45°50′	83°07′
Greenfarm	UNP/LNO	MB	7,18-3-3-W	62 H/4	49°12′	97°51′
Greenfeld	UNP/LNO	SK	15-40-5-W3	73 B/7	52°26′	106°38′
Greenfield	UNP/LNO	PE	Kings	11 L/2	46°11′	62°44′
Greenfield	UNP/LNO	NS	Colchester	11 E/6	45°22′	63°08′
Greenfield	UNP/LNO	NS	Hants	11 E/4	45°04′	63°53′
Greenfield	UNP/LNO	NS	Kings	21 H/1	45°01′	64°20′
Greenfield	UNP/LNO	NS	Queens	21 A/7	44°16′	64°50′
Greenfield	UNP/LNO	NB	Carleton	21 J/5	46°28′	67°41′
Greenfield	UNP/LNO	ON	Glengarry	31 G/7	45°18′	74°46′
Greenfield	UNP/LNO	ON	Leeds	31 C/8	44°28′	76°01′
Greenfield	UNP/LNO	ON	Waterloo	40 P/8	43°18′	80°28′
Greenfield No. 529	MUN2/AZM2	SK		73 F/10	53°40′	109°00′
Greenfield Park	CITY/VIL1	QC	Champlain	31 H/6	45°29′	73°29′
Green Glade	UNP/LNO	AB	6-41-1-W4	73 D/8	52°30′	110°09′

NAME NOM	ENTITY ENTITÉ	LOC 1 LIEU 1	LOC 2 LIEU 2	MAP CARTE	POSITION LAT	LONG
Greenhead Road	UNP/LNO	NS	Halifax	11 D/12	44°38′	63°42′
Greenhill	UNP/LNO	NS	Pictou	11 E/10	45°34′	62°48′
Green Hill - see-voir - Greenhill	UNP/LNO	NS		11 D/13	45°00′	63°56′
Greenhill	UNP/LNO	NS	Hants	11 D/13	45°00′	63°56′
Greenhill	UNP/LNO	NS	Cumberland	21 H/8	45°23′	64°16′
Green Hill	UNP/LNO	NB	York	21 J/7	46°21′	66°41′
Greenhill	UNP/LNO	NB	York	21 J/3	46°04′	67°02′
Greenhill	UNP/LNO	ON	Peterborough	31 D/8	44°18′	78°21′
Greenhill River	RIV/CDE	ON	Algoma	42 B/11	48°44′	83°27′
Greenhills	UNP/LNO	BC	Kootenay	82 J/2	50°01′	114°50′
Green Hills	MTN/MNT	NF		1 L/16	46°54′	54°07′
Greenhorn Lakes	LAKE/LAC	NT	Mackenzie	86 M	67°05′	119°03′
Greenhurst-Thurstonia	UNP/LNO	ON	Victoria	31 D/7	44°28′	78°40′
Greening	UNP/LNO	BC	Cariboo	93 G/1	53°10′	122°23′
Green Island	ISL/ÎLE	NF		2 C/11	48°42′	53°07′
Green Island	ISL/ÎLE	NF		2 C/3	48°12′	53°26′
Green Island	ISL/ÎLE	NF		2 F/12	49°33′	53°49′
Green Island	ISL/ÎLE	NF		2 E/8	49°27′	54°14′
Green Island	ISL/ÎLE	NF		11 I/16	46°53′	56°05′
Green Island	ISL/ÎLE	NS	Shelburne	20 P/5	43°25′	65°41′
Green Island Brook	UNP/LNO	NF		12 P/7	51°24′	56°32′
Green Island Cove	UNP/LNO	NF		12 P/7	51°23′	56°35′
Green Lake	VILG/VILG	SK	19-61-12-W3	73 J/5	54°17′	107°47′
Green Lake	UNP/LNO	ON	Renfrew	31 F/11	45°40′	77°08′
Green Lake	LAKE/LAC	SK		73 J/4	54°10′	107°43′
Green Lake	LAKE/LAC	BC	Lillooet	92 P/6	51°25′	121°13′
Green Lake	LAKE/LAC	BC	New Westminster	92 J/2	50°09′	122°56′
Greenland	UNP/LNO	NF		1 N/11	47°34′	53°11′
Greenland	UNP/LNO	NS	Annapolis	21 A/12	44°35′	65°35′
Greenland	UNP/LNO	MB	8,9-8-6-E	62 H/10	49°38′	96°44′
Greenlands	UNP/LNO	ON	Carleton	31 F/8	45°29′	76°03′
Green Lane	UNP/LNO	ON	Prescott	31 G/10	45°34′	74°38′
Greenlay	UNP/LNO	QC	Le Val-Saint-François	31 H/9	45°34′	72°01′
Greenleys Corners	UNP/LNO	ON	Northumberland	31 C/4	44°04′	77°55′
Greenly's Corners	UNP/LNO	ON	Lanark	31 C/16	44°54′	76°16′
Green Meadows	UNP/LNO	PE	Kings	11 L/7	46°22′	62°44′
Greenmount	UNP/LNO	PE	Prince	21 I/16	46°54′	64°03′
Green Mountain	UNP/LNO	NB	York	21 G/13	45°47′	67°46′
Greenmount-Montrose	VILG/VILG	PE	Prince	21 I/16	46°52′	64°02′
Green Oak	UNP/LNO	MB	9-14-8-E	62 I/1	50°10′	96°27′
Green Oaks	UNP/LNO	NS	Colchester	11 E/6	45°15′	63°26′
Greenock	MUN2/AZM2	ON	Bruce	41 A/3	44°10′	81°20′
Greenock	UNP/LNO	NB	Charlotte	21 G/6	45°20′	67°07′
Greenock	UNP/LNO	ON	Bruce	41 A/3	44°06′	81°15′
Greenough	UNP/LNO	NS	Halifax	11 D/12	44°41′	63°30′
Greenough Point	CAPE/CAP	ON	Bruce	41 A/14	44°58′	81°26′
Green Park	UNP/LNO	ON	Wellington	40 P/16	43°52′	80°28′
Green Point	UNP/LNO	NF		12 H/12	49°41′	57°58′
Green Point	UNP/LNO	NB	Gloucester	21 P/13	47°51′	65°46′
Greenpoint	UNP/LNO	ON	Prince Edward	31 C/3	44°09′	77°04′
Green Point	CAPE/CAP	NF		2 E/5	49°24′	55°40′
Green Point	CAPE/CAP	NF		12 I/1	50°04′	56°04′
Green Point	CAPE/CAP	NF		12 H/12	49°41′	57°58′
Green Point	CAPE/CAP	NS	Lunenburg	21 A/1	44°12′	64°27′
Green Point	CAPE/CAP	NS	Shelburne	20 P/6	43°29′	65°25′
Green Ridge	UNP/LNO	MB	28-2-4-E	62 H/2	49°10′	97°00′
Green River	UNP/LNO	NB	Madawaska	21 N/8	47°19′	68°09′
Green River	UNP/LNO	ON	Ontario	30 M/14	43°53′	79°11′
Green River	UNP/LNO	BC	Lillooet	92 J/2	50°13′	122°53′
Green River - also-aussi - Verte, Rivière	RIV/CDE	NB	Madawaska	21 N/8	47°18′	68°09′
Green River	RIV/CDE	BC	Lillooet	92 J/7	50°18′	122°45′
Green River	RIV/CDE	YT		105 A/9	60°37′	128°11′
Green Road	UNP/LNO	PE	Queens	11 L/3	46°12′	63°23′
Green Road	UNP/LNO	NB	Carleton	21 J/4	46°05′	67°45′
Green Rock	SHL/H-FD	NS	Shelburne	20 P/15	43°46′	64°56′
Greens Brook	UNP/LNO	NS	Pictou	11 E/8	45°26′	62°13′
Greens Corner	UNP/LNO	ON	Norfolk	40 I/16	42°48′	80°25′
Greens Corners	UNP/LNO	ON	Welland	30 M/3	43°05′	79°07′
Green's Creek	RIV/CDE	ON	Carleton	31 G/5	45°28′	75°34′
Green's Harbour	UNP/LNO	NF		1 N/11	47°38′	53°30′
Greenshield Lake	LAKE/LAC	NT	Franklin	26 O	67°05′	66°45′
Greenshields	UNP/LNO	QC	Le Val-Saint-François	31 H/9	45°42′	72°03′
Greenshields	UNP/LNO	AB	14-44-6-W4	73 D/15	52°47′	110°46′
Greenside Acres	UNP/LNO	ON	Wentworth	30 M/4	43°13′	79°59′
Greens Landing	UNP/LNO	NB	Charlotte	21 B/10	44°38′	66°49′

NAME NOM	ENTITY ENTITÉ	LOC 1 LIEU 1	LOC 2 LIEU 2	MAP CARTE	POSITION	
					LAT	LONG
Greens, Le	UNP/LNO	QC	Brome-Missisquoi	31 H/3	45°02'	73°05'
Greens Point	UNP/LNO	NS	Pictou	11 E/10	45°38'	62°39'
Greens Point	UNP/LNO	NB	Charlotte	21 G/2	45°03'	66°53'
Greenspond	TOWN/VIL2	NF		2 F/4	49°04'	53°34'
Greenspond Island	ISL/ÎLE	NF		2 F/4	49°05'	53°35'
Greenstone Mountain	MTN/MNT	BC	Kamloops Division Yale	92 I/10	50°36'	120°38'
Greenstreet	UNP/LNO	SK	6-52-26-W3	73 F/5	53°28'	109°49'
Greenstreet Lake	LAKE/LAC	SK	52-26-W3	73 F/5	53°28'	109°49'
Greensville	UNP/LNO	ON	Wentworth	30 M/5	43°17'	80°00'
Greenvale	UNP/LNO	PE	Kings	11 L/8	46°23'	62°11'
Greenvale	UNP/LNO	PE	Queens	11 L/6	46°20'	63°19'
Greenvale	UNP/LNO	NS	Pictou	11 E/9	45°30'	62°29'
Green Valley	UNP/LNO	ON	Glengarry	31 G/7	45°16'	74°36'
Greenview	UNP/LNO	ON	Hastings	31 F/4	45°15'	77°49'
Greenview No. 16, Municipal District of	MUN1/AZM1	AB	64-1-W6	83 L/9	54°38'	118°00'
Greenville	UNP/LNO	NS	Yarmouth	20 O/16	43°51'	66°02'
Greenville	UNP/LNO	BC	Cassiar	103 P/4	55°02'	129°34'
Greenville Station	UNP/LNO	NS	Cumberland	11 E/12	45°39'	63°40'
Greenwald	UNP/LNO	MB	30-15-8-E	62 I/8	50°19'	96°29'
Greenwater Lake	UNP/LNO	SK	40,41-11-W2	63 D/12	52°32'	103°30'
Greenwater Lake	LAKE/LAC	ON	Thunder Bay	52 B/9	48°34'	90°26'
Greenwater Lake	LAKE/LAC	SK	41-11-W2	63 D/12	52°31'	103°30'
Greenway	UNP/LNO	ON	Middlesex	40 P/4	43°14'	81°43'
Greenway	UNP/LNO	MB	2-5-13-W	62 G/6	49°22'	99°07'
Greenway Sound	CHAN/CHEN	BC	Range 1 Coast	92 L/15	50°51'	126°46'
Greenwich	UNP/LNO	PE	Kings	11 L/7	46°26'	62°38'
Greenwich	UNP/LNO	NS	Kings	21 H/1	45°05'	64°24'
Greenwich	GEOG/GÉOG	NB	Kings	21 G/9	45°32'	66°07'
Greenwich Hill	UNP/LNO	NB	Kings	21 G/8	45°27'	66°10'
Greenwich Lake	LAKE/LAC	ON	Thunder Bay	52 A/15	48°48'	88°51'
Greenwold	UNP/LNO	NS	Antigonish	11 F/12	45°37'	61°58'
Greenwood	CITY/VIL1	BC	Similkameen Division Yale	82 E/2	49°06'	118°41'
Greenwood	VILG/VILG	NS	Kings	21 A/15	44°59'	64°54'
Greenwood	UNP/LNO	NS	Pictou	11 E/10	45°33'	62°34'
Greenwood	UNP/LNO	NS	Shelburne	20 P/11	43°34'	65°23'
Greenwood	UNP/LNO	NB	Saint John	21 H/5	45°19'	65°57'
Greenwood	UNP/LNO	ON	Renfrew	31 F/14	45°46'	77°01'
Greenwood	UNP/LNO	ON	Ontario	30 M/14	43°56'	79°03'
Greenwood Heights	UNP/LNO	NS	Halifax	11 D/12	44°39'	63°44'
Greenwood Island 3	IR/RI	BC	Yale Division Yale	92 H/6	49°23'	121°27'
Greenwood Lake	LAKE/LAC	NS	Shelburne	20 P/11	43°36'	65°25'
Greer Mount	UNP/LNO	QC	Pontiac	31 F/16	45°45'	76°28'
Gregan	UNP/LNO	NB	Northumberland	21 P/3	47°04'	65°03'
Gregg	UNP/LNO	MB	3-12-14-W	62 G/14	49°59'	99°18'
Gregg Settlement	UNP/LNO	NB	Carleton	21 J/5	46°27'	67°42'
Gregherd	UNP/LNO	SK	32-24-18-W2	72 P/1	51°05'	104°30'
Gregoire Lake - see-voir - Willow Lake	LAKE/LAC	AB		74 D/6	56°28'	111°08'
Gregoire Lake 176	IR/RI	AB		74 D/6	56°25'	111°09'
Gregoire Lake 176A	IR/RI	AB	10-56-8-W4	74 D/6	56°27'	111°12'
Gregoire Lake 176B	IR/RI	AB	24-56-8-W4	74 D/6	56°28'	111°08'
Gregoire Lake Provincial Park	PARK/PARC	AB	86-8-W4	74 D/6	56°29'	111°11'
Gregoire Lakes	LAKE/LAC	NT	Keewatin	65 G	61°45'	99°52'
Grégoires Mill	UNP/LNO	ON	Cochrane	42 H/5	49°17'	81°57'
Gregory	UNP/LNO	ON	Muskoka	31 E/4	45°08'	79°39'
Gregory Island	ISL/ÎLE	BC	Range 1 Coast	92 L/15	50°52'	126°34'
Gregorys Mill	UNP/LNO	MB	34-6-18-W	62 G/12	49°31'	99°50'
Greig Beach	UNP/LNO	SK	20-63-18-W3	73 K/7	54°27'	108°41'
Greig Lake	VILG/VILG	SK	17-63-18-3	73 K/7	54°26'	108°42'
Greig Lake	LAKE/LAC	SK	17-63-18-3	73 K/7	54°27'	108°43'
Greiner Lake	LAKE/LAC	NT	Franklin	77 D	69°12'	104°55'
Grenadier Island	UNP/LNO	ON	Leeds	31 B/5	44°24'	75°53'
Grenadier Island	ISL/ÎLE	ON	Leeds	31 B/5	44°24'	75°52'
Grenfell	TOWN/VIL2	SK	8-17-7-W2	62 L/7	50°25'	102°56'
Grenfell	UNP/LNO	ON	Simcoe	31 D/5	44°21'	79°48'
Grenfell Beach	UNP/LNO	SK		62 L/10	50°36'	102°46'
Grenfell Glen	UNP/LNO	ON	Carleton	31 G/5	45°19'	75°44'
Grenfell Heights	UNP/LNO	NF		2 D/13	48°57'	55°38'
Grenfell Sound	CHAN/CHEN	NT	Franklin	25 A/8	60°17'	64°27'
Grenville	TOWN/VIL2	QC	Argenteuil	31 G/10	45°38'	74°36'
Grenville	VILG/VILG	QC	Argenteuil	31 G/10	45°43'	74°40'
Grenville	UNP/LNO	QC	Le Fjord-du-Saguenay	22 D/8	48°24'	70°17'
Grenville	GEOG/GÉOG	ON		31 B/13	44°50'	75°40'
Grenville Bay	UNP/LNO	QC	Argenteuil	31 G/10	45°38'	74°36'
Grenville Channel	CHAN/CHEN	BC	Range 4 Coast	103 H/12	53°37'	129°43'
Grenville Lake	LAKE/LAC	NT	Mackenzie	86 B/15	64°55'	114°45'

NAME NOM	ENTITY ENTITÉ	LOC 1 LIEU 1	LOC 2 LIEU 2	MAP CARTE	POSITION LAT	LONG
Grenville, Mount	MTN/MNT	BC	Range 1 Coast	92 K/15	50°58′	124°32′
Grenville Park	UNP/LNO	ON	Frontenac	31 C/2	44°14′	76°32′
Gresham	UNP/LNO	ON	Bruce	41 A/6	44°17′	81°24′
Grès, Les	UNP/LNO	QC	Francheville	31 I/7	46°28′	72°46′
Greta Lake	LAKE/LAC	ON	Thunder Bay	42 E/14	49°59′	87°01′
Gretna	VILG/VILG	MB	5-1-1-W	62 H/4	49°00′	97°34′
Gretna	UNP/LNO	ON	Lennox and Addington	31 C/2	44°11′	76°59′
Greville Bay	BAY/BAIE	NS	Cumberland	21 H/7	45°22′	64°35′
Grewatsch Creek	RIV/CDE	BC	Peace River	94 H/4	57°14′	121°45′
Grew Lake	LAKE/LAC	AB	91-20,21-W4	84 A/14	56°54′	113°12′
Grey	MUN1/AZM1	ON	Grey	41 A/7	44°20′	80°45′
Grey	MUN2/AZM2	ON	Huron	40 P/11	43°44′	81°09′
Grey	MUN2/AZM2	MB		62 G/9	49°43′	98°05′
Grey	UNP/LNO	AB	27-56-5-W6	83 E/15	53°53′	118°40′
Grey	GEOG/GÉOG	ON		41 A/7	44°20′	80°45′
Grey Goose Island	ISL/ÎLE	NT	Franklin	33 E	53°54′	79°54′
Grey Hunter Peak	MTN/MNT	YT		105 M/4	63°08′	135°38′
Grey Island	ISL/ÎLE	NS	Shelburne	20 P/11	43°36′	65°18′
Grey Island	ISL/ÎLE	SK		74 G/8	57°25′	106°21′
Grey Islands	ISL/ÎLE	NF		2 L/13	50°50′	55°35′
Grey Islands Harbour	UNP/LNO	NF		2 L/12	50°43′	55°36′
Grey, Mount	MTN/MNT	BC	Barclay	92 C/15	48°59′	124°42′
Grey, Point	CAPE/CAP	BC	New Westminster	92 G/6	49°16′	123°16′
Grey River	UNP/LNO	NF		11 P/11	47°35′	57°06′
Grey River	RIV/CDE	NF		11 P/11	47°34′	57°07′
Grey River Point	CAPE/CAP	NF		11 P/11	47°34′	57°07′
Grey River Rocks	SHL/H-FD	NF		11 P/6	47°28′	57°06′
Grey Rock	UNP/LNO	QC	Brome-Missisquoi	31 H/2	45°05′	72°33′
Greystone Heights	UNP/LNO	SK		73 B/2	52°07′	106°37′
Greywillow Point	CAPE/CAP	AB	118-1-W4	74 M/8	59°17′	110°02′
Gribbell Island	ISL/ÎLE	BC	Range 4 Coast	103 H/6	53°25′	129°01′
Gribble Island 10	IR/RI	BC	Range 4 Coast	103 H/6	53°21′	129°08′
Grief Island 2	IR/RI	BC	Range 3 Coast	103 A/8	52°17′	128°13′
Grief Point	CAPE/CAP	BC	New Westminster	92 F/15	49°48′	124°31′
Grief Point	CAPE/CAP	BC	Range 4 Coast	103 G/8	53°16′	130°05′
Griersville	UNP/LNO	ON	Grey	41 A/10	44°32′	80°34′
Griesbach	UNP/LNO	AB	9-54-22-W4	83 H/11	53°39′	113°11′
Grieves Corners	UNP/LNO	ON	Lennox and Addington	31 C/6	44°21′	77°01′
Griff	UNP/LNO	ON	Thunder Bay	52 A/12	48°41′	89°49′
Griffin	HAM/HAM	SK	28-8-11-W2	62 E/11	49°40′	103°26′
Griffin	UNP/LNO	QC	Memphrémagog	31 H/1	45°03′	72°10′
Griffin Bay	BAY/BAIE	NT	Franklin	25 J	62°49′	67°10′
Griffin Cove	BAY/BAIE	NS	Digby	21 A/12	44°34′	65°59′
Griffin Creek	UNP/LNO	AB	16-81-25-W5	84 C/4	56°01′	117°51′
Griffin Inlet	BAY/BAIE	NT	Franklin	58 G	75°07′	92°10′
Griffin Lake	LAKE/LAC	ON	Cochrane	42 B/16	48°55′	82°23′
Griffin Lake	LAKE/LAC	NT	Keewatin	65 G	61°17′	98°47′
Griffin, Mount	MTN/MNT	BC	Kamloops Division Yale	82 L/15	50°56′	118°34′
Griffin No. 66	MUN2/AZM2	SK		62 E/11	49°40′	103°25′
Griffis Corners	UNP/LNO	ON	Northumberland	31 C/4	44°02′	77°54′
Griffith	UNP/LNO	ON	Renfrew	31 F/3	45°15′	77°10′
Griffith	UNP/LNO	BC	Kootenay	82 N/6	51°27′	117°29′
Griffith and Matawachan - see-voir - Griffith and Matawatchan	MUN2/AZM2	ON		31 F/3	45°15′	77°08′
Griffith and Matawatchan	MUN2/AZM2	ON	Renfrew	31 F/3	45°15′	77°08′
Griffith Island	ISL/ÎLE	ON	Grey	41 A/15	44°50′	80°55′
Griffith Island	ISL/ÎLE	NT	Franklin	58 F	74°35′	95°30′
Griffiths Point	CAPE/CAP	NT	Franklin	99 A	76°05′	123°02′
Griffon, Lac au	LAKE/LAC	QC	Caniapiscau	23 C/2	52°05′	68°51′
Grifton	UNP/LNO	MB	29-27-23-W	62 N/7	51°20′	100°39′
Grillade, La	UNP/LNO	QC	Bellechasse	21 L/9	46°39′	70°29′
Grill Lake	LAKE/LAC	SK	37-22-W3	73 C/3	52°12′	109°07′
Grimes Lake	LAKE/LAC	MB		64 J/12	58°34′	99°35′
Grimmer	GEOG/GÉOG	NB	Restigouche	21 O/11	47°43′	67°25′
Grimmington Bay	BAY/BAIE	NT	Keewatin	33 E	53°14′	78°56′
Grimmonds Beach	UNP/LNO	ON	Elgin	40 I/11	42°40′	81°13′
Grimms Settlement	UNP/LNO	NS	Lunenburg	21 A/8	44°21′	64°23′
Grimsby	TOWN/VIL2	ON	Lincoln	30 M/4	43°12′	79°34′
Grimsby Beach	UNP/LNO	ON	Lincoln	30 M/4	43°12′	79°32′
Grimsby Centre	UNP/LNO	ON	Lincoln	30 M/4	43°08′	79°35′
Grimshaw	TOWN/VIL2	AB	17-83-23-W5	84 C/4	56°11′	117°36′
Grimsthorpe	UNP/LNO	ON	Manitoulin	41 G/9	45°43′	82°19′
Grimston	UNP/LNO	ON	Grey	41 A/6	44°25′	81°05′
Grinder Creek	RIV/CDE	BC	Lillooet	92 O/8	51°22′	122°14′
Grindrod	UNP/LNO	BC	Kamloops Division Yale	82 L/11	50°38′	119°07′
Grindstone Head	CAPE/CAP	NF		2 C/4	48°13′	53°56′

NAME NOM	ENTITY ENTITÉ	LOC 1 LIEU 1	LOC 2 LIEU 2	MAP CARTE	POSITION LAT	LONG
Grindstone Island	ISL/ÎLE	NB	Albert	21 H/10	45°43'	64°37'
Grindstone, Lac	LAKE/LAC	QC	Témiscamingue	31 L/15	46°49'	78°42'
Grindstone Point	CAPE/CAP	NB	Gloucester	21 P/14	47°45'	65°22'
Grindstone Point	CAPE/CAP	MB	18-27-7-E	62 P/7	51°21'	96°36'
Grinnell, Cape	CAPE/CAP	NT	Franklin	58 G	75°09'	92°21'
Grinnell Glacier	GLAC/GLAC	NT	Franklin	25 J	62°34'	66°45'
Grinnell Lake	LAKE/LAC	NT	Franklin	47 C	69°37'	84°14'
Grinnell Peninsula	CAPE/CAP	NT	Franklin	59 B	76°40'	95°00'
Grinnell Ridge	SEAU/SMER	—		7951	77°13'	99°40'
Gripes Nest	UNP/LNO	NF		1 K/15	46°54'	52°55'
Grippen Lake	LAKE/LAC	ON	Leeds	31 C/9	44°30'	76°09'
Griquet	UNP/LNO	NF		2 M/11	51°32'	55°28'
Grise Fiord	HAM/HAM	NT	Franklin	49 A/5	76°25'	82°54'
Grise Fiord	BAY/BAIE	NT	Franklin	49 A/12	76°35'	83°13'
Grist Lake	LAKE/LAC	AB	73,74-3,4-W4	73 M/8	55°22'	110°28'
Griswold	UNP/LNO	MB	25-9-23-W	62 F/16	49°47'	100°28'
Grizzle Bear Lake	LAKE/LAC	NT	Mackenzie	86 A/2	64°12'	112°58'
Grizzly	UNP/LNO	AB	10-61-22-W5	83 K/6	54°15'	117°12'
Grizzly Bear Hills	MTN/MNT	SK		74 C/3	56°00'	109°20'
Grizzly Bear Mountain	MTN/MNT	NT	Franklin	96 H	65°20'	121°00'
Grizzly Bear's Head 110 and Lean Man 111	IR/RI	SK		73 C/9	52°33'	108°15'
Grizzly Bear Telegraph Station Provincial Historic Site (Undeveloped)	PARK/PARC	AB	48-5-W5	73 E/2	53°09'	110°43'
Grizzly Mountain	MTN/MNT	BC	Kamloops Division Yale	92 P/9	51°42'	120°15'
Groais Island	UNP/LNO	NF		2 L/12	50°43'	55°36'
Groais Island	ISL/ÎLE	NF		2 L/13	50°57'	55°36'
Grole	UNP/LNO	NF		11 P/9	47°31'	56°07'
Grollier Lake	LAKE/LAC	SK		74 P/11	59°43'	105°28'
Grondine, Point	CAPE/CAP	ON	Manitoulin	41 H/14	45°55'	81°08'
Grondines	VILG/VILG	QC	Portneuf	31 I/9	46°36'	72°03'
Grondines-Est	UNP/LNO	QC	Portneuf	31 I/9	46°37'	72°01'
Grondines-Ouest	UNP/LNO	QC	Portneuf	31 I/9	46°36'	72°04'
Grondines-Station	UNP/LNO	QC	Portneuf	31 I/9	46°38'	72°04'
Gronlid	HAM/HAM	SK	32-47-17-W2	73 H/1	53°06'	104°28'
Grono Road	UNP/LNO	NS	Halifax	11 D/14	44°59'	63°26'
Gros Cacouna, Le	CAPE/CAP	QC	Rivière-du-Loup	21 N/13	47°57'	69°30'
Gros-Cap	UNP/LNO	QC	Les Îles-de-la-Madeleine	11 N/5	47°21'	61°53'
Gros Cap	UNP/LNO	ON	Algoma	41 K/10	46°32'	84°34'
Gros Cap 49	IR/RI	ON	Algoma	41 N/15	47°59'	84°54'
Gros Cap Indian Village 49A	IR/RI	ON	Algoma	41 N/15	48°00'	84°55'
Gros Cap, Le	CAPE/CAP	QC	Les Îles-de-la-Madeleine	11 N/4	47°13'	62°00'
Gros-Mécatina	VILG/VILG	QC	Côte-Nord-du-Golfe-Saint-Laurent	12 J/15	50°50'	58°58'
Gros Mécatina, Archipel du	ISL/ÎLE	QC	Côte-Nord-du-Golfe-Saint-Laurent	12 J/11	50°40'	59°00'
Gros Mécatina, Cap du	CAPE/CAP	QC	Côte-Nord-du-Golfe-Saint-Laurent	12 J/11	50°45'	59°00'
Gros Mécatina, Île du	ISL/ÎLE	QC	Côte-Nord-du-Golfe-Saint-Laurent	12 J/15	50°48'	58°52'
Gros Mécatina, Lac du	LAKE/LAC	QC	Côte-Nord-du-Golfe-Saint-Laurent	12 J/14	50°52'	59°05'
Gros Mécatina, Rivière du	RIV/CDE	QC	Côte-Nord-du-Golfe-Saint-Laurent	12 J/14	50°46'	59°05'
Grosmont	UNP/LNO	AB	10-68-24-W4	83 I/13	54°51'	113°33'
Gros-Morne	UNP/LNO	QC	Denis-Riverin	22 H/5	49°15'	65°33'
Gros Morne	MTN/MNT	NF		12 H/12	49°36'	57°47'
Gros Morne National Park - also-aussi - Gros-Morne, Parc national du	PARK/PARC	NF		12 H/12	49°41'	57°44'
Gros Morne National Park World Heritage Site - also-aussi - Parc du Gros-Morne, Site du patrimoine mondial du	PARK/PARC	NF		12 H/12	49°41'	57°44'
Gros-Morne, Parc national du - also-aussi - Gros Morne National Park	PARK/PARC	NF		12 H/12	49°41'	57°44'
Gros-Pin, Le	UNP/LNO	QC	Montmagny	21 M/2	47°02'	70°34'
Grosse Boule, La	ISL/ÎLE	QC	Sept-Rivières	22 J/1	50°08'	66°17'
Grosse-Île	VILG/VILG	QC	Les Îles-de-la-Madeleine	11 N/12	47°37'	61°31'
Grosse-Île	UNP/LNO	QC	Le Fjord-du-Saguenay	22 D/1	48°15'	70°01'
Grosse-Île	UNP/LNO	QC	Montmagny	21 M/2	47°02'	70°40'
Grosse Île and the Irish Memorial National Historic Site - also-aussi - Grosse-Île-et-le-Mémorial-des-Irlandais, Lieu historique national de la	PARK/PARC	QC	Montmagny	21 M/2	47°02'	70°40'
Grosse-Île-et-le-Mémorial-des-Irlandais, Lieu historique national de la - also-aussi - Grosse Île and the Irish Memorial National Historic Site	PARK/PARC	QC	Montmagny	21 M/2	47°02'	70°40'
Grosse Île, La	ISL/ÎLE	QC	Les Îles-de-la-Madeleine	11 N/12	47°37'	61°31'
Grosse Île, La	ISL/ÎLE	QC	Montmagny	21 M/2	47°02'	70°40'
Grosse-Île-Nord	UNP/LNO	QC	Les Îles-de-la-Madeleine	11 N/12	47°38'	61°31'
Grosse Isle	UNP/LNO	MB	6-13-1-E	62 I/3	50°04'	97°27'
Grosses Coques	UNP/LNO	NS	Digby	21 B/8	44°21'	66°06'
Grosses-Roches	VILG/VILG	QC	Matane	22 B/14	48°56'	67°10'
Gross Island	ISL/ÎLE	NT	Franklin	25 I	62°02'	65°53'
Grosswerder	UNP/LNO	SK	10-37-27-W3	73 C/4	52°10'	109°46'
Grosvenor	UNP/LNO	NS	Guysborough	11 F/12	45°37'	61°31'
Grosvenor Island	ISL/ÎLE	NT	Mackenzie	69 C	77°05'	103°52'

NAME NOM	ENTITY ENTITÉ	LOC 1 LIEU 1	LOC 2 LIEU 2	MAP CARTE	POSITION LAT	POSITION LONG
Grosvenor Park	UNP/LNO	SK		73 B/2	52°07′	106°38′
Gros-Violon, Le	UNP/LNO	QC	Minganie	12 L/3	50°14′	63°20′
Groswater Bay	BAY/BAIE	NF		13 I/5	54°20′	57°40′
Grotte-des-Fées, La	UNP/LNO	QC	Arthabaska	21 E/13	45°57′	71°45′
Grotte, La	UNP/LNO	QC	Argenteuil	31 G/9	45°40′	74°22′
Grouard	UNP/LNO	AB	19-75-14-W5	83 N/9	55°31′	116°09′
Grouard Lake	LAKE/LAC	NT	Mackenzie	86 F/5	65°24′	117°57′
Grouard Mission	UNP/LNO	AB	31-75-14-W5	83 N/9	55°33′	116°09′
Groulx, Monts	MTN/MNT	QC	Caniapiscau	22 O/12	51°37′	67°37′
Groundbirch	UNP/LNO	BC	Peace River	93 P/15	55°47′	120°55′
Groundhog Creek	RIV/CDE	BC	Lillooet	92 O/11	51°32′	123°07′
Groundhog Lake	LAKE/LAC	ON	Sudbury	42 B/1	48°06′	82°15′
Groundhog River	UNP/LNO	ON	Sudbury	42 B/1	48°08′	82°14′
Groundhog River	RIV/CDE	ON	Cochrane	42 H/12	49°43′	81°58′
Grouse Island	ISL/ÎLE	SK		74 N/7	59°19′	108°48′
Grouse (Moul) Creek	RIV/CDE	BC	Kamloops Division Yale	92 P/16	51°50′	120°03′
Grove Creek	UNP/LNO	QC	Pontiac	31 F/16	45°54′	76°16′
Grovedale	UNP/LNO	AB	4-70-6-W6	83 M/2	55°03′	118°52′
Grove Hamlet	UNP/LNO	NB	Westmorland	21 I/2	46°06′	64°44′
Grove Hill	UNP/LNO	NB	Saint John	21 H/5	45°24′	65°44′
Grove Hill	UNP/LNO	QC	Communauté urbaine de Montréal	31 H/5	45°27′	73°42′
Grove Lake	LAKE/LAC	SK		74 P/8	59°28′	104°19′
Grove Park	UNP/LNO	ON	Muskoka	31 E/2	45°14′	78°59′
Grove Park	UNP/LNO	SK	22-18-1-W2	62 L/9	50°32′	102°03′
Grovesend	UNP/LNO	ON	Elgin	40 I/10	42°40′	80°56′
Groves Point	UNP/LNO	NS	Cape Breton	11 K/1	46°14′	60°20′
Groveton	UNP/LNO	ON	Grenville	31 B/13	44°53′	75°34′
Grub Road	UNP/LNO	NB	Albert	21 H/14	45°59′	65°01′
Gruenthal	UNP/LNO	SK	28-40-4-W3	73 B/7	52°28′	106°31′
Grues, Île aux	ISL/ÎLE	QC	Montmagny	21 M/2	47°04′	70°33′
Grumbler	UNP/LNO	NT	Mackenzie	85 C	60°07′	116°45′
Grund	UNP/LNO	MB	10-6-14-W	62 G/6	49°28′	99°16′
Grunthal	UNP/LNO	MB	21-5-5-E	62 H/7	49°24′	96°51′
Guagus Lake	LAKE/LAC	NB	Northumberland	21 O/1	47°01′	66°21′
Guay, Lac	LAKE/LAC	QC	Témiscamingue	31 M/3	47°13′	79°02′
Guaytown	UNP/LNO	ON	Glengarry	31 G/7	45°20′	74°39′
Guéguen, Lac	LAKE/LAC	QC	Vallée-de-l'Or	32 C/3	48°06′	77°13′
Guelph	CITY/VIL1	ON	Wellington	40 P/9	43°33′	80°15′
Guelph	MUN2/AZM2	ON	Wellington	40 P/9	43°35′	80°21′
Guelph Junction	UNP/LNO	ON	Halton	30 M/5	43°28′	80°00′
Guelph Junction	UNP/LNO	ON	Wellington	40 P/9	43°32′	80°16′
Guemes, Mount	MTN/MNT	BC	Clayoquot	92 F/5	49°22′	125°49′
Guénette	UNP/LNO	QC	Antoine-Labelle	31 J/11	46°32′	75°15′
Guenyveau, Lac	LAKE/LAC	QC	Kativik	24 L/14	58°51′	71°00′
Guérard, Lac	LAKE/LAC	QC	Kativik	24 A/5	56°20′	65°30′
Guérin	VILG/VILG	QC	Témiscamingue	31 M/11	47°40′	79°15′
Guérin	UNP/LNO	QC	Témiscamingue	31 M/11	47°40′	79°19′
Guerin	UNP/LNO	ON	Peterborough	31 D/8	44°21′	78°10′
Guernesé, Lac	LAKE/LAC	QC	Minganie	12 O/16	51°46′	58°02′
Guernsey	VILG/VILG	SK	34-33-23-W2	72 P/14	51°53′	105°11′
Guernsey Cove	UNP/LNO	PE	Kings	11 E/15	45°59′	62°30′
Guers, Lac	LAKE/LAC	QC	Kativik	24 G/10	57°34′	66°44′
Guhthe Tah 12	IR/RI	BC		104 G/14	57°54′	131°10′
Guichon Creek	RIV/CDE	BC	Kamloops Division Yale	92 I/2	50°09′	120°53′
Guichon, Mount	MTN/MNT	BC	Kamloops Division Yale	92 I/7	50°22′	120°41′
Guigues	UNP/LNO	QC	Témiscamingue	31 M/6	47°28′	79°26′
Guildford	UNP/LNO	BC	New Westminster	92 G/2	49°12′	122°48′
Guilds	UNP/LNO	ON	Kent	40 I/5	42°21′	81°55′
Guildwood Village	UNP/LNO	ON	York	30 M/11	43°44′	79°12′
Guillaume-Delisle, Lac	LAKE/LAC	QC	Kativik	34 C/8	56°15′	76°17′
Guillemard Bay	BAY/BAIE	NT	Franklin	67 H	71°35′	98°00′
Guillemot, Lac	LAKE/LAC	QC	Caniapiscau	23 F/10	53°45′	68°49′
Guillette-aux-Frênes	UNP/LNO	QC	Nicolet-Yamaska	31 I/2	46°12′	72°39′
Guilletville	UNP/LNO	ON	Sudbury	41 I/11	46°35′	81°00′
Guimond-Village	UNP/LNO	NB	Kent	21 I/15	46°46′	64°57′
Guinea	UNP/LNO	NS	Annapolis	21 A/12	44°39′	65°35′
Guinecourt, Lac	LAKE/LAC	QC	Manicouagan	22 K/14	50°55′	69°16′
Guines, Lac - see-voir - Guines Lake	LAKE/LAC	NF		13 C/3	52°07′	61°24′
Guines Lake	LAKE/LAC	NF		13 C/3	52°07′	61°24′
Guiney	UNP/LNO	ON	Renfrew	31 F/6	45°18′	77°26′
Guises Beach	UNP/LNO	SK	22-53-27-W2	73 H/12	53°35′	105°54′
Guité	UNP/LNO	QC	Avignon	22 B/1	48°11′	66°01′
Gulada 3A	IR/RI	BC	Kamloops Division Yale	92 I/6	50°19′	121°24′
Gulatch Lake	LAKE/LAC	BC	Lillooet	92 P/12	51°44′	121°56′
Gulch	UNP/LNO	NF		1 K/13	46°54′	53°36′

NAME / NOM	ENTITY / ENTITÉ	LOC 1 / LIEU 1	LOC 2 / LIEU 2	MAP / CARTE	POSITION LAT	POSITION LONG
Gulch Cape	CAPE/CAP	NF		14 M/3	59°03′	63°08′
Gulch Cove	BAY/BAIE	NF		11 P/11	47°36′	57°01′
Gulch Island	ISL/ÎLE	NF		2 C/13	48°51′	53°36′
Gulf Islands	ISL/ÎLE	BC	Cowichan	92 B/13	48°57′	123°32′
Gulf of Georgia Cannery, Lieu historique national - also-aussi - Gulf of Georgia Cannery National Historic Site	PARK/PARC	BC	New Westminster	92 G/3	49°08′	123°12′
Gulf of Georgia Cannery National Historic Site - also-aussi - Gulf of Georgia Cannery, Lieu historique national	PARK/PARC	BC	New Westminster	92 G/3	49°08′	123°12′
Gull Bay	UNP/LNO	ON	Thunder Bay	52 H/14	49°48′	89°06′
Gull Bay	BAY/BAIE	ON	Thunder Bay	52 H/14	49°45′	89°00′
Gullbridge	UNP/LNO	NF		12 H/1	49°12′	56°09′
Gull Cove	BAY/BAIE	NF		1 L/16	46°50′	54°00′
Gull Creek	UNP/LNO	ON	Lennox and Addington	31 C/10	44°35′	77°00′
Gull Creek	RIV/CDE	SK	55-19-W2	73 H/15	53°45′	104°44′
Gull Harbour	UNP/LNO	MB		62 P/2	51°12′	96°37′
Gullies	UNP/LNO	NF		1 N/11	47°39′	53°17′
Gull Island	UNP/LNO	NF		1 N/14	47°57′	53°03′
Gull Island	ISL/ÎLE	NF		1 N/7	47°16′	52°46′
Gull Island	ISL/ÎLE	NF		2 E/14	50°00′	55°22′
Gull Island	ISL/ÎLE	NF		2 E/5	49°27′	55°33′
Gull Island	ISL/ÎLE	NT	Keewatin	33 D/6	52°18′	79°02′
Gull Island Point	CAPE/CAP	NF		1 K/12	46°42′	53°39′
Gulliver Lake	LAKE/LAC	ON	Kenora	52 G/3	49°10′	91°19′
Gulliver River	RIV/CDE	ON	Kenora	52 G/11	49°33′	91°19′
Gullivers Cove	UNP/LNO	NS	Digby	21 A/12	44°36′	65°55′
Gullivers Head	CAPE/CAP	NS	Digby	21 A/12	44°37′	65°56′
Gull Lake	TOWN/VIL2	SK	13-19-W3	72 K/1	50°06′	108°29′
Gull Lake	VILG/VILG	AB	22,23,26-40-28-W4	83 A/5	52°28′	113°57′
Gull Lake	LAKE/LAC	NF		2 D/14	48°56′	55°22′
Gull Lake	LAKE/LAC	NF		13 C/14	52°58′	61°20′
Gull Lake	LAKE/LAC	ON	Haliburton	31 D/15	44°51′	78°47′
Gull Lake	LAKE/LAC	ON	Nipissing	41 I/16	46°54′	80°12′
Gull Lake	LAKE/LAC	ON	Kenora	52 O/5	51°18′	91°58′
Gull Lake	LAKE/LAC	AB	40,41-28-W4	83 A/12	52°34′	114°00′
Gull Lake No. 139	MUN2/AZM2	SK		72 K/2	50°10′	108°40′
Gull Pond	LAKE/LAC	NF		1 N/7	47°18′	52°52′
Gull Pond	LAKE/LAC	NF		2 C/5	48°17′	53°54′
Gull Pond	LAKE/LAC	NF		2 D/9	48°41′	54°11′
Gull Pond	LAKE/LAC	NF		2 D/16	48°56′	54°13′
Gull Pond	LAKE/LAC	NF		12 H/9	49°34′	56°23′
Gull Pond	LAKE/LAC	NF		12 H/16	49°48′	56°25′
Gull River	RIV/CDE	ON	Victoria	31 D/10	44°38′	78°49′
Gull River	RIV/CDE	ON	Thunder Bay	52 H/14	49°50′	89°06′
Gull River 55	IR/RI	ON	Thunder Bay	52 H/14	49°49′	89°08′
Gull Rock	UNP/LNO	ON	Muskoka	31 E/4	45°13′	79°36′
Gull Rock	SHL/H-FD	NS	Shelburne	20 P/11	43°39′	65°06′
Gull Rock	SHL/H-FD	NS	Digby	21 B/1	44°13′	66°23′
Gullrock Lake	LAKE/LAC	ON	Kenora	52 K/13	50°58′	93°40′
Gulls Marsh	UNP/LNO	NF		12 H/13	49°47′	57°53′
Gullwing Lake	LAKE/LAC	ON	Kenora	52 F/15	49°55′	92°35′
Gully, The	UNP/LNO	QC	Côte-Nord-du-Golfe-Saint-Laurent	12 P/12	51°34′	57°44′
Gully, The - also-aussi - Goulet, Le	SEAU/SMER	—		4013	44°08′	59°12′
Gul-mak 8	IR/RI	BC	Cassiar	93 M/5	55°27′	127°37′
Gulp Pond	LAKE/LAC	NF		12 A/8	48°28′	56°03′
Gulquac Lake	LAKE/LAC	NB	Victoria	21 J/15	46°57′	66°56′
Gulquac River	RIV/CDE	NB	Victoria	21 J/14	46°59′	67°16′
Gun-a-chal 5	IR/RI	BC	Cassiar	93 M/5	55°23′	127°37′
Gun Creek	RIV/CDE	BC	Lillooet	92 J/15	50°54′	122°46′
Gundahoo River	RIV/CDE	BC	Cassiar	94 M/2	59°09′	126°54′
Gundy	UNP/LNO	BC	Peace River	93 P/9	55°36′	120°00′
Gundy Lake	LAKE/LAC	ON	Kenora	52 E/14	49°45′	95°02′
Gunflint Lake	LAKE/LAC	ON	Thunder Bay	52 B/2	48°06′	90°41′
Gunisao Lake	LAKE/LAC	MB		63 H/9	53°32′	96°14′
Gunisao River	RIV/CDE	MB		63 H/13	53°56′	97°53′
Gun Lake	LAKE/LAC	ON	Kenora	52 E/15	49°57′	94°39′
Gun Lake	LAKE/LAC	BC	Lillooet	92 J/15	50°52′	122°53′
Gunn	UNP/LNO	AB	2-55-3-W5	83 G/9	53°44′	114°20′
Gunnar	UNP/LNO	SK		74 N/7	59°23′	108°53′
Gunne	UNP/LNO	ON	Kenora	52 F/14	49°49′	93°17′
Gunners Cove	UNP/LNO	NF		2 M/11	51°31′	55°27′
Gunning Cove	UNP/LNO	NS	Shelburne	20 P/11	43°41′	65°21′
Gunningsville	UNP/LNO	NB	Albert	21 I/2	46°04′	64°47′
Gunnworth	UNP/LNO	SK	26-27-16-W3	72 N/8	51°20′	108°09′
Gunridge	UNP/LNO	NF		1 N/7	47°19′	52°47′
Gunter	UNP/LNO	ON	Hastings	31 C/13	44°53′	77°33′
Gunters - see-voir - Coytown	UNP/LNO	NB		21 G/16	45°50′	66°12′
Gunters	UNP/LNO	ON	Nipissing	31 E/8	45°23′	78°04′

NAME / NOM	ENTITY / ENTITÉ	LOC 1 / LIEU 1	LOC 2 / LIEU 2	MAP / CARTE	POSITION LAT	POSITION LONG
Gunton	UNP/LNO	MB	33-15-2-E	62 I/6	50°19′	97°16′
Guoyskun 22	IR/RI	BC	Queen Charlotte	103 K/3	54°13′	133°02′
Gurd Island	ISL/ÎLE	BC	Range 5 Coast	103 G/15	53°53′	130°37′
Gurney	UNP/LNO	ON	Thunder Bay	42 D/13	48°56′	87°53′
Gurneyville	UNP/LNO	AB	31-59-5-W4	73 L/2	54°08′	110°45′
Gushie Point	CAPE/CAP	NT	Keewatin	34 D	56°26′	78°56′
Gussetts Cove	UNP/LNO	NF		1 N/14	47°51′	53°05′
Gustaf Adolf Trough	SEAU/SMER	—		7953	78°35′	106°00′
Gustafsen Lake	LAKE/LAC	BC	Lillooet	92 P/12	51°32′	121°43′
Gustin Grove	UNP/LNO	ON	Lambton	40 O/1	43°09′	82°03′
Gutah	UNP/LNO	BC	Peace River	94 H/14	57°49′	121°06′
Gutah Creek	RIV/CDE	BC	Peace River	94 I/4	58°02′	121°31′
Gutelius	UNP/LNO	ON	Algoma	42 C/8	48°21′	84°12′
Guthrie	UNP/LNO	QC	Brome-Missisquoi	31 H/2	45°04′	72°56′
Guthrie	UNP/LNO	ON	Simcoe	31 D/5	44°28′	79°33′
Guthrie Lake	LAKE/LAC	MB		63 N/7	55°16′	100°37′
Guy	UNP/LNO	AB	1-76-21-W5	83 N/11	55°33′	117°07′
Guy Canyon	SEAU/SMER	—		8010	43°30′	49°20′
Guyenne	UNP/LNO	QC	Abitibi	32 D/16	48°47′	78°28′
Guyer, Lac	LAKE/LAC	QC	Jamésie	33 G/11	53°32′	75°10′
Guyon Island	ISL/ÎLE	NS	Cape Breton	11 F/16	45°46′	60°07′
Guysborough	MUN1/AZM1	NS	Guysborough	11 F/5	45°23′	61°30′
Guysborough	UNP/LNO	NS	Guysborough	11 F/5	45°23′	61°30′
Guysborough	GEOG/GÉOG	NS	Guysborough	11 F/5	45°16′	61°56′
Guysborough Intervale	UNP/LNO	NS	Guysborough	11 F/5	45°27′	61°37′
Gwaii Haanas National Park Reserve - also-aussi - Gwaii Haanas, Réserve de parc national	PARK/PARC	BC	Queen Charlotte	103 B/6	52°21′	131°26′
Gwaii Haanas, Réserve de parc national - also-aussi - Gwaii Haanas National Park Reserve	PARK/PARC	BC	Queen Charlotte	103 B/6	52°21′	131°26′
Gwayasdums 1	IR/RI	BC	Range 1 Coast	92 L/10	50°42′	126°36′
Gwen Lake 3	IR/RI	BC	Kamloops Division Yale	92 I/2	50°01′	120°46′
Gwillim Lake	LAKE/LAC	BC	Peace River	93 P/6	55°21′	121°20′
Gwimmauz 52	IR/RI	BC	Cassiar	103 P/7	55°29′	128°55′
Gwinaha 44	IR/RI	BC	Cassiar	103 P/3	55°11′	129°14′
Gwindebilk 51	IR/RI	BC	Cassiar	103 P/6	55°25′	129°01′
Gwingag 53	IR/RI	BC	Cassiar	103 P/10	55°30′	128°55′
Gwinkbawaueast 54	IR/RI	BC	Cassiar	103 P/7	55°28′	128°56′
Gwynne	UNP/LNO	AB	24-46-23-W4	83 A/14	52°59′	113°11′
Gye	UNP/LNO	SK	35-4-27-W2	72 H/5	49°21′	105°32′
Gyproc	UNP/LNO	BC	New Westminster	92 G/2	49°13′	122°53′
Gypsum Lake	LAKE/LAC	MB	33-8-W	62 O/15	51°51′	98°31′
Gypsum Mines	UNP/LNO	NS	Hants	21 A/16	44°59′	64°04′
Gypsum Point	CAPE/CAP	NT	Mackenzie	85 G	61°53′	114°35′
Gypsumville	UNP/LNO	MB		62 O/15	51°46′	98°38′
Gyrfalcon Islands	ISL/ÎLE	NT	Franklin	24 N/2	59°05′	68°57′

H

NAME / NOM	ENTITY / ENTITÉ	LOC 1 / LIEU 1	LOC 2 / LIEU 2	MAP / CARTE	POSITION LAT	POSITION LONG
Haakon Fiord	BAY/BAIE	NT	Franklin	69 F/16	78°50′	100°45′
Haakon River	RIV/CDE	NT	Franklin	69 F/10	78°48′	101°03′
Habay	UNP/LNO	AB	14-113-5-W6	84 L/15	58°50′	118°44′
Habermehl	UNP/LNO	ON	Grey	41 A/3	44°13′	81°01′
Habitant	UNP/LNO	NS	Kings	21 H/1	45°09′	64°24′
Hache, Lac la	LAKE/LAC	BC	Lillooet	92 P/13	51°50′	121°31′
Haché Road	UNP/LNO	NB	Gloucester	21 P/10	47°42′	64°56′
Hacheyville	UNP/LNO	NB	Gloucester	21 P/11	47°35′	65°03′
Hacienda	UNP/LNO	MB		62 H/14	49°52′	97°22′
Hackett	UNP/LNO	AB	36-36-18-W4	83 A/1	52°08′	112°27′
Hackett Lake	LAKE/LAC	SK	59-7-W3	73 J/2	54°05′	106°57′
Hackett River	RIV/CDE	BC	Cassiar	104 J/5	58°16′	131°49′
Hacketts Cove	UNP/LNO	NS	Halifax	11 D/12	44°34′	63°55′
Hadashville	UNP/LNO	MB	8-12-E	52 E/12	49°41′	95°54′
Haddington Range	MTN/MNT	NT	Franklin	59 B	76°33′	92°35′
Haddo	UNP/LNO	ON	Dundas	31 B/14	44°52′	75°22′
Haddock	UNP/LNO	AB	2-56-14-W5	83 G/13	53°49′	115°59′
Haddock Channel - also-aussi - Églefin, Chenal de l'	SEAU/SMER	—		4016	45°30′	54°20′
Haddon Hill	UNP/LNO	NS	Lunenburg	21 A/9	44°33′	64°15′
Hadès, Collines	MTN/MNT	QC	Kativik	24 H/3	57°00′	65°08′
Hadley Bay	BAY/BAIE	NT	Franklin	78 B	72°30′	108°12′
Hadleyville	UNP/LNO	NS	Guysborough	11 F/6	45°28′	61°17′
Hadlow	UNP/LNO	QC	Desjardins	21 L/14	46°46′	71°13′
Hafford	TOWN/VIL2	SK	43-10-W3	73 B/11	52°43′	107°21′
Hagar	MUN2/AZM2	ON	Sudbury	41 I/8	46°29′	80°29′
Hagar	UNP/LNO	ON	Sudbury	41 I/8	46°27′	80°25′
Hagarty and Richards	MUN2/AZM2	ON	Renfrew	31 F/11	45°36′	77°30′

NAME NOM	ENTITY ENTITÉ	LOC 1 LIEU 1	LOC 2 LIEU 2	MAP CARTE	POSITION LAT	LONG
Hagen	HAM/HAM	SK	3-46A-25-W2	73 A/13	52°56'	105°33'
Hagensborg	UNP/LNO	BC	Range 3 Coast	93 D/7	52°23'	126°33'
Hagerman	MUN2/AZM2	ON	Parry Sound	31 E/12	45°36'	79°55'
Hagerman Corners - see-voir - Hagerman's Corners	UNP/LNO	ON		30 M/14	43°51'	79°18'
Hagerman's Corners	UNP/LNO	ON	York	30 M/14	43°51'	79°18'
Hagersville	UNP/LNO	ON	Brant	40 I/16	42°58'	80°03'
Hagey	UNP/LNO	ON	Waterloo	40 P/8	43°25'	80°22'
Haggard Creek	RIV/CDE	BC	Kamloops Division Yale	82 M/4	51°15'	119°56'
Haggerty Creek	RIV/CDE	ON	Lambton	40 I/12	42°42'	81°58'
Haggertys Cove	UNP/LNO	NB	Charlotte	21 G/2	45°08'	66°31'
Hagles Corners	UNP/LNO	ON	Oxford	40 P/2	43°01'	80°50'
Hague	TOWN/VIL2	SK	7-41-3-W3	73 B/8	52°31'	106°25'
Hague Creek	RIV/CDE	SK	68-18-W2	73 I/15	54°52'	104°38'
Hagwilget	UNP/LNO	BC	Cassiar	93 M/5	55°15'	127°36'
Hagwilget 1	IR/RI	BC	Cassiar	93 M/5	55°16'	127°36'
Ha! Ha!, Baie des	BAY/BAIE	QC	Côte-Nord-du-Golfe-Saint-Laurent	12 J/15	50°58'	58°57'
Ha! Ha!, Baie des	BAY/BAIE	QC	Le Fjord-du-Saguenay	22 D/7	48°21'	70°49'
Ha Ha Bay	BAY/BAIE	NF		2 M/12	51°35'	55°44'
Ha! Ha!, Lac	LAKE/LAC	QC	Le Fjord-du-Saguenay	22 D/2	48°02'	70°51'
Ha! Ha!, Rivière	RIV/CDE	QC	Le Fjord-du-Saguenay	22 D/7	48°19'	70°52'
Haida Channel	SEAU/SMER	—		15798A	49°15'	129°00'
Haida Ridge	SEAU/SMER	—		15798A	49°52'	128°39'
Haig	UNP/LNO	BC	Yale Division Yale	92 H/6	49°24'	121°27'
Haight	UNP/LNO	AB	30-50-16-W4	83 H/8	53°21'	112°19'
Haig Lake	LAKE/LAC	AB	91-13,14-W5	84 C/16	56°54'	116°06'
Haig, Mount	MTN/MNT	AB/BC		82 G/8	49°17'	114°27'
Haig River	RIV/CDE	AB	103-1-W6	84 E/16	57°59'	118°00'
Haig-Thomas Island	ISL/ÎLE	NT	Franklin	59 F	78°14'	94°30'
Haihte Lake	LAKE/LAC	BC	Rupert	92 L/8	50°21'	126°02'
Haileybury	TOWN/VIL2	ON	Timiskaming	31 M/5	47°27'	79°38'
Hailsham	UNP/LNO	SK	36-52-9-W3	73 G/11	53°32'	107°11'
Haina	UNP/LNO	BC	Queen Charlotte	103 F/1	53°13'	132°02'
Haines Island 8	IR/RI	BC	Barclay	92 C/14	48°50'	125°12'
Haines Junction	VILG/VILG	YT		115 A/13	60°45'	137°30'
Haines Lake	UNP/LNO	ON	Parry Sound	31 E/5	45°20'	79°56'
Hainesville	UNP/LNO	NB	York	21 J/3	46°07'	67°09'
Hainsville	UNP/LNO	ON	Dundas	31 B/14	44°54'	75°24'
Hairy Hill	UNP/LNO	AB	23-55-14-W4	73 E/13	53°46'	111°58'
Hak	UNP/LNO	SK	14-13-W3	72 J/4	50°06'	107°43'
Hakai Passage	CHAN/CHEN	BC	Range 2 Coast	102 P/9	51°43'	128°04'
Halach	UNP/LNO	AB	20-61-25-W4	83 I/5	54°18'	113°43'
Halalt 2	IR/RI	BC	Chemainus	92 B/13	48°53'	123°41'
Halalt Island 1	IR/RI	BC	Chemainus	92 B/13	48°54'	123°40'
Halbrite	VILG/VILG	SK	21-6-12-W2	62 E/5	49°30'	103°33'
Halbstadt	UNP/LNO	MB	22,23-1-1-E	62 H/3	49°03'	97°22'
Halcomb	UNP/LNO	NB	Northumberland	21 I/13	46°56'	65°57'
Halcourt	UNP/LNO	AB	6-7-10-W6	83 M/4	55°07'	119°31'
Halcreek	UNP/LNO	AB	4-62-25-W4	83 I/5	54°20'	113°40'
Halcro	UNP/LNO	SK	46-26-W2	73 H/4	53°02'	105°42'
Halcro 150C	IR/RI	AB		83 N/9	55°36'	116°11'
Halcrow	UNP/LNO	MB	12-60-22-W	63 K/2	54°11'	100°37'
Haldane Hill	UNP/LNO	ON	Parry Sound	31 E/6	45°25'	79°25'
Haldane, Mount	MTN/MNT	YT		105 M/13	63°52'	135°50'
Haldane River	RIV/CDE	NT	Mackenzie	96 I	66°50'	121°12'
Haldimand	TOWN/VIL2	ON	Haldimand	30 M/4	43°00'	79°50'
Haldimand	MUN2/AZM2	ON	Northumberland	31 D/1	44°05'	78°02'
Haldimand	GEOG/GÉOG	ON		30 L/13	42°47'	79°44'
Haldimand Canyon	SEAU/SMER	—		4045	44°00'	57°58'
Haldimand, Cap	CAPE/CAP	QC	La Côte-de-Gaspé	22 A/16	48°48'	64°23'
Haldimand East	UNP/LNO	QC	La Côte-de-Gaspé	22 A/16	48°47'	64°24'
Haldimand-Norfolk	MUN1/AZM1	ON	Haldimand	40 I/9	42°43'	80°00'
Haldimand West	UNP/LNO	QC	La Côte-de-Gaspé	22 A/16	48°47'	64°26'
Hale	UNP/LNO	NB	Carleton	21 J/5	46°20'	67°33'
Hale	UNP/LNO	ON	Algoma	42 G/5	49°21'	83°58'
Hale Lake	LAKE/LAC	MB	88-8,9-E	64 A/9	56°37'	96°10'
Hale Mountain	MTN/MNT	BC	Cassiar	104 M/9	59°32'	134°21'
Hales Landing - see-voir - Herb Lake Landing	UNP/LNO	MB		63 J/12	54°39'	99°47'
Halet	UNP/LNO	QC	Vallée-de-l'Or	32 D/1	48°07'	78°00'
Haley Lake	LAKE/LAC	ON	Lanark	31 F/1	45°02'	76°16'
Haley Station	UNP/LNO	ON	Renfrew	31 F/10	45°34'	76°47'
Half Island Cove	UNP/LNO	NS	Guysborough	11 F/6	45°21'	61°12'
Half Moon Bay	VILG/VILG	AB		83 B/8	52°21'	114°10'
Halfmoon Bay	UNP/LNO	BC	New Westminster	92 G/12	49°31'	123°55'
Half Moon Pit	UNP/LNO	NB	York	21 J/6	46°29'	67°02'
Halfway	UNP/LNO	NB	Restigouche	21 O/16	47°49'	66°05'

NAME NOM	ENTITY ENTITÉ	LOC 1 LIEU 1	LOC 2 LIEU 2	MAP CARTE	POSITION LAT	LONG
Halfway	UNP/LNO	ON	Renfrew	31 F/5	45°25'	77°35'
Halfway Brook	UNP/LNO	NS	Colchester	11 E/3	45°14'	63°05'
Half Way Cabin	UNP/LNO	QC	Côte-Nord-du-Golfe-Saint-Laurent	12 O/2	51°02'	58°53'
Halfway Cove	UNP/LNO	NS	Guysborough	11 F/6	45°21'	61°22'
Halfway Cove Lake	LAKE/LAC	NS	Guysborough	11 F/6	45°18'	61°23'
Halfway Depot	UNP/LNO	NB	Madawaska	21 N/9	47°35'	68°18'
Halfway House	UNP/LNO	NF		1 N/14	47°48'	53°17'
Halfway House Corner	UNP/LNO	ON	Norfolk	40 I/16	42°47'	80°17'
Halfway Inlet	BAY/BAIE	ON	Rainy River	52 C/14	48°49'	93°30'
Halfway Lake	UNP/LNO	AB	25-59-24-W4	83 I/3	54°08'	113°27'
Halfway Lake	LAKE/LAC	MB		53 L/15	54°50'	94°43'
Halfway Lake	LAKE/LAC	MB	69,70,71-6,7-W	63 O/16	55°04'	98°24'
Halfway Point	UNP/LNO	NF		12 B/16	48°59'	58°06'
Halfway Point	UNP/LNO	ON	Bruce	41 A/14	44°54'	81°01'
Halfway Point	CAPE/CAP	ON	Cochrane	42 P/15	51°54'	80°48'
Halfway Point-Benoit's Cove-John's Beach-Frenchman's Cove - see-voir - Humber Arm South	TOWN/VIL2	NF		12 G/1	49°01'	58°09'
Halfway Pond	LAKE/LAC	NF		2 C/6	48°27'	53°12'
Halfway Ranch	UNP/LNO	BC	Peace River	94 B/8	56°30'	122°02'
Halfway River	UNP/LNO	NS	Cumberland	21 H/9	45°31'	64°21'
Halfway River	RIV/CDE	NS	Cumberland	21 H/9	45°30'	64°20'
Halfway River	RIV/CDE	MB	73-5-W	63 O/8	55°20'	98°06'
Halfway River	RIV/CDE	BC	Kootenay	82 K/5	50°26'	117°54'
Halfway River	RIV/CDE	BC	Peace River	94 A/3	56°13'	121°26'
Halfway River 168	IR/RI	BC	Peace River	94 A/5	56°27'	121°50'
Halfway Tucks	UNP/LNO	NF		1 K/12	46°43'	53°36'
Halhalaeden 14	IR/RI	BC	Kamloops Division Yale	92 I/5	50°18'	121°38'
Halhalaeden 14A	IR/RI	BC	Kamloops Division Yale	92 I/5	50°18'	121°37'
Haliburton	MUN1/AZM1	ON	Haliburton	31 E/1	45°10'	78°30'
Haliburton	UNP/LNO	PE	Prince	21 I/9	46°43'	64°21'
Haliburton	UNP/LNO	NS	Pictou	11 E/10	45°41'	62°45'
Haliburton	UNP/LNO	ON	Haliburton	31 E/2	45°03'	78°31'
Haliburton	GEOG/GÉOG	ON		31 E/1	45°10'	78°30'
Haliburton Lake	LAKE/LAC	ON	Haliburton	31 E/1	45°12'	78°24'
Halibut Channel - also-aussi - Flétan, Chenal du	SEAU/SMER	—		4016	46°00'	55°15'
Halicz	UNP/LNO	MB	3-27-21-W	62 N/8	51°18'	100°20'
Halifax	MUN1/AZM1	NS	Halifax	11 D/13	44°52'	63°43'
Halifax	UNP/LNO	NS	Halifax	11 D/12	44°39'	63°36'
Halifax	GEOG/GÉOG	NS		11 D/13	44°52'	63°43'
Halifax, Base des Forces canadiennes - also-aussi - Halifax, Canadian Forces Base	MIL/MIL	NS	Halifax	11 D/12	44°39'	63°35'
Halifax, Canadian Forces Base - also-aussi - Halifax, Base des Forces canadiennes	MIL/MIL	NS	Halifax	11 D/12	44°39'	63°35'
Halifax Citadel National Historic Site - also-aussi - Citadelle-d'Halifax, Lieu historique national de la	PARK/PARC	NS	Halifax	11 D/12	44°39'	63°35'
Halifax Harbour	BAY/BAIE	NS	Halifax	11 D/12	44°38'	63°33'
Halifax-Nord	VILG/VILG	QC	L'Érable	21 L/4	46°08'	71°42'
Halkett	UNP/LNO	SK	5-3-8-W2	62 E/3	49°11'	103°03'
Halkett Lake	LAKE/LAC	SK	54-1-W3	73 G/9	53°39'	106°06'
Halkirk	VILG/VILG	AB	24-38-16-W4	83 A/8	52°17'	112°09'
Hall	UNP/LNO	QC	Le Haut-Saint-François	21 E/12	45°31'	71°33'
Hall	UNP/LNO	ON	Haldimand	30 M/4	43°00'	79°57'
Hall	UNP/LNO	BC	Kamloops Division Yale	82 F/6	49°23'	117°14'
Hallam	UNP/LNO	SK	26-38-28-W3	73 C/5	52°18'	109°54'
Hallam Peak	MTN/MNT	BC	Kootenay	83 D/2	52°12'	118°45'
Hall Basin - also-aussi - Hall, Bassin	CHAN/CHEN	NT	Franklin	120 C/9	81°30'	63°00'
Hall, Bassin - also-aussi - Hall Basin	CHAN/CHEN	NT	Franklin	120 C/9	81°30'	63°00'
Hall Bay	BAY/BAIE	NT	Franklin	25 C	60°54'	69°42'
Hall Beach	HAM/HAM	NT	Franklin	47 A	68°47'	81°14'
Hallboro	UNP/LNO	MB	34-13-15-W	62 J/3	50°09'	99°27'
Hallebourg	UNP/LNO	ON	Cochrane	42 G/12	49°40'	83°31'
Hallecks	UNP/LNO	ON	Leeds	31 B/12	44°33'	75°46'
Hallerton	UNP/LNO	QC	Les Jardins-de-Napierville	31 H/4	45°04'	73°32'
Hallett Lake	LAKE/LAC	BC	Range 4 Coast	93 F/15	53°48'	124°47'
Hall Glen	UNP/LNO	ON	Peterborough	31 D/9	44°31'	78°08'
Halliday	UNP/LNO	BC	Range 5 Coast	103 I/7	54°29'	128°36'
Halliday Lake	LAKE/LAC	NT	Mackenzie	75 F	61°21'	108°56'
Hall Island	ISL/ÎLE	NT	Franklin	25 I	62°32'	64°12'
Hall Lake	LAKE/LAC	BC	Cassiar	104 N/15	59°51'	132°31'
Hall Lake	LAKE/LAC	NT	Franklin	47 A	68°41'	82°17'
Hall Landing	UNP/LNO	ON	Northumberland	31 D/1	44°09'	78°16'
Hall, Mount	MTN/MNT	BC	Cowichan	92 B/13	48°55'	123°53'
Hallnor	UNP/LNO	ON	Cochrane	42 A/11	48°31'	81°09'
Hallonquist	UNP/LNO	SK	25-13-10-W3	72 J/3	50°07'	107°15'
Halloway	UNP/LNO	ON	Hastings	31 C/6	44°17'	77°28'
Hallowell	MUN2/AZM2	ON	Prince Edward	31 C/3	44°00'	77°15'

NAME NOM	ENTITY ENTITÉ	LOC 1 LIEU 1	LOC 2 LIEU 2	MAP CARTE	POSITION LAT	LONG
Hallowell	UNP/LNO	ON	Prince Edward	30 N/14	43°58'	77°17'
Hall Peninsula	CAPE/CAP	NT	Franklin	25 O	63°30'	66°00'
Hall Point	CAPE/CAP	NT	Franklin	47 A	68°45'	81°13'
Hall, Rivière	RIV/CDE	QC	Bonaventure	22 A/3	48°05'	65°26'
Halls Bay	BAY/BAIE	NF		2 E/12	49°30'	56°00'
Halls Corner	UNP/LNO	NB	Carleton	21 J/12	46°35'	67°37'
Halls Harbour	UNP/LNO	NS	Kings	21 H/2	45°12'	64°37'
Halls Hill	UNP/LNO	NB	Westmorland	21 H/16	45°58'	64°11'
Halls Lake	UNP/LNO	ON	Haliburton	31 E/2	45°07'	78°46'
Halls Lake	LAKE/LAC	ON	Haliburton	31 E/2	45°06'	78°45'
Halls Mills	UNP/LNO	ON	Lanark	31 F/1	45°11'	76°24'
Halls Town	UNP/LNO	NF		1 N/11	47°32'	53°19'
Hallville	UNP/LNO	ON	Dundas	31 G/4	45°04'	75°31'
Halowis 5	IR/RI	BC	Range 2 Coast	92 M/6	51°18'	127°03'
Halpenny	UNP/LNO	ON	Lanark	31 F/1	45°07'	76°17'
Halstead Beach	UNP/LNO	ON	Northumberland	31 D/1	44°06'	78°17'
Halsteads Bay	UNP/LNO	ON	Leeds	31 C/8	44°21'	76°05'
Halston	UNP/LNO	ON	Hastings	31 C/6	44°19'	77°17'
Halton	MUN1/AZM1	ON	Halton	30 M/5	43°30'	79°53'
Halton	GEOG/GÉOG	ON		30 M/5	43°30'	79°53'
Halton Hills	TOWN/VIL2	ON	Halton	30 M/12	43°37'	79°56'
Haltonville	UNP/LNO	ON	Halton	40 P/9	43°32'	80°02'
Halverson	UNP/LNO	QC	Les Collines-de-l'Outaouais	31 F/9	45°42'	76°12'
Halverson Ridge	MTN/MNT	AB	92,93-8,9,10-W5	84 E/3	57°03'	119°21'
Halvorgate	UNP/LNO	SK	24-19-6-W3	72 J/10	50°38'	106°42'
Hamburg	UNP/LNO	MB	16-3-3-W	62 H/4	49°13'	97°48'
Hamelin Creek	RIV/CDE	AB	16-81-6-W6	84 D/2	56°02'	118°52'
Hamer Bay	UNP/LNO	ON	Parry Sound	31 E/4	45°14'	79°47'
Hamill Creek	RIV/CDE	BC	Kootenay	82 K/2	50°12'	116°57'
Hamill, Mount	MTN/MNT	BC	Kootenay	82 K/2	50°13'	116°36'
Hamilton	CITY/VIL1	ON	Wentworth	30 M/4	43°15'	79°51'
Hamilton	MUN2/AZM2	ON	Northumberland	31 D/1	44°03'	78°14'
Hamilton	UNP/LNO	PE	Prince	11 L/5	46°30'	63°42'
Hamilton, Banc - also-aussi - Hamilton Bank	SEAU/SMER	—		8048	54°00'	54°45'
Hamilton Bank - also-aussi - Hamilton, Banc	SEAU/SMER	—		8048	54°00'	54°45'
Hamilton Beach	UNP/LNO	ON	Wentworth	30 M/5	43°17'	79°47'
Hamilton Branch	RIV/CDE	NS	Shelburne	20 P/13	43°46'	65°31'
Hamilton Corner	UNP/LNO	ON	Wellington	40 P/9	43°31'	80°12'
Hamilton Creek 2	IR/RI	BC	Kamloops Division Yale	92 I/2	50°09'	120°31'
Hamilton Creek 7	IR/RI	BC	Kamloops Division Yale	92 I/2	50°04'	120°32'
Hamilton Gault, Mount	MTN/MNT	NT	Mackenzie	95 E	61°42'	126°34'
Hamilton Harbour	BAY/BAIE	ON	Wentworth	30 M/5	43°17'	79°50'
Hamilton Heights	UNP/LNO	ON	Waterloo	40 P/7	43°23'	80°42'
Hamilton Heights	UNP/LNO	MB		62 G/13	49°53'	99°58'
Hamilton Inlet	BAY/BAIE	NF		13 J/1	54°00'	57°30'
Hamilton Island	ISL/ÎLE	NT	Franklin	68 E	74°12'	99°11'
Hamilton Point	CAPE/CAP	NT	Franklin	68 B	72°25'	101°56'
Hamilton Point 7	IR/RI	BC	Barclay	92 C/14	48°50'	125°11'
Hamiltonsfield	UNP/LNO	ON	Renfrew	31 F/14	45°49'	77°09'
Hamilton Sound	CHAN/CHEN	NF		2 E/9	49°30'	54°15'
Hamilton Spur	SEAU/SMER	—		813	55°40'	52°30'
Hamilton-Wentworth	MUN1/AZM1	ON	Wentworth	30 M/4	43°15'	80°00'
Hamiota	VILG/VILG	MB	8-14-23-W	62 K/2	50°11'	100°36'
Hamiota	MUN2/AZM2	MB	8-14-23-W	62 K/2	50°10'	100°36'
Hamlen Bay	BAY/BAIE	NT	Franklin	25 O	63°09'	66°33'
Hamlet	UNP/LNO	ON	Simcoe	31 D/14	44°47'	79°24'
Hamlet	UNP/LNO	AB	26-25-24-W4	82 P/3	51°10'	113°14'
Hamlin	UNP/LNO	SK	18-45-16-W3	73 C/16	52°52'	108°19'
Hamlin	UNP/LNO	AB	5-58-13-W4	73 E/13	53°58'	111°54'
Hammertown	UNP/LNO	ON	York	30 M/13	43°56'	79°45'
Hammil Lake	LAKE/LAC	BC	New Westminster	92 F/16	49°50'	124°28'
Hammond	UNP/LNO	ON	Russell	31 G/6	45°26'	75°14'
Hammond	GEOG/GÉOG	NB	Kings	21 H/11	45°35'	65°23'
Hammond River	UNP/LNO	NB	Kings	21 H/5	45°28'	65°55'
Hammond River	RIV/CDE	NB	Kings	21 H/12	45°30'	65°54'
Hammonds Plains	UNP/LNO	NS	Halifax	11 D/12	44°44'	63°47'
Hammonds Plains Road	UNP/LNO	NS	Halifax	11 D/12	44°43'	63°44'
Hammondvale	UNP/LNO	NB	Kings	21 H/11	45°34'	65°30'
Hammone, Lac	LAKE/LAC	QC	Minganie	12 P/11	51°44'	57°18'
Hammtown	UNP/LNO	NB	Queens	21 H/13	45°51'	65°55'
Ham-Nord	VILG/VILG	QC	Arthabaska	21 E/13	45°54'	71°39'
Hampden	VILG/VILG	NF		12 H/10	49°33'	56°51'
Hampden	VILG/VILG	QC	Le Haut-Saint-François	21 E/11	45°30'	71°15'
Hampden	UNP/LNO	ON	Grey	41 A/2	44°07'	80°55'
Hampelsfield	UNP/LNO	ON	Renfrew	31 F/14	45°49'	77°08'

NAME NOM	ENTITY ENTITÉ	LOC 1 LIEU 1	LOC 2 LIEU 2	MAP CARTE	POSITION LAT	LONG
Hampshire	VILG/VILG	PE	Queens	11 L/6	46°17′	63°16′
Hampshire	UNP/LNO	PE	Queens	11 L/6	46°17′	63°17′
Hampshire Mills	UNP/LNO	ON	Simcoe	31 D/11	44°42′	79°27′
Hampstead	CITY/VIL1	QC	Communauté urbaine de Montréal	31 H/5	45°29′	73°38′
Hampstead	UNP/LNO	NB	Queens	21 G/9	45°37′	66°05′
Hampstead	UNP/LNO	ON	Perth	40 P/7	43°27′	80°50′
Hampstead	GEOG/GÉOG	NB	Queens	21 G/9	45°34′	66°10′
Hampton	TOWN/VIL2	NB	Kings	21 H/12	45°32′	65°51′
Hampton	UNP/LNO	PE	Queens	11 L/3	46°13′	63°28′
Hampton	UNP/LNO	NS	Annapolis	21 A/14	44°54′	65°21′
Hampton	UNP/LNO	ON	Durham	30 M/15	43°58′	78°45′
Hampton	GEOG/GÉOG	NB	Kings	21 H/5	45°27′	65°50′
Hampton Heights	UNP/LNO	ON	Wentworth	30 M/4	43°13′	79°50′
Hampton Station	UNP/LNO	NB	Kings	21 H/12	45°32′	65°50′
Ham-Sud	UNP/LNO	QC	Asbestos	21 E/13	45°46′	71°36′
Hamton	UNP/LNO	SK	23-28-3-W2	62 M/8	51°26′	102°20′
Hamtown Corner	UNP/LNO	NB	York	21 J/2	46°07′	66°46′
Hanatsa 6	IR/RI	BC	Range 1 Coast	92 K/12	50°32′	125°58′
Hanbury	UNP/LNO	ON	Timiskaming	31 M/12	47°36′	79°40′
Hanbury Island	ISL/ÎLE	NT	Keewatin	55 O	63°32′	90°49′
Hanbury River	RIV/CDE	NT	Mackenzie	75 P	63°37′	104°34′
Hanceville	UNP/LNO	BC	Lillooet	92 O/14	51°55′	123°03′
Hanctin, Lac	LAKE/LAC	QC	Caniapiscau	23 C/15	52°47′	68°30′
Handel	VILG/VILG	SK	6-36-19-W3	73 C/2	52°04′	108°42′
Handhills Lake	LAKE/LAC	AB	29-15,16-W4	82 P/9	51°30′	112°07′
Handsworth	UNP/LNO	SK	25-10-8-W2	62 E/15	49°51′	102°57′
Haney	UNP/LNO	BC	New Westminster	92 G/2	49°13′	122°36′
Haney, Mount	MTN/MNT	BC	Cassiar	104 K/13	58°56′	133°43′
Haneytown	UNP/LNO	NB	Sunbury	21 G/16	45°48′	66°28′
Hanford Brook	UNP/LNO	NB	Saint John	21 H/5	45°28′	65°38′
Hankin Peak	MTN/MNT	BC	Cassiar	104 G/2	57°12′	130°38′
Hanlan	UNP/LNO	ON	Peel	30 M/12	43°39′	79°39′
Hanley	TOWN/VIL2	SK	1-31-4-W3	72 O/9	51°38′	106°26′
Hanlon	UNP/LNO	AB	17-54-2-W6	83 E/9	53°40′	118°16′
Hanmer	UNP/LNO	ON	Sudbury	41 I/10	46°39′	80°56′
Hanna	TOWN/VIL2	AB	9-31-14-W4	72 M/12	51°38′	111°54′
Hannah Bay	BAY/BAIE	NT	Keewatin	32 M/4	51°15′	79°50′
Hannah Cove	UNP/LNO	NF		12 H/10	49°37′	56°50′
Hannah Lake	LAKE/LAC	ON	Sudbury	41 I/4	46°12′	81°34′
Hannah Lake	LAKE/LAC	MB		54 K/6	58°22′	93°26′
Hannah Lake	LAKE/LAC	SK		64 M/4	59°06′	103°34′
Hannamville	UNP/LNO	NS	Annapolis	21 A/11	44°43′	65°12′
Hanover	TOWN/VIL2	ON	Bruce	41 A/3	44°09′	81°02′
Hanover	MUN2/AZM2	MB		62 H/7	49°28′	96°50′
Hanover Lake	LAKE/LAC	ON	Thunder Bay	42 L/6	50°22′	87°08′
Hansard	UNP/LNO	BC	Cariboo	93 I/4	54°05′	121°52′
Hansen, Cape	CAPE/CAP	NT	Franklin	67 F	70°30′	102°36′
Hansen Lagoon	LAKE/LAC	BC	Rupert	102 I/16	50°46′	128°21′
Hansen Point	CAPE/CAP	NT	Franklin	340 F	82°30′	82°33′
Hansford	UNP/LNO	NS	Cumberland	11 E/12	45°43′	63°46′
Hansine Lake	LAKE/LAC	NT	Keewatin	46 F	65°35′	85°40′
Hanson 13 - see-voir - Nan Tl'At 13	IR/RI	BC		93 K/11	54°31′	125°11′
Hanson Island	ISL/ÎLE	BC	Rupert	92 L/10	50°34′	126°44′
Hanson Lake	LAKE/LAC	SK		63 L/10	54°42′	102°50′
Hansteen Lake	LAKE/LAC	NT	Franklin	57 C	69°47′	94°10′
Hants	GEOG/GÉOG	NS		11 E/4	45°02′	63°52′
Hants Border	UNP/LNO	NS	Kings	21 H/1	45°04′	64°11′
Hant's Harbour	TOWN/VIL2	NF		2 C/3	48°01′	53°16′
Hantsport	TOWN/VIL2	NS	Hants	21 H/1	45°04′	64°10′
Hantzsch Bay	BAY/BAIE	NT	Franklin	36 P	67°34′	72°31′
Hantzsch River	RIV/CDE	NT	Franklin	36 P	67°32′	72°25′
Hanway Lake	LAKE/LAC	NT	Keewatin	55 N/8	63°27′	92°16′
Hanwell	UNP/LNO	NB	York	21 G/15	45°53′	66°47′
Happotiyik Lake	LAKE/LAC	NT	Keewatin	55 L	62°30′	94°22′
Happy Adventure	VILG/VILG	NF		2 C/12	48°38′	53°46′
Happy Hollow	UNP/LNO	ON	Prescott	31 G/10	45°32′	74°38′
Happy Hollow	UNP/LNO	AB	4-64-4-W4	73 L/10	54°30′	110°33′
Happy Isle Lake	LAKE/LAC	ON	Nipissing	31 E/10	45°45′	78°30′
Happyland	UNP/LNO	ON	Simcoe	31 D/11	44°40′	79°25′
Happyland No. 231	MUN2/AZM2	SK		72 K/12	50°45′	109°35′
Happy Mountains	UNP/LNO	QC	La Vallée-de-la-Gatineau	31 K/1	46°13′	76°08′
Happy Valley	UNP/LNO	ON	York	30 M/13	43°59′	79°36′
Happy Valley	UNP/LNO	BC	Metchosin	92 B/5	48°25′	123°32′
Happy Valley-Goose Bay	TOWN/VIL2	NF		13 F/8	53°19′	60°20′
Happy Valley No. 10	MUN2/AZM2	SK		72 H/3	49°10′	105°05′

NAME NOM	ENTITY ENTITÉ	LOC 1 LIEU 1	LOC 2 LIEU 2	MAP CARTE	POSITION LAT	POSITION LONG
Hara Lake	LAKE/LAC	SK		64 M/1	59°07′	102°03′
Harbledown Island	ISL/ÎLE	BC	Range 1 Coast	92 L/10	50°34′	126°35′
Harbottle Lake	LAKE/LAC	MB		64 P/3	59°08′	97°22′
Harbour Breton	TOWN/VIL2	NF		1 M/5	47°29′	55°48′
Harbour Buffett	UNP/LNO	NF		1 M/9	47°31′	54°05′
Harbour Centre	UNP/LNO	NS	Antigonish	11 F/12	45°41′	61°55′
Harbour Chines	UNP/LNO	BC	New Westminster	92 G/7	49°16′	122°51′
Harbour Deep	UNP/LNO	NF		12 I/7	50°22′	56°31′
Harbour Fiord	BAY/BAIE	NT	Franklin	49 B	76°31′	84°08′
Harbour Grace	TOWN/VIL2	NF		1 N/11	47°41′	53°14′
Harbour Grace South	UNP/LNO	NF		1 N/11	47°41′	53°13′
Harbour Island	UNP/LNO	NF		1 M/9	47°33′	54°16′
Harbour Island	ISL/ÎLE	NS	Guysborough	11 F/4	45°08′	61°36′
Harbour Le Cou	UNP/LNO	NF		11 O/10	47°37′	58°41′
Harbour Main	UNP/LNO	NF		1 N/6	47°26′	53°10′
Harbour Main-Chapel Cove-Lakeview	TOWN/VIL2	NF		1 N/6	47°25′	53°10′
Harbour Mille	UNP/LNO	NF		1 M/10	47°36′	54°52′
Harbour Mille-Little Harbour East	UNP/LNO	NF		1 M/10	47°35′	54°52′
Harbour My God Point	CAPE/CAP	NF		1 M/6	47°21′	55°18′
Harbour Round	UNP/LNO	NF		2 E/13	49°55′	55°44′
Harbourview	UNP/LNO	NS	Victoria	11 K/7	46°16′	60°37′
Harbourview	UNP/LNO	NS	Inverness	11 F/13	45°59′	61°31′
Harbour View South	UNP/LNO	MB		62 H/14	49°55′	97°02′
Harbour Village	UNP/LNO	BC	New Westminster	92 G/7	49°16′	122°49′
Harbourville	UNP/LNO	NS	Kings	21 H/2	45°09′	64°49′
Harburn	UNP/LNO	ON	Haliburton	31 E/1	45°08′	78°25′
Harcourt	UNP/LNO	NF		2 C/4	48°12′	53°52′
Harcourt	UNP/LNO	NB	Kent	21 I/6	46°28′	65°15′
Harcourt	UNP/LNO	ON	Haliburton	31 E/1	45°05′	78°09′
Harcourt	GEOG/GÉOG	NB	Kent	21 I/5	46°27′	65°30′
Harcourt Cameron Ridge	SEAU/SMER	—		801	43°45′	60°10′
Harcourt-Monroe-Waterville	UNP/LNO	NF		2 C/4	48°12′	53°52′
Harcus	UNP/LNO	MB	17-20-10-W	62 J/10	50°43′	98°50′
Hardene	UNP/LNO	SK	30-27-28-W3	72 N/5	51°20′	109°55′
Hardieville	UNP/LNO	AB	9-21-W4	82 H/10	49°45′	112°51′
Hardiman Bay	BAY/BAIE	ON	Sudbury	42 B/1	48°02′	82°14′
Hardiman Lake	LAKE/LAC	ON	Sudbury	41 O/16	47°59′	82°09′
Harding	UNP/LNO	MB	3,10-12-23-W	62 F/15	49°59′	100°32′
Hardinge Bay	BAY/BAIE	NT	Franklin	99 A	76°28′	121°40′
Hardinge Mountains	MTN/MNT	NT	Franklin	99 A	76°10′	121°14′
Harding Lake	LAKE/LAC	MB		64 B/1	56°12′	98°22′
Harding Lake	LAKE/LAC	NT	Mackenzie	85 I/6	62°21′	113°22′
Harding Point	CAPE/CAP	NT	Franklin	68 G	75°12′	100°32′
Harding River	RIV/CDE	NT	Mackenzie	87 B/15	68°54′	117°06′
Hardings Island	ISL/ÎLE	NS	Shelburne	20 P/10	43°44′	64°58′
Hardings Point	UNP/LNO	NB	Kings	21 G/8	45°21′	66°13′
Hardington	UNP/LNO	ON		30 M/12	43°43′	79°30′
Hardingville	UNP/LNO	NB	Saint John	21 H/5	45°25′	65°40′
Hardisty	TOWN/VIL2	AB	6-43-9-W4	73 D/11	52°40′	111°18′
Hardisty Island	ISL/ÎLE	NT	Mackenzie	85 G	61°40′	114°37′
Hardisty Lake	LAKE/LAC	NT	Mackenzie	86 C	64°37′	117°45′
Hardrock	UNP/LNO	ON	Thunder Bay	42 E/10	49°43′	86°53′
Hardrock Townsite	UNP/LNO	ON	Thunder Bay	42 E/10	49°41′	86°55′
Hardwicke	UNP/LNO	NB	Northumberland	21 P/3	47°05′	65°01′
Hardwicke	GEOG/GÉOG	NB	Northumberland	21 P/3	47°02′	65°03′
Hardwicke Island	UNP/LNO	BC	Range 1 Coast	92 K/5	50°25′	125°55′
Hardwicke Island	ISL/ÎLE	BC	Range 1 Coast	92 K/5	50°26′	125°51′
Hardwood Hill	UNP/LNO	NS	Cape Breton	11 K/1	46°07′	60°11′
Hardwood Hill	UNP/LNO	NS	Pictou	11 E/10	45°39′	62°49′
Hardwood Hill	UNP/LNO	QC	Le Val-Saint-François	21 E/12	45°37′	71°56′
Hardwood Islands	ISL/ÎLE	ON	Nipissing	41 I/8	46°18′	80°04′
Hardwood Lake	UNP/LNO	ON	Renfrew	31 F/3	45°13′	77°26′
Hardwood Lands	UNP/LNO	NS	Hants	11 E/4	45°02′	63°31′
Hardwood Ridge	UNP/LNO	NB	Sunbury	21 J/1	46°09′	66°02′
Hardwood Settlement	UNP/LNO	NB	Northumberland	21 P/2	47°03′	64°56′
Hardy	VILG/VILG	SK	23-6-21-W2	72 H/7	49°29′	104°44′
Hardy	UNP/LNO	ON	Westmorland	21 I/1	46°04′	64°02′
Hardy Bay	BAY/BAIE	BC	Rupert	92 L/11	50°44′	127°28′
Hardy Bay	BAY/BAIE	NT	Franklin	88 H	75°04′	115°20′
Hardy Creek	RIV/CDE	ON	Lambton	40 I/13	42°52′	81°52′
Hardy Inlet	BAY/BAIE	BC	Range 2 Coast	92 M/12	51°42′	127°33′
Hardy Island	ISL/ÎLE	BC	New Westminster	92 F/9	49°44′	124°12′
Hardy Lake	LAKE/LAC	NT	Mackenzie	76 C	64°52′	109°50′
Hardy's Cove	UNP/LNO	NF		1 M/12	47°40′	55°40′
Hare Bay	TOWN/VIL2	NF		2 D/16	48°51′	54°01′

NAME NOM	ENTITY ENTITÉ	LOC 1 LIEU 1	LOC 2 LIEU 2	MAP CARTE	POSITION	
					LAT	LONG
Hare Bay	BAY/BAIE	NF		2 E/9	49°40′	54°17′
Hare Bay	BAY/BAIE	NF		2 M/5	51°15′	55°45′
Hare Bay	BAY/BAIE	NF		11 P/10	47°40′	56°32′
Hare Bay Head	CAPE/CAP	NF		2 E/9	49°40′	54°19′
Hare Fiord	BAY/BAIE	NT	Franklin	340 C/3	81°01′	85°30′
Hare Harbour	UNP/LNO	NF		1 M/11	47°35′	55°08′
Hare Harbour	UNP/LNO	NF		13 H/15	53°45′	56°44′
Hare Hill	MTN/MNT	NF		1 M/6	47°23′	55°11′
Hare Hill	MTN/MNT	NF		12 B/9	48°39′	58°07′
Hare Indian River	RIV/CDE	NT	Mackenzie	106 I	66°18′	128°37′
Hare Island	ISL/ÎLE	NF		2 E/9	49°34′	54°29′
Hares Islands	ISL/ÎLE	NF		13 O/5	55°21′	59°38′
Harewood	UNP/LNO	NB	Westmorland	21 I/3	46°04′	65°16′
Harfred	UNP/LNO	ON	Nipissing	31 L/5	46°24′	79°51′
Hargrave	UNP/LNO	MB	14-11-27-W	62 F/14	49°55′	101°04′
Hargrave Lake	LAKE/LAC	MB		63 J/5	54°29′	99°40′
Hargrave, Point	CAPE/CAP	NT	Keewatin	46 M	67°22′	87°28′
Hargrave River	RIV/CDE	MB		63 J/7	54°24′	98°48′
Hargreaves - see-voir - Springfield Ranch	UNP/LNO	BC		93 B/8	52°16′	122°15′
Hargwen	UNP/LNO	AB	36-52-22-W5	83 F/11	53°32′	117°06′
Harkaway	UNP/LNO	ON	Grey	41 A/7	44°25′	80°40′
Harkin Bay	BAY/BAIE	NT	Franklin	36 D	64°50′	78°07′
Harlaka	UNP/LNO	QC	Desjardins	21 L/14	46°49′	71°07′
Harlan	UNP/LNO	SK	21-53-27-W3	73 F/12	53°36′	109°55′
Harlands Landing	UNP/LNO	NF		23 H/8	53°29′	64°30′
Harlech	UNP/LNO	AB	4-41-14-W5	83 B/12	52°31′	115°58′
Harlem	UNP/LNO	ON	Leeds	31 C/9	44°40′	76°08′
Harley	MUN2/AZM2	ON	Timiskaming	31 M/12	47°38′	79°41′
Harley	UNP/LNO	ON	Brant	40 P/1	43°04′	80°29′
Harley Road	UNP/LNO	NB	Queens	21 I/4	46°13′	65°49′
Harlington	UNP/LNO	MB	19-35-28-W	63 C/3	52°02′	101°27′
Harlock	UNP/LNO	ON	Huron	40 P/11	43°41′	81°23′
Harlowe	UNP/LNO	ON	Frontenac	31 C/14	44°48′	77°05′
Harmac	UNP/LNO	BC	Cedar	92 G/4	49°08′	123°51′
Harmattan	UNP/LNO	AB	24-32-4-W5	82 O/16	51°46′	114°25′
Harmer	UNP/LNO	BC	Kootenay	82 G/15	49°50′	114°51′
Harmon Lake	LAKE/LAC	ON	Thunder Bay	52 G/16	49°56′	90°13′
Harmon, Port	BAY/BAIE	NF		12 B/10	48°32′	58°32′
Harmon Valley	UNP/LNO	AB	12-82-19-W5	84 C/2	56°07′	116°50′
Harmony	UNP/LNO	PE	Prince	21 I/9	46°31′	64°03′
Harmony	UNP/LNO	NS	Colchester	11 E/6	45°20′	63°13′
Harmony	UNP/LNO	NS	Kings	21 A/15	44°57′	64°52′
Harmony	UNP/LNO	ON	Dundas	31 G/3	45°08′	75°25′
Harmony	UNP/LNO	ON	Ontario	30 M/15	43°54′	78°50′
Harmony	UNP/LNO	ON	Perth	40 P/7	43°19′	80°57′
Harmony	UNP/LNO	ON	Algoma	41 K/1	46°13′	84°03′
Harmony Beach	UNP/LNO	ON	Algoma	41 K/16	46°51′	84°22′
Harmony Hall II	UNP/LNO	ON	Wentworth	30 M/4	43°13′	79°58′
Harmony Junction	UNP/LNO	PE	Kings	11 L/8	46°24′	62°15′
Harmony Lake	LAKE/LAC	NS	Queens	21 A/6	44°24′	65°06′
Harmony Mills	UNP/LNO	NS	Queens	21 A/6	44°24′	65°04′
Harmony Park	UNP/LNO	NS	Halifax	11 D/12	44°43′	63°43′
Harmony Road	UNP/LNO	NS	Colchester	11 E/6	45°21′	63°14′
Harmsworth	UNP/LNO	MB	33-11-26-W	62 F/15	49°58′	100°59′
Harney's Corner	UNP/LNO	QC	Pontiac	31 F/15	45°53′	76°57′
Harnum Point	UNP/LNO	NF		1 N/12	47°34′	53°34′
Harold Price Creek	RIV/CDE	BC	Cassiar	93 M/6	55°17′	127°10′
Haro Strait	CHAN/CHEN	BC	Victoria	92 B/11	48°35′	123°19′
Harp Cove	BAY/BAIE	NT	Franklin	25 B/5	60°20′	67°57′
Harpellville	UNP/LNO	NS	Guysborough	11 F/4	45°07′	61°47′
Harper	UNP/LNO	PE	Prince	21 I/16	46°56′	64°05′
Harper	UNP/LNO	ON	Lanark	31 C/16	44°55′	76°21′
Harper Corners	UNP/LNO	ON	Wentworth	30 M/5	43°22′	79°59′
Harper Creek	RIV/CDE	AB	106-24-W4	84 I/4	58°15′	113°57′
Harper Creek	RIV/CDE	BC	Kamloops Division Yale	82 M/5	51°19′	119°53′
Harper Islands	ISL/ÎLE	NT	Franklin	25 I	62°21′	64°40′
Harper Lake	LAKE/LAC	SK	17-53-20-W2	73 H/10	53°35′	104°55′
Harper Lake	LAKE/LAC	SK		74 N/12	59°40′	109°47′
Harper, Mount	MTN/MNT	YT		116 B/12	64°40′	139°52′
Harper Settlement	UNP/LNO	NB	Kings	21 H/14	45°52′	65°19′
Harpers Lake	LAKE/LAC	NS	Shelburne	20 P/14	43°48′	65°28′
Harperville	UNP/LNO	MB	21-16-2-W	62 I/5	50°24′	97°40′
Harp Lake	LAKE/LAC	NF		13 N/4	55°05′	61°50′
Harpoon Brook	RIV/CDE	NF		12 A/15	48°46′	56°33′
Harpoon Hill	MTN/MNT	NF		12 A/10	48°35′	56°37′

NAME NOM	ENTITY ENTITÉ	LOC 1 LIEU 1	LOC 2 LIEU 2	MAP CARTE	POSITION LAT	LONG
Harp Peninsula	CAPE/CAP	NF		14 L/2	58°10′	62°30′
Harptree	UNP/LNO	SK	22-4-26-W2	72 H/6	49°19′	105°25′
Harpurhey	UNP/LNO	ON	Huron	40 P/11	43°34′	81°25′
Harricana, Rivière - also-aussi - Harricanaw River	RIV/CDE	QC	Jamésie	32 M/4	51°10′	79°45′
Harricanaw River - also-aussi - Harricana, Rivière	RIV/CDE	ON	Cochrane	32 M/4	51°10′	79°45′
Harricott	UNP/LNO	NF		1 N/4	47°10′	53°32′
Harriets Corners	UNP/LNO	ON	Renfrew	31 F/6	45°25′	77°27′
Harrietsfield	UNP/LNO	NS	Halifax	11 D/12	44°34′	63°38′
Harrietsville	UNP/LNO	ON	Middlesex	40 I/14	42°55′	81°00′
Harrigan Cove	UNP/LNO	NS	Halifax	11 D/16	44°56′	62°18′
Harrington	VILG/VILG	QC	Argenteuil	31 G/15	45°50′	74°40′
Harrington	UNP/LNO	PE	Queens	11 L/6	46°21′	63°10′
Harrington	UNP/LNO	NS	Digby	21 B/1	44°06′	66°04′
Harrington	UNP/LNO	ON	Oxford	40 P/2	43°15′	80°59′
Harrington Harbour	UNP/LNO	QC	Côte-Nord-du-Golfe-Saint-Laurent	12 J/11	50°30′	59°29′
Harrington, Îles	ISL/ÎLE	QC	Côte-Nord-du-Golfe-Saint-Laurent	12 J/6	50°29′	59°28′
Harriott Lake	LAKE/LAC	SK		64 D/2	56°12′	102°45′
Harriott River	RIV/CDE	SK	6-7-32	64 D/6	56°15′	103°05′
Harris	VILG/VILG	SK	12-32-12-W3	72 O/12	51°44′	107°35′
Harris	MUN2/AZM2	ON	Timiskaming	31 M/12	47°33′	79°34′
Harris 3	IR/RI	BC	Osoyoos Division Yale	82 L/6	50°23′	119°14′
Harris Brook Settlement	UNP/LNO	NB	Northumberland	21 I/13	46°55′	65°58′
Harrisburg	UNP/LNO	ON	Brant	40 P/1	43°14′	80°13′
Harris Creek	RIV/CDE	BC	Osoyoos Division Yale	82 L/3	50°12′	119°00′
Harris Creek	RIV/CDE	BC	Renfrew	92 C/9	48°35′	124°16′
Harris Hill	UNP/LNO	ON	Rainy River	52 D/15	48°57′	94°32′
Harris Island	UNP/LNO	NS	Yarmouth	20 O/9	43°39′	66°02′
Harris Lake	UNP/LNO	ON	Parry Sound	41 H/9	45°42′	80°23′
Harris Lake	LAKE/LAC	ON	Kenora	52 F/3	49°11′	93°13′
Harris No. 316	MUN2/AZM2	SK		72 O/11	51°45′	107°28′
Harrison	MUN2/AZM2	MB		62 K/8	50°28′	100°05′
Harrison	UNP/LNO	NF		12 A/13	48°59′	57°47′
Harrison Bank	SEAU/SMER	—		8047	55°03′	56°40′
Harrison Brook Settlement	UNP/LNO	NB	Madawaska	21 O/4	47°13′	67°55′
Harrison, Cape	CAPE/CAP	NF		13 I/13	54°56′	57°57′
Harrison Hot Springs	VILG/VILG	BC	New Westminster	92 H/5	49°18′	121°47′
Harrison Island	ISL/ÎLE	NT	Keewatin	34 L/8	58°24′	78°08′
Harrison Islands	ISL/ÎLE	NT	Franklin	57 D	69°20′	90°30′
Harrison Lake	LAKE/LAC	NS	Cumberland	21 H/9	45°42′	64°16′
Harrison Lake	LAKE/LAC	BC	New Westminster	92 H/12	49°33′	121°50′
Harrison Mills	UNP/LNO	BC	New Westminster	92 H/5	49°15′	121°57′
Harrison Point	CAPE/CAP	NT	Franklin	68 C	73°22′	101°17′
Harrison River	RIV/CDE	BC	New Westminster	92 H/4	49°13′	121°57′
Harrison River	RIV/CDE	NT	Mackenzie	86 K	66°28′	117°28′
Harrison Road	UNP/LNO	NS	Cumberland	21 H/9	45°45′	64°16′
Harrisons Corners	UNP/LNO	ON	Stormont	31 G/2	45°05′	74°54′
Harrison Settlement	UNP/LNO	NS	Cumberland	21 H/9	45°31′	64°23′
Harrison Settlement	UNP/LNO	NB	Albert	21 H/14	45°53′	65°02′
Harris Point	UNP/LNO	NF		2 E/8	49°17′	54°29′
Harriston	TOWN/VIL2	ON	Wellington	40 P/15	43°54′	80°53′
Harriston	UNP/LNO	NS	Lunenburg	21 A/16	44°46′	64°28′
Harriston Junction	UNP/LNO	ON	Wellington	40 P/15	43°55′	80°53′
Harrisville	UNP/LNO	NB	Westmorland	21 I/2	46°07′	64°43′
Harrogate	UNP/LNO	BC	Kootenay	82 K/16	50°59′	116°27′
Harrop	UNP/LNO	BC	Kootenay	82 F/11	49°36′	117°04′
Harrop Lake	LAKE/LAC	MB		53 D/12	52°38′	96°00′
Harrow	TOWN/VIL2	ON	Essex	40 J/2	42°02′	82°55′
Harrowby	UNP/LNO	MB	28-20-29-W	62 K/14	50°45′	101°27′
Harrowby Bay	BAY/BAIE	NT	Mackenzie	97 F	70°13′	127°56′
Harrowsmith	UNP/LNO	ON	Frontenac	31 C/7	44°24′	76°40′
Harry Lake	LAKE/LAC	SK	75-10-W3	73 O/11	55°30′	107°24′
Harrys Brook	UNP/LNO	NF		12 B/9	48°40′	58°16′
Harry's Corner	UNP/LNO	ON	Ontario	31 D/11	44°35′	79°18′
Harry's Harbour	UNP/LNO	NF		2 E/12	49°42′	55°55′
Harrys River	RIV/CDE	NF		12 B/9	48°30′	58°25′
Harstone	UNP/LNO	ON	Thunder Bay	52 A/5	48°21′	89°38′
Hart	UNP/LNO	SK	5-3-27-W2	72 H/4	49°11′	105°36′
Hart Butte No. 11	MUN2/AZM2	SK		72 H/3	49°10′	105°32′
Harte	UNP/LNO	MB	4-12-15-W	62 G/14	49°59′	99°28′
Hartell	UNP/LNO	AB	17-19-2-W5	82 J/9	50°36′	114°14′
Harten Corner	UNP/LNO	NB	Carleton	21 J/3	46°09′	67°25′
Hartfell	UNP/LNO	ON	Parry Sound	31 E/11	45°44′	79°20′
Hartfield	UNP/LNO	NB	York	21 J/3	46°01′	67°19′
Hartford	UNP/LNO	NS	Cumberland	11 E/13	45°45′	63°38′
Hartford	UNP/LNO	NB	Carleton	21 J/4	46°11′	67°39′

NAME NOM	ENTITY ENTITÉ	LOC 1 LIEU 1	LOC 2 LIEU 2	MAP CARTE	POSITION	
					LAT	LONG
Hartford	UNP/LNO	ON	Haldimand	40 P/1	43°00'	80°10'
Hart Highlands	UNP/LNO	BC	Cariboo	93 G/15	53°59'	122°48'
Hartington	UNP/LNO	ON	Frontenac	31 C/7	44°26'	76°40'
Hartin Settlement	UNP/LNO	NB	York	21 G/13	45°54'	67°32'
Hart-Jaune, Barrage	MISC/DIV	QC	Caniapiscau	22 O/13	51°49'	67°48'
Hart Jaune, Rivière	RIV/CDE	QC	Caniapiscau	22 N/9	51°31'	68°20'
Hartland	TOWN/VIL2	NB	Carleton	21 J/5	46°18'	67°32'
Hartlen Point	CAPE/CAP	NS	Halifax	11 D/11	44°35'	63°27'
Hartley	UNP/LNO	ON	Victoria	31 D/7	44°26'	78°54'
Hartley Bay	UNP/LNO	ON	Sudbury	41 I/2	46°02'	80°45'
Hartley Bay	UNP/LNO	BC	Range 4 Coast	103 H/6	53°25'	129°15'
Hartley Settlement	UNP/LNO	NB	Carleton	21 J/5	46°27'	67°45'
Hartleyville	UNP/LNO	AB	5-5-27-W4	82 H/5	49°22'	113°37'
Hartlin Settlement	UNP/LNO	NS	Halifax	11 D/14	44°46'	63°00'
Hart, Mount	MTN/MNT	YT		115 N/16	63°55'	140°25'
Hartney	TOWN/VIL2	MB	16-6-23-W	62 F/7	49°29'	100°31'
Hartney Junction	UNP/LNO	MB	6-6-15-W	62 G/6	49°27'	99°30'
Hart Ranges	MTN/MNT	BC	Cariboo	93 O/1	55°00'	122°00'
Hart River	RIV/CDE	YT		116 H/16	65°51'	136°23'
Hartshorn	UNP/LNO	AB	22-34-17-W4	82 P/16	51°56'	112°20'
Hartsmere	UNP/LNO	ON	Hastings	31 F/4	45°06'	77°32'
Hartsville	UNP/LNO	PE	Queens	11 L/6	46°19'	63°24'
Hartville	UNP/LNO	NS	Hants	21 A/16	44°57'	64°02'
Hartwell	UNP/LNO	SK	33-51-20-W3	73 P/7	53°27'	108°54'
Harty	UNP/LNO	ON	Cochrane	42 G/7	49°29'	82°41'
Hartz Mountains	MTN/MNT	NT	Franklin	48 D	73°30'	83°00'
Harvey	VILG/VILG	NB	York	21 G/11	45°44'	67°00'
Harvey	MUN2/AZM2	ON	Peterborough	31 D/9	44°36'	78°24'
Harvey	UNP/LNO	NB	Albert	21 H/10	45°43'	64°43'
Harvey	UNP/LNO	ON	Thunder Bay	52 J/1	50°14'	90°25'
Harvey	UNP/LNO	BC	Cariboo	83 D/14	52°57'	119°27'
Harvey	GEOG/GÉOG	NB	Albert	21 H/10	45°40'	64°48'
Harvey Bank	UNP/LNO	NB	Albert	21 H/10	45°44'	64°42'
Harvie Heights	UNP/LNO	AB	7,18-25-10-W5	82 O/3	51°07'	115°23'
Harwich	MUN2/AZM2	ON	Kent	40 I/5	42°22'	82°00'
Harwill	UNP/LNO	MB	33-26-2-W	62 P/5	51°18'	97°41'
Harwood	UNP/LNO	ON	Northumberland	31 D/1	44°08'	78°11'
Harwood Island	ISL/ÎLE	BC	New Westminster	92 F/15	49°52'	124°39'
Harwood Island 2	IR/RI	BC	New Westminster	92 F/15	49°52'	124°39'
Harwood Plains	UNP/LNO	ON	Carleton	31 G/5	45°23'	75°58'
Hasbala Lake	LAKE/LAC	MB/SK		64 M/16	59°57'	102°01'
Haseltine Mill	UNP/LNO	QC	Coaticook	21 E/5	45°18'	71°42'
Haseville	UNP/LNO	QC	Brome-Missisquoi	31 H/1	45°14'	72°56'
Haskett	UNP/LNO	MB	8-1-4-W	62 H/4	49°01'	97°58'
Haslam Creek	RIV/CDE	BC	New Westminster	92 F/9	49°36'	124°01'
Haslam Lake	LAKE/LAC	BC	New Westminster	92 F/16	49°55'	124°25'
Hasler Flat	UNP/LNO	BC	Peace River	93 P/12	55°36'	121°58'
Hassan	UNP/LNO	SK	3-34-4-W2	62 M/16	51°53'	102°29'
Hasse Lake Provincial Park	PARK/PARC	AB	14-52-2-W5	83 G/8	53°30'	114°11'
Hassel Sound	CHAN/CHEN	NT	Franklin	69 E	78°18'	98°46'
Hassett	UNP/LNO	NS	Digby	21 A/5	44°21'	65°56'
Hasté, Lac	LAKE/LAC	QC	Caniapiscau	23 F/1	53°07'	68°27'
Hastings	VILG/VILG	ON	Peterborough	31 C/5	44°18'	77°57'
Hastings	MUN1/AZM1	ON	Hastings	31 C/12	44°45'	77°40'
Hastings	UNP/LNO	NS	Cumberland	21 H/16	45°50'	64°07'
Hastings	UNP/LNO	NS	Annapolis	21 A/10	44°39'	64°52'
Hastings	GEOG/GÉOG	ON		31 C/12	44°45'	77°40'
Hastings Arm	BAY/BAIE	BC	Cassiar	103 P/5	55°30'	129°47'
Hastings Lake	LAKE/LAC	AB	51-20-W4	83 H/7	53°25'	112°55'
Hastings-Sunrise	UNP/LNO	BC	New Westminster	92 G/6	49°17'	123°02'
Haswell Point	CAPE/CAP	NT	Franklin	98 B	72°41'	125°07'
Hat, Cape	CAPE/CAP	NF		2 L/4	50°02'	55°56'
Hatchet Cove	UNP/LNO	NF		2 C/4	48°02'	53°48'
Hatchet Harbour	UNP/LNO	NF		2 E/10	49°38'	54°40'
Hatchet Lake	UNP/LNO	NS	Halifax	11 D/12	44°34'	63°43'
Hatchet Lake	LAKE/LAC	SK		64 L/12	58°38'	103°40'
Hatchley	UNP/LNO	ON	Brant	40 P/2	43°02'	80°32'
Hatch Point 12	IR/RI	BC	Shawnigan	92 B/12	48°41'	123°32'
Hat Creek	RIV/CDE	BC	Kamloops Division Yale	92 I/14	50°53'	121°24'
Hatfield	UNP/LNO	SK	27-28-22-W2	72 P/6	51°26'	105°01'
Hatfield Point	UNP/LNO	NB	Kings	21 H/12	45°39'	65°52'
Hathaway	UNP/LNO	MB	32-4-22-W	62 F/8	49°20'	100°25'
Hathaway Creek	RIV/CDE	BC	Rupert	92 L/12	50°35'	127°46'
Hathaway Lake	LAKE/LAC	BC	Lillooet	92 P/10	51°40'	120°50'
Hatherleigh	UNP/LNO	SK	36-46-15-W3	73 F/1	53°01'	108°02'

NAME NOM	ENTITY ENTITÉ	LOC 1 LIEU 1	LOC 2 LIEU 2	MAP CARTE	POSITION LAT	LONG
Hatherton	UNP/LNO	ON	Grey	41 A/8	44°16′	80°22′
Hat Island	ISL/ÎLE	NT	Franklin	67 B	68°19′	100°07′
Hatley	VILG/VILG	QC	Memphrémagog	21 E/4	45°11′	71°56′
Hatley	VILG/VILG	QC	Memphrémagog	21 E/5	45°16′	71°57′
Hatley Centre	UNP/LNO	QC	Memphrémagog	21 E/4	45°14′	71°57′
Hatton	UNP/LNO	SK	36-12-29-W3	72 K/4	50°03′	109°50′
Hattonford	UNP/LNO	AB	27-55-12-W5	83 G/13	53°46′	115°42′
Hatton Headland	CAPE/CAP	NT	Franklin	25 H/7	61°19′	64°47′
Hatzic	UNP/LNO	BC	New Westminster	92 G/1	49°09′	122°15′
Haughton, Cape	CAPE/CAP	NT	Franklin	67 H	71°48′	99°46′
Haughton Dome	MTN/MNT	NT	Franklin	58 H	75°24′	89°28′
Haultain	UNP/LNO	ON	Peterborough	31 D/9	44°37′	78°08′
Haultain	UNP/LNO	SK	34-4-W3	72 O/15	51°58′	106°34′
Haultain	UNP/LNO	SK		73 B/2	52°07′	106°39′
Haultain Lake	LAKE/LAC	SK		74 B/16	56°50′	106°22′
Haultain River	RIV/CDE	SK	79-5-W3	73 O/15	55°51′	106°46′
Haut-Bertrand	UNP/LNO	NB	Gloucester	21 P/11	47°43′	65°07′
Haut-Caraquet	UNP/LNO	NB	Gloucester	21 P/14	47°46′	65°03′
Haut-de-Champlain, Le	UNP/LNO	QC	Francheville	31 I/8	46°26′	72°22′
Haut-de-la-Chute, Le	UNP/LNO	QC	Vaudreuil-Soulanges	31 G/8	45°29′	74°23′
Haut-de-la-Côte	UNP/LNO	QC	Lajemmerais	31 H/14	45°46′	73°23′
Haute	UNP/LNO	MB	32-7-16-E	52 E/11	49°37′	95°22′
Haute-Aboujagane	UNP/LNO	NB	Westmorland	21 I/1	46°09′	64°24′
Haute, Isle	ISL/ÎLE	NS	Cumberland	21 H/7	45°15′	65°00′
Hautes-Terres-du-Cap-Breton, Parc national des - also-aussi - Cape Breton Highlands National Park	PARK/PARC	NS	Victoria	11 K/10	46°45′	60°39′
Hauteurs-de-Queenston, Lieu historique national des - also-aussi - Queenston Heights National Historic Site	PARK/PARC	QC	Lincoln	30 M/3	43°10′	79°03′
Hauteurs, Les	UNP/LNO	QC	La Rivière-du-Nord	31 G/16	45°52′	74°00′
Haute-Ville	UNP/LNO	QC	Communauté urbaine de Québec	21 L/14	46°49′	71°14′
Haut-Lamèque	UNP/LNO	NB	Gloucester	21 P/15	47°47′	64°37′
Haut-Paquetville	UNP/LNO	NB	Gloucester	21 P/11	47°40′	65°09′
Haut-Saint-Antoine	UNP/LNO	NB	Kent	21 I/7	46°22′	64°47′
Haut-Sainte-Rose	UNP/LNO	NB	Gloucester	21 P/10	47°37′	65°00′
Haut-Saint-Isidore	UNP/LNO	NB	Gloucester	21 P/11	47°33′	65°06′
Haut-Saint-Simon	UNP/LNO	NB	Gloucester	21 P/10	47°44′	64°50′
Haut-Shippegan	UNP/LNO	NB	Gloucester	21 P/10	47°45′	64°46′
Havelock	VILG/VILG	QC	Le Haut-Saint-Laurent	31 H/4	45°00′	73°45′
Havelock	VILG/VILG	ON	Peterborough	31 C/5	44°26′	77°53′
Havelock	UNP/LNO	NS	Digby	21 A/5	44°18′	65°55′
Havelock	UNP/LNO	NB	Kings	21 H/14	46°00′	65°19′
Havelock	UNP/LNO	QC	Le Haut-Saint-Laurent	31 H/4	45°03′	73°45′
Havelock	GEOG/GÉOG	NB	Kings	21 H/14	45°55′	65°24′
Haven, Cape	CAPE/CAP	NT	Franklin	25 I	62°54′	64°36′
Havendale	UNP/LNO	NS	Guysborough	11 F/5	45°27′	61°35′
Haven, Le	UNP/LNO	QC	Les Collines-de-l'Outaouais	31 F/9	45°38′	76°13′
Havenside	UNP/LNO	NS	Cape Breton	11 G/13	45°55′	59°57′
Havergal	UNP/LNO	ON	Hastings	31 F/4	45°14′	77°37′
Havik Lake	LAKE/LAC	ON	Kenora	52 K/4	50°07′	93°58′
Havilah	UNP/LNO	ON	Algoma	41 J/5	46°28′	83°43′
Haviland Bay	BAY/BAIE	NT	Franklin	46 K	66°32′	85°30′
Havilland	UNP/LNO	ON	Algoma	41 K/16	46°49′	84°24′
Havre-Aubert	UNP/LNO	QC	Les Îles-de-la-Madeleine	11 N/4	47°14′	61°51′
Havre Aubert, Île du	ISL/ÎLE	QC	Les Îles-de-la-Madeleine	11 N/4	47°14′	61°57′
Havre aux Basques, Baie du	LAKE/LAC	QC	Les Îles-de-la-Madeleine	11 N/5	47°17′	61°57′
Havre-aux-Maisons	VILG/VILG	QC	Les Îles-de-la-Madeleine	11 N/5	47°24′	61°49′
Havre aux Maisons, Île du	ISL/ÎLE	QC	Les Îles-de-la-Madeleine	11 N/5	47°25′	61°47′
Havre-Bayfield	UNP/LNO	QC	Côte-Nord-du-Golfe-Saint-Laurent	12 O/1	51°13′	58°23′
Havre Boucher	VILG/VILG	NS	Antigonish	11 F/12	45°41′	61°32′
Havre Boucher Station	UNP/LNO	NS	Antigonish	11 F/12	45°41′	61°32′
Havre, Île du	ISL/ÎLE	QC	Minganie	12 L/4	50°13′	63°37′
Havre-Saint-Pierre	VILG/VILG	QC	Minganie	12 L/4	50°14′	63°36′
Hawarden	VILG/VILG	SK	23-28-5-W3	72 O/7	51°25′	106°36′
Hawcos Pond	LAKE/LAC	NF		1 N/6	47°18′	53°18′
Hawes, Cape	CAPE/CAP	NT	Franklin	59 A/7	76°18′	89°17′
Hawkcliff Lake	LAKE/LAC	ON	Kenora	52 F/12	49°38′	93°31′
Hawke Bay	BAY/BAIE	NF		3 E/4	53°01′	56°00′
Hawke Harbour	UNP/LNO	NF		3 E/4	53°03′	55°49′
Hawke Island	ISL/ÎLE	NF		3 E/4	53°04′	55°50′
Hawker	UNP/LNO	NS	Richmond	11 F/10	45°38′	60°59′
Hawker	UNP/LNO	SK	36-6-W3	73 B/2	52°05′	106°49′
Hawke River	RIV/CDE	NF		13 H/1	53°02′	56°11′
Hawkes	UNP/LNO	ON	Leeds	31 B/12	44°41′	75°55′
Hawke Saddle	SEAU/SMER	—		814A	53°00′	53°10′
Hawke's Bay	TOWN/VIL2	NF		12 I/11	50°36′	57°10′
Hawkesbury	TOWN/VIL2	ON	Prescott	31 G/10	45°36′	74°37′
Hawkesbury Island	ISL/ÎLE	BC	Range 4 Coast	103 H/11	53°35′	129°04′

NAME NOM	ENTITY ENTITÉ	LOC 1 LIEU 1	LOC 2 LIEU 2	MAP CARTE	POSITION LAT	POSITION LONG
Hawkes Point	CAPE/CAP	NT	Franklin	68 C	73°05'	101°55'
Hawkestone	UNP/LNO	ON	Simcoe	31 D/6	44°30'	79°28'
Hawkestone Beach	UNP/LNO	ON	Simcoe	31 D/6	44°29'	79°28'
Hawkesville	UNP/LNO	ON	Waterloo	40 P/10	43°33'	80°38'
Hawkeye	UNP/LNO	SK	50-7-W3	73 G/7	53°18'	106°57'
Hawk Hill Lake	LAKE/LAC	NT	Keewatin	65 G	61°06'	98°40'
Hawk Hills	UNP/LNO	AB	13-95-22-W5	84 F/3	57°14'	117°28'
Hawkins Corner	UNP/LNO	NB	York	21 J/3	46°09'	67°13'
Hawkins Corners	UNP/LNO	ON	Simcoe	31 D/11	44°43'	79°22'
Hawkins Lake	LAKE/LAC	SK		74 P/9	59°44'	104°25'
Hawkins Lake	LAKE/LAC	BC	Lillooet	92 P/15	51°51'	120°55'
Hawk Junction	UNP/LNO	ON	Algoma	42 C/2	48°05'	84°34'
Hawk Lake	UNP/LNO	ON	Kenora	52 F/13	49°48'	93°59'
Hawk Lake	LAKE/LAC	ON	Kenora	52 F/13	49°47'	93°59'
Hawkrock River	RIV/CDE	SK		74 P/3	59°00'	105°02'
Hawks	UNP/LNO	BC	Cariboo	93 B/8	52°19'	122°16'
Hawks, Cape	CAPE/CAP	NT	Franklin	39 H	79°32'	73°06'
Hawks Creek	RIV/CDE	BC	Cariboo	93 B/8	52°18'	122°17'
Hawkshaw	UNP/LNO	NB	York	21 G/14	45°58'	67°14'
Hawley	UNP/LNO	ON	Lennox and Addington	31 C/2	44°11'	76°52'
Hawley's Corner	UNP/LNO	QC	Le Haut-Richelieu	31 H/3	45°05'	73°12'
Hawleys Hill	UNP/LNO	NS	Inverness	11 K/3	46°05'	61°22'
Hawoods	UNP/LNO	SK	36-8-W3	73 B/3	52°07'	107°06'
Haworth Lake	LAKE/LAC	BC	Cassiar	94 F/14	57°48'	125°06'
Hawthorne	UNP/LNO	NS	Inverness	11 F/14	45°58'	61°28'
Hawthorne	UNP/LNO	ON	Carleton	31 G/5	45°23'	75°36'
Hawthorne Cottage National Historic Site - also-aussi - Cottage-Hawthorne, Lieu historique national du	PARK/PARC	NF		1 N/11	47°33'	53°13'
Hawtrey	UNP/LNO	ON	Oxford	40 I/15	42°55'	80°31'
Hay	MUN2/AZM2	ON	Huron	40 P/5	43°24'	81°36'
Hay	UNP/LNO	ON	Huron	40 P/6	43°22'	81°29'
Hay Bay	UNP/LNO	ON	Lennox and Addington	31 C/3	44°09'	77°01'
Hay Bay	BAY/BAIE	ON	Lennox and Addington	31 C/2	44°10'	76°56'
Hayburn	UNP/LNO	ON	Lennox and Addington	31 C/2	44°09'	76°58'
Hay Camp	UNP/LNO	AB	15-121-9-W4	74 M/11	59°31'	111°28'
Hay, Cape	CAPE/CAP	NT	Franklin	38 C	73°44'	79°58'
Hay, Cape	CAPE/CAP	NT	Keewatin	56 M	67°55'	95°34'
Hay, Cape	CAPE/CAP	NT	Franklin	88 E	74°25'	113°04'
Hay Cove	UNP/LNO	NS	Richmond	11 F/10	45°44'	60°44'
Haycroft	UNP/LNO	ON	Essex	40 J/7	42°17'	82°33'
Hayden Ridge	UNP/LNO	NB	Carleton	21 J/11	46°32'	67°16'
Haydon	UNP/LNO	ON	Durham	31 D/2	44°01'	78°45'
Hayes Corners	UNP/LNO	ON	Leeds	31 B/12	44°36'	75°55'
Hayes Corners	UNP/LNO	ON	Parry Sound	31 E/5	45°17'	79°50'
Hayes Creek	RIV/CDE	ON	Cochrane	42 P/8	51°21'	80°29'
Hayes Creek	RIV/CDE	BC	Similkameen Division Yale	92 H/8	49°28'	120°22'
Hayes Fiord	BAY/BAIE	NT	Franklin	39 G	79°02'	76°45'
Hayesland	UNP/LNO	ON	Wentworth	40 P/8	43°19'	80°01'
Hayes Peak	MTN/MNT	YT		105 C/6	60°24'	133°18'
Hayes River	RIV/CDE	MB		54 F/1	57°03'	92°11'
Hayes River	RIV/CDE	NT	Keewatin	56 M	67°08'	95°17'
Hayesville	UNP/LNO	NB	York	21 J/10	46°31'	66°31'
Hayfield	UNP/LNO	MB	24-8-20-W	62 F/9	49°41'	100°04'
Hayfield	UNP/LNO	AB	27-71-11-W6	83 M/4	55°10'	119°36'
Hay Grounds 80B	IR/RI	SK		72 I/16	50°47'	104°10'
Hay Island	ISL/ÎLE	ON	Bruce	41 A/15	44°53'	80°58'
Hay Island	ISL/ÎLE	ON	Kenora	52 E/9	49°39'	94°24'
Hay Islands	ISL/ÎLE	NT	Franklin	68 C	73°40'	101°07'
Haylahte 3	IR/RI	BC	Rupert	92 L/8	50°28'	126°16'
Hay Lake	LAKE/LAC	ON	Nipissing	31 E/8	45°22'	78°11'
Hay Lake	LAKE/LAC	SK	11-25-W3	72 F/14	49°57'	109°22'
Hay Lake	LAKE/LAC	AB	113-5-W6	84 L/15	58°51'	118°50'
Hay Lake 209	IR/RI	AB	112-5-W5	84 L/15	58°45'	118°44'
Hay Lakes	VILG/VILG	AB	6-49-21-W4	83 H/3	53°12'	113°03'
Hay Lakes Telegraph Station Provincial Historic Site (Undeveloped)	PARK/PARC	AB	48-21-W4	83 H/3	53°11'	113°02'
Hayland	UNP/LNO	MB	13-23-10-W	62 J/15	50°59'	98°44'
Haylmore Creek	RIV/CDE	BC	Lillooet	92 J/9	50°32'	122°29'
Hayman Hill	UNP/LNO	NB	Charlotte	21 G/6	45°15'	67°20'
Hay Meadow 1	IR/RI	BC	Kamloops Division Yale	92 I/11	50°36'	121°23'
Hay, Mount	MTN/MNT	BC	Cassiar	114 P/3	59°14'	137°06'
Hayne	UNP/LNO	NB	York	21 J/3	46°06'	67°01'
Haynes	UNP/LNO	AB	4-39-24-W4	83 A/6	52°19'	113°24'
Haynes Lake	LAKE/LAC	NF		2 D/14	48°45'	55°28'
Hay Point	CAPE/CAP	NT	Franklin	88 B	72°24'	118°32'
Hay Ranch 2	IR/RI	BC	Cariboo	93 B/9	52°33'	122°22'
Hay River	TOWN/VIL2	NT	Mackenzie	85 B/13	60°49'	115°48'

NAME NOM	ENTITY ENTITÉ	LOC 1 LIEU 1	LOC 2 LIEU 2	MAP CARTE	POSITION	
					LAT	LONG
Hay River	RIV/CDE	NT/AB/BC		85 B/13	60°52′	115°44′
Hay River Dene 1	IR/RI	NT	Mackenzie	85 B/13	60°48′	115°44′
Hays	UNP/LNO	AB	24-13-4-W4	72 L/4	50°06′	111°48′
Haysport	UNP/LNO	BC	Range 5 Coast	103 J/1	54°10′	130°00′
Hays River	UNP/LNO	NS	Inverness	11 K/3	46°06′	61°15′
Hay's Shore	UNP/LNO	ON	Lanark	31 F/1	45°06′	76°10′
Haystack	UNP/LNO	NF		1 M/9	47°38′	54°05′
Haysville	UNP/LNO	ON	Waterloo	40 P/7	43°21′	80°39′
Hayter	UNP/LNO	AB	17-39-1-W4	73 D/8	52°22′	110°07′
Hayter Peninsula	CAPE/CAP	ON	Kenora	52 E/8	49°24′	94°13′
Hayward	UNP/LNO	BC	Somenos	92 B/13	48°48′	123°43′
Hayward Cove	UNP/LNO	NF		2 E/10	49°33′	54°53′
Haywards Cove	UNP/LNO	NF		2 C/13	48°52′	53°39′
Haywood	UNP/LNO	MB	22-8-6-W	62 G/9	49°40′	98°12′
Haywood Lake	LAKE/LAC	NT	Mackenzie	75 M/7	63°27′	110°30′
Haywood, Mont	MTN/MNT	QC	Kativik	24 I/9	58°36′	64°13′
Haywood, Mount	MTN/MNT	NT	Mackenzie	95 N/11	63°45′	125°03′
Hazel	UNP/LNO	MB	36-10-9-E	62 H/16	49°53′	96°15′
Hazelbrook	VILG/VILG	PE	Queens	11 L/3	46°13′	63°00′
Hazelbrook	UNP/LNO	PE	Queens	11 L/2	46°13′	62°59′
Hazel Cliffe	UNP/LNO	SK	27-18-33-W	62 K/12	50°34′	101°58′
Hazel Creek	RIV/CDE	MB	26-11-8-E	62 H/16	49°57′	96°24′
Hazeldale	UNP/LNO	NS	Victoria	11 K/2	46°01′	60°55′
Hazeldean	UNP/LNO	NB	Victoria	21 J/13	46°57′	67°32′
Hazeldean	UNP/LNO	ON	Carleton	31 G/5	45°18′	75°53′
Hazel Dell	HAM/HAM	SK	35-35-7-W2	62 M/15	51°59′	102°59′
Hazel Dell No. 335	MUN2/AZM2	SK		63 D/2	52°05′	103°00′
Hazeldine	UNP/LNO	AB	18-53-3-W4	73 E/9	53°35′	110°27′
Hazel Glen	UNP/LNO	NS	Pictou	11 E/10	45°32′	62°43′
Hazelglen	UNP/LNO	MB	19-12-7-E	62 I/2	50°01′	96°38′
Hazelgrove	UNP/LNO	PE	Queens	11 L/6	46°22′	63°24′
Hazel Hill	UNP/LNO	NS	Guysborough	11 F/6	45°20′	61°02′
Hazell	UNP/LNO	AB	7-8-5-W5	82 G/10	49°38′	114°40′
Hazelmere	UNP/LNO	AB	3-70-12-W6	83 M/4	55°02′	119°44′
Hazelmere	UNP/LNO	BC	New Westminster	92 G/2	49°02′	122°43′
Hazelridge	UNP/LNO	MB	33-11-6-E	62 H/15	49°58′	96°43′
Hazelton	VILG/VILG	BC	Cassiar	93 M/5	55°15′	127°40′
Hazelton	UNP/LNO	NB	Northumberland	21 J/9	46°34′	66°08′
Hazelton Mountains	MTN/MNT	BC	Range 5 Coast	103 I/9	54°35′	128°00′
Hazelwood	UNP/LNO	SK	19-11-4-W2	62 E/15	49°56′	102°32′
Hazelwood No. 94	MUN2/AZM2	SK		62 E/15	49°55′	102°40′
Hazen	UNP/LNO	NB	Restigouche	21 O/6	47°29′	67°26′
Hazen Camp	UNP/LNO	NT	Franklin	120 C	81°49′	71°20′
Hazen, Lake	LAKE/LAC	NT	Franklin	120 C	81°48′	71°01′
Hazenmore	VILG/VILG	SK	34-8-9-W3	72 G/11	49°42′	107°08′
Hazen Strait	CHAN/CHEN	NT	Franklin	79 B	77°00′	110°00′
Hazlet	VILG/VILG	SK	6-17-19-W3	72 K/7	50°24′	108°36′
Hazzards Corners	UNP/LNO	ON	Hastings	31 C/11	44°34′	77°28′
Head Brook	RIV/CDE	NF		14 D/2	56°09′	62°44′
Head, Clara and Maria	MUN2/AZM2	ON	Renfrew	31 L/1	46°11′	78°00′
Headford	UNP/LNO	ON	York	30 M/14	43°53′	79°23′
Head Harbour	UNP/LNO	NF		2 E/5	49°29′	55°41′
Headingley	MUN2/AZM2	MB		62 H/14	49°52′	97°23′
Headingley	UNP/LNO	MB		62 H/14	49°53′	97°25′
Headingley	GEOG/GÉOG	MB		62 H/14	49°52′	97°23′
Head Lake	UNP/LNO	ON	Victoria	31 D/10	44°43′	78°56′
Head Lake	LAKE/LAC	ON	Victoria	31 D/10	44°44′	78°55′
Head, Mount	MTN/MNT	AB	17-5-W5	82 J/7	50°26′	114°39′
Head of Bay D'Espoir	UNP/LNO	NF		1 M/13	47°56′	55°45′
Head of Cardigan	UNP/LNO	PE	Kings	11 L/7	46°15′	62°41′
Head of Chezzetcook	UNP/LNO	NS	Halifax	11 D/11	44°45′	63°15′
Head of Hillsborough	UNP/LNO	PE	Kings	11 L/7	46°22′	62°47′
Head of Jeddore	UNP/LNO	NS	Halifax	11 D/14	44°47′	63°04′
Head of Loch Lomond	UNP/LNO	NS	Richmond	11 F/10	45°44′	60°36′
Head of Millstream	UNP/LNO	NB	Kings	21 H/13	45°53′	65°32′
Head of Montague	UNP/LNO	PE	Kings	11 L/2	46°10′	62°44′
Head of St. Margarets Bay	UNP/LNO	NS	Halifax	11 D/12	44°41′	63°55′
Head of Wallace Bay	UNP/LNO	NS	Cumberland	11 E/13	45°49′	63°35′
Headquarters	UNP/LNO	BC	Comox	92 F/14	49°46′	125°07′
Head River	RIV/CDE	ON	Ontario	31 D/11	44°44′	79°15′
Head-Smashed-In Buffalo Jump Provincial Historic Site (Developed)	PARK/PARC	AB	9-27-W4	82 H/12	49°43′	113°39′
Head-Smashed-In Buffalo Jump Provincial Historic Site World Heritage Site - also-aussi - Head-Smashed-In Buffalo Jump (site historique provincial), Site du patrimoine mondial	PARK/PARC	AB		82 H/12	49°43′	113°39′

NAME NOM	ENTITY ENTITÉ	LOC 1 LIEU 1	LOC 2 LIEU 2	MAP CARTE	POSITION LAT	LONG
Head-Smashed-In Buffalo Jump (site historique provincial), Site du patrimoine mondial - also-aussi - Head-Smashed-In Buffalo Jump Provincial Historic Site World Heritage Site	PARK/PARC	AB		82 H/12	49°43′	113°39′
Headwall Creek	RIV/CDE	BC	Range 1 Coast	92 K/9	50°42′	124°13′
Headwind, Lac	LAKE/LAC	QC	Kativik	35 B/9	60°33′	74°26′
Heakamie Glacier	GLAC/GLAC	BC	Range 2 Coast	92 N/2	51°05′	124°42′
Healey Falls	UNP/LNO	ON	Northumberland	31 C/5	44°23′	77°46′
Healey Lake	LAKE/LAC	ON	Parry Sound	31 E/4	45°10′	79°55′
Healey Lake	LAKE/LAC	NT	Mackenzie	76 B	64°20′	106°45′
Healey's Heath	UNP/LNO	ON	Carleton	31 G/4	45°14′	75°55′
Health Bay	UNP/LNO	BC	Range 1 Coast	92 L/10	50°42′	126°36′
Heaman	UNP/LNO	MB		63 N/14	55°55′	101°17′
Hearne	UNP/LNO	SK	19-13-23-W2	72 I/3	50°06′	105°08′
Hearne Bay	BAY/BAIE	NT/MB		65 B/3	60°10′	99°18′
Hearne, Cape	CAPE/CAP	NT	Mackenzie	87 A	68°11′	114°44′
Hearne Lake	LAKE/LAC	NT	Mackenzie	85 I/6	62°19′	113°10′
Hearne Point	CAPE/CAP	NT	Franklin	78 F	74°43′	110°33′
Hearst	TOWN/VIL2	ON	Cochrane	42 G/12	49°41′	83°40′
Hearst Junction	UNP/LNO	ON	Cochrane	42 G/12	49°42′	83°42′
Heart Lake	UNP/LNO	AB	34-16-W4	82 P/16	51°55′	112°15′
Heart Lake	LAKE/LAC	MB	19,30-13-14-E	52 L/4	50°06′	95°40′
Heart Lake	LAKE/LAC	AB	70-10-W4	73 M/4	55°02′	111°30′
Heart Lake	LAKE/LAC	AB	1-34-17-W4	82 P/16	51°53′	112°16′
Heart Lake 167	IR/RI	AB	69,70-10,11-W4	73 M/4	55°00′	111°30′
Heart River	UNP/LNO	AB	13-76-17-W5	83 N/10	55°35′	116°30′
Heart River	RIV/CDE	AB	29-83-21-W5	84 C/3	56°14′	117°17′
Heart River Settlement	UNP/LNO	AB	76-15-W5	83 N/9	55°36′	116°13′
Heart's Content	TOWN/VIL2	NF		1 N/14	47°53′	53°22′
Heart's Delight	UNP/LNO	NF		1 N/14	47°46′	53°28′
Heart's Delight-Islington	TOWN/VIL2	NF		1 N/14	47°46′	53°29′
Heart's Desire	TOWN/VIL2	NF		1 N/14	47°49′	53°27′
Hearts Hill	UNP/LNO	SK	33-36-26-W3	73 C/4	52°09′	109°40′
Heart's Hill No. 352	MUN2/AZM2	SK		73 C/4	52°00′	109°45′
Hearts Point	CAPE/CAP	NF		1 N/7	47°25′	52°42′
Heaslip	UNP/LNO	ON	Timiskaming	31 M/13	47°48′	79°48′
Heaslip	UNP/LNO	MB	18-6-19-W	62 F/8	49°28′	100°01′
Heatburg	UNP/LNO	AB	3-39-23-W4	83 A/6	52°19′	113°14′
Heater Point	CAPE/CAP	BC	Rupert	92 L/5	50°17′	127°52′
Heath	UNP/LNO	AB	13-44-5-W4	73 D/15	52°48′	110°36′
Heathbell	UNP/LNO	NS	Pictou	11 E/10	45°41′	62°51′
Heathcote	UNP/LNO	ON	Grey	41 A/8	44°30′	80°29′
Heathcote Lake	LAKE/LAC	ON	Thunder Bay	52 J/8	50°17′	90°23′
Heather	UNP/LNO	ON	Algoma	41 J/3	46°12′	83°04′
Heather Beach	UNP/LNO	NS	Cumberland	11 E/13	45°53′	63°46′
Heatherdale	UNP/LNO	PE	Kings	11 L/2	46°07′	62°42′
Heatherton	UNP/LNO	NF		12 B/7	48°17′	58°45′
Heatherton	UNP/LNO	NS	Antigonish	11 F/12	45°35′	61°47′
Heathland	UNP/LNO	NB	Charlotte	21 G/3	45°14′	67°18′
Heath Point	UNP/LNO	QC	Minganie	12 F/4	49°05′	61°42′
Heath, Pointe	CAPE/CAP	QC	Minganie	12 F/4	49°05′	61°42′
Heath Steele	UNP/LNO	NB	Northumberland	21 O/8	47°17′	66°04′
Heathton	UNP/LNO	QC	Coaticook	21 E/4	45°03′	71°58′
Heaven Lake	LAKE/LAC	ON	Thunder Bay	52 H/5	49°17′	89°36′
Hebb Lake	LAKE/LAC	NS	Lunenburg	21 A/7	44°21′	64°34′
Hebbs Cross	UNP/LNO	NS	Lunenburg	21 A/7	44°18′	64°34′
Hebbville	VILG/VILG	NS	Lunenburg	21 A/7	44°21′	64°32′
Hébécourt, Lac	LAKE/LAC	QC	Abitibi-Ouest	32 D/11	48°30′	79°23′
Heber River	RIV/CDE	BC	Nootka	92 E/16	49°46′	126°03′
Hébert	UNP/LNO	NB	Kent	21 I/6	46°05′	65°05′
Hébert	UNP/LNO	QC	Le Fjord-du-Saguenay	22 D/7	48°16′	70°30′
Hébert, Lac	LAKE/LAC	QC	Jamésie	32 G/3	49°12′	75°18′
Hébert, Lac	LAKE/LAC	QC	Jamésie	32 E/15	49°53′	78°39′
Hébert, Lac	LAKE/LAC	QC	Rouyn-Noranda	32 D/4	48°02′	79°30′
Hébert, River	RIV/CDE	NS	Cumberland	21 H/16	45°45′	64°20′
Hébertville	VILG/VILG	QC	Lac-Saint-Jean-Est	22 D/5	48°24′	71°41′
Hébertville-Station	TOWN/VIL2	QC	Lac-Saint-Jean-Est	22 D/5	48°27′	71°40′
Hebron	UNP/LNO	NF		14 L/2	58°12′	62°38′
Hebron	UNP/LNO	PE	Prince	21 I/9	46°38′	64°16′
Hebron	UNP/LNO	NS	Yarmouth	20 O/16	43°53′	66°05′
Hebron	UNP/LNO	NB	Albert	21 H/10	45°38′	64°54′
Hebron Fiord	BAY/BAIE	NF		14 L/2	58°09′	62°45′
Hecate	UNP/LNO	BC	Nootka	92 E/15	49°51′	126°45′
Hecate 17	IR/RI	BC	Nootka	92 E/15	49°55′	126°47′
Hecate Channel	CHAN/CHEN	BC	Nootka	92 E/15	49°52′	126°45′
Hecate Island	ISL/ÎLE	BC	Range 2 Coast	102 P/9	51°42′	128°02′
Hecate Strait	CHAN/CHEN	BC	Queen Charlotte	103 G	53°30′	131°10′
Heckle Seamount	SEAU/SMER	—		15789A	48°28′	130°08′

NAME / NOM	ENTITY / ENTITÉ	LOC 1 / LIEU 1	LOC 2 / LIEU 2	MAP / CARTE	POSITION LAT	POSITION LONG
Heckle Seamount Chain	SEAU/SMER	—		15789A	48°20'	129°53'
Heckmans Island	UNP/LNO	NS	Lunenburg	21 A/8	44°23'	64°15'
Hecks Corners	UNP/LNO	QC	Le Haut-Richelieu	31 H/3	45°04'	73°12'
Heck Seamount	SEAU/SMER	—		3000	48°25'	129°28'
Heck Seamount Chain	SEAU/SMER	—		15789A	48°30'	129°30'
Heckston	UNP/LNO	ON	Grenville	31 B/13	44°58'	75°32'
Hecla	UNP/LNO	MB		62 P/2	51°08'	96°40'
Hecla and Fury Islands	ISL/ÎLE	NT	Franklin	57 E	70°05'	90°31'
Hecla and Griper Bank	SEAU/SMER	—		7217	71°15'	69°35'
Hecla and Griper Bay	BAY/BAIE	NT	Franklin	79 B	76°02'	111°30'
Hecla and Griper Trough	SEAU/SMER	—		7054	71°01'	70°15'
Hecla, Cape	CAPE/CAP	NT	Franklin	120 F	82°54'	64°52'
Hecla Island	ISL/ÎLE	MB		62 P/2	51°07'	96°43'
Hectanooga	UNP/LNO	NS	Digby	21 B/1	44°06'	66°02'
Hector	UNP/LNO	BC	Kootenay	82 N/8	51°26'	116°20'
Hector Island	ISL/ÎLE	NT	Franklin	35 P	63°39'	72°25'
Hector Lake	LAKE/LAC	ON	Kenora	42 M/12	51°45'	87°43'
Hector Lake	LAKE/LAC	ON	Kenora	52 F/6	49°19'	93°20'
Hector, Mount	MTN/MNT	AB	30-17-W5	82 N/9	51°35'	116°15'
Heddery Creek	RIV/CDE	SK		74 B/6	56°30'	107°30'
Heddery Lake	LAKE/LAC	SK		74 B/12	56°41'	107°44'
Hedgeville	UNP/LNO	NS	Pictou	11 E/15	45°45'	63°00'
Hedley	UNP/LNO	BC	Similkameen Division Yale	92 H/8	49°21'	120°04'
Hedley Creek	RIV/CDE	BC	Similkameen Division Yale	92 H/8	49°21'	120°05'
Heffley Creek	UNP/LNO	BC	Kamloops Division Yale	92 I/16	50°52'	120°16'
Heffley Lake	LAKE/LAC	BC	Kamloops Division Yale	92 I/16	50°50'	120°04'
Hefty Peak	MTN/MNT	BC	Cassiar	104 M/6	59°28'	135°05'
Heger, Mount	MTN/MNT	BC	Kamloops Division Yale	92 P/9	51°39'	120°29'
Heidelberg	UNP/LNO	ON	Waterloo	40 P/10	43°31'	80°37'
Heim Peninsula	CAPE/CAP	NT	Franklin	49 B	76°32'	84°30'
Heinsburg	UNP/LNO	AB	22-55-4-W4	73 E/15	53°46'	110°31'
Heisler	VILG/VILG	AB	2-43-16-W4	83 A/9	52°41'	112°13'
Hekkla	UNP/LNO	ON	Muskoka	31 E/5	45°17'	79°33'
Heldar	UNP/LNO	AB	22-58-7-W5	83 J/2	54°01'	114°57'
Helena Island	ISL/ÎLE	NT	Franklin	69 B	76°39'	101°04'
Helena Lake	UNP/LNO	SK	52-16-W3	73 F/8	53°30'	108°15'
Helena Lake	LAKE/LAC	BC	Lillooet	92 P/13	51°47'	121°38'
Helen Bay	BAY/BAIE	ON	Manitoulin	41 G/15	45°50'	82°38'
Helene Lake	LAKE/LAC	SK	52-15-W3	73 F/9	53°33'	108°12'
Helen Falls	FALL/CHUT	NT	Mackenzie	75 P	63°39'	104°43'
Helen Haven	BAY/BAIE	NT	Franklin	58 G	75°19'	93°45'
Helen Island	ISL/ÎLE	NT	Franklin	57 A	68°45'	89°55'
Helen Junction	UNP/LNO	ON	Algoma	42 C/2	48°02'	84°46'
Helen Lake	LAKE/LAC	ON	Thunder Bay	52 H/1	49°05'	88°15'
Helen Mine	UNP/LNO	ON	Algoma	42 C/2	48°02'	84°44'
Helika Lake	LAKE/LAC	NT	Keewatin	55 L	62°25'	94°02'
Helina	UNP/LNO	AB	32-63-10-W4	73 L/6	54°29'	111°29'
Helldiver Lake	LAKE/LAC	SK	53-31-W	63 F/12	53°35'	101°55'
Heller Creek	RIV/CDE	BC	Kamloops Division Yale	92 P/2	51°01'	120°47'
Hell Gate	CHAN/CHEN	NT	Franklin	59 A/10	76°42'	89°44'
Hells Gate	UNP/LNO	BC	Yale Division Yale	92 H/14	49°47'	121°27'
Helmcken Falls	FALL/CHUT	BC	Kamloops Division Yale	92 P/16	51°57'	120°11'
Helmcken Island	ISL/ÎLE	BC	Range 1 Coast	92 K/5	50°24'	125°52'
Helmcken Land District	GEOG/GÉOG	BC		92 B	48°41'	123°47'
Helmer Lake	LAKE/LAC	SK		74 O/4	59°13'	107°33'
Helmsdale	UNP/LNO	AB	36-25-6-W4	72 M/2	51°11'	110°42'
Helmsdale	UNP/LNO	AB	2-28-1-W5	82 O/8	51°22'	114°02'
Helston	UNP/LNO	MB	25-13-13-W	62 J/3	50°08'	99°07'
Hemaruka	UNP/LNO	AB	33-32-8-W4	72 M/14	51°47'	111°06'
Hematite	UNP/LNO	ON	Rainy River	52 B/14	48°45'	91°23'
Hemford	UNP/LNO	NS	Lunenburg	21 A/10	44°30'	64°47'
Heming Lake	UNP/LNO	MB	12-68-25-W	63 K/14	54°53'	101°08'
Hemison	UNP/LNO	QC	Bellechasse	21 L/10	46°31'	70°44'
Hemlo	UNP/LNO	ON	Thunder Bay	42 C/12	48°41'	85°59'
Hemlock	UNP/LNO	ON	Norfolk	40 I/10	42°37'	80°42'
Hemlock Corners	UNP/LNO	ON	Grenville	31 B/13	44°50'	75°49'
Hemlock Creek	RIV/CDE	NS	Shelburne	20 P/14	43°53'	65°30'
Hemlock Downs	UNP/LNO	ON	Frontenac	31 C/8	44°18'	76°28'
Hemlock Valley	UNP/LNO	BC	New Westminster	92 H/5	49°23'	121°55'
Hemloe Island	ISL/ÎLE	NS	Guysborough	11 F/4	45°01'	61°59'
Hemmingford	TOWN/VIL2	QC	Les Jardins-de-Napierville	31 H/4	45°03'	73°35'
Hemmingford	VILG/VILG	QC	Les Jardins-de-Napierville	31 H/4	45°05'	73°35'
Hemming Lake	LAKE/LAC	BC	Range 1 Coast	92 K/6	50°24'	125°25'
Hemmings Falls	UNP/LNO	QC	Drummond	31 H/16	45°52'	72°27'
Hemphill, Cape	CAPE/CAP	NT	Franklin	89 A	76°56'	115°42'

NAME NOM	ENTITY ENTITÉ	LOC 1 LIEU 1	LOC 2 LIEU 2	MAP CARTE	POSITION LAT	LONG
Hemphill Corner	UNP/LNO	NB	Carleton	21 J/6	46°27′	67°22′
Hemstock Mills	UNP/LNO	ON	Grey	41 A/7	44°26′	80°55′
Hénault, Lac	LAKE/LAC	QC	Témiscamingue	31 N/5	47°21′	77°49′
Henday	UNP/LNO	AB	25,36-34-1-W5	82 O/16	51°57′	114°01′
Henday Lake	LAKE/LAC	SK		74 I/8	58°19′	104°13′
Henderson	UNP/LNO	ON	Frontenac	31 C/15	44°47′	76°59′
Henderson Inlet	BAY/BAIE	NT	Franklin	25 J	62°14′	66°10′
Henderson Lake	LAKE/LAC	ON	Sudbury	41 O/14	47°55′	83°19′
Henderson Lake	LAKE/LAC	BC	Clayoquot	92 F/3	49°06′	125°03′
Henderson, Mount	MTN/MNT	BC	Range 5 Coast	103 I/8	54°17′	128°04′
Henderson Place	UNP/LNO	ON	Frontenac	31 C/2	44°14′	76°34′
Hendersons Beach	UNP/LNO	SK	29-25-24-W2	72 P/3	51°10′	105°19′
Henderson Settlement	UNP/LNO	NB	Queens	21 H/12	45°43′	65°56′
Henderson's Ranch 11	IR/RI	BC	Range 4 Coast	103 H/15	53°59′	128°39′
Hendon	HAM/HAM	SK	36-13-W2	63 D/4	52°05′	103°50′
Hendrickson Island	ISL/ÎLE	NT	Franklin	107 C/10	69°30′	133°35′
Hendrie	UNP/LNO	ON	Simcoe	31 D/5	44°29′	79°50′
Hendriksen Strait	CHAN/CHEN	NT	Franklin	69 D	77°50′	96°30′
Henfryn	UNP/LNO	ON	Huron	40 P/11	43°42′	81°05′
Heninga Lake	LAKE/LAC	NT	Keewatin	65 H	61°51′	96°20′
Henley	UNP/LNO	ON	Lincoln	30 M/3	43°11′	79°17′
Henley Harbour	UNP/LNO	NF		2 M/13	51°59′	55°51′
Hennepin	UNP/LNO	QC	Bellechasse	21 L/10	46°31′	70°35′
Hennigar Corner	UNP/LNO	NB	Victoria	21 O/4	47°03′	67°43′
Henribourg	UNP/LNO	SK	16-51-25-W2	73 H/5	53°24′	105°37′
Henri, Cap	CAPE/CAP	QC	Minganie	22 H/16	49°48′	64°23′
Henrietta Island	ISL/ÎLE	NF		13 J/1	54°05′	58°28′
Henrietta Maria, Cape	CAPE/CAP	ON	Kenora	43 O/1	55°09′	82°20′
Henrietta Nesmith Glacier	GLAC/GLAC	NT	Franklin	340 D	81°49′	72°57′
Henri, Mount	MTN/MNT	BC	Cassiar	94 C/10	56°31′	124°43′
Henri, Rivière	RIV/CDE	QC	Lotbinière	21 L/5	46°30′	71°47′
Henry, Cape	CAPE/CAP	BC	Queen Charlotte	103 C/16	52°56′	132°22′
Henry Farm	UNP/LNO	ON	York	30 M/14	43°46′	79°21′
Henry House	UNP/LNO	AB	27-46-1-W6	83 D/16	52°59′	118°04′
Henry Island	ISL/ÎLE	NS	Inverness	11 F/13	45°58′	61°36′
Henry Island	ISL/ÎLE	BC	Range 5 Coast	103 J/2	54°01′	130°40′
Henry Kater, Cape	CAPE/CAP	NT	Franklin	27 D	69°08′	66°46′
Henry Kater Peninsula	CAPE/CAP	NT	Franklin	27 C	69°23′	68°04′
Henrysburg	UNP/LNO	QC	Les Jardins-de-Napierville	31 H/3	45°05′	73°27′
Henrys Corner	UNP/LNO	ON	Prescott	31 G/10	45°34′	74°41′
Henryville	TOWN/VIL2	QC.	Le Haut-Richelieu	31 H/3	45°08′	73°11′
Henryville	VILG/VILG	QC	Le Haut-Richelieu	31 H/3	45°08′	73°13′
Hensall	VILG/VILG	ON	Huron	40 P/6	43°26′	81°30′
Henson Bay	BAY/BAIE	NT	Franklin	560 D	81°52′	89°25′
Hentig, Mount	MTN/MNT	BC	Peace River	94 K/8	58°18′	124°23′
Henvey Inlet	BAY/BAIE	ON	Parry Sound	41 H/15	45°51′	80°38′
Henvey Inlet 2	IR/RI	ON	Parry Sound	41 H/15	45°50′	80°40′
Héon	UNP/LNO	QC	Arthabaska	21 E/13	45°59′	71°44′
Hepburn	VILG/VILG	SK	13-41-6-W3	73 B/10	52°31′	106°44′
Hepburn Island	ISL/ÎLE	NT	Mackenzie	76 M	67°54′	110°56′
Hepburn Lake	LAKE/LAC	MB		53 L/10	54°43′	94°37′
Hepburn Lake	LAKE/LAC	SK		73 P/15	55°54′	104°58′
Hepburn Lake	LAKE/LAC	NT	Mackenzie	86 J	66°19′	115°16′
Hepburn River	RIV/CDE	NT	Mackenzie	86 G	65°50′	114°25′
Heppell	UNP/LNO	QC	La Matapédia	22 B/6	48°19′	67°14′
Hepworth	VILG/VILG	ON	Bruce	41 A/11	44°37′	81°09′
Herbert	TOWN/VIL2	SK	17-9-W3	72 J/6	50°26′	107°13′
Herbert Corners	UNP/LNO	ON	Carleton	31 G/4	45°13′	75°34′
Herbert Inlet	BAY/BAIE	BC	Clayoquot	92 F/5	49°21′	125°58′
Herbert Lake	LAKE/LAC	SK		74 F/9	59°37′	104°19′
Herbert Point	CAPE/CAP	BC	Range 2 Coast	102 P/8	51°29′	128°05′
Herbert River	RIV/CDE	NS	Hants	21 H/1	45°00′	64°02′
Herb Lake	UNP/LNO	MB	67-16-W	63 J/13	54°47′	99°47′
Herb Lake Landing	UNP/LNO	MB	65-16-W1	63 J/12	54°39′	99°47′
Herblet Lake	LAKE/LAC	MB		63 J/13	54°56′	99°54′
Herchmer	UNP/LNO	MB		54 E/8	57°22′	94°10′
Herdman	UNP/LNO	QC	Le Haut-Saint-Laurent	31 G/1	45°02′	74°06′
Hereford	UNP/LNO	QC	Coaticook	21 E/4	45°01′	71°34′
Hereford Hill	UNP/LNO	QC	Coaticook	21 E/4	45°03′	71°33′
Hereford, Mont	MTN/MNT	QC	Coaticook	21 E/4	45°05′	71°36′
Hereward	UNP/LNO	ON	Dufferin	40 P/16	43°50′	80°19′
Héricart, Baie	BAY/BAIE	NT	Franklin	25 E	61°03′	70°25′
Heriot Bay	UNP/LNO	BC	Sayward	92 K/3	50°06′	125°13′
Heritage Lake	LAKE/LAC	SK	57-22-W2	73 H/14	53°56′	105°09′
Heritage Park	UNP/LNO	ON	York	30 M/13	43°56′	79°32′

NAME NOM	ENTITY ENTITÉ	LOC 1 LIEU 1	LOC 2 LIEU 2	MAP CARTE	POSITION LAT	LONG
Heritage Park	UNP/LNO	ON	Waterloo	40 P/8	43°27′	80°27′
Heritage Park	UNP/LNO	MB		62 H/14	49°53′	97°17′
Herman Lake	LAKE/LAC	SK	62,63-13-W2	63 L/5	54°25′	103°53′
Hermann River	RIV/CDE	NT	Keewatin	56 L	66°14′	96°07′
Hermans Island	UNP/LNO	NS	Lunenburg	21 A/8	44°25′	64°20′
Hermanville	UNP/LNO	PE	Kings	11 L/8	46°28′	62°17′
Hermitage	UNP/LNO	NF		1 M/12	47°33′	55°56′
Hermitage	UNP/LNO	PE	Queens	11 L/2	46°13′	62°50′
Hermitage Bay	BAY/BAIE	NF		1 M/12	47°35′	56°06′
Hermitage Channel	SEAU/SMER	—		15076A	47°00′	57°30′
Hermitage, Chenal d'	SEAU/SMER	—		802	47°00′	57°30′
Hermitage-Sandyville	VILG/VILG	NF		1 M/12	47°32′	55°56′
Hermit Lake	UNP/LNO	AB	32-71-7-W6	83 M/3	55°12′	119°02′
Hermon	UNP/LNO	ON	Hastings	31 F/4	45°07′	77°38′
Hernando Island	ISL/ÎLE	BC	Sayward	92 F/15	49°59′	124°55′
Hérodier, Lac	LAKE/LAC	QC	Kativik	24 F/7	57°21′	68°43′
Heron Bay	UNP/LNO	ON	Thunder Bay	42 D/9	48°40′	86°17′
Heron Bay	BAY/BAIE	ON	Thunder Bay	42 D/9	48°39′	86°19′
Heron Channel	CHAN/CHEN	NB	Restigouche	21 O/16	48°00′	66°15′
Heron Island	UNP/LNO	NB	Restigouche	21 O/16	47°59′	66°09′
Heron Island	ISL/ÎLE	NB	Restigouche	21 O/16	48°00′	66°09′
Heron Lake	LAKE/LAC	ON	Rainy River	52 C/15	48°56′	92°40′
Héron, Pointe au	CAPE/CAP	QC	Jamésie	33 E/2	53°01′	78°59′
Hérons, Île aux	ISL/ÎLE	QC	Communauté urbaine de Montréal	31 H/5	45°25′	73°35′
Hérouxville	VILG/VILG	QC	Mékinac	31 I/10	46°40′	72°37′
Herrick Creek	RIV/CDE	BC	Cariboo	93 I/6	54°12′	121°29′
Herrick Lake	LAKE/LAC	ON	Thunder Bay	42 C/12	48°35′	85°55′
Herrick Low Lake	LAKE/LAC	SK	32,33-24-W3	72 N/14	51°48′	109°20′
Herring Cove	UNP/LNO	NS	Halifax	11 D/12	44°34′	63°34′
Herring Cove	BAY/BAIE	NB	Charlotte	21 B/10	44°44′	66°51′
Herring Cove Lake	LAKE/LAC	NS	Queens	21 A/2	44°08′	64°43′
Herring Head	CAPE/CAP	NF		2 E/10	49°40′	54°32′
Herring Neck	UNP/LNO	NF		2 E/10	49°38′	54°37′
Herring Neck	UNP/LNO	NF		2 E/10	49°38′	54°37′
Herringville	UNP/LNO	QC	Le Haut-Saint-François	21 E/6	45°28′	71°25′
Herriot	UNP/LNO	MB	13-85-25-W	64 C/6	56°22′	101°16′
Herriot Creek	RIV/CDE	MB		54 L/9	58°33′	94°18′
Herrons Corners	UNP/LNO	ON	Grenville	31 B/12	44°44′	75°43′
Herrons Mills	UNP/LNO	ON	Lanark	31 F/1	45°03′	76°24′
Herronton	UNP/LNO	AB	20-19-25-W4	82 I/11	50°38′	113°25′
Herschel	VILG/VILG	SK	9-31-17-W3	72 N/9	51°38′	108°21′
Herschel	MUN2/AZM2	ON	Hastings	31 E/1	45°09′	78°00′
Herschel	UNP/LNO	YT		117 D/11	69°34′	138°54′
Herschel, Cape	CAPE/CAP	NT	Franklin	39 E	78°35′	74°35′
Herschel Island	ISL/ÎLE	YT		117 D/12	69°35′	139°05′
Hersey Corner	UNP/LNO	NB	Queens	21 G/16	45°50′	66°17′
Hersonville	UNP/LNO	NB	Charlotte	21 G/2	45°01′	66°58′
Hervé, Lac	LAKE/LAC	QC	Jamésie	23 L/6	54°27′	71°14′
Hervey-Jonction	UNP/LNO	QC	Mékinac	31 I/16	46°51′	72°28′
Herzel	UNP/LNO	SK	30-23-12-W2	62 M/4	51°01′	103°41′
Hesketh	UNP/LNO	AB	12-29-22-W4	82 P/7	51°28′	112°58′
Hespeler	UNP/LNO	ON	Waterloo	40 P/8	43°26′	80°19′
Hespero	UNP/LNO	AB	1-39-4-W5	83 B/8	52°20′	114°27′
Hesquiat	UNP/LNO	BC	Clayoquot	92 E/8	49°24′	126°28′
Hesquiat 1	IR/RI	BC	Clayoquot	92 E/8	49°24′	126°28′
Hesquiat Harbour	BAY/BAIE	BC	Clayoquot	92 E/8	49°26′	126°27′
Hesquiat Lake	LAKE/LAC	BC	Clayoquot	92 E/8	49°30′	126°24′
Hesquiat Peninsula	CAPE/CAP	BC	Clayoquot	92 E/7	49°24′	126°30′
Hesquis 10A	IR/RI	BC	Nootka	92 E/15	49°53′	126°52′
Hess Mountains	MTN/MNT	YT		105 O/5	63°30′	131°30′
Hesson	UNP/LNO	ON	Perth	40 P/10	43°38′	80°48′
Hess River	RIV/CDE	YT		105 N/12	63°33′	133°59′
Héva	UNP/LNO	QC	Vallée-de-l'Or	32 D/1	48°11′	78°14′
Heward	VILG/VILG	SK	15-9-9-W2	62 E/11	49°44′	103°09′
Hewett, Cape	CAPE/CAP	NT	Franklin	27 E	70°15′	67°47′
Hewett Lake	LAKE/LAC	SK	57-26-W3	73 F/13	53°56′	109°46′
Hewitt	UNP/LNO	NB	Charlotte	21 G/6	45°18′	67°06′
Hewitt Landing	UNP/LNO	SK	34-52-27-W3	73 F/12	53°33′	109°53′
Heyden	UNP/LNO	ON	Algoma	41 K/9	46°39′	84°18′
Heydon Bay	UNP/LNO	BC	Range 1 Coast	92 K/12	50°35′	125°35′
Heydon Lake	LAKE/LAC	BC	Range 1 Coast	92 K/12	50°32′	125°40′
Heytesbury, Cape	CAPE/CAP	NT	Franklin	57 G	71°37′	93°41′
Heywood Island	ISL/ÎLE	ON	Manitoulin	41 H/13	45°56′	81°46′
Heyworth	UNP/LNO	QC	Les Collines-de-l'Outaouais	31 G/12	45°30′	75°58′
Hiam	UNP/LNO	ON	Renfrew	31 F/14	45°48′	77°12′

NAME NOM	ENTITY ENTITÉ	LOC 1 LIEU 1	LOC 2 LIEU 2	MAP CARTE	POSITION LAT	LONG
Hiawatha	UNP/LNO	ON	Peterborough	31 D/1	44°11′	78°13′
Hiawatha First Nation 36	IR/RI	ON	Peterborough	31 D/1	44°11′	78°13′
Hiawatha Park	UNP/LNO	ON	Carleton	31 G/5	45°28′	75°33′
Hibbard	UNP/LNO	QC	Le Haut-Saint-Maurice	31 O/16	47°52′	74°02′
Hibben Island	ISL/ÎLE	BC	Queen Charlotte	103 C/16	52°59′	132°17′
Hibbert	MUN2/AZM2	ON	Perth	40 P/6	43°28′	81°20′
Hibbs Cove	UNP/LNO	NF		1 N/11	47°36′	53°11′
Hibernia	UNP/LNO	NS	Queens	21 A/7	44°20′	64°59′
Hickethier Ranch	UNP/LNO	BC	Peace River	94 B/9	56°31′	122°13′
Hickey	UNP/LNO	MB	9-1-15-E	52 E/4	49°02′	95°31′
Hickey Settlement	UNP/LNO	NB	Restigouche	21 O/16	47°55′	66°06′
Hickey Settlement	UNP/LNO	ON	Hastings	31 F/4	45°10′	77°54′
Hickman, Mount	MTN/MNT	BC	Cassiar	104 G/6	57°16′	131°06′
Hickman's Harbour	UNP/LNO	NF		2 C/4	48°06′	53°44′
Hickory Beach	UNP/LNO	ON	Victoria	31 D/7	44°29′	78°41′
Hickory Beach	UNP/LNO	ON	Haldimand	40 I/16	42°48′	80°04′
Hickory Corner	UNP/LNO	ON	Middlesex	40 P/4	43°00′	81°33′
Hickory Creek	RIV/CDE	ON	Lambton	40 O/1	43°07′	82°05′
Hicks	UNP/LNO	BC	Yale Division Yale	92 H/14	49°50′	121°26′
Hicks Lake	LAKE/LAC	NT	Keewatin	65 F	61°25′	100°00′
Hickson	UNP/LNO	ON	Oxford	40 P/2	43°14′	80°48′
Hickson Lake	LAKE/LAC	SK		74 A/8	56°19′	104°22′
Hicksville	UNP/LNO	NB	Westmorland	21 I/3	46°01′	65°18′
Hidden Bay	BAY/BAIE	SK		64 L/4	58°06′	103°44′
Hidden Lake	LAKE/LAC	BC	Kamloops Division Yale	82 L/10	50°34′	118°49′
Hidden Lake	LAKE/LAC	NT	Mackenzie	85 I/12	62°33′	113°33′
Hidden Valley	UNP/LNO	ON	Muskoka	31 E/6	45°21′	79°07′
Hiellen 2	IR/RI	BC	Queen Charlotte	103 J/4	54°04′	131°47′
Higgins, Mount	MTN/MNT	YT		116 I/2	66°09′	136°33′
Higgins Road	UNP/LNO	PE	Prince	21 I/9	46°31′	64°05′
Higginsville	UNP/LNO	NS	Halifax	11 E/3	45°02′	63°04′
High Bank	UNP/LNO	PE	Kings	11 E/15	45°58′	62°37′
Highbank	UNP/LNO	NB	Northumberland	21 P/4	47°05′	65°36′
Highbank Lake	LAKE/LAC	ON	Kenora	43 D/8	52°19′	86°11′
High Bar 1	IR/RI	BC	Lillooet	92 O/1	51°06′	122°00′
High Bar 1A	IR/RI	BC	Lillooet	92 O/1	51°06′	122°00′
High Bar 2	IR/RI	BC	Lillooet	92 P/4	51°05′	121°58′
High Beach	UNP/LNO	NF		1 L/13	46°53′	55°54′
High Bluff	UNP/LNO	MB	13-12-6-W	62 J/1	50°01′	98°09′
High Bluff	GEOG/GÉOG	MB		62 G/16	49°58′	98°09′
Highbury	UNP/LNO	NS	Kings	21 H/1	45°03′	64°29′
High Capes	CAPE/CAP	NS	Inverness	11 K/15	46°59′	60°39′
Highfall, Ruisseau	RIV/CDE	QC	Kativik	24 K/1	58°01′	68°30′
High Falls	UNP/LNO	QC	Papineau	31 G/13	45°53′	75°38′
High Falls	UNP/LNO	ON	Frontenac	31 C/15	44°57′	76°37′
High Falls	UNP/LNO	ON	Sudbury	41 I/5	46°23′	81°34′
High Falls	FALL/CHUT	ON	Sudbury	41 I/11	46°36′	81°23′
Highfield	UNP/LNO	PE	Queens	11 L/6	46°17′	63°10′
Highfield - see-voir - Belmont	UNP/LNO	NS		21 H/1	45°03′	64°06′
Highfield	UNP/LNO	NB	Queens	21 H/13	45°50′	65°45′
Highfield	UNP/LNO	ON	York	30 M/12	43°43′	79°35′
Highfield Reservoir	LAKE/LAC	SK	15-10,11-W3	72 J/6	50°18′	107°23′
High Forest	UNP/LNO	QC	Le Haut-Saint-François	21 E/5	45°18′	71°36′
Highgate	VILG/VILG	ON	Kent	40 I/5	42°30′	81°49′
Highgate	UNP/LNO	SK	17-45-17-W3	73 C/16	52°52′	108°25′
High Gate Park	UNP/LNO	ON	Frontenac	31 C/2	44°15′	76°36′
High Head	UNP/LNO	NS	Lunenburg	21 A/8	44°22′	64°30′
High Hill	UNP/LNO	SK	20-38-10-W2	63 D/6	52°17′	103°23′
High Hill Lake	LAKE/LAC	MB		53 M/12	55°34′	95°41′
High Hill River	RIV/CDE	MB	22-79-18-E	53 M/15	55°51′	94°42′
High Lake	LAKE/LAC	ON/MB		52 E/11	49°42′	95°07′
Highland	UNP/LNO	ON	Timiskaming	31 M/12	47°36′	79°49′
Highland Acres	UNP/LNO	NS	Halifax	11 D/11	44°40′	63°29′
Highland Beach	UNP/LNO	ON	Ontario	31 D/2	44°07′	78°57′
Highland Creek	UNP/LNO	ON	York	30 M/14	43°47′	79°10′
Highland Glen	UNP/LNO	ON	Lambton	40 O/1	43°06′	82°07′
Highland Glen	UNP/LNO	MB	12-13-5-E	62 I/2	50°05′	96°47′
Highland Grove	UNP/LNO	ON	Haliburton	31 E/1	45°04′	78°05′
Highland Hill	UNP/LNO	NS	Victoria	11 F/15	45°58′	60°52′
Highland Lake	LAKE/LAC	NT	Mackenzie	95 J	62°49′	122°21′
Highland Land District	GEOG/GÉOG	BC		92 B	48°31′	123°30′
Highland Park	UNP/LNO	MB	62 G/13		49°53′	99°57′
Highland Park	UNP/LNO	SK		72 I/7	50°28′	104°37′
Highland Park	UNP/LNO	AB	16-82-6-W6	84 D/2	56°06′	118°52′
Highland Park Survey	UNP/LNO	ON	Wentworth	30 M/5	43°16′	79°58′

NAME NOM	ENTITY ENTITÉ	LOC 1 LIEU 1	LOC 2 LIEU 2	MAP CARTE	POSITION LAT	POSITION LONG
Highland Point	UNP/LNO	ON	Simcoe	31 D/13	44°47′	79°56′
Highland Ranch	UNP/LNO	AB	32-33-24-W4	82 P/14	51°52′	113°21′
Highlands	UNP/LNO	NF		12 B/2	48°10′	58°56′
Highlands	UNP/LNO	NB	Carleton	21 J/6	46°30′	67°23′
Highlands, District of	MUN1/AZM1	BC	Highland	92 B/12	48°31′	123°30′
Highlands River	RIV/CDE	NF		12 B/2	48°12′	58°54′
Highland Village	UNP/LNO	NS	Colchester	11 E/5	45°24′	63°39′
High Level	TOWN/VIL2	AB	110-19-W5	84 K/11	58°31′	117°08′
High Park	UNP/LNO	ON	York	30 M/11	43°39′	79°28′
High Park	UNP/LNO	ON	Lambton	40 J/16	42°59′	82°22′
High Park	UNP/LNO	SK		72 I/5	50°23′	105°32′
High Point	UNP/LNO	SK	20-23-14-W3	72 J/13	50°59′	107°56′
High Prairie	TOWN/VIL2	AB	25-74-17-W5	83 N/8	55°26′	116°29′
Highridge	UNP/LNO	AB	30-58-1-W5	83 J/1	54°03′	114°08′
High River	TOWN/VIL2	AB	6-19-28-W4	82 I/12	50°35′	113°52′
Highrock	UNP/LNO	MB		63 N/16	55°49′	100°24′
Highrock 199	IR/RI	MB		63 N/16	55°55′	100°29′
Highrock Lake	LAKE/LAC	MB		63 N/16	55°47′	100°30′
Highrock Lake	LAKE/LAC	SK		74 H/4	57°05′	105°32′
Highstone Lake	LAKE/LAC	ON	Kenora	52 J/6	50°27′	91°27′
High Tor	UNP/LNO	SK	40-10-W2	63 D/6	52°28′	103°18′
Highvale	UNP/LNO	AB	34-51-4-W5	83 G/7	53°27′	114°30′
Highview Survey	UNP/LNO	ON	Halton	30 M/5	43°22′	79°52′
Highwater	UNP/LNO	QC	Memphrémagog	31 H/1	45°01′	72°26′
Highway	UNP/LNO	AB	31-56-10-W5	83 G/14	53°53′	115°29′
Highwind Lake	LAKE/LAC	ON	Kenora	52 F/12	49°42′	93°55′
Highwood River	RIV/CDE	AB	26-21-28-W4	82 I/13	50°49′	113°47′
Hihium Creek	RIV/CDE	BC	Lillooet	92 P/3	51°04′	121°21′
Hihium Lake	LAKE/LAC	BC	Kamloops Division Yale	92 P/3	51°03′	121°07′
Hihium Lake 6	IR/RI	BC	Kamloops Division Yale	92 P/3	51°04′	121°09′
Hihium Lake 6A	IR/RI	BC	Kamloops Division Yale	92 P/3	51°04′	121°09′
Hihium Lake 6B	IR/RI	BC	Kamloops Division Yale	92 P/3	51°03′	121°05′
Hilbre	UNP/LNO	MB	24-29-9-W	62 O/10	51°30′	98°36′
Hilda	UNP/LNO	ON	Algoma	42 C/9	48°37′	84°16′
Hilda	UNP/LNO	AB	35-17-1-W4	72 L/8	50°28′	110°03′
Hildegarde	UNP/LNO	NB	Westmorland	21 I/2	46°07′	64°51′
Hilden	UNP/LNO	NS	Colchester	11 E/6	45°18′	63°18′
Hillandale	UNP/LNO	NB	Kings	21 G/8	45°20′	66°13′
Hillandale	UNP/LNO	NB	Victoria	21 J/12	46°43′	67°44′
Hillandale	UNP/LNO	SK	9-5-13-W3	72 G/5	49°22′	107°41′
Hillaton	UNP/LNO	NS	Kings	21 H/1	45°09′	64°26′
Hillbank	UNP/LNO	BC	Shawnigan	92 B/12	48°43′	123°39′
Hillcrest	UNP/LNO	NS	Antigonish	11 E/8	45°28′	62°04′
Hillcrest	UNP/LNO	ON	Leeds	31 B/12	44°33′	75°44′
Hillcrest	UNP/LNO	ON	Prince Edward	31 C/3	44°00′	77°27′
Hillcrest	UNP/LNO	ON	Norfolk	40 I/16	42°50′	80°20′
Hill Crest	UNP/LNO	SK		72 I/5	50°24′	105°31′
Hillcrest	UNP/LNO	AB	20-7-3-W5	82 G/9	49°35′	114°23′
Hillcrest	UNP/LNO	BC	Sahtlam	92 B/13	48°48′	123°48′
Hillcrest	UNP/LNO	YT		105 D/11	60°43′	135°05′
Hillcrest Village	UNP/LNO	ON	York	30 M/14	43°48′	79°22′
Hilldale Corner	UNP/LNO	NB	Victoria	21 J/13	46°58′	67°36′
Hillendale	UNP/LNO	ON	Frontenac	31 C/2	44°15′	76°31′
Hillgrade	UNP/LNO	NF		2 E/10	49°34′	54°42′
Hillgrove	UNP/LNO	NS	Digby	21 A/12	44°33′	65°47′
Hillgrove	UNP/LNO	NB	Westmorland	21 H/14	45°55′	65°14′
Hill Head	UNP/LNO	QC	Argenteuil	31 G/9	45°41′	74°17′
Hillhead Corners	UNP/LNO	ON	Victoria	31 D/7	44°19′	78°41′
Hillhurst	UNP/LNO	NB	Kings	21 G/8	45°25′	66°00′
Hillhurst	UNP/LNO	QC	Coaticook	21 E/4	45°12′	71°50′
Hilliard	MUN2/AZM2	ON	Timiskaming	31 M/12	47°41′	79°41′
Hilliard	UNP/LNO	AB	5-54-17-W4	83 H/9	53°39′	112°29′
Hilliard's Bay Provincial Park	PARK/PARC	AB	75-13,14-W5	83 N/8	55°30′	116°00′
Hilliardton	UNP/LNO	ON	Timiskaming	31 M/12	47°44′	79°42′
Hillier	MUN2/AZM2	ON	Prince Edward	31 C/3	44°00′	77°25′
Hillier	UNP/LNO	ON	Prince Edward	30 N/14	43°58′	77°27′
Hilliers	UNP/LNO	BC	Cameron	92 F/8	49°18′	124°29′
Hill Island	ISL/ÎLE	NT	Franklin	25 N/10	63°38′	68°40′
Hill Island Lake	LAKE/LAC	NT	Mackenzie	75 C	60°29′	109°50′
Hill Lake - see-voir - Hill's Lake	UNP/LNO	ON		41 P/9	47°44′	80°02′
Hill Lake	LAKE/LAC	ON	Thunder Bay	52 J/10	50°33′	90°46′
Hill Lake	LAKE/LAC	ON	Kenora	52 F/6	49°17′	93°27′
Hillman	UNP/LNO	NB	Carleton	21 J/4	46°01′	67°32′
Hillman Bay	BAY/BAIE	SK		73 O/9	55°32′	106°29′
Hillmond	UNP/LNO	SK	25-51-26-W3	73 F/5	53°26′	109°42′

NAME NOM	ENTITY ENTITÉ	LOC 1 LIEU 1	LOC 2 LIEU 2	MAP CARTE	POSITION LAT	LONG
Hillock Lake	LAKE/LAC	ON	Kenora	52 F/12	49°40'	93°54'
Hills	UNP/LNO	BC	Kootenay	82 K/3	50°06'	117°29'
Hillsboro	UNP/LNO	NS	Inverness	11 K/3	46°04'	61°21'
Hillsborough	VILG/VILG	NB	Albert	21 H/15	45°56'	64°39'
Hillsborough	GEOG/GÉOG	NB	Albert	21 H/15	45°53'	64°47'
Hillsborough Bay	BAY/BAIE	PE	Queens	11 L/3	46°08'	63°05'
Hillsborough Beach	UNP/LNO	ON	Lambton	40 O/1	43°07'	82°05'
Hillsborough No. 132	MUN2/AZM2	SK		72 I/4	50°10'	105°50'
Hillsborough Park	UNP/LNO	PE	Queens	11 L/6	46°16'	63°06'
Hillsburg	MUN2/AZM2	MB		62 N/6	51°20'	101°00'
Hillsburgh	UNP/LNO	ON	Wellington	40 P/16	43°47'	80°09'
Hillsburn	UNP/LNO	NS	Annapolis	21 A/13	44°48'	65°34'
Hillsdale	UNP/LNO	NS	Inverness	11 F/14	45°56'	61°25'
Hillsdale	UNP/LNO	NB	Kings	21 H/12	45°32'	65°34'
Hillsdale	UNP/LNO	ON	Simcoe	31 D/12	44°35'	79°45'
Hillsdale	UNP/LNO	SK		72 I/7	50°25'	104°37'
Hillsdale No. 440	MUN2/AZM2	SK		73 C/14	52°50'	109°20'
Hillsdale Road	UNP/LNO	NS	Cape Breton	11 F/16	45°57'	60°18'
Hillsdown	UNP/LNO	AB	6-38-25-W4	83 A/4	52°13'	113°34'
Hills Green	UNP/LNO	ON	Huron	40 P/5	43°28'	81°35'
Hillside	UNP/LNO	NS	Cape Breton	11 K/1	46°01'	60°08'
Hillside	UNP/LNO	NS	Pictou	11 E/10	45°37'	62°38'
Hillside	UNP/LNO	NB	Albert	21 H/14	45°47'	65°01'
Hillside	UNP/LNO	NB	Victoria	21 J/13	46°46'	67°33'
Hillside	UNP/LNO	QC	Brome-Missisquoi	31 H/2	45°05'	72°45'
Hillside	UNP/LNO	ON	Muskoka	31 E/6	45°21'	79°05'
Hillside	UNP/LNO	SK	24-30-32-W	62 N/12	51°37'	101°52'
Hillside	UNP/LNO	SK	23-47-15-W3	73 F/1	53°04'	108°04'
Hillside Beach	UNP/LNO	MB	27-19-7-E	62 I/10	50°40'	96°34'
Hillside Boularderie	UNP/LNO	NS	Cape Breton	11 K/1	46°14'	60°23'
Hill's Lake	UNP/LNO	ON	Timiskaming	41 P/9	47°44'	80°02'
Hills, Lake of the	LAKE/LAC	NF		12 A/11	48°32'	57°23'
Hill's Landing	UNP/LNO	ON	Cochrane	42 A/11	48°32'	81°03'
Hillsport	UNP/LNO	ON	Thunder Bay	42 F/5	49°27'	85°33'
Hill Spring	VILG/VILG	AB	18-4-27-W4	82 H/5	49°17'	113°38'
Hills Road	UNP/LNO	NS	Cape Breton	11 K/1	46°02'	60°06'
Hills Siding	UNP/LNO	ON	Parry Sound	31 L/3	46°09'	79°19'
Hillsvale	UNP/LNO	NS	Hants	11 D/13	44°58'	63°53'
Hilltop	UNP/LNO	MB	19-17-17-W	62 J/5	50°28'	99°49'
Hilltop Lake	LAKE/LAC	NT	Mackenzie	75 M/6	63°21'	111°02'
Hilltown	UNP/LNO	NS	Digby	21 A/5	44°19'	65°54'
Hillview	UNP/LNO	NF		2 C/4	48°02'	53°55'
Hillview	UNP/LNO	ON	Frontenac	31 C/2	44°14'	76°36'
Hillview	UNP/LNO	ON	Timiskaming	31 M/12	47°32'	79°47'
Hilly Grove	UNP/LNO	ON	Manitoulin	41 H/12	45°41'	81°52'
Hilton	MUN2/AZM2	ON	Algoma	41 J/4	46°13'	83°53'
Hilton	UNP/LNO	ON	Northumberland	31 C/4	44°05'	77°46'
Hilton	UNP/LNO	MB	26-6-16-W	62 G/12	49°30'	99°32'
Hilton Beach	VILG/VILG	ON	Algoma	41 J/5	46°15'	83°53'
Himsworth North - see-voir - North Himsworth	MUN2/AZM2	ON		31 L/3	46°10'	79°23'
Himsworth South - see-voir - South Himsworth	MUN2/AZM2	ON		31 L/3	46°10'	79°20'
Hinch	UNP/LNO	ON	Lennox and Addington	31 C/7	44°22'	76°56'
Hinchinbrooke	VILG/VILG	QC	Le Haut-Saint-Laurent	31 G/1	45°03'	74°06'
Hinchinbrooke	MUN2/AZM2	ON	Frontenac	31 C/10	44°35'	76°45'
Hinchliffe	UNP/LNO	SK	4-36-5-W2	63 D/2	52°04'	102°39'
Hinde Lake	LAKE/LAC	NT	Mackenzie	65 E	61°11'	103°38'
Hindon Hill	UNP/LNO	ON	Haliburton	31 E/2	45°03'	78°48'
Hinds Brook	RIV/CDE	NF		12 H/3	49°05'	57°13'
Hinds Lake	LAKE/LAC	NF		12 H/3	48°58'	57°00'
Hines Creek	VILG/VILG	AB	32-83-4-W6	84 D/2	56°15'	118°36'
Hines Creek	RIV/CDE	AB	7-80-4-W6	83 M/15	55°55'	118°37'
Hines Lake	LAKE/LAC	SK		73 G/7	53°23'	106°57'
Hink's Corners	UNP/LNO	ON	Oxford	40 I/15	42°59'	80°39'
Hinton	TOWN/VIL2	AB	51-24,25-W5	83 F/5	53°24'	117°35'
Hinton, Mount	MTN/MNT	YT		105 M/14	63°52'	135°08'
Hippa	UNP/LNO	BC	Queen Charlotte	103 F/10	53°32'	132°57'
Hippa Island	ISL/ÎLE	BC	Queen Charlotte	103 F/10	53°32'	132°59'
Hirsch	UNP/LNO	SK	3-3-5-W2	62 E/2	49°11'	102°36'
Hislop Lake	LAKE/LAC	NT	Mackenzie	85 N/7	63°31'	116°55'
Hisnit 4	IR/RI	BC	Rupert	92 L/3	50°11'	127°28'
Hisnit 7	IR/RI	BC	Nootka	92 E/15	49°45'	126°31'
Hisnit Fishery 34	IR/RI	BC	Clayoquot	92 E/8	49°24'	126°20'
Historic Dunvegan Provincial Historic Site (Developed)	PARK/PARC	AB	80-4-W6	83 M/15	55°54'	118°37'
Hitchcock	HAM/HAM	SK	23-3-9-W2	62 E/3	49°14'	103°07'
Hitchcock Bay	HAM/HAM	SK	13,14-24-7-W3	72 O/2	51°03'	106°52'

NAME NOM	ENTITY ENTITÉ	LOC 1 LIEU 1	LOC 2 LIEU 2	MAP CARTE	POSITION LAT	LONG
Hiuihill Creek	RIV/CDE	BC	Kamloops Division Yale	82 L/13	50°55′	119°38′
Hiukitak River	RIV/CDE	NT	Mackenzie	76 O	67°08′	107°15′
Hiusta Meadow	UNP/LNO	BC	Cassiar	104 J/2	58°03′	130°57′
Hiusta's Meadow 2	IR/RI	BC	Cassiar	104 J/2	58°03′	130°56′
Hiver, Lac de l'	LAKE/LAC	QC	Jamésie	23 L/4	54°03′	71°56′
Hives Lake	LAKE/LAC	SK		73 P/3	55°10′	105°25′
Hixon	UNP/LNO	BC	Cariboo	93 G/7	53°24′	122°34′
Hixon	UNP/LNO	BC	Cariboo	93 G/7	53°25′	122°35′
Hjalmar Lake	LAKE/LAC	NT	Mackenzie	75 F	61°33′	109°25′
Hjalmarson Lake	LAKE/LAC	MB		64 F/11	57°41′	101°14′
Hkusam	UNP/LNO	BC	Sayward	92 K/5	50°23′	125°55′
Hleepte 14	IR/RI	BC	Nootka	92 E/9	49°40′	126°22′
Hnausa	UNP/LNO	MB	21-22-4-E	62 I/15	50°54′	97°00′
Hoadley	UNP/LNO	AB	34-44-3-W5	83 B/16	52°51′	114°22′
Hoards	UNP/LNO	ON	Northumberland	31 C/5	44°17′	77°40′
Hoards Creek	RIV/CDE	ON	Northumberland	31 C/5	44°17′	77°39′
Hoare Bay	BAY/BAIE	NT	Franklin	16 E	65°17′	63°05′
Hoare, Cape	CAPE/CAP	NT	Franklin	88 H	75°04′	113°55′
Hoarfrost River	RIV/CDE	NT	Mackenzie	75 K	62°52′	109°16′
Hoasic	UNP/LNO	ON	Dundas	31 B/14	44°59′	75°09′
Hoath Head	UNP/LNO	ON	Grey	41 A/10	44°32′	80°51′
Hobart Island	ISL/ÎLE	NT	Franklin	36 A	64°11′	73°20′
Hobbema	UNP/LNO	AB	29-44-24-W4	83 A/14	52°50′	113°27′
Hobiton Lake	LAKE/LAC	BC	Barclay	92 C/10	48°45′	124°49′
Hobson, Cape	CAPE/CAP	NT	Franklin	67 H	71°25′	96°07′
Hobson Lake	LAKE/LAC	BC	Kamloops Division Yale	93 A/8	52°30′	120°20′
Hochelaga, Archipel d'	ISL/ÎLE	QC	Communauté urbaine de Montréal	31 H/12	45°33′	73°39′
Hochfeld	UNP/LNO	MB	28,33-1-4-W	62 H/4	49°05′	97°56′
Hochstadt	UNP/LNO	MB	16,17-6-5-E	62 H/7	49°28′	96°52′
Hochstadt	UNP/LNO	SK	26-40-4-W3	73 B/8	52°28′	106°29′
Hockin	UNP/LNO	MB	34-72-3-W	63 P/5	55°17′	97°50′
Hocking Lake	LAKE/LAC	SK		74 O/1	59°03′	106°05′
Hockley	UNP/LNO	ON	Simcoe	31 D/4	44°01′	79°58′
Hockley Valley	UNP/LNO	ON	Peel	30 M/13	43°55′	79°50′
Hocquart	UNP/LNO	QC	Rivière-du-Loup	21 N/14	47°53′	69°03′
Hoctor	UNP/LNO	MB	36-10-13-E	52 E/13	49°52′	95°42′
Hodda	UNP/LNO	BC	Cariboo	93 J/15	54°55′	122°40′
Hodderville	UNP/LNO	NF		2 C/11	48°32′	53°18′
Hodge's Cove	UNP/LNO	NF		2 C/4	48°01′	53°45′
Hodges Hill	MTN/MNT	NF		2 E/4	49°04′	55°53′
Hodgeville	VILG/VILG	SK	25-13-8-W3	72 J/2	50°07′	106°58′
Hodgin	UNP/LNO	NB	Gloucester	21 P/13	47°54′	65°53′
Hodgins	UNP/LNO	QC	Pontiac	31 F/9	45°43′	76°24′
Hodgkins Seamount	SEAU/SMER	—		3000	53°31′	136°05′
Hodgson	UNP/LNO	ON	Renfrew	31 L/8	46°17′	78°24′
Hodgson	UNP/LNO	MB		62 P/4	51°13′	97°34′
Hodson	UNP/LNO	NS	Pictou	11 E/10	45°44′	62°58′
Hoegs Corner	UNP/LNO	NS	Colchester	11 E/5	45°26′	63°46′
Hoey	HAM/HAM	SK	12-45A-27-W2	73 A/13	52°52′	105°48′
Hoeya Head	CAPE/CAP	BC	Range 1 Coast	92 K/12	50°41′	125°59′
Hoeya Sound	BAY/BAIE	BC	Range 1 Coast	92 K/12	50°42′	125°58′
Hoey, Cape	CAPE/CAP	NT	Franklin	25 P	63°09′	64°48′
Hoff	UNP/LNO	AB	55-4-W6	83 E/16	53°47′	118°27′
Hoffer	UNP/LNO	SK	18-2-14-W2	62 E/4	49°07′	103°52′
Hoffman	UNP/LNO	ON	Renfrew	31 F/14	45°53′	77°15′
Hogan Island	ISL/ÎLE	BC	Range 5 Coast	103 J/9	54°39′	130°25′
Hogan Lake	LAKE/LAC	ON	Nipissing	31 E/15	45°52′	78°30′
Hogan's Pond	UNP/LNO	NF		1 N/10	47°35′	52°51′
Hogarth	UNP/LNO	ON	Thunder Bay	52 H/1	49°11′	88°16′
Hogarth Island	ISL/ÎLE	NT	Mackenzie	86 K/5	66°18′	117°55′
Hogarth, Point	CAPE/CAP	NT	Franklin	59 B	76°10′	92°47′
Hoge, Mount	MTN/MNT	YT		115 G/3	61°14′	139°24′
Hogem Ranges	MTN/MNT	BC	Cassiar	93 M/16	55°50′	126°00′
Hogg	UNP/LNO	ON	Grey	41 A/10	44°41′	80°56′
Hogg Lake	LAKE/LAC	MB		64 H/8	57°17′	96°09′
Hogg, Mount	MTN/MNT	YT		105 F/8	61°21′	132°14′
Hog Island	ISL/ÎLE	PE	Prince	11 L/12	46°36′	63°48′
Hog Island	ISL/ÎLE	NS	Yarmouth	20 P/12	43°43′	65°53′
Hogs Back	UNP/LNO	ON	Carleton	31 G/5	45°22′	75°42′
Hohoae Island	ISL/ÎLE	BC	Rupert	92 L/3	50°03′	127°13′
Hoiss 8	IR/RI	BC	Nootka	92 E/10	49°42′	126°34′
Hoke Point 10B	IR/RI	BC	Nootka	92 E/15	49°53′	126°52′
Holachten 8	IR/RI	BC	New Westminster	92 G/1	49°13′	122°02′
Holbein	HAM/HAM	SK	14-49-2-W3	73 G/1	53°14′	106°12′
Holberg	UNP/LNO	BC	Rupert	102 I/9	50°39′	128°01′

NAME NOM	ENTITY ENTITÉ	LOC 1 LIEU 1	LOC 2 LIEU 2	MAP CARTE	POSITION LAT	LONG
Holberg Inlet	BAY/BAIE	BC	Rupert	92 L/12	50°36′	127°44′
Holborn	UNP/LNO	AB	33-51-1-W5	83 G/8	53°27′	114°04′
Holbrook	UNP/LNO	ON	Oxford	40 P/2	43°01′	80°42′
Holden	VILG/VILG	AB	14-49-16-W4	83 H/1	53°14′	112°14′
Holden Lake	LAKE/LAC	NS	Lunenburg	21 A/9	44°39′	64°28′
Holderville	UNP/LNO	NB	Kings	21 G/8	45°26′	66°09′
Holdfast	VILG/VILG	SK	15-23-25-W2	72 I/14	50°58′	105°25′
Hole in the Wall	CHAN/CHEN	BC	Sayward	92 K/6	50°19′	125°10′
Hole or Hollow Water 10	IR/RI	MB		62 P/1	51°10′	96°17′
Holford	UNP/LNO	ON	Grey	41 A/7	44°20′	80°49′
Holgar Lake	LAKE/LAC	SK		74 G/8	57°19′	106°07′
Holiday	UNP/LNO	ON	Oxford	40 P/2	43°08′	80°59′
Holiday Harbour	UNP/LNO	ON	Kent	40 J/1	42°05′	82°27′
Holiday Hill	UNP/LNO	NF		1 N/5	47°28′	53°32′
Holiday Park	UNP/LNO	SK		73 B/2	52°06′	106°42′
Holinshead Lake	LAKE/LAC	ON	Thunder Bay	52 H/12	49°39′	89°40′
Holland	MUN2/AZM2	ON	Grey	41 A/7	44°25′	80°48′
Holland	UNP/LNO	ON	Leeds	31 B/5	44°25′	75°57′
Holland	UNP/LNO	MB	27-7-11-W	62 G/10	49°36′	98°53′
Holland Centre	UNP/LNO	ON	Grey	41 A/7	44°24′	80°48′
Holland Harbour	UNP/LNO	NS	Guysborough	11 F/4	45°05′	61°47′
Holland Harbour	BAY/BAIE	NS	Guysborough	11 F/4	45°05′	61°46′
Holland Landing	UNP/LNO	ON	York	31 D/3	44°06′	79°29′
Holland Marsh	VEGL/VÉGB	ON	Simcoe	31 D/4	44°08′	79°33′
Holland Mills	UNP/LNO	QC	Les Collines-de-l'Outaouais	31 G/13	45°47′	75°39′
Holland River	RIV/CDE	ON	Simcoe	31 D/4	44°12′	79°31′
Holleford	UNP/LNO	ON	Frontenac	31 C/7	44°27′	76°37′
Hollen	UNP/LNO	ON	Wellington	40 P/10	43°43′	80°43′
Holliday	UNP/LNO	QC	Kamouraska	21 N/5	47°19′	69°47′
Holliston	UNP/LNO	SK		73 B/2	52°07′	106°38′
Hollist Point	CAPE/CAP	NT	Franklin	68 B	72°55′	101°31′
Holloway	UNP/LNO	SK	1-6-12-W2	62 E/6	49°26′	103°30′
Holloway	UNP/LNO	AB	25-52-19-W5	83 F/10	53°31′	116°39′
Hollow Glen	UNP/LNO	QC	Les Collines-de-l'Outaouais	31 G/5	45°29′	75°53′
Hollow Lake	UNP/LNO	AB	4-61-19-W4	83 I/2	54°15′	112°47′
Hollow Water	UNP/LNO	MB	4,5-26-9-E	62 P/1	51°12′	96°18′
Holly	UNP/LNO	ON	Simcoe	31 D/5	44°20′	79°43′
Hollyburn	UNP/LNO	BC	New Westminster	92 G/6	49°20′	123°09′
Holly Park	UNP/LNO	ON	York	30 M/13	43°56′	79°42′
Holman	HAM/HAM	NT	Franklin	87 F/10	70°44′	117°45′
Holmedale	UNP/LNO	ON	Brant	40 P/1	43°09′	80°17′
Holmer, Lac	LAKE/LAC	QC	Jamésie	23 L/4	54°07′	71°40′
*Holmes	UNP/LNO	SK	20-47-26-W2	73 H/4	53°07′	105°47′
Holmes Crossing	UNP/LNO	AB	31-61-5-W5	83 J/7	54°19′	114°44′
Holmes Lake	LAKE/LAC	MB	5-21-2-W	62 I/13	50°47′	97°42′
Holmes Point	UNP/LNO	ON	York	31 D/6	44°20′	79°14′
Holmes River	RIV/CDE	BC	Cariboo	93 H/8	53°15′	120°04′
Holmesville	UNP/LNO	NB	Carleton	21 J/12	46°35′	67°37′
Holmesville	UNP/LNO	ON	Huron	40 P/12	43°39′	81°36′
Holmfield	UNP/LNO	MB	24-2-16-W	62 G/3	49°08′	99°29′
Holmur	UNP/LNO	ON	Parry Sound	31 E/5	45°18′	79°57′
Holmwood	UNP/LNO	BC	Kamloops Division Yale	82 L/12	50°37′	119°57′
Holstein	UNP/LNO	ON	Grey	41 A/2	44°03′	80°45′
Holt	UNP/LNO	ON	York	31 D/3	44°07′	79°20′
Holton	UNP/LNO	NF		13 I/11	54°35′	57°16′
Holton	UNP/LNO	QC	Les Jardins-de-Napierville	31 H/4	45°08′	73°39′
Holton Heights	UNP/LNO	ON	Halton	30 M/5	43°28′	79°41′
Holton Island	ISL/ÎLE	NF		13 I/11	54°37′	57°18′
Holtry Creek	RIV/CDE	BC	Range 3 Coast	93 C/6	52°27′	125°15′
Holtville	UNP/LNO	NB	Northumberland	21 J/9	46°31′	66°29′
Holtyre	UNP/LNO	ON	Cochrane	42 A/8	48°28′	80°17′
Holy Cross Lake 3	IR/RI	BC	Range 4 Coast	93 F/11	53°43′	125°02′
Holyoke	UNP/LNO	AB	36-59-5-W4	73 L/2	54°08′	110°37′
Holyrood	TOWN/VIL2	NF		1 N/6	47°23′	53°08′
Holyrood	UNP/LNO	ON	Bruce	41 A/3	44°02′	81°28′
Holyrood Bay	BAY/BAIE	NF		1 K/13	46°46′	53°38′
Holyrood Pond	LAKE/LAC	NF		1 K/13	46°52′	53°34′
Homais 2	IR/RI	BC	Clayoquot	92 E/7	49°24′	126°34′
Homalco 1	IR/RI	BC	Range 1 Coast	92 K/15	50°57′	124°53′
Homalco 2	IR/RI	BC	Range 1 Coast	92 K/15	50°58′	124°52′
Homalco 2A	IR/RI	BC	Range 1 Coast	92 K/15	50°58′	124°52′
Homalco 9	IR/RI	BC	Comox	92 F/14	49°57′	125°14′
Homan Bay	BAY/BAIE	NT	Franklin	67 F	70°31′	102°51′
Homards, Baie des	BAY/BAIE	QC	Sept-Rivières	22 G/14	49°50′	67°05′
Homathko Icefield	GLAC/GLAC	BC	Range 2 Coast	92 N/2	51°07′	124°35′

NAME NOM	ENTITY ENTITÉ	LOC 1 LIEU 1	LOC 2 LIEU 2	MAP CARTE	POSITION LAT	LONG
Homathko River	RIV/CDE	BC	Range 1 Coast	92 K/15	50°55′	124°51′
Homayno 2	IR/RI	BC	Range 1 Coast	92 K/12	50°35′	125°34′
Home Bay	BAY/BAIE	NT	Franklin	27 A	68°45′	67°10′
Homebrook	UNP/LNO	MB	14-32-11-W	62 O/10	51°44′	98°53′
Home, Cape	CAPE/CAP	NT	Franklin	48 F	74°32′	83°36′
Homefield	UNP/LNO	SK	25,26-9-W2	62 M/3	51°13′	103°13′
Homeglen	UNP/LNO	AB	22-44-1-W5	83 B/16	52°48′	114°05′
Home Island	ISL/ÎLE	NF		25 A/1	60°10′	64°14′
Home Pond	LAKE/LAC	NF		2 D/16	48°58′	54°18′
Homer	UNP/LNO	ON	Lincoln	30 M/3	43°10′	79°11′
Homestead	UNP/LNO	AB	20-75-9-W6	83 M/11	55°31′	119°22′
Homestead-Motherwell, Lieu historique national du - also-aussi - Motherwell Homestead National Historic Site	PARK/PARC	SK		62 L/11	50°43′	103°26′
Homewood	UNP/LNO	MB	30-6-3-W1	62 H/12	49°31′	97°52′
Homfray Channel	CHAN/CHEN	BC	Range 1 Coast	92 K/2	50°15′	124°38′
Homfray Creek	UNP/LNO	BC	Range 1 Coast	92 K/7	50°18′	124°38′
Hominka River	RIV/CDE	BC	Cariboo	93 J/9	54°38′	122°05′
Homitan 8	IR/RI	BC	Barclay	92 C/15	48°46′	124°44′
Hondo	UNP/LNO	AB	23-70-1-W5	83 O/1	55°04′	114°02′
Hone	UNP/LNO	MB	22-83-25-W	64 C/3	56°13′	101°19′
Hone River	RIV/CDE	NT	Franklin	26 D	64°34′	70°26′
Honeydale	UNP/LNO	NB	Charlotte	21 G/6	45°22′	67°12′
Honey Harbour	UNP/LNO	ON	Muskoka	31 D/13	44°52′	79°49′
Honeyman Island	ISL/ÎLE	NT	Franklin	47 C	69°05′	85°18′
Honeymoon	UNP/LNO	SK	24-50-25-W2	73 H/5	53°19′	105°32′
Honeymoon Bay	UNP/LNO	BC	Cowichan Lake	92 C/16	48°49′	124°10′
Honey's Beach	UNP/LNO	ON	Ontario	31 D/2	44°08′	78°56′
Honeywell Corners	UNP/LNO	ON	Hastings	31 C/3	44°14′	77°22′
Honeywood	UNP/LNO	ON	Dufferin	41 A/1	44°13′	80°11′
Honfleur	VILG/VILG	QC	Bellechasse	21 L/10	46°39′	70°53′
Honguedo, Détroit d'	CHAN/CHEN	QC	La Côte-de-Gaspé	22 H/8	49°15′	64°00′
Honora	UNP/LNO	ON	Manitoulin	41 G/16	45°54′	82°07′
Honoréville	UNP/LNO	QC	Le Haut-Richelieu	31 H/6	45°22′	73°02′
Hood	UNP/LNO	ON	Lanark	31 F/1	45°03′	76°29′
Hood	UNP/LNO	SK	36-32-20-W3	72 N/15	51°47′	108°43′
Hoodoo No. 401	MUN2/AZM2	SK		73 A/12	52°35′	105°35′
Hood River	RIV/CDE	NT	Mackenzie	76 N	67°26′	108°53′
Hooker Bay	BAY/BAIE	NT	Franklin	68 G	75°23′	100°35′
Hooker Lake	LAKE/LAC	ON	Kenora	52 J/11	50°35′	91°01′
Hooker Lake	LAKE/LAC	NT	Mackenzie	86 F	65°51′	117°24′
Hook Point	CAPE/CAP	ON	Kenora	43 J/16	54°53′	82°13′
Hoole Canyon	VALL/VALL	YT		105 F/16	61°50′	132°02′
Hoole River	RIV/CDE	YT		105 G/12	61°45′	131°43′
Hoomak Lake	LAKE/LAC	BC	Rupert	92 L/2	50°12′	126°31′
Hoonees 2	IR/RI	BC	Range 3 Coast	93 D/5	52°19′	127°58′
Hoop and Holler Bend	UNP/LNO	MB	11-6-W	62 G/16	49°56′	98°13′
Hoop Cove	UNP/LNO	NF		1 M/11	47°38′	55°06′
Hooper, Cape	CAPE/CAP	NT	Franklin	27 A	68°27′	66°40′
Hooper Inlet	BAY/BAIE	NT	Franklin	47 D	69°18′	81°46′
Hooper Island	ISL/ÎLE	NT	Mackenzie	107 C	69°41′	134°53′
Hooper, Mount	MTN/MNT	BC	Dunsmuir	92 F/2	49°01′	124°31′
Hooper Point	CAPE/CAP	BC	Range 5 Coast	103 J/2	54°13′	130°47′
Hooping Harbour	UNP/LNO	NF		12 I/9	50°37′	56°16′
Hooping Harbour	BAY/BAIE	NF		12 I/9	50°37′	56°13′
Hoosier	UNP/LNO	SK	3-31-27-W3	72 N/12	51°38′	109°44′
Hootalinqua	UNP/LNO	YT		105 E/10	61°35′	134°54′
Hope	VILG/VILG	QC	Bonaventure	22 A/3	48°03′	65°12′
Hope	MUN1/AZM1	BC	Yale Division Yale	92 H/6	49°23′	121°26′
Hope	MUN2/AZM2	ON	Northumberland	31 D/1	44°01′	78°24′
Hope	UNP/LNO	ON	York	30 M/13	43°53′	79°31′
Hope 1	IR/RI	BC	Yale Division Yale	92 H/6	49°23′	121°26′
Hopeall	UNP/LNO	NF		1 N/12	47°37′	53°31′
Hopeall Bay	BAY/BAIE	NF		1 N/12	47°38′	53°32′
Hopeall Head	CAPE/CAP	NF		1 N/12	47°38′	53°34′
Hope Bay	UNP/LNO	ON	Bruce	41 A/14	44°54′	81°10′
Hope Bay	UNP/LNO	BC	Cowichan	92 B/14	48°48′	123°16′
Hope Bay	BAY/BAIE	ON	Bruce	41 A/14	44°55′	81°08′
Hope Bay	BAY/BAIE	NT	Franklin	77 A	68°09′	106°47′
Hope, Cape	CAPE/CAP	NT	Mackenzie	87 B/16	69°00′	116°15′
Hopedale	VILG/VILG	NF		13 N/8	55°28′	60°13′
Hopedale Mission National Historic Site - also-aussi - Mission-de-Hopedale, Lieu historique national de la	PARK/PARC	NF		13 N/8	53°27′	60°13′
Hopedale Saddle	SEAU/SMER	—		8047	55°55′	58°30′
Hopefield	UNP/LNO	PE	Kings	11 L/2	46°00′	62°41′
Hopefield	UNP/LNO	ON	Renfrew	31 F/5	45°28′	77°32′
Hope Island	ISL/ÎLE	ON	Simcoe	41 A/16	44°54′	80°11′
Hope Island	ISL/ÎLE	BC	Rupert	92 L/13	50°55′	127°54′

NAME NOM	ENTITY ENTITÉ	LOC 1 LIEU 1	LOC 2 LIEU 2	MAP CARTE	POSITION LAT	LONG
Hope Island 1	IR/RI	BC	Rupert	92 L/13	50°55′	127°54′
Hope Lake	LAKE/LAC	ON	Kenora	52 F/5	49°24′	93°46′
Hopeness	UNP/LNO	ON	Bruce	41 A/14	44°56′	81°10′
Hope River	UNP/LNO	PE	Queens	11 L/6	46°26′	63°24′
Hopes Advance Bay	BAY/BAIE	NT	Franklin	24 N/5	59°21′	69°35′
Hopes Advance, Cap	CLF/ESC	QC	Kativik	25 F/4	61°04′	69°34′
Hope Town	VILG/VILG	QC	Bonaventure	22 A/3	48°03′	65°10′
Hopetown	UNP/LNO	ON	Lanark	31 F/1	45°05′	76°27′
Hopetown	UNP/LNO	BC	Range 1 Coast	92 L/15	50°55′	126°49′
Hopetown 10A	IR/RI	BC	Range 1 Coast	92 L/15	50°55′	126°49′
Hope Valley	UNP/LNO	AB	19-46-4-W4	73 D/15	52°58′	110°35′
Hopeville	UNP/LNO	ON	Grey	41 A/2	44°07′	80°33′
Hopewell	UNP/LNO	NF		1 N/6	47°29′	53°03′
Hopewell	UNP/LNO	NS	Pictou	11 E/7	45°29′	62°42′
Hopewell	GEOG/GÉOG	NB	Albert	21 H/15	45°50′	64°43′
Hopewell Cape	UNP/LNO	NB	Albert	21 H/15	45°51′	64°35′
Hopewell Hill	UNP/LNO	NB	Albert	21 H/15	45°46′	64°41′
Hopewell Islands	ISL/ÎLE	NT	Keewatin	34 L/8	58°23′	78°06′
Hopewell Sound	CHAN/CHEN	NT	Keewatin	34 L/8	58°24′	78°05′
Hopington	UNP/LNO	BC	New Westminster	92 G/2	49°05′	122°33′
Hopkins Bay	BAY/BAIE	ON	Bruce	41 H/4	45°11′	81°40′
Hopkins Corners	UNP/LNO	ON	Wentworth	30 M/5	43°17′	79°56′
Hopkins Court	UNP/LNO	ON	Wentworth	30 M/5	43°17′	79°56′
Hopkins Inlet	BAY/BAIE	NT	Franklin	47 C	69°11′	85°15′
Hopkins Landing	UNP/LNO	BC	New Westminster	92 G/6	49°26′	123°29′
Hopkins Survey	UNP/LNO	ON	Wentworth	30 M/5	43°17′	79°56′
Hoppenderry	UNP/LNO	NS	Guysborough	11 F/5	45°25′	61°53′
Hoppner Inlet	BAY/BAIE	NT	Franklin	46 J	66°48′	83°55′
Hoppner River	RIV/CDE	NT	Mackenzie	87 B	68°59′	117°44′
Hopton Lake	LAKE/LAC	NT	Keewatin	65 A	60°39′	96°58′
Horburg	UNP/LNO	AB	6-40-9-W5	83 B/6	52°25′	115°17′
Horen	UNP/LNO	AB	18-52-5-W5	83 G/7	53°29′	114°44′
Horizon	UNP/LNO	SK	31-6-24-W2	72 H/11	49°31′	105°13′
Horizon Channel	SEAU/SMER	—		5.03	50°25′	140°30′
Hornaday River	RIV/CDE	AB	120-9-W4	74 M/6	59°26′	111°28′
Hornaday River	RIV/CDE	NT	Mackenzie	97 D	69°19′	123°48′
Hornbeck	UNP/LNO	AB	2-53-19-W5	83 F/10	53°34′	116°41′
Hornby	UNP/LNO	ON	Halton	30 M/12	43°34′	79°50′
Hornby Bay	BAY/BAIE	NT	Mackenzie	86 L	66°28′	118°05′
Hornby Island	UNP/LNO	BC	Nanaimo	92 F/10	49°31′	124°38′
Hornby Island	UNP/LNO	BC	Nanaimo	92 F/10	49°31′	124°42′
Hornby Island	ISL/ÎLE	BC	Nanaimo	92 F/10	49°32′	124°40′
Hornby Station	UNP/LNO	ON	Halton	30 M/12	43°34′	79°49′
Horndean	UNP/LNO	MB	9,10-3-2-W	62 H/4	49°12′	97°39′
Horne	UNP/LNO	ON	Thunder Bay	52 A/13	48°46′	89°51′
Horne Lake	LAKE/LAC	BC	Alberni	92 F/7	49°20′	124°42′
Hornell Heights	UNP/LNO	ON	Nipissing	31 L/6	46°22′	79°25′
Hornell Lake	LAKE/LAC	NT	Mackenzie	85 L	62°20′	119°25′
Hornepayne	MUN2/AZM2	ON	Algoma	42 F/7	49°15′	84°47′
Hornepayne	UNP/LNO	ON	Algoma	42 F/2	49°13′	84°47′
Horner Lake	LAKE/LAC	ON	Algoma	41 J/12	46°40′	83°32′
Horne Settlement	UNP/LNO	NS	Hants	11 D/13	44°57′	63°34′
Hornes Road	UNP/LNO	NS	Cape Breton	11 K/1	46°03′	60°02′
Hornet Creek	RIV/CDE	BC	Yale Division Yale	92 H/12	49°36′	121°49′
Horning's Mills	UNP/LNO	ON	Dufferin	41 A/1	44°09′	80°12′
Horn Lake	LAKE/LAC	ON	Parry Sound	31 E/11	45°40′	79°30′
Horn Lake	LAKE/LAC	ON	Parry Sound	31 E/5	45°23′	79°36′
Horn Peak	MTN/MNT	YT		105 O/11	63°35′	131°08′
Horn Plateau	PLN/PLNE	NT	Mackenzie	85 L	62°15′	119°15′
Horn River	RIV/CDE	NT	Mackenzie	85 E	61°30′	118°01′
Horod	UNP/LNO	MB	26-19-21-W	62 K/9	50°39′	100°18′
Horsburgh Point	CAPE/CAP	ON	Manitoulin	41 H/12	45°42′	81°39′
Horse Chops	CAPE/CAP	NF		2 C/6	48°21′	53°12′
Horse Collar Junction	UNP/LNO	ON	Rainy River	52 C/9	48°44′	92°26′
Horse Creek	UNP/LNO	SK	28-3-7-W3	72 G/2	49°15′	106°54′
Horse Creek	UNP/LNO	BC	Kootenay	82 N/2	51°12′	116°51′
Horsefly	UNP/LNO	BC	Cariboo	93 A/6	52°20′	121°25′
Horsefly Lake	LAKE/LAC	BC	Cariboo	93 A/6	52°23′	121°10′
Horsefly Lake Reservoir	LAKE/LAC	AB	9-16-W4	82 H/9	49°43′	112°04′
Horsefly River	RIV/CDE	BC	Cariboo	93 A/6	52°28′	121°23′
Horse Head	UNP/LNO	SK	34-56-20-W3	73 F/15	53°54′	108°52′
Horsehead Creek	RIV/CDE	SK	59-20-W3	73 K/2	54°04′	108°58′
Horse Island	ISL/ÎLE	MB		63 G/6	53°19′	99°06′
Horse Islands	UNP/LNO	NF		2 L/4	50°12′	55°44′
Horse Islands	ISL/ÎLE	NF		2 L/4	50°13′	55°48′

NAME NOM	ENTITY ENTITÉ	LOC 1 LIEU 1	LOC 2 LIEU 2	MAP CARTE	POSITION LAT	LONG
Horse Lake	LAKE/LAC	BC	Lillooet	92 P/11	51°35′	121°07′
Horse Lakes 152B	IR/RI	AB	26-73-12-W6	83 M/5	55°21′	119°43′
Horse River	RIV/CDE	AB	89-9-W4	74 D/11	56°43′	111°23′
Horseshoe Bay	VILG/VILG	AB	24-59-10-W4	73 L/3	54°07′	111°22′
Horseshoe Bay	HAM/HAM	SK	29,30,31,32-53-18-3-W1	73 F/10	53°37′	108°38′
Horseshoe Bay	UNP/LNO	ON	Algoma	41 K/15	46°49′	84°30′
Horseshoe Bay	UNP/LNO	BC	New Westminster	92 G/6	49°22′	123°16′
Horseshoe Falls	FALL/CHUT	ON	Welland	30 M/3	43°05′	79°05′
Horseshoe Lake	UNP/LNO	ON	Haliburton	31 D/15	45°00′	78°42′
Horseshoe Lake	UNP/LNO	ON	Parry Sound	31 E/5	45°18′	79°51′
Horseshoe Lake	UNP/LNO	AB	16-34-27-W4	82 P/13	51°56′	113°47′
Horseshoe Lake	LAKE/LAC	ON	Haliburton	31 D/15	44°59′	78°41′
Horseshoe Lake	LAKE/LAC	ON	Kenora	53 B/2	52°14′	90°46′
Horseshoe Lake	LAKE/LAC	MB	13,14-15-E	52 L/3	50°08′	95°26′
Horseshoe Lake	LAKE/LAC	MB		53 D/4	52°11′	95°49′
Horseshoe Lake	LAKE/LAC	AB	39-6-W4	73 D/7	52°21′	110°45′
Horseshoe Lake	LAKE/LAC	BC	New Westminster	92 F/16	49°54′	124°17′
Horseshoe Valley	UNP/LNO	ON	Simcoe	31 D/12	44°33′	79°40′
Horsethief Creek	RIV/CDE	BC	Kootenay	82 K/9	50°34′	116°03′
Horsey	UNP/LNO	ON	Algoma	42 G/5	49°26′	83°54′
Horsfall Island	ISL/ÎLE	BC	Range 3 Coast	103 A/1	52°11′	128°18′
Horsham	UNP/LNO	SK	11-17-29-W3	72 K/5	50°25′	109°53′
Horton	MUN2/AZM2	ON	Renfrew	31 F/10	45°30′	76°40′
Horton 35	IR/RI	NS	Kings	21 H/1	45°03′	64°14′
Horton Lake	LAKE/LAC	NT	Mackenzie	96 O	67°29′	122°31′
Horton Landing	UNP/LNO	NS	Kings	21 H/1	45°07′	64°17′
Horton River	RIV/CDE	NT	Mackenzie	97 A	69°56′	126°48′
Hortons Creek	UNP/LNO	NB	Northumberland	21 P/3	47°02′	65°10′
Hortonville	UNP/LNO	NS	Kings	21 H/1	45°07′	64°17′
Horwood	UNP/LNO	NF		2 E/7	49°27′	54°32′
Horwood Lake	UNP/LNO	ON	Sudbury	42 B/1	48°05′	82°10′
Horwood Lake	LAKE/LAC	ON	Sudbury	42 B/1	48°00′	82°20′
Horwood North - see-voir - Stoneville	UNP/LNO	NF		2 E/7	49°28′	54°33′
Horwood Peninsula	CAPE/CAP	ON	Sudbury	42 B/1	48°01′	82°18′
Hosea Lake	LAKE/LAC	ON	Kenora	53 O/16	55°58′	90°16′
Hoselaw	UNP/LNO	AB	18-60-6-W4	73 L/2	54°11′	110°54′
Hoskyn Channel	CHAN/CHEN	BC	Sayward	92 K/3	50°11′	125°08′
Hosmer	UNP/LNO	BC	Kootenay	82 G/10	49°35′	114°57′
Hospital Bay	BAY/BAIE	NT	Franklin	79 E	78°55′	105°00′
Hospital Hill	UNP/LNO	BC	New Westminster	92 G/11	49°42′	123°09′
Hospital Pond	LAKE/LAC	NF		12 A/7	48°21′	56°53′
Hostile Lake	LAKE/LAC	NT	Mackenzie	75 B	60°55′	106°18′
Hotchkiss	UNP/LNO	AB	13-93-23-W5	84 F/4	57°04′	117°33′
Hotchkiss River	RIV/CDE	AB	93-22-W5	84 F/3	57°02′	117°28′
Hôtel-Dalvay-by-the-Sea, Lieu historique national de l' - also-aussi - Dalvay-by-the-Sea Hotel National Historic Site	PARK/PARC	PE	Queens	11 L/6	46°25′	63°04′
Hotel Lake	LAKE/LAC	NT	Mackenzie	75 D	60°25′	110°05′
Hotham	UNP/LNO	ON	Parry Sound	31 L/4	46°03′	79°37′
Hotham, Cape	CAPE/CAP	NT	Franklin	58 F	74°41′	93°28′
Hotham Sound	BAY/BAIE	BC	New Westminster	92 F/16	49°52′	124°02′
Hotnarko Lake	LAKE/LAC	BC	Range 3 Coast	93 C/5	52°28′	125°37′
Hot Springs Cove	UNP/LNO	BC	Clayoquot	92 E/8	49°22′	126°16′
Hotspur	UNP/LNO	ON	Haliburton	31 D/16	44°56′	78°18′
Hottah Lake	LAKE/LAC	NT	Mackenzie	86 E	65°04′	118°30′
Houël, Lac	LAKE/LAC	QC	Kativik	24 G/8	57°15′	66°21′
Hough Lake	UNP/LNO	ON	Timiskaming	41 P/16	47°56′	80°02′
Houghton Centre	UNP/LNO	ON	Norfolk	40 I/10	42°36′	80°40′
Houghton Lake	LAKE/LAC	ON	Thunder Bay	52 J/7	50°20′	90°55′
Houghton Lake	LAKE/LAC	SK	39,40-22-W2	73 A/6	52°23′	105°08′
Houpsitas 6	IR/RI	BC	Rupert	92 L/3	50°02′	127°22′
House Island	ISL/ÎLE	NT	Keewatin	44 P	59°20′	80°35′
House Mountain	MTN/MNT	BC	Range 1 Coast	92 K/15	50°53′	124°57′
House River	RIV/CDE	AB	18-83-16-W4	84 A/2	56°12′	112°30′
House River Indian Cemetery 178	IR/RI	AB	18-83-16-W4	84 A/2	56°12′	112°30′
Houseys Rapids	UNP/LNO	ON	Muskoka	31 D/14	44°52′	79°13′
Houston	MUN1/AZM1	BC	Range 5 Coast	93 L/7	54°24′	126°40′
Houston Point	CAPE/CAP	NT	Keewatin	43 H/3	53°11′	81°07′
Houston Stewart Channel	CHAN/CHEN	BC	Queen Charlotte	103 B/3	52°09′	131°07′
Hoved Island	ISL/ÎLE	NT	Franklin	49 C	77°32′	85°09′
Hovgaard Islands	ISL/ÎLE	NT	Franklin	57 B	68°29′	95°44′
Howard	MUN2/AZM2	ON	Kent	40 I/5	42°29′	81°55′
Howard	UNP/LNO	NB	Northumberland	21 I/12	46°40′	65°47′
Howard Brook	UNP/LNO	NB	Carleton	21 J/6	46°23′	67°20′
Howard Creek	RIV/CDE	SK	20-51-22-W2	73 H/6	53°25′	105°13′
Howard Lake	LAKE/LAC	NT	Mackenzie	75 I/4	62°15′	105°57′
*Howden	UNP/LNO	MB	28-15-15-W	62 J/6	50°18′	99°29′

NAME NOM	ENTITY ENTITÉ	LOC 1 LIEU 1	LOC 2 LIEU 2	MAP CARTE	POSITION LAT	LONG
Howdenvale	UNP/LNO	ON	Bruce	41 A/14	44°49'	81°18'
Howe Bay	UNP/LNO	PE	Kings	11 L/8	46°18'	62°25'
Howe Bay	BAY/BAIE	PE	Kings	11 L/8	46°18'	62°22'
Howe, Cape	CAPE/CAP	NT	Franklin	25 P	63°05'	64°45'
Howeet 8	IR/RI	BC	Range 3 Coast	103 A/1	52°03'	128°04'
Howe Island	MUN2/AZM2	ON	Frontenac	31 C/8	44°15'	76°15'
Howe Island	ISL/ÎLE	ON	Frontenac	31 C/8	44°16'	76°17'
Howell Point	CAPE/CAP	MB		63 G/11	53°35'	99°02'
Howells River	RIV/CDE	NF		23 J/10	54°35'	66°40'
Howe Point	CAPE/CAP	PE	Kings	11 L/8	46°18'	62°20'
Howes Corners	UNP/LNO	ON	Simcoe	31 D/12	44°45'	79°56'
Howe Sound	BAY/BAIE	BC	New Westminster	92 G/6	49°25'	123°23'
Howick	TOWN/VIL2	QC	Le Haut-Saint-Laurent	31 H/4	45°11'	73°51'
Howick	MUN2/AZM2	ON	Huron	40 P/14	43°53'	81°05'
Howie Centre	UNP/LNO	NS	Cape Breton	11 K/1	46°05'	60°16'
Howlan	UNP/LNO	PE	Prince	21 I/9	46°44'	64°13'
Howland	MUN2/AZM2	ON	Manitoulin	41 G/16	45°53'	82°00'
Howland	UNP/LNO	ON	Haliburton	31 D/15	44°49'	78°39'
Howland Ridge	UNP/LNO	NB	York	21 J/3	46°09'	67°10'
Howley	TOWN/VIL2	NF		12 H/3	49°10'	57°07'
Howley, Mount	MTN/MNT	NF		12 B/8	48°16'	58°26'
Howser	UNP/LNO	BC	Kootenay	82 K/7	50°18'	116°57'
Howser Creek	RIV/CDE	BC	Kootenay	82 K/7	50°27'	116°55'
Hoyle	UNP/LNO	ON	Cochrane	42 A/11	48°33'	81°03'
Hoyle Bay	BAY/BAIE	NT	Franklin	79 B	76°39'	109°35'
Hoyles Canyon	SEAU/SMER	—		8010	43°38'	49°13'
Hoylestown	UNP/LNO	NF		1 N/10	47°35'	52°42'
Hoyt	UNP/LNO	NB	Sunbury	21 G/10	45°35'	66°33'
Hoyt Station	UNP/LNO	NB	Sunbury	21 G/10	45°34'	66°32'
Hozameen Range	MTN/MNT	BC	Yale Division Yale	92 H/2	49°15'	121°00'
Hozier Islands	ISL/ÎLE	NT	Franklin	26 A	64°08'	64°35'
Huallen	UNP/LNO	AB	22-71-9-W6	83 M/3	55°10'	119°17'
Huard	UNP/LNO	QC	Bonaventure	22 A/3	48°08'	65°07'
Huard, Lac	LAKE/LAC	SK	55-11-W3	73 G/12	53°45'	107°37'
Huaskin Lake	LAKE/LAC	BC	Range 1 Coast	92 L/15	50°58'	126°49'
Hub	UNP/LNO	NS	Cape Breton	11 J/4	46°13'	59°57'
Hubalta	UNP/LNO	AB	14-24-29-W4	82 P/4	51°02'	113°57'
Hubbard	VILG/VILG	SK	5-25-10-W2	62 M/3	51°08'	103°22'
Hubbard Glacier	GLAC/GLAC	YT		115 B/6	60°21'	139°23'
Hubbard, Lac	LAKE/LAC	QC	Caniapiscau	23 I/15	54°48'	64°30'
Hubbard, Mount	MTN/MNT	YT		115 B/6	60°19'	139°04'
Hubbard, Pointe	CAPE/CAP	QC	Kativik	24 J/16	58°50'	66°28'
Hubbards	UNP/LNO	NS	Halifax	21 A/9	44°38'	64°04'
Hubbards Point	UNP/LNO	NS	Yarmouth	20 P/13	43°50'	65°59'
Hubbart Point	CAPE/CAP	MB		54 M/7	59°21'	94°40'
Hubbell	UNP/LNO	MB	15-5-9-W	62 G/7	49°25'	98°35'
Hubbs	UNP/LNO	ON	Prince Edward	30 N/14	43°57'	77°25'
Huberdeau	VILG/VILG	QC	Les Laurentides	31 G/15	45°58'	74°38'
Hubert	UNP/LNO	ON	Algoma	41 N/8	47°18'	84°26'
Hubert	UNP/LNO	BC	Range 5 Coast	93 L/10	54°39'	126°59'
Huble	UNP/LNO	BC	Cariboo	93 G/15	53°48'	122°39'
Hubley	UNP/LNO	NS	Halifax	11 D/12	44°40'	63°49'
Hubley Mill Lake Road	UNP/LNO	NS	Halifax	11 D/12	44°41'	63°52'
Hubley Station - see-voir - Hubley	UNP/LNO	NS		11 D/12	44°40'	63°49'
Hubrey	UNP/LNO	ON	Middlesex	40 I/14	42°54'	81°10'
Hub-toul 2A	IR/RI	BC	Rupert	92 L/4	50°06'	127°35'
Huckabones Corners	UNP/LNO	ON	Renfrew	31 F/11	45°42'	77°05'
Huckson Corners	UNP/LNO	ON	Algoma	41 K/9	46°32'	84°19'
Hudson	CITY/VIL1	QC	Vaudreuil-Soulanges	31 G/8	45°27'	74°09'
Hudson	MUN2/AZM2	ON	Timiskaming	31 M/12	47°34'	79°50'
Hudson	UNP/LNO	ON	Kenora	52 K/1	50°05'	92°10'
Hudson Acres	UNP/LNO	QC	Vaudreuil-Soulanges	31 G/8	45°26'	74°09'
Hudson, Baie d' - also-aussi - **Hudson Bay**	BAY/BAIE	NT	Keewatin	MCR130	60°00'	86°00'
Hudson Basin	SEAU/SMER	—		1399A	59°00'	87°00'
Hudson Bay	TOWN/VIL2	SK		63 D/16	52°51'	102°23'
Hudson Bay - also-aussi - **Hudson, Baie d'**	BAY/BAIE	NT	Keewatin	MCR130	60°00'	86°00'
Hudson Bay Mountain	MTN/MNT	BC	Range 5 Coast	93 L/14	54°49'	127°20'
Hudson Bay No. 394	MUN2/AZM2	SK		63 D/16	52°59'	102°13'
Hudson Bay Park	UNP/LNO	SK		73 B/2	52°09'	106°41'
Hudson Channel	SEAU/SMER	—		1399A	62°20'	71°00'
Hudson, Détroit d' - also-aussi - **Hudson Strait**	CHAN/CHEN	NT	Franklin	25 L	62°00'	70°00'
Hudson Island	ISL/ÎLE	NT	Franklin	25 I	62°32'	64°18'
Hudson's Hope	MUN1/AZM1	BC	Peace River	94 A/4	56°00'	122°00'
Hudson Strait - also-aussi - **Hudson, Détroit d'**	CHAN/CHEN	NT	Franklin	25 L	62°00'	70°00'
Hudwin Lake	LAKE/LAC	MB		53 E/4	53°12'	95°41'

NAME NOM	ENTITY ENTITÉ	LOC 1 LIEU 1	LOC 2 LIEU 2	MAP CARTE	POSITION LAT	LONG
Huffman Corners	UNP/LNO	ON	Kent	40 J/8	42°23′	82°03′
Huff's Corners	UNP/LNO	ON	Prince Edward	31 C/3	44°01′	77°18′
Huffs Corners	UNP/LNO	ON	Lambton	40 J/9	42°39′	82°05′
Huff Wharf	UNP/LNO	ON	Lennox and Addington	31 C/3	44°08′	77°03′
Hugel	UNP/LNO	ON	Nipissing	41 I/8	46°30′	80°18′
Huggett	UNP/LNO	AB	18-50-1-W5	83 G/8	53°19′	114°08′
Hughenden	VILG/VILG	AB	8-41-7-W4	73 D/10	52°31′	110°59′
Hughes	UNP/LNO	ON	Hastings	31 F/4	45°06′	77°58′
Hughes	UNP/LNO	MB	35-10-16-W	62 G/13	49°53′	99°33′
Hughes Brook	VILG/VILG	NF		12 A/13	49°00′	57°53′
Hughes Lake	LAKE/LAC	NF		12 H/4	49°04′	57°43′
Hughes Range	MTN/MNT	BC	Kootenay	82 G/11	49°38′	115°28′
Hughes River	RIV/CDE	MB		64 C/16	56°46′	100°01′
Hughson Bay	BAY/BAIE	ON	Manitoulin	41 G/9	45°37′	82°12′
Hughton	UNP/LNO	SK	20-26-14-W3	72 O/4	51°14′	107°55′
Hugonard	UNP/LNO	SK	15-21-12-W2	62 L/13	50°48′	103°35′
Huit Milles, Lac des	LAKE/LAC	QC	La Matapédia	22 B/6	48°28′	67°05′
Hulatt	UNP/LNO	BC	Cariboo	93 G/13	53°58′	123°45′
Hulbert	UNP/LNO	ON	Dundas	31 B/14	44°58′	75°23′
Hulcross	UNP/LNO	BC	Peace River	93 O/9	55°38′	122°07′
Hull	CITY/VIL1	QC	Communauté urbaine de l'Outaouais	31 G/5	45°26′	75°44′
Hull	UNP/LNO	ON	Sudbury	41 I/11	46°34′	81°12′
Hullcar	UNP/LNO	BC	Kamloops Division Yale	82 L/11	50°30′	119°16′
Hullett	MUN2/AZM2	ON	Huron	40 P/11	43°40′	81°25′
Humamilt Lake	LAKE/LAC	BC	Kamloops Division Yale	82 M/6	51°17′	119°06′
Humber	UNP/LNO	ON	Peel	30 M/13	43°54′	79°49′
Humber Arm	BAY/BAIE	NF		12 G/1	49°00′	58°05′
Humber Arm South	TOWN/VIL2	NF		12 G/1	49°01′	58°09′
Humber Bay	UNP/LNO	ON	York	30 M/11	43°38′	79°29′
Humber Bay	BAY/BAIE	ON	York	30 M/11	43°38′	79°27′
Humber Canal	UNP/LNO	NF		12 H/3	49°12′	57°21′
Humber Grove	UNP/LNO	ON	Peel	30 M/13	43°54′	79°48′
Humberlea	UNP/LNO	ON	York	30 M/12	43°43′	79°32′
Humber Park	UNP/LNO	NS	Halifax	11 D/11	44°42′	63°29′
Humber River	RIV/CDE	NF		12 A/13	48°58′	57°54′
Humber River	RIV/CDE	ON	York	30 M/11	43°38′	79°28′
Humberside	UNP/LNO	ON	York	30 M/11	43°39′	79°29′
Humberstone	UNP/LNO	ON	Welland	30 L/14	42°54′	79°15′
Humber Summit	UNP/LNO	ON	York	30 M/13	43°46′	79°34′
Humber Valley	UNP/LNO	ON	York	30 M/12	43°40′	79°32′
Humber Village	UNP/LNO	NF		12 A/13	48°59′	57°46′
Humboldt	TOWN/VIL2	SK		73 A/3	52°12′	105°07′
Humboldt Bay	BAY/BAIE	ON	Thunder Bay	52 H/16	49°58′	88°06′
Humboldt Channel	CHAN/CHEN	NT	Franklin	67 D	69°27′	96°30′
Humboldt No. 370	MUN2/AZM2	SK		73 A/3	52°15′	105°10′
Hume	UNP/LNO	ON	Thunder Bay	52 A/5	48°26′	89°35′
Hume	UNP/LNO	SK	19-8-12-W2	62 E/12	49°40′	103°37′
Hume River	RIV/CDE	NT	Mackenzie	106 I	66°01′	129°09′
Humes Rear	UNP/LNO	NS	Victoria	11 K/2	46°04′	60°57′
Humhampt 6	IR/RI	BC	Kamloops Division Yale	92 I/4	50°10′	121°35′
Humhampt 6A	IR/RI	BC	Kamloops Division Yale	92 I/4	50°10′	121°35′
Hummerston	UNP/LNO	MB	22-13-14-W	62 J/3	50°07′	99°19′
Humphrey	MUN2/AZM2	ON	Parry Sound	31 E/4	45°15′	79°44′
Humphrey	UNP/LNO	NB	Westmorland	21 I/2	46°07′	64°46′
Humphrey	UNP/LNO	ON	Parry Sound	31 E/5	45°17′	79°46′
Humphrey Corner	UNP/LNO	NB	Sunbury	21 I/4	46°11′	65°59′
Humphreys Mills	UNP/LNO	NB	Westmorland	21 I/2	46°06′	64°46′
Humphries Head	CAPE/CAP	NT	Franklin	88 G	75°48′	116°49′
Humpy Lake	LAKE/LAC	NT	Mackenzie	86 A/11	64°40′	113°25′
Humqui, Lac	LAKE/LAC	QC	La Matapédia	22 B/5	48°18′	67°34′
Humqui, Rivière	RIV/CDE	QC	La Matapédia	22 B/6	48°28′	67°26′
Hunaechin Creek	RIV/CDE	BC	New Westminster	92 J/4	50°13′	123°59′
Hunakwa Lake	LAKE/LAC	BC	Kamloops Division Yale	82 M/2	51°10′	118°55′
Hundred Mile Landing	UNP/LNO	YT		105 C/12	60°43′	133°40′
Hungerford	MUN2/AZM2	ON	Hastings	31 C/6	44°26′	77°15′
Hungerford	UNP/LNO	ON	Hastings	31 C/11	44°32′	77°12′
Hungerford Point	CAPE/CAP	ON	Manitoulin	41 H/12	45°31′	81°51′
Hungry Bay	UNP/LNO	QC	Beauharnois-Salaberry	31 G/1	45°13′	74°10′
Hungry Bay	BAY/BAIE	ON	Hastings	31 C/3	44°10′	77°13′
Hungry Creek	RIV/CDE	YT		106 E/11	65°36′	135°28′
Hungry Grove Pond	LAKE/LAC	NF		1 M/14	47°55′	55°06′
Hungry Hill	MTN/MNT	NF		12 A/10	48°42′	56°34′
Hunlen Falls	FALL/CHUT	BC	Range 3 Coast	93 C/5	52°17′	125°46′
Hunta	UNP/LNO	ON	Cochrane	42 H/3	49°06′	81°16′
Hunter Bay	BAY/BAIE	SK		73 P/1	55°10′	104°30′

NAME NOM	ENTITY ENTITÉ	LOC 1 LIEU 1	LOC 2 LIEU 2	MAP CARTE	POSITION	
					LAT	LONG
Hunter, Cape	CAPE/CAP	NT	Franklin	37 H	71°40′	72°30′
Hunter Creek	RIV/CDE	SK		74 I/5	58°19′	105°57′
Hunter Island	ISL/ÎLE	BC	Range 2 Coast	92 M/13	51°57′	128°00′
Hunter Lake	LAKE/LAC	ON	Sudbury	41 I/2	46°08′	80°56′
Hunter Mills	UNP/LNO	QC	Brome-Missisquoi	31 H/2	45°04′	72°52′
Hunter Point	CAPE/CAP	BC	Queen Charlotte	103 F/7	53°15′	132°43′
Hunter River	VILG/VILG	PE	Queens	11 L/6	46°21′	63°21′
Hunter River	UNP/LNO	PE	Queens	11 L/6	46°21′	63°21′
Hunters Corner	UNP/LNO	NB	Carleton	21 J/5	46°26′	67°40′
Hunters Home	UNP/LNO	NB	Queens	21 I/4	46°02′	65°37′
Hunters Mountain	UNP/LNO	NS	Victoria	11 K/2	46°07′	60°52′
Hunter's Point	UNP/LNO	QC	Témiscamingue	31 L/15	47°00′	78°48′
Hunters Point	CAPE/CAP	MB		63 F/2	53°02′	100°56′
Hunters Range	MTN/MNT	BC	Kamloops Division Yale	82 L/15	50°47′	118°47′
Hunterstown	UNP/LNO	QC	Maskinongé	31 I/6	46°27′	73°01′
Huntingdon	CITY/VIL1	QC	Le Haut-Saint-Laurent	31 G/1	45°05′	74°10′
Huntingdon	MUN2/AZM2	ON	Hastings	31 C/6	44°24′	77°28′
Huntingdon	UNP/LNO	BC	New Westminster	92 G/1	49°00′	122°16′
Huntingdon Island	ISL/ÎLE	NF		13 H/15	53°47′	56°55′
Huntingford	UNP/LNO	ON	Oxford	40 P/2	43°12′	80°47′
Hunting Lake	LAKE/LAC	SK	57-16-W3	73 F/16	53°58′	108°16′
Hunting River	RIV/CDE	MB		64 A/8	56°23′	96°08′
Huntington	UNP/LNO	NS	Cape Breton	11 F/16	45°56′	60°18′
Huntington	UNP/LNO	BC	Range 5 Coast	93 L/11	54°42′	127°05′
Huntingville	UNP/LNO	QC	Sherbrooke	21 E/5	45°20′	71°51′
Hunt Island	ISL/ÎLE	ON	Thunder Bay	52 I/2	50°06′	88°39′
Hunt Lake	LAKE/LAC	SK		73 P/7	55°24′	104°41′
Huntley	UNP/LNO	PE	Prince	21 I/16	46°51′	64°05′
Huntley	UNP/LNO	ON	Carleton	31 G/5	45°18′	75°58′
Hunt, Mount	MTN/MNT	YT		105 H/6	61°29′	129°13′
Huntoon	UNP/LNO	SK	12-7-10-W2	62 E/11	49°33′	103°14′
Hunt River	RIV/CDE	NF		13 N/10	55°34′	60°40′
Hunts Inlet	UNP/LNO	BC	Range 5 Coast	103 J/1	54°04′	130°26′
Hunts Landing	UNP/LNO	NS	Queens	20 P/15	43°57′	64°46′
Hunts Point	UNP/LNO	NS	Queens	20 P/15	43°57′	64°47′
Hunts Ponds	LAKE/LAC	NF		2 D/15	48°49′	54°49′
Huntsville	TOWN/VIL2	ON	Muskoka	31 E/6	45°20′	79°13′
Hupel	UNP/LNO	BC	Kamloops Division Yale	82 L/10	50°37′	118°46′
Hurault, Lac	LAKE/LAC	QC	Jamésie	23 L/7	54°15′	70°48′
Hurd, Cape	CAPE/CAP	ON	Bruce	41 H/4	45°13′	81°44′
Hurdman's Bridge	UNP/LNO	ON	Carleton	31 G/5	45°25′	75°40′
Hurds Lake	UNP/LNO	ON	Renfrew	31 F/7	45°24′	76°41′
Hurds Lake	LAKE/LAC	ON	Renfrew	31 F/7	45°24′	76°40′
Hurdville	UNP/LNO	ON	Parry Sound	31 E/5	45°27′	79°55′
Hurdy	UNP/LNO	AB	30-60-14-W5	83 K/1	54°12′	116°06′
Hureauville	UNP/LNO	NS	Richmond	11 F/11	45°38′	61°14′
Hurkett	UNP/LNO	ON	Algoma	52 A/16	48°50′	88°28′
Hurlett	UNP/LNO	NB	York	21 J/2	46°06′	66°43′
Hurley Corner	UNP/LNO	NB	York	21 G/10	45°45′	66°55′
Hurley River	RIV/CDE	BC	Lillooet	92 J/15	50°51′	122°51′
Hurloc Head	CAPE/CAP	NF		2 C/12	48°34′	53°43′
Huron	MUN1/AZM1	ON	Huron	40 P/11	43°40′	81°30′
Huron	MUN2/AZM2	ON	Bruce	41 A/4	44°05′	81°37′
Huron	GEOG/GÉOG	ON		40 P/11	43°40′	81°30′
Hurondale	UNP/LNO	ON	Huron	40 P/6	43°24′	81°28′
Huron Heights	UNP/LNO	ON	Middlesex	40 P/3	43°01′	81°12′
Huron Heights	UNP/LNO	ON	Lambton	40 O/1	43°02′	82°13′
Huronian	UNP/LNO	ON	Thunder Bay	52 B/10	48°43′	90°44′
Huron, Lac	LAKE/LAC	QC	Rimouski-Neigette	22 C/1	48°11′	68°14′
Huron, Lac - also-aussi - **Huron, Lake**	LAKE/LAC	ON		41 G	44°30′	82°15′
Huron, Lake - also-aussi - **Huron, Lac**	LAKE/LAC	ON		41 G	44°30′	82°15′
Huron No. 223	MUN2/AZM2	SK		72 J/16	51°00′	106°15′
Huron Park	UNP/LNO	ON	Huron	40 P/6	43°17′	81°29′
Huron Ridge	UNP/LNO	ON	Bruce	41 A/4	44°11′	81°38′
Hurons, Rivière des	RIV/CDE	QC	La Jacques-Cartier	21 L/14	46°57′	71°23′
Huronville	UNP/LNO	SK	28-12-10-W2	62 L/3	50°01′	103°18′
Hurricane Creek	RIV/CDE	BC	Cassiar	104 N/7	59°16′	132°37′
Hurst Island	ISL/ÎLE	BC	Rupert	92 L/13	50°50′	127°35′
Hurst, Lac	LAKE/LAC	QC	Kativik	23 O/10	55°30′	66°53′
Hurwitz Lake	LAKE/LAC	NT	Keewatin	65 A	60°51′	98°00′
Husavik	UNP/LNO	MB	21-18-4-E	62 I/10	50°34′	97°00′
Huscroft	UNP/LNO	BC	Kootenay	82 F/1	49°01′	116°28′
Huskisson	GEOG/GÉOG	NB	Kent	21 I/11	46°35′	65°30′
Husky Channel	CHAN/CHEN	NT	Mackenzie	107 B/4	68°08′	135°16′
Husky Island	ISL/ÎLE	NT	Keewatin	34 E/7	57°29′	78°37′

NAME NOM	ENTITY ENTITÉ	LOC 1 LIEU 1	LOC 2 LIEU 2	MAP CARTE	POSITION LAT	LONG
Huson Lake	LAKE/LAC	BC	Rupert	92 L/7	50°16′	126°57′
Hussar	VILG/VILG	AB	14-24-20-W4	82 P/2	51°03′	112°41′
Hustalen 1	IR/RI	BC	Kamloops Division Yale	82 L/13	50°58′	119°39′
Hustan Lake - see-voir - Huson Lake	LAKE/LAC	BC		92 L/7	50°16′	126°57′
Hutchins Corners	UNP/LNO	ON	Grenville	31 B/13	44°55′	75°42′
Hutchison	UNP/LNO	BC	Cariboo	93 G/14	53°58′	123°20′
Hutchison Bay	BAY/BAIE	NT	Mackenzie	107 C	69°44′	132°12′
Hutchisons Corners	UNP/LNO	ON	Grey	41 A/7	44°21′	80°34′
Hutch Lake	UNP/LNO	AB	23-112-20-W5	84 K/11	58°45′	117°16′
Hut Point	CAPE/CAP	NT	Keewatin	45 N	63°17′	84°35′
Hutte Sauvage, Lac de la	LAKE/LAC	QC	Kativik	24 A/2	56°10′	64°45′
Hutton	UNP/LNO	AB	6-24-14-W4	72 M/4	51°02′	111°56′
Hutton	UNP/LNO	BC	Cariboo	93 H/13	53°59′	121°37′
Hutton Heights	UNP/LNO	ON	Huron	40 P/14	43°52′	81°20′
Huttonville	UNP/LNO	ON	Peel	30 M/12	43°38′	79°48′
Huxley	UNP/LNO	AB	17-34-23-W4	82 P/14	51°56′	113°14′
Huxley Island	ISL/ÎLE	BC	Queen Charlotte	103 B/6	52°27′	131°22′
Hvitland Peninsula	CAPE/CAP	NT	Franklin	560 D	81°15′	88°00′
Hyannas	UNP/LNO	NS	Inverness	11 K/3	46°05′	61°15′
Hyas	VILG/VILG	SK	5-34-2-W2	62 M/16	51°54′	102°16′
Hyatt's Mills	UNP/LNO	QC	Coaticook	21 E/4	45°12′	71°46′
Hybla	UNP/LNO	ON	Hastings	31 F/4	45°10′	77°51′
Hybord	UNP/LNO	MB	28-48-13-W	63 G/3	53°10′	99°17′
Hyde	UNP/LNO	SK	21-19-7-W2	62 L/10	50°39′	102°54′
Hyde Creek	UNP/LNO	BC	Rupert	92 L/11	50°35′	127°00′
Hyde Inlet	BAY/BAIE	NT	Franklin	48 E	75°02′	80°00′
Hyde Lake	LAKE/LAC	NT	Keewatin	55 D	60°36′	95°17′
Hyde Park	UNP/LNO	ON	Middlesex	40 I/14	42°59′	81°20′
Hyde Park	UNP/LNO	ON	Middlesex	40 I/14	43°00′	81°20′
Hydraulic	UNP/LNO	BC	Cariboo	93 A/12	52°37′	121°42′
Hydraulic Lake	LAKE/LAC	BC	Similkameen Division Yale	82 E/14	49°46′	119°11′
Hydro	UNP/LNO	ON	Nipissing	31 F/13	45°54′	77°53′
Hydro	UNP/LNO	BC	New Westminster	92 G/2	49°10′	122°33′
Hydro Glen	UNP/LNO	ON	Simcoe	31 D/13	44°51′	79°30′
Hydrostone	UNP/LNO	NS	Halifax	11 D/12	44°39′	63°36′
Hyland Post	UNP/LNO	BC	Cassiar	104 H/9	57°39′	128°09′
Hyland Ranch	UNP/LNO	BC	Cassiar	104 J/3	58°10′	131°29′
Hyland River	RIV/CDE	BC/YT		104 P/16	59°52′	128°11′
Hylo	UNP/LNO	AB	4-66-15-W4	83 I/9	54°41′	112°13′
Hymers	UNP/LNO	ON	Thunder Bay	52 A/5	48°18′	89°43′
Hyndford	UNP/LNO	ON	Renfrew	31 F/7	45°29′	76°59′
Hyndman	UNP/LNO	ON	Grenville	31 B/13	44°56′	75°30′
Hyndman Lake	LAKE/LAC	NT	Mackenzie	107 A/4	68°15′	131°10′
Hyperite Point	CAPE/CAP	NT	Franklin	59 E	78°09′	88°53′
Hythe	VILG/VILG	AB	13-73-11-W6	83 M/5	55°20′	119°33′

I

NAME NOM	ENTITY ENTITÉ	LOC 1 LIEU 1	LOC 2 LIEU 2	MAP CARTE	POSITION LAT	LONG
Iakgwas 69	IR/RI	BC	Range 4 Coast	103 H/12	53°40′	129°43′
Iakvas 68	IR/RI	BC	Range 4 Coast	103 H/13	53°52′	129°30′
Iakwulgyiyaps 78	IR/RI	BC	Range 5 Coast	103 I/6	54°15′	129°11′
Ian Calder Lake	LAKE/LAC	NT	Keewatin	66 I	66°28′	97°22′
Ian Lake	LAKE/LAC	BC	Queen Charlotte	103 F/10	53°45′	132°35′
Ibbett Bay	BAY/BAIE	NT	Franklin	88 H	75°50′	115°45′
Iberville	CITY/VIL1	QC	Le Haut-Richelieu	31 H/6	45°18′	73°14′
Iberville-Junction	UNP/LNO	QC	Le Haut-Richelieu	31 H/6	45°19′	73°14′
Ibex River	RIV/CDE	YT		105 D/13	60°50′	135°48′
Ibex Valley	HAM/HAM	YT		105 D/13	60°50′	135°38′
Ibsen	UNP/LNO	SK	28-10-17-W2	72 H/16	49°51′	104°15′
Ibstone	UNP/LNO	SK	35-41-17-W3	73 C/9	52°34′	108°18′
Iceberg Glacier	GLAC/GLAC	NT	Franklin	59 G	79°35′	92°15′
Iceberg Point	CAPE/CAP	NT	Franklin	340 B	80°19′	86°22′
Ice Chest Mountain	MTN/MNT	YT		115 P/12	63°31′	137°35′
Icefield Ranges	MTN/MNT	YT		115 F/2	61°13′	140°35′
Ice Lake	UNP/LNO	ON	Manitoulin	41 G/16	45°54′	82°22′
Ice Lake	LAKE/LAC	ON	Manitoulin	41 G/16	45°53′	82°23′
Icelandic River	RIV/CDE	MB	34-23-4-E	62 P/2	51°02′	96°58′
Icewall Creek	RIV/CDE	BC	Range 1 Coast	92 K/16	50°50′	124°30′
Iconoclast Mountain	MTN/MNT	BC	Kootenay	82 N/5	51°27′	117°45′
Icy Arm	BAY/BAIE	NT	Franklin	37 H	71°42′	75°07′
Icy River	RIV/CDE	NT	Mackenzie	76 C	64°33′	108°30′
Ida	UNP/LNO	ON	Durham	31 D/1	44°13′	78°29′
Ida Bay	BAY/BAIE	NT	Franklin	120 C	81°31′	68°35′
Ida Hill	UNP/LNO	ON	Frontenac	31 C/8	44°22′	76°24′
Idamay	UNP/LNO	AB	22-33-7-W4	72 M/15	51°51′	110°54′

NAME NOM	ENTITY ENTITÉ	LOC 1 LIEU 1	LOC 2 LIEU 2	MAP CARTE	POSITION LAT	LONG
Ida, Mount	MTN/MNT	BC	Kamloops Division Yale	82 L/11	50°38′	119°19′
Iddesleigh	UNP/LNO	AB	34-20-10-W4	72 L/11	50°44′	111°18′
Ideal	UNP/LNO	MB	30-17-2-W	62 I/5	50°29′	97°44′
Ideal Lake	LAKE/LAC	BC	Osoyoos Division Yale	82 L/3	50°01′	119°06′
Idjuniving Island	ISL/ÎLE	NT	Franklin	26 P/15	67°54′	64°45′
Idylwild	UNP/LNO	ON	Waterloo	40 P/8	43°25′	80°21′
Iffley	UNP/LNO	SK	19-46-15-W3	73 C/16	52°59′	108°10′
Igelstrom Lake	LAKE/LAC	ON	Kenora	53 J/4	54°08′	91°47′
Iggiak	UNP/LNO	NF		14 C/5	56°16′	61°40′
Ightkeany 32	IR/RI	BC	Cassiar	103 P/3	55°03′	129°27′
Igissivik	UNP/LNO	QC	Kativik	25 F/4	61°03′	69°38′
Igloolik	HAM/HAM	NT	Franklin	47 D	69°23′	81°48′
Igloo Point	CAPE/CAP	NT	Keewatin	55 K	62°22′	92°06′
Iglosiatik Island	ISL/ÎLE	NF		14 C/3	56°14′	61°08′
Iglosoataliksoak	UNP/LNO	NF		13 N/8	55°16′	60°22′
Iglosuatiliratsuk	UNP/LNO	NF		14 C/13	56°48′	61°41′
Iglusuaktalialuk Island	ISL/ÎLE	NF		14 F/5	57°20′	61°43′
Ignace	MUN2/AZM2	ON	Kenora	52 G/5	49°25′	91°41′
Ignace	UNP/LNO	ON	Kenora	52 G/5	49°25′	91°40′
Ignace, Rivière	RIV/CDE	QC	La Vallée-de-la-Gatineau	31 K/9	46°36′	76°21′
Ignerit Point	CAPE/CAP	NT	Franklin	37 C	69°38′	77°10′
Ihch'Az Uz Ta Tsoh 44	IR/RI	BC	Range 5 Coast	93 K/11	54°35′	125°08′
Ikaluit	UNP/LNO	NT	Franklin	25 N/10	63°44′	68°31′
Ikanyo Island	ISL/ÎLE	NT	Mackenzie	96 J	66°16′	123°18′
Ikinialuk	UNP/LNO	QC	Kativik	34 K/5	58°16′	77°37′
Ikirtuuq, Lac	LAKE/LAC	QC	Kativik	24 E/11	57°37′	71°09′
Ikkudliayuk Fiord	BAY/BAIE	NF		25 A/1	60°07′	64°26′
Ikpik Bay	BAY/BAIE	NT	Franklin	37 C	69°13′	76°10′
Ikpit Bay	BAY/BAIE	NT	Franklin	26 G	65°21′	67°12′
Ikshenigwolk 3	IR/RI	BC	Range 5 Coast	103 I/9	54°45′	128°16′
Iktotat, Rivière	RIV/CDE	QC	Kativik	35 C/13	60°50′	77°31′
Iktuksasuk 7	IR/RI	BC	Barclay	92 C/10	48°42′	124°51′
Ikualavik	UNP/LNO	QC	Kativik	24 K/2	58°01′	68°39′
Ilclo 12	IR/RI	BC	Barclay	92 C/15	48°49′	124°41′
Ilderton	UNP/LNO	ON	Middlesex	40 P/3	43°04′	81°24′
Île-à-Corriveau, L'	UNP/LNO	QC	Les Etchemins	21 L/9	46°31′	70°09′
Île-à-la-Crosse	VILG/VILG	SK		73 O/5	55°27′	107°53′
Ile a la Crosse 192E	IR/RI	SK		73 O/5	55°28′	107°48′
Île-à-la-Crosse, Lac	LAKE/LAC	SK		73 O/12	55°40′	107°45′
Île Anthony (Moresby-Sud), Site du patrimoine mondial de l' - also-aussi - Anthony Island (South Moresby) World Heritage Site	PARK/PARC	BC		103 B/3	52°06′	131°13′
Île au Castor, Lac de l'	LAKE/LAC	QC	Minganie	12 O/10	51°37′	58°53′
Île-aux-Sternes, Réserve écologique de l'	PARK/PARC	QC	Francheville	31 I/7	46°17′	72°38′
Île-Beaubears, Lieu historique national de l' - also-aussi - Beaubears Island National Historic Site	PARK/PARC	NB	Northumberland	21 I/13	46°58′	65°34′
Île-Bonaventure-et-du-Rocher-Percé, Parc de conservation de l'	PARK/PARC	QC	Pabok	22 A/9	48°30′	64°10′
Île-Brion, Réserve écologique de l'	PARK/PARC	QC	Les Îles-de-la-Madeleine	11 N/14	47°48′	61°28′
Île-d'Anticosti, Réserve faunique de l'	PARK/PARC	QC	Minganie	12 E/11	49°30′	63°00′
Île-d'Ellesmere, Réserve de parc national de l' - also-aussi - Ellesmere Island National Park Reserve	PARK/PARC	NT	Franklin	340 E/1	82°13′	72°13′
Île de Sable, Banc de l' - also-aussi - Sable Island Bank	SEAU/SMER	—		8007	43°45′	60°45′
Île-de-Sainte-Hélène, L'	UNP/LNO	QC	Lotbinière	21 L/6	46°27′	71°25′
Ile des Chênes	UNP/LNO	MB	4-9-4-E	62 H/10	49°43′	96°59′
Île d'Orléans, Chenal de l'	CHAN/CHEN	QC	La Côte-de-Beaupré	21 L/14	46°58′	71°00′
Île-du-Prince-Édouard - also-aussi - **Prince Edward Island**	PROV/PROV	PE		MCR77	46°30′	63°00′
Île-du-Prince-Édouard, Parc national de l' - also-aussi - Prince Edward Island National Park	PARK/PARC	PE	Queens	11 L/6	46°26′	63°12′
Île-du-Vieux-Fort, L'	UNP/LNO	QC	Côte-Nord-du-Golfe-Saint-Laurent	12 P/5	51°22′	57°47′
Île-Georges, Lieu historique national de l' - also-aussi - Georges Island National Historic Site	PARK/PARC	NS	Halifax	11 D/12	44°38′	63°34′
Île-Grassy, Lieu historique national de l' - also-aussi - Grassy Island National Historic Site	PARK/PARC	NS	Guysborough	11 F/7	45°20′	60°58′
Île-Juillet, Barrage de l'	MISC/DIV	QC	Vaudreuil-Soulanges	31 G/8	45°18′	74°04′
Île-Maligne, Barrage de l'	MISC/DIV	QC	Lac-Saint-Jean-Est	22 D/12	48°35′	71°38′
Île-Navy, Lieu historique national de l' - also-aussi - Navy Island National Historic Site	PARK/PARC	ON	Welland	30 M/3	43°03′	79°01′
Île-Saint-Éloi, L'	UNP/LNO	QC	Francheville	31 I/8	46°28′	72°15′
Îles-Avelle-Wight-et-Hiam, Réserve écologique des	PARK/PARC	QC	Vaudreuil-Soulanges	31 H/5	45°24′	74°00′
Îles-de-Boucherville, Parc de récréation des	PARK/PARC	QC	Lajemmerais	31 H/11	45°37′	73°29′
Îles-de-la-Baie-Georgienne, Parc national des - also-aussi - Georgian Bay Islands National Park	PARK/PARC	ON	Muskoka	31 D/13	44°53′	79°52′

NAME NOM	ENTITY ENTITÉ	LOC 1 LIEU 1	LOC 2 LIEU 2	MAP CARTE	POSITION LAT	LONG
Îles-du-Saint-Laurent, Parc national des - also-aussi - St. Lawrence Islands National Park	PARK/PARC	ON	Leeds	31 B/5	44°27'	75°52'
Îles, Grand lac des	LAKE/LAC	QC	Matawinie	31 I/12	46°43'	73°30'
Îles, Lac des	LAKE/LAC	QC	Le Granit	21 E/14	45°48'	71°11'
Îles, Lac des	LAKE/LAC	QC	Antoine-Labelle	31 J/5	46°27'	75°32'
Îles, Lac des	LAKE/LAC	ON	Thunder Bay	52 H/4	49°12'	89°37'
Îles, Lac des	LAKE/LAC	SK		73 K/6	54°26'	109°25'
Îles, Les	UNP/LNO	QC	Le Haut-Saint-Maurice	31 P/10	47°42'	72°31'
Île-Verte, L'	UNP/LNO	QC	Côte-Nord-du-Golfe-Saint-Laurent	12 P/6	51°23'	57°12'
Île-Verte, L'	UNP/LNO	QC	Francheville	31 I/9	46°34'	72°11'
Île Verte, Lac de l'	LAKE/LAC	QC	Le Fjord-du-Saguenay	22 E/1	49°10'	70°09'
Ilford	UNP/LNO	MB	81-12-E	54 D/4	56°04'	95°36'
Ilfracombe	UNP/LNO	ON	Muskoka	31 E/6	45°24'	79°23'
Ilikok Island	ISL/ÎLE	NT	Franklin	16 E	65°17'	63°15'
Illecillewaet	UNP/LNO	BC	Kootenay	82 N/4	51°11'	117°45'
Illecillewaet Névé	GLAC/GLAC	BC	Kootenay	82 N/3	51°13'	117°25'
Illerbrun	UNP/LNO	SK	36-11-18-W3	72 F/16	49°56'	108°21'
Illingworth	UNP/LNO	AB	21-13-11-W4	72 L/3	50°07'	111°27'
Illiniatissivik	UNP/LNO	QC	Kativik	24 J/5	58°16'	67°53'
Illualuttalik	UNP/LNO	QC	Kativik	24 G/3	57°10'	67°12'
Illuvertalik Island	ISL/ÎLE	NF		14 L/1	58°08'	62°25'
Illuviniit	UNP/LNO	QC	Kativik	35 F/8	61°28'	76°21'
Illuvinirtalik	UNP/LNO	QC	Kativik	35 F/9	61°31'	76°02'
Ilthpaya 8	IR/RI	BC	Clayoquot	92 F/4	49°07'	125°39'
Iluikoyak Island	ISL/ÎLE	NF		13 N/15	55°54'	61°00'
Imigen Island	ISL/ÎLE	NT	Franklin	26 G	65°58'	66°58'
Imikula Lake	LAKE/LAC	NT	Keewatin	65 I	62°02'	97°40'
Imkusiyan 65	IR/RI	BC	Range 5 Coast	103 I/4	54°11'	129°44'
Imperial	TOWN/VIL2	SK	34-27-25-W2	72 P/6	51°21'	105°26'
Imperial Beach	UNP/LNO	SK	27-24-W2	72 P/6	51°21'	105°15'
Imperial Eagle Channel	CHAN/CHEN	BC	Barclay	92 C/14	48°54'	125°12'
Imperial Mills	UNP/LNO	AB	27-69-12-W4	73 L/13	55°00'	111°44'
Imperial River	RIV/CDE	NT	Mackenzie	96 E	65°14'	127°34'
Imperoyal	UNP/LNO	NS	Halifax	11 D/12	44°38'	63°32'
Improvement District No. 4	MUN2/AZM2	AB		82 H/4	49°05'	113°54'
Improvement District No. 5 - see-voir - Kanaskis Improvement District	MUN2/AZM2	AB		82 J/10	50°42'	114°53'
Improvement District No. 6 - see-voir - Crowsnest Pass	MUN2/AZM2	AB		82 G/9	49°44'	114°18'
Improvement District No. 9	MUN2/AZM2	AB		82 N/9	51°34'	116°04'
Improvement District No. 12	MUN2/AZM2	AB		83 C/13	52°45'	117°54'
Improvement District No. 12 - see-voir - Jasper Improvement District	MUN2/AZM2	AB		83 D/16	52°54'	118°10'
Improvement District No. 124 - see-voir - Lesser Slave River No. 124, Municipal District of	MUN2/AZM2	AB		83 O/1	55°14'	114°20'
Improvement District No. 125 - see-voir - Big Lakes No. 125, Municipal District of	MUN2/AZM2	AB		83 N/8	55°17'	116°00'
Improvement District No. 13	MUN2/AZM2	AB		83 H/10	53°36'	112°53'
Improvement District No. 131 - see-voir - East Peace No. 131, Municipal District of	MUN2/AZM2	AB		84 C/9	56°38'	116°04'
Improvement District No. 14 - see-voir - Yellowhead No. 94, Municipal District of	MUN2/AZM2	AB		83 F/5	53°28'	117°38'
Improvement District No. 143 - see-voir - Wood Buffalo	MUN2/AZM2	AB		84 H/9	57°40'	112°00'
Improvement District No. 15 - see-voir - Woodlands No. 15, Municipal District of	MUN2/AZM2	AB		83 J/6	54°16'	115°24'
Improvement District No. 16 - see-voir - Greenview No. 16, Municipal District of	MUN2/AZM2	AB		83 L/9	54°37'	118°19'
Improvement District No. 17 - see-voir - Opportunity No. 17, Municipal District of	MUN2/AZM2	AB		84 A/4	56°15'	113°48'
Improvement District No. 19 - see-voir - Birch Hills No. 19, Municipal District of	MUN2/AZM2	AB		83 M/9	55°43'	118°05'
Improvement District No. 20 - see-voir - Saddle Hills No. 20, Municipal District of	MUN2/AZM2	AB		83 M/14	55°51'	119°20'
Improvement District No. 21 - see-voir - Clear Hills No. 21, Municipal District of	MUN2/AZM2	AB		84 D/11	56°46'	119°02'
Improvement District No. 22 - see-voir - Northern Lights No. 22, Municipal District of	MUN2/AZM2	AB		84 F/5	57°28'	118°00'
Improvement District No. 23 - see-voir - Mackenzie No. 23, Municipal District of	MUN2/AZM2	AB		84 K/11	58°41'	117°03'
Improvement District No. 24	MUN2/AZM2	AB		84 P/3	59°02'	113°19'
Improvement District No. 25	MUN2/AZM2	AB		83 E/11	53°41'	119°08'
Improvement District No. 40 - see-voir - Pincher Creek No. 9, Municipal District of	MUN2/AZM2	AB		82 G/8	49°28'	114°30'
Improvement District No. 97 - see-voir - Yellowhead No. 94, Municipal District of	MUN2/AZM2	AB		83 F/5	53°28'	117°38'
Inchkeith	UNP/LNO	SK	15-13-4-W2	62 L/1	50°05'	102°28'
Inch Park	UNP/LNO	ON	Wentworth	30 M/4	43°15'	79°52'
Incomappleux River	RIV/CDE	BC	Kootenay	82 K/12	50°45'	117°43'

NAME NOM	ENTITY ENTITÉ	LOC 1 LIEU 1	LOC 2 LIEU 2	MAP CARTE	POSITION	
					LAT	LONG
Indata Lake	LAKE/LAC	BC	Cassiar	93 N/6	55°21′	125°16′
Independent	UNP/LNO	NF		13 H/15	53°51′	56°54′
Indi	UNP/LNO	SK	9-32-4-W3	72 O/10	51°44′	106°31′
Indian	UNP/LNO	ON	Renfrew	31 F/14	45°45′	77°27′
Indian Arm	BAY/BAIE	NF		2 C/5	48°27′	53°33′
Indian Arm	BAY/BAIE	NF		2 E/7	49°19′	54°55′
Indian Arm	BAY/BAIE	BC	New Westminster	92 G/7	49°22′	122°53′
Indian Arm Brook	RIV/CDE	NF		2 E/7	49°17′	54°56′
Indian Arm Pond	LAKE/LAC	NF		2 E/5	49°07′	55°02′
Indian Bay	UNP/LNO	NF		2 F/4	49°02′	53°51′
Indian Bay	UNP/LNO	MB		52 E/11	49°38′	95°12′
Indian Bay	BAY/BAIE	NF		2 F/4	49°01′	53°48′
Indian Bay	BAY/BAIE	NS	Cape Breton	11 K/1	46°14′	60°02′
Indian Bay	BAY/BAIE	ON/MB		52 E/11	49°38′	95°08′
Indian Bay Big Pond	LAKE/LAC	NF		2 E/1	49°04′	54°07′
Indian Bay (Parsons Point)	VILG/VILG	NF		2 F/4	49°03′	53°52′
Indian Bay Pond	LAKE/LAC	NF		2 E/1	49°04′	54°16′
Indian Birch	UNP/LNO	MB	9-41-24-W	63 C/10	52°31′	100°52′
Indian Brook	UNP/LNO	NS	Victoria	11 K/7	46°23′	60°32′
Indian Brook	RIV/CDE	NF		12 H/8	49°29′	56°05′
Indian Brook	RIV/CDE	NS	Victoria	11 K/7	46°22′	60°31′
Indian Brook 14	IR/RI	NS	Hants	11 E/3	45°05′	63°30′
Indian Burying Place	UNP/LNO	NF		2 E/13	49°50′	55°44′
Indian Cabins	UNP/LNO	AB	15-125-18-W5	84 N/14	59°52′	117°02′
Indian Cove	UNP/LNO	NF		2 E/10	49°36′	54°40′
Indian Creek	RIV/CDE	ON	Lanark	31 F/8	45°17′	76°17′
Indian Falls Depot	UNP/LNO	NB	Northumberland	21 O/8	47°23′	66°19′
Indian Gardens 8	IR/RI	MB		62 G/10	49°44′	98°35′
Indian Harbour	UNP/LNO	NF		1 M/8	47°29′	54°12′
Indian Harbour	UNP/LNO	NF		13 H/15	53°48′	57°00′
Indian Harbour	UNP/LNO	NF		13 I/6	54°27′	57°12′
Indian Harbour	UNP/LNO	NF		11 O/9	47°39′	58°25′
Indian Harbour	UNP/LNO	NS	Halifax	11 D/12	44°31′	63°56′
Indian Harbour	BAY/BAIE	NS	Guysborough	11 F/4	45°06′	61°50′
Indian Harbour Lake	UNP/LNO	NS	Guysborough	11 F/4	45°08′	61°53′
Indian Harbour Point	CAPE/CAP	ON	Manitoulin	41 H/5	45°26′	81°48′
Indian Head	TOWN/VIL2	SK	24-18-13-W2	62 L/12	50°32′	103°40′
Indian Head No. 156	MUN2/AZM2	SK		62 L/5	50°30′	103°35′
Indian Head Range	MTN/MNT	NF		12 B/9	48°38′	58°27′
Indian Hill Lake	LAKE/LAC	NT	Mackenzie	75 M/7	63°17′	110°50′
Indian Island	UNP/LNO	NB	Charlotte	21 B/15	44°55′	66°58′
Indian Island	ISL/ÎLE	NF		11 O/10	47°39′	58°30′
Indian Island	ISL/ÎLE	NS	Lunenburg	21 A/1	44°10′	64°24′
Indian Island 28	IR/RI	NB	Kent	21 I/10	46°42′	64°46′
Indian Island 30	IR/RI	BC	Clayoquot	92 F/4	49°07′	125°46′
Indian Lake	LAKE/LAC	NB	Sunbury	21 G/16	45°57′	66°17′
Indian Lake	LAKE/LAC	NB	York	21 J/3	46°12′	67°15′
Indian Lake	LAKE/LAC	ON	Sudbury	41 O/1	47°07′	82°08′
Indian Lake	LAKE/LAC	ON	Kenora	52 G/12	49°34′	91°40′
Indian Lake	LAKE/LAC	ON	Kenora	52 F/13	49°55′	93°32′
Indian Lake	LAKE/LAC	ON	Kenora	52 L/1	50°14′	94°05′
Indian Landing	UNP/LNO	ON	Renfrew	31 F/14	45°55′	77°17′
Indian Mountain	UNP/LNO	NB	Westmorland	21 I/2	46°10′	64°56′
Indian Mountain Lake	LAKE/LAC	NT	Mackenzie	75 M/2	63°08′	111°00′
Indianola Beach	UNP/LNO	ON	York	31 D/3	44°14′	79°28′
Indian Path	UNP/LNO	NS	Lunenburg	21 A/8	44°19′	64°20′
Indian Point	UNP/LNO	NS	Lunenburg	21 A/8	44°27′	64°19′
Indian Point	UNP/LNO	ON	Halton	30 M/5	43°19′	79°49′
Indian Point 1	IR/RI	NB	Northumberland	21 I/13	46°58′	65°48′
Indian Point - Golden Sands	HAM/HAM	SK	20,21-53-18-3	73 F/10	53°35′	108°36′
Indian Pond	UNP/LNO	NF		1 N/6	47°28′	53°05′
Indian Pond	LAKE/LAC	NF		12 H/8	49°28′	56°25′
Indian Ranch	IR/RI	NB	Restigouche	22 B/1	48°04′	66°23′
Indian Reserve	UNP/LNO	ON	Nipissing	31 L/5	46°22′	79°50′
Indian River	UNP/LNO	PE	Prince	11 L/5	46°29′	63°41′
Indian River	UNP/LNO	ON	Peterborough	31 D/8	44°20′	78°09′
Indian River	RIV/CDE	ON	Lanark	31 F/8	45°15′	76°15′
Indian River	RIV/CDE	ON	Renfrew	31 F/14	45°49′	77°07′
Indian River	RIV/CDE	ON	Peterborough	31 D/1	44°14′	78°09′
Indian River	RIV/CDE	BC	New Westminster	92 G/7	49°28′	122°53′
Indian River	RIV/CDE	YT		115 O/13	63°47′	139°44′
Indian River 1	IR/RI	ON	Muskoka	31 E/4	45°07′	79°35′
Indian Springs	UNP/LNO	MB	17-5-11-W	62 G/7	49°23′	98°55′
Indian Tickle	UNP/LNO	NF		13 H/9	53°34′	56°02′
Indiantown	UNP/LNO	NB	Saint John	21 G/8	45°17′	66°05′

NAME / NOM	ENTITY / ENTITÉ	LOC 1 / LIEU 1	LOC 2 / LIEU 2	MAP / CARTE	POSITION LAT	POSITION LONG
Indian Village	UNP/LNO	NB	Carleton	21 J/4	46°07′	67°34′
Indicateur, Lac	LAKE/LAC	QC	Jamésie	22 M/13	51°55′	71°49′
Indigo	UNP/LNO	MB	35-10-14-E	52 E/13	49°53′	95°34′
Indin Lake	LAKE/LAC	NT	Mackenzie	86 B/3	64°15′	115°13′
Indin River	RIV/CDE	NT	Mackenzie	86 B/6	64°17′	115°04′
Indus	UNP/LNO	AB	35-22-28-W4	82 I/13	50°55′	113°47′
Ingalls Head	UNP/LNO	NB	Charlotte	21 B/10	44°40′	66°46′
Ingalls Lake	LAKE/LAC	NT	Mackenzie	75 A	60°15′	104°57′
Ingelow	UNP/LNO	MB	9-12-16-W	62 G/13	49°59′	99°37′
Ingenika Mine	UNP/LNO	BC	Cassiar	94 C/11	56°42′	125°11′
Ingenika Point	IR/RI	BC	Cassiar	94 C/15	56°47′	124°54′
Ingenika River	RIV/CDE	BC	Cassiar	94 C/11	56°45′	125°02′
Ingersoll	TOWN/VIL2	ON	Oxford	40 P/2	43°02′	80°53′
Ingle	UNP/LNO	ON	Lennox and Addington	31 C/6	44°26′	77°02′
Inglefield Mountains	MTN/MNT	NT	Franklin	39 C	77°35′	79°20′
Inglenook	UNP/LNO	SK	33-27-23-W3	72 N/6	51°21′	109°10′
Ingleside	UNP/LNO	NB	Kings	21 G/8	45°20′	66°12′
Ingleside	UNP/LNO	ON	Stormont	31 G/2	45°00′	75°00′
Ingleside Heights	UNP/LNO	NB	Kings	21 G/8	45°20′	66°12′
Inglewood	UNP/LNO	NS	Annapolis	21 A/14	44°51′	65°19′
Inglewood	UNP/LNO	ON	Peel	30 M/13	43°47′	79°56′
Inglis	UNP/LNO	MB	36-22-28-W	62 K/14	50°57′	101°15′
Inglis Bay	BAY/BAIE	NT	Franklin	16 E	65°48′	62°33′
Inglis Bay	BAY/BAIE	NT	Keewatin	57 B	68°35′	93°39′
Inglis Falls	UNP/LNO	ON	Grey	41 A/10	44°32′	80°56′
Inglisville	UNP/LNO	NS	Annapolis	21 A/14	44°51′	65°07′
Ingnit Fiord	BAY/BAIE	NT	Franklin	16 E	65°48′	62°40′
Ingoldsby	UNP/LNO	ON	Haliburton	31 D/15	44°57′	78°37′
Ingolf	UNP/LNO	ON	Kenora	52 E/14	49°48′	95°07′
Ingomar	UNP/LNO	NS	Shelburne	20 P/11	43°34′	65°22′
Ingonish	UNP/LNO	NS	Victoria	11 K/9	46°42′	60°22′
Ingonish Beach	UNP/LNO	NS	Victoria	11 K/9	46°38′	60°25′
Ingonish Centre	UNP/LNO	NS	Victoria	11 K/9	46°40′	60°24′
Ingonish Ferry	UNP/LNO	NS	Victoria	11 K/9	46°38′	60°24′
Ingonish Island	ISL/ÎLE	NS	Victoria	11 K/9	46°41′	60°20′
Ingonish River	RIV/CDE	NS	Victoria	11 K/9	46°38′	60°26′
Ingonish Trough	SEAU/SMER	—		801-A	46°45′	60°15′
Ingornachoix Bay	BAY/BAIE	NF		12 I/11	50°40′	57°21′
Ingraham Bay	BAY/BAIE	BC	Queen Charlotte	103 F/14	53°49′	133°06′
Ingramport	UNP/LNO	NS	Halifax	11 D/12	44°40′	63°57′
Ingray Lake	LAKE/LAC	NT	Mackenzie	86 C/1	64°15′	116°09′
Ingrid, Cape	CAPE/CAP	NT	Franklin	49 E	78°55′	81°45′
Inhabitants Bay	BAY/BAIE	NS	Richmond	11 F/11	45°34′	61°15′
Inhabitants, River	RIV/CDE	NS	Richmond	11 F/11	45°36′	61°13′
Inholmes	UNP/LNO	ON	Parry Sound	31 E/12	45°30′	79°47′
Inkahtsaph 6	IR/RI	BC	Yale Division Yale	92 H/13	50°00′	121°30′
Inkaneep	UNP/LNO	BC	Similkameen Division Yale	82 E/4	49°07′	119°30′
Inkaneep Creek	RIV/CDE	BC	Similkameen Division Yale	82 E/4	49°04′	119°30′
Inkerman	UNP/LNO	NB	Gloucester	21 P/10	47°40′	64°50′
Inkerman	UNP/LNO	ON	Dundas	31 G/3	45°02′	75°24′
Inkerman	GEOG/GÉOG	NB	Gloucester	21 P/10	47°38′	64°55′
Inkerman Ferry	UNP/LNO	NB	Gloucester	21 P/10	47°41′	64°49′
Inkitsaph	UNP/LNO	BC	Yale Division Yale	92 I/4	50°00′	121°31′
Inklin	UNP/LNO	BC	Cassiar	104 K/14	58°55′	133°08′
Inklin River	RIV/CDE	BC	Cassiar	104 K/14	58°54′	133°08′
Inkluckcheen 21B	IR/RI	BC	Kamloops Division Yale	92 I/5	50°17′	121°36′
Inkluckcheen 21	IR/RI	BC	Kamloops Division Yale	92 I/5	50°16′	121°35′
Inklyuhkinatko 2	IR/RI	BC	Kamloops Division Yale	92 I/4	50°11′	121°35′
Inkster	UNP/LNO	SK	34,35-49-15-W2	73 H/8	53°16′	104°06′
Inlailawatash 4	IR/RI	BC	New Westminster	92 G/7	49°28′	122°53′
Inlailawatash 4A	IR/RI	BC	New Westminster	92 G/7	49°29′	122°53′
Inland	UNP/LNO	AB	20-51-15-W4	83 H/8	53°25′	112°11′
Inland Lake	LAKE/LAC	MB	38-16-W	63 B/5	52°17′	99°41′
Inland Lake	LAKE/LAC	BC	New Westminster	92 F/16	49°56′	124°29′
Inlet	UNP/LNO	QC	Papineau	31 G/14	45°47′	75°19′
Inlet Baddeck	UNP/LNO	NS	Victoria	11 K/2	46°05′	60°49′
Inman	UNP/LNO	NB	Victoria	21 J/12	46°41′	67°43′
Inman River	RIV/CDE	NT	Mackenzie	87 C/3	69°08′	118°27′
Inner Basin	BAY/BAIE	BC	Nootka	92 E/15	49°48′	126°47′
Inner Bay	BAY/BAIE	ON	Norfolk	40 I/9	42°37′	80°24′
Inner Browne Bay	BAY/BAIE	NT	Franklin	68 A	72°58′	98°20′
Inner Gooseberry Islands	ISL/ÎLE	NF		2 C/13	48°53′	53°38′
Innerkip	UNP/LNO	ON	Oxford	40 P/2	43°13′	80°42′
Inner Pond	LAKE/LAC	NF		12 I/3	50°09′	57°25′
Innes	UNP/LNO	SK	31-7-10-W2	62 E/11	49°36′	103°21′

NAME NOM	ENTITY ENTITÉ	LOC 1 LIEU 1	LOC 2 LIEU 2	MAP CARTE	POSITION LAT	LONG
Innes Island	ISL/ÎLE	ON	Algoma	41 J/1	46°04′	82°21′
Innes Point	CAPE/CAP	NT	Franklin	58 F	74°48′	92°04′
Innetalling Island	ISL/ÎLE	NT	Keewatin	33 M/14	55°56′	79°00′
Innisfail	TOWN/VIL2	AB	21-35-28-W4	83 A/4	52°02′	113°57′
Innisfil	TOWN/VIL2	ON	Simcoe	31 D/5	44°18′	79°39′
Innisfil Heights	UNP/LNO	ON	Simcoe	31 D/5	44°17′	79°40′
Innisfil Park	UNP/LNO	ON	Simcoe	31 D/5	44°19′	79°32′
Innisfree	VILG/VILG	AB	3-51-11-W4	73 E/5	53°22′	111°32′
Innisville	UNP/LNO	ON	Lanark	31 F/1	45°03′	76°15′
Innuksuac, Rivière	RIV/CDE	QC	Kativik	34 L/8	58°27′	78°06′
Inonoaklin Creek	RIV/CDE	BC	Kootenay	82 E/16	49°47′	118°08′
Insinger	VILG/VILG	SK	21-29-8-W2	62 M/11	51°32′	103°05′
Insinger No. 275	MUN2/AZM2	SK		62 M/6	51°30′	103°00′
Instow	UNP/LNO	SK	8-9-17-W2	72 F/9	49°43′	108°17′
Insula Lake	LAKE/LAC	NT	Mackenzie	75 B	60°32′	106°46′
Intata Reach	RIVF/EFLV	BC	Range 4 Coast	93 F/11	53°34′	125°30′
Interior Plateau	PLN/PLNE	BC	Cariboo	93 B/3	52°00′	123°00′
International Bridge - see-voir - Fort Erie	VILG/VILG	ON		30 L/15	42°54′	78°56′
International Peace Garden	PARK/PARC	MB	2,3,4,9,10,11-1-20-W1	62 F/1	49°01′	100°04′
Intervale	UNP/LNO	NB	Westmorland	21 H/14	45°58′	65°12′
Intola	UNP/LNO	ON	Thunder Bay	52 A/6	48°30′	89°24′
Intrepid Bay	BAY/BAIE	NT	Franklin	68 E	74°58′	96°08′
Intrepid Inlet	BAY/BAIE	NT	Franklin	89 B	76°38′	118°05′
Inugsuin Fiord	BAY/BAIE	NT	Franklin	27 C	69°54′	69°15′
Inukjuak	VILG/VILG	QC	Kativik	34 L/8	58°27′	78°06′
Inuksuapik	UNP/LNO	QC	Kativik	25 F/3	61°00′	69°28′
Inuksulik	UNP/LNO	QC	Kativik	25 F/4	61°02′	69°39′
Inuktorfik Lake	LAKE/LAC	NT	Franklin	47 H	71°07′	80°00′
Inungnait Hills	MTN/MNT	NT	Franklin	47 G	71°57′	85°30′
Inussuit Tunirtait	UNP/LNO	QC	Kativik	24 N/13	59°56′	69°40′
Inutsualuit	UNP/LNO	QC	Kativik	35 F/12	61°36′	77°41′
Inutsulialuk	UNP/LNO	QC	Kativik	34 K/13	58°55′	77°54′
Inuvik	TOWN/VIL2	NT	Mackenzie	107 B/7	68°21′	133°43′
Inverarden House National Historic Site - also-aussi - Maison-Inverarden, Lieu historique national de la	PARK/PARC	ON	Stormont	31 G/2	45°02′	74°40′
Inverary	UNP/LNO	ON	Frontenac	31 C/8	44°23′	76°28′
Invererie Heights	UNP/LNO	ON	Elgin	40 I/11	42°40′	81°14′
Invergordon No. 430	MUN2/AZM2	SK		73 A/14	52°50′	105°15′
Inverhaugh	UNP/LNO	ON	Wellington	40 P/9	43°38′	80°26′
Inverhuron	UNP/LNO	ON	Bruce	41 A/5	44°17′	81°35′
Inverlake	UNP/LNO	AB	13-24-27-W4	82 P/4	51°03′	113°38′
Invermay	VILG/VILG	SK	1-33-9-W2	62 M/14	51°48′	103°09′
Invermay	UNP/LNO	ON	Bruce	41 A/6	44°28′	81°09′
Invermay No. 305	MUN2/AZM2	SK		62 M/11	51°45′	103°05′
Invermere	MUN1/AZM1	BC	Kootenay	82 K/9	50°31′	116°02′
Inverness	TOWN/VIL2	QC	L'Érable	21 L/5	46°16′	71°31′
Inverness	VILG/VILG	QC	L'Érable	21 L/5	46°16′	71°31′
Inverness	MUN1/AZM1	NS	Inverness	11 K/6	46°20′	61°05′
Inverness	UNP/LNO	PE	Prince	21 I/9	46°39′	64°02′
Inverness	UNP/LNO	NS	Inverness	11 K/3	46°14′	61°18′
Inverness	GEOG/GÉOG	NS		11 K/6	46°20′	61°05′
Inverness Lodge	UNP/LNO	ON	Muskoka	31 E/3	45°11′	79°29′
Inverside	UNP/LNO	NS	Inverness	11 K/3	46°14′	61°17′
Investigator Island	ISL/ÎLE	NT	Franklin	87 E	70°34′	115°54′
Investigator Point	CAPE/CAP	NT	Franklin	88 F/4	74°13′	119°04′
Invincible Point	CAPE/CAP	NT	Franklin	79 B	76°16′	108°02′
Inwood	UNP/LNO	ON	Lambton	40 I/13	42°49′	81°59′
Inwood	UNP/LNO	MB	2-18-1-W	62 I/11	50°30′	97°30′
Inzana Lake	LAKE/LAC	BC	Range 5 Coast	93 K/15	54°57′	124°36′
Inzana Lake 12	IR/RI	BC	Range 5 Coast	93 K/15	54°59′	124°42′
Ioco	UNP/LNO	BC	New Westminster	92 G/7	49°18′	122°52′
Iona	UNP/LNO	NF		1 N/5	47°26′	53°59′
Iona	UNP/LNO	PE	Queens	11 L/2	46°06′	62°48′
Iona	UNP/LNO	NS	Victoria	11 F/15	45°58′	60°48′
Iona	UNP/LNO	ON	Elgin	40 I/11	42°41′	81°24′
Iona Islands	ISL/ÎLE	NF		1 N/5	47°24′	53°57′
Iona Rear	UNP/LNO	NS	Cape Breton	11 F/15	45°58′	60°51′
Iona Station	UNP/LNO	ON	Elgin	40 I/11	42°43′	81°25′
Ionview	UNP/LNO	ON	York	30 M/11	43°44′	79°16′
Iosegun Lake	LAKE/LAC	AB	63-19,20-W5	83 K/7	54°29′	116°52′
Iosegun River	RIV/CDE	AB	66-21-W5	83 K/11	54°44′	117°11′
Ipiatik River	RIV/CDE	AB	71-7-W4	73 M/3	55°07′	111°03′
Ipiutaq	UNP/LNO	QC	Kativik	25 C/13	60°51′	69°52′
Ipperwash Beach	UNP/LNO	ON	Lambton	40 P/4	43°13′	81°58′
Ippialuit	UNP/LNO	QC	Kativik	35 G/15	61°47′	74°46′
Ippikallak	UNP/LNO	QC	Kativik	24 N/12	59°31′	69°57′

NAME NOM	ENTITY ENTITÉ	LOC 1 LIEU 1	LOC 2 LIEU 2	MAP CARTE	POSITION LAT	LONG
Ipswich	UNP/LNO	MB	5-17-22-W	62 K/8	50°25′	100°29′
Iqaluit	TOWN/VIL2	NT	Franklin	25 N/10	63°45′	68°31′
Iqiattavik	UNP/LNO	QC	Kativik	35 F/16	61°45′	76°23′
Iracard	UNP/LNO	BC	Peace River	93 P/16	55°45′	120°10′
Irby and Mangles Bay	BAY/BAIE	NT	Keewatin	56 M	67°32′	95°20′
Ireland	UNP/LNO	NS	Antigonish	11 E/8	45°27′	62°05′
Ireland	UNP/LNO	ON	Renfrew	31 F/4	45°10′	77°32′
Ireland Creek	RIV/CDE	BC	Osoyoos Division Yale	82 L/7	50°23′	118°47′
Ireland's Eye	UNP/LNO	NF		2 C/3	48°13′	53°30′
Irena	UNP/LNO	ON	Dundas	31 B/14	44°53′	75°19′
Irene Bay	BAY/BAIE	NT	Franklin	49 E	79°00′	81°47′
Irénée-Marie, Réserve écologique	PARK/PARC	QC	Mékinac	31 I/14	46°54′	73°19′
Irène-Fournier, Réserve écologique	PARK/PARC	QC	Matane	22 B/9	48°39′	66°14′
Ireton	UNP/LNO	AB	30-49-25-W4	83 H/5	53°16′	113°39′
Irik Island	ISL/ÎLE	NT	Keewatin	55 K	62°10′	92°30′
Iris	UNP/LNO	PE	Kings	11 L/2	46°01′	62°42′
Irish Cove	UNP/LNO	NS	Cape Breton	11 F/15	45°49′	60°40′
Irish Lake	UNP/LNO	ON	Grey	41 A/7	44°15′	80°38′
Irish Lake	LAKE/LAC	ON	Leeds	31 B/12	44°45′	75°58′
Irish River	RIV/CDE	NB	Saint John	21 H/5	45°21′	65°32′
Irish Settlement	UNP/LNO	NB	Kings	21 H/13	45°46′	65°44′
Irish Settlement	UNP/LNO	NB	Carleton	21 J/4	46°08′	67°45′
Irishtown	UNP/LNO	NF		1 N/7	47°19′	52°49′
Irishtown	UNP/LNO	NF		12 A/13	48°59′	57°59′
Irishtown	UNP/LNO	PE	Queens	11 L/12	46°30′	63°35′
Irishtown	UNP/LNO	NB	Westmorland	21 I/2	46°11′	64°48′
Irishtown Road	UNP/LNO	NS	Cumberland	11 E/13	45°51′	63°38′
Irishtown-Summerside	TOWN/VIL2	NF		12 A/13	48°59′	57°59′
Irish Vale	UNP/LNO	NS	Cape Breton	11 F/15	45°51′	60°39′
Irlande	VILG/VILG	QC	L'Amiante	21 L/3	46°04′	71°29′
Irlande	UNP/LNO	QC	Pabok	22 A/9	48°30′	64°15′
Irma	VILG/VILG	AB	27-45-9-W4	73 D/14	52°55′	111°14′
Iron Bay	UNP/LNO	BC	New Westminster	92 G/7	49°27′	122°52′
Iron Bound Cove	UNP/LNO	NB	Queens	21 I/4	46°09′	65°58′
Ironbound Islands	ISL/ÎLE	NF		13 O/2	55°10′	58°46′
Iron Bridge	VILG/VILG	ON	Algoma	41 J/6	46°17′	83°14′
Iron Creek	RIV/CDE	AB	22-43-9-W4	73 D/11	52°43′	111°14′
Irondale	UNP/LNO	ON	Haliburton	31 D/15	44°52′	78°31′
Iron Gate	UNP/LNO	QC	Pontiac	31 F/9	45°42′	76°28′
Iron Hill	UNP/LNO	QC	Brome-Missisquoi	31 H/7	45°15′	72°38′
Iron Island	ISL/ÎLE	ON	Nipissing	31 L/5	46°16′	79°53′
Iron Mines	UNP/LNO	NS	Inverness	11 F/14	45°56′	61°09′
Iron Mountain	MTN/MNT	BC	Kamloops Division Yale	92 I/2	50°03′	120°45′
Iron Rapids	RAP/RAP	BC	Lillooet	92 O/16	51°52′	122°24′
Iron River	UNP/LNO	AB	18-63-6-W4	73 L/7	54°27′	110°55′
Iron Rock	UNP/LNO	NS	Pictou	11 E/7	45°24′	62°32′
Irons Creek	RIV/CDE	BC/YT		94 M/13	59°59′	127°50′
Ironside	UNP/LNO	QC	Communauté urbaine de l'Outaouais	31 G/5	45°28′	75°44′
Ironsides	UNP/LNO	ON	Haliburton	31 E/1	45°04′	78°11′
Iron Springs	UNP/LNO	AB	21-11-20-W4	82 H/15	49°56′	112°41′
Ironville	UNP/LNO	NS	Cape Breton	11 K/1	46°08′	60°27′
Ironwood Lake	LAKE/LAC	AB	65-10,11-W4	73 L/12	54°36′	111°31′
Iroquois	VILG/VILG	ON	Dundas	31 B/14	44°51′	75°19′
Iroquois	UNP/LNO	NB	Madawaska	21 N/8	47°22′	68°16′
Iroquois Falls	TOWN/VIL2	ON	Cochrane	42 A/15	48°46′	80°41′
Iroquois Lake - see-voir - Pelican Cove	HAM/HAM	SK		73 G/3	53°10′	107°03′
Iroquois Lake	LAKE/LAC	SK	48-7,8-W3	73 G/3	53°10′	107°01′
Iroquois, Pointe	CAPE/CAP	QC	Kamouraska	21 M/8	47°28′	70°02′
Iroquois River	RIV/CDE	NT	Mackenzie	107 A	68°05′	129°26′
Irqatarvik	UNP/LNO	QC	Kativik	33 N/11	55°42′	77°08′
Irricana	VILG/VILG	AB	21-27-26-W4	82 P/5	51°19′	113°37′
Irvine	UNP/LNO	AB	31-11-2-W4	72 E/16	49°57′	110°16′
Irvine	UNP/LNO	NF		1 N/10	47°32′	52°52′
Irvine	UNP/LNO	BC	Kamloops Division Yale	82 M/12	51°39′	119°41′
Irvine Inlet	BAY/BAIE	NT	Franklin	26 G	65°37′	67°42′
Irvines Landing	UNP/LNO	BC	New Westminster	92 F/9	49°38′	124°03′
Irving Bay	BAY/BAIE	NT	Franklin	25 M	63°06′	70°52′
Irving Islands	ISL/ÎLE	NT	Franklin	67 A	68°48′	98°45′
Irving Lake	LAKE/LAC	BC	Clayoquot	92 E/9	49°36′	126°20′
Irving, Mount	MTN/MNT	BC	Cassiar	94 L/3	58°07′	127°06′
Irvington	UNP/LNO	SK	17-46-17-W2	73 A/16	52°58′	104°25′
Isaac Creek	UNP/LNO	YT		115 J/15	62°50′	138°30′
Isaac (Gale Lake) 8	IR/RI	BC	Range 4 Coast	93 E/16	53°59′	126°15′
Isaac Lake	LAKE/LAC	ON	Bruce	41 A/14	44°47′	81°14′
Isaac Lake	LAKE/LAC	BC	Cariboo	93 H/2	53°11′	120°55′

NAME NOM	ENTITY ENTITÉ	LOC 1 LIEU 1	LOC 2 LIEU 2	MAP CARTE	POSITION LAT	POSITION LONG
Isaacs Glen	UNP/LNO	ON	Victoria	31 D/10	44°32'	78°47'
Isaacs Harbour	UNP/LNO	NS	Guysborough	11 F/4	45°11'	61°40'
Isaacs Harbour North	UNP/LNO	NS	Guysborough	11 F/4	45°12'	61°40'
Isabella	UNP/LNO	MB	9-15-25-W	62 K/7	50°16'	100°52'
Isabella Bay	BAY/BAIE	NT	Franklin	27 D	69°37'	67°33'
Isabella, Cape	CAPE/CAP	NT	Franklin	39 E	78°20'	75°00'
Isachsen	UNP/LNO	NT	Franklin	69 F	78°47'	103°30'
Isachsen, Cape	CAPE/CAP	NT	Franklin	79 H	79°20'	105°28'
Isachsen Peninsula	CAPE/CAP	NT	Franklin	79 H	79°10'	104°45'
Isachsen Point	CAPE/CAP	NT	Franklin	77 H/1	71°11'	104°24'
Isadore Harry 12	IR/RI	BC	Lillooet	92 O/16	51°48'	122°04'
Isaiah Corner	UNP/LNO	NB	Albert	21 H/15	45°54'	64°43'
Isbester	UNP/LNO	ON	Algoma	41 J/5	46°25'	83°59'
Isbister River	RIV/CDE	MB		53 E/10	53°42'	94°52'
Isbjorn Strait	CHAN/CHEN	NT	Franklin	37 H	71°38'	73°09'
Ischimaw	UNP/LNO	QC	Jamésie	33 L/16	54°59'	78°19'
Ischimesh Epimishihk	UNP/LNO	QC	Jamésie	32 M/12	51°35'	79°30'
Isham	UNP/LNO	SK	26-24-19-W3	72 N/2	51°05'	108°34'
Ishkheenickh River	RIV/CDE	BC	Range 5 Coast	103 I/13	54°59'	129°38'
Ishkseenickh 33	IR/RI	BC	Range 5 Coast	103 I/13	54°59'	129°37'
Ishkseenickh River 34	IR/RI	BC	Range 5 Coast	103 I/13	54°57'	129°35'
Ishkseenickh River 35	IR/RI	BC	Range 5 Coast	103 I/13	54°54'	129°34'
Ishkseenickh River 36	IR/RI	BC	Range 5 Coast	103 I/13	54°52'	129°34'
Ishkseenickh River 37	IR/RI	BC	Range 5 Coast	103 I/13	54°50'	129°33'
Ishpatina Ridge	MTN/MNT	ON	Timiskaming	41 P/7	47°19'	80°44'
Ishpiming Beach	UNP/LNO	ON	Simcoe	41 A/9	44°45'	80°06'
Isidore, Lac	LAKE/LAC	QC	La Haute-Côte-Nord	22 F/4	49°11'	69°42'
Isidore's Ranch 4	IR/RI	BC	Kootenay	82 G/12	49°33'	115°37'
Isinglass Lake	LAKE/LAC	ON	Kenora	52 F/5	49°21'	93°41'
Isintok Creek	RIV/CDE	BC	Osoyoos Division Yale	82 E/12	49°39'	119°52'
Isis	UNP/LNO	ON	Thunder Bay	42 E/15	49°52'	86°36'
Iskoyaskweyau Point	CAPE/CAP	ON	Cochrane	32 M/5	51°25'	79°41'
Iskut	UNP/LNO	BC	Cassiar	104 H/13	57°50'	129°59'
Iskut 6	IR/RI	BC	Cassiar	104 G/16	57°50'	130°00'
Iskut River	RIV/CDE	BC	Cassiar	104 B/13	56°45'	131°47'
Iskwao Creek	RIV/CDE	SK	24-22-1-W3	72 J/16	50°53'	106°01'
Iskwatam Lake	LAKE/LAC	SK		63 M/11	55°34'	103°04'
Iskwatikan Lake	LAKE/LAC	SK		73 P/8	55°22'	104°24'
Iskwatimich Aysinakuch	UNP/LNO	QC	Kativik	33 N/2	55°08'	76°58'
Island 14A	IR/RI	BC	Range 3 Coast	103 A/1	52°09'	128°07'
Island Beach	UNP/LNO	MB	16,21-17-7-E	62 I/7	50°28'	96°34'
Island Brook	UNP/LNO	QC	Le Haut-Saint-François	21 E/6	45°23'	71°29'
Island Cache	UNP/LNO	BC	Cariboo	93 G/15	53°55'	122°44'
Island, Chute	FALL/CHUT	QC	Jamésie	33 C/4	52°11'	77°48'
Island Cove	UNP/LNO	NF		2 C/4	48°00'	53°46'
Island East River	UNP/LNO	NS	Pictou	11 E/7	45°28'	62°40'
Island Falls	UNP/LNO	ON	Cochrane	42 H/11	49°35'	81°23'
Island Falls	UNP/LNO	SK		63 M/9	55°32'	102°21'
Island Grove	UNP/LNO	ON	York	31 D/6	44°18'	79°28'
Island Harbour	UNP/LNO	NF		2 E/9	49°37'	54°19'
Island Harbour	UNP/LNO	NF		13 H/15	53°45'	56°47'
Island Lake	VILG/VILG	AB	35-67-24-W4	83 I/13	54°51'	113°33'
Island Lake	UNP/LNO	ON	Sudbury	41 O/12	47°42'	83°34'
Island Lake	UNP/LNO	ON	Algoma	41 K/9	46°40'	84°16'
Island Lake	UNP/LNO	MB		53 E/15	53°52'	94°40'
Island Lake	LAKE/LAC	NB	Northumberland	21 P/5	47°16'	66°00'
Island Lake	LAKE/LAC	NB	Victoria	21 J/15	46°59'	66°50'
Island Lake	LAKE/LAC	ON	Parry Sound	41 H/16	45°48'	80°04'
Island Lake	LAKE/LAC	ON	Thunder Bay	52 B/7	48°23'	90°57'
Island Lake	LAKE/LAC	ON	Kenora	52 E/16	49°48'	94°20'
Island Lake	LAKE/LAC	MB		53 E/16	53°47'	94°25'
Island Lake	LAKE/LAC	NT	Mackenzie	75 P	63°21'	105°39'
Island Lake 22	IR/RI	MB		53 E/15	53°51'	94°56'
Island Lake 22A	IR/RI	MB		53 E/15	53°52'	94°38'
Island Lakes	UNP/LNO	MB		62 H/14	49°50'	97°04'
Island Lake South	VILG/VILG	AB	24-67-24-W4	83 I/13	54°50'	113°32'
Island Point	UNP/LNO	NS	Victoria	11 K/2	46°07'	60°34'
Island Point	CAPE/CAP	NF		2 E/12	49°36'	55°48'
Island Pond	LAKE/LAC	NF		2 D/1	48°06'	54°17'
Island Pond	LAKE/LAC	NF		2 E/8	49°19'	54°18'
Island Pond	LAKE/LAC	NF		2 D/7	48°27'	54°39'
Island Pond	LAKE/LAC	NF		2 E/2	49°03'	54°58'
Island Pond	LAKE/LAC	NF		2 D/13	48°54'	55°36'
Island Pond	LAKE/LAC	NF		12 A/8	48°25'	56°23'
Island Pond	LAKE/LAC	NF		12 A/12	48°32'	57°50'

NAME NOM	ENTITY ENTITÉ	LOC 1 LIEU 1	LOC 2 LIEU 2	MAP CARTE	POSITION LAT	LONG
Island Pond West	LAKE/LAC	NF		2 D/2	48°09'	54°32'
Island River	RIV/CDE	NT	Mackenzie	95 A	60°26'	121°14'
Islands, Bay of	BAY/BAIE	NF		12 G/1	49°10'	58°14'
Islands, Bay of	BAY/BAIE	NF		13 O/4	55°09'	59°49'
Islands, Bay of	BAY/BAIE	ON	Manitoulin	41 I/4	46°05'	81°49'
Islands in the Trent Waters 36A	IR/RI	ON	Peterborough	31 D/8	44°30'	78°15'
Island View	VILG/VILG	SK	21-23-23-W2	72 I/14	50°58'	105°10'
Island View	UNP/LNO	NS	Cape Breton	11 F/15	45°59'	60°33'
Island View	UNP/LNO	NB	York	21 G/15	45°58'	66°48'
Island View Beach	UNP/LNO	ON	York	31 D/6	44°20'	79°16'
Island View Heights	UNP/LNO	NB	Saint John	21 G/1	45°14'	66°07'
Islay	UNP/LNO	ON	Victoria	31 D/7	44°28'	78°52'
Islay	UNP/LNO	AB	9-51-4-W4	73 E/7	53°24'	110°33'
Isle aux Morts	TOWN/VIL2	NF		11 O/10	47°35'	58°59'
Isle aux Morts Harbour	BAY/BAIE	NF		11 O/10	47°35'	59°00'
Isle aux Morts River	RIV/CDE	NF		11 O/11	47°35'	59°00'
Isle Lake	LAKE/LAC	AB	53,54-5,6-W5	83 G/10	53°38'	114°44'
Isle of Skye	UNP/LNO	QC	Le Haut-Saint-Laurent	31 G/1	45°03'	74°27'
Isle Pierre	UNP/LNO	BC	Cariboo	93 G/14	53°57'	123°15'
Isle Valen	UNP/LNO	NF		1 M/8	47°29'	54°24'
Islington	UNP/LNO	NF		1 N/14	47°46'	53°29'
Islington	UNP/LNO	ON	York	30 M/12	43°38'	79°33'
Islington 29	IR/RI	ON	Kenora	52 L/2	50°10'	94°58'
Isolillock Peak	MTN/MNT	BC	Yale Division Yale	92 H/6	49°18'	121°29'
Isortoq Fiord	BAY/BAIE	NT	Franklin	37 C	69°55'	77°05'
Isortoq River	RIV/CDE	NT	Franklin	37 C	69°58'	77°00'
Ispas	UNP/LNO	AB	36-56-13-W4	73 E/13	53°53'	111°48'
Ispatinow Island	ISL/ÎLE	SK		74 G/7	57°30'	106°37'
Issoudun	UNP/LNO	QC	Lotbinière	21 L/12	46°35'	71°37'
Isthmus Bay	BAY/BAIE	ON	Bruce	41 A/14	44°59'	81°15'
Istuyakamikw	UNP/LNO	QC	Kativik	33 O/14	55°58'	75°15'
Isurtuq River	RIV/CDE	NT	Franklin	26 K	66°40'	69°54'
Isurtuup Sijjaapingit	UNP/LNO	QC	Kativik	24 N/13	59°48'	69°51'
Italia Lake	LAKE/LAC	BC	Kamloops Division Yale	92 P/16	51°50'	120°23'
Italy Cross	UNP/LNO	NS	Lunenburg	21 A/7	44°16'	64°33'
Itaska Beach	VILG/VILG	AB	21,28-47-1-W5	83 G/1	53°04'	114°05'
Itchen Lake	LAKE/LAC	NT	Mackenzie	86 H	65°33'	112°50'
Ithingo Lake	LAKE/LAC	SK		74 B/13	56°50'	107°32'
Itirbilung Fiord	BAY/BAIE	NT	Franklin	27 C	69°18'	68°40'
Itivirk Bay	BAY/BAIE	NT	Franklin	25 K	62°42'	69°30'
Itomamis, Lac	LAKE/LAC	QC	Caniapiscau	23 C/14	52°54'	69°28'
Itomamo, Lac	LAKE/LAC	QC	Le Fjord-du-Saguenay	22 E/1	49°11'	70°28'
Itsi Range	MTN/MNT	YT		105 J/16	62°55'	130°10'
Ittatsoo 1	IR/RI	BC	Clayoquot	92 C/13	48°56'	125°32'
Ittilliarsuk	UNP/LNO	NF		13 N/1	55°15'	60°04'
Ituna	TOWN/VIL2	SK	21-25-11-W2	62 M/3	51°10'	103°30'
Ituna Bon Accord No. 246	MUN2/AZM2	SK		62 M/5	51°15'	103°30'
Ivan	UNP/LNO	ON	Middlesex	40 P/3	43°01'	81°28'
Ivanhoe	UNP/LNO	NF		2 C/4	48°12'	53°31'
Ivanhoe	UNP/LNO	ON	Hastings	31 C/6	44°24'	77°28'
Ivanhoe Lake	LAKE/LAC	ON	Sudbury	42 B/2	48°06'	82°35'
Ivanhoe Lake	LAKE/LAC	NT	Keewatin	75 B	60°30'	106°25'
Ivanhoe River	RIV/CDE	ON	Cochrane	42 B/9	48°40'	82°11'
Ivanhoe Station	UNP/LNO	ON	Hastings	31 C/6	44°25'	77°27'
Ives	UNP/LNO	QC	Le Haut-Saint-François	21 E/12	45°41'	71°36'
Ivik Island	ISL/ÎLE	NT	Franklin	24 N	59°56'	69°39'
Ivisarak Lake	LAKE/LAC	NT	Franklin	47 F	70°34'	86°17'
Ivry	UNP/LNO	QC	Les Laurentides	31 J/1	46°05'	74°20'
Ivry, Lac	LAKE/LAC	QC	Côte-Nord-du-Golfe-Saint-Laurent	12 O/2	51°10'	58°57'
Ivry-sur-le-Lac	VILG/VILG	QC	Les Laurentides	31 J/1	46°04'	74°22'
Ivujivik	VILG/VILG	QC	Kativik	35 K/5	62°25'	77°55'
Ivvavik National Park - also-aussi - Ivvavik, Parc national	PARK/PARC	YT		117 D/4	69°06'	139°30'
Ivvavik, Parc national - also-aussi - Ivvavik National Park	PARK/PARC	YT		117 D/4	69°06'	139°30'
Ivy	UNP/LNO	ON	Simcoe	31 D/5	44°17'	79°46'
Ivy Lea	UNP/LNO	ON	Leeds	31 C/8	44°22'	76°01'

J

Jaab Lake	LAKE/LAC	ON	Cochrane	42 O/2	51°10'	82°58'
Jacam	UNP/LNO	MB	86-20-E	54 D/8	56°27'	94°23'
Jack, Cape	CAPE/CAP	NS	Antigonish	11 F/12	45°41'	61°34'

NAME NOM	ENTITY ENTITÉ	LOC 1 LIEU 1	LOC 2 LIEU 2	MAP CARTE	POSITION LAT	LONG
Jack Fish	UNP/LNO	ON	Thunder Bay	42 D/15	48°47′	86°58′
Jackfish	UNP/LNO	AB	35-108-6-W4	74 L/7	58°26′	110°54′
Jackfish Bay	BAY/BAIE	ON	Thunder Bay	42 D/15	48°48′	86°59′
Jackfish Channel	CHAN/CHEN	ON	Thunder Bay	42 D/10	48°45′	87°00′
Jackfish Creek	RIV/CDE	AB	1-63-5-W4	73 L/7	54°25′	110°37′
Jackfish Lake	UNP/LNO	SK	18-48-17-W3	73 F/1	53°09′	108°29′
Jackfish Lake	LAKE/LAC	ON	Rainy River	52 C/13	48°56′	93°35′
Jackfish Lake	LAKE/LAC	MB	16,17-10,11-W	62 J/7	50°28′	98°52′
Jackfish Lake	LAKE/LAC	SK	47-17-W3	73 F/1	53°04′	108°24′
Jackfish Point 214	IR/RI	AB	10-123-4-W6	84 M/10	59°42′	118°36′
Jackfish River	UNP/LNO	AB	18-115-17-W4	84 I/15	59°00′	112°52′
Jackfish River	RIV/CDE	AB	116-17-W4	84 P/2	59°04′	112°53′
Jackhead	UNP/LNO	MB	7,18-34-2-E	62 P/14	51°55′	97°19′
Jackhead 43	IR/RI	MB		62 P/14	51°54′	97°18′
Jackhead 43A	IR/RI	MB		62 P/14	51°53′	97°20′
Jackhead Harbour	UNP/LNO	MB	33-2-E	62 P/14	51°52′	97°16′
Jack Ladder	UNP/LNO	NF		12 H/5	49°20′	57°32′
Jack Lake	UNP/LNO	ON	Peterborough	31 D/9	44°43′	78°04′
Jack Lake	UNP/LNO	ON	Simcoe	31 D/5	44°27′	80°00′
Jack Lake	LAKE/LAC	ON	Peterborough	31 D/9	44°42′	78°02′
Jackman	UNP/LNO	BC	Cariboo	83 D/14	52°57′	119°23′
Jackman Canyon	SEAU/SMER	—		8010	43°14′	49°26′
Jackman Sound	CHAN/CHEN	NT	Franklin	25 J	62°20′	66°25′
Jackpine	UNP/LNO	ON	Thunder Bay	52 A/4	48°08′	89°54′
Jackpine River	RIV/CDE	ON	Algoma	42 C/1	48°02′	84°12′
Jackpine River	RIV/CDE	ON	Thunder Bay	42 D/13	48°58′	88°00′
Jackpine River	RIV/CDE	AB	54-10-W6	83 E/11	53°41′	119°25′
Jackpot Creek	RIV/CDE	AB	125-18-W5	84 N/14	59°52′	117°02′
Jackrabbit, Réserve écologique	PARK/PARC	QC	Les Laurentides	31 J/1	46°01′	74°29′
Jack's Island	ISL/ÎLE	NF		2 E/10	49°38′	54°32′
Jacks Lake	LAKE/LAC	NB	Northumberland	21 J/15	46°58′	66°39′
Jackson	UNP/LNO	ON	Grey	41 A/11	44°33′	81°03′
Jackson	UNP/LNO	AB	13-40-27-W4	83 A/5	52°26′	113°46′
Jackson Bay	UNP/LNO	BC	Range 1 Coast	92 K/12	50°31′	125°45′
Jacksonboro	UNP/LNO	ON	Cochrane	42 H/5	49°15′	81°39′
Jacksonburg	UNP/LNO	ON	Norfolk	40 I/10	42°35′	80°38′
Jackson Creek	RIV/CDE	MB/SK		62 F/7	49°18′	100°54′
Jackson Falls	UNP/LNO	NB	Carleton	21 J/4	46°14′	67°45′
Jackson Heights	UNP/LNO	ON	Peterborough	31 D/8	44°19′	78°21′
Jackson Inlet	BAY/BAIE	NT	Franklin	58 D	73°18′	88°47′
Jackson Island	ISL/ÎLE	NT	Franklin	26 A	64°33′	65°10′
Jacksons	UNP/LNO	BC	Cassiar	104 G/12	57°37′	131°41′
Jackson's Arm	VILG/VILG	NF		12 H/15	49°52′	56°47′
Jackson's Cove	UNP/LNO	NF		2 E/12	49°41′	56°00′
Jackson's Cove-Langdon's Cove-Silverdale	UNP/LNO	NF		2 E/12	49°41′	56°00′
Jacksons Point	UNP/LNO	NS	Cumberland	21 H/16	46°00′	64°02′
Jacksons Point	UNP/LNO	ON	York	31 D/6	44°20′	79°22′
Jacksontown	UNP/LNO	NB	Carleton	21 J/5	46°16′	67°38′
Jacksonville	UNP/LNO	NS	Richmond	11 F/10	45°40′	60°52′
Jacksonville	UNP/LNO	NB	Carleton	21 J/4	46°12′	67°37′
Jackville	UNP/LNO	AB	36-29-3-W5	82 O/9	51°32′	114°18′
Jacob Island	ISL/ÎLE	NT	Keewatin	32 M/11	51°45′	79°15′
Jacobs	UNP/LNO	ON	Thunder Bay	52 I/4	50°15′	89°50′
Jacobs Lake	LAKE/LAC	NT	Keewatin	65 H	61°26′	97°01′
Jaco-Hughes	UNP/LNO	QC	Matane	22 B/14	48°56′	67°13′
Jacola	UNP/LNO	QC	Vallée-de-l'Or	32 C/4	48°06′	77°49′
Jacques-Cartier	UNP/LNO	QC	Portneuf	21 L/12	46°40′	71°45′
Jacques-Cartier, Baie de	BAY/BAIE	QC	Côte-Nord-du-Golfe-Saint-Laurent	12 O/8	51°16′	58°16′
Jacques-Cartier, Détroit de	CHAN/CHEN	QC	Minganie	12 L/4	50°00′	63°30′
Jacques-Cartier, Lac	LAKE/LAC	QC	La Côte-de-Beaupré	21 M/11	47°35′	71°13′
Jacques-Cartier, Mont	MTN/MNT	QC	Denis-Riverin	22 A/13	48°59′	65°57′
Jacques-Cartier, Parc de conservation de la	PARK/PARC	QC	La Côte-de-Beaupré	21 M/6	47°20′	71°21′
Jacques-Cartier, Petit lac	LAKE/LAC	QC	La Côte-de-Beaupré	21 M/5	47°24′	71°32′
Jacques-Cartier, Rivière	RIV/CDE	QC	Portneuf	21 L/12	46°40′	71°45′
Jacques Fontaine	UNP/LNO	NF		1 M/10	47°31′	54°56′
Jacques Island	ISL/ÎLE	NF		11 O/9	47°39′	58°20′
Jacques, Lac à	LAKE/LAC	NT	Mackenzie	96 L	66°10′	127°24′
Jacques Range	MTN/MNT	NT	Mackenzie	96 E/16	65°58′	126°50′
Jacques-Rousseau, Mont	MTN/MNT	QC	Kativik	24 P/7	59°17′	64°34′
Jacquet River	UNP/LNO	NB	Restigouche	21 P/13	47°55′	66°00′
Jacquet River	RIV/CDE	NB	Restigouche	21 O/16	47°55′	66°01′
Jade City	UNP/LNO	BC	Cassiar	104 P/5	59°16′	129°38′
Jadel Lake	LAKE/LAC	MB/ON		52 L/3	50°03′	95°08′
Jaffa	UNP/LNO	ON	Elgin	40 I/11	42°44′	81°02′
Jaffray	UNP/LNO	BC	Kootenay	82 G/6	49°23′	115°18′

NAME NOM	ENTITY ENTITÉ	LOC 1 LIEU 1	LOC 2 LIEU 2	MAP CARTE	POSITION LAT	LONG
Jaffray and Melick - see-voir - Jaffray Melick	TOWN/VIL2	ON		52 E/16	49°50′	94°25′
Jaffray Melick	TOWN/VIL2	ON	Kenora	52 E/16	49°50′	94°25′
Jailletville	UNP/LNO	NB	Kent	21 I/6	46°25′	65°02′
Jakeman Glacier	GLAC/GLAC	NT	Franklin	49 A	76°29′	80°41′
Jakes Corner	UNP/LNO	YT		105 C/5	60°20′	133°58′
Jakes Landing	UNP/LNO	NS	Annapolis	21 A/6	44°24′	65°13′
Jalbert	UNP/LNO	NB	Madawaska	21 N/8	47°24′	68°15′
Jaleslie	UNP/LNO	BC	Kamloops Division Yale	92 I/15	50°47′	120°43′
Jalna	UNP/LNO	AB	55,56-7,8-W5	83 G/14	53°48′	115°02′
Jalobert, Baie	BAY/BAIE	QC	Minganie	12 L/8	50°16′	62°25′
Jalobert, Lac	LAKE/LAC	QC	Le Fjord-du-Saguenay	22 D/10	48°39′	70°35′
Jalun 14	IR/RI	BC	Queen Charlotte	103 K/2	54°08′	132°48′
Jambon, Pointe	CAPE/CAP	QC	Sept-Rivières	22 G/15	49°55′	66°58′
Jambons, Pointe aux	CAPE/CAP	QC	Sept-Rivières	22 J/2	50°02′	66°44′
James	MUN2/AZM2	ON	Timiskaming	41 P/9	47°40′	80°20′
James	UNP/LNO	ON	Thunder Bay	52 B/16	48°56′	90°05′
James Anderson, Cape	CAPE/CAP	NT	Keewatin	47 B	68°12′	87°55′
James, Baie - also-aussi - **James Bay**	BAY/BAIE	NT	Keewatin	43 H	53°30′	80°30′
James Bay	UNP/LNO	BC	Victoria	92 B/6	48°25′	123°23′
James Bay	BAY/BAIE	ON	Manitoulin	41 H/12	45°42′	81°40′
James Bay - also-aussi - **James, Baie**	BAY/BAIE	NT	Keewatin	43 H	53°30′	80°30′
James,Cape	CAPE/CAP	NT	Franklin	340 A	80°51′	79°28′
James Creek	RIV/CDE	AB	124-18-W5	84 N/15	59°48′	116°57′
James Island	ISL/ÎLE	NF		2 F/12	49°35′	53°47′
James Lake	LAKE/LAC	MB		64 G/4	57°15′	99°46′
James Lake	LAKE/LAC	MB		63 N/6	55°27′	101°28′
James Lake	LAKE/LAC	NT	Mackenzie	85 K	63°00′	116°26′
James-Little, Réserve écologique	PARK/PARC	QC	Pontiac	31 K/4	46°11′	77°37′
James Louie 3A	IR/RI	BC	Cariboo	93 A/4	52°10′	121°57′
Jameson	UNP/LNO	SK	4-17-17-W2	72 I/8	50°24′	104°17′
Jameson Bay	BAY/BAIE	NT	Franklin	89 B	76°30′	116°50′
Jameson Islands	ISL/ÎLE	NT	Franklin	77 B	68°06′	109°57′
Jameson (Ragged Point), Cape	CAPE/CAP	NT	Franklin	38 A	72°05′	74°14′
James River	UNP/LNO	NS	Antigonish	11 E/9	45°34′	62°07′
James River	RIV/CDE	AB	13-34-5-W5	82 O/15	51°54′	114°34′
James River	RIV/CDE	NT	Mackenzie	76 N	67°13′	108°47′
James River Bridge	UNP/LNO	AB	27-34-5-W5	82 O/15	51°56′	114°38′
James Ross Bay	BAY/BAIE	NT	Franklin	120 F	82°50′	64°25′
James Ross, Cape	CAPE/CAP	NT	Franklin	88 E	74°42′	114°25′
James Ross River	RIV/CDE	NT	Franklin	120 F	82°48′	64°40′
James Ross Strait	CHAN/CHEN	NT	Franklin	67 D	69°40′	96°10′
James Settlement	UNP/LNO	NS	Halifax	11 D/15	44°48′	62°43′
James Smith 100	IR/RI	SK		73 H/2	53°07′	104°52′
Jamestown	UNP/LNO	NF		2 C/5	48°26′	53°48′
Jamestown	UNP/LNO	ON	Huron	40 P/14	43°49′	81°12′
Jamesville	UNP/LNO	NS	Victoria	11 F/15	45°57′	60°51′
Jamesville	UNP/LNO	ON	Lanark	31 C/16	44°54′	76°15′
Jamesville West	UNP/LNO	NS	Victoria	11 F/15	45°57′	60°52′
Jamieson Creek	RIV/CDE	BC	Kamloops Division Yale	92 I/16	50°53′	120°16′
Jamot	UNP/LNO	ON	Sudbury	41 I/2	46°06′	80°34′
Jamyn, Lac	LAKE/LAC	QC	Minganie	12 O/9	51°40′	58°02′
Janet	UNP/LNO	AB	5-24-28-W4	82 P/4	51°01′	113°52′
Janet Head	CAPE/CAP	ON	Manitoulin	41 G/16	45°57′	82°29′
Janet Lake	LAKE/LAC	YT		105 M/12	63°41′	135°31′
Janetville	UNP/LNO	ON	Durham	31 D/2	44°13′	78°43′
Janeville	UNP/LNO	NB	Gloucester	21 P/11	47°41′	65°26′
Janeville	UNP/LNO	NB	Gloucester	21 P/11	47°41′	65°27′
Jan Lake	UNP/LNO	SK		63 L/15	54°54′	102°49′
Jan Lake	LAKE/LAC	SK		63 L/15	54°56′	102°55′
Jannière, Lac	LAKE/LAC	QC	Caniapiscau	23 I/16	54°53′	64°00′
J-Anomaly Ridge	SEAU/SMER	—		NK22 B	40°30′	51°00′
Janow Corners	UNP/LNO	SK	7-51-23-W2	73 H/6	53°24′	105°22′
Jans Bay	VILG/VILG	SK	71-14-W3	73 N/1	55°09′	108°08′
Jansen	VILG/VILG	SK	36-32-20-W2	72 P/15	51°47′	104°43′
Jansen Lake	LAKE/LAC	SK		72 P/15	51°54′	104°45′
Janvier 194	IR/RI	AB	16,17-80-5-W4	73 M/15	55°56′	110°44′
Janvrin Harbour	UNP/LNO	NS	Richmond	11 F/11	45°32′	61°10′
Janvrin Island	ISL/ÎLE	NS	Richmond	11 F/11	45°32′	61°10′
Jardin-des-Jésuites, Le	UNP/LNO	QC	La Haute-Côte-Nord	22 C/4	48°08′	69°41′
Jardine Brook	UNP/LNO	NB	Victoria	21 O/5	47°27′	67°30′
Jardine Brook	RIV/CDE	NB	Restigouche	21 O/12	47°36′	67°34′
Jardineville	UNP/LNO	NB	Kent	21 I/10	46°39′	64°51′
Jardins, Lac des	LAKE/LAC	QC	Témiscamingue	31 L/9	46°39′	78°17′
Jardins, Les	UNP/LNO	QC	Charlevoix-Est	21 M/16	47°50′	70°09′
Jarnac	UNP/LNO	QC	Papineau	31 G/14	45°47′	75°14′

NAME NOM	ENTITY ENTITÉ	LOC 1 LIEU 1	LOC 2 LIEU 2	MAP CARTE	POSITION LAT	LONG
Jaroslaw	UNP/LNO	MB	35-21-3-E	62 I/14	50°51′	97°04′
Jarratt	UNP/LNO	ON	Simcoe	31 D/12	44°36′	79°34′
Jarrow	UNP/LNO	AB	4-46-10-W4	73 D/14	52°57′	111°24′
Jarvie	UNP/LNO	AB	15-63-27-W4	83 I/5	54°27′	113°59′
Jarvis	UNP/LNO	ON	Haldimand	40 I/16	42°53′	80°06′
Jarvis Bay	VILG/VILG	AB	4-39-1-W5	83 B/8	52°19′	114°04′
Jarvis Bay Provincial Park	PARK/PARC	AB	9-39-1-W5	83 B/8	52°21′	114°05′
Jarvis Glacier	GLAC/GLAC	BC	Cassiar	114 P/7	59°27′	136°32′
Jarvis Lake	LAKE/LAC	ON	Hastings	31 C/12	44°31′	77°34′
Jarvis Lake	LAKE/LAC	NT	Mackenzie	75 H	61°40′	104°49′
Jarvis River	UNP/LNO	ON	Thunder Bay	52 A/3	48°10′	89°28′
Jarvis River	RIV/CDE	YT		115 B/16	60°46′	138°09′
Jasmin	HAM/HAM	SK	9-26-12-W2	62 M/4	51°14′	103°39′
Jasper	UNP/LNO	ON	Leeds	31 B/13	44°50′	75°56′
Jasper	UNP/LNO	AB	16-45-1-W6	83 D/16	52°53′	118°05′
Jasper House, Lieu historique national - also-aussi - Jasper House National Historic Site	PARK/PARC	AB		83 F/4	53°09′	117°59′
Jasper House National Historic Site - also-aussi - Jasper House, Lieu historique national	PARK/PARC	AB		83 F/4	53°09′	117°59′
Jasper Improvement District	MUN2/AZM2	AB		83 D/16	52°54′	118°10′
Jasper in Québec	UNP/LNO	QC	Matawinie	31 J/8	46°16′	74°13′
Jasper National Park - also-aussi - Jasper, Parc national	PARK/PARC	AB		83 D/16	52°59′	118°06′
Jasper, Parc national - also-aussi - Jasper National Park	PARK/PARC	AB		83 D/16	52°59′	118°06′
Jasper Park Information Centre National Historic Site - also-aussi - Centre-d'Accueil-du-Parc-Jasper, Lieu historique national du	PARK/PARC	AB		83 D/16	52°53′	118°05′
Jasper Park Lodge	UNP/LNO	AB	15-45-1-W6	83 D/16	52°53′	118°03′
Jaune, Rivière	RIV/CDE	QC	Kamouraska	21 N/4	47°12′	69°47′
Java	UNP/LNO	SK	30-15-14-W3	72 J/5	50°17′	107°56′
Ja We Yah's 99	IR/RI	BC		103 H/16	53°45′	128°28′
Jayem	UNP/LNO	BC	Nanoose	92 F/8	49°15′	124°08′
Jays	UNP/LNO	SK	32-28-5-W3	72 O/7	51°27′	106°40′
J.-Clovis-Laflamme, Réserve écologique	PARK/PARC	QC	Le Domaine-du-Roy	32 A/7	48°21′	72°34′
Jean Baptiste 28	IR/RI	BC	Range 5 Coast	93 L/11	54°44′	127°01′
Jean Baptiste Gambler 183	IR/RI	AB	30-72-21-W4	83 P/6	55°16′	113°13′
Jean-Charles-Bonenfant, Mont	MTN/MNT	QC	La Côte-de-Beaupré	21 M/11	47°42′	71°14′
Jean Côté	UNP/LNO	AB	36-79-22-W5	83 N/14	55°54′	117°09′
Jean de Baie	UNP/LNO	NF		1 M/3	47°13′	55°04′
Jean-Dechêne	UNP/LNO	QC	Le Fjord-du-Saguenay	22 D/6	48°24′	71°11′
Jean de Gaunt Island	UNP/LNO	NF		1 M/9	47°32′	54°17′
Jean de Gaunt Island	ISL/ÎLE	NF		1 M/9	47°31′	54°17′
Jeanette Bay	BAY/BAIE	NF		13 I/12	54°45′	58°00′
Jeanette Lake	LAKE/LAC	ON	Kenora	52 N/1	51°05′	92°12′
Jean, Lake	LAKE/LAC	ON	Thunder Bay	42 E/5	49°23′	87°53′
Jean-Larose, Rivière	RIV/CDE	QC	La Côte-de-Beaupré	21 M/2	47°04′	70°54′
Jean Marie River	UNP/LNO	NT	Mackenzie	95 H/10	61°31′	120°38′
Jean Marie River	RIV/CDE	NT	Mackenzie	95 H	61°32′	120°38′
Jeanne-d'Arc	UNP/LNO	QC	Communauté urbaine de l'Outaouais	31 G/12	45°32′	75°38′
Jeanne-Mance	UNP/LNO	NB	Gloucester	21 P/6	47°21′	65°26′
Jeannette	UNP/LNO	ON	Kent	40 J/8	42°18′	82°22′
Jeannette Lake	LAKE/LAC	SK	64-17-W3	73 K/10	54°33′	108°32′
Jeannettes Creek	UNP/LNO	ON	Kent	40 J/8	42°19′	82°25′
Jeannettes Creek	RIV/CDE	ON	Kent	40 J/8	42°20′	82°25′
Jeannin, Lac	LAKE/LAC	QC	Kativik	24 B/8	56°29′	66°55′
Jean-Noël	UNP/LNO	QC	Charlevoix-Est	21 M/9	47°37′	70°13′
Jeannotte, Rivière	RIV/CDE	QC	Portneuf	31 P/8	47°17′	72°15′
Jean-Peré, Lac	LAKE/LAC	QC	La Vallée-de-la-Gatineau	31 N/2	47°04′	76°38′
Jean-Talon, Pointe	CAPE/CAP	QC	Kativik	25 E/1	61°05′	70°08′
Jedburgh	VILG/VILG	SK	1-27-8-W2	62 M/6	51°18′	103°00′
Jeddore Harbour	BAY/BAIE	NS	Halifax	11 D/14	44°45′	63°02′
Jeddore Head	CAPE/CAP	NS	Halifax	11 D/11	44°41′	63°03′
Jeddore Lake	LAKE/LAC	NF		2 D/4	48°04′	55°54′
Jeddore Oyster Ponds	UNP/LNO	NS	Halifax	11 D/14	44°47′	63°01′
Jedediah Island	ISL/ÎLE	BC	Nanaimo	92 F/8	49°30′	124°12′
Jedway	UNP/LNO	BC	Queen Charlotte	103 B/6	52°18′	131°13′
Jefferson	UNP/LNO	NS	Cape Breton	11 K/1	46°08′	60°16′
Jefferson	UNP/LNO	ON	York	30 M/14	43°55′	79°27′
Jeffrey	UNP/LNO	AB	18-59-24-W4	83 I/4	54°07′	113°34′
Jeffrey's	UNP/LNO	NF		12 B/2	48°14′	58°51′
Jeffries Corner	UNP/LNO	NB	Kings	21 H/11	45°38′	65°30′
Jekyll Lake	LAKE/LAC	NT	Franklin	57 C	69°45′	93°40′
Jellicoe	UNP/LNO	ON	Thunder Bay	42 E/12	49°41′	87°31′
Jellicoe	UNP/LNO	BC	Kamloops Division Yale	92 H/9	49°41′	120°17′
Jelly	UNP/LNO	ON	Thunder Bay	52 A/6	48°23′	89°29′
Jellyby	UNP/LNO	ON	Leeds	31 B/12	44°44′	75°49′
Jemseg	UNP/LNO	NB	Queens	21 G/16	45°50′	66°07′

NAME NOM	ENTITY ENTITÉ	LOC 1 LIEU 1	LOC 2 LIEU 2	MAP CARTE	POSITION LAT	POSITION LONG
Jenkins Cove	UNP/LNO	NF		2 E/10	48°40′	54°45′
Jenkins Island	ISL/ÎLE	BC	Nanaimo	92 F/8	49°27′	124°18′
Jennejohn Lake	LAKE/LAC	NT	Mackenzie	85 I	62°25′	113°44′
Jenne Lake	LAKE/LAC	NT	Mackenzie	65 D	60°31′	103°35′
Jenner	UNP/LNO	AB	33-20-9-W4	72 L/11	50°45′	111°11′
Jenness Island	ISL/ÎLE	NT	Franklin	89 E	78°17′	113°55′
Jennings River	RIV/CDE	BC	Cassiar	104 N/9	59°40′	132°09′
Jennings River 8	IR/RI	BC	Cassiar	104 N/9	59°41′	132°09′
Jenny Lind Island	ISL/ÎLE	NT	Franklin	67 B	68°43′	101°58′
Jenpeg	UNP/LNO	MB	17-64-4-W	63 J/9	54°32′	98°02′
Jensen	UNP/LNO	AB	6-11-10-W4	72 E/14	49°52′	111°21′
Jensen, Cape	CAPE/CAP	NT	Franklin	37 C	69°44′	77°36′
Jensen, Cape	CAPE/CAP	NT	Franklin	67 F	70°24′	102°13′
Jensen Creek	UNP/LNO	YT		115 O/15	63°46′	138°32′
Jens Munk Island	ISL/ÎLE	NT	Franklin	47 D	69°39′	80°04′
Jérémie, Lac	LAKE/LAC	QC	Kativik	34 O/9	59°37′	74°08′
Jericho	UNP/LNO	NB	Carleton	21 J/6	46°22′	67°28′
Jericho	UNP/LNO	ON	Lambton	40 P/4	43°08′	81°55′
Jermain, Cape	CAPE/CAP	NT	Franklin	46 P	67°46′	81°44′
Jermyn	UNP/LNO	ON	Peterborough	31 D/8	44°19′	78°10′
Jerome	UNP/LNO	ON	Sudbury	41 O/9	47°37′	82°14′
Jerry, Lac	LAKE/LAC	QC	Témiscouata	21 N/7	47°25′	68°47′
Jerrys Nose	UNP/LNO	NF		12 B/10	48°31′	58°56′
Jersey	UNP/LNO	NS	Cumberland	11 E/12	45°40′	63°44′
Jersey	UNP/LNO	ON	York	31 D/3	44°13′	79°26′
Jersey	UNP/LNO	BC	Kootenay	82 F/3	49°06′	117°14′
Jersey Cove	UNP/LNO	NS	Victoria	11 K/7	46°18′	60°33′
Jersey Cove	UNP/LNO	QC	La Côte-de-Gaspé	22 A/16	48°53′	64°14′
Jersey Harbour	UNP/LNO	NF		1 M/5	47°29′	55°46′
Jersey Mills	UNP/LNO	QC	Beauce-Sartigan	21 L/2	46°06′	70°39′
Jerseyside	UNP/LNO	NF		1 N/5	47°16′	53°58′
Jerseyville	UNP/LNO	ON	Wentworth	40 P/1	43°12′	80°07′
Jervis Inlet	BAY/BAIE	BC	New Westminster	92 F/9	49°45′	124°10′
Jervis Island	ISL/ÎLE	BC	Nanaimo	92 F/9	49°31′	124°14′
Jervoise River	RIV/CDE	NT	Mackenzie	66 E	65°25′	103°16′
Jesmond	UNP/LNO	BC	Lillooet	92 P/5	51°15′	121°57′
Jesse Bay	BAY/BAIE	NT	Franklin	98 A	72°14′	120°06′
Jesse Lake	LAKE/LAC	BC	Range 4 Coast	103 H/15	53°53′	128°53′
Jessica Lake	LAKE/LAC	MB	12-15-E	52 E/13	50°00′	95°30′
Jessie Lake	LAKE/LAC	ON	Thunder Bay	52 H/1	49°12′	88°21′
Jessie Point	CAPE/CAP	ON	Manitoulin	41 G/16	45°59′	82°21′
Jessopville	UNP/LNO	ON	Dufferin	41 A/1	44°03′	80°20′
Jessups Falls	UNP/LNO	ON	Prescott	31 G/11	45°34′	75°04′
Jésus, Île	ISL/ÎLE	QC	Laval	31 H/12	45°35′	73°45′
Jetait	UNP/LNO	MB		64 C/3	56°03′	101°18′
Jetée-à-Chabot, La	UNP/LNO	QC	Le Fjord-du-Saguenay	22 D/6	48°18′	71°19′
Jetée-de-l'Iroquois	UNP/LNO	QC	Antoine-Labelle	31 J/14	46°54′	75°10′
Jetée-Plate, La	UNP/LNO	QC	Le Centre-de-la-Mauricie	31 I/10	46°38′	72°58′
Jetée-Raquette	UNP/LNO	QC	La Haute-Côte-Nord	22 F/4	49°14′	69°55′
Jeune Landing	UNP/LNO	BC	Rupert	92 L/6	50°26′	127°29′
Jevins	UNP/LNO	ON	Muskoka	31 D/14	44°54′	79°21′
Jewakwa Glacier	GLAC/GLAC	BC	Range 2 Coast	92 N/2	51°08′	124°46′
Jewakwa Mountain	MTN/MNT	BC	Range 2 Coast	92 N/2	51°09′	124°53′
Jewakwa River	RIV/CDE	BC	Range 2 Coast	92 N/2	51°04′	124°59′
Jewel Lake	LAKE/LAC	BC	Similkameen Division Yale	82 E/2	49°10′	118°37′
Jewellville	UNP/LNO	ON	Renfrew	31 F/5	45°20′	77°32′
Jewett Lake	LAKE/LAC	SK		74 A/2	56°08′	104°38′
Jewetts Mills	UNP/LNO	NB	York	21 G/15	45°59′	66°54′
J. Gordon Island	ISL/ÎLE	NT	Keewatin	44 P	59°40′	80°33′
Jiaviniup Narsanga	UNP/LNO	QC	Kativik	34 C/2	56°01′	76°40′
Jim Brown Creek	RIV/CDE	BC	New Westminster	92 K/1	50°14′	124°21′
Jim Creek	RIV/CDE	BC	Lillooet	92 P/15	51°50′	120°43′
Jim Lake	UNP/LNO	QC	Pontiac	31 K/2	46°06′	76°46′
Jim Lake	LAKE/LAC	BC	Lillooet	92 P/6	51°24′	121°07′
Jim Lake	LAKE/LAC	NT	Mackenzie	75 I	62°24′	104°35′
Jim Myles Garden	UNP/LNO	NF		1 M/10	47°41′	54°43′
Jim's Cove	UNP/LNO	NF		2 E/12	49°31′	55°38′
Jimtown	UNP/LNO	NS	Antigonish	11 F/12	45°42′	61°54′
Jinikkut	UNP/LNO	QC	Kativik	35 F/16	61°55′	76°16′
Joannès	UNP/LNO	QC	Rouyn-Noranda	32 D/2	48°13′	78°41′
Joannès, Lac	LAKE/LAC	QC	Rouyn-Noranda	32 D/2	48°11′	78°41′
Jobrin	UNP/LNO	ON	Cochrane	42 L/1	50°07′	86°07′
Job's Cove	UNP/LNO	NF		1 N/14	47°59′	53°01′
Job's Room	UNP/LNO	NF		12 P/7	51°28′	56°57′
Joburke	UNP/LNO	ON	Sudbury	42 B/1	48°09′	82°16′

NAME NOM	ENTITY ENTITÉ	LOC 1 LIEU 1	LOC 2 LIEU 2	MAP CARTE	POSITION LAT	LONG
Jocelyn	MUN2/AZM2	ON	Algoma	41 J/4	46°09'	83°56'
Jocko	UNP/LNO	ON	Nipissing	31 L/11	46°38'	79°26'
Jocko Point	CAPE/CAP	ON	Nipissing	31 L/5	46°19'	79°46'
Jocko River	RIV/CDE	ON	Nipissing	31 L/11	46°34'	79°00'
Jock River	RIV/CDE	ON	Carleton	31 G/5	45°16'	75°42'
Jockvale	UNP/LNO	ON	Carleton	31 G/5	45°16'	75°45'
Joe Batt's Arm	UNP/LNO	NF		2 E/9	49°44'	54°10'
Joe Batt's Arm	BAY/BAIE	NF		2 E/9	49°44'	54°10'
Joe Batt's Arm-Barr'd Islands-Shoal Bay	TOWN/VIL2	NF		2 E/9	49°43'	54°11'
Joe Batt's Point	CAPE/CAP	NF		2 E/16	49°45'	54°09'
Joe Batts Pond	LAKE/LAC	NF		2 D/15	48°58'	54°46'
Joe Creek	RIV/CDE	YT		117 C/1	69°03'	140°28'
Joe Glodes Brook	RIV/CDE	NF		12 A/16	48°52'	56°27'
Joe Glodes Pond	LAKE/LAC	NF		12 H/1	49°00'	56°21'
Joe Mountain	MTN/MNT	YT		105 D/15	60°57'	134°43'
Joes Lake	UNP/LNO	ON	Lanark	31 F/2	45°08'	76°38'
Joes Lake	LAKE/LAC	NF		12 H/1	49°04'	56°05'
Joeyaska 2	IR/RI	BC	Kamloops Division Yale	92 I/2	50°06'	120°45'
Joffre	UNP/LNO	AB	9-39-25-W4	83 A/5	52°20'	113°32'
Joffre Creek	RIV/CDE	BC	Lillooet	92 J/7	50°18'	122°35'
Joffre, Mount	MTN/MNT	AB/BC		82 J/11	50°32'	115°12'
Joggin Bridge	UNP/LNO	NS	Digby	21 A/12	44°36'	65°44'
Joggins	UNP/LNO	NS	Cumberland	21 H/9	45°41'	64°26'
Jog Lake	LAKE/LAC	ON	Cochrane	42 K/6	50°24'	85°20'
Jogues	UNP/LNO	QC	Les Maskoutains	31 H/7	45°29'	72°49'
Jogues	UNP/LNO	ON	Cochrane	42 G/12	49°36'	83°45'
Jogues, Lac	LAKE/LAC	QC	Kativik	24 F/2	57°08'	68°42'
Johan-Beetz, Baie	BAY/BAIE	QC	Minganie	12 L/7	50°17'	62°48'
Johan Peninsula	CAPE/CAP	NT	Franklin	39 E	78°42'	75°30'
Johansen Bay	BAY/BAIE	NT	Franklin	77 B/12	68°34'	111°05'
John Bay	BAY/BAIE	NS	Pictou	11 E/14	45°46'	63°05'
John, Cape	CAPE/CAP	NF		11 O/14	47°58'	59°19'
John, Cape	CAPE/CAP	NS	Pictou	11 E/14	45°48'	63°08'
John Creek	RIV/CDE	ON	Sudbury	41 I/5	46°23'	81°41'
John D'Or Prairie	UNP/LNO	AB	30-109-7-W5	84 J/6	58°30'	115°08'
John D'Or Prairie 215	IR/RI	AB	109,110-7-W5	84 J/11	58°31'	115°05'
John Dyer, Cape	CAPE/CAP	NT	Franklin	68 C	73°30'	101°37'
John Halkett Island	ISL/ÎLE	NT	Franklin	67 C	69°58'	100°51'
John Hart Lake	LAKE/LAC	BC	Sayward	92 K/3	50°02'	125°22'
John Island	ISL/ÎLE	ON	Algoma	41 J/2	46°10'	82°36'
John Jay, Mount	MTN/MNT	BC	Cassiar	104 B/1	56°08'	130°26'
Johnke, Cape	CAPE/CAP	NT	Franklin	77 H/9	71°35'	104°20'
John, La	UNP/LNO	QC	Matane	22 B/11	48°39'	67°16'
Johnny Hoe River	RIV/CDE	NT	Mackenzie	96 A	64°49'	121°23'
Johnny-Pitre, Le	UNP/LNO	QC	Pabok	22 A/10	48°38'	64°39'
John Richardson Bay	BAY/BAIE	NT	Franklin	120 B	80°10'	71°21'
John, River	RIV/CDE	NS	Pictou	11 E/14	45°45'	63°04'
John's Beach	UNP/LNO	NF		12 G/1	49°02'	58°09'
Johnsborough	UNP/LNO	SK	15-19-25-W3	72 K/11	50°36'	109°23'
Johns Island	ISL/ÎLE	NS	Shelburne	20 P/12	43°33'	65°48'
Johns Island	ISL/ÎLE	NT	Franklin	120 C	81°49'	71°04'
Johnson	MUN2/AZM2	ON	Algoma	41 J/5	46°23'	83°53'
Johnson	UNP/LNO	ON	Timiskaming	31 M/5	47°16'	79°45'
Johnson	UNP/LNO	ON	Grey	41 A/10	44°40'	80°48'
Johnson	UNP/LNO	MB	34-75-1-W	63 P/12	55°33'	97°32'
Johnson	UNP/LNO	MB	20-19-28-W	62 K/11	50°39'	101°20'
Johnson	UNP/LNO	BC	Cariboo	93 A/4	52°00'	121°53'
Johnson	UNP/LNO	BC	New Westminster	92 G/7	49°25'	122°51'
Johnson Beach	UNP/LNO	QC	Roussillon	31 H/5	45°24'	73°44'
Johnson Creek	RIV/CDE	YT		116 O/13	67°51'	139°49'
Johnson Croft	UNP/LNO	NB	Kings	21 G/8	45°30'	66°09'
Johnson Heights	UNP/LNO	BC	New Westminster	92 G/2	49°11'	122°48'
Johnson Island	ISL/ÎLE	NT	Keewatin	34 D	56°43'	79°32'
Johnsonkank	UNP/LNO	MB		53 F/13	53°45'	93°52'
Johnson Lake	LAKE/LAC	BC	Kamloops Division Yale	82 M/4	51°10'	119°45'
Johnson Mills - see-voir - Johnson's Mills	UNP/LNO	NB		21 H/16	45°47'	64°30'
Johnson Point	CAPE/CAP	NT	Franklin	38 G	75°23'	79°28'
Johnson Point	CAPE/CAP	NT	Franklin	88 B	72°46'	118°26'
Johnson River	RIV/CDE	NT	Mackenzie	95 O	63°43'	123°55'
Johnsons Crossing	UNP/LNO	YT		105 C/6	60°29'	133°18'
Johnson Settlement	UNP/LNO	NB	Charlotte	21 G/2	45°14'	66°57'
Johnson Settlement	UNP/LNO	NB	York	21 G/14	45°57'	67°27'
Johnsons Landing	UNP/LNO	ON	Thunder Bay	52 A/10	48°34'	88°38'
Johnsons Landing	UNP/LNO	BC	Kootenay	82 K/2	50°05'	116°53'
Johnson's Mills	UNP/LNO	NB	Westmorland	21 H/16	45°47'	64°30'

NAME NOM	ENTITY ENTITÉ	LOC 1 LIEU 1	LOC 2 LIEU 2	MAP CARTE	POSITION LAT	LONG
Johnsons Point	CAPE/CAP	NS	Pictou	11 E/14	45°48′	63°02′
John's Pond	UNP/LNO	NF		1 N/4	47°08′	53°37′
Johnston	GEOG/GÉOG	NB	Queens	21 H/13	45°50′	65°50′
Johnston Corners	UNP/LNO	ON	Carleton	31 G/5	45°17′	75°36′
Johnstone Strait	CHAN/CHEN	BC	Range 1 Coast	92 L/8	50°27′	126°00′
Johnston Island	ISL/ÎLE	SK		74 N/7	59°21′	108°56′
Johnston Point Road	UNP/LNO	NB	Westmorland	21 I/1	46°09′	64°05′
Johnstons River	UNP/LNO	PE	Queens	11 L/6	46°16′	63°01′
Johnstown	UNP/LNO	NS	Richmond	11 F/15	45°47′	60°44′
Johnstown	UNP/LNO	ON	Grenville	31 B/11	44°44′	75°28′
Johnstown	UNP/LNO	ON	Hastings	31 C/4	44°09′	77°33′
Johnville	UNP/LNO	NB	Carleton	21 J/12	46°34′	67°33′
Johnville	UNP/LNO	QC	Le Haut-Saint-François	21 E/5	45°20′	71°45′
Johny's Cabin	UNP/LNO	QC	Côte-Nord-du-Golfe-Saint-Laurent	12 P/11	51°34′	57°21′
Johny Sticks 2	IR/RI	BC	Lillooet	92 O/16	51°50′	122°10′
Joint Lake	LAKE/LAC	MB		53 L/6	54°23′	95°25′
Joir River - also-aussi - Joir, Rivière	RIV/CDE	NF		12 N/16	51°59′	60°12′
Joir, Rivière - also-aussi - Joir River	RIV/CDE	QC	Minganie	12 N/16	51°59′	60°12′
Jokel Fiord	BAY/BAIE	NT	Franklin	39 F	78°52′	78°05′
Jolicoeur, Rivière	RIV/CDE	QC	Jamésie	33 D/2	52°01′	78°42′
Jolicure	UNP/LNO	NB	Westmorland	21 H/16	45°57′	64°13′
Joliette	CITY/VIL	QC	Joliette	31 I/3	46°01′	73°27′
Joliette	MUN1/AZM1	QC	Joliette	31 I/3	46°01′	73°27′
Joliffs Brook	UNP/LNO	NB	Kings	21 H/12	45°44′	65°46′
Joli, Lake	LAKE/LAC	NS	Digby	21 A/5	44°28′	65°33′
Joli, Port	BAY/BAIE	NS	Queens	20 P/15	43°50′	64°53′
Jolliet, Lac	LAKE/LAC	QC	Jamésie	32 N/10	51°33′	76°54′
Jollimore	UNP/LNO	NS	Halifax	11 D/12	44°37′	63°36′
Jolly Lake	LAKE/LAC	NT	Mackenzie	76 D/4	64°08′	111°55′
Joly	MUN2/AZM2	ON	Parry Sound	31 E/14	45°47′	79°15′
Joly	UNP/LNO	QC	Lotbinière	21 L/5	46°29′	71°40′
Jonathan's Pond	LAKE/LAC	NF		2 E/2	49°01′	54°32′
Joncas, Lac	LAKE/LAC	QC	Pontiac	31 N/4	47°09′	77°40′
Jonchée, Lac	LAKE/LAC	QC	Minganie	12 N/7	51°21′	60°55′
Jones	UNP/LNO	ON	Kenora	52 E/16	49°59′	94°05′
Jones, Cape	CAPE/CAP	NT	Keewatin	55 J	62°36′	91°52′
Jones Creek	RIV/CDE	BC	Cariboo	93 A/4	52°04′	121°56′
Jones Crossing	UNP/LNO	NB	Northumberland	21 I/13	46°58′	65°36′
Jones Falls	UNP/LNO	ON	Leeds	31 C/9	44°33′	76°14′
Jones Forks	UNP/LNO	NB	York	21 J/2	46°05′	66°52′
Jones Landing	UNP/LNO	ON	Algoma	41 K/16	46°54′	84°23′
Jones Landing	UNP/LNO	NT	Mackenzie	95 J	62°50′	123°13′
Jones Sound	CHAN/CHEN	NT	Franklin	48 G	76°00′	86°00′
Jones Trough	SEAU/SMER	—		5.17	76°00′	86°00′
Jonesville	UNP/LNO	ON	Thunder Bay	42 E/10	49°42′	86°57′
Jonquière	CITY/VIL1	QC	Le Fjord-du-Saguenay	22 D/6	48°25′	71°13′
Jonquière-Nord	UNP/LNO	QC	Le Fjord-du-Saguenay	22 D/6	48°26′	71°16′
Jordan	UNP/LNO	ON	Lincoln	30 M/3	43°09′	79°23′
Jordan	UNP/LNO	MB	12-5-5-W	62 G/8	49°22′	98°00′
Jordan Basin - also-aussi - Jordan, Bassin	SEAU/SMER	—		4011	43°30′	67°30′
Jordan, Bassin - also-aussi - Jordan Basin	SEAU/SMER	—		4011	43°30′	67°30′
Jordan Bay	UNP/LNO	NS	Shelburne	20 P/11	43°42′	65°14′
Jordan Branch	UNP/LNO	NS	Shelburne	20 P/14	43°47′	65°16′
Jordan Falls	UNP/LNO	NS	Shelburne	20 P/14	43°49′	65°14′
Jordan Ferry	UNP/LNO	NS	Shelburne	20 P/11	43°45′	65°14′
Jordan Harbour	UNP/LNO	ON	Lincoln	30 M/3	43°11′	79°23′
Jordan Hill	UNP/LNO	QC	Le Haut-Saint-François	21 E/5	45°21′	71°39′
Jordan Lake	LAKE/LAC	NS	Queens	21 A/3	44°05′	65°14′
Jordan Lake	LAKE/LAC	MB		64 F/9	57°37′	100°18′
Jordan Mountain	UNP/LNO	NB	Kings	21 H/14	45°51′	65°28′
Jordan River	UNP/LNO	SK	18-48-10-W2	63 E/3	53°08′	103°28′
Jordan River	RIV/CDE	NS	Shelburne	20 P/14	43°46′	65°14′
Jordan River	RIV/CDE	SK	36-48-11-W2	63 E/3	53°11′	103°29′
Jordan River	RIV/CDE	BC	Renfrew	92 C/8	48°25′	124°03′
Jordan Station	UNP/LNO	ON	Lincoln	30 M/3	43°10′	79°22′
Jordantown	UNP/LNO	NS	Digby	21 A/12	44°35′	65°47′
Jordanville	UNP/LNO	NS	Guysborough	11 F/4	45°09′	61°55′
Jorgens	UNP/LNO	ON	Renfrew	31 F/14	45°55′	77°20′
Josephburg	UNP/LNO	AB	32-54-21-W4	83 H/11	53°43′	113°05′
Joseph Creek	RIV/CDE	BC	Kamloops Division Yale	92 P/8	51°29′	120°10′
Joseph Good, Cape	CAPE/CAP	NT	Franklin	120 B	80°15′	69°55′
Joseph Henry, Cape	CAPE/CAP	NT	Franklin	120 E	82°49′	63°30′
Josephine	UNP/LNO	ON	Algoma	42 C/2	48°07′	84°37′
Josephine Bay	BAY/BAIE	NT	Franklin	57 C	69°36′	94°40′
Josephine River	RIV/CDE	NT	Keewatin	55 O	63°02′	90°41′

NAME NOM	ENTITY ENTITÉ	LOC 1 LIEU 1	LOC 2 LIEU 2	MAP CARTE	POSITION LAT	LONG
Joseph, Lac	LAKE/LAC	NF		23 A/14	52°45'	65°18'
Joseph, Lac	LAKE/LAC	QC	L'Érable	21 L/4	46°12'	71°32'
Joseph, Lake	LAKE/LAC	ON	Muskoka	31 E/4	45°10'	79°44'
Joseph Lake	LAKE/LAC	AB	50-21,22-W4	83 H/6	53°17'	113°04'
Joseph, Petit lac	LAKE/LAC	NF		23 A/11	52°36'	65°05'
Joseph, Pointe	CAPE/CAP	QC	Minganie	12 E/8	49°24'	62°08'
Joseph, Rivière	RIV/CDE	QC	Sept-Rivières	22 J/16	50°58'	66°21'
Josephsburg	UNP/LNO	ON	Waterloo	40 P/7	43°28'	80°40'
Jost Lake	LAKE/LAC	NT	Mackenzie	75 H	61°13'	104°35'
Joubert Creek - also-aussi - +Joubert, Ruisseau	RIV/CDE	MB		62 H/6	49°27'	97°01'
+Joubert, Ruisseau - also-aussi - Joubert Creek	RIV/CDE	MB		62 H/6	49°27'	97°01'
Jourimain Island	ISL/ÎLE	NB	Westmorland	11 L/4	46°09'	63°49'
Journois	UNP/LNO	NF		12 B/7	48°21'	58°41'
Joussard	UNP/LNO	AB	33-73-13-W5	83 O/5	55°24'	115°57'
Joutel	UNP/LNO	QC	Jamésie	32 E/8	49°27'	78°17'
Joy Bay	BAY/BAIE	NT	Franklin	25 E/5	61°30'	71°40'
Joy, Cape	CAPE/CAP	NT	Franklin	48 D	73°39'	83°13'
Joyce	UNP/LNO	NF		12 B/7	48°23'	58°36'
Joyceville	UNP/LNO	ON	Frontenac	31 C/8	44°22'	76°20'
Joy Hill	UNP/LNO	QC	Brome-Missisquoi	31 H/2	45°03'	72°49'
Joy Island	ISL/ÎLE	NT	Keewatin	43 P	55°54'	80°07'
Joyland Beach	UNP/LNO	ON	Ontario	31 D/11	44°34'	79°19'
Joynt	UNP/LNO	QC	Les Collines-de-l'Outaouais	31 F/16	45°45'	76°01'
Juan de Fuca Abyssal Plain	SEAU/SMER	—		15789A	48°45'	130°00'
Juan de Fuca Canyon	SEAU/SMER	—		3602	48°04'	125°20'
Juan de Fuca, Détroit de - also-aussi - Juan de Fuca Strait	CHAN/CHEN	BC		92 B/5	48°20'	123°56'
Juan de Fuca Ridge	SEAU/SMER	—		5.07	46°40'	129°20'
Juan de Fuca Strait - also-aussi - Juan de Fuca, Détroit de	CHAN/CHEN	BC		92 B/5	48°20'	123°56'
Juan Perez Sound	BAY/BAIE	BC	Queen Charlotte	103 B/6	52°30'	131°25'
Jubilee	UNP/LNO	NS	Victoria	11 F/15	45°59'	60°55'
Jubilee	UNP/LNO	NS	Cumberland	21 H/9	45°43'	64°19'
Jubilee Island	ISL/ÎLE	NT	Franklin	36 A	64°20'	73°45'
Jubilee Lake	LAKE/LAC	NF		2 D/3	48°03'	55°11'
Jubilee Mountain	MTN/MNT	YT		105 D/1	60°12'	134°07'
Judah	UNP/LNO	AB	35-82-22-W5	84 C/3	56°09'	117°19'
Juddhaven	UNP/LNO	ON	Muskoka	31 E/4	45°12'	79°37'
Judd's Mills	UNP/LNO	QC	Coaticook	31 H/1	45°02'	72°04'
Jude Island	ISL/ÎLE	NF		1 M/2	47°15'	54°49'
Judes Point	UNP/LNO	PE	Prince	21 I/16	46°57'	64°00'
Judge	UNP/LNO	ON	Timiskaming	31 M/12	47°37'	79°32'
Judge Daly Promontory	CAPE/CAP	NT	Franklin	120 C	81°15'	67°00'
Judge Howay, Mount	MTN/MNT	BC	New Westminster	92 G/9	49°30'	122°19'
Judgeville	UNP/LNO	ON	Leeds	31 C/16	44°46'	76°03'
Judique	UNP/LNO	NS	Inverness	11 F/14	45°52'	61°29'
Judique Intervale	UNP/LNO	NS	Inverness	11 F/14	45°55'	61°29'
Judique North	UNP/LNO	NS	Inverness	11 F/14	45°54'	61°29'
Judique South	UNP/LNO	NS	Inverness	11 F/14	45°51'	61°29'
Judith-De Brésoles, Réserve écologique	PARK/PARC	QC	Le Haut-Saint-Maurice	31 P/9	47°36'	72°19'
Judith Island	ISL/ÎLE	NT	Mackenzie	96 E	65°27'	127°32'
Judson	UNP/LNO	AB	34-6-18-W4	82 H/9	49°32'	112°21'
Juet, Lac	LAKE/LAC	QC	Kativik	35 F/1	61°02'	76°20'
Jugeborg Fiord	BAY/BAIE	NT	Franklin	560 D	81°14'	89°30'
Jugwees (Minette Bay) 5	IR/RI	BC	Range 5 Coast	103 I/2	54°02'	128°37'
Juillet, Lac	LAKE/LAC	QC	Caniapiscau	23 I/16	54°47'	64°00'
Jukes Canyon	SEAU/SMER	—		8010	43°20'	51°55'
Jules	UNP/LNO	QC	La Vallée-de-la-Gatineau	31 G/13	45°57'	75°50'
Jules-Allard, Barrage	MISC/DIV	QC	L'Amiante	21 E/14	45°57'	71°17'
Jules-Léger, Lac	LAKE/LAC	QC	Jamésie	23 D/7	52°52'	70°56'
Julia Bay	BAY/BAIE	ON	Manitoulin	41 G/15	45°56'	82°32'
Julian, Lac	LAKE/LAC	QC	Jamésie	33 K/5	54°26'	77°55'
Julian Peak	MTN/MNT	BC	Range 1 Coast	92 K/8	50°28'	124°17'
Julia Point	CAPE/CAP	ON	Manitoulin	41 G/15	45°58'	82°37'
Julien	UNP/LNO	QC	Portneuf	21 L/12	46°40'	71°59'
Juliet Creek	RIV/CDE	BC	Yale Division Yale	92 H/11	49°44'	121°01'
July Lake	LAKE/LAC	BC	Peace River	94 P/15	59°46'	120°34'
July Mountain	MTN/MNT	BC	Yale Division Yale	92 H/11	49°42'	121°05'
Jumbo Gardens	UNP/LNO	ON	Thunder Bay	52 A/6	48°27'	89°15'
Jumbo Mountain	MTN/MNT	BC	Kootenay	82 K/7	50°24'	116°34'
Jump Creek	RIV/CDE	BC	Dunsmuir	92 F/1	49°02'	124°10'
Jumper Brook	RIV/CDE	NF		2 E/7	49°21'	54°45'
Jumpers Brook	UNP/LNO	NF		2 E/3	49°02'	55°24'
Jumpers Brook	RIV/CDE	NF		2 E/3	49°02'	55°24'
Jumping Lake	LAKE/LAC	SK	44,45-24,25-W2	73 A/14	52°51'	105°27'
Jumpingpound Creek	RIV/CDE	AB	4-26-4-W5	82 O/2	51°11'	114°30'
Junction Bay	BAY/BAIE	NT	Keewatin	45 P	63°42'	80°28'

NAME NOM	ENTITY ENTITÉ	LOC 1 LIEU 1	LOC 2 LIEU 2	MAP CARTE	POSITION LAT	LONG
Junction Brook	UNP/LNO	NF		12 H/3	49°13′	57°24′
June	UNP/LNO	AB	36-40-26-W4	83 A/5	52°29′	113°36′
Juneau Icefield	GLAC/GLAC	BC	Cassiar	104 L/16	58°55′	134°15′
Junetown	UNP/LNO	ON	Leeds	31 B/12	44°30′	75°56′
Jungersen Bay	BAY/BAIE	NT	Franklin	47 G	71°31′	84°38′
Jungersen River	RIV/CDE	NT	Franklin	47 G	71°26′	84°40′
Juniata	UNP/LNO	SK	36-10-W3	73 B/3	52°05′	107°20′
Juniper	UNP/LNO	NB	Carleton	21 J/11	46°33′	67°13′
Juniper	UNP/LNO	SK	27-8-W3	72 O/6	51°19′	107°08′
Juniper Island	UNP/LNO	ON	Peterborough	31 D/9	44°33′	78°09′
Juniper Mountain	UNP/LNO	NS	Cape Breton	11 F/16	45°57′	60°15′
Juniper Ridge	UNP/LNO	BC	Kamloops Division Yale	92 I/9	50°40′	120°15′
Juniper Station	UNP/LNO	NB	Carleton	21 J/11	46°33′	67°10′
Juniper Stump	UNP/LNO	NF		1 N/11	47°30′	53°18′
Junius Lake	LAKE/LAC	NT	Mackenzie	86 K	66°27′	116°43′
Juno	UNP/LNO	MB	10,11,14,15-10-12-E	52 E/13	49°50′	95°52′
Juno	UNP/LNO	AB	18-10-12-W4	72 E/13	49°49′	111°36′
Junor	UNP/LNO	SK	5-53-13-3	73 G/12	53°33′	107°53′
Jupitagon	UNP/LNO	QC	Minganie	22 I/7	50°17′	64°35′
Jupiter Bay	BAY/BAIE	NT	Mackenzie	96 H	65°19′	121°33′
Jupiter, Rivière	RIV/CDE	QC	Minganie	12 E/5	49°29′	63°36′
Jura	UNP/LNO	ON	Lambton	40 P/4	43°06′	81°54′
Jura	UNP/LNO	BC	Kamloops Division Yale	92 H/9	49°32′	120°27′
Juskatla	UNP/LNO	BC	Queen Charlotte	103 F/9	53°37′	132°19′
Juskatla Inlet	BAY/BAIE	BC	Queen Charlotte	103 F/9	53°37′	132°25′
Jus K'Ay Tl'Oh 32	IR/RI	BC	Range 5 Coast	93 K/11	54°39′	125°02′
Justasons Corner	UNP/LNO	NB	Charlotte	21 G/2	45°06′	66°46′
Justice	UNP/LNO	MB	12-12-18-W	62 G/13	50°00′	99°48′
Juvenile Settlement	UNP/LNO	NB	Sunbury	21 G/10	45°32′	66°37′

K

NAME NOM	ENTITY ENTITÉ	LOC 1 LIEU 1	LOC 2 LIEU 2	MAP CARTE	POSITION LAT	LONG
Kaaitukameshtesht	UNP/LNO	QC	Sept-Rivières	22 O/7	51°26′	66°59′
Kaaitukupitak	UNP/LNO	QC	Kativik	23 P/15	55°53′	64°45′
Kaamechiiwaapuukanuch Patistahwaakan	UNP/LNO	QC	Jamésie	32 I/12	50°44′	73°32′
Kaaviup Kangia	UNP/LNO	QC	Kativik	24 N/13	59°46′	69°33′
Kaawiipuuskasich	UNP/LNO	QC	Jamésie	32 I/5	50°24′	73°46′
Kabaigon	UNP/LNO	ON	Thunder Bay	52 B/9	48°40′	90°16′
Kabania Lake	LAKE/LAC	ON	Kenora	53 A/1	52°12′	88°20′
Kabenung Lake	LAKE/LAC	ON	Algoma	42 C/7	48°16′	84°59′
Kabika River	RIV/CDE	ON	Cochrane	32 E/5	49°25′	79°47′
Kabinakagami Lake	LAKE/LAC	ON	Algoma	42 C/16	48°54′	84°25′
Kabinakagami River	RIV/CDE	ON	Cochrane	42 K/8	50°25′	84°20′
Kabinakagamisis Lake	LAKE/LAC	ON	Algoma	42 F/1	49°03′	84°27′
Kabitotikwia Lake	LAKE/LAC	ON	Thunder Bay	52 H/11	49°36′	89°14′
Kaboni	UNP/LNO	ON	Manitoulin	41 H/12	45°43′	81°43′
Kâcâgigamiktikweyak	UNP/LNO	QC	Jamésie	32 F/6	49°29′	77°03′
Kacheposit	UNP/LNO	MB		63 A/2	52°12′	96°32′
Kachimumiskwanuch	UNP/LNO	QC	Jamésie	33 D/7	52°15′	78°31′
Kachisikuntanuch	UNP/LNO	QC	Jamésie	33 D/7	52°17′	78°34′
Kachiyaskunusi, Lac	LAKE/LAC	QC	Jamésie	33 J/9	54°45′	74°06′
Kadis 11	IR/RI	BC	Range 1 Coast	92 L/15	50°50′	126°56′
Kaegudeck Lake	LAKE/LAC	NF		2 D/3	48°07′	55°12′
Kagami Island	ISL/ÎLE	ON	Thunder Bay	52 P/4	51°13′	89°46′
Kagawong	UNP/LNO	ON	Manitoulin	41 G/16	45°54′	82°15′
Kagawong, Lake	LAKE/LAC	ON	Manitoulin	41 G/16	45°49′	82°18′
Kagianagami Lake	LAKE/LAC	ON	Thunder Bay	42 L/13	50°57′	87°50′
Kagiano Lake	LAKE/LAC	ON	Thunder Bay	42 E/8	49°16′	86°26′
Kaglik Lake	LAKE/LAC	NT	Mackenzie	107 D	69°25′	129°50′
Kagloryuak River	RIV/CDE	NT	Franklin	77 F	70°17′	111°30′
Kahas 7	IR/RI	BC	Range 4 Coast	103 H/3	53°04′	129°07′
Kahihikuahtet	UNP/LNO	QC	Minganie	12 L/5	50°28′	63°57′
Kahipetnaniskat	UNP/LNO	QC	Côte-Nord-du-Golfe-Saint-Laurent	12 K/2	50°13′	60°47′
Kahipitaukaw	UNP/LNO	QC	Kativik	33 O/3	55°12′	75°03′
Kahkaykay 6	IR/RI	BC	Range 1 Coast	92 K/2	50°03′	124°45′
Kahkewistahaw 72	IR/RI	SK		62 L/7	50°30′	102°32′
Kahmoose 4	IR/RI	BC	Yale Division Yale	92 H/14	49°58′	121°29′
Kahnawake 14	IR/RI	QC	Roussillon	31 H/5	45°25′	73°41′
Kahntah	UNP/LNO	BC	Peace River	94 I/7	58°21′	120°54′
Kahntah 3	IR/RI	BC	Peace River	94 I/7	58°21′	120°56′
Kahntah River	RIV/CDE	BC	Peace River	94 I/7	58°22′	120°55′
Kahochella Peninsula	CAPE/CAP	NT	Mackenzie	75 L	62°48′	110°05′
Kahshe Lake	UNP/LNO	ON	Muskoka	31 D/14	44°50′	79°18′
Kahshe Lake	LAKE/LAC	ON	Muskoka	31 D/14	44°50′	79°18′

NAME NOM	ENTITY ENTITÉ	LOC 1 LIEU 1	LOC 2 LIEU 2	MAP CARTE	POSITION LAT	LONG
Kaiahkautshenant	UNP/LNO	QC	Côte-Nord-du-Golfe-Saint-Laurent	12 K/2	50°13′	60°54′
Kaiakuanakanti Uta	UNP/LNO	QC	Minganie	12 O/7	51°28′	58°42′
Kaiashashkupat	UNP/LNO	QC	Le Fjord-du-Saguenay	22 M/16	51°53′	70°06′
Kaiashkons Lake	LAKE/LAC	ON	Rainy River	52 F/3	49°04′	93°24′
Kaiatauehikau	UNP/LNO	QC	Côte-Nord-du-Golfe-Saint-Laurent	12 K/2	50°14′	60°52′
Kaikalahun 25	IR/RI	BC	New Westminster	92 G/11	49°31′	123°29′
Kains Lake	LAKE/LAC	BC	Rupert	92 L/12	50°42′	127°41′
Kaipit Creek	RIV/CDE	BC	Rupert	92 L/7	50°16′	126°48′
Kaipit Lake	LAKE/LAC	BC	Rupert	92 L/2	50°08′	126°46′
Kaipokok	UNP/LNO	NF		13 O/4	55°04′	59°35′
Kaipokok Bay	BAY/BAIE	NF		13 J/12	55°00′	59°35′
Kaipokok River	RIV/CDE	NF		13 K/16	54°45′	60°04′
Kairolik Fiord	BAY/BAIE	NT	Franklin	16 E	65°30′	63°30′
Kaisun	UNP/LNO	BC	Queen Charlotte	103 F/1	53°02′	132°27′
Kai-too-kwis 15	IR/RI	BC	Range 2 Coast	92 M/3	51°11′	127°05′
Kajustus 10	IR/RI	BC	Range 3 Coast	103 A/1	52°09′	128°03′
Kakabeka Falls	UNP/LNO	ON	Thunder Bay	52 A/5	48°24′	89°37′
Kakabeka Falls	FALL/CHUT	ON	Thunder Bay	52 A/5	48°24′	89°38′
Kakactanowok	UNP/LNO	QC	Le Haut-Saint-Maurice	32 B/15	48°50′	74°48′
Kakagi Lake	LAKE/LAC	ON	Kenora	52 F/4	49°13′	93°53′
Kakalatza 6	IR/RI	BC	Sahtlam	92 B/13	48°46′	123°52′
Kakapawanis	UNP/LNO	MB		64 G/4	57°07′	99°30′
Kakatshu Etahit	UNP/LNO	QC	Côte-Nord-du-Golfe-Saint-Laurent	12 K/2	50°13′	60°44′
Kakawis	UNP/LNO	BC	Clayoquot	92 F/4	49°11′	125°55′
Kaketsa Mountain	MTN/MNT	BC	Cassiar	104 J/4	58°13′	131°49′
Kakiattukallak, Lac	LAKE/LAC	QC	Kativik	24 E/12	57°42′	71°40′
Kakiddi Lake	LAKE/LAC	BC	Cassiar	104 G/9	57°39′	130°23′
Kakinagimak Lake	LAKE/LAC	SK		63 M/1	55°12′	102°17′
Kakisa	UNP/LNO	NT	Mackenzie	85 C/14	60°56′	117°25′
Kakisa Lake	LAKE/LAC	NT	Mackenzie	85 C	60°56′	117°43′
Kakisa River	RIV/CDE	NT/AB		85 F/3	61°04′	117°09′
Kaku Hipu Kakustshenan	UNP/LNO	QC	Minganie	12 O/9	51°35′	58°22′
Kakuian Ekutnt	UNP/LNO	QC	Minganie	22 I/8	50°27′	64°01′
Kakuskanus, Lac	LAKE/LAC	QC	La Haute-Côte-Nord	22 F/4	49°14′	70°00′
Kakustshenan	UNP/LNO	QC	Côte-Nord-du-Golfe-Saint-Laurent	12 O/2	51°10′	58°41′
Kakwa River	RIV/CDE	AB/BC		83 L/9	54°37′	118°28′
Kakweiken River	RIV/CDE	BC	Range 1 Coast	92 L/16	50°49′	126°01′
Kakweken 4	IR/RI	BC	Range 1 Coast	92 L/16	50°48′	126°02′
Kaladar	UNP/LNO	ON	Lennox and Addington	31 C/11	44°39′	77°07′
Kaladar, Anglesea and Effingham	MUN2/AZM2	ON	Lennox and Addington	31 C/14	44°47′	77°15′
Kalamalka	UNP/LNO	BC	Osoyoos Division Yale	82 L/3	50°11′	119°20′
Kalamalka Lake	LAKE/LAC	BC	Osoyoos Division Yale	82 L/3	50°10′	119°21′
Kaleden	UNP/LNO	BC	Similkameen Division Yale	82 E/5	49°24′	119°36′
Kaleet River	RIV/CDE	NT	Keewatin	66 P	67°40′	97°11′
Kaleida	UNP/LNO	MB	16-2-8-W	62 G/1	49°08′	98°28′
Kaleland	UNP/LNO	AB	10-55-13-W4	73 E/12	53°44′	111°52′
Kalium	UNP/LNO	SK	27-17-24-W2	72 I/6	50°27′	105°13′
Kalliecahoolie Lake	LAKE/LAC	MB		53 L/3	54°14′	95°29′
Kallum	UNP/LNO	BC	Range 5 Coast	103 I/10	54°31′	128°39′
Kalone Peak	MTN/MNT	BC	Range 3 Coast	93 D/10	52°38′	126°37′
Kalyna	UNP/LNO	SK	15-50-24-W2	73 H/6	53°18′	105°26′
Kalzas River	RIV/CDE	YT		105 L/14	62°53′	135°28′
Kalzas Twins	MTN/MNT	YT		105 M/7	63°16′	134°42′
Kama	UNP/LNO	ON	Thunder Bay	52 A/16	48°58′	88°01′
Kâmanek Minitik	UNP/LNO	QC	Témiscamingue	31 N/5	47°18′	77°55′
Kamaniskeg Lake	LAKE/LAC	ON	Hastings	31 F/5	45°25′	77°41′
Kamanitutaukach	UNP/LNO	QC	Jamésie	32 N/8	51°27′	76°08′
Kamarsuk	UNP/LNO	NF		14 C/5	56°17′	61°36′
Kamarvik Harbour	BAY/BAIE	NT	Keewatin	46 D	64°43′	87°29′
Kamaskawak	UNP/LNO	MB		63 A/1	52°11′	96°10′
Kamatisiusich	UNP/LNO	QC	Kativik	24 E/9	57°35′	70°05′
Kamatshiskueut Uhakamehim	UNP/LNO	QC	Minganie	12 M/11	51°32′	63°04′
Kamatsi Lake	LAKE/LAC	SK		64 D/1	56°10′	102°15′
Kamikuapiskat	UNP/LNO	QC	Minganie	22 I/8	50°19′	64°15′
Kamilukuak Lake	LAKE/LAC	NT	Keewatin	65 K	62°02′	101°40′
Kamilukuak River	RIV/CDE	NT	Keewatin	65 K	62°43′	101°31′
Kaminak Lake	LAKE/LAC	NT	Keewatin	55 L	62°10′	95°00′
Kaminichikapwanaskwaniuch	UNP/LNO	QC	Kativik	24 B/9	56°45′	66°19′
Kâminikacik	UNP/LNO	QC	Vallée-de-l'Or	31 N/11	47°35′	77°23′
Kaminikatau	UNP/LNO	QC	Kativik	24 G/6	57°20′	67°21′
Kaministiquia	UNP/LNO	ON	Thunder Bay	52 A/12	48°32′	89°34′
Kaministnahkuteht	UNP/LNO	QC	Minganie	22 I/8	50°27′	64°11′
Kaminuaskuiast	UNP/LNO	QC	Minganie	12 P/13	51°48′	57°43′
Kaminuriak Lake - see-voir - Qamanirjuaq Lake	LAKE/LAC	NT		55 L/13	62°57′	95°46′
Kamishkushikanuts	UNP/LNO	QC	Manicouagan	22 F/2	49°02′	68°37′

NAME NOM	ENTITY ENTITÉ	LOC 1 LIEU 1	LOC 2 LIEU 2	MAP CARTE	POSITION LAT	LONG
Kamiskotia	UNP/LNO	ON	Cochrane	42 A/12	48°35'	81°37'
Kamiskotia Lake	LAKE/LAC	ON	Cochrane	42 A/12	48°34'	81°38'
Kamiskotia River	RIV/CDE	ON	Cochrane	42 A/12	48°34'	81°31'
Kamitshetshistatshuna	UNP/LNO	QC	Kativik	24 A/2	56°03'	64°44'
Kamitusanikanuch	UNP/LNO	QC	Kativik	24 F/3	57°07'	69°14'
Kamloops	CITY/VIL1	BC	Kamloops Division Yale	92 I/9	50°40'	120°19'
Kamloops 1	IR/RI	BC	Kamloops Division Yale	92 I/9	50°43'	120°16'
Kamloops 2	IR/RI	BC	Kamloops Division Yale	92 I/8	50°29'	120°15'
Kamloops 3	IR/RI	BC	Kamloops Division Yale	92 I/8	50°28'	120°16'
Kamloops 4	IR/RI	BC	Kamloops Division Yale	92 P/1	51°01'	120°15'
Kamloops 5	IR/RI	BC	Kamloops Division Yale	92 I/16	50°51'	120°05'
Kamloops Division Yale Land District	GEOG/GÉOG	BC		82 L	50°40'	119°55'
Kamloops Junction	UNP/LNO	BC	Kamloops Division Yale	92 I/9	50°43'	120°21'
Kamloops Lake	LAKE/LAC	BC	Kamloops Division Yale	92 I/10	50°44'	120°38'
Kamouraska	VILG/VILG	QC	Kamouraska	21 N/12	47°34'	69°52'
Kamouraska	MUN1/AZM1	QC	Kamouraska	21 N/12	47°32'	69°49'
Kamouraska, Îles de	ISL/ÎLE	QC	Kamouraska	21 N/12	47°36'	69°53'
Kamouraska-Moulin	UNP/LNO	QC	Kamouraska	21 N/12	47°33'	69°50'
Kampanikkut Illuqarvinga	UNP/LNO	QC	Kativik	34 C/1	56°07'	76°04'
Kamsack	TOWN/VIL2	SK		62 N/12	51°34'	101°54'
Kamsack Beach	UNP/LNO	SK	28-30-30-W	62 N/12	51°38'	101°39'
Kamuchawie Lake	LAKE/LAC	MB/SK		64 C/5	56°18'	101°59'
Kamusikupaw	UNP/LNO	QC	Jamésie	33 K/15	54°53'	76°38'
Kanaaupscow	UNP/LNO	QC	Jamésie	33 K/2	54°01'	76°30'
Kanaaupscow, Rivière	RIV/CDE	QC	Jamésie	33 K/1	54°15'	76°11'
Kanairiktok Bay	BAY/BAIE	NF		13 O/4	55°10'	60°05'
Kanairiktok River	RIV/CDE	NF		13 N/1	55°01'	60°18'
Kanaka	UNP/LNO	BC	Kamloops Division Yale	92 I/4	50°07'	121°34'
Kanaka Bar	UNP/LNO	BC	Kamloops Division Yale	92 I/4	50°07'	121°34'
Kanaka Bar 1A	IR/RI	BC	Kamloops Division Yale	92 I/4	50°07'	121°34'
Kanaka Bar 2	IR/RI	BC	Kamloops Division Yale	92 I/4	50°07'	121°34'
Kananaskis	UNP/LNO	AB	31-24-8-W5	82 O/3	51°04'	115°08'
Kananaskis River	RIV/CDE	AB	24-8-W5	82 O/3	51°06'	115°04'
Kananaskis Village	UNP/LNO	AB	35-22-9-W5	82 J/14	50°55'	115°09'
Kanaskis Improvement District	MUN2/AZM2	AB		82 J/10	50°42'	114°53'
Kanasuta, Rivière	RIV/CDE	QC	Abitibi-Ouest	32 D/6	48°27'	79°19'
Kanata	CITY/VIL1	ON	Carleton	31 G/5	45°18'	75°55'
Kanawana	UNP/LNO	QC	Les Pays-d'en-Haut	31 G/16	45°51'	74°11'
Kandahar	HAM/HAM	SK	21-32-17-W2	72 P/16	51°46'	104°21'
Kane	UNP/LNO	MB	6-5-2-W	62 H/5	49°21'	97°44'
Kane Basin - also-aussi - Kane, Bassin	CHAN/CHEN	NT	Franklin	39 H	79°05'	73°05'
Kane, Bassin - also-aussi - Kane Basin	CHAN/CHEN	NT	Franklin	39 H	79°05'	73°05'
Kanesatake	UNP/LNO	QC	Deux-Montagnes	31 G/8	45°29'	74°07'
Kaneville	UNP/LNO	NS	Cape Breton	11 K/8	46°15'	60°06'
Kangalaksiorvik Fiord	BAY/BAIE	NF		14 M/5	59°25'	64°00'
Kangeeak Point	CAPE/CAP	NT	Franklin	26 P	67°58'	64°44'
Kange River	RIV/CDE	NT	Franklin	88 C	73°33'	116°11'
Kangert Fiord	BAY/BAIE	NT	Franklin	16 M	67°05'	63°30'
Kangilo Fiord	BAY/BAIE	NT	Franklin	26 J	66°18'	67°36'
Kangiqsualujjuaq	VILG/VILG	QC	Kativik	24 I/12	58°41'	65°57'
Kangiqsujuaq	VILG/VILG	QC	Kativik	25 E/12	61°36'	71°58'
Kangiriaraapik	UNP/LNO	QC	Kativik	34 K/4	58°10'	77°31'
Kangirsuk	VILG/VILG	QC	Kativik	25 D/1	60°01'	70°02'
Kangok Fiord	BAY/BAIE	NT	Franklin	27 B	68°37'	68°25'
Kanguk Peninsula	CAPE/CAP	NT	Franklin	59 G	79°15'	92°15'
Kanim Lake	LAKE/LAC	BC	Clayoquot	92 E/8	49°24'	126°20'
Kanish Bay	BAY/BAIE	BC	Sayward	92 K/3	50°15'	125°20'
Kânitawigamitek	UNP/LNO	QC	Vallée-de-l'Or	31 N/14	47°50'	77°05'
Kannata Valley	VILG/VILG	SK	18-21-21-W2	72 I/15	50°47'	104°54'
Kano Inlet	BAY/BAIE	BC	Queen Charlotte	103 F/7	53°10'	132°39'
Kanuchuan Lake	LAKE/LAC	ON	Kenora	43 D/13	52°55'	87°44'
Kanuekaput Ushkui	UNP/LNO	QC	Sept-Rivières	22 O/2	51°13'	66°58'
Kanuhpiamiskat	UNP/LNO	QC	Minganie	12 O/7	51°30'	58°41'
Kaoowinch 10	IR/RI	BC	Rupert	92 L/3	50°09'	127°16'
Kaouk 13	IR/RI	BC	Rupert	92 L/3	50°04'	127°06'
Kaouk Mountain	MTN/MNT	BC	Rupert	92 L/2	50°02'	126°52'
Kaouk River	RIV/CDE	BC	Rupert	92 L/3	50°04'	127°06'
Kâpakebîhâk	UNP/LNO	QC	Jamésie	32 F/6	49°24'	77°19'
Kapaneewekamik Place	UNP/LNO	MB		53 E/15	53°59'	94°47'
Kapapikwamischipiyiu	UNP/LNO	QC	Kativik	24 G/3	57°04'	67°10'
Kapapustitshepanianit	UNP/LNO	QC	Kativik	24 A/14	56°55'	65°00'
Kapasiwin	VILG/VILG	AB	31-52-3-W5	83 G/9	53°33'	114°27'
Kapeeseewinik	UNP/LNO	MB		53 L/12	54°33'	95°58'
Kapeikwaskokapwitc	UNP/LNO	QC	Le Haut-Saint-Maurice	31 P/13	47°49'	73°53'
Kapenakahkueu Uhtukuan	UNP/LNO	QC	Côte-Nord-du-Golfe-Saint-Laurent	12 K/8	50°17'	60°18'

NAME NOM	ENTITY ENTITÉ	LOC 1 LIEU 1	LOC 2 LIEU 2	MAP CARTE	POSITION LAT	LONG
Kapesakosi Lake	LAKE/LAC	ON	Kenora	52 F/6	49°25'	93°20'
Kapikik Lake	LAKE/LAC	ON	Kenora	52 O/12	51°32'	91°57'
Kapikotongwa Lake	LAKE/LAC	ON	Thunder Bay	42 L/11	50°44'	87°06'
Kapikotongwa River	RIV/CDE	ON	Thunder Bay	42 L/10	50°39'	86°43'
Kâpimabikâk	UNP/LNO	QC	Vallée-de-l'Or	32 C/9	48°31'	76°10'
Kapimhyamakach Kachiteuhumakach	UNP/LNO	QC	Jamésie	32 K/11	50°41'	77°30'
Kapiskau River	RIV/CDE	ON	Kenora	43 A/13	52°47'	81°57'
Kapistauchisitanuch	UNP/LNO	QC	Kativik	33 O/13	55°52'	75°39'
Kapitwau Uniwaatikwan	UNP/LNO	QC	Kativik	23 O/15	55°51'	66°55'
Kaposvar Creek	RIV/CDE	SK	11-18-33-W	62 K/12	50°31'	101°55'
Kappan Mountain	MTN/MNT	BC	Range 3 Coast	93 C/5	52°19'	125°30'
Kapuskasing	TOWN/VIL2	ON	Cochrane	42 G/8	49°25'	82°26'
Kapuskasing Lake	LAKE/LAC	ON	Algoma	42 B/7	48°30'	82°57'
Kapuskasing River	RIV/CDE	ON	Cochrane	42 G/16	49°49'	82°00'
Kapuskaypachik	UNP/LNO	MB		64 K/3	58°09'	101°19'
Karalash Corners	UNP/LNO	ON	Algoma	41 K/16	46°47'	84°22'
Karloske River	RIV/CDE	MB		53 N/12	55°41'	93°55'
Karlukwees 1	IR/RI	BC	Range 1 Coast	92 L/9	50°35'	126°30'
Karrak River	RIV/CDE	NT	Keewatin	66 N	67°39'	100°27'
Kars	UNP/LNO	NB	Kings	21 H/12	45°36'	65°59'
Kars	UNP/LNO	ON	Carleton	31 G/4	45°09'	75°39'
Kars	GEOG/GÉOG	NB	Kings	21 H/12	45°38'	65°58'
Karsakuwigamak Lake	LAKE/LAC	MB		64 B/5	56°23'	99°31'
Karsdale	UNP/LNO	NS	Annapolis	21 A/12	44°42'	65°39'
Kasabonika	UNP/LNO	ON	Kenora	53 H/10	53°32'	88°37'
Kasabonika Lake	LAKE/LAC	ON	Kenora	53 H/10	53°35'	88°35'
Kasabonika Lake	IR/RI	ON	Kenora	53 H/10	53°35'	88°39'
Kasasitistin	UNP/LNO	QC	Kativik	24 B/1	56°10'	66°18'
Kasasway Lake	LAKE/LAC	ON	Sudbury	41 P/13	47°55'	81°56'
Kasba Lake	LAKE/LAC	NT	Mackenzie	65 D	60°18'	102°07'
Kasha	UNP/LNO	AB	16-40-27-W4	83 A/5	52°27'	113°50'
Kashabowie	UNP/LNO	ON	Thunder Bay	52 B/9	48°39'	90°27'
Kashabowie Lake	LAKE/LAC	ON	Thunder Bay	52 B/9	48°43'	90°23'
Kashagawigamog Lake	LAKE/LAC	ON	Haliburton	31 D/15	44°59'	78°36'
Kashaweogama Lake	LAKE/LAC	ON	Thunder Bay	52 J/7	50°25'	90°45'
Kashechewan	UNP/LNO	ON	Kenora	43 A/5	52°18'	81°37'
Kashegaba Lake	LAKE/LAC	ON	Parry Sound	41 H/9	45°42'	80°08'
Kashipiautshemus	UNP/LNO	QC	Manicouagan	22 F/10	49°36'	68°51'
Kashishibog Lake	LAKE/LAC	ON	Thunder Bay	52 H/13	49°48'	89°56'
Kashittle 9	IR/RI	BC	Rupert	92 L/3	50°11'	127°18'
Kashutl Inlet	BAY/BAIE	BC	Rupert	92 L/3	50°09'	127°18'
Kashwakamak Lake	LAKE/LAC	ON	Frontenac	31 C/14	44°52'	77°01'
Kasika 36	IR/RI	BC	Range 5 Coast	103 J/8	54°23'	130°05'
Kasika 71	IR/RI	BC	Range 5 Coast	103 I/6	54°18'	129°24'
Kasika 72	IR/RI	BC	Range 5 Coast	103 I/6	54°19'	129°24'
Kasikatunakun	UNP/LNO	QC	Kativik	33 P/10	55°45'	72°58'
Kasiks River 29	IR/RI	BC	Range 5 Coast	103 I/5	54°20'	129°31'
Kasil	UNP/LNO	QC	Les Laurentides	31 G/15	45°59'	74°45'
Kaskattama River	RIV/CDE	MB		54 G/1	57°03'	90°04'
Kaskawulsh Glacier	GLAC/GLAC	YT		115 B/14	60°45'	139°06'
Kaskawulsh River	RIV/CDE	YT		115 A/12	60°39'	137°49'
Kaslo	VILG/VILG	BC	Kootenay	82 F/15	49°55'	116°55'
Kasmere Lake	LAKE/LAC	MB		64 N/11	59°34'	101°09'
Kasshabog Lake	UNP/LNO	ON	Peterborough	31 C/12	44°38'	77°58'
Kasshabog Lake	LAKE/LAC	ON	Peterborough	31 C/12	44°38'	77°58'
Kaste 6	IR/RI	BC	Queen Charlotte	103 G/4	53°10'	131°48'
Kastunaniuch	UNP/LNO	QC	Kativik	24 C/14	56°56'	69°06'
Kasungatak Island	ISL/ÎLE	NF		13 N/15	55°59'	60°54'
Kaszuby	UNP/LNO	ON	Renfrew	31 F/5	45°26'	77°35'
Katah Creek	RIV/CDE	BC	Peace River	94 H/13	57°57'	121°31'
Katattulialuk, Chute	FALL/CHUT	QC	Kativik	34 B/4	56°11'	75°56'
Katchewanooka Lake	LAKE/LAC	ON	Peterborough	31 D/8	44°27'	78°16'
Kateen River 39	IR/RI	BC	Range 5 Coast	103 I/12	54°39'	129°48'
Kate Harbour	BAY/BAIE	NF		2 C/5	48°29'	53°35'
Katepwa Beach	VILG/VILG	SK	9-20-12-W2	62 L/12	50°42'	103°38'
Katepwa South	VILG/VILG	SK	32-19-12-W2	62 L/12	50°40'	103°38'
Kater, Cape	CAPE/CAP	NT	Franklin	57 H	71°57'	90°04'
Kater Point	CAPE/CAP	NT	Mackenzie	76 N	67°44'	109°01'
Kater Trough	SEAU/SMER	—		7053	69°30'	66°45'
Kates Needle	MTN/MNT	BC	Cassiar	104 F/1	57°03'	132°03'
Katevale	UNP/LNO	QC	Memphrémagog	31 H/1	45°15'	72°03'
Kathawachaga Lake	LAKE/LAC	NT	Mackenzie	76 L	66°13'	110°46'
Kathleen	UNP/LNO	AB	35-76-19-W5	83 N/10	55°37'	116°50'
Kathleen Lake	LAKE/LAC	BC	Rupert	92 L/6	50°24'	127°17'
Kathleen Lakes	LAKE/LAC	YT		115 A/11	60°33'	137°23'

NAME NOM	ENTITY ENTITÉ	LOC 1 LIEU 1	LOC 2 LIEU 2	MAP CARTE	POSITION LAT	LONG
Kathleen, Mount	MTN/MNT	BC	Kamloops Division Yale	92 H/16	49°46′	120°03′
Kathmae Siding	UNP/LNO	ON	Renfrew	31 F/14	45°46′	77°02′
Kathmore	UNP/LNO	ON	Nipissing	31 F/13	45°49′	77°38′
Kathrintal Colony	UNP/LNO	SK	14-16-17-W2	72 I/8	50°21′	104°14′
Kathyrn	UNP/LNO	AB	16-26-27-W4	82 P/4	51°13′	113°42′
Katimiagamak Lake	LAKE/LAC	ON	Kenora	52 F/4	49°07′	93°43′
Katimik Lake	LAKE/LAC	MB	45-13,14-W	63 B/14	52°53′	99°22′
Katit 1	IR/RI	BC	Range 2 Coast	92 M/11	51°41′	127°12′
Kativik	GEOG/GÉOG	QC	Kativik	24 L/6	58°29′	71°29′
Katrime	UNP/LNO	MB	8-13-10-W	62 J/2	50°05′	98°47′
Katrine	UNP/LNO	ON	Parry Sound	31 E/11	45°34′	79°21′
Katseyedie River	RIV/CDE	NT	Mackenzie	96 J	66°32′	123°09′
Kattaktoc, Cap	CAPE/CAP	QC	Kativik	24 P/5	59°17′	65°44′
Kattiniq	UNP/LNO	QC	Kativik	35 H/12	61°43′	73°42′
Katz	UNP/LNO	BC	Yale Division Yale	92 H/5	49°22′	121°33′
Katzie 1	IR/RI	BC	New Westminster	92 G/2	49°12′	122°40′
Katzie 2	IR/RI	BC	New Westminster	92 G/2	49°12′	122°39′
Kauahtshuahk	UNP/LNO	QC	Minganie	12 L/12	50°33′	63°53′
Kauapukueht Kaiapit	UNP/LNO	QC	Côte-Nord-du-Golfe-Saint-Laurent	12 K/7	50°18′	60°39′
Kauapushishkat	UNP/LNO	QC	Le Fjord-du-Saguenay	22 M/9	51°39′	70°24′
Kauashetshuak	UNP/LNO	QC	Minganie	12 O/10	51°42′	58°48′
Kauitshinanut Kapatshuss	UNP/LNO	QC	Manicouagan	22 M/9	51°35′	70°00′
Kauk Bight	UNP/LNO	NF		14 C/12	56°30′	61°43′
Kaumajet Mountains	MTN/MNT	NF		14 F/13	57°48′	61°51′
Kaupashkueiat	UNP/LNO	QC	Manicouagan	22 N/3	51°11′	69°01′
Kaussishkashk Kauitshinanut	UNP/LNO	QC	Manicouagan	22 M/9	51°35′	70°00′
Kaustiskach	UNP/LNO	QC	Jamésie	32 L/16	50°49′	78°27′
Kaususwapaskau	UNP/LNO	QC	Kativik	24 E/9	57°37′	70°17′
Kauwinch River	RIV/CDE	BC	Rupert	92 L/3	50°09′	127°16′
Kavanagh	UNP/LNO	AB	36-48-25-W4	83 H/4	53°11′	113°31′
Kawa	UNP/LNO	ON	Thunder Bay	52 I/4	50°14′	89°59′
Kawagama Lake	LAKE/LAC	ON	Haliburton	31 E/7	45°18′	78°45′
Kawages 4	IR/RI	BC	Range 1 Coast	92 L/15	50°52′	126°31′
Kawartha Heights	UNP/LNO	ON	Peterborough	31 D/8	44°17′	78°22′
Kawartha Hideaway	UNP/LNO	ON	Peterborough	31 D/8	44°30′	78°25′
Kawartha Park	UNP/LNO	ON	Peterborough	31 D/9	44°32′	78°12′
Kawasachuun	UNP/LNO	QC	Kativik	24 F/3	57°03′	69°14′
Kawashkagama Lake	LAKE/LAC	ON	Thunder Bay	42 L/2	50°12′	86°55′
Kawastaguta, Baie	BAY/BAIE	QC	Témiscamingue	31 N/11	47°42′	77°26′
Kawawaymog Lake	LAKE/LAC	ON	Nipissing	31 E/14	45°55′	79°10′
Kawaweogama Lake	LAKE/LAC	ON	Thunder Bay	52 J/1	50°12′	90°10′
Kaweenakumik Lake	LAKE/LAC	MB	44,45-14,15-W	63 B/13	52°50′	99°30′
Kawene	UNP/LNO	ON	Rainy River	52 B/14	48°45′	91°13′
Kawigamog Lake	LAKE/LAC	ON	Parry Sound	41 H/16	45°53′	80°16′
Kawinogans River	RIV/CDE	ON	Kenora	52 P/12	51°39′	89°55′
Kawipapach Michiwap	UNP/LNO	QC	Kativik	24 F/3	57°12′	69°18′
Kawkawa Lake 16	IR/RI	BC	Yale Division Yale	92 H/6	49°23′	121°24′
Kawnipi Lake	LAKE/LAC	ON	Rainy River	52 B/6	48°23′	91°15′
Kayak Island	ISL/ÎLE	NT	Keewatin	55 K	62°13′	92°28′
Kaybob	UNP/LNO	AB	1-62-20-W5	83 K/7	54°20′	116°51′
Kaye, Cape	CAPE/CAP	NT	Franklin	58 A	72°11′	89°53′
Kayedon Lake	LAKE/LAC	ON	Thunder Bay	42 L/14	50°48′	87°01′
Kayel 8	IR/RI	BC	Range 4 Coast	103 H/3	53°04′	129°10′
Kaykaip 7	IR/RI	BC	Yale Division Yale	92 H/6	49°29′	121°25′
K'Ay Noo 47	IR/RI	BC	Range 5 Coast	93 K/10	54°40′	124°55′
Kayouk 8	IR/RI	BC	Rupert	92 L/3	50°08′	127°18′
Kay Point	CAPE/CAP	YT		117 D/6	69°18′	138°23′
Kay Point	CAPE/CAP	NT	Franklin	78 H	75°07′	104°55′
Kay Settlement	UNP/LNO	NB	Westmorland	21 H/14	45°59′	65°05′
Kayville	HAM/HAM	SK	11-9-24-W2	72 H/11	49°44′	105°09′
Kazabazua	VILG/VILG	QC	La Vallée-de-la-Gatineau	31 F/16	45°57′	76°01′
Kazabazua Station	UNP/LNO	QC	La Vallée-de-la-Gatineau	31 F/16	45°57′	76°03′
Kazan Lake	LAKE/LAC	SK		73 N/9	55°35′	108°20′
Kazan River	RIV/CDE	NT	Keewatin	56 D/3	64°03′	95°29′
Kazchek Lake	LAKE/LAC	BC	Range 5 Coast	93 K/14	54°58′	125°01′
Kdad-eesh 4	IR/RI	BC	Range 3 Coast	103 A/11	52°44′	129°17′
Keadon Park	UNP/LNO	ON	Haldimand	40 I/16	42°48′	80°05′
Keady	UNP/LNO	ON	Grey	41 A/6	44°28′	81°02′
Kean Point	CAPE/CAP	NT	Franklin	67 B	68°53′	102°27′
Kearney	TOWN/VIL2	ON	Parry Sound	31 E/11	45°33′	79°13′
Kearney	UNP/LNO	SK	27-17-19-W2	72 I/7	50°28′	104°32′
Kearney Head	CAPE/CAP	NF		1 M/9	47°34′	54°05′
Kearney Lake	UNP/LNO	NS	Halifax	11 D/12	44°41′	63°41′
Kearns	UNP/LNO	ON	Timiskaming	32 D/4	48°09′	79°34′
Keary Lake	LAKE/LAC	BC	Lillooet	92 J/15	50°46′	122°30′

NAME NOM	ENTITY ENTITÉ	LOC 1 LIEU 1	LOC 2 LIEU 2	MAP CARTE	POSITION LAT	LONG
Keating	UNP/LNO	BC	South Saanich	92 B/11	48°34′	123°24′
Keating, Lac	LAKE/LAC	QC	Kativik	23 O/8	55°21′	66°30′
Keatings Corner	UNP/LNO	NB	Kings	21 G/8	45°25′	66°14′
Keatley	UNP/LNO	SK	24-44-11-W3	73 B/14	52°48′	107°28′
Keats Island	UNP/LNO	BC	New Westminster	92 G/6	49°24′	123°29′
Keats Island	ISL/ÎLE	BC	New Westminster	92 G/6	49°24′	123°28′
Keats Point	CAPE/CAP	NT	Franklin	97 D	69°49′	121°53′
Kebaowek - see-voir - Eagle Village First Nation-Kipawa	IR/RI	QC		31 L/15	46°47′	78°59′
Kebskwasheshi Lake	LAKE/LAC	ON	Sudbury	41 O/7	47°23′	82°55′
Kechika Ranges	MTN/MNT	BC	Cassiar	94 L/11	58°45′	127°30′
Kechika River	RIV/CDE	BC	Cassiar	94 M/11	59°38′	127°09′
Kecil Lake	LAKE/LAC	ON	Algoma	41 J/8	46°16′	82°18′
Keddys Corner	UNP/LNO	NS	Kings	21 H/2	45°07′	64°34′
Kedgemakooge	UNP/LNO	NS	Annapolis	21 A/6	44°24′	65°14′
Kedgwick	VILG/VILG	NB	Restigouche	21 O/11	47°39′	67°21′
Kedgwick, Grand lac	LAKE/LAC	QC	Rimouski-Neigette	22 C/1	48°06′	68°06′
Kedgwick River	UNP/LNO	NB	Restigouche	21 O/11	47°40′	67°29′
Kedgwick River	RIV/CDE	NB	Restigouche	21 O/11	47°40′	67°29′
Kedgwick, Rivière - also-aussi - North Branch Kedgwick River	RIV/CDE	QC	La Mitis	21 O/13	47°54′	67°55′
Kedleston	UNP/LNO	SK	34-21-23-W2	72 I/14	50°50′	105°06′
Kedleston	UNP/LNO	BC	Osoyoos Division Yale	82 L/6	50°19′	119°11′
Kedleston Beach	UNP/LNO	SK	25,32-21-23-W2	72 I/14	50°49′	105°04′
Keeble	UNP/LNO	NS	Colchester	11 E/11	45°41′	63°11′
Keecekiltum 2	IR/RI	BC	Range 1 Coast	92 L/9	50°33′	126°16′
Keecha 11	IR/RI	BC	Range 4 Coast	103 H/5	53°18′	129°50′
Keefe Lake	LAKE/LAC	SK		74 H/10	57°38′	104°39′
Keefe Road - see-voir - Back Lots	UNP/LNO	NB		21 P/4	47°03′	65°31′
Keefers	UNP/LNO	BC	Yale Division Yale	92 I/4	50°01′	121°32′
Keego	UNP/LNO	ON	Thunder Bay	52 B/10	48°42′	90°36′
Keeha Bay	BAY/BAIE	BC	Barclay	92 C/14	48°47′	125°10′
Keeka Lake	LAKE/LAC	NT	Franklin	36 G	65°05′	74°20′
Keele Peak	MTN/MNT	YT		105 O/8	63°26′	130°19′
Keeler	VILG/VILG	SK	7-20-28-W2	72 I/12	50°41′	105°53′
Keele Range	MTN/MNT	YT		116 K/15	66°50′	141°00′
Keele River	RIV/CDE	NT	Mackenzie	96 C	64°25′	124°48′
Keelerville	UNP/LNO	ON	Frontenac	31 C/8	44°28′	76°21′
Keelesdale	UNP/LNO	ON	York	30 M/11	43°42′	79°29′
Keeley Lake	LAKE/LAC	SK	68-14-W3	73 K/16	54°54′	108°08′
Keeley River	RIV/CDE	SK		73 N/1	55°08′	108°06′
Keels	VILG/VILG	NF		2 C/11	48°36′	53°24′
Keemle	UNP/LNO	ON	Thunder Bay	42 E/14	49°45′	87°12′
Keenan Siding	UNP/LNO	NB	Northumberland	21 I/12	46°42′	65°48′
Keenansville	UNP/LNO	ON	Simcoe	31 D/4	44°03′	79°52′
Keene	HAM/HAM	ON	Peterborough	31 D/1	44°15′	78°10′
Keene Siding	UNP/LNO	QC	Le Granit	21 E/10	45°32′	70°44′
Keeper River	RIV/CDE	ON	Kenora	52 M/14	51°59′	95°05′
Keephills	UNP/LNO	AB	34-51-3-W5	83 G/8	53°27′	114°21′
Keep Lake	LAKE/LAC	SK		63 M/1	55°07′	102°15′
Keeseekoose 66	IR/RI	SK		62 N/12	51°43′	101°58′
Keeseekoose 66A	IR/RI	SK		62 N/13	51°45′	101°56′
Keeseekoowenin	UNP/LNO	MB	9,15,16-18-21-W	62 K/9	50°33′	100°18′
Keeseekoowenin 61	IR/RI	MB	9,15,16-18-21-W	62 K/9	50°33′	100°18′
Keeshan 9	IR/RI	BC	Barclay	92 C/14	48°49′	125°10′
Keeshata Falls	FALL/CHUT	MB		52 M/6	51°20′	95°23′
Keewatin	TOWN/VIL2	ON	Kenora	52 E/15	49°46′	94°34′
Keewatin, District de - also-aussi - **Keewatin, District of**	GEOG/GÉOG	NT		MCR130	65°00′	95°00′
Keewatin, District of - also-aussi - **Keewatin, District de**	GEOG/GÉOG	NT		MCR130	65°00′	95°00′
Keewatin River	RIV/CDE	MB	30-86-21-W	64 C/7	56°29′	100°46′
Keewaydin	UNP/LNO	ON	Nipissing	41 P/1	47°05′	80°06′
Keezhik Lake	LAKE/LAC	ON	Kenora	52 P/9	51°45′	88°30′
Kegaska	UNP/LNO	QC	Côte-Nord-du-Golfe-Saint-Laurent	12 K/3	50°11′	61°16′
Kegaska, Lac	LAKE/LAC	QC	Minganie	12 K/6	50°20′	61°25′
Kegaska, Rivière	RIV/CDE	QC	Minganie	12 K/3	50°11′	61°21′
Keg Creek Cabin	UNP/LNO	QC	La Côte-de-Gaspé	22 A/14	48°51′	65°04′
Kegeshook Lake	LAKE/LAC	NS	Yarmouth	20 P/13	43°58′	65°48′
Keg Lake	LAKE/LAC	SK		73 P/8	55°24′	104°03′
Keg Lake	LAKE/LAC	SK	53-7-W3	73 G/11	53°37′	107°03′
Keglo Bay	BAY/BAIE	NT	Franklin	24 P	59°05′	65°48′
Keg River	UNP/LNO	AB	1-101-23-W5	84 F/12	57°45′	117°38′
Keg River	UNP/LNO	AB	23-101-23-W5	84 F/13	57°47′	117°40′
Keg River	UNP/LNO	AB	21-101-24-W5	84 F/13	57°48′	117°52′
Keg River	RIV/CDE	AB	102-19,20-W5	84 F/14	57°54′	117°07′

NAME NOM	ENTITY ENTITÉ	LOC 1 LIEU 1	LOC 2 LIEU 2	MAP CARTE	POSITION LAT	LONG
Keg River Metis Settlement - see-voir - Paddle Prairie Metis Settlement	UNP/LNO	AB		84 F/14	57°55′	117°20′
Kegworth	UNP/LNO	SK	15-14-8-W2	62 L/3	50°11′	103°01′
Kehiwin 123	IR/RI	AB	16-59-6-W4	73 L/2	54°07′	110°50′
Keho Lake	LAKE/LAC	AB	11-22,23-W4	82 H/15	49°57′	112°59′
Keirsteadville	UNP/LNO	NB	Kings	21 H/12	45°39′	65°51′
Keith	UNP/LNO	AB	5-25-2-W5	82 O/1	51°06′	114°15′
Keith Arm	BAY/BAIE	NT	Mackenzie	96 G	65°20′	122°15′
Keith Bay	BAY/BAIE	NT	Keewatin	57 A	68°17′	88°16′
Keith Island	ISL/ÎLE	NT	Mackenzie	75 L	62°04′	111°50′
Keith Island 7	IR/RI	BC	Barclay	92 C/14	48°55′	125°17′
Keith Lake	LAKE/LAC	SK		73 P/14	55°59′	105°12′
Keithley Creek	UNP/LNO	BC	Cariboo	93 A/14	52°46′	121°25′
Keith-Lynn	UNP/LNO	BC	New Westminster	92 G/6	49°19′	123°04′
Kejimkujik, Annexe côtière du parc national - also-aussi - Kejimkujik National Park Seaside Adjunct	PARK/PARC	NS		20 P/15	43°52′	64°50′
Kejimkujik Lake	LAKE/LAC	NS	Annapolis	21 A/6	44°23′	65°15′
Kejimkujik, Lieu historique national de - also-aussi - Kejimkujik National Historic Site	PARK/PARC	NS	Annapolis	21 A/6	44°23′	65°18′
Kejimkujik National Historic Site - also-aussi - Kejimkujik, Lieu historique national de	PARK/PARC	NS	Annapolis	21 A/6	44°23′	65°18′
Kejimkujik National Park - also-aussi - Kejimkujik, Parc national	PARK/PARC	NS	Annapolis	21 A/6	44°23′	65°18′
Kejimkujik National Park Seaside Adjunct - also-aussi - Kejimkujik, Annexe côtière du parc national	PARK/PARC	NS		20 P/15	43°52′	64°50′
Kejimkujik, Parc national - also-aussi - Kejimkujik National Park	PARK/PARC	NS	Annapolis	21 A/6	44°23′	65°18′
Kekek, Rivière	RIV/CDE	QC	Vallée-de-l'Or	32 B/5	48°24′	75°48′
Kekertal Island	ISL/ÎLE	NT	Franklin	27 A	68°35′	67°48′
Kekertaluk Island	ISL/ÎLE	NT	Franklin	16 E	65°32′	63°12′
Kekertaluk Island	ISL/ÎLE	NT	Franklin	27 A	68°12′	66°24′
Kekertelung Island	ISL/ÎLE	NT	Franklin	26 J	66°21′	66°44′
Kekerten	UNP/LNO	NT	Franklin	26 H	65°43′	65°50′
Kekertukdjuak Island	ISL/ÎLE	NT	Franklin	26 H	65°52′	65°35′
Keld	UNP/LNO	MB	32-23-20-W	62 N/1	51°02′	100°15′
Keldon	UNP/LNO	ON	Grey	41 A/1	44°02′	80°23′
Kelfield	VILG/VILG	SK	27-34-19-W3	72 N/15	51°57′	108°37′
Keller Bridge	UNP/LNO	ON	Hastings	31 C/12	44°37′	77°32′
Keller Lake	LAKE/LAC	SK		74 B/2	56°04′	106°47′
Keller Lake	LAKE/LAC	NT	Mackenzie	95 P	63°57′	121°35′
Kellers	UNP/LNO	ON	Northumberland	31 C/5	44°23′	77°48′
Kellett	UNP/LNO	MB		54 E/8	57°27′	94°12′
Kellett, Cape	CAPE/CAP	NT	Franklin	97 G	71°58′	126°00′
Kellett River	RIV/CDE	NT	Keewatin	57 A	68°20′	90°07′
Kellett River	RIV/CDE	NT	Franklin	98 B	72°05′	125°42′
Kellett Strait	CHAN/CHEN	NT	Franklin	88 G	75°45′	117°30′
Kelleys Cove	UNP/LNO	NS	Yarmouth	20 O/16	43°47′	66°07′
Kelligrews	UNP/LNO	NF		1 N/11	47°30′	53°01′
Kelliher	VILG/VILG	SK	34-26-13-W2	62 M/5	51°16′	103°44′
Kelloe	UNP/LNO	MB	3-17-24-W	62 K/7	50°29′	100°46′
Kellross No. 247	MUN2/AZM2	SK		62 M/4	51°15′	103°55′
Kelly	UNP/LNO	QC	Bonaventure	22 A/3	48°07′	65°08′
Kelly	UNP/LNO	QC	L'Érable	21 L/5	46°15′	71°44′
Kelly	UNP/LNO	ON	Thunder Bay	52 G/1	49°01′	90°12′
Kelly Bay	BAY/BAIE	SK		74 I/1	58°13′	104°28′
Kelly Creek 3	IR/RI	BC	Lillooet	92 I/13	50°58′	121°53′
Kelly Lake	UNP/LNO	BC	Peace River	93 P/8	55°15′	120°02′
Kelly Lake	UNP/LNO	BC	Lillooet	92 P/4	51°01′	121°46′
Kelly Lake	LAKE/LAC	ON	Sudbury	41 I/6	46°27′	81°05′
Kelly Lake	LAKE/LAC	NT	Mackenzie	96 E	65°24′	126°15′
Kelly Newton	UNP/LNO	QC	La Vallée-de-la-Gatineau	31 G/13	45°58′	75°49′
Kelly River	RIV/CDE	BC	Similkameen Division Yale	82 E/6	49°17′	119°02′
Kelly Road	UNP/LNO	PE	Prince	21 I/9	46°43′	64°08′
Kellys Corner	UNP/LNO	ON	Renfrew	31 F/10	45°33′	77°00′
Kellys Cross	UNP/LNO	PE	Queens	11 L/6	46°16′	63°27′
Kellys Island	ISL/ÎLE	NF		1 N/11	47°33′	53°01′
*Kelly Station	UNP/LNO	ON	Middlesex	40 P/3	43°10′	81°08′
Kelowna	CITY/VIL1	BC	Osoyoos Division Yale	82 E/14	49°53′	119°29′
Kelp Head	CAPE/CAP	BC	Range 2 Coast	92 M/5	51°22′	127°47′
Kelp Point	CAPE/CAP	BC	Range 4 Coast	103 G/8	53°23′	130°19′
Kelsall River	RIV/CDE	BC	Cassiar	114 P/9	59°38′	136°15′
Kelsey	UNP/LNO	MB	24-81-6-E	64 A/2	56°02′	96°32′
Kelsey	UNP/LNO	AB	4-45-18-W4	83 A/15	52°51′	112°33′
*Kelsey Bay	UNP/LNO	BC	Sayward	92 K/5	50°33′	125°58′
Kelsey Creek	RIV/CDE	MB		54 K/3	58°05′	93°02′
Kelsey Creek	RIV/CDE	SK	29-51-16-W2	73 H/8	53°25′	104°18′

NAME NOM	ENTITY ENTITÉ	LOC 1 LIEU 1	LOC 2 LIEU 2	MAP CARTE	POSITION LAT	LONG
Kelsey Lake	LAKE/LAC	MB	53-24-W	63 F/11	53°39′	101°03′
Kelso	UNP/LNO	ON	Halton	30 M/12	43°30′	79°57′
Kelso	UNP/LNO	ON	Cochrane	42 A/10	48°41′	80°45′
Kelso	UNP/LNO	SK	32-11-33-W	62 F/13	49°58′	101°57′
Kelstern	UNP/LNO	SK	6-14-6-W3	72 J/2	50°09′	106°48′
Keltic Lodge	UNP/LNO	NS	Victoria	11 K/9	46°39′	60°24′
Keltie Inlet	BAY/BAIE	NT	Franklin	36 A	64°28′	73°20′
Kelvin	UNP/LNO	ON	Brant	40 I/16	43°00′	80°27′
Kelvin	UNP/LNO	BC	New Westminster	92 G/2	49°13′	122°56′
Kelvin Grove	UNP/LNO	PE	Prince	11 L/5	46°25′	63°39′
Kelvingrove	UNP/LNO	QC	Le Haut-Saint-Laurent	31 G/1	45°03′	74°13′
Kelvington	TOWN/VIL2	SK		63 D/4	52°10′	103°32′
Kelvington No. 366	MUN2/AZM2	SK		63 D/3	52°15′	103°30′
Kelvin Island	ISL/ÎLE	ON	Thunder Bay	52 H/15	49°51′	88°40′
Kelwood	UNP/LNO	MB	11-19-15-W	62 J/11	50°37′	99°28′
Kemano	UNP/LNO	BC	Range 4 Coast	93 E/12	53°34′	127°57′
Kemano - see-voir - Kemano Beach	UNP/LNO	BC		103 H/8	53°29′	128°07′
Kemano 17	IR/RI	BC	Range 4 Coast	103 H/8	53°29′	128°09′
Kemano Beach	UNP/LNO	BC	Range 4 Coast	103 H/8	53°29′	128°07′
Kemano River	RIV/CDE	BC	Range 4 Coast	103 H/8	53°29′	128°08′
Kemble	UNP/LNO	ON	Grey	41 A/10	44°44′	80°56′
Kemnay	UNP/LNO	MB	16-10-20-W	62 F/16	49°51′	100°08′
Kempark	UNP/LNO	ON	Carleton	31 G/5	45°20′	75°36′
Kempenfelt Bay	BAY/BAIE	ON	Simcoe	31 D/5	44°25′	79°35′
Kemp River	UNP/LNO	AB	34-98-22-W5	84 F/11	57°33′	117°30′
Kemp River	RIV/CDE	AB	101-22-W5	84 F/12	57°45′	117°35′
Kemps Point	CAPE/CAP	NS	Richmond	11 F/10	45°37′	60°31′
Kempt	UNP/LNO	NS	Queens	21 A/6	44°26′	65°07′
Kempt Back Lake	LAKE/LAC	NS	Yarmouth	21 A/4	44°04′	65°51′
Kempt Head	UNP/LNO	NS	Victoria	11 K/2	46°05′	60°39′
Kempt Head	CAPE/CAP	NS	Victoria	11 K/2	46°04′	60°40′
Kempt, Lac	LAKE/LAC	QC	Matawinie	31 O/8	47°26′	74°16′
Kempt, Lac	LAKE/LAC	QC	Matawinie	31 J/16	46°55′	74°18′
Kempton Bay	BAY/BAIE	SK		64 L/2	58°14′	103°00′
Kempton Lake	LAKE/LAC	NS	Queens	21 A/3	44°07′	65°00′
Kemptown	UNP/LNO	NS	Colchester	11 E/6	45°28′	63°05′
Kempt, Rivière	RIV/CDE	QC	Bonaventure	22 B/2	48°00′	66°46′
Kempt Road	UNP/LNO	NS	Richmond	11 F/11	45°39′	61°10′
Kempt Shore	UNP/LNO	NS	Hants	21 H/1	45°07′	64°12′
Kemptville	TOWN/VIL2	ON	Grenville	31 G/4	45°01′	75°38′
Kemptville	UNP/LNO	NS	Yarmouth	21 A/4	44°03′	65°50′
Kemsquit 1	IR/RI	BC	Range 3 Coast	93 D/15	52°49′	126°58′
Kenabeek	UNP/LNO	ON	Timiskaming	31 M/12	47°39′	79°59′
Kenabutch	UNP/LNO	ON	Algoma	41 J/1	46°12′	82°29′
Kenamu River	RIV/CDE	NF		13 G/5	53°29′	59°55′
Kenaston	VILG/VILG	SK	19-29-2-W3	72 O/8	51°30′	106°17′
Kendal	VILG/VILG	SK	17-15-12-W2	62 L/5	50°15′	103°37′
Kendal	UNP/LNO	ON	Durham	31 D/2	44°02′	78°32′
Kendall, Cape	CAPE/CAP	NT	Keewatin	45 M	63°36′	87°12′
Kendall, Cape	CAPE/CAP	NT	Mackenzie	87 A	68°01′	115°05′
Kendall Island	ISL/ÎLE	NT	Mackenzie	107 C	69°29′	135°17′
Kendall Ridge	SEAU/SMER	—		1399A	62°30′	88°20′
Kendall River	RIV/CDE	NT	Mackenzie	86 N	67°07′	116°07′
Kendall Strait	CHAN/CHEN	NT	Franklin	25 J	62°10′	66°00′
Kendry	UNP/LNO	ON	Peterborough	31 D/1	44°13′	78°24′
Keneden Park	UNP/LNO	ON	Victoria	31 D/7	44°21′	78°31′
Kenemich River	RIV/CDE	NF		13 G/5	53°29′	59°50′
Kenhill Beach	UNP/LNO	ON	Victoria	31 D/7	44°29′	78°39′
Kenilworth	UNP/LNO	ON	Wellington	40 P/15	43°53′	80°38′
Kenilworth Lake	LAKE/LAC	AB	50-4-W4	73 E/7	53°20′	110°32′
Kenlis	UNP/LNO	SK	27-19-11-W2	62 L/11	50°41′	103°27′
Kenloch	UNP/LNO	NS	Inverness	11 K/3	46°11′	61°16′
Kenmore	UNP/LNO	ON	Carleton	31 G/3	45°14′	75°25′
Kennaway	UNP/LNO	ON	Haliburton	31 E/1	45°10′	78°10′
Kennebec	MUN2/AZM2	ON	Frontenac	31 C/11	44°43′	77°00′
Kennebecasis Bay	BAY/BAIE	NB	Kings	21 G/8	45°23′	66°02′
Kennebecasis Park	UNP/LNO	NB	Kings	21 G/8	45°21′	66°02′
Kennebecasis River	RIV/CDE	NB	Saint John	21 G/8	45°19′	66°08′
Kennebec Lake	LAKE/LAC	ON	Frontenac	31 C/10	44°44′	76°58′
Kennedy	VILG/VILG	SK	22-12-3-W2	62 L/1	50°01′	102°21′
Kennedy	UNP/LNO	BC	Cariboo	93 O/2	55°07′	122°48′
Kennedy	UNP/LNO	BC	New Westminster	92 G/2	49°10′	122°53′
Kennedy Acres	UNP/LNO	ON	Lambton	40 O/1	43°02′	82°13′
Kennedy Bay	UNP/LNO	ON	Victoria	31 D/7	44°28′	78°42′
Kennedy Bight	BAY/BAIE	NF		3 D/4	52°08′	55°42′

NAME NOM	ENTITY ENTITÉ	LOC 1 LIEU 1	LOC 2 LIEU 2	MAP CARTE	POSITION LAT	LONG
Kennedy Channel - also-aussi - Kennedy, Passage	CHAN/CHEN	NT	Franklin	120 B/15	80°55′	66°30′
Kennedy Head	CAPE/CAP	NF		3 D/4	52°08′	55°42′
Kennedy Island	ISL/ÎLE	BC	Range 5 Coast	103 J/1	54°02′	130°11′
Kennedy Lake	LAKE/LAC	ON	Sudbury	41 I/13	46°51′	81°50′
Kennedy Lake	LAKE/LAC	SK	53-7-W2	63 E/10	53°35′	102°56′
Kennedy Lake	LAKE/LAC	BC	Clayoquot	92 F/4	49°04′	125°34′
Kennedy Lakes	LAKE/LAC	NB	Northumberland	21 J/15	46°51′	66°30′
Kennedy, Mount	MTN/MNT	BC	Range 1 Coast	92 K/13	50°50′	125°33′
Kennedy, Mount	MTN/MNT	YT		115 B/7	60°20′	138°58′
Kennedy Park	UNP/LNO	ON	York	30 M/11	43°43′	79°16′
Kennedy, Passage - also-aussi - Kennedy Channel	CHAN/CHEN	NT	Franklin	120 B/15	80°55′	66°30′
Kennedy River	RIV/CDE	BC	Clayoquot	92 F/4	49°08′	125°40′
Kennedys	UNP/LNO	ON	Parry Sound	31 E/11	45°41′	79°24′
Kennell	UNP/LNO	SK	30-20-19-W2	72 I/10	50°44′	104°39′
Kennetcook	UNP/LNO	NS	Hants	11 E/4	45°11′	63°44′
Kennetcook River	RIV/CDE	NS	Hants	21 H/1	45°03′	64°08′
Kenneth	UNP/LNO	NB	Carleton	21 J/11	46°35′	67°25′
Kenney Dam	MISC/DIV	BC	Range 4 Coast	93 F/10	53°34′	124°57′
Kennicott	UNP/LNO	ON	Perth	40 P/11	43°33′	81°07′
Kennisis Lake	UNP/LNO	ON	Haliburton	31 E/2	45°13′	78°36′
Kennisis Lake	LAKE/LAC	ON	Haliburton	31 E/2	45°13′	78°38′
Kenny, Mount	MTN/MNT	BC	Peace River	94 B/13	56°56′	123°49′
Kenny Point	CAPE/CAP	ON	Algoma	41 J/1	46°03′	82°22′
Kennyville	UNP/LNO	QC	La Vallée-de-la-Gatineau	31 J/4	46°05′	75°51′
Kenny Woods	UNP/LNO	AB	14-105-9-W4	74 L/3	58°07′	111°23′
Kénogami	UNP/LNO	QC	Le Fjord-du-Saguenay	22 D/6	48°25′	71°15′
Kénogami, Lac	LAKE/LAC	QC	Le Fjord-du-Saguenay	22 D/6	48°20′	71°23′
Kenogami Lake	UNP/LNO	ON	Timiskaming	42 A/1	48°06′	80°12′
Kenogami Lake	LAKE/LAC	ON	Timiskaming	42 A/1	48°06′	80°14′
Kenogami Lake Station	UNP/LNO	ON	Timiskaming	42 A/1	48°06′	80°10′
Kenogaming Lake	LAKE/LAC	ON	Sudbury	42 A/4	48°05′	81°55′
Kenogami River	RIV/CDE	ON	Cochrane	42 N/1	51°06′	84°28′
Kenogamisis Lake	LAKE/LAC	ON	Thunder Bay	42 E/10	49°42′	86°53′
Kenogamissi Lake	LAKE/LAC	ON	Timiskaming	42 A/4	48°11′	81°33′
Keno Hill	UNP/LNO	YT		105 M/14	63°55′	135°18′
Kenora	TOWN/VIL2	ON	Kenora	52 E/16	49°47′	94°29′
Kenora	GEOG/GÉOG	ON		53 I/1	54°00′	88°00′
Kenora 38B	IR/RI	ON	Kenora	52 E/9	49°43′	94°25′
Kenosee Lake	VILG/VILG	SK	24-10-3-W2M	62 E/16	49°50′	102°17′
Kenosee Park	UNP/LNO	SK	24-10-3-W2	62 E/16	49°50′	102°18′
Kenrei Park	UNP/LNO	ON	Victoria	31 D/7	44°24′	78°45′
Kensal Park	UNP/LNO	ON	Middlesex	40 I/14	42°58′	81°17′
Kensington	TOWN/VIL2	PE	Prince	11 L/5	46°26′	63°39′
Kensington	UNP/LNO	QC	Le Haut-Saint-Laurent	31 G/1	45°01′	74°18′
Kensington-Cedar Cottage	UNP/LNO	BC	New Westminster	92 G/3	49°15′	123°04′
Kenstone Beach	UNP/LNO	ON	Victoria	31 D/10	44°31′	78°34′
Kent	MUN1/AZM1	ON	Kent	40 J/8	42°25′	82°10′
Kent	MUN1/AZM1	BC	New Westminster	92 H/4	49°17′	121°45′
Kent	UNP/LNO	NS	Halifax	11 E/3	45°06′	63°01′
Kent	UNP/LNO	ON	Grey	41 A/10	44°36′	80°36′
Kent	GEOG/GÉOG	NB		21 I/11	46°35′	65°15′
Kent	GEOG/GÉOG	NB	Carleton	21 J/11	46°35′	67°20′
Kent	GEOG/GÉOG	ON		40 J/8	42°25′	82°10′
Kent Bay	BAY/BAIE	NT	Franklin	67 D	69°57′	96°08′
Kent Bridge	UNP/LNO	ON	Kent	40 J/9	42°31′	82°04′
Kent Centre	UNP/LNO	ON	Kent	40 J/8	42°23′	82°06′
Kent Gardens	UNP/LNO	ON	Halton	30 M/5	43°27′	79°42′
Kent Island	ISL/ÎLE	NB	Charlotte	21 B/10	44°35′	66°45′
Kent Junction	UNP/LNO	NB	Kent	21 I/11	46°35′	65°20′
Kent Lake	UNP/LNO	NB	Kent	21 I/11	46°38′	65°06′
Kent Lake Siding	UNP/LNO	NB	Kent	21 I/11	46°37′	65°06′
Kenton	UNP/LNO	MB	6-12-23-W	62 F/15	49°59′	100°37′
Kent Park	UNP/LNO	NS	Halifax	11 D/12	44°41′	63°41′
Kent Peninsula	CAPE/CAP	NT	Mackenzie	77 A	68°30′	107°00′
Kentvale	UNP/LNO	ON	Algoma	41 K/1	46°12′	84°02′
Kentville	TOWN/VIL2	NS	Kings	21 H/1	45°05′	64°30′
Kenville	UNP/LNO	MB	13-35-28-W	63 C/3	52°00′	101°19′
Kenville West	UNP/LNO	MB	11-35-28-W	62 N/14	51°59′	101°21′
Kenwell	UNP/LNO	ON	Thunder Bay	42 E/11	49°44′	87°04′
Kenyon	MUN2/AZM2	ON	Glengarry	31 G/7	45°20′	74°45′
Kenyon Lake	LAKE/LAC	MB		53 K/14	54°49′	93°07′
Kenzie	UNP/LNO	AB	29-75-18-W5	83 N/10	55°31′	116°45′
Kenzieville	UNP/LNO	NS	Pictou	11 E/9	45°35′	62°18′
Keogh 2	IR/RI	BC	Range 1 Coast	92 K/12	50°40′	125°43′
Keogh 3	IR/RI	BC	Range 1 Coast	92 L/15	50°57′	126°38′

NAME / NOM	ENTITY / ENTITÉ	LOC 1 / LIEU 1	LOC 2 / LIEU 2	MAP / CARTE	POSITION LAT	POSITION LONG
Keogh 6	IR/RI	BC	Rupert	92 L/11	50°41′	127°21′
Keogh Lake	LAKE/LAC	BC	Rupert	92 L/6	50°30′	127°10′
Keogh River	RIV/CDE	BC	Rupert	92 L/11	50°41′	127°20′
Keoma	UNP/LNO	AB	13-26-27-W4	82 P/4	51°13′	113°39′
Keom Cho 38	IR/RI	BC	Range 5 Coast	93 K/10	54°36′	124°49′
Kepenkeck Lake	LAKE/LAC	NF		2 D/7	48°18′	54°55′
Kepimits Lake	LAKE/LAC	NF		23 A/10	52°45′	64°56′
Kepler	UNP/LNO	ON	Frontenac	31 C/7	44°21′	76°34′
Keppel	MUN2/AZM2	ON	Grey	41 A/11	44°42′	81°01′
Keppel	UNP/LNO	SK	19-35-12-W3	73 B/4	52°02′	107°44′
Keppel Lake	LAKE/LAC	SK	39,40-17-W3	73 C/8	52°24′	108°20′
Keppoch	UNP/LNO	PE	Queens	11 L/3	46°12′	63°07′
Keppoch	UNP/LNO	NS	Inverness	11 K/3	46°12′	61°06′
Kequesta 1	IR/RI	BC	Range 2 Coast	92 M/3	51°06′	127°28′
Kerbodot, Lac	LAKE/LAC	QC	Caniapiscau	23 G/5	53°27′	67°45′
Keremeos	VILG/VILG	BC	Similkameen Division Yale	82 E/4	49°03′	119°50′
Keremeos Creek	RIV/CDE	BC	Similkameen Division Yale	82 E/4	49°10′	119°47′
Keremeos Forks 12 & 12A	IR/RI	BC	Similkameen Division Yale	82 E/5	49°18′	119°49′
Kerensky	UNP/LNO	AB	13-58-22-W4	83 I/3	54°01′	113°08′
Kergus, Lac	LAKE/LAC	QC	La Haute-Côte-Nord	22 C/12	48°36′	69°45′
Kergwenan	UNP/LNO	MB	31-22-15-W	62 J/13	50°57′	99°32′
Kerleys Harbour	UNP/LNO	NF		2 C/6	48°17′	53°28′
Kerman Lake	LAKE/LAC	MB		64 I/11	58°43′	97°28′
Kermode, Mount	MTN/MNT	BC	Queen Charlotte	103 B/13	52°57′	131°51′
Kernertut, Cap	CAPE/CAP	QC	Kativik	24 J/10	58°30′	66°56′
Kern Park	UNP/LNO	MB		62 H/15	49°54′	97°00′
Kerns	MUN2/AZM2	ON	Timiskaming	31 M/12	47°37′	79°48′
Kerouard Islands	ISL/ÎLE	BC	Queen Charlotte	102 O/14	51°55′	131°00′
Kerr Creek	UNP/LNO	BC	Similkameen Division Yale	82 E/2	49°03′	118°45′
Kerrisdale	UNP/LNO	BC	New Westminster	92 G/3	49°13′	123°09′
Kerr Lake	UNP/LNO	ON	Timiskaming	31 M/5	47°23′	79°39′
Kerr Line	UNP/LNO	ON	Renfrew	31 F/10	45°39′	76°45′
Kerrobert	TOWN/VIL2	SK		72 N/14	51°55′	109°08′
Kerrowgare	UNP/LNO	NS	Pictou	11 E/8	45°24′	62°26′
Kerrs Lake	UNP/LNO	MB	35-17-17-W	62 J/12	50°30′	99°42′
Kerrs Mill Road	UNP/LNO	NS	Cumberland	11 E/13	45°47′	63°33′
Kerrs Point	CAPE/CAP	NS	Inverness	11 K/15	46°51′	60°46′
Kerrs Ridge	UNP/LNO	NB	Charlotte	21 G/3	45°13′	67°01′
Kerry	UNP/LNO	MB	5-10,11-E	62 H/8	49°24′	96°06′
Kersey	UNP/LNO	AB	13-28-28-W4	82 P/5	51°24′	113°49′
Kersley	UNP/LNO	BC	Cariboo	93 B/16	52°49′	122°25′
Kertch	UNP/LNO	ON	Lambton	40 J/16	42°59′	82°03′
Kerwood	UNP/LNO	ON	Middlesex	40 I/13	42°56′	81°45′
Kesagami Lake	LAKE/LAC	ON	Cochrane	42 I/8	50°23′	80°15′
Kesagami River	RIV/CDE	ON	Cochrane	32 M/4	51°09′	79°47′
Kesatasew River	RIV/CDE	SK	67-24-W3	73 K/13	54°47′	109°34′
Keseechewun Lake	LAKE/LAC	SK		64 M/10	59°45′	102°41′
Keskarrah Lake	LAKE/LAC	NT	Mackenzie	86 J	66°03′	115°15′
Kessock	UNP/LNO	SK	2-26-33-W2	62 N/4	51°13′	102°00′
Keswar 16	IR/RI	BC	Range 4 Coast	103 G/9	53°39′	130°20′
Keswick	UNP/LNO	NB	York	21 J/2	46°00′	66°50′
Keswick	UNP/LNO	ON	York	31 D/3	44°15′	79°28′
Keswick Beach	UNP/LNO	ON	York	31 D/3	44°14′	79°29′
Keswick Ridge	UNP/LNO	NB	York	21 G/15	46°00′	66°53′
Keswick River	RIV/CDE	NB	York	21 G/15	45°59′	66°50′
Ketai 28	IR/RI	BC	Range 4 Coast	103 H/12	53°38′	129°59′
Ketchen	HAM/HAM	SK	8-35-6-W2	62 M/15	52°00′	102°49′
Ketchen	UNP/LNO	QC	Témiscamingue	31 L/11	46°41′	79°04′
Ketch Harbour	UNP/LNO	NS	Halifax	11 D/5	44°29′	63°33′
Ketchum Ridge	UNP/LNO	NB	Carleton	21 J/6	46°28′	67°28′
Ketepec	UNP/LNO	NB	Saint John	21 G/8	45°17′	66°10′
Ketoneda 7	IR/RI	BC	Range 5 Coast	103 I/16	54°50′	128°19′
Ketoria, Cape	CAPE/CAP	NT	Franklin	36 G	65°26′	75°13′
Kettleby	UNP/LNO	ON	York	31 D/4	44°01′	79°34′
Kettle Canyon	SEAU/SMER	—		8010	44°02′	49°07′
Kettle Cove	UNP/LNO	NF		2 E/10	49°36′	54°43′
Kettle Creek	RIV/CDE	ON	Elgin	40 I/11	42°38′	81°13′
Kettlehut	UNP/LNO	SK	10-20-4-W3	72 J/9	50°41′	106°29′
Kettle Lake	LAKE/LAC	MB	81,82-16,17-E	54 D/2	56°06′	94°56′
Kettle Point	UNP/LNO	ON	Lambton	40 O/1	43°11′	82°01′
Kettle Point	CAPE/CAP	ON	Lambton	40 O/1	43°13′	82°01′
Kettle Point 44	IR/RI	ON	Lambton	40 O/1	43°12′	82°01′
Kettle Rapids	UNP/LNO	MB	85-19-E	54 D/7	56°25′	94°32′
Kettle River	RIV/CDE	MB		54 A/14	56°55′	89°23′
Kettle River	RIV/CDE	MB	20-85-19-E	54 D/7	56°23′	94°34′

NAME NOM	ENTITY ENTITÉ	LOC 1 LIEU 1	LOC 2 LIEU 2	MAP CARTE	POSITION LAT	LONG
Kettle River	RIV/CDE	BC	Similkameen Division Yale	82 E/1	49°00'	118°12'
Kettle's Beach	UNP/LNO	ON	Simcoe	31 D/13	44°51'	79°59'
Kettlestone Bay	BAY/BAIE	NT	Keewatin	35 F	61°12'	77°44'
Kettle Valley	UNP/LNO	BC	Similkameen Division Yale	82 E/2	49°03'	118°56'
Ketyet River	RIV/CDE	NT	Keewatin	56 D/2	64°14'	94°46'
Kevisville	UNP/LNO	AB	25-35-4-W5	83 B/1	52°02'	114°26'
Kew	UNP/LNO	AB	30-20-3-W5	82 J/9	50°44'	114°25'
Kewagama	UNP/LNO	QC	Rouyn-Noranda	32 D/1	48°14'	78°24'
Keward	UNP/LNO	ON	Grey	41 A/7	44°27'	80°58'
Kewstoke	UNP/LNO	NS	Inverness	11 F/14	45°59'	61°13'
Keyano	UNP/LNO	QC	Jamésie	33 H/13	53°50'	73°32'
Keyarka 17	IR/RI	BC	Range 4 Coast	103 G/9	53°36'	130°22'
Keyes	UNP/LNO	MB	36-14-13-W	62 J/3	50°15'	99°07'
Key Harbour	UNP/LNO	ON	Parry Sound	41 H/15	45°53'	80°43'
Key Harbour	BAY/BAIE	ON	Parry Sound	41 H/15	45°53'	80°45'
Key Junction	UNP/LNO	ON	Parry Sound	41 H/15	45°59'	80°43'
Key Point	CAPE/CAP	NT	Franklin	79 A	76°14'	104°16'
Key River	UNP/LNO	ON	Parry Sound	41 H/15	45°54'	80°34'
Key River	RIV/CDE	ON	Parry Sound	41 H/15	45°53'	80°44'
Keyser	UNP/LNO	ON	Middlesex	40 P/4	43°03'	81°44'
Keys Lake	LAKE/LAC	ON	Kenora	52 L/1	50°02'	94°01'
Keys No. 303	MUN2/AZM2	SK		62 M/9	51°45'	102°15'
Keyson	UNP/LNO	ON	Cochrane	42 A/11	48°34'	81°03'
Keystone	UNP/LNO	AB	19-48-3-W5	83 G/1	53°09'	114°26'
Keystone Camps	UNP/LNO	ON	Nipissing	31 L/4	46°12'	79°52'
Keystown	UNP/LNO	SK	36-17-23-W2	72 I/6	50°28'	105°03'
Key West	UNP/LNO	SK	27-8-23-W2	72 H/11	49°41'	105°02'
Key West No. 70	MUN2/AZM2	SK		72 H/10	49°40'	105°00'
Khartoum	UNP/LNO	QC	Memphrémagog	31 H/8	45°22'	72°18'
Khartoum Lake	LAKE/LAC	BC	New Westminster	92 F/16	49°53'	124°06'
Khartum	UNP/LNO	ON	Renfrew	31 F/6	45°16'	77°06'
Khazisela 7	IR/RI	BC	Range 2 Coast	92 M/4	51°06'	127°31'
Khedive	VILG/VILG	SK	4-8-19-W2	72 H/10	49°37'	104°31'
Khikkertarsoak South Island	ISL/ÎLE	NF		14 F/6	57°30'	61°29'
Khiva	UNP/LNO	ON	Huron	40 P/5	43°17'	81°37'
Khrana 4	IR/RI	BC	Queen Charlotte	103 F/1	53°13'	132°02'
Khtada Lake	LAKE/LAC	BC	Range 5 Coast	103 I/3	54°08'	129°28'
Khtahda 10	IR/RI	BC	Range 5 Coast	103 I/4	54°11'	129°36'
Khutzemateen 49	IR/RI	BC	Range 5 Coast	103 I/12	54°38'	129°53'
Khutzeymateen Inlet	BAY/BAIE	BC	Range 5 Coast	103 J/9	54°39'	130°04'
Khyex 8	IR/RI	BC	Range 5 Coast	103 I/4	54°14'	129°48'
Khyex River	RIV/CDE	BC	Range 5 Coast	103 I/4	54°14'	129°48'
Kiamika	VILG/VILG	QC	Antoine-Labelle	31 J/6	46°25'	75°20'
Kiamika	UNP/LNO	QC	Antoine-Labelle	31 J/6	46°25'	75°23'
Kiamika, Réservoir	LAKE/LAC	QC	Antoine-Labelle	31 J/11	46°40'	75°04'
Kichha 10	IR/RI	BC	Barclay	92 C/14	48°47'	125°11'
Kicking Horse Pass	VALL/VALL	AB/BC		82 N/8	51°27'	116°17'
Kicking Horse Pass National Historic Site - also-aussi - Col-Kicking Horse, Lieu historique national du	PARK/PARC	AB/BC		82 N/8	51°27'	116°17'
Kidd	UNP/LNO	BC	Cariboo	93 H/10	53°43'	120°58'
Kidney Island	ISL/ÎLE	NT	Keewatin	34 E	57°33'	79°45'
Kidprice Lake	LAKE/LAC	BC	Range 4 Coast	93 E/14	53°55'	127°27'
Kierkoski	UNP/LNO	QC	La Vallée-du-Richelieu	31 H/11	45°39'	73°08'
Kierstead Mountain	UNP/LNO	NB	Kings	21 H/13	45°48'	65°40'
Kiglapait, Cape	CAPE/CAP	NF		14 F/3	57°06'	61°22'
Kiglapait Mountains	MTN/MNT	NF		14 F/4	57°06'	61°35'
Kiglikavik Lake	LAKE/LAC	NT	Mackenzie	86 I/14	66°49'	113°10'
Kikastan Islands	ISL/ÎLE	NT	Franklin	26 H	65°46'	65°50'
Kikendatch, Baie	BAY/BAIE	QC	Le Haut-Saint-Maurice	32 B/8	48°23'	74°10'
Kikerk Lake	LAKE/LAC	NT	Mackenzie	86 P	67°18'	113°12'
Kikiktaksoak Island	ISL/ÎLE	NF		14 F/6	57°16'	61°30'
Kikiktaluk Island	ISL/ÎLE	NT	Franklin	26 B	64°55'	66°10'
Kikino	UNP/LNO	AB	18-63-14-W4	83 I/8	54°27'	112°08'
Kikino Metis Settlement	UNP/LNO	AB		83 I/8	54°24'	112°09'
Kikkertaksoak Islands	ISL/ÎLE	NF		13 N/9	55°43'	60°10'
Kikkertavak Island	ISL/ÎLE	NF		13 J/15	54°58'	58°42'
Kikkertavak Island	ISL/ÎLE	NF		13 N/8	55°22'	60°09'
Kikkertavak Island	ISL/ÎLE	NF		14 C/5	56°22'	61°35'
Kikkertoksoak Islands	ISL/ÎLE	NT	Franklin	24 P/4	59°05'	65°51'
Kikupegh Pond	LAKE/LAC	NF		12 A/1	48°10'	56°05'
Kikwissi, Lac	LAKE/LAC	QC	Témiscamingue	31 L/15	46°59'	78°33'
Kilbella Bay	UNP/LNO	BC	Range 2 Coast	92 M/11	51°42'	127°20'
Kilbella River	RIV/CDE	BC	Range 2 Coast	92 M/11	51°43'	127°21'
Kilbride	UNP/LNO	NF		1 N/10	47°32'	52°45'
Kilbride	UNP/LNO	ON	Halton	30 M/5	43°25'	79°56'
Kilburn	UNP/LNO	NB	Victoria	21 J/12	46°38'	67°42'

NAME NOM	ENTITY ENTITÉ	LOC 1 LIEU 1	LOC 2 LIEU 2	MAP CARTE	POSITION LAT	LONG
Kilburn	UNP/LNO	ON	Cochrane	42 A/10	48°41′	80°48′
Kilburn Lake	LAKE/LAC	NB	York	21 G/14	45°48′	67°21′
Kilburn Mills	UNP/LNO	QC	Coaticook	21 E/4	45°05′	71°56′
Kilchult 3	IR/RI	BC	Lillooet	92 I/12	50°37′	121°51′
Kil-cona Park	UNP/LNO	MB		62 H/14	49°56′	97°01′
Kilcoo Camp	UNP/LNO	ON	Haliburton	31 D/15	44°51′	78°46′
Kildala Arm	UNP/LNO	BC	Range 4 Coast	103 H/16	53°50′	128°29′
Kildala Arm	BAY/BAIE	BC	Range 4 Coast	103 H/15	53°51′	128°34′
Kildala River	RIV/CDE	BC	Range 4 Coast	103 H/16	53°48′	128°28′
Kildala River (Thala) 10	IR/RI	BC	Range 4 Coast	103 H/16	53°48′	128°27′
Kildare, Cape	CAPE/CAP	PE	Prince	11 L/13	46°53′	63°59′
Kildare Capes	UNP/LNO	PE	Prince	11 L/13	46°54′	63°59′
Kildare River	RIV/CDE	PE	Prince	21 I/16	46°48′	64°03′
Kildonan	UNP/LNO	MB	11-3-E	62 H/14	49°57′	97°06′
Kildonan	UNP/LNO	BC	Clayoquot	92 F/3	49°00′	125°00′
Kildonan	GEOG/GÉOG	MB		62 H/14	49°57′	97°07′
Kilekale Lake	LAKE/LAC	NT	Mackenzie	96 J	66°39′	123°59′
Kilfoil	UNP/LNO	NB	Carleton	21 J/12	46°36′	67°30′
Kilgard	UNP/LNO	BC	New Westminster	92 G/1	49°04′	122°12′
Kilgorie	UNP/LNO	ON	Dufferin	41 A/1	44°10′	80°09′
Kilian Island	ISL/ÎLE	NT	Franklin	78 D	73°35′	107°53′
Kilian Lake	LAKE/LAC	NT	Franklin	78 B	72°10′	111°35′
Kilkenny	UNP/LNO	MB	3-24-3-W1	62 P/4	51°02′	97°47′
Kilkerran	UNP/LNO	BC	Peace River	93 P/16	55°50′	120°16′
Killala Lake	LAKE/LAC	ON	Thunder Bay	42 E/2	49°05′	86°32′
Killaloe	VILG/VILG	ON	Renfrew	31 F/11	45°33′	77°25′
Killaloe - see-voir - Old Killaloe	UNP/LNO	ON		31 F/11	45°32′	77°25′
Killaloe Station - see-voir - Killaloe	VILG/VILG	ON		31 F/11	45°33′	77°25′
Killaly	VILG/VILG	SK	31-20-6-W2	62 L/15	50°45′	102°50′
Killam	TOWN/VIL2	AB	17-44-13-W4	73 D/13	52°47′	111°51′
Killams Mills	UNP/LNO	NB	Westmorland	21 I/3	46°01′	65°14′
Killarney	TOWN/VIL2	MB		62 G/4	49°11′	99°40′
Killarney	UNP/LNO	NS	Halifax	11 D/12	44°44′	63°41′
Killarney	UNP/LNO	ON	Manitoulin	41 H/13	45°58′	81°31′
Killarney	UNP/LNO	BC	New Westminster	92 G/3	49°13′	123°02′
Killarney Bay	BAY/BAIE	ON	Manitoulin	41 H/13	45°59′	81°33′
Killarney Beach	UNP/LNO	ON	Simcoe	31 D/5	44°16′	79°33′
Killarney Beach - see-voir - Killiney Beach	UNP/LNO	BC		82 L/4	50°11′	119°30′
Killarney Lake	UNP/LNO	AB	34-41-1-W4	73 D/9	52°34′	110°04′
Killarney, Lake	LAKE/LAC	NS	Cumberland	11 E/13	45°51′	63°51′
Killarney Lake	LAKE/LAC	ON	Manitoulin	41 I/3	46°04′	81°22′
Killarney Lake	LAKE/LAC	AB	41,42-1-W4	73 D/9	52°35′	110°06′
Killarney Road	UNP/LNO	NB	York	21 J/2	46°01′	66°38′
Killbear Park	UNP/LNO	ON	Parry Sound	41 H/8	45°21′	80°14′
Killdeer	UNP/LNO	SK	9-2-3-W3	72 G/1	49°07′	106°21′
Killean	UNP/LNO	ON	Wellington	40 P/8	43°25′	80°14′
Killiney Beach	UNP/LNO	BC	Osoyoos Division Yale	82 L/4	50°11′	119°30′
Killiniq	UNP/LNO	QC	Kativik	25 A/7	60°25′	64°50′
Killiniq Island	ISL/ÎLE	NF		25 A/7	60°21′	64°32′
Killiniq Island	ISL/ÎLE	NT	Franklin	25 A/7	60°25′	64°38′
Killock Bay	BAY/BAIE	SK		64 L/11	58°33′	103°12′
Killoween	UNP/LNO	NB	Carleton	21 J/12	46°37′	67°33′
Killy	UNP/LNO	BC	Cariboo	93 J/7	54°30′	122°40′
Kilmanagh	UNP/LNO	ON	Peel	30 M/13	43°50′	79°53′
Kilmar	UNP/LNO	QC	Argenteuil	31 G/15	45°46′	74°37′
Kilmarnock	UNP/LNO	NB	Carleton	21 J/3	46°04′	67°29′
Kilmarnock	UNP/LNO	ON	Lanark	31 B/13	44°53′	75°55′
Kilmartin	UNP/LNO	ON	Middlesex	40 I/13	42°47′	81°46′
Kilmaurs	UNP/LNO	ON	Carleton	31 F/8	45°28′	76°07′
Kilmuir	UNP/LNO	PE	Kings	11 L/2	46°07′	62°40′
Kil-pah-las 3	IR/RI	BC	Cowichan	92 B/12	48°44′	123°36′
Kilronan	UNP/LNO	SK	12-54-24-W3	73 F/11	53°39′	109°24′
Kilroy Crescent	UNP/LNO	QC	Communauté urbaine de l'Outaouais	31 G/5	45°26′	75°49′
Kilrush	UNP/LNO	ON	Nipissing	31 L/3	46°06′	79°03′
Kilsyth	UNP/LNO	ON	Grey	41 A/11	44°31′	81°01′
Kilsyth	UNP/LNO	AB	1-65-2-W5	83 J/9	54°36′	114°09′
Kiltala 2	IR/RI	BC	Range 2 Coast	92 M/11	51°43′	127°21′
Kiltarlity	UNP/LNO	NS	Inverness	11 K/3	46°13′	61°10′
Kilty Switch	UNP/LNO	ON	Muskoka	31 D/14	45°00′	79°19′
Kilvert Lake	LAKE/LAC	ON	Kenora	52 E/9	49°42′	94°02′
Kilwinning	UNP/LNO	SK	33-47-5-W3	73 G/2	53°06′	106°40′
Kilworth	UNP/LNO	ON	Middlesex	40 I/14	42°58′	81°23′
Kilworthy	UNP/LNO	ON	Muskoka	31 D/14	44°51′	79°21′
Kimakto Peninsula	CAPE/CAP	NT	Franklin	47 F	70°17′	88°00′
Kimball	UNP/LNO	ON	Lambton	40 J/16	42°49′	82°21′

NAME NOM	ENTITY ENTITÉ	LOC 1 LIEU 1	LOC 2 LIEU 2	MAP CARTE	POSITION LAT	LONG
Kimball	UNP/LNO	AB	31-1-24-W4	82 H/3	49°05′	113°12′
Kimberley	CITY/VIL1	BC	Kootenay	82 G/12	49°41′	115°59′
Kimberley	UNP/LNO	ON	Grey	41 A/7	44°23′	80°32′
Kimberley Park	UNP/LNO	ON	Peterborough	31 D/8	44°26′	78°25′
Kimbo	UNP/LNO	ON	Lincoln	30 M/4	43°07′	79°36′
Kimiwan Lake	LAKE/LAC	AB	78-19-W5	83 N/15	55°45′	116°55′
Kimmirut	HAM/HAM	NT	Franklin	25 K/13	62°51′	69°52′
Kimowin River	RIV/CDE	SK/AB		74 C/3	56°14′	109°14′
Kimsquit	UNP/LNO	BC	Range 3 Coast	93 D/15	52°50′	126°57′
Kimsquit River	RIV/CDE	BC	Range 3 Coast	93 D/14	52°53′	127°05′
Kinaskan Lake	LAKE/LAC	BC	Cassiar	104 G/9	57°36′	130°08′
Kinbasket Lake	LAKE/LAC	BC	Cariboo	83 D/1	52°08′	118°27′
Kinbrook Island Provincial Park	PARK/PARC	AB	16,17-14,15-W4	72 L/5	50°27′	111°54′
Kinburn	UNP/LNO	ON	Carleton	31 F/8	45°23′	76°11′
Kinburn	UNP/LNO	ON	Huron	40 P/11	43°38′	81°25′
Kincaid	VILG/VILG	SK	22-8-8-W3	72 G/11	49°40′	107°00′
Kincardine	TOWN/VIL2	ON	Bruce	41 A/4	44°11′	81°38′
Kincardine	MUN2/AZM2	ON	Bruce	41 A/4	44°13′	81°30′
Kincardine	UNP/LNO	NB	Victoria	21 J/12	46°38′	67°40′
Kincolith	UNP/LNO	BC	Range 5 Coast	103 I/13	54°59′	129°57′
Kincolith 14	IR/RI	BC	Range 5 Coast	103 I/13	55°00′	129°57′
Kincolith 14A	IR/RI	BC	Cassiar	103 I/13	55°00′	129°58′
Kincorth	UNP/LNO	SK	14-12-28-W3	72 F/13	49°59′	109°43′
Kindakun Point	CAPE/CAP	BC	Queen Charlotte	103 F/7	53°19′	132°45′
Kindersley	TOWN/VIL2	SK		72 N/6	51°28′	109°10′
Kindersley No. 290	MUN2/AZM2	SK		72 N/6	51°30′	109°10′
Kindiogami Lake	LAKE/LAC	ON	Algoma	41 J/15	46°50′	82°57′
*Kinert	UNP/LNO	BC	Kootenay	82 F/1	49°08′	116°15′
King	MUN2/AZM2	ON	York	30 M/13	43°58′	79°35′
King	UNP/LNO	ON	York	30 M/13	43°56′	79°32′
Kingarf	UNP/LNO	ON	Bruce	41 A/3	44°09′	81°26′
Kingarut Hill	MTN/MNT	NT	Franklin	47 G	71°36′	85°49′
King Charles Cape	CAPE/CAP	NT	Franklin	36 C	64°14′	77°21′
King Christian Island	ISL/ÎLE	NT	Franklin	69 C	77°48′	101°40′
King City	UNP/LNO	ON	York	30 M/13	43°56′	79°32′
Kingcome	UNP/LNO	BC	Range 1 Coast	92 L/16	50°58′	126°11′
Kingcome Inlet	UNP/LNO	BC	Range 1 Coast	92 L/16	50°57′	126°12′
Kingcome Inlet	BAY/BAIE	BC	Range 1 Coast	92 L/16	50°55′	126°20′
Kingcome River	RIV/CDE	BC	Range 1 Coast	92 L/16	50°56′	126°12′
King Creek	UNP/LNO	ON	York	30 M/13	43°54′	79°37′
King Edward, Mount	MTN/MNT	AB/BC		83 C/4	52°09′	117°31′
King Edward Point	CAPE/CAP	NT	Franklin	49 A	76°08′	81°03′
Kingfisher	UNP/LNO	BC	Kamloops Division Yale	82 L/10	50°37′	118°44′
Kingfisher Creek	RIV/CDE	BC	Kamloops Division Yale	82 L/10	50°37′	118°45′
Kingfisher Lake	UNP/LNO	ON	Kenora	53 H/4	53°02′	89°50′
Kingfisher Lake	LAKE/LAC	ON	Kenora	53 H/4	53°05′	89°49′
Kingfisher Lake 1	IR/RI	ON	Kenora	53 H/4	53°02′	89°51′
King George Islands	ISL/ÎLE	NT	Keewatin	34 E	57°20′	78°25′
King George IV Lake	LAKE/LAC	NF		12 A/4	48°13′	57°53′
King George, Mount	MTN/MNT	BC	Kootenay	82 J/11	50°36′	115°24′
King George No. 256	MUN2/AZM2	SK		72 O/3	51°11′	107°25′
King George Sound	CHAN/CHEN	NT	Franklin	35 I	61°57′	72°24′
Kinghorn	UNP/LNO	ON	York	30 M/13	43°55′	79°34′
Kinghorn	UNP/LNO	ON	Thunder Bay	42 E/11	49°44′	87°21′
Kinghorn Island	ISL/ÎLE	BC	New Westminster	92 K/2	50°05′	124°51′
Kinghurst	UNP/LNO	ON	Grey	41 A/7	44°19′	80°56′
King Island	ISL/ÎLE	NF		1 M/9	47°36′	54°12′
King Island	ISL/ÎLE	BC	Range 3 Coast	93 D/4	52°15′	127°35′
King Kirkland	UNP/LNO	ON	Timiskaming	32 D/4	48°10′	79°57′
King Kirkland Station	UNP/LNO	ON	Timiskaming	32 D/4	48°09′	79°57′
Kingkown Inlet	BAY/BAIE	BC	Range 4 Coast	103 G/9	53°31′	130°25′
Kinglake	UNP/LNO	ON	Norfolk	40 I/10	42°42′	80°42′
King Lake	LAKE/LAC	NT	Mackenzie	75 E	61°05′	110°35′
Kinglet, Lac	LAKE/LAC	QC	Jamésie	33 J/11	54°44′	75°06′
Kingman	UNP/LNO	AB	8-49-19-W4	83 H/2	53°13′	112°45′
Kingman's	UNP/LNO	NF		1 K/15	46°58′	52°56′
Kingnait Fiord	BAY/BAIE	NT	Franklin	26 I	66°03′	64°58′
Kingnait Range	MTN/MNT	NT	Keewatin	36 C	64°30′	77°10′
Kingnelling Fiord	BAY/BAIE	NT	Franklin	26 P	67°27′	64°15′
Kingora River	RIV/CDE	NT	Franklin	47 A	68°36′	82°40′
King Peak	MTN/MNT	YT		115 C/10	60°35′	140°39′
King Pitt	UNP/LNO	ON	Frontenac	31 C/1	44°15′	76°24′
King Point	CAPE/CAP	YT		117 D/2	69°06′	137°59′
King Point	CAPE/CAP	NT	Franklin	78 H	75°28′	105°34′
Kingross	UNP/LNO	NS	Inverness	11 K/7	46°27′	60°55′

NAME NOM	ENTITY ENTITÉ	LOC 1 LIEU 1	LOC 2 LIEU 2	MAP CARTE	POSITION LAT	LONG
Kings	MUN1/AZM1	NS	Kings	21 H/2	45°02′	64°40′
Kings	GEOG/GÉOG	PE		11 L/1	46°15′	62°30′
Kings	GEOG/GÉOG	NS		21 H/2	45°02′	64°40′
Kings	GEOG/GÉOG	NB		21 H/12	45°40′	65°45′
Kingsboro	UNP/LNO	PE	Kings	11 L/8	46°24′	62°07′
Kingsbridge	UNP/LNO	ON	Huron	40 P/13	43°56′	81°42′
Kingsburg	UNP/LNO	NS	Lunenburg	21 A/8	44°17′	64°16′
Kingsbury	TOWN/VIL2	QC	Le Val-Saint-François	31 H/9	45°35′	72°09′
Kingsclear	UNP/LNO	NB	York	21 G/15	45°53′	66°55′
Kingsclear	GEOG/GÉOG	NB	York	21 G/15	45°53′	66°50′
Kingsclear 6	IR/RI	NB	York	21 G/15	45°56′	66°50′
Kingscote	UNP/LNO	ON	Grey	41 A/1	44°03′	80°28′
Kingscote Lake	LAKE/LAC	ON	Haliburton	31 E/1	45°12′	78°13′
Kingscourt	UNP/LNO	ON	Frontenac	31 C/7	44°15′	76°30′
King's Cove	VILG/VILG	NF		2 C/11	48°34′	53°20′
Kings Cove	UNP/LNO	NF		3 D/12	52°34′	55°45′
Kings Cove	UNP/LNO	NF		2 E/12	49°42′	55°54′
Kingscroft	UNP/LNO	QC	Coaticook	21 E/4	45°09′	71°58′
Kingscross Estates	UNP/LNO	ON	York	30 M/13	43°56′	79°33′
Kingsdale	UNP/LNO	ON	Waterloo	40 P/7	43°28′	80°31′
Kingsey	VILG/VILG	QC	Drummond	31 H/16	45°48′	72°12′
Kingsey Falls	TOWN/VIL2	QC	Arthabaska	31 H/16	45°51′	72°04′
Kingsey Falls	VILG/VILG	QC	Arthabaska	31 H/16	45°51′	72°04′
Kingsey Station	UNP/LNO	QC	Asbestos	31 H/16	45°50′	72°00′
Kingsford	MUN2/AZM2	ON	Rainy River	52 D/16	48°47′	94°00′
Kingsford	UNP/LNO	ON	Hastings	31 C/6	44°17′	77°05′
Kingsford	UNP/LNO	SK	5-4-6-W2	62 E/7	49°16′	102°47′
King's Forest	UNP/LNO	ON	Wentworth	30 M/4	43°13′	79°49′
Kingsgate	UNP/LNO	BC	Kootenay	82 F/1	49°00′	116°11′
Kings Harbour Brook	RIV/CDE	NF		11 P/12	47°38′	57°34′
Kings Head	UNP/LNO	NS	Pictou	11 E/10	45°39′	62°32′
Kingsland	UNP/LNO	SK	2-33-16-W3	72 N/16	51°46′	108°08′
Kingsley	UNP/LNO	NB	York	21 J/2	46°03′	66°45′
Kingsley	UNP/LNO	MB	26-4-10-W	62 G/7	49°20′	98°42′
Kingsley Lake	LAKE/LAC	SK/MB		64 K/12	58°34′	102°01′
Kingsley Neighbourhood	UNP/LNO	QC	Le Haut-Saint-François	21 E/5	45°20′	71°38′
Kingsley No. 124	MUN2/AZM2	SK		62 L/2	50°10′	102°35′
Kingsmere Lake	LAKE/LAC	SK		73 J/1	54°06′	106°27′
Kingsmill	UNP/LNO	ON	Elgin	40 I/14	42°48′	81°02′
Kings Mines	UNP/LNO	NB	Queens	21 I/4	46°08′	65°54′
King's Point	TOWN/VIL2	NF		12 H/9	49°35′	56°11′
Kingsport	UNP/LNO	NS	Kings	21 H/1	45°10′	64°22′
Kings Rest	UNP/LNO	NS	Colchester	11 E/5	45°24′	63°46′
Kingston	CITY/VIL1	ON	Frontenac	31 C/1	44°14′	76°30′
Kingston	VILG/VILG	PE	Queens	11 L/6	46°16′	63°19′
Kingston	VILG/VILG	NS	Kings	21 A/15	44°59′	64°57′
Kingston	MUN2/AZM2	ON	Frontenac	31 C/7	44°18′	76°34′
Kingston	UNP/LNO	NF		1 N/14	47°49′	53°07′
Kingston	UNP/LNO	PE	Queens	11 L/6	46°16′	63°17′
Kingston	UNP/LNO	NB	Kings	21 H/12	45°30′	65°58′
Kingston	GEOG/GÉOG	NB	Kings	21 G/8	45°28′	66°03′
Kingston, Base des Forces canadiennes - also-aussi - Kingston, Canadian Forces Base	MIL/MIL	ON	Frontenac	31 C/8	44°15′	76°27′
Kingston, Canadian Forces Base - also-aussi - Kingston, Base des Forces canadiennes	MIL/MIL	ON	Frontenac	31 C/8	44°15′	76°27′
Kingston Corner	UNP/LNO	NB	Kings	21 H/12	45°31′	65°58′
Kingston Crescent	UNP/LNO	MB		62 H/14	49°51′	97°08′
Kingston Lake	LAKE/LAC	SK		64 L/16	58°58′	102°30′
Kingston Martello Towers National Historic Site - also-aussi - Tours-Martello-de-Kingston, Lieu historique national des	PARK/PARC	ON	Frontenac	31 C/1	44°14′	76°29′
Kingston Mills	UNP/LNO	ON	Frontenac	31 C/8	44°17′	76°27′
Kingston Mountain	MTN/MNT	YT		105 E/5	61°16′	135°54′
Kingston Station	UNP/LNO	ON	Frontenac	31 C/8	44°15′	76°29′
Kingston Village	UNP/LNO	NS	Kings	21 A/15	44°58′	64°56′
Kingsvale	UNP/LNO	BC	Yale Division Yale	92 H/15	49°54′	120°55′
Kingsview Village	UNP/LNO	ON	York	30 M/12	43°42′	79°33′
Kingsville	TOWN/VIL2	ON	Essex	40 J/2	42°02′	82°45′
Kingsville	UNP/LNO	NS	Inverness	11 F/14	45°47′	61°19′
Kingsway Park	UNP/LNO	SK		72 I/5	50°22′	105°33′
Kings Wharf	UNP/LNO	ON	Victoria	31 D/7	44°26′	78°31′
Kingswood Acres	UNP/LNO	ON	Simcoe	41 A/16	44°47′	80°08′
Kinguk Lake	LAKE/LAC	NT	Franklin	36 B	64°40′	75°30′
Kingurutik Lake	LAKE/LAC	NF		14 D/16	56°49′	62°20′
Kingurutik River	RIV/CDE	NF		14 D/15	56°49′	62°33′
Kingwell	UNP/LNO	NF		1 M/9	47°33′	54°06′
King William Island	ISL/ÎLE	NT	Franklin	67 D/2	69°10′	97°25′
Kingwood	UNP/LNO	ON	Waterloo	40 P/10	43°31′	80°50′
Kinhop	UNP/LNO	SK	33-32-11-W3	72 O/13	51°47′	107°30′

NAME NOM	ENTITY ENTITÉ	LOC 1 LIEU 1	LOC 2 LIEU 2	MAP CARTE	POSITION LAT	LONG
Kinhuron	UNP/LNO	ON	Bruce	41 A/4	44°14′	81°36′
Kinikinik	UNP/LNO	AB	5-65-21-W4	83 I/11	54°35′	113°00′
Kininvie	UNP/LNO	AB	29-16-11-W4	72 L/6	50°22′	111°28′
Kinistin 91	IR/RI	SK		73 A/9	52°37′	104°13′
Kinistin 91A	IR/RI	SK		73 A/8	52°29′	104°14′
Kinistino	TOWN/VIL2	SK	45-21-W2	73 A/14	52°57′	105°02′
Kinistino 91 - see-voir - Kinistin 91	IR/RI	SK		73 A/9	52°37′	104°13′
Kinistino 91A - see-voir - Kinistin 91A	IR/RI	SK		73 A/8	52°29′	104°14′
Kinistino No. 459	MUN2/AZM2	SK		73 H/2	53°00′	104°55′
Kinkora	VILG/VILG	PE	Prince	11 L/5	46°19′	63°36′
Kinkora	UNP/LNO	PE	Prince	11 L/5	46°19′	63°36′
Kinkora	UNP/LNO	ON	Perth	40 P/6	43°28′	81°04′
Kinley	VILG/VILG	SK	6-36-10-W3	73 B/3	52°04′	107°26′
Kinley Point	CAPE/CAP	NT	Franklin	340 A	80°51′	78°54′
Kinloch	UNP/LNO	SK	40-10-W2	63 D/6	52°24′	103°26′
Kinlock	UNP/LNO	PE	Queens	11 L/3	46°12′	63°05′
Kinloss	MUN2/AZM2	ON	Bruce	41 A/3	44°00′	81°29′
Kinloss	UNP/LNO	ON	Bruce	41 A/3	44°06′	81°25′
Kinlough	UNP/LNO	ON	Bruce	41 A/3	44°04′	81°27′
Kinmakanksk 6	IR/RI	BC	Range 3 Coast	103 A/10	52°42′	128°57′
Kinmelit 20	IR/RI	BC	Cassiar	103 P/5	55°17′	129°51′
Kinmount	UNP/LNO	ON	Victoria	31 D/15	44°47′	78°39′
Kinnaird	UNP/LNO	ON	Lambton	40 P/4	43°08′	81°58′
Kinnaird Lake	LAKE/LAC	AB	66,67-10-W4	73 L/12	54°47′	111°31′
Kinnamax 15	IR/RI	BC	Range 5 Coast	103 J/16	54°47′	130°09′
Kinnear River	RIV/CDE	NB	Westmorland	21 I/1	46°11′	64°24′
Kinnear Settlement	UNP/LNO	NB	Westmorland	21 H/14	45°58′	65°16′
Kinnear's Mills	VILG/VILG	QC	L'Amiante	21 L/3	46°13′	71°23′
Kinniwabi Lake	LAKE/LAC	ON	Algoma	41 N/16	47°55′	84°20′
Kinogama	UNP/LNO	ON	Sudbury	41 O/11	47°39′	83°02′
Kinojévis, Rivière	RIV/CDE	QC	Rouyn-Noranda	31 M/15	47°55′	78°39′
Kinoosao	HAM/HAM	SK		64 E/1	57°05′	102°01′
Kinosheo River	RIV/CDE	ON	Cochrane	43 A/3	52°08′	81°25′
Kinosis	UNP/LNO	AB	84-7-W4	74 D/7	56°20′	110°58′
Kinosota	UNP/LNO	MB	22-10,11-W	62 J/15	50°54′	98°52′
Kinross	UNP/LNO	PE	Queens	11 L/2	46°09′	62°49′
Kinsac	UNP/LNO	NS	Halifax	11 D/13	44°50′	63°40′
Kinsale	UNP/LNO	ON	Ontario	30 M/14	43°56′	79°02′
Kinsella	UNP/LNO	AB	27-46-11-W4	73 E/4	53°00′	111°32′
Kinskuch River	RIV/CDE	BC	Cassiar	103 P/10	55°31′	128°55′
Kinsman Lake	LAKE/LAC	MB		64 J/7	58°19′	98°49′
Kinsmans Corner	UNP/LNO	NS	Kings	21 H/2	45°06′	64°39′
Kintail	UNP/LNO	ON	Huron	40 P/13	43°58′	81°42′
Kintore	UNP/LNO	ON	Oxford	40 P/3	43°08′	81°02′
Kintyre	UNP/LNO	ON	Elgin	40 I/12	42°34′	81°45′
Kinushseo River	RIV/CDE	ON	Kenora	43 O/4	55°15′	83°45′
Kinusisipi	UNP/LNO	MB		63 H/13	53°57′	97°52′
Kinuso	VILG/VILG	AB	23-73-10-W5	83 O/6	55°20′	115°25′
Kinwow Bay	BAY/BAIE	MB		62 P/13	52°00′	97°34′
Kinyug 57	IR/RI	BC	Cassiar	103 P/7	55°30′	128°54′
Kioosta 15	IR/RI	BC	Queen Charlotte	103 K/3	54°11′	133°01′
Kioshkokwi Lake	LAKE/LAC	ON	Nipissing	31 L/2	46°05′	78°53′
Kiosk	UNP/LNO	ON	Nipissing	31 L/2	46°05′	78°53′
Kiowana Beach	UNP/LNO	ON	Grey	41 A/10	44°39′	80°38′
Kipabiskau	UNP/LNO	SK	41-16-W2	73 A/9	52°34′	104°11′
Kipahigan Lake	LAKE/LAC	MB/SK		63 N/5	55°19′	102°54′
Kipawa	VILG/VILG	QC	Témiscamingue	31 L/15	46°47′	78°59′
Kipawa, Baie de	BAY/BAIE	QC	Témiscamingue	31 L/16	46°56′	78°00′
Kipawa, Lac	LAKE/LAC	QC	Témiscamingue	31 L/14	46°55′	79°00′
Kipawa, Rivière	RIV/CDE	QC	Témiscamingue	31 M/3	47°03′	79°23′
Kipisa	UNP/LNO	NT	Franklin	26 G	65°12′	66°57′
Kipisako River	RIV/CDE	NT	Franklin	88 B	72°51′	119°44′
Kipling	TOWN/VIL2	SK	21-13-5-W2	62 L/2	50°06′	102°38′
Kipling	UNP/LNO	ON	Nipissing	41 I/8	46°30′	80°13′
Kipling Heights	UNP/LNO	ON	York	30 M/12	43°44′	79°34′
Kipp	UNP/LNO	AB	29-9-22-W4	82 H/15	49°45′	112°57′
Kippase 2	IR/RI	BC	Rupert	92 L/11	50°41′	127°25′
Kippen	UNP/LNO	ON	Huron	40 P/5	43°28′	81°31′
Kippen Cove	BAY/BAIE	NF		2 E/9	49°38′	54°07′
Kippens	TOWN/VIL2	NF		12 B/10	48°33′	58°38′
Kirby	UNP/LNO	ON	Durham	31 D/2	44°01′	78°37′
Kirby Lake	LAKE/LAC	AB	74,75-5,6-W4	73 M/7	55°28′	110°46′
Kirby Point 6	IR/RI	BC	Rupert	92 C/14	48°51′	125°12′
Kirby's Corner	UNP/LNO	ON	Algoma	41 K/9	46°44′	84°17′
Kirby's Cove	UNP/LNO	NF		1 M/3	47°02′	55°10′

NAME / NOM	ENTITY / ENTITÉ	LOC 1 / LIEU 1	LOC 2 / LIEU 2	MAP / CARTE	POSITION LAT	POSITION LONG
Kirchoffer River	RIV/CDE	NT	Keewatin	46 B	64°07′	83°27′
Kirk	UNP/LNO	ON	Nipissing	41 I/8	46°26′	80°12′
Kirkcaldy	UNP/LNO	AB	9-16-24-W4	82 I/6	50°20′	113°14′
Kirkcaldy Heights	UNP/LNO	MB		62 G/13	49°52′	99°57′
Kirk Cove	UNP/LNO	ON	Frontenac	31 C/15	44°48′	76°59′
Kirkdale	UNP/LNO	QC	Drummond	31 H/9	45°42′	72°13′
Kirke	UNP/LNO	ON	Cochrane	42 A/16	48°55′	80°14′
Kirkella	UNP/LNO	MB	22-12-29-W	62 K/3	50°01′	101°22′
Kirkfield	UNP/LNO	ON	Victoria	31 D/10	44°34′	78°59′
Kirkfield Park	UNP/LNO	MB		62 H/14	49°52′	97°17′
Kirkhill	UNP/LNO	NS	Cumberland	21 H/8	45°25′	64°22′
Kirkhill	UNP/LNO	ON	Glengarry	31 G/7	45°25′	74°39′
Kirk, Île	ISL/ÎLE	QC	Jamésie	32 K/15	50°55′	76°55′
Kirk Lake	LAKE/LAC	NT	Mackenzie	75 N	63°43′	109°05′
Kirkland	CITY/VIL1	QC	Communauté urbaine de Montréal	31 H/5	45°27′	73°52′
Kirkland	UNP/LNO	NB	Carleton	21 G/13	45°58′	67°43′
Kirkland Creek	RIV/CDE	YT		115 H/9	61°45′	136°02′
Kirkland Lake	TOWN/VIL2	ON	Timiskaming	42 A/1	48°09′	80°02′
Kirkman Creek	UNP/LNO	YT		115 J/14	63°00′	139°23′
Kirkmount	UNP/LNO	NS	Pictou	11 E/10	45°31′	62°35′
Kirkness	UNP/LNO	MB		62 I/2	50°05′	96°52′
Kirkness Lake	LAKE/LAC	ON	Kenora	52 N/12	51°32′	93°56′
Kirkpatrick	UNP/LNO	AB	24-29-21-W4	82 P/7	51°30′	112°50′
Kirkpatrick Lake	LAKE/LAC	ON	Algoma	41 J/11	46°39′	83°05′
Kirkpatrick Lake	LAKE/LAC	AB	33,34-9,10-W4	72 M/14	51°52′	111°18′
Kirks Ferry	UNP/LNO	QC	Les Collines-de-l'Outaouais	31 G/12	45°32′	75°49′
Kirkton	UNP/LNO	ON	Huron	40 P/6	43°20′	81°19′
Kirkwall	UNP/LNO	ON	Wentworth	40 P/8	43°21′	80°10′
Kirkwood	UNP/LNO	NB	Northumberland	21 I/13	46°54′	65°37′
Kiron	UNP/LNO	AB	33-45-19-W4	83 A/15	52°57′	112°42′
Kirriemuir	UNP/LNO	AB	13-34-3-W4	72 M/16	51°56′	110°18′
Kirwan	UNP/LNO	QC	Témiscamingue	31 M/6	47°28′	79°21′
Kisameet 7	IR/RI	BC	Range 2 Coast	92 M/13	51°58′	127°53′
Kis-an-usko 7	IR/RI	BC	Cassiar	93 M/5	55°26′	127°36′
Kisbey	VILG/VILG	SK	18-8-5-W2	62 E/10	49°39′	102°40′
Kischiayamweekemow	UNP/LNO	MB		54 K/4	58°10′	93°58′
Kisgegas	IR/RI	BC	Cassiar	93 M/12	55°43′	127°35′
Kishikas River	RIV/CDE	ON	Kenora	53 B/12	52°45′	91°43′
Kishkutena Lake	LAKE/LAC	ON	Rainy River	52 F/4	49°03′	93°46′
Kishnacous 29	IR/RI	BC	Clayoquot	92 E/9	49°31′	126°18′
Kiskatinaw	UNP/LNO	BC	Peace River	93 P/15	55°46′	120°34′
Kiskatinaw River	RIV/CDE	BC	Peace River	94 A/1	56°05′	120°10′
Kiski Lake	LAKE/LAC	MB	66,67-10-W	63 J/15	54°45′	98°55′
Kiskissink	MUN2/AZM2	QC	Le Haut-Saint-Maurice	31 P/16	47°56′	72°09′
Kiskissink	UNP/LNO	QC	Le Haut-Saint-Maurice	31 P/16	47°56′	72°09′
Kiskittogisu Lake	LAKE/LAC	MB		63 J/8	54°16′	98°14′
Kiskitto Lake	LAKE/LAC	MB	61-78-W	63 J/7	54°16′	98°30′
Kispiox	UNP/LNO	BC	Cassiar	93 M/5	55°21′	127°41′
Kispiox 1	IR/RI	BC	Cassiar	93 M/15	55°22′	127°41′
Kispiox Range	MTN/MNT	BC	Cassiar	93 M/5	55°20′	127°55′
Kispiox River	RIV/CDE	BC	Cassiar	93 M/5	55°21′	127°42′
Kisseynew Lake	LAKE/LAC	MB/SK		63 K/13	54°57′	101°36′
Kissick	UNP/LNO	BC	Kamloops Division Yale	92 I/9	50°43′	120°29′
Kississing Lake	LAKE/LAC	MB		63 N/3	55°10′	101°20′
Kississing River	RIV/CDE	MB		63 N/10	55°34′	100°48′
Kistigan Lake	LAKE/LAC	MB		53 K/10	54°38′	92°34′
Kitako Lake	LAKE/LAC	SK	40-16-W2	73 A/8	52°28′	104°13′
Kitamaat 1	IR/RI	BC	Range 5 Coast	103 I/2	54°02′	128°40′
Kitamaat 2	IR/RI	BC	Range 4 Coast	103 H/15	53°58′	128°39′
Kitamaat Village	UNP/LNO	BC	Range 4 Coast	103 H/15	53°59′	128°39′
Kitasa 7	IR/RI	BC	Range 4 Coast	103 H/15	53°54′	128°47′
Kitaskino	UNP/LNO	QC	Le Domaine-du-Roy	32 B/16	48°55′	74°22′
Kitasoo 1	IR/RI	BC	Range 3 Coast	103 A/10	52°36′	128°32′
Kitchener	CITY/VIL1	ON	Waterloo	40 P/8	43°27′	80°29′
Kitchener	UNP/LNO	BC	Kootenay	82 F/1	49°10′	116°20′
Kitchener, Cape	CAPE/CAP	NF		13 O/2	55°04′	58°49′
Kitchener Lake	LAKE/LAC	BC	Cassiar	94 E/3	57°04′	127°28′
Kitchener, Mount	MTN/MNT	AB	37-24-W5	83 C/3	52°13′	117°20′
Kitchener, Mount	MTN/MNT	BC	Cassiar	104 G/13	57°47′	131°57′
Kitchie Lake	LAKE/LAC	ON	Kenora	43 D/7	52°26′	86°31′
Kitchigama, Rivière	RIV/CDE	QC	Jamésie	32 M/2	51°05′	78°43′
Kitchiokonim Place	UNP/LNO	MB		53 E/16	53°55′	94°20′
Kitchisakik	UNP/LNO	MB		53 K/11	54°40′	93°20′
Kitchuses	UNP/LNO	NF		1 N/6	47°27′	53°11′
Kitciôbickacik	UNP/LNO	QC	Vallée-de-l'Or	32 C/3	48°13′	77°20′

NAME NOM	ENTITY ENTITÉ	LOC 1 LIEU 1	LOC 2 LIEU 2	MAP CARTE	POSITION LAT	LONG
Kiteen River	RIV/CDE	BC	Cassiar	103 P/10	55°31′	128°48′
Kitiga Lake	LAKE/LAC	NT	Franklin	77 D	69°15′	105°40′
Kitigan	UNP/LNO	ON	Cochrane	42 G/8	49°23′	82°18′
Kitigan Zibi	IR/RI	QC	La Vallée-de-la-Gatineau	31 K/8	46°22′	76°04′
Kitimat	MUN1/AZM1	BC	Range 5 Coast	103 I/2	54°03′	128°39′
Kitimat Arm	BAY/BAIE	BC	Range 4 Coast	103 H/15	53°55′	128°42′
Kitimat Ranges	MTN/MNT	BC	Range 4 Coast	103 H/15	53°50′	128°30′
Kitimat River	RIV/CDE	BC	Range 5 Coast	103 I/2	54°00′	128°40′
Kitimat-Stikine	MUN1/AZM1	BC	Cassiar	103 P/7	55°20′	129°00′
Kitkahta 1	IR/RI	BC	Range 4 Coast	103 H/11	53°38′	129°16′
Kitkatla	UNP/LNO	BC	Range 4 Coast	103 G/16	53°48′	130°26′
Kitkiata Inlet	BAY/BAIE	BC	Range 4 Coast	103 H/11	53°38′	129°17′
Kitladamax 1A	IR/RI	BC	Cassiar	103 P/6	55°17′	129°07′
Kitlawaoo 10	IR/RI	BC	Range 4 Coast	103 H/4	53°15′	129°47′
Kitley	MUN2/AZM2	ON	Grenville	31 B/13	44°45′	75°59′
Kitlope 16	IR/RI	BC	Range 4 Coast	93 E/4	53°15′	127°53′
Kitlope River	RIV/CDE	BC	Range 4 Coast	93 E/4	53°15′	127°52′
Kitsakie 156B	IR/RI	SK		73 P/3	55°05′	105°19′
Kitsault	UNP/LNO	BC	Cassiar	103 P/6	55°28′	129°29′
Kitsault River	RIV/CDE	BC	Cassiar	103 P/6	55°29′	129°28′
Kitscoty	VILG/VILG	AB	26-50-3-W4	73 E/8	53°20′	110°20′
Kitseguecla	UNP/LNO	BC	Cassiar	93 M/4	55°05′	127°50′
Kitseguecla 1 - see-voir - Gitsegukla 1	IR/RI	BC		93 M/4	55°05′	127°49′
Kitsegukla Logging 3 - see-voir - Gitsegukla Logging 3	IR/RI	BC		93 M/4	55°05′	127°50′
Kitselas	UNP/LNO	BC	Range 5 Coast	103 I/9	54°34′	128°27′
Kitselas 1	IR/RI	BC	Range 5 Coast	103 I/9	54°37′	128°25′
Kitsemenlagan 19	IR/RI	BC	Range 4 Coast	103 H/12	53°30′	129°52′
Kitsemenlagan 19A	IR/RI	BC	Range 4 Coast	103 H/12	53°30′	129°52′
Kitsilano	UNP/LNO	BC	New Westminster	92 G/6	49°16′	123°10′
Kits-ka-haws 6	IR/RI	BC	Cassiar	103 P/1	55°05′	128°12′
Kitson River	RIV/CDE	NT	Franklin	89 A	76°10′	112°25′
Kitsumkalum	UNP/LNO	BC	Range 5 Coast	103 I/10	54°31′	128°38′
Kitsumkalum Lake	LAKE/LAC	BC	Range 5 Coast	103 I/15	54°47′	128°47′
Kitsumkalum River	RIV/CDE	BC	Range 5 Coast	103 I/10	54°31′	128°40′
Kitsumkaylum 1	IR/RI	BC	Range 5 Coast	103 I/10	54°32′	128°40′
Kittigazuit	UNP/LNO	NT	Mackenzie	107 C	69°20′	133°42′
Kitty's Brook	UNP/LNO	NF		12 H/2	49°11′	56°54′
Kitwancool 1 - see-voir - Gitanyow 1	IR/RI	BC		103 P/8	55°16′	128°04′
Kitwancool 2 - see-voir - Gitanyow 2	IR/RI	BC		103 P/1	55°10′	128°02′
Kitwancool 3A - see-voir - Gitanyow 3A	IR/RI	BC		103 P/8	55°19′	128°06′
Kitwancool Lake	LAKE/LAC	BC	Cassiar	103 P/8	55°22′	128°07′
Kitwanga	UNP/LNO	BC	Cassiar	103 P/1	55°06′	128°04′
Kitwanga Fort National Historic Site - also-aussi - Fort-Kitwanga, Lieu historique national du	PARK/PARC	BC	Cassiar	103 P/1	55°07′	128°01′
Kitwilluchsilt (Canyon City) 7 - see-voir - Gitwinksihlkw 7	IR/RI	BC		103 P/3	55°12′	129°13′
Kitzowit 20	IR/RI	BC	Kamloops Division Yale	92 I/4	50°12′	121°34′
Kiusta	UNP/LNO	BC	Queen Charlotte	103 K/3	54°10′	133°01′
Kivikoski	UNP/LNO	ON	Thunder Bay	52 A/11	48°30′	89°20′
Kivimaa-Moonlight Bay	VILG/VILG	SK	25-53-19-W3	73 F/10	53°36′	108°40′
Kivimaa's Moonlight Bay - see-voir - Kivimaa-Moonlight Bay	HAM/HAM	SK		73 F/10	53°36′	108°40′
Kivitoo	UNP/LNO	NT	Franklin	26 P	67°56′	64°52′
Kiwigana River	RIV/CDE	BC	Peace River	94 O/3	59°14′	123°10′
Kiyiu Lake	LAKE/LAC	SK	30-21-W3	72 N/10	51°36′	108°53′
Kiyuk Lake	LAKE/LAC	NT	Keewatin	65 C	60°27′	100°30′
Kjer, Cape	CAPE/CAP	NT	Franklin	57 D	69°42′	91°03′
Klagookchew 4 - see-voir - Klagookchew 9	IR/RI	BC		93 L/2	54°01′	126°38′
Klagookchew 9	IR/RI	BC	Range 5 Coast	93 L/2	54°01′	126°38′
Klahkamich 17	IR/RI	BC	Kamloops Division Yale	92 I/4	50°14′	121°35′
Klahkowit 5	IR/RI	BC	Kamloops Division Yale	92 I/6	50°19′	121°24′
Klahoose 1	IR/RI	BC	Range 1 Coast	92 K/9	50°31′	124°19′
Klakelse 86	IR/RI	BC	Range 5 Coast	103 I/7	54°25′	128°49′
Klaklacum 12	IR/RI	BC	Yale Division Yale	92 H/6	49°25′	121°25′
Klaklakama Lakes	LAKE/LAC	BC	Rupert	92 L/1	50°09′	126°27′
Klanawa River	RIV/CDE	BC	Barclay	92 C/10	48°42′	124°57′
Klappan River	RIV/CDE	BC	Cassiar	104 H/13	57°57′	129°40′
Klapthlon 5	IR/RI	BC	Range 4 Coast	103 G/16	53°54′	130°09′
Klapthlon 5A	IR/RI	BC	Range 4 Coast	103 G/16	53°54′	130°01′
Klashwun Point	CAPE/CAP	BC	Queen Charlotte	103 K/2	54°09′	132°40′
Klaskino Inlet	BAY/BAIE	BC	Rupert	92 L/5	50°18′	127°50′
Klaskish 3	IR/RI	BC	Rupert	92 L/4	50°14′	127°45′
Klaskish Inlet	BAY/BAIE	BC	Rupert	92 L/4	50°15′	127°46′
Klaskish River	RIV/CDE	BC	Rupert	92 L/5	50°16′	127°43′
Klastline River	RIV/CDE	BC	Cassiar	104 J/2	58°03′	130°47′
Klattasine Glacier	GLAC/GLAC	BC	Range 2 Coast	92 N/2	51°11′	124°48′
Klawli River	RIV/CDE	BC	Cassiar	93 N/2	55°12′	124°45′
Klaza River	RIV/CDE	YT		115 J/1	62°06′	138°29′

NAME NOM	ENTITY ENTITÉ	LOC 1 LIEU 1	LOC 2 LIEU 2	MAP CARTE	POSITION LAT	LONG
Kleczkowski, Lac	LAKE/LAC	QC	Minganie	12 L/14	50°49′	63°27′
Kledo Creek	RIV/CDE	BC	Peace River	94 J/14	58°50′	123°25′
Kleecoot	UNP/LNO	BC	Alberni	92 F/7	49°18′	124°57′
Kleefeld	UNP/LNO	MB	20,29,32-6-5-E	62 H/10	49°30′	96°52′
Kleena Kleene	UNP/LNO	BC	Range 2 Coast	92 N/15	51°57′	124°50′
Kleetlekut 22	IR/RI	BC	Kamloops Division Yale	92 I/5	50°16′	121°34′
Kleetlekut 22A	IR/RI	BC	Kamloops Division Yale	92 I/4	50°15′	121°34′
Klehkoot 2	IR/RI	BC	Alberni	92 F/7	49°18′	124°53′
Kleinburg	UNP/LNO	ON	York	30 M/13	43°50′	79°38′
Kleinburg Station	UNP/LNO	ON	York	30 M/13	43°50′	79°39′
Kleindale	UNP/LNO	BC	New Westminster	92 G/12	49°38′	123°58′
Klemtu	UNP/LNO	BC	Range 3 Coast	103 A/10	52°35′	128°31′
Klengenberg Bay	BAY/BAIE	NT	Franklin	87 A	68°10′	115°07′
Klesilkwa River	RIV/CDE	BC	Yale Division Yale	92 H/3	49°07′	121°10′
Kleskun Hill	UNP/LNO	AB	24-72-4-W6	83 M/8	55°15′	118°29′
Klewaduska (Cataract) 6	IR/RI	BC	Cassiar	94 D/2	56°13′	126°54′
Kleybolte Peninsula	CAPE/CAP	NT	Franklin	560 D	81°45′	91°00′
Kleykleyhous 5	IR/RI	BC	Clayoquot	92 F/2	49°04′	124°53′
Klickkumcheen 18	IR/RI	BC	Kamloops Division Yale	92 I/4	50°14′	121°35′
Klickseewy 7	IR/RI	BC	Rupert	92 L/11	50°36′	127°10′
Klie's Beach	UNP/LNO	ON	Essex	40 G/15	41°59′	82°55′
Klinaklini Glacier	GLAC/GLAC	BC	Range 2 Coast	92 N/5	51°28′	125°47′
Klinaklini River	RIV/CDE	BC	Range 2 Coast	92 N/4	51°06′	125°43′
Klinkit Creek	RIV/CDE	BC	Cassiar	104 O/6	59°26′	131°21′
Klintonel	UNP/LNO	SK	34-8-22-W3	72 F/10	49°41′	108°55′
Klite River	RIV/CDE	BC	Range 1 Coast	92 K/9	50°31′	124°20′
Klitsis 16	IR/RI	BC	Nootka	92 E/15	49°56′	126°54′
Kloch Lake	LAKE/LAC	BC	Cassiar	93 N/3	55°03′	125°03′
Klock	UNP/LNO	ON	Nipissing	31 L/8	46°18′	78°30′
Klock, Baie	BAY/BAIE	QC	Témiscamingue	31 M/10	47°35′	78°44′
Kloklowuck 7	IR/RI	BC	Kamloops Division Yale	92 I/6	50°22′	121°14′
Klondike	UNP/LNO	YT		116 B/3	64°03′	139°26′
Klondike River	RIV/CDE	YT		116 B/3	64°03′	139°26′
Klondike Settlement	UNP/LNO	NB	Sunbury	21 G/10	45°40′	66°41′
Klondyke	UNP/LNO	ON	Essex	40 J/2	42°05′	82°46′
Klotassin River	RIV/CDE	YT		115 J/12	62°34′	139°31′
Klotz, Lac	LAKE/LAC	QC	Kativik	35 A/12	60°32′	73°40′
Klotz Lake	LAKE/LAC	ON	Thunder Bay	42 F/13	49°48′	85°52′
Klotz, Mount	MTN/MNT	YT		116 F/8	65°23′	140°06′
Kloyadingli 2	IR/RI	BC	Range 4 Coast	93 F/1	53°07′	124°23′
Klua	UNP/LNO	BC	Peace River	94 J/9	58°38′	122°30′
Kluachon Lake 1	IR/RI	BC	Cassiar	104 G/16	57°50′	130°00′
Klua Creek	RIV/CDE	BC	Peace River	94 J/9	58°32′	122°13′
Klua Lakes	LAKE/LAC	BC	Peace River	94 J/1	58°07′	122°18′
Kluane Glacier	GLAC/GLAC	YT		115 B/14	60°53′	139°19′
Kluane Lake	LAKE/LAC	YT		115 G/2	61°15′	138°43′
Kluane National Park Reserve - also-aussi - Kluane, Réserve de parc national	PARK/PARC	YT		115 B/11	60°45′	139°30′
Kluane Ranges	MTN/MNT	YT		115 G/1	61°07′	138°23′
Kluane, Réserve de parc national - also-aussi - Kluane National Park Reserve	PARK/PARC	YT		115 B/11	60°45′	139°30′
Kluane River	RIV/CDE	YT		115 G/13	61°53′	139°43′
Kluane/Wrangell-St. Elias/Glacier Bay/Tatshenshini-Alsek, Site du patrimoine mondial - also-aussi - Kluane/Wrangell-St. Elias/Glacier Bay/Tatshenshini-Alsek World Heritage Site	PARK/PARC	YT/BC		114 P/11	60°15′	138°45′
Kluane/Wrangell-St. Elias/Glacier Bay/Tatshenshini-Alsek World Heritage Site - also-aussi - Kluane/Wrangell-St. Elias/Glacier Bay/Tatshenshini-Alsek, Site du patrimoine mondial	PARK/PARC	YT/BC		114 P/11	60°15′	138°45′
Kluayetz Creek	RIV/CDE	BC	Cassiar	104 H/7	57°16′	128°41′
Klueys Bay	UNP/LNO	ON	Muskoka	31 D/14	44°51′	79°18′
Klukeville	UNP/LNO	QC	Pontiac	31 F/16	45°57′	76°27′
Klukshu	UNP/LNO	YT		115 A/6	60°18′	137°00′
Klusha Creek	RIV/CDE	YT		115 H/9	61°44′	136°02′
Kluskus 1	IR/RI	BC	Range 4 Coast	93 F/1	53°06′	124°29′
Kluskus 14	IR/RI	BC	Range 4 Coast	93 F/1	53°07′	124°18′
Klutlan Glacier	GLAC/GLAC	YT		115 F/7	61°30′	140°36′
Klutschak Peninsula	CAPE/CAP	NT	Keewatin	66 O	67°55′	98°30′
Kluziai Island	ISL/ÎLE	NT	Mackenzie	75 L	62°50′	110°00′
Knamadeek 52	IR/RI	BC	Range 5 Coast	103 J/9	54°32′	130°16′
Knames 45	IR/RI	BC	Range 5 Coast	103 J/16	54°47′	130°07′
Knames 46	IR/RI	BC	Range 5 Coast	103 J/16	54°47′	130°07′
Knapp Lake	LAKE/LAC	BC	Range 4 Coast	93 F/14	53°49′	125°19′
Knapp Lake 6	IR/RI	BC	Range 4 Coast	93 F/14	53°48′	125°14′
Kneehill	UNP/LNO	AB	9-29-20-W4	82 P/7	51°28′	112°44′
Kneehill No. 48, Municipal District of	MUN1/AZM1	AB	32-23-W4	82 P/11	51°40′	113°16′

NAME NOM	ENTITY ENTITÉ	LOC 1 LIEU 1	LOC 2 LIEU 2	MAP CARTE	POSITION
					LAT	LONG
Kneehills Creek	RIV/CDE	AB	24-29-21-W4	82 P/7	51°30'	112°50'
Knee Hill Valley	UNP/LNO	AB	6-35-26-W4	82 P/13	51°58'	113°42'
Knee Lake	LAKE/LAC	MB		53 M/2	55°03'	94°44'
Knee Lake	LAKE/LAC	SK		73 O/14	55°51'	107°00'
Knee Lake 192B	IR/RI	SK		73 O/14	55°53'	107°15'
Kneeland Bay	BAY/BAIE	NT	Franklin	25 J	62°58'	67°30'
Knewstubb Lake	LAKE/LAC	BC	Range 4 Coast	93 F/10	53°31'	124°49'
Knickerbocker Inlet	BAY/BAIE	ON	Kenora	52 E/8	49°23'	94°18'
Knife Creek	RIV/CDE	BC	Cariboo	93 A/4	52°01'	121°52'
Knife Delta	CAPE/CAP	MB		54 L/15	58°54'	94°42'
Knife Lake	LAKE/LAC	ON	Rainy River	52 B/3	48°06'	91°12'
Knife Lake	LAKE/LAC	ON	Kenora	53 G/14	53°47'	91°20'
Knife Lake	LAKE/LAC	MB		53 L/9	54°33'	94°12'
Knife Point	CAPE/CAP	NT	Mackenzie	96 J	66°09'	123°14'
Knight	UNP/LNO	AB	1-60-18-W5	83 K/2	54°09'	116°33'
Knight Inlet	BAY/BAIE	BC	Range 2 Coast	92 K/13	50°47'	125°38'
Knight Islands	ISL/ÎLE	NT	Franklin	25 A/10	60°34'	64°35'
Knights Cove	UNP/LNO	NF		2 C/11	48°32'	53°19'
Knights Island	ISL/ÎLE	NF		2 E/7	49°25'	54°56'
Knightville	UNP/LNO	NB	Kings	21 H/14	45°52'	65°22'
Knob Hill	UNP/LNO	AB	22-46-3-W5	83 B/16	52°59'	114°21'
Knob Hill	MTN/MNT	BC	Rupert	102 I/16	50°46'	128°04'
Knob Lake Junction	UNP/LNO	NF		23 J/15	54°45'	66°47'
Knockholt	UNP/LNO	BC	Range 5 Coast	93 L/7	54°27'	126°34'
Knokmolks 67	IR/RI	BC	Range 4 Coast	103 H/13	53°56'	129°40'
Knollys	UNP/LNO	SK	20-6-22-W3	72 F/7	49°29'	108°56'
Knorr, Cape	CAPE/CAP	NT	Franklin	29 G	79°53'	70°54'
Knorr Creek	RIV/CDE	YT		106 E/7	65°22'	134°39'
Knot Lakes	LAKE/LAC	BC	Range 2 Coast	92 N/13	51°57'	125°43'
Knowles Lake	LAKE/LAC	NT	Mackenzie	75 H	61°35'	105°02'
Knowlesville	UNP/LNO	NB	Carleton	21 J/6	46°27'	67°23'
Knowlton	UNP/LNO	QC	Brome-Missisquoi	31 H/2	45°13'	72°31'
Knowlton Lake	LAKE/LAC	ON	Frontenac	31 C/7	44°27'	76°37'
Knowlton Landing	UNP/LNO	QC	Memphrémagog	31 H/1	45°09'	72°18'
Knox	UNP/LNO	MB	11-12-19-W	62 G/13	50°00'	99°58'
Knoxbridge	UNP/LNO	QC	Pabok	22 A/8	48°28'	64°20'
Knox, Cape	CAPE/CAP	BC	Queen Charlotte	103 K/3	54°11'	133°05'
Knoxford	UNP/LNO	NB	Carleton	21 J/5	46°30'	67°44'
Knox Lake	LAKE/LAC	NF		23 I/14	54°46'	65°19'
Knox Lake	LAKE/LAC	BC	Cariboo	93 B/1	52°13'	122°27'
Knox Landing	UNP/LNO	QC	Pontiac	31 F/8	45°29'	76°23'
Knoydart	UNP/LNO	NS	Pictou	11 E/9	45°43'	62°15'
Knud Inlet	BAY/BAIE	NT	Franklin	67 A	68°27'	97°33'
Knud Peninsula	CAPE/CAP	NT	Franklin	39 G	79°06'	77°08'
Knudsens Corner	UNP/LNO	ON	Thunder Bay	52 A/10	48°33'	88°40'
Knutsford	UNP/LNO	PE	Prince	21 I/9	46°42'	64°17'
Knutsford	UNP/LNO	BC	Kamloops Division Yale	92 I/9	50°37'	120°20'
Koanclikulluk	UNP/LNO	NF		13 N/8	55°18'	60°24'
Kobes	UNP/LNO	BC	Peace River	94 A/12	56°38'	121°39'
Koch Creek	RIV/CDE	BC	Kootenay	82 F/12	49°36'	117°44'
Koch Island	ISL/ÎLE	NT	Franklin	37 C	69°38'	78°20'
Kodiak Seamount	SEAU/SMER	—		5.03	56°52'	149°15'
Kodjidîk	UNP/LNO	QC	Vallée-de-l'Or	32 C/3	48°07'	77°09'
Kodjidji	UNP/LNO	QC	Abitibi	32 D/16	48°53'	78°29'
Koeye Lake	LAKE/LAC	BC	Range 2 Coast	92 M/13	51°47'	127°42'
Kogaluc, Lac	LAKE/LAC	QC	Kativik	34 N/11	59°37'	77°28'
Kogaluc, Rivière	RIV/CDE	QC	Kativik	34 N/12	59°40'	77°35'
Kogaluk Bay	BAY/BAIE	NT	Keewatin	34 N	59°22'	77°50'
Kogaluk River	RIV/CDE	NF		14 C/4	56°12'	61°44'
Kogalu River	RIV/CDE	NT	Franklin	27 F	70°42'	69°00'
Kognak River	RIV/CDE	NT	Keewatin	65 H	61°05'	97°12'
Kogtok River	RIV/CDE	NT	Keewatin	65 H	61°58'	96°23'
Kohler	UNP/LNO	ON	Haldimand	30 L/13	42°54'	79°52'
Kohlmeister, Lac	LAKE/LAC	QC	Kativik	24 K/1	58°10'	68°00'
Kohn Lake	LAKE/LAC	SK		64 M/8	59°17'	102°29'
Koidern	UNP/LNO	YT		115 F/16	61°59'	140°30'
Koidern Mountain	MTN/MNT	YT		115 K/1	62°04'	140°21'
Kokanee Peak	MTN/MNT	BC	Kootenay	82 F/11	49°44'	117°08'
Kokeragi Point	CAPE/CAP	NT	Mackenzie	96 G	65°48'	122°08'
Kokish	UNP/LNO	BC	Rupert	92 L/10	50°32'	126°51'
Kokish River	RIV/CDE	BC	Rupert	92 L/10	50°32'	126°52'
Koko Platz	UNP/LNO	MB		62 G/16	49°57'	98°18'
Koksilah	UNP/LNO	BC	Quamichan	92 B/13	48°46'	123°41'
Koksoak, Rivière	RIV/CDE	QC	Kativik	24 K/9	58°32'	68°10'
Koktac, Rivière	RIV/CDE	QC	Kativik	34 M/1	59°03'	78°14'

NAME NOM	ENTITY ENTITÉ	LOC 1 LIEU 1	LOC 2 LIEU 2	MAP CARTE	POSITION	
					LAT	LONG
Ko-kwi-iss 14	IR/RI	BC	Range 2 Coast	92 M/3	51°09′	127°06′
Kokyet 1	IR/RI	BC	Range 3 Coast	103 A/8	52°17′	128°12′
Kola	UNP/LNO	MB	21-10-29-W	62 F/14	49°51′	101°22′
Kolapore	UNP/LNO	ON	Grey	41 A/8	44°25′	80°24′
Kolbec	UNP/LNO	NS	Cumberland	11 E/13	45°46′	63°49′
Koluktoo Bay	BAY/BAIE	NT	Franklin	48 A	72°05′	80°50′
Komaktorvik Fiord	BAY/BAIE	NF		14 M/5	59°17′	63°44′
Komakuk Beach	BCH/PLAG	YT		117 C/9	69°37′	140°09′
Komarno	UNP/LNO	MB	33-17-2-E	62 I/11	50°30′	97°15′
Komo	UNP/LNO	BC	Yale Division Yale	92 H/14	49°50′	121°25′
Komoka	UNP/LNO	ON	Middlesex	40 I/14	42°57′	81°26′
Komoka Station	UNP/LNO	ON	Middlesex	40 I/14	42°57′	81°27′
Kondiaronk, Lac	LAKE/LAC	QC	Pontiac	31 K/15	46°56′	76°45′
Kongut, Rivière	RIV/CDE	QC	Kativik	34 L/8	58°24′	78°03′
Konigus Creek	RIV/CDE	BC	Cassiar	104 A/15	56°51′	128°49′
Konni Lake	LAKE/LAC	BC	Lillooet	92 O/5	51°28′	123°54′
Konth River	RIV/CDE	NT	Mackenzie	75 D	60°40′	111°46′
Koocanusa, Lake	LAKE/LAC	BC	Kootenay	82 G/3	49°10′	115°13′
Kookipi Creek	RIV/CDE	BC	Yale Division Yale	92 I/4	50°00′	121°38′
Koona Lake	LAKE/LAC	MB		64 N/10	59°44′	100°38′
Koonwats 7	IR/RI	BC	Cassiar	103 P/1	55°01′	128°18′
Kooryet 12	IR/RI	BC	Range 4 Coast	103 H/5	53°21′	129°52′
Kootenay 1	IR/RI	BC	Kootenay	82 G/12	49°37′	115°42′
Kootenay Bay	UNP/LNO	BC	Kootenay	82 F/10	49°41′	116°52′
Kootenay Boundary	MUN1/AZM1	BC	Similkameen Division Yale	82 E/7	49°20′	118°45′
Kootenay Crossing	UNP/LNO	BC	Kootenay	82 K/16	50°53′	116°03′
Kootenay Lake	LAKE/LAC	BC	Kootenay	82 F/10	49°40′	116°50′
Kootenay Land District	GEOG/GÉOG	BC		82 K	50°40′	116°55′
Kootenay Landing	UNP/LNO	BC	Kootenay	82 F/7	49°15′	116°41′
Kootenay National Park - also-aussi - Kootenay, Parc national	PARK/PARC	BC	Kootenay	82 K/16	50°57′	116°02′
Kootenay, Parc national - also-aussi - Kootenay National Park	PARK/PARC	BC	Kootenay	82 K/16	50°57′	116°02′
Kootenay Ranges	MTN/MNT	BC	Kootenay	82 G/11	50°30′	115°50′
Kootenay River	RIV/CDE	BC	Kootenay	82 F/5	49°19′	117°39′
Kootowis 4	IR/RI	BC	Clayoquot	92 F/4	49°06′	125°43′
Kootyuk Point	CAPE/CAP	NT	Franklin	37 C	69°17′	78°14′
Kopchitchin 2	IR/RI	BC	Yale Division Yale	92 H/14	49°53′	121°27′
Kopka River	RIV/CDE	ON	Thunder Bay	52 I/3	50°04′	89°01′
Kopp's Kove	HAM/HAM	SK	35-52-19-W3	73 F/10	53°31′	108°41′
Koprino Harbour	BAY/BAIE	BC	Rupert	92 L/5	50°30′	127°51′
Koqui 6	IR/RI	BC	Range 3 Coast	103 A/1	52°14′	128°22′
Korah	UNP/LNO	ON	Algoma	41 K/9	46°33′	84°24′
Korak Bay	BAY/BAIE	NT	Keewatin	35 C	60°43′	77°45′
Kormak	UNP/LNO	ON	Sudbury	41 O/10	47°38′	82°59′
Koroc, Rivière	RIV/CDE	QC	Kativik	24 I/13	58°51′	65°47′
Kosapachekaywinasinne	UNP/LNO	MB	35-84-22-W	64 C/7	56°20′	100°49′
Kosapechekanesik	UNP/LNO	MB	25-85-28-W	64 C/5	56°24′	101°44′
Kose 9	IR/RI	BC	Queen Charlotte	103 F/15	53°54′	132°42′
Koshlong Lake	LAKE/LAC	ON	Haliburton	31 D/16	44°58′	78°29′
Koskaecodde Lake	LAKE/LAC	NF		2 D/3	48°00′	55°20′
Kossuth	UNP/LNO	ON	Waterloo	40 P/8	43°27′	80°22′
Kostal Lake	LAKE/LAC	BC	Kamloops Division Yale	83 D/4	52°10′	119°59′
Koster	UNP/LNO	BC	Lillooet	92 P/6	51°15′	121°25′
Kotaneelee Range	MTN/MNT	NT/YT		95 C/9	60°32′	124°12′
Kotaneelee River	RIV/CDE	NT	Mackenzie	95 B	60°11′	123°42′
Kotcho Lake	LAKE/LAC	BC	Peace River	94 P/3	59°04′	121°09′
Kotcho River	RIV/CDE	BC	Peace River	94 I/16	58°45′	120°10′
Kotowakan	UNP/LNO	QC	Le Haut-Saint-Maurice	31 P/13	47°53′	73°50′
Kotsine (Skutsil) 2	IR/RI	BC	Cassiar	93 M/16	55°49′	126°26′
Kotsinta Creek	RIV/CDE	BC	Cassiar	104 A/8	56°25′	128°26′
Kotuko Point	CAPE/CAP	NT	Franklin	37 A	68°32′	75°26′
Kouchibouguac	UNP/LNO	NB	Kent	21 I/14	46°48′	65°03′
Kouchibouguac Bay	BAY/BAIE	NB	Kent	21 I/15	46°51′	64°56′
Kouchibouguacis River	RIV/CDE	NB	Kent	21 I/15	46°47′	64°54′
Kouchibouguac National Park - also-aussi - Kouchibouguac, Parc national	PARK/PARC	NB	Kent	21 I/15	46°52′	64°59′
Kouchibouguac, Parc national - also-aussi - Kouchibouguac National Park	PARK/PARC	NB	Kent	21 I/15	46°52′	64°59′
Kouchibouguac River	RIV/CDE	NB	Kent	21 I/15	46°50′	64°56′
Koukdjuak River	RIV/CDE	NT	Franklin	36 I	66°43′	73°00′
Kovik Bay	BAY/BAIE	NT	Franklin	35 F	61°33′	77°40′
Kovik, Rivière	RIV/CDE	QC	Kativik	35 F/12	61°35′	77°36′
Kowesas River	RIV/CDE	BC	Range 4 Coast	103 H/8	53°20′	128°08′
Kowkash	UNP/LNO	ON	Thunder Bay	42 L/3	50°14′	87°13′
Kowtain 17	IR/RI	BC	New Westminster	92 G/11	49°44′	123°08′
Krabbé, Cape	CAPE/CAP	NT	Franklin	89 C	77°30′	116°01′
Krabbé Point	CAPE/CAP	NT	Franklin	68 E	74°02′	98°46′
Kraft	UNP/LNO	BC	Kootenay	82 F/5	49°20′	117°44′

NAME NOM	ENTITY ENTITÉ	LOC 1 LIEU 1	LOC 2 LIEU 2	MAP CARTE	POSITION LAT	LONG
Krag Mountains	MTN/MNT	NT	Franklin	47 H	71°53'	80°25'
Krakow	UNP/LNO	AB	15-55-17-W4	83 H/9	53°45'	112°26'
Kramer - see-voir - Kramer Subdivision	UNP/LNO	ON		31 F/14	45°52'	77°14'
Kramer Subdivision	UNP/LNO	ON	Renfrew	31 F/14	45°52'	77°14'
Krans Corners	UNP/LNO	QC	Brome-Missisquoi	31 H/2	45°04'	72°54'
Krasne	UNP/LNO	SK	36-29-16-W2	72 P/9	51°34'	104°09'
Krestova	UNP/LNO	BC	Kootenay	82 F/5	49°27'	117°35'
Krieger Mountains	MTN/MNT	NT	Franklin	340 B	80°54'	82°40'
Kristnes	UNP/LNO	SK	28-32-12-W2	62 M/13	51°46'	103°40'
Kristoffer Bay	BAY/BAIE	NT	Franklin	69 F	78°05'	102°00'
Kronau	HAM/HAM	SK	33-15-17-W2	72 I/8	50°18'	104°18'
Kronsgart	UNP/LNO	MB	6-4-3-W	62 H/5	49°17'	97°51'
Kronstal - see-voir - Kronsthal	UNP/LNO	MB		62 H/4	49°02'	97°44'
Kronsthal	UNP/LNO	MB	18-1-2-W1	62 H/4	49°02'	97°44'
Krueger Island	ISL/ÎLE	NT	Franklin	560 D	81°35'	91°43'
Krugerdorf	UNP/LNO	ON	Timiskaming	31 M/13	47°56'	79°54'
Krusenstern, Cape	CAPE/CAP	NT	Mackenzie	87 A	68°24'	113°54'
Krusenstern Lake	LAKE/LAC	NT	Franklin	57 F	69°56'	92°49'
Krydor	VILG/VILG	SK	15-44-8-W3	73 B/14	52°47'	107°04'
Ksabasn 50	IR/RI	BC	Range 5 Coast	103 J/9	54°36'	130°23'
Ksadagamks 43	IR/RI	BC	Range 5 Coast	103 J/16	54°46'	130°27'
Ksadsks 44	IR/RI	BC	Range 5 Coast	103 J/10	54°43'	130°31'
Ksagwisgwas 62	IR/RI	BC	Range 5 Coast	103 I/5	54°21'	129°47'
Ksagwisgwas 63	IR/RI	BC	Range 5 Coast	103 I/5	54°18'	129°45'
Ksames 85	IR/RI	BC	Range 5 Coast	103 I/7	54°24'	128°55'
'Ksan	UNP/LNO	BC	Cassiar	93 M/4	55°15'	127°40'
Kshaoom 23	IR/RI	BC	Range 5 Coast	103 J/1	54°08'	130°09'
Kshish 4	IR/RI	BC	Range 5 Coast	103 I/9	54°34'	128°28'
Kshish 4B	IR/RI	BC	Range 5 Coast	103 I/9	54°34'	128°28'
Kshwan 27	IR/RI	BC	Cassiar	103 P/12	55°38'	129°48'
Kshwan 27A	IR/RI	BC	Cassiar	103 P/12	55°38'	129°48'
Kshwan Mountain	MTN/MNT	BC	Cassiar	103 P/12	55°41'	129°45'
Ksilamisk 89	IR/RI	BC	Cassiar	103 P/3	55°14'	129°06'
Ksituan	UNP/LNO	AB	34-79-7-W6	83 M/14	55°54'	119°01'
Ksituan River	RIV/CDE	AB	11-80-5-W6	83 M/15	55°56'	118°40'
Ksoo-gun-ya 2A	IR/RI	BC	Cassiar	93 M/5	55°17'	127°37'
Kstus 83	IR/RI	BC	Range 5 Coast	103 I/6	54°25'	129°05'
Kstus 84	IR/RI	BC	Range 5 Coast	103 I/6	54°27'	129°07'
Ksui-la-das 6	IR/RI	BC	Rupert	92 L/10	50°35'	126°48'
Ktamgaodzen 51	IR/RI	BC	Range 5 Coast	103 J/9	54°37'	130°22'
Ktsinet 23	IR/RI	BC	Cassiar	103 P/5	55°23'	129°41'
Kuaste (Mud Bay)(Kildala Arm) 8	IR/RI	BC	Range 4 Coast	103 H/15	53°52'	128°41'
Kuekuatsheu Kutukuaniutshuahp	UNP/LNO	QC	Minganie	12 O/15	51°51'	58°41'
Kugaituk River	RIV/CDE	NT	Franklin	77 H/5	71°23'	107°43'
Kugaluk River	RIV/CDE	NT	Franklin	87 C	69°38'	116°50'
Kugaluk River	RIV/CDE	NT	Mackenzie	107 D	69°08'	130°58'
Kugaryuak River	RIV/CDE	NT	Mackenzie	86 P	67°42'	113°18'
Kugluktuk	HAM/HAM	NT	Mackenzie	86 O/14	67°50'	115°06'
Kugmallit Bay	BAY/BAIE	NT	Franklin	107 C	69°33'	133°35'
Kugmallit Pingos	SEAU/SMER	—		7651	70°45'	132°40'
Kugmallit Valley	SEAU/SMER	—		7663	70°30'	133°45'
Kugong Island	ISL/ÎLE	NT	Keewatin	34 D	56°18'	79°50'
Kuhryville	UNP/LNO	ON	Perth	40 P/11	43°31'	81°01'
Kuhushan Point	CAPE/CAP	BC	Comox	92 F/14	49°53'	125°07'
Kukagami Lake	LAKE/LAC	ON	Sudbury	41 I/10	46°44'	80°33'
Kukaluk River	RIV/CDE	NT	Franklin	47 E	70°08'	80°43'
Kukamaw, Lac	LAKE/LAC	QC	Jamésie	33 J/1	54°13'	74°27'
Kukatush	UNP/LNO	ON	Sudbury	42 B/1	48°08'	82°12'
Kukukus Lake	LAKE/LAC	ON	Kenora	52 G/13	49°47'	91°41'
Kukwapa 5	IR/RI	BC	Range 1 Coast	92 L/15	50°46'	126°38'
Kul 18	IR/RI	BC	Range 4 Coast	103 G/7	53°29'	130°38'
Kuldekduma 7	IR/RI	BC	Rupert	92 L/10	50°35'	126°51'
Kuldo	UNP/LNO	BC	Cassiar	93 M/13	55°52'	127°54'
Kuldo Creek	RIV/CDE	BC	Cassiar	93 M/13	55°50'	127°55'
Kuldoe 1	IR/RI	BC	Cassiar	93 M/13	55°52'	127°54'
Kulish	UNP/LNO	MB	12-30-23-W	62 N/10	51°34'	100°33'
Kulkayu (Hartley Bay) 4	IR/RI	BC	Range 4 Coast	103 H/6	53°25'	129°16'
Kulkayu (Hartley Bay) 4A	IR/RI	BC	Range 4 Coast	103 H/6	53°25'	129°15'
Kull Island	ISL/ÎLE	NT	Franklin	57 D	69°33'	90°19'
Kulspai 6	IR/RI	BC	Range 5 Coast	103 I/7	54°30'	128°35'
Kultah 4	IR/RI	BC	Rupert	92 L/12	50°33'	127°33'
Kumcheen 1	IR/RI	BC	Kamloops Division Yale	92 I/6	50°26'	121°19'
Kumdis Island	ISL/ÎLE	BC	Queen Charlotte	103 F/9	53°45'	132°10'
Kumlien Fiord	BAY/BAIE	NT	Franklin	26 H	65°24'	64°45'
Kummel Lake	LAKE/LAC	NT	Keewatin	56 C	64°08'	92°45'

NAME / NOM	ENTITY / ENTITÉ	LOC 1 / LIEU 1	LOC 2 / LIEU 2	MAP / CARTE	POSITION LAT	POSITION LONG
Kumowdah 3	IR/RI	BC	Range 4 Coast	103 H/12	53°33'	129°33'
Kumpfville	UNP/LNO	ON	Wellington	40 P/10	43°41'	80°45'
Kunakun Point	CAPE/CAP	BC	Queen Charlotte	103 F/7	53°28'	132°54'
Kunda Park	UNP/LNO	ON	Welland	30 M/3	43°02'	79°17'
Kung	UNP/LNO	BC	Queen Charlotte	103 K/2	54°03'	132°34'
Kung 11	IR/RI	BC	Queen Charlotte	103 K/2	54°03'	132°34'
Kunga Island	ISL/ÎLE	BC	Queen Charlotte	103 B/13	52°46'	131°34'
Kunghit Island	ISL/ÎLE	BC	Queen Charlotte	103 B/3	52°06'	131°05'
Kunhunoan 13	IR/RI	BC	Range 4 Coast	103 H/3	53°13'	129°18'
Kunsoot 9	IR/RI	BC	Range 3 Coast	103 A/1	52°09'	128°01'
Kunstamis 2	IR/RI	BC	Range 1 Coast	92 L/15	50°56'	126°53'
Kunstamis 2A	IR/RI	BC	Range 1 Coast	92 L/15	50°56'	126°53'
Kunwak River	RIV/CDE	NT	Keewatin	65 P	63°40'	97°03'
Kupchynalth 1	IR/RI	BC	Kamloops Division Yale	92 I/4	50°08'	121°33'
Kupchynalth 2	IR/RI	BC	Kamloops Division Yale	92 I/4	50°08'	121°34'
Kuper Island	ISL/ÎLE	BC	Cowichan	92 B/13	48°58'	123°39'
Kuper Island 7	IR/RI	BC	Chemainus	92 B/13	48°58'	123°38'
Kuroki	HAM/HAM	SK	34-33-11-W2	62 M/14	51°52'	103°29'
Kurtzville	UNP/LNO	ON	Perth	40 P/15	43°48'	81°00'
Kusawak Range	MTN/MNT	BC	Cassiar	114 P/9	59°43'	136°28'
Kusawa Lake	LAKE/LAC	YT		115 A/8	60°21'	136°22'
Kushog Lake	LAKE/LAC	ON	Kenora	52 F/12	49°44'	93°58'
Kushya Creek 7	IR/RI	BC	Range 4 Coast	93 F/2	53°05'	124°40'
Kushya Creek 12	IR/RI	BC	Range 4 Coast	93 F/2	53°05'	124°39'
Kuskanax Creek	RIV/CDE	BC	Kootenay	82 K/4	50°15'	117°49'
Kuskonook	UNP/LNO	BC	Kootenay	82 F/7	49°18'	116°39'
Kustra Lake	LAKE/LAC	MB		64 F/16	57°54'	100°17'
Kutawa	UNP/LNO	SK	28-16-W2	72 P/8	51°25'	104°13'
Kutawanis	UNP/LNO	QC	Jamésie	33 D/15	52°59'	78°55'
Kutawa No. 278	MUN2/AZM2	SK		72 P/8	51°25'	104°20'
Kutcho Creek	RIV/CDE	BC	Cassiar	104 I/10	58°31'	128°45'
Kutcous Point 33	IR/RI	BC	Clayoquot	92 E/1	49°15'	126°05'
Kuthlalth 3	IR/RI	BC	Yale Division Yale	92 H/11	49°34'	121°24'
Kuthlo 18	IR/RI	BC	Range 2 Coast	92 M/2	51°04'	126°39'
Kuugaarjuk River	RIV/CDE	NT	Franklin	77 A	68°16'	105°02'
Kuujjuaq	VILG/VILG	QC	Kativik	24 K/1	58°06'	68°24'
Kuujjuarapik	VILG/VILG	QC	Kativik	33 N/5	55°17'	77°45'
Kuujjua River	RIV/CDE	NT	Franklin	87 G	71°16'	116°49'
Kuuk Avinninga	UNP/LNO	QC	Kativik	34 K/12	58°37'	77°40'
Kuuk River	RIV/CDE	NT	Franklin	87 E	70°34'	112°38'
Kuusamo	UNP/LNO	AB	5-26-38-2-W5	83 B/8	52°18'	114°11'
Kuuvik Lake	LAKE/LAC	NT	Mackenzie	76 K	66°29'	109°20'
Kuuviup Paanga	UNP/LNO	QC	Kativik	35 F/12	61°34'	77°39'
Kuuviup Sitjangit	UNP/LNO	QC	Kativik	35 F/9	61°35'	76°03'
Kuz Che 5	IR/RI	BC	Range 5 Coast	93 K/15	54°47'	124°53'
Kuzkwa River	RIV/CDE	BC	Range 5 Coast	93 K/15	54°47'	124°52'
Kwadacha River	RIV/CDE	BC	Cassiar	94 F/5	57°25'	125°36'
Kwakiutl Canyon	SEAU/SMER	—		3604	50°22'	128°18'
Kwakiutl Ridge	SEAU/SMER	—		19308A	50°13'	128°22'
Kwalate Point	CAPE/CAP	BC	Range 1 Coast	92 K/13	50°47'	125°39'
Kwatlena 4	IR/RI	BC	Range 3 Coast	93 D/3	52°06'	127°21'
Kwatna Inlet	BAY/BAIE	BC	Range 3 Coast	93 D/3	52°06'	127°30'
Kwatna River	RIV/CDE	BC	Range 3 Coast	93 D/3	52°06'	127°23'
Kwa-tsa-lix 4	IR/RI	BC	Range 5 Coast	103 I/16	54°54'	128°23'
Kwatse 3	IR/RI	BC	Range 1 Coast	92 K/12	50°41'	125°45'
Kwatsi Bay	BAY/BAIE	BC	Range 1 Coast	92 L/16	50°51'	126°15'
Kwawkwawapilt 6	IR/RI	BC	New Westminster	92 H/4	49°10'	121°59'
Kwejinne Lake	LAKE/LAC	NT	Mackenzie	85 O	63°44'	115°53'
Kwetabohigan River	RIV/CDE	ON	Cochrane	42 P/2	51°09'	80°50'
Kwetahkis 9	IR/RI	BC	Range 1 Coast	92 L/14	50°58'	127°13'
Kwikoit Creek	RIV/CDE	BC	Kamloops Division Yale	82 M/3	51°01'	119°27'
Kwinamuck 49	IR/RI	BC	Cassiar	103 P/6	55°22'	129°02'
Kwinitsa	UNP/LNO	BC	Range 5 Coast	103 I/4	54°15'	129°33'
Kwinkwaga Lake	LAKE/LAC	ON	Thunder Bay	42 C/14	48°48'	85°20'
Kwoiek Creek	RIV/CDE	BC	Kamloops Division Yale	92 I/4	50°06'	121°34'
Kwoiek Needle	MTN/MNT	BC	Yale Division Yale	92 I/4	50°05'	121°48'
Kwokullie Lake	LAKE/LAC	BC	Peace River	94 P/7	59°16'	120°59'
Kwum Kwum	IR/RI	BC	New Westminster	92 G/11	49°35'	123°17'
Kyak Bay	BAY/BAIE	NT	Franklin	25 C	60°03'	69°47'
Kyarti 3	IR/RI	BC	Range 3 Coast	103 A/8	52°18'	128°12'
Kyaska Lake	LAKE/LAC	SK		64 D/1	56°16'	102°28'
Kyex 64	IR/RI	BC	Range 5 Coast	103 I/5	54°16'	129°47'
Kye-Yaa-La 1	IR/RI	BC	Range 1 Coast	92 L/10	50°42'	126°37'
Kyidagwis 2	IR/RI	BC	Range 2 Coast	92 M/2	51°01'	126°33'
Kyimla 11	IR/RI	BC	Range 1 Coast	92 L/9	50°44'	126°09'

NAME NOM	ENTITY ENTITÉ	LOC 1 LIEU 1	LOC 2 LIEU 2	MAP CARTE	POSITION LAT	LONG
Kykinalko 2	IR/RI	BC	Kamloops Division Yale	92 I/6	50°16′	121°23′
Kyklo Creek	RIV/CDE	BC	Peace River	94 I/10	58°40′	120°50′
Kyle	TOWN/VIL2	SK	32-21-15-W3	72 K/16	50°50′	108°02′
Kylemore	HAM/HAM	SK	9-34-12-W2	62 M/14	51°54′	103°38′
Kynoch	UNP/LNO	ON	Algoma	41 J/6	46°27′	83°16′
Kynoch Inlet	BAY/BAIE	BC	Range 3 Coast	93 D/12	52°45′	128°00′
Kynocks	UNP/LNO	YT		105 E/5	61°16′	135°58′
Kytes Hill	UNP/LNO	NS	Cape Breton	11 K/1	46°09′	60°08′
Kyuquot	UNP/LNO	BC	Rupert	92 L/3	50°02′	127°22′
Kyuquot Canyon	SEAU/SMER	—		3604	49°50′	127°40′
Kyuquot Channel	CHAN/CHEN	BC	Rupert	92 E/14	49°59′	127°15′
Kyuquot Sound	CHAN/CHEN	BC	Rupert	92 L/3	50°04′	127°13′
Kzimeng 82	IR/RI	BC	Cassiar	103 P/3	55°14′	129°09′

L

NAME NOM	ENTITY ENTITÉ	LOC 1 LIEU 1	LOC 2 LIEU 2	MAP CARTE	POSITION LAT	LONG
La Baie	CITY/VIL1	QC	Le Fjord-du-Saguenay	22 D/7	48°20′	70°52′
La Baie	UNP/LNO	QC	Les Îles-de-la-Madeleine	11 N/4	47°14′	61°52′
La Baleine	VILG/VILG	QC	Charlevoix	21 M/8	47°24′	70°21′
La Barre	UNP/LNO	QC	Lac-Saint-Jean-Est	22 D/5	48°27′	71°36′
La Barrière	UNP/LNO	QC	Matawinie	31 I/5	46°25′	73°43′
L'Abattis	UNP/LNO	QC	Le Fjord-du-Saguenay	22 D/7	48°24′	70°35′
La Baume, Lac	LAKE/LAC	QC	Jamésie	23 L/10	54°39′	70°49′
Labelle	VILG/VILG	QC	Les Laurentides	31 J/7	46°17′	74°44′
LaBelle	UNP/LNO	NS	Queens	21 A/7	44°19′	64°50′
Laberge	UNP/LNO	QC	Beauharnois-Salaberry	31 H/5	45°17′	73°48′
Laberge	UNP/LNO	QC	Les Laurentides	31 J/1	46°07′	74°26′
Laberge, Lake	LAKE/LAC	YT		105 E/3	61°11′	135°12′
La Biche Range	MTN/MNT	YT/NT		95 C/10	60°33′	124°33′
La Biche River	RIV/CDE	AB	31-69-18-W4	83 P/2	55°01′	112°44′
La Biche River	RIV/CDE	BC/YT		94 O/13	59°55′	123°52′
La Bolduc, Monts	MTN/MNT	QC	La Côte-de-Gaspé	22 A/14	48°53′	65°05′
La Bostonnais	VILG/VILG	QC	Le Haut-Saint-Maurice	31 P/10	47°31′	72°42′
Labouchere Channel	CHAN/CHEN	BC	Range 3 Coast	93 D/6	52°24′	127°14′
Labouchere Passage	CHAN/CHEN	BC	Range 1 Coast	92 L/14	50°48′	127°03′
La Bouille, Lac	LAKE/LAC	QC	Caniapiscau	23 C/2	52°09′	68°46′
Labrador	GEOG/GÉOG	NF		13 K/5	54°20′	61°45′
Labrador Basin - also-aussi - Labrador, Bassin du	SEAU/SMER	—		5001	55°00′	47°00′
Labrador, Bassin du - also-aussi - Labrador Basin	SEAU/SMER	—		5001	55°00′	47°00′
Labrador City	TOWN/VIL2	NF		23 B/15	52°57′	66°55′
Labrador Continental Margin	SEAU/SMER	—			56°00′	56°00′
Labrador Marginal Trough	SEAU/SMER	—		8047	55°00′	58°00′
Labrador, Mer du - also-aussi - **Labrador Sea**	SEA/MER	NF		MCR130	55°00′	56°00′
Labrador Rise	SEAU/SMER	—		813	57°00′	55°00′
Labrador Sea - also-aussi - **Labrador, Mer du**	SEA/MER	NF		MCR130	55°00′	56°00′
Labrador Shelf	SEAU/SMER	—		813	56°00′	58°00′
Labrador Slope	SEAU/SMER	—		813	56°20′	57°30′
La Branche	UNP/LNO	QC	La Jacques-Cartier	21 M/3	47°02′	71°11′
Labrecque	VILG/VILG	QC	Lac-Saint-Jean-Est	22 D/12	48°40′	71°32′
Labrecque	UNP/LNO	QC	La Jacques-Cartier	21 M/3	47°00′	71°25′
Labrecque, Lac	LAKE/LAC	QC	Lac-Saint-Jean-Est	22 D/12	48°41′	71°30′
Labrie	UNP/LNO	QC	Bellechasse	21 L/15	46°48′	70°56′
Labrieville	UNP/LNO	QC	La Haute-Côte-Nord	22 F/5	49°18′	69°34′
Labrieville-Sud	UNP/LNO	QC	La Haute-Côte-Nord	22 F/3	49°10′	69°13′
La Broquerie	MUN2/AZM2	MB		62 H/7	49°21′	96°57′
La Broquerie	UNP/LNO	MB	31-6-8-E	62 H/9	49°31′	96°30′
Labuma	UNP/LNO	AB	10-39-27-W4	83 A/5	52°20′	113°48′
La Butte-aux-Puces	UNP/LNO	QC	Portneuf	21 L/12	46°43′	71°51′
La Butte Creek	RIV/CDE	AB	120-9-W4	74 M/6	59°25′	111°26′
Labyrinth Bay	BAY/BAIE	ON	Kenora	52 E/10	49°35′	94°50′
Labyrinth Bay	BAY/BAIE	NT	Mackenzie	77 A	68°25′	105°17′
Labyrinth Lake	LAKE/LAC	NT	Franklin	75 B	60°44′	106°23′
Lac-à-Beauce	UNP/LNO	QC	Le Haut-Saint-Maurice	31 P/7	47°19′	72°46′
Lac-à-Belley	UNP/LNO	QC	Le Domaine-du-Roy	32 A/8	48°22′	72°06′
Lac-Achouakan	MUN2/AZM2	QC	Lac-Saint-Jean-Est	22 D/4	48°07′	71°39′
Lac-à-Dave	UNP/LNO	QC	Beauce-Sartigan	21 E/16	45°57′	70°26′
Lacadena	HAM/HAM	SK	17-23-17-W3	72 K/16	50°57′	108°20′
Lacadena No. 228	MUN2/AZM2	SK	72 K/16		50°50′	108°10′
L'Acadie	VILG/VILG	QC	Le Haut-Richelieu	31 H/6	45°19′	73°21′
L'Acadie, Rivière	RIV/CDE	QC	La Vallée-du-Richelieu	31 H/6	45°25′	73°16′
Lac-à-Dîner	UNP/LNO	QC	Maria-Chapdelaine	22 E/4	49°02′	71°37′
Lac-à-Foin	UNP/LNO	QC	Antoine-Labelle	31 J/4	46°11′	75°41′
Lac-à-Foin	UNP/LNO	QC	Antoine-Labelle	31 J/4	46°11′	75°41′

NAME NOM	ENTITY ENTITÉ	LOC 1 LIEU 1	LOC 2 LIEU 2	MAP CARTE	POSITION LAT	LONG
Lac-Akonapwehikan	MUN2/AZM2	QC	Antoine-Labelle	31 O/9	47°30′	74°29′
Lac-à-la-Croix	VILG/VILG	QC	Lac-Saint-Jean-Est	22 D/5	48°24′	71°47′
Lac-à-la-Croix	MUN2/AZM2	QC	La Mitis	22 B/5	48°18′	67°47′
Lac-Alain	UNP/LNO	QC	Portneuf	21 L/13	46°57′	71°50′
Lac-à-la-Loutre	UNP/LNO	QC	Les Laurentides	31 G/15	46°00′	74°39′
Lac-à-la-Tortue	VILG/VILG	QC	Le Centre-de-la-Mauricie	31 I/10	46°37′	72°38′
Lac-à-la-Tortue, Réserve écologique de	PARK/PARC	QC	Le Centre-de-la-Mauricie	31 I/10	46°33′	72°40′
Lac-à-la-Truite	UNP/LNO	QC	Les Laurentides	31 J/1	46°02′	74°15′
Lac-à-l'Eau-Claire	UNP/LNO	QC	Le Centre-de-la-Mauricie	31 I/11	46°32′	73°05′
Lac-à-l'Esturgeon	UNP/LNO	QC	La Vallée-de-la-Gatineau	31 K/1	46°08′	76°05′
Lac-Alfred	MUN2/AZM2	QC	La Matapédia	22 B/5	48°25′	67°48′
La Canadienne, Pointe	CAPE/CAP	ON	Thunder Bay	42 C/4	48°02′	85°55′
La Carrière	UNP/LNO	QC	Les Maskoutains	31 H/10	45°35′	72°53′
La Carrière	UNP/LNO	QC	Argenteuil	31 G/9	45°41′	74°26′
Lac-Ashuapmushuan	MUN2/AZM2	QC	Le Domaine-du-Roy	32 H/4	49°10′	73°45′
Lac-au-Brochet	MUN2/AZM2	QC	La Haute-Côte-Nord	22 F/12	49°40′	69°36′
Lac-au-Saumon	TOWN/VIL2	QC	La Matapédia	22 B/6	48°25′	67°21′
Lac-au-Saumon	UNP/LNO	QC	La Matapédia	22 B/6	48°25′	67°21′
Lac-aux-Bleuets	UNP/LNO	QC	Le Fjord-du-Saguenay	22 D/6	48°26′	71°21′
Lac-aux-Brochets	UNP/LNO	QC	Le Haut-Saint-Maurice	31 P/2	47°13′	72°41′
Lac-aux-Ours	UNP/LNO	QC	Les Laurentides	31 J/1	46°12′	74°29′
Lac-aux-Sables	VILG/VILG	QC	Mékinac	31 I/16	46°52′	72°24′
Lac-Bachelor	UNP/LNO	QC	Jamésie	32 F/9	49°32′	76°07′
Lac Baker	VILG/VILG	NB	Madawaska	21 N/7	47°20′	68°39′
Lac-Baker - see-voir - Lac Baker	VILG/VILG	NB		21 N/7	47°20′	68°39′
Lac-Baker	GEOG/GÉOG	NB	Madawaska	21 N/7	47°20′	68°37′
Lac-Baribeau	UNP/LNO	QC	Matawinie	31 J/8	46°21′	74°10′
Lac-Bazinet	MUN2/AZM2	QC	Antoine-Labelle	31 O/7	47°27′	74°46′
Lac-Beaudry	UNP/LNO	QC	Montcalm	31 H/13	45°59′	73°56′
Lac-Beauport	VILG/VILG	QC	La Jacques-Cartier	21 L/14	46°58′	71°18′
Lac-Beaven	UNP/LNO	QC	Les Laurentides	31 G/15	45°58′	74°36′
Lac-Bécancour	UNP/LNO	QC	L'Amiante	21 L/3	46°04′	71°15′
Lac Bellevue	UNP/LNO	AB	7-56-9-W4	73 E/14	53°49′	111°20′
Lac-Berlinguet	MUN2/AZM2	QC	Le Haut-Saint-Maurice	32 B/9	48°41′	74°07′
Lac-Bertrand	UNP/LNO	QC	La Rivière-du-Nord	31 H/13	45°52′	73°59′
Lac-Bitobig	UNP/LNO	QC	La Vallée-de-la-Gatineau	31 J/5	46°16′	75°55′
Lac-Blanc	MUN2/AZM2	QC	Portneuf	31 P/8	47°17′	72°01′
Lac-Blanc	UNP/LNO	QC	Portneuf	31 I/16	46°49′	72°16′
Lac-Blanc	UNP/LNO	QC	Antoine-Labelle	31 J/7	46°22′	74°58′
Lac-Blouin	UNP/LNO	QC	Vallée-de-l'Or	32 C/4	48°09′	77°43′
Lac-Boisbouscache	MUN2/AZM2	QC	Les Basques	22 C/2	48°08′	68°50′
Lac-Boissonneault	UNP/LNO	QC	Le Val-Saint-François	21 E/12	45°36′	71°55′
Lac-Bouchette	VILG/VILG	QC	Le Domaine-du-Roy	32 A/8	48°15′	72°11′
Lac-Bouchette	UNP/LNO	QC	Les Pays-d'en-Haut	31 G/16	45°55′	74°15′
Lac-Boulé	MUN2/AZM2	QC	Mékinac	31 I/13	46°53′	73°37′
Lac, Branche du	RIV/CDE	QC	Matane	22 B/9	48°40′	66°12′
Lac-Breton	UNP/LNO	QC	Les Pays-d'en-Haut	31 G/16	45°52′	74°14′
Lac-Bricault	MUN2/AZM2	QC	Vallée-de-l'Or	31 N/16	47°45′	76°23′
Lac Brochet	UNP/LNO	MB		64 K/11	58°37′	101°29′
Lac Brochet 197A	IR/RI	MB		64 K/11	58°37′	101°30′
Lac-Brome	CITY/VIL1	QC	Brome-Missisquoi	31 H/2	45°13′	72°31′
Lac-Brompton-Sud	UNP/LNO	QC	Memphrémagog	31 H/8	45°23′	72°09′
Lac-Caché	UNP/LNO	QC	Jamésie	32 G/16	49°49′	74°26′
Lac-Cameron	UNP/LNO	QC	Les Laurentides	31 J/2	46°07′	74°50′
Lac-Cameron	UNP/LNO	QC	Jamésie	32 F/7	49°18′	76°53′
Lac-Campion	UNP/LNO	QC	Antoine-Labelle	31 J/4	46°07′	75°38′
Lac-Caribou	UNP/LNO	QC	Les Laurentides	31 J/1	46°03′	74°26′
Lac-Caribou	UNP/LNO	QC	Les Laurentides	31 J/7	46°17′	74°42′
Lac-Caroline	UNP/LNO	QC	Argenteuil	31 G/16	45°46′	74°14′
Lac-Carré	UNP/LNO	QC	Les Laurentides	31 J/1	46°08′	74°29′
Lac-Carroll	UNP/LNO	QC	La Rivière-du-Nord	31 G/16	45°47′	74°11′
Lac-Casault	MUN2/AZM2	QC	La Matapédia	22 B/11	48°30′	67°09′
Lac-Castagnier	UNP/LNO	QC	Abitibi	32 C/12	48°43′	77°45′
Lac-Castor	UNP/LNO	QC	Antoine-Labelle	31 J/7	46°22′	74°53′
Lac-Caugnawana	UNP/LNO	QC	Témiscamingue	31 L/9	46°32′	78°18′
Lac-Cayamant	UNP/LNO	QC	La Vallée-de-la-Gatineau	31 K/1	46°08′	76°15′
Lac-Chanoine	UNP/LNO	QC	Matawinie	31 I/4	46°10′	73°41′
Lac-Chantal	UNP/LNO	QC	Les Pays-d'en-Haut	31 G/16	45°58′	74°22′
Lac-Chapleau	UNP/LNO	QC	Les Pays-d'en-Haut	31 G/16	45°54′	74°25′
Lac-Chapleau	UNP/LNO	QC	Les Laurentides	31 J/2	46°15′	74°56′
Lac-Charlebois	UNP/LNO	QC	Les Pays-d'en-Haut	31 J/1	46°05′	74°03′
Lac-Charlebois	UNP/LNO	QC	Papineau	31 G/14	45°45′	75°04′
Lac-Chat	UNP/LNO	QC	Le Haut-Saint-Maurice	31 P/2	47°10′	72°39′
Lac-Chaud	UNP/LNO	QC	Antoine-Labelle	31 J/7	46°25′	74°46′
Lac-Chevreuils	UNP/LNO	QC	Les Pays-d'en-Haut	31 G/16	45°54′	74°19′

NAME / NOM	ENTITY / ENTITÉ	LOC 1 / LIEU 1	LOC 2 / LIEU 2	MAP / CARTE	POSITION LAT	LONG
Lac-Chicobi	MUN2/AZM2	QC	Abitibi	32 D/15	48°53′	78°30′
Lac-Clair	UNP/LNO	QC	Le Haut-Saint-Maurice	31 P/10	47°42′	72°48′
Lac-Clair	UNP/LNO	QC	Matawinie	31 I/4	46°05′	73°48′
Lac-Clef	UNP/LNO	QC	Matawinie	31 J/8	46°23′	74°13′
Lac-Corbeau	UNP/LNO	QC	Matawinie	31 I/5	46°19′	73°31′
Lac-Cornu	UNP/LNO	QC	Les Pays-d'en-Haut	31 G/16	45°58′	74°23′
Lac-Cristal	UNP/LNO	QC	Montcalm	31 H/13	45°59′	73°53′
Lac-Croche	MUN2/AZM2	QC	La Jacques-Cartier	21 M/5	47°24′	71°47′
Lac-Cyprès	UNP/LNO	QC	Le Domaine-du-Roy	32 A/5	48°27′	73°41′
Lac-Danford	UNP/LNO	QC	La Vallée-de-la-Gatineau	31 F/16	45°57′	76°08′
Lac-Darey	UNP/LNO	QC	Le Haut-Saint-Maurice	31 P/11	47°40′	73°09′
Lac-David	UNP/LNO	QC	Matawinie	31 I/4	46°05′	73°57′
Lac-David	UNP/LNO	QC	Antoine-Labelle	31 J/11	46°35′	75°13′
Lac-De La Bidière	MUN2/AZM2	QC	Antoine-Labelle	30 O/6	47°26′	75°05′
Lac-Delage	CITY/VIL1	QC	La Jacques-Cartier	21 L/14	46°58′	71°24′
Lac-de-la-Maison-de-Pierre	MUN2/AZM2	QC	Antoine-Labelle	31 J/15	46°53′	74°42′
Lac-de-la-Pomme	MUN2/AZM2	QC	Antoine-Labelle	31 O/2	47°11′	74°31′
Lac-Deligny	UNP/LNO	QC	D'Autray	31 I/6	46°23′	73°18′
Lac-de-l'Orignal	UNP/LNO	QC	Les Laurentides	31 J/1	46°12′	74°19′
Lac-des-Aigles	VILG/VILG	QC	Témiscouata	21 N/15	47°59′	68°41′
Lac-des-Aulnes	UNP/LNO	QC	Matawinie	31 J/8	46°22′	74°11′
Lac-des-Becs-Scie	UNP/LNO	QC	Les Pays-d'en-Haut	31 G/16	45°51′	74°13′
Lac-des-Chats	UNP/LNO	QC	Les Pays-d'en-Haut	31 G/16	45°51′	74°14′
Lac-Deschênes	UNP/LNO	QC	Charlevoix-Est	21 M/16	47°57′	70°04′
Lac-des-Cinq	MUN2/AZM2	QC	Le Centre-de-la-Mauricie	31 I/15	46°51′	72°59′
Lac-des-Commissaires	UNP/LNO	QC	Le Domaine-du-Roy	32 A/1	48°09′	72°14′
Lac des Cygnes, Mont du	MTN/MNT	QC	Charlevoix	21 M/10	47°40′	70°36′
Lac-des-Dix-Milles	MUN2/AZM2	QC	Matawinie	31 J/8	46°27′	74°23′
Lac-des-Eaux-Mortes	MUN2/AZM2	QC	La Mitis	22 C/1	48°14′	68°05′
Lac-des-Échos	UNP/LNO	QC	Rimouski-Neigette	22 C/1	48°01′	68°23′
Lac-des-Écorces	TOWN/VIL2	QC	Antoine-Labelle	31 J/11	46°34′	75°22′
Lac-des-Écorces	MUN2/AZM2	QC	Papineau	31 G/14	45°54′	75°19′
Lac-des-Français	UNP/LNO	QC	Matawinie	31 I/4	46°08′	73°38′
Lac-des-Îles	UNP/LNO	QC	Antoine-Labelle	31 J/5	46°24′	75°32′
Lac-des-Loups	UNP/LNO	QC	Les Collines-de-l'Outaouais	31 F/9	45°41′	76°13′
Lac-des-Lys	UNP/LNO	NB	Restigouche	21 O/15	47°58′	66°38′
Lac-Desmarais	UNP/LNO	QC	Les Laurentides	31 J/2	46°10′	74°38′
Lac des Mille Lacs 22A1	IR/RI	ON	Thunder Bay	52 B/16	48°53′	90°22′
Lac-des-Moires	MUN2/AZM2	QC	Le Haut-Saint-Maurice	31 P/9	47°42′	72°02′
Lac-des-Neiges	UNP/LNO	QC	La Côte-de-Beaupré	21 M/6	47°29′	71°02′
Lac-des-Perdrix	UNP/LNO	QC	La Rivière-du-Nord	31 H/13	45°50′	73°56′
Lac-des-Piles	UNP/LNO	QC	Le Centre-de-la-Mauricie	31 I/10	46°39′	72°47′
Lac-Despinassy	MUN2/AZM2	QC	Abitibi	32 C/14	48°47′	77°20′
Lac-des-Pins	UNP/LNO	QC	Les Laurentides	31 G/16	45°55′	74°30′
Lac-des-Plages	VILG/VILG	QC	Papineau	31 J/2	46°00′	74°54′
Lac-des-Plaines	UNP/LNO	QC	L'Islet	21 M/1	47°04′	70°08′
Lac-des-Seize-Îles	VILG/VILG	QC	Les Pays-d'en-Haut	31 G/16	45°54′	74°28′
Lac-des-Sources	UNP/LNO	QC	La Rivière-du-Nord	31 G/16	45°57′	74°03′
Lac-Devenyns	MUN2/AZM2	QC	Matawinie	31 P/4	47°05′	73°50′
Lac-Dion	UNP/LNO	QC	Bellechasse	21 L/10	46°39′	70°40′
Lac-Doré	UNP/LNO	QC	Jamésie	32 G/16	49°52′	74°23′
Lac-Douaire	MUN2/AZM2	QC	Antoine-Labelle	30 O/4	47°10′	75°48′
Lac-Drolet	VILG/VILG	QC	Le Granit	21 E/10	45°43′	70°51′
Lac du Bonnet	VILG/VILG	MB	17-15-11-E	62 I/8	50°15′	96°04′
Lac du Bonnet	MUN2/AZM2	MB		62 I/8	50°15′	96°10′
Lac-du-Brochet	UNP/LNO	QC	La Vallée-de-la-Gatineau	31 G/13	45°55′	75°50′
Lac-du-Camp	UNP/LNO	QC	Antoine-Labelle	31 J/5	46°18′	75°39′
Lac-du-Cerf	VILG/VILG	QC	Antoine-Labelle	31 J/5	46°18′	75°30′
Lac-Dufault	VILG/VILG	QC	Rouyn-Noranda	32 D/6	48°18′	79°02′
Lac-Duffy	UNP/LNO	QC	Montcalm	31 I/4	46°01′	73°55′
Lac-Dufresne	UNP/LNO	QC	Les Laurentides	31 J/1	46°12′	74°13′
Lac-du-Marcheur	UNP/LNO	QC	Matawinie	31 J/1	46°11′	74°02′
Lac-du-Milieu	UNP/LNO	QC	Portneuf	31 P/1	47°01′	72°10′
Lac-Duparquet	MUN2/AZM2	QC	Abitibi-Ouest	32 D/6	48°28′	79°16′
Lac-du-Pin-Rouge	UNP/LNO	QC	La Rivière-du-Nord	31 G/16	45°58′	74°03′
Lac-du-Taureau	MUN2/AZM2	QC	Matawinie	31 O/7	47°15′	74°39′
Lac-Écho	UNP/LNO	QC	Papineau	31 G/14	45°53′	75°26′
Lac-Édouard	VILG/VILG	QC	Le Haut-Saint-Maurice	31 P/9	47°39′	72°16′
Lac-en-Coeur	UNP/LNO	QC	La Rivière-du-Nord	31 G/16	45°58′	74°01′
Lac-Équerre	UNP/LNO	QC	Les Laurentides	31 J/7	46°17′	74°59′
Lac-Ernest	MUN2/AZM2	QC	Antoine-Labelle	31 J/3	46°11′	75°12′
Lac-Etchemin	CITY/VIL1	QC	Les Etchemins	21 L/7	46°24′	70°30′
Lac-Filion	UNP/LNO	QC	La Rivière-du-Nord	31 G/16	45°49′	74°06′
Lac-Fortune	UNP/LNO	QC	Rouyn-Noranda	32 D/3	48°11′	79°18′
Lac-Fouillac	MUN2/AZM2	QC	Vallée-de-l'Or	32 D/1	48°02′	78°18′

NAME / NOM	ENTITY / ENTITÉ	LOC 1 / LIEU 1	LOC 2 / LIEU 2	MAP / CARTE	POSITION LAT	POSITION LONG
Lac-Fournelle	UNP/LNO	QC	La Rivière-du-Nord	31 G/16	45°55′	74°03′
Lac-Français	UNP/LNO	QC	Les Laurentides	31 J/1	46°10′	74°28′
Lac-Frontière	VILG/VILG	QC	Montmagny	21 L/9	46°42′	70°00′
Lac-Gareau	UNP/LNO	QC	La Vallée-de-la-Gatineau	31 K/1	46°06′	76°08′
Lac-Gatineau	UNP/LNO	QC	Antoine-Labelle	31 J/12	46°34′	75°43′
Lac-Gauthier	UNP/LNO	QC	Les Laurentides	31 J/2	46°10′	74°31′
Lac-Gauvin	UNP/LNO	QC	Abitibi	32 D/9	48°36′	78°11′
Lac-Gélinas	UNP/LNO	QC	Les Laurentides	31 J/2	46°10′	74°38′
Lac-Gémont	UNP/LNO	QC	Les Pays-d'en-Haut	31 G/16	45°55′	74°23′
Lac-Gervais	UNP/LNO	QC	Les Laurentides	31 J/7	46°16′	74°41′
Lac-Goth	UNP/LNO	QC	Le Fjord-du-Saguenay	22 D/7	48°18′	70°41′
Lac-Granet	MUN2/AZM2	QC	Vallée-de-l'Or	31 N/13	47°47′	77°31′
Lac-Grosleau	UNP/LNO	QC	Papineau	31 G/14	45°50′	75°05′
La Chapelle	UNP/LNO	QC	Mirabel	31 G/9	45°45′	74°00′
Lachenaie	CITY/VIL1	QC	Les Moulins	31 H/12	45°42′	73°33′
La Chevrotière	UNP/LNO	QC	Portneuf	31 I/9	46°39′	72°01′
La Chevrotière, Lac	LAKE/LAC	QC	Kativik	34 I/14	58°45′	73°18′
Lachine	CITY/VIL1	QC	Communauté urbaine de Montréal	31 H/5	45°26′	73°41′
Lachine Canal - also-aussi - Lachine, Canal de	PARK/PARC	QC	Communauté urbaine de Montréal	31 H/5	45°28′	73°37′
Lachine, Canal de - also-aussi - Lachine Canal	PARK/PARC	QC	Communauté urbaine de Montréal	31 H/5	45°28′	73°37′
Lachine, Rapides de	RAP/RAP	QC	Communauté urbaine de Montréal	31 H/5	45°25′	73°36′
Lachkaltsap 9	IR/RI	BC	Cassiar	103 P/4	55°03′	129°33′
Lachkul-jeets 6	IR/RI	BC	Range 4 Coast	103 H/6	53°16′	129°19′
Lachmach 16	IR/RI	BC	Range 5 Coast	103 I/5	54°18′	129°59′
Lachtesk 12	IR/RI	BC	Range 5 Coast	103 I/13	54°58′	129°42′
Lachtesk 12A	IR/RI	BC	Range 5 Coast	103 I/13	54°58′	129°40′
Lac-Huguette	UNP/LNO	QC	Les Pays-d'en-Haut	31 G/16	45°58′	74°21′
Lac-Humqui	UNP/LNO	QC	La Matapédia	22 B/5	48°19′	67°35′
Lac-Huron	MUN2/AZM2	QC	Rimouski-Neigette	22 C/1	48°12′	68°14′
Lachute	CITY/VIL1	QC	Argenteuil	31 G/9	45°39′	74°20′
Lac, Île du	ISL/ÎLE	QC	Côte-Nord-du-Golfe-Saint-Laurent	12 K/1	50°11′	60°05′
Lac-Jacques-Cartier	MUN2/AZM2	QC	La Côte-de-Beaupré	21 M/11	47°35′	71°13′
Lac-Jérôme	MUN2/AZM2	QC	Minganie	12 L/13	50°51′	63°33′
Lac-Joannès	UNP/LNO	QC	Rouyn-Noranda	32 D/2	48°12′	78°41′
Lac-Johanne	UNP/LNO	QC	Les Pays-d'en-Haut	31 G/16	45°50′	74°08′
Lac John	IR/RI	QC	Caniapiscau	23 J/15	54°49′	66°47′
Lac-Jolicoeur	UNP/LNO	QC	Les Laurentides	31 J/2	46°07′	74°32′
Lac-Juillet	MUN2/AZM2	QC	Caniapiscau	23 I/16	54°47′	64°00′
Lac-Kataway	UNP/LNO	QC	Matawinie	31 J/9	46°42′	74°01′
Lackaway 2	IR/RI	BC	New Westminster	92 G/1	49°08′	122°03′
Lac-Keatley	UNP/LNO	QC	Argenteuil	31 G/15	45°47′	74°36′
Lac-Kénogami	VILG/VILG	QC	Le Fjord-du-Saguenay	22 D/6	48°23′	71°24′
Lackzuswadda 9	IR/RI	BC	Range 3 Coast	103 A/14	52°54′	129°09′
Lac-Labelle	UNP/LNO	QC	Les Laurentides	31 J/7	46°16′	74°50′
Lac La Biche	TOWN/VIL2	AB	6-67-13-W4	73 L/13	54°46′	111°58′
Lac La Biche Mission	UNP/LNO	AB	29-67-14-W4	83 I/16	54°49′	112°06′
Lac-Labonté	UNP/LNO	QC	Le Fjord-du-Saguenay	22 D/11	48°35′	71°26′
Lac-Labrie	UNP/LNO	QC	Sept-Rivières	22 J/2	50°11′	66°41′
Lac la Croix	UNP/LNO	ON	Rainy River	52 C/8	48°22′	92°10′
Lac la Hache	UNP/LNO	BC	Lillooet	92 P/14	51°49′	121°28′
Lac la Hache	UNP/LNO	BC	Lillooet	92 P/14	51°48′	121°29′
Lac la Hache 220	IR/RI	SK		64 L/3	58°10′	103°00′
Lac-Lajoie	UNP/LNO	QC	Matawinie	31 J/8	46°25′	74°17′
Lac la Martre - see-voir - Wha Ti	HAM/HAM	NT		85 N/3	63°08′	117°16′
Lac-La Motte	UNP/LNO	QC	Abitibi	32 D/8	48°26′	78°04′
Lac-Lamoureux	UNP/LNO	QC	Les Laurentides	31 J/2	46°09′	74°38′
Lac la Nonne	UNP/LNO	AB	12-57-3-W5	83 G/16	53°55′	114°18′
Lac-Laperrière	UNP/LNO	QC	Témiscamingue	31 M/6	47°18′	79°27′
Lac-Lapeyrère	MUN2/AZM2	QC	Portneuf	31 P/1	47°13′	72°22′
Lac-Laplaine	UNP/LNO	QC	Les Moulins	31 H/13	45°46′	73°41′
Lac la Ronge 156	IR/RI	SK		73 P/3	55°04′	105°19′
Lac-Lasalle	UNP/LNO	QC	Matawinie	31 I/5	46°24′	73°42′
Lac-Laurel	UNP/LNO	QC	Les Pays-d'en-Haut	31 G/16	45°52′	74°28′
Lac-Légaré	UNP/LNO	QC	Témiscouata	21 N/7	47°29′	68°49′
Lac-Legendre	MUN2/AZM2	QC	Matawinie	31 J/9	46°41′	74°22′
Lac Le Jeune	UNP/LNO	BC	Kamloops Division Yale	92 I/8	50°29′	120°30′
Lac-Lenôtre	MUN2/AZM2	QC	La Vallée-de-la-Gatineau	31 N/8	47°21′	76°02′
La Cloche Creek	RIV/CDE	ON	Sudbury	41 J/1	46°10′	82°05′
La Cloche Lake	LAKE/LAC	ON	Sudbury	41 J/1	46°10′	82°04′
La Cloche Mountains	MTN/MNT	ON	Algoma	41 I/4	46°08′	81°45′
Lac-Loïs	UNP/LNO	QC	Abitibi-Ouest	32 D/10	48°34′	78°50′
Lac-Long	UNP/LNO	QC	La Vallée-de-la-Gatineau	31 K/1	46°13′	76°07′
Lac-Long-Nord	UNP/LNO	QC	Matawinie	31 I/4	46°10′	73°40′
Lac-Long-Sud	UNP/LNO	QC	Matawinie	31 I/4	46°09′	73°40′
Lac-Louisa	UNP/LNO	QC	Argenteuil	31 G/16	45°46′	74°25′

NAME NOM	ENTITY ENTITÉ	LOC 1 LIEU 1	LOC 2 LIEU 2	MAP CARTE	POSITION LAT	LONG
Laclu	UNP/LNO	ON	Kenora	52 E/15	49°46'	94°41'
Laclu	UNP/LNO	ON	Kenora	52 E/15	49°47'	94°42'
Lac-MacDonald	UNP/LNO	QC	Argenteuil	31 G/15	45°52'	74°35'
Lac-Maggie	UNP/LNO	QC	Le Domaine-du-Roy	32 A/1	48°15'	72°05'
Lac-Malakisis, Réserve écologique du	PARK/PARC	QC	Témiscamingue	31 L/10	46°42'	78°39'
Lac-Manitou-Sud	UNP/LNO	QC	Les Laurentides	31 J/1	46°03'	74°21'
Lac-Marguerite	MUN2/AZM2	QC	Antoine-Labelle	31 O/4	47°02'	75°48'
Lac-Marmette	UNP/LNO	QC	Vallée-de-l'Or	31 N/13	47°58'	77°51'
Lac-Marsan	UNP/LNO	QC	Antoine-Labelle	31 J/7	46°21'	74°51'
Lac-Masketsi	MUN2/AZM2	QC	Mékinac	31 P/2	47°00'	72°33'
Lac-Masketsi	UNP/LNO	QC	Mékinac	31 P/2	47°00'	72°33'
Lac-Maskinongé	UNP/LNO	QC	Les Laurentides	31 J/2	46°05'	74°36'
Lac-Matapédia	MUN2/AZM2	QC	La Matapédia	22 B/12	48°33'	67°34'
Lac-Matawin	MUN2/AZM2	QC	Matawinie	31 J/16	46°49'	74°18'
Lac-McGregor	UNP/LNO	QC	Les Collines-de-l'Outaouais	31 G/12	45°39'	75°39'
Lac-Mégantic	CITY/VIL1	QC	Le Granit	21 E/10	45°35'	70°53'
Lac-Minaki	MUN2/AZM2	QC	Matawinie	31 I/14	46°53'	73°29'
Lac-Mingo	MUN2/AZM2	QC	Vallée-de-l'Or	31 O/13	47°50'	75°42'
Lac-Ministuk	MUN2/AZM2	QC	Le Fjord-du-Saguenay	22 D/3	48°06'	71°19'
Lac-Miroir	UNP/LNO	QC	Les Pays-d'en-Haut	31 G/16	45°53'	74°21'
Lac-Mitis	UNP/LNO	QC	La Mitis	22 B/5	48°19'	67°54'
Lac-Moncouche	MUN2/AZM2	QC	Lac-Saint-Jean-Est	21 M/13	47°57'	71°58'
Lac-Mondor	UNP/LNO	QC	Le Centre-de-la-Mauricie	31 I/10	46°37'	72°46'
Lac-Montanier	MUN2/AZM2	QC	Rouyn-Noranda	32 D/2	48°03'	78°31'
Lac-Moore	UNP/LNO	QC	Les Laurentides	31 J/2	46°12'	74°37'
Lac-Morin	UNP/LNO	QC	La Jacques-Cartier	21 L/14	46°59'	71°18'
Lac-Moselle	MUN2/AZM2	QC	La Vallée-de-la-Gatineau	31 O/12	47°31'	75°35'
Lac-Nilgaut	MUN2/AZM2	QC	Pontiac	31 K/11	46°36'	77°15'
Lac-Nominingue	VILG/VILG	QC	Antoine-Labelle	31 J/6	46°24'	75°02'
Lac-Normand	MUN2/AZM2	QC	Mékinac	31 P/3	47°05'	73°14'
Lac-Notre-Dame	UNP/LNO	QC	Les Pays-d'en-Haut	31 G/16	45°52'	74°22'
Lacolle	TOWN/VIL2	QC	Le Haut-Richelieu	31 H/3	45°05'	73°22'
La Colonie	UNP/LNO	QC	Denis-Riverin	22 G/1	49°12'	66°04'
Lacombe	TOWN/VIL2	AB	30-40-26-W4	83 A/5	52°28'	113°44'
Lacombe County	MUN1/AZM1	AB		83 A/5	52°27'	113°43'
Lacombe, Lac	LAKE/LAC	QC	Minganie	12 M/6	51°20'	63°02'
Lacombe No. 14, County of - see-voir - Lacombe County	MUN1/AZM1	AB		83 A/5	52°27'	113°43'
La Conception	VILG/VILG	QC	Les Laurentides	31 J/2	46°09'	74°42'
La Conception-Station	UNP/LNO	QC	Les Laurentides	31 J/2	46°12'	74°41'
Laconia	UNP/LNO	NS	Lunenburg	21 A/7	44°20'	64°39'
Lacordaire	UNP/LNO	SK	18-1-29-W2	72 H/4	49°02'	105°52'
La Corey	UNP/LNO	AB	13-63-6-W4	73 L/7	54°27'	110°46'
La Corne	VILG/VILG	QC	Abitibi	32 C/5	48°21'	78°00'
La Corniche	UNP/LNO	QC	Matawinie	31 J/8	46°17'	74°13'
Lac-Oscar	MUN2/AZM2	QC	Antoine-Labelle	31 O/6	47°17'	75°12'
Lacoste	UNP/LNO	QC	Antoine-Labelle	31 J/7	46°27'	74°56'
La Côte-de-Beaupré	MUN1/AZM1	QC	La Côte-de-Beaupré	21 M/2	47°03'	70°54'
La Côte-de-Gaspé	MUN1/AZM1	QC	La Côte-de-Gaspé	22 H/2	49°10'	64°55'
Lac-Ouareau	UNP/LNO	QC	Matawinie	31 J/8	46°19'	74°07'
La Coulée	UNP/LNO	QC	Le Fjord-du-Saguenay	22 D/1	48°11'	70°03'
La Coulée	UNP/LNO	MB	16-8-7-E	62 H/10	49°40'	96°35'
La Course, Lac	LAKE/LAC	SK	32,33-31,32-W	62 N/13	51°47'	101°52'
Lac-Pellerin	MUN2/AZM2	QC	Le Haut-Saint-Maurice	31 O/15	47°47'	74°37'
Lac Pelletier	UNP/LNO	SK	21-11-14-W3	72 G/13	49°56'	107°51'
Lac Pelletier No. 107	MUN2/AZM2	SK		72 G/13	49°55'	107°50'
Lac-Pemichangan	UNP/LNO	QC	La Vallée-de-la-Gatineau	31 J/4	46°02'	75°52'
Lac-Pérodeau	UNP/LNO	QC	Antoine-Labelle	31 J/14	46°46'	75°09'
Lac-Pikauba	MUN2/AZM2	QC	Charlevoix	21 M/14	47°48'	71°07'
Lac-Pilon	UNP/LNO	QC	Les Pays-d'en-Haut	31 G/16	46°00'	74°01'
Lac-Pimbina	UNP/LNO	QC	Matawinie	31 J/8	46°22'	74°14'
Lac-Pinault	UNP/LNO	QC	La Matapédia	22 B/11	48°32'	67°19'
Lac-Pitre	UNP/LNO	QC	La Matapédia	22 B/6	48°28'	67°20'
Lac-Poisson-Blanc	UNP/LNO	QC	La Vallée-de-la-Gatineau	31 J/4	46°04'	75°55'
Lac-Poulin	TOWN/VIL2	QC	Beauce-Sartigan	21 L/2	46°06'	70°49'
Lac-Provost	UNP/LNO	QC	Matawinie	31 J/8	46°23'	74°15'
Lac-Pythonga	MUN2/AZM2	QC	La Vallée-de-la-Gatineau	31 K/8	46°23'	76°26'
Lac-Quentin	MUN2/AZM2	QC	Vallée-de-l'Or	31 N/16	47°49'	76°06'
Lac-Raquette	UNP/LNO	QC	Les Etchemins	21 L/7	46°22'	70°30'
Lac-Relique	UNP/LNO	QC	Jamésie	32 G/12	49°37'	75°40'
Lac-Renaud	UNP/LNO	QC	Les Pays-d'en-Haut	31 G/16	45°56'	74°12'
La Crête	UNP/LNO	AB	9-106-15-W5	84 K/1	58°11'	116°24'
Lac-Rimouski	UNP/LNO	QC	Rimouski-Neigette	22 C/1	48°01'	68°12'
Lac-Robert	UNP/LNO	QC	Argenteuil	31 G/16	45°48'	74°08'
La Croche	UNP/LNO	QC	Le Haut-Saint-Maurice	31 P/10	47°36'	72°44'
Lac-Rocher	UNP/LNO	QC	Joliette	31 I/4	46°10'	73°32'

NAME NOM	ENTITY ENTITÉ	LOC 1 LIEU 1	LOC 2 LIEU 2	MAP CARTE	POSITION LAT	LONG
Lacroix	UNP/LNO	QC	Beauce-Sartigan	21 L/2	46°08'	70°41'
Lacroix, Lac	LAKE/LAC	QC	Jamésie	32 B/14	49°00'	75°25'
Lacroixville	UNP/LNO	QC	La Vallée-de-la-Gatineau	31 K/1	46°06'	76°02'
Lac-Rose	UNP/LNO	QC	Bécancour	31 I/8	46°21'	72°10'
Lac-Rossignol	UNP/LNO	QC	Les Laurentides	31 J/1	46°10'	74°27'
Lac-Rouge-Nord	UNP/LNO	QC	Matawinie	31 I/4	46°11'	73°42'
Lac-Saguay	TOWN/VIL2	QC	Antoine-Labelle	31 J/11	46°32'	75°09'
Lac-Saguay	UNP/LNO	QC	Antoine-Labelle	31 J/6	46°30'	75°09'
Lac-Saint-Amour	UNP/LNO	QC	Les Pays-d'en-Haut	31 G/16	45°51'	74°07'
Lac-Saint-Charles	VILG/VILG	QC	Communauté urbaine de Québec	21 L/14	46°54'	71°23'
Lac-Sainte-Anne	UNP/LNO	QC	Manicouagan	22 J/4	50°06'	67°57'
Lac Ste. Anne	UNP/LNO	AB	30-54-3-W5	83 G/9	53°41'	114°26'
Lac Ste. Anne County	MUN1/AZM1	AB		83 G/15	53°51'	114°42'
Lac Ste. Anne No. 28, County of - see-voir - Lac Ste. Anne County	MUN1/AZM1	AB		83 G/15	53°51'	114°42'
Lac Ste. Anne Settlement	UNP/LNO	AB	54-4,5-W5	83 G/9	53°40'	114°25'
Lac-Sainte-Marie	VILG/VILG	QC	La Vallée-de-la-Gatineau	31 G/13	45°57'	75°57'
Lac-Ste-Thérèse	UNP/LNO	ON	Cochrane	42 G/13	49°47'	83°39'
Lac-Saint-François-Xavier	UNP/LNO	QC	Les Pays-d'en-Haut	31 G/16	45°53'	74°22'
Lac-Saint-Germains	UNP/LNO	QC	Le Fjord-du-Saguenay	22 D/7	48°27'	70°38'
Lac-Saint-Jean-Est	MUN1/AZM1	QC	Lac-Saint-Jean-Est	22 D/12	48°33'	71°39'
Lac-Saint-Joseph	CITY/VIL1	QC	La Jacques-Cartier	21 L/13	46°55'	71°39'
Lac-Saint-Louis	UNP/LNO	QC	Matawinie	31 I/12	46°33'	73°48'
Lac-Saint-Paul	VILG/VILG	QC	Antoine-Labelle	31 J/11	46°44'	75°19'
Lac Saint-Pierre, Archipel du	ISL/ÎLE	QC	D'Autray	31 I/3	46°06'	73°04'
Lacs-Albanel-Mistassini-et-Waconichi, Réserve faunique des	PARK/PARC	QC	Jamésie	32 O/1	51°08'	74°25'
Lac-Salé	UNP/LNO	QC	Côte-Nord-du-Golfe-Saint-Laurent	12 J/15	50°53'	58°58'
Lac-Santé	MUN2/AZM2	QC	Matawinie	31 J/9	46°37'	74°29'
Lac-Sarrazin	UNP/LNO	QC	Les Laurentides	31 J/1	46°07'	74°12'
Lac-Sébastien	UNP/LNO	QC	Le Fjord-du-Saguenay	22 D/11	48°39'	71°08'
Lac-Sec, Le	UNP/LNO	QC	La Côte-de-Gaspé	22 A/15	48°46'	64°51'
Lac-Sergent	CITY/VIL1	QC	Portneuf	21 L/13	46°51'	71°44'
Lac Seul	UNP/LNO	ON	Kenora	52 K/8	50°20'	92°16'
Lac Seul 28	IR/RI	ON	Kenora	52 K/1	50°14'	92°15'
Lac-Simon	VILG/VILG	QC	Papineau	31 G/14	45°54'	75°06'
Lac-Simon	UNP/LNO	QC	Les Laurentides	31 J/2	46°09'	74°44'
Lac Simon	IR/RI	QC	Vallée-de-l'Or	32 C/3	48°03'	77°21'
Lac-Spectacles	UNP/LNO	QC	Les Pays-d'en-Haut	31 G/15	45°48'	74°32'
Lacs, Riviere des	RIV/CDE	SK	4-1-2-W2	62 E/1	49°00'	102°13'
Lac-Stoke	UNP/LNO	QC	Le Val-Saint-François	21 E/12	45°31'	71°49'
Lac-Supérieur	VILG/VILG	QC	Les Laurentides	31 J/1	46°12'	74°28'
Lac-Surimau	MUN2/AZM2	QC	Rouyn-Noranda	32 D/1	48°08'	78°19'
Lacs-Waterton, Parc national des - also-aussi - Waterton Lakes National Park	PARK/PARC	AB		82 H/4	49°05'	113°52'
Lac-Thibeault	UNP/LNO	QC	Témiscouata	21 N/7	47°24'	68°44'
Lac-Tire	UNP/LNO	QC	Matawinie	31 J/8	46°20'	74°14'
Lac-Tourlay	MUN2/AZM2	QC	Le Haut-Saint-Maurice	21 M/13	47°50'	71°58'
Lac-Tremblant-Nord	VILG/VILG	QC	Les Laurentides	31 J/2	46°13'	74°37'
Lac-Unique	UNP/LNO	NB	Madawaska	21 N/7	47°19'	68°44'
Lacusta Lake	LAKE/LAC	NT	Mackenzie	75 A	60°02'	105°09'
Lac-Vacher	MUN2/AZM2	QC	Caniapiscau	23 J/15	54°55'	66°55'
Lac-Vert	HAM/HAM	SK	2-41-18-W2	73 A/9	52°30'	104°30'
Lac-Vert	UNP/LNO	QC	Bellechasse	21 L/10	46°41'	70°43'
Lac-Vert	UNP/LNO	QC	Les Pays-d'en-Haut	31 G/16	45°57'	74°20'
Lac-Vert	UNP/LNO	QC	La Vallée-de-la-Gatineau	31 G/13	46°00'	75°48'
Lac-Vert-Nord	UNP/LNO	QC	Matawinie	31 I/4	46°11'	73°43'
Lac-Vert-Sud	UNP/LNO	QC	Matawinie	31 I/4	46°11'	73°43'
Lac-Vingt-Sous	UNP/LNO	QC	Les Pays-d'en-Haut	31 G/16	45°57'	74°22'
Lac-Wagwabika	MUN2/AZM2	QC	Antoine-Labelle	31 O/10	47°37'	74°39'
Lac-Walker	MUN2/AZM2	QC	Sept-Rivières	22 J/6	50°16'	67°09'
Lac-Wapizagonke	MUN2/AZM2	QC	Le Centre-de-la-Mauricie	31 I/11	46°43'	73°02'
Lac-Wentworth	UNP/LNO	QC	Les Pays-d'en-Haut	31 G/16	45°50'	74°20'
Lac-William	UNP/LNO	QC	L'Érable	21 L/4	46°09'	71°35'
Lacy Island	ISL/ÎLE	NT	Franklin	25 A/10	60°46'	64°36'
Ladder Lake	LAKE/LAC	SK	56-7-W3	73 G/15	53°50'	107°00'
Ladder Valley	UNP/LNO	SK	55-6-W3	73 G/15	53°46'	106°54'
Ladd's Mills	UNP/LNO	QC	Coaticook	21 E/4	45°06'	71°49'
Laderoute Lake	LAKE/LAC	NT	Keewatin	65 B	60°02'	99°25'
Ladle Cove	UNP/LNO	NF		2 E/8	49°28'	54°03'
Ladle Point	CAPE/CAP	NF		2 E/8	49°29'	54°04'
Ladner	UNP/LNO	BC	New Westminster	92 G/3	49°05'	123°05'
La Doré	VILG/VILG	QC	Le Domaine-du-Roy	32 A/10	48°43'	72°39'
Ladue River	RIV/CDE	YT		115 N/1	63°10'	140°20'
La Durantaye	VILG/VILG	QC	Bellechasse	21 L/15	46°50'	70°51'
Lady Ann Strait	CHAN/CHEN	NT	Franklin	38 G/12	75°40'	79°50'
Lady Bank	UNP/LNO	ON	Grey	41 A/8	44°22'	80°26'
Lady Cove	UNP/LNO	NF		2 C/4	48°06'	53°51'

NAME NOM	ENTITY ENTITÉ	LOC 1 LIEU 1	LOC 2 LIEU 2	MAP CARTE	POSITION LAT	LONG
Lady Douglas Island	ISL/ÎLE	BC	Range 3 Coast	103 A/8	52°20′	128°26′
Lady Evelyn Falls	FALL/CHUT	NT	Mackenzie	85 C	60°57′	117°20′
Lady Evelyn Lake	LAKE/LAC	ON	Timiskaming	41 P/8	47°20′	80°10′
Lady Fane	UNP/LNO	PE	Queens	11 L/5	46°17′	63°31′
Lady Franklin Bay	BAY/BAIE	NT	Franklin	120 C	81°35′	64°30′
Lady Franklin Island	ISL/ÎLE	NT	Franklin	15 L	62°55′	63°42′
Lady Franklin Point	CAPE/CAP	NT	Franklin	87 A	68°29′	113°15′
Lady Grey Lake	LAKE/LAC	NT	Mackenzie	75 D/15	60°54′	110°32′
Lady Lake	HAM/HAM	SK	26-35-5-W2	63 D/2	52°02′	102°37′
Lady Melville Lake	LAKE/LAC	NT	Keewatin	57 C	69°08′	92°30′
Lady Parry Island	ISL/ÎLE	NT	Franklin	57 E	70°10′	90°48′
Lady Pond	LAKE/LAC	NF		2 C/4	48°14′	53°43′
Lady Richardson Bay	BAY/BAIE	NT	Franklin	87 C/9	69°32′	116°37′
Lady Simpson, Cape	CAPE/CAP	NT	Franklin	47 B	68°12′	85°53′
Lady Slipper	VILG/VILG	PE	Prince	21 I/9	46°36′	64°01′
Ladysmith	TOWN/VIL2	BC	Oyster	92 B/13	48°59′	123°49′
Ladysmith	UNP/LNO	QC	Pontiac	31 F/16	45°46′	76°23′
Ladysmith	UNP/LNO	ON	Lambton	40 J/16	42°47′	82°24′
Ladysmith	UNP/LNO	MB	1-10-11-W	62 G/15	49°48′	98°49′
Ladywood	UNP/LNO	MB	7-14-8-E	62 I/1	50°11′	96°30′
La Ferme	UNP/LNO	QC	Beauharnois-Salaberry	31 H/4	45°15′	73°48′
Laferté	UNP/LNO	QC	Abitibi-Ouest	32 D/10	48°35′	78°48′
Laferte River	RIV/CDE	NT	Mackenzie	85 F	61°53′	117°44′
Lafferty	UNP/LNO	BC	Kootenay	82 E/1	49°08′	118°11′
Laflamme, Lac	LAKE/LAC	QC	Le Fjord-du-Saguenay	22 D/16	48°56′	70°21′
Laflamme, Lac	LAKE/LAC	QC	Kativik	35 H/5	61°20′	73°43′
Laflamme, Rivière	RIV/CDE	QC	Jamésie	32 F/6	49°18′	77°10′
Lafleche	TOWN/VIL2	SK	2-9-5-W3	72 G/10	49°43′	106°35′
Laflèche	UNP/LNO	QC	Champlain	31 H/6	45°30′	73°28′
Lafond	UNP/LNO	AB	6-57-10-W4	73 E/14	53°53′	111°29′
Lafond Creek	RIV/CDE	AB	93-7-W5	84 G/3	57°03′	115°05′
Lafontaine	TOWN/VIL2	QC	La Rivière-du-Nord	31 G/16	45°49′	74°01′
Lafontaine	UNP/LNO	ON	Simcoe	41 A/16	44°45′	80°04′
Lafontaine Beach	UNP/LNO	ON	Simcoe	41 A/9	44°45′	80°06′
Laforce	VILG/VILG	QC	Témiscamingue	31 M/10	47°32′	78°44′
Laforest	UNP/LNO	ON	Sudbury	41 P/3	47°02′	81°13′
La Forest, Lac	LAKE/LAC	QC	Kativik	23 M/3	55°10′	71°03′
Laforge, Rivière	RIV/CDE	QC	Jamésie	33 I/3	54°10′	73°14′
La Fourche	UNP/LNO	QC	Montcalm	31 H/13	45°56′	73°43′
La Fresnière	UNP/LNO	QC	Deux-Montagnes	31 H/12	45°34′	73°59′
La Gabelle, Barrage	MISC/DIV	QC	Francheville	31 I/7	46°27′	72°44′
Lagacé	UNP/LNO	QC	Avignon	22 B/2	48°01′	66°56′
Lagacéville	UNP/LNO	NB	Northumberland	21 P/3	47°14′	65°10′
La Galissonnière, Lac	LAKE/LAC	QC	Minganie	12 M/8	51°25′	62°00′
Laggan	UNP/LNO	NS	Pictou	11 E/9	45°32′	62°20′
Laggan	UNP/LNO	ON	Glengarry	31 G/7	45°23′	74°42′
Lagins 5	IR/RI	BC	Queen Charlotte	103 F/1	53°13′	132°20′
La Glace	UNP/LNO	AB	10-74-8-W6	83 M/6	55°24′	119°09′
La Glacière	UNP/LNO	QC	Matawinie	31 I/5	46°30′	73°44′
Lagoon City	UNP/LNO	ON	Simcoe	31 D/11	44°33′	79°13′
La Grande-Acadie	UNP/LNO	QC	Maskinongé	31 I/7	46°19′	72°52′
La Grande-Barbue	UNP/LNO	QC	Rouville	31 H/7	45°25′	72°58′
La Grand-Mare	UNP/LNO	QC	Pabok	22 A/9	48°35′	64°18′
La Grave	UNP/LNO	QC	Les Îles-de-la-Madeleine	11 N/4	47°13′	61°50′
La Grosse-Roche	UNP/LNO	QC	Le Granit	21 E/10	45°36′	70°56′
La Guadeloupe	TOWN/VIL2	QC	Beauce-Sartigan	21 E/15	45°57′	70°56′
Lahaieville	UNP/LNO	AB	14-67-24-W4	83 I/13	54°48′	113°33′
La Haute-Côte-Nord	MUN1/AZM1	QC	La Haute-Côte-Nord	22 C/11	48°34′	69°14′
La Haute-Yamaska	MUN1/AZM1	QC	La Haute-Yamaska	31 H/7	45°24′	72°44′
LaHave	UNP/LNO	NS	Lunenburg	21 A/8	44°18′	64°22′
LaHave, Banc de - also-aussi - LaHave Bank	SEAU/SMER	—		4012	43°11′	64°05′
LaHave Bank - also-aussi - LaHave, Banc de	SEAU/SMER	—		4012	43°11′	64°05′
LaHave Basin - also-aussi - LaHave, Bassin de	SEAU/SMER	—		4012	43°43′	63°51′
LaHave, Bassin de - also-aussi - LaHave Basin	SEAU/SMER	—		4012	43°43′	63°51′
LaHave, Cape	CAPE/CAP	NS	Lunenburg	21 A/1	44°11′	64°21′
LaHave Island	UNP/LNO	NS	Lunenburg	21 A/1	44°14′	64°22′
LaHave Islands	ISL/ÎLE	NS	Lunenburg	21 A/1	44°13′	64°22′
LaHave River	RIV/CDE	NS	Lunenburg	21 A/8	44°16′	64°20′
La Hêtrière	UNP/LNO	NB	Westmorland	21 I/2	46°01′	64°36′
La Hune Bay	BAY/BAIE	NF		11 P/10	47°36′	56°52′
La Hune, Cape	CAPE/CAP	NF		11 P/10	47°32′	56°51′
Laidlaw	UNP/LNO	BC	Yale Division Yale	92 H/5	49°19′	121°36′
Laird	VILG/VILG	SK	24-43-5-W3	73 B/10	52°43′	106°35′
Laird	MUN2/AZM2	ON	Algoma	41 K/8	46°24′	84°03′
Laird	UNP/LNO	ON	Algoma	41 K/8	46°24′	84°04′

NAME NOM	ENTITY ENTITÉ	LOC 1 LIEU 1	LOC 2 LIEU 2	MAP CARTE	POSITION LAT	LONG
Laird Island	ISL/ÎLE	SK		74 N/14	59°47′	109°03′
Laird No. 404	MUN2/AZM2	SK		73 B/10	52°35′	106°40′
La Jacques-Cartier	MUN1/AZM1	QC	La Jacques-Cartier	21 M/4	47°02′	71°35′
La Jannaye, Lac	LAKE/LAC	QC	Caniapiscau	23 G/12	53°38′	67°36′
Lajemmerais	MUN1/AZM1	QC	Lajemmerais	31 H/11	45°41′	73°26′
Lajeunesse Bridge	UNP/LNO	ON	Kenora	52 E/16	49°50′	94°21′
Lajord	UNP/LNO	SK	9-15-16-W2	72 I/1	50°14′	104°09′
Lajord No. 128	MUN2/AZM2	SK	9-15-16-W2	72 I/1	50°10′	104°15′
La Justone, Lac	LAKE/LAC	QC	Caniapiscau	23 C/16	52°53′	68°27′
Lakahahmen 11	IR/RI	BC	New Westminster	92 G/1	49°12′	122°05′
Lakata 41	IR/RI	BC	Range 5 Coast	103 I/13	54°58′	129°39′
Lakbelak 38	IR/RI	BC	Range 5 Coast	103 I/13	54°49′	129°34′
Lakbelak Creek 39	IR/RI	BC	Range 5 Coast	103 I/13	54°48′	129°38′
Lakbelak Lake 40	IR/RI	BC	Range 5 Coast	103 I/13	54°48′	129°40′
Lake	UNP/LNO	ON	Hastings	31 C/13	44°46′	77°53′
Lake Alma	VILG/VILG	SK	22-2-17-W2	72 H/1	49°09′	104°12′
Lake Alma No. 8	MUN2/AZM2	SK		72 H/1	49°10′	104°15′
Lake Annis	UNP/LNO	NS	Yarmouth	21 B/1	44°03′	66°00′
Lake Athabasca - see-voir - Athabasca, Lake	LAKE/LAC					
Lake Audy	UNP/LNO	MB	8-20-20-W	62 K/9	50°43′	100°14′
Lake Bernard	UNP/LNO	ON	Parry Sound	31 E/11	45°42′	79°24′
Lake Brook	RIV/CDE	NT	Keewatin	45 P	63°34′	81°32′
Lake Buntzen	UNP/LNO	BC	New Westminster	92 G/7	49°22′	122°52′
Lakeburn	UNP/LNO	NB	Westmorland	21 I/2	46°06′	64°41′
Lake Centre	UNP/LNO	NS	Lunenburg	21 A/8	44°19′	64°29′
Lake Charles	UNP/LNO	ON	Grey	41 A/14	44°46′	81°01′
Lake Charlotte	UNP/LNO	NS	Halifax	11 D/15	44°46′	62°57′
Lake Clear	UNP/LNO	ON	Renfrew	31 F/6	45°28′	77°16′
Lake Country, District of	MUN1/AZM1	BC	Osoyoos Division Yale	82 L/3	50°07′	119°22′
Lake Cowichan	VILG/VILG	BC	Cowichan	92 C/16	48°49′	124°03′
Lake Creek	RIV/CDE	YT		116 A/11	64°38′	137°10′
Lake Creek	RIV/CDE	YT		115 P/5	63°29′	137°54′
Lake Dalrymple	UNP/LNO	ON	Victoria	31 D/11	44°40′	79°06′
Lakedell	UNP/LNO	AB	24-46-1-W5	83 B/16	52°58′	114°04′
Lake Doré	UNP/LNO	ON	Renfrew	31 F/11	45°38′	77°04′
Lake Doucette	UNP/LNO	NS	Digby	21 B/1	44°03′	66°09′
Lake Echo	UNP/LNO	NS	Halifax	11 D/11	44°44′	63°23′
Lake Edward	UNP/LNO	NB	Victoria	21 J/13	46°55′	67°39′
Lake Egmont	UNP/LNO	NS	Halifax	11 D/14	44°58′	63°19′
Lake Eliza	UNP/LNO	AB	5-56-8-W4	73 E/14	53°48′	111°10′
Lake Erie - see-voir - Erie, Lake	LAKE/LAC					
Lake Erie Country Club	UNP/LNO	ON	Essex	40 J/3	42°02′	83°02′
Lake Errock	UNP/LNO	BC	New Westminster	92 G/1	49°13′	122°01′
Lakefield	VILG/VILG	ON	Peterborough	31 D/8	44°26′	78°16′
Lakefield	UNP/LNO	QC	Argenteuil	31 G/16	45°45′	74°15′
Lake Four	UNP/LNO	SK	27-54-6-W3	73 G/10	53°42′	106°47′
Lake Francis	UNP/LNO	MB	28-15-3-W	62 I/5	50°18′	97°48′
Lake George	UNP/LNO	NS	Kings	21 A/15	44°55′	64°42′
Lake George	UNP/LNO	NS	Yarmouth	21 B/1	44°01′	66°04′
Lake George	UNP/LNO	NB	York	21 G/14	45°51′	67°02′
Lake Harbour - see-voir - Kimmirut	HAM/HAM	NT		25 K/13	62°51′	69°53′
Lake Helen 53A	IR/RI	ON	Thunder Bay	52 H/1	49°01′	88°13′
Lake Hill	UNP/LNO	BC	Victoria	92 B/6	48°28′	123°22′
Lake Huron - see-voir - Huron, Lake	LAKE/LAC					
Lake Huron Highland	UNP/LNO	ON	Bruce	41 A/4	44°15′	81°36′
Lakehurst	UNP/LNO	ON	Peterborough	31 D/9	44°32′	78°26′
Lake Isle	UNP/LNO	AB	8-54-5-W5	83 G/10	53°39′	114°43′
Lake Johnston No. 102	MUN2/AZM2	SK		72 H/13	49°55′	105°50′
Lake Joseph	UNP/LNO	ON	Parry Sound	31 E/4	45°11′	79°47′
Lake Kathlyn	UNP/LNO	BC	Range 5 Coast	93 L/14	54°49′	127°13′
Lake Killarney	UNP/LNO	NS	Cumberland	11 E/13	45°51′	63°52′
Lake Laberge 1	IR/RI	YT		105 D/14	60°57′	135°06′
Lakeland	UNP/LNO	NB	Northumberland	21 I/14	46°49′	65°29′
Lakeland	UNP/LNO	MB	8-15-9-W	62 J/7	50°16′	98°40′
Lakeland Acres	UNP/LNO	ON	Frontenac	31 C/2	44°13′	76°35′
Lake Land District	GEOG/GÉOG	BC		92 B	48°31′	123°25′
Lakeland No. 521	MUN2/AZM2	SK		73 H/12	53°40′	105°59′
Lakeland Point	UNP/LNO	ON	Frontenac	31 C/2	44°13′	76°34′
Lakeland Provincial Park	PARK/PARC	AB	65,66,67-10,11,12-W4	73 L/13	54°45′	111°33′
Lakelands	UNP/LNO	NS	Hants	11 D/13	44°55′	63°53′
Lakelands	UNP/LNO	NS	Cumberland	21 H/8	45°28′	64°20′
Lake La Rose	UNP/LNO	NS	Annapolis	21 A/11	44°42′	65°26′
Lake Lenore	VILG/VILG	SK	32-39-21-W2	73 A/7	52°24′	104°59′
Lake Lenore No. 399	MUN2/AZM2	SK		73 A/7	52°30′	104°45′
Lakelet	UNP/LNO	ON	Huron	40 P/14	43°57′	81°04′

NAME NOM	ENTITY ENTITÉ	LOC 1 LIEU 1	LOC 2 LIEU 2	MAP CARTE	POSITION LAT	POSITION LONG
Lake Louise	UNP/LNO	AB	28-28-16-W5	82 N/8	51°26′	116°11′
Lakelse	UNP/LNO	BC	Range 5 Coast	103 I/7	54°23′	128°38′
Lakelse 25	IR/RI	BC	Range 5 Coast	103 I/7	54°23′	128°37′
Lakelse Lake	UNP/LNO	BC	Range 5 Coast	103 I/7	54°22′	128°33′
Lakelse Lake	LAKE/LAC	BC	Range 5 Coast	103 I/7	54°23′	128°33′
Lake Majeau	UNP/LNO	AB	19-56-3-W5	83 G/16	53°52′	114°26′
Lake Major	UNP/LNO	NS	Halifax	11 D/11	44°43′	63°28′
Lakeman Island	ISL/ÎLE	NF		2 C/13	48°50′	53°47′
Lake Manitoba - see-voir - Manitoba, Lake	LAKE/LAC					
Lake Midway	UNP/LNO	NS	Digby	21 B/9	44°32′	66°03′
Lakenheath	UNP/LNO	SK	12-7-3-W3	72 G/9	49°32′	106°17′
Lake Nipigon - see-voir - Nipigon, Lake	LAKE/LAC					
Lake Nipissing - see-voir - Nipissing, Lake	LAKE/LAC					
Lake of Bays	MUN2/AZM2	ON	Muskoka	31 E/6	45°15′	79°00′
Lake of The Rivers No. 72	MUN2/AZM2	SK		72 H/12	49°40′	105°50′
Lake of the Woods	UNP/LNO	NS	Halifax	11 D/12	44°40′	63°48′
Lake of the Woods - see-voir - Woods, Lake of the	LAKE/LAC					
Lake of the Woods 31B	IR/RI	ON	Kenora	52 E/10	49°30′	94°51′
Lake of the Woods 31C	IR/RI	ON	Kenora	52 E/7	49°19′	94°49′
Lake of the Woods 31G	IR/RI	ON	Kenora	52 E/7	49°22′	94°59′
Lake of the Woods 31H	IR/RI	ON	Kenora	52 E/2	49°07′	94°43′
Lake of the Woods 34	IR/RI	ON	Kenora	52 E/7	49°18′	94°35′
Lake of the Woods 35J	IR/RI	ON	Kenora	52 E/1	49°13′	94°25′
Lake of the Woods 37	IR/RI	ON	Kenora	52 E/7	49°22′	94°52′
Lake of the Woods 37B	IR/RI	ON	Kenora	52 E/7	49°19′	94°48′
Lake Ontario - see-voir - Ontario, Lake	LAKE/LAC					
Lake on the Mountain	UNP/LNO	ON	Prince Edward	31 C/3	44°02′	77°04′
Lake Opinicon	UNP/LNO	ON	Frontenac	31 C/9	44°32′	76°22′
Lake Park	UNP/LNO	ON	Lanark	31 F/1	45°07′	76°10′
Lake Park	UNP/LNO	SK	9-47-23-W2	73 H/3	53°03′	105°18′
Lake Paul	UNP/LNO	NS	Kings	21 A/15	44°52′	64°41′
Lake Pleasant	UNP/LNO	NS	Annapolis	21 A/10	44°37′	64°53′
Lakeport	UNP/LNO	ON	Northumberland	30 N/13	43°59′	77°54′
Lake Ramsay	UNP/LNO	NS	Lunenburg	21 A/15	44°45′	64°31′
Lakeridge	UNP/LNO	SK		73 B/2	52°06′	106°35′
Lake River	UNP/LNO	ON	Kenora	43 J/7	54°22′	82°31′
Lake Road	UNP/LNO	NS	Colchester	11 E/11	45°41′	63°29′
Lake Road	UNP/LNO	NS	Hants	11 E/5	45°17′	63°44′
Lake Road	UNP/LNO	NB	Westmorland	21 I/1	46°07′	64°10′
Lake Road	UNP/LNO	NB	York	21 G/14	45°48′	67°03′
Lake Road Corner	UNP/LNO	NS	Cumberland	21 H/8	45°28′	64°20′
Lake Rosalind	UNP/LNO	ON	Bruce	41 A/3	44°10′	81°04′
Lake St. Martin	UNP/LNO	MB	32-7,8-W	62 O/9	51°45′	98°25′
Lake St. Peter	UNP/LNO	ON	Hastings	31 E/8	45°18′	78°02′
Lake Saskatoon	UNP/LNO	AB	11-72-8-W6	83 M/3	55°14′	119°07′
Lakesend	UNP/LNO	AB	21-38-8-W4	73 D/6	52°17′	111°04′
Lakeshore Heights	UNP/LNO	MB	32-17-7-E	62 I/7	50°30′	96°36′
Lakeshore Village	UNP/LNO	ON	Waterloo	40 P/7	43°29′	80°33′
Lakeside	UNP/LNO	NS	Halifax	11 D/12	44°38′	63°42′
Lakeside	UNP/LNO	NS	Yarmouth	20 O/16	43°53′	66°07′
Lakeside	UNP/LNO	NB	Kings	21 H/12	45°30′	65°51′
Lakeside	UNP/LNO	QC	Communauté urbaine de Montréal	31 H/5	45°27′	73°48′
Lakeside	UNP/LNO	ON	Oxford	40 P/3	43°12′	81°01′
Lakeside	UNP/LNO	SK	32-19-12-W2	62 L/12	50°41′	103°39′
Lakeside Beach	UNP/LNO	ON	Ontario	31 D/2	44°09′	78°55′
Lakeside Meadows	UNP/LNO	MB		62 H/14	49°55′	97°02′
Lakeside No. 338	MUN2/AZM2	SK		73 A/1	52°00′	104°20′
Lake Siding	UNP/LNO	NF		12 H/3	49°10′	57°27′
Lake Simcoe - see-voir - Simcoe, Lake	LAKE/LAC					
Lake's Mill	UNP/LNO	QC	Le Haut-Saint-François	21 E/5	45°23′	71°35′
Lake Stream	RIV/CDE	NB	Kent	21 I/5	46°20′	65°36′
Lake Stream Lake	LAKE/LAC	NB	Queens	21 I/3	46°13′	65°29′
Lake Superior - see-voir - Superior, Lake	LAKE/LAC					
Lake Timiskaming - see-voir - Timiskaming, Lake	LAKE/LAC					
Laketon	UNP/LNO	NB	Kent	21 I/14	46°51′	65°08′
Laketon	UNP/LNO	BC	Cassiar	104 J/9	58°42′	130°06′
Laketown 3	IR/RI	BC	Range 4 Coast	93 F/16	53°56′	124°12′
Lake Traverse	UNP/LNO	ON	Nipissing	31 E/16	45°57′	78°03′
Lake Traverse	UNP/LNO	ON	Nipissing	31 E/16	45°57′	78°05′
Lake Uist	UNP/LNO	NS	Richmond	11 F/15	45°46′	60°37′
Lakevale	UNP/LNO	NS	Antigonish	11 F/13	45°47′	61°55′
Lake Valley	UNP/LNO	SK	26-19-1-W3	72 J/9	50°38′	106°01′
Lake Verde	UNP/LNO	PE	Queens	11 L/2	46°14′	62°53′
Lakeview	VILG/VILG	AB	12-53-4-W5	83 G/9	53°34′	114°27′
Lakeview	HAM/HAM	SK	9-47-17-3	73 F/1	53°02′	108°26′

NAME NOM	ENTITY ENTITÉ	LOC 1 LIEU 1	LOC 2 LIEU 2	MAP CARTE	POSITION LAT	LONG
Lakeview	MUN2/AZM2	MB		62 J/7	50°20′	98°45′
Lakeview	UNP/LNO	NF		1 N/6	47°24′	53°09′
Lakeview	UNP/LNO	NS	Halifax	11 D/13	44°46′	63°38′
Lakeview	UNP/LNO	NS	Kings	21 A/15	44°46′	64°45′
Lakeview	UNP/LNO	NS	Queens	21 A/6	44°23′	65°03′
Lakeview	UNP/LNO	NB	Westmorland	21 I/2	46°04′	64°50′
Lakeview	UNP/LNO	NB	Queens	21 H/13	45°52′	65°57′
Lake View	UNP/LNO	QC	La Jacques-Cartier	21 L/13	46°54′	71°37′
Lakeview	UNP/LNO	QC	Argenteuil	31 G/15	45°53′	74°34′
Lakeview	UNP/LNO	ON	Simcoe	31 D/5	44°27′	79°31′
Lakeview	UNP/LNO	ON	Peel	30 M/12	43°35′	79°34′
Lakeview	UNP/LNO	ON	Elgin	40 I/10	42°40′	80°53′
Lakeview	UNP/LNO	SK		72 I/7	50°26′	104°37′
Lakeview	UNP/LNO	SK		73 B/2	52°06′	106°36′
Lakeview Beach	UNP/LNO	ON	Ontario	31 D/11	44°35′	79°08′
Lake View Beach	UNP/LNO	SK	8-20-12-W2	62 L/12	50°42′	103°39′
Lakeview Estates	UNP/LNO	ON	Victoria	31 D/7	44°27′	78°31′
Lakeview Heights	UNP/LNO	ON	Stormont	31 G/2	45°02′	74°51′
Lakeview Heights	UNP/LNO	BC	Osoyoos Division Yale	82 E/13	49°52′	119°32′
Lakeview Mountain	MTN/MNT	BC	Similkameen Division Yale	92 H/1	49°03′	120°09′
Lakeview No. 337	MUN2/AZM2	SK		63 D/4	52°00′	103°55′
Lakeview Park	UNP/LNO	ON	Ontario	30 M/15	43°52′	78°50′
Lakeview-Terrasse	UNP/LNO	QC	Communauté urbaine de l'Outaouais	31 G/5	45°24′	75°48′
Lakeville	UNP/LNO	PE	Kings	11 L/8	46°28′	62°06′
Lakeville	UNP/LNO	NS	Kings	21 H/2	45°06′	64°37′
Lakeville	UNP/LNO	NB	Westmorland	21 I/2	46°08′	64°41′
Lakeville	UNP/LNO	NB	Carleton	21 J/5	46°20′	67°41′
Lakeville Corner	UNP/LNO	NB	Sunbury	21 G/16	45°54′	66°15′
Lake Wasaw	UNP/LNO	ON	Rainy River	52 C/12	48°43′	93°39′
Lake William	UNP/LNO	NS	Lunenburg	21 A/10	44°35′	64°40′
Lake Winnipeg - see-voir - Winnipeg, Lake	LAKE/LAC					
Lake Winnipegosis - see-voir - Winnipegosis, Lake	LAKE/LAC					
Lakewood	UNP/LNO	NB	Saint John	21 H/5	45°19′	65°58′
Lakewood	UNP/LNO	ON	Muskoka	31 E/3	45°00′	79°05′
Lakewood	UNP/LNO	MB		62 H/14	49°50′	97°19′
Lakewood	UNP/LNO	SK		72 I/7	50°30′	104°40′
Lakewood Beach	UNP/LNO	ON	Essex	40 J/3	42°02′	83°04′
Lakewood Heights	UNP/LNO	NB	Saint John	21 H/5	45°18′	65°59′
Lakgeas 87	IR/RI	BC	Range 5 Coast	103 I/7	54°24′	128°38′
Lakitusaki River	RIV/CDE	ON	Kenora	43 J/8	54°21′	82°25′
Lakksgamal 85	IR/RI	BC	Cassiar	103 P/3	55°13′	129°09′
Lakksgamal 86	IR/RI	BC	Cassiar	103 P/3	55°13′	129°09′
Lakksgamal 88	IR/RI	BC	Cassiar	103 P/3	55°13′	129°09′
Lakway Cemetery 3	IR/RI	BC	New Westminster	92 G/1	49°09′	122°03′
Lalemant	MUN2/AZM2	QC	Le Fjord-du-Saguenay	22 D/2	48°03′	70°38′
Lalement	UNP/LNO	QC	L'Islet	21 N/4	47°00′	69°54′
Laliberté, Rivière	RIV/CDE	QC	Manicouagan	22 F/2	49°05′	68°57′
Lally Cove	UNP/LNO	NF		1 M/11	47°39′	55°22′
La Loche	VILG/VILG	SK		74 C/6	56°29′	109°26′
La Loche 221 - see-voir - Clearwater River Dene Band 221	IR/RI	SK		74 C/5	56°20′	109°35′
La Loche 222 - see-voir - Clearwater River Dene Band 222	IR/RI	SK		74 C/7	56°23′	108°54′
La Loche 223 - see-voir - Clearwater River Dene Band 223	IR/RI	SK		74 C/2	56°05′	108°45′
La Loche, Lac	LAKE/LAC	SK		74 C/5	56°28′	109°30′
La Loche Lakes	LAKE/LAC	NT	Mackenzie	75 E	62°00′	110°53′
La Loche River	RIV/CDE	SK		74 C/3	56°09′	109°08′
La Loche River	RIV/CDE	NT	Mackenzie	85 H	61°38′	112°13′
La Loche West	UNP/LNO	SK		74 C/5	56°29′	109°39′
Lalonde, Lac	LAKE/LAC	QC	Vallée-de-l'Or	31 N/5	47°16′	77°48′
L'Alverne	UNP/LNO	QC	Avignon	22 B/2	48°08′	66°42′
L'Amable	UNP/LNO	ON	Hastings	31 F/4	45°01′	77°47′
L'Amable	UNP/LNO	ON	Nipissing	31 E/8	45°37′	78°06′
La Macaza	VILG/VILG	QC	Antoine-Labelle	31 J/7	46°23′	74°46′
La Malbaie	UNP/LNO	QC	Charlevoix-Est	21 M/9	47°39′	70°09′
La Malbaie — Pointe-au-Pic	CITY/VIL1	QC	Charlevoix-Est	21 M/9	47°39′	70°09′
Lamaline	TOWN/VIL2	NF		1 L/13	46°52′	55°49′
La Manche	UNP/LNO	NF		1 N/2	47°10′	52°52′
La Manche	UNP/LNO	NF		1 N/12	47°42′	53°57′
La Manche River	RIV/CDE	NF		1 N/2	47°10′	52°52′
La Manche Siding	UNP/LNO	NF		1 N/12	47°42′	53°54′
Lamarche	VILG/VILG	QC	Lac-Saint-Jean-Est	22 D/14	48°48′	71°26′
La Mare	UNP/LNO	QC	Charlevoix	21 M/7	47°28′	70°32′
La Martine	UNP/LNO	QC	Le Domaine-du-Roy	32 A/8	48°21′	72°01′
La Martinière, Pointe de	CAPE/CAP	QC	Desjardins	21 L/14	46°50′	71°07′
La Martre	VILG/VILG	QC	Denis-Riverin	22 G/1	49°10′	66°10′
La Matapédia	MUN1/AZM1	QC	La Matapédia	22 B/5	48°18′	67°34′

NAME NOM	ENTITY ENTITÉ	LOC 1 LIEU 1	LOC 2 LIEU 2	MAP CARTE	POSITION	
					LAT	LONG
Lamaune	UNP/LNO	ON	Thunder Bay	52 I/8	50°16′	88°15′
La Mauricie National Park - also-aussi - Mauricie, Parc national de la	PARK/PARC	QC	Le Centre-de-la-Mauricie	31 I/15	46°48′	72°58′
Lambert	UNP/LNO	ON	Perth	40 P/10	43°35′	81°00′
Lambert Channel	CHAN/CHEN	BC	Nanaimo	92 F/7	49°30′	124°42′
Lambert Island	ISL/ÎLE	NT	Franklin	87 A	68°39′	114°06′
Lambert, Lac	LAKE/LAC	QC	La Vallée-de-la-Gatineau	31 N/8	47°18′	76°02′
Lamberts Cove	UNP/LNO	NB	Charlotte	21 G/2	45°01′	66°56′
Lambertville	UNP/LNO	NB	Charlotte	21 G/2	45°01′	66°57′
Lambeth	UNP/LNO	ON	Middlesex	40 I/14	42°54′	81°18′
Lamb Island 5	IR/RI	BC	Metchosin	92 B/5	48°20′	123°37′
Lambly Creek	RIV/CDE	BC	Osoyoos Division Yale	82 E/13	49°56′	119°30′
Lamb, Roche	SEAU/SMER	—		802	46°28′	54°02′
Lamb Rock	SEAU/SMER	—		4817	46°28′	54°02′
Lambs Corners	UNP/LNO	ON	Haldimand	40 I/16	42°49′	80°01′
Lambton	VILG/VILG	QC	Le Granit	21 E/14	45°50′	71°05′
Lambton	MUN1/AZM1	ON	Lambton	40 J/9	42°45′	82°05′
Lambton	GEOG/GÉOG	ON		40 J/9	42°45′	82°05′
Lambton, Cape	CAPE/CAP	NT	Franklin	97 H	71°05′	123°09′
Lambton Mills	UNP/LNO	ON	York	30 M/12	43°39′	79°31′
Lambton Park	UNP/LNO	AB	26-52-24-W4	83 H/11	53°31′	113°25′
Lamèque	TOWN/VIL2	NB	Gloucester	21 P/15	47°47′	64°38′
Lamèque, Île	ISL/ÎLE	NB	Gloucester	21 P/15	47°50′	64°38′
La Merisière	UNP/LNO	QC	Les Etchemins	21 L/1	46°11′	70°26′
Lamerton	UNP/LNO	AB	4-41-22-W4	83 A/6	52°30′	113°05′
L'Amiante	MUN1/AZM1	QC	L'Amiante	21 L/3	46°05′	71°18′
La Miche	UNP/LNO	QC	La Côte-de-Beaupré	21 M/2	47°05′	70°50′
La Minerve	VILG/VILG	QC	Les Laurentides	31 J/7	46°16′	74°56′
La Mitis	MUN1/AZM1	QC	La Mitis	22 C/9	48°32′	68°05′
Lamlash	UNP/LNO	ON	Grey	41 A/2	44°13′	80°58′
Lammermoor	UNP/LNO	ON	Lanark	31 F/2	45°06′	76°32′
Lamming Mills	UNP/LNO	BC	Cariboo	93 H/8	53°21′	120°16′
La Moinerie, Lac	LAKE/LAC	QC	Kativik	24 G/7	57°26′	66°36′
Lamont	TOWN/VIL2	AB	55-19-W4	83 H/15	53°46′	112°48′
La Montagne	UNP/LNO	NB	Westmorland	21 H/15	46°00′	64°37′
La Montagne	UNP/LNO	QC	Les Îles-de-la-Madeleine	11 N/4	47°15′	61°57′
La Montagne	UNP/LNO	QC	Pontiac	31 F/10	45°40′	76°40′
La Montée	UNP/LNO	QC	Pabok	22 A/8	48°25′	64°21′
Lamont No. 30, County of	MUN1/AZM1	AB	54-13-W4	83 H/15	53°46′	112°33′
La Morandière	VILG/VILG	QC	Abitibi	32 C/12	48°37′	77°38′
Lamoreaux Corner	UNP/LNO	NB	Carleton	21 J/5	46°28′	67°41′
La Mothe, Lac	LAKE/LAC	QC	Le Fjord-du-Saguenay	22 D/14	48°46′	71°09′
La Motte	VILG/VILG	QC	Abitibi	32 D/8	48°20′	78°07′
La Motte, Lac	LAKE/LAC	QC	Abitibi	32 D/8	48°24′	78°03′
Lamoureux	UNP/LNO	AB	4-55-22-W4	83 H/11	53°43′	113°15′
Lampard	UNP/LNO	SK	19-34-18-W2	72 P/15	51°56′	104°33′
Lampedo	UNP/LNO	NB	Victoria	21 J/11	46°43′	67°16′
Lampidoes Passage	CHAN/CHEN	NF		1 M/12	47°45′	56°00′
Lampman	TOWN/VIL2	SK	16-5-6-W2	62 E/7	49°23′	102°45′
Lamprey	UNP/LNO	MB		54 L/8	58°19′	94°09′
La Muir, Lake	LAKE/LAC	ON	Nipissing	31 E/15	45°50′	78°35′
Lamy	UNP/LNO	QC	Rivière-du-Loup	21 N/14	47°47′	69°06′
Lamy-Sud	UNP/LNO	QC	Témiscouata	21 N/14	47°46′	69°04′
Lanark	VILG/VILG	ON	Lanark	31 F/1	45°01′	76°22′
Lanark	MUN1/AZM1	ON	Lanark	31 F/1	45°05′	76°20′
Lanark	MUN2/AZM2	ON	Lanark	31 F/1	45°06′	76°21′
Lanark	UNP/LNO	NS	Antigonish	11 F/12	45°39′	61°56′
Lanark	GEOG/GÉOG	ON		31 F/1	45°05′	76°20′
Lanas 4	IR/RI	BC	Queen Charlotte	103 F/9	53°39′	132°13′
La Nation	UNP/LNO	QC	Papineau	31 G/14	45°47′	75°04′
Lanaudière	MUN1/AZM1	QC	Matawinie	31 I/13	46°46′	73°50′
Lancaster	VILG/VILG	ON	Glengarry	31 G/2	45°08′	74°30′
Lancaster	MUN2/AZM2	ON	Glengarry	31 G/2	45°15′	74°30′
Lancaster	UNP/LNO	NF		2 C/11	48°40′	53°03′
Lancaster Park	UNP/LNO	AB	21-54-24-W4	83 H/11	53°40′	113°29′
Lancaster Sound	CHAN/CHEN	NT	Franklin	48 E	74°13′	84°00′
Lancaster Trough	SEAU/SMER	—		7000	74°00′	85°30′
Lance Cove	UNP/LNO	NF		1 N/10	47°36′	52°59′
Lance Cove	UNP/LNO	NF		1 N/6	47°28′	53°04′
Lance Cove	UNP/LNO	NF		2 C/11	48°40′	53°05′
Lance Cove	BAY/BAIE	NF		1 L/16	46°48′	54°05′
Lancelot	UNP/LNO	ON	Muskoka	31 E/6	45°16′	79°21′
Lance, Point	CAPE/CAP	NF		1 L/16	46°47′	54°04′
Lancer	VILG/VILG	SK	20-21-21-W3	72 K/15	50°48′	108°53′
Lance River	RIV/CDE	NF		1 L/16	46°48′	54°04′
L'Ancienne-Lorette	CITY/VIL1	QC	Communauté urbaine de Québec	21 L/14	46°48′	71°21′

NAME NOM	ENTITY ENTITÉ	LOC 1 LIEU 1	LOC 2 LIEU 2	MAP CARTE	POSITION LAT	LONG
Landerkin	UNP/LNO	ON	Grey	41 A/2	44°01′	80°37′
Landing Lake	LAKE/LAC	MB		63 P/6	55°17′	97°26′
Landing, Le	UNP/LNO	QC	Pontiac	31 F/14	45°52′	77°09′
Landing Place	UNP/LNO	QC	Témiscamingue	31 M/14	47°47′	79°15′
Landis	VILG/VILG	SK	24-37-18-W3	73 C/1	52°12′	108°27′
Landmark	UNP/LNO	MB	22,23-8-5-E	62 H/10	49°40′	96°49′
Landon Lake - see-voir - Louis Lake	LAKE/LAC	AB		73 E/10	53°43′	110°49′
Landreville	UNP/LNO	QC	Beauharnois-Salaberry	31 G/1	45°10′	74°02′
Landreville, Mount	MTN/MNT	YT		106 F/2	65°09′	132°52′
Landrienne	VILG/VILG	QC	Abitibi	32 C/12	48°33′	77°57′
Landry	UNP/LNO	NB	Gloucester	21 P/10	47°40′	64°57′
Landry, Cape	CAPE/CAP	NT	Franklin	57 E	70°40′	89°02′
Landry Creek	RIV/CDE	NT	Mackenzie	95 K	62°56′	125°12′
Landry Crossing	UNP/LNO	ON	Renfrew	31 F/14	45°58′	77°22′
Landry, Lac	LAKE/LAC	QC	Minganie	12 K/12	50°37′	61°32′
Landry Lake	LAKE/LAC	MB	56-23-W	63 F/15	53°48′	100°52′
Landscape	UNP/LNO	SK	13-6-27-W2	72 H/5	49°29′	105°30′
Landseer	UNP/LNO	MB	13-7-12-W	62 G/10	49°35′	98°58′
Lands End	UNP/LNO	NB	Kings	21 G/8	45°21′	66°11′
Lands End	CAPE/CAP	NT	Franklin	99 A	76°22′	122°37′
Lanes	UNP/LNO	ON	Huron	40 P/13	43°57′	81°37′
Lanesville	UNP/LNO	NS	Colchester	11 E/3	45°08′	63°14′
Lanezi Lake	LAKE/LAC	BC	Cariboo	93 H/2	53°04′	120°55′
Lanfine	UNP/LNO	AB	7-28-5-W4	72 M/7	51°23′	110°42′
Lang	VILG/VILG	SK	23-11-18-W2	72 H/16	49°55′	104°22′
Lang	UNP/LNO	ON	Peterborough	31 D/8	44°16′	78°10′
Langara Island	ISL/ÎLE	BC	Queen Charlotte	103 K/3	54°14′	133°02′
Langbank	HAM/HAM	SK	12,13-3-W2	62 L/1	50°03′	102°18′
Lang Bay	UNP/LNO	BC	New Westminster	92 F/16	49°47′	124°21′
Langdale	UNP/LNO	BC	New Westminster	92 G/6	49°26′	123°28′
Langdon	UNP/LNO	ON	Algoma	42 C/16	48°59′	84°05′
Langdon	UNP/LNO	AB	23-23-27-W4	82 I/13	50°58′	113°40′
Langdon's Cove	UNP/LNO	NF		2 E/12	49°42′	55°59′
L'Ange-Gardien	TOWN/VIL2	QC	Rouville	31 H/7	45°21′	72°56′
L'Ange-Gardien	VILG/VILG	QC	La Côte-de-Beaupré	21 L/14	46°55′	71°06′
L'Ange-Gardien	VILG/VILG	QC	Les Collines-de-l'Outaouais	31 G/11	45°38′	75°28′
L'Ange-Gardien	UNP/LNO	ON	Prescott	31 G/10	45°35′	74°46′
Langelier	VILG/VILG	QC	Le Haut-Saint-Maurice	31 P/10	47°38′	72°46′
Langenburg	TOWN/VIL2	SK	27-21-31-W	62 K/13	50°51′	101°43′
Langenburg No. 181	MUN2/AZM2	SK		62 K/12	50°45′	101°45′
Langford	MUN1/AZM1	BC	Esquimalt	92 B/5	48°27′	123°30′
Langford	MUN2/AZM2	MB		62 J/3	50°10′	99°25′
Langford	UNP/LNO	ON	Brant	40 P/1	43°10′	80°08′
Langford Park	UNP/LNO	AB	15-53-4-W5	83 G/10	53°35′	114°31′
Langham	TOWN/VIL2	SK	16-39-7-W3	73 B/7	52°22′	106°58′
Langlade	UNP/LNO	QC	Vallée-de-l'Or	32 B/4	48°14′	75°59′
Lang Lake	LAKE/LAC	BC	Lillooet	92 P/14	51°58′	121°02′
Langley	CITY/VIL1	BC	New Westminster	92 G/2	49°06′	122°39′
Langley	MUN1/AZM1	BC	New Westminster	92 G/2	49°05′	122°35′
Langley 2	IR/RI	BC	New Westminster	92 G/1	49°11′	122°25′
Langley 3	IR/RI	BC	New Westminster	92 G/1	49°11′	122°25′
Langley 4	IR/RI	BC	New Westminster	92 G/1	49°11′	122°24′
Langley 5	IR/RI	BC	New Westminster	92 G/2	49°11′	122°32′
Langley Island	ISL/ÎLE	NT	Mackenzie	107 C	69°00′	135°15′
Langley Point	CAPE/CAP	NT	Franklin	68 G	75°10′	103°35′
Langman	UNP/LNO	ON	Simcoe	31 D/12	44°32′	79°58′
Langruth	UNP/LNO	MB	20-16-9-W	62 J/7	50°23′	98°40′
Langs Crossing	UNP/LNO	MB	4-6-18-W	62 G/5	49°28′	99°51′
Langside	UNP/LNO	ON	Bruce	40 P/14	43°58′	81°26′
Langstaff	UNP/LNO	ON	York	30 M/14	43°50′	79°25′
Langton	UNP/LNO	ON	Norfolk	40 I/10	42°45′	80°35′
Langton Bay	BAY/BAIE	NT	Franklin	97 C	69°23′	125°25′
Langue-de-Chatte, La	UNP/LNO	QC	Montmagny	21 L/16	46°45′	70°05′
Languedoc	UNP/LNO	QC	Abitibi-Ouest	32 D/15	48°48′	78°42′
Laniel	UNP/LNO	QC	Témiscamingue	31 M/3	47°03′	79°16′
Lanigan	TOWN/VIL2	SK	22-23-22-W2	72 P/14	51°51′	105°02′
Lanigan Creek	RIV/CDE	SK	28-23-W2	72 P/11	51°23′	105°13′
Laniwci	UNP/LNO	SK	35-40-2-W3	73 B/8	52°29′	106°11′
L'Annonciation	TOWN/VIL2	QC	Antoine-Labelle	31 J/7	46°25′	74°52′
Lanoieville	UNP/LNO	QC	Les Maskoutains	31 H/15	45°51′	72°53′
Lanoraie	UNP/LNO	QC	D'Autray	31 H/14	45°58′	73°13′
Lanoraie	UNP/LNO	QC	Joliette	31 H/14	45°59′	73°19′
Lanoraie-d'Autray	VILG/VILG	QC	D'Autray	31 H/14	45°58′	73°13′
La Normandie	UNP/LNO	QC	Montmagny	21 L/15	46°57′	70°33′
La Nouvelle-Beauce	MUN1/AZM1	QC	La Nouvelle-Beauce	21 L/6	46°27′	71°02′

NAME NOM	ENTITY ENTITÉ	LOC 1 LIEU 1	LOC 2 LIEU 2	MAP CARTE	POSITION LAT	LONG
Lansberg Siding	UNP/LNO	NS	Colchester	11 E/7	45°26'	62°57'
Lansdowne	MUN2/AZM2	MB		62 J/6	50°20'	99°15'
Lansdowne	UNP/LNO	NS	Digby	21 A/12	44°35'	65°43'
Lansdowne	UNP/LNO	NB	Carleton	21 J/5	46°23'	67°31'
Lansdowne	UNP/LNO	ON	Leeds	31 C/8	44°24'	76°01'
Lansdowne	UNP/LNO	YT		105 D/7	60°16'	134°46'
Lansdowne House	UNP/LNO	ON	Kenora	43 D/4	52°14'	87°53'
Lansdowne Lake	LAKE/LAC	SK		74 G/10	57°33'	106°56'
Lansdowne Station	UNP/LNO	NS	Pictou	11 E/7	45°26'	62°49'
L'Anse-à-Baril	UNP/LNO	QC	Matawinie	31 I/5	46°18'	73°33'
L'Anse-à-Beaufils	UNP/LNO	QC	Pabok	22 A/8	48°28'	64°19'
L'Anse-à-Benjamin	UNP/LNO	QC	Le Fjord-du-Saguenay	22 D/7	48°22'	70°52'
L'Anse-à-Brillant	UNP/LNO	QC	La Côte-de-Gaspé	22 A/9	48°44'	64°19'
L'Anse-à-Fugère	UNP/LNO	QC	La Côte-de-Gaspé	22 A/16	48°58'	64°22'
L'Anse-à-Gilles	UNP/LNO	QC	L'Islet	21 M/1	47°04'	70°26'
L'Anse-à-Jean	UNP/LNO	QC	Denis-Riverin	22 G/1	49°11'	66°20'
L'Anse-à-la-Cabane	UNP/LNO	QC	Les Îles-de-la-Madeleine	11 N/4	47°13'	61°59'
L'Anse-à-la-Croix	UNP/LNO	QC	Matane	22 B/14	48°54'	67°17'
L'Anse-à-l'Eau	UNP/LNO	NF		1 M/3	47°01'	55°13'
L'Anse-à-Mercier	UNP/LNO	QC	La Côte-de-Gaspé	22 H/3	49°14'	65°06'
L'Anse-Amour	UNP/LNO	NF		12 P/7	51°28'	56°52'
L'Anse-au-Clair	VILG/VILG	NF		12 P/6	51°25'	57°05'
L'Anse-au-Diable	UNP/LNO	NF		12 P/10	51°34'	56°45'
L'Anse-au-Griffon	UNP/LNO	QC	La Côte-de-Gaspé	22 A/16	48°56'	64°18'
L'Anse-au-Griffon-Nord	UNP/LNO	QC	La Côte-de-Gaspé	22 A/16	48°56'	64°19'
L'Anse-au-Loup	VILG/VILG	NF		12 P/10	51°31'	56°50'
L'Anse-au-Loup	UNP/LNO	NF		1 M/4	47°05'	55°42'
L'Anse-au-Persil	UNP/LNO	QC	Rivière-du-Loup	21 N/13	47°52'	69°32'
L'Anse-au-Sac	UNP/LNO	QC	Charlevoix-Est	21 M/9	47°31'	70°12'
L'Anse-aux-Canards	UNP/LNO	QC	Pabok	22 A/7	48°18'	64°43'
L'Anse-aux-Canons	UNP/LNO	QC	La Côte-de-Gaspé	22 H/2	49°12'	64°55'
L'Anse-aux-Cousins	UNP/LNO	QC	La Côte-de-Gaspé	22 A/15	48°51'	64°31'
L'Anse-aux-Gascons	UNP/LNO	QC	Pabok	22 A/2	48°11'	64°51'
L'Anse aux Meadows	UNP/LNO	NF		2 M/12	51°36'	55°32'
L'Anse aux Meadows, Lieu historique national de - also-aussi - L'Anse aux Meadows National Historic Site	PARK/PARC	NF		2 M/12	51°36'	55°32'
L'Anse aux Meadows National Historic Site - also-aussi - L'Anse aux Meadows, Lieu historique national de	PARK/PARC	NF		2 M/12	51°36'	55°32'
L'Anse aux Meadows National Historic Site World Heritage Site - also-aussi - Lieu historique national de L'Anse aux Meadows, Site du patrimoine mondial du	PARK/PARC	NF		2 M/12	51°36'	55°32'
L'Anse-à-Valleau	UNP/LNO	QC	La Côte-de-Gaspé	22 H/2	49°05'	64°33'
L'Anse-Creuse	UNP/LNO	QC	La Haute-Côte-Nord	22 C/4	48°12'	69°52'
L'Anse-de-Cap-Santé	UNP/LNO	QC	Portneuf	21 L/12	46°41'	71°50'
L'Anse-de-l'Église	UNP/LNO	QC	Denis-Riverin	22 G/1	49°09'	66°26'
L'Anse-de-Roche	UNP/LNO	QC	La Haute-Côte-Nord	22 C/4	48°13'	69°52'
L'Anse-du-Portage	UNP/LNO	QC	Côte-Nord-du-Golfe-Saint-Laurent	12 O/1	51°14'	58°19'
L'Anse-McInnes	UNP/LNO	QC	Pabok	22 A/2	48°11'	64°56'
L'Anse-Mercier	UNP/LNO	QC	Bellechasse	21 L/15	46°53'	70°52'
L'Anse-Pleureuse	UNP/LNO	QC	Denis-Riverin	22 H/4	49°15'	65°39'
L'Anse-Sainte-Anne-des-Monts	UNP/LNO	QC	Denis-Riverin	22 G/2	49°07'	66°31'
L'Anse-Saint-Jean	VILG/VILG	QC	Le Fjord-du-Saguenay	22 D/1	48°14'	70°12'
L'Anse-Victoria	UNP/LNO	QC	Communauté urbaine de Québec	21 L/14	46°45'	71°17'
Lansing	UNP/LNO	ON	York	30 M/14	43°46'	79°25'
Lansing	UNP/LNO	YT		105 N/11	63°45'	133°28'
Lansing Range	MTN/MNT	YT		105 N/15	63°46'	132°53'
Lansing River	RIV/CDE	YT		105 N/11	63°45'	133°28'
Lantier	VILG/VILG	QC	Les Laurentides	31 J/1	46°09'	74°15'
Lantz	UNP/LNO	NS	Hants	11 D/14	44°59'	63°29'
Lantzville	UNP/LNO	BC	Wellington	92 F/8	49°15'	124°04'
Lanyan, Lac	LAKE/LAC	QC	Kativik	35 F/6	61°25'	77°08'
Lanz Island	ISL/ÎLE	BC	Rupert	102 I/15	50°49'	128°41'
Lanz Point	HAM/HAM	SK	4,9-16-W3	73 F/1	53°02'	108°17'
La Palestine	UNP/LNO	QC	Le Haut-Richelieu	31 H/3	45°03'	73°10'
Lapalmes	UNP/LNO	ON	Sudbury	41 P/3	47°14'	81°25'
La Passe	UNP/LNO	ON	Renfrew	31 F/15	45°49'	76°46'
La Patrie	TOWN/VIL2	QC	Le Haut-Saint-François	21 E/6	45°24'	71°15'
La Pause, Lac	LAKE/LAC	QC	Abitibi	32 D/7	48°22'	78°32'
La Pêche	VILG/VILG	QC	Les Collines-de-l'Outaouais	31 G/12	45°41'	75°59'
La Pérouse	UNP/LNO	MB	14-72-4-W	63 P/4	55°14'	97°58'
La Pérouse Bay	BAY/BAIE	MB		54 K/11	58°45'	93°25'
La Petite-Acadie	UNP/LNO	QC	Maskinongé	31 I/7	46°19'	72°52'
La Petite-Barbue	UNP/LNO	QC	Rouville	31 H/7	45°24'	72°56'
La Petite-Floride	UNP/LNO	QC	Bécancour	31 I/8	46°22'	72°27'
La Petite-France	UNP/LNO	QC	Pabok	22 A/8	48°25'	64°29'
La Petite-France	UNP/LNO	QC	Le Haut-Richelieu	31 H/3	45°06'	73°15'

NAME NOM	ENTITY ENTITÉ	LOC 1 LIEU 1	LOC 2 LIEU 2	MAP CARTE	POSITION LAT	LONG
La Petite-Gaspésie	UNP/LNO	QC	L'Islet	21 M/1	47°07′	70°23′
La Petite-Minerve	UNP/LNO	QC	Les Laurentides	31 J/7	46°18′	74°50′
La Petite-Rivière	UNP/LNO	QC	Maskinongé	31 I/7	46°18′	72°49′
Lapeyrère, Lac	LAKE/LAC	QC	Portneuf	31 P/1	47°13′	72°22′
Lapierre House	UNP/LNO	YT		116 P/6	67°24′	137°01′
Lapin, Lac au	LAKE/LAC	QC	Témiscamingue	31 M/9	47°30′	78°22′
La Plaine	CITY/VIL1	QC	Les Moulins	31 H/13	45°47′	73°46′
La Plaine	UNP/LNO	QC	Lotbinière	21 L/12	46°38′	71°35′
La Plaine	UNP/LNO	SK	7-43-2-W3	73 B/9	52°44′	106°16′
Lapland	UNP/LNO	NS	Lunenburg	21 A/7	44°18′	64°41′
LaPlante	UNP/LNO	NB	Gloucester	21 P/13	47°46′	65°47′
La Plonge 192	IR/RI	SK		73 O/4	55°14′	107°34′
La Pocatière	CITY/VIL1	QC	Kamouraska	21 M/8	47°22′	70°02′
La Poile	UNP/LNO	NF		11 O/9	47°41′	58°24′
La Poile Bay	BAY/BAIE	NF		11 O/9	47°43′	58°21′
La Poile River	RIV/CDE	NF		11 O/16	47°48′	58°19′
La Pointe	UNP/LNO	NS	Inverness	11 K/11	46°37′	61°03′
Lapointe	UNP/LNO	QC	Témiscouata	21 N/10	47°31′	68°41′
Lapointe	UNP/LNO	QC	La Côte-de-Beaupré	21 M/2	47°01′	70°57′
La Pointe-à-Carcy	UNP/LNO	QC	Communauté urbaine de Québec	21 L/14	46°49′	71°12′
Lapointe, Lac	LAKE/LAC	QC	Caniapiscau	23 F/7	53°27′	68°35′
Lapointe Settlement	UNP/LNO	NB	Restigouche	21 O/16	47°55′	66°05′
Lapointe-Station	UNP/LNO	QC	Kamouraska	21 N/5	47°26′	69°36′
Laporte	HAM/HAM	SK	13-26-26-W3	72 N/4	51°13′	109°30′
Laporte, Mount	MTN/MNT	YT		95 E/4	61°14′	127°42′
La Potherie, Cap	CAPE/CAP	QC	Kativik	35 H/16	61°48′	72°07′
La Potherie, Lac	LAKE/LAC	QC	Kativik	34 I/16	58°50′	72°24′
Lappe	UNP/LNO	ON	Thunder Bay	52 A/11	48°34′	89°21′
La Prairie	CITY/VIL1	QC	Roussillon	31 H/6	45°25′	73°30′
La Prairie	UNP/LNO	NS	Inverness	11 K/10	46°38′	60°58′
La Présentation	VILG/VILG	QC	Les Maskoutains	31 H/11	45°40′	73°03′
La Providence	UNP/LNO	QC	Les Maskoutains	31 H/10	45°37′	72°57′
La Pulpe	UNP/LNO	QC	Rimouski-Neigette	22 C/7	48°25′	68°33′
La Rallonge	UNP/LNO	QC	Les Basques	22 C/3	48°01′	69°00′
La Ratière	UNP/LNO	QC	Le Fjord-du-Saguenay	22 D/6	48°25′	71°21′
L'Archevêque	UNP/LNO	NS	Richmond	11 F/10	45°38′	60°35′
Larchwood	UNP/LNO	ON	Sudbury	41 I/11	46°35′	81°18′
Larcom Island	ISL/ÎLE	BC	Cassiar	103 P/5	55°26′	129°44′
Lardeau	UNP/LNO	BC	Kootenay	82 K/2	50°09′	116°57′
Lardeau River	RIV/CDE	BC	Kootenay	82 K/2	50°15′	116°57′
Larder Lake	MUN2/AZM2	ON	Timiskaming	32 D/4	48°05′	79°40′
Larder Lake	UNP/LNO	ON	Timiskaming	32 D/4	48°06′	79°43′
Larder Lake	LAKE/LAC	ON	Timiskaming	32 D/4	48°05′	79°38′
Larder River	RIV/CDE	ON	Timiskaming	31 M/13	47°50′	79°49′
L'Ardoise	UNP/LNO	NS	Richmond	11 F/10	45°37′	60°45′
L'Ardoise West	UNP/LNO	NS	Richmond	11 F/10	45°37′	60°46′
La Rédemption	VILG/VILG	QC	La Mitis	22 B/5	48°27′	67°53′
Laredo Channel	CHAN/CHEN	BC	Range 3 Coast	103 A/10	52°42′	129°03′
Laredo Inlet	BAY/BAIE	BC	Range 3 Coast	103 A/15	52°48′	128°44′
Laredo Sound	CHAN/CHEN	BC	Range 3 Coast	103 A/7	52°29′	128°53′
La Reine	VILG/VILG	QC	Abitibi-Ouest	32 D/13	48°52′	79°30′
La Renouche	UNP/LNO	ON	Prescott	31 G/9	45°33′	74°29′
La Résurrection	UNP/LNO	QC	Témiscouata	21 N/10	47°35′	68°59′
L'Argent, Cape	CAPE/CAP	NF		2 C/11	48°39′	53°02′
Largepike Lake	LAKE/LAC	NT	Mackenzie	75 D	60°05′	110°20′
Largie	UNP/LNO	ON	Elgin	40 I/12	42°42′	81°34′
Largs	UNP/LNO	MB	8-15-18-W	62 J/5	50°16′	99°56′
Laribosière, Lac	LAKE/LAC	QC	Jamésie	23 E/12	53°39′	71°45′
La Richardière	UNP/LNO	QC	Rivière-du-Loup	22 C/3	48°02′	69°25′
Larive, Lac	LAKE/LAC	QC	Pontiac	31 N/3	47°04′	77°26′
La Rivière	UNP/LNO	MB	25-3-10-W	62 G/2	49°14′	98°41′
La Rivière-du-Nord	MUN1/AZM1	QC	La Rivière-du-Nord	31 G/16	45°49′	74°01′
Larkhall	UNP/LNO	MB	30-9-10-E	62 H/16	49°47′	96°12′
Lark Harbour	VILG/VILG	NF		12 G/1	49°06′	58°23′
Larkhaven	UNP/LNO	SK		73 B/2	52°10′	106°41′
Larkhill	UNP/LNO	MB		62 G/13	49°50′	99°59′
Larkin	UNP/LNO	BC	Osoyoos Division Yale	82 L/6	50°22′	119°14′
Larkin Point	CAPE/CAP	NF		11 O/14	47°46′	59°20′
Larkins	UNP/LNO	ON	Hastings	31 C/6	44°27′	77°11′
Larkspur	VILG/VILG	AB	5-63-25-W4	83 I/5	54°25′	113°46′
Laroche	UNP/LNO	QC	Brome-Missisquoi	31 H/7	45°17′	72°36′
La Rochelle	UNP/LNO	QC	L'Érable	21 L/4	46°08′	71°47′
Larochelle	UNP/LNO	QC	Asbestos	21 E/13	45°48′	71°53′
Larochelle	UNP/LNO	QC	Bécancour	31 I/7	46°16′	72°30′
La Rochelle	UNP/LNO	MB		62 H/7	49°21′	96°59′

NAME NOM	ENTITY ENTITÉ	LOC 1 LIEU 1	LOC 2 LIEU 2	MAP CARTE	POSITION LAT	POSITION LONG
Larocque	UNP/LNO	ON	Cochrane	42 H/3	49°08′	81°02′
Larocque, Lac	LAKE/LAC	QC	Caniapiscau	22 N/13	51°51′	69°35′
La Romaine	UNP/LNO	QC	Côte-Nord-du-Golfe-Saint-Laurent	12 K/2	50°13′	60°40′
La Ronge	TOWN/VIL2	SK		73 P/3	55°06′	105°17′
Larouche	VILG/VILG	QC	Le Fjord-du-Saguenay	22 D/5	48°27′	71°31′
Larrimac	UNP/LNO	QC	Les Collines-de-l'Outaouais	31 G/12	45°33′	75°50′
Larrys River	UNP/LNO	NS	Guysborough	11 F/3	45°13′	61°23′
Larsen, Cape	CAPE/CAP	NT	Franklin	87 C	69°47′	117°15′
Larsen Island	ISL/ÎLE	BC	Range 4 Coast	103 G/10	53°37′	130°33′
Larsen Sound	CHAN/CHEN	NT	Franklin	67 E	70°30′	98°45′
Larson	UNP/LNO	ON	Thunder Bay	52 G/1	49°05′	90°18′
Larsons Landing	UNP/LNO	BC	New Westminster	92 F/15	49°59′	124°41′
LaRue Mills	UNP/LNO	ON	Leeds	31 B/5	44°26′	75°53′
Larus Lake	LAKE/LAC	ON	Kenora	52 M/7	51°17′	94°40′
Lasal Bay - see-voir - Wee Too Beach	HAM/HAM	SK		72 I/14	50°56′	105°10′
La Salette	UNP/LNO	ON	Norfolk	40 I/15	42°54′	80°30′
LaSalle	CITY/VIL1	QC	Communauté urbaine de Montréal	31 H/5	45°26′	73°38′
LaSalle	TOWN/VIL2	ON	Essex	40 J/3	42°13′	83°03′
La Salle	UNP/LNO	ON	Halton	30 M/5	43°19′	79°50′
La Salle	UNP/LNO	ON	Essex	40 J/3	42°14′	83°06′
La Salle	UNP/LNO	MB	28-8-2-E	62 H/11	49°42′	97°16′
La Salle, Lac	LAKE/LAC	QC	Portneuf	31 P/8	47°15′	72°07′
La Salle, Lac	LAKE/LAC	QC	Jamésie	33 H/7	53°20′	72°55′
LaSalle Park	UNP/LNO	ON	Frontenac	31 C/2	44°13′	76°34′
La Salle River - also-aussi - +La Salle, Rivière	RIV/CDE	MB	9-3-E	62 H/14	49°45′	97°08′
+La Salle, Rivière - also-aussi - La Salle River	RIV/CDE	MB		62 H/14	49°45′	97°08′
La Sarre	CITY/VIL1	QC	Abitibi-Ouest	32 D/14	48°48′	79°12′
La Sarre, Baie	BAY/BAIE	QC	Abitibi-Ouest	32 D/11	48°41′	79°18′
La Sarre, Rivière	RIV/CDE	QC	Abitibi-Ouest	32 D/11	48°43′	79°16′
La Savonnière, Lac	LAKE/LAC	QC	Jamésie	33 H/8	53°27′	72°23′
Lascelles	UNP/LNO	QC	Les Collines-de-l'Outaouais	31 G/12	45°42′	75°48′
L'Ascension	VILG/VILG	QC	Antoine-Labelle	31 J/10	46°33′	74°50′
L'Ascension	UNP/LNO	QC	Lac-Saint-Jean-Est	22 D/12	48°42′	71°40′
L'Ascension-de-Notre-Seigneur	VILG/VILG	QC	Lac-Saint-Jean-Est	22 D/12	48°42′	71°41′
L'Ascension-de-Patapédia	VILG/VILG	QC	Avignon	21 O/14	47°56′	67°15′
La Scie	TOWN/VIL2	NF		2 E/13	49°57′	55°36′
La Scie Harbour	BAY/BAIE	NF		2 E/13	49°57′	55°36′
Laseine	UNP/LNO	ON	Rainy River	52 C/16	48°45′	92°13′
Lash	UNP/LNO	ON	Kenora	52 F/14	49°59′	93°19′
Lasha	UNP/LNO	BC	Kamloops Division Yale	92 I/4	50°15′	121°34′
Lashburn	TOWN/VIL2	SK	8-48-25-W3	73 F/4	53°08′	109°36′
Laskay	UNP/LNO	ON	York	30 M/13	43°55′	79°35′
Laskeek Bay	BAY/BAIE	BC	Queen Charlotte	103 B/13	52°49′	131°35′
La Société	UNP/LNO	QC	Les Basques	21 N/15	47°59′	68°59′
La Sorbière, Lac	LAKE/LAC	QC	Le Fjord-du-Saguenay	22 E/7	49°21′	70°40′
La Souricière	UNP/LNO	QC	Pabok	22 A/9	48°36′	64°25′
Lasqueti Island	ISL/ÎLE	BC	Nanaimo	92 F/8	49°29′	124°16′
L'Assomption	CITY/VIL1	QC	L'Assomption	31 H/14	45°50′	73°25′
L'Assomption	MUN1/AZM1	QC	L'Assomption	31 H/14	45°48′	73°26′
L'Assomption, Rivière	RIV/CDE	QC	L'Assomption	31 H/11	45°43′	73°29′
Lasswade	UNP/LNO	ON	Peterborough	31 C/13	44°46′	77°57′
La Station	UNP/LNO	QC	Francheville	31 I/9	46°31′	72°16′
Last Lake	UNP/LNO	AB	25-83-26-W5	84 C/4	56°13′	117°57′
Last Lake	LAKE/LAC	MB	3,10,15,22-22-12-W	62 J/14	50°53′	99°03′
Lastman Lake	LAKE/LAC	BC	Lillooet	92 O/5	51°20′	123°40′
Last Mountain	UNP/LNO	SK	3-26-20-W2	72 P/2	51°12′	104°44′
Last Mountain Lake	LAKE/LAC	SK		72 P/3	51°05′	105°14′
Last Mountain Lake 80A	IR/RI	SK		72 I/14	50°46′	105°02′
Last Mountain Valley No. 250	MUN2/AZM2	SK		72 P/2	51°15′	105°00′
La Tabatière	UNP/LNO	QC	Côte-Nord-du-Golfe-Saint-Laurent	12 J/15	50°50′	58°58′
Lataignant, Lac	LAKE/LAC	QC	Jamésie	23 E/14	53°55′	71°20′
Latchford	TOWN/VIL2	ON	Timiskaming	31 M/5	47°20′	79°49′
Latchford Bridge	UNP/LNO	ON	Renfrew	31 F/6	45°18′	77°28′
Laterrière	CITY/VIL1	QC	Le Fjord-du-Saguenay	22 D/6	48°18′	71°07′
Laterrière-Bassin	UNP/LNO	QC	Le Fjord-du-Saguenay	22 D/6	48°19′	71°08′
La Tête-de-l'Île	UNP/LNO	QC	Pontiac	31 F/14	45°53′	77°07′
Latewhos Creek	RIV/CDE	BC	Osoyoos Division Yale	82 L/7	50°28′	118°44′
Lathom	UNP/LNO	AB	29-20-17-W4	82 I/9	50°43′	112°20′
Latimer	UNP/LNO	ON	Frontenac	31 C/7	44°22′	76°31′
Latimer Lake	UNP/LNO	NB	Saint John	21 H/5	45°18′	65°55′
Latimer Lake	LAKE/LAC	NT	Mackenzie	65 D	60°38′	102°44′
Latornell	UNP/LNO	AB	12-65-3-W6	83 L/9	54°37′	118°19′
Latornell River	RIV/CDE	AB	69-27-W5	83 K/13	54°58′	118°00′
La Tourette, Rivière	RIV/CDE	QC	Le Fjord-du-Saguenay	22 E/16	49°48′	70°05′
Latourette, Rivière	RIV/CDE	QC	Kativik	25 D/16	60°53′	70°09′

NAME NOM	ENTITY ENTITÉ	LOC 1 LIEU 1	LOC 2 LIEU 2	MAP CARTE	POSITION LAT	LONG
La Tour, Port	BAY/BAIE	NS	Shelburne	20 P/6	43°30′	65°27′
La Trappe	UNP/LNO	QC	Deux-Montagnes	31 G/8	45°30′	74°02′
La Trinité-des-Monts	VILG/VILG	QC	Rimouski-Neigette	22 C/1	48°08′	68°28′
LaTrobe Bay	BAY/BAIE	NT	Franklin	57 C	69°03′	95°55′
La Tse Cho Diz 33	IR/RI	BC	Range 5 Coast	93 K/11	54°38′	125°01′
Latta	UNP/LNO	ON	Hastings	31 C/6	44°18′	77°20′
Latties Brook	UNP/LNO	NS	Hants	11 E/4	45°14′	63°34′
Lattkaloup 9	IR/RI	BC	Range 3 Coast	103 A/10	52°42′	128°44′
Latulipe	UNP/LNO	QC	Témiscamingue	31 M/6	47°26′	79°02′
Latulipe-et-Gaboury	VILG/VILG	QC	Témiscamingue	31 M/6.	47°24′	79°00′
La Tuque	CITY/VIL1	QC	Le Haut-Saint-Maurice	31 P/7	47°26′	72°47′
Lauchlan River	RIV/CDE	NT	Franklin	77 B	68°57′	108°32′
Lauder	UNP/LNO	MB	17-5-24-W	62 F/7	49°23′	100°41′
Lauderbach	UNP/LNO	ON	Grey	41 A/2	44°00′	80°58′
Laughland Lake	LAKE/LAC	NT	Keewatin	56 K/2	66°07′	92°45′
Laumet, Lac	LAKE/LAC	QC	Jamésie	23 E/16	53°55′	70°07′
Launay	VILG/VILG	QC	Abitibi	32 D/10	48°39′	78°32′
Launching Place	UNP/LNO	PE	Kings	11 L/1	46°13′	62°26′
Launching Point	CAPE/CAP	PE	Kings	11 L/1	46°13′	62°25′
Laundrie Lake	LAKE/LAC	ON	Sudbury	41 P/2	47°07′	80°52′
Laura	UNP/LNO	SK	19-33-9-W3	72 O/14	51°51′	107°16′
Lauréat	UNP/LNO	QC	Pontiac	31 F/16	45°55′	76°22′
Laure-Gaudreault, Mont	MTN/MNT	QC	Le Fjord-du-Saguenay	22 D/1	48°08′	70°18′
Laurel	UNP/LNO	QC	Les Pays-d'en-Haut	31 G/16	45°51′	74°28′
Laurel	UNP/LNO	ON	Dufferin	40 P/16	43°57′	80°13′
Laurel-Station	UNP/LNO	QC	Les Pays-d'en-Haut	31 G/16	45°53′	74°25′
Laurence	UNP/LNO	QC	Montcalm	31 H/13	45°54′	73°34′
Laurenceton	UNP/LNO	NF		2 E/3	49°12′	55°17′
Laurent	UNP/LNO	QC	Portneuf	31 P/1	47°09′	72°17′
Laurentia Beach	UNP/LNO	MB	16,17-4-W	62 I/5	50°25′	97°58′
Laurentian Belaire	UNP/LNO	BC	New Westminster	92 G/7	49°15′	122°50′
Laurentian Channel - also-aussi - Laurentien, Chenal	SEAU/SMER	—		801	48°30′	62°00′
Laurentian Fan - also-aussi - Laurentien, Cône	SEAU/SMER	—		802	44°00′	56°30′
Laurentian Hills	UNP/LNO	ON	Waterloo	40 P/8	43°25′	80°30′
Laurentian Mountains - also-aussi - **Laurentides, Les**	MTN/MNT	QC	Le Fjord-du-Saguenay	22 D/3	48°00′	71°00′
Laurentian View	UNP/LNO	ON	Carleton	31 G/5	45°23′	75°44′
Laurentian View	UNP/LNO	ON	Renfrew	31 F/14	45°53′	77°14′
Laurentides	CITY/VIL1	QC	Montcalm	31 H/13	45°51′	73°46′
Laurentides	MUN1/AZM1	QC	Antoine-Labelle	31 J/7	46°26′	74°59′
Laurentides	UNP/LNO	QC	Portneuf	31 P/1	47°08′	72°17′
Laurentides, Les - also-aussi - **Laurentian Mountains**	MTN/MNT	QC	Le Fjord-du-Saguenay	22 D/3	48°00′	71°00′
Laurentides, Réserve faunique des	PARK/PARC	QC	La Côte-de-Beaupré	21 M/14	47°45′	71°15′
Laurentien	UNP/LNO	ON	Sudbury	41 I/11	46°35′	81°00′
Laurentien, Chenal - also-aussi - Laurentian Channel	SEAU/SMER	—		801	48°30′	62°00′
Laurentien, Cône - also-aussi - Laurentian Fan	SEAU/SMER	—		802	44°00′	56°30′
Laurent, Lac	LAKE/LAC	QC	Le Fjord-du-Saguenay	22 D/7	48°28′	70°45′
Lauretta	UNP/LNO	PE	Prince	21 I/16	46°51′	64°09′
Lauretta	UNP/LNO	BC	Kootenay	82 N/4	51°05′	117°55′
Laurie Lake	LAKE/LAC	MB/SK		64 C/12	56°35′	101°57′
Laurier	UNP/LNO	MB	12-22-16-W	62 J/13	50°53′	99°34′
Laurier House National Historic Site - also-aussi - Maison-Laurier, Lieu historique national de la	PARK/PARC	ON	Carleton	31 G/5	45°26′	75°41′
Laurie River	UNP/LNO	MB		64 C/3	56°14′	101°00′
Laurie River	UNP/LNO	MB	84-25-W	64 C/3	56°15′	101°18′
Laurie River	RIV/CDE	MB		64 C/2	56°13′	100°44′
Laurier Lake	LAKE/LAC	AB	56-4-W4	73 E/15	53°52′	110°32′
Laurier, Mount	MTN/MNT	BC	Peace River	94 B/14	56°47′	123°29′
Laurier No. 38	MUN2/AZM2	SK		72 H/8	49°25′	104°10′
Laurier-Station	TOWN/VIL2	QC	Lotbinière	21 L/12	46°32′	71°38′
Laurierville	TOWN/VIL2	QC	L'Érable	21 L/5	46°18′	71°39′
Laurin	UNP/LNO	ON	Simcoe	41 A/16	44°47′	80°05′
Lauriston	UNP/LNO	ON	Grey	41 A/7	44°18′	80°44′
Lauvergot	UNP/LNO	NB	Northumberland	21 P/6	47°18′	65°11′
Lauzon	UNP/LNO	QC	Desjardins	21 L/14	46°50′	71°10′
Lauzon Lake	LAKE/LAC	ON	Algoma	41 J/2	46°12′	82°50′
Laval	CITY/VIL1	QC	Laval	31 H/12	45°35′	73°45′
Laval	MUN1/AZM1	QC	Laval	31 H/12	45°35′	73°45′
Laval	MUN1/AZM1	QC	Laval	31 H/12	45°35′	73°45′
Laval	UNP/LNO	QC	Bécancour	31 I/7	46°20′	72°31′
Lava Lake	LAKE/LAC	BC	Cassiar	103 P/2	55°03′	128°58′
Laval, Baie	BAY/BAIE	QC	La Haute-Côte-Nord	22 C/14	48°46′	69°03′
Laval-des-Rapides	UNP/LNO	QC	Laval	31 H/12	45°33′	73°42′
Laval, Lac	LAKE/LAC	QC	La Haute-Côte-Nord	22 F/3	49°00′	69°10′
La Vallee	MUN2/AZM2	ON	Rainy River	52 C/12	48°41′	93°40′
La Vallée	UNP/LNO	ON	Rainy River	52 C/12	48°37′	93°39′
La Vallée-de-la-Gatineau	MUN1/AZM1	QC	La Vallée-de-la-Gatineau	31 K/9	46°32′	76°03′

NAME NOM	ENTITY ENTITÉ	LOC 1 LIEU 1	LOC 2 LIEU 2	MAP CARTE	POSITION LAT	POSITION LONG
La Vallée-du-Richelieu	MUN1/AZM1	QC	La Vallée-du-Richelieu	31 H/11	45°34′	73°12′
Lavallée Lake	LAKE/LAC	SK	61-4-W3	73 J/7	54°17′	106°34′
La Vallée River	RIV/CDE	ON	Rainy River	52 C/12	48°32′	93°38′
Laval-Ouest	UNP/LNO	QC	Laval	31 H/12	45°33′	73°52′
Laval, Rivière	RIV/CDE	QC	La Haute-Côte-Nord	22 C/14	48°46′	69°03′
Laval-sur-le-Lac	UNP/LNO	QC	Laval	31 H/12	45°32′	73°52′
Lavaltrie	TOWN/VIL2	QC	D'Autray	31 H/14	45°53′	73°17′
Lavaltrie-Station	UNP/LNO	QC	Joliette	31 H/14	45°56′	73°23′
Lavant	UNP/LNO	ON	Lanark	31 F/2	45°04′	76°39′
Lavant, Dalhousie and North Sherbrooke	MUN2/AZM2	ON	Lanark	31 F/2	45°03′	76°37′
Lavant Station	UNP/LNO	ON	Lanark	31 F/2	45°03′	76°42′
Lavender	UNP/LNO	ON	Dufferin	41 A/8	44°16′	80°09′
Lavender Peak	MTN/MNT	BC	Cassiar	103 P/11	55°39′	129°19′
Lavenham	UNP/LNO	MB	35-9-10-W	62 G/15	49°48′	98°43′
L'Avenir	VILG/VILG	QC	Drummond	31 H/16	45°46′	72°18′
Laventure	UNP/LNO	SK	2-52-11-W3	73 G/5	53°28′	107°31′
Laverdière	UNP/LNO	QC	La Côte-de-Beaupré	21 L/14	46°58′	71°02′
La Vérendrye, Réserve faunique	PARK/PARC	QC	La Vallée-de-la-Gatineau	31 N/6	47°20′	77°00′
Laverlochère	VILG/VILG	QC	Témiscamingue	31 M/6	47°26′	79°18′
La Vernière	UNP/LNO	QC	Les Îles-de-la-Madeleine	11 N/5	47°22′	61°54′
Lavesta	UNP/LNO	AB	21-43-3-W5	83 B/9	52°43′	114°23′
Lavieille, Lake	LAKE/LAC	ON	Nipissing	31 E/16	45°51′	78°14′
Lavigne	UNP/LNO	ON	Nipissing	41 I/8	46°20′	80°10′
Lavillette	UNP/LNO	NB	Northumberland	21 P/6	47°16′	65°19′
Lavington	UNP/LNO	BC	Osoyoos Division Yale	82 L/3	50°14′	119°06′
Lavinia	UNP/LNO	MB	13-15-24-W	62 K/7	50°16′	100°40′
La Visitation	UNP/LNO	QC	Nicolet-Yamaska	31 I/2	46°08′	72°36′
La Visitation-de-l'Île-Dupas	VILG/VILG	QC	D'Autray	31 I/3	46°05′	73°09′
La Visitation-de-Yamaska	VILG/VILG	QC	Nicolet-Yamaska	31 I/2	46°08′	72°36′
Lavoie	UNP/LNO	QC	La Mitis	22 C/9	48°34′	68°15′
Lavoie	UNP/LNO	QC	Acton	31 H/10	45°37′	72°33′
Lavoie	UNP/LNO	QC	Francheville	31 I/7	46°23′	72°45′
Lavoie Bay	BAY/BAIE	SK		73 O/7	55°23′	106°47′
Lavoy	VILG/VILG	AB	4-52-13-W4	73 E/5	53°27′	111°52′
Lawabiskau River	RIV/CDE	ON	Cochrane	43 A/3	52°03′	81°04′
Lawagamau Lake	LAKE/LAC	ON	Cochrane	42 H/16	49°50′	80°05′
Lawagamau River	RIV/CDE	ON	Cochrane	32 M/4	51°04′	79°44′
Lawanth 5	IR/RI	BC	Range 1 Coast	92 L/15	50°57′	126°52′
Lawashi River	RIV/CDE	ON	Kenora	43 B/16	52°53′	82°12′
Lawford Islands	ISL/ÎLE	NT	Mackenzie	86 P	67°56′	113°05′
Lawford Lake	LAKE/LAC	MB		63 I/7	54°30′	96°42′
Lawford River	RIV/CDE	MB		63 I/9	54°36′	96°01′
Lawledge	UNP/LNO	MB		54 D/16	56°57′	94°07′
Lawless Creek	RIV/CDE	BC	Yale Division Yale	92 H/10	49°32′	120°50′
Lawn	TOWN/VIL2	NF		1 L/13	46°57′	55°32′
Lawn	UNP/LNO	QC	Pontiac	31 F/10	45°41′	76°33′
Lawn Bay	BAY/BAIE	NF		1 L/13	46°52′	55°34′
Lawn Head	CAPE/CAP	NF		1 L/14	46°53′	55°29′
Lawnhill	UNP/LNO	BC	Queen Charlotte	103 G/5	53°24′	131°55′
Lawn Point	CAPE/CAP	BC	Rupert	92 L/5	50°20′	127°58′
Lawn Point	CAPE/CAP	BC	Queen Charlotte	103 G/5	53°26′	131°55′
Lawrence	MUN2/AZM2	MB		62 O/5	51°20′	99°30′
Lawrence Bay	BAY/BAIE	SK		64 D/10	56°38′	102°53′
Lawrence, Cape	CAPE/CAP	NT	Franklin	120 B	80°23′	69°26′
Lawrence Colony	UNP/LNO	QC	Le Haut-Saint-François	21 E/6	45°25′	71°24′
Lawrence Harbour	BAY/BAIE	NF		2 E/6	49°25′	55°11′
Lawrence Heights	UNP/LNO	ON	York	30 M/11	43°43′	79°27′
Lawrence Lake	LAKE/LAC	ON	Kenora	52 F/6	49°17′	93°23′
Lawrence Lake	LAKE/LAC	SK	61-7-W3	73 J/3	54°15′	107°02′
Lawrence Lake	LAKE/LAC	AB	69-24,25-W4	83 I/13	54°58′	113°42′
Lawrence Manor	UNP/LNO	ON	York	30 M/11	43°43′	79°26′
Lawrence Park	UNP/LNO	ON	Frontenac	31 C/2	44°14′	76°37′
Lawrence Park	UNP/LNO	ON	York	30 M/11	43°43′	79°25′
Lawrence Point	CAPE/CAP	BC	Range 1 Coast	92 K/6	50°27′	125°06′
Lawrence Pond	UNP/LNO	NF		1 N/6	47°28′	53°03′
Lawrence Station	UNP/LNO	NB	Charlotte	21 G/6	45°26′	67°11′
Lawrence Station	UNP/LNO	ON	Elgin	40 I/14	42°45′	81°25′
Lawrencetown	VILG/VILG	NS	Annapolis	21 A/14	44°53′	65°10′
Lawrencetown	UNP/LNO	NS	Halifax	11 D/11	44°39′	63°21′
Lawrenceville	TOWN/VIL2	QC	Le Val-Saint-François	31 H/8	45°25′	72°21′
Lawson	UNP/LNO	SK	9-22-5-W3	72 J/15	50°51′	106°39′
Lawson Heights	UNP/LNO	SK		73 B/2	52°10′	106°37′
Lawson Island	ISL/ÎLE	NT	Franklin	25 A	60°37′	64°40′
Lawson Quarry	UNP/LNO	ON	Sudbury	41 I/4	46°07′	81°44′
Lawton	UNP/LNO	AB	27-58-4-W5	83 J/1	54°03′	114°29′

NAME NOM	ENTITY ENTITÉ	LOC 1 LIEU 1	LOC 2 LIEU 2	MAP CARTE	POSITION LAT	LONG
Lawtonia No. 135	MUN2/AZM2	SK		72 J/2	50°10′	107°00′
Lawton's Corners	UNP/LNO	ON	Elgin	40 I/11	42°42′	81°07′
Lax Kw'alaams	UNP/LNO	BC	Range 5 Coast	103 J/9	54°33′	130°26′
Lax Kw'a laams 1	IR/RI	BC	Range 5 Coast	103 J/9	54°34′	130°24′
Laxton, Digby and Longford	MUN2/AZM2	ON	Victoria	31 D/14	44°50′	79°00′
Layco	UNP/LNO	SK	19-31-10-W2	62 M/11	51°42′	103°25′
Layland	UNP/LNO	MB	2-10-6-W	62 G/16	49°48′	98°10′
Lay, Mount	MTN/MNT	BC	Cassiar	94 C/12	56°33′	125°33′
Layton	UNP/LNO	ON	Ontario	31 D/3	44°13′	79°00′
Lazo	UNP/LNO	BC	Comox	92 F/10	49°43′	124°54′
Lazo, Cape	CAPE/CAP	BC	Comox	92 F/10	49°42′	124°52′
Leach Bay	BAY/BAIE	NT	Franklin	25 O	63°02′	67°40′
Leach Island	ISL/ÎLE	ON	Algoma	41 N/7	47°28′	84°57′
Leach Lake	UNP/LNO	QC	Pontiac	31 F/16	45°48′	76°29′
Leacross	UNP/LNO	SK	7-47-14-W2	73 H/1	53°03′	104°03′
Leadbury	UNP/LNO	ON	Huron	40 P/11	43°39′	81°19′
Lead Cove	UNP/LNO	NF		2 C/3	48°03′	53°05′
Leader	TOWN/VIL2	SK		72 K/13	50°53′	109°33′
Leading Tickles East	UNP/LNO	NF		2 E/6	49°30′	55°25′
Leading Tickles South	UNP/LNO	NF		2 E/6	49°30′	55°27′
Leading Tickles West	VILG/VILG	NF		2 E/11	49°30′	55°28′
Lead Mines	UNP/LNO	NF		1 N/12	47°41′	53°56′
Leadville	UNP/LNO	QC	Memphrémagog	31 H/1	45°01′	72°17′
Leaf Bay	BAY/BAIE	NT	Franklin	25 K	58°56′	69°05′
Leaf Lake	LAKE/LAC	SK	46,47-1,2-W2	63 E/1	53°01′	102°08′
Leaf Rapids	TOWN/VIL2	MB	85,86,87-13,14,15,16,17-W	64 B/5	56°28′	99°45′
Leah Point	CAPE/CAP	NT	Franklin	57 H	71°31′	90°02′
Leahurst	UNP/LNO	AB	26-39-19-W4	83 A/7	52°23′	112°38′
Leakville	UNP/LNO	SK	27-13-26-W2	72 I/3	50°07′	105°29′
Leaman	UNP/LNO	AB	36-53-11-W5	83 G/11	53°37′	115°29′
Leamington	TOWN/VIL2	ON	Essex	40 J/2	42°03′	82°36′
Leamington	UNP/LNO	NS	Cumberland	21 H/9	45°36′	64°05′
Leanchoil	UNP/LNO	BC	Kootenay	82 N/2	51°13′	116°37′
Lea Park	UNP/LNO	AB	14-54-3-W4	73 E/9	53°39′	110°20′
Leards Mill	UNP/LNO	PE	Kings	11 L/7	46°18′	62°43′
Learned Plain	UNP/LNO	QC	Le Haut-Saint-François	21 E/5	45°26′	71°33′
Lears Cove	UNP/LNO	NF		1 L/16	46°51′	54°11′
Learys	UNP/LNO	MB	13-6-8-W	62 G/8	49°29′	98°25′
Leaside	UNP/LNO	ON	York	30 M/11	43°42′	79°22′
Leaside Beach	UNP/LNO	MB	20-31-5-E	62 P/10	51°41′	96°51′
Leask	VILG/VILG	SK	1-47-6-W3	73 G/2	53°01′	106°45′
Leaskdale	UNP/LNO	ON	Ontario	31 D/3	44°12′	79°10′
Leask No. 464	MUN2/AZM2	SK		73 G/2	53°00′	106°50′
Leatherdale Landing	UNP/LNO	ON	Rainy River	52 C/10	48°32′	92°34′
Leather River	RIV/CDE	SK	48-13-W2	63 E/4	53°07′	103°54′
Leavitt	UNP/LNO	AB	31-2-26-W4	82 H/3	49°10′	113°27′
Leavitt Bay	BAY/BAIE	SK		74 G/6	57°16′	107°01′
Leavitt's Mill	UNP/LNO	QC	Coaticook	21 E/5	45°17′	71°40′
Lebahdo	UNP/LNO	BC	Kootenay	82 F/12	49°36′	117°35′
Lebanon	UNP/LNO	ON	Wellington	40 P/10	43°42′	80°50′
Le Barbier, Lac	LAKE/LAC	QC	La Haute-Côte-Nord	22 F/6	49°26′	69°18′
Le Bas-de-la-Paroisse	UNP/LNO	QC	Les Chutes-de-la-Chaudière	21 L/11	46°44′	71°19′
Le Bas-de-la-Paroisse	UNP/LNO	QC	Lotbinière	21 L/12	46°40′	71°32′
Le Bas-de-Sainte-Anne	UNP/LNO	QC	Francheville	31 I/9	46°35′	72°08′
Le Bas-Richelieu	MUN1/AZM1	QC	Le Bas-Richelieu	31 H/14	45°58′	73°00′
Le Bassin	UNP/LNO	QC	Roussillon	31 H/5	45°22′	73°45′
Lebel-sur-Quévillon	CITY/VIL1	QC	Jamésie	32 F/2	49°03′	76°59′
Le Bic	VILG/VILG	QC	Rimouski-Neigette	22 C/7	48°22′	68°42′
LeBlanc	UNP/LNO	NB	Westmorland	21 I/1	46°10′	64°16′
LeBlanc Bay	BAY/BAIE	SK		73 O/3	55°07′	107°24′
LeBlanc Lake	LAKE/LAC	SK		74 O/8	59°21′	106°08′
LeBlanc Lake	LAKE/LAC	SK		74 N/10	59°40′	108°42′
LeBlancville	UNP/LNO	NB	Westmorland	21 I/7	46°16′	64°47′
Le Bois-Clair	UNP/LNO	QC	Lotbinière	21 L/12	46°39′	71°31′
Le Bout-du-Banc	UNP/LNO	QC	Denis-Riverin	22 H/4	49°13′	65°53′
Le Bouthillier	UNP/LNO	NB	Gloucester	21 P/15	47°48′	64°55′
Lebret	VILG/VILG	SK	2-21-13-W2	62 L/13	50°45′	103°42′
Le Breton, Lac	LAKE/LAC	QC	Le Fjord-du-Saguenay	22 D/10	48°42′	70°33′
Lebrix Lake	LAKE/LAC	MB		63 H/11	53°45′	97°03′
Lebrun	UNP/LNO	QC	Maskinongé	31 I/3	46°14′	73°04′
Le Centre-de-la-Mauricie	MUN1/AZM1	QC	Le Centre-de-la-Mauricie	31 I/10	46°36′	72°49′
L'Échouerie	UNP/LNO	QC	Les Îles-de-la-Madeleine	11 N/5	47°24′	61°47′
Leckie Park	UNP/LNO	ON	Wentworth	30 M/4	43°11′	79°47′
Leclair	UNP/LNO	QC	Pontiac	31 F/15	45°54′	76°40′
Leclercville	TOWN/VIL2	QC	Lotbinière	21 L/12	46°34′	72°00′

NAME NOM	ENTITY ENTITÉ	LOC 1 LIEU 1	LOC 2 LIEU 2	MAP CARTE	POSITION LAT	LONG
Le Cocq, Lac	LAKE/LAC	QC	Caniapiscau	23 C/1	52°14′	68°13′
Le Coin	UNP/LNO	QC	Le Granit	21 E/7	45°29′	70°56′
Le Coin-chez-Brault	UNP/LNO	QC	Brome-Missisquoi	31 H/3	45°02′	73°01′
Le Coin-chez-Desranleau	UNP/LNO	QC	Brome-Missisquoi	31 H/3	45°04′	73°01′
Le Coin-des-Anglais	UNP/LNO	QC	Matawinie	31 J/1	46°05′	74°01′
Lecointre, Lac	LAKE/LAC	QC	La Vallée-de-la-Gatineau	31 O/5	47°21′	75°37′
Le Cordon	UNP/LNO	QC	Montcalm	31 H/13	45°59′	73°40′
Leddy	UNP/LNO	AB	11-85-23-W5	84 C/5	56°22′	117°31′
Le Dépôt	UNP/LNO	QC	Les Jardins-de-Napierville	31 H/4	45°12′	73°35′
Le Dépôt	UNP/LNO	QC	Vaudreuil-Soulanges	31 G/8	45°23′	74°06′
Ledge Creek	RIV/CDE	BC	Kootenay	82 K/5	50°29′	118°00′
Ledgerwoods Corner	UNP/LNO	ON	Renfrew	31 F/10	45°43′	76°50′
Le Domaine	UNP/LNO	QC	La Vallée-de-la-Gatineau	31 N/2	47°02′	76°32′
Le Domaine-de-la-Pêche-au-Saumon	UNP/LNO	QC	Beauharnois-Salaberry	31 H/5	45°15′	73°48′
Le Domaine-du-Roy	MUN1/AZM1	QC	Le Domaine-du-Roy	32 A/8	48°29′	72°21′
Le Doré, Lac	LAKE/LAC	QC	Minganie	12 N/6	51°17′	61°23′
Leduc	CITY/VIL1	AB	49-25-W4	83 H/5	53°16′	113°33′
Leduc No. 25, County of	MUN1/AZM1	AB	49-26-W4	83 H/4	53°14′	113°48′
Ledwyn	UNP/LNO	MB	17-23-3-E	62 I/14	51°00′	97°08′
Lee	UNP/LNO	ON	Thunder Bay	52 A/5	48°26′	89°33′
Leeburn	UNP/LNO	ON	Algoma	41 J/5	46°28′	83°49′
Leech	UNP/LNO	NB	Gloucester	21 P/7	47°27′	64°59′
Leech Lake	LAKE/LAC	MB	28,33-24-27-W	62 N/3	51°07′	101°12′
Leech Lake	LAKE/LAC	SK	24-4-W2	62 M/1	51°05′	102°28′
Leechtown	UNP/LNO	BC	Malahat	92 B/5	48°29′	123°43′
Lee Creek	UNP/LNO	BC	Kamloops Division Yale	82 L/13	50°54′	119°32′
Lee Creek	RIV/CDE	AB	23-3-25-W4	82 H/3	49°13′	113°16′
Leedale	UNP/LNO	AB	35-41-4-W5	83 B/9	52°35′	114°29′
Leeds	UNP/LNO	ON	Leeds	31 C/9	44°31′	76°11′
Leeds	GEOG/GÉOG	ON		31 B/12	44°35′	76°00′
Leeds and Grenville, United Counties of	MUN1/AZM1	ON	Grenville	31 B/13	44°50′	75°40′
Lee Point	CAPE/CAP	NT	Franklin	49 A	76°24′	82°16′
Lee River	UNP/LNO	MB	15-12-E	52 L/5	50°17′	95°52′
Lee River Falls	UNP/LNO	MB	3-16-12-E	52 L/5	50°19′	95°52′
Lee's Corner	UNP/LNO	QC	Le Haut-Saint-Laurent	31 G/1	45°03′	74°20′
Lees Corner	UNP/LNO	BC	Lillooet	92 O/14	51°56′	123°06′
Lee Settlement	UNP/LNO	NB	Charlotte	21 G/7	45°16′	66°49′
Lee Valley	UNP/LNO	ON	Sudbury	41 I/4	46°12′	81°56′
Leeville	UNP/LNO	ON	Timiskaming	41 P/9	47°40′	80°10′
Lefaives Corners	UNP/LNO	ON	Simcoe	31 D/12	44°44′	79°59′
Lefaivre	UNP/LNO	ON	Prescott	31 G/10	45°38′	74°54′
Le Faubourg	UNP/LNO	QC	Portneuf	31 I/9	46°36′	72°04′
Lefebvre	VILG/VILG	QC	Drummond	31 H/9	45°43′	72°25′
Le Fer, Lac	LAKE/LAC	QC	Kativik	23 O/6	55°18′	67°20′
Le Feuvre Inlet	BAY/BAIE	NT	Franklin	68 A	72°18′	96°46′
Leffert Glacier	GLAC/GLAC	NT	Franklin	39 E/12	78°41′	75°02′
Lefferts Island	ISL/ÎLE	NT	Franklin	25 I	62°31′	65°04′
Le Fjord-du-Saguenay	MUN1/AZM1	QC	Le Fjord-du-Saguenay	22 D/7	48°20′	70°52′
Lefrançois	UNP/LNO	QC	La Côte-de-Beaupré	21 L/14	46°59′	71°01′
Le Frappe-Sacre	UNP/LNO	QC	Portneuf	31 I/9	46°37′	72°01′
Lefroy	UNP/LNO	ON	Simcoe	31 D/5	44°16′	79°34′
Lefroy Bay	BAY/BAIE	NT	Franklin	46 M	67°31′	86°33′
Lefroy, Rivière	RIV/CDE	QC	Kativik	24 N/12	59°42′	69°39′
Leftrook Lake	LAKE/LAC	MB		64 B/2	56°04′	98°38′
Legal	VILG/VILG	AB	24-57-25-W4	83 H/13	53°57′	113°35′
Le Gal, Lac	LAKE/LAC	QC	Minganie	12 K/5	50°22′	61°55′
Legarde River	RIV/CDE	ON	Cochrane	42 K/11	50°32′	85°30′
Le Gardeur	CITY/VIL1	QC	L'Assomption	31 H/14	45°45′	73°28′
Le Gardeur, Lac	LAKE/LAC	QC	Jamésie	32 K/15	50°57′	76°30′
Légaré, Lac	LAKE/LAC	QC	Matawinie	31 I/13	46°58′	73°57′
Legend	UNP/LNO	AB	19-6-12-W4	72 E/5	49°29′	111°36′
Legend Lake	LAKE/LAC	AB	96,97-18,19-W4	84 H/7	57°24′	112°55′
Le Gendre, Lac	LAKE/LAC	QC	Kativik	24 G/1	57°10′	66°25′
Le Gentilhomme, Lac	LAKE/LAC	QC	Caniapiscau	23 B/10	52°36′	66°53′
Légerville	UNP/LNO	NB	Kent	21 I/6	46°18′	65°00′
Leggat Lake	LAKE/LAC	ON	Frontenac	31 C/10	44°43′	76°43′
Leggatt	UNP/LNO	QC	La Mitis	22 C/9	48°38′	68°04′
Leggatt	UNP/LNO	ON	Dufferin	40 P/16	43°58′	80°21′
Legge	UNP/LNO	ON	Leeds	31 C/8	44°21′	76°08′
Legoff, Lac	LAKE/LAC	QC	Jamésie	32 N/1	51°05′	76°12′
Le Goulet	VILG/VILG	NB	Gloucester	21 P/10	47°42′	64°43′
Leg Pond	LAKE/LAC	NF		12 I/15	50°54′	56°48′
Legrand	UNP/LNO	BC	Cariboo	93 H/8	53°25′	120°23′
Le Grand-Ruisseau	UNP/LNO	QC	Maskinongé	31 I/7	46°20′	72°51′
Le Grand-Sainte-Marie	UNP/LNO	QC	Francheville	31 I/9	46°33′	72°14′

NAME NOM	ENTITY ENTITÉ	LOC 1 LIEU 1	LOC 2 LIEU 2	MAP CARTE	POSITION LAT	LONG
Le Grand-Sault	UNP/LNO	QC	Beauce-Sartigan	21 L/2	46°03′	70°39′
Le Grand-Village	UNP/LNO	QC	Communauté urbaine de Québec	21 L/14	46°46′	71°29′
Le Granit	MUN1/AZM1	QC	Le Granit	21 E/10	45°35′	70°53′
Le Haut-de-la-Paroisse	UNP/LNO	QC	Les Chutes-de-la-Chaudière	21 L/11	46°41′	71°27′
Le Haut-de-la-Paroisse	UNP/LNO	QC	Lotbinière	21 L/12	46°38′	71°37′
Le Haut-Richelieu	MUN1/AZM1	QC	Le Haut-Richelieu	31 H/3	45°12′	73°14′
Le Haut-Saint-François	MUN1/AZM1	QC	Le Haut-Saint-François	21 E/5	45°28′	71°38′
Le Haut-Saint-Laurent	MUN1/AZM1	QC	Le Haut-Saint-Laurent	31 G/1	45°05′	74°10′
Le Haut-Saint-Maurice	MUN1/AZM1	QC	Le Haut-Saint-Maurice	31 P/7	47°26′	72°47′
Lehigh	UNP/LNO	AB	31-27-18-W4	82 P/7	51°21′	112°32′
Lehighs Corners	UNP/LNO	ON	Leeds	31 B/12	44°43′	75°57′
Leiblin Park	UNP/LNO	NS	Halifax	11 D/12	44°36′	63°37′
Leicester	UNP/LNO	AB	3-78-16-W5	83 N/9	55°43′	116°24′
Leif, Lac	LAKE/LAC	QC	Kativik	23 P/9	55°40′	64°08′
Leifur	UNP/LNO	MB	23,26-20-10-W	62 J/10	50°45′	98°46′
Leigh	UNP/LNO	ON	Thunder Bay	42 F/6	49°22′	85°15′
Leighmore	UNP/LNO	AB	5-71-11-W6	83 M/4	55°07′	119°38′
Leighton	UNP/LNO	MB	13-3-24-W	62 F/2	49°13′	100°36′
Leinan	UNP/LNO	SK	5-18-13-W3	72 J/5	50°29′	107°46′
Leipzig	UNP/LNO	SK	17-37-19-W3	73 C/2	52°11′	108°41′
Leismer	UNP/LNO	AB	17-78-7-W4	73 M/11	55°45′	111°03′
Leitch Collieries Provincial Historic Site (Developed)	PARK/PARC	AB	15-7-3-W5	82 G/9	49°34′	114°19′
Leitches Creek	UNP/LNO	NS	Cape Breton	11 K/1	46°09′	60°20′
Leitches Creek Station	UNP/LNO	NS	Cape Breton	11 K/1	46°10′	60°18′
Leith	UNP/LNO	ON	Grey	41 A/10	44°37′	80°53′
Leith Peninsula	CAPE/CAP	NT	Mackenzie	86 E	65°38′	119°15′
Leith, Point	CAPE/CAP	NT	Mackenzie	86 E	65°45′	119°46′
Leitrim	UNP/LNO	ON	Carleton	31 G/5	45°20′	75°36′
Lejac	UNP/LNO	BC	Range 5 Coast	93 K/2	54°03′	124°45′
Lejeune	VILG/VILG	QC	Témiscouata	21 N/15	47°46′	68°34′
Lejeune	UNP/LNO	QC	Témiscouata	21 N/15	47°46′	68°34′
Le Jeune, Lac	LAKE/LAC	BC	Kamloops Division Yale	92 I/8	50°29′	120°29′
Le Lac	UNP/LNO	NB	Westmorland	21 H/15	46°00′	64°32′
Lelachen 6	IR/RI	BC	New Westminster	92 G/16	49°47′	122°12′
Leland	UNP/LNO	ON	Frontenac	31 C/8	44°27′	76°26′
Leland Lakes	LAKE/LAC	AB/NT		74 M/14	59°51′	111°00′
LeMare Lake	LAKE/LAC	BC	Rupert	92 L/5	50°25′	127°53′
Le Marié, Lac	LAKE/LAC	QC	Le Fjord-du-Saguenay	22 D/15	48°45′	70°34′
Lemay	UNP/LNO	QC	La Vallée-de-la-Gatineau	31 G/13	45°59′	75°55′
Lemay, Lac	LAKE/LAC	QC	Manicouagan	22 K/9	50°36′	68°25′
Lemay, Rivière	RIV/CDE	QC	Manicouagan	22 K/7	50°25′	68°36′
Lemberg	TOWN/VIL2	SK	21-20-9-W2	62 L/11	50°44′	103°12′
Le Méandre	UNP/LNO	QC	Beauharnois-Salaberry	31 H/4	45°15′	73°48′
Lemesurier	UNP/LNO	QC	L'Amiante	21 L/3	46°15′	71°17′
Lemieux	VILG/VILG	QC	Bécancour	31 I/8	46°18′	72°07′
Lemieux	UNP/LNO	QC	Portneuf	31 P/1	47°07′	72°16′
Lemieux	UNP/LNO	ON	Prescott	31 G/6	45°24′	75°04′
Lemieux Creek	RIV/CDE	BC	Kamloops Division Yale	92 P/8	51°25′	120°12′
Lemieux Islands	ISL/ÎLE	NT	Franklin	25 P	63°40′	64°20′
Leminster	UNP/LNO	NS	Hants	21 A/16	44°49′	64°18′
Lemmens Inlet	BAY/BAIE	BC	Clayoquot	92 F/4	49°12′	125°52′
Le Moine, Bay	BAY/BAIE	NF		11 O/10	47°39′	58°38′
Le Moine, Cap	CAPE/CAP	NS	Inverness	11 K/11	46°31′	61°04′
Lemoine, Lac	LAKE/LAC	QC	Maria-Chapdelaine	22 E/6	49°23′	71°20′
Lemoine, Lac	LAKE/LAC	QC	Vallée-de-l'Or	32 C/4	48°00′	78°00′
Lemon Creek	UNP/LNO	BC	Kootenay	82 F/11	49°42′	117°29′
Lemonville	UNP/LNO	ON	York	30 M/14	43°59′	79°18′
Lemoray	UNP/LNO	BC	Peace River	93 O/9	55°32′	122°29′
Lemotte's Lake	LAKE/LAC	NF		2 D/13	48°54′	55°45′
Le Moulin	UNP/LNO	QC	Les Îles-de-la-Madeleine	11 N/4	47°13′	61°57′
LeMoyne	CITY/VIL1	QC	Champlain	31 H/6	45°30′	73°30′
Le Moyne	UNP/LNO	QC	La Côte-de-Beaupré	21 L/14	46°57′	71°03′
Le Moyne, Lac	LAKE/LAC	QC	Kativik	24 F/1	57°03′	68°23′
Lempriere	UNP/LNO	BC	Kamloops Division Yale	83 D/6	52°27′	119°08′
Lempriere Creek	RIV/CDE	BC	Kamloops Division Yale	83 D/6	52°29′	119°12′
Lemsford	UNP/LNO	SK	9-22-23-W3	72 K/14	50°51′	109°07′
Lena	UNP/LNO	MB	27-1-17-W	62 G/4	49°04′	99°40′
Lenarthur	UNP/LNO	AB	4-87-7-W4	74 D/1	56°31′	111°03′
Leney	UNP/LNO	SK	30-35-11-W3	73 B/4	52°02′	107°33′
Lennard	UNP/LNO	MB	13,24-23-28-W	62 K/14	51°00′	101°16′
Lennie River	RIV/CDE	NT	Franklin	98 B	72°17′	125°29′
Lennon	UNP/LNO	ON	Algoma	42 F/7	49°17′	84°51′
Lennox	UNP/LNO	NS	Richmond	11 F/11	45°35′	61°02′
Lennox and Addington	MUN1/AZM1	ON	Lennox and Addington	31 C/7	44°30′	77°00′
Lennox and Addington	GEOG/GÉOG	ON		31 C/7	44°30′	77°00′

NAME NOM	ENTITY ENTITÉ	LOC 1 LIEU 1	LOC 2 LIEU 2	MAP CARTE	POSITION LAT	LONG
Lennox Island	UNP/LNO	PE	Prince	11 L/12	46°36′	63°51′
Lennox Island 1	IR/RI	PE	Prince	11 L/12	46°38′	63°48′
Lennox Passage	UNP/LNO	NS	Richmond	11 F/11	45°35′	61°05′
Lennox Passage	CHAN/CHEN	NS	Richmond	11 F/11	45°35′	61°04′
Lennoxville	CITY/VIL1	QC	Sherbrooke	21 E/5	45°22′	71°51′
Lenore	UNP/LNO	MB	30-11-24-W	62 F/15	49°58′	100°45′
Lenore Lake	LAKE/LAC	SK		73 A/7	52°30′	104°59′
Lenormand, Lac	LAKE/LAC	QC	Kativik	33 O/9	55°31′	74°00′
Lenôtre, Lac	LAKE/LAC	QC	La Vallée-de-la-Gatineau	31 N/8	47°21′	76°02′
Lens	UNP/LNO	ON	Lennox and Addington	31 C/7	44°26′	76°56′
Lens	UNP/LNO	SK	42-8-W2	63 D/11	52°37′	103°04′
Lenswood	UNP/LNO	MB	2-39-25-W	63 C/7	52°19′	100°57′
Lenvale	UNP/LNO	SK	32-46-18-W2	73 H/2	53°01′	104°34′
Lenzie	UNP/LNO	AB	10-9-22-W4	82 H/10	49°43′	112°55′
Leo	UNP/LNO	AB	34-35-17-W4	83 A/1	52°03′	112°22′
Leo Creek	UNP/LNO	BC	Cassiar	93 N/4	55°05′	125°34′
Leofnard	UNP/LNO	SK	19-41-26-W2	73 A/12	52°33′	105°43′
Leon	UNP/LNO	MB	9-10-18-W	62 G/13	49°49′	99°51′
Leon 14	IR/RI	BC	Range 4 Coast	93 F/6	53°28′	125°04′
Leonard	UNP/LNO	ON	Russell	31 G/6	45°25′	75°21′
Léonard-de-Matapédia	UNP/LNO	QC	Avignon	21 O/14	47°57′	67°01′
Leonard Island	ISL/ÎLE	NT	Keewatin	34 K	58°12′	77°37′
Leonard Lake	LAKE/LAC	ON	Muskoka	31 E/3	45°04′	79°27′
Leonard Lake	LAKE/LAC	SK	61-2-W2	·63 L/8	54°18′	102°13′
Leonards Beach	UNP/LNO	ON	Simcoe	31 D/5	44°20′	79°32′
Leonardville	UNP/LNO	NB	Charlotte	21 B/15	44°58′	66°57′
Leon Creek	RIV/CDE	BC	Lillooet	92 P/4	51°00′	121°55′
Leon Creek 2	IR/RI	BC	Lillooet	92 I/13	51°00′	121°55′
Leon Creek 2A	IR/RI	BC	Lillooet	92 I/13	51°00′	121°55′
Leopold Island	ISL/ÎLE	NT	Franklin	16 D	64°58′	63°23′
Leopold M'Clintock, Cape	CAPE/CAP	NT	Franklin	89 C	77°33′	116°20′
Leopold, Port	MISC/DIV	NT	Franklin	58 D	73°51′	90°20′
Leoville	VILG/VILG	SK	3-54-11-W3	73 G/12	53°38′	107°33′
Leoville	UNP/LNO	PE	Prince	21 I/16	46°55′	64°08′
Leoville Hills	MTN/MNT	SK	54-10-W3	73 G/11	53°40′	107°26′
Lepage	UNP/LNO	QC	Thérèse-De Blainville	31 H/12	45°44′	73°49′
Lepage	UNP/LNO	ON	Cochrane	42 G/7	49°28′	82°36′
Lepellé, Rivière	RIV/CDE	QC	Kativik	34 P/16	59°57′	72°24′
Le Pensie	UNP/LNO	MB		64 K/6	58°27′	101°10′
Le Petit-Brûlé	UNP/LNO	QC	Mirabel	31 G/9	45°36′	74°02′
Le Petit-Canada	UNP/LNO	QC	Témiscamingue	31 L/11	46°44′	79°05′
Le Petit-Canton	UNP/LNO	QC	Bellechasse	21 L/15	46°52′	70°47′
Le Petit-Ouest	UNP/LNO	QC	Pabok	22 A/7	48°22′	64°39′
Le Petit-Poste	UNP/LNO	QC	Maskinongé	31 I/6	46°20′	73°04′
Le Petit-Sainte-Marie	UNP/LNO	QC	Francheville	31 I/9	46°35′	72°15′
Le Petit-Saint-Marcellin	UNP/LNO	QC	Rimouski-Neigette	22 C/8	48°23′	68°14′
Le Petit-Village	UNP/LNO	QC	Communauté urbaine de Québec	21 L/12	46°44′	71°32′
Le Petit-Village	UNP/LNO	QC	Maskinongé	31 I/7	46°17′	72°54′
Le Pied-de-l'Île	UNP/LNO	QC	Pontiac	31 F/15	45°51′	77°00′
Lepine	UNP/LNO	SK	19-42-25-W2	73 A/12	52°38′	105°35′
L'Épiphanie	CITY/VIL1	QC	L'Assomption	31 H/14	45°51′	73°29′
L'Épiphanie	VILG/VILG	QC	L'Assomption	31 H/14	45°51′	73°29′
Le Plateau	UNP/LNO	QC	Charlevoix-Est	21 N/12	47°44′	70°00′
Le Pré	UNP/LNO	QC	Les Îles-de-la-Madeleine	11 N/5	47°25′	61°48′
Lepreau	UNP/LNO	NB	Charlotte	21 G/1	45°10′	66°28′
Lepreau	GEOG/GÉOG	NB	Charlotte	21 G/2	45°13′	66°32′
Lepreau, Point	CAPE/CAP	NB	Charlotte	21 G/1	45°04′	66°27′
Lepreau River	RIV/CDE	NB	Charlotte	21 G/1	45°10′	66°28′
Le Précieux-Sang	UNP/LNO	QC	Bécancour	31 I/8	46°18′	72°24′
Lequille	UNP/LNO	NS	Annapolis	21 A/11	44°44′	65°29′
L'Érable	MUN1/AZM1	QC	L'Érable	21 L/5	46°15′	71°45′
Le Radar	UNP/LNO	QC	Lotbinière	21 L/6	46°20′	71°09′
Le Rageois, Lac	LAKE/LAC	QC	Caniapiscau	23 F/3	53°14′	69°08′
Le Remous	UNP/LNO	QC	Charlevoix-Est	21 M/9	47°43′	70°00′
Le Renversé	UNP/LNO	QC	Matane	22 B/11	48°42′	67°20′
Le Rocher	UNP/LNO	QC	Le Haut-Saint-Laurent	31 H/4	45°06′	73°54′
Le Rocher-Fendu	UNP/LNO	QC	Pontiac	31 F/10	45°44′	76°43′
Leross	VILG/VILG	SK	11-27A-14-W2	62 M/5	51°01′	103°52′
Leroy	TOWN/VIL2	SK	13-35-20-W2	73 A/2	52°00′	104°44′
Le Roy, Lac	LAKE/LAC	QC	Kativik	34 J/11	58°37′	75°22′
Leroy No. 339	MUN2/AZM2	SK		73 A/2	52°00′	104°45′
Lerwick	UNP/LNO	NB	Victoria	21 J/13	46°51′	67°37′
Léry	CITY/VIL1	QC	Roussillon	31 H/5	45°21′	73°48′
Lesage	UNP/LNO	QC	La Rivière-du-Nord	31 G/16	45°51′	74°04′
Les Basques	MUN1/AZM1	QC	Les Basques	22 C/3	48°06′	69°04′

NAME NOM	ENTITY ENTITÉ	LOC 1 LIEU 1	LOC 2 LIEU 2	MAP CARTE	POSITION	
					LAT	LONG
Les Boules	VILG/VILG	QC	La Mitis	22 B/12	48°41′	67°58′
Les Buissons	UNP/LNO	QC	Manicouagan	22 F/1	49°06′	68°23′
Les Caps	UNP/LNO	QC	Les Îles-de-la-Madeleine	11 N/5	47°24′	61°56′
Les Cèdres	VILG/VILG	QC	Vaudreuil-Soulanges	31 G/8	45°18′	74°03′
Les Cèdres	UNP/LNO	QC	Communauté urbaine de l'Outaouais	31 G/5	45°24′	75°52′
Les Chenaux	UNP/LNO	QC	La Côte-de-Beaupré	21 M/2	47°11′	70°44′
Les Chenaux	UNP/LNO	QC	Vaudreuil-Soulanges	31 G/8	45°25′	74°01′
Les Chutes-de-la-Chaudière	MUN1/AZM1	QC	Les Chutes-de-la-Chaudière	21 L/11	46°42′	71°17′
Les Collines-de-l'Outaouais	MUN1/AZM1	QC	Les Collines-de-l'Outaouais	31 G/12	45°33′	75°52′
Les Coteaux	VILG/VILG	QC	Vaudreuil-Soulanges	31 G/8	45°15′	74°13′
Les Côtes-du-Portage	UNP/LNO	QC	Denis-Riverin	22 H/5	49°15′	65°34′
Lescot, Lac	LAKE/LAC	QC	Témiscamingue	31 M/1	47°14′	78°26′
Les Dalles	UNP/LNO	QC	Montcalm	31 H/13	45°59′	73°31′
Lesdiguières, Lac	LAKE/LAC	QC	Kativik	35 B/10	60°39′	74°50′
Les Éboulements	VILG/VILG	QC	Charlevoix	21 M/8	47°29′	70°19′
Les Éboulements-Centre	UNP/LNO	QC	Charlevoix	21 M/8	47°28′	70°20′
Les Éboulements-Est	UNP/LNO	QC	Charlevoix	21 M/9	47°30′	70°16′
Le Secteur-des-Lacs	UNP/LNO	QC	Arthabaska	21 E/13	45°48′	71°55′
Les Écureuils	UNP/LNO	QC	Portneuf	21 L/12	46°40′	71°42′
Les Escoumins	VILG/VILG	QC	La Haute-Côte-Nord	22 C/6	48°21′	69°24′
Les Etchemins	MUN1/AZM1	QC	Les Etchemins	21 L/8	46°24′	70°21′
Les Étroits	UNP/LNO	QC	Témiscouata	21 N/7	47°23′	68°54′
Les Étroits-Nord	UNP/LNO	QC	Témiscouata	21 N/7	47°26′	68°54′
Les Fonds	UNP/LNO	QC	Lotbinière	21 L/12	46°39′	71°36′
Les Grands-Déserts	UNP/LNO	QC	Communauté urbaine de Québec	21 L/14	46°48′	71°25′
Les Grèves	UNP/LNO	QC	Le Bas-Richelieu	31 H/14	45°59′	73°11′
Les Hauteurs	VILG/VILG	QC	La Mitis	22 C/8	48°23′	68°07′
Les Hauteurs-de-Rimouski	UNP/LNO	QC	La Mitis	22 C/8	48°23′	68°07′
Les Hurons	UNP/LNO	QC	Rouville	31 H/6	45°29′	73°13′
Les Îles-de-la-Madeleine	MUN1/AZM1	QC	Les Îles-de-la-Madeleine	11 N/5	47°24′	61°48′
Les Îles-Laval	UNP/LNO	QC	Laval	31 H/12	45°31′	73°51′
Les Îles-Sainte-Marie	UNP/LNO	QC	Côte-Nord-du-Golfe-Saint-Laurent	12 J/5	50°19′	59°39′
Les Îlets	UNP/LNO	QC	Matane	22 B/14	48°59′	67°01′
Les Îlets	UNP/LNO	QC	La Haute-Côte-Nord	22 C/6	48°25′	69°21′
Les Îlets-Jérémie	UNP/LNO	QC	La Haute-Côte-Nord	22 C/15	48°53′	68°48′
Les Îlots-de-Newport	UNP/LNO	QC	Pabok	22 A/7	48°15′	64°46′
Les Islets-Caribou	UNP/LNO	QC	Manicouagan	22 G/6	49°30′	67°14′
Les Jardins-de-Napierville	MUN1/AZM1	QC	Les Jardins-de-Napierville	31 H/4	45°10′	73°31′
Leskard	UNP/LNO	ON	Durham	31 D/2	44°02′	78°39′
Les Laurentides	MUN1/AZM1	QC	Les Laurentides	31 J/2	46°07′	74°36′
Leslie	VILG/VILG	SK	13-31-13-W2	62 M/12	51°42′	103°42′
Leslie	UNP/LNO	QC	Les Îles-de-la-Madeleine	11 N/12	47°37′	61°31′
Leslie-Clapham-et-Huddersfield	VILG/VILG	QC	Pontiac	31 F/16	45°56′	76°29′
Leslieville	UNP/LNO	AB	26-39-5-W5	83 B/7	52°23′	114°36′
Les Maskoutains	MUN1/AZM1	QC	Les Maskoutains	31 H/10	45°37′	72°57′
Les Méchins	VILG/VILG	QC	Matane	22 G/2	49°00′	66°59′
Les Moulins	MUN1/AZM1	QC	Les Moulins	31 H/13	45°45′	73°36′
Les Pays-d'en-Haut	MUN1/AZM1	QC	Les Pays-d'en-Haut	31 G/16	45°57′	74°08′
L'Espérance	UNP/LNO	QC	Montmagny	21 L/16	46°55′	70°15′
Les Petites-Terres	UNP/LNO	QC	Maskinongé	31 I/7	46°17′	72°52′
Les Prairies	UNP/LNO	QC	Montmagny	21 L/15	46°51′	70°39′
Les Prairies	UNP/LNO	QC	Le Fjord-du-Saguenay	22 D/11	48°32′	71°21′
Les Quarante	UNP/LNO	QC	Pabok	22 A/7	48°24′	64°35′
Les Quatre-Chemins-de-la-Huitième	UNP/LNO	QC	Bellechasse	21 L/10	46°37′	70°46′
Les Rapides	UNP/LNO	NB	Madawaska	21 N/7	47°16′	68°36′
Lessard, Lac	LAKE/LAC	QC	La Haute-Côte-Nord	22 F/3	49°08′	69°10′
Less Crossing	UNP/LNO	MB	12-4-E	62 I/2	50°04′	97°00′
Les Sept-Lacs	UNP/LNO	QC	Manicouagan	22 K/10	50°38′	68°50′
Lesser Slave Lake	LAKE/LAC	AB	75-10-W5	83 O/6	55°27′	115°27′
Lesser Slave Lake Provincial Park	PARK/PARC	AB	73,74,75-5,6,7-W5	83 O/7	55°26′	114°49′
Lesser Slave Lake Settlement	UNP/LNO	AB	75-14-W5	83 N/9	55°32′	116°07′
Lesser Slave River	RIV/CDE	AB	71-1-W5	83 O/1	55°10′	114°03′
Lesser Slave River No. 124, Municipal District of	MUN1/AZM1	AB		83 O/1	55°14′	114°20′
Les Souliers-Verts	UNP/LNO	QC	Asbestos	21 E/13	45°45′	71°46′
Lestage, Rivière	RIV/CDE	QC	Kativik	25 D/4	60°10′	71°30′
Lester Beach	UNP/LNO	MB	18,19-7-E	62 I/10	50°35′	96°35′
Lester Creek	RIV/CDE	SK	72-20-W3	73 N/2	55°13′	108°59′
Lesterdale	UNP/LNO	NS	Guysborough	11 F/5	45°27′	61°32′
Lester Jones, Mount	MTN/MNT	BC	Cassiar	104 K/11	58°43′	133°14′
Lester Pearson, Mount	MTN/MNT	BC	Cariboo	83 D/13	52°47′	119°33′
Lestock	VILG/VILG	SK	6-27-14-W2	62 M/12	51°19′	103°59′
Les Trois-Ruisseaux	UNP/LNO	QC	La Côte-de-Gaspé	22 A/16	48°55′	64°16′
Lesueur, Lac	LAKE/LAC	QC	Antoine-Labelle	31 O/6	47°27′	75°18′
Letang	UNP/LNO	NB	Charlotte	21 G/2	45°05′	66°51′
Letang	UNP/LNO	QC	Témiscamingue	31 L/11	46°44′	79°04′

NAME NOM	ENTITY ENTITÉ	LOC 1 LIEU 1	LOC 2 LIEU 2	MAP CARTE	POSITION LAT	LONG
L'Étang-des-Caps	UNP/LNO	QC	Les Îles-de-la-Madeleine	11 N/4	47°14'	62°00'
L'Étang-du-Nord	VILG/VILG	QC	Les Îles-de-la-Madeleine	11 N/5	47°22'	61°57'
L'Étape	UNP/LNO	QC	La Côte-de-Beaupré	21 M/11	47°34'	71°14'
Letellier	UNP/LNO	MB	19,20-2-2-E	62 H/3	49°08'	97°18'
Letete	UNP/LNO	NB	Charlotte	21 G/2	45°04'	66°54'
Lethbridge	CITY/VIL1	AB	8,9-21-W4	82 H/10	49°42'	112°49'
Lethbridge	UNP/LNO	NF		2 C/5	48°22'	53°52'
Lethbridge No. 26, County of	MUN1/AZM1	AB	10-21-W4	82 H/15	49°50'	112°48'
Le Tort, Lacs	LAKE/LAC	QC	Minganie	12 N/10	51°38'	60°32'
Le Trou-à-Balle	UNP/LNO	QC	Avignon	22 B/1	48°10'	66°24'
Le Trou-de-Chat	UNP/LNO	QC	Pabok	22 A/9	48°32'	64°13'
Lett	UNP/LNO	SK	27-37-16-W3	73 C/1	52°12'	108°11'
Letterbreen	UNP/LNO	ON	Grey	41 A/2	44°01'	80°47'
Letterkenny	UNP/LNO	ON	Renfrew	31 F/6	45°22'	77°25'
Letts Corners	UNP/LNO	ON	Renfrew	31 F/11	45°35'	77°06'
Letty Harbour	UNP/LNO	NT	Franklin	97 C	69°51'	124°26'
Levack	UNP/LNO	ON	Sudbury	41 I/11	46°38'	81°23'
Levack	UNP/LNO	ON	Sudbury	41 I/11	46°36'	81°24'
Le Val-Saint-François	MUN1/AZM1	QC	Le Val-Saint-François	31 H/9	45°34'	72°01'
Levasseur Inlet	BAY/BAIE	NT	Franklin	48 B	72°35'	85°35'
Levasseur, Lac	LAKE/LAC	QC	Le Haut-Saint-Maurice	32 B/8	48°28'	74°00'
Leven	UNP/LNO	MB	4-74-1-W	63 P/5	55°23'	97°33'
Levergood Beach	UNP/LNO	ON	Essex	40 J/2	42°01'	83°00'
Lever Lake	LAKE/LAC	NT	Mackenzie	86 F	65°24'	117°16'
Leverrier, Lac	LAKE/LAC	QC	L'Islet	21 K/13	46°47'	69°59'
Leverville	UNP/LNO	NB	Charlotte	21 G/6	45°18'	67°08'
Levesque	UNP/LNO	NB	Madawaska	21 N/8	47°26'	68°16'
Levesque Settlement	UNP/LNO	NB	Madawaska	21 O/4	47°08'	67°45'
Le Vieux-Port	UNP/LNO	QC	Communauté urbaine de Montréal	31 H/12	45°30'	73°33'
Le Village-de-la-Madeleine	UNP/LNO	QC	Portneuf	21 L/12	46°44'	71°40'
Le Village-d'Orvilliers	UNP/LNO	QC	Francheville	31 I/9	46°36'	72°10'
Le Village-Saint-Jean	UNP/LNO	QC	Portneuf	21 L/12	46°44'	71°40'
Leville	UNP/LNO	NS	Lunenburg	21 A/9	44°45'	64°25'
Levine	UNP/LNO	MB	10-12-20-W	62 K/1	50°00'	100°08'
Lévis	CITY/VIL1	QC	Desjardins	21 L/14	46°48'	71°11'
Lévis	UNP/LNO	QC	Desjardins	21 L/14	46°48'	71°11'
Levis, Lac	LAKE/LAC	NT	Mackenzie	85 K	62°37'	117°58'
Levuka	UNP/LNO	SK	23-14-25-W2	72 I/3	50°11'	105°24'
Levvel, Cape	CAPE/CAP	NT	Franklin	59 F	78°59'	94°20'
Lévy, Pointe de	CAPE/CAP	QC	Desjardins	21 L/14	46°49'	71°10'
Lewaseechjeech Brook	RIV/CDE	NF		12 A/12	48°38'	57°57'
Lewes	UNP/LNO	PE	Queens	11 L/2	46°03'	62°45'
Lewes Island	ISL/ÎLE	NT	Franklin	76 N	67°56'	109°00'
Lewin's Cove	VILG/VILG	NF		1 M/3	47°05'	55°13'
Lewis	UNP/LNO	MB	31,32-10-11-E	62 H/16	49°53'	96°04'
Lewis	UNP/LNO	YT		105 D/7	60°20'	134°49'
Lewis Bay West	UNP/LNO	NS	Cape Breton	11 F/16	45°51'	60°21'
Lewis Cass, Mount	MTN/MNT	BC	Cassiar	104 B/6	56°25'	131°05'
Lewis Channel	CHAN/CHEN	BC	Sayward	92 K/2	50°11'	124°56'
Lewis Corners	UNP/LNO	ON	Middlesex	40 I/13	42°46'	81°37'
Lewis Cove Road	UNP/LNO	NS	Richmond	11 F/10	45°39'	60°42'
Lewis Creek	RIV/CDE	SK	3-27-24-W2	72 P/6	51°17'	105°17'
Lewisham	UNP/LNO	ON	Muskoka	31 D/14	44°52'	79°07'
Lewis Head	CAPE/CAP	NF		2 C/13	48°58'	53°45'
Lewis Hills	MTN/MNT	NF		12 B/15	48°48'	58°30'
Lewis Island	ISL/ÎLE	NF		2 C/13	48°58'	53°48'
Lewis Lake	UNP/LNO	NS	Halifax	11 D/13	44°49'	63°46'
Lewis Lake	UNP/LNO	NS	Halifax	11 D/12	44°41'	63°51'
Lewis Lake	LAKE/LAC	NF		2 E/5	49°17'	55°32'
Lewis Lake	LAKE/LAC	ON	Kenora	52 J/6	50°18'	91°05'
Lewis Lake	LAKE/LAC	BC	New Westminster	92 F/16	49°58'	124°21'
Lewis Mountain	UNP/LNO	NS	Inverness	11 K/3	46°01'	61°04'
Lewis Mountain	UNP/LNO	NB	Westmorland	21 I/3	46°03'	65°10'
Lewis Point	UNP/LNO	PE	Queens	11 L/6	46°15'	63°10'
Lewis Point	CAPE/CAP	BC	Rupert	92 L/10	50°33'	126°51'
Lewis Pond	LAKE/LAC	NF		2 D/14	48°58'	55°12'
Lewisporte	TOWN/VIL2	NF		2 E/3	49°15'	55°03'
Lewistown	UNP/LNO	NS	Digby	21 A/5	44°28'	65°57'
Lewisville	UNP/LNO	NB	Westmorland	21 I/2	46°06'	64°46'
Lewvan	UNP/LNO	SK	15-12-16-W2	72 I/1	50°00'	104°06'
Lexau Ranch	UNP/LNO	BC	Peace River	94 B/9	56°31'	122°07'
Leybourne Islands	ISL/ÎLE	NT	Franklin	26 A	64°16'	64°40'
Leyland	UNP/LNO	AB	8-47-23-W5	83 F/3	53°02'	117°19'
Leyson Point	CAPE/CAP	NT	Keewatin	45 P	63°27'	80°56'
Lezbye 6	IR/RI	BC	Range 3 Coast	92 N/8	51°25'	124°04'

NAME NOM	ENTITY ENTITÉ	LOC 1 LIEU 1	LOC 2 LIEU 2	MAP CARTE	POSITION LAT	LONG
L'Hebert, Port	BAY/BAIE	NS	Queens	20 P/15	43°50′	64°57′
Lhoh Cho 29	IR/RI	BC	Range 5 Coast	93 K/16	54°46′	124°13′
Liard Range	MTN/MNT	NT	Mackenzie	95 B/12	60°45′	123°58′
Liard River	UNP/LNO	BC	Cassiar	94 M/8	59°25′	126°05′
Liard River	RIV/CDE	NT/BC/YT		95 H/14	61°51′	121°19′
Liard River 3	IR/RI	BC	Cassiar	104 P/15	59°55′	128°30′
Libau	UNP/LNO	MB	9,16-15-6-E	62 I/7	50°16′	96°43′
Libby Lake	LAKE/LAC	NT	Mackenzie	87 B	68°14′	117°26′
Libbytown	UNP/LNO	QC	Coaticook	21 E/4	45°08′	72°00′
Liberté, Cap	CAPE/CAP	QC	Le Fjord-du-Saguenay	22 D/8	48°20′	70°17′
Liberty	VILG/VILG	SK	21-25-25-W2	72 P/3	51°08′	105°26′
Licford	UNP/LNO	NB	Victoria	21 J/14	46°47′	67°30′
Lichen Mountain	MTN/MNT	BC	Kamloops Division Yale	82 M/3	51°09′	119°16′
Lichteneger, Lac	LAKE/LAC	QC	Jamésie	33 B/6	52°15′	75°13′
Liddon Gulf	BAY/BAIE	NT	Franklin	88 H	75°03′	113°00′
Lido Plage	UNP/LNO	MB		62 H/13	49°53′	97°31′
Lidstone	UNP/LNO	MB	29-35-26-W	63 C/3	52°02′	101°10′
Liebenthal	UNP/LNO	SK	4-20-26-W3	72 K/12	50°40′	109°22′
Liége River	RIV/CDE	AB	30-90-24-W4	84 A/13	56°50′	113°49′
Liersch	UNP/LNO	BC	Cariboo	93 J/6	54°25′	123°21′
Lieu-de-Roches	UNP/LNO	QC	Beauce-Sartigan	21 L/2	46°04′	70°50′
Lieu historique national de L'Anse aux Meadows, Site du patrimoine mondial du - also-aussi - L'Anse aux Meadows National Historic Site World Heritage Site	PARK/PARC	NF		2 M/12	51°36′	55°32′
Lieury	UNP/LNO	ON	Middlesex	40 P/4	43°12′	81°36′
Lièvre, Rivière du	RIV/CDE	QC	Communauté urbaine de l'Outaouais	31 G/11	45°31′	75°26′
Lièvre, Ruisseau du	RIV/CDE	QC	Le Haut-Saint-Maurice	31 O/16	47°57′	74°04′
Lièvres, Île aux	ISL/ÎLE	QC	Kamouraska	21 N/13	47°51′	69°44′
Lifford	UNP/LNO	ON	Durham	31 D/2	44°11′	78°39′
Li Fiord	BAY/BAIE	NT	Franklin	560 A	80°05′	95°25′
Lighthouse Point	UNP/LNO	BC	Cowichan	92 B/14	48°52′	123°17′
Lighthouse Point	CAPE/CAP	NS	Cape Breton	11 G/13	45°54′	59°57′
Lighthouse Point	CAPE/CAP	ON	Essex	40 G/15	41°50′	82°38′
Lighthouse Road	UNP/LNO	NS	Digby	21 A/12	44°38′	65°46′
Lightning Creek	RIV/CDE	SK	2-3-32-W	62 F/4	49°11′	101°42′
Lightning Creek	RIV/CDE	BC	Cariboo	93 G/1	53°01′	122°06′
Light, The	UNP/LNO	QC	Côte-Nord-du-Golfe-Saint-Laurent	12 P/6	51°22′	57°11′
Lightwoods	UNP/LNO	SK	4-42-15-W2	73 A/9	52°35′	104°05′
Ligny-Saint-Flochel	UNP/LNO	QC	Pabok	22 A/8	48°24′	64°28′
Likely	UNP/LNO	BC	Cariboo	93 A/12	52°37′	121°33′
Lilac	UNP/LNO	SK	32-42-13-W3	73 B/12	52°40′	107°50′
L'Île-à-Lafond	UNP/LNO	QC	Francheville	31 I/9	46°34′	72°12′
L'Île-au-Canot	UNP/LNO	QC	Montmagny	21 M/2	47°05′	70°34′
L'Île-au-Pigeon	UNP/LNO	QC	Côte-Nord-du-Golfe-Saint-Laurent	12 P/5	51°24′	57°39′
L'Île-aux-Castors	UNP/LNO	QC	D'Autray	31 I/3	46°05′	73°09′
L'Île-aux-Chats	UNP/LNO	QC	Argenteuil	31 G/9	45°35′	74°23′
L'Île-aux-Coudres	VILG/VILG	QC	Charlevoix	21 M/8	47°24′	70°25′
L'Île-aux-Noix	UNP/LNO	QC	Le Haut-Richelieu	31 H/3	45°08′	73°17′
L'Île-aux-Oies	UNP/LNO	QC	Montmagny	21 M/1	47°08′	70°28′
L'Île-Bizard	CITY/VIL1	QC	Communauté urbaine de Montréal	31 H/5	45°30′	73°54′
L'Île-Bouchard	UNP/LNO	QC	L'Assomption	31 H/14	45°49′	73°21′
L'Île-Cadieux	CITY/VIL1	QC	Vaudreuil-Soulanges	31 G/8	45°26′	74°01′
L'Île-d'Anticosti	VILG/VILG	QC	Minganie	12 E/11	49°30′	63°00′
L'Île-d'Embarras	UNP/LNO	QC	Le Bas-Richelieu	31 I/2	46°05′	72°58′
L'Île-d'Entrée	TOWN/VIL2	QC	Les Îles-de-la-Madeleine	11 N/5	47°16′	61°42′
L'Île-des-Esquimaux	UNP/LNO	QC	Côte-Nord-du-Golfe-Saint-Laurent	12 P/5	51°25′	57°43′
L'Île-des-Pins	UNP/LNO	QC	Francheville	31 I/9	46°34′	72°13′
L'Île-d'Orléans	MUN1/AZM1	QC	L'Île-d'Orléans	21 L/15	46°55′	70°54′
L'Île-Dorval	CITY/VIL1	QC	Communauté urbaine de Montréal	31 H/5	45°26′	73°45′
L'Île-du-Collège	UNP/LNO	QC	Témiscamingue	31 M/5	47°23′	79°31′
L'Île-du-Grand-Calumet	UNP/LNO	QC	Pontiac	31 F/10	45°43′	76°37′
L'Île-du-Havre-Aubert	VILG/VILG	QC	Les Îles-de-la-Madeleine	11 N/4	47°14′	61°57′
L'Île-du-Moine	UNP/LNO	QC	Le Bas-Richelieu	31 I/3	46°04′	73°01′
L'Île-du-Sable	UNP/LNO	QC	Francheville	31 I/9	46°34′	72°10′
L'Île-Enchanteresse	UNP/LNO	QC	La Jacques-Cartier	21 L/14	46°58′	71°12′
L'Île-Madame	UNP/LNO	QC	D'Autray	31 I/3	46°05′	73°05′
L'Île-Merrill	UNP/LNO	QC	Jamésie	32 G/16	49°52′	74°20′
L'Île-Michon	UNP/LNO	QC	Minganie	12 L/1	50°14′	62°02′
L'Île-Nepawa	UNP/LNO	QC	Abitibi-Ouest	32 D/11	48°41′	79°27′
L'Île-Perrot	CITY/VIL1	QC	Vaudreuil-Soulanges	31 H/5	45°23′	73°57′
L'Île-Perrot-Nord	UNP/LNO	QC	Vaudreuil-Soulanges	31 H/5	45°24′	73°59′
L'Île-Saint-Amour	UNP/LNO	QC	D'Autray	31 I/3	46°04′	73°08′
L'Île-Sainte-Thérèse	UNP/LNO	QC	Le Haut-Richelieu	31 H/6	45°22′	73°15′
L'Île-Saint-Régis	UNP/LNO	QC	Le Haut-Saint-Laurent	31 G/2	45°01′	74°39′
L'Île-Siscoe	UNP/LNO	QC	Vallée-de-l'Or	32 C/4	48°09′	77°52′
Lille	UNP/LNO	SK	23-25-16-W3	72 N/1	51°09′	108°08′
Lillestrom	UNP/LNO	SK	13-15-29-W2	72 I/5	50°16′	105°52′

NAME / NOM	ENTITY / ENTITÉ	LOC 1 / LIEU 1	LOC 2 / LIEU 2	MAP / CARTE	POSITION LAT	POSITION LONG
Lillesve	UNP/LNO	MB	20-3-W	62 I/12	50°44′	97°44′
Lillian Lake	LAKE/LAC	BC	Clayoquot	92 E/9	49°34′	126°15′
Lillico Point	CAPE/CAP	NT	Keewatin	34 D	56°32′	79°32′
Lillies	UNP/LNO	ON	Leeds	31 B/12	44°35′	75°50′
Lillooet	VILG/VILG	BC	Lillooet	92 I/12	50°41′	121°56′
Lillooet 1	IR/RI	BC	Lillooet	92 I/12	50°42′	121°56′
Lillooet 1A	IR/RI	BC	Lillooet	92 I/12	50°43′	121°56′
Lillooet Glacier	GLAC/GLAC	BC	Lillooet	92 J/12	50°45′	123°45′
Lillooet Lake	LAKE/LAC	BC	Lillooet	92 J/1	50°15′	122°30′
Lillooet Land District	GEOG/GÉOG	BC		92 O	51°13′	122°40′
Lillooet Ranges	MTN/MNT	BC	Yale Division Yale	92 H/13	49°53′	121°50′
Lillooet River	RIV/CDE	BC	New Westminster	92 G/9	49°45′	122°09′
Lilly Canyon	SEAU/SMER	—		8010	44°50′	49°20′
Lily Bay	UNP/LNO	MB	34-20-6-W	62 J/16	50°46′	98°14′
Lilydale	UNP/LNO	NS	Lunenburg	21 A/8	44°24′	64°21′
Lilydale	UNP/LNO	SK	1-46-24-W3	73 C/14	52°56′	109°22′
Lilyfield	UNP/LNO	MB	8,16-12-2-E	62 I/3	50°00′	97°17′
Lily Lake	UNP/LNO	BC	Range 4 Coast	93 F/15	53°55′	124°33′
Lily Oak	UNP/LNO	ON	Grey	41 A/7	44°25′	80°43′
Lily Plain	UNP/LNO	SK	28-48-1-W3	73 G/1	53°10′	106°05′
Limberlost Lodge	UNP/LNO	ON	Muskoka	31 E/6	45°24′	79°00′
Limbour	UNP/LNO	QC	Communauté urbaine de l'Outaouais	31 G/5	45°29′	75°45′
Lime	UNP/LNO	BC	Lillooet	92 P/4	51°03′	121°41′
Lime Hill	UNP/LNO	NS	Inverness	11 F/14	45°47′	61°07′
Limehouse	UNP/LNO	ON	Halton	30 M/12	43°38′	79°58′
Limekiln	UNP/LNO	NB	York	21 J/7	46°16′	66°47′
Lime Kiln	UNP/LNO	QC	Memphrémagog	31 H/1	45°04′	72°14′
Lime Lake	UNP/LNO	ON	Hastings	31 C/6	44°24′	77°09′
Lime Lake	LAKE/LAC	ON	Hastings	31 C/6	44°24′	77°07′
Limer	UNP/LNO	ON	Algoma	41 N/15	47°58′	84°32′
Limerick	VILG/VILG	SK	18-8-2-W3	72 G/9	49°39′	106°16′
Limerick	MUN2/AZM2	ON	Hastings	31 C/13	44°55′	77°42′
Limerick	UNP/LNO	NB	Restigouche	21 O/11	47°34′	67°20′
Limerick	UNP/LNO	ON	Dundas	31 G/3	45°05′	75°11′
Limerick Lake	LAKE/LAC	ON	Hastings	31 C/13	44°53′	77°37′
Lime Ridge	UNP/LNO	QC	Le Haut-Saint-François	21 E/12	45°37′	71°36′
Limerock	UNP/LNO	NS	Pictou	11 E/10	45°33′	62°51′
Limestone	UNP/LNO	NB	Carleton	21 J/4	46°02′	67°41′
Limestone	UNP/LNO	NB	Victoria	21 J/13	46°55′	67°42′
Limestone	UNP/LNO	MB	1-87-21-E	54 D/9	56°31′	94°08′
Limestone Bay	BAY/BAIE	MB		63 G/15	53°50′	98°53′
Limestone Bay	BAY/BAIE	MB	50,61-18,19-W	63 K/1	54°14′	100°10′
Limestone Island	ISL/ÎLE	NT	Franklin	58 F	74°02′	95°14′
Limestone Lake	LAKE/LAC	MB		54 D/12	56°35′	95°55′
Limestone Lake	LAKE/LAC	SK	64-8,9-W2	63 L/11	54°38′	103°13′
Limestone Point	CAPE/CAP	MB		63 G/15	53°48′	98°51′
Limestone Point	CAPE/CAP	NT	Mackenzie	86 L	66°58′	119°45′
Limestone Point Lake	LAKE/LAC	MB		63 N/2	55°07′	100°32′
Limestone River	RIV/CDE	MB	87-21-E	54 D/9	56°31′	94°07′
L'Immaculée-Conception	UNP/LNO	QC	Avignon	21 O/14	47°57′	67°08′
Limoges	UNP/LNO	ON	Russell	31 G/6	45°20′	75°15′
Limoilou	UNP/LNO	QC	Communauté urbaine de Québec	21 L/14	46°50′	71°14′
Linacre	UNP/LNO	SK	34-17-27-W3	72 K/5	50°29′	109°38′
Linacy	UNP/LNO	NS	Pictou	11 E/10	45°35′	62°36′
Linaluk Island	ISL/ÎLE	NT	Franklin	87 E	70°18′	113°04′
Linaria	UNP/LNO	AB	24-61-2-W5	83 J/8	54°19′	114°08′
Linbarr Lake	LAKE/LAC	ON	Algoma	42 F/3	49°14′	85°07′
Lincoln	TOWN/VIL2	ON	Lincoln	30 M/3	43°10′	79°29′
Lincoln	UNP/LNO	NB	York	21 G/15	45°54′	66°35′
Lincoln	UNP/LNO	AB	36-65-24-W4	83 I/12	54°40′	113°30′
Lincoln	GEOG/GÉOG	NB	Sunbury	21 G/15	45°49′	66°35′
Lincoln	GEOG/GÉOG	ON		30 M/3	43°00′	79°15′
Lincoln Bay	BAY/BAIE	NT	Franklin	120 E	82°07′	61°50′
Lincoln, Mer de - also-aussi - Lincoln Sea	SEA/MER	NT	Franklin	120 E/11	82°30′	62°00′
Lincoln Park	UNP/LNO	BC	New Westminster	92 G/7	49°17′	122°45′
Lincoln Sea - also-aussi - Lincoln, Mer de	SEA/MER	NT	Franklin	120 E/11	82°30′	62°00′
Lincolnville	UNP/LNO	NS	Guysborough	11 F/12	45°30′	61°33′
Lincolnville	UNP/LNO	ON	York	31 D/3	44°01′	79°14′
Lind	UNP/LNO	ON	Perth	40 P/3	43°15′	81°09′
Lindale	UNP/LNO	AB	21-49-5-W5	83 G/7	53°15′	114°39′
Lindbergh	UNP/LNO	AB	34-56-5-W4	73 E/15	53°53′	110°40′
Lindbrook	UNP/LNO	AB	12-51-20-W4	83 H/7	53°24′	112°49′
Lindell	UNP/LNO	BC	New Westminster	92 G/1	49°01′	122°03′
Lindell Beach	UNP/LNO	BC	New Westminster	92 G/1	49°02′	122°01′
Lindeman	UNP/LNO	BC	Cassiar	104 M/14	59°47′	135°05′

NAME NOM	ENTITY ENTITÉ	LOC 1 LIEU 1	LOC 2 LIEU 2	MAP CARTE	POSITION LAT	LONG
Linden	VILG/VILG	AB	30-25-W4	82 P/11	51°36′	113°28′
Linden	UNP/LNO	NS	Cumberland	11 E/13	45°53′	63°50′
Linden	UNP/LNO	MB	17,20-8-5-E	62 H/10	49°40′	96°53′
Linden Beach	UNP/LNO	ON	Essex	40 J/2	42°01′	82°45′
Lindenkohl Basin	SEAU/SMER	—		8005	42°30′	67°50′
Linden Lanes	UNP/LNO	MB		62 G/13	49°50′	99°59′
Linden Valley	UNP/LNO	ON	Victoria	31 D/7	44°22′	78°52′
Lindenwood	UNP/LNO	ON	Grey	41 A/10	44°41′	80°59′
Linden Woods	UNP/LNO	MB		62 H/14	49°50′	97°11′
Lindenwoods - see-voir - Linden Woods	UNP/LNO	MB		62 H/14	49°50′	97°11′
Lindequist	UNP/LNO	SK	33-43-17-W3	73 C/16	52°45′	108°25′
Lindsay	TOWN/VIL2	ON	Victoria	31 D/7	44°21′	78°44′
Lindsay	MUN2/AZM2	ON	Bruce	41 H/3	45°05′	81°22′
Lindsay	UNP/LNO	NB	Carleton	21 J/5	46°15′	67°42′
Lindsay Lake	UNP/LNO	NS	Halifax	11 E/3	45°03′	63°01′
Lindsley Bay	BAY/BAIE	NT	Mackenzie	86 K	66°08′	117°46′
Lindstrom Lake	LAKE/LAC	SK		63 M/6	55°22′	103°27′
Lindstrom Peninsula	CAPE/CAP	NT	Franklin	49 A	76°36′	83°40′
Lindys	UNP/LNO	NB	Kings	21 H/14	45°48′	65°19′
Lineboro	UNP/LNO	QC	Memphrémagog	31 H/1	45°00′	72°10′
Line Creek	UNP/LNO	BC	Kootenay	82 G/15	49°52′	114°51′
Lingan	UNP/LNO	NS	Cape Breton	11 K/1	46°14′	60°03′
Lingan Bay	BAY/BAIE	NS	Cape Breton	11 K/1	46°13′	60°03′
Lingan Road	UNP/LNO	NS	Cape Breton	11 K/1	46°11′	60°08′
Lingham Lake	LAKE/LAC	ON	Hastings	31 C/14	44°46′	77°25′
Lingley	UNP/LNO	NB	Kings	21 G/8	45°22′	66°15′
Lingman Lake	UNP/LNO	ON	Kenora	53 F/15	53°51′	92°54′
Lingwick	VILG/VILG	QC	Le Haut-Saint-François	21 E/11	45°35′	71°20′
Link Lake	LAKE/LAC	BC	Range 3 Coast	93 D/5	52°25′	127°40′
Linklater	UNP/LNO	MB	11-7-28-W	62 F/11	49°34′	101°11′
Linklater Lake	LAKE/LAC	ON	Thunder Bay	52 I/10	50°33′	88°48′
Linkletter	VILG/VILG	PE	Prince	11 L/5	46°25′	63°50′
Linko	UNP/LNO	ON	Thunder Bay	52 A/13	48°53′	89°59′
Links Mills	UNP/LNO	ON	Lennox and Addington	31 C/2	44°13′	76°46′
Lintlaw	VILG/VILG	SK	6-36-9-W2	63 D/3	52°04′	103°14′
Linton	MUN2/AZM2	QC	Portneuf	31 P/8	47°15′	72°15′
Linton	UNP/LNO	QC	Portneuf	31 P/8	47°15′	72°15′
Linton	UNP/LNO	ON	York	30 M/13	43°56′	79°40′
Linton Corner	UNP/LNO	NB	Victoria	21 J/14	46°53′	67°25′
Linwood	UNP/LNO	NS	Antigonish	11 F/12	45°39′	61°35′
Linwood	UNP/LNO	NS	Antigonish	11 F/12	45°38′	61°35′
Linwood	UNP/LNO	ON	Waterloo	40 P/10	43°35′	80°43′
Lionel-Cinq-Mars, Réserve écologique	PARK/PARC	QC	Lotbinière	21 L/12	46°31′	71°46′
Lions Bay	VILG/VILG	BC	New Westminster	92 G/6	49°27′	123°14′
Lions Den	BAY/BAIE	NF		2 C/12	48°33′	53°47′
Lion's Head	VILG/VILG	ON	Bruce	41 A/14	44°59′	81°15′
Liot Point	CAPE/CAP	NT	Franklin	98 C	73°06′	124°53′
Lipp's Beach	HAM/HAM	SK	8-23-23-W2	72 I/14	50°56′	105°10′
Lippy Point	CAPE/CAP	BC	Rupert	102 I/8	50°28′	128°06′
Lipsett	UNP/LNO	SK	10-44-19-W2	73 A/15	52°47′	104°41′
*Lipsett	UNP/LNO	BC	Kootenay	82 F/1	49°07′	116°27′
Lipsett Lake	LAKE/LAC	ON	Sudbury	42 B/3	48°15′	83°20′
Lipton	VILG/VILG	SK	26-22-14-W2	62 L/13	50°54′	103°51′
Lipton No. 217	MUN2/AZM2	SK		62 L/13	51°00′	103°55′
Lisbon	UNP/LNO	ON	Waterloo	40 P/7	43°28′	80°47′
Lisburn	UNP/LNO	AB	23-56-6-W5	83 G/15	53°51′	114°46′
Liscomb	UNP/LNO	NS	Guysborough	11 F/4	45°01′	62°00′
Liscomb Harbour	BAY/BAIE	NS	Guysborough	11 E/1	45°00′	62°02′
Liscomb Island	ISL/ÎLE	NS	Guysborough	11 C/13	44°59′	61°57′
Liscomb Mills	UNP/LNO	NS	Guysborough	11 E/1	45°00′	62°05′
Liscomb Point	CAPE/CAP	NS	Guysborough	11 C/13	44°59′	61°59′
Liscomb River	RIV/CDE	NS	Guysborough	11 E/1	45°00′	62°06′
Lisgar	UNP/LNO	ON	Peel	30 M/12	43°36′	79°47′
Lisgar Station	UNP/LNO	QC	Drummond	31 H/9	45°39′	72°17′
*Lisgar Station	UNP/LNO	ON		30 M/12	43°36′	79°46′
Lish-Leesh-Tum 17	IR/RI	BC	Kamloops Division Yale	92 I/6	50°26′	121°20′
Lisieux	HAM/HAM	SK	9-4-30-W2	72 H/5	49°17′	105°58′
Lisle	UNP/LNO	ON	Simcoe	31 D/5	44°16′	79°59′
L'Isle-aux-Allumettes	VILG/VILG	QC	Pontiac	31 F/14	45°53′	77°07′
L'Isle-aux-Allumettes-Partie-Est	VILG/VILG	QC	Pontiac	31 F/14	45°51′	77°01′
L'Isle-aux-Grues	UNP/LNO	QC	Montmagny	21 M/2	47°04′	70°33′
L'Isle-Maligne	UNP/LNO	QC	Lac-Saint-Jean-Est	22 D/12	48°35′	71°38′
L'Islet	CITY/VIL1	QC	L'Islet	21 M/1	47°06′	70°21′
L'Islet	MUN1/AZM1	QC	L'Islet	21 N/4	47°06′	69°59′
L'Islet-sur-Mer	VILG/VILG	QC	L'Islet	21 M/1	47°08′	70°22′

NAME NOM	ENTITY ENTITÉ	LOC 1 LIEU 1	LOC 2 LIEU 2	MAP CARTE	POSITION LAT	LONG
L'Isle-Verte	TOWN/VIL2	QC	Rivière-du-Loup	22 C/3	48°01′	69°20′
L'Isle-Verte-Ouest	UNP/LNO	QC	Rivière-du-Loup	22 C/3	48°00′	69°21′
Lismore	UNP/LNO	NS	Pictou	11 E/9	45°42′	62°16′
Lisson Settlement	UNP/LNO	NB	Kings	21 H/11	45°37′	65°25′
Listen Lake	LAKE/LAC	SK	62-5-W3	73 J/7	54°21′	106°42′
Lister	UNP/LNO	BC	Kootenay	82 F/1	49°03′	116°28′
Lister Rapids Park	UNP/LNO	MB		62 H/14	49°59′	97°03′
Listerville	UNP/LNO	NB	Carleton	21 J/12	46°34′	67°46′
Liston Island	ISL/ÎLE	NT	Franklin	87 A	68°53′	114°25′
Listowel	TOWN/VIL2	ON	Perth	40 P/10	43°44′	80°57′
Listuguj 1	IR/RI	QC	Avignon	22 B/2	48°03′	66°45′
Litchfield	VILG/VILG	QC	Pontiac	31 F/10	45°45′	76°35′
Litchfield	UNP/LNO	NS	Annapolis	21 A/13	44°47′	65°36′
Little Abitibi Lake	LAKE/LAC	ON	Cochrane	42 H/7	49°24′	80°33′
Little Abitibi River	RIV/CDE	ON	Cochrane	42 I/5	50°29′	81°32′
Little Anse	UNP/LNO	NS	Richmond	11 F/7	45°29′	60°56′
Little Atlin Lake	LAKE/LAC	YT		105 C/5	60°15′	133°58′
Little Ausable River	RIV/CDE	ON	Middlesex	40 P/4	43°11′	81°32′
Little Aylmer	UNP/LNO	ON	Elgin	40 I/15	42°49′	80°59′
Little Barachois Brook	RIV/CDE	NF		12 B/8	48°27′	58°26′
Little Barachois River	RIV/CDE	NF		1 N/4	47°01′	53°48′
Little Barasway	UNP/LNO	NF		1 M/1	47°11′	54°03′
Little Bartibog	UNP/LNO	NB	Northumberland	21 P/3	47°08′	65°27′
Little Bass River	UNP/LNO	NS	Colchester	11 E/5	45°24′	63°48′
Little Bay	VILG/VILG	NF		2 E/12	49°36′	55°57′
Little Bay	UNP/LNO	NF		1 M/3	47°10′	55°06′
Little Bay	UNP/LNO	NF		11 P/9	47°37′	56°02′
Little Bay	BAY/BAIE	NF		11 P/10	47°38′	56°40′
Little Bay Arm	BAY/BAIE	NF		2 E/12	49°35′	55°58′
Little Bay East	VILG/VILG	NF		1 M/10	47°33′	54°51′
Little Bay Head	CAPE/CAP	NF		11 O/11	47°35′	59°05′
Little Bay Island	ISL/ÎLE	NF		2 E/12	49°39′	55°48′
Little Bay Islands	VILG/VILG	NF		2 E/12	49°39′	55°47′
Little Bay West	UNP/LNO	NF		1 M/12	47°30′	55°43′
Little Beach	UNP/LNO	NB	Saint John	21 H/6	45°23′	65°28′
Little Bear Cape	CAPE/CAP	NT	Franklin	59 D	77°40′	88°14′
Little Bear Creek	RIV/CDE	ON	Kent	40 J/9	42°32′	82°24′
Little Bear Lake	LAKE/LAC	SK	61,62-18-W2	73 I/7	54°20′	104°35′
Little Bear River	RIV/CDE	NT	Mackenzie	96 C	64°55′	125°54′
Little Beaver River	RIV/CDE	MB		54 E/12	57°44′	95°30′
Little Black Bear 84	IR/RI	SK		62 M/3	51°00′	103°23′
Little Black Island	ISL/ÎLE	NF		2 E/10	49°32′	54°58′
Little Black River	UNP/LNO	MB	32,33-21-9-E	62 I/16	50°50′	96°19′
Little Bona	UNP/LNO	NF		1 M/7	47°22′	54°34′
Little Bone 73A - see-voir - Little Bone 74B	IR/RI	SK		62 M/1	51°01′	102°28′
Little Bone 74B	IR/RI	SK	23-4-W2	62 M/1	51°01′	102°28′
Little Bow Provincial Park	PARK/PARC	AB	2-15-22-W4	82 I/2	50°13′	112°56′
Little Bow River	RIV/CDE	AB	2-11-19-W4	82 H/16	49°53′	112°29′
Little Branch	UNP/LNO	NB	Northumberland	21 P/3	47°00′	65°13′
Little Bras d'Or	UNP/LNO	NS	Cape Breton	11 K/1	46°14′	60°17′
Little Bras d'Or South Side	UNP/LNO	NS	Cape Breton	11 K/8	46°17′	60°18′
Little Brehat	UNP/LNO	NF		2 M/5	51°27′	55°29′
Little Bridge Creek	RIV/CDE	SK	19-48-14-W2	73 H/1	53°09′	104°02′
Little Bridge Creek	RIV/CDE	BC	Lillooet	92 P/11	51°39′	121°16′
Little Britain	UNP/LNO	ON	Victoria	31 D/7	44°17′	78°52′
Little Britain	UNP/LNO	ON	Sudbury	41 I/6	46°30′	81°01′
Little Britain	UNP/LNO	MB		62 I/2	50°06′	96°57′
Little Brockville	UNP/LNO	ON	Grenville	31 C/9	44°35′	76°09′
Little Brook	UNP/LNO	NS	Digby	21 B/8	44°18′	66°07′
Little Brook Station	UNP/LNO	NS	Digby	21 B/8	44°17′	66°06′
Little Brule	UNP/LNO	NF		1 M/9	47°40′	54°07′
Little Buffalo	UNP/LNO	ON	Brant	40 P/1	43°00′	80°10′
Little Buffalo	UNP/LNO	SK	50-13-W3	73 G/5	53°58′	107°53′
Little Buffalo	UNP/LNO	AB	11-86-14-W5M	84 C/8	56°26′	116°07′
Little Buffalo River	UNP/LNO	NT	Mackenzie	85 H	61°00′	113°45′
Little Buffalo River	RIV/CDE	BC/AB		94 I/8	58°21′	120°13′
Little Buffalo River	RIV/CDE	NT/AB		85 H/4	61°00′	113°46′
Little Bullhead	UNP/LNO	MB	21-31-5-E	62 P/10	51°40′	96°50′
Little Burnt Bay	TOWN/VIL2	NF		2 E/6	47°20′	55°05′
Little Cadotte River	RIV/CDE	AB	88-20-W5	84 C/11	56°41′	117°06′
Little Cape	CAPE/CAP	NF		1 M/5	47°16′	55°50′
Little Cape	CAPE/CAP	ON	Kenora	43 O/5	55°17′	83°42′
Little Catalina	TOWN/VIL2	NF		2 C/11	48°33′	53°02′
Little Cedar Brook	RIV/CDE	NB	Victoria	21 O/6	47°20′	67°11′
Little Chaudière Dam	MISC/DIV	ON	Nipissing	41 I/1	46°09′	80°08′

NAME NOM	ENTITY ENTITÉ	LOC 1 LIEU 1	LOC 2 LIEU 2	MAP CARTE	POSITION	
					LAT	LONG
Little Chicago	UNP/LNO	NT	Mackenzie	106 O	67°12′	130°15′
Little Churchill River	RIV/CDE	MB		54 E/11	57°30′	95°22′
Little Clarke Lake	LAKE/LAC	SK	63-6,7-W3	73 J/7	54°28′	106°55′
Little Codroy Pond	LAKE/LAC	NF		11 O/14	47°50′	59°06′
Little Codroy River	RIV/CDE	NF		11 O/14	47°46′	59°19′
Little Colinet Island	ISL/ÎLE	NF		1 N/4	47°03′	53°40′
Little Cornwallis Island	ISL/ÎLE	NT	Franklin	68 H	75°30′	96°30′
Littlecote Channel	CHAN/CHEN	NT	Franklin	26 A	64°37′	65°35′
Little Creek	RIV/CDE	ON	Lennox and Addington	31 C/2	44°11′	76°56′
Little Current	TOWN/VIL2	ON	Manitoulin	41 H/13	45°58′	81°56′
Little Current River	RIV/CDE	ON	Cochrane	42 K/15	50°57′	84°36′
Little Cygnet Lake	LAKE/LAC	MB		54 D/15	56°51′	94°53′
Little Dam	UNP/LNO	QC	La Jacques-Cartier	21 L/13	46°53′	71°31′
Little Denier	ISL/ÎLE	NF		2 C/12	48°41′	53°36′
Little Denier Island	ISL/ÎLE	NF		2 E/12	49°33′	55°33′
Little Divide No. 18 South, Improvement District of *- see-voir - Bonnyville No. 87, Municipal District of*	MUN2/AZM2	AB		73 L/16	54°41′	110°37′
Little Doctor Lake	LAKE/LAC	NT	Mackenzie	95 G	61°53′	123°16′
Little Dover	UNP/LNO	NB	Westmorland	21 I/2	46°00′	64°38′
Little Dover (White) Island	ISL/ÎLE	NS	Guysborough	11 F/7	45°16′	60°59′
Little Duck Lake	LAKE/LAC	MB		64 P/5	59°27′	97°44′
Little Dyke	UNP/LNO	NS	Colchester	11 E/5	45°23′	63°33′
Little Egypt	UNP/LNO	ON	Bruce	41 A/3	44°05′	81°22′
Little Egypt Road	UNP/LNO	NS	Pictou	11 E/10	45°38′	62°37′
Little Ekwan River	RIV/CDE	ON	Kenora	43 F/9	53°33′	84°25′
Little Emmeline Lake	LAKE/LAC	SK	69-4-W3	73 J/15	54°58′	106°30′
Little Fishery	UNP/LNO	QC	Côte-Nord-du-Golfe-Saint-Laurent	12 J/15	50°50′	58°58′
Little Fishery	UNP/LNO	AB	12-112-22-W4	84 I/12	58°42′	113°33′
Little Fishing Lake	HAM/HAM	SK	56-24-W3	73 F/13	53°51′	109°33′
Little Fish Lake	LAKE/LAC	AB	28-16,17-W4	82 P/8	51°22′	112°14′
Little Fish Lake Provincial Park	PARK/PARC	AB	4,9-28-16-W4	82 P/8	51°22′	112°12′
Little Flatstone Lake	LAKE/LAC	SK		74 B/4	56°06′	107°42′
Little Fogo Islands	ISL/ÎLE	NF		2 E/16	49°49′	54°07′
Little Forehead Lake	LAKE/LAC	NT	Mackenzie	86 A	64°47′	113°15′
Little Forks	UNP/LNO	NS	Cumberland	21 H/9	45°42′	64°09′
Little Forks Stream	RIV/CDE	NB	Kent	21 I/5	46°22′	65°31′
Little Fort	UNP/LNO	BC	Kamloops Division Yale	92 P/8	51°25′	120°12′
Little French River	RIV/CDE	ON	Nipissing	41 I/1	46°09′	80°02′
Little Gander Pond	LAKE/LAC	NF		2 D/6	48°25′	55°13′
Little Garia Bay	BAY/BAIE	NF		11 O/10	47°39′	58°35′
Little Gaspereau	UNP/LNO	NB	Gloucester	21 P/10	47°33′	64°57′
Little Gem	UNP/LNO	AB	18-32-7-W4	72 M/10	51°44′	110°58′
Little Germany	UNP/LNO	ON	Northumberland	31 D/1	44°13′	78°05′
Little Germany	UNP/LNO	ON	Grey	41 A/8	44°24′	80°26′
Little Gold	UNP/LNO	YT		116 C/2	64°05′	141°00′
Little Grand Lake	LAKE/LAC	NF		12 A/12	48°35′	57°50′
Little Grand Rapids	UNP/LNO	MB	35-14-E	53 D/3	52°02′	95°28′
Little Grand Rapids 14	IR/RI	MB	35-14-E	53 D/3	52°00′	95°25′
Little Green Lake	LAKE/LAC	BC	Lillooet	92 P/6	51°26′	121°03′
Little Gull Lake	LAKE/LAC	NF		2 D/6	48°22′	55°29′
Little Gull River	RIV/CDE	NF		2 D/12	48°30′	55°32′
Little Harbour	UNP/LNO	NF		2 E/10	49°38′	54°43′
Little Harbour	UNP/LNO	NF		1 M/7	47°23′	54°48′
Little Harbour	UNP/LNO	NF		12 H/3	49°08′	57°29′
Little Harbour	UNP/LNO	PE	Kings	11 L/8	46°22′	62°11′
Little Harbour	UNP/LNO	NS	Richmond	11 F/10	45°35′	60°44′
Little Harbour	UNP/LNO	NS	Pictou	11 E/10	45°39′	62°33′
Little Harbour	UNP/LNO	NS	Halifax	11 D/10	44°43′	62°51′
Little Harbour	UNP/LNO	NS	Shelburne	20 P/11	43°43′	65°02′
Little Harbour Deep	UNP/LNO	NF		12 I/2	50°15′	56°33′
Little Harbour Deep River	RIV/CDE	NF		12 I/2	50°15′	56°34′
Little Harbour East	UNP/LNO	NF		1 N/12	47°39′	53°56′
Little Harbour East	UNP/LNO	NF		1 M/10	47°36′	54°52′
Little Harbour River	RIV/CDE	NF		1 N/3	47°08′	53°29′
Little Harbour Road	UNP/LNO	NS	Pictou	11 E/10	45°37′	62°35′
Little Hawk Lake	UNP/LNO	ON	Haliburton	31 E/2	45°08′	78°44′
Little Heart's Ease	UNP/LNO	NF		2 C/4	48°01′	53°42′
Little Hills 158	IR/RI	SK		73 P/3	55°03′	105°25′
Little Hills 158A	IR/RI	SK		73 P/3	55°02′	105°28′
Little Hills 158B	IR/RI	SK		73 P/3	55°01′	105°25′
Little Hope Island	ISL/ÎLE	NS	Queens	20 P/15	43°49′	64°47′
Little Hyland River	RIV/CDE	YT		105 H/9	61°38′	128°20′
Little Island Cove	UNP/LNO	NF		1 N/5	47°26′	53°33′
Little Joe Glodes Pond	LAKE/LAC	NF		12 H/1	49°01′	56°22′
Little Judique	UNP/LNO	NS	Inverness	11 F/14	45°57′	61°29′
Little Judique Ponds	UNP/LNO	NS	Inverness	11 F/13	45°57′	61°31′

NAME / NOM	ENTITY / ENTITÉ	LOC 1 / LIEU 1	LOC 2 / LIEU 2	MAP / CARTE	POSITION LAT	LONG
Little Keele River	RIV/CDE	NT	Mackenzie	96 D	64°42′	126°57′
Little Key River	RIV/CDE	ON	Parry Sound	41 H/15	45°54′	80°32′
Little Klappan River	RIV/CDE	BC	Cassiar	104 H/11	57°35′	129°26′
Little La Cloche Island	ISL/ÎLE	ON	Manitoulin	41 I/4	46°00′	81°45′
Little Lake	UNP/LNO	NB	Sunbury	21 G/10	45°35′	66°52′
Little Lake	UNP/LNO	ON	Simcoe	31 D/5	44°25′	79°40′
Little Lake	UNP/LNO	ON	Wellington	40 P/8	43°25′	80°15′
Little Lake	LAKE/LAC	ON	Northumberland	31 C/4	44°03′	77°49′
Little Lake	LAKE/LAC	ON	Simcoe	31 D/5	44°25′	79°40′
Little Lawn Harbour	BAY/BAIE	NF		1 L/14	46°55′	55°29′
Little Lepreau	UNP/LNO	NB	Charlotte	21 G/1	45°08′	66°27′
Little Limestone Lake	LAKE/LAC	MB		54 D/10	56°39′	94°58′
Little Limestone Lake	LAKE/LAC	MB	55-13-W	63 G/11	53°45′	99°20′
Little Liscomb	UNP/LNO	NS	Guysborough	11 F/4	45°02′	61°58′
Little Liscomb River	RIV/CDE	NS	Guysborough	11 E/1	45°05′	62°08′
Little Longlac	UNP/LNO	ON	Thunder Bay	42 E/10	49°41′	86°59′
Little Long Rapids	UNP/LNO	ON	Cochrane	42 J/1	50°00′	82°10′
Little Lorraine	UNP/LNO	NS	Cape Breton	11 G/13	45°57′	59°52′
Little Mabou	UNP/LNO	NS	Inverness	11 K/4	46°03′	61°31′
Little Magaguadavic Lake	LAKE/LAC	NB	York	21 G/14	45°48′	67°13′
Little Main Restigouche River	RIV/CDE	NB	Restigouche	21 O/11	47°40′	67°30′
Little Maitland River	RIV/CDE	ON	Huron	40 P/14	43°51′	81°18′
Little Manitou Lake	LAKE/LAC	SK	32-25,26-W2	72 P/12	51°44′	105°30′
Little Manitou Lake	LAKE/LAC	SK	42-25,26-W3	73 C/12	52°37′	109°37′
Little Marten Lake	LAKE/LAC	NT	Mackenzie	86 A	64°40′	113°00′
Little Mecatina River - also-aussi - Petit Mécatina, Rivière du	RIV/CDE	NF		12 J/11	50°40′	59°25′
Little Michinappi Lake	LAKE/LAC	NF		13 J/11	54°32′	59°29′
Little Missinaibi Lake	LAKE/LAC	ON	Sudbury	42 B/4	48°13′	83°38′
Little Mortier Bay	BAY/BAIE	NF		1 M/3	47°05′	55°06′
Little Mushamush Lake	LAKE/LAC	NS	Lunenburg	21 A/9	44°31′	64°28′
Little Nahanni River	RIV/CDE	NT	Mackenzie	105 I	62°29′	128°37′
Little Narrows	UNP/LNO	NS	Victoria	11 F/15	45°59′	60°59′
Little Nictau Lake	LAKE/LAC	NB	Restigouche	21 O/7	47°25′	66°51′
Little Nut Lake	LAKE/LAC	SK	38,39-11-W2	63 D/5	52°20′	103°30′
Little Ocean Pond	LAKE/LAC	NF		2 E/1	49°13′	54°11′
Little Otter Creek	RIV/CDE	ON	Elgin	40 I/10	42°44′	80°50′
Little Oyster River	RIV/CDE	BC	Comox	92 F/14	49°53′	125°11′
Little Paradise	UNP/LNO	NF		1 M/8	47°22′	54°35′
Little Partridge River	RIV/CDE	MB/NT		64 N/11	59°41′	101°17′
Little Passage	CHAN/CHEN	NF		1 M/12	47°39′	55°56′
Little Pic River	RIV/CDE	ON	Thunder Bay	42 D/15	48°48′	86°38′
Little Pine and Lucky Man 116	IR/RI	SK		73 C/14	52°55′	109°04′
Little Plate Island	ISL/ÎLE	NF		11 P/1	47°11′	56°04′
Little Playgreen Lake	LAKE/LAC	MB		63 H/13	54°00′	97°55′
Little Point	CAPE/CAP	NT	Franklin	67 D	69°10′	99°16′
Little Point	CAPE/CAP	NT	Franklin	78 H	75°02′	106°13′
Little Pond	UNP/LNO	PE	Kings	11 L/8	46°17′	62°25′
Little Pond	UNP/LNO	NS	Cape Breton	11 K/8	46°17′	60°16′
Little Port Elgin	UNP/LNO	ON	Bruce	41 A/14	44°53′	81°03′
Little Port Head	CAPE/CAP	NF		12 G/1	49°06′	58°26′
Little Port L'Hebert	UNP/LNO	NS	Shelburne	20 P/15	43°46′	64°57′
Little Pumbly Cove	UNP/LNO	NF		12 H/10	49°43′	56°43′
Little Quill Lake	LAKE/LAC	SK		72 P/16	51°55′	104°05′
Little Quirke Lake	LAKE/LAC	ON	Algoma	41 J/10	46°32′	82°36′
Little Quirpon	UNP/LNO	NF		2 M/11	51°35′	55°27′
Little Rancheria River	RIV/CDE	YT/BC		105 A/4	60°12′	129°33′
Little Rapids	UNP/LNO	NF		12 A/13	48°59′	57°44′
Little Rapids	UNP/LNO	ON	Algoma	41 J/5	46°18′	83°33′
Little Rattling Brook	RIV/CDE	NF		2 D/13	48°57′	55°36′
Little Red Deer River	RIV/CDE	AB	6-36-1-W5	83 B/1	52°04′	114°09′
Little Red Indian Pond	LAKE/LAC	NF		12 A/16	48°54′	56°15′
Little Red River	UNP/LNO	AB	28-108-5-W5	84 J/7	58°24′	114°46′
Little Red River 106C	IR/RI	SK		73 H/5	53°30′	105°57′
Little Red River 106D	IR/RI	SK		73 G/9	53°34′	106°03′
Little Ridge	UNP/LNO	NB	Albert	21 H/10	45°39′	64°45′
Little Ridge	UNP/LNO	MB	18-9-W	62 J/10	50°33′	98°42′
Little River	UNP/LNO	NS	Victoria	11 K/8	46°26′	60°28′
Little River	UNP/LNO	NS	Cumberland	11 E/13	45°47′	63°55′
Little River	UNP/LNO	NS	Digby	21 B/8	44°27′	66°09′
Little River	UNP/LNO	NB	Albert	21 H/15	45°54′	64°59′
Little River	UNP/LNO	BC	Comox	92 F/10	49°44′	124°55′
Little River	UNP/LNO	YT		105 D/13	60°54′	135°42′
Little River	RIV/CDE	NF		1 M/13	47°47′	55°49′
Little River	RIV/CDE	NB	Gloucester	21 P/12	47°36′	65°40′
Little River	RIV/CDE	NB	Sunbury	21 G/16	45°57′	66°16′

NAME	ENTITY	LOC 1	LOC 2	MAP	POSITION	
NOM	ENTITÉ	LIEU 1	LIEU 2	CARTE	LAT	LONG
Little River	RIV/CDE	NB	Victoria	21 O/4	47°03′	67°44′
Little River Harbour	UNP/LNO	NS	Yarmouth	20 O/9	43°43′	66°02′
Little River Lake	LAKE/LAC	NS	Kings	21 A/16	44°57′	64°28′
Little Rocky Lake	LAKE/LAC	NT	Mackenzie	65 L	62°21′	102°12′
Little Sachigo Lake	LAKE/LAC	ON	Kenora	53 K/1	54°09′	92°11′
Little St. Lawrence	UNP/LNO	NF		1 L/14	46°56′	55°21′
Little St. Lawrence River	RIV/CDE	NF		1 L/14	46°56′	55°22′
Little Salmon	UNP/LNO	YT		105 L/4	62°03′	135°41′
Little Salmonier	UNP/LNO	NF		1 M/3	47°04′	55°11′
Little Salmonier River	RIV/CDE	NF		1 N/4	47°02′	53°45′
Little Salmon Lake	LAKE/LAC	YT		105 L/2	62°11′	134°40′
Little Salmon River	RIV/CDE	NB	Saint John	21 H/6	45°28′	65°17′
Little Salmon River	RIV/CDE	YT		105 L/4	62°03′	135°40′
Little Salmon River 10	IR/RI	YT		105 L/4	62°03′	135°40′
Little Sand Lake	LAKE/LAC	ON	Kenora	52 L/2	50°02′	94°41′
Little Sand Lake	LAKE/LAC	MB		64 G/15	57°48′	98°33′
Little Sands	UNP/LNO	PE	Kings	11 E/15	45°58′	62°39′
Little Sandy Pond	LAKE/LAC	NF		12 H/1	49°07′	56°23′
Little Saskatchewan	UNP/LNO	MB	31-8-W	62 O/10	51°41′	98°34′
Little Saskatchewan 48	IR/RI	MB		62 O/10	51°41′	98°35′
Little Saskatchewan 48B	IR/RI	MB		62 O/9	51°39′	98°25′
Little Saskatchewan River	RIV/CDE	MB	33-10-20-W	62 F/16	49°52′	100°07′
Littles Corners	UNP/LNO	ON	Waterloo	40 P/8	43°21′	80°16′
Little Seal River	RIV/CDE	MB		54 M/2	59°12′	94°47′
Little Seldom	UNP/LNO	NF		2 E/9	49°36′	54°12′
Little Shemogue	UNP/LNO	NB	Westmorland	21 I/1	46°07′	64°01′
Little Shemogue Harbour	BAY/BAIE	NB	Westmorland	21 I/1	46°10′	64°05′
Little Shippegan	UNP/LNO	NB	Gloucester	21 P/15	47°53′	64°36′
Little Shuswap Lake	LAKE/LAC	BC	Kamloops Division Yale	82 L/13	50°51′	119°38′
Little Sled Lake	LAKE/LAC	SK		73 J/5	54°26′	107°30′
Little Smoky	UNP/LNO	AB	29-74-19-W5	83 N/7	55°26′	116°52′
Little Smoky	UNP/LNO	AB	66-21,22-W5	83 K/11	54°44′	117°11′
Little Smoky River	RIV/CDE	AB	15-77-24-W5	83 N/12	55°40′	117°38′
Little Southwest Miramichi River	RIV/CDE	NB	Northumberland	21 I/13	46°57′	65°50′
Littles Point	CAPE/CAP	ON	Essex	40 G/15	41°59′	82°55′
Little Springs 8	IR/RI	BC	Lillooet	92 O/16	51°51′	122°05′
Little Springs 18	IR/RI	BC	Lillooet	92 O/16	51°52′	122°05′
Little Stull Lake	LAKE/LAC	MB		53 K/10	54°33′	92°41′
Little Sturgeon Island	ISL/ÎLE	MB		63 A/4	52°11′	97°47′
Little Sturgeon River	RIV/CDE	ON	Nipissing	31 L/5	46°22′	79°45′
Little Swan River	HAM/HAM	SK	36-39-2-W2	63 D/8	52°24′	102°10′
Little Tancook	UNP/LNO	NS	Lunenburg	21 A/8	44°28′	64°08′
Little Teslin Lake	UNP/LNO	YT		105 C/6	60°29′	133°28′
Little Toba River	RIV/CDE	BC	Range 1 Coast	92 K/9	50°31′	124°12′
Little Tobique River	RIV/CDE	NB	Victoria	21 O/3	47°15′	67°09′
Little Touchwood Hills	MTN/MNT	SK		72 P/8	51°16′	104°12′
Little Tracadie	UNP/LNO	NB	Gloucester	21 P/10	47°32′	64°57′
Little Traverse, The	BAY/BAIE	ON	Kenora	52 E/7	49°15′	94°43′
Little Trout Lake	LAKE/LAC	ON	Kenora	52 N/3	51°04′	93°17′
Little Trout Lake	LAKE/LAC	ON	Kenora	52 F/4	49°09′	93°45′
Little Turtle Lake	LAKE/LAC	ON	Rainy River	52 C/15	48°47′	92°40′
Little Turtle River	RIV/CDE	ON	Rainy River	52 C/15	48°46′	92°36′
Little Vermilion Lake	LAKE/LAC	ON	Kenora	52 N/5	51°16′	93°50′
Little Wawa Lake	LAKE/LAC	ON	Sudbury	41 O/13	47°51′	83°50′
Little White Lake	LAKE/LAC	BC	Lillooet	92 P/5	51°17′	121°41′
Little White Mountain	MTN/MNT	BC	Similkameen Division Yale	82 E/11	49°42′	119°20′
Little White River	RIV/CDE	ON	Algoma	41 J/6	46°23′	83°20′
Little Whiteshell Lake	LAKE/LAC	MB	12-16-E	52 L/3	50°02′	95°21′
Littlewood	UNP/LNO	ON	Middlesex	40 I/14	42°51′	81°20′
Little Woody	UNP/LNO	SK	13-4-29-W2	72 H/5	49°18′	105°47′
Little Yoho Brook	RIV/CDE	NB	Sunbury	21 G/10	45°41′	66°46′
Little Zeballos	UNP/LNO	BC	Nootka	92 E/15	49°57′	126°49′
Livain, Lac à	LAKE/LAC	NB	Kent	21 I/15	46°57′	64°55′
Livelong	HAM/HAM	SK	35-51-19-W3	73 F/7	53°27′	108°42′
Lively	UNP/LNO	ON	Sudbury	41 I/6	46°26′	81°09′
Livernois, Rivière	RIV/CDE	QC	Le Haut-Saint-Maurice	31 P/6	47°18′	73°29′
Liverpool	UNP/LNO	NS	Queens	21 A/2	44°02′	64°43′
Liverpool	UNP/LNO	ON	Ontario	30 M/14	43°50′	79°05′
Liverpool Bay	BAY/BAIE	NT	Franklin	107 D	69°54′	129°30′
Liverpool, Cape	CAPE/CAP	NT	Franklin	38 C	73°40′	78°06′
Living Springs	UNP/LNO	ON	Wellington	40 P/16	43°45′	80°24′
Livingston	UNP/LNO	NF		23 G/16	53°56′	66°27′
Livingstone	UNP/LNO	ON	Algoma	41 J/6	46°15′	83°26′
Livingstone	UNP/LNO	BC	New Westminster	92 G/2	49°08′	122°35′
Livingstone	UNP/LNO	YT		105 E/8	61°20′	134°20′

NAME NOM	ENTITY ENTITÉ	LOC 1 LIEU 1	LOC 2 LIEU 2	MAP CARTE	POSITION	
					LAT	LONG
Livingstone Cove	UNP/LNO	NS	Antigonish	11 F/13	45°52′	61°59′
Livingstone Creek	UNP/LNO	ON	Algoma	41 J/6	46°16′	83°28′
Livingstone Fiord	BAY/BAIE	NT	Franklin	26 J	66°03′	67°45′
Livingstone Lake	LAKE/LAC	SK		74 J/11	58°37′	107°16′
Livingstone Point	CAPE/CAP	NS	Antigonish	11 F/13	45°52′	61°59′
Livingstone River	RIV/CDE	NT	Franklin	25 N	63°07′	69°44′
Livingston No. 331	MUN2/AZM2	SK		63 C/4	52°05′	101°55′
Lizard Head Mountain	MTN/MNT	BC	Kamloops Division Yale	92 P/16	51°46′	120°11′
Lizard Lake	UNP/LNO	SK	34-38-14-W3	73 B/5	52°19′	107°56′
Lizard Point	CAPE/CAP	BC	Rupert	92 L/10	50°40′	126°53′
Lizard Point 62	IR/RI	MB		62 K/10	50°41′	100°56′
Lizotte	UNP/LNO	QC	Le Domaine-du-Roy	32 A/1	48°06′	72°11′
Lizzie Lake	LAKE/LAC	BC	New Westminster	92 J/1	50°08′	122°23′
Llewellyn Glacier	GLAC/GLAC	BC	Cassiar	104 M/1	59°05′	134°05′
Lloy	UNP/LNO	NS	Halifax	11 D/11	44°39′	63°20′
Lloyd	UNP/LNO	ON	Lanark	31 F/1	45°09′	76°20′
Lloyd Lake	LAKE/LAC	ON	Timiskaming	41 P/14	47°51′	81°00′
Lloyd Lake	LAKE/LAC	MB	15,21-77-2-E	63 P/11	55°41′	97°14′
Lloyd Lake	LAKE/LAC	SK		74 F/7	57°22′	108°57′
Lloydminster	CITY/VIL1	SK	35-49-28-W3	73 F/5	53°17′	110°00′
Lloydminster	CITY/VIL1	AB	1-50-1-W4	73 E/8	53°17′	110°00′
Lloyd Point	CAPE/CAP	NT	Franklin	36 D	64°26′	78°02′
Lloyds	UNP/LNO	NS	Kings	21 H/2	45°01′	64°39′
Lloyds Hill	UNP/LNO	AB	22-37-6-W4	73 D/2	52°12′	110°48′
Lloyds Lake	LAKE/LAC	NF		12 A/5	48°23′	57°31′
Lloyds River	RIV/CDE	NF		12 A/11	48°33′	57°13′
Lloydtown	UNP/LNO	ON	York	30 M/13	43°59′	79°42′
*Loasby	UNP/LNO	BC	Kootenay	82 F/2	49°10′	116°33′
Lobbville	UNP/LNO	MB	28-13-13W	62 J/3	50°08′	99°12′
Lobo	MUN2/AZM2	ON	Middlesex	40 P/3	43°02′	81°30′
Lobo	UNP/LNO	ON	Middlesex	40 P/3	43°00′	81°26′
Lobo Siding	UNP/LNO	ON	Middlesex	40 I/14	42°59′	81°23′
Lobster Cove	UNP/LNO	NF		12 H/12	49°37′	57°57′
Lobster Harbour	UNP/LNO	NF		2 E/10	49°36′	54°41′
Lobster Point	CAPE/CAP	NF		2 M/5	51°18′	55°36′
Lobstick	UNP/LNO	AB	30-53-8-W5	83 G/11	53°36′	115°10′
Lobstick Bay	BAY/BAIE	ON	Kenora	52 F/5	49°25′	93°55′
Lobstick Island	ISL/ÎLE	SK		74 N/5	59°30′	109°40′
Lobstick River	RIV/CDE	AB	29-53-7-W5	83 G/10	53°37′	115°00′
Lobstick Settlement	UNP/LNO	AB	58-18-W4	83 I/2	54°02′	112°36′
Lochaber	VILG/VILG	QC	Papineau	31 G/11	45°38′	75°13′
Lochaber	UNP/LNO	NS	Antigonish	11 E/8	45°25′	62°02′
Lochaber	UNP/LNO	QC	Papineau	31 G/11	45°35′	75°19′
Lochaber Lake	LAKE/LAC	NS	Antigonish	11 E/8	45°25′	62°02′
Lochaber Mines	UNP/LNO	NS	Halifax	11 E/1	45°00′	62°28′
Lochaber-Partie-Ouest	VILG/VILG	QC	Papineau	31 G/11	45°37′	75°18′
Lochalsh	UNP/LNO	ON	Huron	41 A/4	44°01′	81°39′
Lochalsh	UNP/LNO	ON	Algoma	42 C/8	48°21′	84°16′
Loch Broom	UNP/LNO	NS	Pictou	11 E/10	45°39′	62°45′
Lochearn	UNP/LNO	AB	21-39-7-W5	83 B/7	52°22′	114°58′
Lochiel	MUN2/AZM2	ON	Glengarry	31 G/7	45°25′	74°36′
Lochiel	UNP/LNO	ON	Glengarry	31 G/7	45°23′	74°37′
Lochinvar	UNP/LNO	ON	Glengarry	31 G/7	45°27′	74°40′
Lochinvar	UNP/LNO	AB	15-41-26-W4	83 A/12	52°32′	113°40′
Loch Katrine	UNP/LNO	NS	Antigonish	11 F/5	45°26′	61°56′
Loch Leven	UNP/LNO	NF		12 B/2	48°10′	58°52′
Lochlin	UNP/LNO	ON	Haliburton	31 D/15	44°56′	78°34′
Loch Lomond	UNP/LNO	NS	Richmond	11 F/15	45°46′	60°34′
Loch Lomond	UNP/LNO	NB	Saint John	21 H/5	45°21′	65°52′
Loch Lomond West	UNP/LNO	NS	Richmond	11 F/15	45°45′	60°37′
Loch Point	CAPE/CAP	NT	Franklin	88 D	73°10′	113°57′
Lochside	UNP/LNO	NS	Richmond	11 F/15	45°46′	60°40′
Lochside	UNP/LNO	NS	Richmond	11 F/10	45°33′	60°59′
Lochview Road	UNP/LNO	NS	Halifax	11 D/13	44°49′	63°37′
Lochwinnoch	UNP/LNO	ON	Renfrew	31 F/7	45°29′	76°32′
Locke Bay	BAY/BAIE	ON	Kenora	52 E/15	49°50′	94°38′
Lockeport	TOWN/VIL2	NS	Shelburne	20 P/11	43°42′	65°07′
Lockeport	UNP/LNO	BC	Queen Charlotte	103 B/12	52°43′	131°50′
Lockeport Station	UNP/LNO	NS	Shelburne	20 P/11	43°44′	65°06′
Lockerby	UNP/LNO	ON	Sudbury	41 I/6	46°28′	81°00′
Lockerby	UNP/LNO	ON	Bruce	41 A/6	44°19′	81°14′
Locke Road	UNP/LNO	PE	Prince	21 I/9	46°43′	64°19′
Locker Point	CAPE/CAP	NT	Mackenzie	87 A	68°15′	113°59′
Lockers Bay	BAY/BAIE	NF		2 C/13	48°54′	53°57′
Lockers Flat Island	ISL/ÎLE	NF		2 C/13	48°53′	53°50′

NAME NOM	ENTITY ENTITÉ	LOC 1 LIEU 1	LOC 2 LIEU 2	MAP CARTE	POSITION LAT	LONG
Lockers Reach	RIVF/EFLV	NF		2 C/13	48°55′	53°49′
Lockhart Lake	LAKE/LAC	NT	Mackenzie	75 M	63°40′	112°05′
Lockhart River	RIV/CDE	NT	Mackenzie	75 K	62°48′	108°54′
Lockharts Mill	UNP/LNO	NB	Carleton	21 J/5	46°29′	67°33′
Lockhartville	UNP/LNO	NS	Kings	21 H/1	45°05′	64°13′
Lock Island	ISL/ÎLE	NT	Franklin	68 D	73°18′	97°10′
Lockport	UNP/LNO	MB		62 I/2	50°05′	96°57′
Lock's Cove	UNP/LNO	NF		2 M/5	51°20′	55°57′
Locks Cove	UNP/LNO	NF		11 P/10	47°38′	56°31′
Locks Harbour	UNP/LNO	NF		2 E/5	49°27′	55°30′
Locksley	UNP/LNO	ON	Renfrew	31 F/11	45°44′	77°08′
Lockstead	UNP/LNO	NB	Northumberland	21 I/13	46°46′	65°52′
Lockston	UNP/LNO	NF		2 C/6	48°24′	53°23′
Lockton	UNP/LNO	ON	Peel	30 M/13	43°55′	79°52′
Lockwood	VILG/VILG	SK	11-31-22-W2	72 P/11	51°39′	105°01′
Lockwood, Cape	CAPE/CAP	NT	Franklin	340 B	80°16′	84°04′
Lockwood Lake	LAKE/LAC	SK	76-22-W3	73 N/11	55°36′	109°17′
Lockwood Park	UNP/LNO	ON	Middlesex	40 I/14	42°52′	81°19′
Locust Hill	UNP/LNO	ON	York	30 M/14	43°53′	79°12′
Lodge	UNP/LNO	AB	24-39-7-W5	83 B/7	52°22′	114°54′
Lodge Bay	UNP/LNO	NF		3 D/4	52°14′	55°51′
Lodge Creek	RIV/CDE	SK/AB		72 F/4	49°00′	109°43′
Lodge, Mount	MTN/MNT	BC	Cassiar	114 P/4	59°07′	137°32′
Lodgepole	UNP/LNO	AB	31-47-9-W5	83 G/3	53°06′	115°19′
Lodgeroom Corners	UNP/LNO	ON	Hastings	31 C/6	44°28′	77°22′
Lodges	UNP/LNO	NF		1 N/12	47°33′	53°38′
Lodi	UNP/LNO	ON	Stormont	31 G/3	45°13′	75°01′
Lo-Ellen	UNP/LNO	ON	Sudbury	41 I/7	46°27′	80°59′
Lofthouse Point	CAPE/CAP	NT	Keewatin	56 D/2	64°08′	94°53′
Logan	MUN2/AZM2	ON	Perth	40 P/11	43°32′	81°09′
Logan Canyon	SEAU/SMER	—		8007	43°15′	59°50′
Logan, Cuvettes - also-aussi - Logan Troughs	SEAU/SMER	—		801-A	47°38′	59°54′
Logan Glacier	GLAC/GLAC	YT		115 C/15	60°47′	140°30′
Logan Island	ISL/ÎLE	ON	Thunder Bay	52 I/1	50°07′	88°27′
Logan Lake	MUN1/AZM1	BC	Kamloops Division Yale	92 I/7	50°30′	120°48′
Logan Lake	LAKE/LAC	NB	Northumberland	21 O/2	47°06′	66°43′
Logan Lake	LAKE/LAC	ON	Victoria	31 D/15	44°52′	78°59′
Logan Lake	LAKE/LAC	AB	126-3-W4	74 M/16	59°57′	110°24′
Logan Lake	LAKE/LAC	AB	70,71-9,10-W4	73 M/3	55°05′	111°21′
Logan, Mont	MTN/MNT	QC	Matane	22 B/15	48°53′	66°38′
Logan, Mount	MTN/MNT	YT		115 C/9	60°34′	140°23′
Logan Mountains	MTN/MNT	YT/NT		105 H/10	61°45′	128°38′
Logan, Port	MISC/DIV	NT	Franklin	57 G	71°24′	93°06′
Logan River	RIV/CDE	AB	71-12-W4	73 M/4	55°09′	111°42′
Logan's 6	IR/RI	BC	Kamloops Division Yale	92 H/15	49°59′	120°33′
Logans Point	CAPE/CAP	NS	Pictou	11 E/10	45°43′	62°38′
Logan Subdivision	UNP/LNO	NS	Pictou	11 E/10	45°37′	62°37′
Logan Troughs - also-aussi - Logan, Cuvettes	SEAU/SMER	—		801-A	47°38′	59°54′
Loganville	UNP/LNO	NS	Pictou	11 E/11	45°37′	63°03′
Log Cabin	UNP/LNO	BC	Cassiar	104 M/15	59°46′	134°57′
Log Creek	RIV/CDE	BC	Yale Division Yale	92 I/4	50°01′	121°38′
Loggiecroft	UNP/LNO	NB	Kent	21 I/15	46°50′	64°56′
Loggie Lodge	UNP/LNO	NB	Northumberland	21 J/15	46°58′	66°32′
Loggieville	UNP/LNO	NB	Northumberland	21 P/3	47°04′	65°23′
Login Bay	BAY/BAIE	NT	Keewatin	57 A	68°40′	89°44′
Log Valley	UNP/LNO	SK	23-20-8-W3	72 J/11	50°42′	107°01′
Logy Bay	UNP/LNO	NF		1 N/10	47°38′	52°41′
Logy Bay-Middle Cove-Outer Cove	TOWN/VIL2	NF		1 N/10	47°38′	52°41′
Lohbiee 3	IR/RI	BC	Lillooet	92 O/5	51°08′	123°56′
L'Oiseau-Bleu	UNP/LNO	QC	Asbestos	21 E/13	45°48′	71°55′
Lois Island	ISL/ÎLE	NT	Franklin	49 H	79°05′	83°53′
Loïs, Lac	LAKE/LAC	QC	Abitibi-Ouest	32 D/10	48°34′	78°44′
Lois Lake	LAKE/LAC	BC	New Westminster	92 F/16	49°51′	124°14′
Lokken, Mount	MTN/MNT	YT		105 E/16	62°00′	134°24′
Lokla 4	IR/RI	BC	Lillooet	92 J/7	50°23′	122°43′
Loks Land	ISL/ÎLE	NT	Franklin	25 I	62°26′	64°38′
Lola Lake	LAKE/LAC	ON	Algoma	42 C/7	48°22′	84°38′
Lolo, Mount	MTN/MNT	BC	Kamloops Division Yale	92 I/16	50°48′	120°07′
Lombardy	UNP/LNO	ON	Leeds	31 C/16	44°49′	76°05′
Lombell	UNP/LNO	AB	5-59-9-W5	83 J/3	54°05′	115°18′
Lombrette	UNP/LNO	QC	La Côte-de-Beaupré	21 M/2	47°10′	70°45′
Lombrette, Rivière	RIV/CDE	QC	La Côte-de-Beaupré	21 M/2	47°08′	70°48′
Lomier, Lac	LAKE/LAC	QC	Jamésie	33 L/16	54°51′	78°15′
Lomond	VILG/VILG	AB	14-16-20-W4	82 I/7	50°21′	112°39′
Lomond	UNP/LNO	NF		12 H/5	49°28′	57°46′

NAME / NOM	ENTITY / ENTITÉ	LOC 1 / LIEU 1	LOC 2 / LIEU 2	MAP / CARTE	POSITION LAT	LONG
Lomond, Loch	LAKE/LAC	NS	Richmond	11 F/10	45°45′	60°36′
Lomond, Loch	LAKE/LAC	NB	Saint John	21 H/5	45°22′	65°52′
Lomond, Loch	LAKE/LAC	ON	Thunder Bay	52 A/3	48°15′	89°20′
Lomond No. 37	MUN2/AZM2	SK		62 E/5	49°25′	103°50′
Lona Bay	BAY/BAIE	NT	Franklin	36 C	64°20′	77°35′
Londesborough	UNP/LNO	ON	Huron	40 P/11	43°42′	81°29′
London	CITY/VIL1	ON	Middlesex	40 I/14	42°59′	81°14′
London	MUN2/AZM2	ON	Middlesex	40 P/3	43°05′	81°19′
Londonderry	UNP/LNO	NS	Colchester	11 E/5	45°29′	63°36′
Londonderry	UNP/LNO	NB	Kings	21 H/11	45°35′	65°24′
Londonderry Station	UNP/LNO	NS	Colchester	11 E/5	45°28′	63°34′
London Settlement	UNP/LNO	NB	Queens	21 G/9	45°39′	66°02′
Lonebutte	UNP/LNO	AB	32-27-15-W4	82 P/8	51°21′	112°09′
Lone Butte	UNP/LNO	BC	Lillooet	92 P/11	51°33′	121°12′
Lonebutte Bay	BAY/BAIE	NT	Franklin	36 D/8	64°28′	78°02′
Lone Cabin Creek	RIV/CDE	BC	Lillooet	92 O/8	51°19′	122°14′
Lone Island Lake	LAKE/LAC	MB	12-16-E	52 L/3	50°01′	95°24′
Lone Lake	LAKE/LAC	NT	Mackenzie	65 D	60°42′	103°49′
Lonely Bay	BAY/BAIE	NT	Mackenzie	85 G	61°45′	115°23′
Lonely Island	ISL/ÎLE	ON	Manitoulin	41 H/11	45°34′	81°28′
Lonely Lake	UNP/LNO	MB	24-25-12-W	62 O/3	51°10′	99°02′
Lonely Lake	LAKE/LAC	MB		62 O/3	51°09′	99°05′
Lonely Point	CAPE/CAP	ON	Manitoulin	41 G/9	45°41′	82°21′
Lone Pine	UNP/LNO	ON	Rainy River	52 B/13	48°46′	91°37′
Lone Pine	UNP/LNO	AB	27-61-8-W5	83 J/6	54°18′	115°07′
Lonepine Creek	RIV/CDE	AB	19-30-25-W4	82 P/12	51°34′	113°30′
Lone Prairie	UNP/LNO	BC	Peace River	93 P/11	55°34′	121°23′
Lone Rock	HAM/HAM	SK	15-47-27-W3	73 F/4	53°03′	109°53′
Lonesand	UNP/LNO	MB	22-3-9-E	62 H/1	49°13′	96°18′
Lonesome Butte	UNP/LNO	SK	35-1-4-W3	72 G/1	49°05′	106°27′
Lonesome Cove	UNP/LNO	NF		12 P/7	51°24′	56°33′
Lone Spruce	UNP/LNO	MB	8-18-10-W	62 J/10	50°32′	98°49′
Lone Spruce	UNP/LNO	SK	12-34-8-W2	62 M/15	51°55′	103°00′
Lone Tree No. 18	MUN2/AZM2	SK		72 F/1	49°10′	108°10′
Long Bay	UNP/LNO	ON	Manitoulin	41 G/16	45°48′	82°24′
Long Bay	BAY/BAIE	ON	Kenora	52 E/8	49°28′	94°10′
Long Beach	UNP/LNO	NF		1 N/14	47°57′	53°03′
Long Beach	UNP/LNO	NF		1 K/11	46°38′	53°08′
Long Beach	UNP/LNO	NF		2 C/5	48°26′	53°34′
Long Beach	UNP/LNO	NF		1 N/13	48°00′	53°49′
Long Beach	UNP/LNO	NS	Cape Breton	11 J/4	46°09′	59°51′
Long Beach	UNP/LNO	ON	Victoria	31 D/7	44°27′	78°44′
Long Beach	UNP/LNO	ON	Welland	30 L/14	42°52′	79°23′
Longbeach	UNP/LNO	BC	Kootenay	82 F/11	49°37′	117°05′
Longbeak Point	CAPE/CAP	BC	Nanaimo	92 F/10	49°37′	124°50′
Long Body Creek	UNP/LNO	MB	23,26-32-6-E	62 P/15	51°46′	96°39′
Longbow Lake	UNP/LNO	ON	Kenora	52 E/9	49°43′	94°20′
Longbow Lake	LAKE/LAC	ON	Kenora	52 E/9	49°43′	94°19′
Long Branch	UNP/LNO	ON	York	30 M/12	43°35′	79°32′
Longburn	UNP/LNO	MB	23-13-8-W	62 J/1	50°07′	98°28′
Long Cove	UNP/LNO	NF		1 N/12	47°34′	53°40′
Long Cove	UNP/LNO	NF		1 M/3	47°04′	55°11′
Long Creek	UNP/LNO	PE	Queens	11 L/3	46°10′	63°16′
Long Creek	UNP/LNO	NB	Queens	21 H/13	45°53′	65°46′
Long Creek	RIV/CDE	SK	15-2-8-W2	62 E/2	49°07′	102°59′
Longfellow Inlet	BAY/BAIE	NT	Franklin	67 A	68°10′	98°20′
Longford	UNP/LNO	ON	Ontario	31 D/11	44°40′	79°20′
Longford Point	CAPE/CAP	NT	Franklin	68 G	75°45′	103°13′
Long Grade	UNP/LNO	NF		11 O/11	47°37′	59°12′
Long Gull Pond	LAKE/LAC	NF		12 B/9	48°34′	58°26′
Long Harbour	UNP/LNO	NF		1 N/5	47°26′	53°48′
Long Harbour	UNP/LNO	BC	Saltspring Island	92 B/14	48°51′	123°27′
Long Harbour	BAY/BAIE	NF		1 M/11	47°42′	55°03′
Long Harbour Head	CAPE/CAP	NF		1 N/5	47°23′	53°56′
Long Harbour-Mount Arlington Heights	TOWN/VIL2	NF		1 N/5	47°26′	53°51′
Long Harbour River	RIV/CDE	NF		1 M/15	47°48′	54°56′
Long Harbour Station	UNP/LNO	NF		1 N/5	47°28′	53°44′
Long Hill	UNP/LNO	NS	Victoria	11 K/2	46°07′	60°42′
Longhope	UNP/LNO	SK	27-50-18-W3	73 F/7	53°20′	108°34′
Long Island	ISL/ÎLE	NF		1 M/8	47°30′	54°06′
Long Island	ISL/ÎLE	NF		1 M/7	47°20′	54°40′
Long Island	ISL/ÎLE	NF		2 E/6	49°26′	55°02′
Long Island	ISL/ÎLE	NF		2 D/14	48°50′	55°03′
Long Island	ISL/ÎLE	NF		2 E/12	49°36′	55°42′
Long Island	ISL/ÎLE	NF		11 P/9	47°39′	56°00′

NAME NOM	ENTITY ENTITÉ	LOC 1 LIEU 1	LOC 2 LIEU 2	MAP CARTE	POSITION LAT	LONG
Long Island	ISL/ÎLE	NF		13 O/3	55°07′	59°25′
Long Island	ISL/ÎLE	NS	Halifax	11 D/10	44°41′	62°54′
Long Island	ISL/ÎLE	NS	Digby	21 B/8	44°20′	66°16′
Long Island	ISL/ÎLE	NB	Kings	21 G/8	45°23′	66°02′
Long Island	ISL/ÎLE	NB	Charlotte	21 B/10	44°44′	66°43′
Long Island	ISL/ÎLE	SK		74 N/7	59°16′	108°52′
Long Island	ISL/ÎLE	BC	New Westminster	92 H/5	49°29′	121°50′
Long Island	ISL/ÎLE	NT	Keewatin	33 L	54°52′	79°25′
Long Island Bay	BAY/BAIE	NB	Charlotte	21 B/10	44°45′	66°45′
Long Island Bay	BAY/BAIE	MB		62 O/13	51°48′	99°41′
Long Island Lake	LAKE/LAC	BC	Kamloops Division Yale	92 P/8	51°29′	120°25′
Long Island Main	UNP/LNO	NS	Cape Breton	11 K/1	46°12′	60°23′
Long Island Point	CAPE/CAP	NF		1 M/9	47°42′	54°05′
Long Islands	ISL/ÎLE	NF		2 C/12	48°35′	53°40′
Long Island Sound	CHAN/CHEN	NT	Keewatin	33 L/14	54°48′	79°22′
Long Island Tickle	CHAN/CHEN	NF		2 E/12	49°34′	55°40′
Longlac	TOWN/VIL2	ON	Thunder Bay	42 E/15	49°48′	86°31′
Long, Lac	LAKE/LAC	QC	Témiscouata	21 N/7	47°24′	68°55′
Long Lake	UNP/LNO	ON	Frontenac	31 C/10	44°41′	76°46′
Long Lake	UNP/LNO	MB	22-15-E	52 L/14	50°52′	95°23′
Long Lake	LAKE/LAC	NF		12 A/6	48°26′	57°11′
Long Lake	LAKE/LAC	NS	Halifax	11 E/2	45°00′	62°58′
Long Lake	LAKE/LAC	NS	Annapolis	21 A/11	44°39′	65°14′
Long Lake	LAKE/LAC	NB	Victoria	21 O/2	47°02′	66°54′
Long Lake	LAKE/LAC	ON	Frontenac	31 C/10	44°40′	76°46′
Long Lake	LAKE/LAC	ON	Simcoe	31 D/14	44°47′	79°29′
Long Lake	LAKE/LAC	ON	Muskoka	31 E/6	45°20′	79°30′
Long Lake	LAKE/LAC	ON	Sudbury	41 I/6	46°22′	81°05′
Long Lake	LAKE/LAC	ON	Thunder Bay	42 E/7	49°30′	86°50′
Long Lake	LAKE/LAC	BC	Lillooet	92 P/5	51°24′	121°57′
Long Lake	LAKE/LAC	BC	Range 2 Coast	92 M/3	51°14′	127°08′
Long Lake 58	IR/RI	ON	Thunder Bay	42 E/15	49°47′	86°32′
Long Lake 77 - see-voir - Ginoogaming First Nation 77	IR/RI	ON		42 E/10	49°44′	86°31′
Long Lake Provincial Park	PARK/PARC	AB	63-19-W4	83 I/7	54°27′	112°46′
Longlaketon No. 219	MUN2/AZM2	SK		72 I/15	50°55′	104°35′
Longland, Chute	FALL/CHUT	QC	Kativik	34 F/7	57°28′	76°43′
Longland, Rivière	RIV/CDE	QC	Kativik	34 F/7	57°27′	76°44′
Long Ledge	SHL/H-FD	NF		12 B/15	48°53′	58°41′
Longlegged Lake	LAKE/LAC	ON	Kenora	52 L/16	50°45′	94°05′
Longley	UNP/LNO	NB	Victoria	21 J/14	46°50′	67°18′
Longmoor	UNP/LNO	ON	Halton	30 M/5	43°22′	79°46′
Long Mountain	MTN/MNT	BC	Osoyoos Division Yale	82 L/3	50°05′	119°15′
Long Neck Island 9	IR/RI	BC	Metchosin	92 B/5	48°19′	123°36′
Long Plain	UNP/LNO	MB	22,27,28-10-8-W	62 G/16	49°51′	98°29′
Long Plain 6	IR/RI	MB		62 G/16	49°50′	98°29′
Long Point	UNP/LNO	NF		12 B/10	48°46′	58°48′
Long Point	UNP/LNO	NS	Inverness	11 F/14	45°49′	61°29′
Long Point	UNP/LNO	NB	Kings	21 H/12	45°36′	65°54′
Long Point	UNP/LNO	ON	Leeds	31 C/9	44°30′	76°07′
Long Point	UNP/LNO	ON	Victoria	31 D/10	44°33′	78°52′
Long Point	UNP/LNO	ON	Norfolk	40 I/9	42°35′	80°25′
Long Point	CAPE/CAP	NF		1 N/7	47°23′	52°43′
Long Point	CAPE/CAP	NF		1 M/8	47°24′	54°12′
Long Point	CAPE/CAP	NF		13 I/4	54°06′	57°58′
Long Point	CAPE/CAP	NF		12 A/15	48°47′	58°46′
Long Point	CAPE/CAP	NF		13 G/11	53°42′	59°19′
Long Point	CAPE/CAP	NS	Victoria	11 K/16	46°51′	60°18′
Long Point	CAPE/CAP	NS	Inverness	11 F/14	45°48′	61°29′
Long Point	CAPE/CAP	ON	Frontenac	31 C/1	44°06′	76°29′
Long Point	CAPE/CAP	ON	Prince Edward	30 N/15	43°56′	76°54′
Long Point	CAPE/CAP	ON	Norfolk	40 I/9	42°34′	80°15′
Long Point	CAPE/CAP	ON	Grey	41 A/9	44°32′	80°18′
Long Point	CAPE/CAP	ON	Cochrane	42 P/8	51°20′	80°23′
Long Point	CAPE/CAP	MB		63 G/2	53°02′	98°40′
Long Point	CAPE/CAP	MB	14-41-23-W	63 C/10	52°31′	100°40′
Long Point	CAPE/CAP	NT	Franklin	77 D	69°06′	105°26′
Long Point	CAPE/CAP	NT	Franklin	89 A	76°11′	112°22′
Long Point Bay	BAY/BAIE	ON	Norfolk	40 I/9	42°40′	80°10′
Long Point Island	ISL/ÎLE	ON	Kenora	52 E/8	49°26′	94°07′
Long Pond	UNP/LNO	NF		1 N/10	47°31′	52°58′
Long Pond	LAKE/LAC	NF		2 D/16	48°53′	54°10′
Long Pond	LAKE/LAC	NF		1 M/16	47°53′	54°24′
Long Pond	LAKE/LAC	NF		12 H/1	49°12′	56°02′
Long Pond	LAKE/LAC	NF		12 B/8	48°23′	58°06′
Long Pond Ground	UNP/LNO	QC	Côte-Nord-du-Golfe-Saint-Laurent	12 P/5	51°29′	57°50′

NAME NOM	ENTITY ENTITÉ	LOC 1 LIEU 1	LOC 2 LIEU 2	MAP CARTE	POSITION LAT	LONG
Longpre Lake	LAKE/LAC	NT	Keewatin	65 A	60°42′	97°38′
Longrais, Lac	LAKE/LAC	QC	Caniapiscau	23 K/1	54°08′	68°22′
Long Range Mountains	MTN/MNT	NF		12 H/14	50°00′	57°00′
Long Reach	UNP/LNO	NB	Kings	21 G/8	45°28′	66°06′
Long Reach	RIVF/EFLV	NB	Kings	21 G/8	45°26′	66°09′
Long Reach	RIVF/EFLV	ON	Prince Edward	31 C/3	44°08′	77°04′
Long Reach Island	ISL/ÎLE	NF		2 C/12	48°44′	53°51′
Long River	UNP/LNO	PE	Queens	11 L/5	46°29′	63°33′
Long Sault	UNP/LNO	ON	Stormont	31 G/2	45°02′	74°53′
Longs Creek	UNP/LNO	NB	York	21 G/15	45°52′	66°56′
Long Settlement	UNP/LNO	NB	Carleton	21 J/5	46°24′	67°45′
Long Spruce	UNP/LNO	MB	22-85-20-E	54 D/8	56°23′	94°22′
Longtinville	UNP/LNO	ON	Russell	31 G/6	45°16′	75°11′
Longtom Lake	LAKE/LAC	NT	Mackenzie	86 F	65°10′	117°50′
Long Tunnel 5	IR/RI	BC	Yale Division Yale	92 H/11	49°44′	121°26′
Long Tunnel 5A	IR/RI	BC	Yale Division Yale	92 H/11	49°44′	121°27′
Long Tusket Lake	LAKE/LAC	NS	Digby	21 A/5	44°21′	65°46′
Longue-Pointe	VILG/VILG	QC	Minganie	22 I/8	50°16′	64°09′
Longue Pointe, La	CAPE/CAP	QC	Côte-Nord-du-Golfe-Saint-Laurent	12 P/6	51°25′	57°12′
Longue Pointe, La	CAPE/CAP	QC	Minganie	22 I/8	50°15′	64°10′
Longue Pointe, La	CAPE/CAP	QC	Jamésie	33 D/10	52°45′	78°52′
Longueuil	CITY/VIL1	QC	Champlain	31 H/11	45°32′	73°30′
Longueuil	MUN2/AZM2	ON	Prescott	31 G/10	45°35′	74°45′
Longview	VILG/VILG	AB	20-18-2-W5	82 J/9	50°32′	114°14′
Longwood	UNP/LNO	ON	Middlesex	40 I/13	42°51′	81°34′
Longworth	UNP/LNO	BC	Cariboo	93 H/14	53°55′	121°28′
Loni Beach	UNP/LNO	MB	20-19-4-E	62 I/10	50°39′	96°59′
Lonira	UNP/LNO	AB	4-59-10-W5	83 J/3	54°05′	115°26′
Lonsdale	UNP/LNO	ON	Hastings	31 C/6	44°16′	77°08′
Lonsdale Station	UNP/LNO	ON	Hastings	31 C/6	44°15′	77°10′
Lookout, Cape	CAPE/CAP	ON	Kenora	43 O/5	55°18′	83°56′
Looma	UNP/LNO	AB	35-50-23-W4	83 H/6	53°22′	113°15′
Loomis	UNP/LNO	SK	14-3-21-W3	72 F/2	49°13′	108°44′
Loon	UNP/LNO	ON	Thunder Bay	52 A/10	48°38′	88°46′
Loon Bay	UNP/LNO	NF		2 E/7	49°16′	54°50′
Loon Bay	BAY/BAIE	NF		2 E/7	49°20′	54°50′
Loon Creek	RIV/CDE	BC	Lillooet	92 P/3	51°02′	121°26′
Loonhaunt Lake	LAKE/LAC	ON	Rainy River	52 F/3	49°01′	93°30′
Loonhead Lake	LAKE/LAC	MB	69-20-W	63 K/16	54°57′	100°29′
Loon Lake	VILG/VILG	SK	58-22-W3	73 K/3	54°02′	109°10′
Loon Lake	UNP/LNO	AB	17-87-9-W5	84 B/11	56°33′	115°24′
Loon Lake	UNP/LNO	BC	Lillooet	92 P/3	51°05′	121°18′
Loon Lake	LAKE/LAC	NS	Guysborough	11 F/5	45°17′	61°33′
Loon Lake	LAKE/LAC	ON	Manitoulin	41 G/14	45°53′	83°02′
Loon Lake	LAKE/LAC	MB/SK		63 N/13	55°51′	101°58′
Loon Lake	LAKE/LAC	BC	Lillooet	92 P/3	51°06′	121°15′
Loon Lake	LAKE/LAC	NT	Mackenzie	106 I	66°37′	128°43′
Loon Lake 4	IR/RI	BC	Lillooet	92 P/3	51°05′	121°20′
Loon Lake 10	IR/RI	BC	Lillooet	92 P/13	51°52′	121°58′
Loon Lake No. 561	MUN2/AZM2	SK		73 F/14	53°57′	109°21′
Loon, Pointe	CAPE/CAP	QC	Jamésie	33 D/2	52°03′	78°42′
Loon River	UNP/LNO	SK	59-21-W3	73 K/3	54°07′	109°02′
Loon River	RIV/CDE	MB		63 N/13	55°53′	101°58′
Loon River	RIV/CDE	SK	20-51-22-W2	73 H/6	53°25′	105°13′
Loon River	RIV/CDE	AB	87-10-W5	84 G/3	57°08′	115°03′
Loon Straits	UNP/LNO	MB		62 P/10	51°32′	96°35′
Loos	UNP/LNO	BC	Cariboo	93 H/10	53°36′	120°42′
Loose Lake	LAKE/LAC	BC	Range 1 Coast	92 L/16	50°45′	126°23′
Loquin, Lac	LAKE/LAC	QC	Kativik	24 B/15	56°47′	66°43′
Lorado	UNP/LNO	SK	74 N/7		59°30′	108°40′
Loran	UNP/LNO	NF		3 D/4	52°15′	55°36′
Loranger	UNP/LNO	QC	Antoine-Labelle	31 J/6	46°26′	75°04′
Loranger Island	ISL/ÎLE	SK		64 E/14	57°57′	103°25′
Lord Creek	RIV/CDE	YT		116 O/11	67°33′	139°09′
Lord Lindsay River	RIV/CDE	NT	Franklin	57 F	70°08′	92°25′
Lord Mayor Bay	BAY/BAIE	NT	Franklin	57 C	69°44′	92°02′
Lord River	RIV/CDE	BC	Lillooet	92 O/4	51°09′	123°33′
Lord's Cove	VILG/VILG	NF		1 L/13	46°53′	55°40′
Lords Cove	UNP/LNO	NB	Charlotte	21 G/2	45°00′	66°57′
Lord Selkirk	UNP/LNO	MB		62 H/14	49°57′	97°12′
Lord Selkirk Park	UNP/LNO	MB		62 H/14	49°55′	97°08′
Lord Selkirk - West Kildonan	VILG/VILG	MB		62 H/14	49°57′	97°09′
Lords Mills	UNP/LNO	ON	Grenville	31 B/12	44°43′	75°38′
Lordsvale	UNP/LNO	QC	Les Collines-de-l'Outaouais	31 G/12	45°44′	75°55′
Loreburn	VILG/VILG	SK	23-26-5-W3	72 O/2	51°13′	106°36′

NAME NOM	ENTITY ENTITÉ	LOC 1 LIEU 1	LOC 2 LIEU 2	MAP CARTE	POSITION	
					LAT	LONG
Loreburn	UNP/LNO	NF		2 C/4	48°03′	53°43′
Loreburn No. 254	MUN2/AZM2	SK		72 O/2	51°15′	106°35′
Loree	UNP/LNO	ON	Grey	41 A/9	44°30′	80°24′
L'Orée-des-Bois	UNP/LNO	QC	Le Fjord-du-Saguenay	22 D/6	48°25′	71°17′
Lorens, Lac	LAKE/LAC	QC	Minganie	12 N/7	51°19′	60°39′
Lorenzo	UNP/LNO	SK	24-46-10-W3	73 B/14	52°59′	107°20′
Lorette	UNP/LNO	MB	33-9-5-E	62 H/15	49°47′	96°51′
Lorette	UNP/LNO	MB		62 H/10	49°44′	96°52′
Lorette	GEOG/GÉOG	MB		62 H/10	49°45′	96°50′
Lorette 7 - see-voir - Village des Hurons, Wendake	IR/RI	QC		21 L/14	46°51′	71°21′
Lorette 7A - see-voir - Village des Hurons, Wendake	IR/RI	QC		21 L/14	46°51′	71°21′
Lorette, Rivière	RIV/CDE	QC	Communauté urbaine de Québec	21 L/14	46°49′	71°19′
Loretteville	CITY/VIL1	QC	Communauté urbaine de Québec	21 L/14	46°51′	71°21′
Loretto	UNP/LNO	NF		12 B/11	48°30′	59°09′
Loretto	UNP/LNO	ON	Simcoe	31 D/4	44°03′	79°53′
Lories	UNP/LNO	NF		1 L/13	46°54′	55°56′
L'Orignal	VILG/VILG	ON	Prescott	31 G/10	45°37′	74°42′
Lorillard River	RIV/CDE	NT	Keewatin	56 B	64°08′	90°06′
Lorimer Lake	UNP/LNO	ON	Parry Sound	31 E/12	45°33′	79°59′
Lorimer Lake	LAKE/LAC	ON	Parry Sound	31 E/12	45°32′	79°58′
Lorimer Lake	LAKE/LAC	SK	71-7-W3	73 O/3	55°08′	107°02′
Loring	UNP/LNO	ON	Parry Sound	31 E/13	45°56′	80°00′
Lorin, Lac	LAKE/LAC	QC	Jamésie	33 K/3	54°08′	77°00′
Lorin Meadow 9	IR/RI	BC	Cariboo	93 B/10	52°40′	122°35′
Lorlie	UNP/LNO	SK	26-21-10-W2	62 L/14	50°50′	103°17′
Lorna Lake	LAKE/LAC	BC	Lillooet	92 O/3	51°07′	123°10′
Lorne	MUN2/AZM2	MB		62 G/7	49°25′	98°45′
Lorne	UNP/LNO	NS	Pictou	11 E/7	45°26′	62°42′
Lorne	UNP/LNO	NB	Restigouche	21 O/16	47°53′	66°08′
Lorne	UNP/LNO	ON	Glengarry	31 G/7	45°23′	74°36′
Lorne	UNP/LNO	ON	Bruce	41 A/4	44°14′	81°36′
Lorne	UNP/LNO	ON	Sudbury	41 I/5	46°18′	81°42′
Lorne	UNP/LNO	YT		105 D/7	60°18′	134°48′
Lorne	GEOG/GÉOG	NB	Victoria	21 O/3	47°08′	67°10′
Lorne Beach	UNP/LNO	ON	Bruce	41 A/4	44°14′	81°36′
Lorne Lake	LAKE/LAC	ON	Manitoulin	41 G/15	45°47′	82°37′
Lorne, Mount	MTN/MNT	YT		105 D/7	60°28′	134°42′
Lorne Park	UNP/LNO	ON	Peel	30 M/12	43°32′	79°37′
Lorne Park Estates	UNP/LNO	ON	Peel	30 M/12	43°32′	79°36′
Lornevale	UNP/LNO	NS	Colchester	11 E/5	45°28′	63°41′
Lorne Valley	VILG/VILG	PE	Kings	11 L/7	46°16′	62°41′
Lorne Valley	UNP/LNO	PE	Kings	11 L/7	46°16′	62°41′
Lorneville	UNP/LNO	NS	Cumberland	11 E/13	45°59′	63°57′
Lorneville	UNP/LNO	NB	Saint John	21 G/1	45°11′	66°09′
Lorneville	UNP/LNO	ON	Victoria	31 D/6	44°25′	79°00′
Lorrain	UNP/LNO	ON	Timiskaming	31 M/5	47°22′	79°46′
Lorraine	CITY/VIL1	QC	Thérèse-De Blainville	31 H/12	45°41′	73°47′
Lorraine	UNP/LNO	ON	Welland	30 L/14	42°52′	79°13′
Lorraine	UNP/LNO	AB	12-39-12-W4	73 D/5	52°20′	111°35′
Lorrain Lake	LAKE/LAC	ON	Timiskaming	31 M/4	47°06′	79°37′
Lorrain Valley	UNP/LNO	ON	Timiskaming	31 M/5	47°16′	79°30′
Lorrainville	VILG/VILG	QC	Témiscamingue	31 M/6	47°21′	79°21′
Loseman Lake	LAKE/LAC	AB	68-3-W4	73 L/16	54°54′	110°26′
Losier Settlement	UNP/LNO	NB	Gloucester	21 P/10	47°34′	64°56′
Loss Creek	RIV/CDE	BC	Renfrew	92 C/8	48°29′	124°16′
Lost Channel	UNP/LNO	ON	Hastings	31 C/6	44°25′	77°19′
Lost Channel	UNP/LNO	ON	Parry Sound	41 H/16	45°53′	80°19′
Lost Creek	RIV/CDE	ON	Rainy River	52 C/13	48°47′	93°33′
Lost Lake	LAKE/LAC	ON	Kenora	52 K/1	50°07′	92°11′
Lost Lake	LAKE/LAC	SK	67-19-W3	73 K/15	54°48′	108°52′
Lost Nation	UNP/LNO	ON	Renfrew	31 F/6	45°23′	77°24′
Lost Pond	LAKE/LAC	NF		12 A/10	48°34′	56°42′
Lost Reindeer Lakes	LAKE/LAC	NT	Mackenzie	107 B	68°06′	132°30′
Lost River	UNP/LNO	QC	Argenteuil	31 G/15	45°50′	74°33′
Lost River	UNP/LNO	SK	31-49-16-2	73 H/8	53°16′	104°20′
Lost River, Le	UNP/LNO	QC	Argenteuil	31 G/15	45°50′	74°31′
Lost River No. 313	MUN2/AZM2	SK		72 O/9	51°45′	106°10′
Lost Shoe Creek	RIV/CDE	BC	Clayoquot	92 F/4	49°00′	125°38′
Lost Valley Creek	RIV/CDE	BC	Lillooet	92 J/9	50°40′	122°20′
Lot 11 and Area	VILG/VILG	PE	Prince	11 L/12	46°40′	63°58′
Lotbinière	VILG/VILG	QC	Lotbinière	21 L/12	46°37′	71°56′
Lotbinière	MUN1/AZM1	QC	Lotbinière	21 L/12	46°31′	71°36′
Lothian	UNP/LNO	ON	Huron	40 P/13	43°59′	81°38′
Lothian	UNP/LNO	SK	29-28-W2	72 P/5	51°27′	105°50′
Lothrop	UNP/LNO	AB	29-80-1-W6	83 M/16	55°57′	118°08′

NAME NOM	ENTITY ENTITÉ	LOC 1 LIEU 1	LOC 2 LIEU 2	MAP CARTE	POSITION LAT	POSITION LONG
Lots-Renversés	UNP/LNO	QC	Témiscouata	21 N/10	47°40′	68°40′
Lottie Lake	LAKE/LAC	AB	58,59-11-W4	73 L/4	54°04′	111°35′
Lotus	UNP/LNO	ON	Durham	31 D/2	44°07′	78°42′
Loudin, Lac	LAKE/LAC	QC	Kativik	24 D/8	56°16′	70°18′
Loudoun Canyon	SEAU/SMER	—		3602	48°40′	126°13′
Loudoun Channel	CHAN/CHEN	BC	Barclay	92 C/14	48°56′	125°23′
Louet, Lac	LAKE/LAC	QC	Kativik	23 M/5	55°18′	71°45′
Loughborough	MUN2/AZM2	ON	Frontenac	31 C/7	44°27′	76°31′
Loughborough 3	IR/RI	BC	Range 1 Coast	92 K/12	50°31′	125°33′
Loughborough Inlet	BAY/BAIE	BC	Range 1 Coast	92 K/12	50°31′	125°32′
Loughborough Lake	LAKE/LAC	ON	Frontenac	31 C/8	44°27′	76°25′
Loughbreeze	UNP/LNO	ON	Northumberland	30 N/13	43°59′	77°52′
Lougheed	VILG/VILG	AB	33-43-11-W4	73 D/12	52°44′	111°33′
Lougheed Basin	SEAU/SMER	—		7951	77°30′	108°30′
Lougheed Island	ISL/ÎLE	NT	Franklin	79 D	77°26′	105°06′
Louisa	UNP/LNO	QC	Argenteuil	31 G/16	45°46′	74°22′
Louisa, Lake	LAKE/LAC	ON	Haliburton	31 E/8	45°28′	78°29′
Louisa Lake	LAKE/LAC	ON	Rainy River	52 B/3	48°09′	91°19′
Louis-Babel, Réserve écologique	PARK/PARC	QC	Manicouagan	22 N/7	51°27′	68°42′
Louisbourg	UNP/LNO	NS	Cape Breton	11 G/13	45°55′	59°58′
Louisbourg Road	UNP/LNO	NS	Cape Breton	11 F/16	45°56′	60°00′
Louis Bull 138B	IR/RI	AB	45-25-W4	83 A/13	52°55′	113°34′
Louis Creek	UNP/LNO	BC	Kamloops Division Yale	92 P/1	51°08′	120°07′
Louis Creek	RIV/CDE	BC	Kamloops Division Yale	92 P/1	51°08′	120°08′
Louis Creek 4	IR/RI	BC	Kamloops Division Yale	92 P/1	51°08′	120°07′
Louisdale	UNP/LNO	NS	Richmond	11 F/11	45°36′	61°04′
Louise	MUN2/AZM2	MB		62 G/2	49°10′	98°54′
Louise	UNP/LNO	ON	Grey	41 A/7	44°16′	80°59′
Louise Falls	FALL/CHUT	NT	Mackenzie	85 C	60°30′	116°13′
Louise Fiord	BAY/BAIE	NT	Franklin	69 F	78°58′	102°36′
Louise Island	ISL/ÎLE	BC	Queen Charlotte	103 B/13	52°59′	131°47′
Louise, Lac	LAKE/LAC	QC	Le Haut-Saint-François	21 E/11	45°43′	71°25′
Louiseville	CITY/VIL1	QC	Maskinongé	31 I/7	46°15′	72°57′
Louis Head	UNP/LNO	NS	Shelburne	20 P/11	43°45′	65°01′
Louis-Hémon, Mont	MTN/MNT	QC	La Côte-de-Beaupré	21 M/11	47°36′	71°13′
Louis-Joseph-Papineau, Lieu historique national - also-aussi - Louis-Joseph Papineau National Historic Site	PARK/PARC	QC	Communauté urbaine de Montréal	31 H/12	45°31′	73°33′
Louis-Joseph Papineau National Historic Site - also-aussi - Louis-Joseph-Papineau, Lieu historique national	PARK/PARC	QC	Communauté urbaine de Montréal	31 H/12	45°31′	73°33′
Louis, Lac	LAKE/LAC	QC	Kativik	23 O/11	55°32′	67°06′
Louis Lake	LAKE/LAC	NB	Northumberland	21 J/15	46°51′	66°36′
Louis Lake	LAKE/LAC	AB	3-55-6-W4	73 E/10	53°43′	110°49′
Louis Napoleon, Cape	CAPE/CAP	NT	Franklin	39 H	79°39′	72°15′
Louison Lake	LAKE/LAC	NT	Mackenzie	75 F	61°39′	109°02′
Louis-Ovide-Brunet, Réserve écologique	PARK/PARC	QC	Le Domaine-du-Roy	32 A/8	48°16′	72°05′
Louis Point	CAPE/CAP	BC	Queen Charlotte	103 F/11	53°41′	133°02′
Louis, Port	BAY/BAIE	BC	Queen Charlotte	103 F/10	53°42′	132°58′
Louis St-Laurent, Mount	MTN/MNT	BC	Cariboo	83 D/13	52°45′	119°47′
Louis Squinas Ranch 14	IR/RI	BC	Range 3 Coast	93 C/11	52°35′	125°27′
Louis-S.-St-Laurent, Lieu historique national - also-aussi - Louis S. St. Laurent National Historic Site	PARK/PARC	QC	Coaticook	21 E/4	45°14′	71°50′
Louis S. St. Laurent National Historic Site - also-aussi - Louis-S.-St-Laurent, Lieu historique national	PARK/PARC	QC	Coaticook	21 E/4	45°14′	71°50′
Louisville	UNP/LNO	NS	Pictou	11 E/11	45°44′	63°07′
Louisville	UNP/LNO	ON	Kent	40 J/8	42°28′	82°07′
Louis-XIV, Pointe	CAPE/CAP	QC	Jamésie	33 L/12	54°38′	79°45′
Louis-Zéphirin-Rousseau, Réserve écologique	PARK/PARC	QC	Antoine-Labelle	31 J/5	46°16′	75°47′
Lount Lake	LAKE/LAC	ON	Kenora	52 L/1	50°10′	94°19′
Loup Marin, Lac au	LAKE/LAC	QC	Manicouagan	22 F/7	49°19′	68°43′
Loup, Rivière du	RIV/CDE	QC	Rivière-du-Loup	21 N/13	47°51′	69°33′
Loup, Rivière du	RIV/CDE	QC	Beauce-Sartigan	21 L/2	46°05′	70°39′
Loup, Rivière du	RIV/CDE	QC	Maskinongé	31 I/2	46°13′	72°55′
Loups, Baie des	BAY/BAIE	QC	Côte-Nord-du-Golfe-Saint-Laurent	12 K/1	50°14′	60°13′
Loups, Lac des	LAKE/LAC	QC	Témiscamingue	31 M/1	47°04′	78°18′
Loups Marins, Lacs des	LAKE/LAC	QC	Kativik	34 A/12	56°30′	73°45′
Loups Marins, Petit lac des	LAKE/LAC	QC	Kativik	34 A/3	56°07′	73°15′
Lourdes	VILG/VILG	NF		12 B/11	48°39′	59°00′
Lourdes	UNP/LNO	NS	Pictou	11 E/10	45°34′	62°39′
Lourdes	UNP/LNO	QC	L'Érable	21 L/5	46°20′	71°49′
Lourdes-de-Blanc-Sablon	UNP/LNO	QC	Côte-Nord-du-Golfe-Saint-Laurent	12 P/6	51°25′	57°12′
Lousana	UNP/LNO	AB	23-36-23-W4	83 A/3	52°07′	113°10′
Loutre, Lac à la	LAKE/LAC	QC	La Haute-Côte-Nord	22 C/13	48°50′	69°39′
Loutre, Rivière à la	RIV/CDE	QC	Minganie	12 E/12	49°37′	63°48′

NAME NOM	ENTITY ENTITÉ	LOC 1 LIEU 1	LOC 2 LIEU 2	MAP CARTE	POSITION LAT	LONG
Loutres, Lac aux	LAKE/LAC	QC	Vallée-de-l'Or	32 B/13	48°57′	75°47′
Loutres, Rivière aux	RIV/CDE	QC	Kamouraska	21 N/12	47°34′	69°39′
Louvicourt	UNP/LNO	QC	Vallée-de-l'Or	32 C/3	48°04′	77°23′
Lovat	UNP/LNO	NS	Pictou	11 E/10	45°31′	62°51′
Lovat	UNP/LNO	ON	Bruce	41 A/6	44°16′	81°20′
Love	VILG/VILG	SK	16-52-15-W2	73 H/8	53°29′	104°10′
Lovekin	UNP/LNO	ON	Durham	30 M/15	43°54′	78°33′
*Lovell	UNP/LNO	BC	Cassiar	93 M/9	55°36′	126°04′
Lovell Lake	LAKE/LAC	SK		63 M/3	55°07′	103°15′
Lovering	UNP/LNO	ON	Simcoe	31 D/13	44°45′	79°36′
Lovering, Lac	LAKE/LAC	QC	Memphrémagog	31 H/1	45°10′	72°09′
Loverna	VILG/VILG	SK	13-31-29-W3	72 N/12	51°40′	110°00′
Lovett	UNP/LNO	ON	Northumberland	31 C/4	44°02′	77°40′
Low	VILG/VILG	QC	La Vallée-de-la-Gatineau	31 G/13	45°49′	75°57′
Lowbanks	UNP/LNO	ON	Haldimand	30 L/14	42°52′	79°27′
Low Bush	UNP/LNO	ON	Cochrane	42 A/16	48°55′	80°09′
Low Bush River	UNP/LNO	ON	Cochrane	42 A/16	48°55′	80°10′
Low Bush River	RIV/CDE	ON	Cochrane	42 A/16	48°55′	80°08′
Low, Cape	CAPE/CAP	NT	Keewatin	45 N	63°07′	85°18′
Lowden Lake	LAKE/LAC	AB	36,37-19-W4	83 A/2	52°09′	112°42′
Lowe Farm	UNP/LNO	MB	6-5-1-W	62 H/5	49°21′	97°35′
Lowell Glacier	GLAC/GLAC	YT		115 B/8	60°18′	138°15′
Lowell Glacier - see-voir - Dusty Glacier	GLAC/GLAC	YT		115 B/8	60°24′	138°23′
Lowe, Mount	MTN/MNT	BC	Range 2 Coast	92 N/3	51°08′	125°29′
Lower Anfield	UNP/LNO	NB	Victoria	21 J/14	46°55′	67°29′
Lower Argyle	UNP/LNO	NS	Yarmouth	20 P/12	43°44′	65°50′
Lower Arrow Lake	LAKE/LAC	BC	Kootenay	82 E/9	49°45′	118°05′
Lower Barnaby	UNP/LNO	NB	Northumberland	21 I/13	46°53′	65°34′
Lower Barneys River	UNP/LNO	NS	Pictou	11 E/9	45°40′	62°21′
Lower Bedeque	UNP/LNO	PE	Prince	11 L/5	46°21′	63°46′
Lower Beverley Lake	LAKE/LAC	ON	Leeds	31 C/9	44°36′	76°08′
Lower Blomidon	UNP/LNO	NS	Kings	21 H/1	45°15′	64°22′
Lower Bloomfield	UNP/LNO	NB	Carleton	21 J/5	46°17′	67°44′
Lower Blue Mountain	MTN/MNT	NB	Victoria	21 O/3	47°04′	67°14′
Lower Branch	UNP/LNO	NS	Lunenburg	21 A/7	44°25′	64°35′
Lower Brighton	UNP/LNO	NB	Carleton	21 J/5	46°15′	67°30′
Lower Burlington	UNP/LNO	NS	Hants	21 H/1	45°05′	64°08′
Lower Burton	UNP/LNO	NB	Sunbury	21 G/16	45°52′	66°22′
Lower Caledonia	UNP/LNO	NS	Guysborough	11 E/8	45°17′	62°17′
Lower California	UNP/LNO	NB	Victoria	21 J/13	46°51′	67°46′
Lower Cambridge	UNP/LNO	NB	Queens	21 G/9	45°44′	66°05′
Lower Canard	UNP/LNO	NS	Kings	21 H/1	45°08′	64°23′
Lower Cape	UNP/LNO	NB	Albert	21 H/15	45°49′	64°36′
*Lower Capilano	UNP/LNO	BC	New Westminster	92 G/6	49°19′	123°07′
Lower Caverhill	UNP/LNO	NB	York	21 J/3	46°02′	67°08′
Lower Chatham Head	UNP/LNO	NB	Northumberland	21 P/4	47°01′	65°32′
Lower China Creek	UNP/LNO	BC	Kootenay	82 F/4	49°13′	117°41′
Lower Clarks Harbour	UNP/LNO	NS	Shelburne	20 P/5	43°26′	65°37′
Lower Coast	UNP/LNO	NF		1 K/11	46°43′	53°23′
Lower Concession	UNP/LNO	NS	Digby	21 B/1	44°15′	66°05′
Lower Cove	UNP/LNO	NF		12 B/11	48°31′	59°00′
Lower Cove	UNP/LNO	NS	Cumberland	21 H/9	45°43′	64°26′
Lower Cove	UNP/LNO	NB	Kings	21 H/12	45°42′	65°34′
Lower Coverdale	UNP/LNO	NB	Albert	21 I/2	46°02′	64°43′
Lower Dacre	UNP/LNO	ON	Renfrew	31 F/7	45°22′	76°57′
Lower Darnley	UNP/LNO	PE	Prince	11 L/12	46°33′	63°39′
Lower Debert	UNP/LNO	NS	Colchester	11 E/5	45°23′	63°31′
Lower Derby	UNP/LNO	NB	Northumberland	21 I/13	46°56′	65°37′
Lower Durham	UNP/LNO	NB	York	21 J/2	46°08′	66°32′
Lower East Chezzetcook	UNP/LNO	NS	Halifax	11 D/11	44°42′	63°13′
Lower East Pubnico	UNP/LNO	NS	Yarmouth	20 P/12	43°36′	65°46′
Lower Economy	UNP/LNO	NS	Colchester	11 E/5	45°24′	63°59′
Lower Eel Brook	UNP/LNO	NS	Yarmouth	20 P/13	43°50′	65°55′
Lower Fishpot Lake 24A	IR/RI	BC	Cariboo	93 B/13	52°58′	123°48′
Lower Five Islands	UNP/LNO	NS	Colchester	21 H/8	45°25′	64°05′
Lower Flodden	UNP/LNO	QC	Sherbrooke	31 H/9	45°32′	72°14′
Lower Fort Garry, Lieu historique national de - also-aussi - Lower Fort Garry National Historic Site	PARK/PARC	MB		62 I/2	50°07′	96°56′
Lower Fort Garry National Historic Site - also-aussi - Lower Fort Garry, Lieu historique national de	PARK/PARC	MB		62 I/2	50°07′	96°56′
Lower Foster Lake	LAKE/LAC	SK		74 A/11	56°33′	105°23′
Lower Freetown	UNP/LNO	PE	Prince	11 L/5	46°22′	63°40′
Lower Gagetown	UNP/LNO	NB	Queens	21 G/9	45°44′	66°08′
Lower Garry Lake	LAKE/LAC	NT	Keewatin	66 F	65°52′	99°36′
Lower Glencoe	UNP/LNO	NS	Guysborough	11 F/5	45°25′	61°43′
Lower Grant Road	UNP/LNO	NS	Lunenburg	21 A/9	44°34′	64°18′
Lower Greenfield	UNP/LNO	NB	Carleton	21 J/5	46°29′	67°39′

NAME NOM	ENTITY ENTITÉ	LOC 1 LIEU 1	LOC 2 LIEU 2	MAP CARTE	POSITION LAT	LONG
Lower Greenville	UNP/LNO	NS	Cumberland	11 E/12	45°38′	63°37′
Lower Gulf Shore	UNP/LNO	NS	Cumberland	11 E/13	45°52′	63°33′
Lower Hainesville	UNP/LNO	NB	York	21 J/3	46°06′	67°03′
Lower Hamilton	UNP/LNO	PE	Prince	11 L/12	46°30′	63°42′
Lower Harmony	UNP/LNO	NS	Colchester	11 E/6	45°21′	63°10′
Lower Hat Creek 2	IR/RI	BC	Kamloops Division Yale	92 I/13	50°53′	121°30′
Lower Hillsdale	UNP/LNO	NS	Inverness	11 F/14	45°55′	61°26′
Lower Holleford	UNP/LNO	ON	Frontenac	31 C/7	44°27′	76°37′
Lower Island Cove	UNP/LNO	NF		2 C/2	48°00′	52°59′
Lower Jemseg	UNP/LNO	NB	Queens	21 G/16	45°47′	66°06′
Lower Jordan Bay	UNP/LNO	NS	Shelburne	20 P/11	43°41′	65°15′
Lower Kars	UNP/LNO	NB	Kings	21 H/12	45°35′	65°59′
Lower Kingston	UNP/LNO	NB	Kings	21 H/12	45°30′	65°59′
Lower Kintore	UNP/LNO	NB	Victoria	21 J/12	46°40′	67°39′
Lower Kootenay 1A	IR/RI	BC	Kootenay	82 F/2	49°02′	116°32′
Lower Kootenay 1B	IR/RI	BC	Kootenay	82 F/2	49°05′	116°33′
Lower Kootenay 1C	IR/RI	BC	Kootenay	82 F/2	49°06′	116°35′
Lower Kootenay 2	IR/RI	BC	Kootenay	82 F/2	49°07′	116°34′
Lower Kootenay 3	IR/RI	BC	Kootenay	82 F/2	49°08′	116°35′
Lower Kootenay 4	IR/RI	BC	Kootenay	82 F/2	49°09′	116°36′
Lower Kootenay 5	IR/RI	BC	Kootenay	82 F/2	49°10′	116°35′
Lower Laberge	UNP/LNO	YT		105 E/6	61°24′	135°14′
Lower LaHave	UNP/LNO	NS	Lunenburg	21 A/8	44°17′	64°20′
Lower Lance Cove	UNP/LNO	NF		2 C/4	48°09′	53°42′
Lower Langside	UNP/LNO	ON	Bruce	40 P/14	43°59′	81°24′
Lower L'Ardoise	UNP/LNO	NS	Richmond	11 F/10	45°36′	60°44′
Lower Lincoln	UNP/LNO	NB	Sunbury	21 G/15	45°52′	66°31′
Lower Line Queensbury	UNP/LNO	NB	York	21 G/15	45°55′	66°55′
Lower Little Ridge	UNP/LNO	NB	Charlotte	21 G/3	45°12′	67°24′
Lower Lonsdale	UNP/LNO	BC	New Westminster	92 G/6	49°19′	123°04′
Lower Maccan	UNP/LNO	NS	Cumberland	21 H/16	45°46′	64°18′
Lower Macdougall Lake	LAKE/LAC	NT	Keewatin	66 G	66°00′	98°37′
Lower Main River	UNP/LNO	NB	Kent	21 I/10	46°34′	64°59′
Lower Malpeque	UNP/LNO	PE	Prince	11 L/12	46°32′	63°42′
Lower Manitou Lake	LAKE/LAC	ON	Kenora	52 F/7	49°15′	93°00′
Lower Mazinaw Lake	LAKE/LAC	ON	Frontenac	31 C/14	44°52′	77°11′
Lower Meaghers Grant	UNP/LNO	NS	Halifax	11 D/14	44°55′	63°13′
Lower Melbourne	UNP/LNO	NS	Yarmouth	20 O/16	43°45′	66°04′
Lower Middle River	UNP/LNO	NS	Victoria	11 K/2	46°08′	60°55′
Lower Middleton	UNP/LNO	NS	Annapolis	21 A/14	44°56′	65°05′
Lower Midland	UNP/LNO	NB	Kings	21 H/12	45°38′	65°49′
Lower Millstream	UNP/LNO	NB	Kings	21 H/12	45°44′	65°37′
Lower Minnipuka Lake	LAKE/LAC	ON	Algoma	42 B/13	48°54′	83°48′
Lower Montague	VILG/VILG	PE	Kings	11 L/2	46°10′	62°36′
Lower Montague	UNP/LNO	PE	Kings	11 L/2	46°10′	62°34′
Lower Mount Thom	UNP/LNO	NS	Pictou	11 E/10	45°31′	62°57′
Lower Napan	UNP/LNO	NB	Northumberland	21 P/3	47°03′	65°21′
Lower Neguac	UNP/LNO	NB	Northumberland	21 P/6	47°16′	65°04′
Lower New Annan	UNP/LNO	PE	Prince	11 L/5	46°26′	63°43′
Lower Newcastle	UNP/LNO	NB	Northumberland	21 P/3	47°05′	65°24′
Lower New Cornwall	UNP/LNO	NS	Lunenburg	21 A/8	44°29′	64°28′
Lower Newtown	UNP/LNO	PE	Queens	11 L/2	46°07′	62°52′
Lower Nicola	UNP/LNO	BC	Kamloops Division Yale	92 I/2	50°09′	120°53′
Lower Nine Mile River	UNP/LNO	NS	Hants	11 E/4	45°01′	63°33′
Lower Northampton	UNP/LNO	NB	Carleton	21 J/4	46°03′	67°32′
Lower Northfield	UNP/LNO	NS	Lunenburg	21 A/7	44°28′	64°34′
Lower North Grant	UNP/LNO	NS	Antigonish	11 E/9	45°39′	62°01′
Lower Norton	UNP/LNO	NB	Kings	21 H/12	45°32′	65°52′
Lower Ohio	UNP/LNO	NS	Shelburne	20 P/14	43°51′	65°22′
Lower Onslow	UNP/LNO	NS	Colchester	11 E/6	45°23′	63°24′
Lower Perth	UNP/LNO	NB	Victoria	21 J/12	46°42′	67°43′
Lower Pleasant Valley	UNP/LNO	NS	Colchester	11 E/6	45°16′	63°21′
Lower Point	CAPE/CAP	NS	Cumberland	21 H/10	45°37′	64°35′
Lower Portage	UNP/LNO	NB	Victoria	21 J/13	46°55′	67°43′
Lower Post	UNP/LNO	BC	Cassiar	104 P/16	59°56′	128°30′
Lower Prince William	UNP/LNO	NB	York	21 G/15	45°53′	67°00′
Lower Prospect	UNP/LNO	NS	Halifax	11 D/5	44°27′	63°44′
Lower Queensbury	UNP/LNO	NB	York	21 G/15	45°54′	66°58′
Lower Red Cove	BAY/BAIE	NF		1 K/13	46°51′	53°58′
Lower Rideau Lake	LAKE/LAC	ON	Lanark	31 C/16	44°51′	76°07′
Lower Ridge	UNP/LNO	NB	Kings	21 H/14	45°58′	65°22′
Lower River Hébert	UNP/LNO	NS	Cumberland	21 H/9	45°43′	64°21′
Lower River Inhabitants	UNP/LNO	NS	Richmond	11 F/11	45°37′	61°15′
Lower Rockport	UNP/LNO	NB	Westmorland	21 H/10	45°44′	64°31′
Lower Rollo Bay	UNP/LNO	PE	Kings	11 L/8	46°21′	62°18′

NAME NOM	ENTITY ENTITÉ	LOC 1 LIEU 1	LOC 2 LIEU 2	MAP CARTE	POSITION	
					LAT	LONG
Lower Rose Bay	UNP/LNO	NS	Lunenburg	21 A/8	44°17′	64°17′
Lower Royalton	UNP/LNO	NB	Carleton	21 J/5	46°28′	67°46′
Lower Sackville	UNP/LNO	NS	Halifax	11 D/13	44°45′	63°40′
Lower Saint-Charles	UNP/LNO	NB	Kent	21 I/10	46°42′	64°58′
Lower St. Esprit	UNP/LNO	NS	Richmond	11 F/9	45°40′	60°29′
Lower St. Marys	UNP/LNO	NB	York	21 G/15	45°56′	66°36′
Lower Sandy Point	UNP/LNO	NS	Shelburne	20 P/11	43°41′	65°18′
Lower Saulnierville	UNP/LNO	NS	Digby	21 B/1	44°14′	66°08′
Lower Savage Islands	ISL/ÎLE	NT	Franklin	25 H	61°48′	65°48′
Lower Selma	UNP/LNO	NS	Hants	11 E/5	45°19′	63°36′
Lower Shag Harbour	UNP/LNO	NS	Shelburne	20 P/12	43°30′	65°41′
Lower Shawniken 4A	IR/RI	BC	Kamloops Division Yale	92 I/6	50°25′	121°22′
Lower Shinimicas	UNP/LNO	NS	Cumberland	11 E/13	45°54′	63°54′
Lower Ship Harbour	UNP/LNO	NS	Halifax	11 D/15	44°47′	62°50′
Lower Similkameen 2	IR/RI	BC	Similkameen Division Yale	82 E/4	49°07′	119°45′
Lower South River	UNP/LNO	NS	Antigonish	11 F/12	45°36′	61°55′
Lower Springfield	UNP/LNO	NS	Antigonish	11 F/5	45°30′	61°53′
Lower Stafford	UNP/LNO	ON	Renfrew	31 F/11	45°42′	77°01′
Lower Stoneridge	UNP/LNO	NB	York	21 J/2	46°04′	66°55′
Lower Sturgeon	UNP/LNO	ON	Cochrane	42 A/14	48°49′	81°29′
Lower Thérien Lake	LAKE/LAC	AB	57-10-W4	73 E/14	53°55′	111°23′
Lower Three Fathom Harbour	UNP/LNO	NS	Halifax	11 D/11	44°38′	63°17′
Lower Tower Hill	UNP/LNO	NB	Charlotte	21 G/6	45°18′	67°11′
Lower Truro	UNP/LNO	NS	Colchester	11 E/6	45°21′	63°22′
Lower Tryon	UNP/LNO	PE	Prince	11 L/4	46°13′	63°33′
Lower Turtle Creek	UNP/LNO	NB	Albert	21 I/2	46°01′	64°53′
Lower Twin Lake	LAKE/LAC	ON	Thunder Bay	42 L/2	50°11′	86°33′
Lower Vaughan	UNP/LNO	NS	Hants	21 A/16	44°50′	64°15′
Lower Waddy Lake	LAKE/LAC	SK		64 D/4	56°10′	103°48′
Lower Wakefield	UNP/LNO	NB	Carleton	21 J/4	46°13′	67°32′
Lower Washabuck	UNP/LNO	NS	Victoria	11 K/2	46°04′	60°46′
Lower Waterville	UNP/LNO	NB	Carleton	21 J/4	46°15′	67°35′
Lower Wedgeport	UNP/LNO	NS	Yarmouth	20 P/12	43°43′	65°59′
Lower Wentworth	UNP/LNO	NS	Cumberland	11 E/12	45°42′	63°33′
Lower West Jeddore	UNP/LNO	NS	Halifax	11 D/11	44°42′	63°01′
Lower West Pubnico	UNP/LNO	NS	Yarmouth	20 P/12	43°38′	65°48′
Lower West River	UNP/LNO	NS	Antigonish	11 E/9	45°37′	62°01′
Lower Whitehead	UNP/LNO	NS	Guysborough	11 F/3	45°13′	61°11′
Lower Windsor	UNP/LNO	NB	Carleton	21 J/6	46°22′	67°25′
Lower Wingham	UNP/LNO	ON	Huron	40 P/14	43°54′	81°20′
Lower Wolfville	UNP/LNO	NS	Kings	21 H/1	45°06′	64°20′
Lower Woods Harbour	UNP/LNO	NS	Shelburne	20 P/12	43°31′	65°44′
Lower Woodstock	UNP/LNO	NB	Carleton	21 J/4	46°07′	67°35′
Low Forest	UNP/LNO	QC	Le Haut-Saint-François	21 E/5	45°20′	71°37′
Low, Lac	LAKE/LAC	QC	Jamésie	33 C/8	52°29′	76°17′
Lowland	UNP/LNO	MB	6-15-9-E	62 I/8	50°15′	96°21′
Low Landing	UNP/LNO	NS	Queens	21 A/6	44°16′	65°09′
Low Point	UNP/LNO	NF		2 C/2	48°04′	52°57′
Low Point	UNP/LNO	PE	Prince	11 L/12	46°35′	63°52′
Low Point	UNP/LNO	NS	Inverness	11 F/11	45°43′	61°27′
Low Point	CAPE/CAP	NS	Cape Breton	11 K/8	46°16′	60°08′
Low Point	CAPE/CAP	NT	Franklin	48 D	73°09′	80°35′
Low Point	CAPE/CAP	NT	Keewatin	55 N	63°51′	92°44′
Low Shoal Island	ISL/ÎLE	ON	Cochrane	32 L/13	50°58′	79°33′
Lowther	UNP/LNO	ON	Cochrane	42 G/11	49°34′	83°01′
Lowther	UNP/LNO	ON	Kenora	52 E/15	49°46′	94°54′
Lowther Island	ISL/ÎLE	NT	Franklin	68 E	74°33′	97°30′
Lowther Lake	LAKE/LAC	SK	59,60-13-W3	73 J/4	54°09′	107°51′
Lowville	UNP/LNO	ON	Halton	30 M/5	43°26′	79°54′
Low Water Lake	LAKE/LAC	ON	Sudbury	41 P/4	47°09′	81°42′
Loyal	UNP/LNO	ON	Huron	40 P/13	43°47′	81°40′
Loyalist	UNP/LNO	PE	Queens	11 L/6	46°18′	63°14′
Loyalist	UNP/LNO	AB	9-35-7-W4	72 M/15	51°58′	110°57′
Loyalist Park	UNP/LNO	ON	Leeds	31 B/12	44°37′	75°43′
Lozeau, Lac	LAKE/LAC	QC	Minganie	13 D/4	52°06′	63°50′
Lubicon Lake	UNP/LNO	AB	17-85-13-W5	84 B/5	56°22′	115°52′
Lubicon Lake	LAKE/LAC	AB	85-12,13-W5	84 B/5	56°23′	115°56′
Lubicon River	RIV/CDE	AB	87-10-W5	84 B/5	56°29′	115°27′
Lubin	UNP/LNO	BC	Cariboo	83 D/14	52°53′	119°19′
Lucan	VILG/VILG	ON	Middlesex	40 P/3	43°11′	81°24′
Lucan Crossing	UNP/LNO	ON	Middlesex	40 P/3	43°10′	81°26′
Lucania, Mount	MTN/MNT	YT		115 F/1	61°01′	140°28′
Lucas	UNP/LNO	BC	Range 5 Coast	93 L/1	54°27′	126°32′
Lucasville	UNP/LNO	NS	Halifax	11 D/13	44°46′	63°43′
Lucasville	UNP/LNO	ON	Lambton	40 J/16	42°56′	82°21′

NAME NOM	ENTITY ENTITÉ	LOC 1 LIEU 1	LOC 2 LIEU 2	MAP CARTE	POSITION LAT	POSITION LONG
Lucerne	UNP/LNO	QC	Communauté urbaine de l'Outaouais	31 G/5	45°24′	75°49′
Lucerne	UNP/LNO	BC	Cariboo	83 D/15	52°51′	118°33′
Luceville	TOWN/VIL2	QC	La Mitis	22 C/9	48°32′	68°22′
Lucie, Lac	LAKE/LAC	QC	Jamésie	32 L/8	50°23′	78°27′
Lucille	UNP/LNO	ON	Dufferin	30 M/13	43°59′	79°59′
Luck Lake	LAKE/LAC	SK		72 O/3	51°05′	107°05′
Lucknow	VILG/VILG	ON	Bruce	40 P/13	43°57′	81°31′
Lucky Brook Ground	UNP/LNO	QC	Minganie	12 P/13	51°53′	57°48′
Lucky Lake	VILG/VILG	SK	25-23-9-W3	72 J/14	50°59′	107°08′
Lucky Man	IR/RI	SK	26-33-46-9	73 G/3	55°00′	107°14′
Lucky Rock	UNP/LNO	QC	Abitibi-Ouest	32 D/6	48°26′	79°19′
Luc, Pointe à	CAPE/CAP	QC	Sept-Rivières	22 G/14	49°49′	67°03′
Lucy Lake	LAKE/LAC	ON	Thunder Bay	42 L/6	50°19′	87°10′
Lucyville	UNP/LNO	NF		13 J/16	54°47′	58°26′
Ludgate	UNP/LNO	ON	Parry Sound	41 H/15	45°53′	80°32′
Ludgate Lake	LAKE/LAC	NB	Saint John	21 G/1	45°12′	66°13′
Ludlow	UNP/LNO	NB	Northumberland	21 J/8	46°29′	66°21′
Ludlow	GEOG/GÉOG	NB	Northumberland	21 J/9	46°37′	66°23′
Ludlow Rich, Cape	CAPE/CAP	NT	Franklin	89 D	77°18′	115°21′
Ludwig, Cape	CAPE/CAP	NT	Franklin	59 C	77°57′	95°07′
Lueck Mill	UNP/LNO	ON	Grey	41 A/7	44°23′	80°54′
Luemat Lake	LAKE/LAC	NT	Mackenzie	97 B	68°47′	126°32′
Lugar	UNP/LNO	NB	Gloucester	21 P/12	47°40′	65°49′
Luigi d'Abruzzi Cape	CAPE/CAP	NT	Franklin	57 B	68°40′	95°32′
Luke	UNP/LNO	MB	21-84-17-E	54 D/7	56°18′	94°51′
Luke's Arm	UNP/LNO	NF		2 E/10	49°31′	54°51′
Lukseetsissum 9	IR/RI	BC	Yale Division Yale	92 H/5	49°21′	121°37′
Lulu 5	IR/RI	BC	Similkameen Division Yale	92 H/8	49°24′	120°14′
Lulu Island	ISL/ÎLE	BC	New Westminster	92 G/3	49°10′	123°06′
Lulu, Lake	LAKE/LAC	ON	Kenora	52 E/15	49°46′	94°42′
Lumberton	UNP/LNO	BC	Kootenay	82 G/5	49°25′	115°52′
Lumby	VILG/VILG	BC	Osoyoos Division Yale	82 L/2	50°15′	118°58′
Lumby Junction	UNP/LNO	BC	Osoyoos Division Yale	82 L/3	50°14′	119°16′
Lumina	UNP/LNO	ON	Muskoka	31 E/6	45°17′	79°01′
Lumley	UNP/LNO	ON	Huron	40 P/6	43°23′	81°25′
Lumsden	TOWN/VIL2	NF		2 F/5	49°18′	53°36′
Lumsden	TOWN/VIL2	SK	33-19-21-W2	72 I/10	50°39′	104°52′
Lumsden Beach	VILG/VILG	SK	7-21-21-W2	72 I/15	50°46′	104°54′
Lumsden Dam	UNP/LNO	NS	Kings	21 H/1	45°02′	64°24′
Lumsden No. 189	MUN2/AZM2	SK		72 I/10	50°38′	104°50′
Lumsden Road	UNP/LNO	NB	Northumberland	21 P/4	47°05′	65°47′
Lunan Lake	LAKE/LAC	NT	Keewatin	56 C	64°51′	93°00′
Lunar	UNP/LNO	ON	Algoma	41 K/16	46°54′	84°12′
Lund	UNP/LNO	BC	New Westminster	92 F/15	49°58′	124°46′
Lundar	UNP/LNO	MB	1-20-5-W	62 J/9	50°42′	98°02′
Lundar Beach	UNP/LNO	MB	19-20-6-W	62 J/9	50°44′	98°17′
Lundbreck	UNP/LNO	AB	25,26-7-2-W5	82 G/9	49°35′	114°10′
Lundgren	UNP/LNO	BC	New Westminster	92 G/1	49°10′	122°29′
Lundy	UNP/LNO	NS	Guysborough	11 F/5	45°17′	61°30′
Lundys Corners	UNP/LNO	ON	Renfrew	31 F/7	45°26′	76°31′
Lundy's Lane	UNP/LNO	ON	Welland	30 M/3	43°06′	79°06′
Lunenburg	TOWN/VIL2	NS	Lunenburg	21 A/8	44°23′	64°19′
Lunenburg	MUN1/AZM1	NS	Lunenburg	21 A/7	44°26′	64°36′
Lunenburg	UNP/LNO	ON	Stormont	31 G/2	45°03′	74°57′
Lunenburg	GEOG/GÉOG	NS		21 A/9	44°32′	64°30′
Lunenburg Bay	BAY/BAIE	NS	Lunenburg	21 A/8	44°21′	64°16′
Lunge Lodge	UNP/LNO	ON	Nipissing	41 I/1	46°10′	80°01′
Lunnford	UNP/LNO	AB	1-59-3-W5	83 J/1	54°04′	114°19′
Lupin	UNP/LNO	NT	Mackenzie	76 E	65°46′	111°13′
Lupton Channel	CHAN/CHEN	NT	Franklin	25 I	62°33′	64°50′
Lure	UNP/LNO	AB	9-37-11-W4	73 D/4	52°10′	111°30′
Lurgan	UNP/LNO	SK	26-45-15-W2	73 A/16	52°54′	104°04′
Lurgan Beach	UNP/LNO	ON	Bruce	41 A/4	44°05′	81°44′
Luscar	UNP/LNO	AB	23-47-24-W5	83 F/3	53°04′	117°24′
Luseland	TOWN/VIL2	SK	8-36-24-W3	73 C/3	52°05′	109°24′
Lushes Bight	UNP/LNO	NF		2 E/12	49°36′	55°43′
Lushes Bight-Beaumont-Beaumont North	VILG/VILG	NF		2 E/12	49°37′	55°42′
Lusignan, Lac	LAKE/LAC	QC	Matawinie	31 J/9	46°41′	74°09′
Lusk	UNP/LNO	QC	Les Collines-de-l'Outaouais	31 F/9	45°30′	76°00′
Luskville	UNP/LNO	QC	Les Collines-de-l'Outaouais	31 F/9	45°32′	76°01′
Lussier	UNP/LNO	QC	Matawinie	31 J/8	46°17′	74°10′
Lussier River	RIV/CDE	BC	Kootenay	82 G/13	49°54′	115°44′
Lust Subdivision	UNP/LNO	BC	Cariboo	93 B/16	52°57′	122°26′
Lutes Mountain	UNP/LNO	NB	Westmorland	21 I/2	46°08′	64°54′
Lutesville	UNP/LNO	NB	Westmorland	21 I/2	46°06′	64°55′

NAME NOM	ENTITY ENTITÉ	LOC 1 LIEU 1	LOC 2 LIEU 2	MAP CARTE	POSITION LAT	LONG
Luther Lake	LAKE/LAC	ON	Dufferin	40 P/16	43°56'	80°26'
Luton	UNP/LNO	ON	Elgin	40 I/10	42°44'	80°58'
Lutose	UNP/LNO	AB	120-19,20-W5	84 N/6	59°25'	117°16'
Łutselk'e	UNP/LNO	NT	Mackenzie	75 L/7	62°24'	110°44'
Lutterworth	MUN2/AZM2	ON	Haliburton	31 D/15	44°50'	78°45'
Lutterworth	UNP/LNO	ON	Haliburton	31 D/15	44°53'	78°45'
Luxana Bay	BAY/BAIE	BC	Queen Charlotte	103 B/3	52°03'	131°03'
Luxemburg	UNP/LNO	ON	Waterloo	40 P/7	43°24'	80°42'
Luxor	UNP/LNO	BC	Kootenay	82 K/16	50°46'	116°13'
Luxton	UNP/LNO	SK	8-5-6-W2	62 E/7	49°22'	102°46'
Luxton	UNP/LNO	BC	Esquimalt	92 B/5	48°26'	123°32'
Lyacksun 3	IR/RI	BC	Cedar	92 G/4	49°06'	123°40'
Lyal Island	ISL/ÎLE	ON	Bruce	41 A/14	44°57'	81°24'
Lyall Point	CAPE/CAP	NT	Franklin	79 A	76°41'	104°15'
Lyalta	UNP/LNO	AB	8-25-26-W4	82 P/4	51°07'	113°36'
Lyddal	UNP/LNO	MB	2-70-7-W	63 O/1	55°02'	98°25'
Lydgate	UNP/LNO	NS	Shelburne	20 P/11	43°43'	65°08'
Lydiatt	UNP/LNO	MB	8,9-12-8-E	62 H/16	49°59'	96°27'
Lyell Icefield	GLAC/GLAC	AB/BC		82 N/14	51°56'	117°04'
Lyell Island	ISL/ÎLE	BC	Queen Charlotte	103 B/11	52°40'	131°30'
Lyell, Mount	MTN/MNT	AB/BC		82 N/14	51°57'	117°06'
Lyle Lake	LAKE/LAC	AB	72-17-W4	83 P/1	55°13'	112°30'
Lyleton	UNP/LNO	MB	21-1-28-W	62 F/3	49°03'	101°11'
Lyman Point	CAPE/CAP	BC	Queen Charlotte	103 B/2	52°05'	130°56'
Lymburn	UNP/LNO	AB	21-73-12-W6	83 M/5	55°21'	119°47'
Lyn	UNP/LNO	ON	Leeds	31 B/12	44°35'	75°47'
Lynbrook Heights	UNP/LNO	SK		72 I/5	50°24'	105°33'
Lynch Corner	UNP/LNO	NB	Kings	21 G/9	45°30'	66°10'
Lynch Creek	RIV/CDE	BC	Similkameen Division Yale	82 E/1	49°15'	118°26'
Lynche River	UNP/LNO	NS	Richmond	11 F/10	45°39'	60°49'
Lynch, Lac	LAKE/LAC	QC	Les Collines-de-l'Outaouais	31 G/12	45°39'	75°33'
Lyndale	UNP/LNO	PE	Queens	11 L/2	46°09'	62°47'
Lyndale	UNP/LNO	ON	Elgin	40 I/14	42°45'	81°11'
Lynden	UNP/LNO	ON	Wentworth	40 P/1	43°14'	80°09'
Lyndhurst	UNP/LNO	ON	Leeds	31 C/9	44°33'	76°08'
Lyndon	UNP/LNO	AB	34-12-29-W4	82 I/4	50°02'	113°53'
Lynedoch	UNP/LNO	ON	Norfolk	40 I/16	42°48'	80°30'
Lynhurst	UNP/LNO	ON	Elgin	40 I/14	42°47'	81°12'
Lynn	UNP/LNO	NS	Colchester	21 H/8	45°28'	64°06'
Lynnfield	UNP/LNO	NB	Charlotte	21 G/6	45°24'	67°18'
Lynn Lake	MUN2/AZM2	MB		64 C/14	56°50'	101°05'
Lynn Lake	UNP/LNO	MB		64 C/14	56°51'	101°03'
Lynnmour	UNP/LNO	BC	New Westminster	92 G/6	49°19'	123°02'
Lynn River	RIV/CDE	ON	Norfolk	40 I/16	42°47'	80°12'
Lynn Valley	UNP/LNO	ON	Norfolk	40 I/16	42°48'	80°16'
Lynn Valley	UNP/LNO	BC	New Westminster	92 G/6	49°20'	123°02'
Lynnville	UNP/LNO	ON	Norfolk	40 I/16	42°53'	80°22'
Lynton	UNP/LNO	AB	8-88-7-W4	74 D/11	56°37'	111°06'
Lynx	UNP/LNO	ON	Cochrane	42 K/4	50°06'	85°57'
Lynx Bay	BAY/BAIE	MB		53 L/13	54°46'	95°58'
Lynx Bay	BAY/BAIE	MB		63 A/4	52°08'	97°39'
Lynx Creek	UNP/LNO	BC	Peace River	94 A/4	56°04'	121°50'
Lynx Lake	LAKE/LAC	NT	Mackenzie	75 J	62°25'	106°15'
Lynx Point	CAPE/CAP	MB		63 A/4	52°09'	97°35'
Lyon, Cape	CAPE/CAP	NT	Franklin	97 D	69°50'	122°57'
Lyon Inlet	BAY/BAIE	NT	Franklin	46 J/12	66°32'	83°53'
Lyons	UNP/LNO	ON	Elgin	40 I/15	42°51'	80°59'
Lyons	UNP/LNO	SK	35-26-8-W3	72 O/6	51°16'	107°01'
Lyons Brook	UNP/LNO	NS	Pictou	11 E/10	45°40'	62°47'
Lyonshall	UNP/LNO	MB	33,34-2-18-W	62 G/4	49°10'	99°49'
Lyons Point	CAPE/CAP	NT	Franklin	68 D	73°51'	97°11'
Lypps Beach	UNP/LNO	ON	Essex	40 J/2	42°01'	82°59'
Lys, Baie des	BAY/BAIE	QC	Témiscamingue	31 M/9	47°38'	78°10'
Lys Creek	RIV/CDE	BC	Kamloops Division Yale	83 D/2	52°24'	119°44'
Lyster	VILG/VILG	QC	L'Érable	21 L/5	46°22'	71°37'
Lyster, Lac	LAKE/LAC	QC	Coaticook	21 E/4	45°02'	71°54'
Lythmore	UNP/LNO	ON	Haldimand	30 L/13	42°58'	79°55'
Lyttleton	UNP/LNO	NB	Northumberland	21 I/13	46°56'	65°55'
Lytton	VILG/VILG	QC	La Vallée-de-la-Gatineau	31 K/9	46°39'	76°02'
Lytton	VILG/VILG	BC	Kamloops Division Yale	92 I/4	50°14'	121°34'
Lytton 3A	IR/RI	BC	Kamloops Division Yale	92 I/5	50°21'	121°40'
Lytton 4A	IR/RI	BC	Kamloops Division Yale	92 I/5	50°27'	121°43'
Lytton 4B	IR/RI	BC	Kamloops Division Yale	92 I/5	50°27'	121°43'
Lytton 4C	IR/RI	BC	Kamloops Division Yale	92 I/5	50°27'	121°43'
Lytton 4D	IR/RI	BC	Kamloops Division Yale	92 I/5	50°28'	121°43'

NAME NOM	ENTITY ENTITÉ	LOC 1 LIEU 1	LOC 2 LIEU 2	MAP CARTE	POSITION	
					LAT	LONG
Lytton 4E	IR/RI	BC	Kamloops Division Yale	92 I/5	50°26'	121°42'
Lytton 4F	IR/RI	BC	Kamloops Division Yale	92 I/5	50°25'	121°42'
Lytton 5A	IR/RI	BC	Kamloops Division Yale	92 I/12	50°31'	121°45'
Lytton 6B	IR/RI	BC	Lillooet	92 I/12	50°34'	121°46'
Lytton 9A	IR/RI	BC	Kamloops Division Yale	92 I/5	50°18'	121°39'
Lytton 9B	IR/RI	BC	Kamloops Division Yale	92 I/5	50°16'	121°37'
Lytton 13A	IR/RI	BC	Kamloops Division Yale	92 I/5	50°24'	121°41'
Lytton 21A	IR/RI	BC	Kamloops Division Yale	92 I/5	50°17'	121°35'
Lytton 26A	IR/RI	BC	Kamloops Division Yale	92 I/4	50°11'	121°36'
Lytton 27B	IR/RI	BC	Kamloops Division Yale	92 I/4	50°14'	121°36'
Lytton 31	IR/RI	BC	Kamloops Division Yale	92 I/4	50°12'	121°36'
Lytton 32	IR/RI	BC	Kamloops Division Yale	92 I/5	50°25'	121°41'
Lytton 33	IR/RI	BC	Kamloops Division Yale	92 I/5	50°25'	121°43'

M

NAME	ENTITY	LOC 1	LOC 2	MAP	LAT	LONG
Maahpe 4	IR/RI	BC	Clayoquot	92 E/8	49°29'	126°26'
Mabee's Corners	UNP/LNO	ON	Norfolk	40 I/15	42°47'	80°41'
Mabel	UNP/LNO	QC	Argenteuil	31 G/9	45°39'	74°28'
Mabella	UNP/LNO	ON	Thunder Bay	52 A/12	48°36'	89°59'
Mabel Lake	UNP/LNO	BC	Osoyoos Division Yale	82 L/7	50°19'	118°48'
Mabel Lake	LAKE/LAC	BC	Osoyoos Division Yale	82 L/10	50°31'	118°44'
Maberly	UNP/LNO	NF		2 C/11	48°37'	53°01'
Maberly	UNP/LNO	ON	Lanark	31 C/15	44°50'	76°32'
Mabille, Lac - also-aussi - Mabille Lake	LAKE/LAC	QC	Minganie	12 M/15	52°00'	62°56'
Mabille Lake - also-aussi - Mabille, Lac	LAKE/LAC	NF		12 M/15	52°00'	62°56'
Mabou	UNP/LNO	NS	Inverness	11 K/3	46°04'	61°23'
Mabou, Cape	CAPE/CAP	NS	Inverness	11 K/3	46°09'	61°22'
Mabou Harbour	UNP/LNO	NS	Inverness	11 K/3	46°05'	61°25'
Mabou Harbour	BAY/BAIE	NS	Inverness	11 K/3	46°05'	61°27'
Mabou Harbour Mouth	UNP/LNO	NS	Inverness	11 K/3	46°05'	61°27'
Mabou Mines	UNP/LNO	NS	Inverness	11 K/3	46°07'	61°28'
Mabou Station	UNP/LNO	NS	Inverness	11 K/3	46°04'	61°24'
Mabretou, Lac - see-voir - Mabretou Lake	LAKE/LAC	NF		13 C/5	52°17'	61°43'
Mabretou Lake	LAKE/LAC	NF		13 C/5	52°17'	61°43'
Macabee	UNP/LNO	NB	Restigouche	21 O/15	47°55'	66°38'
Macalister	UNP/LNO	BC	Cariboo	93 B/8	52°27'	122°24'
Macalister	UNP/LNO	BC	Cariboo	93 B/8	52°29'	122°25'
MacAllister Lake	LAKE/LAC	SK	77-6-W3	73 O/10	55°40'	106°54'
Macallum Lake	LAKE/LAC	SK	69,70-16-W3	73 N/1	55°02'	108°25'
MacAlpine Lake	LAKE/LAC	NT	Mackenzie	66 L	66°32'	102°45'
Macamic	CITY/VIL1	QC	Abitibi-Ouest	32 D/14	48°45'	79°00'
Macamic	VILG/VILG	QC	Abitibi-Ouest	32 D/14	48°45'	79°00'
Macamic, Lac	LAKE/LAC	QC	Abitibi-Ouest	32 D/15	48°48'	78°59'
MacArthur Siding	UNP/LNO	AB	36-54-25-W4	83 H/12	53°43'	113°33'
MacAskill	UNP/LNO	ON	Thunder Bay	52 H/1	49°08'	88°18'
MacAskills Brook	RIV/CDE	NS	Cape Breton	11 J/4	46°09'	59°57'
Macaulay, Mount	MTN/MNT	YT		115 F/2	61°13'	140°31'
MacAulays Hill	UNP/LNO	NS	Victoria	11 K/2	46°08'	60°41'
MacBains Corner	UNP/LNO	NS	Colchester	11 E/11	45°38'	63°07'
Maccan	UNP/LNO	NS	Cumberland	21 H/9	45°43'	64°15'
Maccan River	RIV/CDE	NS	Cumberland	21 H/16	45°46'	64°20'
Maccles	UNP/LNO	NF		2 D/9	48°38'	54°08'
Maccles Lake	LAKE/LAC	NF		2 D/9	48°37'	54°13'
MacColl Island	ISL/ÎLE	NT	Franklin	25 A	60°38'	64°42'
MacCormicks Corner	UNP/LNO	NS	Inverness	11 K/3	46°09'	61°16'
Macculloch, Cape	CAPE/CAP	NT	Franklin	38 A	72°29'	75°09'
Macdiarmid	UNP/LNO	ON	Thunder Bay	52 H/8	49°26'	88°08'
Macdonald	MUN2/AZM2	MB		62 H/11	49°40'	97°30'
Macdonald	UNP/LNO	MB	35-12-8-W	62 J/1	50°03'	98°28'
Macdonald	UNP/LNO	BC	Kootenay	82 N/5	51°17'	117°30'
MacDonald Bay	UNP/LNO	ON	Peterborough	31 C/12	44°39'	77°56'
MacDonald Beach	UNP/LNO	ON	Ontario	31 D/11	44°35'	79°19'
Macdonald Creek	RIV/CDE	SK	32-10-W3	72 O/11	51°43'	107°23'
Macdonald Falls	FALL/CHUT	NT	Mackenzie	75 P	63°45'	104°45'
Macdonald Island	ISL/ÎLE	NT	Franklin	35 P	63°42'	72°40'
MacDonald, Lac	LAKE/LAC	QC	La Haute-Côte-Nord	22 C/14	48°56'	69°02'
MacDonald Lake	LAKE/LAC	SK		74 O/10	59°38'	107°00'
Macdonald, Meredith and Aberdeen Additional	MUN2/AZM2	ON	Algoma	41 J/5	46°28'	83°56'
Macdonald Range	MTN/MNT	BC	Kootenay	82 G/2	49°07'	114°45'
MacDonald River	RIV/CDE	NT	Franklin	37 D	69°31'	75°25'
MacDonalds Glen	UNP/LNO	NS	Inverness	11 K/3	46°08'	61°27'
MacDonalds Grove	UNP/LNO	ON	Stormont	31 G/7	45°18'	74°54'

NAME NOM	ENTITY ENTITÉ	LOC 1 LIEU 1	LOC 2 LIEU 2	MAP CARTE	POSITION LAT	LONG
MacDonalds Point	UNP/LNO	NB	Queens	21 G/9	45°43′	66°03′
MacDonnel, Cape	CAPE/CAP	NT	Mackenzie	96 I	66°24′	120°32′
MacDougall	UNP/LNO	PE	Prince	11 L/12	46°30′	63°56′
MacDougall	UNP/LNO	NB	Westmorland	21 I/7	46°16′	64°42′
Macdougall Point	CAPE/CAP	NT	Franklin	79 B	76°27′	110°28′
Macdowall	HAM/HAM	SK	13-46-1-W3	73 G/1	53°01′	106°01′
MacDowell	UNP/LNO	ON	Kenora	53 C/2	52°13′	92°44′
MacDowell Lake	LAKE/LAC	ON	Kenora	53 C/2	52°15′	92°42′
MacDowell River	RIV/CDE	ON	Kenora	53 B/13	52°45′	91°59′
Macduff	UNP/LNO	ON	Algoma	42 F/1	49°11′	84°17′
Mace	UNP/LNO	ON	Cochrane	32 D/13	48°56′	79°56′
Maces Bay	UNP/LNO	NB	Charlotte	21 G/1	45°06′	66°29′
Maces Bay	BAY/BAIE	NB	Charlotte	21 G/2	45°06′	66°32′
Maceys Bay	UNP/LNO	ON	Muskoka	31 D/13	44°50′	79°46′
MacFarlane River	RIV/CDE	SK		74 O/4	59°12′	107°58′
MacGillivrays Bridge	UNP/LNO	ON	Glengarry	31 G/2	45°09′	74°39′
MacGregor	VILG/VILG	MB	33-11-10-W	62 G/15	49°58′	98°47′
MacGregor Cove	BAY/BAIE	ON	Algoma	41 N/7	47°18′	84°36′
MacGregors Mal Bay	LAKE/LAC	NB	Gloucester	21 P/16	47°59′	64°29′
Machar	MUN2/AZM2	ON	Parry Sound	31 E/14	45°53′	79°30′
Machault, Lac	LAKE/LAC	QC	Kativik	13 M/12	55°33′	63°55′
Machawaian Lake	LAKE/LAC	ON	Kenora	52 P/16	51°52′	88°08′
Machete Lake	LAKE/LAC	BC	Lillooet	92 P/7	51°23′	120°34′
Machias Seal Island	ISL/ÎLE	NB	Charlotte	21 B/11	44°30′	67°06′
Machichi River	RIV/CDE	MB		54 F/1	57°03′	92°06′
Machin	MUN2/AZM2	ON	Kenora	52 F/11	49°44′	93°13′
Machisatat	UNP/LNO	QC	Kativik	34 A/11	56°36′	73°17′
Machmell River	RIV/CDE	BC	Range 2 Coast	92 M/10	51°39′	126°42′
Machta 16	IR/RI	BC	Rupert	92 L/3	50°00′	127°09′
Machum Lake	LAKE/LAC	NT	Keewatin	55 N	63°16′	92°36′
MacInnis Lake	LAKE/LAC	NT	Mackenzie	75 E	61°21′	110°12′
MacIntosh Mill	UNP/LNO	NB	Carleton	21 J/11	46°31′	67°27′
MacIntyre Lake	UNP/LNO	NS	Inverness	11 F/11	45°39′	61°17′
MacIntyre Lake	LAKE/LAC	SK		74 G/8	57°26′	106°07′
MacIsaacs Point	CAPE/CAP	NS	Antigonish	11 F/12	45°44′	61°53′
MacIvors Point	CAPE/CAP	PE	Queens	11 L/3	46°11′	63°27′
Macjack River	RIV/CDE	BC	Rupert	102 I/9	50°35′	128°14′
Mack	UNP/LNO	ON	Thunder Bay	52 G/1	49°09′	90°23′
MacKay	UNP/LNO	AB	8-54-11-W5	83 G/12	53°39′	115°35′
MacKay-Bennett Seamount	SEAU/SMER	—		NK22 B	41°21′	48°57′
Mackay, Cape	CAPE/CAP	NT	Franklin	89 E	78°20′	113°17′
MacKay Lake	LAKE/LAC	SK		73 P/7	55°27′	104°56′
MacKay Lake	LAKE/LAC	NT	Mackenzie	75 M	63°55′	110°25′
MacKay Point	CAPE/CAP	NS	Victoria	11 K/2	46°04′	60°44′
MacKay River	RIV/CDE	AB	94-11-W4	74 E/4	57°10′	111°38′
MacKay River	RIV/CDE	BC	Cariboo	93 A/7	52°23′	120°44′
MacKays Corner	UNP/LNO	NS	Pictou	11 E/15	45°46′	62°49′
Mackdale	UNP/LNO	NS	Inverness	11 F/11	45°41′	61°21′
Mackenzie	MUN1/AZM1	BC	Cariboo	93 O/6	55°18′	123°10′
Mackenzie	UNP/LNO	ON	Thunder Bay	52 A/10	48°33′	88°58′
MacKenzie Bay	BAY/BAIE	SK		74 G/7	57°25′	106°58′
Mackenzie Bay	BAY/BAIE	YT		117 D/3	69°13′	138°00′
Mackenzie Delta	CAPE/CAP	NT/YT		107 B/6	68°26′	134°30′
Mackenzie, District de - also-aussi - **Mackenzie, District of**	GEOG/GÉOG	NT		MCR130	65°00′	111°30′
Mackenzie, District of - also-aussi - **Mackenzie, District de**	GEOG/GÉOG	NT		MCR130	65°00′	111°30′
Mackenzie, Fleuve - also-aussi - **Mackenzie River**	RIV/CDE	NT	Mackenzie	107 C	69°21′	133°54′
Mackenzie, Havre	BAY/BAIE	QC	Côte-Nord-du-Golfe-Saint-Laurent	12 K/2	50°14′	60°45′
Mackenzie King Island	ISL/ÎLE	NT	Franklin	79 C	77°45′	112°00′
Mackenzie King, Mount	MTN/MNT	BC	Cariboo	83 D/13	52°46′	119°46′
MacKenzie Lake	LAKE/LAC	SK		64 E/15	57°50′	102°43′
MacKenzie Lake	LAKE/LAC	SK		74 N/14	59°57′	109°10′
MacKenzie Lake	LAKE/LAC	NT	Keewatin	55 L	62°39′	95°45′
Mackenzie Mountains	MTN/MNT	NT/YT		95 M/13	63°53′	127°45′
Mackenzie No. 23, Municipal District of	MUN1/AZM1	AB		84 K/11	58°41′	117°03′
Mackenzie River - also-aussi - **Mackenzie, Fleuve**	RIV/CDE	NT	Mackenzie	107 C	69°21′	133°54′
Mackenzie Spot	SEAU/SMER	—		8007	43°58′	62°25′
MacKenzies River	RIV/CDE	NS	Inverness	11 K/15	46°49′	60°50′
MacKerracher Lake	LAKE/LAC	MB		64 G/6	57°30′	99°21′
Mackey	UNP/LNO	ON	Renfrew	31 K/4	46°10′	77°48′
Mackid	UNP/LNO	SK	27-11-27-W3	72 F/13	49°56′	109°37′
Mackies	UNP/LNO	ON	Thunder Bay	52 B/1	48°14′	90°04′
Mackin	UNP/LNO	BC	Cariboo	93 B/8	52°15′	122°15′
Mackin Creek	RIV/CDE	BC	Cariboo	93 B/8	52°22′	122°23′
Mackinnon, Cap	CAPE/CAP	QC	Côte-Nord-du-Golfe-Saint-Laurent	12 J/11	50°31′	59°21′
MacKinnons Brook	UNP/LNO	NS	Inverness	11 K/3	46°10′	61°26′

NAME NOM	ENTITY ENTITÉ	LOC 1 LIEU 1	LOC 2 LIEU 2	MAP CARTE	POSITION LAT	LONG
Mackintosh Bay	BAY/BAIE	NT	Mackenzie	96 J	66°08'	123°05'
Mack Lake	LAKE/LAC	MB		54 L/4	58°02'	95°30'
Macklin	TOWN/VIL2	SK	3-39-28-W3	73 C/5	52°20'	109°56'
Mackode Nigapi	UNP/LNO	QC	Jamésie	32 E/8	49°18'	78°09'
Macksville	UNP/LNO	ON	Middlesex	40 I/13	42°49'	81°41'
MacLarens Landing	UNP/LNO	ON	Carleton	31 F/9	45°31'	76°10'
Maclean Park	UNP/LNO	ON	Frontenac	31 C/8	44°16'	76°28'
MacLean Settlement	UNP/LNO	NB	York	21 J/2	46°05'	66°50'
Maclean Strait	CHAN/CHEN	NT	Franklin	69 C	77°30'	103°30'
MacLellan Lake	LAKE/LAC	NT	Mackenzie	75 M	63°15'	110°02'
MacLennan	UNP/LNO	ON	Algoma	41 K/8	46°21'	84°02'
MacLeod	UNP/LNO	ON	Thunder Bay	42 E/10	49°41'	86°57'
MacLeod Lake	LAKE/LAC	MB		64 P/4	59°11'	97°34'
MacLeod Settlement	UNP/LNO	NS	Inverness	11 F/14	45°56'	61°21'
Macleod's Fort (St. Mary's II) Provincial Historic Site (Undeveloped)	PARK/PARC	AB	83-21-W5	84 C/3	56°10'	117°22'
MacLeods Point	UNP/LNO	NS	Victoria	11 K/2	46°14'	60°36'
Maclure, Lac	LAKE/LAC	QC	La Haute-Côte-Nord	22 C/5	48°28'	69°48'
MacMillan Lake	LAKE/LAC	MB		64 N/8	59°25'	100°18'
Macmillan Pass	VALL/VALL	YT/NT		105 O/1	63°15'	130°02'
Macmillan River	RIV/CDE	YT		105 L/13	62°52'	135°54'
MacMullin Lake	LAKE/LAC	NS	Cape Breton	11 F/16	45°47'	60°19'
MacNab Park	UNP/LNO	SK	8-37-5-W3	73 B/2	52°10'	106°41'
MacNeill	UNP/LNO	BC	Lillooet	92 J/9	50°41'	122°02'
MacNeils Vale	UNP/LNO	NS	Victoria	11 K/2	46°01'	60°49'
MacNutt	VILG/VILG	SK	22-24-30-W	62 N/4	51°05'	101°36'
Macoah 1	IR/RI	BC	Clayoquot	92 C/14	50°00'	125°23'
Macormick Bay	BAY/BAIE	NT	Franklin	58 G	75°22'	92°23'
Macoun	VILG/VILG	SK	22-4-10-W2	62 E/6	49°19'	103°16'
Macoun Islands	ISL/ÎLE	ON	Thunder Bay	52 H/9	49°36'	88°20'
Macoun Lake	LAKE/LAC	SK		64 D/12	56°32'	103°50'
Macpès, Grand lac	LAKE/LAC	QC	Rimouski-Neigette	22 C/8	48°18'	68°29'
MacPhees Corner	UNP/LNO	NS	Hants	11 E/4	45°07'	63°32'
MacPherson Lake	UNP/LNO	NS	Guysborough	11 F/6	45°26'	61°25'
MacQuoid Lake	LAKE/LAC	NT	Keewatin	55 M	63°25'	94°40'
MacRae	UNP/LNO	YT		105 D/10	60°38'	135°00'
Macrorie	VILG/VILG	SK	20-27-8-W3	72 O/6	51°20'	107°05'
Macs Island	ISL/ÎLE	NB	Charlotte	21 G/2	45°03'	66°56'
Macson	UNP/LNO	AB	10-12-5-W4	72 E/15	49°58'	110°36'
Mactaquac	UNP/LNO	NB	York	21 G/15	45°57'	66°53'
Mactaquac Dam	MISC/DIV	NB	York	21 G/15	45°57'	66°52'
Mactaquac Lake	LAKE/LAC	NB	York	21 G/14	46°00'	67°18'
Mactaquac Stream	RIV/CDE	NB	York	21 J/2	46°01'	66°58'
Mactavish, Mount	MTN/MNT	NT	Keewatin	57 A	68°06'	88°42'
MacTier	UNP/LNO	ON	Muskoka	31 E/4	45°08'	79°47'
Macton	UNP/LNO	ON	Wellington	40 P/10	43°37'	80°41'
Macville	UNP/LNO	ON	Peel	30 M/13	43°51'	79°47'
Macworth	UNP/LNO	SK	33-2-4-W3	72 G/1	49°10'	106°29'
Madame, Île	ISL/ÎLE	QC	L'Île-d'Orléans	21 L/15	46°58'	70°48'
Madame, Isle	ISL/ÎLE	NS	Richmond	11 F/11	45°33'	61°03'
Madashack Lake	LAKE/LAC	NS	Yarmouth	20 P/13	43°47'	65°39'
Madawaska	UNP/LNO	ON	Nipissing	31 F/12	45°30'	77°59'
Madawaska	GEOG/GÉOG	NB	Madawaska	21 N/9	47°38'	68°08'
Madawaska	GEOG/GÉOG	NB		21 N/8	47°25'	68°15'
Madawaska Lake	LAKE/LAC	ON	Haliburton	31 E/8	45°20'	78°23'
Madawaska River - also-aussi - Madawaska, Rivière	RIV/CDE	NB	Madawaska	21 N/8	47°22'	68°19'
Madawaska River	RIV/CDE	ON	Renfrew	31 F/8	45°27'	76°21'
Madawaska, Rivière - also-aussi - Madawaska River	RIV/CDE	QC/NB		21 N/8	47°22'	68°19'
Madden	UNP/LNO	AB	31-28-2-W5	82 O/8	51°26'	114°17'
Maddington	VILG/VILG	QC	Arthabaska	31 I/1	46°13'	72°08'
Maddington Falls	UNP/LNO	QC	Arthabaska	31 I/1	46°13'	72°08'
Mad Dog Lake	LAKE/LAC	NF		12 G/1	49°02'	58°15'
Maddox Cove	UNP/LNO	NF		1 N/7	47°28'	52°42'
Madeira Park	UNP/LNO	BC	New Westminster	92 F/9	49°37'	124°01'
Madeleine, Cap de la	CAPE/CAP	QC	Denis-Riverin	22 H/6	49°15'	65°19'
Madeleine-Centre	UNP/LNO	QC	Denis-Riverin	22 H/3	49°15'	65°21'
Madeleine, Îles de la	ISL/ÎLE	QC	Les Îles-de-la-Madeleine	11 N/12	47°30'	61°45'
Madeleine, Lac	LAKE/LAC	QC	Denis-Riverin	22 A/13	48°52'	65°51'
Madeleine, Rivière	RIV/CDE	QC	Denis-Riverin	22 H/3	49°15'	65°20'
Maders Cove	UNP/LNO	NS	Lunenburg	21 A/8	44°26'	64°21'
Madge Lake	LAKE/LAC	SK	30,31-30-W	62 N/12	51°40'	101°38'
Madigans	UNP/LNO	ON	Parry Sound	41 H/8	45°30'	80°15'
Madison	VILG/VILG	SK	16-26-22-W3	72 N/3	51°13'	109°01'
Madoc	VILG/VILG	ON	Hastings	31 C/11	44°30'	77°28'
Madoc	MUN2/AZM2	ON	Hastings	31 C/12	44°35'	77°30'
Madoc	UNP/LNO	ON	Peel	30 M/12	43°42'	79°45'

NAME NOM	ENTITY ENTITÉ	LOC 1 LIEU 1	LOC 2 LIEU 2	MAP CARTE	POSITION LAT	LONG
Madoc Junction	UNP/LNO	ON	Hastings	31 C/6	44°19'	77°28'
Madran	UNP/LNO	NB	Gloucester	21 P/13	47°49'	65°46'
Madrid	UNP/LNO	SK	32-16-24-W2	72 I/6	50°23'	105°16'
Madril, La	UNP/LNO	QC	L'Islet	21 L/16	46°54'	70°06'
Mad River	RIV/CDE	ON	Simcoe	31 D/5	44°24'	79°54'
Mad River	RIV/CDE	BC	Kamloops Division Yale	82 M/12	51°40'	119°37'
Madsen	UNP/LNO	ON	Kenora	52 K/13	50°58'	93°55'
Maecks Subdivision	UNP/LNO	ON	Parry Sound	31 E/14	45°50'	79°23'
Mafeking	UNP/LNO	ON	Huron	40 P/13	43°55'	81°36'
Mafeking	UNP/LNO	MB	43-26-W	63 C/11	52°41'	101°07'
Magaguadavic	UNP/LNO	NB	York	21 G/14	45°46'	67°10'
Magaguadavic Lake	LAKE/LAC	NB	York	21 G/11	45°43'	67°12'
Magaguadavic River	RIV/CDE	NB	Charlotte	21 G/2	45°07'	66°54'
Magaguadavic Siding	UNP/LNO	NB	York	21 G/11	45°41'	67°12'
Maganasipi, Lac	LAKE/LAC	QC	Témiscamingue	31 L/9	46°32'	78°23'
Maganktoon 56	IR/RI	BC	Range 5 Coast	103 I/5	54°19'	129°59'
Magdalen Shallows	SEAU/SMER	—		1399A	47°25'	62°45'
Magenta	UNP/LNO	QC	Rouville	31 H/7	45°17'	72°53'
Maggie Lake	LAKE/LAC	BC	Clayoquot	92 F/3	49°01'	125°26'
Maggotty Point	CAPE/CAP	NF		1 K/13	46°58'	53°49'
Magill Lake	LAKE/LAC	MB		53 L/10	54°45'	94°57'
Maginot	UNP/LNO	MB		62 H/14	49°52'	97°05'
Magiss Lake	LAKE/LAC	ON	Kenora	53 B/13	52°59'	91°40'
Magloire, Lac	LAKE/LAC	AB	79-21-W5	83 N/14	55°52'	117°10'
Magna Bay	UNP/LNO	BC	Kamloops Division Yale	82 L/14	50°58'	119°17'
Magnet	UNP/LNO	MB	15-27-15-W	62 O/5	51°19'	99°30'
Magnetawan	VILG/VILG	ON	Parry Sound	31 E/12	45°40'	79°39'
Magnetawan 1	IR/RI	ON	Parry Sound	41 H/16	45°45'	80°28'
Magnetawan River	RIV/CDE	ON	Parry Sound	41 H/15	45°46'	80°37'
Magnetic Hill	UNP/LNO	NB	Westmorland	21 I/2	46°08'	64°54'
Magnetic Point	CAPE/CAP	NT	Franklin	26 L	66°18'	70°38'
Magnet Island	ISL/ÎLE	NT	Keewatin	35 C	60°16'	77°37'
Magnet Point	CAPE/CAP	ON	Thunder Bay	52 A/7	48°25'	88°35'
Magnolia	UNP/LNO	AB	30-53-6-W5	83 G/10	53°37'	114°52'
Magnolia Bridge	UNP/LNO	AB	19-53-6-W5	83 G/10	53°35'	114°52'
Magnum Mine	UNP/LNO	BC	Peace River	94 K/11	58°30'	125°10'
Magog	CITY/VIL1	QC	Memphrémagog	31 H/8	45°16'	72°08'
Magog	VILG/VILG	QC	Memphrémagog	31 H/1	45°15'	72°10'
Magog, Lac	LAKE/LAC	QC	Memphrémagog	31 H/8	45°18'	72°02'
Magoon Point	UNP/LNO	QC	Memphrémagog	31 H/1	45°06'	72°15'
Magpie	UNP/LNO	QC	Minganie	22 I/8	50°19'	64°30'
Magpie	UNP/LNO	ON	Algoma	42 C/2	48°06'	84°42'
Magpie, Baie de	BAY/BAIE	QC	Minganie	22 I/8	50°17'	64°27'
Magpie, Lac	LAKE/LAC	QC	Minganie	22 P/2	51°00'	64°41'
Magpie Mine	UNP/LNO	ON	Algoma	42 C/2	48°13'	84°43'
Magpie Ouest, Rivière	RIV/CDE	QC	Minganie	22 P/2	51°02'	64°42'
Magpie River	RIV/CDE	ON	Algoma	41 N/15	47°56'	84°50'
Magpie, Rivière	RIV/CDE	QC	Minganie	22 I/8	50°19'	64°27'
Magrath	TOWN/VIL2	AB	5-22-W4	82 H/7	49°25'	112°52'
Maguire, Cape	CAPE/CAP	NT	Franklin	57 G	71°33'	95°56'
Maguire, Lac	LAKE/LAC	QC	Kativik	34 I/6	58°15'	73°25'
Magundy	UNP/LNO	NB	York	21 G/14	45°49'	67°07'
Magundy River	RIV/CDE	YT		105 L/1	62°11'	134°21'
Maguse Lake	LAKE/LAC	NT	Keewatin	55 E	61°37'	95°10'
Maguse Point	CAPE/CAP	NT	Keewatin	55 F/5	61°20'	93°50'
Maguse River	UNP/LNO	NT	Keewatin	55 E	61°17'	94°04'
Maguse River	RIV/CDE	NT	Keewatin	55 E	61°17'	94°04'
Magusi River - also-aussi - Magusi, Rivière	RIV/CDE	ON	Cochrane	32 D/6	48°27'	79°21'
Magusi, Rivière - also-aussi - Magusi River	RIV/CDE	QC	Abitibi-Ouest	32 D/6	48°27'	79°21'
Magwekstala 10	IR/RI	BC	Range 1 Coast	92 L/15	50°55'	126°46'
Magyar	UNP/LNO	SK	2-26-16-W2	72 P/1	51°11'	104°08'
Mahaska	UNP/LNO	AB	56,57-13-W5	83 G/13	53°53'	115°56'
Mahatta Creek	RIV/CDE	BC	Rupert	92 L/5	50°27'	127°52'
Mahatta River	UNP/LNO	BC	Rupert	92 L/5	50°28'	127°48'
Maher	UNP/LNO	ON	Cochrane	42 H/6	49°27'	81°09'
Mahers	UNP/LNO	NF		1 N/6	47°24'	53°22'
Mahigan Lake	LAKE/LAC	SK	66-4-W3	73 J/9	54°42'	106°30'
Mahinaikanapeu Umehkanam	UNP/LNO	QC	Côte-Nord-du-Golfe-Saint-Laurent	12 K/8	50°17'	60°19'
Mahmalillikullah 1	IR/RI	BC	Range 1 Coast	92 L/10	50°37'	126°34'
Mahone Bay	TOWN/VIL2	NS	Lunenburg	21 A/8	44°27'	64°23'
Mahone Bay	BAY/BAIE	NS	Lunenburg	21 A/8	44°30'	64°13'
Mahoneys Beach	UNP/LNO	NS	Antigonish	11 F/12	45°42'	61°54'
Mahoneys Corner	UNP/LNO	NS	Cumberland	11 E/12	45°41'	63°38'
Mahon, Lac	LAKE/LAC	QC	Les Collines-de-l'Outaouais	31 F/9	45°41'	76°01'
Mahony Lake	LAKE/LAC	NT	Mackenzie	96 F	65°30'	125°20'

NAME NOM	ENTITY ENTITÉ	LOC 1 LIEU 1	LOC 2 LIEU 2	MAP CARTE	POSITION LAT	LONG
Mahood Falls	UNP/LNO	BC	Lillooet	92 P/15	51°50′	120°39′
Mahood Lake	LAKE/LAC	BC	Kamloops Division Yale	92 P/16	51°55′	120°24′
Mahope 3	IR/RI	BC	Rupert	92 L/4	50°08′	127°35′
Mahpahkum 4	IR/RI	BC	Range 1 Coast	92 L/14	50°53′	127°28′
Mah-te-nicht 8	IR/RI	BC	Rupert	92 L/5	50°28′	127°52′
Mahtihk Niapaut	UNP/LNO	QC	Minganie	12 L/4	50°13′	63°48′
Maiangowi Settlement	UNP/LNO	ON	Manitoulin	41 H/13	45°46′	81°43′
Maicasagi, Lac	LAKE/LAC	QC	Jamésie	32 F/15	49°56′	76°39′
Maicasagi, Rivière	RIV/CDE	QC	Jamésie	32 F/15	49°57′	76°33′
Maiden Island	ISL/ÎLE	NT	Franklin	35 I	62°01′	72°25′
Maidens	UNP/LNO	ON	Timiskaming	31 M/3	47°13′	79°27′
Maidmonts Island	ISL/ÎLE	NF		14 L/7	58°22′	62°35′
Maidstone	TOWN/VIL2	SK	47-23-W3	73 F/3	53°06′	109°17′
Maidstone	MUN2/AZM2	ON	Essex	40 J/2	42°15′	82°47′
Maidstone	UNP/LNO	NF		12 B/2	48°12′	58°53′
Maidstone	UNP/LNO	ON	Essex	40 J/2	42°13′	82°53′
Maidstone Lake	LAKE/LAC	SK	46,47-23-W3	73 F/3	53°02′	109°17′
Maikan Sakaikan Ecitacikewapan	UNP/LNO	QC	Témiscamingue	31 M/1	47°03′	78°21′
Mailhot	UNP/LNO	QC	L'Érable	21 L/4	46°11′	71°41′
Maillard	UNP/LNO	QC	Charlevoix	21 M/7	47°20′	70°33′
Maillardville	UNP/LNO	BC	New Westminster	92 G/2	49°14′	122°53′
Maillou House National Historic Site - also-aussi - Maison-Maillou, Lieu historique national de la	PARK/PARC	QC	Communauté urbaine de Québec	21 L/14	46°49′	71°11′
Main-à-Dieu	UNP/LNO	NS	Cape Breton	11 J/4	46°00′	59°51′
Main Brook	TOWN/VIL2	NF		12 P/1	51°11′	56°01′
Main Brook	RIV/CDE	NF		1 M/3	47°06′	55°17′
Main Centre	HAM/HAM	SK	5-19-10-W3	72 J/11	50°35′	107°21′
Main Channel	CHAN/CHEN	ON	Bruce	41 H/5	45°21′	81°45′
Main Channel (French River)	CHAN/CHEN	ON	Parry Sound	41 I/2	46°01′	80°50′
Main Duck Island	ISL/ÎLE	ON	Prince Edward	30 N/15	43°56′	76°37′
Maine, Golfe du - also-aussi - Maine, Gulf of	BAY/BAIE	—			44°00′	66°30′
Maine, Gulf of - also-aussi - Maine, Golfe du	BAY/BAIE	—			44°00′	66°30′
Mainguy Lake	LAKE/LAC	BC	Lillooet	92 O/12	51°33′	123°55′
Main Lake	LAKE/LAC	BC	Sayward	92 K/3	50°13′	125°13′
Mainland	UNP/LNO	NF		12 B/11	48°34′	59°11′
Mainland River	RIV/CDE	MB		53 E/14	53°58′	95°05′
Main Point	UNP/LNO	NF		2 E/8	49°20′	54°26′
Main Point-Davidsville	UNP/LNO	NF		2 E/8	49°21′	54°26′
Main River	RIV/CDE	NF		12 H/15	49°46′	56°54′
Mains Lake	LAKE/LAC	NB	Northumberland	21 J/16	46°56′	66°29′
Mainstream	UNP/LNO	NB	Carleton	21 J/6	46°20′	67°24′
Mainsville	UNP/LNO	ON	Grenville	31 B/14	44°49′	75°26′
Mair	UNP/LNO	SK	17-9-32-W	62 F/12	49°44′	101°48′
Mair Mills	UNP/LNO	ON	Simcoe	41 A/8	44°30′	80°17′
Maison commémorative Bethune, Lieu historique national de la - also-aussi - Bethune Memorial House National Historic Site	PARK/PARC	ON		31 D/14	44°55′	79°23′
Maison de Pierre, Lac de la	LAKE/LAC	QC	Antoine-Labelle	31 J/15	46°53′	74°42′
Maison-de-Sir-John-Johnson, Lieu historique national de la - also-aussi - Sir John Johnson House National Historic Site	PARK/PARC	ON	Glengarry	31 G/2	45°09′	74°35′
Maison-des-Mines, La	UNP/LNO	QC	Beauce-Sartigan	21 E/16	45°58′	70°28′
Maison-Inverarden, Lieu historique national de la - also-aussi - Inverarden House National Historic Site	PARK/PARC	ON	Stormont	31 G/2	45°02′	74°40′
Maison-Laurier, Lieu historique national de la - also-aussi - Laurier House National Historic Site	PARK/PARC	ON	Carleton	31 G/5	45°26′	75°41′
Maison-Maillou, Lieu historique national de la - also-aussi - Maillou House National Historic Site	PARK/PARC	QC	Communauté urbaine de Québec	21 L/14	46°49′	71°11′
Maisonnette	VILG/VILG	NB	Gloucester	21 P/14	47°49′	65°00′
Maison-Riel, Lieu historique national de la - also-aussi - Riel House National Historic Site	PARK/PARC	MB		62 H/14	49°49′	97°08′
Maison-Saint-Bernard	UNP/LNO	QC	Bellechasse	21 L/10	46°39′	70°39′
Maisons-de-Cèdre	UNP/LNO	QC	Les Pays-d'en-Haut	31 G/16	45°58′	74°09′
Maitland	UNP/LNO	NS	Hants	11 E/5	45°19′	63°30′
Maitland	UNP/LNO	NS	Lunenburg	21 A/8	44°26′	64°28′
Maitland	UNP/LNO	ON	Grenville	31 B/12	44°38′	75°37′
Maitland Bridge	UNP/LNO	NS	Annapolis	21 A/6	44°27′	65°12′
Maitland Forks	UNP/LNO	NS	Lunenburg	21 A/8	44°26′	64°30′
Maitland Island	ISL/ÎLE	BC	Range 4 Coast	103 H/10	53°43′	128°58′
Maitland Point	CAPE/CAP	NT	Mackenzie	107 E	70°09′	128°12′
Maitland River	RIV/CDE	ON	Huron	40 P/12	43°45′	81°43′
Maitland Station	UNP/LNO	NS	Lunenburg	21 A/8	44°26′	64°28′
Majeau Lake	LAKE/LAC	AB	57-3,4-W5	83 G/16	53°54′	114°25′
Majestic	UNP/LNO	AB	31-21-6-W4	72 L/15	50°51′	110°50′
Major	VILG/VILG	SK	34-33-26-W3	72 N/13	51°52′	109°37′
Major, Lake	LAKE/LAC	NS	Halifax	11 D/11	44°45′	63°30′
Majorville	UNP/LNO	AB	27-19-20-W4	82 I/10	50°38′	112°42′
Maka 8	IR/RI	BC	Kamloops Division Yale	92 I/5	50°16′	121°33′

NAME / NOM	ENTITY / ENTITÉ	LOC 1 / LIEU 1	LOC 2 / LIEU 2	MAP / CARTE	POSITION LAT	POSITION LONG
Maka Creek	RIV/CDE	BC	Yale Division Yale	92 H/14	49°58′	121°05′
Makada Lake	LAKE/LAC	ON	Sudbury	41 I/6	46°22′	81°10′
Makaoo 120	IR/RI	AB/SK		73 E/9	53°40′	110°03′
Makaroff	UNP/LNO	MB	21-27-29-W	62 N/5	51°21′	101°31′
Makataewaukawauk	UNP/LNO	ON	Bruce	41 A/15	44°57′	80°58′
Makepeace	UNP/LNO	AB	8-23-19-W4	82 I/15	50°56′	112°37′
Makinak	UNP/LNO	MB	17-23-16-W	62 J/13	50°59′	99°40′
Makinson	UNP/LNO	BC	Kootenay	82 K/4	50°04′	117°55′
Makinson Inlet	BAY/BAIE	NT	Franklin	39 C	77°16′	79°40′
Makinsons	UNP/LNO	NF		1 N/6	47°29′	53°19′
Makkovik	VILG/VILG	NF		13 O/3	55°05′	59°11′
Makkovik Bay	BAY/BAIE	NF		13 O/3	55°06′	59°14′
Makkovik, Cape	CAPE/CAP	NF		13 O/3	55°14′	59°09′
Makkovik River	RIV/CDE	NF		13 J/14	54°59′	59°25′
Maklaksadagmaks 41	IR/RI	BC	Range 5 Coast	103 J/16	54°47′	130°26′
Maklaksadagmaks 42	IR/RI	BC	Range 5 Coast	103 J/16	54°50′	130°29′
Makobe Lake	LAKE/LAC	ON	Timiskaming	41 P/8	47°26′	80°25′
Makobe River	RIV/CDE	ON	Timiskaming	41 P/9	47°44′	80°20′
Makokibatan Lake	LAKE/LAC	ON	Kenora	42 M/6	51°17′	87°20′
Makoop Lake	LAKE/LAC	ON	Kenora	53 G/7	53°24′	90°50′
Makoop River	RIV/CDE	ON	Kenora	53 G/15	53°47′	90°50′
Maktak Fiord	BAY/BAIE	NT	Franklin	26 P	67°19′	64°23′
Makwa	VILG/VILG	SK	58-20-W3	73 K/2	54°00′	108°55′
Makwa	UNP/LNO	ON	Sudbury	41 P/12	47°33′	81°41′
Makwa Lake	LAKE/LAC	SK		73 K/3	54°04′	109°15′
Makwa Lake 129	IR/RI	SK		73 F/14	54°00′	109°19′
Makwa Lake 129A	IR/RI	SK		73 K/3	54°02′	109°04′
Makwa Lake 129B	IR/RI	SK		73 K/3	54°02′	109°13′
Makwa Lake 129C	IR/RI	SK		73 K/3	54°02′	109°05′
Makwa River	RIV/CDE	SK	61-19-W3	73 K/2	54°15′	108°42′
Malachan 11	IR/RI	BC	Renfrew	92 C/15	48°49′	124°40′
Malachi	UNP/LNO	ON	Kenora	52 E/15	49°56′	94°59′
Malachi Lake	LAKE/LAC	ON	Kenora	52 E/14	49°53′	95°00′
Malagash	UNP/LNO	NS	Cumberland	11 E/14	45°46′	63°23′
Malagash Mine	UNP/LNO	NS	Cumberland	11 E/14	45°47′	63°20′
Malagash Point	UNP/LNO	NS	Cumberland	11 E/14	45°48′	63°16′
Malagash Point	CAPE/CAP	NS	Cumberland	11 E/14	45°48′	63°14′
Malagash Station	UNP/LNO	NS	Cumberland	11 E/14	45°45′	63°25′
Malagawatch	UNP/LNO	NS	Inverness	11 F/15	45°50′	60°59′
Malagawatch 4	IR/RI	NS	Inverness	11 F/15	45°53′	61°00′
Malahat	UNP/LNO	BC	Malahat	92 B/12	48°33′	123°34′
Malahat	UNP/LNO	BC	Malahat	92 B/12	48°34′	123°35′
Malahat 11	IR/RI	BC	Malahat	92 B/12	48°37′	123°31′
Malahat Land District	GEOG/GÉOG	BC		92 B	48°33′	123°48′
Malahide	MUN2/AZM2	ON	Elgin	40 I/10	42°45′	80°58′
Malahide	UNP/LNO	ON	Elgin	40 I/10	42°44′	80°54′
Malakoff	UNP/LNO	NB	Westmorland	21 I/2	46°08′	64°32′
Malakoff	UNP/LNO	ON	Carleton	31 G/4	45°06′	75°46′
Malakwa	UNP/LNO	BC	Kamloops Division Yale	82 L/15	50°56′	118°48′
Malartic	CITY/VIL1	QC	Vallée-de-l'Or	32 D/1	48°08′	78°08′
Malartic, Lac	LAKE/LAC	QC	Vallée-de-l'Or	32 D/8	48°15′	78°07′
Malaspina Strait	CHAN/CHEN	BC	New Westminster	92 F/9	49°40′	124°15′
Malauze	UNP/LNO	NB	Restigouche	21 O/15	47°57′	66°45′
Malay Falls	UNP/LNO	NS	Halifax	11 D/16	44°59′	62°29′
Malbaie, La	BAY/BAIE	QC	Pabok	22 A/9	48°35′	64°14′
Malbaie, Lac	LAKE/LAC	QC	La Côte-de-Beaupré	21 M/11	47°34′	71°00′
Malbaie, Rivière	RIV/CDE	QC	Pabok	22 A/9	48°37′	64°19′
Malbaie, Rivière	RIV/CDE	QC	Charlevoix-Est	21 M/9	47°39′	70°09′
Mal-Bay	UNP/LNO	QC	Pabok	22 A/9	48°37′	64°12′
Mal Bay	BAY/BAIE	NF		1 M/11	47°38′	55°10′
Mal Bay Brook	RIV/CDE	NF		1 M/11	47°42′	55°08′
Malcolm	UNP/LNO	ON	Bruce	41 A/3	44°14′	81°06′
Malcolm Island	ISL/ÎLE	SK		64 D/16	57°00′	102°08′
Malcolm Island	ISL/ÎLE	BC	Rupert	92 L/10	50°39′	126°59′
Malcolm Island 8	IR/RI	BC	Rupert	92 L/11	50°38′	127°08′
Malcolm Point	CAPE/CAP	BC	Rupert	92 L/11	50°40′	127°06′
Malcolm River	RIV/CDE	YT		117 D/12	69°33′	139°37′
Malden	MUN2/AZM2	ON	Essex	40 J/3	42°05′	83°02′
Malden	UNP/LNO	NB	Westmorland	11 L/4	46°06′	63°53′
Malden Centre	UNP/LNO	ON	Essex	40 J/3	42°03′	83°02′
Maldigues Bay	BAY/BAIE	NF		12 I/14	51°00′	57°03′
Maleb	UNP/LNO	AB	24-8-10-W4	72 E/11	49°40′	111°15′
Male Otter, Lac	LAKE/LAC	QC	Jamésie	23 L/1	54°07′	70°07′
Malfait, Lac	LAKE/LAC	NT	Mackenzie	86 C	64°38′	117°57′
Malherbe	UNP/LNO	QC	Le Fjord-du-Saguenay	22 D/6	48°19′	71°03′

NAME NOM	ENTITY ENTITÉ	LOC 1 LIEU 1	LOC 2 LIEU 2	MAP CARTE	POSITION LAT	POSITION LONG
Malibu	UNP/LNO	BC	New Westminster	92 J/4	50°10'	123°51'
Malignant Cove	UNP/LNO	NS	Antigonish	11 E/16	45°47'	62°05'
Maligne Lake	LAKE/LAC	AB	42,43-25-W5	83 C/12	52°40'	117°31'
Maligne River	RIV/CDE	AB	45-1-W6	83 D/16	52°56'	118°02'
Malim Creek	RIV/CDE	BC	Range 2 Coast	92 N/1	51°04'	124°20'
Maliotenam 27A	IR/RI	QC	Caniapiscau	22 J/1	50°13'	66°11'
Maliseet	UNP/LNO	NB	Victoria	21 J/13	46°46'	67°42'
Malksope 7	IR/RI	BC	Rupert	92 L/3	50°08'	127°25'
Malksope Inlet	BAY/BAIE	BC	Rupert	92 L/3	50°07'	127°28'
Mallaig	UNP/LNO	AB	25-60-10-W4	73 L/3	54°13'	111°22'
Mallard	UNP/LNO	MB	34-15-W	62 O/13	51°57'	99°34'
Mallard Lake	LAKE/LAC	SK	65-19-W3	73 K/10	54°38'	108°45'
Mall Bay	UNP/LNO	NF		1 K/13	46°59'	53°35'
Mallery Lake	LAKE/LAC	NT	Keewatin	65 O	63°59'	98°23'
Mallet Lake	LAKE/LAC	NT	Mackenzie	65 E	61°12'	102°16'
Malley Lake	LAKE/LAC	NT	Mackenzie	75 N	63°35'	108°02'
Mallik Island	ISL/ÎLE	NT	Franklin	36 C	64°14'	76°38'
Malloch, Cape	CAPE/CAP	NT	Franklin	79 F	78°46'	110°43'
Mallorytown	UNP/LNO	ON	Leeds	31 B/5	44°29'	75°53'
Mallorytown Landing	UNP/LNO	ON	Leeds	31 B/5	44°27'	75°52'
Mallow	UNP/LNO	AB	16-22-16-W4	82 I/16	50°52'	112°10'
Malloy Lake	LAKE/LAC	MB	12-15-E	52 L/3	50°01'	95°27'
Malmaison	UNP/LNO	QC	Brome-Missisquoi	31 H/3	45°09'	73°04'
Malmgren	UNP/LNO	SK	15-31-14-W3	72 O/12	51°40'	107°55'
Malmo	UNP/LNO	AB	14-44-23-W4	83 A/14	52°47'	113°13'
Malobès, Grand lac	LAKE/LAC	QC	Rimouski-Neigette	22 C/7	48°16'	68°52'
Malone	UNP/LNO	ON	Hastings	31 C/12	44°34'	77°36'
Malonton	UNP/LNO	MB	26-18-2-E	62 I/11	50°34'	97°13'
Malouin, Rivière	RIV/CDE	QC	Jamésie	32 L/11	50°42'	79°19'
Malpeque	UNP/LNO	PE	Prince	11 L/12	46°32'	63°41'
Malpeque Bay	VILG/VILG	PE	Prince	11 L/12	46°31'	63°39'
Malpeque Bay	BAY/BAIE	PE	Prince	11 L/12	46°32'	63°47'
Maltais	UNP/LNO	NB	Restigouche	21 O/15	47°56'	66°37'
Maltampec	UNP/LNO	NB	Gloucester	21 P/11	47°40'	65°00'
Malton	UNP/LNO	ON	Peel	30 M/12	43°42'	79°38'
Malvern	UNP/LNO	ON	York	30 M/14	43°48'	79°13'
Malvern West	UNP/LNO	ON	York	30 M/14	43°47'	79°15'
Malvina	UNP/LNO	QC	Le Haut-Saint-François	21 E/3	45°11'	71°27'
Malwood	UNP/LNO	ON	Carleton	31 G/5	45°24'	76°00'
Mamainse Point	CAPE/CAP	ON	Algoma	41 N/2	47°02'	84°47'
Mamakwash Lake	LAKE/LAC	ON	Kenora	52 N/10	51°38'	92°56'
Mamalilaculla	UNP/LNO	BC	Range 1 Coast	92 L/10	50°37'	126°35'
Mamawi Lake	LAKE/LAC	AB	110,111-9-W4	74 L/11	58°38'	111°28'
Mameigwess Lake	LAKE/LAC	ON	Kenora	43 D/12	52°35'	87°50'
Mameigwess Lake	LAKE/LAC	ON	Kenora	52 G/12	49°34'	91°49'
Mamen, Cape	CAPE/CAP	NT	Franklin	79 C	77°37'	110°03'
Ma-Me-O Beach	VILG/VILG	AB	14-46-28-W4	83 A/13	52°58'	113°59'
Ma-Me-O Beach Provincial Park	PARK/PARC	AB	14-46-28-W4	83 A/13	52°59'	113°57'
Mamit Lake	LAKE/LAC	BC	Kamloops Division Yale	92 I/7	50°23'	120°48'
Mammamattawa	UNP/LNO	ON	Cochrane	42 K/8	50°25'	84°22'
Mammin River 25	IR/RI	BC	Queen Charlotte	103 F/9	53°37'	132°19'
Mamozekel River	RIV/CDE	NB	Victoria	21 O/3	47°15'	67°09'
Mamquam Icefield	GLAC/GLAC	BC	New Westminster	92 G/15	49°48'	122°51'
Mamquam Lake	LAKE/LAC	BC	New Westminster	92 G/15	49°49'	122°55'
Mamquam Mountain	MTN/MNT	BC	New Westminster	92 G/15	49°46'	122°51'
Mamquam River	RIV/CDE	BC	New Westminster	92 G/11	49°44'	123°09'
Manassette Lake	UNP/LNO	NS	Guysborough	11 F/6	45°26'	61°20'
Manatinaw Hill	MTN/MNT	SK	44-27-W2	73 A/13	52°47'	105°51'
Manawan Lake	LAKE/LAC	SK		63 M/6	55°24'	103°14'
Manawan Lake	LAKE/LAC	AB	56,57-25-W4	83 H/13	53°54'	113°41'
Manbert	UNP/LNO	ON	Parry Sound	41 H/9	45°38'	80°26'
Manche-d'Épée	UNP/LNO	QC	Denis-Riverin	22 H/6	49°15'	65°26'
Manche-d'Épée, Réserve écologique de	PARK/PARC	QC	Denis-Riverin	22 H/3	49°13'	65°27'
Manchester	UNP/LNO	NS	Guysborough	11 F/6	45°27'	61°28'
Manchester	UNP/LNO	ON	Ontario	31 D/2	44°05'	78°59'
Manchester Lake	LAKE/LAC	NT	Mackenzie	75 G	61°28'	107°29'
Mandalay West	UNP/LNO	MB		62 H/14	49°57'	97°11'
Mandaumin	UNP/LNO	ON	Lambton	40 J/16	42°57'	82°14'
Manders	UNP/LNO	ON	Rainy River	52 D/9	48°40'	94°04'
Mandreville Lake	LAKE/LAC	NT	Keewatin	55 L	62°46'	95°14'
Manful Bight	BAY/BAIE	NF		2 E/14	49°57'	55°29'
Manganese Mines	UNP/LNO	NS	Colchester	11 E/6	45°25'	63°10'
Mangnuc, Lac	LAKE/LAC	QC	Kativik	34 N/7	59°28'	76°38'
Manhard	UNP/LNO	ON	Grenville	31 B/12	44°41'	75°44'
Manhattan Beach	UNP/LNO	MB	8-5-16-W	62 G/5	49°23'	99°36'

NAME / NOM	ENTITY / ENTITÉ	LOC 1 / LIEU 1	LOC 2 / LIEU 2	MAP / CARTE	POSITION LAT	LONG
Manibridge	UNP/LNO	MB	22-66-10-W	63 J/10	54°44′	98°52′
Manic-Cinq	UNP/LNO	QC	Manicouagan	22 K/10	50°38′	68°44′
Manic-Deux, Barrage	MISC/DIV	QC	Manicouagan	22 F/8	49°19′	68°21′
Manic Deux, Réservoir	LAKE/LAC	QC	Manicouagan	22 F/8	49°25′	68°25′
Manico Point	CAPE/CAP	NT	Keewatin	45 N	63°33′	85°38′
Manicouagan	MUN1/AZM1	QC	Manicouagan	22 F/1	49°13′	68°09′
Manicouagan, Péninsule de	CAPE/CAP	QC	Manicouagan	22 F/1	49°08′	68°20′
Manicouagan, Petite rivière	RIV/CDE	QC	Caniapiscau	22 O/13	51°55′	67°42′
Manicouagan, Petit lac	LAKE/LAC	QC	Caniapiscau	22 O/13	51°50′	67°38′
Manicouagan, Pointe	CAPE/CAP	QC	Manicouagan	22 F/1	49°06′	68°12′
Manicouagan, Réservoir	LAKE/LAC	QC	Manicouagan	22 N/2	51°08′	68°45′
Manicouagan, Rivière	RIV/CDE	QC	Manicouagan	22 F/1	49°11′	68°12′
Manic Trois, Réservoir	LAKE/LAC	QC	Manicouagan	22 K/2	50°00′	68°40′
Manic-Un, Barrage	MISC/DIV	QC	Manicouagan	22 F/1	49°12′	68°20′
Manigotagan	UNP/LNO	MB		62 P/1	51°07′	96°18′
Manigotagan River	RIV/CDE	MB/ON		62 P/1	51°07′	96°20′
Manigotagan Settlement	GEOG/GÉOG	MB		62 P/1	51°07′	96°18′
Maniittur Cape	CAPE/CAP	NT	Franklin	25 K	62°33′	69°25′
Manikanis	UNP/LNO	QC	Kativik	24 B/3	56°13′	67°24′
Manilla	UNP/LNO	ON	Victoria	31 D/7	44°18′	79°00′
Manion Corners	UNP/LNO	ON	Carleton	31 F/8	45°15′	76°04′
Manion Lake	LAKE/LAC	ON	Rainy River	52 C/16	48°54′	92°19′
Manir	UNP/LNO	AB	4-78-4-W6	83 M/10	55°44′	118°33′
Manirainnaat	UNP/LNO	QC	Kativik	25 C/12	60°35′	69°51′
Manistikwan Lake - see-voir - Big Island Lake	LAKE/LAC	MB		63 K/13	54°45′	101°46′
Manistuueu	UNP/LNO	QC	Kativik	24 A/7	56°27′	64°47′
Manitoba	PROV/PROV	MB		MCR27	55°00′	97°00′
Manitoba House Settlement	GEOG/GÉOG	MB		62 J/15	50°52′	98°52′
Manitoba, Lac - also-aussi - **Manitoba, Lake**	LAKE/LAC	MB		62 J/15	50°59′	98°48′
Manitoba, Lake - also-aussi - **Manitoba, Lac**	LAKE/LAC	MB		62 J/15	50°59′	98°48′
Manitoba, Le	UNP/LNO	QC	Denis-Riverin	22 G/1	49°04′	66°30′
Manitou	VILG/VILG	MB	30-3-8-W	62 G/2	49°14′	98°32′
Manitou	UNP/LNO	QC	Minganie	22 I/6	50°18′	65°15′
Manitou Beach	VILG/VILG	SK	2-32-25-W2	72 P/11	51°43′	105°26′
Manitou Dock	UNP/LNO	ON	Parry Sound	41 H/1	45°07′	80°07′
Manitou Falls	UNP/LNO	ON	Kenora	52 K/11	50°35′	93°26′
Manitou Island	ISL/ÎLE	NT	Mackenzie	96 G	65°02′	122°17′
Manitou Island	ISL/ÎLE	NT	Mackenzie	106 I	66°17′	128°40′
Manitou Islands	ISL/ÎLE	ON	Nipissing	31 L/5	46°15′	79°35′
Manitou, Lac	LAKE/LAC	QC	Minganie	12 L/5	50°29′	63°54′
Manitou, Lac	LAKE/LAC	QC	Minganie	22 I/14	50°53′	65°17′
Manitou Lake	LAKE/LAC	ON	Nipissing	31 L/2	46°01′	79°00′
Manitou Lake	LAKE/LAC	ON	Manitoulin	41 G/16	45°47′	82°00′
Manitou Lake	LAKE/LAC	SK		73 C/12	52°43′	109°43′
Manitou Lake No. 442	MUN2/AZM2	SK		73 C/13	52°50′	109°45′
Manitoulin	GEOG/GÉOG	ON		41 G/9	45°45′	82°30′
Manitoulin Island	ISL/ÎLE	ON	Manitoulin	41 G/16	45°50′	82°20′
Manitounuk Sound	CHAN/CHEN	NT	Keewatin	33 N	55°30′	77°25′
Manitou Park	UNP/LNO	ON	Algoma	41 K/9	46°32′	84°16′
Manitou Rapids 11	IR/RI	ON	Rainy River	52 C/12	48°39′	93°55′
Manitou River	RIV/CDE	ON	Manitoulin	41 G/9	45°36′	82°06′
Manitou, Rivière	RIV/CDE	QC	Minganie	22 I/8	50°18′	64°01′
Manitou, Rivière	RIV/CDE	QC	Minganie	22 I/6	50°18′	65°15′
Manitou Sound	BAY/BAIE	ON	Rainy River	52 C/14	48°54′	93°19′
Manitou Stretch	RIVF/EFLV	ON	Kenora	52 F/3	49°09′	93°07′
Manitouwabing Lake	LAKE/LAC	ON	Parry Sound	31 E/5	45°29′	79°54′
Manitouwadge	MUN2/AZM2	ON	Thunder Bay	42 F/4	49°08′	85°50′
Manitouwadge	UNP/LNO	ON	Thunder Bay	42 F/4	49°07′	85°50′
Manitowaning	UNP/LNO	ON	Manitoulin	41 H/12	45°45′	81°49′
Manitowaning Bay	BAY/BAIE	ON	Manitoulin	41 H/13	45°48′	81°48′
Manitowik Lake	LAKE/LAC	ON	Algoma	42 C/1	48°10′	84°24′
Manitung Island	ISL/ÎLE	NT	Franklin	27 A	68°08′	65°38′
Maniwaki	CITY/VIL1	QC	La Vallée-de-la-Gatineau	31 J/5	46°23′	75°58′
Maniwaki 18 - see-voir - Kitigan Zibi	IR/RI	QC		31 K/8	46°22′	76°04′
Mankota	VILG/VILG	SK	30-5-8-W3	72 G/6	49°25′	107°04′
Mankota No. 45	MUN2/AZM2	SK		72 G/6	49°25′	107°00′
Manley	UNP/LNO	ON	Huron	40 P/11	43°36′	81°14′
Manlius	UNP/LNO	MB		62 H/14	49°59′	97°02′
Manly Corner	UNP/LNO	AB	16-53-2-W5	83 G/9	53°34′	114°13′
Mann	UNP/LNO	QC	Avignon	22 B/2	48°05′	66°43′
Mann Creek	RIV/CDE	BC	Kamloops Division Yale	92 P/9	51°34′	120°08′
Manners Sutton	UNP/LNO	NB	York	21 G/11	45°41′	67°02′
Manners Sutton	GEOG/GÉOG	NB	York	21 G/11	45°38′	67°05′
Mannessier, Lac	LAKE/LAC	QC	Kativik	23 M/7	55°25′	70°40′
Manneville	UNP/LNO	QC	Abitibi	32 D/9	48°33′	78°26′

NAME NOM	ENTITY ENTITÉ	LOC 1 LIEU 1	LOC 2 LIEU 2	MAP CARTE	POSITION LAT	LONG
Mannheim	UNP/LNO	ON	Waterloo	40 P/7	43°24'	80°33'
Mannhurst	UNP/LNO	NB	Kings	21 H/14	45°57'	65°17'
Manning	TOWN/VIL2	AB	28-91-23-W5	84 C/13	56°55'	117°37'
Manning	UNP/LNO	BC	Yale Division Yale	92 H/10	49°38'	120°47'
Manning, Cape	CAPE/CAP	NT	Franklin	98 H	75°51'	122°20'
Manning Park	UNP/LNO	BC	Yale Division Yale	92 H/2	49°04'	120°47'
Mann Lake	LAKE/LAC	SK	37,38-6-W2	63 D/2	52°15'	102°45'
Mann Mountain Settlement	UNP/LNO	NB	Restigouche	21 O/15	47°56'	66°58'
Mann, Ruisseau	RIV/CDE	QC	Avignon	22 B/1	48°10'	66°22'
Mann Settlement	UNP/LNO	QC	Avignon	22 B/3	48°00'	67°01'
Mann Siding	UNP/LNO	NB	Restigouche	21 O/11	47°44'	67°13'
Mannville	VILG/VILG	AB	25-50-9-W4	73 E/6	53°20'	111°10'
Man of War Cove	UNP/LNO	NF		12 B/10	48°32'	58°48'
Man of War Point	CAPE/CAP	NF		13 I/11	54°31'	57°15'
Manoir-Papineau, Lieu historique national du - also-aussi - Manoir Papineau National Historic Site	PARK/PARC	QC	Papineau	31 G/10	45°39'	74°57'
Manoir Papineau National Historic Site - also-aussi - Manoir-Papineau, Lieu historique national du	PARK/PARC	QC	Papineau	31 G/10	45°39'	74°57'
Manola	UNP/LNO	AB	16-59-2-W5	83 J/1	54°06'	114°14'
Manomin	UNP/LNO	ON	Rainy River	52 C/13	48°54'	93°46'
Manomin Lake	LAKE/LAC	ON	Kenora	52 F/13	49°46'	93°45'
Manor	VILG/VILG	SK	33-7-1-W2	62 E/9	49°36'	102°05'
Manor Park	UNP/LNO	ON	Carleton	31 G/5	45°28'	75°39'
Manor Park	UNP/LNO	ON	Middlesex	40 I/14	42°58'	81°16'
Manotick	UNP/LNO	ON	Carleton	31 G/4	45°13'	75°41'
Manotick Station	UNP/LNO	ON	Carleton	31 G/5	45°15'	75°37'
Manouane	UNP/LNO	QC	Le Haut-Saint-Maurice	31 P/13	47°53'	73°48'
Manouane, Lac	LAKE/LAC	QC	Le Fjord-du-Saguenay	22 L/10	50°41'	70°45'
Manouane, Lac	LAKE/LAC	QC	Le Haut-Saint-Maurice	31 O/9	47°34'	74°07'
Manouane, Petite rivière	RIV/CDE	QC	Le Fjord-du-Saguenay	22 E/15	49°58'	70°54'
Manouane, Rivière	RIV/CDE	QC	Le Fjord-du-Saguenay	22 E/11	49°30'	71°11'
Manouane, Rivière	RIV/CDE	QC	Le Haut-Saint-Maurice	31 P/13	47°54'	73°48'
Manouanis, Lac	LAKE/LAC	QC	Le Fjord-du-Saguenay	22 L/16	50°50'	70°19'
Manouanis, Rivière	RIV/CDE	QC	Le Fjord-du-Saguenay	22 L/16	50°54'	70°16'
Man O'War Peak	MTN/MNT	NF		14 C/13	56°58'	61°40'
Man Peak	MTN/MNT	NF		2 C/13	48°49'	53°58'
Man River	RIV/CDE	SK	52-6-W2	63 E/7	53°29'	102°50'
Manseau	TOWN/VIL2	QC	Bécancour	31 I/8	46°22'	72°00'
Mansel Bank	SEAU/SMER	—		1399A	61°15'	80°15'
Mansel Island	ISL/ÎLE	NT	Keewatin	35 E	62°00'	79°50'
Mansewood	UNP/LNO	ON	Halton	30 M/12	43°33'	79°54'
Mansfield	UNP/LNO	NS	Cumberland	11 E/13	45°48'	63°56'
Mansfield	UNP/LNO	ON	Carleton	31 G/4	45°12'	75°54'
Mansfield	UNP/LNO	ON	Renfrew	31 F/8	45°26'	76°22'
Mansfield	UNP/LNO	ON	Dufferin	41 A/1	44°10'	80°02'
Mansfield-et-Pontefract	VILG/VILG	QC	Pontiac	31 K/2	46°02'	76°44'
Manson	UNP/LNO	MB	27-13-29-W	62 K/3	50°08'	101°22'
Manson Creek	UNP/LNO	BC	Cassiar	93 N/9	55°40'	124°29'
Manson Icefield	GLAC/GLAC	NT	Franklin	39 B	76°40'	79°40'
Manson Passage	CHAN/CHEN	BC	New Westminster	92 F/15	49°57'	124°53'
Manson Point	CAPE/CAP	NT	Franklin	89 B	76°05'	119°04'
Manson River	RIV/CDE	BC	Cariboo	93 O/12	55°43'	123°53'
Mansons Landing	UNP/LNO	BC	Sayward	92 K/2	50°04'	124°59'
Mansonville	UNP/LNO	QC	Memphrémagog	31 H/1	45°03'	72°23'
Mansur	UNP/LNO	SK	12-9-14-W2	62 E/12	49°43'	103°46'
Mansville	UNP/LNO	QC	Brome-Missisquoi	31 H/2	45°10'	72°36'
Mantagao Lake	LAKE/LAC	MB	27,28-4-W	62 P/5	51°21'	98°00'
Mantagao River	RIV/CDE	MB	33-3-W	62 P/13	51°52'	97°47'
Mantario	VILG/VILG	SK	34-26-27-W3	72 N/5	51°16'	109°42'
Mantario Lake	LAKE/LAC	MB/ON		52 L/3	50°00'	95°11'
Mantic Lake	LAKE/LAC	NT	Mackenzie	75 I	62°20'	104°27'
Mantle Glacier	GLAC/GLAC	BC	Range 2 Coast	92 N/7	51°18'	124°36'
Mantua	UNP/LNO	NS	Hants	21 H/1	45°00'	64°03'
Manuan 26 - see-voir - Communauté Atikamekw de Manawan	IR/RI	QC		31 O/1	47°13'	74°23'
Manuel Lake	LAKE/LAC	NT	Mackenzie	106 I	66°58'	128°54'
Manuels	UNP/LNO	NF		1 N/10	47°31'	52°57'
Manuels	UNP/LNO	NB	Northumberland	21 P/2	47°02'	64°59'
Manuels Cove	UNP/LNO	NF		2 E/10	49°36'	54°44'
Manuels River	RIV/CDE	NF		1 N/10	47°32'	52°57'
Manvers	MUN2/AZM2	ON	Victoria	31 D/2	44°10'	78°40'
Manvers	UNP/LNO	ON	Durham	31 D/2	44°08'	78°35'
Manvers, Port	BAY/BAIE	NF		14 C/14	56°58'	61°27'
Manyberries	UNP/LNO	AB	24-5-6-W4	72 E/7	49°24'	110°42'
Manyberries Creek	RIV/CDE	AB	4,5-7-W4	72 E/9	49°20'	110°53'
Many Island Lake	LAKE/LAC	AB/SK		72 L/1	50°07'	110°02'
Manzer	UNP/LNO	NB	York	21 J/2	46°04'	66°36'
Manzo Nagano, Mount	MTN/MNT	BC	Range 2 Coast	92 M/10	51°37'	126°57'

NAME NOM	ENTITY ENTITÉ	LOC 1 LIEU 1	LOC 2 LIEU 2	MAP CARTE	POSITION LAT	LONG
Mapes	UNP/LNO	BC	Range 4 Coast	93 G/13	53°53′	123°52′
Maple	UNP/LNO	ON	York	30 M/13	43°51′	79°31′
Maple	UNP/LNO	ON	Halton	30 M/5	43°20′	79°49′
Maple Bay	UNP/LNO	BC	Comiaken	92 B/13	48°49′	123°37′
Maple Beach	UNP/LNO	ON	Ontario	31 D/6	44°22′	79°11′
Maple Brook	UNP/LNO	NS	Inverness	11 F/14	45°49′	61°17′
Maple Bush No. 224	MUN2/AZM2	SK		72 J/15	51°00′	106°40′
Maple Creek	TOWN/VIL2	SK	15-11-26-W3	72 F/14	49°55′	109°29′
Maple Creek	RIV/CDE	SK	15-25-W3	72 K/3	50°14′	109°24′
Maple Creek No. 111	MUN2/AZM2	SK		72 F/13	49°55′	109°30′
Mapledale	UNP/LNO	NB	Carleton	21 J/4	46°06′	67°40′
Mapledale	UNP/LNO	QC	Brome-Missisquoi	31 H/2	45°14′	72°47′
Maple Glen	UNP/LNO	NB	Northumberland	21 P/4	47°02′	65°43′
Maple Green	UNP/LNO	NB	Restigouche	22 B/2	48°02′	66°32′
Maple Grove	CITY/VIL1	QC	Beauharnois-Salaberry	31 H/5	45°19′	73°50′
Maple Grove	UNP/LNO	NS	Hants	11 E/5	45°16′	63°32′
Maple Grove	UNP/LNO	NB	York	21 J/7	46°22′	66°43′
Maple Grove	UNP/LNO	QC	L'Amiante	21 L/4	46°05′	71°32′
Maple Grove	UNP/LNO	ON	Leeds	31 C/8	44°22′	76°12′
Maple Grove	UNP/LNO	ON	Durham	30 M/15	43°55′	78°44′
Maplegrove	UNP/LNO	ON	Simcoe	31 D/5	44°24′	79°32′
Maple Grove	UNP/LNO	ON	Dufferin	41 A/1	44°03′	80°17′
Maple Grove	UNP/LNO	ON	Brant	40 P/1	43°04′	80°20′
Maple Grove	UNP/LNO	ON	Middlesex	40 P/3	43°10′	81°18′
Maple Grove Station	UNP/LNO	NB	York	21 J/7	46°24′	66°46′
Maple Hill	UNP/LNO	PE	Queens	11 L/7	46°21′	62°52′
Maple Hill	UNP/LNO	ON	Frontenac	31 C/8	44°24′	76°21′
Maple Hill	UNP/LNO	ON	York	31 D/3	44°11′	79°25′
Maple Hill	UNP/LNO	ON	Bruce	41 A/3	44°09′	81°05′
Maple Hills	UNP/LNO	ON	Waterloo	40 P/7	43°27′	80°33′
Maplehurst	UNP/LNO	NB	Carleton	21 J/12	46°36′	67°42′
Maple Island	UNP/LNO	ON	Parry Sound	31 E/12	45°42′	79°52′
Maple Lake	UNP/LNO	ON	Haliburton	31 E/2	45°05′	78°40′
Maple Lake	LAKE/LAC	ON	Haliburton	31 E/2	45°06′	78°40′
Maple Lake	LAKE/LAC	MB	6,7-25-W	62 F/10	49°32′	100°50′
Maple Lake Park	UNP/LNO	ON	Oxford	40 P/2	43°13′	80°39′
Maple Lane	UNP/LNO	ON	Wentworth	30 M/4	43°12′	79°59′
Maple Lane	UNP/LNO	ON	Grey	41 A/2	44°04′	80°38′
Maple Lane Annex	UNP/LNO	ON	Wentworth	30 M/4	43°12′	79°59′
Maple Lawn	UNP/LNO	ON	Frontenac	31 C/8	44°18′	76°28′
Maple Leaf	UNP/LNO	QC	Le Haut-Saint-François	21 E/6	45°20′	71°29′
Maple Leaf	UNP/LNO	ON	Hastings	31 F/5	45°16′	77°50′
Maplemore	UNP/LNO	QC	Le Haut-Saint-Laurent	31 G/1	45°05′	74°19′
Maple Mountain	MTN/MNT	ON	Timiskaming	41 P/8	47°25′	80°20′
Maple Park	UNP/LNO	ON	Welland	30 M/3	43°00′	79°17′
Maple Plains	UNP/LNO	PE	Prince	11 L/5	46°17′	63°34′
Maple Point 11	IR/RI	BC	Range 4 Coast	103 H/3	53°06′	129°12′
Maple Ridge	MUN1/AZM1	BC	New Westminster	92 G/8	49°16′	122°30′
Maple Ridge	UNP/LNO	NB	York	21 J/3	46°06′	67°13′
Maple Ridge	UNP/LNO	QC	Vaudreuil-Soulanges	31 G/8	45°24′	74°10′
Maple Ridge	UNP/LNO	QC	Pontiac	31 F/9	45°33′	76°24′
Maple Ridge	UNP/LNO	ON	Dundas	31 G/3	45°05′	75°18′
Maple Ridge	UNP/LNO	ON	Muskoka	31 E/2	45°13′	78°58′
Maples	UNP/LNO	MB	4-10-26-W	62 F/15	49°48′	100°57′
Mapleton	UNP/LNO	NS	Cumberland	21 H/9	45°35′	64°09′
Mapleton	UNP/LNO	NB	Westmorland	21 I/2	46°08′	64°50′
Mapleton	UNP/LNO	NB	Albert	21 H/14	45°50′	65°03′
Mapleton	UNP/LNO	ON	Elgin	40 I/14	42°49′	81°04′
Mapleton Place	UNP/LNO	NB	Westmorland	21 I/2	46°07′	64°46′
Maple Valley	UNP/LNO	ON	Simcoe	31 D/11	44°44′	79°28′
Maple Valley	UNP/LNO	ON	Simcoe	41 A/8	44°16′	80°14′
Mapleview	UNP/LNO	NB	Victoria	21 J/14	46°58′	67°24′
Maple View	UNP/LNO	ON	Northumberland	31 C/4	44°15′	77°40′
Maplewood	UNP/LNO	PE	Queens	11 L/6	46°17′	63°27′
Maplewood	UNP/LNO	NS	Lunenburg	21 A/10	44°38′	64°37′
Maplewood	UNP/LNO	NB	York	21 J/3	46°11′	67°14′
Maplewood	UNP/LNO	ON	Oxford	40 P/7	43°16′	80°54′
Maplewood	UNP/LNO	BC	New Westminster	92 G/6	49°18′	123°00′
Mapova	UNP/LNO	AB	25-61-22-W4	83 I/6	54°18′	113°09′
Maquapit Lake	UNP/LNO	NB	Queens	21 G/16	45°56′	66°11′
Maquapit Lake	LAKE/LAC	NB	Queens	21 G/16	45°55′	66°11′
Maquatua, Rivière	RIV/CDE	QC	Jamésie	33 D/15	53°00′	78°50′
Maquazneecht Island 17	IR/RI	BC	Rupert	92 L/12	50°33′	127°33′
Maquereau, Pointe au	CAPE/CAP	QC	Pabok	22 A/2	48°12′	64°47′
Maquilla Peak	MTN/MNT	BC	Rupert	92 L/1	50°07′	126°20′

NAME NOM	ENTITY ENTITÉ	LOC 1 LIEU 1	LOC 2 LIEU 2	MAP CARTE	POSITION LAT	LONG
Maquinna Point	CAPE/CAP	BC	Nootka	92 E/10	49°35′	126°40′
Mar	UNP/LNO	ON	Bruce	41 A/14	44°49′	81°13′
Mara	UNP/LNO	BC	Kamloops Division Yale	82 L/11	50°41′	119°04′
Mara Beach	UNP/LNO	ON	Ontario	31 D/11	44°31′	79°12′
Maraiche Lake	LAKE/LAC	SK	63,64-1-W2	63 L/8	54°28′	102°01′
Marais, Le	UNP/LNO	QC	Avignon	22 B/1	48°13′	66°16′
Marais, Les	UNP/LNO	QC	La Matapédia	22 B/6	48°28′	67°14′
+Marais River - also-aussi - Marais, Rivière aux	RIV/CDE	MB		62 H/3	49°09′	97°17′
Marais, Rivière aux - also-aussi - +Marais River	RIV/CDE	MB	2-2-E	62 H/3	49°09′	97°17′
Mara Lake	LAKE/LAC	BC	Kamloops Division Yale	82 L/14	50°47′	119°00′
Mara River	RIV/CDE	NT	Mackenzie	76 F	66°34′	108°56′
Marathon	TOWN/VIL2	ON	Thunder Bay	42 D/9	48°45′	86°26′
Marathon	UNP/LNO	ON	Carleton	31 F/8	45°21′	76°08′
Marathon	UNP/LNO	ON	Thunder Bay	42 D/9	48°43′	86°23′
Marathon Village	UNP/LNO	ON	Carleton	31 F/8	45°22′	76°07′
Marble Canyon 3	IR/RI	BC	Kamloops Division Yale	92 I/13	50°49′	121°40′
Marble Dome	MTN/MNT	BC	Cassiar	104 N/15	59°49′	132°58′
Marblehead	UNP/LNO	BC	Kootenay	82 K/2	50°15′	116°58′
Marble Hill	UNP/LNO	NS	Inverness	11 K/4	46°02′	61°32′
Marble Island	ISL/ÎLE	NT	Keewatin	55 J	62°41′	91°08′
Marble Lake	LAKE/LAC	NF		23 J/8	54°25′	66°25′
Marble Mountain	UNP/LNO	NS	Inverness	11 F/14	45°49′	61°03′
Marble Mountain Ski Area	UNP/LNO	NF		12 A/13	48°57′	57°50′
Marble Rock	UNP/LNO	ON	Leeds	31 C/8	44°24′	76°09′
Marbleton	UNP/LNO	QC	Le Haut-Saint-François	21 E/12	45°37′	71°35′
Marbleton Station	UNP/LNO	QC	Le Haut-Saint-François	21 E/12	45°36′	71°34′
Marbre, Antre de	CAVE/CAV	QC	Jamésie	32 P/2	51°04′	72°54′
Marburg	UNP/LNO	ON	Norfolk	40 I/16	42°50′	80°10′
Marceau, Lac	LAKE/LAC	QC	Sept-Rivières	22 O/7	51°25′	66°41′
Marcelin	VILG/VILG	SK	34-45-6-W3	73 B/15	52°55′	106°47′
Marcel, Lac	LAKE/LAC	QC	Kativik	24 C/16	56°50′	68°08′
Marcelle-Gauvreau, Réserve écologique	PARK/PARC	QC	Le Fjord-du-Saguenay	22 D/8	48°21′	70°02′
Marcel-Raymond, Réserve écologique	PARK/PARC	QC	Le Haut-Richelieu	31 H/3	45°07′	73°15′
Marcelville	UNP/LNO	NB	Northumberland	21 I/12	46°40′	65°32′
Marchand	VILG/VILG	QC	Antoine-Labelle	31 J/7	46°23′	74°51′
Marchand	UNP/LNO	QC	Francheville	31 I/7	46°24′	72°43′
Marchand	UNP/LNO	MB	1-6-8-E	62 H/8	49°27′	96°23′
Marchantgrove	UNP/LNO	SK	33-50-3-W3	73 G/8	53°22′	106°23′
Marchel Lake	LAKE/LAC	SK		63 M/7	55°22′	102°44′
Marches-du-Géant, Les	UNP/LNO	QC	Manicouagan	22 N/8	51°29′	68°07′
Marches Point	UNP/LNO	NF		12 B/6	48°30′	59°08′
Marchhurst	UNP/LNO	ON	Carleton	31 G/5	45°22′	75°59′
Marchington Lake	LAKE/LAC	ON	Kenora	52 J/3	50°12′	91°20′
Marchmont	UNP/LNO	ON	Simcoe	31 D/12	44°37′	79°30′
Marchwell	UNP/LNO	SK	10-21-30-W	62 K/13	50°48′	101°35′
Marcil	UNP/LNO	QC	Pabok	22 A/3	48°08′	65°02′
Marc, Île	ISL/ÎLE	NT	Franklin	68 G	75°51′	103°35′
Marc Lake	LAKE/LAC	NF		13 D/5	52°25′	63°59′
Marco	UNP/LNO	MB	22-20-23-W	62 K/10	50°44′	100°36′
Marconi, Lieu historique national - also-aussi - Marconi National Historic Site	PARK/PARC	NS	Cape Breton	11 J/4	46°13′	59°57′
Marconi National Historic Site - also-aussi - Marconi, Lieu historique national	PARK/PARC	NS	Cape Breton	11 J/4	46°13′	59°57′
Marconi Towers	UNP/LNO	NS	Cape Breton	11 J/4	46°10′	59°58′
Marcopeet Islands	ISL/ÎLE	NT	Keewatin	34 E	57°55′	79°39′
Marcotte	UNP/LNO	QC	Abitibi-Ouest	32 D/14	49°00′	79°21′
Marden	UNP/LNO	ON	Wellington	40 P/9	43°36′	80°18′
Marean Lake	UNP/LNO	SK	12-41-12-W2	63 D/12	52°31′	103°36′
Mare-du-Sault	UNP/LNO	QC	La Côte-de-Beaupré	21 M/6	47°25′	71°11′
Marelan	UNP/LNO	QC	Argenteuil	31 G/10	45°38′	74°33′
Marengo	VILG/VILG	SK	18-29-27-W3	72 N/5	51°29′	109°47′
Marentette Beach	UNP/LNO	ON	Essex	40 G/15	42°00′	82°30′
Mares-Noires, Les	UNP/LNO	QC	Bécancour	31 I/8	46°21′	72°26′
Marest, Lac	LAKE/LAC	QC	Jamésie	33 K/15	54°45′	76°35′
Mareuil	UNP/LNO	QC	Drummond	31 H/16	45°49′	72°09′
Margach	UNP/LNO	ON	Kenora	52 E/16	49°46′	94°21′
Margaree	UNP/LNO	NF		11 O/11	47°34′	59°03′
Margaree	UNP/LNO	NS	Inverness	11 K/6	46°24′	61°05′
Margaree 25	IR/RI	NS	Inverness	11 K/6	46°21′	61°05′
Margaree Brook	UNP/LNO	NS	Inverness	11 K/6	46°18′	61°05′
Margaree Centre	UNP/LNO	NS	Inverness	11 K/6	46°21′	61°00′
Margaree Forks	UNP/LNO	NS	Inverness	11 K/6	46°20′	61°05′
Margaree Harbour	UNP/LNO	NS	Inverness	11 K/6	46°26′	61°07′
Margaree Island (Sea Wolf Island)	ISL/ÎLE	NS	Inverness	11 K/6	46°21′	61°16′
Margaree River	RIV/CDE	NS	Inverness	11 K/6	46°26′	61°06′
Margaree Valley	UNP/LNO	NS	Inverness	11 K/7	46°21′	60°58′
Margaret	UNP/LNO	MB	21-5-18-W	62 G/5	49°24′	99°51′

NAME NOM	ENTITY ENTITÉ	LOC 1 LIEU 1	LOC 2 LIEU 2	MAP CARTE	POSITION LAT	LONG
Margaret, Cape	CAPE/CAP	NT	Franklin	57 E	70°09′	91°31′
Margaret Hamilton Lake	LAKE/LAC	NF		23 J/8	54°20′	66°30′
Margaret Island	ISL/ÎLE	NT	Franklin	59 B	76°04′	94°46′
Margaret Lake	LAKE/LAC	AB	114-9-W5	84 J/14	58°56′	115°25′
Margaret Lake	LAKE/LAC	NT	Mackenzie	75 N	63°40′	109°47′
Margaret Lake	LAKE/LAC	NT	Mackenzie	86 C	64°30′	117°08′
Margaret Park	UNP/LNO	MB		62 H/14	49°57′	97°07′
Margaretsville	UNP/LNO	NS	Annapolis	21 H/3	45°03′	65°04′
Margate	UNP/LNO	PE	Prince	11 L/5	46°28′	63°35′
Margie	UNP/LNO	AB	28-74-9-W4	73 M/6	55°26′	111°20′
Margo	VILG/VILG	SK	15-33-10-W2	62 M/14	51°49′	103°20′
Margo Lake	UNP/LNO	ON	Thunder Bay	42 E/16	49°48′	86°20′
Marguerite	UNP/LNO	BC	Cariboo	93 B/9	52°30′	122°26′
Marguerite Lake	LAKE/LAC	AB	65-5,6-W4	73 L/10	54°37′	110°45′
Marguerite Lake	LAKE/LAC	BC	Cariboo	93 A/5	52°24′	121°59′
Marguerite River	RIV/CDE	AB/SK		74 E/11	57°36′	111°05′
Maria	VILG/VILG	QC	Avignon	22 A/4	48°10′	65°59′
Maria 2 - see-voir - Gesgapegiag 2	IR/RI	QC	Avignon	22 A/4	48°12′	65°56′
Maria-Chapdelaine	MUN1/AZM1	QC	Maria-Chapdelaine	32 A/16	48°59′	72°17′
Maria-Chapdelaine, Lac	LAKE/LAC	QC	Le Fjord-du-Saguenay	22 E/2	49°12′	70°37′
Maria-de-Kent	UNP/LNO	NB	Kent	21 I/7	46°27′	64°47′
Maria Lake	LAKE/LAC	ON	Kenora	53 A/13	53°00′	89°38′
Maria Lake	LAKE/LAC	MB		64 K/10	58°43′	100°40′
Mariana Lake	UNP/LNO	AB	19-80-13-W4	83 P/16	55°57′	112°01′
Marian Lake	LAKE/LAC	NT	Mackenzie	85 K	63°00′	116°15′
Marian River	RIV/CDE	NT	Mackenzie	85 N	63°04′	116°21′
Maria-Ouest	UNP/LNO	QC	Avignon	22 B/1	48°09′	66°03′
Maria Point	CAPE/CAP	NT	Franklin	79 A	76°31′	104°35′
Mariapolis	UNP/LNO	MB	2-5-12-W	62 G/7	49°22′	98°59′
Mariatown	UNP/LNO	ON	Dundas	31 B/14	44°53′	75°12′
Maribelli Lake	LAKE/LAC	SK		74 A/1	56°13′	104°26′
Maricourt	VILG/VILG	QC	Le Val-Saint-François	31 H/9	45°30′	72°15′
Maricourt	UNP/LNO	QC	Le Val-Saint-François	31 H/9	45°34′	72°16′
Maricourt, Lac	LAKE/LAC	QC	Vallée-de-l'Or	32 C/9	48°37′	76°04′
Marie	UNP/LNO	PE	Kings	11 L/7	46°24′	62°39′
Marie Bay	BAY/BAIE	NT	Franklin	89 A	76°13′	115°20′
Marie-Claire, Lac	LAKE/LAC	QC	Côte-Nord-du-Golfe-Saint-Laurent	12 K/6	50°19′	61°04′
Marie Heights	CAPE/CAP	NT	Franklin	89 A	76°17′	115°40′
Marie Hill	UNP/LNO	SK	30-50-24-W3	73 F/6	53°20′	109°29′
Marie-Jean-Eudes, Réserve écologique	PARK/PARC	QC	Maskinongé	31 I/11	46°42′	73°09′
Marie Joseph	UNP/LNO	NS	Guysborough	11 D/16	44°58′	62°05′
Marie Lake	LAKE/LAC	AB	65-2,3-W4	73 L/9	54°38′	110°18′
Marie-Le Franc, Lac	LAKE/LAC	QC	Les Laurentides	31 J/2	46°08′	75°00′
Marienthal	UNP/LNO	SK	1-1-12-W2	62 E/3	49°00′	103°30′
Marie-Reine	UNP/LNO	AB	6-82-21-W5	84 C/3	56°04′	117°17′
Marieton	UNP/LNO	SK	24-22-23-W2	72 I/14	50°53′	105°05′
Marieval	UNP/LNO	SK		62 L/10	50°35′	102°39′
Marieville	CITY/VIL1	QC	Rouville	31 H/6	45°26′	73°10′
Marigold	UNP/LNO	BC	Victoria	92 B/6	48°28′	123°24′
Marigot, Le	UNP/LNO	QC	Francheville	31 I/9	46°31′	72°15′
Mari Lake	LAKE/LAC	SK		63 M/1	55°05′	102°00′
Marilla	UNP/LNO	BC	Range 4 Coast	93 F/12	53°42′	125°51′
Marina	UNP/LNO	AB	2-87-8-W6	84 D/6	56°30′	119°10′
Marina Estates	UNP/LNO	ON	York	31 D/6	44°20′	79°13′
Marina Island	ISL/ÎLE	BC	Sayward	92 K/3	50°04′	125°03′
Marina Peninsula	CAPE/CAP	NT	Franklin	38 G	75°52′	78°57′
Marina Veilleux	UNP/LNO	ON	Cochrane	42 G/13	49°48′	83°43′
Marinette	UNP/LNO	NS	Halifax	11 D/15	44°58′	62°39′
Maringouin, Cape	CAPE/CAP	NB	Westmorland	21 H/10	45°44′	64°33′
Marion Bridge	UNP/LNO	NS	Cape Breton	11 F/16	45°59′	60°13′
Marion Bridge Road	UNP/LNO	NS	Cape Breton	11 F/16	45°58′	60°14′
Marion, Lac	LAKE/LAC	QC	Pontiac	31 K/13	46°53′	77°47′
Marion Lake	LAKE/LAC	MB	11-17-E	52 E/14	49°54′	95°10′
Marion Lake	LAKE/LAC	AB	37-17,18-W4	83 A/1	52°12′	112°28′
Marion Lake	LAKE/LAC	NT	Mackenzie	106 J	66°48′	130°35′
Marion's Corner	UNP/LNO	QC	Pontiac	31 F/14	45°54′	77°04′
Marionville	UNP/LNO	ON	Russell	31 G/3	45°11′	75°21′
Mariposa	MUN2/AZM2	ON	Victoria	31 D/7	44°19′	78°55′
Mariposa	UNP/LNO	ON	Victoria	31 D/7	44°18′	78°52′
Mariposa Beach	UNP/LNO	ON	Ontario	31 D/11	44°39′	79°21′
Mariposa Brook	RIV/CDE	ON	Victoria	31 D/7	44°17′	78°45′
Mariposa No. 350	MUN2/AZM2	SK		73 C/3	52°00′	109°00′
Maritana	UNP/LNO	QC	Le Haut-Saint-Laurent	31 H/4	45°02′	73°52′
Marjorie Hills	MTN/MNT	NT	Keewatin	66 B	64°18′	99°25′
Marjorie Lake	LAKE/LAC	NT	Keewatin	66 B	64°09′	99°12′

NAME NOM	ENTITY ENTITÉ	LOC 1 LIEU 1	LOC 2 LIEU 2	MAP CARTE	POSITION LAT	LONG
Markale 14	IR/RI	BC	Rupert	92 L/3	50°04′	127°10′
Markale Passage	CHAN/CHEN	BC	Rupert	92 L/3	50°04′	127°12′
Mark Crossing	UNP/LNO	QC	La Vallée-de-la-Gatineau	31 K/1	46°02′	76°06′
Markdale	VILG/VILG	ON	Grey	41 A/7	44°19′	80°39′
Markerville	UNP/LNO	AB	26-36-2-W5	83 B/1	52°07′	114°10′
Markham	TOWN/VIL2	ON	York	30 M/14	43°52′	79°16′
Markham Bay	BAY/BAIE	NT	Franklin	25 M	63°30′	71°48′
Markham Fiord	BAY/BAIE	NT	Franklin	120 F	82°59′	71°28′
Markham Lake	LAKE/LAC	NT	Mackenzie	65 L	62°30′	102°37′
Markham Strait	CHAN/CHEN	NT	Franklin	67 B	68°40′	100°40′
Markhamville	UNP/LNO	NB	Kings	21 H/11	45°37′	65°27′
Mark Hill	UNP/LNO	NB	Charlotte	21 B/10	44°40′	66°48′
Markinch	VILG/VILG	SK	7-23-17-W2	72 I/16	50°56′	104°22′
Mark Lake	LAKE/LAC	ON	Kenora	52 E/16	49°56′	94°03′
Markland	UNP/LNO	NF		1 N/5	47°23′	53°33′
Markland	UNP/LNO	MB	19-2-W	62 I/12	50°38′	97°44′
Markland Woods	UNP/LNO	ON	York	30 M/12	43°38′	79°35′
Markstay	UNP/LNO	ON	Sudbury	41 I/7	46°29′	80°32′
Marktosis	UNP/LNO	BC	Clayoquot	92 E/8	49°17′	126°03′
Marktosis 15	IR/RI	BC	Clayoquot	92 E/8	49°17′	126°03′
Marlbank	UNP/LNO	ON	Hastings	31 C/6	44°26′	77°06′
Marlboro	UNP/LNO	AB	6-53-19-W5	83 F/10	53°33′	116°45′
Marlin	UNP/LNO	SK	24-49-17-W3	73 F/1	53°15′	108°21′
Marlington	UNP/LNO	QC	Memphrémagog	31 H/1	45°03′	72°12′
Marmion	UNP/LNO	ON	Grey	41 A/6	44°23′	81°03′
Marmion Lake	LAKE/LAC	ON	Rainy River	52 B/13	48°53′	91°31′
Marmites-de-Géants, Les	UNP/LNO	QC	Témiscamingue	31 M/3	47°03′	79°23′
Marmora	VILG/VILG	ON	Hastings	31 C/5	44°29′	77°41′
Marmora and Lake	MUN2/AZM2	ON	Hastings	31 C/12	44°38′	77°45′
Marmora Station	UNP/LNO	ON	Hastings	31 C/5	44°30′	77°39′
Marne	UNP/LNO	NB	York	21 G/14	45°54′	67°29′
Marne	UNP/LNO	BC	Lillooet	92 J/9	50°38′	122°25′
Marne Lake	LAKE/LAC	ON	Sudbury	41 P/14	47°47′	81°20′
Marnoch	UNP/LNO	ON	Huron	40 P/14	43°50′	81°26′
Maroon Hill	UNP/LNO	NS	Halifax	11 D/13	44°48′	63°43′
Marpole	UNP/LNO	BC	New Westminster	92 G/3	49°12′	123°08′
Marquette	UNP/LNO	MB	6-13-2-W	62 I/4	50°04′	97°44′
Marquette, Lac	LAKE/LAC	QC	Le Domaine-du-Roy	32 A/13	48°54′	73°54′
Marquis	VILG/VILG	SK	20-19-27-W2	72 I/12	50°38′	105°43′
Marquise	UNP/LNO	NF		1 N/5	47°17′	54°00′
Marquis No. 191	MUN2/AZM2	SK		72 I/12	50°40′	105°45′
Marralik, Rivière	RIV/CDE	QC	Kativik	24 J/6	58°16′	67°24′
Marriott	UNP/LNO	SK	1-33-15-W3	72 N/16	51°48′	108°01′
Marriott No. 317	MUN2/AZM2	SK		72 O/12	51°45′	107°55′
Marriotts Cove	UNP/LNO	NS	Lunenburg	21 A/9	44°33′	64°16′
Marron Valley	UNP/LNO	BC	Similkameen Division Yale	82 E/5	49°22′	119°40′
Marrs Island	ISL/ÎLE	NS	Halifax	11 D/5	44°26′	63°44′
Marrtown	UNP/LNO	NB	Kings	21 H/13	45°51′	65°40′
Marsac, Lac	LAKE/LAC	QC	Caniapiscau	23 C/4	52°12′	69°58′
Marsal, Lac	LAKE/LAC	QC	Minganie	22 P/7	51°15′	64°41′
Marsboro	UNP/LNO	QC	Le Granit	21 E/10	45°33′	70°57′
Marsdale	UNP/LNO	ON	Lincoln	30 M/3	43°08′	79°15′
Marsden	VILG/VILG	SK	35-44-27-W3	73 C/13	52°51′	109°49′
Marsh	UNP/LNO	NS	Pictou	11 E/9	45°30′	62°16′
Marshall	VILG/VILG	SK	49-26-W3	73 F/4	53°11′	109°47′
Marshall Bay	UNP/LNO	ON	Carleton	31 F/8	45°26′	76°18′
Marshall Flowage	LAKE/LAC	NS	Halifax	11 E/1	45°02′	62°30′
Marshall Lake	LAKE/LAC	ON	Thunder Bay	42 L/6	50°25′	87°30′
Marshall Lake	LAKE/LAC	BC	Lillooet	92 J/15	50°55′	122°35′
Marshall Park	UNP/LNO	ON	Nipissing	31 L/6	46°17′	79°26′
Marshall Point	CAPE/CAP	BC	Texada Island	92 F/15	49°47′	124°38′
Marshall School Junction	UNP/LNO	BC	Texada Island	92 F/10	49°43′	124°31′
Marshall's Corners	UNP/LNO	ON	Timiskaming	31 M/13	47°50′	79°39′
Marshalls Crossing	UNP/LNO	NS	Pictou	11 E/10	45°39′	62°38′
Marshalltown	UNP/LNO	NS	Digby	21 A/12	44°35′	65°48′
Marsh Brook	UNP/LNO	NS	Inverness	11 K/6	46°22′	61°00′
Marshdale	UNP/LNO	NS	Pictou	11 E/7	45°28′	62°43′
Marshes (West Bay)	UNP/LNO	NS	Inverness	11 F/14	45°45′	61°10′
Marshfield	UNP/LNO	PE	Queens	11 L/6	46°18′	63°04′
Marshfield	UNP/LNO	ON	Essex	40 J/2	42°05′	82°55′
Marsh Hill	UNP/LNO	ON	Ontario	31 D/3	44°09′	79°04′
Marsh Junction	UNP/LNO	NB	Westmorland	21 I/2	46°04′	64°50′
Marsh Lake	UNP/LNO	YT		105 D/9	60°31′	134°20′
Marsh Lake	LAKE/LAC	YT		105 D/8	60°27′	134°18′
Marsh Point	CAPE/CAP	NS	Inverness	11 K/6	46°18′	61°16′

NAME NOM	ENTITY ENTITÉ	LOC 1 LIEU 1	LOC 2 LIEU 2	MAP CARTE	POSITION LAT	LONG
Marsh Point	CAPE/CAP	MB		54 F/1	57°04′	92°12′
Marsh River - also-aussi - +Marsh, Rivière	RIV/CDE	MB		62 H/11	49°34′	97°08′
+Marsh, Rivière - also-aussi - Marsh River	RIV/CDE	MB		62 H/11	49°34′	97°08′
Marshville	UNP/LNO	NS	Pictou	11 E/14	45°45′	63°07′
Marshville	UNP/LNO	ON	Welland	30 L/14	42°57′	79°23′
Marshy Creek	RIV/CDE	SK	27-42-9-W3	73 B/11	52°39′	107°14′
Marshy Hope	UNP/LNO	NS	Pictou	11 E/9	45°35′	62°12′
Marshy Point	CAPE/CAP	MB	18-5-W	62 J/9	50°32′	98°07′
Marsilly, Lac	LAKE/LAC	QC	Jamésie	23 L/8	54°26′	70°10′
Mars Island	ISL/ÎLE	BC	Range 1 Coast	92 L/10	50°43′	126°39′
Marsoui	TOWN/VIL2	QC	Denis-Riverin	22 G/1	49°13′	66°04′
Mars, Rivière à	RIV/CDE	QC	Le Fjord-du-Saguenay	22 D/7	48°20′	70°53′
Marston	VILG/VILG	QC	Le Granit	21 E/11	45°30′	71°00′
Marston	UNP/LNO	ON	Norfolk	40 I/10	42°42′	80°37′
Marsville	UNP/LNO	ON	Dufferin	40 P/16	43°50′	80°13′
Martel	UNP/LNO	BC	Kamloops Division Yale	92 I/6	50°30′	121°18′
Martell Lake	LAKE/LAC	NT	Keewatin	55 M	63°52′	95°21′
Martels Corners	UNP/LNO	ON	Russell	31 G/6	45°22′	75°07′
Marten Falls 65	IR/RI	ON	Kenora	42 N/12	51°40′	85°55′
Marten Lake	UNP/LNO	BC	Range 5 Coast	93 K/1	54°01′	124°25′
Marten Lake	LAKE/LAC	ON	Nipissing	31 L/12	46°43′	79°47′
Marten River	UNP/LNO	ON	Nipissing	31 L/12	46°44′	79°49′
Marten River	UNP/LNO	AB	33-86-14-W5	84 C/9	56°30′	116°10′
Marten River	RIV/CDE	NT	Mackenzie	75 C	60°44′	109°05′
Martensville	TOWN/VIL2	SK	21,28-38-5-W3	73 B/7	52°17′	106°40′
Marter	UNP/LNO	ON	Timiskaming	31 M/13	47°53′	79°48′
Marte, Rivière à la	RIV/CDE	QC	Jamésie	32 N/8	51°22′	76°22′
Marthaville	UNP/LNO	ON	Lambton	40 J/16	42°54′	82°10′
Marticot Island	ISL/ÎLE	NF		1 M/7	47°20′	54°35′
Martin	UNP/LNO	QC	Bonaventure	22 A/3	48°07′	65°06′
Martin	UNP/LNO	ON	Kenora	52 G/6	49°15′	91°08′
Martin-Corner	UNP/LNO	QC	La Haute-Yamaska	31 H/7	45°25′	72°31′
Martindale	UNP/LNO	QC	La Vallée-de-la-Gatineau	31 G/13	45°50′	75°57′
Martindale Heights	UNP/LNO	ON	Lincoln	30 M/3	43°10′	79°16′
Martineau	UNP/LNO	QC	Montmagny	21 L/15	46°51′	70°39′
Martineau, Cape	CAPE/CAP	NT	Franklin	46 J	66°11′	83°40′
Martineau River	RIV/CDE	AB/SK		73 L/9	54°38′	110°03′
Martin Farm	UNP/LNO	ON	Simcoe	31 D/12	44°32′	79°34′
Martin Grove Gardens	UNP/LNO	ON	York	30 M/12	43°42′	79°34′
Martin Head	CAPE/CAP	NB	Saint John	21 H/6	45°29′	65°11′
Martin Hills	MTN/MNT	NT	Mackenzie	95 G	61°47′	122°15′
Martin House	UNP/LNO	NT	Mackenzie	106 K/14	66°47′	133°06′
Martinique	UNP/LNO	NS	Richmond	11 F/11	45°35′	61°03′
Martin Island	ISL/ÎLE	NF		14 E/8	57°29′	62°16′
Martin Lake	LAKE/LAC	NF		2 D/12	48°43′	55°34′
Martin Lake	LAKE/LAC	BC	Range 2 Coast	92 N/15	51°57′	124°35′
Martin Lake	LAKE/LAC	BC	Range 1 Coast	92 K/12	50°39′	125°47′
Martin, Mount	MTN/MNT	YT		95 C/1	60°08′	124°09′
Martin No. 122	MUN2/AZM2	SK		62 K/4	50°12′	101°50′
Martinon	UNP/LNO	NB	Saint John	21 G/8	45°17′	66°12′
Martin-Pêcheur, Le	UNP/LNO	QC	Maskinongé	31 I/7	46°16′	72°49′
Martin Prairie	UNP/LNO	BC	Kamloops Division Yale	82 L/12	50°40′	119°49′
Martin River	RIV/CDE	NT	Mackenzie	95 H	61°55′	121°35′
Martins	UNP/LNO	ON	Muskoka	31 E/6	45°17′	79°19′
Martins Brook	UNP/LNO	NS	Lunenburg	21 A/8	44°25′	64°21′
Martins Corner	UNP/LNO	ON	Renfrew	31 F/7	45°28′	76°54′
Martins Corners	UNP/LNO	ON	Russell	31 G/11	45°30′	75°27′
Martin Siding	UNP/LNO	NB	Madawaska	21 O/4	47°06′	67°51′
Martins Landing	UNP/LNO	ON	Hastings	31 C/13	44°52′	77°39′
Martinson	UNP/LNO	BC	Yale Division Yale	92 H/14	49°55′	121°27′
Martinson's Beach	HAM/HAM	SK	33-47-17-W3	73 F/1	53°06′	108°26′
Martins Point	UNP/LNO	NS	Lunenburg	21 A/8	44°29′	64°19′
Martins River	UNP/LNO	NS	Lunenburg	21 A/8	44°29′	64°20′
Martins River	RIV/CDE	NS	Lunenburg	21 A/8	44°29′	64°19′
Martintown	UNP/LNO	ON	Glengarry	31 G/2	45°09′	74°42′
Martinvale	UNP/LNO	PE	Kings	11 L/7	46°18′	62°39′
Martinville	VILG/VILG	QC	Coaticook	21 E/5	45°16′	71°43′
Martinville	UNP/LNO	ON	Simcoe	31 D/12	44°35′	79°42′
Martock	UNP/LNO	NS	Hants	21 A/16	44°57′	64°10′
Martre, Lac la	LAKE/LAC	NT	Mackenzie	85 N	63°15′	117°55′
Martres, Lac des	LAKE/LAC	QC	Charlevoix	21 M/15	47°50′	70°39′
Martyrs Shrine	UNP/LNO	ON	Simcoe	31 D/12	44°44′	79°50′
Marvelville	UNP/LNO	ON	Russell	31 G/3	45°13′	75°22′
Marvin Heights	UNP/LNO	ON	Peel	30 M/12	43°43′	79°39′
Marvins Island	UNP/LNO	NS	Lunenburg	21 A/9	44°33′	64°18′

NAME NOM	ENTITY ENTITÉ	LOC 1 LIEU 1	LOC 2 LIEU 2	MAP CARTE	POSITION LAT	LONG
Marwayne	VILG/VILG	AB	26-52-3-W4	73 E/9	53°32′	110°20′
Mary Ann Lake	LAKE/LAC	NF		2 E/4	49°06′	55°54′
Maryborough	MUN2/AZM2	ON	Wellington	40 P/10	43°45′	80°45′
Mary Cove 12	IR/RI	BC	Range 3 Coast	103 A/9	52°37′	128°27′
Marydale	UNP/LNO	NS	Antigonish	11 F/12	45°32′	61°50′
Maryen, Lac	LAKE/LAC	QC	Minganie	12 N/8	51°20′	60°28′
Maryfield	VILG/VILG	SK	17-10-30-W	62 F/13	49°50′	101°32′
Maryfield No. 91	MUN2/AZM2	SK		62 F/13	49°53′	101°33′
Mary Frances Lake	LAKE/LAC	NT	Mackenzie	75 O	63°19′	106°13′
Mary Frances River	RIV/CDE	NT	Mackenzie	75 P	63°01′	104°53′
Marygrove	UNP/LNO	ON	Simcoe	31 D/13	44°50′	79°54′
Maryhill	UNP/LNO	ON	Waterloo	40 P/9	43°32′	80°23′
Mary Hill	UNP/LNO	BC	New Westminster	92 G/2	49°14′	122°47′
Mary Jones Bay	BAY/BAIE	NT	Franklin	57 E	70°19′	91°57′
Mary Lake	LAKE/LAC	ON	Muskoka	31 E/3	45°15′	79°15′
Mary Lake	LAKE/LAC	NT	Mackenzie	65 L	62°23′	103°31′
Maryland	UNP/LNO	QC	Pontiac	31 F/9	45°34′	76°22′
Mary March	UNP/LNO	NF		12 A/15	49°00′	56°33′
Mary March's Brook	RIV/CDE	NF		12 A/15	48°50′	56°30′
Marysburg	UNP/LNO	SK	38-22-W2	73 A/6	52°19′	105°05′
Mary's Harbour	VILG/VILG	NF		3 D/5	52°19′	55°50′
Marys Point	CAPE/CAP	NB	Albert	21 H/10	45°43′	64°39′
Marystown	TOWN/VIL2	NF		1 M/3	47°10′	55°09′
Marysvale	UNP/LNO	NF		1 N/6	47°30′	53°13′
Marysville	UNP/LNO	NB	York	21 G/15	45°59′	66°35′
Marysville	UNP/LNO	ON	Frontenac	31 C/1	44°11′	76°26′
Marysville	UNP/LNO	ON	Hastings	31 C/3	44°14′	77°06′
Marysville	UNP/LNO	BC	Kootenay	82 G/12	49°38′	115°57′
Maryvale	UNP/LNO	NS	Antigonish	11 E/9	45°44′	62°03′
Maryvale	UNP/LNO	ON	York	30 M/14	43°46′	79°18′
Maryville	UNP/LNO	NS	Inverness	11 F/13	45°56′	61°31′
Maryville	UNP/LNO	SK	9-47-17-W2	73 H/1	53°03′	104°25′
Marywood Meadows	UNP/LNO	ON	Halton	30 M/12	43°39′	79°56′
Mascarene	UNP/LNO	NB	Charlotte	21 G/2	45°06′	66°54′
Mascouche	CITY/VIL1	QC	Les Moulins	31 H/13	45°45′	73°36′
Mascouche, Rivière	RIV/CDE	QC	Les Moulins	31 H/12	45°42′	73°37′
Masefield	UNP/LNO	SK	27-2-14-W3	72 G/4	49°09′	107°48′
Maseres, Lac	LAKE/LAC	QC	Vallée-de-l'Or	32 B/13	48°50′	75°57′
Mashagama Lake	LAKE/LAC	ON	Algoma	41 J/14	46°55′	83°21′
Mashkode	UNP/LNO	ON	Algoma	41 N/1	47°02′	84°06′
Mashteuiatsh	IR/RI	QC	Le Domaine-du-Roy	32 A/9	48°34′	72°14′
Masit 13	IR/RI	BC	Barclay	92 C/11	48°45′	125°07′
Maskawata	UNP/LNO	MB	29-10-23-W	62 F/15	49°51′	100°35′
Maskinongé	TOWN/VIL2	QC	Maskinongé	31 I/3	46°14′	73°01′
Maskinongé	MUN1/AZM1	QC	Maskinongé	31 I/7	46°19′	72°56′
Maskinongé, Lac	LAKE/LAC	QC	D'Autray	31 I/6	46°19′	73°23′
Maskinonge Lake	LAKE/LAC	ON	Sudbury	41 I/16	46°47′	80°27′
Maskinonge Park	UNP/LNO	ON	York	31 D/3	44°14′	79°28′
Maskinongé, Rivière	RIV/CDE	QC	Maskinongé	31 I/3	46°10′	73°01′
Mason Creek	UNP/LNO	BC	Cassiar	94 G/7	57°20′	122°47′
Mason Lake	LAKE/LAC	ON	Kenora	52 E/7	49°29′	94°55′
Mason Landing	UNP/LNO	YT		105 E/7	61°26′	134°39′
Mason Point	UNP/LNO	NS	Inverness	11 K/3	46°08′	61°14′
Mason River	RIV/CDE	NT	Mackenzie	107 D/16	69°56′	128°20′
Masons Beach	UNP/LNO	NS	Lunenburg	21 A/8	44°22′	64°20′
Masons Cove	UNP/LNO	NF		2 E/6	49°19′	55°02′
Masons Point	UNP/LNO	NS	Halifax	11 D/12	44°40′	63°55′
Masons Pond	LAKE/LAC	NF		2 D/9	48°43′	54°22′
Masonville	UNP/LNO	QC	Matawinie	31 I/4	46°02′	73°44′
Masonville	UNP/LNO	ON	Middlesex	40 P/3	43°02′	81°16′
Massacre Butte Provincial Historic Site (Undeveloped)	PARK/PARC	AB	7-1-W5	82 G/9	49°36′	114°04′
Massanoga	UNP/LNO	ON	Lennox and Addington	31 C/14	44°58′	77°17′
Massawippi	UNP/LNO	QC	Memphrémagog	21 E/4	45°11′	71°59′
Massawippi, Lac	LAKE/LAC	QC	Memphrémagog	31 H/1	45°13′	72°00′
Massé, Lac	LAKE/LAC	QC	Manicouagan	22 F/8	49°19′	68°00′
Masset	VILG/VILG	BC	Queen Charlotte	103 K/1	54°01′	132°06′
Masset	UNP/LNO	BC	Queen Charlotte	103 K/1	54°01′	132°09′
Masset 1	IR/RI	BC	Queen Charlotte	103 K/1	54°02′	132°10′
Masset Inlet	BAY/BAIE	BC	Queen Charlotte	103 F/9	53°43′	132°20′
Masset Sound	CHAN/CHEN	BC	Queen Charlotte	103 F/16	53°55′	132°07′
Massey	TOWN/VIL2	ON	Sudbury	41 J/1	46°12′	82°05′
Massey Drive	TOWN/VIL2	NF		12 A/13	48°56′	57°54′
Massey Island	ISL/ÎLE	NT	Franklin	69 B	76°00′	103°00′
Massey Place	UNP/LNO	SK		73 B/2	52°08′	106°43′
Massey Sound	CHAN/CHEN	NT	Franklin	59 F	78°30′	94°00′

NAME NOM	ENTITY ENTITÉ	LOC 1 LIEU 1	LOC 2 LIEU 2	MAP CARTE	POSITION LAT	LONG
Massie	UNP/LNO	ON	Grey	41 A/7	44°28′	80°48′
Massinahigan River	RIV/CDE	SK	73-5-W3	73 O/7	55°20′	106°45′
Massive	UNP/LNO	AB	17-26-13-W5	82 O/4	51°13′	115°47′
Masson-Angers	CITY/VIL1	QC	Communauté urbaine de l'Outaouais	31 G/11	45°32′	75°25′
Masstown	UNP/LNO	NS	Colchester	11 E/6	45°23′	63°29′
Massueville	TOWN/VIL2	QC	Le Bas-Richelieu	31 H/15	45°55′	72°56′
Masters Head	CAPE/CAP	NF		1 N/12	47°43′	53°50′
Mastigouche Nord, Rivière	RIV/CDE	QC	D'Autray	31 I/6	46°25′	73°25′
Mastigouche, Réserve faunique	PARK/PARC	QC	Matawinie	31 I/12	46°40′	73°30′
Mastigouche, Rivière	RIV/CDE	QC	D'Autray	31 I/6	46°20′	73°24′
Matachewan	MUN2/AZM2	ON	Timiskaming	41 P/15	47°57′	80°48′
Matachewan	UNP/LNO	ON	Timiskaming	41 P/15	47°56′	80°39′
Matachewan 72	IR/RI	ON	Timiskaming	42 A/2	48°05′	80°38′
Matador	UNP/LNO	SK	24-21-15-W3	72 J/13	50°48′	107°57′
Matagami	CITY/VIL1	QC	Jamésie	32 F/13	49°45′	77°38′
Matagami, Lac	LAKE/LAC	QC	Jamésie	32 F/13	49°53′	77°30′
Matagami Mine	UNP/LNO	QC	Jamésie	32 F/12	49°44′	77°45′
Matago	UNP/LNO	MB	11-76-2-E	63 P/11	55°34′	97°11′
Matamec	UNP/LNO	QC	Sept-Rivières	22 I/5	50°17′	65°58′
Matamec, Lac	LAKE/LAC	QC	Sept-Rivières	22 I/5	50°22′	65°54′
Matamec, Réserve écologique de la	PARK/PARC	QC	Sept-Rivières	22 I/5	50°22′	65°54′
Matamec, Rivière	RIV/CDE	QC	Sept-Rivières	22 I/5	50°17′	65°58′
Matane	CITY/VIL1	QC	Matane	22 B/13	48°51′	67°32′
Matane	MUN1/AZM1	QC	Matane	22 B/14	48°51′	67°17′
Matane-Est	UNP/LNO	QC	Matane	22 B/14	48°51′	67°29′
Matane, Lac	LAKE/LAC	QC	Matane	22 B/10	48°42′	66°59′
Matane, Petite rivière	RIV/CDE	QC	Matane	22 B/11	48°43′	67°24′
Matane, Réserve faunique de	PARK/PARC	QC	Matane	22 B/10	48°44′	66°55′
Matane, Rivière	RIV/CDE	QC	Matane	22 B/13	48°51′	67°32′
Matane, Rivière	RIV/CDE	QC	La Matapédia	22 B/12	48°35′	67°35′
Matane-sur-Mer	UNP/LNO	QC	Matane	22 B/13	48°50′	67°35′
Matapédia	VILG/VILG	QC	Avignon	21 O/15	47°58′	66°57′
Matapédia, Lac	LAKE/LAC	QC	La Matapédia	22 B/12	48°33′	67°34′
Matapédia-Ouest	UNP/LNO	QC	Avignon	21 O/15	47°56′	66°58′
Matapédia, Rivière	RIV/CDE	QC	Avignon	21 O/15	47°58′	66°57′
Matapédia, Vallée de la	VALL/VALL	QC	La Matapédia	22 B/3	48°10′	67°10′
Matateto River	RIV/CDE	ON	Kenora	43 F/9	53°33′	84°28′
Matawackweak Sakahikan Ecitacikewapan	UNP/LNO	QC	Témiscamingue	31 M/1	47°02′	78°11′
Matawak	UNP/LNO	MB		53 K/11	54°35′	93°24′
Matawa Place	UNP/LNO	MB		53 D/12	52°36′	95°44′
Matawatchan	UNP/LNO	ON	Renfrew	31 F/3	45°09′	77°07′
Matawinie	MUN1/AZM1	QC	Matawinie	31 I/5	46°16′	73°47′
Matawin, Rivière	RIV/CDE	QC	Le Centre-de-la-Mauricie	31 I/15	46°54′	72°56′
Matchedash - see-voir - Severn	MUN2/AZM2	ON		31 D/13	44°49′	79°35′
Matchedash Bay	BAY/BAIE	ON	Simcoe	31 D/12	44°44′	79°40′
Matchee	UNP/LNO	SK	27-59-15-W3	73 K/1	54°49′	108°10′
Matchi-Manitou	MUN2/AZM2	QC	Vallée-de-l'Or	32 C/3	48°01′	77°03′
Matchi-Manitou, Lac	LAKE/LAC	QC	Vallée-de-l'Or	32 C/3	48°01′	77°03′
Matchinameigus Lake	LAKE/LAC	ON	Algoma	42 C/1	48°09′	84°08′
Matchlee 13	IR/RI	BC	Nootka	92 E/9	49°37′	126°03′
Matchlee Mountain	MTN/MNT	BC	Nootka	92 F/12	49°38′	125°58′
Mates Corner	UNP/LNO	NB	Westmorland	21 I/1	46°08′	64°08′
Mathe Point	CAPE/CAP	NT	Franklin	57 E	70°27′	88°37′
Mather	UNP/LNO	MB	6-2-13-W	62 G/3	49°06′	99°11′
Mathers Corners	UNP/LNO	ON	Peterborough	31 D/1	44°14′	78°12′
Matheson	UNP/LNO	ON	Cochrane	42 A/9	48°32′	80°28′
Matheson Island	UNP/LNO	MB		62 P/10	51°44′	96°55′
Mathevet, Lac	LAKE/LAC	QC	Manicouagan	22 N/1	51°07′	68°07′
Mathias Landing	UNP/LNO	NB	Northumberland	21 O/8	47°23′	66°23′
Mathieson Channel	CHAN/CHEN	BC	Range 3 Coast	103 A/9	52°38′	128°11′
Matilda	MUN2/AZM2	ON	Dundas	31 B/14	44°54′	75°19′
Matilpi	UNP/LNO	BC	Range 1 Coast	92 L/9	50°33′	126°11′
Matimekosh	IR/RI	QC	Caniapiscau	23 J/15	54°49′	66°49′
Matinenda Lake	LAKE/LAC	ON	Algoma	41 J/7	46°22′	82°57′
Matlahaw Point	CAPE/CAP	BC	Clayoquot	92 E/8	49°23′	126°29′
Matlaten 4	IR/RI	BC	Range 1 Coast	92 K/5	50°28′	125°32′
Matlock	UNP/LNO	MB	3,10-17-4E	62 I/7	50°26′	96°58′
Matlset Narrows	CHAN/CHEN	BC	Clayoquot	92 F/4	49°14′	125°48′
Matonipi, Lac	LAKE/LAC	QC	Caniapiscau	22 N/13	51°52′	69°48′
Matonipi, Rivière	RIV/CDE	QC	Manicouagan	22 N/5	51°21′	69°45′
Matonipis, Lac	LAKE/LAC	QC	Caniapiscau	22 N/13	51°50′	69°40′
Matsayno 5	IR/RI	BC	Range 1 Coast	92 K/11	50°32′	125°20′
Matse River	RIV/CDE	NF		13 B/3	52°03′	59°27′
Matshishkam	UNP/LNO	QC	Kativik	24 I/4	58°07′	65°47′
Matshukueu Hikuanupunan	UNP/LNO	QC	Minganie	12 O/15	51°55′	58°43′

NAME NOM	ENTITY ENTITÉ	LOC 1 LIEU 1	LOC 2 LIEU 2	MAP CARTE	POSITION LAT	LONG
Matsiu Creek	RIV/CDE	BC	Range 1 Coast	92 K/12	50°42′	125°50′
Matson Creek	RIV/CDE	YT		115 N/9	63°43′	140°12′
Matsqui	MUN1/AZM1	BC	New Westminster	92 G/1	49°05′	122°21′
Matsqui	UNP/LNO	BC	New Westminster	92 G/1	49°07′	122°18′
Matsqui 4	IR/RI	BC	New Westminster	92 G/1	49°00′	122°28′
Matsqui Main 2	IR/RI	BC	New Westminster	92 G/1	49°07′	122°21′
Mattabi	UNP/LNO	ON	Kenora	52 G/11	49°44′	91°10′
Mattagami 71	IR/RI	ON	Sudbury	41 P/13	47°51′	81°31′
Mattagami Lake	LAKE/LAC	ON	Sudbury	41 P/13	47°52′	81°35′
Mattagami Landing	UNP/LNO	ON	Sudbury	41 P/11	47°44′	81°29′
Mattagami River	RIV/CDE	ON	Cochrane	42 I/11	50°44′	81°29′
Mattatall Lake	LAKE/LAC	NS	Cumberland	11 E/11	45°41′	63°29′
Mattawa	TOWN/VIL2	ON	Nipissing	31 L/7	46°19′	78°42′
Mattawa Lake	LAKE/LAC	ON	Kenora	52 G/10	49°42′	90°58′
Mattawan	MUN2/AZM2	ON	Nipissing	31 L/7	46°22′	78°48′
Mattawishkwia River	RIV/CDE	ON	Cochrane	42 G/14	49°54′	83°12′
Mattawitchewan River	RIV/CDE	ON	Cochrane	42 G/6	49°22′	83°27′
Mattberry Lake	LAKE/LAC	NT	Mackenzie	86 B/4	64°05′	115°54′
Mattes	UNP/LNO	SK	52-6-W3	73 G/7	53°28′	106°49′
Matthews	UNP/LNO	NB	Northumberland	21 I/13	46°56′	65°55′
Matthews Crossing	UNP/LNO	AB	24-54-7-W5	83 G/10	53°41′	114°54′
Matthews Lake	LAKE/LAC	ON	Algoma	42 C/14	48°56′	85°06′
Matthews Pond	LAKE/LAC	NF		2 C/5	48°19′	53°52′
Matthews Pond	LAKE/LAC	NF		2 D/4	48°11′	55°42′
Matthiasville	UNP/LNO	ON	Muskoka	31 D/14	44°59′	79°12′
Mattice	UNP/LNO	ON	Cochrane	42 G/11	49°37′	83°16′
Mattice-Val Côté	MUN2/AZM2	ON	Cochrane	42 G/11	49°39′	83°17′
Mattie Settlement	UNP/LNO	NS	Guysborough	11 F/12	45°35′	61°33′
Mattis Point	UNP/LNO	NF		12 B/8	48°29′	58°24′
Matty Island	ISL/ÎLE	NT	Franklin	57 C	69°29′	95°40′
Matzhiwin	UNP/LNO	AB	32-21-15-W4	82 I/16	50°50′	112°03′
Maud Bight	BAY/BAIE	NT	Franklin	38 C	73°39′	79°14′
Maude, Lac	LAKE/LAC	QC	Vallée-de-l'Or	32 C/8	48°21′	76°14′
Maud Lake	LAKE/LAC	ON	Kenora	52 E/7	49°27′	94°31′
Maufelly Bay	BAY/BAIE	NT	Mackenzie	75 N	63°27′	108°25′
Maugerville	UNP/LNO	NB	Sunbury	21 G/16	45°52′	66°27′
Maugerville	GEOG/GÉOG	NB	Sunbury	21 J/1	46°10′	66°17′
Maundy Thursday, Cape	CAPE/CAP	NT	Franklin	59 F	78°28′	92°59′
Maunoir, Lac	LAKE/LAC	NT	Mackenzie	96 N	67°29′	124°55′
Maupertuis, Lac	LAKE/LAC	QC	Maria-Chapdelaine	22 L/5	50°26′	71°45′
Maurelle Island	ISL/ÎLE	BC	Sayward	92 K/6	50°17′	125°09′
Maurepas, Promontoire	CAPE/CAP	QC	Kativik	35 J/7	62°15′	74°58′
Maurice Point	CAPE/CAP	SK		74 N/5	59°21′	109°50′
Maurice Point	CAPE/CAP	NT	Keewatin	45 O	63°40′	83°56′
Maurice, Sommet de	MTN/MNT	QC	Charlevoix	21 M/15	47°48′	70°52′
Mauriceville	UNP/LNO	QC	La Côte-de-Beaupré	21 M/6	47°16′	71°02′
Mauricie — Bois-Francs	MUN1/AZM1	QC	Mékinac	31 P/2	47°09′	72°56′
Mauricie, Parc national de la - also-aussi - La Mauricie National Park	PARK/PARC	QC	Le Centre-de-la-Mauricie	31 I/15	46°48′	72°58′
Maury Channel	CHAN/CHEN	NT	Franklin	58 G	75°41′	94°30′
Mauvais Bois, Lac	LAKE/LAC	QC	Manicouagan	22 K/8	50°28′	68°18′
Mauvais Rocher 5	IR/RI	BC	Kamloops Division Yale	92 I/14	50°47′	121°05′
Mauves, Baie des	BAY/BAIE	QC	Le Fjord-du-Saguenay	22 L/10	50°43′	70°35′
Mavillette	UNP/LNO	NS	Digby	21 B/1	44°06′	66°11′
Mavis Mills	UNP/LNO	NB	York	21 J/7	46°24′	66°39′
Mavor Island	ISL/ÎLE	NT	Keewatin	34 D	56°05′	78°52′
Mawcook	UNP/LNO	QC	La Haute-Yamaska	31 H/7	45°27′	72°47′
Mawdesley Lake	LAKE/LAC	MB	58-21,22,23-W	63 K/2	54°02′	100°38′
Mawer	UNP/LNO	SK	5-21-3-W3	72 J/9	50°45′	106°24′
Maxan Creek 5	IR/RI	BC	Range 5 Coast	93 L/8	54°20′	126°08′
Maxan Lake	LAKE/LAC	BC	Range 5 Coast	93 L/8	54°18′	126°05′
Maxan Lake 3	IR/RI	BC	Range 5 Coast	93 L/8	54°21′	126°10′
Maxan Lake 4	IR/RI	BC	Range 5 Coast	93 L/8	54°19′	126°07′
Maxhamish Lake	LAKE/LAC	BC	Peace River	94 O/14	59°52′	123°18′
Maxim	UNP/LNO	SK	21-4-15-W2	62 E/5	49°19′	103°58′
Maxim Creek 11A - see-voir - Foxy Creek 6	IR/RI	BC		93 L/8	54°20′	126°08′
Maxim Creek 11A - see-voir - Maxan Creek 5	IR/RI	BC		93 L/8	54°20′	126°08′
Maximeville	UNP/LNO	PE	Prince	21 I/8	46°26′	64°08′
Maxim Lake 11 - see-voir - Maxan Lake 4	IR/RI	BC		93 L/8	54°19′	126°07′
Maxim Lake 12A - see-voir - Maxan Lake 3	IR/RI	BC		93 L/8	54°21′	126°10′
Max Lake	LAKE/LAC	MB		53 L/12	54°33′	95°58′
Maxstone	UNP/LNO	SK	23-6-1-W3	72 G/8	49°30′	106°02′
Maxville	VILG/VILG	ON	Glengarry	31 G/7	45°17′	74°51′
Maxwell	UNP/LNO	NB	York	21 G/13	45°54′	67°42′
Maxwell	UNP/LNO	ON	Hastings	31 F/4	45°06′	77°50′
Maxwell	UNP/LNO	ON	Grey	41 A/8	44°18′	80°24′

NAME NOM	ENTITY ENTITÉ	LOC 1 LIEU 1	LOC 2 LIEU 2	MAP CARTE	POSITION LAT	LONG
Maxwell Bay	BAY/BAIE	NT	Franklin	58 E	74°40′	88°49′
Maxwell Crossing	UNP/LNO	NB	Charlotte	21 G/3	45°15′	67°16′
Maxwell, Lac	LAKE/LAC	QC	Minganie	12 P/12	51°42′	57°32′
Maxwells	UNP/LNO	ON	Haliburton	31 D/16	44°53′	78°29′
Maxwellton	UNP/LNO	NS	Digby	21 B/1	44°10′	66°03′
Maybank	UNP/LNO	QC	Le Haut-Saint-Laurent	31 G/1	45°04′	74°24′
Maybank	UNP/LNO	MB		62 H/14	49°50′	97°09′
Mayberry	UNP/LNO	SK	36-12-27-W2	72 I/4	50°02′	105°33′
Mayer Lake	LAKE/LAC	BC	Queen Charlotte	103 F/9	53°41′	132°03′
Mayerthorpe	TOWN/VIL2	AB	28-57-8-W5	83 G/14	53°57′	115°08′
Mayerville	UNP/LNO	ON	Russell	31 G/6	45°16′	75°04′
Mayfair	HAM/HAM	SK	19-46-11-W3	73 B/13	52°59′	107°36′
Mayfair	UNP/LNO	ON	Middlesex	40 I/13	42°47′	81°35′
Mayfair	UNP/LNO	SK		73 B/2	52°09′	106°40′
Mayfair	UNP/LNO	BC	New Westminster	92 G/2	49°14′	122°49′
Mayfeld	UNP/LNO	MB	23-13-12-W	62 J/2	50°07′	99°00′
Mayfield	UNP/LNO	PE	Queens	11 L/6	46°27′	63°21′
Mayfield	UNP/LNO	NB	Charlotte	21 G/3	45°13′	67°19′
Mayfield	UNP/LNO	ON	Peel	30 M/13	43°46′	79°48′
Mayfield No. 406	MUN2/AZM2	SK		73 B/12	52°35′	107°40′
Mayflower	UNP/LNO	NS	Digby	21 B/1	44°05′	66°07′
Mayhew	UNP/LNO	ON	Renfrew	31 F/7	45°28′	76°37′
Mayhews Landing	UNP/LNO	ON	Renfrew	31 F/5	45°20′	77°35′
May Inlet	BAY/BAIE	NT	Franklin	69 B	76°15′	100°45′
May Lake	LAKE/LAC	ON	Algoma	41 J/8	46°25′	82°29′
May Lake	LAKE/LAC	SK		64 D/5	56°21′	103°45′
May Lake	LAKE/LAC	AB	66-3-W4	73 L/9	54°42′	110°23′
May Lake	LAKE/LAC	BC	Sayward	92 K/6	50°19′	125°08′
Maymont	VILG/VILG	SK	30-41-12-W3	73 B/12	52°34′	107°42′
Maymont Beach	HAM/HAM	SK	19-47-16-W3	73 F/1	53°04′	108°20′
May, Mount	MTN/MNT	AB	58-13-W6	83 L/4	54°03′	119°55′
Maynard	UNP/LNO	ON	Grenville	31 B/12	44°43′	75°35′
Maynard Lake	LAKE/LAC	ON	Kenora	52 K/5	50°22′	93°54′
Maynard Lake	LAKE/LAC	SK		63 M/4	55°02′	103°56′
Maynard Lake	LAKE/LAC	BC	Rupert	92 L/6	50°24′	127°13′
Mayne	UNP/LNO	BC	Cowichan	92 B/14	48°51′	123°18′
Mayne Corners	UNP/LNO	ON	Perth	40 P/14	43°49′	81°01′
Mayne Island	ISL/ÎLE	BC	Cowichan	92 B/14	48°51′	123°17′
Mayne Island 6	IR/RI	BC	Cowichan	92 B/14	48°51′	123°19′
Mayne Passage	CHAN/CHEN	BC	Range 1 Coast	92 K/5	50°24′	125°31′
Maynooth	UNP/LNO	ON	Hastings	31 F/4	45°14′	77°57′
Maynooth Station	UNP/LNO	ON	Hastings	31 F/4	45°14′	77°55′
Mayo	VILG/VILG	QC	Papineau	31 G/11	45°40′	75°21′
Mayo	VILG/VILG	YT		105 M/12	63°36′	135°54′
Mayo	MUN2/AZM2	ON	Hastings	31 F/4	45°05′	77°36′
Mayo Lake	LAKE/LAC	ON	Hastings	31 F/4	45°02′	77°35′
Mayo Lake	LAKE/LAC	YT		105 M/14	63°45′	135°02′
Mayook	UNP/LNO	BC	Kootenay	82 G/5	49°29′	115°34′
Mayo River	RIV/CDE	YT		105 M/12	63°35′	135°54′
May Point	CAPE/CAP	NT	Franklin	49 G	79°16′	85°54′
May River	RIV/CDE	AB	77-9-W4	73 M/11	55°43′	111°22′
Mayson Lake	LAKE/LAC	SK		74 G/14	57°55′	107°10′
Mayson Lake	LAKE/LAC	BC	Kamloops Division Yale	92 P/1	51°14′	120°25′
Mayton	UNP/LNO	AB	23-33-27-W4	82 P/13	51°50′	113°44′
Mayview	UNP/LNO	SK	27-52-2-W3	73 G/9	53°31′	106°12′
Maywood	UNP/LNO	ON	Wentworth	30 M/4	43°14′	79°59′
Mazana, Lac	LAKE/LAC	QC	Antoine-Labelle	31 O/2	47°08′	74°31′
Mazana, Rivière	RIV/CDE	QC	Antoine-Labelle	31 O/2	47°09′	74°53′
Maze Lake	LAKE/LAC	NT	Keewatin	55 K	62°23′	93°30′
Maze Lake	LAKE/LAC	NT	Mackenzie	75 P	63°53′	105°57′
Mazenod	VILG/VILG	SK	33-10-2-W3	72 G/16	49°52′	106°13′
Mazenod Lake	LAKE/LAC	NT	Mackenzie	85 N	63°42′	117°00′
Mazeppa	UNP/LNO	AB	30-19-27-W4	82 I/12	50°38′	113°44′
Mazerolle Settlement	UNP/LNO	NB	York	21 G/15	45°53′	66°51′
McAbee	UNP/LNO	BC	Kamloops Division Yale	92 I/14	50°47′	121°08′
McAdam	VILG/VILG	NB	York	21 G/11	45°36′	67°20′
McAdam	GEOG/GÉOG	NB	York	21 G/11	45°40′	67°23′
McAdams Lake	UNP/LNO	NS	Cape Breton	11 K/1	46°02′	60°27′
McAleese Lake	LAKE/LAC	NT	Keewatin	65 B	60°19′	98°40′
McAlpine	UNP/LNO	ON	Prescott	31 G/10	45°32′	74°42′
McAlpine Corners	UNP/LNO	ON	Hastings	31 F/4	45°14′	77°52′
McAlpines	UNP/LNO	NB	Queens	21 G/9	45°43′	66°06′
McAndrew	UNP/LNO	NF		1 N/5	47°17′	53°59′
McArras Brook	UNP/LNO	NS	Antigonish	11 E/9	45°44′	62°12′
McArthur Falls	UNP/LNO	MB	3-17-11-E	52 L/5	50°24′	96°00′

NAME NOM	ENTITY ENTITÉ	LOC 1 LIEU 1	LOC 2 LIEU 2	MAP CARTE	POSITION LAT	LONG
McArthur Lake	LAKE/LAC	SK		63 M/1	55°15′	102°24′
McArthur Lake	LAKE/LAC	NT	Mackenzie	75 G	61°35′	106°50′
McArthur Peak	MTN/MNT	YT		115 C/9	60°36′	140°13′
McArthurs Mills	UNP/LNO	ON	Hastings	31 F/4	45°08′	77°35′
McAuley	UNP/LNO	MB	10-15-29-W	62 K/6	50°16′	101°23′
McAvoy Lake	LAKE/LAC	NT	Mackenzie	76 N	67°19′	109°31′
McBean	UNP/LNO	QC	La Vallée-de-la-Gatineau	31 J/4	46°04′	75°59′
McBean Bay	BAY/BAIE	NT	Franklin	58 A	72°38′	89°35′
McBean Harbour	UNP/LNO	ON	Algoma	41 J/1	46°08′	82°11′
McBeth Fiord	BAY/BAIE	NT	Franklin	27 C	69°32′	69°10′
McBeth Point	CAPE/CAP	MB		63 A/3	52°08′	97°30′
McBeth River	RIV/CDE	NT	Franklin	27 C	69°32′	70°02′
McBride	VILG/VILG	BC	Cariboo	93 H/8	53°18′	120°10′
McBride Lake	LAKE/LAC	BC	Range 5 Coast	93 L/3	54°04′	127°19′
McBride River	RIV/CDE	BC	Cassiar	104 H/14	57°58′	129°17′
McCabe	UNP/LNO	BC	Cariboo	83 D/14	52°56′	119°24′
McCabe Creek	UNP/LNO	YT		115 I/10	62°32′	136°46′
McCabe Lake	LAKE/LAC	ON	Algoma	41 J/7	46°25′	82°34′
McCafferty Landing	UNP/LNO	MB		63 J/13	54°50′	99°44′
McCain Settlement	UNP/LNO	NB	Kings	21 H/12	45°40′	65°32′
McCall	UNP/LNO	BC	Range 5 Coast	93 K/1	54°03′	124°09′
McCallum	UNP/LNO	NF		11 P/9	47°38′	56°14′
McCallum Lake	LAKE/LAC	MB		64 C/4	56°05′	101°45′
McCallum Settlement	UNP/LNO	NS	Colchester	11 E/6	45°29′	63°15′
McCann	UNP/LNO	NB	Northumberland	21 I/13	46°48′	65°48′
McCann Lake	LAKE/LAC	NT	Mackenzie	75 G	61°14′	106°30′
McCann's Shore	UNP/LNO	ON	Lanark	31 F/1	45°06′	76°11′
McCarleys Corners	UNP/LNO	ON	Grenville	31 B/13	44°55′	75°32′
McCarthy Lake	LAKE/LAC	ON	Algoma	41 J/8	46°19′	82°28′
McCarthy Park	UNP/LNO	SK		72 I/7	50°29′	104°40′
McCartney's Flat 4	IR/RI	BC	Lillooet	92 I/12	50°39′	121°54′
McCauley Island	ISL/ÎLE	BC	Range 4 Coast	103 G/9	53°40′	130°15′
McClarty Lake	LAKE/LAC	MB	63-19-20-W	63 K/8	54°28′	100°21′
McClelland Lake	LAKE/LAC	AB	97,98-8,9-W4	74 E/6	57°29′	111°20′
McClures Mills	UNP/LNO	NS	Colchester	11 E/6	45°21′	63°18′
McCluskey	UNP/LNO	NB	Victoria	21 J/13	46°58′	67°46′
McCluskeys Corners	UNP/LNO	ON	Thunder Bay	52 A/6	48°18′	89°28′
McConechy Lake	LAKE/LAC	SK	55,56-25-W2	73 H/13	53°48′	105°40′
McConnel	UNP/LNO	BC	Kootenay	82 F/1	49°09′	116°20′
McConnell	UNP/LNO	MB	12-15-23-W	62 K/7	50°16′	100°32′
*McConnell Creek	UNP/LNO	BC	Cassiar	94 D/16	56°53′	126°30′
McConnell Island	ISL/ÎLE	NT	Franklin	89 D	77°39′	113°16′
McConnell Range	MTN/MNT	NT	Mackenzie	96 C	64°14′	124°15′
McConnell River	RIV/CDE	YT		105 F/8	61°17′	132°30′
McConnell River	RIV/CDE	NT	Keewatin	55 D	60°51′	94°21′
McCool	UNP/LNO	ON	Timiskaming	31 M/12	47°38′	79°53′
McCord	HAM/HAM	SK	36-5-7-W3	72 G/7	49°26′	106°50′
McCormack Island	ISL/ÎLE	NT	Keewatin	34 L	58°36′	78°38′
McCormick	UNP/LNO	ON	Glengarry	31 G/7	45°21′	74°36′
McCormick, Barrage	MISC/DIV	QC	Manicouagan	22 F/1	49°12′	68°19′
McCormick Inlet	BAY/BAIE	NT	Franklin	78 G	75°51′	111°56′
McCourt Lake	LAKE/LAC	NT	Keewatin	65 F	61°11′	100°15′
McCourts Corner	UNP/LNO	QC	Le Val-Saint-François	31 H/9	45°36′	72°01′
McCoy Head	CAPE/CAP	NB	Saint John	21 H/5	45°15′	65°44′
McCoy Islands	ISL/ÎLE	ON	Parry Sound	41 H/8	45°27′	80°29′
McCoy Lake	LAKE/LAC	ON	Kenora	53 C/9	52°35′	92°19′
McCracken	UNP/LNO	BC	Kamloops Division Yale	92 I/9	50°40′	120°13′
McCracken Landing	UNP/LNO	ON	Northumberland	31 D/1	44°15′	78°04′
McCrackens Landing	UNP/LNO	ON	Peterborough	31 D/9	44°32′	78°09′
McCrackins Beach	UNP/LNO	ON	Victoria	31 D/11	44°41′	79°06′
McCrae	UNP/LNO	ON	Hastings	31 C/14	44°58′	77°27′
McCraney Lake	LAKE/LAC	ON	Nipissing	31 E/10	45°34′	78°54′
McCraney No. 282	MUN2/AZM2	SK		72 P/5	51°30′	105°55′
McCrary Isthmus	CAPE/CAP	NT	Keewatin	66 P	67°38′	96°45′
McCreadyville	UNP/LNO	NS	Cape Breton	11 K/8	46°19′	60°18′
McCrea Heights	UNP/LNO	ON	Sudbury	41 I/10	46°35′	80°59′
McCrea Lake	LAKE/LAC	ON	Thunder Bay	52 J/16	50°52′	90°18′
McCrea River	RIV/CDE	NT	Mackenzie	85 I	62°58′	113°55′
McCreary	VILG/VILG	MB		62 J/14	50°46′	99°30′
McCreary	MUN2/AZM2	MB		62 J/14	50°45′	99°20′
McCrearys	UNP/LNO	ON	Lanark	31 F/1	45°07′	76°13′
McCreary's Shore	UNP/LNO	ON	Lanark	31 F/1	45°01′	76°13′
McCreight Lake	LAKE/LAC	BC	Sayward	92 K/5	50°18′	125°39′
McCrimmon	UNP/LNO	ON	Glengarry	31 G/7	45°25′	74°44′
McCrosson and Tovell	MUN2/AZM2	ON	Rainy River	52 D/16	48°58′	94°19′

NAME NOM	ENTITY ENTITÉ	LOC 1 LIEU 1	LOC 2 LIEU 2	MAP CARTE	POSITION LAT	LONG
McCulloch	UNP/LNO	BC	Similkameen Division Yale	82 E/14	49°48'	119°11'
McCulloughs Landing	UNP/LNO	ON	Lanark	31 F/1	45°01'	76°13'
McCully	UNP/LNO	NB	Kings	21 H/14	45°46'	65°25'
McCurdys Corner	UNP/LNO	NS	Colchester	11 E/6	45°23'	63°18'
McCusker Lake	LAKE/LAC	ON	Kenora	52 M/10	51°39'	94°39'
McCusker Lake	LAKE/LAC	MB	82-11,12-E	54 D/4	56°05'	95°45'
McCusker Lake	LAKE/LAC	SK	72-18-W3	73 N/7	55°16'	108°44'
McCusker, Mount	MTN/MNT	BC	Peace River	94 G/4	57°05'	123°55'
McCusker River	RIV/CDE	SK	75-18-W3	73 N/10	55°32'	108°39'
McDame	UNP/LNO	BC	Cassiar	104 P/3	59°11'	129°14'
McDame Creek	RIV/CDE	BC	Cassiar	104 P/3	59°11'	129°14'
McDames Creek 2	IR/RI	BC	Cassiar	104 P/3	59°11'	129°14'
McDiarmid Lake	LAKE/LAC	ON	Cochrane	32 D/5	48°28'	79°33'
McDiarmid's Shore	UNP/LNO	ON	Lanark	31 F/1	45°08'	76°10'
McDonald	UNP/LNO	MB		62 I/2	50°05'	96°58'
McDonald Bay	BAY/BAIE	SK		73 O/10	55°41'	106°30'
McDonald Corner	UNP/LNO	NB	Queens	21 H/13	45°47'	66°00'
McDonald Court	UNP/LNO	ON	Wentworth	30 M/5	43°19'	79°55'
McDonald Hills	UNP/LNO	SK	5-25-15-W2	72 P/1	51°06'	104°05'
McDonald Lake	LAKE/LAC	NT	Mackenzie	75 L	62°07'	111°13'
McDonald Lake 1	IR/RI	BC	Cassiar	104 N/12	59°44'	133°33'
McDonalds Corners	UNP/LNO	ON	Lanark	31 C/15	44°57'	76°32'
McDonalds Landing	UNP/LNO	BC	Range 4 Coast	93 L/1	54°00'	126°02'
McDougal Creek	RIV/CDE	SK	60-12-W2	63 L/4	54°10'	103°47'
McDougall	MUN2/AZM2	ON	Parry Sound	41 H/8	45°24'	80°00'
McDougall	UNP/LNO	ON	Renfrew	31 F/7	45°28'	76°50'
McDougall Lake	LAKE/LAC	NB	Charlotte	21 G/7	45°19'	66°46'
McDougall Lake	LAKE/LAC	BC	Kamloops Division Yale	83 D/4	52°13'	119°54'
McDougall Mills	UNP/LNO	ON	Kenora	52 J/4	50°10'	91°32'
McDougall Pass	VALL/VALL	NT/YT		116 P/9	67°43'	136°25'
McDougalls Landing	UNP/LNO	MB	35-9-17-E	52 E/14	49°48'	95°10'
McDougall Sound	CHAN/CHEN	NT	Franklin	68 H	75°10'	97°00'
McEachern	UNP/LNO	SK	34-1-8-W3	72 G/3	49°05'	107°00'
McElhanney	UNP/LNO	SK	42,43-7-W2	63 D/10	52°40'	102°57'
McEvoy Lake	LAKE/LAC	YT		105 G/16	61°48'	130°14'
McEvoy, Mount	MTN/MNT	BC	Cassiar	104 A/16	56°46'	128°19'
McFarlane Lake	UNP/LNO	ON	Sudbury	41 I/7	46°26'	80°57'
McFerson - see-voir - Pronto East	UNP/LNO	ON		41 J/2	46°12'	82°44'
McGarry	MUN2/AZM2	ON	Timiskaming	32 D/4	48°09'	79°38'
McGary Flats	UNP/LNO	ON	Hastings	31 F/4	45°10'	77°58'
McGavock Lake	LAKE/LAC	MB		64 C/11	56°32'	101°24'
McGaw	UNP/LNO	ON	Huron	40 P/12	43°45'	81°38'
McGee	UNP/LNO	SK	19-29-16-W3	72 N/9	51°30'	108°15'
McGerrigle, Monts	MTN/MNT	QC	Denis-Riverin	22 A/13	48°57'	65°57'
McGill Bay	BAY/BAIE	NT	Mackenzie	96 J	66°34'	122°27'
McGillivray	MUN2/AZM2	ON	Middlesex	40 P/4	43°13'	81°35'
McGillivray	UNP/LNO	BC	Lillooet	92 J/9	50°37'	122°26'
McGillivray Bay	BAY/BAIE	NT	Franklin	67 A	68°25'	98°05'
McGillivray, Lac	LAKE/LAC	QC	Pontiac	31 K/3	46°04'	77°07'
McGillivray Lake	LAKE/LAC	BC	Kamloops Division Yale	82 L/13	50°51'	119°50'
McGillivray Range	MTN/MNT	BC	Kootenay	82 G/4	49°15'	115°33'
McGill, Lac	LAKE/LAC	QC	Le Haut-Saint-François	21 E/11	45°35'	71°17'
McGinleys Corner	UNP/LNO	NB	Westmorland	21 H/15	45°50'	64°35'
McGinnis Creek	UNP/LNO	ON	Rainy River	52 D/15	48°51'	94°39'
McGiverin Lake	LAKE/LAC	ON	Algoma	41 I/8	46°18'	82°43'
McGivney	UNP/LNO	NB	York	21 J/7	46°22'	66°34'
McGlennon Point	CAPE/CAP	ON	Northumberland	30 N/13	43°58'	77°56'
McGowans Corner	UNP/LNO	NB	Sunbury	21 G/16	45°53'	66°18'
McGrath	UNP/LNO	ON	Renfrew	31 F/6	45°29'	77°06'
McGrath Corner	UNP/LNO	NB	Carleton	21 J/5	46°29'	67°44'
McGraths Cove	UNP/LNO	NS	Halifax	11 D/12	44°30'	63°51'
McGraths Mountain	UNP/LNO	NS	Pictou	11 E/9	45°32'	62°22'
McGraw Brook	UNP/LNO	NB	Northumberland	21 J/16	46°49'	66°07'
McGregor	UNP/LNO	ON	Essex	40 J/2	42°09'	82°58'
McGregor	UNP/LNO	BC	Cariboo	93 I/4	54°05'	121°50'
McGregor Bay	UNP/LNO	ON	Manitoulin	41 I/4	46°05'	81°40'
McGregor Bay	BAY/BAIE	ON	Manitoulin	41 I/4	46°05'	81°40'
McGregor Brook	UNP/LNO	NB	Kings	21 H/13	45°46'	65°32'
McGregor Creek	RIV/CDE	ON	Kent	40 J/8	42°24'	82°11'
McGregor Junction	UNP/LNO	ON	Essex	40 J/2	42°09'	82°57'
McGregor, Lac	LAKE/LAC	QC	Les Collines-de-l'Outaouais	31 G/12	45°39'	75°39'
McGregor Lake	LAKE/LAC	AB	15,16,17,18-21-W4	82 I/7	50°25'	112°52'
McGregor Lake	LAKE/LAC	NT	Mackenzie	86 J	66°53'	115°14'
McGregor River	RIV/CDE	BC	Cariboo	93 J/1	54°11'	122°02'
McGuire	UNP/LNO	ON	Renfrew	31 F/14	45°51'	77°12'

NAME NOM	ENTITY ENTITÉ	LOC 1 LIEU 1	LOC 2 LIEU 2	MAP CARTE	POSITION LAT	LONG
McGuire	UNP/LNO	BC	New Westminster	92 J/3	50°03′	123°06′
McGuire Settlement	UNP/LNO	ON	Lennox and Addington	31 C/11	44°32′	77°04′
McInnes Lake	LAKE/LAC	ON	Kenora	53 C/4	52°13′	93°45′
McInnes, Mount	MTN/MNT	BC	Kamloops Division Yale	92 I/2	50°05′	120°58′
McInnes River	RIV/CDE	ON	Kenora	53 C/12	52°38′	93°47′
McInnis	UNP/LNO	ON	Cochrane	42 H/11	49°32′	81°26′
McIntosh	UNP/LNO	ON	Bruce	40 P/14	43°58′	81°06′
McIntosh	UNP/LNO	ON	Kenora	52 F/13	49°59′	93°36′
McIntosh Bay	BAY/BAIE	ON	Kenora	52 K/4	50°03′	93°37′
McIntosh Bay	BAY/BAIE	ON	Kenora	53 D/9	52°35′	94°07′
McIntosh Lake	LAKE/LAC	ON	Nipissing	31 E/10	45°40′	78°46′
McIntosh Lake	LAKE/LAC	SK		73 P/11	55°45′	105°08′
McIntosh Lakes	LAKE/LAC	BC	Cariboo	93 A/3	52°08′	121°29′
McIntosh Mills	UNP/LNO	ON	Leeds	31 B/12	44°33′	75°54′
McIntosh Springs	UNP/LNO	ON	Cochrane	42 A/10	48°38′	80°52′
McIntyre	UNP/LNO	ON	Lennox and Addington	31 C/2	44°13′	76°48′
McIntyre	UNP/LNO	ON	Grey	41 A/8	44°18′	80°18′
McIntyre Bay	BAY/BAIE	ON	Thunder Bay	52 H/7	49°27′	88°40′
McIntyre Bay	BAY/BAIE	BC	Queen Charlotte	103 J/4	54°05′	132°00′
McIntyres Mountain	UNP/LNO	NS	Inverness	11 F/14	45°47′	61°22′
McIver	UNP/LNO	ON	Bruce	41 A/14	44°52′	81°06′
McIver's	VILG/VILG	NF		12 G/1	49°05′	58°08′
McIvor River	RIV/CDE	AB	107-13-W4	84 I/8	58°18′	112°03′
McKague	UNP/LNO	SK	15-42-14-W2	63 D/12	52°37′	103°56′
McKay Island	ISL/ÎLE	BC	Clayoquot	92 E/8	49°19′	126°03′
McKay Lake	LAKE/LAC	NF		23 H/12	53°44′	65°37′
McKay Lake	LAKE/LAC	ON	Thunder Bay	42 E/9	49°37′	86°25′
McKay Meadow 4	IR/RI	BC	Cariboo	93 B/10	52°30′	122°37′
McKay's	UNP/LNO	NF		12 B/2	48°14′	58°49′
McKays Corner	UNP/LNO	NS	Cape Breton	11 J/4	46°11′	59°59′
McKay's Corners	UNP/LNO	ON	Kent	40 I/5	42°27′	82°00′
McKay Section	UNP/LNO	NS	Hants	11 E/4	45°00′	63°58′
McKay Siding	UNP/LNO	NS	Colchester	11 E/3	45°10′	63°19′
McKays Point	CAPE/CAP	NS	Inverness	11 F/13	45°54′	61°31′
McKay's Waterfront	UNP/LNO	ON	Carleton	31 F/9	45°31′	76°12′
McKeaghan	UNP/LNO	NB	Carleton	21 J/5	46°23′	67°40′
McKeand River	RIV/CDE	NT	Franklin	26 G	65°34′	67°55′
McKearney Ranch	UNP/LNO	BC	Peace River	94 B/9	56°38′	122°28′
McKee	UNP/LNO	QC	Pontiac	31 F/9	45°34′	76°26′
McKeens Corner	UNP/LNO	NB	York	21 G/15	45°58′	66°51′
McKees Camp	UNP/LNO	ON	Sudbury	41 P/3	47°06′	81°16′
McKees Mills	UNP/LNO	NB	Kent	21 I/7	46°25′	64°44′
McKellar	MUN2/AZM2	ON	Parry Sound	31 E/5	45°30′	79°50′
McKellar	UNP/LNO	ON	Parry Sound	31 E/12	45°30′	79°55′
McKellar Bay	BAY/BAIE	NT	Franklin	25 K	62°45′	69°30′
McKellar Lake	LAKE/LAC	ON	Kenora	52 K/4	50°06′	93°50′
McKellar Park	UNP/LNO	ON	Carleton	31 G/5	45°23′	75°46′
McKendrick	UNP/LNO	NB	Restigouche	21 O/15	47°56′	66°40′
McKendrick Lake	LAKE/LAC	NB	Northumberland	21 J/16	46°51′	66°22′
McKenna	UNP/LNO	NB	Carleton	21 J/4	46°13′	67°31′
McKenzie Bay	BAY/BAIE	ON	Kenora	52 K/10	50°30′	92°47′
McKenzie Bay	BAY/BAIE	ON	Kenora	52 F/11	49°45′	93°23′
McKenzie Corner	UNP/LNO	NB	Carleton	21 J/4	46°06′	67°43′
McKenzie Creek	RIV/CDE	ON	Haldimand	30 M/4	43°01′	79°54′
McKenzie Island	UNP/LNO	ON	Kenora	52 N/4	51°05′	93°48′
McKenzie Lake	UNP/LNO	ON	Nipissing	31 E/8	45°23′	78°01′
McKenzie Lake	LAKE/LAC	ON	Nipissing	31 E/8	45°22′	78°01′
McKenzie Lake	LAKE/LAC	ON	Rainy River	52 B/6	48°28′	91°04′
McKenzie Lake	LAKE/LAC	SK	60-4-W2	63 L/1	54°12′	102°30′
McKerrow	UNP/LNO	ON	Sudbury	41 I/5	46°17′	81°46′
McKiel Lake	LAKE/LAC	NB	York	21 J/10	46°36′	66°58′
McKillop	MUN2/AZM2	ON	Huron	40 P/11	43°36′	81°17′
McKillop No. 220	MUN2/AZM2	SK		72 I/14	51°00′	105°00′
McKim	UNP/LNO	SK	9-24-5-W2	62 M/2	51°03′	102°39′
McKinlay Lake	LAKE/LAC	NT	Mackenzie	75 L	62°53′	111°33′
McKinley Bay	BAY/BAIE	NT	Franklin	340 D	81°08′	79°12′
McKinley Bay	BAY/BAIE	NT	Franklin	107 D	69°56′	131°10′
McKinley Creek	RIV/CDE	BC	Cariboo	93 A/6	52°17′	121°04′
McKinley Lake	LAKE/LAC	BC	Cariboo	93 A/7	52°16′	120°57′
McKinley Landing	UNP/LNO	BC	Osoyoos Division Yale	82 E/14	49°58′	119°27′
McKinleyville	UNP/LNO	NB	Northumberland	21 I/13	46°52′	65°40′
McKinney Creek	RIV/CDE	BC	Similkameen Division Yale	82 E/3	49°04′	119°13′
McKinnons Harbour	UNP/LNO	NS	Victoria	11 F/15	45°56′	60°53′
McKirdy	UNP/LNO	ON	Thunder Bay	52 H/8	49°16′	88°09′
McKnight Lake	LAKE/LAC	MB		64 C/3	56°05′	101°10′

NAME NOM	ENTITY ENTITÉ	LOC 1 LIEU 1	LOC 2 LIEU 2	MAP CARTE	POSITION LAT	LONG
McKusky Creek	RIV/CDE	BC	Cariboo	93 A/7	52°21′	120°51′
McLaren	UNP/LNO	SK	4-50-23-W3	73 F/6	53°17′	109°18′
McLaren Lake	LAKE/LAC	NT	Mackenzie	86 K	66°37′	116°54′
McLaren's Bay	UNP/LNO	ON	Nipissing	31 L/14	46°51′	79°15′
McLaren's Beach	UNP/LNO	ON	Ontario	31 D/2	44°09′	78°51′
McLarens Settlement	UNP/LNO	ON	Renfrew	31 F/10	45°37′	76°42′
McLaughlin	UNP/LNO	NB	Victoria	21 J/14	46°54′	67°29′
McLaughlin	UNP/LNO	AB	25-46-2-W4	73 D/16	52°59′	110°10′
McLaughlin River	RIV/CDE	MB		63 H/13	53°47′	97°39′
McLean	VILG/VILG	SK	18-15,16-W2	72 I/9	50°31′	104°04′
McLean	UNP/LNO	ON	Frontenac	31 C/10	44°39′	76°50′
McLean Bay	BAY/BAIE	NT	Mackenzie	75 L	62°22′	110°22′
McLean Lake	LAKE/LAC	SK		74 C/6	56°27′	109°15′
McLean Lake	LAKE/LAC	BC	Kamloops Division Yale	92 I/14	50°47′	121°25′
McLean Peninsula	CAPE/CAP	ON	Nipissing	41 I/16	46°53′	80°06′
McLean Ranch	UNP/LNO	BC	Peace River	94 B/9	56°31′	122°09′
McLean Settlement	UNP/LNO	NB	Kent	21 I/7	46°22′	64°57′
McLean's Lake 3	IR/RI	BC	Kamloops Division Yale	92 I/14	50°47′	121°24′
McLeanville	UNP/LNO	ON	Leeds	31 B/13	44°47′	75°39′
McLeary Point	CAPE/CAP	NT	Keewatin	34 D	56°10′	78°40′
McLeese Lake	UNP/LNO	BC	Cariboo	93 B/8	52°25′	122°18′
McLeese Lake	LAKE/LAC	BC	Cariboo	93 B/8	52°25′	122°18′
McLellans Brook	UNP/LNO	NS	Pictou	11 E/10	45°32′	62°36′
McLellans Mountain	UNP/LNO	NS	Pictou	11 E/10	45°30′	62°33′
McLennan	TOWN/VIL2	AB	32-77-19-W5	83 N/10	55°42′	116°54′
McLennan, Lac	LAKE/LAC	QC	La Vallée-de-la-Gatineau	31 O/5	47°26′	75°47′
McLennan Lake	UNP/LNO	SK		73 P/16	55°55′	104°18′
McLennan's Beach	UNP/LNO	ON	Ontario	31 D/6	44°25′	79°10′
McLeod	UNP/LNO	BC	Cassiar	93 M/4	55°14′	127°40′
McLeod Bay	BAY/BAIE	NT	Mackenzie	75 L	62°53′	110°15′
McLeod Hill	UNP/LNO	NB	York	21 J/2	46°01′	66°41′
McLeod Lake	UNP/LNO	BC	Cariboo	93 J/14	54°59′	123°02′
McLeod Lake	LAKE/LAC	BC	Cariboo	93 J/15	54°55′	122°58′
McLeod Lake 1	IR/RI	BC	Cariboo	93 J/14	54°59′	123°03′
McLeod Lake 5	IR/RI	BC	Cariboo	93 J/15	54°57′	122°59′
McLeod No. 185	MUN2/AZM2	SK		62 L/11	50°45′	103°05′
McLeod River	UNP/LNO	AB	7-52-18-W5	83 F/7	53°28′	116°38′
McLeod River	RIV/CDE	AB	59-12-W5	83 J/4	54°09′	115°42′
McLeods	UNP/LNO	NB	Restigouche	22 B/2	48°01′	66°34′
McLeod's	UNP/LNO	QC	Le Granit	21 E/11	45°33′	71°11′
McLeods Crossing	UNP/LNO	NS	Cape Breton	11 J/4	46°11′	60°00′
McLeod Valley	UNP/LNO	AB	2-55-14-W5	83 G/12	53°43′	115°59′
McLeodville	UNP/LNO	ON	Peel	40 P/16	43°53′	80°03′
M'Clintock	UNP/LNO	MB		54 E/16	57°48′	94°13′
M'Clintock, Cape	CAPE/CAP	NT	Franklin	29 G	79°59′	70°39′
M'Clintock Channel	CHAN/CHEN	NT	Franklin	67 G	72°00′	102°00′
M'Clintock Inlet	BAY/BAIE	NT	Franklin	340 E	82°45′	76°30′
M'Clintock Point	CAPE/CAP	NT	Franklin	67 C	69°10′	100°08′
M'Clintock Point	CAPE/CAP	NT	Franklin	89 C	77°23′	117°52′
M'Clintock River	RIV/CDE	YT		105 D/9	60°34′	134°29′
M'Clintock Valley	SEAU/SMER	—		5.17	72°30′	103°30′
McLoughlin Bay	BAY/BAIE	NT	Keewatin	66 O	67°51′	98°35′
McLure	UNP/LNO	BC	Kamloops Division Yale	92 P/1	51°03′	120°14′
M'Clure Bay	BAY/BAIE	NT	Franklin	58 C	73°37′	95°38′
M'Clure, Cape	CAPE/CAP	NT	Franklin	98 E	74°32′	121°17′
M'Clure Strait	CHAN/CHEN	NT	Franklin	88 F	74°30′	119°00′
McLurg Creek	RIV/CDE	SK	72-5-W3	73 O/2	55°13′	106°41′
McMahon	UNP/LNO	SK	10-13-12-W3	72 J/4	50°05′	107°33′
McManus Siding	UNP/LNO	NB	Madawaska	21 O/4	47°04′	67°43′
McMaster, Mount	MTN/MNT	BC	Cassiar	104 N/6	59°21′	133°11′
McMasterville	VILG/VILG	QC	La Vallée-du-Richelieu	31 H/11	45°33′	73°16′
McMichael	UNP/LNO	SK	32-44-19-W2	73 A/15	52°50′	104°44′
McMillan	UNP/LNO	ON	Simcoe	31 D/12	44°44′	79°49′
McMillan Island 6	IR/RI	BC	New Westminster	92 G/2	49°11′	122°34′
McMillan Lake	LAKE/LAC	MB		64 C/13	56°57′	101°42′
McMillan Lake	LAKE/LAC	AB	74-18-W4	83 P/7	55°26′	112°40′
McMillans Corners	UNP/LNO	ON	Stormont	31 G/2	45°10′	74°51′
McMinn	UNP/LNO	NB	Charlotte	21 G/6	45°17′	67°04′
McMonagle Corner	UNP/LNO	NB	Carleton	21 J/5	46°30′	67°40′
McMorran	UNP/LNO	SK	27-20-W3	72 N/7	51°19′	108°45′
McMunn	UNP/LNO	MB	2-8-13-E	52 E/12	49°38′	95°42′
McMurchy Settlement	UNP/LNO	ON	Grey	41 A/8	44°29′	80°17′
McMurdo	UNP/LNO	BC	Kootenay	82 N/2	51°08′	116°46′
McMurphy	UNP/LNO	BC	Kamloops Division Yale	82 M/11	51°40′	119°24′
McMurrich	MUN2/AZM2	ON	Parry Sound	31 E/6	45°28′	79°29′

NAME / NOM	ENTITY / ENTITÉ	LOC 1 / LIEU 1	LOC 2 / LIEU 2	MAP / CARTE	POSITION LAT	POSITION LONG
McMurrich	UNP/LNO	ON	Parry Sound	31 E/6	45°26′	79°26′
McNab	MUN2/AZM2	ON	Renfrew	31 F/7	45°25′	76°30′
McNab	UNP/LNO	ON	Lincoln	30 M/3	43°13′	79°11′
McNab	UNP/LNO	AB	1-5-18-W4	82 H/8	49°21′	112°17′
McNab Creek	UNP/LNO	BC	New Westminster	92 G/11	49°33′	123°24′
McNab, Lac	LAKE/LAC	QC	Jamésie	33 C/14	52°53′	77°27′
McNabs Island	UNP/LNO	NS	Halifax	11 D/12	44°37′	63°32′
McNabs Island	ISL/ÎLE	NS	Halifax	11 D/12	44°37′	63°32′
McNairn	UNP/LNO	NB	Kent	21 I/7	46°27′	64°50′
McNallys	UNP/LNO	NB	York	21 G/15	45°54′	66°55′
McNamara, Mount	MTN/MNT	BC	Cassiar	94 E/11	57°40′	127°14′
McNamee	UNP/LNO	NB	Northumberland	21 J/9	46°30′	66°18′
McNaught	UNP/LNO	ON	Huron	40 P/11	43°38′	81°11′
McNaughton	UNP/LNO	NS	Antigonish	11 F/5	45°28′	61°54′
McNaughton Lake	LAKE/LAC	NT	Keewatin	66 O	67°20′	98°25′
McNaughton River	RIV/CDE	NT	Keewatin	66 O	67°47′	98°30′
McNaughton Shore	UNP/LNO	ON	Lanark	31 F/1	45°02′	76°11′
McNeil	UNP/LNO	QC	Les Laurentides	31 J/1	46°01′	74°11′
McNeill	UNP/LNO	AB	12-20-1-W4	72 L/9	50°41′	110°02′
McNeil Lake	LAKE/LAC	BC	Cariboo	93 A/2	52°04′	120°38′
McNeills Mills	UNP/LNO	PE	Prince	11 L/12	46°38′	63°58′
McNeil River	RIV/CDE	YT		105 F/1	61°10′	132°17′
McNeish	UNP/LNO	NB	Restigouche	22 B/1	48°04′	66°25′
McNulty Creek	RIV/CDE	BC	Similkameen Division Yale	92 H/8	49°24′	120°05′
McNutts Island	UNP/LNO	NS	Shelburne	20 P/11	43°39′	65°18′
McNutts Island	ISL/ÎLE	NS	Shelburne	20 P/11	43°38′	65°17′
McOrmond Lake	LAKE/LAC	SK	59-4-W2	63 L/2	54°07′	102°33′
McParlon Lake	LAKE/LAC	ON	Cochrane	42 I/2	50°09′	80°42′
McPhadyen River	RIV/CDE	NF		23 J/2	54°06′	66°30′
McPhail Cove	UNP/LNO	SK	27-53-27-W2	73 H/12	53°36′	105°54′
McPhail Creek	RIV/CDE	BC	Yale Division Yale	92 H/15	49°47′	120°48′
McPherson Island	ISL/ÎLE	ON	Kenora	52 E/7	49°20′	94°40′
McPherson Lake	LAKE/LAC	YT		105 H/13	61°54′	129°34′
McPhersons Mills	UNP/LNO	NS	Pictou	11 E/10	45°32′	62°31′
McQuaby Lake	LAKE/LAC	ON	Parry Sound	31 L/4	46°02′	79°34′
McQuade	UNP/LNO	NB	Westmorland	21 I/2	46°13′	64°50′
McQueen	UNP/LNO	ON	Algoma	41 K/9	46°34′	84°23′
McQuesten	UNP/LNO	YT		115 P/11	63°33′	137°24′
McQuesten 3	IR/RI	YT		115 P/11	63°34′	137°28′
McQuesten Lake	LAKE/LAC	YT		106 D/3	64°07′	135°19′
McQuesten River	RIV/CDE	YT		115 P/11	63°33′	137°26′
McRae	UNP/LNO	AB	10-62-12-W4	73 L/5	54°21′	111°42′
McRae Lake	LAKE/LAC	NT	Keewatin	65 O	63°32′	99°01′
McRae Point	CAPE/CAP	ON	Bruce	41 A/5	44°16′	81°31′
McReynolds	UNP/LNO	ON	Grenville	31 B/13	44°53′	75°37′
McRoberts Corner	UNP/LNO	ON	Grenville	31 B/13	44°50′	75°39′
McTaggart	VILG/VILG	SK	17-9-15-W2	72 H/9	49°44′	104°01′
McTaggart Lake	LAKE/LAC	SK		74 K/7	58°02′	108°25′
McTavish	UNP/LNO	MB	10,11-6-1-E	62 H/6	49°28′	97°22′
McTavish Arm	BAY/BAIE	NT	Mackenzie	86 L	66°06′	119°00′
McTavish, Cape	CAPE/CAP	NT	Franklin	46 M	67°41′	86°32′
McTavish Island	ISL/ÎLE	NT	Keewatin	34 F	57°32′	76°53′
McTavish Lake	LAKE/LAC	MB	30-21-22-W	62 K/15	50°50′	100°31′
McTavish Lake	LAKE/LAC	SK		73 P/14	55°55′	105°18′
McTavish Point	CAPE/CAP	NT	Keewatin	66 N	67°47′	101°04′
McVeigh	UNP/LNO	MB		64 C/11	56°42′	101°14′
McVicar	UNP/LNO	ON	Bruce	41 H/3	45°09′	81°28′
McVicar Arm	BAY/BAIE	NT	Mackenzie	96 H	65°20′	120°10′
McVitties	UNP/LNO	ON	Sudbury	41 I/7	46°17′	80°51′
McWatters	VILG/VILG	QC	Rouyn-Noranda	32 D/2	48°13′	78°55′
Meacham	VILG/VILG	SK	23-36-27-W2	73 A/4	52°06′	105°45′
Meachen	UNP/LNO	BC	Kootenay	82 F/9	49°37′	116°16′
Mead	UNP/LNO	ON	Cochrane	42 G/5	49°28′	83°52′
Meadow	UNP/LNO	NS	Victoria	11 K/7	46°19′	60°40′
Meadow	UNP/LNO	NB	Albert	21 H/14	45°48′	65°01′
Meadow Bank	VILG/VILG	PE	Queens	11 L/3	46°12′	63°14′
Meadow Bank	UNP/LNO	PE	Queens	11 L/3	46°12′	63°14′
Meadowbank, Mount	MTN/MNT	NT	Keewatin	66 I	66°09′	96°58′
Meadowbank River	RIV/CDE	NT	Keewatin	66 H	65°59′	97°10′
Meadow Brook	UNP/LNO	NB	Westmorland	21 I/2	46°06′	64°35′
Meadowbrook	UNP/LNO	AB	35-63-25-W4	83 I/5	54°29′	113°38′
Meadowbrook	UNP/LNO	BC	New Westminster	92 G/7	49°16′	122°47′
Meadow Brook Lake	LAKE/LAC	NB	Northumberland	21 I/5	46°25′	65°48′
Meadow Creek	UNP/LNO	BC	Kootenay	82 K/2	50°14′	116°59′
Meadow Creek	RIV/CDE	BC	Kamloops Division Yale	92 I/7	50°28′	120°49′

NAME NOM	ENTITY ENTITÉ	LOC 1 LIEU 1	LOC 2 LIEU 2	MAP CARTE	POSITION LAT	LONG
Meadow Creek 3	IR/RI	BC	Kamloops Division Yale	82 L/13	50°49′	119°32′
Meadow Green	UNP/LNO	NS	Antigonish	11 F/12	45°33′	61°49′
Meadow Green	UNP/LNO	SK		73 B/2	52°07′	106°43′
Meadow Lake	TOWN/VIL2	SK		73 K/1	54°08′	108°26′
Meadow Lake	LAKE/LAC	SK	52,53-5,6-W2	63 E/10	53°33′	102°45′
Meadow Lake	LAKE/LAC	SK	59-16-W3	73 K/1	54°07′	108°20′
Meadow Lake	LAKE/LAC	BC	Lillooet	92 P/5	51°22′	121°46′
Meadow Lake 105	IR/RI	SK		73 K/1	54°10′	108°24′
Meadow Lake 105A	IR/RI	SK		73 K/2	54°03′	108°31′
Meadow Lake No. 588	MUN2/AZM2	SK		73 K/1	54°01′	108°19′
Meadowlands	UNP/LNO	ON	Carleton	31 G/5	45°21′	75°45′
Meadowlands	UNP/LNO	MB	18-30-16-W	62 O/12	51°34′	99°42′
Meadow Lea	UNP/LNO	MB	30-13-2-W	62 I/4	50°07′	97°44′
Meadowood	UNP/LNO	MB		62 H/14	49°50′	97°06′
Meadowood Park - see-voir - Meadowood	UNP/LNO	MB		62 H/14	49°50′	97°06′
Meadow Park	UNP/LNO	ON	Algoma	41 K/9	46°31′	84°17′
Meadow Portage	UNP/LNO	MB	24-31-16-W	62 O/12	51°40′	99°36′
Meadow River	RIV/CDE	SK	61-15-W3	73 K/8	54°18′	108°11′
Meadow, Rivière	RIV/CDE	QC	Avignon	22 B/4	48°03′	67°35′
Meadows	VILG/VILG	NF		12 B/16	48°59′	58°03′
Meadows	UNP/LNO	MB	19-12-1-W	62 I/4	50°02′	97°36′
Meadows	UNP/LNO	MB		62 G/13	49°50′	99°58′
Meadows	UNP/LNO	BC	Kootenay	82 F/3	49°11′	117°24′
Meadows	UNP/LNO	BC	Cassiar	104 M/11	59°41′	135°04′
Meadowside	UNP/LNO	ON	Nipissing	31 L/5	46°23′	79°45′
Meadow Springs	UNP/LNO	NS	Pictou	11 E/9	45°30′	62°22′
Meadows Road	UNP/LNO	NS	Cape Breton	11 K/1	46°02′	60°18′
Meadows West	UNP/LNO	MB		62 H/14	49°57′	97°12′
Meadowvale	UNP/LNO	NS	Colchester	11 E/3	45°10′	63°03′
Meadowvale	UNP/LNO	NS	Annapolis	21 A/15	44°57′	64°59′
Meadowvale	UNP/LNO	MB	12-10-5-E	62 H/15	49°50′	96°47′
Meadowvale South	UNP/LNO	ON	Peel	30 M/12	43°36′	79°44′
Meadowvale Station	UNP/LNO	ON	Peel	30 M/12	43°37′	79°44′
Meadowvale Village	UNP/LNO	ON	Peel	30 M/12	43°38′	79°44′
Meadowvale West	UNP/LNO	ON	Peel	30 M/12	43°36′	79°46′
Meadowview	UNP/LNO	AB	33-57-5-W5	83 G/15	53°59′	114°40′
Meadowville	UNP/LNO	NS	Pictou	11 E/10	45°42′	62°55′
Meadow Wood	UNP/LNO	ON	Peel	30 M/12	43°31′	79°37′
Meaford	TOWN/VIL2	ON	Grey	41 A/10	44°36′	80°35′
Meager Creek	RIV/CDE	BC	Lillooet	92 J/11	50°37′	123°24′
Meagher	UNP/LNO	NS	Halifax	11 D/14	44°56′	63°15′
Meagher	UNP/LNO	NS	Queens	21 A/6	44°24′	65°03′
Meaghers Grant	UNP/LNO	NS	Halifax	11 D/14	44°56′	63°14′
Meagwan 8	IR/RI	BC	Queen Charlotte	103 K/1	54°07′	132°18′
Mealy Mountains	MTN/MNT	NF		13 G/6	53°23′	59°28′
Meander River	UNP/LNO	AB	32-115-22-W5	84 N/4	59°02′	117°42′
Meanlaw 24	IR/RI	BC	Range 5 Coast	103 J/1	54°11′	130°02′
Meanook	UNP/LNO	AB	31-64-22-W4	83 I/11	54°34′	113°20′
Meares Island	ISL/ÎLE	BC	Clayoquot	92 F/4	49°11′	125°50′
Mearns	UNP/LNO	AB	28-56-26-W4	83 H/13	53°52′	113°48′
Mears	UNP/LNO	MB	21,22,27,28-21-24-W1	62 K/15	50°49′	100°45′
Meat Cove	UNP/LNO	NS	Victoria	11 N/2	47°02′	60°34′
Meath	UNP/LNO	ON	Renfrew	31 F/10	45°44′	76°59′
Meath Park	VILG/VILG	SK	31-51-23-W2	73 H/6	53°26′	105°22′
Meaux	UNP/LNO	QC	Témiscamingue	31 M/11	47°34′	79°29′
Mécatina, Banc de	SEAU/SMER	—		811A	50°40′	58°20′
Mécatina, Cuvette de	SEAU/SMER	—		811A	51°10′	58°10′
Mecham, Cape	CAPE/CAP	NT	Franklin	98 H	75°44′	121°04′
Mecham River	RIV/CDE	NT	Franklin	78 G	75°04′	108°47′
Mechanic Settlement	UNP/LNO	NB	Kings	21 H/11	45°44′	65°12′
Méchins, Cap des	CAPE/CAP	QC	Matane	22 G/2	49°01′	66°57′
Medard	UNP/LNO	MB	12-69-8-W	63 J/15	54°58′	98°32′
Medford	UNP/LNO	NS	Kings	21 H/1	45°11′	64°22′
Medford	UNP/LNO	NB	Victoria	21 J/13	46°52′	67°41′
Medicine Hat	CITY/VIL1	AB	12-5-W4	72 L/2	50°03′	110°40′
Medicine Lake	LAKE/LAC	AB	44,45-26,27-W5	83 C/13	52°51′	117°46′
Medicine Lodge	UNP/LNO	AB	34-52-21-W5	83 F/11	53°34′	117°01′
Medicine River	RIV/CDE	AB	5-36-1-W5	83 B/1	52°04′	114°06′
Medika	UNP/LNO	MB	15-9-12-E	52 E/12	49°44′	95°53′
Medina	UNP/LNO	ON	Oxford	40 P/3	43°11′	81°03′
Medina Corners	UNP/LNO	ON	Brant	40 P/1	43°01′	80°09′
Meditation Lake	LAKE/LAC	MB	13-15-E	52 L/3	50°06′	95°27′
Medley River	RIV/CDE	AB	11-65-2-W4	73 L/9	54°36′	110°11′
Medonnegonix Lake	LAKE/LAC	NF		1 M/14	47°59′	55°24′
Medonte - see-voir - Oro-Medonte	MUN2/AZM2	ON		31 D/12	44°35′	79°36′

NAME NOM	ENTITY ENTITÉ	LOC 1 LIEU 1	LOC 2 LIEU 2	MAP CARTE	POSITION LAT	LONG
Medonte	UNP/LNO	ON	Simcoe	31 D/12	44°42'	79°36'
Medora	UNP/LNO	ON	Muskoka	31 E/4	45°03'	79°39'
Medora	UNP/LNO	MB	31-3-24-W	62 F/7	49°15'	100°42'
Medstead	VILG/VILG	SK	11-50-14-W3	73 F/8	53°18'	108°04'
Medstead No. 497	MUN2/AZM2	SK		73 F/8	53°20'	108°00'
Meductic	VILG/VILG	NB	York	21 G/14	46°00'	67°29'
Meduxnekeag River	RIV/CDE	NB	Carleton	21 J/4	46°09'	67°34'
Medway	UNP/LNO	NS	Queens	21 A/2	44°08'	64°38'
Medway Creek	RIV/CDE	ON	Middlesex	40 P/3	43°01'	81°16'
Medway Head	CAPE/CAP	NS	Queens	21 A/2	44°06'	64°32'
Medway Heights	UNP/LNO	ON	Middlesex	40 P/3	43°01'	81°18'
Medway River	RIV/CDE	NS	Queens	21 A/2	44°08'	64°36'
Medway River 11	IR/RI	NS	Queens	21 A/7	44°16'	64°50'
Meech, Lac	LAKE/LAC	QC	Les Collines-de-l'Outaouais	31 G/12	45°32'	75°53'
Meech, Ruisseau	RIV/CDE	QC	Les Collines-de-l'Outaouais	31 G/12	45°36'	75°53'
Meehaus, Mount	MTN/MNT	BC	Cassiar	104 J/2	58°02'	130°34'
Meek Lake	LAKE/LAC	BC	Cassiar	104 I/14	58°58'	129°27'
Meek Point	CAPE/CAP	NT	Franklin	98 B	72°52'	125°07'
Meekwap Lake	LAKE/LAC	AB	65-18-W5	83 K/10	54°40'	116°38'
Meelpaeg Lake	LAKE/LAC	NF		12 A/2	48°15'	56°33'
Meenans Corner	UNP/LNO	NB	Kings	21 H/5	45°27'	65°56'
Meeting Creek	UNP/LNO	AB	5-43-19-W4	83 A/10	52°41'	112°44'
Meeting Creek	RIV/CDE	AB	25-41-17-W4	83 A/9	52°33'	112°20'
Meeting Lake	UNP/LNO	SK	30-48-11-W3	73 G/4	53°10'	107°35'
Meeting Lake	LAKE/LAC	SK	48,49-12-W3	73 G/4	53°11'	107°39'
Meeting Lake No. 466	MUN2/AZM2	SK		73 G/3	53°00'	107°20'
Meetoos	UNP/LNO	SK	57-13-W3	73 G/13	53°56'	107°56'
Meetup 2	IR/RI	BC	Range 1 Coast	92 L/16	50°47'	126°22'
Meeyomoot Lake	LAKE/LAC	SK	63-22-W2	73 I/6	54°32'	105°15'
Meeyomoot River	RIV/CDE	SK	68-21-W2	73 I/14	54°53'	105°08'
Mégantic, Lac	LAKE/LAC	QC	Le Granit	21 E/10	45°32'	70°53'
Mégantic, Mont	MTN/MNT	QC	Le Haut-Saint-François	21 E/6	45°28'	71°09'
Mega River	RIV/CDE	AB	113-7-W6	84 L/14	58°50'	119°09'
Megin Lake	LAKE/LAC	BC	Clayoquot	92 E/8	49°29'	126°04'
Mégiscane	UNP/LNO	QC	Vallée-de-l'Or	32 C/6	48°20'	77°05'
Mégiscane, Lac	LAKE/LAC	QC	Vallée-de-l'Or	32 B/12	48°35'	75°55'
Mégiscane, Rivière	RIV/CDE	QC	Abitibi	32 C/6	48°28'	77°08'
Mehan	UNP/LNO	SK	36-26-4-W2	62 M/8	51°18'	102°27'
Meharry	UNP/LNO	MB	1-26-25-W	62 N/2	51°13'	100°51'
Mehatl Creek	RIV/CDE	BC	New Westminster	92 H/13	49°56'	121°57'
Meighen Ice Cap	GLAC/GLAC	NT	Franklin	69 H	80°00'	99°15'
Meighen Island	ISL/ÎLE	NT	Franklin	69 G	79°55'	99°30'
Meigs Corners	UNP/LNO	QC	Brome-Missisquoi	31 H/2	45°07'	72°51'
Meikle Creek	RIV/CDE	BC	Peace River	93 P/6	55°21'	121°22'
Meikle River	RIV/CDE	AB	94-21-W5	84 F/3	57°10'	117°22'
Meilleur River	RIV/CDE	NT	Mackenzie	95 C	61°16'	124°33'
Meilleurs Bay	UNP/LNO	ON	Renfrew	31 K/4	46°10'	77°38'
Meiseners Section	UNP/LNO	NS	Lunenburg	21 A/10	44°36'	64°46'
Meisners Island	ISL/ÎLE	NS	Lunenburg	21 A/9	44°32'	64°14'
Meister River	RIV/CDE	YT		105 A/6	60°19'	129°28'
Mekatina	UNP/LNO	ON	Algoma	41 N/1	47°05'	84°05'
Mékinac	MUN1/AZM1	QC	Mékinac	31 I/15	46°49'	72°31'
Mékinac, Lac	LAKE/LAC	QC	Mékinac	31 P/2	47°04'	72°41'
Melançon	UNP/LNO	QC	Maria-Chapdelaine	32 H/1	49°05'	72°21'
Melancthon	MUN2/AZM2	ON	Dufferin	41 A/1	44°09'	80°17'
Melancthon	UNP/LNO	ON	Dufferin	41 A/1	44°07'	80°16'
Melanson	UNP/LNO	NS	Kings	21 H/1	45°04'	64°19'
Melanson Settlement	UNP/LNO	NB	Westmorland	21 I/2	46°05'	64°39'
Melaval	UNP/LNO	SK	35-8-4-W3	72 G/9	49°41'	106°27'
Melba	UNP/LNO	SK	13-17-4-W3	72 J/8	50°26'	106°25'
Melbern Glacier	GLAC/GLAC	BC	Cassiar	114 P/6	59°18'	137°27'
Melboro	UNP/LNO	QC	Le Val-Saint-François	31 H/9	45°35'	72°11'
Melbourne	TOWN/VIL2	QC	Le Val-Saint-François	31 H/9	45°39'	72°09'
Melbourne	VILG/VILG	QC	Le Val-Saint-François	31 H/9	45°35'	72°10'
Melbourne	UNP/LNO	NS	Yarmouth	20 O/16	43°47'	66°03'
Melbourne	UNP/LNO	ON	Middlesex	40 I/13	42°49'	81°33'
Melbourne	UNP/LNO	MB	32-10-13-W	62 G/14	49°52'	99°11'
Melbourne Island	ISL/ÎLE	NT	Franklin	77 A	68°30'	104°45'
Melbourne Ridge	UNP/LNO	QC	Le Val-Saint-François	31 H/9	45°33'	72°13'
Melchett Lake	LAKE/LAC	ON	Thunder Bay	42 L/11	50°42'	87°02'
Meldrum	UNP/LNO	BC	Cariboo	93 B/1	52°12'	122°15'
Meldrum Bay	UNP/LNO	ON	Manitoulin	41 G/14	45°56'	83°07'
Meldrum Bay	BAY/BAIE	ON	Manitoulin	41 G/14	45°56'	83°06'
Meldrum Creek	UNP/LNO	BC	Cariboo	93 B/1	52°06'	122°20'
Meldrum Creek	RIV/CDE	BC	Cariboo	93 B/1	52°14'	122°29'

NAME NOM	ENTITY ENTITÉ	LOC 1 LIEU 1	LOC 2 LIEU 2	MAP CARTE	POSITION LAT	LONG
Meldrum Lake	LAKE/LAC	BC	Cariboo	93 B/2	52°12'	122°32'
Melduf	UNP/LNO	ON	Simcoe	31 D/12	44°43'	79°46'
Meleb	UNP/LNO	MB	14-20-2-E	62 I/11	50°44'	97°13'
Mélèzes, Les	UNP/LNO	QC	Jamésie	33 C/2	52°13'	76°37'
Mélèzes, Rivière aux	RIV/CDE	QC	Kativik	24 F/11	57°40'	69°29'
Melford	UNP/LNO	NS	Inverness	11 F/14	45°52'	61°16'
Melfort	CITY/VIL1	SK		73 A/15	52°52'	104°37'
Melgund	UNP/LNO	ON	Thunder Bay	42 D/9	48°41'	86°11'
Meliadine Lake	LAKE/LAC	NT	Keewatin	55 N/1	63°05'	92°15'
Melissa	UNP/LNO	ON	Muskoka	31 E/6	45°25'	79°14'
Melita	TOWN/VIL2	MB	1-4-27-W	62 F/7	49°16'	101°00'
Mellenville	UNP/LNO	MB		62 G/16	49°57'	98°18'
Mellon	UNP/LNO	QC	Pontiac	31 F/15	45°54'	76°51'
Mellor	UNP/LNO	NT	Mackenzie	85 B	60°43'	114°57'
Mellowdale	UNP/LNO	AB	21-60-3-W5	83 J/1	54°13'	114°24'
Melnice	UNP/LNO	MB	7-17-4-E	62 I/6	50°27'	97°03'
Melocheville	TOWN/VIL2	QC	Beauharnois-Salaberry	31 H/5	45°19'	73°56'
Melrose	VILG/VILG	NF		2 C/6	48°29'	53°04'
Melrose	UNP/LNO	NS	Guysborough	11 E/8	45°16'	62°03'
Melrose	UNP/LNO	NB	Westmorland	11 L/4	46°06'	63°57'
Melrose	UNP/LNO	ON	Hastings	31 C/6	44°15'	77°12'
Melrose	UNP/LNO	ON	Middlesex	40 I/14	43°00'	81°24'
Melrose	UNP/LNO	MB	36-12-5-E	62 I/2	50°03'	96°47'
Melrose Gardens	UNP/LNO	ON	Cochrane	42 A/6	48°29'	81°21'
Melrose Hill	UNP/LNO	NS	Inverness	11 K/3	46°05'	61°18'
Melvern Square	UNP/LNO	NS	Annapolis	21 A/15	44°59'	64°59'
Melville	CITY/VIL1	SK		62 L/15	50°55'	102°48'
Melville	UNP/LNO	PE	Queens	11 L/2	46°01'	62°50'
Melville	UNP/LNO	NS	Pictou	11 E/14	45°48'	63°02'
Melville	UNP/LNO	ON	Prince Edward	31 C/3	44°01'	77°25'
Melville	UNP/LNO	ON	Peel	40 P/16	43°53'	80°04'
Melville Beach	VILG/VILG	SK	12-19-6-W2	62 L/10	50°37'	102°44'
Melville Cove	UNP/LNO	NS	Halifax	11 D/12	44°38'	63°37'
Melville Creek	RIV/CDE	NT	Mackenzie	86 O	67°16'	115°31'
Melville Hills	MTN/MNT	NT	Mackenzie	97 C	69°15'	122°00'
Melville Island	ISL/ÎLE	BC	Range 5 Coast	103 J/7	54°23'	130°45'
Melville Island	ISL/ÎLE	NT	Franklin	78 G	75°30'	111°30'
Melville, Lake	LAKE/LAC	NF		13 G/12	53°40'	59°40'
Melville Peninsula	CAPE/CAP	NT	Franklin	46 N	68°00'	84°00'
Melville Sound	CHAN/CHEN	NT	Mackenzie	77 A	68°10'	107°00'
Melville Sound	BAY/BAIE	ON	Bruce	41 A/14	44°56'	81°05'
Melvin Creek	RIV/CDE	BC	Cassiar	104 N/2	59°15'	133°41'
Melvin Lake	LAKE/LAC	MB		64 F/1	57°09'	100°14'
Melvin, Mount	MTN/MNT	BC	Cassiar	94 C/13	56°52'	125°55'
Melvin River	RIV/CDE	AB	117-21-W5	84 N/4	59°11'	117°31'
Melvin Settlement	UNP/LNO	ON	Dundas	31 G/3	45°08'	75°19'
Membertou 28B	IR/RI	NS	Cape Breton	11 K/1	46°07'	60°12'
Memekay River	RIV/CDE	BC	Sayward	92 K/4	50°14'	125°47'
Memel Settlement	UNP/LNO	NB	Albert	21 H/15	45°49'	64°41'
Memesagamesing Lake	LAKE/LAC	ON	Parry Sound	31 E/13	46°00'	80°00'
Memewin, Lac	LAKE/LAC	QC	Témiscamingue	31 L/7	46°28'	78°42'
Memphrémagog	MUN1/AZM1	QC	Memphrémagog	31 H/8	45°16'	72°05'
Memphrémagog, Lac	LAKE/LAC	QC	Memphrémagog	31 H/1	45°08'	72°16'
Memramcook	VILG/VILG	NB	Westmorland	21 H/15	45°58'	64°36'
Memramcook	UNP/LNO	NB	Westmorland	21 I/2	46°00'	64°33'
Memramcook East	UNP/LNO	NB	Westmorland	21 I/2	46°01'	64°31'
Memramcook River	RIV/CDE	NB	Westmorland	21 H/15	45°52'	64°33'
Memramcook West	UNP/LNO	NB	Westmorland	21 I/2	46°02'	64°35'
Menaik	UNP/LNO	AB	35-43-25-W4	83 A/13	52°45'	113°31'
Menako Lakes	LAKE/LAC	ON	Kenora	53 B/1	52°05'	90°11'
Ménard	UNP/LNO	QC	Les Etchemins	21 L/9	46°33'	70°16'
Ménard	UNP/LNO	QC	Le Haut-Richelieu	31 H/6	45°18'	73°19'
Ménardville	UNP/LNO	QC	Le Haut-Richelieu	31 H/6	45°17'	73°04'
Ménascouagama, Lac	LAKE/LAC	QC	Minganie	12 N/4	51°13'	61°52'
Menchikoff Bay	BAY/BAIE	NT	Franklin	57 G	71°39'	93°44'
Mendenhall Landing	UNP/LNO	YT		115 A/16	60°45'	136°02'
Mendenhall River	RIV/CDE	YT		115 A/16	60°45'	136°02'
Mendham	VILG/VILG	SK	10-21-27-W3	72 K/13	50°46'	109°40'
Meneset	UNP/LNO	ON	Huron	40 P/13	43°46'	81°43'
Menie	UNP/LNO	ON	Northumberland	31 C/5	44°19'	77°42'
Menihek	UNP/LNO	NF		23 J/7	54°28'	66°36'
Menihek Lakes	LAKE/LAC	NF		23 J/7	54°15'	66°32'
Menisino	UNP/LNO	MB	35-1-10-E	62 H/1	49°05'	96°08'
Ménistouc, Lac	LAKE/LAC	QC	Caniapiscau	23 B/16	52°52'	66°29'
Menneval	UNP/LNO	NB	Restigouche	21 O/14	47°48'	67°11'

NAME NOM	ENTITY ENTITÉ	LOC 1 LIEU 1	LOC 2 LIEU 2	MAP CARTE	POSITION LAT	LONG
Mennon	UNP/LNO	SK	10-40-6-W3	73 B/7	52°26′	106°46′
Mennonite Corner	UNP/LNO	ON	Perth	40 P/7	43°25′	80°49′
Menoke Beach	UNP/LNO	ON	Simcoe	31 D/11	44°41′	79°24′
Menouow, Lac	LAKE/LAC	QC	Jamésie	33 C/16	52°47′	76°10′
Menteith	UNP/LNO	MB	7-7-22-W	62 F/9	49°34′	100°27′
Mentmore	UNP/LNO	MB	26-13-16-W	62 J/4	50°08′	99°34′
Menton, Lac au	LAKE/LAC	QC	Le Fjord-du-Saguenay	22 E/7	49°24′	70°34′
Menzie	UNP/LNO	MB	7-18-22-W	62 K/9	50°32′	100°29′
Menzie, Mount	MTN/MNT	YT		105 K/12	62°44′	133°56′
Menzies Bay	BAY/BAIE	BC	Sayward	92 K/3	50°07′	125°23′
Menzies Lake	LAKE/LAC	NB	Saint John	21 G/1	45°14′	66°14′
Menzies, Mount	MTN/MNT	BC	Sayward	92 K/3	50°14′	125°30′
Meota	VILG/VILG	SK	8-47-17-W3	73 F/1	53°02′	108°27′
Meota No. 468	MUN2/AZM2	SK		73 F/1	53°00′	108°25′
Merasheen	UNP/LNO	NF		1 M/8	47°25′	54°21′
Merasheen Island	ISL/ÎLE	NF		1 M/8	47°25′	54°15′
Mercer's Cove	UNP/LNO	NF		1 N/11	47°36′	53°14′
Mercer's Cove	UNP/LNO	NF		1 M/5	47°16′	55°53′
Mercer Settlement	UNP/LNO	NB	Kings	21 H/12	45°41′	65°42′
Merchant Lake	LAKE/LAC	ON	Nipissing	31 E/15	45°46′	78°31′
Merchants Bay	BAY/BAIE	NT	Franklin	16 M	67°10′	62°50′
Mercier	CITY/VIL1	QC	Roussillon	31 H/5	45°19′	73°45′
Mercier	UNP/LNO	QC	Rouyn-Noranda	32 D/2	48°14′	78°59′
Mercier-de-Caplan	UNP/LNO	QC	Bonaventure	22 A/4	48°11′	65°36′
Mercoal	UNP/LNO	AB	24-48-22-W5	83 F/3	53°10′	117°05′
Mercutio Lake	LAKE/LAC	ON	Rainy River	52 B/14	48°50′	91°05′
Mercy Bay	BAY/BAIE	NT	Franklin	88 F	74°05′	119°00′
Mercy, Cape	CAPE/CAP	NT	Franklin	16 D	64°53′	63°32′
Meredith Settlement	UNP/LNO	NB	Charlotte	21 G/6	45°27′	67°16′
Merid	UNP/LNO	SK	33-28-28-W3	72 N/5	51°26′	109°54′
Meridian Island	ISL/ÎLE	NT	Mackenzie	85 F	61°21′	117°48′
Meridian Lake	LAKE/LAC	NT	Mackenzie	75 K	62°36′	109°25′
Meridian River	RIV/CDE	MB		64 A/3	56°05′	97°27′
Merigomish	UNP/LNO	NS	Pictou	11 E/9	45°38′	62°26′
Merigomish Harbour	BAY/BAIE	NS	Pictou	11 E/9	45°38′	62°27′
Merigomish Harbour 31	IR/RI	NS	Pictou	11 E/9	45°37′	62°30′
Merivale	UNP/LNO	ON	Carleton	31 G/5	45°19′	75°43′
Merivale Gardens	UNP/LNO	ON	Carleton	31 G/5	45°19′	75°44′
Merivale Station	UNP/LNO	ON	Carleton	31 G/5	45°18′	75°44′
Merland	UNP/LNO	NS	Antigonish	11 F/12	45°35′	61°40′
Merle	UNP/LNO	SK	41-12-W2	63 D/12	52°32′	103°41′
Merlin	UNP/LNO	ON	Kent	40 J/1	42°14′	82°14′
Mermaid	UNP/LNO	PE	Queens	11 L/6	46°16′	63°02′
Merrickville	VILG/VILG	ON	Lanark	31 B/13	44°55′	75°50′
Merridale	UNP/LNO	MB	33-27-27-W	62 N/6	51°21′	101°13′
Merrill, Mount	MTN/MNT	YT		95 C/2	60°08′	124°42′
Merritt	CITY/VIL1	BC	Kamloops Division Yale	92 I/2	50°07′	120°48′
Merritton	UNP/LNO	ON	Lincoln	30 M/3	43°09′	79°13′
Merritt's Harbour	UNP/LNO	NF		2 E/10	49°38′	54°39′
Merryflat	UNP/LNO	SK	14-6-29-W3	72 F/5	49°28′	109°48′
Merry Island	ISL/ÎLE	NT	Keewatin	33 N	55°29′	77°31′
Merryweather Lake	LAKE/LAC	AB	119-20-W4	84 P/6	59°21′	113°21′
Merry Widow Mountain	MTN/MNT	BC	Rupert	92 L/6	50°20′	127°17′
Mersea	MUN2/AZM2	ON	Essex	40 J/2	42°06′	82°32′
Mersereau Stream	RIV/CDE	NB	Sunbury	21 G/10	45°38′	66°34′
Mersey Point	UNP/LNO	NS	Queens	21 A/2	44°02′	64°41′
Mersey River	RIV/CDE	NS	Queens	21 A/2	44°02′	64°43′
Merton	UNP/LNO	BC	Cariboo	93 J/6	54°21′	123°04′
Mertz's Corner	UNP/LNO	ON	Simcoe	31 D/12	44°40′	79°51′
Merville	UNP/LNO	BC	Comox	92 F/14	49°47′	125°03′
Mervin	VILG/VILG	SK	21-50-20-W3	73 F/7	53°20′	108°53′
Mervin No. 499	MUN2/AZM2	SK		73 F/7	53°20′	108°55′
Mesachie Lake	UNP/LNO	BC	Cowichan Lake	92 C/16	48°49′	124°07′
Mésaconane, Pointe	CAPE/CAP	QC	Jamésie	32 M/12	51°32′	79°32′
Mesa Lake	LAKE/LAC	NT	Mackenzie	86 B	64°50′	115°10′
Mesgouez, Lac	LAKE/LAC	QC	Jamésie	32 O/6	51°24′	75°05′
Mesilinka River	RIV/CDE	BC	Cassiar	94 C/1	56°08′	124°29′
Meskanaw	HAM/HAM	SK	11-44-22-W2	73 A/14	52°47′	105°05′
Meskanu	UNP/LNO	QC	Jamésie	32 M/10	51°31′	78°43′
Meslilloet Mountain	MTN/MNT	BC	New Westminster	92 G/10	49°34′	122°50′
Mesomikenda Lake	LAKE/LAC	ON	Sudbury	41 P/12	47°40′	81°53′
Mesplet, Lac	LAKE/LAC	QC	Vallée-de-l'Or	32 B/13	48°47′	75°47′
Mess Creek	RIV/CDE	BC	Cassiar	104 G/14	57°53′	131°13′
Messines	VILG/VILG	QC	La Vallée-de-la-Gatineau	31 K/1	46°14′	76°01′
Messiter	UNP/LNO	BC	Kamloops Division Yale	82 M/14	51°56′	119°21′

NAME NOM	ENTITY ENTITÉ	LOC 1 LIEU 1	LOC 2 LIEU 2	MAP CARTE	POSITION LAT	LONG
Mestao, Lac	LAKE/LAC	QC	Manicouagan	22 K/14	50°48′	69°18′
Meszah Peak	MTN/MNT	BC	Cassiar	104 J/6	58°28′	131°27′
Métabetchouan	CITY/VIL1	QC	Lac-Saint-Jean-Est	22 D/5	48°26′	71°52′
Métabetchouane, Rivière	RIV/CDE	QC	Le Domaine-du-Roy	22 D/5	48°25′	71°58′
Metagama	UNP/LNO	ON	Sudbury	41 P/4	47°05′	81°57′
Meta Incognita Peninsula	CAPE/CAP	NT	Franklin	25 K	62°45′	68°30′
Meta Lake	LAKE/LAC	ON	Thunder Bay	42 L/11	50°31′	87°24′
Meta Pond	LAKE/LAC	NF		2 D/2	48°05′	54°50′
Métascouac, Lac	LAKE/LAC	QC	La Côte-de-Beaupré	21 M/13	47°50′	71°50′
Metawatikwa	UNP/LNO	QC	Jamésie	33 C/10	52°40′	76°50′
Metcalfe	MUN2/AZM2	ON	Middlesex	40 I/13	42°52′	81°44′
Metcalfe	UNP/LNO	ON	Carleton	31 G/3	45°14′	75°28′
Metchin River	RIV/CDE	NF		13 E/6	53°19′	63°22′
Metchosin	MUN1/AZM1	BC	Metchosin	92 B/5	48°23′	123°32′
Metchosin Land District	GEOG/GÉOG	BC		92 B	48°23′	123°33′
Meteghan	UNP/LNO	NS	Digby	21 B/1	44°11′	66°10′
Meteghan Centre	UNP/LNO	NS	Digby	21 B/1	44°12′	66°09′
Meteghan River	UNP/LNO	NS	Digby	21 B/1	44°13′	66°09′
Meteghan Station	UNP/LNO	NS	Digby	21 B/1	44°12′	66°05′
Meteorologist Peninsula	CAPE/CAP	NT	Franklin	69 D	78°00′	100°00′
Methven	UNP/LNO	MB	32-7-17-W	62 G/12	49°37′	99°44′
Metigoshe	UNP/LNO	MB	3,4-1-22-W	62 F/1	49°00′	100°21′
Metigoshe Lake	LAKE/LAC	MB	4-1-22-W	62 F/1	49°00′	100°22′
Metikewap	UNP/LNO	MB	55-24-W	63 F/10	53°44′	101°00′
Metinota	VILG/VILG	SK	47-17-W3	73 F/1	53°02′	108°24′
Metionga Lake	LAKE/LAC	ON	Thunder Bay	52 G/9	49°43′	90°28′
Metis	UNP/LNO	AB	11-106-21-W5	84 K/3	58°12′	117°21′
Metiskow	UNP/LNO	AB	3-40-5-W4	73 D/7	52°24′	110°38′
Métis-sur-Mer	TOWN/VIL2	QC	La Mitis	22 B/12	48°40′	68°00′
Metlakatla	UNP/LNO	BC	Range 5 Coast	103 J/8	54°20′	130°26′
Metropolitan	UNP/LNO	ON	Perth	40 P/6	43°16′	81°19′
Metropolitan Toronto	MUN1/AZM1	ON	York	30 M/11	43°42′	79°25′
Metrotown	UNP/LNO	BC	New Westminster	92 G/2	49°14′	123°00′
Metso A Choot 23	IR/RI	BC	Cassiar	93 N/3	55°11′	125°25′
Metz	UNP/LNO	ON	Wellington	40 P/16	43°49′	80°27′
Meux Creek	RIV/CDE	ON	Grey	41 A/3	44°07′	81°01′
Mewassin	UNP/LNO	AB	31-51-2-W5	83 G/8	53°27′	114°18′
Mewatha Beach	VILG/VILG	AB	12-65-19-W4	83 I/10	54°37′	112°44′
Meyakumew Lake	LAKE/LAC	SK		73 I/13	54°55′	105°55′
Me-yan-law 47	IR/RI	BC	Range 5 Coast	103 J/9	54°43′	130°18′
Meyanlow 58	IR/RI	BC	Range 5 Coast	103 I/12	54°30′	129°59′
Meyersburg	UNP/LNO	ON	Northumberland	31 C/4	44°15′	77°49′
Meyronne	VILG/VILG	SK	24-8-7-W3	72 G/10	49°39′	106°50′
Meziadin Junction	UNP/LNO	BC	Cassiar	104 A/3	56°06′	129°18′
Meziadin Lake	LAKE/LAC	BC	Cassiar	104 A/3	56°03′	129°17′
Miami	UNP/LNO	MB	8-5-6-W	62 G/8	49°22′	98°15′
Miami Beach	UNP/LNO	ON	York	31 D/3	44°13′	79°29′
Mica Bay	BAY/BAIE	ON	Algoma	41 N/2	47°06′	84°43′
Mica Creek	UNP/LNO	BC	Kootenay	83 D/2	52°00′	118°34′
Mica Creek	RIV/CDE	YT		115 I/15	62°44′	136°34′
Micer Matakan	UNP/LNO	QC	Le Haut-Saint-Maurice	31 O/9	47°36′	74°02′
Michael Keen Canyon	SEAU/SMER	—		802	46°06′	46°08′
Michael, Lake	LAKE/LAC	NF		13 J/9	54°36′	58°27′
Michael Lake	LAKE/LAC	SK		64 E/13	57°51′	104°00′
Michael Point	CAPE/CAP	NT	Franklin	25 K	62°32′	69°20′
Michael's Bay	UNP/LNO	ON	Manitoulin	41 G/9	45°36′	82°06′
Michael's Bay	BAY/BAIE	ON	Manitoulin	41 G/9	45°35′	82°07′
Michael's Harbour	UNP/LNO	NF		2 E/7	49°18′	54°59′
Michaels River	RIV/CDE	NF		13 B/3	52°06′	59°26′
Michaud, Point	CAPE/CAP	NS	Richmond	11 F/10	45°34′	60°41′
Michaudville	UNP/LNO	QC	Les Maskoutains	31 H/14	45°50′	73°04′
Michel - see-voir - Michel Village	UNP/LNO	SK		73 N/14	55°59′	109°06′
Michel, Lake	LAKE/LAC	NF		12 I/6	50°16′	57°01′
Michelle Creek 22	IR/RI	BC	Cariboo	93 B/13	52°54′	123°39′
Michelle Creek 23	IR/RI	BC	Cariboo	93 B/13	52°54′	123°39′
Michell Pierre 12	IR/RI	BC	Cassiar	93 M/1	55°02′	126°22′
Michelsen, Cape	CAPE/CAP	NT	Franklin	67 F	70°42′	103°03′
Michel Village	HAM/HAM	SK	81-20-W3	73 N/14	55°59′	109°06′
Michener, Mount	MTN/MNT	AB	29-37-17-W5	83 C/1	52°12′	116°23′
Michichi	UNP/LNO	AB	19-30-18-W4	82 P/10	51°35′	112°32′
Michikinabish Lake	LAKE/LAC	MB		53 L/11	54°45′	95°25′
Michipicoten	MUN2/AZM2	ON	Algoma	42 C/2	48°05′	84°49′
Michipicoten	UNP/LNO	ON	Algoma	41 N/15	47°58′	84°54′
Michipicoten Bay	BAY/BAIE	ON	Algoma	41 N/15	47°57′	84°53′
Michipicoten Island	ISL/ÎLE	ON	Thunder Bay	41 N/12	47°45′	85°45′

NAME NOM	ENTITY ENTITÉ	LOC 1 LIEU 1	LOC 2 LIEU 2	MAP CARTE	POSITION LAT	LONG
Michipicoten River	UNP/LNO	ON	Algoma	41 N/15	47°56′	84°49′
Michipicoten River	RIV/CDE	ON	Algoma	41 N/15	47°56′	84°51′
Micklesham, Cape	CAPE/CAP	NT	Franklin	16 E	65°31′	62°30′
Micksburg	UNP/LNO	ON	Renfrew	31 F/11	45°40′	77°02′
Micmac	UNP/LNO	NS	Pictou	11 E/10	45°37′	62°31′
Micmac	UNP/LNO	NS	Hants	11 E/3	45°06′	63°29′
Micmac Lake	LAKE/LAC	NF		12 H/9	49°36′	56°26′
Micmac Village	UNP/LNO	NS	Halifax	11 D/12	44°41′	63°33′
Micocoulier, Réserve écologique du	PARK/PARC	QC	Vaudreuil-Soulanges	31 G/8	45°17′	74°11′
Micoua	UNP/LNO	QC	Manicouagan	22 F/10	49°42′	68°46′
Micoua	UNP/LNO	QC	Manicouagan	22 F/15	49°46′	68°49′
Mictikwatik	UNP/LNO	QC	Antoine-Labelle	31 O/7	47°26′	74°31′
Midale	TOWN/VIL2	SK	22-5-11-W2	62 E/6	49°24′	103°24′
Midbay Bank	SEAU/SMER	—		5449	59°45′	85°20′
Midbay Shoal	SEAU/SMER	—		5449	59°45′	85°20′
Middle Amherst Cove	UNP/LNO	NF		2 C/11	48°34′	53°13′
Middle Arm	VILG/VILG	NF		12 H/9	49°42′	56°06′
Middle Arm	UNP/LNO	NF		1 N/6	47°26′	53°12′
Middle Arm	UNP/LNO	NF		12 H/16	49°51′	56°26′
Middle Arm	BAY/BAIE	NF		2 C/12	48°42′	54°00′
Middle Arm	BAY/BAIE	NF		2 E/8	49°24′	54°15′
Middle Arm	BAY/BAIE	NF		12 H/9	49°42′	56°05′
Middle Arm	BAY/BAIE	NF		12 H/16	49°53′	56°27′
Middle Arm	BAY/BAIE	NF		12 G/1	49°08′	58°02′
Middle Aspy River	RIV/CDE	NS	Victoria	11 K/16	46°53′	60°29′
Middle Bank - also-aussi - Milieu, Banc du	SEAU/SMER	—		8007	44°35′	60°35′
Middle Barachois River	RIV/CDE	NF		12 B/2	48°15′	58°50′
Middle Barneys River	UNP/LNO	NS	Pictou	11 E/9	45°31′	62°19′
Middle Bay	UNP/LNO	QC	Côte-Nord-du-Golfe-Saint-Laurent	12 P/6	51°28′	57°30′
Middle Beaverbank	UNP/LNO	NS	Halifax	11 D/13	44°51′	63°41′
Middleboro	UNP/LNO	NS	Cumberland	11 E/13	45°46′	63°34′
Middlebro	UNP/LNO	MB	7-1-16-E	52 E/3	49°01′	95°26′
Middle Brook	UNP/LNO	NF		2 D/16	48°48′	54°13′
Middle Cape	UNP/LNO	NS	Cape Breton	11 F/15	45°52′	60°36′
Middle Caraquet	UNP/LNO	NB	Gloucester	21 P/15	47°48′	64°52′
Middle Channel	CHAN/CHEN	NT	Mackenzie	107 C	69°21′	135°33′
Middle Church - see-voir - Middlechurch	UNP/LNO	MB		62 H/14	49°59′	97°04′
Middlechurch	UNP/LNO	MB		62 H/14	49°59′	97°04′
Middle Clyde River	UNP/LNO	NS	Shelburne	20 P/13	43°51′	65°31′
Middle Country Harbour	UNP/LNO	NS	Guysborough	11 F/4	45°14′	61°46′
Middle Cove	UNP/LNO	NF		1 N/10	47°39′	52°42′
Middle Coverdale	UNP/LNO	NB	Albert	21 I/2	46°03′	64°51′
Middle Creek	UNP/LNO	AB	7-56-4-W4	73 E/15	53°49′	110°34′
Middle Creek	RIV/CDE	SK/AB		72 F/4	49°06′	109°49′
Middle Duck Island	ISL/ÎLE	ON	Manitoulin	41 G/10	45°43′	82°55′
Middle East Pubnico	UNP/LNO	NS	Shelburne	20 P/12	43°39′	65°46′
Middlefield	UNP/LNO	NS	Queens	21 A/2	44°13′	64°53′
Middle Fiord	BAY/BAIE	NT	Franklin	59 G	79°37′	95°00′
Middle Foster Lake	LAKE/LAC	SK		74 A/11	56°38′	105°25′
Middlegate	UNP/LNO	BC	New Westminster	92 G/2	49°13′	122°57′
Middle Gull Pond	LAKE/LAC	NF		1 N/6	47°22′	53°18′
Middle Gut	UNP/LNO	NF		1 K/13	46°47′	53°38′
Middle Hainesville	UNP/LNO	NB	York	21 J/3	46°04′	67°05′
Middle Head	CAPE/CAP	NF		1 L/14	46°54′	55°22′
Middle Head	CAPE/CAP	NS	Victoria	11 K/9	46°39′	60°22′
Middle House	UNP/LNO	NF		13 J/2	54°12′	58°36′
Middle Island	ISL/ÎLE	ON	Essex	40 G/10	41°41′	82°41′
Middle Kouchibouguac	UNP/LNO	NB	Kent	21 I/15	46°48′	64°59′
Middle LaHave	UNP/LNO	NS	Lunenburg	21 A/8	44°19′	64°24′
Middle Lake	VILG/VILG	SK	31-40-23-W2	73 A/6	52°29′	105°18′
Middle Lake	LAKE/LAC	SK	41-22,23-W2	73 A/11	52°34′	105°10′
Middle Lake	LAKE/LAC	NT	Franklin	57 C	69°37′	93°18′
Middle Landing	UNP/LNO	NB	Gloucester	21 P/5	47°27′	65°42′
Middle Manchester	UNP/LNO	NS	Guysborough	11 F/6	45°26′	61°27′
Middlemarch	UNP/LNO	ON	Elgin	40 I/14	42°45′	81°16′
Middle Melford	UNP/LNO	NS	Guysborough	11 F/11	45°32′	61°19′
Middlemiss	UNP/LNO	ON	Middlesex	40 I/14	42°46′	81°30′
Middle Musquodoboit	UNP/LNO	NS	Halifax	11 E/3	45°03′	63°09′
Middle New Cornwall	UNP/LNO	NS	Lunenburg	21 A/10	44°30′	64°32′
Middle Ohio	UNP/LNO	NS	Shelburne	20 P/14	43°56′	65°24′
Middle Pereaux	UNP/LNO	NS	Kings	21 H/1	45°11′	64°24′
Middle Point	CAPE/CAP	NT	Franklin	78 G	75°53′	111°33′
Middle Pond	LAKE/LAC	NF		2 D/1	48°08′	54°27′
Middleport	UNP/LNO	ON	Brant	40 P/1	43°06′	80°04′
Middle Porters Lake	UNP/LNO	NS	Halifax	11 D/11	44°42′	63°18′

NAME / NOM	ENTITY / ENTITÉ	LOC 1 / LIEU 1	LOC 2 / LIEU 2	MAP / CARTE	POSITION LAT	POSITION LONG
Middle Ridge	SEAU/SMER	—		15787A	48°35'	128°35'
Middle Ridge	MTN/MNT	NF		2 D/3	48°20'	55°15'
Middle River	UNP/LNO	NS	Victoria	11 K/2	46°09'	60°55'
Middle River	UNP/LNO	NS	Lunenburg	21 A/9	44°34'	64°18'
Middle River	UNP/LNO	BC	Range 5 Coast	93 K/14	54°52'	125°07'
Middle River	RIV/CDE	NS	Victoria	11 K/2	46°05'	60°55'
Middle River	RIV/CDE	NB	Gloucester	21 P/12	47°36'	65°40'
Middle River	RIV/CDE	BC	Range 5 Coast	93 K/14	54°52'	125°07'
Middle River Framboise	RIV/CDE	NS	Richmond	11 F/9	45°44'	60°22'
Middle Sackville	UNP/LNO	NS	Halifax	11 D/13	44°47'	63°42'
Middle Sackville	UNP/LNO	NB	Westmorland	21 H/16	45°55'	64°22'
Middle Sand Hills, The	MTN/MNT	AB	18,19-3,4-W4	72 L/9	50°35'	110°23'
Middle Savage Islands	ISL/ÎLE	NT	Franklin	25 J	62°09'	67°57'
Middlesex	MUN1/AZM1	ON	Middlesex	40 I/14	43°00'	81°25'
Middlesex	UNP/LNO	NB	Albert	21 H/14	45°58'	65°01'
Middlesex	GEOG/GÉOG	ON		40 I/14	43°00'	81°25'
Middle Sister Island	ISL/ÎLE	ON	Essex	40 G/15	41°52'	82°59'
Middle Southampton	UNP/LNO	NB	York	21 G/14	45°58'	67°24'
Middle Stewiacke	UNP/LNO	NS	Colchester	11 E/3	45°13'	63°08'
Middle Thames River	RIV/CDE	ON	Oxford	40 I/15	42°59'	80°58'
Middleton	TOWN/VIL2	NS	Annapolis	21 A/14	44°57'	65°04'
Middleton	UNP/LNO	PE	Prince	11 L/5	46°19'	63°39'
Middleton	UNP/LNO	NS	Antigonish	11 F/5	45°26'	61°59'
Middleton	UNP/LNO	NS	Colchester	11 E/11	45°43'	63°11'
Middleton	UNP/LNO	NB	Westmorland	21 H/15	45°55'	64°31'
Middleton	UNP/LNO	ON	Thunder Bay	42 D/15	48°48'	86°39'
Middleton Corner	UNP/LNO	NS	Colchester	11 E/11	45°43'	63°10'
Middleton Island	ISL/ÎLE	SK		74 G/9	57°36'	106°23'
Middleton Lake	LAKE/LAC	NF		2 E/4	49°02'	55°58'
Middle Valley	SEAU/SMER	—		15787A	48°37'	128°43'
Middle Village	UNP/LNO	NS	Halifax	11 D/12	44°30'	63°53'
Middleville	UNP/LNO	ON	Lanark	31 F/1	45°06'	76°24'
Middle West Pubnico	UNP/LNO	NS	Yarmouth	20 P/12	43°39'	65°48'
Middlewood	UNP/LNO	NS	Lunenburg	21 A/2	44°14'	64°34'
Midgell	UNP/LNO	PE	Kings	11 L/7	46°25'	62°39'
Midgell River	RIV/CDE	PE	Kings	11 L/7	46°25'	62°38'
Midgic	UNP/LNO	NB	Westmorland	21 H/16	45°59'	64°18'
Midhurst	UNP/LNO	ON	Simcoe	31 D/5	44°27'	79°44'
Midhurst Station	UNP/LNO	ON	Simcoe	31 D/5	44°26'	79°45'
Midland	TOWN/VIL2	ON	Simcoe	31 D/12	44°45'	79°53'
Midland	UNP/LNO	NB	Albert	21 H/14	45°47'	65°08'
Midland	UNP/LNO	NB	Kings	21 H/12	45°39'	65°47'
Midland	UNP/LNO	NB	Queens	21 I/4	46°08'	65°59'
Midland	UNP/LNO	MB		62 H/14	49°54'	97°11'
Midland Bay	BAY/BAIE	ON	Simcoe	31 D/13	44°46'	79°51'
Midland Point	UNP/LNO	ON	Simcoe	31 D/13	44°47'	79°53'
Midland Provincial Park	PARK/PARC	AB	29-20-W4	82 P/7	51°29'	112°46'
Midlothian	UNP/LNO	ON	Parry Sound	31 E/12	45°37'	79°33'
Midnapore	UNP/LNO	AB	22,23-1-W5	82 J/16	50°55'	114°05'
Midnight Lake	UNP/LNO	SK	1-52-17-W3	73 F/8	53°27'	108°23'
Midnight Lake	LAKE/LAC	SK	52-16-W3	73 F/8	53°30'	108°21'
Midshipman Bay	BAY/BAIE	NT	Franklin	68 H	75°16'	96°10'
Midsummer Island	ISL/ÎLE	BC	Range 1 Coast	92 L/10	50°39'	126°39'
Midville Branch	UNP/LNO	NS	Lunenburg	21 A/7	44°25'	64°38'
Midway	VILG/VILG	BC	Similkameen Division Yale	82 E/2	49°01'	118°46'
Midway	UNP/LNO	NB	Albert	21 H/10	45°41'	64°46'
Midway Crossing	UNP/LNO	ON	Renfrew	31 F/14	45°55'	77°19'
Midway Range	MTN/MNT	BC	Similkameen Division Yale	82 E/10	49°30'	118°40'
Midwood	UNP/LNO	NB	Saint John	21 G/8	45°16'	66°01'
Miertsching Lake	LAKE/LAC	NT	Franklin	46 N	67°13'	85°25'
Miette	UNP/LNO	AB	7-49-27-W5	83 F/4	53°13'	117°57'
Miette Hotsprings	UNP/LNO	AB	8-48-26-W5	83 F/4	53°08'	117°46'
Mignon-Corner	UNP/LNO	QC	Vaudreuil-Soulanges	31 G/8	45°26'	74°05'
Migration Lake	LAKE/LAC	NT	Mackenzie	76 C	64°58'	108°51'
Miguasha	UNP/LNO	QC	Avignon	22 B/1	48°05'	66°17'
Miguasha-Ouest	UNP/LNO	QC	Avignon	22 B/1	48°06'	66°20'
Miguasha, Parc de conservation de	PARK/PARC	QC	Avignon	22 B/1	48°06'	66°22'
Miguasha, Pointe de	CAPE/CAP	QC	Avignon	22 B/1	48°04'	66°18'
Miguels Lake	LAKE/LAC	NF		2 D/12	48°41'	55°34'
Miguick	UNP/LNO	QC	Portneuf	31 P/1	47°13'	72°15'
Mijinemungshing Lake	LAKE/LAC	ON	Algoma	41 N/10	47°42'	84°42'
Mikado	HAM/HAM	SK	19-30-2-W2	62 M/9	51°37'	102°16'
Mikkola	UNP/LNO	ON	Sudbury	41 I/6	46°26'	81°08'
Mikkwa River	RIV/CDE	AB	108-5-W5	84 J/7	58°25'	114°46'
Mikwasiskwaw Umitukap Aytakunich	UNP/LNO	QC	Jamésie	33 D/15	52°59'	78°57'

NAME / NOM	ENTITY / ENTITÉ	LOC 1 / LIEU 1	LOC 2 / LIEU 2	MAP / CARTE	POSITION LAT	POSITION LONG
Milan	VILG/VILG	QC	Le Granit	21 E/11	45°36′	71°08′
Milate	UNP/LNO	ON	Sudbury	41 I/6	46°29′	81°08′
Milaty	UNP/LNO	SK	5-18-17-W2	72 I/8	50°29′	104°19′
Milbanke Sound	CHAN/CHEN	BC	Range 3 Coast	103 A/7	52°19′	128°33′
Milberta	UNP/LNO	ON	Timiskaming	31 M/12	47°36′	79°48′
Milburn	UNP/LNO	PE	Kings	11 L/7	46°22′	62°38′
Milburn	UNP/LNO	PE	Prince	21 I/9	46°40′	64°16′
Milburn	UNP/LNO	ON	Frontenac	31 C/8	44°25′	76°22′
Milby	UNP/LNO	QC	Sherbrooke	21 E/5	45°19′	71°49′
Milden	VILG/VILG	SK	17-29-11-W3	72 O/5	51°29′	107°31′
Milden Lake	LAKE/LAC	SK	28-11-W3	72 O/6	51°23′	107°26′
Milden No. 286	MUN2/AZM2	SK		72 O/5	51°25′	107°32′
Mildmay	VILG/VILG	ON	Bruce	41 A/3	44°03′	81°07′
Mildred	UNP/LNO	SK	50-10-W3	73 G/6	53°21′	107°20′
Mildred Lake	UNP/LNO	AB	6-93-10-W4	74 E/4	57°02′	111°36′
Mileage 56	UNP/LNO	ON	Thunder Bay	52 H/1	49°13′	88°13′
Mile Corner	UNP/LNO	ON	Elgin	40 I/15	42°49′	80°56′
Mile Lake	LAKE/LAC	ON	Renfrew	31 F/2	45°14′	76°42′
Miles Bay	BAY/BAIE	ON	Kenora	52 E/8	49°15′	94°20′
Miles, Cape	CAPE/CAP	NT	Franklin	47 C	69°19′	85°29′
Miles Cove	VILG/VILG	NF		2 E/12	49°32′	55°47′
Mile 62 1/2	UNP/LNO	BC	Peace River	94 A/6	56°23′	121°05′
Milestone	TOWN/VIL2	SK	15-12-19-W2	72 H/15	49°59′	104°31′
Milford	UNP/LNO	NS	Annapolis	21 A/11	44°36′	65°25′
Milford	UNP/LNO	NB	Saint John	21 G/8	45°16′	66°06′
Milford	UNP/LNO	ON	Prince Edward	30 N/14	43°56′	77°05′
Milford Bay	UNP/LNO	ON	Muskoka	31 E/3	45°05′	79°29′
Milford Haven	UNP/LNO	NS	Guysborough	11 F/5	45°26′	61°31′
Milford Haven	UNP/LNO	ON	Algoma	41 J/4	46°10′	83°50′
Milford Station	UNP/LNO	NS	Hants	11 E/3	45°03′	63°26′
Miliakdjuin Island	ISL/ÎLE	NT	Franklin	26 H	65°33′	65°31′
Milieu, Banc du - also-aussi - Middle Bank	SEAU/SMER	—		8007	44°35′	60°35′
Milieu, Rivière du	RIV/CDE	QC	Lac-Saint-Jean-Est	22 D/4	48°14′	71°44′
Milieu, Rivière du	RIV/CDE	QC	Matawinie	31 I/13	46°47′	73°56′
Militia Point	UNP/LNO	NS	Inverness	11 F/15	45°51′	60°56′
Militia Point	CAPE/CAP	NS	Inverness	11 F/15	45°50′	60°57′
Milkish	UNP/LNO	NB	Kings	21 G/8	45°23′	66°08′
Milk River	TOWN/VIL2	AB	28-2-16-W4	82 H/1	49°09′	112°05′
Milk River	RIV/CDE	AB	1-1-15-W4	72 E/2	49°00′	110°33′
Milk River Ridge	MTN/MNT	AB	3,4-18,19,20,21-W4	82 H/1	49°15′	112°30′
Milk River Ridge Reservoir	LAKE/LAC	AB	4,5-19,20-W4	82 H/7	49°22′	112°35′
Millar	UNP/LNO	ON	Thunder Bay	52 A/5	48°28′	89°33′
Millar Channel	RIV/CDE	BC	Clayoquot	92 E/8	49°19′	126°04′
Millar Hill	UNP/LNO	ON	Muskoka	31 E/6	45°23′	79°01′
Millars Corner	UNP/LNO	ON	Renfrew	31 F/10	45°40′	76°46′
Millars Corners	UNP/LNO	ON	Grenville	31 B/13	44°57′	75°35′
Millarton	UNP/LNO	ON	Bruce	41 A/4	44°09′	81°34′
Millarville	UNP/LNO	AB	3-21-3-W5	82 J/16	50°45′	114°19′
Millbank	UNP/LNO	NB	Northumberland	21 P/3	47°03′	65°28′
Millbank	UNP/LNO	ON	Perth	40 P/10	43°34′	80°50′
Mill Bay	UNP/LNO	BC	Shawnigan	92 B/12	48°39′	123°33′
Mill Bay	UNP/LNO	BC	Range 5 Coast	103 I/13	54°59′	129°53′
Millbridge	UNP/LNO	ON	Hastings	31 C/12	44°41′	77°36′
Millbrook	VILG/VILG	ON	Peterborough	31 D/1	44°09′	78°27′
Millbrook	UNP/LNO	NS	Pictou	11 E/10	45°31′	62°49′
Millbrook	UNP/LNO	NS	Colchester	11 E/6	45°20′	63°18′
Mill Brook	UNP/LNO	NS	Colchester	11 E/11	45°40′	63°22′
Millbrook	UNP/LNO	MB	20-10-6-E	62 H/15	49°51′	96°44′
Millbrook 27	IR/RI	NS	Colchester	11 E/6	45°20′	63°18′
Millcove	UNP/LNO	PE	Queens	11 L/6	46°21′	63°02′
Mill Cove	UNP/LNO	NS	Lunenburg	21 A/9	44°35′	64°04′
Mill Cove	UNP/LNO	NB	Queens	21 G/16	45°53′	66°00′
Mill Creek	UNP/LNO	NS	Cape Breton	11 K/8	46°17′	60°18′
Mill Creek	UNP/LNO	NS	Cumberland	21 H/16	45°46′	64°23′
Mill Creek	RIV/CDE	ON	Bruce	41 A/6	44°27′	81°22′
Milldale	UNP/LNO	ON	Oxford	40 I/15	42°57′	80°35′
Mille-Carré, Le	UNP/LNO	QC	Les Collines-de-l'Outaouais	31 G/12	45°42′	75°41′
Mille Îles, Rivière des	RIV/CDE	QC	Les Moulins	31 H/12	45°42′	73°32′
Mille-Isles	VILG/VILG	QC	Argenteuil	31 G/16	45°49′	74°13′
Mille Lacs, Lac des	LAKE/LAC	ON	Thunder Bay	52 B/16	48°50′	90°30′
Millerand	UNP/LNO	ON	Nipissing	41 I/8	46°22′	80°09′
Miller Creek	UNP/LNO	NS	Hants	21 H/1	45°01′	64°04′
Millerdale	UNP/LNO	SK	6-33-21-W3	72 N/15	51°47′	108°59′
Millerd Lake	LAKE/LAC	ON	Sudbury	41 I/7	46°16′	80°57′
Millerfield	UNP/LNO	AB	36-27-18-W4	82 P/8	51°21′	112°25′

NAME / NOM	ENTITY / ENTITÉ	LOC 1 / LIEU 1	LOC 2 / LIEU 2	MAP / CARTE	POSITION LAT	POSITION LONG
Miller Island	ISL/ÎLE	NT	Franklin	120 C	81°34'	66°35'
Miller Lake	UNP/LNO	ON	Bruce	41 H/3	45°06'	81°26'
Miller Lake	LAKE/LAC	ON	Bruce	41 H/4	45°06'	81°23'
Miller Lake	LAKE/LAC	SK	13-52-21-W3	73 F/7	53°29'	108°57'
Miller Lake East	UNP/LNO	ON	Bruce	41 H/3	45°06'	81°23'
Miller Lake West	UNP/LNO	ON	Bruce	41 H/3	45°06'	81°24'
Miller Line Cache	UNP/LNO	NB	Madawaska	21 O/5	47°21'	67°52'
Miller Road	UNP/LNO	NS	Cumberland	11 E/13	45°50'	63°37'
Millers Corner	UNP/LNO	NS	Hants	11 E/4	45°11'	63°41'
Millers Corner	UNP/LNO	NS	Cumberland	21 H/9	45°38'	64°05'
Millers Corner	UNP/LNO	ON	Lennox and Addington	31 C/2	44°11'	76°50'
Miller Seamount	SEAU/SMER	—		5.03	53°30'	144°20'
Miller's Hill	UNP/LNO	SK	24-48-26-W2	73 H/4	53°12'	105°40'
Millers Landing	UNP/LNO	BC	New Westminster	92 G/6	49°24'	123°19'
Miller's Passage	UNP/LNO	NF		1 M/12	47°31'	55°39'
Millerton	UNP/LNO	NB	Northumberland	21 I/13	46°54'	65°38'
Millertown	VILG/VILG	NF		12 A/15	48°49'	56°33'
Millertown Junction	UNP/LNO	NF		12 H/1	49°01'	56°20'
Millerville	UNP/LNO	NB	Restigouche	21 O/14	47°49'	67°01'
Millet	TOWN/VIL2	AB	32-47-24-W4	83 H/3	53°06'	113°28'
Milleton	UNP/LNO	SK	34-50-23-W3	73 F/6	53°21'	109°18'
Mille-Vaches, Baie de	BAY/BAIE	QC	La Haute-Côte-Nord	22 C/11	48°34'	69°13'
Millfield	UNP/LNO	QC	L'Amiante	21 L/3	46°12'	71°29'
Millgrove	UNP/LNO	ON	Wentworth	30 M/5	43°20'	79°58'
Mill Grove Station - see-voir - Millgrove Station	UNP/LNO	ON		30 M/5	43°22'	79°56'
Millgrove Station	UNP/LNO	ON	Wentworth	30 M/5	43°22'	79°56'
Millhaven	UNP/LNO	ON	Lennox and Addington	31 C/2	44°12'	76°45'
Millhaven Creek	RIV/CDE	ON	Lennox and Addington	31 C/2	44°12'	76°45'
Millicent	UNP/LNO	AB	20-20-13-W4	72 L/12	50°42'	111°46'
Millidge	UNP/LNO	ON	Kenora	52 K/2	50°00'	92°42'
Millidgeville	UNP/LNO	NB	Saint John	21 G/8	45°18'	66°06'
Milligan Creek	RIV/CDE	BC	Peace River	94 A/15	56°51'	120°48'
Milliken	UNP/LNO	ON	York	30 M/14	43°49'	79°18'
Millington	UNP/LNO	QC	Memphrémagog	31 H/1	45°12'	72°17'
Million	UNP/LNO	MB	17-27-16-W	62 O/5	51°18'	99°41'
Mill Island	ISL/ÎLE	NT	Franklin	35 N	64°00'	77°47'
Mill Lake	LAKE/LAC	ON	Parry Sound	41 H/8	45°22'	80°00'
Mill Pond	UNP/LNO	NS	Cape Breton	11 K/8	46°18'	60°21'
Mill River East	UNP/LNO	PE	Prince	21 I/16	46°46'	64°08'
Mill Road	UNP/LNO	PE	Prince	21 I/9	46°45'	64°08'
Mill Road	UNP/LNO	NS	Lunenburg	21 A/16	44°47'	64°27'
Mill Road	UNP/LNO	NB	Queens	21 G/16	45°47'	66°13'
Mills Corners	UNP/LNO	ON	Carleton	31 G/4	45°10'	75°48'
Mill Section	UNP/LNO	NS	Hants	21 A/16	44°54'	64°12'
Mill Settlement West	UNP/LNO	NB	Sunbury	21 G/10	45°34'	66°36'
Mills Lake	LAKE/LAC	NT	Mackenzie	85 E	61°30'	118°15'
Mills Point	UNP/LNO	PE	Prince	11 L/5	46°27'	63°43'
Mills Siding	UNP/LNO	NF		2 C/4	48°12'	53°58'
Millstream	UNP/LNO	NS	Pictou	11 E/7	45°27'	62°39'
Millstream	UNP/LNO	QC	Avignon	22 B/3	48°03'	67°06'
Millstream	UNP/LNO	BC	Highland	92 B/5	48°30'	123°31'
Millstream River	RIV/CDE	NB	Gloucester	21 P/12	47°42'	65°42'
Millsville	UNP/LNO	NS	Pictou	11 E/10	45°37'	62°55'
Milltown	UNP/LNO	NF		1 M/13	47°54'	55°46'
Milltown	UNP/LNO	NB	Charlotte	21 G/3	45°10'	67°18'
Milltown	UNP/LNO	ON	Hastings	31 C/3	44°12'	77°12'
Milltown Cross	UNP/LNO	PE	Kings	11 L/2	46°06'	62°37'
Milltown-Head of Bay D'Espoir	TOWN/VIL2	NF		1 M/13	47°55'	55°45'
Millvale	UNP/LNO	PE	Queens	11 L/6	46°25'	63°25'
Millvale	UNP/LNO	NS	Cumberland	11 E/12	45°37'	63°49'
Mill Valley	UNP/LNO	PE	Prince	11 L/5	46°24'	63°38'
Millview	UNP/LNO	PE	Queens	11 L/2	46°12'	62°52'
Millview	UNP/LNO	NS	Halifax	11 D/12	44°43'	63°40'
Mill Village	UNP/LNO	NS	Hants	11 E/3	45°05'	63°26'
Mill Village	UNP/LNO	NS	Queens	21 A/2	44°09'	64°39'
Millville	VILG/VILG	NB	York	21 J/3	46°08'	67°12'
Millville	UNP/LNO	NF		11 O/14	47°51'	59°21'
Millville	UNP/LNO	NS	Kings	21 H/2	45°00'	64°49'
Millville Boularderie	UNP/LNO	NS	Cape Breton	11 K/8	46°16'	60°20'
Millwater	UNP/LNO	MB	3-65-28-W	63 K/12	54°36'	101°37'
Millwood	UNP/LNO	ON	Algoma	41 N/9	47°41'	84°30'
Millwood	UNP/LNO	MB	2-20-29-W	62 K/11	50°42'	101°24'
Milly	UNP/LNO	SK	12-5-7-W3	72 G/7	49°23'	106°50'
Milne Fiord	BAY/BAIE	NT	Franklin	340 F	82°38'	81°27'
Milne Glacier	GLAC/GLAC	NT	Franklin	340 E	82°24'	80°00'

NAME NOM	ENTITY ENTITÉ	LOC 1 LIEU 1	LOC 2 LIEU 2	MAP CARTE	POSITION LAT	LONG
Milne Inlet	BAY/BAIE	NT	Franklin	48 A	72°20′	80°30′
Milne Island	ISL/ÎLE	NT	Franklin	68 H	75°37′	96°53′
Milne Point	CAPE/CAP	NT	Franklin	68 C	73°50′	100°51′
Milner	UNP/LNO	BC	New Westminster	92 G/2	49°08′	122°37′
Milner Lake	LAKE/LAC	NF		23 G/15	53°54′	66°51′
Milner Ridge	UNP/LNO	MB	12-14-9-E	62 I/1	50°10′	96°14′
Milnerton	UNP/LNO	AB	12-35-26-W4	82 P/13	51°59′	113°36′
Milnes Landing	UNP/LNO	BC	Sooke	92 B/5	48°23′	123°42′
Milnet	UNP/LNO	ON	Sudbury	41 I/15	46°50′	80°57′
Milnikek	UNP/LNO	QC	La Matapédia	22 B/3	48°08′	67°09′
Milnikek, Rivière	RIV/CDE	QC	La Matapédia	22 B/3	48°08′	67°09′
Milo	VILG/VILG	AB	31-18-21-W4	82 I/10	50°34′	112°53′
Milo	UNP/LNO	PE	Prince	21 I/9	46°39′	64°14′
Milsap	UNP/LNO	ON	Lennox and Addington	31 C/7	44°22′	76°52′
Milton	TOWN/VIL2	ON	Halton	30 M/12	43°31′	79°53′
Milton	UNP/LNO	NF		2 C/4	48°13′	53°58′
Milton	UNP/LNO	NS	Queens	21 A/2	44°04′	64°45′
Milton	UNP/LNO	NS	Yarmouth	20 O/16	43°51′	66°07′
Milton-Est	UNP/LNO	QC	La Haute-Yamaska	31 H/7	45°29′	72°46′
Milton Heights	UNP/LNO	ON	Halton	30 M/12	43°31′	79°56′
Milton Highlands	UNP/LNO	NS	Yarmouth	20 O/16	43°51′	66°07′
Milton Lake	LAKE/LAC	SK		64 M/5	59°30′	103°52′
Milton No. 292	MUN2/AZM2	SK		72 N/5	51°30′	109°45′
Milton Spur	UNP/LNO	ON	Halton	30 M/12	43°32′	79°54′
Milton Station	UNP/LNO	PE	Queens	11 L/6	46°18′	63°13′
Miltonvale Park	VILG/VILG	PE	Queens	11 L/6	46°19′	63°13′
Milverton	VILG/VILG	ON	Perth	40 P/10	43°34′	80°55′
Mimenuh Mountain	MTN/MNT	BC	Kamloops Division Yale	92 I/3	50°11′	121°13′
Mimico	UNP/LNO	ON	York	30 M/11	43°37′	79°30′
Mimico Beach	UNP/LNO	ON	York	30 M/11	43°37′	79°29′
Miminegash	VILG/VILG	PE	Prince	21 I/16	46°53′	64°14′
Miminegash	UNP/LNO	PE	Prince	21 I/16	46°53′	64°14′
Miminiska Lake	LAKE/LAC	ON	Thunder Bay	52 P/10	51°35′	88°37′
Mimosa	UNP/LNO	ON	Wellington	40 P/9	43°44′	80°13′
Minago River	RIV/CDE	MB		63 J/9	54°33′	98°12′
Minahico	UNP/LNO	ON	Rainy River	52 E/1	49°02′	94°22′
Minaker River	RIV/CDE	BC	Peace River	94 G/14	57°52′	123°01′
Minaki	UNP/LNO	ON	Kenora	52 E/15	49°59′	94°40′
Mina, Lac	LAKE/LAC	QC	Kativik	24 A/4	56°06′	65°30′
Minamkeak Lake	LAKE/LAC	NS	Lunenburg	21 A/7	44°17′	64°36′
Minard	UNP/LNO	SK	17-5-6-W2	62 E/7	49°23′	102°47′
Minaret	UNP/LNO	AB	18-32-1-W5	82 O/9	51°44′	114°08′
Minas Basin	BAY/BAIE	NS	Cumberland	21 H/1	45°10′	64°10′
Minas Channel	CHAN/CHEN	NS	Cumberland	21 H/2	45°15′	64°45′
Minasville	UNP/LNO	NS	Hants	11 E/5	45°17′	63°49′
Minataree	UNP/LNO	ON	Thunder Bay	52 I/1	50°14′	88°04′
Minaty Bay	UNP/LNO	BC	New Westminster	92 G/11	49°37′	123°13′
Minburn	VILG/VILG	AB	14-50-10-W4	73 E/6	53°19′	111°22′
Minburn No. 27, County of	MUN1/AZM1	AB	51-12-W4	73 E/5	53°25′	111°39′
Mindemoya	UNP/LNO	ON	Manitoulin	41 G/9	45°44′	82°10′
Mindemoya Lake	LAKE/LAC	ON	Manitoulin	41 G/16	45°45′	82°13′
Minden	UNP/LNO	ON	Haliburton	31 D/15	44°55′	78°43′
Mindoka	UNP/LNO	ON	Timiskaming	31 M/13	47°59′	79°56′
Mine-Bateman-Bay	UNP/LNO	QC	Jamésie	32 G/16	49°54′	74°15′
Mine-Blackburn	UNP/LNO	QC	Les Collines-de-l'Outaouais	31 G/12	45°38′	75°37′
Mine-Bruneau	UNP/LNO	QC	Jamésie	32 G/16	49°56′	74°15′
Mine-Canadian-Merrill	UNP/LNO	QC	Jamésie	32 G/16	49°52′	74°20′
Mine Centre	UNP/LNO	ON	Rainy River	52 C/15	48°45′	92°37′
Mine-Chib-Kayrand	UNP/LNO	QC	Jamésie	32 G/16	49°52′	74°21′
Mine-Copper-Cliff	UNP/LNO	QC	Jamésie	32 G/16	49°54′	74°18′
Mine-de-Mica	UNP/LNO	QC	Les Collines-de-l'Outaouais	31 G/13	45°50′	75°36′
Mine-Grandroy	UNP/LNO	QC	Jamésie	32 G/16	49°56′	74°12′
Mine-Jaculet	UNP/LNO	QC	Jamésie	32 G/16	49°54′	74°16′
Mine-Koko-Creek	UNP/LNO	QC	Jamésie	32 G/16	49°53′	74°20′
Mine, Lac de la	LAKE/LAC	QC	Minganie	22 I/15	50°51′	64°43′
Mine-Lemoine	UNP/LNO	QC	Jamésie	32 G/16	49°46′	74°06′
Mine-Merrill	UNP/LNO	QC	Jamésie	32 G/16	49°52′	74°20′
Mine-Norbeau	UNP/LNO	QC	Jamésie	32 G/16	49°57′	74°19′
Mine-Obalski	UNP/LNO	QC	Jamésie	32 G/16	49°52′	74°24′
Mine-Québec-Chibougamau	UNP/LNO	QC	Jamésie	32 G/16	49°53′	74°18′
Minerai, Pointe au	CAPE/CAP	QC	Minganie	22 I/7	50°16′	64°58′
Mineral	UNP/LNO	NB	Carleton	21 J/12	46°35′	67°37′
Mineral Springs	UNP/LNO	ON	Wentworth	40 P/1	43°14′	80°01′
Mine-Robitaille	UNP/LNO	QC	Jamésie	32 G/15	49°47′	74°52′
Miner River	RIV/CDE	YT		116 J/9	66°30′	138°25′

NAME NOM	ENTITY ENTITÉ	LOC 1 LIEU 1	LOC 2 LIEU 2	MAP CARTE	POSITION LAT	POSITION LONG
Miner River	RIV/CDE	NT	Mackenzie	107 D	69°08′	130°58′
Miners Bay	UNP/LNO	ON	Haliburton	31 D/15	44°49′	78°46′
Miners Range	MTN/MNT	YT		105 E/4	61°09′	135°41′
Minesing	UNP/LNO	ON	Simcoe	31 D/5	44°26′	79°50′
Minesville	UNP/LNO	NS	Halifax	11 D/11	44°41′	63°22′
Minet's Point	UNP/LNO	ON	Simcoe	31 D/5	44°23′	79°40′
Minett	UNP/LNO	ON	Muskoka	31 E/4	45°10′	79°39′
Mineurs, Ruisseau des	RIV/CDE	QC	La Matapédia	22 B/9	48°38′	66°24′
Mingan	UNP/LNO	QC	Minganie	22 I/8	50°18′	64°02′
Mingan Archipelago National Park Reserve - also-aussi - Archipel-de-Mingan, Réserve de parc national de l'	PARK/PARC	QC	Minganie	12 L/3	50°13′	63°10′
Mingan, Archipel de	ISL/ÎLE	QC	Minganie	12 L/4	50°13′	63°35′
Mingan, Bancs de	SEAU/SMER	—		811A	50°10′	64°00′
Mingan, Chenal de	CHAN/CHEN	QC	Minganie	12 L/4	50°15′	63°50′
Mingan	IR/RI	QC	Minganie	22 I/8	50°18′	64°02′
Minganie	MUN1/AZM1	QC	Minganie	12 L/4	50°14′	63°36′
Mingan, Îles de	ISL/ÎLE	QC	Minganie	12 L/4	50°13′	63°50′
Mingan, Rivière	RIV/CDE	QC	Minganie	12 L/5	50°18′	63°59′
Mingo Lake	LAKE/LAC	NT	Franklin	36 A	64°35′	72°10′
Mingré, Lac	LAKE/LAC	QC	Caniapiscau	23 G/6	53°18′	67°07′
Ming's Bight	VILG/VILG	NF		12 H/16	49°59′	56°03′
Ming's Bight	BAY/BAIE	NF		12 H/16	50°00′	56°00′
Minia Seamount	SEAU/SMER	—			40°22′	51°33′
Miniota	MUN2/AZM2	MB		62 K/2	50°10′	100°55′
Miniota	UNP/LNO	MB	31-13-26-W	62 K/3	50°09′	101°02′
Minipi Lake	LAKE/LAC	NF		13 C/7	52°25′	60°45′
Minipi River	RIV/CDE	NF		13 C/13	52°52′	61°37′
Minisinakwa Lake	LAKE/LAC	ON	Sudbury	41 P/12	47°39′	81°44′
Miniss Lake	LAKE/LAC	ON	Thunder Bay	52 J/15	50°48′	90°50′
Ministers Island	ISL/ÎLE	NB	Charlotte	21 G/3	45°06′	67°02′
Ministic Lake	LAKE/LAC	ON	Sudbury	41 I/12	46°34′	81°34′
Ministik Beach	UNP/LNO	SK	24-30-30-W	62 N/12	51°38′	101°38′
Ministik Creek	RIV/CDE	ON	Cochrane	42 I/1	50°13′	80°24′
Ministik Creek	RIV/CDE	ON	Kenora	43 N/12	55°36′	85°44′
Ministik Lake	LAKE/LAC	AB	50-21-W4	83 H/6	53°21′	113°01′
Ministikwan 161	IR/RI	SK		73 F/13	54°00′	109°40′
Ministikwan 161A	IR/RI	SK		73 K/4	54°10′	109°45′
Ministikwan Lake	LAKE/LAC	SK	58-25-W3	73 K/4	54°01′	109°39′
Minitonas	VILG/VILG	MB	36-26-W	63 C/3	52°05′	101°02′
Minitonas	MUN2/AZM2	MB		63 C/2	52°10′	101°00′
Mink Brook	UNP/LNO	NB	Charlotte	21 G/1	45°09′	66°29′
Mink Cove	UNP/LNO	NS	Digby	21 B/8	44°28′	66°06′
Mink Creek	UNP/LNO	MB	27-28-22-W	62 N/8	51°25′	100°29′
Mink Creek	RIV/CDE	ON	Hastings	31 E/1	45°12′	78°09′
Mink Creek	RIV/CDE	MB	9-15-14-W	62 J/6	50°16′	99°20′
Mink Creek	RIV/CDE	MB	30-28-18-W	62 O/5	51°26′	99°58′
Mink Island	ISL/ÎLE	BC	New Westminster	92 K/2	50°06′	124°46′
Mink Islands	ISL/ÎLE	ON	Parry Sound	41 H/8	45°22′	80°25′
Mink Lake	UNP/LNO	ON	Renfrew	31 F/11	45°33′	77°03′
Mink Lake	UNP/LNO	ON	Nipissing	31 L/2	46°03′	78°46′
Mink Lake	LAKE/LAC	NS	Shelburne	21 A/3	44°09′	65°26′
Mink Lake	LAKE/LAC	ON	Renfrew	31 F/11	45°33′	77°03′
Mink Lake	LAKE/LAC	ON	Kenora	52 K/4	50°08′	93°30′
Mink Lake	LAKE/LAC	AB	91-21-W4	84 A/14	56°54′	113°17′
Mink Lake	LAKE/LAC	AB	81-11-W5	84 B/4	56°01′	115°36′
Mink Lake	LAKE/LAC	NT	Mackenzie	85 F	61°54′	117°40′
Minnedosa	TOWN/VIL2	MB	15-18-W	62 J/4	50°15′	99°51′
Minnedosa Beach	UNP/LNO	MB	1,12-15-18-W	62 J/5	50°15′	99°49′
Minnehaha	UNP/LNO	SK	34-49-18-W3	73 F/7	53°17′	108°33′
Minnewakan	UNP/LNO	MB	14-20-6-W	62 J/9	50°43′	98°11′
Minnewanka, Lake	LAKE/LAC	AB	26,27-10,11-W5	82 O/6	51°15′	115°23′
Minniehill	UNP/LNO	ON	Grey	41 A/10	44°33′	80°36′
Minnie Lake	LAKE/LAC	BC	Kamloops Division Yale	92 I/1	50°01′	120°25′
Minnipuka	UNP/LNO	ON	Algoma	42 B/13	48°54′	83°51′
Minnitaki	UNP/LNO	ON	Kenora	52 F/14	49°49′	93°06′
Minnitaki Lake	LAKE/LAC	ON	Kenora	52 F/16	49°58′	92°00′
Minnow Lake	UNP/LNO	ON	Sudbury	41 I/7	46°29′	80°56′
Minnow Lake	LAKE/LAC	SK		73 K/8	54°28′	108°07′
Minoahchak 230 - see-voir - Minoahchak 74C	IR/RI	SK		62 M/1	51°03′	102°25′
Minoahchak 74C	IR/RI	SK		62 M/1	51°03′	102°25′
Minowukaw Beach	UNP/LNO	SK	26-55-22-W2	73 H/14	53°47′	105°10′
Minstrel Island	UNP/LNO	BC	Range 1 Coast	92 L/9	50°37′	126°18′
Minstrel Island	ISL/ÎLE	BC	Range 1 Coast	92 L/9	50°37′	126°19′
Mintlaw	UNP/LNO	AB	34-37-28-W4	83 A/4	52°13′	113°54′
Minto	VILG/VILG	NB	Sunbury	21 J/1	46°05′	66°04′
Minto	MUN2/AZM2	ON	Wellington	40 P/15	43°55′	80°51′

NAME NOM	ENTITY ENTITÉ	LOC 1 LIEU 1	LOC 2 LIEU 2	MAP CARTE	POSITION LAT	LONG
Minto	MUN2/AZM2	MB		62 J/5	50°20'	99°45'
Minto	UNP/LNO	ON	Hastings	31 C/5	44°22'	77°32'
Minto	UNP/LNO	ON	Wellington	40 P/15	43°55'	80°49'
Minto	UNP/LNO	MB	19-5-19-W	62 F/8	49°24'	100°01'
Minto	UNP/LNO	YT		105 D/7	60°23'	134°49'
Minto	UNP/LNO	YT		115 I/10	62°35'	136°52'
Minto Bridge	UNP/LNO	YT		105 M/12	63°42'	135°52'
Minto Head	CAPE/CAP	NT	Franklin	68 C	73°05'	102°17'
Minto Inlet	BAY/BAIE	NT	Franklin	87 G	71°20'	117°00'
Minto Islands	ISL/ÎLE	NT	Franklin	77 A	68°34'	105°15'
Minto, Lac	LAKE/LAC	QC	Kativik	34 G/3	57°13'	75°00'
Minto Landing	UNP/LNO	BC	New Westminster	92 H/4	49°12'	121°57'
Minto, Mount	MTN/MNT	BC	Cassiar	104 N/13	59°56'	133°54'
Minton	VILG/VILG	SK	35-2-20-W2	72 H/2	49°10'	104°35'
Minton	UNP/LNO	QC	Memphrémagog	21 E/5	45°17'	71°59'
Minturn Bay	BAY/BAIE	NT	Franklin	25 J	62°47'	67°03'
Minudie	UNP/LNO	NS	Cumberland	21 H/16	45°46'	64°21'
Miocene	UNP/LNO	BC	Cariboo	93 A/4	52°15'	121°46'
Miquelon	UNP/LNO	QC	Jamésie	32 F/8	49°24'	76°27'
Miquelon Lake Provincial Park	PARK/PARC	AB	49-20-W4	83 H/2	53°15'	112°53'
Miquelon Lakes	LAKE/LAC	AB	49-20,21-W4	83 H/2	53°15'	112°53'
Mira Bay	BAY/BAIE	NS	Cape Breton	11 J/4	46°02'	59°56'
Mirabel	CITY/VIL1	QC	Mirabel	31 G/9	45°39'	74°05'
Mirabel	MUN1/AZM1	QC	Mirabel	31 G/9	45°39'	74°05'
Miracle Valley	UNP/LNO	BC	New Westminster	92 G/8	49°15'	122°15'
Mirage Bay	BAY/BAIE	NT	Franklin	26 L	66°55'	71°00'
Mira Gut	UNP/LNO	NS	Cape Breton	11 J/4	46°02'	59°58'
Miramichi	CITY/VIL1	NB	Northumberland	21 P/3	47°00'	65°28'
Miramichi	UNP/LNO	NS	Inverness	11 K/3	46°02'	61°19'
Miramichi	UNP/LNO	NB	Northumberland	21 P/3	47°02'	65°11'
Miramichi Bay	BAY/BAIE	NB	Northumberland	21 P/2	47°08'	64°58'
Miramichi Inner Bay	BAY/BAIE	NB	Northumberland	21 P/3	47°08'	65°12'
Miramichi Lake	LAKE/LAC	NB	York	21 J/7	46°27'	66°59'
Miramichi River	RIV/CDE	NB	Northumberland	21 P/3	47°05'	65°22'
Mira River	RIV/CDE	NS	Cape Breton	11 J/4	46°02'	59°58'
Mira Road	UNP/LNO	NS	Cape Breton	11 K/1	46°06'	60°06'
Mirasty Lake	LAKE/LAC	SK	63-8-W3	73 J/6	54°29'	107°10'
Mire Lake	LAKE/LAC	MB	33-13-W	62 O/14	51°52'	99°16'
Mirepoix, Lac	LAKE/LAC	QC	Le Fjord-du-Saguenay	22 E/2	49°02'	70°32'
Miron	UNP/LNO	QC	Témiscamingue	31 M/6	47°17'	79°25'
Mirond Lake	LAKE/LAC	SK		63 M/2	55°06'	102°47'
Mirond Lake 184E	IR/RI	SK		63 M/2	55°10'	102°47'
Mirror	VILG/VILG	AB	28-40-22-W4	83 A/6	52°28'	113°07'
Mirror Lake	UNP/LNO	BC	Kootenay	82 F/15	49°53'	116°54'
Mirror River	RIV/CDE	SK		74 F/10	57°33'	108°52'
Mirwins Park	UNP/LNO	ON	Kent	40 J/9	42°35'	82°27'
Miry Creek	RIV/CDE	SK	21-18-W3	72 K/16	50°48'	108°29'
Miry Creek No. 229	MUN2/AZM2	SK		72 K/10	50°45'	108°45'
Misaine, Banc de - also-aussi - Misaine Bank	SEAU/SMER	—		8008	45°15'	58°45'
Misaine Bank - also-aussi - Misaine, Banc de	SEAU/SMER	—		8008	45°15'	58°45'
Misamikwash Lake	LAKE/LAC	ON	Kenora	53 A/13	52°59'	89°55'
Misask, Rivière	RIV/CDE	QC	Jamésie	33 A/9	52°32'	72°27'
Misaw Lake	LAKE/LAC	SK		64 M/15	59°52'	102°30'
Miscou Banks	SEAU/SMER	—		4024	48°05'	64°15'
Miscou Centre	UNP/LNO	NB	Gloucester	21 P/15	47°57'	64°34'
Miscouche	VILG/VILG	PE	Prince	11 L/5	46°26'	63°52'
Miscou Gully	CHAN/CHEN	NB	Gloucester	21 P/16	47°55'	64°30'
Miscou Harbour	UNP/LNO	NB	Gloucester	21 P/15	47°54'	64°35'
Miscou Harbour	BAY/BAIE	NB	Gloucester	21 P/15	47°53'	64°33'
Miscou Island	ISL/ÎLE	NB	Gloucester	21 P/15	47°57'	64°32'
Miscou Lighthouse	UNP/LNO	NB	Gloucester	22 A/2	48°01'	64°31'
Miscou Plains	UNP/LNO	NB	Gloucester	21 P/15	47°59'	64°32'
Misehkow River	RIV/CDE	ON	Thunder Bay	52 P/6	51°26'	89°11'
Misekumaw Lake	LAKE/LAC	SK		64 M/4	59°10'	103°40'
Misèle, Lac	LAKE/LAC	QC	Jamésie	23 E/11	53°33'	71°07'
Misère	UNP/LNO	QC	Charlevoix	21 M/8	47°28'	70°24'
Misery Bay	BAY/BAIE	ON	Manitoulin	41 G/15	45°47'	82°44'
Misery Point	CAPE/CAP	ON	Manitoulin	41 G/15	45°47'	82°45'
Misgatlee (Foch Lagoon) 14	IR/RI	BC	Range 4 Coast	103 H/14	53°50'	129°05'
Mishamattawa River	RIV/CDE	ON	Kenora	43 N/3	55°10'	85°18'
Mishibishu Lake	LAKE/LAC	ON	Thunder Bay	42 C/3	48°05'	85°25'
Mishwamakan River	RIV/CDE	ON	Kenora	53 G/9	53°38'	90°12'
Misikeyask Lake	LAKE/LAC	ON	Kenora	53 G/16	53°55'	90°20'
Misinchinka Ranges	MTN/MNT	BC	Cariboo	93 O/2	55°10'	122°30'
Miskokway Lake	LAKE/LAC	ON	Parry Sound	41 H/9	45°39'	80°14'

NAME NOM	ENTITY ENTITÉ	LOC 1 LIEU 1	LOC 2 LIEU 2	MAP CARTE	POSITION LAT	POSITION LONG
Miskwabi Lake	LAKE/LAC	ON	Haliburton	31 E/1	45°03'	78°19'
Mispec	UNP/LNO	NB	Saint John	21 H/4	45°13'	65°57'
Mispec Point	CAPE/CAP	NB	Saint John	21 H/4	45°12'	65°59'
Mispec River	RIV/CDE	NB	Saint John	21 H/4	45°13'	65°57'
Misquamaebin Lake	LAKE/LAC	ON	Kenora	53 G/6	53°30'	91°05'
Missanabie	UNP/LNO	ON	Algoma	42 C/8	48°19'	84°05'
Missanabie 62	IR/RI	ON	Algoma	42 C/8	48°19'	84°07'
Missawawi Lake	LAKE/LAC	AB	66-15-W4	83 I/9	54°42'	112°12'
Missezula Lake	LAKE/LAC	BC	Kamloops Division Yale	92 H/15	49°47'	120°31'
Missezula Mountain	MTN/MNT	BC	Kamloops Division Yale	92 H/10	49°41'	120°32'
Missi Island	ISL/ÎLE	MB		63 F/15	53°48'	100°53'
Missi Island	ISL/ÎLE	SK		63 L/9	54°41'	102°12'
Missi Lake	LAKE/LAC	SK		74 A/8	56°29'	104°11'
Missinaibi Lake	LAKE/LAC	ON	Algoma	42 B/5	48°23'	83°40'
Missinaibi River	RIV/CDE	ON	Cochrane	42 I/11	50°44'	81°29'
Missinipe	HAM/HAM	SK		73 P/10	55°36'	104°46'
Mission	MUN1/AZM1	BC	New Westminster	92 G/1	49°14'	122°20'
Mission	UNP/LNO	BC	New Westminster	92 G/1	49°08'	122°18'
Mission	UNP/LNO	BC	New Westminster	92 G/1	49°08'	122°18'
Mission 1	IR/RI	BC	New Westminster	92 G/6	49°19'	123°06'
Mission 5	IR/RI	BC	Lillooet	92 J/9	50°42'	122°17'
Mission Beach	UNP/LNO	AB	30-47-1-W5	83 G/2	53°05'	114°07'
Mission City - see-voir - Mission	UNP/LNO	BC		92 G/1	49°08'	122°18'
Mission Creek	RIV/CDE	BC	Osoyoos Division Yale	82 E/14	49°51'	119°29'
Mission Creek 8	IR/RI	BC	Osoyoos Division Yale	82 E/14	49°51'	119°28'
Mission-de-Hopedale, Lieu historique national de la - also-aussi - Hopedale Mission National Historic Site	PARK/PARC	NF		13 N/8	53°27'	60°13'
Mission Gardens	UNP/LNO	MB		62 H/14	49°53'	97°02'
Mission Group	ISL/ÎLE	BC	Rupert	92 L/3	50°00'	127°24'
Mission Island 2	IR/RI	BC	Rupert	92 L/3	50°01'	127°23'
Missionnaire, Lac du	LAKE/LAC	QC	Mékinac	31 I/15	46°55'	72°34'
Mission-Saint-Louis	UNP/LNO	QC	Avignon	22 B/1	48°10'	66°15'
Mission-Saint-Louis, Lieu historique national de la - also-aussi - Saint-Louis Mission National Historic Site	PARK/PARC	ON	Simcoe	31 D/12	44°43'	79°46'
Missipuskiow River	RIV/CDE	SK	56-9-W2	63 E/14	53°53'	103°18'
Missisa Lake	LAKE/LAC	ON	Kenora	43 C/6	52°18'	85°12'
Missisa River	RIV/CDE	ON	Kenora	43 F/2	53°01'	84°53'
Missisicabi, Rivière	RIV/CDE	ON/QC		32 M/5	51°15'	79°40'
Missisquoi, Baie	BAY/BAIE	QC	Le Haut-Richelieu	31 H/3	45°03'	73°08'
Missisquoi, Rivière	RIV/CDE	QC	Brome-Missisquoi	31 H/2	45°01'	72°35'
Mississagagon Lake	LAKE/LAC	ON	Frontenac	31 C/14	44°52'	77°05'
Mississagi River 8	IR/RI	ON	Algoma	41 J/2	46°13'	83°00'
Mississagi Bay	BAY/BAIE	ON	Algoma	41 J/3	46°11'	83°06'
Mississagi Island	ISL/ÎLE	ON	Algoma	41 J/3	46°07'	83°00'
Mississagi River	RIV/CDE	ON	Algoma	41 J/3	46°10'	83°01'
Mississagi Strait	CHAN/CHEN	ON	Manitoulin	41 G/14	45°56'	83°13'
Mississagua Lake	LAKE/LAC	ON	Peterborough	31 D/9	44°42'	78°19'
Mississagua Landing	UNP/LNO	ON	Peterborough	31 D/9	44°42'	78°21'
Mississagua River	RIV/CDE	ON	Peterborough	31 D/9	44°33'	78°20'
Mississauga	CITY/VIL1	ON	Peel	30 M/12	43°35'	79°39'
Mississauga	UNP/LNO	ON	Algoma	41 J/3	46°12'	83°02'
Mississauga Beach	UNP/LNO	ON	Lincoln	30 M/6	43°16'	79°05'
Mississauga's of Scugog Island 34	IR/RI	ON	Ontario	31 D/2	44°11'	78°54'
Mississauga Valley	UNP/LNO	ON	Peel	30 M/12	43°37'	79°36'
Mississippi Lake	LAKE/LAC	ON	Lanark	31 F/1	45°05'	76°10'
Mississippi River	RIV/CDE	ON	Carleton	31 F/8	45°26'	76°17'
Mississippi Station	UNP/LNO	ON	Frontenac	31 C/15	44°55'	76°41'
Missonga	UNP/LNO	ON	Sudbury	42 B/7	48°23'	82°41'
Missouri	UNP/LNO	ON	Frontenac	31 C/8	44°25'	76°29'
Missouri Coteau, The	CLF/ESC	SK		72 H/14	50°00'	105°00'
Mistachagagane, Lac	LAKE/LAC	QC	Manicouagan	22 K/16	50°58'	68°06'
Mistahayo Lake	LAKE/LAC	ON	Kenora	54 A/3	56°11'	89°19'
Mistahini	UNP/LNO	QC	Côte-Nord-du-Golfe-Saint-Laurent	12 K/7	50°18'	60°39'
Mistake Bay	BAY/BAIE	NT	Keewatin	34 M	59°08'	78°12'
Mistake Bay	BAY/BAIE	NT	Keewatin	55 K	62°09'	92°55'
Mistake Creek	RIV/CDE	NT	Keewatin	56 A	64°15'	88°02'
Mistaken Cove	UNP/LNO	NF		12 P/7	51°19'	56°43'
Mistaken Point	CAPE/CAP	NF		1 K/11	46°37'	53°10'
Mistamahkuhua	UNP/LNO	QC	Minganie	12 K/7	50°22'	60°44'
Mistango River	RIV/CDE	ON	Cochrane	42 A/15	48°47'	80°30'
Mistanipisipou, Rivière	RIV/CDE	QC	Minganie	12 N/12	51°32'	61°50'
Mistaouac, Lac	LAKE/LAC	QC	Jamésie	32 E/7	49°25'	78°41'
Mistaouac, Rivière	RIV/CDE	QC	Jamésie	32 E/10	49°44'	78°56'
Mistassibi Nord-Est, Rivière	RIV/CDE	QC	Maria-Chapdelaine	22 E/12	49°31'	71°56'
Mistassibi, Rivière	RIV/CDE	QC	Maria-Chapdelaine	32 A/16	48°53'	72°13'
Mistassini	CITY/VIL1	QC	Maria-Chapdelaine	32 A/16	48°53'	72°12'
Mistassini	VILG/VILG	QC	Jamésie	32 J/8	50°19'	74°01'

NAME / NOM	ENTITY / ENTITÉ	LOC 1 / LIEU 1	LOC 2 / LIEU 2	MAP / CARTE	POSITION LAT	POSITION LONG
Mistassini, Lac	LAKE/LAC	QC	Jamésie	32 P/4	51°00'	73°37'
Mistassini, Rivière	RIV/CDE	QC	Le Domaine-du-Roy	32 A/9	48°42'	72°19'
Mistastin Lake	LAKE/LAC	NF		13 M/14	55°54'	63°20'
Mistastin River	RIV/CDE	NF		14 D/2	56°09'	62°50'
Mistatim	VILG/VILG	SK	15-45-10-W2	63 D/14	52°52'	103°22'
Mistawasis	UNP/LNO	SK		73 G/2	53°11'	106°48'
Mistawasis 103	IR/RI	SK		73 G/2	53°10'	106°47'
Mistawasis Creek	RIV/CDE	SK	49-6-W3	73 G/7	53°17'	106°44'
Mistawasis Lake	LAKE/LAC	SK	47-9-W3	73 G/3	53°05'	107°15'
Mistigougèche, Lac	LAKE/LAC	QC	La Mitis	22 B/4	48°08'	67°58'
Mistik	IR/RI	SK		63 L/14	54°54'	103°23'
Mistikokan River	RIV/CDE	MB		54 G/4	57°09'	91°36'
Mistikukamik	UNP/LNO	QC	Jamésie	33 D/8	52°16'	78°29'
Mistinibi, Lac	LAKE/LAC	QC	Kativik	23 P/16	55°56'	64°15'
Mistinic, Lac	LAKE/LAC	QC	Caniapiscau	23 C/10	52°40'	69°00'
Mistinikon Lake	LAKE/LAC	ON	Timiskaming	41 P/15	47°56'	80°44'
Mistinippi Lake	LAKE/LAC	NF		13 K/14	54°45'	61°20'
Mistiutshimau	UNP/LNO	QC	Kativik	24 A/7	56°26'	64°46'
Mistohay Lake	LAKE/LAC	SK	63-21-W3	73 K/6	54°27'	109°05'
Mistouk, Rivière	RIV/CDE	QC	Lac-Saint-Jean-Est	22 D/12	48°38'	71°41'
Mistuhekasookun	UNP/LNO	MB		64 A/9	56°40'	96°05'
Mistusinne	VILG/VILG	SK	20,29-24-4-W3	72 O/2	51°04'	106°32'
Misty Icefield	GLAC/GLAC	BC	New Westminster	92 G/15	49°49'	122°37'
Misty Lake	LAKE/LAC	ON	Nipissing	31 E/10	45°42'	78°47'
Misty Lake	LAKE/LAC	MB		64 K/13	58°53'	101°40'
Mitchell	TOWN/VIL2	ON	Perth	40 P/6	43°28'	81°12'
Mitchell	UNP/LNO	QC	Drummond	31 I/1	46°01'	72°25'
Mitchell	UNP/LNO	MB	6-7-6-E	62 H/10	49°32'	96°46'
Mitchell Bay	UNP/LNO	NS	Halifax	11 D/16	44°57'	62°11'
Mitchell Bay	UNP/LNO	BC	Rupert	92 L/10	50°38'	126°51'
Mitchell Heights	UNP/LNO	ON	Elgin	40 I/11	42°40'	81°14'
Mitchell Lake	LAKE/LAC	NB	Northumberland	21 O/2	47°04'	66°40'
Mitchell Lake	LAKE/LAC	BC	Cariboo	93 A/15	52°52'	120°38'
Mitchell's Bay	UNP/LNO	ON	Kent	40 J/8	42°23'	82°24'
Mitchell's Bay	BAY/BAIE	ON	Kent	40 J/8	42°27'	82°26'
Mitchells Brook	UNP/LNO	NF		1 N/4	47°08'	53°31'
Mitchells Corner	UNP/LNO	NB	Albert	21 H/11	45°37'	65°01'
Mitchell's Corners	UNP/LNO	ON	Durham	30 M/15	43°57'	78°48'
Mitchell Settlement	UNP/LNO	NB	Restigouche	21 P/13	47°52'	66°00'
Mitchell's Point	CAPE/CAP	ON	Kent	40 J/8	42°27'	82°26'
Mitchell Square	UNP/LNO	ON	Simcoe	31 D/12	44°31'	79°32'
Mitchellton	UNP/LNO	SK	25-11-28-W2	72 H/13	49°56'	105°42'
Mitchellview	UNP/LNO	SK	16-33-6-W2	62 M/15	51°50'	102°47'
Mitchellville	UNP/LNO	ON	Leeds	31 B/5	44°25'	75°59'
Mitchinamecus, Réservoir	LAKE/LAC	QC	Antoine-Labelle	31 O/6	47°21'	75°04'
Mitchinamecus, Rivière	RIV/CDE	QC	Antoine-Labelle	31 O/3	47°04'	75°07'
Mitford	UNP/LNO	AB	7-26-4-W5	82 O/2	51°13'	114°34'
Mitis, Baie	BAY/BAIE	QC	La Mitis	22 C/9	48°38'	68°06'
Mitishto River	RIV/CDE	MB	67-10-W	63 J/15	54°50'	98°58'
Mitis, Lac	LAKE/LAC	QC	La Mitis	22 B/5	48°17'	67°45'
Mitis, Pointe	CAPE/CAP	QC	La Mitis	22 C/9	48°41'	68°02'
Mitis, Rivière	RIV/CDE	QC	La Mitis	22 C/9	48°38'	68°08'
Mitlenatch Island	ISL/ÎLE	BC	Sayward	92 F/14	49°57'	125°00'
Mitsue	UNP/LNO	AB	30-72-4-W5	83 O/7	55°16'	114°37'
Mitusach	UNP/LNO	QC	Kativik	33 N/2	55°05'	76°32'
Miworth	UNP/LNO	BC	Cariboo	93 G/15	53°57'	122°56'
Mnjikaning First Nation 32	IR/RI	ON	Ontario	31 D/11	44°42'	79°19'
Moak Lake	UNP/LNO	MB	7-80-1-W	63 P/13	55°55'	97°36'
Moar Bay	BAY/BAIE	NT	Keewatin	33 D	52°48'	78°48'
Moar Lake	LAKE/LAC	MB/ON		52 M/14	52°00'	95°11'
Moberly	UNP/LNO	BC	Kootenay	82 N/6	51°23'	117°01'
Moberly Lake	UNP/LNO	BC	Peace River	93 P/13	55°50'	121°44'
Moberly Lake	LAKE/LAC	BC	Peace River	93 P/13	55°50'	121°45'
Moberly River	RIV/CDE	BC	Peace River	94 A/2	56°12'	120°56'
Mobert	UNP/LNO	ON	Thunder Bay	42 C/12	48°41'	85°38'
Mobert Creek	RIV/CDE	ON	Thunder Bay	42 C/13	48°53'	85°53'
Mobile	UNP/LNO	NF		1 N/2	47°15'	52°51'
Mobile Big Pond	LAKE/LAC	NF		1 N/6	47°16'	53°02'
Mobile River	RIV/CDE	NF		1 N/2	47°15'	52°50'
Moccasin Pond	LAKE/LAC	NF		2 E/1	49°08'	54°04'
Mochelle	UNP/LNO	NS	Annapolis	21 A/14	44°45'	65°28'
Mocodome, Cape	CAPE/CAP	NS	Guysborough	11 F/4	45°05'	61°39'
Model Farm	UNP/LNO	NB	Kings	21 H/5	45°26'	65°56'
Modeste, Mount	MTN/MNT	BC	Malahat	92 C/9	48°38'	124°06'
Modsley Lake	LAKE/LAC	NB	York	21 G/11	45°38'	67°21'

NAME NOM	ENTITY ENTITÉ	LOC 1 LIEU 1	LOC 2 LIEU 2	MAP CARTE	POSITION LAT	LONG
Moes River	UNP/LNO	QC	Coaticook	21 E/4	45°14′	71°47′
Moes, Rivière	RIV/CDE	QC	Sherbrooke	21 E/5	45°19′	71°49′
Moffat	UNP/LNO	ON	Halton	40 P/9	43°31′	80°03′
Moffat	UNP/LNO	SK	26-15-10-W2	62 L/6	50°18′	103°16′
Moffat	UNP/LNO	BC	Cariboo	93 B/9	52°33′	122°27′
Moffat Creek	RIV/CDE	BC	Cariboo	93 A/6	52°20′	121°25′
Moffat Lakes	LAKE/LAC	BC	Cariboo	93 A/3	52°08′	121°03′
Moffatt, Lac	LAKE/LAC	QC	Le Haut-Saint-François	21 E/11	45°34′	71°19′
Moffet	VILG/VILG	QC	Témiscamingue	31 M/10	47°32′	78°57′
Moffet Inlet	BAY/BAIE	NT	Franklin	48 B	72°06′	84°30′
Mogg Bay	BAY/BAIE	NT	Franklin	47 D	69°15′	82°08′
Moha	UNP/LNO	BC	Lillooet	92 J/16	50°52′	122°10′
Mohannes	UNP/LNO	NB	Charlotte	21 G/3	45°09′	67°21′
Mohawk Lake	LAKE/LAC	NT	Mackenzie	86 A	64°01′	112°07′
Mohawk Meadows	UNP/LNO	ON	Wentworth	30 M/4	43°14′	79°57′
Mohr	UNP/LNO	QC	Les Collines-de-l'Outaouais	31 F/9	45°32′	76°10′
Mohr Corners	UNP/LNO	ON	Carleton	31 F/8	45°25′	76°15′
Mohr's Beach	HAM/HAM	SK	23-22-23-W3	72 I/14	50°53′	105°06′
Mohun Lake	LAKE/LAC	BC	Sayward	92 K/3	50°07′	125°30′
Moira	UNP/LNO	ON	Hastings	31 C/6	44°21′	77°24′
Moira Lake	LAKE/LAC	ON	Hastings	31 C/6	44°30′	77°27′
Moira Lake	LAKE/LAC	BC	Kamloops Division Yale	92 P/16	51°48′	120°12′
Moira River	RIV/CDE	ON	Hastings	31 C/3	44°09′	77°23′
Moisie	CITY/VIL1	QC	Sept-Rivières	22 J/1	50°11′	66°05′
Moisie, Baie de	BAY/BAIE	QC	Sept-Rivières	22 I/5	50°16′	65°56′
Moisie, Rivière	RIV/CDE	QC	Sept-Rivières	22 J/1	50°12′	66°04′
Moisie-Salmon-Club	UNP/LNO	QC	Sept-Rivières	22 J/8	50°17′	66°12′
Mojikit Lake	LAKE/LAC	ON	Thunder Bay	52 I/9	50°40′	88°15′
Moketas Island	ISL/ÎLE	BC	Rupert	92 L/3	50°05′	127°13′
Mokka Fiord	BAY/BAIE	NT	Franklin	49 G	79°35′	87°15′
Mokomon	UNP/LNO	ON	Thunder Bay	52 A/5	48°29′	89°38′
Molanosa	UNP/LNO	SK	63-24-W2	73 I/12	54°30′	105°33′
Molanosa Lake	LAKE/LAC	SK	64-23,24-W2	73 I/11	54°32′	105°29′
Molega	UNP/LNO	NS	Queens	21 A/7	44°20′	64°54′
Molega Lake	LAKE/LAC	NS	Queens	21 A/7	44°22′	64°51′
Molesworth	UNP/LNO	ON	Huron	40 P/14	43°47′	81°04′
Molewood	UNP/LNO	SK	21-48-15-W3	73 F/1	53°09′	108°09′
Moline	UNP/LNO	MB	8-14-20-W	62 K/1	50°11′	100°11′
Mollet, Lacs	LAKE/LAC	QC	Kativik	33 O/9	55°37′	74°25′
Molliers	UNP/LNO	NF		1 M/4	47°06′	55°40′
Molliers Point	CAPE/CAP	NF		1 M/4	47°07′	55°41′
Mollyguajeck Lake	LAKE/LAC	NF		2 D/7	48°21′	54°33′
Molson	UNP/LNO	MB	21-12-9-E	62 I/1	50°01′	96°18′
Molson Lake	LAKE/LAC	NF		23 G/8	53°22′	66°16′
Molson Lake	LAKE/LAC	MB		63 I/2	54°12′	96°45′
Molson Landing	UNP/LNO	QC	Memphrémagog	31 H/1	45°05′	72°16′
Molson River	RIV/CDE	MB		63 I/2	54°11′	96°58′
Moltke	UNP/LNO	ON	Bruce	41 A/3	44°03′	81°00′
Molus River	UNP/LNO	NB	Kent	21 I/11	46°34′	65°05′
Momich Lake	LAKE/LAC	BC	Kamloops Division Yale	82 M/6	51°19′	119°21′
Monarch	UNP/LNO	AB	7-10-23-W4	82 H/14	49°48′	113°07′
Monarch Icefield	GLAC/GLAC	BC	Range 2 Coast	92 M/16	51°57′	126°02′
Monarch Mountain	MTN/MNT	BC	Range 2 Coast	92 N/13	51°54′	125°53′
Monarchvale	UNP/LNO	SK	19-37-14-W3	73 B/4	52°12′	107°59′
Monashee Creek	RIV/CDE	BC	Osoyoos Division Yale	82 L/2	50°14′	118°33′
Monashee Mountains	MTN/MNT	BC	Kamloops Division Yale	82 L/15	51°00′	119°00′
Monastery	UNP/LNO	NS	Antigonish	11 F/12	45°36′	61°36′
Monchy	UNP/LNO	NF		2 D/15	48°58′	54°48′
Monchy	UNP/LNO	SK	8-1-14-W3	72 G/4	49°01′	107°50′
Monck	UNP/LNO	ON	Wellington	40 P/16	43°58′	80°29′
Monck Road	UNP/LNO	ON	Hastings	31 F/4	45°01′	78°00′
Moncouche, Lac	LAKE/LAC	QC	Le Fjord-du-Saguenay	22 D/15	48°46′	70°41′
Moncrieff	UNP/LNO	ON	Huron	40 P/11	43°39′	81°09′
Moncton	CITY/VIL1	NB	Westmorland	21 I/2	46°06′	64°47′
Moncton	GEOG/GÉOG	NB	Westmorland	21 I/2	46°10′	64°50′
Moncton Road	UNP/LNO	NB	Westmorland	21 I/2	46°12′	64°37′
Mondonac, Lac	LAKE/LAC	QC	Le Haut-Saint-Maurice	31 P/5	47°24′	73°58′
Mondou	UNP/LNO	SK	25-24-16-W3	72 N/1	51°04′	108°07′
Monet	UNP/LNO	QC	Vallée-de-l'Or	32 B/4	48°10′	75°39′
Monet No. 257	MUN2/AZM2	SK		72 N/1	51°15′	108°00′
Monetville	UNP/LNO	ON	Sudbury	41 I/1	46°10′	80°22′
Moneymore	UNP/LNO	ON	Hastings	31 C/6	44°23′	77°15′
Money Point	CAPE/CAP	NS	Victoria	11 N/1	47°02′	60°24′
Monger, Îles	ISL/ÎLE	QC	Côte-Nord-du-Golfe-Saint-Laurent	12 O/2	51°05′	58°45′
Mongolia	UNP/LNO	ON	York	30 M/14	43°56′	79°13′

NAME NOM	ENTITY ENTITÉ	LOC 1 LIEU 1	LOC 2 LIEU 2	MAP CARTE	POSITION LAT	LONG
Mongus Lake	LAKE/LAC	ON	Kenora	52 F/4	49°15′	93°46′
Monias	UNP/LNO	BC	Peace River	94 A/3	56°03′	121°15′
Monitor	UNP/LNO	AB	6-35-4-W4	72 M/15	51°58′	110°34′
Monitor Creek	RIV/CDE	AB	35-4-W4	72 M/16	52°00′	110°28′
Monk	UNP/LNO	QC	L'Islet	21 N/4	47°06′	69°59′
Monkland	UNP/LNO	QC	Communauté urbaine de Montréal	31 H/12	45°32′	73°42′
Monkland	UNP/LNO	ON	Stormont	31 G/2	45°12′	74°52′
Monkman Pass	VALL/VALL	BC	Cariboo	93 I/11	54°33′	121°15′
Monks Head	UNP/LNO	NS	Antigonish	11 F/12	45°39′	61°50′
Monks Head	CAPE/CAP	NS	Antigonish	11 F/12	45°40′	61°50′
Monkstown	UNP/LNO	NF		1 M/9	47°35′	54°26′
Monkton	UNP/LNO	ON	Perth	40 P/11	43°35′	81°05′
Monmouth	MUN2/AZM2	ON	Haliburton	31 D/16	44°58′	78°15′
Monmouth Mountain	MTN/MNT	BC	Lillooet	92 J/13	50°59′	123°47′
Monnery River	RIV/CDE	SK	52-25-W3	73 F/5	53°30′	109°34′
Monnoir	UNP/LNO	QC	Rouville	31 H/6	45°25′	73°07′
Mono	MUN2/AZM2	ON	Dufferin	40 P/16	44°00′	80°05′
Mono Centre	UNP/LNO	ON	Dufferin	41 A/1	44°02′	80°04′
Mono Hills	MTN/MNT	ON	Dufferin	41 A/1	44°03′	80°02′
Mono Mills	UNP/LNO	ON	Peel	30 M/13	43°57′	79°58′
Monominto	UNP/LNO	MB	2-10-7-E	62 H/15	49°48′	96°31′
Monominto	UNP/LNO	MB	10-10-7-E	62 H/15	49°49′	96°34′
Mono Road	UNP/LNO	ON	Peel	30 M/13	43°51′	79°51′
Monquart	UNP/LNO	NB	Carleton	21 J/12	46°33′	67°36′
Monquart Stream	RIV/CDE	NB	Carleton	21 J/12	46°31′	67°36′
Monroe	UNP/LNO	NF		2 C/4	48°12′	53°48′
Mons	UNP/LNO	BC	New Westminster	92 J/2	50°08′	122°57′
Mons Creek	RIV/CDE	ON	Algoma	42 G/3	49°01′	83°06′
Monsell	UNP/LNO	ON	Muskoka	31 E/3	45°04′	79°12′
Montagnais Point	CAPE/CAP	NF		13 F/9	53°34′	60°05′
Montagne-de-la-Croix	UNP/LNO	NB	Madawaska	21 N/8	47°21′	68°02′
Montagne-des-Chênes, La	UNP/LNO	QC	Drummond	31 H/16	45°51′	72°17′
Montagne-des-Roy	UNP/LNO	NB	Madawaska	21 O/5	47°22′	68°00′
Montagne-des-Therrien	UNP/LNO	NB	Madawaska	21 N/8	47°23′	68°07′
Montagne du Pin, Lac de la	LAKE/LAC	QC	Jamésie	33 G/13	53°58′	75°40′
Montagne-Ronde	UNP/LNO	QC	Rivière-du-Loup	21 N/14	47°51′	69°06′
Montagnes Blanches, Rivière des	RIV/CDE	QC	Le Fjord-du-Saguenay	22 L/15	50°48′	70°34′
Montagnes, Lac des	LAKE/LAC	QC	Jamésie	32 O/12	51°40′	75°55′
Montagneuse River	RIV/CDE	AB	6-84-6-W6	84 D/2	56°15′	118°57′
Montague	TOWN/VIL2	PE	Kings	11 L/2	46°10′	62°39′
Montague	MUN2/AZM2	ON	Lanark	31 B/13	44°59′	75°59′
Montague	UNP/LNO	YT		115 H/16	61°47′	136°01′
Montague Gold Mines	UNP/LNO	NS	Halifax	11 D/12	44°43′	63°31′
Montague Harbour	UNP/LNO	BC	Cowichan	92 B/14	48°53′	123°23′
Montague Lake	LAKE/LAC	SK	6-29-W2	72 H/5	49°28′	105°49′
Mont-Albert	MUN2/AZM2	QC	Denis-Riverin	22 B/16	48°55′	66°11′
Mont-Alexandre	MUN2/AZM2	QC	Pabok	22 A/11	48°37′	65°09′
Montana 139	IR/RI	AB	43-24-W4	83 A/11	52°44′	113°26′
Montana Lake	LAKE/LAC	BC	Lillooet	92 P/7	51°26′	120°39′
Mont-Apica	MUN2/AZM2	QC	Lac-Saint-Jean-Est	21 M/14	47°59′	71°26′
Mont-Apica	UNP/LNO	QC	Lac-Saint-Jean-Est	21 M/14	47°58′	71°25′
Montauban, Lac	LAKE/LAC	QC	Portneuf	31 I/16	46°52′	72°10′
Montauban-les-Mines	UNP/LNO	QC	Mékinac	31 I/16	46°50′	72°21′
Montavista	UNP/LNO	NS	Hants	11 D/13	44°57′	63°36′
Montbeillard	VILG/VILG	QC	Rouyn-Noranda	32 D/3	48°02′	79°15′
Montbeillard, Lac	LAKE/LAC	QC	Rouyn-Noranda	32 D/3	48°06′	79°07′
Mont-Brun	UNP/LNO	QC	Rouyn-Noranda	32 D/7	48°22′	78°43′
Montcalm	VILG/VILG	QC	Les Laurentides	31 G/15	45°58′	74°30′
Montcalm	MUN1/AZM1	QC	Montcalm	31 H/13	45°54′	73°40′
Montcalm	MUN2/AZM2	MB		62 H/3	49°10′	97°20′
Montcalm	UNP/LNO	QC	Montcalm	31 I/4	46°01′	73°37′
Mont-Carmel	VILG/VILG	QC	Kamouraska	21 N/5	47°26′	69°52′
Mont-Carrier	UNP/LNO	QC	Le Val-Saint-François	21 E/2	45°32′	71°53′
Montcerf	VILG/VILG	QC	La Vallée-de-la-Gatineau	31 K/9	46°32′	76°03′
Montcevelles, Lac	LAKE/LAC	QC	Minganie	12 N/2	51°07′	60°38′
Mont-Dufresne	UNP/LNO	QC	Le Val-Saint-François	21 E/5	45°28′	71°50′
Monteagle	MUN2/AZM2	ON	Hastings	31 F/4	45°13′	77°50′
Monteagle	UNP/LNO	NB	Westmorland	21 I/3	46°05′	65°06′
Monteagle Valley	UNP/LNO	ON	Hastings	31 F/4	45°11′	77°47′
Montebello	TOWN/VIL2	QC	Papineau	31 G/10	45°39′	74°56′
Montebello	UNP/LNO	ON	Lincoln	30 M/3	43°09′	79°15′
Monte Creek	UNP/LNO	BC	Kamloops Division Yale	82 L/12	50°39′	119°57′
Monteith	UNP/LNO	ON	Cochrane	42 A/10	48°39′	80°41′
Monteith, Mount	MTN/MNT	BC	Peace River	93 O/10	55°45′	122°30′
Monte Lake	UNP/LNO	BC	Kamloops Division Yale	82 L/12	50°32′	119°50′

NAME NOM	ENTITY ENTITÉ	LOC 1 LIEU 1	LOC 2 LIEU 2	MAP CARTE	POSITION LAT	LONG
Monte Lake	LAKE/LAC	BC	Kamloops Division Yale	82 L/5	50°30'	119°50'
Mont-Élie	MUN2/AZM2	QC	Charlevoix-Est	21 M/16	47°56'	70°21'
Montérégie	MUN1/AZM1	QC	Rouville	31 H/6	45°23'	73°06'
Montérégiennes, Collines	MTN/MNT	QC	Rouville	31 H/6	45°28'	73°03'
Montfort	UNP/LNO	QC	Les Pays-d'en-Haut	31 G/16	45°53'	74°20'
Mont-Gabriel	UNP/LNO	QC	Les Pays-d'en-Haut	31 G/16	45°55'	74°10'
Montgomery Crossing	UNP/LNO	ON	Renfrew	31 F/14	45°55'	77°18'
Montgomery Lake	LAKE/LAC	NT	Keewatin	65 H	61°28'.	97°45'
Montgomery Park	UNP/LNO	ON	Lanark	31 F/1	45°08'	76°11'
Montgomery Place	UNP/LNO	SK		73 B/2	52°07'	106°44'
Monticello	UNP/LNO	PE	Kings	11 L/8	46°28'	62°27'
Monticello	UNP/LNO	ON	Dufferin	40 P/16	43°59'	80°24'
Montigny	UNP/LNO	QC	Antoine-Labelle	31 J/6	46°24'	75°07'
Montjoie	UNP/LNO	QC	Sherbrooke	31 H/8	45°24'	72°06'
Mont-Joie	UNP/LNO	QC	Vaudreuil-Soulanges	31 G/8	45°17'	74°24'
Montjoie, Lac	LAKE/LAC	QC	Le Val-Saint-François	31 H/8	45°24'	72°06'
Montjoie, Lac	LAKE/LAC	QC	Antoine-Labelle	31 J/6	46°17'	75°08'
Mont-Joli	CITY/VIL1	QC	La Mitis	22 C/9	48°35'	68°11'
Mont-Laurier	CITY/VIL1	QC	Antoine-Labelle	31 J/12	46°33'	75°30'
Mont-Lebel	VILG/VILG	QC	Rimouski-Neigette	22 C/8	48°20'	68°25'
Mont-Louis	UNP/LNO	QC	Denis-Riverin	22 H/4	49°15'	65°44'
Mont-Louis, Rivière de	RIV/CDE	QC	Denis-Riverin	22 H/4	49°14'	65°44'
Montmagny	CITY/VIL1	QC	Montmagny	21 L/15	46°59'	70°33'
Montmagny	MUN1/AZM1	QC	Montmagny	21 L/16	46°50'	70°24'
Montmartre No. 126	MUN2/AZM2	SK	33-14-11-W2	62 L/3	50°14'	103°27'
Montmartre	VILG/VILG	SK	33-14-11-W2	62 L/3	50°10'	103°25'
Mont-Mégantic, Parc de conservation du	PARK/PARC	QC	Le Haut-Saint-François	21 E/6	45°27'	71°09'
Montmorency	UNP/LNO	QC	Communauté urbaine de Québec	21 L/14	46°52'	71°09'
Montmorency, Chute	FALL/CHUT	QC	La Côte-de-Beaupré	21 L/14	46°53'	71°09'
Montmorency, Rivière	RIV/CDE	QC	La Côte-de-Beaupré	21 L/14	46°53'	71°09'
Mont-Murray	UNP/LNO	QC	Charlevoix-Est	21 M/9	47°41'	70°05'
Mont Nebo	UNP/LNO	SK	50-6-W3	73 G/7	53°17'	106°51'
Montney	UNP/LNO	BC	Peace River	94 A/7	56°27'	120°55'
Mont-Orford	UNP/LNO	QC	Memphrémagog	31 H/8	45°18'	72°16'
Mont-Orford, Parc de récréation du	PARK/PARC	QC	Memphrémagog	31 H/8	45°20'	72°13'
Montours Lake	LAKE/LAC	NT	Mackenzie	75 N	63°59'	109°07'
Montpellier	VILG/VILG	QC	Papineau	31 G/14	45°51'	75°10'
Montréal	CITY/VIL1	QC	Communauté urbaine de Montréal	31 H/12	45°30'	73°36'
Montréal	MUN1/AZM1	QC	Communauté urbaine de Montréal	31 H/12	45°30'	73°41'
Montréal, Base des Forces canadiennes - also-aussi - Montréal, Canadian Forces Base	MIL/MIL	QC	Champlain	31 H/11	45°30'	73°26'
Montréal, Canadian Forces Base - also-aussi - Montréal, Base des Forces canadiennes	MIL/MIL	QC	Champlain	31 H/11	45°30'	73°26'
Montréal, Communauté urbaine de	MUN1/AZM1	QC	Communauté urbaine de Montréal	31 H/12	45°30'	73°41'
Montréal-Est	CITY/VIL1	QC	Communauté urbaine de Montréal	31 H/12	45°38'	73°31'
Montreal Falls	UNP/LNO	ON	Algoma	41 N/8	47°16'	84°26'
Montréal, Île de	ISL/ÎLE	QC	Communauté urbaine de Montréal	31 H/12	45°30'	73°40'
Montreal Island	ISL/ÎLE	ON	Algoma	41 N/7	47°19'	84°44'
Montreal Island	ISL/ÎLE	NT	Franklin	66 P	67°49'	96°05'
Montreal Lake	UNP/LNO	SK		73 I/4	54°03'	105°46'
Montreal Lake	LAKE/LAC	SK		73 I/5	54°20'	105°40'
Montreal Lake 106	IR/RI	SK		73 I/4	54°05'	105°49'
Montreal Lake 106B	IR/RI	SK		73 G/9	53°32'	106°03'
Montréal-Nord	CITY/VIL1	QC	Communauté urbaine de Montréal	31 H/12	45°36'	73°38'
Montréal-Ouest	CITY/VIL1	QC	Communauté urbaine de Montréal	31 H/5	45°27'	73°39'
Montreal Point	CAPE/CAP	MB		63 H/12	53°37'	97°50'
Montreal River	RIV/CDE	ON	Timiskaming	31 M/3	47°08'	79°27'
Montreal River	RIV/CDE	ON	Algoma	41 N/2	47°14'	84°39'
Montreal River	RIV/CDE	SK		73 P/3	55°05'	105°19'
Montreal River Harbour	UNP/LNO	ON	Algoma	41 N/2	47°14'	84°39'
Montresor River	RIV/CDE	NT	Keewatin	56 L/12	66°32'	95°49'
Mont-Revelstoke, Parc national du - also-aussi - Mount Revelstoke National Park	PARK/PARC	BC	Kootenay	82 M/1	51°06'	118°04'
Mont-Riding, Parc national du - also-aussi - Riding Mountain National Park	PARK/PARC	MB		62 K/16	50°53'	100°15'
Montrock	UNP/LNO	ON	Cochrane	42 A/15	48°46'	80°41'
Mont-Rolland	TOWN/VIL2	QC	Les Pays-d'en-Haut	31 G/16	45°57'	74°07'
Montrose	VILG/VILG	BC	Kootenay	82 F/4	49°05'	117°35'
Montrose	UNP/LNO	PE	Prince	21 I/16	46°52'	64°04'
Montrose	UNP/LNO	NS	Colchester	11 E/5	45°25'	63°42'
Montrose	UNP/LNO	ON	Welland	30 M/3	43°03'	79°08'
Montrose Creek	RIV/CDE	BC	Range 1 Coast	92 K/9	50°37'	124°11'
Montrose Junction	UNP/LNO	ON	Welland	30 M/3	43°04'	79°05'
Montrose No. 315	MUN2/AZM2	SK		72 O/10	51°45'	107°00'
Mont-Royal	CITY/VIL1	QC	Communauté urbaine de Montréal	31 H/12	45°31'	73°39'
Mont-Saint-Bruno, Parc de conservation du	PARK/PARC	QC	La Vallée-du-Richelieu	31 H/11	45°33'	73°19'
Mont-Sainte-Adèle	UNP/LNO	QC	Les Pays-d'en-Haut	31 G/16	45°56'	74°11'
Mont-Sainte-Anne, Parc du	PARK/PARC	QC	La Côte-de-Beaupré	21 M/2	47°06'	70°55'
Mont-Saint-Grégoire	VILG/VILG	QC	Le Haut-Richelieu	31 H/6	45°20'	73°10'

NAME / NOM	ENTITY / ENTITÉ	LOC 1 / LIEU 1	LOC 2 / LIEU 2	MAP / CARTE	POSITION LAT	POSITION LONG
Mont-Saint-Hilaire	CITY/VIL1	QC	La Vallée-du-Richelieu	31 H/11	45°34′	73°12′
Mont-Saint-Hilaire, Réserve de la biosphère du	PARK/PARC	QC	La Vallée-du-Richelieu	31 H/11	45°33′	73°10′
Mont-Saint-Michel	VILG/VILG	QC	Antoine-Labelle	31 J/14	46°47′	75°20′
Mont-Saint-Pierre	TOWN/VIL2	QC	Denis-Riverin	22 H/4	49°13′	65°49′
Mont-Saint-Pierre, Anse de	BAY/BAIE	QC	Denis-Riverin	22 H/4	49°14′	65°48′
Monts, Pointe des	CAPE/CAP	QC	Manicouagan	22 G/6	49°19′	67°23′
Monts-Valin, Parc de conservation des	PARK/PARC	QC	Le Fjord-du-Saguenay	22 D/10	48°37′	70°48′
Mont-Tremblant	VILG/VILG	QC	Les Laurentides	31 J/2	46°13′	74°36′
Mont-Tremblant, Parc de récréation du	PARK/PARC	QC	Matawinie	31 J/8	46°26′	74°21′
Mont-Tremblant-Village	UNP/LNO	QC	Les Laurentides	31 J/2	46°12′	74°38′
Mont-Valin	MUN2/AZM2	QC	Le Fjord-du-Saguenay	22 D/10	48°37′	70°48′
Montviel, Lac	LAKE/LAC	QC	Jamésie	23 E/16	53°47′	70°15′
Mont-Wright	UNP/LNO	QC	Caniapiscau	23 B/14	52°46′	67°20′
Monument	UNP/LNO	NB	Carleton	21 G/13	45°57′	67°46′
Monumental Island	ISL/ÎLE	NT	Franklin	15 L	62°46′	63°51′
Monument Bay	BAY/BAIE	ON	Kenora	52 E/7	49°27′	94°55′
Monument Brook	RIV/CDE	NB	York	21 G/13	45°50′	67°46′
Monument Corner	UNP/LNO	ON	Manitoulin	41 G/9	45°43′	82°15′
Monument Corners	UNP/LNO	ON	Bruce	41 H/3	45°03′	81°19′
Moodie	UNP/LNO	MB	23-2-12-E	52 E/4	49°09′	95°53′
Moodie Island	ISL/ÎLE	NT	Franklin	26 A	64°37′	65°26′
Moodie, Mount	MTN/MNT	BC	Cassiar	94 C/8	56°18′	124°13′
Moody Bay	BAY/BAIE	SK		63 L/9	54°31′	102°24′
Moodys Corner	UNP/LNO	NS	Digby	21 A/4	44°09′	65°56′
Moonbeam	MUN2/AZM2	ON	Cochrane	42 G/8	49°23′	82°10′
Moonbeam	UNP/LNO	ON	Cochrane	42 G/8	49°21′	82°09′
Moon Island	ISL/ÎLE	ON	Parry Sound	41 H/1	45°09′	80°02′
Moon Lake	UNP/LNO	AB	34-51-7-W5	83 G/7	53°27′	114°57′
Moon Lake	LAKE/LAC	ON	Algoma	41 J/7	46°24′	82°54′
Moon Lake	LAKE/LAC	NT	Mackenzie	96 E	65°37′	127°27′
Moon River	UNP/LNO	ON	Muskoka	31 E/4	45°06′	79°57′
Moon River	RIV/CDE	ON	Parry Sound	31 E/4	45°08′	79°59′
Moons Beach	UNP/LNO	ON	Simcoe	31 D/11	44°33′	79°25′
Moons Corners	UNP/LNO	ON	Frontenac	31 C/7	44°24′	76°35′
Moonshine Lake Provincial Park	PARK/PARC	AB	79-8-W6	83 M/14	55°53′	119°13′
Moonstone	UNP/LNO	ON	Simcoe	31 D/12	44°39′	79°40′
Moorcrest	UNP/LNO	QC	Les Moulins	31 H/13	45°45′	73°38′
Moore	MUN2/AZM2	ON	Lambton	40 J/16	42°51′	82°21′
Moore Bay	BAY/BAIE	NT	Franklin	89 D	77°07′	115°52′
Moore Centre	UNP/LNO	ON	Lambton	40 J/16	42°50′	82°21′
Moore Creek	RIV/CDE	BC	Kamloops Division Yale	92 I/1	50°15′	120°27′
Moore Dale	UNP/LNO	MB	31-25-12-W	62 O/3	51°13′	99°09′
Moore Falls	UNP/LNO	ON	Haliburton	31 D/15	44°48′	78°48′
Moorefield	UNP/LNO	NB	Northumberland	21 P/3	47°03′	65°29′
Moorefield	UNP/LNO	ON	Wellington	40 P/15	43°46′	80°45′
Moore Island	ISL/ÎLE	NT	Keewatin	34 D	56°20′	79°33′
Moore Islands	ISL/ÎLE	BC	Range 3 Coast	103 A/11	52°40′	129°25′
Moore Lake	LAKE/LAC	ON	Nipissing	31 E/8	45°26′	78°01′
Moore Lake - see-voir - Crane Lake	LAKE/LAC	AB		73 L/10	54°31′	110°31′
Moore, Mount	MTN/MNT	BC	Similkameen Division Yale	82 E/15	49°53′	118°49′
Moore Park	UNP/LNO	ON	York	30 M/11	43°42′	79°23′
Moore Park	UNP/LNO	ON	Halton	30 M/12	43°39′	79°56′
Moore Park	UNP/LNO	MB	6-13-17-W	62 J/4	50°04′	99°47′
Moore Peak	MTN/MNT	BC	Kamloops Division Yale	92 I/12	50°44′	121°42′
Moore Point	CAPE/CAP	ON	Ontario	30 M/14	43°48′	79°03′
Mooresburg	UNP/LNO	ON	Grey	41 A/7	44°20′	80°59′
Moores Corners	UNP/LNO	ON	Carleton	31 G/4	45°08′	75°46′
Moore's Cove	UNP/LNO	NF		2 E/11	49°30′	55°18′
Moore's Crossing	UNP/LNO	QC	Brome-Missisquoi	31 H/3	45°04′	73°02′
Moores Harbour	UNP/LNO	NF		14 F/12	57°32′	61°45′
Moores Lake	UNP/LNO	ON	Renfrew	31 F/7	45°27′	76°50′
Moores Mills	UNP/LNO	NB	Charlotte	21 G/6	45°18′	67°17′
Mooresville	UNP/LNO	ON	Middlesex	40 P/3	43°14′	81°27′
Mooretown	UNP/LNO	ON	Lambton	40 J/16	42°51′	82°28′
Mooring Cove	UNP/LNO	NF		1 M/3	47°12′	55°07′
Moor Lake	UNP/LNO	ON	Renfrew	31 K/4	46°08′	77°41′
Mooscana	UNP/LNO	SK		72 I/5	50°24′	105°30′
Moose Bay	HAM/HAM	SK	7-19-5-W2	62 L/10	50°37′	102°41′
Moose Bay	UNP/LNO	MB	3-28-17-W	62 O/5	51°22′	99°46′
Moose Brook	UNP/LNO	NS	Hants	11 E/5	45°17′	63°50′
Moose Channel	RIV/CDE	YT/NT		117 A/16	68°52′	136°42′
Moose Creek	UNP/LNO	ON	Stormont	31 G/7	45°15′	74°58′
Moose Creek No. 33	MUN2/AZM2	SK		62 E/8	49°25′	102°10′
Moose Factory	UNP/LNO	ON	Cochrane	42 P/7	51°16′	80°37′
Moose Factory 68	IR/RI	ON	Cochrane	42 P/2	51°07′	80°36′

NAME NOM	ENTITY ENTITÉ	LOC 1 LIEU 1	LOC 2 LIEU 2	MAP CARTE	POSITION LAT	LONG
Moose Falls	FALL/CHUT	MB		63 A/2	52°12′	96°33′
Moose Harbour	UNP/LNO	NS	Queens	21 A/2	44°01′	64°40′
Moosehead	UNP/LNO	NS	Halifax	11 D/16	44°57′	62°16′
Moose Head	CAPE/CAP	NS	Guysborough	11 F/6	45°24′	61°26′
Moose Heights	UNP/LNO	BC	Cariboo	93 G/1	53°05′	122°30′
Moosehide	UNP/LNO	YT		116 B/3	64°06′	139°26′
Moosehide Creek 2	IR/RI	YT		116 B/3	64°06′	139°26′
Moose Hill	UNP/LNO	NS	Queens	21 A/2	44°04′	64°44′
Moose Hill	UNP/LNO	ON	Thunder Bay	52 A/6	48°15′	89°29′
Moosehorn	UNP/LNO	MB	31-26-7-W	62 O/8	51°17′	98°25′
Moosehorn Creek	RIV/CDE	NB	Kings	21 H/12	45°36′	65°43′
Moose Horn River	RIV/CDE	NT	Mackenzie	95 M	63°36′	126°20′
Moose Island	ISL/ÎLE	MB		62 P/11	51°40′	97°10′
Moose Island	ISL/ÎLE	MB		63 N/3	55°12′	101°28′
Moose Island	ISL/ÎLE	SK		74 N/8	59°27′	108°20′
Moose Jaw	CITY/VIL1	SK		72 I/5	50°24′	105°32′
Moose Jaw No. 161	MUN2/AZM2	SK		72 I/5	50°25′	105°30′
Moose Jaw River	RIV/CDE	SK	31-18-24-W2	72 I/11	50°34′	105°18′
Moose Lake	UNP/LNO	MB	11,12,13-3-16-E	52 E/3	49°12′	95°18′
Moose Lake	UNP/LNO	MB		63 F/9	53°42′	100°19′
Moose Lake	LAKE/LAC	NB	York	21 J/15	46°51′	66°47′
Moose Lake	LAKE/LAC	ON	Cochrane	42 A/10	48°30′	80°44′
Moose Lake	LAKE/LAC	ON	Sudbury	41 I/4	46°08′	81°52′
Moose Lake	LAKE/LAC	MB	3-16-E	52 E/3	49°13′	95°19′
Moose Lake	LAKE/LAC	MB	29-4-E	62 P/10	51°30′	96°58′
Moose Lake	LAKE/LAC	AB	60,61-6,7-W4	73 L/2	54°15′	110°55′
Moose Lake 31A	IR/RI	MB		63 F/9	53°43′	100°20′
Moose Lake 31C	IR/RI	MB		63 F/9	53°45′	100°10′
Moose Lake 31G	IR/RI	MB		63 F/16	53°52′	100°20′
Moose Lake 31J	IR/RI	MB		63 G/14	53°46′	99°18′
Moose Lake Provincial Park	PARK/PARC	AB	61-7-W4	73 L/7	54°16′	110°56′
Mooseland	UNP/LNO	NS	Halifax	11 D/15	44°57′	62°48′
Mooseland Lake	LAKE/LAC	ON	Thunder Bay	52 G/8	49°25′	90°00′
Mooselanka Beach	UNP/LNO	ON	Simcoe	31 D/5	44°22′	79°32′
Moose Meadows 4	IR/RI	NB	Restigouche	21 O/9	47°44′	66°25′
Moose Mountain	UNP/LNO	NB	Carleton	21 J/12	46°37′	67°37′
Moose Mountain	MTN/MNT	SK	9-4,5-W2	62 E/15	49°47′	102°35′
Moose Mountain Creek	RIV/CDE	SK	15-3-2-W2	62 E/1	49°13′	102°12′
Moose Mountain Lake	LAKE/LAC	SK	11-8,9-W2	62 E/14	49°55′	103°05′
Moose Mountain No. 63	MUN2/AZM2	SK		62 E/9	49°40′	102°10′
Moose Nose Lake	LAKE/LAC	MB	81,82-11,12-E	54 D/4	56°03′	95°42′
Mooseocoot	IR/RI	MB		54 D/4	56°04′	95°37′
Moose Point 79	IR/RI	ON	Muskoka	41 H/1	45°03′	80°00′
Moose Portage	UNP/LNO	AB	12-72-26-W4	83 P/4	55°13′	113°52′
Moose Range	UNP/LNO	SK	16-49-12-W2	63 E/4	53°14′	103°42′
Moose Range	UNP/LNO	SK	5-49-12-W3	73 G/4	53°12′	107°43′
Moose Range No. 486	MUN2/AZM2	SK		63 E/6	53°20′	103°20′
Moose River	UNP/LNO	NS	Pictou	11 E/8	45°29′	62°22′
Moose River	UNP/LNO	NS	Cumberland	21 H/8	45°25′	64°11′
Moose River	UNP/LNO	QC	Acton	31 H/9	45°39′	72°25′
Moose River	UNP/LNO	ON	Cochrane	42 I/14	50°48′	81°17′
Moose River	RIV/CDE	ON	Cochrane	42 P/8	51°20′	80°24′
Moose River Gold Mines	UNP/LNO	NS	Halifax	11 D/15	44°59′	62°57′
Moose Valley	UNP/LNO	SK	32-11-5-W2	62 E/15	49°57′	102°39′
Moose Wallow	UNP/LNO	AB	23-60-7-W5	83 J/2	54°12′	114°57′
Moosh 4	IR/RI	BC	Kamloops Division Yale	92 I/1	50°08′	121°34′
Moosomin	TOWN/VIL2	SK		62 K/4	50°08′	101°40′
Moosomin 112A	IR/RI	SK		73 C/16	52°58′	108°11′
Moosomin 112B	IR/RI	SK		73 F/1	53°07′	108°15′
Moosomin 112E	IR/RI	SK		73 F/9	53°33′	108°10′
Moosomin 112F	IR/RI	SK		73 F/9	53°36′	108°06′
Moosomin Lake	LAKE/LAC	SK	12,13-31,32-W	62 K/4	50°04′	101°42′
Moosomin No. 121	MUN2/AZM2	SK		62 K/4	50°12′	101°35′
Moosonee	UNP/LNO	ON	Cochrane	42 P/7	51°17′	80°39′
Moostissoostikwan	UNP/LNO	MB	19-56-26-W	63 F/14	53°51′	101°19′
Mooyah 16	IR/RI	BC	Clayoquot	92 E/9	49°38′	126°27′
Mooyah Bay	UNP/LNO	BC	Clayoquot	92 E/9	49°38′	126°27′
Moquin	UNP/LNO	QC	Le Fjord-du-Saguenay	22 D/6	48°26′	71°26′
Moraine Lake	LAKE/LAC	NT	Mackenzie	75 O	64°00′	106°04′
Moraine Point	CAPE/CAP	NT	Mackenzie	85 G	61°36′	115°38′
Morais	UNP/LNO	NB	Gloucester	21 P/15	47°46′	64°48′
Moran	UNP/LNO	BC	Lillooet	92 I/13	50°55′	121°51′
Morand Lake	LAKE/LAC	MB		64 J/4	58°08′	99°47′
Morar	UNP/LNO	NS	Antigonish	11 F/13	45°51′	61°59′
Morass Point	CAPE/CAP	MB	38-15-W	63 B/8	52°18′	98°14′

NAME NOM	ENTITY ENTITÉ	LOC 1 LIEU 1	LOC 2 LIEU 2	MAP CARTE	POSITION LAT	LONG
Moravian 47	IR/RI	ON	Kent	40 I/12	42°33'	81°52'
Moraviantown	UNP/LNO	ON	Kent	40 I/12	42°35'	81°54'
Moray	UNP/LNO	ON	Middlesex	40 P/4	43°12'	81°40'
Morden	TOWN/VIL2	MB		62 G/1	49°12'	98°06'
Morden	UNP/LNO	NS	Kings	21 H/2	45°06'	64°57'
Mordolphin	UNP/LNO	ON	Simcoe	31 D/13	44°48'	79°37'
Morecambe	UNP/LNO	AB	18-54-10-W4	73 E/11	53°40'	111°28'
More Creek	RIV/CDE	BC	Cassiar	104 G/1	57°02'	130°21'
Morehead	UNP/LNO	QC	Pontiac	31 F/10	45°41'	76°34'
Morehouse Corner	UNP/LNO	NB	York	21 J/2	46°04'	66°57'
Morel	UNP/LNO	ON	Nipissing	31 L/7	46°16'	78°47'
Moreland	UNP/LNO	SK	12-9-20-W2	72 H/10	49°44'	104°36'
Morell	VILG/VILG	PE	Kings	11 L/7	46°25'	62°42'
Morell 2	IR/RI	PE	Kings	11 L/7	46°22'	62°43'
Morell East	UNP/LNO	PE	Kings	11 L/7	46°23'	62°40'
Morell Lake	LAKE/LAC	SK		64 E/12	57°37'	103°46'
Moresby Camp	UNP/LNO	BC	Queen Charlotte	103 F/1	53°03'	132°02'
Moresby Channel	SEAU/SMER	—		5.03	50°15'	134°30'
Moresby Island	ISL/ÎLE	BC	Cowichan	92 B/11	48°43'	123°19'
Moresby Island	ISL/ÎLE	BC	Queen Charlotte	103 B/5	52°25'	131°30'
Moreton's Harbour	UNP/LNO	NF		2 E/10	49°34'	54°52'
Morewood	UNP/LNO	ON	Dundas	31 G/3	45°11'	75°17'
Morey	UNP/LNO	BC	Cariboo	83 D/14	52°59'	119°17'
Morgan	UNP/LNO	ON	Kenora	52 F/14	49°58'	93°14'
Morgan Arm	BAY/BAIE	NF		11 P/10	47°43'	56°31'
Morgan Brook	RIV/CDE	NF		11 P/10	47°43'	56°31'
Morgan's Corner	UNP/LNO	QC	Brome-Missisquoi	31 H/3	45°05'	73°03'
Morgans Point	UNP/LNO	ON	Welland	30 L/14	42°52'	79°20'
Morgans Point	CAPE/CAP	ON	Welland	30 L/14	42°51'	79°21'
Morganston	UNP/LNO	ON	Northumberland	31 C/4	44°09'	77°52'
Morganville	UNP/LNO	NS	Digby	21 A/12	44°32'	65°37'
Moriah, Mount	MTN/MNT	NF		12 B/16	48°58'	58°03'
Moriarty, Mount	MTN/MNT	BC	Dunsmuir	92 F/1	49°08'	124°27'
Morice Lake	LAKE/LAC	BC	Range 4 Coast	93 E/13	53°59'	127°37'
Morice River	RIV/CDE	BC	Range 5 Coast	93 L/7	54°25'	126°45'
Moricetown	UNP/LNO	BC	Cassiar	93 M/3	55°02'	127°20'
Moricetown 1	IR/RI	BC	Cassiar	93 M/3	55°01'	127°19'
Morien	UNP/LNO	NS	Cape Breton	11 J/4	46°08'	59°53'
Morien Bay	BAY/BAIE	NS	Cape Breton	11 J/4	46°08'	59°51'
Morien Hill	UNP/LNO	NS	Cape Breton	11 J/4	46°11'	59°57'
Morien Junction	UNP/LNO	NS	Cape Breton	11 J/4	46°08'	59°55'
Morigeau	UNP/LNO	QC	Montmagny	21 L/15	46°53'	70°40'
Morin	UNP/LNO	QC	Bellechasse	21 L/15	46°48'	70°49'
Morin Creek	UNP/LNO	SK	58-19-W3	73 K/2	54°02'	108°44'
Morin-Heights	VILG/VILG	QC	Les Pays-d'en-Haut	31 G/16	45°54'	74°15'
Morin, Lac	LAKE/LAC	QC	Kamouraska	21 N/12	47°38'	69°32'
Morin Lake	LAKE/LAC	MB		63 N/11	55°35'	101°23'
Morin Lake	LAKE/LAC	SK		73 P/4	55°10'	105°50'
Morin Lake 217	IR/RI	SK		73 P/4	55°07'	105°46'
Morin, Mount	MTN/MNT	YT		105 D/1	60°01'	134°18'
Morin Point	CAPE/CAP	NT	Franklin	57 H	71°19'	89°48'
Morin River	RIV/CDE	NT	Franklin	88 C	73°59'	116°34'
Morinus	UNP/LNO	ON	Muskoka	31 E/4	45°10'	79°38'
Morin Village	UNP/LNO	ON	Sudbury	41 P/6	47°28'	81°26'
Morinville	TOWN/VIL2	AB	55,56-25-W4	83 H/13	53°48'	113°39'
Morisset-Station	UNP/LNO	QC	Les Etchemins	21 L/7	46°15'	70°32'
Morkill River	RIV/CDE	BC	Cariboo	93 H/10	53°36'	120°42'
Morley	MUN2/AZM2	ON	Rainy River	52 D/9	48°44'	94°12'
Morley	UNP/LNO	ON	Grey	41 A/10	44°39'	80°45'
Morley	UNP/LNO	AB	25-25-7-W5	82 O/2	51°09'	114°52'
Morley, Mount	MTN/MNT	YT		105 C/1	60°05'	132°12'
Morley River	UNP/LNO	YT		105 C/1	60°01'	132°10'
Morley River	RIV/CDE	YT		105 C/1	60°06'	132°29'
Morleys Siding	UNP/LNO	NF		2 C/5	48°19'	53°55'
Morleyville Settlement	UNP/LNO	AB	26-6-W5	82 O/2	51°12'	114°46'
Morna	UNP/LNO	NB	Saint John	21 G/8	45°17'	66°11'
Morna Heights	UNP/LNO	NB	Saint John	21 G/8	45°17'	66°10'
Morneau	UNP/LNO	SK	53-9-W3	73 G/11	53°35'	107°15'
Morning Lake	LAKE/LAC	AB	8-44-3-W4	73 D/16	52°46'	110°24'
Morningside	UNP/LNO	SK		72 I/6	50°24'	105°29'
Morningside	UNP/LNO	AB	35-41-26-W4	83 A/12	52°35'	113°38'
Mornington	MUN2/AZM2	ON	Perth	40 P/10	43°37'	80°51'
Morpeth	UNP/LNO	ON	Kent	40 I/5	42°23'	81°51'
Morrell	UNP/LNO	NB	Victoria	21 J/13	46°51'	67°42'
Morrin	VILG/VILG	AB	15-31-20-W4	82 P/10	51°40'	112°47'

NAME NOM	ENTITY ENTITÉ	LOC 1 LIEU 1	LOC 2 LIEU 2	MAP CARTE	POSITION LAT	POSITION LONG
Morris	TOWN/VIL2	MB		62 H/6	49°21′	97°22′
Morris	MUN2/AZM2	ON	Huron	40 P/14	43°46′	81°17′
Morris	MUN2/AZM2	MB		62 H/6	49°24′	97°28′
Morrisburg	VILG/VILG	ON	Dundas	31 B/14	44°54′	75°11′
Morrisburg Station	UNP/LNO	ON	Dundas	31 B/14	44°55′	75°12′
Morris Channel	CHAN/CHEN	NF		2 C/12	48°44′	53°47′
Morrisdale	UNP/LNO	NB	Kings	21 G/8	45°23′	66°13′
Morrisey Point	CAPE/CAP	NT	Franklin	37 B	68°50′	79°15′
Morrish	UNP/LNO	ON	Durham	30 M/16	43°58′	78°24′
Morris Island	UNP/LNO	NS	Yarmouth	20 P/13	43°46′	65°56′
Morris Island	ISL/ÎLE	NF		2 C/12	48°45′	53°45′
Morris Jesup Ridge	SEAU/SMER	—		7000	84°30′	26°00′
Morris Lake	LAKE/LAC	YT		105 B/5	60°27′	131°40′
Morris No. 312	MUN2/AZM2	SK		72 P/12	51°45′	105°50′
Morrison	UNP/LNO	QC	Les Laurentides	31 J/2	46°07′	74°31′
Morrison	UNP/LNO	QC	Les Laurentides	31 G/15	45°58′	74°35′
Morrison Cove	UNP/LNO	NB	Northumberland	21 P/3	47°01′	65°30′
Morrison Lake	UNP/LNO	ON	Muskoka	31 D/14	44°52′	79°27′
Morrison Lake	LAKE/LAC	ON	Muskoka	31 D/14	44°52′	79°27′
Morrison Lake	LAKE/LAC	ON	Algoma	41 O/4	47°00′	83°49′
Morrison Lake	LAKE/LAC	MB	47-13-W	63 G/3	53°02′	99°17′
Morrison Lake	LAKE/LAC	BC	Cassiar	93 M/1	55°14′	126°22′
Morrison Landing	UNP/LNO	ON	Muskoka	31 D/14	44°51′	79°28′
Morrison River Landing	UNP/LNO	ON	Algoma	42 F/2	49°12′	84°33′
Morrison Road	UNP/LNO	NS	Cape Breton	11 K/1	46°06′	60°01′
Morris River	RIV/CDE	ON	Kenora	53 B/2	52°12′	90°46′
Morris River - also-aussi - +Morris, Rivière	RIV/CDE	MB		62 H/6	49°21′	97°21′
+Morris, Rivière - also-aussi - Morris River	RIV/CDE	MB		62 H/6	49°21′	97°21′
Morrissey	UNP/LNO	BC	Kootenay	82 G/6	49°23′	115°01′
Morriston	UNP/LNO	ON	Wellington	40 P/8	43°27′	80°07′
Morristown	UNP/LNO	NS	Antigonish	11 F/12	45°44′	61°54′
Morristown	UNP/LNO	NS	Kings	21 A/15	44°59′	64°46′
Morrisville	VILG/VILG	NF		1 M/13	47°52′	55°46′
Morrisville	UNP/LNO	ON	Manitoulin	41 G/15	45°54′	82°51′
Morrogh Creek	RIV/CDE	ON	Lambton	40 I/13	42°50′	81°51′
Morse	TOWN/VIL2	SK	9-17-8-W3	72 J/6	50°25′	107°03′
Morse	UNP/LNO	QC	Le Val-Saint-François	31 H/9	45°36′	72°05′
Morse No. 165	MUN2/AZM2	SK		72 J/6	50°25′	107°00′
Morse, Pointe du	CAPE/CAP	QC	Jamésie	33 E/11	53°35′	79°04′
Morse River	RIV/CDE	NT	Keewatin	66 F/10	65°44′	100°41′
Morse's Line	UNP/LNO	QC	Brome-Missisquoi	31 H/2	45°01′	72°59′
Morson	MUN2/AZM2	ON	Rainy River	52 E/1	49°01′	94°17′
Morson	UNP/LNO	ON	Rainy River	52 E/1	49°06′	94°19′
Morteen 9	IR/RI	BC	New Westminster	92 G/16	49°55′	122°22′
Mortier	UNP/LNO	NF		1 M/3	47°05′	55°07′
Mortier Bay	BAY/BAIE	NF		1 M/3	47°11′	55°06′
Mortier Head	CAPE/CAP	NF		1 M/3	47°05′	55°05′
Mortimer	UNP/LNO	NB	Kent	21 I/6	46°29′	65°16′
Mortimers Point	UNP/LNO	ON	Muskoka	31 E/4	45°03′	79°34′
Mort, Lac du	LAKE/LAC	NT	Mackenzie	75 M	63°02′	111°15′
Mortlach	VILG/VILG	SK	22-17-1-W3	72 J/8	50°27′	106°04′
Morton	MUN2/AZM2	MB		62 F/1	49°11′	100°06′
Morton	UNP/LNO	ON	Leeds	31 C/9	44°32′	76°12′
Morton	UNP/LNO	ON	York	31 D/3	44°14′	79°28′
Morton Seamount	SEAU/SMER	—		5.03	50°20′	142°40′
Morven	UNP/LNO	ON	Lennox and Addington	31 C/2	44°14′	76°51′
Morweena	UNP/LNO	MB	21-23-1-E	62 I/14	51°00′	97°25′
Mosa	MUN2/AZM2	ON	Middlesex	40 I/12	42°44′	81°46′
Mosambik Lake	LAKE/LAC	ON	Algoma	42 C/10	48°42′	84°32′
Mosborough	UNP/LNO	ON	Wellington	40 P/9	43°31′	80°20′
Moscow	UNP/LNO	ON	Lennox and Addington	31 C/7	44°26′	76°48′
Mose Ambrose	UNP/LNO	NF		1 M/5	47°28′	55°31′
Moseley	UNP/LNO	SK	38-22-W2	73 A/6	52°18′	105°02′
Moser River	UNP/LNO	NS	Halifax	11 D/16	44°58′	62°15′
Moser River	RIV/CDE	NS	Halifax	11 D/16	44°58′	62°15′
Moserville	UNP/LNO	ON	Perth	40 P/7	43°30′	80°58′
Moses Inlet	BAY/BAIE	BC	Range 2 Coast	92 M/14	51°46′	127°25′
Moses Oates, Cape	CAPE/CAP	NT	Franklin	35 I	62°37′	73°56′
Mosher	UNP/LNO	ON	Algoma	42 C/9	48°42′	84°12′
Mosher Lake	LAKE/LAC	NT	Mackenzie	85 O	63°05′	115°27′
Mosher River	RIV/CDE	NB	Saint John	21 H/5	45°20′	65°32′
Moshers Corner	UNP/LNO	NS	Annapolis	21 H/3	45°00′	65°07′
Moshers Island	UNP/LNO	NS	Lunenburg	21 A/1	44°14′	64°19′
Mosherville	UNP/LNO	NS	Hants	11 E/4	45°04′	63°58′
Moshikopaw Lake	LAKE/LAC	ON	Kenora	43 L/5	54°22′	87°33′

NAME NOM	ENTITY ENTITÉ	LOC 1 LIEU 1	LOC 2 LIEU 2	MAP CARTE	POSITION LAT	LONG
Mosley Creek	RIV/CDE	BC	Range 2 Coast	92 N/7	51°18′	124°51′
Mosque	UNP/LNO	BC	Cassiar	94 D/5	56°29′	127°32′
Mosque River	RIV/CDE	BC	Cassiar	94 D/12	56°31′	127°34′
Mosquito	UNP/LNO	NF		1 K/13	46°59′	53°41′
Mosquito 109	IR/RI	SK		73 C/9	52°31′	108°15′
Mosquito Bay	BAY/BAIE	NT	Keewatin	35 C	60°37′	77°55′
Mosquito Berry Hill	MTN/MNT	NT	Mackenzie	96 B	64°52′	122°20′
Mosquito Creek	RIV/CDE	AB	7-15-25-W4	82 I/3	50°14′	113°25′
Mosquito Creek 5	IR/RI	BC	Cassiar	104 I/16	58°56′	128°15′
Mosquito Lake	LAKE/LAC	BC	Kootenay	82 L/8	50°19′	118°04′
Mosquito Lake	LAKE/LAC	NT	Mackenzie	65 L	62°36′	103°22′
Mos Sakik	UNP/LNO	QC	Pontiac	31 N/4	47°01′	77°51′
Mossbank	TOWN/VIL2	SK	11-29,30-W2	72 H/13	49°56′	105°58′
Mossey River	MUN2/AZM2	MB		62 O/12	51°40′	100°00′
Moss Glen	UNP/LNO	NB	Kings	21 G/8	45°26′	66°02′
Mosside	UNP/LNO	AB	32-58-4-W5	83 J/2	54°04′	114°34′
Mossington Park	UNP/LNO	ON	York	31 D/6	44°19′	79°21′
Moss Lake	LAKE/LAC	MB	5,6-10-14-E	52 E/13	49°48′	95°40′
Moss Lake	LAKE/LAC	MB		64 G/10	57°38′	98°41′
Mossleigh	UNP/LNO	AB	30-20-24-W4	82 I/11	50°43′	113°20′
Mossley	UNP/LNO	ON	Middlesex	40 I/14	42°57′	81°01′
Mossman	UNP/LNO	NS	Lunenburg	21 A/7	44°27′	64°35′
Mossman Corner	UNP/LNO	NS	Lunenburg	21 A/7	44°26′	64°35′
Moss Mine	UNP/LNO	QC	Les Collines-de-l'Outaouais	31 F/9	45°34′	76°15′
Moss, Point	CAPE/CAP	NT	Franklin	120 F	82°58′	67°09′
Moss Spur	UNP/LNO	MB	3,10-12-10-E	62 H/16	49°59′	96°08′
Mossy Point	CAPE/CAP	MB		63 A/11	52°38′	97°13′
Mossy River	RIV/CDE	MB	11-31-18-W	62 O/12	51°39′	99°55′
Mossy River	RIV/CDE	SK	59-7-W2	63 L/2	54°05′	102°58′
Mossyvale	UNP/LNO	SK	21-53-11-W2	63 E/12	53°36′	103°35′
Mostoos Hills	MTN/MNT	SK		73 K/14	54°50′	109°10′
Motase Lake	LAKE/LAC	BC	Cassiar	94 D/3	56°02′	127°03′
Motase Peak	MTN/MNT	BC	Cassiar	94 D/3	56°05′	127°11′
Motherwell	UNP/LNO	ON	Perth	40 P/6	43°21′	81°11′
Motherwell Homestead National Historic Site - also-aussi - Homestead-Motherwell, Lieu historique national du	PARK/PARC	SK		62 L/11	50°43′	103°26′
Motion Bay	BAY/BAIE	NF		1 N/7	47°27′	52°40′
Motion Head	CAPE/CAP	NF		1 N/7	47°26′	52°40′
Motts Mills	UNP/LNO	ON	Leeds	31 C/16	44°47′	76°02′
Mouat, Cape	CAPE/CAP	NT	Franklin	39 C	77°36′	77°41′
Mouchalagane, Rivière	RIV/CDE	QC	Caniapiscau	22 N/11	51°36′	69°07′
Moul Creek - see-voir - Grouse (Moul) Creek	RIV/CDE	BC		92 P/16	51°50′	120°03′
Mould Bay	BAY/BAIE	NT	Franklin	89 B	76°12′	119°25′
Moulin-à-Albert	UNP/LNO	QC	Témiscouata	21 N/6	47°27′	69°10′
Moulin-à-Baude	UNP/LNO	QC	La Haute-Côte-Nord	22 C/4	48°09′	69°41′
Moulin-à-Beaudry, Le	UNP/LNO	QC	Pabok	22 A/10	48°41′	64°46′
Moulin-à-Gagnon, Le	UNP/LNO	QC	Pabok	22 A/10	48°38′	64°38′
Moulin-à-Nadeau, Le	UNP/LNO	QC	Pabok	22 A/10	48°35′	64°35′
Moulin-à-Pelletier, Le	UNP/LNO	QC	La Matapédia	22 B/10	48°35′	66°52′
Moulin-à-Vénéran	UNP/LNO	QC	Témiscouata	21 N/6	47°28′	69°09′
Moulin-Beaudoin	UNP/LNO	QC	Lotbinière	21 L/5	46°28′	71°32′
Moulin-Caron	UNP/LNO	QC	Rouyn-Noranda	32 D/2	48°07′	78°58′
Moulin-Couture	UNP/LNO	QC	La Mitis	22 C/9	48°35′	68°07′
Moulin-Dufour	UNP/LNO	QC	Kamouraska	21 N/12	47°31′	69°50′
Moulin-du-Seigneur, Le	UNP/LNO	QC	Rivière-du-Loup	21 N/14	47°55′	69°22′
Moulin-Gosselin	UNP/LNO	QC	Les Chutes-de-la-Chaudière	21 L/11	46°41′	71°16′
Moulin-Goulet	UNP/LNO	QC	Bellechasse	21 L/10	46°38′	70°43′
Moulin-Lajoie	UNP/LNO	QC	Kamouraska	21 N/12	47°32′	69°49′
Moulin-Legendre	UNP/LNO	QC	Le Granit	21 E/11	45°43′	71°10′
Moulin-Morneault	UNP/LNO	NB	Madawaska	21 N/8	47°27′	68°21′
Moulin-Plamondon	UNP/LNO	QC	Asbestos	21 E/13	45°45′	71°45′
Moulin, Rivière du	RIV/CDE	QC	Avignon	22 B/3	48°04′	67°06′
Moulin, Rivière du	RIV/CDE	QC	Le Fjord-du-Saguenay	22 D/6	48°26′	71°02′
Moulin, Ruisseau du	RIV/CDE	QC	Communauté urbaine de Québec	21 L/14	46°50′	71°13′
Moulin-Samson	UNP/LNO	QC	Asbestos	21 E/13	45°46′	71°48′
Moulin-Tourville	UNP/LNO	QC	Maskinongé	31 I/2	46°15′	72°56′
Moulin-Vallière	UNP/LNO	QC	La Côte-de-Beaupré	21 L/14	46°58′	71°12′
Moulton Bay	BAY/BAIE	ON	Haldimand	30 L/14	42°52′	79°27′
Moulton Hill	UNP/LNO	QC	Sherbrooke	21 E/5	45°23′	71°50′
Moulton Station	UNP/LNO	ON	Haldimand	30 L/13	42°57′	79°33′
Mound	UNP/LNO	AB	32-33-4-W5	82 O/15	51°51′	114°31′
Mountain	MUN2/AZM2	ON	Dundas	31 G/3	45°03′	75°19′
Mountain	MUN2/AZM2	MB		63 C/2	52°13′	100°44′
Mountain	UNP/LNO	ON	Dundas	31 G/3	45°02′	75°30′
Mountain Brook	UNP/LNO	NB	Restigouche	21 O/16	47°59′	66°21′
Mountain Cabin	UNP/LNO	SK		63 E/9	53°36′	102°06′

NAME NOM	ENTITY ENTITÉ	LOC 1 LIEU 1	LOC 2 LIEU 2	MAP CARTE	POSITION LAT	LONG
Mountain Chutes	UNP/LNO	ON	Timiskaming	41 P/9	47°39'	80°10'
Mountain Front	UNP/LNO	NS	Kings	21 H/2	45°09'	64°36'
Mountain Gardens	UNP/LNO	ON	Halton	30 M/5	43°21'	79°49'
Mountain Grove	UNP/LNO	ON	Frontenac	31 C/10	44°44'	76°51'
Mountain Lake	UNP/LNO	ON	Timiskaming	41 P/9	47°39'	80°13'
Mountain Lake	LAKE/LAC	ON	Haliburton	31 D/15	44°59'	78°43'
Mountain Lake	LAKE/LAC	ON	Grey	41 A/10	44°43'	80°41'
Mountain Lake	LAKE/LAC	ON	Grey	41 A/11	44°42'	81°03'
Mountain Lake	LAKE/LAC	SK		73 P/7	55°29'	104°30'
Mountain Lake	LAKE/LAC	NT	Keewatin	65 G	61°12'	98°35'
Mountain Lake	LAKE/LAC	NT	Mackenzie	75 A	60°54'	105°20'
Mountain Land District	GEOG/GÉOG	BC		92 F	49°10'	124°02'
Mountain Park	UNP/LNO	AB	33-45-23-W5	83 C/14	52°55'	117°16'
Mountain Ranches	UNP/LNO	QC	Vaudreuil-Soulanges	31 G/8	45°28'	74°15'
Mountain River	RIV/CDE	NT	Mackenzie	106 H	65°41'	128°50'
Mountain Road	UNP/LNO	NS	Pictou	11 E/11	45°42'	63°06'
Mountain Road	UNP/LNO	MB	18-17-16-W	62 J/5	50°27'	99°39'
Mountainside	UNP/LNO	MB	24-2-22-W	62 F/1	49°09'	100°17'
Mountains, Lake of the	LAKE/LAC	ON	Sudbury	41 I/5	46°20'	81°42'
Mountains, Lake of the	LAKE/LAC	BC	Rupert	92 L/13	50°46'	127°47'
Mountain Station	UNP/LNO	BC	Kootenay	82 F/6	49°29'	117°17'
Mountain View	UNP/LNO	NB	Carleton	21 J/6	46°19'	67°20'
Mountain View	UNP/LNO	ON	Prince Edward	31 C/3	44°04'	77°22'
Mountain View	UNP/LNO	ON	Renfrew	31 K/3	46°04'	77°28'
Mountain View	UNP/LNO	AB	19-2-27-W4	82 H/4	49°08'	113°36'
Mountain View Beach	UNP/LNO	ON	Simcoe	31 D/12	44°39'	79°59'
Mountain View No. 17, County of	MUN1/AZM1	AB	30-2-W5	82 O/9	51°41'	114°14'
Mountain View No. 318	MUN2/AZM2	SK		72 N/9	51°45'	108°20'
Mountairy Lake	LAKE/LAC	ON	Thunder Bay	52 G/16	49°50'	90°23'
Mount Albert	UNP/LNO	ON	York	31 D/3	44°08'	79°19'
Mount Albion	UNP/LNO	PE	Queens	11 L/2	46°14'	62°57'
Mount Albion	UNP/LNO	ON	Wentworth	30 M/4	43°12'	79°48'
Mount Arlington Heights	UNP/LNO	NF		1 N/5	47°26'	53°52'
Mount Auburn	UNP/LNO	NS	Richmond	11 F/15	45°46'	60°42'
Mount Baldy	UNP/LNO	BC	Similkameen Division Yale	82 E/3	49°09'	119°14'
Mountbatten 76A	IR/RI	ON	Sudbury	41 O/11	47°43'	83°03'
Mount Brydges	UNP/LNO	ON	Middlesex	40 I/14	42°54'	81°29'
Mount Buchanan	UNP/LNO	PE	Queens	11 L/2	46°05'	62°56'
Mount Carmel	UNP/LNO	NF		1 N/3	47°09'	53°29'
Mount Carmel	UNP/LNO	PE	Prince	21 I/8	46°24'	64°02'
Mount Carmel	UNP/LNO	ON	Prince Edward	31 C/3	44°08'	77°05'
Mount Carmel	UNP/LNO	ON	Ontario	31 D/2	44°02'	78°54'
Mount Carmel	UNP/LNO	ON	Haldimand	30 L/13	42°56'	79°31'
Mount Carmel	UNP/LNO	ON	Huron	40 P/5	43°16'	81°37'
Mount Carmel	UNP/LNO	ON	Essex	40 J/2	42°06'	82°36'
Mount Carmel-Mitchells Brook-St. Catherines	TOWN/VIL2	NF		1 N/4	47°09'	53°29'
Mount Carmel Pond	LAKE/LAC	NF		1 N/3	47°08'	53°06'
Mount Cashel	UNP/LNO	NF		1 N/10	47°35'	52°43'
Mount Charles	UNP/LNO	ON	Peel	30 M/12	43°41'	79°40'
Mount Chesney	UNP/LNO	ON	Frontenac	31 C/8	44°20'	76°27'
Mount Currie	UNP/LNO	BC	Lillooet	92 J/7	50°19'	122°43'
Mount Currie 1	IR/RI	BC	Lillooet	92 J/7	50°19'	122°43'
Mount Currie 2	IR/RI	BC	Lillooet	92 J/7	50°18'	122°44'
Mount Currie 6	IR/RI	BC	Lillooet	92 J/7	50°19'	122°40'
Mount Currie 7	IR/RI	BC	Lillooet	92 J/7	50°21'	122°42'
Mount Currie 8	IR/RI	BC	Lillooet	92 J/7	50°18'	122°42'
Mount Currie 10	IR/RI	BC	Lillooet	92 J/7	50°19'	122°43'
Mount Dennis	UNP/LNO	ON	York	30 M/11	43°41'	79°29'
Mount Denson	UNP/LNO	NS	Hants	21 H/1	45°03'	64°10'
Mount Elgin	UNP/LNO	ON	Oxford	40 I/15	42°57'	80°47'
Mount Forest	TOWN/VIL2	ON	Grey	40 P/15	43°59'	80°44'
Mount Gardner	UNP/LNO	BC	New Westminster	92 G/6	49°24'	123°23'
Mount Hanley	UNP/LNO	NS	Annapolis	21 A/14	44°58'	65°10'
Mount Healy	UNP/LNO	ON	Haldimand	30 M/4	43°00'	79°53'
Mount Hebron	UNP/LNO	NB	Kings	21 H/13	45°49'	65°30'
Mount Herbert	UNP/LNO	PE	Queens	11 L/3	46°14'	63°02'
Mount Hope	UNP/LNO	PE	Kings	11 L/8	46°22'	62°30'
Mount Hope	UNP/LNO	NB	York	21 J/2	46°03'	66°30'
Mount Hope	UNP/LNO	ON	Wentworth	30 M/4	43°09'	79°55'
Mount Hope	UNP/LNO	ON	Bruce	41 A/6	44°25'	81°14'
Mount Hope No. 279	MUN2/AZM2	SK		72 P/7	51°30'	104°45'
Mount Horeb	UNP/LNO	ON	Victoria	31 D/7	44°15'	78°39'
Mount Irwin	UNP/LNO	ON	Peterborough	31 D/15	44°45'	78°32'
Mount Joy	UNP/LNO	ON	York	30 M/14	43°53'	79°16'
Mountjoy	UNP/LNO	ON	Cochrane	42 A/6	48°29'	81°22'

NAME NOM	ENTITY ENTITÉ	LOC 1 LIEU 1	LOC 2 LIEU 2	MAP CARTE	POSITION LAT	LONG
Mount Julian	UNP/LNO	ON	Peterborough	31 D/9	44°34′	78°09′
Mount Lehman	UNP/LNO	BC	New Westminster	92 G/1	49°07′	122°23′
Mount Lorne	HAM/HAM	YT		105 D/7	60°26′	134°56′
Mount Loyal	UNP/LNO	QC	Matawinie	31 I/4	46°03′	73°48′
Mount MacDonald	UNP/LNO	ON	Timiskaming	41 P/16	47°47′	80°08′
Mount Maple	UNP/LNO	QC	Argenteuil	31 G/9	45°41′	74°29′
Mount Mellick	UNP/LNO	PE	Queens	11 L/2	46°12′	62°57′
Mount Merrit	UNP/LNO	NS	Queens	21 A/6	44°26′	65°05′
Mount Middleton	UNP/LNO	NB	Kings	21 H/13	45°47′	65°33′
Mount Misery Pond	LAKE/LAC	NF		1 K/14	46°50′	53°25′
Mount Moriah	TOWN/VIL2	NF		12 B/16	48°58′	58°02′
Mount Nemo	UNP/LNO	ON	Halton	30 M/5	43°24′	79°53′
Mount Pearl	CITY/VIL1	NF		1 N/10	47°31′	52°47′
Mount Pisgah	UNP/LNO	NB	Kings	21 H/14	45°49′	65°25′
Mount Pleasant	UNP/LNO	PE	Prince	21 I/9	46°35′	64°01′
Mount Pleasant	UNP/LNO	NS	Inverness	11 K/3	46°14′	61°07′
Mount Pleasant	UNP/LNO	NS	Cumberland	11 E/13	45°48′	63°51′
Mount Pleasant	UNP/LNO	NS	Lunenburg	21 A/8	44°17′	64°26′
Mount Pleasant	UNP/LNO	NS	Queens	21 A/2	44°02′	64°42′
Mount Pleasant	UNP/LNO	NS	Digby	21 A/12	44°39′	65°47′
Mount Pleasant	UNP/LNO	NB	Carleton	21 J/6	46°24′	67°29′
Mount Pleasant	UNP/LNO	ON	Lennox and Addington	31 C/3	44°15′	77°02′
Mount Pleasant	UNP/LNO	ON	Hastings	31 C/5	44°18′	77°37′
Mount Pleasant	UNP/LNO	ON	Durham	31 D/8	44°16′	78°30′
Mount Pleasant	UNP/LNO	ON	York	31 D/3	44°14′	79°24′
Mount Pleasant	UNP/LNO	ON	Peel	30 M/12	43°40′	79°49′
Mount Pleasant	UNP/LNO	ON	Brant	40 P/1	43°05′	80°19′
Mount Pleasant	UNP/LNO	ON	Perth	40 P/6	43°22′	81°16′
Mount Pleasant	UNP/LNO	SK	17-25-W2	72 I/6	50°28′	105°24′
Mount Pleasant	UNP/LNO	BC	New Westminster	92 G/6	49°16′	123°06′
Mount Pleasant No. 2	MUN2/AZM2	SK		62 F/4	49°10′	101°50′
Mount Prospect	UNP/LNO	NB	Kings	21 H/5	45°28′	65°46′
Mount Revelstoke National Park - also-aussi - Mont-Revelstoke, Parc national du	PARK/PARC	BC	Kootenay	82 M/1	51°06′	118°04′
Mount Robson	UNP/LNO	BC	Cariboo	83 E/3	53°02′	119°14′
Mount Rose	UNP/LNO	NS	Annapolis	21 A/14	44°55′	65°15′
Mount Royal	UNP/LNO	PE	Prince	21 I/9	46°41′	64°16′
Mount Royal	UNP/LNO	SK		72 I/7	50°28′	104°40′
Mount Royal	UNP/LNO	SK		73 B/2	52°08′	106°42′
Mount Royal West	UNP/LNO	SK		73 B/2	52°08′	106°43′
Mount St. Louis	UNP/LNO	ON	Simcoe	31 D/12	44°36′	79°43′
Mount St. Patrick	UNP/LNO	ON	Renfrew	31 F/7	45°20′	76°53′
Mount Salem	UNP/LNO	ON	Elgin	40 I/10	42°43′	80°56′
Mountsberg	UNP/LNO	ON	Wentworth	40 P/8	43°26′	80°02′
Mount Sheer	UNP/LNO	BC	New Westminster	92 G/11	49°37′	123°08′
Mount Stephen	UNP/LNO	ON	Simcoe	31 D/12	44°45′	79°34′
Mount Stewart	VILG/VILG	PE	Queens	11 L/7	46°22′	62°52′
Mount Temple Seamount	SEAU/SMER	—		NK22 B	41°32′	51°09′
Mount Thom	UNP/LNO	NS	Pictou	11 E/11	45°31′	63°00′
Mount Uniacke	UNP/LNO	NS	Hants	11 D/13	44°54′	63°50′
Mount Uniacke Gold District	UNP/LNO	NS	Hants	11 D/13	44°56′	63°48′
Mount Valley	UNP/LNO	AB	24-70-13-W6	83 M/4	55°05′	119°50′
Mount Vernon	UNP/LNO	PE	Queens	11 L/2	46°01′	62°45′
Mount Vernon	UNP/LNO	ON	Brant	40 P/1	43°07′	80°24′
Mount Vernon	UNP/LNO	ON	Elgin	40 I/15	42°53′	80°56′
Mount View	UNP/LNO	NB	Westmorland	21 H/16	45°57′	64°23′
Mount View	UNP/LNO	ON	Wellington	40 P/16	43°54′	80°26′
Mountville	UNP/LNO	NS	Pictou	11 E/10	45°32′	62°37′
Mountville	UNP/LNO	NB	Albert	21 H/15	45°48′	64°37′
Mount Waddington	MUN1/AZM1	BC	Range 1 Coast	92 L/15	50°45′	127°00′
Mount Whatley	UNP/LNO	NB	Westmorland	21 H/16	45°53′	64°16′
Mount William	UNP/LNO	NS	Pictou	11 E/10	45°35′	62°43′
Mount Young	UNP/LNO	NS	Inverness	11 K/3	46°07′	61°16′
Mount Zion	UNP/LNO	ON	Northumberland	31 C/4	44°09′	77°37′
Mount Zion	UNP/LNO	ON	Ontario	30 M/14	43°58′	79°04′
Mourier, Lac	LAKE/LAC	QC	Vallée-de-l'Or	31 M/16	47°59′	78°11′
Mourier, Ruisseau	RIV/CDE	QC	Bonaventure	22 A/11	48°31′	65°28′
Mouse Island	UNP/LNO	NF		11 O/11	47°34′	59°10′
Mousseau, Lac	LAKE/LAC	QC	Les Collines-de-l'Outaouais	31 G/12	45°34′	75°57′
Mousseauville	UNP/LNO	QC	Bonaventure	22 A/4	48°08′	65°42′
Moutcha 5	IR/RI	BC	Nootka	92 E/16	49°47′	126°26′
Mouton, Port	BAY/BAIE	NS	Queens	20 P/15	43°56′	64°47′
Mouy, Lac	LAKE/LAC	QC	Jamésie	23 E/9	53°33′	70°04′
Mowat	UNP/LNO	ON	Parry Sound	41 H/16	45°51′	80°28′
Mowat Island	ISL/ÎLE	NT	Keewatin	34 C	56°58′	76°40′
Mowat Landing	UNP/LNO	ON	Timiskaming	31 M/5	47°28′	79°58′

NAME / NOM	ENTITY / ENTITÉ	LOC 1 / LIEU 1	LOC 2 / LIEU 2	MAP / CARTE	POSITION LAT	POSITION LONG
Mowbray	UNP/LNO	MB	4-1-8-W	62 G/1	49°00'	98°29'
Mow Creek	RIV/CDE	BC	Kamloops Division Yale	92 P/2	51°02'	120°45'
Mowhokam Creek	RIV/CDE	BC	Yale Division Yale	92 I/4	50°02'	121°32'
Moxam's Landing	UNP/LNO	ON	Sudbury	41 I/6	46°22'	81°05'
Moyehai 23	IR/RI	BC	Clayoquot	92 F/5	49°25'	125°55'
Moyeha Mountain	MTN/MNT	BC	Clayoquot	92 F/12	49°31'	125°44'
Moyeha River	RIV/CDE	BC	Clayoquot	92 F/5	49°25'	125°55'
Moyen, Lac	LAKE/LAC	QC	Kativik	13 M/4	55°11'	63°48'
Moyer, Lac	LAKE/LAC	QC	Kativik	24 D/2	56°05'	70°43'
Moyie	UNP/LNO	BC	Kootenay	82 G/5	49°18'	115°50'
Moyie Lake	LAKE/LAC	BC	Kootenay	82 G/5	49°20'	115°50'
Moyie River	RIV/CDE	BC	Kootenay	82 F/1	49°00'	116°11'
Moyle Bay	BAY/BAIE	NT	Franklin	46 K	66°17'	84°13'
Mozart	HAM/HAM	SK	25-32-15-W2	62 M/13	51°47'	104°00'
Mozhabong Lake	LAKE/LAC	ON	Algoma	41 J/16	46°57'	82°05'
Muchalat Inlet	BAY/BAIE	BC	Clayoquot	92 E/9	49°39'	126°14'
Muchalat Lake	LAKE/LAC	BC	Nootka	92 E/16	49°52'	126°11'
Muchalat River	RIV/CDE	BC	Nootka	92 E/16	49°51'	126°06'
Mud Bay	UNP/LNO	BC	New Westminster	92 G/2	49°06'	122°53'
Mud Bay	UNP/LNO	BC	Newcastle	92 F/7	49°28'	124°48'
Mud Bay	BAY/BAIE	BC	New Westminster	92 G/2	49°05'	122°53'
Mud Creek	RIV/CDE	BC	Kamloops Division Yale	83 D/3	52°07'	119°12'
Muddy Bay	UNP/LNO	NF		13 H/11	53°39'	57°03'
Muddy Brook	UNP/LNO	NF		2 D/8	48°23'	54°12'
Muddy Creek	UNP/LNO	PE	Prince	11 L/5	46°25'	63°58'
Muddy Hole	UNP/LNO	NF		11 P/9	47°37'	56°21'
Muddy Hole Bay	BAY/BAIE	NF		11 P/12	47°40'	57°59'
Muddy Lake	LAKE/LAC	SK	38,39-22,23-W3	73 C/6	52°19'	109°06'
Muddy Point	CAPE/CAP	NF		2 F/5	49°27'	53°56'
Muddy River 1	IR/RI	BC	Cassiar	94 M/11	59°38'	127°08'
Mudge Bay	BAY/BAIE	ON	Manitoulin	41 G/16	45°56'	82°16'
Mudge, Cape	CAPE/CAP	NT	Franklin	78 G	75°54'	110°03'
Mudie Lake	UNP/LNO	SK	13-60-26-W3	73 K/4	54°11'	109°47'
Mudie Lake	LAKE/LAC	SK	60-25-W3	73 K/4	54°13'	109°45'
Mud Island	ISL/ÎLE	NS	Shelburne	20 P/5	43°29'	65°59'
Mudjatik River	RIV/CDE	SK		74 B/4	56°01'	107°36'
Mud Lake	UNP/LNO	NF		13 F/8	53°19'	60°10'
Mud Lake	UNP/LNO	ON	Renfrew	31 F/11	45°34'	77°11'
Mud Lake	LAKE/LAC	ON	Ontario	31 D/11	44°40'	79°18'
Mud Lake	LAKE/LAC	ON	Manitoulin	41 G/16	45°47'	82°26'
Mud Lake	LAKE/LAC	BC	Kamloops Division Yale	83 D/3	52°08'	119°14'
Mud River	UNP/LNO	ON	Thunder Bay	52 I/7	50°19'	88°31'
Mud River	UNP/LNO	BC	Cariboo	93 G/14	53°46'	123°01'
Mud Turtle Lake	LAKE/LAC	MB	10,11-11-14-E	52 E/13	49°54'	95°35'
Muenster	VILG/VILG	SK	19-37-21-W2	73 A/2	52°12'	105°00'
Mugford, Cape	CAPE/CAP	NF		14 F/13	57°50'	61°43'
Muhigan Falls	FALL/CHUT	MB		63 J/10	54°41'	98°36'
Muingmak Island	ISL/ÎLE	NT	Franklin	16 E	65°17'	63°01'
Muir	UNP/LNO	ON	Oxford	40 P/2	43°07'	80°36'
Muir	UNP/LNO	MB	14-13-11-W	62 J/2	50°06'	98°52'
Muir Creek	RIV/CDE	BC	Malahat	92 B/5	48°23'	123°52'
Muirkirk	UNP/LNO	ON	Kent	40 I/12	42°31'	81°46'
Muketei River	RIV/CDE	ON	Kenora	43 F/3	53°08'	85°19'
Mukluk Channel	SEAU/SMER	—		5.03	49°00'	140°30'
Mukutawa River	RIV/CDE	MB		63 H/3	53°10'	97°25'
Mulcuish Lake	LAKE/LAC	NS	Cape Breton	11 F/16	45°45'	60°13'
Muldrew Lake	UNP/LNO	ON	Muskoka	31 D/14	44°53'	79°25'
Mule, Lac la	LAKE/LAC	QC	Sept-Rivières	22 P/12	51°33'	65°35'
Mulgrave	TOWN/VIL2	NS	Guysborough	11 F/11	45°37'	61°23'
Mulgrave	UNP/LNO	ON	Welland	30 L/14	42°54'	79°06'
Mulgrave-et-Derry	VILG/VILG	QC	Papineau	31 G/14	45°47'	75°22'
Mulgrave, Lake	LAKE/LAC	NS	Halifax	11 E/2	45°02'	62°35'
Mulgrave, Lake	LAKE/LAC	NS	Annapolis	21 A/12	44°30'	65°29'
Mulgrave Park	UNP/LNO	NS	Halifax	11 D/12	44°40'	63°36'
Mulhern	UNP/LNO	ON	Welland	30 M/3	43°06'	79°09'
Mulhurst	UNP/LNO	AB	15-47-28-W4	83 H/4	53°03'	113°59'
Mull	UNP/LNO	ON	Kent	40 I/5	42°24'	81°59'
Müller Ice Cap	GLAC/GLAC	NT	Franklin	59 H	79°47'	91°30'
Mullifarry	UNP/LNO	ON	Middlesex	40 I/13	42°59'	81°42'
Mulligan Bay	BAY/BAIE	NF		13 G/13	53°50'	59°50'
Mulligan Ferry	UNP/LNO	QC	La Vallée-de-la-Gatineau	31 K/1	46°01'	76°01'
Mulligan River	RIV/CDE	NF		13 G/13	53°49'	59°53'
Mullingar	HAM/HAM	SK	27-47-12-W3	73 G/4	53°05'	107°40'
Mullins Cove	BAY/BAIE	NF		13 H/9	53°44'	56°25'
Mullin Stream Lake	LAKE/LAC	NB	Northumberland	21 O/1	47°01'	66°18'

NAME NOM	ENTITY ENTITÉ	LOC 1 LIEU 1	LOC 2 LIEU 2	MAP CARTE	POSITION LAT	LONG
Mulloys	UNP/LNO	ON	Dundas	31 G/3	45°05′	75°24′
Mull River	UNP/LNO	NS	Inverness	11 K/3	46°02′	61°20′
Mulmur	MUN2/AZM2	ON	Dufferin	41 A/1	44°11′	80°06′
Mulmur	UNP/LNO	ON	Dufferin	41 A/1	44°07′	80°01′
Mulmur Hills	MTN/MNT	ON	Dufferin	41 A/1	44°10′	80°04′
Mulock	UNP/LNO	ON	Nipissing	31 L/6	46°27′	79°22′
Mulock	UNP/LNO	ON	Grey	41 A/2	44°13′	80°55′
Mulvihill	UNP/LNO	MB	12-23-6-W	62 J/16	50°58′	98°11′
Muncey	UNP/LNO	ON	Middlesex	40 I/14	42°49′	81°28′
Muncey 1 - see-voir - Munsee-Delaware Nation 1	IR/RI	ON		40 I/14	42°48′	81°29′
Muncho Lake	UNP/LNO	BC	Peace River	94 K/13	58°56′	125°46′
Muncho Lake	LAKE/LAC	BC	Peace River	94 K/13	58°59′	125°47′
Mundare	TOWN/VIL2	AB	19-53-16-W4	83 H/9	53°36′	112°20′
Mundleville	UNP/LNO	NB	Kent	21 I/10	46°35′	64°55′
Mundy Harbour	BAY/BAIE	NT	Franklin	57 E	70°12′	91°40′
Munekun Lake	LAKE/LAC	ON	Kenora	53 G/6	53°25′	91°15′
Muniac	UNP/LNO	NB	Victoria	21 J/12	46°37′	67°42′
Munk	UNP/LNO	MB		53 M/13	55°59′	96°00′
Munn, Cape	CAPE/CAP	NT	Keewatin	46 F	65°55′	85°30′
Munn Lake	LAKE/LAC	NT	Mackenzie	75 N	69°39′	109°58′
Munns Road	UNP/LNO	PE	Kings	11 L/8	46°25′	62°05′
Munro	UNP/LNO	ON	Perth	40 P/6	43°25′	81°15′
Munro	UNP/LNO	BC	Kamloops Division Yale	92 I/10	50°44′	120°42′
Munroe	UNP/LNO	MB	36-12-15-W	62 J/3	50°03′	99°24′
Munroe	UNP/LNO	BC	Kamloops Division Yale	92 I/11	50°34′	121°18′
Munroe Bay	BAY/BAIE	SK		74 B/13	56°50′	107°42′
Munroe Lake	LAKE/LAC	MB		64 O/2	59°12′	98°33′
Munroes Island	ISL/ÎLE	NS	Pictou	11 E/10	45°44′	62°40′
Munroes Mills	UNP/LNO	ON	Glengarry	31 G/2	45°12′	74°42′
Munro Lake	LAKE/LAC	MB		53 L/11	54°38′	95°14′
Munsee-Delaware Nation 1	IR/RI	ON	Middlesex	40 I/14	42°48′	81°29′
Munson	VILG/VILG	AB	15-30-20-W4	82 P/10	51°34′	112°45′
Munsons Landing	UNP/LNO	NB	Northumberland	21 J/16	46°50′	66°01′
Munster	UNP/LNO	ON	Carleton	31 G/4	45°10′	75°56′
Munuscong Lake	LAKE/LAC	ON	Algoma	41 K/1	46°10′	84°04′
Murailles, Bras des	RIV/CDE	QC	Le Fjord-du-Saguenay	22 D/8	48°24′	70°17′
Murchison	UNP/LNO	ON	Nipissing	31 E/9	45°30′	78°02′
Murchison, Cape	CAPE/CAP	NT	Franklin	25 P	63°16′	64°03′
Murchison Island	ISL/ÎLE	ON	Thunder Bay	52 H/16	50°00′	88°21′
Murchison Island	ISL/ÎLE	BC	Queen Charlotte	103 B/11	52°36′	131°23′
Murchison, Mount	MTN/MNT	AB	34-19-W5	82 N/15	51°55′	116°39′
Murchison, Mount	MTN/MNT	BC	New Westminster	92 G/11	49°43′	123°15′
Murchison Promontory	CAPE/CAP	NT	Franklin	57 G	71°58′	94°57′
Murchison River	RIV/CDE	NT	Keewatin	57 B	68°35′	93°35′
Murchyville	UNP/LNO	NS	Halifax	11 D/14	45°00′	63°08′
Murdale	UNP/LNO	BC	Peace River	94 A/7	56°22′	120°52′
Murdale	UNP/LNO	BC	Peace River	94 A/11	56°32′	121°00′
Murder Island	ISL/ÎLE	NS	Yarmouth	20 O/9	43°40′	66°04′
Murdoch, Lac	LAKE/LAC	QC	Kativik	23 O/10	55°33′	66°42′
Murdoch, Rivière	RIV/CDE	QC	Kativik	23 O/15	55°52′	66°55′
Murdochville	CITY/VIL1	QC	La Côte-de-Gaspé	22 A/14	48°58′	65°30′
Murdock Lake	LAKE/LAC	NT	Mackenzie	75 N	63°37′	109°27′
Murdock River	RIV/CDE	ON	Sudbury	41 I/2	46°03′	80°36′
Mureau, Lac	LAKE/LAC	QC	Jamésie	33 J/14	54°55′	75°13′
Muriel	UNP/LNO	AB	10-57-6-W4	73 E/15	53°54′	110°49′
Muriel Lake	UNP/LNO	AB	25-60-4-W4	73 L/2	54°13′	110°37′
Muriel Lake	LAKE/LAC	AB	59,60-5-W4	73 L/2	54°09′	110°40′
Murillo	UNP/LNO	ON	Thunder Bay	52 A/5	48°25′	89°30′
Murky Lake	LAKE/LAC	ON	Thunder Bay	42 L/2	50°05′	86°53′
Murky Lake	LAKE/LAC	NT	Mackenzie	75 L	62°19′	110°54′
Murphy Beach	UNP/LNO	ON	Ontario	31 D/11	44°35′	79°19′
Murphy Corner	UNP/LNO	NB	Carleton	21 J/12	46°35′	67°31′
Murphy Corners	UNP/LNO	ON	Hastings	31 C/13	44°49′	77°43′
Murphy Cove	UNP/LNO	NS	Halifax	11 D/15	44°47′	62°45′
Murphy Creek	UNP/LNO	SK	36-48-17-W2	73 H/1	53°11′	104°21′
Murphy (Eagle) Lake - see-voir - Eagle (Murphy) Lake	LAKE/LAC	BC		93 A/3	52°03′	121°14′
Murphy Lake	UNP/LNO	NS	Kings	21 A/15	44°55′	64°32′
Murphy Lake	LAKE/LAC	BC	Lillooet	92 P/13	51°55′	121°49′
Murphy, Mount	MTN/MNT	YT		105 C/13	61°00′	133°35′
Murphys	UNP/LNO	SK	45-13-W2	63 D/13	52°51′	103°46′
Murphys Cove	UNP/LNO	NF		1 M/8	47°27′	54°28′
Murphy Settlement	UNP/LNO	NB	Kent	21 I/7	46°28′	64°55′
Murray	MUN2/AZM2	ON	Northumberland	31 C/4	44°11′	77°44′
Murray	UNP/LNO	NS	Victoria	11 K/7	46°17′	60°36′
Murray Bay	BAY/BAIE	NT	Franklin	57 G	71°46′	93°54′

NAME NOM	ENTITY ENTITÉ	LOC 1 LIEU 1	LOC 2 LIEU 2	MAP CARTE	POSITION LAT	LONG
Murray, Cape	CAPE/CAP	NT	Franklin	89 D	77°58′	115°06′
Murray Corner	UNP/LNO	NB	Westmorland	11 L/4	46°10′	63°58′
Murray Creek	RIV/CDE	BC	Kamloops Division Yale	92 I/6	50°25′	121°22′
Murraydale	UNP/LNO	SK	35-8-25-W3	72 F/11	49°42′	109°17′
Murray Harbour	VILG/VILG	PE	Kings	11 L/2	46°00′	62°31′
Murray Harbour	BAY/BAIE	PE	Kings	11 L/2	46°02′	62°30′
Murray Harbour North	UNP/LNO	PE	Kings	11 L/1	46°03′	62°30′
Murray Head	CAPE/CAP	PE	Kings	11 L/1	46°01′	62°27′
Murray Hill	UNP/LNO	ON	Peterborough	31 D/8	44°16′	78°26′
Murray Ice Cap	GLAC/GLAC	NT	Franklin	120 C	81°21′	69°24′
Murray Inlet	BAY/BAIE	NT	Franklin	88 H	75°15′	114°00′
Murray Island	ISL/ÎLE	NT	Franklin	77 B	68°26′	111°05′
Murray Lake	LAKE/LAC	ON	Algoma	42 C/1	48°14′	84°09′
Murray Lake	LAKE/LAC	MB		53 L/8	54°23′	94°23′
Murray Lake	LAKE/LAC	SK	47-16-W3	73 F/1	53°03′	108°18′
Murray Lake	LAKE/LAC	BC	Yale Division Yale	92 H/14	49°48′	121°00′
Murray Lake 4	IR/RI	BC	Range 4 Coast	93 F/11	53°40′	125°06′
Murray Maxwell Bay	BAY/BAIE	NT	Franklin	47 D	69°57′	80°40′
Murray Mine	UNP/LNO	ON	Sudbury	41 I/11	46°31′	81°04′
Murray, Mount	MTN/MNT	YT		105 A/15	60°53′	128°49′
Murray Mountain	MTN/MNT	NS	Victoria	11 K/7	46°18′	60°35′
Murray Park	UNP/LNO	MB		62 H/14	49°54′	97°17′
Murray Point	UNP/LNO	SK	53-27-W2	73 H/12	53°37′	105°56′
Murray Point	CAPE/CAP	NT	Franklin	77 B	68°34′	110°19′
Murray River	VILG/VILG	PE	Kings	11 L/2	46°01′	62°37′
Murray River	RIV/CDE	BC	Peace River	93 P/11	55°43′	121°13′
Murray Road	UNP/LNO	PE	Prince	11 L/12	46°42′	63°59′
Murray Road	UNP/LNO	NB	Westmorland	11 L/4	46°09′	63°58′
Murray Settlement	UNP/LNO	NB	Northumberland	21 I/14	46°50′	65°26′
Murrays Siding	UNP/LNO	NS	Colchester	11 E/6	45°22′	63°12′
Murrayville	UNP/LNO	BC	New Westminster	92 G/2	49°05′	122°37′
Murr Basin	SEAU/SMER	—		15146A	44°33′	67°14′
Murrell	UNP/LNO	QC	Pontiac	31 F/10	45°38′	76°36′
Murtle Lake	LAKE/LAC	BC	Kamloops Division Yale	83 D/4	52°08′	119°38′
Murtle River	RIV/CDE	BC	Kamloops Division Yale	92 P/16	51°55′	120°12′
Murvale	UNP/LNO	ON	Frontenac	31 C/7	44°22′	76°39′
*Murvale Station	UNP/LNO	ON	Frontenac	31 C/7	44°22′	76°38′
Musclow	UNP/LNO	ON	Hastings	31 F/4	45°08′	77°48′
Musclow Lake	LAKE/LAC	ON	Kenora	52 M/7	51°24′	94°57′
Muscote Bay	BAY/BAIE	ON	Prince Edward	31 C/3	44°06′	77°18′
Muscow	UNP/LNO	SK	32-20-14-W2	62 L/12	50°45′	103°55′
Muscowpetung 80	IR/RI	SK		72 I/16	50°46′	104°15′
Musée-du-Parc-Banff, Lieu historique national du - also-aussi - Banff Park Museum National Historic Site	PARK/PARC	AB		82 O/4	51°10′	115°34′
Musgrave Harbour	TOWN/VIL2	NF		2 F/5	49°27′	53°58′
Musgrave Landing	UNP/LNO	BC	Saltspring Island	92 B/12	48°45′	123°33′
Musgravetown	TOWN/VIL2	NF		2 C/5	48°25′	53°53′
Mushaboom	UNP/LNO	NS	Halifax	11 D/15	44°51′	62°32′
Mushaboom Harbour	BAY/BAIE	NS	Halifax	11 D/15	44°51′	62°33′
Mushkin 5	IR/RI	BC	Sayward	92 K/6	50°21′	125°08′
Mushkin 5A	IR/RI	BC	Sayward	92 K/6	50°21′	125°09′
Mush Lake	LAKE/LAC	YT		115 A/6	60°18′	137°26′
Mushpauk Lake	LAKE/LAC	NS	Yarmouth	20 P/13	43°51′	65°48′
Musidora	UNP/LNO	AB	29-54-11-W4	73 E/12	53°42′	111°35′
Musk	UNP/LNO	ON	Sudbury	41 O/13	47°57′	83°40′
Muskaboo Creek	RIV/CDE	BC	Cassiar	104 A/10	56°38′	128°33′
Muskasenda Lake	LAKE/LAC	ON	Sudbury	42 A/3	48°06′	81°18′
Muskeegan	UNP/LNO	SK	5-44-7-W2	63 D/10	52°46′	102°59′
Muskeg Bay	BAY/BAIE	ON	Kenora	52 F/11	49°37′	93°19′
Muskeg Lake	LAKE/LAC	ON	Thunder Bay	52 B/16	49°00′	90°02′
Muskeg Lake 102 - see-voir - Asimakaniseckan Askiy 102A	IR/RI	SK		73 B/15	53°00′	106°54′
Muskeg River	UNP/LNO	AB	15-57-5-W6	83 E/15	53°55′	118°39′
Muskeg River	RIV/CDE	SK		73 K/13	54°47′	109°38′
Muskeg River	RIV/CDE	AB	58-8-W6	83 L/3	54°01′	119°03′
Muskeg River	RIV/CDE	BC	Cariboo	93 J/6	54°24′	123°11′
Muskeg River	RIV/CDE	NT	Mackenzie	95 B	60°19′	123°21′
Muskeg River 20C	IR/RI	SK		63 L/2	54°04′	102°39′
Muskiki Lake	LAKE/LAC	SK	38,39-26,27-W2	73 A/5	52°20′	105°45′
Muskiki Springs	UNP/LNO	SK	4-39-26-W2	73 A/5	52°19′	105°42′
Musk Lake	LAKE/LAC	MB/ON		52 L/3	50°07′	95°09′
Muskoday 99 - see-voir - Muskoday First Nation	IR/RI	SK		73 H/3	53°06′	105°30′
Muskoday First Nation	IR/RI	SK		73 H/3	53°06′	105°30′
Muskoka	MUN1/AZM1	ON	Muskoka	31 E/3	45°10′	79°30′
Muskoka	UNP/LNO	ON	Muskoka	31 D/14	44°54′	79°22′
Muskoka	GEOG/GÉOG	ON		31 E/3	45°05′	79°03′
Muskoka Beach	UNP/LNO	ON	Muskoka	31 D/14	44°58′	79°22′

NAME NOM	ENTITY ENTITÉ	LOC 1 LIEU 1	LOC 2 LIEU 2	MAP CARTE	POSITION LAT	LONG
Muskoka Falls	UNP/LNO	ON	Muskoka	31 D/14	45°00′	79°18′
Muskoka, Lake	LAKE/LAC	ON	Muskoka	31 D/14	45°00′	79°25′
Muskoka Lakes	MUN2/AZM2	ON	Muskoka	31 E/4	45°10′	79°35′
Muskoka Lodge	UNP/LNO	ON	Muskoka	31 E/3	45°14′	79°14′
Muskosung Lake	LAKE/LAC	ON	Nipissing	41 I/8	46°29′	80°03′
Muskowekwan 85	IR/RI	SK		72 P/8	51°19′	104°07′
Muskowekwan 85A	IR/RI	SK	11-28-17	72 P/8	51°23′	104°19′
Muskox Fiord	BAY/BAIE	NT	Franklin	49 B	76°30′	87°27′
Muskox Hill	MTN/MNT	NT	Franklin	68 A	72°48′	97°25′
Muskox Lake	LAKE/LAC	NT	Mackenzie	76 C	64°38′	108°14′
Muskox River	RIV/CDE	NT	Franklin	88 C	73°49′	119°55′
Muskrat Dam	UNP/LNO	ON	Kenora	53 G/5	53°24′	91°45′
Muskrat Dam Lake	LAKE/LAC	ON	Kenora	53 G/5	53°25′	91°40′
Muskrat Dam Lake	IR/RI	ON	Kenora	53 G/5	53°25′	91°40′
Muskrat Falls	FALL/CHUT	NF		13 F/2	53°15′	60°47′
Muskrat Lake	LAKE/LAC	ON	Renfrew	31 F/10	45°40′	76°55′
Muskwa	UNP/LNO	BC	Peace River	94 J/15	58°45′	122°41′
Muskwa Lake	LAKE/LAC	AB	82,83-4,5-W5	84 B/2	56°09′	114°38′
Muskwa Ranges	MTN/MNT	BC	Peace River	94 F/14	58°00′	125°00′
Muskwa River	RIV/CDE	AB	1-84-25-W4	84 A/4	56°15′	113°48′
Muskwa River	RIV/CDE	BC	Peace River	94 J/15	58°48′	122°33′
Muskwesi River	RIV/CDE	MB		64 G/10	57°37′	98°35′
Musquanousse, Lac	LAKE/LAC	QC	Côte-Nord-du-Golfe-Saint-Laurent	12 K/6	50°22′	61°05′
Musquaro	UNP/LNO	QC	Côte-Nord-du-Golfe-Saint-Laurent	12 K/3	50°13′	61°04′
Musquaro, Lac	LAKE/LAC	QC	Minganie	12 K/11	50°25′	61°05′
Musquaro, Pointe	CAPE/CAP	QC	Côte-Nord-du-Golfe-Saint-Laurent	12 K/3	50°11′	61°04′
Musquaro, Rivière	RIV/CDE	QC	Côte-Nord-du-Golfe-Saint-Laurent	12 K/3	50°13′	61°04′
Musquash	UNP/LNO	NB	Saint John	21 G/1	45°11′	66°20′
Musquash	GEOG/GÉOG	NB	Saint John	21 G/1	45°10′	66°21′
Musquash Harbour	BAY/BAIE	NB	Saint John	21 G/1	45°10′	66°15′
Musquash Head	CAPE/CAP	NB	Saint John	21 G/1	45°08′	66°14′
Musquash Lake	LAKE/LAC	NB	York	21 G/12	45°41′	67°38′
Musqueam 2	IR/RI	BC	New Westminster	92 G/3	49°14′	123°13′
Musqueam 4	IR/RI	BC	New Westminster	92 G/3	49°04′	123°08′
Musquodoboit Harbour	UNP/LNO	NS	Halifax	11 D/14	44°47′	63°09′
Musquodoboit Harbour	BAY/BAIE	NS	Halifax	11 D/11	44°44′	63°07′
Musquodoboit River	RIV/CDE	NS	Halifax	11 D/14	44°47′	63°08′
Mussel Inlet	BAY/BAIE	BC	Range 3 Coast	103 A/16	52°54′	128°07′
Musselman Lake - see-voir - Musselman's Lake	UNP/LNO	ON		31 D/3	44°02′	79°16′
Musselman's Lake	UNP/LNO	ON	York	31 D/3	44°02′	79°16′
Musselyville	UNP/LNO	QC	Bonaventure	22 A/4	48°11′	65°40′
Mustard Lake	LAKE/LAC	NT	Mackenzie	95 H	62°00′	120°05′
Muswabik Lake	LAKE/LAC	ON	Cochrane	42 N/11	51°35′	85°05′
Muswabik River	RIV/CDE	ON	Kenora	42 N/6	51°24′	85°03′
Mutchler	UNP/LNO	SK	7-45-3-W2	63 D/16	52°52′	102°25′
Mutrie	UNP/LNO	SK	13-10,11-W2	62 L/3	50°05′	103°23′
Mutton Bay	UNP/LNO	QC	Côte-Nord-du-Golfe-Saint-Laurent	12 J/14	50°46′	59°02′
Mutton Bay	BAY/BAIE	NF		1 K/11	46°42′	53°22′
Mutton, Cape	CAPE/CAP	NF		1 K/11	46°41′	53°21′
Muttonville	UNP/LNO	ON	Dundas	31 B/14	44°55′	75°14′
Muzhikoba Creek	RIV/CDE	ON	Kenora	43 L/3	54°10′	87°26′
Muzroll Brook	RIV/CDE	NB	Northumberland	21 I/12	46°32′	65°51′
Muzroll Lake	LAKE/LAC	NB	Northumberland	21 J/8	46°26′	66°12′
Mye, Mount	MTN/MNT	YT		105 K/6	62°19′	133°06′
Myers Cave	UNP/LNO	ON	Frontenac	31 C/14	44°50′	77°08′
Myers Point	UNP/LNO	NS	Halifax	11 D/14	44°46′	63°03′
Mylor Peninsula	CAPE/CAP	BC	Range 5 Coast	103 J/16	54°55′	130°04′
Myo Creek	RIV/CDE	SK	14-57-W3	73 G/13	53°54′	107°59′
Myra	UNP/LNO	MB	36-12-22-W	62 K/1	50°03′	100°22′
Myra	UNP/LNO	BC	Similkameen Division Yale	82 E/14	49°48′	119°19′
Myrehall	UNP/LNO	ON	Hastings	31 C/6	44°20′	77°14′
Myre Lake	LAKE/LAC	MB		54 D/15	56°53′	94°49′
Myrnam	VILG/VILG	AB	14-54-9-W4	73 E/11	53°40′	111°14′
Myrtle	UNP/LNO	ON	Ontario	31 D/2	44°00′	78°58′
Myrtle	UNP/LNO	MB	32-4-3-W	62 H/5	49°21′	97°50′
Myrtle Point	UNP/LNO	BC	New Westminster	92 F/16	49°48′	124°29′
Myrtle Station	UNP/LNO	ON	Ontario	31 D/2	44°01′	78°59′
Mystery Lake	MUN2/AZM2	MB		63 P/12	55°34′	97°59′
Mystery Lake	UNP/LNO	AB	1-60-7-W5	83 J/2	54°10′	114°55′
Mystery Lake	LAKE/LAC	NT	Mackenzie	85 I/7	62°15′	112°32′
Mystic	UNP/LNO	QC	Brome-Missisquoi	31 H/2	45°09′	72°59′

NAME NOM	ENTITY ENTITÉ	LOC 1 LIEU 1	LOC 2 LIEU 2	MAP CARTE	POSITION LAT	LONG

N

NAME NOM	ENTITY ENTITÉ	LOC 1 LIEU 1	LOC 2 LIEU 2	MAP CARTE	LAT	LONG
Nabakwasi Lake	LAKE/LAC	ON	Sudbury	41 P/11	47°33'	81°27'
Nabesche River	RIV/CDE	BC	Peace River	94 B/3	56°07'	123°10'
Nabisipi, Pointe	CAPE/CAP	QC	Minganie	12 L/1	50°14'	62°13'
Nabisipi, Rivière	RIV/CDE	QC	Minganie	12 L/1	50°14'	62°13'
Nabukjuak Bay	BAY/BAIE	NT	Franklin	36 F	65°24'	77°25'
Nachicapau, Lac	LAKE/LAC	QC	Kativik	24 C/9	56°40'	68°05'
Nachvak Fiord	BAY/BAIE	NF		14 M/4	59°03'	63°45'
Nackawic	TOWN/VIL2	NB	York	21 G/14	46°00'	67°15'
Nackawic Stream	RIV/CDE	NB	York	21 J/3	46°00'	67°15'
Nacmine	UNP/LNO	AB	8-29-20-W4	82 P/7	51°28'	112°47'
Naco	UNP/LNO	AB	33-31-6-W4	72 M/10	51°42'	110°48'
Nadaleen Mountain	MTN/MNT	YT		106 C/6	64°15'	133°04'
Nadaleen Range	MTN/MNT	YT		106 C/3	64°12'	133°08'
Nadaleen River	RIV/CDE	YT		105 N/13	63°58'	133°40'
Nadeauville	UNP/LNO	SK	5-16-21-W3	72 K/7	50°19'	108°51'
Naden 10	IR/RI	BC	Queen Charlotte	103 F/15	53°57'	132°41'
Naden 23	IR/RI	BC	Queen Charlotte	103 F/15	53°58'	132°42'
Naden Harbour	UNP/LNO	BC	Queen Charlotte	103 K/2	54°00'	132°39'
Naden Harbour	BAY/BAIE	BC	Queen Charlotte	103 F/15	54°00'	132°36'
Nadila Creek	RIV/CDE	BC	Lillooet	92 O/11	51°30'	123°06'
Nadina Lake	LAKE/LAC	BC	Range 4 Coast	93 E/14	53°54'	127°02'
Nadina River	RIV/CDE	BC	Range 4 Coast	93 E/15	53°59'	126°31'
Naena Point	CAPE/CAP	BC	Range 1 Coast	92 K/12	50°43'	125°43'
Nagagami Lake	LAKE/LAC	ON	Algoma	42 F/6	49°25'	85°01'
Nagagami River	RIV/CDE	ON	Cochrane	42 K/8	50°23'	84°20'
Nagagamisis Lake	LAKE/LAC	ON	Algoma	42 F/7	49°28'	84°40'
Nagasin Lake	LAKE/LAC	ON	Sudbury	41 O/12	47°44'	83°37'
Nagas Point	CAPE/CAP	BC	Queen Charlotte	103 B/3	52°11'	131°22'
Nagle Lake	LAKE/LAC	SK		74 A/3	56°07'	105°21'
Nagvaak Lake	LAKE/LAC	NT	Franklin	46 O	67°33'	83°39'
Nagvaraaluk, Lac	LAKE/LAC	QC	Kativik	25 D/10	60°44'	70°55'
Nahamanak 7	IR/RI	BC	Yale Division Yale	92 I/4	50°08'	121°35'
Nahanni Butte	UNP/LNO	NT	Mackenzie	95 G/3	61°02'	123°23'
Nahanni Butte	MTN/MNT	NT	Mackenzie	95 G	61°05'	123°23'
Nahanni Mountain	MTN/MNT	NT	Mackenzie	95 J	62°05'	123°20'
Nahanni National Park Reserve - also-aussi - Nahanni, Réserve de parc national	PARK/PARC	NT	Mackenzie	95 F/12	61°36'	125°41'
Nahanni National Park World Heritage Site - also-aussi - Parc national Nahanni, Site du patrimoine mondial du	PARK/PARC	NT		95 F/12	61°36'	125°41'
Nahanni Range	MTN/MNT	NT	Mackenzie	95 G	61°30'	123°20'
Nahanni, Réserve de parc national - also-aussi - Nahanni National Park Reserve	PARK/PARC	NT	Mackenzie	95 F/12	61°36'	125°41'
Nahatlatch Lake	LAKE/LAC	BC	Yale Division Yale	92 H/13	49°59'	121°46'
Nahatlatch River	RIV/CDE	BC	Yale Division Yale	92 H/13	49°59'	121°31'
Nahili Lake	LAKE/LAC	MB		64 N/16	59°45'	100°11'
Nahlin River	RIV/CDE	BC	Cassiar	104 K/16	58°47'	132°05'
Nahlouza Lake	LAKE/LAC	BC	Range 4 Coast	93 E/1	53°05'	126°10'
Nahlquonate 2	IR/RI	BC	Cariboo	93 G/6	53°18'	123°11'
Nahma	UNP/LNO	ON	Cochrane	42 H/2	49°01'	80°58'
Nahmint	UNP/LNO	BC	Clayoquot	92 F/2	49°03'	124°52'
Nahmint Lake	LAKE/LAC	BC	Clayoquot	92 F/2	49°08'	125°00'
Nahmint River	RIV/CDE	BC	Clayoquot	92 F/2	49°04'	124°53'
Nahun	UNP/LNO	BC	Osoyoos Division Yale	82 L/3	50°05'	119°30'
Nahwitti 4	IR/RI	BC	Rupert	102 I/16	50°52'	128°03'
Nahwitti Lake	LAKE/LAC	BC	Rupert	92 L/12	50°42'	127°51'
Nahwitti River	RIV/CDE	BC	Rupert	102 I/16	50°52'	128°00'
Naicam	TOWN/VIL2	SK	2-40-18-W2	73 A/8	52°25'	104°30'
Nail Pond	VILG/VILG	PE	Prince	21 I/16	46°59'	64°04'
Nail Pond	UNP/LNO	PE	Prince	21 I/16	46°59'	64°04'
Nain	TOWN/VIL2	NF		14 C/12	56°32'	61°41'
Nain Bank	SEAU/SMER	—		5001	57°00'	60°00'
Nain Bay	BAY/BAIE	NF		14 C/12	56°36'	62°00'
Nainlin Brook	RIV/CDE	NT	Mackenzie	96 D	64°14'	127°18'
Nairn	MUN2/AZM2	ON	Sudbury	41 I/5	46°20'	81°36'
Nairn	UNP/LNO	ON	Middlesex	40 P/4	43°07'	81°34'
Nairn - see-voir - Nairn Centre	UNP/LNO	ON		41 I/5	46°20'	81°35'
Nairn Centre	UNP/LNO	ON	Sudbury	41 I/5	46°20'	81°35'
Nairn, Lac	LAKE/LAC	QC	Charlevoix-Est	21 M/9	47°41'	70°21'
Naisberry	UNP/LNO	SK	12-45-18-W2	73 A/16	52°52'	104°29'
Naiscoot	UNP/LNO	ON	Parry Sound	41 H/9	45°40'	80°27'
Naiscoot River	RIV/CDE	ON	Parry Sound	41 H/10	45°38'	80°34'
Naiscoutaing 17A	IR/RI	ON	Parry Sound	41 H/9	45°40'	80°29'

NAME NOM	ENTITY ENTITÉ	LOC 1 LIEU 1	LOC 2 LIEU 2	MAP CARTE	POSITION	
					LAT	LONG
Nak'a Lat 39	IR/RI	BC	Range 5 Coast	93 K/11	54°42′	125°13′
Nakamistshetshuant	UNP/LNO	QC	Minganie	12 K/12	50°43′	61°39′
Nakamun	UNP/LNO	AB	21-56-2-W5	83 G/16	53°52′	114°14′
Nakamun Park	VILG/VILG	AB	34-56-2-W5	83 G/16	53°53′	114°12′
Nakina	MUN2/AZM2	ON	Thunder Bay	42 L/2	50°10′	86°39′
Nakina	UNP/LNO	ON	Thunder Bay	42 L/2	50°10′	86°42′
*Nakina	UNP/LNO	BC	Cassiar	104 N/2	59°13′	132°47′
Nakina River	RIV/CDE	BC	Cassiar	104 K/14	58°54′	133°08′
Nakoma	UNP/LNO	ON	Wentworth	30 M/4	43°13′	80°00′
Nakusp	VILG/VILG	BC	Kootenay	82 K/4	50°15′	117°48′
Nakvak Brook	RIV/CDE	NF		14 L/6	58°30′	63°19′
Na-kwockto 2	IR/RI	BC	Range 2 Coast	92 M/3	51°05′	127°28′
Nalaisk Mountain	MTN/MNT	NB	Northumberland	21 O/2	47°12′	66°45′
Naltesby Lake	LAKE/LAC	BC	Cariboo	93 G/11	53°38′	123°30′
Namaka	UNP/LNO	AB	16-23-24-W4	82 I/14	50°57′	113°17′
Namakan Lake	LAKE/LAC	ON	Rainy River	52 C/7	48°27′	92°35′
Namakan River	RIV/CDE	ON	Rainy River	52 C/8	48°27′	92°27′
Namao	UNP/LNO	AB	33-54-24-W4	83 H/11	53°43′	113°29′
Namaycush Lake	LAKE/LAC	NT	Franklin	77 F	70°49′	108°22′
Namego Lake	LAKE/LAC	ON	Kenora	52 L/1	50°07′	94°29′
Nameigos Lake	LAKE/LAC	ON	Algoma	42 C/15	48°47′	84°43′
Namekus Lake	LAKE/LAC	SK	56-1-W3	73 G/16	53°49′	106°01′
Nameless Cove	UNP/LNO	NF		12 P/7	51°19′	56°44′
Nameless Lake	LAKE/LAC	SK		74 B/13	56°59′	107°33′
Namepi Creek	RIV/CDE	AB	24-58-19-W4	83 I/2	54°02′	112°51′
Namewaminikan River	RIV/CDE	ON	Thunder Bay	52 H/9	49°40′	88°05′
Namew Lake	LAKE/LAC	SK/MB		63 K/4	54°14′	101°55′
Nampa	VILG/VILG	AB	19-81-20-W5	84 C/3	56°02′	117°08′
Namu	UNP/LNO	BC	Range 2 Coast	92 M/13	51°52′	127°52′
Namur	VILG/VILG	QC	Papineau	31 G/15	45°54′	74°56′
Namur Lake	LAKE/LAC	AB	97-17-W4	84 H/7	57°25′	112°40′
Namur Lake 174B	IR/RI	AB	97-17-W4	84 H/7	57°26′	112°37′
Namur River 174A	IR/RI	AB	98-16-W4	84 H/8	57°29′	112°30′
Nânâdônok	UNP/LNO	QC	Vallée-de-l'Or	31 N/14	47°50′	77°21′
Nanaimo	CITY/VIL1	BC	Nanaimo	92 G/4	49°10′	123°56′
Nanaimo	MUN1/AZM1	BC	Nanoose	92 F/1	49°15′	124°20′
Nanaimo Lakes	LAKE/LAC	BC	Dunsmuir	92 F/1	49°06′	124°11′
Nanaimo Land District	GEOG/GÉOG	BC		92 F	49°29′	124°17′
Nanaimo River	RIV/CDE	BC	Nanaimo	92 G/4	49°08′	123°54′
Nanaimo River 2	IR/RI	BC	Nanaimo	92 G/4	49°07′	123°53′
Nanaimo River 3	IR/RI	BC	Cranberry	92 G/4	49°07′	123°53′
Nanaimo River 4	IR/RI	BC	Cranberry	92 G/4	49°07′	123°52′
Nanaimo Town 1	IR/RI	BC	Nanaimo	92 G/4	49°09′	123°56′
Nananahout 1	IR/RI	BC	Kamloops Division Yale	92 I/5	50°26′	121°34′
Nancut - see-voir - Yekooche	UNP/LNO	BC		93 K/11	54°36′	125°05′
Nancut 3 - see-voir - Ye Koo Che 3	IR/RI	BC		93 K/11	54°36′	125°04′
Nango Lake	LAKE/LAC	ON	Kenora	53 B/6	52°30′	91°22′
Nango River	RIV/CDE	ON	Kenora	53 B/10	52°43′	90°57′
Nanika Lake	LAKE/LAC	BC	Range 4 Coast	93 E/12	53°45′	127°40′
Nanika River	RIV/CDE	BC	Range 5 Coast	93 L/3	54°06′	127°28′
Nanisivik	UNP/LNO	NT	Franklin	48 C/1	73°02′	84°33′
Nankai Peak	MTN/MNT	BC	Cassiar	93 M/16	55°58′	126°13′
Nannuit	UNP/LNO	QC	Kativik	24 N/12	59°43′	69°37′
Nannuk Harbour	BAY/BAIE	NT	Franklin	25 G	61°54′	66°24′
Nanook River	RIV/CDE	NT	Franklin	77 H/12	71°36′	107°47′
Nanoose Bay	UNP/LNO	BC	Nanoose	92 F/8	49°16′	124°12′
Nanoose Harbour	BAY/BAIE	BC	Nanaimo	92 F/8	49°16′	124°10′
Nanoose	IR/RI	BC	Nanoose	92 F/1	49°15′	124°07′
Nanoose Land District	GEOG/GÉOG	BC		92 F	49°16′	124°17′
Nansen, Mount	MTN/MNT	YT		115 I/3	62°06′	137°18′
Nansen Sound	CHAN/CHEN	NT	Franklin	560 D	81°00′	90°35′
Nansen Trough	SEAU/SMER	—		850A	82°00′	90°00′
Nantais, Lac	LAKE/LAC	QC	Kativik	35 A/13	60°59′	74°00′
Nantel	UNP/LNO	QC	Les Laurentides	31 J/1	46°06′	74°24′
Nantes	VILG/VILG	QC	Le Granit	21 E/11	45°38′	71°02′
Nanticoke	CITY/VIL1	ON	Norfolk	40 I/16	42°54′	80°11′
Nanticoke	UNP/LNO	ON	Haldimand	40 I/16	42°48′	80°04′
Nanticoke Creek	RIV/CDE	ON	Haldimand	40 I/16	42°47′	80°04′
Nan Tl'At 13	IR/RI	BC	Range 5 Coast	93 K/11	54°31′	125°11′
Nanton	TOWN/VIL2	AB	15-16-28-W4	82 I/5	50°21′	113°46′
Nanton Lake	LAKE/LAC	BC	New Westminster	92 F/16	49°55′	124°19′
Nantucket Island	ISL/ÎLE	NB	Charlotte	21 B/10	44°42′	66°43′
Nantyr	UNP/LNO	ON	Simcoe	31 D/5	44°18′	79°34′
Nantyr Park	UNP/LNO	ON	Simcoe	31 D/5	44°18′	79°32′
Naococane, Lac	LAKE/LAC	QC	Jamésie	23 D/15	52°52′	70°40′

NAME NOM	ENTITY ENTITÉ	LOC 1 LIEU 1	LOC 2 LIEU 2	MAP CARTE	POSITION LAT	LONG
Naongashing	UNP/LNO	ON	Kenora	52 E/7	49°15′	94°31′
Naongashing 31A	IR/RI	ON	Kenora	52 E/8	49°15′	94°30′
Naongashing 35A	IR/RI	ON	Kenora	52 E/8	49°15′	94°30′
Naosap Lake	LAKE/LAC	MB	68-26-W	63 K/14	54°51′	101°23′
Napadogan	UNP/LNO	NB	York	21 J/7	46°25′	66°56′
Napajut Lake	LAKE/LAC	NT	Keewatin	55 E	61°11′	95°25′
Napaktok (Black Duck) Bay	BAY/BAIE	NF		14 L/1	58°01′	62°19′
Napaktulik Lake	LAKE/LAC	NT	Mackenzie	86 I/7	66°20′	113°00′
Napan Bay	UNP/LNO	NB	Northumberland	21 P/3	47°04′	65°18′
Napanee	TOWN/VIL2	ON	Lennox and Addington	31 C/2	44°15′	76°57′
Napanee River	RIV/CDE	ON	Lennox and Addington	31 C/3	44°12′	77°01′
Napatalik Island	ISL/ÎLE	NF		13 N/9	55°38′	60°22′
Napetipi, Baie	BAY/BAIE	QC	Côte-Nord-du-Golfe-Saint-Laurent	12 O/8	51°19′	58°09′
Napetipi, Lac	LAKE/LAC	QC	Côte-Nord-du-Golfe-Saint-Laurent	12 O/8	51°25′	58°04′
Napetipi River - also-aussi - Napetipi, Rivière	RIV/CDE	NF		12 O/8	51°21′	58°08′
Napetipi, Rivière - also-aussi - Napetipi River	RIV/CDE	QC	Côte-Nord-du-Golfe-Saint-Laurent	12 O/8	51°21′	58°08′
Naphan	UNP/LNO	ON	Hastings	31 C/6	44°22′	77°12′
Napier	UNP/LNO	NB	Restigouche	21 O/15	47°48′	66°56′
Napier	UNP/LNO	ON	Middlesex	40 I/13	42°52′	81°46′
Napier Bay	BAY/BAIE	NT	Franklin	69 A	76°59′	96°30′
Napier River	RIV/CDE	NS	Yarmouth	21 A/4	44°08′	65°44′
Napierville	TOWN/VIL2	QC	Les Jardins-de-Napierville	31 H/3	45°11′	73°24′
Napinka	UNP/LNO	MB	19-4-25-W	62 F/7	49°19′	100°50′
Napken Lake	LAKE/LAC	ON	Cochrane	42 N/14	51°53′	85°20′
Naples	UNP/LNO	AB	20-60-2-W5	83 J/1	54°13′	114°16′
Napoiak Channel	CHAN/CHEN	NT	Mackenzie	107 B	68°40′	135°14′
Nappan	UNP/LNO	NS	Cumberland	21 H/16	45°46′	64°14′
Nappan River	RIV/CDE	NS	Cumberland	21 H/16	45°46′	64°15′
Napper Lake	LAKE/LAC	MB		54 K/6	58°21′	93°20′
Napperton	UNP/LNO	ON	Middlesex	40 I/13	42°57′	81°43′
Narakay Islands	ISL/ÎLE	NT	Mackenzie	96 I/9	66°43′	120°03′
Naramata	UNP/LNO	BC	Similkameen Division Yale	82 E/12	49°36′	119°35′
Narcisse	UNP/LNO	MB	34-19-1-W	62 I/12	50°41′	97°32′
Narcisse's Farm 4	IR/RI	BC	Similkameen Division Yale	82 E/4	49°08′	119°46′
Narcosli Creek	UNP/LNO	BC	Cariboo	93 B/10	52°44′	122°32′
Narcosli Creek	RIV/CDE	BC	Cariboo	93 B/16	52°49′	122°28′
Nardin Lake	LAKE/LAC	NT	Mackenzie	85 P	63°30′	113°50′
Nares, Cape	CAPE/CAP	NT	Franklin	120 G	83°30′	71°35′
Nares, Cape	CAPE/CAP	NT	Franklin	88 G	75°37′	119°25′
Nares, Détroit de - also-aussi - Nares Strait	CHAN/CHEN	NT		120 B/4	80°00′	70°00′
Nares Strait - also-aussi - Nares, Détroit de	CHAN/CHEN	NT	Franklin	120 B/4	80°00′	70°00′
Narol	UNP/LNO	MB		62 I/2	50°03′	96°59′
Narpaing Fiord	BAY/BAIE	NT	Franklin	26 P	67°46′	65°30′
Narraway River	RIV/CDE	AB/BC		83 L/12	54°44′	119°55′
Narrow Lake	UNP/LNO	ON	Kenora	52 N/2	51°13′	92°47′
Narrows	UNP/LNO	ON	Leeds	31 B/5	44°24′	75°55′
Narrows Inlet	BAY/BAIE	BC	New Westminster	92 G/12	49°41′	123°49′
Narrows, The	CHAN/CHEN	NF		13 J/1	54°09′	58°25′
Narrows, The	CHAN/CHEN	NF		13 J/2	54°10′	58°39′
Narva	UNP/LNO	ON	Bruce	41 A/3	44°12′	81°21′
Narwhal Mountain	MTN/MNT	NT	Franklin	16 K	66°43′	61°58′
Nasauya Point	CAPE/CAP	NT	Franklin	26 I	66°05′	65°59′
Naseby	UNP/LNO	SK	10-37-16-W3	73 C/1	52°10′	108°13′
Nash Creek	UNP/LNO	NB	Restigouche	21 O/16	47°55′	66°05′
Nashlyn	UNP/LNO	SK	13-3-27-W3	72 F/4	49°12′	109°31′
Nashville	UNP/LNO	ON	York	30 M/13	43°50′	79°40′
Nashwaak	UNP/LNO	NB	York	21 J/2	46°06′	66°36′
Nashwaak Bridge	UNP/LNO	NB	York	21 J/2	46°14′	66°37′
Nashwaak Lake	LAKE/LAC	NB	Carleton	21 J/6	46°28′	67°07′
Nashwaak River	RIV/CDE	NB	York	21 G/15	45°57′	66°37′
Nashwaaksis	UNP/LNO	NB	York	21 G/15	45°59′	66°39′
Nashwaak Village	UNP/LNO	NB	York	21 J/2	46°06′	66°37′
Naskapis	UNP/LNO	QC	Kativik	24 B/15	56°59′	66°40′
Naskaupi River	RIV/CDE	NF		13 F/15	53°47′	60°51′
Nasoga Gulf	BAY/BAIE	BC	Range 5 Coast	103 J/15	54°52′	130°06′
Nasonworth	UNP/LNO	NB	York	21 G/15	45°50′	66°41′
Nasparti Inlet	BAY/BAIE	BC	Rupert	92 L/4	50°08′	127°40′
Nassau	UNP/LNO	ON	Peterborough	31 D/8	44°21′	78°17′
Nass Bay	BAY/BAIE	BC	Range 5 Coast	103 I/13	54°58′	129°54′
Nass Camp	UNP/LNO	BC	Cassiar	103 P/7	55°17′	128°59′
Nass Ranges	MTN/MNT	BC	Cassiar	103 P/1	55°05′	128°30′
Nass River	RIV/CDE	BC	Range 5 Coast	103 I/13	54°59′	129°52′
Nastapoka, Chutes	FALL/CHUT	QC	Kativik	34 C/15	56°55′	76°32′
Nastapoka Islands	ISL/ÎLE	NT	Keewatin	34 C/15	56°55′	76°50′
Nastapoka, Rivière	RIV/CDE	QC	Kativik	34 C/15	56°55′	76°33′

NAME NOM	ENTITY ENTITÉ	LOC 1 LIEU 1	LOC 2 LIEU 2	MAP CARTE	POSITION LAT	LONG
Nastapoka Sound	CHAN/CHEN	NT	Keewatin	34 F	57°00′	76°40′
Natal	UNP/LNO	BC	Kootenay	82 G/10	49°43′	114°51′
Natalie Lake	LAKE/LAC	MB	13-11-E	52 L/4	50°08′	95°58′
Natalkuz Lake	LAKE/LAC	BC	Range 4 Coast	93 F/6	53°27′	125°14′
Natashquan	VILG/VILG	QC	Minganie	12 K/4	50°10′	61°45′
Natashquan	UNP/LNO	QC	Minganie	12 K/4	50°12′	61°49′
Natashquan 1	IR/RI	QC	Minganie	12 K/4	50°08′	61°48′
Natashquan, Banc de	SEAU/SMER	—		4454	50°00′	61°30′
Natashquan Est, Rivière - also-aussi - East Natashquan River	RIV/CDE	QC	Minganie	12 N/5	51°20′	61°40′
Natashquan, Pointe de	CAPE/CAP	QC	Côte-Nord-du-Golfe-Saint-Laurent	12 K/4	50°05′	61°45′
Natashquan River - also-aussi - Natashquan, Rivière	RIV/CDE	NF		12 K/4	50°07′	61°48′
Natashquan, Rivière - also-aussi - Natashquan River	RIV/CDE	QC	Minganie	12 K/4	50°07′	61°48′
Nataweuse Lake	LAKE/LAC	SK		63 M/5	55°17′	103°36′
Natazutlooh 25	IR/RI	BC	Range 5 Coast	93 K/5	54°18′	125°50′
Nathlegalis 3	IR/RI	BC	Range 2 Coast	92 M/5	51°17′	127°39′
Nathorst, Cape	CAPE/CAP	NT	Franklin	69 D	77°47′	99°50′
Natikamaukau	UNP/LNO	QC	Kativik	24 A/7	56°23′	64°46′
*Nation	UNP/LNO	BC	Cassiar	93 N/5	55°23′	125°50′
National Mills	UNP/LNO	MB	27-44-29-W	63 C/13	52°50′	101°35′
Nation Peak	MTN/MNT	BC	Cassiar	104 H/10	57°39′	128°56′
Nation River	RIV/CDE	BC	Cariboo	93 O/5	55°29′	123°32′
Nation Valley	UNP/LNO	ON	Dundas	31 G/3	45°04′	75°17′
Natipi, Lac	LAKE/LAC	QC	Le Fjord-du-Saguenay	22 M/6	51°27′	71°23′
Natirnaaraaluk	UNP/LNO	QC	Kativik	34 K/12	58°39′	77°50′
Native Bay	BAY/BAIE	NT	Keewatin	45 O	63°52′	82°38′
Native Point	CAPE/CAP	NT	Keewatin	45 O	63°44′	82°31′
Natkusiak Peninsula	CAPE/CAP	NT	Franklin	78 B	72°45′	109°45′
Natla River	RIV/CDE	NT	Mackenzie	105 P/9	63°34′	128°05′
Natogami Lake	LAKE/LAC	ON	Cochrane	42 I/2	50°13′	80°34′
Natowite Lake	LAKE/LAC	BC	Cassiar	93 N/4	55°05′	125°58′
Nat River	RIV/CDE	ON	Cochrane	42 B/16	48°48′	82°07′
Natsy Lake	LAKE/LAC	BC	Cariboo	93 B/1	52°14′	122°29′
Natuak, Lac	LAKE/LAC	QC	Kativik	24 E/4	57°13′	71°45′
Naudville	UNP/LNO	QC	Lac-Saint-Jean-Est	22 D/12	48°33′	71°39′
Naufrage	UNP/LNO	PE	Kings	11 L/8	46°28′	62°25′
Naufrage, Pointe au	CAPE/CAP	QC	Minganie	12 E/14	49°50′	63°23′
Naughton	UNP/LNO	ON	Sudbury	41 I/6	46°24′	81°12′
Naugle	UNP/LNO	NS	Halifax	11 D/11	44°40′	63°23′
Nauglers Settlement	UNP/LNO	NS	Halifax	11 D/16	44°59′	62°15′
Nauja Bay	BAY/BAIE	NT	Franklin	37 A	68°43′	75°42′
Nauja Harbour	BAY/BAIE	NT	Franklin	37 A	68°06′	74°13′
Nautley (Fort Fraser) 1	IR/RI	BC	Range 5 Coast	93 K/2	54°05′	124°36′
Nauwigewauk	UNP/LNO	NB	Kings	21 H/5	45°28′	65°54′
Navan	UNP/LNO	ON	Russell	31 G/6	45°25′	75°26′
Navarre	UNP/LNO	QC	Antoine-Labelle	31 J/12	46°30′	75°34′
Navarre	UNP/LNO	AB	22-45-24-W4	83 A/14	52°54′	113°25′
Naver Creek	RIV/CDE	BC	Cariboo	93 G/7	53°26′	122°39′
Navilus	UNP/LNO	ON	Thunder Bay	52 A/6	48°30′	89°07′
Navin	UNP/LNO	MB	20,21-10-4-E	62 H/14	49°51′	97°00′
Navy Board Inlet	BAY/BAIE	NT	Franklin	48 D	73°15′	81°00′
Navy Island	ISL/ÎLE	NB	Charlotte	21 G/3	45°04′	67°03′
Navy Island National Historic Site - also-aussi - Île-Navy, Lieu historique national de l'	PARK/PARC	ON	Welland	30 M/3	43°03′	79°01′
Nayausheeng	UNP/LNO	ON	Bruce	41 A/14	44°57′	81°02′
Nayelles Lake	LAKE/LAC	SK		64 D/5	56°20′	103°50′
Naykikoulth 13	IR/RI	BC	Kamloops Division Yale	92 I/6	50°20′	121°14′
Naylor Hills	MTN/MNT	AB	99-24-W5	84 F/12	57°37′	117°50′
Naylors Landing	UNP/LNO	NT	Mackenzie	95 H/14	61°50′	121°06′
Nazareth	UNP/LNO	QC	Rimouski-Neigette	22 C/7	48°26′	68°33′
Nazco 20	IR/RI	BC	Cariboo	93 B/13	52°57′	123°34′
Nazco 21	IR/RI	BC	Cariboo	93 B/13	52°56′	123°38′
Nazco Cemetery 20A	IR/RI	BC	Cariboo	93 B/13	52°58′	123°34′
Nazko	UNP/LNO	BC	Cariboo	93 G/4	53°00′	123°37′
Nazko River	RIV/CDE	BC	Cariboo	93 G/4	53°08′	123°34′
Ndakdolk 54	IR/RI	BC	Range 5 Coast	103 J/8	54°29′	130°12′
Neagle Lake	LAKE/LAC	SK	66,67-3-W2	63 L/16	54°46′	102°24′
Neakongut Bay	BAY/BAIE	NT	Keewatin	35 C	60°31′	77°40′
Neakunguac, Lac	LAKE/LAC	QC	Kativik	34 N/11	59°31′	77°00′
Neapolis	UNP/LNO	AB	11-31-28-W4	82 P/12	51°39′	113°52′
Necait 6	IR/RI	BC	Lillooet	92 J/9	50°42′	122°17′
Necausley Creek 6	IR/RI	BC	Cariboo	93 B/7	52°29′	122°37′
Nechako	UNP/LNO	BC	Cariboo	93 G/14	53°52′	123°01′
Nechako Centre	UNP/LNO	BC	Range 5 Coast	103 I/2	54°04′	128°38′
Nechako Reservoir	LAKE/LAC	BC	Range 4 Coast	93 E/16	53°45′	126°00′
Nechako River	RIV/CDE	BC	Cariboo	93 G/15	53°55′	122°42′
Neck Point	CAPE/CAP	BC	Wellington	92 G/4	49°14′	123°58′

NAME NOM	ENTITY ENTITÉ	LOC 1 LIEU 1	LOC 2 LIEU 2	MAP CARTE	POSITION LAT	LONG
Necoslie 1 - see-voir - Necoslie (Fort St. James) 1	IR/RI	BC		93 K/8	54°26′	124°15′
Necoslie (Fort St. James) 1	IR/RI	BC	Range 5 Coast	93 K/8	54°26′	124°15′
Necoslie River	RIV/CDE	BC	Range 5 Coast	93 K/8	54°26′	124°15′
Necum Teuch	UNP/LNO	NS	Halifax	11 D/16	44°58′	62°14′
Necum Teuch Bay	BAY/BAIE	NS	Halifax	11 D/16	44°56′	62°14′
Neddick, Cape	CAPE/CAP	NF		1 N/2	47°09′	52°51′
Neddy Harbour	UNP/LNO	NF		12 H/12	49°32′	57°53′
Nédélec	VILG/VILG	QC	Témiscamingue	31 M/11	47°41′	79°26′
Nédélec	UNP/LNO	QC	Témiscamingue	31 M/11	47°41′	79°26′
Nedlouc, Lac	LAKE/LAC	QC	Kativik	34 H/7	57°25′	72°47′
Nedluk Bay	BAY/BAIE	NT	Franklin	26 K	66°15′	68°26′
Nedlukseak Fiord	BAY/BAIE	NT	Franklin	26 O	67°55′	66°22′
Nedlunga Bay	BAY/BAIE	NT	Franklin	26 D	64°50′	71°40′
Nedoats 11	IR/RI	BC	Cassiar	93 M/1	55°03′	126°19′
Nedoats 13	IR/RI	BC	Cassiar	93 M/1	55°03′	126°22′
Neeb	UNP/LNO	SK	23-58-14-W3	73 J/4	54°01′	107°59′
Neebing	MUN2/AZM2	ON	Thunder Bay	52 A/3	48°09′	89°30′
Neebing	UNP/LNO	ON	Thunder Bay	52 A/6	48°22′	89°20′
Neebing Yard	UNP/LNO	ON	Thunder Bay	52 A/6	48°21′	89°20′
Neebish	UNP/LNO	ON	Algoma	41 K/8	46°21′	84°06′
Needa Lake	LAKE/LAC	BC	Lillooet	92 P/10	51°37′	120°43′
Needles	UNP/LNO	BC	Kootenay	82 E/16	49°52′	118°06′
Needley	UNP/LNO	BC	Peace River	94 I/4	58°14′	121°38′
Neekas 4	IR/RI	BC	Range 5 Coast	103 A/8	52°27′	128°09′
Neelby	UNP/LNO	SK	18-13-5-W2	62 L/2	50°05′	102°40′
Neelin	UNP/LNO	MB	19-3-14-W	62 G/3	49°14′	99°21′
Neely	UNP/LNO	SK	20-34-27-W2	72 P/13	51°56′	105°47′
Neely Lake	LAKE/LAC	SK	43-6-W2	63 D/10	52°43′	102°48′
Neepawa	TOWN/VIL2	MB	33-14-15-W	62 J/3	50°14′	99°28′
Neergaard Lake	LAKE/LAC	NT	Franklin	37 F	70°13′	97°58′
Neerlandia	UNP/LNO	AB	34-61-3-W5	83 J/8	54°20′	114°22′
Neerlonakto Island	ISL/ÎLE	NT	Franklin	47 D	69°29′	81°36′
Negassa Lake	LAKE/LAC	MB		64 J/16	58°45′	98°11′
Negro Harbour	BAY/BAIE	NS	Shelburne	20 P/1	43°33′	65°26′
Neguac	VILG/VILG	NB	Northumberland	21 P/3	47°15′	65°05′
Neguac Bay	BAY/BAIE	NB	Northumberland	21 P/3	47°15′	65°01′
Neguac Beach	BCH/PLAG	NB	Northumberland	21 P/3	47°15′	65°00′
Neguaguon Lake 25D	IR/RI	ON	Rainy River	52 C/8	48°23′	92°05′
Negwazu Lake	LAKE/LAC	ON	Algoma	42 C/6	48°28′	85°00′
Nehalliston Creek	RIV/CDE	BC	Kamloops Division Yale	92 P/8	51°28′	120°13′
Nehounlee Lake 13 - see-voir - Nehounlee Lake (Six Mile Lake) 13	IR/RI	BC		93 K/8	54°27′	124°05′
Nehounlee Lake (Six Mile Lake) 13	IR/RI	BC	Range 5 Coast	93 K/8	54°27′	124°05′
Neidpath	UNP/LNO	SK	1-15-10-W3	72 J/3	50°13′	107°15′
Neiges, Lac des	LAKE/LAC	QC	La Côte-de-Beaupré	21 M/6	47°28′	71°02′
Neiges, Rivière des	RIV/CDE	QC	La Côte-de-Beaupré	21 M/3	47°11′	71°06′
Neigette	UNP/LNO	QC	Rimouski-Neigette	22 C/8	48°26′	68°22′
Neigette, Grand lac	LAKE/LAC	QC	La Mitis	22 C/8	48°16′	68°10′
Neigette, Rivière	RIV/CDE	QC	La Mitis	22 C/9	48°32′	68°08′
Neighbour	UNP/LNO	SK	23-6-23-W3	72 F/6	49°29′	109°00′
Neiland Bay	BAY/BAIE	NT	Mackenzie	86 E	65°42′	119°40′
Neilburg	VILG/VILG	SK	31-44-25-W3	73 C/13	52°50′	109°38′
Neil Icecap	GLAC/GLAC	NT	Franklin	340 B	80°48′	82°43′
Neil Peninsula	CAPE/CAP	NT	Franklin	340 B	80°47′	82°50′
Neils Harbour	UNP/LNO	NS	Victoria	11 K/16	46°49′	60°19′
Neiman Lake	LAKE/LAC	SK		74 O/12	59°35′	107°51′
Nejanilini Lake	LAKE/LAC	MB		64 P/12	59°37′	97°47′
Nekalliston 2	IR/RI	BC	Kamloops Division Yale	92 P/8	51°25′	120°12′
Nekaneet 160A	IR/RI	SK		72 F/11	49°45′	109°17′
Neketawak	UNP/LNO	MB		63 H/13	53°47′	97°39′
Nekite 2	IR/RI	BC	Range 2 Coast	92 M/6	51°25′	127°05′
Nekliptum 1	IR/RI	BC	Kamloops Division Yale	92 I/4	50°07′	121°33′
Nekweaga Bay	BAY/BAIE	SK		64 E/13	57°51′	103°40′
Nelles Corners	UNP/LNO	ON	Haldimand	30 L/13	42°56′	79°57′
Nelles Estates	UNP/LNO	ON	Lincoln	30 M/4	43°11′	79°33′
Nellie Lake	UNP/LNO	ON	Cochrane	42 A/15	48°46′	80°48′
Nelson	CITY/VIL1	BC	Kootenay	82 F/6	49°30′	117°17′
Nelson	UNP/LNO	ON	Halton	30 M/5	43°23′	79°50′
Nelson	GEOG/GÉOG	NB	Northumberland	21 I/13	46°50′	65°37′
Nelson Beach	HAM/HAM	SK	29-42-26-2	73 A/12	52°39′	105°42′
Nelson, Fleuve - also-aussi - **Nelson River**	RIV/CDE	MB		54 F/2	57°04′	92°30′
Nelson Forks	UNP/LNO	BC	Peace River	94 N/8	59°30′	124°01′
Nelson Head	CAPE/CAP	NT	Franklin	97 H	71°06′	122°47′
Nelson Hill	MTN/MNT	NT	Keewatin	66 L	66°46′	102°36′
Nelson Hollow	UNP/LNO	NB	Northumberland	21 J/9	46°32′	66°11′
Nelson House	UNP/LNO	MB		63 O/15	55°47′	98°53′

NAME NOM	ENTITY ENTITÉ	LOC 1 LIEU 1	LOC 2 LIEU 2	MAP CARTE	POSITION LAT	LONG
Nelson House 170	IR/RI	MB		63 O/15	55°49'	98°53'
Nelson House 170A	IR/RI	MB		63 O/10	55°45'	98°56'
Nelson House 170B	IR/RI	MB		63 O/15	55°45'	98°52'
Nelson House 170C	IR/RI	MB		63 O/15	55°48'	98°50'
Nelson Island	ISL/ÎLE	BC	New Westminster	92 F/9	49°42'	124°08'
Nelson Junction	UNP/LNO	NB	Northumberland	21 I/13	46°57'	65°35'
Nelson Lake	LAKE/LAC	ON	Thunder Bay	52 B/7	48°27'	90°32'
Nelson Lake	LAKE/LAC	MB		63 N/16	55°46'	100°07'
Nelson Land District	GEOG/GÉOG	BC		92 F	49°34'	125°06'
Nelson-Miramichi	UNP/LNO	NB	Northumberland	21 I/13	46°58'	65°33'
Nelson Park	UNP/LNO	ON	Middlesex	40 I/14	43°00'	81°10'
Nelson, Port	BAY/BAIE	MB	92-9-E2	54 F/2	57°04'	92°30'
Nelson Range	MTN/MNT	BC	Kootenay	82 F/7	49°17'	116°58'
Nelson River - also-aussi - **Nelson, Fleuve**	RIV/CDE	MB		54 F/2	57°04'	92°30'
Nelson River	RIV/CDE	NT	Franklin	97 H	71°13'	122°28'
Nelson, Rivière	RIV/CDE	QC	Communauté urbaine de Québec	21 L/14	46°52'	71°23'
Nelway	UNP/LNO	BC	Kootenay	82 F/3	49°00'	117°17'
Nemaiah Valley	UNP/LNO	BC	Lillooet	92 O/5	51°29'	123°53'
Nemebien River 156C	IR/RI	SK		73 P/6	55°17'	105°10'
Nemegos	UNP/LNO	ON	Sudbury	41 O/11	47°43'	83°12'
Nemegosenda Lake	LAKE/LAC	ON	Sudbury	41 O/14	48°00'	83°07'
Nemegosenda River	RIV/CDE	ON	Algoma	42 B/10	48°32'	82°53'
Nemegos Lake	LAKE/LAC	ON	Sudbury	41 O/11	47°42'	83°15'
Nemeiben Lake	LAKE/LAC	SK		73 P/6	55°20'	105°20'
Némiscachingue, Lac	LAKE/LAC	QC	Antoine-Labelle	31 O/7	47°25'	74°30'
Nemiscau	VILG/VILG	QC	Jamésie	32 N/9	51°43'	76°20'
Nemiscau, Lac	LAKE/LAC	QC	Jamésie	32 N/7	51°26'	76°43'
Nemiscau, Rivière	RIV/CDE	QC	Jamésie	32 N/9	51°31'	76°24'
Nemiskam	UNP/LNO	AB	22-6-10-W4	72 E/6	49°29'	111°16'
Nenagh	UNP/LNO	ON	Grey	41 A/2	44°02'	80°51'
Néo-Écossaise, Plate-forme - also-aussi - Scotian Shelf	SEAU/SMER	—		1399A	44°00'	62°30'
Neola	UNP/LNO	SK	32-35-13-W3	73 B/4	52°02'	107°49'
Nepean	CITY/VIL1	ON	Carleton	31 G/5	45°16'	75°46'
Nepean	UNP/LNO	ON	Carleton	31 G/5	45°20'	75°52'
Nepewassi Lake	LAKE/LAC	ON	Sudbury	41 I/7	46°22'	80°38'
Nephton	UNP/LNO	ON	Peterborough	31 D/9	44°38'	78°00'
Nepisiguit Bay	BAY/BAIE	NB	Restigouche	21 P/13	47°46'	65°32'
Nepisiguit Junction	UNP/LNO	NB	Gloucester	21 P/12	47°33'	65°40'
Nepisiguit Lakes	LAKE/LAC	NB	Northumberland	21 O/7	47°23'	66°46'
Nepisiguit River	RIV/CDE	NB	Gloucester	21 P/12	47°37'	65°38'
Neptune	UNP/LNO	SK	11-5-16-W2	72 H/8	49°22'	104°04'
Neptune Bay	BAY/BAIE	NT	Franklin	26 A	64°34'	65°20'
Neptune, Lac	LAKE/LAC	QC	Jamésie	33 A/11	52°44'	73°03'
Neptune Peak	MTN/MNT	BC	Kootenay	82 M/16	51°53'	118°08'
Nequatque 1	IR/RI	BC	Lillooet	92 J/9	50°33'	122°29'
Nequatque 2	IR/RI	BC	Lillooet	92 J/9	50°32'	122°29'
Nequatque 3	IR/RI	BC	Lillooet	92 J/9	50°32'	122°29'
Nequatque 3A	IR/RI	BC	Lillooet	92 J/9	50°32'	122°29'
Nequatque 4	IR/RI	BC	Lillooet	92 J/10	50°30'	122°33'
Nerepis	UNP/LNO	NB	Kings	21 G/8	45°24'	66°18'
Nerepis River	RIV/CDE	NB	Kings	21 G/8	45°22'	66°15'
Néret, Lac	LAKE/LAC	QC	Jamésie	23 L/15	54°45'	70°44'
Neroutsos Inlet	BAY/BAIE	BC	Rupert	92 L/5	50°24'	127°31'
Nesbitt	UNP/LNO	MB	28-7-18-W	62 G/12	49°36'	99°52'
Nesikep 6	IR/RI	BC	Lillooet	92 I/12	50°33'	121°47'
Nesikep 6A	IR/RI	BC	Lillooet	92 I/12	50°34'	121°47'
Neskainlith 1 - see-voir - Neskonlith 1	IR/RI	BC		82 L/13	50°47'	119°45'
Neskainlith 2 - see-voir - Neskonlith 2	IR/RI	BC		82 L/13	50°46'	119°44'
Nesketahin	UNP/LNO	YT		115 A/3	60°08'	137°03'
Neskonlith 1	IR/RI	BC	Kamloops Division Yale	82 L/13	50°47'	119°45'
Neskonlith 2	IR/RI	BC	Kamloops Division Yale	82 L/13	50°46'	119°44'
Nesselrode, Mount	MTN/MNT	BC	Cassiar	104 L/16	58°57'	134°19'
Nesslin Lake	HAM/HAM	SK		73 G/15	53°56'	106°47'
Nesslin Lake	LAKE/LAC	SK	57-6-W3	73 G/15	53°57'	106°47'
Nestaocano, Rivière	RIV/CDE	QC	Maria-Chapdelaine	32 H/11	49°38'	73°27'
Nesters	UNP/LNO	BC	New Westminster	92 J/2	50°08'	122°57'
Nestledown	UNP/LNO	SK	12-52-5-W3	73 G/7	53°29'	106°36'
Nestleton	UNP/LNO	ON	Durham	31 D/2	44°09'	78°48'
Nestleton Station	UNP/LNO	ON	Durham	31 D/2	44°08'	78°48'
Nestor Falls	UNP/LNO	ON	Kenora	52 F/4	49°07'	93°56'
Nestorville	UNP/LNO	ON	Algoma	41 J/5	46°17'	83°36'
Nestow	UNP/LNO	AB	31-60-24-W4	83 I/4	54°14'	113°36'
Nesuch 3	IR/RI	BC	Lillooet	92 J/7	50°18'	122°38'
Nesuk 4	IR/RI	BC	Nootka	92 E/16	49°45'	126°23'
Neswabin	UNP/LNO	ON	Algoma	42 B/13	49°00'	83°58'

NAME NOM	ENTITY ENTITÉ	LOC 1 LIEU 1	LOC 2 LIEU 2	MAP CARTE	POSITION LAT	LONG
Netalzul Mountain	MTN/MNT	BC	Cassiar	93 M/7	55°17'	126°56'
Netchek, Cape	CAPE/CAP	NT	Keewatin	45 J	62°56'	83°17'
Netherby	UNP/LNO	ON	Welland	30 L/14	42°57'	79°08'
Netherhill	VILG/VILG	SK	11-29-21-W3	72 N/7	51°28'	108°52'
Netherton	UNP/LNO	SK	14-31-9-W2	62 M/11	51°41'	103°11'
Netla	UNP/LNO	NT	Mackenzie	95 B	60°57'	123°16'
Netley	UNP/LNO	MB	10-16-4-E	62 I/7	50°22'	96°57'
Netley Lake	LAKE/LAC	MB		62 I/7	50°19'	96°52'
Netook	UNP/LNO	AB	34-33-1-W5	82 O/16	51°53'	114°03'
Ne-tsaw-greece 10	IR/RI	BC	Cassiar	93 M/1	55°04'	126°29'
Netsilik Lake	LAKE/LAC	NT	Keewatin	57 C	69°15'	93°05'
Netson Creek	RIV/CDE	BC	Cassiar	94 L/15	59°00'	126°52'
Nettell Lake	LAKE/LAC	SK		74 N/13	59°57'	109°32'
Nettichi River	RIV/CDE	ON	Cochrane	43 A/3	52°06'	81°22'
Nettilling Fiord	BAY/BAIE	NT	Franklin	26 K	66°02'	68°12'
Nettilling Lake	LAKE/LAC	NT	Franklin	26 L	66°29'	70°20'
Nettle Island	ISL/ÎLE	BC	Barclay	92 C/14	48°56'	125°15'
Nettle Island 5	IR/RI	BC	Barclay	92 C/14	48°56'	125°14'
Neuanlage	HAM/HAM	SK	23-40-4-W3	73 B/8	52°27'	106°28'
Neubergthal	UNP/LNO	MB	25,26,35,36-1-1-W1	62 H/3	49°04'	97°29'
Neudorf	VILG/VILG	SK	14-20-8-W2	62 L/11	50°43'	103°01'
Neuenburg	UNP/LNO	MB	34,35-1-4-W1	62 H/4	49°05'	97°54'
Neuf Milles, Lac des	LAKE/LAC	QC	Pontiac	31 N/3	47°05'	77°10'
Neuhoffnung	UNP/LNO	SK	35-12-14-W3	72 J/4	50°03'	107°49'
Neuhorst	HAM/HAM	SK	31-39-4-W3	73 B/7	52°24'	106°35'
Neuhorst	UNP/LNO	MB	1-1-3-W	62 H/4	49°00'	97°44'
Neustadt	VILG/VILG	ON	Grey	41 A/2	44°05'	81°00'
Neutral Hills	UNP/LNO	AB	28-37-7-W4	73 D/2	52°14'	110°57'
Neutral Valley	UNP/LNO	AB	32-36-6-W4	73 D/2	52°08'	110°48'
Neuville	TOWN/VIL2	QC	Portneuf	21 L/12	46°42'	71°35'
Nevada Valley	UNP/LNO	NS	Inverness	11 K/3	46°03'	61°16'
Nevers Brook	RIV/CDE	NB	Westmorland	21 I/3	46°05'	65°19'
Nevertouch Lake	LAKE/LAC	BC	Similkameen Division Yale	82 E/15	49°47'	118°46'
Neveton	UNP/LNO	MB	27-19-2-W	62 I/12	50°40'	97°40'
Nevill Bay	BAY/BAIE	NT	Keewatin	55 K	61°59'	93°14'
Neville	VILG/VILG	SK	6-12-12-W3	72 G/13	49°58'	107°38'
Neville, Port	BAY/BAIE	BC	Range 1 Coast	92 L/8	50°30'	126°00'
Nevins Lake	LAKE/LAC	SK		74 O/12	59°32'	107°50'
Nevis	UNP/LNO	AB	1-39-22-W4	83 A/6	52°20'	113°01'
Nevis Junction	UNP/LNO	AB	31-38-21-W4	83 A/6	52°18'	113°01'
New Aberdeen	UNP/LNO	NS	Cape Breton	11 J/4	46°13'	59°58'
New Acadia	UNP/LNO	PE	Kings	11 L/8	46°24'	62°24'
New Aiyansh	UNP/LNO	BC	Cassiar	103 P/3	55°12'	129°05'
New Aiyansh 1	IR/RI	BC	Cassiar	103 P/3	55°12'	129°05'
New Albany	UNP/LNO	NS	Annapolis	21 A/14	44°49'	65°04'
New Albany	UNP/LNO	NS	Annapolis	21 A/6	44°27'	65°05'
New Annan	UNP/LNO	PE	Prince	11 L/5	46°25'	63°43'
New Argyle	UNP/LNO	PE	Queens	11 L/3	46°10'	63°19'
Newark	UNP/LNO	ON	Oxford	40 I/15	42°58'	80°42'
New Avon	UNP/LNO	NB	Sunbury	21 J/1	46°04'	66°06'
Newaygo	UNP/LNO	QC	Les Pays-d'en-Haut	31 G/16	45°53'	74°21'
New Bandon	UNP/LNO	NB	Gloucester	21 P/14	47°45'	65°19'
New Bandon	UNP/LNO	NB	Northumberland	21 J/8	46°30'	66°16'
New Bandon	GEOG/GÉOG	NB	Gloucester	21 P/11	47°42'	65°15'
New Bay	BAY/BAIE	NF		2 E/11	49°30'	55°22'
New Bay Head	CAPE/CAP	NF		2 E/11	49°32'	55°20'
New Bay Pond	LAKE/LAC	NF		2 E/4	49°10'	55°34'
New Bay River	RIV/CDE	NF		2 E/6	49°19'	55°24'
New Bella Bella	UNP/LNO	BC	Range 3 Coast	103 A/1	52°10'	128°09'
New Bercthal - see-voir - **Neubergthal**	UNP/LNO	MB		62 H/3	49°04'	97°29'
Newbliss	UNP/LNO	ON	Leeds	31 B/13	44°48'	75°58'
New Bonaventure	UNP/LNO	NF		2 C/6	48°17'	53°27'
Newboro'	VILG/VILG	ON	Leeds	31 C/9	44°39'	76°19'
Newboro Lake	LAKE/LAC	ON	Leeds	31 C/9	44°38'	76°20'
New Boston	UNP/LNO	NS	Cape Breton	11 F/16	45°58'	60°04'
New Bothwell	UNP/LNO	MB	19,29,30-7-5-E	62 H/10	49°35'	96°53'
Newboyne	UNP/LNO	ON	Leeds	31 C/9	44°44'	76°07'
New Bridge	UNP/LNO	NF		1 N/3	47°08'	53°28'
Newbridge	UNP/LNO	NB	Carleton	21 J/4	46°10'	67°30'
Newbridge	UNP/LNO	ON	Huron	40 P/15	43°51'	80°58'
New Brigden	UNP/LNO	AB	34-31-4-W4	72 M/9	51°42'	110°29'
New Brighton	UNP/LNO	BC	New Westminster	92 G/6	49°27'	123°26'
New Britain	UNP/LNO	NS	Colchester	21 H/8	45°27'	64°02'
Newbrook	UNP/LNO	AB	5-62-20-W4	83 I/7	54°19'	112°57'
New Brunswick - also-aussi - **Nouveau-Brunswick**	PROV/PROV	NB		MCR77	46°30'	66°00'

NAME / NOM	ENTITY / ENTITÉ	LOC 1 / LIEU 1	LOC 2 / LIEU 2	MAP / CARTE	LAT	LONG
Newburg	UNP/LNO	NB	Carleton	21 J/3	46°11′	67°30′
Newburgh	VILG/VILG	ON	Lennox and Addington	31 C/7	44°19′	76°52′
Newburg Junction	UNP/LNO	NB	Carleton	21 J/4	46°11′	67°32′
Newburne	UNP/LNO	NS	Lunenburg	21 A/10	44°36′	64°36′
New Burnt Cove	UNP/LNO	NF		2 C/4	48°11′	53°43′
Newbury	VILG/VILG	ON	Middlesex	40 I/12	42°41′	81°48′
Newbury Station	UNP/LNO	ON	Middlesex	40 I/12	42°41′	81°50′
Newby	UNP/LNO	SK	14-44-22-W3	73 C/14	52°47′	109°06′
New California	UNP/LNO	ON	Essex	40 J/2	42°02′	82°47′
New Campbellton	UNP/LNO	NS	Victoria	11 K/8	46°17′	60°25′
New Canaan	UNP/LNO	NS	Cumberland	21 H/9	45°31′	64°16′
New Canaan	UNP/LNO	NB	Queens	21 I/3	46°05′	65°26′
New Canaan	UNP/LNO	ON	Essex	40 J/2	42°07′	82°57′
New Canada	UNP/LNO	NS	Lunenburg	21 A/7	44°29′	64°41′
New Carlisle	VILG/VILG	QC	Bonaventure	22 A/3	48°01′	65°20′
New Carlisle East	UNP/LNO	QC	Bonaventure	22 A/3	48°01′	65°18′
New Carlisle West	UNP/LNO	QC	Bonaventure	22 A/3	48°00′	65°24′
New Carlow	UNP/LNO	ON	Hastings	31 F/5	45°15′	77°44′
Newcastle - see-voir - Clarington	TOWN/VIL2	ON		30 M/15	43°55′	78°35′
Newcastle	UNP/LNO	NB	Northumberland	21 P/4	47°00′	65°34′
Newcastle	UNP/LNO	BC	Nanaimo	92 G/4	49°11′	123°56′
Newcastle	GEOG/GÉOG	NB	Northumberland	21 P/4	47°10′	65°35′
Newcastle Bridge	UNP/LNO	NB	Queens	21 J/1	46°05′	66°03′
Newcastle Centre	UNP/LNO	NB	Queens	21 I/4	46°05′	65°59′
Newcastle Creek	UNP/LNO	NB	Queens	21 J/1	46°04′	66°01′
Newcastle Creek	RIV/CDE	NB	Queens	21 I/4	46°05′	66°00′
Newcastle Island	ISL/ÎLE	BC	Nanaimo	92 G/4	49°11′	123°56′
Newcastle Land District	GEOG/GÉOG	BC		92 F	49°27′	124°49′
Newcastle Mine	UNP/LNO	AB	10-29-20-W4	82 P/7	51°28′	112°46′
Newcastle Village	UNP/LNO	ON	Durham	30 M/15	43°55′	78°35′
New Chelsea	UNP/LNO	NF		2 C/3	48°02′	53°13′
New Chelsea-New Melbourne-Brownsdale-Sibley's Cove-Lead Cove	UNP/LNO	NF		2 C/3	48°02′	53°10′
New Chester	UNP/LNO	NS	Guysborough	11 E/1	45°02′	62°13′
New Clew	UNP/LNO	BC	Queen Charlotte	103 G/4	53°02′	131°47′
New Clew 10	IR/RI	BC	Queen Charlotte	103 G/4	53°02′	131°47′
Newcomb Corner	UNP/LNO	NS	Halifax	11 E/3	45°04′	63°03′
Newcombe Lake	LAKE/LAC	BC	Range 4 Coast	93 E/14	53°58′	127°11′
Newcombe No. 260	MUN2/AZM2	SK		72 N/3	51°10′	109°10′
Newcombville	UNP/LNO	NS	Lunenburg	21 A/7	44°23′	64°37′
New Country Siding	UNP/LNO	NF		2 C/5	48°21′	53°44′
New Credit	UNP/LNO	ON	Brant	40 I/16	43°00′	80°06′
New Credit 40A	IR/RI	ON	Brant	40 P/1	43°00′	80°05′
Newcross	UNP/LNO	SK	10-36-5-W3	73 B/2	52°04′	106°37′
New Cumberland	UNP/LNO	NS	Lunenburg	21 A/8	44°17′	64°27′
New Currie	UNP/LNO	SK		72 I/5	50°23′	105°34′
Newdale	UNP/LNO	MB	8-16-20-W	62 K/8	50°21′	100°12′
New Dayton	UNP/LNO	AB	33-5-18-W4	82 H/8	49°25′	112°23′
New Denmark	UNP/LNO	NB	Victoria	21 J/13	46°59′	67°36′
New Denmark Corner	UNP/LNO	NB	Victoria	21 J/13	46°57′	67°39′
New Denmark Station	UNP/LNO	NB	Victoria	21 J/13	47°00′	67°35′
New Denver	VILG/VILG	BC	Kootenay	82 F/14	50°00′	117°22′
New Dominion	UNP/LNO	PE	Queens	11 L/3	46°11′	63°14′
New Dominion	UNP/LNO	NS	Cape Breton	11 K/8	46°15′	60°25′
New Dublin	UNP/LNO	ON	Leeds	31 B/12	44°40′	75°48′
New Dundee	UNP/LNO	ON	Waterloo	40 P/7	43°21′	80°31′
New Durham	UNP/LNO	ON	Brant	40 P/2	43°03′	80°34′
New Edinburgh	UNP/LNO	NS	Digby	21 B/8	44°26′	66°01′
Newell, Lake	LAKE/LAC	AB	17-15-W4	72 L/5	50°26′	111°55′
Newell No. 4, County of	MUN1/AZM1	AB	19-15-W4	72 L/12	50°37′	111°57′
Newell Sound	CHAN/CHEN	NT	Franklin	25 O	63°06′	67°53′
Newellton	UNP/LNO	NS	Shelburne	20 P/5	43°28′	65°38′
New Elm	UNP/LNO	NS	Lunenburg	21 A/7	44°24′	64°50′
New England	UNP/LNO	SK	13,14-47A-24-W2	73 H/3	53°03′	105°24′
New England Seamount Chain - also-aussi - Nouvelle-Angleterre, Chaîne de monts de la	SEAU/SMER	—		4006	38°00′	61°00′
New England Settlement	UNP/LNO	NB	Sunbury	21 J/1	46°05′	66°06′
New Ferolle	UNP/LNO	NF		12 P/3	51°01′	57°04′
New Ferolle Peninsula	CAPE/CAP	NF		12 P/3	51°02′	57°05′
New Fish Creek	UNP/LNO	AB	12-73-22-W5	83 N/6	55°18′	117°15′
New Flos	UNP/LNO	ON	Simcoe	31 D/5	44°28′	79°57′
Newfoundland - also-aussi - **Terre-Neuve**	PROV/PROV	NF		MCR77	53°00′	60°00′
Newfoundland Basin - also-aussi - Terre-Neuve, Bassin de	SEAU/SMER	—		802	43°30′	45°00′
Newfoundland Dog Pond	LAKE/LAC	NF		2 D/5	48°16′	55°56′

NAME NOM	ENTITY ENTITÉ	LOC 1 LIEU 1	LOC 2 LIEU 2	MAP CARTE	POSITION	
					LAT	LONG
Newfoundland Ridge - also-aussi - Terre-Neuve, Dorsale de	SEAU/SMER	—		800A	41°30′	49°30′
Newfoundland Seamounts - also-aussi - Terre-Neuve, Chaîne de monts de	SEAU/SMER	—		4001	43°50′	45°00′
Newfoundland Shelf - also-aussi - Terre-Neuve, Plate-forme de	SEAU/SMER	—		802	50°00′	47°00′
Newfoundout	UNP/LNO	ON	Renfrew	31 F/6	45°23′	77°06′
New France	UNP/LNO	NS	Antigonish	11 F/12	45°33′	61°44′
New France	UNP/LNO	NS	Digby	21 A/5	44°19′	65°46′
New Gairloch	UNP/LNO	NS	Pictou	11 E/7	45°29′	62°50′
New Gamebridge Beach	UNP/LNO	ON	Ontario	31 D/11	44°30′	79°12′
Newgate	UNP/LNO	BC	Kootenay	82 G/3	49°02′	115°12′
New Germany	UNP/LNO	NS	Lunenburg	21 A/10	44°33′	64°43′
New Gitsegukla 2	IR/RI	BC	Cassiar	93 M/4	55°10′	127°47′
New Glasgow	TOWN/VIL2	NS	Pictou	11 E/10	45°35′	62°39′
New Glasgow	TOWN/VIL2	QC	La Rivière-du-Nord	31 H/13	45°50′	73°53′
New Glasgow	UNP/LNO	PE	Queens	11 L/6	46°25′	63°21′
New Glasgow	UNP/LNO	ON	Elgin	40 I/12	42°31′	81°38′
New Glasgow Mills	UNP/LNO	PE	Queens	11 L/6	46°26′	63°21′
New Glen	UNP/LNO	NS	Victoria	11 K/2	46°13′	60°46′
New Grafton	UNP/LNO	NS	Queens	21 A/6	44°25′	65°11′
New Hamburg	UNP/LNO	ON	Waterloo	40 P/7	43°23′	80°42′
New Harbour	UNP/LNO	NF		1 N/12	47°35′	53°32′
New Harbour	UNP/LNO	NF		1 M/10	47°36′	54°58′
New Harbour	UNP/LNO	NF		11 P/10	47°36′	56°39′
New Harbour	UNP/LNO	NS	Guysborough	11 F/3	45°10′	61°28′
New Harbour	UNP/LNO	NS	Lunenburg	21 A/8	44°28′	64°05′
New Harbour Cove	BAY/BAIE	NS	Guysborough	11 F/3	45°10′	61°27′
New Harbour East	UNP/LNO	NS	Guysborough	11 F/3	45°12′	61°30′
New Harbour Head	CAPE/CAP	NS	Guysborough	11 F/3	45°09′	61°28′
New Harbour River	RIV/CDE	NS	Guysborough	11 F/3	45°11′	61°28′
New Harbour West	UNP/LNO	NS	Guysborough	11 F/3	45°12′	61°29′
New Harmony	UNP/LNO	PE	Kings	11 L/8	46°25′	62°14′
New Harris Forks	UNP/LNO	NS	Victoria	11 K/8	46°15′	60°30′
New Harris Settlement	UNP/LNO	NS	Victoria	11 K/1	46°15′	60°30′
New Haven	UNP/LNO	PE	Queens	11 L/3	46°13′	63°18′
New Haven	UNP/LNO	NS	Victoria	11 K/16	46°49′	60°20′
New Haven-Riverdale	VILG/VILG	PE	Queens	11 L/3	46°13′	63°20′
New Hazelton	MUN1/AZM1	BC	Cassiar	93 M/4	55°15′	127°35′
Newholm	UNP/LNO	ON	Muskoka	31 E/3	45°14′	79°09′
New Horton	UNP/LNO	NB	Albert	21 H/10	45°40′	64°44′
Newington	UNP/LNO	ON	Stormont	31 G/3	45°07′	75°01′
New Ireland	UNP/LNO	QC	L'Amiante	21 L/4	46°06′	71°31′
New Jersey	UNP/LNO	NB	Northumberland	21 P/3	47°12′	65°11′
New Kitseguecla 2 - see-voir - New Gitsegukla 2	IR/RI	BC		93 M/4	55°10′	127°47′
New Lairg	UNP/LNO	NS	Pictou	11 E/7	45°27′	62°49′
New Lake	LAKE/LAC	NT	Mackenzie	75 K	62°41′	109°28′
Newlands	UNP/LNO	BC	Cariboo	93 J/1	54°06′	122°12′
New Line Road	UNP/LNO	NB	Kings	21 H/11	45°40′	65°29′
New Liskeard	TOWN/VIL2	ON	Timiskaming	31 M/12	47°30′	79°40′
New Lismore	UNP/LNO	QC	La Vallée-de-la-Gatineau	31 K/1	46°13′	76°02′
New London	UNP/LNO	PE	Queens	11 L/5	46°28′	63°31′
New London	UNP/LNO	QC	Le Val-Saint-François	31 H/9	45°39′	72°05′
New London Bay	BAY/BAIE	PE	Queens	11 L/6	46°30′	63°27′
New Lowell	UNP/LNO	ON	Simcoe	31 D/5	44°22′	79°57′
New Lunnon	UNP/LNO	AB	27-55-23-W4	83 H/14	53°47′	113°20′
Newman's Beach	UNP/LNO	ON	Victoria	31 D/2	44°13′	78°52′
Newmans Cove	UNP/LNO	NF		2 C/11	48°35′	53°12′
Newman Smith, Cape	CAPE/CAP	NT	Franklin	48 G	75°40′	85°05′
Newman Sound	BAY/BAIE	NF		2 C/12	48°36′	53°47′
Newmanville	UNP/LNO	ON	Grenville	31 B/13	44°56′	75°46′
Newmarket	TOWN/VIL2	ON	York	31 D/3	44°03′	79°28′
Newmarket	UNP/LNO	NB	York	21 G/15	45°50′	66°56′
New Maryland	VILG/VILG	NB	York	21 G/15	45°53′	66°41′
New Maryland	GEOG/GÉOG	NB	York	21 G/10	45°43′	66°50′
New Melbourne	UNP/LNO	NF		2 C/3	48°03′	53°09′
New Melbourne-Brownsdale-Sibley's Cove-Lead Cove - see-voir - New Chelsea-New Melbourne-Brownsdale-Sibley's Cove-Lead Cove	UNP/LNO	NF		2 C/3	48°02′	53°10′
New Mexico	UNP/LNO	QC	Le Haut-Saint-François	21 E/6	45°21′	71°27′
New Mills	UNP/LNO	NB	Restigouche	21 O/16	47°58′	66°11′
New Minas	VILG/VILG	NS	Kings	21 H/1	45°04′	64°27′
New, Mount	MTN/MNT	BC	Cassiar	94 L/1	58°15′	126°26′
Newnes	UNP/LNO	SK	35-8-15-W	62 E/12	49°42′	103°57′
Newnham Bay	BAY/BAIE	ON	Cochrane	42 I/8	50°16′	80°11′
New Norway	VILG/VILG	AB	11-45-21-W4	83 A/15	52°52′	112°57′
New Osgoode	UNP/LNO	SK	22-46-13-W2	63 D/13	52°59′	103°48′

NAME / NOM	ENTITY / ENTITÉ	LOC 1 / LIEU 1	LOC 2 / LIEU 2	MAP / CARTE	LAT	LONG
New Osnaburgh	UNP/LNO	ON	Kenora	52 O/1	51°14′	90°14′
New Park	UNP/LNO	ON	Durham	31 D/2	44°04′	78°41′
New Perlican	TOWN/VIL2	NF		1 N/14	47°54′	53°21′
New Perth	UNP/LNO	PE	Kings	11 L/2	46°13′	62°42′
Newport	VILG/VILG	QC	Pabok	22 A/7	48°16′	64°45′
Newport	VILG/VILG	QC	Le Haut-Saint-François	21 E/6	45°23′	71°27′
Newport	UNP/LNO	NF		2 F/4	49°03′	53°38′
Newport	UNP/LNO	PE	Kings	11 L/2	46°13′	62°32′
Newport	UNP/LNO	ON	Brant	40 P/1	43°06′	80°14′
Newport Centre	UNP/LNO	QC	Pabok	22 A/7	48°16′	64°45′
Newport Corner	UNP/LNO	NS	Hants	11 D/13	44°58′	63°58′
Newport Landing	UNP/LNO	NS	Hants	21 H/1	45°01′	64°08′
Newport-Ouest	UNP/LNO	QC	Pabok	22 A/2	48°14′	64°46′
Newport Point	UNP/LNO	QC	Pabok	22 A/7	48°17′	64°43′
Newport, Pointe de	CAPE/CAP	QC	Pabok	22 A/7	48°17′	64°43′
Newport Station	UNP/LNO	NS	Hants	21 A/16	44°58′	64°04′
New Post 69	IR/RI	ON	Cochrane	42 H/14	49°52′	81°22′
New Prospect	UNP/LNO	NS	Cumberland	21 H/8	45°26′	64°16′
New Prussia	UNP/LNO	ON	Waterloo	40 P/7	43°27′	80°45′
New Richmond	CITY/VIL1	QC	Bonaventure	22 A/4	48°10′	65°52′
New Richmond Centre	UNP/LNO	QC	Bonaventure	22 A/4	48°10′	65°51′
New Richmond Station	UNP/LNO	QC	Bonaventure	22 A/4	48°10′	65°51′
New Richmond West	UNP/LNO	QC	Bonaventure	22 A/4	48°11′	65°54′
New River	UNP/LNO	NB	Charlotte	21 G/2	45°11′	66°33′
New River	RIV/CDE	NB	Charlotte	21 G/2	45°08′	66°33′
New River Beach	UNP/LNO	NB	Charlotte	21 G/2	45°08′	66°32′
New Rosa	UNP/LNO	MB	27,28-3-5-E	62 H/2	49°14′	96°51′
New Ross	UNP/LNO	NS	Lunenburg	21 A/9	44°44′	64°27′
New Ross 20	IR/RI	NS	Lunenburg	21 A/16	44°51′	64°25′
New Russel - see-voir - New Russell	UNP/LNO	NS		21 A/16	44°46′	64°25′
New Russell	UNP/LNO	NS	Lunenburg	21 A/16	44°46′	16°25′
Newry	UNP/LNO	ON	Perth	40 P/11	43°39′	81°02′
New Salem	UNP/LNO	NS	Cumberland	21 H/7	45°25′	64°47′
New Sarepta	VILG/VILG	AB	34-49-22-W4	83 H/6	53°16′	113°08′
New Sarum	UNP/LNO	ON	Elgin	40 I/14	42°46′	81°05′
New Scotland	UNP/LNO	NB	Westmorland	21 I/2	46°14′	64°57′
New Scotland	UNP/LNO	ON	York	30 M/13	43°57′	79°37′
New Scotland	UNP/LNO	ON	Kent	40 I/5	42°21′	81°53′
New Settlement	UNP/LNO	BC	Kootenay	82 F/5	49°25′	117°37′
New Songhees 1A	IR/RI	BC	Esquimalt	92 B/6	48°27′	123°25′
Newstead	UNP/LNO	MB	5-8-20-W	62 F/9	49°37′	100°09′
New Sudbury	UNP/LNO	ON	Sudbury	41 I/10	46°33′	80°57′
New Tecumseth	TOWN/VIL2	ON	Simcoe	31 D/4	44°05′	79°46′
New Thunderchild 115B	IR/RI	SK		73 F/7	53°30′	108°50′
New Thunderchild 115C	IR/RI	SK		73 F/10	53°36′	108°36′
Newton	UNP/LNO	NF		1 N/10	47°39′	52°44′
Newton	UNP/LNO	PE	Prince	11 L/5	46°20′	63°35′
Newton	UNP/LNO	ON	Perth	40 P/10	43°35′	80°53′
Newton	UNP/LNO	MB	15-11-5-W	62 G/16	49°56′	98°05′
Newton	UNP/LNO	BC	New Westminster	92 G/2	49°08′	122°51′
Newton Brook	UNP/LNO	ON	York	30 M/14	43°47′	79°25′
Newton Fiord	BAY/BAIE	NT	Franklin	25 O	63°05′	66°10′
Newton Lake	LAKE/LAC	NF		2 D/6	48°26′	55°01′
Newton Lake	LAKE/LAC	SK	4-14-W3	72 G/5	49°19′	107°49′
Newton Mills	UNP/LNO	NS	Colchester	11 E/2	45°14′	62°55′
Newton Robinson	UNP/LNO	ON	Simcoe	31 D/4	44°08′	79°41′
Newtonville	UNP/LNO	NS	Kings	21 H/1	45°02′	64°23′
Newtonville	UNP/LNO	ON	Durham	30 M/16	43°56′	78°30′
New Toronto	UNP/LNO	ON	York	30 M/12	43°36′	79°30′
Newtown	UNP/LNO	NF		1 N/6	47°22′	53°11′
*Newtown	UNP/LNO	NF		2 F/4	49°12′	53°31′
Newtown	UNP/LNO	NS	Guysborough	11 E/8	45°22′	62°08′
Newtown	UNP/LNO	NB	Kings	21 H/14	45°50′	65°27′
Newtown Cross	UNP/LNO	PE	Queens	11 L/2	46°08′	62°49′
New Truro Road	UNP/LNO	NS	Colchester	11 E/11	45°40′	63°17′
New Tusket	UNP/LNO	NS	Digby	21 A/5	44°17′	65°54′
New Uhthoff	UNP/LNO	ON	Simcoe	31 D/11	44°41′	79°29′
New Victoria	UNP/LNO	NS	Cape Breton	11 K/1	46°15′	60°08′
Newville	UNP/LNO	NF		2 E/10	49°35′	54°41′
New Wasaga Beach	UNP/LNO	ON	Simcoe	31 D/12	44°34′	80°00′
New Waterford	UNP/LNO	NS	Cape Breton	11 K/1	46°15′	60°05′
New Westminster	CITY/VIL1	BC	New Westminster	92 G/2	49°13′	122°55′
New Westminster Land District	GEOG/GÉOG	BC		92 G	49°44′	123°05′
New-Wes-Valley	TOWN/VIL2	NF		2 F/4	49°09′	53°34′
New World Island	ISL/ÎLE	NF		2 E/10	49°35′	54°40′

NAME NOM	ENTITY ENTITÉ	LOC 1 LIEU 1	LOC 2 LIEU 2	MAP CARTE	POSITION LAT	POSITION LONG
New Yarmouth	UNP/LNO	NS	Cumberland	21 H/7	45°23′	64°50′
New Zealand	UNP/LNO	PE	Kings	11 L/8	46°25′	62°19′
New Zion	UNP/LNO	NB	Sunbury	21 J/1	46°03′	66°06′
Neyaashiinigmiing 27	IR/RI	ON	Bruce	41 A/14	44°55′	81°02′
Ney Harbour	BAY/BAIE	NT	Franklin	25 J	62°52′	67°15′
Ney Lake	LAKE/LAC	ON/MB		53 K/9	54°37′	92°20′
Neys	UNP/LNO	ON	Thunder Bay	42 D/15	48°47′	86°35′
Nezah	UNP/LNO	ON	Thunder Bay	42 E/12	49°40′	87°39′
Nez Croche, Lac	LAKE/LAC	NT	Mackenzie	75 M	63°15′	111°25′
Niagara	MUN1/AZM1	ON	Welland	30 M/3	43°00′	79°15′
Niagara	UNP/LNO	BC	Similkameen Division Yale	82 E/1	49°06′	118°28′
Niagara, Chutes - also-aussi - **Niagara Falls**	FALL/CHUT	ON	Welland	30 M/3	43°05′	79°04′
Niagara Creek	RIV/CDE	BC	Cariboo	93 A/9	52°36′	120°26′
Niagara Escarpment	CLF/ESC	ON	Grey	30 M/13	43°50′	80°00′
Niagara Falls	CITY/VIL1	ON	Welland	30 M/3	43°06′	79°04′
Niagara Falls - also-aussi - **Niagara, Chutes**	FALL/CHUT	ON	Welland	30 M/3	43°05′	79°04′
Niagara Falls Centre	UNP/LNO	ON	Welland	30 M/3	43°06′	79°04′
Niagara Falls South	UNP/LNO	ON	Welland	30 M/3	43°05′	79°06′
Niagara Gardens	UNP/LNO	ON	Lincoln	30 M/3	43°09′	79°13′
Niagara-on-the-Lake	TOWN/VIL2	ON	Lincoln	30 M/3	43°15′	79°04′
Niagara Peninsula	CAPE/CAP	ON	Welland	30 M/3	43°01′	79°21′
Niagara River	RIV/CDE	ON	Lincoln	30 M/6	43°16′	79°03′
Niakwa Park	UNP/LNO	MB		62 H/14	49°52′	97°05′
Niakwa Place	UNP/LNO	MB		62 H/14	49°51′	97°05′
Nias Island	ISL/ÎLE	NT	Keewatin	46 F	65°32′	84°38′
Nias Point	CAPE/CAP	NT	Franklin	78 G	75°35′	110°26′
Niblock	UNP/LNO	ON	Thunder Bay	52 G/2	49°06′	90°42′
Nicabau, Lac	LAKE/LAC	QC	Le Domaine-du-Roy	32 G/8	49°23′	74°08′
Nicabong	UNP/LNO	QC	Pontiac	31 F/14	45°58′	77°08′
Nicette, Lac	LAKE/LAC	QC	La Haute-Côte-Nord	22 C/14	48°57′	69°20′
Nichcotéa, Lac	LAKE/LAC	QC	Vallée-de-l'Or	31 N/3	47°09′	77°03′
Nichicun, Lac	LAKE/LAC	QC	Jamésie	23 E/3	53°05′	71°00′
Nichol	MUN2/AZM2	ON	Wellington	40 P/9	43°40′	80°21′
Nichol	UNP/LNO	BC	Cariboo	93 G/14	53°55′	123°13′
Nicholas Denys	UNP/LNO	NB	Gloucester	21 P/12	47°42′	65°53′
Nichols	UNP/LNO	BC	Cariboo	93 G/15	53°58′	122°42′
Nichols Creek	RIV/CDE	BC	Lillooet	92 J/14	50°51′	123°18′
Nicholson	UNP/LNO	ON	Sudbury	41 O/13	47°57′	83°46′
Nicholson	UNP/LNO	BC	Kootenay	82 N/2	51°15′	116°54′
Nicholson Island	ISL/ÎLE	ON	Prince Edward	30 N/13	43°55′	77°32′
Nicholson Island	ISL/ÎLE	NT	Keewatin	34 F	57°14′	76°45′
Nicholson Island	ISL/ÎLE	NT	Franklin	107 D	69°54′	128°59′
Nicholson Lake	LAKE/LAC	NT	Mackenzie	65 L	62°41′	102°40′
Nicholsons Point	UNP/LNO	ON	Lennox and Addington	31 C/2	44°12′	76°41′
Nicholsville	UNP/LNO	NF		12 H/3	49°11′	57°27′
Nicholsville	UNP/LNO	NS	Kings	21 A/15	44°59′	64°48′
Nickel Centre	TOWN/VIL2	ON	Sudbury	41 I/10	46°34′	80°49′
Nickeldale	UNP/LNO	ON	Sudbury	41 I/10	46°31′	80°59′
Nickel Lake	UNP/LNO	ON	Rainy River	52 C/11	48°42′	93°05′
Nickel Palm 4	IR/RI	BC	Kamloops Division Yale	92 I/5	50°27′	121°42′
Nickel Plate Lake	LAKE/LAC	BC	Similkameen Division Yale	82 E/5	49°25′	119°58′
Nickerson, Banc	SEAU/SMER	—		802	46°26′	53°20′
Nickerson Bank	SEAU/SMER	—		4817	46°26′	53°20′
Nickeyeah 25	IR/RI	BC	Kamloops Division Yale	92 I/4	50°12′	121°35′
Nickey's Nose Cove	UNP/LNO	NF		2 E/12	49°42′	55°57′
Nicklen	UNP/LNO	SK	31-47-14-W2	73 H/1	53°06′	104°02′
Nicklin Lake	LAKE/LAC	MB		64 J/13	58°51′	99°48′
Nickoll Passage	CHAN/CHEN	BC	Range 1 Coast	92 L/9	50°40′	126°14′
Nick Power Cove	BAY/BAIE	NF		11 P/10	47°33′	56°46′
Nicoamen River	RIV/CDE	BC	Kamloops Division Yale	92 I/6	50°16′	121°24′
Nicobi, Lac	LAKE/LAC	QC	Jamésie	32 F/8	49°21′	76°00′
Nicoelton 6	IR/RI	BC	Kamloops Division Yale	92 I/6	50°30′	121°23′
Nicola	UNP/LNO	BC	Kamloops Division Yale	92 I/2	50°10′	120°40′
Nicola Lake	LAKE/LAC	BC	Kamloops Division Yale	92 I/2	50°10′	120°32′
Nicola Lake 1	IR/RI	BC	Kamloops Division Yale	92 I/1	50°13′	120°27′
Nicol-Albert, Mont	MTN/MNT	QC	Matane	22 B/15	48°50′	66°46′
Nicola Mameet 1	IR/RI	BC	Kamloops Division Yale	92 I/2	50°10′	120°50′
Nicola River	RIV/CDE	BC	Kamloops Division Yale	92 I/6	50°26′	121°19′
Nicolay, Mount	MTN/MNT	NT	Franklin	59 C	77°47′	94°51′
Nicolet	CITY/VIL1	QC	Nicolet-Yamaska	31 I/2	46°13′	72°37′
Nicolet, Lac	LAKE/LAC	QC	Arthabaska	21 E/13	45°50′	71°33′
Nicolet, Rivière	RIV/CDE	QC	Nicolet-Yamaska	31 I/7	46°15′	72°39′
Nicolet-Sud	VILG/VILG	QC	Nicolet-Yamaska	31 I/2	46°13′	72°36′
Nicolet Sud-Ouest, Rivière	RIV/CDE	QC	Nicolet-Yamaska	31 I/2	46°13′	72°36′
Nicolet-Yamaska	MUN1/AZM1	QC	Nicolet-Yamaska	31 I/2	46°04′	72°50′

NAME / NOM	ENTITY / ENTITÉ	LOC 1 / LIEU 1	LOC 2 / LIEU 2	MAP / CARTE	POSITION LAT	POSITION LONG
Nicol Lake	LAKE/LAC	NT	Keewatin	65 E	61°37'	103°28'
Nicolston	UNP/LNO	ON	Simcoe	31 D/4	44°10'	79°49'
Nicomekl River	RIV/CDE	BC	New Westminster	92 G/2	49°04'	122°52'
Nicomen	UNP/LNO	BC	New Westminster	92 G/1	49°11'	122°07'
Nicomen 1	IR/RI	BC	Kamloops Division Yale	92 I/6	50°16'	121°24'
Nicomen Island	ISL/ÎLE	BC	New Westminster	92 G/1	49°10'	122°07'
Nictau	UNP/LNO	NB	Victoria	21 O/3	47°14'	67°09'
Nictau Lake	LAKE/LAC	NB	Restigouche	21 O/7	47°25'	66°53'
Nictaux	UNP/LNO	NS	Annapolis	21 A/14	44°56'	65°03'
Nictaux East	UNP/LNO	NS	Annapolis	21 A/14	44°56'	65°02'
Nictaux Falls	UNP/LNO	NS	Annapolis	21 A/14	44°55'	65°02'
Nictaux River	RIV/CDE	NS	Annapolis	21 A/14	44°56'	65°04'
Nictaux South	UNP/LNO	NS	Annapolis	21 A/14	44°52'	65°02'
Nictaux West	UNP/LNO	NS	Annapolis	21 A/14	44°55'	65°04'
Niddrie	UNP/LNO	ON	Kenora	52 K/3	50°00'	93°05'
Nier	UNP/LNO	AB	23-28-2-W5	82 O/8	51°25'	114°10'
Nies Beach	UNP/LNO	SK	13,14-53-27-W2	73 H/12	53°34'	105°51'
Nig	UNP/LNO	BC	Peace River	94 H/3	57°07'	121°29'
Nigadoo	VILG/VILG	NB	Gloucester	21 P/12	47°44'	65°44'
Nigadoo River	RIV/CDE	NB	Gloucester	21 P/12	47°45'	65°43'
Nigei Island	ISL/ÎLE	BC	Rupert	92 L/13	50°53'	127°45'
Niger Sound	BAY/BAIE	NF		3 D/4	52°10'	55°38'
Night	UNP/LNO	AB	14-23-2-W5	82 J/16	50°57'	114°11'
Night Hawk Centre	UNP/LNO	ON	Cochrane	42 A/10	48°33'	80°57'
Night Hawk Lake	LAKE/LAC	ON	Cochrane	42 A/7	48°28'	80°58'
Nightingale	UNP/LNO	AB	30-25-24-W4	82 P/3	51°10'	113°20'
Nijadluk Harbour	BAY/BAIE	NT	Franklin	26 H	65°05'	64°03'
Nikip Lake	LAKE/LAC	ON	Kenora	53 B/13	52°53'	91°53'
Nikwikwaia Creek	RIV/CDE	BC	Kamloops Division Yale	82 L/13	50°56'	119°39'
Nile	UNP/LNO	ON	Huron	40 P/13	43°48'	81°37'
Niles Corners	UNP/LNO	ON	Prince Edward	30 N/14	43°58'	77°25'
Nilestown	UNP/LNO	ON	Middlesex	40 I/14	42°58'	81°06'
Nilgaut, Lac	LAKE/LAC	QC	Pontiac	31 K/11	46°36'	77°15'
Nilkitkwa River	RIV/CDE	BC	Cassiar	93 M/7	55°27'	126°42'
Nilrem	UNP/LNO	AB	1-41-9-W4	73 D/11	52°30'	111°10'
Nimpkish	UNP/LNO	BC	Rupert	92 L/7	50°20'	126°55'
Nimpkish 2	IR/RI	BC	Rupert	92 L/10	50°34'	126°56'
Nimpkish Heights	UNP/LNO	BC	Rupert	92 L/11	50°34'	127°00'
Nimpkish Lake	LAKE/LAC	BC	Rupert	92 L/7	50°24'	126°58'
Nimpkish River	RIV/CDE	BC	Rupert	92 L/10	50°34'	126°59'
Nimpo Lake	UNP/LNO	BC	Range 3 Coast	93 C/6	52°20'	125°09'
Nimpo Lake	LAKE/LAC	BC	Range 3 Coast	93 C/6	52°21'	125°12'
Nina Bang Lake	LAKE/LAC	NT	Franklin	37 F	70°52'	79°24'
Ninastoko	UNP/LNO	AB	24-3-26-W4	82 H/3	49°14'	113°23'
Ninawawe, Lac	LAKE/LAC	QC	Kativik	24 B/9	56°36'	66°12'
Nine Holes	UNP/LNO	QC	Memphrémagog	31 H/1	45°07'	72°28'
Nine Mile Creek	UNP/LNO	PE	Queens	11 L/3	46°09'	63°14'
Nine Mile Creek	RIV/CDE	BC	Range 2 Coast	92 N/1	51°12'	124°11'
Nine Mile Creek 4	IR/RI	BC	Similkameen Division Yale	92 H/8	49°26'	120°18'
Nine Mile River	UNP/LNO	NS	Hants	11 E/4	45°02'	63°35'
Nine Mile River	RIV/CDE	ON	Huron	40 P/13	43°53'	81°44'
Ninette	UNP/LNO	MB	24-5-17-W	62 G/5	49°24'	99°38'
93 Mile	UNP/LNO	BC	Lillooet	92 P/11	51°34'	121°20'
Nineveh	UNP/LNO	NS	Victoria	11 F/15	45°57'	60°58'
Nineveh	UNP/LNO	NS	Lunenburg	21 A/7	44°29'	64°48'
Ninga	UNP/LNO	MB	19-3-18-W	62 G/4	49°14'	99°53'
Ninstints	UNP/LNO	BC	Queen Charlotte	103 B/3	52°06'	131°13'
Ninstints, Lieu historique national de - also-aussi - Ninstints National Historic Site	PARK/PARC	BC	Queen Charlotte	103 B/3	52°06'	131°13'
Ninstints National Historic Site - also-aussi - Ninstints, Lieu historique national de	PARK/PARC	BC	Queen Charlotte	103 B/3	52°06'	131°13'
Niobe	UNP/LNO	AB	3-36-28-W4	83 A/4	52°03'	113°54'
Niobe	UNP/LNO	AB	13-73-8-W6	83 M/6	55°20'	119°05'
Nipawin	TOWN/VIL2	SK		73 H/8	53°22'	104°00'
Nipawin No. 487	MUN2/AZM2	SK		73 H/1	53°15'	104°20'
Nipekamew Lake	LAKE/LAC	SK	62,63-20-W2	73 I/7	54°24'	104°58'
Nipekamew River	RIV/CDE	SK	59-19-W2	73 I/15	54°59'	104°52'
Nipew Lake	LAKE/LAC	SK		73 P/10	55°41'	105°00'
Nipigon	MUN2/AZM2	ON	Thunder Bay	52 H/1	49°00'	88°20'
Nipigon	UNP/LNO	ON	Thunder Bay	52 H/1	49°01'	88°16'
Nipigon Bay	BAY/BAIE	ON	Thunder Bay	42 D/13	48°53'	87°50'
Nipigon, Lac - also-aussi - **Nipigon, Lake**	LAKE/LAC	ON	Thunder Bay	52 H/15	49°50'	88°30'
Nipigon, Lake - also-aussi - **Nipigon, Lac**	LAKE/LAC	ON	Thunder Bay	52 H/15	49°50'	88°30'
Nipigon River	RIV/CDE	ON	Thunder Bay	52 A/16	48°57'	88°14'
Nipi Katakuat	UNP/LNO	QC	La Haute-Côte-Nord	22 C/15	48°54'	68°43'
Nipi, Lac	LAKE/LAC	QC	La Haute-Côte-Nord	22 F/2	49°04'	68°48'
Nipin Lake	LAKE/LAC	SK	72,73-23-W3	73 N/6	55°17'	109°26'

NAME NOM	ENTITY ENTITÉ	LOC 1 LIEU 1	LOC 2 LIEU 2	MAP CARTE	POSITION LAT	LONG
Nipin River	RIV/CDE	SK	78-20-W3	73 N/14	55°46′	109°02′
Nipi, Rivière	RIV/CDE	QC	Manicouagan	22 C/15	48°57′	68°46′
Nipirqanaup Paangani	UNP/LNO	QC	Kativik	24 N/5	59°20′	69°33′
Nipishish Lake	LAKE/LAC	NF		13 K/2	54°12′	60°45′
Nipisi Lake	LAKE/LAC	AB	78-6,7-W5	83 O/15	55°47′	114°57′
Nipisi River	RIV/CDE	AB	82-5-W5	84 B/2	56°08′	114°38′
Nipissing	MUN2/AZM2	ON	Parry Sound	31 L/4	46°05′	79°33′
Nipissing	UNP/LNO	ON	Parry Sound	31 L/4	46°06′	79°31′
Nipissing	GEOG/GÉOG	ON		31 L/2	46°00′	79°00′
Nipissing 10	IR/RI	ON	Nipissing	31 L/5	46°20′	79°45′
Nipissing Beach	UNP/LNO	ON	Parry Sound	31 L/4	46°11′	79°30′
Nipissing Junction	UNP/LNO	ON	Nipissing	31 L/6	46°16′	79°23′
Nipissing, Lac - also-aussi - **Nipissing, Lake**	LAKE/LAC	ON	Nipissing	31 L/5	46°17′	80°00′
Nipissing, Lake - also-aussi - **Nipissing, Lac**	LAKE/LAC	ON	Nipissing	31 L/5	46°17′	80°00′
Nipissing River	RIV/CDE	ON	Nipissing	31 L/2	46°00′	78°31′
Nipissis, Lac	LAKE/LAC	QC	Sept-Rivières	22 O/1	51°02′	66°10′
Nipissis, Rivière	RIV/CDE	QC	Sept-Rivières	22 J/8	50°30′	66°06′
Nipisso, Lac	LAKE/LAC	QC	Sept-Rivières	22 I/13	50°52′	65°49′
Nipisso, Rivière	RIV/CDE	QC	Sept-Rivières	22 I/12	50°39′	65°59′
Nippers Harbour	VILG/VILG	NF		2 E/13	49°48′	55°52′
Nipple, The	MTN/MNT	BC	Yale Division Yale	92 H/13	49°57′	121°35′
Nisbet	UNP/LNO	AB	11-34-28-W4	82 P/13	51°55′	113°53′
Nishanocknawnak 35	IR/RI	BC	Range 5 Coast	103 J/8	54°26′	130°07′
Niska Lake	LAKE/LAC	MB		64 F/11	57°44′	101°17′
Niska Lake	LAKE/LAC	SK		73 N/10	55°35′	108°38′
Niskibi River	RIV/CDE	ON	Kenora	54 A/8	56°29′	88°09′
Niskonlith Lake	LAKE/LAC	BC	Kamloops Division Yale	82 L/13	50°52′	119°47′
Nisku	UNP/LNO	AB	26-50-25-W4	83 H/5	53°20′	113°32′
Nisling Range	MTN/MNT	YT		115 G/15	61°55′	138°40′
Nisling River	RIV/CDE	YT		115 J/6	62°29′	139°29′
Nistowiak Lake	LAKE/LAC	SK		73 P/8	55°25′	104°20′
Nisutlin 14	IR/RI	YT		105 C/2	60°13′	132°34′
Nisutlin River	RIV/CDE	YT		105 C/2	60°14′	132°34′
Nitassinan	UNP/LNO	QC	Caniapiscau	23 B/14	52°50′	67°12′
Nitatshun Nutapushuanan	UNP/LNO	QC	Sept-Rivières	22 O/2	51°08′	66°59′
Nitchequon	UNP/LNO	QC	Jamésie	23 E/2	53°12′	70°54′
Niteal	UNP/LNO	BC	Peace River	94 I/4	58°05′	121°32′
Niteal Creek	RIV/CDE	BC	Peace River	94 I/4	58°12′	121°39′
Nithburg	UNP/LNO	ON	Perth	40 P/7	43°28′	80°49′
Nith Grove	UNP/LNO	ON	Muskoka	31 E/3	45°12′	79°04′
Nith River	RIV/CDE	ON	Brant	40 P/1	43°12′	80°23′
Nitinat Canyon	SEAU/SMER	—		3602	48°15′	125°40′
Nitinat Lake	LAKE/LAC	BC	Barclay	92 C/10	48°45′	124°45′
Nitinat River	RIV/CDE	BC	Renfrew	92 C/15	48°49′	124°41′
Niton	UNP/LNO	AB	18-54-12-W5	83 G/12	53°40′	115°46′
Niton Junction	UNP/LNO	AB	31-53-12-W5	83 G/12	53°37′	115°46′
Nitro	UNP/LNO	ON	Sudbury	41 I/13	46°51′	81°44′
Niven River	RIV/CDE	BC	Cassiar	94 D/15	56°54′	126°54′
Niverville	TOWN/VIL2	MB	30-7-4E	62 H/11	49°36′	97°03′
Niwelin Lake	LAKE/LAC	NT	Mackenzie	96 N	67°53′	125°55′
Niweme	UNP/LNO	ON	Parry Sound	41 H/9	45°36′	80°24′
Nixon	UNP/LNO	NB	Albert	21 H/15	45°57′	64°56′
Nixon	UNP/LNO	ON	Norfolk	40 I/16	42°51′	80°24′
Nkaih 10	IR/RI	BC	Kamloops Division Yale	92 I/5	50°19′	121°39′
Noaxe Creek	RIV/CDE	BC	Lillooet	92 O/2	51°01′	122°45′
Nobbs Siding	UNP/LNO	ON	Hastings	31 F/4	45°00′	77°44′
Nobel	UNP/LNO	ON	Parry Sound	41 H/8	45°25′	80°06′
Nober	UNP/LNO	ON	Norfolk	40 I/16	42°56′	80°10′
Nobleford	VILG/VILG	AB	3-11-23-W4	82 H/14	49°53′	113°03′
Noble Inlet	BAY/BAIE	NT	Franklin	25 J	62°04′	66°05′
Nobleton	UNP/LNO	ON	York	30 M/13	43°54′	79°40′
Nobleville	UNP/LNO	SK	40-12-W2	63 D/5	52°26′	103°37′
Nocten 19	IR/RI	BC	Kamloops Division Yale	92 I/5	50°16′	121°31′
No-Cut 5	IR/RI	BC	Cassiar	93 M/7	55°21′	126°39′
Nodales Channel	CHAN/CHEN	BC	Sayward	92 K/6	50°24′	125°20′
Noddy Bay	UNP/LNO	NF		2 M/11	51°35′	55°29′
Noddy Island	ISL/ÎLE	NS	Yarmouth	20 P/5	43°27′	65°59′
Nodier, Lac	LAKE/LAC	QC	Témiscamingue	31 M/9	47°38′	78°26′
Noeick River	RIV/CDE	BC	Range 3 Coast	93 D/2	52°02′	126°40′
Noel	UNP/LNO	NS	Hants	11 E/5	45°18′	63°45′
Noel Bay	BAY/BAIE	NS	Hants	11 E/5	45°19′	63°45′
Noel Creek	RIV/CDE	BC	Lillooet	92 J/15	50°46′	122°49′
Noel Harbour	BAY/BAIE	NT	Franklin	25 M	63°07′	70°56′
Noel Lake	LAKE/LAC	NS	Hants	11 E/5	45°16′	63°44′
Noell Lake	LAKE/LAC	NT	Mackenzie	107 B	68°32′	133°34′

NAME NOM	ENTITY ENTITÉ	LOC 1 LIEU 1	LOC 2 LIEU 2	MAP CARTE	POSITION	
					LAT	LONG
Noel Paul's Brook	RIV/CDE	NF		12 A/16	48°49′	56°19′
Noel Road	UNP/LNO	NS	Hants	11 E/4	45°12′	63°45′
Noel Shore	UNP/LNO	NS	Hants	11 E/5	45°19′	63°39′
Noels Pond	UNP/LNO	NF		12 B/10	48°34′	58°31′
Noëlville	UNP/LNO	ON	Sudbury	41 I/1	46°08′	80°26′
Noggin Cove	UNP/LNO	NF		2 E/8	49°25′	54°19′
Noggin Cove	BAY/BAIE	NF		2 E/8	49°25′	54°19′
Nogies Creek	UNP/LNO	ON	Peterborough	31 D/9	44°35′	78°30′
Nogold Creek	RIV/CDE	YT		105 M/6	63°26′	135°06′
Nohomeen 23	IR/RI	BC	Kamloops Division Yale	92 I/4	50°15′	121°36′
Noice Peninsula	CAPE/CAP	NT	Franklin	79 E	78°25′	104°00′
Noinville	UNP/LNO	NB	Kent	21 I/11	46°39′	65°22′
Noirclair, Lac	LAKE/LAC	QC	Minganie	12 K/9	50°38′	60°23′
Noire, Grande rivière	RIV/CDE	QC	L'Islet	21 K/13	46°54′	69°48′
Noire, Pointe	CAPE/CAP	QC	Charlevoix-Est	22 C/4	48°07′	69°43′
Noire, Rivière	RIV/CDE	QC	Charlevoix-Est	21 N/13	47°51′	69°53′
Noire, Rivière	RIV/CDE	QC	Bellechasse	21 L/15	46°46′	70°40′
Noire, Rivière	RIV/CDE	QC	Les Chutes-de-la-Chaudière	21 L/11	46°36′	71°22′
Noire, Rivière	RIV/CDE	QC	Les Maskoutains	31 H/10	45°33′	72°58′
Noire, Rivière	RIV/CDE	QC	Pontiac	31 F/15	45°54′	76°57′
Noir, Lac	LAKE/LAC	QC	Bonaventure	22 A/3	48°03′	65°19′
Noisy Creek	RIV/CDE	YT		106 E/15	65°53′	134°56′
Noisy River	RIV/CDE	ON	Simcoe	41 A/8	44°19′	80°09′
Noix, Île aux	ISL/ÎLE	QC	Le Haut-Richelieu	31 H/3	45°07′	73°16′
Nojack	UNP/LNO	AB	28,29-53-11-W5	83 G/12	53°37′	115°35′
Nokomis	TOWN/VIL2	SK	27-29-22-W2	72 P/11	51°30′	105°00′
Nokomis Lake	LAKE/LAC	SK		64 E/2	57°00′	103°00′
Nolalu	UNP/LNO	ON	Thunder Bay	52 A/5	48°17′	89°49′
Nolans Corners	UNP/LNO	ON	Lanark	31 B/13	44°57′	75°59′
Noman Lake	LAKE/LAC	NT	Mackenzie	75 K	62°15′	108°55′
Nomansland Point	CAPE/CAP	ON	Cochrane	43 A/3	52°03′	81°05′
Nominingue, Lac	LAKE/LAC	QC	Antoine-Labelle	31 J/7	46°26′	74°59′
Nonacho Lake	LAKE/LAC	NT	Mackenzie	75 F	61°59′	109°28′
Nonias Lake	LAKE/LAC	NS	Yarmouth	20 P/13	43°47′	65°44′
Nonne, Lac la	LAKE/LAC	AB	57-2,3-W5	83 G/16	53°56′	114°19′
Nonsuch	UNP/LNO	MB	20-82-14-E	54 D/3	56°08′	95°23′
Nooaitch 10	IR/RI	BC	Kamloops Division Yale	92 I/3	50°12′	121°05′
Nooaitch Grass 9	IR/RI	BC	Kamloops Division Yale	92 I/3	50°11′	121°01′
Noodleook Fiord	BAY/BAIE	NF		24 P/16	59°55′	64°27′
Noo Kat 42	IR/RI	BC	Range 5 Coast	93 K/14	54°49′	125°08′
Noomut River	RIV/CDE	NT	Keewatin	65 H	61°45′	96°15′
Noonan	UNP/LNO	NB	Sunbury	21 G/15	45°58′	66°32′
Noonan Stream	RIV/CDE	NB	Sunbury	21 G/16	45°54′	66°25′
Noonla 6	IR/RI	BC	Range 3 Coast	93 K/1	54°02′	124°04′
Nooseseck 2	IR/RI	BC	Range 3 Coast	93 D/7	52°20′	126°59′
Noota 4	IR/RI	BC	Range 3 Coast	93 D/5	52°29′	127°45′
Nootka	UNP/LNO	BC	Nootka	92 E/10	49°37′	126°37′
Nootka Island	ISL/ÎLE	BC	Nootka	92 E/10	49°45′	126°45′
Nootka Land District	GEOG/GÉOG	BC		92 E	49°50′	126°16′
Nootka Ridge	SEAU/SMER	—		15796A	49°12′	127°35′
Nootka Sound	BAY/BAIE	BC	Nootka	92 E/10	49°36′	126°34′
Nora	UNP/LNO	SK	20-39-13-W2	63 D/5	52°23′	103°50′
Noral	UNP/LNO	AB	28-65-16-W4	83 I/9	54°39′	112°22′
Nora Lake	LAKE/LAC	MB	10-17-E	52 E/14	49°52′	95°13′
Noralee	UNP/LNO	BC	Range 4 Coast	93 E/16	53°59′	126°26′
Norberry	UNP/LNO	MB		62 H/14	49°51′	97°07′
Norbert River	RIV/CDE	SK		73 O/15	55°59′	106°32′
Norbertville	TOWN/VIL2	QC	Arthabaska	21 L/4	46°06′	71°49′
Norbestos	UNP/LNO	QC	Arthabaska	21 E/13	45°49′	71°51′
Norboro	UNP/LNO	PE	Prince	11 L/5	46°25′	63°35′
Norbuck	UNP/LNO	AB	35-46-4-W5	83 G/1	53°01′	114°29′
Norbury	UNP/LNO	SK	49-10-W3	73 G/6	53°16′	107°25′
Norcan Lake	LAKE/LAC	ON	Frontenac	31 F/2	45°10′	76°52′
Norco	UNP/LNO	SK	16-33-27-W2	72 P/13	51°49′	105°46′
Norcran	UNP/LNO	MB	16-11-4-E	62 H/15	49°55′	97°00′
Nord, Baie du	BAY/BAIE	QC	Jamésie	32 F/14	49°57′	77°28′
Nordbye Lake	LAKE/LAC	SK		64 M/3	59°04′	103°30′
Nord, Chenal du	CHAN/CHEN	QC	Charlevoix-Est	21 M/9	47°35′	70°05′
Nord-du-Québec	MUN1/AZM1	QC	Kativik	34 B/1	56°10′	74°25′
Nordegg	UNP/LNO	AB	27-40-15-W5	83 C/8	52°28′	116°05′
Nordegg River	RIV/CDE	AB	45-10-W5	83 B/14	52°53′	115°19′
Nordenskiold, Cape	CAPE/CAP	NT	Franklin	57 G	71°21′	92°57′
Nordenskiöld Islands	ISL/ÎLE	NT	Franklin	67 B	68°28′	100°50′
Nordenskiold River	RIV/CDE	YT		115 I/1	62°06′	136°18′
Nord-Est, Chenal - also-aussi - Northeast Channel	SEAU/SMER	—		8005	42°10′	65°50′

NAME / NOM	ENTITY / ENTITÉ	LOC 1 / LIEU 1	LOC 2 / LIEU 2	MAP / CARTE	POSITION LAT	POSITION LONG
Nord-Est, Lac du	LAKE/LAC	QC	Sept-Rivières	22 J/11	50°44′	67°28′
Nordet, Le	UNP/LNO	QC	L'Érable	21 L/5	46°23′	71°31′
Nord, Grand lac du	LAKE/LAC	QC	Sept-Rivières	22 J/14	50°54′	67°06′
Nordic Townsite	UNP/LNO	ON	Algoma	41 J/7	46°23′	82°35′
Nordin	UNP/LNO	NB	Northumberland	21 P/4	47°01′	65°32′
Nord-Ouest, Bassin du	BAY/BAIE	QC	La Côte-de-Gaspé	22 A/15	48°52′	64°32′
Nord-Ouest, Pointe	CAPE/CAP	QC	La Côte-de-Gaspé	22 A/16	48°57′	64°18′
Nord-Ouest, Territoires du - also-aussi - **Northwest Territories**	TERR/TERR	NT		MCR130	70°00′	95°00′
Nord, Petit lac du	LAKE/LAC	QC	Sept-Rivières	22 J/14	50°50′	67°09′
Nord, Pointe	CAPE/CAP	QC	Minganie	22 H/16	49°57′	64°09′
Nord, Rivière du	RIV/CDE	QC	Argenteuil	31 G/9	45°31′	74°20′
Nord, Rivière du	RIV/CDE	QC	Kativik	34 C/9	56°34′	76°23′
Nordstrand Point	CAPE/CAP	NT	Franklin	59 A	76°59′	88°58′
Norembega	UNP/LNO	ON	Cochrane	42 A/15	48°59′	80°43′
Norem, Cape	CAPE/CAP	NT	Franklin	79 C	77°28′	110°23′
Norfolk	MUN2/AZM2	ON	Norfolk	40 I/10	42°43′	80°35′
Norfolk	UNP/LNO	AB	16-24-27-W4	82 P/4	51°02′	113°43′
Norfolk	GEOG/GÉOG	ON		40 I/9	42°35′	80°24′
Norfolk Inlet	BAY/BAIE	NT	Franklin	59 A	76°28′	91°05′
Norgate	UNP/LNO	MB	34-19-15-W	62 J/11	50°41′	99°28′
Norgate	UNP/LNO	BC	New Westminster	92 G/6	49°19′	123°07′
Norgate, Secteur	UNP/LNO	QC	Communauté urbaine de Montréal	31 H/12	45°31′	73°42′
Norge	UNP/LNO	SK	32-6-10-W3	72 G/11	49°30′	107°18′
Norglenwold	VILG/VILG	AB	5,6-39-1-W5	83 B/8	52°19′	114°07′
Norham	UNP/LNO	ON	Northumberland	31 C/4	44°11′	77°52′
Norlake	UNP/LNO	BC	Cariboo	93 B/1	52°09′	122°11′
Norland	UNP/LNO	ON	Victoria	31 D/10	44°43′	78°49′
Norma	UNP/LNO	AB	31-54-14-W4	83 H/9	53°43′	112°03′
Norman	UNP/LNO	ON	Elgin	40 I/11	42°44′	81°12′
Norman	UNP/LNO	MB	5-13-22-W	62 K/1	50°04′	100°27′
Normanby	MUN2/AZM2	ON	Grey	41 A/2	44°04′	80°54′
Norman, Cape	CAPE/CAP	NF		2 M/12	51°38′	55°54′
Normandale	UNP/LNO	ON	Norfolk	40 I/9	42°43′	80°19′
Normandeau	UNP/LNO	AB	34-64-12-W4	73 L/12	54°32′	111°41′
Normandie	UNP/LNO	NB	Kent	21 I/7	46°29′	64°59′
Normandin	CITY/VIL1	QC	Maria-Chapdelaine	32 A/15	48°50′	72°32′
Normandin, Rivière	RIV/CDE	QC	Le Domaine-du-Roy	32 H/4	49°12′	73°48′
Normand, Lac	LAKE/LAC	QC	Mékinac	31 P/3	47°05′	73°14′
Normand Park	UNP/LNO	MB		62 H/14	49°48′	97°07′
Normand, Pointe	CAPE/CAP	QC	Kativik	34 K/4	58°10′	77°32′
Normandville	UNP/LNO	AB	27-79-22-W5	83 N/14	55°52′	117°22′
Normandy Heights	UNP/LNO	SK		72 I/7	50°26′	104°38′
Normanhurst	UNP/LNO	ON	Wentworth	30 M/4	43°14′	79°48′
Norman Range	MTN/MNT	NT	Mackenzie	96 E/6	65°20′	127°00′
Norman's Cove	UNP/LNO	NF		1 N/12	47°33′	53°40′
Norman's Cove-Long Cove	TOWN/VIL2	NF		1 N/12	47°34′	53°40′
Normanview	UNP/LNO	SK		72 I/7	50°29′	104°40′
Normanview West	UNP/LNO	SK		72 I/7	50°29′	104°41′
Norman Wells	TOWN/VIL2	NT	Mackenzie	96 E	65°17′	126°50′
Normétal	VILG/VILG	QC	Abitibi-Ouest	32 D/14	49°00′	79°22′
Norquay	TOWN/VIL2	SK	4-34-1-W2	62 M/16	51°53′	102°05′
Norran Island	ISL/ÎLE	ON	Cochrane	42 O/11	51°33′	83°19′
Norrie	UNP/LNO	QC	Vallée-de-l'Or	32 D/1	48°08′	78°05′
Norris Arm	TOWN/VIL2	NF		2 E/3	49°05′	55°15′
Norris Arm	BAY/BAIE	NF		2 E/3	49°06′	55°15′
Norris Arm North	UNP/LNO	NF		2 E/3	49°07′	55°15′
Norris Beach	VILG/VILG	AB	13-46-1-W5	83 B/16	52°59′	114°01′
Norrish Creek	RIV/CDE	BC	New Westminster	92 G/1	49°14′	122°08′
Norris Lake	UNP/LNO	MB	15-17-1-E	62 I/6	50°27′	97°24′
Norris Lake	LAKE/LAC	MB	52-16-W	63 G/5	53°29′	99°42′
Norris Point	VILG/VILG	NF		12 H/12	49°31′	57°53′
Norris Point	UNP/LNO	NF		12 H/12	49°31′	57°53′
Norsemans Pond	LAKE/LAC	NF		2 D/1	48°10′	54°28′
North Ainslie	UNP/LNO	NS	Inverness	11 K/3	46°11′	61°12′
North Algona	MUN2/AZM2	ON	Renfrew	31 F/11	45°37′	77°20′
North Alton	UNP/LNO	NS	Kings	21 H/2	45°03′	64°31′
Northam	UNP/LNO	PE	Prince	11 L/12	46°33′	63°58′
Northampton	UNP/LNO	NB	Carleton	21 J/4	46°04′	67°33′
Northampton	GEOG/GÉOG	NB	Carleton	21 J/3	46°08′	67°28′
North Appin Station	UNP/LNO	ON	Middlesex	40 I/13	42°48′	81°40′
North Arm	BAY/BAIE	NF		12 G/1	49°12′	58°02′
North Arm	BAY/BAIE	ON	Thunder Bay	52 J/2	50°09′	90°42′
North Arm	BAY/BAIE	BC	Cariboo	93 A/10	52°40′	120°55′
North Arm	BAY/BAIE	BC	New Westminster	92 G/3	49°12′	123°05′
North Arm	BAY/BAIE	NT	Franklin	38 B	72°04′	76°01′

NAME NOM	ENTITY ENTITÉ	LOC 1 LIEU 1	LOC 2 LIEU 2	MAP CARTE	POSITION	
					LAT	LONG
North Arm	BAY/BAIE	NT	Mackenzie	85 J	62°30′	115°20′
North Arm Mountain	MTN/MNT	NF		12 H/4	49°14′	57°59′
North Aspy River	RIV/CDE	NS	Victoria	11 K/15	46°54′	60°31′
North Augusta	UNP/LNO	ON	Grenville	31 B/13	44°46′	75°44′
North Aulatsivik Island	ISL/ÎLE	NF		24 P/16	59°46′	64°05′
Northbank	UNP/LNO	AB	25-58-18-W4	83 I/2	54°02′	112°33′
North Barrière Lake	LAKE/LAC	BC	Kamloops Division Yale	82 M/5	51°20′	119°50′
North Battleford	CITY/VIL1	SK		73 C/16	52°47′	108°17′
North Battleford No. 437	MUN2/AZM2	SK		73 C/16	52°50′	108°05′
North Bay	CITY/VIL1	ON	Nipissing	31 L/6	46°19′	79°28′
North Bay	UNP/LNO	NF		11 O/16	47°48′	58°20′
North Bay	BAY/BAIE	NF		1 M/11	47°42′	55°25′
North Bay	BAY/BAIE	NF		11 O/16	47°47′	58°20′
North Bay	BAY/BAIE	ON	Essex	40 G/15	41°49′	82°40′
North Bay	BAY/BAIE	SK		73 P/6	55°23′	105°25′
North Bay	BAY/BAIE	NT	Franklin	25 K	62°40′	69°50′
North Bay	BAY/BAIE	NT	Franklin	26 E	65°22′	71°40′
North Bay 5	IR/RI	BC	Kamloops Division Yale	82 L/14	50°47′	119°19′
North Bay Ingonish	BAY/BAIE	NS	Victoria	11 K/9	46°40′	60°23′
North Bedeque	UNP/LNO	PE	Prince	11 L/5	46°22′	63°43′
North Bend	UNP/LNO	BC	Yale Division Yale	92 H/14	49°53′	121°27′
North Bentinck Arm	BAY/BAIE	BC	Range 3 Coast	93 D/7	52°22′	126°53′
North Big Salmon River	RIV/CDE	YT		105 E/15	61°46′	134°37′
North Bill	CAPE/CAP	NF		2 F/5	49°17′	53°30′
North Bill	CAPE/CAP	NF		2 E/12	49°41′	55°51′
North Bloomfield	UNP/LNO	NS	Pictou	11 E/9	45°31′	62°27′
North Blue River	RIV/CDE	BC	Kamloops Division Yale	83 D/3	52°05′	119°25′
Northbluff Point	CAPE/CAP	ON	Cochrane	42 P/8	51°30′	80°27′
North Boat Harbour	UNP/LNO	NF		2 M/12	51°35′	55°59′
North Bonaparte	UNP/LNO	BC	Lillooet	92 P/7	51°24′	120°55′
North Branch	UNP/LNO	NB	Westmorland	21 I/3	46°12′	65°13′
North Branch	UNP/LNO	ON	Glengarry	31 G/2	45°09′	74°45′
North Branch	UNP/LNO	ON	Rainy River	52 D/16	48°52′	94°10′
North Branch Big Sevogle River	RIV/CDE	NB	Northumberland	21 P/4	47°06′	65°56′
North Branch Gulquac River	RIV/CDE	NB	Victoria	21 J/14	46°59′	67°16′
North Branch Kedgwick River - also-aussi - Kedgwick, Rivière	RIV/CDE	NB	Restigouche	21 O/13	47°54′	67°55′
North Branch Lake	LAKE/LAC	NS	Guysborough	11 F/5	45°23′	61°42′
North Branch Muskoka River	RIV/CDE	ON	Muskoka	31 E/3	45°02′	79°19′
North Branch Renous River	RIV/CDE	NB	Northumberland	21 J/16	46°47′	66°11′
North Branch Southwest Miramichi River	RIV/CDE	NB	Carleton	21 J/11	46°31′	67°09′
North Branch Tomogonops River	RIV/CDE	NB	Northumberland	21 P/5	47°15′	65°55′
Northbrook	UNP/LNO	ON	Lennox and Addington	31 C/11	44°44′	77°10′
North Brookfield	UNP/LNO	NS	Queens	21 A/7	44°24′	64°57′
North Broughton Island	ISL/ÎLE	BC	Range 1 Coast	92 L/15	50°51′	126°48′
North Bruce	UNP/LNO	ON	Bruce	41 A/6	44°23′	81°26′
North Buck Lake	LAKE/LAC	AB	65,66-17,18-W4	83 I/10	54°41′	112°32′
North Bulkley	UNP/LNO	BC	Range 5 Coast	93 L/8	54°29′	126°29′
North Burgess	MUN2/AZM2	ON	Lanark	31 C/16	44°47′	76°18′
North Buxton	UNP/LNO	ON	Kent	40 J/8	42°18′	82°14′
North Cains	UNP/LNO	NB	York	21 J/8	46°20′	66°25′
North Campbell River	UNP/LNO	BC	Sayward	92 K/3	50°03′	125°16′
North Cape	CAPE/CAP	PE	Prince	11 M/4	47°04′	64°00′
North, Cape	CAPE/CAP	NS	Victoria	11 N/1	47°02′	60°25′
North Cape Highlands	UNP/LNO	NS	Inverness	11 K/3	46°11′	61°21′
North Caribou Lake	LAKE/LAC	ON	Kenora	53 B/15	52°50′	90°40′
North Caribou Lake	LAKE/LAC	NT	Mackenzie	107 B	68°06′	132°43′
North Carleton	UNP/LNO	PE	Prince	11 L/5	46°17′	63°42′
North Castor River	RIV/CDE	ON	Carleton	31 G/6	45°15′	75°23′
North Channel	CHAN/CHEN	ON	Lennox and Addington	31 C/2	44°11′	76°40′
North Channel	CHAN/CHEN	ON	Parry Sound	41 H/15	45°46′	80°39′
North Channel	CHAN/CHEN	ON	Algoma	41 G/15	46°00′	82°45′
North Channel	CHAN/CHEN	ON	Kenora	43 D/3	52°05′	87°06′
North Channel	CHAN/CHEN	NT	Keewatin	56 D/2	64°07′	94°31′
North Channel (French River)	CHAN/CHEN	ON	Sudbury	41 I/2	46°06′	80°34′
North Chegoggin	UNP/LNO	NS	Yarmouth	20 O/16	43°53′	66°08′
North Clarendon	UNP/LNO	QC	Pontiac	31 F/9	45°42′	76°30′
North Cobalt	UNP/LNO	ON	Timiskaming	31 M/5	47°26′	79°39′
North Colesdale Park	HAM/HAM	SK		72 I/14	50°58′	105°09′
North Cooking Lake	UNP/LNO	AB	6-52-20-W4	83 H/7	53°28′	112°58′
Northcote	UNP/LNO	ON	Renfrew	31 F/10	45°31′	76°49′
North Cove	UNP/LNO	NF		13 H/16	53°47′	56°29′
North Cowichan	MUN1/AZM1	BC	Somenos	92 B/13	48°51′	123°41′
Northcrest	UNP/LNO	ON	Middlesex	40 P/3	43°02′	81°17′
North Crosby	MUN2/AZM2	ON	Grenville	31 C/9	44°43′	76°24′
North Cypress	MUN2/AZM2	MB		62 G/14	49°55′	99°21′

NAME / NOM	ENTITY / ENTITÉ	LOC 1 / LIEU 1	LOC 2 / LIEU 2	MAP / CARTE	POSITION LAT	POSITION LONG
Northdale	UNP/LNO	ON	Middlesex	40 P/3	43°02′	81°15′
North Delta	UNP/LNO	BC	New Westminster	92 G/2	49°10′	122°55′
North Devon	UNP/LNO	NB	York	21 G/15	45°58′	66°38′
North Dorchester	MUN2/AZM2	ON	Middlesex	40 I/14	42°56′	81°00′
North Driftwood River	RIV/CDE	ON	Cochrane	42 H/6	49°24′	81°18′
North Duck River	RIV/CDE	MB	18-37-19-W	63 C/1	52°11′	100°11′
North Dumfries	MUN2/AZM2	ON	Waterloo	40 P/8	43°19′	80°24′
North Earltown	UNP/LNO	NS	Colchester	11 E/11	45°37′	63°08′
Northeast Arm	BAY/BAIE	NF		2 C/12	48°39′	53°53′
Northeast Arm	BAY/BAIE	NF		1 M/5	47°29′	55°47′
Northeast Arm	BAY/BAIE	NF		11 P/11	47°40′	57°02′
Northeast Arm	BAY/BAIE	NF		11 O/16	47°45′	58°17′
Northeast Arm	BAY/BAIE	NB	Queens	21 I/4	46°04′	65°57′
Northeast Arm	BAY/BAIE	ON	Nipissing	31 M/4	47°01′	79°55′
Northeast Arm - see-voir - Beaton Arm	BAY/BAIE	BC		82 K/12	50°43′	117°48′
Northeast Arm Harbour Deep	UNP/LNO	NF		12 I/8	50°24′	56°29′
Northeast Bay	BAY/BAIE	ON	Cochrane	32 D/13	48°55′	79°55′
North East Brook	RIV/CDE	NF		1 M/11	47°44′	55°22′
Northeast Channel - also-aussi - Nord-Est, Chenal	SEAU/SMER	—		8005	42°10′	65°50′
North East Croque	UNP/LNO	NF		2 M/4	51°04′	55°48′
Northeast Crouse	UNP/LNO	NF		2 L/13	50°56′	55°51′
North East Harbour	UNP/LNO	NS	Shelburne	20 P/11	43°33′	65°23′
Northeast Harbour Buffett	UNP/LNO	NF		1 M/9	47°32′	54°04′
North Easthope	MUN2/AZM2	ON	Perth	40 P/7	43°23′	80°50′
Northeast Mabou	UNP/LNO	NS	Inverness	11 K/3	46°06′	61°24′
North East Margaree	UNP/LNO	NS	Inverness	11 K/6	46°20′	61°00′
Northeast Margaree River	RIV/CDE	NS	Inverness	11 K/6	46°20′	61°05′
Northeast Newfoundland Rise	SEAU/SMER	—		813	52°00′	48°00′
Northeast Newfoundland Shelf	SEAU/SMER	—		8015	51°00′	52°30′
Northeast Newfoundland Slope	SEAU/SMER	—		813	51°30′	50°30′
North East Point	UNP/LNO	NS	Shelburne	20 P/12	43°31′	65°36′
Northeast Point	CAPE/CAP	NF		3 D/3	52°01′	55°17′
Northeast Point	CAPE/CAP	NS	Victoria	11 N/1	47°13′	60°08′
Northeast Point	CAPE/CAP	ON	Manitoulin	41 H/12	45°32′	81°42′
Northeast Point	CAPE/CAP	NT	Franklin	59 C	77°44′	93°17′
Northeast River	RIV/CDE	NF		1 N/5	47°16′	53°51′
North Echo - see-voir - Fort San	VILG/VILG	SK		62 L/13	50°48′	103°49′
North Ekfrid	UNP/LNO	ON	Middlesex	40 I/13	42°51′	81°39′
North Elmsley	MUN2/AZM2	ON	Lanark	31 C/16	44°55′	76°09′
North End	UNP/LNO	ON	Wentworth	30 M/5	43°16′	79°52′
North End	UNP/LNO	MB		62 H/14	49°55′	97°09′
North End	CAPE/CAP	NF		2 E/9	49°41′	54°26′
North Enmore	UNP/LNO	PE	Prince	21 I/9	46°36′	64°03′
Norther Head	CAPE/CAP	NF		1 L/16	46°52′	54°12′
Northern	UNP/LNO	NF		12 H/3	49°11′	57°20′
Northern Arm	TOWN/VIL2	NF		2 E/3	49°10′	55°23′
Northern Arm	BAY/BAIE	NF		2 E/3	49°10′	55°22′
Northern Arm	BAY/BAIE	NF		11 P/9	47°42′	56°08′
Northern Arm Brook	RIV/CDE	NF		2 E/3	49°09′	55°23′
Northern Bay	UNP/LNO	NF		1 N/14	47°57′	53°04′
Northern Bight	UNP/LNO	NF		2 D/1	48°01′	54°00′
Northern Cat Island	ISL/ÎLE	NF		2 F/5	49°20′	53°36′
Northern Harbour	UNP/LNO	NB	Charlotte	21 B/15	44°59′	67°00′
Northern Head	CAPE/CAP	NS	Cape Breton	11 J/4	46°10′	59°49′
Northern Head	CAPE/CAP	NB	Charlotte	21 B/15	44°48′	66°47′
Northern Heights	UNP/LNO	ON	Sudbury	41 I/11	46°31′	81°15′
Northern Indian Lake	LAKE/LAC	MB		64 H/6	57°20′	97°15′
Northern Light	UNP/LNO	SK	22-44-25-W2	73 A/13	52°48′	105°32′
Northern Light Lake	LAKE/LAC	ON	Thunder Bay	52 B/7	48°16′	90°39′
Northern Lights No. 22, Municipal District of	MUN1/AZM1	AB		84 F/5	57°33′	118°00′
Northern Peninsula	CAPE/CAP	ON	Kenora	52 E/10	49°40′	94°36′
Northern Pine	UNP/LNO	SK	63-25-W3	73 K/5	54°27′	109°42′
Northern Spur	SEAU/SMER	—		4099	44°08′	60°48′
Northern Valley	UNP/LNO	AB	33-55-6-W4	73 E/15	53°47′	110°50′
Norther Point	CAPE/CAP	NF		2 C/6	48°24′	53°08′
Northesk	GEOG/GÉOG	NB	Northumberland	21 O/1	47°15′	66°15′
North Esk Boom	UNP/LNO	NB	Northumberland	21 I/13	46°58′	65°41′
North Etomami River	RIV/CDE	MB		63 A/7	52°20′	96°53′
Northfield	VILG/VILG	QC	La Vallée-de-la-Gatineau	31 J/4	46°06′	75°54′
Northfield	UNP/LNO	NS	Hants	11 E/5	45°15′	63°41′
Northfield	UNP/LNO	NS	Lunenburg	21 A/7	44°28′	64°37′
Northfield	UNP/LNO	NS	Annapolis	21 A/6	44°27′	65°08′
Northfield	UNP/LNO	ON	Stormont	31 G/2	45°07′	74°55′
Northfield	UNP/LNO	ON	Brant	40 P/1	43°01′	80°28′
Northfield	UNP/LNO	ON	Cochrane	42 G/8	49°25′	82°25′

NAME NOM	ENTITY ENTITÉ	LOC 1 LIEU 1	LOC 2 LIEU 2	MAP CARTE	POSITION LAT	LONG
Northfield	UNP/LNO	BC	Nanaimo	92 G/4	49°11′	123°59′
Northfield	GEOG/GÉOG	NB	Sunbury	21 J/1	46°13′	66°00′
Northfield Station	UNP/LNO	ON	Stormont	31 G/2	45°06′	74°57′
North Fiord	BAY/BAIE	NT	Franklin	69 H	79°56′	96°25′
North Fork Pass	VALL/VALL	YT		116 B/9	64°34′	138°15′
North Forks	UNP/LNO	NB	Sunbury	21 I/4	46°13′	65°58′
North Fourchu	UNP/LNO	NS	Richmond	11 F/9	45°43′	60°15′
North Framboise	UNP/LNO	NS	Richmond	11 F/9	45°44′	60°23′
North Fredericksburgh	MUN2/AZM2	ON	Lennox and Addington	31 C/2	44°11′	77°00′
North French River	RIV/CDE	ON	Cochrane	42 P/2	51°08′	80°43′
North Galiano	UNP/LNO	BC	Cowichan	92 B/13	49°00′	123°35′
Northgate	UNP/LNO	SK	6-1-2-W2	62 E/1	49°00′	102°16′
North Georgetown	UNP/LNO	QC	Le Haut-Saint-Laurent	31 H/4	45°12′	73°52′
North Glanford	UNP/LNO	ON	Wentworth	30 M/4	43°11′	79°54′
North Glen	UNP/LNO	NS	Cape Breton	11 F/16	45°51′	60°30′
North Glencoe Station	UNP/LNO	ON	Middlesex	40 I/13	42°46′	81°44′
North Gower	UNP/LNO	ON	Carleton	31 G/4	45°08′	75°43′
North Grand Pré	UNP/LNO	NS	Kings	21 H/1	45°08′	64°19′
North Grant	UNP/LNO	NS	Antigonish	11 E/9	45°40′	62°02′
North Great Rattling Brook	RIV/CDE	NF		2 D/12	48°37′	55°46′
North Greville	UNP/LNO	NS	Cumberland	21 H/7	45°25′	64°33′
North Grove	VILG/VILG	SK	9,16,17,20-20-26-W	72 I/12	50°41′	105°33′
North Hall	UNP/LNO	ON	Elgin	40 I/15	42°48′	80°49′
North Harbour	UNP/LNO	NF		1 N/4	47°09′	53°40′
North Harbour	UNP/LNO	NF		1 M/16	47°51′	54°06′
North Harbour	BAY/BAIE	NF		1 N/4	47°08′	53°40′
North Harbour	BAY/BAIE	NF		1 M/16	47°51′	54°05′
North Harbour	BAY/BAIE	NS	Victoria	11 K/16	46°55′	60°29′
North Harbour Point	CAPE/CAP	NF		1 N/4	47°06′	53°40′
North Harbour South	UNP/LNO	NF		1 N/4	47°09′	53°39′
North Hatley	TOWN/VIL2	QC	Memphrémagog	21 E/5	45°17′	71°58′
North Head	UNP/LNO	NB	Charlotte	21 B/15	44°46′	66°45′
North Head	CAPE/CAP	NF		1 N/7	47°29′	52°38′
North Head	CAPE/CAP	NF		1 N/7	47°19′	52°45′
North Head	CAPE/CAP	NF		2 C/11	48°33′	53°00′
North Head	CAPE/CAP	NF		2 E/11	49°33′	55°10′
North Head	CAPE/CAP	NF		13 H/9	53°43′	56°24′
North Head	CAPE/CAP	NF		14 L/14	58°55′	63°08′
North Henik Lake	LAKE/LAC	NT	Keewatin	65 H	61°44′	97°40′
North Himsworth	MUN2/AZM2	ON	Parry Sound	31 L/3	46°10′	79°23′
North Intervale	UNP/LNO	NS	Guysborough	11 F/5	45°29′	61°39′
North Island	ISL/ÎLE	ON	Kenora	52 E/2	49°15′	94°34′
North Junction	UNP/LNO	MB	20-25-19-W	62 N/1	51°11′	100°07′
North Kamloops	UNP/LNO	BC	Kamloops Division Yale	92 I/9	50°42′	120°22′
North Kemptville	UNP/LNO	NS	Yarmouth	21 A/4	44°05′	65°50′
North Kent Island	ISL/ÎLE	NT	Franklin	59 A	76°40′	90°08′
North Kildonan	UNP/LNO	MB		62 H/14	49°56′	97°05′
North Kingston	UNP/LNO	NS	Kings	21 H/2	45°01′	64°58′
North Klondike River	RIV/CDE	YT		115 O/15	63°58′	138°41′
North Knife Lake	UNP/LNO	MB		64 I/3	58°13′	97°05′
North Knife Lake	LAKE/LAC	MB		64 I/3	58°05′	97°05′
North Knife River	RIV/CDE	MB		54 L/15	58°57′	94°37′
North Lake	UNP/LNO	PE	Kings	11 L/8	46°27′	62°03′
North Lake	UNP/LNO	NB	York	21 G/13	45°50′	67°44′
North Lake	GEOG/GÉOG	NB	York	21 G/13	45°45′	67°40′
North Lake	LAKE/LAC	NF		12 A/12	48°31′	57°54′
North Lake	LAKE/LAC	NB	York	21 G/13	45°49′	67°45′
North Lake	LAKE/LAC	ON	Thunder Bay	52 B/2	48°07′	90°32′
North Lakevale	UNP/LNO	NS	Antigonish	11 F/13	45°46′	61°57′
North Lancaster	UNP/LNO	ON	Glengarry	31 G/1	45°13′	74°29′
North Lancaster	UNP/LNO	ON	Glengarry	31 G/1	45°15′	74°30′
Northland	UNP/LNO	ON	Algoma	41 K/9	46°43′	84°08′
Northlands Park	UNP/LNO	ON	Timiskaming	32 D/4	48°08′	79°52′
Northleigh	UNP/LNO	AB	34-50-6-W5	83 G/7	53°22′	114°48′
North Limestone Island	ISL/ÎLE	ON	Parry Sound	41 H/7	45°25′	80°32′
North Little River Lake	LAKE/LAC	NB	Northumberland	21 O/8	47°16′	66°09′
North Lochaber	UNP/LNO	NS	Antigonish	11 E/8	45°27′	62°01′
North Lonsdale	UNP/LNO	BC	New Westminster	92 G/6	49°20′	123°04′
North Low	UNP/LNO	QC	La Vallée-de-la-Gatineau	31 G/13	45°51′	75°57′
North Lunenburg	UNP/LNO	ON	Stormont	31 G/2	45°04′	74°58′
North Macmillan River	RIV/CDE	YT		105 N/3	63°03′	133°18′
North Magnetawan	UNP/LNO	ON	Parry Sound	41 H/9	45°44′	80°19′
North Main	UNP/LNO	MB		62 H/14	49°58′	97°05′
Northmark	UNP/LNO	AB	20-76-6-W6	83 M/10	55°36′	118°54′
North Marysburgh	MUN2/AZM2	ON	Prince Edward	31 C/3	44°01′	77°00′

NAME NOM	ENTITY ENTITÉ	LOC 1 LIEU 1	LOC 2 LIEU 2	MAP CARTE	POSITION LAT	LONG
North McIntyre	UNP/LNO	ON	Thunder Bay	52 A/6	48°28′	89°18′
North McQuesten River	RIV/CDE	YT		115 P/16	63°50′	136°20′
North Medford	UNP/LNO	NS	Kings	21 H/1	45°11′	64°22′
North Middleboro	UNP/LNO	NS	Cumberland	11 E/13	45°47′	63°35′
North Milk River	RIV/CDE	AB	20-2-18-W4	82 H/1	49°08′	112°23′
North Milton	UNP/LNO	PE	Queens	11 L/6	46°20′	63°13′
Northminster	UNP/LNO	SK	4-51-27-W3	73 F/5	53°22′	109°56′
North Minto	UNP/LNO	NB	Sunbury	21 J/1	46°06′	66°05′
North Monaghan	MUN2/AZM2	ON	Peterborough	31 D/8	44°20′	78°24′
North Monetville	UNP/LNO	ON	Sudbury	41 I/1	46°11′	80°19′
North Moose Lake	LAKE/LAC	MB	2-59-19W	63 K/1	54°05′	100°12′
North Mountain	MTN/MNT	NS	Inverness	11 F/14	45°49′	61°05′
North Mountain	MTN/MNT	NS	Annapolis	21 A/14	44°58′	65°00′
North Muskego River	RIV/CDE	ON	Cochrane	42 H/4	49°14′	81°39′
North Nahanni River	RIV/CDE	NT	Mackenzie	95 J	62°15′	123°20′
North Nation Mills	UNP/LNO	QC	Papineau	31 G/11	45°38′	75°08′
North Nechako	UNP/LNO	BC	Cariboo	93 G/15	53°56′	122°46′
North Noel Road	UNP/LNO	NS	Hants	11 E/4	45°14′	63°45′
North Norfolk	MUN2/AZM2	MB		62 G/15	49°55′	98°50′
North Ogden	UNP/LNO	NS	Guysborough	11 F/5	45°22′	61°40′
North Okanagan	MUN1/AZM1	BC	Osoyoos Division Yale	82 L/7	50°25′	118°45′
North Onslow	UNP/LNO	QC	Les Collines-de-l'Outaouais	31 F/9	45°36′	76°16′
North Ooglit Islands	ISL/ÎLE	NT	Franklin	47 A	68°59′	81°09′
North Opuskiamishes River	RIV/CDE	MB		53 N/9	55°32′	92°11′
North Oshawa	UNP/LNO	ON	Ontario	30 M/15	43°56′	78°53′
North Pangnirtung Fiord	BAY/BAIE	NT	Franklin	26 P	67°09′	64°17′
North Parcel of Beaton River 204	IR/RI	BC	Peace River	94 A/10	56°44′	120°49′
North Park	UNP/LNO	ON	York	30 M/11	43°43′	79°29′
North Park	UNP/LNO	SK		73 B/2	52°09′	106°39′
North Parry	UNP/LNO	ON	Parry Sound	41 H/8	45°21′	80°03′
North Pelham	UNP/LNO	ON	Welland	30 M/3	43°04′	79°21′
North Pender Island	ISL/ÎLE	BC	Cowichan	92 B/14	48°47′	123°17′
North Penetangore River	RIV/CDE	ON	Bruce	41 A/4	44°11′	81°39′
North Peninsula	CAPE/CAP	ON	Thunder Bay	52 I/1	50°10′	88°20′
North Pine	UNP/LNO	BC	Peace River	94 A/7	56°26′	120°43′
North Pine River	RIV/CDE	MB	2-34-21-W	62 N/16	51°54′	100°19′
North Plantagenet	MUN2/AZM2	ON	Prescott	31 G/11	45°31′	75°01′
North Point	CAPE/CAP	NS	Digby	21 B/8	44°17′	66°21′
North Point Douglas	UNP/LNO	MB		62 H/14	49°55′	97°08′
North Pole Stream	RIV/CDE	NB	Northumberland	21 J/16	46°58′	66°28′
North Pond	LAKE/LAC	NF		2 F/4	49°08′	53°49′
North Pond	LAKE/LAC	NF		2 D/9	48°43′	54°30′
North Pond Heights	UNP/LNO	NF		1 N/10	47°39′	52°44′
North Poplar	UNP/LNO	BC	New Westminster	92 G/1	49°02′	122°20′
*Northport	VILG/VILG	PE	Prince	21 I/16	46°48′	64°05′
Northport	UNP/LNO	NS	Cumberland	11 E/13	45°56′	63°52′
North Port	UNP/LNO	ON	Prince Edward	31 C/3	44°08′	77°11′
North Portage	UNP/LNO	ON	Muskoka	31 E/6	45°20′	79°05′
North Portal	VILG/VILG	SK	1-1-5-W2	62 E/2	49°00′	102°33′
North Preston	UNP/LNO	NS	Halifax	11 D/14	44°45′	63°28′
North Qu'Appelle No. 187	MUN2/AZM2	SK		62 L/12	50°45′	103°55′
North Ram River	RIV/CDE	AB	38-12-W5	83 B/5	52°16′	115°38′
North Range	UNP/LNO	NS	Digby	21 A/12	44°30′	65°51′
North Red Deer	UNP/LNO	AB	20-38-27-W4	83 A/5	52°17′	113°49′
North Renous	UNP/LNO	NB	Northumberland	21 I/13	46°48′	65°51′
North Renous Lake	LAKE/LAC	NB	Northumberland	21 J/15	46°55′	66°35′
North Ridge	UNP/LNO	NB	Carleton	21 J/11	46°33′	67°18′
North Ridge	UNP/LNO	ON	Essex	40 J/2	42°09′	82°46′
Northridge	UNP/LNO	BC	New Westminster	92 G/11	49°42′	123°08′
North River	VILG/VILG	NF		1 N/11	47°33′	53°19′
North River - see-voir - Cornwall	VILG/VILG	PE		11 L/3	46°14′	63°13′
North River	UNP/LNO	NF		13 H/14	53°49′	57°06′
North River	UNP/LNO	PE	Queens	11 L/6	46°16′	63°12′
North River	UNP/LNO	NS	Colchester	11 E/6	45°25′	63°15′
North River	UNP/LNO	NS	Lunenburg	21 A/10	44°37′	64°46′
North River	UNP/LNO	MB		54 L/15	58°53′	94°41′
North River	RIV/CDE	NF		13 H/14	53°49′	57°05′
North River	RIV/CDE	NF		14 E/9	57°31′	62°33′
North River	RIV/CDE	NS	Victoria	11 K/7	46°18′	60°37′
North River	RIV/CDE	NS	Colchester	11 E/6	45°23′	63°18′
North River	RIV/CDE	NB	Westmorland	21 H/14	45°56′	65°11′
North River	RIV/CDE	ON	Simcoe	31 D/12	44°44′	79°39′
North River Bridge	UNP/LNO	NS	Victoria	11 K/7	46°18′	60°37′
North River Centre	UNP/LNO	NS	Victoria	11 K/7	46°17′	60°37′
North River Dam	UNP/LNO	QC	Témiscamingue	31 L/15	46°51′	78°47′

NAME NOM	ENTITY ENTITÉ	LOC 1 LIEU 1	LOC 2 LIEU 2	MAP CARTE	POSITION LAT	LONG
North River Heights	UNP/LNO	MB		62 H/14	49°52′	97°11′
North Riverside	UNP/LNO	NS	Guysborough	11 F/5	45°27′	61°32′
North Road	UNP/LNO	NB	Charlotte	21 B/15	44°55′	66°57′
North Road 19	IR/RI	BC	Range 5 Coast	93 K/8	54°27′	124°11′
North Rock	SHL/H-FD	NB	Charlotte	21 B/11	44°32′	67°05′
North Rogersville	UNP/LNO	NB	Northumberland	21 I/14	46°46′	65°27′
North Rosetown	UNP/LNO	SK	13-30-15-W3	72 O/12	51°34′	107°59′
Northrups Corner	UNP/LNO	NB	Kings	21 H/13	45°46′	65°46′
North Russell	UNP/LNO	ON	Russell	31 G/6	45°18′	75°23′
North Rustico	VILG/VILG	PE	Queens	11 L/6	46°27′	63°19′
North Rustico Harbour	UNP/LNO	PE	Queens	11 L/6	46°28′	63°18′
North Saanich	MUN1/AZM1	BC	North Saanich	92 B/11	48°40′	123°25′
North Saanich Land District	GEOG/GÉOG	BC		92 B	48°39′	123°26′
North Sailing Lake	LAKE/LAC	MB	23-14-15-E	52 L/3	50°11′	95°27′
North St. Boniface	UNP/LNO	MB		62 H/14	49°54′	97°07′
North St. Eleanors	UNP/LNO	PE	Prince	11 L/5	46°27′	63°49′
North Salem	UNP/LNO	NS	Hants	11 E/3	45°08′	63°28′
North Salmon River	RIV/CDE	NF		12 A/1	48°13′	56°02′
North Samson Island	ISL/ÎLE	NF		2 E/7	49°30′	54°57′
North Saskatchewan River - also-aussi - **Saskatchewan Nord, Rivière**	RIV/CDE	SK/AB		73 H/3	53°15′	105°05′
North Saskatoon	UNP/LNO	SK	37-5-W3	73 B/2	52°11′	106°39′
North Saugeen River	RIV/CDE	ON	Bruce	41 A/5	44°19′	81°16′
Norths Corner	UNP/LNO	NS	Kings	21 H/1	45°11′	64°25′
North Scot Lake	LAKE/LAC	ON	Kenora	52 E/14	49°59′	95°03′
North Seal River	RIV/CDE	MB		64 J/16	58°50′	98°06′
North Seguin	UNP/LNO	ON	Parry Sound	31 E/5	45°30′	79°42′
North Shoal Lake	LAKE/LAC	MB	17,18-2-W	62 I/5	50°29′	97°39′
North Shore	VILG/VILG	PE	Queens	11 L/6	46°23′	63°07′
North Shore	UNP/LNO	NF		2 D/9	48°41′	54°02′
North Shore	UNP/LNO	NS	Victoria	11 K/8	46°25′	60°28′
North Shore	UNP/LNO	NS	Cumberland	11 E/14	45°47′	63°21′
North Shore Fishing Lake	HAM/HAM	SK	33-11-W2	62 M/13	51°51′	103°31′
Northside	HAM/HAM	SK	28-52-26-W2	73 H/12	53°31′	105°46′
North Side	UNP/LNO	NF		1 K/15	46°58′	52°56′
Northside	UNP/LNO	NF		1 N/12	47°36′	53°56′
Northside East Bay	UNP/LNO	NS	Cape Breton	11 K/1	46°00′	60°26′
North Side Whycocomagh Bay	UNP/LNO	NS	Inverness	11 F/14	45°59′	61°02′
North Spicer Island	ISL/ÎLE	NT	Franklin	37 B	68°33′	78°45′
North Spirit Lake	UNP/LNO	ON	Kenora	53 C/6	52°31′	93°01′
North Spirit Lake	LAKE/LAC	ON	Kenora	53 C/10	52°31′	92°55′
North Spirit Lake	IR/RI	ON	Kenora	53 C/11	52°31′	93°01′
North Stag Islands	ISL/ÎLE	NF		13 I/3	54°05′	57°12′
North Star	UNP/LNO	SK	9-47-19-W2	73 H/2	53°02′	104°44′
North Star	UNP/LNO	AB	32-90-23-W5	84 C/13	56°51′	117°38′
North Star	UNP/LNO	BC	Kootenay	82 G/12	49°33′	115°45′
North Star Harbour	BAY/BAIE	NT	Franklin	98 B/15	72°51′	125°07′
North Star Mountain	MTN/MNT	BC	Cariboo	93 H/7	53°20′	120°54′
North Steady Pond	LAKE/LAC	NF		2 D/4	48°13′	55°48′
North Stukely	UNP/LNO	QC	Le Val-Saint-François	31 H/8	45°24′	72°20′
North Sutton	UNP/LNO	QC	Brome-Missisquoi	31 H/2	45°09′	72°40′
North Sydenham River	RIV/CDE	ON	Kent	40 J/9	42°36′	82°23′
North Sydney	UNP/LNO	NS	Cape Breton	11 K/1	46°13′	60°15′
North Tacla Lake 7	IR/RI	BC	Cassiar	93 N/5	55°29′	125°58′
North Tacla Lake 7A	IR/RI	BC	Cassiar	93 N/5	55°30′	125°59′
North Tacla Lake 12	IR/RI	BC	Cassiar	93 N/15	55°48′	124°38′
North Tacla Lake (Bates Creek) 10	IR/RI	BC	Cassiar	93 M/9	55°42′	126°14′
North Tacla Lake (North Meadow) 11A	IR/RI	BC	Cassiar	93 M/9	55°42′	126°16′
North Tacla Lake (West Landing) 8	IR/RI	BC	Cassiar	93 N/5	55°28′	126°01′
North Tay	UNP/LNO	NB	York	21 J/2	46°14′	66°52′
North Tea Lake	LAKE/LAC	ON	Nipissing	31 E/14	45°57′	79°03′
North Tetagouche	UNP/LNO	NB	Gloucester	21 P/12	47°38′	65°47′
North Thames River	RIV/CDE	ON	Middlesex	40 I/14	42°59′	81°15′
North Thamesville	UNP/LNO	ON	Kent	40 I/12	42°34′	82°00′
North Thompson 1	IR/RI	BC	Kamloops Division Yale	92 P/8	51°17′	120°10′
North Thompson River	RIV/CDE	BC	Kamloops Division Yale	92 I/9	50°41′	120°21′
North Tilley	UNP/LNO	NB	Victoria	21 J/13	46°51′	67°40′
North Toronto	UNP/LNO	ON	York	30 M/11	43°41′	79°23′
North Transcona	UNP/LNO	MB		62 H/14	49°55′	97°00′
North Tryon	UNP/LNO	PE	Prince	11 L/5	46°15′	63°33′
North Twillingate Island	ISL/ÎLE	NF		2 E/10	49°40′	54°48′
North Twin	MTN/MNT	AB	37-25-W5	83 C/3	52°14′	117°26′
North Twin Island	ISL/ÎLE	NT	Keewatin	33 E	53°18′	80°00′
North Twin Lake	LAKE/LAC	NF		2 E/5	49°16′	55°56′
Northumberland	MUN1/AZM1	ON	Northumberland	31 D/1	44°10′	78°00′
Northumberland	GEOG/GÉOG	NB		21 J/16	46°55′	66°00′

NAME NOM	ENTITY ENTITÉ	LOC 1 LIEU 1	LOC 2 LIEU 2	MAP CARTE	POSITION LAT	LONG
Northumberland	GEOG/GÉOG	ON		31 C/4	44°10′	78°00′
Northumberland, Détroit de - also-aussi - **Northumberland Strait**	CHAN/CHEN	PE/NB/NS		11 L/4	46°09′	63°39′
Northumberland Sound	CHAN/CHEN	NT	Franklin	69 A	76°49′	96°40′
Northumberland Strait - also-aussi - **Northumberland, Détroit de**	CHAN/CHEN	PE/NB/NS		11 L/4	46°09′	63°39′
North Valley	UNP/LNO	NF		1 N/11	47°33′	53°19′
North Valley	UNP/LNO	ON	Stormont	31 G/3	45°03′	75°03′
North Vancouver	CITY/VIL1	BC	New Westminster	92 G/6	49°19′	123°04′
North Vancouver	MUN1/AZM1	BC	New Westminster	92 G/6	49°22′	123°04′
North Vermilion Settlement	UNP/LNO	AB	108-13-W5	84 K/8	58°24′	116°02′
North View	UNP/LNO	NB	Victoria	21 J/14	46°58′	67°26′
Northville	UNP/LNO	NS	Kings	21 H/2	45°09′	64°34′
North Wabasca Lake	LAKE/LAC	AB	80,81-25,26-W4	83 P/13	56°09′	113°55′
North Wallace	UNP/LNO	NS	Cumberland	11 E/14	45°50′	63°29′
North Wallace Bay	UNP/LNO	NS	Cumberland	11 E/13	45°50′	63°34′
North Ward	UNP/LNO	ON	Elgin	40 I/11	42°41′	81°13′
North Washagami Lake	LAKE/LAC	ON	Kenora	43 K/6	54°30′	85°03′
North Washagami River	RIV/CDE	ON	Kenora	43 F/15	53°47′	84°59′
Northway	UNP/LNO	SK	21-46A-25-W2	73 A/13	52°59′	105°35′
Northwest	UNP/LNO	NS	Lunenburg	21 A/4	44°24′	64°21′
Northwest Angle 33B	IR/RI	ON	Kenora	52 E/6	49°23′	95°00′
Northwest Angle 34C	IR/RI	MB		52 E/6	49°22′	95°11′
Northwest Angle 34C & 37B	IR/RI	ON	Kenora	52 E/6	49°24′	95°09′
Northwest Angle 37C	IR/RI	MB		52 E/6	49°22′	95°10′
North West Arm	UNP/LNO	NF		1 N/11	47°35′	53°17′
North West Arm	UNP/LNO	NF		2 F/4	49°08′	53°38′
North West Arm	UNP/LNO	NS	Cape Breton	11 K/1	46°09′	60°17′
Northwest Arm	BAY/BAIE	NF		2 C/5	48°27′	53°41′
Northwest Arm	BAY/BAIE	NF		2 C/12	48°45′	53°59′
Northwest Arm	BAY/BAIE	NF		12 P/8	51°21′	56°04′
Northwest Arm	BAY/BAIE	NF		11 P/10	47°42′	56°33′
North West Arm	BAY/BAIE	NS	Cape Breton	11 K/1	46°11′	60°16′
Northwest Arm	BAY/BAIE	BC	Cassiar	93 N/4	55°13′	125°55′
Northwest Atlantic Mid-Ocean Canyon	SEAU/SMER	—		814A	50°00′	41°00′
Northwest Basin	UNP/LNO	ON	Simcoe	31 D/13	44°48′	79°57′
Northwest Bay	UNP/LNO	ON	Rainy River	52 C/13	48°51′	93°34′
Northwest Bay	BAY/BAIE	ON	Cochrane	42 A/16	48°54′	80°06′
Northwest Bay	BAY/BAIE	ON	Rainy River	52 C/13	48°50′	93°34′
Northwest Bay	BAY/BAIE	BC	Nanoose	92 F/8	49°19′	124°13′
Northwest Bridge	UNP/LNO	NB	Northumberland	21 I/13	46°58′	65°35′
North West Brook	UNP/LNO	NF		2 C/4	48°01′	53°58′
Northwest Brook	RIV/CDE	NF		1 K/14	46°45′	53°23′
Northwest Brook	RIV/CDE	NF		2 D/9	48°44′	54°03′
Northwest Brook	RIV/CDE	NF		2 D/16	48°52′	54°08′
Northwest Brook	RIV/CDE	NF		11 O/16	47°48′	58°20′
Northwest Brook	RIV/CDE	NF		11 O/10	47°42′	58°34′
Northwest Burnt Island	ISL/ÎLE	ON	Manitoulin	41 H/13	45°54′	81°38′
Northwest, Cape	CAPE/CAP	NT	Franklin	560 B	80°21′	96°36′
Northwest Cove	UNP/LNO	NS	Lunenburg	21 A/9	44°32′	64°01′
Northwestern Explorer Rift Valley	SEAU/SMER	—		19400A	50°20′	130°10′
Northwest Gander River	RIV/CDE	NF		2 D/14	48°52′	55°01′
North West Harbour	UNP/LNO	NS	Shelburne	20 P/11	43°34′	65°25′
Northwest Head	CAPE/CAP	NF		1 M/5	47°16′	55°58′
Northwest Island	ISL/ÎLE	NF		11 P/11	47°31′	57°24′
Northwest Millstream	RIV/CDE	NB	Northumberland	21 I/13	46°58′	65°42′
Northwest Miramichi River	RIV/CDE	NB	Northumberland	21 I/13	46°58′	65°35′
Northwest Point	UNP/LNO	MB	13-5-17-E	52 E/6	49°24′	95°10′
Northwest Point	CAPE/CAP	NT	Mackenzie	85 G	61°42′	115°30′
Northwest Pond	LAKE/LAC	NF		2 C/5	48°23′	53°55′
Northwest Pond	LAKE/LAC	NF		2 F/4	49°00′	53°56′
North West River	TOWN/VIL2	NF		13 F/9	53°32′	60°08′
Northwest River	RIV/CDE	NF		2 D/8	48°24′	54°12′
Northwest Territories - also-aussi - **Nord-Ouest, Territoires du**	TERR/TERR	NT		MCR130	70°00′	95°00′
Northwest Upsalquitch River	RIV/CDE	NB	Restigouche	21 O/10	47°40′	66°42′
North Weyburn	HAM/HAM	SK	35-8-14-W2	62 E/12	49°41′	103°49′
North Williamston	UNP/LNO	NS	Annapolis	21 A/14	44°54′	65°08′
North Wiltshire	VILG/VILG	PE	Queens	11 L/6	46°18′	63°19′
North Wiltshire	UNP/LNO	PE	Queens	11 L/6	46°18′	63°20′
North Winchester	UNP/LNO	ON	Dundas	31 G/3	45°11′	75°15′
North Wind Lake	LAKE/LAC	ON	Thunder Bay	42 E/13	49°52′	87°57′
Northwind Ridge	SEAU/SMER	—		800A	77°00′	156°00′
Northwood	UNP/LNO	ON	Kent	40 J/8	42°29′	82°03′
North Woodlands	UNP/LNO	BC	New Westminster	92 G/7	49°21′	122°55′
Northwood Park	UNP/LNO	ON	Peel	30 M/12	43°41′	79°47′
Northwoods Camp	UNP/LNO	ON	Nipissing	41 I/16	46°50′	80°08′
North Woodslee	UNP/LNO	ON	Essex	40 J/2	42°13′	82°43′

NAME NOM	ENTITY ENTITÉ	LOC 1 LIEU 1	LOC 2 LIEU 2	MAP CARTE	POSITION LAT	LONG
North Woolwich	UNP/LNO	ON	Waterloo	40 P/10	43°39′	80°33′
North York	CITY/VIL1	ON	York	30 M/14	43°46′	79°25′
Norton	VILG/VILG	NB	Kings	21 H/12	45°38′	65°42′
Norton	UNP/LNO	BC	New Westminster	92 G/1	49°01′	122°11′
Norton	GEOG/GÉOG	NB	Kings	21 H/12	45°37′	65°45′
Norton, Cape	CAPE/CAP	NT	Franklin	67 D	69°14′	96°02′
Norton Creek	UNP/LNO	QC	Les Jardins-de-Napierville	31 H/4	45°10′	73°43′
Nortondale	UNP/LNO	NB	York	21 J/3	46°07′	67°16′
Norton Lake	LAKE/LAC	MB		54 K/12	58°42′	93°34′
Norton No. 69	MUN2/AZM2	SK		72 H/10	49°40′	104°35′
Norton Shaw, Cape	CAPE/CAP	NT	Franklin	39 B	76°28′	78°23′
Norval	UNP/LNO	ON	Halton	30 M/12	43°39′	79°51′
Norval Station	UNP/LNO	ON	Halton	30 M/12	43°40′	79°52′
Norvern Shores	UNP/LNO	ON	Muskoka	31 E/6	45°20′	79°20′
Norway	UNP/LNO	PE	Prince	21 P/1	47°00′	64°02′
Norway Bay	UNP/LNO	QC	Pontiac	31 F/9	45°31′	76°25′
Norway Bay	BAY/BAIE	NT	Franklin	77 H/1	71°06′	104°28′
Norway House	UNP/LNO	MB		63 H/13	53°59′	97°49′
Norway House 17	IR/RI	MB		63 I/4	54°01′	97°45′
Norway House 17A	IR/RI	MB		63 I/4	54°15′	97°36′
Norway House 17B	IR/RI	MB		63 I/4	54°14′	97°36′
Norway House Settlement	GEOG/GÉOG	MB		63 H/13	53°57′	97°53′
Norway Island	ISL/ÎLE	NT	Franklin	98 C	73°41′	124°40′
Norway Lake	LAKE/LAC	ON	Renfrew	31 F/7	45°20′	76°43′
Norway Point	UNP/LNO	ON	Muskoka	31 E/3	45°13′	79°01′
Norwegian Bay	BAY/BAIE	NT	Franklin	59 D	77°30′	90°30′
Norwich	MUN2/AZM2	ON	Oxford	40 P/2	43°00′	80°40′
Norwich	UNP/LNO	ON	Oxford	40 I/15	42°59′	80°36′
Norwood	VILG/VILG	ON	Peterborough	31 C/5	44°23′	77°59′
Norwood	UNP/LNO	NS	Digby	21 B/1	44°04′	66°01′
Norwood	UNP/LNO	MB		62 H/14	49°53′	97°07′
Norwood East	UNP/LNO	MB		62 H/14	49°53′	97°07′
Norwood West	UNP/LNO	MB		62 H/14	49°53′	97°08′
Nosbonsing	UNP/LNO	ON	Nipissing	31 L/3	46°14′	79°13′
Nosbonsing, Lake	LAKE/LAC	ON	Nipissing	31 L/3	46°12′	79°13′
Nose Creek	RIV/CDE	AB	68-11-W6	83 L/13	54°52′	119°38′
Nose Hill	MTN/MNT	AB	37-8,9-W4	73 D/3	52°10′	111°10′
Nose Lake	LAKE/LAC	NT	Mackenzie	76 F/7	65°25′	108°55′
Nose of the Bank	SEAU/SMER	—			46°45′	47°30′
Nostetuko River	RIV/CDE	BC	Range 2 Coast	92 N/8	51°26′	124°29′
Notakwanon River	RIV/CDE	NF		14 C/4	56°02′	61°31′
Notawassi, Lac	LAKE/LAC	QC	Antoine-Labelle	31 O/4	47°06′	75°30′
Notch Hill	UNP/LNO	BC	Kamloops Division Yale	82 L/14	50°51′	119°26′
Notchtop Peak	MTN/MNT	BC	Cassiar	94 D/5	56°28′	127°40′
Notigi	UNP/LNO	MB	30-79-12-W	63 O/14	55°52′	99°19′
Notigi Lake	LAKE/LAC	MB	80-12,13-W	63 O/14	55°56′	99°18′
Notikewin	UNP/LNO	AB	16-92-23-W5	84 C/13	56°59′	117°38′
Notikewin Provincial Park	PARK/PARC	AB	94,95-19,20-W5	84 F/3	57°14′	117°08′
Notikewin River	RIV/CDE	AB	95-20-W5	84 F/6	57°17′	117°08′
Notman	UNP/LNO	ON	Kenora	52 G/5	49°22′	91°34′
Notre-Dame	UNP/LNO	NB	Kent	21 I/7	46°19′	64°43′
Notre-Dame-Auxiliatrice-de-Buckland	VILG/VILG	QC	Bellechasse	21 L/10	46°37′	70°33′
Notre Dame Bay	BAY/BAIE	NF		2 E/14	49°45′	55°00′
Notre Dame Channel - also-aussi - Notre-Dame, Chenal	SEAU/SMER	—		8015	50°00′	54°30′
Notre-Dame, Chenal - also-aussi - Notre Dame Channel	SEAU/SMER	—		8015	50°00′	54°30′
Notre-Dame-de-Bon-Secours	VILG/VILG	QC	Rouville	31 H/6	45°24′	73°13′
Notre-Dame-de-Bon-Secours-Partie-Nord	VILG/VILG	QC	Papineau	31 G/10	45°42′	74°52′
Notre-Dame-de-Ham	VILG/VILG	QC	Arthabaska	21 E/13	45°55′	71°44′
Notre-Dame-de-la-Merci	VILG/VILG	QC	Matawinie	31 J/1	46°14′	74°03′
Notre-Dame-de-la-Paix	VILG/VILG	QC	Papineau	31 G/15	45°49′	74°58′
Notre-Dame-de-la-Salette	VILG/VILG	QC	Les Collines-de-l'Outaouais	31 G/13	45°46′	75°35′
Notre-Dame-de-l'Île-Perrot	VILG/VILG	QC	Vaudreuil-Soulanges	31 H/5	45°22′	73°56′
Notre-Dame-de-l'Isle-Verte	UNP/LNO	QC	Rivière-du-Loup	22 C/3	48°00′	69°27′
Notre-Dame-de-Lorette	VILG/VILG	QC	Maria-Chapdelaine	32 H/1	49°05′	72°21′
Notre-Dame-de-Lourdes	VILG/VILG	QC	L'Érable	21 L/5	46°19′	71°49′
Notre-Dame-de-Lourdes	VILG/VILG	QC	Joliette	31 I/3	46°06′	73°26′
Notre Dame de Lourdes	VILG/VILG	MB	36,1-6,7-9-W	62 G/10	49°32′	98°33′
Notre-Dame-de-Lourdes	UNP/LNO	NB	Madawaska	21 O/5	47°15′	67°56′
Notre-Dame-de-Lourdes	GEOG/GÉOG	NB	Madawaska	21 O/5	47°22′	67°50′
Notre-Dame-de-Montauban	VILG/VILG	QC	Mékinac	31 I/16	46°52′	72°20′
Notre-Dame-de-Pierreville	VILG/VILG	QC	Nicolet-Yamaska	31 I/2	46°06′	72°53′
Notre-Dame-de-Pontmain	VILG/VILG	QC	Antoine-Labelle	31 J/5	46°17′	75°38′
Notre-Dame-de-Portneuf	VILG/VILG	QC	Portneuf	21 L/12	46°44′	71°55′
Notre-Dame-de-Saint-Hyacinthe	VILG/VILG	QC	Les Maskoutains	31 H/10	45°37′	72°56′
Notre-Dame-des-Anges	VILG/VILG	QC	Communauté urbaine de Québec	21 L/14	46°49′	71°14′

NAME / NOM	ENTITY / ENTITÉ	LOC 1 / LIEU 1	LOC 2 / LIEU 2	MAP / CARTE	POSITION LAT	POSITION LONG
Notre-Dame-des-Anges	UNP/LNO	QC	Mékinac	31 I/16	46°53′	72°19′
Notre-Dame-des-Bois	VILG/VILG	QC	Le Granit	21 E/6	45°24′	71°04′
Notre-Dame-des-Champs	UNP/LNO	ON	Carleton	31 G/6	45°26′	75°29′
Notre-Dame-des-Érables	UNP/LNO	NB	Gloucester	21 P/11	47°38′	65°14′
Notre-Dame-des-Laurentides	UNP/LNO	QC	Communauté urbaine de Québec	21 L/14	46°55′	71°21′
Notre-Dame-des-Mères	UNP/LNO	QC	Sherbrooke	21 E/12	45°31′	71°54′
Notre-Dame-des-Monts	VILG/VILG	QC	Charlevoix-Est	21 M/9	47°40′	70°23′
Notre-Dame-des-Neiges-des-Trois-Pistoles	VILG/VILG	QC	Les Basques	22 C/3	48°07′	69°10′
Notre-Dame-des-Pins	VILG/VILG	QC	Beauce-Sartigan	21 L/2	46°11′	70°43′
Notre-Dame-des-Prairies	VILG/VILG	QC	Joliette	31 I/3	46°03′	73°26′
Notre-Dame-des-Sept-Douleurs	VILG/VILG	QC	Rivière-du-Loup	22 C/3	48°00′	69°27′
Notre-Dame-de-Stanbridge	VILG/VILG	QC	Brome-Missisquoi	31 H/3	45°10′	73°02′
Notre-Dame-du-Bon-Conseil	TOWN/VIL2	QC	Drummond	31 I/1	46°00′	72°21′
Notre-Dame-du-Bon-Conseil	VILG/VILG	QC	Drummond	31 I/1	46°00′	72°21′
Notre-Dame-du-Lac	CITY/VIL1	QC	Témiscouata	21 N/10	47°36′	68°48′
Notre Dame du Lac	UNP/LNO	ON	Nipissing	41 I/8	46°18′	80°11′
Notre-Dame-du-Laus	VILG/VILG	QC	Antoine-Labelle	31 J/4	46°05′	75°37′
Notre-Dame-du-Mont-Carmel	VILG/VILG	QC	Le Centre-de-la-Mauricie	31 I/7	46°29′	72°39′
Notre-Dame-du-Mont-Carmel	VILG/VILG	QC	Le Haut-Richelieu	31 H/3	45°05′	73°22′
Notre-Dame-du-Nord	VILG/VILG	QC	Témiscamingue	31 M/11	47°36′	79°29′
Notre-Dame-du-Portage	VILG/VILG	QC	Rivière-du-Loup	21 N/13	47°46′	69°37′
Notre-Dame-du-Rosaire	VILG/VILG	QC	Montmagny	21 L/16	46°50′	70°24′
Notre-Dame-du-Rosaire	UNP/LNO	QC	Lac-Saint-Jean-Est	22 D/14	48°48′	71°26′
Notre-Dame-du-Sacré-Coeur-d'Issoudun	VILG/VILG	QC	Lotbinière	21 L/12	46°35′	71°37′
Notre-Dame-du-Saguenay	UNP/LNO	QC	Le Fjord-du-Saguenay	22 D/8	48°19′	70°19′
Notre Dame Junction	UNP/LNO	NF		2 E/3	49°08′	55°05′
Notre-Dame, Monts	MTN/MNT	QC	La Mitis	22 C/1	48°10′	68°00′
Notre-Dame, Ruisseau	RIV/CDE	QC	Lajemmerais	31 H/11	45°41′	73°27′
Nottawa	UNP/LNO	ON	Simcoe	41 A/8	44°27′	80°13′
Nottawasaga - see-voir - Clearview	MUN2/AZM2	ON		41 A/8	44°24′	80°04′
Nottawasaga Bay	BAY/BAIE	ON	Grey	41 A/9	44°35′	80°15′
Nottawasaga River	RIV/CDE	ON	Simcoe	41 A/9	44°32′	80°00′
Nottaway, Rivière	RIV/CDE	QC	Jamésie	32 M/7	51°22′	78°55′
Nottingham	UNP/LNO	SK	15-5-32-W	62 F/5	49°24′	101°43′
Nottingham Island	UNP/LNO	NT	Franklin	35 N	63°07′	77°56′
Nottingham Island	ISL/ÎLE	NT	Franklin	35 N	63°20′	77°55′
Notukeu	UNP/LNO	SK	4-4-27-W3	72 F/5	49°17′	109°35′
Notukeu Creek	RIV/CDE	SK	27-11-4-W3	72 G/16	49°56′	106°29′
Nouel, Lac	LAKE/LAC	QC	Minganie	22 I/15	50°49′	64°33′
Noueux, Ruisseau	RIV/CDE	QC	Communauté urbaine de l'Outaouais	31 G/12	45°32′	75°38′
Nourse	UNP/LNO	MB	1-11-8-E	62 H/16	49°53′	96°23′
Nouveau-Brunswick - also-aussi - **New Brunswick**	PROV/PROV	NB		MCR77	46°30′	66°00′
Nouveau, Lac	LAKE/LAC	QC	Caniapiscau	23 F/14	53°57′	69°01′
Nouveau-Québec	GEOG/GÉOG	QC	Jamésie	34 A/16	57°00′	72°00′
Nouveau-Québec, Cratère du	CRAT/CRAT	QC	Kativik	35 H/5	61°17′	73°40′
Nouvel, Lacs	LAKE/LAC	QC	Manicouagan	22 K/2	50°03′	68°52′
Nouvelle	VILG/VILG	QC	Avignon	22 B/1	48°08′	66°19′
Nouvelle-Angleterre, Chaîne de monts de la - also-aussi - New England Seamount Chain	SEAU/SMER	—		4006	38°00′	61°00′
Nouvelle, Baie	BAY/BAIE	QC	Le Fjord-du-Saguenay	22 L/10	50°37′	70°52′
Nouvelle-Écosse - also-aussi - **Nova Scotia**	PROV/PROV	NS		MCR77	45°00′	63°00′
Nouvelle-France, Cap de	CAPE/CAP	QC	Kativik	35 I/5	62°28′	73°40′
Nouvelle-Ouest	UNP/LNO	QC	Avignon	22 B/1	48°09′	66°22′
Nouvelle, Petite rivière	RIV/CDE	QC	Avignon	22 B/7	48°18′	66°31′
Nouvelle, Rivière	RIV/CDE	QC	Bonaventure	22 A/5	48°16′	65°43′
Nouvelle, Rivière	RIV/CDE	QC	Avignon	22 B/1	48°07′	66°17′
Novar	UNP/LNO	ON	Parry Sound	31 E/6	45°27′	79°15′
Nova Scotia - also-aussi - **Nouvelle-Écosse**	PROV/PROV	NS		MCR77	45°00′	63°00′
Nova Zembla Island	ISL/ÎLE	NT	Franklin	38 A	72°11′	74°50′
Novereau, Lac	LAKE/LAC	QC	Kativik	23 M/8	55°17′	70°15′
Novra	UNP/LNO	MB	13-41-26-W	63 C/11	52°32′	101°04′
Nowashe Creek	RIV/CDE	ON	Kenora	43 J/1	54°06′	82°18′
Nowashe Lake	LAKE/LAC	ON	Kenora	43 G/14	53°48′	83°08′
Nowell Channel	CHAN/CHEN	BC	Range 1 Coast	92 L/15	50°47′	126°48′
Nowlanville	UNP/LNO	NB	Northumberland	21 I/13	46°57′	65°31′
Nowleye Lake	LAKE/LAC	NT	Keewatin	65 K	62°23′	101°05′
Nowyak Lake	LAKE/LAC	NT	Keewatin	65 G	61°50′	98°21′
Noyan	VILG/VILG	QC	Le Haut-Richelieu	31 H/3	45°04′	73°18′
Noyée, La	MTN/MNT	QC	Charlevoix-Est	21 M/16	47°46′	70°28′
Noyé, Le	UNP/LNO	QC	La Jacques-Cartier	21 L/13	46°54′	71°31′
Noyes Crossing	UNP/LNO	AB	8-55-1-W5	83 G/9	53°44′	114°06′
Noyrot, Lac	LAKE/LAC	QC	Minganie	12 O/7	51°25′	58°50′
Nuchaquis 2	IR/RI	BC	Barclay	92 C/14	48°56′	125°03′
Nuchatl 1	IR/RI	BC	Nootka	92 E/15	49°49′	126°58′
Nuchatl 2	IR/RI	BC	Nootka	92 E/15	49°48′	126°58′
Nuchatlitz	UNP/LNO	BC	Nootka	92 E/15	49°48′	126°58′

NAME NOM	ENTITY ENTITÉ	LOC 1 LIEU 1	LOC 2 LIEU 2	MAP CARTE	POSITION LAT	LONG
Nuchatlitz Inlet	BAY/BAIE	BC	Nootka	92 E/15	49°46′	126°56′
Nude Creek	RIV/CDE	BC	Range 2 Coast	92 N/7	51°23′	124°45′
Nudell Bush	UNP/LNO	ON	Dundas	31 B/14	44°58′	75°06′
Nudlukta Inlet	BAY/BAIE	NT	Franklin	57 G	71°44′	94°18′
Nudlung Fiord	BAY/BAIE	NT	Franklin	27 A	68°21′	67°27′
Nue de Mingan, Île	ISL/ÎLE	QC	Minganie	22 I/1	50°13′	64°07′
Nueltin Lake	LAKE/LAC	NT/MB		65 B/5	60°20′	99°35′
Nugent	UNP/LNO	AB	11-44-3-W5	83 B/16	52°48′	114°18′
Nuggetville	UNP/LNO	NF		1 N/5	47°20′	53°34′
Nukko Lake	UNP/LNO	BC	Cariboo	93 J/2	54°05′	122°59′
Nukvuk Lake	LAKE/LAC	NT	Franklin	36 G	65°01′	75°55′
Nuliarvik	UNP/LNO	QC	Kativik	25 F/4	61°01′	69°40′
Nulki	UNP/LNO	BC	Range 4 Coast	93 F/16	53°55′	124°12′
Nulki Lake	LAKE/LAC	BC	Range 4 Coast	93 F/16	53°55′	124°09′
Nullualuk, Lac	LAKE/LAC	QC	Kativik	24 E/15	57°53′	70°51′
Nuluarniavik, Lac	LAKE/LAC	QC	Kativik	34 K/5	58°20′	77°37′
Numabin Bay	BAY/BAIE	SK		64 D/11	56°36′	103°07′
Numao Lake	LAKE/LAC	MB	14-14-E	52 L/4	50°10′	95°38′
Numas Islands	ISL/ÎLE	BC	Range 1 Coast	92 L/14	50°46′	127°06′
Numogate	UNP/LNO	ON	Lanark	31 C/16	44°57′	76°02′
Numukamis 1	IR/RI	BC	Barclay	92 C/14	48°54′	125°00′
Nunainnaq	UNP/LNO	QC	Kativik	34 K/15	58°52′	76°41′
Nunaksaluk Island	ISL/ÎLE	NF		13 N/16	55°49′	60°20′
Nunalik	UNP/LNO	QC	Kativik	25 C/12	60°39′	69°57′
Nunalla	UNP/LNO	MB		54 M/15	59°55′	94°50′
Nunavut (effective/en vigueur 1/4/99)	TERR/TERR	NT		57 E/3	70°10′	90°44′
Nungesser Lake	LAKE/LAC	ON	Kenora	52 N/5	51°28′	93°30′
Nunim Lake	LAKE/LAC	SK		64 M/8	59°28′	102°25′
Nunn Lake	LAKE/LAC	SK		73 P/1	55°15′	104°20′
Nursery	UNP/LNO	BC	Similkameen Division Yale	82 E/1	49°01′	118°24′
Nutak	UNP/LNO	NF		14 F/5	57°28′	61°52′
Nutana	UNP/LNO	SK		73 B/2	52°07′	106°39′
Nutana Park South	UNP/LNO	SK		73 B/2	52°06′	106°38′
Nutapushuanan	UNP/LNO	QC	Sept-Rivières	22 O/2	51°10′	66°59′
Nutarawit Lake	LAKE/LAC	NT	Keewatin	65 O	63°02′	98°10′
Nutimesanu	UNP/LNO	QC	Jamésie	32 M/9	51°31′	78°06′
Nutimik Lake	UNP/LNO	MB	14-13,14-E	52 L/4	50°09′	95°41′
Nut Island	ISL/ÎLE	ON	Lennox and Addington	31 C/2	44°06′	76°44′
Nut Lake	LAKE/LAC	SK		63 D/5	52°22′	103°42′
Nut Lake 90 - see-voir - Yellowquill 90	IR/RI	SK		63 D/5	52°22′	103°39′
Nut Mountain	HAM/HAM	SK	28-36-10-W2	63 D/3	52°08′	103°23′
Nuttby	UNP/LNO	NS	Colchester	11 E/11	45°32′	63°12′
Nuttlude Lake	LAKE/LAC	BC	Cassiar	104 G/9	57°43′	130°26′
Nutt's Corners	UNP/LNO	QC	Le Haut-Richelieu	31 H/3	45°03′	73°12′
Nutzotin Mountains	MTN/MNT	YT		115 K/2	62°00′	140°55′
Nuuautin 2	IR/RI	BC	Kamloops Division Yale	92 I/5	50°16′	121°35′
Nuuautin 2A	IR/RI	BC	Kamloops Division Yale	92 I/4	50°15′	121°35′
Nuuautin 2B	IR/RI	BC	Kamloops Division Yale	92 I/5	50°16′	121°35′
Nuvorak Point	CAPE/CAP	NT	Mackenzie	107 E	70°09′	130°23′
Nuvuk Islands	ISL/ÎLE	NT	Franklin	35 L/8	62°24′	78°03′
Nuvuk Point	CAPE/CAP	NT	Franklin	26 H	65°05′	64°33′
Nuvuk Point	CAPE/CAP	NT	Keewatin	46 E	65°08′	86°56′
Nuvulik	UNP/LNO	QC	Kativik	25 C/12	60°41′	69°52′
Nuwata	UNP/LNO	NT	Franklin	36 F	65°08′	77°37′
Nyanza	UNP/LNO	NS	Victoria	11 K/2	46°05′	60°54′
Nyanza Bay	BAY/BAIE	NS	Victoria	11 K/2	46°05′	60°53′
Nyarling River	RIV/CDE	NT	Mackenzie	85 A	60°41′	113°23′
Nyeboe Fiord	BAY/BAIE	NT	Franklin	47 F	70°25′	86°30′
Nyel, Lac	LAKE/LAC	QC	Minganie	12 N/2	51°11′	60°47′
Nym Lake	LAKE/LAC	ON	Rainy River	52 B/11	48°42′	91°26′

O

Oak	UNP/LNO	NB	Carleton	21 J/4	46°01′	67°39′
Oak Acres	UNP/LNO	ON	Lambton	40 O/1	43°00′	82°23′
Oakbank	UNP/LNO	MB	21,22-11-5-E	62 H/15	49°57′	96°51′
Oak Bay	MUN1/AZM1	BC	Victoria	92 B/6	48°27′	123°18′
Oak Bay	UNP/LNO	NB	Charlotte	21 G/3	45°14′	67°12′
Oak Bay	UNP/LNO	QC	Avignon	22 B/2	48°03′	66°38′
Oak Bay	BAY/BAIE	NB	Charlotte	21 G/3	45°12′	67°10′
Oak Bluff	UNP/LNO	MB	25-9-1-E	62 H/14	49°46′	97°19′
Oak Bluff Station	UNP/LNO	MB	25-9-1-E	62 H/14	49°46′	97°21′
Oak Brae	UNP/LNO	MB	36-28-18-W	62 O/5	51°27′	99°52′
Oakburn	UNP/LNO	MB	28-18-23-W	62 K/10	50°34′	100°35′
Oakdale	UNP/LNO	ON	Lambton	40 J/9	42°43′	82°02′

NAME NOM	ENTITY ENTITÉ	LOC 1 LIEU 1	LOC 2 LIEU 2	MAP CARTE	POSITION LAT	LONG
Oakdale No. 320	MUN2/AZM2	SK		72 N/11	51°45′	109°15′
Oakdene Point	UNP/LNO	ON	Victoria	31 D/2	44°13′	78°48′
Oakfield	UNP/LNO	NS	Cape Breton	11 K/1	46°00′	60°09′
Oakfield	UNP/LNO	NS	Halifax	11 D/13	44°54′	63°35′
Oak Flats	UNP/LNO	ON	Frontenac	31 C/10	44°33′	76°44′
Oakgrove	UNP/LNO	ON	Renfrew	31 F/7	45°28′	76°49′
Oak Haven	UNP/LNO	NB	Charlotte	21 G/3	45°12′	67°12′
Oak Heights	UNP/LNO	ON	Northumberland	31 C/4	44°09′	77°59′
Oak Hill	UNP/LNO	NS	Lunenburg	21 A/7	44°24′	64°30′
Oak Hill	UNP/LNO	NB	Charlotte	21 G/6	45°20′	67°20′
Oakhill	UNP/LNO	ON	Wentworth	30 M/4	43°14′	80°00′
Oakhill Forest	UNP/LNO	ON	Welland	30 L/14	42°54′	79°02′
Oak Hills	UNP/LNO	BC	Kamloops Division Yale	92 I/9	50°45′	120°21′
Oak Island	ISL/ÎLE	NS	Cumberland	11 E/14	45°51′	63°24′
Oak Island	ISL/ÎLE	NS	Lunenburg	21 A/9	44°31′	64°18′
Oak Island Settlement	GEOG/GÉOG	MB		62 H/10	49°41′	96°56′
Oak Lake	TOWN/VIL2	MB	23-9-24-W	62 F/15	49°46′	100°38′
Oak Lake	UNP/LNO	ON	Hastings	31 C/5	44°16′	77°31′
Oak Lake	UNP/LNO	ON	Peterborough	31 C/12	44°36′	77°53′
Oak Lake	LAKE/LAC	ON	Hastings	31 C/5	44°16′	77°31′
Oak Lake	LAKE/LAC	ON	Kenora	52 K/5	50°26′	93°50′
Oak Lake	LAKE/LAC	MB	3,4,5-9-10-E	62 H/9	49°43′	96°10′
Oak Lake	LAKE/LAC	MB	8-24,25-W	62 F/10	49°40′	100°45′
Oak Lake 59	IR/RI	MB		62 F/10	49°37′	100°56′
Oak Lake 59A	IR/RI	MB		62 F/10	49°42′	100°56′
Oak Lake Beach	UNP/LNO	MB	19,30-8-24-W	62 F/10	49°41′	100°43′
Oak Lake Reserve	UNP/LNO	MB	7,8-26-W	62 F/10	49°37′	100°57′
Oakland	MUN2/AZM2	ON	Brant	40 P/1	43°03′	80°20′
Oakland	MUN2/AZM2	MB		62 G/12	49°37′	99°51′
Oakland	UNP/LNO	NS	Lunenburg	21 A/8	44°27′	64°22′
Oakland	UNP/LNO	NB	Carleton	21 J/5	46°24′	67°34′
Oakland	UNP/LNO	ON	Brant	40 P/1	43°02′	80°20′
Oakland	UNP/LNO	ON	Essex	40 J/2	42°09′	82°36′
Oakland	UNP/LNO	MB	14-13-7-W	62 J/1	50°06′	98°19′
Oakland Lake	LAKE/LAC	NS	Digby	21 A/4	44°15′	65°36′
Oak Leaf	UNP/LNO	ON	Leeds	31 C/9	44°35′	76°02′
Oak Mountain	UNP/LNO	NB	Carleton	21 J/4	46°01′	67°39′
Oakner	UNP/LNO	MB	8-13-23-W	62 K/2	50°05′	100°35′
Oak Orchard	UNP/LNO	ON	Peterborough	31 D/8	44°28′	78°26′
Oak Park	UNP/LNO	NS	Shelburne	20 P/12	43°35′	65°38′
Oak Park Lake	LAKE/LAC	NS	Shelburne	20 P/12	43°36′	65°40′
Oak Point	UNP/LNO	NB	Northumberland	21 P/3	47°07′	65°16′
Oak Point	UNP/LNO	NB	Kings	21 G/9	45°31′	66°05′
Oak Point	UNP/LNO	MB	17,18-5-W	62 J/9	50°30′	98°02′
Oak Point Settlement	GEOG/GÉOG	MB		62 J/8	50°30′	98°00′
Oakridge	UNP/LNO	ON	York	30 M/11	43°42′	79°17′
Oakridge	UNP/LNO	BC	New Westminster	92 G/3	49°14′	123°07′
Oakridge Acres	UNP/LNO	ON	Middlesex	40 I/14	42°58′	81°18′
Oakridge Park	UNP/LNO	ON	Middlesex	40 I/14	42°59′	81°20′
Oak Ridges	UNP/LNO	ON	York	30 M/14	43°56′	79°27′
Oak River	UNP/LNO	MB	28-13-22-W	62 K/1	50°08′	100°26′
Oak River	RIV/CDE	MB	10-23-W	62 F/16	49°51′	100°28′
Oakshela	UNP/LNO	SK	34-16-6-W2	62 L/7	50°24′	102°46′
Oak Valley	UNP/LNO	ON	Dundas	31 G/3	45°00′	75°22′
Oakview	UNP/LNO	MB	1-24-9-W	62 O/2	51°05′	98°38′
Oakview Beach	UNP/LNO	ON	Simcoe	41 A/8	44°29′	80°03′
Oakville	TOWN/VIL2	ON	Halton	30 M/5	43°27′	79°41′
Oakville	UNP/LNO	NB	Carleton	21 J/4	46°15′	67°45′
Oakville	UNP/LNO	MB	18,19-11-4-W	62 H/13	49°56′	98°00′
Oakwood	UNP/LNO	ON	Victoria	31 D/7	44°20′	78°53′
Oakwood	UNP/LNO	ON	York	30 M/11	43°41′	79°26′
Oakwood Corners	UNP/LNO	ON	Lambton	40 O/1	43°00′	82°23′
Oasis	UNP/LNO	BC	Kootenay	82 F/4	49°08′	117°45′
Oatland	UNP/LNO	ON	Algoma	42 B/7	48°28′	82°48′
Oatswish 13	IR/RI	BC	Range 3 Coast	103 A/16	52°56′	128°08′
Oba	UNP/LNO	ON	Algoma	42 F/1	49°04′	84°06′
Obabika Lake	LAKE/LAC	ON	Nipissing	41 P/1	47°05′	80°17′
Obabikong 35B	IR/RI	ON	Kenora	52 E/8	49°15′	94°15′
Obabikon Lake	LAKE/LAC	ON	Kenora	52 E/8	49°16′	94°14′
Ôbacigwâtikokâk	UNP/LNO	QC	Témiscamingue	31 N/12	47°34′	77°32′
Obadjiwan 15E	IR/RI	ON	Algoma	41 K/15	46°55′	84°32′
Obakamiga Lake	LAKE/LAC	ON	Algoma	42 F/3	49°09′	85°09′
Oba Lake	LAKE/LAC	ON	Algoma	42 C/9	48°40′	84°16′
Obalski	UNP/LNO	QC	Jamésie	32 G/9	49°45′	74°24′
Obalski, Lac	LAKE/LAC	QC	Abitibi	32 C/12	48°44′	77°58′

NAME NOM	ENTITY ENTITÉ	LOC 1 LIEU 1	LOC 2 LIEU 2	MAP CARTE	POSITION LAT	LONG
Obamsca, Lac	LAKE/LAC	QC	Jamésie	32 L/8	50°24′	78°16′
Obamsca, Rivière	RIV/CDE	QC	Jamésie	32 L/15	50°50′	78°50′
Oban	UNP/LNO	NS	Richmond	11 F/10	45°44′	60°55′
Oban	UNP/LNO	SK	31-36-15-W3	73 C/1	52°08′	108°08′
Oba River	RIV/CDE	ON	Algoma	42 C/16	48°55′	84°17′
Obaska	UNP/LNO	QC	Vallée-de-l'Or	32 C/3	48°13′	77°21′
Obatogamau, Lacs	LAKE/LAC	QC	Jamésie	32 G/9	49°35′	74°28′
Obatogamau, Rivière	RIV/CDE	QC	Jamésie	32 G/13	49°48′	75°30′
Obed	UNP/LNO	AB	6-53-22-W5	83 F/11	53°33′	117°14′
Obedjiwan	MUN2/AZM2	QC	Le Haut-Saint-Maurice	32 B/10	48°40′	74°56′
Obedjiwan 28	IR/RI	QC	Le Haut-Saint-Maurice	32 B/10	48°40′	74°56′
Oberlin	UNP/LNO	AB	23-38-21-W4	83 A/7	52°17′	112°54′
Oberon	UNP/LNO	MB	29-12-15-W	62 J/3	50°03′	99°29′
Obonga Lake	LAKE/LAC	ON	Thunder Bay	52 H/14	49°57′	89°22′
Obre Lake	LAKE/LAC	NT	Mackenzie	65 D	60°22′	103°03′
O'Brien	UNP/LNO	NF		2 E/2	49°03′	55°00′
O'Brien	UNP/LNO	ON	Timiskaming	31 M/5	47°24′	79°40′
O'Brien	UNP/LNO	ON	Timiskaming	41 P/10	47°41′	80°44′
O'Brien	UNP/LNO	ON	Algoma	42 C/11	48°31′	85°08′
O'Brien, Cape	CAPE/CAP	NT	Franklin	59 C	77°27′	95°13′
O'Brien Lake	LAKE/LAC	NF		2 E/2	49°04′	55°00′
O'Brien Provincial Park	PARK/PARC	AB	15,23-70-6-W6	83 M/2	55°04′	118°49′
O'Briens Landing	UNP/LNO	ON	Kenora	52 G/14	49°50′	91°11′
Observation, Baie	BAY/BAIE	QC	Minganie	12 E/10	49°40′	62°45′
Observation, Cap	CAPE/CAP	QC	Minganie	12 E/10	49°40′	62°42′
Observation Point	CAPE/CAP	NT	Franklin	107 E	70°39′	128°15′
Observatory Inlet	BAY/BAIE	BC	Cassiar	103 P/4	55°15′	129°49′
Obstruction Island	ISL/ÎLE	BC	Clayoquot	92 E/8	49°24′	126°05′
Obstruction Mountain	MTN/MNT	AB	39-21-W5	83 C/7	52°23′	116°53′
Occosh 8	IR/RI	BC	Nootka	92 E/14	49°57′	127°03′
Ocean Eagle Point	CAPE/CAP	NT	Franklin	37 B	68°39′	78°54′
Ocean Falls	UNP/LNO	BC	Range 3 Coast	93 D/5	52°21′	127°42′
Ocean Grove	UNP/LNO	BC	Comox	92 F/14	49°57′	125°12′
Ocean Lake	LAKE/LAC	NS	Guysborough	11 F/4	45°15′	61°37′
Ocean Man 69	IR/RI	SK		62 E/14	49°51′	103°03′
Ocean Man 69A	IR/RI	SK		62 E/14	49°54′	103°09′
Ocean Man 69B	IR/RI	SK		62 E/14	49°53′	103°09′
Ocean Man 69C	IR/RI	SK		62 E/14	49°53′	103°04′
Ocean Man 69D	IR/RI	SK		62 E/15	49°50′	102°54′
Ocean Man 69E	IR/RI	SK		62 E/15	49°50′	102°56′
Ocean Man 69F	IR/RI	SK		62 E/15	49°48′	102°55′
Ocean Man 69G	IR/RI	SK		62 E/15	49°51′	102°56′
Ocean Man 69H	IR/RI	SK		62 E/14	49°51′	103°52′
Ocean Man 69I	IR/RI	SK		62 E/15	49°52′	102°55′
Ocean Park	UNP/LNO	BC	New Westminster	92 G/2	49°02′	122°52′
Ocean Pond	UNP/LNO	NF		1 N/6	47°25′	53°25′
Ocean Pond	LAKE/LAC	NF		1 N/6	47°25′	53°27′
Ocean Pond	LAKE/LAC	NF		2 C/5	48°19′	53°39′
Ocean Pond	LAKE/LAC	NF		2 E/1	49°11′	54°12′
Ocean Pond	LAKE/LAC	NF		2 D/2	48°13′	54°31′
Oceanview	UNP/LNO	NS	Cape Breton	11 F/16	45°53′	60°09′
Ochak Lake	LAKE/LAC	SK		64 M/5	59°16′	103°49′
Ochapowace 71	IR/RI	SK		62 L/8	50°29′	102°25′
Ochapowace 71-5	IR/RI	SK	15-17-1-W2	62 L/8	50°26′	102°04′
Ochapowace 71-6	IR/RI	SK	15-18-2-W2	62 L/9	50°02′	102°12′
Ochapowace 71-7	IR/RI	SK	31-18-3-W2	62 L/9	50°21′	102°45′
Ochapowace 71-8	IR/RI	SK	31-18-3-W2	62 L/9	50°34′	102°24′
Ochapowace 71-9	IR/RI	SK	2-17-1-W2	62 L/8	50°24′	102°02′
O'Chiese 203	IR/RI	AB	43-9,10-W5	83 B/14	52°48′	115°20′
O'Chiese Cemetery 203A	IR/RI	AB	26-37-8-W5	83 B/3	52°12′	115°02′
Ochre Beach	UNP/LNO	MB	4-25-17-W	62 O/4	51°08′	99°48′
Ochre Pit Cove	UNP/LNO	NF		1 N/14	47°55′	53°04′
Ochre River	MUN2/AZM2	MB		62 O/4	51°00′	99°40′
Ochre River	UNP/LNO	MB	10-24-17-W	62 O/4	51°04′	99°47′
Ochre River	RIV/CDE	MB	24-17-W	62 O/4	51°07′	99°45′
Ochre River	RIV/CDE	NT	Mackenzie	95 O	63°28′	123°42′
Oclucje 7	IR/RI	BC	Nootka	92 E/15	49°59′	126°56′
O'Connell Lake	LAKE/LAC	BC	Rupert	92 L/5	50°24′	127°43′
O'Connor	MUN2/AZM2	ON	Thunder Bay	52 A/5	48°20′	89°41′
O'Connor	UNP/LNO	ON	Algoma	41 N/10	47°35′	84°31′
O'Connor	UNP/LNO	ON	Thunder Bay	52 A/5	48°22′	89°42′
O'Connor Lake	LAKE/LAC	NT	Mackenzie	75 E	61°18′	111°52′
Oconto	UNP/LNO	ON	Frontenac	31 C/10	44°43′	76°40′
Octave, Rivière	RIV/CDE	QC	Jamésie	32 E/1	49°05′	78°08′
Odanah	MUN2/AZM2	MB		62 J/4	50°08′	99°45′

NAME NOM	ENTITY ENTITÉ	LOC 1 LIEU 1	LOC 2 LIEU 2	MAP CARTE	POSITION LAT	LONG
Odanak 12	IR/RI	QC	Nicolet-Yamaska	31 I/2	46°04′	72°50′
O'Day	UNP/LNO	MB		54 E/9	57°35′	94°12′
Odei River	RIV/CDE	MB	82-4-E	64 A/2	56°06′	96°54′
Odell	UNP/LNO	NB	Victoria	21 J/14	46°49′	67°26′
O'Dell	UNP/LNO	BC	Cariboo	93 J/7	54°16′	122°38′
O'Dell Lake	LAKE/LAC	ON	Kenora	52 E/7	49°25′	94°33′
Odell River	UNP/LNO	NB	Victoria	21 J/14	46°49′	67°26′
Odell River	RIV/CDE	NB	Victoria	21 J/14	46°49′	67°26′
Odelltown	UNP/LNO	QC	Le Haut-Richelieu	31 H/3	45°02′	73°23′
Odena	UNP/LNO	ON	Algoma	41 K/9	46°35′	84°19′
Odenback	UNP/LNO	ON	Nipissing	31 E/16	45°59′	78°19′
Oderin	UNP/LNO	NF		1 M/7	47°18′	54°48′
Oderin Island	ISL/ÎLE	NF		1 M/7	47°17′	54°48′
Odessa	VILG/VILG	SK	30-15-13-W2	62 L/5	50°17′	103°47′
Odessa	UNP/LNO	ON	Lennox and Addington	31 C/7	44°17′	76°43′
Odessa Lake	LAKE/LAC	ON	Lennox and Addington	31 C/7	44°19′	76°41′
Odhill	UNP/LNO	MB	36-70-6-W	63 O/1	55°06′	98°14′
Odin Lake	LAKE/LAC	NT	Mackenzie	75 B	60°38′	106°23′
Odin, Mount	MTN/MNT	BC	Kootenay	82 L/9	50°33′	118°08′
Odin, Mount	MTN/MNT	NT	Franklin	26 I	66°33′	65°26′
Odlum Junction	UNP/LNO	NB	Westmorland	21 I/2	46°06′	64°52′
O'Donnell Landing	UNP/LNO	ON	Victoria	31 D/7	44°18′	78°44′
O'Donnell Point	CAPE/CAP	ON	Muskoka	41 H/1	45°05′	80°06′
O'Donnells	UNP/LNO	NF		1 N/4	47°04′	53°34′
O'Donnells	UNP/LNO	NB	Northumberland	21 J/9	46°31′	66°16′
O'Donnel River	RIV/CDE	BC	Cassiar	104 N/6	59°23′	133°36′
Oeufs, Lac des	LAKE/LAC	QC	Jamésie	33 I/9	54°33′	72°27′
Offer Gooseberry Island	ISL/ÎLE	NF		2 C/13	48°56′	53°32′
Offer Wadham Island	ISL/ÎLE	NF		2 F/12	49°35′	53°46′
Officier, Lac de l'	LAKE/LAC	QC	La Vallée-de-la-Gatineau	31 N/3	47°05′	77°00′
Off Lake	LAKE/LAC	ON	Rainy River	52 C/13	48°54′	93°49′
Off Lake Corner	UNP/LNO	ON	Rainy River	52 C/13	48°48′	93°52′
Oftedal Lake	LAKE/LAC	NT	Keewatin	65 H	61°39′	97°58′
Ogahalla	UNP/LNO	ON	Cochrane	42 K/4	50°06′	85°50′
Ogaki	UNP/LNO	ON	Thunder Bay	52 I/5	50°16′	89°36′
Ogascanane, Lac	LAKE/LAC	QC	Témiscamingue	31 M/1	47°05′	78°25′
Ogden	VILG/VILG	QC	Memphrémagog	31 H/1	45°03′	72°08′
Ogden	UNP/LNO	NS	Guysborough	11 F/5	45°21′	61°38′
Ogden	UNP/LNO	AB	25-23-1-W5	82 J/16	51°00′	114°00′
Ogden	UNP/LNO	BC	Lillooet	92 J/15	50°47′	122°49′
Ogden Bay	BAY/BAIE	NT	Keewatin	66 N	67°44′	101°30′
Ogden Channel	CHAN/CHEN	BC	Range 4 Coast	103 G/16	53°52′	130°18′
Ogden Mill	UNP/LNO	NB	Westmorland	21 H/16	45°55′	64°23′
Ogden, Mount	MTN/MNT	BC	Cassiar	104 K/6	58°26′	133°22′
Ogden Point	CAPE/CAP	ON	Northumberland	30 N/13	43°59′	77°53′
Ogden's Beach	UNP/LNO	ON	Simcoe	31 D/13	44°45′	79°51′
Ogdensburg	UNP/LNO	QC	Argenteuil	31 G/10	45°40′	74°31′
Ogema	TOWN/VIL2	SK	22-7-22-W2	72 H/10	49°35′	104°55′
Ogidaki	UNP/LNO	ON	Algoma	41 K/16	46°58′	84°12′
Ogidaki Mountain	MTN/MNT	ON	Algoma	41 J/13	46°59′	83°59′
Ogilvie	UNP/LNO	NS	Kings	21 H/2	45°08′	64°51′
Ogilvie	UNP/LNO	MB	20-15-12-W	62 J/6	50°18′	99°05′
Ogilvie	UNP/LNO	YT		115 O/12	63°34′	139°45′
Ogilvie Island	ISL/ÎLE	NT	Mackenzie	96 E	65°25′	127°27′
Ogilvie, Mount	MTN/MNT	BC	Cassiar	104 L/16	58°51′	134°15′
Ogilvie Mountains	MTN/MNT	YT		116 B/9	64°35′	138°15′
Ogilvie River	RIV/CDE	YT		116 H/14	65°51′	137°15′
Ogle	UNP/LNO	SK	23-6-1-W3	72 G/8	49°29′	106°02′
Ogle Point	CAPE/CAP	NT	Keewatin	57 B	68°18′	95°53′
Ogoki	UNP/LNO	ON	Cochrane	42 N/12	51°38′	85°57′
Ogoki Lake	LAKE/LAC	ON	Thunder Bay	42 L/14	50°50′	87°10′
Ogoki Reservoir	LAKE/LAC	ON	Thunder Bay	52 I/16	50°48′	88°18′
Ogoki River	RIV/CDE	ON	Cochrane	42 N/12	51°38′	85°57′
O'Grady Settlement	UNP/LNO	ON	Renfrew	31 F/6	45°30′	77°29′
Ohamil 1	IR/RI	BC	Yale Division Yale	92 H/5	49°20′	121°36′
Ohaton	UNP/LNO	AB	14-46-19-W4	83 A/15	52°58′	112°40′
Ohio	UNP/LNO	NS	Antigonish	11 E/9	45°31′	62°04′
Ohio	UNP/LNO	NS	Digby	21 B/8	44°23′	66°01′
Ohio	UNP/LNO	NS	Yarmouth	20 O/16	43°55′	66°04′
Ohio-Du-Barachois	UNP/LNO	NB	Westmorland	21 I/1	46°13′	64°29′
Ohio River	RIV/CDE	NS	Antigonish	11 E/9	45°33′	62°05′
Ohsweken	UNP/LNO	ON	Brant	40 P/1	43°04′	80°07′
Oies, Cap aux	CAPE/CAP	QC	Charlevoix	21 M/8	47°29′	70°14′
Oies, Île aux	ISL/ÎLE	QC	Montmagny	21 M/1	47°07′	70°29′
Oil City	UNP/LNO	ON	Lambton	40 J/16	42°48′	82°07′

NAME NOM	ENTITY ENTITÉ	LOC 1 LIEU 1	LOC 2 LIEU 2	MAP CARTE	POSITION LAT	POSITION LONG
Oil Springs	VILG/VILG	ON	Lambton	40 J/16	42°47′	82°07′
Oinimitis 14	IR/RI	BC	Clayoquot	92 F/5	49°21′	125°46′
Oiseau Bay	BAY/BAIE	ON	Thunder Bay	42 D/8	48°23′	86°12′
Oiseau Point	CAPE/CAP	ON	Thunder Bay	42 D/8	48°23′	86°12′
Oiseaux, Rochers aux	ISL/ÎLE	QC	Les Îles-de-la-Madeleine	11 N/14	47°51′	61°10′
Ojibway	UNP/LNO	ON	Essex	40 J/6	42°16′	83°05′
Ojibway Island	UNP/LNO	ON	Parry Sound	41 H/9	45°32′	80°28′
Oka	VILG/VILG	QC	Deux-Montagnes	31 G/8	45°28′	74°05′
Oka	VILG/VILG	QC	Deux-Montagnes	31 G/8	45°30′	74°05′
Okak	UNP/LNO	NF		14 F/12	57°33′	61°58′
Okak Bank	SEAU/SMER	—		5001	58°00′	60°30′
Okak Bay	BAY/BAIE	NF		14 E/8	57°28′	62°20′
Okak Islands	ISL/ÎLE	NF		14 F/6	57°30′	61°50′
Okalik Bay	BAY/BAIE	NT	Franklin	26 A	64°02′	65°00′
Okalik Island	ISL/ÎLE	NT	Franklin	26 A	64°05′	64°57′
Okanagan 1	IR/RI	BC	Osoyoos Division Yale	82 L/6	50°21′	119°19′
Okanagan Centre	UNP/LNO	BC	Osoyoos Division Yale	82 L/3	50°03′	119°27′
Okanagan Falls	UNP/LNO	BC	Similkameen Division Yale	82 E/5	49°21′	119°34′
Okanagan Lake	LAKE/LAC	BC	Osoyoos Division Yale	82 E/12	49°45′	119°44′
Okanagan Landing	UNP/LNO	BC	Osoyoos Division Yale	82 L/3	50°14′	119°21′
Okanagan Mission	UNP/LNO	BC	Osoyoos Division Yale	82 E/14	49°49′	119°29′
Okanagan Range	MTN/MNT	BC	Similkameen Division Yale	92 H/1	49°05′	120°10′
Okanagan River	RIV/CDE	BC	Similkameen Division Yale	82 E/4	49°05′	119°31′
Okanagan-Similkameen	MUN1/AZM1	BC	Similkameen Division Yale	82 E/5	49°25′	120°00′
Okanese 82	IR/RI	SK		62 L/14	50°55′	103°23′
Okaopéo, Lac	LAKE/LAC	QC	Manicouagan	22 K/7	50°22′	68°55′
Oka, Parc de récréation d′	PARK/PARC	QC	Deux-Montagnes	31 G/8	45°28′	74°03′
Oka-sur-la-Montagne	UNP/LNO	QC	Deux-Montagnes	31 G/9	45°30′	74°04′
Okawakenda Lake	LAKE/LAC	ON	Sudbury	41 P/11	47°39′	81°17′
O Kay Wha Cho 26	IR/RI	BC	Range 5 Coast	93 K/14	54°56′	125°16′
Oke	UNP/LNO	AB	27-49-21-W5	83 F/7	53°16′	116°59′
Oke 10	IR/RI	BC	Nootka	92 E/15	49°53′	126°51′
Okeamin 5	IR/RI	BC	Clayoquot	92 F/4	49°08′	125°40′
O′Keefe	UNP/LNO	BC	Osoyoos Division Yale	82 L/6	50°24′	119°19′
Oke Lake	LAKE/LAC	ON	Cochrane	42 A/13	48°56′	81°53′
Okema Beach	UNP/LNO	SK	29-53-27-W2	73 H/12	53°36′	105°57′
Okemasis 96 and Beardy′s 97 - see-voir - Beardy′s 97 and Okemasis 96	IR/RI	SK		73 B/16	52°48′	106°28′
Okemasis Lake	LAKE/LAC	SK	45-2,3-W3	73 B/16	52°54′	106°17′
Okeover Inlet	BAY/BAIE	BC	New Westminster	92 F/15	50°00′	124°42′
Okikendawt Island	ISL/ÎLE	ON	Parry Sound	41 I/1	46°07′	80°05′
Okikodoski, Baie - also-aussi - Okikodosik Bay	BAY/BAIE	QC	Abitibi-Ouest	32 D/13	48°47′	79°53′
Okikodosik Bay - also-aussi - Okikodoski, Baie	BAY/BAIE	ON	Cochrane	32 D/13	48°47′	79°53′
Okipwatsikew Lake	LAKE/LAC	SK		63 M/9	55°41′	102°12′
Okisollo Channel	CHAN/CHEN	BC	Sayward	92 K/6	50°17′	125°12′
Okla	HAM/HAM	SK	35-8-W2	63 D/3	52°01′	103°06′
Okno	UNP/LNO	MB	12-24-2-E	62 P/3	51°03′	97°12′
Okoa Bay	BAY/BAIE	NT	Franklin	26 P	67°55′	65°55′
Okolli Island	ISL/ÎLE	NT	Franklin	36 C	64°10′	76°37′
Okotoks	TOWN/VIL2	AB	28-20-29-W4	82 I/12	50°44′	113°59′
Okse Bay	BAY/BAIE	NT	Franklin	49 C	77°07′	87°30′
Oktwanch River	RIV/CDE	BC	Nootka	92 E/16	49°53′	126°10′
Olalla	UNP/LNO	BC	Similkameen Division Yale	82 E/5	49°16′	119°50′
Olcott	UNP/LNO	ON	Rainy River	52 B/13	48°45′	91°30′
Old Altona	UNP/LNO	MB	5-2-1-W	62 H/4	49°06′	97°34′
Old Barns	UNP/LNO	NS	Colchester	11 E/6	45°21′	63°24′
Old Bella Bella	UNP/LNO	BC	Range 3 Coast	103 A/1	52°09′	128°07′
Old Bonaventure	UNP/LNO	NF		2 C/6	48°17′	53°26′
Old Canoe Lake	LAKE/LAC	NT	Mackenzie	75 M	63°28′	111°30′
Oldcastle	UNP/LNO	ON	Essex	40 J/2	42°14′	82°56′
Old Channel	CHAN/CHEN	SK	56,57-3,7-W2	63 E/14	53°56′	102°43′
Old Chelsea	UNP/LNO	QC	Les Collines-de-l′Outaouais	31 G/12	45°30′	75°49′
Old Clemenes 16	IR/RI	BC	Lillooet	92 O/9	51°43′	122°21′
Old Cobequid Road	UNP/LNO	NS	Halifax	11 D/13	44°46′	63°39′
Old Country Meadow 4	IR/RI	BC	Range 4 Coast	93 F/16	53°56′	124°13′
Old Crow	UNP/LNO	YT		116 O/12	67°34′	139°50′
Old Crow Range	MTN/MNT	YT		116 N/10	67°43′	140°30′
Old Crow River	RIV/CDE	YT		116 O/12	67°35′	139°48′
Old Cut	UNP/LNO	ON	Norfolk	40 I/9	42°35′	80°24′
Old Dans Landing	UNP/LNO	NB	Northumberland	21 P/6	47°20′	65°12′
Olden	MUN2/AZM2	ON	Frontenac	31 C/15	44°45′	76°46′
Oldenberg	UNP/LNO	MB	22,27-12-11-E	62 I/1	50°01′	96°01′
Old England	UNP/LNO	MB		62 I/2	50°07′	96°55′
Old Entrance	UNP/LNO	AB	2-51-26-W5	83 F/5	53°22′	117°43′
Old Factory Bay	BAY/BAIE	NT	Keewatin	33 D	52°36′	78°45′
Old Ferolle Island	ISL/ÎLE	NF		12 P/2	51°05′	56°54′

NAME NOM	ENTITY ENTITÉ	LOC 1 LIEU 1	LOC 2 LIEU 2	MAP CARTE	POSITION LAT	LONG
Oldfield	UNP/LNO	ON	Kent	40 J/9	42°33′	82°19′
Old Fort	UNP/LNO	ON	Simcoe	31 D/12	44°44′	79°50′
Old Fort	UNP/LNO	BC	Peace River	94 A/2	56°12′	120°49′
Old Fort	UNP/LNO	BC	Cassiar	93 M/1	55°02′	126°19′
Old Fort 157B	IR/RI	SK		73 P/7	55°17′	104°36′
Old Fort 217	IR/RI	AB	108-9-W4	74 L/6	58°25′	111°29′
Old Fort Bay	BAY/BAIE	AB	111-3-W4	74 L/9	58°38′	110°25′
Old Fort Erie	UNP/LNO	ON	Welland	30 L/15	42°55′	78°56′
Old Fort Nelson	UNP/LNO	BC	Peace River	94 J/15	58°49′	122°33′
Old Fort Providence	UNP/LNO	NT	Mackenzie	85 J/8	62°16′	114°10′
Old Fort Rae	UNP/LNO	NT	Mackenzie	85 J	62°39′	115°50′
Old Fort River	RIV/CDE	AB/SK		74 L/9	58°36′	110°24′
Old Glenridge	UNP/LNO	ON	Lincoln	30 M/3	43°10′	79°14′
Old Glory Mountain	MTN/MNT	BC	Kootenay	82 F/4	49°09′	117°55′
Oldham	UNP/LNO	NS	Halifax	11 D/14	44°55′	63°30′
Old-Harry	UNP/LNO	QC	Les Îles-de-la-Madeleine	11 N/11	47°34′	61°29′
Old Hogem	UNP/LNO	BC	Cassiar	93 N/14	55°46′	125°27′
Old Holland Road	UNP/LNO	NS	Halifax	11 D/13	44°51′	63°36′
Old Horton Channel	CHAN/CHEN	NT	Mackenzie	97 F	70°14′	127°33′
Old Kildonan	UNP/LNO	MB		62 H/14	49°57′	97°06′
Old Killaloe	UNP/LNO	ON	Renfrew	31 F/11	45°32′	77°25′
Old Main Centre	UNP/LNO	SK	4-19-10-W3	72 J/11	50°34′	107°21′
Oldman Creek	RIV/CDE	AB	60-14-W5	83 K/1	54°11′	116°03′
Oldman Lake	LAKE/LAC	SK		74 O/12	59°43′	107°37′
Oldman Lake	LAKE/LAC	AB	56-4-W5	83 G/15	53°52′	114°32′
Old Man Lake	LAKE/LAC	NT	Mackenzie	107 B	68°58′	132°17′
Oldman River	RIV/CDE	MB		64 H/6	57°27′	97°12′
Oldman River	RIV/CDE	SK		74 N/8	59°28′	108°05′
Oldman River	RIV/CDE	AB	27-11-13-W4	72 E/13	49°57′	111°42′
Old Mans Pond	LAKE/LAC	NF		12 B/16	48°46′	58°10′
Old Mill	UNP/LNO	ON	York	30 M/11	43°39′	79°30′
Old Mine Centre	UNP/LNO	ON	Rainy River	52 C/10	48°42′	92°37′
Old Perlican	TOWN/VIL2	NF		2 C/3	48°05′	53°01′
Old Post No. 43	MUN2/AZM2	SK		72 G/8	49°20′	106°10′
Old Remo	UNP/LNO	BC	Range 5 Coast	103 I/7	54°28′	128°43′
Old Ridge	UNP/LNO	NB	Charlotte	21 G/3	45°15′	67°17′
Old Road Crossing	UNP/LNO	ON	Renfrew	31 F/14	45°55′	77°19′
Olds	TOWN/VIL2	AB	32-32-1-W5	82 O/16	51°47′	114°06′
Old Settler, The	MTN/MNT	BC	Yale Division Yale	92 H/12	49°31′	121°37′
Old Shop	UNP/LNO	NF		1 N/12	47°32′	53°35′
Old Sow Point	CAPE/CAP	NF		1 N/11	47°43′	53°10′
Old Spring Bay	UNP/LNO	ON	Manitoulin	41 G/9	45°45′	82°15′
Old Stittsville	UNP/LNO	ON	Carleton	31 G/5	45°16′	75°56′
Old Tabusintac Gully	CHAN/CHEN	NB	Northumberland	21 P/7	47°20′	64°56′
Old Thor Lake	UNP/LNO	ON	Sudbury	41 P/3	47°07′	81°16′
Old Town	UNP/LNO	BC	Kootenay	82 G/12	49°33′	115°58′
Old Town Lunenburg World Heritage Site - also-aussi - Vieux-Lunenburg, Site du patrimoine mondial du	PARK/PARC	NS		21 A/8	44°23′	64°19′
Old Tracadie Gully	CHAN/CHEN	NB	Gloucester	21 P/10	47°33′	64°51′
Old Tuxedo	UNP/LNO	MB		62 H/14	49°52′	97°13′
Old Wives	UNP/LNO	SK	30-14-30-W2	72 J/1	50°12′	106°00′
Old Wives Lake	LAKE/LAC	SK		72 I/4	50°06′	106°00′
Old Woman's River	UNP/LNO	ON	Bruce	41 A/14	44°58′	81°21′
O'Leary	VILG/VILG	PE	Prince	21 I/9	46°43′	64°14′
O'Leary Lake	LAKE/LAC	SK	60,61-2-W2	63 L/1	54°14′	102°14′
Olga	UNP/LNO	SK	16-5-23-W3	72 F/6	49°23′	109°03′
Olga, Lac	LAKE/LAC	QC	Jamésie	32 F/14	49°47′	77°15′
Olha	UNP/LNO	MB	26,35-19-23-W	62 K/10	50°40′	100°33′
Olinda	UNP/LNO	ON	Essex	40 J/2	42°05′	82°40′
Oliphant	UNP/LNO	ON	Bruce	41 A/11	44°44′	81°16′
Olive	UNP/LNO	ON	Rainy River	52 C/15	48°46′	92°42′
Oliver	TOWN/VIL2	BC	Similkameen Division Yale	82 E/4	49°11′	119°33′
Oliver	MUN2/AZM2	ON	Thunder Bay	52 A/5	48°27′	89°30′
Oliver	UNP/LNO	NS	Colchester	11 E/11	45°39′	63°19′
Oliver	UNP/LNO	ON	Oxford	40 P/3	43°09′	81°05′
Oliver	UNP/LNO	ON	Essex	40 J/3	42°14′	83°00′
Oliver	UNP/LNO	AB	5-54-23-W4	83 H/11	53°38′	113°22′
Oliver Corner	UNP/LNO	QC	Memphrémagog	31 H/1	45°12′	72°13′
Oliver Creek	RIV/CDE	BC	Kamloops Division Yale	82 M/14	51°52′	119°07′
Oliver Lake	LAKE/LAC	SK		64 D/14	56°56′	103°22′
Oliver Sound	CHAN/CHEN	NT	Franklin	38 B	72°15′	77°44′
Olivet	UNP/LNO	ON	Wellington	40 P/15	43°51′	80°40′
Olomane Ouest, Rivière	RIV/CDE	QC	Minganie	12 N/2	51°05′	60°45′
Olomane, Rivière	RIV/CDE	QC	Côte-Nord-du-Golfe-Saint-Laurent	12 K/2	50°14′	60°38′
Olscamps	UNP/LNO	QC	Mékinac	31 P/2	47°03′	72°56′
Olson	UNP/LNO	BC	Kootenay	82 G/10	49°39′	114°55′

NAME NOM	ENTITY ENTITÉ	LOC 1 LIEU 1	LOC 2 LIEU 2	MAP CARTE	POSITION LAT	LONG
Omagh	UNP/LNO	ON	Halton	30 M/12	43°30′	79°49′
Omaktai	UNP/LNO	AB	34-3-27-W4	82 H/5	49°15′	113°34′
Oman Lake	LAKE/LAC	SK		74 O/10	59°42′	106°45′
Oman Lake	LAKE/LAC	NT	Mackenzie	65 L	62°17′	103°15′
Omarolluk Sound	CHAN/CHEN	NT	Keewatin	34 D	56°03′	79°02′
Ombabika	UNP/LNO	ON	Thunder Bay	42 L/4	50°14′	87°54′
Ombabika Bay	BAY/BAIE	ON	Thunder Bay	52 I/1	50°12′	88°15′
Omeedjilawh Camp	UNP/LNO	ON	Bruce	41 A/14	44°53′	81°01′
Omemee	VILG/VILG	ON	Victoria	31 D/7	44°18′	78°33′
Omer	UNP/LNO	QC	Pontiac	31 F/16	45°55′	76°27′
Omerville	TOWN/VIL2	QC	Memphrémagog	31 H/8	45°17′	72°07′
Omineca 1	IR/RI	BC	Range 4 Coast	93 F/13	54°00′	125°52′
Omineca Mountains	MTN/MNT	BC	Cassiar	94 C	56°30′	125°30′
Omineca River	RIV/CDE	BC	Cassiar	94 C/1	56°07′	124°29′
Omineeseenowenik	UNP/LNO	MB		53 K/4	54°09′	93°30′
Ominicetla Creek	RIV/CDE	BC	Cassiar	93 N/13	55°55′	125°46′
Ominuk, Lac	LAKE/LAC	QC	Jamésie	33 L/11	54°34′	79°20′
Ommanney Bay	BAY/BAIE	NT	Franklin	68 B	73°00′	101°00′
Omoah 9	IR/RI	BC	Barclay	92 C/14	48°52′	125°18′
O'Morrow	UNP/LNO	AB	29-68-19-W4	83 I/15	54°54′	112°52′
Ompah	UNP/LNO	ON	Frontenac	31 F/2	45°01′	76°50′
Onadsilth 9	IR/RI	BC	Clayoquot	92 F/4	49°14′	125°36′
Onagon	UNP/LNO	ON	Cochrane	42 A/10	48°44′	80°43′
Onah	UNP/LNO	MB	1-10-16-W	62 G/13	49°48′	99°31′
Onakawana	UNP/LNO	ON	Cochrane	42 I/11	50°36′	81°27′
Onamakawash Lake	LAKE/LAC	ON	Thunder Bay	52 I/5	50°18′	89°35′
Onaman Lake	LAKE/LAC	ON	Thunder Bay	42 L/3	50°00′	87°26′
Onaman River	RIV/CDE	ON	Thunder Bay	52 H/16	49°59′	88°00′
Onanole	UNP/LNO	MB	7-19-18-W	62 J/12	50°37′	99°58′
Onaping	UNP/LNO	ON	Sudbury	41 I/11	46°37′	81°25′
Onaping	UNP/LNO	ON	Thunder Bay	52 I/6	50°17′	89°11′
Onaping Falls	TOWN/VIL2	ON	Sudbury	41 I/11	46°36′	81°22′
Onaping Lake	LAKE/LAC	ON	Sudbury	41 P/4	47°04′	81°30′
Onaping River	RIV/CDE	ON	Sudbury	41 I/11	46°37′	81°18′
Onatchiway, Barrage	MISC/DIV	QC	Le Fjord-du-Saguenay	22 D/14	48°53′	71°02′
Onatchiway, Lac	LAKE/LAC	QC	Le Fjord-du-Saguenay	22 E/3	49°00′	71°03′
Onatchiway, Petit lac	LAKE/LAC	QC	Le Fjord-du-Saguenay	22 E/3	49°07′	71°02′
One Arrow 95	IR/RI	SK		73 B/9	52°45′	106°01′
Onefour	UNP/LNO	AB	15-2-4-W4	72 E/1	49°07′	110°28′
100 Mile House	MUN1/AZM1	BC	Lillooet	92 P/11	51°39′	121°17′
105 Mile House	UNP/LNO	BC	Lillooet	92 P/11	51°42′	121°19′
111 Mile House	UNP/LNO	BC	Lillooet	92 P/14	51°46′	121°23′
114 Mile House	UNP/LNO	BC	Lillooet	92 P/14	51°48′	121°26′
122 Mile House	UNP/LNO	BC	Lillooet	92 P/13	51°51′	121°36′
127 Mile House	UNP/LNO	BC	Lillooet	92 P/13	51°53′	121°40′
141 Mile House	UNP/LNO	BC	Cariboo	93 A/4	52°00′	121°51′
150 Mile House	UNP/LNO	BC	Cariboo	93 A/4	52°07′	121°51′
105 Mile Post 2	IR/RI	BC	Kamloops Division Yale	92 I/11	50°44′	121°19′
108 Mile Ranch	UNP/LNO	BC	Lillooet	92 P/11	51°45′	121°21′
Oneida 41	IR/RI	ON	Middlesex	40 I/14	42°50′	81°25′
O'Neil	UNP/LNO	NB	Westmorland	21 I/2	46°12′	64°52′
O'Neil	UNP/LNO	QC	Le Haut-Saint-Laurent	31 G/1	45°06′	74°17′
O'Neil Lake	LAKE/LAC	NT	Keewatin	55 L	62°28′	95°16′
One Man Lake 29	IR/RI	ON	Kenora	52 L/7	50°21′	94°45′
One Mile 6	IR/RI	BC	Clayoquot	92 H/10	49°36′	120°34′
One Mile Point 1	IR/RI	BC	Cassiar	104 J/16	58°48′	130°05′
Onhda Lake	LAKE/LAC	NT	Mackenzie	106 P/3	67°08′	129°16′
Onion Creek	RIV/CDE	YT		115 J/2	62°12′	138°58′
Onion Lake	UNP/LNO	SK		73 F/12	53°43′	110°00′
Onion Lake	LAKE/LAC	ON	Thunder Bay	52 A/11	48°40′	89°09′
Onistagane, Lac	LAKE/LAC	QC	Maria-Chapdelaine	22 L/11	50°42′	71°19′
Onondaga	MUN2/AZM2	ON	Brant	40 P/1	43°08′	80°05′
Onondaga	UNP/LNO	ON	Brant	40 P/1	43°07′	80°07′
Ononette	UNP/LNO	NB	Kings	21 G/8	45°20′	66°13′
Onoway	VILG/VILG	AB	35-54-2-W5	83 G/9	53°42′	114°12′
Onslow	UNP/LNO	NS	Colchester	11 E/6	45°23′	63°18′
Onslow Corners	UNP/LNO	QC	Les Collines-de-l'Outaouais	31 F/9	45°37′	76°18′
Onslow Mountain	UNP/LNO	NS	Colchester	11 E/6	45°25′	63°19′
Ontaratue River	RIV/CDE	NT	Mackenzie	106 J	66°45′	130°02′
Ontario	PROV/PROV	ON		MCR39	49°15′	84°30′
Ontario	GEOG/GÉOG	ON		31 D/3	44°15′	79°05′
Ontario, Lac - also-aussi - **Ontario, Lake**	LAKE/LAC	ON		30 M/16	43°45′	78°00′
Ontario, Lake - also-aussi - **Ontario, Lac**	LAKE/LAC	ON		30 M/16	43°45′	78°00′
Onward	UNP/LNO	SK	15-34-24-W3	72 N/14	51°55′	109°19′
Onward	UNP/LNO	BC	Cariboo	93 A/4	52°04′	122°00′

NAME / NOM	ENTITY / ENTITÉ	LOC 1 / LIEU 1	LOC 2 / LIEU 2	MAP / CARTE	POSITION LAT	POSITION LONG
Oobloyah Bay	BAY/BAIE	NT	Franklin	340 B	80°47′	83°20′
Oona River	UNP/LNO	BC	Range 5 Coast	103 G/16	53°57′	130°15′
Oo-oolth 8	IR/RI	BC	Clayoquot	92 C/13	49°00′	125°40′
Ootischenia	UNP/LNO	BC	Kootenay	82 F/5	49°17′	117°38′
Ootsa Lake	UNP/LNO	BC	Range 4 Coast	93 E/16	53°48′	126°03′
Ootsa Lake	LAKE/LAC	BC	Range 4 Coast	93 E/16	53°47′	126°15′
Opachuanau Lake	LAKE/LAC	MB		64 B/12	56°44′	99°37′
Opakopa Lake	LAKE/LAC	ON	Kenora	53 B/13	52°54′	91°32′
Opal	UNP/LNO	AB	9-58-22-W4	83 H/14	53°59′	113°13′
Opapimiskan Lake	LAKE/LAC	ON	Kenora	53 B/9	52°37′	90°24′
Opasatica, Lac	LAKE/LAC	QC	Rouyn-Noranda	32 D/3	48°05′	79°18′
Opasatika	MUN2/AZM2	ON	Cochrane	42 G/10	49°31′	82°57′
Opasatika	UNP/LNO	ON	Cochrane	42 G/10	49°32′	82°52′
Opasatika Lake	LAKE/LAC	ON	Algoma	42 G/3	49°04′	83°06′
Opasatika River	RIV/CDE	ON	Cochrane	42 J/8	50°24′	82°22′
Opaskwayak Cree Nation 21A	IR/RI	MB		63 F/14	53°48′	101°14′
Opaskwayak Cree Nation 21B	IR/RI	MB		63 F/14	53°50′	101°13′
Opaskwayak Cree Nation 21C	IR/RI	MB		63 F/14	53°49′	101°16′
Opaskwayak Cree Nation 21D	IR/RI	MB		63 F/14	53°50′	101°17′
Opaskwayak Cree Nation 21E	IR/RI	MB		63 F/14	53°52′	101°20′
Opaskwayak Cree Nation 21F	IR/RI	MB		63 F/14	53°52′	101°22′
Opaskwayak Cree Nation 21G	IR/RI	MB		63 F/14	53°56′	101°23′
Opaskwayak Cree Nation 21I	IR/RI	MB		63 F/14	53°49′	101°19′
Opaskwayak Cree Nation 21J	IR/RI	MB		63 F/14	53°50′	101°19′
Opaskwayak Cree Nation 21K	IR/RI	MB		63 F/14	53°50′	101°22′
Opaskwayak Cree Nation 21L	IR/RI	MB		63 K/4	54°06′	101°34′
Opaskwayak Cree Nation 21N	IR/RI	MB		63 F/14	53°48′	101°23′
Opaskwayak Cree Nation 21P	IR/RI	MB		63 F/14	53°53′	101°28′
Opaskwayak Cree Nation 27A	IR/RI	SK		63 F/12	53°39′	102°00′
Opaskwayak Cree Nation Root Lake 23I	IR/RI	MB		63 F/14	54°00′	101°21′
Opaskwayak Cree Nation Salt Channel 21D	IR/RI	MB		63 F/12	53°44′	101°42′
Opasquia	UNP/LNO	ON	Kenora	53 F/5	53°16′	93°35′
Opasquia Lake	LAKE/LAC	ON	Kenora	53 F/5	53°18′	93°34′
Opataca, Lac	LAKE/LAC	QC	Jamésie	32 J/7	50°22′	74°55′
Opataouaga, Lac	LAKE/LAC	QC	Jamésie	32 K/7	50°22′	76°43′
Opatseeah 13	IR/RI	BC	Renfrew	92 C/15	48°50′	124°40′
Opawakoscikan 201	IR/RI	SK		73 H/4	53°12′	105°47′
Opawica, Île	ISL/ÎLE	QC	Jamésie	32 G/12	49°35′	75°59′
Opawica, Lac	LAKE/LAC	QC	Jamésie	32 G/12	49°35′	75°55′
Opawica, Rivière	RIV/CDE	QC	Jamésie	32 G/12	49°42′	75°58′
Opeepeesway Lake	LAKE/LAC	ON	Sudbury	41 O/9	47°37′	82°15′
Opekamank	UNP/LNO	MB		63 A/10	52°45′	96°43′
Opémisca, Lac	LAKE/LAC	QC	Jamésie	32 G/15	49°56′	74°52′
Opemit 4	IR/RI	BC	Nootka	92 E/15	49°49′	126°58′
Open Bay	BAY/BAIE	NF		3 E/5	53°21′	55°52′
Open Bay 8	IR/RI	BC	Sayward	92 K/3	50°09′	125°13′
Open Hall	UNP/LNO	NF		2 C/11	48°33′	53°29′
Open Hall-Red Cliffe	UNP/LNO	NF		2 C/11	48°34′	53°30′
Openit 27	IR/RI	BC	Clayoquot	92 E/8	49°22′	126°16′
Openshaw	UNP/LNO	SK	26-2-3-W2	62 E/1	49°09′	102°19′
Opeongo	UNP/LNO	ON	Nipissing	31 F/12	45°34′	77°53′
Opeongo Lake	LAKE/LAC	ON	Nipissing	31 E/9	45°42′	78°23′
*Opeongo Lodge	UNP/LNO	ON	Nipissing	31 E/9	45°39′	78°23′
Opeongo River	RIV/CDE	ON	Nipissing	31 F/12	45°30′	77°57′
Opescal Lake	LAKE/LAC	NT/SK		75 A/2	60°02′	104°55′
Ophir	UNP/LNO	ON	Algoma	41 J/5	46°28′	83°44′
Ophir	UNP/LNO	MB	30-10-17-E	52 E/14	49°52′	95°15′
Opichuan River	RIV/CDE	ON	Thunder Bay	42 M/5	51°19′	87°41′
Opikeigen Lake	LAKE/LAC	ON	Kenora	52 P/9	51°40′	88°04′
Opikinimika Lake	LAKE/LAC	ON	Sudbury	41 P/6	47°22′	81°25′
Opiminegoka Lake	LAKE/LAC	MB		63 I/9	54°35′	96°00′
Opinaca, Lac	LAKE/LAC	QC	Jamésie	33 C/9	52°39′	76°20′
Opinaca, Petit lac	LAKE/LAC	QC	Jamésie	33 C/7	52°23′	76°40′
Opinaca, Réservoir	LAKE/LAC	QC	Jamésie	33 C/9	52°39′	76°20′
Opinaca, Rivière	RIV/CDE	QC	Jamésie	33 D/1	52°14′	78°02′
Opingiviksuak Island	ISL/ÎLE	NF		14 F/5	57°26′	61°32′
Opinicon Lake	LAKE/LAC	ON	Frontenac	31 C/9	44°34′	76°19′
Opinnagau Lake	LAKE/LAC	ON	Kenora	43 F/16	53°55′	84°22′
Opinnagau River	RIV/CDE	ON	Kenora	43 J/1	54°12′	82°25′
Opiscotéo, Lac	LAKE/LAC	QC	Caniapiscau	23 F/1	53°10′	68°10′
Opiscotiche, Lac	LAKE/LAC	QC	Caniapiscau	23 G/4	53°10′	67°50′
Opitoune, Lac	LAKE/LAC	QC	Le Fjord-du-Saguenay	22 L/9	50°41′	70°30′
Opitsat	UNP/LNO	BC	Clayoquot	92 F/4	49°10′	125°55′
Opitsat 1	IR/RI	BC	Clayoquot	92 F/4	49°11′	125°55′
Opocopa	UNP/LNO	NF		23 G/2	53°03′	66°37′

NAME / NOM	ENTITY / ENTITÉ	LOC 1 / LIEU 1	LOC 2 / LIEU 2	MAP / CARTE	POSITION LAT	POSITION LONG
Opocopa, Lac	LAKE/LAC	QC	Caniapiscau	23 B/10	52°38′	66°34′
Opportunity No. 17, Municipal District of	MUN1/AZM1	AB		84 A/4	56°15′	113°48′
Opposite Island	ISL/ÎLE	NT	Keewatin	46 G	65°47′	83°25′
Oppy Lake	LAKE/LAC	BC	Range 4 Coast	93 E/1	53°04′	126°24′
Ops	MUN2/AZM2	ON	Victoria	31 D/7	44°19′	78°44′
Ops	UNP/LNO	ON	Victoria	31 D/7	44°20′	78°48′
Optic Lake	UNP/LNO	MB	31-66-25-W	63 K/14	54°45′	101°14′
Opuntia Lake	LAKE/LAC	SK	32,33-19-W3	72 N/15	51°49′	108°35′
Orange Corners	UNP/LNO	ON	Victoria	31 D/8	44°18′	78°28′
Orangedale	UNP/LNO	NS	Inverness	11 F/14	45°54′	61°06′
Orangedale East	UNP/LNO	NS	Inverness	11 F/14	45°56′	61°04′
Orange Hill	UNP/LNO	NB	Saint John	21 H/5	45°22′	65°32′
Orangeville	TOWN/VIL2	ON	Dufferin	40 P/16	43°55′	80°06′
Oranmore	UNP/LNO	ON	Parry Sound	31 E/12	45°35′	79°42′
Orcadia	UNP/LNO	SK	26-26-5-W2	62 M/7	51°16′	102°37′
Or, Cape d'	CAPE/CAP	NS	Cumberland	21 H/7	45°18′	64°46′
Orchard	UNP/LNO	ON	Halton	30 M/5	43°24′	79°48′
Orchard Beach	UNP/LNO	ON	York	31 D/6	44°15′	79°29′
Orchard Beach	UNP/LNO	ON	Elgin	40 I/11	42°40′	81°12′
Orchard Grove	UNP/LNO	ON	York	31 D/6	44°16′	79°29′
Orchard Heights	UNP/LNO	ON	Peel	30 M/12	43°35′	79°36′
Orchard Park	UNP/LNO	ON	Welland	30 M/3	43°07′	79°06′
Orchard Park	UNP/LNO	ON	Middlesex	40 P/3	43°00′	81°18′
Orchard Point	UNP/LNO	ON	Simcoe	31 D/11	44°36′	79°22′
Orchards Point	CAPE/CAP	BC	Rupert	92 L/4	50°13′	127°48′
Orchards Corner	UNP/LNO	NB	Carleton	21 J/5	46°28′	67°44′
Orchardside	UNP/LNO	ON	Dundas	31 G/3	45°03′	75°12′
Orchardville	UNP/LNO	ON	Grey	41 A/2	44°04′	80°47′
Ordale	UNP/LNO	SK	32-49-5-W3	73 G/7	53°16′	106°42′
O'Regan's	UNP/LNO	NF		11 O/14	47°52′	59°14′
Oregon	UNP/LNO	NS	Victoria	11 K/7	46°19′	60°39′
Oregon Jack Creek 2	IR/RI	BC	Kamloops Division Yale	92 I/11	50°39′	121°27′
Oregon Jack Creek 3	IR/RI	BC	Kamloops Division Yale	92 I/11	50°37′	121°19′
Oregon Jack Creek 5	IR/RI	BC	Kamloops Division Yale	92 I/11	50°36′	121°19′
O'Reilly Island	ISL/ÎLE	NT	Franklin	67 A/3	68°02′	99°00′
O'Reilly's Bridge	UNP/LNO	ON	Welland	30 L/14	42°58′	79°19′
Oreway	UNP/LNO	NF		23 A/12	52°34′	65°53′
Orford	VILG/VILG	QC	Memphrémagog	31 H/8	45°23′	72°12′
Orford	MUN2/AZM2	ON	Kent	40 I/12	42°31′	81°49′
Orford Bay 4	IR/RI	BC	Range 1 Coast	92 K/10	50°37′	124°51′
Orford Lake	UNP/LNO	QC	Memphrémagog	31 H/8	45°18′	72°17′
Orford, Mont	MTN/MNT	QC	Memphrémagog	31 H/8	45°19′	72°15′
Orford River	RIV/CDE	BC	Range 1 Coast	92 K/10	50°36′	124°52′
Oriel	UNP/LNO	ON	Oxford	40 P/2	43°04′	80°39′
Orient	UNP/LNO	ON	Russell	31 G/11	45°33′	75°11′
Orient Bay	UNP/LNO	ON	Thunder Bay	52 H/8	49°22′	88°08′
Orient, Pointe	CAPE/CAP	QC	La Haute-Côte-Nord	22 C/15	48°46′	68°59′
Orignal, Baie à l'	BAY/BAIE	QC	Rouyn-Noranda	32 D/3	48°05′	79°17′
Orignal, Baie de l'	BAY/BAIE	QC	Témiscamingue	31 N/4	47°01′	77°51′
Orignaux, Rivière aux	RIV/CDE	QC	Bécancour	31 I/8	46°26′	72°14′
Orillia	CITY/VIL1	ON	Simcoe	31 D/11	44°37′	79°25′
Oriole Parkway	UNP/LNO	ON	Kent	40 J/8	42°23′	82°13′
Orion	UNP/LNO	AB	7-6-6-W4	72 E/7	49°27′	110°49′
Orkney	HAM/HAM	SK	23-2-15-W3	72 G/4	49°08′	107°55′
Orkney Beach	UNP/LNO	ON	Ontario	31 D/11	44°35′	79°20′
Orkney No. 244	MUN2/AZM2	SK		62 M/7	51°15′	102°35′
Orland	UNP/LNO	ON	Northumberland	31 C/4	44°08′	77°47′
Orléans	UNP/LNO	ON	Carleton	31 G/5	45°28′	75°31′
Orléans, Île d'	ISL/ÎLE	QC	L'Île-d'Orléans	21 L/15	46°55′	70°58′
Orley	UNP/LNO	SK	13-45-11-W2	63 D/14	52°53′	103°28′
Orlo	UNP/LNO	QC	La Vallée-de-la-Gatineau	31 K/1	46°12′	76°03′
Orloff Lake	LAKE/LAC	AB	73,74-23,24-W4	83 P/5	55°22′	113°30′
Orlomah Beach	UNP/LNO	BC	New Westminster	92 G/7	49°22′	122°53′
Ormeaux	UNP/LNO	SK	52-7-W3	73 G/10	53°31′	106°59′
Ormiston	HAM/HAM	SK	18-9-25-W2	72 H/11	49°44′	105°24′
Ormond	UNP/LNO	ON	Dundas	31 G/3	45°09′	75°24′
Ormond Beach	UNP/LNO	ON	Elgin	40 I/11	42°39′	81°02′
Ormonde Creek 8	IR/RI	BC	Range 5 Coast	93 K/2	54°12′	124°41′
Ormonde Island	ISL/ÎLE	NT	Franklin	47 D	69°46′	82°40′
Ormsby	UNP/LNO	ON	Hastings	31 C/13	44°53′	77°45′
Ormstown	TOWN/VIL2	QC	Le Haut-Saint-Laurent	31 H/4	45°08′	74°00′
Oro - see-voir - Oro-Medonte	MUN2/AZM2	ON		31 D/12	44°35′	79°36′
Oro Beach	UNP/LNO	ON	Simcoe	31 D/5	44°27′	79°30′
Orok	UNP/LNO	MB	26-57-25-W	63 F/14	53°57′	101°03′
Oro Lea Beach	UNP/LNO	ON	Simcoe	31 D/5	44°26′	79°32′

NAME NOM	ENTITY ENTITÉ	LOC 1 LIEU 1	LOC 2 LIEU 2	MAP CARTE	POSITION LAT	LONG
Orolow	UNP/LNO	SK	27-42-8-W3	73 B/14	52°38′	107°04′
Oro-Medonte	MUN2/AZM2	ON	Simcoe	31 D/12	44°35′	79°36′
Oromocto	TOWN/VIL2	NB	Sunbury	21 G/16	45°51′	66°29′
Oromocto 26	IR/RI	NB	Sunbury	21 G/16	45°51′	66°29′
Oromocto Island	ISL/ÎLE	NB	Sunbury	21 G/16	45°52′	66°29′
Oromocto Lake	LAKE/LAC	NB	York	21 G/10	45°35′	67°00′
Oromocto River	RIV/CDE	NB	Sunbury	21 G/16	45°51′	66°29′
Oromocto West	UNP/LNO	NB	Sunbury	21 G/15	45°50′	66°31′
Orono	UNP/LNO	ON	Durham	30 M/15	43°59′	78°37′
Oro Park	UNP/LNO	ON	Simcoe	31 D/6	44°27′	79°30′
Oro Station	UNP/LNO	ON	Simcoe	31 D/5	44°27′	79°31′
Orphan Bank - also-aussi - Orphelin, Banc de l'	SEAU/SMER	—		801	48°18′	63°10′
Orphan, Dôme - also-aussi - Orphan Knoll	SEAU/SMER	—		800A	50°30′	46°30′
Orphan Knoll - also-aussi - Orphan, Dôme	SEAU/SMER	—		800A	50°30′	46°30′
Orphelin, Banc de l' - also-aussi - Orphan Bank	SEAU/SMER	—		801	48°18′	63°10′
Orpheus Lake	LAKE/LAC	NT	Mackenzie	75 B	60°58′	106°32′
Orr Lake	UNP/LNO	ON	Simcoe	31 D/12	44°36′	79°47′
Orr Lake	LAKE/LAC	ON	Simcoe	31 D/12	44°36′	79°48′
Orr Lake	LAKE/LAC	MB		64 A/3	56°06′	97°12′
Orr's Lake	UNP/LNO	ON	Waterloo	40 P/8	43°22′	80°22′
Orrville	UNP/LNO	ON	Parry Sound	31 E/5	45°23′	79°46′
Orsainville	UNP/LNO	QC	Communauté urbaine de Québec	21 L/14	46°53′	71°17′
Orsogna, Lac	LAKE/LAC	QC	Minganie	12 O/3	51°04′	59°19′
Ortell, Mount	MTN/MNT	YT		105 N/15	63°58′	132°49′
Orton	UNP/LNO	ON	Wellington	40 P/16	43°47′	80°14′
Ortona, Lac	LAKE/LAC	QC	Minganie	12 O/3	51°09′	59°26′
Orton Island	ISL/ÎLE	NF		14 C/14	56°52′	61°05′
Ortonville	UNP/LNO	NB	Victoria	21 J/13	46°58′	67°41′
Orwell	UNP/LNO	PE	Queens	11 L/2	46°09′	62°50′
Orwell	UNP/LNO	ON	Elgin	40 I/14	42°46′	81°02′
Orwell Bay	BAY/BAIE	PE	Queens	11 L/2	46°06′	62°56′
Orwell Cove	UNP/LNO	PE	Queens	11 L/2	46°08′	62°52′
Ory	UNP/LNO	QC	Pabok	22 A/8	48°27′	64°21′
Osaca	UNP/LNO	ON	Durham	31 D/1	44°00′	78°26′
Osage	VILG/VILG	SK	33-11-12-W2	62 E/13	49°57′	103°35′
Osaquan	UNP/LNO	ON	Kenora	52 G/5	49°27′	91°44′
Osawin	UNP/LNO	ON	Thunder Bay	42 F/6	49°25′	85°24′
Osawin River	RIV/CDE	ON	Cochrane	42 F/14	49°45′	85°19′
Osbon Bay	BAY/BAIE	NT	Franklin	25 I	62°29′	64°23′
Osborn	UNP/LNO	BC	Peace River	94 A/9	56°36′	120°23′
Osborn Bay	UNP/LNO	BC	Chemainus	92 B/13	48°53′	123°41′
Osborn, Cape	CAPE/CAP	NT	Franklin	58 G	75°26′	92°25′
Osborne	UNP/LNO	ON	Nipissing	31 L/11	46°41′	79°29′
Osborne	UNP/LNO	ON	Lambton	40 J/16	42°55′	82°16′
Osborne	UNP/LNO	MB	2,3-7-1-E	62 H/11	49°33′	97°22′
Osborne Corner	UNP/LNO	NB	Albert	21 H/15	45°54′	64°48′
Osborne Corners	UNP/LNO	ON	Brant	40 P/1	43°14′	80°17′
Osborne Harbour	UNP/LNO	NS	Shelburne	20 P/11	43°43′	65°07′
Osborne Lake	UNP/LNO	MB	7-69-15-W	63 J/13	54°58′	99°44′
Osborne Village	UNP/LNO	MB		62 H/14	49°53′	97°09′
Osborn, Mount	MTN/MNT	YT		116 F/15	65°46′	140°49′
Osborn Range	MTN/MNT	NT	Franklin	340 D	81°25′	78°25′
Osborn River	RIV/CDE	BC/AB		94 A/9	56°34′	120°29′
Osbourne Bay	BAY/BAIE	ON	Kenora	52 F/11	49°34′	93°02′
Oscar	UNP/LNO	ON	Thunder Bay	52 G/7	49°18′	90°43′
Oscar Bay	BAY/BAIE	NT	Franklin	57 C	69°46′	95°40′
Oscar Lake	UNP/LNO	SK	4-46-9-W3	73 B/14	52°56′	107°16′
Oscar Peak	MTN/MNT	BC	Range 5 Coast	103 I/14	54°56′	129°03′
Osceola	UNP/LNO	ON	Renfrew	31 F/10	45°37′	76°57′
Oschawwinna 3	IR/RI	BC	Range 5 Coast	93 L/14	54°56′	127°16′
Osgoode	MUN2/AZM2	ON	Carleton	31 G/4	45°11′	75°32′
Osgoode	UNP/LNO	ON	Carleton	31 G/4	45°08′	75°36′
Osgood, Rivière	RIV/CDE	QC	L'Amiante	21 L/6	46°18′	71°23′
Oshawa	CITY/VIL1	ON	Ontario	30 M/15	43°54′	78°51′
Oshinow Lake	LAKE/LAC	BC	Clayoquot	92 F/6	49°27′	125°20′
Osilinka River	RIV/CDE	BC	Cassiar	94 C/2	56°05′	124°33′
Oskélanéo	UNP/LNO	QC	Le Haut-Saint-Maurice	32 B/3	48°07′	75°12′
Oskélanéo, Lac	LAKE/LAC	QC	Le Haut-Saint-Maurice	32 B/3	48°07′	75°11′
Oskondaga	UNP/LNO	ON	Thunder Bay	52 A/12	48°45′	89°51′
Osland	UNP/LNO	BC	Range 5 Coast	103 J/1	54°08′	130°10′
Osler	TOWN/VIL2	SK	20-39-4-W3	73 B/7	52°22′	106°33′
Osler Bluff	MTN/MNT	ON	Grey	41 A/8	44°27′	80°17′
Osmond	UNP/LNO	NF		11 O/11	47°37′	59°16′
Osmonton Arm	BAY/BAIE	NF		2 E/6	49°27′	55°24′
Osnabruck	MUN2/AZM2	ON	Stormont	31 G/3	45°05′	75°01′

NAME NOM	ENTITY ENTITÉ	LOC 1 LIEU 1	LOC 2 LIEU 2	MAP CARTE	POSITION LAT	LONG
Osnabruck Centre	UNP/LNO	ON	Stormont	31 G/3	45°02′	75°00′
Osnaburgh 63A	IR/RI	ON	Thunder Bay	52 O/1	51°03′	90°15′
Osnaburgh 63B	IR/RI	ON	Kenora	52 O/1	51°13′	90°11′
Osnaburgh House	UNP/LNO	ON	Kenora	52 O/1	51°08′	90°16′
Osnaburgh Lake	LAKE/LAC	ON	Kenora	52 O/1	51°09′	90°09′
Oso	MUN2/AZM2	ON	Frontenac	31 C/15	44°48′	76°39′
Oso	UNP/LNO	ON	Frontenac	31 C/15	44°49′	76°41′
Osoyoos	TOWN/VIL2	BC	Similkameen Division Yale	82 E/3	49°02′	119°27′
Osoyoos 1	IR/RI	BC	Similkameen Division Yale	82 E/3	49°10′	119°30′
Osoyoos 3	IR/RI	BC	Similkameen Division Yale	82 E/3	49°04′	119°26′
Osoyoos Division Yale Land District	GEOG/GÉOG	BC		82 L	50°05′	119°10′
Osoyoos Lake	LAKE/LAC	BC	Similkameen Division Yale	82 E/3	49°02′	119°27′
Ospika River	RIV/CDE	BC	Cassiar	94 B/5	56°19′	123°57′
Osprey	MUN2/AZM2	ON	Grey	41 A/8	44°19′	80°20′
Osprey Lake	UNP/LNO	BC	Osoyoos Division Yale	92 H/9	49°43′	120°11′
Ospringe	UNP/LNO	ON	Wellington	40 P/9	43°42′	80°07′
Ospwagan Lake	LAKE/LAC	MB	76-4-W	63 O/9	55°35′	98°02′
Ossant, Lac	LAKE/LAC	QC	Kativik	33 P/1	55°03′	72°20′
Osseo	UNP/LNO	ON	Timiskaming	41 P/9	47°38′	80°05′
Osseo	UNP/LNO	ON	Timiskaming	41 P/9	47°39′	80°05′
Ossokmanuan Reservoir	LAKE/LAC	NF		23 H/11	53°31′	65°06′
Ossossane Beach	UNP/LNO	ON	Simcoe	31 D/12	44°40′	79°59′
Ostaboningue, Lac	LAKE/LAC	QC	Témiscamingue	31 M/2	47°08′	78°52′
Ostenfeld	UNP/LNO	MB	6-10-8-E	62 H/16	49°48′	96°29′
Osten Lake	LAKE/LAC	SK	59-5-W3	73 J/2	54°05′	106°44′
Osterwick	UNP/LNO	MB	31-1-4-W	62 H/4	49°05′	98°00′
Ostrander	UNP/LNO	ON	Oxford	40 I/15	42°54′	80°45′
Ostrea Lake	UNP/LNO	NS	Halifax	11 D/11	44°43′	63°05′
Ostrom	UNP/LNO	ON	Sudbury	41 P/5	47°27′	81°37′
Ostryhon Corners	UNP/LNO	ON	Welland	30 L/14	42°53′	79°21′
O'Sullivan, Lac	LAKE/LAC	QC	La Vallée-de-la-Gatineau	31 O/12	47°34′	76°00′
O'Sullivan Lake	LAKE/LAC	ON	Thunder Bay	42 L/6	50°25′	87°02′
O'Sullivan, Rivière	RIV/CDE	QC	Jamésie	32 F/8	49°28′	76°28′
Oswald	UNP/LNO	MB	20-14-1-W	62 I/4	50°13′	97°33′
Oswald Lake	LAKE/LAC	ON	Sudbury	42 B/8	48°21′	82°20′
Oswald Lake	LAKE/LAC	NT	Mackenzie	75 C	60°30′	108°09′
Oswego Creek	RIV/CDE	ON	Welland	30 L/13	42°59′	79°33′
Oswego Park	UNP/LNO	ON	Haldimand	30 L/13	42°59′	79°34′
Otakus Lake	LAKE/LAC	ON	Kenora	52 F/5	49°30′	93°58′
Otasawian River	RIV/CDE	ON	Cochrane	42 K/1	50°13′	84°18′
Otauwau River	RIV/CDE	AB	33-72-3-W5	83 O/8	55°16′	114°25′
Otelnuk, Lac	LAKE/LAC	QC	Kativik	24 C/1	56°09′	68°12′
Othello	UNP/LNO	BC	Yale Division Yale	92 H/6	49°23′	121°21′
Otherside River	RIV/CDE	SK		74 O/7	59°16′	106°55′
Otish, Monts	MTN/MNT	QC	Jamésie	23 D/7	52°18′	70°37′
Otis, Lac	LAKE/LAC	QC	Le Fjord-du-Saguenay	22 D/7	48°18′	70°39′
Otnabog Lake	LAKE/LAC	NB	Queens	21 G/9	45°42′	66°07′
Otonabee	MUN2/AZM2	ON	Peterborough	31 D/8	44°15′	78°14′
Otonabee River	RIV/CDE	ON	Northumberland	31 D/1	44°09′	78°14′
Otoreke	UNP/LNO	QC	Les Pays-d'en-Haut	31 G/16	45°59′	74°20′
Otoskwin River	RIV/CDE	ON	Kenora	53 A/1	52°13′	88°06′
Otosquen	UNP/LNO	SK	1-50-1-W2	63 E/8	53°17′	102°01′
O-tsaw-las 5	IR/RI	BC	Rupert	92 L/11	50°32′	127°01′
Ottarasko Creek	RIV/CDE	BC	Range 2 Coast	92 N/8	51°26′	124°28′
Ottarasko Mountain	MTN/MNT	BC	Range 2 Coast	92 N/10	51°31′	124°43′
Ottawa	CITY/VIL1	ON	Carleton	31 G/5	45°25′	75°42′
Ottawa, Base des Forces canadiennes - also-aussi - Ottawa, Canadian Forces Base	MIL/MIL	ON	Carleton	31 G/5	45°20′	75°40′
Ottawa Brook	UNP/LNO	NS	Victoria	11 F/15	45°56′	60°56′
Ottawa, Canadian Forces Base - also-aussi - Ottawa, Base des Forces canadiennes	MIL/MIL	ON	Carleton	31 G/5	45°20′	75°40′
Ottawa-Carleton	MUN1/AZM1	ON	Carleton	31 G/5	45°20′	75°35′
Ottawa East	UNP/LNO	ON	Carleton	31 G/5	45°25′	75°41′
Ottawa Islands	ISL/ÎLE	NT	Keewatin	44 P	59°35′	80°16′
Ottawa River - also-aussi - **Outaouais, Rivière des**	RIV/CDE	QC/ON		31 H/5	45°20′	73°55′
Ottawa South	UNP/LNO	ON	Carleton	31 G/5	45°24′	75°42′
Otter	UNP/LNO	ON	Nipissing	31 L/12	46°44′	79°31′
Otter	UNP/LNO	ON	Algoma	42 C/8	48°24′	84°24′
Otter	UNP/LNO	AB	10-23-2-W5	82 J/16	50°56′	114°12′
Otter Bay	UNP/LNO	BC	Cowichan	92 B/14	48°48′	123°19′
Otter Bay	BAY/BAIE	NF		11 O/10	47°36′	58°56′
Otter Brook	UNP/LNO	NS	Colchester	11 E/3	45°14′	63°03′
Otterburne	UNP/LNO	MB		62 H/6	49°30′	97°03′
Otterburn Park	CITY/VIL1	QC	La Vallée-du-Richelieu	31 H/11	45°32′	73°13′
Otterbury	UNP/LNO	NF		1 N/10	47°33′	52°54′
Otterbury	UNP/LNO	NF		1 N/11	47°41′	53°15′
Otterbury	UNP/LNO	NF		1 N/11	47°33′	53°16′

NAME NOM	ENTITY ENTITÉ	LOC 1 LIEU 1	LOC 2 LIEU 2	MAP CARTE	POSITION LAT	LONG
Otter Cove	UNP/LNO	NB	Charlotte	21 B/15	44°56′	66°55′
Otter Creek	UNP/LNO	ON	Hastings	31 C/11	44°31′	77°13′
Otter Creek	UNP/LNO	ON	Bruce	41 A/3	44°05′	81°08′
Otter Creek	RIV/CDE	SK	57-9-W3	73 G/14	53°57′	107°12′
Otter Creek	RIV/CDE	BC	Yale Division Yale	92 H/10	49°32′	120°45′
Otter Creek	RIV/CDE	YT		105 J/6	62°28′	131°19′
Otterdale	UNP/LNO	ON	Thunder Bay	42 F/12	49°32′	85°41′
Otter Falls	UNP/LNO	MB	6-14-13-E	52 L/4	50°09′	95°49′
Otter Head	CAPE/CAP	ON	Thunder Bay	42 D/1	48°05′	86°02′
Otter Head	CAPE/CAP	ON	Thunder Bay	52 H/8	49°27′	88°27′
Otter Island	ISL/ÎLE	NF		2 E/12	49°37′	55°54′
Otter Island	ISL/ÎLE	ON	Thunder Bay	42 D/1	48°07′	86°04′
Otter Lake	UNP/LNO	QC	Pontiac	31 F/16	45°51′	76°26′
Otter Lake	UNP/LNO	ON	Parry Sound	31 E/5	45°17′	79°56′
Otter Lake	LAKE/LAC	NF		13 K/6	54°15′	61°00′
Otter Lake	LAKE/LAC	ON	Leeds	31 C/16	44°47′	76°07′
Otter Lake	LAKE/LAC	MB	6,7-25-2-E	62 P/3	51°09′	97°18′
Otter Lake	LAKE/LAC	MB	17,18-18-W	62 J/12	50°30′	99°50′
Otter Lake	LAKE/LAC	SK		73 P/10	55°35′	104°39′
Otter Lake	LAKE/LAC	SK	56-10-W3	73 G/14	53°49′	107°25′
Otter Lake	LAKE/LAC	AB	73-24-W4	83 P/5	55°21′	113°35′
Otter Lake	LAKE/LAC	BC	Yale Division Yale	92 H/10	49°35′	120°46′
Otter Lake	LAKE/LAC	YT		105 J/8	62°30′	130°25′
Otter Lake	LAKE/LAC	NT	Keewatin	65 G	61°08′	98°05′
Otter Lake 2	IR/RI	BC	Osoyoos Division Yale	82 L/6	50°24′	119°15′
Otter Land District	GEOG/GÉOG	BC		92 B	48°25′	123°45′
Ottermere	UNP/LNO	ON	Kenora	52 E/15	49°55′	94°56′
Otter Point	CAPE/CAP	BC	Otter	92 B/5	48°21′	123°49′
Otter Pond	LAKE/LAC	NF		1 M/15	47°59′	54°36′
Otter Rapids	UNP/LNO	ON	Cochrane	42 I/4	50°11′	81°39′
Otter River	RIV/CDE	ON	Kenora	53 I/7	54°20′	88°33′
Otterskin Lake	LAKE/LAC	ON	Kenora	52 F/4	49°14′	93°34′
Otter's Point	UNP/LNO	NF		11 O/9	47°41′	58°01′
Ottertail	UNP/LNO	BC	Kootenay	82 N/7	51°19′	116°33′
Ottertail Lake	LAKE/LAC	ON	Rainy River	52 C/13	48°57′	93°42′
Ottertail River	RIV/CDE	ON	Thunder Bay	42 L/13	50°47′	87°45′
Otterville	UNP/LNO	ON	Oxford	40 I/15	42°55′	80°36′
Otthon	HAM/HAM	SK	26-24-5-W2	62 M/2	51°06′	102°36′
Ottman - Murray Beach	HAM/HAM	SK	10,11-33-11-W3	62 M/14	51°49′	103°28′
Otto	UNP/LNO	MB	28-19-3-W	62 I/12	50°39′	97°49′
Otto Fiord	BAY/BAIE	NT	Franklin	340 C	81°02′	87°00′
Otto Glacier	GLAC/GLAC	NT	Franklin	340 C	81°21′	84°09′
Otty Glen	UNP/LNO	NB	Kings	21 H/5	45°27′	65°57′
Otty Lake	LAKE/LAC	ON	Lanark	31 C/16	44°51′	76°13′
Otukamamoan Lake	LAKE/LAC	ON	Rainy River	52 C/15	48°58′	92°51′
Otway	UNP/LNO	AB	22-39-7-W5	83 B/7	52°22′	114°55′
Otway	UNP/LNO	BC	Cariboo	93 G/15	53°58′	122°51′
Ouagama, Lac	LAKE/LAC	QC	Jamésie	32 K/11	50°38′	77°07′
Ouapetec, Rivière	RIV/CDE	QC	Sept-Rivières	22 J/16	50°52′	66°28′
Ouapitagone, Île de	ISL/ÎLE	QC	Côte-Nord-du-Golfe-Saint-Laurent	12 K/1	50°13′	60°02′
Ouareau, Lac	LAKE/LAC	QC	Matawinie	31 J/8	46°17′	74°09′
Ouasiemsca, Rivière	RIV/CDE	QC	Maria-Chapdelaine	32 H/1	49°00′	72°29′
Ouchton 3	IR/RI	BC	Rupert	102 I/16	50°46′	128°25′
Ouelle, Rivière	RIV/CDE	QC	Kamouraska	21 M/8	47°26′	70°03′
Ouellette	UNP/LNO	ON	Sudbury	41 I/2	46°06′	80°30′
Ouescapis, Lac	LAKE/LAC	QC	Jamésie	32 K/3	50°14′	77°00′
Ouest, Chenal de l'	CHAN/CHEN	QC	Jamésie	32 F/6	49°19′	77°21′
Ouest, Dune de l'	MTN/MNT	QC	Les Îles-de-la-Madeleine	11 N/5	47°18′	61°58′
Ouest, Pointe de l'	CAPE/CAP	QC	Minganie	22 H/15	49°52′	64°31′
Ouiatchouan, Rivière	RIV/CDE	QC	Le Domaine-du-Roy	32 A/8	48°27′	72°10′
Ouimet	UNP/LNO	ON	Thunder Bay	52 A/15	48°45′	88°35′
Ouimet Canyon	VALL/VALL	ON	Thunder Bay	52 A/15	48°47′	88°40′
Oulton Lake	LAKE/LAC	NT	Mackenzie	75 D	60°47′	111°20′
Oungah	UNP/LNO	ON	Kent	40 I/8	42°29′	82°17′
Oungre	HAM/HAM	SK	21-2-14-W2	62 E/4	49°09′	103°48′
Ououkinsh 5	IR/RI	BC	Rupert	92 L/3	50°11′	127°26′
Ououkinsh Canyon	SEAU/SMER	—		3604	50°00′	127°50′
Ououkinsh Inlet	BAY/BAIE	BC	Rupert	92 L/3	50°10′	127°28′
Our Harbour	UNP/LNO	NF		11 P/12	47°36′	57°36′
Ours, Cap de l'	CAPE/CAP	QC	Minganie	12 E/9	49°33′	62°27′
Ours, Grand lac de l' - also-aussi - **Great Bear Lake**	LAKE/LAC	NT	Mackenzie	96 H	65°50′	120°45′
Ours, Lac à l'	LAKE/LAC	QC	Minganie	12 L/6	50°24′	63°05′
Ours, Lac d'	LAKE/LAC	QC	Pontiac	31 F/15	45°51′	76°32′
Ours Noir, Pointe à l'	CAPE/CAP	QC	Jamésie	32 M/11	51°32′	79°06′
Ours, Rivière à l'	RIV/CDE	QC	Le Fjord-du-Saguenay	22 D/11	48°33′	71°20′

NAME NOM	ENTITY ENTITÉ	LOC 1 LIEU 1	LOC 2 LIEU 2	MAP CARTE	POSITION LAT	LONG
Ours, Rivière aux	RIV/CDE	QC	La Haute-Côte-Nord	22 C/13	48°45′	69°39′
Ous 17	IR/RI	BC	Nootka	92 E/9	49°38′	126°22′
Ouse River	RIV/CDE	ON	Peterborough	31 D/8	44°16′	78°03′
Oustic	UNP/LNO	ON	Wellington	40 P/9	43°42′	80°15′
Outaouais	MUN1/AZM1	QC	La Vallée-de-la-Gatineau	31 K/8	46°16′	76°19′
Outaouais, Communauté urbaine de l'	MUN1/AZM1	QC	Communauté urbaine de l'Outaouais	31 G/12	45°35′	75°49′
Outaouais, Rivière des - also-aussi - **Ottawa River**	RIV/CDE	QC/ON		31 H/5	45°20′	73°55′
Outardes, Baie aux	BAY/BAIE	QC	Manicouagan	22 F/2	49°02′	68°30′
Outardes Quatre, Réservoir	LAKE/LAC	QC	Manicouagan	22 F/15	49°50′	68°58′
Outardes, Rivière aux	RIV/CDE	QC	Manicouagan	22 F/1	49°04′	68°28′
Outardes-Trois, Barrage	MISC/DIV	QC	Manicouagan	22 F/10	49°34′	68°48′
Outcrop Point	CAPE/CAP	NT	Franklin	37 B	68°20′	76°18′
Outer Bald Tusket Island	ISL/ÎLE	NS	Yarmouth	20 O/9	43°36′	66°01′
Outer Cove	UNP/LNO	NF		1 N/10	47°39′	52°41′
Outer Duck Island	ISL/ÎLE	ON	Manitoulin	41 G/10	45°39′	82°55′
Outer Island	ISL/ÎLE	NS	Shelburne	20 P/5	43°28′	65°45′
Outer Wood Island	ISL/ÎLE	NB	Charlotte	21 B/10	44°37′	66°49′
Outlet	UNP/LNO	ON	Leeds	31 C/8	44°29′	76°03′
Outlet - see-voir - The Outlet	UNP/LNO	ON		30 N/14	43°54′	77°13′
Outlet Bay	BAY/BAIE	NT	Keewatin	65 N	62°25′	100°45′
Outlook	TOWN/VIL2	SK	29-8-W3	72 O/6	51°30′	107°03′
Outlook	UNP/LNO	ON	Algoma	41 J/4	46°10′	83°59′
Outram	UNP/LNO	NS	Annapolis	21 A/14	44°57′	65°13′
Outram	UNP/LNO	SK	9-2-10-W2	62 E/3	49°09′	103°19′
Outram Lakes	LAKE/LAC	NT	Mackenzie	76 C	64°02′	109°25′
Outram, Mount	MTN/MNT	BC	Yale Division Yale	92 H/6	49°17′	121°10′
Outremont	CITY/VIL1	QC	Communauté urbaine de Montréal	31 H/12	45°31′	73°37′
Outs 3	IR/RI	BC	Clayoquot	92 C/14	48°59′	125°11′
Ouvry	UNP/LNO	ON	Kent	40 J/1	42°13′	82°08′
Ovens Point	CAPE/CAP	NS	Lunenburg	21 A/8	44°19′	64°15′
Overbrook	UNP/LNO	ON	Carleton	31 G/5	45°26′	75°40′
Overby Lake	LAKE/LAC	MB		64 J/16	58°55′	98°24′
Overflow	UNP/LNO	ON	Rainy River	52 B/13	48°46′	91°41′
Overflow Bay	BAY/BAIE	MB		63 F/2	53°05′	101°00′
Overflowing River	UNP/LNO	MB	18-48-25-W	63 F/3	53°08′	101°06′
Overflowing River	RIV/CDE	MB/SK		63 F/3	53°08′	101°05′
Overlea	UNP/LNO	AB	25-72-4-W5	83 O/8	55°16′	114°29′
Overlord Mountain	MTN/MNT	BC	New Westminster	92 J/2	50°01′	122°49′
Overstoneville	UNP/LNO	MB	32-1-5-E	62 H/2	49°05′	96°53′
Overton	UNP/LNO	NS	Yarmouth	20 O/16	43°51′	66°09′
Overton	UNP/LNO	MB	2-23-8-W	62 J/16	50°57′	98°29′
Owaissa	UNP/LNO	ON	Nipissing	31 M/4	47°09′	79°46′
Owakonze	UNP/LNO	ON	Thunder Bay	52 B/10	48°44′	90°50′
Owen	UNP/LNO	AB	10-57-6-W6	83 E/15	53°55′	118°48′
Owen Bay	UNP/LNO	BC	Sayward	92 K/6	50°19′	125°13′
Owenbrook	UNP/LNO	ON	Peterborough	31 C/13	44°48′	77°56′
Owen Channel	CHAN/CHEN	ON	Manitoulin	41 H/12	45°31′	81°48′
Owendale	UNP/LNO	AB	36-1-24-W4	82 H/3	49°05′	113°05′
Owen Lake	LAKE/LAC	BC	Cariboo	93 B/2	52°15′	122°54′
Owen Lake	LAKE/LAC	NT	Franklin	57 F	70°29′	92°31′
Owen Point	CAPE/CAP	NT	Franklin	58 G	75°59′	92°35′
Owen Sound	CITY/VIL1	ON	Grey	41 A/10	44°34′	80°56′
Owen Sound	BAY/BAIE	ON	Grey	41 A/10	44°40′	80°54′
Owens Peak	MTN/MNT	BC	Cassiar	104 F/15	57°47′	132°40′
Owh-wis-too-a-wan 10	IR/RI	BC	Range 2 Coast	92 M/2	51°05′	126°46′
Owikeno Lake	LAKE/LAC	BC	Range 2 Coast	92 M/10	51°41′	126°55′
Owl Creek	UNP/LNO	BC	Lillooet	92 J/7	50°21′	122°44′
Owl Lake	LAKE/LAC	ON	Thunder Bay	42 D/14	49°00′	87°00′
Owl River	UNP/LNO	AB	23-68-13-W4	73 L/13	54°54′	111°53′
Owl River	RIV/CDE	MB		54 F/15	57°51′	92°45′
Owl River	RIV/CDE	AB	68-13-W4	73 L/13	54°54′	111°57′
Owlseye	UNP/LNO	AB	4-59-10-W4	73 L/3	54°04′	111°26′
Owls Head Harbour	UNP/LNO	NS	Halifax	11 D/10	44°44′	62°50′
Owl's Head, Mont	MTN/MNT	QC	Memphrémagog	31 H/1	45°04′	72°18′
Owossitsa 6	IR/RI	BC	Nootka	92 E/15	49°50′	126°55′
Owun 24	IR/RI	BC	Queen Charlotte	103 F/10	53°39′	132°31′
Oxarat	UNP/LNO	SK	33-5-27-W3	72 F/5	49°26′	109°35′
Oxbow	TOWN/VIL2	SK	23-3-2-W2	62 E/1	49°14′	102°10′
Oxbow	UNP/LNO	NB	Victoria	21 O/3	47°01′	67°18′
Oxbow Park	UNP/LNO	ON	Simcoe	41 A/8	44°29′	80°04′
Oxdrift	UNP/LNO	ON	Kenora	52 F/15	49°49′	92°59′
Oxenden	UNP/LNO	ON	Grey	41 A/14	44°46′	81°05′
Oxford	TOWN/VIL2	NS	Cumberland	11 E/12	45°44′	63°52′
Oxford	MUN1/AZM1	ON	Oxford	40 P/2	43°08′	80°50′
Oxford	GEOG/GÉOG	ON		40 P/2	43°08′	80°50′

NAME NOM	ENTITY ENTITÉ	LOC 1 LIEU 1	LOC 2 LIEU 2	MAP CARTE	POSITION	
					LAT	LONG
Oxford Centre	UNP/LNO	ON	Oxford	40 P/2	43°06′	80°41′
Oxford Heights	UNP/LNO	BC	New Westminster	92 G/7	49°17′	122°46′
Oxford House	UNP/LNO	MB		53 L/14	54°57′	95°16′
Oxford House 24	IR/RI	MB		53 L/14	54°55′	95°20′
Oxford Junction	UNP/LNO	NS	Cumberland	11 E/12	45°42′	63°53′
Oxford Lake	LAKE/LAC	MB		53 L/13	54°51′	95°38′
Oxford Mills	UNP/LNO	ON	Grenville	31 B/13	44°58′	75°41′
Oxford, Mount	MTN/MNT	NT	Franklin	340 E	82°10′	73°10′
Oxford-on-Rideau	MUN2/AZM2	ON	Leeds	31 B/13	44°57′	75°40′
Oxford-Park	UNP/LNO	ON	Middlesex	40 I/14	42°59′	81°16′
Oxford Station	UNP/LNO	ON	Grenville	31 B/13	44°56′	75°37′
Oxley	UNP/LNO	ON	Essex	40 G/15	42°00′	82°53′
Oxmead	UNP/LNO	ON	Grey	41 A/10	44°35′	80°38′
Oxtongue River	RIV/CDE	ON	Muskoka	31 E/6	45°19′	79°01′
Oxville	UNP/LNO	AB	10-46-2-W4	73 D/16	52°57′	110°13′
O-ya-kum-la 11	IR/RI	BC	Rupert	102 I/8	50°29′	128°01′
Oyama	UNP/LNO	BC	Osoyoos Division Yale	82 L/3	50°07′	119°22′
Oyama Lake	LAKE/LAC	BC	Osoyoos Division Yale	82 L/3	50°07′	119°16′
Oyees 9	IR/RI	BC	Renfrew	92 C/10	48°43′	124°47′
Oyen	TOWN/VIL2	AB	34-27-4-W4	72 M/8	51°22′	110°28′
Oyster Bay	BAY/BAIE	BC	Comox	92 F/14	49°54′	125°10′
Oyster Bay 12	IR/RI	BC	Oyster	92 G/4	49°01′	123°51′
Oyster Bed Bridge	UNP/LNO	PE	Queens	11 L/6	46°23′	63°14′
Oyster Land District	GEOG/GÉOG	BC		92 B	49°00′	123°49′
Oyster River	UNP/LNO	BC	Comox	92 F/14	49°52′	125°08′
Oyster River	RIV/CDE	BC	Comox	92 F/14	49°52′	125°07′
Ozada	UNP/LNO	AB	13-25-8-W5	82 O/2	51°07′	114°58′
Ozanam	UNP/LNO	QC	L'Islet	21 M/8	47°16′	70°13′
Ozerna	UNP/LNO	MB	1-17-20-W	62 K/8	50°26′	100°06′
Ozhiski Lake	LAKE/LAC	ON	Kenora	53 A/1	52°01′	88°30′

P

NAME NOM	ENTITY ENTITÉ	LOC 1 LIEU 1	LOC 2 LIEU 2	MAP CARTE	POSITION	
Pa-aat 6	IR/RI	BC	Range 4 Coast	103 G/16	53°49′	130°01′
Paalik	UNP/LNO	QC	Kativik	35 F/12	61°36′	77°40′
Pabineau 11	IR/RI	NB	Gloucester	21 P/12	47°32′	65°40′
Pabok	MUN1/AZM1	QC	Pabok	22 A/7	48°22′	64°37′
Pabos	VILG/VILG	QC	Pabok	22 A/7	48°22′	64°37′
Pabos Mills	VILG/VILG	QC	Pabok	22 A/7	48°18′	64°42′
Pa-cat'l-lin-ne 3	IR/RI	BC	Rupert	92 L/12	50°38′	127°59′
Paces Lake	LAKE/LAC	NS	Halifax	11 D/14	44°49′	63°13′
Pacheena 1	IR/RI	BC	Renfrew	92 C/9	48°34′	124°23′
Pachena Bay	BAY/BAIE	BC	Barclay	92 C/14	48°47′	125°08′
Pachena Point	CAPE/CAP	BC	Barclay	92 C/11	48°43′	125°06′
Pachena River	RIV/CDE	BC	Barclay	92 C/14	48°48′	125°08′
Pacific	UNP/LNO	BC	Range 5 Coast	103 I/16	54°46′	128°15′
Pacific Heights	UNP/LNO	SK		73 B/2	52°08′	106°44′
Pacific Junction	UNP/LNO	NB	Westmorland	21 I/2	46°08′	64°59′
Pacific Ocean - also-aussi - **Pacifique, Océan**	SEA/MER	—				
Pacific Park	UNP/LNO	SK		72 I/5	50°23′	105°34′
Pacific Ranges	MTN/MNT	BC	Range 1 Coast	92 K/16	50°48′	124°25′
Pacific Rim National Park Reserve - also-aussi - Pacific Rim, Réserve de parc national	PARK/PARC	BC	Clayoquot	92 C/13	49°04′	125°40′
Pacific Rim, Réserve de parc national - also-aussi - Pacific Rim National Park Reserve	PARK/PARC	BC	Clayoquot	92 C/13	49°04′	125°40′
Pacifique, Océan - also-aussi - **Pacific Ocean**	SEA/MER	—				
Packers Mountain	MTN/MNT	YT		105 E/13	61°50′	135°32′
Packington	VILG/VILG	QC	Témiscouata	21 N/7	47°29′	68°47′
Pack River 2	IR/RI	BC	Cariboo	93 O/3	55°01′	123°03′
Packs Harbour	UNP/LNO	NF		13 H/15	53°51′	56°59′
Pacquet	VILG/VILG	NF		2 E/13	49°59′	55°53′
Pacquet Brook	RIV/CDE	NF		2 E/13	49°58′	55°53′
Pacquet Harbour	BAY/BAIE	NF		2 E/13	49°59′	55°52′
Paddle Prairie	UNP/LNO	AB	18-103-21-W5	84 F/14	57°57′	117°29′
Paddle Prairie Metis Settlement	UNP/LNO	AB		84 F/13	57°55′	117°32′
Paddle River	RIV/CDE	AB	15-59-2-W5	83 J/1	54°05′	114°15′
Paddling Lake	UNP/LNO	SK	26-49-8-W3	73 G/3	53°15′	107°04′
Paddling Lake	LAKE/LAC	SK		73 B/15	52°57′	106°56′
Paddock's Bight	UNP/LNO	NF		2 E/12	49°34′	55°47′
Paddockwood	VILG/VILG	SK	25-52-25-W2	73 H/12	53°31′	105°34′
Paddockwood Junction	UNP/LNO	SK	49-26-W2	73 H/4	53°13′	105°46′
Paddockwood No. 520	MUN2/AZM2	SK		73 H/12	53°39′	105°33′
Padille Pond	LAKE/LAC	NF		12 A/5	48°29′	57°33′
Padle Fiord	BAY/BAIE	NT	Franklin	16 L	66°55′	63°25′

NAME NOM	ENTITY ENTITÉ	LOC 1 LIEU 1	LOC 2 LIEU 2	MAP CARTE	POSITION LAT	LONG
Padlei	UNP/LNO	NT	Keewatin	65 H	61°55′	96°40′
Padle River	RIV/CDE	NT	Franklin	16 L	66°49′	63°50′
Padliak Inlet	BAY/BAIE	NT	Franklin	67 C	69°15′	103°03′
Padloping Island	UNP/LNO	NT	Franklin	16 M	67°02′	62°44′
Padloping Island	ISL/ÎLE	NT	Franklin	16 M	67°06′	62°38′
Padoue	VILG/VILG	QC	La Mitis	22 B/12	48°35′	67°59′
Padstow	UNP/LNO	AB	14-56-8-W5	83 G/14	53°50′	115°05′
Pagashi River	RIV/CDE	ON	Kenora	42 O/11	51°40′	83°14′
Pagato Lake	LAKE/LAC	SK		64 D/1	56°08′	102°30′
Pagato River	RIV/CDE	SK		63 M/16	55°53′	102°08′
Pageant	UNP/LNO	AB	5-18-21-W4	82 I/7	50°29′	112°51′
Paget	UNP/LNO	ON	Sudbury	41 I/2	46°14′	80°44′
Paget Point	CAPE/CAP	NT	Franklin	39 E	78°08′	75°35′
Pagoda Peak	MTN/MNT	BC	Range 2 Coast	92 N/7	51°30′	124°52′
Paguchi Lake	LAKE/LAC	ON	Kenora	52 G/12	49°34′	91°32′
Pagwa	UNP/LNO	ON	Cochrane	42 K/3	50°01′	85°16′
Pagwachuan Lake	LAKE/LAC	ON	Thunder Bay	42 E/9	49°43′	86°05′
Pagwachuan River	RIV/CDE	ON	Cochrane	42 K/2	50°12′	84°43′
Pagwa River	UNP/LNO	ON	Cochrane	42 K/3	50°01′	85°13′
Pahas 3	IR/RI	BC	Range 1 Coast	92 L/14	50°54′	127°18′
Pahonan	UNP/LNO	SK	16-48-21-W2	73 H/2	53°08′	105°00′
Pahtauau Tshuap	UNP/LNO	QC	Minganie	12 L/5	50°18′	63°57′
Paimpont, Lac	LAKE/LAC	QC	Minganie	12 K/5	50°28′	61°34′
Pain Court	UNP/LNO	ON	Kent	40 J/8	42°25′	82°19′
Paincourt - see-voir - **Pain Court**	UNP/LNO	ON		40 J/8	42°25′	82°19′
Pain de Sucre, Le	UNP/LNO	QC	Communauté urbaine de Montréal	31 H/12	45°30′	73°54′
Painsec	UNP/LNO	NB	Westmorland	21 I/2	46°06′	64°38′
Pain-Sec	UNP/LNO	QC	Bellechasse	21 L/10	46°36′	70°33′
Painsec Junction	UNP/LNO	NB	Westmorland	21 I/2	46°08′	64°40′
Painswick	UNP/LNO	ON	Simcoe	31 D/5	44°21′	79°40′
Paintearth Creek	RIV/CDE	AB	4-40-13-W4	73 D/5	52°24′	111°49′
Paintearth No. 18, County of	MUN1/AZM1	AB	37-12-W4	73 D/4	52°13′	111°42′
Painted Rock Island	ISL/ÎLE	ON	Kenora	52 E/1	49°11′	94°29′
Paint Hills Bay	BAY/BAIE	NT	Keewatin	33 D	52°57′	78°54′
Paint Lake	UNP/LNO	MB	75-4-W	63 O/9	55°30′	98°00′
Paint Lake	LAKE/LAC	MB	74,75-3,4-W	63 P/5	55°28′	97°57′
Paipoonge	MUN2/AZM2	ON	Thunder Bay	52 A/6	48°20′	89°30′
Paisley	VILG/VILG	ON	Bruce	41 A/6	44°18′	81°16′
Paisley Brook	UNP/LNO	SK	21-1-23-W2	72 H/3	49°04′	105°01′
Paix, Rivière de la - also-aussi - **Peace River**	RIV/CDE	AB/BC		74 L/14	59°00′	111°25′
Pakan	UNP/LNO	AB	12-58-17-W4	83 I/1	54°01′	112°23′
Pakashan 150D	IR/RI	AB	76-15-W5	83 N/9	55°37′	116°16′
Pakashkan Lake	LAKE/LAC	ON	Thunder Bay	52 G/8	49°21′	90°15′
Pakenham	MUN2/AZM2	ON	Lanark	31 F/8	45°19′	76°20′
Pakenham	UNP/LNO	ON	Lanark	31 F/8	45°20′	76°17′
Pakeshkag River	RIV/CDE	ON	Parry Sound	41 H/15	45°59′	80°32′
Pakesley	UNP/LNO	ON	Parry Sound	41 H/15	45°55′	80°31′
Pakitahokansik	UNP/LNO	MB		53 L/14	54°48′	95°28′
Pakowki	UNP/LNO	AB	12-6-8-W4	72 E/7	49°28′	110°57′
Pakowki Lake	LAKE/LAC	AB	4,5-7,8-W4	72 E/7	49°20′	110°55′
Pakuashipi	UNP/LNO	QC	Côte-Nord-du-Golfe-Saint-Laurent	12 O/2	51°14′	58°40′
Pakwa Lake	LAKE/LAC	MB	67,68-10-W	63 J/15	54°52′	98°53′
Pakwash Lake	LAKE/LAC	ON	Kenora	52 K/11	50°45′	93°30′
Pakwaw Lake	UNP/LNO	SK	52-5-W2	63 E/7	53°29′	102°38′
Palairet, Lac	LAKE/LAC	QC	Maria-Chapdelaine	22 M/4	51°09′	71°42′
Palander Strait	CHAN/CHEN	NT	Franklin	67 B	68°33′	100°45′
Paldi	UNP/LNO	BC	Sahtlam	92 B/13	48°47′	123°51′
Palermo	UNP/LNO	ON	Halton	30 M/5	43°26′	79°47′
Palfrey Lake	LAKE/LAC	NB	York	21 G/11	45°39′	67°29′
Palgrave	UNP/LNO	ON	Peel	30 M/13	43°57′	79°50′
Palgrave Station	UNP/LNO	ON		30 M/13	43°58′	79°49′
Palisade	UNP/LNO	SK	33-5-24-W3	72 F/6	49°25′	109°10′
Palling	UNP/LNO	BC	Range 5 Coast	93 K/5	54°21′	125°53′
Palling	UNP/LNO	BC	Range 5 Coast	93 K/5	54°21′	125°55′
Palling 1	IR/RI	BC	Range 5 Coast	93 K/5	54°20′	125°55′
Palliser	UNP/LNO	BC	Kootenay	82 N/7	51°15′	116°43′
Palliser Heights	UNP/LNO	SK		72 I/5	50°24′	105°34′
Palliser River	RIV/CDE	BC	Kootenay	82 J/5	50°28′	115°40′
Palmarolle	VILG/VILG	QC	Abitibi-Ouest	32 D/11	48°40′	79°12′
Palm Beach	UNP/LNO	ON	Simcoe	31 D/6	44°28′	79°29′
Palmer	VILG/VILG	SK	33-10-3-W3	72 G/16	49°51′	106°21′
Palmer	UNP/LNO	ON	Halton	30 M/5	43°22′	79°49′
Palmer	UNP/LNO	BC	Esquimalt	92 B/6	48°28′	123°27′
Palmer Bay	BAY/BAIE	NT	Franklin	46 I	66°43′	82°20′
Palmer Point	CAPE/CAP	NT	Franklin	78 E	74°56′	107°56′

NAME NOM	ENTITY ENTITÉ	LOC 1 LIEU 1	LOC 2 LIEU 2	MAP CARTE	POSITION LAT	LONG
Palmer Rapids	UNP/LNO	ON	Renfrew	31 F/5	45°19′	77°31′
Palmer, Rivière	RIV/CDE	QC	Lotbinière	21 L/6	46°19′	71°27′
Palmer Road	UNP/LNO	PE	Prince	21 I/16	46°55′	64°09′
Palmerston	TOWN/VIL2	ON	Wellington	40 P/15	43°50′	80°51′
Palmerston and North and South Canonto	MUN2/AZM2	ON	Frontenac	31 F/2	45°05′	76°40′
Palmerston, Cape	CAPE/CAP	BC	Rupert	102 I/9	50°36′	128°18′
Palmerston, Cape	CAPE/CAP	NT	Franklin	57 F	70°46′	92°40′
Palmerston Lake	LAKE/LAC	ON	Frontenac	31 F/2	45°01′	76°51′
Palmerston, Mount	MTN/MNT	BC	Rupert	92 L/8	50°25′	126°20′
Palmquist	UNP/LNO	ON	Cochrane	42 F/15	49°48′	84°33′
Palmyra	UNP/LNO	ON	Kent	40 I/5	42°26′	81°47′
Palo	UNP/LNO	SK	12-37-17-W3	73 C/1	52°10′	108°18′
Palomar	UNP/LNO	ON	Sudbury	42 B/1	48°10′	82°16′
Palsen River	RIV/CDE	MB/ON		53 D/14	52°51′	95°15′
Pambrun	UNP/LNO	SK	28-11-11-W3	72 G/14	49°56′	107°27′
Pambrun, Lac	LAKE/LAC	QC	Le Fjord-du-Saguenay	22 M/10	51°42′	70°44′
Pamdenec	UNP/LNO	NB	Kings	21 G/8	45°19′	66°12′
Pamemen, Lac	LAKE/LAC	QC	Jamésie	33 B/16	52°45′	74°20′
Pamigamachi, Lac	LAKE/LAC	QC	Jamésie	33 K/3	54°10′	77°28′
Pamiok Island	ISL/ÎLE	NT	Franklin	25 C	60°04′	69°35′
Pamour	UNP/LNO	ON	Cochrane	42 A/11	48°31′	81°07′
Pamouscachiou-Deux, Barrage	MISC/DIV	QC	Le Fjord-du-Saguenay	22 E/10	49°31′	70°55′
Pamouscachiou-Un, Barrage	MISC/DIV	QC	Le Fjord-du-Saguenay	22 E/7	49°20′	70°58′
Panache, Lake	LAKE/LAC	ON	Sudbury	41 I/6	46°15′	81°20′
Panache, Rivière au	RIV/CDE	QC	Jamésie	32 F/1	49°09′	76°07′
Panalik Point	CAPE/CAP	NT	Keewatin	46 K	66°04′	85°58′
Pancake Bay	BAY/BAIE	ON	Algoma	41 K/15	46°57′	84°41′
Panchia Lake	LAKE/LAC	NF		23 H/2	53°08′	64°40′
Pandora Island	ISL/ÎLE	NT	Franklin	68 A	72°48′	96°48′
Pandora Peak	MTN/MNT	BC	Renfrew	92 C/9	48°34′	124°27′
Pangburn	UNP/LNO	NB	Queens	21 I/4	46°13′	65°34′
Pangertot Peninsula	CAPE/CAP	NT	Keewatin	55 K	62°36′	92°10′
Pangis	UNP/LNO	ON	Algoma	41 N/1	47°08′	84°07′
Pangman	VILG/VILG	SK	16-8-20-W2	72 H/10	49°39′	104°40′
Pangnik Lake	LAKE/LAC	NT	Franklin	36 B	64°42′	75°08′
Pangnikto Lake	LAKE/LAC	NT	Keewatin	57 C	69°31′	92°58′
Pangnirtung	HAM/HAM	NT	Franklin	26 I	66°09′	65°43′
Pangnirtung Fiord	BAY/BAIE	NT	Franklin	26 I	66°07′	65°38′
Panmure	UNP/LNO	ON	Carleton	31 F/8	45°19′	76°11′
Panmure Island	UNP/LNO	PE	Kings	11 L/1	46°08′	62°29′
Panmure Island	ISL/ÎLE	PE	Kings	11 L/1	46°08′	62°29′
Panny River	RIV/CDE	AB	94-6-W5	84 G/2	57°08′	114°51′
Panorama	UNP/LNO	BC	Kootenay	82 K/8	50°28′	116°14′
Panorama Lake	LAKE/LAC	ON	Rainy River	52 C/13	48°58′	93°49′
Panorama Ridge	UNP/LNO	BC	New Westminster	92 G/2	49°06′	122°51′
Pansy	UNP/LNO	MB	22-4-6-E	62 H/7	49°20′	96°43′
Pantage Lake	LAKE/LAC	BC	Cariboo	93 G/3	53°12′	123°05′
Panther Falls	FALL/CHUT	AB	37-22-W5	83 C/3	52°11′	117°03′
Panton	UNP/LNO	SK	54-12-W3	73 G/12	53°39′	107°38′
Panuke Lake	LAKE/LAC	NS	Halifax	21 A/16	44°48′	64°07′
Panuke Road	UNP/LNO	NS	Hants	21 A/16	44°57′	64°05′
Papakamistikw	UNP/LNO	QC	Jamésie	32 L/15	50°49′	78°49′
Papanakies Lake	LAKE/LAC	NT	Mackenzie	75 M	63°14′	110°19′
Papaonga River	RIV/CDE	ON	Kenora	52 K/15	50°52′	92°45′
Papekwatchin 4	IR/RI	BC	New Westminster	92 G/1	49°09′	122°07′
Papiit	UNP/LNO	QC	Kativik	35 F/6	61°28′	77°12′
Papikwan River	RIV/CDE	SK	17-50-9-W2	63 E/6	53°19′	103°17′
Papinachois	UNP/LNO	QC	Manicouagan	22 F/2	49°00′	68°38′
Papinachois, Rivière de	RIV/CDE	QC	Manicouagan	22 F/2	49°00′	68°38′
Papineau	MUN1/AZM1	QC	Papineau	31 G/14	45°53′	75°03′
Papineau - see-voir - Papineau-Cameron	MUN2/AZM2	ON		31 L/2	46°14′	78°34′
Papineau-Cameron	MUN2/AZM2	ON	Nipissing	31 L/2	46°14′	78°34′
Papineau-Labelle, Réserve faunique de	PARK/PARC	QC	Antoine-Labelle	31 J/3	46°10′	75°19′
Papineau, Lac	LAKE/LAC	QC	Argenteuil	31 G/15	45°49′	74°46′
Papineau Lake	LAKE/LAC	ON	Hastings	31 F/5	45°21′	77°49′
Papineauville	TOWN/VIL2	QC	Papineau	31 G/11	45°37′	75°01′
Papsilqua 2	IR/RI	BC	Yale Division Yale	92 H/11	49°41′	121°24′
Papsilqua 2A	IR/RI	BC	Yale Division Yale	92 H/11	49°41′	121°24′
Papsilqua 2B	IR/RI	BC	Yale Division Yale	92 H/11	49°42′	121°24′
Papsilqua 13	IR/RI	BC	Kamloops Division Yale	92 I/6	50°19′	121°09′
Papyum 27	IR/RI	BC	Kamloops Division Yale	92 I/4	50°14′	121°35′
Papyum 27A	IR/RI	BC	Kamloops Division Yale	92 I/4	50°14′	121°36′
Papyum Graveyard 27C	IR/RI	BC	Kamloops Division Yale	92 I/4	50°14′	121°35′
Paquet Bay	BAY/BAIE	NT	Franklin	38 B	72°00′	78°25′
Paquette	UNP/LNO	QC	Coaticook	21 E/3	45°08′	71°28′

NAME NOM	ENTITY ENTITÉ	LOC 1 LIEU 1	LOC 2 LIEU 2	MAP CARTE	POSITION	
					LAT	LONG
Paquette Corners	UNP/LNO	ON	Essex	40 J/2	42°11′	82°58′
Paquetville	VILG/VILG	NB	Gloucester	21 P/11	47°40′	65°06′
Paquetville	GEOG/GÉOG	NB	Gloucester	21 P/11	47°40′	65°12′
Paquin	UNP/LNO	QC	Témiscamingue	31 M/11	47°38′	79°19′
Paquin Lake	LAKE/LAC	SK	61-5-W3	73 J/2	54°15′	106°40′
Paradis	UNP/LNO	QC	Vallée-de-l'Or	32 C/2	48°13′	76°35′
Paradis Bay	UNP/LNO	ON	Timiskaming	31 M/5	47°20′	79°32′
Paradis-des-Chênes	UNP/LNO	QC	Brome-Missisquoi	31 H/2	45°10′	72°45′
Paradise	TOWN/VIL2	NF		1 N/10	47°32′	52°53′
Paradise	UNP/LNO	NF		1 N/10	47°32′	52°52′
Paradise	UNP/LNO	NF		2 E/10	49°40′	54°47′
Paradise	UNP/LNO	NF		13 N/9	55°31′	60°05′
Paradise	UNP/LNO	NS	Annapolis	21 A/14	44°52′	65°13′
Paradise Beach	UNP/LNO	ON	York	31 D/6	44°19′	79°26′
Paradise Brook	RIV/CDE	NS	Annapolis	21 A/14	44°52′	65°13′
Paradise Hill	VILG/VILG	SK	52-24-W3	73 F/11	53°32′	109°38′
Paradise Lake	LAKE/LAC	NS	Annapolis	21 A/14	44°46′	65°10′
Paradise Lake	LAKE/LAC	BC	Kamloops Division Yale	92 H/16	49°55′	120°17′
Paradise Point	UNP/LNO	NF		13 H/6	53°25′	57°16′
Paradise Point	UNP/LNO	ON	Simcoe	31 D/13	44°46′	79°49′
Paradise Point	UNP/LNO	BC	Kamloops Division Yale	82 L/14	50°48′	119°10′
Paradise River	UNP/LNO	NF		13 H/6	53°27′	57°17′
Paradise River	RIV/CDE	NF		1 M/9	47°37′	54°26′
Paradise River	RIV/CDE	NF		13 H/6	53°26′	57°17′
Paradise-St. Thomas - see-voir - Paradise	TOWN/VIL2	NF		1 N/10	47°32′	52°53′
Paradise Sound	BAY/BAIE	NF		1 M/7	47°24′	54°36′
Paradise Valley	VILG/VILG	AB	6-47-2-W4	73 E/1	53°02′	110°17′
Paradise Valley	UNP/LNO	BC	New Westminster	92 G/14	49°49′	123°09′
Paradis, Lac	LAKE/LAC	QC	Manicouagan	22 K/15	50°47′	68°51′
Paradis, Lac	LAKE/LAC	QC	La Haute-Côte-Nord	22 C/5	48°17′	69°43′
Paradis-Marin, Le	UNP/LNO	QC	La Haute-Côte-Nord	22 C/6	48°17′	69°28′
Paragon Lake	LAKE/LAC	MB		64 I/6	58°19′	97°13′
Parallel Creek	RIV/CDE	AB	19-78-17-W4	83 P/15	55°46′	112°38′
Paramé, Lac	LAKE/LAC	QC	Côte-Nord-du-Golfe-Saint-Laurent	12 O/8	51°28′	58°08′
Parc-Belvoir	UNP/LNO	QC	Les Laurentides	31 J/1	46°01′	74°21′
Parc-Bon-Air	UNP/LNO	QC	La Jacques-Cartier	21 L/13	46°48′	71°33′
Parc-de-la-Chaudière	UNP/LNO	QC	La Nouvelle-Beauce	21 L/11	46°32′	71°07′
Parc-de-l'Artillerie, Lieu historique national du - also-aussi - Artillery Park National Historic Site	PARK/PARC	QC	Communauté urbaine de Québec	21 L/14	46°49′	71°13′
Parc du Gros-Morne, Site du patrimoine mondial du - also-aussi - Gros Morne National Park World Heritage Site	PARK/PARC	NF		12 H/12	49°41′	57°44′
Parc international de la paix Waterton-Glacier, Site du patrimoine mondial du - also-aussi - Waterton-Glacier International Peace Park World Heritage Site	PARK/PARC	AB		82 H/4	49°00′	113°50′
Parc La Salle	UNP/LNO	MB		62 H/14	49°46′	97°10′
Parc national Nahanni, Site du patrimoine mondial du - also-aussi - Nahanni National Park World Heritage Site	PARK/PARC	NT		95 F/12	61°36′	125°41′
Parc national Wood Buffalo, Site du patrimoine mondial du - also-aussi - Wood Buffalo National Park World Heritage Site	PARK/PARC	AB/NT		84 H/9	59°25′	113°00′
Parc provincial Dinosaur, Site du patrimoine mondial du - also-aussi - Dinosaur Provincial Park World Heritage Site	PARK/PARC	AB		72 L/13	50°47′	111°30′
Parcs des montagnes Rocheuses canadiennes, Site du patrimoine mondial des - also-aussi - The Canadian Rocky Mountain Parks World Heritage Site	PARK/PARC	BC/AB		83 C/3	52°02′	117°07′
Parc-Stanley, Lieu historique national du - also-aussi - Stanley Park National Historic Site	PARK/PARC	BC	New Westminster	92 G/6	49°18′	123°09′
Pardee	UNP/LNO	ON	Sudbury	41 O/13	47°55′	83°37′
Pardee	UNP/LNO	ON	Thunder Bay	52 A/4	48°08′	89°35′
Pardy Island	UNP/LNO	NF		1 M/3	47°02′	55°09′
Paré	UNP/LNO	QC	Portneuf	21 L/12	46°38′	71°58′
Parent	TOWN/VIL2	QC	Le Haut-Saint-Maurice	31 O/15	47°55′	74°37′
Parent, Lac	LAKE/LAC	QC	Abitibi	32 C/11	48°38′	77°03′
Parham	UNP/LNO	ON	Frontenac	31 C/10	44°39′	76°43′
Paris	TOWN/VIL2	ON	Brant	40 P/1	43°12′	80°23′
Paris	UNP/LNO	YT		115 O/15	63°49′	138°39′
Parisienne, Île	ISL/ÎLE	ON	Algoma	41 K/10	46°41′	84°44′
Paris, Sommet de	MTN/MNT	QC	Charlevoix	21 M/15	47°46′	70°50′
Parisville	VILG/VILG	QC	Bécancour	31 I/9	46°31′	72°04′
Parisville	UNP/LNO	QC	Bécancour	31 I/9	46°31′	72°04′
Park	MUN2/AZM2	MB		62 K/10	50°43′	100°31′
Park Beach	UNP/LNO	ON	Muskoka	31 E/4	45°01′	79°36′
Parkbeg	UNP/LNO	SK	19-17-2-W3	72 J/8	50°27′	106°16′
Parkbend	UNP/LNO	AB	30-3-27-W4	82 H/4	49°15′	113°37′

NAME NOM	ENTITY ENTITÉ	LOC 1 LIEU 1	LOC 2 LIEU 2	MAP CARTE	POSITION LAT	LONG
Park Bluff	UNP/LNO	SK	49-16-W3	73 F/1	53°13′	108°13′
Park Corner	UNP/LNO	PE	Queens	11 L/12	46°32′	63°34′
Park Court	UNP/LNO	AB	34-54-7-W5	83 G/10	53°43′	114°58′
Parkdale	UNP/LNO	PE	Queens	11 L/6	46°15′	63°07′
Parkdale	UNP/LNO	NS	Halifax	11 D/12	44°39′	63°43′
Parkdale	UNP/LNO	NS	Lunenburg	21 A/10	44°39′	64°38′
Parkdale	UNP/LNO	ON	York	30 M/11	43°39′	79°27′
Parkdale	UNP/LNO	MB	12-4-E	62 I/3	50°03′	97°02′
Parkdale Boulevard	UNP/LNO	SK		72 I/5	50°26′	105°33′
Parkdale Gardens	UNP/LNO	BC	New Westminster	92 G/3	49°06′	123°03′
Parkdale Heights	UNP/LNO	MB		62 G/13	49°49′	99°59′
Parkdale No. 498	MUN2/AZM2	SK		73 F/8	53°25′	108°20′
Parke Hills	MTN/MNT	NT	Keewatin	57 A	68°21′	89°50′
Parker	UNP/LNO	QC	Les Collines-de-l'Outaouais	31 F/9	45°32′	76°04′
Parker	UNP/LNO	ON	Wellington	40 P/15	43°46′	80°35′
Parker Bay	BAY/BAIE	NT	Franklin	67 B	68°48′	103°10′
Parker, Cape	CAPE/CAP	NT	Franklin	38 G	75°13′	79°30′
Parker Hill	UNP/LNO	QC	Le Haut-Saint-François	21 E/5	45°19′	71°32′
Parker Island	ISL/ÎLE	BC	Cowichan	92 B/14	48°53′	123°25′
Parker Lake	LAKE/LAC	SK		73 N/8	55°20′	108°19′
Parker Lake	LAKE/LAC	NT	Keewatin	55 M	63°31′	95°18′
Parker Landing	UNP/LNO	ON	Bruce	41 A/14	45°57′	81°21′
Parker Point	CAPE/CAP	SK		74 N/8	59°28′	108°11′
Parker Ridge	UNP/LNO	NB	York	21 J/7	46°27′	66°31′
Parker River	RIV/CDE	NT	Franklin	88 D	73°40′	115°35′
Parker Road	UNP/LNO	NS	Kings	21 H/2	45°03′	64°49′
Parkers Corners	UNP/LNO	ON	Prescott	31 G/7	45°26′	74°56′
Parkers Cove	VILG/VILG	NF		1 M/7	47°24′	54°52′
Parkers Cove	UNP/LNO	NS	Annapolis	21 A/13	44°49′	65°31′
Parkersville	UNP/LNO	ON	Muskoka	31 E/3	45°11′	79°19′
Parkerview	UNP/LNO	SK	21-27-9-W2	62 M/6	51°21′	103°14′
Park Farm	UNP/LNO	AB	4-43-6-W4	73 D/10	52°41′	110°48′
Park Head	UNP/LNO	ON	Bruce	41 A/11	44°36′	81°09′
Parkhill	TOWN/VIL2	ON	Middlesex	40 P/4	43°09′	81°41′
Parkhill Creek	RIV/CDE	ON	Middlesex	40 P/4	43°13′	81°47′
Parkhurst	UNP/LNO	QC	Lotbinière	21 L/6	46°25′	71°17′
Parkindale	UNP/LNO	NB	Albert	21 H/15	45°52′	64°59′
Parkins, Cape	CAPE/CAP	BC	Rupert	102 I/8	50°27′	128°03′
Parkinson	UNP/LNO	ON	Algoma	41 J/6	46°22′	83°16′
Park Lake	LAKE/LAC	SK		63 M/4	55°07′	103°49′
Park Lake Provincial Park	PARK/PARC	AB	9-10-22-W4	82 H/15	49°48′	112°55′
Parkland	UNP/LNO	AB	16-15-27-W4	82 I/5	50°15′	113°39′
Parkland	UNP/LNO	BC	Peace River	93 P/15	55°55′	120°34′
Parkland Beach	VILG/VILG	AB	10-42-1-W5	83 B/9	52°36′	114°04′
Parkland Beach	HAM/HAM	SK	53-19-3W	73 F/10	53°33′	108°42′
Parkland County	MUN1/AZM1	AB		83 G/8	53°29′	114°22′
Parkland No. 31, County of - see-voir - Parkland County	MUN1/AZM1	AB		83 G/8	53°29′	114°22′
Parkman	UNP/LNO	SK	4-9-33-W	62 F/12	49°43′	101°54′
Parkmount	UNP/LNO	MB	28-11-4-E	62 H/15	49°57′	96°59′
Park Mountain	MTN/MNT	BC	Osoyoos Division Yale	82 L/7	50°28′	118°35′
Parkridge	UNP/LNO	SK		73 B/2	52°07′	106°45′
Park Rill	RIV/CDE	BC	Similkameen Division Yale	82 E/4	49°12′	119°33′
Park Royal	UNP/LNO	ON	Peel	30 M/12	43°31′	79°39′
Park Royal	UNP/LNO	BC	New Westminster	92 G/6	49°20′	123°09′
Parks Corner	UNP/LNO	MB	31,32-13-23-W	62 K/2	50°08′	100°36′
Parks Creek	RIV/CDE	ON	Hastings	31 C/6	44°17′	77°20′
Parkside	VILG/VILG	SK	28-48-4-W3	73 G/2	53°10′	106°33′
Parkside Beach	UNP/LNO	ON	Simcoe	31 D/6	44°28′	79°29′
Park Siding	UNP/LNO	BC	Kootenay	82 F/3	49°10′	117°30′
Parks Lake	LAKE/LAC	ON	Thunder Bay	42 E/5	49°27′	87°38′
Parksville	CITY/VIL1	BC	Nanoose	92 F/8	49°19′	124°19′
Park Valley	UNP/LNO	SK	12-54-6-W3	73 G/10	53°39′	106°46′
Parkview	HAM/HAM	SK	18,19-19-25-W2	72 I/11	50°37′	105°27′
Parkview Heights	UNP/LNO	ON	Wentworth	30 M/4	43°13′	80°00′
Parkview Hill	UNP/LNO	ON	York	30 M/11	43°42′	79°19′
Parkway	UNP/LNO	ON	Waterloo	40 P/8	43°25′	80°27′
Parkway East	UNP/LNO	ON	York	30 M/14	43°46′	79°20′
Parkway West	UNP/LNO	ON	York	30 M/14	43°45′	79°20′
Parkwood	UNP/LNO	ON	Sudbury	41 I/10	46°39′	80°59′
Parkwood Hills	UNP/LNO	ON	Carleton	31 G/5	45°22′	75°44′
Parlee	UNP/LNO	MB	15-77-2-W	63 P/12	55°40′	97°41′
Parlee Brook	UNP/LNO	NB	Kings	21 H/11	45°40′	65°25′
Parleeville	UNP/LNO	NB	Kings	21 H/12	45°42′	65°41′
Parliament Place	UNP/LNO	SK		72 I/7	50°25′	104°38′
Parmacheene	UNP/LNO	ON	Thunder Bay	52 H/1	49°04′	88°19′

NAME / NOM	ENTITY / ENTITÉ	LOC 1 / LIEU 1	LOC 2 / LIEU 2	MAP / CARTE	LAT	LONG
Parr Bay	BAY/BAIE	NT	Franklin	120 G	83°03'	69°26'
Parrish Glacier	GLAC/GLAC	NT	Franklin	39 G	79°36'	77°11'
Parr Lake	LAKE/LAC	NS	Yarmouth	21 A/4	44°05'	65°54'
Parrott Lakes	LAKE/LAC	BC	Range 5 Coast	93 L/2	54°07'	126°36'
Parrsboro	TOWN/VIL2	NS	Cumberland	21 H/8	45°24'	64°20'
Parry	HAM/HAM	SK	1-10-21-W2	72 H/15	49°47'	104°44'
Parry Bay	BAY/BAIE	NT	Franklin	47 A	68°06'	81°40'
Parry Bay	BAY/BAIE	NT	Mackenzie	77 A	68°15'	107°25'
Parry, Cape	CAPE/CAP	NT	Mackenzie	97 F	70°12'	124°31'
Parry Channel	CHAN/CHEN	NT	Franklin	68 F	74°20'	102°00'
Parry Falls	FALL/CHUT	NT	Mackenzie	75 K	62°53'	108°40'
Parry Island	UNP/LNO	ON	Parry Sound	41 H/8	45°19'	80°04'
Parry Island	ISL/ÎLE	ON	Parry Sound	41 H/8	45°15'	80°09'
Parry Island 16 - see-voir - Parry Island First Nation	IR/RI	ON		41 H/8	45°18'	80°08'
Parry Island First Nation	IR/RI	ON	Parry Sound	41 H/8	45°18'	80°08'
Parry Islands	ISL/ÎLE	NT	Franklin	78 H	75°30'	106°00'
Parry, Lac	LAKE/LAC	QC	Kativik	34 O/11	59°44'	75°20'
Parry Passage	CHAN/CHEN	BC	Queen Charlotte	103 K/3	54°11'	133°01'
Parry Peninsula	CAPE/CAP	NT	Mackenzie	97 C	69°45'	124°45'
Parry Point	CAPE/CAP	NT	Franklin	36 P	67°59'	72°57'
Parry, Port	BAY/BAIE	NT	Franklin	67 D	69°39'	97°25'
Parry Sound	TOWN/VIL2	ON	Parry Sound	41 H/8	45°21'	80°02'
Parry Sound	GEOG/GÉOG	ON		31 E/13	45°45'	79°50'
Parry Sound	BAY/BAIE	ON	Parry Sound	41 H/8	45°22'	80°08'
Parsnip 5	IR/RI	BC	Cariboo	93 O/2	55°08'	122°55'
Parsnip River	RIV/CDE	BC	Cariboo	93 O/3	55°10'	123°03'
Parsnips 5 - see-voir - Parsnip 5	IR/RI	BC		93 O/2	55°08'	122°55'
Parson	UNP/LNO	BC	Kootenay	82 N/2	51°04'	116°38'
Parson Bay	BAY/BAIE	BC	Range 1 Coast	92 L/10	50°34'	126°39'
Parsons Creek	RIV/CDE	BC	Barclay	92 C/15	48°59'	124°51'
Parsons Harbour	UNP/LNO	NF		11 P/10	47°36'	56°39'
Parsons Lake	LAKE/LAC	NT	Mackenzie	107 B	68°57'	133°39'
Parsons Point	UNP/LNO	NF		2 F/4	49°02'	53°52'
Parson's Pond	VILG/VILG	NF		12 I/4	50°02'	57°43'
Parsons Pond	LAKE/LAC	NF		2 D/9	48°38'	54°22'
Parsons Pond	LAKE/LAC	NF		12 H/13	49°59'	57°37'
Parthia	UNP/LNO	ON	Cochrane	42 G/11	49°36'	83°11'
Partridge Bay	BAY/BAIE	NF		3 E/4	53°12'	55°50'
Partridge Breast Lake	LAKE/LAC	MB		64 H/5	57°21'	97°56'
Partridge Creek	RIV/CDE	ON	Lennox and Addington	31 C/11	44°44'	77°14'
Partridge Falls	FALL/CHUT	ON	Thunder Bay	52 A/4	48°00'	89°51'
Partridge Island	ISL/ÎLE	ON	Kenora	43 M/13	55°59'	87°37'
Partridge Island	ISL/ÎLE	NT	Keewatin	44 D	56°02'	87°33'
Partridge Point	CAPE/CAP	NF		12 I/1	50°10'	56°10'
Partridge Ponds Ground	UNP/LNO	QC	Minganie	12 P/12	51°39'	57°58'
Partridge River	RIV/CDE	ON	Cochrane	42 P/8	51°19'	80°18'
Partridge Valley	UNP/LNO	NB	Queens	21 H/13	45°57'	65°52'
Pasadena	TOWN/VIL2	NF		12 H/4	49°01'	57°36'
Pasayten River	RIV/CDE	BC	Similkameen Division Yale	92 H/2	49°09'	120°35'
Pascagama, Lac	LAKE/LAC	QC	Vallée-de-l'Or	32 B/12	48°34'	75°36'
Pascagama, Rivière	RIV/CDE	QC	Vallée-de-l'Or	32 B/12	48°38'	75°34'
Pascal	UNP/LNO	SK	29-52-8-W3	73 G/11	53°31'	107°08'
Pascalis	UNP/LNO	QC	Vallée-de-l'Or	32 C/3	48°09'	77°29'
Pascalis, Lac	LAKE/LAC	QC	Vallée-de-l'Or	32 C/6	48°16'	77°24'
Pascobac	UNP/LNO	NB	Kings	21 H/12	45°42'	65°44'
Pascopee	UNP/LNO	ON	Thunder Bay	52 I/6	50°15'	89°19'
Pas d'Eau, Lac	LAKE/LAC	NF		23 A/12	52°33'	65°35'
Pasfield Lake	LAKE/LAC	SK		74 I/6	58°24'	105°20'
Pashashibou, Baie	BAY/BAIE	QC	Minganie	12 L/8	50°16'	62°20'
Pashilqua 2	IR/RI	BC	Lillooet	92 I/12	50°39'	121°55'
Pashilqua 2A	IR/RI	BC	Lillooet	92 I/12	50°39'	121°56'
Pashkokogan Lake	LAKE/LAC	ON	Thunder Bay	52 J/16	50°59'	90°17'
Paska Lake	LAKE/LAC	BC	Kamloops Division Yale	92 I/10	50°31'	120°39'
Paskwachi Bay	BAY/BAIE	MB/SK		64 F/5	57°17'	101°57'
Pasley Bay	BAY/BAIE	NT	Franklin	67 E	70°35'	96°12'
Pasley Island	UNP/LNO	BC	New Westminster	92 G/6	49°22'	123°27'
Pasley River	RIV/CDE	NT	Franklin	57 F	70°32'	95°47'
Paspébiac	VILG/VILG	QC	Bonaventure	22 A/3	48°02'	65°15'
Paspébiac, Baie de	BAY/BAIE	QC	Bonaventure	22 A/3	48°01'	65°16'
Paspébiac-Est	UNP/LNO	QC	Bonaventure	22 A/3	48°02'	65°12'
Paspébiac-Ouest	VILG/VILG	QC	Bonaventure	22 A/3	48°01'	65°16'
Paspébiac, Pointe de	CAPE/CAP	QC	Bonaventure	22 A/3	48°01'	65°15'
Paspébiac, Rivière	RIV/CDE	QC	Bonaventure	22 A/3	48°04'	65°09'
Pas Perdus, Lac des	LAKE/LAC	QC	Charlevoix	21 M/11	47°43'	71°04'
Pasqua	UNP/LNO	SK	28-16-25-W2	72 I/6	50°22'	105°23'

NAME NOM	ENTITY ENTITÉ	LOC 1 LIEU 1	LOC 2 LIEU 2	MAP CARTE	POSITION LAT	POSITION LONG
Pasqua 79	IR/RI	SK		62 L/12	50°45′	104°00′
Pasqua Lake	HAM/HAM	SK	21-14,15-2	62 L/13	50°47′	103°57′
Pasquatchai River	RIV/CDE	MB/ON		53 O/4	55°15′	91°31′
Pasquia Hills	MTN/MNT	SK		63 E/2	53°13′	102°37′
Pasquia River	RIV/CDE	MB/SK		63 F/14	53°50′	101°16′
Pasquia Settlement	GEOG/GÉOG	MB	54,55-27,28,29-W	63 F/13	53°45′	101°38′
Passage Point	CAPE/CAP	NF		1 M/12	47°37′	55°52′
Passamaquoddy Bay	BAY/BAIE	NB	Charlotte	21 G/2	45°06′	66°59′
Passchendaele	UNP/LNO	NS	Cape Breton	11 J/4	46°11′	59°58′
Pass Creek	UNP/LNO	AB	35-60-20-W5	83 K/2	54°13′	116°53′
Pass Creek	UNP/LNO	BC	Kootenay	82 F/5	49°23′	117°40′
Passe-Gagnon	UNP/LNO	QC	Côte-Nord-du-Golfe-Saint-Laurent	12 O/2	51°07′	58°34′
Passekeag	UNP/LNO	NB	Kings	21 H/12	45°33′	65°46′
Passe, La	CHAN/CHEN	QC	Les Îles-de-la-Madeleine	11 N/5	47°16′	61°44′
Passerelle, La	UNP/LNO	QC	Charlevoix-Est	21 M/16	47°47′	70°22′
Pass Island	UNP/LNO	NF		11 P/8	47°30′	56°12′
Pass Lake	UNP/LNO	ON	Thunder Bay	52 A/10	48°34′	88°44′
Passmore	UNP/LNO	NB	Northumberland	21 I/13	46°56′	65°34′
Passmore	UNP/LNO	BC	Kootenay	82 F/12	49°32′	117°39′
Pass Peak	MTN/MNT	YT		105 F/10	61°34′	132°50′
Pastecho River	RIV/CDE	AB		84 B/1	56°07′	114°15′
Pasteur, Lac	LAKE/LAC	QC	Sept-Rivières	22 J/2	50°13′	66°58′
Pas Trail	UNP/LNO	SK	22-52-12-W2	63 E/12	53°31′	103°41′
Paswegin	UNP/LNO	SK	8-35-14-W2	62 M/13	51°59′	103°58′
Patamisk, Lac	LAKE/LAC	QC	Jamésie	23 D/14	52°53′	71°05′
Patapedia River - also-aussi - Patapédia, Rivière	RIV/CDE	NB	Restigouche	21 O/14	47°51′	67°23′
Patapédia, Rivière - also-aussi - Patapedia River	RIV/CDE	QC	Avignon	21 O/14	47°51′	67°23′
Patate, Rivière à la	RIV/CDE	QC	Minganie	12 E/10	49°42′	62°55′
Patchepawapoka River	RIV/CDE	ON	Kenora	43 J/1	54°06′	82°20′
Patch, The	SEAU/SMER	—		4013	44°17′	62°18′
Pat Creek	RIV/CDE	BC	Kootenay	82 K/10	50°32′	116°52′
Patelin-Leroux	UNP/LNO	QC	Les Laurentides	31 J/2	46°09′	74°45′
Paterson	UNP/LNO	MB	5-63-17-W	63 J/5	54°26′	100°00′
Paterson	UNP/LNO	BC	Kootenay	82 F/4	49°00′	117°50′
Paterson Inlet	BAY/BAIE	NT	Franklin	37 H	71°30′	73°25′
Paterson Lake	LAKE/LAC	BC	Sayward	92 K/4	50°04′	125°39′
Pateyville	UNP/LNO	NF		2 M/5	51°21′	55°34′
Path End	UNP/LNO	NF		1 K/15	46°51′	52°57′
Path End	UNP/LNO	NF		1 K/13	46°54′	53°33′
Path End	UNP/LNO	NF		1 N/13	47°52′	53°57′
Path End	UNP/LNO	NF		1 M/3	47°03′	55°10′
Pathlow	HAM/HAM	SK	23-43-20-W2	73 A/10	52°43′	104°48′
Patience Lake	LAKE/LAC	SK	36-3-W3	73 B/1	52°07′	106°20′
Patricia	UNP/LNO	AB	13-20-13-W4	72 L/12	50°42′	111°40′
Patricia Bay	BAY/BAIE	NT	Franklin	27 F	70°25′	68°35′
Patrick	UNP/LNO	SK	11-22-13-W2	62 L/13	50°52′	103°42′
Patrick Point	CAPE/CAP	ON	Elgin	40 I/11	42°35′	81°28′
Patrick's Cove	UNP/LNO	NF		1 M/1	47°02′	54°07′
Patrick's Cove-Angels Cove	UNP/LNO	NF		1 M/1	47°02′	54°07′
Patricks Harbour	UNP/LNO	NF		11 P/9	47°41′	56°01′
Patricks Pond	LAKE/LAC	NF		12 H/1	49°01′	56°26′
Patrickton	UNP/LNO	QC	Bonaventure	22 A/4	48°14′	65°57′
Patrieville	UNP/LNO	NB	Madawaska	21 N/8	47°29′	68°25′
Pattee	UNP/LNO	SK	34-17-22-W2	72 I/7	50°28′	104°56′
Pattee Island	ISL/ÎLE	NT	Keewatin	44 P	59°40′	80°26′
Patten River	RIV/CDE	ON	Cochrane	32 E/5	49°27′	79°32′
Patterson	UNP/LNO	NB	Sunbury	21 G/10	45°33′	66°32′
Patterson	UNP/LNO	QC	Les Collines-de-l'Outaouais	31 G/12	45°36′	75°54′
Patterson	UNP/LNO	ON	York	30 M/14	43°52′	79°28′
Patterson Island	ISL/ÎLE	ON	Thunder Bay	42 D/10	48°39′	87°00′
Patterson Island	ISL/ÎLE	NT	Franklin	69 C	77°03′	103°41′
Patterson Lake	LAKE/LAC	ON	Lanark	31 F/2	45°00′	76°32′
Patterson Lake	LAKE/LAC	SK		64 M/16	59°56′	102°18′
Patterson Lake	LAKE/LAC	SK		74 F/11	57°39′	109°20′
Patterson, Mount	MTN/MNT	YT		106 D/2	64°04′	134°40′
Pattersons Corners	UNP/LNO	ON	Grenville	31 B/13	44°55′	75°40′
Patterson Siding	UNP/LNO	NB	Northumberland	21 P/4	47°05′	65°35′
Patton	UNP/LNO	ON	Algoma	41 J/6	46°17′	83°11′
Patton Seamount	SEAU/SMER	—		5.03	54°40′	150°30′
Pattullo, Mount	MTN/MNT	BC	Cassiar	104 A/4	56°14′	129°39′
Patuanak	HAM/HAM	SK		73 O/13	55°55′	107°43′
Patukami, Lac	LAKE/LAC	QC	Jamésie	33 J/4	54°13′	75°54′
Paudash	UNP/LNO	ON	Hastings	31 C/13	45°00′	77°58′
Paudash Lake	UNP/LNO	ON	Haliburton	31 D/16	45°00′	78°01′
Paudash Lake	LAKE/LAC	ON	Haliburton	31 D/16	44°58′	78°03′

NAME NOM	ENTITY ENTITÉ	LOC 1 LIEU 1	LOC 2 LIEU 2	MAP CARTE	POSITION LAT	LONG
Paugan Falls	UNP/LNO	QC	La Vallée-de-la-Gatineau	31 G/13	45°48'	75°56'
Paugh Lake	UNP/LNO	ON	Renfrew	31 F/12	45°34'	77°39'
Paugh Lake	LAKE/LAC	ON	Renfrew	31 F/12	45°35'	77°42'
Pauingassi	UNP/LNO	MB		53 D/3	52°09'	95°22'
Pauingassi First Nation	IR/RI	MB		53 D/3	52°10'	95°23'
Paukeanum 3	IR/RI	BC	Sayward	92 K/2	50°03'	124°59'
Pauktorvik Island	ISL/ÎLE	NT	Franklin	24 K/9	58°42'	68°20'
Paulatuk	HAM/HAM	NT	Mackenzie	97 C/8	69°21'	124°04'
Paul Bay	BAY/BAIE	NT	Keewatin	33 L	54°01'	79°00'
Paul Creek	RIV/CDE	BC	Similkameen Division Yale	92 H/1	49°15'	120°01'
Paul Island	ISL/ÎLE	NF		14 C/6	56°30'	61°25'
Paul, Lac à	LAKE/LAC	QC	Le Fjord-du-Saguenay	22 E/15	49°53'	70°46'
Paul Lake	LAKE/LAC	BC	Kamloops Division Yale	92 I/9	50°44'	120°07'
Paull Lake	LAKE/LAC	SK		74 A/2	56°08'	104°48'
Paull River	RIV/CDE	SK		73 P/14	55°49'	105°07'
Paul Revere Ridge	SEAU/SMER	—		15798A	50°08'	129°33'
Paul River	RIV/CDE	BC	Cassiar	94 F/6	57°19'	125°27'
Paul's 6	IR/RI	BC	Yale Division Yale	92 H/14	49°48'	121°27'
Paul's Basin 2	IR/RI	BC	Yale Division Yale	92 H/15	49°58'	120°57'
Pauls Lake	LAKE/LAC	NF		12 H/1	49°06'	56°04'
Paulson	UNP/LNO	MB	33-24-18-W	62 O/4	51°07'	99°56'
Paulson	UNP/LNO	BC	Similkameen Division Yale	82 E/1	49°12'	118°07'
Pauls Pond	LAKE/LAC	NF		2 D/11	48°40'	55°08'
Paungassi - see-voir - Pauingassi	UNP/LNO	MB		53 D/3	52°09'	95°22'
Pavey	UNP/LNO	BC	Cassiar	104 M/15	59°56'	134°55'
Pavilion	UNP/LNO	BC	Lillooet	92 I/13	50°52'	121°50'
Pavilion	UNP/LNO	BC	Lillooet	92 I/13	50°53'	121°50'
Pavilion 1	IR/RI	BC	Lillooet	92 I/13	50°53'	121°51'
Pavilion 1A	IR/RI	BC	Lillooet	92 I/13	50°55'	121°54'
Pavilion 3A	IR/RI	BC	Kamloops Division Yale	92 I/13	50°49'	121°39'
Pavilion 4	IR/RI	BC	Kamloops Division Yale	92 I/13	50°49'	121°39'
Pavilion Lake	LAKE/LAC	BC	Lillooet	92 I/13	50°52'	121°44'
Pavillon, Rivière du	RIV/CDE	QC	Minganie	12 E/2	49°11'	62°54'
Pavy, Lac	LAKE/LAC	QC	Kativik	34 O/1	59°08'	74°23'
Pawala 5	IR/RI	BC	Range 1 Coast	92 K/12	50°37'	125°55'
Pawistik	UNP/LNO	MB		63 N/11	55°42'	101°13'
Paxson	UNP/LNO	AB	6-66-20-W4	83 I/11	54°41'	113°00'
Payne	UNP/LNO	ON	Renfrew	31 F/7	45°30'	76°45'
Payne	UNP/LNO	ON	Lambton	40 J/16	42°51'	82°25'
Payne Bay	BAY/BAIE	NT	Franklin	25 C	60°02'	69°40'
Payne, Lac	LAKE/LAC	QC	Kativik	34 O/8	59°25'	74°00'
Payne River	RIV/CDE	ON	Russell	31 G/3	45°14'	75°08'
Paynes	UNP/LNO	ON	Elgin	40 I/14	42°48'	81°16'
Paynes Mills	UNP/LNO	ON	Elgin	40 I/14	42°47'	81°17'
Paynton	VILG/VILG	SK	35-46-21-W3	73 F/2	53°01'	108°56'
Paynton No. 470	MUN2/AZM2	SK		73 F/2	53°00'	108°55'
Paypeeshek River	RIV/CDE	ON	Cochrane	42 B/9	48°37'	82°21'
Pays Plat	UNP/LNO	ON	Thunder Bay	42 D/13	48°52'	87°35'
Pays Plat 51	IR/RI	ON	Thunder Bay	42 D/13	48°53'	87°34'
Payuk	UNP/LNO	MB	8-65-27-W	63 K/12	54°37'	101°30'
Peabody	UNP/LNO	QC	Memphrémagog	31 H/1	45°05'	72°23'
Peabody	UNP/LNO	ON	Bruce	41 A/6	44°21'	81°01'
Peace Grove	UNP/LNO	AB	27-84-5-W6	84 D/7	56°18'	118°43'
Peace No. 135, Municipal District of	MUN1/AZM1	AB	82-24-W5	84 C/4	56°08'	117°45'
Peace Point	UNP/LNO	AB	35-116-15-W4	84 P/1	59°07'	112°27'
Peace Reach	RIVF/EFLV	BC	Cariboo	94 B/2	56°05'	123°00'
Peace River	TOWN/VIL2	AB	83,84-21-W5	84 C/3	56°15'	117°17'
Peace River	MUN1/AZM1	BC	Peace River	94 B/10	56°40'	122°45'
Peace River - also-aussi - **Paix, Rivière de la**	RIV/CDE	AB/BC		74 L/14	59°00'	111°25'
Peace River Land District	GEOG/GÉOG	BC		94 G	57°25'	122°10'
Peace River-Liard - see-voir - Peace River	MUN1/AZM1	BC		94 B/10	56°40'	122°45'
Peace River-Liard - see-voir - Fort Nelson-Liard	MUN1/AZM1	BC		94 O/4	59°00'	123°45'
Peaches Cove	UNP/LNO	NF		1 M/9	47°40'	54°04'
Peachland	MUN1/AZM1	BC	Osoyoos Division Yale	82 E/13	49°46'	119°44'
Peachland Creek	RIV/CDE	BC	Osoyoos Division Yale	82 E/12	49°44'	119°46'
Peachytown	UNP/LNO	NF		1 N/10	47°30'	52°59'
Peacock	UNP/LNO	AB	9-13-23-W4	82 I/3	50°05'	113°05'
Peacock Hills	MTN/MNT	NT	Mackenzie	76 L	66°05'	110°45'
Peacock Point	UNP/LNO	ON	Haldimand	30 L/13	42°47'	79°59'
Peacock Point	CAPE/CAP	ON	Haldimand	30 L/13	42°47'	79°59'
Peakes	UNP/LNO	PE	Kings	11 L/7	46°18'	62°47'
Peakes Road	UNP/LNO	PE	Kings	11 L/7	46°19'	62°44'
Pearce	UNP/LNO	AB	1-10-25-W4	82 H/14	49°48'	113°16'
Pearce Lake	LAKE/LAC	NT	Keewatin	56 J	66°32'	90°02'
Pearceley	UNP/LNO	ON	Parry Sound	31 E/12	45°44'	79°31'

NAME NOM	ENTITY ENTITÉ	LOC 1 LIEU 1	LOC 2 LIEU 2	MAP CARTE	POSITION LAT	LONG
Pearce Point	CAPE/CAP	NT	Mackenzie	97 D	69°49'	122°44'
Pearceton	UNP/LNO	QC	Brome-Missisquoi	31 H/2	45°09'	72°53'
Pearkes, Mount	MTN/MNT	BC	New Westminster	92 J/4	50°09'	123°44'
Pearl	UNP/LNO	ON	Thunder Bay	52 A/10	48°40'	88°40'
Pearl (Big) Island	ISL/ÎLE	NF		12 G/1	49°13'	58°16'
Pearl (Green) Island	ISL/ÎLE	NS	Lunenburg	21 A/8	44°23'	64°03'
Pearl Lake	UNP/LNO	ON	Bruce	41 A/3	44°12'	81°03'
Pearse Island	ISL/ÎLE	BC	Range 5 Coast	103 J/15	54°52'	130°20'
Pearse Island 43	IR/RI	BC	Cassiar	103 O/1	55°01'	130°11'
Pearse Islands	ISL/ÎLE	BC	Rupert	92 L/10	50°35'	126°52'
Pearse Peninsula	CAPE/CAP	BC	Range 1 Coast	92 L/15	50°47'	126°33'
Pearse Strait	CHAN/CHEN	NT	Franklin	69 B	76°03'	103°11'
Pearson	UNP/LNO	ON	Timiskaming	31 M/12	47°38'	79°34'
Pearson Creek	RIV/CDE	BC	Osoyoos Division Yale	82 E/14	49°53'	119°04'
Pearson Lake	LAKE/LAC	MB		64 A/3	56°15'	97°15'
Pearsonville	UNP/LNO	NB	Kings	21 H/13	45°48'	65°43'
Peary Channel	CHAN/CHEN	NT	Franklin	69 G	79°40'	101°30'
Peary Trough	SEAU/SMER	—		NT1216	79°30'	99°00'
Peas Brook	UNP/LNO	NS	Guysborough	11 F/6	45°21'	61°20'
Pease Lake	LAKE/LAC	SK	63-4-W3	73 J/8	54°25'	106°28'
Peases Island	ISL/ÎLE	NS	Yarmouth	20 O/9	43°38'	66°02'
Peavey	UNP/LNO	AB	34-56-25-W4	83 H/13	53°53'	113°38'
Peavine	UNP/LNO	AB	1-59-7-W5	83 J/2	54°05'	114°54'
Peavine Metis Settlement	UNP/LNO	AB		83 N/16	55°52'	116°17'
Peawanuck	UNP/LNO	ON	Kenora	43 N/3	55°01'	85°25'
Pebble Baye	VILG/VILG	SK	31-48-7-3	73 G/3	53°11'	107°00'
Pebble Beach	UNP/LNO	MB	19-23-7-W	62 J/16	51°00'	98°27'
Pebble Island	ISL/ÎLE	NT	Keewatin	33 D	52°45'	79°10'
Pebonishewi Lake	LAKE/LAC	ON	Sudbury	41 O/9	47°43'	82°03'
Pêche-à-l'Anguille, La	UNP/LNO	QC	Rimouski-Neigette	22 C/7	48°16'	68°33'
Pêche-Blanche, La	UNP/LNO	QC	Le Fjord-du-Saguenay	22 D/7	48°27'	70°53'
Pêche-du-Curé, La	UNP/LNO	QC	La Haute-Côte-Nord	22 C/4	48°08'	69°42'
Peche Island	ISL/ÎLE	ON	Essex	40 J/7	42°21'	82°56'
Pêche, Lac la	LAKE/LAC	QC	Les Collines-de-l'Outaouais	31 F/9	45°38'	76°11'
Pêche, Rivière la	RIV/CDE	QC	Jamésie	33 D/8	52°15'	78°26'
Peckford Island	ISL/ÎLE	NF		2 F/12	49°33'	53°51'
Peck Lake	LAKE/LAC	SK	57-25-W3	73 F/13	53°54'	109°36'
Peck Meadow Corner	UNP/LNO	NS	Kings	21 H/1	45°00'	64°22'
Pecors Lake	LAKE/LAC	ON	Algoma	41 J/8	46°22'	82°28'
Pecten	UNP/LNO	AB	21-4-30-W4	82 H/5	49°18'	113°59'
Pecten Harbour	BAY/BAIE	NT	Keewatin	35 F	61°04'	77°51'
Pedder Point	CAPE/CAP	NT	Franklin	88 G	75°30'	118°34'
Peddie Point	CAPE/CAP	NT	Franklin	88 E	74°47'	114°05'
Pedley	UNP/LNO	AB	3-52-24-W5	83 F/6	53°28'	117°27'
Peeagwon Creek	RIV/CDE	ON	Kenora	53 A/15	52°47'	88°41'
Peebles	HAM/HAM	SK	7-14-7-W2	62 L/2	50°10'	102°57'
Peejay	UNP/LNO	BC	Peace River	94 A/15	56°53'	120°37'
Peekaboo Corner	UNP/LNO	NB	Kings	21 H/12	45°39'	65°43'
Peekaboo Point	UNP/LNO	ON	Simcoe	31 D/13	44°49'	79°55'
Peel	MUN1/AZM1	ON	Peel	30 M/12	43°45'	79°47'
Peel	MUN2/AZM2	ON	Wellington	40 P/10	43°43'	80°36'
Peel	UNP/LNO	NB	Carleton	21 J/5	46°21'	67°33'
Peel	GEOG/GÉOG	NB	Carleton	21 J/5	46°25'	67°32'
Peel	GEOG/GÉOG	ON		30 M/12	43°45'	79°47'
Peel, Cape	CAPE/CAP	NT	Franklin	77 D/4	69°03'	107°16'
Peel Channel	CHAN/CHEN	NT	Mackenzie	107 B	68°13'	135°00'
Peel Inlet	BAY/BAIE	NT	Franklin	67 D	69°08'	96°10'
Peel Island	ISL/ÎLE	BC	Rupert	92 L/11	50°44'	127°24'
Peel Point	CAPE/CAP	NT	Franklin	88 D	73°22'	114°30'
Peel River	RIV/CDE	NT/YT		106 M/10	67°42'	134°32'
Peel Sound	CHAN/CHEN	NT	Franklin	68 D	73°00'	96°20'
Peel Village	UNP/LNO	ON	Peel	30 M/12	43°40'	79°44'
Peepabun	UNP/LNO	ON	Dufferin	40 P/16	43°53'	80°23'
Peepeekisis 81	IR/RI	SK		62 L/14	50°52'	103°23'
Peerless	UNP/LNO	SK	62-22-W3	73 K/6	54°21'	109°14'
Peerless Lake	UNP/LNO	AB	33-88-4-W5	84 B/10	56°40'	114°35'
Peerless Lake	LAKE/LAC	AB	88-5-W5	84 B/10	56°37'	114°40'
Peers	UNP/LNO	AB	16-54-14-W5	83 G/12	53°40'	116°00'
Peesane	UNP/LNO	SK	12-45-12-W2	63 D/13	52°52'	103°36'
Pefferlaw	UNP/LNO	ON	York	31 D/6	44°19'	79°12'
Pefferlaw Brook	RIV/CDE	ON	York	31 D/6	44°20'	79°13'
Peffers	UNP/LNO	ON	Perth	40 P/10	43°37'	80°54'
Peggys Cove	UNP/LNO	NS	Halifax	11 D/5	44°29'	63°55'
Peggys Point	CAPE/CAP	NS	Halifax	11 D/5	44°29'	63°55'
Pegleg 3	IR/RI	BC	Kamloops Division Yale	92 I/4	50°07'	121°33'

NAME NOM	ENTITY ENTITÉ	LOC 1 LIEU 1	LOC 2 LIEU 2	MAP CARTE	POSITION LAT	LONG
Pegleg 3A	IR/RI	BC	Kamloops Division Yale	92 I/4	50°07′	121°33′
Peguis	UNP/LNO	MB		62 I/2	50°13′	96°50′
Peguis	UNP/LNO	MB	5-27-1-W	62 P/5	51°18′	97°34′
Peguis 1B	IR/RI	MB		62 P/5	51°18′	97°35′
Peguis 1C	IR/RI	MB		62 P/11	51°32′	97°18′
Peguis 1D	IR/RI	MB	20-15-5-E1	62 I/7	50°53′	96°52′
Peguis 1E	IR/RI	MB	17-15-5-E1	62 I/7	50°17′	96°52′
Peguis 1F	IR/RI	MB	17-15-5-E1	62 I/7	50°16′	96°52′
Peguis 1G	IR/RI	MB	10-15-5-E1	62 I/7	50°17′	96°50′
Peguis 1H	IR/RI	MB	22,23-14-5-E1	62 I/2	50°13′	96°49′
Peguis 1I	IR/RI	MB	15-14-5-E1	62 I/2	50°12′	96°50′
Peigan 147	IR/RI	AB	7-27-W4	82 H/12	49°34′	113°37′
Peigan Timber Limit 147B	IR/RI	AB	9-30-W4	82 H/12	49°45′	113°58′
Pekagoning Lake	LAKE/LAC	ON	Kenora	52 F/1	49°09′	92°11′
Pékans, Rivière aux	RIV/CDE	QC	Caniapiscau	23 B/2	52°12′	66°49′
Pekisko	UNP/LNO	AB	13-17-2-W5	82 J/8	50°26′	114°10′
Pelee	MUN2/AZM2	ON	Essex	40 G/15	41°47′	82°40′
Pelée - see-voir - Pelee	MUN2/AZM2	ON	Essex	40 G/15	41°47′	82°40′
Pelee Island	UNP/LNO	ON	Essex	40 G/15	41°45′	82°41′
Pelee Island	ISL/ÎLE	ON	Essex	40 G/15	41°47′	82°40′
Pelee Island South	UNP/LNO	ON	Essex	40 G/10	41°45′	82°38′
Pelee Passage	CHAN/CHEN	ON	Essex	40 G/15	41°52′	82°35′
Pelee, Point	CAPE/CAP	ON	Essex	40 G/15	41°54′	82°31′
Pelerin	UNP/LNO	NB	Kent	21 I/7	46°22′	64°49′
Pèlerins, Les	ISL/ÎLE	QC	Kamouraska	21 N/12	47°44′	69°44′
Pelham	TOWN/VIL2	ON	Welland	30 M/3	43°03′	79°21′
Pelham	UNP/LNO	ON	Lincoln	30 M/3	43°09′	79°16′
Pelham Centre	UNP/LNO	ON	Welland	30 M/3	43°02′	79°20′
Pelham Corners	UNP/LNO	ON	Welland	30 M/3	43°01′	79°18′
Pelham Union	UNP/LNO	ON	Welland	30 M/3	43°05′	79°23′
Pelican	UNP/LNO	ON	Kenora	52 K/1	50°07′	92°02′
Pelican Bay	BAY/BAIE	MB		63 C/16	52°45′	100°22′
Pelican Cove	HAM/HAM	SK		73 G/3	53°10′	107°03′
Pélican, Lac du	LAKE/LAC	QC	Kativik	34 P/13	59°47′	73°35′
Pelican Lake	LAKE/LAC	ON	Kenora	52 J/4	50°07′	91°58′
Pelican Lake	LAKE/LAC	MB		63 H/16	53°49′	96°08′
Pelican Lake	LAKE/LAC	MB	4,5-16-W	62 G/5	49°20′	99°34′
Pelican Lake	LAKE/LAC	MB		63 C/8	52°28′	100°20′
Pelican Lake	LAKE/LAC	MB	19-31-26-W	62 N/11	51°40′	101°08′
Pelican Lake	LAKE/LAC	SK		63 M/2	55°08′	103°00′
Pelican Lake	LAKE/LAC	SK		72 J/9	50°32′	106°00′
Pelican Lake	LAKE/LAC	AB	20-45-3-W4	73 D/16	52°53′	110°24′
Pelican Lake	LAKE/LAC	AB	78,79-21,22-W4	83 P/14	55°48′	113°15′
Pelican Lake	LAKE/LAC	AB	1-70-25-W5	83 N/4	55°02′	117°40′
Pelican Mountain	MTN/MNT	AB	76-23,24,25-W4	83 P/12	55°35′	113°40′
Pelican Narrows	VILG/VILG	SK		63 M/2	55°10′	102°56′
Pelican Narrows	VILG/VILG	AB	7-61-6-W4	73 L/7	54°15′	110°53′
Pelican Narrows 184B	IR/RI	SK		63 M/2	55°10′	102°54′
Pelican Point	HAM/HAM	SK	17-47-16-W3	73 F/1	53°03′	108°19′
Pelican Pointe	VILG/VILG	SK	19,30-21-22-W2	72 I/14	50°48′	105°02′
Pelican Portage	UNP/LNO	AB	30-78-17-W4	83 P/15	55°48′	112°37′
Pelicanpouch Lake	LAKE/LAC	ON	Kenora	52 E/15	49°52′	94°52′
Pelican Rapids	UNP/LNO	MB		63 C/10	52°45′	100°42′
Pelican River	RIV/CDE	AB	79-17-W4	83 P/15	55°50′	112°39′
Pelican Settlement	UNP/LNO	AB	78-17-W4	83 P/15	55°48′	112°39′
Pellatt Lake	LAKE/LAC	NT	Mackenzie	76 F	65°04′	109°42′
Pellegrin	UNP/LNO	QC	Pabok	22 A/7	48°30′	64°50′
Pellerin	UNP/LNO	QC	L'Islet	21 M/1	47°10′	70°05′
Pelletier	UNP/LNO	QC	Matane	22 B/14	48°45′	67°26′
Pelletier	UNP/LNO	QC	Témiscouata	21 N/11	47°33′	69°25′
Pelletier Bridge	UNP/LNO	ON	Kenora	52 E/16	49°49′	94°24′
Pelletier Lake	LAKE/LAC	MB		64 A/10	56°30′	96°58′
Pelletiers Mill	UNP/LNO	NB	Madawaska	21 N/2	47°14′	68°46′
Pell Inlet	BAY/BAIE	NT	Franklin	68 G	75°48′	102°26′
Pel-looth'l kai 17	IR/RI	BC	Range 2 Coast	92 M/2	51°07′	126°55′
Pelly	VILG/VILG	SK	27-33-32-W	62 N/13	51°52′	101°56′
Pelly Bay	HAM/HAM	NT	Keewatin	57 A	68°32′	89°50′
Pelly Bay	BAY/BAIE	NT	Keewatin	57 A	68°53′	90°05′
Pelly Creek	RIV/CDE	BC	Cassiar	94 C/14	56°46′	125°27′
Pelly Crossing	UNP/LNO	YT		115 I/15	62°49′	136°34′
Pelly Island	ISL/ÎLE	NT	Mackenzie	107 C	69°36′	135°30′
Pelly Lake	LAKE/LAC	BC	Cassiar	94 C/14	56°52′	125°24′
Pelly Lake	LAKE/LAC	NT	Keewatin	66 F	65°55′	101°20′
Pelly Lakes	UNP/LNO	YT		105 J/1	62°04′	130°14′
Pelly Mountains	MTN/MNT	YT		105 F/10	61°40′	132°30′

NAME NOM	ENTITY ENTITÉ	LOC 1 LIEU 1	LOC 2 LIEU 2	MAP CARTE	POSITION	
					LAT	LONG
Pelly Point	CAPE/CAP	NT	Franklin	67 F	70°12′	101°01′
Pelly River	RIV/CDE	YT		115 I/14	62°47′	137°20′
Peltoma Lake	LAKE/LAC	NB	Sunbury	21 G/10	45°33′	66°53′
Pelton	UNP/LNO	ON	Essex	40 J/2	42°15′	82°58′
Pemache River	RIV/CDE	ON	Sudbury	41 O/12	47°35′	83°42′
Pemberton	VILG/VILG	BC	Lillooet	92 J/7	50°19′	122°48′
Pemberton Heights	UNP/LNO	BC	New Westminster	92 G/6	49°20′	123°07′
Pemberton Icefield	GLAC/GLAC	BC	Lillooet	92 J/6	50°22′	123°22′
Pemberton Meadows	UNP/LNO	BC	Lillooet	92 J/7	50°26′	122°55′
Pemberton Ridge	UNP/LNO	NB	York	21 G/12	45°43′	67°45′
Pembina	MUN2/AZM2	MB		62 G/1	49°10′	98°29′
Pembina	UNP/LNO	AB	18-48-8-W5	83 G/3	53°08′	115°09′
Pembina Forks	UNP/LNO	AB	5-46-19-W5	83 C/15	52°59′	116°39′
Pembina Heights	UNP/LNO	AB	24-60-2-W5	83 J/11	54°13′	114°09′
Pembina Hills	MTN/MNT	MB		62 G/8	49°21′	98°24′
Pembina River - also-aussi - +Pembina, Rivière	RIV/CDE	MB	1-6-W	62 G/1	49°00′	98°12′
Pembina River	RIV/CDE	AB	30-66-2-W5	83 J/9	54°45′	114°17′
Pembina River Provincial Park	PARK/PARC	AB	29-53-7-W5	83 G/10	53°36′	115°00′
+Pembina, Rivière - also-aussi - Pembina River	RIV/CDE	MB	1-6-W	62 G/1	49°00′	98°12′
Pembridge	UNP/LNO	AB	10-57-5-W5	83 G/15	53°54′	114°40′
Pembroke	CITY/VIL1	ON	Renfrew	31 F/14	45°49′	77°07′
Pembroke	MUN2/AZM2	ON	Renfrew	31 F/14	45°48′	77°04′
Pembroke	UNP/LNO	PE	Kings	11 L/1	46°05′	62°29′
Pembroke	UNP/LNO	NS	Colchester	11 E/7	45°16′	62°56′
Pembroke	UNP/LNO	NS	Hants	21 H/1	45°13′	64°04′
Pembroke	UNP/LNO	NS	Yarmouth	20 O/16	43°52′	66°10′
Pembroke	UNP/LNO	NB	Carleton	21 J/4	46°11′	67°32′
Pembroke - see-voir - Stafford and Pembroke	MUN2/AZM2	ON		31 F/11	45°44′	77°35′
Pembroke, Cape	CAPE/CAP	NT	Keewatin	45 J	62°56′	81°55′
Pembroke Junction	UNP/LNO	ON	Renfrew	31 F/14	45°48′	77°07′
Pembroke Lake	LAKE/LAC	NS	Inverness	11 K/7	46°30′	60°59′
Pembroke River	RIV/CDE	NS	Colchester	11 E/2	45°13′	62°58′
Pemburton Hill	UNP/LNO	AB	20-50-2-W5	83 G/8	53°20′	114°15′
Pemichangan, Lac	LAKE/LAC	QC	La Vallée-de-la-Gatineau	31 J/4	46°04′	75°51′
Pemichigamau Lake	LAKE/LAC	MB		64 B/5	56°16′	99°33′
Pemmican Point	CAPE/CAP	NT	Franklin	87 G	71°35′	118°25′
Pemmican Portage	UNP/LNO	SK	57-2-W2	63 E/16	53°56′	102°17′
Pémonca	UNP/LNO	QC	Le Domaine-du-Roy	32 A/15	48°46′	72°42′
Pemukan	UNP/LNO	AB	1-35-4-W4	72 M/16	51°58′	110°27′
Pemynoos 9	IR/RI	BC	Kamloops Division Yale	92 I/6	50°30′	121°16′
Penassi Lake	LAKE/LAC	ON	Kenora	52 G/14	49°57′	91°11′
Pend-d'Oreille River	RIV/CDE	BC	Kootenay	82 F/4	49°00′	117°37′
Pendennis	UNP/LNO	MB	5-12-20-W	62 F/16	49°59′	100°11′
Pender Island	UNP/LNO	BC	Cowichan	92 B/14	48°47′	123°17′
Pender Island 8	IR/RI	BC	Cowichan	92 B/11	48°45′	123°14′
Pendleton	UNP/LNO	ON	Prescott	31 G/6	45°27′	75°04′
Pendleton Bay	UNP/LNO	BC	Range 5 Coast	93 K/12	54°31′	125°43′
Pendleton Lakes	LAKE/LAC	BC	Kamloops Division Yale	92 P/16	51°57′	120°26′
Pendrell Sound	BAY/BAIE	BC	New Westminster	92 K/2	50°15′	124°43′
Pendryl	UNP/LNO	AB	15-46-5-W5	83 B/15	52°58′	114°39′
Peneece 11	IR/RI	BC	Range 2 Coast	92 M/2	51°07′	126°42′
Peneetle 22	IR/RI	BC	Clayoquot	92 F/5	49°18′	125°57′
Penequani	UNP/LNO	ON	Thunder Bay	42 L/4	50°14′	87°47′
Penetang	UNP/LNO	ON	Simcoe	31 D/13	44°47′	79°55′
Penetang Harbour	BAY/BAIE	ON	Simcoe	31 D/13	44°47′	79°56′
Penetangore River	RIV/CDE	ON	Bruce	41 A/4	44°11′	81°39′
Penetanguishene	TOWN/VIL2	ON	Simcoe	31 D/13	44°47′	79°55′
Penetanguishene	UNP/LNO	NF		1 N/10	47°36′	52°45′
Pengelly Landing	UNP/LNO	ON	Northumberland	31 D/1	44°08′	78°18′
Penguin Arm	UNP/LNO	NF		12 H/4	49°10′	57°59′
Penguin Islands	ISL/ÎLE	NF		2 F/5	49°27′	53°48′
Penguin Islands	ISL/ÎLE	NF		11 P/6	47°23′	57°00′
Penhall	UNP/LNO	ON	Cochrane	42 G/12	49°44′	83°56′
Penhold	TOWN/VIL2	AB	36-36-28-W4	83 A/4	52°08′	113°52′
Penhurst	UNP/LNO	ON	Algoma	42 F/1	49°12′	84°26′
Peninsula Lake	LAKE/LAC	ON	Muskoka	31 E/6	45°20′	79°06′
Peninsular Park	UNP/LNO	ON	Simcoe	31 D/5	44°23′	79°33′
Péninsule-Bruce, Parc national de la - also-aussi - Bruce Peninsula National Park	PARK/PARC	ON	Bruce	41 H/4	45°14′	81°36′
Penkill	UNP/LNO	SK	27-19-W3	72 N/7	51°19′	108°38′
Pen Lake	LAKE/LAC	ON	Haliburton	31 E/8	45°27′	78°23′
Penn	UNP/LNO	SK	22-54-12-W3	73 G/12	53°40′	107°42′
Pennal 19	IR/RI	NS	Lunenburg	21 A/16	44°48′	64°26′
Pennant	VILG/VILG	SK	23-18-17-W3	72 K/9	50°32′	108°14′
Pennant Bay	BAY/BAIE	NS	Halifax	11 D/5	44°27′	63°41′
Pennant Point	CAPE/CAP	NS	Halifax	11 D/5	44°26′	63°39′

NAME / NOM	ENTITY / ENTITÉ	LOC 1 / LIEU 1	LOC 2 / LIEU 2	MAP / CARTE	LAT	LONG
Pennask Lake	LAKE/LAC	BC	Kamloops Division Yale	92 H/16	50°00′	120°07′
Pennask Mountain	MTN/MNT	BC	Kamloops Division Yale	92 H/16	49°53′	120°07′
Penney's Room	UNP/LNO	QC	Côte-Nord-du-Golfe-Saint-Laurent	12 P/6	51°24′	57°09′
Pennfield	UNP/LNO	NB	Charlotte	21 G/2	45°06′	66°44′
Pennfield	GEOG/GÉOG	NB	Charlotte	21 G/2	45°07′	66°41′
Pennfield Corner	UNP/LNO	NB	Charlotte	21 G/2	45°07′	66°44′
Pennfield Ridge	UNP/LNO	NB	Charlotte	21 G/2	45°07′	66°41′
Pennfield Station	UNP/LNO	NB	Charlotte	21 G/2	45°07′	66°40′
Penniac	UNP/LNO	NB	York	21 J/2	46°02′	66°34′
Pennington	UNP/LNO	BC	Cassiar	104 M/15	59°59′	134°54′
Pennlyn	UNP/LNO	NB	Queens	21 I/4	46°06′	65°53′
Penny	UNP/LNO	BC	Cariboo	93 H/14	53°51′	121°17′
Pennycutaway River	RIV/CDE	MB	89-9-E2	54 C/10	56°43′	92°42′
Penny Ice Cap	GLAC/GLAC	NT	Franklin	26 O	67°17′	66°13′
Penny Strait	CHAN/CHEN	NT	Franklin	69 A	76°30′	97°00′
Peno	UNP/LNO	AB	18-57-18-W4	83 H/15	53°55′	112°41′
Penobsquis	UNP/LNO	NB	Kings	21 H/14	45°47′	65°23′
Penouille	UNP/LNO	QC	La Côte-de-Gaspé	22 A/16	48°51′	64°25′
Penouille, Presqu'île de	CAPE/CAP	QC	La Côte-de-Gaspé	22 A/16	48°51′	64°26′
Penrhyn, Cape	CAPE/CAP	NT	Franklin	46 P	67°27′	81°12′
Pense	VILG/VILG	SK	9-17-22-W2	72 I/7	50°25′	104°59′
Pense No. 160	MUN2/AZM2	SK		72 I/6	50°25′	105°00′
Pensons Arm	UNP/LNO	NF		3 D/12	52°41′	55°54′
Pentecôte, Lac	LAKE/LAC	QC	Sept-Rivières	22 G/14	49°53′	67°20′
Pentecôte, Rivière	RIV/CDE	QC	Sept-Rivières	22 G/14	49°47′	67°10′
Pentenemis Kaiapis	UNP/LNO	QC	Côte-Nord-du-Golfe-Saint-Laurent	12 K/2	50°12′	60°57′
Pentice Ice Caps	GLAC/GLAC	BC	Cassiar	114 P/11	59°20′	137°23′
Penticton	CITY/VIL1	BC	Similkameen Division Yale	82 E/5	49°30′	119°35′
Penticton 1	IR/RI	BC	Osoyoos Division Yale	82 E/12	49°30′	119°40′
Penticton 3A	IR/RI	BC	Osoyoos Division Yale	82 E/12	49°34′	119°47′
Penticton Creek	RIV/CDE	BC	Similkameen Division Yale	82 E/5	49°30′	119°35′
Pentledge 2	IR/RI	BC	Comox	92 F/10	49°42′	125°00′
Pentz	UNP/LNO	NS	Lunenburg	21 A/8	44°18′	64°23′
Penville	UNP/LNO	ON	Simcoe	31 D/4	44°03′	79°43′
Penylan Lake	LAKE/LAC	NT	Mackenzie	75 G	61°50′	106°20′
Penzance	VILG/VILG	SK	21-24-25-W2	72 P/3	51°04′	105°26′
Penzance Lake	LAKE/LAC	NT	Mackenzie	75 B	60°29′	107°20′
Peonan Creek	RIV/CDE	SK		73 H/2	53°09′	104°52′
Peonan Point	CAPE/CAP	MB		62 O/7	51°29′	98°58′
Peony Farm	UNP/LNO	MB		62 G/16	49°59′	98°16′
Peoria	UNP/LNO	AB	36-73-3-W6	83 M/9	55°37′	118°17′
Pepaw River	RIV/CDE	SK	4-43-3-W2	63 D/9	52°40′	102°22′
Perbeck	UNP/LNO	AB	32-34-22-W4	82 P/14	51°58′	113°06′
Percé	CITY/VIL1	QC	Pabok	22 A/9	48°32′	64°13′
Percé	UNP/LNO	QC	Pabok	22 A/8	48°28′	64°19′
Percé, Rocher	ISL/ÎLE	QC	Pabok	22 A/9	48°31′	64°12′
Perches, Lac des	LAKE/LAC	QC	La Haute-Côte-Nord	22 C/12	48°39′	69°39′
Perch Lake	LAKE/LAC	ON	Manitoulin	41 G/16	45°54′	82°00′
Perch Lake	LAKE/LAC	ON	Kenora	52 L/2	50°04′	94°32′
Perch River	RIV/CDE	SK		74 P/2	59°07′	104°51′
Percival	HAM/HAM	SK	19-16-3-W2	62 L/8	50°22′	102°25′
Percival Bay	BAY/BAIE	PE	Prince	21 I/9	46°36′	64°06′
Percy	MUN2/AZM2	ON	Northumberland	31 C/4	44°14′	77°55′
Percy Boom	UNP/LNO	ON	Northumberland	31 C/4	44°14′	77°48′
Percy Lake	LAKE/LAC	ON	Haliburton	31 E/1	45°12′	78°22′
Percy Reach	RIVF/EFLV	ON	Northumberland	31 C/4	44°14′	77°47′
Perdrix-Garden	UNP/LNO	QC	Minganie	12 P/11	51°41′	57°22′
Perdrix, Rivière de la	RIV/CDE	QC	Jamésie	32 E/7	49°21′	78°51′
Perdrix, Rivière des	RIV/CDE	QC	Montmagny	21 L/15	46°59′	70°31′
Perdue	VILG/VILG	SK	32-35-11-W3	73 B/4	52°04′	107°33′
Perdue No. 346	MUN2/AZM2	SK		73 B/3	52°00′	107°30′
Perdu, Lac	LAKE/LAC	QC	Sept-Rivières	22 J/13	50°47′	67°33′
Perdu, Lac	LAKE/LAC	QC	Le Fjord-du-Saguenay	22 L/9	50°43′	70°14′
Pereaux	UNP/LNO	NS	Kings	21 H/1	45°10′	64°24′
Peregrine Point	CAPE/CAP	NT	Franklin	36 F	65°26′	76°49′
Péré, Lac	LAKE/LAC	QC	Jamésie	23 E/9	53°43′	70°27′
Père-Louis-Marie, Réserve écologique du	PARK/PARC	QC	La Vallée-de-la-Gatineau	31 J/4	46°13′	75°50′
Péribonka	VILG/VILG	QC	Maria-Chapdelaine	32 A/16	48°46′	72°03′
Péribonka, Lac	LAKE/LAC	QC	Le Fjord-du-Saguenay	22 L/3	50°07′	71°15′
Péribonka, Rivière	RIV/CDE	QC	Lac-Saint-Jean-Est	32 A/9	48°45′	72°05′
Périgny	UNP/LNO	QC	La Côte-de-Beaupré	21 L/15	47°00′	71°00′
Périgord	UNP/LNO	SK	39-11-W2	63 D/5	52°21′	103°34′
Perivale	UNP/LNO	ON	Manitoulin	41 G/16	45°46′	82°19′
Perkins	UNP/LNO	QC	Les Collines-de-l'Outaouais	31 G/12	45°36′	75°37′
Perkinsfield	UNP/LNO	ON	Simcoe	31 D/12	44°42′	79°57′

NAME NOM	ENTITY ENTITÉ	LOC 1 LIEU 1	LOC 2 LIEU 2	MAP CARTE	POSITION LAT	LONG
Perkins Landing	UNP/LNO	QC	Memphrémagog	31 H/1	45°05'	72°18'
Perles, Rivière aux	RIV/CDE	QC	Kamouraska	21 N/12	47°33'	69°51'
Perley Island	ISL/ÎLE	NT	Keewatin	44 P	59°40'	80°16'
Perley Island	ISL/ÎLE	NT	Franklin	560 B	80°11'	99°15'
Perlson Lake	LAKE/LAC	NT	Mackenzie	75 M	63°08'	111°55'
Perm	UNP/LNO	ON	Dufferin	41 A/1	44°10'	80°04'
Perotte	UNP/LNO	NS	Annapolis	21 A/11	44°41'	65°24'
Pérou, Le	UNP/LNO	QC	Francheville	31 I/9	46°39'	72°14'
Perow	UNP/LNO	BC	Range 5 Coast	93 L/9	54°31'	126°26'
Perras	UNP/LNO	QC	La Vallée-de-la-Gatineau	31 K/1	46°04'	76°06'
Perrault	UNP/LNO	ON	Renfrew	31 F/6	45°27'	77°03'
Perrault Falls	UNP/LNO	ON	Kenora	52 K/6	50°19'	93°11'
Perrault Lake	LAKE/LAC	ON	Kenora	52 K/6	50°18'	93°08'
Perrets 11	IR/RI	BC	New Westminster	92 G/6	49°53'	122°17'
Perretton	UNP/LNO	ON	Renfrew	31 F/15	45°46'	76°57'
Perrins Corners	UNP/LNO	ON	Grenville	31 B/13	44°46'	75°38'
Perron	UNP/LNO	QC	Vallée-de-l'Or	32 C/4	48°10'	77°33'
Perrot, Île	ISL/ÎLE	QC	Vaudreuil-Soulanges	31 H/5	45°22'	73°57'
Perry	MUN2/AZM2	ON	Parry Sound	31 E/6	45°29'	79°17'
Perry	UNP/LNO	ON	Welland	30 L/14	42°58'	79°26'
Perry	UNP/LNO	ON	Algoma	41 N/15	47°54'	84°32'
Perryboro	UNP/LNO	QC	Coaticook	21 E/4	45°07'	71°38'
Perry Island	UNP/LNO	NT	Franklin	66 M	67°48'	102°33'
Perry Island	ISL/ÎLE	NT	Mackenzie	96 E	65°29'	127°43'
Perry Point	UNP/LNO	NB	Kings	21 H/5	45°29'	65°57'
Perry River	RIV/CDE	BC	Kamloops Division Yale	82 L/15	50°59'	118°41'
Perry River	RIV/CDE	NT	Keewatin	66 M	67°43'	102°14'
Perrys	UNP/LNO	BC	Kootenay	82 F/12	49°40'	117°31'
Perry's Corners	UNP/LNO	ON	Oxford	40 P/7	43°18'	80°32'
Perry's Cove	UNP/LNO	NF		1 N/14	47°48'	53°09'
Perry Settlement	UNP/LNO	NB	Kings	21 H/14	45°55'	65°27'
Perry Siding - see-voir - Perrys	UNP/LNO	BC		82 F/12	49°40'	117°31'
Perrys Lane	UNP/LNO	ON	Oxford	40 P/2	43°09'	80°46'
Perrytown	UNP/LNO	ON	Durham	31 D/1	44°02'	78°23'
Perryvale	UNP/LNO	AB	22-63-23-W4	83 I/6	54°28'	113°23'
Perseverance Point	CAPE/CAP	NT	Franklin	98 H	75°54'	122°40'
Person Lake	LAKE/LAC	NT	Mackenzie	75 F	61°46'	108°17'
Perth	TOWN/VIL2	ON	Lanark	31 C/16	44°54'	76°15'
Perth	MUN1/AZM1	ON	Perth	40 P/6	43°30'	81°05'
Perth	GEOG/GÉOG	NB	Victoria	21 J/12	46°43'	67°37'
Perth	GEOG/GÉOG	ON		40 P/6	43°30'	81°05'
Perth-Andover	VILG/VILG	NB	Victoria	21 J/13	46°45'	67°42'
Perth Park	UNP/LNO	ON	Wentworth	30 M/4	43°13'	79°59'
Perth Road	UNP/LNO	ON	Frontenac	31 C/8	44°28'	76°29'
Perthuis	UNP/LNO	QC	Portneuf	31 I/16	46°56'	72°07'
Peru	UNP/LNO	ON	Halton	30 M/12	43°31'	79°55'
Pesika Creek	RIV/CDE	BC	Cassiar	94 C/14	56°59'	125°02'
Peskawa Lake	LAKE/LAC	NS	Digby	21 A/6	44°19'	65°22'
Peskowesk Lake	LAKE/LAC	NS	Annapolis	21 A/6	44°19'	65°17'
Petabec Lakes	LAKE/LAC	SK	55-2-W2	63 E/9	53°44'	102°11'
Petaguishene Beach	UNP/LNO	ON	Simcoe	31 D/13	44°48'	79°57'
Petaigan	UNP/LNO	SK	33-51-11-W2	63 E/5	53°26'	103°34'
Petain	UNP/LNO	NS	Halifax	11 D/11	44°42'	63°17'
Petawaga, Lac	LAKE/LAC	QC	Antoine-Labelle	31 O/4	47°03'	75°52'
Petawanga Lake	LAKE/LAC	ON	Thunder Bay	52 P/8	51°29'	88°25'
Petawawa	VILG/VILG	ON	Renfrew	31 F/14	45°54'	77°17'
Petawawa	MUN2/AZM2	ON	Renfrew	31 F/14	45°54'	77°19'
Petawawa, Base des Forces canadiennes - also-aussi - Petawawa, Canadian Forces Base	MIL/MIL	ON	Renfrew	31 F/14	45°55'	77°18'
Petawawa, Canadian Forces Base - also-aussi - Petawawa, Base des Forces canadiennes	MIL/MIL	ON	Renfrew	31 F/14	45°55'	77°18'
Petawawa Point	UNP/LNO	ON	Renfrew	31 F/14	45°55'	77°15'
Petawawa River	RIV/CDE	ON	Renfrew	31 F/14	45°55'	77°15'
Peter	UNP/LNO	ON	York	31 D/3	44°13'	79°26'
Peter Alec 6 - see-voir - Gaichbin 8	IR/RI	BC		93 L/2	54°02'	126°40'
Peterbell	UNP/LNO	ON	Algoma	42 B/11	48°36'	83°21'
Peterborough	CITY/VIL1	ON	Peterborough	31 D/8	44°18'	78°19'
Peterborough	MUN1/AZM1	ON	Peterborough	31 D/9	44°33'	78°15'
Peterborough	GEOG/GÉOG	ON		31 D/9	44°33'	78°15'
Peterhead Inlet	BAY/BAIE	NT	Franklin	25 N	63°45'	68°39'
Peter Hope Lake	LAKE/LAC	BC	Kamloops Division Yale	92 I/8	50°18'	120°19'
Peter Lake	LAKE/LAC	SK		64 E/4	57°15'	103°53'
Peter Lake	LAKE/LAC	NT	Keewatin	55 N	63°08'	92°48'
Peterlong Lake	LAKE/LAC	ON	Sudbury	42 A/3	48°05'	81°25'
Peter Lougheed Provincial Park	PARK/PARC	AB	18,19,20,21-7,8,9,10-W5	82 J/11	50°42'	115°10'
Peter Pond Lake	LAKE/LAC	SK		73 N/15	55°55'	108°44'
Peter Pond Lake 193	IR/RI	SK		73 N/14	55°55'	109°00'

NAME NOM	ENTITY ENTITÉ	LOC 1 LIEU 1	LOC 2 LIEU 2	MAP CARTE	POSITION LAT	LONG
Peter Richards, Cape	CAPE/CAP	NT	Franklin	87 G	71°28′	118°18′
Peters 1	IR/RI	BC	Yale Division Yale	92 H/5	49°18′	121°39′
Peters 1A	IR/RI	BC	Yale Division Yale	92 H/5	49°18′	121°39′
Peters 2	IR/RI	BC	Yale Division Yale	92 H/5	49°19′	121°39′
Petersburg	UNP/LNO	ON	Waterloo	40 P/7	43°25′	80°35′
Peters Corners	UNP/LNO	ON	Wentworth	40 P/8	43°17′	80°04′
Petersfield	UNP/LNO	MB	27-15-4-E	62 I/7	50°18′	96°58′
Peters, Lac	LAKE/LAC	QC	Kativik	24 M/10	59°41′	70°53′
Peters Lake	LAKE/LAC	BC	Osoyoos Division Yale	82 L/9	50°30′	118°14′
Peters Mills	UNP/LNO	NB	Kent	21 I/10	46°40′	64°48′
Peterson	UNP/LNO	SK	20-37-26-W2	73 A/4	52°11′	105°41′
Peterson	UNP/LNO	BC	Cariboo	83 D/14	52°55′	119°23′
Peterson Corner	UNP/LNO	ON	Haliburton	31 E/2	45°02′	78°45′
Peterson Creek	RIV/CDE	BC	Kamloops Division Yale	92 P/1	51°12′	120°09′
Peters Point	CAPE/CAP	NT	Franklin	25 J	62°25′	66°20′
Peters Pond	LAKE/LAC	NF		2 E/3	49°05′	55°26′
Peters Ridge	SEAU/SMER	—		3000	50°33′	138°00′
Peter's River	UNP/LNO	NF		1 K/13	46°46′	53°36′
Peters River	UNP/LNO	NB	Gloucester	21 P/12	47°40′	65°42′
Peter's River	RIV/CDE	NF		1 K/13	46°46′	53°37′
Peters River	RIV/CDE	NF		2 E/3	49°07′	55°22′
Peters Road	UNP/LNO	PE	Kings	11 L/2	46°04′	62°34′
Peter Strides Pond	LAKE/LAC	NF		12 A/4	48°11′	57°40′
Petersville	GEOG/GÉOG	NB	Queens	21 G/9	45°30′	66°25′
Peterview	TOWN/VIL2	NF		2 E/3	49°07′	55°21′
Peterville	UNP/LNO	PE	Prince	21 I/16	46°56′	64°06′
Pete Suckers 13	IR/RI	BC	Lillooet	92 O/16	51°47′	122°04′
Pethei Peninsula	CAPE/CAP	NT	Mackenzie	75 L	62°40′	111°00′
Pethericks Corners	UNP/LNO	ON	Northumberland	31 C/5	44°21′	77°44′
Petherton	UNP/LNO	ON	Wellington	40 P/15	43°52′	80°36′
Petit-Aigle, Le	UNP/LNO	QC	La Vallée-de-la-Gatineau	31 K/1	46°12′	76°13′
Petit-Bécancour	UNP/LNO	QC	Arthabaska	21 L/4	46°08′	71°59′
Petit-Bégin	UNP/LNO	QC	Le Fjord-du-Saguenay	22 D/11	48°39′	71°21′
Petit-Bois-de-l'Ail, Le	UNP/LNO	QC	Portneuf	21 L/12	46°43′	71°49′
Petit-Canot, Le	UNP/LNO	QC	Le Fjord-du-Saguenay	22 D/14	48°50′	71°07′
Petit-Cap	UNP/LNO	NB	Westmorland	21 I/1	46°12′	64°10′
Petit-Cap	UNP/LNO	QC	La Côte-de-Gaspé	22 H/1	49°02′	64°27′
Petit-Cap	UNP/LNO	QC	La Côte-de-Beaupré	21 M/2	47°04′	70°48′
Petit-Carleton	UNP/LNO	QC	Avignon	22 B/1	48°07′	66°05′
Petit-Cascapédia	UNP/LNO	QC	Bonaventure	22 A/4	48°11′	65°50′
Petit-Cherbourg	UNP/LNO	QC	Matane	22 B/14	48°54′	67°08′
Petit-Chertsey	UNP/LNO	QC	Matawinie	31 I/4	46°10′	73°48′
Petit-Chockpish	UNP/LNO	NB	Kent	21 I/10	46°36′	64°45′
Petitcodiac	VILG/VILG	NB	Westmorland	21 H/14	45°56′	65°10′
Petitcodiac East	UNP/LNO	NB	Westmorland	21 H/14	45°57′	65°10′
Petitcodiac River	RIV/CDE	NB	Westmorland	21 H/15	45°51′	64°34′
Petit-de-Grat	UNP/LNO	NS	Richmond	11 F/10	45°30′	60°58′
Petit-de-Grat Harbour	BAY/BAIE	NS	Richmond	11 F/7	45°29′	60°59′
Petit-de-Grat Island	ISL/ÎLE	NS	Richmond	11 F/10	45°31′	60°56′
Petite-Aldouane	UNP/LNO	NB	Kent	21 I/10	46°43′	64°54′
Petite-Allemagne	UNP/LNO	QC	Les Laurentides	31 J/7	46°17′	74°59′
Petite-Angleterre, La	UNP/LNO	QC	Le Haut-Saint-François	21 E/6	45°22′	71°14′
Petite-Anse	UNP/LNO	QC	La Côte-de-Gaspé	22 H/2	49°11′	64°52′
Petite-Belgique, La	UNP/LNO	QC	Arthabaska	21 L/5	46°17′	71°58′
Petite-Ferme, La	UNP/LNO	QC	La Côte-de-Beaupré	21 M/2	47°04′	70°48′
Petite-Ferme-Loken, La	UNP/LNO	QC	Le Haut-Saint-Maurice	31 P/6	47°28′	73°15′
Petite-Lamèque	UNP/LNO	NB	Gloucester	21 P/15	47°49′	64°42′
Petite-Martine, La	UNP/LNO	QC	Le Domaine-du-Roy	32 A/8	48°23′	72°01′
Petite-Mine, La	UNP/LNO	QC	Papineau	31 G/11	45°43′	75°28′
Petite-Montagne, La	UNP/LNO	QC	Les Îles-de-la-Madeleine	11 N/4	47°14′	61°56′
Petite Nation, Rivière de la	RIV/CDE	QC	Papineau	31 G/11	45°35′	75°06′
Petite-Prairie, La	UNP/LNO	QC	Témiscamingue	31 M/6	47°17′	79°18′
Petite-Réserve	UNP/LNO	NB	Restigouche	21 O/11	47°40′	67°23′
Petite Rivière - see-voir - Petite Rivière Bridge	UNP/LNO	NS		21 A/1	44°14′	64°27′
Petite-Rivière	UNP/LNO	QC	Charlevoix	21 M/7	47°18′	70°34′
Petite-Rivière-à-la-Truite	UNP/LNO	NB	Madawaska	21 N/7	47°24′	68°31′
Petite-Rivière-au-Renard	UNP/LNO	QC	La Côte-de-Gaspé	22 H/1	49°01′	64°25′
Petite Rivière Bridge	UNP/LNO	NS	Lunenburg	21 A/1	44°14′	64°27′
Petite-Rivière-de-l'Ile	UNP/LNO	NB	Gloucester	21 P/15	47°52′	64°38′
Petite-Rivière-Est	UNP/LNO	QC	Pabok	22 A/8	48°25′	64°25′
Petite-Rivière-Ouest	UNP/LNO	QC	Pabok	22 A/7	48°23′	64°33′
Petite-Rivière-Pabos	UNP/LNO	QC	Pabok	22 A/7	48°23′	64°36′
Petite-Rivière-Saint-François	VILG/VILG	QC	Charlevoix	21 M/7	47°18′	70°34′
Petites	UNP/LNO	NF		11 O/10	47°37′	58°38′
Petites-Bergeronnes	UNP/LNO	QC	La Haute-Côte-Nord	22 C/4	48°14′	69°36′

NAME / NOM	ENTITY / ENTITÉ	LOC 1 / LIEU 1	LOC 2 / LIEU 2	MAP / CARTE	POSITION LAT	POSITION LONG
Petites-Piles, Les	UNP/LNO	QC	Le Centre-de-la-Mauricie	31 I/10	46°39′	72°42′
Petit Étang	UNP/LNO	NS	Inverness	11 K/10	46°39′	60°58′
Petite-Tourelle	UNP/LNO	QC	Denis-Riverin	22 G/1	49°10′	66°22′
Petite-Vallée	VILG/VILG	QC	La Côte-de-Gaspé	22 H/3	49°13′	65°02′
Petit-Fond, Le	UNP/LNO	QC	Le Granit	21 E/10	45°31′	70°54′
Petit-Fonds	UNP/LNO	QC	Denis-Riverin	22 G/2	49°04′	66°40′
Petit Forte	UNP/LNO	NF		1 M/7	47°24′	54°40′
Petit-Gaspé	UNP/LNO	QC	La Côte-de-Gaspé	22 A/16	48°48′	64°15′
Petit-Glaude, Le	UNP/LNO	QC	Le Fjord-du-Saguenay	22 D/7	48°25′	70°44′
Petit Jardin	UNP/LNO	NF		12 B/6	48°28′	59°14′
Petit-Kinnears	UNP/LNO	QC	L'Érable	21 L/6	46°15′	71°29′
Petit-Lac	UNP/LNO	QC	L'Amiante	21 L/3	46°04′	71°07′
Petit-Lac-Long	UNP/LNO	QC	Les Laurentides	31 J/1	46°08′	74°18′
Petit-Lac-Magog	UNP/LNO	QC	Sherbrooke	31 H/8	45°20′	72°02′
Petit-Lac-Sainte-Anne	MUN2/AZM2	QC	Kamouraska	21 N/4	47°12′	69°48′
Petit-Lac-Wayagamac	MUN2/AZM2	QC	Le Haut-Saint-Maurice	31 P/7	47°23′	72°31′
Petit-Large	UNP/LNO	NB	Kent	21 I/15	46°47′	64°59′
Petit-Mai	UNP/LNO	QC	Manicouagan	22 G/6	49°26′	67°16′
Petit-Maine, Le	UNP/LNO	QC	Montmagny	21 L/9	46°36′	70°02′
Petit-Matane	VILG/VILG	QC	Matane	22 B/14	48°52′	67°27′
Petit-Mécatina	MUN2/AZM2	QC	Minganie	12 N/9	51°30′	60°00′
Petit Mécatina, Île du	ISL/ÎLE	QC	Côte-Nord-du-Golfe-Saint-Laurent	12 J/11	50°33′	59°20′
Petit Mécatina, Rivière du - also-aussi - Little Mecatina River	RIV/CDE	QC	Côte-Nord-du-Golfe-Saint-Laurent	12 J/11	50°40′	59°25′
Petit-Métis	UNP/LNO	QC	La Mitis	22 C/9	48°37′	68°01′
Petit-Mexique, Le	UNP/LNO	QC	Le Haut-Richelieu	31 H/3	45°09′	73°21′
Petit-Montréal, Le	UNP/LNO	QC	Pabok	22 A/9	48°32′	64°20′
Petit-Montréal, Le	UNP/LNO	QC	Bonaventure	22 A/5	48°17′	65°58′
Petit-Montréal, Le	UNP/LNO	QC	Vallée-de-l'Or	32 C/6	48°27′	77°19′
Petit-Nicolet	UNP/LNO	QC	Asbestos	21 E/13	45°48′	71°59′
Petit-Nord, Le	UNP/LNO	QC	Les Etchemins	21 L/9	46°31′	70°22′
Petit-Nord, Le	UNP/LNO	QC	Le Fjord-du-Saguenay	22 D/7	48°25′	70°40′
Petitot River	RIV/CDE	NT/AB/BC		95 B/3	60°14′	123°29′
Petit-Ouest	UNP/LNO	NB	Restigouche	21 O/11	47°37′	67°25′
Petit-Pabos	UNP/LNO	QC	Pabok	22 A/7	48°23′	64°35′
Petit Pabos, Rivière du	RIV/CDE	QC	Pabok	22 A/7	48°23′	64°36′
Petit-Paquetville	UNP/LNO	NB	Gloucester	21 P/11	47°42′	65°05′
Petit-Paradis, Le	UNP/LNO	QC	La Haute-Côte-Nord	22 C/11	48°34′	69°15′
Petit Passage	CHAN/CHEN	NS	Digby	21 B/8	44°24′	66°13′
Petit-Poisson-Blanc	UNP/LNO	QC	La Vallée-de-la-Gatineau	31 J/4	46°00′	75°55′
Petit-Pré	UNP/LNO	QC	La Côte-de-Beaupré	21 L/14	46°56′	71°04′
Petit Pré, Rivière du	RIV/CDE	QC	La Côte-de-Beaupré	21 L/14	46°56′	71°03′
Petit-Québec	UNP/LNO	QC	Le Haut-Saint-François	21 E/6	45°26′	71°17′
Petit-Québec	UNP/LNO	QC	Abitibi-Ouest	32 D/11	48°36′	79°29′
Petit-Québec, Le	UNP/LNO	QC	Pabok	22 A/9	48°31′	64°19′
Petit-Rainbow, Le	UNP/LNO	QC	Jamésie	32 G/16	49°51′	74°21′
Petit Rocher	VILG/VILG	NB	Gloucester	21 P/13	47°47′	65°43′
Petit-Rocher - see-voir - Petit Rocher	VILG/VILG	NB		21 P/13	47°47′	65°43′
Petit-Rocher, Le	UNP/LNO	QC	Le Domaine-du-Roy	32 A/8	48°19′	72°13′
Petit-Rocher-Nord	UNP/LNO	NB	Gloucester	21 P/13	47°48′	65°44′
Petit-Rocher-Sud	UNP/LNO	NB	Gloucester	21 P/13	47°46′	65°43′
Petit-Saguenay	VILG/VILG	QC	Le Fjord-du-Saguenay	22 D/1	48°13′	70°04′
Petit Saguenay, Rivière	RIV/CDE	QC	Le Fjord-du-Saguenay	22 D/1	48°14′	70°06′
Petit-Saint-Jean, Le	UNP/LNO	QC	Les Chutes-de-la-Chaudière	21 L/11	46°40′	71°20′
Petit-Saint-Louis	UNP/LNO	QC	Bécancour	31 I/8	46°18′	72°19′
Petits-Capucins	UNP/LNO	QC	Denis-Riverin	22 G/2	49°04′	66°48′
Petits-Escoumins	UNP/LNO	QC	La Haute-Côte-Nord	22 C/6	48°26′	69°19′
Petitsikapau Lake	LAKE/LAC	NF		23 J/9	54°37′	66°25′
Petit-Six, Le	UNP/LNO	QC	Lac-Saint-Jean-Est	22 D/12	48°31′	71°37′
Petits-Méchins	UNP/LNO	QC	Matane	22 G/2	49°01′	66°55′
Petley	UNP/LNO	NF		2 C/4	48°09′	53°45′
Petlura	UNP/LNO	MB	11,14-24-26-W	62 N/3	51°04′	101°01′
Petownikip Lake	LAKE/LAC	ON	Kenora	53 C/16	52°56′	92°02′
Petrel	UNP/LNO	MB	36-11-15-W	62 G/14	49°58′	99°24′
Petrel Channel	CHAN/CHEN	BC	Range 4 Coast	103 G/9	53°41′	130°07′
Petrel Junction	UNP/LNO	MB	1-12-15-W	62 G/14	49°59′	99°24′
Petre, Point	CAPE/CAP	ON	Prince Edward	30 N/14	43°50′	77°09′
Petries	UNP/LNO	NF		12 B/16	48°58′	58°01′
Petrie Shore	UNP/LNO	ON	Lanark	31 F/1	45°05′	76°10′
Petrofka	UNP/LNO	SK	43-7-W3	73 B/10	52°40′	106°53′
Petrolia	TOWN/VIL2	ON	Lambton	40 J/16	42°52′	82°09′
Petry	UNP/LNO	ON	Thunder Bay	52 G/7	49°20′	90°50′
Pettapiece	UNP/LNO	MB	18-13-20-W	62 K/1	50°06′	100°12′
Pettigrew Settlement	UNP/LNO	NS	Cumberland	21 H/9	45°32′	64°21′
Petty Harbour	UNP/LNO	NF		1 N/7	47°28′	52°43′
Petty Harbour	UNP/LNO	NF		3 D/5	52°24′	55°40′

NAME NOM	ENTITY ENTITÉ	LOC 1 LIEU 1	LOC 2 LIEU 2	MAP CARTE	POSITION	
					LAT	LONG
Petty Harbour-Maddox Cove	TOWN/VIL2	NF		1 N/7	47°28′	52°43′
Petworth	UNP/LNO	ON	Lennox and Addington	31 C/7	44°25′	76°46′
Peuplier, Pointe du	CAPE/CAP	QC	Jamésie	32 M/10	51°31′	78°50′
Peuplier, Rivière du	RIV/CDE	QC	Jamésie	33 D/15	52°47′	78°43′
Pevensey	UNP/LNO	ON	Parry Sound	31 E/11	45°42′	79°20′
Peveril	UNP/LNO	QC	Vaudreuil-Soulanges	31 G/8	45°19′	74°26′
Peyton, Mount	MTN/MNT	NF		2 D/14	48°57′	55°06′
Peytons Brook	RIV/CDE	NF		1 N/7	47°20′	52°56′
Phantom Beach	UNP/LNO	SK	26-66-30-W	63 K/12	54°44′	101°52′
Phantom Lake	LAKE/LAC	BC	New Westminster	92 G/14	49°52′	123°30′
Phare-de-Fisgard, Lieu historique national du - also-aussi - Fisgard Lighthouse National Historic Site	PARK/PARC	BC	Esquimalt	92 B/6	48°26′	123°27′
Phare-de-la-Pointe-Clark, Lieu historique national du - also-aussi - Point Clark Lighthouse National Historic Site	PARK/PARC	ON	Bruce	41 A/4	44°04′	81°45′
Phare-de-l'Île-Bois Blanc, Lieu historique national du - also-aussi - Bois Blanc Island Lighthouse National Historic Site	PARK/PARC	ON	Essex	40 J/3	42°05′	83°07′
Phare-de-Pointe-au-Père, Lieu historique national du - also-aussi - Pointe-au-Père Lighthouse National Historic Site	PARK/PARC	QC	Rimouski-Neigette	22 C/9	48°31′	68°28′
Phayre, Mount	MTN/MNT	NT	Franklin	87 G	71°28′	118°15′
Pheasant Creek	RIV/CDE	SK	9-19A-11-W2	62 L/11	50°35′	103°28′
Pheasant Forks	UNP/LNO	SK	22-21-9-W2	62 L/14	50°49′	103°10′
Pheasant Hills	MTN/MNT	SK		62 L/11	50°45′	103°10′
Pheasant Rump Nakota	IR/RI	SK		62 E/16	49°45′	102°15′
Phelan	UNP/LNO	BC	Range 5 Coast	103 J/1	54°12′	130°16′
Phelan Lake	LAKE/LAC	SK		63 M/1	55°15′	102°09′
Phelans	UNP/LNO	ON	Sudbury	41 I/11	46°35′	81°22′
Phelps Lake	LAKE/LAC	SK		64 M/3	59°15′	103°15′
Phelps, Mount	MTN/MNT	YT		106 F/4	65°04′	133°57′
Phelpston	UNP/LNO	ON	Simcoe	31 D/12	44°31′	79°51′
Philémon	UNP/LNO	QC	La Vallée-de-la-Gatineau	31 J/12	46°39′	75°51′
Phililloo Lake	LAKE/LAC	BC	Lillooet	92 P/13	51°50′	121°42′
Philion Lake	LAKE/LAC	SK	65-5-W3	73 J/10	54°36′	106°39′
Philip Creek	RIV/CDE	BC	Cariboo	93 O/5	55°18′	123°39′
Philip Edward Island	ISL/ÎLE	ON	Manitoulin	41 H/14	45°58′	81°15′
Philipot, Lac	LAKE/LAC	QC	Minganie	12 N/7	51°30′	60°47′
Philippe, Lac	LAKE/LAC	QC	Les Collines-de-l'Outaouais	31 G/12	45°36′	75°59′
Philip, River	RIV/CDE	NS	Cumberland	11 E/13	45°51′	63°44′
Philips	UNP/LNO	AB	12-47-12-W4	73 E/4	53°03′	111°38′
Philipsburg	TOWN/VIL2	QC	Brome-Missisquoi	31 H/3	45°02′	73°05′
Philips Harbour	UNP/LNO	NS	Guysborough	11 F/6	45°21′	61°14′
Philipsville	UNP/LNO	ON	Leeds	31 C/9	44°38′	76°09′
Phillips Arm	UNP/LNO	BC	Range 1 Coast	92 K/11	50°33′	125°21′
Phillips Arm	BAY/BAIE	BC	Range 1 Coast	92 K/11	50°31′	125°24′
Phillips Bay	BAY/BAIE	YT		117 D/6	69°17′	138°30′
Phillips Beach	HAM/HAM	SK	26-56-7-W3	73 G/11	53°52′	106°56′
Phillips Brook	RIV/CDE	NF		11 O/9	47°44′	58°07′
Phillipsburg	UNP/LNO	ON	Waterloo	40 P/7	43°25′	80°44′
Phillips, Cape	CAPE/CAP	NT	Franklin	58 G	75°36′	94°18′
Phillips Creek	RIV/CDE	NT	Franklin	47 H	71°53′	80°56′
Phillips Head	UNP/LNO	NF		2 E/3	49°14′	55°18′
Phillips Inlet	BAY/BAIE	NT	Franklin	340 F	82°05′	86°10′
Phillips Lake	LAKE/LAC	BC	Range 1 Coast	92 K/11	50°35′	125°22′
Phillips Point	CAPE/CAP	NT	Franklin	39 B	76°06′	78°48′
Phillips River	RIV/CDE	BC	Range 1 Coast	92 K/11	50°33′	125°22′
Phillipston	UNP/LNO	ON	Hastings	31 C/6	44°19′	77°24′
Phillipstown	UNP/LNO	NB	Queens	21 H/13	45°57′	65°45′
Philomena	UNP/LNO	AB	27-71-11-W4	73 M/4	55°10′	111°38′
Philomène, Baie	BAY/BAIE	QC	La Vallée-de-la-Gatineau	31 J/12	46°42′	75°50′
Philpot, Lac	LAKE/LAC	QC	Kativik	35 B/5	60°27′	75°58′
Philpots Island	ISL/ÎLE	NT	Franklin	38 F/13	74°57′	79°58′
Phinneys Cove	UNP/LNO	NS	Annapolis	21 A/14	44°53′	65°24′
Phippen	UNP/LNO	SK	13-40-21-W3	73 C/7	52°27′	108°53′
Phipps	UNP/LNO	QC	Vallée-de-l'Or	32 C/6	48°20′	77°07′
Phipps	UNP/LNO	BC	Similkameen Division Yale	82 E/2	49°06′	118°35′
Phoenix	ISL/ÎLE	NS	Halifax	11 D/15	44°47′	62°37′
Phoenix Island	RIV/CDE	QC	Jamésie	33 L/12	54°31′	79°30′
Phoque, Rivière au	LAKE/LAC	QC	Le Fjord-du-Saguenay	22 M/7	51°16′	70°54′
Piacouadie, Lac	RIV/CDE	QC	Jamésie	33 L/3	54°02′	79°02′
Piagochioui, Rivière	VILG/VILG	SK	7-12-23-W3	72 F/14	49°59′	109°07′
Piapot	IR/RI	SK		72 I/9	50°45′	104°26′
Piapot 75	MUN2/AZM2	SK		72 F/14	49°55′	109°05′
Piapot No. 110	LAKE/LAC	QC	Minganie	12 L/7	50°29′	62°52′
Piashti, Lac	UNP/LNO	QC	Le Fjord-du-Saguenay	22 D/6	48°22′	71°17′
Pibrac						

NAME NOM	ENTITY ENTITÉ	LOC 1 LIEU 1	LOC 2 LIEU 2	MAP CARTE	POSITION LAT	LONG
Pibrac, Barrages	MISC/DIV	QC	Le Fjord-du-Saguenay	22 D/6	48°22′	71°16′
Pibroch	UNP/LNO	AB	5-61-26-W4	83 I/5	54°15′	113°52′
Picadilly	UNP/LNO	NB	Kings	21 H/11	45°43′	65°24′
Picadilly-Abrahams Cove - see-voir - Piccadilly Slant-Abrahams Cove	UNP/LNO	NF		12 B/10	48°32′	58°55′
Picanoc, Rivière	RIV/CDE	QC	La Vallée-de-la-Gatineau	31 K/1	46°04′	76°03′
Picard	MUN2/AZM2	QC	Kamouraska	21 N/12	47°30′	69°31′
Picard	UNP/LNO	QC	Kamouraska	21 N/12	47°30′	69°31′
Picardie	UNP/LNO	QC	Francheville	31 I/8	46°28′	72°19′
Piccadilly	UNP/LNO	NF		12 B/10	48°33′	58°55′
Piccadilly	UNP/LNO	NB	Victoria	21 J/13	46°49′	67°30′
Piccadilly	UNP/LNO	ON	Frontenac	31 C/10	44°31′	76°41′
Piccadilly Bay	BAY/BAIE	NF		12 B/10	48°34′	58°53′
Piccadilly Head	UNP/LNO	NF		12 B/10	48°36′	58°56′
Piccadilly Slant	UNP/LNO	NF		12 B/10	48°34′	58°55′
Piccadilly Slant-Abrahams Cove	UNP/LNO	NF		12 B/10	48°33′	58°55′
Piccaire	UNP/LNO	NF		1 M/12	47°37′	55°56′
Pichanikap	UNP/LNO	QC	Jamésie	33 J/16	54°54′	74°20′
Piché Lake	LAKE/LAC	AB	70-11-W4	73 M/4	55°02′	111°37′
Pichogen River	RIV/CDE	ON	Algoma	42 G/4	49°08′	83°59′
Pic Island	ISL/ÎLE	ON	Thunder Bay	42 D/10	48°43′	86°37′
Pickardville	UNP/LNO	AB	25,36-58-27-W4	83 I/4	54°03′	113°53′
Pickerel	UNP/LNO	ON	Parry Sound	41 H/15	45°59′	80°32′
Pickerel Lake	UNP/LNO	ON	Parry Sound	31 E/11	45°40′	79°18′
Pickerel Lake	LAKE/LAC	ON	Parry Sound	31 E/11	45°41′	79°18′
Pickerel Lake	LAKE/LAC	ON	Rainy River	52 B/11	48°37′	91°19′
Pickerel Lake	LAKE/LAC	ON	Kenora	52 E/15	49°48′	94°52′
Pickerel Point	UNP/LNO	ON	Victoria	31 D/7	44°25′	78°45′
Pickerel River	UNP/LNO	ON	Parry Sound	41 I/2	46°00′	80°44′
Pickerel River	RIV/CDE	ON	Parry Sound	41 H/15	45°55′	80°46′
Pickering	TOWN/VIL2	ON	Ontario	30 M/14	43°54′	79°08′
Pickering - see-voir - Pickering Village	UNP/LNO	ON		30 M/14	43°51′	79°03′
Pickering Beach	UNP/LNO	ON	Ontario	30 M/15	43°50′	78°59′
Pickering Village	UNP/LNO	ON	Ontario	30 M/14	43°51′	79°03′
Pick Eyes	UNP/LNO	NF		1 N/11	47°36′	53°11′
Pickle Crow	UNP/LNO	ON	Kenora	52 O/8	51°30′	90°04′
Pickle Lake	MUN2/AZM2	ON	Kenora	52 O/8	51°28′	90°10′
Pickle Lake	UNP/LNO	ON	Kenora	52 O/8	51°28′	90°12′
Pickle Lake	LAKE/LAC	ON	Kenora	52 O/8	51°28′	90°15′
Pic Mobert North	IR/RI	ON	Thunder Bay	42 C/12	48°40′	85°40′
Pic Mobert South	IR/RI	ON	Thunder Bay	42 C/12	48°40′	85°40′
Picnic Grove	UNP/LNO	ON	Glengarry	31 G/1	45°11′	74°28′
Picoudi	UNP/LNO	QC	Le Bas-Richelieu	31 I/2	46°00′	72°59′
Pic River	UNP/LNO	ON	Thunder Bay	42 D/9	48°36′	86°18′
Pic River	RIV/CDE	ON	Thunder Bay	42 D/9	48°36′	86°18′
Pic River 50	IR/RI	ON	Thunder Bay	42 D/9	48°37′	86°15′
Picton	TOWN/VIL2	ON	Prince Edward	31 C/3	44°00′	77°08′
Pictou	TOWN/VIL2	NS	Pictou	11 E/10	45°41′	62°43′
Pictou	MUN1/AZM1	NS	Pictou	11 E/10	45°30′	62°35′
Pictou	GEOG/GÉOG	NS		11 E/10	45°30′	62°35′
Pictou Harbour	BAY/BAIE	NS	Pictou	11 E/10	45°40′	62°43′
Pictou Island	UNP/LNO	NS	Pictou	11 E/15	45°48′	62°33′
Pictou Island	ISL/ÎLE	NS	Pictou	11 E/15	45°49′	62°33′
Pictou Landing	UNP/LNO	NS	Pictou	11 E/10	45°40′	62°41′
Picture Butte	TOWN/VIL2	AB	2-11-21-W4	82 H/15	49°53′	112°47′
Pidgeon	UNP/LNO	QC	L'Érable	21 L/4	46°11′	71°39′
Pidgeon Cove-St Barbe	UNP/LNO	NF		12 P/2	51°12′	56°47′
Pièce-des-Guérets, La	UNP/LNO	QC	Vaudreuil-Soulanges	31 G/8	45°28′	74°19′
Pièce-Perdue, La	UNP/LNO	QC	Antoine-Labelle	31 J/3	46°10′	75°30′
Pied-de-la-Montagne	UNP/LNO	QC	Joliette	31 I/4	46°08′	73°34′
Pied-des-Monts, Le	UNP/LNO	QC	Charlevoix	21 M/10	47°39′	70°37′
Pied-du-Calumet	UNP/LNO	QC	Pontiac	31 F/10	45°40′	76°38′
Pied-du-Lac	UNP/LNO	QC	Témiscouata	21 N/6	47°28′	69°00′
Piedmont	VILG/VILG	QC	Les Pays-d'en-Haut	31 G/16	45°54′	74°08′
Piedmont	UNP/LNO	NS	Pictou	11 E/9	45°36′	62°22′
Pie Island	ISL/ÎLE	ON	Thunder Bay	52 A/3	48°15′	89°06′
Pierard	UNP/LNO	SK	26-46-15-W3	73 C/16	52°59′	108°04′
Pierce Lake	LAKE/LAC	ON/MB		53 K/2	54°10′	92°58′
Pierce Lake	LAKE/LAC	SK		73 K/5	54°30′	109°42′
Pierceland	VILG/VILG	SK	62-26-W3	73 K/5	54°20′	109°46′
Piercemont	UNP/LNO	NB	Carleton	21 J/12	46°34′	67°38′
Pierces Corners	UNP/LNO	ON	Carleton	31 G/4	45°06′	75°45′
Pierre-à-Chaux, La	UNP/LNO	QC	Avignon	22 B/1	48°09′	66°18′
Pierrefonds	CITY/VIL1	QC	Communauté urbaine de Montréal	31 H/5	45°29′	73°52′
Pierre Lake	LAKE/LAC	ON	Cochrane	42 H/7	49°30′	80°45′
Pierre, Rivière à	RIV/CDE	QC	Portneuf	31 I/16	46°58′	72°16′

NAME NOM	ENTITY ENTITÉ	LOC 1 LIEU 1	LOC 2 LIEU 2	MAP CARTE	POSITION LAT	LONG
Pierres, Lac	LAKE/LAC	QC	Minganie	22 P/11	51°30′	65°09′
Pierreville	TOWN/VIL2	QC	Nicolet-Yamaska	31 I/2	46°04′	72°49′
Pierron, Lac	LAKE/LAC	QC	Matawinie	31 J/16	46°53′	74°20′
Piers Island	ISL/ÎLE	BC	Cowichan	92 B/11	48°42′	123°25′
Pierson	UNP/LNO	MB	1-3-29-W	62 F/3	49°11′	101°16′
Pieter, Banc de - also-aussi - Pieter Bank	SEAU/SMER	—		811A	48°00′	63°06′
Pieter Bank - also-aussi - Pieter, Banc de	SEAU/SMER	—		811A	48°00′	63°06′
Pieville	UNP/LNO	QC	Témiscamingue	31 M/6	47°19′	79°13′
Pigeon Bay	BAY/BAIE	ON	Essex	40 J/2	42°01′	82°41′
Pigeon Bay	BAY/BAIE	MB		63 A/6	52°17′	97°05′
Pigeon Cove	UNP/LNO	NF		12 P/2	51°12′	56°47′
Pigeon Cove	BAY/BAIE	NF		12 I/8	50°26′	56°22′
Pigeon Falls	FALL/CHUT	ON	Thunder Bay	52 A/4	48°00′	89°36′
Pigeon Head	CAPE/CAP	NF		12 B/11	48°31′	59°01′
Pigeon Hill	UNP/LNO	NB	Gloucester	21 P/15	47°51′	64°31′
Pigeon Hill	UNP/LNO	QC	Brome-Missisquoi	31 H/2	45°03′	72°56′
Pigeon Island	ISL/ÎLE	NF		2 E/9	49°43′	54°03′
Pigeon Lake	UNP/LNO	MB		62 H/13	49°57′	97°36′
Pigeon Lake	LAKE/LAC	ON	Victoria	31 D/8	44°27′	78°30′
Pigeon Lake	LAKE/LAC	ON	Timiskaming	41 P/11	47°43′	81°03′
Pigeon Lake	LAKE/LAC	AB	46-1-W5	83 G/1	53°01′	114°02′
Pigeon Lake 138A	IR/RI	AB	46-28-W4	83 A/13	52°59′	113°58′
Pigeon Lake Provincial Park	PARK/PARC	AB	47-1,2-W5	83 G/1	53°01′	114°08′
Pigeon Mountain - see-voir - Dead Man's Flats	UNP/LNO	AB		82 O/3	51°02′	115°16′
Pigeon Point	CAPE/CAP	MB		63 A/3	52°15′	97°07′
Pigeon River	UNP/LNO	ON	Thunder Bay	52 A/4	48°01′	89°42′
Pigeon River	RIV/CDE	ON	Victoria	31 D/7	44°21′	78°33′
Pigeon River	RIV/CDE	ON	Thunder Bay	52 A/4	48°00′	89°34′
Pigeon River	RIV/CDE	MB		63 A/3	52°15′	97°01′
Pigeon River 13A	IR/RI	MB		63 A/2	52°14′	96°59′
Pikangikum	UNP/LNO	ON	Kenora	52 M/16	51°49′	94°00′
Pikangikum 14	IR/RI	ON	Kenora	52 N/13	51°48′	93°58′
Pikangikum Lake	LAKE/LAC	ON	Kenora	52 M/16	51°48′	94°00′
Pikauba, Lac	LAKE/LAC	QC	Charlevoix	21 M/14	47°48′	71°07′
Pikauba, Petite rivière	RIV/CDE	QC	Le Fjord-du-Saguenay	22 D/3	48°10′	71°27′
Pike Bay	UNP/LNO	ON	Bruce	41 A/14	44°53′	81°19′
Pike Bay	BAY/BAIE	ON	Bruce	41 A/14	44°52′	81°21′
Pike Creek	UNP/LNO	ON	Essex	40 J/7	42°18′	82°50′
Pike Island	ISL/ÎLE	NT	Franklin	25 N	63°15′	68°00′
Pike Lake	UNP/LNO	SK	34-6-W3	72 O/15	51°54′	106°49′
Pike Lake	LAKE/LAC	ON	Leeds	31 C/16	44°47′	76°21′
Pike, Mount	MTN/MNT	BC	Yale Division Yale	92 H/10	49°43′	120°40′
Pike, Mount	MTN/MNT	YT		105 I/4	62°11′	129°39′
Pike River	UNP/LNO	QC	Brome-Missisquoi	31 H/3	45°07′	73°04′
Pikes Arm	UNP/LNO	NF		2 E/10	49°39′	54°35′
Pikes Peak	UNP/LNO	SK	30-50-23-W3	73 F/6	53°19′	109°21′
Pikitigushi River	RIV/CDE	ON	Thunder Bay	52 I/7	50°15′	88°35′
Pikogan	IR/RI	QC	Abitibi	32 D/9	48°36′	78°07′
Piksimanik River	RIV/CDE	NT	Keewatin	56 H/9	65°38′	88°24′
Pikwitonei	UNP/LNO	MB	13-76-2-E	63 P/11	55°35′	97°09′
Pikwitonei Lake	LAKE/LAC	MB	75,76-3,4-E	63 P/11	55°33′	97°03′
Pilektuak Island	ISL/ÎLE	NT	Franklin	27 A	68°20′	66°30′
Piles, Lac des	LAKE/LAC	QC	Le Centre-de-la-Mauricie	31 I/10	46°39′	72°48′
Pilger	VILG/VILG	SK	9-40-23-W2	73 A/6	52°25′	105°16′
Piling Bay	BAY/BAIE	NT	Franklin	37 A	68°53′	74°47′
Piling Lake	LAKE/LAC	NT	Franklin	37 D	69°03′	74°49′
Pilkington	MUN2/AZM2	ON	Wellington	40 P/9	43°39′	80°28′
Pillet, Lac	LAKE/LAC	QC	Minganie	12 K/16	50°46′	60°25′
Pilley's Island	VILG/VILG	NF		2 E/12	49°31′	55°44′
Pilley's Island	ISL/ÎLE	NF		2 E/12	49°32′	55°43′
Pilley's Tickle	CHAN/CHEN	NF		2 E/5	49°30′	55°42′
Pilot Butte	TOWN/VIL2	SK	33-17-18-W2	72 I/8	50°28′	104°25′
Pilot Lake	LAKE/LAC	NT	Mackenzie	75 D	60°17′	111°00′
Pilot Mound	VILG/VILG	MB	9-3-11-W	62 G/2	49°12′	98°54′
Pilot Mountain	MTN/MNT	YT		105 E/4	61°02′	135°32′
Pimainus Creek	RIV/CDE	BC	Kamloops Division Yale	92 I/6	50°28′	121°18′
Pim Island	ISL/ÎLE	NT	Franklin	39 E/11	78°44′	74°25′
Pinacle, Le	MTN/MNT	QC	Brome-Missisquoi	31 H/2	45°03′	72°44′
Pinacle-Nord	UNP/LNO	QC	Brome-Missisquoi	31 H/2	45°04′	72°44′
Pinantan Lake	UNP/LNO	BC	Kamloops Division Yale	92 I/9	50°43′	120°02′
Pinaus Lake	LAKE/LAC	BC	Osoyoos Division Yale	82 L/5	50°25′	119°36′
Pinawa	MUN2/AZM2	MB		52 L/11	50°11′	95°58′
Pinawa	UNP/LNO	MB	3-14-12-E	52 L/4	50°09′	95°53′
Pinawa Bay	UNP/LNO	MB	6,7-16-13-E	52 L/5	50°19′	95°48′
Pinawa Channel	CHAN/CHEN	MB		52 L/5	50°15′	95°55′

NAME NOM	ENTITY ENTITÉ	LOC 1 LIEU 1	LOC 2 LIEU 2	MAP CARTE	POSITION LAT	LONG
Pincebec	UNP/LNO	QC	Maskinongé	31 I/6	46°30'	73°06'
Pinchard's Bight	BAY/BAIE	NF		2 F/4	49°13'	53°31'
Pinchards Island	UNP/LNO	NF		2 F/3	49°12'	53°29'
Pinchards Island	ISL/ÎLE	NF		2 F/3	49°12'	53°29'
Pincher	UNP/LNO	AB	1-7-30-W4	82 H/12	49°32'	113°56'
Pincher Creek	TOWN/VIL2	AB	6-30-W4	82 H/5	49°29'	113°57'
Pincher Creek No. 9, Municipal District of	MUN1/AZM1	AB	6-1-W5	82 G/8	49°29'	114°03'
Pinchgut Lake	LAKE/LAC	NF		12 A/13	48°49'	57°59'
Pinchgut Point	CAPE/CAP	NF		1 N/12	47°36'	53°56'
Pinchi	UNP/LNO	BC	Range 5 Coast	93 K/9	54°34'	124°30'
Pinchie 2 - see-voir - Binche 2	IR/RI	BC		93 K/9	54°34'	124°30'
Pinchie Lake 7 - see-voir - Binche Bun 7	IR/RI	BC		93 K/9	54°37'	124°26'
Pinchie Lake 7A - see-voir - Tes Gha La 7A	IR/RI	BC		93 K/9	54°37'	124°24'
Pinchie Lake 10 - see-voir - Binche 10	IR/RI	BC		93 K/9	54°35'	124°16'
Pinchie Lake 12 - see-voir - Binche 12	IR/RI	BC		93 K/9	54°37'	124°27'
Pinchi Lake	UNP/LNO	BC	Range 5 Coast	93 K/9	54°38'	124°25'
Pinchi Lake	LAKE/LAC	BC	Range 5 Coast	93 K/9	54°35'	124°20'
Pincourt	CITY/VIL1	QC	Vaudreuil-Soulanges	31 H/5	45°23'	73°59'
Pincourt	UNP/LNO	QC	Lotbinière	21 L/12	46°39'	71°34'
Pincourt	UNP/LNO	QC	Les Moulins	31 H/12	45°44'	73°41'
Pinder	UNP/LNO	NB	York	21 J/3	46°03'	67°14'
Pinder Peak	MTN/MNT	BC	Rupert	92 L/2	50°12'	126°56'
Pine	UNP/LNO	ON	Kenora	52 F/13	49°48'	93°48'
Pineal Lake	UNP/LNO	ON	Sudbury	41 O/12	47°31'	83°37'
Pineau	UNP/LNO	NB	Kent	21 I/11	46°42'	65°20'
Pine Beach	UNP/LNO	QC	Communauté urbaine de Montréal	31 H/5	45°27'	73°46'
Pine Beach	UNP/LNO	ON	York	31 D/3	44°13'	79°28'
Pine Bluff	UNP/LNO	MB	52-22-W	63 F/10	53°31'	100°40'
Pine Bluff 20A	IR/RI	SK		63 L/2	54°07'	102°53'
Pine Bluff 20B	IR/RI	SK		63 L/2	54°07'	102°53'
Pine, Cape	CAPE/CAP	NF		1 K/12	46°37'	53°32'
Pine Cove	UNP/LNO	SK	10,15-59-22-W3	73 K/3	54°06'	109°13'
Pine Creek	UNP/LNO	MB	17-35-19-W	63 C/1	52°00'	100°09'
Pine Creek	RIV/CDE	MB	4-1-12-E	52 E/4	49°00'	95°56'
Pine Creek	RIV/CDE	MB	29-18-10-E	62 I/9	50°34'	96°10'
Pine Creek	RIV/CDE	MB		63 I/4	54°07'	97°40'
Pine Creek	RIV/CDE	MB	1-14-10-W	62 J/2	50°10'	98°43'
Pine Creek	RIV/CDE	AB	3-69-17-W4	83 I/15	54°56'	112°31'
Pine Creek	RIV/CDE	YT		116 I/13	66°51'	137°52'
Pine Creek	RIV/CDE	NT	Mackenzie	85 L	62°36'	119°05'
Pine Creek 66A	IR/RI	MB		63 C/1	52°04'	100°12'
Pine Creek Settlement	GEOG/GÉOG	MB	35-20-W	62 N/16	51°59'	100°09'
Pine Creek Station	UNP/LNO	MB	23-12-12-W	62 J/3	50°02'	99°00'
Pinecrest	UNP/LNO	ON	Wentworth	30 M/4	43°13'	79°58'
Pinecrest	UNP/LNO	ON	Sudbury	41 I/11	46°38'	81°01'
Pine Crest Point	UNP/LNO	ON	Welland	30 L/14	42°52'	79°11'
Pine Croft	UNP/LNO	QC	La Rivière-du-Nord	31 H/13	45°54'	73°57'
Pinedale	UNP/LNO	ON	Ontario	31 D/3	44°15'	79°00'
Pine Dock	UNP/LNO	MB	3-31-5-E	62 P/10	51°39'	96°48'
Pine Falls	UNP/LNO	MB	25-18-9-E	62 I/9	50°34'	96°13'
Pine Glen	UNP/LNO	NB	Albert	21 I/2	46°02'	64°46'
Pineglen	UNP/LNO	ON	Carleton	31 G/5	45°19'	75°43'
Pineglen Annex	UNP/LNO	ON	Carleton	31 G/5	45°20'	75°42'
Pine Grove	UNP/LNO	NS	Colchester	11 E/3	45°02'	63°23'
Pine Grove	UNP/LNO	NS	Lunenburg	21 A/7	44°25'	64°31'
Pine Grove	UNP/LNO	ON	Glengarry	31 G/7	45°24'	74°41'
Pine Grove	UNP/LNO	ON	Frontenac	31 C/8	44°25'	76°16'
Pine Grove	UNP/LNO	ON	Lanark	31 F/1	45°03'	76°20'
Pinegrove	UNP/LNO	ON	Renfrew	31 F/8	45°26'	76°24'
Pinegrove	UNP/LNO	ON	Lennox and Addington	31 C/6	44°22'	77°03'
Pine Grove	UNP/LNO	ON	York	30 M/13	43°48'	79°35'
Pine Grove	UNP/LNO	ON	Norfolk	40 I/16	42°47'	80°27'
Pinegrove	UNP/LNO	BC	Cariboo	93 H/4	53°04'	121°57'
Pine Hill	UNP/LNO	QC	Argenteuil	31 G/9	45°44'	74°29'
Pine Hill	UNP/LNO	ON	Glengarry	31 G/2	45°14'	74°32'
Pine Hill	UNP/LNO	ON	Frontenac	31 C/8	44°20'	76°22'
Pinehouse	VILG/VILG	SK	75-4-W3	73 O/10	55°31'	106°34'
Pinehouse Lake - see-voir - Pinehouse	VILG/VILG	SK		73 O/10	55°31'	106°34'
Pinehouse Lake	LAKE/LAC	SK		73 O/10	55°32'	106°35'
Pinehurst	UNP/LNO	NS	Lunenburg	21 A/7	44°30'	64°39'
Pinehurst	UNP/LNO	ON	Kent	40 J/8	42°26'	82°02'
Pinehurst Lake	LAKE/LAC	AB	65,66-9,10-W4	73 L/11	54°39'	111°25'
Pinehurst Park	UNP/LNO	ON	Brant	40 P/8	43°16'	80°24'
Pineimuta River	RIV/CDE	ON	Kenora	53 A/2	52°08'	88°33'
Pine Island	ISL/ÎLE	SK		63 L/1	54°02'	102°27'

NAME NOM	ENTITY ENTITÉ	LOC 1 LIEU 1	LOC 2 LIEU 2	MAP CARTE	POSITION LAT	LONG
Pine Junction	UNP/LNO	NT	Mackenzie	85 B/12	60°45′	115°52′
Pine Lake	UNP/LNO	AB	22-36-25-W4	83 A/3	52°07′	113°29′
Pine Lake	LAKE/LAC	ON	Frontenac	31 C/15	44°54′	76°53′
Pine Lake	LAKE/LAC	AB	36-24,25-W4	83 A/3	52°04′	113°27′
Pine Lodge	UNP/LNO	QC	Pontiac	31 F/9	45°31′	76°27′
Pine Meadows	UNP/LNO	ON	Renfrew	31 F/14	45°53′	77°15′
Pine Orchard	UNP/LNO	ON	York	31 D/3	44°03′	79°22′
Pine Orchard Station	UNP/LNO	ON	York	31 D/3	44°04′	79°21′
Pine Point	UNP/LNO	ON	Ontario	31 D/2	44°09′	78°52′
Pine Point	UNP/LNO	ON	York	30 M/12	43°43′	79°33′
Pine Point	UNP/LNO	NT	Mackenzie	85 B/16	60°50′	114°28′
Pine Point	CAPE/CAP	ON	Thunder Bay	52 A/3	48°02′	89°27′
Pine Point	CAPE/CAP	NT	Mackenzie	85 G	61°01′	114°15′
Pine Portage	UNP/LNO	ON	Thunder Bay	52 H/8	49°18′	88°19′
Pine Ridge	UNP/LNO	NB	Kent	21 I/6	46°29′	65°03′
Pine Ridge	UNP/LNO	ON	Renfrew	31 F/14	45°51′	77°12′
Pine Ridge	UNP/LNO	MB	15-12-5-E	62 I/2	50°00′	96°50′
Pine River	UNP/LNO	ON	Bruce	41 A/4	44°07′	81°40′
Pine River	UNP/LNO	MB	32,33-32-22-W	62 N/15	51°47′	100°32′
Pine River	UNP/LNO	SK	80-10-W3	73 O/14	55°57′	107°26′
Pine River	RIV/CDE	ON	Simcoe	31 D/5	44°20′	79°52′
Pine River	RIV/CDE	ON	Bruce	41 A/4	44°05′	81°44′
Pine River	RIV/CDE	SK		74 I/13	58°50′	105°48′
Pine River	RIV/CDE	BC	Peace River	94 A/2	56°08′	120°42′
Pines Cove	UNP/LNO	NF		12 P/7	51°22′	56°36′
Pine Springs	UNP/LNO	ON	Haliburton	31 E/2	45°08′	78°50′
Pinesul	UNP/LNO	BC	Peace River	93 P/12	55°36′	121°59′
Pine Tree	UNP/LNO	NS	Pictou	11 E/10	45°36′	62°33′
Pine Tree Harbour	BAY/BAIE	ON	Bruce	41 H/3	45°04′	81°30′
Pinette	UNP/LNO	PE	Queens	11 L/2	46°03′	62°54′
Pinette Point	CAPE/CAP	PE	Queens	11 L/2	46°02′	62°56′
Pinevale	UNP/LNO	NS	Antigonish	11 F/12	45°31′	61°59′
Pine Valley	UNP/LNO	ON	Renfrew	31 F/10	45°34′	76°58′
Pine Valley	UNP/LNO	BC	Cariboo	93 B/1	52°10′	122°05′
Pine Valley	UNP/LNO	BC	Peace River	93 O/9	55°38′	122°07′
Pineview	UNP/LNO	BC	Peace River	94 A/7	56°20′	120°46′
Pineview	UNP/LNO	BC	Cariboo	93 G/15	53°50′	122°39′
Pineville	UNP/LNO	NB	Northumberland	21 I/13	46°49′	65°54′
Pinewood	UNP/LNO	ON	Nipissing	31 L/6	46°19′	79°29′
Pinewood	UNP/LNO	ON	Rainy River	52 D/9	48°43′	94°18′
Pinewood River	RIV/CDE	ON	Rainy River	52 D/9	48°43′	94°19′
Piney	MUN2/AZM2	MB		52 E/4	49°14′	95°55′
Piney	UNP/LNO	MB	30-1-12-E	52 E/4	49°05′	95°59′
Pinger Point	CAPE/CAP	NT	Franklin	47 D	69°06′	81°16′
Pinginak	UNP/LNO	NF		13 N/8	55°20′	60°24′
Pingle	UNP/LNO	AB	8-80-6-W4	73 M/15	55°55′	110°55′
Pingston Creek	RIV/CDE	BC	Kootenay	82 K/5	50°26′	117°57′
Pinguet	UNP/LNO	QC	L'Islet	21 M/1	47°14′	70°06′
Pinguksoak, Mount	MTN/MNT	NF		14 L/6	58°25′	63°15′
Pinkerton	UNP/LNO	ON	Simcoe	31 D/4	44°09′	79°39′
Pinkerton	UNP/LNO	ON	Bruce	41 A/3	44°13′	81°16′
Pinkham	UNP/LNO	SK	28-28-25-W3	72 N/6	51°26′	109°27′
Pinkie	UNP/LNO	SK	21-17-20-W2	72 I/7	50°26′	104°42′
Pink Mountain	UNP/LNO	BC	Peace River	94 G/2	57°02′	122°31′
Pink Mountain	MTN/MNT	BC	Peace River	94 G/2	57°04′	122°52′
Pinkneys Point	UNP/LNO	NS	Yarmouth	20 O/9	43°43′	66°04′
Pink River	RIV/CDE	SK		64 D/13	56°50′	103°50′
Pinkut Lake 23	IR/RI	BC	Range 5 Coast	93 K/5	54°25′	125°35′
Pinnacle Islands	ISL/ÎLE	NT	Franklin	35 I	62°04′	72°24′
Pinnacles, The	MTN/MNT	BC	Kootenay	82 L/1	50°13′	118°15′
Pinniquine	UNP/LNO	NB	Madawaska	21 N/7	47°23′	68°33′
Pin-Rigide, Réserve écologique du	PARK/PARC	QC	Le Haut-Saint-Laurent	31 H/4	45°06′	73°52′
Pin, Rivière du	RIV/CDE	QC	Bellechasse	21 L/15	46°45′	70°30′
Pinsent	UNP/LNO	NF		2 E/8	49°26′	54°03′
Pins, Pointe aux	CAPE/CAP	ON	Kent	40 I/5	42°17′	81°51′
Pins, Rivière aux	RIV/CDE	QC	La Jacques-Cartier	21 L/13	46°54′	71°38′
Pins, Rivière des	RIV/CDE	QC	Arthabaska	31 I/1	46°00′	72°03′
Pintendre	VILG/VILG	QC	Desjardins	21 L/14	46°45′	71°08′
Pinto	UNP/LNO	SK	25-1-6-W2	62 E/2	49°04′	102°42′
Pinto Creek	RIV/CDE	SK	24-8-6-W3	72 G/10	49°40′	106°41′
Pinto Creek	RIV/CDE	AB	56-25-W5	83 F/13	53°51′	117°35′
Pinto Creek	RIV/CDE	AB	69-10-W6	83 L/14	54°58′	119°28′
Pinto Creek No. 75	MUN2/AZM2	SK		72 G/10	49°40′	107°00′
Pinus Lake	LAKE/LAC	ON	Rainy River	52 F/4	49°04′	93°53′
Pinware	VILG/VILG	NF		12 P/10	51°37′	56°42′

NAME NOM	ENTITY ENTITÉ	LOC 1 LIEU 1	LOC 2 LIEU 2	MAP CARTE	POSITION LAT	LONG
Pinware Bay	BAY/BAIE	NF		12 P/10	51°37′	56°41′
Pinware River	RIV/CDE	NF		12 P/10	51°38′	56°41′
Pioneer	UNP/LNO	AB	13-55-15-W5	83 F/16	53°46′	116°08′
Pioneer Bay	BAY/BAIE	NT	Franklin	68 E	75°00′	96°30′
Pioneer Island	ISL/ÎLE	NT	Franklin	69 A	76°57′	96°57′
Pioneer Mine	UNP/LNO	BC	Lillooet	92 J/15	50°46′	122°47′
Pioneer Peak	MTN/MNT	NT	Franklin	27 F	70°28′	70°50′
Pioneer Village	UNP/LNO	SK		72 I/7	50°27′	104°39′
Pionniers, Parc des	PARK/PARC	QC	Lajemmerais	31 H/14	45°47′	73°22′
Piopolis	VILG/VILG	QC	Le Granit	21 E/7	45°29′	70°54′
Pipers Cove	UNP/LNO	NS	Cape Breton	11 F/15	45°56′	60°45′
Pipers Cove	BAY/BAIE	NS	Cape Breton	11 F/15	45°55′	60°44′
Pipers Glen	UNP/LNO	NS	Inverness	11 K/3	46°12′	61°07′
Pipers Hole River	RIV/CDE	NF		1 M/16	47°55′	54°16′
Piperville	UNP/LNO	ON	Carleton	31 G/5	45°21′	75°31′
Pipestem Inlet	BAY/BAIE	BC	Clayoquot	92 F/3	49°02′	125°15′
Pipestone	MUN2/AZM2	MB		62 F/11	49°40′	101°10′
Pipestone	UNP/LNO	MB	9-7-26-W	62 F/10	49°33′	100°57′
Pipestone	UNP/LNO	AB	18-47-26-W4	83 H/4	53°03′	113°47′
Pipestone Bay	BAY/BAIE	ON	Kenora	52 M/1	51°04′	94°13′
Pipestone Creek	UNP/LNO	AB	14-70-8-W6	83 M/3	55°04′	119°06′
Pipestone Creek	RIV/CDE	MB/SK		62 F/10	49°41′	100°48′
Pipestone Creek	RIV/CDE	AB	20-46-22-W4	83 A/14	52°58′	113°09′
Pipestone Lake	LAKE/LAC	ON	Rainy River	52 F/4	49°05′	93°35′
Pipestone Lake	LAKE/LAC	MB		63 I/12	54°31′	97°39′
Pipestone Lake	LAKE/LAC	SK		74 G/15	57°54′	106°35′
Pipestone River	RIV/CDE	ON	Kenora	53 A/14	52°53′	89°23′
Pipestone River	RIV/CDE	ON	Rainy River	52 C/10	48°33′	92°33′
Pipestone River	RIV/CDE	SK		74 I/12	58°38′	105°45′
Pipichicau, Rivière	RIV/CDE	QC	Caniapiscau	22 N/14	51°58′	69°23′
Pipmuacan, Réservoir	LAKE/LAC	QC	Le Fjord-du-Saguenay	22 E/9	49°40′	70°20′
Piponshewanik	UNP/LNO	MB		53 K/3	54°06′	93°29′
Pipowitan River	RIV/CDE	ON	Kenora	44 D/4	56°08′	87°38′
Pipseul 3	IR/RI	BC	Kamloops Division Yale	92 I/7	50°28′	120°48′
Pipun	UNP/LNO	MB	34-67-9-W	63 J/15	54°50′	98°45′
Pirate Harbour	UNP/LNO	NS	Guysborough	11 F/11	45°35′	61°23′
Piraube, Lac	LAKE/LAC	QC	Maria-Chapdelaine	22 L/12	50°32′	71°42′
Pirmez Creek	UNP/LNO	AB	18-24-3-W5	82 O/1	51°02′	114°24′
Pirogue	UNP/LNO	NB	Kent	21 I/10	46°41′	64°49′
Piscatosine, Lac	LAKE/LAC	QC	Antoine-Labelle	31 J/13	46°54′	75°36′
Pisces Canyon	SEAU/SMER	—		3605	50°33′	128°35′
Pischu Amakwayitach	UNP/LNO	QC	Jamésie	33 D/7	52°28′	78°31′
Pisew Lake	LAKE/LAC	SK	72-1-W3	73 O/1	55°15′	106°03′
Piskahegan Stream	RIV/CDE	NB	Charlotte	21 G/7	45°23′	66°54′
Pisquid	UNP/LNO	PE	Queens	11 L/7	46°20′	62°51′
Pisquid West	UNP/LNO	PE	Queens	11 L/7	46°20′	62°53′
Pis-Sec	UNP/LNO	QC	Le Fjord-du-Saguenay	22 D/1	48°08′	70°01′
Piste-Chilkoot, Lieu historique national de la - also-aussi - Chilkoot Trail National Historic Site	PARK/PARC	BC	Cassiar	104 M/15	59°45′	134°58′
Pistol Bay	BAY/BAIE	NT	Keewatin	55 K	62°25′	92°41′
Pistoles, Les	UNP/LNO	QC	Bellechasse	21 L/10	46°37′	70°39′
Pistolet Bay	BAY/BAIE	NF		2 M/5	51°35′	55°45′
Pitaga	UNP/LNO	NF		23 A/5	52°27′	65°48′
Pit-à-Grenon	UNP/LNO	QC	Le Haut-Richelieu	31 H/3	45°05′	73°21′
Pit-à-Lebeau	UNP/LNO	QC	La Rivière-du-Nord	31 G/16	45°46′	74°01′
Pitchers Farm	UNP/LNO	NS	Antigonish	11 F/12	45°33′	61°58′
Pit-chez-Gosselin	UNP/LNO	QC	L'Île-d'Orléans	21 L/14	46°52′	71°05′
Pitchforth Fiord	BAY/BAIE	NT	Franklin	27 B	68°58′	68°10′
Pitchimi Lake	LAKE/LAC	AB	115-11-W5	84 J/15	59°00′	114°46′
Pit-de-la-Mer	UNP/LNO	QC	Le Fjord-du-Saguenay	22 D/6	48°27′	71°06′
Pitlochrie	UNP/LNO	AB	35-69-12-W4	73 M/4	55°02′	111°44′
Pitlochry	UNP/LNO	MB	2-14-23-W2	62 K/2	50°09′	100°31′
Pitman	UNP/LNO	SK	7-15-22-W2	72 I/3	50°15′	105°02′
Pitman	UNP/LNO	BC	Range 5 Coast	103 I/9	54°42′	128°19′
Pitman River	RIV/CDE	BC	Cassiar	104 H/15	57°59′	128°30′
Pitmans Pond	LAKE/LAC	NF		2 C/3	48°00′	53°12′
Pitquah	UNP/LNO	BC	Kamloops Division Yale	92 I/6	50°15′	121°29′
Pit Siding	UNP/LNO	MB	5,9-80-8-E	63 P/16	55°55′	96°19′
Pitt Island	ISL/ÎLE	BC	Range 4 Coast	103 H/12	53°30′	129°47′
Pitt Island 27	IR/RI	BC	Range 4 Coast	103 G/9	53°38′	130°03′
Pitt Lake	LAKE/LAC	BC	New Westminster	92 G/7	49°25′	122°33′
Pitt Lake 4	IR/RI	BC	New Westminster	92 G/7	49°21′	122°36′
Pitt Meadows	MUN1/AZM1	BC	New Westminster	92 G/2	49°15′	122°42′
Pitt Meadows	UNP/LNO	BC	New Westminster	92 G/2	49°14′	122°41′
Pitt, Mount	MTN/MNT	BC	New Westminster	92 G/15	49°53′	122°42′
Pitt River	RIV/CDE	BC	New Westminster	92 G/2	49°14′	122°46′

NAME NOM	ENTITY ENTITÉ	LOC 1 LIEU 1	LOC 2 LIEU 2	MAP CARTE	POSITION LAT	LONG
Pittsburgh	MUN2/AZM2	ON	Frontenac	31 C/8	44°21′	76°18′
Pitts Ferry	UNP/LNO	ON	Frontenac	31 C/8	44°17′	76°20′
Pitts Harbour	UNP/LNO	NF		3 D/4	52°01′	55°54′
Pitts, Mount	MTN/MNT	YT		115 I/12	62°35′	137°35′
Pitt Sound Island	ISL/ÎLE	NF		2 C/13	48°52′	53°44′
Pitt Sound Reach	RIVF/EFLV	NF		2 C/13	48°53′	53°46′
Pitts Pond	LAKE/LAC	NF		2 D/8	48°28′	54°12′
Pittston	UNP/LNO	ON	Grenville	31 B/14	44°51′	75°27′
Pittville No. 169	MUN2/AZM2	SK		72 K/7	50°25′	108°40′
Pitukupi Lake	LAKE/LAC	ON	Cochrane	42 K/9	50°40′	84°07′
Pitz Lake	LAKE/LAC	NT	Keewatin	65 P	63°57′	96°32′
Piusville	UNP/LNO	PE	Prince	21 I/16	46°47′	64°12′
Pivabiska, Lac	LAKE/LAC	ON	Cochrane	42 G/13	49°49′	83°43′
Pivabiska Lake - see-voir - Pivabiska, Lac	LAKE/LAC	ON		42 G/13	49°49′	83°43′
Pivabiska River	RIV/CDE	ON	Cochrane	42 J/2	50°13′	82°52′
Pivot	UNP/LNO	AB	11-17-1-W4	72 L/8	50°25′	110°02′
Piwei River	RIV/CDE	SK	9-40-5-W2	63 D/7	52°26′	102°41′
Pixie Beach	UNP/LNO	BC	Osoyoos Division Yale	82 L/3	50°04′	119°27′
Piyagoskogau Lake	LAKE/LAC	ON	Cochrane	42 I/1	50°14′	80°25′
Piyami	UNP/LNO	AB	30-10-21-W4	82 H/15	49°51′	112°50′
Place-aux-Français	UNP/LNO	QC	Manicouagan	22 G/11	49°33′	67°14′
Place-Joseph	UNP/LNO	QC	Les Moulins	31 H/13	45°45′	73°41′
Place-Laurentienne	UNP/LNO	QC	La Jacques-Cartier	21 L/13	46°49′	71°34′
Placentia	TOWN/VIL2	NF		1 N/4	47°14′	53°58′
Placentia Bay	BAY/BAIE	NF		1 N/5	47°00′	54°30′
Placentia Junction	UNP/LNO	NF		1 N/5	47°23′	53°40′
Placentia Sound	BAY/BAIE	NF		1 N/5	47°20′	53°56′
Place-Quoibion	UNP/LNO	QC	Le Haut-Richelieu	31 H/3	45°11′	73°15′
Placer Mountain	MTN/MNT	BC	Yale Division Yale	92 H/1	49°08′	120°25′
Plage-Brunet	UNP/LNO	QC	Le Haut-Richelieu	31 H/3	45°10′	73°15′
Plage-Chartrand	UNP/LNO	QC	Laval	31 H/12	45°40′	73°35′
Plage-des-Ours	UNP/LNO	QC	Montmagny	21 L/16	46°45′	70°05′
Plage-Ferguson	UNP/LNO	QC	Sept-Rivières	22 J/1	50°13′	66°17′
Plage-Idéale	UNP/LNO	QC	Laval	31 H/12	45°39′	73°46′
Plage-Jacques-Cartier	UNP/LNO	QC	Laval	31 H/12	45°39′	73°46′
Plage-Labelle	UNP/LNO	QC	Le Haut-Richelieu	31 H/3	45°12′	73°15′
Plage-Larocque	UNP/LNO	QC	Deux-Montagnes	31 H/12	45°31′	73°57′
Plage-Levesque	UNP/LNO	QC	Sept-Rivières	22 J/1	50°13′	66°14′
Plage-Monaghan	UNP/LNO	QC	Sept-Rivières	22 J/1	50°12′	66°19′
Plage-Mon-Repos	UNP/LNO	QC	Laval	31 H/12	45°32′	73°45′
Plage-Moreau	UNP/LNO	QC	Le Haut-Richelieu	31 H/3	45°11′	73°15′
Plage-Normandin	UNP/LNO	QC	Vallée-de-l'Or	32 D/1	48°14′	78°09′
Plage-Orange	UNP/LNO	QC	Vallée-de-l'Or	32 D/1	48°14′	78°08′
Plage-Rouge	UNP/LNO	QC	Le Haut-Richelieu	31 H/3	45°12′	73°15′
Plage-Routhier	UNP/LNO	QC	Sept-Rivières	22 J/1	50°13′	66°15′
Plage-Sainte-Marguerite	UNP/LNO	QC	Sept-Rivières	22 J/2	50°09′	66°33′
Plage-Saint-François	UNP/LNO	QC	Le Haut-Saint-Laurent	31 G/1	45°11′	74°13′
Plage-Somerville	UNP/LNO	QC	Le Haut-Saint-Laurent	31 G/1	45°05′	74°26′
Plage-Youville	UNP/LNO	QC	Deux-Montagnes	31 H/12	45°31′	73°57′
Plaine-à-Thomas, La	UNP/LNO	QC	Pabok	22 A/10	48°38′	64°36′
Plainfield	UNP/LNO	NS	Pictou	11 E/10	45°39′	62°55′
Plainfield	UNP/LNO	ON	Hastings	31 C/6	44°17′	77°21′
Plain Lake	LAKE/LAC	AB	53-12-W4	73 E/12	53°37′	111°42′
Plain, Le	UNP/LNO	QC	Pabok	22 A/8	48°25′	64°24′
Plain View	UNP/LNO	SK	33-24-7-W2	62 M/2	51°06′	102°57′
Plainville	UNP/LNO	ON	Northumberland	31 D/1	44°05′	78°14′
Plaisance	VILG/VILG	QC	Papineau	31 G/11	45°37′	75°07′
Plaisance, Baie de	BAY/BAIE	QC	Les Îles-de-la-Madeleine	11 N/5	47°18′	61°53′
Plaisance, Réserve faunique de	PARK/PARC	QC	Papineau	31 G/11	45°36′	75°08′
Plaister Mines	UNP/LNO	NS	Victoria	11 K/2	46°07′	60°39′
Plamondon	VILG/VILG	AB	2-68-16-W4	83 I/16	54°51′	112°19′
Planet	UNP/LNO	ON	Thunder Bay	52 B/10	48°41′	90°32′
Planinshek Lake	LAKE/LAC	SK		63 M/12	55°33′	103°46′
Plantagenet	VILG/VILG	ON	Prescott	31 G/10	45°32′	75°00′
Plantagenet Station	UNP/LNO	ON	Prescott	31 G/10	45°31′	74°59′
Plante, Rivière des	RIV/CDE	QC	Robert-Cliche	21 L/7	46°16′	70°49′
Plan-Vautrin	UNP/LNO	QC	Avignon	22 B/1	48°12′	66°18′
Plaqué-des-Landry, Le	UNP/LNO	QC	Denis-Riverin	22 G/2	49°02′	66°42′
Plaque-Verte, La	UNP/LNO	QC	Les Îles-de-la-Madeleine	11 N/5	47°24′	61°46′
Plassey	UNP/LNO	SK	6-32-26-W2	72 P/12	51°43′	105°40′
Plaster Cove	UNP/LNO	NS	Victoria	11 F/15	45°58′	60°49′
Plaster Rock	VILG/VILG	NB	Victoria	21 J/14	46°54′	67°24′
Plateau	UNP/LNO	NS	Inverness	11 K/11	46°36′	61°00′
Plateau Mountain	MTN/MNT	YT		105 N/4	63°06′	133°56′
Plate Cove East	VILG/VILG	NF		2 C/11	48°31′	53°29′

NAME NOM	ENTITY ENTITÉ	LOC 1 LIEU 1	LOC 2 LIEU 2	MAP CARTE	POSITION	
					LAT	LONG
Plate Cove West	VILG/VILG	NF		2 C/5	48°30′	53°30′
Platier, Le - also-aussi - Southeast Shoal	SEAU/SMER	—		8010	44°08′	49°45′
Platine, La	UNP/LNO	QC	Le Bas-Richelieu	31 I/3	46°04′	73°03′
Plat, Lac	LAKE/LAC	QC	La Haute-Côte-Nord	22 C/13	48°52′	69°53′
Plato	UNP/LNO	SK	27-25-18-W3	72 N/1	51°10′	108°27′
Platon, Pointe	CAPE/CAP	QC	Lotbinière	21 L/12	46°40′	71°51′
Plattsville	UNP/LNO	ON	Oxford	40 P/7	43°18′	80°37′
Plavin Homestead Provincial Historic Site (Undeveloped)	PARK/PARC	AB	28-90-23-W4	84 C/13	56°50′	117°38′
Player	UNP/LNO	SK	26-14-4-W3	72 J/4	50°12′	107°49′
Playfair Point	CAPE/CAP	NT	Franklin	68 G	75°21′	100°48′
Playfairville	UNP/LNO	ON	Lanark	31 C/16	44°58′	76°25′
Playgreen Lake	LAKE/LAC	MB		63 J/1	54°02′	98°14′
Playmor Junction	UNP/LNO	BC	Kootenay	82 F/5	49°27′	117°32′
Pleasant Bay	UNP/LNO	NS	Inverness	11 K/15	46°49′	60°48′
Pleasant Bay	BAY/BAIE	NS	Inverness	11 K/15	46°50′	60°48′
Pleasant Camp	UNP/LNO	BC	Cassiar	114 P/9	59°30′	136°28′
Pleasant Corners	UNP/LNO	ON	Prescott	31 G/10	45°33′	74°38′
Pleasant Creek	RIV/CDE	YT		105 N/12	63°31′	133°55′
Pleasantdale	VILG/VILG	SK	34-41-18-W2	73 A/10	52°35′	104°30′
Pleasantdale No. 398	MUN2/AZM2	SK		73 A/8	52°30′	104°25′
Pleasantfield	UNP/LNO	NS	Queens	21 A/2	44°14′	64°54′
Pleasant Grove	VILG/VILG	PE	Queens	11 L/6	46°22′	63°04′
Pleasant Grove	UNP/LNO	PE	Queens	11 L/6	46°22′	63°04′
Pleasant Harbour	UNP/LNO	NS	Halifax	11 D/15	44°47′	62°44′
Pleasant Hill	UNP/LNO	NS	Inverness	11 F/11	45°38′	61°22′
Pleasant Hill	UNP/LNO	QC	Le Haut-Saint-François	21 E/5	45°20′	71°31′
Pleasant Hill	UNP/LNO	SK		73 B/2	52°08′	106°42′
Pleasant Hills	UNP/LNO	NS	Colchester	11 E/5	45°26′	63°51′
Pleasant Hill West	UNP/LNO	SK		73 B/2	52°08′	106°43′
Pleasant Home	UNP/LNO	MB	20-17-3-E	62 I/6	50°28′	97°10′
Pleasant Inlet	BAY/BAIE	NT	Franklin	25 K	62°48′	69°59′
Pleasant Lake	UNP/LNO	NS	Yarmouth	20 O/16	43°51′	66°01′
Pleasant Park	UNP/LNO	ON	Essex	40 J/2	42°13′	82°49′
Pleasant Point	UNP/LNO	NS	Halifax	11 D/11	44°41′	63°04′
Pleasant Point	UNP/LNO	NS	Shelburne	20 P/11	43°43′	65°06′
Pleasant Point	UNP/LNO	ON	Victoria	31 D/7	44°27′	78°43′
Pleasant Point	UNP/LNO	MB	4-10-13-W	62 G/14	49°48′	99°11′
Pleasant Point	CAPE/CAP	ON	Prince Edward	31 C/2	44°07′	76°51′
Pleasant Ridge	UNP/LNO	NB	Northumberland	21 I/11	46°44′	65°28′
Pleasant Ridge	UNP/LNO	NB	Kings	21 H/13	45°49′	65°37′
Pleasant Ridge	UNP/LNO	NB	Charlotte	21 G/7	45°23′	66°58′
Pleasant River	UNP/LNO	NS	Queens	21 A/7	44°26′	64°53′
Pleasantside	UNP/LNO	BC	New Westminster	92 G/7	49°18′	122°51′
Pleasant Vale	UNP/LNO	NB	Albert	21 H/14	45°51′	65°00′
Pleasant Valley	UNP/LNO	PE	Queens	11 L/6	46°22′	63°29′
Pleasant Valley	UNP/LNO	NS	Antigonish	11 E/9	45°41′	62°04′
Pleasant Valley	UNP/LNO	NS	Pictou	11 E/10	45°33′	62°47′
Pleasant Valley	UNP/LNO	NS	Halifax	11 E/2	45°07′	62°53′
Pleasant Valley	UNP/LNO	NS	Colchester	11 E/3	45°15′	63°20′
Pleasant Valley	UNP/LNO	NS	Yarmouth	20 P/13	43°59′	65°58′
Pleasant Valley	UNP/LNO	NB	York	21 J/2	46°13′	66°37′
Pleasant Valley	UNP/LNO	ON	Stormont	31 G/3	45°02′	75°03′
Pleasant Valley	UNP/LNO	ON	Dundas	31 B/14	44°57′	75°27′
Pleasant Valley	UNP/LNO	ON	Renfrew	31 F/15	45°47′	76°51′
Pleasant Valley	UNP/LNO	ON	Wentworth	30 M/5	43°15′	79°58′
Pleasant Valley	UNP/LNO	ON	Manitoulin	41 G/16	45°52′	82°20′
Pleasant Valley	UNP/LNO	ON	Essex	40 J/2	42°03′	82°52′
Pleasant Valley	UNP/LNO	SK	10-44-19-W2	73 A/15	52°47′	104°41′
Pleasant Valley No. 288	MUN2/AZM2	SK		72 N/8	51°30′	108°15′
Pleasantview	UNP/LNO	NF		2 E/6	49°22′	55°19′
Pleasant View	UNP/LNO	PE	Prince	21 I/16	46°55′	64°12′
Pleasant View	UNP/LNO	ON	Renfrew	31 F/14	45°49′	77°05′
Pleasant View	UNP/LNO	SK		72 I/5	50°23′	105°32′
Pleasant View Survey	UNP/LNO	ON	Wentworth	30 M/5	43°18′	79°55′
Pleasant Villa	UNP/LNO	NB	Queens	21 G/9	45°42′	66°10′
Pleasantville	UNP/LNO	NF		1 N/10	47°35′	52°41′
Pleasantville	UNP/LNO	NS	Lunenburg	21 A/8	44°20′	64°26′
Pleasantville	UNP/LNO	ON	York	31 D/3	44°03′	79°24′
Pledger Lake	LAKE/LAC	ON	Cochrane	42 J/13	50°53′	83°42′
Plenty	VILG/VILG	SK	33-32-19-W3	72 N/15	51°47′	108°38′
Plessisville	CITY/VIL1	QC	L'Érable	21 L/4	46°13′	71°47′
Plessisville	VILG/VILG	QC	L'Érable	21 L/4	46°14′	71°45′
Plétipi, Lac	LAKE/LAC	QC	Le Fjord-du-Saguenay	22 M/9	51°41′	70°06′
Pleureuse, Pointe	CAPE/CAP	QC	Denis-Riverin	22 H/5	49°15′	65°38′
Plevna	UNP/LNO	ON	Frontenac	31 C/15	44°58′	76°59′

NAME NOM	ENTITY ENTITÉ	LOC 1 LIEU 1	LOC 2 LIEU 2	MAP CARTE	POSITION LAT	LONG
Plonge, Lac la	LAKE/LAC	SK		73 O/3	55°08′	107°20′
Plongeon, Lac au	LAKE/LAC	QC	Charlevoix-Est	21 M/16	47°51′	70°08′
Plourde	UNP/LNO	QC	La Mitis	22 B/12	48°41′	67°57′
Plover Islands	ISL/ÎLE	NT	Franklin	25 C	60°18′	69°35′
Plover Lake	LAKE/LAC	AB	29-10,11-W4	72 M/6	51°29′	111°23′
Plover Mills	UNP/LNO	ON	Middlesex	40 P/3	43°09′	81°12′
Pluie, Lac à la - also-aussi - **Rainy Lake**	LAKE/LAC	ON	Rainy River	52 C/11	48°42′	93°10′
Pluie, Rivière à la - also-aussi - **Rainy River**	RIV/CDE	ON	Rainy River	52 D/15	48°50′	94°41′
Plumas	UNP/LNO	MB	20-16-12-W	62 J/6	50°23′	99°05′
Plum Coulee	VILG/VILG	MB	2,11-3-3-W	62 H/4	49°11′	97°46′
Plum Creek	RIV/CDE	MB	33-7-21-W	62 F/9	49°37′	100°15′
Plum Hollow	UNP/LNO	ON	Leeds	31 C/9	44°40′	76°02′
Plum Lakes	LAKE/LAC	MB	7,8-24,25-W	62 F/10	49°38′	100°44′
Plummer	UNP/LNO	ON	Algoma	41 J/5	46°24′	83°48′
Plummer Additional	MUN2/AZM2	ON	Algoma	41 J/5	46°23′	83°45′
Plumper Harbour	UNP/LNO	BC	Nootka	92 E/10	49°41′	126°38′
Plumper Islands	ISL/ÎLE	BC	Rupert	92 L/10	50°35′	126°47′
Plumper Sound	BAY/BAIE	BC	Cowichan	92 B/14	48°46′	123°13′
Plum Point	UNP/LNO	NF		12 P/2	51°04′	56°53′
Plum Point	CAPE/CAP	ON	Elgin	40 I/11	42°36′	81°24′
Plumweseep	UNP/LNO	NB	Kings	21 H/14	45°45′	65°28′
Plunkett	VILG/VILG	SK	11-34-25-W2	72 P/14	51°55′	105°27′
Pluton, Dôme	MTN/MNT	QC	Jamésie	32 G/14	49°52′	75°29′
Plymouth	UNP/LNO	NS	Pictou	11 E/10	45°33′	62°39′
Plymouth	UNP/LNO	NS	Yarmouth	20 O/16	43°48′	66°01′
Plymouth	UNP/LNO	NB	Carleton	21 J/4	46°10′	67°40′
Plymouth Park	UNP/LNO	NS	Pictou	11 E/10	45°33′	62°39′
Plympton	MUN2/AZM2	ON	Lambton	40 O/1	43°01′	82°06′
Plympton	UNP/LNO	NS	Digby	21 A/12	44°30′	65°55′
Plympton Station	UNP/LNO	NS	Digby	21 A/5	44°29′	65°54′
Pocahontas	UNP/LNO	AB	6-49-27-W5	83 F/4	53°12′	117°55′
Pocket Knife Lake	LAKE/LAC	NF		13 K/6	54°24′	61°18′
Pockwock	UNP/LNO	NS	Halifax	11 D/13	44°46′	63°51′
Pockwock Lake	LAKE/LAC	NS	Halifax	11 D/13	44°47′	63°50′
Pocologan	UNP/LNO	NB	Charlotte	21 G/2	45°08′	66°35′
Pocologan River	RIV/CDE	NB	Charlotte	21 G/2	45°07′	66°35′
Poe	UNP/LNO	AB	30-49-16-W4	83 H/8	53°16′	112°20′
Pogamasing	UNP/LNO	ON	Sudbury	41 I/13	46°55′	81°46′
Pogamasing Lake	LAKE/LAC	ON	Sudbury	41 I/13	46°58′	81°50′
Pohénégamook	CITY/VIL1	QC	Témiscouata	21 N/11	47°31′	69°16′
Pohénégamook, Lac	LAKE/LAC	QC	Témiscouata	21 N/6	47°29′	69°16′
Poillon, Cape	CAPE/CAP	NT	Franklin	25 O	63°08′	67°52′
Poilu	UNP/LNO	ON	Thunder Bay	42 L/2	50°03′	86°40′
Poilu Lake	LAKE/LAC	ON	Thunder Bay	42 L/2	50°01′	86°41′
Poincaré, Lac	LAKE/LAC	QC	Minganie	12 O/9	51°44′	58°19′
Point Abino	UNP/LNO	ON	Welland	30 L/14	42°51′	79°06′
Point Aconi	UNP/LNO	NS	Cape Breton	11 K/8	46°20′	60°18′
Point Alexander	UNP/LNO	ON	Renfrew	31 K/4	46°08′	77°34′
Point Alexandria	UNP/LNO	ON	Frontenac	31 C/1	44°08′	76°21′
Point Alison	VILG/VILG	AB	2-53-4-W5	83 G/9	53°33′	114°29′
Point Anne	UNP/LNO	ON	Hastings	31 C/3	44°09′	77°18′
Point au Gaul	VILG/VILG	NF		1 L/13	46°52′	55°45′
Point au Mal	UNP/LNO	NF		12 B/10	48°39′	58°39′
Point aux Carr	UNP/LNO	NB	Northumberland	21 P/3	47°05′	65°13′
Point Brule	UNP/LNO	AB	13-104-9-W4	74 L/3	58°01′	111°20′
Point Clark	UNP/LNO	ON	Bruce	41 A/4	44°04′	81°45′
Point Clark Lighthouse National Historic Site - also-aussi - Phare-de-la-Pointe-Clark, Lieu historique national du	PARK/PARC	ON	Bruce	41 A/4	44°04′	81°45′
Point Comfort	UNP/LNO	QC	La Vallée-de-la-Gatineau	31 J/4	46°05′	75°51′
Point Cross	UNP/LNO	NS	Inverness	11 K/11	46°35′	61°01′
Point de Bute	UNP/LNO	NB	Westmorland	21 H/16	45°54′	64°15′
Point Deroche	UNP/LNO	PE	Queens	11 L/7	46°25′	62°55′
Point Douglas	UNP/LNO	MB		62 H/14	49°54′	97°07′
Point-du-Jour	UNP/LNO	QC	Les Maskoutains	31 H/10	45°41′	72°59′
Pointe-à-Boisvert	UNP/LNO	QC	La Haute-Côte-Nord	22 C/11	48°34′	69°11′
Pointe-à-Bouleau	UNP/LNO	NB	Gloucester	21 P/10	47°30′	64°53′
Pointe-à-la-Croix	VILG/VILG	QC	Avignon	22 B/2	48°01′	66°41′
Pointe-à-la-Frégate	UNP/LNO	QC	La Côte-de-Gaspé	22 H/2	49°12′	64°56′
Pointe-à-la-Garde	UNP/LNO	QC	Avignon	22 B/2	48°05′	66°32′
Pointe à l'Aurore	UNP/LNO	NF		2 M/4	51°06′	55°45′
Pointe-Alexandre	UNP/LNO	NB	Gloucester	21 P/15	47°48′	64°40′
Pointe-à-Mailhot, La	UNP/LNO	QC	L'Érable	21 L/4	46°11′	71°44′
Pointe-à-Maurier	UNP/LNO	QC	Côte-Nord-du-Golfe-Saint-Laurent	12 J/5	50°20′	59°48′
Pointe-Antoine	UNP/LNO	QC	Témiscamingue	31 L/14	46°52′	79°14′
Pointe-à-Poulin	UNP/LNO	QC	Manicouagan	22 G/6	49°24′	67°19′
Pointe au Baril	UNP/LNO	ON	Parry Sound	41 H/10	45°34′	80°30′

NAME NOM	ENTITY ENTITÉ	LOC 1 LIEU 1	LOC 2 LIEU 2	MAP CARTE	POSITION LAT	LONG
Pointe au Baril Station	UNP/LNO	ON	Parry Sound	41 H/9	45°36'	80°22'
Pointe-au-Bouleau	UNP/LNO	QC	Charlevoix-Est	22 C/4	48°05'	69°44'
Pointe-au-Chêne	UNP/LNO	QC	Argenteuil	31 G/10	45°39'	74°45'
Pointe-au-Père	CITY/VIL1	QC	Rimouski-Neigette	22 C/9	48°31'	68°28'
Pointe-au-Père Lighthouse National Historic Site - also-aussi - Phare-de-Pointe-au-Père, Lieu historique national du	PARK/PARC	QC	Rimouski-Neigette	22 C/9	48°31'	68°28'
Pointe-au-Pic	UNP/LNO	QC	Charlevoix-Est	21 M/9	47°38'	70°09'
Pointe-au-Renard	UNP/LNO	QC	Vaudreuil-Soulanges	31 H/5	45°21'	73°59'
Pointe-au-Sable	UNP/LNO	QC	Argenteuil	31 G/9	45°31'	74°18'
Pointe-aux-Anglais	UNP/LNO	QC	Sept-Rivières	22 G/11	49°41'	67°10'
Pointe-aux-Anglais	UNP/LNO	QC	Deux-Montagnes	31 G/8	45°30'	74°10'
Pointe-aux-Loups	UNP/LNO	QC	Les Îles-de-la-Madeleine	11 N/12	47°32'	61°43'
Pointe-aux-Orignaux	UNP/LNO	QC	Kamouraska	21 M/8	47°29'	70°01'
Pointe-aux-Outardes	TOWN/VIL2	QC	Manicouagan	22 F/1	49°03'	68°26'
Pointe aux Pins	UNP/LNO	ON	Algoma	41 K/8	46°29'	84°28'
Pointe-aux-Trembles	VILG/VILG	QC	Portneuf	21 L/12	46°44'	71°35'
Pointe-aux-Trembles	UNP/LNO	QC	Communauté urbaine de Montréal	31 H/12	45°39'	73°30'
Pointe-Basse	UNP/LNO	QC	Les Îles-de-la-Madeleine	11 N/5	47°24'	61°47'
Pointe-Blanche, La	UNP/LNO	QC	Témiscouata	21 N/7	47°20'	68°59'
Pointe-Bourg	UNP/LNO	QC	Avignon	22 B/1	48°06'	66°04'
Pointe-Brûlé	UNP/LNO	NB	Gloucester	21 P/15	47°45'	64°44'
Pointe-Calumet	TOWN/VIL2	QC	Deux-Montagnes	31 H/12	45°30'	73°58'
Pointe-Canot	UNP/LNO	NB	Gloucester	21 P/15	47°50'	64°42'
Pointe-Carleton	UNP/LNO	QC	Minganie	12 E/10	49°44'	62°56'
Pointe-Castagner	UNP/LNO	QC	Le Haut-Saint-Laurent	31 G/1	45°09'	74°21'
Pointe-Cavagnal	UNP/LNO	QC	Vaudreuil-Soulanges	31 G/8	45°26'	74°04'
Pointe-Chambord	UNP/LNO	QC	Le Domaine-du-Roy	32 A/8	48°28'	72°05'
Pointe-Claire	CITY/VIL1	QC	Communauté urbaine de Montréal	31 H/5	45°26'	73°50'
Pointe-de-l'Orignal	UNP/LNO	QC	Les Chutes-de-la-Chaudière	21 L/11	46°39'	71°19'
Pointe-de-l'Ouest	UNP/LNO	QC	Minganie	22 H/15	49°52'	64°31'
Pointe-de-Rivière-du-Loup	UNP/LNO	QC	Rivière-du-Loup	21 N/13	47°51'	69°34'
Pointe-de-Rivière-Ouelle	UNP/LNO	QC	Kamouraska	21 M/8	47°26'	70°03'
Pointe-des-Cascades	TOWN/VIL2	QC	Vaudreuil-Soulanges	31 H/5	45°20'	73°58'
Pointe-des-Cascades, Barrage de	MISC/DIV	QC	Vaudreuil-Soulanges	31 H/5	45°19'	73°57'
Pointe-des-Cèdres	UNP/LNO	QC	Témiscamingue	31 M/6	47°18'	79°28'
Pointe des Chênes	UNP/LNO	ON	Algoma	41 K/7	46°28'	84°30'
Pointe des Chênes Park	UNP/LNO	ON	Algoma	41 K/7	46°30'	84°32'
Pointe-des-Monts	UNP/LNO	QC	Manicouagan	22 G/6	49°19'	67°23'
Pointed Mountain	MTN/MNT	NT	Mackenzie	95 B	60°22'	123°55'
Pointe du Bois	UNP/LNO	MB	36-15-14-E	52 L/5	50°18'	95°33'
Pointe-du-Buisson, Barrage de la	MISC/DIV	QC	Beauharnois-Salaberry	31 H/5	45°19'	73°59'
Pointe-du-Chêne	UNP/LNO	NB	Westmorland	21 I/2	46°14'	64°32'
Pointe-du-Domaine	UNP/LNO	QC	Vaudreuil-Soulanges	31 H/5	45°23'	73°54'
Pointe-du-Lac	VILG/VILG	QC	Francheville	31 I/7	46°17'	72°42'
Pointe-du-Marigot	UNP/LNO	QC	Champlain	31 H/11	45°34'	73°30'
Pointe-du-Moulin	UNP/LNO	QC	Vaudreuil-Soulanges	31 H/5	45°22'	73°52'
Point Edward	VILG/VILG	ON	Lambton	40 J/16	43°00'	82°24'
Point Edward	UNP/LNO	NS	Cape Breton	11 K/1	46°10'	60°16'
Pointe-Fortin, La	UNP/LNO	QC	Le Haut-Richelieu	31 H/3	45°08'	73°10'
Pointe-Fortune	TOWN/VIL2	QC/ON		31 G/9	45°34'	74°23'
Pointe-Gatineau	UNP/LNO	QC	Communauté urbaine de l'Outaouais	31 G/5	45°28'	75°42'
Pointe-Heath, Réserve écologique de la	PARK/PARC	QC	Minganie	12 F/4	49°06'	61°44'
Pointe-Jaune	UNP/LNO	QC	La Côte-de-Gaspé	22 H/2	49°04'	64°31'
Pointe, La	UNP/LNO	QC	Le Haut-Saint-François	21 E/3	45°12'	71°27'
Pointe, Lac de la	LAKE/LAC	QC	Jamésie	23 D/10	52°39'	70°30'
Pointe-Lebel	TOWN/VIL2	QC	Manicouagan	22 F/1	49°10'	68°12'
Pointe-Leblanc	UNP/LNO	QC	Le Haut-Saint-Laurent	31 G/1	45°05'	74°26'
Pointe-Leggatt	UNP/LNO	QC	La Mitis	22 C/9	48°40'	68°04'
Pointe Louise	UNP/LNO	ON	Algoma	41 K/7	46°28'	84°28'
Pointe-Marie	UNP/LNO	QC	Lajemmerais	31 H/14	45°45'	73°23'
Pointe-Martel	UNP/LNO	QC	Témiscamingue	31 M/3	47°09'	79°23'
Pointe-McGinnis	UNP/LNO	QC	Le Haut-Richelieu	31 H/3	45°13'	73°07'
Pointe-Meloche	UNP/LNO	QC	Beauharnois-Salaberry	31 G/8	45°18'	74°07'
Pointe-Navarre	UNP/LNO	QC	La Côte-de-Gaspé	22 A/15	48°52'	64°33'
Pointe-Noire	UNP/LNO	QC	Sept-Rivières	22 J/1	50°09'	66°29'
Point Enragée	UNP/LNO	NF		1 M/6	47°23'	55°17'
Pointe-Parent	UNP/LNO	QC	Minganie	12 K/4	50°08'	61°47'
Pointe-Pelée, Parc national de la - also-aussi - Point Pelee National Park	PARK/PARC	ON	Essex	40 G/15	41°58'	82°31'
Pointe-Piché	UNP/LNO	QC	Témiscamingue	31 M/5	47°27'	79°32'
Pointe-Platon	UNP/LNO	QC	Lotbinière	21 L/12	46°40'	71°52'
Pointe-Platon, Réserve écologique de	PARK/PARC	QC	Lotbinière	21 L/12	46°40'	71°51'
Pointe Riche Peninsula	CAPE/CAP	NF		12 I/11	50°42'	57°23'
Pointer Lake	LAKE/LAC	SK		63 M/12	55°38'	103°45'
Pointe-Rocheuse	UNP/LNO	NB	Gloucester	21 P/15	47°47'	64°58'
Pointe-Rocheuse	UNP/LNO	QC	Côte-Nord-du-Golfe-Saint-Laurent	12 P/6	51°28'	57°25'
Pointe-Rouge	UNP/LNO	QC	L'Islet	21 M/8	47°20'	70°06'

NAME NOM	ENTITY ENTITÉ	LOC 1 LIEU 1	LOC 2 LIEU 2	MAP CARTE	POSITION LAT	POSITION LONG
Pointe-Saint-Gilles	UNP/LNO	QC	Lotbinière	21 L/11	46°36′	71°22′
Pointe-Saint-Pierre	UNP/LNO	QC	Pabok	22 A/9	48°38′	64°10′
Pointe-Sapin	UNP/LNO	NB	Kent	21 I/15	46°58′	64°50′
Pointe-Sapin-Centre	UNP/LNO	NB	Kent	21 I/15	46°57′	64°52′
Pointe-Sauvage	UNP/LNO	NB	Gloucester	21 P/10	47°44′	64°41′
Pointes, Les	UNP/LNO	QC	Bellechasse	21 L/10	46°39′	70°30′
Pointes, Les	UNP/LNO	QC	Arthabaska	21 E/13	45°58′	71°52′
Pointe-Taillon, Parc de conservation de la	PARK/PARC	QC	Lac-Saint-Jean-Est	22 D/12	48°42′	71°58′
Pointe-Verte	VILG/VILG	NB	Gloucester	21 P/13	47°51′	65°46′
Point Gardiner	UNP/LNO	NB	Northumberland	21 P/3	47°04′	65°06′
Point Grondine 3	IR/RI	ON	Manitoulin	41 H/14	45°58′	81°08′
Point Hill	UNP/LNO	NS	Cumberland	21 H/7	45°21′	64°48′
Point La Haye	UNP/LNO	NF		1 K/13	46°54′	53°36′
Point Lake	LAKE/LAC	NT	Mackenzie	86 H/3	65°15′	113°04′
Point Lance	VILG/VILG	NF		1 L/16	46°49′	54°05′
Point La Nim	UNP/LNO	NB	Restigouche	22 B/1	48°04′	66°27′
Point Leamington	TOWN/VIL2	NF		2 E/6	49°20′	55°24′
Point May	VILG/VILG	NF		1 L/13	46°54′	55°56′
Point Michaud	UNP/LNO	NS	Richmond	11 F/10	45°35′	60°41′
Point of Bay	VILG/VILG	NF		2 E/6	49°15′	55°15′
Point of Mara Beach	UNP/LNO	ON	Ontario	31 D/11	44°31′	79°12′
Point Park	UNP/LNO	NB	Albert	21 I/2	46°05′	64°46′
Point Pelee National Park - also-aussi - Pointe-Pelée, Parc national de la	PARK/PARC	ON	Essex	40 G/15	41°58′	82°31′
Point Pleasant	UNP/LNO	PE	Kings	11 L/2	46°03′	62°34′
Point Pleasant	UNP/LNO	ON	Frontenac	31 C/2	44°13′	76°34′
Point Pleasant	UNP/LNO	ON	Peterborough	31 D/9	44°34′	78°27′
Point Prim	UNP/LNO	PE	Queens	11 L/2	46°04′	62°59′
Point Rosie	UNP/LNO	NF		1 M/6	47°23′	55°17′
Point Tupper	UNP/LNO	NS	Richmond	11 F/11	45°36′	61°22′
Point Verde	UNP/LNO	NF		1 M/1	47°14′	54°00′
Point Wolfe River	RIV/CDE	NB	Albert	21 H/11	45°33′	65°01′
Poirier	UNP/LNO	NB	Kent	21 I/7	46°17′	64°48′
Poirierville	UNP/LNO	NS	Richmond	11 F/10	45°35′	60°56′
Poison Creek 17	IR/RI	BC	Range 5 Coast	93 K/4	54°14′	125°47′
Poison Creek 17A	IR/RI	BC	Range 5 Coast	93 K/4	54°13′	125°47′
Poissant	UNP/LNO	QC	Antoine-Labelle	31 J/14	46°46′	75°16′
Poisson-Blanc	UNP/LNO	QC	Le Domaine-du-Roy	32 A/14	49°00′	73°18′
Poisson Blanc, Lac du	LAKE/LAC	QC	Antoine-Labelle	31 G/13	46°00′	75°44′
Poissons, Rivière aux	RIV/CDE	NF		23 A/14	52°53′	65°13′
Poitras Siding	UNP/LNO	NB	Madawaska	21 O/4	47°05′	67°49′
Poivre, Lac au	LAKE/LAC	QC	Le Fjord-du-Saguenay	22 E/2	49°05′	70°49′
Pokei Lake	LAKE/LAC	ON	Algoma	42 C/6	48°25′	85°14′
Pokemouche	UNP/LNO	NB	Gloucester	21 P/10	47°40′	64°53′
Pokemouche 13	IR/RI	NB	Gloucester	21 P/10	47°39′	64°59′
Pokemouche Gully	CHAN/CHEN	NB	Gloucester	21 P/10	47°39′	64°47′
Pokemouche Landing	UNP/LNO	NB	Gloucester	21 P/11	47°31′	65°13′
Pokemouche River	RIV/CDE	NB	Gloucester	21 P/10	47°40′	64°48′
Pokeshaw	UNP/LNO	NB	Gloucester	21 P/14	47°47′	65°15′
Pokesudie	UNP/LNO	NB	Gloucester	21 P/15	47°48′	64°46′
Pokesudie Island	ISL/ÎLE	NB	Gloucester	21 P/15	47°48′	64°47′
Pokheitsk 10	IR/RI	BC	Kamloops Division Yale	92 I/11	50°32′	121°17′
Pokiok	UNP/LNO	NB	Saint John	21 G/8	45°17′	66°06′
Pokiok	UNP/LNO	NB	York	21 G/14	45°57′	67°15′
Pokiok Settlement	UNP/LNO	NB	York	21 G/14	45°53′	67°05′
Poland	UNP/LNO	ON	Lanark	31 F/2	45°04′	76°33′
Poland	UNP/LNO	ON	Thunder Bay	52 B/16	48°56′	90°07′
Polaris	UNP/LNO	NT	Franklin	68 H	75°24′	96°53′
Polecat Point	CAPE/CAP	NT	Franklin	37 C	69°09′	77°17′
Pole Hill	UNP/LNO	NB	Carleton	21 J/6	46°17′	67°24′
Pole Island 14	IR/RI	BC	Range 3 Coast	103 A/1	52°11′	128°06′
Poletica, Mount	MTN/MNT	BC	Cassiar	104 M/1	59°08′	134°29′
Polette, Lac	LAKE/LAC	QC	La Haute-Côte-Nord	22 C/5	48°25′	69°41′
Police Island	ISL/ÎLE	NT	Mackenzie	96 C	64°51′	125°11′
Police Meadow 2	IR/RI	BC	Cassiar	94 C/15	56°47′	124°47′
Police Outpost Provincial Park	PARK/PARC	AB	6-1-26-W4	82 H/3	49°00′	113°28′
Pollards Point	UNP/LNO	NF		12 H/10	49°45′	56°54′
Pollett River	UNP/LNO	NB	Westmorland	21 H/14	45°53′	65°06′
Pollett River	RIV/CDE	NB	Westmorland	21 H/14	46°00′	65°05′
Polley	UNP/LNO	BC	Lillooet	92 I/12	50°43′	121°55′
Pollock Point	CAPE/CAP	NS	Lunenburg	21 A/1	44°08′	64°30′
Pollockville	UNP/LNO	AB	3-25-12-W4	72 M/4	51°06′	111°35′
Polonais, Lac des	LAKE/LAC	QC	Antoine-Labelle	31 O/3	47°01′	75°22′
Polonia	UNP/LNO	MB	21-16-16-W	62 J/5	50°23′	99°37′
Polson Park	UNP/LNO	ON	Frontenac	31 C/2	44°14′	76°32′
Polsons Brook	UNP/LNO	NS	Antigonish	11 F/5	45°27′	61°53′

NAME NOM	ENTITY ENTITÉ	LOC 1 LIEU 1	LOC 2 LIEU 2	MAP CARTE	POSITION LAT	LONG
Polwarth	UNP/LNO	SK	30-51-5-W3	73 G/7	53°26′	106°44′
Polynia Islands	ISL/ÎLE	NT	Franklin	89 D	77°40′	115°54′
Pomeroy	UNP/LNO	NB	Charlotte	21 G/7	45°24′	66°55′
Pomeroy	UNP/LNO	MB	24-5-5-W	62 G/8	49°24′	98°00′
Pomeroy Ridge	UNP/LNO	NB	Charlotte	21 G/6	45°17′	67°25′
Pomialuk Bay	BAY/BAIE	NF		13 J/15	54°47′	58°32′
Pommerel Lake	LAKE/LAC	NF		13 D/5	52°20′	63°39′
Pommeroy, Lac	LAKE/LAC	QC	Témiscamingue	31 M/2	47°04′	78°39′
Pommes, Rivière aux	RIV/CDE	QC	Portneuf	21 L/12	46°42′	71°44′
Pomona	UNP/LNO	ON	Grey	41 A/2	44°14′	80°39′
Pompes, Les	UNP/LNO	QC	L'Amiante	21 L/3	46°04′	71°12′
Pomquet	UNP/LNO	NS	Antigonish	11 F/12	45°38′	61°51′
Pomquet and Afton 23	IR/RI	NS	Antigonish	11 F/12	45°35′	61°45′
Pomquet Forks	UNP/LNO	NS	Antigonish	11 F/12	45°35′	61°48′
Pomquet Island	ISL/ÎLE	NS	Antigonish	11 F/12	45°39′	61°45′
Pomquet Station	UNP/LNO	NS	Antigonish	11 F/12	45°37′	61°49′
Ponask Lake	LAKE/LAC	ON	Kenora	53 F/16	53°58′	92°35′
Ponask River	RIV/CDE	ON	Kenora	53 J/7	54°18′	92°38′
Ponass Lake No. 367	MUN2/AZM2	SK		63 D/4	52°15′	104°00′
Ponass Lakes	LAKE/LAC	SK		63 D/5	52°16′	103°58′
Poncheville	UNP/LNO	QC	Matane	22 B/14	48°52′	67°28′
Poncheville, Lac	LAKE/LAC	QC	Jamésie	32 K/2	50°10′	76°55′
Pond Cove	UNP/LNO	NF		12 P/2	51°08′	56°52′
Pond Inlet	HAM/HAM	NT	Franklin	38 B	72°42′	77°59′
Pond Inlet	BAY/BAIE	NT	Franklin	38 B	72°48′	77°00′
Pond, La	UNP/LNO	QC	Bonaventure	22 A/6	48°16′	65°24′
Pond Mills	UNP/LNO	ON	Middlesex	40 I/14	42°57′	81°12′
Pondosy Lake	LAKE/LAC	BC	Range 4 Coast	93 E/2	53°12′	126°53′
Ponds	UNP/LNO	NS	Pictou	11 E/9	45°41′	62°18′
Ponds, Island of	ISL/ÎLE	NF		3 E/5	53°28′	55°53′
Pond Trough	SEAU/SMER	—		5.17	72°48′	77°30′
Pondville	UNP/LNO	NS	Richmond	11 F/10	45°32′	60°59′
Pondville South	UNP/LNO	NS	Richmond	11 F/10	45°32′	60°59′
Ponemah	UNP/LNO	MB	22,23-27-4E	62 I/7	50°28′	96°57′
Ponemah Beach	UNP/LNO	MB	22-17-4-E	62 I/7	50°28′	96°57′
Ponhook Lake	LAKE/LAC	NS	Queens	21 A/7	44°19′	64°53′
Ponhook Lake 10	IR/RI	NS	Queens	21 A/2	44°10′	65°00′
Ponoka	TOWN/VIL2	AB	4-43-25-W4	83 A/12	52°42′	113°35′
Ponoka No. 3, County of	MUN1/AZM1	AB	43-27-W4	83 A/12	52°43′	113°52′
Ponsonby	UNP/LNO	ON	Wellington	40 P/9	43°38′	80°22′
Pons, Rivière	RIV/CDE	QC	Kativik	24 C/2	56°07′	68°53′
Pont-à-Léo, Le	UNP/LNO	QC	Les Îles-de-la-Madeleine	11 N/12	47°37′	61°34′
Pont-Arnaud	UNP/LNO	QC	Le Fjord-du-Saguenay	22 D/6	48°25′	71°07′
Pontax, Rivière	RIV/CDE	QC	Jamésie	32 M/10	51°37′	78°50′
Pontbriand	VILG/VILG	QC	L'Amiante	21 L/3	46°09′	71°15′
Pontbriand, Baie	BAY/BAIE	QC	Minganie	12 L/7	50°16′	62°33′
Pontchartrain, Promontoire	CAPE/CAP	QC	Kativik	35 J/6	62°16′	75°15′
Pont-Château	UNP/LNO	QC	Vaudreuil-Soulanges	31 G/8	45°20′	74°12′
Pont-de-la-Noreau	UNP/LNO	QC	Portneuf	21 L/12	46°43′	71°51′
Pont-du-Gouvernement	UNP/LNO	QC	Matawinie	31 I/4	46°07′	73°51′
Pont-du-Milieu	UNP/LNO	NB	Kent	21 I/11	46°43′	65°01′
Pont-du-Séminaire, Le	UNP/LNO	QC	Charlevoix-Est	21 M/9	47°39′	70°29′
Ponteix	TOWN/VIL2	SK	19-9-11-W3	72 G/11	49°45′	107°29′
Pontgravé	UNP/LNO	NB	Northumberland	21 P/7	47°25′	64°57′
Pontiac	VILG/VILG	QC	Les Collines-de-l'Outaouais	31 F/9	45°35′	76°08′
Pontiac	MUN1/AZM1	QC	Pontiac	31 K/2	46°03′	76°55′
Pontiac Station	UNP/LNO	QC	Pontiac	31 F/8	45°28′	76°20′
Pont-Lafrance	UNP/LNO	NB	Gloucester	21 P/7	47°27′	64°59′
Pont-Landry	UNP/LNO	NB	Gloucester	21 P/10	47°35′	64°57′
Pont-Laval	UNP/LNO	QC	La Haute-Côte-Nord	22 C/14	48°49′	69°02′
Pont-Mousseau	UNP/LNO	QC	Montcalm	31 H/13	45°52′	73°39′
Ponton	UNP/LNO	MB	23-65-12-W	63 J/11	54°39′	99°10′
Ponton River	RIV/CDE	AB	109-14-W5	84 K/8	58°27′	116°11′
Pontrilas	UNP/LNO	SK	7-49-14-W2	73 H/1	53°13′	104°02′
Pont-Rouge	CITY/VIL1	QC	Portneuf	21 L/13	46°45′	71°42′
Pont-Viau	UNP/LNO	QC	Laval	31 H/12	45°34′	73°41′
Pontypool	UNP/LNO	ON	Durham	31 D/2	44°06′	78°38′
Poodiac	UNP/LNO	NB	Kings	21 H/12	45°35′	65°32′
Pooeyelth 3	IR/RI	BC	Kamloops Division Yale	92 I/4	50°10′	121°35′
Poohbah Lake	LAKE/LAC	ON	Rainy River	52 B/5	48°23′	91°41′
Poole	UNP/LNO	ON	Perth	40 P/10	43°31′	80°52′
Poole Point	CAPE/CAP	NT	Franklin	36 N	67°45′	77°17′
Pooles Corner	UNP/LNO	PE	Kings	11 L/2	46°13′	62°39′
Pooles Resort	UNP/LNO	ON	Leeds	31 B/5	44°26′	75°53′
Pooley Island	ISL/ÎLE	BC	Range 3 Coast	103 A/9	52°43′	128°14′

NAME / NOM	ENTITY / ENTITÉ	LOC 1 / LIEU 1	LOC 2 / LIEU 2	MAP / CARTE	POSITION LAT	POSITION LONG
Pool's Cove	VILG/VILG	NF		1 M/11	47°41′	55°26′
Pool's Island	UNP/LNO	NF		2 F/4	49°07′	53°36′
Poorfish Lake	LAKE/LAC	NT	Keewatin	65 C	60°16′	100°48′
Poorman 88	IR/RI	SK		72 P/8	51°30′	104°24′
Pope	UNP/LNO	MB	20-13-24-W	62 K/2	50°07′	100°44′
Pope Landing	UNP/LNO	BC	New Westminster	92 F/9	49°37′	124°03′
Popelogan Depot	UNP/LNO	NB	Restigouche	21 O/10	47°45′	66°44′
Popes Harbour	UNP/LNO	NF		2 C/4	48°14′	53°33′
Popes Harbour	UNP/LNO	NS	Halifax	11 D/15	44°49′	62°39′
Popes Harbour Pond	LAKE/LAC	NF		2 C/5	48°15′	53°36′
Popham Bay	BAY/BAIE	ON	Northumberland	31 C/4	44°00′	77°45′
Popham Bay	BAY/BAIE	NT	Franklin	26 A	64°13′	65°10′
Popham Point	CAPE/CAP	ON	Manitoulin	41 H/14	45°56′	81°12′
Popkum	UNP/LNO	BC	Yale Division Yale	92 H/4	49°12′	121°44′
Popkum 1	IR/RI	BC	Yale Division Yale	92 H/4	49°12′	121°43′
Popkum 2	IR/RI	BC	Yale Division Yale	92 H/4	49°11′	121°45′
Poplar	UNP/LNO	ON	Manitoulin	41 G/16	45°46′	82°28′
Poplar Bay	VILG/VILG	AB	46,47-1-W5	83 G/1	53°00′	114°06′
Poplar Bay	UNP/LNO	MB	29,30-16-13-E	52 L/5	50°22′	95°47′
Poplar Creek	UNP/LNO	BC	Kootenay	82 K/6	50°25′	117°08′
Poplar Dale	UNP/LNO	ON	Algoma	41 J/12	46°31′	83°44′
Poplarfield	UNP/LNO	MB	12-22-2-W	62 I/13	50°53′	97°36′
Poplar Grove	UNP/LNO	PE	Prince	11 L/12	46°39′	63°56′
Poplar Grove	UNP/LNO	NS	Hants	21 H/1	45°01′	64°05′
Poplar Grove	UNP/LNO	ON	Frontenac	31 C/1	44°15′	76°25′
Poplar Grove	UNP/LNO	SK	4-14-2-W2	62 L/1	50°08′	102°13′
Poplar Grove	UNP/LNO	BC	Similkameen Division Yale	82 E/12	49°32′	119°34′
Poplar Hill	UNP/LNO	NS	Pictou	11 E/10	45°43′	62°55′
Poplar Hill	UNP/LNO	ON	Middlesex	40 P/4	43°00′	81°31′
Poplar Hill	UNP/LNO	ON	Kenora	53 D/1	52°05′	94°18′
Poplar Hill	UNP/LNO	AB	27-73-9-W6	83 M/6	55°21′	119°18′
Poplar Hill	IR/RI	ON	Kenora	53 D/1	52°05′	94°18′
Poplar Island	ISL/ÎLE	ON	Kenora	52 E/7	49°17′	94°42′
Poplar Lodge	UNP/LNO	ON	Thunder Bay	52 H/9	49°38′	88°05′
Poplar Park	UNP/LNO	MB	34-15-6-E	62 I/7	50°19′	96°40′
Poplar Point	UNP/LNO	PE	Kings	11 L/8	46°17′	62°29′
Poplar Point	UNP/LNO	MB		62 I/4	50°03′	97°59′
Poplar Point	GEOG/GÉOG	MB		62 J/1	50°05′	98°01′
Poplar Point	CAPE/CAP	MB		63 A/14	52°57′	97°28′
Poplar Point Bay	BAY/BAIE	MB		63 F/7	53°22′	100°41′
Poplar Rapids River	RIV/CDE	ON	Cochrane	42 H/12	49°35′	81°48′
Poplar Ridge	UNP/LNO	AB	11-80-7-W6	83 M/15	55°56′	118°59′
Poplar River	UNP/LNO	MB	46-2-E	63 A/14	53°00′	97°17′
Poplar River	RIV/CDE	ON	Cochrane	42 O/13	51°49′	83°42′
Poplar River	RIV/CDE	MB		63 A/14	53°00′	97°18′
Poplar River	RIV/CDE	SK	1-1-29-W2	72 H/4	49°00′	105°46′
Poplar River	RIV/CDE	NT	Mackenzie	95 H	61°22′	120°52′
Poplar River 16	IR/RI	MB		63 A/14	53°00′	97°17′
Poplar Valley No. 12	MUN2/AZM2	SK		72 H/4	49°10′	105°50′
Poplarville	UNP/LNO	MB	46-2-E1	63 A/14	52°59′	97°14′
Popple Depot	UNP/LNO	NB	Northumberland	21 O/7	47°24′	66°30′
Poquiosin & Skamain 13	IR/RI	BC	New Westminster	92 G/14	49°47′	123°10′
Por-à-Vaches, Le	UNP/LNO	QC	Vaudreuil-Soulanges	31 G/8	45°18′	74°10′
Porcher Island	UNP/LNO	BC	Range 5 Coast	103 J/1	54°05′	130°23′
Porcher Island	ISL/ÎLE	BC	Range 5 Coast	103 G/15	53°58′	130°25′
Porc-Pic	UNP/LNO	QC	Rimouski-Neigette	22 C/7	48°16′	68°56′
Porcupine	UNP/LNO	ON	Cochrane	42 A/6	48°30′	81°10′
Porcupine Bay	BAY/BAIE	NF		3 E/5	53°25′	55°55′
Porcupine, Cape	CAPE/CAP	NF		13 H/14	53°56′	57°08′
Porcupine Hills	MTN/MNT	SK/MB		63 C/5	52°30′	101°40′
Porcupine No. 395	MUN2/AZM2	SK		63 D/10	52°40′	102°55′
Porcupine Plain	TOWN/VIL2	SK	8-42-9-W2	63 D/11	52°36′	103°15′
Porcupine River	RIV/CDE	SK		74 P/2	59°11′	104°46′
Porcupine River	RIV/CDE	YT		116 N/7	67°25′	141°00′
Porcupine River	RIV/CDE	NT	Mackenzie	96 G	65°03′	123°43′
Porcus Lake	LAKE/LAC	ON	Kenora	52 F/12	49°43′	93°52′
Porden Point	CAPE/CAP	NT	Franklin	59 B	76°15′	93°38′
Porée, Lac	LAKE/LAC	QC	Caniapiscau	23 K/13	54°47′	69°40′
Pork Island	ISL/ÎLE	NF		2 C/13	48°59′	53°44′
Pork Peninsula	CAPE/CAP	NT	Keewatin	55 K	62°24′	92°20′
Porlock	UNP/LNO	ON	Sudbury	41 I/2	46°12′	80°49′
Porquis Junction	UNP/LNO	ON	Cochrane	42 A/10	48°42′	80°47′
Portage	UNP/LNO	PE	Prince	21 I/9	46°40′	64°04′
Portage	UNP/LNO	NS	Cape Breton	11 K/1	46°02′	60°20′
Portage, Baie du	BAY/BAIE	QC	Le Fjord-du-Saguenay	22 L/15	50°46′	70°58′

NAME NOM	ENTITY ENTITÉ	LOC 1 LIEU 1	LOC 2 LIEU 2	MAP CARTE	POSITION LAT	LONG
Portage Bay	BAY/BAIE	ON	Kenora	52 F/11	49°43′	93°20′
Portage Bay	BAY/BAIE	MB		62 O/10	51°33′	98°50′
Portage Bay	BAY/BAIE	NT	Mackenzie	75 M	63°48′	111°02′
Portage-de-la-Nation	UNP/LNO	QC	Papineau	31 G/11	45°40′	75°01′
Portage-des-Roches, Barrage de	MISC/DIV	QC	Le Fjord-du-Saguenay	22 D/6	48°19′	71°13′
Portage-des-Roches-Nord	UNP/LNO	QC	Le Fjord-du-Saguenay	22 D/6	48°18′	71°11′
Portage-des-Roches-Sud	UNP/LNO	QC	Le Fjord-du-Saguenay	22 D/6	48°18′	71°10′
Portage-du-Cap	UNP/LNO	QC	Les Îles-de-la-Madeleine	11 N/4	47°14′	61°54′
Portage-du-Fort	TOWN/VIL2	QC	Pontiac	31 F/10	45°36′	76°40′
Portage-du-Lac	UNP/LNO	NB	Madawaska	21 N/7	47°19′	68°36′
Portage Gully	CHAN/CHEN	NB	Northumberland	21 P/3	47°12′	65°02′
Portage Island	ISL/ÎLE	NB	Northumberland	21 P/3	47°11′	65°03′
Portage Junction	UNP/LNO	MB		62 H/14	49°51′	97°09′
Portage, Lac du	LAKE/LAC	QC	Matane	22 B/12	48°39′	67°36′
Portage, Lac du	LAKE/LAC	QC	Beauce-Sartigan	21 E/16	45°56′	70°16′
Portage Lake	LAKE/LAC	NF		12 A/5	48°27′	57°31′
Portage Lake	LAKE/LAC	NF		12 B/1	48°14′	58°05′
Portage-Lapointe	UNP/LNO	QC	Le Fjord-du-Saguenay	22 D/11	48°33′	71°15′
Portage la Prairie	CITY/VIL1	MB	11,12-6,7-W	62 G/16	49°58′	98°18′
Portage la Prairie	MUN2/AZM2	MB		62 G/16	50°00′	98°16′
Portage la Prairie	GEOG/GÉOG	MB		62 G/16	49°57′	98°20′
Portage, Le	UNP/LNO	QC	Matane	22 B/13	48°50′	67°34′
Portage, Le	UNP/LNO	QC	Deux-Montagnes	31 G/8	45°29′	74°00′
Portage-Moïse	UNP/LNO	QC	Rouyn-Noranda	32 D/1	48°01′	78°19′
Portage Park	UNP/LNO	ON	Simcoe	31 D/14	44°46′	79°54′
Portage, Rivière du	RIV/CDE	QC	Le Fjord-du-Saguenay	22 D/1	48°10′	70°03′
Portage-Saint-Hélier	UNP/LNO	QC	La Côte-de-Gaspé	22 H/2	49°06′	64°40′
Portage Vale	UNP/LNO	NB	Kings	21 H/14	45°50′	65°14′
Port Alberni	CITY/VIL1	BC	Alberni	92 F/2	49°15′	124°48′
Port Albert	UNP/LNO	NF		2 E/10	49°33′	54°32′
Port Albert	UNP/LNO	ON	Huron	40 P/13	43°53′	81°43′
Port Albert Peninsula	CAPE/CAP	NF		2 E/9	49°33′	54°30′
Port Albion	UNP/LNO	BC	Clayoquot	92 C/13	48°57′	125°33′
Port-Alfred	UNP/LNO	QC	Le Fjord-du-Saguenay	22 D/7	48°19′	70°53′
Port Alice	VILG/VILG	BC	Rupert	92 L/6	50°23′	127°27′
Port Alma	UNP/LNO	ON	Kent	40 J/1	42°11′	82°15′
Port Anne	UNP/LNO	NF		1 M/7	47°23′	54°42′
Port Anson	VILG/VILG	NF		2 E/12	49°32′	55°50′
Port Anson	UNP/LNO	ON	Parry Sound	31 E/12	45°36′	79°37′
Portapique	UNP/LNO	NS	Colchester	11 E/5	45°24′	63°42′
Portapique Mountain	UNP/LNO	NS	Colchester	11 E/5	45°26′	63°45′
Portapique River	RIV/CDE	NS	Colchester	11 E/5	45°24′	63°43′
Port au Bras	VILG/VILG	NF		1 M/3	47°03′	55°08′
Port au Choix	TOWN/VIL2	NF		12 I/11	50°43′	57°22′
Port au Choix, Lieu historique national de - also-aussi - Port au Choix National Historic Site	PARK/PARC	NF		12 I/11	50°43′	57°23′
Port au Choix National Historic Site - also-aussi - Port au Choix, Lieu historique national de	PARK/PARC	NF		12 I/11	50°43′	57°23′
Port-au-Persil	UNP/LNO	QC	Charlevoix-Est	21 N/13	47°48′	69°54′
Port au Port	UNP/LNO	NF		12 B/10	48°33′	58°43′
Port au Port Bay	BAY/BAIE	NF		12 B/10	48°40′	58°47′
Port au Port East	VILG/VILG	NF		12 B/10	48°33′	58°43′
Port au Port Peninsula	CAPE/CAP	NF		12 B/6	48°35′	59°00′
Port au Port West-Aguathuna-Felix Cove	TOWN/VIL2	NF		12 B/10	48°33′	58°46′
Port-au-Saumon	UNP/LNO	QC	Charlevoix-Est	21 N/13	47°46′	69°57′
Port-aux-Quilles	UNP/LNO	QC	Charlevoix-Est	21 N/13	47°55′	69°52′
Port Ban	UNP/LNO	NS	Inverness	11 K/3	46°12′	61°23′
Port Bickerton	UNP/LNO	NS	Guysborough	11 F/4	45°06′	61°43′
Port Blandford	TOWN/VIL2	NF		2 D/8	48°21′	54°10′
Port Bolster	UNP/LNO	ON	York	31 D/6	44°20′	79°12′
Port Britain	UNP/LNO	ON	Durham	30 M/16	43°56′	78°22′
Port Bruce	UNP/LNO	ON	Elgin	40 I/11	42°39′	81°01′
Port Burwell	VILG/VILG	ON	Elgin	40 I/10	42°39′	80°49′
Port Burwell	UNP/LNO	NT	Franklin	25 A	60°25′	64°50′
Port Caledonia	UNP/LNO	NS	Cape Breton	11 J/4	46°11′	59°55′
Port Carling	UNP/LNO	ON	Muskoka	31 E/4	45°07′	79°35′
Port Carmen	UNP/LNO	ON	Parry Sound	31 E/12	45°39′	79°35′
Port-Cartier	CITY/VIL1	QC	Sept-Rivières	22 J/2	50°01′	66°52′
Port-Cartier-Ouest	UNP/LNO	QC	Sept-Rivières	22 J/2	50°01′	66°53′
Port Clements	VILG/VILG	BC	Queen Charlotte	103 F/9	53°41′	132°11′
Port Clyde	UNP/LNO	NS	Shelburne	20 P/11	43°36′	65°28′
Port Cockburn	UNP/LNO	ON	Parry Sound	31 E/5	45°15′	79°46′
Port Colborne	CITY/VIL1	ON	Welland	30 L/14	42°54′	79°14′
Port Coquitlam	CITY/VIL1	BC	New Westminster	92 G/7	49°16′	122°46′
Port Credit	UNP/LNO	ON	Peel	30 M/12	43°33′	79°35′
Port Crewe	UNP/LNO	ON	Kent	40 J/1	42°11′	82°12′
Port Cunnington	UNP/LNO	ON	Muskoka	31 E/6	45°16′	79°02′

NAME NOM	ENTITY ENTITÉ	LOC 1 LIEU 1	LOC 2 LIEU 2	MAP CARTE	POSITION LAT	LONG
Port Dalhousie	UNP/LNO	ON	Lincoln	30 M/3	43°12′	79°16′
Port-Daniel	VILG/VILG	QC	Pabok	22 A/2	48°11′	64°58′
Port-Daniel	UNP/LNO	QC	Pabok	22 A/2	48°11′	64°58′
Port-Daniel, Baie de	BAY/BAIE	QC	Pabok	22 A/2	48°10′	64°57′
Port-Daniel-Centre	UNP/LNO	QC	Pabok	22 A/2	48°09′	64°59′
Port-Daniel-Est	UNP/LNO	QC	Pabok	22 A/2	48°11′	64°58′
Port-Daniel-Ouest	UNP/LNO	QC	Pabok	22 A/3	48°07′	65°01′
Port-Daniel, Petite rivière	RIV/CDE	QC	Pabok	22 A/2	48°11′	64°58′
Port-Daniel, Réserve faunique de	PARK/PARC	QC	Pabok	22 A/7	48°17′	64°57′
Port-Daniel, Rivière	RIV/CDE	QC	Pabok	22 A/2	48°11′	64°58′
Port Darlington	UNP/LNO	ON	Durham	30 M/15	43°53′	78°40′
Port Davidson	UNP/LNO	ON	Lincoln	30 L/13	42°59′	79°34′
Port de Grave	UNP/LNO	NF		1 N/11	47°35′	53°13′
Port Desire	UNP/LNO	BC	Barclay	92 C/14	48°50′	125°08′
Port Douglas	UNP/LNO	BC	New Westminster	92 G/16	49°46′	122°10′
Port Dover	UNP/LNO	ON	Norfolk	40 I/16	42°47′	80°12′
Port Dufferin	UNP/LNO	NS	Halifax	11 D/16	44°55′	62°23′
Port Dufferin West	UNP/LNO	NS	Halifax	11 D/16	44°54′	62°24′
Porteau	UNP/LNO	BC	New Westminster	92 G/11	49°33′	123°14′
Porte-de-Caotibi, La	UNP/LNO	QC	Sept-Rivières	22 J/5	50°20′	67°37′
Porte-des-Bouleaux, La	UNP/LNO	QC	Manicouagan	22 N/8	51°29′	68°10′
Port Edward	MUN1/AZM1	BC	Range 5 Coast	103 J/1	54°13′	130°17′
Port Elgin	TOWN/VIL2	ON	Bruce	41 A/6	44°26′	81°24′
Port Elgin	VILG/VILG	NB	Westmorland	21 I/1	46°03′	64°05′
Port Elmsley	UNP/LNO	ON	Lanark	31 C/16	44°53′	76°07′
Porten Settlement	UNP/LNO	NB	Carleton	21 G/13	45°57′	67°32′
Porteous	UNP/LNO	BC	Kootenay	82 G/12	49°36′	115°53′
Porter	UNP/LNO	NS	Halifax	11 D/11	44°44′	63°17′
Porter	UNP/LNO	SK	13-42-17-W3	73 C/9	52°37′	108°19′
Porter Brook	UNP/LNO	NB	Northumberland	21 J/8	46°29′	66°28′
Porter, Cape	CAPE/CAP	NT	Keewatin	57 C	69°10′	94°18′
Porter Cove	UNP/LNO	NB	Northumberland	21 J/8	46°29′	66°22′
Porter Creek	UNP/LNO	YT		105 D/14	60°46′	135°09′
Porter Lake	LAKE/LAC	SK		74 B/6	56°20′	107°20′
Porter Lake	LAKE/LAC	AB	44-3-W4	73 D/16	52°48′	110°18′
Porter Lake	LAKE/LAC	NT	Mackenzie	75 F	61°41′	108°05′
Porter Landing	UNP/LNO	BC	Cassiar	104 J/16	58°48′	130°06′
Porter Road	UNP/LNO	NB	Saint John	21 H/5	45°26′	65°38′
Porter's Hill	UNP/LNO	ON	Huron	40 P/12	43°38′	81°39′
Porters Lake	UNP/LNO	NS	Halifax	11 D/11	44°44′	63°19′
Porters Lake	LAKE/LAC	NS	Halifax	11 D/11	44°45′	63°18′
Porters Lake	LAKE/LAC	NS	Digby	21 A/5	44°30′	65°48′
Porterville	UNP/LNO	NF		2 E/6	49°15′	55°11′
Portes de l'Enfer, Les	VALL/VALL	QC	La Côte-de-Beaupré	21 M/11	47°44′	71°16′
Port Essington	UNP/LNO	BC	Range 5 Coast	103 I/4	54°09′	129°58′
Port Essington	IR/RI	BC	Range 5 Coast	103 I/4	54°09′	129°58′
Port Felix	UNP/LNO	NS	Guysborough	11 F/3	45°15′	61°13′
Port Felix East	UNP/LNO	NS	Guysborough	11 F/6	45°15′	61°12′
Port Findlay	UNP/LNO	ON	Algoma	41 K/8	46°19′	84°01′
Port Franks	UNP/LNO	ON	Lambton	40 P/4	43°13′	81°54′
Port George	UNP/LNO	NS	Annapolis	21 H/3	45°00′	65°09′
Port Glasgow	UNP/LNO	ON	Elgin	40 I/12	42°30′	81°37′
Port Granby	UNP/LNO	ON	Durham	30 M/16	43°54′	78°28′
Port Greville	UNP/LNO	NS	Cumberland	21 H/7	45°24′	64°33′
Port Guichon	UNP/LNO	BC	New Westminster	92 G/3	49°05′	123°06′
Port Hammond	UNP/LNO	BC	New Westminster	92 G/2	49°12′	122°39′
Port Hardy	MUN1/AZM1	BC	Rupert	92 L/11	50°42′	127°25′
Port Hastings	UNP/LNO	NS	Inverness	11 F/11	45°39′	61°24′
Port Hawkesbury	TOWN/VIL2	NS	Inverness	11 F/11	45°37′	61°21′
Port Hilford	UNP/LNO	NS	Guysborough	11 F/4	45°06′	61°50′
Port Hill	UNP/LNO	PE	Prince	11 L/12	46°35′	63°53′
Port Hill Station	UNP/LNO	PE	Prince	11 L/12	46°35′	63°57′
Port Hood	UNP/LNO	NS	Inverness	11 K/4	46°01′	61°32′
Port Hood Island	UNP/LNO	NS	Inverness	11 K/4	46°01′	61°34′
Port Hood Island	ISL/ÎLE	NS	Inverness	11 K/4	46°01′	61°35′
Port Hood Station	UNP/LNO	NS	Inverness	11 K/4	46°00′	61°32′
Port Hope	TOWN/VIL2	ON	Durham	30 M/16	43°57′	78°18′
Port Hope Simpson	VILG/VILG	NF		13 A/9	52°33′	56°18′
Port Howe	UNP/LNO	NS	Cumberland	11 E/13	45°51′	63°45′
Portia	UNP/LNO	MB	17-22-12-W	62 J/14	50°54′	99°06′
Portier Pass 5	IR/RI	BC	Cedar	92 G/4	49°01′	123°36′
Port Joli	UNP/LNO	NS	Queens	20 P/15	43°52′	64°54′
Port Joli Head	CAPE/CAP	NS	Queens	20 P/15	43°49′	64°50′
Port Kells	UNP/LNO	BC	New Westminster	92 G/2	49°10′	122°42′
Port Kirwan	VILG/VILG	NF		1 K/15	46°58′	52°55′

NAME NOM	ENTITY ENTITÉ	LOC 1 LIEU 1	LOC 2 LIEU 2	MAP CARTE	POSITION LAT	LONG
Port Lambton	UNP/LNO	ON	Lambton	40 J/10	42°39′	82°30′
Portland	MUN2/AZM2	ON	Frontenac	31 C/7	44°27′	76°42′
Portland	UNP/LNO	NF		2 C/5	48°25′	53°49′
Portland	UNP/LNO	ON	Leeds	31 C/9	44°42′	76°12′
Portland Canal	CHAN/CHEN	BC	Cassiar	103 P/5	55°27′	130°02′
Portland Creek	UNP/LNO	NF		12 I/4	50°10′	57°37′
Portland Creek Pond	LAKE/LAC	NF		12 I/4	50°11′	57°32′
Portland Inlet	BAY/BAIE	BC	Range 5 Coast	103 J/9	54°44′	130°24′
Portland Island	ISL/ÎLE	BC	Cowichan	92 B/11	48°44′	123°22′
Portland-Ouest	UNP/LNO	QC	Les Collines-de-l'Outaouais	31 G/13	45°47′	75°42′
Portland Point	CAPE/CAP	BC	Clayoquot	92 F/4	49°04′	125°49′
Port La Tour	UNP/LNO	NS	Shelburne	20 P/6	43°30′	65°29′
Port Law	UNP/LNO	ON	Grey	41 A/8	44°16′	80°27′
Port Lewis	UNP/LNO	QC	Le Haut-Saint-Laurent	31 G/1	45°10′	74°17′
Port L'Hebert	UNP/LNO	NS	Shelburne	20 P/15	43°48′	64°56′
Portlock	UNP/LNO	ON	Algoma	41 J/5	46°20′	83°53′
Port Loring	UNP/LNO	ON	Parry Sound	31 E/13	45°55′	79°59′
Port Lorne	UNP/LNO	NS	Annapolis	21 A/14	44°57′	65°16′
Port Maitland	UNP/LNO	NS	Yarmouth	20 O/16	43°59′	66°09′
Port Maitland	UNP/LNO	ON	Haldimand	30 L/13	42°52′	79°34′
Port Malcolm	UNP/LNO	NS	Richmond	11 F/11	45°35′	61°17′
Port Mann	UNP/LNO	BC	New Westminster	92 G/2	49°12′	122°49′
Port McNeill	TOWN/VIL2	BC	Rupert	92 L/11	50°35′	127°06′
Port McNicoll	UNP/LNO	ON	Simcoe	31 D/12	44°45′	79°49′
Port Medway	UNP/LNO	NS	Queens	21 A/2	44°08′	64°35′
Port Mellon	UNP/LNO	BC	New Westminster	92 G/11	49°31′	123°29′
Port-Menier	UNP/LNO	QC	Minganie	22 H/16	49°49′	64°21′
Port Metcalf	UNP/LNO	ON	Frontenac	31 C/1	44°14′	76°11′
Port Milford	UNP/LNO	ON	Prince Edward	30 N/14	43°56′	77°03′
Port Moody	CITY/VIL1	BC	New Westminster	92 G/7	49°17′	122°51′
Port Morien	UNP/LNO	NS	Cape Breton	11 J/4	46°08′	59°52′
Port Mouton	UNP/LNO	NS	Queens	20 P/15	43°56′	64°51′
Port Mouton Head	CAPE/CAP	NS	Queens	20 P/15	43°52′	64°47′
Port Mouton Island	ISL/ÎLE	NS	Queens	20 P/15	43°54′	64°46′
Port Nelson	UNP/LNO	NF		2 F/4	49°05′	53°37′
Port Nelson	UNP/LNO	ON	Halton	30 M/5	43°20′	79°46′
Port Nelson	UNP/LNO	MB		54 F/2	57°03′	92°36′
Portneuf	CITY/VIL1	QC	Portneuf	21 L/12	46°42′	71°53′
Portneuf	MUN1/AZM1	QC	Portneuf	21 L/13	46°53′	71°55′
Portneuf Est, Rivière	RIV/CDE	QC	La Haute-Côte-Nord	22 C/13	48°49′	69°47′
Portneuf, Lac	LAKE/LAC	QC	Le Fjord-du-Saguenay	22 E/1	49°08′	70°18′
Portneuf, Réserve faunique de	PARK/PARC	QC	Portneuf	31 P/1	47°09′	72°17′
Portneuf, Rivière	RIV/CDE	QC	La Haute-Côte-Nord	22 C/11	48°38′	69°05′
Portneuf-Station	UNP/LNO	QC	Portneuf	21 L/12	46°43′	71°53′
Portneuf-sur-Mer	UNP/LNO	QC	La Haute-Côte-Nord	22 C/11	48°37′	69°06′
Port Neville	UNP/LNO	BC	Range 1 Coast	92 L/8	50°30′	126°05′
Port Neville 4	IR/RI	BC	Range 1 Coast	92 K/12	50°34′	125°56′
Portobello	UNP/LNO	NS	Halifax	11 D/12	44°44′	63°33′
Porto Rico	UNP/LNO	BC	Kootenay	82 F/6	49°20′	117°14′
Port Perry	UNP/LNO	ON	Ontario	31 D/2	44°06′	78°57′
Port Philip	UNP/LNO	NS	Cumberland	11 E/13	45°51′	63°44′
Portree	UNP/LNO	NS	Inverness	11 K/7	46°24′	60°58′
Portreeve	UNP/LNO	SK	32-21-22-W3	72 K/14	50°50′	109°01′
Port Renfrew	UNP/LNO	BC	Renfrew	92 C/9	48°33′	124°25′
Port Rexton	VILG/VILG	NF		2 C/6	48°24′	53°20′
Port Rexton	UNP/LNO	NF		2 C/6	48°23′	53°20′
Port Richmond	UNP/LNO	NS	Richmond	11 F/11	45°36′	61°16′
Port Robinson	UNP/LNO	ON	Welland	30 M/3	43°02′	79°13′
Port Rowan	UNP/LNO	ON	Norfolk	40 I/9	42°37′	80°28′
Port Royal	UNP/LNO	NF		1 M/9	47°32′	54°06′
Port Royal	UNP/LNO	NS	Richmond	11 F/11	45°32′	61°06′
Port Royal	UNP/LNO	NS	Annapolis	21 A/12	44°43′	65°36′
Port Royal	UNP/LNO	ON	Norfolk	40 I/9	42°36′	80°29′
Port-Royal, Lieu historique national de - also-aussi - 　Port-Royal National Historic Site	PARK/PARC	NS	Annapolis	21 A/12	44°43′	65°37′
Port-Royal National Historic Site - also-aussi - 　Port-Royal, Lieu historique national de	PARK/PARC	NS	Annapolis	21 A/12	44°43′	65°37′
Port Ryerse	UNP/LNO	ON	Norfolk	40 I/16	42°45′	80°15′
Port-Saint-François	UNP/LNO	QC	Nicolet-Yamaska	31 I/7	46°16′	72°37′
Port-Saint-Servan	UNP/LNO	QC	Côte-Nord-du-Golfe-Saint-Laurent	12 O/8	51°19′	58°02′
Port Sandfield	UNP/LNO	ON	Muskoka	31 E/4	45°07′	79°37′
Port Saunders	TOWN/VIL2	NF		12 I/11	50°39′	57°18′
Port Saxon	UNP/LNO	NS	Shelburne	20 P/11	43°35′	65°26′
Port Severn	UNP/LNO	ON	Simcoe	31 D/14	44°48′	79°43′
Port Shoreham	UNP/LNO	NS	Guysborough	11 F/6	45°25′	61°25′
Port Simpson - see-voir - Lax Kw'alaams	UNP/LNO	BC		103 J/9	54°33′	130°26′
Port Simpson 1 - see-voir - Lax K'wa laams 1	IR/RI	BC		103 J/9	54°34′	130°26′

NAME NOM	ENTITY ENTITÉ	LOC 1 LIEU 1	LOC 2 LIEU 2	MAP CARTE	POSITION LAT	POSITION LONG
Portsmouth	UNP/LNO	ON	Frontenac	31 C/2	44°13′	76°31′
Port Stanley	VILG/VILG	ON	Elgin	40 I/11	42°40′	81°13′
Port Stanton	UNP/LNO	ON	Simcoe	31 D/14	44°48′	79°25′
Port Sydney	UNP/LNO	ON	Muskoka	31 E/3	45°13′	79°17′
Port Talbot	UNP/LNO	ON	Elgin	40 I/11	42°39′	81°21′
Portugal Cove	UNP/LNO	NF		1 N/10	47°38′	52°51′
Portugal Cove Brook	RIV/CDE	NF		1 K/11	46°43′	53°16′
Portugal Cove-St. Philip's	TOWN/VIL2	NF		1 N/10	47°38′	52°50′
Portugal Cove-St. Phillips-Hogan's Pond - see-voir - Portugal Cove-St. Philip's	TOWN/VIL2	NF		1 N/10	47°38′	52°50′
Portugal Cove South	VILG/VILG	NF		1 K/11	46°42′	53°16′
Portuguese Cove	UNP/LNO	NS	Halifax	11 D/12	44°31′	63°32′
Port Union	TOWN/VIL2	NF		2 C/6	48°30′	53°05′
Port Union	UNP/LNO	ON	Ontario	30 M/14	43°46′	79°08′
Port View Beach	UNP/LNO	ON	Ontario	31 D/2	44°07′	78°55′
Port Wade	UNP/LNO	NS	Annapolis	21 A/12	44°41′	65°43′
Port Wallace	UNP/LNO	NS	Halifax	11 D/12	44°42′	63°33′
Port Washington	UNP/LNO	BC	Cowichan	92 B/14	48°49′	123°19′
Port Weller	UNP/LNO	ON	Lincoln	30 M/3	43°13′	79°14′
Port Weller East	UNP/LNO	ON	Lincoln	30 M/5	43°14′	79°13′
Port Whitby	UNP/LNO	ON	Ontario	30 M/15	43°51′	78°56′
Port Williams	VILG/VILG	NS	Kings	21 H/1	45°06′	64°25′
Poser	UNP/LNO	BC	Cariboo	93 H/8	53°26′	120°25′
Poshkokagan Lake	LAKE/LAC	ON	Thunder Bay	52 H/6	49°16′	89°18′
Poshkokagan River	RIV/CDE	ON	Thunder Bay	52 H/11	49°32′	89°02′
Postans	UNP/LNO	ON	Thunder Bay	52 B/9	48°40′	90°22′
Poste, Baie du	BAY/BAIE	QC	Jamésie	32 I/5	50°19′	73°51′
Poste-Canton-Blais	UNP/LNO	QC	La Matapédia	22 B/11	48°34′	67°11′
Poste-de-Chibougamau	UNP/LNO	QC	Jamésie	32 G/16	49°52′	74°17′
Poste-de-la-Baleine	VILG/VILG	QC	Jamésie	33 N/5	55°15′	77°45′
Poste-des-Villeneuve	UNP/LNO	QC	Le Fjord-du-Saguenay	22 D/7	48°21′	70°44′
Poste-de-Yale	UNP/LNO	QC	Maskinongé	31 I/6	46°19′	73°08′
Poste, Rivière du	RIV/CDE	QC	Matawinie	31 I/13	46°52′	73°54′
Poste-Saint-Martin	UNP/LNO	QC	Le Fjord-du-Saguenay	22 D/7	48°26′	70°57′
Postill	UNP/LNO	BC	Osoyoos Division Yale	82 E/14	49°58′	119°23′
Postill Lake	LAKE/LAC	BC	Osoyoos Division Yale	82 E/14	49°59′	119°12′
Post River	RIV/CDE	NT	Keewatin	46 B	64°07′	83°10′
Postville	VILG/VILG	NF		13 J/13	54°54′	59°47′
Potagannissing Bay	BAY/BAIE	ON	Algoma	41 J/4	46°04′	83°55′
Potato Lake	LAKE/LAC	SK	54-1-W2	63 E/9	53°42′	102°07′
Potato Point 3	IR/RI	BC	Range 1 Coast	92 K/15	50°56′	124°52′
Potato River 156A	IR/RI	SK	Range 1 Coast	73 P/3	55°01′	105°15′
Pothier Lake	LAKE/LAC	MB	62,63-25-W	63 K/6	54°25′	101°09′
Pothole Creek	RIV/CDE	BC	Kamloops Division Yale	92 H/15	49°58′	120°33′
Pottageville	UNP/LNO	ON	York	30 M/13	43°59′	79°37′
Potter	UNP/LNO	ON	Cochrane	42 A/15	48°52′	80°51′
Potter	UNP/LNO	BC	Lillooet	92 P/11	51°31′	121°11′
Potter Island	ISL/ÎLE	NT	Franklin	25 I	62°07′	65°55′
Pottersburg	UNP/LNO	ON	Middlesex	40 I/14	43°00′	81°11′
Potters Landing	UNP/LNO	ON	Muskoka	31 D/13	44°59′	79°49′
Pottles Bay	BAY/BAIE	NF		13 I/5	54°29′	57°30′
Potton	VILG/VILG	QC	Memphrémagog	31 H/1	45°05′	72°22′
Potton Springs	UNP/LNO	QC	Memphrémagog	31 H/1	45°09′	72°22′
Potts Lake	LAKE/LAC	AB	123,124-3-W4	74 M/9	59°45′	110°28′
Pottsville	UNP/LNO	ON	Cochrane	42 A/6	48°30′	81°11′
Potvin Island	ISL/ÎLE	ON	Sudbury	41 I/2	46°02′	80°45′
Pouce Coupe	VILG/VILG	BC	Peace River	93 P/9	55°43′	120°08′
Pouce Coupé River	RIV/CDE	AB/BC		84 D/4	56°08′	119°53′
Pouce Coupé River	RIV/CDE	BC	Peace River	93 P/16	55°53′	120°00′
Pouch Cove	TOWN/VIL2	NF		1 N/10	47°45′	52°47′
Pouch Cove	UNP/LNO	NF		1 N/15	47°46′	52°46′
Pouch Cove	BAY/BAIE	NF		1 N/15	47°46′	52°45′
Poudrière, La	UNP/LNO	QC	Le Val-Saint-François	21 E/12	45°35′	71°59′
Poulamon	UNP/LNO	NS	Richmond	11 F/11	45°35′	61°01′
Poularies	VILG/VILG	QC	Abitibi-Ouest	32 D/10	48°40′	78°59′
Poulin-De Courval, Lac	LAKE/LAC	QC	Le Fjord-du-Saguenay	22 D/16	48°52′	70°27′
Pouliot	UNP/LNO	QC	Les Basques	22 C/3	48°04′	69°13′
Poulter, Lac	LAKE/LAC	QC	La Vallée-de-la-Gatineau	31 N/2	47°06′	76°44′
Pouncet Island	ISL/ÎLE	NT	Franklin	57 F	70°33′	92°03′
Pound Cove	UNP/LNO	NF		2 F/4	49°10′	53°33′
Pound Cove	UNP/LNO	NF		12 H/15	49°47′	56°38′
*Poundmaker	UNP/LNO	SK	8-44-21-W3	73 C/14	52°46′	109°00′
Poundmaker 114	IR/RI	SK		73 C/15	52°51′	108°56′
Poupore	UNP/LNO	QC	Les Collines-de-l'Outaouais	31 G/12	45°42′	75°32′
Poupore	UNP/LNO	BC	Kootenay	82 F/4	49°13′	117°41′
Pouterel, Lac	LAKE/LAC	QC	Caniapiscau	23 G/12	53°32′	67°35′

NAME NOM	ENTITY ENTITÉ	LOC 1 LIEU 1	LOC 2 LIEU 2	MAP CARTE	POSITION LAT	LONG
Poutrincourt, Lac	LAKE/LAC	QC	Le Domaine-du-Roy	32 G/1	49°11′	74°07′
Povungnituk Bay	BAY/BAIE	NT	Keewatin	34 N	59°52′	77°35′
Powassan	TOWN/VIL2	ON	Parry Sound	31 L/3	46°05′	79°22′
Powder Hill Pond	LAKE/LAC	NF		2 F/4	49°11′	53°40′
Powderhorn Lake	LAKE/LAC	NF		12 H/1	49°06′	56°07′
Powder Lake	LAKE/LAC	NT	Mackenzie	75 F	61°05′	109°15′
Powell	UNP/LNO	MB	36-44-28-W	63 C/14	52°50′	101°24′
Powell Inlet	BAY/BAIE	NT	Franklin	48 F	74°35′	85°28′
Powell Lake	LAKE/LAC	BC	New Westminster	92 K/1	50°05′	124°25′
Powell River	MUN1/AZM1	BC	New Westminster	92 F/15	50°00′	124°30′
Powell River	MUN1/AZM1	BC	New Westminster	92 F/15	49°51′	124°32′
Powell River	RIV/CDE	BC	New Westminster	92 F/15	49°52′	124°34′
Powells Corners	UNP/LNO	ON	Norfolk	40 I/16	42°49′	80°29′
Power Glen	UNP/LNO	ON	Lincoln	30 M/3	43°07′	79°16′
Powers Addition	UNP/LNO	BC	Kamloops Division Yale	92 I/9	50°41′	120°21′
Powerscourt	UNP/LNO	QC	Le Haut-Saint-Laurent	31 G/1	45°00′	74°09′
Powers Creek	UNP/LNO	NB	Madawaska	21 O/4	47°05′	67°49′
Powers Creek	RIV/CDE	BC	Osoyoos Division Yale	82 E/13	49°49′	119°37′
Powerview	VILG/VILG	MB	18-10-E	62 I/9	50°34′	96°12′
Powles Corners	UNP/LNO	ON	Victoria	31 D/7	44°29′	78°45′
Powles Head	CAPE/CAP	NF		1 K/11	46°41′	53°24′
Powm Beach	HAM/HAM	SK	14-53-19-W3	73 F/10	53°34′	108°42′
Pownal	UNP/LNO	PE	Queens	11 L/2	46°12′	62°59′
Pownal Bay	BAY/BAIE	PE	Queens	11 L/2	46°10′	62°58′
Poyam 9	IR/RI	BC	New Westminster	92 G/14	49°59′	123°19′
Poyser	UNP/LNO	SK	27-40-23-W3	73 C/6	52°28′	109°13′
Prairie Bee Lake	LAKE/LAC	ON	Sudbury	41 O/13	47°54′	83°54′
Prairie Creek	RIV/CDE	AB	39-7-W5	83 B/7	52°20′	114°55′
Prairie Creek	RIV/CDE	NT	Mackenzie	95 F	61°15′	124°27′
Prairiedale No. 321	MUN2/AZM2	SK		72 N/11	51°45′	109°30′
Prairie Echo	UNP/LNO	AB	22-76-16-W5	83 N/9	55°36′	116°23′
Prairie Grove	UNP/LNO	MB	3-10-4-W	62 H/15	49°48′	96°58′
Prairie Heights	UNP/LNO	SK		72 I/5	50°23′	105°34′
Prairie, La	UNP/LNO	QC	Sept-Rivières	22 J/1	50°06′	66°23′
Prairie, La	UNP/LNO	QC	La Côte-de-Beaupré	21 M/2	47°07′	70°39′
Prairie No. 408	MUN2/AZM2	SK		73 C/9	52°35′	108°15′
Prairie River	HAM/HAM	SK	8-45-7-W2	63 D/15	52°52′	102°59′
Prairie Rose No. 309	MUN2/AZM2	SK		72 P/10	51°45′	104°45′
Prairie Siding	UNP/LNO	ON	Kent	40 J/8	42°21′	82°19′
Prairies, Lac des	LAKE/LAC	QC	Le Fjord-du-Saguenay	22 L/9	50°35′	70°17′
Prairies, Lake of the	LAKE/LAC	MB/SK		62 N/3	51°08′	101°26′
Prairies, Les	UNP/LNO	QC	Minganie	12 P/12	51°42′	57°48′
Prairies, Les	UNP/LNO	QC	Charlevoix	21 M/7	47°21′	70°32′
Prairies, Les	UNP/LNO	QC	Beauce-Sartigan	21 L/2	46°04′	70°54′
Prairies, Parc national des - also-aussi - Grasslands National Park	PARK/PARC	SK		72 G/3	49°07′	107°26′
Prairies, Rivière des	RIV/CDE	QC	Les Moulins	31 H/11	45°43′	73°29′
Prairie Valley	UNP/LNO	BC	Osoyoos Division Yale	82 E/12	49°35′	119°42′
Prairie View	UNP/LNO	SK	6-18-11-W3	72 J/11	50°31′	107°20′
Praslin, Lac	LAKE/LAC	QC	Manicouagan	22 K/4	50°02′	69°49′
Pratt	UNP/LNO	MB	4-10-11-W	62 G/15	49°48′	98°55′
Pratt	UNP/LNO	BC	New Westminster	92 G/2	49°06′	122°43′
Pratt Guyot	SEAU/SMER	—		5.03	56°10′	142°30′
Pratt, Mount	MTN/MNT	BC	Range 1 Coast	92 K/11	50°40′	125°22′
Pratts Camp	UNP/LNO	NB	Northumberland	21 J/15	46°57′	66°36′
Prawda	UNP/LNO	MB	7-8-13-E	52 E/12	49°39′	95°48′
Prayer River	UNP/LNO	MB	80-20-W	63 N/16	55°55′	100°26′
Preble Island	ISL/ÎLE	NT	Mackenzie	85 H	61°39′	112°28′
Precious Corners	UNP/LNO	ON	Northumberland	31 D/1	44°01′	78°12′
Pré-d'en-Haut	UNP/LNO	NB	Westmorland	21 H/15	45°58′	64°38′
Preeceville	TOWN/VIL2	SK	32-34-5-W2	62 M/15	51°57′	102°40′
Preeceville No. 334	MUN2/AZM2	SK		63 D/2	52°05′	102°40′
Préfontaine	UNP/LNO	QC	Les Laurentides	31 J/1	46°02′	74°15′
Prefontaine, Cape	CAPE/CAP	NT	Keewatin	45 J	63°00′	82°15′
Preissac	VILG/VILG	QC	Abitibi	32 D/8	48°24′	78°22′
Preissac, Lac	LAKE/LAC	QC	Rouyn-Noranda	32 D/8	48°20′	78°20′
Prelate	VILG/VILG	SK	9-22-25-W3	72 K/14	50°51′	109°24′
Prelude Lake	LAKE/LAC	NT	Mackenzie	85 I	62°34′	113°55′
Premier	UNP/LNO	BC	Cassiar	104 B/1	56°03′	130°01′
Premier Lake	UNP/LNO	BC	Kootenay	82 G/13	49°57′	115°39′
Premier Lake	LAKE/LAC	SK		74 O/16	59°53′	106°05′

Premier-Puits-de-Pétrole-de-l'Ouest-Canadien, Lieu
  historique national du - also-aussi - First Oil Well
  in Western Canada National Historic Site
	PARK/PARC	AB		82 H/4	49°04′	113°59′

Prendergast	UNP/LNO	SK	59-14-W3	73 K/1	54°06′	108°04′
Preneveau	UNP/LNO	ON	Peterborough	31 C/5	44°26′	77°48′
Prentiss	UNP/LNO	AB	24-39-26-W4	83 A/5	52°22′	113°38′
Pré-Ste-Marie	UNP/LNO	SK	42-12-W2	63 D/12	52°37′	103°40′

NAME NOM	ENTITY ENTITÉ	LOC 1 LIEU 1	LOC 2 LIEU 2	MAP CARTE	POSITION LAT	LONG
Presbytère-St. Andrew's, Lieu historique national du - also-aussi - St. Andrew's Rectory National Historic Site	PARK/PARC	MB		62 I/2	50°04′	96°59′
Prescott	TOWN/VIL2	ON	Grenville	31 B/12	44°43′	75°31′
Prescott	GEOG/GÉOG	ON		31 G/10	45°30′	74°45′
Prescott and Russell, United Counties of	MUN1/AZM1	ON	Russell	31 G/6	45°25′	75°15′
Prescott Island	ISL/ÎLE	BC	Range 5 Coast	103 J/2	54°06′	130°36′
Prescott Island	ISL/ÎLE	NT	Franklin	68 D	73°03′	96°50′
Prespatou	UNP/LNO	BC	Peace River	94 A/14	56°56′	121°03′
Presque	UNP/LNO	NF		1 M/8	47°25′	54°30′
Presqu'ile Bay	BAY/BAIE	ON	Northumberland	31 C/4	44°01′	77°42′
Presqu'île, La	UNP/LNO	QC	Les Maskoutains	31 H/10	45°31′	72°57′
Presqu'île Point	UNP/LNO	ON	Northumberland	30 N/13	44°00′	77°41′
Press	UNP/LNO	QC	Vallée-de-l'Or	32 C/2	48°15′	76°44′
Press Lake	LAKE/LAC	ON	Kenora	52 G/14	49°47′	91°28′
Pressure Point	CAPE/CAP	NT	Franklin	58 C	73°59′	95°18′
Prestfoss	UNP/LNO	SK	10-47-21-W2	73 H/2	53°02′	104°58′
Preston	UNP/LNO	NS	Halifax	11 D/11	44°43′	63°26′
Preston	UNP/LNO	ON	Waterloo	40 P/8	43°23′	80°21′
Preston East	UNP/LNO	ON	Cochrane	42 A/6	48°27′	81°14′
Preston Lake	UNP/LNO	ON	York	30 M/14	43°59′	79°23′
Preston Lake	LAKE/LAC	SK		74 F/6	57°25′	109°08′
Prestonvale	UNP/LNO	ON	Lanark	31 F/1	45°01′	76°17′
Prestville	UNP/LNO	AB	7-78-4-W6	83 M/10	55°44′	118°37′
Pretty Girl Lake	LAKE/LAC	BC	Clayoquot	92 E/9	49°30′	126°12′
Pretty River	RIV/CDE	ON	Simcoe	41 A/9	44°30′	80°13′
Pretty Valley	UNP/LNO	MB	34,35-27-W	62 N/14	51°58′	101°15′
Prével	UNP/LNO	QC	Pabok	22 A/9	48°41′	64°15′
Prévert, Lac	LAKE/LAC	QC	Manicouagan	22 G/5	49°27′	67°33′
Prevo	UNP/LNO	AB	1-39-1-W5	83 B/8	52°20′	114°01′
Prévost	VILG/VILG	QC	La Rivière-du-Nord	31 G/16	45°52′	74°05′
Prévost-Gilbert, Rivière	RIV/CDE	QC	L'Amiante	21 L/2	46°08′	70°56′
Prevost Island	ISL/ÎLE	BC	Cowichan	92 B/14	48°50′	123°23′
Prevost River	RIV/CDE	YT		105 J/11	62°36′	131°10′
Priam Lake	LAKE/LAC	ON	Kenora	52 F/6	49°21′	93°20′
Price	TOWN/VIL2	QC	La Mitis	22 C/9	48°36′	68°07′
Price	UNP/LNO	NB	Albert	21 I/2	46°01′	65°00′
Price	UNP/LNO	ON	Algoma	42 C/16	48°45′	84°12′
Price Island	ISL/ÎLE	BC	Range 3 Coast	103 A/7	52°24′	128°42′
Price Road	UNP/LNO	NB	Victoria	21 O/4	47°01′	67°41′
Prices Corner	UNP/LNO	ON	Simcoe	31 D/12	44°38′	79°31′
Prices Corner	UNP/LNO	ON	Dufferin	40 P/16	43°49′	80°14′
Price Settlement	UNP/LNO	NB	Northumberland	21 P/6	47°19′	65°06′
Priceville	UNP/LNO	NB	Northumberland	21 J/9	46°31′	66°17′
Priceville	UNP/LNO	ON	Grey	41 A/2	44°12′	80°38′
Pricket Point	CAPE/CAP	NT	Keewatin	35 N	63°27′	76°32′
Priddis	UNP/LNO	AB	22-22-3-W5	82 J/16	50°53′	114°20′
Prides Landing	UNP/LNO	NB	Sunbury	21 G/10	45°40′	66°35′
Priestley, Mount	MTN/MNT	BC	Cassiar	103 P/2	55°14′	128°52′
Priest Pond	UNP/LNO	PE	Kings	11 L/8	46°29′	62°11′
Priest's Valley 6	IR/RI	BC	Osoyoos Division Yale	82 L/3	50°15′	119°20′
Priestville	UNP/LNO	NS	Pictou	11 E/10	45°34′	62°38′
Primate	VILG/VILG	SK	17-38-27-W3	73 C/5	52°16′	109°49′
Prime	UNP/LNO	NB	Madawaska	21 N/8	47°17′	68°05′
Primeau Lake	LAKE/LAC	SK		73 O/14	55°53′	107°12′
Primeau Lake 192F	IR/RI	SK	79,80-8,9-W3	73 O/14	55°55′	107°15′
Prime Brook	UNP/LNO	NS	Cape Breton	11 K/1	46°07′	60°12′
Primore, La	UNP/LNO	QC	Matane	22 B/15	48°58′	66°42′
Prim, Point	CAPE/CAP	PE	Queens	11 L/3	46°03′	63°02′
Prim, Point	CAPE/CAP	NS	Digby	21 A/12	44°41′	65°47′
Primrose	UNP/LNO	PE	Kings	11 L/7	46°18′	62°33′
Primrose	UNP/LNO	NB	Saint John	21 H/5	45°25′	65°46′
Primrose	UNP/LNO	ON	Dufferin	41 A/1	44°06′	80°08′
Primrose Island	ISL/ÎLE	NT	Keewatin	55 N	63°53′	93°00′
Primrose Lake	LAKE/LAC	SK/AB		73 K/13	54°55′	109°44′
Primrose River	RIV/CDE	YT/BC		115 A/8	60°28′	136°06′
Prince	HAM/HAM	SK	14-46-17-W3	73 C/16	52°58′	108°23′
Prince	MUN2/AZM2	ON	Algoma	41 K/10	46°35′	84°32′
Prince	GEOG/GÉOG	PE		21 I/9	46°45′	64°05′
Prince Albert	CITY/VIL1	SK		73 H/4	53°12′	105°46′
Prince Albert	UNP/LNO	NS	Annapolis	21 H/3	45°00′	65°03′
Prince Albert	UNP/LNO	ON	Ontario	31 D/2	44°05′	78°58′
Prince Albert Hills	MTN/MNT	NT	Franklin	47 B	68°30′	84°45′
Prince Albert National Park - also-aussi - Prince Albert, Parc national de	PARK/PARC	SK		73 G/16	53°57′	106°22′
Prince Albert No. 461	MUN2/AZM2	SK		73 H/4	53°05′	105°40′
Prince Albert, Parc national de - also-aussi - Prince Albert National Park	PARK/PARC	SK		73 G/16	53°57′	106°22′
Prince Albert Peninsula	CAPE/CAP	NT	Franklin	88 B	72°30′	117°00′

NAME NOM	ENTITY ENTITÉ	LOC 1 LIEU 1	LOC 2 LIEU 2	MAP CARTE	POSITION LAT	LONG
Prince Albert Settlement	UNP/LNO	SK	47-1-W3	73 H/4	53°10′	105°52′
Prince Albert Sound	CHAN/CHEN	NT	Franklin	87 E/5	70°25′	115°00′
Prince Alfred Bay	BAY/BAIE	NT	Franklin	59 B	76°19′	93°22′
Prince Alfred, Cape	CAPE/CAP	NT	Franklin	98 F	74°20′	124°46′
Prince Charles Island	ISL/ÎLE	NT	Franklin	36 N	67°47′	76°12′
Princedale	UNP/LNO	NS	Annapolis	21 A/12	44°39′	65°31′
Prince-de-Galles, Cap du	CAPE/CAP	QC	Kativik	25 E/12	61°36′	71°31′
Prince Edward	MUN1/AZM1	ON	Prince Edward	31 C/3	44°00′	77°15′
Prince Edward	GEOG/GÉOG	ON		31 C/3	44°00′	77°15′
Prince Edward Bay	BAY/BAIE	ON	Prince Edward	30 N/15	43°57′	77°00′
Prince Edward Island - also-aussi - **Île-du-Prince-Édouard**	PROV/PROV	PE		MCR77	46°30′	63°00′
Prince Edward Island	ISL/ÎLE	PE		MCR77	46°30′	63°00′
Prince Edward Island National Park - also-aussi - Île-du-Prince-Édouard, Parc national de l′	PARK/PARC	PE	Queens	11 L/6	46°26′	63°12′
Prince Edward Point	CAPE/CAP	ON	Prince Edward	30 N/15	43°56′	76°52′
Prince George	CITY/VIL1	BC	Cariboo	93 G/15	53°55′	122°45′
Prince Gustaf Adolf Sea	SEA/MER	NT	Franklin	79 E	78°30′	107°00′
Prince Leboo Island 32	IR/RI	BC	Range 5 Coast	103 J/7	54°27′	130°58′
Prince Leopold Island	ISL/ÎLE	NT	Franklin	58 D	74°02′	90°05′
Prince of Wales	UNP/LNO	NB	Saint John	21 G/1	45°12′	66°16′
Prince of Wales, Cape	CAPE/CAP	NT	Franklin	25 E	61°37′	71°30′

Prince of Wales Fort National Historic Site
  - also-aussi - Fort-Prince-de-Galles, Lieu historique
  national du
	PARK/PARC	MB		54 L/16	58°48′	94°13′

Prince of Wales Icefield	GLAC/GLAC	NT	Franklin	39 F	78°15′	79°00′
Prince of Wales Island	ISL/ÎLE	NT	Franklin	68 A	72°40′	99°00′
Prince of Wales Mountains	MTN/MNT	NT	Franklin	39 F	78°33′	78°40′
Prince of Wales Reach	RIVF/EFLV	BC	New Westminster	92 G/13	49°54′	123°55′
Prince of Wales Strait	CHAN/CHEN	NT	Franklin	88 B	72°41′	118°25′

Prince of Wales Tower National Historic Site
  - also-aussi - Tour-Prince-de-Galles, Lieu historique
  national de la
	PARK/PARC	NS	Halifax	11 D/12	44°37′	63°34′

Prince Patrick Island	ISL/ÎLE	NT	Franklin	89 B	76°45′	119°30′
Princeport	UNP/LNO	NS	Colchester	11 E/6	45°17′	63°28′
Princeport Road	UNP/LNO	NS	Colchester	11 E/6	45°18′	63°26′
Prince Regent Inlet	BAY/BAIE	NT	Franklin	58 D	73°00′	90°30′
Prince Regent Valley	SEAU/SMER	—		5.17	72°30′	91°00′
Prince Rupert	CITY/VIL1	BC	Range 5 Coast	103 J/8	54°19′	130°19′
Princes Lodge	UNP/LNO	NS	Halifax	11 D/12	44°42′	63°40′
Princess	UNP/LNO	AB	11-20-12-W4	72 L/12	50°41′	111°34′
Princess Anne Manor	UNP/LNO	ON	York	30 M/12	43°41′	79°33′
Princess Harbour	UNP/LNO	MB	33-5-E	62 P/15	51°52′	96°52′
Princess Louisa Inlet	BAY/BAIE	BC	New Westminster	92 J/4	50°11′	123°48′
Princess Margaret	UNP/LNO	ON	York	30 M/12	43°40′	79°33′
Princess Margaret Range	MTN/MNT	NT	Franklin	59 H	79°41′	90°30′
Princess Marie Bay	BAY/BAIE	NT	Franklin	39 G	79°20′	76°00′
Princess Mary Lake	LAKE/LAC	NT	Keewatin	65 P	63°57′	97°35′
Princess Park	UNP/LNO	NB	Queens	21 G/16	45°57′	66°04′
Princess Royal Channel	CHAN/CHEN	BC	Range 4 Coast	103 A/15	53°10′	128°40′
Princess Royal Island	ISL/ÎLE	BC	Range 3 Coast	103 A/10	52°55′	128°50′
Princess Royal Island	ISL/ÎLE	NT	Franklin	59 B	76°56′	94°19′
Princess Royal Reach	RIVF/EFLV	BC	New Westminster	92 J/4	50°02′	123°52′
Princeton	TOWN/VIL2	BC	Yale Division Yale	92 H/7	49°28′	120°31′
Princeton	UNP/LNO	NF		2 C/5	48°25′	53°36′
Princeton	UNP/LNO	ON	Oxford	40 P/2	43°10′	80°32′
Princetown	GEOG/GÉOG	PE	Prince	11 L/12	46°33′	63°41′
Princeville	CITY/VIL1	QC	L′Érable	21 L/4	46°10′	71°53′
Princeville	VILG/VILG	QC	L′Érable	21 L/4	46°10′	71°53′
Princeville	UNP/LNO	NS	Inverness	11 F/14	45°46′	61°18′
Prince William	UNP/LNO	NB	York	21 G/14	45°55′	67°03′
Prince William	GEOG/GÉOG	NB	York	21 G/14	45°48′	67°08′
Prince William Station	UNP/LNO	NB	York	21 G/11	45°42′	67°07′
Principe Channel	CHAN/CHEN	BC	Range 4 Coast	103 H/5	53°29′	129°59′
Pringle	UNP/LNO	ON	Thunder Bay	42 D/9	48°41′	86°03′
Prinham	UNP/LNO	SK	31-45-16-W3	73 C/16	52°56′	108°22′
Priory Park	UNP/LNO	ON	Wellington	40 P/9	43°31′	80°15′
Prise, Lac la	LAKE/LAC	NT	Mackenzie	75 N	63°04′	108°44′
Pritchard	UNP/LNO	BC	Kamloops Division Yale	82 L/12	50°41′	119°49′
Pritchetts	UNP/LNO	NF		2 D/16	48°50′	54°17′
Pritzler Harbour	BAY/BAIE	NT	Franklin	25 J	62°07′	67°21′
Privert, Lac	LAKE/LAC	QC	Kativik	24 B/8	56°15′	66°16′
Procter	UNP/LNO	BC	Kootenay	82 F/10	49°37′	116°57′
Profits Corner	UNP/LNO	PE	Prince	21 I/16	46°54′	64°05′
Profitts Point	CAPE/CAP	PE	Prince	11 L/12	46°34′	63°40′
Progress	UNP/LNO	BC	Peace River	93 P/15	55°47′	120°43′
Progress No. 351	MUN2/AZM2	SK		73 C/3	52°00′	109°15′
Progreston	UNP/LNO	ON	Wentworth	30 M/5	43°24′	79°58′

NAME NOM	ENTITY ENTITÉ	LOC 1 LIEU 1	LOC 2 LIEU 2	MAP CARTE	POSITION LAT	POSITION LONG
Projet-Laplante	UNP/LNO	QC	Le Haut-Saint-Laurent	31 H/4	45°01'	73°50'
Promise Island	ISL/ÎLE	NT	Keewatin	55 O	63°22'	90°32'
Promontory	UNP/LNO	BC	New Westminster	92 H/4	49°06'	121°56'
Prongua	UNP/LNO	SK	33-43-18-W3	73 C/10	52°44'	108°33'
Prophet Beach	UNP/LNO	ON	Ontario	31 D/11	44°32'	79°12'
Prophet River	UNP/LNO	BC	Peace River	94 J/2	58°05'	122°42'
Prophet River	RIV/CDE	BC	Peace River	94 J/15	58°46'	122°44'
Prophet River 4	IR/RI	BC	Peace River	94 J/2	58°05'	122°42'
Prospect	UNP/LNO	NS	Halifax	11 D/5	44°28'	63°47'
Prospect	UNP/LNO	NS	Kings	21 H/2	45°02'	64°37'
Prospect	UNP/LNO	ON	Lanark	31 G/4	45°06'	75°58'
Prospect	UNP/LNO	ON	Ontario	31 D/2	44°02'	78°59'
Prospect Bay	BAY/BAIE	NS	Halifax	11 D/12	44°31'	63°47'
Prospect Creek	RIV/CDE	BC	Yale Division Yale	92 I/3	50°01'	121°04'
Prospect Hill	UNP/LNO	ON	Perth	40 P/3	43°13'	81°14'
Prospect Lake	UNP/LNO	BC	Lake	92 B/11	48°31'	123°26'
Prospector	UNP/LNO	MB	27-57-26-W	63 F/14	53°58'	101°15'
Prospector Mountain	MTN/MNT	YT		115 I/5	62°27'	137°48'
Prospect Valley	UNP/LNO	AB	45-2,3-W4	73 D/16	52°51'	110°17'
Prosperity	UNP/LNO	ON	Huron	40 P/13	43°50'	81°33'
Prosperous Lake	LAKE/LAC	NT	Mackenzie	85 J/9	62°36'	114°12'
Prosser Brook	UNP/LNO	NB	Albert	21 H/15	45°50'	64°57'
Proton	MUN2/AZM2	ON	Grey	41 A/1	44°06'	80°30'
Proton Station	UNP/LNO	ON	Grey	41 A/1	44°12'	80°29'
Proulx	UNP/LNO	ON	Prescott	31 G/7	45°27'	74°46'
Proulx Lake	LAKE/LAC	ON	Nipissing	31 E/16	45°46'	78°24'
Proulx Lake	LAKE/LAC	MB	33-13-W	62 O/14	51°50'	99°14'
Proulxville	UNP/LNO	QC	Mékinac	31 I/10	46°40'	72°30'
Provancher	UNP/LNO	QC	Avignon	22 B/1	48°13'	66°26'
Providence Bay	UNP/LNO	ON	Manitoulin	41 G/9	45°40'	82°16'
Providence, Cape	CAPE/CAP	NT	Franklin	88 E	74°26'	112°17'
Providence, Lake	LAKE/LAC	NT	Mackenzie	76 D	64°42'	111°55'
Providence Point	CAPE/CAP	ON	Manitoulin	41 G/9	45°39'	82°16'
Province Hill	UNP/LNO	QC	Memphrémagog	31 H/1	45°01'	72°21'
Province House, Lieu historique national - also-aussi - Province House National Historic Site	PARK/PARC	PE	Queens	11 L/3	46°14'	63°08'
Province House National Historic Site - also-aussi - Province House, Lieu historique national	PARK/PARC	PE	Queens	11 L/3	46°14'	63°08'
Province, Île de la	ISL/ÎLE	QC	Memphrémagog	31 H/1	45°01'	72°14'
Provost	TOWN/VIL2	AB	17-39-2-W4	73 D/8	52°21'	110°16'
Provost No. 52, Municipal District of	MUN1/AZM1	AB	39-5-W4	73 D/7	52°24'	110°38'
Prowseton	UNP/LNO	NF		1 M/9	47°41'	54°19'
Prud'homme	VILG/VILG	SK	12-39-28-W2	73 A/5	52°20'	105°54'
Prusse, La	UNP/LNO	QC	Montmagny	21 L/9	46°39'	70°03'
Pryce Channel	CHAN/CHEN	BC	Range 1 Coast	92 K/7	50°18'	124°50'
Pryors Beach	UNP/LNO	SK	28,33-25-24-W2	72 P/3	51°10'	105°18'
Psacelay 77	IR/RI	BC	Range 5 Coast	103 I/6	54°17'	129°11'
Ptarmigan Fiord	BAY/BAIE	NT	Franklin	26 B	64°47'	66°07'
Ptarmigan Lake	LAKE/LAC	NT	Mackenzie	75 O	63°36'	107°26'
Ptarmigan Mountain	MTN/MNT	YT		115 I/9	62°43'	136°08'
P'tit-Brick, Le	UNP/LNO	QC	Les Îles-de-la-Madeleine	11 N/12	47°34'	61°39'
P'tit-Havre, Le	UNP/LNO	QC	Les Îles-de-la-Madeleine	11 N/5	47°29'	61°46'
Ptolemy, Mount	MTN/MNT	AB/BC		82 G/10	49°33'	114°37'
Public Landing	UNP/LNO	NB	Kings	21 G/8	45°25'	66°12'
Pubnico	UNP/LNO	NS	Yarmouth	20 P/12	43°42'	65°47'
Pubnico Harbour	BAY/BAIE	NS	Yarmouth	20 P/12	43°38'	65°47'
Pubnico Point	CAPE/CAP	NS	Yarmouth	20 P/12	43°36'	65°48'
Puce	UNP/LNO	ON	Essex	40 J/7	42°18'	82°47'
Puckahn	UNP/LNO	SK		73 H/4	53°02'	105°32'
Puckatholetchin 11	IR/RI	BC	Yale Division Yale	92 H/6	49°27'	121°26'
Puddle Pond	LAKE/LAC	NF		12 A/5	48°28'	57°35'
Pudla Inlet	BAY/BAIE	NT	Franklin	36 C	64°20'	76°15'
Puffer	UNP/LNO	AB	22-39-10-W4	73 D/6	52°22'	111°22'
Pugh Island	ISL/ÎLE	NT	Franklin	25 N/1	63°14'	68°06'
Pughs Crossing	UNP/LNO	NB	York	21 J/2	46°03'	66°51'
Pugwash	VILG/VILG	NS	Cumberland	11 E/13	45°51'	63°40'
Pugwash Harbour	BAY/BAIE	NS	Cumberland	11 E/13	45°52'	63°41'
Pugwash Junction	UNP/LNO	NS	Cumberland	11 E/13	45°48'	63°38'
Pugwash Point	UNP/LNO	NS	Cumberland	11 E/13	45°52'	63°40'
Pugwash River	UNP/LNO	NS	Cumberland	11 E/13	45°48'	63°42'
Pugwash River	RIV/CDE	NS	Cumberland	11 E/13	45°51'	63°40'
Puisseaux, Lac	LAKE/LAC	QC	Jamésie	23 E/11	53°35'	71°05'
Puits-d'Huile, Le	UNP/LNO	QC	Pabok	22 A/10	48°40'	64°48'
Pukaist Creek	RIV/CDE	BC	Kamloops Division Yale	92 I/11	50°30'	121°17'
Pukaskwa Depot	UNP/LNO	ON	Thunder Bay	42 C/4	48°02'	85°55'
Pukaskwa National Park - also-aussi - Pukaskwa, Parc national	PARK/PARC	ON	Thunder Bay	42 C/5	48°15'	85°55'
Pukaskwa, Parc national - also-aussi - Pukaskwa National Park	PARK/PARC	ON	Thunder Bay	42 C/5	48°15'	85°55'

NAME / NOM	ENTITY / ENTITÉ	LOC 1 / LIEU 1	LOC 2 / LIEU 2	MAP / CARTE	POSITION LAT	POSITION LONG
Pukaskwa River	RIV/CDE	ON	Thunder Bay	42 C/4	48°00′	85°53′
Pukatawagan	UNP/LNO	MB		63 N/14	55°46′	101°12′
Pukatawagan	UNP/LNO	MB		63 N/11	55°45′	101°19′
Pukatawagan 198	IR/RI	MB		63 N/11	55°45′	101°17′
Pukatawagan Lake	LAKE/LAC	MB		63 N/14	55°45′	101°19′
Pukeashun Mountain	MTN/MNT	BC	Kamloops Division Yale	82 M/3	51°12′	119°14′
Pulberry	UNP/LNO	MB		62 H/14	49°50′	97°07′
Pulcah 15	IR/RI	BC	Rupert	92 L/12	50°32′	127°59′
Pullen	UNP/LNO	ON	Cochrane	42 H/4	49°12′	81°33′
Pullen Island	ISL/ÎLE	NT	Mackenzie	107 C	69°46′	134°23′
Pullen Pingos	SEAU/SMER	—		7651	70°30′	135°30′
Pullen Strait	CHAN/CHEN	NT	Franklin	58 G	75°30′	96°00′
Pulp River	UNP/LNO	MB	36-32-21-W	62 N/16	51°48′	100°18′
Pulteney	UNP/LNO	AB	15-13-27-W4	82 I/4	50°05′	113°36′
Pumbly Cove	UNP/LNO	NF		12 H/10	49°44′	56°41′
Punchaw	UNP/LNO	BC	Cariboo	93 G/6	53°26′	123°11′
Pungak Lake	LAKE/LAC	NT	Keewatin	56 C	64°13′	92°39′
Punkeydoodles Corners	UNP/LNO	ON	Waterloo	40 P/7	43°21′	80°44′
Punngavialuk	UNP/LNO	QC	Kativik	34 C/2	56°10′	76°35′
Punngaviapik	UNP/LNO	QC	Kativik	34 C/2	56°10′	76°39′
Punnichy	VILG/VILG	SK	2-28-17-W2	72 P/8	51°23′	104°18′
Puntledge	UNP/LNO	BC	Comox	92 F/11	49°40′	125°03′
Puntledge River	RIV/CDE	BC	Comox	92 F/10	49°42′	125°00′
Puntzi Lake	LAKE/LAC	BC	Range 3 Coast	93 C/1	52°12′	124°00′
Puntzi Lake 2	IR/RI	BC	Range 3 Coast	93 C/1	52°13′	124°04′
Purbeck's Cove	UNP/LNO	NF		12 H/10	49°45′	56°39′
Purbrook	UNP/LNO	ON	Muskoka	31 E/3	45°02′	79°09′
Purcell Bay	BAY/BAIE	NT	Franklin	69 B	76°20′	100°20′
Purcell Lake	LAKE/LAC	ON	Cochrane	42 N/11	51°33′	85°25′
Purcell Mountains	MTN/MNT	BC	Kootenay	82 K/2	50°00′	116°30′
Purcell Point	CAPE/CAP	BC	Range 1 Coast	92 K/15	50°48′	124°55′
Purcells Cove	UNP/LNO	NS	Halifax	11 D/12	44°37′	63°34′
Purcell's Harbour	UNP/LNO	NF		2 E/10	49°37′	54°42′
Purchase Bay	BAY/BAIE	NT	Franklin	88 G	75°35′	116°00′
Purden Lake	LAKE/LAC	BC	Cariboo	93 H/13	53°55′	121°55′
Purdy	UNP/LNO	ON	Hastings	31 F/5	45°20′	77°44′
Purdy Corners	UNP/LNO	ON	Northumberland	31 C/4	44°01′	77°54′
Purdys Corner	UNP/LNO	NB	Saint John	21 G/1	45°15′	66°07′
Purlbrook	UNP/LNO	NS	Antigonish	11 E/9	45°34′	62°02′
Purple Grove	UNP/LNO	ON	Bruce	41 A/4	44°05′	81°31′
Purple Hill	UNP/LNO	ON	Durham	31 D/2	44°04′	78°51′
Purple Hill	UNP/LNO	ON	Dufferin	40 P/16	43°55′	80°05′
Purple Springs	UNP/LNO	AB	18-10-14-W4	72 E/13	49°49′	111°54′
Purple Valley	UNP/LNO	ON	Bruce	41 A/14	44°50′	81°05′
Purpleville	UNP/LNO	ON	York	30 M/13	43°51′	79°35′
Pursuit Point	CAPE/CAP	NT	Franklin	37 C	69°20′	78°44′
Purtuniq	UNP/LNO	QC	Kativik	35 H/13	61°49′	73°57′
Purves	UNP/LNO	MB	15-2-10-W	62 G/2	49°08′	98°44′
Pusey	UNP/LNO	ON	Haliburton	31 E/1	45°03′	78°13′
Pushthrough	UNP/LNO	NF		11 P/9	47°39′	56°10′
Puskiakiwenin 122	IR/RI	AB	57-4-W4	73 E/16	53°57′	110°27′
Puskuta Lake	LAKE/LAC	ON	Algoma	42 B/13	48°52′	83°34′
Puskwakau River	RIV/CDE	SK	64-11-W2	63 L/12	54°33′	103°34′
Puskwaskau Lake	LAKE/LAC	AB	72-24-W5	83 N/4	55°15′	117°39′
Puskwaskau River	RIV/CDE	AB	12-75-2-W6	83 M/8	55°29′	118°10′
Puslinch	MUN2/AZM2	ON	Wellington	40 P/8	43°28′	80°10′
Puslinch	UNP/LNO	ON	Wellington	40 P/8	43°26′	80°05′
Puslinch Lake	LAKE/LAC	ON	Wellington	40 P/8	43°25′	80°16′
Pusticamica, Lac	LAKE/LAC	QC	Jamésie	32 F/8	49°21′	76°23′
Putahow Lake	LAKE/LAC	MB		64 N/15	59°54′	100°40′
Putahow River	RIV/CDE	MB/NT		64 N/16	59°52′	100°07′
Putkwa 14	IR/RI	BC	Kamloops Division Yale	92 I/6	50°15′	121°29′
Putnam	UNP/LNO	ON	Middlesex	40 I/15	43°00′	80°57′
Putnam Island	ISL/ÎLE	NT	Franklin	35 N	63°59′	77°32′
Puvirnituq	VILG/VILG	QC	Kativik	35 C/3	60°02′	77°17′
Puvirnituq, Lac de	LAKE/LAC	QC	Kativik	35 C/3	60°05′	77°07′
Puvirnituq, Monts de	MTN/MNT	QC	Kativik	35 G/6	61°22′	75°05′
Puvirnituq, Rivière de	RIV/CDE	QC	Kativik	35 C/3	60°03′	77°13′
Puyjalon, Lac	LAKE/LAC	QC	Minganie	12 L/11	50°30′	63°25′
Pye Lake	LAKE/LAC	BC	Sayward	92 K/5	50°17′	125°35′
Pym	UNP/LNO	SK	23-30-14-W3	72 O/12	51°35′	107°52′
Pym Point	CAPE/CAP	NT	Franklin	79 A	76°24′	104°28′
Pynns	UNP/LNO	NF		12 H/4	49°06′	57°33′
Pyramid	UNP/LNO	BC	Kamloops Division Yale	83 D/6	52°21′	119°11′
Pyroxene Mountain	MTN/MNT	YT		115 O/1	63°01′	138°21′
Pythonga, Lac	LAKE/LAC	QC	La Vallée-de-la-Gatineau	31 K/8	46°23′	76°26′

NAME NOM	ENTITY ENTITÉ	LOC 1 LIEU 1	LOC 2 LIEU 2	MAP CARTE	POSITION LAT	LONG
			Q			
Qairtuinaq	UNP/LNO	QC	Kativik	34 K/3	58°07′	77°24′
Qajakkuvik	UNP/LNO	QC	Kativik	24 N/13	59°53′	69°40′
Qalluviartuuq, Lac	LAKE/LAC	QC	Kativik	34 O/10	59°43′	74°50′
Qamanirjuaq Lake	LAKE/LAC	NT	Keewatin	55 L/13	62°57′	95°46′
Qarliik Sijjangit	UNP/LNO	QC	Kativik	24 N/12	59°36′	69°47′
Qarmait	UNP/LNO	QC	Kativik	24 N/12	59°38′	69°31′
Qattaujavinaaluit	UNP/LNO	QC	Kativik	35 G/11	61°32′	75°20′
Qattaujaviniit	UNP/LNO	QC	Kativik	35 F/8	61°24′	76°10′
Qijunniavik	UNP/LNO	QC	Jamésie	33 N/5	55°17′	77°42′
Qijuttavik	UNP/LNO	QC	Kativik	24 N/13	59°46′	69°34′
Qijuttaviup Inussutalinga	UNP/LNO	QC	Kativik	24 N/13	59°46′	69°34′
Qikirtajuaq Island	ISL/ÎLE	NT	Franklin	24 J/5	58°20′	67°36′
Qikirtaluup Kuunga, Rivière	RIV/CDE	QC	Kativik	34 K/3	58°01′	77°12′
Qikirtartuuq Lake	LAKE/LAC	NT	Franklin	87 D/10	69°36′	113°10′
Qilalugalik, Lac	LAKE/LAC	QC	Kativik	34 J/12	58°41′	75°59′
Qilalugarsiuviup, Chute	FALL/CHUT	QC	Kativik	33 N/15	55°58′	76°40′
Qimmitaarvik	UNP/LNO	QC	Kativik	35 F/9	61°34′	76°06′
Qingaaluk	UNP/LNO	QC	Kativik	34 C/2	56°10′	76°35′
Qirniraujaq, Pointe	CAPE/CAP	QC	Kativik	24 K/9	58°35′	68°01′
Quaal 3	IR/RI	BC	Range 4 Coast	103 H/11	53°39′	129°20′
Quaal 3A	IR/RI	BC	Range 4 Coast	103 H/11	53°38′	129°17′
Quaaout 1	IR/RI	BC	Kamloops Division Yale	82 L/13	50°53′	119°35′
Quabbin	UNP/LNO	ON	Leeds	31 B/5	44°28′	75°55′
Quaco Bay	BAY/BAIE	NB	Saint John	21 H/5	45°20′	65°32′
Quaco Head	CAPE/CAP	NB	Saint John	21 H/5	45°19′	65°32′
Quaco Road	UNP/LNO	NB	Saint John	21 H/5	45°23′	65°46′
Quadeville	UNP/LNO	ON	Renfrew	31 F/6	45°19′	77°23′
Quadra	UNP/LNO	MB	29-13-25-W	62 K/2	50°08′	100°51′
Quadra Island	ISL/ÎLE	BC	Sayward	92 K/3	50°12′	125°15′
Quaee 7	IR/RI	BC	Range 1 Coast	92 L/16	50°58′	126°11′
Quai-à-Mousse	UNP/LNO	QC	Rivière-du-Loup	22 C/3	48°01′	69°21′
Quai-de-la-Pipe	UNP/LNO	QC	Lac-Saint-Jean-Est	22 D/12	48°39′	71°50′
Quai-de-Rivière-Ouelle	UNP/LNO	QC	Kamouraska	21 M/8	47°29′	70°01′
Quai-de-Saint-Juste	UNP/LNO	QC	Témiscouata	21 N/10	47°38′	68°47′
Quai-des-Brown	UNP/LNO	QC	Manicouagan	22 C/15	48°56′	68°42′
Quai-des-Paroissiens	UNP/LNO	QC	Les Laurentides	31 J/2	46°00′	74°34′
Quai-Dupré, Le	UNP/LNO	QC	Mékinac	31 I/16	46°53′	72°22′
Quai-Franquelin	UNP/LNO	QC	Manicouagan	22 G/5	49°17′	67°55′
Quajon Fiord	BAY/BAIE	NT	Franklin	26 P	67°42′	65°10′
Quaker	UNP/LNO	ON	York	30 M/14	43°57′	79°24′
Quaker Brook	UNP/LNO	NB	Victoria	21 J/13	46°46′	67°38′
Quaker Hat	ISL/ÎLE	NF		13 I/11	54°44′	57°21′
Qualark 4	IR/RI	BC	Yale Division Yale	92 H/11	49°32′	121°25′
Qualcho Lake	LAKE/LAC	BC	Range 4 Coast	93 F/4	53°02′	125°52′
Qualicum Bay	UNP/LNO	BC	Newcastle	92 F/7	49°24′	124°38′
Qualicum Beach	TOWN/VIL2	BC	Newcastle	92 F/8	49°21′	124°26′
Qualicum	IR/RI	BC	Newcastle	92 F/7	49°24′	124°37′
Qualicum River	RIV/CDE	BC	Newcastle	92 F/7	49°24′	124°37′
Quamichan Lake	LAKE/LAC	BC	Comiaken	92 B/13	48°48′	123°40′
Quamichan Land District	GEOG/GÉOG	BC		92 B	48°46′	123°44′
Quanatulik	UNP/LNO	QC	Kativik	24 J/5	58°20′	67°40′
Quaniwsom 2	IR/RI	BC	Range 1 Coast	92 K/8	50°29′	124°24′
Quan-skum-ksin-mich-mich 4	IR/RI	BC	Cassiar	93 M/5	55°23′	127°39′
Quantock	UNP/LNO	SK	5-3-1-W3	72 G/1	49°11′	106°06′
Quantz Lake	LAKE/LAC	ON	Cochrane	42 N/3	51°10′	85°23′
Quantztown	UNP/LNO	ON	York	30 M/14	43°53′	79°18′
Qu'Appelle	TOWN/VIL2	SK	21-18-14-W2	62 L/12	50°33′	103°53′
Qu'Appelle River	RIV/CDE	MB/SK		62 K/6	50°27′	101°19′
Qu'Appelle Valley Dam	MISC/DIV	SK	23-4-3	72 J/16	50°59′	106°26′
Qu'Appelle Village	UNP/LNO	SK		72 I/7	50°25′	104°36′
Quaqtaq	VILG/VILG	QC	Kativik	25 F/4	61°02′	69°37′
Quarante-Six, Le	UNP/LNO	QC	La Matapédia	22 B/10	48°40′	66°39′
Quarindale	UNP/LNO	ON	Wellington	40 P/10	43°41′	80°45′
Quarman Point	CAPE/CAP	NT	Franklin	47 A	68°31′	81°33′
Quarries	UNP/LNO	NB	Queens	21 G/9	45°36′	66°04′
Quarries	UNP/LNO	ON	Carleton	31 G/5	45°27′	75°38′
Quarry	UNP/LNO	NF		12 H/2	49°03′	56°35′
Quarry St. Anns	UNP/LNO	NS	Victoria	11 K/7	46°15′	60°39′
Quarryville	UNP/LNO	NB	Northumberland	21 I/13	46°50′	65°47′
Quartcha 3	IR/RI	BC	Range 3 Coast	93 D/12	52°31′	127°50′
Quartier-De Quen	UNP/LNO	QC	Lac-Saint-Jean-Est	22 D/12	48°34′	71°38′
Quartier-Saint-Georges	UNP/LNO	QC	Lac-Saint-Jean-Est	22 D/12	48°34′	71°40′

NAME / NOM	ENTITY / ENTITÉ	LOC 1 / LIEU 1	LOC 2 / LIEU 2	MAP / CARTE	POSITION LAT	POSITION LONG
Quartier-Saint-Thomas	UNP/LNO	QC	Kamouraska	21 N/12	47°35′	69°39′
Quartzite Lake	LAKE/LAC	NT	Keewatin	55 L	62°22′	94°32′
Quartz Lake	LAKE/LAC	NT	Franklin	47 E/16	70°57′	80°42′
Quatam River	RIV/CDE	BC	Range 1 Coast	92 K/7	50°23′	124°56′
Quathiaski Cove	UNP/LNO	BC	Sayward	92 K/3	50°03′	125°13′
Quatlenemo 5	IR/RI	BC	Lillooet	92 I/12	50°41′	121°48′
Quatleyo 12	IR/RI	BC	Rupert	102 I/9	50°30′	128°05′
Quatorze-Arpents, Les	UNP/LNO	QC	Lac-Saint-Jean-Est	22 D/12	48°31′	71°45′
Quatre-Cents-Pieds, Le	UNP/LNO	QC	Témiscouata	21 N/6	47°27′	69°07′
Quatre-Chemins	UNP/LNO	QC	Les Etchemins	21 L/1	46°10′	70°24′
Quatre-Chemins	UNP/LNO	QC	Les Etchemins	21 L/2	46°14′	70°31′
Quatre-Chemins	UNP/LNO	QC	La Nouvelle-Beauce	21 L/11	46°35′	71°04′
Quatre-Chemins	UNP/LNO	QC	Le Bas-Richelieu	31 H/14	45°50′	73°08′
Quatre-Chemins, Le	UNP/LNO	QC	Les Chutes-de-la-Chaudière	21 L/11	46°41′	71°22′
Quatre-Chemins, Les	UNP/LNO	QC	L'Islet	21 K/13	46°49′	69°58′
Quatre-Chemins, Les	UNP/LNO	QC	Les Pays-d'en-Haut	31 G/16	45°58′	74°03′
Quatre-Coins	UNP/LNO	NB	Victoria	21 O/4	47°03′	67°40′
Quatre-Coins	UNP/LNO	NB	Madawaska	21 N/8	47°25′	68°28′
Quatre-Coins, Le	UNP/LNO	QC	Mirabel	31 G/9	45°38′	74°15′
Quatre-Coins, Les	UNP/LNO	QC	Sherbrooke	21 E/5	45°22′	71°54′
Quatre Fourches	UNP/LNO	AB	21-111-8-W4	74 L/11	58°38′	111°17′
Quatre-Fourches, Les	UNP/LNO	QC	La Vallée-de-la-Gatineau	31 J/5	46°23′	75°55′
Quatre-Milles	UNP/LNO	NB	Restigouche	21 O/11	47°40′	67°25′
Quatse Lake	LAKE/LAC	BC	Rupert	92 L/12	50°38′	127°34′
Quatsino	UNP/LNO	BC	Rupert	92 L/12	50°32′	127°39′
Quatsino Canyon	SEAU/SMER	—		3604	50°15′	128°07′
Quatsino Sound	BAY/BAIE	BC	Rupert	92 L/5	50°30′	127°35′
Quatsino Subdivision 18	IR/RI	BC	Rupert	92 L/12	50°37′	127°34′
Quattishe 1	IR/RI	BC	Rupert	92 L/12	50°32′	127°35′
Quaw	UNP/LNO	BC	Cariboo	93 J/2	54°04′	122°36′
Quay 4	IR/RI	BC	Range 1 Coast	92 L/15	50°58′	126°42′
Quckwa 7	IR/RI	BC	Range 3 Coast	103 A/10	52°33′	128°42′
Quebec - also-aussi - **Québec**	PROV/PROV	QC		MCR42	52°00′	72°00′
Québec - also-aussi - **Quebec**	PROV/PROV	QC		MCR42	52°00′	72°00′
Québec	CITY/VIL1	QC	Communauté urbaine de Québec	21 L/14	46°49′	71°14′
Québec	MUN1/AZM1	QC	La Côte-de-Beaupré	21 M/6	47°22′	71°18′
Québec, Communauté urbaine de	MUN1/AZM1	QC	Communauté urbaine de Québec	21 L/14	46°51′	71°21′
Quebec Harbour	UNP/LNO	ON	Thunder Bay	41 N/12	47°43′	85°47′
Québec, Sommet de	MTN/MNT	QC	Charlevoix	21 M/15	47°46′	70°50′
Queen Bess, Mount	MTN/MNT	BC	Range 2 Coast	92 N/7	51°16′	124°34′
Queen, Cape	CAPE/CAP	NT	Franklin	36 D	64°42′	78°18′
Queen Charlotte Channel	CHAN/CHEN	BC	New Westminster	92 G/6	49°22′	123°18′
Queen Charlotte City	UNP/LNO	BC	Queen Charlotte	103 F/8	53°15′	132°05′
Queen Charlotte Fan	SEAU/SMER	—		19410A	51°30′	131°20′
Queen Charlotte Islands - also-aussi - Reine-Charlotte, Îles de la	ISL/ÎLE	BC	Queen Charlotte	103 C/16	53°00′	132°00′
Queen Charlotte Land District	GEOG/GÉOG	BC		103 F	53°20′	132°10′
Queen Charlotte Mountains	MTN/MNT	BC	Queen Charlotte	103 C/16	53°00′	132°00′
Queen Charlotte Shelf	SEAU/SMER	—		3002	53°30′	131°45′
Queen Charlotte Slope	SEAU/SMER	—		3002	52°45′	132°30′
Queen Charlotte Sound	BAY/BAIE	BC	Range 2 Coast	102 P/8	51°30′	128°30′
Queen Charlotte Strait	CHAN/CHEN	BC	Range 1 Coast	92 L/11	50°45′	127°15′
Queen Charlotte Terrace	SEAU/SMER	—		3002	52°45′	132°30′
Queen Charlotte Trough	SEAU/SMER	—		5.03	53°00′	133°30′
Queen Elizabeth Foreland	CAPE/CAP	NT	Franklin	25 I	62°23′	64°28′
Queen Elizabeth Islands - also-aussi - Reine-Élisabeth, Îles de la	ISL/ÎLE	NT	Franklin	59 F/4	78°00′	95°00′
Queen Elizabeth Provincial Park, Lac Cardinal	PARK/PARC	AB	22,27-83-24-W5	84 C/4	56°13′	117°41′
Queen Elizabeth Ranges	MTN/MNT	AB	42,43,44-24,25,26-W5	83 C/12	52°45′	117°37′
Queen Elizabeth Rise	SEAU/SMER	—		7000	82°00′	110°30′
Queen Elizabeth Shelf	SEAU/SMER	—		7000	80°30′	100°00′
Queen Elizabeth Slope	SEAU/SMER	—		7000	80°15′	105°00′
Queen Mary, Mount	MTN/MNT	YT		115 B/12	60°38′	139°43′
Queen Maud Gulf	BAY/BAIE	NT	Franklin	67 B	68°20′	102°00′
Queens	MUN1/AZM1	NS	Queens	21 A/3	44°14′	65°00′
Queens	GEOG/GÉOG	PE		11 L/6	46°17′	63°15′
Queens	GEOG/GÉOG	NS		21 A/3	44°14′	65°00′
Queens	GEOG/GÉOG	NB		21 G/16	45°50′	66°00′
Queens Acres	UNP/LNO	ON	Lennox and Addington	31 C/2	44°14′	76°39′
Queens Bay	UNP/LNO	BC	Kamloops Division Yale	82 F/10	49°39′	116°56′
Queensborough	UNP/LNO	ON	Hastings	31 C/11	44°35′	77°25′
Queensborough	UNP/LNO	BC	New Westminster	92 G/2	49°11′	122°56′
Queensbury	GEOG/GÉOG	NB	York	21 J/3	46°00′	67°05′
Queens Cape	CAPE/CAP	NT	Franklin	26 H	65°10′	64°43′
Queens Channel	CHAN/CHEN	NT	Franklin	59 B/4	76°11′	96°00′
Queen's Cove	UNP/LNO	NF		2 C/4	48°01′	53°56′
Queens Cove	UNP/LNO	BC	Nootka	92 E/15	49°53′	126°59′

NAME NOM	ENTITY ENTITÉ	LOC 1 LIEU 1	LOC 2 LIEU 2	MAP CARTE	POSITION LAT	LONG
Queens Lake	LAKE/LAC	NB	Queens	21 G/8	45°24′	66°26′
Queensland	UNP/LNO	NS	Halifax	21 A/9	44°38′	64°02′
Queens Line	UNP/LNO	ON	Renfrew	31 F/10	45°38′	76°46′
Queens Park	UNP/LNO	BC	New Westminster	92 G/2	49°13′	122°54′
Queensport	UNP/LNO	NS	Guysborough	11 F/6	45°20′	61°16′
Queens Reach	RIVF/EFLV	BC	New Westminster	92 J/4	50°10′	123°53′
Queens Sound	CHAN/CHEN	BC	Range 2 Coast	102 P/16	51°56′	128°21′
Queenston	UNP/LNO	ON	Lincoln	30 M/3	43°10′	79°03′
Queenston Heights National Historic Site - also-aussi - Hauteurs-de-Queenston, Lieu historique national des	PARK/PARC	QC	Lincoln	30 M/3	43°10′	79°03′
Queenstown	UNP/LNO	NB	Queens	21 G/9	45°41′	66°07′
Queenstown	UNP/LNO	AB	26-19-22-W4	82 I/10	50°38′	112°56′
Queens Valley	UNP/LNO	MB	34-10-7-E	62 H/15	49°53′	96°34′
Queensville	UNP/LNO	NS	Inverness	11 F/11	45°44′	61°22′
Queensville	UNP/LNO	ON	York	31 D/3	44°08′	79°28′
Queensway Gardens	UNP/LNO	ON	Welland	30 M/3	43°06′	79°07′
Queesidaquah 4	IR/RI	BC	Renfrew	92 C/9	48°35′	124°16′
Queest Mountain	MTN/MNT	BC	Kamloops Division Yale	82 L/15	50°59′	118°52′
Quennell Lake	LAKE/LAC	BC	Cedar	92 G/4	49°05′	123°49′
Quénonisca, Lac	LAKE/LAC	QC	Jamésie	32 K/10	50°36′	76°33′
Quentin Lake	LAKE/LAC	BC	Cassiar	94 F/14	57°51′	125°10′
Quequa 6	IR/RI	BC	New Westminster	92 K/2	50°12′	124°56′
Quernbiter Fiord	BAY/BAIE	NT	Franklin	37 H	71°36′	75°02′
Querrin	UNP/LNO	SK	1-9-22-W2	72 H/10	49°43′	104°52′
Querry	UNP/LNO	QC	Bonaventure	22 A/4	48°11′	65°47′
Quesnel	CITY/VIL1	BC	Cariboo	93 B/15	53°00′	122°30′
Quesnel 1	IR/RI	BC	Cariboo	93 B/16	52°58′	122°29′
Quesnel Forks	UNP/LNO	BC	Cariboo	93 A/12	52°40′	121°40′
Quesnel Lake	LAKE/LAC	BC	Cariboo	93 A/10	52°30′	121°00′
Quesnel River	RIV/CDE	BC	Cariboo	93 B/16	52°58′	122°30′
Quesnel View	UNP/LNO	BC	Cariboo	93 B/15	52°57′	122°31′
Quetachou, Baie	BAY/BAIE	QC	Minganie	12 L/7	50°17′	62°45′
Quetico	UNP/LNO	ON	Thunder Bay	52 B/10	48°44′	90°55′
Quetico Lake	LAKE/LAC	ON	Rainy River	52 B/12	48°34′	91°55′
Quévillon, Lac	LAKE/LAC	QC	Jamésie	32 F/2	49°04′	76°57′
Queylus	UNP/LNO	QC	La Côte-de-Beaupré	21 M/2	47°03′	70°52′
Quibell	UNP/LNO	ON	Kenora	52 F/14	49°57′	93°26′
Quick	UNP/LNO	BC	Range 5 Coast	93 L/10	54°37′	126°54′
Quiddy River	RIV/CDE	NB	Saint John	21 H/6	45°29′	65°12′
Quidi Vidi	UNP/LNO	NF		1 N/10	47°35′	52°41′
Quiet Lake	LAKE/LAC	YT		105 F/3	61°05′	133°05′
Quigley	UNP/LNO	AB	27-82-6-W4	74 D/2	56°07′	110°53′
Quilchena	UNP/LNO	BC	Kamloops Division Yale	92 I/2	50°10′	120°30′
Quilchena Creek	RIV/CDE	BC	Kamloops Division Yale	92 I/2	50°10′	120°31′
Quill Creek	UNP/LNO	YT		115 G/11	61°31′	139°20′
Quilliam Bay	BAY/BAIE	NT	Franklin	47 D	69°30′	82°45′
Quill Lake	VILG/VILG	SK	36-16-W2	73 A/1	52°04′	104°15′
Quimper	UNP/LNO	SK	27-7-11-W3	72 G/11	49°35′	107°25′
Quinan	UNP/LNO	NS	Yarmouth	20 P/13	43°55′	65°50′
Quinan Lake	LAKE/LAC	NS	Yarmouth	20 P/13	43°51′	65°41′
Quinaquilth 4	IR/RI	BC	Clayoquot	92 F/3	49°03′	125°08′
Quinchien	UNP/LNO	QC	Vaudreuil-Soulanges	31 G/8	45°22′	74°00′
Quincy Adams, Mount	MTN/MNT	BC	Cassiar	114 I/13	58°54′	137°30′
Quin-e-ex 8	IR/RI	BC	Rupert	92 L/4	50°05′	127°47′
Quinn	UNP/LNO	ON	Kent	40 J/1	42°13′	82°23′
Quinn, Lac	LAKE/LAC	QC	Antoine-Labelle	31 J/5	46°29′	75°45′
Quinn Lake	LAKE/LAC	NF		12 A/7	48°29′	56°51′
Quinn Lake	LAKE/LAC	MB		64 I/11	58°33′	97°15′
Quinn Settlement	UNP/LNO	ON	Lanark	31 F/1	45°05′	76°17′
Quinnville	UNP/LNO	QC	Communauté urbaine de l'Outaouais	31 G/12	45°33′	75°41′
Quinogag 61	IR/RI	BC	Cassiar	103 P/3	55°13′	129°09′
Quinsam	UNP/LNO	BC	Sayward	92 K/3	50°01′	125°16′
Quinsam 12	IR/RI	BC	Sayward	92 K/3	50°01′	125°18′
Quinsam Lake	LAKE/LAC	BC	Comox	92 F/14	49°57′	125°23′
Quinsam River	RIV/CDE	BC	Sayward	92 K/3	50°02′	125°18′
Quinte, Bay of	BAY/BAIE	ON	Hastings	31 C/3	44°09′	77°15′
Quintette Mountain	MTN/MNT	BC	Peace River	93 I/15	54°51′	120°53′
Quinton	VILG/VILG	SK	12-28-18-W2	72 P/8	51°23′	104°24′
Quinton Heights	UNP/LNO	NB	Saint John	21 G/1	45°15′	66°07′
Quinze, Barrage des	MISC/DIV	QC	Témiscamingue	31 M/11	47°33′	79°14′
Quinze, Lac des	LAKE/LAC	QC	Témiscamingue	31 M/11	47°35′	79°05′
Quinze-Milles	UNP/LNO	QC	Le Haut-Saint-Maurice	32 A/4	48°04′	73°48′
Quirke Lake	LAKE/LAC	ON	Algoma	41 J/7	46°28′	82°33′
Quirpon	UNP/LNO	NF		2 M/11	51°35′	55°26′
Quirpon Island	ISL/ÎLE	NF		2 M/11	51°37′	55°26′
Quisibis	UNP/LNO	NB	Madawaska	21 N/8	47°15′	68°03′

NAME NOM	ENTITY ENTITÉ	LOC 1 LIEU 1	LOC 2 LIEU 2	MAP CARTE	POSITION LAT	LONG
Quisibis Mountain	MTN/MNT	NB	Madawaska	21 O/5	47°25′	67°58′
Quisibis, Rivière	RIV/CDE	NB	Madawaska	21 N/8	47°15′	68°03′
Quisitis 9	IR/RI	BC	Clayoquot	92 F/4	49°01′	125°40′
Quisitis Point	CAPE/CAP	BC	Clayoquot	92 C/13	48°59′	125°40′
Quispamsis	TOWN/VIL2	NB	Kings	21 H/5	45°25′	65°58′
Quitting Lake	LAKE/LAC	AB	88,89-3-W5	84 B/9	56°41′	114°20′
Qullisaq	UNP/LNO	QC	Kativik	35 G/16	61°56′	74°29′
Qullisaq	UNP/LNO	QC	Kativik	35 G/15	61°47′	74°59′
Qullutunga, Chute	FALL/CHUT	QC	Kativik	34 N/11	59°35′	77°06′
Quoddy Narrows	CHAN/CHEN	NB	Charlotte	21 B/15	44°49′	66°57′
Quoddy River	RIV/CDE	NS	Halifax	11 D/16	44°55′	62°21′
Quoich River	RIV/CDE	NT	Keewatin	55 N/13	64°00′	93°30′
Quorn	UNP/LNO	ON	Thunder Bay	52 G/7	49°25′	90°55′
Quortsowe 13	IR/RI	BC	Clayoquot	92 F/5	49°16′	125°44′
Quottoon Inlet	BAY/BAIE	BC	Range 5 Coast	103 J/8	54°28′	130°04′
Qurlutuq, Chute	FALL/CHUT	QC	Kativik	33 N/5	55°17′	77°35′
Qurlutuq, Rivière	RIV/CDE	QC	Kativik	24 J/7	58°27′	66°49′
Quunnguq Lake	LAKE/LAC	NT	Franklin	87 D	69°55′	112°35′
Quyon	UNP/LNO	QC	Les Collines-de-l'Outaouais	31 F/9	45°31′	76°14′
Quyon Ferry Landing	UNP/LNO	ON	Carleton	31 F/9	45°31′	76°13′
Quyon, Rivière	RIV/CDE	QC	Les Collines-de-l'Outaouais	31 F/9	45°31′	76°13′

R

NAME NOM	ENTITY ENTITÉ	LOC 1 LIEU 1	LOC 2 LIEU 2	MAP CARTE	POSITION LAT	LONG
Raanes Peninsula	CAPE/CAP	NT	Franklin	49 F	78°30′	86°00′
Rabbabou Bay	BAY/BAIE	SK		64 L/7	58°24′	102°45′
Rabbit Creek	RIV/CDE	SK	53-4-W3	73 G/9	53°34′	106°30′
Rabbit Island	ISL/ÎLE	ON	Manitoulin	41 H/12	45°38′	81°39′
Rabbit Island	ISL/ÎLE	NT	Franklin	97 F	70°05′	125°06′
Rabbit Lake	VILG/VILG	SK	13-48-13-W3	73 G/4	53°08′	107°46′
Rabbit Lake	LAKE/LAC	ON	Nipissing	31 M/4	47°00′	79°38′
Rabbit Lake	LAKE/LAC	SK	42-7,8-W3	73 B/11	52°37′	107°01′
Rabbit Point	CAPE/CAP	MB		62 P/15	51°52′	96°53′
Rabbit River	RIV/CDE	ON	Cochrane	42 J/8	50°28′	82°17′
Rabbit River	RIV/CDE	BC	Cassiar	94 M/11	59°36′	127°05′
Rabbitskin River	RIV/CDE	NT	Mackenzie	95 H	61°47′	120°42′
Rabbit Town	UNP/LNO	NF		1 N/10	47°34′	52°44′
Raby Head	CAPE/CAP	ON	Durham	30 M/15	43°52′	78°43′
Raccoon Lake	LAKE/LAC	NT	Mackenzie	85 K	62°52′	117°43′
Raccourci, Lac du	LAKE/LAC	QC	La Haute-Côte-Nord	22 F/6	49°20′	69°07′
Race, Cape	CAPE/CAP	NF		1 K/11	46°40′	53°05′
Race Horse Camp	UNP/LNO	ON	Renfrew	31 F/14	45°55′	77°28′
Racine	VILG/VILG	QC	Le Val-Saint-François	31 H/9	45°30′	72°15′
Racine	UNP/LNO	QC	Le Fjord-du-Saguenay	22 D/6	48°27′	71°15′
Racine de Bouleau, Rivière de la	RIV/CDE	QC	Caniapiscau	22 N/10	51°14′	68°34′
Racine Lake	LAKE/LAC	ON	Sudbury	42 B/3	48°02′	83°20′
Racine-sur-le-Lac	UNP/LNO	QC	Maria-Chapdelaine	32 A/9	48°44′	72°12′
Racing Island	ISL/ÎLE	NT	Franklin	97 C	69°54′	124°25′
Racing River	RIV/CDE	BC	Peace River	94 K/14	58°55′	125°03′
Rackety	UNP/LNO	ON	Haliburton	31 D/15	44°52′	78°47′
Rackham	UNP/LNO	MB	17-18-19-W	62 K/9	50°32′	100°04′
Rackla River	RIV/CDE	YT		106 D/1	64°07′	134°24′
Radcliffe	MUN2/AZM2	ON	Renfrew	31 F/5	45°22′	77°35′
Radford	UNP/LNO	QC	Pontiac	31 F/10	45°38′	76°33′
Radford Lake	LAKE/LAC	NT	Mackenzie	75 P	63°24′	105°34′
Radford River	RIV/CDE	NT	Mackenzie	75 P	63°39′	104°42′
Radiant	UNP/LNO	ON	Nipissing	31 E/16	45°59′	78°17′
Radisson	TOWN/VIL2	SK	20-40-10-W3	73 B/6	52°28′	107°24′
Radisson	UNP/LNO	QC	Vaudreuil-Soulanges	31 G/8	45°27′	74°12′
Radisson	UNP/LNO	QC	Jamésie	33 F/13	53°48′	77°37′
Radisson Lake	LAKE/LAC	ON	Timiskaming	42 A/2	48°12′	80°45′
Radisson Lake	LAKE/LAC	SK	40,41-10-W3	73 B/6	52°29′	107°25′
Radisson, Pointe	CAPE/CAP	QC	Kativik	35 I/6	62°18′	73°12′
Radium	UNP/LNO	BC	Kootenay	82 K/9	50°37′	116°06′
Radium Hot Springs	VILG/VILG	BC	Kootenay	82 K/9	50°37′	116°04′
Radmore Harbour	BAY/BAIE	NT	Franklin	120 B	80°28′	70°30′
Radnor	UNP/LNO	AB	18-26-5-W5	82 O/2	51°13′	114°42′
Radnor-des-Forges	UNP/LNO	QC	Francheville	31 I/7	46°30′	72°32′
Radstock Bay	BAY/BAIE	NT	Franklin	58 E	74°45′	91°00′
Radville	TOWN/VIL2	SK	12-6-18-W2	72 H/8	49°27′	104°17′
Radway	UNP/LNO	AB	32-58-20-W4	83 I/2	54°04′	112°57′
Rae	UNP/LNO	NT	Franklin	85 K/16	62°50′	116°03′
Rae Creek	RIV/CDE	YT		116 A/14	64°53′	137°01′
Rae-Edzo	HAM/HAM	NT	Mackenzie	85 K/16	62°48′	116°03′
Rae Isthmus	CAPE/CAP	NT	Franklin	46 L	66°48′	87°00′

NAME NOM	ENTITY ENTITÉ	LOC 1 LIEU 1	LOC 2 LIEU 2	MAP CARTE	POSITION LAT	LONG
Rae Lake	LAKE/LAC	MB	21-12-17-E	52 L/3	50°01'	95°14'
Rae Lake	LAKE/LAC	NT	Mackenzie	86 C	64°10'	117°20'
Rae Lakes	UNP/LNO	NT	Mackenzie	86 C/3	64°07'	117°21'
Rae, Mount	MTN/MNT	AB	19-8-W5	82 J/10	50°37'	114°59'
Rae River	RIV/CDE	NT	Mackenzie	86 O	67°55'	115°32'
Rae Strait	CHAN/CHEN	NT	Franklin	57 B	68°50'	94°51'
Rafael Point	CAPE/CAP	BC	Clayoquot	92 E/8	49°17'	126°14'
Rafale, La	UNP/LNO	QC	La Matapédia	22 B/9	48°34'	66°09'
Rafferty	UNP/LNO	SK	23-2-10-W2	62 E/3	49°09'	103°15'
Raft Cove	BAY/BAIE	BC	Rupert	102 I/9	50°35'	128°15'
Rafter	UNP/LNO	MB		63 N/11	55°37'	101°09'
Raft River	RIV/CDE	BC	Kamloops Division Yale	82 M/12	51°38'	119°59'
Rafuse Island	ISL/ÎLE	NS	Lunenburg	21 A/8	44°27'	64°14'
Ragged Harbour	BAY/BAIE	NF		2 F/5	49°27'	53°59'
Ragged Harbour River	RIV/CDE	NF		2 E/8	49°26'	54°03'
Ragged Head	CAPE/CAP	NF		1 L/13	46°54'	55°34'
Ragged Head	CAPE/CAP	NS	Guysborough	11 F/6	45°25'	61°23'
Ragged Islands	ISL/ÎLE	NF		13 J/16	55°00'	58°15'
Ragged Lake	LAKE/LAC	NS	Halifax	11 D/5	44°30'	63°40'
Ragged Point	CAPE/CAP	NF		2 E/8	49°28'	54°01'
Ragged Point	CAPE/CAP	NS	Cumberland	21 H/10	45°40'	64°31'
Ragged, Pointe	CAPE/CAP	QC	Kativik	24 K/16	58°49'	68°24'
Ragged Range	MTN/MNT	NT	Mackenzie	95 E	61°44'	127°15'
Ragged Reef	UNP/LNO	NS	Cumberland	21 H/9	45°40'	64°28'
Ragged Wood Lake	LAKE/LAC	ON	Kenora	52 J/11	50°31'	91°13'
Raglan	MUN2/AZM2	ON	Renfrew	31 F/3	45°15'	77°30'
Raglan	UNP/LNO	ON	Ontario	31 D/2	44°01'	78°55'
Raglan	UNP/LNO	ON	Kent	40 I/5	42°18'	81°55'
Raglan Range	MTN/MNT	NT	Franklin	88 H	75°58'	112°30'
Ragueneau	VILG/VILG	QC	Manicouagan	22 F/2	49°04'	68°32'
Rail	UNP/LNO	QC	Pabok	22 A/8	48°26'	64°22'
Rail Creek	RIV/CDE	BC	Lillooet	92 P/14	51°48'	121°21'
Rail Lake	LAKE/LAC	BC	Lillooet	92 P/14	51°57'	121°28'
Railton	UNP/LNO	ON	Frontenac	31 C/7	44°23'	76°34'
Raimbault, Lac	LAKE/LAC	QC	Caniapiscau	23 F/1	53°13'	68°21'
Rainbow	UNP/LNO	AB	29-17-W4	82 P/8	51°28'	112°23'
Rainbow Haven	UNP/LNO	NS	Halifax	11 D/11	44°38'	63°25'
Rainbow Lake	TOWN/VIL2	AB	109-9-W6	84 L/6	58°30'	119°23'
Rainbow Lodge	UNP/LNO	QC	Jamésie	32 G/16	49°54'	74°14'
Rainbow Mountain	MTN/MNT	BC	New Westminster	92 J/3	50°11'	123°03'
Rainbow River	RIV/CDE	BC	Cassiar	94 L/2	58°15'	126°33'
Rainham Centre	UNP/LNO	ON	Haldimand	30 L/13	42°50'	79°51'
Rainier	UNP/LNO	AB	26-16-16-W4	82 I/8	50°22'	112°05'
Rainville	VILG/VILG	QC	Brome-Missisquoi	31 H/7	45°17'	72°58'
Rainy Hollow	UNP/LNO	BC	Cassiar	114 P/10	59°33'	136°32'
Rainy Lake	LAKE/LAC	NF		2 D/3	48°13'	55°04'
Rainy Lake	LAKE/LAC	NF		12 A/14	48°51'	57°19'
Rainy Lake	LAKE/LAC	ON	Parry Sound	31 E/11	45°32'	79°30'
Rainy Lake - also-aussi - **Pluie, Lac à la**	LAKE/LAC	ON	Rainy River	52 C/11	48°42'	93°10'
Rainy Lake 17A	IR/RI	ON	Rainy River	52 C/13	48°50'	93°36'
Rainy Lake 17B	IR/RI	ON	Rainy River	52 C/13	48°51'	93°47'
Rainy Lake 18C	IR/RI	ON	Rainy River	52 C/11	48°43'	93°26'
Rainy Lake 26A	IR/RI	ON	Rainy River	52 C/10	48°45'	92°55'
Rainy Lake 26B	IR/RI	ON	Rainy River	52 C/15	48°49'	92°57'
Rainy Lake 26C	IR/RI	ON	Rainy River	52 C/15	48°50'	92°46'
Rainy River	TOWN/VIL2	ON	Rainy River	52 D/10	48°43'	94°34'
Rainy River	GEOG/GÉOG	ON		52 C/7	48°30'	92°30'
Rainy River - also-aussi - **Pluie, Rivière à la**	RIV/CDE	ON	Rainy River	52 D/15	48°50'	94°41'
Raisin River	RIV/CDE	ON	Glengarry	31 G/1	45°08'	74°30'
Raith	UNP/LNO	ON	Thunder Bay	52 A/13	48°50'	89°56'
Rajah, The	MTN/MNT	AB	49-4-W6	83 E/7	53°16'	118°33'
Rak	UNP/LNO	SK	39-2-W3	73 B/8	52°23'	106°10'
Raleigh	VILG/VILG	NF		2 M/12	51°34'	55°44'
Raleigh	MUN2/AZM2	ON	Kent	40 J/8	42°18'	82°10'
Raleigh	UNP/LNO	ON	Kenora	52 G/5	49°29'	91°56'
Raleigh Lake	LAKE/LAC	ON	Kenora	52 G/5	49°25'	91°55'
Raleigh, Mount	MTN/MNT	BC	Range 1 Coast	92 K/16	50°55'	124°16'
Raleigh, Mount	MTN/MNT	NT	Franklin	16 L	66°31'	62°17'
Raley	UNP/LNO	AB	16-4-24-W4	82 H/6	49°17'	113°11'
Ralleau, Lac	LAKE/LAC	QC	Kativik	24 J/2	58°00'	66°40'
Ralls Island	UNP/LNO	MB	56-25-W	63 F/14	53°50'	101°06'
Ralph	UNP/LNO	SK	22-7-13-W2	62 E/12	49°34'	103°41'
Ralston	UNP/LNO	MB	12-9-23-W	62 F/9	49°44'	100°28'
Ralston	UNP/LNO	AB	10-15-9-W5	72 L/3	50°15'	111°10'
Rama	VILG/VILG	SK	19-32-7-W2	62 M/15	51°46'	103°00'

NAME NOM	ENTITY ENTITÉ	LOC 1 LIEU 1	LOC 2 LIEU 2	MAP CARTE	POSITION LAT	LONG
Rama - see-voir - Ramara	MUN2/AZM2	ON		31 D/11	44°38′	79°14′
Rama 32 - see-voir - Mnjikaning First Nation 32	IR/RI	ON		31 D/11	44°42′	79°19′
Rama First Nation 32 - see-voir - Mnjikaning First Nation 32	IR/RI	ON		31 D/11	44°42′	79°19′
Ramage	UNP/LNO	BC	Kamloops Division Yale	92 I/16	50°59′	120°14′
Ramah Bay	BAY/BAIE	NF		14 L/14	58°52′	63°13′
Ramara	MUN2/AZM2	ON	Simcoe	31 D/11	44°38′	79°14′
Rama Road	UNP/LNO	ON	Ontario	31 D/11	44°38′	79°19′
Rambau, Lac	LAKE/LAC	QC	Jamésie	23 E/9	53°43′	70°14′
Rambler	UNP/LNO	NF		12 H/16	49°53′	56°05′
Ramea	TOWN/VIL2	NF		11 P/11	47°31′	57°23′
Ramea Islands	ISL/ÎLE	NF		11 P/11	47°31′	57°22′
Ramea Southeast Rocks	SHL/H-FD	NF		11 P/6	47°28′	57°17′
Rameau	UNP/LNO	QC	Pabok	22 A/9	48°31′	64°27′
Ram Falls	FALL/CHUT	AB	18-36-13-W5	83 B/4	52°05′	115°50′
Ram Island	ISL/ÎLE	NS	Shelburne	20 P/11	43°41′	65°02′
Rammelsberg, Cape	CAPE/CAP	NT	Franklin	25 N	63°26′	68°23′
Ramore	UNP/LNO	ON	Cochrane	42 A/8	48°26′	80°20′
Rampart House	UNP/LNO	YT		116 N/7	67°25′	140°59′
Ramparts River	RIV/CDE	NT	Mackenzie	106 I	66°11′	129°02′
Ram River	RIV/CDE	AB	39-10-W5	83 B/6	52°23′	115°25′
Ram River	RIV/CDE	NT	Mackenzie	95 J	62°01′	123°41′
Ramsay	MUN2/AZM2	ON	Lanark	31 F/1	45°12′	76°14′
Ramsay Arm	BAY/BAIE	BC	Range 1 Coast	92 K/7	50°23′	124°58′
Ramsay Island	ISL/ÎLE	BC	Queen Charlotte	103 B/11	52°34′	131°24′
Ramsay Island	ISL/ÎLE	NT	Franklin	87 G	71°34′	119°09′
Ramsay Lodge	UNP/LNO	NB	Northumberland	21 J/16	46°59′	66°29′
Ramsay River	RIV/CDE	NT	Franklin	25 M	63°09′	70°52′
Ramsay Sheds	UNP/LNO	NB	Restigouche	21 O/10	47°34′	66°32′
Ramsayville	UNP/LNO	ON	Carleton	31 G/5	45°23′	75°34′
Ramsey	UNP/LNO	ON	Sudbury	41 O/8	47°26′	82°20′
Ramsey Lake	LAKE/LAC	ON	Sudbury	41 I/7	46°29′	80°57′
Ramsey Lake	LAKE/LAC	ON	Sudbury	41 O/1	47°13′	82°15′
Ramseys	UNP/LNO	NS	Colchester	11 E/3	45°05′	63°15′
Ramusio, Lac	LAKE/LAC	QC	Kativik	13 M/4	55°03′	63°42′
Ranch	UNP/LNO	AB	27-70-26-W4	83 P/4	55°05′	113°53′
Ranch-Bar U, Lieu historique national du - also-aussi - Bar U Ranch National Historic Site	PARK/PARC	AB	8-17-2-W5	82 J/8	50°25′	114°15′
Rancheria	UNP/LNO	YT		105 B/2	60°05′	130°36′
Rancheria River	RIV/CDE	YT		105 A/3	60°13′	129°08′
Ranchero	UNP/LNO	BC	Kamloops Division Yale	82 L/11	50°39′	119°12′
Ranch Lake	LAKE/LAC	SK	40,41-20-W2	73 A/7	52°30′	104°46′
Ranchland No. 6, Improvement District of - see-voir - Ranchland No. 66, Municipal District of	MUN2/AZM2	AB	82 G/16		49°56′	114°25′
Ranchland No. 66, Municipal District of	MUN1/AZM1	AB		82 G/16	49°56′	114°25′
Ranch Park	UNP/LNO	BC	New Westminster	92 G/7	49°16′	122°49′
Rand	UNP/LNO	ON	Algoma	41 N/1	47°12′	84°21′
Randall	UNP/LNO	ON	Simcoe	31 D/4	44°08′	79°46′
Randall Corner	UNP/LNO	NB	Sunbury	21 G/16	45°55′	66°16′
Randall River	RIV/CDE	SK	69-2-W3	73 J/16	54°57′	106°18′
Randboro	UNP/LNO	QC	Le Haut-Saint-François	21 E/5	45°20′	71°32′
Randolph	UNP/LNO	NB	Saint John	21 G/8	45°16′	66°07′
Randolph	UNP/LNO	ON	Simcoe	41 A/16	44°46′	80°02′
Randolph	UNP/LNO	MB	10-7-5-E	62 H/10	49°33′	96°50′
Random Head Harbour	BAY/BAIE	NF		2 C/4	48°06′	53°34′
Random Heights	UNP/LNO	NF		2 C/4	48°11′	53°56′
Random Island	ISL/ÎLE	NF		2 C/4	48°08′	53°44′
Random Island West	UNP/LNO	NF		2 C/4	48°08′	53°53′
Random Sound	BAY/BAIE	NF		2 C/4	48°04′	53°36′
Randwick	UNP/LNO	ON	Dufferin	41 A/8	44°15′	80°03′
Ranelagh	UNP/LNO	ON	Norfolk	40 I/16	42°59′	80°30′
Ranfurly	UNP/LNO	AB	15-51-12-W4	73 E/5	53°25′	111°41′
Rang-Cinq-Et-Six	UNP/LNO	NB	Restigouche	21 O/12	47°32′	67°30′
Rang-de-l'Aiguille, Le	UNP/LNO	QC	Matane	22 B/12	48°38′	67°33′
Rang-des-Bossé	UNP/LNO	NB	Madawaska	21 N/8	47°28′	68°20′
Rang-des-Bourgoin	UNP/LNO	NB	Madawaska	21 O/4	47°07′	67°49′
Rang-des-Collin	UNP/LNO	NB	Madawaska	21 N/7	47°20′	68°41′
Rang-des-Couturier	UNP/LNO	NB	Madawaska	21 N/8	47°27′	68°20′
Rang-des-Deschêne	UNP/LNO	NB	Madawaska	21 N/8	47°16′	68°00′
Rang-des-Lavoie	UNP/LNO	NB	Madawaska	21 N/8	47°24′	68°16′
Rang-des-Morneault	UNP/LNO	NB	Madawaska	21 N/7	47°22′	68°33′
Rang-Dix	UNP/LNO	NB	Restigouche	21 O/11	47°33′	67°26′
Rang-Dix-Huit	UNP/LNO	NB	Restigouche	21 O/11	47°31′	67°17′
Rang-Double-Nord	UNP/LNO	NB	Restigouche	21 O/11	47°39′	67°23′
Rang-Double-Sud	UNP/LNO	NB	Restigouche	21 O/11	47°38′	67°23′
Rang-Douze-Nord	UNP/LNO	NB	Restigouche	21 O/11	47°33′	67°24′
Rang-Douze-Sud	UNP/LNO	NB	Restigouche	21 O/6	47°29′	67°24′
Range 13	IR/RI	BC	Similkameen Division Yale	82 E/4	49°08′	119°50′

NAME NOM	ENTITY ENTITÉ	LOC 1 LIEU 1	LOC 2 LIEU 2	MAP CARTE	POSITION LAT	LONG
Range 1 Coast Land District	GEOG/GÉOG	BC		92 K	50°40′	125°35′
Range 2 Coast Land District	GEOG/GÉOG	BC		92 M	51°25′	125°10′
Range 3 Coast Land District	GEOG/GÉOG	BC		93 D	52°25′	126°25′
Range 4 Coast Land District	GEOG/GÉOG	BC		93 E	53°40′	127°45′
Range 5 Coast Land District	GEOG/GÉOG	BC		93 L	54°35′	127°40′
Range Creek	RIV/CDE	BC	Kamloops Division Yale	92 I/1	50°11′	120°10′
Ranger	UNP/LNO	SK	28-53-12-W3	73 G/12	53°35′	107°42′
Ranger Brook	RIV/CDE	NT	Keewatin	45 N	63°07′	85°18′
Ranger Lake	UNP/LNO	ON	Algoma	41 J/13	46°52′	83°35′
Ranger Lake	LAKE/LAC	ON	Algoma	41 J/13	46°54′	83°34′
Ranger River	RIV/CDE	NT	Franklin	26 J	66°37′	67°32′
Rangeton	UNP/LNO	AB	13-55-8-W5	83 G/14	53°45′	115°03′
Rangeview	UNP/LNO	SK	18-3-25-W3	72 F/3	49°12′	109°21′
Rangifer Mountain	MTN/MNT	YT		105 E/16	61°47′	134°03′
Rang-Quatorze	UNP/LNO	NB	Restigouche	21 O/6	47°30′	67°21′
Rang-Quatre, Le	UNP/LNO	QC	Denis-Riverin	22 G/2	49°02′	66°48′
Rang-Saint-David	UNP/LNO	QC	Témiscouata	21 N/7	47°24′	68°52′
Rang-Saint-Georges	UNP/LNO	NB	Gloucester	21 P/11	47°39′	65°06′
Rang-Saint-Grégoire	UNP/LNO	QC	Témiscouata	21 N/10	47°42′	68°41′
Rang-Saint-Joseph	UNP/LNO	NB	Madawaska	21 N/7	47°19′	68°33′
Rang-Saint-Laurent	UNP/LNO	QC	Avignon	22 B/1	48°10′	66°19′
Rang-Saint-Paul	UNP/LNO	QC	Pabok	22 A/9	48°35′	64°18′
Rang-Seize	UNP/LNO	NB	Restigouche	21 O/11	47°30′	67°19′
Rang-Sept	UNP/LNO	NB	Restigouche	21 O/11	47°40′	67°20′
Rang-Sept-et-Huit	UNP/LNO	NB	Restigouche	21 O/11	47°31′	67°28′
Rankin	UNP/LNO	ON	Renfrew	31 F/11	45°41′	77°06′
Rankin	UNP/LNO	ON	Nipissing	31 L/7	46°18′	78°34′
Rankin Inlet	HAM/HAM	NT	Keewatin	55 K	62°49′	92°05′
Rankin Inlet	BAY/BAIE	NT	Keewatin	55 J	62°44′	91°59′
Rankin Location 15D	IR/RI	ON	Algoma	41 K/9	46°33′	84°15′
Rankinville	UNP/LNO	NS	Inverness	11 K/3	46°04′	61°22′
Rannoch	UNP/LNO	ON	Perth	40 P/6	43°16′	81°11′
Ranoke	UNP/LNO	ON	Cochrane	42 I/5	50°26′	81°35′
Rantem	UNP/LNO	NF		1 N/12	47°42′	53°52′
Rantem Station	UNP/LNO	NF		1 N/12	47°40′	53°53′
Raoul-Blanchard, Mont	MTN/MNT	QC	La Côte-de-Beaupré	21 M/7	47°19′	70°50′
Raper, Cape	CAPE/CAP	NT	Franklin	27 D	69°44′	67°06′
Raphoe	UNP/LNO	ON	Sudbury	41 I/14	46°56′	81°04′
Rapid City	TOWN/VIL2	MB	20,29-13-19-W	62 K/1	50°07′	100°02′
Rapide-Blanc	UNP/LNO	QC	Le Haut-Saint-Maurice	31 P/15	47°48′	72°58′
Rapide-Danseur	VILG/VILG	QC	Abitibi-Ouest	32 D/11	48°33′	79°18′
Rapide-des-Cèdres	UNP/LNO	QC	Jamésie	32 F/3	49°01′	77°04′
Rapide-des-Chiens	UNP/LNO	QC	Antoine-Labelle	31 J/11	46°43′	75°24′
Rapide-des-Pins	UNP/LNO	QC	Antoine-Labelle	31 J/11	46°43′	75°23′
Rapide-Deux	UNP/LNO	QC	Rouyn-Noranda	31 M/15	47°56′	78°34′
Rapide-Deux, Barrage de	MISC/DIV	QC	Rouyn-Noranda	31 M/15	47°56′	78°34′
Rapide-Deux, Le	UNP/LNO	QC	Rouyn-Noranda	31 M/9	47°44′	78°15′
Rapide-Douze, Le	UNP/LNO	QC	Vallée-de-l'Or	31 M/9	47°42′	78°13′
Rapide-du-Cheval-Blanc	UNP/LNO	QC	Antoine-Labelle	31 J/13	46°51′	75°56′
Rapide-du-Cheval-Gris	UNP/LNO	QC	Antoine-Labelle	31 J/13	46°54′	75°59′
Rapide-du-Fort	UNP/LNO	QC	Antoine-Labelle	31 J/4	46°08′	75°41′
Rapide, Le	UNP/LNO	QC	Minganie	12 L/3	50°14′	63°12′
Rapide, Le	UNP/LNO	QC	Antoine-Labelle	31 J/13	46°49′	75°53′
Rapide-Mascouche	UNP/LNO	QC	Les Moulins	31 H/13	45°46′	73°40′
Rapides-de-la-Vache-Caille	UNP/LNO	QC	Lac-Saint-Jean-Est	22 D/12	48°32′	71°37′
Rapides-des-Cèdres	MUN2/AZM2	QC	Rouyn-Noranda	31 M/16	47°52′	78°27′
Rapides-des-Joachims	VILG/VILG	QC	Pontiac	31 K/4	46°12′	77°41′
Rapides-du-Diable	UNP/LNO	QC	Manicouagan	22 F/9	49°44′	68°18′
Rapides-du-Rocher-Fendu	UNP/LNO	QC	Pontiac	31 F/10	45°38′	76°41′
Rapide-Sept	UNP/LNO	QC	Rouyn-Noranda	31 M/16	47°46′	78°19′
Rapide-Sept, Barrage de	MISC/DIV	QC	Rouyn-Noranda	31 M/16	47°46′	78°19′
Rapides, Grand lac des	LAKE/LAC	QC	Sept-Rivières	22 J/8	50°30′	66°26′
Rapides, Lac des	LAKE/LAC	QC	Sept-Rivières	22 J/8	50°19′	66°26′
Rapide-Treize, Le	UNP/LNO	QC	Témiscamingue	31 M/9	47°41′	78°07′
Rapid Lake	IR/RI	QC	La Vallée-de-la-Gatineau	31 N/7	47°15′	76°42′
Rapid River	RIV/CDE	BC	Cassiar	104 P/6	59°19′	129°01′
Rapids Depot	UNP/LNO	NB	Restigouche	21 O/13	47°49′	67°44′
Rapid Valley	UNP/LNO	ON	Leeds	31 C/8	44°26′	76°01′
Rapid View	UNP/LNO	SK	32-59-19-W3	73 K/2	54°09′	108°49′
Rapson Bay	BAY/BAIE	ON	Kenora	53 K/8	54°24′	92°27′
Rasmussen Basin	BAY/BAIE	NT	Franklin	57 B/6	68°26′	94°46′
Raspberry	UNP/LNO	BC	Kootenay	82 F/5	49°20′	117°39′
Ratchford Creek	RIV/CDE	BC	Kamloops Division Yale	82 M/7	51°19′	118°52′
Ratcliffe	UNP/LNO	SK	6-2-15-W2	62 E/4	49°06′	103°59′
Rat Creek	RIV/CDE	AB	12-48-11-W5	83 G/3	53°08′	115°28′

NAME / NOM	ENTITY / ENTITÉ	LOC 1 / LIEU 1	LOC 2 / LIEU 2	MAP / CARTE	POSITION LAT	POSITION LONG
Rathburn	UNP/LNO	ON	Ontario	31 D/11	44°39′	79°16′
Ratho	UNP/LNO	ON	Oxford	40 P/7	43°17′	80°43′
Rathouse Bay	BAY/BAIE	ON	Kenora	53 C/14	52°55′	93°25′
Rathwell	UNP/LNO	MB	7-8-8-W	62 G/10	49°39′	98°33′
Rathwell's Shore	UNP/LNO	ON	Lanark	31 F/1	45°07′	76°11′
Rat Lake	LAKE/LAC	MB		53 L/11	54°40′	95°30′
Rat Lake	LAKE/LAC	MB		64 B/4	56°10′	99°39′
Rat Lake	LAKE/LAC	SK	46-5-W2	63 D/15	52°59′	102°41′
Ratner	UNP/LNO	SK	29-48-16-W2	73 H/1	53°10′	104°18′
Rat Portage 38A	IR/RI	ON	Kenora	52 E/10	49°41′	94°33′
Rat Portage Bay	BAY/BAIE	ON	Kenora	52 E/10	49°44′	94°32′
Rat Rapids	UNP/LNO	ON	Kenora	52 O/1	51°11′	90°14′
Rat River	UNP/LNO	NT	Mackenzie	85 H	61°07′	112°37′
Rat River - also-aussi - +Rats, Rivière aux	RIV/CDE	MB		62 H/11	49°35′	97°08′
Rat River	RIV/CDE	MB	77-11-W	63 O/11	55°42′	99°04′
Rat River	RIV/CDE	NT/YT		106 M/10	67°37′	134°52′
Rat River Settlement	GEOG/GÉOG	MB		62 H/7	49°29′	97°00′
Rats, Rivière aux	RIV/CDE	QC	Maria-Chapdelaine	32 A/16	48°54′	72°14′
Rats, Rivière aux	RIV/CDE	QC	Le Haut-Saint-Maurice	31 P/2	47°13′	72°53′
+Rats, Rivière aux - also-aussi - Rat River	RIV/CDE	MB		62 H/11	49°35′	97°08′
Ratter and Dunnet	MUN2/AZM2	ON	Sudbury	41 I/8	46°27′	80°20′
Ratter Corner	UNP/LNO	NB	Kings	21 H/12	45°38′	65°35′
Rattlesnake Harbour	UNP/LNO	ON	Norfolk	40 I/16	42°53′	80°25′
Rattling Brook	UNP/LNO	NF		2 E/3	49°04′	55°19′
Rattling Brook	UNP/LNO	NF		12 H/9	49°38′	56°10′
Rattling Brook	RIV/CDE	NF		2 E/3	49°04′	55°18′
Rattling Brook Depot	UNP/LNO	NF		2 D/13	48°58′	55°32′
Rattling Lake	LAKE/LAC	NF		2 E/3	49°01′	55°18′
Rattray Park Estates	UNP/LNO	ON	Peel	30 M/12	43°31′	79°36′
Ratzburg	UNP/LNO	ON	Perth	40 P/7	43°25′	80°47′
Ratz, Mount	MTN/MNT	BC	Cassiar	104 F/8	57°24′	132°18′
Raude, Lac	LAKE/LAC	QC	Kativik	23 P/8	55°15′	64°17′
Raudot	UNP/LNO	QC	Les Basques	21 N/15	47°58′	68°56′
Raush River	RIV/CDE	BC	Cariboo	93 H/1	53°12′	120°00′
Raush Valley	UNP/LNO	BC	Cariboo	83 E/4	53°11′	119°59′
Ravage, Le	UNP/LNO	QC	Rivière-du-Loup	21 N/15	47°49′	68°52′
Raven	UNP/LNO	AB	14-36-4-W5	83 B/1	52°05′	114°29′
Ravendale	UNP/LNO	SK	3-53-10-W2	63 E/11	53°33′	103°24′
Ravenhead	UNP/LNO	SK	46-11-W3	73 B/13	52°59′	107°31′
Raven Lake	LAKE/LAC	NT	Mackenzie	106 P	67°49′	128°22′
Ravenna	UNP/LNO	ON	Grey	41 A/8	44°28′	80°25′
Raven River	RIV/CDE	AB	28-35-3-W5	83 B/1	52°02′	114°22′
Ravenscliff - see-voir - Ravenscliffe	UNP/LNO	ON		31 E/6	45°22′	79°17′
Ravenscliffe	UNP/LNO	ON	Muskoka	31 E/6	45°22′	79°17′
Ravenscrag	UNP/LNO	SK	19-6-23-W3	72 F/6	49°30′	109°06′
Ravenshoe	UNP/LNO	ON	York	31 D/3	44°12′	79°24′
Ravens Throat River	RIV/CDE	NT	Mackenzie	95 N	63°31′	125°50′
Ravensview	UNP/LNO	ON	Frontenac	31 C/1	44°14′	76°25′
Ravenswood	UNP/LNO	ON	Lambton	40 P/4	43°11′	81°58′
Ravensworth	UNP/LNO	ON	Parry Sound	31 E/11	45°35′	79°07′
Ravignan-Nord	UNP/LNO	QC	Les Etchemins	21 L/8	46°18′	70°20′
Ravine	UNP/LNO	AB	19-54-9-W5	83 G/11	53°41′	115°20′
Rawalpindi Lake	LAKE/LAC	NT	Mackenzie	86 G	65°02′	114°37′
Rawcliffe	UNP/LNO	QC	Argenteuil	31 G/10	45°41′	74°33′
Rawdon	TOWN/VIL2	QC	Matawinie	31 I/4	46°03′	73°43′
Rawdon	VILG/VILG	QC	Matawinie	31 I/4	46°05′	73°45′
Rawdon	MUN2/AZM2	ON	Hastings	31 C/5	44°22′	77°36′
Rawdon Gold Mines	UNP/LNO	NS	Hants	11 E/4	45°03′	63°46′
Rawebb	UNP/LNO	MB	25-61-20-W	63 K/8	54°18′	100°19′
Rawhide Lake	LAKE/LAC	ON	Algoma	41 J/10	46°39′	82°37′
Rawlings Bay	BAY/BAIE	NT	Franklin	120 B	80°19′	70°00′
Rawlinson Hills	MTN/MNT	NT	Franklin	68 B	72°56′	102°10′
Rawlison	UNP/LNO	BC	New Westminster	92 G/2	49°09′	122°34′
Rawson Island	ISL/ÎLE	NT	Franklin	35 P	63°57′	72°54′
Ray, Cape	CAPE/CAP	NF		11 O/11	47°37′	59°19′
Rayfield River	RIV/CDE	BC	Lillooet	92 P/6	51°15′	121°06′
Ray Lake	LAKE/LAC	BC	Kamloops Division Yale	93 A/1	52°14′	120°04′
Ray Lake	LAKE/LAC	NT	Keewatin	65 H	61°02′	96°16′
Rayleigh	UNP/LNO	BC	Kamloops Division Yale	92 I/16	50°49′	120°18′
Raymond	TOWN/VIL2	AB	6-20-W4	82 H/7	49°27′	112°39′
Raymond	UNP/LNO	ON	Muskoka	31 E/3	45°12′	79°26′
Raymond Peak	MTN/MNT	BC	Cassiar	104 M/12	59°40′	135°58′
Raymond Point	UNP/LNO	NF		1 M/12	47°42′	55°56′
Raymonds Corners	UNP/LNO	ON	Frontenac	31 C/8	44°29′	76°29′
Raymore	TOWN/VIL2	SK	19-28-18-W2	72 P/7	51°25′	104°31′

NAME NOM	ENTITY ENTITÉ	LOC 1 LIEU 1	LOC 2 LIEU 2	MAP CARTE	POSITION LAT	LONG
Raynards Lake	LAKE/LAC	NS	Yarmouth	20 P/13	43°58′	65°55′
Raynardton	UNP/LNO	NS	Yarmouth	20 P/13	43°55′	65°58′
Raynor Group	ISL/ÎLE	BC	Range 1 Coast	92 L/14	50°53′	127°14′
Rayside	UNP/LNO	ON	Oxford	40 P/2	43°05′	80°55′
Rayside-Balfour	TOWN/VIL2	ON	Sudbury	41 I/11	46°37′	81°13′
Raza Island	ISL/ÎLE	BC	New Westminster	92 K/6	50°18′	125°00′
Raza Passage	CHAN/CHEN	BC	Range 1 Coast	92 K/6	50°20′	125°00′
Reaboro	UNP/LNO	ON	Victoria	31 D/7	44°19′	78°38′
Reaburn	UNP/LNO	MB	13-3,4-W	62 I/4	50°05′	97°52′
Reach, The	RIVF/EFLV	NF		2 E/7	49°24′	54°41′
Read	UNP/LNO	ON	Hastings	31 C/6	44°18′	77°12′
Read Bay	BAY/BAIE	NT	Franklin	58 G	75°03′	93°35′
Reader Lake	LAKE/LAC	MB	57-26,27-W	63 F/14	53°56′	101°21′
Readford	UNP/LNO	YT		115 O/14	63°47′	139°07′
Reading	UNP/LNO	ON	Dufferin	40 P/16	43°50′	80°13′
Read Island	UNP/LNO	BC	Sayward	92 K/3	50°11′	125°05′
Read Island	UNP/LNO	NT	Franklin	87 D/2	69°12′	113°50′
Read Island	ISL/ÎLE	BC	Sayward	92 K/3	50°14′	125°05′
Readlyn	UNP/LNO	SK	30-7-27-W2	72 H/12	49°35′	105°39′
Reads Corner	UNP/LNO	PE	Prince	11 L/5	46°24′	63°45′
Rear Balls Creek	UNP/LNO	NS	Cape Breton	11 K/1	46°08′	60°20′
Rear Big Hill	UNP/LNO	NS	Victoria	11 K/2	46°10′	60°40′
Rear Big Pond	UNP/LNO	NS	Cape Breton	11 F/16	45°55′	60°29′
Rear Black River	UNP/LNO	NS	Richmond	11 F/11	45°41′	61°08′
Rear Boisdale	UNP/LNO	NS	Cape Breton	11 K/1	46°03′	60°28′
Rear Christmas Island	UNP/LNO	NS	Cape Breton	11 F/15	45°58′	60°43′
Rear Dunvegan	UNP/LNO	NS	Inverness	11 K/6	46°20′	61°12′
Rear Estmere	UNP/LNO	NS	Victoria	11 F/15	45°57′	60°58′
Rear Forks	UNP/LNO	NS	Victoria	11 K/2	46°12′	60°45′
Rear Judique Chapel	UNP/LNO	NS	Inverness	11 F/14	45°52′	61°28′
Rear Judique South	UNP/LNO	NS	Inverness	11 F/14	45°51′	61°25′
Rear Little River	UNP/LNO	NS	Victoria	11 K/8	46°26′	60°29′
Rear Monastery	UNP/LNO	NS	Antigonish	11 F/12	45°35′	61°37′
Rear of East Bay	UNP/LNO	NS	Cape Breton	11 F/16	45°59′	60°22′
Rear of Leeds and Lansdowne	MUN2/AZM2	ON	Grenville	31 C/9	44°31′	76°07′
Rear of Yonge and Escott	MUN2/AZM2	ON	Grenville	31 B/12	44°36′	75°57′
Reay	UNP/LNO	ON	Muskoka	31 D/14	44°57′	79°18′
Reba	UNP/LNO	ON	Thunder Bay	52 G/7	49°29′	90°51′
Rébéca	UNP/LNO	QC	Charlevoix-Est	21 M/9	47°39′	70°26′
Rebecca Spit	CAPE/CAP	BC	Sayward	92 K/3	50°06′	125°11′
Rebesca Lake	LAKE/LAC	NT	Mackenzie	86 C	64°32′	116°22′
Reboul, Rivière	RIV/CDE	QC	Bonaventure	22 A/6	48°24′	65°29′
Reciprocity No. 32	MUN2/AZM2	SK		62 F/5	49°25′	101°50′
Reclaim	UNP/LNO	BC	New Westminster	92 G/1	49°01′	122°06′
Recluse, Lac	LAKE/LAC	QC	Sept-Rivières	22 P/4	51°11′	65°36′
Rectory Hill	UNP/LNO	QC	L'Érable	21 L/5	46°19′	71°31′
Recul-à-Rankin	UNP/LNO	QC	Kamouraska	21 N/12	47°37′	69°46′
Redan	UNP/LNO	ON	Leeds	31 B/12	44°43′	75°54′
Red Bank	UNP/LNO	NB	Northumberland	21 I/13	46°56′	65°49′
Redbank	UNP/LNO	NB	Queens	21 I/4	46°11′	65°50′
Red Bank 4	IR/RI	NB	Northumberland	21 I/13	46°55′	65°53′
Red Bank 7	IR/RI	NB	Northumberland	21 I/13	46°58′	65°55′
Red Bay	VILG/VILG	NF		12 P/9	51°44′	56°25′
Red Bay	UNP/LNO	ON	Bruce	41 A/14	44°48′	81°17′
Red Bay	BAY/BAIE	NF		12 P/9	51°44′	56°25′
Redberry	UNP/LNO	SK	34-43-9-W3	73 B/11	52°45′	107°14′
Redberry Lake	LAKE/LAC	SK		73 B/11	52°42′	107°10′
Redberry No. 435	MUN2/AZM2	SK		73 B/11	52°45′	107°10′
Redberry Park	UNP/LNO	SK	36-41-9-W3	73 B/11	52°35′	107°15′
Red Bluff	UNP/LNO	BC	Cariboo	93 B/16	52°58′	122°28′
Red Bluff 88	IR/RI	BC	Range 5 Coast	103 I/13	54°59′	129°42′
Red Bluff Lake	LAKE/LAC	BC	Range 4 Coast	103 H/5	53°28′	129°36′
Redbridge	UNP/LNO	ON	Nipissing	31 L/6	46°23′	79°16′
Red Brook	UNP/LNO	NF		12 B/6	48°30′	59°10′
Redburn No. 130	MUN2/AZM2	SK		72 I/3	50°10′	105°05′
Red Cedar Lake	LAKE/LAC	ON	Nipissing	31 L/13	46°45′	79°54′
Redcliff	TOWN/VIL2	AB	8-13-6-W4	72 L/2	50°05′	110°47′
Red Cliff	UNP/LNO	NF		2 C/11	48°34′	53°29′
Red Cliff	UNP/LNO	NF		2 D/13	48°57′	55°46′
Redcliff Island	ISL/ÎLE	NT	Mackenzie	75 L	62°22′	111°15′
Red Cliff Pond	LAKE/LAC	NF		1 M/14	47°57′	55°09′
Red Cliff Pond	LAKE/LAC	NF		2 E/13	49°53′	55°43′
Red Cliff (Red Bluff) 13	IR/RI	BC	Cassiar	103 P/4	55°00′	129°45′
Red Cove	UNP/LNO	NF		1 M/12	47°32′	55°37′
Red Creek	RIV/CDE	BC	Kamloops Division Yale	92 H/9	49°31′	120°24′

NAME NOM	ENTITY ENTITÉ	LOC 1 LIEU 1	LOC 2 LIEU 2	MAP CARTE	POSITION LAT	LONG
Red Cross	UNP/LNO	SK	34-54-24-W3	73 F/11	53°43′	109°27′
Red Cross Lake	LAKE/LAC	MB		53 N/2	55°06′	92°53′
Red Deer	CITY/VIL1	AB	16-38-27-W4	83 A/5	52°16′	113°48′
Red Deer Creek	RIV/CDE	BC	Peace River	93 I/9	54°41′	120°15′
Red Deer Hill	UNP/LNO	SK	18-46-26-W2	73 H/4	53°01′	105°48′
Red Deer Junction	UNP/LNO	AB	11-39-27-W4	83 A/5	52°21′	113°46′
Red Deer Lake	UNP/LNO	MB	21-45-28-W	63 C/14	52°54′	101°28′
Red Deer Lake	LAKE/LAC	ON	Sudbury	41 I/7	46°24′	80°45′
Red Deer Lake	LAKE/LAC	ON	Kenora	52 L/1	50°01′	94°10′
Red Deer Lake	LAKE/LAC	MB		63 C/14	52°57′	101°22′
Red Deer Lake	LAKE/LAC	AB	15,16-3-W4	72 L/8	50°17′	110°23′
Red Deer Lake	LAKE/LAC	AB	43-21,22-W4	83 A/11	52°43′	113°02′
Red Deer No. 23, County of	MUN1/AZM1	AB	36-27-W4	83 A/4	52°06′	113°47′
Red Deer Point	CAPE/CAP	MB	32,33,34,35-18-W	62 O/13	51°52′	99°58′
Red Deer River	RIV/CDE	MB/SK		63 C/14	52°54′	101°01′
Red Deer River	RIV/CDE	SK/AB		72 K/13	50°55′	109°54′
Reddendale	UNP/LNO	ON	Frontenac	31 C/2	44°14′	76°34′
Redding Creek	RIV/CDE	BC	Kootenay	82 F/9	49°38′	116°18′
Redditt	UNP/LNO	ON	Kenora	52 E/16	49°59′	94°24′
Red Earth	UNP/LNO	SK		63 E/7	53°29′	102°52′
Red Earth 29	IR/RI	SK		63 E/7	53°27′	102°52′
Red Earth Creek	UNP/LNO	AB	18-87-8-W5	84 B/11	56°33′	115°15′
Red Earth Creek	RIV/CDE	SK	52-6-W2	63 E/7	53°28′	102°50′
Red Earth Lake	LAKE/LAC	MB	54-22,23-W	63 F/10	53°41′	100°41′
Redfern Lake	LAKE/LAC	BC	Peace River	94 G/5	57°21′	123°54′
Redfield	UNP/LNO	SK	12-46-13-W3	73 B/13	52°57′	107°45′
Redgrave	UNP/LNO	BC	Kootenay	82 N/11	51°31′	117°17′
Redgut Bay	BAY/BAIE	ON	Rainy River	52 C/15	48°47′	92°52′
Red Harbour	VILG/VILG	NF		1 M/7	47°18′	54°59′
Red Harbour Head	CAPE/CAP	NF		1 M/7	47°17′	54°58′
Red Head	UNP/LNO	NB	Saint John	21 G/8	45°15′	66°01′
Red Head	CAPE/CAP	NF		1 K/13	46°55′	53°53′
Red Head	CAPE/CAP	NS	Richmond	11 F/10	45°37′	60°38′
Red Head	CAPE/CAP	NS	Guysborough	11 F/6	45°29′	61°14′
Red Head	CAPE/CAP	NS	Colchester	21 H/8	45°23′	64°02′
Red Head Cove	UNP/LNO	NF		2 C/2	48°08′	52°54′
Red Head River	RIV/CDE	NF		1 K/13	46°57′	53°52′
Redhorse Lake	LAKE/LAC	ON	Frontenac	31 F/2	45°06′	76°48′
Red House	UNP/LNO	PE	Kings	11 L/8	46°20′	62°24′
Redickville	UNP/LNO	ON	Dufferin	41 A/1	44°13′	80°13′
Red Indian Brook	RIV/CDE	NF		12 H/12	48°44′	57°40′
Red Indian Lake	LAKE/LAC	NF		12 A/10	48°45′	56°45′
Red Island	UNP/LNO	NF		1 M/8	47°24′	54°09′
Red Island	UNP/LNO	NF		11 P/12	47°38′	57°30′
Red Island	ISL/ÎLE	NF		1 M/8	47°23′	54°10′
Red Island	ISL/ÎLE	NF		12 B/11	48°34′	59°14′
Red Islands	UNP/LNO	NS	Richmond	11 F/15	45°46′	60°44′
Red Islands	ISL/ÎLE	NS	Richmond	11 F/15	45°48′	60°46′
Red Jacket	UNP/LNO	SK	21-14-32-W	62 K/4	50°12′	101°47′
Redknife Hills	MTN/MNT	NT	Mackenzie	85 D	60°33′	120°00′
Redknife River	RIV/CDE	NT	Mackenzie	85 E	61°13′	119°22′
Red Lake	MUN2/AZM2	ON	Kenora	52 K/13	51°00′	93°50′
Red Lake	UNP/LNO	ON	Kenora	52 N/4	51°01′	93°50′
Red Lake	LAKE/LAC	ON	Kenora	52 N/4	51°03′	93°57′
Red Lake	LAKE/LAC	BC	Kamloops Division Yale	92 I/15	50°53′	120°47′
Red Lake Road	UNP/LNO	ON	Kenora	52 F/14	49°58′	93°22′
Redland	UNP/LNO	AB	10-27-22-W4	82 P/6	51°18′	113°00′
Red Landing Head	CAPE/CAP	NF		1 M/6	47°16′	55°00′
Red Lodge Provincial Park	PARK/PARC	AB	29-34-2-W5	82 O/16	51°57′	114°15′
Redman Head	CAPE/CAP	NS	Guysborough	11 F/4	45°01′	61°57′
Red Mill	UNP/LNO	QC	Francheville	31 I/8	46°25′	72°28′
Redmond	UNP/LNO	ON	Thunder Bay	42 L/4	50°14′	87°32′
Redmondville	UNP/LNO	NB	Northumberland	21 I/14	46°56′	65°15′
Red Mountain	MTN/MNT	BC	Lillooet	92 O/2	51°12′	122°33′
Red Mountain	MTN/MNT	YT		115 P/15	63°58′	136°42′
Rednersville	UNP/LNO	ON	Prince Edward	31 C/3	44°07′	77°27′
Redore	UNP/LNO	NF		23 J/10	54°39′	66°40′
Redoute-York, Lieu historique national de la - also-aussi - York Redoubt National Historic Site	PARK/PARC	NS	Halifax	11 D/12	44°36′	63°33′
Red Pass	UNP/LNO	BC	Cariboo	83 D/14	52°59′	119°00′
Red Pheasant	UNP/LNO	SK	20-40-16-W3	73 C/8	52°27′	108°16′
Red Pheasant 108	IR/RI	SK		73 C/8	52°29′	108°08′
Red Pillar, The	MTN/MNT	BC	Clayoquot	92 F/11	49°32′	125°23′
Red Point	UNP/LNO	NF		3 E/5	53°30′	55°53′
Red Point	UNP/LNO	PE	Kings	11 L/8	46°23′	62°08′
Red Point	UNP/LNO	NS	Victoria	11 F/15	45°56′	60°54′

NAME NOM	ENTITY ENTITÉ	LOC 1 LIEU 1	LOC 2 LIEU 2	MAP CARTE	POSITION LAT	LONG
Red Point	CAPE/CAP	NS	Richmond	11 F/10	45°35′	60°45′
Red Point East	UNP/LNO	NS	Victoria	11 F/15	45°56′	60°53′
Red Rapids	UNP/LNO	NB	Victoria	21 J/13	46°47′	67°31′
Red River	UNP/LNO	NS	Inverness	11 K/15	46°51′	60°46′
Red River	RIV/CDE	NS	Inverness	11 K/15	46°51′	60°46′
Red River - also-aussi - **Rouge, Rivière**	RIV/CDE	MB		62 I/7	50°24′	96°49′
Red River	RIV/CDE	BC	Cassiar	94 M/5	59°28′	127°40′
Red River	RIV/CDE	YT		105 C/9	60°44′	132°07′
Red River	RIV/CDE	NT	Keewatin	65 C	60°33′	100°08′
Red River Floodway - also-aussi - +Rivière Rouge, Canal de dérivation de la	MISC/DIV	MB		62 I/2	50°05′	96°56′
Red Rock	MUN2/AZM2	ON	Thunder Bay	52 A/16	48°55′	88°15′
Red Rock	UNP/LNO	NB	Northumberland	21 J/16	46°47′	66°29′
Red Rock	UNP/LNO	NB	York	21 J/7	46°15′	66°41′
Red Rock	UNP/LNO	ON	Algoma	41 K/10	46°38′	84°31′
Red Rock	UNP/LNO	ON	Thunder Bay	52 A/16	48°56′	88°15′
Red Rock	UNP/LNO	BC	Cariboo	93 G/10	53°41′	122°40′
Red Rock 53	IR/RI	ON	Thunder Bay	52 H/1	49°05′	88°15′
Red Rock Lake	UNP/LNO	MB	12-15-E	52 E/13	49°59′	95°31′
Red Rock Lake	LAKE/LAC	NB	Charlotte	21 G/2	45°15′	66°44′
Redrock Lake	LAKE/LAC	NT	Mackenzie	86 G	65°28′	114°10′
Red Rock Point	CAPE/CAP	NF		13 I/12	54°41′	57°45′
Red Rocks	UNP/LNO	NF		11 O/11	47°40′	59°18′
Redroofs	UNP/LNO	BC	New Westminster	92 G/5	49°30′	123°55′
Red Rose	UNP/LNO	MB	3-29-1-W	62 P/5	51°28′	97°32′
Red Rose	UNP/LNO	BC	Cassiar	93 M/4	55°08′	127°37′
*Redsand	UNP/LNO	BC	Kamloops Division Yale	83 D/3	52°10′	119°16′
Red Star	UNP/LNO	AB	8-81-2-W6	84 D/1	56°01′	118°16′
Redstone	UNP/LNO	BC	Cariboo	93 B/4	52°08′	123°42′
Redstone Cemetery 1B	IR/RI	BC	Cariboo	93 B/4	52°08′	123°57′
Redstone Flat 1	IR/RI	BC	Cariboo	93 B/4	52°08′	123°58′
Redstone Flat 1A	IR/RI	BC	Cariboo	93 B/4	52°09′	123°58′
Redstone Lake	LAKE/LAC	ON	Haliburton	31 E/2	45°11′	78°32′
Redstone River	RIV/CDE	ON	Cochrane	42 A/6	48°27′	81°02′
Redstone River	RIV/CDE	NT	Mackenzie	96 C	64°17′	124°33′
Red Sucker Lake	UNP/LNO	MB		53 K/4	54°10′	93°34′
Red Sucker Lake	LAKE/LAC	MB		53 K/4	54°09′	93°40′
Red Sucker Lake 1976	IR/RI	MB		53 K/4	54°10′	93°34′
Red Sucker River	RIV/CDE	MB/ON		53 N/7	55°19′	92°30′
Redvers	TOWN/VIL2	SK	13-7-32-W	62 F/12	49°34′	101°42′
Redwater	TOWN/VIL2	AB	30-57-21-W4	83 H/14	53°57′	113°06′
Redwater	UNP/LNO	ON	Nipissing	31 L/13	46°54′	79°39′
Redwater Creek 30	IR/RI	BC	Cariboo	93 G/4	53°01′	123°47′
Redwater River	RIV/CDE	AB	57-20-W4	83 H/15	53°53′	112°58′
Red Willow	UNP/LNO	AB	19-40-18-W4	83 A/7	52°27′	112°34′
Redwillow Creek	RIV/CDE	SK	50-9-W2	63 E/6	53°18′	103°17′
Redwillow River	RIV/CDE	AB/BC		83 M/3	55°02′	119°18′
Red Wine River	RIV/CDE	NF		13 F/14	53°55′	61°00′
Red Wing	UNP/LNO	ON	Grey	41 A/8	44°27′	80°27′
Redwood	UNP/LNO	ON	Muskoka	31 E/4	45°07′	79°40′
Reeces Corners	UNP/LNO	ON	Lambton	40 J/16	42°59′	82°07′
Reeder	UNP/LNO	MB	19-13-27-W	62 K/3	50°06′	101°09′
Reed Lake	LAKE/LAC	MB	65,66-20,21-W	63 K/9	54°38′	100°30′
Reed Lake	LAKE/LAC	SK	16,17-8,9-W3	72 J/6	50°24′	107°05′
Reed River	RIV/CDE	MB	20-2-17-E	52 E/3	49°09′	95°17′
Reed River 36A	IR/RI	MB		52 E/3	49°08′	95°18′
Reeds Bay	BAY/BAIE	ON	Frontenac	31 C/1	44°08′	76°28′
Reedsdale	UNP/LNO	QC	L'Érable	21 L/6	46°16′	71°28′
Reeds Island - see-voir - St. Almo	UNP/LNO	NB		21 J/14	46°51′	67°26′
Reeds Point	UNP/LNO	NB	Kings	21 H/5	45°27′	65°59′
Reedy Creek	UNP/LNO	MB	33-22-11-W	62 J/15	50°57′	98°56′
Reedy Lake	LAKE/LAC	MB	38-9-W	63 B/7	52°17′	98°41′
Reef Icefield	GLAC/GLAC	BC/AB		83 E/3	53°08′	119°01′
Reef Island	ISL/ÎLE	BC	Queen Charlotte	103 B/13	52°52′	131°31′
Reefs Harbour	UNP/LNO	NF		12 P/3	51°01′	57°01′
Rees	UNP/LNO	NB	Queens	21 H/13	45°59′	65°59′
Reesor	UNP/LNO	ON	Cochrane	42 G/11	49°35′	83°07′
Reesor Siding	UNP/LNO	ON	Cochrane	42 G/11	49°34′	83°05′
Reeve	UNP/LNO	MB	13-20-15W	62 J/11	50°43′	99°25′
Reeve Craig	UNP/LNO	ON	Carleton	31 G/4	45°06′	75°38′
Reeves Harbour	BAY/BAIE	NT	Franklin	25 L	62°32′	70°21′
Reflex Lakes	LAKE/LAC	AB/SK		73 D/9	52°40′	110°00′
Reford	UNP/LNO	SK	5-39-19-W3	73 C/7	52°19′	108°43′
Reford No. 379	MUN2/AZM2	SK		73 C/7	52°15′	108°35′
Refuge Cove	UNP/LNO	BC	New Westminster	92 K/2	50°07′	124°50′
Refuge Cove 6	IR/RI	BC	Clayoquot	92 E/8	49°22′	126°16′

NAME NOM	ENTITY ENTITÉ	LOC 1 LIEU 1	LOC 2 LIEU 2	MAP CARTE	POSITION	
					LAT	LONG
Refuge-du-Col-Abbot, Lieu historique national du - also-aussi - Abbot Pass Refuge Cabin National Historic Site	PARK/PARC	AB		82 N/8	51°22′	116°17′
Refuge Lagoon	LAKE/LAC	BC	New Westminster	92 K/2	50°08′	124°50′
Regal Heights	UNP/LNO	SK		72 I/5	50°24′	105°34′
Regan	UNP/LNO	ON	Thunder Bay	42 C/12	48°41′	85°37′
Regan Lake	LAKE/LAC	NT	Mackenzie	76 G	65°04′	107°47′
Reg Christie Creek	RIV/CDE	BC	Kamloops Division Yale	82 M/12	51°36′	119°41′
Regent	UNP/LNO	ON	Algoma	41 N/1	47°14′	84°24′
Regent	UNP/LNO	MB	36-4-22-W	62 F/8	49°20′	100°19′
Regent Park	UNP/LNO	ON	York	30 M/11	43°40′	79°22′
Regent Park	UNP/LNO	MB		62 H/14	49°54′	97°01′
Regent Park	UNP/LNO	SK		72 I/7	50°28′	104°39′
Reggie Libby Place	UNP/LNO	QC	Pontiac	31 F/15	45°55′	76°57′
Regina	CITY/VIL1	SK		72 I/7	50°27′	104°37′
Regina Bay	BAY/BAIE	ON	Kenora	52 E/8	49°25′	94°02′
Regina Beach	TOWN/VIL2	SK	21-21-22-W2	72 I/15	50°47′	105°00′
Regina's Market Square	UNP/LNO	SK		72 I/7	50°27′	104°37′
Regway	UNP/LNO	SK	2-1-20-W2	72 H/2	49°00′	104°34′
Reid	UNP/LNO	NS	Halifax	11 E/3	45°05′	63°04′
Reid Bay	BAY/BAIE	NT	Franklin	16 L	66°57′	62°02′
Reid Island	ISL/ÎLE	BC	Cowichan	92 B/13	49°00′	123°37′
Reid Lake	UNP/LNO	BC	Cariboo	93 G/14	53°58′	123°06′
Reid Lake	LAKE/LAC	SK		72 K/1	50°01′	108°09′
Reid Lake	LAKE/LAC	NT	Mackenzie	75 M	63°45′	110°00′
Reid Point	CAPE/CAP	NT	Franklin	37 C	69°01′	76°37′
Reid Point	CAPE/CAP	NT	Franklin	57 G	71°21′	95°35′
Reid's Corners	UNP/LNO	ON	Bruce	41 A/4	44°04′	81°42′
Reids Fishing Room	UNP/LNO	NF		1 N/12	47°31′	53°40′
Reid's Mill	UNP/LNO	ON	Waterloo	40 P/8	43°19′	80°27′
Reids Mills	UNP/LNO	ON	Dundas	31 G/4	45°06′	75°33′
Reids Room	UNP/LNO	NF		1 N/12	47°34′	53°34′
Reidsville	UNP/LNO	ON	Waterloo	40 P/8	43°19′	80°26′
Reidville	VILG/VILG	NF		12 H/3	49°14′	57°23′
Reidville	UNP/LNO	QC	Memphrémagog	21 E/5	45°17′	71°58′
Reidville	UNP/LNO	ON	Lennox and Addington	31 C/7	44°26′	76°56′
Reindeer Cape	CAPE/CAP	NT	Franklin	79 E	78°47′	104°58′
Reindeer Island	ISL/ÎLE	MB		63 B/8	52°25′	98°00′
Reindeer Lake	LAKE/LAC	SK/MB		64 E/1	57°14′	102°16′
Reindeer Lake	LAKE/LAC	NT	Mackenzie	85 P	63°53′	113°35′
Reindeer Mountain	MTN/MNT	YT		115 O/11	63°37′	139°22′
Reindeer Peninsula	CAPE/CAP	NT	Franklin	79 E	78°53′	104°35′
Reindeer River	RIV/CDE	SK		63 M/11	55°36′	103°11′
Reindeer Station	UNP/LNO	NT	Mackenzie	107 B/11	68°42′	134°08′
Reine-Charlotte, Îles de la - also-aussi - **Queen Charlotte Islands**	ISL/ÎLE	BC	Queen Charlotte	102 O/14	53°00′	132°00′
Reine-Élisabeth, Îles de la - also-aussi - **Queen Elizabeth Islands**	ISL/ÎLE	NT	Franklin	59 F/4	78°00′	95°00′
Reinfeld	UNP/LNO	MB	1,2-3-4-W	62 H/4	49°11′	97°53′
Reinland	UNP/LNO	MB	13-1-4-W	62 H/4	49°03′	97°52′
Reita Lake	LAKE/LAC	AB	59-3,4-W4	73 L/1	54°08′	110°25′
Relay	UNP/LNO	ON	Cochrane	42 H/13	49°59′	81°37′
Relay Creek	RIV/CDE	BC	Lillooet	92 O/2	51°03′	122°47′
Relay Mountain	MTN/MNT	BC	Lillooet	92 O/2	51°08′	122°59′
Relessey	UNP/LNO	ON	Dufferin	41 A/1	44°03′	80°02′
Relfe River	RIV/CDE	NT	Franklin	98 F	74°01′	124°22′
Reliance	UNP/LNO	SK	32-4-10-W3	72 G/6	49°21′	107°19′
Reliance	UNP/LNO	NT	Mackenzie	75 K/11	62°43′	109°10′
Reliance Bay	BAY/BAIE	NT	Franklin	68 C	73°48′	100°05′
Reliance Mountain	MTN/MNT	BC	Range 2 Coast	92 N/7	51°21′	124°42′
Remac	UNP/LNO	BC	Kootenay	82 F/3	49°02′	117°23′
Remblais-de-Southwold, Lieu historique national des - also-aussi - Southwold Earthworks National Historic Site	PARK/PARC	ON	Elgin	40 I/11	42°41′	81°21′
Rembrandt	UNP/LNO	MB	11-21-2-E	62 I/14	50°48′	97°13′
Remicks	UNP/LNO	ON	Thunder Bay	52 B/1	48°11′	90°08′
Rémigny	VILG/VILG	QC	Témiscamingue	31 M/14	47°46′	79°12′
Rémigny, Lac	LAKE/LAC	QC	Témiscamingue	31 M/14	47°51′	79°12′
Remi Lake	LAKE/LAC	ON	Cochrane	42 G/8	49°26′	82°10′
Remington Park	UNP/LNO	ON	Essex	40 J/6	42°17′	83°01′
Remi River	RIV/CDE	ON	Cochrane	42 G/9	49°43′	82°11′
Remo	UNP/LNO	BC	Range 5 Coast	103 I/7	54°29′	128°43′
Remote Mountain	MTN/MNT	BC	Range 2 Coast	92 N/5	51°28′	125°31′
Remote Peninsula	CAPE/CAP	NT	Franklin	27 F	70°51′	71°00′
Remous, Le	UNP/LNO	QC	Les Chutes-de-la-Chaudière	21 L/11	46°37′	71°14′
Renabie	UNP/LNO	ON	Sudbury	42 B/5	48°23′	83°53′
Renard, Lac à	LAKE/LAC	QC	Minganie	22 I/10	50°35′	64°35′
Renard, Lac du	LAKE/LAC	QC	Minganie	12 E/1	49°13′	62°00′

NAME NOM	ENTITY ENTITÉ	LOC 1 LIEU 1	LOC 2 LIEU 2	MAP CARTE	POSITION LAT	LONG
Renard, Pointe au	CAPE/CAP	QC	La Côte-de-Gaspé	22 A/16	49°00′	64°23′
Renard, Rivière au	RIV/CDE	QC	La Côte-de-Gaspé	22 A/16	49°00′	64°24′
Renard, Rivière du	RIV/CDE	QC	Minganie	12 F/5	49°17′	61°50′
Renards, Pointe aux	CAPE/CAP	NB	Kent	21 I/7	46°22′	64°34′
Renata	UNP/LNO	BC	Kootenay	82 E/8	49°26′	118°06′
Renata Creek	RIV/CDE	BC	Kootenay	82 E/8	49°26′	118°06′
Renauds Mills	UNP/LNO	NB	Kent	21 I/7	46°22′	64°43′
Rencontre Bay	BAY/BAIE	NF		11 P/10	47°37′	56°41′
Rencontre Brook	RIV/CDE	NF		1 M/11	47°38′	55°13′
Rencontre East	VILG/VILG	NF		1 M/11	47°38′	55°13′
Rencontre Islands	ISL/ÎLE	NF		1 M/11	47°38′	55°14′
Rencontre Lake	LAKE/LAC	NF		1 M/11	47°41′	55°12′
Rencontre West	UNP/LNO	NF		11 P/10	47°37′	56°41′
Rendel, Cape	CAPE/CAP	NT	Franklin	67 H	71°16′	96°28′
Rendell Creek	RIV/CDE	BC	Similkameen Division Yale	82 E/10	49°37′	118°46′
Rendu Glacier	GLAC/GLAC	BC		114 P/2	59°07′	136°55′
Reneault	UNP/LNO	QC	Rouyn-Noranda	32 D/6	48°28′	79°02′
René-Levasseur, Île	ISL/ÎLE	QC	Manicouagan	22 N/7	51°20′	68°40′
Renews	UNP/LNO	NF		1 K/15	46°56′	52°56′
Renews-Cappahayden	VILG/VILG	NF		1 K/15	46°54′	52°57′
Renews Harbour	BAY/BAIE	NF		1 K/15	46°55′	52°56′
Renews Head	CAPE/CAP	NF		1 K/15	46°54′	52°55′
Renforth	VILG/VILG	NB	Kings	21 G/8	45°22′	66°01′
Renforth	UNP/LNO	ON	Wentworth	30 M/4	43°10′	79°57′
Renfrew	TOWN/VIL2	ON	Renfrew	31 F/7	45°28′	76°41′
Renfrew	MUN1/AZM1	ON	Renfrew	31 F/6	45°30′	77°05′
Renfrew	UNP/LNO	NS	Hants	11 E/4	45°00′	63°38′
Renfrew	GEOG/GÉOG	ON		31 F/6	45°30′	77°05′
Renfrew-Collingwood	UNP/LNO	BC	New Westminster	92 G/3	49°15′	123°02′
Renfrew Junction	UNP/LNO	ON	Renfrew	31 F/7	45°28′	76°42′
Renfrew Land District	GEOG/GÉOG	BC		92 C	48°40′	124°25′
Renison	UNP/LNO	ON	Cochrane	42 I/14	50°58′	81°07′
Rennell, Cape	CAPE/CAP	NT	Franklin	58 F	74°11′	93°28′
Rennell Sound	CHAN/CHEN	BC	Queen Charlotte	103 F/7	53°24′	132°44′
Rennie	UNP/LNO	MB	24-10-14-E	52 E/13	49°51′	95°33′
Rennie Lake	LAKE/LAC	ON	Sudbury	42 B/5	48°23′	83°58′
Rennie Lake	LAKE/LAC	NT	Mackenzie	75 H	61°32′	105°35′
Rennie River	RIV/CDE	MB	33-13-14-E	52 L/4	50°07′	95°38′
Rennies Road	UNP/LNO	PE	Queens	11 L/6	46°22′	63°21′
Rennison Island	ISL/ÎLE	BC	Range 3 Coast	103 A/14	52°50′	129°20′
Reno	UNP/LNO	AB	1-81-20-W5	83 N/15	56°00′	117°00′
Renommée, Pointe à la	CAPE/CAP	QC	La Côte-de-Gaspé	22 H/2	49°07′	64°36′
Reno No. 51	MUN2/AZM2	SK		72 F/6	49°25′	109°25′
Renouard, Lac	LAKE/LAC	QC	La Haute-Côte-Nord	22 F/11	49°33′	69°19′
Renouf Island	ISL/ÎLE	NT	Keewatin	34 D	56°35′	79°08′
Renous	UNP/LNO	NB	Northumberland	21 I/13	46°49′	65°48′
Renous 12	IR/RI	NB	Northumberland	21 I/13	46°49′	65°47′
Renous River	RIV/CDE	NB	Northumberland	21 I/13	46°49′	65°47′
Renown	UNP/LNO	SK	1-31-26-W2	72 P/12	51°38′	105°33′
Rens Fiord	BAY/BAIE	NT	Franklin	560 D	81°10′	93°40′
Renton	UNP/LNO	ON	Norfolk	40 I/16	42°51′	80°14′
Renversy	UNP/LNO	QC	Maskinongé	31 I/6	46°24′	73°01′
Renwer	UNP/LNO	MB	15-36-24-W	63 C/2	52°06′	100°49′
Renwick	UNP/LNO	ON	Kent	40 J/1	42°09′	82°23′
Repentigny	CITY/VIL1	QC	L'Assomption	31 H/11	45°44′	73°28′
Repulse Bay	HAM/HAM	NT	Franklin	46 L	66°32′	86°15′
Repulse Bay	BAY/BAIE	NT	Franklin	46 K	66°20′	86°00′
Requisite Channel	CHAN/CHEN	NT	Keewatin	67 B	68°21′	100°25′
Reserve	UNP/LNO	SK	27-40-5-W2	63 D/7	52°28′	102°39′
Réserve, La	UNP/LNO	QC	Les Basques	21 N/15	47°59′	68°52′
Reserve Mines	UNP/LNO	NS	Cape Breton	11 K/1	46°11′	60°01′
Reserve Rows	UNP/LNO	NS	Cape Breton	11 K/1	46°11′	60°01′
Réservoir-Dozois	MUN2/AZM2	QC	Vallée-de-l'Or	31 N/11	47°30′	77°05′
Resolute	HAM/HAM	NT	Franklin	58 F/11	74°42′	94°50′
Resolution Bay	BAY/BAIE	NT	Mackenzie	85 H	61°06′	113°52′
Resolution Island	UNP/LNO	NT	Franklin	25 H	61°18′	64°53′
Resolution Island	ISL/ÎLE	NT	Franklin	25 H	61°30′	65°00′
Resolution, Lac	LAKE/LAC	QC	Kativik	23 P/8	55°16′	64°29′
Resor Island	ISL/ÎLE	NT	Franklin	25 N	63°15′	68°04′
Resource	UNP/LNO	SK	27-43-18-W2	73 A/10	52°44′	104°32′
Reste-de-Cacouna, Le	UNP/LNO	QC	Rivière-du-Loup	21 N/14	47°53′	69°27′
Resthaven Icefield	GLAC/GLAC	AB	51-10,11-W6	83 E/6	53°26′	119°28′
Restigouche	UNP/LNO	QC	Avignon	22 B/2	48°01′	66°42′
Restigouche	GEOG/GÉOG	NB		21 O/11	47°40′	67°00′
Restigouche 1 - see-voir - Listuguj 1	IR/RI	QC		22 B/2	48°03′	66°45′

NAME NOM	ENTITY ENTITÉ	LOC 1 LIEU 1	LOC 2 LIEU 2	MAP CARTE	POSITION LAT	LONG
Restigouche River - also-aussi - **Ristigouche, Rivière**	RIV/CDE	NB/QC		22 B/1	48°04′	66°20′
Restless Bight	BAY/BAIE	BC	Rupert	92 L/5	50°22′	127°58′
Reston	UNP/LNO	MB	9-7-27-W	62 F/11	49°33′	101°06′
Restoule	UNP/LNO	ON	Parry Sound	31 L/4	46°02′	79°44′
Restoule Lake	LAKE/LAC	ON	Parry Sound	31 L/4	46°03′	79°46′
Retallack	UNP/LNO	BC	Kootenay	82 K/3	50°03′	117°08′
Retaskit	UNP/LNO	BC	Lillooet	92 J/9	50°42′	122°06′
Retlaw	UNP/LNO	AB	9-13-17-W4	82 I/1	50°04′	112°16′
Retreat Passage	CHAN/CHEN	BC	Range 1 Coast	92 L/10	50°42′	126°36′
Revelstoke	CITY/VIL1	BC	Kootenay	82 L/16	50°59′	118°12′
Revelstoke, Lake	LAKE/LAC	BC	Kootenay	82 M/8	51°30′	118°29′
Revenue	UNP/LNO	SK	35-37-21-W3	73 C/2	52°14′	108°54′
Rev. George McDougall Provincial Historic Site (Undeveloped)	PARK/PARC	AB	33-25-1-W5	82 O/1	51°10′	114°06′
Revillon Island	ISL/ÎLE	NT	Keewatin	43 P	55°56′	80°09′
Reward	HAM/HAM	SK	28-38-24-W3	73 C/6	52°17′	109°22′
Rex	UNP/LNO	SK	33-51-27-W3	73 F/5	53°27′	109°56′
Rexdale	UNP/LNO	ON	York	30 M/12	43°43′	79°33′
Rexons Cove	UNP/LNO	NF		3 D/12	52°35′	55°53′
Rexton	VILG/VILG	NB	Kent	21 I/10	46°39′	64°52′
Reykjavik	UNP/LNO	MB	35-25-11-W	62 O/2	51°12′	98°54′
Reynaud	HAM/HAM	SK	19-42-24-W2	73 A/11	52°38′	105°26′
Reynolds	MUN2/AZM2	MB		52 E/12	49°43′	95°56′
Reynolds Creek	RIV/CDE	ON	Middlesex	40 I/15	43°00′	80°58′
Reynoldscroft	UNP/LNO	NS	Shelburne	20 P/11	43°32′	65°27′
Rheault	UNP/LNO	ON	Sudbury	41 I/7	46°24′	81°00′
Rhein	VILG/VILG	SK	23-27-2-W2	62 M/8	51°21′	102°12′
Rheinfeld	UNP/LNO	SK	27-13-12-W3	72 J/4	50°07′	107°34′
Rheinland	UNP/LNO	SK	31-39-4-W3	73 B/7	52°25′	106°30′
Rhineland	MUN2/AZM2	MB		62 H/4	49°10′	97°40′
Rhineland	UNP/LNO	SK	13-14-13-W3	72 J/4	50°10′	107°39′
Rhodena	UNP/LNO	NS	Inverness	11 F/14	45°46′	61°24′
Rhodes	UNP/LNO	ON	Kent	40 J/8	42°20′	82°14′
Rhodes	UNP/LNO	MB	11-3-18-W	62 G/4	49°12′	99°48′
Rhodes Corner	UNP/LNO	NS	Lunenburg	21 A/8	44°23′	64°25′
Rhone	UNP/LNO	BC	Similkameen Division Yale	82 E/3	49°14′	119°01′
Rhyl	UNP/LNO	SK	21-36-10-W3	73 B/3	52°06′	107°22′
Rib Lake	UNP/LNO	ON	Nipissing	31 M/4	47°11′	79°43′
Rib Lake	LAKE/LAC	ON	Nipissing	31 M/4	47°13′	79°43′
Ribot	UNP/LNO	QC	Les Collines-de-l'Outaouais	31 G/11	45°33′	75°30′
Ribstone	UNP/LNO	AB	17-43-2-W4	73 D/9	52°42′	110°15′
Ribstone Creek	RIV/CDE	AB	9-45-1-W4	73 D/16	52°52′	110°05′
Ribstone Heritage Monument Provincial Historic Site (Undeveloped)	PARK/PARC	AB	25-46-12-W4	73 D/13	52°59′	111°37′
Ribstone Lake	LAKE/LAC	AB	43,44-5-W4	73 D/15	52°46′	110°39′
Riceburg	UNP/LNO	QC	Brome-Missisquoi	31 H/2	45°08′	72°56′
Rice Lake	UNP/LNO	ON	Kenora	52 E/14	49°53′	95°07′
Rice Lake	LAKE/LAC	ON	Peterborough	31 D/1	44°12′	78°10′
Rice Lake	LAKE/LAC	ON	Sudbury	41 O/9	47°43′	82°08′
Rice Lake	LAKE/LAC	ON	Kenora	52 E/14	49°52′	95°07′
Rice Lake	LAKE/LAC	SK	35,36-8-W3	73 B/3	52°03′	107°07′
Rice Point	UNP/LNO	PE	Queens	11 L/3	46°08′	63°15′
Riceton	HAM/HAM	SK	30-13-17-W2	72 I/1	50°07′	104°19′
Riceville	UNP/LNO	NB	Carleton	21 J/4	46°00′	67°31′
Riceville	UNP/LNO	NB	Madawaska	21 N/8	47°21′	68°27′
Riceville	UNP/LNO	ON	Prescott	31 G/7	45°26′	74°57′
Richan	UNP/LNO	ON	Kenora	52 F/15	49°59′	92°49′
Richard	VILG/VILG	SK	8-43-12-W3	73 B/12	52°42′	107°40′
Richard Collinson, Cape	CAPE/CAP	NT	Franklin	68 B	72°46′	102°45′
Richard Collinson Inlet	BAY/BAIE	NT	Franklin	88 A	72°46′	113°54′
Richard Lake	LAKE/LAC	NT	Keewatin	55 O/13	63°52′	91°46′
Richards Bay	BAY/BAIE	NT	Franklin	47 D	69°35′	82°25′
Richards, Cape	CAPE/CAP	NT	Franklin	340 E	82°59′	79°17′
Richard's Harbour	UNP/LNO	NF		11 P/9	47°37′	56°24′
Richards Island	ISL/ÎLE	NF		2 C/12	48°40′	53°37′
Richards Island	ISL/ÎLE	NT	Franklin	107 C	69°20′	134°30′
Richards Lake	LAKE/LAC	SK		74 O/3	59°10′	107°10′
Richards Landing	UNP/LNO	ON	Algoma	41 K/8	46°17′	84°02′
Richardson	UNP/LNO	NB	Charlotte	21 B/15	45°00′	66°57′
Richardson	UNP/LNO	ON	Kent	40 J/8	42°23′	82°07′
Richardson	UNP/LNO	SK	32-16-18-W2	72 I/8	50°23′	104°27′
Richardson Bay	BAY/BAIE	SK		64 L/7	58°28′	102°54′
Richardson, Cape	CAPE/CAP	NT	Franklin	120 E	82°34′	62°55′
Richardson, Cape	CAPE/CAP	NT	Franklin	47 B	68°47′	85°32′
Richardson Island	ISL/ÎLE	NT	Mackenzie	86 E	65°45′	118°21′
Richardson Islands	ISL/ÎLE	NT	Franklin	77 B	68°33′	110°45′
Richardson Lake	LAKE/LAC	AB	108-6,7-W4	74 L/6	58°23′	111°02′

NAME NOM	ENTITY ENTITÉ	LOC 1 LIEU 1	LOC 2 LIEU 2	MAP CARTE	POSITION LAT	LONG
Richardson, Mont	MTN/MNT	QC	Denis-Riverin	22 B/16	48°56′	66°01′
Richardson Mountains	MTN/MNT	YT/NT		116 P/7	67°23′	136°45′
Richardson Point	CAPE/CAP	NT	Keewatin	67 A	68°20′	96°23′
Richardson River	RIV/CDE	AB/SK		74 L/6	58°25′	111°14′
Richardson River	RIV/CDE	NT	Mackenzie	86 O	67°55′	115°31′
Richards Point	CAPE/CAP	NT	Franklin	99 A	76°34′	121°20′
Richardsville	UNP/LNO	NB	Restigouche	22 B/2	48°00′	66°38′
Richard-Village	UNP/LNO	NB	Kent	21 I/14	46°48′	65°16′
Rich Bar	UNP/LNO	BC	Cariboo	93 B/16	52°55′	122°27′
Rich Bar 4	IR/RI	BC	Cariboo	93 B/16	52°56′	122°29′
Rich, Cape	CAPE/CAP	ON	Grey	41 A/10	44°43′	80°38′
Richdale	UNP/LNO	AB	34-30-12-W4	72 M/12	51°37′	111°36′
Richelieu	CITY/VIL1	QC	Rouville	31 H/6	45°27′	73°15′
Richelieu, Rapides	RAP/RAP	QC	Lotbinière	21 L/12	46°39′	71°55′
Richelieu, Rivière	RIV/CDE	QC	Le Bas-Richelieu	31 I/3	46°03′	73°07′
Richer	UNP/LNO	MB	16,17-8-8-E	62 H/9	49°39′	96°27′
Richfield	UNP/LNO	NS	Digby	21 A/4	44°07′	65°56′
Rich Hill	UNP/LNO	ON	Simcoe	31 D/4	44°00′	79°46′
Richibucto	TOWN/VIL2	NB	Kent	21 I/10	46°41′	64°52′
Richibucto	GEOG/GÉOG	NB	Kent	21 I/10	46°38′	64°52′
Richibucto 15	IR/RI	NB	Kent	21 I/10	46°35′	65°00′
Richibucto Cape	CAPE/CAP	NB	Kent	21 I/10	46°40′	64°43′
Richibucto Harbour	BAY/BAIE	NB	Kent	21 I/10	46°42′	64°50′
Richibucto River	RIV/CDE	NB	Kent	21 I/10	46°42′	64°51′
Richibucto-Village	UNP/LNO	NB	Kent	21 I/10	46°39′	64°45′
Rich Lake	UNP/LNO	AB	5-64-11-W4	73 L/12	54°30′	111°37′
Rich Lake	LAKE/LAC	AB	64-11-W4	73 L/12	54°32′	111°33′
Richland	UNP/LNO	MB	10-6,7-E	62 H/15	49°50′	96°38′
Richlea	UNP/LNO	SK	4-26-19-W3	72 N/2	51°11′	108°35′
Richmond	CITY/VIL1	QC	Le Val-Saint-François	31 H/9	45°40′	72°09′
Richmond	CITY/VIL1	BC	New Westminster	92 G/3	49°10′	123°07′
Richmond	VILG/VILG	PE	Prince	11 L/12	46°31′	63°59′
Richmond	MUN1/AZM1	NS	Richmond	11 F/10	45°39′	60°46′
Richmond	MUN2/AZM2	ON	Lennox and Addington	31 C/6	44°19′	77°03′
Richmond	UNP/LNO	PE	Prince	11 L/12	46°30′	63°59′
Richmond	UNP/LNO	NS	Cumberland	11 E/14	45°45′	63°28′
Richmond	UNP/LNO	ON	Carleton	31 G/4	45°11′	75°50′
Richmond	UNP/LNO	ON	Elgin	40 I/15	42°46′	80°51′
Richmond	UNP/LNO	SK	15-37-5-W3	73 B/2	52°11′	106°38′
Richmond	GEOG/GÉOG	NS		11 F/10	45°39′	60°46′
Richmond	GEOG/GÉOG	NB	Carleton	21 J/4	46°07′	67°43′
Richmond Corner	UNP/LNO	NB	Carleton	21 J/4	46°09′	67°42′
Richmond Heights	UNP/LNO	SK		73 B/2	52°09′	106°39′
Richmond Hill	TOWN/VIL2	ON	York	30 M/14	43°52′	79°27′
Richmond Lakes	UNP/LNO	MB		62 H/14	49°46′	97°10′
Richmond Park	UNP/LNO	MB		62 G/13	49°49′	99°58′
Richmond Road	UNP/LNO	NS	Yarmouth	20 O/16	43°59′	66°07′
Richmond West	UNP/LNO	MB		62 H/14	49°47′	97°10′
Richmound	VILG/VILG	SK	23-17-28-W3	72 K/5	50°27′	109°45′
Richvale	UNP/LNO	ON	York	30 M/14	43°51′	79°26′
Rich Valley	UNP/LNO	AB	22-56-3-W5	83 G/16	53°51′	114°21′
Richview Gardens	UNP/LNO	ON	York	30 M/12	43°41′	79°33′
Richwood	UNP/LNO	ON	Oxford	40 P/2	43°13′	80°30′
Ricinus	UNP/LNO	AB	9-36-7-W5	83 B/2	52°05′	114°57′
Ricketts Bridge	UNP/LNO	NF		1 N/10	47°36′	52°44′
Ricketts, Cape	CAPE/CAP	NT	Franklin	58 E	74°38′	91°17′
Riddell River	RIV/CDE	YT		105 K/16	62°51′	132°25′
Rideau	MUN2/AZM2	ON	Carleton	31 G/4	45°08′	75°41′
Rideau Canal - also-aussi - Rideau, Canal	PARK/PARC	ON	Leeds	31 C/16	44°54′	76°04′
Rideau, Canal - also-aussi - Rideau Canal	PARK/PARC	ON	Leeds	31 C/16	44°54′	76°04′
Rideau Ferry	UNP/LNO	ON	Leeds	31 C/16	44°51′	76°09′
Rideau Heights	UNP/LNO	ON	Frontenac	31 C/8	44°16′	76°29′
Rideau Heights	UNP/LNO	SK		72 I/5	50°26′	105°33′
Rideau River	RIV/CDE	ON	Carleton	31 G/5	45°27′	75°42′
Rideout Island	ISL/ÎLE	NT	Franklin	76 O	67°17′	107°39′
Rider	UNP/LNO	BC	Cariboo	93 H/7	53°29′	120°32′
Ridgeclough	UNP/LNO	AB	2-46-1-W4	73 D/16	52°56′	110°02′
Ridgedale	VILG/VILG	SK	17-47-15-W2	73 H/1	53°04′	104°09′
Ridgedale	UNP/LNO	BC	New Westminster	92 G/1	49°07′	122°15′
Ridgehill	UNP/LNO	ON	Peel	30 M/12	43°41′	79°46′
Ridgemount	UNP/LNO	ON	Welland	30 L/14	42°56′	79°01′
Ridge Point	UNP/LNO	QC	Côte-Nord-du-Golfe-Saint-Laurent	22 I/7	50°17′	64°38′
Ridge River	RIV/CDE	ON	Cochrane	42 K/8	50°25′	84°20′
Ridgetown	TOWN/VIL2	ON	Kent	40 I/5	42°26′	81°54′
Ridgeville	UNP/LNO	ON	Welland	30 M/3	43°02′	79°19′

NAME NOM	ENTITY ENTITÉ	LOC 1 LIEU 1	LOC 2 LIEU 2	MAP CARTE	POSITION LAT	LONG
Ridgeville	UNP/LNO	MB	28,29-1-4-E	62 H/3	49°04'	97°01'
Ridgeway	UNP/LNO	ON	Welland	30 L/14	42°53'	79°03'
Ridgewood	UNP/LNO	ON	Welland	30 L/14	42°54'	79°02'
Ridgewood	UNP/LNO	ON	Peel	30 M/12	43°43'	79°38'
Riding Mountain	UNP/LNO	MB	10-18-15-W	62 J/11	50°32'	99°28'
Riding Mountain	MTN/MNT	MB	4,9-20-16-W	62 J/12	50°42'	99°38'
Riding Mountain National Park - also-aussi - Mont-Riding, Parc national du	PARK/PARC	MB		62 K/16	50°53'	100°15'
Riding Mountain Park East Gate Registration Complex National Historic Site - also-aussi - Centre-d'Inscription-de-l'Entrée-Est-du-Parc-du- Mont-Riding, Lieu historique national du	PARK/PARC	MB	19,20-16-W1	62 J/12	50°41'	99°33'
Ridley	UNP/LNO	BC	Range 5 Coast	103 J/1	54°15'	130°19'
Ridley Heights	UNP/LNO	ON	Lincoln	30 M/3	43°09'	79°16'
Ridpath	UNP/LNO	SK	29-16-W3	72 N/9	51°31'	108°07'
Riel	VILG/VILG	MB		62 H/14	49°48'	97°05'
Riel	UNP/LNO	MB		62 H/14	49°49'	97°07'
Riel House National Historic Site - also-aussi - Maison-Riel, Lieu historique national de la	PARK/PARC	MB		62 H/14	49°49'	97°08'
Rife	UNP/LNO	AB	17-60-7-W4	73 L/3	54°10'	111°00'
Rigaud	VILG/VILG	QC	Vaudreuil-Soulanges	31 G/8	45°29'	74°18'
Rigaud, Montagne de	MTN/MNT	QC	Vaudreuil-Soulanges	31 G/8	45°27'	74°18'
Rigaud River - also-aussi - Rigaud, Rivière	RIV/CDE	ON	Prescott	31 G/8	45°30'	74°19'
Rigaud, Rivière - also-aussi - Rigaud River	RIV/CDE	QC	Vaudreuil-Soulanges	31 G/8	45°30'	74°19'
Rigby Bay	BAY/BAIE	NT	Franklin	58 E	74°34'	90°03'
Right Hand Branch Tobique River	RIV/CDE	NB	Victoria	21 O/3	47°15'	67°09'
Rignold	UNP/LNO	MB	21-12-8-W	62 J/2	50°01'	98°31'
Rigolet	VILG/VILG	NF		13 J/1	54°11'	58°26'
Rikitakikok	UNP/LNO	QC	Le Haut-Saint-Maurice	32 B/14	48°55'	75°00'
Riley	UNP/LNO	BC	Kootenay	82 G/12	49°35'	115°43'
Riley Brook	UNP/LNO	NB	Victoria	21 O/3	47°10'	67°13'
Riley Creek 1B	IR/RI	BC	Lillooet	92 I/12	50°36'	121°51'
Riley Lake	UNP/LNO	ON	Muskoka	31 D/14	44°50'	79°12'
Riley Lake	LAKE/LAC	ON	Muskoka	31 D/14	44°50'	79°11'
Riley Park	UNP/LNO	BC	New Westminster	92 G/3	49°15'	123°06'
Rimbey	TOWN/VIL2	AB	28-42-2-W5	83 B/9	52°38'	114°14'
Rimington	UNP/LNO	ON	Hastings	31 C/11	44°36'	77°28'
Rimouski	CITY/VIL1	QC	Rimouski-Neigette	22 C/7	48°26'	68°33'
Rimouski-Est	TOWN/VIL2	QC	Rimouski-Neigette	22 C/7	48°28'	68°31'
Rimouski-Neigette	MUN1/AZM1	QC	Rimouski-Neigette	22 C/7	48°20'	68°40'
Rimouski, Petite rivière	RIV/CDE	QC	Rimouski-Neigette	22 C/7	48°20'	68°32'
Rimouski, Réserve faunique de	PARK/PARC	QC	Rimouski-Neigette	22 C/1	48°03'	68°15'
Rimouski River - also-aussi - Rimouski, Rivière	RIV/CDE	NB	Restigouche	22 C/7	48°27'	68°32'
Rimouski, Rivière - also-aussi - Rimouski River	RIV/CDE	QC	Rimouski-Neigette	22 C/7	48°27'	68°32'
Rineland - see-voir - Rheinland	UNP/LNO	SK		73 B/7	52°25'	106°30'
Ringold	UNP/LNO	ON	Kent	40 J/8	42°21'	82°17'
Ring Point	CAPE/CAP	BC	Range 4 Coast	103 H/4	53°13'	129°36'
Rings Corner	UNP/LNO	NB	Westmorland	21 I/2	46°13'	64°31'
Ringwood	UNP/LNO	ON	York	30 M/14	43°58'	79°17'
Rio Grande	UNP/LNO	NB	Gloucester	21 P/12	47°34'	65°47'
Rio Grande	UNP/LNO	AB	36-70-12-W6	83 M/4	55°06'	119°42'
Riondel	UNP/LNO	BC	Kootenay	82 F/15	49°46'	116°51'
Riou	UNP/LNO	QC	Les Basques	22 C/2	48°03'	69°00'
Riou Lake	LAKE/LAC	SK		74 O/1	59°07'	106°25'
Rioulx Creek	RIV/CDE	BC	Kootenay	82 L/8	50°17'	118°02'
Rioux	UNP/LNO	NF		2 D/1	48°12'	54°02'
Ripault, Lac	LAKE/LAC	QC	Minganie	12 M/10	51°33'	62°51'
Ripault, Lac	LAKE/LAC	QC	Charlevoix	21 M/7	47°28'	70°45'
Ripley	UNP/LNO	ON	Bruce	41 A/4	44°04'	81°35'
Ripley Loop	UNP/LNO	NS	Cumberland	11 E/13	45°49'	63°51'
Ripon	TOWN/VIL2	QC	Papineau	31 G/14	45°47'	75°06'
Ripon	VILG/VILG	QC	Papineau	31 G/14	45°48'	75°09'
Ripple	UNP/LNO	ON	Thunder Bay	42 D/15	48°48'	86°44'
Ripple Mountain	MTN/MNT	BC	Kootenay	82 F/3	49°02'	117°05'
Ripples	UNP/LNO	NB	Sunbury	21 G/16	46°00'	66°13'
Risborough	VILG/VILG	QC	Le Granit	21 E/10	45°45'	70°42'
Riske Creek	UNP/LNO	BC	Lillooet	92 O/15	51°58'	122°31'
Riske Creek	RIV/CDE	BC	Lillooet	92 O/16	51°53'	122°24'
Ristigouche-Partie-Sud-Est	VILG/VILG	QC	Avignon	22 B/2	48°03'	66°52'
Ristigouche, Réserve écologique de	PARK/PARC	QC	Avignon	22 B/2	48°02'	66°53'
Ristigouche, Rivière - also-aussi - **Restigouche River**	RIV/CDE	QC/NB		22 B/1	48°04'	66°20'
Ristigouche, Secteur	UNP/LNO	QC	Avignon	21 O/15	47°59'	66°56'
Ritchance	UNP/LNO	ON	Prescott	31 G/10	45°34'	74°48'
Ritchie	UNP/LNO	NB	York	21 G/14	45°58'	67°22'
Ritchie	UNP/LNO	SK	36-5-23-W2	72 H/7	49°25'	104°58'
Ritchie	UNP/LNO	BC	Range 5 Coast	103 I/16	54°55'	128°23'
Ritchie Lake	UNP/LNO	NB	Kings	21 H/5	45°25'	65°59'

NAME NOM	ENTITY ENTITÉ	LOC 1 LIEU 1	LOC 2 LIEU 2	MAP CARTE	POSITION LAT	LONG
Ritch Island	ISL/ÎLE	NT	Mackenzie	86 L	66°52′	119°18′
Ritchot	MUN2/AZM2	MB		62 H/11	49°42′	97°05′
Ritchot	UNP/LNO	MB		62 H/14	49°48′	97°07′
Rivard	UNP/LNO	QC	Coaticook	21 E/4	45°09′	71°40′
Riverbank	UNP/LNO	NB	Kings	21 H/12	45°40′	65°39′
Riverbank	UNP/LNO	NB	Carleton	21 J/5	46°24′	67°36′
Riverbank	UNP/LNO	ON	Wellington	40 P/15	43°49′	80°37′
Riverbend	UNP/LNO	QC	Lac-Saint-Jean-Est	22 D/12	48°34′	71°39′
Riverbend	UNP/LNO	MB		62 H/14	49°58′	97°06′
Riverbend	UNP/LNO	AB	15-54-23-W4	83 H/11	53°40′	113°18′
River Bennet	UNP/LNO	NS	Victoria	11 K/7	46°20′	60°32′
River Bourgeois	UNP/LNO	NS	Richmond	11 F/10	45°38′	60°57′
River Brook	UNP/LNO	NF		12 B/2	48°08′	58°48′
River Canard	UNP/LNO	ON	Essex	40 J/3	42°11′	83°05′
River Centre	UNP/LNO	NS	Inverness	11 F/14	45°59′	61°26′
River Charlo	UNP/LNO	NB	Restigouche	21 O/16	47°59′	66°17′
Rivercourse	UNP/LNO	AB	34-46-1-W4	73 E/1	53°01′	110°03′
Rivercrest	UNP/LNO	MB		62 I/3	50°00′	97°03′
Riverdale	UNP/LNO	NF		1 N/6	47°30′	53°01′
Riverdale	UNP/LNO	PE	Queens	11 L/3	46°14′	63°21′
Riverdale	UNP/LNO	NS	Digby	21 A/5	44°21′	65°52′
Riverdale	UNP/LNO	ON	Stormont	31 G/2	45°01′	74°46′
Riverdale	UNP/LNO	ON	York	30 M/11	43°40′	79°21′
Riverdale	UNP/LNO	MB		62 H/14	49°58′	97°04′
Riverdale	UNP/LNO	MB	14-14-19-W	62 J/4	50°11′	99°58′
Riverdale	UNP/LNO	YT		105 D/11	60°42′	135°01′
River de Chute	UNP/LNO	NB	Victoria	21 J/12	46°36′	67°44′
River de Chute Siding	UNP/LNO	NB	Carleton	21 J/12	46°36′	67°43′
River Denys	UNP/LNO	NS	Inverness	11 F/14	45°50′	61°10′
River Denys Centre	UNP/LNO	NS	Inverness	11 F/14	45°52′	61°14′
River Denys Road	UNP/LNO	NS	Inverness	11 F/14	45°52′	61°19′
River Drive Park	UNP/LNO	ON	York	31 D/4	44°08′	79°31′
River East	UNP/LNO	MB		62 H/14	49°57′	97°04′
Riverfield	UNP/LNO	QC	Le Haut-Saint-Laurent	31 H/4	45°09′	73°49′
River Glade	UNP/LNO	NB	Westmorland	21 H/14	45°59′	65°07′
Rivergrove	UNP/LNO	MB		62 H/14	49°57′	97°05′
Riverhead	VILG/VILG	NF		1 K/13	46°58′	53°31′
Riverhead	UNP/LNO	NF		1 K/15	46°59′	52°58′
Riverhead	UNP/LNO	NF		1 N/14	47°53′	53°05′
Riverhead	UNP/LNO	NF		1 N/11	47°32′	53°12′
Riverhead	UNP/LNO	NF		1 N/11	47°40′	53°16′
Riverhead	UNP/LNO	NF		1 K/14	46°46′	53°21′
River Head	UNP/LNO	NS	Queens	20 P/15	43°56′	64°50′
Riverhead	UNP/LNO	NS	Shelburne	20 P/12	43°34′	65°36′
Riverhead Brook	RIV/CDE	NF		2 D/10	48°38′	54°34′
River Hebert	VILG/VILG	NS	Cumberland	21 H/9	45°41′	64°23′
River Hebert East (Strathcona)	UNP/LNO	NS	Cumberland	21 H/9	45°42′	64°21′
River Heights	UNP/LNO	ON	Cochrane	42 G/8	49°26′	82°26′
River Heights	UNP/LNO	MB		62 H/14	49°52′	97°11′
Riverheights	UNP/LNO	MB		62 G/13	49°51′	100°00′
River Heights	UNP/LNO	SK		72 I/7	50°26′	104°38′
River Heights	UNP/LNO	SK		73 B/2	52°10′	106°38′
River Hills	UNP/LNO	MB	22-13-11-E	62 I/1	50°05′	96°02′
Riverhurst	VILG/VILG	SK	26-22-7-W3	72 J/15	50°54′	106°52′
River John	UNP/LNO	NS	Pictou	11 E/11	45°45′	63°03′
River Jordan	UNP/LNO	BC	Renfrew	92 C/8	48°25′	124°03′
Riverland	UNP/LNO	MB	15-15-11-E	52 L/5	50°15′	96°00′
River of Ponds	VILG/VILG	NF		12 I/11	50°32′	57°24′
River of Ponds Lake	LAKE/LAC	NF		12 I/11	50°30′	57°20′
River Park	UNP/LNO	SK		72 I/5	50°23′	105°32′
River Park South	UNP/LNO	MB		62 H/14	49°49′	97°06′
River Philip	UNP/LNO	NS	Cumberland	11 E/12	45°41′	63°54′
River Philip Centre	UNP/LNO	NS	Cumberland	11 E/12	45°38′	63°56′
Riverport	UNP/LNO	NS	Lunenburg	21 A/8	44°18′	64°20′
River Ryan	UNP/LNO	NS	Cape Breton	11 K/1	46°13′	60°05′
Rivers	TOWN/VIL2	MB	23-12-21-W	62 K/1	50°02′	100°14′
Riversdale	UNP/LNO	NS	Colchester	11 E/6	45°25′	63°03′
Riversdale	UNP/LNO	NS	Queens	21 A/2	44°11′	64°41′
Riversdale	UNP/LNO	ON	Bruce	41 A/3	44°05′	81°20′
Riversdale	UNP/LNO	SK		73 B/2	52°08′	106°41′
Riversdale South	UNP/LNO	SK		73 B/2	52°07′	106°41′
Riverside	MUN2/AZM2	MB		62 G/5	49°20′	99°45′
Riverside	UNP/LNO	NS	Inverness	11 F/11	45°42′	61°15′
Riverside	UNP/LNO	NS	Colchester	11 E/3	45°10′	63°23′
Riverside	UNP/LNO	NS	Hants	21 H/1	45°06′	64°07′

NAME NOM	ENTITY ENTITÉ	LOC 1 LIEU 1	LOC 2 LIEU 2	MAP CARTE	POSITION LAT	LONG
Riverside	UNP/LNO	ON	Ontario	30 M/14	43°52′	79°04′
Riverside	UNP/LNO	ON	Simcoe	31 D/12	44°41′	79°48′
Riverside	UNP/LNO	ON	Middlesex	40 I/13	42°46′	81°32′
Riverside	UNP/LNO	ON	Essex	40 J/7	42°20′	82°57′
Riverside	UNP/LNO	MB		62 I/3	50°01′	97°04′
Riverside	UNP/LNO	MB	20,29-5-1-E	62 H/6	49°25′	97°25′
Riverside	UNP/LNO	BC	New Westminster	92 G/1	49°07′	122°18′
Riverside-Albert	VILG/VILG	NB	Albert	21 H/15	45°45′	64°44′
Riverside Beach	UNP/LNO	NS	Cumberland	21 H/8	45°23′	64°18′
Riverside Corner	UNP/LNO	NS	Hants	11 E/4	45°08′	63°47′
Riverside Estates	HAM/HAM	SK	31-35-5-W3	73 B/2	52°03′	106°42′
Riverside Heights	UNP/LNO	ON	Dundas	31 B/14	44°56′	75°08′
Riverside No. 168	MUN2/AZM2	SK		72 K/8	50°30′	108°15′
Riverside Trailer Park	UNP/LNO	ON	Kent	40 J/8	42°26′	82°09′
Rivers Inlet	UNP/LNO	BC	Range 2 Coast	92 M/11	51°41′	127°15′
Rivers Inlet	BAY/BAIE	BC	Range 2 Coast	92 M/5	51°28′	127°35′
Rivers, Lake of the	LAKE/LAC	SK		72 H/13	49°49′	105°44′
River Springs	UNP/LNO	BC	New Westminster	92 G/7	49°17′	122°46′
Riverstone	UNP/LNO	SK	32-47-15-W2	73 H/1	53°06′	104°09′
Riverstown	UNP/LNO	ON	Wellington	40 P/15	43°56′	80°40′
River Tillard	UNP/LNO	NS	Richmond	11 F/10	45°39′	60°55′
Riverton	VILG/VILG	MB	23-4-E	62 I/15	51°00′	97°00′
Riverton	UNP/LNO	PE	Kings	11 L/7	46°18′	62°41′
Riverton	UNP/LNO	NS	Pictou	11 E/10	45°31′	62°40′
Riverton Heights	UNP/LNO	NS	Pictou	11 E/10	45°33′	62°40′
Rivervale	UNP/LNO	BC	Kootenay	82 F/4	49°07′	117°44′
River Valley	UNP/LNO	ON	Hastings	31 C/5	44°16′	77°33′
River Valley	UNP/LNO	ON	Nipissing	41 I/9	46°35′	80°11′
Riverview	TOWN/VIL2	NB	Albert	21 I/2	46°04′	64°48′
Riverview	UNP/LNO	NS	Pictou	11 E/10	45°35′	62°39′
Riverview	UNP/LNO	NS	Cumberland	11 E/13	45°48′	63°47′
River View	UNP/LNO	NB	Albert	21 H/14	45°45′	65°05′
Riverview	UNP/LNO	ON	Renfrew	31 F/14	45°51′	77°12′
Riverview	UNP/LNO	ON	Peel	30 M/12	43°36′	79°43′
Riverview	UNP/LNO	ON	Dufferin	41 A/1	44°06′	80°22′
Riverview	UNP/LNO	MB		62 H/14	49°52′	97°08′
River View	UNP/LNO	SK		72 I/5	50°23′	105°33′
Riverview	UNP/LNO	AB	23-56-5-W4	73 E/15	53°52′	110°39′
Riverview Beach	UNP/LNO	ON	York	31 D/6	44°20′	79°13′
Riverview Heights	UNP/LNO	NB	Albert	21 I/2	46°04′	64°49′
Riverview Heights	UNP/LNO	NB	Kings	21 H/5	45°27′	65°59′
Riverview Heights	UNP/LNO	ON	Grenville	31 B/12	44°42′	75°32′
Riverville	UNP/LNO	NS	Inverness	11 K/3	46°08′	61°20′
River West Park	UNP/LNO	MB		62 H/14	49°52′	97°19′
Rivett Lake	LAKE/LAC	NT	Mackenzie	75 M	63°18′	111°50′
Rivière-à-Claude	VILG/VILG	QC	Denis-Riverin	22 H/4	49°13′	65°54′
Rivière-à-la-Chaloupe	UNP/LNO	QC	Minganie	22 I/6	50°17′	65°07′
Rivière-à-la-Truite	UNP/LNO	NB	Madawaska	21 N/7	47°27′	68°31′
Rivière-à-Pierre	VILG/VILG	QC	Portneuf	31 I/16	46°59′	72°11′
Rivière-au-Portage	UNP/LNO	NB	Kent	21 I/15	46°56′	64°55′
Rivière-au-Renard	UNP/LNO	QC	La Côte-de-Gaspé	22 A/16	49°00′	64°23′
Rivière-au-Renard-Ouest	UNP/LNO	QC	La Côte-de-Gaspé	22 A/16	49°00′	64°24′
Rivière-au-Tonnerre	VILG/VILG	QC	Minganie	22 I/7	50°16′	64°47′
Rivière-aux-Graines	UNP/LNO	QC	Minganie	22 I/6	50°17′	65°11′
Rivière-aux-Outardes	MUN2/AZM2	QC	Manicouagan	22 K/6	50°15′	69°00′
Rivière-aux-Rats	UNP/LNO	QC	Le Haut-Saint-Maurice	31 P/2	47°13′	72°53′
Rivière-Barry	UNP/LNO	QC	Pontiac	31 F/15	45°46′	76°44′
Rivière-Beaudette	VILG/VILG	QC	Vaudreuil-Soulanges	31 G/1	45°14′	74°20′
Rivière-Bell	UNP/LNO	QC	Jamésie	32 F/13	49°47′	77°38′
Rivière-Bersimis	UNP/LNO	QC	La Haute-Côte-Nord	22 C/15	48°56′	68°42′
Rivière-Blanche	UNP/LNO	QC	Matane	22 B/13	48°47′	67°42′
Rivière-Bleue	VILG/VILG	QC	Témiscouata	21 N/6	47°26′	69°03′
Rivière-Boisvert	UNP/LNO	QC	Le Domaine-du-Roy	32 G/9	49°30′	74°11′
Rivière-Bonaventure	MUN2/AZM2	QC	Bonaventure	22 A/12	48°30′	65°36′
Rivière-Bonaventure	UNP/LNO	QC	Bonaventure	22 A/3	48°04′	65°27′
Rivière-Bonjour	MUN2/AZM2	QC	Matane	22 B/15	48°46′	66°55′
Rivière-Brochu	UNP/LNO	QC	Sept-Rivières	22 J/2	50°06′	66°42′
Rivière-Cabano	UNP/LNO	QC	Témiscouata	21 N/10	47°33′	68°57′
Rivière-Caplan	UNP/LNO	QC	Bonaventure	22 A/4	48°07′	65°44′
Rivière-Cascapédia, Réserve faunique de la	PARK/PARC	QC	Matane	22 B/9	48°40′	66°12′
Rivière-Cazeau	UNP/LNO	QC	La Côte-de-Beaupré	21 L/14	46°57′	71°03′
Rivière-Chalifour	UNP/LNO	QC	Jamésie	32 I/5	50°24′	73°41′
Rivière-Coupée	UNP/LNO	QC	Acton	31 H/10	45°39′	72°35′
Rivière-Creuse	UNP/LNO	QC	Témiscouata	21 N/10	47°35′	68°47′
Rivière-Croche	UNP/LNO	QC	Le Haut-Saint-Maurice	31 P/10	47°32′	72°46′

NAME NOM	ENTITY ENTITÉ	LOC 1 LIEU 1	LOC 2 LIEU 2	MAP CARTE	POSITION LAT	LONG
Rivière-de-la-Savane	MUN2/AZM2	QC	Mékinac	31 P/4	47°03′	73°38′
Rivière-des-Caches	UNP/LNO	NB	Northumberland	21 P/3	47°14′	65°07′
Rivière-des-Caps	UNP/LNO	QC	Rivière-du-Loup	21 N/12	47°44′	69°38′
Rivière-des-Fèves	UNP/LNO	QC	Beauharnois-Salaberry	31 H/4	45°12′	73°46′
Rivière-des-Hurons	UNP/LNO	QC	Rouville	31 H/6	45°30′	73°09′
Rivière-des-Plante	UNP/LNO	QC	Robert-Cliche	21 L/7	46°15′	70°49′
Rivière-des-Prairies	UNP/LNO	QC	Communauté urbaine de Montréal	31 H/12	45°39′	73°35′
Rivière-des-Roches	UNP/LNO	QC	La Côte-de-Beaupré	21 M/2	47°08′	70°50′
Rivière-du-Loup	CITY/VIL1	QC	Rivière-du-Loup	21 N/13	47°50′	69°32′
Rivière-du-Loup	MUN1/AZM1	QC	Rivière-du-Loup	21 N/14	47°54′	69°20′
Rivière-du-Moulin	UNP/LNO	QC	Le Fjord-du-Saguenay	22 D/6	48°26′	71°02′
Rivière-du-Moulin, Réserve écologique de la	PARK/PARC	QC	Lotbinière	21 L/12	46°39′	71°54′
Rivière-du-Nord	UNP/LNO	QC	Le Haut-Saint-François	21 E/6	45°21′	71°25′
Rivière-du-Portage	UNP/LNO	NB	Northumberland	21 P/7	47°25′	64°56′
Rivière-Éperlan	UNP/LNO	QC	La Haute-Côte-Nord	22 C/11	48°35′	69°13′
Rivière-Éternité	VILG/VILG	QC	Le Fjord-du-Saguenay	22 D/8	48°15′	70°25′
Rivière-Gilbert	UNP/LNO	QC	Robert-Cliche	21 L/2	46°12′	70°44′
Rivière-Hâtée	UNP/LNO	QC	Rimouski-Neigette	22 C/7	48°24′	68°38′
Rivière-Héva	VILG/VILG	QC	Vallée-de-l'Or	32 D/1	48°14′	78°13′
Rivière-Kipawa	MUN2/AZM2	QC	Témiscamingue	31 M/2	47°00′	78°35′
Rivière-Koksoak	MUN2/AZM2	QC	Kativik	24 F/3	57°10′	69°20′
Rivière-Lafleur	UNP/LNO	QC	L'Île-d'Orléans	21 L/15	46°54′	70°56′
Rivière-La Guerre	UNP/LNO	QC	Le Haut-Saint-Laurent	31 G/1	45°07′	74°18′
Rivière-la-Madeleine	UNP/LNO	QC	Denis-Riverin	22 H/3	49°14′	65°18′
Rivière-Loïs	UNP/LNO	QC	Abitibi-Ouest	32 D/10	48°41′	79°00′
Rivière-Mailloux	UNP/LNO	QC	Charlevoix-Est	21 M/9	47°39′	70°09′
Rivière-Malbaie	VILG/VILG	QC	Charlevoix-Est	21 M/9	47°40′	70°09′
Rivière-Manie	UNP/LNO	QC	Kamouraska	21 N/5	47°24′	69°39′
Rivière-Matane	UNP/LNO	QC	Matane	22 B/11	48°39′	67°20′
Rivière-Matawin	UNP/LNO	QC	Mékinac	31 I/15	46°55′	72°56′
Rivière-Mékinac	UNP/LNO	QC	Mékinac	31 I/15	46°50′	72°46′
Rivière-Metgermette-Nord	UNP/LNO	QC	Les Etchemins	21 L/1	46°06′	70°21′
Rivière-Mistassini	MUN2/AZM2	QC	Maria-Chapdelaine	32 H/15	49°55′	72°50′
Rivière-Mont-Louis	UNP/LNO	QC	Denis-Riverin	22 H/4	49°12′	65°44′
Rivière-Morris	UNP/LNO	QC	La Côte-de-Gaspé	22 A/16	48°58′	64°28′
Rivière-Mouchalagane	MUN2/AZM2	QC	Caniapiscau	23 C/7	52°20′	68°30′
Rivière-Nipissis	MUN2/AZM2	QC	Sept-Rivières	22 P/5	51°15′	65°55′
Rivière-Noire	UNP/LNO	QC	Charlevoix-Est	21 N/13	47°51′	69°53′
Rivière-Noire	UNP/LNO	QC	Matawinie	31 I/5	46°18′	73°33′
Rivière-Nord	UNP/LNO	QC	Beauharnois-Salaberry	31 H/5	45°16′	73°54′
Rivière-Nouvelle	MUN2/AZM2	QC	Avignon	22 B/8	48°18′	66°29′
Rivière-Ojima	MUN2/AZM2	QC	Abitibi-Ouest	32 D/15	48°50′	78°42′
Rivière-Ouelle	VILG/VILG	QC	Kamouraska	21 M/8	47°26′	70°01′
Rivière-Ouelle-Station	UNP/LNO	QC	Kamouraska	21 N/5	47°26′	69°57′
Rivière-Paspébiac	UNP/LNO	QC	Bonaventure	22 A/3	48°03′	65°16′
Rivière-Patapédia-Est	MUN2/AZM2	QC	La Matapédia	22 B/4	48°07′	67°39′
Rivière-Pentecôte	VILG/VILG	QC	Sept-Rivières	22 G/14	49°47′	67°10′
Rivière-Petit-Saguenay, Réserve faunique de la	PARK/PARC	QC	Le Fjord-du-Saguenay	22 D/1	48°10′	70°03′
Rivière-Pigou	UNP/LNO	QC	Sept-Rivières	22 I/5	50°16′	65°35′
Rivière-Plate	UNP/LNO	QC	Rivière-du-Loup	21 N/15	47°52′	68°58′
Rivière-Port-Daniel	UNP/LNO	QC	Pabok	22 A/2	48°12′	64°58′
Rivière-Portneuf	UNP/LNO	QC	La Haute-Côte-Nord	22 C/11	48°38′	69°06′
Rivière Qui Barre	UNP/LNO	AB	30-55-26-W4	83 H/13	53°47′	113°52′
+Rivière Rouge, Canal de dérivation de la - also-aussi - Red River Floodway	MISC/DIV	MB		62 I/2	50°05′	96°56′
Rivière-Sainte-Anne, Réserve faunique de la	PARK/PARC	QC	Denis-Riverin	22 G/1	49°05′	66°30′
Rivière-Sainte-Marguerite	UNP/LNO	QC	La Haute-Côte-Nord	22 C/5	48°15′	69°52′
Rivière-Sainte-Marguerite-en-Bas	UNP/LNO	QC	Sept-Rivières	22 J/2	50°08′	66°37′
Rivière-Saint-François	UNP/LNO	QC	Drummond	31 H/16	45°48′	72°16′
Rivière-Saint-Jean	VILG/VILG	QC	Minganie	22 I/8	50°18′	64°20′
Rivière-Saint-Jean	MUN2/AZM2	QC	La Côte-de-Gaspé	22 A/15	48°50′	64°55′
Rivière-Saint-Jean, Réserve faunique de la	PARK/PARC	QC	La Côte-de-Gaspé	22 A/11	48°43′	65°06′
Rivière-Saint-Paul	UNP/LNO	QC	Côte-Nord-du-Golfe-Saint-Laurent	12 P/5	51°28′	57°43′
Rivières-Matapédia-et-Patapédia, Réserve faunique des	PARK/PARC	QC	La Matapédia	22 B/6	48°24′	67°14′
Rivière-Susie	UNP/LNO	QC	Vallée-de-l'Or	32 B/4	48°12′	75°45′
Rivière-Thompson	UNP/LNO	QC	Vallée-de-l'Or	32 C/4	48°05′	77°53′
Rivière-Trois-Pistoles	UNP/LNO	QC	Les Basques	22 C/3	48°06′	69°13′
Rivière-Turgeon	UNP/LNO	QC	Abitibi-Ouest	32 E/3	49°00′	79°10′
Rivière-Vaseuse	MUN2/AZM2	QC	La Matapédia	22 B/3	48°13′	67°28′
Rivière-Verte	VILG/VILG	NB	Madawaska	21 N/8	47°19′	68°09′
Rivière-Verte	UNP/LNO	QC	Rivière-du-Loup	21 N/14	47°47′	69°27′
Rivière-Verte	GEOG/GÉOG	NB	Madawaska	21 N/8	47°30′	68°00′
Rivière Veuve	UNP/LNO	ON	Sudbury	41 I/9	46°32′	80°25′
Rivière-Wedding	UNP/LNO	QC	Jamésie	32 F/3	49°12′	77°08′
Rivière-Windigo	MUN2/AZM2	QC	Le Haut-Saint-Maurice	31 P/13	47°55′	73°50′
Rivington	UNP/LNO	QC	Argenteuil	31 G/15	45°48′	74°41′

NAME NOM	ENTITY ENTITÉ	LOC 1 LIEU 1	LOC 2 LIEU 2	MAP CARTE	POSITION LAT	POSITION LONG
Rivulet	UNP/LNO	NS	Inverness	11 K/7	46°23'	60°57'
Roach	UNP/LNO	NB	York	21 G/10	45°40'	66°56'
Roachvale	UNP/LNO	NS	Guysborough	11 F/5	45°21'	61°33'
Roachville	UNP/LNO	NB	Kings	21 H/12	45°44'	65°32'
Roadene	UNP/LNO	SK	12-18-21-W3	72 K/10	50°30'	108°45'
Road Point	CAPE/CAP	NF		12 B/10	48°41'	58°41'
Roaring Bull Point	CAPE/CAP	NS	Pictou	11 E/10	45°41'	62°34'
Roaring River	RIV/CDE	MB	37-25-W	63 C/3	52°13'	101°02'
Robb	UNP/LNO	AB	15-49-21-W5	83 F/2	53°13'	116°58'
*Robbins	UNP/LNO	BC	Kamloops Division Yale	82 L/12	50°38'	119°59'
*Robbins Range	UNP/LNO	BC	Kamloops Division Yale	82 L/12	50°36'	120°00'
Robb Lake	LAKE/LAC	NT	Mackenzie	86 F	65°22'	116°02'
Robbtown	UNP/LNO	ON	Grey	41 A/2	44°02'	80°41'
Robe Noire, Lac de la	LAKE/LAC	QC	Minganie	12 L/10	50°42'	62°42'
Roberge	UNP/LNO	QC	Arthabaska	21 E/13	45°58'	71°48'
Robert	UNP/LNO	NF		12 I/16	50°47'	56°02'
Roberta	UNP/LNO	NS	Richmond	11 F/15	45°45'	60°53'
Robert-Bourassa, Barrage	MISC/DIV	QC	Jamésie	33 F/14	53°47'	77°27'
Robert-Bourassa, Centrale	MISC/DIV	QC	Jamésie	33 F/13	53°47'	77°32'
Robert-Bourassa, Réservoir	LAKE/LAC	QC	Jamésie	33 F/11	53°45'	77°00'
Robert Brown, Cape	CAPE/CAP	NT	Franklin	46 P	67°35'	81°21'
Robert, Cap	CAPE/CAP	QC	Minganie	12 E/8	49°29'	62°20'
Robert-Cliche	MUN1/AZM1	QC	Robert-Cliche	21 L/2	46°12'	70°49'
Robert, Lac	LAKE/LAC	QC	Jamésie	32 G/1	49°14'	74°23'
Robert, Mount	MTN/MNT	BC	Peace River	93 P/6	55°28'	121°29'
Robert Peel Inlet	BAY/BAIE	NT	Franklin	26 G	65°00'	66°56'
Roberts	UNP/LNO	ON	Sudbury	41 O/8	47°20'	82°12'
Robert's Arm	TOWN/VIL2	NF		2 E/5	49°29'	55°49'
Roberts Bay	BAY/BAIE	ON	Manitoulin	41 H/12	45°35'	81°54'
Roberts, Cape	CAPE/CAP	ON	Manitoulin	41 G/15	46°00'	82°49'
Roberts Creek	UNP/LNO	BC	New Westminster	92 G/5	49°25'	123°39'
Roberts Island	UNP/LNO	NS	Yarmouth	20 P/13	43°47'	65°53'
Roberts, Lac	LAKE/LAC	QC	Kativik	25 D/8	60°23'	70°26'
Roberts Lake	LAKE/LAC	BC	Sayward	92 K/4	50°13'	125°32'
Robertson Bay	BAY/BAIE	NT	Keewatin	34 D	55°58'	79°39'
Robertson, Lac	LAKE/LAC	QC	Minganie	12 O/3	51°00'	59°11'
Robertson Lake	LAKE/LAC	AB	120-18-W4	84 P/6	59°28'	113°00'
Robertson Point	CAPE/CAP	NT	Franklin	78 H	75°12'	105°48'
Robertson River	RIV/CDE	BC	Cowichan Lake	92 C/16	48°49'	124°08'
Robertson River	RIV/CDE	NT	Franklin	48 A	72°05'	81°01'
Robertson's Shore	UNP/LNO	ON	Lanark	31 F/1	45°01'	76°12'
Robertsonville	TOWN/VIL2	QC	L'Amiante	21 L/3	46°09'	71°13'
Robertsville	UNP/LNO	ON	Frontenac	31 C/15	44°54'	76°41'
Robertville	UNP/LNO	NB	Gloucester	21 P/12	47°42'	65°46'
Roberval	CITY/VIL1	QC	Le Domaine-du-Roy	32 A/9	48°31'	72°13'
Robeson Channel - also-aussi - Robeson, Détroit de	CHAN/CHEN	NT	Franklin	120 E/3	82°00'	61°30'
Robeson, Détroit de - also-aussi - Robeson Channel	CHAN/CHEN	NT		120 E/3	82°00'	61°30'
Robford	UNP/LNO	ON	Thunder Bay	52 A/16	48°57'	88°18'
Robichaud	UNP/LNO	NB	Westmorland	21 I/1	46°13'	64°23'
Robichaud	UNP/LNO	QC	Bonaventure	22 A/4	48°06'	65°40'
Robichaud Settlement	UNP/LNO	NB	Northumberland	21 P/6	47°15'	65°08'
Robidoux	UNP/LNO	QC	Bonaventure	22 A/5	48°16'	65°40'
Robillard Island	ISL/ÎLE	NT	Franklin	98 C	73°54'	124°28'
Robin Creek	UNP/LNO	BC	Range 5 Coast	93 L/10	54°36'	126°52'
Robinhood	UNP/LNO	SK	1-50-16-W3	73 F/8	53°17'	108°12'
Robinhood Bay	BAY/BAIE	NF		2 C/6	48°22'	53°19'
Robinhood Bay	BAY/BAIE	NT	Keewatin	55 N/9	63°45'	92°01'
Robin Landing	UNP/LNO	ON	Northumberland	31 D/1	44°13'	78°05'
Robins	UNP/LNO	NS	Richmond	11 F/11	45°30'	61°00'
Robinson	UNP/LNO	NB	Restigouche	21 O/11	47°43'	67°13'
Robinson	UNP/LNO	ON	Kenora	52 J/3	50°11'	91°18'
Robinson	UNP/LNO	AB	34-56-7-W5	83 G/15	53°53'	114°58'
Robinson	UNP/LNO	YT		105 D/7	60°27'	134°51'
Robinson Bight	UNP/LNO	NF		2 C/4	48°06'	53°48'
Robinson Corner	UNP/LNO	NS	Kings	21 H/1	45°03'	64°17'
Robinson Falls	FALL/CHUT	MB		63 I/8	54°24'	96°19'
Robinson Lake	LAKE/LAC	ON	Kenora	52 F/12	49°38'	93°59'
Robinsons	UNP/LNO	NF		12 B/2	48°15'	58°49'
Robinsons Corner	UNP/LNO	NS	Lunenburg	21 A/9	44°33'	64°15'
Robinson Sound	CHAN/CHEN	NT	Franklin	25 P	63°23'	64°25'
Robinsons River	RIV/CDE	NF		12 B/2	48°15'	58°49'
Robinson Subdivision	UNP/LNO	ON	Sudbury	41 I/6	46°28'	81°02'
Robinsonville	UNP/LNO	NB	Restigouche	21 O/15	47°52'	66°57'
Robin's Point	UNP/LNO	ON	Simcoe	31 D/13	44°46'	79°45'
Robitaille	UNP/LNO	QC	Avignon	22 B/1	48°06'	66°16'

NAME NOM	ENTITY ENTITÉ	LOC 1 LIEU 1	LOC 2 LIEU 2	MAP CARTE	POSITION LAT	LONG
Roblaytin	UNP/LNO	MB	66-24-W	63 K/10	54°45′	100°57′
Roblin	TOWN/VIL2	MB	26-28-W	62 N/3	51°14′	101°21′
Roblin	MUN2/AZM2	MB		62 G/3	49°06′	99°17′
Roblin	UNP/LNO	ON	Lennox and Addington	31 C/6	44°23′	77°01′
Roblindale	UNP/LNO	ON	Lennox and Addington	31 C/6	44°22′	77°01′
Roblin Lake	LAKE/LAC	ON	Prince Edward	31 C/3	44°03′	77°25′
Roblin Mills	UNP/LNO	ON	Prince Edward	31 C/3	44°07′	77°05′
Roblin Park	UNP/LNO	MB		62 H/14	49°51′	97°17′
Rob Roy	UNP/LNO	ON	Grey	41 A/8	44°23′	80°19′
Robsart	VILG/VILG	SK	10-5-25-W3	72 F/6	49°23′	109°17′
Robson	UNP/LNO	QC	Drummond	31 H/16	45°52′	72°11′
Robson	UNP/LNO	BC	Kootenay	82 F/5	49°20′	117°41′
Robson, Mount	MTN/MNT	BC	Cariboo	83 E/3	53°07′	119°09′
Robson West	UNP/LNO	BC	Kootenay	82 F/5	49°20′	117°42′
Rocanville	TOWN/VIL2	SK	21-16-31-W	62 K/5	50°23′	101°42′
Rocanville No. 151	MUN2/AZM2	SK		62 K/5	50°25′	101°45′
Roc-d'Or	UNP/LNO	QC	Vallée-de-l'Or	32 D/1	48°10′	78°08′
Roche-à-Boily, La	UNP/LNO	QC	Le Haut-Saint-Maurice	31 P/10	47°37′	72°53′
Roche-à-Maillot, La	UNP/LNO	QC	Bécancour	31 I/9	46°34′	72°04′
Rochebaucourt	VILG/VILG	QC	Abitibi	32 C/12	48°41′	77°30′
Roche-Blanche, La	UNP/LNO	QC	La Vallée-de-la-Gatineau	31 J/13	46°47′	75°58′
Roche-du-Diable, La	UNP/LNO	QC	Bellechasse	21 L/10	46°41′	70°48′
Rochefort	UNP/LNO	ON	Renfrew	31 F/6	45°30′	77°24′
Rochefort, Lac	LAKE/LAC	QC	Kativik	34 I/6	58°27′	73°15′
Roche, La	UNP/LNO	QC	Charlevoix	21 M/10	47°41′	70°50′
Roche Lake	LAKE/LAC	BC	Kamloops Division Yale	92 I/8	50°28′	120°09′
Roche Percee	VILG/VILG	SK	30-1-6-W2	62 E/2	49°04′	102°48′
Roche-Plate	UNP/LNO	QC	La Jacques-Cartier	21 L/14	46°57′	71°22′
Roche-Plate, La	UNP/LNO	QC	La Jacques-Cartier	31 P/8	47°25′	72°09′
Roche-Pleureuse, La	UNP/LNO	QC	Charlevoix	21 M/8	47°25′	70°20′
Roche Point	CAPE/CAP	NT	Franklin	79 B	76°43′	109°30′
Roche, Pointe de	CAPE/CAP	NT	Mackenzie	85 C	60°53′	116°07′
Rocher Bay	BAY/BAIE	NB	Albert	21 H/10	45°36′	64°51′
Rocher-de-la-Chapelle	UNP/LNO	QC	Montmagny	21 L/15	46°57′	70°35′
Rocher Fendu	UNP/LNO	ON	Renfrew	31 F/15	45°45′	76°48′
Rocher-Fendu, Le	UNP/LNO	QC	Vaudreuil-Soulanges	31 H/5	45°20′	73°58′
Rocher, Lac	LAKE/LAC	QC	Jamésie	32 K/9	50°36′	76°26′
Rocher, Lac du	LAKE/LAC	NT	Mackenzie	75 M	63°27′	111°25′
Rocher, Le	UNP/LNO	QC	Robert-Cliche	21 L/2	46°15′	70°49′
Rocher-Noir	UNP/LNO	QC	Montmagny	21 L/15	46°57′	70°31′
Rocher-Percé	UNP/LNO	QC	Le Domaine-du-Roy	32 A/8	48°26′	72°02′
Rocher River	UNP/LNO	NT	Mackenzie	85 H	61°23′	112°44′
Rochers, Baie des	BAY/BAIE	QC	Côte-Nord-du-Golfe-Saint-Laurent	12 J/11	50°37′	59°18′
Rochers-du-Cormoran	UNP/LNO	QC	Côte-Nord-du-Golfe-Saint-Laurent	12 K/1	50°10′	60°04′
Rochers, Rivière aux	RIV/CDE	QC	Sept-Rivières	22 J/2	50°01′	66°52′
Roches, Baie des	BAY/BAIE	QC	Le Fjord-du-Saguenay	22 L/10	50°35′	70°44′
Roches, Lac des	LAKE/LAC	BC	Lillooet	92 P/7	51°29′	120°34′
Roches Point	UNP/LNO	ON	York	31 D/5	44°16′	79°30′
Rochester	MUN2/AZM2	ON	Essex	40 J/7	42°15′	82°40′
Rochester	UNP/LNO	AB	24-62-24-W4	83 I/6	54°22′	113°27′
Rochette	UNP/LNO	QC	Charlevoix-Est	21 M/9	47°35′	70°16′
Rocheuses, Montagnes - also-aussi - **Rocky Mountains**	MTN/MNT	BC/AB		93 I/2	54°00′	120°47′
Rocheville	UNP/LNO	NB	Gloucester	21 P/11	47°40′	65°18′
Rochfort Bridge	UNP/LNO	AB	7-57-7-W5	83 G/14	53°55′	115°02′
Rochon Lake	LAKE/LAC	MB		53 L/1	54°14′	94°23′
Rochon Lake	LAKE/LAC	NT	Mackenzie	65 C	60°49′	101°55′
Rochon Sands	VILG/VILG	AB	19-40-20-W4	83 A/7	52°27′	112°53′
Rochon Sands Provincial Park	PARK/PARC	AB	40-20,21-W4	83 A/7	52°28′	112°53′
Rock Barra	UNP/LNO	PE	Kings	11 L/8	46°28′	62°14′
Rock Bay	UNP/LNO	BC	Sayward	92 K/6	50°20′	125°29′
Rockburn	UNP/LNO	QC	Le Haut-Saint-Laurent	31 G/1	45°01′	74°01′
Rock Chapel	UNP/LNO	ON	Wentworth	30 M/5	43°18′	79°56′
Rockcliffe Park	VILG/VILG	ON	Carleton	31 G/5	45°27′	75°41′
Rockcliffe Survey	UNP/LNO	ON	Wentworth	30 M/5	43°19′	79°54′
Rock Creek	UNP/LNO	BC	Similkameen Division Yale	82 E/2	49°03′	119°00′
Rock Creek	UNP/LNO	YT		116 B/3	64°04′	139°05′
Rock Creek	RIV/CDE	SK	5-1-6-W3	72 G/2	49°00′	106°47′
Rock Creek	RIV/CDE	BC	Similkameen Division Yale	82 E/2	49°03′	119°00′
Rockcroft	UNP/LNO	ON	Peterborough	31 D/9	44°39′	78°23′
Rockcut	UNP/LNO	ON	Wellington	40 P/9	43°37′	80°09′
Rockdale	UNP/LNO	NS	Richmond	11 F/10	45°37′	60°48′
Rockdale	UNP/LNO	ON	Prescott	31 G/11	45°30′	75°03′
Rockdale	UNP/LNO	ON	Peterborough	31 C/12	44°31′	77°48′
Rock Dell	UNP/LNO	SK	22-25-7-W2	62 M/2	51°11′	102°54′
Rock Elm	UNP/LNO	NS	Cape Breton	11 F/16	45°55′	60°20′

NAME / NOM	ENTITY / ENTITÉ	LOC 1 / LIEU 1	LOC 2 / LIEU 2	MAP / CARTE	POSITION LAT	POSITION LONG
Rockfield	UNP/LNO	NS	Pictou	11 E/10	45°37′	62°51′
Rockfield	UNP/LNO	ON	Leeds	31 B/5	44°28′	75°57′
Rockford	UNP/LNO	ON	Norfolk	40 I/16	42°55′	80°10′
Rockford	UNP/LNO	ON	Grey	41 A/10	44°31′	80°55′
Rockford	UNP/LNO	SK	10-37-7-W2	63 D/2	52°10′	102°56′
Rock Forest	CITY/VIL1	QC	Sherbrooke	21 E/5	45°21′	71°59′
Rockglen	TOWN/VIL2	SK	2-3-30-W2	72 H/4	49°11′	105°57′
Rock Harbour	UNP/LNO	NF		1 M/3	47°11′	55°03′
Rockhaven	VILG/VILG	SK	5-43-20-W3	73 C/10	52°40′	108°52′
Rockhaven	UNP/LNO	QC	La Vallée-de-la-Gatineau	31 K/1	46°14′	76°02′
Rockhouse Island	ISL/ÎLE	NT	Keewatin	55 O	63°28′	90°40′
Rockhurst	UNP/LNO	QC	Les Collines-de-l'Outaouais	31 G/12	45°38′	75°56′
Rockingham	UNP/LNO	NS	Halifax	11 D/12	44°41′	63°39′
Rockingham	UNP/LNO	ON	Renfrew	31 F/6	45°24′	77°29′
Rockinghorse Lake	LAKE/LAC	NT	Mackenzie	86 H/16	65°53′	112°18′
Rock in the Woods	UNP/LNO	QC	Côte-Nord-du-Golfe-Saint-Laurent	12 P/5	51°27′	57°52′
Rock Island	UNP/LNO	QC	Memphrémagog	31 H/1	45°00′	72°06′
Rock Island	ISL/ÎLE	NT	Franklin	27 A	68°24′	66°43′
Rock Island Lake	LAKE/LAC	AB	56-1,2-W4	73 E/16	53°51′	110°07′
Rock Island Lake	LAKE/LAC	AB	75-22,23-W4	83 P/6	55°30′	113°23′
*Rock Lake	UNP/LNO	ON	Haliburton	31 E/9	45°31′	78°25′
Rock Lake	UNP/LNO	ON	Algoma	41 J/5	46°26′	83°44′
Rock Lake	LAKE/LAC	ON	Haliburton	31 E/9	45°31′	78°24′
Rock Lake	LAKE/LAC	ON	Sudbury	41 I/5	46°19′	81°40′
Rock Lake	LAKE/LAC	ON	Algoma	41 J/5	46°26′	83°46′
Rock Lake	LAKE/LAC	MB	3-13,14-W	62 G/3	49°13′	99°12′
Rockland	TOWN/VIL2	ON	Russell	31 G/11	45°33′	75°18′
Rockland	UNP/LNO	NS	Kings	21 H/2	45°00′	64°42′
Rockland	UNP/LNO	NS	Shelburne	20 P/11	43°44′	65°05′
Rockland	UNP/LNO	QC	Le Val-Saint-François	31 H/9	45°34′	72°08′
Rockland East	UNP/LNO	ON	Russell	31 G/11	45°33′	75°16′
Rockley	UNP/LNO	NS	Cumberland	11 E/13	45°50′	63°45′
Rocklin	UNP/LNO	NS	Pictou	11 E/7	45°30′	62°47′
Rocklyn	UNP/LNO	ON	Grey	41 A/7	44°28′	80°35′
Rock Mills	UNP/LNO	ON	Grey	41 A/8	44°17′	80°29′
Rocknest Bay	BAY/BAIE	NT	Mackenzie	76 C	64°10′	108°11′
Rocknest Lake	LAKE/LAC	NT	Mackenzie	86 G	65°39′	114°23′
Rockport	UNP/LNO	NB	Westmorland	21 H/9	45°44′	64°30′
Rockport	UNP/LNO	ON	Leeds	31 B/5	44°22′	75°56′
Rock Ridge	UNP/LNO	MB	18-34-15-W1	62 O/13	51°55′	99°35′
Rock River	RIV/CDE	YT		95 D/3	60°07′	127°07′
Rock River	RIV/CDE	YT		116 P/6	67°17′	137°06′
Rocksand River	RIV/CDE	ON	Kenora	53 P/1	55°09′	88°28′
Rocks, Bay of	BAY/BAIE	NS	Richmond	11 F/10	45°32′	60°57′
Rockside	UNP/LNO	ON	Peel	30 M/13	43°45′	79°58′
Rock's Mills	UNP/LNO	ON	Oxford	40 I/15	42°53′	80°40′
Rocksprings	UNP/LNO	ON	Leeds	31 B/12	44°44′	75°52′
Rockton	UNP/LNO	ON	Wentworth	40 P/8	43°17′	80°07′
Rockville	UNP/LNO	NS	Yarmouth	20 O/16	43°47′	66°07′
Rockville	UNP/LNO	NB	Kings	21 H/11	45°41′	65°26′
Rockville	UNP/LNO	ON	Manitoulin	41 G/16	45°50′	82°04′
Rockville Notch	UNP/LNO	NS	Kings	21 A/15	44°57′	64°54′
Rock Wall Dock	UNP/LNO	QC	Témiscamingue	31 M/9	47°40′	78°05′
Rockway	UNP/LNO	ON	Lincoln	30 M/3	43°06′	79°20′
Rockway	UNP/LNO	ON	Waterloo	40 P/8	43°26′	80°29′
Rockway Valley	UNP/LNO	QC	Les Laurentides	31 G/15	45°59′	74°43′
Rockwell Stream	RIV/CDE	NB	Sunbury	21 G/15	45°47′	66°31′
Rockwood	MUN2/AZM2	MB		62 I/3	50°15′	97°20′
Rockwood	UNP/LNO	ON	Wellington	40 P/9	43°37′	80°08′
Rockwood	UNP/LNO	MB	16-13-2-E1	62 I/3	50°06′	97°16′
Rockwynn	UNP/LNO	ON	Parry Sound	31 E/12	45°38′	79°34′
Rocky Bay	UNP/LNO	NS	Richmond	11 F/10	45°33′	60°57′
Rocky Bay	BAY/BAIE	NF		2 E/8	49°26′	54°15′
Rocky Bay	BAY/BAIE	NF		3 E/5	53°29′	56°00′
Rocky Bay 1	IR/RI	ON	Thunder Bay	52 H/8	49°26′	88°08′
Rocky Brook	RIV/CDE	NB	York	21 J/10	46°36′	66°38′
Rocky Corner	UNP/LNO	NB	Saint John	21 H/4	45°13′	65°59′
Rocky Corner	UNP/LNO	NB	Charlotte	21 B/15	44°47′	66°46′
Rocky Cove	BAY/BAIE	NF		13 I/5	54°23′	57°52′
Rocky Cove	BAY/BAIE	NF		13 J/15	54°48′	58°36′
Rockyford	VILG/VILG	AB	22-26-23-W4	82 P/3	51°14′	113°08′
Rocky Ford	UNP/LNO	AB	9-44-8-W4	73 D/14	52°47′	111°07′
Rocky Harbour	VILG/VILG	NF		12 H/12	49°36′	57°55′
Rocky Harbour	UNP/LNO	NF		12 H/12	49°36′	57°55′
Rocky Inlet	UNP/LNO	ON	Rainy River	52 C/11	48°41′	93°16′

NAME NOM	ENTITY ENTITÉ	LOC 1 LIEU 1	LOC 2 LIEU 2	MAP CARTE	POSITION	
					LAT	LONG
Rocky Island Lake	LAKE/LAC	ON	Algoma	41 J/14	46°55′	83°04′
Rocky Lake	LAKE/LAC	MB	59,60-27,28-W	63 K/4	54°09′	101°30′
Rocky Lake 21L - see-voir - **Opaskwayak Cree Nation 21L**	IR/RI	MB		63 K/4	54°06′	101°34′
Rocky Lane	UNP/LNO	AB	16-109-14-W5	84 K/8	58°27′	116°17′
Rocky Mountain	UNP/LNO	NS	Pictou	11 E/8	45°24′	62°15′
Rocky Mountain Foothills	MTN/MNT	AB/BC		83 E/14	52°59′	119°12′
Rocky Mountain House	TOWN/VIL2	AB	22-39-7-W5	83 B/7	52°22′	114°55′
Rocky Mountain House, Lieu historique national - also-aussi - Rocky Mountain House National Historic Site	PARK/PARC	AB		83 B/7	52°22′	114°58′
Rocky Mountain House National Historic Site - also-aussi - Rocky Mountain House, Lieu historique national	PARK/PARC	AB		83 B/7	52°22′	114°58′
Rocky Mountains - also-aussi - **Rocheuses, Montagnes**	MTN/MNT	BC/AB		93 I/2	54°00′	120°47′
Rocky Mountain Trench	VALL/VALL	BC	Cariboo	93 J/9	54°30′	122°30′
Rocky Point	UNP/LNO	PE	Queens	11 L/3	46°12′	63°09′
Rocky Point	CAPE/CAP	NF		2 E/8	49°28′	54°10′
Rocky Point 3	IR/RI	PE	Queens	11 L/3	46°12′	63°09′
Rocky Pond	LAKE/LAC	NF		2 C/5	48°21′	53°40′
Rocky Pond	LAKE/LAC	NF		2 E/7	49°17′	54°40′
Rocky Pond	LAKE/LAC	NF		2 E/4	49°10′	55°59′
Rocky Pond	LAKE/LAC	NF		12 H/8	49°18′	56°02′
Rocky Rapids	UNP/LNO	AB	4-50-7-W5	83 G/7	53°17′	114°57′
Rocky Ridge	UNP/LNO	NS	Inverness	11 K/3	46°02′	61°29′
Rocky Ridge	MTN/MNT	NF		11 O/16	47°53′	58°10′
Rocky Ridge Pond	LAKE/LAC	NF		2 F/4	49°10′	53°49′
Rocky Ridge Pond	LAKE/LAC	NF		12 A/4	48°02′	57°51′
Rocky River	RIV/CDE	NF		1 N/4	47°13′	53°34′
Rocky River	RIV/CDE	AB	48-28-W5	83 F/4	53°08′	117°59′
Rocky Saugeen	UNP/LNO	ON	Grey	41 A/2	44°14′	80°50′
Rocky Saugeen River	RIV/CDE	ON	Grey	41 A/2	44°12′	80°53′
Rocky View	UNP/LNO	AB	2-26-29-W4	82 P/4	51°11′	113°56′
Rockyview	UNP/LNO	BC	Kootenay	82 G/5	49°30′	115°47′
Rocky View No. 44, Municipal District of	MUN1/AZM1	AB	26-1-W5	82 O/1	51°11′	114°04′
Rodayer, Lac	LAKE/LAC	QC	Jamésie	32 K/13	50°52′	77°42′
Roddick	UNP/LNO	SK	18-45-1-W3	73 B/16	52°55′	106°08′
Roddickton	TOWN/VIL2	NF		12 I/16	50°52′	56°08′
Roderick	UNP/LNO	ON	Muskoka	31 E/4	45°03′	79°41′
Roderick Island	ISL/ÎLE	BC	Range 3 Coast	103 A/9	52°38′	128°22′
Roderick Lake	LAKE/LAC	ON	Kenora	52 M/9	51°34′	94°23′
Rodgerdale	UNP/LNO	QC	Argenteuil	31 G/9	45°34′	74°18′
Rodgers	UNP/LNO	SK	20-13-2-W3	72 J/1	50°06′	106°14′
Rodgers Cove	UNP/LNO	NF		2 E/7	49°18′	54°30′
Rodgers No. 133	MUN2/AZM2	SK		72 J/1	50°10′	106°10′
Rodney	UNP/LNO	NS	Cumberland	21 H/9	45°36′	64°02′
Rodney	UNP/LNO	ON	Elgin	40 I/12	42°34′	81°41′
Rodney, Mount	MTN/MNT	BC	Range 1 Coast	92 K/15	50°51′	124°47′
Rodney Pond	LAKE/LAC	NF		2 D/15	48°49′	54°38′
Roeberta Park	UNP/LNO	ON	Simcoe	31 D/5	44°26′	79°32′
Roebuck	UNP/LNO	ON	Grenville	31 B/13	44°48′	75°37′
Roe Lake	UNP/LNO	BC	Lillooet	92 P/10	51°31′	120°50′
Roe Lake	LAKE/LAC	MB		64 B/8	56°20′	98°06′
Roe Lake	LAKE/LAC	SK		74 B/13	56°55′	107°56′
Roes Welcome Channel	SEAU/SMER	—		1399A	64°00′	87°30′
Roes Welcome Sound	CHAN/CHEN	NT	Franklin	46 E	65°01′	86°40′
Roger, Cape	CAPE/CAP	NF		1 M/7	47°21′	54°44′
Roger, Lac	LAKE/LAC	QC	Témiscamingue	31 M/15	47°50′	78°51′
Roger Lake	LAKE/LAC	NB	Northumberland	21 O/8	47°21′	66°06′
Roger Lake	LAKE/LAC	BC	Lillooet	92 P/15	51°54′	120°55′
Roger Point	CAPE/CAP	NS	Pictou	11 E/15	45°48′	62°33′
Rogers	UNP/LNO	NS	Pictou	11 E/10	45°43′	62°59′
Rogers	UNP/LNO	MB	8-19-22-W	62 K/9	50°37′	100°29′
Rogers	UNP/LNO	BC	Kootenay	82 N/6	51°30′	117°29′
Rogers Creek	RIV/CDE	ON	Haldimand	30 L/13	42°58′	79°53′
Rogers Creek	RIV/CDE	BC	New Westminster	92 G/16	49°59′	122°27′
Rogers Head	CAPE/CAP	NB	Saint John	21 H/5	45°18′	65°35′
Rogers Hill	UNP/LNO	NS	Pictou	11 E/10	45°37′	62°52′
Rogers Hill Cross Roads	UNP/LNO	NS	Pictou	11 E/10	45°38′	62°50′
Rogers Island	ISL/ÎLE	NT	Franklin	25 P/2	63°13′	64°42′
Rogerson Lake	LAKE/LAC	NF		12 A/10	48°31′	56°46′
Rogers Pass	UNP/LNO	BC	Kootenay	82 N/5	51°18′	117°31′
Rogers Pass National Historic Site - also-aussi - Col-Rogers, Lieu historique national du	PARK/PARC	BC	Kootenay	82 N/5	51°18′	117°31′
Rogers Point	CAPE/CAP	NF		2 E/9	49°35′	54°19′
Rogersville	VILG/VILG	NB	Northumberland	21 I/11	46°44′	65°26′
Rogersville	GEOG/GÉOG	NB	Northumberland	21 I/14	46°45′	65°30′
Roggan, Lac	LAKE/LAC	QC	Jamésie	33 K/4	54°08′	77°49′

NAME / NOM	ENTITY / ENTITÉ	LOC 1 / LIEU 1	LOC 2 / LIEU 2	MAP / CARTE	POSITION LAT	POSITION LONG
Roggan River	UNP/LNO	QC	Jamésie	33 L/6	54°24′	79°25′
Roggan, Rivière	RIV/CDE	QC	Jamésie	33 L/6	54°25′	79°28′
Rognons, Lac aux	LAKE/LAC	QC	La Jacques-Cartier	21 M/12	47°31′	71°44′
Rogue Range	MTN/MNT	YT		105 O/11	63°35′	131°09′
Rogue River	RIV/CDE	YT		105 N/8	63°24′	132°30′
Rogues Harbour	BAY/BAIE	NF		2 E/13	49°46′	55°54′
Rohallion	UNP/LNO	ON	Victoria	31 D/11	44°35′	79°02′
Rohault, Lac	LAKE/LAC	QC	Le Domaine-du-Roy	32 G/8	49°22′	74°20′
Roix Road	UNP/LNO	NB	Charlotte	21 G/6	45°15′	67°07′
Rokeby	UNP/LNO	ON	Lambton	40 I/13	42°51′	81°49′
Rokeby	UNP/LNO	SK	3-25-3-W2	62 M/1	51°08′	102°20′
Roland	MUN2/AZM2	MB		62 H/5	49°20′	97°55′
Roland	UNP/LNO	MB	4-5-4-W	62 H/5	49°22′	97°56′
Rolette, La	UNP/LNO	QC	Montmagny	21 L/9	46°41′	70°14′
Rolfe Lake	LAKE/LAC	NT	Mackenzie	75 M	63°05′	111°45′
Rolla	UNP/LNO	BC	Peace River	93 P/16	55°54′	120°08′
Rolland-Germain, Réserve écologique	PARK/PARC	QC	La Vallée-de-la-Gatineau	31 K/9	46°40′	76°05′
Rollet	VILG/VILG	QC	Rouyn-Noranda	31 M/14	47°55′	79°15′
Rolling Cove	BAY/BAIE	NF		2 C/11	48°33′	53°20′
Rollingdam	UNP/LNO	NB	Charlotte	21 G/6	45°19′	67°05′
Rolling Hills	UNP/LNO	AB	6-15-13-W4	72 L/4	50°13′	111°46′
Rolling Pond	LAKE/LAC	NF		2 D/11	48°40′	55°28′
Rolling River	UNP/LNO	MB	14,23-17-19-W	62 J/5	50°27′	99°59′
Rolling River 67	IR/RI	MB		62 K/8	50°28′	100°00′
Rollo Bay	UNP/LNO	PE	Kings	11 L/8	46°22′	62°20′
Rollo Bay	BAY/BAIE	PE	Kings	11 L/8	46°20′	62°19′
Rollo Lake	LAKE/LAC	ON	Sudbury	41 O/15	47°53′	82°39′
Rolly View	UNP/LNO	AB	29-49-23-W4	83 H/3	53°15′	113°20′
Rolph, Buchanan, Wylie and McKay	MUN2/AZM2	ON	Renfrew	31 F/13	45°58′	77°30′
Rolphton	UNP/LNO	ON	Renfrew	31 K/4	46°10′	77°42′
Roma	UNP/LNO	AB	21-83-22-W5	84 C/3	56°13′	117°25′
Romaine 2	IR/RI	QC	Côte-Nord-du-Golfe-Saint-Laurent	12 K/2	50°13′	60°40′
Romaine, Lac	LAKE/LAC	QC	La Haute-Côte-Nord	22 C/11	48°31′	69°25′
Romaine, Rivière	RIV/CDE	QC	Minganie	12 L/5	50°18′	63°48′
Romaines	UNP/LNO	NF		12 B/10	48°33′	58°41′
Romaines Brook	RIV/CDE	NF		12 B/10	48°33′	58°40′
Romaines, Les	UNP/LNO	QC	La Haute-Côte-Nord	22 C/6	48°29′	69°17′
Roma Junction	UNP/LNO	AB	30-83-22-W5	84 C/3	56°14′	117°29′
Romance	UNP/LNO	SK	2-36-19-W2	73 A/2	52°04′	104°37′
Romanet, Lac	LAKE/LAC	QC	Kativik	24 B/5	56°15′	67°45′
Roman Valley	UNP/LNO	NS	Guysborough	11 F/5	45°27′	61°45′
Romford	UNP/LNO	ON	Sudbury	41 I/7	46°29′	80°52′
Romieu	UNP/LNO	QC	Matane	22 B/15	49°00′	66°47′
Romieu-Sud	UNP/LNO	QC	Matane	22 B/15	48°58′	66°48′
Romney	MUN2/AZM2	ON	Kent	40 J/1	42°10′	82°24′
Ronalane	UNP/LNO	AB	9-13-12-W4	72 L/4	50°04′	111°35′
Ronan	UNP/LNO	AB	15-56-9-W5	83 G/14	53°50′	115°16′
Ronayne, Mount	MTN/MNT	BC	Lillooet	92 J/7	50°28′	122°49′
Roncott	UNP/LNO	SK	12-5-25-W2	72 H/6	49°22′	105°15′
Rondeau Bay	BAY/BAIE	ON	Kent	40 I/5	42°18′	81°53′
Rondeau Bay Estates	UNP/LNO	ON	Kent	40 I/5	42°20′	81°52′
Rondeau Park	UNP/LNO	ON	Kent	40 I/5	42°19′	81°51′
Ronde, Cap	CAPE/CAP	NS	Richmond	11 F/10	45°35′	60°53′
Rond, Lac	LAKE/LAC	QC	Sept-Rivières	22 J/11	50°40′	67°27′
Rond, Lac	LAKE/LAC	QC	Témiscouata	21 N/10	47°45′	68°50′
Rond, Lac	LAKE/LAC	QC	Le Fjord-du-Saguenay	22 E/7	49°16′	70°39′
Rond, Lac	LAKE/LAC	QC	La Vallée-de-la-Gatineau	31 K/9	46°39′	76°15′
Rondon, Cape	CAPE/CAP	NT	Franklin	79 D	77°19′	104°25′
Ronge, Lac la	LAKE/LAC	SK		73 P/2	55°10′	105°00′
Rooney	UNP/LNO	QC	Pontiac	31 F/16	45°47′	76°27′
Roosevelt Campobello International Park - also-aussi - Roosevelt Campobello, Parc international	PARK/PARC	NB	Charlotte	21 B/15	44°51′	66°57′
Roosevelt Campobello, Parc international - also-aussi - Roosevelt Campobello International Park	PARK/PARC	NB	Charlotte	21 B/15	44°51′	66°57′
Roosville	UNP/LNO	BC	Kootenay	82 G/3	49°00′	115°03′
Rooth	UNP/LNO	NB	York	21 G/10	45°41′	66°50′
Root Lake	UNP/LNO	MB	31-58-26-W	63 K/3	54°04′	101°18′
Root Lake	LAKE/LAC	MB	58,59-26,27-W	63 K/3	54°04′	101°23′
Root Lake 23I - see-voir - Opaskwayak Cree Nation Root Lake 23I	IR/RI	MB		63 F/14	54°00′	101°21′
Root River	RIV/CDE	NT	Mackenzie	95 J/6	62°26′	123°18′
Roper Bay	BAY/BAIE	SK		74 A/5	56°28′	105°41′
Roper's Meadow 14	IR/RI	BC	Lillooet	92 O/16	51°47′	122°09′
Roquemaure	VILG/VILG	QC	Abitibi-Ouest	32 D/11	48°36′	79°24′
Rorey Lake	LAKE/LAC	NT	Mackenzie	106 I	66°55′	128°24′

NAME NOM	ENTITY ENTITÉ	LOC 1 LIEU 1	LOC 2 LIEU 2	MAP CARTE	POSITION LAT	LONG
Rorke Lake	LAKE/LAC	MB/ON		53 K/10	54°34′	92°33′
Rorketon	UNP/LNO	MB	12-28-16-W	62 O/5	51°23′	99°35′
Roros	UNP/LNO	AB	45-2-W4	73 D/16	52°52′	110°12′
Rosa	UNP/LNO	MB	26,27-3-5-E	62 H/2	49°15′	96°50′
Rosaireville	UNP/LNO	NB	Northumberland	21 I/14	46°49′	65°18′
Rosalind	VILG/VILG	AB	17-44-17-W4	83 A/16	52°47′	112°27′
Rosanna	UNP/LNO	ON	Oxford	40 I/15	42°53′	80°38′
Rosborough Settlement	UNP/LNO	NB	York	21 G/14	45°54′	67°05′
Roscoe	UNP/LNO	SK	33-44-31-W	63 C/13	52°50′	101°54′
Roscoe Inlet	BAY/BAIE	BC	Range 3 Coast	93 D/5	52°25′	127°54′
Roscoe River	RIV/CDE	NT	Franklin	97 D	69°40′	120°57′
Rose	UNP/LNO	NS	Cumberland	11 E/12	45°36′	63°46′
Roseau Rapids 2A	IR/RI	MB		62 H/2	49°13′	96°56′
Roseau River	UNP/LNO	MB	2-3-5-E	62 H/2	49°11′	96°50′
Roseau River	RIV/CDE	MB		62 H/3	49°09′	97°15′
Roseau River 2	IR/RI	MB		62 H/3	49°10′	97°16′
Roseau River Reserve	UNP/LNO	MB	15,22-2-2-E	62 H/3	49°08′	97°15′
Rosebank	UNP/LNO	PE	Queens	11 L/3	46°13′	63°07′
Rosebank	UNP/LNO	PE	Prince	21 I/16	46°48′	64°09′
Rosebank	UNP/LNO	ON	Renfrew	31 F/10	45°31′	76°47′
Rosebank	UNP/LNO	ON	Ontario	30 M/14	43°48′	79°08′
Rosebank	UNP/LNO	MB	8-5-5-W	62 G/8	49°22′	98°07′
Rosebank Station	UNP/LNO	ON	Ontario	30 M/14	43°47′	79°07′
Rose Bay	UNP/LNO	NS	Lunenburg	21 A/8	44°18′	64°18′
Rose Bay Junction	UNP/LNO	NF		23 G/1	53°03′	66°12′
Roseberry	UNP/LNO	PE	Queens	11 L/2	46°02′	62°52′
Roseberry River	RIV/CDE	ON	Kenora	53 C/15	52°56′	92°44′
Rosebery	UNP/LNO	BC	Kootenay	82 K/3	50°02′	117°25′
Roseblade Lake	LAKE/LAC	NT	Keewatin	65 H	61°07′	97°02′
Rose Blanche	UNP/LNO	NF		11 O/10	47°37′	58°41′
Rose Blanche, Banc de la - also-aussi - Rose Blanche Bank	SEAU/SMER	—		15078A	47°25′	58°50′
Rose Blanche Bank - also-aussi - Rose Blanche, Banc de la	SEAU/SMER	—		15078A	47°25′	58°50′
Rose Blanche Brook	RIV/CDE	NF		11 O/10	47°37′	58°42′
Rose Blanche-Harbour Le Cou	TOWN/VIL2	NF		11 O/10	47°37′	58°41′
Rose Bridge	UNP/LNO	QC	La Côte-de-Gaspé	22 A/15	48°52′	64°30′
Rosebud	UNP/LNO	AB	18-27-21-W4	82 P/7	51°18′	112°57′
Rosebud Creek	RIV/CDE	YT		115 O/8	63°17′	138°26′
Rosebud River	RIV/CDE	AB	28-28-19-W4	82 P/7	51°25′	112°38′
Roseburn	UNP/LNO	NS	Inverness	11 K/3	46°01′	61°14′
Rosedale	MUN2/AZM2	MB		62 J/5	50°20′	99°30′
Rosedale	UNP/LNO	NF		2 C/12	48°41′	53°58′
Rosedale	UNP/LNO	NS	Inverness	11 F/14	45°59′	61°16′
Rosedale	UNP/LNO	NB	Carleton	21 J/4	46°15′	67°33′
Rosedale	UNP/LNO	ON	Lanark	31 B/13	44°54′	75°56′
Rosedale	UNP/LNO	ON	Frontenac	31 C/7	44°26′	76°35′
Rosedale	UNP/LNO	ON	Victoria	31 D/10	44°34′	78°48′
Rosedale	UNP/LNO	ON	York	30 M/11	43°41′	79°24′
Rosedale	UNP/LNO	ON	Wentworth	30 M/4	43°13′	79°48′
Rosedale	UNP/LNO	AB	29-28-19-W4	82 P/7	51°25′	112°38′
Rosedale	UNP/LNO	BC	New Westminster	92 H/4	49°11′	121°48′
Rosedale No. 283	MUN2/AZM2	SK		72 O/9	51°35′	106°30′
Rosedale Point	UNP/LNO	ON	Thunder Bay	42 E/16	49°42′	86°57′
Rosedale Terrace	UNP/LNO	ON	Stormont	31 G/2	45°04′	74°47′
Rosedene	UNP/LNO	ON	Lincoln	30 M/3	43°04′	79°25′
Rosée, Lac	LAKE/LAC	QC	Jamésie	33 A/13	52°46′	73°42′
Rosefield	UNP/LNO	SK	33-1-12-W3	72 G/4	49°05′	107°32′
Rosegrove	UNP/LNO	ON	Timiskaming	32 D/4	48°02′	79°59′
Rosegrove Beach	UNP/LNO	ON	Timiskaming	42 A/1	48°02′	80°02′
Rosehall	UNP/LNO	ON	Prince Edward	30 N/14	43°57′	77°25′
Rose Harbour	UNP/LNO	BC	Queen Charlotte	103 B/3	52°09′	131°05′
Rosehaven	UNP/LNO	ON	Dundas	31 G/3	45°01′	75°25′
Rosehill	UNP/LNO	PE	Prince	11 L/5	46°28′	63°52′
Rose Hill	UNP/LNO	ON	Lennox and Addington	31 F/3	45°09′	77°13′
Rosehill	UNP/LNO	ON	Peel	40 P/16	43°55′	80°02′
Rose Hill Estates	UNP/LNO	ON	Welland	30 L/15	42°53′	78°59′
Rose Island	UNP/LNO	ON	Hastings	31 C/13	44°52′	77°56′
Rose Island	ISL/ÎLE	ON	Parry Sound	41 H/8	45°19′	80°13′
Roseisle	UNP/LNO	MB	21-6-7-W	62 G/8	49°30′	98°21′
Rose Lake	UNP/LNO	BC	Range 5 Coast	93 L/8	54°24′	126°02′
Rose Lake	LAKE/LAC	BC	Cariboo	93 A/4	52°15′	121°46′
Roseland	UNP/LNO	NS	Colchester	11 E/3	45°06′	63°16′
Roseland	UNP/LNO	ON	Halton	30 M/5	43°20′	79°47′
Roseland	UNP/LNO	ON	Essex	40 J/7	42°15′	83°00′
Roseland	UNP/LNO	MB	31-9-19-W	62 F/16	49°48′	100°05′
Roselea	UNP/LNO	AB	1-59-6-W5	83 J/2	54°05′	114°46′

NAME NOM	ENTITY ENTITÉ	LOC 1 LIEU 1	LOC 2 LIEU 2	MAP CARTE	POSITION LAT	LONG
Rose Lynn	UNP/LNO	AB	30-28-12-W4	72 M/5	51°25'	111°41'
Rosemary	VILG/VILG	AB	1-21-16-W4	82 I/16	50°46'	112°05'
Rosemère	CITY/VIL1	QC	Thérèse-De Blainville	31 H/12	45°38'	73°48'
Rosemont	UNP/LNO	ON	Simcoe	31 D/4	44°07'	80°00'
Rosemont	UNP/LNO	SK		72 I/7	50°28'	104°40'
Rosemont	UNP/LNO	SK		72 I/5	50°24'	105°32'
Rosemound	UNP/LNO	SK	43-21-W3	73 C/15	52°45'	108°55'
Rosemount	UNP/LNO	ON	Waterloo	40 P/8	43°27'	80°28'
Rose Mountain	MTN/MNT	YT		105 K/5	62°21'	133°37'
Rosemount No. 378	MUN2/AZM2	SK		73 C/1	52°15'	108°15'
Rosenburg	UNP/LNO	MB	23-24-2-E	62 P/3	51°06'	97°12'
Rosendale	UNP/LNO	ON	Waterloo	40 P/8	43°30'	80°27'
Roseneath	UNP/LNO	PE	Kings	11 L/2	46°13'	62°37'
Roseneath	UNP/LNO	ON	Northumberland	31 D/1	44°12'	78°03'
Rosenfeld	UNP/LNO	MB	8,9-3-1-W	62 H/4	49°12'	97°33'
Rosengard	UNP/LNO	MB	12-6-5-E	62 H/7	49°28'	96°48'
Rosengart	UNP/LNO	MB	7-1-3-W	62 H/4	49°01'	97°52'
Rosengart	UNP/LNO	SK	15-14-13-W3	72 J/4	50°11'	107°43'
Rosenheim	UNP/LNO	AB	14-37-2-W4	73 D/1	52°10'	110°10'
Rosenhof	UNP/LNO	SK	34-14-12-W3	72 J/4	50°13'	107°34'
Rosenort	UNP/LNO	MB	7,8-6-1-E	62 H/6	49°28'	97°26'
Rosenort	UNP/LNO	SK	3-14-12-W3	72 J/4	50°08'	107°35'
Rosenthal	UNP/LNO	ON	Renfrew	31 F/6	45°22'	77°28'
Rose Point	UNP/LNO	ON	Parry Sound	41 H/8	45°19'	80°03'
Rose Point	CAPE/CAP	NS	Lunenburg	21 A/8	44°14'	64°14'
Rose Point	CAPE/CAP	BC	Queen Charlotte	103 J/4	54°11'	131°39'
Rose Prairie	UNP/LNO	BC	Peace River	94 A/10	56°30'	120°47'
Roseray	UNP/LNO	SK	25-17-19-W3	72 K/8	50°28'	108°29'
Rosetown	TOWN/VIL2	SK		72 O/12	51°33'	108°00'
Rosetown	UNP/LNO	MB	13,24-1-3-W	62 H/4	49°03'	97°45'
Rosetta	UNP/LNO	ON	Lanark	31 F/1	45°07'	76°20'
Rosevale	UNP/LNO	NB	Albert	21 H/15	45°51'	64°51'
Rose Valley	TOWN/VIL2	SK	28-38-13-W2	63 D/5	52°18'	103°49'
Rose Valley	UNP/LNO	PE	Queens	11 L/6	46°19'	63°30'
Rosevear	UNP/LNO	AB	16-54-15-W5	83 F/9	53°40'	116°09'
Roseville	UNP/LNO	PE	Prince	21 I/16	46°49'	64°15'
Roseville	UNP/LNO	ON	Ontario	31 D/3	44°05'	79°11'
Roseville	UNP/LNO	ON	Waterloo	40 P/8	43°21'	80°29'
Roseway	UNP/LNO	NS	Shelburne	20 P/11	43°38'	65°21'
Roseway, Banc - also-aussi - Roseway Bank	SEAU/SMER	—		8006	43°25'	64°40'
Roseway Bank - also-aussi - Roseway, Banc	SEAU/SMER	—		8006	43°25'	64°40'
Roseway Basin - also-aussi - Roseway, Bassin	SEAU/SMER	—		8006	43°10'	65°10'
Roseway, Bassin - also-aussi - Roseway Basin	SEAU/SMER	—		8006	43°10'	65°10'
Roseway, Cape	CAPE/CAP	NS	Shelburne	20 P/11	43°37'	65°16'
Roseway Lake	LAKE/LAC	NS	Shelburne	21 A/3	44°10'	65°24'
Roseway River	RIV/CDE	NS	Shelburne	20 P/14	43°46'	65°20'
Rosewood	UNP/LNO	MB	13,23-9-6-E	62 H/15	49°45'	96°40'
Rosiers, Cap des	CAPE/CAP	QC	La Côte-de-Gaspé	22 A/16	48°51'	64°12'
Rosiers, Rivière aux	RIV/CDE	QC	Manicouagan	22 F/2	49°04'	68°35'
Rosita Lake	LAKE/LAC	BC	Cariboo	93 B/6	52°25'	123°10'
Roslin	UNP/LNO	NS	Cumberland	11 E/13	45°46'	63°47'
Roslin	UNP/LNO	ON	Hastings	31 C/6	44°21'	77°20'
Roslyn	UNP/LNO	MB		62 H/14	49°53'	97°09'
Roslyn Lake	LAKE/LAC	ON	Thunder Bay	42 E/6	49°19'	87°28'
Rosnel	UNP/LNO	ON	Kenora	52 J/4	50°10'	91°35'
Ross	MUN2/AZM2	ON	Renfrew	31 F/10	45°37'	76°46'
Ross	UNP/LNO	NB	York	21 J/2	46°13'	66°37'
Ross	UNP/LNO	MB	22-9-8-E	62 H/16	49°46'	96°26'
Ross Bay	UNP/LNO	NF		23 B/16	52°55'	66°12'
Ross Bay	BAY/BAIE	NT	Franklin	46 K	66°52'	85°00'
Ross Bay Junction	UNP/LNO	NF		23 G/1	53°03'	66°12'
Rossburn	VILG/VILG	MB	36-19-25-W	62 K/10	50°40'	100°49'
Rossburn	MUN2/AZM2	MB		62 K/10	50°44'	100°44'
Rossburn Junction	UNP/LNO	MB	21-15-15-W	62 J/6	50°18'	99°29'
Rossclair	UNP/LNO	ON	Muskoka	31 E/4	45°04'	79°33'
Ross Corner	UNP/LNO	PE	Prince	11 L/5	46°22'	63°43'
Ross Corner	UNP/LNO	NS	Kings	21 H/2	45°09'	64°39'
Ross Corner	UNP/LNO	NB	Albert	21 H/11	45°44'	65°01'
Ross Creek	RIV/CDE	AB	33-12-5-W4	72 L/2	50°02'	110°38'
Ross Creek	RIV/CDE	BC	Kamloops Division Yale	82 L/14	50°58'	119°14'
Rossdale	UNP/LNO	MB	24-14-3-E	62 I/3	50°05'	97°00'
Rosseau	VILG/VILG	ON	Parry Sound	31 E/5	45°16'	79°39'
Rosseau Falls	UNP/LNO	ON	Muskoka	31 E/4	45°14'	79°36'
Rosseau, Lake	LAKE/LAC	ON	Muskoka	31 E/4	45°10'	79°35'
Rosseau Road	UNP/LNO	ON	Parry Sound	31 E/5	45°17'	79°52'

NAME NOM	ENTITY ENTITÉ	LOC 1 LIEU 1	LOC 2 LIEU 2	MAP CARTE	POSITION LAT	POSITION LONG
Rosse Bay	BAY/BAIE	NT	Franklin	39 E	78°40′	74°35′
Rosse, Cape	CAPE/CAP	NT	Franklin	68 E	74°54′	96°19′
Rossendale	UNP/LNO	NS	Cumberland	11 E/13	45°48′	63°49′
Rossendale	UNP/LNO	MB	10-10-9-W	62 G/15	49°50′	98°37′
Rosser	MUN2/AZM2	MB		62 H/14	49°55′	97°28′
Rosser	UNP/LNO	MB	6,7-12-1-E	62 H/14	49°59′	97°27′
Rosser Heights	UNP/LNO	MB		62 H/14	49°56′	97°12′
Ross Ferry	UNP/LNO	NS	Victoria	11 K/2	46°08′	60°35′
Ross Haven	VILG/VILG	AB	8-55-3-W5	83 G/9	53°44′	114°24′
Ross Hills	MTN/MNT	NT	Keewatin	57 B	68°45′	92°27′
Rossignol, Lac	LAKE/LAC	QC	Jamésie	33 A/12	52°43′	73°40′
Rossignol, Lake	LAKE/LAC	NS	Queens	21 A/3	44°12′	65°05′
Rossington	UNP/LNO	AB	4-60-1-W5	83 J/1	54°10′	114°03′
Ross Inlet	BAY/BAIE	NT	Franklin	46 M	67°10′	87°16′
Ross Island	ISL/ÎLE	NB	Charlotte	21 B/10	44°40′	66°44′
Ross Island	ISL/ÎLE	MB		63 I/4	54°11′	97°55′
Ross Island	ISL/ÎLE	NT	Keewatin	34 C	56°13′	76°45′
Ross Junction	UNP/LNO	SK	22-30-3-W2	62 M/9	51°37′	102°21′
Ross Lake	LAKE/LAC	SK	62-12-W3	73 J/5	54°21′	107°47′
Ross Lake	LAKE/LAC	BC	Cariboo	93 B/2	52°08′	122°51′
Ross Lake	LAKE/LAC	NT	Mackenzie	85 I/11	62°41′	113°15′
Rossland	CITY/VIL1	BC	Kootenay	82 F/4	49°05′	117°48′
Rossland Range	MTN/MNT	BC	Kootenay	82 F/4	49°11′	117°54′
Rosslyn Village	UNP/LNO	ON	Thunder Bay	52 A/6	48°22′	89°27′
Rossmere	UNP/LNO	ON	Thunder Bay	52 B/9	48°39′	90°08′
Rossmere	UNP/LNO	MB		62 H/14	49°56′	97°06′
Rossmore	UNP/LNO	ON	Prince Edward	31 C/3	44°08′	77°23′
Rossmount	UNP/LNO	ON	Northumberland	31 D/1	44°03′	78°18′
Ross Park	UNP/LNO	SK		72 I/5	50°24′	105°31′
Ross Peak	UNP/LNO	BC	Kootenay	82 N/5	51°15′	117°36′
Ross Peninsula	CAPE/CAP	NT	Keewatin	57 D	69°35′	91°20′
Ross Point	CAPE/CAP	NT	Franklin	78 E	74°55′	107°15′
Rossport	UNP/LNO	ON	Thunder Bay	42 D/13	48°50′	87°31′
Ross River	UNP/LNO	YT		105 F/16	61°59′	132°26′
Ross River	RIV/CDE	YT		105 F/16	61°59′	132°25′
Ross Spur	UNP/LNO	BC	Kootenay	82 F/3	49°11′	117°28′
Rossville	UNP/LNO	NB	York	21 J/3	46°01′	67°16′
Rossville	UNP/LNO	MB	58-3-W	63 H/13	54°00′	97°47′
Rossway	UNP/LNO	NS	Digby	21 A/12	44°35′	65°55′
Rosswood	UNP/LNO	BC	Range 5 Coast	103 I/15	54°48′	128°46′
Rosthern	TOWN/VIL2	SK	35-42-3-W3	73 B/9	52°40′	106°20′
Rosthern No. 403	MUN2/AZM2	SK		73 B/9	52°40′	106°20′
Rostock	UNP/LNO	ON	Perth	40 P/6	43°29′	81°01′
Rostrevor	UNP/LNO	ON	Muskoka	31 E/4	45°11′	79°33′
Rosyth	UNP/LNO	AB	22-42-9-W4	73 D/11	52°38′	111°13′
Rotave	UNP/LNO	SK	24-13-31-W	62 K/4	50°06′	101°35′
Rothermere	UNP/LNO	SK	13-49-12-W3	73 G/4	53°13′	107°36′
Rothesay	TOWN/VIL2	NB	Kings	21 H/5	45°23′	66°00′
Rothesay	GEOG/GÉOG	NB	Kings	21 H/5	45°24′	65°55′
Rothesay Park	UNP/LNO	SK		72 I/5	50°23′	105°31′
Rothsay	UNP/LNO	ON	Wellington	40 P/9	43°48′	80°42′
Rothwell	UNP/LNO	NB	Queens	21 J/1	46°04′	66°04′
Rothwell Heights	UNP/LNO	ON	Carleton	31 G/5	45°27′	75°37′
Rothwell Place	UNP/LNO	SK		72 I/7	50°27′	104°34′
Rôti Bay	BAY/BAIE	NF		11 O/9	47°40′	58°18′
Rôti Brook	RIV/CDE	NF		11 O/9	47°41′	58°16′
Rottenfish River	RIV/CDE	ON	Kenora	53 F/9	53°41′	92°19′
Rouge	UNP/LNO	ON	York	30 M/14	43°48′	79°10′
Rouge, Cape	CAPE/CAP	NF		13 I/12	54°40′	57°32′
Rouge Harbour	UNP/LNO	NF		2 E/13	49°46′	55°55′
Rouge Hill	UNP/LNO	ON	Ontario	30 M/14	43°48′	79°08′
Rouge-Matawin, Réserve faunique	PARK/PARC	QC	Antoine-Labelle	31 J/15	46°51′	74°31′
Rougemont	TOWN/VIL2	QC	Rouville	31 H/6	45°26′	73°03′
Rougemont, Lac	LAKE/LAC	QC	Kativik	24 K/4	58°03′	69°40′
Rougemont, Mont	MTN/MNT	QC	Rouville	31 H/6	45°28′	73°03′
Rouge Park	UNP/LNO	ON	Ontario	30 M/14	43°48′	79°10′
Rouge, Pointe	CAPE/CAP	QC	Manicouagan	22 G/5	49°18′	67°40′
Rouge River	RIV/CDE	ON	Ontario	30 M/14	43°48′	79°07′
Rouge, Rivière	RIV/CDE	QC	Argenteuil	31 G/10	45°39′	74°41′
Rouge, Rivière - also-aussi - **Red River**	RIV/CDE	MB		62 I/7	50°24′	96°49′
Rouget, Lac	LAKE/LAC	QC	Jamésie	33 H/6	53°22′	73°15′
Rouge-Valley	UNP/LNO	QC	Argenteuil	31 G/15	45°55′	74°39′
Roughrock Lake	LAKE/LAC	ON	Kenora	52 L/2	50°06′	94°46′
Rough Top	MTN/MNT	YT		115 P/3	63°10′	137°20′
Rough Waters	UNP/LNO	NB	Gloucester	21 P/12	47°35′	65°39′

NAME / NOM	ENTITY / ENTITÉ	LOC 1 / LIEU 1	LOC 2 / LIEU 2	MAP / CARTE	POSITION LAT	LONG
Roulante Lake	LAKE/LAC	NT	Mackenzie	86 A	64°34′	113°45′
Rouleau	TOWN/VIL2	SK	23-14-22-W2	72 I/2	50°11′	104°56′
Rouleau-Siding	UNP/LNO	QC	Vallée-de-l'Or	32 B/4	48°12′	75°54′
Roulier	MUN2/AZM2	QC	Témiscamingue	31 M/14	47°46′	79°25′
Roulier	UNP/LNO	QC	Témiscamingue	31 M/14	47°46′	79°25′
Roulston Corner	UNP/LNO	NS	Hants	11 E/4	45°06′	63°39′
Roundabout	UNP/LNO	NF		1 L/13	46°55′	55°35′
Round Bay	UNP/LNO	NS	Shelburne	20 P/11	43°36′	65°21′
Round Cove	UNP/LNO	NF		1 M/12	47°39′	55°43′
Roundeyed, Lac	LAKE/LAC	QC	Jamésie	23 E/11	53°30′	71°00′
Round Harbour	UNP/LNO	NF		2 E/13	49°51′	55°40′
Round Harbour	UNP/LNO	NF		11 P/9	47°37′	56°00′
Round Head	CAPE/CAP	NF		2 E/9	49°45′	54°06′
Round Head	CAPE/CAP	NF		12 B/11	48°38′	59°03′
Round Hill	UNP/LNO	NS	Annapolis	21 A/14	44°46′	65°24′
Round Hill	UNP/LNO	AB	30-48-18-W4	83 H/2	53°10′	112°38′
Round Hill	MTN/MNT	NF		11 P/12	47°43′	57°58′
Round Hill No. 467	MUN2/AZM2	SK		73 B/13	53°00′	108°00′
Round Island	UNP/LNO	NS	Cape Breton	11 J/4	46°03′	59°56′
Round Island	ISL/ÎLE	NS	Lunenburg	21 A/9	44°31′	64°18′
Round Island	ISL/ÎLE	NS	Yarmouth	20 P/12	43°30′	65°59′
Round Lake	UNP/LNO	ON	Peterborough	31 C/12	44°31′	77°53′
Round Lake	UNP/LNO	BC	Range 5 Coast	93 L/10	54°40′	126°55′
Round Lake	LAKE/LAC	NF		12 P/2	51°08′	56°32′
Round Lake	LAKE/LAC	ON	Renfrew	31 F/11	45°38′	77°30′
Round Lake	LAKE/LAC	ON	Peterborough	31 C/5	44°30′	77°53′
Round Lake	LAKE/LAC	ON	Timiskaming	42 A/1	48°01′	80°02′
Round Lake	LAKE/LAC	ON	Parry Sound	41 H/9	45°31′	80°08′
Round Lake	LAKE/LAC	SK		62 L/9	50°32′	102°22′
Round Lake Centre	UNP/LNO	ON	Renfrew	31 F/12	45°37′	77°32′
Round Plains	UNP/LNO	ON	Norfolk	40 I/16	42°56′	80°20′
Round Pond	LAKE/LAC	NF		2 C/6	48°18′	53°26′
Round Pond	LAKE/LAC	NF		2 D/4	48°11′	56°00′
Round Prairie	UNP/LNO	BC	Kootenay	82 J/2	50°04′	114°55′
Round Valley	UNP/LNO	AB	28-50-7-W5	83 G/7	53°21′	114°57′
Round Valley No. 410	MUN2/AZM2	SK		73 C/11	52°35′	109°10′
Rounthwaite	UNP/LNO	MB	24-8-18-W	62 G/12	49°40′	99°48′
Rousseau	UNP/LNO	QC	Mékinac	31 I/16	46°56′	72°17′
Roussillon	MUN1/AZM1	QC	Roussillon	31 H/5	45°22′	73°34′
Route-du-Sault	UNP/LNO	QC	Témiscouata	21 N/10	47°40′	68°52′
Route Lake	LAKE/LAC	ON	Kenora	52 K/2	50°04′	92°38′
Routhier	UNP/LNO	ON	Prescott	31 G/7	45°29′	74°47′
Routhierville	MUN2/AZM2	QC	La Matapédia	22 B/3	48°11′	67°09′
Routhierville	UNP/LNO	QC	La Matapédia	22 B/3	48°11′	67°09′
Routledge	UNP/LNO	MB	34-9-25-W	62 F/15	49°48′	100°48′
Rouvière, Lac	LAKE/LAC	NT	Mackenzie	86 N	67°12′	117°23′
Rouville	MUN1/AZM1	QC	Rouville	31 H/6	45°26′	73°03′
Rouvray, Lac	LAKE/LAC	QC	Le Fjord-du-Saguenay	22 E/7	49°18′	70°49′
Rouyn-Noranda	CITY/VIL1	QC	Rouyn-Noranda	32 D/3	48°14′	79°01′
Rouyn-Noranda	MUN1/AZM1	QC	Rouyn-Noranda	32 D/6	48°15′	79°02′
Rowan Lake	LAKE/LAC	ON	Kenora	52 F/5	49°18′	93°32′
Rowan Mills	UNP/LNO	ON	Norfolk	40 I/10	42°37′	80°32′
Rowatt	UNP/LNO	SK	18-16-19-W2	72 I/7	50°20′	104°37′
Rowdy Lake	LAKE/LAC	ON	Kenora	52 L/9	50°33′	94°29′
Rowena	UNP/LNO	NB	Victoria	21 J/13	46°47′	67°38′
Rowena	UNP/LNO	ON	Dundas	31 B/14	44°54′	75°17′
Rowland	UNP/LNO	ON	Hastings	31 F/4	45°08′	77°37′
Rowletta	UNP/LNO	SK	10-19-29-W2	72 I/12	50°35′	105°56′
Rowley	UNP/LNO	AB	21-32-20-W4	82 P/15	51°46′	112°47′
Rowley Island	ISL/ÎLE	NT	Franklin	37 C	69°06′	78°52′
Rowley Lake	LAKE/LAC	NT	Mackenzie	75 A	60°30′	104°25′
Rowley River	RIV/CDE	NT	Franklin	37 F	70°15′	77°47′
Rowlinson Creek	RIV/CDE	YT		115 I/1	62°03′	136°17′
Rows Corners	UNP/LNO	ON	Leeds	31 B/12	44°38′	75°42′
Rowsell Harbour	BAY/BAIE	NF		14 L/14	58°58′	63°14′
Roxana	UNP/LNO	AB	24-78-20-W5	83 N/15	55°47′	116°58′
Roxboro	CITY/VIL1	QC	Communauté urbaine de Montréal	31 H/12	45°31′	73°48′
Roxboro	UNP/LNO	ON	Huron	40 P/11	43°35′	81°24′
Roxborough	MUN2/AZM2	ON	Stormont	31 G/2	45°14′	74°57′
Roxbourgh	UNP/LNO	ON	Muskoka	31 E/3	45°03′	79°16′
Roxbury	UNP/LNO	PE	Prince	21 I/9	46°43′	64°06′
Roxbury	UNP/LNO	NS	Annapolis	21 A/14	44°48′	65°10′
Roxham	UNP/LNO	QC	Les Jardins-de-Napierville	31 H/4	45°02′	73°31′
Roxton	VILG/VILG	QC	Acton	31 H/10	45°33′	72°31′
Roxton-Est	UNP/LNO	QC	Acton	31 H/9	45°31′	72°29′

NAME NOM	ENTITY ENTITÉ	LOC 1 LIEU 1	LOC 2 LIEU 2	MAP CARTE	POSITION LAT	LONG
Roxton Falls	TOWN/VIL2	QC	Acton	31 H/10	45°34'	72°31'
Roxton, Lac	LAKE/LAC	QC	La Haute-Yamaska	31 H/7	45°28'	72°39'
Roxton Pond	TOWN/VIL2	QC	La Haute-Yamaska	31 H/7	45°29'	72°40'
Roxton Pond	VILG/VILG	QC	La Haute-Yamaska	31 H/7	45°28'	72°38'
Roxton-Sud	UNP/LNO	QC	La Haute-Yamaska	31 H/7	45°29'	72°36'
Roxville	UNP/LNO	NS	Digby	21 A/12	44°36'	65°52'
Roy	UNP/LNO	NB	Kent	21 I/7	46°25'	64°47'
Roy	UNP/LNO	BC	Range 1 Coast	92 K/12	50°31'	125°32'
Royal	UNP/LNO	ON	Welland	30 M/3	43°06'	79°07'
Royal Beach	UNP/LNO	ON	York	31 D/6	44°20'	79°17'
Royal Geographical Society Islands	ISL/ÎLE	NT	Franklin	67 B/16	68°56'	100°15'
Royal Lake	UNP/LNO	SK	36-47-7-W3	73 G/2	53°06'	106°54'
Royal, Mont	MTN/MNT	QC	Communauté urbaine de Montréal	31 H/12	45°30'	73°36'
Royal, Mount	MTN/MNT	ON	Thunder Bay	52 H/15	49°55'	88°48'
Royal Oak	UNP/LNO	BC	Lake	92 B/6	48°29'	123°23'
Royal Oak Creek	RIV/CDE	ON	Bruce	41 A/4	44°06'	81°41'
Royal Park	UNP/LNO	AB	31-52-15-W4	83 H/9	53°32'	112°12'
Royal Road	UNP/LNO	NB	York	21 J/2	46°02'	66°42'
Royal Society Fiord	BAY/BAIE	NT	Franklin	37 H	71°24'	74°00'
Royalties	UNP/LNO	AB	28-18-2-W5	82 J/9	50°33'	114°14'
Royalton	UNP/LNO	NB	Carleton	21 J/5	46°29'	67°46'
Royalty Junction	UNP/LNO	PE	Queens	11 L/6	46°18'	63°09'
Royce	UNP/LNO	AB	26-83-6-W6	84 D/2	56°13'	118°50'
Roydale	UNP/LNO	AB	3-58-7-W5	83 G/15	53°59'	114°58'
Royer	UNP/LNO	SK	22-9-7-W3	72 G/10	49°44'	106°52'
Royer Cove	BAY/BAIE	NT	Franklin	25 O	63°12'	66°48'
Roy Island	ISL/ÎLE	NS	Pictou	11 E/10	45°39'	62°32'
Roy, Lac	LAKE/LAC	QC	La Haute-Côte-Nord	22 F/13	49°45'	69°54'
Roy, Lac	LAKE/LAC	QC	Jamésie	32 G/2	49°07'	74°46'
Roy Settlement	UNP/LNO	NB	Gloucester	21 P/12	47°38'	65°36'
Royston	UNP/LNO	BC	Nelson	92 F/10	49°39'	124°57'
Roytal	UNP/LNO	AB	16-12-5-W4	72 E/15	49°59'	110°40'
Royville	UNP/LNO	QC	Acton	31 H/15	45°45'	72°40'
Roz, Lac	LAKE/LAC	QC	Jamésie	33 I/15	54°50'	72°55'
Ruau, Île au	ISL/ÎLE	QC	L'Île-d'Orléans	21 M/2	47°01'	70°44'
Ruby	UNP/LNO	ON	Renfrew	31 F/11	45°32'	77°20'
Ruby Beach	UNP/LNO	SK	15-46-3-W2	63 D/16	52°58'	102°21'
Ruby Creek	UNP/LNO	BC	Yale Division Yale	92 H/5	49°21'	121°36'
Ruby Creek 2	IR/RI	BC	Yale Division Yale	92 H/5	49°22'	121°37'
Ruby Lake	LAKE/LAC	BC	New Westminster	92 G/12	49°43'	123°59'
Ruby Mine	UNP/LNO	ON	Renfrew	31 F/3	45°12'	77°22'
Ruby Range	MTN/MNT	YT		115 G/8	61°25'	138°15'
Ruddell	VILG/VILG	SK	7-42-13-W3	73 B/12	52°36'	107°51'
Ruddock	UNP/LNO	MB		63 N/7	55°16'	100°56'
Rudy No. 284	MUN2/AZM2	SK		72 O/7	51°30'	106°55'
Ruel	UNP/LNO	ON	Sudbury	41 P/6	47°16'	81°28'
Ruffin, Lac	LAKE/LAC	QC	Minganie	12 M/2	51°10'	62°35'
Rufford	UNP/LNO	MB	33-13-18W	62 J/4	50°09'	99°54'
Rufus	UNP/LNO	SK	17-17-21-W2	72 I/7	50°26'	104°52'
Rufus Lake	LAKE/LAC	ON	Algoma	42 G/3	49°09'	83°05'
Rufus Lake	LAKE/LAC	NT	Mackenzie	107 D	69°35'	129°59'
Rufus River	RIV/CDE	NT	Franklin	97 H	71°25'	123°35'
Rugby	UNP/LNO	ON	Simcoe	31 D/11	44°34'	79°30'
Rugby	UNP/LNO	MB		62 H/14	49°55'	97°10'
Rugby Lake	LAKE/LAC	ON	Kenora	52 F/15	49°57'	92°58'
Ruggles River	RIV/CDE	NT	Franklin	120 C	81°42'	69°18'
Ruin Point	CAPE/CAP	NT	Keewatin	45 O	63°46'	83°36'
Ruis Lake	LAKE/LAC	AB	108,109-23-W4	84 I/5	58°25'	113°48'
Ruisseau-à-la-Loutre	UNP/LNO	QC	Matane	22 B/14	48°57'	67°09'
Ruisseau-à-l'Eau-Chaude	UNP/LNO	QC	Bellechasse	21 L/10	46°30'	70°39'
Ruisseau-à-Rebours	UNP/LNO	QC	Denis-Riverin	22 H/4	49°14'	65°56'
Ruisseau-à-Sem	UNP/LNO	QC	Matane	22 B/14	48°58'	67°04'
Ruisseau-Blanc	UNP/LNO	QC	Minganie	12 E/13	49°51'	63°41'
Ruisseau-Castor	UNP/LNO	QC	Denis-Riverin	22 G/1	49°11'	66°20'
Ruisseau-de-l'Indien, Réserve écologique du	PARK/PARC	QC	Pontiac	31 K/3	46°07'	77°29'
Ruisseau-des-Anges	UNP/LNO	QC	Montcalm	31 H/13	45°48'	73°40'
Ruisseau-des-Mineurs	MUN2/AZM2	QC	La Matapédia	22 B/10	48°35'	66°40'
Ruisseau-des-Olives	UNP/LNO	QC	Denis-Riverin	22 H/4	49°15'	65°40'
Ruisseau-Ferguson	MUN2/AZM2	QC	Avignon	22 B/4	48°05'	67°30'
Ruisseau-Gagnon	UNP/LNO	QC	Matane	22 B/11	48°43'	67°25'
Ruisseau-Jureux	UNP/LNO	QC	Charlevoix-Est	21 M/9	47°33'	70°12'
Ruisseau-Leblanc	UNP/LNO	QC	Bonaventure	22 A/4	48°05'	65°38'
Ruisseau-Noir	UNP/LNO	QC	Les Basques	21 N/15	47°57'	68°51'
Ruisseau-Vacher	UNP/LNO	QC	Montcalm	31 H/13	45°56'	73°32'
Ruisseau-Vert	UNP/LNO	QC	Manicouagan	22 F/1	49°04'	68°28'

NAME NOM	ENTITY ENTITÉ	LOC 1 LIEU 1	LOC 2 LIEU 2	MAP CARTE	POSITION	
					LAT	LONG
Ruisseaux, Les	UNP/LNO	QC	Les Îles-de-la-Madeleine	11 N/11	47°35′	61°29′
Ruiters Corners	UNP/LNO	QC	Memphrémagog	31 H/1	45°03′	72°07′
Rumble Beach	UNP/LNO	BC	Rupert	92 L/6	50°26′	127°29′
Rummelhardt	UNP/LNO	ON	Waterloo	40 P/7	43°27′	80°34′
Rumpelville	UNP/LNO	QC	L'Amiante	21 L/3	46°11′	71°10′
Rumsey	UNP/LNO	AB	24-33-21-W4	82 P/15	51°51′	112°51′
Rumsey Cairn Provincial Historic Site (Undeveloped)	PARK/PARC	AB	3-33-21-W4	82 P/15	51°48′	112°53′
Runciman	UNP/LNO	SK	24-46-15-W2	73 A/16	52°59′	104°03′
Runnymede	HAM/HAM	SK	6-29-30-W	62 N/5	51°29′	101°42′
Runnymede	UNP/LNO	QC	Avignon	21 O/15	47°54′	66°57′
Runnymede	UNP/LNO	ON	York	30 M/11	43°41′	79°29′
Rupert	UNP/LNO	QC	Les Collines-de-l'Outaouais	31 G/12	45°41′	75°59′
Rupert	UNP/LNO	BC	Cassiar	104 M/9	59°36′	134°11′
Rupert Bay	BAY/BAIE	NT	Keewatin	32 M	51°32′	78°58′
Rupert Creek	RIV/CDE	MB		54 F/10	57°32′	92°33′
Rupert Inlet	BAY/BAIE	BC	Rupert	92 L	50°35′	127°30′
Rupert Land District	GEOG/GÉOG	BC		92 L	50°20′	127°05′
Rupert, Rivière	RIV/CDE	QC	Jamésie	32 M/7	51°30′	78°45′
Rural	UNP/LNO	SK	23-34-23-W3	72 N/14	51°56′	109°09′
Rusagonis	UNP/LNO	NB	Sunbury	21 G/15	45°48′	66°37′
Rusagonis Station	UNP/LNO	NB	Sunbury	21 G/15	45°46′	66°35′
Ruscom River	RIV/CDE	ON	Essex	40 J/7	42°18′	82°37′
Ruscom Station	UNP/LNO	ON	Essex	40 J/2	42°13′	82°39′
Rush Lake	VILG/VILG	SK	1-17-11-W3	72 J/6	50°24′	107°24′
Rush Lake	LAKE/LAC	ON	Sudbury	41 O/16	47°47′	82°11′
Rushmere	UNP/LNO	BC	Kootenay	82 J/5	50°24′	115°56′
Rushoon	VILG/VILG	NF		1 M/7	47°21′	54°55′
Rush Point	UNP/LNO	ON	Peterborough	31 C/5	44°28′	77°53′
Rushton Island 90	IR/RI	BC	Range 5 Coast	103 J/7	54°16′	130°49′
Rushville	UNP/LNO	SK	31-30-15-W2	72 P/9	51°39′	104°07′
Rushy Pond	UNP/LNO	NF		2 D/13	48°57′	55°48′
Rushy Pond	LAKE/LAC	NF		2 D/13	48°57′	55°43′
Ruskin	UNP/LNO	BC	New Westminster	92 G/1	49°12′	122°26′
Ruskview	UNP/LNO	ON	Dufferin	41 A/1	44°14′	80°07′
Russel Bay	BAY/BAIE	NT	Mackenzie	96 G	65°29′	122°53′
Russeldale	UNP/LNO	ON	Perth	40 P/6	43°23′	81°16′
Russel Island	ISL/ÎLE	ON	Bruce	41 H/5	45°16′	81°42′
Russell	TOWN/VIL2	MB		62 K/14	50°47′	101°17′
Russell	MUN2/AZM2	ON	Russell	31 G/6	45°18′	75°19′
Russell	MUN2/AZM2	MB		62 K/11	50°44′	101°22′
Russell	UNP/LNO	NF		12 A/13	48°58′	57°48′
Russell	UNP/LNO	NB	Gloucester	21 P/5	47°22′	65°38′
Russell	UNP/LNO	ON	Russell	31 G/6	45°15′	75°22′
Russell	GEOG/GÉOG	ON		31 G/6	45°25′	75°15′
Russell, Cape	CAPE/CAP	BC	Rupert	102 I/9	50°41′	128°22′
Russell, Cape	CAPE/CAP	NT	Franklin	88 G	75°15′	117°40′
Russell Channel	CHAN/CHEN	BC	Clayoquot	92 E/1	49°14′	126°06′
Russell Creek	RIV/CDE	SK	9-11-10-W3	72 G/14	49°54′	107°19′
Russell Inlet	BAY/BAIE	NT	Franklin	107 E	70°08′	130°00′
Russell Island	ISL/ÎLE	NT	Franklin	68 D	74°00′	98°25′
Russell, Lac	LAKE/LAC	QC	Témiscamingue	31 K/12	46°37′	77°54′
Russell Lake	LAKE/LAC	MB		64 C/4	56°15′	101°31′
Russell Lake	LAKE/LAC	SK	68-2-W2	63 L/16	54°55′	102°12′
Russell Lake	LAKE/LAC	SK		74 H/6	57°26′	105°20′
Russell Lake	LAKE/LAC	SK	49-18-W3	73 F/2	53°14′	108°35′
Russell Lake	LAKE/LAC	NT	Mackenzie	85 O	63°00′	115°47′
Russell Landing	UNP/LNO	ON	Haliburton	31 E/7	45°16′	78°49′
Russell Point	CAPE/CAP	NT	Franklin	88 D	73°32′	115°18′
Russell Pond	LAKE/LAC	NF		2 D/16	48°56′	54°09′
Russell Range	MTN/MNT	YT		105 N/3	63°13′	133°10′
Russelltown	UNP/LNO	NB	Northumberland	21 J/9	46°33′	66°10′
Russellville	UNP/LNO	NB	Northumberland	21 P/3	47°07′	65°23′
Russel, Mount	MTN/MNT	BC	Cassiar	94 F/4	57°08′	125°45′
Russels Cove	BAY/BAIE	NF		2 C/3	48°04′	53°06′
Russeltown Flats	UNP/LNO	QC	Le Haut-Saint-Laurent	31 H/4	45°04′	73°46′
Russick Lake	LAKE/LAC	MB		63 N/5	55°21′	101°39′
Rustico Island	ISL/ÎLE	PE	Queens	11 L/6	46°27′	63°15′
Rusticoville	UNP/LNO	PE	Queens	11 L/6	46°26′	63°19′
Rusty Lake	LAKE/LAC	MB		64 B/12	56°34′	99°37′
Rusylvia	UNP/LNO	AB	28-53-6-W4	73 E/10	53°37′	110°50′
Rutan	UNP/LNO	SK	22-35-27-W2	73 A/4	52°01′	105°46′
Ruthenia	UNP/LNO	MB	28-21-25-W	62 K/15	50°51′	100°55′
Rutherford	UNP/LNO	ON	Lambton	40 J/9	42°39′	82°08′
Rutherford and George Island	MUN2/AZM2	ON	Manitoulin	41 H/13	45°58′	81°31′
Rutherford, Cape	CAPE/CAP	NT	Franklin	39 E	78°50′	74°48′

NAME NOM	ENTITY ENTITÉ	LOC 1 LIEU 1	LOC 2 LIEU 2	MAP CARTE	POSITION	
					LAT	LONG
Rutherford Creek	RIV/CDE	BC	Lillooet	92 J/7	50°17′	122°51′
Rutherford House Provincial Historic Site (Developed)	PARK/PARC	AB		83 H/11	53°32′	113°22′
Rutherglen	UNP/LNO	ON	Nipissing	31 L/6	46°16′	79°03′
Ruthilda	VILG/VILG	SK	3-34-18-W3	72 N/16	51°54′	108°28′
Ruth Lake	LAKE/LAC	ON	Parry Sound	31 L/4	46°01′	79°31′
Ruth Lake	LAKE/LAC	BC	Lillooet	92 P/14	51°50′	121°04′
Ruthledge	UNP/LNO	QC	Les Collines-de-l'Outaouais	31 F/9	45°39′	76°19′
Ruthven	UNP/LNO	ON	Essex	40 J/2	42°03′	82°40′
Rutland	UNP/LNO	SK	9-41-25-W3	73 C/12	52°31′	109°32′
Rutland	UNP/LNO	BC	Osoyoos Division Yale	82 E/14	49°54′	119°23′
Rutledge Lake	LAKE/LAC	NT	Mackenzie	75 E	61°33′	110°47′
Rutledge River	RIV/CDE	NT	Mackenzie	85 H	61°04′	112°01′
Ruttan Mine	UNP/LNO	MB	86-14-W	64 B/5	56°29′	99°39′
Rutter	UNP/LNO	ON	Sudbury	41 I/2	46°06′	80°40′
Ruzé, Lac	LAKE/LAC	QC	Côte-Nord-du-Golfe-Saint-Laurent	12 O/3	51°10′	59°02′
Ryan	UNP/LNO	BC	Kootenay	82 F/1	49°08′	116°02′
Ryan Lake	LAKE/LAC	MB		64 J/10	58°34′	98°46′
Ryan Premises National Historic Site - also-aussi - Établissement-Ryan, Lieu historique national de l'	PARK/PARC	NF		2 C/11	48°39′	53°07′
Ryan River	RIV/CDE	BC	Lillooet	92 J/7	50°22′	122°50′
Ryans Bay	BAY/BAIE	NF		24 P/9	59°35′	64°03′
Ryans Brook	RIV/CDE	NF		11 O/14	47°51′	59°14′
Ryan's Corner	UNP/LNO	QC	Pontiac	31 F/15	45°50′	76°57′
Ryanville	UNP/LNO	QC	La Vallée-de-la-Gatineau	31 G/13	45°56′	75°54′
Ryckmans	UNP/LNO	ON	Wentworth	30 M/4	43°12′	79°53′
Ryckmans Corners	UNP/LNO	ON	Wentworth	30 M/4	43°12′	79°53′
Rycroft	VILG/VILG	AB	16-78-5-W6	83 M/15	55°45′	118°43′
Rydal Bank	UNP/LNO	ON	Algoma	41 J/5	46°22′	83°45′
Ryder Lake	UNP/LNO	BC	New Westminster	92 H/4	49°06′	121°53′
Ryders Brook	RIV/CDE	NF		2 C/4	48°14′	53°56′
Ryderville	UNP/LNO	ON	Lincoln	30 M/3	43°11′	79°13′
Rye	UNP/LNO	ON	Parry Sound	31 E/13	45°52′	79°37′
Ryerson	MUN2/AZM2	ON	Parry Sound	31 E/12	45°35′	79°30′
Ryerson	UNP/LNO	ON	Algoma	42 C/7	48°29′	84°43′
Ryerson	UNP/LNO	SK	31-9-31-W	62 F/13	49°47′	101°40′
Rykerts	UNP/LNO	BC	Kootenay	82 F/1	49°00′	116°30′
Ryland	UNP/LNO	ON	Cochrane	42 G/12	49°43′	83°47′
Ryley	VILG/VILG	AB	4-50-17-W4	83 H/8	53°17′	112°26′
Rylstone	UNP/LNO	ON	Hastings	31 C/5	44°23′	77°42′
Rymal	UNP/LNO	ON	Wentworth	30 M/4	43°11′	79°50′

S

Saagoombahlah 6	IR/RI	BC	Range 2 Coast	92 M/4	51°05′	127°31′
Saaiyouck 6	IR/RI	BC	Range 1 Coast	92 K/6	50°25′	125°10′
Saanich	MUN1/AZM1	BC	South Saanich	92 B/11	48°33′	123°22′
Saanich Inlet	BAY/BAIE	BC	Cowichan	92 B/11	48°37′	123°30′
Saanichton	UNP/LNO	BC	South Saanich	92 B/11	48°36′	123°25′
Sabaskong Bay	BAY/BAIE	ON	Kenora	52 E/1	49°09′	94°09′
Sabaskong Bay 32C	IR/RI	ON	Kenora	52 E/1	49°10′	94°11′
Sabaskong Bay 35C	IR/RI	ON	Kenora	52 E/1	49°11′	94°05′
Sabaskong Bay 35D	IR/RI	ON	Kenora	52 F/4	49°10′	93°55′
Sabaskong Bay 35F	IR/RI	ON	Kenora	52 E/1	49°08′	94°05′
Sabaskong Bay 35H	IR/RI	ON	Kenora	52 E/1	49°10′	94°11′
Sabaskong Peninsula	CAPE/CAP	ON	Kenora	52 E/1	49°08′	94°00′
Sabaskosing Bay	BAY/BAIE	ON	Kenora	52 E/7	49°20′	94°39′
Sabbies River	RIV/CDE	NB	Northumberland	21 I/12	46°35′	65°44′
Sabine	UNP/LNO	AB	26-37-19-W4	83 A/2	52°12′	112°36′
Sabine Bay	BAY/BAIE	NT	Franklin	25 I	62°40′	65°19′
Sabine Bay	BAY/BAIE	NT	Franklin	78 G	75°39′	109°30′
Sabine, Cape	CAPE/CAP	NT	Franklin	39 E	78°43′	74°07′
Sabine Channel	CHAN/CHEN	BC	Texada Island	92 F/8	49°30′	124°11′
Sabine Island	ISL/ÎLE	NT	Franklin	46 M	67°38′	86°37′
Sabine, Lac	LAKE/LAC	QC	Kativik	34 I/10	58°44′	72°35′
Sabine Peninsula	CAPE/CAP	NT	Franklin	79 B	76°20′	109°30′
Sabine River	RIV/CDE	NT	Franklin	78 G	75°31′	108°51′
Sable	UNP/LNO	ON	Middlesex	40 P/4	43°05′	81°44′
Sable, Baie au	BAY/BAIE	QC	La Vallée-de-la-Gatineau	31 J/12	46°41′	75°47′
Sable, Cape	CAPE/CAP	NS	Shelburne	20 P/5	43°24′	65°37′
Sable, Île de - also-aussi - **Sable Island**	ISL/ÎLE	NS	Halifax	10 O/13	43°57′	59°55′
Sable Island - also-aussi - **Sable, Île de**	ISL/ÎLE	NS	Halifax	10 O/13	43°57′	59°55′
Sable Island Bank - also-aussi - Île de Sable, Banc de l'	SEAU/SMER	—		8007	43°45′	60°45′
Sable Islands	ISL/ÎLE	ON	Rainy River	52 D/15	48°55′	94°39′

NAME NOM	ENTITY ENTITÉ	LOC 1 LIEU 1	LOC 2 LIEU 2	MAP CARTE	POSITION LAT	LONG
Sable, Lac du	LAKE/LAC	QC	Caniapiscau	23 J/5	54°22′	67°50′
Sable River	UNP/LNO	NS	Shelburne	20 P/14	43°51′	65°03′
Sable River	RIV/CDE	NS	Shelburne	20 P/14	43°45′	65°00′
Sable River Station	UNP/LNO	NS	Shelburne	20 P/14	43°49′	65°03′
Sable River West	UNP/LNO	NS	Shelburne	20 P/14	43°49′	65°03′
Sable, Rivière du	RIV/CDE	QC	Kativik	23 N/9	55°30′	68°21′
Sables, Baie des	BAY/BAIE	QC	Minganie	12 E/6	49°19′	63°18′
Sables, Lac aux	LAKE/LAC	ON	Algoma	41 J/16	46°47′	82°20′
Sables, Lac des	LAKE/LAC	QC	La Haute-Côte-Nord	22 C/5	48°18′	69°41′
Sables, Les	UNP/LNO	QC	Lac-Saint-Jean-Est	22 D/5	48°20′	71°42′
Sables, Les	UNP/LNO	QC	Le Domaine-du-Roy	32 A/8	48°26′	72°07′
Sables, Réservoir aux	LAKE/LAC	QC	Antoine-Labelle	31 J/4	46°10′	75°41′
Sables, River aux	RIV/CDE	ON	Sudbury	41 J/1	46°13′	82°03′
Sables, Rivière aux	RIV/CDE	QC	Le Fjord-du-Saguenay	22 E/7	49°23′	70°30′
Sables, Rivière aux	RIV/CDE	QC	Le Fjord-du-Saguenay	22 D/6	48°27′	71°15′
Sabomin Lake	LAKE/LAC	MB	72-2-E	63 P/6	55°15′	97°15′
Sabourin, Lac	LAKE/LAC	QC	Vallée-de-l'Or	31 N/13	47°58′	77°41′
Sabourin Lake	LAKE/LAC	ON	Kenora	53 F/12	53°36′	93°49′
Sabourin Lake	LAKE/LAC	ON	Kenora	52 M/7	51°20′	94°49′
Sabourins Crossing	UNP/LNO	ON	Grenville	31 G/4	45°05′	75°37′
Sabrevois	UNP/LNO	QC	Le Haut-Richelieu	31 H/3	45°12′	73°14′
Sacacomie, Lac	LAKE/LAC	QC	Maskinongé	31 I/11	46°31′	73°14′
Sachawil 5	IR/RI	BC	Barclay	92 C/14	48°51′	125°10′
Sachigo Lake	UNP/LNO	ON	Kenora	53 F/16	53°52′	92°10′
Sachigo Lake	LAKE/LAC	ON	Kenora	53 F/16	53°49′	92°08′
Sachigo Lake 1	IR/RI	ON	Kenora	53 F/16	53°50′	92°10′
Sachigo Lake 2	IR/RI	ON	Kenora	53 F/16	53°58′	92°30′
Sachigo Lake 3	IR/RI	ON	Kenora	53 F/9	53°45′	92°20′
Sachigo River	RIV/CDE	ON	Kenora	53 P/2	55°06′	88°58′
Sachsa 4	IR/RI	BC	Barclay	92 C/14	48°50′	125°06′
Sachs Harbour	HAM/HAM	NT	Franklin	97 G/15	71°59′	125°14′
Sachs River	RIV/CDE	NT	Franklin	97 G/15	71°59′	125°07′
Sachteen 2	IR/RI	BC	New Westminster	92 G/16	49°59′	122°27′
Sachteen 2A	IR/RI	BC	New Westminster	92 G/16	49°58′	122°26′
Sackanitecla 2	IR/RI	BC	Range 4 Coast	93 F/1	53°54′	124°06′
Sackum 3	IR/RI	BC	Kamloops Division Yale	92 I/6	50°19′	121°24′
Sackville	TOWN/VIL2	NB	Westmorland	21 H/16	45°54′	64°22′
Sackville	GEOG/GÉOG	NB	Westmorland	21 I/1	46°00′	64°23′
Sackville Spur	SEAU/SMER	—		8012	48°15′	46°30′
Sacré-Coeur	VILG/VILG	QC	La Haute-Côte-Nord	22 C/4	48°14′	69°48′
Sacré-Coeur	UNP/LNO	QC	Rimouski-Neigette	22 C/7	48°26′	68°35′
Sacré-Coeur-de-Crabtree	VILG/VILG	QC	Joliette	31 H/14	45°58′	73°29′
Sacré-Coeur-de-Jésus	VILG/VILG	QC	L'Amiante	21 L/3	46°13′	71°05′
Sacré-Coeur-de-Marie-Partie-Sud	VILG/VILG	QC	L'Amiante	21 L/3	46°08′	71°11′
Sacré-Coeur-Deslandes	UNP/LNO	QC	Denis-Riverin	22 G/1	49°04′	66°18′
Sacred Bay	BAY/BAIE	NF		2 M/12	51°36′	55°36′
Saddle Back Pond	LAKE/LAC	NF		2 C/5	48°20′	53°30′
Saddlebrook	UNP/LNO	QC	Vaudreuil-Soulanges	31 G/8	45°26′	74°10′
Saddle (Burnt) River	RIV/CDE	AB	6-80-1-W6	83 M/16	55°55′	118°08′
Saddle Hills	MTN/MNT	AB	75-6-7,8-W6	83 M/11	55°31′	119°05′
Saddle Hills No. 20, Municipal District of	MUN1/AZM1	AB	79-9-W6	83 M/14	55°51′	119°20′
Saddle Horse 2	IR/RI	BC	Lillooet	92 O/14	51°48′	123°03′
Saddle, La	UNP/LNO	QC	Les Îles-de-la-Madeleine	11 N/14	47°48′	61°26′
Saddle Lake	UNP/LNO	AB	34-57-12-W4	73 E/13	53°58′	111°41′
Saddle Lake	LAKE/LAC	MB	14-16-E	52 L/3	50°11′	95°21′
Saddle Lake	LAKE/LAC	AB	58-11.12-W4	73 L/4	54°01′	111°40′
Saddle Lake	LAKE/LAC	NT	Mackenzie	85 N	63°56′	116°29′
Saddle Lake 125	IR/RI	AB	58-12-W4	73 E/13	53°59′	111°42′
Saddle, Mont	MTN/MNT	QC	Le Granit	21 E/6	45°21′	71°01′
Saddle Rock	UNP/LNO	BC	Yale Division Yale	92 H/11	49°38′	121°24′
Saddle Rock 9	IR/RI	BC	Yale Division Yale	92 H/11	49°38′	121°24′
Sadene Lake	LAKE/LAC	NT	Franklin	97 B	68°52′	126°37′
Sadler Lake	LAKE/LAC	SK		63 M/5	55°17′	103°45′
Sadler Point	CAPE/CAP	BC	Queen Charlotte	103 K/3	54°06′	133°06′
Sadowa	UNP/LNO	ON	Victoria	31 D/14	44°45′	79°09′
Safe Harbour	UNP/LNO	NF		2 F/4	49°06′	53°37′
Saffray, Lac	LAKE/LAC	QC	Kativik	24 G/11	57°35′	67°04′
Sagamok	UNP/LNO	ON	Algoma	41 J/1	46°09′	82°07′
Sagamok 5	IR/RI	ON	Algoma	41 J/1	46°10′	82°15′
Saganaga Lake	UNP/LNO	ON	Thunder Bay	52 B/2	48°14′	90°52′
Saganaga Lake	LAKE/LAC	ON	Thunder Bay	52 B/2	48°14′	90°55′
Saganagons Lake	LAKE/LAC	ON	Rainy River	52 B/7	48°17′	90°58′
Saganash Lake	LAKE/LAC	ON	Cochrane	42 G/2	49°04′	82°35′
Saganash River	RIV/CDE	ON	Cochrane	42 G/8	49°22′	82°28′
Sagard	MUN2/AZM2	QC	Charlevoix-Est	22 D/1	48°03′	70°06′

NAME NOM	ENTITY ENTITÉ	LOC 1 LIEU 1	LOC 2 LIEU 2	MAP CARTE	POSITION LAT	POSITION LONG
Sagard	UNP/LNO	QC	Charlevoix-Est	22 D/1	48°02′	70°04′
Sagathun	UNP/LNO	SK	2-14-26-W3	72 K/3	50°08′	109°28′
Sagawitchewan River	RIV/CDE	MB/ON		53 F/12	53°44′	93°41′
Sage	UNP/LNO	ON	Nipissing	31 L/6	46°19′	79°25′
Sagehill	UNP/LNO	SK	22-38-27-W2	73 A/5	52°17′	105°46′
Sagemace Bay	BAY/BAIE	MB		62 N/16	51°54′	100°03′
Saginaw	UNP/LNO	ON	Ontario	31 D/6	44°21′	79°03′
Sagittarius Channel	SEAU/SMER	—		5.03	49°00′	159°25′
Saglarsuk Bay	BAY/BAIE	NF		24 P/16	59°57′	64°15′
Saglek Bank	SEAU/SMER	—		5001	59°20′	62°00′
Saglek Bay	BAY/BAIE	NF		14 L/10	58°30′	63°00′
Sagona Island	UNP/LNO	NF		1 M/5	47°22′	55°47′
Sagona Island	ISL/ÎLE	NF		1 M/5	47°22′	55°48′
Saguenay, Fjord du	BAY/BAIE	QC	La Haute-Côte-Nord	22 C/4	48°08′	69°44′
Saguenay — Lac-Saint-Jean	MUN1/AZM1	QC	Maria-Chapdelaine	22 E/13	49°52′	71°45′
Saguenay, Parc de conservation du	PARK/PARC	QC	Le Fjord-du-Saguenay	22 D/8	48°17′	70°17′
Saguenay River - also-aussi - **Saguenay, Rivière**	RIV/CDE	QC	La Haute-Côte-Nord	22 C/4	48°08′	69°42′
Saguenay, Rivière - also-aussi - **Saguenay River**	RIV/CDE	QC	La Haute-Côte-Nord	22 C/4	48°08′	69°42′
Saguenay — Saint-Laurent, Parc marin du - also-aussi - Saguenay—St. Lawrence Marine Park	PARK/PARC	QC	La Haute-Côte-Nord	22 C/4	48°08′	69°44′
Saguenay—St. Lawrence Marine Park - also-aussi - Saguenay — Saint-Laurent, Parc marin du	PARK/PARC	QC	La Haute-Côte-Nord	22 C/4	48°08′	69°44′
Sagwa	UNP/LNO	NB	Kings	21 G/8	45°22′	66°16′
Sahali	UNP/LNO	BC	Kamloops Division Yale	92 I/9	50°39′	120°20′
Sahanatien	UNP/LNO	ON	Muskoka	31 D/13	44°59′	79°45′
Sahara Heights	UNP/LNO	BC	Alberni	92 F/7	49°15′	124°47′
Sahdoanah Creek	RIV/CDE	BC	Peace River	94 P/11	59°36′	121°13′
Sahhacum 1	IR/RI	BC	New Westminster	92 G/1	49°05′	122°17′
Sahhaltkum 4	IR/RI	BC	Kamloops Division Yale	82 L/13	50°49′	119°45′
Sahtaneh River	RIV/CDE	BC	Peace River	94 O/1	59°02′	122°27′
Sahtlam	UNP/LNO	BC	Sahtlam	92 B/13	48°46′	123°48′
Sahtlam	UNP/LNO	BC	Cowichan Lake	92 B/13	48°48′	123°54′
Sahtlam Land District	GEOG/GÉOG	BC		92 B	48°46′	123°50′
Sailing Lake	LAKE/LAC	MB	14-11-16-E	52 E/14	49°56′	95°19′
Sailors Encampment	UNP/LNO	ON	Algoma	41 K/8	46°16′	84°06′
Saindon, Lacs	LAKE/LAC	QC	Kativik	33 P/12	55°36′	73°30′
Sainsbury Point	CAPE/CAP	NT	Franklin	33 M	55°40′	79°13′
Saint-Achillée	UNP/LNO	QC	La Côte-de-Beaupré	21 M/3	47°03′	71°02′
Saint-Adalbert	VILG/VILG	QC	L'Islet	21 K/13	46°52′	69°54′
Saint-Adélard	UNP/LNO	QC	Bonaventure	22 A/3	48°08′	65°25′
Saint-Adelme	VILG/VILG	QC	Matane	22 B/14	48°49′	67°19′
Saint-Adelme-Sud	UNP/LNO	QC	Matane	22 B/14	48°50′	67°15′
Saint-Adelphe	VILG/VILG	QC	Mékinac	31 I/9	46°44′	72°26′
Saint-Adolphe	UNP/LNO	QC	La Jacques-Cartier	21 M/3	47°04′	71°19′
St. Adolphe	UNP/LNO	MB		62 H/11	49°40′	97°07′
Saint-Adolphe-de-Dudswell	UNP/LNO	QC	Le Haut-Saint-François	21 E/12	45°38′	71°36′
Saint-Adolphe-d'Howard	VILG/VILG	QC	Les Pays-d'en-Haut	31 G/16	45°58′	74°20′
Saint-Adrien	VILG/VILG	QC	Asbestos	21 E/13	45°49′	71°43′
Saint-Adrien-d'Irlande	VILG/VILG	QC	L'Amiante	21 L/3	46°07′	71°27′
Saint-Agapit	VILG/VILG	QC	Lotbinière	21 L/11	46°34′	71°26′
St. Agatha	UNP/LNO	ON	Waterloo	40 P/7	43°26′	80°36′
Saint-Agricole	UNP/LNO	QC	La Matapédia	22 B/12	48°20′	67°37′
Saint-Aimé	VILG/VILG	QC	Le Bas-Richelieu	31 H/15	45°55′	72°56′
Saint-Aimé-des-Lacs	VILG/VILG	QC	Charlevoix-Est	21 M/9	47°41′	70°18′
Saint-Aimé-du-Lac-des-Îles	VILG/VILG	QC	Antoine-Labelle	31 J/5	46°24′	75°32′
Saint-Alban	VILG/VILG	QC	Portneuf	31 I/9	46°43′	72°05′
St. Alban's	TOWN/VIL2	NF		1 M/14	47°52′	55°51′
St. Albert	CITY/VIL1	AB	4-54-25-W4	83 H/12	53°38′	113°38′
Saint-Albert	UNP/LNO	QC	Arthabaska	31 I/1	46°00′	72°05′
St-Albert	UNP/LNO	ON	Russell	31 G/6	45°15′	75°07′
Saint-Albert-de-Warwick	VILG/VILG	QC	Arthabaska	31 I/1	46°00′	72°05′
St. Albert Settlement	UNP/LNO	AB	53,54-25-W4	83 H/12	53°38′	113°37′
St. Aldwyn	UNP/LNO	SK	17-13-W3	72 J/5	50°26′	107°42′
Saint-Alexandre	VILG/VILG	QC	Kamouraska	21 N/12	47°41′	69°38′
Saint-Alexandre	VILG/VILG	QC	Le Haut-Richelieu	31 H/3	45°14′	73°07′
Saint-Alexandre-des-Lacs	VILG/VILG	QC	La Matapédia	22 B/6	48°28′	67°18′
Saint-Alexis	TOWN/VIL2	QC	Montcalm	31 H/13	45°56′	73°37′
Saint-Alexis	VILG/VILG	QC	Montcalm	31 H/13	45°56′	73°37′
Saint-Alexis	UNP/LNO	QC	Avignon	22 B/3	48°01′	67°02′
Saint-Alexis-de-Matapédia	VILG/VILG	QC	Avignon	21 O/14	47°58′	67°03′
Saint-Alexis-des-Monts	VILG/VILG	QC	Maskinongé	31 I/6	46°28′	73°08′
Saint-Alexis-Station	UNP/LNO	QC	Montcalm	31 H/13	45°57′	73°35′
Saint-Alfred	VILG/VILG	QC	Robert-Cliche	21 L/2	46°09′	70°50′
St. Almo	UNP/LNO	NB	Victoria	21 J/14	46°51′	67°26′
St. Alphege	UNP/LNO	SK	26-39-19-W3	73 C/7	52°23′	108°37′
Saint-Alphonse	VILG/VILG	QC	Bonaventure	22 A/4	48°11′	65°38′
Saint-Alphonse	VILG/VILG	QC	La Haute-Yamaska	31 H/7	45°20′	72°49′

NAME NOM	ENTITY ENTITÉ	LOC 1 LIEU 1	LOC 2 LIEU 2	MAP CARTE	POSITION LAT	LONG
St. Alphonse	UNP/LNO	NS	Digby	21 B/1	44°08′	66°11′
St. Alphonse	UNP/LNO	MB	34-5-12-W	62 G/6	49°26′	99°00′
Saint-Alphonse-de-Caplan	UNP/LNO	QC	Bonaventure	22 A/4	48°11′	65°38′
Saint-Alphonse-de-Granby	UNP/LNO	QC	La Haute-Yamaska	31 H/7	45°20′	72°49′
Saint-Alphonse-Rodriguez	VILG/VILG	QC	Matawinie	31 I/4	46°11′	73°42′
Saint-Amable	VILG/VILG	QC	Lajemmerais	31 H/11	45°39′	73°18′
Saint-Amand	UNP/LNO	NB	Madawaska	21 O/4	47°09′	67°46′
Saint-Amateur	UNP/LNO	NB	Gloucester	21 P/11	47°41′	65°11′
Saint-Ambroise	VILG/VILG	QC	Le Fjord-du-Saguenay	22 D/11	48°33′	71°20′
St. Ambroise	UNP/LNO	MB	11-15-5-W	62 J/8	50°15′	98°02′
Saint-Ambroise-de-Kildare	VILG/VILG	QC	Joliette	31 I/4	46°05′	73°33′
Saint-Amédée	UNP/LNO	QC	Papineau	31 G/10	45°42′	74°59′
Saint-Amédée-de-Péribonka	UNP/LNO	QC	Maria-Chapdelaine	32 A/16	48°49′	72°03′
St-Amour	UNP/LNO	ON	Prescott	31 G/7	45°26′	74°50′
Saint-Amour, Lac	LAKE/LAC	QC	La Vallée-de-la-Gatineau	31 N/8	47°18′	76°22′
Saint-Anaclet	UNP/LNO	QC	Rimouski-Neigette	22 C/8	48°29′	68°25′
Saint-Anaclet-de-Lessard	VILG/VILG	QC	Rimouski-Neigette	22 C/8	48°29′	68°25′
St. André	VILG/VILG	NB	Madawaska	21 O/4	47°06′	67°46′
Saint-André	VILG/VILG	QC	Kamouraska	21 N/12	47°41′	69°44′
Saint-André	GEOG/GÉOG	NB	Madawaska	21 O/4	47°08′	67°45′
Saint-André-Avellin	TOWN/VIL2	QC	Papineau	31 G/11	45°43′	75°04′
Saint-André-Avellin	VILG/VILG	QC	Papineau	31 G/11	45°42′	75°06′
Saint-André-d'Acton	VILG/VILG	QC	Acton	31 H/10	45°38′	72°34′
Saint-André-d'Argenteuil	VILG/VILG	QC	Argenteuil	31 G/9	45°36′	74°19′
Saint-André-de-Restigouche	VILG/VILG	QC	Avignon	22 B/2	48°04′	66°57′
Saint-André-de-Shédiac	UNP/LNO	NB	Westmorland	21 I/1	46°11′	64°19′
Saint-André-du-Lac-Saint-Jean	TOWN/VIL2	QC	Le Domaine-du-Roy	22 D/5	48°19′	71°59′
Saint-André-Est	TOWN/VIL2	QC	Argenteuil	31 G/9	45°34′	74°20′
Saint-André-Station	UNP/LNO	QC	Kamouraska	21 N/12	47°38′	69°41′
St. Andrew, Lake	LAKE/LAC	MB	30-32-1-E	62 P/11	51°41′	97°23′
Saint Andrews	TOWN/VIL2	NB	Charlotte	21 G/3	45°05′	67°03′
St. Andrews	MUN2/AZM2	MB		62 I/2	50°15′	97°00′
St. Andrew's	UNP/LNO	NF		11 O/14	47°47′	59°16′
St. Andrews	UNP/LNO	PE	Queens	11 L/7	46°23′	62°51′
St. Andrews	UNP/LNO	NS	Antigonish	11 F/12	45°33′	61°53′
St. Andrews	UNP/LNO	ON	Stormont	31 G/2	45°06′	74°47′
St. Andrews	UNP/LNO	MB		62 I/2	50°04′	96°59′
Saint Andrews	GEOG/GÉOG	NB	Charlotte	21 G/3	45°07′	67°05′
St. Andrews	GEOG/GÉOG	MB		62 I/2	50°04′	96°59′
St. Andrews Blockhouse National Historic Site - also-aussi - Blockhaus-de-St. Andrews, Lieu historique national du	PARK/PARC	NB	Charlotte	21 G/3	45°05′	67°04′
St. Andrews Channel	UNP/LNO	NS	Cape Breton	11 F/15	45°55′	60°31′
St. Andrews Channel	CHAN/CHEN	NS	Cape Breton	11 K/2	46°08′	60°30′
St. Andrews No. 287	MUN2/AZM2	SK		72 O/5	51°30′	107°55′
St. Andrew's Rectory National Historic Site - also-aussi - Presbytère-St. Andrew's, Lieu historique national du	PARK/PARC	MB		62 I/2	50°04′	96°59′
Saint-Ange-Gardien	VILG/VILG	QC	Rouville	31 H/7	45°21′	72°54′
Saint-Anicet	VILG/VILG	QC	Le Haut-Saint-Laurent	31 G/1	45°07′	74°21′
St. Ann	UNP/LNO	PE	Queens	11 L/6	46°26′	63°24′
St. Annes	UNP/LNO	NF		1 M/8	47°26′	54°28′
St. Anns	UNP/LNO	NS	Victoria	11 K/2	46°12′	60°36′
St. Anns	UNP/LNO	ON	Lincoln	30 M/4	43°05′	79°30′
St. Anns Bank - also-aussi - Sainte-Anne, Banc de	SEAU/SMER	—		4022	46°00′	59°30′
St. Anns Bay	BAY/BAIE	NS	Victoria	11 K/7	46°20′	60°30′
St. Anns Harbour	BAY/BAIE	NS	Victoria	11 K/2	46°15′	60°35′
Saint-Anselme	TOWN/VIL2	QC	Bellechasse	21 L/10	46°38′	70°58′
Saint-Anselme	VILG/VILG	QC	Bellechasse	21 L/10	46°35′	71°00′
Saint-Anselme	UNP/LNO	NB	Westmorland	21 I/2	46°04′	64°43′
St. Anthony	TOWN/VIL2	NF		2 M/5	51°22′	55°35′
St. Anthony	UNP/LNO	PE	Prince	21 I/9	46°44′	64°11′
St. Anthony Basin	SEAU/SMER	—		813	51°55′	53°30′
St. Anthony Bight	UNP/LNO	NF		2 M/5	51°23′	55°33′
St. Anthony, Cape	CAPE/CAP	NF		2 M/5	51°21′	55°31′
St. Anthony Lake	LAKE/LAC	ON	Timiskaming	31 M/13	47°58′	79°43′
Saint-Antoine	CITY/VIL1	QC	La Rivière-du-Nord	31 H/13	45°46′	73°59′
Saint-Antoine	VILG/VILG	NB	Kent	21 I/7	46°22′	64°45′
Saint-Antoine	UNP/LNO	QC	Le Fjord-du-Saguenay	22 D/1	48°09′	70°02′
St. Antoine	UNP/LNO	SK	32-5-31-W	62 F/5	49°26′	101°38′
Saint-Antoine-Abbé	UNP/LNO	QC	Le Haut-Saint-Laurent	31 H/4	45°03′	73°53′
Saint-Antoine-de-Lavaltrie	VILG/VILG	QC	D'Autray	31 H/14	45°53′	73°17′
Saint-Antoine-de-l'Isle-aux-Grues	VILG/VILG	QC	Montmagny	21 M/2	47°04′	70°33′
Saint-Antoine-des-Laurentides	UNP/LNO	QC	Mirabel	31 H/13	45°45′	73°58′
Saint-Antoine-de-Tilly	VILG/VILG	QC	Lotbinière	21 L/12	46°40′	71°35′
Saint-Antoine-sur-Richelieu	VILG/VILG	QC	La Vallée-du-Richelieu	31 H/14	45°47′	73°11′
Saint-Antonin	VILG/VILG	QC	Rivière-du-Loup	21 N/14	47°46′	69°29′
Saint-Apollinaire	VILG/VILG	QC	Lotbinière	21 L/12	46°37′	71°31′
Saint-Armand	VILG/VILG	QC	Brome-Missisquoi	31 H/3	45°02′	73°03′

NAME NOM	ENTITY ENTITÉ	LOC 1 LIEU 1	LOC 2 LIEU 2	MAP CARTE	POSITION LAT	LONG
Saint-Armand-Centre	UNP/LNO	QC	Brome-Missisquoi	31 H/2	45°03′	72°53′
St. Arnaud Hills	MTN/MNT	NT	Franklin	78 G	75°50′	108°35′
Saint-Arsène	VILG/VILG	QC	Rivière-du-Loup	21 N/14	47°55′	69°26′
Saint-Arsène	UNP/LNO	QC	Lajemmerais	31 H/14	45°58′	73°11′
Saint-Arthur	UNP/LNO	NB	Restigouche	21 O/15	47°53′	66°46′
Saint-Athanase	VILG/VILG	QC	Témiscouata	21 N/6	47°26′	69°25′
Saint-Athanase	VILG/VILG	QC	Le Haut-Richelieu	31 H/6	45°18′	73°14′
Saint-Athanase	UNP/LNO	NB	Kent	21 I/11	46°43′	65°24′
Saint-Aubert	VILG/VILG	QC	L'Islet	21 M/1	47°11′	70°13′
Saint-Aubin	UNP/LNO	NB	Restigouche	21 O/15	47°58′	66°35′
St. Aubyn Bay	BAY/BAIE	ON	Parry Sound	41 H/8	45°21′	80°15′
St. Aubyn Lake	LAKE/LAC	BC	Sayward	92 K/6	50°21′	125°14′
Saint-Augustin	VILG/VILG	QC	Côte-Nord-du-Golfe-Saint-Laurent	12 O/2	51°13′	58°39′
Saint-Augustin	VILG/VILG	QC	Maria-Chapdelaine	22 D/13	48°48′	71°57′
Saint-Augustin	UNP/LNO	QC	Côte-Nord-du-Golfe-Saint-Laurent	12 O/2	51°13′	58°39′
Saint-Augustin	UNP/LNO	QC	Communauté urbaine de Québec	21 L/11	46°45′	71°28′
Saint-Augustin	UNP/LNO	QC	Mirabel	31 H/12	45°38′	73°59′
Saint-Augustin, Baie	BAY/BAIE	QC	Côte-Nord-du-Golfe-Saint-Laurent	12 O/2	51°12′	58°35′
Saint-Augustin-de-Desmaures	VILG/VILG	QC	Communauté urbaine de Québec	21 L/11	46°45′	71°28′
Saint-Augustin-de-Woburn	VILG/VILG	QC	Le Granit	21 E/7	45°23′	70°51′
St. Augustine	UNP/LNO	ON	Huron	40 P/13	43°51′	81°30′
Saint-Augustin, Lac	LAKE/LAC	QC	Communauté urbaine de Québec	21 L/14	46°45′	71°23′
Saint-Augustin Nord-Ouest, Rivière	RIV/CDE	QC	Côte-Nord-du-Golfe-Saint-Laurent	12 O/7	51°15′	58°41′
St. Augustin River - also-aussi - Saint-Augustin, Rivière	RIV/CDE	NF		12 O/2	51°13′	58°38′
Saint-Augustin, Rivière - also-aussi - St. Augustin River	RIV/CDE	QC	Côte-Nord-du-Golfe-Saint-Laurent	12 O/2	51°13′	58°38′
St Barbe	UNP/LNO	NF		12 P/2	51°12′	56°46′
St. Barbe Bay	BAY/BAIE	NF		12 P/2	51°13′	56°47′
Saint-Barnabé	VILG/VILG	QC	Maskinongé	31 I/7	46°24′	72°53′
Saint-Barnabé, Île	ISL/ÎLE	QC	Rimouski-Neigette	22 C/7	48°28′	68°34′
Saint-Barnabé-Nord	UNP/LNO	QC	Maskinongé	31 I/7	46°24′	72°53′
Saint-Barnabé-Sud	VILG/VILG	QC	Les Maskoutains	31 H/10	45°44′	72°55′
Saint-Barnabé-Sud	UNP/LNO	QC	Les Maskoutains	31 H/10	45°44′	72°55′
Saint-Barthélemy	VILG/VILG	QC	D'Autray	31 I/3	46°11′	73°08′
Saint-Barthélemy-Station	UNP/LNO	QC	D'Autray	31 I/3	46°11′	73°06′
Saint-Basile	TOWN/VIL2	NB	Madawaska	21 N/8	47°21′	68°14′
Saint-Basile	VILG/VILG	QC	Portneuf	21 L/13	46°45′	71°49′
Saint-Basile	GEOG/GÉOG	NB	Madawaska	21 N/8	47°23′	68°13′
St. Basile 10	IR/RI	NB	Madawaska	21 N/8	47°22′	68°18′
Saint-Basile-de-Tableau	UNP/LNO	QC	Le Fjord-du-Saguenay	22 D/8	48°22′	70°28′
Saint-Basile-le-Grand	CITY/VIL1	QC	La Vallée-du-Richelieu	31 H/11	45°32′	73°17′
Saint-Basile-Station	UNP/LNO	QC	Portneuf	21 L/12	46°43′	71°50′
Saint-Basile-Sud	TOWN/VIL2	QC	Portneuf	21 L/13	46°45′	71°49′
Saint-Bède	UNP/LNO	QC	Matane	22 B/15	48°57′	66°47′
St. Benedict	VILG/VILG	SK	33-41-24-W2	73 A/11	52°34′	105°23′
Saint-Benjamin	VILG/VILG	QC	Les Etchemins	21 L/7	46°17′	70°36′
Saint-Benoît	UNP/LNO	QC	Mirabel	31 G/9	45°34′	74°06′
Saint-Benoît-de-Matapédia	UNP/LNO	QC	Avignon	21 O/14	48°00′	67°06′
Saint-Benoît-du-Lac	VILG/VILG	QC	Memphrémagog	31 H/1	45°10′	72°16′
Saint-Benoît-Labre	VILG/VILG	QC	Beauce-Sartigan	21 L/2	46°04′	70°48′
St. Benoni	UNP/LNO	NS	Digby	21 B/1	44°13′	66°08′
Saint-Bernard	VILG/VILG	QC	La Nouvelle-Beauce	21 L/6	46°30′	71°08′
St. Bernard	UNP/LNO	NS	Digby	21 B/8	44°24′	66°03′
Saint-Bernard-de-Lacolle	VILG/VILG	QC	Les Jardins-de-Napierville	31 H/3	45°05′	73°25′
Saint-Bernard-des-Lacs	UNP/LNO	QC	Denis-Riverin	22 G/1	49°02′	66°22′
Saint-Bernard, Île	ISL/ÎLE	QC	Roussillon	31 H/5	45°23′	73°45′
St-Bernardin	UNP/LNO	ON	Prescott	31 G/7	45°27′	74°48′
Saint-Bernard, Lac	LAKE/LAC	QC	Maskinongé	31 I/11	46°34′	73°18′
Saint-Bernard-Partie-Sud	VILG/VILG	QC	Les Maskoutains	31 H/14	45°50′	73°04′
St. Bernard's	UNP/LNO	NF		1 M/10	47°32′	54°57′
St. Bernard's-Jacques Fontaine	TOWN/VIL2	NF		1 M/10	47°31′	54°55′
Saint-Bernard-sur-Mer	UNP/LNO	QC	Charlevoix	21 M/8	47°25′	70°23′
Saint-Blaise-sur-Richelieu	VILG/VILG	QC	Le Haut-Richelieu	31 H/3	45°13′	73°17′
Saint-Bonaventure	VILG/VILG	QC	Drummond	31 H/15	45°58′	72°41′
St. Boniface	UNP/LNO	MB		62 H/14	49°53′	97°05′
St. Boniface	GEOG/GÉOG	MB		62 H/14	49°54′	97°08′
Saint-Boniface-de-Shawinigan	TOWN/VIL2	QC	Le Centre-de-la-Mauricie	31 I/10	46°30′	72°49′
St. Boniface - St. Vital - see-voir - Riel	VILG/VILG	MB		62 H/14	49°48′	97°05′
St. Boswells	UNP/LNO	SK	36-12-7-W3	72 J/2	50°03′	106°50′
St. Brendan's	VILG/VILG	NF		2 C/13	48°52′	53°40′
St. Bride, Mount	MTN/MNT	AB	29-14-W5	82 O/12	51°30′	115°57′
St. Bride's	VILG/VILG	NF		1 L/16	46°55′	54°10′
St. Brides	UNP/LNO	AB	10-58-11-W4	73 E/13	53°59′	111°33′
St. Brieux	VILG/VILG	SK	24-42-21-W2	73 A/10	52°38′	104°54′
Saint-Bruno	VILG/VILG	QC	Lac-Saint-Jean-Est	22 D/5	48°28′	71°39′
Saint-Bruno	UNP/LNO	QC	Le Fjord-du-Saguenay	22 D/7	48°17′	70°49′

NAME NOM	ENTITY ENTITÉ	LOC 1 LIEU 1	LOC 2 LIEU 2	MAP CARTE	POSITION LAT	LONG
Saint-Bruno	UNP/LNO	QC	La Vallée-du-Richelieu	31 H/11	45°31′	73°20′
Saint-Bruno-de-Guigues	VILG/VILG	QC	Témiscamingue	31 M/6	47°28′	79°26′
Saint-Bruno-de-Kamouraska	VILG/VILG	QC	Kamouraska	21 N/5	47°27′	69°45′
Saint-Bruno-de-Montarville	CITY/VIL1	QC	La Vallée-du-Richelieu	31 H/11	45°32′	73°21′
Saint-Bruno, Mont	MTN/MNT	QC	La Vallée-du-Richelieu	31 H/11	45°33′	73°19′
Saint-Cajetan	UNP/LNO	QC	La Vallée-de-la-Gatineau	31 J/12	46°32′	75°49′
Saint-Calixte	VILG/VILG	QC	Montcalm	31 H/13	45°57′	73°51′
Saint-Calixte-de-Kilkenny	UNP/LNO	QC	Montcalm	31 H/13	45°57′	73°51′
Saint-Calixte-Nord	UNP/LNO	QC	Montcalm	31 H/13	45°59′	73°55′
Saint-Camille	VILG/VILG	QC	Asbestos	21 E/12	45°41′	71°42′
Saint-Camille	UNP/LNO	NB	Kent	21 I/15	47°00′	64°50′
Saint-Camille	UNP/LNO	QC	Les Etchemins	21 L/8	46°29′	70°12′
Saint-Camille-de-Bellechasse	UNP/LNO	QC	Les Etchemins	21 L/8	46°29′	70°13′
Saint-Camille-de-Lellis	VILG/VILG	QC	Les Etchemins	21 L/8	46°27′	70°11′
Saint-Canut	UNP/LNO	QC	Mirabel	31 G/9	45°43′	74°05′
St. Carols	UNP/LNO	NF		2 M/5	51°23′	55°30′
Saint-Casimir	VILG/VILG	QC	Portneuf	31 I/9	46°39′	72°07′
Saint-Casimir	VILG/VILG	QC	Portneuf	31 I/9	46°40′	72°09′
Saint-Cassien-des-Caps	UNP/LNO	QC	Charlevoix	21 M/7	47°21′	70°37′
St. Catharines	CITY/VIL1	ON	Lincoln	30 M/3	43°10′	79°15′
St. Catherine's	UNP/LNO	NF		1 N/3	47°11′	53°24′
St. Catherines	UNP/LNO	PE	Kings	11 L/8	46°22′	62°12′
St. Catherines	UNP/LNO	PE	Queens	11 L/3	46°12′	63°18′
St. Catherines River	UNP/LNO	NS	Queens	20 P/15	43°51′	64°52′
Saint-Célestin	TOWN/VIL2	QC	Nicolet-Yamaska	31 I/1	46°13′	72°26′
Saint-Célestin	VILG/VILG	QC	Nicolet-Yamaska	31 I/1	46°13′	72°26′
Saint-Célestin-Station	UNP/LNO	QC	Nicolet-Yamaska	31 I/1	46°14′	72°25′
Saint-Césaire	CITY/VIL1	QC	Rouville	31 H/6	45°25′	73°00′
Saint-Césaire	VILG/VILG	QC	Rouville	31 H/6	45°25′	73°00′
St. Chads	UNP/LNO	NF		2 C/12	48°42′	53°47′
St. Charles	UNP/LNO	PE	Kings	11 L/8	46°24′	62°26′
Saint-Charles	UNP/LNO	NB	Kent	21 I/10	46°40′	64°59′
Saint-Charles	UNP/LNO	QC	Pabok	22 A/7	48°27′	64°38′
Saint-Charles	UNP/LNO	QC	Le Fjord-du-Saguenay	22 D/6	48°30′	71°24′
St. Charles	UNP/LNO	ON	Sudbury	41 I/8	46°22′	80°25′
St. Charles	UNP/LNO	MB		62 H/14	49°53′	97°19′
Saint-Charles	GEOG/GÉOG	NB	Kent	21 I/11	46°40′	65°00′
St. Charles	GEOG/GÉOG	MB		62 H/14	49°52′	97°18′
Saint-Charles-Borromée	VILG/VILG	QC	Joliette	31 I/3	46°03′	73°28′
St. Charles Creek	RIV/CDE	NT	Mackenzie	96 C	64°59′	124°54′
Saint-Charles-de-Bellechasse	VILG/VILG	QC	Bellechasse	21 L/15	46°46′	70°57′
Saint-Charles-de-Bourget	VILG/VILG	QC	Le Fjord-du-Saguenay	22 D/11	48°34′	71°23′
Saint-Charles-de-Drummond	VILG/VILG	QC	Drummond	31 H/16	45°54′	72°28′
Saint-Charles-de-Mandeville	VILG/VILG	QC	D'Autray	31 I/6	46°22′	73°21′
Saint-Charles-de-Montcalm	UNP/LNO	QC	Matawinie	31 I/4	46°06′	73°56′
Saint-Charles-Garnier	VILG/VILG	QC	La Mitis	22 C/8	48°20′	68°03′
Saint-Charles, Lac	LAKE/LAC	QC	Communauté urbaine de Québec	21 L/14	46°56′	71°23′
Saint-Charles-Nord	UNP/LNO	NB	Kent	21 I/11	46°39′	65°02′
Saint-Charles, Pointe	CAPE/CAP	QC	Sept-Rivières	22 I/5	50°15′	65°49′
Saint-Charles, Rivière	RIV/CDE	NB	Kent	21 I/10	46°43′	64°55′
Saint-Charles, Rivière	RIV/CDE	QC	Communauté urbaine de Québec	21 L/14	46°49′	71°13′
Saint-Charles, Rivière	RIV/CDE	QC	Lajemmerais	31 H/11	45°41′	73°27′
Saint-Charles Station	UNP/LNO	NB	Kent	21 I/10	46°39′	64°58′
Saint-Charles-sur-Richelieu	VILG/VILG	QC	La Vallée-du-Richelieu	31 H/11	45°41′	73°11′
Saint-Chrétien	UNP/LNO	QC	Charlevoix-Est	21 N/13	47°49′	69°56′
Saint-Christophe-d'Arthabaska	VILG/VILG	QC	Arthabaska	21 L/4	46°02′	71°53′
St. Christopher	UNP/LNO	ON	Durham	31 D/2	44°11′	78°47′
Saint-Chrysostome	TOWN/VIL2	QC	Le Haut-Saint-Laurent	31 H/4	45°06′	73°46′
St. Chrysostome	UNP/LNO	PE	Prince	21 I/9	46°31′	64°06′
St. Clair Beach	VILG/VILG	ON	Essex	40 J/7	42°19′	82°51′
St. Clair, Lake - also-aussi - **Sainte-Claire, Lac**	LAKE/LAC	ON	Essex	40 J/7	42°28′	82°40′
St. Clair River	RIV/CDE	ON	Lambton	40 J/10	42°33′	82°40′
Saint-Claude	VILG/VILG	QC	Le Val-Saint-François	21 E/12	45°40′	71°59′
St. Claude	VILG/VILG	MB	15-8-7-W	62 G/9	49°40′	98°21′
Saint-Claude-Nord	UNP/LNO	QC	Le Val-Saint-François	31 H/9	45°40′	72°00′
Saint-Clément	VILG/VILG	QC	Les Basques	21 N/14	47°55′	69°06′
St. Clements	MUN2/AZM2	MB		62 I/2	50°10′	96°45′
St. Clements	UNP/LNO	ON	Waterloo	40 P/10	43°31′	80°39′
St. Clements	GEOG/GÉOG	MB		62 I/2	50°08′	96°52′
Saint-Cléophas	VILG/VILG	QC	La Matapédia	22 B/5	48°29′	67°45′
Saint-Cléophas	VILG/VILG	QC	D'Autray	31 I/3	46°14′	73°25′
Saint-Clet	VILG/VILG	QC	Vaudreuil-Soulanges	31 G/8	45°21′	74°13′
St. Cloud	UNP/LNO	ON	Sudbury	41 I/7	46°24′	80°48′
Saint-Colomban	VILG/VILG	QC	La Rivière-du-Nord	31 G/9	45°44′	74°08′
St. Columba	UNP/LNO	NS	Victoria	11 F/15	45°59′	60°51′

NAME / NOM	ENTITY / ENTITÉ	LOC 1 / LIEU 1	LOC 2 / LIEU 2	MAP / CARTE	POSITION LAT	LONG
St. Columban	UNP/LNO	ON	Huron	40 P/11	43°32′	81°19′
Saint-Côme	VILG/VILG	QC	Matawinie	31 I/5	46°16′	73°47′
Saint-Côme — Linière	VILG/VILG	QC	Beauce-Sartigan	21 L/2	46°05′	70°31′
Saint-Conrad	UNP/LNO	QC	Avignon	22 B/2	48°08′	66°48′
Saint-Constant	CITY/VIL1	QC	Roussillon	31 H/5	45°22′	73°34′
St. Croix	UNP/LNO	NS	Hants	21 A/16	44°58′	64°02′
St. Croix	UNP/LNO	NB	York	21 G/11	45°34′	67°26′
Saint Croix	GEOG/GÉOG	NB	Charlotte	21 G/3	45°12′	67°08′
St. Croix 34	IR/RI	NS	Hants	21 A/16	44°54′	64°04′
St. Croix Bay	BAY/BAIE	NF		1 N/5	47°26′	53°52′
St. Croix Cove	UNP/LNO	NS	Annapolis	21 A/14	44°55′	65°18′
St. Croix Cove	BAY/BAIE	NS	Annapolis	21 A/14	44°55′	65°19′
St. Croix River	RIV/CDE	NB	Charlotte	21 G/3	45°05′	67°06′
Saint-Cuthbert	VILG/VILG	QC	D'Autray	31 I/3	46°09′	73°14′
Saint-Cyprien	VILG/VILG	QC	Rivière-du-Loup	21 N/14	47°54′	69°01′
Saint-Cyprien	VILG/VILG	QC	Les Etchemins	21 L/8	46°21′	70°16′
Saint-Cyprien-de-Napierville	VILG/VILG	QC	Les Jardins-de-Napierville	31 H/3	45°11′	73°25′
Saint-Cyr	UNP/LNO	QC	Le Val-Saint-François	31 H/9	45°43′	72°03′
Saint-Cyriac	UNP/LNO	QC	Le Fjord-du-Saguenay	22 D/6	48°20′	71°22′
Saint-Cyrille	UNP/LNO	NB	Kent	21 I/7	46°23′	64°55′
Saint-Cyrille-de-Lessard	VILG/VILG	QC	L'Islet	21 M/1	47°02′	70°17′
Saint-Cyrille-de-L'Islet	UNP/LNO	QC	L'Islet	21 M/1	47°02′	70°17′
Saint-Cyrille-de-Wendover	VILG/VILG	QC	Drummond	31 H/16	45°56′	72°26′
Saint-Cyr, Lac	LAKE/LAC	QC	Vallée-de-l'Or	32 B/12	48°44′	75°42′
St. Cyr Lake	UNP/LNO	SK	60-14-W3	73 K/1	54°13′	108°04′
Saint Cyr Lake	LAKE/LAC	SK		73 K/1	54°15′	108°06′
St. Cyr, Mount	MTN/MNT	YT		105 F/6	61°21′	133°09′
St. Cyr Range	MTN/MNT	YT		105 G/5	61°30′	132°00′
Saint-Cyr, Rivière	RIV/CDE	QC	Jamésie	32 G/6	49°19′	75°19′
Saint-Damase	TOWN/VIL2	QC	Les Maskoutains	31 H/11	45°31′	73°01′
Saint-Damase	VILG/VILG	QC	La Matapédia	22 B/12	48°40′	67°50′
Saint-Damase	VILG/VILG	QC	Les Maskoutains	31 H/11	45°31′	73°01′
Saint-Damase-de-L'Islet	VILG/VILG	QC	L'Islet	21 M/1	47°12′	70°08′
Saint-Damase-des-Aulnaies	UNP/LNO	QC	L'Islet	21 M/1	47°12′	70°08′
Saint-Damien	VILG/VILG	QC	Matawinie	31 I/6	46°20′	73°29′
Saint-Damien	UNP/LNO	NB	Kent	21 I/7	46°20′	64°49′
Saint-Damien-de-Buckland	VILG/VILG	QC	Bellechasse	21 L/10	46°38′	70°40′
Saint-Damien-Station	UNP/LNO	QC	Bellechasse	21 L/10	46°37′	70°43′
Saint-Daniel	UNP/LNO	QC	L'Amiante	21 L/3	46°01′	71°11′
Saint-David	VILG/VILG	QC	Le Bas-Richelieu	31 H/15	45°57′	72°51′
Saint-David	UNP/LNO	NB	Kent	21 I/7	46°25′	64°45′
Saint David	GEOG/GÉOG	NB	Charlotte	21 G/6	45°18′	67°12′
St. David, Cape	CAPE/CAP	NT	Franklin	25 P	63°58′	64°37′
Saint-David-de-Falardeau	VILG/VILG	QC	Le Fjord-du-Saguenay	22 D/11	48°37′	71°07′
Saint-David-de-l'Auberivière	UNP/LNO	QC	Desjardins	21 L/14	46°47′	71°12′
Saint-David-d'Yamaska	UNP/LNO	QC	Le Bas-Richelieu	31 H/15	45°57′	72°51′
St. David, Lake	LAKE/LAC	MB	31,32-1-W	62 P/12	51°41′	97°30′
St. David Ridge	UNP/LNO	NB	Charlotte	21 G/6	45°16′	67°15′
St. David's	UNP/LNO	NF		12 B/2	48°12′	58°52′
St. Davids	UNP/LNO	ON	Prescott	31 G/9	45°31′	74°28′
St. Davids	UNP/LNO	ON	Lincoln	30 M/3	43°10′	79°07′
Saint-Denis	TOWN/VIL2	QC	La Vallée-du-Richelieu	31 H/14	45°47′	73°09′
Saint-Denis	VILG/VILG	QC	Kamouraska	21 N/12	47°30′	69°56′
Saint-Denis	VILG/VILG	QC	La Vallée-du-Richelieu	31 H/14	45°47′	73°09′
St-Denis	UNP/LNO	SK	4-37-1-W3	73 B/1	52°09′	106°07′
Saint-Denis-de-Brompton	VILG/VILG	QC	Le Val-Saint-François	31 H/8	45°27′	72°05′
Saint-Denis, Rivière	RIV/CDE	QC	Kamouraska	21 N/5	47°29′	69°48′
Saint-Didace	VILG/VILG	QC	D'Autray	31 I/6	46°20′	73°17′
Saint-Dominique	VILG/VILG	QC	Les Maskoutains	31 H/10	45°34′	72°51′
Saint-Dominique	UNP/LNO	QC	Vaudreuil-Soulanges	31 G/8	45°20′	74°08′
Saint-Dominique-du-Rosaire	VILG/VILG	QC	Abitibi	32 D/16	48°46′	78°07′
Saint-Donat	VILG/VILG	QC	La Mitis	22 C/8	48°30′	68°16′
Saint-Donat	VILG/VILG	QC	Matawinie	31 J/8	46°19′	74°13′
Saint-Donat-de-Montcalm	UNP/LNO	QC	Matawinie	31 J/8	46°19′	74°13′
Sainte-Adélaïde-de-Pabos	UNP/LNO	QC	Pabok	22 A/7	48°22′	64°37′
Sainte-Adèle	CITY/VIL1	QC	Les Pays-d'en-Haut	31 G/16	45°57′	74°08′
Sainte-Adèle-en-Bas	UNP/LNO	QC	Les Pays-d'en-Haut	31 G/16	45°57′	74°09′
Sainte-Adèle-en-Haut	UNP/LNO	QC	Les Pays-d'en-Haut	31 G/16	45°57′	74°08′
Sainte-Adèle-Nord	UNP/LNO	QC	Les Pays-d'en-Haut	31 G/16	45°58′	74°09′
Sainte-Agathe	TOWN/VIL2	QC	Lotbinière	21 L/6	46°23′	71°25′
Sainte-Agathe	VILG/VILG	QC	Lotbinière	21 L/6	46°23′	71°25′
Ste. Agathe	UNP/LNO	MB		62 H/11	49°34′	97°11′
Ste. Agathe	GEOG/GÉOG	MB		62 H/9	49°19′	97°20′
Sainte-Agathe-des-Monts	CITY/VIL1	QC	Les Laurentides	31 J/1	46°03′	74°17′
Sainte-Agathe-Nord	VILG/VILG	QC	Les Laurentides	31 J/1	46°04′	74°19′

NAME NOM	ENTITY ENTITÉ	LOC 1 LIEU 1	LOC 2 LIEU 2	MAP CARTE	POSITION LAT	LONG
Sainte-Agathe-Sud	TOWN/VIL2	QC	Les Laurentides	31 J/1	46°02′	74°16′
Sainte-Agnès	VILG/VILG	QC	Charlevoix-Est	21 M/9	47°40′	70°16′
Sainte-Agnès-de-Bellecombe	UNP/LNO	QC	Rouyn-Noranda	32 D/2	48°06′	78°56′
Sainte-Agnès-de-Charlevoix	UNP/LNO	QC	Charlevoix-Est	21 M/9	47°40′	70°16′
Sainte-Agnès-de-Dundee	UNP/LNO	QC	Le Haut-Saint-Laurent	31 G/1	45°01′	74°24′
Ste. Amélie	UNP/LNO	MB	16-23-14-W	62 J/14	50°59′	99°23′
Sainte-Anastasie	UNP/LNO	QC	L'Érable	21 L/5	46°22′	71°35′
Sainte-Angèle-de-Mérici	VILG/VILG	QC	La Mitis	22 C/9	48°32′	68°05′
Sainte-Angèle-de-Monnoir	VILG/VILG	QC	Rouville	31 H/6	45°23′	73°06′
Sainte-Angèle-de-Prémont	VILG/VILG	QC	Maskinongé	31 I/6	46°22′	73°03′
Sainte-Angélique	VILG/VILG	QC	Papineau	31 G/11	45°39′	75°01′
Ste. Anne	VILG/VILG	MB		62 H/10	49°40′	96°39′
Ste. Anne	MUN2/AZM2	MB		62 H/10	49°35′	96°30′
Sainte-Anne	UNP/LNO	NB	Gloucester	21 P/12	47°38′	65°43′
Sainte-Anne	GEOG/GÉOG	NB	Madawaska	21 O/5	47°25′	67°57′
Ste. Anne	GEOG/GÉOG	MB		62 H/10	49°40′	96°39′
Sainte-Anne, Anse	BAY/BAIE	QC	Kamouraska	21 M/8	47°20′	70°05′
Sainte-Anne, Baie	BAY/BAIE	NB	Northumberland	21 P/2	47°04′	64°59′
Sainte-Anne, Banc de - also-aussi - St. Anns Bank	SEAU/SMER	—		4022	46°00′	59°30′
Sainte-Anne, Barrage	MISC/DIV	QC	Manicouagan	22 J/4	50°06′	67°57′
Sainte-Anne, Chute	FALL/CHUT	QC	La Côte-de-Beaupré	21 M/2	47°04′	70°53′
Sainte-Anne-de-Beaupré	CITY/VIL1	QC	La Côte-de-Beaupré	21 M/2	47°01′	70°56′
Sainte-Anne-de-Bellevue	CITY/VIL1	QC	Communauté urbaine de Montréal	31 H/5	45°25′	73°56′
Sainte-Anne-de-Bellevue Canal - also-aussi - Sainte-Anne-de-Bellevue, Canal de	PARK/PARC	QC	Communauté urbaine de Montréal	31 H/5	45°24′	73°57′
Sainte-Anne-de-Bellevue, Canal de - also-aussi - Sainte-Anne-de-Bellevue Canal	PARK/PARC	QC	Communauté urbaine de Montréal	31 H/5	45°24′	73°57′
Sainte-Anne-de-Kent	UNP/LNO	NB	Kent	21 I/10	46°33′	64°46′
Sainte-Anne-de-la-Pérade	VILG/VILG	QC	Francheville	31 I/9	46°35′	72°12′
Sainte-Anne-de-la-Pocatière	VILG/VILG	QC	Kamouraska	21 M/8	47°21′	70°00′
Sainte-Anne-de-la-Rochelle	VILG/VILG	QC	Le Val-Saint-François	31 H/8	45°24′	72°24′
Sainte-Anne-de-Madawaska	VILG/VILG	NB	Madawaska	21 N/8	47°15′	68°02′
Sainte-Anne-de-Portneuf	VILG/VILG	QC	La Haute-Côte-Nord	22 C/11	48°37′	69°06′
Ste-Anne-de-Prescott	UNP/LNO	ON	Prescott	31 G/8	45°27′	74°28′
Sainte-Anne-de-Sabrevois	VILG/VILG	QC	Le Haut-Richelieu	31 H/3	45°13′	73°13′
Sainte-Anne-des-Lacs	VILG/VILG	QC	Les Pays-d'en-Haut	31 G/16	45°51′	74°08′
Sainte-Anne-des-Monts	CITY/VIL1	QC	Denis-Riverin	22 G/1	49°08′	66°30′
Sainte-Anne-de-Sorel	VILG/VILG	QC	Le Bas-Richelieu	31 I/3	46°03′	73°04′
Sainte-Anne-des-Plaines	CITY/VIL1	QC	Thérèse-De Blainville	31 H/13	45°46′	73°49′
Sainte-Anne-du-Bocage	UNP/LNO	NB	Gloucester	21 P/14	47°46′	65°01′
Sainte-Anne-du-Lac	TOWN/VIL2	QC	L'Amiante	21 L/3	46°05′	71°12′
Sainte-Anne-du-Lac	VILG/VILG	QC	Antoine-Labelle	31 J/14	46°53′	75°20′
Ste. Anne du Ruisseau	UNP/LNO	NS	Yarmouth	20 P/13	43°50′	65°56′
Sainte-Anne-du-Sault	VILG/VILG	QC	Arthabaska	31 I/1	46°12′	72°02′
Sainte-Anne, Lac	LAKE/LAC	QC	Denis-Riverin	22 B/16	48°48′	66°03′
Sainte-Anne, Lac	LAKE/LAC	QC	Manicouagan	22 J/4	50°05′	67°50′
Sainte-Anne, Lac	LAKE/LAC	QC	L'Islet	21 N/4	47°11′	69°49′
Sainte-Anne, Lac	LAKE/LAC	QC	La Jacques-Cartier	21 M/5	47°17′	71°40′
Ste. Anne, Lac	LAKE/LAC	AB	54,55-3,4-W5	83 G/9	53°42′	114°25′
Sainte-Anne, Mont	MTN/MNT	QC	La Côte-de-Beaupré	21 M/2	47°05′	70°56′
Sainte-Anne-Ouest	UNP/LNO	QC	La Côte-de-Beaupré	21 M/2	47°00′	70°58′
Sainte-Anne, Petit lac	LAKE/LAC	QC	Kamouraska	21 N/4	47°12′	69°48′
Sainte-Anne, Pointe	CAPE/CAP	QC	Denis-Riverin	22 G/2	49°08′	66°33′
Sainte-Anne, Rivière	RIV/CDE	QC	Denis-Riverin	22 G/2	49°08′	66°30′
Sainte-Anne, Rivière	RIV/CDE	QC	La Côte-de-Beaupré	21 M/2	47°02′	70°53′
Sainte-Anne, Rivière	RIV/CDE	QC	Francheville	31 I/9	46°33′	72°12′
Sainte-Apolline	UNP/LNO	QC	Montmagny	21 L/16	46°48′	70°12′
Sainte-Apolline-de-Patton	VILG/VILG	QC	Montmagny	21 L/16	46°48′	70°12′
Sainte-Apolline-Station	UNP/LNO	QC	Montmagny	21 L/16	46°53′	70°18′
Sainte-Aurélie	VILG/VILG	QC	Les Etchemins	21 L/1	46°11′	70°22′
Sainte-Barbe	VILG/VILG	QC	Le Haut-Saint-Laurent	31 G/1	45°10′	74°12′
Sainte-Béatrix	VILG/VILG	QC	Matawinie	31 I/4	46°12′	73°37′
Sainte-Blandine	VILG/VILG	QC	Rimouski-Neigette	22 C/8	48°22′	68°28′
Sainte-Brigide-d'Iberville	VILG/VILG	QC	Le Haut-Richelieu	31 H/6	45°19′	73°04′
Sainte-Brigitte-de-Laval	VILG/VILG	QC	La Jacques-Cartier	21 M/3	47°00′	71°12′
Sainte-Brigitte-des-Saults	VILG/VILG	QC	Drummond	31 I/1	46°02′	72°29′
Sainte-Catherine	CITY/VIL1	QC	Roussillon	31 H/5	45°24′	73°35′
Sainte-Catherine-de-Hatley	VILG/VILG	QC	Memphrémagog	31 H/1	45°15′	72°03′
Sainte-Catherine-de-la-Jacques-Cartier	VILG/VILG	QC	La Jacques-Cartier	21 L/13	46°51′	71°37′
Sainte-Cécile	UNP/LNO	NB	Gloucester	21 P/15	47°52′	64°40′
Sainte-Cécile-de-Lévrard	VILG/VILG	QC	Bécancour	31 I/8	46°28′	72°10′
Sainte-Cécile-de-Masham	UNP/LNO	QC	Les Collines-de-l'Outaouais	31 F/9	45°39′	76°02′
Sainte-Cécile-de-Milton	VILG/VILG	QC	La Haute-Yamaska	31 H/7	45°29′	72°45′
Sainte-Cécile-de-Whitton	VILG/VILG	QC	Le Granit	21 E/10	45°40′	70°56′
Sainte-Cécile, Mont	MTN/MNT	QC	Le Granit	21 E/10	45°42′	70°58′
Sainte-Cécile-Station	UNP/LNO	QC	Le Granit	21 E/10	45°41′	70°57′
Sainte-Christine	VILG/VILG	QC	Acton	31 H/9	45°37′	72°25′

NAME / NOM	ENTITY / ENTITÉ	LOC 1 / LIEU 1	LOC 2 / LIEU 2	MAP / CARTE	LAT	LONG
Sainte-Christine-d'Auvergne	VILG/VILG	QC	Portneuf	21 L/13	46°49′	71°58′
Sainte-Claire	VILG/VILG	QC	Bellechasse	21 L/10	46°36′	70°52′
Sainte-Claire-de-Bonaventure	UNP/LNO	QC	Bonaventure	22 A/4	48°12′	65°38′
Sainte-Claire, Lac - also-aussi - **St. Clair, Lake**	LAKE/LAC	ON	Essex	40 J/7	42°28′	82°40′
Saint-Éclanche	UNP/LNO	QC	L'Amiante	21 L/3	46°03′	71°09′
Sainte-Clothilde-de-Horton	VILG/VILG	QC	Arthabaska	31 H/16	45°59′	72°14′
Sainte-Clotilde-de-Beauce	VILG/VILG	QC	L'Amiante	21 L/3	46°08′	71°02′
Sainte-Clotilde-de-Châteauguay	VILG/VILG	QC	Les Jardins-de-Napierville	31 H/4	45°09′	73°41′
Sainte-Clotilde-de-Horton	TOWN/VIL2	QC	Arthabaska	31 H/16	45°59′	72°14′
Sainte-Croix	TOWN/VIL2	QC	Lotbinière	21 L/12	46°37′	71°44′
Sainte-Croix	VILG/VILG	QC	Lotbinière	21 L/12	46°37′	71°44′
Sainte-Croix-Est	UNP/LNO	QC	Lotbinière	21 L/12	46°38′	71°39′
Ste. Croix, Lac	LAKE/LAC	NT	Mackenzie	86 C	64°18′	117°14′
Saint-Edgar	UNP/LNO	QC	Bonaventure	22 A/4	48°14′	65°44′
Saint-Edmond	VILG/VILG	QC	La Matapédia	22 B/6	48°24′	67°23′
Saint-Edmond	VILG/VILG	QC	Maria-Chapdelaine	32 A/15	48°54′	72°33′
Saint-Edmond	UNP/LNO	QC	D'Autray	31 I/6	46°16′	73°16′
Saint-Edmond	UNP/LNO	QC	Vallée-de-l'Or	32 C/4	48°12′	77°49′
Saint-Edmond-de-Grantham	VILG/VILG	QC	Drummond	31 H/15	45°53′	72°40′
Saint-Edmond-de-Pabos	UNP/LNO	QC	Pabok	22 A/7	48°27′	64°44′
Saint-Edmond-les-Plaines	UNP/LNO	QC	Maria-Chapdelaine	32 A/15	48°54′	72°33′
St. Edmunds	MUN2/AZM2	ON	Bruce	41 H/4	45°12′	81°35′
Sainte-Dorothée	UNP/LNO	QC	Laval	31 H/12	45°32′	73°49′
Sainte-Dorothée-Station	UNP/LNO	QC	Laval	31 H/12	45°31′	73°51′
Saint-Édouard	VILG/VILG	QC	Les Jardins-de-Napierville	31 H/4	45°14′	73°31′
Saint-Édouard	UNP/LNO	QC	Lotbinière	21 L/12	46°34′	71°50′
Saint-Édouard	UNP/LNO	QC	Les Maskoutains	31 H/10	45°41′	72°48′
St. Edouard	UNP/LNO	AB	4-58-8-W4	73 E/14	53°59′	111°08′
Saint-Édouard-de-Fabre	VILG/VILG	QC	Témiscamingue	31 M/3	47°12′	79°22′
Saint-Édouard-de-Frampton	VILG/VILG	QC	La Nouvelle-Beauce	21 L/7	46°28′	70°48′
Saint-Édouard-de-Kent	UNP/LNO	NB	Kent	21 I/10	46°33′	64°43′
Saint-Édouard-de-Lotbinière	VILG/VILG	QC	Lotbinière	21 L/12	46°34′	71°50′
Saint-Édouard-de-Maskinongé	VILG/VILG	QC	Maskinongé	31 I/6	46°20′	73°09′
St. Edward	UNP/LNO	PE	Prince	21 I/16	46°53′	64°11′
Sainte-Edwidge	UNP/LNO	QC	Coaticook	21 E/4	45°12′	71°41′
Sainte-Edwidge-de-Clifton	VILG/VILG	QC	Coaticook	21 E/4	45°12′	71°41′
Sainte-Élisabeth	VILG/VILG	QC	D'Autray	31 I/3	46°05′	73°21′
Sainte-Élisabeth-de-Proulx	UNP/LNO	QC	Maria-Chapdelaine	32 A/16	48°58′	72°04′
Sainte-Élisabeth-de-Warwick	VILG/VILG	QC	Arthabaska	31 H/16	45°55′	72°05′
Ste. Elizabeth	UNP/LNO	MB	4-2,3-E	62 H/6	49°20′	97°11′
Sainte-Émélie-de-l'Énergie	VILG/VILG	QC	Matawinie	31 I/5	46°19′	73°39′
Sainte-Emmélie	VILG/VILG	QC	Lotbinière	21 L/12	46°31′	71°53′
Sainte-Eulalie	VILG/VILG	QC	Nicolet-Yamaska	31 I/1	46°06′	72°15′
Sainte-Euphémie	UNP/LNO	QC	Montmagny	21 L/16	46°46′	70°26′
Sainte-Euphémie-sur-Rivière-du-Sud	VILG/VILG	QC	Montmagny	21 L/16	46°46′	70°26′
Sainte-Famille	VILG/VILG	QC	L'Île-d'Orléans	21 L/15	46°58′	70°58′
Sainte-Félicité	VILG/VILG	QC	Matane	22 B/14	48°54′	67°20′
Sainte-Félicité	VILG/VILG	QC	L'Islet	21 K/13	46°57′	69°56′
Sainte-Félicité-Ouest	UNP/LNO	QC	Matane	22 B/14	48°53′	67°24′
Sainte-Flavie	VILG/VILG	QC	La Mitis	22 C/9	48°37′	68°14′
Sainte-Flore	UNP/LNO	QC	Le Centre-de-la-Mauricie	31 I/10	46°37′	72°44′
Sainte-Florence	VILG/VILG	QC	La Matapédia	22 B/6	48°16′	67°15′
Sainte-Foy	CITY/VIL1	QC	Communauté urbaine de Québec	21 L/14	46°47′	71°17′
Sainte-Françoise	VILG/VILG	QC	Les Basques	22 C/3	48°06′	69°04′
Sainte-Françoise	VILG/VILG	QC	Bécancour	21 L/5	46°27′	71°59′
Sainte-Geneviève	CITY/VIL1	QC	Communauté urbaine de Montréal	31 H/5	45°29′	73°52′
Sainte-Geneviève	UNP/LNO	QC	Communauté urbaine de Montréal	31 H/12	45°31′	73°49′
Ste-Geneviève	UNP/LNO	MB	13,14-9-7-E	62 H/10	49°45′	96°31′
Ste. Geneviève Bay	BAY/BAIE	NF		12 P/2	51°09′	56°49′
Sainte-Geneviève-de-Batiscan	VILG/VILG	QC	Francheville	31 I/9	46°32′	72°20′
Sainte-Geneviève-de-Berthier	VILG/VILG	QC	D'Autray	31 I/3	46°05′	73°13′
Sainte-Geneviève, Île	ISL/ÎLE	QC	Minganie	12 L/3	50°15′	63°04′
Sainte-Germaine	UNP/LNO	QC	Abitibi-Ouest	32 D/11	48°36′	79°07′
Sainte-Germaine-Boulé	VILG/VILG	QC	Abitibi-Ouest	32 D/11	48°36′	79°07′
Sainte-Germaine-de-l'Anse-aux-Gascons	VILG/VILG	QC	Pabok	22 A/2	48°52′	64°52′
Sainte-Germaine-du-Lac-Etchemin	VILG/VILG	QC	Les Etchemins	21 L/7	46°24′	70°31′
Sainte-Germaine-Station	UNP/LNO	QC	Les Etchemins	21 L/8	46°22′	70°26′
Sainte-Gertrude	UNP/LNO	QC	Bécancour	31 I/8	46°18′	72°17′
Sainte-Gertrude	UNP/LNO	QC	Abitibi	32 D/9	48°31′	78°18′
Sainte-Gertrude-Manneville	VILG/VILG	QC	Abitibi	32 D/9	48°32′	78°22′
Sainte-Hedwidge	VILG/VILG	QC	Le Domaine-du-Roy	32 A/8	48°29′	72°21′
Sainte-Hedwidge-de-Roberval	UNP/LNO	QC	Le Domaine-du-Roy	32 A/8	48°29′	72°21′
Sainte-Hélène	VILG/VILG	QC	Kamouraska	21 N/12	47°36′	69°44′
Sainte-Hélène	UNP/LNO	QC	Abitibi-Ouest	32 D/11	48°45′	79°18′
Sainte-Hélène-de-Bagot	VILG/VILG	QC	Les Maskoutains	31 H/10	45°44′	72°44′

NAME NOM	ENTITY ENTITÉ	LOC 1 LIEU 1	LOC 2 LIEU 2	MAP CARTE	POSITION LAT	LONG
Sainte-Hélène-de-Breakeyville	VILG/VILG	QC	Les Chutes-de-la-Chaudière	21 L/11	46°40′	71°14′
Sainte-Hélène-de-Chester	UNP/LNO	QC	Arthabaska	21 L/4	46°02′	71°42′
Sainte-Hélène-de-la-Croix	UNP/LNO	QC	Bonaventure	22 A/3	48°02′	65°26′
Sainte-Hélène-de-Mancebourg	VILG/VILG	QC	Abitibi-Ouest	32 D/11	48°44′	79°18′
Sainte-Hélène, Île	ISL/ÎLE	QC	Communauté urbaine de Montréal	31 H/12	45°31′	73°32′
Sainte-Hénédine	VILG/VILG	QC	La Nouvelle-Beauce	21 L/10	46°33′	70°59′
Sainte-Irène	VILG/VILG	QC	La Matapédia	22 B/5	48°26′	67°36′
Sainte-Jeanne-d'Arc	TOWN/VIL2	QC	Maria-Chapdelaine	32 A/16	48°52′	72°05′
Sainte-Jeanne-d'Arc	VILG/VILG	QC	La Mitis	22 B/5	48°30′	67°57′
Sainte-Jeanne-d'Arc	UNP/LNO	QC	Drummond	31 H/9	45°43′	72°25′
Sainte-Julie	CITY/VIL1	QC	Lajemmerais	31 H/11	45°35′	73°20′
Sainte-Julie	VILG/VILG	QC	L'Érable	21 L/5	46°19′	71°40′
Sainte-Julie-de-Verchères	UNP/LNO	QC	Lajemmerais	31 H/11	45°35′	73°20′
Sainte-Julienne	VILG/VILG	QC	Montcalm	31 H/13	45°58′	73°43′
Sainte-Julie-Station	UNP/LNO	QC	L'Érable	21 L/5	46°19′	71°40′
Sainte-Justine	VILG/VILG	QC	Les Etchemins	21 L/8	46°24′	70°21′
Sainte-Justine-de-Newton	VILG/VILG	QC	Vaudreuil-Soulanges	31 G/8	45°22′	74°25′
Sainte-Justine-Station	UNP/LNO	QC	Les Etchemins	21 L/8	46°25′	70°22′
Sainte-Justine-Station	UNP/LNO	QC	Vaudreuil-Soulanges	31 G/8	45°22′	74°25′
St. Eleanors - see-voir - Summerside	VILG/VILG	PE		11 L/5	46°24′	63°47′
St. Eleanors	UNP/LNO	PE	Prince	11 L/5	46°25′	63°49′
St. Eleanors Station	UNP/LNO	PE	Prince	11 L/5	46°25′	63°49′
Saint-Éleuthère	UNP/LNO	QC	Témiscouata	21 N/6	47°29′	69°17′
St. Elias, Mount	MTN/MNT	YT		115 C/7	60°18′	140°56′
St. Elias Mountains	MTN/MNT	YT/BC		115 B/7	60°23′	138°45′
St. Elias Mountains	MTN/MNT	YT		115 B/11	60°33′	139°28′
Saint-Élie	VILG/VILG	QC	Le Centre-de-la-Mauricie	31 I/7	46°29′	72°58′
Saint-Élie-d'Orford	VILG/VILG	QC	Sherbrooke	31 H/8	45°23′	72°04′
St. Elmo	UNP/LNO	ON	Glengarry	31 G/7	45°19′	74°52′
St. Elmo	UNP/LNO	ON	Muskoka	31 E/3	45°01′	79°24′
Saint-Éloi	VILG/VILG	QC	Les Basques	22 C/3	48°02′	69°14′
Saint-Éloi-Station	UNP/LNO	QC	Rivière-du-Loup	22 C/3	48°04′	69°16′
Sainte-Louise	VILG/VILG	QC	L'Islet	21 M/8	47°17′	70°08′
Sainte-Louise	UNP/LNO	NB	Gloucester	21 P/12	47°41′	65°48′
Sainte-Louise-Station	UNP/LNO	QC	L'Islet	21 M/8	47°17′	70°08′
Saint-Elphège	VILG/VILG	QC	Nicolet-Yamaska	31 I/2	46°03′	72°42′
Sainte-Luce	VILG/VILG	QC	La Mitis	22 C/9	48°33′	68°23′
Sainte-Lucie-de-Beauregard	VILG/VILG	QC	Montmagny	21 L/9	46°44′	70°01′
Sainte-Lucie-des-Laurentides	VILG/VILG	QC	Les Laurentides	31 J/1	46°08′	74°11′
Saint-Elzéar	VILG/VILG	QC	Bonaventure	22 A/3	48°09′	65°24′
Saint-Elzéar	VILG/VILG	QC	Témiscouata	21 N/11	47°35′	69°06′
Saint-Elzéar	VILG/VILG	QC	La Nouvelle-Beauce	21 L/6	46°24′	71°04′
Sainte-Madeleine	TOWN/VIL2	QC	Les Maskoutains	31 H/11	45°36′	73°06′
Sainte-Madeleine-de-la-Rivière-Madeleine	VILG/VILG	QC	Denis-Riverin	22 H/3	49°14′	65°18′
Sainte-Marcelline-de-Kildare	VILG/VILG	QC	Matawinie	31 I/4	46°07′	73°36′
Sainte-Marguerite	VILG/VILG	QC	La Matapédia	22 B/6	48°18′	67°05′
Sainte-Marguerite	VILG/VILG	QC	La Nouvelle-Beauce	21 L/10	46°31′	70°56′
Sainte-Marguerite	UNP/LNO	QC	Les Pays-d'en-Haut	31 J/1	46°02′	74°04′
Sainte-Marguerite, Baie	BAY/BAIE	QC	Sept-Rivières	22 J/2	50°06′	66°37′
Sainte-Marguerite, Barrage	MISC/DIV	QC	Sept-Rivières	22 J/2	50°13′	66°40′
Sainte-Marguerite-de-Lingwick	UNP/LNO	QC	Le Haut-Saint-François	21 E/11	45°36′	71°21′
Sainte-Marguerite-du-Lac-Masson	VILG/VILG	QC	Les Pays-d'en-Haut	31 J/1	46°03′	74°05′
Sainte-Marguerite, Île	ISL/ÎLE	QC	Montmagny	21 M/2	47°02′	70°37′
Sainte-Marguerite-Marie	UNP/LNO	QC	La Matapédia	22 B/6	48°19′	67°05′
Sainte-Marguerite-Marie	UNP/LNO	QC	Maria-Chapdelaine	32 A/16	48°49′	72°13′
Sainte-Marguerite, Mont	MTN/MNT	QC	Lotbinière	21 L/6	46°20′	71°08′
Sainte-Marguerite-Nord	UNP/LNO	QC	La Matapédia	22 B/6	48°20′	67°02′
Sainte-Marguerite Nord-Est, Rivière	RIV/CDE	QC	La Haute-Côte-Nord	22 C/5	48°16′	69°55′
Sainte-Marguerite, Rivière	RIV/CDE	QC	Sept-Rivières	22 J/2	50°09′	66°36′
Sainte-Marguerite, Rivière	RIV/CDE	QC	La Haute-Côte-Nord	22 C/5	48°16′	69°57′
Sainte-Marguerite-Station	UNP/LNO	QC	Les Pays-d'en-Haut	31 G/16	45°59′	74°07′
Sainte-Marie	CITY/VIL1	QC	La Nouvelle-Beauce	21 L/6	46°27′	71°02′
Sainte-Marie, Cap	CAPE/CAP	QC	Minganie	12 E/12	49°40′	63°55′
Sainte-Marie, Courant	RIVF/EFLV	QC	Communauté urbaine de Montréal	31 H/12	45°31′	73°33′
Sainte-Marie-de-Blandford	VILG/VILG	QC	Bécancour	31 I/8	46°19′	72°11′
Sainte-Marie-de-Charlevoix	UNP/LNO	QC	Charlevoix	21 M/9	47°31′	70°23′
Sainte-Marie-de-Kent	UNP/LNO	NB	Kent	21 I/7	46°25′	64°49′
Sainte-Marie-de-Laval	UNP/LNO	QC	Laval	31 H/12	45°41′	73°41′
Sainte-Marie-de-Monnoir	VILG/VILG	QC	Rouville	31 H/6	45°26′	73°10′
Sainte-Marie, Île	ISL/ÎLE	QC	Jamésie	32 P/7	51°17′	72°53′
Sainte-Marie, Île	ISL/ÎLE	QC	La Vallée-de-la-Gatineau	31 K/1	46°13′	76°03′
Sainte-Marie, Îles	ISL/ÎLE	QC	Côte-Nord-du-Golfe-Saint-Laurent	12 J/5	50°19′	59°39′
Sainte-Marie-Madeleine	VILG/VILG	QC	Les Maskoutains	31 H/11	45°36′	73°06′
Sainte-Marie-Saint-Raphaël	VILG/VILG	NB	Gloucester	21 P/15	47°47′	64°34′
Sainte-Marie-Salomé	VILG/VILG	QC	Montcalm	31 H/14	45°56′	73°30′

NAME NOM	ENTITY ENTITÉ	LOC 1 LIEU 1	LOC 2 LIEU 2	MAP CARTE	POSITION LAT	LONG
Sainte-Marie-sur-Mer	UNP/LNO	NB	Gloucester	21 P/15	47°47′	64°34′
Sainte-Marthe	VILG/VILG	QC	Vaudreuil-Soulanges	31 G/8	45°24′	74°18′
Sainte-Marthe-du-Cap	VILG/VILG	QC	Francheville	31 I/8	46°23′	72°28′
Ste-Marthe-Rocanville	UNP/LNO	SK	10-17-30-W	62 K/5	50°26′	101°33′
Sainte-Marthe-sur-le-Lac	CITY/VIL1	QC	Deux-Montagnes	31 H/12	45°32′	73°56′
Sainte-Martine	VILG/VILG	QC	Beauharnois-Salaberry	31 H/5	45°15′	73°48′
Sainte-Mathilde	UNP/LNO	QC	Charlevoix-Est	21 M/9	47°41′	70°06′
Sainte-Mélanie	VILG/VILG	QC	Joliette	31 I/4	46°08′	73°31′
Saint-Émile	CITY/VIL1	QC	Communauté urbaine de Québec	21 L/14	46°52′	71°20′
Saint-Émile-de-Suffolk	VILG/VILG	QC	Papineau	31 G/15	45°56′	74°55′
Sainte-Monique	VILG/VILG	QC	Lac-Saint-Jean-Est	22 D/12	48°44′	71°51′
Sainte-Monique	VILG/VILG	QC	Nicolet-Yamaska	31 I/2	46°10′	72°32′
Sainte-Monique	UNP/LNO	QC	Mirabel	31 H/12	45°40′	74°00′
Sainte-Odile-sur-Rimouski	VILG/VILG	QC	Rimouski-Neigette	22 C/6	48°26′	68°33′
Sainte-Paule	VILG/VILG	QC	Matane	22 B/12	48°40′	67°33′
Sainte-Perpétue	VILG/VILG	QC	L'Islet	21 N/4	47°03′	69°56′
Sainte-Perpétue	VILG/VILG	QC	Nicolet-Yamaska	31 I/1	46°05′	72°28′
Sainte-Perpétue-Station	UNP/LNO	QC	Nicolet-Yamaska	31 I/1	46°03′	72°24′
Sainte-Pétronille	TOWN/VIL2	QC	L'Île-d'Orléans	21 L/14	46°51′	71°08′
Sainte-Philomène-de-Fortierville	VILG/VILG	QC	Bécancour	31 I/8	46°29′	72°02′
Saint-Éphrem-de-Beauce	VILG/VILG	QC	Beauce-Sartigan	21 L/2	46°04′	70°57′
Saint-Éphrem-de-Tring	TOWN/VIL2	QC	Beauce-Sartigan	21 L/2	46°04′	70°57′
Saint-Éphrem-d'Upton	VILG/VILG	QC	Acton	31 H/10	45°39′	72°40′
Saint-Éphrem-Station	UNP/LNO	QC	Beauce-Sartigan	21 L/2	46°04′	70°55′
Saint-Épiphane	VILG/VILG	QC	Rivière-du-Loup	21 N/14	47°54′	69°20′
Sainte-Praxède	VILG/VILG	QC	L'Amiante	21 E/14	45°54′	71°15′
Sainte-Rita	VILG/VILG	QC	Les Basques	21 N/15	47°57′	68°55′
Ste. Rita	UNP/LNO	MB	33,34-10-9-E	62 H/16	49°53′	96°18′
Sainte-Rosalie	TOWN/VIL2	QC	Les Maskoutains	31 H/10	45°38′	72°54′
Sainte-Rosalie	VILG/VILG	QC	Les Maskoutains	31 H/10	45°38′	72°54′
Sainte-Rosalie-Jonction	UNP/LNO	QC	Les Maskoutains	31 H/10	45°38′	72°55′
Ste. Rose	MUN2/AZM2	MB		62 J/14	51°00′	99°25′
Sainte-Rose	UNP/LNO	QC	Laval	31 H/12	45°37′	73°47′
Sainte-Rose	UNP/LNO	QC	Abitibi-Ouest	32 D/10	48°40′	78°59′
Ste-Rose-de-Prescott	UNP/LNO	ON	Prescott	31 G/7	45°22′	74°59′
Sainte-Rose-de-Watford	VILG/VILG	QC	Les Etchemins	21 L/8	46°19′	70°25′
Ste. Rose du Lac	VILG/VILG	MB	24-15-W	62 O/4	51°04′	99°31′
Sainte-Rose-du-Nord	VILG/VILG	QC	Le Fjord-du-Saguenay	22 D/7	48°23′	70°35′
Sainte-Rose-Gloucester	UNP/LNO	NB	Gloucester	21 P/10	47°37′	64°56′
Sainte-Rose-Station	UNP/LNO	QC	Les Etchemins	21 L/8	46°19′	70°29′
Sainte-Rosette	UNP/LNO	NB	Gloucester	21 P/12	47°43′	65°48′
Sainte-Sabine	VILG/VILG	QC	Les Etchemins	21 L/8	46°29′	70°21′
Sainte-Sabine	VILG/VILG	QC	Brome-Missisquoi	31 H/3	45°14′	73°01′
Sainte-Sabine-Station	UNP/LNO	QC	Les Etchemins	21 L/8	46°27′	70°17′
Sainte-Scholastique	UNP/LNO	QC	Mirabel	31 G/9	45°39′	74°05′
Sainte-Séraphine	VILG/VILG	QC	Arthabaska	31 H/16	45°55′	72°11′
Sainte-Sophie	VILG/VILG	QC	L'Érable	21 L/4	46°09′	71°43′
Sainte-Sophie	VILG/VILG	QC	La Rivière-du-Nord	31 H/13	45°49′	73°54′
Sainte-Sophie-de-Lévrard	VILG/VILG	QC	Bécancour	31 I/8	46°26′	72°07′
Sainte-Sophie-de-Mégantic	UNP/LNO	QC	L'Érable	21 L/4	46°09′	71°42′
Saint-Esprit	VILG/VILG	QC	Montcalm	31 H/13	45°54′	73°40′
St. Esprit	UNP/LNO	NS	Richmond	11 F/10	45°38′	60°32′
St. Esprit Island	ISL/ÎLE	NS	Richmond	11 F/9	45°37′	60°29′
St. Esprit Lake	LAKE/LAC	NS	Richmond	11 F/9	45°39′	60°30′
Sainte-Thècle	VILG/VILG	QC	Mékinac	31 I/15	46°49′	72°30′
Sainte-Thècle-Station	UNP/LNO	QC	Mékinac	31 I/16	46°48′	72°30′
Sainte-Thérèse	CITY/VIL1	QC	Thérèse-De Blainville	31 H/12	45°38′	73°51′
Sainte-Thérèse-de-Gaspé	VILG/VILG	QC	Pabok	22 A/8	48°25′	64°25′
Sainte-Thérèse-de-Gaspé-Station	UNP/LNO	QC	Pabok	22 A/8	48°25′	64°23′
Sainte-Thérèse-de-Gatineau	UNP/LNO	QC	La Vallée-de-la-Gatineau	31 J/5	46°18′	75°52′
Sainte-Thérèse-de-la-Gatineau	VILG/VILG	QC	La Vallée-de-la-Gatineau	31 J/5	46°18′	75°52′
Sainte-Thérèse-de-Lisieux	UNP/LNO	QC	Communauté urbaine de Québec	21 L/14	46°54′	71°12′
Sainte-Thérèse, Île	ISL/ÎLE	QC	Lajemmerais	31 H/11	45°41′	73°28′
Ste. Thérèse, Lac	LAKE/LAC	NT	Mackenzie	96 A	64°40′	121°35′
Saint-Étienne	UNP/LNO	QC	Le Fjord-du-Saguenay	22 C/4	48°12′	69°56′
Saint-Étienne-de-Beauharnois	VILG/VILG	QC	Beauharnois-Salaberry	31 H/4	45°15′	73°55′
Saint-Étienne-de-Beaumont	VILG/VILG	QC	Bellechasse	21 L/14	46°49′	71°00′
Saint-Étienne-de-Bolton	VILG/VILG	QC	Memphrémagog	31 H/8	45°16′	72°22′
Saint-Étienne-de-Lauzon	VILG/VILG	QC	Les Chutes-de-la-Chaudière	21 L/11	46°39′	71°18′
Saint-Étienne-de-Ristigouche	UNP/LNO	QC	Avignon	22 B/2	48°04′	66°52′
Saint-Étienne-des-Grès	VILG/VILG	QC	Francheville	31 I/7	46°26′	72°46′
Saint-Eugène	VILG/VILG	QC	L'Islet	21 M/1	47°05′	70°20′
Saint-Eugène	VILG/VILG	QC	Maria-Chapdelaine	32 A/16	48°59′	72°17′
Saint-Eugène	VILG/VILG	QC	Drummond	31 H/15	45°48′	72°42′
St-Eugène	UNP/LNO	ON	Prescott	31 G/8	45°30′	74°28′

NAME NOM	ENTITY ENTITÉ	LOC 1 LIEU 1	LOC 2 LIEU 2	MAP CARTE	POSITION LAT	LONG
Saint-Eugène-de-Chazel	UNP/LNO	QC	Abitibi-Ouest	32 D/15	48°57′	78°58′
Saint-Eugène-de-Grantham	UNP/LNO	QC	Drummond	31 H/15	45°48′	72°42′
Saint-Eugène-de-Guigues	VILG/VILG	QC	Témiscamingue	31 M/11	47°31′	79°21′
Saint-Eugène-de-Ladrière	VILG/VILG	QC	Rimouski-Neigette	22 C/7	48°15′	68°48′
St. Eugene Mission	UNP/LNO	BC	Kootenay	82 G/12	49°35′	115°45′
Sainte-Ursule	VILG/VILG	QC	Maskinongé	31 I/6	46°17′	73°02′
Sainte-Ursule, Chutes de	FALL/CHUT	QC	Maskinongé	31 I/6	46°18′	73°06′
Saint-Eusèbe	VILG/VILG	QC	Témiscouata	21 N/10	47°33′	68°55′
Saint-Eusèbe-Ouest	UNP/LNO	QC	Témiscouata	21 N/7	47°30′	68°57′
Saint-Eustache	CITY/VIL1	QC	Deux-Montagnes	31 H/12	45°34′	73°54′
St. Eustache	UNP/LNO	MB	2,3-12-3-W	62 H/13	49°59′	97°47′
Saint-Évariste-de-Forsyth.	VILG/VILG	QC	Beauce-Sartigan	21 E/15	45°56′	70°57′
Sainte-Véronique	TOWN/VIL2	QC	Antoine-Labelle	31 J/10	46°31′	74°59′
Sainte-Victoire	UNP/LNO	QC	Le Bas-Richelieu	31 H/14	45°57′	73°05′
Sainte-Victoire-de-Sorel	VILG/VILG	QC	Le Bas-Richelieu	31 H/14	45°57′	73°05′
Saint-Fabien	VILG/VILG	QC	Rimouski-Neigette	22 C/7	48°18′	68°52′
Saint-Fabien	UNP/LNO	NB	Kent	21 I/7	46°26′	64°53′
Saint-Fabien-de-Panet	VILG/VILG	QC	Montmagny	21 L/9	46°39′	70°09′
Saint-Fabien-sur-Mer	UNP/LNO	QC	Rimouski-Neigette	22 C/7	48°19′	68°52′
Saint-Faustin	UNP/LNO	QC	Les Laurentides	31 J/1	46°07′	74°29′
Saint-Faustin — Lac-Carré	VILG/VILG	QC	Les Laurentides	31 J/1	46°07′	74°29′
Saint-Félicien	CITY/VIL1	QC	Le Domaine-du-Roy	32 A/9	48°39′	72°27′
St. Felix	VILG/VILG	PE	Prince	21 I/16	46°56′	64°02′
St. Felix	UNP/LNO	PE	Prince	21 I/16	46°56′	64°01′
Saint-Félix-de-Dalquier	VILG/VILG	QC	Abitibi	32 D/9	48°41′	78°07′
Saint-Félix-de-Kingsey	UNP/LNO	QC	Drummond	31 H/16	45°48′	72°12′
Saint-Félix-de-Valois	TOWN/VIL2	QC	Matawinie	31 I/3	46°10′	73°26′
Saint-Félix-de-Valois	VILG/VILG	QC	Matawinie	31 I/3	46°10′	73°26′
Saint-Félix-d'Otis	VILG/VILG	QC	Le Fjord-du-Saguenay	22 D/7	48°16′	70°37′
Saint-Ferdinand	VILG/VILG	QC	L'Érable	21 L/4	46°06′	71°35′
Saint-Ferréol-les-Neiges	VILG/VILG	QC	La Côte-de-Beaupré	21 M/2	47°07′	70°51′
Saint-Fiacre	UNP/LNO	QC	Le Fjord-du-Saguenay	22 D/1	48°15′	70°11′
Saint-Fidèle	UNP/LNO	QC	Charlevoix-Est	21 N/12	47°44′	69°59′
Saint-Fidèle-de-Mont-Murray	VILG/VILG	QC	Charlevoix-Est	21 N/12	47°44′	69°59′
Saintfield	UNP/LNO	ON	Ontario	31 D/3	44°11′	79°02′
St. Fintan's	UNP/LNO	NF		12 B/2	48°11′	58°51′
Saint-Flavien	TOWN/VIL2	QC	Lotbinière	21 L/12	46°31′	71°36′
Saint-Flavien	VILG/VILG	QC	Lotbinière	21 L/12	46°31′	71°36′
Saint-Fond, Rivière	RIV/CDE	QC	Kativik	24 N/5	59°29′	69°45′
Saint-Fortunat	VILG/VILG	QC	L'Amiante	21 E/13	45°58′	71°36′
St. Francis	UNP/LNO	AB	2-50-3-W5	83 G/8	53°17′	114°20′
St. Francis, Cape	CAPE/CAP	NF		1 N/15	47°49′	52°47′
St. Francis Harbour	UNP/LNO	NS	Guysborough	11 F/6	45°27′	61°19′
St. Francis Harbour River	RIV/CDE	NS	Guysborough	11 F/6	45°27′	61°19′
St. Francis, Lake - also-aussi - Saint-François, Lac	LAKE/LAC	ON	Glengarry	31 G/1	45°10′	74°22′
St. Francis River - also-aussi - Saint-François, Rivière	RIV/CDE	NB	Madawaska	21 N/2	47°11′	68°54′
Saint-François	VILG/VILG	QC	L'Île-d'Orléans	21 M/2	47°00′	70°49′
Saint-François	UNP/LNO	QC	Laval	31 H/12	45°40′	73°37′
Saint-François	GEOG/GÉOG	NB	Madawaska	21 N/7	47°17′	68°53′
Saint-François-d'Assise	VILG/VILG	QC	Avignon	21 O/14	47°59′	67°10′
Saint-François-de-Beauce	VILG/VILG	QC	Robert-Cliche	21 L/7	46°16′	70°46′
Saint-François-de-Kent	UNP/LNO	NB	Kent	21 I/7	46°27′	64°41′
Saint-François-de-la-Rivière-du-Sud	VILG/VILG	QC	Montmagny	21 L/15	46°53′	70°43′
Saint-François de Madawaska	VILG/VILG	NB	Madawaska	21 N/2	47°15′	68°42′
Saint-François-de-Madawaska - see-voir - Saint-François de Madawaska	VILG/VILG	NB		21 N/2	47°15′	68°42′
Saint-François-de-Masham	UNP/LNO	QC	Les Collines-de-l'Outaouais	31 F/9	45°38′	76°04′
Saint-François-de-Pabos	VILG/VILG	QC	Pabok	22 A/7	48°23′	64°39′
Saint-François-de-Sales	VILG/VILG	QC	Le Domaine-du-Roy	32 A/8	48°19′	72°08′
Saint-François-du-Lac	TOWN/VIL2	QC	Nicolet-Yamaska	31 I/2	46°04′	72°50′
Saint-François-du-Lac	VILG/VILG	QC	Nicolet-Yamaska	31 I/2	46°04′	72°50′
Saint-François, Lac	LAKE/LAC	QC	Rivière-du-Loup	21 N/14	47°45′	69°19′
Saint-François, Lac	LAKE/LAC	QC	Le Granit	21 E/14	45°54′	71°10′
Saint-François, Lac - also-aussi - St. Francis, Lake	LAKE/LAC	QC	Le Haut-Saint-Laurent	31 G/1	45°10′	74°22′
Saint-François-Ouest	VILG/VILG	QC	Robert-Cliche	21 L/2	46°12′	70°49′
Saint-François, Rivière - also-aussi - St. Francis River	RIV/CDE	NB/QC		12 N/2	47°11′	68°54′
Saint-François, Rivière	RIV/CDE	QC	Nicolet-Yamaska	31 I/2	46°07′	72°56′
Saint-François-Station	UNP/LNO	QC	Montmagny	21 L/15	46°54′	70°42′
St. François Xavier	MUN2/AZM2	MB		62 H/13	49°55′	97°40′
St. François Xavier	UNP/LNO	MB		62 H/13	49°55′	97°33′
St. François Xavier	GEOG/GÉOG	MB		62 H/13	49°55′	97°33′
Saint-François-Xavier-de-Brompton	VILG/VILG	QC	Le Val-Saint-François	31 H/9	45°32′	72°03′
Saint-François-Xavier-de-Viger	VILG/VILG	QC	Rivière-du-Loup	21 N/14	47°51′	69°15′
Saint-Frédéric	VILG/VILG	QC	Robert-Cliche	21 L/7	46°18′	70°58′
Saint-Front	UNP/LNO	SK	24-39-16-W2	73 A/8	52°22′	104°10′
Saint-Fulgence	VILG/VILG	QC	Le Fjord-du-Saguenay	22 D/7	48°27′	70°54′

NAME NOM	ENTITY ENTITÉ	LOC 1 LIEU 1	LOC 2 LIEU 2	MAP CARTE	POSITION LAT	LONG
Saint-Gabriel	CITY/VIL1	QC	D'Autray	31 I/6	46°18′	73°23′
Saint-Gabriel	VILG/VILG	QC	La Mitis	22 C/8	48°25′	68°10′
Saint-Gabriel-de-Brandon	VILG/VILG	QC	D'Autray	31 I/6	46°16′	73°23′
Saint-Gabriel-de-Gaspé	UNP/LNO	QC	Pabok	22 A/10	48°31′	64°32′
Saint-Gabriel-de-Kamouraska	UNP/LNO	QC	Kamouraska	21 N/5	47°23′	69°56′
Saint-Gabriel-de-Kent	UNP/LNO	NB	Kent	21 I/10	46°31′	64°49′
Saint-Gabriel-de-Valcartier	VILG/VILG	QC	La Jacques-Cartier	21 L/14	46°56′	71°28′
Saint-Gabriel-Lalemant	VILG/VILG	QC	Kamouraska	21 N/5	47°23′	69°56′
Saint-Gédéon	TOWN/VIL2	QC	Beauce-Sartigan	21 E/15	45°51′	70°38′
Saint-Gédéon	VILG/VILG	QC	Beauce-Sartigan	21 E/15	45°51′	70°38′
Saint-Gédéon	VILG/VILG	QC	Lac-Saint-Jean-Est	22 D/5	48°30′	71°46′
St. George	TOWN/VIL2	NB	Charlotte	21 G/2	45°08′	66°50′
St. George	UNP/LNO	ON	Brant	40 P/1	43°15′	80°15′
Saint George	GEOG/GÉOG	NB	Charlotte	21 G/7	45°17′	66°50′
St. George, Cape	CAPE/CAP	NF		12 B/6	48°28′	59°16′
St. George, Lake	LAKE/LAC	MB	31,32-1-E	62 P/11	51°44′	97°26′
Saint-Georges	CITY/VIL1	QC	Beauce-Sartigan	21 L/2	46°07′	70°40′
St. George's	TOWN/VIL2	NF		12 B/8	48°26′	58°29′
Saint-Georges	TOWN/VIL2	QC	Le Centre-de-la-Mauricie	31 I/10	46°37′	72°40′
St. Georges	UNP/LNO	PE	Kings	11 L/8	46°16′	62°29′
Saint-Georges	UNP/LNO	QC	Pabok	22 A/9	48°39′	64°14′
St-Georges	UNP/LNO	MB	16-18-10-E	62 I/9	50°32′	96°09′
St. George's Bay	BAY/BAIE	NF		12 B/7	48°24′	58°53′
St. Georges Bay	BAY/BAIE	NS	Antigonish	11 F/12	45°45′	61°45′
St. Georges Channel	UNP/LNO	NS	Richmond	11 F/11	45°43′	61°03′
Saint-Georges-de-Bagot	UNP/LNO	QC	Les Maskoutains	31 H/10	45°40′	72°50′
Saint-Georges-de-Cacouna	TOWN/VIL2	QC	Rivière-du-Loup	21 N/13	47°55′	69°30′
Saint-Georges-de-Cacouna	VILG/VILG	QC	Rivière-du-Loup	21 N/13	47°55′	69°30′
Saint-Georges-de-Clarenceville	VILG/VILG	QC	Le Haut-Richelieu	31 H/3	45°04′	73°15′
Saint-Georges-de-Malbaie	UNP/LNO	QC	Pabok	22 A/9	48°39′	64°13′
Saint-Georges-de-Windsor	VILG/VILG	QC	Asbestos	21 E/12	45°42′	71°50′
Saint-Georges-Est	VILG/VILG	QC	Beauce-Sartigan	21 L/2	46°07′	70°40′
St. George's Harbour	BAY/BAIE	NF		12 B/8	48°26′	53°29′
St. George's Hill	HAM/HAM	SK	79-19-W3	73 N/15	55°53′	108°57′
St. George's River	RIV/CDE	NF		12 B/8	48°29′	58°26′
St. George Trough	SEAU/SMER	—		801-A	48°10′	59°26′
Saint-Gérard	TOWN/VIL2	QC	Le Haut-Saint-François	21 E/14	45°46′	71°25′
Saint-Gérard-des-Laurentides	VILG/VILG	QC	Le Centre-de-la-Mauricie	31 I/10	46°36′	72°49′
Saint-Gérard-d'Yamaska	UNP/LNO	QC	Le Bas-Richelieu	31 I/2	46°00′	72°50′
Saint-Gérard-Majella	VILG/VILG	QC	Le Bas-Richelieu	31 I/2	46°00′	72°50′
Saint-Gérard-Majella	VILG/VILG	QC	L'Assomption	31 H/14	45°54′	73°26′
Saint-Germain	VILG/VILG	QC	Kamouraska	21 N/12	47°35′	69°48′
St. Germain	UNP/LNO	MB		62 H/14	49°46′	97°08′
Saint-Germain-de-Grantham	VILG/VILG	QC	Drummond	31 H/15	45°50′	72°34′
Saint-Germain-de-Grantham	VILG/VILG	QC	Drummond	31 H/15	45°50′	72°34′
Saint-Germain, Rivière	RIV/CDE	QC	Drummond	31 H/16	45°54′	72°30′
Saint-Germains, Grand lac	LAKE/LAC	QC	Le Fjord-du-Saguenay	22 D/7	48°26′	70°36′
Saint-Gervais	VILG/VILG	QC	Bellechasse	21 L/10	46°43′	70°53′
Saint-Gervais	UNP/LNO	QC	Bellechasse	21 L/10	46°43′	70°53′
Saint-Gilbert	VILG/VILG	QC	Portneuf	21 L/12	46°43′	72°00′
St. Gilbert	UNP/LNO	PE	Prince	21 I/8	46°29′	64°03′
Saint-Gilles	VILG/VILG	QC	Lotbinière	21 L/11	46°31′	71°22′
Saint-Godefroi	VILG/VILG	QC	Bonaventure	22 A/3	48°05′	65°07′
Saint-Grégoire	UNP/LNO	NB	Kent	21 I/7	46°25′	64°42′
Saint-Grégoire	UNP/LNO	QC	Bécancour	31 I/7	46°16′	72°31′
Saint-Grégoire-de-Greenlay	TOWN/VIL2	QC	Le Val-Saint-François	31 H/9	45°34′	72°01′
Saint-Grégoire, Mont	MTN/MNT	QC	Le Haut-Richelieu	31 H/6	45°21′	73°09′
St. Gregor	VILG/VILG	SK	17-37-20-W2	73 A/2	52°11′	104°50′
St. Gregory, Cape	CAPE/CAP	NF		12 G/8	49°24′	58°14′
Saint-Guillaume	VILG/VILG	QC	Drummond	31 H/15	45°53′	72°46′
Saint-Guillaume-de-Granada	UNP/LNO	QC	Rouyn-Noranda	32 D/2	48°10′	79°00′
Saint-Guillaume-Nord	MUN2/AZM2	QC	Matawinie	31 J/9	46°36′	74°06′
Saint-Guillaume-Nord	UNP/LNO	QC	Matawinie	31 J/9	46°36′	74°06′
Saint-Guy	VILG/VILG	QC	Les Basques	22 C/2	48°02′	68°47′
St. Hans, Mount	MTN/MNT	NT	Franklin	38 B	72°53′	76°19′
St. Helens	UNP/LNO	ON	Huron	40 P/13	43°54′	81°30′
Saint-Henri	VILG/VILG	QC	Desjardins	21 L/11	46°42′	71°04′
Saint-Henri-de-Taillon	VILG/VILG	QC	Lac-Saint-Jean-Est	22 D/12	48°40′	71°50′
Saint-Hermas	UNP/LNO	QC	Mirabel	31 G/9	45°36′	74°11′
Saint-Herménégilde	VILG/VILG	QC	Coaticook	21 E/4	45°06′	71°40′
Saint-Hilaire - see-voir - St. Hilaire	VILG/VILG	NB		21 N/8	47°18′	68°24′
St. Hilaire	VILG/VILG	NB	Madawaska	21 N/8	47°18′	68°24′
Saint-Hilaire	UNP/LNO	QC	La Vallée-du-Richelieu	31 H/11	45°33′	73°12′
Saint-Hilaire	GEOG/GÉOG	NB	Madawaska	21 N/8	47°20′	68°27′
Saint-Hilaire-de-Dorset	VILG/VILG	QC	Beauce-Sartigan	21 E/15	45°52′	70°51′

NAME NOM	ENTITY ENTITÉ	LOC 1 LIEU 1	LOC 2 LIEU 2	MAP CARTE	POSITION LAT	LONG
Saint-Hilaire-Est	UNP/LNO	QC	La Vallée-du-Richelieu	31 H/11	45°34'	73°12'
Saint-Hilaire, Mont	MTN/MNT	QC	La Vallée-du-Richelieu	31 H/11	45°33'	73°10'
Saint-Hilarion	VILG/VILG	QC	Charlevoix	21 M/9	47°34'	70°24'
Saint-Hilarion-du-Lac	UNP/LNO	QC	Charlevoix	21 M/9	47°34'	70°26'
Saint-Hilarion-Nord	UNP/LNO	QC	Charlevoix	21 M/9	47°36'	70°24'
Saint-Hippolyte	VILG/VILG	QC	La Rivière-du-Nord	31 G/16	45°56'	74°01'
Saint Hippolyte	UNP/LNO	SK	5-48-19-W3	73 F/2	53°07'	108°44'
Saint-Honoré	VILG/VILG	QC	Témiscouata	21 N/11	47°42'	69°08'
Saint-Honoré	VILG/VILG	QC	Beauce-Sartigan	21 E/15	45°58'	70°50'
Saint-Honoré	VILG/VILG	QC	Le Fjord-du-Saguenay	22 D/11	48°32'	71°05'
Saint-Honoré-Station	UNP/LNO	QC	Témiscouata	21 N/11	47°43'	69°08'
Saint-Hubert	CITY/VIL1	QC	Champlain	31 H/11	45°30'	73°25'
St. Hubert	VILG/VILG	QC	Rivière-du-Loup	21 N/14	47°49'	69°09'
St. Hubert	UNP/LNO	PE	Prince	21 I/9	46°30'	64°02'
St. Hubert Mission	UNP/LNO	SK	33-14-3-W2	62 L/1	50°13'	102°21'
Saint-Hugues	VILG/VILG	QC	Les Maskoutains	31 H/15	45°48'	72°52'
Saint-Hyacinthe	CITY/VIL1	QC	Les Maskoutains	31 H/10	45°37'	72°57'
Saint-Hyacinthe-le-Confesseur	VILG/VILG	QC	Les Maskoutains	31 H/10	45°37'	72°57'
Saint-Hyacinthe-Station	UNP/LNO	QC	Les Maskoutains	31 H/10	45°38'	72°56'
Saint-Ignace	UNP/LNO	NB	Kent	21 I/11	46°42'	65°05'
Saint-Ignace	UNP/LNO	QC	La Côte-de-Beaupré	21 M/3	47°02'	71°03'
Saint-Ignace-de-Loyola	VILG/VILG	QC	D'Autray	31 I/3	46°04'	73°08'
Saint-Ignace-de-Stanbridge	VILG/VILG	QC	Brome-Missisquoi	31 H/2	45°10'	72°57'
Saint-Ignace-du-Lac	UNP/LNO	QC	Matawinie	31 I/12	46°43'	73°48'
Saint-Ignace, Île	ISL/ÎLE	QC	D'Autray	31 I/3	46°05'	73°07'
St. Ignace Island	ISL/ÎLE	ON	Thunder Bay	42 D/13	48°45'	87°55'
Saint-Ignace Siding	UNP/LNO	NB	Kent	21 I/11	46°38'	65°09'
Saint-Irénée	VILG/VILG	QC	Charlevoix-Est	21 M/9	47°34'	70°12'
Saint-Irénée	UNP/LNO	NB	Gloucester	21 P/11	47°30'	65°00'
Saint-Irénée-les-Bains	UNP/LNO	QC	Charlevoix-Est	21 M/9	47°33'	70°13'
Saint-Isidore	VILG/VILG	NB	Gloucester	21 P/11	47°33'	65°03'
Saint-Isidore	VILG/VILG	QC	La Nouvelle-Beauce	21 L/11	46°35'	71°06'
Saint-Isidore	VILG/VILG	QC	Roussillon	31 H/5	45°18'	73°41'
St. Isidore	VILG/VILG	ON	Prescott	31 G/7	45°23'	74°54'
St. Isidore	UNP/LNO	AB	21-83-20-W5	84 C/3	56°12'	117°06'
Saint-Isidore	GEOG/GÉOG	NB	Gloucester	21 P/11	47°35'	65°05'
Saint-Isidore-d'Auckland	VILG/VILG	QC	Le Haut-Saint-François	21 E/5	45°16'	71°31'
St-Isidore-de-Bellevue	HAM/HAM	SK	44-27,28-W2	73 A/13	52°47'	105°55'
Saint-Isidore-de-Gaspé	UNP/LNO	QC	Pabok	22 A/8	48°27'	64°27'
St. Isidore de Prescott - see-voir - St. Isidore	VILG/VILG	ON		31 G/7	45°23'	74°54'
St. Ives	UNP/LNO	ON	Middlesex	40 P/3	43°09'	81°10'
St. Ives	UNP/LNO	BC	Kamloops Division Yale	82 L/14	50°59'	119°06'
St. Jacobs	UNP/LNO	ON	Waterloo	40 P/10	43°32'	80°33'
Saint-Jacques	TOWN/VIL2	QC	Montcalm	31 H/13	45°57'	73°34'
Saint-Jacques	VILG/VILG	NB	Madawaska	21 N/8	47°26'	68°23'
Saint-Jacques	VILG/VILG	QC	Montcalm	31 H/13	45°57'	73°34'
St. Jacques	UNP/LNO	NF		1 M/6	47°29'	55°55'
Saint-Jacques	GEOG/GÉOG	NB	Madawaska	21 N/8	47°26'	68°27'
St. Jacques-Coomb's Cove	TOWN/VIL2	NF		1 M/5	47°28'	55°31'
Saint-Jacques-de-Horton	VILG/VILG	QC	Arthabaska	31 H/16	46°00'	72°12'
Saint-Jacques-de-Leeds	VILG/VILG	QC	L'Amiante	21 L/6	46°17'	71°21'
Saint-Jacques, Lac	LAKE/LAC	QC	Le Fjord-du-Saguenay	22 E/6	49°28'	71°08'
Saint-Jacques-le-Majeur-de-Causapscal	VILG/VILG	QC	La Matapédia	22 B/6	48°23'	67°15'
Saint-Jacques-le-Majeur-de-Wolfestown	VILG/VILG	QC	L'Amiante	21 E/13	45°56'	71°30'
Saint-Jacques-le-Mineur	VILG/VILG	QC	Les Jardins-de-Napierville	31 H/6	45°17'	73°25'
Saint-Jacques, Rivière	RIV/CDE	QC	Roussillon	31 H/6	45°26'	73°29'
St. James	UNP/LNO	MB		62 H/14	49°53'	97°15'
Saint James	GEOG/GÉOG	NB	Charlotte	21 G/6	45°23'	67°20'
St. James	GEOG/GÉOG	MB		62 H/14	49°54'	97°09'
St. James - Assiniboia - see-voir - Assiniboia	VILG/VILG	MB		62 H/14	49°52'	97°16'
St. James - Assiniboia - see-voir - Headingley	VILG/VILG	MB		62 H/14	49°52'	97°23'
St. James, Cape	CAPE/CAP	BC	Queen Charlotte	102 O/14	51°56'	131°01'
St. James Junction	UNP/LNO	MB		62 H/14	49°51'	97°12'
St. James Town	UNP/LNO	ON	York	30 M/11	43°40'	79°22'
Saint-Janvier	UNP/LNO	QC	Mirabel	31 H/12	45°42'	73°56'
Saint-Janvier-de-Joly	VILG/VILG	QC	Lotbinière	21 L/5	46°29'	71°40'
Saint-Jean	VILG/VILG	QC	L'Île-d'Orléans	21 L/15	46°55'	70°54'
Saint-Jean, Anse	BAY/BAIE	QC	Le Fjord-du-Saguenay	22 D/1	48°15'	70°12'
Saint-Jean-Baptiste	VILG/VILG	QC	La Mitis	22 C/9	48°34'	68°13'
Saint-Jean-Baptiste	VILG/VILG	QC	Rouville	31 H/11	45°31'	73°07'
Saint-Jean-Baptiste	UNP/LNO	NB	Kent	21 I/7	46°29'	64°42'
Saint-Jean-Baptiste	UNP/LNO	QC	L'Islet	21 M/1	47°07'	70°11'
St. Jean Baptiste	UNP/LNO	MB	3,4-1-E	62 H/6	49°16'	97°20'
Saint-Jean-Baptiste-de-l'Isle-Verte	VILG/VILG	QC	Rivière-du-Loup	22 C/3	48°01'	69°20'
Saint-Jean-Baptiste-de-Nicolet	VILG/VILG	QC	Nicolet-Yamaska	31 I/2	46°15'	72°36'

NAME NOM	ENTITY ENTITÉ	LOC 1 LIEU 1	LOC 2 LIEU 2	MAP CARTE	POSITION	
					LAT	LONG
Saint-Jean-Baptiste-de-Restigouche	UNP/LNO	NB	Restigouche	21 O/14	47°46′	67°13′
Saint-Jean-Baptiste-de-Rouville	UNP/LNO	QC	Rouville	31 H/11	45°31′	73°07′
Saint-Jean, Base des Forces canadiennes - also-aussi - Saint-Jean, Canadian Forces Base	MIL/MIL	QC	Le Haut-Richelieu	31 H/6	45°18′	73°17′
Saint-Jean, Canadian Forces Base - also-aussi - Saint-Jean, Base des Forces canadiennes	MIL/MIL	QC	Le Haut-Richelieu	31 H/6	45°18′	73°17′
Saint-Jean-Chrysostome	CITY/VIL1	QC	Les Chutes-de-la-Chaudière	21 L/11	46°43′	71°12′
Saint-Jean-Chrysostome	VILG/VILG	QC	Le Haut-Saint-Laurent	31 H/4	45°07′	73°47′
Saint-Jean-de-Brébeuf	VILG/VILG	QC	L'Amiante	21 L/3	46°11′	71°28′
Saint-Jean-de-Cherbourg	VILG/VILG	QC	Matane	22 B/14	48°51′	67°07′
Saint-Jean-de-Dieu	VILG/VILG	QC	Les Basques	22 C/3	48°00′	69°03′
Saint-Jean-de-la-Lande	VILG/VILG	QC	Témiscouata	21 N/7	47°26′	68°41′
Saint-Jean-de-la-Lande	VILG/VILG	QC	Beauce-Sartigan	21 L/2	46°03′	70°42′
Saint-Jean-de-Matapédia	UNP/LNO	QC	Avignon	21 O/14	47°58′	67°13′
Saint-Jean-de-Matha	VILG/VILG	QC	Matawinie	31 I/4	46°14′	73°32′
Saint-Jean-des-Piles	VILG/VILG	QC	Le Centre-de-la-Mauricie	31 I/10	46°41′	72°44′
Saint-Jean-Eudes	UNP/LNO	QC	Le Fjord-du-Saguenay	22 D/6	48°26′	71°08′
Saint-Jean, Lac	LAKE/LAC	QC	Les Basques	21 N/15	47°59′	68°51′
Saint-Jean, Lac	LAKE/LAC	QC	Lac-Saint-Jean-Est	32 A/9	48°36′	72°02′
Saint-Jean Nord-Est, Rivière	RIV/CDE	QC	Minganie	22 I/9	50°41′	64°03′
Saint-Jean-Port-Joli	VILG/VILG	QC	L'Islet	21 M/1	47°13′	70°16′
Saint-Jean-Port-Joli-Station	UNP/LNO	QC	L'Islet	21 M/1	47°12′	70°15′
Saint-Jean, Rivière - also-aussi - **Saint John River**	RIV/CDE	NB	Saint John	21 G/8	45°16′	66°04′
Saint-Jean, Rivière	RIV/CDE	QC	Minganie	22 I/8	50°17′	64°20′
Saint-Jean, Rivière	RIV/CDE	QC	La Côte-de-Gaspé	22 A/16	48°46′	64°27′
Saint-Jean, Rivière	RIV/CDE	QC	Le Fjord-du-Saguenay	22 D/1	48°14′	70°12′
Saint-Jean Sud-Ouest, Rivière	RIV/CDE	QC	Les Etchemins	21 L/8	46°25′	70°03′
Saint-Jean-sur-le-Lac	UNP/LNO	QC	Antoine-Labelle	31 J/12	46°33′	75°35′
Saint-Jean-sur-Richelieu	CITY/VIL1	QC	Le Haut-Richelieu	31 H/6	45°19′	73°16′
Saint-Jean-Vianney	UNP/LNO	QC	Le Granit	21 E/10	45°34′	70°50′
Saint-Jean-Vianney	UNP/LNO	QC	Le Fjord-du-Saguenay	22 D/6	48°28′	71°14′
Saint-Jérôme	CITY/VIL1	QC	La Rivière-du-Nord	31 G/16	45°47′	74°00′
Saint-Jérôme-de-Matane	VILG/VILG	QC	Matane	22 B/13	48°49′	67°32′
Saint-Joachim	VILG/VILG	QC	La Côte-de-Beaupré	21 M/2	47°03′	70°51′
St. Joachim	UNP/LNO	ON	Essex	40 J/7	42°16′	82°38′
Saint-Joachim-de-Courval	VILG/VILG	QC	Drummond	31 H/15	45°58′	72°33′
Saint-Joachim-de-Shefford	VILG/VILG	QC	La Haute-Yamaska	31 H/7	45°27′	72°32′
St. Joachim Station	UNP/LNO	ON	Essex	40 J/7	42°17′	82°38′
Saint Joe 10	IR/RI	BC	Range 3 Coast	103 A/15	52°52′	128°41′
Saint-Jogues	UNP/LNO	QC	Bonaventure	22 A/3	48°10′	65°15′
Saint-Jogues-Sud	UNP/LNO	QC	Bonaventure	22 A/3	48°09′	65°14′
Saint John	CITY/VIL1	NB	Saint John	21 G/8	45°16′	66°03′
Saint John	GEOG/GÉOG	NB		21 H/5	45°20′	65°50′
St. John	GEOG/GÉOG	MB		62 H/14	49°54′	97°09′
St. John Bay	BAY/BAIE	NF		12 I/14	50°55′	57°09′
St. John, Cape	CAPE/CAP	NF		2 L/4	50°00′	55°32′
Saint John East	UNP/LNO	NB	Saint John	21 G/8	45°17′	66°02′
Saint John Harbour	BAY/BAIE	NB	Saint John	21 G/1	45°15′	66°02′
St. John Island	UNP/LNO	NF		12 I/14	50°49′	57°14′
St. John Island	ISL/ÎLE	NF		12 I/14	50°49′	57°14′
St. John, Lake	LAKE/LAC	NF		2 D/7	48°23′	54°41′
St. John Point	CAPE/CAP	BC	Nanaimo	92 F/10	49°31′	124°35′
Saint John River - also-aussi - **Saint-Jean, Rivière**	RIV/CDE	NB	Saint John	21 G/8	45°16′	66°04′
St. John's	CITY/VIL1	NF		1 N/10	47°34′	52°44′
St. Johns	UNP/LNO	ON	Welland	30 M/3	43°05′	79°16′
St. Johns	UNP/LNO	ON	Brant	40 P/1	43°04′	80°05′
St. Johns	UNP/LNO	MB		62 H/14	49°56′	97°08′
St. John's Bay	UNP/LNO	NF		1 M/5	47°28′	55°36′
St. John's Bay	BAY/BAIE	NF		1 N/10	47°34′	52°38′
St. John's Bay	BAY/BAIE	NF		2 E/6	49°20′	55°07′
St. John's Bay	BAY/BAIE	NF		1 M/5	47°25′	55°38′
St. John's, Canadian Forces Station - also-aussi - St. John's, Station des Forces canadiennes	MIL/MIL	NF		1 N/10	47°35′	52°41′
St. John's Head	CAPE/CAP	NF		1 M/5	47°26′	55°40′
St. John's Metropolitan Area	MUN1/AZM1	NF		1 N/10	47°34′	52°46′
St. John's, Station des Forces canadiennes - also-aussi - St. John's, Canadian Forces Station	MIL/MIL	NF		1 N/10	47°35′	52°41′
Saint John West	UNP/LNO	NB	Saint John	21 G/8	45°15′	66°04′
St. Jones Head	CAPE/CAP	NF		1 N/13	47°58′	53°40′
St. Jones Within	UNP/LNO	NF		2 C/4	48°03′	53°45′
St. Jones Without	UNP/LNO	NF		1 N/13	47°55′	53°42′
St. Joseph	MUN2/AZM2	ON	Algoma	41 K/1	46°15′	84°00′
St. Joseph	UNP/LNO	NS	Antigonish	11 E/9	45°32′	62°05′
St. Joseph	UNP/LNO	NS	Digby	21 B/8	44°16′	66°01′
Saint-Joseph	UNP/LNO	NB	Westmorland	21 H/15	45°59′	64°34′
Saint-Joseph	UNP/LNO	NB	Kent	21 I/11	46°36′	65°15′
Saint-Joseph	UNP/LNO	QC	Les Maskoutains	31 H/10	45°38′	72°56′
Saint-Joseph	UNP/LNO	QC	Pontiac	31 F/14	45°51′	77°00′
St. Joseph	UNP/LNO	ON	Huron	40 P/5	43°25′	81°42′

NAME NOM	ENTITY ENTITÉ	LOC 1 LIEU 1	LOC 2 LIEU 2	MAP CARTE	POSITION LAT	LONG
St. Joseph	UNP/LNO	MB	21,22-2-1-E	62 H/3	49°08'	97°23'
Saint-Joseph	GEOG/GÉOG	NB	Madawaska	21 N/9	47°35'	68°18'
St. Joseph Channel	CHAN/CHEN	ON	Algoma	41 J/5	46°15'	83°46'
Saint-Joseph-de-Beauce	CITY/VIL1	QC	Robert-Cliche	21 L/7	46°18'	70°53'
Saint-Joseph-de-Beauce	VILG/VILG	QC	Robert-Cliche	21 L/7	46°18'	70°53'
Saint-Joseph-de-Blandford	VILG/VILG	QC	Bécancour	31 I/8	46°22'	72°00'
Saint-Joseph-de-Cléricy	VILG/VILG	QC	Rouyn-Noranda	32 D/7	48°22'	78°52'
Saint-Joseph-de-Coleraine	VILG/VILG	QC	L'Amiante	21 E/14	45°58'	71°22'
Saint-Joseph-de-Ham-Sud	VILG/VILG	QC	Asbestos	21 E/13	45°46'	71°36'
Saint-Joseph-de-Kamouraska	VILG/VILG	QC	Kamouraska	21 N/12	47°37'	69°38'
Saint-Joseph-de-Kent	UNP/LNO	NB	Kent	21 I/7	46°27'	64°45'
Saint-Joseph-de-Lanoraie	VILG/VILG	QC	D'Autray	31 H/14	45°58'	73°13'
Saint-Joseph-de-la-Pointe-de-Lévy	VILG/VILG	QC	Desjardins	21 L/14	46°48'	71°05'
Saint-Joseph-de-la-Rive	TOWN/VIL2	QC	Charlevoix	21 M/8	47°27'	70°22'
Saint-Joseph-de-Lepage	VILG/VILG	QC	La Mitis	22 C/9	48°35'	68°10'
Saint-Joseph-de-Madawaska	UNP/LNO	NB	Madawaska	21 N/8	47°27'	68°19'
Saint-Joseph-de-Maskinongé	VILG/VILG	QC	Maskinongé	31 I/3	46°12'	73°02'
Saint-Joseph-de-Matapédia	UNP/LNO	QC	Avignon	21 O/14	47°56'	67°06'
Saint-Joseph-de-Mékinac	UNP/LNO	QC	Mékinac	31 I/15	46°55'	72°42'
Saint-Joseph-des-Érables	VILG/VILG	QC	Robert-Cliche	21 L/7	46°17'	70°55'
Saint-Joseph-des-Monts	UNP/LNO	QC	Denis-Riverin	22 G/1	49°02'	66°28'
Saint-Joseph-de-Sorel	CITY/VIL1	QC	Le Bas-Richelieu	31 I/3	46°02'	73°07'
Saint-Joseph-du-Lac	VILG/VILG	QC	Deux-Montagnes	31 G/9	45°32'	74°00'
St. Joseph du Moine	UNP/LNO	NS	Inverness	11 K/11	46°32'	61°03'
St. Joseph Island	ISL/ÎLE	ON	Algoma	41 J/4	46°13'	83°57'
Saint-Joseph, Lac	LAKE/LAC	QC	La Jacques-Cartier	21 L/13	46°54'	71°38'
St. Joseph, Lake	LAKE/LAC	ON	Thunder Bay	52 O/2	51°05'	90°35'
St. Joseph Mission	UNP/LNO	BC	Cariboo	93 A/4	52°04'	121°57'
St. Joseph's	VILG/VILG	NF		1 N/4	47°07'	53°31'
St. Joseph's	HAM/HAM	SK	5-18-16-W2	72 I/8	50°30'	104°11'
St. Joseph's	UNP/LNO	NF		1 M/7	47°23'	54°46'
St. Josephs Colony - see-voir - St. Joseph's	UNP/LNO	SK		72 I/8	50°30'	104°11'
St. Joseph's Cove	UNP/LNO	NF		1 M/13	47°55'	55°48'
St. Josephs Cove	UNP/LNO	NF		12 H/5	49°29'	57°56'
St. Joseph's Cove-St. Veronica's	UNP/LNO	NF		1 M/13	47°56'	55°47'
St. Joseph's Industrial School Provincial Historic Site (Undeveloped)	PARK/PARC	AB	SE27-21-28-W4	82 I/13	50°48'	113°47'
Saint-Jovite	CITY/VIL1	QC	Les Laurentides	31 J/2	46°07'	74°36'
Saint-Jovite	VILG/VILG	QC	Les Laurentides	31 J/2	46°07'	74°36'
Saint-Jovite-Station	UNP/LNO	QC	Les Laurentides	31 J/2	46°08'	74°35'
Saint-Jude	VILG/VILG	QC	Les Maskoutains	31 H/15	45°46'	72°59'
St. Judes	UNP/LNO	NF		12 H/3	49°09'	57°28'
Saint-Jules	VILG/VILG	QC	Bonaventure	22 A/5	48°15'	65°55'
Saint-Jules	VILG/VILG	QC	Robert-Cliche	21 L/2	46°13'	70°57'
Saint-Jules-de-Beauce	UNP/LNO	QC	Robert-Cliche	21 L/2	46°13'	70°57'
Saint-Jules-de-Cascapédia	UNP/LNO	QC	Bonaventure	22 A/5	48°15'	65°55'
Saint-Julien	VILG/VILG	QC	L'Amiante	21 E/13	46°00'	71°32'
St-Julien	UNP/LNO	SK	21-43-27-W2	73 A/12	52°43'	105°52'
St. Julien Island	ISL/ÎLE	NF		2 M/4	51°06'	55°43'
St. Julien's	UNP/LNO	NF		2 M/4	51°06'	55°45'
Saint-Just-de-Bretenières	VILG/VILG	QC	Montmagny	21 L/9	46°34'	70°06'
Saint-Juste-du-Lac	VILG/VILG	QC	Témiscouata	21 N/10	47°39'	68°45'
Saint-Justin	VILG/VILG	QC	Maskinongé	31 I/6	46°15'	73°05'
St. Kyran's	UNP/LNO	NF		1 M/8	47°28'	54°27'
St. Labre	UNP/LNO	MB	27,28-4-11-E	62 H/8	49°20'	96°02'
St. Labre Creek	RIV/CDE	MB	22-6-12-E	52 E/12	49°30'	95°54'
Saint-Lambert	CITY/VIL1	QC	Champlain	31 H/12	45°30'	73°30'
Saint-Lambert	VILG/VILG	QC	Abitibi-Ouest	32 D/14	48°57'	79°28'
Saint-Lambert-de-Lauzon	VILG/VILG	QC	Les Chutes-de-la-Chaudière	21 L/11	46°35'	71°12'
Saint-Lambert-de-Lévis	UNP/LNO	QC	Les Chutes-de-la-Chaudière	21 L/11	46°35'	71°13'
Saint-Laurent	CITY/VIL1	QC	Communauté urbaine de Montréal	31 H/12	45°30'	73°40'
Saint-Laurent	VILG/VILG	QC	L'Île-d'Orléans	21 L/14	46°52'	71°01'
St. Laurent	MUN2/AZM2	MB		62 I/5	50°20'	97°50'
Saint-Laurent	UNP/LNO	NB	Gloucester	21 P/12	47°44'	65°47'
St. Laurent	UNP/LNO	MB	16-4-W	62 I/5	50°25'	97°56'
St. Laurent	GEOG/GÉOG	MB		62 I/5	50°23'	97°56'
Saint-Laurent, Baie	BAY/BAIE	QC	Minganie	12 L/6	50°16'	63°06'
Saint-Laurent, Cape	CAPE/CAP	NB	Westmorland	11 L/4	46°04'	63°54'
Saint-Laurent-du-Fleuve	UNP/LNO	QC	Lajemmerais	31 H/14	45°56'	73°12'
Saint-Laurent, Fleuve - also-aussi - **St. Lawrence River**	RIV/CDE	QC/ON		22 H/10	49°40'	64°30'
Saint-Laurent, Golfe du - also-aussi - **St. Lawrence, Gulf of**	BAY/BAIE	NB/NF/NS/QC/PE		12 C/9	48°41'	60°01'
St-Laurent-Grandin	UNP/LNO	SK	16-44-1-W3	73 B/16	52°50'	106°05'
St. Lawrence	TOWN/VIL2	NF		1 L/14	46°55'	55°24'
St. Lawrence	UNP/LNO	PE	Prince	21 I/16	46°51'	64°13'
St. Lawrence, Bay	BAY/BAIE	NS	Victoria	11 N/1	47°01'	60°29'
St. Lawrence, Cape	CAPE/CAP	NS	Inverness	11 N/2	47°03'	60°36'

NAME NOM	ENTITY ENTITÉ	LOC 1 LIEU 1	LOC 2 LIEU 2	MAP CARTE	POSITION LAT	LONG
St. Lawrence, Gulf of - also-aussi - **Saint-Laurent, Golfe du**	BAY/BAIE	NB/NF/NS/QC/PE		12 C/9	48°41′	60°01′
St. Lawrence Islands National Park - also-aussi - Îles-du-Saint-Laurent, Parc national des	PARK/PARC	ON	Leeds	31 B/5	44°27′	75°52′
St. Lawrence River - see-voir - Little St. Lawrence River	RIV/CDE	NF		1 L/14	46°56′	55°22′
St. Lawrence River - also-aussi - **Saint-Laurent, Fleuve**	RIV/CDE	QC/ON		22 H/10	49°40′	64°30′
St. Lawrence Woods	UNP/LNO	ON	Frontenac	31 C/1	44°14′	76°25′
Saint-Lazare	VILG/VILG	QC	Vaudreuil-Soulanges	31 G/8	45°24′	74°08′
St-Lazare	VILG/VILG	MB	17-17-28-W	62 K/6	50°27′	101°18′
Saint-Lazare	UNP/LNO	NB	Kent	21 I/7	46°25′	64°54′
Saint-Lazare-de-Bellechasse	VILG/VILG	QC	Bellechasse	21 L/10	46°39′	70°48′
Saint-Léandre	VILG/VILG	QC	Matane	22 B/12	48°44′	67°36′
Saint-Léolin	VILG/VILG	NB	Gloucester	21 P/14	47°46′	65°10′
Saint-Léon	UNP/LNO	QC	Rimouski-Neigette	22 C/7	48°22′	68°31′
Saint-Léon	UNP/LNO	QC	La Côte-de-Beaupré	21 M/2	47°10′	70°48′
Saint-Léon	UNP/LNO	QC	Maskinongé	31 I/7	46°19′	72°56′
St. Leon	UNP/LNO	MB	3-5-9-W	62 G/7	49°22′	98°35′
Saint-Léonard	CITY/VIL1	QC	Communauté urbaine de Montréal	31 H/12	45°35′	73°35′
Saint-Léonard - see-voir - St. Leonard	TOWN/VIL2	NB		21 O/4	47°10′	67°56′
St. Leonard	TOWN/VIL2	NB	Madawaska	21 O/4	47°10′	67°56′
Saint-Léonard	GEOG/GÉOG	NB	Madawaska	21 O/5	47°15′	67°52′
Saint-Léonard-d'Aston	VILG/VILG	QC	Nicolet-Yamaska	31 I/1	46°06′	72°22′
Saint-Léonard-de-Portneuf	VILG/VILG	QC	Portneuf	21 L/13	46°53′	71°55′
Saint-Léonard-Parent	UNP/LNO	NB	Madawaska	21 O/4	47°09′	67°54′
St. Leonards	UNP/LNO	NF		1 M/8	47°28′	54°27′
Saint-Léon-de-Standon	VILG/VILG	QC	Bellechasse	21 L/7	46°29′	70°37′
Saint-Léon-le-Grand	VILG/VILG	QC	La Matapédia	22 B/5	48°23′	67°30′
Saint-Léon-le-Grand	VILG/VILG	QC	Maskinongé	31 I/7	46°19′	72°56′
St. Lewis	VILG/VILG	NF		3 D/5	52°22′	55°41′
St. Lewis, Cape	CAPE/CAP	NF		3 D/5	52°22′	55°38′
St. Lewis Inlet	BAY/BAIE	NF		3 D/5	52°20′	55°49′
St. Lewis River	RIV/CDE	NF		13 A/8	52°27′	56°14′
St. Lewis Sound	CHAN/CHEN	NF		3 D/5	52°20′	55°40′
Saint-Liboire	VILG/VILG	QC	Les Maskoutains	31 H/10	45°39′	72°46′
Saint-Liguori	VILG/VILG	QC	Montcalm	31 I/4	46°01′	73°34′
Saint-Lin	VILG/VILG	QC	Montcalm	31 H/13	45°51′	73°46′
St. Lina	UNP/LNO	AB	20-61-10-W4	73 L/6	54°18′	111°27′
St. Louis	VILG/VILG	PE	Prince	21 I/16	46°53′	64°09′
Saint-Louis	VILG/VILG	QC	Les Maskoutains	31 H/15	45°51′	72°59′
St. Louis	VILG/VILG	SK	12-45-27-W2	73 A/13	52°55′	105°49′
Saint-Louis	GEOG/GÉOG	NB	Kent	21 I/11	46°40′	65°10′
Saint-Louis, Baie de	BAY/BAIE	NB	Kent	21 I/15	46°45′	64°53′
Saint-Louis-de-Bagot	UNP/LNO	QC	Le Fjord-du-Saguenay	22 D/7	48°21′	71°00′
Saint-Louis-de-Blandford	VILG/VILG	QC	Arthabaska	31 I/8	46°15′	72°00′
Saint-Louis-de-Bonsecours	UNP/LNO	QC	Les Maskoutains	31 H/15	45°51′	72°59′
Saint-Louis-de-Champlain	UNP/LNO	QC	Francheville	31 I/7	46°25′	72°36′
Saint-Louis-de-France	CITY/VIL1	QC	Francheville	31 I/7	46°25′	72°36′
Saint-Louis-de-Gonzague	VILG/VILG	QC	Les Etchemins	21 L/8	46°16′	70°20′
Saint-Louis-de-Gonzague	VILG/VILG	QC	Beauharnois-Salaberry	31 H/4	45°12′	73°59′
Saint-Louis-de-Gonzague-du-Cap-Tourmente	VILG/VILG	QC	La Côte-de-Beaupré	21 M/2	47°04′	70°50′
Saint-Louis de Kent	VILG/VILG	NB	Kent	21 I/10	46°44′	64°58′
Saint-Louis-de-Kent - see-voir - Saint-Louis de Kent	VILG/VILG	NB		21 I/10	46°44′	64°58′
Saint-Louis-de-Masham	UNP/LNO	QC	Les Collines-de-l'Outaouais	31 F/9	45°40′	76°08′
Saint-Louis-de-Terrebonne	UNP/LNO	QC	Les Moulins	31 H/12	45°42′	73°47′
Saint-Louis-du-Ha! Ha!	VILG/VILG	QC	Témiscouata	21 N/10	47°40′	68°59′
Saint-Louis, Île	ISL/ÎLE	QC	Le Fjord-du-Saguenay	22 D/1	48°15′	70°01′
Saint-Louis, Lac	LAKE/LAC	QC	Roussillon	31 H/5	45°24′	73°48′
Saint-Louis Mission National Historic Site - also-aussi - Mission-Saint-Louis, Lieu historique national de la	PARK/PARC	ON	Simcoe	31 D/12	44°43′	79°46′
St. Louis No. 431	MUN2/AZM2	SK		73 A/13	52°50′	105°45′
Saint-Luc	CITY/VIL1	QC	Le Haut-Richelieu	31 H/6	45°22′	73°18′
Saint-Luc	VILG/VILG	QC	Matane	22 B/14	48°48′	67°28′
Saint-Luc	VILG/VILG	QC	Les Etchemins	21 L/9	46°31′	70°29′
Saint-Luc	UNP/LNO	NB	Kent	21 I/11	46°44′	65°11′
Saint-Luc-de-Matane	UNP/LNO	QC	Matane	22 B/14	48°48′	67°28′
Saint-Luc-de-Vincennes	VILG/VILG	QC	Francheville	31 I/8	46°30′	72°25′
Saint-Lucien	VILG/VILG	QC	Drummond	31 H/16	45°52′	72°16′
Saint-Ludger	TOWN/VIL2	QC	Le Granit	21 E/10	45°45′	70°42′
Saint-Ludger-de-Milot	VILG/VILG	QC	Lac-Saint-Jean-Est	22 D/13	48°54′	71°49′
St. Luke	UNP/LNO	SK	16-17-2-W2	62 L/8	50°26′	102°14′
St. Lunaire	UNP/LNO	NF		2 M/11	51°30′	55°29′
St. Lunaire Bay	BAY/BAIE	NF		2 M/5	51°30′	55°30′
St. Lunaire-Griquet	TOWN/VIL2	NF		2 M/11	51°31′	55°28′
St. Lupicin	UNP/LNO	MB	9-6-8-W	62 G/8	49°28′	98°29′
Saint-Magloire	UNP/LNO	QC	Les Etchemins	21 L/9	46°35′	70°17′

NAME NOM	ENTITY ENTITÉ	LOC 1 LIEU 1	LOC 2 LIEU 2	MAP CARTE	POSITION LAT	LONG
Saint-Magloire-de-Bellechasse	VILG/VILG	QC	Les Etchemins	21 L/9	46°35′	70°17′
Saint-Majorique	UNP/LNO	QC	Drummond	31 H/15	45°56′	72°35′
Saint-Majorique-de-Grantham	VILG/VILG	QC	Drummond	31 H/15	45°56′	72°35′
Saint-Malachie	VILG/VILG	QC	Bellechasse	21 L/10	46°32′	70°46′
Saint-Malachie-d'Ormstown	VILG/VILG	QC	Le Haut-Saint-Laurent	31 H/4	45°07′	73°59′
Saint-Malachie-Station	UNP/LNO	QC	Bellechasse	21 L/10	46°32′	70°47′
Saint-Malo	VILG/VILG	QC	Le Haut-Saint-François	21 E/4	45°12′	71°30′
St. Malo	UNP/LNO	MB		62 H/7	49°19′	96°57′
St. Malo Settlement	GEOG/GÉOG	MB	4,5-4E	62 H/7	49°20′	96°57′
Saint-Marc-de-Figuery	VILG/VILG	QC	Abitibi	32 D/8	48°28′	78°03′
Saint-Marc-de-Latour	UNP/LNO	QC	La Haute-Côte-Nord	22 C/15	48°49′	68°58′
Saint-Marc-des-Carrières	TOWN/VIL2	QC	Portneuf	31 I/9	46°41′	72°03′
Saint-Marc-du-Lac-Long	VILG/VILG	QC	Témiscouata	21 N/7	47°23′	68°54′
Saint-Marcel	VILG/VILG	QC	L'Islet	21 L/16	46°54′	70°04′
Saint-Marcel	UNP/LNO	NB	Kent	21 I/7	46°19′	64°35′
Saint-Marcel-de-Richelieu	VILG/VILG	QC	Les Maskoutains	31 H/15	45°52′	72°54′
Saint-Marcellin	VILG/VILG	QC	Rimouski-Neigette	22 C/8	48°20′	68°18′
Saint-Marc-sur-Richelieu	VILG/VILG	QC	La Vallée-du-Richelieu	31 H/11	45°41′	73°12′
St. Margaret Bay	BAY/BAIE	NF		12 P/3	51°01′	57°00′
St. Margarets	UNP/LNO	PE	Kings	11 L/8	46°27′	62°23′
St. Margarets	UNP/LNO	NB	Northumberland	21 I/14	46°54′	65°12′
St. Margarets Bay	BAY/BAIE	NS	Halifax	21 A/9	44°35′	64°00′
St. Margaret Village	UNP/LNO	NS	Victoria	11 K/16	46°59′	60°29′
St. Marks	UNP/LNO	MB	22-14-5-W	62 J/1	50°12′	98°03′
Saint-Martin	VILG/VILG	QC	Beauce-Sartigan	21 E/15	45°58′	70°39′
St. Martin	UNP/LNO	NS	Digby	21 B/1	44°10′	66°08′
St. Martin	UNP/LNO	MB	4-32-9-W	62 O/10	51°43′	98°41′
Saint-Martin-de-Kent	UNP/LNO	NB	Kent	21 I/7	46°21′	64°40′
Saint-Martin-de-Restigouche	UNP/LNO	NB	Restigouche	21 O/11	47°34′	67°20′
St. Martin Junction	UNP/LNO	MB	31,32-9,10-W	62 O/10	51°43′	98°44′
St. Martin, Lake	LAKE/LAC	MB		62 O/9	51°37′	98°29′
St. Martins	VILG/VILG	NB	Saint John	21 H/5	45°21′	65°32′
Saint Martins	GEOG/GÉOG	NB	Saint John	21 H/6	45°26′	65°25′
St. Mary	UNP/LNO	NB	Gloucester	21 P/12	47°36′	65°38′
Saint Mary	GEOG/GÉOG	NB	Kent	21 I/7	46°23′	64°53′
St. Mary Reservoir	LAKE/LAC	AB	4-24,25-W4	82 H/6	49°20′	113°11′
St. Mary River	RIV/CDE	AB	8-22-W4	82 H/10	49°37′	112°52′
St. Mary River	RIV/CDE	BC	Kootenay	82 G/12	49°37′	115°39′
St. Marys	TOWN/VIL2	ON	Perth	40 P/6	43°15′	81°08′
St. Mary's	VILG/VILG	NF		1 K/13	46°55′	53°35′
St. Mary's	MUN1/AZM1	NS	Guysborough	11 E/1	45°12′	62°11′
St. Marys	UNP/LNO	NS	Richmond	11 F/11	45°50′	61°06′
Saint Marys	GEOG/GÉOG	NB	York	21 J/1	46°10′	66°25′
Saint Mary's 1A	IR/RI	BC	Kootenay	82 G/12	49°35′	115°45′
St. Mary's 24	IR/RI	NB	York	21 G/15	45°58′	66°38′
St. Mary's Bay	BAY/BAIE	NF		1 K/12	46°50′	53°45′
St. Marys Bay	BAY/BAIE	PE	Kings	11 L/1	46°07′	62°29′
St. Marys Bay	BAY/BAIE	NS	Digby	21 B/8	44°25′	66°10′
St. Mary's, Cape	CAPE/CAP	NF		1 L/16	46°49′	54°12′
St. Marys, Cape	CAPE/CAP	NS	Guysborough	11 F/4	45°03′	61°52′
St. Marys, Cape	CAPE/CAP	NS	Digby	21 B/1	44°05′	66°13′
St. Mary's Harbour	BAY/BAIE	NF		1 K/13	46°56′	53°35′
St. Marys Junction	UNP/LNO	ON	Perth	40 P/6	43°17′	81°07′
St. Marys River	UNP/LNO	NS	Guysborough	11 F/4	45°05′	61°56′
St. Marys River	RIV/CDE	NS	Guysborough	11 F/4	45°02′	61°53′
St. Marys River	RIV/CDE	ON	Algoma	41 J/5	46°15′	83°46′
St. Marys Road	UNP/LNO	PE	Kings	11 L/2	46°05′	62°37′
Saint-Mathias-de-Bonneterre	UNP/LNO	QC	Le Haut-Saint-François	21 E/6	45°18′	71°24′
Saint-Mathias-sur-Richelieu	VILG/VILG	QC	Rouville	31 H/6	45°28′	73°16′
Saint-Mathieu	VILG/VILG	QC	Le Centre-de-la-Mauricie	31 I/10	46°34′	72°55′
Saint-Mathieu	VILG/VILG	QC	Roussillon	31 H/5	45°19′	73°31′
Saint-Mathieu	UNP/LNO	QC	Les Basques	22 C/2	48°11′	68°59′
Saint-Mathieu-de-Beloeil	VILG/VILG	QC	La Vallée-du-Richelieu	31 H/11	45°34′	73°12′
Saint-Mathieu-de-Rioux	VILG/VILG	QC	Les Basques	22 C/2	48°11′	68°59′
Saint-Mathieu-d'Harricana	VILG/VILG	QC	Abitibi	32 D/8	48°28′	78°08′
Saint-Mathieu, Lac	LAKE/LAC	QC	Les Basques	22 C/3	48°09′	69°01′
Saint-Maure	UNP/LNO	NB	Restigouche	21 O/16	47°57′	66°28′
Saint-Maurice	VILG/VILG	QC	Francheville	31 I/7	46°28′	72°32′
Saint-Maurice	UNP/LNO	NB	Kent	21 I/7	46°29′	64°48′
Saint-Maurice-de-Dalquier	UNP/LNO	QC	Abitibi	32 C/12	48°39′	77°59′
Saint-Maurice-de-l'Échouerie	UNP/LNO	QC	La Côte-de-Gaspé	22 H/1	49°03′	64°29′
Saint-Maurice, Réserve faunique du	PARK/PARC	QC	Mékinac	31 P/3	47°05′	73°15′
Saint-Maurice, Rivière	RIV/CDE	QC	Francheville	31 I/7	46°21′	72°32′
Saint-Maxime-du-Mont-Louis	VILG/VILG	QC	Denis-Riverin	22 H/4	49°14′	65°44′
Saint-Médard	VILG/VILG	QC	Les Basques	22 C/2	48°02′	68°54′

NAME NOM	ENTITY ENTITÉ	LOC 1 LIEU 1	LOC 2 LIEU 2	MAP CARTE	POSITION LAT	POSITION LONG
Saint-Méthode	VILG/VILG	QC	Le Domaine-du-Roy	32 A/9	48°44'	72°25'
Saint-Méthode-de-Frontenac	VILG/VILG	QC	L'Amiante	21 L/3	46°03'	71°05'
St. Michael	UNP/LNO	AB	9-56-18-W4	83 H/15	53°50'	112°38'
St. Michael, Lake	LAKE/LAC	MB	33,34-1-W	62 P/13	51°54'	97°30'
St. Michaels	UNP/LNO	NF		1 N/2	47°11'	52°51'
St. Michaels Bay	BAY/BAIE	NF		3 D/12	52°43'	55°54'
Saint-Michel	VILG/VILG	QC	Les Jardins-de-Napierville	31 H/4	45°14'	73°34'
Saint-Michel-de-Bellechasse	VILG/VILG	QC	Bellechasse	21 L/15	46°52'	70°55'
Saint-Michel-de-Rougemont	VILG/VILG	QC	Rouville	31 H/6	45°26'	73°04'
Saint-Michel-des-Saints	VILG/VILG	QC	Matawinie	31 I/12	46°41'	73°55'
Saint-Michel-de-Wentworth	UNP/LNO	QC	Les Pays-d'en-Haut	31 G/16	45°46'	74°29'
Saint-Michel-du-Squatec	VILG/VILG	QC	Témiscouata	21 N/15	47°53'	68°43'
Saint-Michel-d'Yamaska	VILG/VILG	QC	Le Bas-Richelieu	31 I/2	46°00'	72°55'
Saint-Michel, Lac	LAKE/LAC	QC	La Côte-de-Beaupré	21 M/7	47°18'	70°54'
Saint-Modeste	VILG/VILG	QC	Rivière-du-Loup	21 N/14	47°50'	69°24'
Saint-Modeste-Station	UNP/LNO	QC	Rivière-du-Loup	21 N/14	47°48'	69°24'
Saint-Moïse	VILG/VILG	QC	La Matapédia	22 B/12	48°31'	67°51'
Saint-Narcisse	VILG/VILG	QC	Francheville	31 I/9	46°34'	72°28'
Saint-Narcisse	UNP/LNO	QC	Lotbinière	21 L/6	46°29'	71°14'
Saint-Narcisse-de-Beaurivage	VILG/VILG	QC	Lotbinière	21 L/6	46°29'	71°14'
Saint-Narcisse-de-Rimouski	VILG/VILG	QC	Rimouski-Neigette	22 C/8	48°17'	68°26'
Saint-Nazaire	VILG/VILG	QC	Lac-Saint-Jean-Est	22 D/12	48°35'	71°32'
Saint-Nazaire-d'Acton	VILG/VILG	QC	Acton	31 H/10	45°44'	72°37'
Saint-Nazaire-de-Berry	UNP/LNO	QC	Abitibi	32 D/9	48°43'	78°15'
Saint-Nazaire-de-Dorchester	VILG/VILG	QC	Bellechasse	21 L/10	46°33'	70°40'
Saint-Nérée	VILG/VILG	QC	Bellechasse	21 L/10	46°44'	70°43'
Saint-Nérée-Station	UNP/LNO	QC	Bellechasse	21 L/10	46°41'	70°40'
Saint-Nicéphore	VILG/VILG	QC	Drummond	31 H/16	45°50'	72°25'
St. Nicholas	VILG/VILG	PE	Prince	11 L/5	46°25'	63°57'
St. Nicholas	UNP/LNO	PE	Prince	11 L/5	46°26'	63°57'
Saint-Nicolas	UNP/LNO	QC	La Côte-de-Beaupré	21 M/2	47°09'	70°51'
Saint-Nicolas	UNP/LNO	QC	Les Chutes-de-la-Chaudière	21 L/11	46°42'	71°24'
Saint-Nicolas-Est	UNP/LNO	QC	La Rivière-du-Nord	31 G/16	45°45'	74°05'
Saint-Nicolas-Ouest	UNP/LNO	QC	La Rivière-du-Nord	31 G/16	45°45'	74°07'
Saint-Nicolas, Pointe	CAPE/CAP	QC	Manicouagan	22 G/5	49°18'	67°46'
Saint Ninian	UNP/LNO	NS	Inverness	11 F/14	45°57'	61°26'
Saint-Noël	TOWN/VIL2	QC	La Matapédia	22 B/12	48°35'	67°50'
St. Nora Lake	LAKE/LAC	ON	Haliburton	31 E/2	45°09'	78°50'
Saint-Norbert	VILG/VILG	QC	D'Autray	31 I/3	46°10'	73°19'
Saint-Norbert	UNP/LNO	NB	Kent	21 I/7	46°28'	64°58'
St. Norbert	UNP/LNO	MB		62 H/14	49°46'	97°09'
St. Norbert	GEOG/GÉOG	MB		62 H/11	49°44'	97°08'
Saint-Norbert-d'Arthabaska	VILG/VILG	QC	Arthabaska	21 L/4	46°06'	71°51'
Saint-Norbert-de-Mont-Brun	VILG/VILG	QC	Rouyn-Noranda	32 D/7	48°24'	78°40'
Saint-Octave-de-l'Avenir	UNP/LNO	QC	Denis-Riverin	22 B/15	49°00'	66°33'
Saint-Octave-de-Métis	VILG/VILG	QC	La Mitis	22 C/9	48°36'	68°05'
Saint-Odilon	UNP/LNO	QC	Robert-Cliche	21 L/7	46°22'	70°41'
Saint-Odilon-de-Cranbourne	VILG/VILG	QC	Robert-Cliche	21 L/7	46°22'	70°41'
St. Ola	UNP/LNO	ON	Hastings	31 C/13	44°51'	77°36'
Saint-Olivier	UNP/LNO	NB	Kent	21 I/15	46°45'	64°56'
Saint-Omer	VILG/VILG	QC	Avignon	22 B/1	48°07'	66°13'
Saint-Omer	VILG/VILG	QC	L'Islet	21 N/4	47°03'	69°44'
Saint-Onésime	UNP/LNO	QC	Kamouraska	21 N/5	47°19'	69°59'
Saint-Onésime-d'Ixworth	VILG/VILG	QC	Kamouraska	21 N/5	47°18'	69°56'
St-Onge	UNP/LNO	ON	Russell	31 G/6	45°16'	75°17'
Saint-Onge, Lac	LAKE/LAC	QC	La Haute-Côte-Nord	22 C/6	48°25'	69°25'
St. Ouens	UNP/LNO	MB	33-12-8-E	62 I/1	50°03'	96°27'
Saint-Ours	CITY/VIL1	QC	Le Bas-Richelieu	31 H/14	45°53'	73°09'
Saint-Ours Canal - also-aussi - Saint-Ours, Canal de	PARK/PARC	QC	Le Bas-Richelieu	31 H/14	45°52'	73°09'
Saint-Ours, Canal de - also-aussi - Saint-Ours Canal	PARK/PARC	QC	Le Bas-Richelieu	31 H/14	45°52'	73°09'
Saint-Pacôme	VILG/VILG	QC	Kamouraska	21 N/5	47°24'	69°57'
Saint-Pacôme-Station	UNP/LNO	QC	Kamouraska	21 N/5	47°25'	69°58'
Saint-Pamphile	CITY/VIL1	QC	L'Islet	21 K/13	46°58'	69°47'
Saint-Pancrace, Anse	BAY/BAIE	QC	Manicouagan	22 F/8	49°17'	68°03'
Saint-Pancrace, Pointe	CAPE/CAP	QC	Manicouagan	22 F/8	49°15'	68°05'
Saint-Pascal	CITY/VIL1	QC	Kamouraska	21 N/12	47°32'	69°49'
Saint-Pascal	VILG/VILG	QC	Kamouraska	21 N/12	47°32'	69°49'
St-Pascal	UNP/LNO	ON	Russell	31 G/6	45°30'	75°09'
Saint-Patrice	UNP/LNO	QC	Rivière-du-Loup	21 N/13	47°49'	69°34'
Saint-Patrice-de-Beaurivage	VILG/VILG	QC	Lotbinière	21 L/6	46°25'	71°14'
Saint-Patrice-de-la-Rivière-du-Loup	VILG/VILG	QC	Rivière-du-Loup	21 N/13	47°49'	69°34'
Saint-Patrice-de-Sherrington	VILG/VILG	QC	Les Jardins-de-Napierville	31 H/4	45°10'	73°31'
Saint-Patrice, Lac	LAKE/LAC	QC	Pontiac	31 K/6	46°22'	77°20'
Saint Patrick	GEOG/GÉOG	NB	Charlotte	21 G/3	45°12'	67°00'
St. Patrick Bay	BAY/BAIE	NT	Franklin	120 C	81°47'	64°09'

NAME NOM	ENTITY ENTITÉ	LOC 1 LIEU 1	LOC 2 LIEU 2	MAP CARTE	POSITION LAT	POSITION LONG
St. Patrick Road	UNP/LNO	PE	Kings	11 L/7	46°20′	62°47′
St. Patricks	UNP/LNO	NF		2 E/12	49°34′	55°59′
St. Patricks	UNP/LNO	PE	Queens	11 L/6	46°24′	63°23′
St. Patricks Channel	UNP/LNO	NS	Victoria	11 K/2	46°03′	60°55′
St. Patricks Channel	CHAN/CHEN	NS	Victoria	11 K/2	46°03′	60°51′
St. Paul	TOWN/VIL2	AB	8-58-9-W4	73 E/14	53°59′	111°17′
Saint-Paul	VILG/VILG	QC	Joliette	31 H/14	45°59′	73°27′
Saint-Paul	UNP/LNO	NB	Kent	21 I/6	46°20′	65°00′
Saint-Paul	UNP/LNO	QC	Rouville	31 H/7	45°26′	72°53′
Saint-Paul	GEOG/GÉOG	NB	Kent	21 I/6	46°22′	65°00′
Saint-Paul, Baie	BAY/BAIE	QC	Charlevoix	21 M/8	47°25′	70°29′
Saint-Paul-d'Abbotsford	VILG/VILG	QC	Rouville	31 H/7	45°26′	72°53′
Saint-Paul-de-Châteauguay	VILG/VILG	QC	Beauharnois-Salaberry	31 H/5	45°16′	73°46′
Saint-Paul-de-la-Croix	VILG/VILG	QC	Rivière-du-Loup	21 N/14	47°57′	69°12′
Saint-Paul-de-l'Île-aux-Noix	VILG/VILG	QC	Le Haut-Richelieu	31 H/3	45°08′	73°17′
Saint-Paul-de-Montminy	VILG/VILG	QC	Montmagny	21 L/9	46°44′	70°22′
Saint-Paul-d'Industrie	UNP/LNO	QC	Joliette	31 H/14	45°59′	73°27′
Saint-Paul-du-Nord	VILG/VILG	QC	La Haute-Côte-Nord	22 C/11	48°34′	69°14′
Saint-Paul-Est	UNP/LNO	QC	Montmagny	21 L/9	46°45′	70°20′
Saint-Paulin	VILG/VILG	QC	Maskinongé	31 I/6	46°25′	73°02′
Saint-Paulin-Dalibaire	UNP/LNO	QC	Matane	22 B/15	48°56′	66°50′
St. Paul Island	ISL/ÎLE	NS	Victoria	11 N/1	47°12′	60°09′
St. Paul Junction	UNP/LNO	AB	31-53-23-W4	83 H/11	53°37′	113°23′
Saint-Paul, Lac	LAKE/LAC	QC	Bécancour	31 I/8	46°18′	72°29′
St. Paul No. 19, County of	MUN1/AZM1	AB	47-10-W4	73 E/14	53°56′	111°19′
St. Paul River - also-aussi - Saint-Paul, Rivière	RIV/CDE	NF		12 P/5	51°27′	57°42′
Saint-Paul, Rivière - also-aussi - St. Paul River	RIV/CDE	QC	Côte-Nord-du-Golfe-Saint-Laurent	12 P/5	51°27′	57°42′
St. Pauls	VILG/VILG	NF		12 H/13	49°52′	57°49′
St. Pauls	UNP/LNO	NS	Pictou	11 E/7	45°25′	62°35′
St. Pauls	UNP/LNO	ON	Simcoe	31 D/5	44°21′	79°38′
St. Pauls	GEOG/GÉOG	MB		62 H/14	50°00′	97°03′
St. Pauls Bay	BAY/BAIE	NF		12 H/13	49°52′	57°48′
St. Pauls Inlet	BAY/BAIE	NF		12 H/13	49°50′	57°45′
St. Pauls Station	UNP/LNO	ON	Perth	40 P/6	43°19′	81°03′
St. Peter and St. Paul	UNP/LNO	PE	Prince	21 I/16	46°55′	64°04′
St. Peter Bay	BAY/BAIE	NF		3 D/4	52°05′	55°47′
St. Peter No. 369	MUN2/AZM2	SK		73 A/2	52°15′	104°50′
St. Peter's	VILG/VILG	NS	Richmond	11 F/10	45°40′	60°52′
St. Peters	GEOG/GÉOG	MB		62 I/2	50°12′	96°50′
St. Peters Bay	VILG/VILG	PE	Kings	11 L/7	46°25′	62°35′
St. Peters Bay	BAY/BAIE	PE	Kings	11 L/7	46°26′	62°40′
St. Peters Bay	BAY/BAIE	NS	Richmond	11 F/10	45°38′	60°53′
St. Peters Canal - also-aussi - St. Peters, Canal de	PARK/PARC	NS		11 F/10	45°39′	60°52′
St. Peters, Canal de - also-aussi - St. Peters Canal	PARK/PARC	NS		11 F/10	45°39′	60°52′
St. Peters Colony	UNP/LNO	SK	7-16-16-W2	72 I/8	50°20′	104°11′
St. Peters Fishing Station 1A	IR/RI	MB		62 I/7	50°24′	96°54′
St. Peters Harbour	UNP/LNO	PE	Kings	11 L/7	46°26′	62°45′
St. Peters Inlet	BAY/BAIE	NS	Richmond	11 F/10	45°42′	60°48′
St. Peters Island	ISL/ÎLE	PE	Queens	11 L/3	46°07′	63°11′
St. Peters Island	ISL/ÎLE	NS	Richmond	11 F/10	45°36′	60°48′
St. Peters Junction	UNP/LNO	NS	Richmond	11 F/11	45°36′	61°18′
St. Peters Pond	LAKE/LAC	NF		3 D/4	52°08′	55°54′
Saint-Philémon	VILG/VILG	QC	Bellechasse	21 L/9	46°41′	70°27′
Saint-Philémon-Nord	UNP/LNO	QC	Bellechasse	21 L/9	46°42′	70°30′
Saint-Philémon-Sud	UNP/LNO	QC	Bellechasse	21 L/9	46°39′	70°24′
Saint-Philibert	VILG/VILG	QC	Beauce-Sartigan	21 L/2	46°08′	70°33′
St. Philip	UNP/LNO	PE	Prince	21 I/9	46°30′	64°04′
Saint-Philippe	VILG/VILG	QC	Roussillon	31 H/6	45°21′	73°28′
Saint-Philippe	UNP/LNO	NB	Westmorland	21 I/2	46°13′	64°42′
Saint-Philippe	UNP/LNO	QC	Argenteuil	31 G/9	45°38′	74°26′
Saint-Philippe-de-La Prairie	UNP/LNO	QC	Roussillon	31 H/6	45°21′	73°28′
Saint-Philippe-de-Néri	VILG/VILG	QC	Kamouraska	21 N/5	47°28′	69°53′
Saint-Philippe-Est	UNP/LNO	QC	Argenteuil	31 G/9	45°38′	74°23′
St. Philips	UNP/LNO	SK	2-32-32-W	62 N/12	51°43′	101°54′
St. Philips No. 301	MUN2/AZM2	SK		62 N/12	51°45′	101°50′
St. Phillips	UNP/LNO	NF		1 N/10	47°36′	52°53′
St. Phillips	UNP/LNO	ON	York	30 M/12	43°42′	79°32′
Saint-Pie	TOWN/VIL2	QC	Les Maskoutains	31 H/10	45°30′	72°54′
Saint-Pie	VILG/VILG	QC	Les Maskoutains	31 H/10	45°30′	72°54′
Saint-Pie	UNP/LNO	QC	Rimouski-Neigette	22 C/8	48°19′	68°20′
Saint-Pie-de-Guire	VILG/VILG	QC	Drummond	31 I/2	46°00′	72°45′
Saint-Pierre	CITY/VIL1	QC	Communauté urbaine de Montréal	31 H/5	45°27′	73°39′
Saint-Pierre	TOWN/VIL2	QC	Joliette	31 I/3	46°01′	73°28′
Saint-Pierre	VILG/VILG	QC	L'Île-d'Orléans	21 L/14	46°53′	71°04′
Saint-Pierre	UNP/LNO	QC	Le Haut-Saint-Laurent	31 H/4	45°07′	73°54′

NAME NOM	ENTITY ENTITÉ	LOC 1 LIEU 1	LOC 2 LIEU 2	MAP CARTE	POSITION LAT	LONG
Saint-Pierre, Banc de - also-aussi - St. Pierre Bank	SEAU/SMER	—		4001	46°00′	56°15′
St. Pierre Bank - also-aussi - Saint-Pierre, Banc de	SEAU/SMER	—		4001	46°00′	56°15′
Saint-Pierre-Baptiste	VILG/VILG	QC	L'Érable	21 L/4	46°12′	71°37′
St. Pierre Channel - also-aussi - Saint-Pierre, Chenal de	SEAU/SMER	—		15066A	46°30′	56°00′
Saint-Pierre, Chenal de - also-aussi - St. Pierre Channel	SEAU/SMER	—		15066A	46°30′	56°00′
Saint-Pierre-de-Broughton	VILG/VILG	QC	L'Amiante	21 L/3	46°15′	71°12′
Saint-Pierre-de-Kent	UNP/LNO	NB	Kent	21 I/10	46°31′	64°46′
Saint-Pierre-de-Lamy	VILG/VILG	QC	Témiscouata	21 N/14	47°47′	69°00′
Saint-Pierre-de-la-Rivière-du-Sud	VILG/VILG	QC	Montmagny	21 L/15	46°55′	70°38′
Saint-Pierre-de-Véronne-à-Pike-River	VILG/VILG	QC	Brome-Missisquoi	31 H/3	45°07′	73°04′
Saint-Pierre-de-Wakefield	UNP/LNO	QC	Les Collines-de-l'Outaouais	31 G/12	45°42′	75°43′
St-Pierre-Jolys	VILG/VILG	MB		62 H/7	49°26′	96°59′
St. Pierre-Jolys - see-voir - St-Pierre-Jolys	VILG/VILG	MB		62 H/7	49°26′	96°59′
Saint-Pierre, Lac	LAKE/LAC	QC	Manicouagan	22 K/1	50°08′	68°26′
Saint-Pierre, Lac	LAKE/LAC	QC	Maskinongé	31 I/2	46°12′	72°50′
Saint-Pierre-les-Becquets	VILG/VILG	QC	Bécancour	31 I/9	46°30′	72°12′
Saint-Pierre-Montmagny	UNP/LNO	QC	Montmagny	21 L/15	46°55′	70°38′
Saint-Pierre, Pointe	CAPE/CAP	QC	Pabok	22 A/9	48°38′	64°10′
St. Pierre Sud	UNP/LNO	MB	10-5-4-E	62 H/7	49°23′	96°59′
St. Pie X	UNP/LNO	ON	Cochrane	42 G/12	49°41′	83°39′
Saint-Placide	VILG/VILG	QC	Deux-Montagnes	31 G/9	45°32′	74°12′
Saint-Placide-de-Charlevoix	UNP/LNO	QC	Charlevoix	21 M/7	47°25′	70°38′
Saint-Placide-Nord	UNP/LNO	QC	Charlevoix	21 M/7	47°28′	70°35′
Saint-Polycarpe	VILG/VILG	QC	Vaudreuil-Soulanges	31 G/8	45°18′	74°18′
Saint-Pons	UNP/LNO	NB	Gloucester	21 P/7	47°29′	64°58′
Saint-Prime	VILG/VILG	QC	Le Domaine-du-Roy	32 A/9	48°35′	72°20′
Saint-Prosper	VILG/VILG	QC	Les Etchemins	21 L/1	46°13′	70°29′
Saint-Prosper	VILG/VILG	QC	Francheville	31 I/9	46°37′	72°17′
Saint-Prosper-de-Dorchester	UNP/LNO	QC	Les Etchemins	21 L/1	46°13′	70°29′
Saint-Quentin	TOWN/VIL2	NB	Restigouche	21 O/11	47°31′	67°23′
Saint-Quentin	GEOG/GÉOG	NB	Restigouche	21 N/16	47°50′	68°00′
Saint-Raphaël	VILG/VILG	QC	Bellechasse	21 L/15	46°48′	70°45′
St. Raphael	UNP/LNO	PE	Prince	21 I/8	46°26′	64°01′
Saint-Raphaël-d'Albertville	VILG/VILG	QC	La Matapédia	22 B/6	48°19′	67°22′
St. Raphael Lake	LAKE/LAC	ON	Kenora	52 J/11	50°43′	91°07′
Saint-Raphaël-Partie-Sud	VILG/VILG	QC	Nicolet-Yamaska	31 I/1	46°10′	72°14′
St. Raphaels	UNP/LNO	ON	Glengarry	31 G/2	45°13′	74°36′
Saint-Raphaël-sur-Mer	UNP/LNO	NB	Gloucester	21 P/15	47°48′	64°34′
Saint-Raymond	CITY/VIL1	QC	Portneuf	21 L/13	46°54′	71°50′
St. Raymond	UNP/LNO	MB	33-7-7-E	62 H/10	49°37′	96°35′
Saint-Rédempteur	CITY/VIL1	QC	Les Chutes-de-la-Chaudière	21 L/11	46°42′	71°17′
Saint-Rédempteur	UNP/LNO	QC	Vaudreuil-Soulanges	31 G/8	45°26′	74°23′
St. Regis 15 - see-voir - Akwesasne 15	IR/RI	QC		31 G/2	45°03′	74°34′
St. Regis Akwesasne 59 - see-voir - Akwesasne 59	IR/RI	ON		31 G/2	45°03′	74°34′
Saint-Rémi	CITY/VIL1	QC	Les Jardins-de-Napierville	31 H/5	45°16′	73°37′
Saint-Rémi-d'Amherst	UNP/LNO	QC	Les Laurentides	31 J/2	46°01′	74°46′
Saint-Rémi-de-Tingwick	VILG/VILG	QC	Arthabaska	21 E/13	45°52′	71°49′
Saint-René	VILG/VILG	QC	Beauce-Sartigan	21 L/2	46°01′	70°37′
Saint-René-de-Matane	VILG/VILG	QC	Matane	22 B/11	48°42′	67°23′
Saint-Robert	VILG/VILG	QC	Le Bas-Richelieu	31 H/14	45°58′	73°00′
Saint-Robert-Bellarmin	VILG/VILG	QC	Le Granit	21 E/15	45°45′	70°35′
St. Roch	UNP/LNO	PE	Prince	21 I/16	46°55′	64°03′
Saint-Roch	UNP/LNO	QC	Rouyn-Noranda	32 D/2	48°01′	78°56′
St. Roch Basin	CHAN/CHEN	NT	Franklin	57 C	69°15′	95°00′
Saint-Roch-de-l'Achigan	VILG/VILG	QC	Montcalm	31 H/13	45°51′	73°36′
Saint-Roch-de-Mékinac	VILG/VILG	QC	Mékinac	31 I/15	46°49′	72°46′
Saint-Roch-de-Richelieu	VILG/VILG	QC	Le Bas-Richelieu	31 H/14	45°53′	73°10′
Saint-Roch-des-Aulnaies	VILG/VILG	QC	L'Islet	21 M/8	47°19′	70°11′
Saint-Roch-Ouest	VILG/VILG	QC	Montcalm	31 H/13	45°51′	73°39′
Saint-Romain	VILG/VILG	QC	Le Granit	21 E/14	45°47′	71°06′
Saint-Romuald	CITY/VIL1	QC	Les Chutes-de-la-Chaudière	21 L/14	46°45′	71°14′
Saint-Rosaire	VILG/VILG	QC	Arthabaska	31 I/1	46°10′	72°02′
St. Rose	UNP/LNO	NS	Inverness	11 K/6	46°21′	61°11′
Saint-Samuel	VILG/VILG	QC	Arthabaska	31 I/1	46°04′	72°13′
Saint-Samuel-de-Horton	UNP/LNO	QC	Arthabaska	31 I/1	46°04′	72°13′
Saint-Samuel-Station	UNP/LNO	QC	Le Granit	21 E/10	45°43′	70°55′
Saints-Anges	VILG/VILG	QC	La Nouvelle-Beauce	21 L/7	46°25′	70°53′
Saint-Sauveur	VILG/VILG	QC	Les Pays-d'en-Haut	31 G/16	45°52′	74°12′
Saint-Sauveur	UNP/LNO	NB	Gloucester	21 P/11	47°31′	65°17′
Saint-Sauveur-des-Monts	TOWN/VIL2	QC	Les Pays-d'en-Haut	31 G/16	45°54′	74°10′
Saint-Sébastien	VILG/VILG	QC	Le Granit	21 E/15	45°47′	70°58′
Saint-Sébastien	VILG/VILG	QC	Le Haut-Richelieu	31 H/3	45°07′	73°09′
Saint-Sébastien, Morne de	MTN/MNT	QC	Le Granit	21 E/15	45°46′	70°55′
Saint-Sévère	VILG/VILG	QC	Maskinongé	31 I/7	46°21′	72°54′
Saint-Séverin	VILG/VILG	QC	Robert-Cliche	21 L/6	46°19′	71°03′

NAME NOM	ENTITY ENTITÉ	LOC 1 LIEU 1	LOC 2 LIEU 2	MAP CARTE	POSITION LAT	LONG
Saint-Séverin	VILG/VILG	QC	Mékinac	31 I/10	46°40′	72°30′
St. Shores	UNP/LNO	NF		1 K/12	46°40′	53°38′
St. Shores Cove	BAY/BAIE	NF		1 K/12	46°40′	53°38′
St. Shotts	VILG/VILG	NF		1 K/12	46°38′	53°35′
St. Shotts River	RIV/CDE	NF		1 K/12	46°38′	53°36′
Saint-Siméon	TOWN/VIL2	QC	Charlevoix-Est	21 N/13	47°50′	69°53′
Saint-Siméon	VILG/VILG	QC	Bonaventure	22 A/4	48°04′	65°34′
Saint-Siméon	VILG/VILG	QC	Charlevoix-Est	21 N/13	47°50′	69°53′
Saint-Siméon-de-Bonaventure	UNP/LNO	QC	Bonaventure	22 A/4	48°04′	65°34′
Saint-Siméon-Est	UNP/LNO	QC	Bonaventure	22 A/4	48°04′	65°32′
Saint-Siméon-Ouest	UNP/LNO	QC	Bonaventure	22 A/4	48°05′	65°36′
Saint-Simon	VILG/VILG	QC	Les Basques	22 C/3	48°12′	69°03′
Saint-Simon	VILG/VILG	QC	Les Maskoutains	31 H/10	45°44′	72°52′
Saint-Simon	UNP/LNO	QC	Les Maskoutains	31 H/10	45°43′	72°51′
Saint-Simon-de-Bagot	UNP/LNO	QC	Les Maskoutains	31 H/10	45°44′	72°52′
Saint-Simon-de-Rimouski	UNP/LNO	QC	Les Basques	22 C/3	48°12′	69°03′
Saint-Simon-les-Mines	VILG/VILG	QC	Beauce-Sartigan	21 L/2	46°13′	70°41′
Saint-Sixte	VILG/VILG	QC	Papineau	31 G/11	45°42′	75°13′
Saints-Martyrs	UNP/LNO	QC	Arthabaska	21 E/13	45°51′	71°32′
Saints-Martyrs-Canadiens	VILG/VILG	QC	Arthabaska	21 E/13	45°51′	71°32′
Saint-Sosime	UNP/LNO	NB	Kent	21 I/6	46°23′	65°15′
Saints Rest	UNP/LNO	NS	Colchester	11 E/5	45°24′	63°47′
Saint-Stanislas	VILG/VILG	QC	Maria-Chapdelaine	32 H/1	49°00′	72°11′
Saint-Stanislas	VILG/VILG	QC	Francheville	31 I/9	46°37′	72°24′
Saint-Stanislas-de-Kostka	VILG/VILG	QC	Beauharnois-Salaberry	31 G/1	45°11′	74°07′
St. Stephen	TOWN/VIL2	NB	Charlotte	21 G/3	45°12′	67°17′
Saint Stephen	GEOG/GÉOG	NB	Charlotte	21 G/3	45°13′	67°20′
St. Stephens	UNP/LNO	NF		1 K/13	46°46′	53°37′
Saint-Sulpice	VILG/VILG	QC	L'Assomption	31 H/14	45°50′	73°21′
Saint-Sylvère	VILG/VILG	QC	Bécancour	31 I/1	46°14′	72°13′
Saint-Sylvestre	TOWN/VIL2	QC	Lotbinière	21 L/6	46°22′	71°14′
Saint-Sylvestre	VILG/VILG	QC	Lotbinière	21 L/6	46°22′	71°14′
Saint-Télesphore	VILG/VILG	QC	Vaudreuil-Soulanges	31 G/8	45°18′	74°23′
Saint-Télesphore	UNP/LNO	QC	Les Chutes-de-la-Chaudière	21 L/14	46°46′	71°13′
St. Teresa	UNP/LNO	NF		12 B/7	48°22′	58°40′
St. Teresa	UNP/LNO	PE	Kings	11 L/7	46°17′	62°45′
Saint-Tharcisius	VILG/VILG	QC	La Matapédia	22 B/11	48°32′	67°20′
Saint-Théodore	UNP/LNO	QC	Matawinie	31 I/4	46°04′	73°54′
Saint-Théodore-d'Acton	VILG/VILG	QC	Acton	31 H/10	45°41′	72°35′
Saint-Théophile	VILG/VILG	QC	Beauce-Sartigan	21 E/16	45°56′	70°29′
St. Theresa Point	UNP/LNO	MB		53 E/15	53°50′	94°51′
St. Thomas	CITY/VIL1	ON	Elgin	40 I/14	42°47′	81°12′
Saint-Thomas	VILG/VILG	QC	Joliette	31 I/3	46°01′	73°21′
St. Thomas	UNP/LNO	NF		1 N/10	47°34′	52°54′
St. Thomas	UNP/LNO	NB	Carleton	21 J/5	46°19′	67°36′
Saint-Thomas	UNP/LNO	QC	Le Fjord-du-Saguenay	22 D/6	48°24′	71°04′
St. Thomas Bay	BAY/BAIE	BC	Range 4 Coast	93 E/7	53°25′	126°54′
Saint-Thomas-d'Aquin	VILG/VILG	QC	Les Maskoutains	31 H/10	45°39′	72°59′
Saint-Thomas-de-Caxton	UNP/LNO	QC	Francheville	31 I/7	46°22′	72°47′
Saint-Thomas-de-Cherbourg	UNP/LNO	QC	Matane	22 B/15	48°53′	66°58′
Saint-Thomas-de-Cloridorme	UNP/LNO	QC	La Côte-de-Gaspé	22 H/2	49°10′	64°57′
Saint-Thomas-de-Kent	UNP/LNO	NB	Kent	21 I/7	46°27′	64°39′
Saint-Thomas-de-Pierreville	VILG/VILG	QC	Nicolet-Yamaska	31 I/2	46°04′	72°49′
Saint-Thomas-de-Soulanges	UNP/LNO	QC	Vaudreuil-Soulanges	31 G/1	45°15′	74°18′
Saint-Thomas-Didyme	VILG/VILG	QC	Maria-Chapdelaine	32 A/15	48°54′	72°40′
Saint-Thuribe	VILG/VILG	QC	Portneuf	31 I/9	46°43′	72°10′
Saint-Timothée	CITY/VIL1	QC	Beauharnois-Salaberry	31 G/8	45°18′	74°02′
St. Timothy	UNP/LNO	PE	Prince	21 I/8	46°25′	64°04′
Saint-Tite	CITY/VIL1	QC	Mékinac	31 I/10	46°44′	72°34′
Saint-Tite	VILG/VILG	QC	Mékinac	31 I/10	46°44′	72°34′
Saint-Tite-des-Caps	VILG/VILG	QC	La Côte-de-Beaupré	21 M/2	47°08′	70°46′
Saint-Ubalde	VILG/VILG	QC	Portneuf	31 I/16	46°45′	72°16′
Saint-Ulric	TOWN/VIL2	QC	Matane	22 B/13	48°47′	67°42′
Saint-Ulric-de-Matane	VILG/VILG	QC	Matane	22 B/13	48°45′	67°41′
Saint-Urbain	VILG/VILG	QC	Charlevoix	21 M/10	47°33′	70°32′
Saint-Urbain-Premier	VILG/VILG	QC	Beauharnois-Salaberry	31 H/4	45°13′	73°44′
Saint-Valentin	VILG/VILG	QC	Le Haut-Richelieu	31 H/3	45°08′	73°19′
Saint-Valère	VILG/VILG	QC	Arthabaska	31 I/1	46°04′	72°06′
Saint-Valérien	VILG/VILG	QC	Rimouski-Neigette	22 C/7	48°20′	68°40′
Saint-Valérien-de-Milton	VILG/VILG	QC	Les Maskoutains	31 H/10	45°34′	72°43′
Saint-Vallier	VILG/VILG	QC	Bellechasse	21 L/15	46°53′	70°49′
Saint-Vallier-Station	UNP/LNO	QC	Bellechasse	21 L/15	46°52′	70°48′
Saint-Venant-de-Paquette	VILG/VILG	QC	Coaticook	21 E/3	45°08′	71°28′
St. Veronica's	UNP/LNO	NF		1 M/13	47°57′	55°47′
Saint-Vianney	VILG/VILG	QC	La Matapédia	22 B/11	48°38′	67°25′

NAME NOM	ENTITY ENTITÉ	LOC 1 LIEU 1	LOC 2 LIEU 2	MAP CARTE	POSITION LAT	LONG
Saint-Viateur	VILG/VILG	QC	D'Autray	31 I/3	46°10′	73°10′
Saint-Victor	TOWN/VIL2	QC	Robert-Cliche	21 L/2	46°09′	70°54′
St. Victor	VILG/VILG	SK	5-6-29-W2	72 H/5	49°26′	105°52′
Saint-Victor, Bras	RIV/CDE	QC	Robert-Cliche	21 L/7	46°16′	70°49′
Saint-Victor-de-Bonaventure	UNP/LNO	QC	Avignon	22 B/2	48°03′	66°59′
Saint-Victor-de-Tring	VILG/VILG	QC	Robert-Cliche	21 L/2	46°09′	70°54′
Saint-Victor-Station	UNP/LNO	QC	Robert-Cliche	21 L/2	46°09′	70°55′
St. Vincent	MUN2/AZM2	ON	Grey	41 A/10	44°37′	80°40′
St. Vincent	UNP/LNO	AB	3-60-9-W4	73 L/3	54°09′	111°16′
St. Vincent Bay	BAY/BAIE	BC	New Westminster	92 F/16	49°49′	124°05′
Saint-Vincent-de-Paul	UNP/LNO	QC	Laval	31 H/12	45°37′	73°39′
St. Vincent's	UNP/LNO	NF		1 K/13	46°48′	53°38′
St. Vincent's-St. Stephen's-Peter's River	TOWN/VIL2	NF		1 K/13	46°46′	53°37′
St. Vital	UNP/LNO	MB		62 H/14	49°48′	97°05′
St. Vital	GEOG/GÉOG	MB		62 H/14	49°49′	97°10′
Saint-Vital-de-Clermont	UNP/LNO	QC	Abitibi-Ouest	32 D/14	48°55′	79°15′
St. Walburg	TOWN/VIL2	SK		73 F/11	53°39′	109°12′
Saint-Wenceslas	VILG/VILG	QC	Nicolet-Yamaska	31 I/1	46°10′	72°20′
Saint-Wilfred	UNP/LNO	NB	Northumberland	21 P/6	47°15′	65°13′
St. Williams	UNP/LNO	ON	Norfolk	40 I/9	42°40′	80°25′
Saint-Yvon	UNP/LNO	QC	La Côte-de-Gaspé	22 H/2	49°10′	64°48′
Saint-Zacharie	VILG/VILG	QC	Les Etchemins	21 L/1	46°08′	70°22′
Saint-Zacharie	UNP/LNO	QC	Le Vai-Saint-François	21 E/12	45°36′	71°57′
Saint-Zénon	VILG/VILG	QC	Matawinie	31 I/12	46°33′	73°49′
Saint-Zénon-du-Lac-Humqui	VILG/VILG	QC	La Matapédia	22 B/5	48°18′	67°35′
Saint-Zéphirin	UNP/LNO	QC	Nicolet-Yamaska	31 I/2	46°04′	72°38′
Saint-Zéphirin-de-Courval	VILG/VILG	QC	Nicolet-Yamaska	31 I/2	46°04′	72°38′
Saint-Zotique	TOWN/VIL2	QC	Vaudreuil-Soulanges	31 G/1	45°15′	74°15′
Sainville River	RIV/CDE	NT	Mackenzie	106 K	66°30′	133°04′
Sakamayack	UNP/LNO	SK		73 O/4	55°07′	107°39′
Sakami	UNP/LNO	QC	Jamésie	33 F/9	53°42′	76°04′
Sakami, Lac	LAKE/LAC	QC	Jamésie	33 F/7	53°15′	76°45′
Sakami, Rivière	RIV/CDE	QC	Jamésie	33 F/10	53°31′	76°40′
Sakiak Fiord	BAY/BAIE	NT	Franklin	16 E	65°42′	62°45′
Sakimay 74	IR/RI	SK		62 L/10	50°33′	102°48′
Sakinaw Lake	LAKE/LAC	BC	New Westminster	92 F/9	49°40′	124°02′
Sakitaw	UNP/LNO	MB	10-77-2-E	63 P/11	55°39′	97°13′
Sâkitawâbîkak	UNP/LNO	QC	Vallée-de-l'Or	31 N/11	47°45′	77°24′
Sakkiak Island	ISL/ÎLE	NT	Franklin	36 C	64°09′	76°33′
Sakwaso Lake	LAKE/LAC	ON	Kenora	53 G/4	53°02′	91°55′
Sakwatamau River	RIV/CDE	AB	60-12-W5	83 J/4	54°10′	115°43′
Salaberry	UNP/LNO	QC	L'Amiante	21 L/3	46°03′	71°26′
Salaberry-de-Valleyfield	CITY/VIL1	QC	Beauharnois-Salaberry	31 G/8	45°15′	74°08′
Salamandre, Lac	LAKE/LAC	QC	Jamésie	32 K/10	50°37′	76°38′
Salaquo (Chilako River) 4	IR/RI	BC	Cariboo	93 G/15	53°53′	122°58′
Salé, Lac	LAKE/LAC	QC	Côte-Nord-du-Golfe-Saint-Laurent	12 K/8	50°19′	60°18′
Salem	UNP/LNO	NS	Cumberland	21 H/16	45°46′	64°07′
Salem	UNP/LNO	NB	Albert	21 H/15	45°55′	64°42′
Salem	UNP/LNO	NB	Kings	21 I/3	46°02′	65°24′
Salem	UNP/LNO	ON	Leeds	31 C/9	44°39′	76°27′
Salem	UNP/LNO	ON	Northumberland	31 C/4	44°01′	77°50′
Salem	UNP/LNO	ON	Durham	30 M/15	43°57′	78°43′
Salem	UNP/LNO	ON	Dufferin	40 P/16	43°57′	80°03′
Salem	UNP/LNO	ON	Wellington	40 P/9	43°42′	80°27′
Salem	UNP/LNO	ON	Bruce	41 A/6	44°21′	81°11′
Salem	UNP/LNO	ON	Bruce	41 A/3	44°03′	81°18′
Salem Corners	UNP/LNO	ON	Victoria	31 D/7	44°17′	78°56′
Salem Road	UNP/LNO	NS	Cape Breton	11 F/15	45°49′	60°34′
Salford	UNP/LNO	ON	Oxford	40 I/15	43°00′	80°50′
Salina	UNP/LNO	NB	Kings	21 H/12	45°32′	65°42′
Saline, La	UNP/LNO	QC	Lajemmerais	31 H/11	45°42′	73°26′
Saline Lake	LAKE/LAC	SK	32,33-9-W2	62 M/14	51°47′	103°12′
Salisbury	VILG/VILG	NB	Westmorland	21 I/3	46°02′	65°03′
Salisbury	GEOG/GÉOG	NB	Westmorland	21 I/3	46°05′	65°10′
Salisbury Island	ISL/ÎLE	NT	Franklin	35 N	63°30′	77°00′
Salkeld Lake	LAKE/LAC	NT	Mackenzie	75 F	61°25′	109°50′
Salle-d'Affinage-de-l'Or-de-Bear Creek, Lieu historique national de la - also-aussi - Gold Room at Bear Creek National Historic Site	PARK/PARC	YT		116 B/3	64°02′	139°14′
Salluit	VILG/VILG	QC	Kativik	35 J/4	62°13′	75°39′
Sally's Cove	VILG/VILG	NF		12 H/12	49°44′	57°56′
Sallysout Creek	RIV/CDE	BC	Cassiar	104 A/8	56°20′	128°28′
Salmo	VILG/VILG	BC	Kootenay	82 F/3	49°12′	117°16′
Salmon Arm	MUN1/AZM1	BC	Kamloops Division Yale	82 L/11	50°42′	119°18′
Salmon Arm	UNP/LNO	BC	Kamloops Division Yale	82 L/11	50°42′	119°16′
Salmon Arm	BAY/BAIE	BC	Kamloops Division Yale	82 L/14	50°46′	119°18′
Salmon Bay	UNP/LNO	QC	Côte-Nord-du-Golfe-Saint-Laurent	12 P/5	51°25′	57°37′

NAME NOM	ENTITY ENTITÉ	LOC 1 LIEU 1	LOC 2 LIEU 2	MAP CARTE	POSITION LAT	LONG
Salmon Bay 3	IR/RI	BC	Range 1 Coast	92 K/7	50°26′	124°39′
Salmon Beach	UNP/LNO	NB	Gloucester	21 P/12	47°40′	65°32′
Salmon Bight	UNP/LNO	NF		3 E/5	53°28′	55°47′
Salmon Brook Lake	LAKE/LAC	NB	Northumberland	21 J/10	46°39′	66°33′
Salmon Channel	CHAN/CHEN	BC	Range 1 Coast	92 L/10	50°43′	126°49′
Salmon Cove	TOWN/VIL2	NF		1 N/14	47°47′	53°10′
Salmon Cove	UNP/LNO	NF		1 N/11	47°33′	53°16′
Salmon Cove Pond	LAKE/LAC	NF		2 C/6	48°26′	53°17′
Salmon Creek	UNP/LNO	NB	Queens	21 H/13	45°49′	65°50′
Salmon Creek	UNP/LNO	NB	Queens	21 I/4	46°12′	65°58′
Salmon Creek 3	IR/RI	BC	Cassiar	104 J/4	58°11′	131°38′
Salmon Fork	RIV/CDE	YT		116 K/10	66°33′	141°00′
Salmonhurst Corner	UNP/LNO	NB	Victoria	21 J/13	46°59′	67°38′
Salmonier	UNP/LNO	NF		1 M/3	47°04′	55°13′
Salmonier Arm	BAY/BAIE	NF		1 N/3	47°08′	53°30′
Salmonier River	RIV/CDE	NF		1 N/3	47°11′	53°24′
Salmonier River	RIV/CDE	NF		1 L/13	46°52′	55°46′
Salmon Inlet	BAY/BAIE	BC	New Westminster	92 G/12	49°39′	123°40′
Salmon Lake	LAKE/LAC	ON	Peterborough	31 D/16	44°49′	78°27′
Salmon Lake	LAKE/LAC	BC	Kamloops Division Yale	82 L/5	50°16′	120°00′
Salmon Lake 7	IR/RI	BC	Kamloops Division Yale	82 L/5	50°17′	119°59′
Salmon Point	UNP/LNO	ON	Prince Edward	30 N/14	43°53′	77°12′
Salmon Point	CAPE/CAP	ON	Prince Edward	30 N/14	43°51′	77°15′
Salmon Pond	LAKE/LAC	NF		2 D/8	48°21′	54°19′
Salmon Pond	LAKE/LAC	NF		2 E/2	49°01′	54°54′
Salmon Pond	LAKE/LAC	NT	Keewatin	46 C	64°14′	84°55′
Salmon River	UNP/LNO	NS	Richmond	11 F/10	45°39′	60°47′
Salmon River	UNP/LNO	NS	Colchester	11 E/6	45°22′	63°15′
Salmon River	UNP/LNO	NS	Digby	21 B/1	44°03′	66°10′
Salmon River	UNP/LNO	NB	Saint John	21 H/6	45°25′	65°24′
Salmon River	RIV/CDE	NF		2 E/2	49°01′	54°54′
Salmon River	RIV/CDE	NF		11 P/16	47°49′	56°00′
Salmon River	RIV/CDE	NF		12 P/1	51°10′	56°01′
Salmon River	RIV/CDE	NS	Cape Breton	11 F/16	45°55′	60°18′
Salmon River	RIV/CDE	NS	Victoria	11 N/1	47°00′	60°30′
Salmon River	RIV/CDE	NS	Guysborough	11 F/6	45°21′	61°28′
Salmon River	RIV/CDE	NS	Colchester	11 E/6	45°22′	63°22′
Salmon River	RIV/CDE	NS	Digby	21 B/1	44°03′	66°10′
Salmon River	RIV/CDE	NB	Queens	21 I/4	46°06′	65°56′
Salmon River	RIV/CDE	NB	Victoria	21 J/13	46°57′	67°40′
Salmon River	RIV/CDE	ON	Hastings	31 C/3	44°11′	77°15′
Salmon River	RIV/CDE	BC	Kamloops Division Yale	82 L/11	50°42′	119°18′
Salmon River	RIV/CDE	BC	Cariboo	93 J/2	54°04′	122°33′
Salmon River	RIV/CDE	BC	Sayward	92 K/5	50°23′	125°57′
Salmon River 1	IR/RI	BC	Kamloops Division Yale	82 L/6	50°30′	119°19′
Salmon River 1	IR/RI	BC	Sayward	92 K/5	50°23′	125°57′
Salmon River Bridge	UNP/LNO	NS	Halifax	11 D/14	44°47′	63°02′
Salmon River Lake	UNP/LNO	NS	Guysborough	11 F/5	45°22′	61°43′
Salmon River Meadow 7	IR/RI	BC	Range 3 Coast	93 C/14	52°58′	125°10′
Salmon River Road	UNP/LNO	NS	Cape Breton	11 F/16	45°54′	60°20′
Salmon Rock	UNP/LNO	NF		12 P/7	51°16′	56°46′
Salmontail Lake	LAKE/LAC	NS	Lunenburg	21 A/15	44°50′	64°33′
Salmon Valley	UNP/LNO	BC	Cariboo	93 J/2	54°07′	122°39′
Salmon Valley	UNP/LNO	BC	Cariboo	93 J/2	54°05′	122°42′
Salmonville	UNP/LNO	ON	Middlesex	40 P/3	43°07′	81°12′
Salmo River	RIV/CDE	BC	Kootenay	82 F/3	49°02′	117°23′
Salomé	UNP/LNO	QC	Montcalm	31 H/14	45°56′	73°28′
Salon-de-Thé-des-Chutes-Twin, Lieu historique national du - also-aussi - Twin Falls Tea House National Historic Site	PARK/PARC	BC	Kootenay	82 N/10	51°33′	116°32′
Salone, Lac	LAKE/LAC	QC	Mékinac	31 P/5	47°22′	73°55′
Saloon	UNP/LNO	BC	Cassiar	104 J/3	58°08′	131°23′
Saltair	UNP/LNO	BC	Oyster	92 B/13	48°57′	123°46′
Saltburn	UNP/LNO	SK	12-23-17-W3	72 K/16	50°57′	108°15′
Salt Channel 21D - see-voir - Opaskwayak Cree Nation Salt Channel 21D	IR/RI	MB		63 F/12	53°44′	101°42′
Saltcoats	TOWN/VIL2	SK	1-24-2-W2	62 M/1	51°02′	102°10′
Saltcoats No. 213	MUN2/AZM2	SK		62 M/1	51°00′	102°15′
Salt Creek	RIV/CDE	ON	Northumberland	31 C/4	44°13′	77°47′
Salter	UNP/LNO	SK	21-38-16-W3	73 C/8	52°17′	108°13′
Salter Head	CAPE/CAP	NS	Hants	11 E/5	45°20′	63°32′
Salter Hill	MTN/MNT	YT		106 L/2	66°09′	134°50′
Salters Brook	RIV/CDE	NS	Queens	21 A/2	44°11′	64°40′
Saltery Bay	UNP/LNO	BC	New Westminster	92 F/16	49°47′	124°11′
Saltford	UNP/LNO	ON	Huron	40 P/13	43°45′	81°42′
Salt Harbour	UNP/LNO	NF		2 E/10	49°39′	54°37′
Salt Plains 195	IR/RI	NT	Mackenzie	85 A/1	60°06′	112°15′
Salt Point	UNP/LNO	MB	21-32-17-W	62 O/13	51°45′	99°49′

NAME NOM	ENTITY ENTITÉ	LOC 1 LIEU 1	LOC 2 LIEU 2	MAP CARTE	POSITION LAT	LONG
Salt Point	CAPE/CAP	MB	32,33-17-W	62 O/13	51°50′	99°46′
Salt Point	CAPE/CAP	MB	44-24-W	63 C/15	52°47′	100°52′
Salt Pond	UNP/LNO	NF		1 M/3	47°06′	55°12′
Salt Pond Cove	UNP/LNO	NF		2 E/6	49°18′	55°02′
Salt Prairie	UNP/LNO	AB	2-77-14-W5	83 N/9	55°38′	116°04′
Salt Prairie Settlement	UNP/LNO	AB	76-14-W5	83 N/9	55°37′	116°07′
Salt River	UNP/LNO	NT	Mackenzie	85 A	60°07′	112°14′
Salt River	RIV/CDE	NT/AB		85 A/1	60°07′	112°14′
Saltspring Island	ISL/ÎLE	BC	Saltspring Island	92 B/11	48°45′	123°29′
Saltspring Island Land District	GEOG/GÉOG	BC		92 B	48°49′	123°29′
Salt Springs	UNP/LNO	NS	Antigonish	11 E/9	45°36′	62°01′
Salt Springs	UNP/LNO	NS	Pictou	11 E/10	45°32′	62°54′
Salt Springs	UNP/LNO	NS	Cumberland	21 H/9	45°40′	64°00′
Salt Springs	UNP/LNO	NB	Kings	21 H/12	45°33′	65°39′
Salt Springs Station	UNP/LNO	NS	Cumberland	21 H/9	45°41′	64°00′
Saltwater Pond	LAKE/LAC	NF		2 E/12	49°34′	55°54′
Salvador	VILG/VILG	SK	9-37-25-W3	73 C/4	52°10′	109°30′
Salvage	TOWN/VIL2	NF		2 C/12	48°41′	53°38′
Salvage Point	CAPE/CAP	NF		2 C/3	48°04′	53°10′
Salvages, The	SHL/H-FD	NS	Shelburne	20 P/6	43°28′	65°23′
Salvail	UNP/LNO	QC	Les Maskoutains	31 H/11	45°40′	73°04′
Salvail, Rivière	RIV/CDE	QC	Les Maskoutains	31 H/15	45°50′	72°58′
Salvation	UNP/LNO	NF		13 N/8	55°28′	60°13′
Salvus	UNP/LNO	BC	Range 5 Coast	103 I/6	54°19′	129°20′
Salvus 26	IR/RI	BC	Range 5 Coast	103 I/6	54°18′	129°24′
Sam Adams 12	IR/RI	BC	Yale Division Yale	92 H/14	49°55′	121°27′
Samahquam 1	IR/RI	BC	New Westminster	92 J/2	50°01′	122°32′
Samandré Lake	LAKE/LAC	NT	Mackenzie	86 G	65°58′	115°16′
Samaqua, Rivière	RIV/CDE	QC	Maria-Chapdelaine	32 H/2	49°09′	72°34′
Samatosum Mountain	MTN/MNT	BC	Kamloops Division Yale	82 M/4	51°09′	119°46′
Sambo Creek	RIV/CDE	YT		105 A/5	60°25′	129°33′
Sambo Lake	LAKE/LAC	YT		105 A/12	60°45′	129°30′
Sambro	UNP/LNO	NS	Halifax	11 D/5	44°28′	63°36′
Sambro, Banc - also-aussi - Sambro Bank	SEAU/SMER	—		8007	43°43′	63°19′
Sambro Bank - also-aussi - Sambro, Banc	SEAU/SMER	—		8007	43°43′	63°19′
Sambro Creek	UNP/LNO	NS	Halifax	11 D/5	44°28′	63°36′
Sambro Head	UNP/LNO	NS	Halifax	11 D/5	44°29′	63°35′
Sambro Island	ISL/ÎLE	NS	Halifax	11 D/5	44°26′	63°34′
Samburg	UNP/LNO	SK	7-50-23-W2	73 H/6	53°18′	105°22′
Sam Ford Fiord	BAY/BAIE	NT	Franklin	27 F	70°30′	71°09′
Samiajij Miawpukek	IR/RI	NF		1 M/13	47°52′	55°45′
Sam Lake	UNP/LNO	ON	Kenora	52 J/4	50°05′	92°00′
Samp Hill	UNP/LNO	NB	Kings	21 H/14	45°59′	65°22′
Sampsons Cove	UNP/LNO	NS	Richmond	11 F/10	45°30′	60°56′
Sampson's Meadow 11	IR/RI	BC	Lillooet	92 O/16	51°48′	122°01′
Sampson's Meadow 11A	IR/RI	BC	Lillooet	92 O/16	51°48′	122°00′
Sampsonville	UNP/LNO	NS	Richmond	11 F/10	45°41′	60°51′
Samson 137	IR/RI	AB	44-24-W4	83 A/14	52°47′	113°22′
Samson 137A	IR/RI	AB	4-44-24-W4	83 A/14	52°45′	113°26′
Samson (Flat) Islands - see-voir - Flat Islands	ISL/ÎLE	NF		2 C/13	48°48′	53°38′
Samson Island	UNP/LNO	NF		2 E/7	49°30′	54°57′
Samson Lake	LAKE/LAC	AB	43,44-23-W4	83 A/11	52°44′	113°13′
Samson, Rivière	RIV/CDE	QC	Beauce-Sartigan	21 E/15	45°48′	70°38′
Samuel-Brisson, Réserve écologique	PARK/PARC	QC	Le Haut-Saint-François	21 E/6	45°29′	71°08′
Samuel Island	ISL/ÎLE	BC	Cowichan	92 B/14	48°49′	123°13′
Sanagak Lake	LAKE/LAC	NT	Franklin	57 F	70°15′	93°35′
Sanborn	UNP/LNO	QC	L'Amiante	21 E/13	45°56′	71°33′
Sanca	UNP/LNO	BC	Kootenay	82 F/7	49°23′	116°44′
San Clara	UNP/LNO	MB	23-29-29-W	62 N/6	51°30′	101°26′
Sanctuary	UNP/LNO	SK	30-23-15-W3	72 K/16	50°59′	108°05′
Sandbank Lake	LAKE/LAC	ON	Cochrane	42 O/2	51°08′	82°41′
Sand Banks	UNP/LNO	ON	Prince Edward	30 N/14	43°54′	77°16′
Sand Bar, Le	UNP/LNO	QC	Les Îles-de-la-Madeleine	11 N/14	47°47′	61°29′
Sand Bay	UNP/LNO	QC	Pontiac	31 F/10	45°32′	76°34′
Sand Bay	UNP/LNO	ON	Algoma	41 K/10	46°44′	84°33′
Sand Bay	BAY/BAIE	NT	Franklin	59 F	78°48′	93°27′
Sand Bay Corner	UNP/LNO	ON	Leeds	31 C/8	44°28′	76°05′
Sand Beach	UNP/LNO	NS	Yarmouth	20 O/16	43°48′	66°00′
Sand Beach	UNP/LNO	SK	23-47-9-W3	73 G/3	53°04′	107°13′
Sand Brook	UNP/LNO	NB	Sunbury	21 G/10	45°30′	66°34′
Sand Brook	RIV/CDE	NB	Charlotte	21 G/7	45°30′	66°36′
Sand Castle Beach	UNP/LNO	ON	Simcoe	41 A/9	44°45′	80°08′
Sand Cove	BAY/BAIE	NS	Cumberland	21 H/10	45°34′	64°39′
Sand Cove Head - see-voir - Sandy Cove Point	CAPE/CAP	NF		1 L/13	46°52′	55°39′
Sandeau, Lac	LAKE/LAC	QC	Témiscamingue	31 M/1	47°10′	78°13′

NAME NOM	ENTITY ENTITÉ	LOC 1 LIEU 1	LOC 2 LIEU 2	MAP CARTE	POSITION LAT	LONG
Sanderson Lake	LAKE/LAC	NT	Mackenzie	75 H	61°20′	104°55′
Sandfield	MUN2/AZM2	ON	Manitoulin	41 G/9	45°44′	82°02′
Sandfield	UNP/LNO	NS	Cape Breton	11 F/16	45°58′	60°16′
Sandfield	UNP/LNO	ON	Manitoulin	41 H/12	45°42′	82°00′
Sandfield Mills	UNP/LNO	ON	Stormont	31 G/2	45°09′	74°46′
Sandfly Lake	LAKE/LAC	SK		73 O/9	55°43′	106°06′
Sandford	UNP/LNO	NS	Yarmouth	20 O/16	43°55′	66°09′
Sandford	UNP/LNO	ON	Ontario	31 D/3	44°08′	79°14′
Sandford Lake	LAKE/LAC	ON	Kenora	52 G/4	49°08′	91°41′
Sandgren	UNP/LNO	SK	16-27-23-W3	72 N/6	51°19′	109°10′
Sand Hill	UNP/LNO	NB	Gloucester	21 P/12	47°38′	65°37′
Sand Hill	UNP/LNO	QC	Le Haut-Saint-François	21 E/5	45°22′	71°45′
Sandhill	UNP/LNO	ON	Peel	30 M/13	43°50′	79°49′
Sand Hill Cove	BAY/BAIE	NF		13 H/9	53°35′	56°20′
Sandhill Creek	RIV/CDE	SK	23-48-15-W2	73 H/1	53°09′	104°05′
Sand Hill River	RIV/CDE	NF		13 H/9	53°35′	56°21′
Sandhurst	UNP/LNO	ON	Lennox and Addington	31 C/2	44°08′	76°53′
Sandhurst Shores	UNP/LNO	ON	Lennox and Addington	31 C/2	44°08′	76°53′
Sandilands	UNP/LNO	MB	22-4-9-E	62 H/8	49°19′	96°18′
Sand Island 4	IR/RI	BC	Range 5 Coast	103 G/16	53°49′	130°23′
Sandison	UNP/LNO	ON	Kent	40 J/8	42°16′	82°08′
Sand Lake	UNP/LNO	NS	Cape Breton	11 J/4	46°08′	59°56′
Sand Lake	UNP/LNO	ON	Parry Sound	31 E/11	45°39′	79°11′
Sand Lake	UNP/LNO	ON	Algoma	41 N/15	47°46′	84°31′
Sand Lake	LAKE/LAC	NS	Cape Breton	11 J/4	46°08′	59°56′
Sand Lake	LAKE/LAC	ON	Leeds	31 C/9	44°34′	76°16′
Sand Lake	LAKE/LAC	ON	Parry Sound	31 E/11	45°37′	79°10′
Sand Lake	LAKE/LAC	ON	Parry Sound	31 L/4	46°06′	79°40′
Sand Lake	LAKE/LAC	NT	Keewatin	66 G	65°15′	99°37′
Sandon	UNP/LNO	BC	Kootenay	82 F/14	49°59′	117°14′
Sandown	UNP/LNO	ON	Prescott	31 G/7	45°27′	74°50′
Sand Pit	UNP/LNO	ON	Sudbury	41 I/10	46°32′	80°55′
Sand Pits	UNP/LNO	NF		1 N/10	47°34′	52°44′
Sand Point	UNP/LNO	NS	Guysborough	11 F/11	45°32′	61°16′
Sand Point	UNP/LNO	NS	Colchester	11 E/11	45°44′	63°17′
Sand Point	UNP/LNO	NB	Kings	21 G/8	45°21′	66°12′
Sand Point	UNP/LNO	ON	Renfrew	31 F/8	45°29′	76°26′
Sand Point	UNP/LNO	BC	Nootka	92 E/15	49°48′	126°39′
Sand Point Beach	HAM/HAM	SK	17-20-26-W2	72 I/12	50°41′	105°34′
Sand Point Lake	LAKE/LAC	ON	Rainy River	52 C/8	48°23′	92°28′
Sandridge	UNP/LNO	MB	35-18-1-W	62 I/11	50°35′	97°30′
Sandringham	VILG/VILG	NF		2 C/12	48°40′	53°50′
Sandringham	UNP/LNO	ON	Stormont	31 G/7	45°18′	74°56′
Sand River	UNP/LNO	NS	Cumberland	21 H/10	45°32′	64°41′
Sand River	RIV/CDE	ON	Algoma	41 N/7	47°26′	84°44′
Sand River	RIV/CDE	MB	14-3-9-E	62 H/1	49°13′	96°17′
Sand River	RIV/CDE	AB	19-62-7-W4	73 L/6	54°23′	111°02′
Sandspit	UNP/LNO	BC	Queen Charlotte	103 G/4	53°15′	131°49′
Sandtown	UNP/LNO	ON	Stormont	31 G/3	45°06′	75°05′
Sandusk	UNP/LNO	ON	Haldimand	40 I/16	42°51′	80°02′
Sandusk Creek	RIV/CDE	ON	Haldimand	30 L/13	42°48′	79°58′
Sandwich	UNP/LNO	ON	Essex	40 J/6	42°17′	83°04′
Sandwich Bay	BAY/BAIE	NF		13 H/11	53°39′	57°14′
Sandwich South	MUN2/AZM2	ON	Essex	40 J/2	42°13′	82°57′
Sandwich West - see-voir - LaSalle	MUN2/AZM2	ON		40 J/3	42°13′	83°03′
Sandwick	UNP/LNO	BC	Comox	92 F/10	49°42′	124°59′
Sandwith	UNP/LNO	SK	8-48-14-W3	73 F/1	53°08′	108°00′
Sandy Bar	CAPE/CAP	MB		63 A/6	52°25′	97°07′
Sandy Bay	VILG/VILG	SK		63 M/9	55°31′	102°19′
Sandy Bay	UNP/LNO	MB	18-9-W	62 J/10	50°33′	98°39′
Sandy Bay	BAY/BAIE	ON	Parry Sound	41 H/15	45°49′	80°40′
Sandy Bay	BAY/BAIE	SK		74 N/3	59°07′	109°23′
Sandy Bay 5	IR/RI	MB		62 J/10	50°33′	98°40′
Sandy Bay Landings	UNP/LNO	NS	Queens	20 P/15	43°49′	64°54′
Sandy Beach	VILG/VILG	SK	17-20-12-W2	62 L/12	50°44′	103°39′
Sandy Beach	VILG/VILG	AB	34,35-55-1-W5	83 G/16	53°48′	114°02′
Sandy Beach	UNP/LNO	NF		1 N/11	47°32′	53°14′
Sandy Beach	UNP/LNO	QC	La Côte-de-Gaspé	22 A/16	48°49′	64°26′
Sandy Beach	UNP/LNO	ON	Renfrew	31 F/8	45°27′	76°22′
Sandy Beach	UNP/LNO	ON	Ontario	31 D/11	44°35′	79°21′
Sandy Beach	UNP/LNO	AB	54-20-W4	83 H/10	53°41′	112°50′
Sandy Brook	RIV/CDE	NF		2 D/13	48°56′	55°46′
Sandy Brook	RIV/CDE	NF		12 H/1	49°04′	56°21′
Sandy Cove	VILG/VILG	NF		2 C/12	48°38′	53°44′
Sandy Cove	UNP/LNO	NS	Halifax	11 D/5	44°28′	63°34′

NAME NOM	ENTITY ENTITÉ	LOC 1 LIEU 1	LOC 2 LIEU 2	MAP CARTE	POSITION LAT	POSITION LONG
Sandy Cove	UNP/LNO	NS	Queens	21 A/2	44°03′	64°42′
Sandy Cove	UNP/LNO	NS	Digby	21 B/8	44°29′	66°05′
Sandy Cove	UNP/LNO	ON	Simcoe	31 D/5	44°22′	79°32′
Sandy Cove	UNP/LNO	ON	Haldimand	40 I/16	42°48′	80°05′
Sandy Cove	UNP/LNO	BC	New Westminster	92 G/6	49°21′	123°14′
Sandy Cove	BAY/BAIE	NF		2 C/12	48°38′	53°44′
Sandy Cove Acres	UNP/LNO	ON	Simcoe	31 D/5	44°21′	79°33′
Sandy Cove Point	CAPE/CAP	NF		1 L/13	46°52′	55°39′
Sandy Cove, St. Barbe North	UNP/LNO	NF		12 P/7	51°21′	56°40′
Sandy Creek	UNP/LNO	QC	Pontiac	31 F/16	45°58′	76°29′
Sandy Falls	UNP/LNO	ON		42 A/11	48°31′	81°27′
Sandy Harbour	UNP/LNO	NF		1 M/9	47°41′	54°19′
Sandy Harbour River	RIV/CDE	NF		1 M/9	47°42′	54°21′
Sandy Harry 4	IR/RI	BC	Lillooet	92 O/16	51°49′	122°06′
Sandy Hill	UNP/LNO	ON	Prescott	31 G/10	45°35′	74°40′
Sandy Hook	UNP/LNO	NF		3 D/12	52°32′	55°48′
Sandy Hook	UNP/LNO	ON	Renfrew	31 F/8	45°27′	76°22′
Sandy Hook	UNP/LNO	MB	16-18-4-E	62 I/10	50°33′	96°59′
Sandy Island	ISL/ÎLE	ON	Nipissing	31 L/4	46°14′	79°53′
Sandy Island	ISL/ÎLE	ON	Parry Sound	41 H/8	45°16′	80°16′
Sandy Lake	UNP/LNO	ON	Kenora	53 F/3	53°03′	93°20′
Sandy Lake	UNP/LNO	MB	9-18-20-W	62 K/9	50°32′	100°11′
Sandy Lake	UNP/LNO	SK		74 B/14	56°59′	107°17′
Sandy Lake	UNP/LNO	AB	5-79-22-W4M	83 P/14	55°49′	113°25′
Sandy Lake	LAKE/LAC	NF		12 H/2	49°15′	57°00′
Sandy Lake	LAKE/LAC	ON	Peterborough	31 D/9	44°32′	78°25′
Sandy Lake	LAKE/LAC	ON	Kenora	53 F/2	53°02′	93°00′
Sandy Lake	LAKE/LAC	SK	77,78-4,5-W3	73 O/10	55°43′	106°39′
Sandy Lake	LAKE/LAC	SK	55-11-W3	73 G/12	53°43′	107°31′
Sandy Lake	LAKE/LAC	AB	44-7-W4	73 D/15	52°49′	111°00′
Sandy Lake	LAKE/LAC	AB	79-22-W4	83 P/14	55°50′	113°25′
Sandy Lake	LAKE/LAC	AB	55,56-1-W5	83 G/16	53°47′	114°02′
Sandy Lake	LAKE/LAC	NT	Mackenzie	75 A	60°52′	105°30′
Sandy Lake	LAKE/LAC	NT	Mackenzie	106 N	67°48′	132°14′
Sandy Lake 88	IR/RI	ON	Kenora	53 F/3	53°04′	93°20′
Sandy Narrows	UNP/LNO	SK		63 M/3	55°05′	103°04′
Sandy Narrows 184C	IR/RI	SK		63 M/3	55°01′	103°03′
Sandy Point	UNP/LNO	NF		1 M/3	47°03′	55°11′
Sandy Point	UNP/LNO	NF		2 E/3	49°13′	55°18′
Sandy Point	UNP/LNO	NF		12 B/7	48°27′	58°30′
Sandy Point	UNP/LNO	NS	Shelburne	20 P/11	43°42′	65°19′
Sandy Point	UNP/LNO	ON	Victoria	31 D/7	44°29′	78°40′
Sandy Point	CAPE/CAP	NF		13 F/8	53°26′	60°02′
Sandy Point	CAPE/CAP	NB	Gloucester	21 P/15	47°55′	64°30′
Sandy Point 221	IR/RI	AB	114-5-W4	74 L/15	58°56′	110°44′
Sandy Point Beach	UNP/LNO	ON	Simcoe	31 D/11	44°34′	79°14′
Sandy Point Road	UNP/LNO	NB	Saint John	21 G/8	45°19′	66°05′
Sandyville	UNP/LNO	NB	York	21 G/15	45°59′	66°36′
Saneraun Hills	MTN/MNT	NT	Franklin	87 H	71°25′	113°25′
Sanford	UNP/LNO	QC	Le Haut-Saint-Maurice	31 P/8	47°29′	72°13′
Sanford	UNP/LNO	MB	19,30-8-1-E	62 H/11	49°41′	97°27′
Sangaree	UNP/LNO	NS	Cape Breton	11 K/1	46°00′	60°06′
Sango Bay	BAY/BAIE	NF		13 N/14	55°52′	61°07′
Sangster Island	ISL/ÎLE	BC	Nanaimo	92 F/8	49°26′	124°12′
Sangsues, Lac aux	LAKE/LAC	QC	Témiscamingue	31 K/5	46°28′	77°56′
Sangudo	VILG/VILG	AB	36-56-7-W5	83 G/15	53°53′	114°54′
Sangumaniq	UNP/LNO	QC	Kativik	24 G/11	57°33′	67°20′
Sanikiluaq	HAM/HAM	NT	Keewatin	34 D	56°32′	79°14′
San Jose 6	IR/RI	BC	Cariboo	93 B/1	52°08′	122°07′
San Josef	UNP/LNO	BC	Rupert	102 I/9	50°40′	128°05′
San Josef Bay	BAY/BAIE	BC	Rupert	102 I/9	50°39′	128°19′
San Josef River	RIV/CDE	BC	Rupert	102 I/9	50°40′	128°16′
San Jose River	RIV/CDE	BC	Cariboo	93 B/1	52°07′	122°02′
San Juan Point	CAPE/CAP	BC	Renfrew	92 C/9	48°32′	124°27′
San Juan, Port	BAY/BAIE	BC	Renfrew	92 C/9	48°33′	124°27′
San Juan River	RIV/CDE	BC	Renfrew	92 C/9	48°34′	124°24′
Sanklksgamal 80	IR/RI	BC	Cassiar	103 P/3	55°13′	129°08′
Sanmaur	UNP/LNO	QC	Le Haut-Saint-Maurice	31 P/13	47°54′	73°48′
Sans Bout, Rivière	RIV/CDE	QC	Maskinongé	31 I/11	46°38′	73°23′
San Simon Point	CAPE/CAP	BC	Renfrew	92 C/8	48°26′	124°06′
Sans Souci	UNP/LNO	ON	Parry Sound	41 H/1	45°10′	80°08′
Sans Souci	UNP/LNO	MB	2-17-4-E	62 I/7	50°26′	96°57′
Santein, Lac	LAKE/LAC	QC	Côte-Nord-du-Golfe-Saint-Laurent	12 O/3	51°06′	59°04′
Santé, Lac	LAKE/LAC	AB	56-11-W4	73 E/13	53°50′	111°35′
Santianna Point	CAPE/CAP	NT	Keewatin	45 J	62°26′	83°59′

NAME NOM	ENTITY ENTITÉ	LOC 1 LIEU 1	LOC 2 LIEU 2	MAP CARTE	POSITION LAT	LONG
Santoy Lake	LAKE/LAC	ON	Thunder Bay	42 D/15	48°52′	86°53′
Saouayane, Pointe	CAPE/CAP	QC	Jamésie	32 M/11	51°40′	79°19′
Saouchten 18	IR/RI	BC	Queen Charlotte	103 K/1	54°01′	132°11′
Saouk 16	IR/RI	BC	Barclay	92 C/15	48°54′	124°35′
Sapawe	UNP/LNO	ON	Rainy River	52 B/14	48°46′	91°20′
Sapin-Court	UNP/LNO	NB	Northumberland	21 I/11	46°43′	65°28′
Sapperton	UNP/LNO	BC	New Westminster	92 G/2	49°13′	122°53′
Sapton	UNP/LNO	MB	21-12-6-E	62 I/2	50°01′	96°42′
Saputing Lake	LAKE/LAC	NT	Franklin	47 F	70°42′	85°25′
Saraguay	UNP/LNO	QC	Communauté urbaine de Montréal	31 H/12	45°31′	73°45′
Sarah, Cape	CAPE/CAP	NT	Franklin	25 I	62°48′	65°32′
Sarah Island	ISL/ÎLE	BC	Range 3 Coast	103 A/15	52°46′	128°30′
Sarah Lake	LAKE/LAC	ON	Rainy River	52 B/4	48°13′	91°35′
Sarah Lake	LAKE/LAC	MB	33-28-W	62 N/14	51°50′	101°21′
Sarah Lake	LAKE/LAC	NT	Mackenzie	85 N	63°45′	117°10′
Saratoga	UNP/LNO	ON	Huron	40 P/13	43°49′	81°34′
Saratoga Beach	UNP/LNO	QC	Laval	31 H/12	45°33′	73°53′
Saratoga Beach	UNP/LNO	BC	Comox	92 F/14	49°52′	125°07′
Sarawak	MUN2/AZM2	ON	Grey	41 A/10	44°39′	80°58′
Sarcee 145	IR/RI	AB	23-2,3,4-W5	82 J/16	50°59′	114°20′
Sarcee Junction	UNP/LNO	AB	33-23-29-W4	82 P/4	51°00′	114°00′
Sarcpa Lake	LAKE/LAC	NT	Franklin	47 A	68°31′	83°16′
Sardis	UNP/LNO	BC	New Westminster	92 H/4	49°08′	121°57′
Sargent Park	UNP/LNO	MB		62 H/14	49°54′	97°11′
Sargent Point	CAPE/CAP	NT	Franklin	48 C	73°52′	86°10′
Sargent Point	CAPE/CAP	NT	Franklin	69 A	76°12′	97°30′
Sarita	UNP/LNO	BC	Barclay	92 C/14	48°53′	125°02′
Sarita River	RIV/CDE	BC	Barclay	92 C/14	48°54′	125°00′
Sarnia	CITY/VIL1	ON	Lambton	40 J/16	42°58′	82°23′
Sarnia 45	IR/RI	ON	Lambton	40 J/16	42°55′	82°28′
Sarnia Beach	HAM/HAM	SK	36-23-24-W2	72 I/14	51°00′	105°13′
Sarnia-Clearwater - see-voir - **Sarnia**	CITY/VIL1	ON		40 J/16	42°58′	82°23′
Sarnia No. 221	MUN2/AZM2	SK		72 I/14	51°00′	105°20′
Sarosto	UNP/LNO	QC	Desjardins	21 L/14	46°47′	71°10′
Sarque 5	IR/RI	BC	Barclay	92 C/10	48°40′	124°47′
Sarsfield	UNP/LNO	ON	Russell	31 G/6	45°27′	75°21′
Sartine Island	ISL/ÎLE	BC	Rupert	102 I/15	50°49′	128°54′
Sarto	UNP/LNO	MB	17,20-5-6-E	62 H/7	49°24′	96°45′
Sarvakallak, Chute	FALL/CHUT	QC	Kativik	34 P/15	59°49′	72°32′
Sasaginnigak Lake	LAKE/LAC	MB		52 M/12	51°36′	95°40′
Saseenos	UNP/LNO	BC	Sooke	92 B/5	48°23′	123°40′
Saseginaga	UNP/LNO	QC	Témiscamingue	31 M/2	47°04′	78°34′
Saseginaga, Lac	LAKE/LAC	QC	Témiscamingue	31 M/2	47°06′	78°34′
Saskatchewan	PROV/PROV	SK		MCR27	54°00′	106°00′
Saskatchewan	MUN2/AZM2	MB		62 K/1	50°10′	100°00′
Saskatchewan Beach	VILG/VILG	SK	24-21-22-W2	72 I/15	50°48′	104°56′
Saskatchewan Landing	UNP/LNO	SK	35-19-15-W3	72 J/4	50°39′	107°59′
Saskatchewan Landing No. 167	MUN2/AZM2	SK		72 J/5	50°30′	107°50′
Saskatchewan Nord, Rivière - also-aussi - **North Saskatchewan River**	RIV/CDE	SK/AB		73 H/3	53°15′	105°05′
Saskatchewan Point	CAPE/CAP	MB		63 A/4	52°09′	97°43′
Saskatchewan River - also-aussi - **Saskatchewan, Rivière**	RIV/CDE	MB/SK		63 G/3	53°11′	99°15′
Saskatchewan River Crossing	UNP/LNO	AB	1-35-20-W5	82 N/15	51°59′	116°45′
Saskatchewan, Rivière - also-aussi - **Saskatchewan River**	RIV/CDE	MB/SK		63 G/3	53°11′	99°15′
Saskatchewan Sud, Rivière - also-aussi - **South Saskatchewan River**	RIV/CDE	SK/AB		73 H/3	53°15′	105°05′
Saskatoon	CITY/VIL1	SK		73 B/2	52°07′	106°38′
Saskatoon Island Provincial Park	PARK/PARC	AB	72-7,8-W6	83 M/3	55°12′	119°05′
Saskeram Lake	LAKE/LAC	MB	56-28-W	63 F/14	53°50′	101°30′
Saskoba Lake	LAKE/LAC	SK/MB		63 K/5	54°27′	101°53′
Saskum Lake	LAKE/LAC	BC	Kamloops Division Yale	82 M/5	51°24′	119°42′
Sasman No. 336	MUN2/AZM2	SK		62 M/13	51°55′	103°35′
Sass River	RIV/CDE	NT	Mackenzie	85 A	60°18′	112°54′
Satah Mountain	MTN/MNT	BC	Range 3 Coast	93 C/7	52°29′	124°42′
Satah River	RIV/CDE	NT/YT		106 M/2	67°04′	134°51′
Satellite Bay	BAY/BAIE	NT	Franklin	89 C	77°23′	117°18′
*Satellite Slopes	UNP/LNO	NS	Pictou	11 E/10	45°32′	62°39′
Satigsun Island	ISL/ÎLE	NT	Franklin	27 A	68°33′	66°41′
Satin Lake	LAKE/LAC	NT	Mackenzie	75 K	62°13′	108°30′
Satsalla River	RIV/CDE	BC	Range 2 Coast	92 M/1	51°08′	126°08′
Satunquin 5	IR/RI	BC	Queen Charlotte	103 F/9	53°40′	132°13′
Saturna	UNP/LNO	BC	Cowichan	92 B/14	48°48′	123°12′
Saturna Island	ISL/ÎLE	BC	Cowichan	92 B/14	48°47′	123°09′
Saturna Island 7	IR/RI	BC	Cowichan	92 B/14	48°47′	123°05′
Sauble Beach	UNP/LNO	ON	Bruce	41 A/11	44°38′	81°16′
Sauble Beach North	UNP/LNO	ON	Bruce	41 A/11	44°39′	81°16′
Sauble Beach South	UNP/LNO	ON	Bruce	41 A/11	44°36′	81°15′

NAME NOM	ENTITY ENTITÉ	LOC 1 LIEU 1	LOC 2 LIEU 2	MAP CARTE	POSITION LAT	LONG
Sauble Falls	UNP/LNO	ON	Bruce	41 A/11	44°40′	81°15′
Sauble River	RIV/CDE	ON	Bruce	41 A/11	44°39′	81°17′
Saubosq, Lac	LAKE/LAC	QC	Minganie	22 P/7	51°30′	64°53′
Saucier	UNP/LNO	QC	La Matapédia	22 B/12	48°35′	67°45′
Saug-A-Gaw-Sing 1	IR/RI	ON	Rainy River	52 E/1	49°07′	94°19′
Saugattalik	UNP/LNO	QC	Kativik	24 K/1	58°08′	68°06′
Saugeen	MUN2/AZM2	ON	Bruce	41 A/6	44°25′	81°24′
Saugeen	UNP/LNO	ON	Grey	41 A/2	44°13′	80°31′
Saugeen 29	IR/RI	ON	Bruce	41 A/11	44°33′	81°20′
Saugeen and Cape Croker Fishing Islands 1	IR/RI	ON	Bruce	41 A/14	44°51′	81°20′
Saugeen Hunting Ground 60A	IR/RI	ON	Bruce	41 H/3	45°10′	81°30′
Saugeen River	RIV/CDE	ON	Bruce	41 A/11	44°30′	81°22′
Saugstad, Mount	MTN/MNT	BC	Range 3 Coast	93 D/7	52°15′	126°31′
Saulnierville	UNP/LNO	NS	Digby	21 B/8	44°16′	66°08′
Saulnierville Station	UNP/LNO	NS	Digby	21 B/1	44°15′	66°06′
Sault-à-la-Puce	UNP/LNO	QC	La Côte-de-Beaupré	21 L/14	46°59′	71°01′
Sault à la Puce, Rivière du	RIV/CDE	QC	La Côte-de-Beaupré	21 L/14	46°59′	71°00′
Sault-au-Cochon	MUN2/AZM2	QC	La Côte-de-Beaupré	21 M/2	47°12′	70°38′
Sault-au-Cochon	UNP/LNO	QC	La Côte-de-Beaupré	21 M/2	47°12′	70°38′
Sault-au-Mouton	TOWN/VIL2	QC	La Haute-Côte-Nord	22 C/11	48°33′	69°15′
Sault au Mouton, Rivière du	RIV/CDE	QC	La Haute-Côte-Nord	22 C/11	48°32′	69°15′
Sault-au-Récollet	UNP/LNO	QC	Communauté urbaine de Montréal	31 H/12	45°35′	73°39′
Sault aux Cochons, Lac du	LAKE/LAC	QC	La Haute-Côte-Nord	22 F/5	49°17′	69°58′
Sault aux Cochons, Rivière du	RIV/CDE	QC	La Haute-Côte-Nord	22 C/11	48°44′	69°04′
Saulteaux	UNP/LNO	AB	13-72-3-W5	83 O/1	55°14′	114°19′
Saulteaux 159	IR/RI	SK		73 F/1	53°08′	108°19′
Saulteaux 159A	IR/RI	SK		73 F/8	53°29′	108°08′
Saulteaux 159B	IR/RI	SK	24-44-16	73 C/16	52°48′	108°12′
Saulteaux River	RIV/CDE	AB	25-72-3-W5	83 O/8	55°16′	114°25′
Sault, Le	UNP/LNO	QC	Les Chutes-de-la-Chaudière	21 L/11	46°39′	71°15′
Sault Ste. Marie	CITY/VIL1	ON	Algoma	41 K/9	46°31′	84°20′
Sault Ste. Marie Canal - also-aussi - Sault Ste. Marie, Canal de	PARK/PARC	ON		41 K/9	46°31′	84°21′
Sault Ste. Marie, Canal de - also-aussi - Sault Ste. Marie Canal	PARK/PARC	ON		41 K/9	46°31′	84°21′
Sault-Saint-Lin	UNP/LNO	QC	Montcalm	31 H/13	45°53′	73°46′
Sault Ship Canal	UNP/LNO	ON	Algoma	41 K/9	46°31′	84°21′
Saumarez	UNP/LNO	NB	Gloucester	21 P/7	47°30′	64°56′
Saumarez	GEOG/GÉOG	NB	Gloucester	21 P/6	47°25′	65°07′
Saumon, Cap au	CAPE/CAP	QC	Charlevoix-Est	21 N/13	47°46′	69°55′
Saumon, Rivière	RIV/CDE	QC	Papineau	31 G/10	45°39′	74°55′
Saumon, Rivière au	RIV/CDE	QC	Le Haut-Saint-François	21 E/11	45°41′	71°27′
Saumons, Rivière aux	RIV/CDE	QC	Minganie	12 E/8	49°25′	62°15′
Saumons, Rivière aux	RIV/CDE	QC	Sherbrooke	21 E/5	45°21′	71°52′
Saumons, Rivière aux	RIV/CDE	QC	Le Domaine-du-Roy	32 A/10	48°42′	72°30′
Saumur, Lac	LAKE/LAC	QC	Minganie	12 M/7	51°16′	62°49′
Saunders	UNP/LNO	AB	24-40-13-W5	83 B/5	52°27′	115°44′
Saunders Cove	UNP/LNO	NF		2 D/9	48°42′	54°01′
Saunders, Lac	LAKE/LAC	QC	Jamésie	33 J/9	54°44′	74°18′
Saunders Lake	LAKE/LAC	SK	62,63-8-W2	63 L/6	54°23′	103°10′
Saunders Point	CAPE/CAP	NT	Keewatin	45 P	63°53′	80°28′
Saunders River	RIV/CDE	NT	Franklin	36 B	64°37′	75°51′
Sauniat, Lac	LAKE/LAC	QC	La Haute-Côte-Nord	22 C/11	48°44′	69°20′
Saunier Creek	RIV/CDE	BC	Similkameen Division Yale	82 E/11	49°32′	119°11′
Saurin	UNP/LNO	ON	Simcoe	31 D/12	44°36′	79°53′
Sautauriski, Lac	LAKE/LAC	QC	La Côte-de-Beaupré	21 M/6	47°22′	71°18′
Sautauriski, Rivière	RIV/CDE	QC	La Jacques-Cartier	21 M/3	47°11′	71°23′
Sauterelles, Lac aux	LAKE/LAC	QC	Minganie	22 P/16	51°59′	64°13′
Sauvage, Lac du	LAKE/LAC	NT	Mackenzie	76 D/12	64°37′	109°58′
Sauvage, Pointe	CAPE/CAP	QC	La Haute-Côte-Nord	22 C/4	48°13′	69°34′
Sauvé	UNP/LNO	QC	Denis-Riverin	22 G/1	49°08′	66°19′
Sauvolles, Lac	LAKE/LAC	QC	Jamésie	33 H/7	53°26′	73°00′
Savage Cove	UNP/LNO	NF		12 P/7	51°20′	56°42′
Savage Harbour	UNP/LNO	PE	Queens	11 L/7	46°25′	62°51′
Savage Harbour	BAY/BAIE	PE	Kings	11 L/7	46°25′	62°50′
Savage Harbour	BAY/BAIE	NT	Franklin	25 H	61°50′	65°45′
Savage Islands	ISL/ÎLE	NT	Keewatin	56 H	65°27′	88°26′
Savage Lake	LAKE/LAC	ON	Sudbury	41 J/8	46°25′	82°00′
Savage Lake	LAKE/LAC	NT	Keewatin	55 L	62°26′	95°22′
Savalette, Rivière	RIV/CDE	QC	Kativik	23 O/16	55°48′	66°00′
Savane, Lac	LAKE/LAC	QC	Charlevoix	21 M/7	47°27′	70°52′
Savane, Rivière	RIV/CDE	QC	Le Fjord-du-Saguenay	22 M/3	51°09′	71°26′
Savanes, Lac des	LAKE/LAC	QC	Le Fjord-du-Saguenay	22 D/9	48°37′	70°01′
Savanna	UNP/LNO	AB	11-8-5-W5	82 G/10	49°38′	114°34′
Savanne	UNP/LNO	ON	Thunder Bay	52 B/16	48°57′	90°15′
Savant Lake	UNP/LNO	ON	Thunder Bay	52 J/2	50°14′	90°43′
Savant Lake	LAKE/LAC	ON	Thunder Bay	52 J/9	50°30′	90°25′

NAME NOM	ENTITY ENTITÉ	LOC 1 LIEU 1	LOC 2 LIEU 2	MAP CARTE	POSITION	
					LAT	LONG
Savard Lake	LAKE/LAC	NT	Keewatin	65 H	61°28′	96°52′
Savary Island	ISL/ÎLE	BC	New Westminster	92 F/15	49°56′	124°49′
Savey 15	IR/RI	BC	Nootka	92 E/15	49°58′	126°56′
Savignon, Lac	LAKE/LAC	QC	Jamésie	33 L/10	54°41′	78°51′
Saville Farm	UNP/LNO	AB	6-44-8-W4	73 D/14	52°46′	111°10′
Savoff	UNP/LNO	ON	Cochrane	42 F/15	49°56′	84°58′
Savona	UNP/LNO	BC	Kamloops Division Yale	92 I/15	50°45′	120°50′
Savona	UNP/LNO	BC	Kamloops Division Yale	92 I/15	50°46′	120°52′
Savory	UNP/LNO	BC	Range 5 Coast	93 K/3	54°06′	125°10′
Savoy Landing	UNP/LNO	NB	Gloucester	21 P/15	47°45′	64°41′
Sawback	UNP/LNO	AB	35-25-13-W5	82 O/4	51°11′	115°43′
Sawbill	UNP/LNO	NF		23 G/9	53°37′	66°21′
Sawbill	UNP/LNO	MB		64 F/12	57°38′	101°43′
Sawbill Lake	LAKE/LAC	NF		23 G/7	53°26′	66°40′
Sawlog Bay	UNP/LNO	ON	Simcoe	31 D/13	44°52′	79°56′
Sawmill Bay	UNP/LNO	NT	Mackenzie	86 E	65°43′	118°54′
Sawmill Bay	BAY/BAIE	NT	Mackenzie	86 E	65°43′	118°49′
Sawmill Mountain	MTN/MNT	NT	Mackenzie	95 B	60°48′	123°40′
Sawn Lake	LAKE/LAC	AB	92-12,13-W5	84 B/13	56°58′	115°55′
Sawridge 150G	IR/RI	AB	72,73-4,5-W5	83 O/7	55°17′	114°41′
Sawridge 150H	IR/RI	AB	73-6-W5	83 O/7	55°18′	114°53′
Sawtooth Mountain	MTN/MNT	NT	Franklin	27 F	70°25′	68°54′
Sawtooth Range	MTN/MNT	NT	Franklin	49 G	79°35′	83°15′
Sawyer Bay	BAY/BAIE	NT	Franklin	39 G	79°19′	77°33′
Sawyer Glacier	GLAC/GLAC	BC	Cassiar	104 F/15	57°56′	132°56′
Sawyers Hill	MTN/MNT	NF		1 N/4	47°11′	53°52′
Sawyerville	TOWN/VIL2	QC	Le Haut-Saint-François	21 E/5	45°20′	71°34′
Saxby Corner	UNP/LNO	QC	La Haute-Yamaska	31 H/7	45°23′	72°38′
Sayabec	VILG/VILG	QC	La Matapédia	22 B/12	48°34′	67°41′
Sayat-Nova, Étang	LAKE/LAC	QC	Memphrémagog	31 H/8	45°19′	72°11′
Sayers Mills	UNP/LNO	ON	Halton	40 P/9	43°33′	80°02′
Say-La-Quas 10	IR/RI	BC	Chemainus	92 B/13	48°54′	123°41′
Sayunei Range	MTN/MNT	NT	Mackenzie	105 P/15	64°00′	128°50′
Sayward	VILG/VILG	BC	Sayward	92 K/5	50°23′	125°58′
Sayward Land District	GEOG/GÉOG	BC		92 K	50°12′	125°32′
Scaia, Mount	MTN/MNT	BC	Similkameen Division Yale	82 E/16	49°52′	118°22′
Scale	UNP/LNO	NB	Sunbury	21 J/1	46°04′	66°07′
Scamakounst 19	IR/RI	BC	Cassiar	103 P/13	55°57′	129°58′
Scandia	UNP/LNO	AB	19-15-15-W4	82 I/8	50°17′	112°02′
Scandinavia	UNP/LNO	MB	7-18-17-W	62 J/12	50°32′	99°48′
Scapa	UNP/LNO	AB	31-33-14-W4	72 M/13	51°52′	111°59′
Scarborough	CITY/VIL1	ON	York	30 M/14	43°47′	79°15′
Scarborough Bluffs	MTN/MNT	ON	York	30 M/11	43°42′	79°14′
Scarborough Station	UNP/LNO	ON	York	30 M/11	43°43′	79°15′
Scarborough Village	UNP/LNO	ON	York	30 M/11	43°45′	79°12′
Scar Creek	RIV/CDE	BC	Range 2 Coast	92 N/3	51°11′	125°02′
Scarlet Park	UNP/LNO	ON	Simcoe	31 D/11	44°43′	79°22′
Scarsdale	UNP/LNO	NS	Lunenburg	21 A/10	44°36′	64°38′
Scarth	UNP/LNO	MB	9-9-26-W	62 F/10	49°44′	100°57′
Scarth River	RIV/CDE	SK	61-14-W2	73 I/8	54°17′	104°06′
Scatarie, Banc - also-aussi - Scatarie Bank	SEAU/SMER	—		4002	45°59′	59°15′
Scatarie Bank - also-aussi - Scatarie, Banc	SEAU/SMER	—		4002	45°59′	59°15′
Scatarie Island	UNP/LNO	NS	Cape Breton	11 J/4	46°02′	59°42′
Scatarie Island	ISL/ÎLE	NS	Cape Breton	11 J/4	46°00′	59°44′
Scaucy 5	IR/RI	BC	Yale Division Yale	92 H/14	49°49′	121°28′
Scenic Lake	LAKE/LAC	ON	Kenora	52 L/1	50°14′	94°13′
Scented Grass Hills	MTN/MNT	NT	Mackenzie	96 J/1	66°08′	122°30′
Scentgrass	UNP/LNO	SK	10-46-16-W3	73 C/16	52°57′	108°15′
Scentgrass Lake	LAKE/LAC	SK	46-15-W3	73 C/16	52°58′	108°09′
Sceptre	VILG/VILG	SK	9-22-24-W3	72 K/14	50°51′	109°15′
Schade Lake	LAKE/LAC	ON	Kenora	53 B/15	52°59′	90°40′
Schade River	RIV/CDE	ON	Kenora	53 G/11	53°37′	91°01′
Schaefer Lakes	LAKE/LAC	NT	Mackenzie	75 D	60°05′	111°23′
Schaltuuch 27	IR/RI	BC	New Westminster	92 G/6	49°24′	123°29′
Schantzenfeld	UNP/LNO	SK	19-13-13-W3	72 J/4	50°06′	107°46′
Schanzenfeld	UNP/LNO	MB	16,21-2-4-W	62 H/4	49°08′	97°57′
Schefferville	CITY/VIL1	QC	Caniapiscau	23 J/15	54°48′	66°50′
Schefferville	VILG/VILG	QC	Kativik	23 O/2	55°10′	66°52′
Schefferville - see-voir - Lac John	IR/RI	QC		23 J/15	54°49′	66°48′
Schei Peninsula	CAPE/CAP	NT	Franklin	340 B	80°15′	88°00′
Schellinger, Mount	MTN/MNT	YT		106 F/7	65°29′	132°39′
Schelowat 1	IR/RI	BC	New Westminster	92 H/4	49°11′	121°50′
Scheltens Lake	LAKE/LAC	AB	70-1-W4	73 M/1	55°05′	110°04′
Schewabik Lake	LAKE/LAC	ON	Sudbury	42 B/3	48°13′	83°10′
Schikaelton 16	IR/RI	BC	Kamloops Division Yale	92 I/6	50°25′	121°21′

NAME NOM	ENTITY ENTITÉ	LOC 1 LIEU 1	LOC 2 LIEU 2	MAP CARTE	POSITION LAT	POSITION LONG
Schindelsteddle	UNP/LNO	ON	Waterloo	40 P/7	43°23'	80°36'
Schistes, Chute aux	FALL/CHUT	QC	Kativik	24 C/11	56°44'	69°01'
Schist Falls	FALL/CHUT	ON	Thunder Bay	42 C/4	48°00'	85°53'
Schist Lake	UNP/LNO	MB	32-65-29-W	63 K/12	54°40'	101°48'
Schistose Lake	LAKE/LAC	ON	Kenora	52 F/4	49°10'	93°37'
Schkam 2	IR/RI	BC	Yale Division Yale	92 H/6	49°24'	121°27'
Schnares Crossing	UNP/LNO	NS	Lunenburg	21 A/8	44°24'	64°21'
Schoenfeld	UNP/LNO	SK	15-13-13-W3	72 J/4	50°06'	107°42'
Schoen Lake	LAKE/LAC	BC	Rupert	92 L/1	50°10'	126°16'
Schoenweise	UNP/LNO	SK	19-40-4-W3	73 B/7	52°27'	106°34'
Schoenwiese	UNP/LNO	MB	16,17-1-3-W	62 H/4	49°02'	97°49'
Schoenwiese	UNP/LNO	SK	34-13-13-W3	72 J/4	50°08'	107°39'
Schomberg	UNP/LNO	ON	York	31 D/4	44°00'	79°41'
Schomberg Heights	UNP/LNO	ON	Simcoe	31 D/4	44°02'	79°43'
Schomberg Point	CAPE/CAP	NT	Franklin	68 G	75°33'	102°47'
Schooner Harbour	BAY/BAIE	NT	Franklin	36 C	64°25'	77°54'
Schooner Point	CAPE/CAP	NF		1 M/4	47°07'	55°37'
Schooner Pond	UNP/LNO	NS	Cape Breton	11 J/4	46°10'	59°50'
Schoppe Ridge	SEAU/SMER	—		5.03	51°10'	139°30'
Schreiber	MUN2/AZM2	ON	Thunder Bay	42 D/14	48°49'	87°15'
Schreiber	UNP/LNO	ON	Thunder Bay	42 D/14	48°48'	87°15'
Schuler	UNP/LNO	AB	9-16-1-W4	72 L/8	50°20'	110°06'
Schultz Lake	LAKE/LAC	ON	Kenora	52 K/3	50°12'	93°25'
Schultz Lake	LAKE/LAC	NT	Keewatin	66 A	64°45'	97°30'
Schumacher	UNP/LNO	ON	Cochrane	42 A/6	48°28'	81°18'
Schutt	UNP/LNO	ON	Renfrew	31 F/3	45°15'	77°28'
Schuyter Point	CAPE/CAP	NT	Franklin	97 H	71°53'	120°21'
Schwandt River	RIV/CDE	NT/SK		64 M	60°07'	102°13'
Schwartz	UNP/LNO	QC	Pontiac	31 F/16	45°48'	76°22'
Schwatka Bay	BAY/BAIE	NT	Franklin	57 B	68°43'	95°39'
Schwitzer	UNP/LNO	MB	22-7-22-W	62 F/9	49°36'	100°22'
Schyan	UNP/LNO	QC	Pontiac	31 K/3	46°11'	77°01'
Schyan, Lac	LAKE/LAC	QC	Pontiac	31 K/6	46°18'	77°11'
Schyan Point	UNP/LNO	QC	Pontiac	31 K/3	46°06'	77°26'
Science Hill	UNP/LNO	ON	Perth	40 P/6	43°18'	81°12'
Scie, Rivière à la	RIV/CDE	QC	Desjardins	21 L/14	46°46'	71°13'
Scimitar Glacier	GLAC/GLAC	BC	Range 2 Coast	92 N/6	51°27'	125°13'
Sclanders	UNP/LNO	SK	34-26-W2	72 P/13	51°57'	105°34'
Sclater	UNP/LNO	MB	23-34-23-W	62 N/15	51°56'	100°37'
Sclater River	RIV/CDE	MB	36-36-20-W	63 C/1	52°08'	100°12'
Scoble West	UNP/LNO	ON	Thunder Bay	52 A/4	48°13'	89°38'
Scollard	UNP/LNO	AB	19-34-20-W4	82 P/15	51°56'	112°50'
Scone	UNP/LNO	ON	Bruce	41 A/6	44°18'	81°05'
Scorch Lake	LAKE/LAC	ON	Sudbury	42 B/8	48°17'	82°15'
Scoresby Bay	BAY/BAIE	NT	Franklin	29 G	79°56'	71°10'
Scoresby, Cape	CAPE/CAP	NT	Franklin	57 G	71°43'	93°41'
Scot Bay	BAY/BAIE	ON	Kenora	52 L/2	50°04'	95°00'
Scotch Bay	UNP/LNO	MB	28-21-7-W	62 J/16	50°50'	98°23'
Scotch Block	UNP/LNO	ON	Halton	30 M/12	43°34'	79°57'
Scotch Block	UNP/LNO	ON	Manitoulin	41 G/14	45°55'	83°21'
Scotch Bush	UNP/LNO	ON	Renfrew	31 F/7	45°26'	76°58'
Scotch Bush	UNP/LNO	ON	Hastings	31 F/4	45°14'	77°58'
Scotch Corners	UNP/LNO	ON	Lanark	31 F/1	45°05'	76°12'
Scotch Creek	UNP/LNO	BC	Kamloops Division Yale	82 L/14	50°54'	119°27'
Scotch Creek	RIV/CDE	BC	Kamloops Division Yale	82 L/13	50°55'	119°30'
Scotch Creek 4	IR/RI	BC	Kamloops Division Yale	82 L/14	50°55'	119°29'
Scotch Fir Point	CAPE/CAP	BC	New Westminster	92 F/9	49°44'	124°16'
Scotchfort	UNP/LNO	PE	Queens	11 L/7	46°21'	62°55'
Scotchfort 4	IR/RI	PE	Queens	11 L/7	46°22'	62°55'
Scotch Hill	UNP/LNO	NS	Inverness	11 K/6	46°24'	61°06'
Scotch Hill	UNP/LNO	NS	Pictou	11 E/10	45°42'	62°49'
Scotch Lake	UNP/LNO	NS	Cape Breton	11 K/1	46°11'	60°22'
Scotch Lake	UNP/LNO	NB	York	21 G/15	45°57'	66°58'
Scotch Lake	LAKE/LAC	ON	Kenora	52 G/3	49°10'	91°10'
Scotch Line	UNP/LNO	ON	Lanark	31 C/16	44°52'	76°16'
Scotch Point	UNP/LNO	ON	Leeds	31 C/16	44°46'	76°10'
Scotch Ridge	UNP/LNO	NB	Charlotte	21 G/6	45°17'	67°24'
Scotch Settlement	UNP/LNO	NB	Westmorland	21 I/2	46°14'	64°45'
Scotch Settlement	UNP/LNO	NB	York	21 G/15	45°59'	66°56'
Scotch Settlement	UNP/LNO	ON	Frontenac	31 C/1	44°13'	76°21'
Scotch Settlement	UNP/LNO	ON	Bruce	41 A/11	44°32'	81°17'
Scotchtown	UNP/LNO	NS	Cape Breton	11 K/1	46°14'	60°06'
Scotchtown	UNP/LNO	NB	Queens	21 G/16	45°54'	66°09'
Scotch Village	UNP/LNO	NS	Hants	11 E/4	45°03'	64°00'
Scotfield	UNP/LNO	AB	10-30-10-W4	72 M/11	51°33'	111°20'

NAME NOM	ENTITY ENTITÉ	LOC 1 LIEU 1	LOC 2 LIEU 2	MAP CARTE	POSITION LAT	LONG
Scotford	UNP/LNO	AB	20-55-21-W4	83 H/14	53°46′	113°05′
Scotia	UNP/LNO	ON	Parry Sound	31 E/11	45°30′	79°18′
Scotia Bay	UNP/LNO	BC	Cassiar	104 N/12	59°36′	133°49′
Scotia Lake	LAKE/LAC	ON	Sudbury	41 P/3	47°04′	81°24′
Scotian Rise	SEAU/SMER	—		1399A	42°00′	60°00′
Scotian Shelf - also-aussi - Néo-Écossaise, Plate-forme	SEAU/SMER	—		1399A	44°00′	62°30′
Scotian Slope	SEAU/SMER	—		1399A	43°00′	61°00′
Scotland	UNP/LNO	ON	Brant	40 P/1	43°01′	80°22′
Scot River	RIV/CDE	ON	Kenora	52 L/3	50°03′	95°01′
Scots Bay	UNP/LNO	NS	Kings	21 H/8	45°18′	64°24′
Scots Bay	BAY/BAIE	NS	Cumberland	21 H/8	45°18′	64°27′
Scots Bay Road	UNP/LNO	NS	Kings	21 H/1	45°14′	64°24′
Scotsburn	UNP/LNO	NS	Pictou	11 E/10	45°39′	62°51′
Scotsguard	UNP/LNO	SK	8-9-16-W3	72 F/9	49°43′	108°09′
Scotstoun Lake	LAKE/LAC	NT	Mackenzie	86 G	65°37′	115°06′
Scotstown	CITY/VIL1	QC	Le Haut-Saint-François	21 E/11	45°32′	71°17′
Scotsville	UNP/LNO	NS	Inverness	11 K/3	46°11′	61°09′
Scotswood	UNP/LNO	AB	13-82-5-W6	84 D/2	56°07′	118°39′
Scott	TOWN/VIL2	SK	21-39-20-W3	73 C/7	52°22′	108°50′
Scott	VILG/VILG	QC	La Nouvelle-Beauce	21 L/11	46°30′	71°04′
Scott	UNP/LNO	ON	Welland	30 M/3	43°06′	79°05′
Scott Bay	BAY/BAIE	NT	Franklin	68 C	73°00′	100°15′
Scott, Cape	CAPE/CAP	BC	Rupert	102 I/16	50°47′	128°26′
Scott, Cape	CAPE/CAP	NT	Franklin	89 A	76°31′	114°41′
Scott Channel	SEAU/SMER	—		19400A	50°00′	133°00′
Scott Channel	CHAN/CHEN	BC	Rupert	102 I/16	50°47′	128°28′
Scott Cove	UNP/LNO	BC	Range 1 Coast	92 L/16	50°46′	126°28′
Scott Falls	FALL/CHUT	NF		23 H/10	53°31′	64°32′
Scottie Creek	RIV/CDE	BC	Kamloops Division Yale	92 I/14	50°57′	121°26′
Scott Inlet	BAY/BAIE	NT	Franklin	27 G	71°05′	71°00′
Scott Island	ISL/ÎLE	NT	Franklin	27 G	71°06′	71°08′
Scott Islands	ISL/ÎLE	BC	Rupert	102 I/15	50°48′	128°50′
Scott Lake	LAKE/LAC	SK/NT		74 O/16	59°57′	106°15′
Scott No. 98	MUN2/AZM2	SK		72 H/16	49°55′	104°15′
Scott Road	UNP/LNO	NB	Westmorland	21 I/3	46°02′	65°06′
Scottsburgh	UNP/LNO	SK	14-14-9-W3	72 J/3	50°10′	107°08′
Scott Seamount	SEAU/SMER	—		5.03	50°20′	141°30′
Scott Seamount Chain	SEAU/SMER	—		19400A	50°40′	131°10′
Scott Settlement	UNP/LNO	ON	Hastings	31 F/4	45°12′	77°58′
Scott Settlement	UNP/LNO	ON	Peterborough	31 D/16	44°51′	78°03′
Scotts Hill	UNP/LNO	MB	3,4-12-12-E	52 E/13	49°58′	95°53′
Scott Siding	UNP/LNO	NB	York	21 G/13	45°55′	67°33′
Scotts Landing	UNP/LNO	ON	Peterborough	31 D/16	44°47′	78°04′
Scottsmore	UNP/LNO	QC	Brome-Missisquoi	31 H/2	45°11′	72°42′
Scottsville	UNP/LNO	ON	Middlesex	40 I/14	42°53′	81°17′
Scott Trough	SEAU/SMER	—		1399A	71°10′	70°35′
Scoudouc	UNP/LNO	NB	Westmorland	21 I/2	46°10′	64°34′
Scout Lake	HAM/HAM	SK	8-5-30-W2	72 H/5	49°22′	106°00′
Scovil	UNP/LNO	NB	Queens	21 G/16	45°46′	66°08′
Scovil	UNP/LNO	ON	Kenora	52 E/16	49°47′	94°13′
Scovil, Mount	MTN/MNT	BC	Cariboo	93 O/3	55°15′	123°26′
Scowban 28	IR/RI	BC	Cassiar	103 P/4	55°03′	129°59′
Scowlitz 1	IR/RI	BC	New Westminster	92 H/4	49°14′	121°56′
Scrabble Hill	UNP/LNO	NS	Colchester	11 E/5	45°26′	63°37′
Scraggy Lake	LAKE/LAC	NS	Halifax	11 D/15	44°57′	62°53′
Scrape Point	CAPE/CAP	NF		2 E/13	49°52′	55°38′
Scrape Shore	UNP/LNO	NF		1 K/12	46°37′	53°33′
Screech Seamount	SEAU/SMER	—		NK23	43°59′	46°41′
Scrip	UNP/LNO	SK	33-37-15-W2	73 A/1	52°14′	104°05′
Scrip Creek	RIV/CDE	BC	Kootenay	82 M/15	51°50′	118°39′
Scriven, Mount	MTN/MNT	BC	Range 1 Coast	92 K/12	50°38′	125°53′
Scroggie Creek	UNP/LNO	YT		115 O/2	63°12′	138°50′
Scroggie Creek	RIV/CDE	YT		115 O/2	63°12′	138°51′
Scruncheon Seamount	SEAU/SMER	—		NK23	43°45′	45°35′
Scudder	UNP/LNO	ON	Essex	40 G/15	41°49′	82°39′
Scud River	RIV/CDE	BC	Cassiar	104 G/5	57°18′	131°50′
Scugog	MUN2/AZM2	ON	Ontario	31 D/2	44°08′	78°55′
Scugog	UNP/LNO	ON	Ontario	31 D/2	44°10′	78°54′
Scugog 34 - see-voir - Mississauga's of Scugog Island 34	IR/RI	ON		31 D/2	44°11′	78°54′
Scugog Centre	UNP/LNO	ON	Ontario	31 D/2	44°09′	78°54′
Scugog, Lake	LAKE/LAC	ON	Ontario	31 D/2	44°10′	78°50′
Scugog Point	UNP/LNO	ON	Durham	31 D/2	44°11′	78°48′
Scugog River	RIV/CDE	ON	Victoria	31 D/7	44°24′	78°45′
Scuitto Lake	LAKE/LAC	BC	Kamloops Division Yale	92 I/9	50°33′	120°08′
Scully	UNP/LNO	ON	Algoma	42 C/9	48°32′	84°20′

NAME NOM	ENTITY ENTITÉ	LOC 1 LIEU 1	LOC 2 LIEU 2	MAP CARTE	POSITION LAT	LONG
Scuttsap 11	IR/RI	BC	Range 5 Coast	103 I/4	54°13′	129°34′
Scuttsap 11A	IR/RI	BC	Range 5 Coast	103 I/4	54°13′	129°34′
Scuzzy Creek	RIV/CDE	BC	Yale Division Yale	92 H/14	49°49′	121°27′
Scuzzy Mountain	MTN/MNT	BC	Yale Division Yale	92 H/13	49°51′	121°38′
Seabird Island	IR/RI	BC	Yale Division Yale	92 H/5	49°16′	121°43′
Seabird Lake	LAKE/LAC	BC	Range 1 Coast	92 K/12	50°31′	125°54′
Sea Breeze	UNP/LNO	ON	Muskoka	31 E/7	45°17′	78°58′
Seabright	UNP/LNO	NS	Halifax	11 D/12	44°37′	63°56′
Seabrook	UNP/LNO	NS	Digby	21 A/12	44°37′	65°48′
Seabrook Lake	LAKE/LAC	ON	Algoma	41 O/3	47°01′	83°17′
Seacliffe	UNP/LNO	ON	Essex	40 J/2	42°02′	82°37′
Seacow Head	CAPE/CAP	PE	Prince	11 L/5	46°19′	63°49′
Seacow Pond	UNP/LNO	PE	Prince	11 M/4	47°02′	64°00′
Seafair	UNP/LNO	BC	New Westminster	92 G/3	49°09′	123°11′
Seafoam	UNP/LNO	NS	Pictou	11 E/15	45°47′	62°58′
Seaford	UNP/LNO	BC	Sayward	92 K/2	50°05′	124°54′
Seaforth	TOWN/VIL2	ON	Huron	40 P/11	43°33′	81°24′
Seaforth	UNP/LNO	NS	Halifax	11 D/11	44°40′	63°16′
Seaforth Channel	CHAN/CHEN	BC	Range 3 Coast	103 A/1	52°14′	128°18′
Seager Wheeler Lake	LAKE/LAC	SK	61-10,11-W2	63 L/5	54°17′	103°31′
Seagram Lakes	LAKE/LAC	SK	41,42-24-W3	73 C/11	52°36′	109°23′
Seagrave	UNP/LNO	ON	Ontario	31 D/2	44°12′	78°57′
Seagrove	UNP/LNO	NS	Cumberland	11 E/13	45°59′	63°59′
Seagull Lake	LAKE/LAC	MB	16-10,11-W	62 J/7	50°23′	98°53′
Seah 5	IR/RI	BC	Kamloops Division Yale	92 I/5	50°30′	121°44′
Seahorse	UNP/LNO	NF		23 A/4	52°11′	65°42′
Seahorse Lake	LAKE/LAC	NF		23 A/4	52°12′	65°48′
Seahorse Lake	LAKE/LAC	NT	Mackenzie	76 D	64°18′	111°15′
Seahorse Point	CAPE/CAP	NT	Keewatin	45 P	63°47′	80°09′
Seaichem 16	IR/RI	BC	New Westminster	92 G/14	49°45′	123°08′
Sea Island	ISL/ÎLE	BC	New Westminster	92 G/3	49°11′	123°10′
Sea Island 3	IR/RI	BC	New Westminster	92 G/3	49°12′	123°12′
Seaks 3	IR/RI	BC	Cassiar	103 P/3	55°13′	129°07′
Seaks 60	IR/RI	BC	Cassiar	103 P/3	55°12′	129°03′
Seal Bay	BAY/BAIE	NF		2 E/5	49°26′	55°32′
Seal Bay	BAY/BAIE	NT	Franklin	67 D	69°29′	98°30′
Seal Bay Brook	RIV/CDE	NF		2 E/5	49°22′	55°35′
Seal Bay Head	CAPE/CAP	NF		2 E/5	49°29′	55°33′
Seal Bight	UNP/LNO	NF		3 D/5	52°27′	55°40′
Seal Brook	RIV/CDE	NF		11 P/12	47°40′	57°41′
Seal Cove	TOWN/VIL2	NF		12 H/16	49°56′	56°23′
Seal Cove	VILG/VILG	NF		11 P/8	47°29′	56°04′
Seal Cove	UNP/LNO	NF		1 N/2	47°11′	52°51′
Seal Cove	UNP/LNO	NF		1 N/6	47°28′	53°05′
Seal Cove	UNP/LNO	NS	Inverness	11 F/14	45°53′	61°06′
Seal Cove	UNP/LNO	NB	Charlotte	21 B/10	44°39′	66°51′
Seal Cove	UNP/LNO	QC	La Côte-de-Gaspé	22 A/9	48°44′	64°20′
Seal Harbour	UNP/LNO	NS	Guysborough	11 F/4	45°09′	61°35′
Sealhole Lake	LAKE/LAC	NT	Keewatin	65 B	60°50′	98°46′
Seal Inlet	BAY/BAIE	BC	Queen Charlotte	103 F/7	53°29′	132°45′
Seal Island	UNP/LNO	NS	Yarmouth	20 O/8	43°24′	66°01′
Seal Island	ISL/ÎLE	NS	Yarmouth	20 O/8	43°25′	66°01′
Seal Island Bight	BAY/BAIE	NF		2 E/14	49°59′	55°30′
Seal Islands Harbour	UNP/LNO	NF		3 E/4	53°13′	55°44′
Seal Lake	LAKE/LAC	NF		13 K/5	54°20′	61°40′
Seal Lake	LAKE/LAC	NT	Mackenzie	76 C	64°40′	108°58′
Seal Point	CAPE/CAP	PE	Prince	21 I/9	46°45′	64°23′
Seal River	UNP/LNO	PE	Kings	11 L/2	46°14′	62°33′
Seal River	UNP/LNO	PE	Queens	11 L/2	46°12′	62°54′
Seal River	RIV/CDE	MB		54 M/2	59°04′	94°48′
Seal Rocks	UNP/LNO	NF		12 B/8	48°26′	58°28′
Seamap Channel	SEAU/SMER	—		5.03	51°45′	162°30′
Sea Otter Harbour	BAY/BAIE	NT	Franklin	98 B	72°36′	125°00′
Sea Otter Island	ISL/ÎLE	NT	Franklin	98 B	72°33′	125°10′
Sea Otter Shoals	SEAU/SMER	—		19318A	51°15′	128°10′
Sea Otter Trough	SEAU/SMER	—		19318A	51°19′	129°00′
Searchmont	UNP/LNO	ON	Algoma	41 K/16	46°47′	84°03′
*Searle	UNP/LNO	MB		62 H/14	49°51′	97°15′
Searle, Cape	CAPE/CAP	NT	Franklin	16 M	67°14′	62°28′
Searletown	UNP/LNO	PE	Prince	11 L/5	46°18′	63°42′
Searston	UNP/LNO	NF		11 O/14	47°50′	59°19′
Searston Bay	BAY/BAIE	NF		11 O/14	47°49′	59°21′
Searsville	UNP/LNO	NB	Kings	21 H/12	45°43′	65°42′
Sea Side	UNP/LNO	NB	Restigouche	21 O/16	47°57′	66°08′
Seaside Park	UNP/LNO	BC	New Westminster	92 G/11	49°31′	123°29′

NAME NOM	ENTITY ENTITÉ	LOC 1 LIEU 1	LOC 2 LIEU 2	MAP CARTE	POSITION LAT	LONG
Seaspunkut 4	IR/RI	BC	Range 5 Coast	93 K/2	54°03'	124°46'
Seaton	UNP/LNO	BC	Cassiar	93 M/3	55°07'	127°21'
Seattle, Mount	MTN/MNT	YT		115 B/3	60°05'	139°12'
Sea View	UNP/LNO	PE	Queens	11 L/12	46°32'	63°36'
Seaview	UNP/LNO	NS	Richmond	11 F/10	45°41'	60°59'
Seaview	UNP/LNO	NB	Saint John	21 G/1	45°10'	66°11'
Seba Beach	VILG/VILG	AB	5,6-53-5-W5	83 G/10	53°33'	114°44'
Sebalhall Creek	RIV/CDE	BC	Rupert	92 L/1	50°05'	126°27'
Sebaskachu Bay	BAY/BAIE	NF		13 F/16	53°45'	60°00'
Sebaskachu River	RIV/CDE	NF		13 F/16	53°46'	60°07'
Sebastopol	MUN2/AZM2	ON	Renfrew	31 F/6	45°24'	77°13'
Sébastopol	UNP/LNO	QC	Memphrémagog	31 H/1	45°08'	72°19'
Sebastopol	UNP/LNO	ON	Perth	40 P/7	43°20'	80°50'
Sebert Lake	LAKE/LAC	ON	Kenora	42 M/16	51°57'	86°05'
Sebright	UNP/LNO	ON	Ontario	31 D/11	44°42'	79°10'
Sebright	UNP/LNO	MB	4,9-13-7-E	62 I/2	50°05'	96°34'
Sebringville	UNP/LNO	ON	Perth	40 P/6	43°24'	81°04'
Sèche, Baie	BAY/BAIE	QC	Kativik	24 K/12	58°39'	69°48'
Sèche, Baie	BAY/BAIE	NT	Franklin	24 K/9	58°33'	68°15'
Séchelles, Lac	LAKE/LAC	QC	Caniapiscau	23 C/6	52°20'	69°12'
Sechelt	MUN1/AZM1	BC	New Westminster	92 G/5	49°28'	123°46'
Sechelt Basin	SEAU/SMER	—		15792A	49°23'	123°40'
Sechelt Creek	RIV/CDE	BC	New Westminster	92 G/12	49°41'	123°33'
Sechelt Indian Government District	UNP/LNO	BC	New Westminster	92 G/5	49°29'	123°45'
Sechelt Inlet	BAY/BAIE	BC	New Westminster	92 G/12	49°36'	123°48'
Sechelt Peninsula	CAPE/CAP	BC	New Westminster	92 G/12	49°40'	123°55'
Sèche, Pointe	CAPE/CAP	QC	La Côte-de-Gaspé	22 H/2	49°10'	64°47'
Seckerton	UNP/LNO	ON	Lambton	40 J/16	42°51'	82°23'
Second Burnt Pond	LAKE/LAC	NF		2 D/16	48°47'	54°29'
Second Cranberry Lake	LAKE/LAC	MB	65-25-W	63 K/11	54°39'	101°41'
Second Double Pond	LAKE/LAC	NF		2 F/4	49°12'	53°59'
Second Eel Lake	LAKE/LAC	NB	York	21 G/13	45°48'	67°38'
Second Falls	UNP/LNO	NB	Charlotte	21 G/2	45°14'	66°51'
Second North River	UNP/LNO	NB	Westmorland	21 I/3	46°04'	65°05'
Secondon, Lac	LAKE/LAC	QC	Kativik	24 B/10	56°36'	66°58'
Second Peninsula	UNP/LNO	NS	Lunenburg	21 A/8	44°24'	64°17'
Second Pond	LAKE/LAC	NF		2 E/7	49°23'	54°38'
Secord	UNP/LNO	ON	Sudbury	41 I/7	46°20'	80°50'
Secretan	UNP/LNO	SK	26-17-4-W3	72 J/8	50°28'	106°28'
Secret Cove	UNP/LNO	BC	New Westminster	92 G/12	49°32'	123°57'
Secteur-Charlevoix	UNP/LNO	QC	Le Fjord-du-Saguenay	22 D/3	48°10'	71°04'
Secteur-Como	UNP/LNO	QC	Vaudreuil-Soulanges	31 G/8	45°26'	74°07'
Sedalia	UNP/LNO	AB	21-31-5-W4	72 M/10	51°41'	110°40'
Seddall	UNP/LNO	BC	Kamloops Division Yale	92 I/6	50°19'	121°24'
Seddons Corner	UNP/LNO	MB	4-13-9-E	62 I/1	50°04'	96°17'
Sedgewick	TOWN/VIL2	AB	9-44-12-W4	73 D/13	52°46'	111°41'
Sedley	VILG/VILG	SK	17-14-15-W2	72 I/1	50°10'	104°00'
Sedores	UNP/LNO	ON	York	31 D/6	44°19'	79°25'
Seebe	UNP/LNO	AB	33-24-8-W5	82 O/3	51°06'	115°04'
Seeber Lake	LAKE/LAC	ON	Kenora	53 F/14	53°51'	93°01'
Seeber River	RIV/CDE	MB/ON		53 K/7	54°25'	92°47'
Seech	UNP/LNO	MB	2-20-22-W	62 K/9	50°41'	100°26'
Seekaskootch 119	IR/RI	SK		73 F/12	53°42'	109°55'
Seektukis 24	IR/RI	BC	Clayoquot	92 E/8	49°22'	126°03'
Seela Pass	VALL/VALL	YT		116 B/10	64°42'	138°53'
Seeley	UNP/LNO	ON	Leeds	31 B/12	44°35'	75°49'
Seeleys Bay	UNP/LNO	ON	Leeds	31 C/8	44°29'	76°14'
Seeleys Cove	UNP/LNO	NB	Charlotte	21 G/2	45°05'	66°39'
Seeney	UNP/LNO	BC	Kootenay	82 N/2	51°03'	116°36'
Seffernsville	UNP/LNO	NS	Lunenburg	21 A/9	44°40'	64°24'
Segise Lake	LAKE/LAC	ON	Kenora	52 K/4	50°08'	93°35'
Seguin Falls	UNP/LNO	ON	Parry Sound	31 E/5	45°25'	79°40'
Seguin Lake	LAKE/LAC	ON	Parry Sound	31 E/12	45°32'	79°41'
Seibert	UNP/LNO	ON	Rainy River	52 C/11	48°39'	93°18'
Seibert Lake	LAKE/LAC	AB	66-9-W4	73 L/11	54°43'	111°19'
Seignelay, Rivière	RIV/CDE	QC	Manicouagan	22 N/11	51°36'	69°06'
Seigneurie-de-Vaudreuil	UNP/LNO	QC	Vaudreuil-Soulanges	31 G/8	45°25'	74°03'
Seine River	RIV/CDE	ON	Rainy River	52 C/10	48°40'	92°49'
Seine River - also-aussi - +Seine, Rivière	RIV/CDE	MB		62 H/14	49°54'	97°07'
Seine River 22A2	IR/RI	ON	Thunder Bay	52 G/2	49°01'	90°53'
Seine River 23A	IR/RI	ON	Rainy River	52 C/9	48°42'	92°27'
Seine River 23B	IR/RI	ON	Rainy River	52 C/10	48°40'	92°47'
Seine River Village	UNP/LNO	ON	Rainy River	52 C/9	48°43'	92°26'
+Seine, Rivière - also-aussi - Seine River	RIV/CDE	MB		62 H/14	49°54'	97°07'
Sekulmun Lake	LAKE/LAC	YT		115 H/5	61°26'	137°33'

NAME / NOM	ENTITY / ENTITÉ	LOC 1 / LIEU 1	LOC 2 / LIEU 2	MAP / CARTE	LAT	LONG
Selby	UNP/LNO	ON	Lennox and Addington	31 C/7	44°18′	76°59′
Seldom	UNP/LNO	NF		2 E/9	49°37′	54°11′
Seldom Come By	UNP/LNO	NF		2 E/9	49°37′	54°11′
Seldom-Little Seldom	TOWN/VIL2	NF		2 E/9	49°36′	54°12′
Self Lake	LAKE/LAC	NT	Mackenzie	86 F	65°18′	117°15′
Selfridge Corner	UNP/LNO	NS	Kings	21 H/2	45°02′	64°53′
Selim	UNP/LNO	ON	Thunder Bay	42 D/14	48°50′	87°24′
Selish Mountain	MTN/MNT	BC	Kamloops Division Yale	92 H/15	49°59′	120°49′
Selkirk	TOWN/VIL2	MB		62 I/2	50°09′	96°53′
Selkirk	UNP/LNO	PE	Kings	11 L/8	46°25′	62°27′
Selkirk	UNP/LNO	ON	Haldimand	30 L/13	42°49′	79°56′
Selkirk Bay	BAY/BAIE	NT	Franklin	47 B	68°13′	85°50′
Selkirk, Cape	CAPE/CAP	NT	Keewatin	57 B	68°22′	94°12′
Selkirk, Cape	CAPE/CAP	NT	Franklin	67 D	69°55′	96°08′
Selkirk Mountains	MTN/MNT	BC	Kootenay	82 K/12	50°30′	117°30′
Sellars	UNP/LNO	ON	Thunder Bay	52 A/5	48°17′	89°45′
Sellarsville	UNP/LNO	QC	Avignon	22 B/2	48°00′	66°52′
Seller Lake	LAKE/LAC	MB		53 L/15	55°00′	94°31′
Sellwood	UNP/LNO	ON	Sudbury	41 I/14	46°51′	81°01′
Sellwood Bay	BAY/BAIE	NT	Franklin	97 C	69°55′	125°00′
Selma	UNP/LNO	NS	Hants	11 E/5	45°19′	63°32′
Selma Park	UNP/LNO	BC	New Westminster	92 G/5	49°28′	123°44′
Seloam Lake	LAKE/LAC	NS	Halifax	11 E/2	45°10′	62°30′
Selous, Mount	MTN/MNT	YT		105 K/16	62°58′	132°30′
Seltat Peak	MTN/MNT	BC	Cassiar	114 P/9	59°36′	136°22′
Selton	UNP/LNO	ON	Leeds	31 B/5	44°22′	75°59′
Selton	UNP/LNO	ON	Kent	40 I/12	42°30′	81°57′
Selwood	UNP/LNO	NB	Restigouche	21 O/16	47°59′	66°25′
Selwyn	UNP/LNO	ON	Peterborough	31 D/8	44°28′	78°19′
Selwyn	UNP/LNO	YT		115 J/16	62°48′	138°17′
Selwyn Inlet	BAY/BAIE	BC	Queen Charlotte	103 B/13	52°52′	131°46′
Selwyn Lake	LAKE/LAC	ON	Thunder Bay	52 G/7	49°27′	90°53′
Selwyn Lake	LAKE/LAC	NT/SK		75 A/1	60°03′	104°29′
Selwyn Mountains	MTN/MNT	YT/NT		105 O	62°07′	129°15′
Semach 2	IR/RI	BC	Rupert	102 I/9	50°40′	128°21′
Semans	VILG/VILG	SK	22-28-20-W2	72 P/7	51°25′	104°44′
Semenof Hills	MTN/MNT	YT		105 E/7	61°27′	134°35′
Semiahmoo Bay	BAY/BAIE	BC	New Westminster	92 G/2	49°01′	122°50′
Semiahmoo	IR/RI	BC	New Westminster	92 G/2	49°00′	122°46′
Seminole Seamount	SEAU/SMER	—		15798A	49°46′	129°50′
Semiwagan Ridge	UNP/LNO	NB	Northumberland	21 I/13	46°52′	65°34′
Semiwagan Stream	RIV/CDE	NB	Northumberland	21 I/13	46°53′	65°36′
Semlin	UNP/LNO	BC	Kamloops Division Yale	92 I/14	50°47′	121°06′
Semmens Lake	LAKE/LAC	MB		53 M/1	55°03′	94°12′
Semmens River	RIV/CDE	MB		53 N/4	55°07′	93°42′
Semple Lake	LAKE/LAC	MB		53 M/4	55°03′	95°37′
Senanus Island 10	IR/RI	BC	Victoria	92 B/11	48°36′	123°29′
Senate	UNP/LNO	SK	3-4-28-W3	72 F/5	49°17′	109°42′
Senator	UNP/LNO	SK	16-46-25-W2	73 H/4	53°03′	105°36′
Sen Bay	BAY/BAIE	ON	Kenora	52 J/5	50°16′	91°46′
Senecal	UNP/LNO	ON	Prescott	31 G/10	45°34′	75°00′
Sénécal, Lac - also-aussi - Senécal Lake	LAKE/LAC	QC	Minganie	13 D/3	52°03′	63°22′
Senécal Lake - also-aussi - Sénécal, Lac	LAKE/LAC	NF		13 D/3	52°03′	63°22′
Sénescoupé, Rivière	RIV/CDE	QC	Les Basques	21 N/14	47°56′	69°05′
Senkiw	UNP/LNO	MB	17-3-5-E	62 H/2	49°12′	96°53′
Senlac	VILG/VILG	SK	32-40-26-W3	73 C/5	52°29′	109°42′
Senlac No. 411	MUN2/AZM2	SK		73 C/12	52°35′	109°45′
Senneterre	CITY/VIL1	QC	Vallée-de-l'Or	32 C/6	48°23′	77°14′
Senneterre	VILG/VILG	QC	Vallée-de-l'Or	32 C/6	48°23′	77°15′
Senneville	TOWN/VIL2	QC	Communauté urbaine de Montréal	31 H/5	45°25′	73°57′
Senneville, Lac	LAKE/LAC	QC	Vallée-de-l'Or	32 C/4	48°14′	77°41′
Sentiers-du-Sommet	UNP/LNO	QC	Les Pays-d'en-Haut	31 J/1	46°02′	74°03′
Sentinel	UNP/LNO	AB	10-8-5-W5	82 G/10	49°38′	114°35′
Sentinel Hill	UNP/LNO	BC	New Westminster	92 G/6	49°20′	123°08′
Sentinel Mountain	MTN/MNT	BC	Cassiar	104 N/6	59°26′	133°26′
Sentinel Peak	MTN/MNT	BC	Cariboo	93 I/13	54°54′	121°58′
Sentry Island	ISL/ÎLE	NT	Keewatin	55 F	61°10′	93°51′
Senyk Lakes	LAKE/LAC	SK	75-7-W3	73 O/6	55°30′	107°01′
Seouls Corners	UNP/LNO	ON	Frontenac	31 C/15	44°47′	76°48′
Separation Lake	LAKE/LAC	ON	Kenora	52 L/1	50°14′	94°24′
Separation Point	UNP/LNO	NF		13 H/11	53°37′	57°25′
Separation, Point	CAPE/CAP	NT	Mackenzie	106 M	67°37′	134°05′
Sept-Chutes	UNP/LNO	QC	La Côte-de-Beaupré	21 M/2	47°07′	70°50′
Sept-Côtes, Les	UNP/LNO	QC	Charlevoix-Est	21 N/13	47°45′	69°58′
Sept-Crans, Les	UNP/LNO	QC	La Côte-de-Beaupré	21 M/2	47°05′	70°59′

NAME NOM	ENTITY ENTITÉ	LOC 1 LIEU 1	LOC 2 LIEU 2	MAP CARTE	POSITION LAT	LONG
September Mountains	MTN/MNT	NT	Mackenzie	86 O	67°11′	115°56′
Sept-Îles	CITY/VIL1	QC	Sept-Rivières	22 J/1	50°12′	66°23′
Sept Îles, Baie des	BAY/BAIE	QC	Sept-Rivières	22 J/1	50°12′	66°28′
Sept Îles, Lac	LAKE/LAC	QC	Portneuf	21 L/13	46°56′	71°45′
Sept Îles, Lac des	LAKE/LAC	QC	Pabok	22 A/7	48°22′	64°48′
Sept-Îles — Port-Cartier, Réserve faunique de	PARK/PARC	QC	Sept-Rivières	22 J/1	50°30′	67°12′
Septimus	UNP/LNO	BC	Peace River	94 A/2	56°10′	120°53′
Sept Milles, Lac	LAKE/LAC	QC	Pontiac	31 K/12	46°42′	77°41′
Sept Milles, Lac des	LAKE/LAC	QC	Le Fjord-du-Saguenay	22 M/2	51°14′	70°44′
Sept-Rivières	MUN1/AZM1	QC	Sept-Rivières	22 J/2	50°08′	66°37′
Sequart Lake	LAKE/LAC	NF		13 D/5	52°26′	63°47′
Serath	UNP/LNO	SK	36-25-19-W2	72 P/2	51°11′	104°31′
Sergent	UNP/LNO	SK	59-14-W3	73 K/1	54°05′	108°00′
Sergent, Lac	LAKE/LAC	QC	Portneuf	21 L/13	46°52′	71°43′
Sérigny, Lac	LAKE/LAC	QC	Kativik	23 N/5	55°22′	69°38′
Sérigny, Rivière	RIV/CDE	QC	Kativik	23 N/15	56°00′	68°40′
Serpent Harbour	BAY/BAIE	ON	Algoma	41 J/2	46°12′	82°39′
Serpentine	UNP/LNO	NF		12 B/16	48°48′	58°09′
Serpentine Lake	LAKE/LAC	NF		12 B/16	48°53′	58°17′
Serpentine Lake	LAKE/LAC	NB	Northumberland	21 O/2	47°07′	66°52′
Serpentine River	RIV/CDE	NF		12 B/15	48°57′	58°30′
Serpentine River	RIV/CDE	NB	Victoria	21 O/2	47°15′	67°00′
Serpent, Lac du	LAKE/LAC	QC	Maria-Chapdelaine	22 E/13	49°49′	71°37′
Serpent River	UNP/LNO	ON	Algoma	41 J/2	46°12′	82°34′
Serpent River	RIV/CDE	ON	Algoma	41 J/2	46°12′	82°38′
Serpent River	RIV/CDE	ON	Kenora	52 N/10	51°36′	92°40′
Serpent River 7	IR/RI	ON	Algoma	41 J/2	46°11′	82°33′
Serpent, Rivière au	RIV/CDE	QC	Maria-Chapdelaine	22 E/11	49°34′	71°13′
Service	UNP/LNO	SK	26-8-1-W2	62 E/9	49°40′	102°02′
Servos	UNP/LNO	ON	Sudbury	41 I/2	46°12′	80°44′
Seseganaga Lake	LAKE/LAC	ON	Thunder Bay	52 G/16	50°00′	90°28′
Sesekinika	UNP/LNO	ON	Timiskaming	42 A/1	48°12′	80°14′
Sesekinika Lake	LAKE/LAC	ON	Timiskaming	42 A/1	48°11′	80°14′
Sesikinaga Lake	LAKE/LAC	ON	Kenora	52 N/1	51°09′	92°09′
Sesitinikastikw	UNP/LNO	QC	Jamésie	32 L/1	50°06′	78°07′
Seskatciwan	UNP/LNO	QC	Le Haut-Saint-Maurice	32 B/10	48°43′	74°56′
Sether, Mount	MTN/MNT	YT		115 P/8	63°20′	136°13′
Seton	UNP/LNO	BC	Lillooet	92 J/9	50°43′	122°17′
Seton Lake	LAKE/LAC	BC	Lillooet	92 J/9	50°41′	122°07′
Seton Lake 5	IR/RI	BC	Lillooet	92 I/12	50°40′	121°59′
Seton Lake 5A	IR/RI	BC	Lillooet	92 J/9	50°43′	122°18′
Seton Portage	UNP/LNO	BC	Lillooet	92 J/9	50°42′	122°17′
Settee Lake	LAKE/LAC	MB		64 H/2	57°03′	96°55′
Settee Lake	LAKE/LAC	SK		73 P/16	55°50′	104°05′
Setting Lake	LAKE/LAC	MB		63 J/15	55°00′	98°37′
Seul, Lac	LAKE/LAC	ON	Kenora	52 K/8	50°20′	92°30′
Seven Islands 27A - see-voir - Maliotenam 27A	IR/RI	QC		22 J/1	50°13′	66°11′
Seven Islands Bay	BAY/BAIE	NF		14 M/5	59°25′	63°45′
Seven Islands Crossing	UNP/LNO	NT	Mackenzie	106 O/5	67°23′	131°56′
Seven Islands (Pt-des-Saubles) 27 - see-voir - Uashat 27	IR/RI	QC		22 J/1	50°13′	66°24′
Sevenmile	UNP/LNO	SK	32-16-27-W2	72 I/5	50°23′	105°41′
Sevenmile Bay	BAY/BAIE	PE	Prince	11 L/5	46°17′	63°45′
Seven Mile Corner	UNP/LNO	BC	Peace River	93 P/16	55°54′	120°19′
Seven Mile Lake	LAKE/LAC	NS	Lunenburg	21 A/7	44°27′	64°46′
Seven Mile Lake	LAKE/LAC	NB	Kings	21 G/1	45°13′	66°27′
Seven Mile Narrows	UNP/LNO	ON	Parry Sound	41 H/8	45°16′	80°07′
Seven Oaks	UNP/LNO	MB		62 H/14	49°56′	97°06′
Sevenoaks	UNP/LNO	BC	Victoria	92 B/6	48°28′	123°23′
Seven Persons	UNP/LNO	AB	4-11-7-W4	72 E/15	49°52′	110°54′
Seven Persons Creek	RIV/CDE	AB	29-12-5-W4	72 L/2	50°02′	110°39′
Seven Sisters Falls	UNP/LNO	MB	27-13-11-E	62 I/1	50°06′	96°01′
Seven Sisters Peaks	MTN/MNT	BC	Range 5 Coast	103 I/16	54°58′	128°12′
70 Mile	UNP/LNO	BC	Lillooet	92 P/6	51°18′	121°24′
70 Mile House	UNP/LNO	BC	Lillooet	92 P/6	51°18′	121°24′
Severn	MUN2/AZM2	ON	Simcoe	31 D/13	44°45′	79°30′
Severn Bridge	UNP/LNO	ON	Muskoka	31 D/14	44°46′	79°20′
Severn Falls	UNP/LNO	ON	Simcoe	31 D/13	44°52′	79°36′
Severn Lake	LAKE/LAC	ON	Kenora	53 G/15	53°54′	90°48′
Severn River	RIV/CDE	ON	Muskoka	31 D/13	44°48′	79°43′
Severn River	RIV/CDE	ON	Kenora	44 D/4	56°02′	87°36′
Severson, Monts	MTN/MNT	QC	Caniapiscau	23 B/14	52°45′	67°15′
Sevestre, Lac	LAKE/LAC	QC	Caniapiscau	23 C/9	52°34′	68°01′
Seville	UNP/LNO	ON	Elgin	40 I/15	42°46′	80°54′
Sevogle	UNP/LNO	NB	Northumberland	21 P/4	47°05′	65°50′
Sewall	UNP/LNO	BC	Queen Charlotte	103 F/16	53°46′	132°18′

NAME NOM	ENTITY ENTITÉ	LOC 1 LIEU 1	LOC 2 LIEU 2	MAP CARTE	POSITION LAT	POSITION LONG
Seward	UNP/LNO	SK	36-14-16-W3	72 K/1	50°13′	108°04′
Seward Glacier	GLAC/GLAC	YT		115 C/8	60°16′	140°18′
Sewell	UNP/LNO	MB	1-4-1-W	62 H/6	49°16′	97°28′
Sewell Inlet	UNP/LNO	BC	Queen Charlotte	103 B/13	52°53′	131°59′
Sewell Ridge	SEAU/SMER	—		4011	42°40′	67°30′
Sewer Copse	UNP/LNO	QC	La Jacques-Cartier	21 L/13	46°54′	71°30′
Sexsmith	TOWN/VIL2	AB	25-73-6-W6	83 M/7	55°21′	118°47′
Seymour	MUN2/AZM2	ON	Northumberland	31 C/5	44°20′	77°47′
Seymour Arm	UNP/LNO	BC	Kamloops Division Yale	82 M/2	51°14′	118°57′
Seymour Arm	BAY/BAIE	BC	Kamloops Division Yale	82 M/2	51°08′	119°00′
Seymour Beach	UNP/LNO	ON	Essex	40 J/2	42°01′	82°59′
Seymour Creek 2	IR/RI	BC	New Westminster	92 G/6	49°18′	123°02′
Seymour Heights	UNP/LNO	BC	New Westminster	92 G/7	49°19′	123°00′
Seymour Inlet	BAY/BAIE	BC	Range 2 Coast	92 M/3	51°04′	127°10′
Seymour Lake	UNP/LNO	BC	Range 5 Coast	93 L/14	54°45′	127°10′
Seymour Land District	GEOG/GÉOG	BC		92 B	48°50′	123°50′
Seymour Landing	UNP/LNO	BC	New Westminster	92 G/6	49°21′	123°21′
Seymour Meadows 19	IR/RI	BC	Range 3 Coast	93 C/1	52°12′	124°27′
Seymour River	RIV/CDE	BC	Kamloops Division Yale	82 M/2	51°15′	118°57′
Seymour River	RIV/CDE	BC	New Westminster	92 G/6	49°18′	123°01′
Seymourville	UNP/LNO	MB	26-9-E	62 P/1	51°11′	96°20′
Shabaqua	UNP/LNO	ON	Thunder Bay	52 A/12	48°35′	89°55′
Shabaqua Corners	UNP/LNO	ON	Thunder Bay	52 A/12	48°36′	89°54′
Shabastic Channel	CHAN/CHEN	ON	Kenora	53 I/12	54°35′	89°40′
Shabo	UNP/LNO	NF		23 G/8	53°19′	66°12′
Shabogamo Lake	LAKE/LAC	NF		23 G/1	53°15′	66°30′
Shabotik River	RIV/CDE	ON	Thunder Bay	42 C/13	48°51′	85°35′
Shabuskwia Lake	LAKE/LAC	ON	Thunder Bay	52 P/2	51°15′	89°00′
Shacabac Lake	LAKE/LAC	ON	Thunder Bay	42 F/13	49°58′	85°55′
Shackan 11	IR/RI	BC	Kamloops Division Yale	92 I/6	50°17′	121°12′
Shack-du-Garde-Feu, Le	UNP/LNO	QC	Antoine-Labelle	31 O/4	47°00′	75°45′
Shackleton	VILG/VILG	SK	8-20-19-W3	72 K/10	50°41′	108°36′
Shad Bay	UNP/LNO	NS	Halifax	11 D/12	44°31′	63°47′
Shad Bay	BAY/BAIE	NS	Halifax	11 D/12	44°31′	63°48′
Shadd Lake	LAKE/LAC	SK		73 P/11	55°41′	105°26′
Shadow Lake	LAKE/LAC	ON	Victoria	31 D/10	44°43′	78°48′
Shady Grove	UNP/LNO	SK	16,17-36-21-W2	73 A/2	52°05′	104°58′
Shady Nook	UNP/LNO	ON	Renfrew	31 F/14	45°46′	77°07′
Shady Valley	UNP/LNO	BC	Cariboo	93 G/15	53°58′	122°43′
Shaftesbury Inlet	BAY/BAIE	NT	Franklin	25 K	62°35′	69°16′
Shaftesbury Settlement	UNP/LNO	AB	83-22-W5	84 C/3	56°10′	117°25′
Shagamu Lake	LAKE/LAC	ON	Kenora	43 M/3	55°05′	87°04′
Shagamu River	RIV/CDE	ON	Kenora	43 M/15	55°52′	86°47′
Shag Harbour	UNP/LNO	NS	Shelburne	20 P/5	43°30′	65°42′
Shag, Île	ISL/ÎLE	QC	Les Îles-de-la-Madeleine	11 N/5	47°29′	61°42′
Shag Island	ISL/ÎLE	NF		12 B/15	48°52′	58°36′
Shag Islands	ISL/ÎLE	NF		2 C/12	48°42′	53°37′
Shagwenaw Lake	LAKE/LAC	SK		73 O/13	55°54′	107°41′
Shakan Creek	RIV/CDE	BC	Kamloops Division Yale	92 I/6	50°17′	121°10′
Shakespeare	UNP/LNO	ON	Perth	40 P/7	43°22′	80°49′
Shakespeare Island	ISL/ÎLE	ON	Thunder Bay	52 H/9	49°38′	88°25′
Shakwa Lake	LAKE/LAC	ON	Algoma	41 I/13	46°46′	81°59′
Shalalth	UNP/LNO	BC	Lillooet	92 J/9	50°44′	122°13′
Shale Banks	UNP/LNO	AB	49-2-W6	83 E/1	53°14′	118°12′
Shaler Mountains	MTN/MNT	NT	Franklin	77 G	71°55′	111°30′
Shallop Cove	UNP/LNO	NF		12 B/7	48°25′	58°32′
Shalloway	UNP/LNO	NF		1 M/3	47°00′	55°10′
Shalloway Brook	RIV/CDE	NF		2 F/5	49°24′	53°49′
Shalloway Cove	UNP/LNO	NF		2 C/13	48°51′	53°41′
Shallow Bay	BAY/BAIE	NT	Mackenzie	107 B	68°50′	135°40′
Shallow Lake	VILG/VILG	ON	Grey	41 A/11	44°36′	81°05′
Shallow Lake	UNP/LNO	ON	Cochrane	42 G/11	49°39′	83°17′
Shallow Lake	LAKE/LAC	SK	65-16-W3	73 K/9	54°37′	108°18′
Shamattawa	UNP/LNO	MB		53 N/16	55°51′	92°05′
Shamattawa 1	IR/RI	MB		53 N/16	55°52′	92°06′
Shamattawa River	RIV/CDE	ON	Kenora	43 N/3	55°01′	85°23′
Sham Bay	BAY/BAIE	NT	Franklin	24 K	58°36′	68°20′
Shamblers Cove	UNP/LNO	NF		2 F/4	49°04′	53°36′
Shames	UNP/LNO	BC	Range 5 Coast	103 I/7	54°25′	128°56′
Shammis Island	ISL/ÎLE	ON	Kenora	52 E/10	49°37′	94°32′
Shampers	UNP/LNO	NB	Kings	21 G/9	45°32′	66°01′
Shamrock	VILG/VILG	SK	9-14-5-W3	72 J/2	50°10′	106°37′
Shamrock	UNP/LNO	PE	Prince	11 L/5	46°19′	63°32′
Shamrock	UNP/LNO	ON	Renfrew	31 F/7	45°23′	76°50′
Shamrock Dome	MTN/MNT	YT		115 O/5	63°16′	139°42′

NAME NOM	ENTITY ENTITÉ	LOC 1 LIEU 1	LOC 2 LIEU 2	MAP CARTE	POSITION LAT	LONG
Shamrock No. 134	MUN2/AZM2	SK		72 J/2	50°10′	106°35′
Shanadithit Brook	RIV/CDE	NF		12 A/11	48°37′	57°07′
Shana Mountain	MTN/MNT	BC	Cassiar	104 K/4	58°51′	133°07′
Shand	UNP/LNO	SK	4-2-7-W2	62 E/2	49°06′	102°53′
Shand Creek	RIV/CDE	SK	8-42-5-W2	63 D/10	52°36′	102°41′
Shandro	UNP/LNO	AB	27-57-15-W4	83 H/16	53°57′	112°10′
Shands	UNP/LNO	ON	Wellington	40 P/9	43°44′	80°21′
Shand's Corner	UNP/LNO	ON	Norfolk	40 I/16	42°50′	80°12′
Shanes	UNP/LNO	ON	Leeds	31 C/16	44°50′	76°01′
Shanick	UNP/LNO	ON	Hastings	31 C/12	44°36′	77°42′
Shaniko	UNP/LNO	ON	Timiskaming	42 A/1	48°07′	80°06′
Shanklin	UNP/LNO	NB	Saint John	21 H/5	45°21′	65°38′
Shanks	UNP/LNO	QC	Sherbrooke	31 H/8	45°18′	72°03′
Shanks Lake	LAKE/LAC	AB	1-21-W4	82 H/2	49°04′	112°43′
Shanly	UNP/LNO	ON	Grenville	31 B/14	44°53′	75°28′
Shannon	VILG/VILG	QC	La Jacques-Cartier	21 L/13	46°53′	71°31′
Shannon	UNP/LNO	NB	Queens	21 H/12	45°42′	65°59′
Shannon	UNP/LNO	BC	New Westminster	92 G/11	49°40′	123°10′
Shannon Bay	UNP/LNO	BC	Queen Charlotte	103 F/9	53°39′	132°30′
Shannon Hall	UNP/LNO	ON	Muskoka	31 E/5	45°18′	79°32′
Shannon Lake	LAKE/LAC	MB		64 O/12	59°33′	99°58′
Shannon Park	UNP/LNO	NS	Halifax	11 D/12	44°41′	63°36′
Shannons Corners	UNP/LNO	ON	Frontenac	31 C/7	44°19′	76°30′
Shannonvale	UNP/LNO	NB	Restigouche	22 B/1	48°01′	66°27′
Shannonville	UNP/LNO	ON	Hastings	31 C/3	44°12′	77°13′
Shanty Bay	UNP/LNO	ON	Simcoe	31 D/5	44°25′	79°36′
Shanty Bay	UNP/LNO	ON	Sudbury	41 I/1	46°11′	80°23′
Shantz	UNP/LNO	AB	27-31-4-W5	82 O/9	51°41′	114°28′
Shapio Lake	LAKE/LAC	NF		13 K/14	55°00′	61°18′
Sharbot Lake	UNP/LNO	ON	Frontenac	31 C/15	44°46′	76°41′
Sharbot Lake	LAKE/LAC	ON	Frontenac	31 C/15	44°46′	76°41′
Sharko Peninsula	CAPE/CAP	NT	Franklin	25 I	62°42′	65°20′
Sharks Cove	UNP/LNO	NF		1 N/11	47°34′	53°13′
Sharon	UNP/LNO	ON	York	31 D/3	44°06′	79°26′
Sharon	UNP/LNO	ON	Middlesex	40 I/14	42°53′	81°22′
Sharp, Cape	CAPE/CAP	PE	Kings	11 L/1	46°06′	62°27′
Sharp, Cape	CAPE/CAP	NS	Cumberland	21 H/8	45°22′	64°23′
Sharpe	UNP/LNO	SK	22-51-25-W2	73 H/5	53°25′	105°36′
Sharpe Lake	LAKE/LAC	MB		53 K/5	54°24′	93°30′
Sharpes Creek	RIV/CDE	ON	Huron	40 P/12	43°43′	81°37′
Sharpewood	UNP/LNO	MB	16-22-3-W	62 I/13	50°53′	97°49′
Sharples	UNP/LNO	AB	17-29-22-W4	82 P/6	51°28′	113°04′
Sharples Lake	LAKE/LAC	NT	Mackenzie	85 P	63°53′	112°59′
Sharp Point	CAPE/CAP	BC	Clayoquot	92 E/8	49°21′	126°16′
Sharps Corners	UNP/LNO	ON	Lennox and Addington	31 C/6	44°20′	77°00′
Sharpstone Lake	LAKE/LAC	ON	Kenora	53 D/2	52°02′	94°57′
Sharpton	UNP/LNO	ON	Frontenac	31 C/7	44°19′	76°40′
Sharrow	UNP/LNO	AB	35-22-2-W4	72 L/16	50°55′	110°11′
Sharun Lake	LAKE/LAC	NT	Mackenzie	85 K	62°05′	117°33′
Shas Dzuhl Koh 35	IR/RI	BC	Range 5 Coast	93 K/7	54°30′	124°59′
Shatford Creek	RIV/CDE	BC	Osoyoos Division Yale	82 E/5	49°28′	119°43′
Shaughnessy	UNP/LNO	AB	30-10-21-W4	82 H/15	49°51′	112°50′
Shaughnessy	UNP/LNO	BC	New Westminster	92 G/3	49°15′	123°08′
Shaughnessy Heights	UNP/LNO	MB		62 H/14	49°56′	97°10′
Shaunavon	TOWN/VIL2	SK		72 F/9	49°39′	108°25′
Shaver	UNP/LNO	AB	23-70-5-W6	83 M/2	55°05′	118°39′
Shaw	UNP/LNO	AB	12-48-22-W5	83 F/3	53°07′	117°07′
Shawanabis Lake	LAKE/LAC	ON	Thunder Bay	52 I/3	50°15′	89°29′
Shawanaga	UNP/LNO	ON	Parry Sound	41 H/9	45°31′	80°17′
Shawanaga 17	IR/RI	ON	Parry Sound	41 H/9	45°31′	80°20′
Shawanaga 17B	IR/RI	ON	Parry Sound	41 H/9	45°31′	80°20′
Shawanaga Inlet	BAY/BAIE	ON	Parry Sound	41 H/9	45°32′	80°24′
Shawanaga Island	ISL/ÎLE	ON	Parry Sound	41 H/9	45°30′	80°26′
Shawanaga Landing	UNP/LNO	ON	Parry Sound	41 H/9	45°31′	80°23′
Shawanaga River	RIV/CDE	ON	Parry Sound	41 H/9	45°33′	80°23′
Shawbridge	UNP/LNO	QC	La Rivière-du-Nord	31 G/16	45°52′	74°05′
Shaw Brook	UNP/LNO	NB	Westmorland	21 I/2	46°13′	64°53′
Shawinigan	CITY/VIL1	QC	Le Centre-de-la-Mauricie	31 I/10	46°33′	72°45′
Shawinigan, Chutes de	FALL/CHUT	QC	Le Centre-de-la-Mauricie	31 I/10	46°32′	72°46′
Shawinigan, Lac	LAKE/LAC	QC	Maskinongé	31 I/11	46°41′	73°09′
Shawinigan-Nord	UNP/LNO	QC	Le Centre-de-la-Mauricie	31 I/10	46°34′	72°46′
Shawinigan, Rivière	RIV/CDE	QC	Le Centre-de-la-Mauricie	31 I/10	46°32′	72°46′
Shawinigan-Sud	CITY/VIL1	QC	Le Centre-de-la-Mauricie	31 I/10	46°31′	72°45′
Shaw Island	UNP/LNO	NS	Lunenburg	21 A/9	44°33′	64°17′
Shaw Lake	LAKE/LAC	SK		64 D/7	56°22′	102°31′

NAME NOM	ENTITY ENTITÉ	LOC 1 LIEU 1	LOC 2 LIEU 2	MAP CARTE	POSITION LAT	LONG
Shawl Bay	UNP/LNO	BC	Range 1 Coast	92 L/15	50°51′	126°33′
Shawmere	UNP/LNO	ON	Sudbury	42 B/7	48°20′	82°33′
Shawmere River	RIV/CDE	ON	Sudbury	42 B/8	48°20′	82°29′
Shawnigan	UNP/LNO	BC	Shawnigan	92 B/12	48°39′	123°38′
Shawnigan Lake	UNP/LNO	BC	Shawnigan	92 B/12	48°39′	123°38′
Shawnigan Lake	LAKE/LAC	BC	Malahat	92 B/12	48°37′	123°38′
Shawnigan Land District	GEOG/GÉOG	BC		92 B	48°41′	123°37′
Shawniken 3	IR/RI	BC	Kamloops Division Yale	92 I/6	50°25′	121°22′
Shawniken 4B	IR/RI	BC	Kamloops Division Yale	92 I/6	50°25′	121°21′
Shaws Bog	UNP/LNO	NS	Hants	21 H/1	45°02′	64°10′
Shawville	TOWN/VIL2	QC	Pontiac	31 F/9	45°36′	76°29′
Shaw Woolen Mill Provincial Historic Site (Undeveloped)	PARK/PARC	AB	SE4-23-1-W5	82 J/16	50°55′	114°04′
Sheahan	UNP/LNO	ON	Sudbury	41 I/13	46°56′	81°48′
Shea Heights	UNP/LNO	NF		1 N/10	47°33′	52°43′
Shearer Dale	UNP/LNO	BC	Peace River	94 A/1	56°04′	120°05′
Shearstown	UNP/LNO	NF		1 N/11	47°35′	53°18′
Shearwater	UNP/LNO	BC	Range 3 Coast	103 A/1	52°09′	128°05′
Shearwater, Base des Forces canadiennes - also-aussi - Shearwater, Canadian Forces Base	MIL/MIL	NS	Halifax	11 D/12	44°38′	63°30′
Shearwater, Canadian Forces Base - also-aussi - Shearwater, Base des Forces canadiennes	MIL/MIL	NS	Halifax	11 D/12	44°38′	63°30′
Shearwater Passage	CHAN/CHEN	BC	New Westminster	92 F/15	49°53′	124°43′
Sheasby Lake	LAKE/LAC	SK	59-26-W3	73 K/4	54°08′	109°53′
Sheatown	UNP/LNO	ON	Leeds	31 B/12	44°34′	75°57′
Sheaves Cove	UNP/LNO	NF		12 B/11	48°31′	59°03′
Shebandowan	UNP/LNO	ON	Thunder Bay	52 B/9	48°38′	90°04′
Shebandowan Lakes	LAKE/LAC	ON	Thunder Bay	52 B/9	48°38′	90°18′
Shebeshekong	UNP/LNO	ON	Parry Sound	41 H/8	45°25′	80°12′
Shebeshekong River	RIV/CDE	ON	Parry Sound	41 H/8	45°25′	80°19′
Shedden	MUN2/AZM2	ON	Algoma	41 J/1	46°14′	82°22′
Shedden	UNP/LNO	ON	Elgin	40 I/11	42°44′	81°21′
Shediac	TOWN/VIL2	NB	Westmorland	21 I/2	46°13′	64°32′
Shediac	GEOG/GÉOG	NB	Westmorland	21 I/1	46°10′	64°30′
Shediac Bay	BAY/BAIE	NB	Westmorland	21 I/7	46°16′	64°30′
Shediac Bridge	UNP/LNO	NB	Westmorland	21 I/7	46°16′	64°35′
Shediac Cape	UNP/LNO	NB	Westmorland	21 I/2	46°14′	64°34′
Shediac Island	ISL/ÎLE	NB	Westmorland	21 I/7	46°16′	64°32′
Shediac Ridge	UNP/LNO	NB	Northumberland	21 I/14	46°46′	65°24′
Shediac River	UNP/LNO	NB	Westmorland	21 I/7	46°16′	64°38′
Shediac River	RIV/CDE	NB	Westmorland	21 I/7	46°16′	64°34′
Shediac, Vallée de - also-aussi - Shediac Valley	SEAU/SMER	—		4024	47°20′	64°25′
Shediac Valley - also-aussi - Shediac, Vallée de	SEAU/SMER	—		4024	47°20′	64°25′
Shedin Creek	RIV/CDE	BC	Cassiar	93 M/12	55°42′	127°36′
Shedin Peak	MTN/MNT	BC	Cassiar	93 M/14	55°56′	127°29′
Shed, La	UNP/LNO	QC	La Haute-Côte-Nord	22 C/11	48°40′	69°15′
Sheemahant River	RIV/CDE	BC	Range 2 Coast	92 M/10	51°45′	126°38′
Sheenboro	UNP/LNO	QC	Pontiac	31 F/14	45°58′	77°14′
Sheen-Esher-Aberdeen-et-Malakoff	VILG/VILG	QC	Pontiac	31 K/3	46°11′	77°28′
Sheep Creek	RIV/CDE	AB/BC		83 L/3	54°05′	119°00′
Sheepherders Junction	UNP/LNO	NS	Pictou	11 E/7	45°22′	62°50′
Sheep Lake	LAKE/LAC	MB	2,3-13-17-E	52 L/3	50°03′	95°11′
Sheep River	RIV/CDE	AB	32-20-28-W4	82 I/12	50°44′	113°51′
Sheerness	UNP/LNO	AB	18-29-12-W4	72 M/5	51°29′	111°41′
Sheerway	UNP/LNO	QC	Pontiac	31 K/12	46°30′	77°46′
Sheet Harbour	UNP/LNO	NS	Halifax	11 D/15	44°55′	62°32′
Sheet Harbour	BAY/BAIE	NS	Halifax	11 D/15	44°53′	62°30′
Sheet Harbour 36	IR/RI	NS	Halifax	11 D/15	44°55′	62°34′
Sheet Harbour Passage	UNP/LNO	NS	Halifax	11 D/16	44°52′	62°27′
Sheet Harbour Road	UNP/LNO	NS	Halifax	11 E/2	45°07′	62°54′
Sheffield	MUN2/AZM2	ON	Lennox and Addington	31 C/11	44°32′	77°00′
Sheffield	UNP/LNO	NB	Sunbury	21 G/16	45°53′	66°20′
Sheffield	UNP/LNO	ON	Wentworth	40 P/8	43°19′	80°12′
Sheffield	GEOG/GÉOG	NB	Sunbury	21 J/1	46°00′	66°15′
Sheffield Lake	LAKE/LAC	NF		12 H/7	49°20′	56°34′
Sheffield Mills	UNP/LNO	NS	Kings	21 H/1	45°09′	64°28′
Shefford	VILG/VILG	QC	La Haute-Yamaska	31 H/7	45°21′	72°34′
Shefford, Mont	MTN/MNT	QC	La Haute-Yamaska	31 H/7	45°22′	72°36′
Shefford-Ouest	UNP/LNO	QC	La Haute-Yamaska	31 H/7	45°19′	72°39′
Sheganny 14	IR/RI	BC	Range 4 Coast	103 H/5	53°27′	129°47′
Shegonla Hills	MTN/MNT	NT	Mackenzie	95 P	63°40′	121°30′
Sheguiandah	UNP/LNO	ON	Manitoulin	41 H/13	45°54′	81°55′
Sheguiandah 24	IR/RI	ON	Manitoulin	41 H/13	45°52′	81°57′
Sheho	VILG/VILG	SK	9-30-9-W2	62 M/11	51°35′	103°13′
Sheila	UNP/LNO	NB	Gloucester	21 P/7	47°29′	64°55′
Shekak	UNP/LNO	ON	Algoma	42 F/2	49°12′	84°34′
Shekak Lake	LAKE/LAC	ON	Algoma	42 F/3	49°05′	85°05′
Shekak River	RIV/CDE	ON	Cochrane	42 F/15	49°49′	84°31′

NAME / NOM	ENTITY / ENTITÉ	LOC 1 / LIEU 1	LOC 2 / LIEU 2	MAP / CARTE	POSITION LAT	POSITION LONG
Shekatika	UNP/LNO	QC	Côte-Nord-du-Golfe-Saint-Laurent	12 O/8	51°17′	58°20′
Shekilie River	RIV/CDE	BC	Peace River	94 I/16	58°47′	120°15′
Shelagyote Peak	MTN/MNT	BC	Cassiar	93 M/14	55°57′	127°12′
Shelagyote River	RIV/CDE	BC	Cassiar	93 M/11	55°37′	127°07′
Shelburne	TOWN/VIL2	NS	Shelburne	20 P/14	43°46′	65°19′
Shelburne	TOWN/VIL2	ON	Dufferin	41 A/1	44°04′	80°12′
Shelburne	MUN1/AZM1	NS	Shelburne	20 P/14	43°51′	65°17′
Shelburne	GEOG/GÉOG	NS		20 P/14	43°50′	65°20′
Shelburne Harbour	BAY/BAIE	NS	Shelburne	20 P/11	43°41′	65°20′
Shelburne River	RIV/CDE	NS	Queens	21 A/3	44°13′	65°13′
Sheldon	UNP/LNO	ON	Simcoe	31 D/4	44°05′	79°59′
Sheldon, Mount	MTN/MNT	YT		105 J/11	62°44′	131°05′
Sheldon's Corners	UNP/LNO	ON	Leeds	31 C/9	44°39′	76°01′
Sheldrake	UNP/LNO	QC	Minganie	22 I/7	50°16′	64°54′
Sheldrake Lake	UNP/LNO	NS	Halifax	11 D/12	44°40′	63°48′
Sheldrake, Rivière	RIV/CDE	QC	Minganie	22 I/7	50°16′	64°55′
Sheldrake, Rivière	RIV/CDE	QC	Kativik	34 C/10	56°38′	76°33′
Shellabear Point	CAPE/CAP	NT	Franklin	88 E	74°53′	113°18′
Shellbrook	TOWN/VIL2	SK	16-49-3-W3	73 G/1	53°13′	106°24′
Shell Brook	RIV/CDE	ON	Kenora	43 M/15	55°55′	86°58′
Shell Brook	RIV/CDE	SK	50-1-W3	73 H/5	53°21′	106°00′
Shellbrook No. 493	MUN2/AZM2	SK		73 G/8	53°25′	106°15′
Shell Camp Lake	LAKE/LAC	NS	Kings	21 A/15	44°50′	64°48′
Shelley	UNP/LNO	MB	1-12-10-E	62 H/16	49°59′	96°06′
Shelley	UNP/LNO	BC	Cariboo	93 J/2	54°00′	122°37′
Shell Island 3	IR/RI	BC	Rupert	92 L/11	50°42′	127°24′
Shell Lake	VILG/VILG	SK	11-50-8-W3	73 G/6	53°18′	107°04′
Shell Lake	LAKE/LAC	SK	49-8-W3	73 G/3	53°13′	107°10′
Shellmouth	MUN2/AZM2	MB		62 K/14	51°00′	101°15′
Shellmouth	UNP/LNO	MB	32-22-29-W	62 K/14	50°56′	101°29′
Shell River	MUN2/AZM2	MB		62 N/6	51°18′	101°24′
Shell River	RIV/CDE	MB	12-23-29-W	62 K/14	50°58′	101°24′
Shell Valley	UNP/LNO	MB	18-24-27-W	62 N/3	51°05′	101°15′
Shelter Bay	UNP/LNO	BC	Kootenay	82 K/12	50°38′	117°56′
Shelter Inlet	BAY/BAIE	BC	Clayoquot	92 E/8	49°24′	126°08′
Shelter Point	UNP/LNO	BC	Comox	92 F/14	49°56′	125°11′
Shelter Point	CAPE/CAP	BC	Comox	92 F/14	49°56′	125°11′
Shemogue	UNP/LNO	NB	Westmorland	21 I/1	46°09′	64°11′
Shemogue Harbour	BAY/BAIE	NB	Westmorland	21 I/1	46°10′	64°09′
Shenley	VILG/VILG	QC	Beauce-Sartigan	21 E/15	45°58′	70°50′
Shenston	UNP/LNO	ON	Rainy River	52 D/9	48°43′	94°03′
Shenstone	UNP/LNO	NB	Albert	21 H/15	45°54′	64°44′
Shep	UNP/LNO	ON	Peel	30 M/12	43°35′	79°33′
Shepard	UNP/LNO	AB	18-23-28-W4	82 I/13	50°57′	113°55′
Shepherd Bay	BAY/BAIE	NT	Keewatin	57 B	68°50′	93°50′
Shepherd, Mount	MTN/MNT	BC	Texada Island	92 F/9	49°32′	124°11′
Shepody	UNP/LNO	NB	Albert	21 H/15	45°46′	64°40′
Shepody Bay	BAY/BAIE	NB	Westmorland	21 H/15	45°45′	64°35′
Sheppard Peak	MTN/MNT	BC	Cassiar	104 F/10	57°41′	132°36′
Sheppardton	UNP/LNO	ON	Huron	40 P/13	43°50′	81°42′
Sheppardville	UNP/LNO	NF		12 H/8	49°27′	56°27′
Shep's Subdivision	UNP/LNO	ON	Waterloo	40 P/8	43°19′	80°19′
Sherard Bay	BAY/BAIE	NT	Franklin	79 B	76°08′	108°07′
Sherard, Cape	CAPE/CAP	NT	Franklin	48 E	74°36′	80°13′
Sherard Head	CAPE/CAP	NT	Franklin	68 D	73°23′	97°07′
Sherard Osborn Island	ISL/ÎLE	NT	Franklin	69 A	76°42′	99°39′
Sherard Osborn Point	CAPE/CAP	NT	Franklin	68 B	72°17′	101°40′
Sheraton	UNP/LNO	BC	Range 5 Coast	93 K/3	54°10′	125°28′
Sheraton Creek 19	IR/RI	BC	Range 5 Coast	93 K/3	54°11′	125°29′
Sherborne, McClintock, Livingstone, Lawrence and Nightingale	MUN2/AZM2	ON	Haliburton	31 E/7	45°24′	78°38′
Sherbrooke	CITY/VIL1	QC	Sherbrooke	21 E/5	45°25′	71°54′
Sherbrooke	VILG/VILG	PE	Prince	11 L/5	46°26′	63°47′
Sherbrooke - see-voir - Summerside	VILG/VILG	PE		11 L/5	46°24′	63°47′
Sherbrooke	MUN1/AZM1	QC	Sherbrooke	21 E/5	45°25′	71°54′
Sherbrooke	UNP/LNO	PE	Prince	11 L/5	46°25′	63°46′
Sherbrooke	UNP/LNO	NS	Guysborough	11 F/4	45°08′	61°59′
Sherbrooke Lake	LAKE/LAC	NS	Lunenburg	21 A/10	44°40′	64°36′
Sherbrooke-Ouest	UNP/LNO	QC	Sherbrooke	21 E/5	45°23′	71°56′
Sherbrooke River	RIV/CDE	NS	Lunenburg	21 A/10	44°43′	64°38′
Shere	UNP/LNO	BC	Cariboo	83 E/4	53°02′	119°35′
Sherer, Mount	MTN/MNT	NT	Franklin	58 A	72°58′	89°09′
Shergrove	UNP/LNO	MB	2-24-13-W	62 O/3	51°03′	99°12′
Sheridan, Cape	CAPE/CAP	NT	Franklin	120 E	82°28′	61°30′
Sheridan Homelands	UNP/LNO	ON	Peel	30 M/12	43°32′	79°40′
Sheridan Lake	LAKE/LAC	BC	Lillooet	92 P/10	51°32′	120°54′

NAME NOM	ENTITY ENTITÉ	LOC 1 LIEU 1	LOC 2 LIEU 2	MAP CARTE	POSITION LAT	LONG
Sheridan Park	UNP/LNO	ON	Leeds	31 B/12	44°37′	75°42′
Sheridan Park	UNP/LNO	ON	Peel	30 M/12	43°31′	79°40′
Sheridan Point	CAPE/CAP	ON	Essex	40 G/15	41°49′	82°41′
Sheringham Point	CAPE/CAP	BC	Renfrew	92 B/5	48°23′	123°55′
Sherks	UNP/LNO	ON	Welland	30 L/14	42°53′	79°08′
Sherkston	UNP/LNO	ON	Welland	30 L/14	42°53′	79°08′
Sherman Basin	BAY/BAIE	NT	Keewatin	66 P	67°47′	97°35′
Sherman Inlet	BAY/BAIE	NT	Franklin	67 A	68°00′	98°21′
Sherose Island	UNP/LNO	NS	Shelburne	20 P/12	43°32′	65°36′
Sherridon	UNP/LNO	MB		63 N/3	55°07′	101°05′
Sherrington	UNP/LNO	QC	Les Jardins-de-Napierville	31 H/4	45°10′	73°31′
Sherritt Junction	UNP/LNO	MB	12-65-27-W	63 K/11	54°37′	101°24′
Sherwood	UNP/LNO	PE	Queens	11 L/6	46°16′	63°08′
Sherwood	UNP/LNO	NS	Lunenburg	21 A/9	44°43′	64°18′
Sherwood	UNP/LNO	ON	York	30 M/13	43°50′	79°31′
Sherwood	UNP/LNO	ON	Algoma	41 J/5	46°17′	83°34′
Sherwood	UNP/LNO	MB	35-16-7-E1	62 I/7	50°23′	96°30′
Sherwood Estates	UNP/LNO	SK		72 I/7	50°30′	104°41′
Sherwood Forest	UNP/LNO	ON	Middlesex	40 P/3	43°00′	81°18′
Sherwood Forrest	UNP/LNO	ON	Peel	30 M/12	43°32′	79°39′
Sherwood Head	CAPE/CAP	NT	Franklin	59 E	78°08′	89°32′
Sherwood Heights	UNP/LNO	NS	Halifax	11 D/12	44°40′	63°40′
Sherwood, Jones and Burns	MUN2/AZM2	ON	Renfrew	31 F/12	45°33′	77°41′
Sherwood Lake	UNP/LNO	ON	Kenora	52 E/15	49°46′	94°53′
Sherwood Lake	LAKE/LAC	NT	Mackenzie	65 D	60°52′	103°22′
Sherwood No. 159	MUN2/AZM2	SK		72 I/7	50°25′	104°40′
Sherwood Park	UNP/LNO	NS	Halifax	11 D/12	44°41′	63°39′
Sherwood Park	UNP/LNO	NB	Kings	21 H/5	45°26′	66°00′
Sherwood Park	UNP/LNO	AB	27-52-23-W4	83 H/11	53°31′	113°19′
Sherwood River	RIV/CDE	ON	Renfrew	31 F/12	45°38′	77°34′
Sherwood Springs	UNP/LNO	ON	Leeds	31 B/12	44°31′	75°47′
Sherwood Village	UNP/LNO	ON	Lambton	40 J/16	42°58′	82°21′
Sheshatsheits	UNP/LNO	NF		13 F/9	53°31′	60°09′
Shesheeb Bay	BAY/BAIE	ON	Thunder Bay	52 A/9	48°40′	88°20′
Shesheep 74A	IR/RI	SK		62 L/10	50°37′	102°45′
Sheshegwaning	UNP/LNO	ON	Manitoulin	41 G/15	45°55′	82°51′
Sheshegwaning 20	IR/RI	ON	Manitoulin	41 G/15	45°56′	82°50′
Sheslay	UNP/LNO	BC	Cassiar	104 J/5	58°16′	131°48′
Sheslay River	RIV/CDE	BC	Cassiar	104 K/16	58°47′	132°06′
Shethanei Lake	LAKE/LAC	MB		64 I/13	58°48′	97°50′
Shetland	UNP/LNO	ON	Lambton	40 I/12	42°42′	81°59′
Shevlin	UNP/LNO	MB	28-25-27-W	62 N/3	51°12′	101°13′
Shewan	UNP/LNO	NB	Carleton	21 J/3	46°13′	67°26′
Shibogama Lake	LAKE/LAC	ON	Kenora	53 H/9	53°35′	88°15′
Shields	VILG/VILG	SK	33-3-W3	72 O/16	51°49′	106°24′
Shields Bay	BAY/BAIE	BC	Queen Charlotte	103 F/8	53°21′	132°29′
Shields Crossing	UNP/LNO	ON	Renfrew	31 F/10	45°40′	76°56′
Shigawake	VILG/VILG	QC	Bonaventure	22 A/3	48°06′	65°05′
Shigawake-Est	UNP/LNO	QC	Bonaventure	22 A/3	48°06′	65°03′
Shikag Lake	LAKE/LAC	ON	Thunder Bay	52 G/10	49°45′	90°45′
Shikwamkwa Lake	LAKE/LAC	ON	Algoma	42 C/1	48°06′	84°08′
Shikwamkwa River	RIV/CDE	ON	Algoma	41 N/15	47°57′	84°31′
Shillabeer Lake	LAKE/LAC	ON	Thunder Bay	52 H/2	49°06′	88°44′
Shillington	UNP/LNO	ON	Cochrane	42 A/10	48°32′	80°41′
Shilo	UNP/LNO	MB	16-17-10-W	62 G/13	49°48′	99°38′
Shiloh	UNP/LNO	ON	Northumberland	31 C/4	44°05′	77°50′
Shiloh	UNP/LNO	ON	Wellington	40 P/9	43°43′	80°16′
Shin Creek	RIV/CDE	NB	Sunbury	21 G/10	45°33′	66°36′
Shingle Creek	UNP/LNO	BC	Osoyoos Division Yale	82 E/12	49°31′	119°48′
Shingle Creek	RIV/CDE	BC	Osoyoos Division Yale	82 E/5	49°29′	119°36′
Shingle Lake	LAKE/LAC	NS	Lunenburg	21 A/7	44°25′	64°48′
Shingle Point	CAPE/CAP	YT		117 A/15	68°59′	137°22′
Shingle Point 4	IR/RI	BC	Nanaimo	92 G/4	49°03′	123°38′
Shingwak Lake	LAKE/LAC	ON	Kenora	52 F/5	49°18′	93°42′
Shinimicas Bridge	UNP/LNO	NS	Cumberland	11 E/13	45°53′	63°54′
Shinimicas River	RIV/CDE	NS	Cumberland	11 E/13	45°56′	63°52′
Shining Bank	UNP/LNO	AB	3-57-14-W5	83 G/13	53°53′	115°59′
Shiningbank Lake	LAKE/LAC	AB	56-14-W5	83 F/6	53°52′	116°01′
Shining Tree	UNP/LNO	ON	Sudbury	41 P/11	47°33′	81°16′
Shinnickburn	UNP/LNO	NB	Northumberland	21 I/12	46°33′	65°50′
Ship Cove	UNP/LNO	NF		1 N/11	47°35′	53°12′
Ship Cove	UNP/LNO	NF		1 M/1	47°06′	54°05′
Ship Cove	UNP/LNO	NF		1 M/3	47°02′	55°11′
Ship Cove	UNP/LNO	NF		2 M/12	51°36′	55°38′
Ship Cove	UNP/LNO	NF		12 B/10	48°31′	58°57′

NAME NOM	ENTITY ENTITÉ	LOC 1 LIEU 1	LOC 2 LIEU 2	MAP CARTE	POSITION LAT	LONG
Ship Cove	BAY/BAIE	NF		12 B/2	48°08′	58°59′
Ship Cove-Lower Cove - see-voir - Ship Cove-Lower Cove-Jerry's Nose	UNP/LNO	NF		12 B/10	48°31′	58°59′
Ship Cove-Lower Cove-Jerry's Nose	UNP/LNO	NF		12 B/10	48°31′	58°59′
Ship Harbour	UNP/LNO	NF		1 N/5	47°22′	53°53′
Ship Harbour	UNP/LNO	NS	Halifax	11 D/15	44°49′	62°53′
Ship Harbour	BAY/BAIE	NF		3 D/12	52°38′	55°47′
Ship Harbour	BAY/BAIE	NS	Halifax	11 D/15	44°48′	62°51′
Ship Harbour Long Lake	LAKE/LAC	NS	Halifax	11 D/14	44°55′	63°02′
Shiphead	UNP/LNO	QC	La Côte-de-Gaspé	22 A/16	48°45′	64°10′
Shipiskan Lake	LAKE/LAC	NF		13 L/9	54°39′	62°19′
Ship Island	UNP/LNO	NF		2 E/10	49°39′	54°36′
Ship Island	ISL/ÎLE	NF		2 C/12	48°45′	53°39′
Shipka	UNP/LNO	ON	Huron	40 P/5	43°17′	81°41′
Shipman	HAM/HAM	SK	11-52-21-W2	73 H/7	53°29′	104°59′
Shipman	UNP/LNO	ON	Lincoln	30 M/3	43°10′	79°15′
Shippagan	TOWN/VIL2	NB	Gloucester	21 P/16	47°44′	64°42′
Shippegan	GEOG/GÉOG	NB	Gloucester	21 P/15	47°50′	64°37′
Shippegan, Baie de	BAY/BAIE	NB	Gloucester	21 P/15	47°48′	64°43′
Shippegan Gully	CHAN/CHEN	NB	Gloucester	21 P/10	47°43′	64°40′
Shippegan Portage	UNP/LNO	NB	Gloucester	21 P/10	47°44′	64°44′
Shippigan	UNP/LNO	NB	Gloucester	21 P/10	47°44′	64°42′
Ship Run	CHAN/CHEN	NF		2 E/11	49°31′	55°08′
Ship Sands Island	ISL/ÎLE	ON	Cochrane	42 P/8	51°21′	80°27′
Shipshaw	VILG/VILG	QC	Le Fjord-du-Saguenay	22 D/6	48°27′	71°14′
Shipshaw, Rivière	RIV/CDE	QC	Le Fjord-du-Saguenay	22 D/6	48°27′	71°12′
Shipton	VILG/VILG	QC	Asbestos	31 H/16	45°45′	72°00′
Shirley	UNP/LNO	ON	Ontario	31 D/2	44°03′	78°54′
Shirley	UNP/LNO	BC	Renfrew	92 B/5	48°23′	123°54′
Shirley Lake	LAKE/LAC	ON	Nipissing	31 E/9	45°41′	78°08′
Shirleys Bay	UNP/LNO	ON	Carleton	31 G/5	45°22′	75°53′
Shisler Point	UNP/LNO	ON	Welland	30 L/14	42°51′	79°08′
Shoal Arm	UNP/LNO	NF		2 E/12	49°36′	55°57′
Shoal Arm	BAY/BAIE	NF		2 E/5	49°25′	55°45′
Shoal Arm Brook	RIV/CDE	NF		2 E/5	49°25′	55°45′
Shoal Bay	UNP/LNO	NF		2 E/9	49°41′	54°12′
Shoal Bay	BAY/BAIE	NF		1 K/13	46°59′	53°38′
Shoal Bay	BAY/BAIE	NF		1 N/13	47°52′	53°45′
Shoal Bay	BAY/BAIE	NF		2 E/9	49°42′	54°13′
Shoal Bay	BAY/BAIE	NF		2 E/8	49°27′	54°29′
Shoal Bay	BAY/BAIE	NF		3 E/5	53°16′	55°48′
Shoal Brook	UNP/LNO	NF		12 H/5	49°28′	57°55′
Shoal Cove	UNP/LNO	NF		12 P/7	51°21′	56°39′
Shoal Cove	UNP/LNO	NF		12 P/3	51°01′	57°02′
Shoal Creek	UNP/LNO	AB	28-61-2-W5	83 J/8	54°18′	114°14′
Shoal Harbour	UNP/LNO	NF		2 C/4	48°11′	53°59′
Shoal Harbour	BAY/BAIE	NT	Franklin	34 N	59°34′	77°49′
Shoal Harbour Pond	LAKE/LAC	NF		2 D/1	48°12′	54°09′
Shoal Harbour River	RIV/CDE	NF		2 C/4	48°11′	53°59′
Shoal Lake	VILG/VILG	MB		62 K/7	50°26′	100°35′
Shoal Lake	MUN2/AZM2	MB		62 K/7	50°28′	100°34′
Shoal Lake	UNP/LNO	ON	Kenora	52 E/11	49°37′	95°07′
Shoal Lake	LAKE/LAC	ON	Rainy River	52 C/10	48°41′	92°38′
Shoal Lake	LAKE/LAC	ON/MB		52 E/11	49°34′	95°03′
Shoal Lake	LAKE/LAC	MB	16,17-23-W	62 K/7	50°24′	100°37′
Shoal Lake	LAKE/LAC	AB	61-3,4-W5	83 J/8	54°17′	114°27′
Shoal Lake 28A	IR/RI	SK		63 E/7	53°30′	102°38′
Shoal Lake 31J	IR/RI	ON	Kenora	52 E/6	49°26′	95°08′
Shoal Lake 34B1	IR/RI	ON	Kenora	52 E/6	49°26′	95°07′
Shoal Lake 34B2	IR/RI	ON	Kenora	52 E/11	49°37′	95°08′
Shoal Lake 37A	IR/RI	MB/ON		52 E/11	49°28′	95°10′
Shoal Lake 39	IR/RI	MB/ON		52 E/6	49°30′	95°09′
Shoal Lake 39A	IR/RI	MB/ON		52 E/11	49°38′	95°06′
Shoal Lake 40	IR/RI	MB/ON		52 E/11	49°37′	95°13′
Shoal Point	UNP/LNO	NF		1 K/14	46°46′	53°22′
Shoal Point	UNP/LNO	NF		11 O/14	47°53′	59°24′
Shoal Point	CAPE/CAP	NF		12 B/10	48°39′	58°50′
Shoal Point	CAPE/CAP	NF		12 B/2	48°09′	58°58′
Shoal Point	CAPE/CAP	NF		11 O/11	47°45′	59°19′
Shoal River	UNP/LNO	MB	43,44-23-W	63 C/10	52°45′	100°41′
Shoal River 65A	IR/RI	MB		63 C/10	52°45′	100°41′
Shoal River 65B	IR/RI	MB		63 C/15	52°50′	100°40′
Shoal River 65F	IR/RI	MB		63 C/15	52°48′	100°39′
Shoalwater Bay	BAY/BAIE	YT		117 A/16	68°55′	136°43′
Shoe Cove	UNP/LNO	NF		1 N/10	47°45′	52°44′
Shoe Cove	UNP/LNO	NF		2 E/13	49°55′	55°33′

NAME / NOM	ENTITY / ENTITÉ	LOC 1 / LIEU 1	LOC 2 / LIEU 2	MAP / CARTE	POSITION LAT	POSITION LONG
Shoe Cove	BAY/BAIE	NF		1 K/15	46°47′	52°59′
Shoe Cove Point	CAPE/CAP	NF		2 F/4	49°02′	53°36′
Shogomoc Lake	LAKE/LAC	NB	York	21 G/14	45°51′	67°19′
Shomeo Point	CAPE/CAP	NT	Franklin	26 H	65°22′	65°04′
Shonts	UNP/LNO	AB	21-50-18-W4	83 H/7	53°20′	112°35′
Shoomart 5	IR/RI	BC	Nootka	92 E/15	49°48′	126°44′
Sho-ook 5	IR/RI	BC	Yale Division Yale	92 H/14	49°59′	121°29′
Shooter Hill	UNP/LNO	SK	24-20-7-W3	72 J/10	50°43′	106°51′
Shoowahtlans (Shawtlans) 4	IR/RI	BC	Range 5 Coast	103 J/8	54°20′	130°51′
Shops	UNP/LNO	BC	New Westminster	92 G/2	49°12′	122°52′
Shoran Bay	BAY/BAIE	NT	Keewatin	45 J	62°10′	83°25′
Shore Acres	UNP/LNO	ON	Simcoe	31 D/4	44°14′	79°32′
Shoreacres	UNP/LNO	ON	Halton	30 M/5	43°22′	79°45′
Shoreacres	UNP/LNO	BC	Kootenay	82 F/5	49°25′	117°32′
Shoreholme	UNP/LNO	BC	Kootenay	82 K/5	50°18′	117°51′
Shore's Cove	UNP/LNO	NF		1 N/2	47°06′	52°56′
Shorncliffe	UNP/LNO	MB	21-24-3-E	62 P/3	51°05′	97°08′
Short Beach	UNP/LNO	NS	Yarmouth	20 O/16	43°56′	66°09′
Shortdale	UNP/LNO	MB	10-26-26-W	62 N/3	51°14′	101°02′
Shortland Canyon	SEAU/SMER	—		4045	43°50′	58°15′
Shorts Creek	RIV/CDE	BC	Osoyoos Division Yale	82 L/4	50°08′	119°30′
Shortts Lake	LAKE/LAC	NS	Colchester	11 E/3	45°13′	63°19′
Shoskhost 7	IR/RI	BC	Kamloops Division Yale	92 I/6	50°16′	121°26′
Shouldice	UNP/LNO	ON	Grey	41 A/11	44°39′	81°02′
Shouldice	UNP/LNO	AB	22-20-22-W4	82 I/10	50°43′	112°59′
Shovel Creek	RIV/CDE	BC	Range 5 Coast	93 K/3	54°08′	125°17′
Shovelnose Mountain	MTN/MNT	BC	Yale Division Yale	92 H/15	49°52′	120°51′
Showers Corners	UNP/LNO	ON	Oxford	40 P/2	43°12′	80°35′
Shpapzchinh 20	IR/RI	BC	Yale Division Yale	92 I/11	50°33′	121°17′
Shredder Seamount	SEAU/SMER	—		NK23	43°46′	43°36′
Shrewsbury	UNP/LNO	QC	Argenteuil	31 G/16	45°47′	74°17′
Shrewsbury	UNP/LNO	ON	Kent	40 I/5	42°18′	81°55′
Shrigley	UNP/LNO	ON	Dufferin	41 A/1	44°13′	80°18′
Shrypttahooks 7	IR/RI	BC	Yale Division Yale	92 H/14	49°49′	121°26′
Shubenacadie	UNP/LNO	NS	Hants	11 E/3	45°05′	63°24′
Shubenacadie 13	IR/RI	NS	Halifax	11 D/13	44°57′	63°37′
Shubenacadie East	UNP/LNO	NS	Colchester	11 E/3	45°06′	63°23′
Shubenacadie Grand Lake	LAKE/LAC	NS	Halifax	11 D/13	44°55′	63°36′
Shubenacadie River	RIV/CDE	NS	Hants	11 E/6	45°19′	63°29′
Shugba Bay	BAY/BAIE	NT	Franklin	36 B	64°40′	74°08′
Shukbuk Bay	BAY/BAIE	NT	Franklin	36 B	64°50′	74°40′
Shulaps Peak	MTN/MNT	BC	Lillooet	92 J/15	50°57′	122°32′
Shulie	UNP/LNO	NS	Cumberland	21 H/10	45°36′	64°34′
Shulie River	RIV/CDE	NS	Cumberland	21 H/10	45°36′	64°34′
Shulus	UNP/LNO	BC	Kamloops Division Yale	92 I/2	50°08′	120°51′
Shumal Creek 81	IR/RI	BC	Cassiar	103 P/3	55°14′	129°09′
Shumal Creek 84	IR/RI	BC	Cassiar	103 P/3	55°15′	129°10′
Shumway Lake	LAKE/LAC	BC	Kamloops Division Yale	92 I/9	50°31′	120°15′
Shunacadie	UNP/LNO	NS	Cape Breton	11 K/2	46°01′	60°39′
Shuniah	MUN2/AZM2	ON	Thunder Bay	52 A/7	48°30′	88°45′
Shuouchten 15	IR/RI	BC	Kamloops Division Yale	92 I/6	50°16′	121°28′
Shushartie	UNP/LNO	BC	Rupert	92 L/13	50°51′	127°51′
Shushartie River	RIV/CDE	BC	Rupert	92 L/13	50°51′	127°52′
Shuswap	UNP/LNO	BC	Kootenay	82 K/9	50°32′	116°01′
Shuswap	UNP/LNO	BC	Kamloops Division Yale	82 L/13	50°47′	119°42′
Shuswap Falls	UNP/LNO	BC	Osoyoos Division Yale	82 L/7	50°18′	118°49′
Shuswap	IR/RI	BC	Kootenay	82 K/9	50°32′	116°02′
Shuswap Lake	LAKE/LAC	BC	Kamloops Division Yale	82 L/14	50°56′	119°17′
Shuswap River	RIV/CDE	BC	Kamloops Division Yale	82 L/11	50°43′	119°03′
Shuttleworth Creek	RIV/CDE	BC	Similkameen Division Yale	82 E/5	49°20′	119°35′
Shutty Bench	UNP/LNO	BC	Kootenay	82 F/15	49°58′	116°55′
Siakin 4	IR/RI	BC	New Westminster	92 K/7	50°17′	124°47′
Sibbald	UNP/LNO	AB	13-28-2-W4	72 M/8	51°23′	110°09′
Sibbeston Lake	LAKE/LAC	NT	Mackenzie	95 G	61°45′	122°45′
Siberia	UNP/LNO	ON	Renfrew	31 F/5	45°28′	77°42′
Sibley Peninsula	CAPE/CAP	ON	Thunder Bay	52 A/7	48°25′	88°45′
Sibleys Cove	UNP/LNO	NF		2 C/3	48°02′	53°06′
Sicamous	MUN1/AZM1	BC	Kamloops Division Yale	82 L/15	50°50′	118°59′
Sicamous 3	IR/RI	BC	Kamloops Division Yale	82 L/14	50°49′	119°00′
Sicintine River	RIV/CDE	BC	Cassiar	94 D/4	56°03′	127°57′
Sidcup	UNP/LNO	AB	30-46-3-W4	73 D/16	52°59′	110°25′
Sideburned Lake	LAKE/LAC	ON	Sudbury	41 O/12	47°45′	83°30′
Siderite Junction	UNP/LNO	ON	Algoma	42 C/2	48°04′	84°43′
Side Saddle Lake	LAKE/LAC	MB	23,24-14-16-E	52 L/3	50°11′	95°18′
Sidewood	UNP/LNO	SK	12-22-W3	72 K/2	50°03′	108°54′

NAME NOM	ENTITY ENTITÉ	LOC 1 LIEU 1	LOC 2 LIEU 2	MAP CARTE	POSITION LAT	LONG
Sidina 6	IR/RI	BC	Cassiar	93 M/5	55°27′	127°37′
Sid Lake	LAKE/LAC	NT	Mackenzie	75 I/8	62°16′	104°04′
Sidmar	UNP/LNO	SK	36-17-21-W2	72 I/7	50°28′	104°46′
Sidney	TOWN/VIL2	BC	North Saanich	92 B/11	48°39′	123°24′
Sidney	MUN2/AZM2	ON	Hastings	31 C/4	44°13′	77°30′
Sidney	UNP/LNO	MB	5-11-12-W	62 G/14	49°54′	99°05′
Sidney Channel	CHAN/CHEN	BC	Cowichan	92 B/11	48°37′	123°20′
Sidney Creek	RIV/CDE	YT		105 C/15	60°46′	132°57′
Sidney Dobson, Mount	MTN/MNT	NT	Mackenzie	95 L	62°01′	127°37′
Sidney Island	ISL/ÎLE	BC	Cowichan	92 B/11	48°37′	123°18′
Sidney Lake	LAKE/LAC	SK	55-25-W3	73 F/13	53°46′	109°37′
Siegas	UNP/LNO	NB	Madawaska	21 O/4	47°13′	67°59′
Siegas Lake Settlement	UNP/LNO	NB	Madawaska	21 O/5	47°19′	67°55′
Siegas, Rivière	RIV/CDE	NB	Madawaska	21 O/4	47°13′	67°59′
Siegs Corner	UNP/LNO	MB	6,7-13-11-E	62 I/1	50°04′	96°04′
Sienna	UNP/LNO	QC	Antoine-Labelle	31 J/10	46°31′	74°49′
Siffleur River	RIV/CDE	AB	36-17-W5	83 C/1	52°04′	116°24′
Sifton	MUN2/AZM2	MB		62 F/10	49°40′	100°40′
Sifton	UNP/LNO	MB	24-27-20-W	62 N/8	51°22′	100°09′
Sifton Junction	UNP/LNO	MB	12-28-20-W	62 N/8	51°23′	100°09′
Sifton Lake	LAKE/LAC	NT	Mackenzie	75 O	63°45′	106°33′
Sifton Pass	VALL/VALL	BC	Cassiar	94 E/16	57°56′	126°11′
Sifton Range	MTN/MNT	YT		115 A/16	60°56′	136°10′
Sifton Ranges	MTN/MNT	BC	Cassiar	94 E/9	57°42′	126°09′
Sight Point	UNP/LNO	NS	Inverness	11 K/3	46°11′	61°25′
Siglavik	UNP/LNO	MB	22-14-17-E	62 I/10	50°36′	97°00′
Siglunes	MUN2/AZM2	MB		62 O/2	51°10′	98°30′
Siglunes	UNP/LNO	MB	23-22-10-W	62 J/15	50°55′	98°44′
Signai	UNP/LNO	QC	Vallée-de-l'Or	32 C/7	48°18′	76°50′
Signal Hill, Lieu historique national de - also-aussi - Signal Hill National Historic Site	PARK/PARC	NF		1 N/10	47°34′	52°41′
Signal Hill National Historic Site - also-aussi - Signal Hill, Lieu historique national de	PARK/PARC	NF		1 N/10	47°34′	52°41′
Signet	UNP/LNO	ON	Grey	41 A/1	44°01′	80°28′
Sigutlat Lake	LAKE/LAC	BC	Range 3 Coast	93 D/16	52°57′	126°13′
Siikuunsiiwan	UNP/LNO	QC	Jamésie	32 I/4	50°11′	73°56′
Sijjaaluit	UNP/LNO	QC	Kativik	24 N/13	59°53′	69°51′
Sijjaapiit	UNP/LNO	QC	Kativik	24 N/12	59°41′	69°53′
Sijjait	UNP/LNO	QC	Kativik	24 M/11	59°42′	71°06′
Sijjait	UNP/LNO	QC	Kativik	24 M/13	59°52′	71°41′
Sijjaruluit	UNP/LNO	QC	Kativik	25 F/3	61°01′	69°29′
Sikachu Lake	LAKE/LAC	SK		73 P/4	55°05′	105°43′
Sikanni	UNP/LNO	BC	Peace River	94 H/14	57°58′	121°11′
Sikanni Chief	UNP/LNO	BC	Peace River	94 G/2	57°14′	122°42′
Sikanni Chief River	RIV/CDE	BC	Peace River	94 I/5	58°17′	121°45′
Sik-e-dakh 2	IR/RI	BC	Cassiar	93 M/5	55°18′	127°41′
Siksika 146	IR/RI	AB	14-21-22-W4	82 I/15	50°47′	112°57′
Siksik Point	CAPE/CAP	NT	Franklin	98 B	72°25′	125°26′
Sikunitakuhp	UNP/LNO	QC	Jamésie	32 M/15	51°59′	78°42′
Silas	UNP/LNO	SK	45-6-W2	63 D/15	52°52′	102°53′
Silberfeld	UNP/LNO	MB	22-1-1-W	62 H/4	49°03′	97°30′
Silcote	UNP/LNO	ON	Grey	41 A/10	44°39′	80°46′
Silcox	UNP/LNO	MB		54 E/1	57°12′	94°10′
Silcox Creek	RIV/CDE	MB		54 F/12	57°35′	93°34′
Silica	UNP/LNO	BC	Kootenay	82 F/4	49°02′	117°51′
Silicon 2	IR/RI	BC	Lillooet	92 J/9	50°42′	122°06′
Sillem Island	ISL/ÎLE	NT	Franklin	27 F	70°56′	71°43′
Sillery	CITY/VIL1	QC	Communauté urbaine de Québec	21 L/14	46°46′	71°15′
Sillikers	UNP/LNO	NB	Northumberland	21 I/13	46°57′	65°53′
Sillsville	UNP/LNO	ON	Lennox and Addington	31 C/2	44°09′	76°55′
Siloam	UNP/LNO	ON	Ontario	31 D/3	44°05′	79°13′
Silsby Lake	LAKE/LAC	MB		53 M/5	55°29′	95°46′
Siltaza Lake	LAKE/LAC	NT	Mackenzie	75 K	62°13′	109°38′
Silton	VILG/VILG	SK	30-21-21-W2	72 I/15	50°48′	104°55′
Silumiut, Cape	CAPE/CAP	NT	Keewatin	55 O	63°38′	90°09′
*Silvene	UNP/LNO	BC	Bright	92 G/4	49°06′	123°54′
Silver	UNP/LNO	MB	35-21-2-E	62 I/14	50°51′	97°13′
Silver Bay	UNP/LNO	ON	Welland	30 L/14	42°52′	79°10′
Silver Bay	UNP/LNO	MB	5-26-8-W	62 O/2	51°13′	98°32′
Silver Beach	VILG/VILG	AB	11-47-28-W4	83 H/4	53°02′	113°58′
Silverberry River	RIV/CDE	NT	Mackenzie	95 M	63°16′	126°22′
Silver Birch Beach	UNP/LNO	ON	Simcoe	41 A/16	44°49′	80°03′
Silver Centre	UNP/LNO	ON	Timiskaming	31 M/4	47°12′	79°30′
Silver City	UNP/LNO	YT		115 G/1	61°02′	138°23′
Silver Corners	UNP/LNO	ON	Perth	40 P/11	43°40′	81°06′
Silver Creek	MUN2/AZM2	MB		62 K/11	50°41′	101°00′
Silver Creek	UNP/LNO	QC	Papineau	31 G/11	45°37′	75°20′

NAME NOM	ENTITY ENTITÉ	LOC 1 LIEU 1	LOC 2 LIEU 2	MAP CARTE	POSITION	
					LAT	LONG
Silver Creek	UNP/LNO	ON	Peel	30 M/13	43°50′	79°56′
Silver Creek	UNP/LNO	ON	Halton	30 M/12	43°40′	79°59′
Silver Creek	UNP/LNO	AB	29-60-16-W5	83 K/1	54°13′	116°21′
Silver Creek	UNP/LNO	BC	Kamloops Division Yale	82 L/11	50°36′	119°22′
Silver Creek	UNP/LNO	BC	Yale Division Yale	92 H/6	49°22′	121°27′
Silverdale	UNP/LNO	NF		2 E/12	49°41′	55°59′
Silverdale	UNP/LNO	ON	Lincoln	30 M/3	43°05′	79°27′
Silverdale	UNP/LNO	BC	New Westminster	92 G/1	49°09′	122°24′
Silver Dollar	UNP/LNO	ON	Kenora	52 G/14	49°48′	91°11′
Silver Falls	UNP/LNO	NB	Saint John	21 G/8	45°18′	66°01′
Silver Falls	UNP/LNO	MB	2-18-10-E	62 I/9	50°31′	96°06′
Silver Falls	UNP/LNO	BC	New Westminster	92 G/7	49°25′	122°53′
Silver Falls Park	UNP/LNO	NB	Saint John	21 G/8	45°18′	66°01′
Silver Fox Island	UNP/LNO	NF		2 F/4	49°01′	53°41′
Silver Fox Island	ISL/ÎLE	NF		2 F/4	49°01′	53°41′
Silver Grove	UNP/LNO	SK	25-46-4-W3	73 B/16	52°59′	106°28′
Silver Harbour	UNP/LNO	ON	Thunder Bay	52 A/10	48°31′	88°56′
Silver Harbour	UNP/LNO	MB	15-21-4-E	62 I/15	50°49′	96°58′
Silver Heights	UNP/LNO	MB		62 H/14	49°53′	97°15′
Silver Heights	UNP/LNO	SK		72 I/6	50°24′	105°29′
Silver Heights	UNP/LNO	AB	3-39-9-W4	73 D/6	52°18′	111°13′
Silver Hill	UNP/LNO	ON	Norfolk	40 I/16	42°45′	80°29′
Silverhill	UNP/LNO	BC	New Westminster	92 G/1	49°11′	122°23′
Silver Hills	UNP/LNO	ON	York	30 M/14	43°46′	79°22′
Silverhope Creek	RIV/CDE	BC	Yale Division Yale	92 H/6	49°22′	121°28′
Silver Islet	UNP/LNO	ON	Thunder Bay	52 A/7	48°20′	88°45′
Silver Lake	UNP/LNO	ON	Renfrew	31 F/11	45°31′	77°16′
Silver Lake	UNP/LNO	ON	Peterborough	31 D/10	44°39′	78°35′
Silver Lake	UNP/LNO	BC	Peace River	94 H/6	57°28′	121°14′
Silver Lake	LAKE/LAC	ON	Frontenac	31 C/15	44°50′	76°36′
Silver Lake	LAKE/LAC	ON	Manitoulin	41 G/15	45°53′	82°54′
Silver Lake	LAKE/LAC	ON	Rainy River	52 F/4	49°05′	93°36′
Silver Lake	LAKE/LAC	ON	Kenora	52 E/16	49°53′	94°11′
Silver Mine	UNP/LNO	NS	Cape Breton	11 F/16	45°52′	60°24′
Silver Mountain	UNP/LNO	ON	Thunder Bay	52 A/5	48°16′	89°53′
Silver Park	UNP/LNO	SK	34-42-18-W2	73 A/10	52°40′	104°31′
Silver Plains	UNP/LNO	MB		62 H/6	49°28′	97°18′
Silver Point	UNP/LNO	NF		12 H/5	49°28′	57°55′
Silver Point Road	UNP/LNO	NS	Lunenburg	21 A/8	44°29′	64°20′
Silver Ridge	UNP/LNO	MB	12-21-11-W	62 J/15	50°48′	98°52′
Silver River	UNP/LNO	BC	Yale Division Yale	92 H/12	49°34′	121°49′
Silver River	RIV/CDE	NS	Digby	21 A/4	44°13′	65°48′
Silver Salmon Lake 5	IR/RI	BC	Cassiar	104 N/3	59°14′	133°13′
Silver Sands	VILG/VILG	AB	3-54-5-W5	83 G/10	53°38′	114°39′
Silvers Corners	UNP/LNO	ON	Frontenac	31 C/7	44°18′	76°32′
Silver Springs	UNP/LNO	AB	24-2-W5	82 O/1	51°06′	114°09′
Silverthorne	UNP/LNO	ON	York	30 M/11	43°41′	79°28′
Silverthrone Glacier	GLAC/GLAC	BC	Range 2 Coast	92 N/5	51°26′	125°53′
Silverthrone Mountain	MTN/MNT	BC	Range 2 Coast	92 M/9	51°31′	126°07′
Silvertip Mountain	MTN/MNT	BC	Yale Division Yale	92 H/3	49°10′	121°13′
Silverton	VILG/VILG	BC	Kootenay	82 F/14	49°57′	117°22′
Silverton	UNP/LNO	MB	33-20-27W	62 K/14	50°46′	101°10′
Silverton Station - see-voir - Silverton	UNP/LNO	MB		62 K/14	50°46′	101°10′
Silver Valley	UNP/LNO	AB	24-81-11-W6	84 D/4	56°02′	119°34′
Silver Valley	UNP/LNO	BC	New Westminster	92 G/7	49°16′	122°34′
Silver Water	UNP/LNO	ON	Manitoulin	41 G/15	45°52′	82°52′
Silverwood	UNP/LNO	NB	York	21 G/15	45°58′	66°46′
Silverwood	UNP/LNO	MB	13-28-29-W	62 N/6	51°25′	101°26′
Silverwood	UNP/LNO	AB	20-77-5-W6	83 M/10	55°41′	118°43′
Silverwood Heights	UNP/LNO	SK		73 B/2	52°11′	106°37′
Silverwood No. 123	MUN2/AZM2	SK		62 L/1	50°10′	102°10′
Silvy, Lac	LAKE/LAC	QC	Jamésie	33 K/9	54°35′	76°12′
Simard	UNP/LNO	ON	Sudbury	41 I/11	46°34′	81°07′
Simard, Lac	LAKE/LAC	QC	Sept-Rivières	22 J/6	50°19′	67°28′
Simard, Lac	LAKE/LAC	QC	Témiscamingue	31 M/10	47°37′	78°41′
Simcoe	TOWN/VIL2	ON	Norfolk	40 I/16	42°50′	80°18′
Simcoe	MUN1/AZM1	ON	Simcoe	31 D/5	44°25′	79°50′
Simcoe	GEOG/GÉOG	ON		31 D/5	44°25′	79°50′
Simcoe Beach	UNP/LNO	ON	Simcoe	31 D/5	44°18′	79°33′
Simcoe Island	UNP/LNO	ON	Frontenac	31 C/2	44°09′	76°32′
Simcoe Island	ISL/ÎLE	ON	Frontenac	31 C/2	44°10′	76°32′
Simcoe, Lake	LAKE/LAC	ON	York	31 D/6	44°25′	79°20′
Simcoe Lodge	UNP/LNO	ON	Ontario	31 D/11	44°36′	79°22′
Simcoeside	UNP/LNO	ON	Simcoe	31 D/6	44°29′	79°28′
Sim Creek 5	IR/RI	BC	Range 3 Coast	92 N/4	51°01′	125°37′

NAME NOM	ENTITY ENTITÉ	LOC 1 LIEU 1	LOC 2 LIEU 2	MAP CARTE	POSITION LAT	LONG
Similkameen Division Yale Land District	GEOG/GÉOG	BC		82 E	49°20'	119°10'
Similkameen River	RIV/CDE	BC	Similkameen Division Yale	82 E/4	49°00'	119°42'
Simmie	HAM/HAM	SK	27-11-16-W3	72 F/16	49°57'	108°06'
Simmons Bay	BAY/BAIE	NT	Franklin	120 C	81°15'	69°20'
Simmons Ice Cap	GLAC/GLAC	NT	Franklin	120 C	81°19'	68°51'
Simmons Lake	LAKE/LAC	BC	Range 1 Coast	92 K/6	50°23'	125°28'
Simmons Peninsula	CAPE/CAP	NT	Franklin	59 A	76°40'	89°07'
Simms Corner	UNP/LNO	NB	Saint John	21 G/8	45°16'	66°06'
Simms Settlement	UNP/LNO	NS	Lunenburg	21 A/9	44°38'	64°05'
Simonds	UNP/LNO	NB	Carleton	21 J/5	46°20'	67°33'
Simonds	GEOG/GÉOG	NB	Saint John	21 H/5	45°20'	65°48'
Simonds	GEOG/GÉOG	NB	Carleton	21 J/5	46°23'	67°35'
Simonet	UNP/LNO	QC	Le Domaine-du-Roy	32 A/8	48°21'	72°05'
Simonet, Lac	LAKE/LAC	QC	Papineau	31 G/14	45°48'	75°04'
Simonette River	RIV/CDE	AB	21-71-2-W6	83 M/1	55°09'	118°15'
Simonhouse	UNP/LNO	MB	7-63-26-W	63 K/6	54°26'	101°23'
Simonhouse Lake	LAKE/LAC	MB	63,64-25,26-W	63 K/11	54°33'	101°09'
Simon, Lac	LAKE/LAC	QC	Papineau	31 G/14	45°57'	75°04'
Simon Lakes	UNP/LNO	AB	29-86-17-W5	84 C/7	56°29'	116°38'
Simons Island	ISL/ÎLE	NT	Keewatin	65 D	60°33'	102°24'
Simons Valley	UNP/LNO	AB	3-26-2-W5	82 O/1	51°11'	114°12'
Simoom Sound	CHAN/CHEN	BC	Range 1 Coast	92 L/15	50°51'	126°30'
Simpson	VILG/VILG	SK	3-29-25-W2	72 P/6	51°27'	105°27'
Simpson Bay	BAY/BAIE	NT	Franklin	87 D	69°05'	114°20'
Simpson Corner	UNP/LNO	NB	Charlotte	21 G/3	45°14'	67°11'
Simpson Corners	UNP/LNO	ON	Wellington	40 P/16	43°46'	80°18'
Simpson Island	ISL/ÎLE	ON	Thunder Bay	42 D/13	48°48'	87°41'
Simpson Islands	ISL/ÎLE	NT	Mackenzie	85 H	61°50'	112°28'
Simpson Lake	LAKE/LAC	YT		105 A/11	60°44'	129°15'
Simpson Lake	LAKE/LAC	NT	Keewatin	57 A	68°35'	91°40'
Simpson Lake	LAKE/LAC	NT	Mackenzie	97 B	68°08'	126°35'
Simpson Peak	MTN/MNT	BC	Cassiar	104 O/11	59°43'	131°28'
Simpson Peninsula	CAPE/CAP	NT	Keewatin	57 A	68°34'	88°45'
Simpson Ranch	UNP/LNO	BC	Peace River	94 B/9	56°36'	122°26'
Simpson Range	MTN/MNT	YT		105 A/13	60°53'	129°55'
Simpson River	RIV/CDE	NT	Keewatin	66 N	67°49'	100°34'
Simpsons	UNP/LNO	ON	Renfrew	31 F/12	45°32'	77°30'
Simpsons Corner	UNP/LNO	NS	Lunenburg	21 A/10	44°33'	64°47'
Simpsons Field	UNP/LNO	NB	Restigouche	21 O/10	47°33'	66°32'
Simpson Strait	CHAN/CHEN	NT	Franklin	67 A/7	68°29'	97°10'
Simpson Tower	MTN/MNT	YT		105 H/6	61°24'	129°29'
Sim River	RIV/CDE	BC	Range 2 Coast	92 N/4	51°01'	125°37'
Sims	UNP/LNO	ON	Rainy River	52 C/11	48°41'	93°09'
Sims Creek	RIV/CDE	BC	Lillooet	92 J/5	50°15'	123°35'
Sims Lake	LAKE/LAC	NF		23 I/4	54°00'	65°55'
Sims Locks	UNP/LNO	ON	Haldimand	30 M/4	43°03'	79°55'
Sinaminda Lake	LAKE/LAC	ON	Algoma	41 I/13	46°53'	81°57'
Sinasac Corners	UNP/LNO	ON	Essex	40 J/2	42°06'	82°58'
Sincennes, Lac	LAKE/LAC	QC	Le Haut-Saint-Maurice	31 P/5	47°30'	73°52'
Sinclair	UNP/LNO	MB	13-7-29-W	62 F/11	49°34'	101°17'
Sinclair Lake	LAKE/LAC	ON	Sudbury	41 P/14	47°51'	81°21'
Sinclair Lake	LAKE/LAC	NT	Mackenzie	75 H	61°54'	104°40'
Sinclair Mills	UNP/LNO	BC	Cariboo	93 I/4	54°01'	121°41'
Sinclair Pass	VALL/VALL	BC	Kootenay	82 J/12	50°40'	115°56'
Sinclair River	RIV/CDE	MB	29-37-25-W	63 C/2	52°13'	101°00'
Sinclair Shore	UNP/LNO	ON	Lanark	31 F/1	45°04'	76°10'
Sinclairville	UNP/LNO	ON	Haldimand	30 M/4	43°03'	79°46'
Sine	UNP/LNO	ON	Hastings	31 C/5	44°20'	77°35'
Singelake	UNP/LNO	ON	Sudbury	42 B/1	48°12'	82°18'
Singer	UNP/LNO	QC	Papineau	31 G/14	45°54'	75°09'
Singer Point	CAPE/CAP	NT	Franklin	25 C	60°35'	68°13'
Singhampton	UNP/LNO	ON	Simcoe	41 A/8	44°21'	80°15'
Sinking Lake	LAKE/LAC	AB	59,60-6-W4	73 L/2	54°09'	110°50'
*Sinkut	UNP/LNO	BC	Range 5 Coast	93 J/4	54°00'	123°52'
Sinkut Lake 8	IR/RI	BC	Range 4 Coast	93 G/13	53°55'	123°58'
Sinkut River	UNP/LNO	BC	Range 4 Coast	93 G/13	53°57'	123°52'
Sinmax Creek	RIV/CDE	BC	Kamloops Division Yale	82 M/4	51°05'	119°47'
Sinnce-tah-lah 2	IR/RI	BC	Cariboo	93 B/15	52°57'	122°30'
Sinnett	UNP/LNO	SK	9-34-21-W2	72 P/15	51°54'	104°55'
Sintaluta	TOWN/VIL2	SK	33-17-11-W2	62 L/6	50°29'	103°27'
Siogak River	RIV/CDE	NT	Franklin	98 A	72°50'	121°40'
Sion	UNP/LNO	AB	36-56-2-W5	83 G/16	53°53'	114°09'
Siorak Brook	RIV/CDE	NF		14 E/9	57°35'	62°06'
Siorarsuk Peninsula	CAPE/CAP	NT	Franklin	47 D	69°55'	81°15'
Sioux Lake	LAKE/LAC	MB		64 J/7	58°23'	98°35'

NAME NOM	ENTITY ENTITÉ	LOC 1 LIEU 1	LOC 2 LIEU 2	MAP CARTE	POSITION LAT	LONG
Sioux Lookout	TOWN/VIL2	ON	Kenora	52 J/4	50°06′	91°55′
Sioux Narrows	MUN2/AZM2	ON	Kenora	52 E/8	49°23′	94°08′
Sioux Narrows	UNP/LNO	ON	Kenora	52 E/8	49°25′	94°06′
Sioux Valley	UNP/LNO	MB	10-23-W	62 F/16	49°51′	100°30′
Sioux Valley 58	IR/RI	MB		62 F/16	49°51′	100°30′
Sipanok Channel	CHAN/CHEN	SK	55-8-W2	63 E/10	53°40′	102°47′
Sipiwesk	UNP/LNO	MB	33-74-1-E	63 P/6	55°27′	97°24′
Sipiwesk Lake	LAKE/LAC	MB		63 P/4	55°05′	97°35′
Sir Alexander, Mount	MTN/MNT	BC	Cariboo	93 H/16	53°56′	120°23′
Sir Allan MacNab, Mount	MTN/MNT	BC	Kamloops Division Yale	83 D/11	52°31′	119°12′
Sirdar	UNP/LNO	BC	Kootenay	82 F/2	49°14′	116°37′
Sir Douglas, Mount	MTN/MNT	AB/BC		82 J/11	50°44′	115°21′
Sirenac	UNP/LNO	QC	Beauharnois-Salaberry	31 G/8	45°15′	74°08′
Sir Francis Drake, Mount	MTN/MNT	BC	Range 1 Coast	92 K/15	50°47′	124°47′
Sir-George-Étienne-Cartier, Lieu historique national de - also-aussi - Sir George-Étienne Cartier National Historic Site	PARK/PARC	QC	Communauté urbaine de Montréal	31 H/12	45°31′	73°33′
Sir George-Étienne Cartier National Historic Site - also-aussi - Sir-George-Étienne-Cartier, Lieu historique national de	PARK/PARC	QC	Communauté urbaine de Montréal	31 H/12	45°31′	73°33′
Sirius Seamount	SEAU/SMER	—		5.03	52°00′	160°50′
Sir James MacBrien, Mount	MTN/MNT	NT	Mackenzie	95 L	62°07′	127°41′
Sir John Johnson House National Historic Site - also-aussi - Maison-de-Sir-John-Johnson, Lieu historique national de la	PARK/PARC	ON	Glengarry	31 G/2	45°09′	74°35′
Sir-John Lake	UNP/LNO	QC	Argenteuil	31 G/9	45°43′	74°17′
Sirko	UNP/LNO	MB	7-1-10-E	62 H/1	49°01′	96°15′
Sirmisarniavik	UNP/LNO	QC	Kativik	25 C/13	60°53′	69°38′
Sirmisartalik	UNP/LNO	QC	Kativik	25 C/12	60°38′	69°48′
Sirois	UNP/LNO	NB	Madawaska	21 N/8	47°17′	68°00′
Sir Richard, Mount	MTN/MNT	BC	New Westminster	92 G/15	49°58′	122°42′
Sir Sandford, Mount	MTN/MNT	BC	Kootenay	82 N/12	51°39′	117°52′
Sir-Wilfrid-Laurier, Lieu historique national de - also-aussi - Sir Wilfrid Laurier National Historic Site	PARK/PARC	QC	Montcalm	31 H/13	45°51′	73°45′
Sir Wilfrid Laurier, Mount	MTN/MNT	BC	Cariboo	83 D/13	52°48′	119°44′
Sir Wilfrid Laurier National Historic Site - also-aussi - Sir-Wilfrid-Laurier, Lieu historique national de	PARK/PARC	QC	Montcalm	31 H/13	45°51′	73°45′
Sir-Wilfrid, Mont	MTN/MNT	QC	Antoine-Labelle	31 J/12	46°41′	75°36′
Sir Winston Churchill Provincial Park	PARK/PARC	AB	67-13,14-W4	73 L/13	54°50′	111°59′
Sisib Lake	LAKE/LAC	MB	36-41-14-W1	63 B/11	52°34′	99°20′
Sisipuk Lake	LAKE/LAC	MB/SK		63 N/12	55°44′	101°51′
Siska Flat 3	IR/RI	BC	Yale Division Yale	92 I/4	50°08′	121°34′
Siska Flat 5A	IR/RI	BC	Yale Division Yale	92 I/4	50°09′	121°34′
Siska Flat 5B	IR/RI	BC	Yale Division Yale	92 I/4	50°09′	121°35′
Siska Flat 8	IR/RI	BC	Kamloops Division Yale	92 I/4	50°08′	121°34′
Sisseney Lake	LAKE/LAC	ON	Timiskaming	41 P/15	47°52′	80°40′
Sissiboo	UNP/LNO	NS	Digby	21 A/5	44°27′	65°54′
Sissiboo Falls	UNP/LNO	NS	Digby	21 A/5	44°26′	65°52′
Sissiboo Grand Lake	LAKE/LAC	NS	Digby	21 A/5	44°24′	65°44′
Sissiboo River	RIV/CDE	NS	Digby	21 B/8	44°26′	66°01′
Sisson	UNP/LNO	NB	Victoria	21 J/14	46°54′	67°26′
Sisson Branch	RIV/CDE	NB	Victoria	21 O/3	47°15′	67°10′
Sisson Branch Reservoir	LAKE/LAC	NB	Victoria	21 O/6	47°18′	67°18′
Sisson Brook	UNP/LNO	NB	Victoria	21 J/14	46°59′	67°22′
Sisson Ridge	UNP/LNO	NB	Victoria	21 J/14	46°55′	67°26′
Sisson Settlement	UNP/LNO	NB	York	21 J/2	46°02′	66°51′
Sisters Islets	ISL/ÎLE	BC	Nanaimo	92 F/8	49°29′	124°26′
Sistonens Corners	UNP/LNO	ON	Thunder Bay	52 A/12	48°32′	89°39′
Sisul Tl'o K'Ut 14	IR/RI	BC	Range 5 Coast	93 K/10	54°39′	124°40′
Sisul Tl'o K'ut 21	IR/RI	BC	Range 5 Coast	93 K/10	54°40′	124°40′
Sitdown Pond	LAKE/LAC	NF		12 A/8	48°22′	56°04′
Sitialuit	UNP/LNO	QC	Kativik	34 K/9	58°40′	76°13′
Sitiapiit	UNP/LNO	QC	Kativik	34 K/8	58°25′	76°10′
Sitidgi Lake	LAKE/LAC	NT	Mackenzie	107 B	68°33′	132°42′
Sitiguluit	UNP/LNO	QC	Kativik	34 K/11	58°41′	77°29′
Sitiit	UNP/LNO	QC	Kativik	25 C/4	60°03′	69°58′
Sitiit	UNP/LNO	QC	Kativik	35 F/9	61°45′	76°02′
Sitiit	UNP/LNO	QC	Kativik	34 K/9	58°43′	76°09′
Sitiit Akianittuit	UNP/LNO	QC	Kativik	35 F/13	61°55′	77°47′
Sitiit Ivigaarittuit	UNP/LNO	QC	Kativik	34 K/10	58°41′	76°40′
Sitiit Siqinirsiq	UNP/LNO	QC	Kativik	35 F/13	61°54′	77°47′
Sitiit Tarrasiq	UNP/LNO	QC	Kativik	35 F/13	61°55′	77°48′
Sititalik	UNP/LNO	QC	Kativik	34 J/15	58°45′	74°58′
Sitkum Creek	RIV/CDE	BC	Osoyoos Division Yale	82 L/8	50°23′	118°27′
Sittakanay Mountain	MTN/MNT	BC	Cassiar	104 K/11	58°34′	133°26′
Situqqaaluk	UNP/LNO	QC	Kativik	34 K/6	58°28′	77°17′
Sivier Island	ISL/ÎLE	NF		2 E/7	49°21′	54°59′

NAME NOM	ENTITY ENTITÉ	LOC 1 LIEU 1	LOC 2 LIEU 2	MAP CARTE	POSITION LAT	LONG
Siwash Creek	RIV/CDE	BC	Kamloops Division Yale	92 H/9	49°40′	120°20′
Siwash Creek	RIV/CDE	YT		95 D/1	60°08′	126°20′
Siwash Mountain	MTN/MNT	BC	Kootenay	82 F/6	49°21′	117°27′
Siwhe Mountain	MTN/MNT	BC	Kamloops Division Yale	92 I/5	50°22′	121°50′
Six Mile Brook	UNP/LNO	NS	Pictou	11 E/10	45°35′	62°54′
Six Mile Corner	UNP/LNO	ON	Kenora	52 F/15	49°47′	92°42′
Six Mile Lake	LAKE/LAC	ON	Muskoka	31 D/13	44°54′	79°43′
Six Mile Meadow 6	IR/RI	BC	Range 5 Coast	93 K/8	54°20′	124°17′
Six Mile Point	UNP/LNO	BC	Kamloops Division Yale	82 L/14	50°46′	119°01′
Six Mile Road	UNP/LNO	NS	Cumberland	11 E/13	45°46′	63°31′
Six-Milles	UNP/LNO	NB	Restigouche	21 O/11	47°40′	67°27′
Six Nations 40	IR/RI	ON	Brant	40 P/1	43°03′	80°05′
Six Nations Corner	UNP/LNO	ON	Brant	40 P/1	43°03′	80°02′
Six Points	UNP/LNO	ON	York	30 M/12	43°38′	79°32′
Six Roads	UNP/LNO	NB	Gloucester	21 P/10	47°37′	64°52′
Sixteen Mile Creek	RIV/CDE	ON	Halton	30 M/5	43°26′	79°40′
Sixtymile	UNP/LNO	YT		116 C/2	64°02′	140°45′
Sixty Mile River	RIV/CDE	YT		115 O/12	63°34′	139°46′
Sixty-Nine Corners	UNP/LNO	ON	Brant	40 P/1	43°02′	80°08′
Skaare Fiord	BAY/BAIE	NT	Franklin	59 E	78°51′	88°05′
Skagit Range	MTN/MNT	BC	Yale Division Yale	92 H/3	49°10′	121°30′
Skagit River	RIV/CDE	BC	Yale Division Yale	92 H/3	49°00′	121°05′
Skaha Lake	LAKE/LAC	BC	Similkameen Division Yale	82 E/5	49°25′	119°35′
Skaigha 2	IR/RI	BC	Queen Charlotte	103 G/5	53°22′	131°56′
Skaro	UNP/LNO	AB	16-57-19-W4	83 H/15	53°55′	112°47′
Skawahlook 1	IR/RI	BC	Yale Division Yale	92 H/5	49°22′	121°35′
Skawahlum 10	IR/RI	BC	Yale Division Yale	92 H/6	49°27′	121°25′
Skaynaneichst 12	IR/RI	BC	Kamloops Division Yale	92 I/6	50°21′	121°16′
Skead	UNP/LNO	ON	Sudbury	41 I/10	46°40′	80°45′
Skedance 8	IR/RI	BC	Queen Charlotte	103 B/13	52°58′	131°37′
Skedans	UNP/LNO	BC	Queen Charlotte	103 B/13	52°58′	131°37′
Skeena	UNP/LNO	BC	Range 5 Coast	103 I/4	54°14′	129°50′
Skeena Crossing	UNP/LNO	BC	Cassiar	93 M/4	55°06′	127°49′
Skeena Mountains	MTN/MNT	BC	Cassiar	104 A/10	56°30′	128°40′
Skeena-Queen Charlotte	MUN1/AZM1	BC		103 F/16	53°45′	132°00′
Skeena River	RIV/CDE	BC	Range 5 Coast	103 J/1	54°01′	130°07′
Skeetchestn	IR/RI	BC	Kamloops Division Yale	92 I/15	50°48′	120°58′
Skeikut 9	IR/RI	BC	Kamloops Division Yale	92 I/6	50°18′	121°17′
Skelding	UNP/LNO	MB	19-11-7-W	62 G/16	49°56′	98°25′
Skeleton Lake	LAKE/LAC	ON	Muskoka	31 E/3	45°15′	79°27′
Skeleton Lake	LAKE/LAC	ON	Timiskaming	31 M/13	47°52′	79°39′
Skelu Bay	BAY/BAIE	BC	Queen Charlotte	103 F/7	53°30′	132°52′
Skemeoskuankin 7 & 8 - see-voir - Chopaka 7	IR/RI	BC		82 E/4	49°03′	119°43′
Skene Bay	BAY/BAIE	NT	Franklin	78 H	75°00′	107°50′
Skerryvore	UNP/LNO	ON	Parry Sound	41 H/9	45°32′	80°23′
Skhpowtz 4	IR/RI	BC	Kamloops Division Yale	92 I/6	50°18′	121°24′
Skibbereen	UNP/LNO	NF		1 N/6	47°23′	53°11′
Skibi Lake	UNP/LNO	ON	Thunder Bay	42 L/10	50°37′	86°57′
Skibo	UNP/LNO	ON	Algoma	41 J/6	46°18′	83°11′
Skidegate - see-voir - Skidegate Landing	UNP/LNO	BC		103 F/1	53°15′	132°01′
Skidegate 1	IR/RI	BC	Queen Charlotte	103 F/8	53°16′	132°00′
Skidegate Inlet	BAY/BAIE	BC	Queen Charlotte	103 G/4	53°14′	132°00′
Skidegate Landing	UNP/LNO	BC	Queen Charlotte	103 F/1	53°15′	132°01′
Skiff	UNP/LNO	AB	26-6-14-W4	72 E/12	49°30′	111°47′
Skiff Island	ISL/ÎLE	ON	Kenora	52 E/7	49°15′	94°38′
Skiff Lake	UNP/LNO	NB	York	21 G/13	45°50′	67°33′
Skiff Lake	LAKE/LAC	NB	York	21 G/13	45°49′	67°31′
Skiffsail Point	CAPE/CAP	NF		1 M/3	47°09′	55°04′
Skihist Mountain	MTN/MNT	BC	Kamloops Division Yale	92 I/4	50°11′	121°54′
Skilak 14	IR/RI	BC	Range 3 Coast	103 A/9	52°43′	128°19′
Skincuttle Inlet	BAY/BAIE	BC	Queen Charlotte	103 B/6	52°20′	131°13′
Skin Lake 15	IR/RI	BC	Range 4 Coast	93 F/13	53°47′	125°55′
Skinner Lake	LAKE/LAC	ON	Kenora	53 B/9	52°41′	90°18′
Skinners Pond	UNP/LNO	PE	Prince	21 I/16	46°58′	64°08′
Skins Lake 16A	IR/RI	BC	Range 4 Coast	93 F/13	54°00′	125°54′
Skins Lake 16B	IR/RI	BC	Range 4 Coast	93 F/13	53°57′	125°39′
Skipness	UNP/LNO	ON	Bruce	41 A/11	44°35′	81°13′
Skir Dhu	UNP/LNO	NS	Victoria	11 K/8	46°29′	60°27′
Sklahhesten 5	IR/RI	BC	New Westminster	92 G/16	49°55′	122°19′
Sklahhesten 5A	IR/RI	BC	New Westminster	92 G/16	49°56′	122°20′
Sklahhesten 5B	IR/RI	BC	New Westminster	92 G/16	49°54′	122°19′
Skoki Ski Lodge National Historic Site - also-aussi - Auberge-de-Ski-Skoki, Lieu historique national de l′	PARK/PARC	AB		82 N/9	51°31′	116°05′
Skonseng, Mount	MTN/MNT	YT		95 D/14	60°57′	127°13′
Skooby Island 48	IR/RI	BC	Range 5 Coast	93 K/11	54°34′	125°14′
Skooks Landing	UNP/LNO	BC	Cassiar	94 M/11	59°37′	127°07′

NAME / NOM	ENTITY / ENTITÉ	LOC 1 / LIEU 1	LOC 2 / LIEU 2	MAP / CARTE	POSITION LAT	LONG
Skookumchuck	UNP/LNO	BC	Kootenay	82 G/13	49°55′	115°44′
Skookumchuck	UNP/LNO	BC	New Westminster	92 G/16	49°56′	122°24′
Skookumchuck 4	IR/RI	BC	New Westminster	92 G/16	49°57′	122°24′
Skookumchuck 4A	IR/RI	BC	New Westminster	92 G/16	49°56′	122°23′
Skookumchuck Creek	RIV/CDE	BC	Kootenay	82 G/13	49°56′	115°46′
Skookum Jim, Mount	MTN/MNT	YT		116 G/3	65°11′	139°02′
Skoonka	UNP/LNO	BC	Kamloops Division Yale	92 I/6	50°22′	121°24′
Skoonkoon 2	IR/RI	BC	Kamloops Division Yale	92 I/6	50°22′	121°24′
Skootamatta Lake	LAKE/LAC	ON	Lennox and Addington	31 C/14	44°50′	77°16′
Skootamatta River	RIV/CDE	ON	Hastings	31 C/11	44°32′	77°20′
Skowishin 7	IR/RI	BC	New Westminster	92 G/14	49°56′	123°18′
Skowishin Graveyard 10	IR/RI	BC	New Westminster	92 G/14	49°55′	123°17′
Skowkale 10	IR/RI	BC	New Westminster	92 H/4	49°08′	121°56′
Skowkale 11	IR/RI	BC	New Westminster	92 H/4	49°08′	121°57′
Skownan	UNP/LNO	MB	34-16-W	62 O/13	51°59′	99°35′
Skowquiltz River 3	IR/RI	BC	Range 3 Coast	93 D/11	52°36′	127°10′
Skraeling Point	CAPE/CAP	NT	Franklin	340 B	80°05′	87°18′
Skrugar Point	CAPE/CAP	NT	Franklin	59 F	78°46′	93°50′
Skruis Point	CAPE/CAP	NT	Franklin	58 H	75°41′	88°46′
Skuet 6	IR/RI	BC	Yale Division Yale	92 H/11	49°42′	121°24′
Skuhun Creek	RIV/CDE	BC	Kamloops Division Yale	92 I/6	50°17′	121°11′
Skukum, Mount	MTN/MNT	YT		105 D/3	60°12′	135°29′
Skull Creek	UNP/LNO	SK	4-11-22-W3	72 F/15	49°53′	108°57′
Skull Hill	MTN/MNT	NF		12 H/1	49°00′	56°15′
Skumalasph 16	IR/RI	BC	New Westminster	92 G/1	49°12′	122°02′
Skuppah 1	IR/RI	BC	Kamloops Division Yale	92 I/4	50°10′	121°34′
Skuppah 2A	IR/RI	BC	Kamloops Division Yale	92 I/4	50°12′	121°35′
Skuppah 2B	IR/RI	BC	Kamloops Division Yale	92 I/4	50°12′	121°35′
Skuppah 3A	IR/RI	BC	Kamloops Division Yale	92 I/4	50°10′	121°35′
Skuppah 4	IR/RI	BC	Kamloops Division Yale	92 I/4	50°10′	121°35′
Skuppah 4A	IR/RI	BC	Kamloops Division Yale	92 I/4	50°10′	121°34′
Skutz 7	IR/RI	BC	Cowichan Lake	92 B/13	48°47′	123°57′
Skutz 8	IR/RI	BC	Cowichan Lake	92 B/13	48°47′	123°57′
Skwah 4	IR/RI	BC	New Westminster	92 H/4	49°11′	121°56′
Skwahla 2	IR/RI	BC	New Westminster	92 H/4	49°11′	121°56′
Skwali 3	IR/RI	BC	New Westminster	92 H/4	49°11′	121°58′
Skwawka River	RIV/CDE	BC	New Westminster	92 J/4	50°13′	123°59′
Skway 5	IR/RI	BC	New Westminster	92 G/1	49°10′	122°00′
Skwayaynope 26	IR/RI	BC	Kamloops Division Yale	92 I/4	50°12′	121°35′
Skweahm 10	IR/RI	BC	New Westminster	92 G/1	49°11′	122°05′
Skybattle Bay	BAY/BAIE	NT	Franklin	79 D	77°09′	105°00′
Skye	UNP/LNO	ON	Glengarry	31 G/7	45°24′	74°48′
Skye Glen	UNP/LNO	NS	Inverness	11 K/3	46°02′	61°12′
Skye Mountain	UNP/LNO	NS	Inverness	11 F/14	45°58′	61°12′
Skye River	RIV/CDE	NS	Inverness	11 F/14	45°58′	61°07′
Skylake	UNP/LNO	MB	35-21-1-E	62 I/14	50°51′	97°22′
Sky Lake	LAKE/LAC	ON	Bruce	41 A/14	44°48′	81°15′
Sky Pilot Mountain	MTN/MNT	BC	New Westminster	92 G/11	49°38′	123°05′
Slab City	UNP/LNO	QC	Le Haut-Saint-François	21 E/5	45°24′	71°36′
Slabtown	UNP/LNO	ON	Renfrew	31 F/11	45°42′	77°06′
Slabtown	UNP/LNO	ON	Perth	40 P/11	43°35′	81°13′
Slade	UNP/LNO	ON	Bruce	41 A/4	44°13′	81°35′
Slate Falls	UNP/LNO	ON	Lennox and Addington	31 F/3	45°11′	77°16′
Slate Falls	UNP/LNO	ON	Kenora	52 O/4	51°10′	91°35′
Slate Islands	ISL/ÎLE	ON	Thunder Bay	42 D/10	48°40′	87°00′
Slate Lake	UNP/LNO	MB	20-17-E	52 L/11	50°43′	95°11′
Slate Mountain	MTN/MNT	YT		105 C/13	60°59′	133°45′
Slater	UNP/LNO	SK		72 I/5	50°23′	105°32′
Slate River Valley	UNP/LNO	ON	Thunder Bay	52 A/6	48°20′	89°28′
Slave Bay	BAY/BAIE	NT	Mackenzie	85 G	61°13′	115°57′
Slave Falls	UNP/LNO	MB	2-15-14-E	52 L/4	50°14′	95°34′
Slave Lake	TOWN/VIL2	AB	31-72-5-W5	83 O/7	55°17′	114°46′
Slave Point	CAPE/CAP	NT	Mackenzie	85 G	61°11′	115°56′
Slave River	RIV/CDE	NT/AB		85 H/5	61°18′	113°40′
Slavey Creek	UNP/LNO	AB	4-118-21-W5	84 N/4	59°13′	117°30′
Slawa	UNP/LNO	AB	21-54-8-W4	73 E/11	53°41′	111°09′
Sled Creek	RIV/CDE	NT	Mackenzie	75 J	62°13′	107°25′
Sled Lake	HAM/HAM	SK		73 J/6	54°26′	107°20′
Sled Lake	LAKE/LAC	SK	63-10-W3	73 J/6	54°27′	107°25′
Sled Lake	LAKE/LAC	NT	Mackenzie	75 J	62°08′	106°50′
Sled River	RIV/CDE	SK		73 J/12	54°40′	107°32′
Sleeman	UNP/LNO	ON	Rainy River	52 D/9	48°43′	94°26′
Sleeper Islands	ISL/ÎLE	NT	Keewatin	34 E	57°30′	79°45′
Sleepy Hollow	HAM/HAM	SK	19-47-16-W3	73 F/1	53°04′	108°19′
Sleetsis 6	IR/RI	BC	Kamloops Division Yale	92 I/6	50°21′	121°24′

NAME NOM	ENTITY ENTITÉ	LOC 1 LIEU 1	LOC 2 LIEU 2	MAP CARTE	POSITION LAT	LONG
Sleigh Pond	LAKE/LAC	NF		2 D/1	48°07′	54°12′
Slemon Lake	LAKE/LAC	NT	Mackenzie	85 N/1	63°13′	116°02′
Slemon Park	UNP/LNO	PE	Prince	11 L/5	46°26′	63°49′
Slesse Creek	RIV/CDE	BC	Yale Division Yale	92 H/4	49°05′	121°42′
Slesse Mountain	MTN/MNT	BC	Yale Division Yale	92 H/4	49°01′	121°36′
Slesse Park	UNP/LNO	BC	New Westminster	92 H/4	49°05′	121°49′
Sleswick	UNP/LNO	ON	Peel	30 M/13	43°55′	79°56′
Sliammon	UNP/LNO	BC	New Westminster	92 F/15	49°54′	124°36′
Sliammon 1	IR/RI	BC	New Westminster	92 F/15	49°54′	124°37′
Sliammon Lake	LAKE/LAC	BC	New Westminster	92 F/15	49°56′	124°34′
Sliding Hills No. 273	MUN2/AZM2	SK		62 M/8	51°30′	102°10′
Slidre Fiord	BAY/BAIE	NT	Franklin	340 B	80°00′	86°15′
Slidre River	RIV/CDE	NT	Franklin	49 G	79°55′	85°18′
Sligo	UNP/LNO	ON	Peel	30 M/13	43°49′	79°58′
Slim Creek	RIV/CDE	BC	Cariboo	93 H/14	53°48′	121°12′
Slim Creek	RIV/CDE	BC	Lillooet	92 J/15	50°57′	122°59′
Slime Peninsula	CAPE/CAP	NT	Franklin	69 E	78°03′	97°30′
Slims River	RIV/CDE	YT		115 B/15	61°00′	138°32′
Slip-à-Frank, Le	UNP/LNO	QC	Les Îles-de-la-Madeleine	11 N/12	47°34′	61°31′
Slip-chez-Cyrice, Le	UNP/LNO	QC	Les Îles-de-la-Madeleine	11 N/12	47°34′	61°32′
Slip-chez-Éloquin, Le	UNP/LNO	QC	Les Îles-de-la-Madeleine	11 N/12	47°34′	61°31′
Slip-chez-Joseph, Le	UNP/LNO	QC	Les Îles-de-la-Madeleine	11 N/12	47°34′	61°31′
Sloane	UNP/LNO	BC	Cassiar	94 D/6	56°20′	127°12′
Sloan River	RIV/CDE	NT	Mackenzie	86 K/6	66°28′	117°28′
Slocan	VILG/VILG	BC	Kootenay	82 F/14	49°46′	117°28′
Slocan City	UNP/LNO	BC	Kootenay	82 F/14	49°46′	117°28′
Slocan Lake	LAKE/LAC	BC	Kootenay	82 F/14	49°54′	117°25′
Slocan Park	UNP/LNO	BC	Kootenay	82 F/12	49°31′	117°37′
Slocan River	RIV/CDE	BC	Kootenay	82 F/5	49°25′	117°31′
Slocomb, Mount	MTN/MNT	BC	Cassiar	94 E/16	57°53′	126°18′
Slok Creek	RIV/CDE	BC	Lillooet	92 I/13	50°51′	121°53′
Sloko River	RIV/CDE	BC	Cassiar	104 N/3	59°01′	133°09′
Slollicum Peak	MTN/MNT	BC	Yale Division Yale	92 H/5	49°25′	121°43′
Slooks 21	IR/RI	BC	Cassiar	103 P/5	55°15′	129°48′
Slope Road	UNP/LNO	NB	Sunbury	21 J/1	46°06′	66°06′
Sloquet Creek	RIV/CDE	BC	New Westminster	92 G/16	49°46′	122°12′
Slosh 1	IR/RI	BC	Lillooet	92 J/9	50°44′	122°13′
Slosh 1A	IR/RI	BC	Lillooet	92 J/9	50°44′	122°12′
Slouce, La	UNP/LNO	QC	Coaticook	21 E/4	45°03′	71°37′
Sluice Point	UNP/LNO	NS	Yarmouth	20 P/13	43°47′	65°58′
Smales	UNP/LNO	SK	34-28-2-W3	72 O/8	51°27′	106°13′
Small Island 4	IR/RI	BC	Range 1 Coast	92 L/9	50°34′	126°29′
Small Lake	LAKE/LAC	MB		64 H/11	57°41′	97°20′
Small Point	UNP/LNO	NF		1 N/14	47°50′	53°06′
Small Point-Broad Cove-Blackhead-Adams Cove	TOWN/VIL2	NF		1 N/14	47°50′	53°06′
Smalltree Lake	LAKE/LAC	NT	Mackenzie	75 A	61°00′	105°00′
Smallwood Reservoir	LAKE/LAC	NF		23 H	54°05′	64°30′
Smart	UNP/LNO	MB	7-12-19-W	62 F/16	50°00′	100°03′
Smart Lake	LAKE/LAC	NT	Mackenzie	75 O	63°30′	106°49′
Smeaton	VILG/VILG	SK	13-52-20-W2	73 H/7	53°30′	104°49′
Smellie	UNP/LNO	QC	Le Haut-Saint-Laurent	31 G/1	45°04′	74°14′
Smelt Brook	UNP/LNO	NS	Victoria	11 K/16	46°52′	60°23′
Smiley	VILG/VILG	SK	3-31-25-W3	72 N/11	51°38′	109°29′
Smith	MUN2/AZM2	ON	Peterborough	31 D/8	44°24′	78°19′
Smith	UNP/LNO	AB	23-71-1-W5	83 O/1	55°10′	114°02′
Smith Arm	BAY/BAIE	NT	Mackenzie	96 J	66°15′	124°00′
Smith Bay	BAY/BAIE	ON	Manitoulin	41 H/13	45°49′	81°38′
Smith Bay	BAY/BAIE	NT	Franklin	39 C	77°04′	78°40′
Smith Bay	BAY/BAIE	NT	Keewatin	65 B	60°35′	99°42′
Smith Bay	BAY/BAIE	NT	Franklin	68 C	73°18′	100°18′
Smith, Cape	CAPE/CAP	ON	Manitoulin	41 H/13	45°48′	81°35′
Smith, Cape	CAPE/CAP	NT	Keewatin	35 D	60°44′	78°41′
Smith Channel	CHAN/CHEN	NT	Franklin	25 P	63°30′	64°50′
Smith Corner	UNP/LNO	NB	Queens	21 H/13	45°47′	65°49′
Smith Cove	UNP/LNO	NS	Halifax	11 D/16	44°58′	62°13′
Smith Creek	RIV/CDE	BC	Similkameen Division Yale	92 H/8	49°23′	120°11′
Smithdale	UNP/LNO	ON	Simcoe	41 A/8	44°21′	80°09′
Smith, Détroit de - also-aussi - Smith Sound	CHAN/CHEN	NT		39 F	78°25′	74°00′
Smithers	TOWN/VIL2	BC	Range 5 Coast	93 L/14	54°47′	127°10′
Smithers Landing	UNP/LNO	BC	Cassiar	93 M/2	55°03′	126°30′
Smithfield	UNP/LNO	NS	Guysborough	11 E/8	45°16′	62°08′
Smithfield	UNP/LNO	NS	Colchester	11 E/6	45°16′	63°05′
Smithfield	UNP/LNO	NB	York	21 G/15	45°48′	66°55′
Smithfield	UNP/LNO	ON	Northumberland	31 C/4	44°04′	77°41′
Smithfield	UNP/LNO	AB	10-53-3-W5	83 G/9	53°34′	114°21′

NAME NOM	ENTITY ENTITÉ	LOC 1 LIEU 1	LOC 2 LIEU 2	MAP CARTE	POSITION	
					LAT	LONG
Smith Hill	UNP/LNO	MB	4-2-16-W1	62 G/4	49°05′	99°33′
Smith Inlet	BAY/BAIE	BC	Range 2 Coast	92 M/6	51°19′	127°25′
Smith Island	ISL/ÎLE	BC	Range 5 Coast	103 J/1	54°09′	130°14′
Smith Island	ISL/ÎLE	NT	Keewatin	35 D/9	60°45′	78°25′
Smith Island	ISL/ÎLE	NT	Franklin	49 A	76°10′	81°22′
Smithmill	UNP/LNO	AB	19-86-24-W5	84 C/5	56°28′	117°47′
Smith Point	CAPE/CAP	NS	Cumberland	11 E/14	45°52′	63°25′
Smith River	UNP/LNO	BC	Cassiar	94 M/16	59°53′	126°26′
Smith River	RIV/CDE	BC/YT		94 M/9	59°33′	126°29′
Smiths	UNP/LNO	MB	35-4-1-W	62 H/5	49°21′	97°30′
Smiths Corner	UNP/LNO	NS	Hants	21 A/16	44°50′	64°14′
Smiths Corner	UNP/LNO	NB	Kent	21 I/11	46°30′	65°10′
Smith's Corners	UNP/LNO	ON	Brant	40 P/1	43°02′	80°12′
Smiths Cove	UNP/LNO	NS	Digby	21 A/12	44°37′	65°42′
Smiths Creek	UNP/LNO	NB	Kings	21 H/14	45°47′	65°29′
Smiths Crossing	UNP/LNO	NB	Northumberland	21 I/13	46°46′	65°48′
Smith Settlement	UNP/LNO	NS	Halifax	11 D/14	44°47′	63°06′
Smith Settlement	UNP/LNO	NB	Westmorland	11 L/4	46°09′	64°00′
Smiths Falls	TOWN/VIL2	ON	Leeds	31 C/16	44°54′	76°01′
Smith's Harbour	UNP/LNO	NF		2 E/12	49°44′	55°58′
Smith's Landing	UNP/LNO	ON	Nipissing	31 L/7	46°25′	78°49′
Smith Sound - also-aussi - Smith, Détroit de	CHAN/CHEN	NT	Franklin	39 E	78°25′	74°00′
Smith Sound	BAY/BAIE	NF		2 C/4	48°10′	53°40′
Smith Sound	BAY/BAIE	BC	Range 2 Coast	92 M/5	51°18′	127°40′
Smiths Pond	LAKE/LAC	NF		2 F/5	49°22′	53°57′
Smithsville	UNP/LNO	NS	Shelburne	20 P/6	43°29′	65°28′
Smithtown	UNP/LNO	NB	Kings	21 H/5	45°28′	65°48′
Smithville	UNP/LNO	NS	Inverness	11 K/3	46°06′	61°20′
Smithville	UNP/LNO	ON	Lincoln	30 M/4	43°06′	79°33′
Smokehouse Creek	RIV/CDE	BC	Range 2 Coast	92 M/6	51°19′	127°03′
Smoke Lake	LAKE/LAC	ON	Nipissing	31 E/10	45°31′	78°41′
Smoke Lake	LAKE/LAC	AB	62-20-W5	83 K/7	54°22′	116°56′
Smokey	UNP/LNO	NF		13 I/6	54°28′	57°14′
Smokey, Cape	CAPE/CAP	NS	Victoria	11 K/9	46°37′	60°22′
Smoking Hills	MTN/MNT	NT	Mackenzie	97 C	69°31′	126°33′
Smoking Tent	UNP/LNO	SK	2-45-1-W2	63 D/16	52°51′	102°03′
Smoky Burn	UNP/LNO	SK	32-50-8-W2	63 E/6	53°22′	103°08′
Smoky Falls	UNP/LNO	ON	Cochrane	42 J/1	50°04′	82°10′
Smoky Heights	UNP/LNO	AB	13-74-3-W6	83 M/8	55°24′	118°18′
Smoky Lake	TOWN/VIL2	AB	22-59-17-W4	83 I/1	54°07′	112°28′
Smoky Lake	LAKE/LAC	AB	59,60-18-W4	83 I/2	54°10′	112°40′
Smoky Lake No. 13, County of	MUN1/AZM1	AB	61-6-W4	83 I/1	54°14′	112°15′
Smoky Ridge	UNP/LNO	SK	45,46-1-W2	63 D/16	52°56′	102°02′
Smoky River	RIV/CDE	AB	18-83-21-W5	84 C/3	56°11′	117°19′
Smoky River No. 130, Municipal District of	MUN1/AZM1	AB	77-21-W5	83 N/11	55°39′	117°11′
Smooth Cove	UNP/LNO	NF		1 N/14	47°55′	53°04′
Smooth Rock	UNP/LNO	ON	Cochrane	42 H/4	49°14′	81°37′
Smooth Rock Falls	TOWN/VIL2	ON	Cochrane	42 H/5	49°17′	81°38′
Smoothrock Lake	LAKE/LAC	ON	Thunder Bay	52 I/11	50°30′	89°30′
Smoothstone Lake	LAKE/LAC	SK		73 J/10	54°40′	106°50′
Smoothstone River	RIV/CDE	SK	73-5-W3	73 O/7	55°19′	106°39′
Smooth Town	UNP/LNO	ON	Brant	40 P/1	43°02′	80°04′
Smoothwater Lake	LAKE/LAC	ON	Timiskaming	41 P/7	47°24′	80°41′
Smuts	UNP/LNO	SK	8-40-1-W3	73 B/8	52°26′	106°07′
Smyth, Cape	CAPE/CAP	NT	Franklin	88 E	74°58′	115°40′
Smythe, Mount	MTN/MNT	BC	Peace River	94 F/15	57°54′	124°53′
Smyth Harbour	BAY/BAIE	NT	Franklin	46 G	65°09′	83°42′
Snack Cove	UNP/LNO	NF		13 H/15	53°48′	56°50′
Snag	UNP/LNO	YT		115 K/8	62°24′	140°22′
Snag Creek	RIV/CDE	YT		115 K/8	62°24′	140°22′
Snag Junction	UNP/LNO	YT		115 K/2	62°14′	140°41′
Snake 5	IR/RI	BC	Peace River	94 O/1	59°03′	122°27′
Snake Bay	BAY/BAIE	ON	Kenora	52 E/8	49°22′	94°02′
Snake Creek	RIV/CDE	ON	Grey	41 A/6	44°20′	81°24′
Snake Falls	UNP/LNO	ON	Kenora	52 K/14	50°50′	93°28′
Snake Indian River	RIV/CDE	AB	48-28-W5	83 F/4	53°11′	117°59′
Snake Island	ISL/ÎLE	NS	Lunenburg	21 A/9	44°32′	64°10′
Snake Island	ISL/ÎLE	ON	York	31 D/6	44°19′	79°29′
Snake Lake	LAKE/LAC	AB	123-1-W5	84 O/9	59°40′	114°09′
Snake River	UNP/LNO	ON	Renfrew	31 F/10	45°41′	76°57′
Snake River	UNP/LNO	BC	Peace River	94 O/1	59°02′	122°27′
Snake River	RIV/CDE	YT		106 E/16	65°59′	134°12′
Snakes Bight	BAY/BAIE	NF		11 O/14	47°57′	59°19′
Snape Island	ISL/ÎLE	NT	Franklin	33 M	55°45′	79°18′
Snare Lake	LAKE/LAC	SK		74 J/5	58°27′	107°44′

NAME NOM	ENTITY ENTITÉ	LOC 1 LIEU 1	LOC 2 LIEU 2	MAP CARTE	POSITION LAT	LONG
Snare Lake	LAKE/LAC	NT	Mackenzie	86 B/1	64°11′	114°22′
Snare Lakes	UNP/LNO	NT	Mackenzie	86 B/1	64°11′	114°11′
Snare River	RIV/CDE	SK		74 J/12	58°36′	107°45′
Snare River	RIV/CDE	NT	Mackenzie	85 O	63°07′	115°53′
Snaring	UNP/LNO	AB	28-47-1-W6	83 E/1	53°05′	118°04′
Snaring River	RIV/CDE	AB	46-1-W6	83 E/1	53°01′	118°05′
Snass Mountain	MTN/MNT	BC	Yale Division Yale	92 H/7	49°16′	120°59′
Snedden	UNP/LNO	ON	Lanark	31 F/8	45°16′	76°14′
Snegamook Lake	LAKE/LAC	NF		13 K/11	54°33′	61°27′
Snelgrove	UNP/LNO	ON	Peel	30 M/12	43°44′	79°49′
Snelgrove Lake	LAKE/LAC	NF		23 I/12	54°37′	65°50′
Sniatyn	UNP/LNO	AB	30-57-16-W4	83 H/16	53°57′	112°22′
Snider	UNP/LNO	ON	Halton	30 M/12	43°31′	79°43′
Snider Mountain	UNP/LNO	NB	Kings	21 H/13	45°50′	65°38′
Snipe Lake	UNP/LNO	SK	29-25-21-W3	72 N/2	51°10′	108°53′
Snipe Lake	LAKE/LAC	SK	26-21-W3	72 N/2	51°13′	108°51′
Snipe Lake	LAKE/LAC	AB	70,71-18,19-W5	83 N/2	55°07′	116°47′
Snipe Lake No. 259	MUN2/AZM2	SK		72 N/2	51°10′	108°35′
Snook Lake	LAKE/LAC	ON	Kenora	52 L/2	50°12′	94°41′
Snooks Arm	UNP/LNO	NF		2 E/13	49°51′	55°42′
Snooks Arm	BAY/BAIE	NF		2 E/13	49°51′	55°42′
Snooks Harbour	UNP/LNO	NF		2 C/4	48°10′	53°53′
Snowball	UNP/LNO	ON	York	30 M/13	43°59′	79°31′
Snowbank River	RIV/CDE	NT	Keewatin	46 E	65°53′	86°22′
Snowbird Lake	LAKE/LAC	NT	Mackenzie	65 D	60°41′	102°56′
Snowcap Creek	RIV/CDE	BC	New Westminster	92 G/16	49°56′	122°24′
Snowcap Lake	LAKE/LAC	BC	New Westminster	92 G/15	49°52′	122°37′
Snowcap Mountain	MTN/MNT	YT		105 L/2	62°09′	134°49′
Snowcrest Mountain	MTN/MNT	BC	Kootenay	82 F/10	49°33′	116°31′
Snowden	HAM/HAM	SK	13-52-19-W2	73 H/7	53°29′	104°41′
Snow Dome	MTN/MNT	AB/BC		83 C/3	52°12′	117°19′
Snowdon	MUN2/AZM2	ON	Haliburton	31 D/15	44°52′	78°36′
Snowdons Corners	UNP/LNO	ON	Grenville	31 B/13	44°51′	75°45′
Snowdrift - see-voir - Łutselk'e	UNP/LNO	NT		75 L/7	62°24′	110°44′
Snowdrift River	RIV/CDE	NT	Mackenzie	75 L/7	62°21′	110°37′
Snowflake	UNP/LNO	MB	19-1-9-W	62 G/2	49°03′	98°40′
Snow Island	ISL/ÎLE	NT	Keewatin	65 N	63°11′	101°55′
Snow Lake	TOWN/VIL2	MB		63 K/16	54°53′	100°02′
Snow, Mont	MTN/MNT	QC	La Jacques-Cartier	21 L/14	46°56′	71°25′
Snow Peak	MTN/MNT	BC	Cassiar	104 J/8	58°28′	130°28′
Snow Road Station	UNP/LNO	ON	Frontenac	31 C/15	44°57′	76°41′
Snowshoe Bay	BAY/BAIE	MB/ON		52 E/11	49°36′	95°10′
Snowshoe Island	ISL/ÎLE	SK		64 L/6	58°22′	103°29′
Snowshoe Peak	MTN/MNT	YT		115 B/9	60°38′	138°19′
Snowshoe Pond	LAKE/LAC	NF		12 A/7	48°21′	56°49′
Snows Pond	LAKE/LAC	NF		1 N/11	47°28′	53°23′
Snowville	UNP/LNO	ON	Manitoulin	41 G/9	45°40′	82°03′
Snowy Mountain	MTN/MNT	BC	Similkameen Division Yale	82 E/4	49°03′	119°52′
Snug Cove	UNP/LNO	AB	19-65-9-W4	73 L/11	54°38′	111°21′
Snug Cove	UNP/LNO	BC	New Westminster	92 G/6	49°23′	123°20′
Snug Harbour	UNP/LNO	NF		3 D/13	52°53′	55°52′
Snug Harbour	UNP/LNO	QC	Memphrémagog	31 H/1	45°13′	72°12′
Snug Harbour	UNP/LNO	ON	Victoria	31 D/7	44°25′	78°44′
Snug Harbour	UNP/LNO	ON	Parry Sound	41 H/8	45°22′	80°18′
Snug Haven	UNP/LNO	ON	Parry Sound	41 H/8	45°22′	80°18′
Snug Lake	LAKE/LAC	NT	Keewatin	55 L	62°22′	94°20′
Snyder	UNP/LNO	ON	Welland	30 L/14	42°58′	79°03′
Snyder	UNP/LNO	BC	Peace River	94 A/14	56°55′	121°23′
Snyder Lake	LAKE/LAC	MB		64 N/5	59°23′	101°40′
Soapstone Mine	UNP/LNO	NS	Inverness	11 F/14	45°59′	61°11′
Sober Island	UNP/LNO	NS	Halifax	11 D/16	44°51′	62°28′
Sober Island	ISL/ÎLE	NS	Halifax	11 D/16	44°50′	62°28′
Société, La	UNP/LNO	QC	Montmagny	21 L/9	46°40′	70°04′
Sockeye	UNP/LNO	BC	Range 5 Coast	103 J/1	54°09′	130°08′
Soda Creek	UNP/LNO	BC	Cariboo	93 B/8	52°21′	122°17′
Soda Creek	UNP/LNO	BC	Cariboo	93 B/8	52°22′	122°19′
Soda Creek 1	IR/RI	BC	Cariboo	93 B/8	52°19′	122°16′
Soeurs, Île des	ISL/ÎLE	QC	Communauté urbaine de Montréal	31 H/5	45°28′	73°33′
Sohm Abyssal Plain - also-aussi - Sohm, Plaine abyssale	SEAU/SMER	—		800A	36°00′	55°00′
Sohm, Plaine abyssale - also-aussi - Sohm Abyssal Plain	SEAU/SMER	—		800A	36°00′	55°00′
Sointula	UNP/LNO	BC	Rupert	92 L/11	50°38′	127°01′
Soissons, Lac	LAKE/LAC	QC	Kativik	24 G/1	57°05′	66°25′
Sokal	UNP/LNO	SK	18-43-27-W2	73 A/12	52°42′	105°54′
Sokatisewin Lake	LAKE/LAC	SK		63 M/8	55°30′	102°25′
Solace Lake	LAKE/LAC	ON	Sudbury	41 P/2	47°11′	80°42′

NAME / NOM	ENTITY / ENTITÉ	LOC 1 / LIEU 1	LOC 2 / LIEU 2	MAP / CARTE	POSITION LAT	LONG
Soldatquo 12	IR/RI	BC	Kamloops Division Yale	92 I/6	50°21′	121°10′
Soldier Lake	LAKE/LAC	NS	Halifax	11 D/13	44°49′	63°34′
Soldier's Cove	UNP/LNO	NF		1 M/16	47°48′	54°13′
Soldiers Cove	UNP/LNO	NS	Richmond	11 F/10	45°42′	60°44′
Soldiers Cove West	UNP/LNO	NS	Richmond	11 F/10	45°42′	60°45′
Solina	UNP/LNO	ON	Durham	30 M/15	43°58′	78°47′
Solmesville	UNP/LNO	ON	Prince Edward	31 C/3	44°09′	77°07′
Solomon	UNP/LNO	AB	23-50-27-W5	83 F/5	53°20′	117°50′
Solomons Temple Islands	ISL/ÎLE	NT	Keewatin	33 D	52°50′	79°09′
Solsgirth	UNP/LNO	MB	30-17-25-W	62 K/7	50°29′	100°55′
Solsqua	UNP/LNO	BC	Kamloops Division Yale	82 L/15	50°52′	118°57′
Somass River	RIV/CDE	BC	Alberni	92 F/2	49°14′	124°49′
Sombra	MUN2/AZM2	ON	Lambton	40 J/9	42°41′	82°21′
Sombra	UNP/LNO	ON	Lambton	40 J/9	42°43′	82°29′
Sombre Mountains	MTN/MNT	NT	Mackenzie	95 K	62°15′	125°45′
Sombrio Point	CAPE/CAP	BC	Renfrew	92 C/8	48°29′	124°17′
Somenos	UNP/LNO	BC	Somenos	92 B/13	48°49′	123°44′
Somenos Land District	GEOG/GÉOG	BC		92 B	48°49′	123°43′
Somerset	VILG/VILG	MB	20-5-9-W	62 G/7	49°25′	98°40′
Somerset	UNP/LNO	NS	Lunenburg	21 A/2	44°14′	64°32′
Somerset	UNP/LNO	NS	Kings	21 H/2	45°04′	64°45′
Somerset Island	ISL/ÎLE	NT	Franklin	58 C	73°15′	93°30′
Somerville	MUN2/AZM2	ON	Victoria	31 D/10	44°41′	78°44′
Somerville	UNP/LNO	NB	Carleton	21 J/5	46°18′	67°32′
Somerville Island	ISL/ÎLE	BC	Range 5 Coast	103 J/9	54°44′	130°17′
Somerville Island	ISL/ÎLE	NT	Franklin	68 E	74°44′	96°11′
Somme	UNP/LNO	MB	16-1-9-E	62 H/1	49°02′	96°19′
Somme	UNP/LNO	SK	32-41-7-W2	63 D/10	52°35′	102°58′
Sommerfeld	UNP/LNO	MB	30-1-1-E	62 H/3	49°04′	97°27′
Sommet, Lac du	LAKE/LAC	QC	Caniapiscau	23 C/14	53°00′	69°23′
Sommet-Vert	UNP/LNO	QC	Les Pays-d'en-Haut	31 J/1	46°02′	74°04′
Songis	UNP/LNO	ON	Nipissing	31 L/6	46°22′	79°12′
Sonningdale	UNP/LNO	SK	28-39-12-W3	73 B/5	52°23′	107°41′
Sonora	UNP/LNO	NS	Guysborough	11 F/4	45°04′	61°54′
Sonora Island	ISL/ÎLE	BC	Sayward	92 K/6	50°22′	125°15′
Sonya	UNP/LNO	ON	Victoria	31 D/2	44°14′	78°57′
Sooke	UNP/LNO	BC	Sooke	92 B/5	48°23′	123°43′
Sooke 1	IR/RI	BC	Sooke	92 B/5	48°23′	123°42′
Sooke 2	IR/RI	BC	Sooke	92 B/5	48°22′	123°45′
Sooke Inlet	BAY/BAIE	BC	Sooke	92 B/5	48°21′	123°43′
Sooke Lake	LAKE/LAC	BC	Malahat	92 B/12	48°33′	123°42′
Sooke Land District	GEOG/GÉOG	BC		92 B	48°22′	123°41′
Sooke River	RIV/CDE	BC	Sooke	92 B/5	48°23′	123°42′
Soo River	RIV/CDE	BC	New Westminster	92 J/7	50°16′	122°52′
Soowahlie 14	IR/RI	BC	New Westminster	92 H/4	49°05′	121°57′
Soper Lake	LAKE/LAC	NT	Franklin	25 K	62°53′	69°54′
Soper River	RIV/CDE	NT	Franklin	25 K	62°54′	69°51′
Sopers	UNP/LNO	NF		12 B/16	48°57′	58°02′
Soperton	UNP/LNO	ON	Leeds	31 C/9	44°36′	76°04′
Sophe 14	IR/RI	BC	Nootka	92 E/15	49°48′	126°50′
Sopher's Landing	UNP/LNO	ON	Muskoka	31 D/14	44°51′	79°24′
Sophiasburgh	MUN2/AZM2	ON	Prince Edward	31 C/3	44°05′	77°13′
Sop's Arm	UNP/LNO	NF		12 H/15	49°46′	56°53′
Sops Arm	BAY/BAIE	NF		2 E/5	49°27′	55°47′
Sops Arm Brook	RIV/CDE	NF		2 E/5	49°26′	55°48′
Sops Island	UNP/LNO	NF		12 H/15	49°46′	56°51′
Sops Island	ISL/ÎLE	NF		12 H/15	49°47′	56°49′
Sops Lake	LAKE/LAC	NF		2 E/5	49°25′	55°50′
Sorcerer Mountain	MTN/MNT	BC	Kootenay	82 N/5	51°27′	117°55′
Sorcier, Lac au	LAKE/LAC	QC	Maskinongé	31 I/11	46°40′	73°24′
Sorehead, Rivière	RIV/CDE	QC	Kativik	35 C/12	60°33′	77°30′
Sorel	CITY/VIL1	QC	Le Bas-Richelieu	31 I/3	46°02′	73°07′
Sorenson's Beach	HAM/HAM	SK	1-22-23-W2	72 I/14	50°50′	105°03′
Sor Fiord	BAY/BAIE	NT	Franklin	49 C	77°20′	84°40′
Sormany	UNP/LNO	NB	Gloucester	21 P/12	47°40′	65°52′
Sorrel Ridge	UNP/LNO	NB	Charlotte	21 G/6	45°22′	67°03′
Sorrento	UNP/LNO	BC	Kamloops Division Yale	82 L/14	50°53′	119°28′
Soscumica, Lac	LAKE/LAC	QC	Jamésie	32 K/6	50°50′	77°27′
Soucy	UNP/LNO	NB	Madawaska	21 N/7	47°20′	68°36′
Soucy	UNP/LNO	QC	Drummond	31 H/15	45°55′	72°44′
Soucyville	UNP/LNO	QC	Avignon	22 B/1	48°08′	66°22′
Soufflets River	RIV/CDE	NF		12 I/7	50°25′	56°31′
Soufflot, Lac	LAKE/LAC	QC	Témiscamingue	31 M/7	47°24′	78°31′
Soulier Lake	LAKE/LAC	SK		74 N/15	59°50′	108°42′
Soulier Lake	LAKE/LAC	NT	Mackenzie	75 D	60°41′	110°08′

NAME NOM	ENTITY ENTITÉ	LOC 1 LIEU 1	LOC 2 LIEU 2	MAP CARTE	POSITION LAT	LONG
Soulis Pond	LAKE/LAC	NF		2 D/16	48°56′	54°21′
Soul Lake	LAKE/LAC	MB	42,43-14-W	63 B/11	52°40′	99°26′
Sounding Creek	RIV/CDE	AB	26-36-4-W4	73 D/1	52°06′	110°28′
Sounding Lake	UNP/LNO	AB	16-36-4-W4	73 D/2	52°06′	110°30′
Sounding Lake	LAKE/LAC	AB	36,37-4-W4	73 D/2	52°08′	110°29′
Sound Island	ISL/ÎLE	NF		1 M/16	47°49′	54°10′
Soup Harbour	BAY/BAIE	ON	Prince Edward	30 N/14	43°51′	77°11′
Source-de-la-Loutre, La	UNP/LNO	QC	Minganie	12 E/12	49°41′	63°43′
Source-de-Saumure-de-la-Chaloupe, La	UNP/LNO	QC	Minganie	12 E/1	49°12′	62°29′
Sourd, Lac du	LAKE/LAC	QC	Antoine-Labelle	31 J/3	46°09′	75°16′
Souris	TOWN/VIL2	PE	Kings	11 L/8	46°21′	62°15′
Souris	TOWN/VIL2	MB	7,8-21-W	62 F/9	49°37′	100°16′
Souris Line Road	UNP/LNO	PE	Kings	11 L/8	46°24′	62°15′
Souris River	UNP/LNO	PE	Kings	11 L/8	46°23′	62°17′
Souris River	UNP/LNO	SK	31-1-2-W2	62 E/1	49°05′	102°16′
Souris River	RIV/CDE	MB	22-8-16-W	62 G/12	49°40′	99°34′
Souris River	RIV/CDE	SK		62 F/4	49°00′	102°00′
Souris Valley	UNP/LNO	SK	36-5-17-W2	72 H/8	49°26′	104°10′
Souris Valley No. 7	MUN2/AZM2	SK		62 E/4	49°10′	103°50′
Souris West	VILG/VILG	PE	Kings	11 L/8	46°21′	62°18′
Souris West	UNP/LNO	PE	Kings	11 L/8	46°22′	62°17′
Sour Spring	UNP/LNO	ON	Brant	40 P/1	43°03′	80°12′
South Algona	MUN2/AZM2	ON	Renfrew	31 F/11	45°30′	77°17′
Southall	UNP/LNO	SK	8-3-13-W2	62 E/4	49°12′	103°43′
South Allan	UNP/LNO	SK	28-32-1-W3	72 O/16	51°46′	106°04′
South Alton	UNP/LNO	NS	Kings	21 H/2	45°01′	64°32′
Southampton	TOWN/VIL2	ON	Bruce	41 A/6	44°29′	81°23′
Southampton	UNP/LNO	PE	Kings	11 L/7	46°23′	62°35′
Southampton	UNP/LNO	NS	Cumberland	21 H/9	45°35′	64°15′
Southampton	UNP/LNO	NB	York	21 G/14	45°58′	67°15′
Southampton	GEOG/GÉOG	NB	York	21 J/3	46°07′	67°18′
Southampton, Cape	CAPE/CAP	NT	Keewatin	45 J	62°08′	83°43′
Southampton Island	ISL/ÎLE	NT	Keewatin	46 C	64°20′	84°40′
Southampton Junction	UNP/LNO	NB	York	21 J/3	46°07′	67°11′
Southarm	UNP/LNO	BC	New Westminster	92 G/3	49°08′	123°06′
South Arm	BAY/BAIE	NF		2 E/6	49°23′	55°18′
South Arm	BAY/BAIE	ON	Nipissing	41 I/16	46°53′	80°04′
South Arm	GLAC/GLAC	YT		115 B/10	60°38′	138°48′
South Athol	UNP/LNO	NS	Cumberland	21 H/9	45°39′	64°14′
South Augusta	UNP/LNO	ON	Grenville	31 B/12	44°39′	75°39′
South Aulatsivik Island	ISL/ÎLE	NF		14 C/11	56°45′	61°30′
Southbank	UNP/LNO	BC	Range 4 Coast	93 K/4	54°01′	125°46′
South Baptiste	VILG/VILG	AB	22-66-24-W4	83 I/12	54°43′	113°34′
South Bar	UNP/LNO	NS	Cape Breton	11 K/1	46°12′	60°11′
South Barnston	UNP/LNO	QC	Coaticook	21 E/4	45°03′	71°59′
South Bathurst	UNP/LNO	NB	Gloucester	21 P/12	47°36′	65°40′
South Bay	UNP/LNO	NB	Saint John	21 G/8	45°15′	66°09′
South Bay	UNP/LNO	ON	Prince Edward	30 N/14	43°55′	77°02′
South Bay	UNP/LNO	ON	Muskoka	31 D/13	44°52′	79°46′
South Bay	UNP/LNO	ON	Kenora	52 N/2	51°07′	92°41′
South Bay	BAY/BAIE	ON	Parry Sound	31 L/4	46°09′	79°34′
South Bay	BAY/BAIE	ON	Cochrane	32 D/12	48°42′	79°58′
South Bay	BAY/BAIE	ON	Manitoulin	41 G/9	45°34′	82°00′
South Bay	BAY/BAIE	ON	Essex	40 G/10	41°44′	82°39′
South Bay	BAY/BAIE	ON	Thunder Bay	52 H/2	49°07′	88°51′
South Bay	BAY/BAIE	MB		64 B/10	56°42′	98°59′
South Bay	BAY/BAIE	SK		73 J/11	54°39′	107°24′
South Bay	BAY/BAIE	SK		73 O/5	55°17′	107°48′
South Bay	BAY/BAIE	NT	Keewatin	45 O	63°58′	83°30′
South Bay Ingonish	BAY/BAIE	NS	Victoria	11 K/9	46°38′	60°23′
South Baymouth	UNP/LNO	ON	Manitoulin	41 G/9	45°33′	82°01′
South Beach	UNP/LNO	ON	Peterborough	31 D/8	44°29′	78°13′
South Beach	UNP/LNO	MB	31-10-15-E	52 E/13	49°53′	95°32′
South Beach	UNP/LNO	MB	9-19-4-E	62 I/10	50°37′	96°59′
South Bentinck	UNP/LNO	BC	Range 3 Coast	93 D/2	52°03′	126°40′
South Bentinck Arm	BAY/BAIE	BC	Range 3 Coast	93 D/2	52°10′	126°50′
South Berwick	UNP/LNO	NS	Kings	21 H/2	45°02′	64°43′
South Bill	CAPE/CAP	NF		2 E/14	49°58′	55°29′
South Bill	CAPE/CAP	NF		2 E/12	49°40′	55°51′
Southboine	UNP/LNO	MB		62 H/14	49°52′	97°18′
South Bolton	UNP/LNO	QC	Memphrémagog	31 H/1	45°09′	72°22′
South Branch	UNP/LNO	NF		11 O/14	47°55′	59°02′
South Branch	UNP/LNO	NS	Colchester	11 E/3	45°10′	63°05′
South Branch	UNP/LNO	NB	Kent	21 I/10	46°32′	64°55′
South Branch	UNP/LNO	NB	Kings	21 H/11	45°45′	65°18′

NAME / NOM	ENTITY / ENTITÉ	LOC 1 / LIEU 1	LOC 2 / LIEU 2	MAP / CARTE	POSITION LAT	POSITION LONG
South Branch	UNP/LNO	ON	Grenville	31 B/13	44°49′	75°42′
South Branch Big Sevogle River	RIV/CDE	NB	Northumberland	21 P/4	47°06′	65°56′
South Branch Kedgwick River	RIV/CDE	NB	Restigouche	21 O/13	47°54′	67°55′
South Branch Muskoka River	RIV/CDE	ON	Muskoka	31 E/3	45°02′	79°19′
South Branch Nepisiguit River	RIV/CDE	NB	Northumberland	21 O/8	47°23′	66°30′
South Branch Renous River	RIV/CDE	NB	Northumberland	21 J/16	46°47′	66°11′
South Brook	TOWN/VIL2	NF		12 H/8	49°26′	56°05′
South Brook	UNP/LNO	NF		12 H/16	49°59′	56°02′
South Brook	UNP/LNO	NF		12 H/4	49°01′	57°36′
South Brook	UNP/LNO	NS	Cumberland	21 H/9	45°33′	64°11′
South Brook	RIV/CDE	NF		12 H/8	49°26′	56°05′
South Brookfield	UNP/LNO	NS	Queens	21 A/7	44°23′	64°58′
South Buxton	UNP/LNO	ON	Kent	40 J/8	42°16′	82°11′
Southby Lake	LAKE/LAC	NT	Mackenzie	75 A	60°38′	105°19′
South Cambie	UNP/LNO	BC	New Westminster	92 G/3	49°15′	123°07′
South Canaan	UNP/LNO	NS	Yarmouth	20 P/13	43°56′	65°53′
South Canoe	UNP/LNO	BC	Kamloops Division Yale	82 L/11	50°42′	119°13′
South Cape	CAPE/CAP	NT	Franklin	49 B	76°18′	84°27′
South Cape Fiord	BAY/BAIE	NT	Franklin	49 B	76°26′	84°53′
South Cape Highlands	UNP/LNO	NS	Inverness	11 K/3	46°09′	61°23′
South Cayuga	UNP/LNO	ON	Haldimand	30 L/13	42°52′	79°43′
South Channel	CHAN/CHEN	NT	Keewatin	56 D/2	64°02′	94°35′
South Charlo River	RIV/CDE	NB	Restigouche	21 O/16	47°59′	66°17′
South Chegoggin	UNP/LNO	NS	Yarmouth	20 O/16	43°52′	66°08′
Southcote	UNP/LNO	ON	Wentworth	30 M/4	43°11′	79°57′
Southcott Pines	UNP/LNO	ON	Lambton	40 P/5	43°18′	81°46′
South Cove	UNP/LNO	NS	Victoria	11 K/2	46°02′	60°54′
South Creek	RIV/CDE	ON	Cochrane	42 G/1	49°09′	82°02′
Southcrest Estates	UNP/LNO	ON	Middlesex	40 I/14	42°57′	81°16′
South Crosby	MUN2/AZM2	ON	Grenville	31 C/9	44°36′	76°14′
South Cross Lake	LAKE/LAC	MB	10-17-E	52 E/14	49°51′	95°15′
South Cypress	MUN2/AZM2	MB		62 G/11	49°40′	99°20′
Southdale	UNP/LNO	NS	Halifax	11 D/12	44°40′	63°32′
Southdale	UNP/LNO	ON	Middlesex	40 I/14	42°57′	81°14′
Southdale	UNP/LNO	MB		62 H/14	49°51′	97°04′
South Dawson	UNP/LNO	BC	Peace River	93 P/9	55°44′	120°21′
South Deerfield	UNP/LNO	NS	Yarmouth	20 P/13	43°56′	65°59′
South Devon	UNP/LNO	NB	York	21 G/15	45°58′	66°37′
South Dildo	UNP/LNO	NF		1 N/12	47°31′	53°33′
South Dorchester	MUN2/AZM2	ON	Elgin	40 I/14	42°52′	81°00′
South Dumfries	MUN2/AZM2	ON	Brant	40 P/1	43°14′	80°20′
South Dummer	UNP/LNO	ON	Peterborough	31 D/8	44°23′	78°03′
Southeast Arm	UNP/LNO	NF		2 E/6	49°28′	55°16′
Southeast Arm	BAY/BAIE	NF		11 P/11	47°36′	57°02′
Southeast Arm	BAY/BAIE	NF		13 H/11	53°33′	57°10′
Southeast Arm	BAY/BAIE	SK		63 L/14	54°46′	103°14′
South East Bight	UNP/LNO	NF		1 M/7	47°23′	54°35′
Southeastern Explorer Rift Valley	SEAU/SMER	—		19308A	50°06′	129°45′
Southeast Grand Banks Rise	SEAU/SMER	—		1399A	44°30′	47°00′
Southeast Grand Banks Slope	SEAU/SMER	—		1399A	44°30′	48°30′
South Easthope	MUN2/AZM2	ON	Perth	40 P/7	43°20′	80°50′
South East Passage	UNP/LNO	NS	Halifax	11 D/11	44°36′	63°28′
Southeast Placentia	UNP/LNO	NF		1 N/4	47°13′	53°56′
Southeast River	RIV/CDE	NF		1 N/4	47°13′	53°55′
Southeast Shoal - also-aussi - Platier, Le	SEAU/SMER	—		8010	44°08′	49°45′
Southeast Upsalquitch River	RIV/CDE	NB	Restigouche	21 O/10	47°40′	66°42′
South Elmsley	MUN2/AZM2	ON	Grenville	31 C/16	44°50′	76°05′
Southend - see-voir - Southend Reindeer	HAM/HAM	SK		64 D/6	56°19′	103°14′
South End	CAPE/CAP	NF		2 E/9	49°34′	54°24′
Southend 200	IR/RI	SK		64 D/6	56°20′	103°12′
Southend Reindeer	HAM/HAM	SK		64 D/6	56°19′	103°14′
Southern Arm	UNP/LNO	NF		2 E/12	49°39′	55°55′
Southern Arm	BAY/BAIE	NF		2 E/12	49°40′	55°55′
Southern Arm	BAY/BAIE	NF		12 H/16	49°55′	56°24′
Southern Bay	UNP/LNO	NF		2 C/5	48°24′	53°38′
Southern Bay	BAY/BAIE	NF		2 C/5	48°26′	53°36′
Southern Harbour	TOWN/VIL2	NF		1 N/12	47°43′	53°58′
Southern Harbour Station	UNP/LNO	NF		1 N/12	47°45′	53°55′
Southern Head	CAPE/CAP	NF		2 C/11	48°37′	53°22′
Southern Head	CAPE/CAP	NF		2 E/6	49°22′	55°05′
Southern Head	CAPE/CAP	NF		2 E/12	49°36′	55°35′
Southern Indian Lake	LAKE/LAC	MB		64 G/1	57°10′	98°30′
Southern Lake	LAKE/LAC	NT	Keewatin	55 L	62°13′	94°20′
Southern Pond	LAKE/LAC	NF		2 E/1	49°02′	54°10′
Southern Pond	LAKE/LAC	NF		12 H/16	49°52′	56°20′

NAME NOM	ENTITY ENTITÉ	LOC 1 LIEU 1	LOC 2 LIEU 2	MAP CARTE	POSITION LAT	LONG
Southern Wolf Island	ISL/ÎLE	NB	Charlotte	21 B/15	44°56′	66°44′
South Esk	UNP/LNO	NB	Northumberland	21 I/13	46°57′	65°41′
Southesk	UNP/LNO	AB	33-19-16-W4	82 I/9	50°39′	112°10′
Southesk	GEOG/GÉOG	NB	Northumberland	21 O/2	47°00′	66°30′
Southey	TOWN/VIL2	SK	7-23-18-W2	72 I/15	50°56′	104°30′
South Farmington	UNP/LNO	NS	Annapolis	21 A/15	44°58′	65°00′
Southfield	UNP/LNO	NB	Kings	21 H/12	45°36′	65°37′
Southfield Road	UNP/LNO	NB	Kings	21 H/12	45°37′	65°40′
South Fiord	BAY/BAIE	NT	Franklin	59 G	79°20′	94°25′
South Fork	UNP/LNO	SK	25-7-21-W3	72 F/10	49°36′	108°43′
South Fork Range	MTN/MNT	YT		105 K/15	62°48′	132°48′
South Fort George	UNP/LNO	BC	Cariboo	93 G/15	53°54′	122°45′
South Fosthall Creek	RIV/CDE	BC	Kootenay	82 L/8	50°22′	118°02′
*South Fraser	UNP/LNO	BC	New Westminster	92 G/3	49°12′	123°06′
South Fredericksburgh	MUN2/AZM2	ON	Lennox and Addington	31 C/2	44°08′	76°57′
South Freetown	UNP/LNO	PE	Prince	11 L/5	46°21′	63°37′
South French Bar Creek	RIV/CDE	BC	Lillooet	92 O/1	51°13′	122°13′
Southgate	UNP/LNO	ON	Middlesex	40 P/3	43°07′	81°22′
Southgate River	RIV/CDE	BC	Range 1 Coast	92 K/15	50°53′	124°47′
South Gillies	UNP/LNO	ON	Thunder Bay	52 A/4	48°14′	89°42′
Southglen	UNP/LNO	MB		62 H/14	49°49′	97°05′
South Gloucester	UNP/LNO	ON	Carleton	31 G/5	45°17′	75°34′
South Gnadenthal	UNP/LNO	SK	12-13-12-W3	72 J/4	50°04′	107°31′
South Gordonsville	UNP/LNO	NB	Carleton	21 J/6	46°26′	67°29′
South Gower	MUN2/AZM2	ON	Leeds	31 G/4	45°00′	75°35′
South Gower	UNP/LNO	ON	Grenville	31 G/4	45°00′	75°33′
South Granville	UNP/LNO	PE	Queens	11 L/6	46°24′	63°28′
South Great Rattling Brook	RIV/CDE	NF		2 D/12	48°37′	55°46′
South Greenfield	UNP/LNO	NB	Carleton	21 J/4	46°12′	67°34′
South Green Island	ISL/ÎLE	NF		13 I/3	54°14′	57°29′
South Greenwood	UNP/LNO	NS	Kings	21 A/15	44°58′	64°54′
South Harbour	UNP/LNO	NS	Victoria	11 K/16	46°52′	60°28′
South Harbour	BAY/BAIE	NS	Victoria	11 K/16	46°52′	60°27′
South Haven	UNP/LNO	NS	Victoria	11 K/2	46°12′	60°35′
South Hazelton	UNP/LNO	BC	Cassiar	93 M/4	55°14′	127°40′
South Head	CAPE/CAP	NF		1 N/7	47°17′	52°46′
South Head	CAPE/CAP	NF		1 N/2	47°00′	52°54′
South Head	CAPE/CAP	NF		2 C/6	48°28′	53°03′
South Head	CAPE/CAP	NF		12 G/1	49°09′	58°22′
South Head	CAPE/CAP	NS	Cape Breton	11 J/4	46°06′	59°51′
South Headingley	UNP/LNO	MB		62 H/14	49°52′	97°25′
South Heart River	RIV/CDE	AB	12-76-15-W5	83 N/9	55°34′	116°11′
South Henik Lake	LAKE/LAC	NT	Keewatin	65 H	61°30′	97°20′
South Himsworth	MUN2/AZM2	ON	Parry Sound	31 L/3	46°00′	79°20′
South Indian Lake	UNP/LNO	MB		64 B/15	56°47′	98°56′
South Ingonish Harbour	UNP/LNO	NS	Victoria	11 K/9	46°38′	60°26′
South Johnville	UNP/LNO	NB	Carleton	21 J/12	46°33′	67°31′
South Junction	UNP/LNO	MB	15-1-13-E	52 E/4	49°02′	95°46′
South Knife Lake	UNP/LNO	MB		64 I/1	58°13′	96°21′
South Knife Lake	LAKE/LAC	MB		64 I/1	58°10′	96°28′
South Knife River	RIV/CDE	MB		54 L/15	58°54′	94°36′
South Knowlesville	UNP/LNO	NB	Carleton	21 J/6	46°26′	67°21′
South Kouchibouguac	UNP/LNO	NB	Kent	21 I/15	46°50′	64°56′
South La Cloche Range	MTN/MNT	ON	Manitoulin	41 I/3	46°03′	81°30′
South Lake	VILG/VILG	SK	8,9-20-26-W2	72 I/12	50°41′	105°34′
South Lake	UNP/LNO	PE	Kings	11 L/8	46°25′	62°03′
South Lake	LAKE/LAC	ON	Leeds	31 C/8	44°26′	76°13′
South Lake Ainslie	UNP/LNO	NS	Inverness	11 K/3	46°03′	61°07′
South Lakeside	UNP/LNO	BC	Cariboo	93 B/1	52°07′	122°06′
South Lakeview	UNP/LNO	SK		72 I/7	50°25′	104°37′
South Lancaster	UNP/LNO	ON	Glengarry	31 G/1	45°08′	74°29′
South Limestone Islands	ISL/ÎLE	ON	Parry Sound	41 H/7	45°23′	80°32′
South Little River Lake	LAKE/LAC	NB	Northumberland	21 O/8	47°15′	66°09′
South Lochaber	UNP/LNO	NS	Guysborough	11 E/8	45°23′	62°03′
South Lowell Glacier - see-voir - Lowell Glacier	GLAC/GLAC	YT		115 B/8	60°18′	138°15′
South Macmillan River	RIV/CDE	YT		105 N/3	63°03′	133°18′
South Magnetawan	UNP/LNO	ON	Parry Sound	41 H/9	45°43′	80°15′
South Maitland	UNP/LNO	NS	Hants	11 E/6	45°15′	63°28′
South Maitland River	RIV/CDE	ON	Huron	40 P/12	43°43′	81°34′
South Manchester	UNP/LNO	NS	Guysborough	11 F/6	45°24′	61°27′
South March	UNP/LNO	ON	Carleton	31 G/5	45°21′	75°56′
South March Station	UNP/LNO	ON	Carleton	31 G/5	45°20′	75°55′
South Marysburgh	MUN2/AZM2	ON	Prince Edward	30 N/14	43°55′	77°02′
South McQuesten River	RIV/CDE	YT		115 P/16	63°50′	136°19′
South Melville	UNP/LNO	PE	Queens	11 L/3	46°14′	63°26′

NAME NOM	ENTITY ENTITÉ	LOC 1 LIEU 1	LOC 2 LIEU 2	MAP CARTE	POSITION LAT	LONG
South Merland	UNP/LNO	NS	Guysborough	11 F/12	45°32′	61°38′
South Middleboro	UNP/LNO	NS	Cumberland	11 E/13	45°45′	63°35′
South Middleton	UNP/LNO	ON	Norfolk	40 I/15	42°47′	80°36′
South Milford	UNP/LNO	NS	Annapolis	21 A/11	44°34′	65°24′
South Mindoka	UNP/LNO	ON	Timiskaming	31 M/13	47°58′	79°55′
Southminster	UNP/LNO	SK	12-49-28-W3	73 F/4	53°13′	109°58′
South Minto	UNP/LNO	NB	Queens	21 J/1	46°04′	66°04′
South Monaghan	MUN2/AZM2	ON	Peterborough	31 D/1	44°10′	78°17′
South Monaghan	UNP/LNO	ON	Northumberland	31 D/1	44°09′	78°22′
South Moose Lake	LAKE/LAC	MB	2-56-18W	63 F/16	53°49′	100°01′
South Mountain	UNP/LNO	ON	Dundas	31 B/14	44°59′	75°27′
South Mountain	MTN/MNT	NS	Annapolis	21 A/15	45°00′	64°45′
South Musquash	UNP/LNO	NB	Saint John	21 G/1	45°11′	66°17′
South Nahanni River	RIV/CDE	NT	Mackenzie	95 G/3	61°03′	123°21′
South Nanaimo River	RIV/CDE	BC	Douglas	92 F/1	49°05′	124°05′
South Napanee	UNP/LNO	ON	Lennox and Addington	31 C/2	44°14′	76°57′
South Nation River	RIV/CDE	ON	Prescott	31 G/11	45°34′	75°06′
South Nelson Road	UNP/LNO	NB	Northumberland	21 I/13	46°58′	65°34′
South Nepa 7	IR/RI	BC	Kamloops Division Yale	92 I/11	50°38′	121°16′
South Norfolk	MUN2/AZM2	MB		62 G/10	49°40′	98°36′
South Ohio	UNP/LNO	NS	Yarmouth	20 O/16	43°55′	66°04′
South Ooglit Island	ISL/ÎLE	NT	Franklin	47 A	68°25′	81°41′
South Oromocto Lake	LAKE/LAC	NB	Charlotte	21 G/7	45°24′	66°38′
South Parcel of Beaton River 204	IR/RI	BC	Peace River	94 A/10	56°43′	120°49′
South Parry	UNP/LNO	ON	Parry Sound	31 E/5	45°20′	80°00′
South Pender Island	ISL/ÎLE	BC	Cowichan	92 B/11	48°45′	123°13′
South Peninsula	CAPE/CAP	ON	Thunder Bay	52 I/1	50°05′	88°12′
South Plantagenet	MUN2/AZM2	ON	Prescott	31 G/7	45°23′	75°00′
South Point	CAPE/CAP	NF		1 K/13	46°57′	53°43′
South Point	CAPE/CAP	NF		1 M/16	47°49′	54°05′
South Point	CAPE/CAP	NF		2 M/14	51°53′	55°23′
South Point Douglas	UNP/LNO	MB		62 H/14	49°54′	97°07′
South Pond	LAKE/LAC	NF		2 E/2	49°07′	54°45′
South Pond	LAKE/LAC	NF		12 H/8	49°23′	56°06′
South Poplar	UNP/LNO	BC	New Westminster	92 G/1	49°01′	122°19′
South Porcupine	UNP/LNO	ON	Cochrane	42 A/6	48°28′	81°13′
Southport - see-voir - Stratford	VILG/VILG	PE		11 L/3	46°13′	63°05′
Southport	UNP/LNO	NF		2 C/4	48°03′	53°38′
Southport	UNP/LNO	PE	Queens	11 L/3	46°14′	63°06′
Southport	UNP/LNO	MB	18-11-6-W	62 G/16	49°55′	98°16′
South Portage	UNP/LNO	NB	York	21 J/7	46°17′	66°36′
South Portage	UNP/LNO	ON	Muskoka	31 E/6	45°19′	79°04′
South Port Morien	UNP/LNO	NS	Cape Breton	11 J/4	46°07′	59°51′
South Pugwash	UNP/LNO	NS	Cumberland	11 E/13	45°50′	63°38′
South Qu'Appelle No. 157	MUN2/AZM2	SK		72 I/8	50°30′	104°00′
South Quinan	UNP/LNO	NS	Yarmouth	20 P/13	43°55′	65°48′
South Range	UNP/LNO	NS	Digby	21 A/5	44°29′	65°48′
South Range Corner	UNP/LNO	NS	Digby	21 A/5	44°28′	65°49′
South Rawdon	UNP/LNO	NS	Hants	11 D/13	45°00′	63°52′
South Ridge	UNP/LNO	NB	Carleton	21 J/11	46°30′	67°18′
South River	TOWN/VIL2	NF		1 N/11	47°33′	53°16′
South River	VILG/VILG	ON	Parry Sound	31 E/14	45°50′	79°23′
South River	UNP/LNO	NB	Gloucester	21 P/10	47°39′	64°52′
South River	RIV/CDE	NS	Antigonish	11 F/12	45°36′	61°55′
South River	RIV/CDE	ON	Parry Sound	31 L/4	46°08′	79°34′
South River Heights	UNP/LNO	MB		62 H/14	49°51′	97°11′
South River Lake	UNP/LNO	NS	Antigonish	11 F/5	45°24′	61°57′
South River Station	UNP/LNO	NS	Antigonish	11 F/12	45°36′	61°54′
South Road Settlement	UNP/LNO	NB	Northumberland	21 J/9	46°34′	66°05′
South Rustico	UNP/LNO	PE	Queens	11 L/6	46°25′	63°18′
South Saanich 1	IR/RI	BC	South Saanich	92 B/11	48°35′	123°27′
South Saanich Land District	GEOG/GÉOG	BC		92 B	48°35′	123°25′
South Saint-Norbert	UNP/LNO	NB	Kent	21 I/7	46°27′	64°57′
South St. Vital	UNP/LNO	MB		62 H/14	49°49′	97°06′
South Salt Springs	UNP/LNO	NS	Antigonish	11 E/9	45°34′	62°00′
South Samson Island	ISL/ÎLE	NF		2 E/7	49°29′	54°56′
South Saskatchewan River - also-aussi - **Saskatchewan Sud, Rivière**	RIV/CDE	SK/AB		73 H/3	53°15′	105°05′
South Saskatoon	UNP/LNO	SK	36-5-W3	73 B/2	52°05′	106°39′
South Saugeen River	RIV/CDE	ON	Bruce	41 A/3	44°09′	81°02′
Souths Bay	BAY/BAIE	NT	Franklin	87 A	68°58′	115°54′
South Scot Lake	LAKE/LAC	ON	Kenora	52 E/14	49°56′	95°03′
South Scots Bay	UNP/LNO	NS	Kings	21 H/8	45°16′	64°24′
South Seal River	RIV/CDE	MB		64 J/16	58°47′	98°08′
South Section	UNP/LNO	NS	Halifax	11 E/3	45°01′	63°10′
South Shalalth	UNP/LNO	BC	Lillooet	92 J/9	50°43′	122°15′

NAME NOM	ENTITY ENTITÉ	LOC 1 LIEU 1	LOC 2 LIEU 2	MAP CARTE	POSITION	
					LAT	LONG
South Sherbrooke	MUN2/AZM2	ON	Lanark	31 C/15	44°49'	76°30'
South Shore	UNP/LNO	NS	Cumberland	11 E/14	45°46'	63°19'
Southside	UNP/LNO	NF		1 N/11	47°34'	53°13'
South Side	UNP/LNO	NF		2 E/3	49°13'	55°02'
South Side	UNP/LNO	NS	Shelburne	20 P/5	43°27'	65°36'
Southside Antigonish Harbour	UNP/LNO	NS	Antigonish	11 F/12	45°40'	61°53'
South Side Basin of River Denys	UNP/LNO	NS	Inverness	11 F/14	45°52'	61°02'
South Side of Baddeck River	UNP/LNO	NS	Victoria	11 K/2	46°09'	60°46'
South Side of Boularderie	UNP/LNO	NS	Victoria	11 K/2	46°10'	60°31'
South Side River Bourgeois	UNP/LNO	NS	Richmond	11 F/10	45°38'	60°58'
South Side River Denys	UNP/LNO	NS	Inverness	11 F/14	45°50'	61°13'
South Side Whycocomagh Bay	UNP/LNO	NS	Inverness	11 F/14	45°56'	61°03'
South Slocan	UNP/LNO	BC	Kootenay	82 F/5	49°28'	117°31'
South Slope	UNP/LNO	BC	New Westminster	92 G/3	49°13'	123°00'
South Spicer Island	ISL/ÎLE	NT	Franklin	37 B	68°16'	79°00'
South Stag Island	ISL/ÎLE	NF		13 I/3	54°01'	57°08'
South Star	UNP/LNO	SK	16-43-16-W2	73 A/9	52°43'	104°15'
South Sumas	UNP/LNO	BC	New Westminster	92 H/4	49°07'	122°00'
South Taylor	UNP/LNO	BC	Peace River	94 A/2	56°06'	120°38'
South Tetagouche	UNP/LNO	NB	Gloucester	21 P/12	47°36'	65°49'
South Thompson River	RIV/CDE	BC	Kamloops Division Yale	92 I/9	50°41'	120°20'
South Tilley	UNP/LNO	NB	Victoria	21 J/13	46°49'	67°37'
South Touchwood	UNP/LNO	SK	13-25-16-W2	72 P/1	51°08'	104°07'
South Transcona	UNP/LNO	MB		62 H/14	49°53'	97°00'
South Tremont	UNP/LNO	NS	Kings	21 A/15	44°56'	64°55'
South Tuxedo	UNP/LNO	MB		62 H/14	49°51'	97°13'
South Tweedside	UNP/LNO	NB	York	21 G/11	45°36'	67°02'
South Tweedsmuir Island	ISL/ÎLE	NT	Franklin	37 A	68°23'	74°15'
South Twillingate Island	ISL/ÎLE	NF		2 E/10	49°38'	54°44'
South Twin	MTN/MNT	AB	37-25-W5	83 C/3	52°12'	117°26'
South Twin Island	ISL/ÎLE	NT	Franklin	33 E	53°07'	79°52'
South Twin Lake	LAKE/LAC	NF		2 E/5	49°16'	55°47'
South Uniacke	UNP/LNO	NS	Hants	11 D/13	44°52'	63°47'
South Valley	UNP/LNO	SK	10-48-22-W2	73 H/3	53°08'	105°08'
South Victoria	UNP/LNO	NS	Cumberland	11 E/12	45°43'	63°41'
South View	VILG/VILG	AB	9-54-5-W5	83 G/10	53°39'	114°40'
Southview Beach	UNP/LNO	ON	Simcoe	31 D/11	44°34'	79°15'
Southview Cove	UNP/LNO	ON	Simcoe	31 D/11	44°33'	79°16'
Southview Estates	UNP/LNO	ON	Victoria	31 D/7	44°27'	78°45'
Southville	UNP/LNO	NS	Digby	21 A/5	44°21'	65°54'
South Wabasca Lake	LAKE/LAC	AB	79,80-24,25-W4	83 P/13	55°55'	113°45'
South Walkerville	UNP/LNO	ON	Essex	40 J/6	42°17'	82°59'
South Wallace Bay	UNP/LNO	NS	Cumberland	11 E/13	45°49'	63°33'
South Waterville	UNP/LNO	NS	Kings	21 H/2	45°01'	64°40'
South Waterville	UNP/LNO	NB	York	21 J/3	46°03'	67°20'
South Wellington	UNP/LNO	BC	Cranberry	92 G/4	49°06'	123°53'
South West Arm	UNP/LNO	NF		2 F/4	49°07'	53°38'
Southwest Arm	BAY/BAIE	NF		2 C/5	48°27'	53°39'
Southwest Arm	BAY/BAIE	NF		2 C/4	48°00'	53°45'
Southwest Arm	BAY/BAIE	NF		1 M/3	47°08'	55°14'
Southwest Arm	BAY/BAIE	NF		2 E/6	49°25'	55°22'
Southwest Arm	BAY/BAIE	NF		12 H/9	49°38'	56°07'
Southwest Brook	RIV/CDE	NF		2 E/3	49°13'	55°03'
Southwest Brook	RIV/CDE	NF		12 B/9	48°31'	58°17'
Southwest, Cape	CAPE/CAP	NT	Franklin	59 F	78°12'	92°02'
Southwest Cove	UNP/LNO	NS	Halifax	11 D/10	44°44'	62°49'
Southwest Cove	UNP/LNO	NS	Lunenburg	21 A/9	44°31'	64°01'
Southwest Croque	UNP/LNO	NF		2 M/4	51°02'	55°48'
Southwest Crouse	UNP/LNO	NF		2 L/13	50°54'	55°54'
Southwest Gander River	RIV/CDE	NF		2 D/15	48°52'	54°55'
Southwest Head	CAPE/CAP	NB	Charlotte	21 B/10	44°36'	66°54'
Southwest Lot 16	UNP/LNO	PE	Prince	11 L/5	46°29'	63°54'
Southwest Mabou	UNP/LNO	NS	Inverness	11 K/3	46°01'	61°27'
Southwest Mabou River	RIV/CDE	NS	Inverness	11 K/3	46°04'	61°26'
South West Margaree	UNP/LNO	NS	Inverness	11 K/6	46°17'	61°09'
Southwest Margaree River	RIV/CDE	NS	Inverness	11 K/6	46°20'	61°05'
*South Westminster	UNP/LNO	BC	New Westminster	92 G/2	49°12'	122°52'
Southwest Miramichi River	RIV/CDE	NB	Northumberland	21 I/13	46°58'	65°35'
South-West Oxford	MUN2/AZM2	ON	Oxford	40 I/15	43°00'	80°48'
Southwest Point	CAPE/CAP	NS	Victoria	11 N/1	47°11'	60°10'
Southwest Pond	LAKE/LAC	NF		2 D/10	48°33'	54°59'
South West Port Mouton	UNP/LNO	NS	Queens	20 P/15	43°54'	64°49'
Southwest Ridge	UNP/LNO	NS	Inverness	11 K/3	46°02'	61°24'
Southwest River	RIV/CDE	NF		2 D/8	48°20'	54°10'
South Wilberforce	UNP/LNO	ON	Haliburton	31 E/1	45°01'	78°13'

NAME NOM	ENTITY ENTITÉ	LOC 1 LIEU 1	LOC 2 LIEU 2	MAP CARTE	POSITION LAT	POSITION LONG
*South Williams Lake	UNP/LNO	BC	Cariboo	93 B/1	52°07′	122°08′
South Williamston	UNP/LNO	NS	Annapolis	21 A/14	44°53′	65°08′
South Windsor	UNP/LNO	ON	Essex	40 J/6	42°16′	83°02′
Southwold	MUN2/AZM2	ON	Elgin	40 I/11	42°43′	81°17′
Southwold	UNP/LNO	ON	Elgin	40 I/14	42°48′	81°23′
Southwold Earthworks National Historic Site - also-aussi - Remblais-de-Southwold, Lieu historique national des	PARK/PARC	ON	Elgin	40 I/11	42°41′	81°21′
South Wolf Island	ISL/ÎLE	NF		3 E/12	53°40′	55°55′
Southwood	UNP/LNO	ON	Muskoka	31 D/13	44°54′	79°30′
Southwood	UNP/LNO	MB		62 H/14	49°49′	97°09′
South Woodslee	UNP/LNO	ON	Essex	40 J/2	42°12′	82°43′
South Wynhurst	UNP/LNO	ON	York	31 D/3	44°13′	79°28′
Sovanco Fracture Zone	SEAU/SMER	—		15789A	48°55′	129°15′
Sovereign	VILG/VILG	SK	26-29-13-W3	72 O/12	51°31′	107°43′
Sovereign Lake	LAKE/LAC	SK/NT		74 P/13	59°57′	105°37′
Sowaqua Creek	RIV/CDE	BC	Yale Division Yale	92 H/6	49°27′	121°16′
Sowchea 3	IR/RI	BC	Range 5 Coast	93 K/8	54°25′	124°24′
Sowchea 3A	IR/RI	BC	Range 5 Coast	93 K/8	54°25′	124°25′
Sowden	UNP/LNO	ON	Kenora	52 G/10	49°35′	90°58′
Sowden Lake	LAKE/LAC	ON	Kenora	52 G/11	49°32′	91°12′
Sowerby	UNP/LNO	ON	Algoma	41 J/6	46°18′	83°24′
*Soyandostar 2	IR/RI	BC	Range 5 Coast	93 K/15	54°52′	125°00′
Soyers Lake	LAKE/LAC	ON	Haliburton	31 E/2	45°01′	78°37′
Spaffordton	UNP/LNO	ON	Frontenac	31 C/7	44°24′	76°31′
Spahats Creek	RIV/CDE	BC	Kamloops Division Yale	92 P/9	51°44′	120°01′
Spahomin Creek	RIV/CDE	BC	Kamloops Division Yale	92 I/1	50°08′	120°16′
Spahomin Creek 4	IR/RI	BC	Kamloops Division Yale	92 I/1	50°04′	120°11′
Spahomin Creek 8	IR/RI	BC	Kamloops Division Yale	92 I/1	50°05′	120°13′
Spaidal	UNP/LNO	ON	Sudbury	41 I/10	46°38′	80°41′
Spakels 17	IR/RI	BC	Range 5 Coast	103 J/9	54°43′	130°13′
Spa Lake	LAKE/LAC	BC	Kamloops Division Yale	82 L/11	50°33′	119°27′
Spalding	VILG/VILG	SK	2-39-18-W2	73 A/8	52°20′	104°30′
Spalding Hill	UNP/LNO	QC	Le Haut-Saint-François	21 E/5	45°26′	71°41′
Spalding No. 368	MUN2/AZM2	SK		73 A/1	52°15′	104°25′
Spallumcheen	MUN1/AZM1	BC	Kamloops Division Yale	82 L/6	50°26′	119°13′
Spanaknok 57	IR/RI	BC	Range 5 Coast	103 J/8	54°28′	130°04′
Spaniard's Bay	TOWN/VIL2	NF		1 N/11	47°37′	53°17′
Spaniard's Bay	UNP/LNO	NF		1 N/11	47°37′	53°17′
Spaniard's Bay	BAY/BAIE	NF		1 N/11	47°38′	53°13′
Spaniard's Bay-Tilton - see-voir - Spaniard's Bay	TOWN/VIL2	NF		1 N/11	47°37′	53°17′
Spaniards Cove	BAY/BAIE	NF		2 C/6	48°18′	53°24′
Spanish	UNP/LNO	ON	Algoma	41 J/1	46°12′	82°21′
Spanish Creek	RIV/CDE	BC	Lillooet	92 P/15	51°58′	120°34′
Spanish River	RIV/CDE	ON	Algoma	41 J/1	46°11′	82°19′
Spanish River 5 - see-voir - Sagamok 5	IR/RI	ON		41 J/1	46°10′	82°15′
Spanish Room	UNP/LNO	NF		1 M/3	47°12′	55°05′
Spanish Ship Bay	UNP/LNO	NS	Guysborough	11 E/1	45°01′	62°01′
Sparbo, Cape	CAPE/CAP	NT	Franklin	48 G	75°49′	84°00′
Spare Point	CAPE/CAP	NF		1 N/11	47°41′	53°11′
Sparkle City	UNP/LNO	ON	Grenville	31 B/12	44°44′	75°32′
Sparkling Lake	LAKE/LAC	ON	Thunder Bay	52 G/16	49°49′	90°10′
Sparks Lake	LAKE/LAC	NT	Mackenzie	75 F	61°12′	109°40′
Spar Lake	LAKE/LAC	NS	Halifax	11 E/1	45°00′	62°22′
Spar Mica	UNP/LNO	QC	Minganie	12 L/7	50°17′	62°46′
Sparrow Lake	UNP/LNO	ON	Muskoka	31 D/14	44°49′	79°22′
Sparrow Lake	LAKE/LAC	ON	Muskoka	31 D/14	44°47′	79°24′
Sparrow Lake	LAKE/LAC	NT	Mackenzie	85 I	62°37′	113°38′
Sparta	UNP/LNO	ON	Elgin	40 I/11	42°42′	81°05′
Sparwood	MUN1/AZM1	BC	Kootenay	82 G/10	49°43′	114°54′
Sparwood	UNP/LNO	BC	Kootenay	82 G/10	49°44′	114°53′
Spa Springs	UNP/LNO	NS	Annapolis	21 A/14	44°58′	65°04′
Spatsizi River	RIV/CDE	BC	Cassiar	104 H/9	57°43′	128°06′
Spatsum	UNP/LNO	BC	Kamloops Division Yale	92 I/11	50°33′	121°18′
Spatsum 11	IR/RI	BC	Kamloops Division Yale	92 I/11	50°34′	121°17′
Spatsum 11A	IR/RI	BC	Kamloops Division Yale	92 I/11	50°35′	121°18′
Spayaks 60	IR/RI	BC	Range 5 Coast	103 J/8	54°22′	130°03′
Spear, Cape	CAPE/CAP	NF		1 N/10	47°31′	52°37′
Spear, Cape	CAPE/CAP	NB	Westmorland	11 L/4	46°05′	63°48′
Spearfish Lake	LAKE/LAC	NT	Mackenzie	75 B	60°46′	107°37′
Spear Harbour	UNP/LNO	NF		3 D/5	52°25′	55°42′
Spearhill	UNP/LNO	MB	23-27-7-W	62 O/8	51°19′	98°21′
Spear Lake	LAKE/LAC	SK		74 B/12	56°37′	107°58′
Spear Point	CAPE/CAP	NF		3 D/5	52°27′	55°38′
Spear Point	CAPE/CAP	NF		12 H/10	49°44′	56°48′
Spectacle Lakes	UNP/LNO	NS	Lunenburg	21 A/8	44°23′	64°23′
Spector Lake	LAKE/LAC	MB		54 B/1	56°02′	90°28′

NAME NOM	ENTITY ENTITÉ	LOC 1 LIEU 1	LOC 2 LIEU 2	MAP CARTE	POSITION LAT	LONG
Spectrum Creek	RIV/CDE	BC	Osoyoos Division Yale	82 L/8	50°29′	118°27′
Spedden	UNP/LNO	AB	34-59-12-W4	73 L/4	54°08′	111°43′
Spednic Lake	LAKE/LAC	NB	York	21 G/12	45°38′	67°38′
Speed River	RIV/CDE	ON	Waterloo	40 P/8	43°23′	80°22′
Speedside	UNP/LNO	ON	Wellington	40 P/9	43°40′	80°17′
Speedwell	UNP/LNO	ON	Wellington	40 P/9	43°33′	80°13′
Speedwell	UNP/LNO	SK	21-52-17-W3	73 F/9	53°30′	108°27′
Speers	VILG/VILG	SK	17-43-11-W3	73 B/12	52°43′	107°34′
Speers Lake	LAKE/LAC	NT	Mackenzie	86 J	66°59′	115°14′
Speersville	UNP/LNO	ON	Peel	30 M/13	43°55′	79°59′
Speerville	UNP/LNO	NB	Carleton	21 J/4	46°03′	67°38′
Spence	UNP/LNO	ON	Parry Sound	31 E/12	45°35′	79°38′
Spence Bay - see-voir - Taloyoak	UNP/LNO	NT		57 C/10	69°32′	93°31′
Spence Bay	BAY/BAIE	NT	Franklin	57 C/7	69°24′	93°50′
Spence Lake	UNP/LNO	MB	30-15,16-W1	62 O/12	51°35′	99°35′
Spence Lake	LAKE/LAC	MB	36,37-14-W	63 B/3	52°09′	99°23′
Spence Lake	LAKE/LAC	MB	29,30-16-W	62 O/12	51°33′	99°36′
Spencer, Cape	CAPE/CAP	NS	Cumberland	21 H/7	45°19′	64°42′
Spencer, Cape	CAPE/CAP	NB	Saint John	21 H/4	45°12′	65°55′
Spencer Island	ISL/ÎLE	NT	Keewatin	33 E	53°30′	79°42′
Spencer Lake	LAKE/LAC	AB	67-9-W4	73 L/14	54°48′	111°15′
Spencer Range	MTN/MNT	NT	Franklin	78 H/13	75°52′	107°25′
Spencers Cove	UNP/LNO	NF		1 M/9	47°40′	54°05′
Spencers Island	UNP/LNO	NS	Cumberland	21 H/7	45°21′	64°43′
Spencerville	UNP/LNO	ON	Grenville	31 B/13	44°51′	75°33′
Spences Bridge	UNP/LNO	BC	Kamloops Division Yale	92 I/6	50°25′	121°21′
Spences Bridge 4	IR/RI	BC	Kamloops Division Yale	92 I/6	50°25′	121°22′
Spences Bridge 4C	IR/RI	BC	Kamloops Division Yale	92 I/6	50°25′	121°20′
Spence Settlement	UNP/LNO	NB	Westmorland	11 L/4	46°09′	63°53′
Speous 8	IR/RI	BC	Kamloops Division Yale	92 I/2	50°08′	121°00′
Sperling	UNP/LNO	MB	29-6-2-W	62 H/12	49°30′	97°42′
Sperling	UNP/LNO	BC	New Westminster	92 G/2	49°08′	122°33′
*Spetch	UNP/LNO	BC	Lillooet	92 J/7	50°22′	122°43′
Speyside	UNP/LNO	ON	Halton	30 M/12	43°35′	79°58′
Speyum 3	IR/RI	BC	Yale Division Yale	92 H/14	49°56′	121°28′
Sphene Lake	LAKE/LAC	ON	Rainy River	52 C/14	48°59′	93°20′
Spicer	UNP/LNO	ON	Northumberland	30 M/16	43°58′	78°05′
Spicer	UNP/LNO	BC	Cariboo	83 D/14	52°53′	119°18′
Spider Bay	BAY/BAIE	ON	Parry Sound	41 H/1	45°13′	80°07′
Spider Island	ISL/ÎLE	BC	Range 2 Coast	102 P/16	51°51′	128°15′
Spier	UNP/LNO	ON	Wellington	40 P/9	43°44′	80°21′
Spillars Cove	UNP/LNO	NF		2 C/11	48°40′	53°04′
Spillars Cove	UNP/LNO	NF		2 M/11	51°36′	55°30′
Spiller Channel	CHAN/CHEN	BC	Range 3 Coast	103 A/8	52°21′	128°11′
Spiller Inlet	BAY/BAIE	BC	Range 3 Coast	103 A/8	52°33′	128°06′
Spillimacheen	UNP/LNO	BC	Kootenay	82 K/16	50°54′	116°22′
Spillimacheen River	RIV/CDE	BC	Kootenay	82 K/16	50°55′	116°24′
Spillway	UNP/LNO	NF		12 H/3	49°10′	57°26′
Spilmouse 4	IR/RI	BC	Lillooet	92 O/8	51°27′	122°00′
Spinel Lake	LAKE/LAC	BC	Cassiar	94 E/16	57°53′	126°18′
Spinney Hill	UNP/LNO	SK	28-40-13-W3	73 B/5	52°28′	107°48′
Spintlum Flat 3	IR/RI	BC	Kamloops Division Yale	92 I/5	50°20′	121°39′
Spirit River	TOWN/VIL2	AB	22-78-6-W6	83 M/15	55°47′	118°50′
Spirit River No. 133, Municipal District of	MUN1/AZM1	AB	78-5-W6	83 M/15	55°46′	118°31′
Spirit River Settlement	UNP/LNO	AB	78-5,6-W6	83 M/10	55°45′	118°47′
Spiritwood	TOWN/VIL2	SK		73 G/5	53°22′	107°31′
Spiritwood Acres	HAM/HAM	SK		62 M/7	51°29′	102°41′
Spiritwood No. 496	MUN2/AZM2	SK		73 G/6	53°25′	107°20′
Spirity Cove	UNP/LNO	NF		12 I/11	50°36′	57°22′
Spitfire Lake	LAKE/LAC	NT	Mackenzie	75 B	60°53′	107°41′
Spit (Kate) Island	ISL/ÎLE	NT	Franklin	69 A	76°50′	97°07′
Spittler Creek	RIV/CDE	ON	Oxford	40 I/15	42°55′	80°36′
Spius Creek	RIV/CDE	BC	Kamloops Division Yale	92 I/3	50°09′	121°01′
Splatt Bay	BAY/BAIE	ON	Haldimand	30 L/13	42°51′	79°36′
Split, Cape	CAPE/CAP	NS	Kings	21 H/8	45°20′	64°30′
Split Island	ISL/ÎLE	NT	Keewatin	34 D	56°51′	79°51′
Split Lake	UNP/LNO	MB	81-11-E	54 D/4	56°01′	95°50′
Split Lake	UNP/LNO	MB		64 A/1	56°15′	96°06′
Split Lake	LAKE/LAC	MB		64 A/1	56°08′	96°15′
Split Lake 171	IR/RI	MB		64 A/1	56°14′	96°12′
Split Lake 171A	IR/RI	MB		64 A/1	56°12′	96°05′
Split Lake 171B	IR/RI	MB		64 A/1	56°06′	96°10′
Split Point	CAPE/CAP	NF		2 C/2	48°06′	52°51′
Splitrock Bay	BAY/BAIE	ON	Kenora	52 E/1	49°05′	94°05′
Splitrock Island	ISL/ÎLE	ON	Kenora	52 E/1	49°13′	94°30′

NAME / NOM	ENTITY / ENTITÉ	LOC 1 / LIEU 1	LOC 2 / LIEU 2	MAP / CARTE	POSITION LAT	POSITION LONG
Splitrock River	RIV/CDE	ON	Rainy River	52 E/1	49°04′	94°04′
Split Seamount	SEAU/SMER	—		5.03	47°39′	128°59′
Spokin Lake	LAKE/LAC	BC	Cariboo	93 A/4	52°10′	121°46′
Spokwan 48	IR/RI	BC	Range 5 Coast	103 J/9	54°42′	130°14′
Spondin	UNP/LNO	AB	27-33-12-W4	72 M/13	51°52′	111°36′
Spoon Cove	UNP/LNO	NF		1 N/11	47°39′	53°12′
Sporting Lake	LAKE/LAC	NS	Digby	21 A/5	44°17′	65°36′
Sporting Mountain	UNP/LNO	NS	Richmond	11 F/10	45°40′	60°59′
Spotswood	UNP/LNO	ON	Renfrew	31 F/15	45°54′	76°55′
Spotted Horse Lake	LAKE/LAC	AB	68-26-W4	83 I/13	54°55′	113°52′
Spotted Island	UNP/LNO	NF		3 E/5	53°30′	55°45′
Spotted Island	ISL/ÎLE	NF		3 E/12	53°31′	55°47′
Spot, The	SEAU/SMER	—		4353	44°42′	62°43′
Spout Cove	UNP/LNO	NF		1 N/14	47°49′	53°08′
Spout Lake	LAKE/LAC	BC	Cariboo	92 P/14	51°59′	121°25′
Spragge	UNP/LNO	ON	Algoma	41 J/2	46°12′	82°40′
Sprague	UNP/LNO	MB	15-1-14-E	52 E/4	49°02′	95°38′
Sprague Creek	RIV/CDE	MB	1-14-W	52 E/4	49°00′	95°40′
Spratt Point	CAPE/CAP	ON	Simcoe	41 A/9	44°36′	80°00′
Spray Lakes Reservoir	LAKE/LAC	AB	22,23-10,11-W5	82 J/14	50°54′	115°20′
Spray River	RIV/CDE	AB	25-12-W5	82 O/4	51°09′	115°34′
Spread Eagle	UNP/LNO	NF		1 N/12	47°32′	53°37′
Spread Eagle	UNP/LNO	NF		1 N/5	47°23′	53°38′
Sprecher	UNP/LNO	ON	Sudbury	41 I/11	46°31′	81°02′
Spring Arbour	UNP/LNO	ON	Norfolk	40 I/10	42°40′	80°32′
Springbank	UNP/LNO	ON	Middlesex	40 P/4	43°04′	81°39′
Spring Bay	HAM/HAM	SK	10-23-23-W2	72 I/14	50°56′	105°08′
Spring Bay	UNP/LNO	ON	Manitoulin	41 G/9	45°44′	82°19′
Springbrook	UNP/LNO	PE	Queens	11 L/5	46°30′	63°31′
Spring Brook	UNP/LNO	NB	Kent	21 I/10	46°31′	64°53′
Springbrook	UNP/LNO	QC	La Nouvelle-Beauce	21 L/10	46°30′	70°50′
Spring Brook	UNP/LNO	ON	Hastings	31 C/5	44°24′	77°36′
Springbrook	UNP/LNO	ON	Peel	30 M/12	43°39′	79°47′
Springburn	UNP/LNO	AB	16-80-19-W5	83 N/15	55°56′	116°55′
Spring Coulee	UNP/LNO	AB	28-4-23-W4	82 H/6	49°20′	113°03′
Spring Creek	UNP/LNO	ON	Parry Sound	31 E/13	45°58′	79°56′
Springdale	TOWN/VIL2	NF		12 H/9	49°30′	56°04′
Springdale	UNP/LNO	NS	Digby	21 B/1	44°03′	66°05′
Springdale	UNP/LNO	NB	Kings	21 H/14	45°46′	65°19′
Springdale	UNP/LNO	AB	35-44-2-W5	83 B/16	52°50′	114°12′
Springdale Park	UNP/LNO	ON	Muskoka	31 E/3	45°06′	79°18′
Springer	MUN2/AZM2	ON	Nipissing	31 L/5	46°24′	79°58′
Springer, Mont	MTN/MNT	QC	Jamésie	32 G/15	49°48′	74°49′
Springfeld	UNP/LNO	SK	5-14-13-W3	72 J/4	50°09′	107°44′
Springfield	VILG/VILG	ON	Elgin	40 I/15	42°50′	80°56′
Springfield	MUN2/AZM2	MB		62 H/15	49°55′	96°45′
Springfield	UNP/LNO	NF		1 N/11	47°31′	53°17′
Springfield	UNP/LNO	PE	Queens	11 L/5	46°23′	63°31′
Springfield	UNP/LNO	NS	Annapolis	21 A/10	44°38′	64°52′
Springfield	UNP/LNO	NB	Kings	21 H/12	45°41′	65°49′
Springfield	UNP/LNO	NB	York	21 J/3	46°01′	67°04′
Springfield	UNP/LNO	NB	Carleton	21 G/13	45°59′	67°32′
Springfield	UNP/LNO	ON	Leeds	31 C/8	44°23′	76°14′
Springfield	UNP/LNO	ON	Middlesex	40 I/13	42°52′	81°40′
Springfield	GEOG/GÉOG	NB	Kings	21 H/12	45°42′	65°50′
Springfield Heights	UNP/LNO	MB		62 H/14	49°56′	97°03′
Springfield Lake	UNP/LNO	NS	Halifax	11 D/13	44°49′	63°45′
Springfield Ranch	UNP/LNO	BC	Cariboo	93 B/8	52°16′	122°15′
Springfield Seamount	SEAU/SMER			3000	48°04′	130°12′
Springfield Settlement	UNP/LNO	NB	Gloucester	21 P/11	47°40′	65°23′
Springfield West	UNP/LNO	PE	Prince	21 I/9	46°41′	64°22′
Springford	UNP/LNO	ON	Oxford	40 I/15	42°55′	80°40′
Springhaven	UNP/LNO	NS	Yarmouth	20 P/13	43°54′	65°52′
Springhill	TOWN/VIL2	NS	Cumberland	21 H/9	45°39′	64°03′
Springhill	UNP/LNO	PE	Prince	21 I/9	46°34′	64°00′
Springhill	UNP/LNO	NB	Kings	21 I/3	46°00′	65°23′
Springhill	UNP/LNO	NB	York	21 G/15	45°58′	66°44′
Spring Hill	UNP/LNO	ON	Carleton	31 G/3	45°12′	75°29′
Springhill	UNP/LNO	MB	23-15-16-W	62 J/5	50°17′	99°35′
Springhill Junction	UNP/LNO	NS	Cumberland	21 H/9	45°42′	64°07′
Springhouse	UNP/LNO	BC	Lillooet	92 O/16	51°58′	122°08′
Springhurst Beach	UNP/LNO	ON	Simcoe	41 A/8	44°29′	80°05′
Spring Lake	LAKE/LAC	BC	Lillooet	92 P/14	51°49′	121°13′
Springmount	UNP/LNO	ON	Grey	41 A/10	44°34′	81°00′
Spring Park	UNP/LNO	PE	Queens	11 L/6	46°16′	63°09′

NAME NOM	ENTITY ENTITÉ	LOC 1 LIEU 1	LOC 2 LIEU 2	MAP CARTE	POSITION	
					LAT	LONG
Spring Passage	CHAN/CHEN	BC	Range 1 Coast	92 L/10	50°39′	126°36′
Spring Point	UNP/LNO	AB	10-9-29-W4	82 H/12	49°43′	113°46′
Springridge	UNP/LNO	AB	12-6-28-W4	82 H/5	49°27′	113°39′
Springside	TOWN/VIL2	SK	23-27-6-W2	62 M/7	51°21′	102°44′
Springside	UNP/LNO	NS	Colchester	11 E/7	45°16′	62°54′
Springside	UNP/LNO	SK	3-32-32-W	62 N/12	51°43′	101°55′
Springstein	UNP/LNO	MB	2-10-1-W	62 H/14	49°48′	97°30′
Springton	UNP/LNO	PE	Queens	11 L/6	46°19′	63°25′
Springtown	UNP/LNO	ON	Renfrew	31 F/7	45°21′	76°40′
Springvale	UNP/LNO	PE	Queens	11 L/6	46°19′	63°15′
Springvale	UNP/LNO	ON	Wentworth	30 M/4	43°13′	79°59′
Springvale	UNP/LNO	ON	Haldimand	40 I/16	42°58′	80°07′
Springvale	UNP/LNO	ON	Lambton	40 P/4	43°10′	81°54′
Spring Valley	UNP/LNO	PE	Prince	11 L/12	46°30′	63°38′
Spring Valley	UNP/LNO	QC	Les Pays-d'en-Haut	31 G/16	45°51′	74°11′
Spring Valley	UNP/LNO	ON	Leeds	31 B/12	44°38′	75°47′
Spring Valley	UNP/LNO	ON	Northumberland	31 C/4	44°03′	77°45′
Spring Valley	UNP/LNO	ON	Wentworth	30 M/4	43°13′	80°00′
Spring Valley	UNP/LNO	SK	30-11-25-W2	72 H/14	49°56′	105°24′
Springville	UNP/LNO	NS	Pictou	11 E/7	45°27′	62°38′
Springville	UNP/LNO	ON	Peterborough	31 D/1	44°14′	78°24′
Springwater	VILG/VILG	SK	4-35-17-W3	72 N/16	51°58′	108°23′
Springwater	MUN2/AZM2	ON	Simcoe	31 D/5	44°30′	79°51′
Springwater Lakes	UNP/LNO	ON	Dufferin	41 A/1	44°08′	80°07′
Spring Well	UNP/LNO	MB	34-15-9-E	62 I/8	50°19′	96°16′
Sproat Lake	UNP/LNO	BC	Alberni	92 F/7	49°17′	124°55′
Sproat Lake	LAKE/LAC	BC	Clayoquot	92 F/6	49°16′	125°00′
Sproatt	UNP/LNO	BC	New Westminster	92 J/3	50°05′	123°02′
Sprott Lake	LAKE/LAC	MB		64 J/5	58°23′	99°40′
Sproule Peninsula	CAPE/CAP	NT	Franklin	89 A	76°22′	114°55′
Spruce Bay	HAM/HAM	SK	9-49-12-W3	73 G/4	53°12′	107°42′
Spruce Bay Heights	UNP/LNO	MB	9-21-4-E	62 I/15	50°47′	96°59′
Spruce Bluff	UNP/LNO	MB	11,12,13,14-25-20-W1	62 N/1	51°09′	100°09′
Spruce Bluff	CLF/ESC	MB	43-18-W	63 C/16	52°45′	100°03′
Spruce Brook	UNP/LNO	NF		12 B/16	48°45′	58°11′
Spruce Brook	UNP/LNO	NB	Gloucester	21 P/11	47°34′	65°07′
Spruce Creek	UNP/LNO	MB	21-24-20-W	62 N/1	51°06′	100°12′
Sprucedale	UNP/LNO	ON	Parry Sound	31 E/6	45°29′	79°28′
Sprucefield	UNP/LNO	AB	8-60-19-W4	83 I/2	54°11′	112°49′
Spruce Green	UNP/LNO	ON	Wellington	40 P/10	43°42′	80°37′
Spruce Grove	CITY/VIL1	AB	3-53-27-W4	83 H/12	53°32′	113°55′
Spruce Hedge	UNP/LNO	ON	Renfrew	31 F/7	45°20′	76°39′
Spruce Home	UNP/LNO	SK	16-51-26-W2	73 H/5	53°24′	105°46′
Spruce Island	ISL/ÎLE	MB		63 F/2	53°03′	100°35′
Spruce Island	ISL/ÎLE	SK		63 E/16	53°57′	102°20′
Spruce Island	ISL/ÎLE	NT	Mackenzie	107 B	68°54′	134°33′
Spruce Lake	VILG/VILG	SK	6-53-21-W3	73 F/11	53°32′	109°05′
Spruce Lake	UNP/LNO	NB	Saint John	21 G/1	45°13′	66°11′
Spruce Lake	LAKE/LAC	ON	Kenora	43 K/6	54°20′	85°01′
Spruce Lake Junction	UNP/LNO	SK	6-53-21-W3	73 F/11	53°33′	109°05′
Spruce Park	UNP/LNO	NF		13 F/8	53°19′	60°23′
Spruce Point	CAPE/CAP	NS	Inverness	11 F/11	45°44′	61°07′
Spruce Pond	LAKE/LAC	NF		12 A/4	48°08′	57°35′
Spruce River	RIV/CDE	ON	Thunder Bay	52 H/7	49°17′	88°51′
Spruce River	RIV/CDE	ON	Kenora	52 P/13	51°48′	89°48′
Spruce River	RIV/CDE	SK	15-49-26-W2	73 H/4	53°13′	105°43′
Spruce Sands	UNP/LNO	MB	4-21-4-E	62 I/15	50°47′	96°59′
Spruce Siding	UNP/LNO	MB	9-9-11-E	62 H/9	49°43′	96°03′
Spruce View	UNP/LNO	AB	11-36-3-W5	83 B/1	52°05′	114°19′
Sprucewood	UNP/LNO	ON	Thunder Bay	52 A/16	48°56′	88°21′
Sprucewoods	UNP/LNO	MB	10-17-W	62 G/13	49°49′	99°39′
Sprucy Cove	UNP/LNO	NF		12 H/10	49°45′	56°52′
Spry	UNP/LNO	ON	Bruce	41 A/14	44°56′	81°20′
Spry Bay	UNP/LNO	NS	Halifax	11 D/15	44°51′	62°37′
Spry Bay	BAY/BAIE	NS	Halifax	11 D/15	44°48′	62°35′
Spry, Cape	CAPE/CAP	PE	Kings	11 L/8	46°15′	62°23′
Spryfield	UNP/LNO	NS	Halifax	11 D/12	44°37′	63°37′
Spry Harbour	UNP/LNO	NS	Halifax	11 D/15	44°50′	62°37′
Spry Lake	LAKE/LAC	ON	Bruce	41 A/11	44°45′	81°15′
Spurfield	UNP/LNO	AB	8-72-2-W5	83 O/1	55°13′	114°16′
Sputinow	UNP/LNO	AB	17-57-2-W4	73 E/16	53°55′	110°15′
Spuzzum	UNP/LNO	BC	Yale Division Yale	92 H/11	49°41′	121°25′
Spuzzum 1	IR/RI	BC	Yale Division Yale	92 H/11	49°40′	121°25′
Spuzzum 1A	IR/RI	BC	Yale Division Yale	92 H/11	49°39′	121°25′
Spuzzum 7	IR/RI	BC	Yale Division Yale	92 H/11	49°39′	121°24′

NAME NOM	ENTITY ENTITÉ	LOC 1 LIEU 1	LOC 2 LIEU 2	MAP CARTE	POSITION LAT	LONG
Spuzzum Creek	RIV/CDE	BC	Yale Division Yale	92 H/11	49°40′	121°25′
Spy Hill	VILG/VILG	SK	2-19-31-W	62 K/12	50°36′	101°41′
Spy Hill No. 152	MUN2/AZM2	SK		62 K/12	50°35′	101°45′
Squaam 2	IR/RI	BC	Kamloops Division Yale	82 M/4	51°05′	119°47′
Squaderee 91	IR/RI	BC	Range 5 Coast	103 J/2	54°08′	130°47′
Squally Channel	CHAN/CHEN	BC	Range 4 Coast	103 H/3	53°08′	129°22′
Squally Point	CAPE/CAP	NS	Cumberland	21 H/7	45°26′	64°55′
Squamish	MUN1/AZM1	BC	New Westminster	92 G/14	49°45′	123°08′
Squamish Dock Station	UNP/LNO	BC	New Westminster	92 G/11	49°41′	123°10′
Squamish Harbour	BAY/BAIE	BC	New Westminster	92 G/11	49°39′	123°14′
Squamish-Lillooet	MUN1/AZM1	BC	Lillooet	92 J/6	50°30′	123°00′
Squamish River	RIV/CDE	BC	New Westminster	92 G/11	49°41′	123°10′
Square Forks, Rivière	RIV/CDE	QC	La Matapédia	22 B/9	48°34′	66°09′
Square Hill	UNP/LNO	SK	6-47-13-W3	73 G/4	53°01′	107°54′
Square Island	ISL/ÎLE	NF		3 D/13	52°45′	55°52′
Square Islands	UNP/LNO	NF		3 D/12	52°44′	55°50′
Square Lake	LAKE/LAC	NB	Westmorland	21 I/1	46°09′	64°14′
Square Lake	LAKE/LAC	NB	Victoria	21 O/2	47°04′	66°56′
Square Lake	LAKE/LAC	AB	68-12,13-W4	73 L/13	54°54′	111°50′
Square Pond	LAKE/LAC	NF		2 D/16	48°47′	54°18′
Squash Lake	LAKE/LAC	NS	Digby	21 A/4	44°10′	65°53′
Squatec	UNP/LNO	QC	Témiscouata	21 N/15	47°53′	68°43′
Squatec, Grand lac	LAKE/LAC	QC	Témiscouata	21 N/10	47°40′	68°34′
Squaw-Hay-One 11	IR/RI	BC	Nanaimo	92 B/13	48°54′	123°42′
Squawk Lake	LAKE/LAC	BC	Cariboo	93 A/4	52°02′	121°35′
Squawkum Creek 3	IR/RI	BC	New Westminster	92 G/1	49°15′	122°00′
Squeah	UNP/LNO	BC	Yale Division Yale	92 H/6	49°30′	121°25′
Squeah 6	IR/RI	BC	Yale Division Yale	92 H/11	49°30′	121°25′
Squiaala 7	IR/RI	BC	New Westminster	92 H/4	49°09′	121°59′
Squiaala 8	IR/RI	BC	New Westminster	92 H/4	49°10′	122°00′
Squianny 10	IR/RI	BC	Kamloops Division Yale	92 I/6	50°21′	121°19′
Squid Cove	UNP/LNO	NS	Lunenburg	21 A/9	44°35′	64°12′
Squilax	UNP/LNO	BC	Kamloops Division Yale	82 L/13	50°52′	119°37′
Squinas 2	IR/RI	BC	Range 3 Coast	93 C/6	52°28′	125°18′
Squingula River	RIV/CDE	BC	Cassiar	94 D/3	56°15′	127°25′
Squire	UNP/LNO	ON	Grey	41 A/10	44°31′	80°59′
Squires Beach	UNP/LNO	ON	Ontario	30 M/14	43°49′	79°03′
Squirrel Cove	UNP/LNO	BC	Sayward	92 K/2	50°07′	124°55′
Squirrel Cove 8	IR/RI	BC	Sayward	92 K/2	50°08′	124°55′
Squirrel Depot	UNP/LNO	ON	Renfrew	31 F/13	45°52′	77°33′
Squirrel Island	ISL/ÎLE	ON	Lambton	40 J/7	42°30′	82°33′
Squirrel River	RIV/CDE	ON	Cochrane	42 K/8	50°24′	84°18′
Squirreltown	UNP/LNO	NS	Annapolis	21 A/14	44°46′	65°02′
Squirrel Town	UNP/LNO	ON	Manitoulin	41 H/12	45°40′	81°53′
S.S. Keno, Lieu historique national - also-aussi - S.S. Keno National Historic Site	PARK/PARC	YT		116 B/3	64°04′	139°26′
S.S. Keno National Historic Site - also-aussi - S.S. Keno, Lieu historique national	PARK/PARC	YT		116 B/3	64°04′	139°26′
S.S. Klondike, Lieu historique national - also-aussi - S.S. Klondike National Historic Site	PARK/PARC	YT		105 D/11	60°44′	135°03′
S.S. Klondike National Historic Site - also-aussi - S.S. Klondike, Lieu historique national	PARK/PARC	YT		105 D/11	60°44′	135°03′
Stackpool	UNP/LNO	ON	Sudbury	41 P/13	47°53′	81°55′
Staffa	UNP/LNO	ON	Perth	40 P/6	43°26′	81°20′
Stafford	MUN2/AZM2	ON	Renfrew	31 F/11	45°41′	77°00′
Stafford	UNP/LNO	ON	Renfrew	31 F/14	45°51′	77°12′
Stafford - see-voir - Stafford and Pembroke	MUN2/AZM2	ON		31 F/11	45°44′	77°35′
Stafford and Pembroke	MUN2/AZM2	ON	Renfrew	31 F/11	45°44′	77°35′
Stafford Lake	LAKE/LAC	BC	Range 1 Coast	92 K/14	50°46′	125°27′
Stafford River	RIV/CDE	BC	Range 1 Coast	92 K/11	50°43′	125°29′
Stage Shore	UNP/LNO	NF		1 K/12	46°38′	53°36′
Stagg Lake	LAKE/LAC	NT	Mackenzie	85 J	62°53′	115°28′
Stag Harbour	UNP/LNO	NF		2 E/9	49°35′	54°17′
Stag Island	ISL/ÎLE	NF		2 E/12	49°39′	55°40′
Stag Island	ISL/ÎLE	NT	Keewatin	32 M/11	51°39′	79°04′
Stag Lake	LAKE/LAC	NF		12 B/16	48°50′	58°02′
Stagsburn	UNP/LNO	QC	La Vallée-de-la-Gatineau	31 F/16	45°47′	76°01′
Staiyahanny 8	IR/RI	BC	Kamloops Division Yale	92 I/4	50°04′	121°33′
Stalin - see-voir - Hansen	GEOG/GÉOG	ON		41 I/3	46°09′	81°22′
Stalk Peak	MTN/MNT	BC	Cassiar	94 E/4	57°08′	127°43′
Stall Lake	UNP/LNO	MB	2-68-17-W	63 J/13	54°51′	99°56′
Stallworthy, Cape	CAPE/CAP	NT	Franklin	560 D	81°23′	93°30′
Stalwart	UNP/LNO	SK	21-26-25-W2	72 P/3	51°14′	105°26′
Stalwart	UNP/LNO	SK	21-26-25-W2	72 P/3	51°14′	105°28′
Stamford	UNP/LNO	ON	Welland	30 M/3	43°08′	79°06′
Stamford Centre	UNP/LNO	ON	Welland	30 M/3	43°07′	79°06′
Stamford Station	UNP/LNO	ON	Welland	30 M/3	43°07′	79°06′
Stamp	UNP/LNO	SK	56-13-W3	73 G/13	53°53′	107°54′
Stamp River	RIV/CDE	BC	Alberni	92 F/7	49°18′	124°53′

NAME NOM	ENTITY ENTITÉ	LOC 1 LIEU 1	LOC 2 LIEU 2	MAP CARTE	POSITION LAT	LONG
Stampville	UNP/LNO	ON	Dundas	31 B/14	44°52′	75°19′
Stanbridge	VILG/VILG	QC	Brome-Missisquoi	31 H/2	45°07′	72°55′
Stanbridge East	UNP/LNO	QC	Brome-Missisquoi	31 H/2	45°07′	72°55′
Stanbridge Lake	LAKE/LAC	NT	Mackenzie	86 J	66°53′	115°04′
Stanbridge Station	VILG/VILG	QC	Brome-Missisquoi	31 H/3	45°07′	73°02′
Stanburne	UNP/LNO	NS	Lunenburg	21 A/10	44°36′	64°43′
Stanbury	UNP/LNO	QC	Brome-Missisquoi	31 H/2	45°12′	72°55′
Stanchel	UNP/LNO	PE	Queens	11 L/6	46°19′	63°27′
Standard	VILG/VILG	AB	3-25-22-W4	82 P/2	51°07′	112°59′
Standard Hill	UNP/LNO	SK	34-49-22-W3	73 F/6	53°17′	109°08′
Standing Buffalo 78	IR/RI	SK		62 L/13	50°50′	103°54′
Standish Lake	LAKE/LAC	AB	68-7,8-W4	73 L/14	54°51′	111°04′
Stand Off	UNP/LNO	AB	9-6-25-W4	82 H/6	49°28′	113°19′
Standoff Fort (Whiskey Post) Provincial Historic Site (Undeveloped)	PARK/PARC	AB	6-25-W5	82 H/6	49°29′	113°19′
Stang Bay	BAY/BAIE	NT	Franklin	560 A	80°30′	89°51′
Stang, Cape	CAPE/CAP	NT	Franklin	77 H/8	71°21′	104°17′
Stanger	UNP/LNO	AB	22-55-6-W5	83 G/15	53°46′	114°49′
Stanhope	MUN2/AZM2	ON	Haliburton	31 E/2	45°07′	78°45′
Stanhope	UNP/LNO	NF		2 E/6	49°17′	55°05′
Stanhope	UNP/LNO	PE	Queens	11 L/6	46°25′	63°06′
Stanhope	UNP/LNO	QC	Coaticook	21 E/4	45°00′	71°48′
Stanhope Bayshore	UNP/LNO	PE	Queens	11 L/6	46°25′	63°07′
Stanhope by the Sea	UNP/LNO	PE	Queens	11 L/6	46°25′	63°07′
Stanjikoming Bay	BAY/BAIE	ON	Rainy River	52 C/11	48°41′	93°23′
Stanley	VILG/VILG	NB	York	21 J/7	46°17′	66°44′
Stanley	MUN2/AZM2	ON	Huron	40 P/12	43°30′	81°36′
Stanley	MUN2/AZM2	MB		62 G/1	49°10′	98°05′
Stanley	UNP/LNO	NS	Hants	11 E/4	45°05′	63°55′
Stanley	UNP/LNO	NS	Cumberland	21 H/16	45°45′	64°05′
Stanley	UNP/LNO	ON	Thunder Bay	52 A/5	48°22′	89°34′
Stanley	UNP/LNO	BC	Cariboo	93 H/4	53°02′	121°43′
Stanley	GEOG/GÉOG	NB	York	21 J/10	46°30′	66°40′
Stanley 157	IR/RI	SK		73 P/7	55°19′	104°34′
Stanley 157A	IR/RI	SK		73 P/8	55°24′	104°22′
Stanley Bridge	UNP/LNO	PE	Queens	11 L/6	46°28′	63°27′
Stanley Corners	UNP/LNO	ON	Carleton	31 G/4	45°14′	75°54′
Stanley Cove	UNP/LNO	NF		11 P/9	47°42′	56°10′
Stanleydale	UNP/LNO	ON	Muskoka	31 E/6	45°21′	79°26′
Stanley Falls	FALL/CHUT	AB	39-24-W5	83 C/6	52°20′	117°19′
Stanley Harbour	BAY/BAIE	NT	Keewatin	46 B	64°42′	82°09′
Stanley House	UNP/LNO	ON	Parry Sound	31 E/4	45°13′	79°44′
Stanley Mission	HAM/HAM	SK		73 P/7	55°25′	104°33′
Stanley Mountain	MTN/MNT	NB	Victoria	21 J/14	46°53′	67°03′
Stanley No. 215	MUN2/AZM2	SK		62 L/15	51°00′	103°00′
Stanley Park	UNP/LNO	ON	Waterloo	40 P/8	43°27′	80°27′
Stanley Park National Historic Site - also-aussi - Parc-Stanley, Lieu historique national du	PARK/PARC	BC	New Westminster	92 G/6	49°18′	123°09′
Stanley Section	UNP/LNO	NS	Lunenburg	21 A/10	44°31′	64°44′
Stanley Smith Glacier	GLAC/GLAC	BC	Lillooet	92 J/13	50°53′	123°50′
Stanleyville	UNP/LNO	NF		12 H/5	49°28′	57°47′
Stanleyville	UNP/LNO	ON	Lanark	31 C/16	44°48′	76°19′
Stanleyville	UNP/LNO	SK	32-47-24-W2	73 H/3	53°09′	105°29′
Stanmore	UNP/LNO	AB	20-30-11-W4	72 M/12	51°35′	111°30′
Stanstead	CITY/VIL1	QC	Memphrémagog	31 H/1	45°01′	72°06′
Stanstead	VILG/VILG	QC	Memphrémagog	31 H/1	45°07′	72°12′
Stanstead-Est	VILG/VILG	QC	Coaticook	31 H/1	45°06′	72°03′
Stanstead Plain	UNP/LNO	QC	Memphrémagog	31 H/1	45°01′	72°06′
Stanton	UNP/LNO	ON	Dufferin	41 A/1	44°09′	80°02′
Stanton	UNP/LNO	NT	Mackenzie	107 D	69°48′	128°41′
Stanwell-Fletcher Lake	LAKE/LAC	NT	Franklin	58 B	72°45′	94°46′
Stanwood	UNP/LNO	ON	Northumberland	31 C/5	44°24′	77°46′
Stapledon	UNP/LNO	ON	Carleton	31 G/4	45°09′	75°54′
Staplehurst	UNP/LNO	AB	33-50-1-W4	73 E/8	53°21′	110°05′
Staples	UNP/LNO	ON	Essex	40 J/2	42°10′	82°36′
Staples Brook	UNP/LNO	NS	Colchester	11 E/6	45°27′	63°24′
Staples River	RIV/CDE	ON	Victoria	31 D/10	44°33′	78°54′
Staples Settlement	UNP/LNO	NB	York	21 J/3	46°04′	67°05′
Stapylton Bay	BAY/BAIE	NT	Mackenzie	87 B/16	68°52′	116°15′
Staqoo 22	IR/RI	BC	Cassiar	103 P/5	55°17′	129°44′
Star	UNP/LNO	ON	Peel	30 M/13	43°53′	79°57′
Star	UNP/LNO	AB	9-56-19-W4	83 H/15	53°49′	112°46′
Starblanket	UNP/LNO	SK		73 G/7	53°23′	106°56′
Star Blanket 83	IR/RI	SK		62 L/14	50°58′	103°23′
Star Blanket 83B	IR/RI	SK	8-21-13-W2	62 L/13	50°46′	103°46′
Starbuck	UNP/LNO	MB	25,26-9-2-W	62 H/13	49°46′	97°37′
Star City	TOWN/VIL2	SK	12-45-17-W2	73 A/16	52°52′	104°20′

NAME NOM	ENTITY ENTITÉ	LOC 1 LIEU 1	LOC 2 LIEU 2	MAP CARTE	POSITION LAT	LONG
Star City No. 428	MUN2/AZM2	SK		73 A/16	52°50′	104°20′
Star Corners	UNP/LNO	ON	Frontenac	31 C/7	44°23′	76°41′
Stardale	UNP/LNO	ON	Prescott	31 G/10	45°32′	74°33′
Starfish Bay	BAY/BAIE	NT	Franklin	49 F	78°12′	84°30′
Starfish Lake	LAKE/LAC	NT	Mackenzie	76 D	64°20′	111°35′
Stark Lake	LAKE/LAC	NT	Mackenzie	75 L	62°28′	110°20′
Starks	UNP/LNO	BC	Cranberry	92 G/4	49°07′	123°55′
Starks Corners	UNP/LNO	QC	Pontiac	31 F/10	45°36′	76°36′
Starkville	UNP/LNO	ON	Durham	30 M/15	44°00′	78°30′
Star Lake	UNP/LNO	MB	9-17-E	52 E/14	49°45′	95°14′
Star Lake	LAKE/LAC	NF		12 A/11	48°34′	57°18′
Starland No. 47, Municipal District of	MUN1/AZM1	AB	31-18-W4	82 P/10	51°40′	112°33′
Starlight	UNP/LNO	AB	14-23-2-W5	82 J/16	50°58′	114°10′
Starnes Fiord	BAY/BAIE	NT	Franklin	49 A	76°37′	82°10′
Starrat	UNP/LNO	ON	Parry Sound	31 E/12	45°33′	79°32′
Starratt-Olsen	UNP/LNO	ON	Kenora	52 K/13	50°57′	93°57′
Starr's Beach	UNP/LNO	ON	Victoria	31 D/2	44°13′	78°50′
Starrs Point	UNP/LNO	NS	Kings	21 H/1	45°07′	64°23′
Starrview Acres	UNP/LNO	ON	Dufferin	40 P/16	43°56′	80°06′
Starvation Lake	LAKE/LAC	NT	Mackenzie	86 A	64°54′	112°45′
Starvation Point	UNP/LNO	QC	La Jacques-Cartier	31 P/8	47°28′	72°10′
States Lake	LAKE/LAC	NB	Restigouche	21 O/13	47°55′	67°46′
Station Bay	BAY/BAIE	NT	Franklin	69 F	78°43′	103°47′
Station-d'Étude-des-Rayons-Cosmiques-du- Mont-Sulphur, Lieu historique national de la - also-aussi - Sulphur Mountain Cosmic Ray Station National Historic Site	PARK/PARC	AB		82 O/4	51°09′	115°35′
Statlu Creek	RIV/CDE	BC	New Westminster	92 H/5	49°21′	122°00′
Stauffer	UNP/LNO	AB	14-37-5-W5	83 B/2	52°10′	114°35′
Staunton	UNP/LNO	ON	Thunder Bay	52 J/2	50°14′	90°31′
Stave Falls	UNP/LNO	BC	New Westminster	92 G/1	49°13′	122°21′
Stave Lake	LAKE/LAC	BC	New Westminster	92 G/8	49°22′	122°18′
Stavely	TOWN/VIL2	AB	8-14-27-W4	82 I/4	50°10′	113°38′
Stave River	RIV/CDE	BC	New Westminster	92 G/1	49°10′	122°25′
Stawamus 24	IR/RI	BC	New Westminster	92 G/11	49°41′	123°09′
Stawamus River	RIV/CDE	BC	New Westminster	92 G/11	49°41′	123°09′
Stayner	UNP/LNO	ON	Simcoe	41 A/8	44°24′	80°04′
Staynerville	UNP/LNO	QC	Argenteuil	31 G/9	45°38′	74°25′
Staynor Hall	UNP/LNO	SK	2-2-23-W3	72 F/2	49°05′	108°59′
Steacie Ice Cap	GLAC/GLAC	NT	Franklin	59 E	78°50′	91°15′
Stead	UNP/LNO	MB	4-17-8-E	62 I/8	50°26′	96°27′
Steady Brook	TOWN/VIL2	NF		12 A/13	48°57′	57°49′
Steady Brook Lake	LAKE/LAC	NF		12 A/13	48°57′	57°41′
Steamboat	UNP/LNO	BC	Peace River	94 J/12	58°41′	123°43′
Steam Mill Village	UNP/LNO	NS	Kings	21 H/2	45°07′	64°31′
Stearing Island - see-voir - Stearin Island	ISL/ÎLE	NF		12 H/13	49°56′	57°50′
Stearin Island	ISL/ÎLE	NF		12 H/13	49°56′	57°50′
Steel	UNP/LNO	QC	Les Collines-de-l'Outaouais	31 F/9	45°34′	76°11′
Steel	UNP/LNO	ON	Thunder Bay	42 D/15	48°47′	86°51′
Steele Glacier	GLAC/GLAC	YT		115 F/8	61°15′	140°10′
Steele Lake	LAKE/LAC	AB	65-25,26-W4	83 I/12	54°39′	113°46′
Steele, Mount	MTN/MNT	YT		115 F/1	61°06′	140°19′
Steeles	UNP/LNO	ON	York	30 M/14	43°49′	79°19′
Steeles Corners	UNP/LNO	ON	York	30 M/14	43°48′	79°25′
Steeles Hill	UNP/LNO	NS	Cape Breton	11 J/4	46°10′	59°59′
Steelhead	UNP/LNO	BC	New Westminster	92 G/1	49°14′	122°19′
Steel Lake	LAKE/LAC	ON	Thunder Bay	42 E/7	49°15′	86°49′
Steelman	UNP/LNO	SK	15-4-5-W2	62 E/7	49°18′	102°36′
Steel River	RIV/CDE	ON	Thunder Bay	42 D/15	48°46′	86°54′
Steels Ferry	UNP/LNO	MB	31-8-13-W	62 G/11	49°42′	99°14′
Steelton	UNP/LNO	ON	Algoma	41 K/9	46°32′	84°20′
Steen	UNP/LNO	SK	4-43-11-W2	63 D/12	52°41′	103°32′
Steenburg Lake	UNP/LNO	ON	Hastings	31 C/13	44°50′	77°42′
Steen River	UNP/LNO	AB	15-122-19-W5	84 N/11	59°38′	117°10′
Steen River	RIV/CDE	AB	122-19-W6	84 N/11	59°35′	117°10′
Steensby Inlet	BAY/BAIE	NT	Franklin	37 F/3	70°15′	78°35′
Steensby Peninsula	CAPE/CAP	NT	Franklin	47 G	71°57′	85°00′
Steepbank River	RIV/CDE	AB	92-10-W4	74 E/3	57°01′	111°28′
Steep Creek	UNP/LNO	NS	Guysborough	11 F/11	45°33′	61°21′
Steeper	UNP/LNO	AB	13-48-22-W5	83 F/3	53°08′	117°05′
Steephill Falls	FALL/CHUT	ON	Algoma	42 C/2	48°05′	84°44′
Steephill Lake	LAKE/LAC	SK		63 M/14	55°58′	103°09′
Steep Rock	UNP/LNO	MB	33-28-10-W	62 O/7	51°27′	98°48′
Steep Rock Junction	UNP/LNO	MB	28-28-8-W	62 O/7	51°26′	98°32′
Steep Rock Lake	UNP/LNO	ON	Rainy River	52 B/13	48°49′	91°39′
Steeprock Lake	LAKE/LAC	MB	30-15-W	62 O/11	51°35′	99°27′
Steeprock River	RIV/CDE	MB	13-44-25-W	63 C/15	52°47′	100°57′
Steevescote	UNP/LNO	NB	Albert	21 H/15	45°56′	64°42′

NAME NOM	ENTITY ENTITÉ	LOC 1 LIEU 1	LOC 2 LIEU 2	MAP CARTE	POSITION LAT	LONG
Steeves Mills	UNP/LNO	NB	Albert	21 H/15	45°56′	64°48′
Steeves Mountain	UNP/LNO	NB	Westmorland	21 I/3	46°05′	65°00′
Steeves Settlement	UNP/LNO	NB	Westmorland	21 I/3	46°01′	65°15′
Stefansson Island	ISL/ÎLE	NT	Franklin	78 D	73°20′	105°45′
Steinbach	TOWN/VIL2	MB		62 H/10	49°32′	96°41′
Stein Lake	LAKE/LAC	BC	Kamloops Division Yale	92 J/1	50°10′	122°11′
Stein Mountain	MTN/MNT	BC	Kamloops Division Yale	92 I/5	50°20′	121°46′
Stein River	RIV/CDE	BC	Kamloops Division Yale	92 I/5	50°17′	121°38′
Stelcam	UNP/LNO	SK	8-16-24-W2	72 I/6	50°20′	105°16′
Stella	UNP/LNO	ON	Lennox and Addington	31 C/2	44°10′	76°42′
Stellako	UNP/LNO	BC	Range 5 Coast	93 K/2	54°04′	124°54′
Stella Lake	LAKE/LAC	BC	Sayward	92 K/5	50°17′	125°31′
Stellaquo 5 - see-voir - Stellaquo (Stella) 1	IR/RI	BC		93 K/2	54°03′	124°55′
Stellaquo (Stella) 1	IR/RI	BC	Range 5 Coast	93 K/2	54°03′	124°55′
Stellarton	TOWN/VIL2	NS	Pictou	11 E/10	45°34′	62°40′
Stenen	VILG/VILG	SK	9-34-3-W2	62 M/16	51°54′	102°23′
Stenkul Fiord	BAY/BAIE	NT	Franklin	49 D	77°25′	83°54′
Stepaside	UNP/LNO	NF		1 M/3	47°02′	55°09′
Stephansson House Provincial Historic Site (Developed)	PARK/PARC	AB	3,10-37-2-W5	83 B/1	52°10′	114°13′
Stephen	MUN2/AZM2	ON	Huron	40 P/5	43°18′	81°36′
Stephen	UNP/LNO	BC	Kootenay	82 N/8	51°27′	116°17′
Stephenfield	UNP/LNO	MB	30-6-6-W	62 G/9	49°30′	98°15′
Stephen Lake	LAKE/LAC	ON	Kenora	52 F/5	49°18′	93°48′
Stephens Bay	UNP/LNO	ON	Muskoka	31 E/3	45°01′	79°21′
Stephens Headland	CAPE/CAP	NT	Franklin	48 B	72°32′	85°37′
Stephens Island	ISL/ÎLE	BC	Range 5 Coast	103 J/2	54°10′	130°46′
Stephens Lake	LAKE/LAC	MB		54 D/6	56°26′	95°07′
Stephensons Pond	LAKE/LAC	NF		11 P/13	47°54′	57°30′
Stephenville	TOWN/VIL2	NF		12 B/10	48°33′	58°35′
Stephenville Crossing	TOWN/VIL2	NF		12 B/9	48°30′	58°26′
Steppes	UNP/LNO	SK	3-8-2-W2	62 E/9	49°37′	102°11′
Stepp Lake	LAKE/LAC	BC	Range 4 Coast	93 E/14	53°57′	127°20′
Stepstone	UNP/LNO	ON	Thunder Bay	52 A/11	48°33′	89°15′
Stequmwhulpa 5	IR/RI	BC	Kamloops Division Yale	82 L/13	50°51′	119°36′
Sterco	UNP/LNO	AB	35-47-20-W5	83 F/2	53°06′	116°49′
Sterlet Lake	LAKE/LAC	NT	Mackenzie	76 C	64°44′	109°28′
Sterling	UNP/LNO	NS	Cape Breton	11 J/4	46°12′	59°57′
Sterns Lake	LAKE/LAC	NT	Keewatin	65 F	61°14′	100°30′
Stettin	UNP/LNO	AB	10-56-1-W5	83 G/16	53°49′	114°04′
Stettler	TOWN/VIL2	AB	5-39-19-W4	83 A/7	52°19′	112°43′
Stettler No. 6, County of	MUN1/AZM1	AB	37-18-W4	83 A/2	52°14′	112°36′
Stevan 4 - see-voir - Tsay Cho 4	IR/RI	BC		93 K/15	54°48′	124°55′
Stevens	UNP/LNO	ON	Thunder Bay	42 F/12	49°33′	85°49′
Stevens Bay	BAY/BAIE	ON	Kenora	52 F/4	49°11′	93°59′
Stevens Head	CAPE/CAP	NT	Franklin	88 G	75°35′	117°12′
Stevens Lake	LAKE/LAC	MB		64 G/14	57°49′	99°13′
Stevens Lakes	LAKE/LAC	BC	Kamloops Division Yale	82 M/13	51°59′	119°46′
Stevenson	UNP/LNO	ON	Kent	40 J/1	42°12′	82°19′
Stevenson Lake	LAKE/LAC	MB		53 E/13	53°55′	95°55′
Stevenson River	RIV/CDE	MB		53 L/3	54°06′	95°14′
Stevensons Village	UNP/LNO	NF		1 N/11	47°41′	53°15′
Stevens Passage	CHAN/CHEN	BC	Nanaimo	92 F/8	49°29′	124°24′
Stevens Roadhouse	UNP/LNO	YT		115 P/4	63°11′	137°59′
Stevensville	UNP/LNO	ON	Welland	30 L/14	42°57′	79°04′
Steveston	UNP/LNO	BC	New Westminster	92 G/3	49°08′	123°11′
Steveville	UNP/LNO	AB	4-22-12-W4	72 L/13	50°50′	111°37′
Stewardson Inlet	UNP/LNO	BC	Clayoquot	92 E/8	49°25′	126°19′
Stewart	MUN1/AZM1	BC	Cassiar	103 P/13	55°56′	129°59′
Stewart	UNP/LNO	AB	13-8-21-W4	82 H/10	49°39′	112°44′
Stewart Creek	RIV/CDE	SK	55-16-W2	73 H/9	53°44′	104°21′
Stewart Crossing	UNP/LNO	ON	Renfrew	31 F/14	45°57′	77°21′
Stewart Crossing	UNP/LNO	YT		115 P/7	63°22′	136°41′
Stewartdale	UNP/LNO	NS	Inverness	11 K/3	46°01′	61°10′
Stewart Farm	UNP/LNO	ON	Renfrew	31 F/14	45°56′	77°22′
Stewartfield	UNP/LNO	AB	19-58-4-W5	83 J/2	54°02′	114°34′
Stewart Hall	UNP/LNO	ON	Peterborough	31 D/1	44°13′	78°19′
Stewart Heights	UNP/LNO	ON	Peterborough	31 D/8	44°20′	78°26′
Stewart Lake	LAKE/LAC	YT		105 A/10	60°38′	128°40′
Stewart Lake	LAKE/LAC	NT	Keewatin	56 I/15	66°45′	88°50′
Stewart Lake	LAKE/LAC	NT	Mackenzie	96 C	64°24′	125°16′
Stewart, Mount	MTN/MNT	YT		115 O/3	63°11′	139°22′
Stewarton	UNP/LNO	NB	Kings	21 H/12	45°44′	65°51′
Stewart Point	CAPE/CAP	NT	Keewatin	66 O	67°46′	98°50′
Stewart Point	CAPE/CAP	NT	Franklin	88 B	72°22′	119°17′
Stewart River	UNP/LNO	YT		115 O/6	63°19′	139°26′

NAME NOM	ENTITY ENTITÉ	LOC 1 LIEU 1	LOC 2 LIEU 2	MAP CARTE	POSITION LAT	LONG
Stewart River	RIV/CDE	YT		115 O/6	63°19'	139°24'
Stewarts Glen	UNP/LNO	ON	Glengarry	31 G/7	45°21'	74°51'
Stewarttown	UNP/LNO	ON	Halton	30 M/12	43°38'	79°56'
Stewarttown Station	UNP/LNO	ON	Halton	30 M/12	43°37'	79°56'
Stewart Valley	VILG/VILG	SK	12-19-14-W3	72 J/12	50°36'	107°48'
Stewartville	UNP/LNO	ON	Renfrew	31 F/8	45°25'	76°30'
Stewiacke	TOWN/VIL2	NS	Colchester	11 E/3	45°08'	63°21'
Stewiacke Cross Roads	UNP/LNO	NS	Colchester	11 E/2	45°14'	62°56'
Stewiacke East	UNP/LNO	NS	Colchester	11 E/3	45°09'	63°18'
Stewiacke River	RIV/CDE	NS	Colchester	11 E/3	45°08'	63°23'
Stickney	UNP/LNO	NB	Carleton	21 J/5	46°23'	67°34'
Stick Point	UNP/LNO	QC	Côte-Nord-du-Golfe-Saint-Laurent	12 P/5	51°25'	57°40'
Stikelan Creek	RIV/CDE	BC	Range 2 Coast	92 N/8	51°28'	124°24'
Stikine	UNP/LNO	BC	Cassiar	104 B/12	56°42'	131°48'
Stikine Ranges	MTN/MNT	BC	Cassiar	104 P/3	59°00'	129°00'
Stikine River	RIV/CDE	BC	Cassiar	104 B/12	56°39'	131°50'
Stikine River 7	IR/RI	BC	Cassiar	104 G/14	57°54'	131°10'
Stilesville	UNP/LNO	NB	Westmorland	21 I/2	46°10'	64°53'
Still Creek	UNP/LNO	BC	New Westminster	92 G/6	49°16'	123°02'
Stillman	UNP/LNO	NS	Pictou	11 E/10	45°33'	62°53'
Still River	UNP/LNO	ON	Parry Sound	41 H/15	45°50'	80°33'
Still River	RIV/CDE	ON	Parry Sound	41 H/15	45°46'	80°33'
Stillwater	UNP/LNO	NS	Guysborough	11 F/4	45°11'	61°59'
Stillwater	UNP/LNO	NS	Hants	11 D/13	44°55'	63°57'
Stillwater	UNP/LNO	BC	Kamloops Division Yale	83 D/4	52°03'	119°57'
Stillwater	UNP/LNO	BC	New Westminster	92 F/16	49°46'	124°18'
Stillwater Lake	UNP/LNO	NS	Halifax	11 D/12	44°42'	63°51'
Stimson	UNP/LNO	ON	Cochrane	42 A/15	48°59'	80°38'
Stimson Diamond	UNP/LNO	ON	Cochrane	42 A/15	48°58'	80°36'
Stinson	UNP/LNO	ON	Sudbury	41 I/10	46°31'	80°41'
Stirling	VILG/VILG	ON	Hastings	31 C/5	44°18'	77°33'
Stirling	VILG/VILG	AB	29-6-19-W4	82 H/10	49°30'	112°31'
Stirling	UNP/LNO	NS	Richmond	11 F/9	45°44'	60°26'
Stirling Arm	BAY/BAIE	BC	Alberni	92 F/2	49°15'	124°55'
Stirling Brook	UNP/LNO	NS	Hants	11 E/5	45°19'	63°34'
Stirling Creek	RIV/CDE	BC	Similkameen Division Yale	82 E/11	49°35'	119°13'
Stirling Falls	UNP/LNO	ON	Parry Sound	31 E/11	45°41'	79°27'
Stirling Island	ISL/ÎLE	BC	Range 2 Coast	102 P/16	51°46'	128°06'
Stirlingville	UNP/LNO	AB	10-30-27-W4	82 P/12	51°34'	113°42'
Stirni Seamount	SEAU/SMER	—		3000	49°07'	132°16'
Stirton	UNP/LNO	ON	Wellington	40 P/10	43°44'	80°42'
Stitt	UNP/LNO	MB	79-6-E	63 P/15	55°50'	96°35'
Stittsville	UNP/LNO	ON	Carleton	31 G/5	45°15'	75°55'
Stivens, Point	CAPE/CAP	NT	Franklin	97 C	69°34'	125°30'
Stlakament 9	IR/RI	BC	Kamloops Division Yale	92 I/4	50°03'	121°33'
St. Lawrence	UNP/LNO	QC	La Matapédia	22 B/6	48°30'	67°29'
Stobart	UNP/LNO	AB	28-22-23-W4	82 I/14	50°54'	113°08'
Stobart Creek	RIV/CDE	BC	Lillooet	92 O/7	51°28'	122°47'
Stock Cove	UNP/LNO	NF		2 C/11	48°32'	53°21'
Stockdale	UNP/LNO	ON	Northumberland	31 C/4	44°12'	77°38'
Stockett	UNP/LNO	BC	Nanaimo	92 G/4	49°08'	123°56'
Stockholm	VILG/VILG	SK	25-19-3-W2	62 L/9	50°39'	102°18'
Stocking Harbour	UNP/LNO	NF		2 E/12	49°44'	55°57'
Stockport	UNP/LNO	MB	10-1-3-E	62 H/3	49°02'	97°07'
Stockport Islands	ISL/ÎLE	NT	Franklin	76 N	67°46'	109°00'
Stockton	UNP/LNO	MB	21-7-15-W	62 G/11	49°35'	99°27'
Stoco	UNP/LNO	ON	Hastings	31 C/6	44°27'	77°17'
Stoco Lake	LAKE/LAC	ON	Hastings	31 C/6	44°28'	77°17'
Stoddart Island	ISL/ÎLE	NS	Shelburne	20 P/5	43°28'	65°43'
Stoddarts	UNP/LNO	NS	Annapolis	21 A/10	44°42'	64°56'
Stoke	VILG/VILG	QC	Le Val-Saint-François	21 E/12	45°32'	71°48'
Stoke	UNP/LNO	QC	Le Val-Saint-François	21 E/12	45°32'	71°48'
Stoke, Monts	MTN/MNT	QC	Le Val-Saint-François	21 E/12	45°33'	71°42'
Stoke-Nord	UNP/LNO	QC	Le Val-Saint-François	21 E/12	45°37'	71°43'
Stoke, Rivière	RIV/CDE	QC	Le Val-Saint-François	21 E/12	45°35'	71°58'
Stokes Bay	UNP/LNO	ON	Bruce	41 H/3	45°00'	81°22'
Stokes Bay	BAY/BAIE	ON	Bruce	41 A/14	44°58'	81°23'
Stokes Point	CAPE/CAP	YT		117 D/6	69°20'	138°43'
Stokes Range	MTN/MNT	NT	Franklin	69 B	76°20'	101°35'
Stokke Creek	RIV/CDE	BC	New Westminster	92 G/9	49°43'	122°02'
Stolberg	UNP/LNO	AB	32-40-13-W5	83 B/5	52°29'	115°49'
Stolz Peninsula	CAPE/CAP	NT	Franklin	49 F	78°52'	87°38'
Stone	UNP/LNO	SK	9-10-21-W3	72 F/15	49°48'	108°47'
Stone 1	IR/RI	BC	Lillooet	92 O/14	51°57'	123°08'
Stone 1A	IR/RI	BC	Lillooet	92 O/14	51°54'	123°08'

NAME / NOM	ENTITY / ENTITÉ	LOC 1 / LIEU 1	LOC 2 / LIEU 2	MAP / CARTE	POSITION LAT	POSITION LONG
Stone 4	IR/RI	BC	Lillooet	92 O/14	51°51′	123°12′
Stonebrook	UNP/LNO	ON	Renfrew	31 F/14	45°45′	77°06′
Stonecliffe	UNP/LNO	ON	Renfrew	31 K/4	46°13′	77°53′
Stone Fence, The	SEAU/SMER	—		8008	44°45′	57°19′
Stonefield	UNP/LNO	QC	Argenteuil	31 G/10	45°36′	74°31′
Stoneham	UNP/LNO	QC	La Jacques-Cartier	21 M/3	47°00′	71°22′
Stoneham-et-Tewkesbury	VILG/VILG	QC	La Jacques-Cartier	21 M/3	47°10′	71°26′
Stonehaven	UNP/LNO	NB	Gloucester	21 P/11	47°45′	65°22′
Stonehenge	UNP/LNO	SK	31-6-1-W3	72 G/9	49°31′	106°07′
Stonehenge No. 73	MUN2/AZM2	SK		72 G/9	49°35′	106°10′
Stonehurst East	UNP/LNO	NS	Lunenburg	21 A/8	44°22′	64°13′
Stonehurst West	UNP/LNO	NS	Lunenburg	21 A/8	44°22′	64°13′
Stone Lake	LAKE/LAC	ON	Thunder Bay	42 L/12	50°35′	87°31′
Stonelaw	UNP/LNO	AB	34-33-18-W4	82 P/16	51°52′	112°29′
Stoneleigh	UNP/LNO	ON	Muskoka	31 E/3	45°06′	79°15′
Stoner	UNP/LNO	BC	Cariboo	93 G/10	53°38′	122°39′
Stoneridge	UNP/LNO	NB	York	21 J/2	46°06′	66°57′
Stoneridge	UNP/LNO	ON	Brant	40 P/1	43°03′	80°04′
Stones Corners	UNP/LNO	ON	Grenville	31 B/12	44°40′	75°38′
Stone's Cove	UNP/LNO	NF		1 M/11	47°35′	55°07′
Stone Valley	UNP/LNO	NF		11 P/9	47°37′	56°02′
Stoneville	UNP/LNO	NF		2 E/7	49°28′	54°33′
Stonewall	TOWN/VIL2	MB	25-13-1-E	62 I/3	50°08′	97°20′
Stoney 142-143-144	IR/RI	AB	25-7-W5	82 O/2	51°10′	114°57′
Stoney 142B	IR/RI	AB	27-6-W5	82 O/7	51°18′	114°46′
Stoney Arm	BAY/BAIE	NF		13 H/9	53°33′	56°10′
Stoneybrook	UNP/LNO	ON	Middlesex	40 P/3	43°02′	81°15′
Stoney Brook	RIV/CDE	NS	Shelburne	20 P/14	43°59′	65°17′
Stoney Creek	CITY/VIL1	ON	Wentworth	30 M/4	43°13′	79°46′
Stoney Creek	UNP/LNO	NB	Albert	21 H/15	46°00′	64°43′
Stoney Creek	UNP/LNO	BC	Kootenay	82 N/6	51°22′	117°27′
Stoney Creek	RIV/CDE	ON	Haldimand	30 L/13	42°49′	79°56′
Stoney Creek Station	UNP/LNO	ON	Wentworth	30 M/4	43°14′	79°45′
Stoneycroft	UNP/LNO	NB	Kings	21 H/5	45°25′	65°58′
Stoney House	UNP/LNO	NF		1 M/1	47°03′	54°06′
Stoney Island	UNP/LNO	NS	Shelburne	20 P/5	43°28′	65°34′
Stoney Point	UNP/LNO	ON	Simcoe	31 D/5	44°16′	79°32′
Stoney Point	UNP/LNO	ON	Essex	40 J/7	42°18′	82°33′
Stoney Point	CAPE/CAP	ON	Essex	40 J/7	42°18′	82°34′
Stony Beach	UNP/LNO	SK	30-17-23-W2	72 I/6	50°28′	105°10′
Stony Brook	RIV/CDE	NF		2 D/13	48°55′	55°40′
Stony Creek	RIV/CDE	MB		52 E/3	49°15′	95°09′
Stony Creek	RIV/CDE	MB/SK		62 F/7	49°29′	100°51′
Stony Creek	RIV/CDE	YT		105 D/13	60°47′	135°58′
Stony Creek 1	IR/RI	BC	Range 4 Coast	93 F/16	53°57′	124°07′
Stony Creek Camp	UNP/LNO	YT		105 D/13	60°48′	136°00′
Stony Creek Station	UNP/LNO	NB	Albert	21 H/15	45°57′	64°45′
Stony Hill	UNP/LNO	MB	25-10-11-E	52 E/13	49°52′	95°58′
Stony Hill	UNP/LNO	MB	18-20-3-W	62 I/12	50°43′	97°51′
Stony Island	ISL/ÎLE	NF		3 D/13	52°59′	55°49′
Stony Lake	LAKE/LAC	NF		2 D/12	48°42′	55°48′
Stony Lake	LAKE/LAC	ON	Peterborough	31 D/9	44°33′	78°06′
Stony Lake	LAKE/LAC	MB		62 O/1	51°00′	98°02′
Stony Lake	LAKE/LAC	MB		64 J/15	58°51′	98°40′
Stony Lake	LAKE/LAC	SK	52-18-W3	73 F/7	53°29′	108°32′
Stony Lake	LAKE/LAC	BC	Cariboo	93 H/5	53°25′	121°53′
Stony Mountain	UNP/LNO	MB	11-13-2-E	62 I/3	50°05′	97°13′
Stony Plain	TOWN/VIL2	AB	36-52-1-W5	83 G/9	53°32′	114°00′
Stony Plain 135	IR/RI	AB	52-26-W4	83 H/5	53°28′	113°45′
Stony Point	CAPE/CAP	NF		1 M/8	47°22′	54°10′
Stony Point	CAPE/CAP	MB	31-24-2-E	62 P/14	51°58′	97°19′
Stony Point 21	IR/RI	MB		63 K/2	54°03′	100°56′
Stony, Pointe	CAPE/CAP	QC	Kativik	24 K/15	58°55′	68°36′
Stony Point (Fishery Bay) 10	IR/RI	BC	Cassiar	103 P/4	55°00′	129°39′
Stony Rapids	HAM/HAM	SK		74 P/5	59°16′	105°50′
Stonyridge	UNP/LNO	ON	Peterborough	31 D/9	44°36′	78°01′
Stonyview	UNP/LNO	SK	34-30-8-W2	62 M/11	51°39′	103°03′
Stonywood	UNP/LNO	ON	Wellington	40 P/15	43°59′	80°31′
Stooping River	RIV/CDE	ON	Cochrane	43 A/4	52°10′	81°52′
Stop 19	UNP/LNO	ON	Welland	30 M/3	43°00′	79°16′
Storeytown	UNP/LNO	NB	Northumberland	21 J/9	46°34′	66°09′
Storie	UNP/LNO	ON	Parry Sound	31 L/3	46°02′	79°27′
Stories Beach	UNP/LNO	BC	Comox	92 F/14	49°55′	125°11′
Stor Island	ISL/ÎLE	NT	Franklin	49 G	78°59′	85°50′
Storis Passage	CHAN/CHEN	NT	Keewatin	67 A/11	68°39′	99°00′

NAME NOM	ENTITY ENTITÉ	LOC 1 LIEU 1	LOC 2 LIEU 2	MAP CARTE	POSITION LAT	POSITION LONG
Storkerson Bay	BAY/BAIE	NT	Franklin	98 B	72°56'	124°50'
Storkerson Peninsula	CAPE/CAP	NT	Franklin	78 A	72°30'	106°30'
Storkerson River	RIV/CDE	NT	Franklin	98 B	72°56'	124°29'
Storkson's Corner	UNP/LNO	ON	Rainy River	52 D/16	48°55'	94°24'
Storm, Cape	CAPE/CAP	NT	Franklin	49 B	76°21'	87°35'
Storm, Lac	LAKE/LAC	QC	Jamésie	32 K/16	50°49'	76°23'
Stormont	UNP/LNO	NS	Guysborough	11 F/4	45°13'	61°44'
Stormont	GEOG/GÉOG	ON		31 G/2	45°10'	75°00'
Stormont, Dundas and Glengarry, United Counties of	MUN1/AZM1	ON	Glengarry	31 G/2	45°15'	74°40'
*Storms	UNP/LNO	BC	Bright	92 G/4	49°02'	123°53'
Storms Corners	UNP/LNO	ON	Lennox and Addington	31 C/2	44°15'	76°49'
Stormy Brook	RIV/CDE	NF		2 D/5	48°22'	55°42'
Stormy Lake	LAKE/LAC	ON	Parry Sound	31 L/4	46°05'	79°46'
Stormy Lake	LAKE/LAC	ON	Kenora	52 F/8	49°23'	92°18'
Stormy Point	CAPE/CAP	NF		11 O/14	47°50'	59°23'
Stornoway	VILG/VILG	QC	Le Granit	21 E/11	45°43'	71°10'
Stornoway	VILG/VILG	SK	35-26-1-W2	62 M/8	51°17'	102°02'
Storrington	MUN2/AZM2	ON	Frontenac	31 C/8	44°26'	76°21'
Storthoaks	VILG/VILG	SK	16-5-31-W	62 F/5	49°23'	101°36'
Storthoaks No. 31	MUN2/AZM2	SK		62 F/5	49°25'	101°30'
Stouffville	UNP/LNO	ON	York	30 M/14	43°58'	79°15'
Stoughton	TOWN/VIL2	SK	28-8-8-W2	62 E/11	49°41'	103°02'
Stout	UNP/LNO	BC	Yale Division Yale	92 H/11	49°39'	121°24'
Stout 8	IR/RI	BC	Yale Division Yale	92 H/11	49°38'	121°23'
Stout Lake	LAKE/LAC	ON	Kenora	53 D/2	52°08'	94°35'
Stove Creek	UNP/LNO	SK	18-37-8-W2	63 D/3	52°11'	103°08'
Stowe	UNP/LNO	AB	31-8-26-W4	82 H/12	49°41'	113°30'
Stowlea	UNP/LNO	SK	21-54-21-W3	73 F/11	53°40'	109°03'
Stoyoma Mountain	MTN/MNT	BC	Yale Division Yale	92 H/14	49°59'	121°13'
Strabane	UNP/LNO	ON	Wentworth	40 P/8	43°22'	80°02'
Strachan	UNP/LNO	AB	7-38-8-W5	83 B/6	52°16'	115°08'
Strachan Creek	UNP/LNO	BC	New Westminster	92 G/6	49°25'	123°14'
Straders Hill	UNP/LNO	ON	Dundas	31 B/14	44°58'	75°18'
Straffordville	UNP/LNO	ON	Elgin	40 I/10	42°45'	80°47'
Straight Lake	LAKE/LAC	ON	Kenora	52 F/11	49°34'	93°18'
Straight River	RIV/CDE	SK		74 O/8	59°27'	106°25'
Strait Lake	LAKE/LAC	BC	Kamloops Division Yale	83 D/4	52°10'	119°34'
Straiton	UNP/LNO	BC	New Westminster	92 G/1	49°05'	122°12'
Straits Bay	BAY/BAIE	NT	Franklin	37 A	68°35'	73°56'
Stralak	UNP/LNO	ON	Sudbury	41 I/13	46°48'	81°41'
Stranby River	RIV/CDE	BC	Rupert	102 I/16	50°50'	128°09'
Strand Bay	BAY/BAIE	NT	Franklin	59 G	79°13'	93°35'
Strand Fiord	BAY/BAIE	NT	Franklin	59 H	79°11'	91°28'
Strange	UNP/LNO	ON	York	30 M/13	43°56'	79°35'
Strange Lake	LAKE/LAC	SK	59-6-W3	73 J/2	54°09'	106°46'
Strangmuir	UNP/LNO	AB	23-22-25-W4	82 I/14	50°53'	113°22'
Stranraer	UNP/LNO	SK	4-32-18-W3	72 N/9	51°43'	108°29'
Strasbourg	TOWN/VIL2	SK	25-24-22-W2	72 P/2	51°04'	104°57'
Strasbourg Beach - see-voir - Island View	HAM/HAM	SK		72 I/14	50°58'	105°10'
Strasburg	UNP/LNO	ON	Waterloo	40 P/8	43°24'	80°27'
Stratford	CITY/VIL1	ON	Perth	40 P/7	43°22'	80°57'
Stratford	TOWN/VIL2	PE	Queens	11 L/3	46°13'	63°05'
Stratford	VILG/VILG	QC	Le Granit	21 E/14	45°47'	71°17'
Strathadam	UNP/LNO	NB	Northumberland	21 I/13	46°58'	65°40'
Strathallan	UNP/LNO	ON	Oxford	40 P/2	43°13'	80°48'
Strathallen	UNP/LNO	SK	36-2-3-W3	72 G/1	49°12'	106°18'
Strathavon	UNP/LNO	ON	Grey	41 A/7	44°29'	80°46'
Strathburn	UNP/LNO	ON	Middlesex	40 I/12	42°43'	81°41'
Strathclair	MUN2/AZM2	MB		62 K/8	50°28'	100°20'
Strathclair	UNP/LNO	MB	35-16-22-W	62 K/8	50°24'	100°24'
Strathcona	MUN2/AZM2	MB		62 G/6	49°20'	99°30'
Strathcona	UNP/LNO	PE	Kings	11 L/7	46°20'	62°34'
Strathcona - see-voir - River Hebert East (Strathcona)	UNP/LNO	NS		21 H/9	45°42'	64°21'
Strathcona	UNP/LNO	ON	Lennox and Addington	31 C/7	44°19'	76°54'
*Strathcona	UNP/LNO	BC	New Westminster	92 G/7	49°19'	122°57'
Strathcona	UNP/LNO	BC	New Westminster	92 G/6	49°17'	123°05'
Strathcona County	MUN1/AZM1	AB		83 H/11	53°35'	113°06'
Strathcona Fiord	BAY/BAIE	NT	Franklin	49 E	78°43'	82°55'
Strathcona Gardens	UNP/LNO	ON	Halton	30 M/5	43°21'	79°46'
Strathcona Islands	ISL/ÎLE	NT	Franklin	25 M	63°01'	71°25'
Strathcona Lodge	UNP/LNO	BC	Shawnigan	92 B/12	48°38'	123°38'
Strathcona No. 20, County of - see-voir - Strathcona County	MUN1/AZM1	AB		83 H/11	53°35'	113°06'
Strathcona Park	UNP/LNO	ON	Frontenac	31 C/7	44°15'	76°31'
Strathcona Park	UNP/LNO	MB	27-4-16-W	62 G/5	49°20'	99°32'
Strathcona Science Park	PARK/PARC	AB	6,7,8-53-23-W4	83 H/11	53°34'	113°22'

NAME NOM	ENTITY ENTITÉ	LOC 1 LIEU 1	LOC 2 LIEU 2	MAP CARTE	POSITION	
					LAT	LONG
Strathcona Sound	CHAN/CHEN	NT	Franklin	48 C/1	73°05′	84°33′
Strathearn	UNP/LNO	ON	Carleton	31 G/5	45°21′	75°56′
Strathgartney	UNP/LNO	PE	Queens	11 L/3	46°13′	63°21′
Strathlorne	UNP/LNO	NS	Inverness	11 K/3	46°11′	61°17′
Strathlorne Station	UNP/LNO	NS	Inverness	11 K/3	46°11′	61°16′
Strathmore	TOWN/VIL2	AB	14-24-25-W4	82 P/3	51°03′	113°23′
Strathmore	UNP/LNO	QC	Communauté urbaine de Montréal	31 H/5	45°27′	73°47′
Strathmore	UNP/LNO	ON	Stormont	31 G/2	45°12′	74°48′
Strathnairn	UNP/LNO	ON	Grey	41 A/10	44°31′	80°40′
Strathnaver	UNP/LNO	BC	Cariboo	93 G/8	53°17′	122°30′
Strathnaver	UNP/LNO	BC	Cariboo	93 G/7	53°21′	122°33′
Strathroy	TOWN/VIL2	ON	Middlesex	40 I/13	42°57′	81°38′
Stratton	UNP/LNO	ON	Rainy River	52 D/9	48°41′	94°10′
Stratton Inlet	BAY/BAIE	NT	Franklin	48 F	74°32′	86°40′
Strawberry, Cape	CAPE/CAP	NF		13 O/3	55°09′	59°02′
Strawberry Creek	RIV/CDE	AB	23-50-1-W5	83 G/8	53°20′	114°03′
Strawberry Hill	UNP/LNO	BC	New Westminster	92 G/2	49°08′	122°53′
Strawberry Island	ISL/ÎLE	ON	Manitoulin	41 H/13	45°56′	81°51′
Strawberry Lakes	LAKE/LAC	SK	16-13-W2	62 L/5	50°21′	103°44′
Strawberry Vale	UNP/LNO	BC	Esquimalt	92 B/6	48°28′	123°25′
Straw Lake	LAKE/LAC	ON	Kenora	52 F/3	49°08′	93°22′
Streak Mountain	MTN/MNT	YT		105 C/12	60°35′	133°39′
Streamstown	UNP/LNO	AB	26-51-2-W4	73 E/8	53°26′	110°11′
Streatfeild Lake	LAKE/LAC	ON	Kenora	43 C/4	52°09′	85°55′
Streatfeild River	RIV/CDE	ON	Kenora	43 C/12	52°38′	85°57′
Streatham	UNP/LNO	BC	Range 4 Coast	93 E/16	53°50′	126°15′
Street Lake	LAKE/LAC	NT	Mackenzie	75 P	63°25′	105°18′
Streets Ridge	UNP/LNO	NS	Cumberland	11 E/12	45°43′	63°39′
Streetsville	UNP/LNO	ON	Peel	30 M/12	43°35′	79°42′
Streetsville Junction	UNP/LNO	ON	Peel	30 M/12	43°36′	79°44′
Strehlow	UNP/LNO	SK	34-4-W3	72 O/15	51°54′	106°31′
Strickland	UNP/LNO	ON	Cochrane	42 H/5	49°17′	81°52′
Strickland Pond	LAKE/LAC	NF		11 O/16	47°48′	58°12′
Striding River	RIV/CDE	SK/NT		74 P/16	59°54′	104°08′
Strome	VILG/VILG	AB	23-44-15-W4	83 A/16	52°48′	112°04′
Stromness	UNP/LNO	ON	Haldimand	30 L/13	42°52′	79°33′
Stromness Bay	BAY/BAIE	NT	Franklin	67 D	68°54′	102°40′
Stronach Mountain	UNP/LNO	NS	Annapolis	21 H/3	45°02′	65°00′
Strong	MUN2/AZM2	ON	Parry Sound	31 E/14	45°45′	79°25′
Strong	UNP/LNO	ON	Parry Sound	31 E/11	45°44′	79°28′
Strong	UNP/LNO	SK	15-30-3-W3	72 O/9	51°34′	106°22′
Strong Corner	UNP/LNO	NB	Carleton	21 J/5	46°21′	67°37′
Strongfield	VILG/VILG	SK	26-27-5-W3	72 O/7	51°20′	106°35′
Strong Island	ISL/ÎLE	NF		2 E/6	49°25′	55°19′
Strong Pine	UNP/LNO	SK	23-50-23-W2	73 H/6	53°19′	105°15′
Strong's Island	UNP/LNO	NF		2 E/7	49°29′	54°47′
Strongville	UNP/LNO	ON	Simcoe	31 D/5	44°25′	79°55′
Stroud	UNP/LNO	ON	Simcoe	31 D/5	44°20′	79°36′
Stroud	UNP/LNO	ON	Simcoe	31 D/5	44°19′	79°37′
Struan	UNP/LNO	SK	1-39-12-W3	73 B/5	52°19′	107°36′
Struthers	UNP/LNO	ON	Thunder Bay	42 C/12	48°41′	85°51′
Strutton Islands	ISL/ÎLE	NT	Keewatin	33 D	52°07′	79°01′
Stry	UNP/LNO	AB	27-58-13-W4	73 L/4	54°03′	111°52′
Stryen 9	IR/RI	BC	Kamloops Division Yale	92 I/5	50°17′	121°38′
Stryker Island	ISL/ÎLE	BC	Range 3 Coast	103 A/1	52°07′	128°21′
Stuart	UNP/LNO	ON	Nipissing	31 E/16	45°56′	78°01′
Stuart Bay	BAY/BAIE	NT	Franklin	69 A	76°09′	99°48′
Stuart Bay 6	IR/RI	BC	Clayoquot	92 C/13	48°55′	125°31′
Stuartburn	MUN2/AZM2	MB		62 H/2	49°08′	96°31′
Stuartburn	UNP/LNO	MB	17,18-2-6-E	62 H/2	49°01′	96°46′
Stuart Channel	CHAN/CHEN	BC	Cowichan	92 B/13	49°00′	123°42′
Stuart Island	UNP/LNO	BC	Range 1 Coast	92 K/6	50°22′	125°08′
Stuart Island	ISL/ÎLE	BC	Range 1 Coast	92 K/6	50°23′	125°08′
Stuart Lake	LAKE/LAC	BC	Range 5 Coast	93 K/10	54°36′	124°40′
Stuart Lake 9 - see-voir - Stuart Lake (Hungry Island) 9	IR/RI	BC		93 K/10	54°30′	124°34′
Stuart Lake 10 - see-voir - Stuart Lake (Dunah Island) 10	IR/RI	BC		93 K/10	54°30′	124°35′
Stuart Lake (Dunah Island) 10	IR/RI	BC	Range 5 Coast	93 K/10	54°30′	124°35′
Stuart Lake (Hungry Island) 9	IR/RI	BC	Range 5 Coast	93 K/10	54°30′	124°34′
Stuart River	RIV/CDE	BC	Cariboo	93 G/13	53°59′	123°32′
Stuarts Lake	LAKE/LAC	NS	Queens	20 P/15	43°54′	64°51′
Stuart Town	UNP/LNO	NB	Charlotte	21 G/2	45°01′	66°56′
Stubborn Head	CAPE/CAP	NS	Hants	21 H/1	45°14′	64°02′
Stubbs Point	CAPE/CAP	NT	Franklin	120 G	83°02′	69°00′
Stuckless Cove	UNP/LNO	NF		12 H/15	49°51′	56°33′
Studholm	GEOG/GÉOG	NB	Kings	21 H/13	45°48′	65°37′

NAME NOM	ENTITY ENTITÉ	LOC 1 LIEU 1	LOC 2 LIEU 2	MAP CARTE	POSITION LAT	LONG
Stuie	UNP/LNO	BC	Range 3 Coast	93 D/8	52°22′	126°04′
Stukely	VILG/VILG	QC	Memphrémagog	31 H/8	45°19′	72°25′
Stukely, Lac	LAKE/LAC	QC	Memphrémagog	31 H/8	45°22′	72°15′
Stukely-Sud	TOWN/VIL2	QC	Memphrémagog	31 H/8	45°19′	72°25′
Stukemapten Lake	LAKE/LAC	BC	Kamloops Division Yale	82 M/6	51°20′	119°14′
Stullawheets 8	IR/RI	BC	Yale Division Yale	92 H/6	49°28′	121°25′
Stull Lake	LAKE/LAC	ON/MB		53 K/7	54°24′	92°37′
Stull River	RIV/CDE	MB/ON		53 N/2	55°10′	92°39′
Stum Lake	LAKE/LAC	BC	Cariboo	93 B/6	52°17′	123°02′
Stump Lake	UNP/LNO	SK	1-53-5-W3	73 G/10	53°33′	106°36′
Stump Lake	UNP/LNO	BC	Kamloops Division Yale	92 I/8	50°23′	120°20′
Stump Lake	LAKE/LAC	BC	Kamloops Division Yale	92 I/8	50°22′	120°22′
Stupart	UNP/LNO	ON	Sudbury	41 P/5	47°21′	81°33′
Stupart River	RIV/CDE	MB		53 N/14	56°00′	93°25′
Stupendous Mountain	MTN/MNT	BC	Range 3 Coast	93 D/8	52°23′	126°12′
Sturdee	UNP/LNO	SK	3-25-3-W2	62 M/1	51°12′	102°22′
Sturdee	UNP/LNO	BC	Kootenay	82 N/6	51°25′	117°29′
Sturdies Bay	UNP/LNO	BC	Cowichan	92 B/14	48°53′	123°19′
Sturge Lake	LAKE/LAC	ON	Thunder Bay	52 H/2	49°07′	88°51′
Sturgeon	UNP/LNO	PE	Kings	11 L/2	46°07′	62°32′
Sturgeon	UNP/LNO	AB	19-55-22-W4	83 H/14	53°46′	113°15′
Sturgeon Bay	UNP/LNO	ON	Simcoe	31 D/12	44°44′	79°44′
Sturgeon Bay	BAY/BAIE	MB		62 P/13	52°00′	97°55′
Sturgeon Beach	UNP/LNO	ON	Simcoe	31 D/12	44°44′	79°44′
Sturgeon Creek	UNP/LNO	MB		62 H/14	49°53′	97°18′
Sturgeon Creek	RIV/CDE	ON	Rainy River	52 D/9	48°39′	94°03′
Sturgeon Falls	TOWN/VIL2	ON	Nipissing	31 L/5	46°22′	79°55′
Sturgeon Falls	FALL/CHUT	MB		63 A/2	52°08′	96°45′
Sturgeon Falls 23	IR/RI	ON	Rainy River	52 C/9	48°45′	92°22′
Sturgeon Heights	UNP/LNO	AB	25-70-25-W5	83 N/4	55°05′	117°40′
Sturgeon Lake	LAKE/LAC	ON	Victoria	31 D/7	44°28′	78°43′
Sturgeon Lake	LAKE/LAC	ON	Thunder Bay	52 G/15	50°00′	90°45′
Sturgeon Lake	LAKE/LAC	ON	Kenora	53 O/7	55°24′	90°55′
Sturgeon Lake	LAKE/LAC	ON	Rainy River	52 B/5	48°29′	91°38′
Sturgeon Lake	LAKE/LAC	AB	70,71-23,24-W5	83 N/4	55°06′	117°32′
Sturgeon Lake 101	IR/RI	SK		73 G/8	53°24′	106°02′
Sturgeon Lake 101A	IR/RI	SK		73 G/8	53°28′	106°21′
Sturgeon Lake 154	IR/RI	AB	70-23-W5	83 N/3	55°03′	117°28′
Sturgeon Lake 154A	IR/RI	AB	71-23-W5	83 N/3	55°08′	117°29′
Sturgeon Lake 154B	IR/RI	AB	69-24-W5	83 K/13	54°59′	117°34′
Sturgeon Landing	HAM/HAM	SK		63 K/5	54°16′	101°49′
Sturgeon No. 90, Municipal District of	MUN1/AZM1	AB	56-25-W4	83 H/13	53°49′	113°31′
Sturgeon Point	VILG/VILG	ON	Victoria	31 D/7	44°28′	78°42′
Sturgeon River	UNP/LNO	ON	Thunder Bay	42 E/11	49°40′	87°20′
Sturgeon River	RIV/CDE	ON	Simcoe	31 D/12	44°44′	79°44′
Sturgeon River	RIV/CDE	ON	Nipissing	31 L/5	46°19′	79°58′
Sturgeon River	RIV/CDE	ON	Kenora	52 L/7	50°22′	94°39′
Sturgeon River	RIV/CDE	MB/ON		53 O/11	55°31′	91°23′
Sturgeon River	RIV/CDE	SK	3-49-27-W2	73 H/4	53°12′	105°52′
Sturgeon River	RIV/CDE	AB	23-55-22-W4	83 H/14	53°46′	113°10′
Sturgeon Valley	UNP/LNO	SK	10-51-2-W3	73 G/8	53°23′	106°12′
Sturgeon Weir 184F	IR/RI	SK		63 K/5	54°17′	101°51′
Sturgeon-weir River	RIV/CDE	SK	13-61-30-W	63 K/5	54°16′	101°49′
Sturges Bourne Islands	ISL/ÎLE	NT	Franklin	46 J	66°03′	83°35′
Sturgis	TOWN/VIL2	SK	20-34-4-W2	62 M/15	51°56′	102°32′
Sturt Point	CAPE/CAP	NT	Franklin	67 B	68°47′	103°25′
Styal	UNP/LNO	AB	28-53-8-W5	83 G/11	53°36′	115°06′
Stygge Glacier	GLAC/GLAC	NT	Franklin	39 F	78°43′	78°24′
Stymiest Road	UNP/LNO	NB	Northumberland	21 P/6	47°18′	65°05′
Styx River	RIV/CDE	ON	Grey	41 A/2	44°11′	80°57′
Success	VILG/VILG	SK	25-17-16-W3	72 K/8	50°27′	108°05′
Success Point	CAPE/CAP	NT	Franklin	79 A	76°36′	104°40′
Suce, La	UNP/LNO	QC	Témiscouata	21 N/6	47°18′	69°03′
Sucker Creek 150A	IR/RI	AB	75-14-W5	83 N/8	55°28′	116°07′
Sucker Creek 23	IR/RI	ON	Manitoulin	41 H/13	45°58′	82°00′
Sucker Creek Landing	UNP/LNO	ON	Sudbury	41 I/1	46°13′	80°19′
Sucker Lake	LAKE/LAC	ON	Manitoulin	41 H/12	45°43′	81°52′
Sucker Lake 2	IR/RI	BC	Cassiar	94 F/5	57°23′	125°35′
Sucker River	RIV/CDE	ON	Cochrane	42 H/6	49°21′	81°06′
Sucker, Ruisseau	RIV/CDE	QC	Jamésie	33 L/15	54°58′	78°34′
Sucwoa 6	IR/RI	BC	Nootka	92 E/16	49°48′	126°29′
Sudbury	CITY/VIL1	ON	Sudbury	41 I/7	46°30′	81°00′
Sudbury	MUN1/AZM1	ON	Sudbury	41 I/10	46°32′	81°00′
Sudbury	UNP/LNO	ON	Sudbury	41 I/10	46°31′	80°54′
Sudbury	GEOG/GÉOG	ON		41 O/1	47°10′	82°00′

NAME / NOM	ENTITY / ENTITÉ	LOC 1 / LIEU 1	LOC 2 / LIEU 2	MAP / CARTE	POSITION LAT	POSITION LONG
Sud, Chenal du	CHAN/CHEN	QC	Kamouraska	21 N/13	47°46′	69°46′
Sud-Ouest, Baie du	BAY/BAIE	QC	Jamésie	32 K/11	50°43′	77°05′
Sud-Ouest, Bassin du	BAY/BAIE	QC	La Côte-de-Gaspé	22 A/15	48°49′	64°30′
Sud-Ouest, Pointe du	CAPE/CAP	QC	Minganie	12 E/5	49°23′	63°36′
Sud-Ouest, Pointe du	CAPE/CAP	QC	Pabok	22 A/2	48°09′	64°57′
Sud-Ouest, Rivière du	RIV/CDE	QC	Rimouski-Neigette	22 C/7	48°21′	68°46′
Sud, Pointe du	CAPE/CAP	QC	Minganie	12 E/1	49°04′	62°15′
Sud, Rivière du	RIV/CDE	QC	Montmagny	21 L/15	46°59′	70°33′
Suette, La	UNP/LNO	QC	Communauté urbaine de Québec	21 L/14	46°47′	71°20′
Suez	UNP/LNO	ON	Sudbury	41 I/10	46°40′	80°55′
Suffield	UNP/LNO	AB	34-14-9-W4	72 L/3	50°12′	111°10′
Suffolk	UNP/LNO	PE	Queens	11 L/6	46°20′	63°04′
Suffren	UNP/LNO	MB	7-21-3-W	62 I/13	50°49′	97°50′
Sugar Brook	UNP/LNO	NB	York	21 G/11	45°44′	67°22′
Sugarcane	UNP/LNO	BC	Cariboo	93 A/4	52°06′	121°59′
Sugar Island 37A	IR/RI	ON	Peterborough	31 D/1	44°13′	78°08′
Sugar Lake	LAKE/LAC	BC	Osoyoos Division Yale	82 L/7	50°24′	118°31′
Sugar Loaf	UNP/LNO	NS	Victoria	11 K/16	46°57′	60°28′
Sugarloaf Head	CAPE/CAP	NF		1 N/10	47°37′	52°39′
Sugarloaf Mountain	MTN/MNT	NS	Inverness	11 K/7	46°25′	60°56′
Sugar Loaf Pond	UNP/LNO	QC	Memphrémagog	31 H/1	45°07′	72°20′
Sugden	UNP/LNO	AB	15-62-11-W4	73 L/5	54°23′	111°33′
Suggi Lake	LAKE/LAC	SK		63 L/7	54°22′	102°47′
Sugluk Inlet	BAY/BAIE	NT	Franklin	35 J	62°15′	75°37′
Sukunka River	RIV/CDE	BC	Peace River	93 P/12	55°37′	121°35′
Sullivan	VILG/VILG	QC	Vallée-de-l'Or	32 C/4	48°07′	77°50′
Sullivan	MUN2/AZM2	ON	Grey	41 A/7	44°22′	80°59′
Sullivan	UNP/LNO	ON	York	30 M/14	43°46′	79°19′
Sullivan	UNP/LNO	BC	New Westminster	92 G/2	49°07′	122°48′
Sullivan Bay	UNP/LNO	BC	Range 1 Coast	92 L/15	50°53′	126°49′
Sullivan Heights	UNP/LNO	BC	New Westminster	92 G/7	49°15′	122°54′
Sullivan Lake	UNP/LNO	AB	18-35-13-W4	73 D/4	52°00′	111°52′
Sullivan Lake	LAKE/LAC	AB	34,37-14,15-W4	83 A/1	52°00′	112°00′
Sullivan Lake	LAKE/LAC	BC	Kamloops Division Yale	92 I/16	50°58′	120°07′
Sullivan River	RIV/CDE	BC	Kootenay	82 N/13	51°58′	117°49′
Sully	UNP/LNO	QC	Témiscouata	21 N/6	47°27′	69°09′
Sulphide	UNP/LNO	ON	Hastings	31 C/11	44°31′	77°14′
Sulphur	UNP/LNO	YT		115 O/15	63°45′	138°53′
Sulphur Bay	BAY/BAIE	NT	Mackenzie	85 G/5	61°24′	115°57′
Sulphur Mountain Cosmic Ray Station National Historic Site - also-aussi - Station-d'Étude-des-Rayons-Cosmiques-du-Mont-Sulphur, Lieu historique national de la	PARK/PARC	AB		82 O/4	51°09′	115°35′
Sulphurous Lake	LAKE/LAC	BC	Lillooet	92 P/10	51°38′	120°50′
Sulphur Point	CAPE/CAP	NT	Mackenzie	85 B	60°56′	114°48′
Sulphur River	RIV/CDE	AB	56-8-W6	83 E/14	53°50′	119°10′
Sultan	UNP/LNO	ON	Sudbury	41 O/10	47°36′	82°45′
Sulut Bay	BAY/BAIE	NT	Franklin	26 A	64°47′	65°40′
Sumallo River	RIV/CDE	BC	Yale Division Yale	92 H/3	49°13′	121°05′
Sumas Cemetery 12	IR/RI	BC	New Westminster	92 G/1	49°08′	122°06′
Sumas River	RIV/CDE	BC	New Westminster	92 G/1	49°09′	122°07′
Summer Beaver	UNP/LNO	ON	Kenora	53 A/10	52°45′	88°31′
Summerberry	HAM/HAM	SK	7-17-8-W2	62 L/6	50°25′	103°06′
Summercove	UNP/LNO	SK	24-4-8-W3	72 G/7	49°19′	106°57′
Summerfield	UNP/LNO	PE	Queens	11 L/5	46°24′	63°33′
Summerfield	UNP/LNO	NB	Kings	21 H/13	45°50′	65°34′
Summerfield	UNP/LNO	NB	Carleton	21 J/12	46°32′	67°41′
Summerfield Beach	HAM/HAM	SK		73 F/1	53°02′	108°19′
Summerford	TOWN/VIL2	NF		2 E/7	49°29′	54°47′
Summerhill	UNP/LNO	ON	Huron	40 P/12	43°41′	81°32′
Summerland	MUN1/AZM1	BC	Osoyoos Division Yale	82 E/12	49°36′	119°40′
Summers Corners	UNP/LNO	ON	Elgin	40 I/15	42°46′	80°56′
Summers Creek	RIV/CDE	BC	Kamloops Division Yale	92 H/10	49°32′	120°31′
Summerside	CITY/VIL1	PE	Prince	11 L/5	46°24′	63°47′
Summerside	UNP/LNO	NF		12 A/13	48°59′	57°59′
Summerside	UNP/LNO	NS	Antigonish	11 F/12	45°36′	61°47′
Summerside 38	IR/RI	NS	Antigonish	11 F/12	45°37′	61°46′
Summerside Harbour	BAY/BAIE	PE	Prince	11 L/5	46°23′	63°48′
Summerstown	UNP/LNO	ON	Glengarry	31 G/2	45°04′	74°33′
Summerstown Station	UNP/LNO	ON	Glengarry	31 G/2	45°05′	74°36′
Summerview	UNP/LNO	AB	21-7-29-W4	82 H/12	49°35′	113°53′
Summerville	UNP/LNO	NF		2 C/5	48°27′	53°33′
Summerville	UNP/LNO	PE	Queens	11 L/2	46°13′	62°46′
Summerville	UNP/LNO	NS	Hants	21 H/1	45°06′	64°10′
Summerville	UNP/LNO	NB	Kings	21 G/8	45°21′	66°06′
Summerville	UNP/LNO	ON	Peel	30 M/12	43°37′	79°34′
Summerville Centre	UNP/LNO	NS	Queens	20 P/15	43°57′	64°49′
*Summerville Station	UNP/LNO	ON		30 M/12	43°37′	79°33′

NAME NOM	ENTITY ENTITÉ	LOC 1 LIEU 1	LOC 2 LIEU 2	MAP CARTE	POSITION LAT	LONG
Summit	UNP/LNO	NB	Restigouche	22 B/1	48°03′	66°27′
Summit	UNP/LNO	NB	Victoria	21 J/11	46°42′	67°14′
Summit	UNP/LNO	QC	Pabok	22 A/9	48°31′	64°20′
Summit	UNP/LNO	QC	Les Laurentides	31 J/1	46°08′	74°27′
Summit	UNP/LNO	ON	Wentworth	40 P/1	43°14′	80°03′
Summit	UNP/LNO	ON	Algoma	41 N/1	47°09′	84°11′
Summit Depot	UNP/LNO	NB	Restigouche	21 N/16	47°47′	68°19′
Summit Lake	UNP/LNO	BC	Kootenay	82 K/4	50°10′	117°40′
Summit Lake	UNP/LNO	BC	Cariboo	93 J/7	54°15′	122°38′
Summit Lake	UNP/LNO	BC	Peace River	94 K/10	58°39′	124°38′
Summit Lake	LAKE/LAC	ON	Thunder Bay	42 L/5	50°25′	87°45′
Summit Lake	LAKE/LAC	BC	Cariboo	93 J/7	54°17′	122°40′
Summit Lake	LAKE/LAC	BC	Cassiar	104 B/1	56°13′	130°05′
Summit Roadhouse	UNP/LNO	YT		115 P/1	63°05′	136°26′
Sunbreaker Cove	VILG/VILG	AB	26-39-2-W5	83 B/8	52°24′	114°11′
Sunbury	UNP/LNO	NB	Sunbury	21 J/1	46°12′	66°10′
Sunbury	UNP/LNO	ON	Frontenac	31 C/8	44°23′	76°26′
Sunbury	UNP/LNO	BC	New Westminster	92 G/2	49°09′	122°59′
Sunbury	GEOG/GÉOG	NB		21 G/16	45°55′	66°20′
Sunchild 202	IR/RI	AB	42-10-W5	83 B/11	52°41′	115°20′
Suncrest	UNP/LNO	BC	New Westminster	92 G/3	49°13′	123°01′
Sundance	UNP/LNO	MB	21-87-22-E	54 D/9	56°32′	94°04′
Sundance	UNP/LNO	AB	36-52-5-W5	83 G/10	53°32′	114°36′
Sundance	UNP/LNO	BC	Peace River	93 P/11	55°43′	121°15′
Sundance Beach	VILG/VILG	AB	29-47-1-W5	83 G/1	53°05′	114°06′
Sunday Cove Island	ISL/ÎLE	NF		2 E/12	49°33′	55°48′
Sunday Inlet	BAY/BAIE	BC	Queen Charlotte	103 B/12	52°39′	131°55′
Sunday Lake	LAKE/LAC	NF		2 D/14	48°51′	55°25′
Sundayman's Meadow 3	IR/RI	BC	Range 4 Coast	93 F/1	53°07′	124°20′
Sunday Peak	MTN/MNT	BC	Cassiar	104 M/9	59°45′	134°06′
Sunderland	UNP/LNO	ON	Ontario	31 D/6	44°16′	79°04′
Sunderland Channel	CHAN/CHEN	BC	Range 1 Coast	92 K/5	50°28′	125°53′
Sundown	UNP/LNO	MB	1-2-9-E	62 H/1	49°06′	96°16′
Sundre	TOWN/VIL2	AB	3-33-5-W5	82 O/15	51°48′	114°38′
Sundridge	VILG/VILG	ON	Parry Sound	31 E/14	45°46′	79°24′
Sundridge	UNP/LNO	NS	Pictou	11 E/10	45°43′	62°51′
Suni	UNP/LNO	ON	Thunder Bay	42 L/3	50°14′	87°20′
Sunken Lake	UNP/LNO	NS	Kings	21 A/16	44°59′	64°26′
Sunkist Beach	UNP/LNO	ON	York	31 D/6	44°20′	79°16′
Sunland	UNP/LNO	AB	1-58-16-W4	83 H/16	53°58′	112°15′
Sunlight Lake	LAKE/LAC	ON	Kenora	52 K/7	50°29′	92°33′
Sunnidale - see-voir - Clearview	MUN2/AZM2	ON		41 A/8	44°24′	80°04′
Sunnidale	UNP/LNO	ON	Simcoe	31 D/5	44°22′	80°00′
Sunnidale Corners	UNP/LNO	ON	Simcoe	41 A/8	44°26′	80°01′
Sunningdale	UNP/LNO	ON	Halton	30 M/5	43°28′	79°43′
Sunningdale	UNP/LNO	SK		72 I/5	50°25′	105°33′
Sunningdale	UNP/LNO	BC	Kootenay	82 F/4	49°07′	117°43′
Sunny Acres	UNP/LNO	NB	Westmorland	21 I/2	46°07′	64°46′
Sunny Acres West	UNP/LNO	NB	Westmorland	21 I/2	46°07′	64°46′
Sunny Bank	UNP/LNO	QC	La Côte-de-Gaspé	22 A/15	48°50′	64°36′
Sunny Brae	UNP/LNO	NS	Pictou	11 E/7	45°24′	62°30′
Sunnybrae - see-voir - Sunny Brae	UNP/LNO	NS		11 E/7	45°24′	62°30′
Sunny Brae	UNP/LNO	NB	Westmorland	21 I/2	46°06′	64°46′
Sunnybrae	UNP/LNO	ON	Northumberland	31 C/5	44°20′	77°55′
Sunnybrae	UNP/LNO	BC	Kamloops Division Yale	82 L/14	50°46′	119°16′
Sunnybrook	UNP/LNO	NS	Lunenburg	21 A/8	44°25′	64°21′
Sunnybrook	UNP/LNO	AB	3-49-2-W5	83 G/1	53°12′	114°13′
Sunny Corner	UNP/LNO	NB	Northumberland	21 I/13	46°56′	65°49′
Sunnydale	UNP/LNO	AB	36-25-5-W4	72 M/2	51°11′	110°35′
Sunnyglen	UNP/LNO	SK	6-39-23-W3	73 C/6	52°19′	109°18′
Sunny Lake	LAKE/LAC	NT	Mackenzie	106 N	67°51′	132°41′
Sunnynook	UNP/LNO	AB	8-27-12-W4	72 M/5	51°17′	111°40′
Sunnyside	TOWN/VIL2	NF		1 N/13	47°51′	53°55′
Sunnyside	UNP/LNO	NF		2 E/10	49°38′	54°37′
Sunnyside	UNP/LNO	NF		13 J/13	54°51′	59°48′
Sunnyside	UNP/LNO	NB	Restigouche	21 O/16	47°51′	66°04′
Sunnyside	UNP/LNO	ON	York	30 M/11	43°38′	79°27′
Sunnyside	UNP/LNO	ON	Simcoe	31 D/13	44°46′	79°54′
Sunnyside	UNP/LNO	SK		72 I/5	50°23′	105°35′
Sunnyside	UNP/LNO	BC	New Westminster	92 G/2	49°03′	122°47′
Sunnyside	UNP/LNO	BC	Range 5 Coast	93 K/10	54°39′	124°44′
Sunnyside Beach	UNP/LNO	SK	11-53-27-W2	73 H/12	53°34′	105°53′
Sunny Slope	UNP/LNO	ON	Parry Sound	31 E/12	45°37′	79°53′
Sunnyslope	UNP/LNO	AB	13-31-26-W4	82 P/12	51°39′	113°33′
Sunnyville	UNP/LNO	NS	Guysborough	11 F/5	45°23′	61°32′

NAME NOM	ENTITY ENTITÉ	LOC 1 LIEU 1	LOC 2 LIEU 2	MAP CARTE	POSITION LAT	POSITION LONG
Sunpoke	UNP/LNO	NB	Sunbury	21 G/15	45°47′	66°35′
Sunrise	UNP/LNO	NS	Victoria	11 K/15	46°52′	60°33′
Sunrise Beach	VILG/VILG	AB	26,34,35-55-1-W5	83 G/16	53°47′	114°03′
Sunrise Beach	UNP/LNO	ON	Ontario	31 D/2	44°10′	78°52′
Sunrise Valley	UNP/LNO	BC	Peace River	93 P/15	55°52′	120°40′
Sunset	UNP/LNO	BC	New Westminster	92 G/3	49°13′	123°05′
Sunset Acres	UNP/LNO	NS	Halifax	11 D/11	44°41′	63°29′
Sunset Bay	UNP/LNO	MB	18-16-13-E	52 L/5	50°20′	95°48′
Sunset Beach	VILG/VILG	AB	26-66-24-W4	83 I/12	54°44′	113°32′
Sunset Beach	HAM/HAM	SK	5-19-5-W2	62 L/10	50°36′	102°40′
Sunset Beach	UNP/LNO	ON	York	31 D/6	44°20′	79°16′
Sunset Beach	UNP/LNO	ON	Muskoka	31 E/3	45°04′	79°29′
Sunset Beach	UNP/LNO	ON	Simcoe	31 D/13	44°46′	79°46′
Sunset Beach	UNP/LNO	ON	Huron	40 P/13	43°47′	81°43′
Sunset Beach	UNP/LNO	ON	Essex	40 J/3	42°03′	83°07′
Sunset Beach	UNP/LNO	MB	5-18-7-E	62 I/10	50°31′	96°36′
Sunset Beach	UNP/LNO	BC	New Westminster	92 G/6	49°24′	123°15′
Sunset Corners	UNP/LNO	ON	Peel	30 M/13	43°46′	79°39′
Sunset Cove	VILG/VILG	SK	28-21-22-W2	72 I/14	50°49′	105°00′
Sunset Creek	RIV/CDE	BC	Kamloops Division Yale	82 M/11	51°39′	119°10′
Sunset House	UNP/LNO	AB	5-71-19-W5	83 N/2	55°07′	116°52′
Sunset Park	UNP/LNO	ON	Nipissing	31 L/6	46°16′	79°27′
Sunset Point	VILG/VILG	AB	26-54-3-W5	83 G/9	53°42′	114°21′
Sunset Prairie	UNP/LNO	BC	Peace River	93 P/15	55°51′	120°46′
Sunset Valley	UNP/LNO	NB	Kings	21 G/8	45°23′	66°17′
Sunset View	UNP/LNO	ON	Ontario	31 D/2	44°09′	78°55′
Sunset View Beach	VILG/VILG	SK	5,6-53-18-W3	73 F/10	53°33′	108°38′
Sunshine	UNP/LNO	ON	Huron	40 P/14	43°47′	81°20′
Sunshine	UNP/LNO	ON	Thunder Bay	52 A/12	48°33′	89°41′
Sunshine	UNP/LNO	BC	New Westminster	92 G/7	49°21′	122°55′
Sunshine Bay	UNP/LNO	BC	Kamloops Division Yale	82 F/11	49°36′	117°00′
Sunshine Coast	MUN1/AZM1	BC	New Westminster	92 J/4	50°00′	123°45′
Sunshine Hills	UNP/LNO	BC	New Westminster	92 G/2	49°07′	122°54′
Sunshine Valley	UNP/LNO	BC	Yale Division Yale	92 H/6	49°16′	121°14′
Sunstrum	UNP/LNO	ON	Kenora	52 K/2	50°03′	92°34′
Sun Valley	VILG/VILG	SK	34-19-26-W2	72 I/12	50°39′	105°32′
Sun Valley	UNP/LNO	BC	New Westminster	92 G/7	49°17′	122°44′
Sunville	UNP/LNO	MB	34-19-13-W	62 J/11	50°40′	99°11′
Sunwapta Falls	FALL/CHUT	AB	41-26-W5	83 C/12	52°32′	117°39′
Sunwapta Pass	VALL/VALL	AB	37-22,23-W5	83 C/3	52°13′	117°10′
Suomi	UNP/LNO	ON	Thunder Bay	52 A/4	48°14′	89°59′
Superb	UNP/LNO	SK	35-33-25-W3	72 N/14	51°53′	109°27′
Supérieur, Lac - also-aussi - **Superior, Lake**	LAKE/LAC	ON		42 D	48°00′	87°00′
Superior Junction	UNP/LNO	ON	Kenora	52 J/4	50°06′	91°45′
Superior, Lake - also-aussi - **Supérieur, Lac**	LAKE/LAC	ON		42 D	48°00′	87°00′
Supreme	UNP/LNO	SK	28-2-26-W3	72 F/3	49°09′	109°25′
Suquash	UNP/LNO	BC	Rupert	92 L/11	50°38′	127°15′
Surbiton	UNP/LNO	SK	9-28-9-W3	72 O/6	51°23′	107°14′
Sureau, Lac	LAKE/LAC	QC	Jamésie	23 E/2	53°01′	70°47′
Surettes Island	UNP/LNO	NS	Yarmouth	20 P/13	43°46′	65°56′
Surf Inlet	BAY/BAIE	BC	Range 3 Coast	103 A/14	52°57′	129°01′
Surge Narrows	UNP/LNO	BC	Sayward	92 K/3	50°14′	125°07′
Surprise	UNP/LNO	SK	20-15-29-W3	72 K/5	50°16′	109°58′
Surprise	UNP/LNO	BC	Cassiar	104 N/11	59°38′	133°25′
Surprise Creek	RIV/CDE	YT		117 B/1	68°14′	140°25′
Surprise Fiord	BAY/BAIE	NT	Franklin	59 E	78°15′	90°00′
Surprise, Lac	LAKE/LAC	QC	Jamésie	32 G/7	49°21′	74°53′
Surprise Lake	LAKE/LAC	BC	Cassiar	104 N/11	59°41′	133°14′
Surprise Valley No. 9	MUN2/AZM2	SK		72 H/2	49°10′	104°35′
Surrey	CITY/VIL1	BC	New Westminster	92 G/2	49°07′	122°45′
Surrey	UNP/LNO	PE	Queens	11 L/2	46°04′	62°49′
Surrey	UNP/LNO	NB	Albert	21 H/15	45°55′	64°38′
Surrey Centre	UNP/LNO	BC	New Westminster	92 G/2	49°07′	122°45′
Surrey Lake	LAKE/LAC	NT	Franklin	77 D/12	69°40′	107°13′
Surveyor Channel	SEAU/SMER	—		5.03	57°15′	145°40′
Surveyor Gap	SEAU/SMER	—		5.03	56°15′	144°50′
Susan Island	ISL/ÎLE	BC	Range 3 Coast	103 A/8	52°30′	128°21′
Susap Creek	RIV/CDE	BC	Similkameen Division Yale	82 E/4	49°06′	119°44′
Susk 17	IR/RI	BC	Queen Charlotte	103 F/14	53°56′	133°08′
Suskwa River	RIV/CDE	BC	Cassiar	93 M/3	55°14′	127°26′
Sussex	TOWN/VIL2	NB	Kings	21 H/12	45°43′	65°31′
Sussex	GEOG/GÉOG	NB	Kings	21 H/12	45°40′	65°33′
Sussex Corner	VILG/VILG	NB	Kings	21 H/11	45°43′	65°29′
Sustut Lake	LAKE/LAC	BC	Cassiar	94 D/9	56°35′	126°27′
Sustut Peak	MTN/MNT	BC	Cassiar	94 D/10	56°35′	126°35′

NAME / NOM	ENTITY / ENTITÉ	LOC 1 / LIEU 1	LOC 2 / LIEU 2	MAP / CARTE	POSITION LAT	POSITION LONG
Sustut River	RIV/CDE	BC	Cassiar	94 D/6	56°19′	127°22′
Sutaquis 18	IR/RI	BC	Clayoquot	92 F/4	49°14′	125°57′
Sutcliffe Lake	LAKE/LAC	NT	Keewatin	65 G	61°44′	99°14′
Sutherland	UNP/LNO	ON	Essex	40 J/6	42°18′	83°04′
Sutherland	UNP/LNO	SK		73 B/2	52°08′	106°36′
Sutherland River	RIV/CDE	BC	Range 5 Coast	93 K/6	54°29′	125°11′
Sutherland Siding	UNP/LNO	NB	York	21 J/7	46°17′	66°41′
Sutherlands River	UNP/LNO	NS	Pictou	11 E/9	45°35′	62°30′
Sutil, Cape	CAPE/CAP	BC	Rupert	102 I/16	50°53′	128°03′
Sutil Channel	CHAN/CHEN	BC	Sayward	92 K/3	50°08′	125°04′
Sutil Point	CAPE/CAP	BC	Sayward	92 K/2	50°01′	124°59′
Sutlahine River	RIV/CDE	BC	Cassiar	104 K/10	58°45′	132°46′
Sutlej Channel	CHAN/CHEN	BC	Range 1 Coast	92 L/15	50°53′	126°44′
Sutorville	UNP/LNO	ON	Lambton	40 I/13	42°54′	81°58′
Sutton	CITY/VIL1	QC	Brome-Missisquoi	31 H/2	45°06′	72°37′
Sutton	VILG/VILG	QC	Brome-Missisquoi	31 H/2	45°05′	72°35′
Sutton	UNP/LNO	ON	York	31 D/6	44°18′	79°22′
Sutton Bay	UNP/LNO	ON	Timiskaming	31 M/12	47°34′	79°35′
Sutton Junction	UNP/LNO	QC	Brome-Missisquoi	31 H/2	45°09′	72°36′
Sutton Lake	LAKE/LAC	ON	Kenora	43 K/7	54°15′	84°44′
Sutton, Monts	MTN/MNT	QC	Brome-Missisquoi	31 H/2	45°05′	72°30′
Sutton No. 103	MUN2/AZM2	SK		72 G/16	49°55′	106°10′
Sutton Range	MTN/MNT	BC	Rupert	92 L/1	50°05′	126°15′
Sutton River	RIV/CDE	ON	Kenora	43 O/4	55°15′	83°45′
Sutton River	RIV/CDE	NT	Franklin	45 O	63°45′	83°47′
Suwannee Lake	LAKE/LAC	MB		64 C/1	56°08′	100°10′
Suzor-Coté, Lac	LAKE/LAC	QC	Le Fjord-du-Saguenay	22 D/3	48°02′	71°27′
Svarte Fiord	BAY/BAIE	NT	Franklin	49 C	77°40′	84°36′
Svarten, Cape	CAPE/CAP	NT	Franklin	48 G	75°37′	87°20′
Svartfjeld Peninsula	CAPE/CAP	NT	Franklin	340 B	80°51′	87°30′
Svendsen Peninsula	CAPE/CAP	NT	Franklin	49 C	77°45′	84°00′
Sverdrup, Cape	CAPE/CAP	NT	Franklin	77 E/16	70°59′	104°18′
Sverdrup Channel	CHAN/CHEN	NT	Franklin	69 H	80°00′	97°45′
Sverdrup Inlet	BAY/BAIE	NT	Franklin	48 G	75°27′	86°12′
Sverdrup Islands	ISL/ÎLE	NT	Franklin	69 E	79°00′	96°00′
Sverre, Cape	CAPE/CAP	NT	Franklin	69 E/14	78°49′	98°12′
Swabs Dock	UNP/LNO	NF		1 M/3	47°08′	55°30′
Swaffield Harbour	BAY/BAIE	NT	Keewatin	35 L	62°23′	79°43′
Swahliseah 14	IR/RI	BC	Yale Division Yale	92 H/6	49°25′	121°25′
Swain Post	UNP/LNO	ON	Kenora	52 N/7	51°17′	92°42′
Swakum Mountain	MTN/MNT	BC	Kamloops Division Yale	92 I/7	50°17′	120°42′
Swale Island	ISL/ÎLE	NF		2 C/12	48°36′	53°45′
Swale Tickle	CHAN/CHEN	NF		2 C/12	48°35′	53°43′
Swallop Creek	RIV/CDE	BC	Range 3 Coast	93 D/10	52°40′	126°58′
Swalwell	UNP/LNO	AB	9-30-24-W4	82 P/11	51°34′	113°19′
Swalwell Lake	LAKE/LAC	BC	Osoyoos Division Yale	82 L/3	50°03′	119°14′
Swamp-Hôtel	UNP/LNO	QC	Pontiac	31 K/1	46°10′	76°19′
Swampy Bay, Rivière	RIV/CDE	QC	Kativik	24 C/14	56°52′	69°04′
Swan 35	IR/RI	BC	Clayoquot	92 E/8	49°22′	126°17′
Swan Bay	BAY/BAIE	MB		64 B/10	56°39′	98°43′
Swan Bay	BAY/BAIE	SK		64 E/7	57°27′	102°50′
Swan Creek	UNP/LNO	NB	Sunbury	21 G/16	45°51′	66°18′
Swan Creek	RIV/CDE	NB	Sunbury	21 G/16	45°51′	66°16′
Swan Crossing	UNP/LNO	ON	Grenville	31 B/13	44°59′	75°42′
Swanger Cove	UNP/LNO	NF		1 M/13	47°53′	55°51′
Swan Hills	TOWN/VIL2	AB	14-66-10-W5	83 J/11	54°43′	115°24′
Swan Hills	MTN/MNT	AB		83 J/12	54°45′	115°45′
Swan Island	ISL/ÎLE	NF		2 E/6	49°28′	55°03′
Swan Lake	UNP/LNO	MB	20-5-10-W	62 G/7	49°25′	98°47′
Swan Lake	LAKE/LAC	ON	Kenora	53 J/6	54°17′	91°12′
Swan Lake	LAKE/LAC	ON	Kenora	52 L/2	50°03′	94°54′
Swan Lake	LAKE/LAC	MB	4,5-11-W	62 G/7	49°22′	98°56′
Swan Lake	LAKE/LAC	MB		63 C/7	52°30′	100°44′
Swan Lake	LAKE/LAC	BC	Osoyoos Division Yale	82 L/6	50°19′	119°15′
Swan Lake	LAKE/LAC	BC	Cassiar	103 P/15	55°47′	128°39′
Swan Lake 3	IR/RI	BC	Lillooet	92 O/16	51°51′	122°07′
Swan Lake 7	IR/RI	MB		62 G/7	49°24′	98°53′
Swan Lake 29	IR/RI	ON	Kenora	52 L/2	50°03′	94°57′
Swan Lake 65C	IR/RI	MB		63 C/10	52°31′	100°52′
Swan Lake Reserve	UNP/LNO	MB	15,16-5-11-W	62 G/7	49°23′	98°53′
Swan Lakes	LAKE/LAC	SK	67,68-4-W3	73 J/15	54°51′	106°33′
Swan Landing	UNP/LNO	AB	14,15-50-27-W5	83 F/5	53°19′	117°51′
Swannell Ranges	MTN/MNT	BC	Cassiar	94 C/5	56°25′	125°40′
Swannell River	RIV/CDE	BC	Cassiar	94 C/11	56°44′	125°06′
Swan Plain	HAM/HAM	SK	36-1-W2	63 D/1	52°07′	102°03′

NAME NOM	ENTITY ENTITÉ	LOC 1 LIEU 1	LOC 2 LIEU 2	MAP CARTE	POSITION	
					LAT	LONG
Swan River	TOWN/VIL2	MB		63 C/3	52°06′	101°16′
Swan River	MUN2/AZM2	MB		63 C/3	52°00′	101°25′
Swan River	RIV/CDE	ON	Kenora	43 G/9	53°35′	82°13′
Swan River	RIV/CDE	MB/SK		63 C/7	52°30′	100°45′
Swan River	RIV/CDE	AB	74-9-W5	83 O/6	55°26′	115°18′
Swan River 150E	IR/RI	AB	73-10-W5	83 O/5	55°22′	115°31′
Swan River Valley	UNP/LNO	MB	SW15-37-27-W	63 C/3	52°11′	101°15′
Swansea	UNP/LNO	NF		1 N/14	47°45′	53°16′
Swansea	UNP/LNO	ON	York	30 M/11	43°38′	79°28′
Swansea	UNP/LNO	BC	Kootenay	82 G/5	49°25′	115°51′
Swanson	UNP/LNO	ON	Algoma	42 C/7	48°29′	84°32′
Swanson	UNP/LNO	SK	36-31-9-W3	72 O/11	51°42′	107°09′
Swanson Channel	CHAN/CHEN	BC	Cowichan	92 B/14	48°46′	123°20′
Swanson Island	ISL/ÎLE	BC	Range 1 Coast	92 L/10	50°37′	126°42′
Swans Shore	UNP/LNO	NB	York	21 G/11	45°38′	67°01′
Swarthmore	UNP/LNO	SK	33-41-21-W3	73 C/10	52°35′	108°59′
Swartz Bay	UNP/LNO	BC	North Saanich	92 B/11	48°41′	123°25′
Swastika	UNP/LNO	ON	Timiskaming	42 A/1	48°06′	80°06′
Sweaburg	UNP/LNO	ON	Oxford	40 P/2	43°04′	80°46′
Sweathouse Creek	UNP/LNO	AB	69-19-W5	83 N/2	55°01′	116°53′
Sweeney Settlement	UNP/LNO	NB	Madawaska	21 N/9	47°31′	68°25′
Sweeneyville	UNP/LNO	NB	Kent	21 I/7	46°20′	64°58′
Sweet Bay	UNP/LNO	NF		2 C/5	48°26′	53°39′
Sweet Bay	BAY/BAIE	NF		2 C/5	48°30′	53°39′
Sweeteen 3	IR/RI	BC	New Westminster	92 G/16	49°58′	122°27′
Sweetgrass	UNP/LNO	SK		73 C/15	52°45′	108°41′
Sweetgrass 113	IR/RI	SK		73 C/15	52°45′	108°42′
Sweetgrass 113A	IR/RI	SK		73 C/15	52°53′	108°38′
Sweetgrass 113B	IR/RI	SK		73 C/15	52°53′	108°48′
Sweetgrass Landing	UNP/LNO	AB	26-114-12-W4	74 L/13	58°55′	111°58′
Sweetland	UNP/LNO	NS	Lunenburg	21 A/7	44°28′	64°31′
Sweetsbridge	UNP/LNO	BC	Kamloops Division Yale	82 L/6	50°27′	119°29′
Sweets Corner	UNP/LNO	NS	Hants	21 A/16	44°59′	64°03′
Sweets Corners	UNP/LNO	ON	Leeds	31 C/9	44°31′	76°10′
Sweets Corners	UNP/LNO	ON	Haldimand	30 L/13	42°50′	79°48′
Sweetwater	UNP/LNO	BC	Peace River	93 P/16	55°55′	120°26′
Swift	UNP/LNO	BC	New Westminster	92 G/14	49°54′	123°10′
*Swift Creek	UNP/LNO	BC	Cariboo	83 D/14	52°51′	119°17′
Swift Current	CITY/VIL1	SK		72 J/5	50°17′	107°48′
Swift Current	UNP/LNO	NF		1 M/16	47°53′	54°12′
Swift Current	BAY/BAIE	NF		1 M/16	47°54′	54°15′
Swift Current Creek	RIV/CDE	SK	27-19-13-W3	72 J/12	50°38′	107°44′
Swift Current No. 137	MUN2/AZM2	SK		72 J/4	50°15′	107°50′
Swift Rapids	UNP/LNO	ON	Simcoe	31 D/13	44°51′	79°33′
Swift River	UNP/LNO	YT		105 B/3	60°00′	131°11′
Swift River	RIV/CDE	BC	Cariboo	93 G/1	53°01′	122°06′
Swift River	RIV/CDE	BC/YT		104 N/16	59°44′	132°11′
Swiftwater	UNP/LNO	BC	Cariboo	83 D/14	52°59′	119°18′
Swinburne	UNP/LNO	SK	32-40-23-W3	73 C/6	52°29′	109°17′
Swinburne, Cape	CAPE/CAP	NT	Franklin	67 H	71°17′	98°41′
Swindle Island	ISL/ÎLE	BC	Range 3 Coast	103 A/7	52°32′	128°35′
Swindon	UNP/LNO	ON	Parry Sound	31 E/6	45°29′	79°12′
Swinnerton Peninsula	CAPE/CAP	NT	Franklin	49 D	77°21′	81°35′
Swinton Park	UNP/LNO	ON	Grey	41 A/2	44°09′	80°35′
Switsemalph 3	IR/RI	BC	Kamloops Division Yale	82 L/11	50°43′	119°20′
Switsemalph 6	IR/RI	BC	Kamloops Division Yale	82 L/11	50°44′	119°19′
Switsemalph 7	IR/RI	BC	Kamloops Division Yale	82 L/11	50°42′	119°18′
Switzerville	UNP/LNO	ON	Lennox and Addington	31 C/7	44°17′	76°51′
Swords	UNP/LNO	ON	Parry Sound	31 E/5	45°21′	79°47′
Sybouts	UNP/LNO	SK	14-1-19-W2	72 H/1	49°02′	104°27′
Sydenham	MUN2/AZM2	ON	Grey	41 A/10	44°36′	80°50′
Sydenham	UNP/LNO	ON	Frontenac	31 C/7	44°25′	76°36′
Sydenham Lake	LAKE/LAC	ON	Frontenac	31 C/7	44°25′	76°33′
Sydenham Place	UNP/LNO	QC	Drummond	31 H/16	45°48′	72°14′
Sydenham River	RIV/CDE	ON	Grey	41 A/10	44°34′	80°57′
Sydenham River	RIV/CDE	ON	Kent	40 J/9	42°33′	82°25′
Sydkap Glacier	GLAC/GLAC	NT	Franklin	49 B	76°36′	85°03′
Sydkap Ice Cap	GLAC/GLAC	NT	Franklin	49 B	76°50′	85°30′
Sydney	UNP/LNO	NS	Cape Breton	11 K/1	46°09′	60°11′
Sydney 28A	IR/RI	NS	Cape Breton	11 K/1	46°10′	60°10′
Sydney Bay	BAY/BAIE	ON	Bruce	41 A/14	44°54′	81°05′
Sydney Cove	UNP/LNO	NF		2 C/13	48°59′	53°45′
Sydney Forks	UNP/LNO	NS	Cape Breton	11 K/1	46°03′	60°18′
Sydney Harbour	BAY/BAIE	NS	Cape Breton	11 K/1	46°13′	60°14′
Sydney Inlet	BAY/BAIE	BC	Clayoquot	92 E/8	49°26′	126°15′

NAME NOM	ENTITY ENTITÉ	LOC 1 LIEU 1	LOC 2 LIEU 2	MAP CARTE	POSITION LAT	LONG
Sydney Lake	LAKE/LAC	ON	Kenora	52 L/9	50°41′	94°25′
Sydney Mines	UNP/LNO	NS	Cape Breton	11 K/1	46°14′	60°14′
Sydney River	UNP/LNO	NS	Cape Breton	11 K/1	46°07′	60°13′
Sydney Webb Point	CAPE/CAP	NT	Franklin	68 B	72°10′	100°55′
Sykeston	UNP/LNO	ON	Lambton	40 J/16	42°53′	82°16′
Sylvan	UNP/LNO	ON	Middlesex	40 P/4	43°09′	81°46′
Sylvan	UNP/LNO	MB	9-24-1-E	62 P/3	51°04′	97°23′
Sylvan Glen	UNP/LNO	AB	30-64-26-W4	83 I/12	54°33′	113°55′
Sylvan Glen Beach	UNP/LNO	ON	Ontario	31 D/11	44°36′	79°07′
Sylvania	HAM/HAM	SK	8-43-14-W2	73 A/9	52°42′	104°00′
Sylvan Lake	TOWN/VIL2	AB	38-1-W5	83 B/8	52°19′	114°05′
Sylvan Lake	LAKE/LAC	AB	39-1,2-W5	83 B/8	52°21′	114°10′
Sylvan Lake	LAKE/LAC	BC	Kootenay	82 G/12	49°31′	115°43′
Sylvan Lake	LAKE/LAC	NT	Mackenzie	75 B	60°55′	106°42′
Sylvan Lake Provincial Park	PARK/PARC	AB	33-38-1-W5	83 B/8	52°19′	114°05′
Sylvan Valley	UNP/LNO	NS	Antigonish	11 E/9	45°38′	62°01′
Sylvan Valley	UNP/LNO	ON	Algoma	41 J/5	46°28′	83°59′
Sylvester	UNP/LNO	NS	Pictou	11 E/10	45°37′	62°46′
Sylvester	UNP/LNO	AB	19-69-11-W6	83 L/13	55°00′	119°41′
Sylvester, Mount	MTN/MNT	NF		2 D/3	48°10′	55°04′
Sylvia Grinnell Lake	LAKE/LAC	NT	Franklin	26 C	64°10′	69°25′
Sylvia Grinnell River	RIV/CDE	NT	Franklin	25 N/10	63°44′	68°34′
Sylvia, Mount	MTN/MNT	BC	Peace River	94 K/1	58°05′	124°28′
Synet	UNP/LNO	QC	Sept-Rivières	22 G/11	49°36′	67°13′
Synton	UNP/LNO	NB	Albert	21 I/2	46°01′	64°58′

T

Ta-a-ack 5	IR/RI	BC	Range 2 Coast	92 M/4	51°02′	127°43′
Tabane Lake	LAKE/LAC	NT	Keewatin	65 C	60°37′	101°48′
Tabasokwia River	RIV/CDE	ON	Kenora	43 E/11	53°39′	87°22′
Taber	TOWN/VIL2	AB	5-10-16-W4	82 H/16	49°49′	112°09′
Taber No. 14, Municipal District of	MUN1/AZM1	AB		82 H/16	49°56′	112°03′
Taber Provincial Park	PARK/PARC	AB	10-16,17-W4	82 H/16	49°49′	112°10′
Tableau-de-Granit, Le	UNP/LNO	QC	Sept-Rivières	22 J/3	50°10′	67°09′
Tableau, Lac du	LAKE/LAC	QC	Le Fjord-du-Saguenay	22 E/1	49°01′	70°06′
Table Bay	UNP/LNO	NF		13 H/10	53°42′	56°42′
Table Bay	BAY/BAIE	NF		13 H/9	53°40′	56°25′
Table, Cap de la	CAPE/CAP	QC	Minganie	12 F/5	49°21′	61°54′
Table Head	UNP/LNO	NS	Cape Breton	11 J/4	46°13′	59°57′
Table Head	UNP/LNO	QC	Minganie	12 F/5	49°21′	61°54′
Table Head	CAPE/CAP	NF		3 D/4	52°05′	55°42′
Table Head	CAPE/CAP	NS	Victoria	11 K/8	46°19′	60°21′
Table Island	ISL/ÎLE	NT	Franklin	59 C	77°12′	95°28′
Tableland	UNP/LNO	SK	20-2-9-W2	62 E/3	49°09′	103°11′
Table Mountain	MTN/MNT	NF		12 B/10	48°37′	58°38′
Table Mountain	MTN/MNT	NF		11 O/11	47°43′	59°14′
Table Mountain	MTN/MNT	NT	Mackenzie	95 O	63°38′	123°29′
Table Point	CAPE/CAP	NF		12 I/5	50°22′	57°32′
Tabor	UNP/LNO	ON	Algoma	41 N/15	47°48′	84°31′
Tabor	UNP/LNO	BC	Cariboo	93 G/15	53°48′	122°43′
Tabusintac	UNP/LNO	NB	Northumberland	21 P/6	47°20′	65°01′
Tabusintac 9	IR/RI	NB	Northumberland	21 P/6	47°20′	65°07′
Tabusintac Bay	BAY/BAIE	NB	Northumberland	21 P/7	47°20′	64°56′
Tabusintac River	RIV/CDE	NB	Northumberland	21 P/7	47°20′	64°58′
Taché	MUN2/AZM2	MB		62 H/10	49°42′	96°40′
Taché	UNP/LNO	ON	Kenora	52 F/9	49°35′	92°10′
Tache 1	IR/RI	BC	Range 5 Coast	93 K/10	54°40′	124°45′
Tacheeda	UNP/LNO	BC	Cariboo	93 J/10	54°41′	122°36′
Taché, Lac	LAKE/LAC	QC	Rimouski-Neigette	22 C/8	48°15′	68°19′
Taché, Lac	LAKE/LAC	NT	Mackenzie	96 A/1	64°02′	120°00′
Tachick Lake	LAKE/LAC	BC	Range 4 Coast	93 F/16	53°58′	124°11′
Tachie	UNP/LNO	BC	Range 5 Coast	93 K/10	54°40′	124°41′
Tachie	UNP/LNO	BC	Range 5 Coast	93 K/10	54°39′	124°45′
Tachie River	RIV/CDE	BC	Range 5 Coast	93 K/15	54°49′	124°58′
Tacks Beach	UNP/LNO	NF		1 M/9	47°34′	54°13′
Tackuan 26	IR/RI	BC	Cassiar	103 P/5	55°27′	129°47′
Tackuan 26A	IR/RI	BC	Cassiar	103 P/5	55°27′	129°48′
Tacla Lake (Ferry Landing) 9	IR/RI	BC	Cassiar	93 M/8	55°19′	126°01′
Tadanac	UNP/LNO	BC	Kootenay	82 F/4	49°07′	117°43′
Tadek Lake	LAKE/LAC	NT	Franklin	96 M	67°02′	127°23′
Tadenet Lake	LAKE/LAC	NT	Franklin	97 B	68°38′	126°05′
Tadinlay 15	IR/RI	BC	Cassiar	93 M/1	55°04′	126°30′

NAME NOM	ENTITY ENTITÉ	LOC 1 LIEU 1	LOC 2 LIEU 2	MAP CARTE	POSITION	
					LAT	LONG
Tadlukotit Hills	MTN/MNT	NT	Franklin	47 G	71°43′	84°49′
Tadmore	HAM/HAM	SK	15-33-4-W2	62 M/16	51°50′	102°29′
Tadoule Lake	UNP/LNO	MB		64 J/9	58°43′	98°29′
Tadoule Lake	LAKE/LAC	MB		64 J/9	58°43′	98°20′
Tadoussac	TOWN/VIL2	QC	La Haute-Côte-Nord	22 C/4	48°09′	69°43′
Tadpole Lake	LAKE/LAC	ON	Kenora	52 F/6	49°28′	93°18′
Ta Duhl' 36	IR/RI	BC	Range 5 Coast	93 K/11	54°36′	125°27′
Taffanel, Lac	LAKE/LAC	QC	Jamésie	23 E/7	53°20′	70°48′
Taft	UNP/LNO	BC	Kamloops Division Yale	82 L/15	50°59′	118°39′
Taft Creek	RIV/CDE	BC	Cassiar	104 A/6	56°30′	129°26′
Tafton	UNP/LNO	ON	Simcoe	31 D/11	44°38′	79°25′
Tagetochlain Lake	LAKE/LAC	BC	Range 4 Coast	93 E/15	54°00′	127°00′
Taggart	UNP/LNO	ON	Kenora	52 K/1	50°05′	92°30′
Taggart Lake	LAKE/LAC	SK		73 J/3	54°08′	107°18′
Taghum	UNP/LNO	BC	Kootenay	82 F/6	49°29′	117°23′
Tagish	UNP/LNO	YT		105 D/8	60°19′	134°16′
Tagish Lake	LAKE/LAC	BC/YT		104 M/16	59°48′	134°14′
Tahaetkun Mountain	MTN/MNT	BC	Kamloops Division Yale	82 L/5	50°16′	119°44′
Tahiapik Mountain	MTN/MNT	NT	Mackenzie	86 N/7	67°18′	116°47′
Tahiryuak Lake	LAKE/LAC	NT	Franklin	87 E/16	70°56′	112°15′
Tahla (Kildala) 4	IR/RI	BC	Range 4 Coast	103 H/16	53°51′	128°29′
Tahlo Lake 24	IR/RI	BC	Cassiar	93 M/8	55°21′	126°29′
Tahltan	UNP/LNO	BC	Cassiar	104 J/2	58°01′	131°00′
Tahltan 1	IR/RI	BC	Cassiar	104 J/2	58°01′	130°59′
Tahltan 10	IR/RI	BC	Cassiar	104 J/2	58°04′	130°47′
Tahltan Forks 5	IR/RI	BC	Cassiar	104 J/3	58°07′	131°20′
Tahltan River	RIV/CDE	BC	Cassiar	104 J/2	58°01′	130°58′
Tahoe Lake	LAKE/LAC	NT	Franklin	77 F/1	70°05′	108°45′
Tahsis	VILG/VILG	BC	Nootka	92 E/15	49°55′	126°40′
Tahsis 11	IR/RI	BC	Nootka	92 E/15	49°55′	126°39′
Tahsish 11	IR/RI	BC	Rupert	92 L/3	50°09′	127°06′
Tahsish Inlet	BAY/BAIE	BC	Rupert	92 L/3	50°06′	127°07′
Tahsis Inlet	BAY/BAIE	BC	Nootka	92 E/10	49°43′	126°37′
Tahsis Mountain	MTN/MNT	BC	Nootka	92 E/15	49°51′	126°37′
Tahsis River	RIV/CDE	BC	Nootka	92 E/15	49°55′	126°40′
Tahtsa Lake	LAKE/LAC	BC	Range 4 Coast	93 E/11	53°42′	127°27′
Tahtsa Reach	RIVF/EFLV	BC	Range 4 Coast	93 E/11	53°42′	127°04′
Tahumming River	RIV/CDE	BC	Range 1 Coast	92 K/8	50°30′	124°23′
Taignoagny Lake	LAKE/LAC	NF		22 P/15	51°58′	64°42′
Tail of the Bank - also-aussi - Grand Banc, Queue du	SEAU/SMER	—		8010	43°13′	50°03′
Tait Lake	LAKE/LAC	MB		63 N/6	55°21′	101°24′
Taitna Lake	LAKE/LAC	NT	Mackenzie	65 E	61°19′	102°20′
Taits Beach	UNP/LNO	ON	Northumberland	31 D/1	44°06′	78°16′
Taits Lake	LAKE/LAC	SK	2-21-W3	72 F/2	49°09′	108°46′
Takakkaw Falls	FALL/CHUT	BC	Kootenay	82 N/8	51°30′	116°28′
Taka Lake	LAKE/LAC	NT	Mackenzie	86 C	64°14′	117°31′
Takhini	UNP/LNO	YT		105 D/11	60°44′	135°06′
Takhini	UNP/LNO	YT		105 D/14	60°51′	135°27′
Takhini Hotspring	UNP/LNO	YT		105 D/14	60°53′	135°22′
Takhini River	RIV/CDE	YT/BC		105 D/14	60°51′	135°11′
Takia River	RIV/CDE	BC	Range 3 Coast	93 D/9	52°45′	126°20′
Takipy	UNP/LNO	MB		63 N/7	55°25′	100°58′
Takla	UNP/LNO	BC	Cassiar	93 N/5	55°28′	125°55′
Takla Lake	LAKE/LAC	BC	Cassiar	93 N/5	55°23′	125°50′
Takla Landing	UNP/LNO	BC	Cassiar	93 N/5	55°29′	125°58′
Tako	UNP/LNO	SK	31-39-22-W3	73 C/6	52°24′	109°01′
Taku	UNP/LNO	BC	Cassiar	104 N/12	59°38′	133°51′
Taku 6	IR/RI	BC	Cassiar	104 N/2	59°07′	133°00′
Taku Arm	BAY/BAIE	BC/YT		104 M/16	59°47′	134°15′
Taku River	RIV/CDE	BC	Cassiar	104 K/12	58°35′	133°39′
Takwa, Rivière	RIV/CDE	QC	Jamésie	32 P/7	51°21′	72°47′
Takysie Lake	UNP/LNO	BC	Range 4 Coast	93 F/13	53°53′	125°52′
Talahaat 16	IR/RI	BC	Range 5 Coast	103 J/16	54°47′	130°07′
Talbot	UNP/LNO	QC	Portneuf	31 P/1	47°05′	72°15′
Talbot	UNP/LNO	ON	Ontario	31 D/11	44°30′	79°07′
Talbot	UNP/LNO	AB	6-38-9-W4	73 D/3	52°14′	111°16′
Talbot Arm	BAY/BAIE	YT		115 G/7	61°30′	138°37′
Talbot Creek	RIV/CDE	ON	Elgin	40 I/11	42°38′	81°22′
Talbot Glacier	GLAC/GLAC	NT	Franklin	39 C	78°00′	78°15′
Talbot Inlet	BAY/BAIE	NT	Franklin	39 C	77°55′	77°40′
Talbot Lake	LAKE/LAC	ON	Victoria	31 D/10	44°42′	78°51′
Talbot Lake	LAKE/LAC	MB		63 J/4	54°05′	99°53′
Talbot River	RIV/CDE	ON	Ontario	31 D/6	44°28′	79°10′
Talbot Trough	SEAU/SMER	—		5.17	77°30′	75°00′
Talbotville Royal	UNP/LNO	ON	Elgin	40 I/14	42°48′	81°15′

NAME / NOM	ENTITY / ENTITÉ	LOC 1 / LIEU 1	LOC 2 / LIEU 2	MAP / CARTE	POSITION LAT	LONG
Talchako Mountain	MTN/MNT	BC	Range 3 Coast	93 D/1	52°06′	126°01′
Talchako River	RIV/CDE	BC	Range 3 Coast	93 D/8	52°23′	126°05′
Talcville	UNP/LNO	NF		1 N/10	47°31′	52°58′
Taleomy 3	IR/RI	BC	Range 3 Coast	93 D/2	52°02′	126°40′
Taliruq, Pointe	CAPE/CAP	QC	Kativik	35 L/8	62°22′	78°05′
Talking, Chute	FALL/CHUT	QC	Jamésie	33 C/4	52°13′	77°53′
Tall Cree 173	IR/RI	AB	2-103-9-W5	84 G/14	57°55′	115°22′
Tall Cree 173A	IR/RI	AB	17-104-10-W5	84 J/4	58°03′	115°37′
Tallheo	UNP/LNO	BC	Range 3 Coast	93 D/7	52°23′	126°50′
Tallman	UNP/LNO	SK	21-44-7-W3	73 B/15	52°48′	106°58′
Tall Pines	UNP/LNO	SK	15-39-5-W2	63 D/7	52°21′	102°39′
Tally Pond	LAKE/LAC	NF		12 A/9	48°37′	56°29′
Talmage	UNP/LNO	SK	35-9-13-W2	62 E/13	49°47′	103°40′
Talon	UNP/LNO	QC	Le Haut-Richelieu	31 H/6	45°22′	73°16′
Talon	UNP/LNO	QC	Communauté urbaine de l'Outaouais	31 G/5	45°29′	75°42′
Talon, Lac	LAKE/LAC	QC	Montmagny	21 L/9	46°43′	70°10′
Talon, Lake	LAKE/LAC	ON	Nipissing	31 L/6	46°18′	79°05′
Taloyoak	HAM/HAM	NT	Keewatin	57 C/10	69°32′	93°31′
Taltapin Lake	LAKE/LAC	BC	Range 5 Coast	93 K/6	54°19′	125°20′
Taltson Lake	LAKE/LAC	NT	Mackenzie	75 E	61°30′	110°15′
Taltson River	RIV/CDE	NT	Mackenzie	85 H	61°24′	112°45′
Talunkwan Island	ISL/ÎLE	BC	Queen Charlotte	103 B/13	52°50′	131°45′
*Talzie	UNP/LNO	NF		23 G/8	53°26′	66°17′
Tamarac Estates	UNP/LNO	ON	Peel	40 P/16	43°56′	80°00′
Tamarack	UNP/LNO	BC	Peace River	94 H/11	57°39′	121°10′
Tamarack Island	ISL/ÎLE	MB		62 P/14	51°49′	97°07′
Tamarack Lake	LAKE/LAC	MB	25,26-13-W	62 O/3	51°13′	99°12′
Tamarack Point	CAPE/CAP	ON	Manitoulin	41 H/12	45°37′	81°43′
Tamarisk	UNP/LNO	BC	New Westminster	92 J/3	50°06′	123°01′
Tamihi Creek	RIV/CDE	BC	New Westminster	92 H/4	49°04′	121°50′
Tammarvi River	RIV/CDE	NT	Mackenzie	66 C	64°29′	101°58′
Tam O'Shanter	UNP/LNO	ON	York	30 M/14	43°47′	79°18′
Tam O'Shanter Ridge	UNP/LNO	NS	Halifax	11 D/12	44°41′	63°32′
Tamworth	UNP/LNO	ON	Lennox and Addington	31 C/7	44°29′	77°00′
Tanakut 4	IR/RI	BC	Lillooet	92 O/5	51°29′	123°51′
Tancook Island	UNP/LNO	NS	Lunenburg	21 A/8	44°28′	64°10′
Tancredia	UNP/LNO	QC	Pontiac	31 F/10	45°43′	76°39′
Tanfield, Cape	CAPE/CAP	NT	Franklin	25 K	62°39′	69°35′
Tangamong Lake	LAKE/LAC	ON	Hastings	31 C/12	44°43′	77°50′
Tangent	UNP/LNO	AB	32-78-24-W5	83 N/13	55°48′	117°40′
Tanghe Creek	RIV/CDE	AB	96-12-W6	84 E/5	57°21′	119°48′
Tangier	UNP/LNO	NS	Halifax	11 D/15	44°48′	62°42′
Tangier Grand Lake	LAKE/LAC	NS	Halifax	11 D/15	44°53′	62°50′
Tangier Harbour	BAY/BAIE	NS	Halifax	11 D/15	44°47′	62°41′
Tangier Lake	LAKE/LAC	NS	Halifax	11 D/15	44°50′	62°44′
Tangleflags	UNP/LNO	SK	16-52-25-W3	73 F/5	53°29′	109°38′
Tanguay	UNP/LNO	QC	Coaticook	21 E/4	45°03′	71°42′
Tanizul 43	IR/RI	BC	Range 5 Coast	93 K/10	54°45′	124°58′
Tankeah 5	IR/RI	BC	Range 3 Coast	103 A/8	52°18′	128°15′
Tankville	UNP/LNO	NB	Westmorland	21 I/2	46°10′	64°47′
Tanner, Mount	MTN/MNT	BC	Similkameen Division Yale	82 E/10	49°39′	118°35′
Tanners Settlement	UNP/LNO	NS	Lunenburg	21 A/8	44°21′	64°22′
Tannin	UNP/LNO	ON	Kenora	52 G/11	49°39′	91°01′
Tanoo 9	IR/RI	BC	Queen Charlotte	103 B/13	52°46′	131°37′
Tanquary Camp	UNP/LNO	NT	Franklin	340 D	81°24′	76°54′
Tanquary Fiord	BAY/BAIE	NT	Franklin	340 D	81°05′	79°45′
Tanquary Glacier	GLAC/GLAC	NT	Franklin	39 F	78°27′	76°12′
Tansley	UNP/LNO	ON	Halton	30 M/5	43°25′	79°48′
Tansleyville	UNP/LNO	ON	Thunder Bay	42 E/12	49°37′	87°56′
Tantallon	VILG/VILG	SK	16-18-32-W	62 K/12	50°32′	101°50′
Tantallon	UNP/LNO	NS	Halifax	11 D/12	44°40′	63°54′
Tantallon Spur	SEAU/SMER	—		NK21 B	43°43′	58°19′
Tantalus, Mount	MTN/MNT	BC	New Westminster	92 G/14	49°49′	123°20′
Tantaré, Lac	LAKE/LAC	QC	La Jacques-Cartier	21 M/4	47°04′	71°33′
Tantaré, Réserve écologique de	PARK/PARC	QC	La Jacques-Cartier	21 M/4	47°04′	71°32′
Tantramar River	RIV/CDE	NB	Westmorland	21 H/16	45°52′	64°20′
Tanu	UNP/LNO	BC	Queen Charlotte	103 B/13	52°46′	131°37′
Tanu Island	ISL/ÎLE	BC	Queen Charlotte	103 B/12	52°45′	131°40′
Tanzilla River	RIV/CDE	BC	Cassiar	104 J/2	58°08′	130°40′
Taoti, Rivière	RIV/CDE	QC	Sept-Rivières	22 O/9	51°41′	66°21′
Tapani, Lac	LAKE/LAC	QC	Antoine-Labelle	31 J/14	46°55′	75°20′
Tapani, Réserve écologique	PARK/PARC	QC	Antoine-Labelle	31 J/14	46°55′	75°20′
Tapley	UNP/LNO	ON	Durham	31 D/2	44°11′	78°30′
Tapley	UNP/LNO	SK		72 I/5	50°22′	105°33′
Tapleytown	UNP/LNO	ON	Wentworth	30 M/4	43°11′	79°44′

NAME / NOM	ENTITY / ENTITÉ	LOC 1 / LIEU 1	LOC 2 / LIEU 2	MAP / CARTE	POSITION LAT	POSITION LONG
Taplow	UNP/LNO	AB	15-30-13-W4	72 M/12	51°33'	111°44'
Tappen	UNP/LNO	BC	Kamloops Division Yale	82 L/14	50°47'	119°20'
Tara	VILG/VILG	ON	Bruce	41 A/6	44°28'	81°09'
Taradale	UNP/LNO	ON	Thunder Bay	42 F/12	49°34'	85°44'
Tarantula Lake	LAKE/LAC	NT	Mackenzie	76 B	64°32'	107°58'
Tarantum	UNP/LNO	PE	Queens	11 L/7	46°17'	62°57'
Tara Siding	UNP/LNO	ON	Bruce	41 A/6	44°28'	81°08'
Tarbert	UNP/LNO	ON	Dufferin	40 P/16	43°56'	80°20'
Tarbot	UNP/LNO	NS	Victoria	11 K/7	46°20'	60°37'
Tarbotvale	UNP/LNO	NS	Victoria	11 K/7	46°21'	60°34'
Tarbutt and Tarbutt Additional	MUN2/AZM2	ON	Algoma	41 J/5	46°23'	84°00'
Targe Creek 15	IR/RI	BC	Range 4 Coast	93 F/10	53°44'	124°57'
Targettville	UNP/LNO	NB	Kent	21 I/11	46°32'	65°02'
Tar Island	UNP/LNO	AB	26-92-10-W4	74 E/3	57°01'	111°29'
Tariujaq Arm	BAY/BAIE	NT	Franklin	37 F	70°35'	79°00'
Tariunnuaq Bay	BAY/BAIE	NT	Keewatin	56 M	67°17'	95°24'
Tarnopol	UNP/LNO	SK	11-43-24-W2	73 A/11	52°42'	105°23'
Tarpon Lake	LAKE/LAC	NT	Mackenzie	76 C	64°45'	109°00'
Tarpon River	RIV/CDE	NT	Mackenzie	76 C	64°54'	108°30'
Tarrionituk Lake	LAKE/LAC	NT	Franklin	26 K	66°20'	68°00'
Tarrtown	UNP/LNO	NB	Carleton	21 J/12	46°33'	67°37'
Tarrys	UNP/LNO	BC	Kootenay	82 F/5	49°23'	117°33'
Tartan	UNP/LNO	ON	Grey	41 A/2	44°08'	80°43'
Tartan Lane	UNP/LNO	NF		1 K/11	46°41'	53°26'
Tarte, La	UNP/LNO	QC	Témiscouata	21 N/6	47°27'	69°01'
Tartigou	UNP/LNO	QC	Matane	22 B/13	48°45'	67°48'
Tartigou, Rivière	RIV/CDE	QC	Matane	22 B/13	48°45'	67°48'
Tartu Inlet	BAY/BAIE	BC	Queen Charlotte	103 F/7	53°27'	132°40'
Tarzwell	UNP/LNO	ON	Timiskaming	42 A/1	48°00'	80°01'
Taschereau	TOWN/VIL2	QC	Abitibi-Ouest	32 D/10	48°40'	78°41'
Taschereau	VILG/VILG	QC	Abitibi-Ouest	32 D/10	48°38'	78°45'
Taseko Lakes	LAKE/LAC	BC	Lillooet	92 O/4	51°15'	123°36'
Taseko Mountain	MTN/MNT	BC	Lillooet	92 O/3	51°14'	123°28'
Taseko River	RIV/CDE	BC	Cariboo	93 B/4	52°00'	123°40'
Tasekyoak Lake	LAKE/LAC	NT	Keewatin	67 A	68°50'	96°38'
Taser Lake	LAKE/LAC	NT	Franklin	47 E	70°47'	81°45'
Tasers Lake	LAKE/LAC	NT	Franklin	46 K	66°58'	85°09'
Tashota	UNP/LNO	ON	Thunder Bay	42 L/4	50°14'	87°40'
Tasialujjuaq, Lac	LAKE/LAC	QC	Kativik	24 M/12	59°40'	71°52'
Tasialuup Itillinga	UNP/LNO	QC	Kativik	34 K/12	58°41'	77°42'
Tasiataq, Lac	LAKE/LAC	QC	Kativik	24 L/13	58°45'	71°45'
Tasiat, Lac	LAKE/LAC	QC	Kativik	34 O/3	59°11'	75°13'
Tasikutaaraaluup Sitialungit	UNP/LNO	QC	Kativik	34 K/10	58°41'	76°35'
Tasin Range	MTN/MNT	YT		105 N/15	63°55'	132°45'
Tasiqanngituq	UNP/LNO	QC	Kativik	34 J/13	58°55'	75°35'
Tasirmiuviup Sijjangit	UNP/LNO	QC	Kativik	24 N/12	59°42'	69°52'
Tasisuak Lake	LAKE/LAC	NF		14 D/10	56°38'	62°45'
Tasiujaq	VILG/VILG	QC	Kativik	24 K/12	58°42'	69°56'
Taskinigup Falls	FALL/CHUT	MB		63 O/9	55°32'	98°30'
Tasmania Islands	ISL/ÎLE	NT	Franklin	67 H	71°16'	96°35'
Tasseriuk Lake	LAKE/LAC	NT	Mackenzie	97 C	69°24'	124°42'
Tassialouc, Lac	LAKE/LAC	QC	Kativik	34 P/4	59°03'	73°59'
Tassijuak Lake	LAKE/LAC	NT	Franklin	87 D	69°03'	112°00'
Tassijuak River	RIV/CDE	NT	Franklin	87 D/2	69°03'	113°30'
Tasu	UNP/LNO	BC	Queen Charlotte	103 C/16	52°46'	132°02'
Tasu Sound	BAY/BAIE	BC	Queen Charlotte	103 B/13	52°47'	132°03'
Tatachikapika Lake	LAKE/LAC	ON	Sudbury	41 P/13	47°52'	81°42'
Ta Ta Creek	UNP/LNO	BC	Kootenay	82 G/13	49°47'	115°47'
Tatagwa	UNP/LNO	SK	17-8-15-W2	72 H/9	49°39'	104°00'
Tatalrose	UNP/LNO	BC	Range 4 Coast	93 F/13	53°59'	125°59'
Tatamagouche	VILG/VILG	NS	Colchester	11 E/11	45°43'	63°18'
Tatamagouche Bay	BAY/BAIE	NS	Colchester	11 E/11	45°45'	63°19'
Tatamagouche Mountain	UNP/LNO	NS	Colchester	11 E/11	45°38'	63°16'
Tatcho Creek 11	IR/RI	BC	Cassiar	104 J/8	58°23'	130°09'
Tatchu 13	IR/RI	BC	Nootka	92 E/14	49°51'	127°08'
Tatchu 13A	IR/RI	BC	Nootka	92 E/14	49°51'	127°09'
Tatchun Hills	MTN/MNT	YT		105 L/3	62°15'	135°30'
Tatchu Point	CAPE/CAP	BC	Nootka	92 E/14	49°51'	127°09'
Tate	UNP/LNO	SK	36-28-21-W2	72 P/7	51°27'	104°50'
Tate Corners	UNP/LNO	ON	Middlesex	40 I/12	42°43'	81°38'
Tatehurst	UNP/LNO	QC	Le Haut-Saint-Laurent	31 G/1	45°08'	74°01'
Tate Lake	LAKE/LAC	NT	Mackenzie	96 C	64°31'	125°21'
Tatelkus Lake 28	IR/RI	BC	Range 4 Coast	93 F/7	53°18'	124°43'
Tatelkuz Lake	LAKE/LAC	BC	Range 4 Coast	93 F/7	53°17'	124°41'
Tatense 16	IR/RI	BC	Queen Charlotte	103 K/2	54°11'	132°59'

NAME NOM	ENTITY ENTITÉ	LOC 1 LIEU 1	LOC 2 LIEU 2	MAP CARTE	POSITION LAT	LONG
Tathlina Lake	LAKE/LAC	NT	Mackenzie	85 C	60°33′	117°32′
Tatinnai Lake	LAKE/LAC	NT	Mackenzie	65 A	60°55′	97°41′
Tatla 1 - see-voir - Tatla East 2	IR/RI	BC		93 E/16	53°59′	126°29′
Tatla 1 - see-voir - Tatla West 11	IR/RI	BC		93 E/16	53°59′	126°30′
Tatla Lake	UNP/LNO	BC	Range 2 Coast	92 N/15	51°54′	124°36′
Tatla Lake	LAKE/LAC	BC	Range 2 Coast	92 N/16	51°58′	124°25′
Tatla't East 2	IR/RI	BC	Range 4 Coast	93 E/16	53°59′	126°29′
Tatlatui Lake	LAKE/LAC	BC	Cassiar	94 D/14	56°55′	127°20′
Tatla West 11	IR/RI	BC	Range 4 Coast	93 E/16	53°59′	126°30′
Tatlayoko Lake	UNP/LNO	BC	Range 2 Coast	92 N/9	51°43′	124°26′
Tatlayoko Lake	LAKE/LAC	BC	Range 2 Coast	92 N/9	51°33′	124°25′
Tatlmain Lake	LAKE/LAC	YT		105 L/12	62°37′	135°59′
Tatlock	UNP/LNO	ON	Lanark	31 F/1	45°10′	76°29′
Tatlow	UNP/LNO	BC	Range 5 Coast	93 L/11	54°42′	127°07′
Tatlow, Mount	MTN/MNT	BC	Lillooet	92 O/5	51°23′	123°52′
Tatnall	UNP/LNO	ON	Algoma	42 C/9	48°41′	84°13′
Tatnam, Cape	CAPE/CAP	MB		54 G/7	57°16′	91°00′
Tatogga	UNP/LNO	BC	Cassiar	104 H/12	57°44′	129°59′
Tatonduk River	RIV/CDE	YT		116 C/15	65°00′	141°00′
Tatpo-oose 10	IR/RI	BC	Sayward	92 K/3	50°14′	125°07′
Tatsadah Lake 14	IR/RI	BC	Cariboo	93 J/5	54°19′	123°55′
Tatsamenie Lake	LAKE/LAC	BC	Cassiar	104 K/8	58°20′	132°20′
Tatselawas 2 - see-voir - Tatselawas (Stuart River) 2	IR/RI	BC		93 K/8	54°18′	124°12′
Tatselawas (Stuart River) 2	IR/RI	BC	Range 5 Coast	93 K/8	54°18′	124°12′
Tatsfield	UNP/LNO	SK	29-44-22-W3	73 C/14	52°49′	109°10′
Tatshenshini River	RIV/CDE	BC/YT		114 P/5	59°29′	137°45′
Tatton	UNP/LNO	BC	Lillooet	92 P/11	51°43′	121°22′
Tattons Corner	UNP/LNO	NB	Charlotte	21 B/15	44°46′	66°46′
Tatui Lake	LAKE/LAC	NT	Mackenzie	96 G/14	65°58′	123°04′
Tatuk Lake	LAKE/LAC	BC	Range 4 Coast	93 F/9	53°32′	124°14′
Tatuk Lake 7	IR/RI	BC	Range 4 Coast	93 F/9	53°33′	124°17′
Taunton	UNP/LNO	ON	Ontario	30 M/15	43°56′	78°49′
Taureau, Réservoir	LAKE/LAC	QC	Matawinie	31 I/13	46°46′	73°50′
Taurus Channel	SEAU/SMER	—		5.03	49°40′	155°00′
Tavani	UNP/LNO	NT	Keewatin	55 K	62°04′	93°06′
Taverna	UNP/LNO	BC	Cariboo	83 D/14	52°58′	119°25′
Taverner Bay	BAY/BAIE	NT	Franklin	36 P	67°12′	72°25′
Tavistock	UNP/LNO	ON	Oxford	40 P/7	43°19′	80°50′
Tawatinaw	UNP/LNO	AB	26-61-24-W4	83 I/6	54°18′	113°29′
Tawatinaw River	RIV/CDE	AB	66-22-W4	83 I/11	54°42′	113°17′
Tawayik Lake	LAKE/LAC	AB	53-20-W4	83 H/10	53°36′	112°53′
Taweel Lake	LAKE/LAC	BC	Kamloops Division Yale	92 P/9	51°38′	120°21′
Tawsig Fiord	BAY/BAIE	NT	Franklin	26 A	64°45′	66°00′
Taxis River	UNP/LNO	NB	York	21 J/8	46°27′	66°28′
Taxis River	RIV/CDE	NB	Northumberland	21 J/8	46°27′	66°25′
Tay	MUN2/AZM2	ON	Simcoe	31 D/12	44°44′	79°46′
Tay	UNP/LNO	BC	Cariboo	93 J/2	54°13′	122°40′
Tay Creek	UNP/LNO	NB	York	21 J/2	46°14′	66°49′
Tay Falls	UNP/LNO	NB	York	21 J/2	46°14′	66°46′
Tay Lake	LAKE/LAC	YT		105 K/8	62°23′	132°03′
Taylor	MUN1/AZM1	BC	Peace River	94 A/2	56°10′	120°41′
Taylor	UNP/LNO	ON	Leeds	31 C/8	44°25′	76°13′
Taylor	UNP/LNO	AB	27-20-W4	82 P/7	51°21′	112°46′
Taylor Beach	HAM/HAM	SK	8-20-12-W2	62 L/12	50°42′	103°39′
Taylor Corners	UNP/LNO	ON	Victoria	31 D/7	44°20′	78°51′
Taylor Island	ISL/ÎLE	NT	Keewatin	34 C	56°45′	76°39′
Taylor Island	ISL/ÎLE	NT	Franklin	67 C	69°09′	101°35′
Taylor Lake	LAKE/LAC	ON	Lanark	31 F/1	45°09′	76°21′
Taylor Lake	LAKE/LAC	NT	Mackenzie	75 N	63°47′	108°42′
Taylor Lake 50	IR/RI	BC	Cassiar	103 P/6	55°28′	129°00′
Taylor Peak	MTN/MNT	BC	Cassiar	104 H/7	57°17′	128°30′
Taylor River	RIV/CDE	BC	Clayoquot	92 F/6	49°17′	125°13′
Taylor River	RIV/CDE	BC	Cassiar	104 A/7	56°20′	128°42′
Taylor's Bay	UNP/LNO	NF		1 L/13	46°53′	55°44′
Taylors Head	UNP/LNO	NS	Halifax	11 D/15	44°49′	62°34′
Taylors Head	CAPE/CAP	NS	Halifax	11 D/15	44°47′	62°33′
Taylorside	UNP/LNO	SK	6-45-20-W2	73 A/15	52°51′	104°53′
Taylors Road	UNP/LNO	NS	Antigonish	11 F/12	45°36′	61°52′
Taylorton	UNP/LNO	SK		62 E/2	49°07′	102°48′
Taylor Village	UNP/LNO	NB	Westmorland	21 H/15	45°56′	64°33′
Taylorville	UNP/LNO	AB	15-1-24-W4	82 H/3	49°02′	113°07′
Tay Mills	UNP/LNO	NB	York	21 J/2	46°11′	66°48′
Taymouth	UNP/LNO	NB	York	21 J/2	46°11′	66°37′
Tay River	RIV/CDE	NB	York	21 J/2	46°11′	66°37′
Tay River	RIV/CDE	ON	Lanark	31 C/16	44°53′	76°07′

NAME NOM	ENTITY ENTITÉ	LOC 1 LIEU 1	LOC 2 LIEU 2	MAP CARTE	POSITION LAT	LONG
Tay River	RIV/CDE	YT		105 L/9	62°34′	134°22′
Tayside	UNP/LNO	ON	Stormont	31 G/7	45°17′	74°58′
Tay Sound	CHAN/CHEN	NT	Franklin	38 B	72°06′	79°00′
Tay Valley	UNP/LNO	NB	York	21 J/2	46°12′	66°41′
Tazin Lake	LAKE/LAC	SK		74 N/14	59°48′	109°05′
Tazin River	RIV/CDE	NT/SK		75 D/7	60°26′	110°45′
Tchaikazan River	RIV/CDE	BC	Lillooet	92 O/4	51°13′	123°36′
Tchaneta River	RIV/CDE	NT	Mackenzie	106 I	66°38′	128°14′
Tchendferi Lake	LAKE/LAC	NT	Mackenzie	96 M	67°14′	127°16′
Tchentlo Lake	LAKE/LAC	BC	Cassiar	93 N/3	55°11′	125°00′
Tchesinkut Lake	UNP/LNO	BC	Range 5 Coast	93 K/4	54°05′	125°44′
Tchesinkut Lake	LAKE/LAC	BC	Range 5 Coast	93 K/4	54°05′	125°35′
Tchitogama, Lac	LAKE/LAC	QC	Lac-Saint-Jean-Est	22 D/14	48°49′	71°23′
Tcîbâtik Sâgik	UNP/LNO	QC	Vallée-de-l'Or	31 N/11	47°32′	77°03′
Tcimotf 1A	IR/RI	BC	Range 3 Coast	103 A/1	52°08′	128°08′
Tcorecik	UNP/LNO	QC	Le Haut-Saint-Maurice	31 O/9	47°39′	74°09′
Tea Cove	UNP/LNO	NF		12 B/10	48°39′	58°58′
Teagues Lake	LAKE/LAC	NB	Gloucester	21 P/11	47°37′	65°25′
Teahans Corner	UNP/LNO	NB	Albert	21 H/10	45°42′	64°58′
Tea Hill	UNP/LNO	PE	Queens	11 L/3	46°13′	63°04′
Teahmit 3	IR/RI	BC	Clayoquot	92 E/8	49°27′	126°29′
Teakerne Arm	UNP/LNO	BC	New Westminster	92 K/2	50°11′	124°49′
Teakerne Arm	BAY/BAIE	BC	New Westminster	92 K/2	50°11′	124°52′
Teakle	UNP/LNO	SK	12-19-9-W3	72 J/11	50°36′	107°07′
Teaquahan River	RIV/CDE	BC	Range 1 Coast	92 K/15	50°56′	124°50′
Tebesjuak Lake	LAKE/LAC	NT	Keewatin	65 O	63°46′	99°00′
Tecumseh	TOWN/VIL2	ON	Essex	40 J/7	42°19′	82°54′
Tecumseh No. 65	MUN2/AZM2	SK		62 E/11	49°40′	103°00′
Tecumseth - see-voir - Bradford West Gwillimbury	MUN2/AZM2	ON		31 D/4	44°07′	79°37′
Tecumseth - see-voir - Innisfil	MUN2/AZM2	ON		31 D/5	44°13′	79°39′
Tecumseth - see-voir - New Tecumseth	MUN2/AZM2	ON		31 D/4	44°05′	79°46′
Tedji Lake	LAKE/LAC	NT	Mackenzie	96 M	67°42′	126°32′
Teeds Mills	UNP/LNO	NB	Carleton	21 J/4	46°06′	67°37′
Tee Lake	UNP/LNO	QC	Témiscamingue	31 J/14	46°45′	79°03′
*Teepee	UNP/LNO	BC	Cassiar	104 M/10	59°38′	134°40′
Teepee Creek	UNP/LNO	AB	5-74-3-W6	83 M/8	55°22′	118°24′
Teequaloose 3	IR/RI	BC	Yale Division Yale	92 H/11	49°42′	121°25′
Teequaloose 3A	IR/RI	BC	Yale Division Yale	92 H/11	49°42′	121°25′
Tees	UNP/LNO	AB	25-40-24-W4	83 A/6	52°28′	113°19′
Teeslee 3 - see-voir - Teeslee 15	IR/RI	BC		93 K/15	54°48′	124°57′
Teeslee 15	IR/RI	BC	Range 5 Coast	93 K/15	54°48′	124°57′
Teeswater	VILG/VILG	ON	Bruce	40 P/14	44°00′	81°17′
Teeswater River	RIV/CDE	ON	Bruce	41 A/6	44°18′	81°16′
Teeta 7	IR/RI	BC	Rupert	92 L/5	50°24′	127°30′
Teeterville	UNP/LNO	ON	Norfolk	40 I/16	42°56′	80°26′
Teggau Lake	LAKE/LAC	ON	Kenora	52 F/12	49°41′	93°38′
Tehek Lake	LAKE/LAC	NT	Keewatin	56 D	64°55′	95°38′
Tehert River	RIV/CDE	NT	Keewatin	56 E	65°02′	95°15′
Tehery Lake	LAKE/LAC	NT	Keewatin	56 C	64°26′	93°06′
Tehkummah	MUN2/AZM2	ON	Manitoulin	41 G/9	45°38′	82°02′
Tehkummah	UNP/LNO	ON	Manitoulin	41 G/9	45°39′	82°01′
Teh Noo'n Che 49	IR/RI	BC	Cassiar	93 N/4	55°05′	125°33′
Tejean Lake	LAKE/LAC	NT	Mackenzie	75 F	61°37′	108°36′
Teko	UNP/LNO	BC	Peace River	94 A/2	56°09′	120°45′
Telachick	UNP/LNO	BC	Cariboo	93 G/14	53°52′	123°12′
Telaise 1	IR/RI	BC		92 L/5	50°20′	127°52′
Telegraph Cove	UNP/LNO	BC	Rupert	92 L/10	50°33′	126°50′
Telegraph Creek	UNP/LNO	BC	Cassiar	104 G/14	57°54′	131°10′
Telegraph Creek 6	IR/RI	BC	Cassiar	104 G/14	57°54′	131°10′
Telegraph Creek 6A	IR/RI	BC	Cassiar	104 G/14	57°54′	131°10′
*Telegraph Point	UNP/LNO	BC	Range 5 Coast	103 I/4	54°11′	129°39′
Telegraph Range	MTN/MNT	BC	Cariboo	93 G/6	53°23′	123°28′
Telfer	UNP/LNO	ON	Middlesex	40 P/3	43°03′	81°24′
Telford	UNP/LNO	NS	Pictou	11 E/9	45°34′	62°28′
Telford	UNP/LNO	MB	18-10-16-E	52 E/14	49°50′	95°23′
Telfordville	UNP/LNO	AB	36-49-2-W5	83 G/8	53°16′	114°10′
Telkwa	VILG/VILG	BC	Range 5 Coast	93 L/11	54°42′	127°03′
Telkwa River	RIV/CDE	BC	Range 5 Coast	93 L/11	54°42′	127°03′
Tellot Glacier	GLAC/GLAC	BC	Range 2 Coast	92 N/6	51°22′	125°05′
Telly Road Crossing	UNP/LNO	NB	Northumberland	21 P/4	47°07′	65°36′
Temagami	MUN2/AZM2	ON	Nipissing	31 M/4	47°04′	79°47′
Temagami	UNP/LNO	ON	Nipissing	31 M/4	47°04′	79°47′
Temagami, Lake	LAKE/LAC	ON	Nipissing	41 P/1	47°00′	80°03′
Temagami North	UNP/LNO	ON	Nipissing	31 M/4	47°07′	79°47′
Témiscamie, Lac	LAKE/LAC	QC	Jamésie	32 P/1	51°10′	72°12′

NAME NOM	ENTITY ENTITÉ	LOC 1 LIEU 1	LOC 2 LIEU 2	MAP CARTE	POSITION LAT	LONG
Témiscamie, Rivière	RIV/CDE	QC	Jamésie	32 I/14	50°59′	73°05′
Témiscaming	CITY/VIL1	QC	Témiscamingue	31 L/11	46°43′	79°06′
Témiscamingue	MUN1/AZM1	QC	Témiscamingue	31 M/11	47°33′	79°14′
Témiscamingue, Lac - also-aussi - **Timiskaming, Lake**	LAKE/LAC	QC/ON		31 M/3	47°15′	79°27′
Témiscouata	MUN1/AZM1	QC	Témiscouata	21 N/10	47°41′	68°53′
Témiscouata, Lac	LAKE/LAC	QC	Témiscouata	21 N/10	47°40′	68°50′
Temperance Bay	BAY/BAIE	NT	Franklin	69 E	78°10′	97°25′
Temperance Vale	UNP/LNO	NB	York	21 J/3	46°04′	67°15′
Temperanceville	UNP/LNO	ON	York	30 M/14	43°56′	79°29′
Tempest	UNP/LNO	AB	21-9-19-W4	82 H/10	49°45′	112°32′
Temple	UNP/LNO	NB	York	21 G/14	45°59′	67°25′
Temple	UNP/LNO	AB	28-15-W5	82 N/8	51°23′	116°06′
Temple Bay	BAY/BAIE	NF		2 M/13	51°59′	55°55′
Temple Hill	UNP/LNO	ON	Grey	41 A/7	44°27′	80°37′
Templeman	UNP/LNO	NF		2 F/4	49°12′	53°33′
Templeman, Mount	MTN/MNT	BC	Kootenay	82 K/11	50°41′	117°12′
Temple, Mount	MTN/MNT	AB	27-16-W5	82 N/8	51°21′	116°13′
Templeton	UNP/LNO	QC	Communauté urbaine de l'Outaouais	31 G/5	45°29′	75°36′
Templeton-Est	UNP/LNO	QC	Communauté urbaine de l'Outaouais	31 G/5	45°30′	75°35′
Templeton-Ouest	UNP/LNO	QC	Communauté urbaine de l'Outaouais	31 G/5	45°29′	75°42′
Tempo	UNP/LNO	ON	Middlesex	40 I/14	42°51′	81°16′
Tenaga	UNP/LNO	QC	Les Collines-de-l'Outaouais	31 G/12	45°32′	75°48′
Tenaka Creek	RIV/CDE	BC	Peace River	94 J/7	58°20′	122°55′
Tenby	UNP/LNO	MB	36-17-13-W	62 J/6	50°30′	99°08′
Tenby Bay	UNP/LNO	ON	Algoma	41 J/4	46°08′	83°56′
Tenlen Lake	LAKE/LAC	NT	Mackenzie	106 O	67°52′	131°05′
Ten Mile	UNP/LNO	BC	Kootenay	82 K/11	50°40′	117°21′
Ten Mile	UNP/LNO	YT		105 D/1	60°10′	134°22′
Tenmile House	UNP/LNO	PE	Queens	11 L/7	46°20′	62°59′
Ten Mile Lake	UNP/LNO	BC	Cariboo	93 G/1	53°05′	122°26′
Ten Mile Lake	LAKE/LAC	NF		2 E/7	49°15′	54°42′
Ten Mile Lake	LAKE/LAC	NF		12 P/2	51°06′	56°42′
Ten Mile Lake	LAKE/LAC	NS	Halifax	11 E/2	45°09′	62°42′
Ten Mile Lake	LAKE/LAC	NS	Queens	21 A/2	44°10′	64°51′
Ten Mile Lake	LAKE/LAC	ON	Algoma	41 J/10	46°31′	82°47′
Ten Mile Point	CAPE/CAP	ON	Manitoulin	41 H/13	45°52′	81°49′
Ten Mile Pond	LAKE/LAC	NF		2 F/4	49°11′	54°00′
Tennants Cove	UNP/LNO	NB	Kings	21 G/9	45°35′	66°00′
Tennent Islands	ISL/ÎLE	NT	Franklin	67 D	69°30′	96°30′
Tennessee	UNP/LNO	QC	Roussillon	31 H/5	45°22′	73°39′
Tennion	UNP/LNO	AB	31-11-19-W4	82 H/15	49°58′	112°35′
Tennycape	UNP/LNO	NS	Hants	11 E/5	45°16′	63°53′
Tenny, Cape	CAPE/CAP	NS	Hants	11 E/5	45°17′	63°53′
Tennyson	UNP/LNO	ON	Lanark	31 F/1	45°02′	76°10′
Tenquille Creek	RIV/CDE	BC	Lillooet	92 J/10	50°32′	122°47′
Tent City	UNP/LNO	ON	Simcoe	31 D/5	44°18′	79°32′
10th Line Shore	UNP/LNO	ON	Lanark	31 F/1	45°06′	76°09′
Tent Island	ISL/ÎLE	YT		117 A/16	68°55′	136°33′
Tent Island	ISL/ÎLE	NT	Keewatin	32 M	51°49′	79°07′
Tent Island 8	IR/RI	BC	Chemainus	92 B/13	48°56′	123°38′
Tent Lake	LAKE/LAC	NT	Mackenzie	75 J	62°25′	107°54′
Teo Lakes	LAKE/LAC	SK		72 N/6	51°30′	109°21′
Tepee Lake	LAKE/LAC	AB	85,86-26-W4	84 A/5	56°24′	114°00′
Tequa 21	IR/RI	BC	Clayoquot	92 E/8	49°17′	126°01′
Terence Bay	UNP/LNO	NS	Halifax	11 D/5	44°28′	63°43′
Terence Bay River	UNP/LNO	NS	Halifax	11 D/5	44°29′	63°44′
Teresa Island	ISL/ÎLE	BC	Cassiar	104 N/5	59°26′	133°47′
Terminal Beach	UNP/LNO	NS	Halifax	11 D/11	44°38′	63°19′
Terminus	UNP/LNO	ON	Lambton	40 J/9	42°41′	82°20′
Term Point	CAPE/CAP	NT	Keewatin	55 K	62°08′	92°28′
Terrace	CITY/VIL1	BC	Range 5 Coast	103 I/10	54°31′	128°36′
Terrace Bay	UNP/LNO	ON	Thunder Bay	42 D/14	48°47′	87°06′
Terrace Creek	RIV/CDE	BC	Osoyoos Division Yale	82 E/13	50°00′	119°37′
Terrace Heights	UNP/LNO	NS	Pictou	11 E/10	45°36′	62°39′
Terrace Hill	UNP/LNO	ON	Brant	40 P/1	43°09′	80°16′
Terrace Mountain	MTN/MNT	BC	Osoyoos Division Yale	82 L/4	50°06′	119°38′
Terra Cotta	UNP/LNO	ON	Peel	30 M/12	43°43′	79°56′
Terrains de L'Évêque	UNP/LNO	NB	Kent	21 I/6	46°17′	65°02′
Terra Nivea	GLAC/GLAC	NT	Franklin	25 J	62°17′	66°31′
Terra Nova	VILG/VILG	NF		2 D/9	48°30′	54°13′
Terra Nova	UNP/LNO	NS	Cape Breton	11 F/15	45°51′	60°32′
Terra Nova	UNP/LNO	ON	Dufferin	41 A/1	44°12′	80°07′
Terra Nova Lake	LAKE/LAC	NF		2 D/9	48°30′	54°18′
Terra Nova National Park - also-aussi - Terra-Nova, Parc national	PARK/PARC	NF		2 C/12	48°32′	53°56′
Terra Nova North River	RIV/CDE	NF		2 D/9	48°31′	54°25′

NAME / NOM	ENTITY / ENTITÉ	LOC 1 / LIEU 1	LOC 2 / LIEU 2	MAP / CARTE	POSITION LAT	POSITION LONG
Terra-Nova, Parc national - also-aussi - Terra Nova National Park	PARK/PARC	NF		2 C/12	48°32′	53°56′
Terra Nova River	RIV/CDE	NF		2 D/9	48°40′	54°00′
Terrasse-Bigras	UNP/LNO	QC	Deux-Montagnes	31 G/8	45°30′	74°08′
Terrasse-Charbonneau	UNP/LNO	QC	Champlain	31 H/11	45°32′	73°30′
Terrasse-Raymond	UNP/LNO	QC	Deux-Montagnes	31 G/8	45°29′	74°08′
Terrasse-Vaudreuil	VILG/VILG	QC	Vaudreuil-Soulanges	31 H/5	45°24′	73°59′
Terra View Heights	UNP/LNO	ON	Peterborough	31 D/8	44°21′	78°19′
Terre-à-Fer	UNP/LNO	QC	Témiscouata	21 N/10	47°43′	68°47′
Terrebonne	CITY/VIL1	QC	Les Moulins	31 H/12	45°42′	73°38′
Terrell No. 101	MUN2/AZM2	SK		72 H/14	49°55′	105°25′
Terrenceville	TOWN/VIL2	NF		1 M/10	47°40′	54°44′
Terre-Neuve - also-aussi - **Newfoundland**	PROV/PROV	NF		MCR77	53°00′	60°00′
Terre-Neuve, Bassin de - also-aussi - Newfoundland Basin	SEAU/SMER	—		802	43°30′	45°00′
Terre-Neuve, Chaîne de monts de - also-aussi - Newfoundland Seamounts	SEAU/SMER	—		4001	43°50′	45°00′
Terre-Neuve, Dorsale de - also-aussi - Newfoundland Ridge	SEAU/SMER	—		800A	41°30′	49°30′
Terre-Neuve, Plate-forme de - also-aussi - Newfoundland Shelf	SEAU/SMER	—		802	50°00′	47°00′
Terre Noire	UNP/LNO	NS	Inverness	11 K/6	46°29′	61°04′
Terres-Rompues	UNP/LNO	QC	Le Fjord-du-Saguenay	22 D/6	48°27′	71°10′
Territoire-Coburn	UNP/LNO	QC	Beauce-Sartigan	21 E/16	45°56′	70°24′
Territok, Cape	CAPE/CAP	NF		14 M/13	59°46′	63°57′
Terror Bay	BAY/BAIE	NT	Franklin	67 A	68°52′	98°57′
Terror Island	ISL/ÎLE	NT	Franklin	98 B	72°50′	125°11′
Terror Point	CAPE/CAP	BC	Range 4 Coast	103 H/4	53°10′	129°58′
Terror Point	CAPE/CAP	NT	Keewatin	46 A	64°07′	80°57′
Terzaghi Dam	MISC/DIV	BC	Lillooet	92 J/16	50°47′	122°13′
Tésécau, Lac	LAKE/LAC	QC	Jamésie	32 O/4	51°02′	75°58′
Tes Gha La 7A	IR/RI	BC	Range 5 Coast	93 K/9	54°37′	124°24′
Tesla Lake	LAKE/LAC	BC	Range 4 Coast	93 E/2	53°08′	126°39′
Teslin	VILG/VILG	YT		105 C/2	60°10′	132°43′
Teslin Crossing	UNP/LNO	YT		105 E/2	61°15′	134°36′
Teslin Lake	UNP/LNO	YT		105 C/2	60°14′	132°55′
Teslin Lake	LAKE/LAC	YT/BC		105 C/1	60°03′	132°30′
Teslin Lake 7	IR/RI	BC	Cassiar	104 N/9	59°34′	132°07′
Teslin Lake 9	IR/RI	BC	Cassiar	104 N/16	59°47′	132°17′
Teslin Post 13	IR/RI	YT		105 C/2	60°10′	132°40′
Teslin River	UNP/LNO	YT		105 C/6	60°29′	133°18′
Teslin River	RIV/CDE	YT/BC		105 E/10	61°34′	134°54′
Tessier	VILG/VILG	SK	1-33-11-W3	72 O/14	51°48′	107°26′
Tessier, Lac	LAKE/LAC	QC	Le Haut-Saint-Maurice	32 B/3	48°12′	75°14′
Tessik Lake	LAKE/LAC	NT	Franklin	36 B	64°49′	75°22′
Teston	UNP/LNO	ON	York	30 M/13	43°52′	79°32′
Testu, Lac	LAKE/LAC	QC	Kativik	24 B/7	56°18′	66°35′
Tetachuck Lake	LAKE/LAC	BC	Range 4 Coast	93 F/5	53°20′	125°50′
Tetagouche River	RIV/CDE	NB	Gloucester	21 P/12	47°38′	65°41′
*Tetana	UNP/LNO	BC	Cassiar	93 M/15	55°56′	126°35′
Tetcho Lake	LAKE/LAC	NT	Mackenzie	95 A	60°25′	120°45′
Tête-à-la-Baleine	UNP/LNO	QC	Côte-Nord-du-Golfe-Saint-Laurent	12 J/11	50°42′	59°19′
Tête Angela Creek	RIV/CDE	BC	Lillooet	92 O/12	51°42′	123°43′
Tête Blanche, Rivière de la	RIV/CDE	QC	Le Fjord-du-Saguenay	22 D/14	48°56′	71°01′
Tête-de-l'Île	UNP/LNO	QC	Le Bas-Richelieu	31 I/3	46°04′	73°04′
Tête d'Ours, Lac	LAKE/LAC	NT	Mackenzie	75 M	63°22′	110°35′
Tête Jaune	UNP/LNO	BC	Cariboo	83 D/13	52°59′	119°30′
Tête Jaune Cache	UNP/LNO	BC	Cariboo	83 D/14	52°59′	119°30′
Tête, Lac de la	LAKE/LAC	QC	Le Haut-Saint-Maurice	32 B/5	48°27′	75°30′
Tétépisca, Lac	LAKE/LAC	QC	Manicouagan	22 N/3	51°04′	69°22′
Tethul River	RIV/CDE	NT/AB		85 A/9	60°35′	112°13′
Tetu Lake	LAKE/LAC	ON	Kenora	52 L/3	50°11′	95°02′
Teulon	VILG/VILG	MB	21-16-2-E	62 I/6	50°23′	97°16′
Teviotdale	UNP/LNO	ON	Wellington	40 P/15	43°51′	80°46′
Tewkesbury	UNP/LNO	QC	La Jacques-Cartier	21 M/3	47°03′	71°26′
Texada Island	ISL/ÎLE	BC	Texada Island	92 F/9	49°40′	124°24′
Texada Island Land District	GEOG/GÉOG	BC		92 F	49°40′	124°23′
Texas	UNP/LNO	QC	Roussillon	31 H/5	45°24′	73°38′
Texas Creek	RIV/CDE	BC	Lillooet	92 I/12	50°34′	121°48′
Tezwa River	RIV/CDE	BC	Range 4 Coast	93 E/4	53°04′	127°48′
Tezzeron Creek	RIV/CDE	BC	Range 5 Coast	93 K/9	54°41′	124°19′
Tezzeron Lake	LAKE/LAC	BC	Range 5 Coast	93 K/9	54°42′	124°25′
Tezzeron Lake 8 - see-voir - Chuz Chun 8	IR/RI	BC		93 K/9	54°38′	124°23′
Tha-anne River	RIV/CDE	NT	Keewatin	55 D	60°31′	94°38′
Thackeray	UNP/LNO	SK	14-41-20-W3	73 C/10	52°31′	108°46′
Thackeray Lake	LAKE/LAC	SK	41-19-W3	73 C/10	52°33′	108°41′
Thackeray Point	CAPE/CAP	NT	Franklin	67 H	71°37′	99°33′

NAME NOM	ENTITY ENTITÉ	LOC 1 LIEU 1	LOC 2 LIEU 2	MAP CARTE	POSITION	
					LAT	LONG
Thaddeus	UNP/LNO	ON	Kenora	52 K/2	50°14'	92°55'
Thaddeus Lake	LAKE/LAC	ON	Kenora	52 K/2	50°11'	92°52'
Thalberg	UNP/LNO	MB	19-16-18-E	62 I/8	50°22'	96°29'
Thalbitzer, Cape	CAPE/CAP	NT	Franklin	37 C	69°53'	78°46'
Thamesford	UNP/LNO	ON	Oxford	40 P/2	43°04'	81°00'
Thames River	RIV/CDE	ON	Kent	40 J/8	42°19'	82°27'
Thames River Siding	UNP/LNO	ON	Elgin	40 I/14	42°46'	81°27'
Thames Road	UNP/LNO	ON	Huron	40 P/6	43°22'	81°25'
Thamesville	VILG/VILG	ON	Kent	40 I/12	42°33'	81°59'
Thaolintoa Lake	LAKE/LAC	NT	Keewatin	65 A	60°54'	96°25'
Thaxted	UNP/LNO	SK	18-46-18-W2	73 A/15	52°58'	104°36'
The Annex	UNP/LNO	ON	York	30 M/11	43°40'	79°24'
The Archipelago	MUN2/AZM2	ON	Parry Sound	41 H/9	45°35'	80°16'
The Back Settlement	UNP/LNO	ON	Algoma	41 J/8	46°15'	82°21'
The Battery	UNP/LNO	NF		1 N/10	47°34'	52°41'
The Battery	UNP/LNO	NF		1 N/11	47°33'	53°12'
The Beaches	UNP/LNO	NF		12 H/10	49°35'	56°50'
The Beaches	UNP/LNO	ON	York	30 M/11	43°40'	79°18'
The Block	UNP/LNO	NF		11 O/14	47°48'	59°20'
The Bluff	UNP/LNO	NB	Westmorland	21 I/2	46°14'	64°30'
The Boyne	UNP/LNO	ON	Dundas	31 G/3	45°07'	75°17'
The Broads	UNP/LNO	NF		1 N/11	47°31'	53°17'
The Brothers 18	IR/RI	NB	Kings	21 G/8	45°18'	66°06'
The Bush	UNP/LNO	ON	Leeds	31 C/9	44°35'	76°12'
The Cache	UNP/LNO	ON	Timiskaming	42 A/5	48°16'	81°34'
The Canadian Rocky Mountain Parks World Heritage Site - also-aussi - Parcs des montagnes Rocheuses canadiennes, Site du patrimoine mondial des	PARK/PARC	AB/BC		83 C/3	52°02'	117°07'
The Cedars	UNP/LNO	NB	Kings	21 G/8	45°29'	66°05'
The Corners	UNP/LNO	MB	18,19-21-W1	62 K/11	50°36'	101°23'
The Cottages	UNP/LNO	ON	Norfolk	40 I/9	42°36'	80°19'
The Dalles 38C	IR/RI	ON	Kenora	52 E/15	49°53'	94°32'
The Delta	UNP/LNO	ON	Wentworth	30 M/4	43°14'	79°49'
The Depot	UNP/LNO	ON	Parry Sound	41 H/16	45°59'	80°06'
Thedford	VILG/VILG	ON	Lambton	40 P/4	43°09'	81°51'
The Dock	UNP/LNO	NF		1 N/11	47°34'	53°15'
The Donovan	UNP/LNO	ON	Sudbury	41 I/6	46°30'	81°00'
The Droke	UNP/LNO	NF		1 M/3	47°04'	55°11'
The Elbow	UNP/LNO	MB	34-62-2-W	63 I/5	54°25'	97°41'
The Falls	UNP/LNO	NS	Colchester	11 E/11	45°38'	63°13'
The Flats	UNP/LNO	NF		1 K/13	46°48'	53°39'
The Forks National Historic Site - also-aussi - Fourche, Lieu historique national de la	PARK/PARC	MB		62 H/14	49°53'	97°08'
The Fort	UNP/LNO	QC	Le Haut-Saint-Laurent	31 H/4	45°03'	73°41'
The Front	UNP/LNO	NF		1 N/10	47°38'	52°56'
The Fur Trade at Lachine National Historic Site - also-aussi - Commerce-de-la-Fourrure-à-Lachine, Lieu historique national du	PARK/PARC	QC		31 H/5	45°26'	73°41'
The Gap No. 39	MUN2/AZM2	SK		72 H/7	49°25'	104°35'
The Glades	UNP/LNO	NB	Westmorland	21 H/14	45°57'	65°05'
The Glebe	UNP/LNO	ON	Carleton	31 G/5	45°24'	75°42'
The Glen	UNP/LNO	ON	Renfrew	31 F/10	45°45'	76°52'
The Golden Mile	UNP/LNO	ON	York	30 M/11	43°44'	79°17'
The Gore	UNP/LNO	ON	Oxford	40 I/15	43°00'	80°33'
The Gore	UNP/LNO	ON	Middlesex	40 I/14	42°59'	81°10'
The Gorge	UNP/LNO	NB	Westmorland	21 I/2	46°10'	64°53'
The Grange	UNP/LNO	ON	Peel	30 M/13	43°47'	79°59'
The Grant	UNP/LNO	NB	Kings	21 H/12	45°40'	65°53'
The Green	UNP/LNO	NF		1 N/10	47°39'	52°57'
The Grove	UNP/LNO	ON	Middlesex	40 P/3	43°02'	81°11'
The Groves	UNP/LNO	NF		1 N/2	47°02'	52°53'
The Gully	UNP/LNO	ON	Northumberland	31 D/1	44°00'	78°04'
The Hawk	UNP/LNO	NS	Shelburne	20 P/5	43°25'	65°37'
The Historic District of Québec World Heritage Site - also-aussi - Arrondissement historique de Québec, Site du patrimoine mondial de l'	PARK/PARC	QC		21 L/14	46°49'	71°13'
The Houser	UNP/LNO	NF		1 N/7	47°15'	52°46'
Theik 2	IR/RI	BC	Cowichan	92 B/12	48°44'	123°38'
The Island	UNP/LNO	ON	Grenville	31 B/13	44°51'	75°35'
The Junction	UNP/LNO	ON	York	30 M/11	43°40'	79°28'
The Junction	UNP/LNO	ON	Oxford	40 I/15	42°58'	80°36'
The Key 65	IR/RI	SK		62 M/9	51°45'	102°08'
The Keys	UNP/LNO	NF		1 N/7	47°18'	52°49'
The Kingsway	UNP/LNO	ON	York	30 M/12	43°39'	79°31'
Thekulthili Lake	LAKE/LAC	NT	Mackenzie	75 E	61°00'	110°06'
The Ledge	UNP/LNO	NB	Charlotte	21 G/3	45°11'	67°12'

NAME NOM	ENTITY ENTITÉ	LOC 1 LIEU 1	LOC 2 LIEU 2	MAP CARTE	POSITION LAT	LONG
The Lodge	UNP/LNO	NS	Lunenburg	21 A/9	44°33′	64°02′
Thelon River	RIV/CDE	NT	Keewatin	66 A/8	64°17′	96°05′
The Lookoff	UNP/LNO	NS	Kings	21 H/1	45°12′	64°25′
The Lots	UNP/LNO	NB	Northumberland	21 I/12	46°41′	65°51′
The Maples	UNP/LNO	ON	Dufferin	40 P/16	43°53′	80°10′
The Maples	UNP/LNO	MB		62 H/14	49°57′	97°10′
The Meadows	UNP/LNO	NS	Pictou	11 E/10	45°36′	62°39′
The Meadows	UNP/LNO	ON	Essex	40 J/3	42°02′	83°00′
The Mines	UNP/LNO	NF		1 N/12	47°35′	53°42′
Thémines, Rivière	RIV/CDE	QC	Caniapiscau	22 N/16	51°49′	68°27′
The Motion	UNP/LNO	NF		1 N/11	47°32′	53°17′
The Narrows	UNP/LNO	NS	Lunenburg	21 A/8	44°28′	64°20′
The Narrows	UNP/LNO	MB	14-24-10-W	62 O/2	51°05′	98°46′
The Narrows 49	IR/RI	MB		62 O/9	51°44′	98°27′
The Narrows 49A	IR/RI	MB		62 O/9	51°43′	98°22′
The Ninth	UNP/LNO	ON	Dundas	31 G/3	45°09′	75°16′
The North Shore	MUN2/AZM2	ON	Algoma	41 J/2	46°08′	82°35′
Théodat, Lac	LAKE/LAC	QC	Jamésie	32 K/16	50°55′	76°10′
Theodore	VILG/VILG	SK	15-28-7-W2	62 M/7	51°26′	102°55′
Theodosia Arm	UNP/LNO	BC	New Westminster	92 K/2	50°04′	124°42′
Theodosia River	RIV/CDE	BC	New Westminster	92 K/2	50°05′	124°39′
The Outlet	UNP/LNO	ON	Prince Edward	30 N/14	43°54′	77°13′
The Pas	TOWN/VIL2	MB		63 F/14	53°50′	101°15′
The Pas 21A - see-voir - Opaskwayak Cree Nation 21A	IR/RI	MB		63 F/14	53°48′	101°14′
The Pas 21B - see-voir - Opaskwayak Cree Nation 21B	IR/RI	MB		63 F/14	53°50′	101°13′
The Pas 21C - see-voir - Opaskwayak Cree Nation 21C	IR/RI	MB		63 F/14	53°49′	101°16′
The Pas 21D - see-voir - Opaskwayak Cree Nation 21D	IR/RI	MB		63 F/14	53°50′	101°17′
The Pas 21E - see-voir - Opaskwayak Cree Nation 21E	IR/RI	MB		63 F/14	53°52′	101°20′
The Pas 21F - see-voir - Opaskwayak Cree Nation 21F	IR/RI	MB		63 F/14	53°52′	101°22′
The Pas 21G - see-voir - Opaskwayak Cree Nation 21G	IR/RI	MB		63 F/14	53°56′	101°23′
The Pas 21I - see-voir - Opaskwayak Cree Nation 21I	IR/RI	MB		63 F/14	53°49′	101°19′
The Pas 21J - see-voir - Opaskwayak Cree Nation 21J	IR/RI	MB		63 F/14	53°50′	101°19′
The Pas 21K - see-voir - Opaskwayak Cree Nation 21K	IR/RI	MB		63 F/14	53°50′	101°22′
The Pas 21N - see-voir - Opaskwayak Cree Nation 21N	IR/RI	MB		63 F/14	53°48′	101°23′
The Pas 21P - see-voir - Opaskwayak Cree Nation 21P	IR/RI	MB		63 F/14	53°53′	101°28′
The Pas Airport	UNP/LNO	MB	57,58-25-W	63 F/14	53°59′	101°05′
The Pines	UNP/LNO	ON	Lennox and Addington	31 C/3	44°07′	77°00′
The Points West Bay	UNP/LNO	NS	Richmond	11 F/15	45°45′	60°58′
The P Patch	UNP/LNO	ON	Algoma	41 K/9	46°32′	84°18′
The Range	UNP/LNO	NB	Queens	21 I/4	46°04′	65°54′
Theresa	UNP/LNO	ON	Thunder Bay	42 E/10	49°42′	86°31′
Thérèse-De Blainville	MUN1/AZM1	QC	Thérèse-De Blainville	31 H/12	45°40′	73°53′
Theriau Lake	LAKE/LAC	SK		74 I/7	58°22′	104°35′
Thériault	UNP/LNO	NB	Gloucester	21 P/11	47°44′	65°03′
Theriault	UNP/LNO	NB	Madawaska	21 N/8	47°17′	68°05′
The Ridge	UNP/LNO	NB	Queens	21 I/4	46°10′	65°49′
The Ridge	UNP/LNO	ON	Hastings	31 C/13	44°48′	77°49′
Therien	UNP/LNO	AB	34-60-9-W4	73 L/3	54°14′	111°16′
The Rock	UNP/LNO	MB		62 I/9	50°34′	96°14′
The Rollway	UNP/LNO	ON	Prescott	31 G/11	45°32′	75°04′
Therrien, Lac	LAKE/LAC	QC	L'Islet	21 M/1	47°02′	70°07′
Thesiger Bay	BAY/BAIE	NT	Franklin	97 G	71°30′	124°05′
The Sixth	UNP/LNO	ON	Dundas	31 G/3	45°00′	75°16′
The Slash	UNP/LNO	ON	Manitoulin	41 H/12	45°37′	81°58′
The Spanish River	MUN2/AZM2	ON	Sudbury	41 J/1	46°12′	82°08′
Thessalon	TOWN/VIL2	ON	Algoma	41 J/5	46°15′	83°34′
Thessalon	MUN2/AZM2	ON	Algoma	41 J/5	46°18′	83°30′
Thessalon 12	IR/RI	ON	Algoma	41 J/3	46°15′	83°25′
The Tannery	UNP/LNO	ON	Lanark	31 F/1	45°13′	76°13′
Thetford Mines	CITY/VIL1	QC	L'Amiante	21 L/3	46°05′	71°18′
Thetford-Partie-Sud	VILG/VILG	QC	L'Amiante	21 L/3	46°04′	71°15′
The Thicket	UNP/LNO	NF		1 N/11	47°39′	53°15′
The Tickles	UNP/LNO	NF		1 M/9	47°31′	54°04′
Thetis Bay	BAY/BAIE	YT		117 D/12	69°34′	139°01′
Thetis Island	UNP/LNO	BC	Cowichan	92 B/13	48°59′	123°41′
Thetis Island	ISL/ÎLE	BC	Cowichan	92 B/13	49°00′	123°41′

NAME NOM	ENTITY ENTITÉ	LOC 1 LIEU 1	LOC 2 LIEU 2	MAP CARTE	POSITION LAT	LONG
Thetis Lake	LAKE/LAC	NT	Mackenzie	85 P	63°43′	113°15′
Thetlaandoa Creek	RIV/CDE	BC	Peace River	94 P/3	59°37′	121°28′
The Two Rivers	UNP/LNO	SK		63 M/14	55°45′	103°09′
Thévenet, Lac	LAKE/LAC	QC	Kativik	24 K/3	58°05′	69°24′
Thévet, Lac	LAKE/LAC	QC	Minganie	22 P/16	51°51′	64°13′
The Willows	UNP/LNO	NB	Northumberland	21 P/3	47°07′	65°16′
Thibaudeau	UNP/LNO	MB		54 E/1	57°04′	94°09′
Thibault	UNP/LNO	NB	Restigouche	21 O/11	47°36′	67°21′
Thibault Island	ISL/ÎLE	ON	Manitoulin	41 G/15	45°46′	82°56′
Thibaut, Lac	LAKE/LAC	QC	Kativik	24 G/5	57°30′	67°51′
Thibeault Terrace	UNP/LNO	ON	Nipissing	31 L/6	46°20′	79°28′
Thibeauville	UNP/LNO	NS	Richmond	11 F/10	45°39′	60°59′
Thiboult Bay	BAY/BAIE	NT	Franklin	57 E	70°58′	89°17′
Thicke Lake	LAKE/LAC	SK		74 O/7	59°28′	106°45′
Thicket Portage	UNP/LNO	MB	15-73-2-W	63 P/5	55°19′	97°41′
Thicksons Point	CAPE/CAP	ON	Ontario	30 M/15	43°51′	78°54′
Thickwood Hills	MTN/MNT	SK		73 G/4	53°05′	107°35′
Thickwood Hills	MTN/MNT	AB	88-15-W4	84 A/9	56°40′	112°10′
Thinahtea Lake	LAKE/LAC	BC	Peace River	94 P/9	59°41′	120°16′
Thirty Mile Lake	LAKE/LAC	NT	Keewatin	65 P	63°36′	96°30′
Thistle	UNP/LNO	ON	Grey	41 A/2	44°09′	80°42′
Thistle Creek	UNP/LNO	YT		115 O/3	63°04′	139°30′
Thistle Lake	LAKE/LAC	NT	Mackenzie	76 C	64°57′	108°39′
Thistlethwaite Lake	LAKE/LAC	NT	Mackenzie	85 P	63°10′	113°34′
Thistletown	UNP/LNO	ON	York	30 M/12	43°44′	79°33′
Thivierge	UNP/LNO	QC	Bonaventure	22 A/3	48°05′	65°29′
Thlewiaza River	RIV/CDE	NT	Keewatin	55 D	60°29′	94°40′
Thluicho Lake	LAKE/LAC	SK		74 N/11	59°43′	109°16′
Thoa River	RIV/CDE	NT	Mackenzie	75 C	60°31′	109°47′
Thode	VILG/VILG	SK	36-32-4-W3	72 O/16	51°47′	106°26′
Thomas	UNP/LNO	QC	Mékinac	31 I/16	46°48′	72°28′
Thomasburg	UNP/LNO	ON	Hastings	31 C/6	44°23′	77°21′
Thomas Falls	FALL/CHUT	NF		23 H/10	53°31′	64°30′
Thomas-Fortin, Réserve écologique	PARK/PARC	QC	Charlevoix	21 M/11	47°42′	71°03′
Thomas Hubbard, Cape	CAPE/CAP	NT	Franklin	560 D	81°22′	94°07′
Thomas Lake	LAKE/LAC	MB		64 A/15	57°00′	96°44′
Thomas Lake	LAKE/LAC	MB		64 F/15	57°57′	100°58′
Thomas Lake	LAKE/LAC	AB	47,48-12-W4	73 E/4	53°07′	111°43′
Thomas Lake	LAKE/LAC	BC	New Westminster	92 G/9	49°34′	122°26′
Thomas Lee Inlet	BAY/BAIE	NT	Franklin	58 H	75°35′	89°05′
Thomas Point	CAPE/CAP	ON	Manitoulin	41 H/12	45°32′	81°57′
Thomas Point 5	IR/RI	BC	Rupert	92 L/11	50°42′	127°23′
Thomas Point 5A	IR/RI	BC	Rupert	92 L/11	50°42′	127°23′
Thomas River	RIV/CDE	NF		13 K/4	54°15′	61°30′
Thomas Squinas Ranch 2A	IR/RI	BC	Range 3 Coast	93 C/6	52°29′	125°19′
Thomas-Sterry-Hunt, Réserve écologique internationale	PARK/PARC	QC	Montmagny	21 L/9	46°31′	70°02′
Thomaston Corner	UNP/LNO	NB	York	21 G/11	45°39′	67°08′
Thomasville	UNP/LNO	NS	Shelburne	20 P/11	43°34′	65°27′
Thom Bay	UNP/LNO	NT	Franklin	57 F	70°09′	92°24′
Thom Bay	BAY/BAIE	NT	Franklin	57 F	70°07′	92°06′
Thomlinson, Mount	MTN/MNT	BC	Cassiar	93 M/11	55°33′	127°29′
Thompson	CITY/VIL1	MB		63 P/12	55°45′	97°51′
Thompson	MUN2/AZM2	ON	Algoma	41 J/3	46°13′	83°09′
Thompson	MUN2/AZM2	MB		62 G/8	49°20′	98°15′
Thompson	UNP/LNO	BC	Kamloops Division Yale	92 I/6	50°16′	121°24′
Thompson	UNP/LNO	BC	New Westminster	92 G/3	49°10′	123°10′
Thompson Corner	UNP/LNO	NB	Kings	21 H/13	45°49′	65°41′
Thompson Glacier	GLAC/GLAC	NT	Franklin	59 H	79°30′	90°35′
Thompson Harbour	BAY/BAIE	NT	Keewatin	35 C	60°14′	77°34′
Thompson Hill	UNP/LNO	ON	Renfrew	31 F/7	45°28′	76°40′
Thompson Island	ISL/ÎLE	ON	Thunder Bay	52 A/3	48°10′	89°11′
Thompson Island	ISL/ÎLE	NT	Franklin	25 N	63°28′	68°29′
Thompson Junction	UNP/LNO	MB	33-74-1-E	63 P/6	55°28′	97°24′
Thompson Landing	UNP/LNO	NT	Mackenzie	75 L	62°55′	110°40′
Thompson, Mount	MTN/MNT	NT	Franklin	340 D	81°15′	76°57′
Thompson-Nicola	MUN1/AZM1	BC	Kamloops Division Yale	92 P/1	51°00′	120°30′
Thompson Point	CAPE/CAP	MB		54 K/7	58°19′	92°59′
Thompson River	RIV/CDE	BC	Kamloops Division Yale	92 I/4	50°14′	121°35′
Thompson Sound	UNP/LNO	BC	Range 1 Coast	92 L/16	50°48′	126°01′
Thompson Sound	CHAN/CHEN	BC	Range 1 Coast	92 L/16	50°47′	126°03′
Thompsonville	UNP/LNO	ON	Simcoe	31 D/4	44°08′	79°50′
Thomsen River	RIV/CDE	NT	Franklin	88 F/4	74°08′	119°45′
Thomson Arm	BAY/BAIE	SK		72 O/2	51°11′	106°49′
Thomson Lake	LAKE/LAC	SK		74 J/8	58°25′	106°08′
Thomson Lake	LAKE/LAC	SK	9,10-5-W3	72 G/10	49°45′	106°36′

NAME NOM	ENTITY ENTITÉ	LOC 1 LIEU 1	LOC 2 LIEU 2	MAP CARTE	POSITION LAT	POSITION LONG
Thomson Station	UNP/LNO	NS	Cumberland	11 E/12	45°41′	63°48′
Thomstown	UNP/LNO	ON	Durham	31 D/1	44°05′	78°24′
Thonokied Lake	LAKE/LAC	NT	Mackenzie	76 C	64°22′	109°40′
Thorah Beach	UNP/LNO	ON	Ontario	31 D/6	44°21′	79°12′
Thorah Island	UNP/LNO	ON	Ontario	31 D/6	44°26′	79°13′
Thorah Island	ISL/ÎLE	ON	Ontario	31 D/6	44°26′	79°14′
Thorburn	UNP/LNO	NS	Pictou	11 E/10	45°34′	62°33′
Thorburn Lake	UNP/LNO	NF		2 D/8	48°16′	54°10′
Thorburn Lake	LAKE/LAC	NF		2 D/8	48°16′	54°09′
Thorburn Road	UNP/LNO	NF		1 N/10	47°35′	52°51′
Thorel House	UNP/LNO	ON	Muskoka	31 E/4	45°10′	79°37′
Thorhild	VILG/VILG	AB	5-60-21-W4	83 I/3	54°10′	113°07′
Thorhild No. 7, County of	MUN1/AZM1	AB	60-21-W4	83 I/3	54°13′	113°03′
Thor Island	ISL/ÎLE	NT	Franklin	69 F	78°12′	103°00′
Thor Lake	UNP/LNO	ON	Sudbury	41 P/3	47°09′	81°18′
Thormanby Islands	ISL/ÎLE	BC	New Westminster	92 G/5	49°30′	124°00′
Thornbrough Channel	CHAN/CHEN	BC	New Westminster	92 G/6	49°29′	123°28′
Thornbury	TOWN/VIL2	ON	Grey	41 A/9	44°34′	80°26′
Thornby	UNP/LNO	QC	Pontiac	31 F/16	45°47′	76°29′
Thorncliff	UNP/LNO	ON	Nipissing	31 L/6	46°16′	79°23′
Thorncliffe	UNP/LNO	ON	York	30 M/11	43°42′	79°21′
Thorncliffe	UNP/LNO	ON	Kent	40 J/9	42°33′	82°07′
Thorncrest Village	UNP/LNO	ON	York	30 M/12	43°40′	79°32′
Thorndale	UNP/LNO	ON	Middlesex	40 P/3	43°06′	81°08′
Thorne	VILG/VILG	QC	Pontiac	31 F/16	45°45′	76°26′
Thorne	UNP/LNO	ON	Nipissing	31 L/11	46°42′	79°06′
Thorne Centre	UNP/LNO	QC	Pontiac	31 F/9	45°44′	76°23′
Thorne, Lac	LAKE/LAC	QC	Pontiac	31 F/9	45°41′	76°22′
Thorne Lake	UNP/LNO	QC	Pontiac	31 F/9	45°41′	76°22′
Thorne River	RIV/CDE	ON	Kenora	53 J/15	54°56′	90°35′
Thornes Cove	UNP/LNO	NS	Annapolis	21 A/12	44°42′	65°41′
Thornetown	UNP/LNO	NB	Queens	21 H/13	45°52′	65°51′
Thornhill	UNP/LNO	NS	Halifax	11 D/12	44°36′	63°37′
Thornhill	UNP/LNO	ON	York	30 M/14	43°48′	79°25′
Thornhill	UNP/LNO	MB	8-3-6-W	62 G/1	49°12′	98°14′
Thornhill	UNP/LNO	BC	Range 5 Coast	103 I/10	54°31′	128°32′
Thornlea	UNP/LNO	NF		1 N/12	47°36′	53°43′
Thornlea	UNP/LNO	ON	York	30 M/14	43°49′	79°24′
Thornloe	VILG/VILG	ON	Timiskaming	31 M/12	47°40′	79°45′
Thornton	UNP/LNO	ON	Simcoe	31 D/5	44°16′	79°43′
Thornton Yard	UNP/LNO	BC	New Westminster	92 G/2	49°13′	122°50′
Thornyhurst	UNP/LNO	ON	Lambton	40 J/9	42°41′	82°25′
Thorold	CITY/VIL1	ON	Welland	30 M/3	43°07′	79°12′
Thorold Park	UNP/LNO	ON	Welland	30 M/3	43°07′	79°13′
Thorold South	UNP/LNO	ON	Welland	30 M/3	43°06′	79°12′
Thoroughfare	UNP/LNO	NF		2 C/4	48°12′	53°33′
Thorpe	UNP/LNO	ON	Lennox and Addington	31 C/7	44°18′	76°46′
Thorsby	VILG/VILG	AB	14-49-1-W5	83 G/1	53°14′	114°03′
Thorstein, Cape	CAPE/CAP	NT	Franklin	69 F	78°07′	103°10′
Thorsteinson Lake	LAKE/LAC	MB		64 H/3	57°15′	97°30′
Thorton Woods	UNP/LNO	ON	Ontario	30 M/15	43°54′	78°54′
Thorvald Peninsula	CAPE/CAP	NT	Franklin	39 F	78°58′	76°30′
Thousand Islands	ISL/ÎLE	ON	Leeds	31 B/5	44°22′	75°55′
Thrasher	UNP/LNO	SK	2-28-15-W3	72 O/5	51°22′	108°00′
Thrasher's Corners	UNP/LNO	ON	Hastings	31 C/6	44°16′	77°22′
Three Arms	UNP/LNO	NF		2 E/12	49°41′	55°54′
Three Bridges	UNP/LNO	ON	Middlesex	40 P/3	43°03′	81°03′
Three Brooks	UNP/LNO	NS	Pictou	11 E/10	45°43′	62°47′
Three Brooks	UNP/LNO	NB	Victoria	21 J/14	46°52′	67°26′
Three Brooks	RIV/CDE	NF		2 D/13	48°56′	55°32′
Three Brothers Mountain	MTN/MNT	BC	Yale Division Yale	92 H/2	49°10′	120°46′
Three Corner Pond	LAKE/LAC	NF		12 H/1	49°12′	56°18′
Three Creeks	UNP/LNO	AB	15-85-20-W5	84 C/6	56°21′	117°05′
Three Day Lake	LAKE/LAC	NT	Mackenzie	96 E	65°09′	126°46′
Three Fathom Harbour	UNP/LNO	NS	Halifax	11 D/11	44°39′	63°17′
Three Forks	UNP/LNO	BC	Kootenay	82 K/3	50°01′	117°17′
Three Hills	TOWN/VIL2	AB	36-31-24-W4	82 P/11	51°42′	113°16′
Threehills Creek	RIV/CDE	AB	3-30-21-W4	82 P/10	51°32′	112°53′
Threehouse	UNP/LNO	MB	4-68-17-W	63 J/13	54°52′	100°00′
Three Islands	ISL/ÎLE	NB	Charlotte	21 B/10	44°35′	66°46′
Three Islands 3	IR/RI	BC	New Westminster	92 G/1	49°07′	122°20′
Three Lakes No. 400	MUN2/AZM2	SK		73 A/6	52°30′	105°15′
Three Mile Lake	LAKE/LAC	ON	Muskoka	31 E/3	45°10′	79°27′
Three Mile Plains	UNP/LNO	NS	Hants	21 A/16	44°58′	64°07′
Three Mile Rock	UNP/LNO	NF		12 I/4	50°00′	57°45′

NAME / NOM	ENTITY / ENTITÉ	LOC 1 / LIEU 1	LOC 2 / LIEU 2	MAP / CARTE	POSITION LAT	POSITION LONG
Threenarrows Lake	LAKE/LAC	ON	Manitoulin	41 I/3	46°05′	81°27′
Threepoint Creek	RIV/CDE	AB	34-20-2-W5	82 J/9	50°44′	114°12′
Threepoint Lake	LAKE/LAC	MB	77,78-10,11-W	63 O/10	55°41′	98°55′
Three Rock Cove	UNP/LNO	NF		12 B/11	48°37′	59°05′
Three Tree Creek	UNP/LNO	NB	Sunbury	21 G/10	45°42′	66°36′
Three Valley	UNP/LNO	BC	Kamloops Division Yale	82 L/16	50°56′	118°28′
Three Wives Lake	LAKE/LAC	NT	Mackenzie	65 E	61°08′	102°47′
Throat River	RIV/CDE	ON	Kenora	52 N/13	51°48′	93°30′
Throat, The	CHAN/CHEN	NT	Franklin	34 F	57°03′	76°40′
Throne	UNP/LNO	AB	31-35-9-W4	73 D/3	52°03′	111°17′
Throoptown	UNP/LNO	ON	Grenville	31 B/13	44°47′	75°41′
Thrum Point	CAPE/CAP	NS	Queens	20 P/15	43°47′	64°54′
Thrums	UNP/LNO	BC	Kootenay	82 F/5	49°20′	117°35′
Thubun Lakes	LAKE/LAC	NT	Mackenzie	75 E	61°32′	111°55′
Thubun River	RIV/CDE	NT	Mackenzie	85 H/7	61°29′	112°34′
Thuchonilini Lake	LAKE/LAC	NT	Keewatin	65 A	60°42′	96°30′
Thudaka Creek	RIV/CDE	BC	Cassiar	94 E/9	57°37′	126°28′
Thule Valley	SEAU/SMER	—		5.17	77°20′	70°00′
Thultue Lake	LAKE/LAC	AB	122-21,22-W4	84 P/12	59°37′	113°40′
Thunder Bay	CITY/VIL1	ON	Thunder Bay	52 A/6	48°24′	89°19′
Thunder Bay	UNP/LNO	ON	Welland	30 L/14	42°53′	79°02′
Thunder Bay	GEOG/GÉOG	ON		52 H/7	49°30′	88°30′
Thunder Bay	BAY/BAIE	ON	Thunder Bay	52 A/6	48°25′	89°00′
Thunder Bay	BAY/BAIE	BC	New Westminster	92 F/16	49°46′	124°16′
Thunder Beach	UNP/LNO	ON	Simcoe	41 A/16	44°48′	80°04′
Thunderbird	UNP/LNO	BC	Range 5 Coast	103 I/7	54°27′	128°38′
Thunder Cape	CAPE/CAP	ON	Thunder Bay	52 A/7	48°18′	88°56′
Thunderchild	UNP/LNO	SK	5-52-20-W3	73 F/7	53°28′	108°56′
Thunderchild 115D	IR/RI	SK		73 F/16	53°48′	108°12′
Thundercloud Creek	RIV/CDE	NT	Mackenzie	95 L	62°49′	126°37′
Thundercloud Range	MTN/MNT	NT	Mackenzie	95 L	62°35′	126°00′
Thunder Creek	UNP/LNO	SK	35-19-5-W3	72 J/10	50°39′	106°35′
Thunder Creek	RIV/CDE	SK	33-16-26-W2	72 I/5	50°23′	105°32′
Thunder Hill	UNP/LNO	MB	10-35-29-W	62 N/13	52°00′	101°31′
Thunderhill Junction	UNP/LNO	MB	36-27-W	63 C/3	52°05′	101°16′
Thunder Hills	MTN/MNT	SK		73 J/9	54°32′	106°15′
Thunder Lake Provincial Park	PARK/PARC	AB	29,30-59-5-W5	83 J/2	54°08′	114°43′
Thunder River	UNP/LNO	BC	Kamloops Division Yale	83 D/3	52°14′	119°12′
Thunder River	RIV/CDE	BC	Kamloops Division Yale	83 D/3	52°13′	119°12′
Thurlow	MUN2/AZM2	ON	Hastings	31 C/6	44°15′	77°21′
Thurlow	UNP/LNO	ON	Hastings	31 C/3	44°11′	77°18′
Thurlow	UNP/LNO	BC	Range 1 Coast	92 K/6	50°27′	125°22′
Thurlow Islands	ISL/ÎLE	BC	Range 1 Coast	92 K/5	50°25′	125°35′
Thurso	CITY/VIL1	QC	Papineau	31 G/11	45°36′	75°15′
Thurston Bay	UNP/LNO	BC	Sayward	92 K/6	50°23′	125°19′
Thurston Harbour	UNP/LNO	BC	Queen Charlotte	103 B/13	52°50′	131°45′
Thurston Lake	LAKE/LAC	AB	126-1-W6	84 M/16	59°56′	118°07′
Thutade Lake	LAKE/LAC	BC	Cassiar	94 D/15	56°53′	126°59′
Thuya Creek	RIV/CDE	BC	Kamloops Division Yale	92 P/8	51°23′	120°11′
Thwaites	UNP/LNO	ON	Timiskaming	31 M/12	47°40′	79°38′
Thwart Island	ISL/ÎLE	NF		2 E/6	49°19′	55°10′
Thwaytes	UNP/LNO	BC	New Westminster	92 G/7	49°23′	122°53′
Thynne, Mount	MTN/MNT	BC	Yale Division Yale	92 H/10	49°42′	120°55′
Tiahn 27	IR/RI	BC	Queen Charlotte	103 F/14	53°47′	133°05′
Tian Head	CAPE/CAP	BC	Queen Charlotte	103 F/14	53°47′	133°07′
Tibbets	UNP/LNO	BC	Range 5 Coast	93 K/3	54°10′	125°28′
Tibbos Hill	UNP/LNO	NF		1 M/5	47°30′	55°36′
Tibériade, Lac	LAKE/LAC	QC	Antoine-Labelle	31 J/10	46°31′	74°59′
Tibielik River	RIV/CDE	NT	Keewatin	66 C	64°41′	100°04′
Tibiska Lake	LAKE/LAC	SK	61-1-W3	73 J/8	54°16′	106°08′
Tiblemont	UNP/LNO	QC	Vallée-de-l'Or	32 C/6	48°19′	77°19′
Tiblemont, Lac	LAKE/LAC	QC	Vallée-de-l'Or	32 C/3	48°14′	77°19′
Ticehurst Corners	UNP/LNO	QC	Memphrémagog	31 H/1	45°05′	72°07′
Tice Lake	LAKE/LAC	MB		64 N/14	59°48′	101°03′
Tichborne	UNP/LNO	ON	Frontenac	31 C/10	44°40′	76°41′
Tichégami, Rivière	RIV/CDE	QC	Jamésie	32 P/13	51°55′	73°44′
Tichfield Junction	UNP/LNO	SK	26-8-W3	72 O/6	51°16′	107°02′
Tickle Bay	BAY/BAIE	NF		1 N/12	47°39′	53°46′
Tickle Cove	UNP/LNO	NF		2 C/11	48°35′	53°29′
Tickle Harbour Point	CAPE/CAP	NF		1 N/12	47°42′	53°42′
Tickle Harbour Station	UNP/LNO	NF		1 N/12	47°35′	53°50′
Tickles	UNP/LNO	NF		1 N/4	47°09′	53°34′
Ticouapé	UNP/LNO	QC	Le Domaine-du-Roy	32 A/9	48°42′	72°29′
Tidal	UNP/LNO	MB		54 L/9	58°40′	94°07′
Tidd, Mount	MTN/MNT	YT		105 J/3	62°09′	131°19′

NAME NOM	ENTITY ENTITÉ	LOC 1 LIEU 1	LOC 2 LIEU 2	MAP CARTE	POSITION LAT	POSITION LONG
Tiddville	UNP/LNO	NS	Digby	21 B/8	44°25′	66°10′
Tideflat Bay	BAY/BAIE	NT	Franklin	37 C	69°12′	78°26′
Tide Head	VILG/VILG	NB	Restigouche	21 O/15	47°59′	66°47′
Tide Lake	LAKE/LAC	ON	Kenora	52 K/5	50°20′	93°58′
Tide Lake	LAKE/LAC	AB	18,19-10-W4	72 L/11	50°33′	111°20′
Tidney River	RIV/CDE	NS	Shelburne	20 P/14	43°50′	65°03′
Tidnish	UNP/LNO	NS	Cumberland	21 H/16	45°59′	64°01′
Tidnish Bridge	UNP/LNO	NS/NB		21 H/16	45°59′	64°02′
Tidnish Bridge	UNP/LNO	NB/NS		21 H/16	45°59′	64°03′
Tidnish Cross Roads	UNP/LNO	NS	Cumberland	21 H/16	45°59′	64°00′
Tidnish River	RIV/CDE	NS	Cumberland	21 H/16	45°59′	64°03′
Tiedemann Glacier	GLAC/GLAC	BC	Range 2 Coast	92 N/6	51°20′	125°03′
Tieland	UNP/LNO	AB	14-67-2-W5	83 J/16	54°48′	114°11′
Tiercel Island	ISL/ÎLE	NT	Franklin	24 K/14	59°00′	69°02′
Tiffin	UNP/LNO	ON	Simcoe	31 D/12	44°45′	79°51′
Tiger Hills	UNP/LNO	SK	31-45-24-W2	73 A/14	52°55′	105°29′
Tiger Hills	MTN/MNT	MB		62 G/6	49°25′	99°20′
Tiger Lily	UNP/LNO	AB	13-60-6-W5	83 J/2	54°11′	114°46′
Tignish	VILG/VILG	PE	Prince	21 I/16	46°57′	64°02′
Tignish	UNP/LNO	PE	Prince	21 I/16	46°57′	64°02′
Tignish Corner	UNP/LNO	PE	Prince	21 I/16	46°57′	64°03′
Tignish Shore	VILG/VILG	PE	Prince	21 I/16	46°57′	64°00′
Tigonankweine Range	MTN/MNT	NT	Mackenzie	96 D/4	64°04′	127°45′
Tiilis - see-voir - Tiilis Landing	UNP/LNO	BC		82 L/14	50°55′	119°05′
Tiilis Landing	UNP/LNO	BC	Kamloops Division Yale	82 L/14	50°55′	119°05′
Tikirartuuq, Lac	LAKE/LAC	QC	Kativik	34 G/4	57°10′	75°55′
Tikkoatokak Bay	BAY/BAIE	NF		14 D/9	56°42′	62°12′
Tilbury	TOWN/VIL2	ON	Kent	40 J/8	42°16′	82°26′
Tilbury	UNP/LNO	BC	New Westminster	92 G/3	49°08′	123°01′
Tilbury Centre - see-voir - Tilbury	VILG/VILG	ON		40 J/8	42°16′	82°26′
Tilbury East	MUN2/AZM2	ON	Kent	40 J/1	42°14′	82°20′
Tilbury North	MUN2/AZM2	ON	Essex	40 J/7	42°17′	82°30′
Tilbury West	MUN2/AZM2	ON	Essex	40 J/2	42°13′	82°33′
Tilchuse River	RIV/CDE	NT	Mackenzie	86 F	65°52′	117°38′
Tilden Lake	UNP/LNO	ON	Nipissing	31 L/12	46°35′	79°38′
Tilgatko 17	IR/RI	BC	Range 3 Coast	93 C/13	52°52′	125°42′
Tillei Lake	LAKE/LAC	YT		105 H/14	61°46′	129°29′
Tilley	VILG/VILG	AB	19-17-12-W4	72 L/5	50°27′	111°39′
Tilley	UNP/LNO	ON	Leeds	31 B/5	44°27′	76°00′
Tilley Road	UNP/LNO	NB	Gloucester	21 P/11	47°32′	65°03′
Tillicum	UNP/LNO	BC	Victoria	92 B/6	48°27′	123°24′
Tillion 4	IR/RI	BC	Cariboo	93 B/1	52°10′	122°17′
Tillsonburg	TOWN/VIL2	ON	Oxford	40 I/15	42°51′	80°44′
Tilly, Lac	LAKE/LAC	QC	Jamésie	33 H/13	53°55′	73°58′
Tilney	UNP/LNO	SK	4-15-25-W2	72 I/3	50°14′	105°24′
Tilston	UNP/LNO	MB	15-5-29-W	62 F/6	49°24′	101°19′
Tilt Cove	VILG/VILG	NF		2 E/13	49°53′	55°38′
Tilt Cove	UNP/LNO	NF		2 E/10	49°33′	54°44′
Tilting	VILG/VILG	NF		2 E/9	49°42′	54°04′
Tilton	UNP/LNO	NF		1 N/11	47°38′	53°18′
Tilts	UNP/LNO	NF		1 L/16	46°48′	54°06′
Timagami Lodge	UNP/LNO	ON	Nipissing	41 I/16	46°58′	80°03′
Timber Bay	HAM/HAM	SK	29-59-25-W2	73 I/4	54°10′	105°42′
Timber Lake	LAKE/LAC	NS	Lunenburg	21 A/9	44°42′	64°10′
Timberlea	UNP/LNO	NS	Halifax	11 D/12	44°40′	63°45′
Timber River	UNP/LNO	NB	Westmorland	21 I/1	46°04′	64°03′
Timberton	UNP/LNO	MB	7-26-25-W	62 N/2	51°14′	100°58′
Timeu	UNP/LNO	AB	6-64-4-W5	83 J/10	54°30′	114°35′
Timeu Creek	RIV/CDE	AB	19-63-3-W5	83 J/8	54°28′	114°27′
Timiskaming	GEOG/GÉOG	ON		41 P/6	47°45′	80°20′
Timiskaming 19	IR/RI	QC	Témiscamingue	31 M/11	47°38′	79°28′
Timiskaming, Lake - also-aussi - **Témiscamingue, Lac**	LAKE/LAC	QC/ON		31 M/3	47°15′	79°27′
Timmins	CITY/VIL1	ON	Cochrane	42 A/6	48°28′	81°20′
Timothy Lake	LAKE/LAC	BC	Lillooet	92 P/14	51°51′	121°16′
Tim River	RIV/CDE	ON	Nipissing	31 E/15	45°47′	78°42′
Tims Harbour	UNP/LNO	NF		2 E/8	49°27′	54°29′
Tincap	UNP/LNO	ON	Leeds	31 B/12	44°37′	75°45′
Tinchebray	UNP/LNO	AB	11-40-14-W4	73 D/5	52°26′	111°56′
Tincup Lake	LAKE/LAC	YT		115 G/14	61°46′	139°14′
Tingin Fiord	BAY/BAIE	NT	Franklin	27 C	69°09′	68°40′
Tingwick	VILG/VILG	QC	Arthabaska	21 E/13	45°53′	71°57′
Tinker	UNP/LNO	NB	Victoria	21 J/13	46°48′	67°46′
Tinmusket 5A	IR/RI	BC	Lillooet	92 P/5	51°23′	121°30′
Tinney Point	CAPE/CAP	NT	Mackenzie	87 C/5	69°21′	119°48′
Tinniswood, Mount	MTN/MNT	BC	Lillooet	92 J/5	50°19′	123°50′

NAME / NOM	ENTITY / ENTITÉ	LOC 1 / LIEU 1	LOC 2 / LIEU 2	MAP / CARTE	POSITION LAT	POSITION LONG
Tintagel	UNP/LNO	BC	Range 5 Coast	93 K/4	54°12′	125°36′
Tintern	UNP/LNO	ON	Lincoln	30 M/3	43°06′	79°25′
Tin Town	UNP/LNO	MB		62 J/1	50°10′	98°12′
Tin Wis	IR/RI	BC	Clayoquot	92 F/4	49°08′	125°54′
Tiny	MUN2/AZM2	ON	Simcoe	31 D/12	44°41′	79°56′
Tiny	UNP/LNO	SK	12-31-5-W2	62 M/10	51°40′	102°36′
Tioga	UNP/LNO	ON	Simcoe	31 D/4	44°13′	79°58′
Tionaga	UNP/LNO	ON	Sudbury	42 B/1	48°05′	82°06′
Tipella	UNP/LNO	BC	New Westminster	92 G/9	49°44′	122°09′
Tipella 7	IR/RI	BC	New Westminster	92 G/16	49°47′	122°13′
Tipitu Pachistuwakan	UNP/LNO	QC	Jamésie	32 M/15	52°00′	78°43′
Tippo River	RIV/CDE	SK	73-5-W3	73 O/7	55°20′	106°44′
Tip Top Mountain	MTN/MNT	ON	Thunder Bay	42 C/5	48°16′	86°00′
Tisdale	TOWN/VIL2	SK	1-45-15-W2	73 A/16	52°51′	104°03′
Tisdale No. 427	MUN2/AZM2	SK		73 A/16	52°50′	104°00′
Tisdall	UNP/LNO	BC	Lillooet	92 J/7	50°17′	122°52′
Tisdall Lake	LAKE/LAC	BC	Cariboo	93 A/3	52°14′	121°01′
Titanic	UNP/LNO	SK	19-44-3-W3	73 B/16	52°52′	106°26′
Titanic Canyon - also-aussi - Titanic, Canyon du	SEAU/SMER	—		NK22 B	41°23′	50°30′
Titanic, Canyon du - also-aussi - Titanic Canyon	SEAU/SMER	—		NK22 B	41°23′	50°30′
Titmarsh Lake	LAKE/LAC	ON	Thunder Bay	52 B/7	48°22′	90°32′
Tittle Road	UNP/LNO	NS	Guysborough	11 F/6	45°20′	61°02′
Titus	UNP/LNO	QC	Le Val-Saint-François	21 E/12	45°31′	71°59′
Titusville	UNP/LNO	NB	Kings	21 H/5	45°29′	65°45′
Tiverton	VILG/VILG	NS	Digby	21 B/8	44°23′	66°13′
Tiverton	VILG/VILG	ON	Bruce	41 A/5	44°16′	81°32′
Tizzard's Harbour	UNP/LNO	NF		2 E/10	49°36′	54°48′
Tlell	UNP/LNO	BC	Queen Charlotte	103 G/12	53°34′	131°56′
Tl'o Ba 22	IR/RI	BC	Range 5 Coast	93 K/15	54°48′	124°41′
Tlogotsho Range	MTN/MNT	NT/YT		95 F/1	61°03′	124°30′
Tlupana Inlet	BAY/BAIE	BC	Nootka	92 E/9	49°43′	126°28′
Tlupana River	RIV/CDE	BC	Nootka	92 E/16	49°45′	126°23′
T Mountain	MTN/MNT	BC	Cassiar	104 F/1	57°13′	132°15′
Toad Lake	LAKE/LAC	ON	Parry Sound	41 H/16	45°54′	80°03′
Toad River	UNP/LNO	BC	Peace River	94 K/14	58°51′	125°14′
Toad River	RIV/CDE	BC	Peace River	94 N/7	59°23′	124°55′
Toanche	UNP/LNO	ON	Simcoe	31 D/13	44°48′	79°57′
Tobacco Lake	UNP/LNO	ON	Manitoulin	41 G/16	45°51′	82°26′
Tobacco Lake	LAKE/LAC	ON	Manitoulin	41 G/16	45°51′	82°27′
Tobacco Plains 2	IR/RI	BC	Kootenay	82 G/3	49°03′	115°06′
Toba Glacier	GLAC/GLAC	BC	Range 1 Coast	92 J/13	50°46′	124°00′
Toba Inlet	BAY/BAIE	BC	Range 1 Coast	92 K/7	50°25′	124°35′
Toba River	RIV/CDE	BC	Range 1 Coast	92 K/8	50°30′	124°21′
Tobeatic Lake	LAKE/LAC	NS	Queens	21 A/3	44°12′	65°17′
Tobermory	UNP/LNO	ON	Bruce	41 H/5	45°15′	81°40′
Tobey	UNP/LNO	SK	31-52-6-W3	73 G/10	53°32′	106°53′
Tobin Lake	VILG/VILG	SK	29-52-12-W2	63 E/12	53°31′	103°44′
Tobin Lake	LAKE/LAC	SK		63 E/11	53°35′	103°30′
Tobique 20	IR/RI	NB	Victoria	21 J/13	46°48′	67°41′
Tobique Narrows	UNP/LNO	NB	Victoria	21 J/13	46°47′	67°41′
Tobique River	RIV/CDE	NB	Victoria	21 J/13	46°46′	67°42′
Toby Creek	UNP/LNO	BC	Kootenay	82 K/8	50°20′	116°25′
Toby Creek	RIV/CDE	BC	Kootenay	82 K/9	50°32′	116°02′
Toby Helenes Meadow 9	IR/RI	BC	Range 3 Coast	93 C/8	52°16′	124°10′
Toby Helenes Meadow 10	IR/RI	BC	Range 3 Coast	93 C/1	52°13′	124°07′
Toby Helenes Meadow 11	IR/RI	BC	Range 3 Coast	93 C/1	52°13′	124°08′
Toby Lake 6	IR/RI	BC	Lillooet	92 P/5	51°23′	121°37′
Toby's Meadow 4	IR/RI	BC	Range 3 Coast	93 C/8	52°18′	124°11′
Tochatwi Bay	BAY/BAIE	NT	Mackenzie	75 L	62°37′	110°10′
Tochatwi Lake	LAKE/LAC	NT	Mackenzie	75 K	62°38′	109°37′
Tochcha Lake	LAKE/LAC	BC	Range 5 Coast	93 K/13	54°57′	125°55′
Tocheri Lake	LAKE/LAC	ON	Algoma	42 F/3	49°03′	85°09′
Tochty	UNP/LNO	BC	Kootenay	82 G/4	49°12′	115°59′
Tod Creek	UNP/LNO	AB	25-9-3-W5	82 G/16	49°46′	114°16′
Todd, Mount	MTN/MNT	BC	Malahat	92 B/12	48°37′	123°56′
Todd Mountain	MTN/MNT	NB	York	21 J/10	46°33′	66°42′
Todds Island	UNP/LNO	NS	Halifax	11 D/12	44°41′	63°54′
Tod Lake	LAKE/LAC	MB		64 C/12	56°34′	101°46′
Tod, Mount	MTN/MNT	BC	Kamloops Division Yale	82 L/13	50°55′	119°56′
Tofield	TOWN/VIL2	AB	1-51-19-W4	83 H/7	53°22′	112°40′
Tofino	MUN1/AZM1	BC	Clayoquot	92 F/4	49°07′	125°53′
Tofino Creek	RIV/CDE	BC	Clayoquot	92 F/4	49°14′	125°36′
Tofino Inlet	BAY/BAIE	BC	Clayoquot	92 F/4	49°09′	125°40′
Togo	VILG/VILG	SK	1-28-30-W	62 N/5	51°24′	101°35′
Toh-quo-eugh 2	IR/RI	BC	Rupert	92 L/12	50°37′	127°52′

NAME NOM	ENTITY ENTITÉ	LOC 1 LIEU 1	LOC 2 LIEU 2	MAP CARTE	POSITION LAT	LONG
Toimela	UNP/LNO	ON	Thunder Bay	52 A/11	48°33′	89°23′
Tokenatch 5	IR/RI	BC	New Westminster	92 F/15	49°58′	124°41′
Toker Point	CAPE/CAP	NT	Mackenzie	107 C	69°39′	132°50′
Toketic	UNP/LNO	BC	Kamloops Division Yale	92 I/11	50°32′	121°17′
Toksee 4	IR/RI	BC	Range 2 Coast	92 M/3	51°14′	127°20′
Toledo	UNP/LNO	ON	Leeds	31 B/12	44°44′	76°00′
Tollendal	UNP/LNO	ON	Simcoe	31 D/5	44°23′	79°39′
Tollgate	UNP/LNO	ON	Oxford	40 P/2	43°10′	80°47′
Tolman	UNP/LNO	AB	14,23-33-22-W4	82 P/14	51°50′	113°01′
Tolmie	UNP/LNO	ON	Bruce	41 A/11	44°37′	81°14′
Tolmie Channel	CHAN/CHEN	BC	Range 3 Coast	103 A/15	52°48′	128°33′
Tolmies Corners	UNP/LNO	ON	Stormont	31 G/2	45°14′	74°57′
Tolsmaville	UNP/LNO	ON	Manitoulin	41 G/14	45°57′	83°19′
Tolsta	UNP/LNO	QC	Le Granit	21 E/11	45°40′	71°13′
Tolstad	UNP/LNO	AB	33-69-4-W6	83 M/2	55°01′	118°34′
Tolstoi	UNP/LNO	MB	35,36-1-5-E	62 H/2	49°04′	96°49′
Tomahawk	UNP/LNO	AB	12-51-6-W5	83 G/7	53°24′	114°46′
Tomasine, Lac	LAKE/LAC	QC	La Vallée-de-la-Gatineau	31 K/9	46°44′	76°19′
Tomasine, Rivière	RIV/CDE	QC	La Vallée-de-la-Gatineau	31 K/9	46°40′	76°16′
Tomawapocokanan	UNP/LNO	QC	Le Haut-Saint-Maurice	32 B/7	48°21′	74°39′
Tom Browne Lake	LAKE/LAC	BC	Range 1 Coast	92 K/12	50°37′	125°45′
Tomelin Bluffs	UNP/LNO	ON	Muskoka	31 E/6	45°16′	79°28′
Tomias Mountain	MTN/MNT	BC	Cassiar	94 E/5	57°26′	127°44′
Tomifobia	UNP/LNO	QC	Memphrémagog	31 H/1	45°03′	72°08′
Tomiko	UNP/LNO	ON	Nipissing	31 L/11	46°34′	79°25′
Tomiko Lake	LAKE/LAC	ON	Nipissing	31 L/12	46°32′	79°49′
Tomiko River	RIV/CDE	ON	Nipissing	31 L/5	46°29′	79°57′
Tom Joe Brook	RIV/CDE	NF		2 D/13	46°57′	55°56′
Tomkinsville	UNP/LNO	NS	Cape Breton	11 K/1	46°11′	60°02′
Tom Longboat Corners	UNP/LNO	ON	Brant	40 P/1	43°05′	80°03′
Tom Luscombe Brook	RIV/CDE	NF		13 J/8	54°21′	58°12′
Tom, Mount	MTN/MNT	BC	Lillooet	92 O/6	51°20′	123°10′
Tommy Jack, Mount	MTN/MNT	BC	Cassiar	94 D/4	56°03′	127°47′
Tommy Lakes	LAKE/LAC	BC	Peace River	94 H/13	57°47′	121°53′
Tommy's Arm River	RIV/CDE	NF		2 E/5	49°28′	55°52′
Tompkins	VILG/VILG	SK	10-13-21-W3	72 K/2	50°04′	108°47′
Tompkins	UNP/LNO	NF		11 O/14	47°48′	59°13′
Tom-Rule's Ground	UNP/LNO	QC	Côte-Nord-du-Golfe-Saint-Laurent	12 P/5	51°28′	57°56′
Tomslake	UNP/LNO	BC	Peace River	93 P/9	55°33′	120°05′
Tomstown	UNP/LNO	ON	Timiskaming	31 M/13	47°48′	79°45′
Tondern	UNP/LNO	ON	Algoma	42 F/6	49°19′	85°00′
Toney Lake	LAKE/LAC	NS	Queens	21 A/2	44°06′	64°58′
Toney Mills	UNP/LNO	NS	Pictou	11 E/15	45°45′	62°55′
Toney River	UNP/LNO	NS	Pictou	11 E/15	45°47′	62°54′
Toniata	UNP/LNO	MB	4,5-9-17-E	52 E/11	49°43′	95°14′
Tonkin	UNP/LNO	SK	25,26-2-W2	62 M/1	51°13′	102°16′
Tonnerre, Pointe au	CAPE/CAP	QC	Minganie	22 I/7	50°16′	64°45′
Toodoggone River	RIV/CDE	BC	Cassiar	94 E/7	57°24′	126°33′
Toogood Arm	UNP/LNO	NF		2 E/10	49°38′	54°36′
Tookoolito Inlet	BAY/BAIE	NT	Franklin	25 P	63°05′	64°45′
Toon 15	IR/RI	BC	Range 5 Coast	103 I/12	54°31′	129°59′
Toops 3	IR/RI	BC	Kamloops Division Yale	82 L/13	50°57′	119°40′
Toosey 1	IR/RI	BC	Lillooet	92 O/16	51°55′	122°29′
Toosey 1A	IR/RI	BC	Lillooet	92 O/15	51°55′	122°32′
Toosey 3	IR/RI	BC	Lillooet	92 O/16	51°53′	122°21′
Toothpick Lake	LAKE/LAC	ON	Kenora	52 L/1	50°07′	94°08′
Tootoowiltena 28	IR/RI	BC	Clayoquot	92 E/8	49°22′	126°14′
Tootyak Lake	LAKE/LAC	NT	Keewatin	55 E	61°52′	95°18′
Toowartz 8	IR/RI	BC	Range 4 Coast	103 H/5	53°19′	129°32′
Topascom Lake	LAKE/LAC	SK		63 M/10	55°41′	102°59′
Topaze Harbour	BAY/BAIE	BC	Range 1 Coast	92 K/12	50°31′	125°48′
Topcliff	UNP/LNO	ON	Grey	41 A/2	44°11′	80°40′
Tophet	UNP/LNO	ON	Sudbury	41 O/11	47°41′	83°07′
Topknot Point	CAPE/CAP	BC	Rupert	102 I/9	50°32′	128°13′
Topland	UNP/LNO	AB	23-62-7-W5	83 J/7	54°22′	114°58′
Topley	UNP/LNO	BC	Range 5 Coast	93 L/9	54°30′	126°18′
Topley Landing	UNP/LNO	BC	Range 5 Coast	93 L/16	54°48′	126°08′
Topping	UNP/LNO	ON	Perth	40 P/10	43°30′	80°52′
Top Pond	LAKE/LAC	NF		11 P/13	47°57′	57°30′
Topsail	UNP/LNO	NF		1 N/10	47°32′	52°56′
Topsails, The	MTN/MNT	NF		12 H/2	49°05′	56°40′
Toquana 4	IR/RI	BC	New Westminster	92 K/2	50°05′	124°39′
Toquart Bay	BAY/BAIE	BC	Clayoquot	92 F/3	49°01′	125°00′
Toquart Lake	LAKE/LAC	BC	Clayoquot	92 F/3	49°05′	125°21′
Torbay	TOWN/VIL2	NF		1 N/10	47°40′	52°44′

NAME / NOM	ENTITY / ENTITÉ	LOC 1 / LIEU 1	LOC 2 / LIEU 2	MAP / CARTE	POSITION LAT	POSITION LONG
Tor Bay	UNP/LNO	NS	Guysborough	11 F/3	45°12′	61°22′
Tor Bay	BAY/BAIE	NF		1 N/10	47°40′	52°42′
Tor Bay	BAY/BAIE	NS	Guysborough	11 F/3	45°14′	61°19′
Torbay Point	CAPE/CAP	NF		1 N/10	47°40′	52°40′
Torbrook	UNP/LNO	NS	Annapolis	21 A/15	44°55′	64°59′
Torbrook East	UNP/LNO	NS	Annapolis	21 A/15	44°56′	64°56′
Torbrook Mines	UNP/LNO	NS	Annapolis	21 A/15	44°56′	64°58′
Torbrook West	UNP/LNO	NS	Annapolis	21 A/14	44°54′	65°01′
Torch Lake	LAKE/LAC	SK	54,55-22,23-W2	73 H/11	53°43′	105°16′
Torch River	UNP/LNO	SK	33-53-15-W2	73 H/9	53°37′	104°09′
Torch River	RIV/CDE	SK	56-8-W2	63 E/14	53°50′	103°05′
Torch River No. 488	MUN2/AZM2	SK		73 H/6	53°30′	104°30′
Torii Mountain	MTN/MNT	BC	Kamloops Division Yale	83 D/7	52°24′	118°56′
Tork 7	IR/RI	BC	Sayward	92 K/2	50°08′	124°56′
Torlea	UNP/LNO	AB	13-48-14-W4	73 E/4	53°08′	111°55′
Tormentine, Cape	CAPE/CAP	NB	Westmorland	11 L/4	46°07′	63°47′
Torment, Lake	LAKE/LAC	NS	Kings	21 A/10	44°44′	64°44′
Tormore	UNP/LNO	ON	Peel	30 M/13	43°51′	79°42′
Tornado Mountain	MTN/MNT	AB/BC		82 G/15	49°58′	114°39′
Tornea	UNP/LNO	SK	1-34-13-W2	62 M/13	51°53′	103°43′
Torngat, Monts - also-aussi - Torngat Mountains	MTN/MNT	QC	Kativik	14 M/4	59°12′	63°53′
Torngat Mountains - also-aussi - Torngat, Monts	MTN/MNT	NF		14 M/4	59°12′	63°53′
Toronto	CITY/VIL1	ON	York	30 M/11	43°39′	79°23′
Toronto	UNP/LNO	PE	Queens	11 L/6	46°27′	63°23′
Toronto Island	ISL/ÎLE	ON	York	30 M/11	43°37′	79°23′
Toronto Lake	LAKE/LAC	ON	Thunder Bay	42 L/5	50°21′	87°48′
Torp Lake	LAKE/LAC	NT	Mackenzie	76 N	67°17′	109°36′
Torpy River	RIV/CDE	BC	Cariboo	93 H/10	53°44′	120°54′
Torquay	VILG/VILG	SK	24-2-12-W2	62 E/3	49°09′	103°30′
Torrance	UNP/LNO	ON	Muskoka	31 D/13	45°00′	79°34′
Torrance Lake	LAKE/LAC	MB		64 G/1	57°03′	98°11′
Torrens, Cape	CAPE/CAP	NT	Franklin	59 D	77°12′	90°08′
Torrent	UNP/LNO	BC	Kootenay	82 G/13	50°00′	115°48′
Torrington	VILG/VILG	AB	34-32-26-W4	82 P/13	51°48′	113°35′
Torryburn	UNP/LNO	NB	Saint John	21 G/8	45°21′	66°01′
Tors Cove	UNP/LNO	NF		1 N/2	47°13′	52°51′
Tortue, Lac	LAKE/LAC	QC	Sept-Rivières	22 I/13	50°55′	65°31′
Tortue, Lac à la	LAKE/LAC	QC	Le Centre-de-la-Mauricie	31 I/10	46°38′	72°37′
Tortue, Rivière	RIV/CDE	QC	Minganie	22 I/6	50°18′	65°23′
Tory Hill	UNP/LNO	ON	Haliburton	31 D/16	44°58′	78°17′
Tosehka (Eagle Bay) 12	IR/RI	BC	Range 4 Coast	103 H/15	53°49′	128°42′
Toslow	UNP/LNO	NF		1 M/8	47°24′	54°29′
Tosorontio - see-voir - Adjala-Tosorontio	MUN2/AZM2	ON		31 D/4	44°08′	79°56′
Tothill	UNP/LNO	AB	23-9-4-W4	72 E/9	49°44′	110°27′
Totnes	UNP/LNO	SK	19-27-18-W3	72 N/7	51°20′	108°31′
Totnes Road	BAY/BAIE	NT	Franklin	16 L	66°22′	62°20′
Totogan Creek	RIV/CDE	ON	Kenora	53 A/2	52°12′	88°42′
Totogan Lake	LAKE/LAC	ON	Kenora	53 A/3	52°05′	89°10′
Tottenham	UNP/LNO	ON	Simcoe	31 D/4	44°01′	79°49′
Totzke	UNP/LNO	SK	20-38-26-W2	73 A/5	52°17′	105°40′
Touak Fiord	BAY/BAIE	NT	Franklin	16 E	65°47′	63°23′
Touchwood	UNP/LNO	SK	27-16-W2	72 P/8	51°21′	104°09′
Touchwood Hills	MTN/MNT	SK		72 P/9	51°34′	104°16′
Touchwood Lake	LAKE/LAC	MB		53 L/7	54°29′	95°00′
Touchwood Lake	LAKE/LAC	AB	67-10-W4	73 L/14	54°49′	111°23′
Touchwood No. 248	MUN2/AZM2	SK		72 P/1	51°15′	104°20′
Touchwood Uplands	PLN/PLNE	SK		62 M/5	51°15′	103°45′
Touladi, Lac	LAKE/LAC	QC	Témiscouata	21 N/10	47°44′	68°46′
Touladi, Petit lac	LAKE/LAC	QC	Témiscouata	21 N/15	47°47′	68°45′
Touladi, Rivière	RIV/CDE	QC	Témiscouata	21 N/10	47°40′	68°48′
Toulnustouc Nord-Est, Rivière	RIV/CDE	QC	Sept-Rivières	22 J/13	50°54′	67°42′
Toulnustouc, Rivière	RIV/CDE	QC	Manicouagan	22 F/9	49°35′	68°24′
Touradi, Grand lac	LAKE/LAC	QC	Rimouski-Neigette	22 C/2	48°07′	68°40′
Touraine	UNP/LNO	QC	Communauté urbaine de l'Outaouais	31 G/5	45°29′	75°44′
Tourbières-de-Lanoraie, Réserve écologique des	PARK/PARC	QC	D'Autray	31 H/14	46°00′	73°18′
Tourbis, Lac	LAKE/LAC	QC	Matawinie	31 O/8	47°17′	74°13′
Tour-Bois-Blanc	UNP/LNO	QC	Sept-Rivières	22 J/3	50°01′	67°00′
Tour-Butney	UNP/LNO	QC	Témiscamingue	31 L/15	46°49′	78°46′
Tour-des-Hauteurs	UNP/LNO	QC	Rimouski-Neigette	22 B/4	48°02′	67°57′
Tour-des-Lacs-George	UNP/LNO	QC	Témiscamingue	31 L/15	46°46′	78°45′
Tour-du-Cinquante-Milles	UNP/LNO	QC	Sept-Rivières	22 G/14	49°46′	67°27′
Tour-du-Nord	UNP/LNO	QC	La Côte-de-Beaupré	21 M/3	47°10′	71°11′
Tourelle	VILG/VILG	QC	Denis-Riverin	22 G/1	49°09′	66°25′
Tour-Fraser	UNP/LNO	QC	Manicouagan	22 F/15	49°49′	68°42′
Tour-Galienne	UNP/LNO	QC	Sept-Rivières	22 J/2	50°13′	66°41′

NAME NOM	ENTITY ENTITÉ	LOC 1 LIEU 1	LOC 2 LIEU 2	MAP CARTE	POSITION LAT	LONG
Tourgis Lake	LAKE/LAC	NT	Mackenzie	76 B	64°41'	106°02'
Tourilli, Rivière	RIV/CDE	QC	La Jacques-Cartier	21 M/4	47°03'	71°40'
Tour-Maher	UNP/LNO	QC	Manicouagan	22 G/5	49°19'	67°57'
Tour-Martello-de-Carleton, Lieu historique national de la - also-aussi - Carleton Martello Tower National Historic Site	PARK/PARC	NB	Saint John	21 G/8	45°15'	66°05'
Tourmente, Cap	CAPE/CAP	QC	La Côte-de-Beaupré	21 M/2	47°05'	70°45'
Tourniquet, Le	UNP/LNO	QC	Lac-Saint-Jean-Est	22 D/11	48°31'	71°29'
Tourond	UNP/LNO	MB	9-7-4-E	62 H/10	49°33'	96°59'
Tour-Patapédia	UNP/LNO	QC	La Mitis	22 B/4	48°10'	67°38'
Tour-Prince-de-Galles, Lieu historique national de la - also-aussi - Prince of Wales Tower National Historic Site	PARK/PARC	NS	Halifax	11 D/12	44°37'	63°34'
Tour-Rita	UNP/LNO	QC	Sept-Rivières	22 J/10	50°34'	66°34'
Tour-Sept-Milles	UNP/LNO	QC	Manicouagan	22 G/5	49°22'	67°40'
Tours-Martello-de-Kingston, Lieu historique national des - also-aussi - Kingston Martello Towers National Historic Site	PARK/PARC	ON	Frontenac	31 C/1	44°14'	76°29'
Tour-Tableau	UNP/LNO	QC	Sept-Rivières	22 J/3	50°10'	67°09'
Tour-Val-Marie	UNP/LNO	QC	La Matapédia	22 B/5	48°25'	67°48'
Tourville	VILG/VILG	QC	L'Islet	21 N/4	47°06'	69°59'
Touten Seamount	SEAU/SMER	—		NK23	43°34'	45°30'
Toutes Aides	UNP/LNO	MB	17-29-15-W	62 O/5	51°29'	99°32'
Touzel, Lac	LAKE/LAC	QC	Minganie	22 I/7	50°21'	64°55'
Towdystan	UNP/LNO	BC	Range 3 Coast	93 C/6	52°16'	125°05'
Towdystan Lake 3	IR/RI	BC	Range 3 Coast	93 C/6	52°17'	125°07'
Tower Lake	UNP/LNO	BC	Peace River	94 A/2	56°01'	120°34'
Tower Mountain	MTN/MNT	NF		24 P/8	59°20'	64°08'
Towincut Mountain	MTN/MNT	BC	Cowichan Lake	92 C/16	48°49'	124°24'
Towinock 2	IR/RI	BC	Lillooet	92 I/12	50°35'	121°51'
Town Lake	UNP/LNO	AB	32-45-3-W5	83 B/16	52°56'	114°25'
Townsend	UNP/LNO	ON	Haldimand	40 I/16	42°54'	80°08'
Townsend	UNP/LNO	BC	New Westminster	92 G/2	49°08'	122°55'
Townsend Centre	UNP/LNO	ON	Norfolk	40 I/16	42°56'	80°15'
Townsend Lake	LAKE/LAC	NT	Keewatin	55 L	62°42'	95°20'
Toyes Hill	UNP/LNO	ON	Dundas	31 B/14	44°59'	75°20'
Tracadie	UNP/LNO	PE	Queens	11 L/7	46°21'	62°58'
Tracadie	UNP/LNO	NS	Antigonish	11 F/12	45°37'	61°40'
Tracadie	UNP/LNO	NB	Gloucester	21 P/10	47°31'	64°54'
Tracadie, Baie de	BAY/BAIE	NB	Gloucester	21 P/10	47°33'	64°53'
Tracadie Bay	BAY/BAIE	PE	Queens	11 L/7	46°23'	63°00'
Tracadie Beach	UNP/LNO	NB	Gloucester	21 P/7	47°27'	64°55'
Tracadie Cross	UNP/LNO	PE	Queens	11 L/7	46°21'	62°58'
Tracadie River	RIV/CDE	NS	Antigonish	11 F/12	45°37'	61°37'
Tracadie Road	UNP/LNO	NS	Guysborough	11 F/5	45°28'	61°31'
Tracadie-Sheila	TOWN/VIL2	NB	Gloucester	21 P/10	47°31'	64°55'
Tracadigache, Baie	BAY/BAIE	QC	Avignon	22 B/1	48°06'	66°12'
Tracadigache, Pointe	CAPE/CAP	QC	Avignon	22 B/1	48°05'	66°07'
Tracard	UNP/LNO	BC	Peace River	93 P/16	55°45'	120°10'
Tracey Mills	UNP/LNO	NB	Carleton	21 J/5	46°26'	67°45'
Tracy	CITY/VIL1	QC	Le Bas-Richelieu	31 I/3	46°01'	73°09'
Tracy	VILG/VILG	NB	Sunbury	21 G/10	45°41'	66°41'
Tracy Depot	UNP/LNO	NB	Restigouche	21 O/13	47°48'	67°32'
Tracyville	UNP/LNO	NB	Sunbury	21 G/10	45°44'	66°40'
Trade Lake	LAKE/LAC	SK		63 M/5	55°22'	103°44'
Traders Cove	UNP/LNO	BC	Osoyoos Division Yale	82 E/14	49°56'	119°30'
Trading River	RIV/CDE	ON	Kenora	52 P/15	51°55'	88°54'
Trafalgar	UNP/LNO	NS	Guysborough	11 E/7	45°17'	62°40'
Trafalgar	UNP/LNO	ON	Halton	30 M/5	43°29'	79°43'
Trafalgar	UNP/LNO	BC	Yale Division Yale	92 H/6	49°26'	121°26'
Trafalgar Flat 13	IR/RI	BC	Yale Division Yale	92 H/6	49°25'	121°25'
Trafalgar Heights	UNP/LNO	ON	Middlesex	40 I/14	43°00'	81°10'
Traffic Mountain	MTN/MNT	YT		105 J/1	62°07'	130°25'
Trail	CITY/VIL1	BC	Kootenay	82 F/4	49°06'	117°42'
Trail Bay	BAY/BAIE	BC	New Westminster	92 G/5	49°28'	123°45'
Trail River	RIV/CDE	YT		106 L/10	66°40'	134°40'
Train Lake	LAKE/LAC	SK		74 O/10	59°43'	106°58'
Trainor Lake	LAKE/LAC	NT	Mackenzie	95 A	60°25'	120°18'
Trait-Carré	UNP/LNO	QC	La Côte-de-Gaspé	22 A/16	48°57'	64°20'
Trait-Carré	UNP/LNO	QC	L'Île-d'Orléans	21 L/14	46°52'	71°05'
Tralee	UNP/LNO	ON	Perth	40 P/10	43°41'	80°50'
Tramore	UNP/LNO	ON	Renfrew	31 F/11	45°37'	77°27'
Tramping Lake	VILG/VILG	SK	33-36-21-W3	73 C/2	52°08'	108°57'
Tramping Lake	LAKE/LAC	SK	35,38-20-W3	73 C/2	52°08'	108°49'
Tramping Lake No. 380	MUN2/AZM2	SK		73 C/2	52°15'	109°00'
Tranquil Creek	RIV/CDE	BC	Clayoquot	92 F/4	49°13'	125°40'
Tranquil Inlet	BAY/BAIE	BC	Clayoquot	92 F/4	49°11'	125°41'
Tranquility	UNP/LNO	ON	Brant	40 P/1	43°11'	80°17'

NAME NOM	ENTITY ENTITÉ	LOC 1 LIEU 1	LOC 2 LIEU 2	MAP CARTE	POSITION LAT	LONG
Tranquille	UNP/LNO	BC	Kamloops Division Yale	92 I/10	50°42′	120°31′
Tranquille	UNP/LNO	BC	Kamloops Division Yale	92 I/10	50°43′	120°31′
Tranquille River	RIV/CDE	BC	Kamloops Division Yale	92 I/10	50°43′	120°32′
Transcona	UNP/LNO	MB		62 H/14	49°54′	97°00′
Transcona	UNP/LNO	SK		72 I/7	50°28′	104°39′
Transfiguration	UNP/LNO	QC	Témiscouata	21 N/15	47°55′	68°47′
Transit Head	CAPE/CAP	BC	Range 1 Coast	92 K/13	50°54′	125°34′
Transition (Kennedy) Bay	BAY/BAIE	NT	Franklin	68 A	72°03′	96°40′
Trapnarrows Lake	LAKE/LAC	ON	Thunder Bay	42 E/5	49°23′	87°32′
Trapper's Landing	UNP/LNO	ON	Thunder Bay	52 J/2	50°12′	90°43′
Trapping Creek	RIV/CDE	BC	Similkameen Division Yale	82 E/11	49°34′	119°04′
Trapp Lake	LAKE/LAC	BC	Kamloops Division Yale	92 I/8	50°28′	120°16′
Trap Point	CAPE/CAP	NT	Mackenzie	77 A	68°53′	105°46′
Travaillant Lake	LAKE/LAC	NT	Mackenzie	106 O	67°42′	131°47′
Travaillant River	RIV/CDE	NT	Mackenzie	106 O	67°28′	131°30′
Travellers Rest	UNP/LNO	PE	Prince	11 L/5	46°25′	63°44′
Travers	UNP/LNO	AB	9-15-19-W4	82 I/2	50°15′	112°33′
Traverse Bay	UNP/LNO	MB	25,36-19-7-E	62 I/9	50°40′	96°29′
Traverse Bay	BAY/BAIE	MB		62 I/9	50°40′	96°25′
Traverse Brook - see-voir - Northwest Brook	RIV/CDE	NF		2 D/16	48°52′	54°08′
Traverse-du-Remous	UNP/LNO	QC	Nicolet-Yamaska	31 I/2	46°02′	72°44′
Traverse, Lake - see-voir - Travers, Lake	LAKE/LAC	ON		31 E/16	46°00′	78°02′
Traverse Landing	UNP/LNO	ON	Sudbury	41 I/6	46°27′	81°28′
Travers, Lake	LAKE/LAC	ON	Nipissing	31 E/16	46°00′	78°02′
Traverspine River	RIV/CDE	NF		13 F/8	53°17′	60°17′
Travers Reservoir	LAKE/LAC	AB	14,15-21,22-W4	82 I/2	50°12′	112°51′
Traverston	UNP/LNO	ON	Grey	41 A/7	44°16′	80°45′
Travor Road	UNP/LNO	QC	Memphrémagog	31 H/1	45°06′	72°22′
Traynor	UNP/LNO	SK	5-38-17-W3	73 C/1	52°14′	108°23′
Traytown	VILG/VILG	NF		2 C/12	48°40′	53°58′
Treadwell	UNP/LNO	ON	Prescott	31 G/11	45°36′	75°00′
Trebell Lake	LAKE/LAC	NT	Keewatin	65 B	60°09′	98°13′
Trécarré-du-Haut-de-la-Paroisse, Le	UNP/LNO	QC	Beauce-Sartigan	21 L/2	46°02′	70°57′
Trecastle	UNP/LNO	ON	Wellington	40 P/15	43°47′	80°48′
Trécesson	VILG/VILG	QC	Abitibi	32 D/9	48°39′	78°19′
Tredcroft Creek	RIV/CDE	BC	Range 2 Coast	92 N/8	51°19′	124°07′
Tree Farm	UNP/LNO	QC	Vaudreuil-Soulanges	31 G/8	45°27′	74°09′
Treelon	UNP/LNO	SK	5-1-18-W3	72 F/1	49°00′	108°23′
Tree River	RIV/CDE	NT	Mackenzie	76 M	67°41′	111°53′
Tree River	RIV/CDE	NT	Mackenzie	106 N/7	67°15′	132°34′
Treesbank	UNP/LNO	MB	5-8-16-W	62 G/12	49°38′	99°37′
Treesbank Ferry	UNP/LNO	MB	17-8-16-W	62 G/12	49°40′	99°36′
Trefoil	UNP/LNO	AB	5-26-16-W4	82 P/1	51°12′	112°11′
Tregarva	UNP/LNO	SK	16-19-20-W2	72 I/10	50°36′	104°43′
Treherne	VILG/VILG	MB	1-8-10-W	62 G/10	49°38′	98°42′
Treize-Milles, Le	UNP/LNO	QC	Pabok	22 A/7	48°24′	64°53′
Tremaine	UNP/LNO	MB	30-13-18-W	62 J/4	50°07′	99°56′
Tremaudan	UNP/LNO	MB	7-57-25-W	63 F/14	53°55′	101°10′
Tremblant, Mont	MTN/MNT	QC	Les Laurentides	31 J/7	46°16′	74°35′
Tremblay	VILG/VILG	QC	Le Fjord-du-Saguenay	22 D/11	48°30′	71°00′
Tremblay	UNP/LNO	NB	Gloucester	21 P/13	47°45′	65°45′
Tremblay	UNP/LNO	BC	Peace River	93 P/15	55°47′	120°51′
Tremblay, Lac	LAKE/LAC	QC	La Haute-Côte-Nord	22 C/13	48°57′	69°44′
Tremblay, Lac	LAKE/LAC	QC	Le Fjord-du-Saguenay	22 D/9	48°41′	70°19′
Tremblay Sound	CHAN/CHEN	NT	Franklin	48 A	72°25′	81°00′
Trembleur	UNP/LNO	BC	Range 5 Coast	93 K/14	54°52′	125°07′
Trembleur Lake	LAKE/LAC	BC	Range 5 Coast	93 K/14	54°49′	125°09′
Trembley	UNP/LNO	ON	Algoma	41 N/15	47°59′	84°50′
Trembowla	UNP/LNO	MB	19,20,29,30-26-20-W	62 N/8	51°16′	100°15′
Tremont	UNP/LNO	NS	Kings	21 A/15	44°57′	64°56′
Trenche	UNP/LNO	QC	Le Haut-Saint-Maurice	31 P/10	47°45′	72°53′
Trenche, Rivière	RIV/CDE	QC	Le Haut-Saint-Maurice	31 P/15	47°50′	72°52′
Trenholm	UNP/LNO	QC	Drummond	31 H/9	45°42′	72°12′
Trente et Un Milles, Lac des	LAKE/LAC	QC	La Vallée-de-la-Gatineau	31 J/4	46°12′	75°49′
Trente-Milles, Le	UNP/LNO	QC	La Matapédia	22 B/10	48°32′	66°47′
Trentham	UNP/LNO	MB	14-5-6-E	62 H/7	49°23′	96°40′
Trenton	CITY/VIL1	ON	Hastings	31 C/4	44°06′	77°35′
Trenton	TOWN/VIL2	NS	Pictou	11 E/10	45°37′	62°38′
Trenton, Base des Forces canadiennes - also-aussi - Trenton, Canadian Forces Base	MIL/MIL	ON	Hastings	31 C/4	44°07′	77°32′
Trenton, Canadian Forces Base - also-aussi - Trenton, Base des Forces canadiennes	MIL/MIL	ON	Hastings	31 C/4	44°07′	77°32′
Trenton Junction	UNP/LNO	ON	Northumberland	31 C/4	44°06′	77°36′
Trent River	UNP/LNO	ON	Northumberland	31 C/5	44°24′	77°52′
Trent River	RIV/CDE	ON	Hastings	31 C/4	44°06′	77°34′
Trent River	RIV/CDE	BC	Nelson	92 F/10	49°39′	124°56′
Trent-Severn, Voie navigable - also-aussi - Trent-Severn Waterway	PARK/PARC	ON	Victoria	31 D/10	44°33′	78°32′

NAME NOM	ENTITY ENTITÉ	LOC 1 LIEU 1	LOC 2 LIEU 2	MAP CARTE	POSITION LAT	LONG
Trent-Severn Waterway - also-aussi - Trent-Severn, Voie navigable	PARK/PARC	ON	Victoria	31 D/10	44°33'	78°32'
Trépanier	UNP/LNO	BC	Osoyoos Division Yale	82 E/13	49°47'	119°42'
Trépanier Creek	RIV/CDE	BC	Osoyoos Division Yale	82 E/13	49°47'	119°43'
Trepassey	TOWN/VIL2	NF		1 K/11	46°44'	53°22'
Trepassey Bay	BAY/BAIE	NF		1 K/12	46°37'	53°30'
Trepassey Harbour	BAY/BAIE	NF		1 K/11	46°43'	53°24'
Treptow Lake	LAKE/LAC	ON	Thunder Bay	42 E/14	49°52'	87°12'
Très-Saint-Rédempteur	VILG/VILG	QC	Vaudreuil-Soulanges	31 G/8	45°26'	74°23'
Très-Saint-Sacrement	VILG/VILG	QC	Le Haut-Saint-Laurent	31 H/4	45°11'	73°51'
Tretheway Creek	RIV/CDE	BC	New Westminster	92 G/9	49°42'	122°05'
Trethewey Lake	LAKE/LAC	ON	Timiskaming	41 P/7	47°26'	80°30'
Treuter Mountains	MTN/MNT	NT	Franklin	48 H	75°40'	82°15'
Trève, Lac la	LAKE/LAC	QC	Jamésie	32 G/13	49°56'	75°30'
Trevelyan	UNP/LNO	ON	Leeds	31 B/12	44°32'	75°56'
Trevessa Beach	HAM/HAM	SK	7-47-16-W3	73 F/1	53°02'	108°20'
Trevor Channel	CHAN/CHEN	BC	Barclay	92 C/14	48°52'	125°08'
Trewdale	UNP/LNO	SK	9-14-4-W3	72 J/2	50°09'	106°30'
Treworgie Canyon	SEAU/SMER	—		8010	43°45'	52°35'
Triangle	UNP/LNO	NF		3 D/13	52°50'	55°51'
Triangle	UNP/LNO	AB	21-74-18-W5	83 N/7	55°26'	116°43'
Triangle Island	ISL/ÎLE	BC	Rupert	102 I/14	50°52'	129°05'
Tribune	VILG/VILG	SK	27-3-14-W2	62 E/4	49°15'	103°49'
Tribune Bay	BAY/BAIE	BC	Nanaimo	92 F/10	49°31'	124°37'
Tribune Channel	CHAN/CHEN	BC	Range 1 Coast	92 L/16	50°48'	126°12'
Trilsbeck Lake	LAKE/LAC	ON	Cochrane	42 K/16	50°48'	84°02'
Trincomali Channel	CHAN/CHEN	BC	Cowichan	92 B/13	48°58'	123°35'
Tring-Jonction	TOWN/VIL2	QC	Robert-Cliche	21 L/7	46°16'	70°59'
Trinité, Cap	CAPE/CAP	QC	Le Fjord-du-Saguenay	22 D/8	48°19'	70°19'
Trinité, Rivière de la	RIV/CDE	QC	Manicouagan	22 G/6	49°25'	67°18'
Trinity	VILG/VILG	NF		2 C/6	48°22'	53°22'
Trinity	UNP/LNO	NF		2 C/13	48°59'	53°55'
Trinity	UNP/LNO	ON	Wentworth	40 P/1	43°10'	80°02'
Trinity Bay	BAY/BAIE	NF		2 C/3	48°00'	53°30'
Trinity Bay	BAY/BAIE	NF		2 C/13	48°59'	53°49'
Trinity Creek	RIV/CDE	BC	Kamloops Division Yale	82 L/10	50°32'	118°58'
Trinity East	UNP/LNO	NF		2 C/6	48°23'	53°20'
Trinity Glacier	GLAC/GLAC	NT	Franklin	39 C	77°58'	78°33'
Trinity Harbour	BAY/BAIE	NF		2 C/6	48°22'	53°21'
Trinity Park	UNP/LNO	MB		62 G/13	49°49'	99°57'
Trinity Pond	LAKE/LAC	NF		2 C/6	48°25'	53°28'
Trinity Valley	UNP/LNO	BC	Osoyoos Division Yale	82 L/7	50°24'	118°55'
Trinny Cove	UNP/LNO	NF		1 N/5	47°29'	53°55'
Trio Mountain	MTN/MNT	BC	Nootka	92 E/16	49°53'	126°00'
Triple Bay Park	UNP/LNO	ON	Simcoe	31 D/13	44°46'	79°50'
Tripp Settlement	UNP/LNO	NB	York	21 J/2	46°01'	66°54'
Triquet, Lac	LAKE/LAC	QC	Minganie	12 J/12	50°42'	59°47'
Tristram	UNP/LNO	AB	14-42-23-W4	83 A/11	52°36'	113°15'
Triton	TOWN/VIL2	NF		2 E/12	49°31'	55°37'
Triton Brook	RIV/CDE	NF		2 D/10	48°38'	54°31'
Triton Island	ISL/ÎLE	NF		2 E/12	49°31'	55°37'
Triton West	UNP/LNO	NF		2 E/12	49°32'	55°37'
Trochu	TOWN/VIL2	AB	17-33-23-W4	82 P/14	51°50'	113°13'
Trodely Island	ISL/ÎLE	NT	Keewatin	33 D	52°15'	79°26'
Troilus, Lac	LAKE/LAC	QC	Jamésie	32 J/15	50°55'	74°30'
Trois-Fourches, Les	UNP/LNO	QC	Pabok	22 A/10	48°36'	64°42'
Trois-Fourches, Les	UNP/LNO	QC	Bellechasse	21 L/9	46°38'	70°28'
Trois-Fourches, Les	UNP/LNO	QC	Lotbinière	21 L/5	46°30'	71°47'
Trois-Lacs	VILG/VILG	QC	Asbestos	21 E/13	45°48'	71°54'
Trois-Pins, Les	UNP/LNO	QC	Deux-Montagnes	31 G/8	45°28'	74°03'
Trois-Pistoles	CITY/VIL1	QC	Les Basques	22 C/3	48°07'	69°10'
Trois Pistoles, Rivière des	RIV/CDE	QC	Les Basques	22 C/3	48°06'	69°13'
Trois-Ponts, Les	UNP/LNO	QC	Arthabaska	21 E/13	45°51'	71°55'
Trois-Rivières	CITY/VIL1	QC	Francheville	31 I/7	46°21'	72°33'
Trois-Rivières-Ouest	CITY/VIL1	QC	Francheville	31 I/7	46°20'	72°36'
Trois-Ruisseaux	UNP/LNO	NB	Westmorland	21 I/1	46°13'	64°13'
Trois-Ruisseaux	UNP/LNO	QC	Minganie	22 H/16	49°55'	64°05'
Trois-Saumons	UNP/LNO	QC	L'Islet	21 M/1	47°10'	70°19'
Trois Saumons, Lac	LAKE/LAC	QC	L'Islet	21 M/1	47°08'	70°11'
Trois-Saumons-Station	UNP/LNO	QC	L'Islet	21 M/1	47°09'	70°18'
Troitsa Lake	LAKE/LAC	BC	Range 4 Coast	93 E/11	53°34'	127°15'
Troitsa Peak	MTN/MNT	BC	Range 4 Coast	93 E/11	53°35'	127°04'
Trold Fiord	BAY/BAIE	NT	Franklin	49 F	78°15'	85°17'
Tromso Fiord	BAY/BAIE	NT	Franklin	37 H	71°12'	73°40'
Tronka Chua Lake	LAKE/LAC	NT	Mackenzie	75 F	61°30'	109°56'
Trophy Mountain	MTN/MNT	BC	Kamloops Division Yale	82 M/13	51°48'	119°52'

NAME NOM	ENTITY ENTITÉ	LOC 1 LIEU 1	LOC 2 LIEU 2	MAP CARTE	POSITION LAT	POSITION LONG
Trossachs	HAM/HAM	SK	10-8-17-W2	72 H/9	49°38′	104°13′
Trottier	UNP/LNO	QC	Arthabaska	21 L/4	46°03′	71°42′
Trou-à-Gardner	UNP/LNO	QC	Kamouraska	21 N/5	47°21′	69°43′
Trou-à-Paradis, Le	UNP/LNO	QC	Avignon	22 B/8	48°25′	66°20′
Trou-à-Pépette	UNP/LNO	QC	Kamouraska	21 N/5	47°23′	69°45′
Troubridge, Mount	MTN/MNT	BC	New Westminster	92 F/16	49°49′	124°10′
Trou-d'Abraham, Le	UNP/LNO	QC	Drummond	31 I/2	46°01′	72°40′
Trou-des-Ours, Le	UNP/LNO	QC	Le Granit	21 E/10	45°32′	70°55′
Trou-des-Roses, Le	UNP/LNO	QC	Francheville	31 I/8	46°27′	72°20′
Trou-des-Valets, Le	UNP/LNO	QC	Nicolet-Yamaska	31 I/2	46°10′	72°45′
Trou-d'Henri, Le	UNP/LNO	QC	Nicolet-Yamaska	31 I/2	46°11′	72°41′
Trou-du-Chat, Le	UNP/LNO	QC	Pabok	22 A/8	48°29′	64°10′
Trou-du-Steamboat, Le	UNP/LNO	QC	Mékinac	31 P/2	47°03′	72°40′
Trou, Le	UNP/LNO	QC	La Haute-Côte-Nord	22 C/4	48°12′	69°47′
Trou, Le	UNP/LNO	QC	L'Assomption	31 H/11	45°44′	73°27′
Trou, Le	UNP/LNO	QC	Vaudreuil-Soulanges	31 G/8	45°24′	74°23′
Troup	UNP/LNO	BC	Kootenay	82 F/11	49°33′	117°14′
Trousers Lake	LAKE/LAC	NB	Victoria	21 O/2	47°00′	66°57′
Trout Brook	UNP/LNO	NS	Cape Breton	11 F/16	45°59′	60°10′
Trout Brook	UNP/LNO	NB	Northumberland	21 P/4	47°07′	65°48′
Trout Brook	RIV/CDE	NF		12 B/9	48°34′	58°22′
Trout Creek	TOWN/VIL2	ON	Parry Sound	31 E/14	45°59′	79°22′
Trout Creek	UNP/LNO	BC	Osoyoos Division Yale	82 E/12	49°34′	119°37′
Trout Creek	RIV/CDE	BC	Osoyoos Division Yale	82 E/12	49°34′	119°37′
Trout Lake	UNP/LNO	ON	Algoma	41 N/1	47°02′	84°06′
Trout Lake	UNP/LNO	AB	34-86-4-W5	84 B/10	56°30′	114°32′
Trout Lake	UNP/LNO	BC	Kootenay	82 K/12	50°39′	117°32′
Trout Lake	UNP/LNO	NT	Mackenzie	95 A/6	60°26′	121°15′
Trout Lake	LAKE/LAC	NS	Annapolis	21 A/14	44°46′	65°04′
Trout Lake	LAKE/LAC	ON	Lennox and Addington	31 F/3	45°09′	77°26′
Trout Lake	LAKE/LAC	ON	Nipissing	31 E/10	45°44′	78°41′
Trout Lake	LAKE/LAC	ON	Nipissing	31 L/6	46°18′	79°20′
Trout Lake	LAKE/LAC	ON	Sudbury	41 I/2	46°13′	80°35′
Trout Lake	LAKE/LAC	ON	Kenora	52 N/3	51°15′	93°15′
Trout Lake	LAKE/LAC	MB		64 G/15	57°53′	98°40′
Trout Lake	LAKE/LAC	SK		73 P/11	55°37′	105°16′
Trout Lake	LAKE/LAC	BC	Kootenay	82 K/11	50°35′	117°27′
Trout Lake	LAKE/LAC	BC	Kootenay	82 K/12	50°39′	117°32′
Trout Lake	LAKE/LAC	NT	Mackenzie	95 A	60°35′	121°19′
Trout Lake Alec 16	IR/RI	BC	Cariboo	93 G/4	53°11′	123°32′
Trout Lake Jonny 15	IR/RI	BC	Cariboo	93 G/4	53°14′	123°34′
Troutlake River	RIV/CDE	ON	Kenora	52 K/14	50°49′	93°27′
Trout Mills	UNP/LNO	ON	Nipissing	31 L/6	46°20′	79°24′
Trout Mountain	MTN/MNT	BC	Kootenay	82 K/12	50°36′	117°35′
Trout River	VILG/VILG	NF		12 G/8	49°29′	58°08′
Trout River	UNP/LNO	QC	Le Haut-Saint-Laurent	31 G/1	45°03′	74°17′
Trout River	UNP/LNO	QC	Le Haut-Saint-Laurent	31 G/1	45°00′	74°19′
Trout River	RIV/CDE	AB	24-84-25-W4	84 A/5	56°17′	113°49′
Trout River	RIV/CDE	BC	Peace River	94 M/8	59°24′	126°01′
Trout River	RIV/CDE	NT	Mackenzie	85 E/5	61°19′	119°51′
Trout River Big Pond	LAKE/LAC	NF		12 G/8	49°25′	58°02′
Trout Stream	UNP/LNO	NB	Gloucester	21 P/10	47°31′	64°58′
Trout Trap Fiord	BAY/BAIE	NF		14 M/5	59°15′	63°32′
Trouty	UNP/LNO	NF		2 C/6	48°20′	53°24′
Trowbridge	UNP/LNO	ON	Perth	40 P/11	43°44′	81°02′
Troy	UNP/LNO	NS	Inverness	11 F/11	45°42′	61°26′
Troy	UNP/LNO	ON	Wentworth	40 P/8	43°16′	80°11′
Troy	UNP/LNO	ON	Kent	40 I/5	42°23′	81°54′
Troyes, Lac	LAKE/LAC	QC	Matawinie	31 O/1	47°11′	74°12′
Truax	UNP/LNO	SK	16-11-22-W2	72 H/15	49°54′	104°57′
Truax, Mount	MTN/MNT	BC	Lillooet	92 J/15	50°49′	122°43′
Truchon, Ruisseau à	RIV/CDE	QC	La Haute-Côte-Nord	22 C/14	48°55′	69°25′
Trudeau	UNP/LNO	ON	Thunder Bay	42 C/12	48°42′	85°46′
Trudel	UNP/LNO	NB	Gloucester	21 P/11	47°41′	65°08′
Trudel	UNP/LNO	QC	Le Granit	21 E/10	45°32′	70°46′
True, Cape	CAPE/CAP	NT	Franklin	25 I	62°32′	65°12′
Truemanville	UNP/LNO	NS	Cumberland	21 H/16	45°52′	64°04′
Truite, Lac à la	LAKE/LAC	QC	Témiscamingue	31 M/8	47°18′	78°16′
Truite, Rivière à la	RIV/CDE	QC	Matane	22 B/11	48°38′	67°07′
Truitt Peak	MTN/MNT	YT		105 L/8	62°16′	134°15′
Truman	UNP/LNO	AB	19-63-8-W4	73 L/6	54°28′	111°12′
Trump Islands	UNP/LNO	NF		2 E/10	49°35′	54°46′
Trunmore Bay	BAY/BAIE	NF		13 H/14	53°53′	57°06′
Truro	TOWN/VIL2	NS	Colchester	11 E/6	45°22′	63°16′
Truro 27A	IR/RI	NS	Colchester	11 E/6	45°19′	63°17′

NAME NOM	ENTITY ENTITÉ	LOC 1 LIEU 1	LOC 2 LIEU 2	MAP CARTE	POSITION LAT	LONG
Truro 27B	IR/RI	NS	Colchester	11 E/6	45°19′	63°17′
Truro 27C	IR/RI	NS	Colchester	11 E/6	45°19′	63°17′
Truro Heights	UNP/LNO	NS	Colchester	11 E/6	45°21′	63°19′
Truro Island	ISL/ÎLE	NT	Franklin	68 H	75°17′	97°11′
Trutch	UNP/LNO	BC	Cassiar	94 G/10	57°44′	122°57′
Trutch Creek	RIV/CDE	BC	Peace River	94 G/16	57°47′	122°11′
Trutch Island	ISL/ÎLE	BC	Range 4 Coast	103 H/4	53°06′	129°41′
Truxton Swell	SEAU/SMER	—		4011	43°05′	67°30′
Trygve, Mount	MTN/MNT	BC	Cassiar	94 D/13	56°59′	127°34′
Tryon	UNP/LNO	PE	Prince	11 L/4	46°14′	63°33′
Tryon, Cape	CAPE/CAP	PE	Queens	11 L/12	46°32′	63°30′
Tryon Settlement	UNP/LNO	NB	Charlotte	21 G/6	45°25′	67°08′
Tsable River	RIV/CDE	BC	Nelson	92 F/10	49°31′	124°50′
Tsacha Lake	LAKE/LAC	BC	Range 4 Coast	93 F/2	53°03′	124°49′
Tsachla Lake 8	IR/RI	BC	Range 4 Coast	93 F/2	53°00′	124°54′
Tsahaheh 1	IR/RI	BC	Alberni	92 F/7	49°16′	124°52′
Tsai-kwi-ee 13	IR/RI	BC	Range 2 Coast	92 M/3	51°10′	127°25′
Tsak 9	IR/RI	BC	Cassiar	93 M/2	55°08′	126°36′
Tsalwor Lake	LAKE/LAC	SK		74 N/11	59°45′	109°25′
Tsarksis 2	IR/RI	BC	Nootka	92 E/10	49°37′	126°46′
Tsaukan 12	IR/RI	BC	Kamloops Division Yale	92 I/5	50°22′	121°41′
Tsawawmuck 1	IR/RI	BC	Yale Division Yale	92 H/14	49°56′	121°28′
Tsawwassen	UNP/LNO	BC	New Westminster	92 G/3	49°01′	123°05′
Tsawwassen	UNP/LNO	BC	New Westminster	92 G/3	49°00′	123°08′
Tsawwassen	IR/RI	BC	New Westminster	92 G/3	49°02′	123°06′
Tsawwassen Beach	UNP/LNO	BC	New Westminster	92 G/3	49°00′	123°05′
Tsawwati 1	IR/RI	BC	Range 2 Coast	92 N/4	51°07′	125°37′
Tsay Cho 4	IR/RI	BC	Range 5 Coast	93 K/15	54°48′	124°55′
Tsaydaychuz Peak	MTN/MNT	BC	Range 4 Coast	93 E/2	53°01′	126°38′
Tsay Keh Dene	UNP/LNO	BC	Cassiar	94 C/15	56°53′	124°58′
Tsayta Lake	LAKE/LAC	BC	Cassiar	93 N/6	55°27′	125°27′
Tsaytis River	RIV/CDE	BC	Range 4 Coast	93 E/4	53°15′	127°52′
Tsaytut Island 1C	IR/RI	BC	Cassiar	94 D/2	56°06′	126°48′
Tsaz Chech 27	IR/RI	BC	Range 5 Coast	93 K/15	55°00′	124°58′
Tsaz Chech 28	IR/RI	BC	Range 5 Coast	93 K/15	54°58′	124°58′
Tsaz Cheh Koh 24	IR/RI	BC	Range 5 Coast	93 K/14	54°58′	125°05′
Tsea River	RIV/CDE	BC	Peace River	94 P/11	59°38′	121°20′
Tseatah 2	IR/RI	BC	New Westminster	92 H/4	49°13′	121°45′
Tse Bay Ha Tine A 34	IR/RI	BC	Range 5 Coast	93 K/11	54°32′	125°06′
Tseepantee Lake	LAKE/LAC	NT	Mackenzie	95 P	63°24′	121°28′
Tseetsum-Sawlasilah 6	IR/RI	BC	Range 2 Coast	92 M/6	51°20′	127°19′
Tsemknawalqan 79	IR/RI	BC	Range 5 Coast	103 I/3	54°12′	129°11′
Tseoowa 4	IR/RI	BC	Clayoquot	92 C/14	48°59′	125°01′
Tshak Penatu Epit	UNP/LNO	QC	Côte-Nord-du-Golfe-Saint-Laurent	12 O/2	51°10′	58°34′
Tshiahahtunekamuk	UNP/LNO	QC	Minganie	22 I/9	50°40′	64°04′
Tshiahkuehihat Peniauiht	UNP/LNO	QC	Minganie	12 L/4	50°14′	64°00′
Tshinuatipish	UNP/LNO	QC	Kativik	24 A/2	56°05′	64°43′
Tsichgass 10	IR/RI	BC	Range 5 Coast	93 L/1	54°03′	126°27′
Tsichgass Lake 2 - see-voir - Tsichgass 10	IR/RI	BC		93 L/1	54°03′	126°27′
Tsiigehtchic	HAM/HAM	NT	Mackenzie	106 N/5	67°27′	133°44′
Tsikwustum Creek	RIV/CDE	BC	Kamloops Division Yale	82 M/6	51°23′	119°25′
Tsikwustum Lake	LAKE/LAC	BC	Kamloops Division Yale	82 M/6	51°25′	119°15′
Tsileuh Creek	RIV/CDE	BC	Yale Division Yale	92 H/14	49°46′	121°27′
Tsimlairen 15	IR/RI	BC	Range 4 Coast	103 H/5	53°30′	129°53′
Tsimmanweenclist 2	IR/RI	BC	Cassiar	103 P/6	55°18′	129°04′
Tsimpsean 2 - see-voir - Lax Kw'a laams 1	IR/RI	BC		103 J/8	54°30′	130°22′
Tsimpsean Peninsula	CAPE/CAP	BC	Range 5 Coast	103 J/8	54°22′	130°15′
Tsimtack 7	IR/RI	BC	Range 4 Coast	103 H/6	53°23′	129°28′
Tsinkahtl 8	IR/RI	BC	Kamloops Division Yale	92 I/6	50°30′	121°17′
Tsinstikeptum 9	IR/RI	BC	Osoyoos Division Yale	82 E/13	49°51′	119°36′
Tsinstikeptum 10	IR/RI	BC	Osoyoos Division Yale	82 E/13	49°53′	119°32′
Tsintahktl 2	IR/RI	BC	Yale Division Yale	92 H/14	49°57′	121°29′
Tsintsunko Lake	LAKE/LAC	BC	Kamloops Division Yale	92 P/1	51°03′	120°30′
Tsintu River	RIV/CDE	NT	Mackenzie	106 I	66°08′	129°02′
Tsirku Glacier	GLAC/GLAC	BC	Cassiar	114 P/7	59°19′	136°37′
Tsitika River	RIV/CDE	BC	Rupert	92 L/7	50°29′	126°35′
Tsitsk 3	IR/RI	BC	Cassiar	93 M/5	55°16′	127°36′
Tsitsutl Peak	MTN/MNT	BC	Range 3 Coast	93 C/12	52°43′	125°47′
Tsoko Lake	LAKE/LAC	NT	Mackenzie	97 B	68°23′	125°32′
Tsolum River	RIV/CDE	BC	Comox	92 F/10	49°42′	124°59′
Tsowenachs 2	IR/RI	BC		92 L/5	50°18′	127°48′
Tsowwin 10	IR/RI	BC	Nootka	92 E/15	49°47′	126°38′
Tsuius Creek	RIV/CDE	BC	Kamloops Division Yale	82 L/10	50°41′	118°38′
Tsu Lake	LAKE/LAC	NT	Mackenzie	75 D	60°40′	111°52′
Tsulquate 4	IR/RI	BC	Rupert	92 L/11	50°44′	127°30′

NAME NOM	ENTITY ENTITÉ	LOC 1 LIEU 1	LOC 2 LIEU 2	MAP CARTE	POSITION LAT	LONG
Tsulquate River	RIV/CDE	BC	Rupert	92 L/11	50°44′	127°30′
Tsuniah Lake	LAKE/LAC	BC	Range 2 Coast	92 N/9	51°33′	124°05′
Tsunnia Lake 5	IR/RI	BC	Range 2 Coast	92 N/9	51°32′	124°09′
Tsun Tine Ah 37	IR/RI	BC	Range 5 Coast	93 K/10	54°44′	124°42′
Tsupmeet (Patcha Creek) 5	IR/RI	BC	Cassiar	94 D/2	56°11′	126°52′
Tsuquanah 2	IR/RI	BC	Barclay	92 C/10	48°41′	124°52′
Tsusiat Lake	LAKE/LAC	BC	Barclay	92 C/10	48°43′	124°53′
Tsussie 6	IR/RI	BC	Chemainus	92 B/13	48°53′	123°41′
Tuadook Lake	LAKE/LAC	NB	Northumberland	21 J/15	46°57′	66°40′
Tuaton Lake	LAKE/LAC	BC	Cassiar	104 H/8	57°17′	128°05′
Tubbs Corners	UNP/LNO	ON	Northumberland	31 C/4	44°03′	77°55′
Tuber Lake	LAKE/LAC	MB	15-16-E	52 L/3	50°14′	95°18′
Tuberose	UNP/LNO	SK	36-22-16-W3	72 K/16	50°55′	108°05′
Tuchialic Bay	BAY/BAIE	NF		13 J/16	54°45′	58°25′
Tuchitua	UNP/LNO	YT		105 A/14	60°55′	129°13′
Tuchitua River	RIV/CDE	YT		105 A/14	60°56′	129°12′
Tuchodi Lakes	LAKE/LAC	BC	Peace River	94 K/1	58°13′	124°30′
Tuchodi River	RIV/CDE	BC	Peace River	94 J/5	58°22′	123°37′
Tucho River	RIV/CDE	BC	Cassiar	104 I/1	58°01′	128°17′
Tucker	UNP/LNO	MB		62 G/16	49°59′	98°13′
Tucker Lake	LAKE/LAC	AB	64-4,5-W4	73 L/10	54°32′	110°37′
Tucker Point	CAPE/CAP	NT	Franklin	59 B	76°45′	93°11′
Tucker Seamount	SEAU/SMER	—		3000	49°48′	133°30′
Tuckersmith	MUN2/AZM2	ON	Huron	40 P/6	43°30′	81°28′
Tuck Inlet 89	IR/RI	BC	Range 5 Coast	103 J/8	54°26′	130°20′
Tuckkwiowhum 1	IR/RI	BC	Yale Division Yale	92 H/14	49°50′	121°26′
Tuckozap 24	IR/RI	BC	Kamloops Division Yale	92 I/4	50°14′	121°35′
Tucks	UNP/LNO	BC	New Westminster	92 G/3	49°12′	123°07′
Tudor	UNP/LNO	AB	33-25-23-W4	82 P/3	51°10′	113°09′
Tudor and Cashel	MUN2/AZM2	ON	Hastings	31 C/13	44°57′	77°30′
Tudor, Lac	LAKE/LAC	QC	Kativik	23 P/14	55°50′	65°25′
Tudyah Lake	LAKE/LAC	BC	Cariboo	93 O/3	55°05′	123°02′
Tuffin Island	ISL/ÎLE	NS	Halifax	11 D/16	44°54′	62°10′
Tuffnell	HAM/HAM	SK	33-30-10-W2	62 M/11	51°39′	103°22′
Tufts Abyssal Plain	SEAU/SMER	—		5.03	47°00′	140°00′
Tufts Cove	UNP/LNO	NS	Halifax	11 D/12	44°41′	63°36′
Tuftsville	UNP/LNO	ON	Hastings	31 C/6	44°19′	77°29′
Tugaske	VILG/VILG	SK	13-22-3-W3	72 J/16	50°52′	106°17′
Tug Pond	LAKE/LAC	NF		2 D/1	48°06′	54°06′
Tugtown	UNP/LNO	NB	York	21 J/10	46°32′	66°32′
Tugwell Creek	RIV/CDE	BC	Otter	92 B/5	48°23′	123°51′
Tugwell Island 21	IR/RI	BC	Range 5 Coast	103 J/7	54°20′	130°30′
Tuitatui Lake	LAKE/LAC	NT	Mackenzie	96 G	65°47′	123°17′
Tukarak Island	ISL/ÎLE	NT	Keewatin	34 D	56°16′	78°45′
Tuktoyaktuk	HAM/HAM	NT	Mackenzie	107 C	69°27′	133°02′
Tuktoyaktuk Peninsula	CAPE/CAP	NT	Mackenzie	107 D	69°45′	131°20′
Tuktut Nogait National Park - also-aussi - Tuktut Nogait, Parc national	PARK/PARC	NT		97 D/2	69°15′	122°00′
Tuktut Nogait, Parc national - also-aussi - Tuktut Nogait National Park	PARK/PARC	NT		97 D/2	69°15′	122°00′
Tulabi Lake	LAKE/LAC	SK	66,67-7-W2	63 L/14	54°46′	103°00′
Tulameen	UNP/LNO	BC	Yale Division Yale	92 H/10	49°33′	120°45′
Tulameen Mountain	MTN/MNT	BC	Yale Division Yale	92 H/6	49°23′	121°07′
Tulameen River	RIV/CDE	BC	Similkameen Division Yale	92 H/7	49°28′	120°30′
Tulemalu Lake	LAKE/LAC	NT	Keewatin	65 J	62°58′	99°25′
Tulita	HAM/HAM	NT	Mackenzie	96 C/13	64°54′	125°35′
Tullamore	UNP/LNO	ON	Peel	30 M/13	43°47′	79°46′
Tullett Point	CAPE/CAP	NT	Franklin	99 A	76°44′	121°12′
Tulliby Lake	UNP/LNO	AB	2-55-2-W4	73 E/9	53°43′	110°11′
Tullis	UNP/LNO	SK	15-24-8-W3	72 O/3	51°03′	107°02′
Tullochgorum	UNP/LNO	QC	Le Haut-Saint-Laurent	31 H/4	45°08′	73°55′
Tully Canyon	SEAU/SMER	—		3602	48°14′	125°12′
Tully Lake	LAKE/LAC	ON	Kenora	52 J/5	50°29′	91°37′
Tullymet No. 216	MUN2/AZM2	SK		62 L/13	51°00′	103°30′
Tulsequah	UNP/LNO	BC	Cassiar	104 K/12	58°38′	133°33′
Tum-bah 5	IR/RI	BC	Cassiar	103 P/1	55°04′	128°02′
Tumbledown Dick Island	ISL/ÎLE	NF		13 I/3	54°09′	57°09′
Tumbler Island	ISL/ÎLE	NF		2 C/13	48°49′	53°45′
Tumbler Ridge	MUN1/AZM1	BC	Peace River	93 P/3	55°03′	121°10′
Tumbler Ridge	UNP/LNO	BC	Peace River	93 P/2	55°08′	121°00′
Tumbo Island	ISL/ÎLE	BC	Cowichan	92 B/14	48°48′	123°04′
Tumeka Lake	LAKE/LAC	BC	Cassiar	104 H/4	57°14′	129°36′
Tummel	UNP/LNO	MB	7-25-28-W	62 N/3	51°08′	101°23′
Tummel River	RIV/CDE	YT		105 L/14	62°45′	135°04′
Tumtum Lake	LAKE/LAC	BC	Kamloops Division Yale	82 M/14	51°52′	119°07′
Tumult Glacier	GLAC/GLAC	BC	Range 2 Coast	92 N/5	51°16′	125°55′
Tunago Lake	LAKE/LAC	NT	Mackenzie	96 K	66°19′	125°50′

NAME NOM	ENTITY ENTITÉ	LOC 1 LIEU 1	LOC 2 LIEU 2	MAP CARTE	POSITION LAT	LONG
Tunaville	UNP/LNO	NB	Charlotte	21 G/2	45°03′	66°48′
Tungsten	UNP/LNO	NT	Mackenzie	105 H/16	61°57′	128°14′
Tunis	UNP/LNO	ON	Cochrane	42 A/15	48°50′	80°50′
Tunkwa Lake	LAKE/LAC	BC	Kamloops Division Yale	92 I/10	50°36′	120°51′
Tunnel 6	IR/RI	BC	Yale Division Yale	92 H/6	49°24′	121°26′
Tunnissugjuak Inlet	BAY/BAIE	NF		25 A/7	60°17′	64°37′
Tunstall	UNP/LNO	SK	9-14-28-W3	72 K/4	50°09′	109°47′
Tunungayualok Island	ISL/ÎLE	NF		14 C/3	56°05′	61°05′
Tununuk	UNP/LNO	NT	Mackenzie	107 C	69°00′	134°40′
Tupialuviniq	UNP/LNO	QC	Kativik	33 M/1	55°01′	78°26′
Tupirviit	UNP/LNO	QC	Kativik	25 C/4	60°10′	69°42′
Tupirviturlik	UNP/LNO	QC	Kativik	34 K/5	58°20′	77°53′
Tupper	UNP/LNO	BC	Peace River	93 P/9	55°30′	120°02′
Tupper Lake	LAKE/LAC	NS	Queens	21 A/7	44°27′	65°00′
Tupperville	UNP/LNO	NS	Annapolis	21 A/14	44°48′	65°22′
Tupperville	UNP/LNO	ON	Kent	40 J/9	42°36′	82°16′
Turbine	UNP/LNO	ON	Sudbury	41 I/5	46°22′	81°31′
Turgeon	UNP/LNO	NB	Gloucester	21 P/13	47°53′	65°51′
Turgeon, Lac	LAKE/LAC	QC	Abitibi-Ouest	32 E/3	49°02′	79°02′
Turgeon, Rivière	RIV/CDE	QC	Jamésie	32 L/2	50°01′	78°56′
Turin	UNP/LNO	ON	Kent	40 I/12	42°31′	81°52′
Turin	UNP/LNO	AB	4-12-19-W4	82 H/15	49°58′	112°31′
Turkey Point	UNP/LNO	ON	Norfolk	40 I/9	42°42′	80°19′
Turkey Point	CAPE/CAP	ON	Norfolk	40 I/9	42°40′	80°21′
Turks Cove	UNP/LNO	NF		1 N/14	47°56′	53°21′
Turks Cove	BAY/BAIE	NF		11 P/11	47°38′	57°27′
Turmoil Lake	LAKE/LAC	NT	Mackenzie	86 F	65°06′	116°15′
Turnagain Point	CAPE/CAP	NT	Mackenzie	77 B	68°38′	108°13′
Turnagain River	RIV/CDE	BC	Cassiar	94 M/4	59°09′	127°35′
Turnavik Islands	ISL/ÎLE	NF		13 O/6	55°17′	59°22′
Turnberry	MUN2/AZM2	ON	Huron	40 P/14	43°52′	81°15′
Turnberry	UNP/LNO	MB	30-51-29-W	63 F/5	53°26′	101°43′
Turnbull	UNP/LNO	MB	26-64-14-W	63 J/11	54°34′	99°29′
Turnbull Island	ISL/ÎLE	ON	Algoma	41 J/2	46°09′	82°46′
Turner	UNP/LNO	ON	Manitoulin	41 H/13	45°59′	81°54′
Turner	UNP/LNO	AB	21-23-1-W5	82 J/16	50°59′	114°05′
Turner, Cape	CAPE/CAP	PE	Queens	11 L/6	46°29′	63°19′
Turner, Mount	MTN/MNT	YT		116 H/8	65°24′	136°14′
Turner Point	CAPE/CAP	NT	Franklin	37 C	69°25′	77°20′
Turners	UNP/LNO	ON	Bruce	41 A/6	44°23′	81°20′
Turner's Bight	UNP/LNO	NF		13 J/1	54°13′	58°07′
Turners Corners	UNP/LNO	ON	Welland	30 M/3	43°04′	79°15′
Turner Settlement	UNP/LNO	NB	Victoria	21 J/13	46°47′	67°46′
Turnertown	UNP/LNO	QC	Memphrémagog	31 H/1	45°14′	72°04′
Turner Valley	TOWN/VIL2	AB	12-20-3-W5	82 J/9	50°40′	114°17′
Turnip Cove	UNP/LNO	NF		1 M/11	47°41′	55°26′
Turnor Lake	HAM/HAM	SK		74 C/7	56°28′	108°41′
Turnor Lake	LAKE/LAC	SK		74 C/10	56°35′	108°35′
Turnor Lake 193B	IR/RI	SK		74 C/7	56°28′	108°41′
Turnor Lake 194	IR/RI	SK		73 N/15	55°54′	108°53′
Turnor Point	CAPE/CAP	SK		74 N/2	59°08′	108°37′
Turnour Island	ISL/ÎLE	BC	Range 1 Coast	92 L/9	50°36′	126°27′
Turn-up Juniper	UNP/LNO	QC	Minganie	12 P/11	51°37′	57°16′
Turret Island	ISL/ÎLE	BC	Barclay	92 C/14	48°54′	125°20′
Turriff	UNP/LNO	ON	Hastings	31 C/13	44°59′	77°45′
Turtle	UNP/LNO	ON	Rainy River	52 C/15	48°45′	92°33′
Turtle Creek	UNP/LNO	NB	Albert	21 H/15	45°58′	64°53′
Turtle Dam	UNP/LNO	QC	Témiscamingue	31 L/15	46°54′	78°52′
Turtleford	TOWN/VIL2	SK	12-51-21-W3	73 F/7	53°23′	108°57′
Turtleford Junction	UNP/LNO	SK	13-51-21-W3	73 F/7	53°24′	108°58′
Turtle Lake	UNP/LNO	ON	Parry Sound	31 E/5	45°19′	79°44′
Turtle Lake	LAKE/LAC	ON	Manitoulin	41 H/13	45°50′	81°53′
Turtle Lake	LAKE/LAC	ON	Algoma	41 J/7	46°16′	82°40′
Turtle Lake	LAKE/LAC	MB	13,14-16-E	52 L/3	50°08′	95°22′
Turtle Lake	LAKE/LAC	SK		73 F/10	53°36′	108°38′
Turtlelake River	RIV/CDE	SK	8-46-18-W3	73 C/15	52°57′	108°34′
Turtle Lake South Bay	HAM/HAM	SK	26-52-19-W3	73 F/10	53°31′	108°42′
Turtle Mountain	MUN2/AZM2	MB		62 G/4	49°10′	99°40′
Turtle Mountain	MTN/MNT	MB		62 F/1	49°00′	100°15′
Turtle Point 12	IR/RI	BC	Range 4 Coast	103 H/6	53°19′	129°16′
Turtle River	RIV/CDE	ON	Kenora	52 F/1	49°02′	92°24′
Turtle River	RIV/CDE	MB	34-24-16-W	62 O/4	51°07′	99°38′
Turtle River No. 469	MUN2/AZM2	SK		73 F/2	53°10′	108°50′
Turtle Valley	UNP/LNO	BC	Kamloops Division Yale	82 L/13	50°49′	119°36′
Turton Lake	LAKE/LAC	NT	Mackenzie	96 E	65°48′	126°57′

NAME NOM	ENTITY ENTITÉ	LOC 1 LIEU 1	LOC 2 LIEU 2	MAP CARTE	POSITION LAT	LONG
Tusket	UNP/LNO	NS	Yarmouth	20 P/13	43°52′	65°58′
Tusket Basin	SEAU/SMER	—		4011	42°50′	66°45′
Tusket Falls	UNP/LNO	NS	Yarmouth	20 P/13	43°53′	65°59′
Tusket Islands	ISL/ÎLE	NS	Yarmouth	20 O/9	43°40′	66°01′
Tutela Heights	UNP/LNO	ON	Brant	40 P/1	43°07′	80°15′
Tutizzi Lake	LAKE/LAC	BC	Cassiar	94 C/5	56°20′	125°45′
*Tutshi	UNP/LNO	BC	Cassiar	104 M/16	59°54′	134°17′
Tutshi Lake	LAKE/LAC	BC	Cassiar	104 M/15	59°56′	134°37′
Tutsieta Lake	LAKE/LAC	NT	Mackenzie	106 O	67°16′	130°00′
Tuttle	UNP/LNO	AB	30-37-27-W4	83 A/4	52°13′	113°50′
Tuttle Point	CAPE/CAP	NT	Franklin	25 E	61°32′	71°36′
Tuttusivik	UNP/LNO	QC	Kativik	34 P/13	59°54′	73°38′
Tutu Creek 4	IR/RI	BC	Cariboo	93 O/6	55°26′	123°12′
Tuurngaup Illuvininga	UNP/LNO	QC	Kativik	34 K/6	58°17′	77°27′
Tuwanek	UNP/LNO	BC	New Westminster	92 G/12	49°33′	123°45′
Tuwasus Creek	RIV/CDE	BC	New Westminster	92 J/2	50°00′	122°30′
Tuxedo	UNP/LNO	MB		62 H/14	49°52′	97°13′
Tuxedo Park	UNP/LNO	SK		72 I/7	50°27′	104°35′
Tuxford	VILG/VILG	SK	5-19-26-W2	72 I/12	50°34′	105°35′
Tuya Lake	LAKE/LAC	BC	Cassiar	104 O/2	59°05′	130°35′
Tuya River	RIV/CDE	BC	Cassiar	104 J/2	58°02′	130°51′
Tuzcha Lake	LAKE/LAC	BC	Lillooet	92 O/5	51°17′	123°42′
Tuzo Wilson Seamounts	SEAU/SMER	—		3744	51°26′	130°55′
Twaal Creek	RIV/CDE	BC	Kamloops Division Yale	92 I/6	50°27′	121°18′
Twan Creek	RIV/CDE	BC	Cariboo	93 B/10	52°34′	122°36′
Tway	HAM/HAM	SK	29-43-24-W2	73 A/11	52°44′	105°26′
Tweed	VILG/VILG	ON	Hastings	31 C/6	44°29′	77°19′
Tweedie	UNP/LNO	NB	Carleton	21 J/12	46°31′	67°40′
Tweedie	UNP/LNO	AB	17-68-12-W4	73 L/13	54°53′	111°47′
Tweedie Brook	UNP/LNO	NB	Kent	21 I/14	46°47′	65°08′
Tweed Island	ISL/ÎLE	NF		12 G/1	49°13′	58°20′
Tweed Lake	LAKE/LAC	NT	Mackenzie	96 K	66°47′	125°53′
Tweedside	UNP/LNO	NB	York	21 G/11	45°38′	67°01′
Tweedside	UNP/LNO	ON	Wentworth	30 M/4	43°10′	79°41′
Tweedsmuir	UNP/LNO	ON	Nipissing	31 L/6	46°17′	79°26′
Tweedsmuir	UNP/LNO	SK	8-53-27-W2	73 H/12	53°34′	105°57′
Tweedsmuir Glacier	GLAC/GLAC	BC/YT		114 O/16	59°52′	138°21′
12 Mile	UNP/LNO	BC	Cassiar	93 N/15	55°49′	124°58′
Twelve Mile Lake	LAKE/LAC	SK		72 G/8	49°29′	106°14′
Twelve Mile Stream	RIV/CDE	NS	Halifax	11 E/2	45°03′	62°30′
Twelve O'Clock Point	UNP/LNO	ON	Northumberland	31 C/4	44°04′	77°36′
Twenty Mile Creek	RIV/CDE	ON	Lincoln	30 M/3	43°10′	79°22′
Twidwell Bend	UNP/LNO	BC	Peace River	93 P/12	55°37′	121°34′
Twigge Lake	LAKE/LAC	SK	63,64-8,-9-W2	63 L/6	54°30′	103°13′
Twillick Brook	RIV/CDE	NF		2 D/4	48°02′	55°35′
Twillingate	TOWN/VIL2	NF		2 E/10	49°39′	54°46′
Twillingate	UNP/LNO	NF		2 E/10	49°39′	54°46′
Twillingate Harbour	BAY/BAIE	NF		2 E/10	49°40′	54°46′
Twin Butte	UNP/LNO	AB	4-4-29-W4	82 H/5	49°16′	113°51′
Twin Butte	UNP/LNO	BC	Kootenay	82 N/4	51°02′	117°59′
Twin City	UNP/LNO	ON	Thunder Bay	52 A/6	48°22′	89°25′
Twin Creeks	UNP/LNO	BC	New Westminster	92 G/6	49°29′	123°29′
Twin Elm	UNP/LNO	ON	Carleton	31 G/4	45°13′	75°48′
Twin Falls	UNP/LNO	NF		23 H/7	53°30′	64°32′
Twin Falls	UNP/LNO	ON	Cochrane	42 A/10	48°45′	80°35′
Twin Falls	FALL/CHUT	BC	Kootenay	82 N/10	51°33′	116°32′
Twin Falls Tea House National Historic Site	PARK/PARC	BC	Kootenay	82 N/10	51°33′	116°32′
- also-aussi - Salon-de-Thé-des-Chutes-Twin, Lieu historique national du						
Twining	UNP/LNO	AB	2-31-24-W4	82 P/11	51°38′	113°17′
Twin Island 10	IR/RI	BC	Esquimalt	92 B/5	48°23′	123°30′
Twin Islands	UNP/LNO	BC	New Westminster	92 G/7	49°21′	122°53′
Twin Islands	ISL/ÎLE	MB	41-23,24-W	63 C/10	52°33′	100°47′
Twin Islands	ISL/ÎLE	BC	Sayward	92 K/2	50°02′	124°56′
Twin Lake	LAKE/LAC	NT	Keewatin	55 N	63°20′	92°24′
Twin Lakes	LAKE/LAC	BC	Similkameen Division Yale	82 E/5	49°19′	119°44′
Twin Lakes Beach	UNP/LNO	MB	15,16-4-W	62 I/5	50°20′	97°58′
Twin Mountain	MTN/MNT	YT		105 F/14	61°50′	133°20′
Twin Rock Valley	UNP/LNO	NS	Inverness	11 K/3	46°09′	61°08′
Twin Valley	UNP/LNO	SK	30-4-29-W2	72 H/5	49°20′	105°54′
Twitya River	RIV/CDE	NT	Mackenzie	106 A	64°10′	128°11′
Two Brooks	UNP/LNO	NB	Victoria	21 O/3	47°04′	67°18′
Two Buttes	MTN/MNT	YT		105 M/6	63°29′	135°23′
Two Creeks	UNP/LNO	MB	19-12-26-W	62 K/3	50°02′	101°02′
Two Creeks	UNP/LNO	AB	29-61-16-W5	83 K/8	54°18′	116°21′
Twoforks River	RIV/CDE	SK		73 J/16	55°00′	106°16′
Two Guns	UNP/LNO	AB	12-23-2-W5	82 J/16	50°57′	114°10′

NAME / NOM	ENTITY / ENTITÉ	LOC 1 / LIEU 1	LOC 2 / LIEU 2	MAP / CARTE	LAT	LONG
Two Guts Pond	LAKE/LAC	NF		12 B/10	48°39'	58°40'
Two Hills	TOWN/VIL2	AB	32-54-12-W4	73 E/12	53°43'	111°45'
Two Hills No. 21, County of	MUN1/AZM1	AB	54-11-W4	73 E/12	53°43'	111°32'
Two Islands	UNP/LNO	NS	Cumberland	21 H/8	45°23'	64°14'
Twomey	UNP/LNO	AB	46-19-W4	83 A/15	52°59'	112°44'
Two Mile	UNP/LNO	BC	Cassiar	93 M/5	55°16'	127°37'
Two Mile Corner	UNP/LNO	ON	Kenora	52 F/15	49°49'	92°51'
Two Mile Creek 16	IR/RI	BC	Kamloops Division Yale	92 I/4	50°15'	121°33'
Two Mile Creek 16A	IR/RI	BC	Kamloops Division Yale	92 I/5	50°15'	121°33'
Two O'Clock	UNP/LNO	ON	Manitoulin	41 H/12	45°44'	81°46'
Twopete Mountain	MTN/MNT	YT		105 K/12	62°41'	133°41'
Two River Lake	LAKE/LAC	ON	Kenora	53 G/14	53°52'	91°27'
Two Rivers	UNP/LNO	NS	Cumberland	21 H/9	45°39'	64°29'
Two Rivers	UNP/LNO	BC	Peace River	94 A/2	56°11'	120°32'
Two Rivers Arm	BAY/BAIE	BC	Clayoquot	92 F/2	49°15'	125°00'
Two Sisters Mountain	MTN/MNT	BC	Cariboo	93 H/4	53°12'	121°32'
Twoyqhalsht 16	IR/RI	BC	Kamloops Division Yale	92 I/6	50°26'	121°20'
Tyandaga	UNP/LNO	ON	Halton	30 M/5	43°21'	79°51'
Tyaughton Creek	RIV/CDE	BC	Lillooet	92 J/15	50°54'	122°37'
Tyaughton Lake	LAKE/LAC	BC	Lillooet	92 J/15	50°57'	122°46'
Tye	UNP/LNO	BC	Kootenay	82 F/7	49°20'	116°48'
Tyee	UNP/LNO	BC	Range 5 Coast	103 I/4	54°12'	129°57'
Tyee Lake	LAKE/LAC	BC	Cariboo	93 B/8	52°23'	122°04'
Tyendinaga	MUN2/AZM2	ON	Hastings	31 C/6	44°18'	77°13'
Tyendinaga 38 - see-voir - Tyendinaga Mohawk Territory	IR/RI	ON		31 C/3	44°12'	77°09'
Tyendinaga Mohawk Territory	IR/RI	ON	Hastings	31 C/3	44°12'	77°09'
Tyers River	RIV/CDE	YT		105 H/3	61°14'	129°15'
Tymgowzan 12	IR/RI	BC	Range 5 Coast	103 J/9	54°38'	130°25'
Tyndall	UNP/LNO	MB	11,12-13-6-E	62 I/2	50°05'	96°40'
Tyndall Park	UNP/LNO	MB		62 H/14	49°56'	97°12'
Tyndal Road	UNP/LNO	NS	Cumberland	21 H/16	45°51'	64°09'
Tynehead	UNP/LNO	BC	New Westminster	92 G/2	49°11'	122°44'
Tynemouth Creek	UNP/LNO	NB	Saint John	21 H/5	45°18'	65°39'
Tyner	HAM/HAM	SK	34-23-18-W3	72 N/1	51°00'	108°25'
Tyneside	UNP/LNO	ON	Haldimand	30 M/4	43°06'	79°53'
Tyne Valley	VILG/VILG	PE	Prince	11 L/12	46°35'	63°56'
Tyotown	UNP/LNO	ON	Glengarry	31 G/2	45°03'	74°39'
Tyranite	UNP/LNO	ON	Timiskaming	41 P/11	47°39'	81°01'
Tyrconnell	UNP/LNO	ON	Elgin	40 I/11	42°36'	81°29'
Tyrone	UNP/LNO	PE	Queens	11 L/6	46°17'	63°21'
Tyrone	UNP/LNO	ON	Durham	31 D/2	44°01'	78°43'
Tyrrell	UNP/LNO	ON	Norfolk	40 I/16	42°52'	80°13'
Tyrrell	UNP/LNO	MB	12-65-13-W	63 J/11	54°36'	99°18'
Tyrrell Arm	BAY/BAIE	NT	Keewatin	65 I	62°27'	97°30'
Tyrrell Falls	FALL/CHUT	NT	Mackenzie	75 K	62°49'	108°51'
Tyrrell Lake	LAKE/LAC	SK	68-1-W2	63 L/16	54°54'	102°07'
Tyrrell Lake	LAKE/LAC	NT	Mackenzie	75 P	63°07'	105°27'
Tyrrell, Mount	MTN/MNT	YT		115 N/9	63°43'	140°04'
Tyson	UNP/LNO	SK	4-14-8-W3	72 J/3	50°08'	107°03'
Tyson Lake	LAKE/LAC	ON	Sudbury	41 I/3	46°07'	81°07'
Tyvan	UNP/LNO	SK	28-12-13-W	62 L/4	50°02'	103°43'
Tzart-lam 5	IR/RI	BC	Sahtlam	92 B/13	48°46'	123°50'
Tzartus Island	ISL/ÎLE	BC	Barclay	92 C/14	48°55'	125°05'
Tzeachten 13	IR/RI	BC	New Westminster	92 H/4	49°07'	121°56'
Tzenzaicut Lake	LAKE/LAC	BC	Cariboo	93 B/10	52°39'	122°51'
Tzeo River	RIV/CDE	BC	Range 2 Coast	92 M/15	51°50'	126°40'
Tzetzi Lake 11	IR/RI	BC	Range 3 Coast	93 C/15	52°59'	125°00'
Tzoonie River	RIV/CDE	BC	New Westminster	92 G/13	49°47'	123°43'
Tzuhalem	UNP/LNO	BC	Cowichan	92 B/13	48°47'	123°39'

U

NAME / NOM	ENTITY / ENTITÉ	LOC 1 / LIEU 1	LOC 2 / LIEU 2	MAP / CARTE	LAT	LONG
Uapinatsheu Mauahunan	UNP/LNO	QC	Côte-Nord-du-Golfe-Saint-Laurent	12 K/8	50°18'	60°17'
Uashat 27	IR/RI	QC	Sept-Rivières	22 J/1	50°13'	66°24'
Uashatuess	UNP/LNO	QC	Sept-Rivières	22 O/2	51°02'	66°56'
Ucausley 4 - see-voir - Ucausley 16	IR/RI	BC		93 K/11	54°34'	125°09'
Ucausley 16	IR/RI	BC	Range 5 Coast	93 K/11	54°34'	125°09'
Uchasumaku Pikwayipanan	UNP/LNO	QC	Kativik	24 D/11	56°31'	71°05'
Uchikwachikanan	UNP/LNO	QC	Jamésie	33 I/14	55°00'	73°27'
Uchi Lake	UNP/LNO	ON	Kenora	52 N/2	51°05'	92°35'
Uchucklesit Inlet	BAY/BAIE	BC	Clayoquot	92 C/14	49°00'	125°00'
Ucluelet	VILG/VILG	BC	Clayoquot	92 C/13	48°56'	125°33'
Ucluth 6	IR/RI	BC	Clayoquot	92 C/13	48°58'	125°36'
Ucona River	RIV/CDE	BC	Nootka	92 E/9	49°43'	126°06'

NAME NOM	ENTITY ENTITÉ	LOC 1 LIEU 1	LOC 2 LIEU 2	MAP CARTE	POSITION LAT	LONG
Udjuktok Bay	BAY/BAIE	NF		13 N/1	55°07′	60°30′
Udney	UNP/LNO	ON	Ontario	31 D/11	44°37′	79°12′
Udora	UNP/LNO	ON	Ontario	31 D/6	44°15′	79°11′
Ueht Ka Tshitaikant	UNP/LNO	QC	Minganie	22 I/8	50°21′	64°14′
Uffington	UNP/LNO	ON	Muskoka	31 D/14	44°59′	79°11′
Ufford	UNP/LNO	ON	Muskoka	31 E/3	45°10′	79°29′
Ugjuktok Fiord	BAY/BAIE	NF		14 L/6	58°25′	63°25′
Uhakakatshihip	UNP/LNO	QC	Côte-Nord-du-Golfe-Saint-Laurent	12 K/2	50°12′	60°37′
Uhakamiskua	UNP/LNO	QC	Minganie	12 O/7	51°29′	58°42′
Uhakatshukua	UNP/LNO	QC	Côte-Nord-du-Golfe-Saint-Laurent	12 O/2	51°13′	58°31′
Uhatnihip	UNP/LNO	QC	Minganie	22 P/9	51°38′	64°15′
Uhatshimatakahp	UNP/LNO	QC	Minganie	12 L/5	50°16′	63°42′
Uhatshinnatshuku	UNP/LNO	QC	Côte-Nord-du-Golfe-Saint-Laurent	12 O/2	51°07′	58°37′
Uhlman Lake	LAKE/LAC	MB		64 B/9	56°41′	98°23′
Uhl's Bay	HAM/HAM	SK	27-23-23-2	72 I/14	50°59′	105°09′
Uhthoff	UNP/LNO	ON	Simcoe	31 D/11	44°41′	79°29′
Uhukanatshehu	UNP/LNO	QC	Minganie	12 L/13	50°48′	63°55′
Uigg	UNP/LNO	PE	Queens	11 L/2	46°10′	62°49′
Uishakutshuakamau	UNP/LNO	QC	Kativik	24 A/7	56°30′	64°45′
Uist, Lake	LAKE/LAC	NS	Richmond	11 F/15	45°48′	60°34′
Uivak, Cape	CAPE/CAP	NF		14 L/7	58°29′	62°34′
Ujarallak	UNP/LNO	QC	Kativik	34 K/8	58°25′	76°23′
Ujuktuk Fiord	BAY/BAIE	NT	Franklin	26 H	65°13′	64°26′
Ukalta	UNP/LNO	AB	34-57-17-W4	83 H/16	53°58′	112°27′
Ukkusikallak	UNP/LNO	QC	Kativik	34 C/2	56°10′	76°36′
Ukraina	UNP/LNO	MB	31-28-20-W	62 N/8	51°27′	100°15′
Ukrainian Cultural Heritage Village Provincial Historic Site (Developed)	PARK/PARC	AB	7-53-19-W4	83 H/10	53°34′	112°48′
Ukunemakak	UNP/LNO	QC	Vallée-de-l'Or	31 N/11	47°37′	77°19′
Ulchen	UNP/LNO	QC	Le Haut-Saint-Laurent	31 H/4	45°01′	73°54′
Ulkatcho	UNP/LNO	BC	Range 3 Coast	93 C/13	53°00′	125°42′
Ulkatcho 1	IR/RI	BC	Range 3 Coast	93 C/13	52°59′	125°42′
Ulkatcho 5	IR/RI	BC	Range 4 Coast	93 E/1	53°04′	126°02′
Ulkatcho 6	IR/RI	BC	Range 4 Coast	93 F/4	53°03′	125°38′
Ulkatcho 13	IR/RI	BC	Range 3 Coast	93 C/6	52°23′	125°02′
Ulkatcho 14A	IR/RI	BC	Range 3 Coast	93 C/6	52°27′	125°16′
Ullasautik	UNP/LNO	QC	Kativik	24 N/13	59°53′	69°40′
Ullin	UNP/LNO	AB	13-39-8-W5	83 B/6	52°22′	115°01′
Ullswater	UNP/LNO	ON	Muskoka	31 E/4	45°13′	79°30′
Ulthakoush 11	IR/RI	BC	Range 3 Coast	103 A/15	52°58′	128°39′
Uluksan Peninsula	CAPE/CAP	NT	Franklin	48 C	73°05′	85°20′
Ulverton	VILG/VILG	QC	Drummond	31 H/9	45°43′	72°14′
Ulvingen Island	ISL/ÎLE	NT	Franklin	59 E	78°20′	88°12′
Umfreville	UNP/LNO	ON	Kenora	52 G/14	49°52′	91°28′
Umfreville Lake	LAKE/LAC	ON	Kenora	52 L/7	50°18′	94°45′
Umiakovik Lake	LAKE/LAC	NF		14 E/7	57°24′	62°50′
Umiarivik	UNP/LNO	QC	Kativik	25 C/4	60°13′	69°36′
Umingmaktok	UNP/LNO	NT	Mackenzie	76 O/12	67°42′	107°57′
Umingmaqautik	UNP/LNO	QC	Kativik	24 K/1	58°09′	68°18′
Umiujaq	VILG/VILG	QC	Kativik	34 C/10	56°33′	76°33′
Umpherville	UNP/LNO	MB	56-26-W	63 F/14	53°50′	101°13′
Unaka	UNP/LNO	ON	Kenora	52 G/11	49°42′	91°06′
Unasaorta 1	IR/RI	BC	Range 4 Coast	93 F/13	53°57′	125°45′
Uncas	UNP/LNO	AB	22-52-21-W4	83 H/6	53°30′	113°01′
Uncha Lake	LAKE/LAC	BC	Range 4 Coast	93 F/13	53°55′	125°37′
Uncha Lake 13A	IR/RI	BC	Range 4 Coast	93 F/13	53°56′	125°40′
Underhill	UNP/LNO	NB	Northumberland	21 I/13	46°45′	65°49′
Underhill	UNP/LNO	MB	33-5-22-W	62 F/8	49°27′	100°23′
Underwood	UNP/LNO	ON	York	30 M/14	43°50′	79°18′
Underwood	UNP/LNO	ON	Bruce	41 A/6	44°18′	81°29′
Undine	UNP/LNO	NB	Victoria	21 J/13	46°58′	67°41′
Undora	UNP/LNO	SK	15-30-23-W2	72 P/11	51°34′	105°10′
Uneven Lake	LAKE/LAC	ON	Thunder Bay	52 H/13	49°58′	89°52′
Ungardlek	UNP/LNO	NF		14 C/14	56°51′	61°23′
Ungava	UNP/LNO	ON	Frontenac	31 C/15	44°48′	76°38′
Ungava, Baie d' - also-aussi - **Ungava Bay**	BAY/BAIE	NT	Franklin	24 O	59°30′	67°30′
Ungava Bay - also-aussi - **Ungava, Baie d'**	BAY/BAIE	NT	Franklin	24 O	59°30′	67°30′
Ungava, Péninsule d'	CAPE/CAP	QC	Kativik	35 B/1	60°00′	74°00′
Ungenuk Lake	LAKE/LAC	NT	Franklin	36 G	65°01′	75°40′
Ungers Corner	UNP/LNO	ON	Norfolk	40 I/9	42°41′	80°25′
Uniacke	UNP/LNO	QC	Vallée-de-l'Or	32 C/5	48°25′	77°31′
Uniacke Hill	UNP/LNO	NB	Westmorland	21 H/16	45°59′	64°06′
Union	UNP/LNO	NS	Colchester	11 E/6	45°24′	63°07′
Union	UNP/LNO	ON	Leeds	31 B/5	44°26′	76°00′
Union	UNP/LNO	ON	Elgin	40 I/11	42°42′	81°12′
Union	UNP/LNO	ON	Essex	40 J/2	42°02′	82°40′

NAME NOM	ENTITY ENTITÉ	LOC 1 LIEU 1	LOC 2 LIEU 2	MAP CARTE	POSITION LAT	LONG
Union Bay	UNP/LNO	BC	Nelson	92 F/10	49°35′	124°53′
Union Bay 4	IR/RI	BC	North Saanich	92 B/11	48°40′	123°27′
Union Bay 31	IR/RI	BC	Range 5 Coast	103 J/9	54°37′	130°21′
Union, Cape	CAPE/CAP	NT	Franklin	120 E	82°14′	61°10′
Union Centre	UNP/LNO	NS	Pictou	11 E/10	45°32′	62°45′
Union Corner	UNP/LNO	PE	Prince	11 L/5	46°23′	64°00′
Union Corner	UNP/LNO	NS	Hants	21 H/1	45°01′	64°01′
Union Corner	UNP/LNO	NB	Carleton	21 J/4	46°03′	67°47′
Union Creek	UNP/LNO	ON	Victoria	31 D/10	44°43′	78°38′
Uniondale	UNP/LNO	ON	Oxford	40 P/3	43°13′	81°04′
Union Dam Flowage	LAKE/LAC	NS	Halifax	11 E/2	45°06′	62°38′
Union Hall	UNP/LNO	ON	Lanark	31 F/1	45°10′	76°18′
Union Island	ISL/ÎLE	BC	Rupert	92 L/3	50°01′	127°16′
Union Island	ISL/ÎLE	NT	Mackenzie	75 E	61°56′	111°56′
Union Jack	UNP/LNO	SK	35-7-15-W2	62 E/12	49°37′	103°57′
Union Mills	UNP/LNO	NB	Charlotte	21 G/3	45°11′	67°18′
Union Point	UNP/LNO	MB		62 H/11	49°31′	97°14′
Union Road	VILG/VILG	PE	Queens	11 L/6	46°20′	63°08′
Union Road	UNP/LNO	PE	Kings	11 L/2	46°11′	62°42′
Union Road	UNP/LNO	PE	Queens	11 L/6	46°20′	63°08′
Union Seamount	SEAU/SMER	—		3000	49°35′	132°45′
Union Settlement	UNP/LNO	NB	Queens	21 H/13	45°55′	65°58′
Union Square	UNP/LNO	NS	Lunenburg	21 A/10	44°33′	64°39′
Unionvale	UNP/LNO	PE	Prince	21 I/9	46°43′	64°11′
Unionville	UNP/LNO	ON	York	30 M/14	43°52′	79°18′
Unipouheos 121	IR/RI	AB	56-3-W4	73 E/16	53°53′	110°21′
United States Range	MTN/MNT	NT	Franklin	120 F	82°25′	68°00′
Unity	TOWN/VIL2	SK	18-40-22-W3	73 C/6	52°27′	109°10′
University	UNP/LNO	SK		72 I/5	50°23′	105°30′
University Gardens	UNP/LNO	ON	Wentworth	30 M/5	43°16′	79°56′
University Heights	UNP/LNO	ON	Middlesex	40 I/14	43°00′	81°17′
University Heights	UNP/LNO	SK		72 I/5	50°24′	105°30′
University Hill	UNP/LNO	BC	New Westminster	92 G/6	49°16′	123°15′
University Park	UNP/LNO	SK		72 I/7	50°26′	104°34′
University Park East	UNP/LNO	SK		72 I/7	50°26′	104°33′
University River - see-voir - Dog River	RIV/CDE	ON		41 N/14	47°58′	85°12′
Unnamed 10	IR/RI	BC	Cassiar	104 N/12	59°34′	133°42′
Uno	UNP/LNO	MB	33-14-27-W	62 K/3	50°14′	101°07′
Uno Park	UNP/LNO	ON	Timiskaming	31 M/12	47°35′	79°45′
Unpukpulquatum 8	IR/RI	BC	Kamloops Division Yale	92 I/6	50°16′	121°25′
Unuk River	RIV/CDE	BC	Cassiar	104 B/7	56°21′	130°44′
Unwin	UNP/LNO	SK	4-46-27-W3	73 C/13	52°56′	109°52′
Unwin Lake	LAKE/LAC	BC	New Westminster	92 K/2	50°07′	124°40′
Upana River	RIV/CDE	BC	Nootka	92 E/16	49°48′	126°04′
Upham	UNP/LNO	NB	Kings	21 H/5	45°29′	65°40′
Upham	GEOG/GÉOG	NB	Kings	21 H/12	45°30′	65°40′
Uphill	UNP/LNO	ON	Victoria	31 D/11	44°44′	79°00′
Uplands	UNP/LNO	ON	Carleton	31 G/5	45°20′	75°38′
Uplands	UNP/LNO	ON	Middlesex	40 P/3	43°02′	81°17′
Uplands	UNP/LNO	SK		72 I/7	50°30′	104°36′
Uplands Park	UNP/LNO	NS	Halifax	11 D/12	44°44′	63°44′
Upper	UNP/LNO	ON	Haldimand	30 L/13	42°53′	79°46′
Upper Afton	UNP/LNO	NS	Antigonish	11 F/12	45°34′	61°41′
Upper Amherst Cove	UNP/LNO	NF		2 C/11	48°33′	53°14′
Upper Arrow Lake	LAKE/LAC	BC	Kootenay	82 K/12	50°35′	117°57′
Upper Balmoral	UNP/LNO	NB	Restigouche	21 O/15	47°57′	66°30′
Upper Barnaby	UNP/LNO	NB	Northumberland	21 I/13	46°53′	65°34′
Upper Barneys River	UNP/LNO	NS	Pictou	11 E/8	45°29′	62°16′
Upper Bass River	UNP/LNO	NS	Colchester	11 E/5	45°26′	63°46′
Upper Beaver River	RIV/CDE	NT	Mackenzie	106 K	66°38′	133°05′
Upper Belleisle	UNP/LNO	NB	Kings	21 H/12	45°44′	65°43′
Upper Beverley Lake	LAKE/LAC	ON	Leeds	31 C/9	44°37′	76°05′
Upper Big Tracadie	UNP/LNO	NS	Guysborough	11 F/12	45°34′	61°36′
Upper Black Island	ISL/ÎLE	NF		2 E/6	49°24′	55°07′
Upper Blackville	UNP/LNO	NB	Northumberland	21 I/12	46°39′	65°52′
Upper Blackville Bridge	UNP/LNO	NB	Northumberland	21 I/12	46°37′	65°53′
Upper Blandford	UNP/LNO	NS	Lunenburg	21 A/9	44°31′	64°07′
Upper Branch	UNP/LNO	NS	Lunenburg	21 A/7	44°27′	64°41′
Upper Brighton	UNP/LNO	NB	Carleton	21 J/5	46°19′	67°33′
Upper Brockway	UNP/LNO	NB	York	21 G/11	45°35′	67°06′
Upper Brookfield	UNP/LNO	NS	Colchester	11 E/6	45°15′	63°15′
Upper Brookside	UNP/LNO	NS	Colchester	11 E/6	45°25′	63°14′
Upper Buctouche	UNP/LNO	NB	Kent	21 I/7	46°24′	64°50′
Upper Burgeo	UNP/LNO	NF		11 P/12	47°36′	57°40′
Upper Burlington	UNP/LNO	NS	Hants	21 H/1	45°03′	64°03′

NAME NOM	ENTITY ENTITÉ	LOC 1 LIEU 1	LOC 2 LIEU 2	MAP CARTE	POSITION LAT	LONG
Upper Burnside	UNP/LNO	NS	Colchester	11 E/7	45°19'	62°59'
Upper California	UNP/LNO	NB	Victoria	21 J/13	46°53'	67°46'
Upper Campbell Lake	LAKE/LAC	BC	Comox	92 F/13	49°56'	125°38'
Upper Canard	UNP/LNO	NS	Kings	21 H/1	45°07'	64°28'
Upper Cape	UNP/LNO	NB	Westmorland	11 L/4	46°03'	63°56'
Upper Carp Lake	LAKE/LAC	NT	Mackenzie	85 P	63°44'	113°45'
Upper Caverhill	UNP/LNO	NB	York	21 J/3	46°03'	67°10'
Upper Charlo	UNP/LNO	NB	Restigouche	22 B/1	48°00'	66°21'
Upper Chelsea	UNP/LNO	NS	Lunenburg	21 A/7	44°20'	64°46'
Upper China Creek	UNP/LNO	BC	Kootenay	82 F/4	49°13'	117°42'
Upper Clarence	UNP/LNO	NS	Annapolis	21 A/14	44°57'	65°10'
Upper Clements	UNP/LNO	NS	Annapolis	21 A/12	44°42'	65°35'
Upper Clyde River	UNP/LNO	NS	Shelburne	20 P/14	43°54'	65°28'
Upper Coverdale	UNP/LNO	NB	Albert	21 I/2	46°03'	64°58'
Upper Crossing	UNP/LNO	NB	Restigouche	21 O/16	47°45'	66°12'
Upper Cumins Lake	LAKE/LAC	SK	75-19-W3	73 N/7	55°30'	108°50'
Upper Cutbank	UNP/LNO	BC	Peace River	93 P/9	55°31'	120°26'
Upper Derby	UNP/LNO	NB	Northumberland	21 I/13	46°51'	65°44'
Upper Dorchester	UNP/LNO	NB	Westmorland	21 H/15	45°57'	64°32'
Upper Dover	UNP/LNO	NB	Westmorland	21 I/2	46°02'	64°41'
Upper Dundee	UNP/LNO	NB	Restigouche	22 B/2	48°00'	66°31'
Upper Durham	UNP/LNO	NB	York	21 J/2	46°09'	66°34'
Upper Dyke Village	UNP/LNO	NS	Kings	21 H/1	45°07'	64°30'
Upper Echo River	RIV/CDE	ON	Algoma	41 J/12	46°34'	83°57'
Upper Economy	UNP/LNO	NS	Colchester	11 E/5	45°23'	63°50'
Upper Falmouth	UNP/LNO	NS	Hants	21 A/16	44°57'	64°14'
Upper Ferry	UNP/LNO	NF		11 O/14	47°51'	59°15'
Upper Foster Lake	LAKE/LAC	SK		74 A/14	56°47'	105°20'
Upper Fraser	UNP/LNO	BC	Cariboo	93 I/4	54°07'	121°56'
Upper Gagetown	UNP/LNO	NB	Queens	21 G/16	45°51'	66°14'
Upper Garry Lake	LAKE/LAC	NT	Keewatin	66 F	65°50'	100°48'
Upper Gaspereau	UNP/LNO	NB	Queens	21 I/5	46°17'	65°52'
Upper Glencoe	UNP/LNO	NS	Inverness	11 F/14	45°57'	61°17'
Upper Golden Grove	UNP/LNO	NB	Kings	21 H/5	45°23'	65°53'
Upper Goose Lake	LAKE/LAC	ON	Kenora	52 N/10	51°43'	92°43'
Upper Goshen	UNP/LNO	NB	Kings	21 H/14	45°46'	65°12'
Upper Grand Mira	UNP/LNO	NS	Cape Breton	11 F/16	45°48'	60°18'
Upper Granville	UNP/LNO	NS	Annapolis	21 A/14	44°50'	65°20'
Upper Greenwich	UNP/LNO	NB	Kings	21 G/9	45°34'	66°02'
Upper Gulf Shore	UNP/LNO	NS	Cumberland	11 E/13	45°52'	63°36'
Upper Gullies	UNP/LNO	NF		1 N/6	47°29'	53°03'
Upper Hainesville	UNP/LNO	NB	York	21 J/3	46°05'	67°09'
Upper Hammonds Plains	UNP/LNO	NS	Halifax	11 D/12	44°45'	63°50'
Upper Harbour Lake	LAKE/LAC	BC	Kamloops Division Yale	82 M/11	51°34'	119°10'
Upper Hat Creek 1	IR/RI	BC	Kamloops Division Yale	92 I/13	50°49'	121°35'
Upper Hay River 212	IR/RI	AB	116-22,23-W5	84 N/4	59°03'	117°46'
Upper Humber River	RIV/CDE	NF		12 H/3	49°11'	57°28'
Upper Indian Pond	LAKE/LAC	NF		12 H/7	49°29'	56°37'
Upper Island Cove	TOWN/VIL2	NF		1 N/11	47°39'	53°13'
Upper Kempt Head	UNP/LNO	NS	Victoria	11 K/2	46°07'	60°38'
Upper Kemptown	UNP/LNO	NS	Colchester	11 E/6	45°29'	63°06'
Upper Kennetcook	UNP/LNO	NS	Hants	11 E/4	45°12'	63°39'
Upper Kent	UNP/LNO	NB	Carleton	21 J/12	46°34'	67°43'
Upper Keswick	UNP/LNO	NB	York	21 J/2	46°03'	66°54'
Upper Kingsburg	UNP/LNO	NS	Lunenburg	21 A/8	44°16'	64°17'
Upper Kintore	UNP/LNO	NB	Victoria	21 J/12	46°43'	67°35'
Upper Kluskus Lake 9	IR/RI	BC	Range 4 Coast	93 F/2	53°05'	124°35'
Upper Knoxford	UNP/LNO	NB	Carleton	21 J/12	46°32'	67°45'
Upper Laberge	UNP/LNO	YT		105 D/14	60°57'	135°06'
Upper LaHave	UNP/LNO	NS	Lunenburg	21 A/8	44°22'	64°27'
Upper Lakeville	UNP/LNO	NS	Halifax	11 D/15	44°47'	62°58'
Upper Lawrencetown	UNP/LNO	NS	Halifax	11 D/11	44°41'	63°27'
Upper Leitches Creek	UNP/LNO	NS	Cape Breton	11 K/1	46°08'	60°23'
Upper Letang	UNP/LNO	NB	Charlotte	21 G/2	45°08'	66°47'
Upper Liard	UNP/LNO	YT		105 A/2	60°03'	128°54'
Upper Linden	UNP/LNO	NS	Cumberland	11 E/13	45°53'	63°50'
Upper Little Ridge	UNP/LNO	NB	Charlotte	21 G/3	45°15'	67°26'
Upper Loch Lomond	UNP/LNO	NB	Saint John	21 H/5	45°22'	65°50'
Upper Loon Lake	LAKE/LAC	BC	Lillooet	92 P/3	51°11'	121°02'
Upper Lynn	UNP/LNO	BC	New Westminster	92 G/6	49°21'	123°02'
Upper Malagash	UNP/LNO	NS	Cumberland	11 E/14	45°46'	63°24'
Upper Manitou Lake	LAKE/LAC	ON	Kenora	52 F/7	49°24'	92°48'
Upper Margaree	UNP/LNO	NS	Inverness	11 K/3	46°13'	61°08'
Upper Maugerville	UNP/LNO	NB	Sunbury	21 G/15	45°54'	66°32'
Upper Mazinaw Lake	LAKE/LAC	ON	Lennox and Addington	31 C/14	44°55'	77°12'

NAME NOM	ENTITY ENTITÉ	LOC 1 LIEU 1	LOC 2 LIEU 2	MAP CARTE	POSITION LAT	LONG
Upper Melbourne	UNP/LNO	QC	Le Val-Saint-François	31 H/9	45°39'	72°09'
Upper Middle River	UNP/LNO	NS	Victoria	11 K/2	46°11'	60°56'
Upper Midland	UNP/LNO	NB	Kings	21 H/12	45°41'	65°46'
Upper Mills	UNP/LNO	NB	York	21 G/11	45°41'	67°05'
Upper Mills	UNP/LNO	NB	Charlotte	21 G/3	45°08'	67°19'
Upper Mount Thom	UNP/LNO	NS	Pictou	11 E/10	45°30'	63°00'
Upper Musquodoboit	UNP/LNO	NS	Halifax	11 E/2	45°08'	62°57'
Upper Napan	UNP/LNO	NB	Northumberland	21 I/14	47°00'	65°26'
Upper Nappan	UNP/LNO	NS	Cumberland	21 H/16	45°47'	64°12'
Upper Nepa 6	IR/RI	BC	Kamloops Division Yale	92 I/11	50°40'	121°16'
Upper New Cornwall	UNP/LNO	NS	Lunenburg	21 A/10	44°31'	64°34'
Upper New Harbour	UNP/LNO	NS	Guysborough	11 F/4	45°13'	61°31'
Upper New Horton	UNP/LNO	NB	Albert	21 H/10	45°41'	64°43'
Upper Nine Mile River	UNP/LNO	NS	Hants	11 E/4	45°05'	63°38'
Upper Northampton	UNP/LNO	NB	Carleton	21 J/4	46°07'	67°33'
Upper Northfield	UNP/LNO	NS	Lunenburg	21 A/10	44°30'	64°37'
Upper North River	UNP/LNO	NS	Colchester	11 E/6	45°29'	63°13'
Upper North Sydney	UNP/LNO	NS	Cape Breton	11 K/1	46°11'	60°16'
Upper Ohio	UNP/LNO	NS	Shelburne	20 P/14	43°59'	65°26'
Upper Onslow	UNP/LNO	NS	Colchester	11 E/6	45°23'	63°17'
Upper Pereaux	UNP/LNO	NS	Kings	21 H/1	45°11'	64°23'
Upper Point de Bute	UNP/LNO	NB	Westmorland	21 H/16	45°55'	64°13'
Upper Pokemouche	UNP/LNO	NB	Gloucester	21 P/10	47°41'	64°53'
Upper Pomquet	UNP/LNO	NS	Antigonish	11 F/12	45°36'	61°49'
Upper Port La Tour	UNP/LNO	NS	Shelburne	20 P/11	43°31'	65°28'
Upper Queensbury	UNP/LNO	NB	York	21 G/14	45°59'	67°12'
Upper Quinsam Lake	LAKE/LAC	BC	Comox	92 F/13	49°53'	125°33'
Upper Rawdon	UNP/LNO	NS	Hants	11 E/4	45°04'	63°43'
Upper Rexton	UNP/LNO	NB	Kent	21 I/10	46°38'	64°56'
Upper Rideau Lake	LAKE/LAC	ON	Leeds	31 C/9	44°41'	76°20'
Upper Ridge	UNP/LNO	NB	Westmorland	21 I/3	46°02'	65°16'
Upper River Denys	UNP/LNO	NS	Inverness	11 F/14	45°54'	61°15'
Upper Rockport	UNP/LNO	NB	Westmorland	21 H/16	45°46'	64°29'
Upper Roslyn Lake	LAKE/LAC	ON	Thunder Bay	42 E/6	49°15'	87°29'
Upper Royalton	UNP/LNO	NB	Carleton	21 J/12	46°31'	67°47'
Upper Sackville	UNP/LNO	NS	Halifax	11 D/13	44°48'	63°44'
Upper Sackville	UNP/LNO	NB	Westmorland	21 H/16	45°56'	64°21'
Upper Saint-Maurice	UNP/LNO	NB	Kent	21 I/7	46°29'	64°51'
Upper Salt Springs	UNP/LNO	NB	Kings	21 H/12	45°34'	65°39'
Upper Savage Islands	ISL/ÎLE	NT	Franklin	25 L	62°36'	70°05'
Upper Sheila	UNP/LNO	NB	Gloucester	21 P/7	47°28'	64°56'
Upper Smithfield	UNP/LNO	NS	Guysborough	11 E/8	45°16'	62°11'
Upper Southampton	UNP/LNO	NB	York	21 J/3	46°00'	67°30'
Upper South River	UNP/LNO	NS	Antigonish	11 F/5	45°28'	61°56'
Upper Southwest Mabou	UNP/LNO	NS	Inverness	11 F/14	45°57'	61°22'
Upper Springfield	UNP/LNO	NS	Antigonish	11 F/5	45°29'	61°50'
Upper Stewiacke	UNP/LNO	NS	Colchester	11 E/2	45°13'	63°00'
Upper Stoneridge	UNP/LNO	NB	York	21 J/2	46°06'	66°57'
Upper Sumas 6	IR/RI	BC	New Westminster	92 G/1	49°03'	122°12'
Upper Tahltan 4	IR/RI	BC	Cassiar	104 J/3	58°09'	131°22'
Upper Tantallon	UNP/LNO	NS	Halifax	11 D/12	44°41'	63°53'
Upper Thérien Lake	LAKE/LAC	AB	57,58-9-W4	73 E/14	53°58'	111°18'
Upper Tilley Road	UNP/LNO	NB	Gloucester	21 P/11	47°31'	65°07'
Upperton	UNP/LNO	NB	Kings	21 H/5	45°29'	65°37'
Upper Tower Hill	UNP/LNO	NB	Charlotte	21 G/6	45°21'	67°10'
Upper Tracy	UNP/LNO	NB	Sunbury	21 G/10	45°40'	66°43'
Upper Trout River Pond - see-voir - Trout River Big Pond	LAKE/LAC	NF		12 G/8	49°25'	58°02'
Upper Tsinkahtl 8A	IR/RI	BC	Kamloops Division Yale	92 I/11	50°31'	121°18'
Upper Twin Lake	LAKE/LAC	ON	Thunder Bay	42 L/2	50°08'	86°37'
Upper Vaughan	UNP/LNO	NS	Hants	21 A/16	44°49'	64°14'
Upper Waddy Lake	LAKE/LAC	SK		64 D/4	56°12'	103°52'
Upper Wards Creek	UNP/LNO	NB	Kings	21 H/12	45°39'	65°31'
Upper Washabuck	UNP/LNO	NS	Victoria	11 K/2	46°02'	60°50'
Upper Waterville	UNP/LNO	NB	Carleton	21 J/5	46°17'	67°37'
Upper Wedgeport	UNP/LNO	NS	Yarmouth	20 P/13	43°45'	65°59'
Upper West Pubnico	UNP/LNO	NS	Yarmouth	20 P/12	43°41'	65°48'
Upper Whitehead	UNP/LNO	NS	Guysborough	11 F/6	45°17'	61°10'
Upper Wicklow	UNP/LNO	NB	Carleton	21 J/12	46°32'	67°39'
Upper Windigo Lake	LAKE/LAC	ON	Kenora	53 B/5	52°30'	91°35'
Upper Woods Harbour	UNP/LNO	NS	Shelburne	20 P/12	43°35'	65°45'
Upper Woodstock	UNP/LNO	NB	Carleton	21 J/4	46°11'	67°34'
Upsala	UNP/LNO	ON	Thunder Bay	52 G/1	49°03'	90°28'
Upsalquitch	UNP/LNO	NB	Restigouche	21 O/15	47°50'	66°53'
Upsalquitch Lake	LAKE/LAC	NB	Northumberland	21 O/8	47°29'	66°30'
Upsalquitch River	RIV/CDE	NB	Restigouche	21 O/15	47°53'	66°57'

NAME NOM	ENTITY ENTITÉ	LOC 1 LIEU 1	LOC 2 LIEU 2	MAP CARTE	POSITION LAT	LONG
Upshall	UNP/LNO	NF		1 N/12	47°40′	53°54′
Upsowis 6	IR/RI	BC	Rupert	92 L/3	50°07′	127°30′
Uptergrove	UNP/LNO	ON	Ontario	31 D/11	44°36′	79°19′
Upton	TOWN/VIL2	QC	Acton	31 H/10	45°39′	72°41′
Upton	UNP/LNO	PE	Kings	11 L/7	46°20′	62°32′
Upwood Point	CAPE/CAP	BC	Texada Island	92 F/8	49°29′	124°07′
Uranium City	HAM/HAM	SK		74 N/10	59°34′	108°37′
Urbainville	UNP/LNO	PE	Prince	21 I/8	46°28′	64°02′
Urban	UNP/LNO	SK	25-36-10-W3	73 B/3	52°07′	107°18′
Urbania	UNP/LNO	NS	Hants	11 E/3	45°13′	63°26′
Ure Creek	RIV/CDE	BC	Lillooet	92 J/7	50°16′	122°35′
Uren	UNP/LNO	SK	33-17-6-W3	72 J/7	50°29′	106°46′
Urling	UNP/LNO	BC	Cariboo	93 H/10	53°41′	120°52′
Urney	UNP/LNO	NB	Kings	21 H/11	45°43′	65°22′
Urquhart	UNP/LNO	BC	Peace River	93 P/16	55°47′	120°25′
Urquhart Lake	LAKE/LAC	NT	Mackenzie	107 C	69°06′	132°03′
Urquhart, Mount	MTN/MNT	BC	Yale Division Yale	92 H/12	49°38′	121°39′
Ursa	UNP/LNO	ON	Haliburton	31 D/16	44°57′	78°23′
Ursula Channel	CHAN/CHEN	BC	Range 4 Coast	103 H/7	53°24′	128°55′
Ursula Lake	LAKE/LAC	NT	Mackenzie	76 D	64°49′	110°27′
Ursus Creek	RIV/CDE	BC	Clayoquot	92 F/5	49°23′	125°45′
Usam Island	ISL/ÎLE	SK		64 L/10	58°33′	102°59′
Usborne	MUN2/AZM2	ON	Huron	40 P/6	43°21′	81°23′
Usborne No. 310	MUN2/AZM2	SK		72 P/11	51°45′	105°10′
Usherville	HAM/HAM	SK	4-38-5-W2	63 D/2	52°14′	102°39′
Usk	UNP/LNO	BC	Range 5 Coast	103 I/9	54°38′	128°25′
Uskahus Achimuwakanut	UNP/LNO	QC	Jamésie	33 J/16	54°51′	74°02′
Uskik Lake	LAKE/LAC	SK		63 M/11	55°32′	103°17′
Usona	UNP/LNO	AB	33-44-26-W4	83 A/13	52°51′	113°43′
Utatnun Kaiahtet Uhakatshuku	UNP/LNO	QC	Côte-Nord-du-Golfe-Saint-Laurent	12 J/5	50°23′	59°50′
Utica	UNP/LNO	ON	Ontario	31 D/3	44°04′	79°01′
Utik Lake	LAKE/LAC	MB		53 M/5	55°16′	95°58′
Utikoomak Lake 155	IR/RI	AB	12-80-11-W5	83 O/13	55°55′	115°35′
Utikoomak Lake 155A	IR/RI	AB	17-80-9-W5	83 O/14	55°56′	115°22′
Utikoomak Lake 155B	IR/RI	AB	23-81-11-W5	84 B/4	56°03′	115°37′
Utik River	LAKE/LAC	MB		53 M/11	55°16′	95°58′
Utikuma Lake	LAKE/LAC	AB	78,79-9,10-W5	83 O/14	55°50′	115°25′
Utikuma Lake Metis Settlement - see-voir - Gift Lake Metis Settlement	UNP/LNO	AB		83 N/16	55°50′	116°00′
Utikuma Lake Metis Settlement - see-voir - Peavine Metis Settlement	UNP/LNO	AB		83 N/16	55°52′	116°17′
Utikuma River	RIV/CDE	AB	83-7-W5	84 B/2	56°10′	114°40′
Utimiskinau Astach	UNP/LNO	QC	Kativik	24 D/3	56°01′	71°03′
Utopia	UNP/LNO	NB	Charlotte	21 G/2	45°09′	66°46′
Utopia	UNP/LNO	ON	Simcoe	31 D/5	44°20′	79°50′
Utopia Centre	UNP/LNO	NB	Charlotte	21 G/2	45°09′	66°44′
Utopia, Lake	LAKE/LAC	NB	Charlotte	21 G/2	45°11′	66°47′
Utshimauat Katipaitsheht Kauitshiht	UNP/LNO	QC	Minganie	12 O/14	51°59′	59°22′
Utterson	UNP/LNO	ON	Muskoka	31 E/3	45°13′	79°20′
Uttoxeter	UNP/LNO	ON	Lambton	40 O/1	43°02′	82°03′
Uxbridge	MUN2/AZM2	ON	Ontario	31 D/3	44°08′	79°11′
Uxbridge	UNP/LNO	ON	Ontario	31 D/3	44°06′	79°07′
Uxbridge Brook	RIV/CDE	ON	York	31 D/6	44°16′	79°12′
Uzta 4 - see-voir - Uzta (Nahounli Creek) 4	IR/RI	BC		93 K/8	54°28′	124°08′
Uzta 7A - see-voir - Uzta (Nahounli Creek) 7A	IR/RI	BC		93 K/8	54°28′	124°07′
Uzta (Nahounli Creek) 4	IR/RI	BC	Range 5 Coast	93 K/8	54°28′	124°08′
Uzta (Nahounli Creek) 7A	IR/RI	BC	Range 5 Coast	93 K/8	54°28′	124°07′
Uztlius Creek	RIV/CDE	BC	Yale Division Yale	92 H/14	49°47′	121°22′

V

NAME NOM	ENTITY ENTITÉ	LOC 1 LIEU 1	LOC 2 LIEU 2	MAP CARTE	POSITION LAT	LONG
Vachell	UNP/LNO	ON	York	31 D/6	44°16′	79°18′
Vachon, Rivière	RIV/CDE	QC	Kativik	25 D/3	60°05′	71°09′
Vade	UNP/LNO	SK	16-35-8-W3	73 B/3	52°01′	107°06′
Vail's Point	CAPE/CAP	ON	Grey	41 A/10	44°44′	80°45′
Val-Alain	VILG/VILG	QC	Lotbinière	21 L/5	46°25′	71°45′
Val Albert	UNP/LNO	ON	Cochrane	42 G/8	49°25′	82°24′
Val-Barrette	TOWN/VIL2	QC	Antoine-Labelle	31 J/11	46°30′	75°21′
Val-Bélair	CITY/VIL1	QC	Communauté urbaine de Québec	21 L/14	46°52′	71°26′
Valbrand	UNP/LNO	SK	23-51-4-W3	73 G/8	53°25′	106°27′
Val-Brillant	VILG/VILG	QC	La Matapédia	22 B/12	48°32′	67°33′
Val Caron	UNP/LNO	ON	Sudbury	41 I/10	46°37′	81°01′
Valcartier, Base des Forces canadiennes - also-aussi - Valcartier, Canadian Forces Base	MIL/MIL	QC	La Jacques-Cartier	21 L/14	46°53′	71°30′

NAME NOM	ENTITY ENTITÉ	LOC 1 LIEU 1	LOC 2 LIEU 2	MAP CARTE	POSITION LAT	LONG
Valcartier, Canadian Forces Base - also-aussi - Valcartier, Base des Forces canadiennes	MIL/MIL	QC	La Jacques-Cartier	21 L/14	46°53′	71°30′
Valcartier-Village	UNP/LNO	QC	La Jacques-Cartier	21 L/14	46°56′	71°28′
Val-Clermont	UNP/LNO	QC	Abitibi-Ouest	32 D/14	48°54′	79°12′
Val-Comeau	UNP/LNO	NB	Gloucester	21 P/7	47°28′	64°53′
Val Côté	UNP/LNO	ON	Cochrane	42 G/11	49°39′	83°24′
Valcourt	CITY/VIL1	QC	Le Val-Saint-François	31 H/8	45°30′	72°19′
Valcourt	VILG/VILG	QC	Le Val-Saint-François	31 H/8	45°30′	72°21′
Val-d'Amour	UNP/LNO	NB	Restigouche	21 O/15	47°57′	66°41′
Val-David	TOWN/VIL2	QC	Les Laurentides	31 J/1	46°02′	74°13′
Val-des-Bois	VILG/VILG	QC	Papineau	31 G/13	45°55′	75°36′
Val-des-Bois	UNP/LNO	QC	Vallée-de-l'Or	32 C/4	48°09′	77°46′
Valdes Island	ISL/ÎLE	BC	Nanaimo	92 G/4	49°05′	123°40′
Val-des-Lacs	VILG/VILG	QC	Les Laurentides	31 J/1	46°11′	74°21′
Val-des-Monts	VILG/VILG	QC	Les Collines-de-l'Outaouais	31 G/12	45°39′	75°40′
Val-d'Espoir	UNP/LNO	QC	Pabok	22 A/9	48°31′	64°24′
Val-d'Espoir-Ouest	UNP/LNO	QC	Pabok	22 A/8	48°30′	64°28′
Val-d'Or	CITY/VIL1	QC	Vallée-de-l'Or	32 C/4	48°06′	77°47′
Valdor	UNP/LNO	QC	Papineau	31 G/11	45°39′	75°11′
Val-Doucet	UNP/LNO	NB	Gloucester	21 P/11	47°37′	65°13′
Val-du-Lac	UNP/LNO	QC	Sherbrooke	31 H/8	45°19′	72°01′
Val-du-Lac	UNP/LNO	QC	Les Collines-de-l'Outaouais	31 G/12	45°44′	75°42′
Val-du-Repos	UNP/LNO	QC	Vallée-de-l'Or	32 C/4	48°11′	77°44′
Vale	UNP/LNO	AB	6-15-3-W4	72 L/1	50°13′	110°24′
Val-Émard	UNP/LNO	QC	La Vallée-de-la-Gatineau	31 J/5	46°28′	75°51′
Valemount	VILG/VILG	BC	Cariboo	83 D/14	52°50′	119°15′
Valencay	UNP/LNO	QC	Papineau	31 G/11	45°44′	75°09′
Valen, Isle	ISL/ÎLE	NF		1 M/8	47°30′	54°23′
Valens	UNP/LNO	ON	Wentworth	40 P/8	43°22′	80°08′
Valentia	UNP/LNO	ON	Victoria	31 D/2	44°15′	78°48′
Vale Perkins	UNP/LNO	QC	Memphrémagog	31 H/1	45°05′	72°18′
Valeport	UNP/LNO	SK	33-20-21-W2	72 I/10	50°45′	104°52′
Valets, Lac	LAKE/LAC	QC	Vallée-de-l'Or	32 C/9	48°32′	76°29′
Valetta	UNP/LNO	ON	Kent	40 J/8	42°15′	82°20′
Val Gagné	UNP/LNO	ON	Cochrane	42 A/10	48°37′	80°38′
Valhalla	UNP/LNO	MB	27-21-4-E	62 I/15	50°50′	96°57′
Valhalla	UNP/LNO	AB	2-75-10-W6	83 M/6	55°28′	119°26′
Valhalla Centre	UNP/LNO	AB	18-74-9-W6	83 M/6	55°24′	119°23′
Valhalla Estate	UNP/LNO	NB	Westmorland	21 I/2	46°07′	64°51′
Valhalla Ranges	MTN/MNT	BC	Kootenay	82 F/13	49°47′	117°43′
Valin	UNP/LNO	QC	Le Fjord-du-Saguenay	22 D/7	48°28′	71°00′
Valin	UNP/LNO	QC	La Côte-de-Beaupré	21 L/14	46°56′	71°03′
Valin, Monts	MTN/MNT	QC	Le Fjord-du-Saguenay	22 D/9	48°34′	70°28′
Valjean	UNP/LNO	SK	25-17-5-W3	72 J/7	50°28′	106°33′
Val-Joli	VILG/VILG	QC	Le Val-Saint-François	21 E/12	45°35′	71°58′
Val-Laflamme	UNP/LNO	QC	Abitibi	32 C/12	48°32′	77°35′
Val-Lambert	UNP/LNO	NB	Madawaska	21 N/7	47°23′	68°32′
Vallant, Rivière	RIV/CDE	QC	Manicouagan	22 F/10	49°42′	68°34′
Vallard, Lac	LAKE/LAC	QC	Caniapiscau	23 C/14	52°48′	69°05′
Vallée-de-l'Or	MUN1/AZM1	QC	Vallée-de-l'Or	32 C/6	48°23′	77°14′
Vallée-du-Ruiter, Réserve écologique de la	PARK/PARC	QC	Memphrémagog	31 H/1	45°06′	72°26′
Vallée-Jonction	VILG/VILG	QC	La Nouvelle-Beauce	21 L/7	46°22′	70°55′
Vallée-Lourdes	UNP/LNO	NB	Gloucester	21 P/12	47°39′	65°42′
Vallentyne	UNP/LNO	ON	Ontario	31 D/6	44°16′	79°08′
Vallerenne, Lac	LAKE/LAC	QC	Kativik	24 D/10	56°33′	70°38′
Valléville	UNP/LNO	QC	Bellechasse	21 L/15	46°51′	70°46′
Valley	UNP/LNO	PE	Queens	11 L/2	46°04′	62°47′
Valley	UNP/LNO	NS	Colchester	11 E/6	45°23′	63°12′
Valley	UNP/LNO	NB	Carleton	21 J/4	46°07′	67°35′
Valley Bay	BAY/BAIE	NF		13 J/2	54°02′	58°58′
Valley Centre	UNP/LNO	SK	6-33-13-W3	72 O/13	51°47′	107°50′
Valleycliffe	UNP/LNO	BC	New Westminster	92 G/11	49°42′	123°08′
Valley Cross Roads	UNP/LNO	NS	Colchester	11 E/6	45°24′	63°12′
Valley East	TOWN/VIL2	ON	Sudbury	41 I/11	46°41′	81°02′
Valleyfield	VILG/VILG	PE	Kings	11 L/2	46°07′	62°43′
Valleyfield	UNP/LNO	NF		2 F/4	49°08′	53°37′
Valleyfield	UNP/LNO	PE	Kings	11 L/2	46°08′	62°44′
Valleyfield Harbour	BAY/BAIE	NF		2 F/4	49°07′	53°37′
Valley Gardens	UNP/LNO	MB		62 H/14	49°55′	97°04′
Valley Green Beach	UNP/LNO	ON	Muskoka	31 E/3	45°06′	79°30′
Valley Mills	UNP/LNO	NS	Inverness	11 F/14	45°51′	61°06′
Valley Park	UNP/LNO	SK	33-6-W3	72 O/15	51°51′	106°47′
Valley Pond	UNP/LNO	NF		2 E/10	49°34′	54°54′
Valley River	UNP/LNO	MB	13-26-20-W	62 N/1	51°15′	100°09′
Valley River	RIV/CDE	MB	34-27-18-W	62 O/5	51°22′	99°55′
Valley River 63A	IR/RI	MB		62 N/2	51°14′	100°56′

NAME / NOM	ENTITY / ENTITÉ	LOC 1 / LIEU 1	LOC 2 / LIEU 2	MAP / CARTE	POSITION LAT	POSITION LONG
Valley River Reserve	UNP/LNO	MB	26-25-W	62 N/2	51°14′	100°58′
Valley Road	UNP/LNO	NS	Cumberland	11 E/12	45°41′	63°55′
Valley Road	UNP/LNO	NB	Charlotte	21 G/3	45°14′	67°16′
Valleys Corners	UNP/LNO	ON	Stormont	31 G/7	45°17′	74°57′
Valley Station	UNP/LNO	NS	Colchester	11 E/6	45°23′	63°12′
Valleyview	TOWN/VIL2	AB	21-70-22-W5	83 N/3	55°04′	117°17′
Valleyview	UNP/LNO	ON	Frontenac	31 C/2	44°15′	76°32′
Valleyview	UNP/LNO	MB		62 G/13	49°51′	99°59′
Valleyview	UNP/LNO	BC	Kamloops Division Yale	92 I/9	50°40′	120°15′
Valley View	UNP/LNO	BC	Peace River	93 P/16	55°59′	120°15′
Valleyview	UNP/LNO	YT		105 D/11	60°44′	135°05′
Valleyview North	UNP/LNO	NB	Westmorland	21 I/2	46°06′	64°45′
Vallican	UNP/LNO	BC	Kootenay	82 F/12	49°34′	117°39′
Vallières-de-Saint-Réal, Mont	MTN/MNT	QC	Denis-Riverin	22 B/16	48°50′	66°03′
Val-Limoges	UNP/LNO	QC	Antoine-Labelle	31 J/12	46°36′	75°44′
Vallon	UNP/LNO	QC	Portneuf	21 L/12	46°43′	71°34′
Val-Marguerite	UNP/LNO	QC	Sept-Rivières	22 J/2	50°09′	66°35′
Val Marie	VILG/VILG	SK	29-3-13-W3	72 G/4	49°14′	107°44′
Val Marie No. 17	MUN2/AZM2	SK		72 G/4	49°10′	107°50′
Val-Melanson	UNP/LNO	NB	Restigouche	21 O/15	47°55′	66°47′
Val-Menaud	UNP/LNO	QC	Le Fjord-du-Saguenay	22 D/6	48°29′	71°24′
Val-Michaud	UNP/LNO	NB	Gloucester	21 P/12	47°41′	65°50′
Val-Morin	VILG/VILG	QC	Les Laurentides	31 J/1	46°00′	74°11′
Valmy, Lac	LAKE/LAC	QC	Vallée-de-l'Or	32 C/8	48°26′	76°14′
Val-Nadeau	UNP/LNO	NB	Madawaska	21 N/7	47°23′	68°35′
Valna Fad	UNP/LNO	NF		1 K/11	46°43′	53°23′
Val Oakes	UNP/LNO	NB	Madawaska	21 N/2	47°13′	68°47′
Valois	UNP/LNO	QC	Communauté urbaine de Montréal	31 H/5	45°27′	73°47′
Val-Ombreuse	UNP/LNO	QC	Antoine-Labelle	31 J/4	46°00′	75°36′
Valor	UNP/LNO	SK	7-8-1-W3	72 G/9	49°38′	106°07′
Valora	UNP/LNO	ON	Kenora	52 G/14	49°46′	91°13′
Val-Paquin	UNP/LNO	QC	Les Collines-de-l'Outaouais	31 G/12	45°44′	75°43′
Val-Paradis	UNP/LNO	QC	Jamésie	32 E/3	49°10′	79°17′
Valparaiso	VILG/VILG	SK	1-45-16-W2	73 A/16	52°51′	104°11′
Val-Piché	UNP/LNO	QC	Abitibi	32 C/14	48°58′	77°03′
Valpy, Mount	MTN/MNT	BC	Range 5 Coast	103 I/6	54°17′	129°03′
Val Quentin	VILG/VILG	AB	16,21-54-3-W5	83 G/9	53°40′	114°23′
Val-Racine	VILG/VILG	QC	Le Granit	21 E/6	45°29′	71°04′
Val-Renard	UNP/LNO	QC	La Côte-de-Gaspé	22 A/16	48°59′	64°25′
Val Rita	UNP/LNO	ON	Cochrane	42 G/7	49°27′	82°33′
Val Rita-Harty	MUN2/AZM2	ON	Cochrane	42 G/10	49°31′	82°38′
Val-Royal	UNP/LNO	QC	Communauté urbaine de Montréal	31 H/12	45°31′	73°42′
Val-Saint-Georges	UNP/LNO	QC	Vallée-de-l'Or	32 C/4	48°15′	77°36′
Val-Saint-Gilles	VILG/VILG	QC	Abitibi-Ouest	32 D/14	48°58′	79°07′
Val-Saint-Michel	UNP/LNO	QC	Communauté urbaine de Québec	21 L/14	46°52′	71°27′
Val-Senneville	VILG/VILG	QC	Vallée-de-l'Or	32 C/4	48°11′	77°39′
Val-Shefford	UNP/LNO	QC	La Haute-Yamaska	31 H/7	45°25′	72°37′
Val Soucy	UNP/LNO	AB	4-58-21-W4	83 H/14	53°59′	113°03′
Val Therese	UNP/LNO	ON	Sudbury	41 I/11	46°39′	81°00′
Val-Viger	UNP/LNO	QC	Antoine-Labelle	31 J/11	46°41′	75°14′
Van Allens	UNP/LNO	ON	Grenville	31 B/13	44°56′	75°34′
Van Anda	UNP/LNO	BC	Texada Island	92 F/15	49°46′	124°33′
Vananda - see-voir - Van Anda	UNP/LNO	BC		92 F/15	49°46′	124°33′
Vanasse, Lac	LAKE/LAC	QC	Kativik	35 G/13	61°50′	75°38′
Vanastra	UNP/LNO	ON	Huron	40 P/12	43°35′	81°32′
Vanbrugh	UNP/LNO	ON	Renfrew	31 F/6	45°26′	77°16′
Van Bruyssel	UNP/LNO	QC	Le Haut-Saint-Maurice	31 P/16	47°56′	72°09′
VanCamp	UNP/LNO	ON	Dundas	31 G/3	45°03′	75°27′
Vance	UNP/LNO	SK	36-35-14-W3	73 B/4	52°03′	107°53′
Vancouver	CITY/VIL1	BC	New Westminster	92 G/3	49°15′	123°07′
Vancouver Gap	SEAU/SMER	—		15798A	49°50′	128°50′
Vancouver, Île de - also-aussi - **Vancouver Island**	ISL/ÎLE	BC	Clayoquot	92 F/12	49°30′	125°30′
Vancouver Island - also-aussi - **Vancouver, Île de**	ISL/ÎLE	BC	Clayoquot	92 F/12	49°30′	125°30′
Vancouver Island Ranges	MTN/MNT	BC	Clayoquot	92 F/12	49°30′	125°30′
Vancouver Island Shelf	SEAU/SMER	—		3001	49°41′	127°10′
Vancouver Island Slope	SEAU/SMER	—		3002	49°20′	127°30′
Vancouver, Mount	MTN/MNT	YT		115 B/5	60°20′	139°41′
Vancouver River	RIV/CDE	BC	New Westminster	92 G/13	49°55′	123°52′
Vandecar	UNP/LNO	ON	Oxford	40 P/2	43°06′	80°37′
Vandekerckhove Lake	LAKE/LAC	MB		64 F/3	57°02′	101°25′
Vandeleur	UNP/LNO	ON	Grey	41 A/7	44°20′	80°34′
Vanderhoof	MUN1/AZM1	BC	Range 5 Coast	93 K/1	54°01′	124°01′
Vandorf	UNP/LNO	ON	York	31 D/3	44°00′	79°24′
Vandry	UNP/LNO	QC	Le Haut-Saint-Maurice	31 P/13	47°52′	73°34′
Vandura	UNP/LNO	SK	20-12-1-W2	62 L/1	50°00′	102°07′

NAME / NOM	ENTITY / ENTITÉ	LOC 1 / LIEU 1	LOC 2 / LIEU 2	MAP / CARTE	POSITION LAT	POSITION LONG
Vandyck Lake	LAKE/LAC	NT	Mackenzie	75 C	60°13′	109°28′
Vanessa	UNP/LNO	ON	Norfolk	40 I/16	42°58′	80°24′
Vanguard	VILG/VILG	SK	15-11-10-W3	72 G/14	49°55′	107°18′
Van Horne	UNP/LNO	ON	Kent	40 J/8	42°26′	82°06′
Vanier	CITY/VIL1	QC	Communauté urbaine de Québec	21 L/14	46°49′	71°15′
Vanier	CITY/VIL1	ON	Carleton	31 G/5	45°26′	75°40′
Vanier, Ile	ISL/ÎLE	NT	Franklin	69 B	76°10′	103°15′
Vankleek Hill	TOWN/VIL2	ON	Prescott	31 G/10	45°31′	74°39′
Vankleek Hill Station	UNP/LNO	ON	Prescott	31 G/10	45°32′	74°39′
Van Koenig Point	CAPE/CAP	NT	Franklin	57 H	71°05′	89°32′
Vankoughnet	UNP/LNO	ON	Muskoka	31 D/14	44°59′	79°03′
Vanneck	UNP/LNO	ON	Middlesex	40 P/3	43°04′	81°26′
Vannes, Lac	LAKE/LAC	QC	Kativik	23 O/15	55°55′	66°45′
Vanrena	UNP/LNO	AB	26-81-4-W6	84 D/2	56°03′	118°31′
Vanscoy	VILG/VILG	SK	17-35-7-W3	73 B/2	52°00′	106°59′
Van Scoy Lake	LAKE/LAC	SK	36-11-W3	73 B/4	52°05′	107°33′
Vanscoy No. 345	MUN2/AZM2	SK		73 B/3	52°00′	107°05′
Vansickle	UNP/LNO	ON	Peterborough	31 C/12	44°37′	77°49′
Vansittart Island	ISL/ÎLE	NT	Franklin	46 F	65°50′	84°00′
Vanstone	UNP/LNO	SK	2-26-5-W2	62 M/2	51°13′	102°36′
Vantage	HAM/HAM	SK	23-10-1-W3	72 G/16	49°50′	106°02′
Vanway	UNP/LNO	BC	Cariboo	93 G/15	53°51′	122°49′
Vanzant's Landing	UNP/LNO	ON	Manitoulin	41 H/13	45°45′	81°53′
Varcoe	UNP/LNO	MB	2-13-19-W	62 J/4	50°04′	99°58′
Vardy	UNP/LNO	ON	Hastings	31 F/4	45°06′	77°47′
Varency	UNP/LNO	ON	Norfolk	40 I/16	42°51′	80°07′
Varennes	CITY/VIL1	QC	Lajemmerais	31 H/11	45°41′	73°26′
Vargas Island	ISL/ÎLE	BC	Clayoquot	92 E/4	49°11′	125°59′
Vargas Island 31	IR/RI	BC	Clayoquot	92 F/4	49°09′	125°58′
Varket Channel	CHAN/CHEN	NF		2 C/13	48°46′	53°40′
Varna	UNP/LNO	ON	Huron	40 P/12	43°32′	81°36′
Varney	UNP/LNO	ON	Grey	41 A/2	44°08′	80°48′
Vars	UNP/LNO	ON	Russell	31 G/6	45°21′	75°21′
Varsity View	UNP/LNO	MB		62 H/14	49°52′	97°15′
Varty Lake	LAKE/LAC	ON	Lennox and Addington	31 C/7	44°23′	76°49′
Vases, Les	UNP/LNO	QC	Arthabaska	21 E/13	45°54′	71°40′
Vaseux Creek	RIV/CDE	BC	Similkameen Division Yale	82 E/4	49°15′	119°32′
Vaseux Lake	LAKE/LAC	BC	Similkameen Division Yale	82 E/5	49°17′	119°32′
Vasey	UNP/LNO	ON	Simcoe	31 D/12	44°40′	79°45′
Vassan	VILG/VILG	QC	Vallée-de-l'Or	32 C/4	48°14′	77°56′
Vassar	UNP/LNO	MB	6-2-13-E	52 E/4	49°06′	95°50′
Vaubois, Lac	LAKE/LAC	QC	Caniapiscau	23 F/15	53°59′	68°58′
Vaucluse	UNP/LNO	QC	L'Assomption	31 H/14	45°54′	73°26′
Vaucroft Beach	UNP/LNO	BC	New Westminster	92 G/12	49°31′	124°00′
Vaudray, Lac	LAKE/LAC	QC	Rouyn-Noranda	32 D/2	48°06′	78°41′
Vaudreuil-Dorion	CITY/VIL1	QC	Vaudreuil-Soulanges	31 G/8	45°24′	74°02′
Vaudreuil-Soulanges	MUN1/AZM1	QC	Vaudreuil-Soulanges	31 G/8	45°21′	74°13′
Vaudreuil-sur-le-Lac	TOWN/VIL2	QC	Vaudreuil-Soulanges	31 G/8	45°25′	74°02′
Vaughan	CITY/VIL1	ON	York	30 M/13	43°50′	79°32′
Vaughan	UNP/LNO	NS	Hants	21 A/16	44°49′	64°15′
Vaughan	UNP/LNO	ON	Lincoln	30 M/4	43°02′	79°33′
Vaughan, Lake	LAKE/LAC	NS	Yarmouth	20 P/13	43°55′	65°58′
Vaughan Survey	UNP/LNO	ON	Norfolk	40 I/16	42°47′	80°08′
Vaulezar, Lac	LAKE/LAC	QC	Jamésie	23 L/12	54°33′	71°50′
Vauquelin	UNP/LNO	QC	Pabok	22 A/9	48°39′	64°23′
Vauquelin, Rivière	RIV/CDE	QC	Jamésie	33 L/15	54°55′	78°44′
Vauréal, Rivière	RIV/CDE	QC	Minganie	12 E/10	49°37′	62°36′
Vautour	UNP/LNO	NB	Kent	21 I/11	46°45′	65°14′
Vautrin	UNP/LNO	QC	Abitibi	32 D/8	48°27′	78°22′
Vauvert	UNP/LNO	QC	Maria-Chapdelaine	32 A/16	48°45′	72°07′
Vauxhall	TOWN/VIL2	AB	10-13-16-W4	82 I/1	50°04′	112°07′
Vavenby	UNP/LNO	BC	Kamloops Division Yale	82 M/12	51°35′	119°43′
Vawn	VILG/VILG	SK	2-48-19-W3	73 F/2	53°07′	108°41′
Vedan Lake	LAKE/LAC	BC	Lillooet	92 O/12	51°33′	123°49′
Vedder Crossing	UNP/LNO	BC	New Westminster	92 H/4	49°06′	121°58′
Vedder River	RIV/CDE	BC	New Westminster	92 G/1	49°08′	122°06′
Vega	UNP/LNO	AB	33-62-3-W5	83 J/8	54°24′	114°23′
Vegreville	TOWN/VIL2	AB	18-52-14-W4	83 H/8	53°30′	112°03′
Veillardville	UNP/LNO	SK	45-4-W2	63 D/15	52°52′	102°32′
Veillette	UNP/LNO	QC	Mékinac	31 I/16	46°55′	72°28′
Veilleux, Rivière	RIV/CDE	QC	Robert-Cliche	21 L/7	46°15′	70°31′
Veilleux's Landing - see-voir - Marina Veilleux	UNP/LNO	ON		42 G/13	49°48′	83°43′
Vein Island	ISL/ÎLE	ON	Thunder Bay	42 D/13	48°47′	87°34′
Vein Lake	LAKE/LAC	ON	Thunder Bay	42 E/1	49°08′	86°19′
Veira Lake	LAKE/LAC	NT	Mackenzie	75 H	61°10′	104°35′

NAME NOM	ENTITY ENTITÉ	LOC 1 LIEU 1	LOC 2 LIEU 2	MAP CARTE	POSITION LAT	LONG
Vellore	UNP/LNO	ON	York	30 M/13	43°50′	79°34′
Venables	UNP/LNO	MB	66-19-W	63 K/16	54°46′	100°15′
Vendée	UNP/LNO	QC	Les Laurentides	31 J/2	46°05′	74°50′
Vendôme	UNP/LNO	QC	Beauharnois-Salaberry	31 H/5	45°16′	73°54′
Vendom Fiord	BAY/BAIE	NT	Franklin	49 D	77°45′	83°00′
Vendremur, Lac	LAKE/LAC	QC	Kativik	24 G/10	57°37′	66°51′
Veneer	UNP/LNO	NB	Madawaska	21 O/5	47°19′	67°43′
Venetian Lake	LAKE/LAC	ON	Sudbury	41 I/14	46°56′	81°15′
Venice	UNP/LNO	AB	11-66-15-W4	83 I/9	54°42′	112°08′
Venise	UNP/LNO	QC	Memphrémagog	31 H/8	45°17′	72°03′
Venise-en-Québec	VILG/VILG	QC	Le Haut-Richelieu	31 H/3	45°05′	73°08′
Venison Creek	RIV/CDE	ON	Norfolk	40 I/10	42°39′	80°33′
Venison Islands	UNP/LNO	NF		3 D/13	52°58′	55°47′
Venlaw	UNP/LNO	MB	22-27-22-W	62 N/8	51°20′	100°29′
Venn	UNP/LNO	SK	34-30-24-W2	72 P/11	51°37′	105°18′
Vennachar	UNP/LNO	ON	Lennox and Addington	31 F/3	45°04′	77°13′
Vennachar Junction	UNP/LNO	ON	Lennox and Addington	31 F/3	45°06′	77°15′
Venosta	UNP/LNO	QC	La Vallée-de-la-Gatineau	31 F/16	45°52′	76°01′
Vent, Butte du	MTN/MNT	QC	Les Îles-de-la-Madeleine	11 N/5	47°23′	61°55′
Ventnor	UNP/LNO	ON	Grenville	31 B/13	44°53′	75°31′
Ventry	UNP/LNO	ON	Grey	41 A/1	44°07′	80°27′
Vents, Lac des	LAKE/LAC	QC	Jamésie	32 G/7	49°28′	74°53′
Vents River	RIV/CDE	BC	Cassiar	94 M/7	59°29′	126°19′
Vera	UNP/LNO	SK	24-41-24-W3	73 C/11	52°33′	109°20′
Vera, Cape	CAPE/CAP	NT	Franklin	59 A	76°14′	89°13′
Vera Lake	LAKE/LAC	NT	Keewatin	65 G	61°09′	99°15′
Verbois	UNP/LNO	QC	Kamouraska	21 N/12	47°40′	69°36′
Verchères	VILG/VILG	QC	Lajemmerais	31 H/14	45°47′	73°21′
Verchères, Îles de	ISL/ÎLE	QC	Lajemmerais	31 H/14	45°48′	73°21′
Verdigris Lake	LAKE/LAC	AB	3,4-15,16-W4	82 H/1	49°14′	112°00′
Verdun	CITY/VIL1	QC	Communauté urbaine de Montréal	31 H/5	45°27′	73°34′
Verdun	UNP/LNO	ON	Bruce	41 A/4	44°03′	81°39′
Veregin	VILG/VILG	SK	9-30-1-W2	62 M/9	51°35′	102°05′
Vereker	UNP/LNO	ON	Essex	40 J/2	42°05′	82°57′
Verendrye	UNP/LNO	SK	17-28-23-W3	72 N/6	51°24′	109°12′
Verger	UNP/LNO	AB	34-22-15-W4	72 L/13	50°56′	112°00′
Verlo	UNP/LNO	SK	6-16-19-W3	72 K/7	50°19′	108°36′
Vermette	UNP/LNO	MB		62 H/14	49°48′	97°04′
Vermette Lake	LAKE/LAC	SK		73 N/11	55°40′	109°05′
Vermette Lake	LAKE/LAC	NT	Mackenzie	75 H	61°22′	105°38′
Vermeulle, Lac	LAKE/LAC	QC	Caniapiscau	23 K/11	54°43′	69°24′
Vermilion	TOWN/VIL2	AB	32-50-6-W4	73 E/7	53°22′	110°51′
Vermilion Bay	UNP/LNO	ON	Kenora	52 F/14	49°51′	93°24′
Vermilion Bay	BAY/BAIE	ON	Kenora	52 F/14	49°50′	93°22′
Vermilion Crossing	UNP/LNO	BC	Kootenay	82 O/4	51°02′	115°59′
Vermilion Forks 1	IR/RI	BC	Similkameen Division Yale	92 H/7	49°28′	120°31′
Vermilion Hills	MTN/MNT	SK		72 J/10	50°43′	106°56′
Vermilion Lake	LAKE/LAC	ON	Sudbury	41 I/11	46°31′	81°24′
Vermilion Lake	LAKE/LAC	ON	Kenora	52 L/2	50°03′	94°34′
Vermilion Lake	LAKE/LAC	AB	125,126-6-W5	84 O/15	59°55′	114°58′
Vermilion Pass	VALL/VALL	BC/AB		82 N/1	51°13′	116°04′
Vermilion Provincial Park	PARK/PARC	AB	50,51-6,7,W4	73 E/7	53°22′	110°55′
Vermilion River	RIV/CDE	ON	Sudbury	41 I/5	46°16′	81°41′
Vermilion River	RIV/CDE	ON	Kenora	52 J/5	50°25′	91°51′
Vermilion River	RIV/CDE	MB	30-25-17-W	62 O/4	51°11′	99°50′
Vermilion River	RIV/CDE	AB	14-54-3-W4	73 E/9	53°39′	110°20′
Vermilion River No. 24, County of	MUN1/AZM1	AB	51-4-W4	73 E/8	53°23′	110°30′
Vermillon	UNP/LNO	QC	Le Haut-Saint-Maurice	31 P/11	47°40′	73°01′
Vermillon, Rivière	RIV/CDE	QC	Le Haut-Saint-Maurice	31 P/10	47°39′	72°57′
Vermilyea Lake	LAKE/LAC	MB		53 L/10	54°32′	94°47′
Vermont, Lac	LAKE/LAC	QC	Le Fjord-du-Saguenay	22 D/14	48°57′	71°09′
Verner	UNP/LNO	ON	Nipissing	41 I/8	46°25′	80°07′
Vernet	UNP/LNO	QC	Papineau	31 G/15	45°52′	74°46′
Vernon	CITY/VIL1	BC	Osoyoos Division Yale	82 L/6	50°16′	119°16′
Vernon	UNP/LNO	ON	Carleton	31 G/3	45°10′	75°28′
Vernon	UNP/LNO	BC	Rupert	92 L/1	50°02′	126°21′
Vernon Bridge	UNP/LNO	PE	Queens	11 L/2	46°10′	62°53′
Vernon Creek	RIV/CDE	BC	Osoyoos Division Yale	82 L/3	50°15′	119°21′
Vernon, Lac	LAKE/LAC	QC	Kativik	34 J/16	58°53′	74°15′
Vernon, Lake	LAKE/LAC	ON	Muskoka	31 E/6	45°20′	79°17′
Vernon Lake	LAKE/LAC	AB	46-10,11-W4	73 D/13	52°57′	111°30′
Vernon Lake	LAKE/LAC	BC	Rupert	92 L/1	50°02′	126°26′
Vernon River	UNP/LNO	PE	Queens	11 L/2	46°12′	62°50′
Vernon Shores	UNP/LNO	ON	Muskoka	31 E/6	45°21′	79°20′
Vernonville	UNP/LNO	ON	Northumberland	31 C/4	44°03′	77°59′

NAME NOM	ENTITY ENTITÉ	LOC 1 LIEU 1	LOC 2 LIEU 2	MAP CARTE	POSITION LAT	LONG
Vern Ritchie Glacier	GLAC/GLAC	BC	Cassiar	114 O/9	59°45′	138°30′
Verona	UNP/LNO	ON	Frontenac	31 C/7	44°29′	76°42′
Véron, Lac	LAKE/LAC	NF		22 P/14	51°48′	65°07′
Verret	VILG/VILG	NB	Madawaska	21 N/8	47°21′	68°23′
Verrill Canyon	SEAU/SMER	—		8007	42°50′	61°15′
Versailles Lake	LAKE/LAC	SK		73 P/16	55°49′	104°21′
Verschoyle	UNP/LNO	ON	Oxford	40 I/15	42°57′	80°51′
Vert, Banc à - also-aussi - Green Bank	SEAU/SMER	—		4016	45°40′	54°40′
Verte, Baie	BAY/BAIE	NF		12 H/16	50°00′	56°08′
Verte, Baie	BAY/BAIE	NB	Westmorland	11 L/4	46°00′	63°55′
Verte, Île	ISL/ÎLE	QC	Rivière-du-Loup	22 C/3	48°02′	69°26′
Verte, Pointe	CAPE/CAP	QC	Pabok	22 A/9	48°37′	64°10′
Verte, Rivière - also-aussi - Green River	RIV/CDE	QC/NB		21 N/8	47°18′	68°09′
Verte, Rivière	RIV/CDE	QC	Rivière-du-Loup	22 C/3	48°01′	69°21′
Vert Island	ISL/ÎLE	ON	Thunder Bay	52 A/16	48°55′	88°03′
Vert Lake	LAKE/LAC	BC	Lillooet	92 O/9	51°39′	122°11′
Verton, Lac	LAKE/LAC	QC	Minganie	12 O/5	51°22′	59°32′
Vertu	UNP/LNO	QC	Communauté urbaine de Montréal	31 H/12	45°31′	73°40′
Verulam	MUN2/AZM2	ON	Victoria	31 D/10	44°33′	78°38′
Verulam	UNP/LNO	SK	3-35-22-W3	72 N/14	51°58′	109°04′
Verulam Park	UNP/LNO	ON	Victoria	31 D/10	44°30′	78°39′
Verwood	UNP/LNO	SK	31-6-27-W2	72 H/12	49°31′	105°37′
Vesey Hamilton, Cape	CAPE/CAP	NT	Franklin	88 F/6	74°17′	118°08′
Vesey Hamilton Island	ISL/ÎLE	NT	Franklin	79 B	76°55′	109°11′
Vesle Fiord	BAY/BAIE	NT	Franklin	49 G	79°08′	84°00′
Vesper	UNP/LNO	SK	20-12-15-W3	72 K/1	50°01′	108°01′
Vespra - see-voir - Springwater	MUN2/AZM2	ON		31 D/5	44°30′	79°51′
Vespra	UNP/LNO	NB	Sunbury	21 G/10	45°41′	66°46′
Vesta	UNP/LNO	ON	Bruce	41 A/6	44°16′	81°10′
Vestfold	UNP/LNO	MB	34-18-3-W	62 I/12	50°35′	97°44′
Vesuvius	UNP/LNO	BC	Saltspring Island	92 B/13	48°53′	123°34′
Veteran	VILG/VILG	AB	17-35-8-W4	73 D/3	52°00′	111°07′
Vetter Peak	MTN/MNT	BC	Cassiar	103 P/3	55°06′	129°12′
Veuve River	RIV/CDE	ON	Nipissing	41 I/8	46°20′	80°02′
Vezina Lake	LAKE/LAC	NF		23 I/14	54°47′	65°13′
Vianney	VILG/VILG	QC	L'Érable	21 L/4	46°04′	71°38′
Vibank	VILG/VILG	SK	12-16-15-W2	62 L/5	50°20′	103°56′
Viceroy	VILG/VILG	SK	12-6-25-W2	72 H/6	49°28′	105°22′
Vickers	UNP/LNO	ON	Grey	41 A/2	44°10′	80°52′
Vickers Heights	UNP/LNO	ON	Thunder Bay	52 A/6	48°21′	89°20′
Vickers Lake	LAKE/LAC	ON	Kenora	52 F/2	49°10′	92°58′
Victoire	UNP/LNO	SK	13-52-8-W3	73 G/6	53°30′	107°02′
Victor	UNP/LNO	MB	16-17-29-W	62 K/6	50°27′	101°26′
Victor	UNP/LNO	AB	33-17-W4	82 P/16	51°48′	112°20′
Victor-A.-Huard, Réserve écologique	PARK/PARC	QC	Le Fjord-du-Saguenay	22 D/3	48°12′	71°14′
Victoria	CITY/VIL1	BC	Victoria	92 B/6	48°26′	123°22′
Victoria	TOWN/VIL2	NF		1 N/14	47°46′	53°14′
Victoria	VILG/VILG	PE	Queens	11 L/3	46°13′	63°29′
Victoria	MUN1/AZM1	NS	Victoria	11 K/10	46°30′	60°35′
Victoria	MUN1/AZM1	ON	Victoria	31 D/10	44°35′	78°50′
Victoria	MUN2/AZM2	MB		62 G/10	49°40′	98°54′
Victoria	UNP/LNO	NS	Cumberland	11 E/12	45°44′	63°41′
Victoria	UNP/LNO	NB	Northumberland	21 P/3	47°02′	65°14′
Victoria	UNP/LNO	ON	Prince Edward	31 C/3	44°04′	77°29′
Victoria	UNP/LNO	ON	Peel	30 M/13	43°46′	79°53′
Victoria	GEOG/GÉOG	NS		11 K/10	46°30′	60°35′
Victoria	GEOG/GÉOG	NB		21 O/3	47°05′	67°20′
Victoria	GEOG/GÉOG	ON		31 D/10	44°35′	78°50′
Victoria and Albert Mountains	MTN/MNT	NT	Franklin	120 B	80°47′	69°54′
Victoria Beach	MUN2/AZM2	MB		62 I/10	50°39′	96°34′
Victoria Beach	UNP/LNO	NS	Annapolis	21 A/12	44°41′	65°45′
Victoria Beach	UNP/LNO	NB	Kings	21 G/8	45°26′	66°10′
Victoria Beach	UNP/LNO	ON	Northumberland	30 N/13	43°59′	77°52′
Victoria Beach	UNP/LNO	MB	9-20-7-E	62 I/10	50°42′	96°34′
Victoria Bridge	UNP/LNO	NS	Cape Breton	11 F/16	45°49′	60°17′
Victoria, Cape	CAPE/CAP	NT	Franklin	67 D	69°52′	96°12′
Victoria Corner	UNP/LNO	NB	Carleton	21 J/5	46°16′	67°31′
Victoria Corners	UNP/LNO	ON	Ontario	31 D/3	44°11′	79°06′
Victoria Corners	UNP/LNO	ON	Grey	41 A/9	44°30′	80°25′
Victoria Cove	UNP/LNO	NF		2 E/8	49°21′	54°30′
Victoria Crescent	UNP/LNO	MB		62 H/14	49°50′	97°08′
Victoria Cross	UNP/LNO	PE	Kings	11 L/2	46°10′	62°42′
Victoria-Fraserview	UNP/LNO	BC	New Westminster	92 G/3	49°13′	123°04′
Victoria, Grand lac	LAKE/LAC	QC	Témiscamingue	31 N/12	47°31′	77°30′
Victoria Harbour	UNP/LNO	NS	Kings	21 H/2	45°07′	64°53′

NAME NOM	ENTITY ENTITÉ	LOC 1 LIEU 1	LOC 2 LIEU 2	MAP CARTE	POSITION LAT	LONG
Victoria Harbour	UNP/LNO	ON	Simcoe	31 D/12	44°44′	79°46′
Victoria Harbour	BAY/BAIE	PE	Queens	11 L/3	46°12′	63°29′
Victoria Head	CAPE/CAP	NT	Franklin	39 H	79°13′	74°25′
Victoria Heights	UNP/LNO	SK		72 I/5	50°24′	105°34′
Victoria Hills	UNP/LNO	ON	Waterloo	40 P/8	43°27′	80°30′
Victoria Island	ISL/ÎLE	NT	Franklin	26 D	64°40′	71°29′
Victoria Island	ISL/ÎLE	NT	Franklin	77 F/14	71°00′	110°00′
Victoria Junction	UNP/LNO	NS	Cape Breton	11 K/1	46°10′	60°07′
Victoria Lake	LAKE/LAC	NF		12 A/6	48°18′	57°22′
Victoria Lake	LAKE/LAC	NB	Charlotte	21 G/7	45°19′	66°37′
Victoria Lake	LAKE/LAC	ON	Nipissing	31 E/9	45°37′	78°01′
Victoria Lake	LAKE/LAC	ON	Timiskaming	32 D/4	48°11′	79°53′
Victoria Lake	LAKE/LAC	BC	Rupert	92 L/6	50°22′	127°23′
Victoria Land District	GEOG/GÉOG	BC		92 B	48°27′	123°20′
Victoria Line	UNP/LNO	NS	Inverness	11 F/14	45°50′	61°18′
Victoria Mills	UNP/LNO	ON	Brant	40 P/1	43°01′	80°13′
Victoria Mine	UNP/LNO	ON	Sudbury	41 I/6	46°24′	81°23′
Victoria Mines	UNP/LNO	NS	Cape Breton	11 K/1	46°14′	60°09′
Victoria Park	UNP/LNO	ON	Simcoe	31 D/12	44°44′	79°48′
Victoria Peak	MTN/MNT	BC	Rupert	92 L/1	50°03′	126°06′
Victoria Plains	UNP/LNO	SK	10-18-19-W2	72 I/10	50°31′	104°32′
Victoria Point	UNP/LNO	ON	Simcoe	31 D/11	44°35′	79°24′
Victoria River	RIV/CDE	NF		12 A/10	48°45′	56°41′
Victoria Road	UNP/LNO	NS	Inverness	11 K/6	46°17′	61°13′
Victoria Road	UNP/LNO	ON	Victoria	31 D/10	44°35′	78°57′
Victoria Settlement	UNP/LNO	AB	58-17-W4	83 I/1	54°00′	112°26′
Victoria Settlement Provincial Historic Site (Developed)	PARK/PARC	AB	12-58-17-W4	83 I/1	54°01′	112°23′
Victoria Springs	UNP/LNO	ON	Peterborough	31 D/9	44°33′	78°18′
Victoria Square	UNP/LNO	ON	York	30 M/14	43°54′	79°22′
Victoria Strait	CHAN/CHEN	NT	Franklin	67 C	69°30′	100°30′
Victoria Vale	UNP/LNO	NS	Annapolis	21 A/14	45°00′	65°04′
Victoria Village	UNP/LNO	ON	York	30 M/11	43°44′	79°19′
Victoriaville	CITY/VIL1	QC	Arthabaska	21 L/4	46°02′	71°55′
Victoria West	UNP/LNO	PE	Prince	21 I/9	46°33′	64°04′
Victor, Lac	LAKE/LAC	QC	Minganie	12 K/12	50°35′	61°50′
Victor-Tremblay, Mont	MTN/MNT	QC	Le Fjord-du-Saguenay	22 D/10	48°38′	70°54′
Victory	UNP/LNO	NS	Annapolis	21 A/11	44°34′	65°28′
Victory Hill	UNP/LNO	ON	Carleton	31 G/5	45°19′	75°42′
Victory Lake	LAKE/LAC	NT	Keewatin	55 L	62°36′	95°31′
Victory Lake	LAKE/LAC	NT	Mackenzie	85 I	62°40′	113°05′
Victory No. 226	MUN2/AZM2	SK		72 J/13	50°50′	107°35′
Victory Point	CAPE/CAP	NT	Franklin	67 D	69°40′	98°18′
Vidal Bay	BAY/BAIE	ON	Manitoulin	41 G/15	45°57′	82°59′
Vidal Island	ISL/ÎLE	ON	Manitoulin	41 G/15	45°58′	82°59′
Vidéo, Mont	MTN/MNT	QC	Abitibi	32 C/5	48°25′	77°47′
Vide-Poche	UNP/LNO	QC	Maskinongé	31 I/7	46°18′	72°51′
Vidette	UNP/LNO	BC	Lillooet	92 P/2	51°10′	120°54′
Vidir	UNP/LNO	MB	30-23-2-E	62 P/3	51°01′	97°18′
Vidora	UNP/LNO	SK	26-4-26-W3	72 F/6	49°20′	109°25′
Vieillard, Lac du	LAKE/LAC	QC	Témiscamingue	31 M/8	47°23′	78°02′
Vieille-Église, La	UNP/LNO	QC	Lotbinière	21 L/12	46°36′	71°57′
Vieille-Maison-Jaune, La	UNP/LNO	QC	Charlevoix	21 M/9	47°31′	70°22′
Vieilles-Écuries, Les	UNP/LNO	QC	Matane	22 B/16	48°47′	66°26′
Vienna	VILG/VILG	ON	Elgin	40 I/10	42°41′	80°48′
Vieux-Arbres, Réserve écologique des	PARK/PARC	QC	Abitibi-Ouest	32 D/6	48°27′	79°17′
Vieux, Bay de	BAY/BAIE	NF		11 P/11	47°38′	57°10′
Vieux-Comptoir	UNP/LNO	QC	Jamésie	33 D/10	52°37′	78°43′
Vieux Comptoir, Lac du	LAKE/LAC	QC	Jamésie	33 C/13	52°47′	77°33′
Vieux Comptoir, Rivière du	RIV/CDE	QC	Jamésie	33 D/10	52°36′	78°42′
Vieux-Fort	UNP/LNO	QC	Côte-Nord-du-Golfe-Saint-Laurent	12 P/5	51°26′	57°49′
Vieux-Fort	UNP/LNO	QC	Témiscamingue	31 M/6	47°17′	79°28′
Vieux Fort, Île du	ISL/ÎLE	QC	Côte-Nord-du-Golfe-Saint-Laurent	12 P/5	51°22′	57°47′
Vieux Fort, Lac du	LAKE/LAC	QC	Côte-Nord-du-Golfe-Saint-Laurent	12 P/5	51°28′	57°51′
Vieux-Lunenburg, Site du patrimoine mondial du - also-aussi - Old Town Lunenburg World Heritage Site	PARK/PARC	NS		21 A/8	44°23′	64°19′
Vieux-Piopolis	UNP/LNO	QC	Le Granit	21 E/10	45°30′	70°55′
Vieuxpont, Lac	LAKE/LAC	QC	Kativik	24 B/7	56°16′	66°45′
Vieux-Poste	UNP/LNO	QC	Côte-Nord-du-Golfe-Saint-Laurent	12 J/15	50°50′	58°57′
Vieux-Poste, Le	UNP/LNO	QC	Manicouagan	22 F/1	49°11′	68°14′
Vieux Poste, Pointe du	CAPE/CAP	QC	Côte-Nord-du-Golfe-Saint-Laurent	12 K/4	50°06′	61°48′
Vieux-Saint-Louis, Le	UNP/LNO	QC	Avignon	22 B/1	48°10′	66°15′
Vieux-Vingt-Neuf, Le	UNP/LNO	QC	Pabok	22 A/7	48°19′	64°50′
Viewfield	UNP/LNO	SK	34-6-9-W2	62 E/11	49°31′	103°09′
Viewlake	UNP/LNO	ON	Durham	31 D/2	44°13′	78°46′
Viewmount	UNP/LNO	NS	Kings	21 H/2	45°05′	64°48′
Viewpoint	UNP/LNO	AB	15-45-20-W4	83 A/15	52°53′	112°49′

NAME NOM	ENTITY ENTITÉ	LOC 1 LIEU 1	LOC 2 LIEU 2	MAP CARTE	POSITION LAT	LONG
View Royal	TOWN/VIL2	BC	Esquimalt	92 B/6	48°28′	123°27′
Vigie, La	UNP/LNO	QC	Pabok	22 A/7	48°25′	64°44′
Vignal, Lac	LAKE/LAC	QC	Caniapiscau	23 F/8	53°18′	68°23′
Vigo	UNP/LNO	ON	Simcoe	31 D/5	44°29′	79°55′
Vigue Creek	RIV/CDE	BC	Osoyoos Division Yale	82 L/9	50°36′	118°24′
Viking	TOWN/VIL2	AB	36-47-13-W4	73 E/4	53°06′	111°46′
Viking Ice Cap	GLAC/GLAC	NT	Franklin	340 D	81°31′	75°40′
Viks Fiord	BAY/BAIE	NT	Franklin	58 H	76°00′	90°53′
Villa-Bellevue, Lieu historique national de la - also-aussi - Bellevue House National Historic Site	PARK/PARC	ON	Frontenac	31 C/2	44°13′	76°30′
Village Bay	UNP/LNO	BC	Cowichan	92 B/14	48°51′	123°19′
Village Bay 7	IR/RI	BC	Sayward	92 K/3	50°10′	125°12′
Village-Blier	UNP/LNO	QC	Témiscouata	21 N/6	47°27′	69°14′
Villagedale	UNP/LNO	NS	Shelburne	20 P/12	43°32′	65°33′
Village-de-la-Belle-Élodie, Le	UNP/LNO	QC	Le Haut-Richelieu	31 H/3	45°09′	73°18′
Village-de-la-Blague	UNP/LNO	QC	Rivière-du-Loup	21 N/12	47°41′	69°31′
Village-de-la-Chute	UNP/LNO	QC	Lac-Saint-Jean-Est	22 D/5	48°25′	71°42′
Village-des-Anglais	UNP/LNO	QC	L'Île-d'Orléans	21 L/14	46°51′	71°02′
Village-des-Arsenault	UNP/LNO	NB	Kent	21 I/10	46°31′	64°50′
Village-des-Aulnaies	UNP/LNO	QC	L'Islet	21 M/8	47°19′	70°09′
Village-des-Belles-Amours	UNP/LNO	QC	L'Islet	21 M/1	47°06′	70°21′
Village-des-Belliveau	UNP/LNO	NB	Kent	21 I/6	46°20′	65°03′
Village-des-Caron	UNP/LNO	QC	Maskinongé	31 I/7	46°18′	72°52′
Village-des-Chutes	UNP/LNO	QC	Arthabaska	21 E/13	45°53′	71°41′
Village-des-Cormier	UNP/LNO	NB	Kent	21 I/7	46°18′	64°56′
Village-des-Couture	UNP/LNO	QC	Desjardins	21 L/14	46°45′	71°09′
Village-des-Crête	UNP/LNO	QC	Francheville	31 I/7	46°18′	72°40′
Village-des-Deschênes	UNP/LNO	QC	Denis-Riverin	22 G/1	49°08′	66°18′
Village-des-Geoffroy	UNP/LNO	QC	Matawinie	31 I/5	46°15′	73°36′
Village des Hurons, Wendake	IR/RI	QC	Communauté urbaine de Québec	21 L/14	46°51′	71°21′
Village-des-Léger	UNP/LNO	NB	Kent	21 I/6	46°22′	65°05′
Village-des-Pères	UNP/LNO	QC	Maria-Chapdelaine	32 A/16	48°53′	72°13′
Village-des-Poirier	UNP/LNO	NB	Gloucester	21 P/14	47°48′	65°03′
Village Green	UNP/LNO	PE	Queens	11 L/2	46°13′	62°56′
Village Island	ISL/ÎLE	BC	Range 1 Coast	92 L/10	50°37′	126°32′
Village Island 1	IR/RI	BC	Rupert	92 L/3	50°01′	127°24′
Village Island 7	IR/RI	BC	Metchosin	92 B/5	48°19′	123°36′
Village, Lacs	LAKE/LAC	QC	Jamésie	33 B/3	52°10′	75°20′
Village-Lafontaine	UNP/LNO	QC	Matawinie	31 I/4	46°07′	73°53′
Village Lanthier	UNP/LNO	ON	Prescott	31 G/10	45°37′	74°46′
Village-La-Prairie	UNP/LNO	NB	Kent	21 I/10	46°36′	64°47′
Village Meadows	UNP/LNO	ON	Peterborough	31 D/8	44°21′	78°19′
Village-Paradis	UNP/LNO	QC	Maria-Chapdelaine	32 A/16	48°53′	72°16′
Village-Saint-Augustin	UNP/LNO	NB	Kent	21 I/6	46°25′	65°09′
Village-Sainte-Catherine, Le	UNP/LNO	QC	Francheville	31 I/9	46°38′	72°13′
Village-Sainte-Croix	UNP/LNO	NB	Kent	21 I/10	46°31′	64°42′
Village-Sainte-Marie	UNP/LNO	QC	Francheville	31 I/8	46°28′	72°20′
Village-Saint-Irénée	UNP/LNO	NB	Kent	21 I/7	46°28′	64°48′
Village-Saint-Jean	UNP/LNO	NB	Kent	21 I/14	46°46′	65°15′
Village-Saint-Laurent	UNP/LNO	NB	Northumberland	21 P/3	47°13′	65°09′
Village-Saint-Nicolas, Le	UNP/LNO	QC	Portneuf	21 L/12	46°43′	71°35′
Village-Saint-Paul	UNP/LNO	NB	Gloucester	21 P/14	47°47′	65°09′
Village-Saint-Pierre	UNP/LNO	NB	Northumberland	21 I/14	46°45′	65°22′
Village-sur-le-Lac	UNP/LNO	QC	Vaudreuil-Soulanges	31 H/5	45°21′	73°54′
Village-Villeneuve	UNP/LNO	QC	Maria-Chapdelaine	32 A/16	48°53′	72°15′
Villa Marie	UNP/LNO	NF		1 N/5	47°18′	53°51′
Villa Nova	UNP/LNO	ON	Norfolk	40 I/16	42°56′	80°12′
Villebois	UNP/LNO	QC	Jamésie	32 E/3	49°06′	79°09′
Villebon, Lac	LAKE/LAC	QC	Vallée-de-l'Or	31 N/14	47°58′	77°19′
Ville-Guay	UNP/LNO	QC	Desjardins	21 L/14	46°50′	71°05′
Ville-Marie	CITY/VIL1	QC	Témiscamingue	31 M/6	47°20′	79°26′
Ville-Marie	UNP/LNO	QC	Desjardins	21 L/14	46°47′	71°01′
Villemontel	UNP/LNO	QC	Abitibi	32 D/9	48°38′	78°22′
Villemontel, Rivière	RIV/CDE	QC	Abitibi	32 D/8	48°28′	78°20′
Villenaud, Lac	LAKE/LAC	QC	Le Fjord-du-Saguenay	22 L/7	50°27′	70°51′
Villeneuve	UNP/LNO	QC	Communauté urbaine de Québec	21 L/14	46°52′	71°10′
Villeneuve	UNP/LNO	AB	18-54-26-W4	83 H/12	53°40′	113°49′
Villeroy	VILG/VILG	QC	L'Érable	21 L/5	46°23′	71°53′
Villette	UNP/LNO	QC	Coaticook	21 E/4	45°04′	71°40′
Villette	UNP/LNO	MB	11-10-20-W	62 F/16	49°49′	100°06′
Villiers	UNP/LNO	ON	Peterborough	31 D/8	44°17′	78°06′
Villiers, Lac	LAKE/LAC	QC	Matawinie	31 O/1	47°08′	74°02′
Vilna	VILG/VILG	AB	20-59-13-W4	73 L/4	54°07′	111°55′
Vilroc	UNP/LNO	QC	Rouyn-Noranda	32 D/3	48°06′	79°16′
Vimont	UNP/LNO	QC	Laval	31 H/12	45°36′	73°43′
Vimy	UNP/LNO	AB	33-58-25-W4	83 I/4	54°04′	113°39′

NAME NOM	ENTITY ENTITÉ	LOC 1 LIEU 1	LOC 2 LIEU 2	MAP CARTE	POSITION LAT	LONG
Vimy-Ridge	UNP/LNO	QC	L'Amiante	21 L/3	46°00′	71°25′
Vimy Ridge	UNP/LNO	ON	Cochrane	42 A/8	48°29′	80°24′
Vimy Ridge	UNP/LNO	MB	24-32-23-W	62 N/15	51°45′	100°36′
Vin, Bay du	BAY/BAIE	NB	Northumberland	21 P/3	47°03′	65°10′
Vincelotte, Lac	LAKE/LAC	QC	Jamésie	33 I/8	54°18′	72°15′
Vincent Lake	LAKE/LAC	ON	Kenora	52 J/11	50°38′	91°00′
Vine	UNP/LNO	ON	Simcoe	31 D/5	44°19′	79°40′
Vinegar Hill	UNP/LNO	NB	Kings	21 H/12	45°37′	65°33′
Vinegar Hill	UNP/LNO	ON	Dundas	31 G/3	45°01′	75°24′
Vinegar Hill	UNP/LNO	ON	York	30 M/14	43°52′	79°15′
Vineland	UNP/LNO	ON	Lincoln	30 M/3	43°09′	79°24′
Vineland Station	UNP/LNO	ON	Lincoln	30 M/3	43°10′	79°24′
Vinemount	UNP/LNO	ON	Wentworth	30 M/4	43°12′	79°41′
Viner Sound	CHAN/CHEN	BC	Range 1 Coast	92 L/16	50°47′	126°24′
Vinet, Lac	LAKE/LAC	QC	Jamésie	23 L/5	54°19′	71°41′
Vinette	UNP/LNO	ON	Russell	31 G/6	45°29′	75°17′
Vingt-Deuxième Mille, Lac du	LAKE/LAC	QC	Minganie	12 L/11	50°34′	63°05′
Vingt-Quatre, Le	UNP/LNO	QC	La Matapédia	22 B/7	48°29′	66°51′
Vinoy	VILG/VILG	QC	Papineau	31 G/14	45°54′	75°01′
Vinsulla	UNP/LNO	BC	Kamloops Division Yale	92 I/16	50°55′	120°14′
Vinton	UNP/LNO	QC	Pontiac	31 F/15	45°47′	76°37′
Viola Bay	BAY/BAIE	NT	Franklin	36 G	65°19′	75°45′
Viola Lake	LAKE/LAC	ON	Kenora	52 E/9	49°33′	94°13′
Viola Lake	LAKE/LAC	BC	Range 1 Coast	92 L/14	50°52′	127°05′
Violet	UNP/LNO	ON	Lennox and Addington	31 C/7	44°16′	76°49′
Violet Grove	UNP/LNO	AB	24-48-8-W5	83 G/3	53°10′	115°02′
Violet Hill	UNP/LNO	ON	Dufferin	41 A/1	44°06′	80°05′
Violette Brook	UNP/LNO	NB	Victoria	21 O/5	47°21′	67°40′
Violette Settlement	UNP/LNO	NB	Madawaska	21 O/4	47°11′	67°51′
Violette Station	UNP/LNO	NB	Victoria	21 O/4	47°02′	67°39′
Virago Sound	CHAN/CHEN	BC	Queen Charlotte	103 K/1	54°05′	132°30′
Virden	TOWN/VIL2	MB	22-10-26-W	62 F/15	49°51′	100°56′
Virgil	UNP/LNO	ON	Lincoln	30 M/3	43°13′	79°08′
Virgin Arm	UNP/LNO	NF		2 E/10	49°32′	54°48′
Virgin Arm-Carter's Cove	UNP/LNO	NF		2 E/10	49°32′	54°47′
Virginia	UNP/LNO	ON	York	31 D/6	44°19′	79°17′
Virginia Beach	UNP/LNO	ON	York	31 D/6	44°20′	79°17′
Virginia East	UNP/LNO	NS	Annapolis	21 A/12	44°38′	65°31′
Virginia Falls	FALL/CHUT	NT	Mackenzie	95 F	61°36′	125°44′
Virginia Park	UNP/LNO	NF		1 N/10	47°36′	52°42′
Virginiatown	UNP/LNO	ON	Timiskaming	32 D/4	48°08′	79°35′
Virgin, Lac	LAKE/LAC	QC	Kativik	25 C/4	60°08′	69°47′
Virgin River	RIV/CDE	SK		74 F/1	57°02′	108°17′
Virgin Rocks	SEAU/SMER	—		4049	46°30′	50°50′
Viscount	VILG/VILG	SK	29-34-26-W2	72 P/13	51°57′	105°39′
Viscount Island	ISL/ÎLE	BC	Range 1 Coast	92 L/9	50°41′	126°13′
Viscount Melville Sound	CHAN/CHEN	NT	Franklin	78 E	74°10′	108°00′
Viscount No. 341	MUN2/AZM2	SK		72 P/13	51°50′	105°35′
Vista	UNP/LNO	MB	11-19-24-W	62 K/10	50°37′	100°43′
Vista Heights	UNP/LNO	ON	Peel	30 M/12	43°34′	79°43′
Vista Lake	LAKE/LAC	ON	Thunder Bay	52 G/15	49°57′	90°34′
Vita	UNP/LNO	MB	15,22-2-7-E	62 H/2	49°08′	96°34′
Vital, Lac	LAKE/LAC	QC	Minganie	22 P/6	51°28′	65°18′
Vital Lake	LAKE/LAC	NT	Mackenzie	75 F	61°33′	108°06′
Vitters Cove	UNP/LNO	NF		1 N/14	47°55′	53°22′
Vittoria	UNP/LNO	ON	Norfolk	40 I/16	42°46′	80°19′
Vittrekwa River	RIV/CDE	NT/YT		106 M/3	67°10′	135°01′
Vivian	UNP/LNO	ON	York	31 D/3	44°04′	79°18′
Vivian	UNP/LNO	MB	32,33-10-8-E	62 H/16	49°53′	96°27′
Vivian Island	ISL/ÎLE	BC	New Westminster	92 F/15	49°50′	124°42′
Vivian Island	ISL/ÎLE	NT	Franklin	68 D	73°15′	97°00′
Vogar	UNP/LNO	MB	33-22-9-W	62 J/15	50°57′	98°39′
Vogel	UNP/LNO	SK	6-14-7-W3	72 J/2	50°09′	106°58′
Voght Creek	RIV/CDE	BC	Kamloops Division Yale	92 H/15	49°54′	120°55′
Voglers Cove	UNP/LNO	NS	Lunenburg	21 A/2	44°09′	64°32′
Voilnadamtk 48	IR/RI	BC	Cassiar	103 P/3	55°13′	129°12′
Voisey Bay	BAY/BAIE	NF		14 C/5	56°15′	61°50′
Voisin, Lac	LAKE/LAC	SK	60-9-W3	73 J/3	54°13′	107°15′
Volcano Mountain	MTN/MNT	YT		115 I/14	62°55′	137°23′
Volga	UNP/LNO	MB	17-30-17-W	62 O/12	51°34′	99°48′
Volmer	UNP/LNO	AB	32-54-25-W4	83 H/12	53°43′	113°40′
Vonda	TOWN/VIL2	SK	4-39-1-W3	73 B/8	52°19′	106°06′
Von Zuben	UNP/LNO	BC	Cariboo	83 D/14	52°51′	119°17′
Vosburg	UNP/LNO	ON	Kent	40 J/8	42°27′	82°07′
Voy's Beach	UNP/LNO	NF		12 G/1	49°02′	58°09′

NAME NOM	ENTITY ENTITÉ	LOC 1 LIEU 1	LOC 2 LIEU 2	MAP CARTE	POSITION LAT	LONG
Vrooman Creek	RIV/CDE	ON	Ontario	31 D/6	44°23′	79°05′
Vroomanton	UNP/LNO	ON	Ontario	31 D/6	44°16′	79°07′
Vuich Creek	RIV/CDE	BC	Yale Division Yale	92 H/7	49°28′	120°59′
Vulcan	TOWN/VIL2	AB	5-17-24-W4	82 I/6	50°24′	113°15′
Vulcan No. 2, County of	MUN1/AZM1	AB	17-22-W4	82 I/7	50°26′	112°58′
Vuntut National Park - also-aussi - Vuntut, Parc national	PARK/PARC	YT		117 A/5	68°25′	139°47′
Vuntut, Parc national - also-aussi - Vuntut National Park	PARK/PARC	YT		117 A/5	68°25′	139°47′
Vydon Acres	UNP/LNO	ON	Carleton	31 F/8	45°27′	76°17′
Vye	UNP/LNO	BC	New Westminster	92 G/1	49°01′	122°16′
Vyner	UNP/LNO	ON	Lambton	40 O/1	43°01′	82°15′

W

NAME NOM	ENTITY ENTITÉ	LOC 1 LIEU 1	LOC 2 LIEU 2	MAP CARTE	POSITION LAT	LONG
Waasagomach	UNP/LNO	MB	57-17,18-E	53 E/15	53°55′	94°57′
Waasis	UNP/LNO	NB	Sunbury	21 G/15	45°50′	66°35′
Waba	UNP/LNO	ON	Renfrew	31 F/8	45°21′	76°27′
Wababimiga Lake	LAKE/LAC	ON	Cochrane	42 L/8	50°20′	86°23′
Waba Creek	RIV/CDE	ON	Renfrew	31 F/8	45°25′	76°20′
Wabagishik Lake	LAKE/LAC	ON	Sudbury	41 I/5	46°18′	81°35′
Wabakimi Lake	LAKE/LAC	ON	Thunder Bay	52 I/12	50°38′	89°45′
Wabamun	VILG/VILG	AB	11-53-4-W5	83 G/9	53°33′	114°28′
Wabamun 133A	IR/RI	AB	52-4-W5	83 G/9	53°31′	114°26′
Wabamun 133B	IR/RI	AB	17-52-3-W5	83 G/9	53°38′	114°26′
Wabamun Lake	LAKE/LAC	AB	52,53-4,5-W5	83 G/10	53°32′	114°35′
Wabamun Lake Provincial Park	PARK/PARC	AB	53-3,4-W5	83 G/9	53°32′	114°26′
Wabana	TOWN/VIL2	NF		1 N/10	47°38′	52°57′
Wabano, Rivière	RIV/CDE	QC	Le Haut-Saint-Maurice	32 B/8	48°21′	74°03′
Wabasca 166	IR/RI	AB	79-23-W4	83 P/13	55°53′	113°31′
Wabasca 166A	IR/RI	AB	80-24,25-W4	83 P/13	55°57′	113°46′
Wabasca 166B	IR/RI	AB	26-81-26-W4	83 P/13	55°58′	113°58′
Wabasca 166C	IR/RI	AB	15-82-25-W4	84 A/4	56°09′	113°50′
Wabasca 166D	IR/RI	AB	79-25-W4	83 P/13	55°55′	113°52′
Wabasca-Desmarais	UNP/LNO	AB	80-25-W4	83 P/13	55°58′	113°51′
Wabasca River	RIV/CDE	AB	108-9,10-W5	84 J/6	58°22′	115°20′
Wabasca Settlement	UNP/LNO	AB	81-25-W4	83 P/13	55°57′	113°50′
Wabash	UNP/LNO	QC	Pontiac	31 F/14	45°52′	77°07′
Wabash	UNP/LNO	ON	Kent	40 J/9	42°34′	82°05′
Wabaskang	UNP/LNO	ON	Kenora	52 K/6	50°26′	93°06′
Wabaskang Lake	LAKE/LAC	ON	Kenora	52 K/6	50°26′	93°13′
Wabassee	UNP/LNO	QC	Antoine-Labelle	31 J/5	46°20′	75°32′
Wabassi River	RIV/CDE	ON	Kenora	42 M/16	51°46′	86°18′
Wabatongushi Lake	LAKE/LAC	ON	Algoma	42 C/8	48°26′	84°13′
Wabauskang 21	IR/RI	ON	Kenora	52 K/6	50°24′	93°11′
Wabeno Lake	LAKE/LAC	SK	61-3-W3	73 J/8	54°19′	106°24′
Wabi	UNP/LNO	BC	Peace River	93 P/11	55°43′	121°24′
Wabigoon	UNP/LNO	ON	Kenora	52 F/10	49°43′	92°35′
Wabigoon Lake	LAKE/LAC	ON	Kenora	52 F/10	49°44′	92°44′
Wabigoon Lake 27	IR/RI	ON	Kenora	52 F/10	49°36′	92°32′
Wabigoon River	RIV/CDE	ON	Kenora	52 F/8	50°16′	93°59′
Wabi-Kon	UNP/LNO	ON	Nipissing	41 I/16	46°57′	80°02′
Wabimeig Lake	LAKE/LAC	ON	Cochrane	42 N/5	51°28′	85°36′
Wabinosh Lake	LAKE/LAC	ON	Thunder Bay	52 I/2	50°05′	89°00′
Wabos	UNP/LNO	ON	Algoma	41 K/16	46°49′	84°07′
Wabowden	UNP/LNO	MB		63 J/15	54°55′	98°38′
Wabozominissing	UNP/LNO	ON	Manitoulin	41 H/13	45°52′	81°42′
Wabron	UNP/LNO	BC	Kamloops Division Yale	82 M/12	51°40′	119°35′
Wabuk Point	CAPE/CAP	ON	Kenora	43 N/6	55°20′	85°05′
Wabush	TOWN/VIL2	NF		23 B/15	52°54′	66°52′
Wabush Lake	LAKE/LAC	NF		23 G/2	53°05′	66°52′
W.A.C. Bennett Dam	MISC/DIV	BC	Peace River	94 B/1	56°01′	122°12′
Wachee	UNP/LNO	SK	26-46-3-W2	63 D/16	52°59′	102°21′
Wachi Creek	RIV/CDE	ON	Kenora	43 N/2	55°14′	84°34′
Wachigabau, Lac	LAKE/LAC	QC	Jamésie	32 G/12	49°32′	75°55′
Waco	UNP/LNO	QC	Sept-Rivières	22 P/5	51°27′	65°37′
Waconichi, Lac	LAKE/LAC	QC	Jamésie	32 J/1	50°08′	74°00′
Wacouno, Lac	LAKE/LAC	QC	Sept-Rivières	22 P/12	51°35′	65°42′
Wacouno, Rivière	RIV/CDE	QC	Sept-Rivières	22 I/13	50°54′	65°57′
Waddell Bay	BAY/BAIE	NT	Franklin	25 O	63°20′	67°00′
Waddens Cove	UNP/LNO	NS	Cape Breton	11 J/4	46°05′	59°52′
Waddington Beach	UNP/LNO	ON	Simcoe	31 D/6	44°30′	79°27′
Waddington Channel	CHAN/CHEN	BC	New Westminster	92 K/2	50°13′	124°43′
Waddington Glacier	GLAC/GLAC	BC	Range 2 Coast	92 N/6	51°19′	125°10′
Waddington, Mount	MTN/MNT	BC	Range 2 Coast	92 N/6	51°23′	125°16′

NAME NOM	ENTITY ENTITÉ	LOC 1 LIEU 1	LOC 2 LIEU 2	MAP CARTE	POSITION LAT	LONG
Wade	UNP/LNO	ON	Kenora	52 E/15	49°57′	94°47′
Wade Corners	UNP/LNO	ON	Northumberland	31 C/4	44°04′	77°46′
Wade Lake	LAKE/LAC	NF		23 I/5	54°20′	65°38′
Wade, Mount	MTN/MNT	BC	Cassiar	114 O/15	59°48′	138°40′
Wadena	TOWN/VIL2	SK	28-34-13-W2	62 M/13	51°57′	103°48′
Wade's Landing	UNP/LNO	ON	Parry Sound	31 L/4	46°07′	79°31′
Wadham Islands	ISL/ÎLE	NF		2 F/12	49°33′	53°51′
Wadhams	UNP/LNO	BC	Range 2 Coast	92 M/12	51°31′	127°30′
Wadin Bay	UNP/LNO	SK		73 P/6	55°16′	105°12′
Wadlin Lake	LAKE/LAC	AB	100,101-10,11-W5	84 G/12	57°44′	115°35′
Wagaming	UNP/LNO	ON	Thunder Bay	52 I/7	50°16′	88°52′
Wagarville	UNP/LNO	ON	Frontenac	31 C/10	44°38′	76°48′
Wager Bay	UNP/LNO	NT	Keewatin	56 G	65°56′	90°49′
Wager Bay	BAY/BAIE	NT	Keewatin	56 H	65°26′	88°40′
Wagmatcook 1	IR/RI	NS	Victoria	11 K/2	46°05′	60°55′
Wagner	UNP/LNO	AB	27-73-7-W5	83 O/7	55°21′	114°59′
Wagner Ranch	UNP/LNO	BC	Peace River	94 B/9	56°31′	122°14′
Wagners Lake	LAKE/LAC	NS	Yarmouth	20 P/13	43°50′	65°36′
Wagram	UNP/LNO	ON	Wellington	40 P/15	43°52′	80°43′
Wahawin	UNP/LNO	ON	Muskoka	31 E/3	45°13′	79°04′
Wahemen, Lac	LAKE/LAC	QC	Jamésie	23 D/11	52°45′	71°15′
Wahkash Creek	RIV/CDE	BC	Range 1 Coast	92 K/13	50°59′	125°32′
Wahkash Point	CAPE/CAP	BC	Range 1 Coast	92 K/13	50°58′	125°32′
Wahleach Island 2	IR/RI	BC	Yale Division Yale	92 H/5	49°20′	121°37′
Wahleach Lake	LAKE/LAC	BC	Yale Division Yale	92 H/4	49°14′	121°37′
Wahnapitae	UNP/LNO	ON	Sudbury	41 I/7	46°29′	80°47′
Wahnapitei 11	IR/RI	ON	Sudbury	41 I/15	46°47′	80°51′
Wahnekewaning Beach	UNP/LNO	ON	Simcoe	41 A/9	44°43′	80°02′
Wahous 19	IR/RI	BC	Clayoquot	92 F/5	49°16′	125°55′
Wahous 20	IR/RI	BC	Clayoquot	92 F/5	49°17′	125°54′
Wahpeton 94A	IR/RI	SK		73 H/5	53°16′	105°51′
Wahpeton 94B	IR/RI	SK		73 H/5	53°16′	105°51′
Wahta Mohawk Territory	IR/RI	ON	Muskoka	31 E/4	45°02′	79°44′
Wahwashkesh	UNP/LNO	ON	Parry Sound	41 H/9	45°43′	80°02′
Wahwashkesh Lake	LAKE/LAC	ON	Parry Sound	41 H/9	45°43′	80°02′
Wainfleet	MUN2/AZM2	ON	Welland	30 L/14	42°55′	79°22′
Wainfleet	UNP/LNO	ON	Welland	30 L/14	42°53′	79°22′
Wainfleet	UNP/LNO	ON	Welland	30 L/14	42°56′	79°23′
Wainwright	TOWN/VIL2	AB	31-44-6-W4	73 D/15	52°49′	110°52′
Wainwright No. 61, Municipal District of	MUN1/AZM1	AB	45-5-W4	73 D/15	52°51′	110°42′
Waiparous	VILG/VILG	AB	7-26-6-W5	82 O/2	51°12′	114°49′
Waite Mine	UNP/LNO	QC	Rouyn-Noranda	32 D/6	48°20′	79°05′
Waitville	UNP/LNO	SK	15-45-24-W2	73 A/14	52°52′	105°24′
Waiwakum 14	IR/RI	BC	New Westminster	92 G/14	49°46′	123°10′
Wakami Lake	LAKE/LAC	ON	Sudbury	41 O/7	47°29′	82°51′
Wakami River	RIV/CDE	ON	Sudbury	41 O/9	47°43′	82°22′
Wakaw	TOWN/VIL2	SK	30-42-26-W2	73 A/12	52°39′	105°44′
Wakaw Lake	VILG/VILG	SK	26,27-42-26-W2	73 A/12	52°38′	105°39′
Wakaw Lake	LAKE/LAC	SK	42,43-25,26-W2	73 A/12	52°40′	105°35′
Wakefield	UNP/LNO	NB	Carleton	21 J/4	46°14′	67°31′
Wakefield	UNP/LNO	QC	Les Collines-de-l'Outaouais	31 G/12	45°38′	75°56′
Wakefield	GEOG/GÉOG	NB	Carleton	21 J/5	46°15′	67°37′
Wakeham	UNP/LNO	QC	La Côte-de-Gaspé	22 A/15	48°50′	64°34′
Wakeham Bay	BAY/BAIE	NT	Franklin	25 E	61°38′	71°58′
Wakely	UNP/LNO	BC	Kootenay	82 N/6	51°24′	117°28′
Wakeman River	RIV/CDE	BC	Range 2 Coast	92 M/2	51°03′	126°32′
Wakeman Sound	CHAN/CHEN	BC	Range 1 Coast	92 L/15	50°59′	126°30′
Wakem Corner	UNP/LNO	NB	Carleton	21 J/5	46°29′	67°41′
Wakems 6	IR/RI	BC	Rupert	92 L/13	50°54′	127°41′
Wakimika Lake	LAKE/LAC	ON	Sudbury	41 P/1	47°09′	80°21′
Wakomata Lake	LAKE/LAC	ON	Algoma	41 J/11	46°34′	83°22′
Wakonassin River	RIV/CDE	ON	Sudbury	41 I/5	46°28′	81°51′
Wakopa	UNP/LNO	MB	32-1-18-W	62 G/4	49°05′	99°51′
Wakuach, Lac	LAKE/LAC	QC	Kativik	23 O/12	55°34′	67°32′
Wakusimi River	RIV/CDE	ON	Cochrane	42 G/1	49°10′	82°04′
Walbran Creek	RIV/CDE	BC	Renfrew	92 C/10	48°35′	124°40′
Walcott	UNP/LNO	BC	Range 5 Coast	93 L/10	54°31′	126°50′
Waldau	UNP/LNO	ON	Waterloo	40 P/7	43°25′	80°34′
Waldeck	VILG/VILG	SK	21-16-12-W3	72 J/5	50°22′	107°36′
Waldeck	UNP/LNO	NS	Annapolis	21 A/12	44°38′	65°38′
Waldeck East	UNP/LNO	NS	Annapolis	21 A/12	44°38′	65°36′
Waldeck West	UNP/LNO	NS	Annapolis	21 A/12	44°37′	65°38′
Waldegrave	UNP/LNO	NS	Colchester	11 E/11	45°43′	63°14′
Waldemar	UNP/LNO	ON	Dufferin	40 P/16	43°53′	80°17′
Walden	TOWN/VIL2	ON	Sudbury	41 I/6	46°23′	81°23′

NAME NOM	ENTITY ENTITÉ	LOC 1 LIEU 1	LOC 2 LIEU 2	MAP CARTE	POSITION LAT	POSITION LONG
Walden	UNP/LNO	NS	Lunenburg	21 A/10	44°36′	64°32′
Walden Place	UNP/LNO	ON	Lambton	40 P/4	43°13′	81°52′
Waldersee	UNP/LNO	MB	21-18-12W	62 J/11	50°34′	99°03′
Waldheim	TOWN/VIL2	SK	16-42-5-W3	73 B/10	52°39′	106°37′
Waldron	VILG/VILG	SK	33-21-4-W2	62 L/15	50°51′	102°31′
Waldron Cove	UNP/LNO	NF		2 E/11	49°31′	55°10′
Waldron River	RIV/CDE	NT	Mackenzie	75 L	62°55′	110°35′
Wales Island	ISL/ÎLE	BC	Range 5 Coast	103 J/9	54°45′	130°29′
Wales Island	ISL/ÎLE	NT	Franklin	25 E	61°52′	72°03′
Wales Island	ISL/ÎLE	NT	Franklin	47 B	68°01′	86°40′
Walford	UNP/LNO	ON	Algoma	41 J/1	46°12′	82°15′
Walhachin	UNP/LNO	BC	Kamloops Division Yale	92 I/15	50°45′	120°59′
Walker	UNP/LNO	BC	Cariboo	93 G/7	53°27′	122°40′
Walker Arm	BAY/BAIE	NT	Franklin	27 F	70°30′	71°39′
Walker Bay	BAY/BAIE	NT	Mackenzie	77 B	68°15′	108°27′
Walker Bay	BAY/BAIE	NT	Franklin	87 G	71°35′	118°10′
Walkerburn	UNP/LNO	MB	22-29-29-W	62 N/11	51°31′	101°29′
Walker, Cape	CAPE/CAP	NT	Franklin	68 E	74°03′	97°37′
Walker Creek	RIV/CDE	SK		74 B/9	56°34′	106°15′
Walker Inlet	BAY/BAIE	NT	Franklin	98 H	76°00′	120°47′
Walker, Lac	LAKE/LAC	QC	Sept-Rivières	22 J/6	50°16′	67°09′
Walker Lake	LAKE/LAC	ON	Sudbury	41 I/4	46°12′	81°30′
Walker Lake	LAKE/LAC	MB/ON		52 M/6	51°29′	95°09′
Walker Lake	LAKE/LAC	MB		63 I/10	54°42′	96°57′
Walker Lake	LAKE/LAC	SK	69-2-W2	63 L/16	54°58′	102°16′
Walker Lake	LAKE/LAC	SK		64 M/5	59°23′	103°50′
Walker Lake	LAKE/LAC	NT	Keewatin	56 J	66°42′	90°40′
Walker, Mount	MTN/MNT	NT	Franklin	58 B	72°03′	94°18′
Walkers	UNP/LNO	ON	Middlesex	40 I/13	42°49′	81°46′
Walkers	UNP/LNO	BC	Kootenay	82 F/10	49°42′	116°52′
Walker Settlement	UNP/LNO	NB	Kings	21 H/11	45°39′	65°23′
Walkers Point	UNP/LNO	ON	Muskoka	31 E/3	45°01′	79°27′
Walkerton	TOWN/VIL2	ON	Bruce	41 A/3	44°07′	81°09′
Walkerville	UNP/LNO	NS	Richmond	11 F/11	45°36′	61°13′
Walkerville	UNP/LNO	ON	Essex	40 J/6	42°19′	83°00′
Walker Woods	UNP/LNO	ON	Lambton	40 P/4	43°14′	81°51′
Walkhouse Point	CAPE/CAP	ON	Manitoulin	41 G/15	45°47′	82°52′
Walkleyburg	UNP/LNO	MB	21-14-6-E	62 I/2	50°12′	96°43′
Wallaback Lake	LAKE/LAC	NS	Lunenburg	21 A/16	44°49′	64°26′
Wallace	MUN2/AZM2	ON	Perth	40 P/10	43°45′	80°54′
Wallace	MUN2/AZM2	MB		62 F/14	49°55′	101°10′
Wallace	UNP/LNO	NS	Cumberland	11 E/14	45°48′	63°29′
Wallace	UNP/LNO	ON	Nipissing	31 E/8	45°23′	78°04′
Wallace	UNP/LNO	ON	Perth	40 P/10	43°45′	80°52′
Wallace	UNP/LNO	SK	33-7-21-W2	72 H/10	49°37′	104°48′
Wallace Bay	UNP/LNO	NS	Cumberland	11 E/13	45°50′	63°35′
Wallace Bridge	UNP/LNO	NS	Cumberland	11 E/13	45°49′	63°31′
Wallace Bridge Station	UNP/LNO	NS	Cumberland	11 E/13	45°48′	63°32′
Wallaceburg	TOWN/VIL2	ON	Kent	40 J/9	42°36′	82°23′
Wallace Cove	UNP/LNO	NB	Charlotte	21 G/2	45°03′	66°48′
Wallace Grant	UNP/LNO	NS	Cumberland	11 E/11	45°44′	63°28′
Wallace Heights	UNP/LNO	NS	Halifax	11 D/12	44°41′	63°36′
Wallace Heights	UNP/LNO	ON	Nipissing	31 L/6	46°20′	79°26′
Wallace Highlands	UNP/LNO	NS	Cumberland	11 E/11	45°43′	63°28′
Wallace Lake	UNP/LNO	MB	31-23-16-E	52 L/14	51°00′	95°21′
Wallace No. 243	MUN2/AZM2	SK		62 M/1	51°15′	102°15′
Wallace Point	UNP/LNO	ON	Peterborough	31 D/1	44°11′	78°20′
Wallace Point	CAPE/CAP	NT	Franklin	88 D	73°25′	115°26′
Wallace Ridge	UNP/LNO	NS	Cumberland	11 E/14	45°47′	63°25′
Wallace River	UNP/LNO	NS	Cumberland	11 E/13	45°48′	63°33′
Wallace River	RIV/CDE	NS	Cumberland	11 E/13	45°49′	63°31′
Wallace River	RIV/CDE	NT	Keewatin	55 F	61°37′	93°41′
Wallace Station	UNP/LNO	NS	Cumberland	11 E/14	45°47′	63°29′
Wallacetown	UNP/LNO	ON	Elgin	40 I/11	42°38′	81°28′
Wallard	UNP/LNO	SK	27-6-11-W3	72 G/6	49°30′	107°25′
Wall Bay	BAY/BAIE	NT	Franklin	67 D	69°49′	98°06′
Wallbridge	UNP/LNO	ON	Hastings	31 C/3	44°13′	77°30′
Wallbrook	UNP/LNO	NS	Kings	21 H/1	45°05′	64°18′
Wallenstein	UNP/LNO	ON	Wellington	40 P/10	43°36′	80°38′
Wall Island	ISL/ÎLE	ON	Manitoulin	41 H/12	45°33′	81°41′
Wallisville	UNP/LNO	SK	3-33-20-W3	72 N/15	51°48′	108°45′
Walls	UNP/LNO	ON	Parry Sound	31 E/6	45°29′	79°21′
Walls Seamount	SEAU/SMER	—		5.03	53°47′	156°00′
Wallubek Lake	LAKE/LAC	NS	Yarmouth	20 P/13	44°00′	65°43′
Wallwort	UNP/LNO	SK	23-41-15-W2	73 A/9	52°33′	104°03′

NAME / NOM	ENTITY / ENTITÉ	LOC 1 / LIEU 1	LOC 2 / LIEU 2	MAP / CARTE	POSITION LAT	POSITION LONG
Walmsley Lake	LAKE/LAC	NT	Mackenzie	75 N	63°25′	108°32′
Walnut	UNP/LNO	ON	Lambton	40 I/13	42°53′	81°54′
Walnut Grove	UNP/LNO	BC	New Westminster	92 G/2	49°11′	122°39′
Walpole	UNP/LNO	SK	36-10-33-W	62 F/13	49°53′	101°50′
Walpole Island	UNP/LNO	ON	Lambton	40 J/10	42°37′	82°31′
Walpole Island	ISL/ÎLE	ON	Lambton	40 J/9	42°33′	82°29′
Walpole Island 46	IR/RI	ON	Lambton	40 J/10	42°33′	82°31′
Walpole No. 92	MUN2/AZM2	SK		62 F/13	49°53′	101°50′
Walrus Island	ISL/ÎLE	NT	Keewatin	45 O	63°16′	83°40′
Walrus Point	CAPE/CAP	NT	Keewatin	33 E	53°42′	79°09′
Walsh	UNP/LNO	NF		2 D/9	48°35′	54°12′
Walsh	UNP/LNO	ON	Norfolk	40 I/9	42°44′	80°22′
Walsh	UNP/LNO	ON	Norfolk	40 I/16	42°46′	80°23′
Walsh	UNP/LNO	AB	35-11-1-W4	72 E/16	49°57′	110°03′
Walsh Acres	UNP/LNO	SK		72 I/7	50°29′	104°39′
Walsh Creek	RIV/CDE	YT		105 E/15	61°55′	134°56′
Walsh Glacier	GLAC/GLAC	YT		115 C/15	60°53′	140°45′
Walsh Lake	LAKE/LAC	SK		64 L/14	58°59′	103°24′
Walsh Lake	LAKE/LAC	SK	76-1-W3	73 O/9	55°36′	106°07′
Walsingham	UNP/LNO	ON	Norfolk	40 I/10	42°41′	80°32′
Walsingham, Cape	CAPE/CAP	NT	Franklin	16 K	66°02′	61°58′
Walter Bathurst, Cape	CAPE/CAP	NT	Franklin	38 C	73°20′	76°43′
Walter Island	ISL/ÎLE	NT	Keewatin	33 E	53°19′	79°40′
Walters Creek - see-voir - Knife Creek	RIV/CDE	BC		93 A/4	52°01′	121°52′
Walters Falls	UNP/LNO	ON	Grey	41 A/7	44°30′	80°43′
Walth 3	IR/RI	BC	Range 4 Coast	103 H/15	53°57′	128°39′
Waltham	UNP/LNO	QC	Pontiac	31 F/15	45°55′	76°55′
Waltham-et-Bryson	VILG/VILG	QC	Pontiac	31 F/15	45°55′	76°55′
Walton	UNP/LNO	NS	Hants	11 E/4	45°14′	64°00′
Walton	UNP/LNO	ON	Huron	40 P/11	43°41′	81°18′
Walton River	RIV/CDE	NS	Hants	21 H/1	45°14′	64°01′
Waltons Lake	UNP/LNO	NB	Kings	21 G/8	45°27′	66°04′
Wampum	UNP/LNO	MB	18-1-13-E	52 E/4	49°03′	95°50′
Wamsley	UNP/LNO	ON	Thunder Bay	52 A/4	48°12′	89°37′
Wanapitei Lake	LAKE/LAC	ON	Sudbury	41 I/10	46°45′	80°45′
Wanapitei River	RIV/CDE	ON	Sudbury	41 I/2	46°02′	80°51′
Wanasing Beach	UNP/LNO	MB	11-20-7-E	62 I/10	50°42′	96°32′
Wanaskuch Bay	BAY/BAIE	SK		74 B/5	56°18′	107°56′
Wanda	UNP/LNO	ON	Algoma	42 C/8	48°23′	84°28′
Wandering River	UNP/LNO	AB	6-72-16-W4	83 P/1	55°12′	112°28′
Wandering River	RIV/CDE	AB	21-70-17-W4	83 P/2	55°05′	112°32′
Wandsworth	UNP/LNO	NF		1 M/3	47°02′	55°12′
Wandsworth	UNP/LNO	SK	28-45-4-W3	73 B/15	52°54′	106°31′
Waneeta Beach	UNP/LNO	ON	Elgin	40 I/11	42°40′	81°01′
Waneta	UNP/LNO	BC	Kootenay	82 F/4	49°00′	117°37′
Waneta Junction	UNP/LNO	BC	Kootenay	82 F/4	49°05′	117°37′
Wanham	VILG/VILG	AB	4-78-3-W6	83 M/9	55°44′	118°24′
Wanikewin	UNP/LNO	ON	Parry Sound	41 H/15	46°00′	80°33′
Wanipigow River	RIV/CDE	MB/ON		62 P/1	51°11′	96°17′
Wanklyn	UNP/LNO	BC	Kootenay	82 G/12	49°35′	115°49′
Wanless	UNP/LNO	MB	12-60-27-W	63 K/3	54°11′	101°22′
Wanstead	UNP/LNO	ON	Lambton	40 J/16	42°57′	82°02′
Wanup	UNP/LNO	ON	Sudbury	41 I/7	46°23′	80°50′
Wapachewunak 192D	IR/RI	SK		73 O/13	55°54′	107°44′
Wapageisi Lake	LAKE/LAC	ON	Kenora	52 F/8	49°18′	92°22′
Wapah	UNP/LNO	MB	18-24-10-W	62 O/2	51°04′	98°52′
Wapaseese River	RIV/CDE	ON	Kenora	53 P/4	55°01′	89°44′
Wapata Lake	LAKE/LAC	SK		74 I/13	58°51′	105°43′
Wapawekka Hills	MTN/MNT	SK		73 I/16	54°47′	104°20′
Wapawekka Lake	LAKE/LAC	SK		73 I/15	54°55′	104°40′
Wapawsik	UNP/LNO	MB	32-81-8-W	64 B/2	56°03′	98°41′
Wapekeka 1	IR/RI	ON	Kenora	53 H/12	53°44′	89°32′
Wapekeka 2	IR/RI	ON	Kenora	53 H/13	53°55′	89°33′
Wapella	TOWN/VIL2	SK	9-15-33-W	62 K/5	50°16′	101°58′
Wapesi Bay	BAY/BAIE	ON	Kenora	52 K/9	50°31′	92°04′
Wapesi Lake	LAKE/LAC	ON	Kenora	52 K/9	50°34′	92°21′
Wapesi River	RIV/CDE	ON	Kenora	52 K/9	50°31′	92°11′
Wa-Pii Moos-Toosis (White Calf) 83A	IR/RI	SK		62 L/13	50°46′	103°43′
Wapikaimaski Lake	LAKE/LAC	ON	Thunder Bay	52 J/1	50°04′	90°10′
Wapikani River	RIV/CDE	MB		53 O/12	55°39′	91°44′
Wapikopa Lake	LAKE/LAC	ON	Kenora	53 A/16	52°57′	88°05′
Wapisew Lake	LAKE/LAC	SK	55-3,4-W2	63 E/16	53°47′	102°29′
Wapiskau River	RIV/CDE	ON	Cochrane	42 P/15	51°51′	80°47′
Wapiskau River	RIV/CDE	SK		64 D/3	56°01′	103°21′
Wapistanschipan	UNP/LNO	QC	Kativik	24 F/8	57°29′	68°22′

NAME NOM	ENTITY ENTITÉ	LOC 1 LIEU 1	LOC 2 LIEU 2	MAP CARTE	POSITION LAT	LONG
Wapisu Lake	LAKE/LAC	MB	78,79-11,12-W	63 O/14	55°47′	99°11′
Wapiti	UNP/LNO	AB	15-69-8-W6	83 L/14	54°58′	119°08′
Wapiti River	RIV/CDE	AB/BC		83 M/1	55°08′	118°18′
Wapiyao Lake	LAKE/LAC	SK		64 M/12	59°45′	103°49′
Wapizagonke, Lac	LAKE/LAC	QC	Le Centre-de-la-Mauricie	31 I/11	46°43′	73°02′
Wappau Lake	LAKE/LAC	AB	75-10,11-W4	73 M/5	55°30′	111°35′
Wappock 26	IR/RI	BC	Clayoquot	92 E/8	49°26′	126°05′
Wapske	UNP/LNO	NB	Victoria	21 J/14	46°53′	67°23′
Wapske River	RIV/CDE	NB	Victoria	21 J/14	46°53′	67°23′
Wapta Icefield	GLAC/GLAC	BC/AB		82 N/10	51°37′	116°34′
Wapusk National Park - also-aussi - Wapusk, Parc national	PARK/PARC	MB		54 F/14	57°46′	93°22′
Wapusk, Parc national - also-aussi - Wapusk National Park	PARK/PARC	MB		54 F/14	57°46′	93°22′
Wapus Lake	LAKE/LAC	SK		64 D/8	56°27′	102°12′
Wapustagamau, Lac	LAKE/LAC	QC	Minganie	12 O/11	51°31′	59°07′
Waputik Icefield	GLAC/GLAC	BC/AB		82 N/9	51°25′	116°33′
Warburg	VILG/VILG	AB	35-48-3-W5	83 G/1	53°11′	114°19′
Warburton	UNP/LNO	ON	Leeds	31 C/8	44°28′	76°03′
Warburton Bay	BAY/BAIE	NT	Mackenzie	75 M	63°50′	111°30′
Ward	UNP/LNO	NB	Westmorland	21 H/16	45°58′	64°19′
Ward Corner	UNP/LNO	NB	Kent	21 I/7	46°25′	64°40′
Warden	TOWN/VIL2	QC	La Haute-Yamaska	31 H/7	45°23′	72°30′
Warden	UNP/LNO	AB	13-38-20-W4	83 A/2	52°16′	112°45′
Ward Hunt Island	ISL/ÎLE	NT	Franklin	340 E	83°06′	74°10′
Ward Inlet	BAY/BAIE	NT	Franklin	25 O	63°30′	67°35′
Wardlow	UNP/LNO	AB	25-22-12-W4	72 L/13	50°54′	111°33′
Wardner	UNP/LNO	BC	Kootenay	82 G/6	49°25′	115°25′
Ward Point	CAPE/CAP	BC	Range 1 Coast	92 K/15	50°53′	124°50′
Ward Point	CAPE/CAP	NT	Franklin	48 H	75°50′	82°22′
Wards Brook	UNP/LNO	NS	Cumberland	21 H/7	45°25′	64°34′
Wards Creek	UNP/LNO	NB	Kings	21 H/12	45°41′	65°31′
Ward Settlement	UNP/LNO	NB	York	21 J/7	46°18′	66°42′
Wards Harbour	UNP/LNO	NF		2 E/12	49°36′	55°53′
Wardsville	VILG/VILG	ON	Middlesex	40 I/12	42°39′	81°45′
Ware	UNP/LNO	BC	Cassiar	94 F/5	57°25′	125°38′
War Eagle Lake	LAKE/LAC	MB	11-14-E	52 E/13	49°56′	95°38′
Wareham	UNP/LNO	NF		2 F/4	49°01′	53°52′
Wareham	UNP/LNO	ON	Grey	41 A/1	44°15′	80°25′
Wareham Island	ISL/ÎLE	NT	Franklin	26 H	65°15′	65°03′
Warell Junction	UNP/LNO	SK		72 I/7	50°28′	104°40′
Warfield	VILG/VILG	BC	Kootenay	82 F/4	49°06′	117°45′
Warina	UNP/LNO	ON	Stormont	31 G/2	45°14′	74°55′
Warings Corner	UNP/LNO	ON	Prince Edward	30 N/14	44°00′	77°11′
Warkworth	UNP/LNO	ON	Northumberland	31 C/4	44°12′	77°53′
Warkworth Lake	LAKE/LAC	MB		54 L/9	58°36′	94°03′
War Lake 4	IR/RI	BC	Cariboo	93 J/14	54°52′	123°18′
Warman	TOWN/VIL2	SK	31-38-4-W3	73 B/7	52°19′	106°34′
Warminster	UNP/LNO	ON	Simcoe	31 D/12	44°38′	79°33′
Warmley	UNP/LNO	SK	7-10-5-W2	62 E/15	49°48′	102°41′
Warn Bay	BAY/BAIE	BC	Clayoquot	92 F/4	49°15′	125°45′
Warneford	UNP/LNO	ON	Thunder Bay	52 H/9	49°34′	88°02′
Warneford River	RIV/CDE	BC	Cassiar	94 F/11	57°36′	125°28′
Warner	VILG/VILG	AB	10-4-17-W4	82 H/8	49°17′	112°12′
Warner	UNP/LNO	ON	Lincoln	30 M/4	43°01′	79°39′
Warner Bay	UNP/LNO	BC	Range 2 Coast	92 M/3	51°03′	127°06′
Warner, Mount	MTN/MNT	BC	Lillooet	92 O/3	51°04′	123°12′
Warner No. 5, County of	MUN1/AZM1	AB	4-16-W4	82 H/8	49°17′	112°07′
Warpath River	RIV/CDE	MB		63 B/8	52°21′	98°25′
Warren	UNP/LNO	NS	Cumberland	21 H/16	45°51′	64°08′
Warren	UNP/LNO	ON	Sudbury	41 I/8	46°27′	80°18′
Warren	UNP/LNO	MB	28-13-1-W	62 I/4	50°08′	97°33′
Warren Brook	RIV/CDE	NS	Victoria	11 K/9	46°43′	60°21′
Warrender Bay	BAY/BAIE	NT	Mackenzie	77 A	68°19′	106°45′
Warrender, Cape	CAPE/CAP	NT	Franklin	48 E	74°28′	81°46′
Warren Grove	VILG/VILG	PE	Queens	11 L/6	46°16′	63°13′
Warren Landing	UNP/LNO	MB		63 H/12	53°42′	97°52′
Warren Point	CAPE/CAP	NT	Mackenzie	107 C	69°46′	132°18′
Warren River	RIV/CDE	NT	Mackenzie	66 E	65°24′	103°22′
Warrensville	UNP/LNO	AB	23-84-24-W5	84 C/5	56°18′	117°40′
Warrensville Centre	UNP/LNO	AB	29,30-84-23-W5	84 C/5	56°18′	117°37′
Warrington Bay	BAY/BAIE	NT	Franklin	88 G	75°10′	116°28′
Warsaw	UNP/LNO	ON	Peterborough	31 D/8	44°26′	78°08′
Warspite	VILG/VILG	AB	10-59-18-W4	83 I/2	54°06′	112°37′
Wartburg	UNP/LNO	ON	Perth	40 P/6	43°27′	81°02′
Wartime	UNP/LNO	SK	26-16-W3	72 N/1	51°13′	108°11′
War Time, Secteur	UNP/LNO	QC	Communauté urbaine de Montréal	31 H/12	45°31′	73°42′

NAME NOM	ENTITY ENTITÉ	LOC 1 LIEU 1	LOC 2 LIEU 2	MAP CARTE	POSITION LAT	LONG
Wart Lake	LAKE/LAC	ON	Algoma	41 N/1	47°10′	84°08′
Wart, The	MTN/MNT	BC	Kamloops Division Yale	92 H/16	49°54′	120°23′
Warwick	CITY/VIL1	QC	Arthabaska	21 E/13	45°56′	71°59′
Warwick	VILG/VILG	QC	Arthabaska	31 H/16	45°58′	72°00′
Warwick	MUN2/AZM2	ON	Lambton	40 P/4	43°01′	81°54′
Warwick	UNP/LNO	ON	Lambton	40 P/4	43°00′	81°56′
Warwick	UNP/LNO	AB	31-53-14-W4	83 H/9	53°38′	112°03′
Warwick, Cape	CAPE/CAP	NT	Franklin	25 H	61°35′	64°37′
Warwick Mountain	UNP/LNO	NS	Colchester	11 E/11	45°37′	63°23′
Warwick Seamount	SEAU/SMER	—		3000	48°04′	132°44′
Warwick Settlement	UNP/LNO	NB	Northumberland	21 I/13	46°53′	65°48′
Wasa	UNP/LNO	BC	Kootenay	82 G/13	49°47′	115°44′
Wasaga Beach	TOWN/VIL2	ON	Simcoe	41 A/9	44°31′	80°01′
Wasagaming	UNP/LNO	MB	30-19-18-W	62 J/12	50°40′	99°58′
Wasaksina Lake	LAKE/LAC	ON	Nipissing	31 L/13	46°56′	79°53′
Wasaw Creek	RIV/CDE	ON	Rainy River	52 C/11	48°42′	93°26′
Wasaw Lake	LAKE/LAC	ON	Rainy River	52 C/12	48°45′	93°35′
Wascana	UNP/LNO	SK	29-17-20-W2	72 I/7	50°27′	104°43′
Wascana Creek	RIV/CDE	SK	31-19-21-W2	72 I/10	50°39′	104°55′
Waseca	VILG/VILG	SK	32-47-24-W3	73 F/3	53°06′	109°28′
Wasekamio Lake	LAKE/LAC	SK		74 C/10	56°45′	108°45′
Wasel	UNP/LNO	AB	2-58-15-W4	83 H/16	53°59′	112°07′
Washabuck Bridge	UNP/LNO	NS	Victoria	11 K/2	46°01′	60°53′
Washabuck Centre	UNP/LNO	NS	Victoria	11 K/2	46°03′	60°48′
Washademoak	UNP/LNO	NB	Queens	21 H/13	45°54′	65°50′
Washademoak Lake	LAKE/LAC	NB	Queens	21 H/13	45°48′	65°58′
Washagami	UNP/LNO	ON	Sudbury	41 I/9	46°38′	80°26′
Washago	UNP/LNO	ON	Ontario	31 D/14	44°45′	79°20′
Washburn	UNP/LNO	ON	Frontenac	31 C/8	44°23′	76°20′
Washburn Lake	LAKE/LAC	NT	Franklin	77 E/4	70°03′	107°30′
Washburns Corners	UNP/LNO	ON	Leeds	31 C/9	44°38′	76°02′
Washicoutai, Archipel de	ISL/ÎLE	QC	Côte-Nord-du-Golfe-Saint-Laurent	12 K/3	50°10′	61°00′
Washicoutai, Lac	LAKE/LAC	QC	Minganie	12 K/7	50°22′	60°50′
Washi Lake	LAKE/LAC	ON	Kenora	42 M/6	51°24′	87°02′
Washington	UNP/LNO	ON	Oxford	40 P/7	43°18′	80°35′
Washington Bay	BAY/BAIE	NT	Franklin	67 A	68°48′	98°20′
Washington, Mount	MTN/MNT	BC	Comox	92 F/14	49°45′	125°18′
Washington Park	UNP/LNO	SK		72 I/7	50°28′	104°37′
Washington Point	CAPE/CAP	NT	Franklin	58 G	75°45′	94°17′
Washow Bay	UNP/LNO	MB	32-24-4-E	62 P/2	51°08′	96°59′
Washow Bay	BAY/BAIE	MB		62 P/7	51°23′	96°49′
Wasi Lake	LAKE/LAC	ON	Nipissing	31 L/3	46°09′	79°14′
Wasing	UNP/LNO	ON	Nipissing	31 L/3	46°05′	79°10′
Waskada	VILG/VILG	MB	5-2-25-W	62 F/2	49°06′	100°48′
Waskahigan River	RIV/CDE	AB	66-22-W5	83 K/14	54°45′	117°13′
Waskaiowaka Lake	LAKE/LAC	MB		64 A/9	56°33′	96°23′
Waskatenau	VILG/VILG	AB	16-59-19-W4	83 I/2	54°07′	112°47′
Waskéga, Baie de	BAY/BAIE	QC	La Vallée-de-la-Gatineau	31 N/7	47°28′	76°30′
Waskesiu Hills	MTN/MNT	SK		73 G/16	53°50′	106°25′
Waskesiu Lake	UNP/LNO	SK	57-1-W3	73 G/16	53°55′	106°05′
Waskesiu Lake	LAKE/LAC	SK		73 G/16	53°58′	106°12′
Waskesiu River	RIV/CDE	SK	10-59-26-W2	73 I/4	54°05′	105°48′
Waskwei Island	ISL/ÎLE	SK		74 C/8	56°22′	108°08′
Waspison Lake	LAKE/LAC	SK/MB		64 L/9	58°39′	102°03′
Wassegam Lake	LAKE/LAC	SK	61-2-W3	73 J/8	54°17′	106°14′
Wastina	UNP/LNO	AB	10-31-8-W4	72 M/11	51°39′	111°03′
Waswanipi	VILG/VILG	QC	Jamésie	32 F/9	49°44′	76°10′
Waswanipi, Lac	LAKE/LAC	QC	Jamésie	32 F/9	49°34′	76°29′
Waswanipi, Rivière	RIV/CDE	QC	Jamésie	32 F/14	49°53′	77°15′
Watabeag	UNP/LNO	ON	Cochrane	42 A/10	48°34′	80°33′
Watabeag Lake	LAKE/LAC	ON	Timiskaming	42 A/7	48°15′	80°33′
Watabeag River	RIV/CDE	ON	Cochrane	42 A/10	48°34′	80°31′
Watagheistic, Île	ISL/ÎLE	QC	Côte-Nord-du-Golfe-Saint-Laurent	12 J/5	50°23′	59°49′
Wataiabei River	RIV/CDE	ON	Cochrane	42 K/15	50°57′	84°40′
Watapi Lake	LAKE/LAC	SK	73-24-W3	73 N/5	55°18′	109°35′
Watch Lake	LAKE/LAC	BC	Lillooet	92 P/6	51°28′	121°06′
Watchman Island	ISL/ÎLE	NF		14 L/1	58°12′	62°07′
Watcomb	UNP/LNO	ON	Kenora	52 G/14	49°50′	91°20′
Watcomb Lake	LAKE/LAC	ON	Kenora	52 G/14	49°51′	91°19′
Waterborough	UNP/LNO	NB	Queens	21 G/16	45°55′	66°00′
Waterborough	GEOG/GÉOG	NB	Queens	21 I/4	46°07′	65°45′
Waterbury Lake	LAKE/LAC	SK		74 I/1	58°10′	104°22′
Watercombe	UNP/LNO	ON	Lennox and Addington	31 C/3	44°07′	77°04′
Waterdown	UNP/LNO	ON	Wentworth	30 M/5	43°20′	79°53′
Waterdown North	UNP/LNO	ON	Wentworth	30 M/5	43°21′	79°53′

NAME NOM	ENTITY ENTITÉ	LOC 1 LIEU 1	LOC 2 LIEU 2	MAP CARTE	POSITION LAT	LONG
Waterfall	UNP/LNO	ON	Sudbury	41 I/7	46°19′	80°50′
Waterford	UNP/LNO	PE	Prince	21 I/16	46°56′	64°10′
Waterford	UNP/LNO	NS	Digby	21 A/12	44°34′	65°58′
Waterford	UNP/LNO	NB	Kings	21 H/11	45°41′	65°22′
Waterford	UNP/LNO	ON	Norfolk	40 I/16	42°56′	80°17′
Waterford	GEOG/GÉOG	NB	Kings	21 H/11	45°40′	65°18′
Waterfound River	RIV/CDE	SK		74 I/16	58°45′	104°06′
Waterhen	UNP/LNO	MB	16-33-15-W	62 O/13	51°50′	99°33′
Waterhen 45	IR/RI	MB		62 O/13	51°57′	99°36′
Waterhen 130	IR/RI	SK		73 K/8	54°28′	108°20′
Waterhen Lake	UNP/LNO	SK		73 K/9	54°31′	108°25′
Waterhen Lake	LAKE/LAC	MB		63 B/4	52°06′	99°34′
Waterhen Lake	LAKE/LAC	SK	57-3-W2	63 E/16	53°54′	102°25′
Waterhen Lake	LAKE/LAC	SK		73 K/8	54°28′	108°25′
Waterhen Reserve	UNP/LNO	MB	36,6-34,35-15,16-W	62 O/13	51°58′	99°36′
Waterhen River	RIV/CDE	SK	65-12-W3	73 J/12	54°38′	107°47′
Waterhole	UNP/LNO	AB	9-81-3-W6	84 D/1	56°01′	118°24′
Watering Chute	UNP/LNO	NF		1 N/14	47°51′	53°23′
Waterloo	CITY/VIL1	QC	La Haute-Yamaska	31 H/7	45°21′	72°31′
Waterloo	CITY/VIL1	ON	Waterloo	40 P/7	43°28′	80°31′
Waterloo	MUN1/AZM1	ON	Waterloo	40 P/7	43°30′	80°30′
Waterloo	UNP/LNO	NS	Lunenburg	21 A/7	44°20′	64°41′
Waterloo	GEOG/GÉOG	ON		40 P/7	43°30′	80°30′
Waterloo Corner	UNP/LNO	NB	Queens	21 H/13	45°48′	65°49′
Waterloo Lake	LAKE/LAC	NS	Annapolis	21 A/10	44°44′	64°59′
Waternish	UNP/LNO	NS	Guysborough	11 E/1	45°12′	62°01′
Waterside	UNP/LNO	PE	Queens	11 L/2	46°12′	62°57′
Waterside	UNP/LNO	NS	Pictou	11 E/15	45°45′	62°46′
Waterside	UNP/LNO	NB	Albert	21 H/10	45°38′	64°50′
Waters Island	ISL/ÎLE	NT	Keewatin	44 P	59°03′	80°36′
Waterton	UNP/LNO	ON	Leeds	31 B/5	44°26′	75°57′
Waterton-Glacier International Peace Park	PARK/PARC	AB		82 H/4	49°00′	113°50′
Waterton-Glacier International Peace Park World Heritage Site - also-aussi - Parc international de la paix Waterton-Glacier, Site du patrimoine mondial du	PARK/PARC	AB		82 H/4	49°00′	113°50′
Waterton Lakes	LAKE/LAC	AB	1-29,30-W4	82 H/4	49°03′	113°54′
Waterton Lakes National Park - also-aussi - Lacs-Waterton, Parc national des	PARK/PARC	AB		82 H/4	49°05′	113°52′
Waterton Park	UNP/LNO	AB	23-1-30-W4	82 H/4	49°03′	113°55′
Waterton Reservoir	LAKE/LAC	AB	4-28-W4	82 H/5	49°18′	113°41′
Waterton River	RIV/CDE	AB	7-25-W4	82 H/11	49°32′	113°16′
Watertown	UNP/LNO	SK	28-24-W2	72 P/6	51°23′	105°16′
Watervale	UNP/LNO	PE	Queens	11 L/7	46°16′	62°54′
Watervale	UNP/LNO	NS	Pictou	11 E/7	45°29′	62°55′
Water Valley	UNP/LNO	AB	27-29-5-W5	82 O/10	51°30′	114°36′
Waterville	CITY/VIL1	QC	Sherbrooke	21 E/5	45°16′	71°54′
Waterville	UNP/LNO	NF		2 C/4	48°12′	53°47′
Waterville	UNP/LNO	NS	Kings	21 H/2	45°03′	64°41′
Waterville	UNP/LNO	NB	Sunbury	21 G/15	45°47′	66°31′
Waterville	UNP/LNO	NB	Carleton	21 J/5	46°16′	67°35′
Watford	VILG/VILG	ON	Lambton	40 I/13	42°57′	81°53′
Watford	UNP/LNO	NS	Lunenburg	21 A/10	44°33′	64°41′
Wathaman Lake	LAKE/LAC	SK		64 D/13	56°55′	103°43′
Wathaman River	RIV/CDE	SK		64 E/7	57°16′	102°59′
Watino	UNP/LNO	AB	35-77-24-W5	83 N/12	55°43′	117°37′
Watistiguam River	RIV/CDE	ON	Cochrane	42 K/3	50°13′	85°13′
Watopeka, Rivière	RIV/CDE	QC	Le Val-Saint-François	31 H/9	45°34′	72°00′
Watrous	TOWN/VIL2	SK	22-31-25-W2	72 P/11	51°40′	105°28′
Watshishou, Lac	LAKE/LAC	QC	Minganie	12 L/10	50°40′	62°31′
Watshishou, Rivière	RIV/CDE	QC	Minganie	12 L/7	50°16′	62°41′
Watson	TOWN/VIL2	SK	28-36-18-W2	73 A/2	52°07′	104°31′
Watson	UNP/LNO	BC	Range 5 Coast	93 K/3	54°09′	125°32′
Watson	UNP/LNO	YT		105 D/2	60°06′	134°50′
Watson Bar Creek	RIV/CDE	BC	Lillooet	92 O/1	51°07′	122°01′
Watson Island	UNP/LNO	BC	Range 5 Coast	103 J/1	54°14′	130°18′
Watson, Lac	LAKE/LAC	QC	Témiscamingue	31 M/1	47°02′	78°16′
Watson Lake	TOWN/VIL2	YT		105 A/2	60°04′	128°42′
Watson Lake	LAKE/LAC	YT		105 A/2	60°06′	128°49′
Watson Point	CAPE/CAP	MB		54 K/13	58°47′	93°32′
Watson River	RIV/CDE	YT		105 D/2	60°11′	134°44′
Watsons	UNP/LNO	ON	Victoria	31 D/10	44°44′	78°41′
Watsons Corners	UNP/LNO	ON	Lanark	31 F/1	45°01′	76°28′
Watson Settlement	UNP/LNO	NB	Carleton	21 J/4	46°11′	67°45′
Watt	UNP/LNO	NB	Charlotte	21 G/6	45°25′	67°10′
Watta 25	IR/RI	BC	Clayoquot	92 E/8	49°27′	126°02′
Watta Lake	LAKE/LAC	NT	Mackenzie	85 I	62°15′	113°04′
Wattenwyle	UNP/LNO	ON	Parry Sound	31 E/13	45°48′	79°35′
Watterson Corners	UNP/LNO	ON	Carleton	31 G/4	45°12′	75°42′

NAME NOM	ENTITY ENTITÉ	LOC 1 LIEU 1	LOC 2 LIEU 2	MAP CARTE	POSITION	
					LAT	LONG
Watterson Lake	LAKE/LAC	NT	Keewatin	65 G	61°14′	99°25′
Watt Junction	UNP/LNO	NB	Charlotte	21 G/6	45°25′	67°10′
Watt Lake	LAKE/LAC	AB	54-14-W4	73 E/12	53°42′	111°56′
Watt, Mount	MTN/MNT	AB	111-21-W5	84 K/11	58°38′	117°29′
Watts	UNP/LNO	AB	17-31-15-W4	82 P/9	51°40′	112°05′
Watts Bay	BAY/BAIE	NT	Franklin	25 J	62°41′	66°55′
Watt Section Sheet Harbour	UNP/LNO	NS	Halifax	11 D/16	44°54′	62°29′
Wattsview	UNP/LNO	MB	23-16-28-W	62 K/6	50°23′	101°14′
Waubamik	UNP/LNO	ON	Parry Sound	41 H/8	45°27′	80°01′
Waubaushene	UNP/LNO	ON	Simcoe	31 D/13	44°45′	79°42′
Waubuno	UNP/LNO	ON	Lambton	40 J/16	42°47′	82°20′
Waubuno Channel	CHAN/CHEN	ON	Parry Sound	41 H/1	45°11′	80°14′
Waubuno Creek	RIV/CDE	ON	Middlesex	40 I/14	42°59′	81°08′
Wauchope	UNP/LNO	SK	28-7-33-W	62 F/12	49°36′	101°54′
Waudby	UNP/LNO	ON	Grey	41 A/7	44°17′	80°47′
Waugh	UNP/LNO	MB		52 E/11	49°38′	95°12′
Waugh	UNP/LNO	AB	19-58-23-W4	83 I/3	54°02′	113°25′
Waugh Creek	RIV/CDE	YT		116 A/14	64°55′	137°02′
Waughs River	UNP/LNO	NS	Colchester	11 E/11	45°42′	63°15′
Waughs River	RIV/CDE	NS	Colchester	11 E/11	45°44′	63°18′
Wauklahegan Lake	LAKE/LAC	NB	York	21 G/11	45°36′	67°22′
Waukwaas Creek	RIV/CDE	BC	Rupert	92 L/11	50°35′	127°25′
Waulp 10	IR/RI	BC	Cassiar	93 M/5	55°29′	127°38′
Waump 16	IR/RI	BC	Range 2 Coast	92 M/2	51°11′	126°55′
Waupoos	UNP/LNO	ON	Prince Edward	31 C/2	44°00′	77°00′
Waupoos East	UNP/LNO	ON	Prince Edward	31 C/2	44°01′	76°58′
Waupoos Island	UNP/LNO	ON	Prince Edward	30 N/15	44°00′	76°59′
Waupoos Island	ISL/ÎLE	ON	Prince Edward	30 N/15	43°59′	76°58′
Wavecrest	UNP/LNO	ON	Welland	30 L/14	42°53′	79°01′
Wavell	UNP/LNO	ON	Cochrane	42 A/8	48°22′	80°14′
Waverley	UNP/LNO	NS	Halifax	11 D/13	44°47′	63°36′
Waverley	UNP/LNO	ON	Simcoe	31 D/12	44°38′	79°49′
Waverley	UNP/LNO	MB		62 G/13	49°50′	99°59′
Waverley Heights	UNP/LNO	MB		62 H/14	49°48′	97°10′
Waverley No. 44	MUN2/AZM2	SK		72 G/7	49°35′	106°35′
Waverly Beach	UNP/LNO	ON	Welland	30 L/15	42°53′	78°56′
Wavey Creek	RIV/CDE	MB	24-15-4-E	62 I/7	50°17′	96°55′
Wavy Lake	LAKE/LAC	ON	Sudbury	41 I/6	46°18′	81°06′
Wavy Lake	LAKE/LAC	AB	45-15-W4	83 A/16	52°52′	112°04′
Wawa	UNP/LNO	ON	Algoma	41 N/15	47°59′	84°47′
Wawagigamau River	RIV/CDE	ON	Cochrane	42 I/10	50°36′	80°55′
Wawagosic, Rivière	RIV/CDE	QC	Jamésie	32 E/14	49°58′	79°06′
Wawaitin Falls	UNP/LNO	ON	Cochrane	42 A/6	48°20′	81°29′
Wawaitin Falls	FALL/CHUT	ON	Timiskaming	42 A/6	48°21′	81°30′
Wawa, Lac	LAKE/LAC	QC	Jamésie	33 K/7	54°17′	76°50′
Wawanesa	VILG/VILG	MB	26-7-17-W	62 G/12	49°36′	99°41′
Wawang Lake	LAKE/LAC	ON	Thunder Bay	52 G/7	49°25′	90°34′
Wawaw Pimi Emichinanuch	UNP/LNO	QC	Jamésie	33 D/10	52°32′	78°38′
Wawbewawa	UNP/LNO	ON	Timiskaming	31 M/13	47°53′	79°54′
Waweig	UNP/LNO	NB	Charlotte	21 G/6	45°15′	67°07′
Waweig Lake	LAKE/LAC	ON	Thunder Bay	52 I/3	50°08′	89°05′
Wawken No. 93	MUN2/AZM2	SK		62 E/16	49°55′	102°10′
Wawong Lake	LAKE/LAC	ON	Thunder Bay	42 L/2	50°14′	86°59′
Wawota	TOWN/VIL2	SK	13-11-1-W2	62 E/16	49°54′	102°02′
Wawwwat'l 12	IR/RI	BC	Range 2 Coast	92 M/2	51°13′	126°40′
Wayagamac, Lac	LAKE/LAC	QC	Le Haut-Saint-Maurice	31 P/7	47°22′	72°39′
Way Bay	BAY/BAIE	NF		23 H/11	53°36′	65°24′
Wayerton	UNP/LNO	NB	Northumberland	21 P/4	47°08′	65°50′
Wayland	UNP/LNO	ON	Sudbury	42 B/4	48°01′	83°49′
Wayne	UNP/LNO	AB	7-28-19-W4	82 P/7	51°23′	112°39′
Wayow Lake	LAKE/LAC	SK		64 M/13	59°54′	103°55′
Ways Mills	UNP/LNO	QC	Coaticook	21 E/4	45°06′	71°58′
Waywayseecappo	UNP/LNO	MB	14-20-25-W	62 K/10	50°43′	100°53′
Weagamow Lake	UNP/LNO	ON	Kenora	53 B/14	52°57′	91°20′
Weagamow Lake	LAKE/LAC	ON	Kenora	53 B/14	52°53′	91°22′
Weagamow Lake 87	IR/RI	ON	Kenora	53 B/14	52°57′	91°16′
Weald	UNP/LNO	AB	51-19-W5	83 F/7	53°23′	116°47′
Weart, Mount	MTN/MNT	BC	New Westminster	92 J/2	50°10′	122°47′
Weasel Creek	UNP/LNO	AB	9-60-20-W4	83 I/2	54°11′	112°55′
Weatherall Bay	BAY/BAIE	NT	Franklin	79 A	76°00′	107°15′
Weaver	UNP/LNO	NB	Victoria	21 J/14	46°56′	67°24′
Weaver Lake	LAKE/LAC	ON	Thunder Bay	52 G/9	49°34′	90°10′
Weaver Lake	LAKE/LAC	MB		63 A/15	52°46′	96°33′
Weaver Lake	LAKE/LAC	BC	New Westminster	92 H/5	49°21′	121°52′
Weaver Settlement	UNP/LNO	NS	Digby	21 A/5	44°23′	65°58′

NAME NOM	ENTITY ENTITÉ	LOC 1 LIEU 1	LOC 2 LIEU 2	MAP CARTE	POSITION LAT	LONG
Weaver Siding	UNP/LNO	NB	Northumberland	21 I/12	46°37'	65°58'
Webb	VILG/VILG	SK	24-14-17-W3	72 K/1	50°11'	108°12'
Webb Bay	BAY/BAIE	NF		14 C/13	56°46'	61°45'
Webber Lake	LAKE/LAC	MB		53 L/8	54°29'	94°00'
Webber Pond	LAKE/LAC	NF		2 D/11	48°42'	55°21'
Webb No. 138	MUN2/AZM2	SK		72 K/1	50°05'	108°15'
Webb Point	CAPE/CAP	NT	Franklin	68 B	72°44'	102°42'
Webbwood	TOWN/VIL2	ON	Sudbury	41 I/5	46°16'	81°53'
Webeck Island	ISL/ÎLE	NF		13 J/16	54°55'	58°03'
Webequie	UNP/LNO	ON	Kenora	43 D/14	52°59'	87°21'
Weber Bay	BAY/BAIE	SK		73 O/3	55°10'	107°27'
Weber, Mount	MTN/MNT	BC	Cassiar	103 P/10	55°32'	128°31'
Weberville	UNP/LNO	AB	24-84-22-W5	84 C/6	56°17'	117°19'
Webster	UNP/LNO	ON	Kenora	52 K/1	50°06'	92°21'
Webster	UNP/LNO	AB	27-74-5-W6	83 M/7	55°26'	118°41'
Webster Creek	RIV/CDE	BC	Cariboo	93 B/7	52°30'	122°44'
Webster Creek 5	IR/RI	BC	Cariboo	93 B/7	52°29'	122°39'
Websters Corner	UNP/LNO	PE	Queens	11 L/7	46°18'	62°57'
Websters Corner	UNP/LNO	NS	Pictou	11 E/7	45°29'	62°31'
Websters Corners	UNP/LNO	BC	New Westminster	92 G/2	49°13'	122°31'
Websterville	UNP/LNO	ON	Simcoe	41 A/8	44°20'	80°08'
Wecho Lake	LAKE/LAC	NT	Mackenzie	85 P	63°58'	113°50'
Wecho River	RIV/CDE	NT	Mackenzie	85 P	63°07'	113°35'
Wedeene	UNP/LNO	BC	Range 5 Coast	103 I/2	54°09'	128°39'
Wedge	UNP/LNO	BC	New Westminster	92 J/2	50°10'	122°55'
Wedge Mountain	MTN/MNT	BC	New Westminster	92 J/2	50°08'	122°48'
Wedge Point	CAPE/CAP	NS	Yarmouth	20 P/12	43°42'	65°59'
Wedgeport	UNP/LNO	NS	Yarmouth	20 P/12	43°44'	65°59'
Wedgewood	UNP/LNO	NS	Halifax	11 D/12	44°41'	63°40'
Wedgewood Park	UNP/LNO	NF		1 N/10	47°36'	53°43'
Wedgwood	UNP/LNO	BC	Cariboo	93 G/13	54°00'	123°30'
Weed Creek	UNP/LNO	AB	15-48-1-W5	83 G/1	53°08'	114°03'
Weedon	VILG/VILG	QC	Le Haut-Saint-François	21 E/11	45°42'	71°27'
Weedon Centre	TOWN/VIL2	QC	Le Haut-Saint-François	21 E/11	45°42'	71°28'
Weedon Lake	LAKE/LAC	BC	Cariboo	93 J/11	54°39'	123°02'
Weed Point	CAPE/CAP	MB	14-27-10-W	62 O/7	51°19'	98°45'
Weekes	VILG/VILG	SK	36-41-7-W2	63 D/10	52°34'	102°52'
Weeks Bay	BAY/BAIE	NT	Franklin	36 P	67°51'	72°47'
Weeks Road	UNP/LNO	NB	Charlotte	21 G/6	45°25'	67°13'
Weesakachak	UNP/LNO	MB		53 F/12	53°45'	93°48'
Wees Beach	UNP/LNO	ON	Lambton	40 O/1	43°01'	82°24'
Weeteeam 3	IR/RI	BC	Range 3 Coast	103 A/11	52°32'	129°03'
Weeteeam Bay	BAY/BAIE	BC	Range 3 Coast	103 A/11	52°31'	129°01'
Wee Too Beach	VILG/VILG	SK	4,9-23-23-W2	72 I/14	50°56'	105°10'
Wee-Too Beach - see-voir - Wee Too Beach	UNP/LNO	SK		72 I/14	50°56'	105°10'
Weewanie	UNP/LNO	BC	Range 4 Coast	103 H/10	53°41'	128°47'
Weggs Island	ISL/ÎLE	NT	Franklin	35 I	62°19'	73°04'
Weiden	UNP/LNO	MB	31-28-16-W	62 O/5	51°27'	99°43'
Weidmann	UNP/LNO	ON	Lambton	40 J/16	42°49'	82°00'
Weikwabinonaw Lake	LAKE/LAC	ON	Thunder Bay	52 B/8	48°19'	90°23'
Weir	UNP/LNO	QC	Les Laurentides	31 G/15	45°57'	74°33'
Weirdale	VILG/VILG	SK	31-51-22-W2	73 H/6	53°27'	105°15'
Weir River	UNP/LNO	MB	19-90-22-E	54 D/16	56°49'	94°06'
Weir River	RIV/CDE	MB	91-5-E2	54 C/14	56°55'	93°21'
Weir's Pond	LAKE/LAC	NF		2 E/1	49°13'	54°23'
Weirstead	UNP/LNO	QC	Pontiac	31 F/9	45°36'	76°22'
Weisbord Acres	UNP/LNO	QC	La Rivière-du-Nord	31 G/16	45°55'	74°03'
Weissenburg	UNP/LNO	ON	Waterloo	40 P/9	43°34'	80°24'
Weissener Lake	LAKE/LAC	BC	Cassiar	94 F/12	57°45'	125°45'
Weissener Lake 3	IR/RI	BC	Cassiar	94 F/12	57°44'	125°45'
Weitzel Lake	LAKE/LAC	SK		74 G/10	57°42'	106°42'
Wekellals 15	IR/RI	BC	Range 4 Coast	93 E/4	53°12'	127°49'
Wekusko	UNP/LNO	MB	1-64-16-W	63 J/12	54°30'	99°45'
Wekusko Lake	LAKE/LAC	MB		63 J/13	54°46'	99°52'
Wekwâgam	UNP/LNO	QC	Vallée-de-l'Or	31 N/14	47°49'	77°20'
Wekweyaukastik River	RIV/CDE	ON	Cochrane	42 I/10	50°43'	80°56'
Welbeck	UNP/LNO	ON	Grey	41 A/7	44°16'	80°54'
Welby	UNP/LNO	SK	9-18-30-W	62 K/12	50°32'	101°34'
Welch	UNP/LNO	NB	Carleton	21 J/11	46°37'	67°14'
Welch Cove	UNP/LNO	NB	Charlotte	21 G/1	45°05'	66°28'
Welch Peak	MTN/MNT	BC	Yale Division Yale	92 H/4	49°09'	121°36'
Welcome	UNP/LNO	ON	Durham	30 M/16	43°58'	78°21'
Welcome Beach	UNP/LNO	BC	New Westminster	92 G/5	49°29'	123°54'
Welcome Islands	ISL/ÎLE	ON	Thunder Bay	52 A/6	48°22'	89°08'
Welcome Lake	LAKE/LAC	ON	Sudbury	41 P/3	47°13'	81°02'

NAME NOM	ENTITY ENTITÉ	LOC 1 LIEU 1	LOC 2 LIEU 2	MAP CARTE	POSITION LAT	LONG
Weld, Cape	CAPE/CAP	NT	Franklin	38 A	72°35'	75°46'
Weldfield	UNP/LNO	NB	Northumberland	21 I/14	46°57'	65°25'
Weldford	GEOG/GÉOG	NB	Kent	21 I/11	46°30'	65°05'
Weld Harbour	BAY/BAIE	NT	Franklin	67 H	71°04'	96°25'
Weldon	VILG/VILG	SK	33-46-22-W2	73 H/3	53°01'	105°08'
Weldon	UNP/LNO	NB	Albert	21 H/15	45°57'	64°40'
Weldon	UNP/LNO	NB	Westmorland	21 I/2	46°06'	64°49'
Welker Guyot	SEAU/SMER	—		5.03	55°07'	140°20'
Welland	CITY/VIL1	ON	Welland	30 L/14	42°59'	79°15'
Welland	GEOG/GÉOG	ON	Welland	30 L/14	43°00'	79°15'
Welland Canal	MISC/DIV	ON	Welland	30 M/3	43°03'	79°13'
Wellandport	UNP/LNO	ON	Lincoln	30 M/3	43°00'	79°29'
Welland River	RIV/CDE	ON	Welland	30 M/3	43°04'	79°03'
Welland South	UNP/LNO	ON	Welland	30 L/14	42°58'	79°16'
Wellbore Channel	CHAN/CHEN	BC	Range 1 Coast	92 K/5	50°27'	125°45'
Wellburn	UNP/LNO	ON	Middlesex	40 P/3	43°11'	81°09'
Weller	UNP/LNO	ON	Frontenac	31 C/2	44°14'	76°30'
Weller Park	UNP/LNO	ON	Lincoln	30 M/3	43°14'	79°13'
Wellers Bay	BAY/BAIE	ON	Northumberland	31 C/4	44°01'	77°36'
Wellesley	MUN2/AZM2	ON	Waterloo	40 P/10	43°33'	80°43'
Wellesley	UNP/LNO	ON	Waterloo	40 P/7	43°28'	80°45'
Wellesley Lake	LAKE/LAC	YT		115 J/5	62°22'	139°50'
Wellesley Park	UNP/LNO	SK		72 I/5	50°23'	105°32'
Welling	UNP/LNO	AB	17-6-21-W4	82 H/7	49°28'	112°47'
Wellington	VILG/VILG	PE	Prince	21 I/8	46°27'	64°00'
Wellington	VILG/VILG	ON	Prince Edward	30 N/14	43°57'	77°21'
Wellington	MUN1/AZM1	ON	Wellington	40 P/15	43°50'	80°30'
Wellington	UNP/LNO	PE	Prince	21 I/8	46°27'	64°00'
Wellington	UNP/LNO	NS	Halifax	11 D/13	44°52'	63°37'
Wellington	UNP/LNO	NS	Queens	21 A/7	44°18'	64°49'
Wellington	UNP/LNO	NS	Yarmouth	20 O/16	43°55'	66°06'
Wellington	UNP/LNO	BC	Wellington	92 F/1	49°12'	124°02'
Wellington	GEOG/GÉOG	NB	Kent	21 I/10	46°30'	64°44'
Wellington	GEOG/GÉOG	ON		40 P/15	43°50'	80°30'
Wellington Bay	BAY/BAIE	NT	Franklin	77 D	69°20'	106°35'
Wellington Centre	UNP/LNO	PE	Prince	11 L/5	46°29'	63°59'
Wellington Channel	CHAN/CHEN	NT	Franklin	58 G	75°28'	93°12'
Wellington Creek	RIV/CDE	ON	Cochrane	42 G/8	49°20'	82°02'
Wellington Land District	GEOG/GÉOG	BC		92 F	49°13'	124°02'
Wellington No. 97	MUN2/AZM2	SK		62 E/13	49°55'	103°50'
Wellington Station	UNP/LNO	NS	Halifax	11 D/13	44°52'	63°37'
Wellington Strait	CHAN/CHEN	NT	Franklin	57 C	69°28'	95°59'
Wellman	UNP/LNO	ON	Hastings	31 C/5	44°20'	77°38'
Wellman Lake	LAKE/LAC	MB	33-25-W	62 N/15	51°49'	100°53'
Wellmans Cove	UNP/LNO	NF		2 E/12	49°34'	55°48'
Wells	UNP/LNO	NB	Kings	21 H/5	45°23'	65°55'
Wells	UNP/LNO	BC	Cariboo	93 H/4	53°06'	121°34'
Wells Cove	BAY/BAIE	BC	Queen Charlotte	103 B/5	52°21'	131°33'
Wells Lake	LAKE/LAC	MB		64 F/2	57°14'	101°00'
Wells Lake	LAKE/LAC	SK	68-5-W2	63 L/15	54°53'	102°38'
Wells Lake	LAKE/LAC	SK	44-27-W3	73 C/13	52°50'	109°51'
Wells Passage	CHAN/CHEN	BC	Range 1 Coast	92 L/15	50°51'	126°55'
Wellwood	UNP/LNO	MB	28-12-14-W	62 J/3	50°02'	99°20'
Welsford	UNP/LNO	NS	Pictou	11 E/11	45°44'	63°03'
Welsford	UNP/LNO	NS	Kings	21 H/2	45°05'	64°46'
Welsford	UNP/LNO	NB	Queens	21 G/8	45°27'	66°20'
Welsford, Cape	CAPE/CAP	NT	Keewatin	46 F	65°29'	84°32'
Welsh	UNP/LNO	ON	Lanark	31 C/16	44°57'	76°03'
Welsh	UNP/LNO	ON	Cochrane	42 A/10	48°43'	80°47'
Welshpool	UNP/LNO	NB	Charlotte	21 B/15	44°53'	66°57'
Welshtown	UNP/LNO	NS	Shelburne	20 P/14	43°50'	65°23'
Welshtown Lake	LAKE/LAC	NS	Shelburne	20 P/14	43°51'	65°24'
Welton Landing	UNP/LNO	NS	Kings	21 A/15	44°59'	64°32'
Weltons Corner	UNP/LNO	NS	Kings	21 H/2	45°03'	64°53'
Welwyn	VILG/VILG	SK	35-15-30-W	62 K/5	50°19'	101°31'
Wembley	TOWN/VIL2	AB	15-71-8-W6	83 M/3	55°09'	119°08'
Wemindji	VILG/VILG	QC	Jamésie	33 D/15	52°55'	78°47'
Wemitogôjî Omîgiwâm	UNP/LNO	QC	Jamésie	32 F/3	49°04'	77°24'
Wemyss	UNP/LNO	ON	Lanark	31 C/16	44°52'	76°23'
Wenasaga River	RIV/CDE	ON	Kenora	52 K/11	50°38'	93°10'
Wendake Beach	UNP/LNO	ON	Simcoe	31 D/12	44°38'	79°59'
Wendigo Beach	UNP/LNO	MB	20-16-12-E	52 L/5	50°21'	95°55'
Wendigo Lake	UNP/LNO	ON	Timiskaming	31 M/13	47°52'	79°46'
Wendover	UNP/LNO	ON	Prescott	31 G/11	45°34'	75°07'
Wenebegon Lake	LAKE/LAC	ON	Sudbury	41 O/6	47°23'	83°06'

NAME NOM	ENTITY ENTITÉ	LOC 1 LIEU 1	LOC 2 LIEU 2	MAP CARTE	POSITION LAT	LONG
Wenebegon River	RIV/CDE	ON	Algoma	41 J/14	46°53′	83°12′
Weneez	UNP/LNO	BC	Range 4 Coast	93 G/13	53°58′	123°59′
Wenham Valley	UNP/LNO	AB	10-47-3-W5	83 G/1	53°03′	114°20′
Wentworth	VILG/VILG	QC	Argenteuil	31 G/16	45°48′	74°22′
Wentworth	UNP/LNO	NS	Cumberland	11 E/12	45°39′	63°33′
Wentworth	GEOG/GÉOG	ON		30 M/4	43°15′	80°00′
Wentworth Centre	UNP/LNO	NS	Cumberland	11 E/12	45°40′	63°33′
Wentworth Creek	UNP/LNO	NS	Hants	21 A/16	44°59′	64°05′
Wentworth Lake	LAKE/LAC	NS	Digby	21 A/4	44°11′	65°56′
Wentworth-Nord	VILG/VILG	QC	Les Pays-d'en-Haut	31 G/16	45°51′	74°27′
Wentworth Station	UNP/LNO	NS	Cumberland	11 E/12	45°37′	63°34′
Wentworth Valley	UNP/LNO	NS	Cumberland	11 E/12	45°36′	63°34′
Wentzel Lake	LAKE/LAC	AB	115-3-W5	84 O/1	59°02′	114°28′
Wentzel Lake	LAKE/LAC	NT	Mackenzie	86 J	66°09′	115°50′
Wentzells Lake	UNP/LNO	NS	Lunenburg	21 A/7	44°29′	64°38′
Wentzel River	RIV/CDE	AB	110-4-W5	84 J/10	58°33′	114°31′
Wentzel River	RIV/CDE	NT	Mackenzie	76 M	67°53′	110°39′
Wepusko Bay	BAY/BAIE	SK		64 E/2	57°07′	102°40′
Werkinellek 11	IR/RI	BC	Range 2 Coast	102 P/16	51°56′	128°29′
Wernecke	UNP/LNO	YT		105 M/14	63°57′	135°16′
Wernecke Mountains	MTN/MNT	YT		106 D/16	64°50′	134°15′
Werner Lake	UNP/LNO	ON	Kenora	52 L/7	50°28′	94°55′
Wernham Lake	LAKE/LAC	MB		64 A/14	56°55′	97°26′
Weslemkoon	UNP/LNO	ON	Lennox and Addington	31 C/14	44°59′	77°25′
Weslemkoon Lake	LAKE/LAC	ON	Lennox and Addington	31 F/3	45°02′	77°25′
Wesley	UNP/LNO	ON	Lennox and Addington	31 C/7	44°22′	76°55′
Wesley	UNP/LNO	ON	Dufferin	41 A/1	44°00′	80°25′
Wesley Corners	UNP/LNO	ON	York	31 D/3	44°01′	79°24′
Wesley Creek	UNP/LNO	AB	31-83-20-W5	84 C/3	56°15′	117°09′
Wesleyville	UNP/LNO	NF		2 F/4	49°09′	53°34′
Wesleyville	UNP/LNO	ON	Durham	30 M/16	43°55′	78°25′
Wesp, Lac	LAKE/LAC	QC	Kativik	34 P/11	59°37′	73°20′
Wessex	UNP/LNO	AB	26-29-1-W5	82 O/9	51°31′	114°03′
Wessonneau, Rivière	RIV/CDE	QC	Le Haut-Saint-Maurice	31 P/2	47°13′	72°54′
West Advocate	UNP/LNO	NS	Cumberland	21 H/7	45°21′	64°49′
West Alba	UNP/LNO	NS	Inverness	11 F/14	45°54′	61°01′
West Amherst	UNP/LNO	NS	Cumberland	21 H/16	45°49′	64°15′
West Apple River	UNP/LNO	NS	Cumberland	21 H/7	45°28′	64°50′
West Arichat	UNP/LNO	NS	Richmond	11 F/11	45°31′	61°05′
West Arm	UNP/LNO	ON	Sudbury	41 I/8	46°16′	80°26′
West Arm	BAY/BAIE	NF		2 E/6	49°23′	55°25′
West Arm	BAY/BAIE	ON	Sudbury	41 I/8	46°16′	80°25′
West Arm Brook	RIV/CDE	NF		2 E/6	49°21′	55°28′
West Arm Tracadie	UNP/LNO	NS	Antigonish	11 F/12	45°38′	61°41′
West Arrowwood Creek	RIV/CDE	AB	9-21-23-W4	82 I/14	50°46′	113°08′
West Baccaro	UNP/LNO	NS	Shelburne	20 P/6	43°28′	65°29′
Westbank	UNP/LNO	BC	Osoyoos Division Yale	82 E/13	49°50′	119°38′
West Baptiste	VILG/VILG	AB	66,67-24-W4	83 I/13	54°45′	113°34′
West Bathurst	UNP/LNO	NB	Gloucester	21 P/12	47°37′	65°40′
West Bay	UNP/LNO	NF		13 I/3	54°08′	57°22′
West Bay	UNP/LNO	NF		12 B/10	48°37′	58°58′
West Bay	UNP/LNO	NF		12 B/10	48°38′	58°58′
West Bay	UNP/LNO	NS	Inverness	11 F/11	45°43′	61°10′
West Bay	UNP/LNO	NS	Cumberland	21 H/8	45°22′	64°23′
West Bay	UNP/LNO	ON	Manitoulin	41 G/16	45°50′	82°10′
West Bay	UNP/LNO	BC	New Westminster	92 G/6	49°20′	123°12′
West Bay	BAY/BAIE	NF		12 B/10	48°37′	58°54′
West Bay	BAY/BAIE	NS	Inverness	11 F/14	45°48′	61°03′
West Bay	BAY/BAIE	ON	Nipissing	41 I/1	46°14′	80°13′
West Bay	BAY/BAIE	ON	Manitoulin	41 I/4	46°04′	81°40′
West Bay	BAY/BAIE	ON	Manitoulin	41 G/16	45°48′	82°12′
West Bay 22	IR/RI	ON	Manitoulin	41 G/16	45°49′	82°10′
West Bay Centre	UNP/LNO	NF		12 B/10	48°36′	58°57′
West Bay Centre	UNP/LNO	NS	Inverness	11 F/11	45°44′	61°12′
West Bay Road	UNP/LNO	NS	Inverness	11 F/11	45°44′	61°15′
West Beach	UNP/LNO	NB	Saint John	21 H/4	45°13′	65°51′
West Becher	UNP/LNO	ON	Lambton	40 J/9	42°39′	82°22′
West Bench	UNP/LNO	BC	Osoyoos Division Yale	82 E/12	49°30′	119°37′
West Bend	VILG/VILG	SK	6-29-12-W2	62 M/5	51°29′	103°41′
West Berlin	UNP/LNO	NS	Queens	21 A/2	44°04′	64°35′
West Black Rock Road	UNP/LNO	NS	Kings	21 H/2	45°09′	64°44′
Westboro	UNP/LNO	ON	Carleton	31 G/5	45°23′	75°45′
Westbourne	MUN2/AZM2	MB		62 J/2	50°15′	98°50′
Westbourne	UNP/LNO	MB	25-13-9-W	62 J/2	50°08′	98°35′
Westbourne Settlement	GEOG/GÉOG	MB		62 J/2	50°08′	98°36′

NAME NOM	ENTITY ENTITÉ	LOC 1 LIEU 1	LOC 2 LIEU 2	MAP CARTE	POSITION LAT	LONG
West Branch	UNP/LNO	NB	Kent	21 I/10	46°32′	64°57′
West Branch Indian Brook	RIV/CDE	NS	Victoria	11 K/7	46°26′	60°33′
West Branch Lake	LAKE/LAC	NS	Pictou	11 E/7	45°22′	62°39′
West Branch River John	UNP/LNO	NS	Pictou	11 E/11	45°38′	63°02′
West Branch Wallace River	RIV/CDE	NS	Cumberland	11 E/12	45°41′	63°33′
West Brant	UNP/LNO	ON	Brant	40 P/1	43°08′	80°17′
Westbridge	UNP/LNO	BC	Similkameen Division Yale	82 E/2	49°10′	118°58′
West Brome	UNP/LNO	QC	Brome-Missisquoi	31 H/2	45°11′	72°40′
West Brook	UNP/LNO	NS	Cumberland	21 H/9	45°33′	64°18′
Westbrook	UNP/LNO	ON	Frontenac	31 C/7	44°16′	76°37′
West Brook	RIV/CDE	NF		12 H/8	49°22′	56°15′
West Brook	RIV/CDE	NS	Queens	21 A/3	44°08′	65°04′
Westbrook Heights	UNP/LNO	ON	Frontenac	31 C/7	44°16′	76°37′
West Brooklyn	UNP/LNO	NS	Kings	21 H/1	45°05′	64°14′
Westbury	VILG/VILG	QC	Le Haut-Saint-François	21 E/12	45°30′	71°40′
West Caledonia	UNP/LNO	NS	Queens	21 A/6	44°22′	65°07′
West Cape	UNP/LNO	PE	Prince	21 I/9	46°41′	64°24′
West Cape Fiord	BAY/BAIE	NT	Franklin	560 A	80°12′	95°30′
West Carleton	MUN2/AZM2	ON	Carleton	31 F/8	45°20′	76°08′
West Catfish Creek	RIV/CDE	ON	Middlesex	40 I/14	42°46′	81°04′
West Channel	CHAN/CHEN	NT	Mackenzie	117 A	68°52′	136°10′
West Chatfield Beach	HAM/HAM	SK	24-47-17-W3	73 F/1	53°04′	108°21′
Westchester Mountain	UNP/LNO	NS	Cumberland	11 E/12	45°34′	63°43′
Westchester Station	UNP/LNO	NS	Cumberland	11 E/12	45°37′	63°40′
Westchester Valley	UNP/LNO	NS	Cumberland	11 E/12	45°36′	63°44′
West Chezzetcook	UNP/LNO	NS	Halifax	11 D/11	44°43′	63°16′
West Churn Creek	RIV/CDE	BC	Lillooet	92 O/7	51°19′	122°40′
West Clifford	UNP/LNO	NS	Lunenburg	21 A/7	44°25′	64°44′
West Coal River	RIV/CDE	YT		95 D/12	60°45′	127°41′
Westcock	UNP/LNO	NB	Westmorland	21 H/16	45°52′	64°22′
West Collette	UNP/LNO	NB	Northumberland	21 I/14	46°46′	65°29′
West Cooks Cove	UNP/LNO	NS	Guysborough	11 F/5	45°22′	61°30′
West Corners	UNP/LNO	ON	Northumberland	31 C/5	44°18′	77°50′
West Coteau Lake	LAKE/LAC	SK	1-19,20-W2	72 H/1	49°02′	104°32′
Westcott	UNP/LNO	AB	35-30-3-W5	82 O/9	51°37′	114°19′
West Cove	VILG/VILG	AB	27,34-54-4-W5	83 G/9	53°42′	114°30′
West Covehead	UNP/LNO	PE	Queens	11 L/6	46°24′	63°08′
West Cracroft Island	ISL/ÎLE	BC	Range 1 Coast	92 L/9	50°33′	126°23′
West Creswell River	RIV/CDE	NT	Franklin	58 B	72°54′	93°30′
Westdale	UNP/LNO	ON	Wentworth	30 M/5	43°16′	79°54′
Westdale	UNP/LNO	MB		62 H/14	49°51′	97°19′
West Dalhousie	UNP/LNO	NS	Annapolis	21 A/11	44°43′	65°14′
West Dawson	UNP/LNO	YT		116 B/3	64°04′	139°27′
West Deane Park	UNP/LNO	ON	York	30 M/12	43°40′	79°35′
West Devon	UNP/LNO	PE	Prince	21 I/9	46°40′	64°07′
West Ditton	UNP/LNO	QC	Le Haut-Saint-François	21 E/6	45°24′	71°18′
West Dover	UNP/LNO	NS	Halifax	11 D/5	44°29′	63°52′
West Dublin	UNP/LNO	NS	Lunenburg	21 A/8	44°15′	64°24′
West Earltown	UNP/LNO	NS	Colchester	11 E/11	45°35′	63°12′
West East River	UNP/LNO	NS	Halifax	11 D/15	44°55′	62°31′
West Elmwood	UNP/LNO	MB		62 H/14	49°55′	97°07′
West Ely	UNP/LNO	QC	Le Val-Saint-François	31 H/8	45°28′	72°24′
West End	VILG/VILG	SK	30-18-3-W2	62 L/9	50°33′	102°25′
Westend	UNP/LNO	NB	Westmorland	21 I/2	46°04′	64°48′
West End	UNP/LNO	MB		62 H/14	49°54′	97°10′
West End	UNP/LNO	BC	New Westminster	92 G/6	49°17′	123°08′
West End	CAPE/CAP	NS	Pictou	11 E/15	45°48′	62°36′
Westerham	UNP/LNO	SK	34-22-27-W3	72 K/13	50°55′	109°39′
West Erinville	UNP/LNO	NS	Guysborough	11 F/5	45°23′	61°45′
Westerly	UNP/LNO	NS	Pictou	11 E/14	45°46′	63°04′
Western Arm	UNP/LNO	NF		12 H/15	49°49′	56°31′
Western Arm	BAY/BAIE	NF		2 E/12	49°41′	55°57′
Western, Banc - also-aussi - Western Bank	SEAU/SMER	—		8007	43°30′	61°45′
Western Bank - also-aussi - Western, Banc	SEAU/SMER	—		8007	43°30′	61°45′
Western Bay	UNP/LNO	NF		1 N/14	47°53′	53°05′
Western Bay Head	CAPE/CAP	NF		1 N/14	47°53′	53°03′
Western Blue Pond	LAKE/LAC	NF		12 I/6	50°21′	57°11′
Western Bradelle Valley	SEAU/SMER	—		4024	48°00′	62°45′
Western Brook Pond	LAKE/LAC	NF		12 I/11	50°36′	57°05′
Western Brook Pond	LAKE/LAC	NF		12 H/13	49°46′	57°49′
Western Channel	CHAN/CHEN	NF		1 M/8	47°23′	54°25′
Western Cove	UNP/LNO	NF		1 M/9	47°41′	54°15′
Western Duck Island	ISL/ÎLE	ON	Manitoulin	41 G/15	45°45′	83°00′
Western Head	UNP/LNO	NF		2 E/10	49°35′	54°54′
Western Head	UNP/LNO	NS	Queens	20 P/15	44°00′	64°40′

NAME NOM	ENTITY ENTITÉ	LOC 1 LIEU 1	LOC 2 LIEU 2	MAP CARTE	POSITION LAT	LONG
Western Head	UNP/LNO	NS	Shelburne	20 P/11	43°41′	65°08′
Western Head	CAPE/CAP	NF		2 C/11	48°37′	53°27′
Western Head	CAPE/CAP	NF		2 E/9	49°38′	54°04′
Western Head	CAPE/CAP	NF		12 G/9	49°33′	58°02′
Western Head	CAPE/CAP	NS	Queens	20 P/15	43°58′	64°40′
Western Head	CAPE/CAP	NS	Shelburne	20 P/11	43°39′	65°08′
Western Hill	UNP/LNO	ON	Lincoln	30 M/3	43°09′	79°15′
Western Indian Island	ISL/ÎLE	NF		2 E/9	49°33′	54°17′
Western Island	ISL/ÎLE	NF		2 L/4	50°12′	55°51′
Western Island 14	IR/RI	BC	Range 4 Coast	93 F/13	53°56′	125°41′
Western Islands	ISL/ÎLE	ON	Parry Sound	41 H/1	45°04′	80°19′
Western Monarch	UNP/LNO	AB	21-27-18-W4	82 P/8	51°20′	112°28′
Western Peninsula	CAPE/CAP	ON	Kenora	52 E/10	49°34′	94°45′
Western Point	CAPE/CAP	NF		12 P/9	51°43′	56°27′
Western River	RIV/CDE	NT	Mackenzie	76 J	66°22′	107°10′
Western Shore	UNP/LNO	NS	Lunenburg	21 A/9	44°32′	64°19′
Westerose	UNP/LNO	AB	9-46-28-W5	83 A/13	52°58′	113°59′
West Essa	UNP/LNO	ON	Simcoe	31 D/4	44°11′	79°52′
Westfield	VILG/VILG	NB	Kings	21 G/8	45°20′	66°14′
Westfield	UNP/LNO	NS	Queens	21 A/6	44°25′	65°01′
Westfield	UNP/LNO	ON	Huron	40 P/14	43°48′	81°28′
Westfield	GEOG/GÉOG	NB	Kings	21 G/8	45°20′	66°20′
Westfield Beach	UNP/LNO	NB	Kings	21 G/8	45°21′	66°14′
Westfield Centre	UNP/LNO	NB	Kings	21 G/8	45°20′	66°14′
West Fiord	BAY/BAIE	NT	Franklin	59 A	76°06′	90°00′
West Flamborough	UNP/LNO	ON	Wentworth	40 P/8	43°16′	80°01′
Westford	UNP/LNO	ON	Bruce	41 A/3	44°03′	81°23′
West Fort William	UNP/LNO	ON	Thunder Bay	52 A/6	48°22′	89°18′
West Franklin	UNP/LNO	ON	York	31 D/3	44°06′	79°19′
West Galloway	UNP/LNO	NB	Kent	21 I/10	46°37′	64°51′
West Garafraxa	MUN2/AZM2	ON	Wellington	40 P/16	43°46′	80°24′
Westgate	UNP/LNO	MB	31-44-29-W	63 C/13	52°50′	101°39′
West Glassville	UNP/LNO	NB	Carleton	21 J/11	46°30′	67°27′
West Glenmont	UNP/LNO	NS	Kings	21 H/2	45°11′	64°32′
West Gore	UNP/LNO	NS	Hants	11 E/4	45°06′	63°46′
West Gravenhurst	UNP/LNO	ON	Muskoka	31 D/14	44°55′	79°25′
West Green Harbour	UNP/LNO	NS	Shelburne	20 P/11	43°43′	65°10′
West Guilford	UNP/LNO	ON	Haliburton	31 E/2	45°07′	78°36′
West Gwillimbury - see-voir - Bradford West Gwillimbury	MUN2/AZM2	ON		31 D/4	44°07′	79°37′
West Gwillimbury - see-voir - Innisfil	MUN2/AZM2	ON		31 D/5	44°18′	79°39′
West Halls Harbour Road	UNP/LNO	NS	Kings	21 H/2	45°10′	64°36′
West Hamilton	UNP/LNO	ON	Wentworth	30 M/4	43°15′	79°55′
Westham Island	ISL/ÎLE	BC	New Westminster	92 G/3	49°05′	123°09′
West Hansford	UNP/LNO	NS	Cumberland	11 E/12	45°43′	63°48′
West Hants	MUN1/AZM1	NS	Hants	21 A/16	45°00′	64°07′
West Hart River	RIV/CDE	YT		116 A/14	64°56′	137°04′
West Havre Boucher	UNP/LNO	NS	Antigonish	11 F/12	45°40′	61°33′
West Hawkesbury	MUN2/AZM2	ON	Prescott	31 G/10	45°34′	74°38′
West Hawk Lake	UNP/LNO	MB	15,16-9-17-E	52 E/11	49°45′	95°12′
West Hawk Lake	LAKE/LAC	ON	Kenora	52 F/8	49°24′	92°09′
West Hawk Lake	LAKE/LAC	MB	9-17-E	52 E/14	49°46′	95°11′
Westhazel	UNP/LNO	SK	50-21-W3	73 F/6	53°20′	109°05′
West Head	UNP/LNO	NS	Shelburne	20 P/5	43°27′	65°39′
West Head	CAPE/CAP	NF		1 M/8	47°24′	54°22′
West Head	CAPE/CAP	NS	Richmond	11 F/9	45°39′	60°25′
Westheath	UNP/LNO	SK		72 I/5	50°23′	105°35′
West Heights	UNP/LNO	BC	New Westminster	92 G/1	49°08′	122°20′
West Hill	UNP/LNO	ON	York	30 M/14	43°46′	79°11′
Westholme	UNP/LNO	BC	Chemainus	92 B/13	48°52′	123°42′
West Humber Estates	UNP/LNO	ON	York	30 M/12	43°43′	79°35′
West Humber River	RIV/CDE	ON	York	30 M/12	43°44′	79°33′
West Huntingdon	UNP/LNO	ON	Hastings	31 C/6	44°21′	77°29′
West Huntingdon Station	UNP/LNO	ON	Hastings	31 C/6	44°20′	77°29′
West Indian Road	UNP/LNO	NS	Hants	11 E/4	45°07′	63°35′
West Inglisville	UNP/LNO	NS	Annapolis	21 A/14	44°51′	65°10′
West Intervale	UNP/LNO	NS	Guysborough	11 F/5	45°27′	61°39′
West Ironbound Island	ISL/ÎLE	NS	Lunenburg	21 A/1	44°14′	64°17′
West Isles	GEOG/GÉOG	NB	Charlotte	21 G/2	45°00′	66°58′
West Jeddore	UNP/LNO	NS	Halifax	11 D/11	44°44′	63°01′
West Kabenung Lake	LAKE/LAC	ON	Algoma	42 C/6	48°16′	85°03′
West Keith	UNP/LNO	QC	Le Haut-Saint-François	21 E/11	45°31′	71°28′
West Kettle River	RIV/CDE	BC	Similkameen Division Yale	82 E/2	49°10′	118°58′
West Kildonan	UNP/LNO	MB		62 H/14	49°57′	97°08′
West Kiskatinaw River	RIV/CDE	BC	Peace River	93 P/8	55°22′	120°18′
West LaHave	UNP/LNO	NS	Lunenburg	21 A/8	44°19′	64°25′

NAME NOM	ENTITY ENTITÉ	LOC 1 LIEU 1	LOC 2 LIEU 2	MAP CARTE	POSITION LAT	LONG
West Lake	UNP/LNO	NF		12 H/1	49°01'	56°12'
West Lake	UNP/LNO	ON	Prince Edward	30 N/14	43°55'	77°16'
West Lake	LAKE/LAC	NF		2 D/13	48°52'	55°56'
West Lake	LAKE/LAC	ON	Prince Edward	30 N/14	43°56'	77°17'
West Lake Ainslie	UNP/LNO	NS	Inverness	11 K/3	46°06'	61°12'
West Lakevale	UNP/LNO	NS	Antigonish	11 F/13	45°46'	61°57'
West Landing	UNP/LNO	NF		1 K/11	46°39'	53°04'
West Landing	UNP/LNO	BC	Cassiar	93 M/8	55°28'	126°00'
*Westlang	UNP/LNO	BC	New Westminster	92 G/2	49°11'	122°40'
West Lawrencetown	UNP/LNO	NS	Halifax	11 D/11	44°40'	63°23'
West Lawrencetown	UNP/LNO	NS	Annapolis	21 A/14	44°52'	65°11'
West Leicester	UNP/LNO	NS	Cumberland	21 H/16	45°47'	64°03'
Westley	UNP/LNO	BC	Kootenay	82 F/5	49°20'	117°46'
West Lincoln	MUN2/AZM2	ON	Lincoln	30 M/4	43°06'	79°34'
West Linden	UNP/LNO	NS	Cumberland	11 E/13	45°53'	63°51'
West Linwood	UNP/LNO	NS	Antigonish	11 F/12	45°38'	61°36'
West Liscomb	UNP/LNO	NS	Guysborough	11 D/16	44°59'	62°06'
West Lochaber	UNP/LNO	NS	Antigonish	11 E/8	45°25'	62°02'
Westlock	TOWN/VIL2	AB	5-60-26-W4	83 I/4	54°09'	113°52'
Westlock No. 92, Municipal District of	MUN1/AZM1	AB	61-26-W4	83 I/5	54°15'	113°51'
West Long Lake	LAKE/LAC	NB	Charlotte	21 G/2	45°21'	66°40'
West Loon Creek	RIV/CDE	SK	24-23-18-W2	72 I/16	50°58'	104°23'
West Lorne	VILG/VILG	ON	Elgin	40 I/12	42°36'	81°36'
West Luther	MUN2/AZM2	ON	Wellington	40 P/15	43°53'	80°30'
West Lynde	UNP/LNO	ON	Ontario	30 M/15	43°52'	78°57'
West Lynn	UNP/LNO	BC	New Westminster	92 G/6	49°20'	123°02'
West Lynne	UNP/LNO	MB		62 H/3	49°00'	97°14'
West Mabou Harbour	UNP/LNO	NS	Inverness	11 K/3	46°04'	61°28'
West McGillivray	UNP/LNO	ON	Middlesex	40 P/4	43°12'	81°34'
Westmeath	MUN2/AZM2	ON	Renfrew	31 F/15	45°46'	76°50'
Westmeath	UNP/LNO	ON	Renfrew	31 F/15	45°49'	76°53'
West Micmac Lake	LAKE/LAC	NF		13 K/9	54°44'	60°10'
West Middle River	UNP/LNO	NS	Victoria	11 K/2	46°10'	60°56'
West Middle Sable	UNP/LNO	NS	Shelburne	20 P/14	43°48'	65°01'
West Midway	UNP/LNO	BC	Similkameen Division Yale	82 E/2	49°01'	118°49'
West Mines	UNP/LNO	NF		1 N/10	47°38'	52°59'
Westminster - see-voir - North Dorchester	TOWN/VIL2	ON		40 I/14	42°56'	81°00'
Westminster - see-voir - Belmont	TOWN/VIL2	ON		40 I/14	42°53'	81°05'
Westminster - see-voir - London	TOWN/VIL2	ON		40 I/14	42°59'	81°14'
Westminster - see-voir - Delaware	TOWN/VIL2	ON		40 I/14	42°52'	81°22'
Westminster	UNP/LNO	ON	Prescott	31 G/6	45°28'	75°00'
West Moberly Lake 168A	IR/RI	BC	Peace River	93 P/13	55°48'	121°55'
West Monkton	UNP/LNO	ON	Perth	40 P/11	43°36'	81°05'
West Montreal River	RIV/CDE	ON	Timiskaming	41 P/15	47°56'	80°39'
West Montrose	UNP/LNO	NS	Colchester	11 E/5	45°25'	63°43'
West Montrose	UNP/LNO	ON	Waterloo	40 P/9	43°35'	80°29'
Westmore	UNP/LNO	SK		72 I/5	50°23'	105°34'
Westmoreland	UNP/LNO	PE	Queens	11 L/6	46°16'	63°29'
Westmorland	GEOG/GÉOG	NB	Westmorland	21 I/1	46°00'	64°10'
Westmorland	GEOG/GÉOG	NB		21 I/2	46°00'	64°40'
Westmorland Heights	UNP/LNO	NB	Saint John	21 G/8	45°17'	66°02'
Westmount	CITY/VIL1	QC	Communauté urbaine de Montréal	31 H/5	45°29'	73°36'
Westmount	UNP/LNO	NS	Cape Breton	11 K/1	46°08'	60°13'
Westmount	UNP/LNO	ON	Peterborough	31 D/8	44°18'	78°21'
Westmount	UNP/LNO	ON	York	30 M/12	43°42'	79°31'
Westmount	UNP/LNO	ON	Waterloo	40 P/7	43°27'	80°32'
Westmount	UNP/LNO	ON	Oxford	40 I/15	42°52'	80°45'
Westmount	UNP/LNO	ON	Middlesex	40 I/14	42°57'	81°17'
Westmount	UNP/LNO	SK		72 I/5	50°23'	105°34'
Westmount	UNP/LNO	SK		73 B/2	52°08'	106°41'
Westmount	UNP/LNO	BC	New Westminster	92 G/6	49°20'	123°13'
West Nadila Creek	RIV/CDE	BC	Lillooet	92 O/6	51°27'	123°09'
West New Annan	UNP/LNO	NS	Colchester	11 E/11	45°38'	63°22'
West Nissouri	MUN2/AZM2	ON	Middlesex	40 P/3	43°08'	81°08'
West Northfield	UNP/LNO	NS	Lunenburg	21 A/7	44°27'	64°35'
Weston	UNP/LNO	NS	Kings	21 H/2	45°04'	64°47'
Weston	UNP/LNO	NB	Carleton	21 J/5	46°17'	67°46'
Weston	UNP/LNO	ON	York	30 M/12	43°43'	79°31'
Weston	UNP/LNO	MB		62 H/14	49°55'	97°11'
Weston, Cape	CAPE/CAP	NT	Franklin	36 F	65°23'	77°29'
Weston Island	ISL/ÎLE	NT	Keewatin	33 D	52°33'	79°36'
West Osgoode	UNP/LNO	ON	Carleton	31 G/4	45°10'	75°34'
Westover	UNP/LNO	QC	Brome-Missisquoi	31 H/2	45°08'	72°36'
Westover	UNP/LNO	ON	Wentworth	40 P/8	43°20'	80°05'
West Paradise	UNP/LNO	NS	Annapolis	21 A/14	44°51'	65°13'

NAME NOM	ENTITY ENTITÉ	LOC 1 LIEU 1	LOC 2 LIEU 2	MAP CARTE	POSITION	
					LAT	LONG
West Pennant	UNP/LNO	NS	Halifax	11 D/5	44°28'	63°39'
West Perch Bay	BAY/BAIE	MB	78-21-W	63 N/15	55°47'	100°37'
West Petpeswick	UNP/LNO	NS	Halifax	11 D/11	44°44'	63°10'
Westphal	UNP/LNO	NS	Halifax	11 D/12	44°41'	63°32'
West Pine Ridge	UNP/LNO	MB	12-4,5-E	62 H/15	50°00'	96°55'
Westplain	UNP/LNO	ON	Lennox and Addington	31 C/6	44°23'	77°04'
West Plains	UNP/LNO	SK	22-5-28-W3	72 F/5	49°25'	109°41'
Westply	UNP/LNO	BC	Cariboo	93 B/16	52°57'	122°29'
West Point	UNP/LNO	NF		11 O/9	47°39'	58°26'
West Point	UNP/LNO	PE	Prince	21 I/9	46°37'	64°23'
West Point	CAPE/CAP	NF		11 P/10	47°34'	56°44'
West Point	CAPE/CAP	PE	Prince	21 I/9	46°37'	64°23'
West Point	CAPE/CAP	NS	Halifax	10 N/16	43°57'	60°06'
West Point	CAPE/CAP	ON	Prince Edward	30 N/14	43°53'	77°17'
West Point Grey	UNP/LNO	BC	New Westminster	92 G/6	49°16'	123°12'
West Pompey Island	ISL/ÎLE	NF		13 J/8	54°19'	58°01'
West Pond	LAKE/LAC	NF		12 H/8	49°24'	56°12'
West Poplar	UNP/LNO	SK	5-1-3-W3	72 G/1	49°00'	106°22'
West Poplar River	RIV/CDE	SK	5-1-3-W3	72 G/1	49°00'	106°22'
Westport	VILG/VILG	NF		12 H/15	49°47'	56°38'
Westport	VILG/VILG	NS	Digby	21 B/8	44°16'	66°21'
Westport	VILG/VILG	ON	Leeds	31 C/9	44°41'	76°24'
West Port Clyde	UNP/LNO	NS	Shelburne	20 P/11	43°35'	65°27'
West Prairie River	RIV/CDE	AB	14-75-17-W5	83 N/7	55°30'	116°31'
West Pubnico	UNP/LNO	NS	Yarmouth	20 P/12	43°40'	65°48'
West Pugwash	UNP/LNO	NS	Cumberland	11 E/13	45°51'	63°42'
West Quaco	UNP/LNO	NB	Saint John	21 H/5	45°20'	65°33'
West Quoddy	UNP/LNO	NS	Halifax	11 D/16	44°55'	62°21'
West Raft River	RIV/CDE	BC	Kamloops Division Yale	82 M/13	51°47'	119°42'
Westray	UNP/LNO	MB	20-53-27-W	63 F/11	53°36'	101°24'
West Redonda Island	ISL/ÎLE	BC	New Westminster	92 K/2	50°13'	124°53'
Westree	UNP/LNO	ON	Sudbury	41 P/5	47°25'	81°33'
Westridge	UNP/LNO	BC	New Westminster	92 G/7	49°17'	122°57'
West River	VILG/VILG	PE	Queens	11 L/3	46°10'	63°18'
West River	UNP/LNO	NS	Antigonish	11 E/9	45°35'	62°02'
West River	UNP/LNO	NB	Albert	21 H/10	45°39'	64°51'
West River	UNP/LNO	ON	Sudbury	41 I/4	46°09'	81°45'
West River	RIV/CDE	PE	Queens	11 L/3	46°13'	63°10'
West River	RIV/CDE	NS	Lunenburg	21 A/10	44°33'	64°45'
West River	RIV/CDE	NT	Franklin	97 C	69°06'	126°18'
West River of Pictou	RIV/CDE	NS	Pictou	11 E/10	45°40'	62°46'
West River St. Marys	RIV/CDE	NS	Guysborough	11 E/8	45°15'	62°04'
West River Sheet Harbour	RIV/CDE	NS	Halifax	11 D/15	44°55'	62°33'
West Riverside	UNP/LNO	ON	Cochrane	42 G/8	49°25'	82°26'
West River Station	UNP/LNO	NS	Pictou	11 E/7	45°27'	62°55'
West Riverview	UNP/LNO	NB	Albert	21 I/2	46°03'	64°48'
West Roachvale	UNP/LNO	NS	Guysborough	11 F/5	45°21'	61°36'
West Road (Blackwater) River	RIV/CDE	BC	Cariboo	93 G/7	53°19'	122°52'
Westroc	UNP/LNO	MB	5-14-9SW	62 J/2	50°09'	98°40'
West Rous Island	ISL/ÎLE	ON	Manitoulin	41 J/1	46°01'	82°02'
West Royalty - see-voir - Charlottetown	VILG/VILG	PE		11 L/3	46°14'	63°08'
West Royalty	UNP/LNO	PE	Queens	11 L/6	46°16'	63°10'
West Sackville	UNP/LNO	NB	Westmorland	21 H/16	45°52'	64°23'
West St. Andrews	UNP/LNO	NS	Colchester	11 E/3	45°06'	63°18'
West St. Modeste	VILG/VILG	NF		12 P/10	51°36'	56°42'
West St. Paul	MUN2/AZM2	MB		62 H/14	50°00'	97°10'
West St. Peters	UNP/LNO	PE	Kings	11 L/7	46°25'	62°47'
West Scotch Settlement	UNP/LNO	NB	Kings	21 H/12	45°41'	65°53'
West Sheet Harbour	UNP/LNO	NS	Halifax	11 D/15	44°55'	62°32'
West Shoal Lake	LAKE/LAC	MB	15,16-2-W	62 I/5	50°20'	97°41'
West Side	UNP/LNO	NS	Yarmouth	20 O/8	43°25'	66°01'
Westside	UNP/LNO	BC	Osoyoos Division Yale	82 E/13	49°53'	119°32'
West Springhill	UNP/LNO	NS	Annapolis	21 A/11	44°35'	65°27'
West Stony Brook	RIV/CDE	NF		2 D/13	48°52'	55°45'
*West Summerland	UNP/LNO	BC	Osoyoos Division Yale	82 E/12	49°35'	119°41'
West Sutton	UNP/LNO	QC	Brome-Missisquoi	31 H/2	45°07'	72°40'
Westsyde	UNP/LNO	BC	Kamloops Division Yale	92 I/16	50°46'	120°21'
West Tarbot	UNP/LNO	NS	Victoria	11 K/7	46°21'	60°36'
West Tatamagouche	UNP/LNO	NS	Colchester	11 E/11	45°43'	63°25'
West Thulean Rise	SEAU/SMER	—		5.04	52°00'	41°00'
West Thurlow Island	ISL/ÎLE	BC	Sayward	92 K/5	50°25'	125°38'
West Toronto - see-voir - The Junction	VILG/VILG	ON		30 M/11	43°40'	79°28'
West Trail	UNP/LNO	BC	Kootenay	82 F/4	49°05'	117°43'
West Valley	SEAU/SMER	—		15787A	48°31'	129°00'
West Vancouver	MUN1/AZM1	BC	New Westminster	92 G/6	49°22'	123°10'

NAME NOM	ENTITY ENTITÉ	LOC 1 LIEU 1	LOC 2 LIEU 2	MAP CARTE	POSITION LAT	LONG
Westview	HAM/HAM	SK	25,36-22-7-W2	62 L/15	50°56′	102°51′
Westview	UNP/LNO	ON	Northumberland	31 C/5	44°21′	77°54′
Westview	UNP/LNO	MB		62 G/13	49°50′	99°59′
Westview	UNP/LNO	SK		73 B/2	52°09′	106°42′
Westview	UNP/LNO	BC	New Westminster	92 F/5	49°50′	124°31′
Westville	TOWN/VIL2	NS	Pictou	11 E/10	45°34′	62°43′
West Waterville	UNP/LNO	NB	York	21 J/3	46°05′	67°21′
West Wawanosh	MUN2/AZM2	ON	Huron	40 P/13	43°53′	81°30′
West Wentworth	UNP/LNO	NS	Cumberland	11 E/12	45°41′	63°36′
Westwick Lakes	LAKE/LAC	BC	Cariboo	93 B/1	52°00′	122°10′
West Williams	MUN2/AZM2	ON	Middlesex	40 P/4	43°07′	81°45′
Westwin	UNP/LNO	MB		62 H/14	49°53′	97°14′
West Winnipeg	UNP/LNO	MB		62 H/14	49°51′	97°25′
Westwold	UNP/LNO	BC	Kamloops Division Yale	82 L/5	50°28′	119°45′
Westwood	UNP/LNO	ON	Carleton	31 F/8	45°21′	76°01′
Westwood	UNP/LNO	ON	Peterborough	31 D/8	44°19′	78°04′
Westwood	UNP/LNO	MB		62 H/14	49°52′	97°18′
Wetalltok Bay	BAY/BAIE	NT	Keewatin	34 D	56°02′	79°14′
Wetaskiwin	CITY/VIL1	AB	14-46-24-W4	83 A/14	52°58′	113°22′
Wetaskiwin No. 10, County of	MUN1/AZM1	AB	46-28-W4	83 B/16	52°58′	114°04′
Wetetnagami, Lac	LAKE/LAC	QC	Vallée-de-l'Or	32 C/16	48°55′	76°15′
Wetetnagami, Rivière	RIV/CDE	QC	Jamésie	32 F/8	49°17′	76°04′
Wetikoweskwattam	UNP/LNO	MB		63 I/9	54°33′	96°04′
Wetstone Point	CAPE/CAP	NF		12 H/3	49°04′	57°16′
Wexford	UNP/LNO	ON	Grenville	31 B/11	44°43′	75°30′
Wexford	UNP/LNO	ON	York	30 M/11	43°45′	79°18′
Wexford Heights	UNP/LNO	ON	York	30 M/11	43°45′	79°17′
Weyakwin	HAM/HAM	SK		73 I/5	54°26′	105°47′
Weyakwin Lake	LAKE/LAC	SK		73 I/5	54°30′	106°00′
Weybridge	UNP/LNO	NF		2 C/4	48°06′	53°53′
Weyburn	CITY/VIL1	SK		62 E/12	49°40′	103°51′
Weyburn Lake	LAKE/LAC	NT	Mackenzie	85 K	63°00′	117°59′
Weyburn No. 67	MUN2/AZM2	SK		62 E/12	49°40′	103°45′
Weygand	UNP/LNO	QC	Pabok	22 A/8	48°29′	64°17′
Weymont	UNP/LNO	QC	Le Haut-Saint-Maurice	31 P/13	47°54′	73°45′
Weymontachie 23 - see-voir - Communauté de Wemotaci	IR/RI	QC		31 P/13	47°54′	73°47′
Weymouth	VILG/VILG	NS	Digby	21 A/5	44°25′	66°00′
Weymouth Falls	UNP/LNO	NS	Digby	21 A/5	44°24′	65°56′
Weymouth Mills	UNP/LNO	NS	Digby	21 A/5	44°25′	65°57′
Weymouth North	UNP/LNO	NS	Digby	21 A/5	44°26′	65°59′
Weynton, Cape	CAPE/CAP	NT	Keewatin	56 P	67°45′	88°07′
Whale Bank - also-aussi - Baleine, Banc de la	SEAU/SMER	—		8011	45°20′	53°20′
Whale Channel	CHAN/CHEN	BC	Range 4 Coast	103 H/3	53°11′	129°08′
Whale Cove	HAM/HAM	NT	Keewatin	55 K	62°10′	92°35′
Whale Cove	UNP/LNO	NF		1 M/3	47°01′	55°10′
Whale Cove	BAY/BAIE	NB	Charlotte	21 B/15	44°47′	66°45′
Whale Deep - also-aussi - Baleine, Trou de la	SEAU/SMER	—		8011	45°20′	52°45′
Whale Island 8	IR/RI	BC	Metchosin	92 B/5	48°19′	123°35′
Whale Lake	LAKE/LAC	NS	Lunenburg	21 A/10	44°34′	64°32′
Whalen Corners	UNP/LNO	ON	Middlesex	40 P/6	43°16′	81°22′
Whalen Lake	LAKE/LAC	BC	Range 4 Coast	103 H/2	53°12′	128°55′
Whale Point	CAPE/CAP	NT	Keewatin	56 A	64°12′	88°02′
Whale's Gulch - see-voir - Valley Pond	UNP/LNO	NF		2 E/10	49°34′	54°54′
Whaletown	UNP/LNO	BC	Sayward	92 K/3	50°06′	125°03′
Whaley's Corners	UNP/LNO	ON	Halton	30 M/12	43°36′	79°48′
Whalley	UNP/LNO	BC	New Westminster	92 G/2	49°12′	122°51′
Wharncliffe	UNP/LNO	ON	Algoma	41 J/6	46°25′	83°24′
Wharton	UNP/LNO	NS	Cumberland	21 H/8	45°25′	64°25′
Wharton Harbour	BAY/BAIE	NT	Franklin	25 M	63°21′	71°43′
Wharton Lake	LAKE/LAC	NT	Franklin	66 B	64°00′	99°50′
Wha T'a Noo 40	IR/RI	BC	Range 5 Coast	93 K/15	54°46′	124°36′
Wha Ti	HAM/HAM	NT	Mackenzie	85 N/3	63°09′	117°16′
Whatshan Lake	LAKE/LAC	BC	Kootenay	82 E/16	49°57′	118°06′
Whatshan Peak	MTN/MNT	BC	Kootenay	82 L/1	50°06′	118°10′
Whatshan River	RIV/CDE	BC	Kootenay	82 E/16	49°52′	118°07′
Wheatland	UNP/LNO	QC	Drummond	31 H/16	45°48′	72°22′
Wheatland	UNP/LNO	MB	16,21-12-21-W	62 K/1	50°01′	100°18′
Wheatland County	MUN1/AZM1	AB		82 P/2	51°04′	112°56′
Wheatland No. 16, County of - see-voir - Wheatland County	MUN1/AZM1	AB		82 P/2	51°04′	112°56′
Wheatlands No. 163	MUN2/AZM2	SK		72 J/8	50°25′	106°15′
Wheatley	VILG/VILG	ON	Essex	40 J/1	42°06′	82°27′
Wheatley River	UNP/LNO	PE	Queens	11 L/6	46°22′	63°17′
Wheaton Settlement	UNP/LNO	NB	Westmorland	21 I/3	46°01′	65°10′
Wheatstone	UNP/LNO	SK	18-9-24-W2	72 H/11	49°44′	105°15′
Wheeler, Lac	LAKE/LAC	QC	Kativik	24 B/11	56°37′	67°25′

NAME NOM	ENTITY ENTITÉ	LOC 1 LIEU 1	LOC 2 LIEU 2	MAP CARTE	POSITION LAT	LONG
Wheeler Lake	LAKE/LAC	NT	Mackenzie	85 O	63°20′	114°52′
Wheeler River	RIV/CDE	SK		74 H/9	57°34′	104°15′
Wheeler, Rivière	RIV/CDE	QC	Kativik	24 G/3	57°04′	67°10′
Whelan	UNP/LNO	SK	58-24-W3	73 K/3	54°02′	109°28′
Whim Road	UNP/LNO	PE	Kings	11 L/2	46°08′	62°36′
Whipple Point	CAPE/CAP	NS	Digby	21 B/1	44°14′	66°24′
Whipsaw Creek	RIV/CDE	BC	Yale Division Yale	92 H/7	49°22′	120°33′
Whirl Creek	RIV/CDE	ON	Perth	40 P/6	43°28′	81°12′
Whirlwind Lake	LAKE/LAC	NT	Mackenzie	75 C	60°15′	108°40′
Whiska Creek No. 106	MUN2/AZM2	SK		72 G/14	49°55′	107°25′
Whiskey Gap	UNP/LNO	AB	16-1-23-W4	82 H/3	49°02′	113°02′
Whiskey Jack - see-voir - Whiskey Jack Landing	MISC/DIV	MB		63 J/8	54°26′	98°00′
Whiskey Jack Lake	LAKE/LAC	MB		64 K/5	58°23′	101°55′
Whiskey Jack Landing	UNP/LNO	MB	9-63-4-W1	63 J/8	54°26′	98°00′
Whiskey Lake	LAKE/LAC	ON	Algoma	41 J/8	46°25′	82°20′
Whisky Creek	UNP/LNO	BC	Newcastle	92 F/7	49°19′	124°30′
Whisky Jack Island	ISL/ÎLE	MB		63 C/16	52°55′	100°17′
Whispering Hills	VILG/VILG	AB	66,67-24-W4	83 I/13	54°46′	113°33′
Whispering Pines 4	IR/RI	BC	Kamloops Division Yale	92 I/16	51°00′	120°14′
Whistler	VILG/VILG	BC	New Westminster	92 J/2	50°07′	122°58′
Whistler	UNP/LNO	BC	New Westminster	92 J/2	50°07′	122°57′
Whistler	UNP/LNO	BC	New Westminster	92 J/2	50°06′	123°00′
Whistler Centre - see-voir - Whistler Creek	UNP/LNO	BC		92 J/2	50°06′	123°00′
Whistler Creek	UNP/LNO	BC	New Westminster	92 J/2	50°06′	123°00′
Whitbourne	TOWN/VIL2	NF		1 N/5	47°25′	53°32′
Whitbourne Canyon	SEAU/SMER	—		8010	43°00′	51°10′
Whitburn	UNP/LNO	AB	21-79-8-W6	83 M/14	55°52′	119°12′
Whitby	TOWN/VIL2	ON	Ontario	30 M/15	43°53′	78°56′
Whitchurch-Stouffville	TOWN/VIL2	ON	York	30 M/14	44°00′	79°19′
White	UNP/LNO	ON	Kenora	52 E/14	49°54′	95°05′
White Bay	BAY/BAIE	NF		12 H/16	50°00′	56°32′
White Bear	HAM/HAM	SK	22-16-W3	72 K/16	50°53′	108°13′
White Bear 70 - see-voir - Pheasant Rump Nakota	IR/RI	SK		62 E/16	49°45′	102°15′
White Bear Bay	BAY/BAIE	NF		11 P/11	47°41′	57°19′
White Bear Bay	BAY/BAIE	NT	Franklin	35 P	63°51′	72°15′
White Bear Island	ISL/ÎLE	NF		14 F/13	57°54′	61°42′
White Bear Islands	ISL/ÎLE	NF		13 I/7	54°28′	56°55′
White Bear Lake	LAKE/LAC	NF		12 A/3	48°05′	57°23′
White Bear Lake	LAKE/LAC	NF		13 J/12	54°36′	59°41′
Whitebear Lake	LAKE/LAC	SK	24,25-15-W3	72 N/1	51°05′	108°05′
Whitebear Point	CAPE/CAP	NT	Mackenzie	67 B	68°10′	103°26′
White Bear River	RIV/CDE	NF		11 P/14	47°47′	57°16′
White Bear River	RIV/CDE	NF		13 H/12	53°35′	57°32′
Whitebeech	UNP/LNO	SK	4,5-36-30-W	63 C/4	52°03′	101°42′
Whitebread	UNP/LNO	ON	Kent	40 J/9	42°38′	82°28′
Whiteburn Mines	UNP/LNO	NS	Queens	21 A/6	44°19′	65°04′
Whitecap	UNP/LNO	SK		72 O/15	51°52′	106°42′
White Cap 94	IR/RI	SK		72 O/15	51°53′	106°44′
White Capes	CAPE/CAP	NS	Inverness	11 K/15	46°47′	60°54′
Whitecap Lake	LAKE/LAC	MB		54 D/14	56°54′	95°14′
Whitecap Mountain	MTN/MNT	BC	Lillooet	92 J/10	50°43′	122°30′
Whitechurch	UNP/LNO	ON	Bruce	40 P/14	43°55′	81°24′
White City	VILG/VILG	SK	23-17-18-W2	72 I/8	50°26′	104°22′
Whiteclay Lake	LAKE/LAC	ON	Thunder Bay	52 I/15	50°53′	88°45′
White Cloud Island	ISL/ÎLE	ON	Grey	41 A/15	44°50′	80°58′
Whitecourt	TOWN/VIL2	AB	35-59-12-W5	83 J/4	54°09′	115°41′
Whitecroft	UNP/LNO	AB	23-52-23-W4	83 H/11	53°31′	113°18′
White Crown Mountain	MTN/MNT	NT	Franklin	59 G	79°56′	92°19′
White Deer	UNP/LNO	QC	Papineau	31 G/13	45°57′	75°38′
Whitedog	UNP/LNO	ON	Kenora	52 L/2	50°08′	94°57′
Whitedog Lake	LAKE/LAC	ON	Kenora	52 L/2	50°09′	94°53′
White Eagle Falls	FALL/CHUT	NT	Mackenzie	86 F	65°36′	117°50′
White Earth Creek	RIV/CDE	AB	36-58-16-W4	83 I/1	54°04′	112°14′
White Elk	UNP/LNO	AB	23-2-W5	82 J/16	50°58′	114°11′
Whitefish	UNP/LNO	ON	Sudbury	41 I/6	46°23′	81°19′
Whitefish Bay	UNP/LNO	ON	Kenora	52 F/5	49°24′	93°58′
Whitefish Bay	BAY/BAIE	ON	Algoma	41 K/10	46°38′	84°33′
Whitefish Bay	BAY/BAIE	ON	Kenora	52 F/10	49°41′	92°41′
Whitefish Bay	BAY/BAIE	ON	Kenora	52 E/8	49°22′	94°08′
Whitefish Bay 32A	IR/RI	ON	Kenora	52 F/5	49°25′	93°57′
Whitefish Bay 33A	IR/RI	ON	Kenora	52 F/5	49°21′	93°58′
Whitefish Bay 34A	IR/RI	ON	Kenora	52 F/5	49°23′	93°59′
Whitefish Falls	UNP/LNO	ON	Sudbury	41 I/4	46°07′	81°44′
Whitefish Lake	LAKE/LAC	ON	Sudbury	41 I/6	46°23′	81°11′
Whitefish Lake	LAKE/LAC	ON	Algoma	42 C/1	48°01′	84°28′

NAME NOM	ENTITY ENTITÉ	LOC 1 LIEU 1	LOC 2 LIEU 2	MAP CARTE	POSITION	
					LAT	LONG
Whitefish Lake	LAKE/LAC	ON	Thunder Bay	52 A/4	48°13′	90°00′
Whitefish Lake	LAKE/LAC	ON	Thunder Bay	52 B/7	48°23′	90°41′
Whitefish Lake	LAKE/LAC	ON	Kenora	52 K/1	50°11′	92°24′
Whitefish Lake	LAKE/LAC	MB		53 N/11	55°33′	93°14′
Whitefish Lake	LAKE/LAC	MB	39-29-W	63 C/5	52°20′	101°37′
Whitefish Lake	LAKE/LAC	AB	62-13-W4	73 L/5	54°22′	111°53′
Whitefish Lake	LAKE/LAC	NT	Keewatin	65 B	60°13′	98°45′
Whitefish Lake	LAKE/LAC	NT	Mackenzie	75 J	62°41′	106°48′
Whitefish Lake 6	IR/RI	ON	Sudbury	41 I/6	46°20′	81°15′
Whitefish Lake 6 - see-voir - Bihlk'a 6	IR/RI	BC		93 K/10	54°34′	124°54′
White Fish Lake 128	IR/RI	AB	61-21-W4	73 L/5	54°18′	111°48′
Whitefish River	RIV/CDE	ON	Cochrane	42 A/7	48°26′	80°56′
Whitefish River	RIV/CDE	ON	Thunder Bay	52 A/5	48°22′	89°35′
Whitefish River	RIV/CDE	YT		95 C/3	60°11′	125°03′
Whitefish River	RIV/CDE	NT	Mackenzie	96 F	65°55′	124°48′
Whitefish River 4	IR/RI	ON	Manitoulin	41 I/4	46°05′	81°45′
Whitefish Station	UNP/LNO	YT		117 A/16	68°54′	136°54′
Whitefish Station	UNP/LNO	NT	Mackenzie	107 C	69°23′	133°37′
White Fox	VILG/VILG	SK		73 H/8	53°27′	104°05′
White Fox River	RIV/CDE	SK	32-52-14-W2	73 H/9	53°32′	104°01′
White Fox River	RIV/CDE	NT	Franklin	98 B	72°28′	124°04′
White Gull	VILG/VILG	AB	11-67-24-W4	83 I/13	54°47′	113°33′
White Gull Creek	RIV/CDE	SK	5-55-16-W2	73 H/9	53°44′	104°21′
White Gull Lake	LAKE/LAC	SK	57-21-W2	73 H/14	53°56′	105°04′
Whitehall	UNP/LNO	ON	Parry Sound	31 E/5	45°29′	79°31′
White Handkerchief, Cape	CAPE/CAP	NF		14 M/6	59°17′	63°23′
Whitehead	MUN2/AZM2	MB		62 F/16	49°47′	100°14′
Whitehead	UNP/LNO	NS	Guysborough	11 F/3	45°14′	61°11′
Whitehead	UNP/LNO	NB	Kings	21 G/8	45°24′	66°04′
White Head	UNP/LNO	NB	Charlotte	21 B/10	44°38′	66°43′
Whitehead Harbour	BAY/BAIE	NS	Guysborough	11 F/3	45°15′	61°10′
White Head Island	ISL/ÎLE	NS	Guysborough	11 F/3	45°12′	61°08′
White Head Island	ISL/ÎLE	NB	Charlotte	21 B/10	44°38′	66°42′
White-Head-Percé	UNP/LNO	QC	Pabok	22 A/8	48°30′	64°15′
Whitehead Pond	LAKE/LAC	NF		2 D/1	48°03′	54°28′
White Heron Lake	LAKE/LAC	SK	34-22-W3	72 N/14	51°54′	109°04′
White Hill	UNP/LNO	NS	Pictou	11 E/7	45°29′	62°45′
White Hills	UNP/LNO	ON	Middlesex	40 P/3	43°00′	81°19′
Whitehills Lake	LAKE/LAC	NT	Keewatin	66 A	64°35′	96°00′
Whitehorse	CITY/VIL1	YT		105 D/11	60°43′	135°03′
Whitehorse 8	IR/RI	YT		105 D/11	60°45′	135°05′
White House	UNP/LNO	NF		12 P/7	51°29′	56°57′
Whitehouse	UNP/LNO	QC	La Côte-de-Gaspé	22 A/14	48°55′	65°10′
White Island	ISL/ÎLE	NF		2 F/12	49°34′	53°54′
White Island	ISL/ÎLE	NT	Keewatin	46 F	65°47′	84°54′
White Lake	UNP/LNO	ON	Renfrew	31 F/7	45°22′	76°30′
White Lake	UNP/LNO	ON	Hastings	31 C/6	44°27′	77°28′
White Lake	UNP/LNO	MB	12-15-E	52 L/4	50°02′	95°31′
White Lake	UNP/LNO	BC	Kamloops Division Yale	82 L/14	50°53′	119°18′
White Lake	LAKE/LAC	ON	Renfrew	31 F/7	45°18′	76°31′
White Lake	LAKE/LAC	ON	Lennox and Addington	31 C/6	44°28′	77°03′
White Lake	LAKE/LAC	ON	Thunder Bay	42 C/13	48°47′	85°37′
White Lake	LAKE/LAC	MB	12-14,15-E	52 L/4	50°02′	95°32′
White Lake	LAKE/LAC	BC	Kamloops Division Yale	82 L/14	50°53′	119°16′
White Lake	LAKE/LAC	BC	Lillooet	92 P/5	51°24′	121°52′
Whitelaw	UNP/LNO	AB	15-82-1-W6	84 D/1	56°07′	118°04′
Whiteman Creek	RIV/CDE	BC	Osoyoos Division Yale	82 L/3	50°14′	119°26′
Whitemouth	MUN2/AZM2	MB		52 E/13	49°58′	95°57′
Whitemouth	UNP/LNO	MB	36-11-11-E	52 E/13	49°57′	95°59′
Whitemouth Lake	LAKE/LAC	MB	3-13-14-E	52 E/4	49°15′	95°41′
Whitemouth River	RIV/CDE	MB	33-13-11-E	62 I/1	50°07′	96°02′
Whitemud Creek	UNP/LNO	AB	1-75-23-W5	83 N/6	55°28′	117°25′
White Mud Falls	UNP/LNO	MB	17-11-E	62 I/8	50°28′	96°04′
Whitemud Falls	FALL/CHUT	MB		63 I/12	54°45′	97°53′
Whitemud Lake	LAKE/LAC	ON	Kenora	52 K/15	50°51′	92°45′
Whitemud Lake	LAKE/LAC	MB		53 M/3	55°08′	95°10′
Whitemud River	RIV/CDE	MB	1-15-9-W	62 J/7	50°15′	98°35′
Whitemud River	RIV/CDE	AB	30-88-20-W5	84 C/11	56°40′	117°10′
White Oak	UNP/LNO	ON	Middlesex	40 I/14	42°54′	81°14′
White Oak Lake	LAKE/LAC	ON	Sudbury	41 I/7	46°18′	81°00′
White Oaks Village	UNP/LNO	ON	Haldimand	40 I/16	42°56′	80°08′
White Otter Lake	LAKE/LAC	ON	Kenora	52 G/4	49°07′	91°52′
White Otter River	RIV/CDE	ON	Thunder Bay	42 E/8	49°19′	86°02′
White Owl Lake	LAKE/LAC	ON	Algoma	41 O/2	47°10′	82°35′
White Partridge Island	ISL/ÎLE	NT	Mackenzie	65 D	60°07′	102°07′

NAME NOM	ENTITY ENTITÉ	LOC 1 LIEU 1	LOC 2 LIEU 2	MAP CARTE	POSITION LAT	LONG
White Partridge Lake	LAKE/LAC	ON	Nipissing	31 E/16	45°50'	78°06'
White Pass	UNP/LNO	BC	Cassiar	104 M/11	59°37'	135°08'
White Pass	VALL/VALL	BC	Cassiar	104 M/11	59°38'	135°08'
White Pigeon	UNP/LNO	ON	Welland	30 M/3	43°00'	79°07'
White Plains	UNP/LNO	MB		62 H/13	49°51'	97°32'
White Point	UNP/LNO	NS	Victoria	11 K/16	46°52'	60°21'
White Point	UNP/LNO	NS	Queens	20 P/15	43°57'	64°44'
White Point	CAPE/CAP	NF		1 M/3	47°11'	55°29'
White Point	CAPE/CAP	NS	Victoria	11 K/16	46°53'	60°21'
White Point	CAPE/CAP	NS	Lunenburg	21 A/9	44°30'	64°00'
White Point	CAPE/CAP	NS	Queens	20 P/15	43°57'	64°44'
White Point	CAPE/CAP	NT	Franklin	560 D	81°12'	90°14'
Whitepool	UNP/LNO	SK	9-33-21-W3	72 N/15	51°49'	108°55'
White Rapids	UNP/LNO	NB	Northumberland	21 I/13	46°48'	65°47'
White River	MUN2/AZM2	ON	Algoma	42 C/11	48°35'	85°15'
White River	UNP/LNO	ON	Algoma	42 C/11	48°36'	85°17'
White River	RIV/CDE	ON	Thunder Bay	42 D/9	48°33'	86°16'
White River	RIV/CDE	BC	Kootenay	82 J/5	50°21'	115°37'
White River	RIV/CDE	BC	Sayward	92 K/5	50°18'	125°54'
White River	RIV/CDE	YT		115 O/4	63°11'	139°36'
White Rock	CITY/VIL1	BC	New Westminster	92 G/2	49°01'	122°48'
White Rock	UNP/LNO	NF		2 C/4	48°11'	53°51'
White Rock	UNP/LNO	NS	Kings	21 H/1	45°03'	64°25'
White Rose	UNP/LNO	ON	York	30 M/14	43°59'	79°25'
Whites	UNP/LNO	ON	Elgin	40 I/11	42°43'	81°12'
Whitesail Lake	LAKE/LAC	BC	Range 4 Coast	93 E/6	53°30'	127°00'
Whitesail Reach	RIVF/EFLV	BC	Range 4 Coast	93 E/10	53°40'	126°42'
Whitesand	UNP/LNO	SK	28-28-5-W2	62 M/7	51°27'	102°40'
Whitesand Bay	BAY/BAIE	MB/SK		64 C/13	56°59'	101°59'
Whitesand	IR/RI	ON	Thunder Bay	52 I/6	50°19'	89°02'
Whitesand River	RIV/CDE	SK	3-30-32-W	62 N/12	51°34'	101°56'
Whitesand River	RIV/CDE	NT/AB		85 B/4	60°11'	115°45'
White Sands	VILG/VILG	AB	24-40-20-W4	83 A/7	52°28'	112°49'
White Sands	UNP/LNO	PE	Kings	11 E/15	45°58'	62°33'
White Sandy River	RIV/CDE	NT	Mackenzie	86 J	66°07'	114°15'
Whites Bluff	UNP/LNO	NB	Kings	21 G/8	45°28'	66°06'
Whites Brook	UNP/LNO	NB	Restigouche	21 O/11	47°41'	67°17'
Whites Brook	RIV/CDE	NB	Restigouche	21 O/14	47°50'	67°23'
Whites Corner	UNP/LNO	NS	Kings	21 H/2	45°09'	64°43'
Whites Cove	UNP/LNO	NB	Queens	21 G/16	45°52'	66°04'
White Settlement	UNP/LNO	NS	Hants	11 E/4	45°13'	63°43'
Whiteshell River	RIV/CDE	MB	7-14-14-E	52 L/4	50°09'	95°40'
Whiteshore Lake	LAKE/LAC	SK	36-16,17-W3	73 C/1	52°07'	108°17'
Whiteside	UNP/LNO	NS	Richmond	11 F/11	45°36'	61°11'
Whiteside	UNP/LNO	ON	Muskoka	31 E/4	45°04'	79°36'
Whites Junction	UNP/LNO	ON	Wellington	40 P/15	43°51'	80°51'
Whites Lake	UNP/LNO	NS	Halifax	11 D/12	44°32'	63°46'
Whites Mills	UNP/LNO	NB	Kings	21 G/8	45°25'	66°06'
Whites Mountain	UNP/LNO	NB	Kings	21 H/14	45°53'	65°26'
White Spruce	UNP/LNO	SK	35-26-5-W2	62 M/7	51°18'	102°35'
Whites Road	UNP/LNO	NF		12 B/9	48°33'	58°25'
Whites Settlement	UNP/LNO	NB	Kent	21 I/7	46°19'	64°39'
White Star	UNP/LNO	SK	16-50-26-W2	73 H/5	53°18'	105°44'
Whitestone	UNP/LNO	ON	Parry Sound	31 E/12	45°41'	79°59'
Whitestone Lake	LAKE/LAC	ON	Parry Sound	31 E/12	45°39'	79°52'
Whitestone Lake	LAKE/LAC	ON	Kenora	52 O/13	51°57'	91°57'
White Stone Lake	LAKE/LAC	MB		64 A/5	56°27'	97°30'
Whitestone River	RIV/CDE	YT		116 J/9	66°30'	138°25'
Whitestone Village	UNP/LNO	YT		116 J/8	66°25'	138°25'
White Strait	CHAN/CHEN	NT	Franklin	25 L	62°50'	70°40'
Whiteswan Lake	LAKE/LAC	BC	Kootenay	82 J/3	50°08'	115°30'
Whiteswan Lakes	LAKE/LAC	SK		73 I/3	54°05'	105°10'
Whitevale	UNP/LNO	ON	Ontario	30 M/14	43°53'	79°09'
White Valley No. 49	MUN2/AZM2	SK	0	72 F/7	49°25'	108°40'
Whitewater	MUN2/AZM2	MB		62 F/8	49°25'	100°05'
White Water	UNP/LNO	NS	Kings	21 H/8	45°15'	64°21'
Whitewater	UNP/LNO	MB	8-3-21-W	62 F/1	49°12'	100°17'
Whitewater Creek	RIV/CDE	SK	1-1-15-W3	72 G/4	49°00'	107°53'
Whitewater Lake	LAKE/LAC	ON	Sudbury	41 I/11	46°32'	81°09'
Whitewater Lake	LAKE/LAC	ON	Thunder Bay	52 I/14	50°48'	89°10'
Whitewater Lake	LAKE/LAC	MB	3,4-21,22-W	62 F/1	49°15'	100°19'
Whitewater Lake	LAKE/LAC	MB	21-21,22-W	62 K/16	50°48'	100°24'
White Water Lily Lake	LAKE/LAC	NT	Mackenzie	96 F	65°46'	124°07'
Whiteway	VILG/VILG	NF		1 N/11	47°41'	53°29'
Whiteway Bay	BAY/BAIE	NF		1 N/12	47°41'	53°30'

NAME NOM	ENTITY ENTITÉ	LOC 1 LIEU 1	LOC 2 LIEU 2	MAP CARTE	POSITION LAT	LONG
Whitewolf Lake	LAKE/LAC	NT	Mackenzie	86 A	64°58′	114°00′
Whitewood	TOWN/VIL2	SK	7-16-2-W2	62 L/8	50°20′	102°16′
Whitewood Grove	UNP/LNO	ON	Timiskaming	31 M/12	47°43′	79°44′
Whitewood Hills	MTN/MNT	SK	44-14-W3	73 B/13	52°50′	107°57′
Whitfield	UNP/LNO	ON	Dufferin	41 A/1	44°09′	80°08′
Whitford	UNP/LNO	AB	30-56-15-W4	83 H/16	53°52′	112°13′
Whitford Lake	LAKE/LAC	AB	56-15,16-W4	83 H/16	53°52′	112°15′
Whithorn	UNP/LNO	MB	29-52-28-W	63 F/12	53°31′	101°33′
Whiting River	RIV/CDE	BC	Cassiar	104 K/3	58°11′	133°13′
Whitkow	UNP/LNO	SK	6-46-13-W3	73 B/13	52°56′	107°52′
Whitla	UNP/LNO	AB	5-11-8-W4	72 E/14	49°52′	111°03′
Whitley Bay	BAY/BAIE	NT	Franklin	25 E	61°22′	71°35′
Whitmore	UNP/LNO	MB	23-43-26-W	63 C/11	52°43′	101°07′
Whitmore Lake	LAKE/LAC	MB		64 N/2	59°04′	100°56′
Whitmore Park	UNP/LNO	SK		72 I/7	50°24′	104°36′
Whitney	UNP/LNO	NB	Northumberland	21 I/13	46°58′	65°44′
Whitney	UNP/LNO	ON	Nipissing	31 E/8	45°30′	78°14′
Whitney	UNP/LNO	AB	18-10-22-W4	82 H/15	49°50′	112°58′
Whitney Inlet	BAY/BAIE	NT	Keewatin	55 O	63°45′	90°00′
Whitney Lakes Provincial Park	PARK/PARC	AB	56-4-W4	73 E/15	53°51′	110°32′
Whitney Pier	UNP/LNO	NS	Cape Breton	11 K/1	46°09′	60°11′
Whitney Pond	LAKE/LAC	NF		2 E/1	49°10′	54°08′
Whitsunday Bay	BAY/BAIE	NT	Franklin	49 F	79°00′	86°55′
Whittier	UNP/LNO	MB		62 H/14	49°54′	97°07′
Whittier Ridge	UNP/LNO	NB	Charlotte	21 G/6	45°19′	67°03′
Whittington	UNP/LNO	ON	Dufferin	40 P/16	43°59′	80°10′
Whittle, Cap	CAPE/CAP	QC	Côte-Nord-du-Golfe-Saint-Laurent	12 K/1	50°11′	60°08′
Whittome	UNP/LNO	SK	35-45-18-W2	73 A/16	52°56′	104°30′
Whitworth 21	IR/RI	QC	Rivière-du-Loup	21 N/11	47°42′	69°17′
Whitworth Peak	MTN/MNT	BC	Yale Division Yale	92 H/3	49°05′	121°13′
Wholdaia Lake	LAKE/LAC	NT	Mackenzie	75 A/9	60°43′	104°10′
Whonnock	UNP/LNO	BC	New Westminster	92 G/1	49°11′	122°28′
Whonnock 1	IR/RI	BC	New Westminster	92 G/1	49°10′	122°28′
Whyac	UNP/LNO	BC	Barclay	92 C/10	48°40′	124°51′
Whycocomagh	UNP/LNO	NS	Inverness	11 F/14	45°59′	61°07′
Whycocomagh 2	IR/RI	NS	Inverness	11 F/14	45°58′	61°09′
Whycocomagh Portage	UNP/LNO	NS	Inverness	11 F/14	45°57′	61°01′
Whycocomagh Reserve	UNP/LNO	NS	Inverness	11 F/14	45°58′	61°08′
Whyeek 4	IR/RI	BC	Kamloops Division Yale	92 I/4	50°07′	121°34′
Whymper, Mount	MTN/MNT	BC	Cowichan Lake	92 C/16	48°57′	124°10′
Whynachts Point	UNP/LNO	NS	Halifax	11 D/12	44°40′	63°54′
Whynotts Settlement	UNP/LNO	NS	Lunenburg	21 A/8	44°24′	64°28′
Whytecliff	UNP/LNO	BC	New Westminster	92 G/6	49°22′	123°17′
Whyte Ridge	UNP/LNO	MB		62 H/14	49°49′	97°12′
Whytewold	UNP/LNO	MB	14,15-17-4E	62 I/7	50°27′	96°57′
Wiah Point	CAPE/CAP	BC	Queen Charlotte	103 K/1	54°07′	132°19′
Wiarton	TOWN/VIL2	ON	Bruce	41 A/11	44°45′	81°09′
Wiau Lake	LAKE/LAC	AB	73,74-9-W4	73 M/6	55°23′	111°18′
Wick	UNP/LNO	ON	Ontario	31 D/3	44°13′	79°02′
Wickaninnish Bay	BAY/BAIE	BC	Clayoquot	92 F/4	49°03′	125°44′
Wicked Point	CAPE/CAP	MB	44-16-W	63 B/15	52°48′	98°49′
Wickenden, Lac	LAKE/LAC	QC	Minganie	12 E/11	49°33′	63°04′
Wickett	UNP/LNO	SK	22-18-17-W3	72 K/9	50°32′	108°16′
Wickham	VILG/VILG	QC	Drummond	31 H/15	45°45′	72°30′
Wickham	UNP/LNO	NB	Queens	21 G/9	45°39′	66°04′
Wickham	UNP/LNO	NB	Carleton	21 J/4	46°03′	67°40′
Wickham	GEOG/GÉOG	NB	Queens	21 G/9	45°42′	66°00′
Wicklow	UNP/LNO	NB	Carleton	21 J/5	46°29′	67°36′
Wicklow	UNP/LNO	ON	Northumberland	30 N/13	44°00′	77°59′
Wicklow	GEOG/GÉOG	NB	Carleton	21 J/12	46°30′	67°40′
Wicksteed - see-voir - Hornepayne	MUN2/AZM2	ON		42 F/7	49°15′	84°47′
Wicksteed Lake	LAKE/LAC	ON	Nipissing	31 L/13	46°46′	79°40′
Wideview	UNP/LNO	SK	22-3-9-W3	72 G/3	49°14′	107°07′
Widewater	UNP/LNO	AB	32-73-7-W5	83 O/6	55°22′	115°02′
Widgeon Lake	LAKE/LAC	BC	New Westminster	92 G/7	49°27′	122°40′
Wiegand Island	ISL/ÎLE	NT	Keewatin	34 D	56°40′	79°12′
Wienerwurst Mountain	MTN/MNT	YT		115 K/15	62°55′	140°56′
Wiggins Mill	UNP/LNO	NB	York	21 J/3	46°03′	67°06′
Wights Corners	UNP/LNO	ON	Leeds	31 B/12	44°39′	75°58′
Wigle	UNP/LNO	ON	Essex	40 J/2	42°06′	82°37′
Wignes Lake	LAKE/LAC	NT	Mackenzie	75 A	60°10′	105°55′
Wigwam Beach	UNP/LNO	QC	Roussillon	31 H/5	45°24′	73°43′
Wigwam Creek	RIV/CDE	ON	Algoma	42 B/15	48°58′	82°50′
Wigwam Inn	UNP/LNO	BC	New Westminster	92 G/7	49°28′	122°53′
Wigwam River	RIV/CDE	BC	Kootenay	82 G/3	49°15′	115°06′

NAME NOM	ENTITY ENTITÉ	LOC 1 LIEU 1	LOC 2 LIEU 2	MAP CARTE	POSITION LAT	LONG
Wigwascence Lake	LAKE/LAC	ON	Kenora	53 A/6	52°27'	89°24'
Wikopi	UNP/LNO	QC	Antoine-Labelle	31 O/7	47°27'	74°32'
Wikwemikong	UNP/LNO	ON	Manitoulin	41 H/13	45°48'	81°43'
Wikwemikonsing	UNP/LNO	ON	Manitoulin	41 H/12	45°43'	81°41'
Wikwemikong Unceded 26	IR/RI	ON	Manitoulin	41 H/12	45°41'	81°43'
Wilbank Bay	BAY/BAIE	NT	Franklin	77 B	68°38'	110°10'
Wilberforce	MUN2/AZM2	ON	Renfrew	31 F/11	45°36'	77°09'
Wilberforce	UNP/LNO	ON	Haliburton	31 E/1	45°02'	78°13'
Wilberforce Falls	FALL/CHUT	NT	Mackenzie	76 N	67°06'	108°47'
Wilberforce Hills	MTN/MNT	NT	Mackenzie	76 N	67°02'	108°34'
Wilber Lake	LAKE/LAC	ON	Renfrew	31 F/11	45°34'	77°11'
Wilbert	UNP/LNO	SK	33-43-22-W3	73 C/14	52°45'	109°09'
Wilbert Hills	MTN/MNT	BC	Similkameen Division Yale	92 H/8	49°20'	120°22'
Wilbur	UNP/LNO	ON	Frontenac	31 F/2	45°01'	76°42'
Wilburn	UNP/LNO	NS	Inverness	11 F/14	45°56'	61°06'
Wilcox	VILG/VILG	SK	19-13-20-W2	72 I/2	50°06'	104°44'
Wilcox Corners	UNP/LNO	ON	Lincoln	30 M/4	43°05'	79°36'
Wilcox Lake	UNP/LNO	ON	Grey	41 A/2	44°13'	80°33'
Wild Bight	UNP/LNO	NF		2 M/12	51°36'	55°54'
Wild Bight	BAY/BAIE	NF		2 E/12	49°36'	55°38'
Wild Bight	BAY/BAIE	NF		2 E/5	49°23'	55°41'
Wild Bight	BAY/BAIE	NF		2 E/13	49°50'	55°43'
Wildbread Bay	BAY/BAIE	NT	Mackenzie	75 L	62°45'	110°05'
Wildcat	UNP/LNO	AB	16-26-5-W5	82 O/2	51°13'	114°39'
Wildcat 12	IR/RI	NS	Queens	21 A/7	44°21'	64°55'
Wild Cove	UNP/LNO	NF		2 E/10	49°40'	54°47'
Wild Cove	UNP/LNO	NF		12 I/9	50°41'	56°10'
Wild Cove	UNP/LNO	NF		12 H/16	50°00'	56°20'
Wild Cove	UNP/LNO	NF		12 H/12	49°32'	57°53'
Wild Cove	BAY/BAIE	NF		2 E/9	49°37'	54°08'
Wild Cove Point	CAPE/CAP	NF		12 H/15	49°50'	56°35'
Wild Cove Pond	LAKE/LAC	NF		12 H/10	49°42'	56°31'
Wild Cove Pond	LAKE/LAC	NF		12 G/1	49°02'	58°25'
Wilde	UNP/LNO	MB	5-78-5-W	63 P/10	55°44'	96°49'
Wildfield	UNP/LNO	ON	Peel	30 M/13	43°49'	79°44'
Wild Goose	UNP/LNO	ON	Thunder Bay	52 A/6	48°29'	89°05'
Wildgoose Lake	LAKE/LAC	ON	Thunder Bay	42 E/11	49°44'	87°11'
Wild Hay	UNP/LNO	AB	12-53-27-W5	83 F/12	53°34'	117°51'
Wildhay River	RIV/CDE	AB	58-23-W5	83 F/14	53°59'	117°16'
Wild Horse	UNP/LNO	AB	4-1-2-W4	72 E/1	49°00'	110°13'
Wilding Lake	LAKE/LAC	NF		12 A/7	48°25'	56°48'
Wild Lake	LAKE/LAC	ON	Kenora	52 E/16	49°58'	94°07'
Wild Lands 15M	IR/RI	ON	Rainy River	52 D/15	48°48'	94°35'
Wildmere	UNP/LNO	AB	12-48-6-W4	73 E/2	53°08'	110°45'
Wildnest Lake	LAKE/LAC	SK		63 L/16	55°00'	102°20'
Wild Point	CAPE/CAP	NF		2 E/9	49°37'	54°07'
Wild Rose	UNP/LNO	SK	50-2-W2	73 G/8	53°18'	106°12'
Wildwood	UNP/LNO	AB	27-53-9-W5	83 G/11	53°37'	115°14'
Wildwood	UNP/LNO	QC	Vaudreuil-Soulanges	31 G/8	45°25'	74°01'
Wildwood	UNP/LNO	ON	Halton	30 M/12	43°40'	79°56'
Wildwood	UNP/LNO	MB		62 H/14	49°51'	97°08'
Wildwood	UNP/LNO	SK		73 B/2	52°07'	106°36'
Wildwood	UNP/LNO	BC	New Westminster	92 F/15	49°54'	124°34'
Wildwood Lake	UNP/LNO	NS	Halifax	11 D/12	44°41'	63°30'
Wildwood Lake	LAKE/LAC	ON	Oxford	40 P/3	43°15'	81°03'
Wile Settlement	UNP/LNO	NS	Hants	21 A/16	44°49'	64°16'
Wileville	UNP/LNO	NS	Lunenburg	21 A/7	44°22'	64°33'
Wiley	UNP/LNO	BC	Range 5 Coast	93 L/9	54°31'	126°20'
Wileys Corner	UNP/LNO	NB	Charlotte	21 G/3	45°07'	67°06'
Wilfrid	UNP/LNO	ON	Ontario	31 D/6	44°19'	79°10'
Wilgar	UNP/LNO	ON	Cochrane	42 K/3	50°02'	85°24'
Wilkes, Cape	CAPE/CAP	NT	Franklin	120 B	80°11'	70°08'
Wilkesport	UNP/LNO	ON	Lambton	40 J/9	42°44'	82°22'
Wilkie	TOWN/VIL2	SK	5-40-19-W3	73 C/7	52°25'	108°42'
Wilkie Point	CAPE/CAP	NT	Franklin	89 B	76°15'	117°18'
Wilkins	UNP/LNO	NS	Queens	20 P/15	43°55'	64°59'
Wilkinson	UNP/LNO	ON	Frontenac	31 C/10	44°32'	76°49'
Wilkinson Creek	RIV/CDE	BC	Similkameen Division Yale	82 E/11	49°30'	119°07'
Wilkinson Mountain	MTN/MNT	NB	Northumberland	21 O/2	47°07'	66°45'
Wilkinson Range	MTN/MNT	YT		105 L/16	62°52'	134°10'
Wilkins Strait	CHAN/CHEN	NT	Franklin	89 E	78°10'	112°00'
Willard	UNP/LNO	MB	30-8-4-E	62 H/11	49°42'	97°03'
Willard Lake	UNP/LNO	ON	Kenora	52 F/13	49°50'	93°58'
Willard Lake	LAKE/LAC	ON	Kenora	52 F/13	49°51'	93°58'
Willbeach	UNP/LNO	MB	83-16-E	54 D/3	56°14'	95°01'

NAME / NOM	ENTITY / ENTITÉ	LOC 1 / LIEU 1	LOC 2 / LIEU 2	MAP / CARTE	POSITION LAT	POSITION LONG
Willen	UNP/LNO	MB	11-14-28-W	62 K/3	50°10′	101°13′
Willersted Inlet	BAY/BAIE	NT	Franklin	57 C	69°20′	93°40′
Willesden Green	UNP/LNO	AB	1-43-5-W5	83 B/10	52°41′	114°35′
Willet Lake	LAKE/LAC	ON	Thunder Bay	42 L/5	50°20′	87°41′
Willetsholme	UNP/LNO	ON	Leeds	31 C/8	44°21′	76°14′
William A. Switzer Provincial Park	PARK/PARC	AB	51,52-26-W5	83 F/5	53°29′	117°48′
William-Baldwin, Réserve écologique	PARK/PARC	QC	Abitibi	32 D/16	48°55′	78°24′
William Head	CAPE/CAP	BC	Metchosin	92 B/5	48°21′	123°32′
William Herschel, Cape	CAPE/CAP	NT	Franklin	58 E	74°35′	89°12′
William, Lac	LAKE/LAC	QC	L'Érable	21 L/4	46°07′	71°34′
William Lake	LAKE/LAC	MB		63 G/14	53°54′	99°22′
William Lake	LAKE/LAC	BC	Rupert	102 I/9	50°44′	128°12′
William McKenzie 151K	IR/RI	AB	81-19-W5	84 C/2	56°01′	116°53′
William Point	CAPE/CAP	SK		74 N/3	59°08′	109°16′
William Poker's Mesh	UNP/LNO	QC	Côte-Nord-du-Golfe-Saint-Laurent	12 O/2	51°15′	58°40′
William River	RIV/CDE	MB	56-10-W	63 G/15	53°52′	98°56′
William River	RIV/CDE	SK		74 N/3	59°08′	109°19′
Williams	UNP/LNO	NF		1 N/7	47°26′	52°46′
Williams 2	IR/RI	BC	New Westminster	92 H/4	49°14′	121°57′
Williams Beach	UNP/LNO	BC	Comox	92 F/14	49°50′	125°03′
Williamsburg	UNP/LNO	NB	York	21 J/7	46°20′	66°47′
Williamsburg	UNP/LNO	ON	Dundas	31 B/14	44°58′	75°15′
Williamsburg	UNP/LNO	ON	Waterloo	40 P/8	43°24′	80°30′
Williamsburgh	MUN2/AZM2	ON	Dundas	31 B/14	45°00′	75°11′
Williamsdale	UNP/LNO	NS	Cumberland	11 E/12	45°36′	63°54′
Williamsford	UNP/LNO	ON	Grey	41 A/7	44°23′	80°52′
Williams Harbour	UNP/LNO	NF		3 D/12	52°33′	55°47′
Williams Lake	CITY/VIL1	BC	Cariboo	93 B/1	52°09′	122°09′
Williams Lake	LAKE/LAC	ON	Kenora	52 O/15	51°48′	90°45′
Williams Lake	LAKE/LAC	ON	Kenora	52 K/2	50°15′	92°50′
Williams Lake	LAKE/LAC	BC	Cariboo	93 B/1	52°07′	122°04′
Williams Lake	LAKE/LAC	NT	Mackenzie	75 O	63°08′	106°10′
Williams Lake 1	IR/RI	BC	Cariboo	93 B/1	52°07′	122°00′
Williams Landing	UNP/LNO	BC	New Westminster	92 G/7	49°26′	122°31′
William-Smith, Cap	CAPE/CAP	QC	Kativik	25 A/7	60°22′	64°51′
Williamson Provincial Park	PARK/PARC	AB	70-24-W5	83 N/4	55°05′	117°33′
Williamsons Landing	UNP/LNO	BC	New Westminster	92 G/6	49°27′	123°28′
Williams Peninsula	CAPE/CAP	NT	Franklin	25 I	62°56′	64°40′
Williams Point	UNP/LNO	NS	Antigonish	11 F/12	45°38′	61°56′
Williams Point	UNP/LNO	ON	Durham	31 D/2	44°10′	78°49′
Williams Point	CAPE/CAP	NT	Franklin	87 C	69°24′	116°30′
Williamsport	UNP/LNO	NF		12 I/9	50°32′	56°19′
Williamsport	UNP/LNO	ON	Muskoka	31 E/6	45°24′	79°10′
Williams Prairie Meadow 1A	IR/RI	BC	Range 5 Coast	93 K/8	54°28′	124°12′
Williamstown	UNP/LNO	NB	Northumberland	21 I/13	46°56′	65°42′
Williamstown	UNP/LNO	NB	Carleton	21 J/5	46°23′	67°42′
Williamstown	UNP/LNO	ON	Glengarry	31 G/2	45°08′	74°35′
Williamstown Lake	LAKE/LAC	NB	Carleton	21 J/5	46°19′	67°42′
Williamswood	UNP/LNO	NS	Halifax	11 D/12	44°31′	63°38′
Willingdon	VILG/VILG	AB	11-56-15-W4	83 H/16	53°50′	112°08′
Willingdon Heights	UNP/LNO	BC	New Westminster	92 G/6	49°17′	123°01′
Willingdon, Mount	MTN/MNT	AB	32-16-W5	82 N/16	51°45′	116°15′
Willis Bay	BAY/BAIE	NT	Franklin	67 H	71°56′	96°35′
Willis Creek	RIV/CDE	BC	Similkameen Division Yale	92 H/8	49°24′	120°25′
Williscroft	UNP/LNO	ON	Bruce	41 A/6	44°23′	81°14′
Willis Island	ISL/ÎLE	NF		2 C/13	48°48′	53°43′
Willis Reach	RIVF/EFLV	NF		2 C/13	48°49′	53°41′
Williston Lake	LAKE/LAC	BC	Cassiar	94 C/1	56°00′	124°00′
Willisville	UNP/LNO	ON	Sudbury	41 I/4	46°08′	81°43′
Willmar	UNP/LNO	SK	22-6-4-W2	62 E/8	49°29′	102°28′
Will, Mount	MTN/MNT	BC	Cassiar	104 H/10	57°33′	128°48′
Willner No. 253	MUN2/AZM2	SK		72 O/1	51°15′	106°20′
Willoughby Point	CAPE/CAP	NT	Franklin	88 A	72°46′	113°36′
Willowbank	UNP/LNO	ON	Leeds	31 C/8	44°19′	76°13′
Willow Bay	UNP/LNO	ON	Welland	30 L/14	42°52′	79°25′
Willow Beach	UNP/LNO	ON	York	31 D/6	44°19′	79°25′
Willow Beach	UNP/LNO	ON	Muskoka	31 E/3	45°03′	79°25′
Willow Beach	UNP/LNO	ON	Essex	40 J/3	42°03′	83°06′
Willowbrook	VILG/VILG	SK	33-25-6-W2	62 M/2	51°12′	102°48′
Willowbrook	UNP/LNO	BC	Similkameen Division Yale	82 E/5	49°16′	119°35′
Willowbrook	UNP/LNO	BC	Peace River	93 P/15	55°49′	120°33′
Willow Brook	RIV/CDE	ON	Dufferin	40 P/16	43°53′	80°17′
Willow Bunch	TOWN/VIL2	SK		72 H/5	49°23′	105°38′
Willow Bunch Lake	LAKE/LAC	SK		72 H/6	49°27′	105°27′
Willow Bunch No. 42	MUN2/AZM2	SK		72 H/5	49°25′	105°40′

NAME NOM	ENTITY ENTITÉ	LOC 1 LIEU 1	LOC 2 LIEU 2	MAP CARTE	POSITION LAT	LONG
Willow Creek	UNP/LNO	SK	6-1-28-W3	72 F/4	49°00'	109°44'
Willow Creek	UNP/LNO	AB	12-28-19-W4	82 P/7	51°23'	112°32'
Willow Creek	RIV/CDE	ON	Simcoe	31 D/5	44°25'	79°54'
Willow Creek	RIV/CDE	ON	Bruce	41 A/6	44°18'	81°16'
Willow Creek	RIV/CDE	AB	9-25-W4	82 H/13	49°46'	113°22'
Willow Creek No. 26, Municipal District of	MUN1/AZM1	AB	12-27-W4	82 H/13	49°58'	113°38'
Willow Creek No. 458	MUN2/AZM2	SK		73 H/1	53°00'	104°20'
Willow Creek Provincial Park	PARK/PARC	AB	13-28-W4	82 I/4	50°07'	113°46'
Willowdale	UNP/LNO	NS	Pictou	11 E/8	45°24'	62°13'
Willowdale	UNP/LNO	NS	Halifax	11 D/11	44°39'	63°29'
Willowdale	UNP/LNO	ON	York	30 M/14	43°46'	79°24'
Willowdale No. 153	MUN2/AZM2	SK		62 L/8	50°25'	102°15'
Willow Grove	UNP/LNO	NB	Saint John	21 H/5	45°20'	65°49'
Willow Grove	UNP/LNO	ON	Haldimand	30 M/4	43°01'	80°00'
Willow Grove	UNP/LNO	ON	Perth	40 P/11	43°31'	81°09'
Willow Hills	MTN/MNT	YT		115 P/2	63°09'	136°51'
Willow Lake	UNP/LNO	ON	Oxford	40 P/2	43°11'	80°47'
Willow Lake	LAKE/LAC	AB	13-86-8-W4	74 D/6	56°28'	111°08'
Willow Lake	LAKE/LAC	NT	Mackenzie	85 L	62°10'	119°08'
Willowlake River	RIV/CDE	NT	Mackenzie	95 J	62°42'	123°08'
Willow Meadow 9	IR/RI	BC	Range 3 Coast	93 C/12	52°45'	125°32'
Willowood	UNP/LNO	ON	Essex	40 J/3	42°03'	83°05'
*Willow Park	UNP/LNO	MB		62 H/14	49°56'	97°11'
Willow Point	UNP/LNO	BC	Kootenay	82 F/11	49°34'	117°14'
Willow Point	CAPE/CAP	MB	19-4-E	62 I/10	50°36'	96°57'
*Willow River	UNP/LNO	BC	Cariboo	93 G/8	53°18'	122°00'
Willow River	UNP/LNO	BC	Cariboo	93 J/1	54°04'	122°28'
Willow River	RIV/CDE	AB	80-25-W4	83 P/13	55°58'	113°55'
Willow River	RIV/CDE	BC	Cariboo	93 J/2	54°05'	122°30'
Willows	UNP/LNO	SK	35-7-29-W2	72 H/12	49°36'	105°51'
Willows Island	ISL/ÎLE	NT	Franklin	25 I	62°47'	65°29'
Willowvale	UNP/LNO	SK	9-2-2-W3	72 G/1	49°06'	106°13'
Willowvale	UNP/LNO	BC	Range 5 Coast	93 K/1	54°02'	124°27'
Willow Valley	UNP/LNO	BC	Peace River	93 P/15	55°51'	120°52'
Willowview	UNP/LNO	MB	13-20-2-W	62 I/12	50°42'	97°36'
Willroy	UNP/LNO	ON	Thunder Bay	42 F/4	49°10'	85°49'
Wilmer	UNP/LNO	ON	Frontenac	31 C/7	44°27'	76°31'
Wilmer	UNP/LNO	BC	Kootenay	82 K/9	50°32'	116°04'
Wilmot - see-voir - Summerside	VILG/VILG	PE		11 L/5	46°24'	63°47'
Wilmot	MUN2/AZM2	ON	Waterloo	40 P/7	43°25'	80°38'
Wilmot	UNP/LNO	PE	Kings	11 L/2	46°01'	62°34'
Wilmot	UNP/LNO	PE	Prince	11 L/5	46°24'	63°46'
Wilmot	UNP/LNO	NS	Annapolis	21 A/14	44°57'	65°01'
Wilmot	UNP/LNO	NB	York	21 G/11	45°40'	67°07'
Wilmot	UNP/LNO	NB	Carleton	21 J/5	46°19'	67°37'
Wilmot	GEOG/GÉOG	NB	Carleton	21 J/5	46°23'	67°40'
Wilmot and Crampton Bay	BAY/BAIE	NT	Franklin	67 A	68°11'	98°45'
Wilmot Centre	UNP/LNO	ON	Waterloo	40 P/7	43°23'	80°38'
Wilmot Islands	ISL/ÎLE	NT	Franklin	77 B	68°11'	109°09'
Wilmot River	RIV/CDE	PE	Prince	11 L/5	46°23'	63°46'
Wilmot Valley	UNP/LNO	PE	Prince	11 L/5	46°24'	63°42'
Wilnaskancaud 3	IR/RI	BC	Range 5 Coast	103 J/8	54°19'	130°16'
Wilno	UNP/LNO	ON	Renfrew	31 F/12	45°31'	77°34'
Wilskaskammel 14	IR/RI	BC	Range 5 Coast	103 J/8	54°27'	130°04'
Wilson	UNP/LNO	QC	L'Amiante	21 L/6	46°19'	71°18'
Wilson	UNP/LNO	ON	Frontenac	31 F/3	45°06'	77°05'
Wilson	UNP/LNO	ON	Timiskaming	41 P/9	47°41'	80°16'
Wilson	UNP/LNO	AB	33-7-20-W4	82 H/10	49°36'	112°39'
Wilson Bay	BAY/BAIE	NT	Keewatin	55 K	62°15'	92°43'
Wilson, Cape	CAPE/CAP	NT	Franklin	46 I	66°59'	81°27'
Wilson Creek	UNP/LNO	BC	New Westminster	92 G/5	49°27'	123°43'
Wilson Heights	UNP/LNO	ON	York	30 M/11	43°44'	79°26'
Wilson Island	ISL/ÎLE	ON	Thunder Bay	42 D/14	48°47'	87°29'
Wilson Island	ISL/ÎLE	NT	Mackenzie	85 H	61°49'	112°50'
Wilson, Lac	LAKE/LAC	QC	Jamésie	32 F/1	49°07'	76°29'
Wilson Lake	LAKE/LAC	NF		13 E/7	53°21'	62°48'
Wilson Lake	LAKE/LAC	NT	Mackenzie	75 K	62°28'	110°00'
Wilson Landing	UNP/LNO	BC	Osoyoos Division Yale	82 E/14	49°59'	119°30'
Wilson, Mount	MTN/MNT	YT/NT		105 I/13	62°53'	129°42'
Wilson Point	UNP/LNO	NB	Gloucester	21 P/16	47°56'	64°29'
Wilson Point	UNP/LNO	ON	Simcoe	31 D/11	44°38'	79°26'
Wilson River	RIV/CDE	MB	36-25-18-W	62 O/4	51°13'	99°51'
Wilson River	RIV/CDE	NT	Keewatin	55 K	62°19'	93°03'
Wilsons Beach	UNP/LNO	NB	Charlotte	21 B/15	44°56'	66°56'
Wilson's Corner	UNP/LNO	QC	Les Collines-de-l'Outaouais	31 G/12	45°37'	75°48'

NAME NOM	ENTITY ENTITÉ	LOC 1 LIEU 1	LOC 2 LIEU 2	MAP CARTE	POSITION LAT	LONG
Wilsons Cove	UNP/LNO	NS	Guysborough	11 E/1	45°00'	62°02'
Wilson's Landing	UNP/LNO	ON	Nipissing	31 L/7	46°24'	78°47'
Wilsonvale	UNP/LNO	QC	Vaudreuil-Soulanges	31 G/8	45°18'	74°11'
Wilsonville	UNP/LNO	ON	Norfolk	40 I/16	43°00'	80°19'
Wilsonwood	UNP/LNO	ON	Kent	40 J/8	42°24'	82°10'
Wilstead	UNP/LNO	ON	Leeds	31 C/8	44°22'	76°06'
Wilton	UNP/LNO	ON	Lennox and Addington	31 C/7	44°19'	76°43'
Wilton Creek	RIV/CDE	ON	Lennox and Addington	31 C/2	44°11'	76°55'
Wiltondale	UNP/LNO	NF		12 H/5	49°24'	57°37'
Wilton Grove	UNP/LNO	ON	Middlesex	40 I/14	42°56'	81°12'
Wilton No. 472	MUN2/AZM2	SK		73 F/4	53°10'	109°45'
Wiltsetown	UNP/LNO	ON	Leeds	31 B/12	44°37'	75°56'
Wiltshire Park	UNP/LNO	ON	Lambton	40 J/16	42°59'	82°22'
Wimapedi Lake	LAKE/LAC	MB		63 O/4	55°11'	99°47'
Wimapedi River	RIV/CDE	MB		63 O/6	55°28'	99°07'
Wimborne	UNP/LNO	AB	26-33-26-W4	82 P/13	51°52'	113°35'
Wimin	UNP/LNO	QC	Kativik	33 N/6	55°27'	77°28'
Wimin Nipi Sipis	UNP/LNO	QC	Kativik	24 F/6	57°30'	69°27'
Wimmer	UNP/LNO	SK	17-36-17-W2	73 A/1	52°06'	104°24'
Winagami	UNP/LNO	AB	31-77-19-W5	83 N/10	55°43'	116°57'
Winagami Lake	LAKE/LAC	AB	76,77-18,19-W5	83 N/10	55°37'	116°44'
Winagami Lake Provincial Park	PARK/PARC	AB	76,77-17,18-W5	83 N/10	55°38'	116°39'
*Winch	UNP/LNO	BC	Kamloops Division Yale	92 I/4	50°13'	121°35'
Winche 7	IR/RI	BC	Clayoquot	92 F/3	49°08'	125°26'
Winchelsea	UNP/LNO	ON	Huron	40 P/6	43°19'	81°23'
Winchelsea Islands	ISL/ÎLE	BC	Nanaimo	92 F/8	49°18'	124°05'
Winchester	VILG/VILG	ON	Dundas	31 G/3	45°06'	75°21'
Winchester	MUN2/AZM2	ON	Dundas	31 G/3	45°08'	75°17'
Winchester	MUN2/AZM2	MB		62 F/1	49°10'	100°30'
Winchester Inlet	BAY/BAIE	NT	Keewatin	55 O	63°55'	90°00'
Winchester Springs	UNP/LNO	ON	Dundas	31 G/3	45°02'	75°18'
Windermere	UNP/LNO	NS	Kings	21 H/2	45°01'	64°45'
Windermere	UNP/LNO	ON	Muskoka	31 E/4	45°10'	79°33'
Windermere	UNP/LNO	BC	Kootenay	82 J/5	50°28'	115°59'
Windermere	UNP/LNO	BC	Kootenay	82 K/9	50°31'	116°02'
Windermere Lake	LAKE/LAC	ON	Sudbury	41 O/13	47°58'	83°47'
Windermere Lake	LAKE/LAC	BC	Kootenay	82 J/5	50°27'	116°00'
Windfall	UNP/LNO	ON	Oxford	40 P/2	43°14'	80°37'
Windfall	UNP/LNO	ON	Essex	40 J/1	42°09'	82°29'
Windfall	UNP/LNO	AB	17-60-15-W5	83 K/1	54°12'	116°13'
Windfall Creek	RIV/CDE	AB	60-15-W5	83 K/1	54°15'	116°10'
Windflower Lake	LAKE/LAC	NT	Mackenzie	85 L	62°52'	118°30'
Windham Centre	UNP/LNO	ON	Norfolk	40 I/16	42°55'	80°25'
Windham Hill	UNP/LNO	NS	Cumberland	11 E/12	45°37'	64°00'
Windigo	UNP/LNO	QC	Le Haut-Saint-Maurice	31 P/14	47°46'	73°20'
Windigo Bay	BAY/BAIE	ON	Thunder Bay	52 I/2	50°13'	88°37'
Windigo Lake	LAKE/LAC	ON	Kenora	53 B/12	52°35'	91°32'
Windigo River	RIV/CDE	ON	Kenora	53 G/5	53°22'	91°48'
Windigo, Rivière	RIV/CDE	QC	Le Haut-Saint-Maurice	31 P/14	47°47'	73°19'
Windon	UNP/LNO	PE	Kings	11 L/7	46°21'	62°43'
Wind River	RIV/CDE	YT		106 E/14	65°51'	135°18'
Windrum Lagoon	LAKE/LAC	NT	Franklin	97 H	71°28'	121°45'
Windsor	CITY/VIL1	QC	Le Val-Saint-François	31 H/9	45°34'	72°00'
Windsor	CITY/VIL1	ON	Essex	40 J/6	42°18'	83°01'
Windsor	TOWN/VIL2	NS	Hants	21 A/16	44°59'	64°08'
Windsor	UNP/LNO	NF		2 D/13	48°57'	55°40'
Windsor	UNP/LNO	NB	Carleton	21 J/6	46°24'	67°25'
Windsor Forks	UNP/LNO	NS	Hants	21 A/16	44°56'	64°11'
Windsor Heights	UNP/LNO	NF		1 N/10	47°37'	52°49'
Windsor Heights	UNP/LNO	ON	Leeds	31 B/12	44°36'	75°42'
Windsor Junction	UNP/LNO	NS	Halifax	11 D/13	44°47'	63°38'
Windsor Lake	LAKE/LAC	NF		1 N/10	47°36'	52°48'
Windsor Lake	LAKE/LAC	BC	New Westminster	92 F/16	50°00'	124°17'
Windsor, Mount	MTN/MNT	NT	Franklin	59 D	77°12'	90°58'
Windsor Park	UNP/LNO	MB		62 H/14	49°52'	97°04'
Windsor Park	UNP/LNO	SK		72 I/5	50°24'	105°30'
Windsor Park	UNP/LNO	BC	New Westminster	92 G/7	49°19'	122°59'
Windsor Place	UNP/LNO	SK		72 I/7	50°28'	104°38'
Windsor Road	UNP/LNO	NS	Lunenburg	21 A/9	44°37'	64°16'
Windsors Mal Bay	LAKE/LAC	NB	Gloucester	21 P/16	47°57'	64°29'
Windsor-Walkerville	UNP/LNO	ON	Essex	40 J/7	42°17'	82°58'
Windthorst	VILG/VILG	SK	25-13-7-W2	62 L/2	50°06'	102°50'
Windward Sands	UNP/LNO	ON	Peterborough	31 D/8	44°27'	78°29'
Windy	UNP/LNO	BC	Peace River	93 P/14	55°57'	121°22'
Windy Arm	BAY/BAIE	YT/BC		105 D/2	60°03'	134°34'

NAME NOM	ENTITY ENTITÉ	LOC 1 LIEU 1	LOC 2 LIEU 2	MAP CARTE	POSITION LAT	LONG
Windygates	UNP/LNO	MB	5-1-7-W	62 G/1	49°00'	98°22'
Windy Lake	UNP/LNO	ON	Sudbury	41 I/11	46°38'	81°28'
Windy Lake	LAKE/LAC	ON	Sudbury	41 I/11	46°36'	81°27'
Windy Lake	LAKE/LAC	MB		53 L/12	54°40'	95°47'
Windy Lake	LAKE/LAC	MB	31,32-8-10-E	62 H/9	49°42'	96°12'
Windy Lake	LAKE/LAC	SK	62-4,5-W2	63 L/7	54°22'	102°35'
Windy Lake	LAKE/LAC	NT	Keewatin	65 C	60°20'	100°02'
Windy Mouth 7	IR/RI	BC	Lillooet	92 P/13	51°51'	121°35'
Windy Point	UNP/LNO	ON	Rainy River	52 C/11	48°41'	93°11'
Windy Point	CAPE/CAP	NF		2 M/4	51°02'	55°47'
Windy Point	CAPE/CAP	ON	Rainy River	52 D/15	48°58'	94°33'
Windy Point	CAPE/CAP	BC	Rupert	92 L/8	50°28'	126°10'
Windy River	RIV/CDE	NT	Keewatin	65 B	60°37'	99°55'
Winefred Lake	LAKE/LAC	AB	75-34-W4	73 M/7	55°30'	110°31'
Winefred River	RIV/CDE	AB	81-4-W4	74 D/2	56°02'	110°36'
Wine Harbour	UNP/LNO	NS	Guysborough	11 F/4	45°05'	61°51'
Wine Harbour Bay	BAY/BAIE	NS	Guysborough	11 F/4	45°03'	61°50'
Wine River	UNP/LNO	NB	Northumberland	21 I/14	46°53'	65°14'
Winfield	UNP/LNO	ON	Wellington	40 P/10	43°40'	80°36'
Winfield	UNP/LNO	AB	18-46-3-W5	83 B/16	52°58'	114°26'
Winfield	UNP/LNO	BC	Osoyoos Division Yale	82 L/3	50°02'	119°24'
Wingard	UNP/LNO	SK	45-3-W3	73 B/16	52°56'	106°25'
Wingdam	UNP/LNO	BC	Cariboo	93 H/4	53°03'	121°58'
Winger	UNP/LNO	ON	Welland	30 L/14	42°57'	79°26'
Wingham	TOWN/VIL2	ON	Huron	40 P/14	43°53'	81°19'
Wingham	UNP/LNO	MB	27-9-5-W1	62 G/16	49°46'	98°03'
Wingham Junction	UNP/LNO	ON	Huron	40 P/14	43°55'	81°15'
Winging Point	CAPE/CAP	NS	Cape Breton	11 F/16	45°47'	60°07'
Wingle	UNP/LNO	ON	Renfrew	31 F/6	45°16'	77°28'
Wing Pond	LAKE/LAC	NF		2 E/1	49°00'	54°08'
Wings	UNP/LNO	ON	Cochrane	42 A/10	48°44'	80°47'
Wings Point	UNP/LNO	NF		2 E/8	49°20'	54°29'
Winisk	UNP/LNO	ON	Kenora	43 N/6	55°16'	85°12'
Winisk 90	IR/RI	ON	Kenora	43 L/6	54°15'	87°15'
Winiskisis Channel	CHAN/CHEN	ON	Kenora	43 E/10	53°45'	86°50'
Winisk Lake	LAKE/LAC	ON	Kenora	43 D/14	52°55'	87°22'
Winisk River	RIV/CDE	ON	Kenora	43 N/6	55°17'	85°05'
Winisk Trough	SEAU/SMER	—		1399A	58°30'	83°00'
Winkler	TOWN/VIL2	MB	4-3-4-W	62 H/4	49°11'	97°56'
Winlaw	UNP/LNO	BC	Kootenay	82 F/12	49°37'	117°34'
Winnange Lake	LAKE/LAC	ON	Kenora	52 F/12	49°44'	93°43'
Winneway	UNP/LNO	QC	Témiscamingue	31 M/10	47°35'	78°34'
Winneway, Rivière	RIV/CDE	QC	Témiscamingue	31 M/10	47°35'	78°35'
Winniandy	UNP/LNO	AB	58-8-W6	83 E/14	53°59'	119°08'
Winnifred	UNP/LNO	AB	17-11-9-W4	72 E/14	49°54'	111°12'
Winnifred Creek	RIV/CDE	BC	Osoyoos Division Yale	82 E/15	49°55'	118°42'
Winnipeg	CITY/VIL1	MB		62 H/14	49°53'	97°09'
Winnipeg Beach	TOWN/VIL2	MB	33,34-17-4-E	62 I/7	50°30'	96°58'
Winnipeg, Lac - also-aussi - **Winnipeg, Lake**	LAKE/LAC	MB		63 A/3	52°08'	97°16'
Winnipeg, Lake - also-aussi - **Winnipeg, Lac**	LAKE/LAC	MB		63 A/3	52°08'	97°16'
Winnipegosis	VILG/VILG	MB		62 O/12	51°39'	99°56'
Winnipegosis, Lac - also-aussi - **Winnipegosis, Lake**	LAKE/LAC	MB		63 B/5	52°29'	99°59'
Winnipegosis, Lake - also-aussi - **Winnipegosis, Lac**	LAKE/LAC	MB		63 B/5	52°29'	99°59'
Winnipeg River - also-aussi - **Winnipeg, Rivière**	RIV/CDE	MB/ON		62 I/9	50°38'	96°19'
Winnipeg, Rivière - also-aussi - **Winnipeg River**	RIV/CDE	MB/ON		62 I/9	50°38'	96°19'
Winnitoba	UNP/LNO	MB	34-10-17-E	52 E/14	49°53'	95°12'
Winokapau Lake	LAKE/LAC	NF		13 E/2	53°10'	62°52'
Winona	UNP/LNO	ON	Wentworth	30 M/4	43°12'	79°39'
Winona Basin	SEAU/SMER	—		19308A	50°30'	129°33'
Winona Park	UNP/LNO	ON	Wentworth	30 M/4	43°13'	79°38'
Winona Ridge	SEAU/SMER	—		19308A	50°17'	129°25'
Winro	UNP/LNO	SK	29-18-13-W2	62 L/12	50°33'	103°45'
Winsloe - see-voir - Charlottetown	VILG/VILG	PE		11 L/3	46°14'	63°08'
Winsloe	UNP/LNO	PE	Queens	11 L/6	46°18'	63°11'
Winsloe North	UNP/LNO	PE	Queens	11 L/6	46°21'	63°12'
Winsloe South	VILG/VILG	PE	Queens	11 L/6	46°19'	63°11'
Winslow	UNP/LNO	ON	Lincoln	30 M/4	43°03'	79°35'
Winslow No. 319	MUN2/AZM2	SK		72 N/10	51°45'	108°50'
Winston	UNP/LNO	NB	Northumberland	21 P/3	47°10'	65°19'
Winston Churchill Range	MTN/MNT	AB	38,39,40-23,24-W5	83 C/6	52°21'	117°28'
Winston, Mount	MTN/MNT	BC	Cassiar	94 L/11	58°40'	127°14'
Winston Park	UNP/LNO	ON	York	30 M/11	43°44'	79°27'
Wintego Lake	LAKE/LAC	SK		63 M/13	55°33'	102°52'
Winter	UNP/LNO	SK	14-42-25-W3	73 C/12	52°37'	109°30'
Winterbourne	UNP/LNO	ON	Waterloo	40 P/9	43°33'	80°28'

NAME / NOM	ENTITY / ENTITÉ	LOC 1 / LIEU 1	LOC 2 / LIEU 2	MAP / CARTE	POSITION LAT	POSITION LONG
Winter Brook	UNP/LNO	NF		2 C/5	48°26′	53°45′
Winter Harbour	UNP/LNO	BC	Rupert	102 I/9	50°31′	128°02′
Winter Harbour	BAY/BAIE	BC	Rupert	92 L/12	50°32′	128°00′
Winter Harbour	BAY/BAIE	NT	Franklin	78 F	74°46′	110°32′
Winterhouse	UNP/LNO	NF		12 B/10	48°42′	58°56′
Winter House Brook	UNP/LNO	NF		12 H/5	49°29′	57°56′
Winterhouse Cove	UNP/LNO	NF		12 H/9	49°44′	56°01′
Wintering Lake	LAKE/LAC	ON	Thunder Bay	42 E/6	49°26′	87°16′
Wintering Lake	LAKE/LAC	ON	Kenora	52 G/11	49°43′	91°18′
Wintering Lake	LAKE/LAC	MB		63 P/5	55°23′	97°43′
Winter Island	ISL/ÎLE	NT	Franklin	46 J/6	66°16′	83°04′
Winter Lake	LAKE/LAC	SK		73 G/10	53°41′	106°53′
Winter Lake	LAKE/LAC	NT	Mackenzie	86 A	64°29′	112°55′
Winterland	VILG/VILG	NF		1 M/3	47°09′	55°18′
Winter River	RIV/CDE	NT	Mackenzie	86 A	64°30′	113°00′
Winter Tickle	CHAN/CHEN	NF		2 E/6	49°23′	55°13′
Winterton	TOWN/VIL2	NF		1 N/14	47°58′	53°20′
Winthorpe	UNP/LNO	SK	23-28-11-W2	62 M/6	51°27′	103°27′
Winthrop	UNP/LNO	ON	Huron	40 P/11	43°37′	81°21′
Winton	UNP/LNO	SK	7-48-23-W2	73 H/3	53°08′	105°22′
Winton Crossing	UNP/LNO	NB	Restigouche	21 O/16	47°46′	66°09′
*Wire Cache	UNP/LNO	BC	Kamloops Division Yale	82 M/11	51°43′	119°22′
Wirral	UNP/LNO	NB	Queens	21 G/9	45°31′	66°29′
Wirral Station	UNP/LNO	NB	Queens	21 G/9	45°31′	66°28′
Wisbeach	UNP/LNO	ON	Lambton	40 P/4	43°00′	81°48′
Wise Creek No. 77	MUN2/AZM2	SK		72 G/12	49°40′	107°50′
Wisemans Corners	UNP/LNO	ON	Parry Sound	31 E/11	45°36′	79°27′
Wiseton	VILG/VILG	SK	17-27-12-W3	72 O/5	51°19′	107°39′
Wishart	VILG/VILG	SK	30-29-14-W2	62 M/12	51°33′	103°59′
Wishart Peninsula	CAPE/CAP	BC	Range 1 Coast	92 L/15	50°32′	126°32′
Wishart Point	UNP/LNO	NB	Northumberland	21 P/7	47°21′	64°59′
Wishingwell Park	UNP/LNO	NF		1 N/10	47°34′	52°44′
Wisla	UNP/LNO	MB	1-19-22-W	62 K/9	50°36′	100°24′
Wistaria	UNP/LNO	BC	Range 4 Coast	93 E/16	53°51′	126°16′
Wiste	UNP/LNO	AB	35-32-7-W4	72 M/15	51°48′	110°53′
Wiswell Inlet	BAY/BAIE	NT	Franklin	25 I	62°55′	65°45′
Witchai Lake	LAKE/LAC	MB	80,81-4,5-E	63 P/15	56°00′	96°49′
Witch Bay	BAY/BAIE	NT	Keewatin	34 L	58°34′	78°23′
Witchekan	UNP/LNO	SK	16-52-11-W3	73 G/5	53°30′	107°34′
Witchekan Lake	LAKE/LAC	SK	52-11-W3	73 G/5	53°26′	107°34′
Witchekan Lake 117	IR/RI	SK		73 G/5	53°29′	107°31′
Witch Lake	LAKE/LAC	BC	Cassiar	93 N/2	55°07′	124°32′
Witegoo River	RIV/CDE	ON	Kenora	53 I/11	54°33′	89°08′
Withers Lake	LAKE/LAC	ON	Kenora	53 J/5	54°22′	91°42′
Withrow	UNP/LNO	AB	28-39-4-W5	83 B/7	52°23′	114°30′
Witless Bay	TOWN/VIL2	NF		1 N/7	47°17′	52°50′
Witless Bay	BAY/BAIE	NF		1 N/7	47°16′	52°48′
Witley	UNP/LNO	SK	25-20-W3	72 N/2	51°07′	108°39′
Wittenburg	UNP/LNO	NS	Colchester	11 E/3	45°06′	63°14′
Wivenhoe	UNP/LNO	MB	83-15-E	54 D/3	56°11′	95°13′
Wiwa Creek	RIV/CDE	SK	12-4-W3	72 J/2	50°02′	106°31′
Wiwa Hill	UNP/LNO	SK	18-13-5-W3	72 J/2	50°05′	106°40′
Wizard Lake	LAKE/LAC	AB	48-27,28-W4	83 H/4	53°07′	113°55′
Wizewood Spur	UNP/LNO	SK	8-45-3-W2	63 D/16	52°52′	102°24′
Woburn	UNP/LNO	QC	Le Granit	21 E/7	45°23′	70°52′
Woburn	UNP/LNO	ON	York	30 M/14	43°46′	79°13′
Wodehouse	UNP/LNO	ON	Grey	41 A/7	44°23′	80°34′
Woermke	UNP/LNO	ON	Renfrew	31 F/6	45°24′	77°14′
Woito	UNP/LNO	ON	Renfrew	31 F/11	45°42′	77°11′
Woking	UNP/LNO	AB	19-76-5-W6	83 M/10	55°35′	118°46′
Wokitsas 14	IR/RI	BC	Barclay	92 C/15	48°50′	124°39′
Wolf	UNP/LNO	AB	14-23-2-W5	82 J/16	50°57′	114°10′
Wolf Bay	UNP/LNO	QC	Côte-Nord-du-Golfe-Saint-Laurent	12 K/8	50°16′	60°08′
Wolf Creek	UNP/LNO	AB	2-54-16-W5	83 F/9	53°38′	116°15′
Wolf Creek - see-voir - Skootamatta River	RIV/CDE	ON		31 C/11	44°32′	77°20′
Wolf Creek	RIV/CDE	AB	54-16-W5	83 F/9	53°38′	116°17′
Wolf Creek 3	IR/RI	BC	Similkameen Division Yale	92 H/8	49°26′	120°19′
Wolfe	UNP/LNO	ON	Renfrew	31 F/6	45°21′	77°19′
Wolfe	UNP/LNO	SK	28-38-18-W3	73 C/7	52°18′	108°30′
Wolfe Creek	RIV/CDE	BC	Similkameen Division Yale	92 H/8	49°22′	120°18′
Wolfe Inlet	BAY/BAIE	PE	Prince	21 I/9	46°37′	64°17′
Wolfe Island	MUN2/AZM2	ON	Frontenac	31 C/1	44°10′	76°25′
Wolfe Island	ISL/ÎLE	ON	Frontenac	31 C/1	44°12′	76°20′
Wolfe Lake	LAKE/LAC	ON	Frontenac	31 C/9	44°41′	76°30′
Wolfenden	UNP/LNO	BC	Kamloops Division Yale	82 M/14	51°59′	119°20′

NAME NOM	ENTITY ENTITÉ	LOC 1 LIEU 1	LOC 2 LIEU 2	MAP CARTE	POSITION LAT	LONG
Wolfenden, Mount	MTN/MNT	BC	Rupert	92 L/5	50°26′	127°34′
Wolfe, Point	CAPE/CAP	NB	Albert	21 H/11	45°32′	65°01′
Wolfes Island	ISL/ÎLE	NS	Halifax	11 D/10	44°44′	62°46′
Wolfes Landing	UNP/LNO	NS	Cape Breton	11 F/16	45°53′	60°03′
Wolf Fiord	BAY/BAIE	NT	Franklin	59 E	78°25′	88°30′
Wolf Lake	LAKE/LAC	NF		12 A/2	48°05′	56°40′
Wolf Lake	LAKE/LAC	AB	66-6,7-W4	73 L/10	54°42′	110°57′
Wolf Lake	LAKE/LAC	BC	Comox	92 F/14	49°46′	125°10′
Wolf Lake	LAKE/LAC	YT		105 B/12	60°40′	131°41′
Wolf Lake	LAKE/LAC	YT		115 F/16	61°57′	140°03′
Wolf Mountain	MTN/MNT	NF		12 A/2	48°08′	56°49′
Wolford	MUN2/AZM2	ON	Leeds	31 B/13	44°51′	75°49′
Wolford Centre	UNP/LNO	ON	Leeds	31 B/13	44°49′	75°49′
Wolford Chapel	UNP/LNO	ON	Grenville	31 B/13	44°52′	75°56′
Wolf Pond	LAKE/LAC	NF		12 H/2	49°05′	56°41′
Wolf River	RIV/CDE	ON	Parry Sound	41 H/16	45°58′	80°09′
Wolf River	RIV/CDE	AB	22-66-8-W4	73 L/11	54°42′	111°09′
Wolf River	RIV/CDE	BC	Nootka	92 F/13	49°47′	125°37′
Wolf River	RIV/CDE	YT		105 C/7	60°17′	132°33′
Wolftown	UNP/LNO	ON	Renfrew	31 F/10	45°35′	76°58′
Wolfville	TOWN/VIL2	NS	Kings	21 H/1	45°05′	64°22′
Wolfville Ridge	UNP/LNO	NS	Kings	21 H/1	45°04′	64°23′
Wôlinak 11	IR/RI	QC	Bécancour	31 I/8	46°19′	72°25′
Wollaston	MUN2/AZM2	ON	Hastings	31 C/13	44°57′	77°50′
Wollaston, Cape	CAPE/CAP	NT	Franklin	87 G	71°07′	118°04′
Wollaston Lake	HAM/HAM	SK		64 L/3	58°07′	103°09′
Wollaston Lake	LAKE/LAC	ON	Hastings	31 C/13	44°51′	77°50′
Wollaston Lake	LAKE/LAC	SK		64 L/3	58°15′	103°15′
Wollaston Peninsula	CAPE/CAP	NT	Franklin	87 D	69°45′	115°00′
Wolley Point	CAPE/CAP	NT	Franklin	98 C	73°03′	124°50′
Wolseley	TOWN/VIL2	SK	11-17-10-W2	62 L/6	50°25′	103°16′
Wolseley	UNP/LNO	ON	Grey	41 A/11	44°44′	81°01′
Wolseley	UNP/LNO	MB		62 H/14	49°53′	97°10′
Wolseley Bay	UNP/LNO	ON	Nipissing	41 I/1	46°06′	80°16′
Wolseley Lake	LAKE/LAC	ON	Rainy River	52 C/8	48°26′	92°05′
Wolseley No. 155	MUN2/AZM2	SK		62 L/6	50°25′	103°10′
Wolseley River	RIV/CDE	ON	Nipissing	41 I/1	46°06′	80°16′
Wolsey, Lake	LAKE/LAC	ON	Manitoulin	41 G/15	45°49′	82°32′
Wolstenholme, Cap	CAPE/CAP	QC	Kativik	35 K/12	62°35′	77°30′
Wolverine	UNP/LNO	SK	2-34-24-W2	72 P/14	51°54′	105°17′
Wolverine	UNP/LNO	BC	Cariboo	93 J/1	54°04′	122°24′
Wolverine Beach	UNP/LNO	ON	Muskoka	31 D/13	44°51′	79°49′
Wolverine Lake	LAKE/LAC	NT	Mackenzie	75 M	63°12′	111°22′
Wolverine No. 340	MUN2/AZM2	SK		73 A/3	52°00′	105°10′
Wolverine River	RIV/CDE	MB		64 I/14	58°55′	97°28′
Wolverine River	RIV/CDE	AB	101-19-W5	84 F/10	57°45′	116°59′
Wolverine River	RIV/CDE	BC	Peace River	93 P/3	55°08′	121°03′
Wolverine River	RIV/CDE	NT	Mackenzie	107 A	68°23′	129°07′
Wolverton	UNP/LNO	ON	Oxford	40 P/7	43°15′	80°32′
Wolves, The	ISL/ÎLE	NB	Charlotte	21 B/15	44°58′	66°43′
Woman Lake	LAKE/LAC	ON	Kenora	52 N/2	51°12′	92°45′
Woman River	UNP/LNO	ON	Sudbury	41 O/10	47°31′	82°38′
Woman River	RIV/CDE	ON	Sudbury	41 O/16	47°50′	82°17′
Woman River	RIV/CDE	ON	Kenora	52 K/14	50°58′	93°03′
Wonderland Lake	LAKE/LAC	ON	Kenora	52 L/1	50°05′	94°08′
Wonowon	UNP/LNO	BC	Peace River	94 A/12	56°44′	121°48′
Wood	UNP/LNO	ON	Rainy River	52 D/9	48°43′	94°29′
Wood Arm	BAY/BAIE	BC	Kootenay	83 D/1	52°08′	118°15′
Wood Bay	UNP/LNO	MB	31-3-10-W	62 G/7	49°15′	98°49′
Wood Bay	BAY/BAIE	NT	Mackenzie	107 D	69°46′	128°55′
Woodbend	UNP/LNO	AB	24-51-26-W4	83 H/5	53°25′	113°41′
Woodbine	UNP/LNO	NS	Cape Breton	11 F/16	46°00′	60°18′
Woodbine Gardens	UNP/LNO	ON	York	30 M/11	43°43′	79°18′
Woodbine Heights	UNP/LNO	ON	York	30 M/11	43°42′	79°19′
Woodbridge	UNP/LNO	ON	York	30 M/13	43°47′	79°36′
Wood Buffalo	MUN1/AZM1	AB	11-100-13-W4	84 H/9	57°40′	112°00′
Wood Buffalo National Park - also-aussi - Wood Buffalo, Parc national	PARK/PARC	AB/NT		84 P/3	59°25′	113°00′
Wood Buffalo National Park World Heritage Site - also-aussi - Parc national Wood Buffalo, Site du patrimoine mondial du	PARK/PARC	AB/NT		84 H/9	59°25′	113°00′
Wood Buffalo, Parc national - also-aussi - Wood Buffalo National Park	PARK/PARC	AB/NT		84 P/3	59°25′	113°00′
Woodburn	UNP/LNO	NS	Pictou	11 E/10	45°37′	62°32′
Woodburn	UNP/LNO	ON	Frontenac	31 C/8	44°21′	76°17′
Woodburn	UNP/LNO	ON	Wentworth	30 M/4	43°08′	79°45′
Woodburn Lake	LAKE/LAC	NT	Keewatin	56 E	65°30′	95°25′
Woodcock	UNP/LNO	BC	Cassiar	103 P/1	55°04′	128°14′
Wood Creek	RIV/CDE	ON	Kenora	43 M/9	55°41′	86°02′

NAME NOM	ENTITY ENTITÉ	LOC 1 LIEU 1	LOC 2 LIEU 2	MAP CARTE	POSITION LAT	LONG
Wood Creek No. 281	MUN2/AZM2	SK		72 P/5	51°30′	105°30′
Wooddale	UNP/LNO	NF		2 E/4	49°03′	53°33′
Woodfibre	UNP/LNO	BC	New Westminster	92 G/11	49°40′	123°15′
Woodfield	UNP/LNO	NS	Pictou	11 E/9	45°31′	62°23′
Woodford	UNP/LNO	ON	Grey	41 A/10	44°35′	80°45′
Woodford Cove	UNP/LNO	NF		2 E/12	49°37′	55°52′
Woodford's	UNP/LNO	NF		1 N/6	47°24′	53°09′
Woodfords Arm	BAY/BAIE	NF		2 E/12	49°31′	55°52′
Woodfords Cut	UNP/LNO	NF		1 N/14	47°50′	53°23′
Woodglen	UNP/LNO	AB	2-47-16-W4	83 H/1	53°01′	112°14′
Woodgreen	UNP/LNO	ON	Middlesex	40 I/12	42°41′	81°43′
Woodgrove	UNP/LNO	AB	20-58-21-W4	83 I/3	54°01′	113°05′
Woodham	UNP/LNO	ON	Perth	40 P/6	43°18′	81°19′
Woodhaven	UNP/LNO	MB		62 H/14	49°52′	97°16′
Woodhaven	UNP/LNO	BC	New Westminster	92 G/7	49°19′	122°54′
Woodhaven Court	UNP/LNO	NB	Westmorland	21 I/2	46°07′	64°52′
Woodhill	UNP/LNO	ON	Peel	30 M/12	43°45′	79°41′
Wood Hill	UNP/LNO	SK	31-48-8-W3	73 G/3	53°12′	107°09′
Woodhouse	UNP/LNO	AB	30-11-26-W4	82 H/13	49°57′	113°32′
Woodhouse Acres	UNP/LNO	ON	Norfolk	40 I/16	42°47′	80°11′
Woodhurst	UNP/LNO	NB	Westmorland	21 H/16	45°57′	64°29′
Woodington	UNP/LNO	ON	Muskoka	31 E/4	45°09′	79°39′
Wood Island	ISL/ÎLE	NB	Charlotte	21 B/10	44°38′	66°50′
Wood Islands	UNP/LNO	PE	Queens	11 E/15	45°58′	62°45′
Wood Islands	ISL/ÎLE	PE	Queens	11 E/15	45°57′	62°45′
Wood Lake	LAKE/LAC	NB	Saint John	21 H/5	45°25′	65°35′
Wood Lake	LAKE/LAC	MB		64 H/5	57°28′	97°45′
Wood Lake	LAKE/LAC	SK		63 M/6	55°17′	103°17′
Wood Lake	LAKE/LAC	BC	Osoyoos Division Yale	82 L/3	50°05′	119°23′
Woodland	UNP/LNO	NB	Charlotte	21 G/2	45°05′	66°43′
Woodland	UNP/LNO	ON	Northumberland	31 C/5	44°23′	77°48′
Woodland	UNP/LNO	ON	Lambton	40 O/1	43°00′	82°23′
Woodland Acres	UNP/LNO	ON	Peterborough	31 D/8	44°22′	78°18′
Woodland Beach	UNP/LNO	ON	Simcoe	31 D/12	44°35′	80°00′
Woodland Cree 226	IR/RI	AB		84 C/16	56°29′	117°15′
Woodland Cree 227	IR/RI	AB	87,88-15,16-W5	84 C/9	56°33′	116°23′
Woodland Cree 228	IR/RI	AB	86,87-13,14-W5	84 C/8	56°29′	116°05′
Wood Landing	UNP/LNO	ON	Muskoka	31 D/13	44°54′	79°47′
Woodlands	MUN2/AZM2	MB		62 I/4	50°10′	97°45′
Woodlands	UNP/LNO	NB	York	21 J/2	46°11′	66°46′
Woodlands	UNP/LNO	ON	Frontenac	31 C/2	44°14′	76°31′
Woodlands	UNP/LNO	MB	22-14-2-W	62 I/4	50°12′	97°40′
Woodlands	UNP/LNO	BC	New Westminster	92 G/7	49°20′	122°55′
Woodlands No. 15, Municipal District of	MUN1/AZM1	AB		83 J/6	54°16′	115°24′
Woodlawn	UNP/LNO	NS	Halifax	11 D/12	44°41′	63°32′
Woodlawn	UNP/LNO	ON	Carleton	31 F/8	45°23′	76°05′
Woodlawn	UNP/LNO	SK		73 B/2	52°09′	106°39′
Woodlawn Heights	UNP/LNO	NS	Halifax	11 D/12	44°41′	63°31′
Woodlawn Park	UNP/LNO	ON	Haldimand	30 L/13	42°48′	79°58′
Woodley	UNP/LNO	SK	28-5-7-W2	62 E/6	49°25′	102°54′
Woodman	UNP/LNO	NB	York	21 J/3	46°09′	67°16′
Woodmans Point	UNP/LNO	NB	Kings	21 G/8	45°22′	66°14′
Wood Meadows	UNP/LNO	SK		72 I/7	50°26′	104°33′
Woodmere	UNP/LNO	BC	Range 5 Coast	93 L/10	54°41′	126°57′
Woodmore	UNP/LNO	MB	20-2-5-E	62 H/2	49°08′	96°53′
Wood, Mount	MTN/MNT	YT		115 F/2	61°14′	140°31′
Wood Mountain	VILG/VILG	SK	8-5-3-W3	72 G/8	49°22′	106°23′
Wood Mountain	MTN/MNT	SK		72 G/1	49°14′	106°30′
Wood Mountain 160	IR/RI	SK		72 G/8	49°19′	106°26′
Woodnorth	UNP/LNO	MB	9-9-27-W	62 F/11	49°44′	101°05′
Woodpecker	UNP/LNO	BC	Cariboo	93 G/10	53°32′	122°39′
Woodpecker	UNP/LNO	BC	Cariboo	93 G/10	53°32′	122°41′
Woodpecker Hall	UNP/LNO	NB	Kings	21 H/12	45°31′	65°49′
Wood Point	UNP/LNO	NB	Westmorland	21 H/16	45°50′	64°23′
Woodridge	UNP/LNO	ON	Leeds	31 B/12	44°33′	75°45′
Woodridge	UNP/LNO	ON	Carleton	31 F/9	45°31′	76°14′
Woodridge	UNP/LNO	MB	3,10-4-10-E	62 H/8	49°17′	96°09′
Wood River	UNP/LNO	SK	5-9-5-W3	72 G/10	49°42′	106°39′
Wood River	RIV/CDE	SK	14-2-W3	72 J/1	50°08′	106°13′
Wood River	RIV/CDE	BC	Kootenay	83 D/1	52°13′	118°11′
Wood River No. 74	MUN2/AZM2	SK		72 G/10	49°40′	106°35′
Woodrous	UNP/LNO	ON	Prince Edward	30 N/14	43°58′	77°10′
Woodrow	VILG/VILG	SK	35-8-6-W3	72 G/10	49°42′	106°43′
Woodrow Beach	UNP/LNO	ON	Lambton	40 O/1	43°01′	82°24′
Woodrowe Shores	UNP/LNO	ON	Lambton	40 O/1	43°01′	82°24′

NAME NOM	ENTITY ENTITÉ	LOC 1 LIEU 1	LOC 2 LIEU 2	MAP CARTE	POSITION LAT	LONG
Woodroyd	UNP/LNO	MB	13-15-1-W	62 I/6	50°17'	97°29'
Woodruff Lake	LAKE/LAC	NT	Franklin	75 A	60°42'	105°40'
Woods	UNP/LNO	ON	Parry Sound	41 H/8	45°29'	80°12'
Woods Bay	UNP/LNO	ON	Parry Sound	31 E/4	45°09'	79°59'
Woods, Cape	CAPE/CAP	NT	Franklin	340 F	82°13'	86°40'
Woodsdale	UNP/LNO	BC	Osoyoos Division Yale	82 L/3	50°03'	119°23'
Woodside	UNP/LNO	NS	Halifax	11 D/12	44°39'	63°33'
Woodside	UNP/LNO	NS	Kings	21 H/1	45°11'	64°27'
Woodside	UNP/LNO	NB	Westmorland	21 I/1	46°05'	64°07'
Woodside	UNP/LNO	NB	Sunbury	21 G/15	45°45'	66°30'
Woodside	UNP/LNO	QC	L'Érable	21 L/4	46°08'	71°35'
Woodside	UNP/LNO	ON	Dufferin	40 P/16	44°00'	80°02'
Woodside	UNP/LNO	MB	16-14-10-W	62 J/2	50°11'	98°47'
Woodside, Lieu historique national - also-aussi - Woodside National Historic Site	PARK/PARC	ON	Waterloo	40 P/8	43°28'	80°30'
Woodside National Historic Site - also-aussi - Woodside, Lieu historique national	PARK/PARC	ON	Waterloo	40 P/8	43°28'	80°30'
Woodside River	RIV/CDE	YT		105 J/2	62°02'	130°33'
Woods Island	ISL/ÎLE	NF		12 G/1	49°06'	58°12'
Woods Lake	LAKE/LAC	NF		23 I/6	54°30'	65°13'
Woods, Lake of the - also-aussi - **Bois, Lac des**	LAKE/LAC	ON/MB		52 E/7	49°16'	94°40'
Woods Landing	UNP/LNO	BC	Kamloops Division Yale	82 M/3	51°04'	119°03'
Woodslee - see-voir - South Woodslee	UNP/LNO	ON		40 J/2	42°12'	82°43'
Woods, Point of the	CAPE/CAP	MB		54 M/2	59°01'	94°46'
Woodstock	CITY/VIL1	ON	Oxford	40 P/2	43°08'	80°45'
Woodstock	TOWN/VIL2	NB	Carleton	21 J/4	46°09'	67°35'
Woodstock	VILG/VILG	NF		2 E/13	49°58'	55°53'
Woodstock	UNP/LNO	NF		1 N/10	47°32'	52°54'
Woodstock	UNP/LNO	PE	Prince	21 I/9	46°43'	64°10'
Woodstock	GEOG/GÉOG	NB	Carleton	21 J/4	46°05'	67°37'
Woodstock Road	UNP/LNO	NB	York	21 J/3	46°08'	67°15'
Woodvale	UNP/LNO	PE	Prince	21 I/16	46°53'	64°05'
Woodview	UNP/LNO	ON	Peterborough	31 D/9	44°35'	78°09'
Woodview	UNP/LNO	ON	Peterborough	31 D/8	44°18'	78°14'
Woodville	VILG/VILG	ON	Victoria	31 D/7	44°24'	78°59'
Woodville	UNP/LNO	NF		11 O/14	47°52'	59°22'
Woodville	UNP/LNO	NS	Hants	11 E/4	45°02'	63°56'
Woodville	UNP/LNO	NS	Kings	21 H/2	45°07'	64°38'
Woodville	UNP/LNO	NB	Madawaska	21 O/4	47°06'	67°43'
Woodville	UNP/LNO	ON	Prince Edward	31 C/3	44°05'	77°05'
Woodville Mills	UNP/LNO	PE	Kings	11 L/2	46°14'	62°31'
Woodward	UNP/LNO	ON	Muskoka	31 D/13	44°56'	79°31'
Woodward Bay	BAY/BAIE	NT	Franklin	39 G	79°24'	77°05'
Woodwards Cove	UNP/LNO	NB	Charlotte	21 B/10	44°42'	66°44'
Woodwards Landing	UNP/LNO	BC	New Westminster	92 G/3	49°07'	123°06'
Woodworth	MUN2/AZM2	MB		62 F/15	49°56'	100°40'
Woody Cove	UNP/LNO	NF		12 H/12	49°36'	57°57'
Woody Island	UNP/LNO	NF		1 M/16	47°47'	54°12'
Woody Island	ISL/ÎLE	NF		1 M/16	47°47'	54°12'
Woody Lake 184D	IR/RI	SK		63 M/3	55°14'	103°11'
Woody Point	VILG/VILG	NF		12 H/5	49°30'	57°56'
Woody River	RIV/CDE	MB/SK		63 C/10	52°31'	100°51'
Woolchester	UNP/LNO	AB	12-10-5-W4	72 E/15	49°49'	110°34'
Wooler	UNP/LNO	ON	Northumberland	31 C/4	44°09'	77°42'
Woolfall Bank	SEAU/SMER	—		8014	46°40'	51°20'
Woolford	UNP/LNO	AB	4-3-24-W4	82 H/3	49°11'	113°08'
Woolford Provincial Park	PARK/PARC	AB	5-3-24-W4	82 H/3	49°11'	113°11'
Woollett, Lac	LAKE/LAC	QC	Jamésie	32 P/5	51°26'	73°47'
Woollings Spur	UNP/LNO	ON	Timiskaming	42 A/1	48°13'	80°15'
Woolwich	MUN2/AZM2	ON	Waterloo	40 P/10	43°35'	80°31'
Woon River	RIV/CDE	NT	Franklin	98 E	74°23'	120°42'
Woosey Lake	LAKE/LAC	MB	67-19-W	63 K/16	54°48'	100°16'
Wootton Peninsula	CAPE/CAP	NT	Franklin	340 F	82°10'	84°36'
Wopmay Lake	LAKE/LAC	NT	Mackenzie	86 F/2	65°07'	116°40'
Wopmay River	RIV/CDE	NT	Mackenzie	86 C	64°32'	117°27'
Worby	UNP/LNO	MB	3-10-12-W	62 G/14	49°49'	99°02'
Worcester	UNP/LNO	SK	18-10-13-W2	62 E/13	49°49'	103°45'
Wordie Bay	BAY/BAIE	NT	Franklin	37 A	68°10'	73°20'
Wordsworth	UNP/LNO	SK	8-7-3-W2	62 E/9	49°33'	102°22'
Work Channel	CHAN/CHEN	BC	Range 5 Coast	103 J/8	54°28'	130°13'
Workman Island	ISL/ÎLE	NT	Mackenzie	86 K	66°14'	117°56'
Worsley	UNP/LNO	AB	36-86-8-W6	84 D/11	56°31'	119°08'
Worth	UNP/LNO	BC	Peace River	94 A/3	56°06'	121°04'
Worthington	MUN2/AZM2	ON	Rainy River	52 D/9	48°42'	94°25'
Worthington	UNP/LNO	ON	Sudbury	41 I/6	46°23'	81°27'
Worthington	UNP/LNO	MB		62 H/14	49°50'	97°06'
Worthington Lake	LAKE/LAC	SK	57-25-W3	73 F/13	53°57'	109°36'

NAME NOM	ENTITY ENTITÉ	LOC 1 LIEU 1	LOC 2 LIEU 2	MAP CARTE	POSITION LAT	LONG
Worth Point	CAPE/CAP	NT	Franklin	98 B	72°16′	125°38′
Woss	UNP/LNO	BC	Rupert	92 L/2	50°13′	126°36′
Woss Lake	LAKE/LAC	BC	Rupert	92 L/2	50°07′	126°36′
Wostok	UNP/LNO	AB	16-56-17-W4	83 H/16	53°51′	112°28′
Wotton	VILG/VILG	QC	Asbestos	21 E/12	45°44′	71°48′
Wouwer Island	ISL/ÎLE	BC	Barclay	92 C/14	48°52′	125°21′
Woyenne 27	IR/RI	BC	Range 5 Coast	93 K/4	54°14′	125°46′
Wreck Cove	UNP/LNO	NF		1 M/5	47°30′	55°36′
Wreck Cove	UNP/LNO	NS	Victoria	11 K/9	46°33′	60°24′
Wreck Cove	BAY/BAIE	NF		2 M/14	51°58′	55°22′
Wreck Cove Lakes	LAKE/LAC	NS	Victoria	11 K/10	46°33′	60°30′
Wreck Cove Point	CAPE/CAP	NS	Victoria	11 K/9	46°31′	60°25′
Wreck Island	ISL/ÎLE	NF		11 P/12	47°39′	57°53′
Wreford No. 280	MUN2/AZM2	SK		72 P/6	51°30′	105°10′
Wrentham	UNP/LNO	AB	36-6-17-W4	82 H/9	49°32′	112°10′
Wright	VILG/VILG	QC	La Vallée-de-la-Gatineau	31 K/1	46°05′	76°04′
Wright	UNP/LNO	BC	Lillooet	92 P/13	51°52′	121°40′
Wright Bay	BAY/BAIE	NT	Franklin	97 C	69°43′	125°12′
Wrightmans Corners	UNP/LNO	ON	Middlesex	40 P/4	43°00′	81°38′
Wright Point	CAPE/CAP	ON	Huron	40 P/13	43°48′	81°44′
Wright River	RIV/CDE	NT	Mackenzie	76 L	66°50′	110°14′
Wrights Cove	UNP/LNO	NS	Halifax	11 D/12	44°41′	63°36′
Wrigley	UNP/LNO	NT	Mackenzie	95 O/5	63°16′	123°37′
Wrigley Corners	UNP/LNO	ON	Waterloo	40 P/8	43°17′	80°22′
Wrigley Creek	RIV/CDE	NT	Mackenzie	95 F	61°34′	125°28′
Wrigley Lake	LAKE/LAC	NT	Mackenzie	95 M	63°51′	126°10′
Wrigley River	RIV/CDE	NT	Mackenzie	95 O	63°15′	123°35′
Writing-On-Stone Provincial Park	PARK/PARC	AB	1-13-W4	72 E/4	49°05′	111°38′
Wrong Lake	LAKE/LAC	MB		63 A/9	52°39′	96°13′
Wrottesley, Cape	CAPE/CAP	NT	Franklin	98 E	74°33′	121°32′
Wrottesley Inlet	BAY/BAIE	NT	Franklin	57 G	71°24′	95°45′
Wrottesley, Mount	MTN/MNT	BC	New Westminster	92 G/11	49°36′	123°21′
Wroxeter	UNP/LNO	ON	Huron	40 P/14	43°52′	81°09′
Wroxton	VILG/VILG	SK	3-26-32-W	62 N/4	51°14′	101°53′
Wuchewun River	RIV/CDE	SK	68-19-W2	73 I/15	54°53′	104°46′
Wudzimagon 61	IR/RI	BC	Range 5 Coast	103 I/5	54°18′	130°00′
Wunehikun Bay	BAY/BAIE	SK		63 M/2	55°11′	102°43′
Wunnumin 1	IR/RI	ON	Kenora	53 A/14	52°52′	89°15′
Wunnumin 2	IR/RI	ON	Kenora	53 A/14	52°52′	89°05′
Wunnumin Lake 86	IR/RI	ON	Kenora	53 A/14	52°54′	89°00′
Wunnummin Lake	UNP/LNO	ON	Kenora	53 A/14	52°56′	89°18′
Wunnummin Lake	LAKE/LAC	ON	Kenora	53 A/14	52°55′	89°10′
Wurtele	UNP/LNO	ON	Cochrane	42 H/6	49°24′	81°04′
Wuskwatim Lake	LAKE/LAC	MB	75,76-7,8-W	63 O/10	55°34′	98°33′
Wya 7	IR/RI	BC	Clayoquot	92 C/13	48°59′	125°37′
Wyah 3	IR/RI	BC	Renfrew	92 C/10	48°40′	124°51′
Wyandot	UNP/LNO	ON	Wellington	40 P/10	43°44′	80°46′
Wyatt	UNP/LNO	SK	6-14-14-W3	72 J/4	50°09′	107°54′
Wyborn	UNP/LNO	ON	Cochrane	42 G/12	49°41′	83°42′
Wychwood Park	UNP/LNO	ON	York	30 M/11	43°41′	79°25′
Wyclese 1	IR/RI	BC	Range 2 Coast	92 M/6	51°17′	127°21′
Wycliffe	UNP/LNO	BC	Kootenay	82 G/12	49°36′	115°52′
Wycott's Flat 6	IR/RI	BC	Lillooet	92 O/9	51°37′	122°19′
Wye	UNP/LNO	MB	1,2-8-14-E	52 E/12	49°37′	95°34′
Wyebridge	UNP/LNO	ON	Simcoe	31 D/12	44°42′	79°53′
Wyeclif	UNP/LNO	AB	19-52-22-W4	83 H/11	53°31′	113°14′
Wyecombe	UNP/LNO	ON	Norfolk	40 I/15	42°47′	80°33′
Wyers Brook	UNP/LNO	NB	Restigouche	21 O/15	47°54′	67°00′
Wyevale	UNP/LNO	ON	Simcoe	31 D/12	44°39′	79°56′
Wykeham Glacier	GLAC/GLAC	NT	Franklin	39 C	77°54′	78°42′
Wyley	UNP/LNO	SK	33-14-10-W2	62 L/3	50°12′	103°18′
Wylie	UNP/LNO	ON	Renfrew	31 K/4	46°04′	77°32′
Wylie Lake	LAKE/LAC	AB	119-2,3-W4	74 M/8	59°19′	110°23′
Wyman	UNP/LNO	QC	Pontiac	31 F/9	45°32′	76°18′
Wyman	UNP/LNO	BC	New Westminster	92 G/3	49°09′	123°01′
Wymark	HAM/HAM	SK	29-13-13-W3	72 J/4	50°07′	107°44′
Wymbolwood Beach	UNP/LNO	ON	Simcoe	31 D/12	44°39′	79°59′
Wynd	UNP/LNO	AB	7-45-1-W6	83 D/16	52°52′	118°08′
Wyndham-Carseland Provincial Park	PARK/PARC	AB	21-25-W4	82 I/14	50°50′	113°26′
Wyndham Hills	UNP/LNO	ON	Brant	40 P/1	43°11′	80°17′
Wynhurst Beach	UNP/LNO	ON	York	31 D/3	44°14′	79°28′
Wynndel	UNP/LNO	BC	Kootenay	82 F/2	49°11′	116°33′
Wynne-Edwards Bay	BAY/BAIE	NT	Franklin	25 J	62°32′	66°36′
Wynniatt Bay	BAY/BAIE	NT	Franklin	78 B	72°45′	111°00′
Wynot	UNP/LNO	SK	30-28-14-W2	62 M/5	51°27′	103°59′

NAME NOM	ENTITY ENTITÉ	LOC 1 LIEU 1	LOC 2 LIEU 2	MAP CARTE	POSITION LAT	LONG
Wynton	UNP/LNO	BC	Cassiar	104 M/15	60°00′	134°40′
Wynyard	TOWN/VIL2	SK	27-32-16-W2	72 P/16	51°46′	104°11′
Wyoming	VILG/VILG	ON	Lambton	40 J/16	42°57′	82°07′
Wyse	UNP/LNO	ON	Nipissing	31 L/11	46°43′	79°07′
Wyses Corner	UNP/LNO	NS	Halifax	11 D/14	44°57′	63°18′
Wyvern	UNP/LNO	NS	Cumberland	11 E/12	45°34′	63°57′

X

Xena	UNP/LNO	SK	3-32-26-W2	72 P/12	51°43′	105°36′

Y

Yaalstrick 1	IR/RI	BC	New Westminster	92 G/1	49°10′	122°03′
Yachisakus Amitapanuch	UNP/LNO	QC	Kativik	33 N/1	55°04′	76°26′
Yaculta	UNP/LNO	BC	Sayward	92 K/3	50°01′	125°12′
Yagan 3	IR/RI	BC	Queen Charlotte	103 J/4	54°04′	131°49′
Yahk	UNP/LNO	BC	Kootenay	82 F/1	49°05′	116°05′
Yahk Mountain	MTN/MNT	BC	Kootenay	82 G/4	49°11′	115°42′
Yaholnitsky Creek	RIV/CDE	SK	68-19-W2	73 I/15	54°53′	104°49′
Yakats 5	IR/RI	BC	Rupert	92 L/3	50°02′	127°24′
Yakoun Lake	LAKE/LAC	BC	Queen Charlotte	103 F/8	53°19′	132°17′
Yakoun River	RIV/CDE	BC	Queen Charlotte	103 F/9	53°39′	132°12′
Yaku	UNP/LNO	BC	Queen Charlotte	103 K/3	54°11′	133°01′
Yakweakwioose 12	IR/RI	BC	New Westminster	92 H/4	49°08′	121°56′
Yaladelassla 4	IR/RI	BC	Range 4 Coast	93 F/1	53°09′	124°21′
Yalakom River	RIV/CDE	BC	Lillooet	92 J/16	50°51′	122°10′
Yale	UNP/LNO	BC	Yale Division Yale	92 H/11	49°33′	121°26′
Yale	UNP/LNO	BC	Yale Division Yale	92 H/11	49°34′	121°26′
Yale 18	IR/RI	BC	Yale Division Yale	92 H/11	49°34′	121°24′
Yale 19	IR/RI	BC	Yale Division Yale	92 H/11	49°34′	121°24′
Yale 20	IR/RI	BC	Yale Division Yale	92 H/11	49°34′	121°24′
Yale 21	IR/RI	BC	Yale Division Yale	92 H/11	49°35′	121°24′
Yale 22	IR/RI	BC	Yale Division Yale	92 H/11	49°35′	121°24′
Yale 23	IR/RI	BC	Yale Division Yale	92 H/11	49°36′	121°25′
Yale 24	IR/RI	BC	Yale Division Yale	92 H/11	49°36′	121°25′
Yale 25	IR/RI	BC	Yale Division Yale	92 H/11	49°36′	121°25′
Yale Division Yale Land District	GEOG/GÉOG	BC		92 H	49°40′	121°15′
Yale Town 1	IR/RI	BC	Yale Division Yale	92 H/11	49°34′	121°26′
Yamachiche	VILG/VILG	QC	Maskinongé	31 I/7	46°16′	72°50′
Yamachiche, Rivière	RIV/CDE	QC	Maskinongé	31 I/7	46°16′	72°49′
Yamaska	TOWN/VIL2	QC	Le Bas-Richelieu	31 I/2	46°00′	72°55′
Yamaska-Est	TOWN/VIL2	QC	Le Bas-Richelieu	31 I/2	46°00′	72°54′
Yamaska, Mont	MTN/MNT	QC	Rouville	31 H/7	45°27′	72°52′
Yamaska Nord, Rivière	RIV/CDE	QC	Brome-Missisquoi	31 H/7	45°17′	72°51′
Yamaska, Parc de récréation de la	PARK/PARC	QC	La Haute-Yamaska	31 H/7	45°25′	72°36′
Yamaska, Rivière	RIV/CDE	QC	Nicolet-Yamaska	31 I/2	46°07′	72°56′
Yamba Lake	LAKE/LAC	NT	Mackenzie	76 D	64°58′	111°20′
Yan 7	IR/RI	BC	Range 5 Coast	103 K/1	54°04′	132°14′
Yandle Lake	LAKE/LAC	NT	Keewatin	65 H	61°52′	96°33′
Yankee Bonnet	UNP/LNO	ON	Peterborough	31 D/8	44°16′	78°19′
Yankee Flats	UNP/LNO	BC	Kamloops Division Yale	82 L/11	50°31′	119°22′
Yankee Line	UNP/LNO	NS	Victoria	11 K/2	46°07′	60°55′
Yankeetown	UNP/LNO	NS	Halifax	11 D/12	44°44′	63°49′
Yarbo	VILG/VILG	SK	1-20-23-W	62 K/12	50°42′	101°56′
Yarker	UNP/LNO	ON	Lennox and Addington	31 C/7	44°23′	76°46′
Yarksis	UNP/LNO	BC	Clayoquot	92 F/4	49°10′	125°58′
Yarksis 11	IR/RI	BC	Clayoquot	92 F/4	49°10′	125°58′
Yarm	UNP/LNO	QC	Pontiac	31 F/9	45°38′	76°28′
Yarmouth	TOWN/VIL2	NS	Yarmouth	20 O/16	43°50′	66°07′
Yarmouth	MUN1/AZM1	NS	Yarmouth	20 O/16	43°57′	66°02′
Yarmouth	MUN2/AZM2	ON	Elgin	40 I/11	42°43′	81°09′
Yarmouth	GEOG/GÉOG	NS		20 P/13	43°55′	65°48′
Yarmouth 33	IR/RI	NS	Yarmouth	20 O/16	43°50′	66°05′
Yarmouth Bar	UNP/LNO	NS	Yarmouth	20 O/16	43°49′	66°09′
Yarmouth Centre	UNP/LNO	ON	Elgin	40 I/14	42°47′	81°07′
Yarrow	UNP/LNO	BC	New Westminster	92 G/1	49°05′	122°03′
Yasinski, Lac	LAKE/LAC	QC	Jamésie	33 F/5	53°16′	77°35′
Yasitkun 21	IR/RI	BC	Queen Charlotte	103 K/3	54°15′	133°04′
Yates	UNP/LNO	AB	32-53-16-W5	83 F/9	53°38′	116°20′

NAME NOM	ENTITY ENTITÉ	LOC 1 LIEU 1	LOC 2 LIEU 2	MAP CARTE	POSITION LAT	LONG
Yates River	RIV/CDE	NT/AB		85 B/4	60°10′	115°51′
Yathkyed Lake	LAKE/LAC	NT	Keewatin	65 J	62°40′	98°00′
Yatisakus, Lac	LAKE/LAC	QC	Jamésie	33 J/6	54°17′	75°29′
Yatsore Lake	LAKE/LAC	NT	Mackenzie	75 D	60°46′	110°16′
Yatton	UNP/LNO	ON	Wellington	40 P/10	43°37′	80°37′
Yatze 13	IR/RI	BC	Queen Charlotte	103 K/2	54°09′	132°39′
Yawaucht 11	IR/RI	BC	Kamloops Division Yale	92 I/5	50°21′	121°40′
Yawkey	UNP/LNO	ON	Essex	40 J/6	42°17′	83°05′
Ycliff	UNP/LNO	ON	Kenora	52 J/3	50°10′	91°08′
Yearley	UNP/LNO	ON	Muskoka	31 E/6	45°22′	79°27′
Yehiniko Creek	RIV/CDE	BC	Cassiar	104 G/14	57°46′	131°26′
Yehiniko Lake	LAKE/LAC	BC	Cassiar	104 G/11	57°34′	131°20′
Ye Koo Che 3	IR/RI	BC	Range 5 Coast	93 K/11	54°36′	125°04′
Ye Koos Lee 11	IR/RI	BC	Range 5 Coast	93 K/11	54°34′	125°16′
Yekwaupsum 18	IR/RI	BC	New Westminster	92 G/11	49°43′	123°09′
Yekwaupsum 19	IR/RI	BC	New Westminster	92 G/11	49°44′	123°09′
Yelakin 4	IR/RI	BC	Yale Division Yale	92 H/11	49°45′	121°25′
Yelakin 4A	IR/RI	BC	Yale Division Yale	92 H/11	49°45′	121°24′
Yellek	UNP/LNO	ON	Nipissing	31 L/5	46°20′	79°35′
Yellertlee 12	IR/RI	BC	Range 2 Coast	102 P/16	51°56′	128°28′
Yellow Bluff	MTN/MNT	NT	Keewatin	46 D	64°22′	87°51′
Yellow Creek	VILG/VILG	SK	34-43-23-W2	73 A/11	52°45′	105°15′
Yellow Girl Bay	BAY/BAIE	ON	Kenora	52 E/8	49°30′	94°16′
Yellow Girl Bay 32B	IR/RI	ON	Kenora	52 E/8	49°30′	94°12′
Yellow Grass	TOWN/VIL2	SK	7-10-16-W2	72 H/16	49°48′	104°10′
Yellowhead	UNP/LNO	BC	Cariboo	83 D/16	52°53′	118°28′
Yellowhead Improvement District No. 14 - see-voir - Yellowhead No. 94, Municipal District of	MUN2/AZM2	AB		83 F/5	53°25′	116°42′
Yellowhead No. 94, Municipal District of	MUN1/AZM1	AB		83 F/7	53°25′	116°42′
Yellowhead Pass	VALL/VALL	BC/AB		83 D/16	52°53′	118°28′
Yellowhead Pass National Historic Site - also-aussi - Col-Yellowhead, Lieu historique national du	PARK/PARC	AB		83 D/16	52°54′	118°28′
Yellowknife	CITY/VIL1	NT	Mackenzie	85 J/8	62°27′	114°21′
Yellowknife Bay	BAY/BAIE	NT	Mackenzie	85 J	62°22′	114°20′
Yellowknife River	RIV/CDE	NT	Mackenzie	85 J	62°31′	114°19′
Yellowquill 90	IR/RI	SK		63 D/5	52°22′	103°39′
Yellowstone	VILG/VILG	AB	9-55-3-W5	83 G/9	53°44′	114°23′
Yeltea Lake	LAKE/LAC	NT	Mackenzie	106 I	66°55′	129°22′
Yelverton	UNP/LNO	ON	Durham	31 D/2	44°10′	78°43′
Yelverton Bay	BAY/BAIE	NT	Franklin	340 F	82°23′	83°18′
Yelverton Inlet	BAY/BAIE	NT	Franklin	340 F	82°09′	81°25′
Yennadon	UNP/LNO	BC	New Westminster	92 G/2	49°14′	122°35′
Yensischuck 3	IR/RI	BC	Range 5 Coast	93 K/2	54°04′	124°33′
Yeo Channel	CHAN/CHEN	ON	Manitoulin	41 H/5	45°24′	81°46′
Yeoford	UNP/LNO	AB	36-46-3-W5	83 G/1	53°01′	114°19′
Yeo Island	ISL/ÎLE	ON	Manitoulin	41 H/5	45°24′	81°47′
Yeo Island	ISL/ÎLE	BC	Range 3 Coast	103 A/8	52°21′	128°08′
Yeo Island 13	IR/RI	BC	Range 3 Coast	103 A/8	52°18′	128°07′
Yeoman	UNP/LNO	SK	15-8-16-W2	72 H/9	49°39′	104°06′
Yeoman Island	ISL/ÎLE	NT	Franklin	48 B	72°16′	85°57′
Yeovil	UNP/LNO	ON	Grey	41 A/2	44°04′	80°41′
Yerexville	UNP/LNO	ON	Prince Edward	31 C/3	44°02′	77°10′
Ymir	UNP/LNO	BC	Kootenay	82 F/6	49°17′	117°13′
Ymir Mountain	MTN/MNT	BC	Kootenay	82 F/6	49°26′	117°07′
Yohetta Lake	LAKE/LAC	BC	Lillooet	92 O/4	51°14′	123°51′
Yoho	UNP/LNO	NB	York	21 G/15	45°47′	66°52′
Yoho	UNP/LNO	BC	Kootenay	82 N/8	51°25′	116°24′
Yoho National Park - also-aussi - Yoho, Parc national	PARK/PARC	BC	Kootenay	82 N/7	51°30′	116°30′
Yoho, Parc national - also-aussi - Yoho National Park	PARK/PARC	BC	Kootenay	82 N/7	51°30′	116°30′
Yoho Stream	RIV/CDE	NB	Sunbury	21 G/10	45°41′	66°45′
Yoke Lake	LAKE/LAC	ON	Kenora	52 F/3	49°08′	93°27′
Yonde	UNP/LNO	ON	Kenora	52 G/13	49°55′	91°33′
Yongehurst	UNP/LNO	ON	York	30 M/14	43°52′	79°26′
Yonge Mills	UNP/LNO	ON	Leeds	31 B/12	44°31′	75°50′
Yonker	UNP/LNO	SK	27-42-26-W3	73 C/12	52°39′	109°40′
Yookwitz 12	IR/RI	BC	New Westminster	92 G/14	49°47′	123°12′
York	CITY/VIL1	ON	York	30 M/11	43°42′	79°27′
York	VILG/VILG	PE	Queens	11 L/6	46°19′	63°06′
York	MUN1/AZM1	ON	York	30 M/14	44°00′	79°28′
York	UNP/LNO	PE	Queens	11 L/6	46°19′	63°06′
York	UNP/LNO	ON	Haldimand	30 M/4	43°01′	79°53′
York	GEOG/GÉOG	NB		21 J/3	46°10′	67°00′
York	GEOG/GÉOG	ON		30 M/14	43°55′	79°25′
York, Cape	CAPE/CAP	NT	Franklin	48 C	73°48′	87°00′
York Centre	UNP/LNO	QC	La Côte-de-Gaspé	22 A/15	48°49′	64°30′
Yorke Settlement	UNP/LNO	NS	Cumberland	21 H/8	45°26′	64°27′
York Factory	UNP/LNO	MB		54 F/1	57°00′	92°18′

NAME NOM	ENTITY ENTITÉ	LOC 1 LIEU 1	LOC 2 LIEU 2	MAP CARTE	POSITION	
					LAT	LONG
York Factory, Lieu historique national - also-aussi - York Factory National Historic Site	PARK/PARC	MB		54 F/1	57°00′	92°18′
York Factory National Historic Site - also-aussi - York Factory, Lieu historique national	PARK/PARC	MB		54 F/1	57°00′	92°18′
York Harbour	VILG/VILG	NF		12 G/1	49°04′	58°23′
York Harbour	BAY/BAIE	NF		12 G/1	49°04′	58°21′
York Height	UNP/LNO	ON	York	30 M/14	43°46′	79°21′
York Landing	UNP/LNO	MB		64 A/1	56°05′	96°06′
York Landing	IR/RI	MB	82-9-E1	64 A/1	56°05′	96°07′
York Mills	UNP/LNO	NB	York	21 G/11	45°40′	67°06′
York Mills	UNP/LNO	ON	York	30 M/11	43°45′	79°25′
York Point	UNP/LNO	PE	Queens	11 L/3	46°13′	63°10′
York Redoubt National Historic Site - also-aussi - Redoute-York, Lieu historique national de la	PARK/PARC	NS	Halifax	11 D/12	44°36′	63°33′
York River	UNP/LNO	ON	Hastings	31 F/4	45°06′	77°53′
York River	RIV/CDE	ON	Renfrew	31 F/5	45°20′	77°35′
York River	RIV/CDE	MB		53 K/4	54°07′	93°46′
York, Rivière	RIV/CDE	QC	La Côte-de-Gaspé	22 A/15	48°49′	64°33′
York Sound	CHAN/CHEN	NT	Franklin	25 J	62°26′	66°30′
Yorkton	CITY/VIL1	SK		62 M/1	51°13′	102°28′
Yorkton Creek	RIV/CDE	SK	32-27-4-W2	62 M/7	51°23′	102°32′
Yorkville	UNP/LNO	ON	York	30 M/11	43°40′	79°23′
Yorston Lake	LAKE/LAC	ON	Sudbury	41 P/2	47°03′	80°32′
Youbou	UNP/LNO	BC	Cowichan Lake	92 C/16	48°52′	124°12′
Youghall	UNP/LNO	NB	Gloucester	21 P/12	47°40′	65°38′
Young	VILG/VILG	SK	27-32-27-W2	72 P/13	51°47′	105°45′
Young Bay	BAY/BAIE	NT	Franklin	68 A	72°43′	96°56′
Young, Cape	CAPE/CAP	NT	Mackenzie	87 B	68°57′	116°58′
Young Inlet	BAY/BAIE	NT	Franklin	69 A	76°33′	99°15′
Young Island	ISL/ÎLE	NT	Franklin	68 E	74°19′	98°40′
Young Islands	ISL/ÎLE	NT	Franklin	76 J	66°58′	108°00′
Young Lake	LAKE/LAC	SK		74 P/10	59°37′	104°34′
Young Lake	LAKE/LAC	BC	Lillooet	92 P/2	51°15′	120°58′
Young Point	UNP/LNO	MB	55-26-W	63 F/14	53°46′	101°14′
Young Point	CAPE/CAP	BC	Nanaimo	92 F/8	49°26′	124°10′
Young Ridge	UNP/LNO	NB	Northumberland	21 I/11	46°45′	65°30′
Youngs Cove	UNP/LNO	NS	Annapolis	21 A/14	44°52′	65°26′
Youngs Cove	UNP/LNO	NB	Queens	21 H/13	45°57′	65°56′
Young's Cove	UNP/LNO	ON	Peterborough	31 D/8	44°27′	78°26′
Youngs Cove Road	UNP/LNO	NB	Queens	21 H/13	45°57′	65°51′
Young's Creek	RIV/CDE	ON	Norfolk	40 I/16	42°45′	80°15′
Youngs Crossing	UNP/LNO	NB	York	21 G/15	45°58′	66°36′
Youngs Harbour	UNP/LNO	ON	York	31 D/3	44°12′	79°29′
Youngs Point	UNP/LNO	ON	Peterborough	31 D/8	44°29′	78°14′
Young's Point Provincial Park	PARK/PARC	AB	70,71-24-W5	83 N/4	55°08′	117°35′
Youngstown	VILG/VILG	AB	33-29-9-W4	72 M/11	51°32′	111°13′
Youngstown	UNP/LNO	ON	Peterborough	31 D/8	44°24′	78°24′
Youngsville	UNP/LNO	ON	Oxford	40 P/2	43°12′	80°56′
Ypres	UNP/LNO	ON	Simcoe	31 D/5	44°16′	79°50′
Yreka	UNP/LNO	BC	Rupert	92 L/5	50°28′	127°33′
Yser, Lac	LAKE/LAC	QC	Vallée-de-l'Or	31 N/15	47°55′	76°52′
Ythier, Lac	LAKE/LAC	QC	Kativik	24 A/5	56°17′	65°57′
Yukon Crossing	UNP/LNO	YT		115 I/8	62°21′	136°29′
Yukon, Fleuve - also-aussi - **Yukon River**	RIV/CDE	YT		116 C/10	64°41′	141°00′
Yukon River - also-aussi - **Yukon, Fleuve**	RIV/CDE	YT		116 C/10	64°41′	141°00′
Yukon, Territoire du - also-aussi - **Yukon Territory**	TERR/TERR	YT		MCR130	63°00′	135°00′
Yukon Territory - also-aussi - **Yukon, Territoire du**	TERR/TERR	YT		MCR130	63°00′	135°00′
Yule	UNP/LNO	ON	Grenville	31 B/13	44°47′	75°52′
Yule Lake	LAKE/LAC	BC	Range 4 Coast	103 H/1	53°02′	128°27′
Yuquot	UNP/LNO	BC	Nootka	92 E/10	49°36′	126°37′
Yuquot 1	IR/RI	BC	Nootka	92 E/10	49°35′	126°37′
Yusezyu River	RIV/CDE	YT		105 H/12	61°33′	129°43′

Z

Zacht 5	IR/RI	BC	Kamloops Division Yale	92 I/4	50°09′	121°34′
Zadow	UNP/LNO	ON	Renfrew	31 F/11	45°33′	77°16′
Zaimoetz 5	IR/RI	BC	Range 5 Coast	103 I/9	54°33′	128°29′
Zaitscullachan 9	IR/RI	BC	New Westminster	92 G/1	49°11′	122°02′
Zakwaski Mountain	MTN/MNT	BC	Kamloops Division Yale	92 I/3	50°09′	121°18′
Zala	UNP/LNO	SK	20-25-16-W2	72 P/1	51°11′	104°09′
Zama Lake	LAKE/LAC	AB	112-7-W6	84 L/11	58°45′	119°05′
Zama Lake 210	IR/RI	AB	112-8-W6	84 L/11	58°44′	119°15′
Zamora	UNP/LNO	BC	Similkameen Division Yale	82 E/2	49°09′	118°59′

NAME NOM	ENTITY ENTITÉ	LOC 1 LIEU 1	LOC 2 LIEU 2	MAP CARTE	POSITION LAT	LONG
Zangeza Bay	BAY/BAIE	SK/MB		64 L/O1	58°03'	102°04'
Zarn	UNP/LNO	ON	Kenora	52 G/13	50°00'	91°38'
Zaulzap 29	IR/RI	BC	Cassiar	103 P/3	55°11'	129°15'
Zaulzap 29A	IR/RI	BC	Cassiar	103 P/3	55°12'	129°15'
Zawale	UNP/LNO	AB	6-56-16-W4	83 H/16	53°48'	112°23'
Zayas Island	ISL/ÎLE	BC	Range 5 Coast	103 J/11	54°36'	131°04'
Zayas Island 32A	IR/RI	BC	Range 5 Coast	103 J/11	54°37'	131°04'
Zbaraz	UNP/LNO	MB	24-23-1-W	62 I/14	51°00'	97°29'
Zealand	UNP/LNO	NB	York	21 J/2	46°03'	66°56'
Zealand	UNP/LNO	ON	Frontenac	31 C/15	44°50'	76°37'
Zealandia	TOWN/VIL2	SK	30-13-W3	72 O/12	51°37'	107°45'
Zeballos	VILG/VILG	BC	Nootka	92 E/15	49°59'	126°51'
Zebulon Lake	LAKE/LAC	NT	Mackenzie	86 F/4	65°03'	117°50'
Zebulon River	RIV/CDE	NT	Mackenzie	86 F	64°58'	118°17'
Zed Lake	LAKE/LAC	MB		64 C/14	56°55'	101°16'
Zehner	UNP/LNO	SK	8-18-18-W2	72 I/9	50°34'	104°28'
Zeke	UNP/LNO	BC	Peace River	94 H/3	57°01'	121°28'
Zelana	UNP/LNO	MB	3,4-30-20-W	62 N/9	51°32'	100°12'
Zelena	UNP/LNO	MB	15-28-28-W	62 N/6	51°24'	101°18'
Zelma	VILG/VILG	SK	21-33-28-W2	72 P/13	51°50'	105°55'
Zenda	UNP/LNO	ON	Oxford	40 I/15	42°59'	80°44'
Zeneta	UNP/LNO	SK	22-20-1-W2	62 L/9	50°44'	102°04'
Zengle Lake	LAKE/LAC	SK		64 E/15	57°55'	102°33'
Zenon Park	VILG/VILG	SK	19-47-12-W2	63 E/4	53°04'	103°45'
Zephyr	UNP/LNO	ON	Ontario	31 D/3	44°12'	79°16'
Zeta	UNP/LNO	ON	Timiskaming	41 P/16	47°49'	80°08'
Zeta Lake	LAKE/LAC	NT	Franklin	77 E/14	70°54'	106°25'
Zhoda	UNP/LNO	MB	12-4-7-E	62 H/7	49°17'	96°31'
Zimagord 3	IR/RI	BC	Range 5 Coast	103 I/7	54°29'	128°44'
Zimmerman	UNP/LNO	ON	Halton	30 M/5	43°25'	79°50'
Zincton	UNP/LNO	BC	Kootenay	82 K/3	50°02'	117°12'
Zinto Lake	LAKE/LAC	NT	Mackenzie	86 C	64°06'	116°25'
Zion	UNP/LNO	ON	Peterborough	31 D/1	44°15'	78°15'
Zion	UNP/LNO	ON	Durham	30 M/16	43°58'	78°26'
Zion	UNP/LNO	ON	Victoria	31 D/7	44°29'	78°49'
Zion	UNP/LNO	ON	Grey	41 A/2	44°14'	80°45'
Zion	UNP/LNO	ON	Grey	41 A/11	44°43'	81°05'
Zion	UNP/LNO	ON	Huron	40 P/13	43°57'	81°33'
Zion Hill	UNP/LNO	ON	Hastings	31 C/6	44°18'	77°25'
Zion Line	UNP/LNO	ON	Renfrew	31 F/10	45°41'	76°51'
Zionville	UNP/LNO	NB	York	21 J/2	46°12'	66°32'
Zionz Lake	LAKE/LAC	ON	Kenora	52 O/5	51°25'	91°52'
Ziska	UNP/LNO	ON	Muskoka	31 E/3	45°04'	79°24'
Zoar	UNP/LNO	NF		14 C/3	56°08'	61°23'
Zoht 4	IR/RI	BC	Kamloops Division Yale	92 I/2	50°11'	120°40'
Zoht 5	IR/RI	BC	Kamloops Division Yale	92 I/2	50°13'	120°37'
Zoht 14	IR/RI	BC	Kamloops Division Yale	92 I/2	50°14'	120°37'
Zone	MUN2/AZM2	ON	Kent	40 I/12	42°37'	81°56'
Zoria	UNP/LNO	MB	34-27-21-W	62 N/8	51°21'	100°20'
Zorra	MUN2/AZM2	ON	Oxford	40 P/2	43°07'	80°54'
Zorra Station	UNP/LNO	ON	Oxford	40 P/2	43°06'	80°53'
Zuber Corners	UNP/LNO	ON	Waterloo	40 P/9	43°35'	80°28'
Zucker Lake	LAKE/LAC	NT	Mackenzie	75 J	62°55'	106°48'
Zurich	VILG/VILG	ON	Huron	40 P/5	43°26'	81°37'
Zymoetz River	RIV/CDE	BC	Range 5 Coast	103 I/9	54°33'	128°29'